ProQuest Statistical Abstract of the United States 2021

ProQuest Statistical Abstract of the United States 2021

Issued December 2020

Published by Rowman & Littlefield
A wholly owned subsidiary of The Rowman & Littlefield Publishing Group, Inc.
4501 Forbes Boulevard, Suite 200, Lanham, Maryland 20706
www.rowman.com, 800-462-6420
6 Tinworth Street, London SE11 5AL, United Kingdom

ISBN 13: 978-1-64143-445-4

Suggested Citation:
ProQuest LLC. ProQuest Statistical Abstract of the United States, 2021. (9th ed.) Bethesda, MD 2020

Preface

The *Statistical Abstract of the United States,* published since 1878, is the best-known statistical reference publication in the country. As a comprehensive collection of statistics on the social, political, and economic conditions of the United States, it is a snapshot of America and its people. In the spring of 2011, the Census Bureau terminated their Statistical Compendia program and production of the *Statistical Abstract.* Since 2012, ProQuest has taken responsibility for curating the data found in this valuable statistical reference tool and publishing it in this print edition and an expanded online edition.

The *ProQuest Statistical Abstract of the United States* is designed to serve as a convenient volume for statistical reference and as a guide to other statistical publications and sources. The latter function is served by the introductory text to each section; source citations appearing below each table; and Appendix I, which is comprised of the *Guide to Sources of Statistics*, including a list of international statistical abstracts, and the *Guide to State Statistical Abstracts.*

Contents—This volume includes a selection of data from many statistical sources, both government and private, as indicated in the source citations at the bottom of every table. Data are obtained from a variety of resources, including PDF documents, Excel data packages, and complex databases. Publications cited as source reports usually contain additional statistical detail and more comprehensive discussions of definitions and concepts. Data not available in written publications issued by the contributing agency but obtained from data files available on the internet or unpublished records are also identified in the source notes. More information on the subjects covered in the tables may generally be obtained from the source.

Except as indicated, figures are for the United States as presently constituted. Although emphasis in the *ProQuest Statistical Abstract* is primarily given to national data, many tables present data for regions and individual states and a smaller number for metropolitan areas and cities. "Appendix II, Metropolitan and Micropolitan Statistical Areas: Concepts, Components, and Population," presents explanatory text, a complete current listing, and 2019 population data for metropolitan and micropolitan areas delineated as of September 2018. Statistics for the Commonwealth of Puerto Rico and for Island Areas of the United States are included in many state tables and are supplemented by information in Section 29.

Statistics in this edition are generally for the most recent year or period available, as of early September 2020. Each year over 1,400 tables are reviewed and evaluated, new tables of current interest are added, continuing series are updated, and less timely data are condensed or eliminated. Text notes and appendices are revised as appropriate.

Changes in this edition—This year ProQuest introduces approximately 40 new tables presenting data on topics that include youth and adult vaccinations, cancer incidence, firearm violence victimizations, maternal mortality, arrests for immigration offenses, women- and minority-owned businesses, nutrient and energy consumption, and COVID-19 cases, hospitalizations, and deaths. For a complete list of new tables, see "New Tables," p. xi.

The *Statistical Abstract* generally presents data on an annual basis. Coverage of the coronavirus disease (COVID-19) pandemic is an exception to this. Table 120 in Section 2: Births, Deaths, Marriages, and Divorces shows cumulative data on COVID-19 deaths; Table 179 in Section 3: Health and Nutrition shows weekly data on coronavirus cases, testing, and hospitalizations. Additionally, monthly employment data has been added to Tables 617, 658, and 659 in Section 12: Labor Force, Employment, and Earnings. The data presented here are intended as an illustration of the progression of the pandemic in the U.S. and to provide information on where to find statistics related to the pandemic. Please refer to the table source notes as a guide to accessing revised and up-to-date data.

Online edition—*ProQuest Statistical Abstract* is also available in an electronic format. This dynamic edition features table-specific capabilities for narrowing results by source, data date, subject, and type of data breakdown. The online edition is updated with new statistical content on a monthly basis, enabling users to access new and revised data in advance of the annual publication of this print edition. The online product functions as a repository for historical trends that cannot fit into the print publication. Users will find spreadsheets that correspond to each table in the book. In many cases, these spreadsheets present expanded coverage of the data shown in print. The online edition is available as a stand-alone product or as a part of ProQuest's Statistical Premium Collection (see inside back cover for details).

Limitations of the data—The contents of this volume were taken from many sources. All data from censuses, surveys, and administrative records are subject to error arising from a number of factors including the following: sampling variability (for statistics based on samples), reporting errors in the data for individual units, incomplete coverage, nonresponse, and imputation and processing errors (see also Appendix III). ProQuest cannot accept responsibility for the accuracy or limitations of the data presented here; however, selection of the material and its proper presentation is the responsibility of ProQuest.

For additional information on data presented—Please consult the source publications available in local libraries and on the internet, or contact the agency or organization indicated in the source notes.

Contents

[Numbers following subject are page numbers]

New and Deleted Tables for the 2021 Edition

New Tables for 2021

Tables Deleted Since the 2020 Edition of the Statistical Abstract

[Tables are deleted for several reasons, including: source data has been discontinued, source data was monographic and new data is not expected to be available, data is believed to be no longer reliable, and data was previously unpublished and cannot be replicated. Some tables have been replaced with tables illustrating similar content. Where applicable, please see reference to new table number]

2020 Table	Section and Table Title	Replaced by...
	Section 1: Population	
Table 82.......	Religious Bodies—Selected Data: 1988 to 2010	
	Section 2: Births, Deaths, Marriages, and Divorces	
Table 105......	Abortions—Number and Rate by Race: 1990 to 2010	
Table 106......	Abortions by Selected Characteristics: 1990 to 2010	Table 105
Table 107......	Abortions—Number and Rate by State of Occurrence: 2000 to 2010	
	Section 3: Health and Nutrition	
Table 160......	Medicaid and Children's Health Insurance Program—Beneficiaries and Payments by Basis of Eligibility and Service Category: 2000 to 2013	
Table 163......	Health Insurance Coverage Status by Selected Characteristics: 2017	Table 164
Table 167......	People Without Health Insurance for the Entire Year by Age, Sex, Race/Ethnicity, and Family Type: 2017	Table 165
Table 203......	Estimated Number of Persons with Stage 3 HIV Infection (AIDS) by Year of Diagnosis, Sex and Transmission Category: 2012 to 2017	Table 205
Table 204......	Estimated Number of Persons Living with HIV Infection Ever Classified as Stage 3 (AIDS) Diagnosis by Selected Characteristics: 2012 to 2016	Table 206
Table 208......	Use of Complementary and Alternative Health Practices Among Adults Age 18 and Over, in the Past 12 Months by Type of Therapy: 2007 and 2012	Table 211
	Section 4: Education	
Table 279......	English as a Second Language (ESL)—Public High School Learners, Programs, and Services by District Characteristics: 2016	Table 284
Table 286......	High School Dropouts by Race and Hispanic Origin: 1980 to 2017	Table 294
	Section 5: Law Enforcement, Courts, and Prisons	
Table 344......	Criminal Victimizations by Age of Victim and Selected Characteristics: 2003 to 2013	
Table 354......	Firearm Violence, Homicides and Nonfatal Victimizations: 1995 to 2011	Table 363
Table 377......	Problem-Solving Courts—Point of Case Entry and Case Outcomes by Type of Court: 2012	
Table 396......	Fire Losses—Total and Per Capita: 1980 to 2016	
	Section 10: National Security and Veterans Affairs	
Table 534......	Military Personnel on Active Duty by Location: 1980 to 2018	
Table 544......	Arms Transfer Agreements with Developing Nations by Supplier Country: 2008 to 2015	
	Section 13: Income, Expenditures, Poverty, and Wealth	
Table 733......	Married-Couple Families—Number and Median Income by Work Experience of Husbands and Wives and Presence of Related Children: 2017	
	Section 15: Business Enterprise	
Table 787......	Employer Firms by Industry and Whether Franchised: 2016	
Table 797......	U.S. Firms—Ownership by Gender, Ethnicity, Race, and Veteran Status: 2012	
Table 798......	Women-Owned Firms by Kind of Business: 2012	Table 802
Table 799......	Minority-Owned Firms by Kind of Business: 2012	Table 803
Table 800......	Hispanic-Owned Firms by Kind of Business: 2012	Table 804
Table 801......	Black-Owned Firms by Kind of Business: 2012	Table 805
Table 802......	Asian–Owned Firms by Kind of Business: 2012	Table 806
Table 803......	Native Hawaiian- and Other Pacific Islander-Owned Firms by Kind of Business: 2012	Table 807
Table 804......	American Indian- and Alaska Native-Owned Firms by Kind of Business: 2012	Table 808
Table 823......	Manufacturing, Mining, and Trade Corporations—Profits and Stockholders' Equity by Industry: 2018	
	Section 16: Science and Technology	
Table 833......	Federal Research and Development (R&D) Budget by Federal Agency: 2010 to 2019	Table 835
Table 848......	Top 20 Metropolitan Areas with the Largest Proportion of Workers in Science and Engineering Occupations: 2014 and 2016	Table 850
	Section 18: Forestry, Fishing, and Mining	
Table 941......	Principal Fuels, Nonmetals, and Metals—World Production, 2000 to 2017, and the U.S. Share, 2017	Table 1389
Table 954......	Crude Petroleum and Natural Gas Extraction Industry Establishments, Employees, and Payroll by State: 2016	Table 944
Table 955......	Natural Gas Liquid Extraction Industry—Establishments, Employees, and Payroll by State: 2016	Table 944
	Section 21: Manufactures	
Table 1039.....	Manufacturing—Selected Industry Statistics by State: 2012	
Table 1055.....	Manufacturing Corporations—Assets and Profits by Asset Size: 2000 to 2018	
	Section 23: Transportation	
Table 1096.....	U.S. Scheduled Airline Industry—Summary: 2007 to 2014	
Table 1110.....	Waterborne Commerce by Type of Commodity: 2000 to 2016	
	Section 24: Information and Communication	
Table 1192.....	Use of Public Libraries, Library Websites, and Library Mobile Applications: 2016	
	Section 25: Banking, Finance, and Insurance	
Table 1247.....	Property and Casualty Insurance—Summary: 2005 to 2016	
	Section 26: Arts, Recreation, and Travel	
Table 1262.....	Personal Participation in Various Arts or Creative Activities by Selected Characteristics: 2012	Table 1258
Table 1267.....	Attendance at/Participation in Various Leisure Activities Including Reading by Selected Characteristics: 2012	Table 1258
Table 1268.....	Household Pet Ownership: 2011	
	Section 27: Accommodation, Food Services, and Other Services	
Table 1306.....	Selected Service Industries—E-Commerce Revenue: 2015 and 2016	Table 1299
	Section 28: Foreign Commerce and Aid	
Table 1333.....	High-technology Products Exports and Imports by World Region and Country: 2007 to 2016	Table 1326
	Section 29: Puerto Rico and the Island Areas	
Table 1345.....	Puerto Rico—Socioeconomic Summary: 1990 to 2018	
Table 1347.....	Puerto Rico—Gross Product and Net Income: 1990 to 2018	
Table 1348.....	Puerto Rico—Transfer Payments: 2000 to 2018	

Guide to Tabular Presentation

Example of Table Structure

Table 1287. Top 20 U.S. Gateway Airports for Nonstop International Air Travel Passengers: 2019

[243,947 represents 243,947,000. International passengers are residents of any country traveling nonstop to and from the United States on U.S. and foreign carriers. The data cover all passengers arriving and departing from U.S. airports on nonstop commercial international flights with 60 seats or more]

Gateway airport	Airport code	Passengers, (1,000)	Gateway airport	Airport code	Passengers, (1,000)
Total, all airports........................	**(X)**	**243,947**	Dallas-Ft. Worth, TX.....................	DFW	9,269
Total, top 20 airports.....................	(X)	216,873	Fort Lauderdale, FL.....................	FLL	8,540
Top 20, percentage of total..............	(X)	88.9	Washington (Dulles), VA................	IAD	8,307
			Boston, MA..............................	BOS	7,882
New York (JFK), NY........................	JFK	33,936	Orlando, FL..............................	MCO	7,057
Los Angeles, CA...........................	LAX	25,402	Seattle-Tacoma, WA.....................	SEA	5,513
Miami, FL...................................	MIA	21,271	Honolulu, HI..............................	HNL	5,279
San Francisco, CA........................	SFO	15,038	Philadelphia, PA.........................	PHL	3,972
Newark, NJ.................................	EWR	14,193	Detroit, MI................................	DTW	3,724
Chicago (O'Hare), IL......................	ORD	13,800	Las Vegas, NV............................	LAS	3,545
Atlanta, GA.................................	ATL	12,455	Charlotte, NC.............................	CLT	3,520
Houston (G. Bush), TX....................	IAH	10,938	Minneapolis-St. Paul, MN..............	MSP	3,232

X Not applicable.

Source: U.S. Department of Transportation, Research and Innovative Technology Administration, Bureau of Transportation Statistics, Office of Airline Information, "T-100 International Segment data," <http://www.transtats.bts.gov/Fields.asp?Table_ID=261>, accessed September 2020.

Headnotes immediately below table titles provide information important for correct interpretation or evaluation of the table as a whole or for a major segment of it.

Footnotes below the bottom rule of tables give information relating to specific items or figures within the table.

Unit indicators show the *specified quantities* in which data items are presented. They are used for two primary reasons. Sometimes data are not available in absolute form and are estimates (as in the case of many surveys). In other cases we round the numbers in order to save space to show more data, as in the case above.

When a table presents data with more than one unit indicator, they are found in the headnotes and column headings (Tables 5 and 29), spanner (Table 38), stub (Table 28), or unit column (Table 255). When the data in a table are shown in the same unit indicator, it is shown as the first part of the headnote (Table 2). If no unit indicator is shown, data presented are in absolute form (Table 1).

Vertical rules are used to separate independent sections of a table (Table 1), or in tables where the stub is continued into one or more additional columns (Table 2).

Averages—An average is a single number or value that is often used to represent the "typical value" of a group of numbers. It is regarded as a measure of "location" or "central tendency" of a group of numbers.

The *arithmetic mean* is the type of average used most frequently. It is derived by summing the individual item values of a particular group and dividing the total by the number of items. The arithmetic mean is often referred to as simply the "mean" or "average."

The *median* of a group of numbers is the middle number or value when each item in the group is arranged according to size (lowest to highest or vice versa); it generally has the same number of items

above it as well as below it. If there is an even number of items in the group, the median is taken to be the average of the two middle numbers.

Per capita (or per person) quantities—a per capita figure represents an average computed for every person in a specified group (or population). It is derived by taking the total for an item (such as income, taxes, or retail sales) and dividing it by the number of persons in the specified population.

Index numbers—An index number is the measure of difference or change, usually expressed as a percent, relating one quantity (the variable) of a specified kind to another quantity of the same kind. Index numbers are widely used to express changes in prices over periods of time, but may also be used to express differences between related subjects for a single point in time.

To compute a price index, a base year or period is selected. The base year price (of the commodity or service) is then designated as the base or reference price to which the prices for other years or periods are related. Many price indexes use the year 1982 as the base year; in tables, this is shown as "1982 = 100." A method expressing the price relationship is: The price of a set of one or more items for a related year (e.g. 1990) **divided by** the price of the same set of items for the base year (e.g. 1982). The result multiplied by 100 provides the index number. When 100 is subtracted from the index number, the result equals the percent change in price from the base year.

Average annual percent change—Unless otherwise stated in the *Abstract* (as in Section 1, Population), average annual percent change is computed by use of a *compound interest formula*. This formula assumes that the rate of change is constant throughout a specified compounding period (1 year for average annual rates of change). The formula is similar to that used to compute the balance of a savings account that receives compound interest. According to this formula, at the end of a compounding period the amount of accrued change (e.g., school enrollment or bank interest) is added to the amount that existed at the beginning of the period. As a result, over time (e.g., with each year or quarter), the same rate of change is applied to a larger and larger figure.

The *exponential formula,* which is based on continuous compounding, is often used to measure population change. It is preferred by population experts because they view population and population-related subjects as changing without interruption, ever ongoing. Both exponential and compound interest formulas assume a constant rate of change. The former, however, applies the amount of change continuously to the base rather than at the end of each compounding period. When the average annual rates are small (e.g., less than 5 percent), both formulas give virtually the same results. For an explanation of these two formulas as they relate to population, see U.S. Census Bureau, *The Methods and Materials of Demography,* Vol. 2, 3d printing (rev.), 1975.

Current and constant dollars—Statistics in some tables in a number of sections are expressed in both current and constant dollars (see, e.g., Table 702 in Section 13, Income, Expenditures, Poverty, and Wealth). Current dollar figures reflect actual prices or costs prevailing during the specified year(s). Constant dollar figures are estimates representing an effort to remove the effects of price changes from statistical series reported in dollar terms. In general, constant dollar series are derived by dividing current dollar estimates by the appropriate price index for the appropriate period (e.g., the Consumer Price Index).

The result is a series as it would presumably exist if prices were the same throughout, as in the base year—in other words, as if the dollar had constant purchasing power. Any changes in this constant dollar series would reflect only changes in real volume of output, income, expenditures, or other measure.

Explanation of Symbols

The following symbols, used in the tables throughout this book, are explained in condensed form in footnotes to the tables where they appear:

— Represents zero or rounds to less than half the unit of measurement shown.

B Base figure too small to meet statistical standards for reliability of a derived figure.

D Figure withheld to avoid disclosure pertaining to a specific organization or individual.

NA Data not enumerated, tabulated, or otherwise available separately.

P Data are preliminary or projected.

S Figure does not meet publication standards for reasons other than that covered by symbol B, above.

X Figure not applicable because column heading and stub line make entry impossible, absurd, or meaningless.

Z Entry would amount to less than half the unit of measurement shown.

In many tables, details will not add to the totals shown because of rounding.

Section 1
Population

This section presents statistics on the growth, distribution, and characteristics of the U.S. population. The principal source of these data is the U.S. Census Bureau, which conducts a decennial census of population, a monthly population survey, a program of population estimates and projections, and a number of other periodic surveys.

Decennial censuses—The U.S. Constitution provides for a census of the population every 10 years, primarily to establish a basis for apportionment of members of the House of Representatives among the states. For over a century after the first census in 1790, the census organization was a temporary one, created only for each decennial census. In 1902, the Census Bureau was established as a permanent federal agency, responsible for enumerating the population and also for compiling statistics on other population and housing characteristics.

Historically, the enumeration of the population has been a complete (100 percent) count. That is, an attempt is made to account for every person, for each person's residence, and for other characteristics (sex, age, family relationships, etc.). In the twentieth century, the questions were divided between a "short" and "long" form. Only a subset of the population was required to answer the long-form questions. The most recent census consisted only of a short form, which included basic questions about age, sex, race, Hispanic origin, household relationship, and owner/renter status. After the 2000 Census, the long form became the American Community Survey (ACS) and continues to collect long-form-type information. The ACS includes not only the basic short-form questions, but also detailed questions about population and housing characteristics. It is a nationwide, continuous sample survey designed to provide communities with reliable and timely demographic, housing, social, and economic data every year. Since its start, the ACS has been providing a continuous stream of updated information for states and local areas. Sample data may be used with confidence where large numbers are involved and assumed to indicate trends and relationships where small numbers are involved.

Current Population Survey (CPS)—The CPS sample is a probability sample designed primarily to produce national and state estimates of labor force characteristics of the civilian non-institutional population 16 years of age and older. The sample consists of independent samples in each state and the District of Columbia, and each state sample is specifically tailored to the demographic and labor market conditions that prevail in that particular state. About 60,000 housing units are required in order to meet the national and State reliability criteria, drawn from 824 sample areas.

The CPS also serves as a vehicle for inquiries on other subjects. Using CPS data, the Census Bureau issues a series of publications under the general title of *Current Population Reports*.

Estimates of population characteristics based on the CPS will not agree with the counts from the census because the CPS and the census use different

procedures for collecting and processing the data for racial groups, the Hispanic population, and other topics. Caution should also be used when comparing estimates for various years because of the periodic introduction of changes into the CPS. Beginning in January 1994, a number of changes were introduced into the CPS that affect all data comparisons with prior years. These changes included the results of a major redesign of the survey questionnaire and collection methodology and the introduction of 1990 census population controls, adjusted for the estimated undercount. Beginning with the 2001 CPS Annual Demographic Supplement, the independent estimates used as control totals for the CPS are based on civilian population benchmarks consistent with Census 2000. In 2003 the name of the March supplement was changed to Annual Social and Economic Supplement (ASEC). Beginning with the 2012 March CPS supplement, the estimates are based on Census 2010 population controls. These changes in population controls had relatively little impact on derived measures such as means, medians, and percent distribution, but did have a significant impact on levels.

In 2002, the ASEC incorporated a significant sample expansion. The sample was expanded primarily to improve state estimates of children's health insurance coverage (CHIP). This sample increase of 19,000 households added to the regular sample of 72,500 households and the Hispanic sample of 6,500 gives a total sample size of about 98,000 households. The 2014 CPS ASEC included redesigned questions for income and health insurance coverage. All of the approximately 98,000 addresses were selected to receive the improved set of health insurance coverage items. The improved income questions were implemented using a split panel design. Approximately 68,000 addresses were selected to receive a set of income questions similar to those used in the 2013 CPS ASEC. The remaining 30,000 addresses were selected to receive the redesigned income questions.

Population estimates and projections—Each year, the United States Census Bureau produces and publishes estimates of the population for the nation, states, counties, state/county equivalents, and Puerto Rico. With each annual release of population estimates, the Population Estimates Program revises and updates the entire time series of estimates from April 1, 2010 to July 1 of the current year, which is referred to as the vintage year. "Vintage" denotes an entire time series created with a consistent population starting point and methodology. The release of a new vintage of estimates supersedes any previous series and incorporates the most up-to-date input data and methodological improvements.

Estimates of the United States population are derived by updating the resident population enumerated in Census 2010 with information on the components of population change: births, deaths, and net international migration. The population estimates base reflects changes to the decennial census population due to the Count Question Resolution program, geographic program revisions, and modifications to the 2010 Census race categories for consistency with the race categories in input data.

Registered births and deaths are estimated from data supplied by the National Center for Health Statistics and the Federal-State Cooperative for Population Estimates (FSCPE). The net international migration component consists of four parts: (1) the net international migration of the foreign born, (2) the net migration of natives to and from the United States, (3) the net migration between the United States and Puerto Rico, and (4) the net overseas movement of the Armed Forces population. Data from the ACS are used to estimate the annual net migration of the foreign-born population. The estimated net migration of the native-born population is produced using the foreign-census method which utilized data from over 80 countries. This work compares estimates of the United States born or United States citizen population living overseas measured by population registers and censuses in other countries at two consecutive time periods. The residual was used to develop estimates of net native migration. Estimates for net migration between Puerto Rico and the U.S. are derived from the ACS and the Puerto Rico Community Survey. Estimates of the net overseas movement of the Armed Forces are derived from data collected by the Defense Manpower Data Center.

Estimates for state and county areas are based on the same components of change data and sources as the national estimates with the addition of net internal migration. Estimates of net internal migration are derived from federal income tax returns from the Internal Revenue Service; group quarters data from the branches of the military, the Department of Veterans Affairs, and the FSCPE; and Medicare data from the Centers for Medicare and Medicaid Services.

Population estimates and projections are available on the Census Bureau Web site, see <census.gov>. These estimates and projections are consistent with official decennial census figures with no adjustment for estimated net census coverage. For details on methodology, see "Methodology for the United States Population Estimates: Vintage 2019," <census.gov/programs-surveys/popest/technical-documentation/methodology.html>.

Immigration—Immigration (migration to a country) is one component of international migration; the other component is emigration (migration *from* a country). In its simplest form, international migration is defined as any movement across a national border. In the United States, federal statistics on international migration are produced primarily by the U.S. Census Bureau and the Office of Immigration Statistics of the U.S. Department of Homeland Security (DHS).

The Census Bureau collects data used to estimate international migration through its decennial censuses and numerous surveys of the U.S. population.

The Office of Immigration Statistics publishes immigration data in annual flow reports and the *Yearbook of Immigration Statistics*. Data for these publications are collected from several administrative data sources including the DS-230 *Application for Immigrant Visa and Alien Registration*, the DS-260 *Electronic Application for Immigrant Visa and Alien Registration* of the U.S. Department of State (used by applicants living abroad), and the I-485 *Application to Register Permanent Residence or Adjust Status* of U.S. Citizenship and Immigration Services (USCIS) for applicants living in the United States.

An immigrant, or lawful permanent resident (LPR), is a foreign national who has been granted lawful permanent residence in the United States. New arrivals are foreign nationals living abroad who apply for an immigrant visa at a consular office of the Department of State, while individuals adjusting status are already living in the United States and file an application for adjustment of status to lawful permanent residence with USCIS. Individuals adjusting status include refugees, asylees, and various classes of nonimmigrants. A refugee is a person outside his or her country of nationality who is unable or unwilling to return to his or her country of nationality because of persecution or a well-founded fear of persecution. An asylee is a person who meets the definition of refugee and is already present in the United States or is seeking admission at a port of entry. Refugees are required to apply for LPR ("green card") status one year after being admitted, and asylees may apply for green card status one year after their grant of asylum.

Nonimmigrants are foreign nationals granted temporary entry into the United States. The major activities for which nonimmigrant admission is authorized include temporary visits for business or pleasure, academic or vocational study, temporary employment, and to act as a representative of a foreign government or international organization. DHS collects information on the characteristics of a proportion of nonimmigrant admissions, those recorded on the I-94/I-94W arrival and departure records.

U.S. immigration law gives preferential immigration status to persons with a close family relationship with a U.S. citizen or legal permanent resident, persons with needed job skills, persons who qualify as refugees or asylees, and persons who are from countries with relatively low levels of immigration to the United States (diversity immigrants). Immigration to the United States can be divided into two general categories: (1) classes of admission subject to the annual worldwide limitation and (2) classes of admission exempt from worldwide limitations. Numerical limits are imposed on visas issued and not on admissions. In 2018, the annual limit for family-sponsored preferences was 226,000 and the limit for employment-based preferences was 140,000 plus any unused visas in the family-sponsored preference classes from the previous year, of which there were 292 from 2017.

The Diversity Visa Program is available to nationals of countries with fewer than 50,000 persons granted LPR status during the preceding five years in the employment-based and family-sponsored preferences and immediate relative classes of admission. The annual diversity visa limit has been 50,000 since 1999.

The number of persons who may be admitted to the United States as refugees each year is established by the President in consultation with Congress. The ceiling was set at 45,000 in 2018. There is no numerical limit on the number of persons who can be granted asylum status in a year.

Classes of admission exempt from the worldwide limitation include immediate relatives of U.S. citizens, refugees and asylees adjusting to permanent residence, and other various classes of special immigrants.

Metropolitan and micropolitan areas—Metropolitan and micropolitan statistical areas (metro and micro areas) are geographic entities delineated by the U.S. Office of Management and Budget (OMB) for use by Federal statistical agencies in collecting, tabulating, and publishing Federal statistics. These areas are the result of the application of published standards to Census Bureau data. Generally, the areas are delineated using the most recent set of standards following each decennial census. Between censuses, the delineations are updated annually to reflect the most recent Census Bureau population estimates. Areas based on the 2010 standards and Census Bureau data were last delineated in March 2020.

The term "Core Based Statistical Area" (CBSA) is a collective term for both metro and micro areas. A metro area contains a core urban area of 50,000 or more population, and a micro area contains an urban core of at least 10,000 (but less than 50,000) population. Each metro or micro area consists of one or more counties and includes the counties containing the core urban area, as well as any adjacent counties that have a high degree of social and economic integration (as measured by commuting to work) with the urban core.

Urban and rural—The Census Bureau's urban-rural classification is fundamentally a delineation of geographical areas, identifying both individual urban areas and the rural areas of the nation. The Census Bureau's urban areas represent densely developed territory, and encompass residential, commercial, and other non-residential urban land uses.

For the 2010 Census, an urban area comprises a densely settled core of census tracts and/or census blocks that meet minimum population density requirements, along with adjacent territory containing non-residential urban land uses as well as territory with low population density included to link outlying densely settled territory with the densely settled core. To qualify as an urban area, the territory identified according to criteria must encompass at least 2,500 people, at least 1,500 of which reside outside institutional group quarters. The Census Bureau identifies two types of urban areas: Urbanized Areas of 50,000 or more people; and Urban Clusters of at least 2,500 and less than 50,000 people. "Rural" encompasses all population, housing, and territory not included within an urban area. For Census 2010, many more geographic entities, including metropolitan areas, counties, and places, contain both urban and rural territory, population, and housing units.

Residence—In determining residence, the Census Bureau counts each person as an inhabitant of a usual place of residence (i.e., the place where one lives and sleeps most of the time). While this place is not necessarily a person's legal residence or voting residence, the use of these different bases of classification would produce the same results in the vast majority of cases.

Race—Census 2000 and 2010 adhere to the federal standards for collecting and presenting data on race and ethnicity as established by the OMB in October 1997. Starting with Census 2000, the OMB requires federal agencies to use a minimum of five race categories: White, Black or African American, American Indian or Alaska Native, Asian, and Native Hawaiian or Other Pacific Islander. Additionally, to collect data on individuals of mixed race parentage, respondents were allowed to select one or more races. For respondents who did not identify with any of these five race categories, the OMB approved and included a sixth category—"Some other race" on the Census 2000 and 2010 questionnaire. The Census 2000 and 2010 question on race included 15 separate response categories and three areas where respondents could write in a more specific race group. The response categories and write-in answers can be combined to create the five minimum OMB race categories plus "Some other race." People who responded to the question on race by indicating only one race are referred to as the *race alone* population, or the group that reported only one race category. Six categories make up this population: White alone, Black or African American alone, American Indian and Alaska Native alone, Asian alone, Native Hawaiian and Other Pacific Islander alone, and Some other race alone. Individuals who chose more than one of the six race categories are referred to as the *Two or More Races* population, or as the group that reported more than one race. Additionally, respondents who reported one race together with those who reported the same race plus one or more other races are combined to create the race alone or in *combination* categories. For example, the *White alone or in combination group* consists of those respondents who reported only White or who reported White combined with one or more other race groups, such as "White and Black or African American," or "White and Asian and American Indian and Alaska Native." Another way to think of the group who reported White alone or in combination is as the total number of people who identified entirely or partially as White. This group is also described as people who reported White, whether or not they reported any other race.

The *alone or in combination* categories are tallies of *responses* rather than *respondents*. That is, the alone or in combination categories are not mutually exclusive. Individuals who reported two races were counted in two separate and distinct alone or in combination race categories, while those who reported three races were counted in three categories, and so on. Consequently, the sum of all alone or in combination categories equals the number of races reported, which exceeds the total population.

The racial categories included in the census questionnaire generally reflect a social definition of race recognized in this country and not an attempt to define race biologically, anthropologically, or genetically. It is also recognized that the categories of the race item include racial and national origin or sociocultural groups. For example, data are available for the American Indian and Alaska Native tribes. A detailed explanation of race can be found at <census.gov/prod/cen2010/doc/sf1.pdf>.

Data for the population by race for April 1, 2000 and 2010, (shown in Tables 8, 10, and 11) are modified counts and are not comparable to Census 2000 and 2010 race categories. These numbers were computed using Census 2000 and 2010 data by race and had been modified to be consistent with the 1997 OMB's "Revisions to the Standards for the Classification of Federal Data on Race and Ethnicity," (Federal Register Notice, Vol. 62, No 210, October 1997). A detailed explanation of the race modification procedure appears at <census.gov/programs-surveys/popest/technical-documentation/research/modified-race-data.html>.

In the CPS and other household sample surveys conducted through personal interview, respondents are asked to classify their race as: (1) White; (2) Black or African American; (3) American Indian or Alaska

Native; (4) Asian; or (5) Native Hawaiian or Other Pacific Islander. Beginning January 2003, respondents were allowed to report more than one race to indicate their mixed racial heritage.

Hispanic population—People who identify with the terms "Hispanic" or "Latino" are those who classify themselves in one of the specific Hispanic or Latino categories listed on the decennial census questionnaire and various Census Bureau survey questionnaires – "Mexican, Mexican American, Chicano" or "Puerto Rican" or "Cuban" – as well as those who indicate that they are "another Hispanic, Latino, or Spanish origin." Origin can be viewed as the heritage, nationality group, lineage, or country of birth of the person or the person's ancestors before their arrival in the United States.

Traditional and current data collection and classification treat race and Hispanic origin as two separate and distinct concepts in accordance with guidelines from the OMB. People who are Hispanic may be of any race and people in each race group may be either Hispanic or Not Hispanic. Also, each person has two attributes, their race (or races) and whether or not they are Hispanic. The overlap of race and Hispanic origin is the main comparability issue. For example, Black Hispanics (Hispanic Blacks) are included in both the number of Blacks and in the number of Hispanics. For further information, see <census.gov/topics/population/race/about.html>.

Foreign-born and native populations—The Census Bureau separates the U.S. resident population into two groups based on whether or not a person was a U.S. citizen or U.S. national at the time of birth. Anyone born in the United States, Puerto Rico, or a U.S. Island Area (such as Guam), or born abroad to a U.S. citizen parent is a U.S. citizen at the time of birth and consequently included in the *native population*. The term *foreign-born population* refers to anyone who is not a U.S. citizen or a U.S. national at birth. This includes naturalized U.S. citizens, legal permanent resident aliens (immigrants), temporary migrants (such as foreign students), humanitarian migrants (such as refugees), and people illegally present in the United States. The Census Bureau provides a variety of demographic, social, economic, geographic, and housing information on the foreign-born population in the United States at <census.gov/topics/population/foreign-born.html>.

Mobility status—The U.S. population is classified according to mobility status on the basis of a comparison between the place of residence of each individual at the time of the survey or census and the place of residence at a specified earlier date. Nonmovers are all persons who were living in the same house or apartment at the end of the period as at the beginning of the period. Movers are all persons who were living in a different house or apartment at the end of the period than at the beginning of the period. Movers are further classified as to whether they were living in the same or different county, state, or region, or were movers from abroad. Movers from abroad include all persons whose place of residence was outside the United States (including Puerto Rico, other U.S. Island Area, or a foreign country) at the beginning of the period.

Living arrangements—Living arrangements refer to residency in households or in group quarters. A "household" comprises all persons who occupy a "housing unit," that is, a house, an apartment or other group of rooms, or a single room that constitutes "separate living quarters." A household includes the related family members and all the unrelated persons, if any, such as lodgers, foster children, or employees who share the housing unit. A person living alone or a group of unrelated persons sharing the same housing unit is also counted as a household. See text, Section 20, Construction and Housing, for definition of housing unit.

All persons not living in housing units are classified as living in group quarters. These individuals may be institutionalized, e.g., under care or custody in juvenile facilities, jails, correctional centers, hospitals, or nursing homes; or they may be residents in noninstitutional group quarters such as college dormitories, group homes, or military barracks.

Householder—The householder is the person, or one of the people, in whose name the home is owned, being bought, or rented. If a home is owned or rented jointly by a married couple, either spouse may be listed first. Two types of householders are distinguished: a family householder and a nonfamily householder. A family householder is a householder living with one or more people related to him or her by birth, marriage, or adoption. The householder and all people in the household related to him or her are family members. A family household may contain people not related to the householder, but those people are not included as part of the householder's family in census tabulations. Thus, the number of family households is equal to the number of families, but family households may include more members than do families.

Nonfamily—A nonfamily householder is a householder living alone or with nonrelatives only.

Subfamily—A subfamily is a married couple with or without children, or a single parent with one or more own never-married children under 18 years old, who does not maintain their own household, but lives in the home of someone else (the householder). Subfamilies are divided into "related" and "unrelated" subfamilies. A related subfamily is related to, but does not include, the householder or the spouse of the householder. Members of a related subfamily are also members of the family with whom they live. The number of related subfamilies, therefore, is not included in the count of families. An unrelated subfamily may include persons such as guests, lodgers, or resident employees and their spouses and/or children; none of whom is related to the householder. The number of unrelated subfamily members is included in the total number of household members, but is not included in the count of family members.

Married couple—A married couple live together in the same household, with or without children and other relatives.

Statistical reliability—For a discussion of statistical collection and estimation, sampling procedures, and measures of statistical reliability applicable to Census Bureau data, see Appendix III.

Figure 1.1
Percent Change in Population for States: April 1, 2000 to April 1, 2010

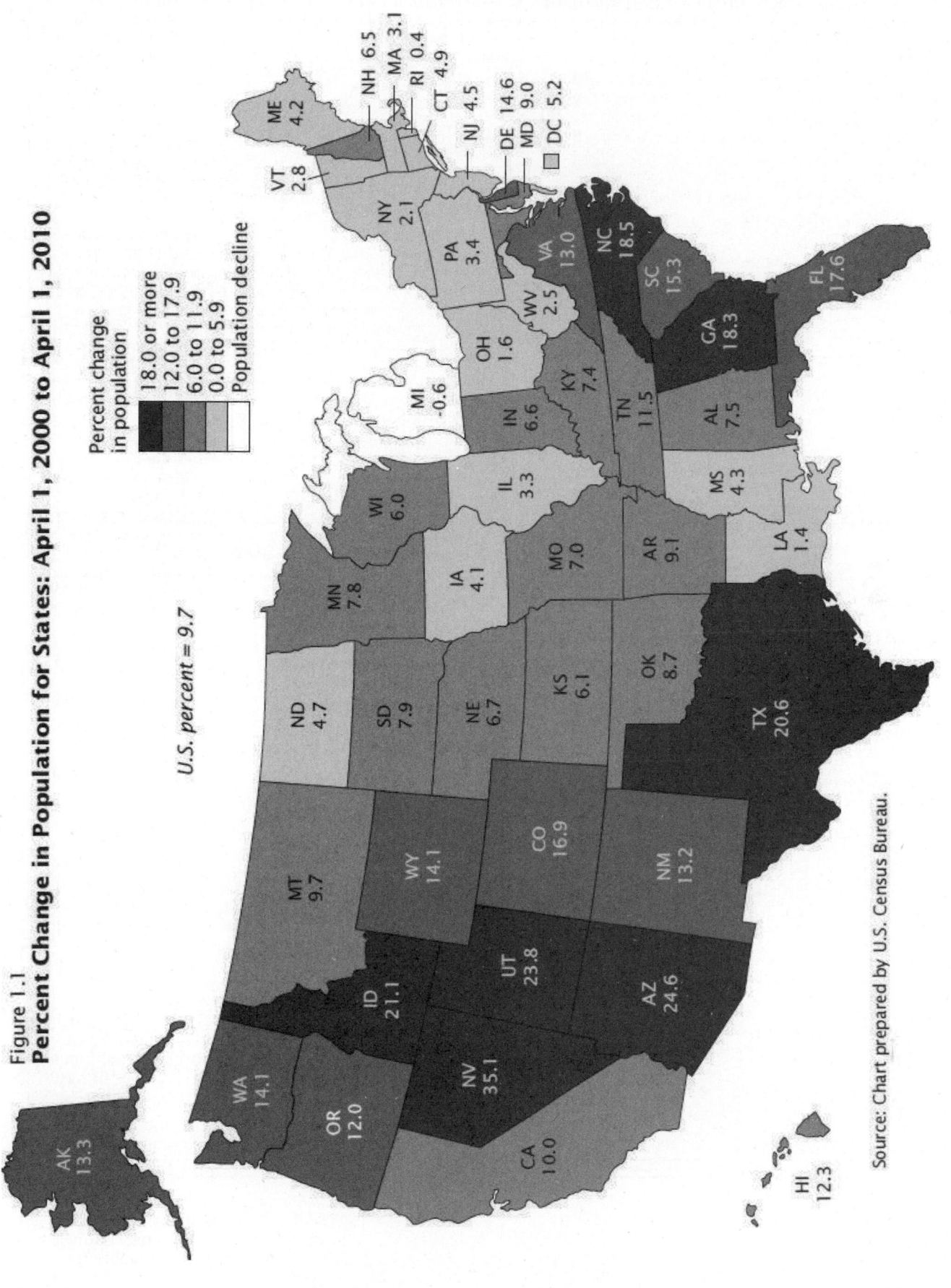

Percent change
in population

- 18.0 or more
- 12.0 to 17.9
- 6.0 to 11.9
- 0.0 to 5.9
- Population decline

U.S. percent = 9.7

AK 13.3
WA 14.1
OR 12.0
NV 35.1
CA 10.0
ID 21.1
UT 23.8
AZ 24.6
MT 9.7
WY 14.1
CO 16.9
NM 13.2
ND 4.7
SD 7.9
NE 6.7
KS 6.1
OK 8.7
TX 20.6
MN 7.8
IA 4.1
MO 7.0
AR 9.1
LA 1.4
WI 6.0
IL 3.3
IN 6.6
MI -0.6
OH 1.6
KY 7.4
TN 11.5
MS 4.3
AL 7.5
GA 18.3
FL 17.6
SC 15.3
NC 18.5
VA 13.0
WV 2.5
PA 3.4
NY 2.1
VT 2.8
ME 4.2
NH 6.5
MA 3.1
RI 0.4
CT 4.9
NJ 4.5
DE 14.6
MD 9.0
DC 5.2
HI 12.3

Source: Chart prepared by U.S. Census Bureau.

Mean Center of Population for the United States: 1790 to 2010

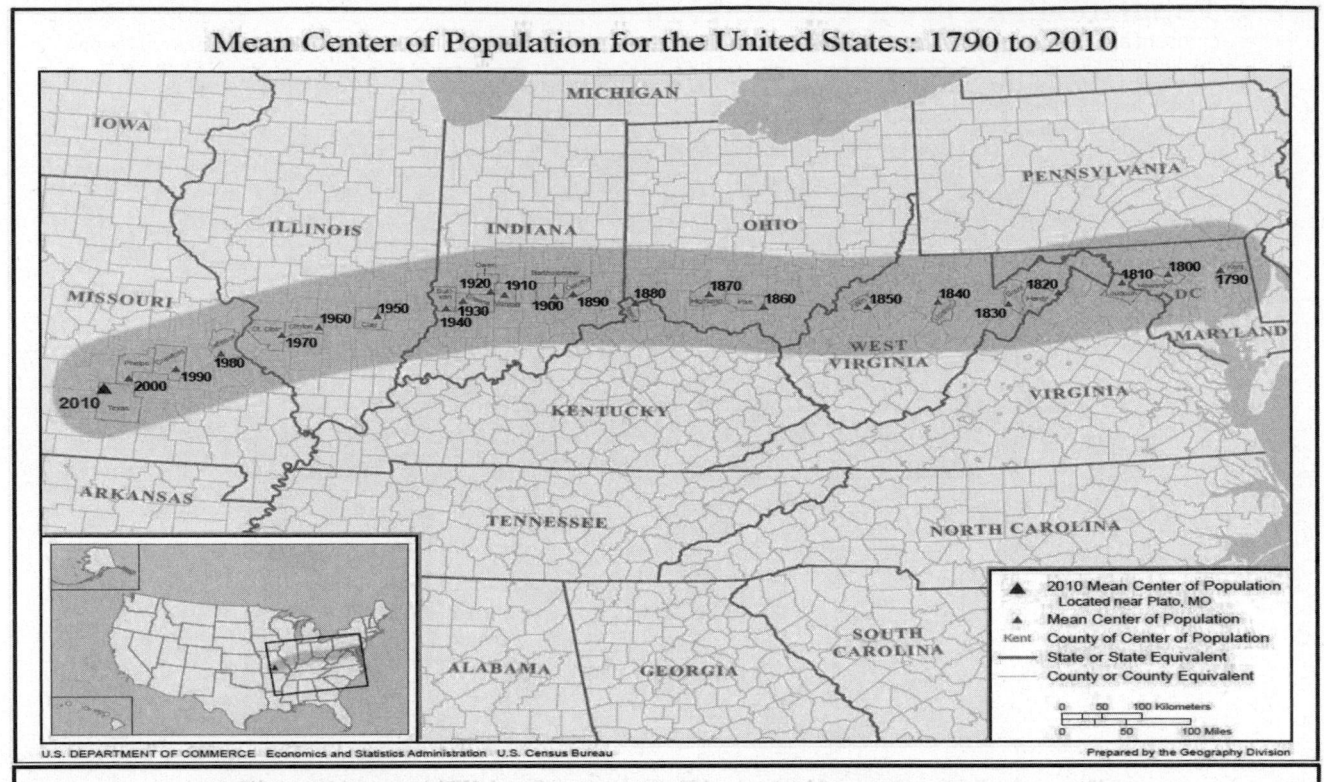

Median Center of Population for the United States: 1880 to 2010

Table 1. Population and Area: 1790 to 2010

[Area figures represent area on indicated date including in some cases considerable areas not then organized or settled, and not covered by the census. Area data include Alaska beginning in 1870 and Hawaii beginning in 1900. Total area figures for 1790 to 1970 have been recalculated on the basis of the remeasurement of states and counties for the 1980 census, but not on the basis of subsequent censuses. The land and water area figures for past censuses have not been adjusted and are not strictly comparable with the total area data for comparable dates because the land areas were derived from different base data, and these values are known to have changed with the construction of reservoirs, draining of lakes, etc. Density figures are based on land area measurements as reported in earlier censuses]

Census date	Resident population				Area (square miles)		
	Number	Per square mile of land area	Increase over preceding census		Total	Land	Water [1]
			Number	Percent			
1790 (Aug. 2)	3,929,214	4.5	(X)	(X)	891,364	864,746	24,065
1800 (Aug. 4)	5,308,483	6.1	1,379,269	35.1	891,364	864,746	24,065
1810 (Aug. 6)	7,239,881	4.3	1,931,398	36.4	1,722,685	1,681,828	34,175
1820 (Aug. 7)	9,638,453	5.5	2,398,572	33.1	1,792,552	1,749,462	38,544
1830 (June 1)	12,866,020	7.4	3,227,567	33.5	1,792,552	1,749,462	38,544
1840 (June 1)	17,069,453	9.8	4,203,433	32.7	1,792,552	1,749,462	38,544
1850 (June 1)	23,191,876	7.9	6,122,423	35.9	2,991,655	2,940,042	52,705
1860 (June 1)	31,443,321	10.6	8,251,445	35.6	3,021,295	2,969,640	52,747
1870 (June 1)	[2] 39,818,449	[2] 11.2	8,375,128	26.6	3,612,299	3,540,705	68,082
1880 (June 1)	50,189,209	14.2	10,370,760	26.0	3,612,299	3,540,705	68,082
1890 (June 1)	62,979,766	17.8	12,790,557	25.5	3,612,299	3,540,705	68,082
1900 (June 1)	76,212,168	21.5	13,232,402	21.0	3,618,770	3,547,314	67,901
1910 (Apr. 15)	92,228,496	26.0	16,016,328	21.0	3,618,770	3,547,045	68,170
1920 (Jan. 1)	106,021,537	29.9	13,793,041	15.0	3,618,770	3,546,931	68,284
1930 (Apr. 1)	123,202,624	34.7	17,181,087	16.2	3,618,770	3,554,608	60,607
1940 (Apr. 1)	132,164,569	37.2	8,961,945	7.3	3,618,770	3,554,608	60,607
1950 (Apr. 1)	151,325,798	42.6	19,161,229	14.5	3,618,770	3,552,206	63,005
1960 (Apr. 1)	179,323,175	50.6	27,997,377	18.5	3,618,770	3,540,911	74,212
1970 (Apr. 1)	203,302,031	57.5	23,978,856	13.4	3,618,770	3,536,855	78,444
1980 (Apr. 1)	[3] 226,542,199	64.0	23,240,168	11.4	3,618,770	3,539,289	79,481
1990 (Apr. 1)	[4] 248,718,302	70.3	22,176,103	9.8	[5] 3,717,796	3,536,278	[5] 181,518
2000 (Apr. 1)	[6] 281,424,603	79.6	32,706,301	13.1	3,794,083	3,537,438	256,645
2010 (Apr. 1)	[7] 308,746,065	87.4	27,321,462	9.7	3,796,742	3,531,905	264,837

X Not applicable. [1] Data for 1790 to 1980 cover inland water only. Data for 1990 comprise Great Lakes, inland, and coastal water. Data for 2000 and 2010 comprise Great Lakes, inland, territorial, and coastal water. [2] Revised to include adjustments for underenumeration in southern states; unrevised number is 38,558,371 (10.9 per square mile). [3] Total population count has been revised since the 1980 census publications. Numbers by age, race, Hispanic origin, and sex have not been corrected. [4] The April 1, 1990, census count includes count question resolution corrections processed through December 1997, and does not include adjustments for census coverage errors. [5] Data reflect corrections made after publication of the results. [6] Reflects modifications to the Census 2000 population as documented in the Count Question Resolution program. [7] Reflects modifications to the Census 2010 population as documented in the Count Question Resolution program (updated February 11, 2014).

Source: U.S. Census Bureau, *Notes and Errata, 2010 Census of Population and Housing*, SF/10-1, 2014; 2000 Census of Population and Housing, *Population and Housing Unit Counts, United States Summary*, Series PHC-3-1, and *Notes and Errata*, (2000), SF/01-ER; *Areas of the United States: 1940*; Area data for 1990: unpublished data from TIGER ®; and Davis, Warren, personal correspondence, U.S. Census Bureau, 23 June 2006.

Table 2. Population: 1970 to 2019

[In thousands (205,052 represents 205,052,000). Estimates as of July 1. Civilian population excludes Armed Forces. For basis of estimates, see text, this section]

Year	Resident population, including Armed Forces overseas	Resident population	Civilian population	Year	Resident population, including Armed Forces overseas	Resident population	Civilian population
1970	205,052	203,984	201,895	1996	269,667	269,394	268,108
1973	211,909	211,357	209,600	1997	272,912	272,647	271,394
1974	213,854	213,342	211,636	1998	276,115	275,854	274,633
1975	215,973	215,465	213,789	1999	279,295	279,040	277,841
1976	218,035	217,563	215,894	2000	(NA)	282,162	(NA)
1977	220,239	219,760	218,106	2001	(NA)	284,969	(NA)
1978	222,585	222,095	220,467	2002	(NA)	287,625	(NA)
1979	225,055	224,567	222,969	2003	(NA)	290,108	(NA)
1980	227,726	227,225	225,621	2004	(NA)	292,805	(NA)
1981	229,966	229,466	227,818	2005	(NA)	295,517	(NA)
1982	232,188	231,664	229,995	2006	(NA)	298,380	(NA)
1983	234,307	233,792	232,097	2007	(NA)	301,231	(NA)
1984	236,348	235,825	234,110	2008	(NA)	304,094	(NA)
1985	238,466	237,924	236,219	2009	(NA)	306,772	(NA)
1986	240,651	240,133	238,412	2010	309,741	309,322	308,086
1987	242,804	242,289	240,550	2011	311,974	311,557	310,339
1988	245,021	244,499	242,817	2012	314,168	313,831	312,591
1989	247,342	246,819	245,131	2013	316,295	315,994	314,751
1990	250,132	249,623	247,983	2014	318,577	318,301	317,075
1991	253,493	252,981	251,370	2015	320,871	320,635	319,439
1992	256,894	256,514	254,929	2016	323,161	322,941	321,739
1993	260,255	259,919	258,446	2017	325,206	324,986	323,795
1994	263,436	263,126	261,714	2018	326,924	326,688	325,501
1995	266,557	266,278	264,927	2019	328,476	328,240	327,053

NA Not available.

Source: U.S. Census Bureau, Population Division, data prior to 2010, <http://www.census.gov/programs-surveys/popest.html>; and 2010 to 2019, "Monthly Population Estimates for the United States: April 1, 2010 to December 1, 2020 (NA-EST2019-01)," <https://www.census.gov/data/tables/time-series/demo/popest/2010s-national-total.html>, accessed January 2020.

Table 3. Resident Population Projections and Components of Change: 2020 to 2060

[In thousands, except as indicated (332,639 represents 332,639,000). As of July 1. The 2017 National Projections are based on the July 1, 2016 population estimates, which are based on the 2010 Census. The projections were produced using a cohort-component method and are based on assumptions about future births, deaths, and net international migration. More information on methodology and assumptions is available at <https://www.census.gov/programs-surveys/popproj/technical-documentation/methodology.html>]

Year	Population			Components of change			
	Total	Numeric change	Percent change [1]	Natural increase	Births	Deaths	Net international migration [2]
2020...............	332,639	2,370	0.7	1,360	4,112	2,752	1,010
2025...............	344,234	2,271	0.7	1,241	4,156	2,915	1,030
2030...............	355,101	2,093	0.6	1,028	4,162	3,134	1,064
2035...............	364,862	1,859	0.5	774	4,166	3,391	1,085
2040...............	373,528	1,657	0.5	558	4,196	3,638	1,098
2045...............	381,390	1,529	0.4	424	4,243	3,819	1,106
2050...............	388,922	1,503	0.4	394	4,304	3,910	1,110
2055...............	396,557	1,548	0.4	437	4,359	3,922	1,112
2060...............	404,483	1,609	0.4	491	4,397	3,906	1,118

[1] Percent change from immediate preceding year. For 2020, change from 2019. [2] Net international migration includes the international migration of both native and foreign-born populations.

Source: U.S. Census Bureau, 2017 National Population Projections Tables, "Table 1. Projected population size and births, deaths, and migration: 2016 to 2060 (NP2017-T1)," September 2018, <census.gov/programs-surveys/popproj/data/tables.html>, accessed April 2020.

Table 4. Resident Population Projections and Components of Change Under High, Low, and Zero Immigration Scenarios: 2025 to 2060

[In thousands. 344,234 represents 344,234,000. As of July 1. Data are from the 2017 National Population Projections Project, and are based on the 2010 Census and official population estimates through 2016. For more information, see <https://www.census.gov/programs-surveys/popproj/technical-documentation/methodology.html>]

Year and scenario	Population	Births	Deaths	Natural increase	Net international migration	Year and scenario	Population	Births	Deaths	Natural increase	Net international migration
MAIN SERIES [1]						HIGH IMMIGRATION					
2025...............	344,234	4,156	2,915	1,241	1,030	2025...............	351,287	4,332	2,929	1,403	1,706
2030...............	355,101	4,162	3,134	1,028	1,064	2030...............	366,552	4,421	3,157	1,264	1,736
2035...............	364,862	4,166	3,391	774	1,085	2035...............	380,999	4,484	3,426	1,058	1,755
2040...............	373,528	4,196	3,638	558	1,098	2040...............	394,536	4,564	3,686	878	1,766
2050...............	388,922	4,304	3,910	394	1,110	2050...............	420,202	4,794	3,994	800	1,767
2060...............	404,483	4,397	3,906	491	1,118	2060...............	446,866	5,027	4,039	988	1,763
LOW IMMIGRATION						ZERO IMMIGRATION					
2025...............	339,532	4,039	2,906	1,133	579	2025...............	330,128	3,805	2,887	917	-322
2030...............	347,467	3,990	3,118	871	616	2030...............	332,198	3,645	3,087	557	-279
2035...............	354,104	3,953	3,368	585	638	2035...............	332,587	3,529	3,323	206	-256
2040...............	359,522	3,951	3,606	345	653	2040...............	331,510	3,461	3,542	-81	-237
2050...............	368,068	3,978	3,855	123	671	2050...............	326,358	3,324	3,743	-419	-206
2060...............	376,226	3,977	3,817	160	687	2060...............	319,706	3,135	3,639	-504	-174

[1] Current expected projections.

Source: U.S. Census Bureau, Population Division, "2017 National Population Projections Tables: Alternative Scenarios," <https://www.census.gov/data/tables/2017/demo/popproj/2017-alternative-summary-tables.html>, accessed February 2020.

Table 5. Components of Population Change: 2010 to 2019

[In thousands, except as indicated (308,758 represents 308,758,000). Resident population]

Period	Population as of beginning of period	Net increase		Births	Deaths	Net international migration [2]	Population as of end of period
		Total	Percent [1]				
April 1, 2010 to July 1, 2010 [3].....................	308,758	564	0.2	988	599	174	309,322
July 1, 2010 to July 1, 2011......................	309,322	2,235	0.7	3,973	2,512	774	311,557
July 1, 2011 to July 1, 2012......................	311,557	2,274	0.7	3,937	2,502	839	313,831
July 1, 2012 to July 1, 2013......................	313,831	2,163	0.7	3,941	2,608	830	315,994
July 1, 2013 to July 1, 2014......................	315,994	2,307	0.7	3,963	2,582	927	318,301
July 1, 2014 to July 1, 2015......................	318,301	2,334	0.7	3,992	2,700	1,042	320,635
July 1, 2015 to July 1, 2016......................	320,635	2,306	0.7	3,963	2,703	1,047	322,941
July 1, 2016 to July 1, 2017......................	322,941	2,044	0.6	3,902	2,788	930	324,986
July 1, 2017 to July 1, 2018......................	324,986	1,702	0.5	3,825	2,824	702	326,688
July 1, 2018 to July 1, 2019......................	326,688	1,552	0.5	3,792	2,835	595	328,240

[1] Percent of population at beginning of period. [2] Net international migration includes the international migration of both native and foreign-born populations. Specifically, it includes: (a) the net international migration of the foreign born, (b) the net migration between the United States and Puerto Rico, (c) the net migration of natives to and from the United States, and (d) the net movement of the Armed Forces population between the United States and overseas. [3] The April 1, 2010 population estimates base reflects changes from the Count Question Resolution program and geographic program revisions.

Source: U.S. Census Bureau, Population Division, "Population, population change, and estimated components of population change: April 1, 2010 to July 1, 2019 (NST-EST2019-alldata)," <https://www.census.gov/data/tables/time-series/demo/popest/2010s-national-total.html>, accessed January 2020.

Table 6. Components of Population Change by Race and Hispanic Origin: 2010 to 2019

[In thousands (19,481 represents 19,481,000). Resident population. Covers period April 1, 2010 to July 1, 2019. The April 1, 2010 population estimates base reflects changes to the Census 2010 population from the Count Question Resolution program and geographic program revisions. Responses of "Some Other Race" from the 2010 Census are modified. This results in differences between the population for specific race categories shown for the 2010 Census population in this table versus those in the original 2010 Census data. Minus sign (-) indicates decrease]

Race and Hispanic origin	April 1, 2010 to July 1, 2019				
	Net increase	Natural increase	Births	Deaths	Net international migration [1]
Total...	**19,481**	**11,622**	**36,275**	**24,654**	**7,860**
One race...	17,323	9,672	34,113	24,441	7,651
White...	8,577	5,455	26,221	20,766	3,121
Black or African American............................	3,821	2,594	5,506	2,912	1,227
American Indian and Alaska Native........................	448	408	589	181	40
Asian...	4,345	1,128	1,694	565	3,217
Native Hawaiian and Other Pacific Islander..................	132	86	103	17	46
Two or more races...................................	2,158	1,950	2,162	213	208
Race alone or in combination: [2]					
White...	10,570	7,273	28,213	20,940	3,297
Black or African American............................	5,004	3,690	6,674	2,983	1,314
American Indian and Alaska Native........................	807	740	1,027	287	67
Asian...	5,185	1,848	2,483	634	3,337
Native Hawaiian and Other Pacific Islander..................	280	216	257	41	64
Hispanic [3]..	10,094	7,724	9,342	1,618	2,370
White alone, not Hispanic.............................	-17	-1,073	18,220	19,293	1,057

[1] Net international migration includes the international migration of both native and foreign-born populations. Specifically, it includes: (a) the net international migration of the foreign born, (b) the net migration between the United States and Puerto Rico, (c) the net migration of natives to and from the United States, and (d) the net movement of the Armed Forces population between the United States and overseas. [2] In combination with one or more other races. The sum of the five race groups adds to more than the total population because individuals may report more than one race. [3] Hispanic origin is considered an ethnicity, not a race. Persons of Hispanic origin may be of any race.

Source: U.S. Census Bureau, Population Division, National Population by Characteristics: 2010-2019, "Estimates of the Components of Resident Population Change by Race and Hispanic Origin for the United States: April 1, 2010 to July 1, 2019," <https://www.census.gov/programs-surveys/popest/data/tables.html>, accessed July 2020.

Table 7. Resident Population by Sex and Age: 2000 to 2019

[In thousands, except as indicated (281,425 represents 281,425,000). Census years as of April 1; all others as of July 1. Excludes Armed Forces overseas]

Age	2000 [1]			2010 [1]			2018			2019		
	Total	Male	Female	Total	Male	Female	Total	Male	Female	Total	Male	Female
Total..................	**281,425**	**138,056**	**143,368**	**308,758**	**151,789**	**156,969**	**326,688**	**160,886**	**165,802**	**328,240**	**161,657**	**166,582**
Under 5 years.........	19,176	9,811	9,365	20,201	10,319	9,882	19,763	10,106	9,657	19,577	10,009	9,567
5 to 9 years...........	20,550	10,523	10,026	20,349	10,390	9,959	20,188	10,313	9,876	20,196	10,323	9,873
10 to 14 years.........	20,528	10,520	10,008	20,677	10,580	10,097	20,869	10,654	10,214	20,798	10,618	10,180
15 to 19 years.........	20,219	10,391	9,828	22,042	11,305	10,737	21,065	10,756	10,309	21,055	10,746	10,309
20 to 24 years.........	18,963	9,688	9,275	21,588	11,015	10,572	21,808	11,166	10,642	21,633	11,065	10,568
25 to 29 years.........	19,382	9,799	9,583	21,103	10,637	10,467	23,511	11,993	11,518	23,509	12,005	11,504
30 to 34 years.........	20,511	10,322	10,189	19,963	9,997	9,966	22,099	11,170	10,929	22,431	11,355	11,077
35 to 39 years.........	22,707	11,319	11,388	20,180	10,043	10,138	21,532	10,773	10,759	21,738	10,885	10,853
40 to 44 years.........	22,442	11,130	11,313	20,892	10,395	10,497	19,681	9,781	9,900	19,922	9,907	10,014
45 to 49 years.........	20,093	9,890	10,203	22,709	11,210	11,500	20,719	10,250	10,468	20,398	10,085	10,312
50 to 54 years.........	17,586	8,608	8,978	22,299	10,934	11,365	20,859	10,265	10,595	20,477	10,087	10,391
55 to 59 years.........	13,469	6,509	6,961	19,665	9,524	10,141	21,918	10,659	11,259	21,877	10,642	11,235
60 to 64 years.........	10,806	5,137	5,669	16,818	8,078	8,741	20,307	9,719	10,588	20,571	9,857	10,714
65 to 74 years.........	18,391	8,303	10,088	21,714	10,097	11,617	30,449	14,225	16,224	31,483	14,700	16,784
75 to 84 years.........	12,361	4,879	7,482	13,062	5,477	7,585	15,376	6,721	8,655	15,970	6,998	8,972
85 years and over. ..	4,240	1,227	3,013	5,495	1,790	3,705	6,544	2,335	4,210	6,605	2,376	4,228
5 to 13 years..........	37,026	18,964	18,062	36,860	18,834	18,026	36,892	18,843	18,050	36,830	18,815	18,014
14 to 17 years.........	16,093	8,285	7,808	17,121	8,792	8,329	16,664	8,500	8,164	16,633	8,484	8,149
18 to 24 years.........	27,141	13,873	13,268	30,674	15,663	15,011	30,373	15,547	14,827	30,219	15,452	14,767
18 years and over. ..	209,130	100,996	108,133	234,576	113,843	120,733	253,368	123,437	129,931	255,200	124,349	130,852
55 years and over. ..	59,267	26,055	33,212	76,755	34,966	41,789	94,594	43,659	50,935	96,507	44,574	51,933
65 years and over. ..	34,992	14,410	20,582	40,271	17,364	22,907	52,369	23,281	29,088	54,058	24,074	29,984
75 years and over. ..	16,601	6,106	10,495	18,557	7,267	11,290	21,920	9,056	12,864	22,575	9,375	13,200
Median age (years)..	35.3	34.0	36.5	37.2	35.8	38.5	38.2	37.0	39.5	38.4	37.2	39.7

[1] The April 1, 2000 and April 1, 2010 population estimates bases reflect changes to the Census 2000 and Census 2010 population from the Count Question Resolution program and geographic program revisions.

Source: U.S. Census Bureau, Current Population Reports, P25-1095; "Intercensal Estimates of the United States Population by Age and Sex, 1990-2000: All Months," September 2002, <https://www.census.gov/data/tables/time-series/demo/popest/intercensal-national.html>; and National Population by Characteristics: 2010-2019, "Annual Estimates of the Resident Population for Selected Age Groups by Sex: April 1, 2010 to July 1, 2019," <https://www.census.gov/programs-surveys/popest/data/tables.html>, accessed July 2020.

Table 8. Resident Population by Sex, Race, and Hispanic Origin: 2000 to 2019

[281,425 represents 281,425,000. Data shown are modified race counts; see text, this section]

Characteristic	Number (1,000)					Percent change	
	2000 [1] (April)	2010 [1] (April)	2015 (July)	2018 (July)	2019 (July)	2000 to 2010	2010 to 2019
BOTH SEXES							
Total	**281,425**	**308,758**	**320,635**	**326,688**	**328,240**	**9.7**	**6.3**
One race	277,527	301,774	312,422	317,767	319,097	8.7	5.7
White	228,106	241,945	247,383	249,961	250,522	6.1	3.5
Black or African American	35,705	40,254	42,532	43,732	44,075	12.7	9.5
American Indian and Alaska Native	2,664	3,740	4,004	4,146	4,188	40.4	12.0
Asian	10,589	15,160	17,753	19,134	19,505	43.2	28.7
Native Hawaiian and Other Pacific Islander	463	675	750	794	807	45.9	19.6
Two or more races	3,898	6,984	8,213	8,921	9,142	79.2	30.9
Race alone or in combination with one or more races:							
White	(NA)	248,076	254,647	257,880	258,646	(NA)	4.3
Black or African American	(NA)	43,217	46,162	47,754	48,221	(NA)	11.6
American Indian and Alaska Native	(NA)	6,139	6,611	6,869	6,946	(NA)	13.1
Asian	(NA)	17,677	20,751	22,406	22,862	(NA)	29.3
Native Hawaiian and Other Pacific Islander	(NA)	1,333	1,493	1,584	1,612	(NA)	21.0
Not Hispanic	246,118	258,279	264,380	267,048	267,667	4.9	3.6
One race	242,712	252,675	257,823	259,948	260,394	4.1	3.1
White	195,577	197,326	197,837	197,535	197,310	0.9	0.0
Black or African American	34,314	37,926	39,863	40,861	41,147	10.5	8.5
American Indian and Alaska Native	2,097	2,263	2,371	2,420	2,435	7.9	7.6
Asian	10,357	14,662	17,198	18,545	18,906	41.6	28.9
Native Hawaiian and Other Pacific Islander	367	497	554	586	596	35.4	19.8
Two or more races	3,406	5,605	6,558	7,100	7,273	64.5	29.8
Race alone or in combination with one or more races:							
White	(NA)	202,237	203,631	203,832	203,768	(NA)	0.8
Black or African American	(NA)	40,287	42,739	44,035	44,420	(NA)	10.3
American Indian and Alaska Native	(NA)	4,042	4,266	4,378	4,411	(NA)	9.1
Asian	(NA)	16,795	19,738	21,316	21,748	(NA)	29.5
Native Hawaiian and Other Pacific Islander	(NA)	1,020	1,140	1,207	1,228	(NA)	20.3
Hispanic [2]	35,306	50,479	56,255	59,640	60,572	43.0	20.0
One race	34,815	49,099	54,600	57,819	58,703	41.0	19.6
White	32,530	44,619	49,546	52,426	53,212	37.2	19.3
Black or African American	1,391	2,328	2,670	2,871	2,928	67.4	25.7
American Indian and Alaska Native	566	1,476	1,633	1,726	1,753	160.6	18.8
Asian	232	498	555	589	599	114.2	20.3
Native Hawaiian and Other Pacific Islander	95	177	196	208	211	85.9	18.9
Two or more races	491	1,380	1,655	1,821	1,869	180.8	35.5
Race alone or in combination with one or more races:							
White	(NA)	45,839	51,016	54,048	54,878	(NA)	19.7
Black or African American	(NA)	2,930	3,424	3,719	3,801	(NA)	29.7
American Indian and Alaska Native	(NA)	2,097	2,345	2,491	2,534	(NA)	20.9
Asian	(NA)	881	1,013	1,090	1,114	(NA)	26.4
Native Hawaiian and Other Pacific Islander	(NA)	312	353	377	385	(NA)	23.3
MALE							
Total	**138,056**	**151,789**	**157,856**	**160,886**	**161,657**	**9.9**	**6.5**
One race	136,146	148,362	153,804	156,472	157,131	9.0	5.9
White	112,478	119,703	122,585	123,908	124,192	6.4	3.8
Black or African American	16,972	19,208	20,357	20,945	21,113	13.2	9.9
American Indian and Alaska Native	1,333	1,890	2,020	2,088	2,109	41.8	11.6
Asian	5,128	7,219	8,460	9,128	9,308	40.8	28.9
Native Hawaiian and Other Pacific Islander	235	343	381	402	409	45.8	19.3
Two or more races	1,910	3,426	4,053	4,413	4,526	79.4	32.1
Race alone or in combination with one or more races:							
White	(NA)	122,721	126,180	127,837	128,225	(NA)	4.5
Black or African American	(NA)	20,635	22,125	22,912	23,144	(NA)	12.2
American Indian and Alaska Native	(NA)	3,055	3,290	3,418	3,456	(NA)	13.1
Asian	(NA)	8,468	9,957	10,764	10,987	(NA)	29.7
Native Hawaiian and Other Pacific Islander	(NA)	668	749	795	809	(NA)	21.2
Not Hispanic	119,894	126,169	129,428	130,777	131,086	5.2	3.9
Hispanic [2]	18,162	25,620	28,429	30,109	30,571	41.1	19.3
FEMALE							
Total	**143,368**	**156,969**	**162,779**	**165,802**	**166,582**	**9.5**	**6.1**
One race	141,381	153,411	158,619	161,294	161,966	8.5	5.6
White	115,628	122,242	124,798	126,053	126,330	5.7	3.3
Black or African American	18,733	21,047	22,175	22,787	22,962	12.4	9.1
American Indian and Alaska Native	1,331	1,850	1,984	2,057	2,079	39.0	12.4
Asian	5,461	7,941	9,292	10,006	10,197	45.4	28.4
Native Hawaiian and Other Pacific Islander	227	332	369	391	398	45.9	20.0
Two or more races	1,987	3,558	4,160	4,507	4,616	79.0	29.7
Race alone or in combination with one or more races:							
White	(NA)	125,355	128,467	130,043	130,421	(NA)	4.0
Black or African American	(NA)	22,582	24,038	24,842	25,078	(NA)	11.1
American Indian and Alaska Native	(NA)	3,084	3,321	3,451	3,490	(NA)	13.2
Asian	(NA)	9,209	10,794	11,642	11,875	(NA)	29.0
Native Hawaiian and Other Pacific Islander	(NA)	665	744	789	803	(NA)	20.8
Not Hispanic	126,224	132,110	134,953	136,271	136,581	4.7	3.4
Hispanic [2]	17,144	24,859	27,826	29,531	30,001	45.0	20.7

NA Not available. [1] The April 1, 2000 and 2010 population estimates base reflect changes to the Census 2000 and 2010 population from the Count Question Resolution program and geographic program revisions. [2] Persons of Hispanic origin may be of any race.

Source: U.S. Census Bureau, Population Division, "Table 2. Intercensal Estimates of the Resident Population by Sex, Race, and Hispanic Origin for the United States: April 1, 2000 to July 1, 2010 (US-EST00INT-02)," September 2011, <https://www.census.gov/data/tables/time-series/demo/popest/intercensal-2000-2010-national.html>; and National Population by Characteristics: 2010-2019, Datasets, "Monthly Population Estimates by Age, Sex, Race, and Hispanic Origin for the United States: April 1, 2010 to July 1, 2019," <https://www.census.gov/data/datasets/time-series/demo/popest/2010s-national-detail.html>, accessed July 2020.

Table 9. Resident Population Projections by Sex and Age: 2020 to 2060

[In thousands, except as indicated (332,639 represents 332,639,000). As of July 1. The 2017 National Projections are based on the July 1, 2016 population estimates, which are based on the 2010 Census. The projections were produced using a cohort-component method and are based on assumptions about future births, deaths, and net international migration. More information on methodology and assumptions is available at <https://www.census.gov/programs-surveys/popproj/technical-documentation/methodology.html>]

Age	2020			2025			2030	2040	2050	2060	Percent distribution				
	Total	Male	Female	Total	Male	Female					2020	2030	2040	2050	2060
Total	**332,639**	**163,904**	**168,735**	**344,234**	**169,738**	**174,497**	**355,101**	**373,528**	**388,922**	**404,483**	**100.0**	**100.0**	**100.0**	**100.0**	**100.0**
FIVE-YEAR AGE GROUPS															
Under 5 years	20,439	10,446	9,993	20,868	10,662	10,205	20,976	21,106	21,610	22,144	6.1	5.9	5.7	5.6	5.5
5 to 9 years	20,200	10,325	9,875	20,721	10,587	10,135	21,163	21,311	21,653	22,261	6.1	6.0	5.7	5.6	5.5
10 to 14 years	20,770	10,604	10,166	20,489	10,476	10,013	21,019	21,599	21,761	22,288	6.2	5.9	5.8	5.6	5.5
15 to 19 years	21,038	10,732	10,306	21,221	10,836	10,385	20,960	21,974	22,159	22,527	6.3	5.9	5.9	5.7	5.6
20 to 24 years	21,899	11,199	10,701	21,910	11,175	10,735	22,146	22,510	23,168	23,384	6.6	6.2	6.0	6.0	5.8
25 to 29 years	23,512	12,029	11,483	22,792	11,627	11,165	22,863	22,978	24,115	24,387	7.1	6.4	6.2	6.2	6.0
30 to 34 years	22,979	11,649	11,330	24,147	12,337	11,810	23,480	23,919	24,412	25,155	6.9	6.6	6.4	6.3	6.2
35 to 39 years	21,922	10,990	10,932	23,326	11,805	11,522	24,527	24,041	24,268	25,470	6.6	6.9	6.4	6.2	6.3
40 to 44 years	20,430	10,168	10,262	22,063	11,027	11,036	23,501	24,129	24,664	25,218	6.1	6.6	6.5	6.3	6.2
45 to 49 years	20,105	9,947	10,157	20,412	10,133	10,279	22,061	24,760	24,382	24,680	6.0	6.2	6.6	6.3	6.1
50 to 54 years	20,510	10,110	10,401	19,855	9,775	10,080	20,197	23,336	24,064	24,681	6.2	5.7	6.2	6.2	6.1
55 to 59 years	21,772	10,599	11,173	20,100	9,831	10,269	19,506	21,562	24,327	24,087	6.5	5.5	5.8	6.3	6.0
60 to 64 years	21,011	10,092	10,919	21,105	10,168	10,937	19,565	19,478	22,664	23,525	6.3	5.5	5.2	5.8	5.8
65 to 69 years	18,030	8,492	9,538	19,978	9,471	10,507	20,144	18,312	20,460	23,269	5.4	5.7	4.9	5.3	5.8
70 to 74 years	14,759	6,837	7,922	16,662	7,701	8,960	18,542	17,567	17,744	20,884	4.4	5.2	4.7	4.6	5.2
75 to 79 years	10,053	4,502	5,551	13,001	5,857	7,144	14,768	16,827	15,592	17,725	3.0	4.2	4.5	4.0	4.4
80 to 84 years	6,508	2,765	3,743	8,136	3,491	4,645	10,609	13,690	13,317	13,779	2.0	3.0	3.7	3.4	3.4
85 to 89 years	3,943	1,529	2,414	4,496	1,785	2,711	5,695	8,707	10,252	9,808	1.2	1.6	2.3	2.6	2.4
90 to 94 years	2,017	684	1,333	2,105	744	1,361	2,455	4,269	5,817	5,957	0.6	0.7	1.1	1.5	1.5
95 to 99 years	649	184	465	729	221	508	784	1,257	2,106	2,666	0.2	0.2	0.3	0.5	0.7
100 years and over	92	21	71	120	30	89	140	196	386	589	(Z)	(Z)	0.1	0.1	0.1
SPECIAL AGE CATEGORIES															
5 to 13 years	36,780	18,789	17,992	37,074	18,947	18,128	38,051	38,568	39,049	40,090	11.1	10.7	10.3	10.0	9.9
14 to 17 years	16,748	8,545	8,203	16,712	8,535	8,177	16,625	17,457	17,566	17,903	5.0	4.7	4.7	4.5	4.4
18 to 24 years	30,380	15,526	14,854	30,554	15,591	14,962	30,612	31,369	32,126	32,467	9.1	8.6	8.4	8.3	8.0
16 years and over	267,049	130,396	136,653	278,019	135,900	142,118	287,784	305,159	319,519	333,323	80.3	81.0	81.7	82.2	82.4
18 years and over	258,672	126,125	132,547	269,580	131,593	137,987	279,449	296,397	310,697	324,346	77.8	78.7	79.4	79.9	80.2
15 to 44 years	131,781	66,768	65,013	135,459	68,806	66,653	137,476	139,551	142,786	146,140	39.6	38.7	37.4	36.7	36.1
55 years and over	98,834	45,705	53,129	106,432	49,299	57,131	112,208	121,865	132,665	142,289	29.7	31.6	32.6	34.1	35.2
65 years and over	56,052	25,014	31,037	65,226	29,301	35,926	73,138	80,827	85,675	94,676	16.9	20.6	21.6	22.0	23.4
75 years and over	23,262	9,685	13,577	28,587	12,128	16,458	34,451	44,946	47,470	50,524	7.0	9.7	12.0	12.2	12.5
85 years and over	6,701	2,418	4,283	7,450	2,780	4,670	9,074	14,430	18,561	19,019	2.0	2.6	3.9	4.8	4.7
Median age (years)[1]	38.5	37.2	39.8	39.3	38.0	40.6	40.1	41.5	42.3	42.9	(X)	(X)	(X)	(X)	(X)

X Not applicable. Z Less than 0.05 percent. [1] For definition of median, see Guide to Tabular Presentation.

Source: U.S. Census Bureau, 2017 National Population Projections Tables, "Table 2. Projected age and sex composition of the population" and "Table 3. Detailed age and sex composition of the population," September 2018, <https://www.census.gov/programs-surveys/popproj/data/tables.html>, accessed April 2020.

Table 10. Resident Population by Race, Hispanic Origin, and Age: 2010 and 2019

[In thousands, except as indicated (308,758 represents 308,758,000). 2010 data as of April 1 and 2019 data as of July 1]

Age	Total 2010[1]	Total 2019	White alone 2010[1]	White alone 2019	Black or African American alone 2010[1]	Black or African American alone 2019	American Indian, Alaska Native alone 2010[1]	American Indian, Alaska Native alone 2019	Asian alone 2010[1]	Asian alone 2019	Native Hawaiian, Other Pacific Islander alone 2010[1]	Native Hawaiian, Other Pacific Islander alone 2019	Two or more races 2010[1]	Two or more races 2019	Hispanic origin[2] 2010[1]	Hispanic origin[2] 2019	Not Hispanic White alone 2010[1]	Not Hispanic White alone 2019
Total	**308,758**	**328,240**	**241,945**	**250,522**	**40,254**	**44,075**	**3,740**	**4,188**	**15,160**	**19,505**	**675**	**807**	**6,984**	**9,142**	**50,479**	**60,572**	**197,326**	**197,310**
FIVE-YEAR AGE GROUPS																		
Under 5 years	20,201	19,577	14,691	14,055	3,055	2,958	330	314	948	1,015	59	58	1,119	1,176	5,114	5,094	10,307	9,697
5 to 9 years	20,349	20,196	15,044	14,518	3,013	3,052	321	324	922	1,073	56	58	944	1,171	4,791	5,244	10,885	10,011
10 to 14 years	20,677	20,798	15,399	15,043	3,155	3,140	318	334	922	1,113	54	62	829	1,107	4,525	5,324	11,449	10,461
15 to 19 years	22,042	21,055	16,347	15,424	3,573	3,149	340	325	999	1,158	60	59	723	940	4,532	5,040	12,387	11,038
20 to 24 years	21,588	21,633	16,247	15,809	3,240	3,299	319	323	1,149	1,305	66	60	566	838	4,322	4,845	12,468	11,575
25 to 29 years	21,103	23,509	16,061	16,986	2,912	3,746	300	347	1,279	1,626	64	69	488	735	4,311	4,939	12,269	12,666
30 to 34 years	19,963	22,431	15,185	16,506	2,744	3,262	275	315	1,284	1,709	56	71	420	569	4,125	4,586	11,534	12,488
35 to 39 years	20,180	21,738	15,473	16,227	2,707	3,004	261	297	1,334	1,646	49	68	357	495	3,856	4,510	12,018	12,258
40 to 44 years	20,892	19,922	16,342	14,977	2,752	2,726	251	266	1,188	1,486	45	56	314	410	3,442	4,147	13,250	11,305
45 to 49 years	22,709	20,398	18,103	15,562	2,902	2,728	255	255	1,105	1,447	43	50	302	355	3,022	3,816	15,387	12,149
50 to 54 years	22,299	20,477	18,009	15,977	2,753	2,679	228	241	1,004	1,231	37	46	268	304	2,442	3,312	15,813	13,008
55 to 59 years	19,665	21,877	16,144	17,427	2,246	2,734	177	239	863	1,143	28	43	207	291	1,841	2,849	14,476	14,873
60 to 64 years	16,818	20,571	14,089	16,626	1,715	2,436	134	203	703	1,023	21	35	156	247	1,372	2,228	12,839	14,625
65 to 69 years	12,436	17,455	10,564	14,346	1,181	1,883	89	152	483	863	14	27	105	184	949	1,640	9,694	12,863
70 to 74 years	9,278	14,028	7,911	11,782	865	1,333	60	108	361	653	9	19	72	133	700	1,182	7,266	10,706
75 to 79 years	7,318	9,653	6,341	8,195	625	862	39	67	255	432	6	11	51	85	511	780	5,867	7,480
80 to 84 years	5,744	6,317	5,079	5,375	430	555	25	41	171	287	4	7	35	52	351	527	4,752	4,889
85 years and over	5,495	6,605	4,918	5,690	386	529	19	35	140	294	3	7	30	50	271	509	4,666	5,217
SPECIAL AGE CATEGORIES																		
Under 18 years	74,182	73,039	54,746	52,758	11,317	10,992	1,168	1,166	3,411	3,882	203	213	3,337	4,028	17,131	18,688	39,890	36,683
Under 5 years	20,201	19,577	14,691	14,055	3,055	2,958	330	314	948	1,015	59	58	1,119	1,176	5,114	5,094	10,307	9,697
5 to 13 years	36,860	36,830	27,331	26,523	5,530	5,576	576	592	1,707	1,960	99	107	1,617	2,071	8,426	9,525	20,002	18,337
14 to 17 years	17,121	16,633	12,724	12,180	2,732	2,458	263	260	756	906	45	48	601	780	3,591	4,068	9,582	8,649
18 to 64 years	194,305	201,142	152,388	152,376	25,450	27,921	2,339	2,618	10,338	13,094	436	523	3,354	4,611	30,566	37,246	125,192	119,471
18 to 24 years	30,674	30,219	22,982	22,089	4,719	4,605	459	454	1,579	1,783	92	83	844	1,204	6,154	6,859	17,606	16,099
25 to 44 years	82,138	87,599	63,061	64,695	11,114	12,739	1,087	1,226	5,084	6,466	214	265	1,578	2,210	15,734	18,182	49,070	48,717
45 to 64 years	81,492	83,323	66,345	65,592	9,617	10,577	793	938	3,675	4,845	130	175	932	1,198	8,678	12,205	58,515	54,655
65 years and over	40,271	54,058	34,812	45,388	3,488	5,163	232	404	1,410	2,529	36	71	293	504	2,782	4,639	32,244	41,156
85 years and over	5,495	6,605	4,918	5,690	386	529	19	35	140	294	3	7	30	50	271	509	4,666	5,217
16 years and over	243,288	263,493	193,656	203,848	30,361	34,313	2,706	3,150	12,130	16,076	495	617	3,939	5,489	35,154	43,888	162,310	164,969
18 years and over	234,576	255,200	187,200	197,764	28,937	33,083	2,571	3,022	11,749	15,623	471	594	3,647	5,115	33,348	41,885	157,436	160,627
15 to 44 years	125,768	130,287	95,655	95,928	17,928	19,186	1,746	1,873	7,232	8,929	341	383	2,867	3,987	24,589	28,066	73,925	71,330
Median age (years)[3]	37.2	38.4	39.0	40.2	32.0	34.1	29.0	31.9	35.1	37.2	28.3	32.6	19.1	21.0	27.3	29.8	42.0	43.7

[1] The April 1, 2010 population estimates base reflects changes to the Census 2010 population from the Count Question Resolution program and geographic program revisions. [2] Hispanic origin is considered an ethnicity, not a race. Persons of Hispanic origin may be of any race. [3] For definition of median, see Guide to Tabular Presentation.

Source: U.S. Census Bureau, National Population by Characteristics: 2010-2019, "Annual Estimates of the Resident Population by Sex, Age, Race, and Hispanic Origin: April 1, 2010 to July 1, 2019," <https://www.census.gov/programs-surveys/popest/data/data-sets.html>, accessed July 2020.

Table 11. Resident Population by Race, Hispanic Origin, and Single Years of Age: 2019

[In thousands, except as indicated (328,240 represents 328,240,000). As of July 1. For derivation of estimates, see text, this section]

Age	Total	Race						Hispanic origin [1]	Non-Hispanic White alone
		White alone	Black or African American alone	American Indian, Alaska Native alone	Asian alone	Native Hawaiian and Other Pacific Islander alone	Two or more races		
Total..............	328,240	250,522	44,075	4,188	19,505	807	9,142	60,572	197,310
Under 5 years old.............	19,577	14,055	2,958	314	1,015	58	1,176	5,094	9,697
Under 1 year old.............	3,783	2,722	571	61	186	11	231	983	1,882
1 year old.................	3,830	2,755	578	62	194	11	230	994	1,904
2 years old.................	3,922	2,817	592	63	203	12	235	1,020	1,945
3 years old.................	3,999	2,868	605	64	211	12	239	1,049	1,970
4 years old.................	4,043	2,894	612	65	221	12	241	1,048	1,997
5 to 9 years old.............	20,196	14,518	3,052	324	1,073	58	1,171	5,244	10,011
5 years old.................	4,028	2,887	611	65	216	12	238	1,037	2,000
6 years old.................	4,017	2,878	608	65	220	12	235	1,034	1,991
7 years old.................	4,022	2,894	608	66	212	11	231	1,041	1,999
8 years old.................	4,066	2,941	612	64	207	11	231	1,069	2,015
9 years old.................	4,062	2,917	613	65	218	12	236	1,063	2,006
10 to 14 years old.............	20,798	15,043	3,140	334	1,113	62	1,107	5,324	10,461
10 years old.................	4,061	2,915	620	65	218	12	230	1,050	2,017
11 years old.................	4,189	3,013	640	67	226	13	231	1,083	2,083
12 years old.................	4,208	3,042	639	68	222	13	224	1,084	2,109
13 years old.................	4,175	3,035	625	67	221	12	214	1,063	2,117
14 years old.................	4,164	3,037	616	67	226	12	206	1,043	2,135
15 to 19 years old.............	21,055	15,424	3,149	325	1,158	59	940	5,040	11,038
15 years old.................	4,175	3,059	612	65	228	12	200	1,022	2,172
16 years old.................	4,150	3,045	609	64	229	12	190	1,007	2,170
17 years old.................	4,142	3,039	621	64	223	12	184	997	2,171
18 years old.................	4,256	3,114	644	65	237	12	184	1,006	2,238
19 years old.................	4,330	3,166	663	66	241	12	182	1,008	2,287
20 to 24 years old.............	21,633	15,809	3,299	323	1,305	60	838	4,845	11,575
20 years old.................	4,270	3,131	649	65	237	12	177	979	2,277
21 years old.................	4,278	3,130	653	65	247	12	171	969	2,284
22 years old.................	4,299	3,143	653	64	260	12	167	963	2,302
23 years old.................	4,342	3,173	655	64	275	12	163	961	2,332
24 years old.................	4,445	3,232	688	65	285	13	160	973	2,380
25 to 29 years old.............	23,509	16,986	3,746	347	1,626	69	735	4,939	12,666
25 years old.................	4,539	3,284	721	67	298	13	157	982	2,423
26 years old.................	4,611	3,328	742	69	308	13	151	987	2,463
27 years old.................	4,734	3,417	759	71	325	14	149	1,001	2,540
28 years old.................	4,819	3,478	768	71	344	15	144	991	2,614
29 years old.................	4,806	3,480	757	69	351	15	135	978	2,627
30 to 34 years old.............	22,431	16,506	3,262	315	1,709	71	569	4,586	12,488
30 years old.................	4,614	3,350	709	66	351	14	125	928	2,539
31 years old.................	4,502	3,298	665	64	342	14	118	920	2,493
32 years old.................	4,422	3,259	638	62	336	14	112	907	2,464
33 years old.................	4,433	3,285	626	62	338	14	108	913	2,484
34 years old.................	4,460	3,314	623	61	342	14	106	918	2,508
35 to 39 years old.............	21,738	16,227	3,004	297	1,646	68	495	4,510	12,258
35 years old.................	4,316	3,209	595	60	338	14	101	892	2,425
36 years old.................	4,372	3,259	601	61	336	14	102	905	2,463
37 years old.................	4,361	3,257	599	59	333	14	99	906	2,460
38 years old.................	4,306	3,226	593	58	318	13	97	891	2,441
39 years old.................	4,382	3,276	616	60	321	14	96	916	2,469
40 to 44 years old.............	19,922	14,977	2,726	266	1,486	56	410	4,147	11,305
40 years old.................	4,105	3,072	573	55	304	12	89	844	2,328
41 years old.................	4,020	3,023	552	54	295	12	86	839	2,282
42 years old.................	3,975	2,990	544	54	293	11	82	830	2,255
43 years old.................	3,854	2,898	523	52	293	11	78	814	2,176
44 years old.................	3,967	2,993	536	52	301	11	75	819	2,263
45 to 49 years old.............	20,398	15,562	2,728	255	1,447	50	355	3,816	12,149
45 years old.................	3,838	2,896	516	50	294	10	72	782	2,197
46 years old.................	3,889	2,935	530	50	294	10	71	769	2,247
47 years old.................	4,058	3,089	547	51	292	10	70	760	2,408
48 years old.................	4,283	3,296	568	52	284	10	72	754	2,622
49 years old.................	4,330	3,346	567	52	284	10	70	750	2,675
50 to 54 years old.............	20,477	15,977	2,679	241	1,231	46	304	3,312	13,008
50 years old.................	4,097	3,182	525	49	267	9	65	697	2,557
51 years old.................	4,004	3,107	526	48	254	9	61	678	2,499
52 years old.................	4,002	3,130	523	47	234	9	59	650	2,547
53 years old.................	4,069	3,177	540	48	237	9	59	642	2,602
54 years old.................	4,306	3,381	565	50	240	9	60	646	2,802
55 to 59 years old.............	21,877	17,427	2,734	239	1,143	43	291	2,849	14,873
55 years old.................	4,375	3,456	558	49	242	9	60	618	2,902
56 years old.................	4,361	3,456	548	48	240	9	59	588	2,929
57 years old.................	4,342	3,469	539	47	220	9	58	564	2,963
58 years old.................	4,386	3,519	538	47	215	8	57	540	3,035
59 years old.................	4,414	3,527	549	47	225	8	57	539	3,043

See footnotes at end of table.

Table 11. Resident Population by Race, Hispanic Origin, and Single Years of Age: 2019-Continued.
See headnote on page 13.

| Age | Total | Race | | | | | | Hispanic origin [1] | Non-Hispanic White alone |
		White alone	Black or African American alone	American Indian, Alaska Native alone	Asian alone	Native Hawaiian and Other Pacific Islander alone	Two or more races		
60 to 64 years old.............	20,571	16,626	2,436	203	1,023	35	247	2,228	14,625
60 years old................	4,253	3,418	520	44	210	8	53	490	2,978
61 years old................	4,215	3,403	501	42	210	7	52	462	2,988
62 years old................	4,157	3,363	493	41	203	7	50	445	2,964
63 years old................	3,996	3,234	469	39	201	7	47	423	2,854
64 years old................	3,951	3,209	453	37	199	6	45	408	2,841
65 to 69 years old.............	17,455	14,346	1,883	152	863	27	184	1,640	12,863
65 years old................	3,775	3,085	421	34	186	6	42	372	2,749
66 years old................	3,618	2,972	391	32	178	6	39	346	2,660
67 years old................	3,464	2,859	366	30	169	5	36	320	2,569
68 years old................	3,345	2,757	359	28	162	5	34	307	2,479
69 years old................	3,252	2,673	346	27	168	5	33	296	2,405
70 to 74 years old.............	14,028	11,782	1,333	108	653	19	133	1,182	10,706
70 years old................	3,137	2,605	317	26	153	5	31	270	2,360
71 years old................	3,083	2,583	298	24	144	4	29	258	2,349
72 years old................	3,191	2,721	279	23	134	4	29	244	2,499
73 years old................	2,334	1,955	222	18	113	3	22	211	1,763
74 years old................	2,283	1,916	217	17	109	3	21	199	1,735
75 to 79 years old.............	9,653	8,195	862	67	432	11	85	780	7,480
75 years old................	2,198	1,861	199	16	99	3	20	181	1,696
76 years old................	2,222	1,903	192	15	91	2	19	171	1,747
77 years old................	1,911	1,624	169	13	87	2	17	152	1,484
78 years old................	1,721	1,457	155	12	79	2	15	141	1,327
79 years old................	1,600	1,350	147	11	76	2	14	135	1,226
80 to 84 years old.............	6,317	5,375	555	41	287	7	52	527	4,889
80 years old................	1,475	1,254	130	10	68	2	12	123	1,141
81 years old................	1,382	1,176	121	9	63	2	11	114	1,071
82 years old................	1,241	1,055	109	8	57	1	10	104	960
83 years old................	1,151	979	102	7	52	1	9	96	890
84 years old................	1,068	911	93	7	47	1	9	90	828
85 to 89 years old.............	3,897	3,348	322	22	171	4	30	316	3,055
85 years old................	922	787	81	6	41	1	7	77	716
86 years old................	857	733	73	5	38	1	7	69	669
87 years old................	779	671	63	4	34	1	6	63	613
88 years old................	703	609	55	4	30	1	5	57	556
89 years old................	636	549	50	3	28	1	5	51	502
90 to 94 years old.............	1,983	1,721	151	10	85	2	15	147	1,584
90 years old................	536	465	41	3	23	1	4	42	426
91 years old................	467	406	35	2	20	(Z)	3	35	373
92 years old................	394	342	30	2	17	(Z)	3	28	316
93 years old................	321	278	25	2	14	(Z)	2	23	257
94 years old................	264	229	20	1	12	(Z)	2	18	212
95 to 99 years old.............	625	539	47	3	30	1	5	40	501
95 years old................	207	180	15	1	9	(Z)	1	14	167
96 years old................	157	136	12	1	8	(Z)	1	10	126
97 years old................	117	101	9	1	6	(Z)	1	7	94
98 years old................	86	74	6	(Z)	4	(Z)	1	5	69
99 years old................	57	48	5	(Z)	3	(Z)	(Z)	4	45
100 years old and over.......	100	83	9	1	7	(Z)	1	6	78
Median age (years) [2].........	38.4	40.2	34.1	31.9	37.2	32.6	21.0	29.8	43.7

Z Less than 500. [1] Persons of Hispanic origin may be of any race. [2] For definition of median, see Guide to Tabular Presentation.

Source: U.S. Census Bureau, National Population by Characteristics: 2010-2019, "2019 Monthly National Population Estimates by Age, Sex, Race, Hispanic Origin, and Population Universe for the United States: April 1, 2010 to December 1, 2020 (NC-EST2019-ALLDATA)," <https://www.census.gov/programs-surveys/popest/data/tables.html>, accessed July 2020.

Table 12. Resident Population Projections by Race, Hispanic Origin, and Age: 2025

[In thousands (344,234 represents 344,234,000). As of July 1. The 2017 National Projections are based on the July 1, 2016 population estimates, which are based on the 2010 Census. The projections were produced using a cohort-component method and are based on assumptions about future births, deaths, and net international migration. More information on methodology and assumptions is available at <https://www.census.gov/programs-surveys/popproj/technical-documentation/methodology.html>]

Age group	Total	White alone	Black or African American alone	American Indian/ Alaska Native alone	Asian alone	Native Hawaiian/ Other Pacific Islander alone	Two or more races	Hispanic origin [1]	Not Hispanic, White alone
Total........................	344,234	258,778	46,906	4,452	22,181	865	11,053	68,484	198,751
Under 5 years................	20,868	14,437	3,276	320	1,243	54	1,537	5,414	9,853
5 to 9 years.................	20,721	14,523	3,227	319	1,228	56	1,368	5,245	10,074
10 to 14 years...............	20,489	14,628	3,097	325	1,185	63	1,192	5,426	9,988
15 to 19 years...............	21,221	15,261	3,183	336	1,230	63	1,147	5,607	10,429
20 to 24 years...............	21,910	15,916	3,192	332	1,427	62	980	5,538	11,076
25 to 29 years...............	22,792	16,481	3,385	331	1,656	62	877	5,424	11,709
30 to 34 years...............	24,147	17,338	3,765	349	1,853	69	773	5,367	12,610
35 to 39 years...............	23,326	17,034	3,425	324	1,866	73	604	4,905	12,720
40 to 44 years...............	22,063	16,426	3,017	297	1,748	69	507	4,628	12,342
45 to 49 years...............	20,412	15,288	2,793	270	1,570	59	431	4,296	11,484
50 to 54 years...............	19,855	15,060	2,647	249	1,492	50	356	3,875	11,591
55 to 59 years...............	20,100	15,614	2,596	233	1,304	45	308	3,373	12,586
60 to 64 years...............	21,105	16,750	2,616	229	1,181	43	287	2,924	14,124
65 to 69 years...............	19,978	16,122	2,347	196	1,031	35	247	2,304	14,051
70 to 74 years...............	16,662	13,701	1,776	143	835	26	181	1,668	12,192
75 to 79 years...............	13,001	10,903	1,224	98	633	18	125	1,158	9,849
80 to 84 years...............	8,136	6,913	708	55	377	10	73	701	6,271
85 to 89 years...............	4,496	3,830	390	29	205	5	38	393	3,469
90 to 94 years...............	2,105	1,813	175	12	86	2	16	175	1,652
95 to 99 years...............	729	636	57	4	26	1	5	55	585
100 years and over.........	120	104	10	1	4	(Z)	1	8	97
SPECIAL CATEGORIES									
5 to 13 years................	37,074	26,178	5,702	580	2,183	107	2,325	9,560	18,048
14 to 17 years...............	16,712	11,989	2,518	263	954	50	938	4,444	8,166
18 to 24 years...............	30,554	22,161	4,479	469	1,934	88	1,424	7,813	15,353
16 years and over...........	278,019	212,226	36,685	3,422	18,288	680	6,718	51,295	166,820
18 years and over...........	269,580	206,174	35,410	3,289	17,801	654	6,252	49,066	162,684
16 to 64 years...............	212,792	158,204	29,998	2,886	15,091	583	6,032	44,833	118,654
55 years and over...........	106,431	86,386	11,899	999	5,682	185	1,281	12,758	74,875
65 years and over...........	65,226	54,022	6,688	537	3,197	97	686	6,461	48,165
75 years and over...........	28,586	24,199	2,565	197	1,331	36	258	2,490	21,923
85 years and over...........	7,450	6,383	633	45	321	8	60	630	5,802

Z Less than 500. [1] Hispanic origin is considered an ethnicity, not a race. Persons of Hispanic origin may be of any race.

Source: U.S. Census Bureau, 2017 National Population Projections Datasets, "Table 1. Projected Population by Single Year of Age, Sex, Race, and Hispanic Origin for the United States: 2016 to 2060," September 2018, <https://census.gov/programs-surveys/popproj/data/datasets.html>, accessed April 2020.

Table 13. Resident Population Projections for Native and Foreign-Born Populations by Age Group: 2020 to 2060

[In thousands (332,639 represents 332,639,000). As of July 1. Based on 2017 National Projections, see headnote Table 12]

Nativity and age group	2020	2025	2030	2035	2040	2045	2050	2055	2060
Total population..............	332,639	344,234	355,101	364,862	373,528	381,390	388,922	396,557	404,483
Under 18 years................	73,967	74,654	75,652	76,664	77,131	77,561	78,225	79,148	80,137
Under 5 years.................	20,439	20,868	20,976	20,993	21,106	21,319	21,610	21,914	22,144
5 to 13 years.................	36,780	37,074	38,051	38,453	38,568	38,715	39,049	39,532	40,090
14 to 17 years................	16,748	16,712	16,625	17,217	17,457	17,527	17,566	17,701	17,903
18 to 64 years................	202,621	204,354	206,311	210,201	215,571	220,995	225,023	227,794	229,670
18 to 24 years................	30,380	30,554	30,612	30,519	31,369	31,943	32,126	32,229	32,467
25 to 44 years................	88,843	92,328	94,370	95,368	95,067	96,054	97,459	98,727	100,230
45 to 64 years................	83,398	81,472	81,329	84,314	89,135	92,998	95,437	96,838	96,973
65 years and over.............	56,052	65,226	73,138	77,997	80,827	82,835	85,675	89,615	94,676
Native population.............	285,936	293,965	301,318	307,758	313,372	318,497	323,612	329,123	335,150
Under 18 years................	71,353	72,145	73,115	74,088	74,469	74,825	75,425	76,294	77,235
Under 5 years.................	20,153	20,592	20,689	20,697	20,801	21,006	21,292	21,591	21,815
5 to 13 years.................	35,462	35,780	36,770	37,123	37,194	37,303	37,603	38,059	38,592
14 to 17 years................	15,738	15,772	15,656	16,268	16,475	16,516	16,530	16,644	16,828
18 to 64 years................	166,549	166,637	167,354	170,136	174,634	179,178	182,350	184,223	185,264
18 to 24 years................	27,225	27,470	27,588	27,433	28,233	28,732	28,837	28,873	29,053
25 to 44 years................	72,200	75,428	77,224	77,935	77,366	78,041	79,107	79,984	81,113
45 to 64 years................	67,124	63,740	62,542	64,767	69,036	72,404	74,406	75,367	75,098
65 years and over.............	48,034	55,182	60,849	63,535	64,268	64,494	65,838	68,606	72,652
Foreign-born population......	46,703	50,270	53,783	57,104	60,156	62,894	65,310	67,434	69,333
Under 18 years................	2,614	2,509	2,537	2,576	2,662	2,736	2,800	2,854	2,902
Under 5 years.................	285	276	286	296	305	312	319	324	329
5 to 13 years.................	1,319	1,294	1,280	1,330	1,374	1,413	1,446	1,473	1,498
14 to 17 years................	1,010	940	970	949	982	1,011	1,036	1,057	1,075
18 to 64 years................	36,072	37,717	38,957	40,066	40,936	41,817	42,673	43,571	44,406
18 to 24 years................	3,155	3,084	3,024	3,086	3,136	3,211	3,289	3,356	3,415
25 to 44 years................	16,643	16,900	17,146	17,433	17,701	18,013	18,352	18,744	19,117
45 to 64 years................	16,273	17,732	18,787	19,547	20,099	20,593	21,031	21,472	21,875
65 years and over.............	8,017	10,044	12,289	14,462	16,559	18,341	19,837	21,009	22,024

Source: U.S. Census Bureau, 2017 National Population Projections Tables, "Table 2. Projected age and sex composition of the population," "Table 9. Age composition of the native-born population," and "Table 10. Age composition of the foreign-born population," September 2018, <https://www.census.gov/programs-surveys/popproj/data/tables.html>, accessed April 2020.

Table 14. Resident Population Projections by Race and Hispanic Origin: 2020 to 2060

[In thousands, except as indicated (332,639 represents 332,639,000). As of July 1. Data shown are modified race counts; see text, this section. The 2017 National Projections are based on the July 1, 2016 population estimates, which are based on the 2010 Census. The projections were produced using a cohort-component method and are based on assumptions about future births, deaths, and net international migration. More information on methodology and assumptions is available at <https://www.census.gov/programs-surveys/popproj/technical-documentation/methodology.html>]

Characteristic	2020	2025	2030	2035	2040	2045	2050	2060
Total	**332,639**	**344,234**	**355,101**	**364,862**	**373,528**	**381,390**	**388,922**	**404,483**
One race	323,069	333,181	342,432	350,454	357,252	363,105	368,473	379,228
White	253,280	258,778	263,453	267,057	269,578	271,249	272,486	275,014
Black or African American	44,734	46,906	49,009	51,002	52,919	54,814	56,725	60,690
American Indian and Alaska Native	4,232	4,452	4,663	4,859	5,038	5,199	5,341	5,583
Asian	20,009	22,181	24,394	26,579	28,718	30,806	32,850	36,815
Native Hawaiian/Other Pacific Islander	813	865	913	958	999	1,038	1,071	1,125
Two or more races	9,570	11,053	12,669	14,408	16,276	18,285	20,450	25,255
Race alone or in combination: [1]								
White	261,811	268,702	274,901	280,151	284,447	288,035	291,344	298,488
Black or African American	49,137	52,177	55,248	58,303	61,383	64,550	67,855	74,984
American Indian and Alaska Native	7,052	7,485	7,910	8,316	8,699	9,060	9,404	10,059
Asian	23,522	26,253	29,074	31,916	34,764	37,614	40,476	46,250
Native Hawaiian/Other Pacific Islander	1,642	1,784	1,928	2,073	2,220	2,368	2,518	2,823
Not Hispanic	**270,326**	**275,750**	**280,293**	**283,632**	**285,912**	**287,564**	**289,125**	**293,267**
One race	262,710	266,968	270,242	272,225	273,055	273,150	273,030	273,450
White	198,571	198,751	197,992	196,105	193,210	189,671	185,954	179,162
Black or African American	41,702	43,548	45,322	46,978	48,550	50,098	51,664	54,949
American Indian and Alaska Native	2,445	2,514	2,575	2,623	2,659	2,683	2,701	2,722
Asian	19,393	21,516	23,678	25,810	27,895	29,928	31,917	35,779
Native Hawaiian/Other Pacific Islander	599	639	676	710	741	769	795	839
Two or more races	7,616	8,783	10,051	11,407	12,857	14,415	16,094	19,816
Race alone or in combination: [1]								
White	205,358	206,638	207,078	206,480	204,970	202,923	200,821	197,620
Black or African American	45,184	47,720	50,263	52,759	55,247	57,798	60,462	66,233
American Indian and Alaska Native	4,457	4,645	4,822	4,978	5,112	5,233	5,347	5,572
Asian	22,366	24,959	27,630	30,308	32,975	35,630	38,285	43,607
Native Hawaiian/Other Pacific Islander	1,246	1,351	1,456	1,559	1,662	1,763	1,865	2,071
Hispanic [2]	**62,313**	**68,484**	**74,807**	**81,230**	**87,616**	**93,826**	**99,798**	**111,216**
One race	60,359	66,214	72,189	78,229	84,197	89,956	95,442	105,777
White	54,709	60,026	65,461	70,952	76,367	81,578	86,532	95,852
Black or African American	3,033	3,358	3,687	4,024	4,368	4,715	5,060	5,740
American Indian and Alaska Native	1,787	1,938	2,088	2,236	2,380	2,515	2,640	2,862
Asian	616	666	716	769	823	878	933	1,036
Native Hawaiian/Other Pacific Islander	214	226	237	248	259	268	277	286
Two or more races	1,954	2,270	2,618	3,000	3,419	3,871	4,355	5,439
Race alone or in combination: [1]								
White	56,454	62,064	67,823	73,671	79,477	85,112	90,523	100,869
Black or African American	3,953	4,457	4,985	5,545	6,135	6,753	7,393	8,751
American Indian and Alaska Native	2,594	2,840	3,089	3,339	3,587	3,827	4,057	4,487
Asian	1,156	1,294	1,444	1,608	1,789	1,984	2,191	2,642
Native Hawaiian/Other Pacific Islander	396	433	472	514	558	605	653	752
PERCENT DISTRIBUTION								
Total	**100.0**	**100.0**	**100.0**	**100.0**	**100.0**	**100.0**	**100.0**	**100.0**
One race	97.1	96.8	96.4	96.1	95.6	95.2	94.7	93.8
White	76.1	75.2	74.2	73.2	72.2	71.1	70.1	68.0
Black or African American	13.5	13.6	13.8	14.0	14.2	14.4	14.6	15.0
American Indian and Alaska Native	1.3	1.3	1.3	1.3	1.4	1.4	1.4	1.4
Asian	6.0	6.4	6.9	7.3	7.7	8.1	8.5	9.1
Native Hawaiian/Other Pacific Islander	0.2	0.3	0.3	0.3	0.3	0.3	0.3	0.3
Two or more races	2.9	3.2	3.6	4.0	4.4	4.8	5.3	6.2
Not Hispanic	**81.3**	**80.1**	**78.9**	**77.7**	**76.5**	**75.4**	**74.3**	**72.5**
One race	79.0	77.6	76.1	74.6	73.1	71.6	70.2	67.6
White	59.7	57.7	55.8	53.8	51.7	49.7	47.8	44.3
Black or African American	12.5	12.7	12.8	12.9	13.0	13.1	13.3	13.6
American Indian and Alaska Native	0.7	0.7	0.7	0.7	0.7	0.7	0.7	0.7
Asian	5.8	6.3	6.7	7.1	7.5	7.9	8.2	8.9
Native Hawaiian/Other Pacific Islander	0.2	0.2	0.2	0.2	0.2	0.2	0.2	0.2
Two or more races	2.3	2.6	2.8	3.1	3.4	3.8	4.1	4.9
Hispanic [2]	**18.7**	**19.9**	**21.1**	**22.3**	**23.5**	**24.6**	**25.7**	**27.5**
One race	18.2	19.2	20.3	21.4	22.5	23.6	24.5	26.2
White	16.5	17.4	18.4	19.5	20.4	21.4	22.3	23.7
Black or African American	0.9	1.0	1.0	1.1	1.2	1.2	1.3	1.4
American Indian and Alaska Native	0.5	0.6	0.6	0.6	0.6	0.7	0.7	0.7
Asian	0.2	0.2	0.2	0.2	0.2	0.2	0.2	0.3
Native Hawaiian/Other Pacific Islander	0.1	0.1	0.1	0.1	0.1	0.1	0.1	0.1
Two or more races	0.6	0.7	0.7	0.8	0.9	1.0	1.1	1.3

[1] In combination with one or more other races. The sum of the five race groups adds to more than the total population because individuals may report more than one race. The original race data from Census 2010 are modified to eliminate the "some other race" category. [2] Persons of Hispanic origin may be of any race.

Source: U.S. Census Bureau, 2017 National Population Projections Datasets, "Table 1. Projected Population by Single Year of Age, Sex, Race, and Hispanic Origin for the United States: 2016 to 2060," September 2018, <https://census.gov/programs-surveys/popproj/data/datasets.html>, accessed April 2020.

Table 15. Resident Population by Region and State: 1990 to 2019

[In thousands (248,791 represents 248,791,000). 1990, 2000, and 2010 data as of April 1; data for other years as of July 1. Insofar as possible, population shown for all years is that of present area of state. See Appendix III]

State and region	1990, estimates base [1]	2000, estimates base [2]	2010, estimates base [3]	2014	2015	2016	2017	2018	2019
United States	**248,791**	**281,425**	**308,758**	**318,301**	**320,635**	**322,941**	**324,986**	**326,688**	**328,240**
Northeast	50,828	53,595	55,318	56,006	56,035	56,042	56,059	56,047	55,983
Midwest	59,669	64,397	66,930	67,745	67,861	67,988	68,127	68,237	68,329
South	85,456	100,235	114,563	119,624	120,997	122,352	123,542	124,569	125,580
West	52,837	63,199	71,947	74,926	75,743	76,560	77,257	77,835	78,347
Alabama	4,040	4,447	4,780	4,842	4,852	4,864	4,874	4,888	4,903
Alaska	550	627	710	736	737	741	740	735	732
Arizona	3,665	5,130	6,392	6,730	6,830	6,941	7,044	7,158	7,279
Arkansas	2,351	2,673	2,916	2,967	2,978	2,990	3,001	3,010	3,018
California	29,811	33,872	37,255	38,597	38,918	39,167	39,358	39,462	39,512
Colorado	3,294	4,302	5,029	5,350	5,451	5,539	5,612	5,691	5,759
Connecticut	3,287	3,406	3,574	3,595	3,587	3,578	3,573	3,572	3,565
Delaware	666	784	898	932	941	949	957	965	974
District of Columbia	607	572	602	662	675	686	695	702	706
Florida	12,938	15,983	18,805	19,846	20,209	20,613	20,964	21,244	21,478
Georgia	6,478	8,187	9,689	10,067	10,178	10,302	10,410	10,511	10,617
Hawaii	1,108	1,211	1,360	1,415	1,422	1,428	1,424	1,421	1,416
Idaho	1,007	1,294	1,568	1,631	1,651	1,682	1,718	1,751	1,787
Illinois	11,431	12,420	12,832	12,884	12,859	12,821	12,779	12,723	12,672
Indiana	5,544	6,081	6,484	6,594	6,608	6,634	6,658	6,695	6,732
Iowa	2,777	2,927	3,047	3,109	3,121	3,131	3,142	3,149	3,155
Kansas	2,478	2,689	2,853	2,900	2,909	2,911	2,909	2,911	2,913
Kentucky	3,687	4,042	4,339	4,414	4,426	4,438	4,452	4,461	4,468
Louisiana	4,222	4,469	4,533	4,644	4,665	4,678	4,671	4,660	4,649
Maine	1,228	1,275	1,328	1,331	1,328	1,331	1,335	1,339	1,344
Maryland	4,781	5,297	5,774	5,957	5,986	6,003	6,024	6,036	6,046
Massachusetts	6,016	6,349	6,548	6,763	6,794	6,824	6,860	6,883	6,893
Michigan	9,295	9,939	9,884	9,930	9,932	9,951	9,973	9,984	9,987
Minnesota	4,376	4,920	5,304	5,451	5,482	5,523	5,566	5,606	5,640
Mississippi	2,575	2,845	2,968	2,990	2,988	2,988	2,989	2,981	2,976
Missouri	5,117	5,597	5,989	6,056	6,072	6,087	6,107	6,122	6,137
Montana	799	902	989	1,022	1,030	1,041	1,052	1,061	1,069
Nebraska	1,578	1,711	1,826	1,879	1,891	1,906	1,916	1,926	1,934
Nevada	1,202	1,998	2,701	2,818	2,867	2,918	2,970	3,027	3,080
New Hampshire	1,109	1,236	1,316	1,333	1,336	1,342	1,349	1,353	1,360
New Jersey	7,748	8,415	8,792	8,865	8,868	8,871	8,886	8,886	8,882
New Mexico	1,515	1,819	2,059	2,090	2,089	2,092	2,092	2,093	2,097
New York	17,991	18,977	19,378	19,651	19,655	19,633	19,590	19,530	19,454
North Carolina	6,632	8,046	9,536	9,933	10,032	10,155	10,268	10,382	10,488
North Dakota	639	642	673	737	754	754	755	758	762
Ohio	10,847	11,353	11,537	11,603	11,618	11,634	11,660	11,676	11,689
Oklahoma	3,146	3,450	3,752	3,878	3,910	3,926	3,931	3,940	3,957
Oregon	2,842	3,422	3,831	3,963	4,016	4,090	4,144	4,182	4,218
Pennsylvania	11,883	12,281	12,703	12,788	12,785	12,782	12,788	12,801	12,802
Rhode Island	1,003	1,048	1,053	1,056	1,056	1,057	1,056	1,058	1,059
South Carolina	3,486	4,012	4,625	4,824	4,892	4,958	5,021	5,084	5,149
South Dakota	696	755	814	849	854	863	873	879	885
Tennessee	4,877	5,689	6,346	6,541	6,591	6,646	6,709	6,772	6,829
Texas	16,986	20,851	25,146	26,964	27,470	27,914	28,295	28,629	28,996
Utah	1,723	2,233	2,764	2,937	2,982	3,042	3,101	3,154	3,206
Vermont	563	609	626	625	625	624	624	624	624
Virginia	6,189	7,079	8,001	8,311	8,362	8,410	8,464	8,501	8,536
Washington	4,867	5,894	6,725	7,055	7,164	7,295	7,423	7,524	7,615
West Virginia	1,793	1,808	1,853	1,849	1,842	1,831	1,817	1,804	1,792
Wisconsin	4,892	5,364	5,687	5,752	5,761	5,773	5,790	5,807	5,822
Wyoming	454	494	564	583	586	584	579	578	579

[1] The April 1, 1990 census counts include corrections processed through August 1997, results of special censuses and test censuses, and do not include adjustments for census coverage errors. [2] The April 1, 2000 population estimates base reflects changes to the Census 2000 population from the Count Question Resolution program, legal boundary updates, and other geographic program revisions. [3] The April 1, 2010 population estimates base reflects changes to the Census 2010 population from the Count Question Resolution program and geographic program revisions.

Source: U.S. Census Bureau, 1990 Census of Population and Housing, Population and Housing Unit Counts (CPH-2); Current Population Reports, P25-1106; "Table CO-EST2001-12-00 - Time Series of Intercensal State Population Estimates: April 1, 1990 to April 1, 2000," April 2002, <http://www2.census.gov/programs-surveys/popest/tables/1990-2000/intercensal/st-co/co-est2001-12-00.pdf>; "Table 1. Intercensal Estimates of the Resident Population for the United States, Regions, States, and Puerto Rico: April 1, 2000 to July 1, 2010 (ST-EST00INT-01)," September 2011, <http://www.census.gov/data/tables/time-series/demo/popest/intercensal-2000-2010-state.html>; and "Table 1. Annual Estimates of the Resident Population for the United States, Regions, States, and Puerto Rico: April 1, 2010 to July 1, 2019 (NST-EST2019-01)," December 2019, <https://www.census.gov/data/tables/time-series/demo/popest/2010s-national-total.html>.

Table 16. State Population—Rank, Percent Change, and Population Density: 1990 to 2019

[As of April 1, except 2019 as of July 1. Insofar as possible, population shown for all years is that of present area of state. For land area by State, see Table 406. Minus sign (-) indicates decrease. See Appendix III]

State	Rank 1990	Rank 2000	Rank 2010	Rank 2019	Percent change 1990 to 2000	Percent change 2000 to 2010	Percent change 2010 to 2019 [2]	Population per square mile of land area [1] 2000	Population per square mile of land area [1] 2010	Population per square mile of land area [1] 2019
United States.........	(X)	(X)	(X)	(X)	**13.1**	**9.7**	**6.3**	**79.7**	**87.4**	**92.9**
Alabama................	22	23	23	24	10.1	7.5	2.6	87.8	94.4	96.8
Alaska..................	49	48	47	48	14.0	13.3	3.0	1.1	1.2	1.3
Arizona................	24	20	16	14	40.0	24.6	13.9	45.2	56.3	64.1
Arkansas..............	33	33	32	33	13.7	9.1	3.5	51.4	56.0	58.0
California..............	1	1	1	1	13.8	10.0	6.1	217.4	239.1	253.6
Colorado...............	26	24	22	21	30.6	16.9	14.5	41.5	48.5	55.6
Connecticut...........	27	29	29	29	3.6	4.9	-0.2	703.3	738.1	736.3
Delaware..............	46	45	45	45	17.6	14.6	8.4	402.1	460.8	499.7
District of Columbia....	(X)	(X)	(X)	(X)	-5.7	5.2	17.3	9,370.6	9,856.2	11,560.2
Florida.................	4	4	4	3	23.5	17.6	14.2	298.0	350.6	400.5
Georgia................	11	10	9	8	26.4	18.3	9.6	142.3	168.4	184.6
Hawaii.................	41	42	40	40	9.3	12.3	4.1	188.6	211.8	220.5
Idaho..................	42	39	39	39	28.5	21.1	14.0	15.7	19.0	21.6
Illinois.................	6	5	5	6	8.6	3.3	-1.2	223.7	231.1	228.2
Indiana................	14	14	15	17	9.7	6.6	3.8	169.7	181.0	187.9
Iowa...................	30	30	30	31	5.4	4.1	3.6	52.4	54.5	56.5
Kansas................	32	32	33	35	8.5	6.1	2.1	32.9	34.9	35.6
Kentucky..............	23	25	26	26	9.6	7.4	3.0	102.4	109.9	113.1
Louisiana..............	21	22	25	25	5.9	1.4	2.5	103.4	104.9	107.6
Maine..................	38	40	41	42	3.8	4.2	1.2	41.3	43.1	43.6
Maryland..............	19	19	19	19	10.8	9.0	4.7	545.6	594.8	622.8
Massachusetts.........	13	13	14	15	5.5	3.1	5.3	814.0	839.4	883.6
Michigan..............	8	8	8	10	6.9	-0.6	1.0	175.8	174.8	176.6
Minnesota.............	20	21	21	22	12.4	7.8	6.3	61.8	66.6	70.8
Mississippi............	31	31	31	34	10.5	4.3	0.3	60.6	63.2	63.4
Missouri...............	15	17	18	18	9.3	7.0	2.5	81.4	87.1	89.3
Montana...............	44	44	44	43	12.9	9.7	8.0	6.2	6.8	7.3
Nebraska..............	36	38	38	37	8.4	6.7	5.9	22.3	23.8	25.2
Nevada................	39	35	35	32	66.3	35.1	14.1	18.2	24.6	28.1
New Hampshire........	40	41	42	41	11.4	6.5	3.3	138.0	147.0	151.9
New Jersey............	9	9	11	11	8.9	4.5	1.0	1,144.2	1,195.5	1,207.8
New Mexico...........	37	36	36	36	20.1	13.2	1.8	15.0	17.0	17.3
New York..............	2	3	3	4	5.5	2.1	0.4	402.7	411.2	412.8
North Carolina.........	10	11	10	9	21.4	18.5	10.0	165.6	196.1	215.7
North Dakota...........	47	47	48	47	0.5	4.7	13.3	9.3	9.7	11.0
Ohio...................	7	7	7	7	4.7	1.6	1.3	277.8	282.3	286.1
Oklahoma..............	28	27	28	28	9.7	8.7	5.5	50.3	54.7	57.7
Oregon................	29	28	27	27	20.4	12.0	10.1	35.6	39.9	43.9
Pennsylvania..........	5	6	6	5	3.4	3.4	0.8	274.5	283.9	286.1
Rhode Island..........	43	43	43	44	4.5	0.4	0.6	1,014.0	1,018.1	1,024.7
South Carolina........	25	26	24	23	15.1	15.3	11.3	133.5	153.9	171.3
South Dakota..........	45	46	46	46	8.5	7.9	8.7	10.0	10.7	11.7
Tennessee.............	17	16	17	16	16.7	11.5	7.6	138.0	153.9	165.6
Texas..................	3	2	2	2	22.8	20.6	15.3	79.8	96.3	111.0
Utah...................	35	34	34	30	29.6	23.8	16.0	27.2	33.6	39.0
Vermont...............	48	49	49	49	8.2	2.8	-0.3	66.1	67.9	67.7
Virginia................	12	12	12	12	14.4	13.0	6.7	179.2	202.6	216.1
Washington............	18	15	13	13	21.1	14.1	13.2	88.7	101.2	114.6
West Virginia..........	34	37	37	38	0.8	2.5	-3.3	75.2	77.1	74.6
Wisconsin.............	16	18	20	20	9.6	6.0	2.4	99.0	105.0	107.5
Wyoming..............	50	50	50	50	8.9	14.1	2.7	5.1	5.8	6.0

X Not applicable. [1] Persons per square mile were calculated on the basis of land area data from the 2010 Census. [2] Based on 2010 population estimates base that reflects changes to the Census 2010 population from the Count Question Resolution program and geographic program revisions.

Source: U.S. Census Bureau, *2000 Census of Population and Housing, PHC-3-1, United States Summary*, 2004, <http://www.census.gov/prod/cen2000/phc3-us-pt1.pdf>; *2010 Census Briefs, Population Distribution and Change: 2000 to 2010,* March 2011, <http://www.census.gov/prod/cen2010/briefs/c2010br-01.pdf>; and "Table 1. Annual Estimates of the Resident Population for the United States, Regions, States, and Puerto Rico: April 1, 2010 to July 1, 2019 (NST-EST2019-01)," December 2019, <https://www.census.gov/data/tables/time-series/demo/popest/2010s-national-total.html>.

Table 17. State and Region Resident Population—Components of Change: 2010 to 2019

[Covers period April 1, 2010 to July 1, 2019. Minus sign (-) indicates net decrease or net outflow]

State and region	Numeric population change [1]	Births	Deaths	Natural increase (births minus deaths)	Net migration Total	Net migration International [2]	Net migration Domestic
United States	**19,481,418**	**36,275,313**	**24,653,755**	**11,621,558**	**7,859,860**	**7,859,860**	**(X)**
Northeast	664,360	5,810,236	4,469,129	1,341,107	-659,918	1,851,164	-2,511,082
Midwest	1,399,279	7,627,933	5,650,699	1,977,234	-563,388	1,102,655	-1,666,043
South	11,017,418	13,996,064	9,611,294	4,384,770	6,596,570	3,156,088	3,440,482
West	6,400,361	8,841,080	4,922,633	3,918,447	2,486,596	1,749,953	736,643
Alabama	123,060	543,396	473,162	70,234	53,493	39,655	13,838
Alaska	21,296	102,219	39,603	62,616	-42,054	16,537	-58,591
Arizona	886,429	783,281	495,142	288,139	595,848	142,125	453,723
Arkansas	101,773	351,712	285,024	66,688	34,584	23,180	11,404
California	2,257,704	4,529,407	2,366,259	2,163,148	109,506	1,021,544	-912,038
Colorado	729,417	605,216	328,372	276,844	447,573	95,710	351,863
Connecticut	-8,860	333,491	278,652	54,839	-63,899	136,392	-200,291
Delaware	75,827	101,672	78,544	23,128	52,765	13,227	39,538
District of Columbia	103,982	87,527	45,721	41,806	61,065	33,805	27,260
Florida	2,673,173	2,025,141	1,758,886	266,255	2,396,653	1,107,039	1,289,614
Georgia	928,694	1,203,841	720,172	483,669	441,756	188,808	252,948
Hawaii	55,565	169,133	102,353	66,780	-10,429	59,793	-70,222
Idaho	219,408	208,785	117,796	90,989	127,605	14,457	113,148
Illinois	-159,751	1,438,187	976,041	462,146	-622,928	242,945	-865,873
Indiana	248,168	766,932	566,619	200,313	50,242	99,099	-48,857
Iowa	108,199	358,277	268,382	89,895	18,712	47,837	-29,125
Kansas	60,191	355,093	237,958	117,135	-56,737	51,058	-107,795
Kentucky	128,340	510,539	418,202	92,337	36,959	50,229	-13,270
Louisiana	115,307	575,059	403,303	171,756	-57,242	44,961	-102,203
Maine	15,854	116,512	127,285	-10,773	27,507	11,551	15,956
Maryland	271,886	670,809	434,837	235,972	39,003	198,996	-159,993
Massachusetts	344,718	663,370	517,296	146,074	202,992	361,770	-158,778
Michigan	102,741	1,043,213	865,959	177,254	-73,053	193,031	-266,084
Minnesota	335,705	637,356	386,868	250,488	88,161	114,414	-26,253
Mississippi	8,019	352,877	284,210	68,667	-61,248	18,949	-80,197
Missouri	148,478	689,089	540,413	148,676	1,943	62,409	-60,466
Montana	79,371	112,063	88,700	23,363	55,715	6,357	49,358
Nebraska	108,103	241,007	147,237	93,770	14,903	35,100	-20,197
Nevada	379,479	330,058	209,080	120,978	256,952	22,389	234,563
New Hampshire	43,249	114,444	106,519	7,925	36,136	26,296	9,840
New Jersey	90,212	952,425	669,805	282,620	-192,493	298,681	-491,174
New Mexico	37,630	236,548	161,869	74,679	-36,933	26,589	-63,522
New York	75,417	2,177,836	1,419,513	758,323	-681,210	698,000	-1,379,210
North Carolina	952,333	1,111,356	803,520	307,836	639,170	163,662	475,508
North Dakota	89,486	97,654	57,147	40,507	47,388	12,724	34,664
Ohio	152,349	1,274,433	1,070,601	203,832	-46,936	170,595	-217,531
Oklahoma	205,389	480,618	359,899	120,719	84,467	56,503	27,964
Oregon	386,658	415,363	320,779	94,584	291,730	58,232	233,498
Pennsylvania	99,121	1,297,472	1,207,095	90,377	17,332	274,060	-256,728
Rhode Island	6,397	100,094	90,425	9,669	-2,877	36,913	-39,790
South Carolina	523,348	529,164	427,079	102,085	418,191	50,964	367,227
South Dakota	70,461	111,921	69,362	42,559	27,672	14,192	13,480
Tennessee	482,898	744,274	601,021	143,253	338,428	79,086	259,342
Texas	3,849,790	3,584,148	1,713,062	1,871,086	1,964,386	818,757	1,145,629
Utah	442,067	467,200	154,759	312,441	130,203	48,077	82,126
Vermont	-1,748	54,592	52,539	2,053	-3,406	7,501	-10,907
Virginia	534,470	941,699	598,377	343,322	190,438	261,541	-71,103
Washington	890,353	813,809	494,595	319,214	571,023	234,772	336,251
West Virginia	-60,871	182,232	206,275	-24,043	-36,298	6,726	-43,024
Wisconsin	135,149	614,771	464,112	150,659	-12,755	59,251	-72,006
Wyoming	14,984	67,998	43,326	24,672	-10,143	3,371	-13,514

X Not applicable. [1] Total population change includes a residual. This residual represents the change in population that cannot be attributed to any specific demographic component. [2] Net international migration includes the international migration of both native and foreign-born populations. Specifically, it includes: (a) the net international migration of the foreign born, (b) the net migration between the United States and Puerto Rico, (c) the net migration of natives to and from the United States, and (d) the net movement of the Armed Forces population between the United States and overseas.

Source: U.S. Census Bureau, Population Division, "Cumulative Estimates of the Components of Resident Population Change for the United States, Regions, States, and Puerto Rico: April 1, 2010 to July 1, 2019 (NST-EST2019-04)," December 2019, <https://www.census.gov/data/tables/time-series/demo/popest/2010s-national-total.html>.

Table 18. Resident Population by Age and State: 2019

[In thousands (328,240,000), unless otherwise noted. As of July 1]

State	Total	Under 5 years	5 to 14 years	15 to 24 years	25 to 34 years	35 to 44 years	45 to 54 years	55 to 64 years	65 to 74 years	75 to 84 years	85 years and over	Median age (years)	Percent 65 years old and over
United States	**328,240**	**19,577**	**40,994**	**42,688**	**45,940**	**41,659**	**40,875**	**42,449**	**31,483**	**15,970**	**6,605**	**38.4**	**16.5**
Alabama	4,903	294	608	636	647	593	617	658	501	257	92	39.4	17.3
Alaska	732	51	101	96	118	96	85	93	61	23	7	35.0	12.5
Arizona	7,279	430	931	974	1,007	896	852	881	752	411	146	38.2	18.0
Arkansas	3,018	188	393	398	397	370	362	386	303	161	60	38.5	17.4
California	39,512	2,384	5,008	5,181	6,053	5,282	4,980	4,787	3,387	1,702	750	37.0	14.8
Colorado	5,759	332	710	743	913	798	706	713	522	230	90	37.1	14.6
Connecticut	3,565	182	409	479	448	427	477	513	353	186	91	41.1	17.7
Delaware	974	55	114	117	129	113	119	138	113	56	20	41.1	19.4
District of Columbia	706	45	67	88	165	109	74	70	50	25	12	34.2	12.4
Florida	21,478	1,140	2,372	2,461	2,799	2,601	2,709	2,898	2,465	1,451	581	42.5	20.9
Georgia	10,617	657	1,413	1,450	1,493	1,381	1,400	1,308	926	440	151	37.1	14.3
Hawaii	1,416	85	168	166	200	182	168	179	152	75	42	39.6	19.0
Idaho	1,787	116	255	242	236	227	202	218	176	85	30	36.9	16.3
Illinois	12,672	747	1,576	1,653	1,758	1,637	1,600	1,658	1,176	600	267	38.6	16.1
Indiana	6,732	418	879	930	891	829	824	875	637	318	131	37.9	16.1
Iowa	3,155	196	408	436	398	385	363	416	311	163	79	38.5	17.5
Kansas	2,913	185	396	413	383	361	328	372	272	138	66	37.1	16.3
Kentucky	4,468	273	560	584	587	551	564	598	448	221	82	39.1	16.8
Louisiana	4,649	301	608	597	658	590	548	605	443	216	82	37.5	15.9
Maine	1,344	64	140	152	163	154	175	212	169	82	34	45.0	21.2
Maryland	6,046	362	748	751	829	782	795	819	562	278	119	39.1	15.9
Massachusetts	6,893	357	751	935	994	848	894	943	673	337	160	39.6	17.0
Michigan	9,987	566	1,197	1,326	1,312	1,166	1,255	1,400	1,038	515	213	39.9	17.7
Minnesota	5,640	352	733	717	763	726	673	756	531	267	123	38.3	16.3
Mississippi	2,976	183	396	403	394	366	362	386	289	145	52	38.0	16.4
Missouri	6,137	368	770	794	826	754	733	831	610	318	134	38.9	17.3
Montana	1,069	61	129	136	138	130	118	150	125	59	23	40.1	19.3
Nebraska	1,934	131	266	268	255	243	216	242	179	90	43	36.8	16.2
Nevada	3,080	186	392	365	453	411	394	383	303	148	45	38.3	16.1
New Hampshire	1,360	64	143	172	173	157	183	214	153	71	30	43.1	18.7
New Jersey	8,882	515	1,084	1,094	1,152	1,138	1,201	1,224	833	440	203	40.1	16.6
New Mexico	2,097	121	272	278	284	255	236	273	224	112	41	38.4	18.0
New York	19,454	1,127	2,219	2,445	2,868	2,430	2,472	2,597	1,860	976	460	39.2	16.9
North Carolina	10,488	610	1,294	1,387	1,416	1,303	1,364	1,362	1,047	515	189	39.1	16.7
North Dakota	762	54	99	109	115	93	78	94	67	34	19	35.3	15.7
Ohio	11,689	691	1,440	1,507	1,554	1,398	1,448	1,605	1,189	601	256	39.5	17.5
Oklahoma	3,957	256	538	540	544	498	454	494	368	193	74	36.9	16.1
Oregon	4,218	228	492	510	604	569	510	539	465	217	85	39.6	18.2
Pennsylvania	12,802	698	1,476	1,603	1,709	1,514	1,604	1,805	1,354	707	332	40.8	18.7
Rhode Island	1,059	55	113	147	148	125	135	150	106	53	28	40.1	17.7
South Carolina	5,149	292	631	655	683	621	641	689	571	275	91	39.9	18.2
South Dakota	885	61	122	117	115	106	95	117	89	42	21	37.4	17.2
Tennessee	6,829	409	845	869	950	848	871	895	681	340	122	39.0	16.7
Texas	28,996	1,991	4,167	4,056	4,277	3,942	3,554	3,275	2,245	1,081	408	35.0	12.9
Utah	3,206	248	527	518	472	443	328	303	219	108	39	31.3	11.4
Vermont	624	29	64	87	74	71	78	95	75	35	14	43.0	20.0
Virginia	8,536	505	1,040	1,113	1,190	1,112	1,100	1,114	802	402	154	38.6	15.9
Washington	7,615	456	936	929	1,172	1,028	924	960	736	340	135	37.8	15.9
West Virginia	1,792	93	203	217	214	214	229	255	217	110	40	42.9	20.5
Wisconsin	5,822	330	714	768	741	713	715	823	595	294	128	39.8	17.5
Wyoming	579	35	77	75	76	74	64	79	61	28	11	38.4	17.1

Source: U.S. Census Bureau, State Population by Characteristics: 2010–2019, State Population by Characteristics: 2010–2019, "Annual Estimates of the Resident Population for Selected Age Groups by Sex: April 1, 2010 to July 1, 2019,"
<https://www.census.gov/programs-surveys/popest/data/tables.html>, accessed July 2020.

Table 19. Age Dependency Ratios by State: 2000 to 2019
[As of April, except 2019 as of July]

State	Age dependency ratio [1]			Child dependency ratio [2]			Old-age dependency ratio [3]		
	2000	2010	2019	2000	2010	2019	2000	2010	2019
United States.........	**61.6**	**58.9**	**63.2**	**41.5**	**38.2**	**36.3**	**20.1**	**20.7**	**26.9**
Alabama................	62.1	59.9	65.4	40.9	37.9	36.7	21.1	22.0	28.7
Alaska.................	56.5	51.8	59.0	47.6	40.0	39.1	8.9	11.7	19.9
Arizona................	65.7	64.7	68.1	44.2	42.0	37.9	21.6	22.7	30.2
Arkansas...............	65.1	63.4	68.2	42.0	39.9	39.0	23.1	23.5	29.2
California..............	61.1	57.1	59.5	44.0	39.2	35.9	17.1	17.9	23.6
Colorado...............	54.5	54.6	57.5	39.5	37.7	34.4	14.9	16.9	23.0
Connecticut............	62.7	58.8	61.5	40.2	36.3	33.0	22.5	22.5	28.5
Delaware...............	60.8	59.5	67.5	39.9	36.6	35.0	20.9	23.0	32.5
District of Columbia....	47.8	39.3	44.0	29.7	23.3	26.1	18.1	15.9	17.8
Florida................	67.7	62.9	68.4	38.3	34.7	33.2	29.5	28.2	35.3
Georgia................	56.5	57.2	61.0	41.5	40.4	38.0	15.0	16.7	23.0
Hawaii.................	60.4	57.9	67.1	39.2	35.3	35.4	21.3	22.7	31.7
Idaho..................	66.1	66.1	70.5	47.4	45.5	42.8	18.7	20.6	27.7
Illinois...............	61.8	58.6	62.2	42.3	38.7	36.1	19.5	19.9	26.2
Indiana................	62.0	60.7	65.1	41.9	39.9	38.4	20.1	20.9	26.6
Iowa...................	66.6	63.3	68.2	41.8	39.0	38.8	24.8	24.3	29.5
Kansas.................	66.0	63.0	67.7	44.0	41.5	40.3	22.0	21.5	27.4
Kentucky...............	59.0	58.5	64.6	39.1	37.4	36.9	19.9	21.1	27.7
Louisiana..............	63.6	58.6	64.8	44.6	39.1	38.6	18.9	19.5	26.3
Maine..................	61.3	57.6	65.9	38.1	32.6	30.7	23.2	25.0	35.2
Maryland...............	58.5	55.5	61.1	40.6	36.4	35.6	17.9	19.1	25.6
Massachusetts..........	59.2	54.9	57.7	37.6	33.6	31.0	21.6	21.4	26.8
Michigan...............	62.3	60.0	64.3	42.4	37.9	35.3	19.9	22.0	29.0
Minnesota..............	61.9	59.0	65.1	42.4	38.5	38.1	19.6	20.5	26.9
Mississippi............	64.8	62.0	66.2	44.9	41.2	39.0	19.9	20.8	27.2
Missouri...............	64.0	60.8	65.7	41.8	38.3	37.0	22.1	22.5	28.7
Montana................	63.7	59.8	68.6	41.7	36.1	36.1	21.9	23.7	32.6
Nebraska...............	66.3	63.0	68.8	43.8	41.0	41.5	22.6	22.0	27.3
Nevada.................	57.6	57.8	62.8	40.4	38.9	36.6	17.3	19.0	26.2
New Hampshire..........	58.8	54.7	59.9	39.8	33.8	30.0	19.0	20.9	29.8
New Jersey.............	61.4	58.7	62.4	40.0	37.3	35.5	21.4	21.4	27.0
New Mexico.............	65.6	62.4	68.6	46.3	40.9	38.3	19.3	21.5	30.4
New York...............	60.3	55.8	60.4	39.6	34.8	33.2	20.7	21.1	27.2
North Carolina.........	57.3	58.4	63.0	38.4	37.9	35.7	19.0	20.5	27.2
North Dakota...........	66.0	58.2	64.9	41.6	35.2	39.0	24.4	22.9	25.9
Ohio...................	63.2	60.6	65.5	41.5	38.0	36.5	21.7	22.6	29.0
Oklahoma...............	64.1	62.1	67.0	42.4	40.2	40.2	21.7	21.9	26.8
Oregon.................	60.1	57.6	63.2	39.6	35.6	33.5	20.5	21.9	29.6
Pennsylvania...........	65.1	59.8	64.7	39.3	35.1	33.9	25.8	24.6	30.8
Rhode Island...........	61.8	55.5	58.6	38.2	33.1	30.6	23.5	22.5	28.0
South Carolina.........	59.4	58.8	66.1	40.1	37.1	35.8	19.3	21.7	30.2
South Dakota...........	70.0	64.5	71.5	45.6	41.0	42.1	24.4	23.6	29.5
Tennessee..............	58.6	58.8	63.5	39.0	37.4	36.2	19.6	21.4	27.4
Texas..................	61.7	60.4	62.3	45.7	43.8	41.4	16.1	16.6	20.9
Utah...................	68.6	68.2	67.9	54.3	53.0	48.8	14.4	15.2	19.2
Vermont................	58.6	54.3	62.1	38.4	31.9	29.6	20.2	22.5	32.5
Virginia...............	55.6	54.7	60.6	38.2	35.9	35.0	17.4	18.9	25.6
Washington.............	58.5	55.8	60.6	40.7	36.6	35.1	17.8	19.2	25.5
West Virginia..........	60.2	58.6	68.2	35.6	33.2	33.7	24.5	25.5	34.4
Wisconsin..............	62.9	59.3	64.5	41.6	37.5	35.8	21.3	21.8	28.7
Wyoming................	60.7	57.4	67.3	41.9	37.8	38.7	18.8	19.6	28.7

[1] The age dependency ratio is derived by dividing the sum of populations age under 18 and age 65 and over by the population age 18-64, and multiplying by 100. [2] The child dependency ratio is derived by dividing the population under age 18 by the population age 18-64, and multiplying by 100. [3] The old-age dependency ratio is derived by dividing the population age 65 and over by the population age 18-64, and multiplying by 100.

Source: U.S. Census Bureau, Census 2010 Briefs, "Age and Sex Composition: 2010," May 2011; and State Population by Characteristics: 2010-2019, "Annual Estimates of the Resident Population for Selected Age Groups by Sex: April 1, 2010 to July 1, 2019," <https://www.census.gov/programs-surveys/popest/data/tables.html>, accessed July 2020.

Table 20. Resident Population by Hispanic Origin and State: 2019

[In thousands, except as indicated (328,240 represents 328,240,000). As of July 1. Hispanic origin is considered an ethnicity, not a race. Persons of Hispanic origin may be of any race]

State	Number (1,000)				Percent		
	Total population	Hispanic or Latino	Total Non-Hispanic	Non-Hispanic White alone	Hispanic or Latino	Total Non-Hispanic	Non-Hispanic White alone
United States.........	**328,240**	**60,572**	**267,667**	**197,310**	**18.5**	**81.5**	**60.1**
Alabama................	4,903	223	4,680	3,201	4.6	95.4	65.3
Alaska..................	732	53	678	440	7.3	92.7	60.2
Arizona................	7,279	2,311	4,968	3,940	31.7	68.3	54.1
Arkansas...............	3,018	237	2,781	2,174	7.8	92.2	72.0
California..............	39,512	15,575	23,937	14,424	39.4	60.6	36.5
Colorado...............	5,759	1,257	4,502	3,896	21.8	78.2	67.7
Connecticut............	3,565	601	2,964	2,350	16.9	83.1	65.9
Delaware...............	974	93	880	600	9.6	90.4	61.7
District of Columbia....	706	79	626	264	11.3	88.7	37.5
Florida.................	21,478	5,664	15,814	11,437	26.4	73.6	53.2
Georgia................	10,617	1,049	9,569	5,523	9.9	90.1	52.0
Hawaii.................	1,416	151	1,265	307	10.7	89.3	21.7
Idaho..................	1,787	229	1,558	1,458	12.8	87.2	81.6
Illinois.................	12,672	2,220	10,452	7,703	17.5	82.5	60.8
Indiana................	6,732	489	6,243	5,279	7.3	92.7	78.4
Iowa...................	3,155	199	2,957	2,683	6.3	93.7	85.0
Kansas................	2,913	356	2,557	2,197	12.2	87.8	75.4
Kentucky..............	4,468	175	4,293	3,759	3.9	96.1	84.1
Louisiana..............	4,649	247	4,402	2,715	5.3	94.7	58.4
Maine.................	1,344	24	1,321	1,250	1.8	98.2	93.0
Maryland..............	6,046	644	5,402	3,026	10.6	89.4	50.0
Massachusetts.........	6,893	855	6,038	4,898	12.4	87.6	71.1
Michigan..............	9,987	528	9,459	7,465	5.3	94.7	74.7
Minnesota.............	5,640	315	5,325	4,460	5.6	94.4	79.1
Mississippi............	2,976	100	2,876	1,678	3.4	96.6	56.4
Missouri...............	6,137	269	5,869	4,858	4.4	95.6	79.1
Montana...............	1,069	43	1,025	918	4.1	95.9	85.9
Nebraska..............	1,934	220	1,715	1,513	11.4	88.6	78.2
Nevada................	3,080	901	2,180	1,484	29.2	70.8	48.2
New Hampshire........	1,360	55	1,305	1,220	4.0	96.0	89.8
New Jersey............	8,882	1,857	7,025	4,851	20.9	79.1	54.6
New Mexico............	2,097	1,033	1,064	773	49.3	50.7	36.8
New York..............	19,454	3,751	15,703	10,755	19.3	80.7	55.3
North Carolina.........	10,488	1,026	9,462	6,567	9.8	90.2	62.6
North Dakota..........	762	32	731	638	4.1	95.9	83.7
Ohio...................	11,689	470	11,219	9,169	4.0	96.0	78.4
Oklahoma..............	3,957	438	3,519	2,572	11.1	88.9	65.0
Oregon................	4,218	567	3,651	3,165	13.4	86.6	75.1
Pennsylvania..........	12,802	1,000	11,802	9,694	7.8	92.2	75.7
Rhode Island..........	1,059	173	887	756	16.3	83.7	71.4
South Carolina........	5,149	307	4,842	3,278	6.0	94.0	63.7
South Dakota..........	885	37	847	721	4.2	95.8	81.5
Tennessee.............	6,829	391	6,438	5,020	5.7	94.3	73.5
Texas.................	28,996	11,526	17,470	11,951	39.7	60.3	41.2
Utah..................	3,206	462	2,744	2,494	14.4	85.6	77.8
Vermont...............	624	13	611	578	2.0	98.0	92.6
Virginia...............	8,536	834	7,701	5,228	9.8	90.2	61.2
Washington............	7,615	992	6,623	5,141	13.0	87.0	67.5
West Virginia..........	1,792	31	1,761	1,649	1.7	98.3	92.0
Wisconsin.............	5,822	413	5,409	4,709	7.1	92.9	80.9
Wyoming..............	579	59	520	484	10.1	89.9	83.7

Source: U.S. Census Bureau, State Population by Characteristics: 2010-2019, "Annual Estimates of the Resident Population by Sex, Race, and Hispanic Origin: April 1, 2010 to July 1, 2019," <https://www.census.gov/programs-surveys/popest/data/tables.html>, accessed August 2020.

Table 21. Resident Population by Race and State: 2019

[In thousands, except as indicated (328,240 represents 328,240,000). As of July 1]

State	Number (1,000)							Percent distribution					
	Total population	White [1]	Black [1]	American Indian [1,2]	Asian [1]	Native Hawaiian [1,3]	Two or more races	White [1]	Black [1]	American Indian [1,2]	Asian [1]	Native Hawaiian [1,3]	Two or more races
U.S.	328,240	250,522	44,075	4,188	19,505	807	9,142	76.3	13.4	1.3	5.9	0.2	2.8
AL	4,903	3,389	1,313	35	74	5	87	69.1	26.8	0.7	1.5	0.1	1.8
AK	732	477	27	114	48	10	55	65.3	3.7	15.6	6.5	1.4	7.5
AZ	7,279	6,013	377	386	269	20	213	82.6	5.2	5.3	3.7	0.3	2.9
AR	3,018	2,385	473	31	50	12	67	79.0	15.7	1.0	1.7	0.4	2.2
CA	39,512	28,425	2,553	650	6,111	200	1,574	71.9	6.5	1.6	15.5	0.5	4.0
CO	5,759	5,007	264	93	203	11	181	86.9	4.6	1.6	3.5	0.2	3.1
CT	3,565	2,842	435	21	177	4	88	79.7	12.2	0.6	5.0	0.1	2.5
DE	974	674	226	7	40	1	27	69.2	23.2	0.7	4.1	0.1	2.7
DC	706	325	324	4	32	1	20	46.0	46.0	0.6	4.5	0.1	2.9
FL	21,478	16,597	3,634	109	635	25	478	77.3	16.9	0.5	3.0	0.1	2.2
GA	10,617	6,392	3,458	56	464	12	235	60.2	32.6	0.5	4.4	0.1	2.2
HI	1,416	361	31	6	532	144	342	25.5	2.2	0.4	37.6	10.1	24.2
ID	1,787	1,662	16	31	28	4	46	93.0	0.9	1.7	1.6	0.2	2.6
IL	12,672	9,727	1,853	76	748	8	261	76.8	14.6	0.6	5.9	0.1	2.1
IN	6,732	5,710	670	28	175	5	145	84.8	9.9	0.4	2.6	0.1	2.2
IA	3,155	2,859	128	17	84	5	62	90.6	4.1	0.5	2.7	0.2	2.0
KS	2,913	2,514	179	35	93	4	89	86.3	6.1	1.2	3.2	0.1	3.1
KY	4,468	3,910	378	13	72	4	90	87.5	8.5	0.3	1.6	0.1	2.0
LA	4,649	2,919	1,525	37	84	3	82	62.8	32.8	0.8	1.8	0.1	1.8
ME	1,344	1,269	23	10	17	(Z)	25	94.4	1.7	0.7	1.3	(Z)	1.8
MD	6,046	3,539	1,879	37	406	7	178	58.5	31.1	0.6	6.7	0.1	2.9
MA	6,893	5,554	622	34	498	7	177	80.6	9.0	0.5	7.2	0.1	2.6
MI	9,987	7,912	1,408	74	336	4	253	79.2	14.1	0.7	3.4	(Z)	2.5
MN	5,640	4,724	396	77	293	4	146	83.8	7.0	1.4	5.2	0.1	2.6
MS	2,976	1,758	1,125	19	33	2	40	59.1	37.8	0.6	1.1	0.1	1.3
MO	6,137	5,086	726	36	133	10	147	82.9	11.8	0.6	2.2	0.2	2.4
MT	1,069	950	6	71	10	1	30	88.9	0.6	6.7	0.9	0.1	2.8
NE	1,934	1,704	101	29	53	2	45	88.1	5.2	1.5	2.7	0.1	2.3
NV	3,080	2,278	316	52	268	25	142	73.9	10.3	1.7	8.7	0.8	4.6
NH	1,360	1,266	24	4	40	1	24	93.1	1.8	0.3	3.0	(Z)	1.8
NJ	8,882	6,389	1,337	55	887	10	203	71.9	15.1	0.6	10.0	0.1	2.3
NM	2,097	1,717	55	230	38	3	55	81.9	2.6	11.0	1.8	0.2	2.6
NY	19,454	13,547	3,421	190	1,753	27	516	69.6	17.6	1.0	9.0	0.1	2.7
NC	10,488	7,399	2,331	166	334	13	245	70.6	22.2	1.6	3.2	0.1	2.3
ND	762	663	26	42	13	1	18	86.9	3.4	5.6	1.7	0.1	2.3
OH	11,689	9,553	1,526	34	291	7	278	81.7	13.1	0.3	2.5	0.1	2.4
OK	3,957	2,927	308	371	94	9	248	74.0	7.8	9.4	2.4	0.2	6.3
OR	4,218	3,655	94	77	205	19	168	86.7	2.2	1.8	4.9	0.5	4.0
PA	12,802	10,447	1,540	51	482	10	272	81.6	12.0	0.4	3.8	0.1	2.1
RI	1,059	886	90	11	40	2	31	83.6	8.5	1.1	3.7	0.2	2.9
SC	5,149	3,532	1,388	28	94	5	101	68.6	27.0	0.5	1.8	0.1	2.0
SD	885	748	20	80	14	1	22	84.6	2.3	9.0	1.5	0.1	2.5
TN	6,829	5,354	1,164	33	134	7	137	78.4	17.1	0.5	2.0	0.1	2.0
TX	28,996	22,806	3,739	295	1,510	43	602	78.7	12.9	1.0	5.2	0.1	2.1
UT	3,206	2,904	48	50	86	34	85	90.6	1.5	1.6	2.7	1.1	2.6
VT	624	588	9	2	12	(Z)	12	94.2	1.4	0.4	1.9	(Z)	2.0
VA	8,536	5,923	1,697	47	590	10	270	69.4	19.9	0.5	6.9	0.1	3.2
WA	7,615	5,978	332	147	728	60	370	78.5	4.4	1.9	9.6	0.8	4.9
WV	1,792	1,675	65	5	15	1	33	93.5	3.6	0.3	0.8	(Z)	1.8
WI	5,822	5,068	391	69	175	3	117	87.0	6.7	1.2	3.0	0.1	2.0
WY	579	535	7	16	7	3	13	92.5	1.3	2.7	1.1	0.1	2.2

Z Less than 500 or 0.05 percent. [1] Data shown for each race alone. [2] Includes Alaska Natives. [3] Includes Other Pacific Islanders.

Source: U.S. Census Bureau, State Population by Characteristics: 2010-2019, "Annual Estimates of the Resident Population by Sex, Race, and Hispanic Origin: April 1, 2010 to July 1, 2019," <https://www.census.gov/programs-surveys/popest/data/tables.html>, accessed August 2020.

Table 22. Large Metropolitan Statistical Areas—Population: 2010 to 2019

[2010 as of April 1. Covers metropolitan statistical areas with population of 250,000 and over in 2019, as delineated by the U.S. Office of Management and Budget as of September 2018. All geographic boundaries for 2010 to 2019 population estimates are defined as of January 1, 2019. For definitions and components of all metropolitan and micropolitan areas, see Appendix II. Minus sign (-) indicates decrease]

Metropolitan statistical area	2010, esti-mates base [1]	2015 (July)	2019 (July)	Change 2010 to 2019 Number	Change 2010 to 2019 Percent	Rank, 2019
Akron, OH..........	703,196	704,382	703,479	283	–	82
Albany-Schenectady-Troy, NY....................	870,713	879,085	880,381	9,668	1.1	63
Albuquerque, NM.....................	887,063	906,026	918,018	30,955	3.5	61
Allentown-Bethlehem-Easton, PA-NJ............	821,273	830,295	844,052	22,779	2.8	70
Amarillo, TX..............	251,935	261,618	265,053	13,118	5.2	185
Anchorage, AK..........	380,821	398,609	396,317	15,496	4.1	137
Ann Arbor, MI..........	345,163	362,975	367,601	22,438	6.5	147
Asheville, NC..........	424,863	444,593	462,680	37,817	8.9	119
Atlanta-Sandy Springs-Alpharetta, GA............	5,286,718	5,686,048	6,020,364	733,646	13.9	9
Atlantic City-Hammonton, NJ.........	274,525	270,153	263,670	-10,855	-4.0	187
Augusta-Richmond County, GA-SC............	564,893	589,574	608,980	44,087	7.8	95
Austin-Round Rock-Georgetown, TX............	1,716,323	2,002,134	2,227,083	510,760	29.8	29
Bakersfield, CA............	839,621	876,031	900,202	60,581	7.2	62
Baltimore-Columbia-Towson, MD............	2,710,598	2,790,053	2,800,053	89,455	3.3	21
Baton Rouge, LA............	825,917	851,167	854,884	28,967	3.5	66
Beaumont-Port Arthur, TX............	388,749	394,825	392,563	3,814	1.0	140
Birmingham-Hoover, AL............	1,061,039	1,079,752	1,090,435	29,396	2.8	50
Boise City, ID............	616,566	674,640	749,202	132,636	21.5	78
Boston-Cambridge-Newton, MA-NH............	4,552,595	4,778,340	4,873,019	320,424	7.0	11
Boulder, CO............	294,560	318,027	326,196	31,636	10.7	155
Bremerton-Silverdale-Port Orchard, WA............	251,143	259,232	271,473	20,330	8.1	180
Bridgeport-Stamford-Norwalk, CT............	916,904	944,943	943,332	26,428	2.9	59
Brownsville-Harlingen, TX............	406,215	419,450	423,163	16,948	4.2	128
Buffalo-Cheektowaga, NY............	1,135,614	1,133,002	1,127,983	-7,631	-0.7	49
Canton-Massillon, OH............	404,425	402,433	397,520	-6,905	-1.7	136
Cape Coral-Fort Myers, FL............	618,755	699,644	770,577	151,822	24.5	76
Cedar Rapids, IA............	257,948	266,312	273,032	15,084	5.8	179
Charleston, WV............	277,985	270,858	257,074	-20,911	-7.5	189
Charleston-North Charleston, SC............	664,645	745,185	802,122	137,477	20.7	74
Charlotte-Concord-Gastonia, NC-SC............	2,243,963	2,447,898	2,636,883	392,920	17.5	22
Chattanooga, TN-GA............	528,126	547,205	565,194	37,068	7.0	100
Chicago-Naperville-Elgin, IL-IN-WI............	9,461,537	9,552,554	9,458,539	-2,998	–	3
Cincinnati, OH-KY-IN............	2,137,713	2,181,427	2,221,208	83,495	3.9	30
Clarksville, TN-KY............	273,942	292,878	307,820	33,878	12.4	164
Cleveland-Elyria, OH............	2,077,277	2,064,012	2,048,449	-28,828	-1.4	34
College Station-Bryan, TX............	228,668	250,567	264,728	36,060	15.8	186
Colorado Springs, CO............	645,612	697,389	745,791	100,179	15.5	79
Columbia, SC............	767,469	809,136	838,433	70,964	9.2	71
Columbus, GA-AL............	308,478	322,772	321,048	12,570	4.1	160
Columbus, OH............	1,902,008	2,027,568	2,122,271	220,263	11.6	32
Corpus Christi, TX............	405,025	427,621	429,024	23,999	5.9	127
Crestview-Fort Walton Beach-Destin, FL............	235,870	260,814	284,809	48,939	20.7	173
Dallas-Fort Worth-Arlington, TX............	6,366,537	7,042,566	7,573,136	1,206,599	19.0	4
Davenport-Moline-Rock Island, IA-IL............	379,681	383,381	379,172	-509	-0.1	144
Dayton-Kettering, OH............	799,280	800,124	807,611	8,331	1.0	73
Deltona-Daytona Beach-Ormond Beach, FL............	590,288	621,166	668,365	78,077	13.2	88
Denver-Aurora-Lakewood, CO............	2,543,608	2,812,896	2,967,239	423,631	16.7	19
Des Moines-West Des Moines, IA............	606,474	659,522	699,292	92,818	15.3	83
Detroit-Warren-Dearborn, MI............	4,296,227	4,309,673	4,319,629	23,402	0.5	14
Duluth, MN-WI............	290,636	289,741	288,732	-1,904	-0.7	170
Durham-Chapel Hill, NC............	564,193	607,706	644,367	80,174	14.2	92
El Paso, TX............	804,109	835,439	844,124	40,015	5.0	69
Erie, PA............	280,584	278,174	269,728	-10,856	-3.9	181
Eugene-Springfield, OR............	351,705	361,946	382,067	30,362	8.6	143
Evansville, IN-KY............	311,548	314,983	315,086	3,538	1.1	162
Fayetteville, NC............	481,011	511,976	526,719	45,708	9.5	108
Fayetteville-Springdale-Rogers, AR............	440,121	491,730	534,904	94,783	21.5	107
Flint, MI............	425,787	410,461	405,813	-19,974	-4.7	134
Fort Collins, CO............	299,630	333,303	356,899	57,269	19.1	150
Fort Smith, AR-OK............	248,240	248,820	250,368	2,128	0.9	192
Fort Wayne, IN............	388,626	400,806	413,263	24,637	6.3	133
Fresno, CA............	930,507	969,488	999,101	68,594	7.4	54
Gainesville, FL............	305,076	316,031	329,128	24,052	7.9	154
Grand Rapids-Kentwood, MI............	993,663	1,044,842	1,077,370	83,707	8.4	51
Greeley, CO............	252,827	285,819	324,492	71,665	28.3	156
Green Bay, WI............	306,241	315,652	322,906	16,665	5.4	158
Greensboro-High Point, NC............	723,923	751,285	771,851	47,928	6.6	75
Greenville-Anderson, SC............	824,031	872,521	920,477	96,446	11.7	60
Gulfport-Biloxi, MS............	388,591	406,604	417,665	29,074	7.5	130
Hagerstown-Martinsburg, MD-WV............	269,146	278,236	288,104	18,958	7.0	171
Harrisburg-Carlisle, PA............	549,444	564,678	577,941	28,497	5.2	98
Hartford-East Hartford-Middletown, CT............	1,212,471	1,211,748	1,204,877	-7,594	-0.6	48
Hickory-Lenoir-Morganton, NC............	365,794	363,346	369,711	3,917	1.1	146
Houston-The Woodlands-Sugar Land, TX............	5,920,487	6,671,808	7,066,141	1,145,654	19.4	5
Huntington-Ashland, WV-KY-OH............	370,899	367,224	355,873	-15,026	-4.1	151
Huntsville, AL............	417,593	444,542	471,824	54,231	13.0	116

See footnotes at end of table.

Table 22. Large Metropolitan Statistical Areas—Population: 2010 to 2019-Continued.

See headnote on page 24.

Metropolitan statistical area	2010, estimates base [1]	2015 (July)	2019 (July)	Change 2010 to 2019 Number	Change 2010 to 2019 Percent	Rank, 2019
Indianapolis-Carmel-Anderson, IN............................	1,888,075	1,986,119	2,074,537	186,462	9.9	33
Jackson, MS..	587,115	597,928	594,806	7,691	1.3	97
Jacksonville, FL..	1,345,594	1,444,638	1,559,514	213,920	15.9	40
Kalamazoo-Portage, MI....................................	250,327	259,676	265,066	14,739	5.9	184
Kansas City, MO-KS.......................................	2,009,355	2,085,913	2,157,990	148,635	7.4	31
Kennewick-Richland, WA...................................	253,328	278,945	299,612	46,284	18.3	166
Killeen-Temple, TX.......................................	405,308	432,583	460,303	54,995	13.6	120
Kingsport-Bristol, TN-VA.................................	309,493	306,279	307,202	-2,291	-0.7	165
Knoxville, TN..	815,025	837,818	869,046	54,021	6.6	64
Lafayette, LA..	466,733	489,507	489,207	22,474	4.8	114
Lakeland-Winter Haven, FL................................	602,073	648,523	724,777	122,704	20.4	81
Lancaster, PA..	519,443	535,811	545,724	26,281	5.1	104
Lansing-East Lansing, MI.................................	534,684	541,271	550,391	15,707	2.9	103
Laredo, TX...	250,304	269,865	276,652	26,348	10.5	176
Las Vegas-Henderson-Paradise, NV.........................	1,951,268	2,096,717	2,266,715	315,447	16.2	28
Lexington-Fayette, KY....................................	472,103	501,469	517,056	44,953	9.5	109
Lincoln, NE..	302,157	323,090	336,374	34,217	11.3	152
Little Rock-North Little Rock-Conway, AR.................	699,790	730,889	742,384	42,594	6.1	80
Longview, TX...	280,007	283,767	286,657	6,650	2.4	172
Los Angeles-Long Beach-Anaheim, CA.......................	12,828,957	13,234,696	13,214,799	385,842	3.0	2
Louisville/Jefferson County, KY-IN.......................	1,202,686	1,246,231	1,265,108	62,422	5.2	46
Lubbock, TX..	290,889	310,001	322,257	31,368	10.8	159
Lynchburg, VA..	252,654	259,447	263,566	10,912	4.3	188
Madison, WI..	605,466	640,198	664,865	59,399	9.8	89
Manchester-Nashua, NH....................................	400,706	408,985	417,025	16,319	4.1	131
McAllen-Edinburg-Mission, TX.............................	774,764	839,667	868,707	93,943	12.1	65
Memphis, TN-MS-AR..	1,316,102	1,334,790	1,346,045	29,943	2.3	43
Merced, CA...	255,796	266,353	277,680	21,884	8.6	175
Miami-Fort Lauderdale-Pompano Beach, FL..................	5,566,274	5,969,135	6,166,488	600,214	10.8	7
Milwaukee-Waukesha, WI...................................	1,555,954	1,576,496	1,575,179	19,225	1.2	39
Minneapolis-St Paul-Bloomington, MN-WI...................	3,333,628	3,503,728	3,640,043	306,415	9.2	16
Mobile, AL...	430,719	431,294	429,536	-1,183	-0.3	126
Modesto, CA..	514,450	533,211	550,660	36,210	7.0	102
Montgomery, AL...	374,540	373,365	373,290	-1,250	-0.3	145
Myrtle Beach-Conway-North Myrtle Beach, SC-NC............	376,575	431,198	496,901	120,326	32.0	111
Naples-Marco Island, FL..................................	321,522	356,041	384,902	63,380	19.7	142
Nashville-Davidson--Murfreesboro--Franklin, TN..........	1,646,183	1,804,671	1,934,317	288,134	17.5	36
New Haven-Milford, CT....................................	862,442	860,186	854,757	-7,685	-0.9	67
New Orleans-Metairie, LA.................................	1,189,891	1,260,281	1,270,530	80,639	6.8	45
New York-Newark-Jersey City, NY-NJ-PA....................	18,896,277	19,320,968	19,216,182	319,905	1.7	1
North Port-Sarasota-Bradenton, FL.......................	702,312	767,309	836,995	134,683	19.2	72
Norwich-New London, CT...................................	274,070	269,636	265,206	-8,864	-3.2	183
Ocala, FL..	331,299	342,182	365,579	34,280	10.3	149
Ogden-Clearfield, UT.....................................	597,162	640,334	683,864	86,702	14.5	85
Oklahoma City, OK..	1,253,002	1,357,178	1,408,950	155,948	12.4	41
Olympia-Lacey-Tumwater, WA...............................	252,260	267,978	290,536	38,276	15.2	168
Omaha-Council Bluffs, NE-IA..............................	865,347	913,073	949,442	84,095	9.7	57
Orlando-Kissimmee-Sanford, FL............................	2,134,399	2,388,509	2,608,147	473,748	22.2	23
Oxnard-Thousand Oaks-Ventura, CA.........................	823,398	845,802	846,006	22,608	2.7	68
Palm Bay-Melbourne-Titusville, FL........................	543,372	565,746	601,942	58,570	10.8	96
Pensacola-Ferry Pass-Brent, FL..........................	448,991	475,537	502,629	53,638	11.9	110
Peoria, IL...	416,253	412,856	400,561	-15,692	-3.8	135
Philadelphia-Camden-Wilmington, PA-NJ-DE-MD..............	5,965,677	6,056,816	6,102,434	136,757	2.3	8
Phoenix-Mesa-Chandler, AZ................................	4,193,129	4,578,519	4,948,203	755,074	18.0	10
Pittsburgh, PA...	2,356,294	2,347,757	2,317,600	-38,694	-1.6	27
Port St Lucie, FL..	424,107	452,841	489,297	65,190	15.4	113
Portland-South Portland, ME..............................	514,108	525,831	538,500	24,392	4.7	105
Portland-Vancouver-Hillsboro, OR-WA......................	2,226,003	2,381,660	2,492,412	266,409	12.0	25
Poughkeepsie-Newburgh-Middletown, NY.....................	670,280	669,842	679,158	8,878	1.3	86
Providence-Warwick, RI-MA................................	1,601,206	1,612,928	1,624,578	23,372	1.5	38
Provo-Orem, UT...	526,885	583,218	648,252	121,367	23.0	91
Raleigh-Cary, NC...	1,130,493	1,271,091	1,390,785	260,292	23.0	42
Reading, PA..	411,570	415,138	421,164	9,594	2.3	129
Reno, NV...	425,442	446,329	475,642	50,200	11.8	115
Richmond, VA...	1,186,471	1,246,665	1,291,900	105,429	8.9	44
Riverside-San Bernardino-Ontario, CA....................	4,224,948	4,461,227	4,650,631	425,683	10.1	13
Roanoke, VA..	308,666	313,152	313,222	4,556	1.5	163
Rochester, NY..	1,079,704	1,077,092	1,069,644	-10,060	-0.9	52
Rockford, IL...	349,431	340,727	336,116	-13,315	-3.8	153
Sacramento-Roseville-Folsom, CA..........................	2,149,150	2,263,121	2,363,730	214,580	10.0	26
Salem, OR..	390,738	408,022	433,903	43,165	11.0	125
Salinas, CA..	415,059	430,552	434,061	19,002	4.6	124
Salisbury, MD-DE...	373,754	393,526	415,726	41,972	11.2	132
Salt Lake City, UT.......................................	1,087,808	1,164,912	1,232,696	144,888	13.3	47
San Antonio-New Braunfels, TX............................	2,142,520	2,379,232	2,550,960	408,440	19.1	24
San Diego-Chula Vista-Carlsbad, CA.......................	3,095,349	3,280,850	3,338,330	242,981	7.8	17
San Francisco-Oakland-Berkeley, CA.......................	4,335,593	4,647,924	4,731,803	396,210	9.1	12
San Jose-Sunnyvale-Santa Clara, CA.......................	1,836,951	1,974,501	1,990,660	153,709	8.4	35

See footnotes at end of table.

Table 22. Large Metropolitan Statistical Areas—Population: 2010 to 2019-Continued.

See headnote on page 24.

Metropolitan statistical area	2010, esti- mates base [1]	2015 (July)	2019 (July)	Change 2010 to 2019 Number	Change 2010 to 2019 Percent	Rank, 2019
San Luis Obispo-Paso Robles, CA.............................	269,597	280,077	283,111	13,514	5.0	174
Santa Cruz-Watsonville, CA....................................	262,350	273,503	273,213	10,863	4.1	178
Santa Maria-Santa Barbara, CA..............................	423,947	442,229	446,499	22,552	5.3	123
Santa Rosa-Petaluma, CA......................................	483,861	500,863	494,336	10,475	2.2	112
Savannah, GA..	347,597	377,827	393,353	45,756	13.2	139
Scranton-Wilkes-Barre, PA....................................	563,604	557,734	553,885	-9,719	-1.7	101
Seattle-Tacoma-Bellevue, WA................................	3,439,808	3,739,654	3,979,845	540,037	15.7	15
Shreveport-Bossier City, LA...................................	398,606	404,000	394,706	-3,900	-1.0	138
Sioux Falls, SD..	228,264	250,012	268,232	39,968	17.5	182
South Bend-Mishawaka, IN-MI................................	319,203	319,703	323,613	4,410	1.4	157
Spartanburg, SC...	284,304	296,558	319,785	35,481	12.5	161
Spokane-Spokane Valley, WA.................................	514,752	532,163	568,521	53,769	10.4	99
Springfield, MA..	693,059	700,688	697,382	4,323	0.6	84
Springfield, MO..	436,756	455,593	470,300	33,544	7.7	117
St Louis, MO-IL...	2,787,751	2,807,503	2,803,228	15,477	0.6	20
Stockton, CA...	685,306	722,271	762,148	76,842	11.2	77
Syracuse, NY...	662,624	657,648	648,593	-14,031	-2.1	90
Tallahassee, FL..	368,771	377,602	387,227	18,456	5.0	141
Tampa-St Petersburg-Clearwater, FL.......................	2,783,485	2,983,928	3,194,831	411,346	14.8	18
Toledo, OH..	651,435	645,973	641,816	-9,619	-1.5	93
Trenton-Princeton, NJ...	367,485	368,124	367,430	-55	–	148
Tucson, AZ..	980,263	1,009,103	1,047,279	67,016	6.8	53
Tulsa, OK..	937,523	980,926	998,626	61,103	6.5	55
Tuscaloosa, AL...	239,214	249,066	252,047	12,833	5.4	190
Urban Honolulu, HI..	953,206	991,064	974,563	21,357	2.2	56
Utica-Rome, NY..	299,329	293,916	289,990	-9,339	-3.1	169
Vallejo, CA..	413,343	433,409	447,643	34,300	8.3	122
Virginia Beach-Norfolk-Newport News, VA-NC.............	1,713,955	1,756,340	1,768,901	54,946	3.2	37
Visalia, CA..	442,182	457,161	466,195	24,013	5.4	118
Waco, TX..	252,766	262,660	273,920	21,154	8.4	177
Washington-Arlington-Alexandria, DC-VA-MD-WV..........	5,649,688	6,093,950	6,280,487	630,799	11.2	6
Wichita, KS...	623,061	635,551	640,218	17,157	2.8	94
Wilmington, NC..	254,879	276,848	297,533	42,654	16.7	167
Winston-Salem, NC...	640,503	656,277	676,008	35,505	5.5	87
Worcester, MA-CT..	916,763	934,604	947,404	30,641	3.3	58
Yakima, WA...	243,240	247,800	250,873	7,633	3.1	191
York-Hanover, PA...	435,015	441,741	449,058	14,043	3.2	121
Youngstown-Warren-Boardman, OH-PA.....................	565,782	548,798	536,081	-29,701	-5.2	106

– Represents or rounds to zero. [1] The April 1, 2010 population estimates base reflects changes to the Census 2010 population from the Count Question Resolution program and geographic program revisions.

Source: U.S. Census Bureau, Metropolitan and Micropolitan Statistical Areas Totals: 2010-2019, "Annual Estimates of the Resident Population: April 1, 2010 to July 1, 2019," and "Cumulative Estimates of Resident Population Change and Rankings: April 1, 2010 to July 1, 2019," March 2020, <census.gov/programs-surveys/popest/data/tables.html>, accessed April 2020.

Table 23. The 50 Largest Metropolitan Statistical Areas in 2019—Components of Population Change: 2010 to 2019

[Covers period April 1, 2010 to July 1, 2019. Covers metropolitan statistical areas as delineated by the U.S. Office of Management and Budget as of September 2018. For definitions and components of all metropolitan and micropolitan areas, see Appendix II. Minus sign (-) indicates decrease or outmigration]

Metropolitan statistical area	Number							Percent change
		Natural increase			Net migration			
	Total change [1]	Total	Births	Deaths	Total	International	Domestic migration	
Atlanta-Sandy Springs-Alpharetta, GA..........	733,646	343,765	673,437	329,672	389,077	144,048	245,029	13.9
Austin-Round Rock-Georgetown, TX...........	510,760	149,806	239,673	89,867	355,902	62,740	293,162	29.8
Baltimore-Columbia-Towson, MD...............	89,455	85,415	309,615	224,200	5,900	63,529	-57,629	3.3
Birmingham-Hoover, AL.......................	29,396	26,658	126,000	99,342	3,387	8,320	-4,933	2.8
Boston-Cambridge-Newton, MA-NH............	320,424	141,612	475,777	334,165	182,147	285,199	-103,052	7.0
Buffalo-Cheektowaga, NY.....................	-7,631	-4	111,885	111,889	-6,892	24,110	-31,002	-0.7
Charlotte-Concord-Gastonia, NC-SC..........	392,920	110,931	281,325	170,394	280,220	49,640	230,580	17.5
Chicago-Naperville-Elgin, IL-IN-WI.............	-2,998	438,246	1,085,985	647,739	-441,506	197,093	-638,599	(-Z)
Cincinnati, OH-KY-IN.........................	83,495	73,617	253,180	179,563	11,213	31,157	-19,944	3.9
Cleveland-Elyria, OH.........................	-28,828	14,479	212,523	198,044	-42,445	36,318	-78,763	-1.4
Columbus, OH................................	220,263	108,626	251,291	142,665	112,154	58,853	53,301	11.6
Dallas-Fort Worth-Arlington, TX................	1,206,599	517,590	903,051	385,461	686,884	237,927	448,957	19.0
Denver-Aurora-Lakewood, CO.................	423,631	162,267	320,151	157,884	257,992	61,997	195,995	16.7
Detroit-Warren-Dearborn, MI.................	23,402	84,753	462,696	377,943	-61,318	110,907	-172,225	0.5
Hartford-East Hartford-Middletown, CT.........	-7,594	13,025	110,209	97,184	-20,759	47,395	-68,154	-0.6
Houston-The Woodlands-Sugar Land, TX......	1,145,654	540,027	889,610	349,583	602,610	333,553	269,057	19.4
Indianapolis-Carmel-Anderson, IN.............	186,462	97,491	246,099	148,608	89,578	43,502	46,076	9.9
Jacksonville, FL..............................	213,920	52,866	167,526	114,660	160,572	34,089	126,483	15.9
Kansas City, MO-KS..........................	148,635	98,218	253,384	155,166	51,716	27,259	24,457	7.4
Las Vegas-Henderson-Paradise, NV...........	315,447	105,372	247,787	142,415	208,889	23,319	185,570	16.2
Los Angeles-Long Beach-Anaheim, CA........	385,842	753,642	1,500,780	747,138	-362,998	377,442	-740,440	3.0
Louisville/Jefferson County, KY-IN..............	62,422	31,671	141,702	110,031	31,536	20,169	11,367	5.2
Memphis, TN-MS-AR..........................	29,943	64,370	170,921	106,551	-34,521	13,637	-48,158	2.3
Miami-Fort Lauderdale-Pompano Beach, FL...	600,214	178,095	626,897	448,802	422,703	615,283	-192,580	10.8
Milwaukee-Waukesha, WI......................	19,225	59,009	182,815	123,806	-39,097	25,298	-64,395	1.2
Minneapolis-St Paul-Bloomington, MN-WI.....	306,415	209,124	419,634	210,510	99,485	87,847	11,638	9.2
Nashville-Davidson-Murfreesboro-Franklin, TN....................................	288,134	88,741	216,969	128,228	197,758	39,422	158,336	17.5
New Orleans-Metairie, LA......................	80,639	43,608	145,792	102,184	36,032	20,800	15,232	6.8
New York-Newark-Jersey City, NY-NJ-PA......	319,905	932,102	2,218,113	1,286,011	-611,662	837,005	-1,448,667	1.7
Oklahoma City, OK...........................	155,948	65,613	171,439	105,826	89,914	24,684	65,230	12.4
Orlando-Kissimmee-Sanford, FL................	473,748	103,875	259,676	155,801	368,588	181,996	186,592	22.2
Philadelphia-Camden-Wilmington, PA-NJ-DE-MD.	136,757	155,315	658,315	503,000	-14,959	156,632	-171,591	2.3
Phoenix-Mesa-Chandler, AZ....................	755,074	247,209	540,924	293,715	505,500	106,785	398,715	18.0
Pittsburgh, PA................................	-38,694	-35,527	218,159	253,686	-1,150	30,654	-31,804	-1.6
Portland-Vancouver-Hillsboro, OR-WA.........	266,409	96,518	253,110	156,592	169,456	47,983	121,473	12.0
Providence-Warwick, RI-MA....................	23,372	13,788	152,794	139,006	10,512.0	49,015	-38,503	1.5
Raleigh-Cary, NC.............................	260,292	78,009	144,250	66,241	180,756	34,019	146,737	23.0
Richmond, VA................................	105,429	39,426	135,249	95,823	66,135	27,868	38,267	8.9
Riverside-San Bernardino-Ontario, CA........	425,683	289,072	560,691	271,619	138,230	26,965	111,265	10.1
Sacramento-Roseville-Folsom, CA.............	214,580	94,910	252,144	157,234	120,948	51,225	69,723	10.0
Salt Lake City, UT............................	144,888	109,213	171,087	61,874	36,389	31,265	5,124	13.3
San Antonio-New Braunfels, TX................	408,440	146,693	300,032	153,339	259,857	45,348	214,509	19.1
San Diego-Chula Vista-Carlsbad, CA..........	242,981	204,933	398,611	193,678	40,821	107,098	-66,277	7.8
San Francisco-Oakland-Berkeley, CA..........	396,210	202,172	477,380	275,208	194,735	231,599	-36,864	9.1
San Jose-Sunnyvale-Santa Clara, CA..........	153,709	126,304	220,891	94,587	28,415	152,520	-124,105	8.4
Seattle-Tacoma-Bellevue, WA..................	540,037	201,727	426,466	224,739	338,123	198,637	139,486	15.7
St Louis, MO-IL..............................	15,477	68,389	310,273	241,884	-52,131	32,872	-85,003	0.6
Tampa-St Petersburg-Clearwater, FL...........	411,346	12,252	294,083	281,831	397,215	104,814	292,401	14.8
Virginia Beach-Norfolk-Newport News, VA-NC..................................	54,946	78,552	209,617	131,065	-23,410	36,319	-59,729	3.2
Washington-Arlington-Alexandria, DC-VA-MD-WV............................	630,799	428,108	743,898	315,790	200,650	326,958	-126,308	11.2

Z represents less than .05 percent. [1] Total population change includes residual. This residual represents the change in population that cannot be attributed to any specific demographic component of change.

Source: U.S. Census Bureau, Metropolitan and Micropolitan Statistical Areas Population Totals: 2010-2019, "Estimates of the Components of Resident Population Change: April 1, 2010 to July 1, 2019," <https://www.census.gov/data/tables/time-series/demo/popest/2010s-total-metro-and-micro-statistical-areas.html>, accessed April 2020.

Table 24. Population by Core Based Statistical Area (CBSA) Status and State: 2019

[328,240 represents 328,240,000. As of July 1. Covers core based statistical areas (metropolitan and micropolitan statistical areas) as delineated by the U.S. Office of Management and Budget as of September 2018. For definitions and components of all metropolitan and micropolitan statistical areas, see Appendix II. Minus sign (-) indicates decrease]

State	Total population, 2019 (1,000)	Inside Core-Based Statistical Area (metropolitan or micropolitan statistical area), 2019				Outside CBSA, 2019		Percent change, 2010–2019		
		Total		Metro-politan (1,000)	Micro-politan (1,000)	Number (1,000)	Percent	Metro-politan	Micro-politan	Outside CBSAs
		Number (1,000)	Percent							
United States.........	**328,240**	**310,081**	**94.5**	**282,829**	**27,253**	**18,158**	**5.5**	**7.5**	**0.4**	**-1.9**
Alabama..............	4,903	4,493	91.6	3,729	765	410	8.4	4.5	-1.6	-5.7
Alaska................	732	539	73.7	493	46	193	26.3	3.1	2.4	2.9
Arizona..............	7,279	7,176	98.6	6,926	250	102	1.4	14.6	1.9	2.0
Arkansas............	3,018	2,522	83.6	1,911	612	495	16.4	7.9	-2.2	-4.7
California............	39,512	39,239	99.3	38,675	564	273	0.7	6.2	-0.7	-1.5
Colorado.............	5,759	5,449	94.6	5,043	406	309	5.4	16.1	5.3	2.6
Connecticut..........	3,565	3,565	100.0	3,385	180	–	–	(Z)	-5.0	(X)
Delaware.............	974	974	100.0	974	–	–	–	8.4	(X)	(X)
District of Columbia....	706	706	100.0	706	–	–	–	17.3	(X)	(X)
Florida...............	21,478	21,157	98.5	20,787	370	321	1.5	14.7	3.6	-1.3
Georgia...............	10,617	9,835	92.6	8,812	1,023	782	7.4	11.4	2.4	0.6
Hawaii................	1,416	1,416	100.0	1,142	274	(Z)	(Z)	3.1	8.6	-4.4
Idaho................	1,787	1,646	92.1	1,327	318	141	7.9	17.4	6.2	2.9
Illinois...............	12,672	12,067	95.2	11,247	820	605	4.8	-0.7	-5.5	-5.8
Indiana...............	6,732	6,295	93.5	5,269	1,027	437	6.5	5.3	-1.0	-1.9
Iowa.................	3,155	2,402	76.1	1,933	468	754	23.9	8.3	-2.6	-3.5
Kansas...............	2,913	2,529	86.8	2,026	503	385	13.2	5.3	-3.5	-5.9
Kentucky.............	4,468	3,569	79.9	2,659	910	898	20.1	5.6	2.2	-3.5
Louisiana.............	4,649	4,351	93.6	3,915	436	297	6.4	3.9	-3.7	-4.6
Maine................	1,344	921	68.5	799	122	423	31.5	3.0	0.1	-1.7
Maryland.............	6,046	5,964	98.6	5,895	69	82	1.4	4.9	-1.8	-1.9
Massachusetts........	6,893	6,881	99.8	6,864	17	11	0.2	5.3	4.8	12.1
Michigan.............	9,987	9,188	92.0	8,185	1,003	799	8.0	1.5	0.2	-2.1
Minnesota............	5,640	5,124	90.9	4,392	732	516	9.1	8.3	1.4	-1.8
Mississippi............	2,976	2,403	80.8	1,440	964	573	19.2	4.6	-3.1	-4.2
Missouri..............	6,137	5,299	86.3	4,603	696	838	13.7	3.8	-0.2	-2.4
Montana..............	1,069	717	67.1	383	335	351	32.9	6.9	15.7	2.7
Nebraska.............	1,934	1,591	82.3	1,265	327	343	17.7	10.5	(Z)	-3.5
Nevada...............	3,080	3,048	98.9	2,798	249	32	1.1	15.1	6.1	-3.1
New Hampshire........	1,360	1,311	96.4	857	453	49	3.6	4.7	0.8	2.3
New Jersey...........	8,882	8,882	100.0	8,882	–	–	–	1.0	(X)	(X)
New Mexico...........	2,097	2,031	96.8	1,411	620	66	3.2	2.9	0.8	-9.8
New York..............	19,454	19,068	98.0	18,095	974	385	2.0	0.8	-4.1	-5.1
North Carolina..........	10,488	9,894	94.3	8,500	1,394	594	5.7	12.6	0.9	-2.3
North Dakota...........	762	563	73.9	380	183	199	26.1	16.2	18.3	4.3
Ohio.................	11,689	11,243	96.2	9,382	1,860	446	3.8	2.2	-1.8	-2.4
Oklahoma.............	3,957	3,385	85.5	2,637	748	572	14.5	8.8	0.7	-2.1
Oregon...............	4,218	4,115	97.6	3,537	578	103	2.4	11.3	4.1	4.7
Pennsylvania..........	12,802	12,430	97.1	11,355	1,075	372	2.9	1.5	-4.2	-4.1
Rhode Island..........	1,059	1,059	100.0	1,059	–	–	–	0.6	(X)	(X)
South Carolina........	5,149	4,860	94.4	4,412	448	288	5.6	14.1	0.2	-7.0
South Dakota..........	885	665	75.2	426	239	219	24.8	15.5	4.6	1.2
Tennessee............	6,829	6,233	91.3	5,343	890	596	8.7	9.1	4.2	0.3
Texas................	28,996	27,606	95.2	25,881	1,726	1,389	4.8	17.1	3.2	2.0
Utah.................	3,206	3,058	95.4	2,871	187	148	4.6	16.6	17.0	4.8
Vermont..............	624	456	73.1	220	236	168	26.9	4.3	-3.2	-1.8
Virginia...............	8,536	7,735	90.6	7,483	252	800	9.4	8.2	-7.4	-1.7
Washington...........	7,615	7,435	97.6	6,834	601	180	2.4	13.9	8.8	6.2
West Virginia..........	1,792	1,450	80.9	1,156	294	342	19.1	-2.0	-3.9	-7.0
Wisconsin............	5,822	5,099	87.6	4,348	751	724	12.4	3.3	(Z)	-0.7
Wyoming..............	579	435	75.1	179	256	144	24.9	7.2	1.3	-0.2

– Represents zero. Z less than 500 or .05 percent. X Not applicable.

Source: U.S. Census Bureau, Metropolitan and Micropolitan Statistical Areas Totals: 2010-2019, "Datasets, CBSA-EST2019-alldata," <https://www.census.gov/data/tables/time-series/demo/popest/2010s-total-metro-and-micro-statistical-areas.html>, accessed April 2020.

Table 25. Population of Incorporated Places With 175,000 or More Inhabitants in 2019: 1990 to 2019

[In thousands, except as indicated (223 represents 223,000). Census years as of April 1; all other years, as of July 1. Data for the 2010 estimates base and July estimates are based on the 2010 Census and reflect changes to the April 1, 2010 population due to the Count Question Resolution program and geographic program revisions. All geographic boundaries for the 2019 population estimates series are defined as of January 1, 2019. For 1990 and 2000, the counts relate to places as defined on January 1, 2010. Minus sign (-) indicates decrease. See Appendix III]

City	Number (1,000)					Percent change			Rank, 2019
	1990	2000	2010, estimates base	2018	2019	1990 to 2000 [1]	2000 to 2010 [1]	2010 to 2019	
Akron, Ohio..........	223	217	199	198	198	-2.7	-8.3	-0.8	125
Albuquerque, New Mexico..........	385	449	546	560	561	16.6	21.7	2.6	32
Amarillo, Texas..........	158	174	191	199	199	10.2	9.8	4.6	118
Anaheim, California..........	267	328	336	351	350	23.0	2.5	4.2	55
Anchorage, Alaska..........	226	260	292	291	288	15.0	12.1	-1.3	69
Arlington, Texas..........	262	333	365	398	399	27.2	9.8	9.2	49
Atlanta, Georgia..........	394	416	427	498	507	5.7	0.8	18.7	37
Augusta-Richmond County, Georgia [2]........	186	200	196	197	198	7.3	-2.0	1.0	123
Aurora, Colorado..........	222	276	325	375	379	24.6	17.6	16.8	54
Aurora, Illinois..........	100	143	198	199	198	43.6	38.4	-0.1	124
Austin, Texas..........	466	657	802	962	979	41.0	20.4	22.1	11
Bakersfield, California..........	175	247	348	382	384	41.2	40.6	10.4	52
Baltimore, Maryland..........	736	651	621	602	593	-11.5	-4.6	-4.4	30
Baton Rouge, Louisiana..........	223	228	229	222	220	2.2	0.7	-4.0	100
Birmingham, Alabama..........	265	243	213	210	209	-8.5	-12.6	-1.5	109
Boise City, Idaho..........	126	186	209	228	229	48.0	10.7	9.3	98
Boston, Massachusetts..........	575	589	618	691	693	2.5	4.8	12.1	21
Brownsville, Texas..........	114	140	175	182	183	22.6	25.3	4.6	141
Buffalo, New York..........	328	293	261	256	255	-10.8	-10.7	-2.3	86
Cape Coral, Florida..........	75	102	154	189	194	36.1	50.9	26.0	132
Chandler, Arizona..........	90	177	236	257	261	96.5	33.7	10.6	81
Charlotte, North Carolina..........	428	541	736	873	886	26.4	35.2	20.4	15
Chattanooga, Tennessee..........	153	156	170	182	183	1.5	7.8	7.3	140
Chesapeake, Virginia..........	152	199	222	242	245	31.1	11.6	10.1	91
Chicago, Illinois..........	2,783	2,896	2,696	2,701	2,694	4.1	-6.9	-0.1	3
Chula Vista, California..........	135	174	244	271	274	28.4	40.5	12.5	75
Cincinnati, Ohio..........	364	331	297	302	304	-9.0	-10.4	2.3	64
Cleveland, Ohio..........	506	478	397	383	381	-5.5	-17.1	-3.9	53
Colorado Springs, Colorado..........	280	361	417	473	478	28.7	15.4	14.6	39
Columbus, Georgia..........	179	186	191	194	196	3.9	2.2	2.7	128
Columbus, Ohio..........	633	711	789	891	899	12.4	10.6	13.9	14
Corpus Christi, Texas..........	258	277	305	326	327	7.4	10.0	7.0	59
Dallas, Texas..........	1,008	1,189	1,198	1,342	1,344	18.0	0.8	12.2	9
Denver, Colorado..........	468	555	600	716	727	18.6	8.2	21.2	19
Des Moines, Iowa..........	193	199	204	216	214	2.8	2.4	4.9	105
Detroit, Michigan..........	1,028	951	714	673	670	-7.5	-25.0	-6.1	24
Durham, North Carolina..........	137	187	230	275	279	36.9	22.1	21.4	74
El Paso, Texas..........	515	564	648	680	682	9.4	15.2	5.2	22
Elk Grove, California..........	(5)	60	153	173	175	(5)	155.1	14.2	149
Fayetteville, North Carolina..........	76	121	201	211	212	59.5	65.7	5.5	108
Fontana, California..........	88	129	196	213	215	47.3	52.1	9.2	104
Fort Lauderdale, Florida..........	149	152	166	182	182	2.1	8.6	10.1	142
Fort Wayne, Indiana..........	173	206	254	267	270	18.9	23.3	6.6	77
Fort Worth, Texas..........	448	535	745	893	910	19.5	38.6	22.1	13
Fremont, California..........	173	203	214	238	241	17.3	5.2	12.6	93
Fresno, California..........	354	428	497	529	532	20.8	15.7	6.9	34
Frisco, Texas..........	6	34	117	188	200	449.3	247.0	71.1	116
Garland, Texas..........	181	216	227	242	240	19.4	5.1	5.7	94
Gilbert, Arizona..........	29	110	208	250	254	276.7	90.0	21.9	87
Glendale, Arizona..........	148	219	226	250	252	48.0	3.6	11.6	88
Glendale, California..........	180	195	192	201	199	8.3	-1.7	4.0	119
Grand Prairie, Texas..........	100	127	175	194	195	27.9	37.6	10.9	130
Grand Rapids, Michigan..........	189	198	188	200	201	4.6	-4.9	6.9	113
Greensboro, North Carolina..........	184	224	269	295	297	21.8	20.4	10.3	67
Henderson, Nevada..........	65	175	257	310	320	170.0	47.0	24.6	61
Hialeah, Florida..........	188	226	225	235	233	20.4	-0.8	3.8	96
Houston, Texas..........	1,631	1,954	2,096	2,319	2,320	19.8	7.5	10.7	4
Huntington Beach, California..........	182	190	191	200	199	4.4	0.2	4.3	120
Huntsville, Alabama..........	160	158	180	198	201	-1.0	13.8	11.2	114
Indianapolis, Indiana [2]..........	731	792	820	871	876	8.3	3.6	6.8	17
Irvine, California..........	110	143	212	282	287	29.7	48.4	35.5	72
Irving, Texas..........	155	192	216	241	240	23.6	12.9	10.9	95
Jacksonville, Florida..........	635	736	822	902	912	15.8	11.7	10.9	12
Jersey City, New Jersey..........	229	240	248	264	262	5.0	3.1	5.8	80
Kansas City, Missouri..........	435	442	460	492	495	1.5	4.1	7.7	38
Knoxville, Tennessee..........	165	174	178	187	188	5.4	2.9	5.3	134
Laredo, Texas..........	123	177	236	261	262	43.7	33.7	11.3	79
Las Vegas, Nevada..........	258	478	584	643	651	85.3	22.0	11.4	27
Lexington-Fayette, Kentucky..........	225	261	296	322	323	15.6	13.5	9.2	60
Lincoln, Nebraska..........	192	226	259	287	289	17.5	14.5	11.7	68
Little Rock, Arkansas..........	176	183	194	197	197	4.2	5.7	2.0	126
Long Beach, California..........	429	462	462	466	463	7.5	0.2	0.1	43
Los Angeles, California..........	3,486	3,695	3,793	3,978	3,980	6.0	2.6	4.9	2
Louisville/Jefferson County, Kentucky [2]........	[3] 270	[3] 256	596	618	618	[3] -4.9	(X)	3.7	29
Lubbock, Texas..........	186	200	230	256	259	7.2	15.0	12.6	83
Madison, Wisconsin..........	191	208	233	258	260	9.1	12.1	11.4	82
McKinney, Texas..........	21	54	131	192	199	155.5	141.2	51.9	121
Memphis, Tennessee..........	610	650	652	651	651	6.5	-0.5	-0.1	28
Mesa, Arizona..........	288	396	440	508	518	37.6	10.8	17.7	35

See footnotes at end of table.

Table 25. Population of Incorporated Places With 175,000 or More Inhabitants in 2019: 1990 to 2019-Continued.

See headnote on page 29.

City	Number (1,000)					Percent change			Rank, 2019
	1990	2000	2010, estimates base	2018	2019	1990 to 2000 [1]	2000 to 2010 [1]	2010 to 2019	
Miami, Florida	359	362	399	463	468	1.1	10.2	17.1	42
Milwaukee, Wisconsin	628	597	594	591	590	-5.0	-0.4	-0.7	31
Minneapolis, Minnesota	368	383	383	425	430	3.9	0.0	12.3	46
Mobile, Alabama	196	199	195	190	189	1.4	-1.9	-3.1	133
Modesto, California	165	189	203	214	215	14.6	6.5	5.9	103
Montgomery, Alabama	188	202	206	199	199	7.5	2.1	-3.4	122
Moreno Valley, California	119	142	193	209	213	19.9	35.8	10.2	106
Nashville-Davidson, Tennessee [2]	488	570	603	667	671	16.7	5.5	11.2	23
New Orleans, Louisiana	497	485	344	391	390	-2.5	-29.1	13.5	50
New York, New York	7,323	8,008	8,175	8,390	8,337	9.4	2.1	2.0	1
Newark, New Jersey	275	274	277	282	282	-0.6	1.3	1.8	73
Newport News, Virginia	171	180	181	179	179	5.1	0.3	-1.0	144
Norfolk, Virginia	261	234	243	244	243	-10.3	3.6	0.0	92
North Las Vegas, Nevada	48	115	217	245	252	141.4	87.9	16.3	89
Oakland, California	372	399	391	429	433	7.3	-2.2	10.8	45
Oceanside, California	128	161	168	176	176	25.7	3.8	4.9	148
Oklahoma City, Oklahoma	445	506	580	648	655	13.8	14.6	12.9	25
Omaha, Nebraska	336	390	459	477	478	16.2	4.9	4.2	40
Ontario, California	133	158	164	181	185	18.6	3.7	12.9	137
Orlando, Florida	165	186	239	286	287	12.9	28.2	20.4	71
Overland Park, Kansas	112	149	173	193	195	33.4	16.3	12.8	129
Oxnard, California	143	170	198	209	209	19.5	16.2	5.5	110
Peoria, Arizona	51	108	154	172	176	113.8	42.2	14.2	147
Philadelphia, Pennsylvania	1,586	1,518	1,526	1,584	1,584	-4.3	0.6	3.8	6
Phoenix, Arizona	983	1,321	1,447	1,655	1,681	34.3	9.4	16.2	5
Pittsburgh, Pennsylvania	370	335	305	301	300	-9.5	-8.6	-1.6	66
Plano, Texas	128	222	260	289	288	73.6	17.0	10.7	70
Port St. Lucie, Florida	56	89	164	195	202	59.2	85.4	22.9	112
Portland, Oregon	439	529	584	651	655	20.6	10.3	12.2	26
Providence, Rhode Island	161	174	178	180	180	8.0	2.5	1.2	143
Raleigh, North Carolina	212	276	404	469	474	30.2	46.3	17.3	41
Rancho Cucamonga, California	101	128	165	177	178	26.0	29.4	7.4	145
Reno, Nevada	134	180	225	250	256	34.8	24.8	13.4	85
Richmond, Virginia	203	198	204	229	230	-2.5	3.2	12.8	97
Riverside, California	227	255	304	330	331	12.6	19.1	9.0	58
Rochester, New York	230	220	211	206	206	-4.6	-4.2	-2.4	111
Sacramento, California	369	407	466	508	514	10.2	14.6	10.1	36
Salt Lake City, Utah	160	182	186	200	201	13.6	2.6	7.6	115
San Antonio, Texas	935	1,145	1,326	1,530	1,547	22.4	16.0	16.7	7
San Bernardino, California	165	185	210	216	216	12.6	13.2	2.5	102
San Diego, California	1,111	1,223	1,302	1,422	1,424	10.2	6.9	9.4	8
San Francisco, California	724	777	805	881	882	7.3	3.7	9.5	16
San Jose, California	782	895	953	1,028	1,022	14.4	5.7	7.3	10
Santa Ana, California	294	338	325	332	332	15.0	-4.0	2.3	57
Santa Clarita, California	111	151	209	214	213	36.5	16.7	2.0	107
Santa Rosa, California	113	148	175	177	177	30.3	13.7	1.0	146
Scottsdale, Arizona	130	203	217	254	258	55.8	7.2	18.7	84
Seattle, Washington	516	563	609	742	754	9.1	8.0	23.8	18
Shreveport, Louisiana	199	200	201	189	187	0.8	-0.4	-6.9	135
Sioux Falls, South Dakota	101	124	154	180	184	22.9	24.1	19.4	139
Spokane, Washington	177	196	209	219	222	10.4	6.8	6.0	99
St. Louis, Missouri	397	348	319	303	301	-12.2	-8.3	-5.9	65
St. Paul, Minnesota	272	287	285	307	308	5.5	-0.7	8.1	63
St. Petersburg, Florida	240	248	245	264	265	3.3	-1.4	8.2	78
Stockton, California	211	244	292	312	313	15.6	19.7	7.0	62
Tacoma, Washington	177	194	198	216	218	9.6	2.5	9.9	101
Tallahassee, Florida	125	151	181	193	195	20.7	20.4	7.4	131
Tampa, Florida	280	303	336	397	400	8.4	10.6	18.9	48
Tempe, Arizona	142	159	162	192	196	11.7	2.0	21.0	127
Toledo, Ohio	333	314	287	275	273	-5.8	-8.4	-5.1	76
Tucson, Arizona	405	487	527	545	548	20.1	6.9	4.1	33
Tulsa, Oklahoma	367	393	392	400	401	7.0	-0.3	2.3	47
Urban Honolulu CDP, Hawaii [4]	(NA)	(NA)	338	347	345	(NA)	(NA)	2.2	56
Vancouver, Washington	46	144	167	183	184	209.5	12.7	10.4	138
Virginia Beach, Virginia	393	425	438	450	450	8.2	3.0	2.8	44
Washington, District of Columbia	607	572	602	702	706	-5.7	5.2	17.3	20
Wichita, Kansas	304	344	382	389	390	13.2	11.1	2.0	51
Winston-Salem, North Carolina	143	186	230	247	248	29.5	23.6	8.0	90
Worcester, Massachusetts	170	173	181	186	185	1.7	4.9	2.5	136
Yonkers, New York	188	196	196	200	200	4.3	-0.1	2.2	117

NA Not available. X Not applicable. [1] Based on census data. [2] Represents the portion of a consolidated city that is not within one or more separately incorporated places. [3] Data are for the incorporated place of Louisville city before consolidation of the city and county governments. [4] CDP=Census Designated Place. [5] Not incorporated.

Source: U.S. Census Bureau, 1990, 2000 and 2010 census data: *Census of Population and Housing, 2010, CPH-2. Population and Housing Unit Counts*; and beginning 2010, City and Town Population Totals: 2010-2019, "Annual Estimates of the Resident Population for Incorporated Places Over 50,000, Ranked by July 1, 2019 Population: April 1, 2010 to July 1, 2019," May 2020, <https://www.census.gov/programs-surveys/popest/data/tables.html>, accessed June 2020.

Table 26. Incorporated Places by Population Size: 1990 to 2019

[153.1 represents 153,100,000. See Appendix III]

Population size	Number of incorporated places				Population (mil.)				Percent of total			
	1990	2000	2010	2019	1990	2000	2010	2019	1990	2000	2010	2019
Total	19,262	19,452	19,540	19,502	153.1	173.5	192.0	206.9	100.0	100.0	100.0	100.0
1,000,000 or more	8	9	9	10	20.0	22.9	23.6	25.9	13.1	13.2	12.3	12.5
500,000 to 999,999	15	20	24	27	10.1	12.9	16.1	18.8	6.6	7.4	8.4	9.1
250,000 to 499,999	41	37	40	52	14.2	13.3	14.0	17.4	9.3	7.7	7.3	8.4
100,000 to 249,999	131	172	200	225	19.1	25.5	30.2	33.0	12.5	14.7	15.7	16.0
50,000 to 99,999	309	363	432	466	21.2	24.9	30.1	32.6	13.8	14.4	15.7	15.8
25,000 to 49,999	567	644	723	741	20.0	22.6	25.2	25.8	13.1	13.0	13.1	12.5
10,000 to 24,999	1,290	1,435	1,542	1,572	20.3	22.6	24.2	24.8	13.3	13.0	12.6	12.0
Under 10,000	16,901	16,772	16,570	16,409	28.2	28.7	28.7	28.5	18.4	16.5	14.9	13.8

Source: U.S. Census Bureau, *1990 Census of Population and Housing, Population and Housing Unit Counts (CPH-2-1)*; *Census 2000 PHC-3, Population and Housing Unit Counts*; *2010 Census Redistricting Data (Public Law 94-171) Summary File*; and City and Town Population Totals: 2010-2019, Incorporated Places and Minor Civil Divisions Datasets, "SUB-EST2019: Subcounty Resident Population Estimates: April 1, 2010 to July 1, 2019," May 2020, <https://www2.census.gov/programs-surveys/popest/datasets/2010-2019/cities/totals/>.

Table 27. Urban and Rural Population by State: 2000 and 2010

[222,361 represents 222,361,000. As of April 1. Resident population. Based on current urban definitions, see text, this section]

State	2000		2010			State	2000		2010		
	Urban (1,000)	Rural (1,000)	Urban Number (1,000)	Urban Percent	Rural (1,000)		Urban (1,000)	Rural (1,000)	Urban Number (1,000)	Urban Percent	Rural (1,000)
U.S.	222,361	59,061	249,253	80.7	59,492	MO	3,883	1,712	4,218	70.4	1,771
AL	2,466	1,981	2,822	59.0	1,958	MT	488	414	553	55.9	436
AK	411	216	469	66.0	241	NE	1,194	518	1,336	73.1	491
AZ	4,524	607	5,741	89.8	651	NV	1,829	170	2,544	94.2	157
AR	1,404	1,269	1,638	56.2	1,278	NH	732	503	794	60.3	523
CA	31,990	1,882	35,374	95.0	1,880	NJ	7,939	475	8,324	94.7	468
CO	3,633	668	4,333	86.2	696	NM	1,364	456	1,594	77.4	465
CT	2,988	418	3,145	88.0	429	NY	16,603	2,374	17,028	87.9	2,350
DE	628	156	748	83.3	150	NC	4,849	3,200	6,302	66.1	3,234
DC	572	0	602	100.0	0	ND	359	283	403	59.9	270
FL	14,270	1,712	17,140	91.2	1,661	OH	8,782	2,571	8,990	77.9	2,547
GA	5,864	2,322	7,272	75.1	2,416	OK	2,255	1,196	2,485	66.2	1,266
HI	1,108	103	1,250	91.9	110	OR	2,694	727	3,104	81.0	727
ID	859	434	1,106	70.6	461	PA	9,464	2,817	9,991	78.7	2,711
IL	10,910	1,510	11,354	88.5	1,477	RI	953	95	955	90.7	98
IN	4,304	1,776	4,697	72.4	1,787	SC	2,427	1,585	3,068	66.3	1,558
IA	1,787	1,139	1,950	64.0	1,096	SD	391	363	461	56.7	353
KS	1,921	768	2,117	74.2	736	TN	3,620	2,069	4,213	66.4	2,133
KY	2,254	1,788	2,533	58.4	1,806	TX	17,204	3,648	21,298	84.7	3,848
LA	3,246	1,223	3,318	73.2	1,216	UT	1,970	263	2,504	90.6	260
ME	513	762	514	38.7	815	VT	232	376	243	38.9	382
MD	4,559	738	5,034	87.2	739	VA	5,170	1,909	6,037	75.5	1,964
MA	5,801	548	6,022	92.0	526	WA	4,831	1,063	5,652	84.1	1,073
MI	7,419	2,519	7,370	74.6	2,514	WV	833	976	903	48.7	950
MN	3,490	1,429	3,886	73.3	1,418	WI	3,664	1,700	3,990	70.2	1,697
MS	1,387	1,457	1,464	49.4	1,503	WY	321	172	365	64.8	199

Source: U.S. Census Bureau, 2000 Census of Population and Housing, *Population and Housing Unit Counts PHC-3*; 2010 Census of Population and Housing, *Population and Housing Unit Counts, CPH-2-1, United States Summary*; and "Percent Urban and Rural in 2010 by State," <https://www.census.gov/programs-surveys/geography/guidance/geo-areas/urban-rural/2010-urban-rural.html>, accessed March 2013.

Table 28. Population in Coastal Counties: 1960 to 2019

[3,537 represents 3,537,000. Data for 1960 to 2010 as of April 1; 2019 data as of July 1. Data for 1960 through 2000 are based on 675 counties in areas as defined by U.S. National Oceanic and Atmospheric Administration, 1992. Beginning 2010, data cover 678 counties and equivalent areas in a coastal watershed; see headnote, Table 29. See Appendix III]

Year	Total	Counties in coastal regions					Balance of United States
		Total	Atlantic	Gulf of Mexico	Great Lakes	Pacific	
Land area, 2010 (1,000 sq. mi.)	3,537	888	147	116	115	510	2,649
POPULATION							
1960 (millions)	179.3	94.6	44.5	8.4	23.7	18.0	84.8
1970 (millions)	203.3	110.0	51.1	10.0	26.0	22.9	93.3
1980 (millions)	226.5	119.8	53.7	13.1	26.0	27.0	106.7
1990 (millions)	248.7	133.4	59.0	15.2	25.9	33.2	115.3
2000 (millions)	281.4	148.3	65.2	18.0	27.3	37.8	133.1
2010 (millions)	308.7	159.7	70.2	20.9	27.2	41.4	149.0
2019 (millions)	328.2	168.9	73.9	23.4	27.2	44.4	159.4
1960 (percent)	100.0	53.0	25.0	5.0	14.0	10.0	47.0
1970 (percent)	100.0	54.0	25.0	5.0	13.0	11.0	46.0
1980 (percent)	100.0	53.0	24.0	6.0	11.0	12.0	47.0
1990 (percent)	100.0	53.6	23.7	6.1	10.4	13.3	46.4
2000 (percent)	100.0	53.0	23.0	6.0	10.0	13.0	47.0
2010 (percent)	100.0	51.7	22.7	6.8	8.8	13.4	48.3
2019 (percent)	100.0	51.4	22.5	7.1	8.3	13.5	48.6

Source: U.S. Census Bureau, U.S. Census of Population: 1960 and 1970; 1980 Census of Population, Vol. 1, Chapter A (PC80-1-A-1), U.S. Summary; 1990 Census of Population and Housing (CPH1); "Annual Estimates of the Resident Population for Counties: April 1, 2000 to July 1, 2009," March 2010 <https://www2.census.gov/programs-surveys/popest/datasets/2000-2009/counties/totals/>; and "County Population Totals: 2010-2019," <https://www.census.gov/programs-surveys/popest/data/tables.html>, accessed July 2020.

Table 29. States With Coastal Watershed Counties—Population and Housing Units, Establishments, and Employees by Coastal Region and State: 2010 to 2019

[308,758 represents 308,758,000. Data for 2010 as of April 1 and reflect population estimates base. Data for 2019 as of July 1. Beginning in 2010, data cover 678 counties and equivalent areas in a coastal watershed. A county is considered a coastal watershed county if one of the following criteria is met: (1) at a minimum, 15 percent of the county's total land area is located within a coastal watershed or (2) a portion of, or an entire county accounts for at least 15 percent of a coastal watershed. The 15 percent rule was selected as an appropriate level for capturing counties with a significant impact on coastal and ocean resources. See Appendix III. Minus sign (-) indicates decrease]

Coastal region and state	Number of counties	Population 2010 (1,000)	Population 2019 Number (1,000)	Population 2019 Percent of state total	Population Percent change 2010–2019	Population Per square mile 2019[1]	Housing units Number 2010 (1,000)	Housing units Number 2019 (1,000)	Housing units Percent change 2010–2019	Housing units Per square mile 2019[1]	Private nonfarm[2] Establishments 2018 (1,000)	Private nonfarm[2] Employees 2018 (1,000)
United States, total	**3,142**	**308,758**	**328,240**	**(X)**	**6.3**	**93**	**131,705**	**139,684**	**6.1**	**39**	**7,912**	**130,881**
Interior U.S.	2,464	149,009	159,380	(X)	7.0	60	64,631	69,042	6.8	26	3,682	64,576
Coastal counties, total	**678**	**159,749**	**168,860**	**(X)**	**5.7**	**190**	**67,074**	**70,643**	**5.3**	**80**	**³ 4,230**	**³ 66,305**
Atlantic	**286**	**70,242**	**73,923**	**(X)**	**5.2**	**502**	**29,916**	**31,373**	**4.9**	**213**	**1,951**	**30,141**
Maine	14	1,239	1,260	94	1.7	62	667	695	4.3	34	39	487
New Hampshire	6	1,073	1,119	82	4.3	266	485	509	4.8	121	31	475
Massachusetts	12	6,318	6,661	97	5.4	1,013	2,712	2,830	4.4	431	174	3,185
Rhode Island	5	1,053	1,059	100	0.6	1,025	463	470	1.5	455	28	437
Connecticut	8	3,574	3,565	100	-0.2	736	1,488	1,525	2.5	315	89	1,502
New York	18	13,952	14,145	73	1.4	1,831	5,601	5,824	4.0	754	426	6,151
New Jersey	20	8,683	8,777	99	1.1	1,254	3,509	3,596	2.5	514	231	3,557
Pennsylvania	12	6,108	6,306	49	3.2	919	2,512	2,596	3.3	378	148	2,754
Delaware	3	898	974	100	8.4	500	406	444	9.3	228	25	398
Maryland	20	5,288	5,536	92	4.7	736	2,176	2,256	3.7	300	127	2,120
District of Columbia	1	602	706	100	17.3	11,570	297	323	8.8	5,292	24	540
Virginia	61	5,426	5,837	68	7.6	421	2,216	2,350	6.1	170	140	2,376
North Carolina	38	2,254	2,353	22	4.4	119	1,078	1,162	7.9	59	47	649
South Carolina	22	1,932	2,197	43	13.7	144	953	1,061	11.3	70	50	695
Georgia	25	945	1,015	10	7.4	86	414	444	7.1	37	21	300
Florida	21	10,896	12,412	58	13.9	666	4,940	5,290	7.1	284	352	4,514
Gulf of Mexico	**144**	**20,888**	**23,389**	**(X)**	**12.0**	**202**	**9,294**	**10,203**	**9.8**	**88**	**509**	**7,759**
Florida	41	7,535	8,667	40	15.0	269	3,887	4,213	8.4	131	206	2,636
Georgia	3	98	95	1	-2.1	60	43	44	2.4	28	2	29
Alabama	8	765	797	16	4.2	91	363	386	6.5	44	17	262
Mississippi	12	629	660	22	5.0	98	280	302	7.9	45	12	187
Louisiana	39	3,574	3,715	80	3.9	142	1,543	1,644	6.5	63	85	1,346
Texas	41	8,288	9,455	33	14.1	236	3,178	3,614	13.7	90	186	3,299
Great Lakes	**158**	**27,191**	**27,150**	**(X)**	**-0.1**	**236**	**12,128**	**12,365**	**2.0**	**107**	**639**	**11,341**
New York	21	3,635	3,567	18	-1.9	167	1,647	1,692	2.8	79	82	1,395
Pennsylvania	1	281	270	2	-3.9	338	119	122	2.3	153	6	116
Ohio	24	4,326	4,258	36	-1.6	404	1,967	1,984	0.9	188	99	1,797
Michigan	74	8,797	8,911	89	1.3	175	4,050	4,140	2.2	81	201	3,442
Indiana	9	1,433	1,445	21	0.9	355	607	626	3.3	154	31	611
Illinois	2	5,898	5,847	46	-0.9	4,209	2,441	2,470	1.2	1,778	154	2,731
Wisconsin	23	2,569	2,602	45	1.3	169	1,165	1,195	2.6	78	59	1,147
Minnesota	4	252	251	4	-0.2	24	132	136	2.7	13	7	102
Pacific	**90**	**41,429**	**44,397**	**(X)**	**7.2**	**87**	**15,737**	**16,702**	**6.1**	**33**	**³ 1,132**	**³ 17,064**
Washington	19	5,229	5,973	78	14.2	242	2,264	2,513	11.0	102	156	2,305
Oregon	12	1,982	2,162	51	9.1	103	895	965	7.8	46	64	880
California	29	32,259	34,226	87	6.1	440	11,803	12,408	5.1	160	861	13,132
Alaska	25	598	620	85	3.7	2	255	266	4.0	1	18	226
Hawaii	5	1,360	1,416	100	4.1	220	520	550	5.9	86	³ 33	³ 521

X Not applicable. ¹ Calculated on the basis of land area data from the 2010 census. ² Covers establishments with payroll. Excludes most government employees, railroad employees, and self-employed persons. Employees are for the week including March 12. ³ Excludes data from Kalawao County, Hawaii.

Source: U.S. Census Bureau, "County Population Totals: 2010–2019" and "National, State, and County Housing Unit Totals: 2010–2019," <https://www.census.gov/programs-surveys/popest/data/tables.html>; and "County Business Patterns," <data.census.gov>; accessed July 2020.

Table 30. Geographic Mobility Status of the Population by Selected Characteristics: 1980 to 2019

[221,641 represents 221,641,000. As of March. For persons 1 year old and over, unless otherwise noted. Based on comparison of place of residence in year shown vs. previous year. Excludes members of the Armed Forces except those living off post or with their families on post. 2011 data based on population controls from Census 2000. 2018 data based on population controls from Census 2010. Based on Current Population Survey, Annual Social and Economic Supplement. See text, this section and Appendix III. For composition of regions, see map, inside front cover]

Mobility period and characteristic	Total persons (1,000)	Non–movers	Percent distribution by geographic mobility						Movers from abroad
			Movers (different house in United States)						
			Total	Same county	Different county				
					Total	Same state	Different state		
1980 to 1981	221,641	82.8	16.6	10.4	6.2	3.4	2.8	0.6
1990 to 1991	244,884	83.0	16.4	10.3	6.1	3.2	2.9	0.6
2000 to 2001	275,611	85.8	13.5	8.0	5.6	2.7	2.8	0.6
2010 to 2011	302,005	88.4	11.3	7.7	3.5	2.0	1.6	0.4
2018 to 2019, total	**320,667**	**90.2**	**9.8**	**5.9**	**3.6**	**2.1**	**1.5**	**0.4**
By age:								
1 to 4 years old	16,047	85.6	14.4	8.7	5.2	3.2	2.0	0.5
5 to 9 years old	20,212	89.6	10.4	6.6	3.5	2.0	1.5	0.4
10 to 14 years old	20,827	91.3	8.7	5.7	2.7	1.7	1.0	0.3
15 to 19 years old	20,849	91.3	8.7	5.4	3.0	1.9	1.1	0.3
20 to 24 years old	21,254	79.6	20.4	12.7	7.0	4.0	3.0	0.7
25 to 29 years old	23,277	79.2	20.8	11.9	8.0	4.5	3.5	0.9
30 to 44 years old	62,959	88.7	11.3	6.8	4.0	2.3	1.7	0.5
45 to 64 years old	82,455	93.9	6.1	3.4	2.4	1.5	1.0	0.2
65 to 74 years old	31,487	96.1	3.9	2.2	1.5	0.9	0.6	0.1
75 to 84 years old	15,407	96.4	3.6	2.1	1.4	0.7	0.7	0.1
85 years old and over	5,893	95.6	4.4	2.6	1.8	1.2	0.6	(NA)
By region:								
Northeast	54,791	92.6	7.4	4.1	2.9	1.7	1.3	0.4
Midwest	66,809	90.2	9.8	5.8	3.8	2.3	1.5	0.2
South	122,228	89.5	10.5	6.2	3.9	2.4	1.5	0.4
West	76,840	89.7	10.3	6.7	3.2	1.6	1.6	0.5
By housing tenure:								
Owner occupied units	214,636	95.1	4.9	2.9	1.9	1.2	0.7	0.1
Renter occupied units	106,031	80.3	19.7	11.9	7.0	3.9	3.1	0.9
Persons 16 years old and over	**259,449**	**90.4**	**9.6**	**5.7**	**3.5**	**2.1**	**1.5**	**0.4**
Civilian labor force	162,709	89.1	10.9	6.6	4.0	2.4	1.6	0.3
Employed	156,416	89.3	10.7	6.5	3.9	2.4	1.6	0.3
Unemployed	6,293	83.3	16.7	9.3	6.9	3.4	3.5	0.5
Armed Forces	922	73.6	26.2	12.3	12.3	3.6	8.7	1.7
Not in labor force	95,818	92.9	7.1	4.1	2.6	1.4	1.2	0.4
By occupation:								
Employed civilians, 16 years old and over	156,416	89.3	10.7	6.5	3.9	2.4	1.6	0.3
Management, business, and financial	26,527	90.3	9.7	5.7	3.8	2.1	1.6	0.3
Professional	37,377	89.1	10.9	6.1	4.5	2.5	1.9	0.4
Service	26,776	88.5	11.5	7.4	3.7	2.3	1.4	0.3
Sales	15,551	89.3	10.7	6.2	4.2	2.5	1.7	0.3
Office and administrative support	17,585	89.0	11.0	6.8	4.0	2.4	1.6	0.1
Farming, fishing, and forestry	1,123	87.5	12.6	7.6	(NA)	1.9	(NA)	2.1
Construction and extraction	8,157	88.7	11.3	7.7	3.1	2.0	1.1	0.5
Installation, maintenance, and repair	4,632	90.2	9.8	5.9	3.6	2.7	0.9	0.3
Production	8,690	89.1	10.9	7.1	3.4	2.5	0.9	0.4
Transportation and material moving	9,998	90.5	9.6	5.8	3.5	2.2	1.3	0.3

– NA Not available.

Source: U.S. Census Bureau, "Geographical Mobility: 2018 to 2019," November 2019, and earlier releases, <https://www.census.gov/topics/population/migration.html>.

Table 31. Movers by Type of Move and Reason for Moving: 2019

[31,371 represents 31,371,000. As of March. For persons 1 year old and over. Based on comparison of place of residence in 2019 vs. 2018. Excludes members of the Armed Forces except those living off post or with their families on post. Based on Current Population Survey, Annual Social and Economic Supplement. See text, this section and Appendix III]

Reason for move	All movers	Intra-county	Inter-county	From abroad	Reason for move	All movers	Intra-county	Inter-county	From abroad
Total (1,000)	**31,371**	**18,833**	**11,401**	**1,137**	**Housing–related reasons**	**40.4**	**51.4**	**25.6**	**6.8**
PERCENT DISTRIBUTION					Wanted to own home/not rent	6.3	7.6	4.7	1.8
Total	100.0	100.0	100.0	100.0	New/better house/apartment	17.0	22.2	10.0	1.6
Family–related reasons	**26.8**	**27.1**	**26.5**	**23.4**	Better neighborhood/less crime	3.0	3.8	2.0	0.3
Change in marital status	5.0	5.2	4.8	3.8	Cheaper housing	6.7	8.5	4.2	1.2
To establish own household	11.4	13.3	9.2	3.4	Foreclosure/eviction	0.7	0.8	0.5	0.3
Other family reasons [1]	10.4	8.7	12.5	16.3	Other housing [1]	6.7	8.5	4.3	1.8
Work–related reasons	**21.2**	**12.5**	**34.5**	**32.1**	**Other reasons**	**11.6**	**8.9**	**13.4**	**37.6**
New job/job transfer	12.1	4.5	23.4	22.6	Attend/leave college	2.6	1.2	3.9	12.4
To look for work/lost job	0.9	0.7	1.2	1.3	Change of climate	0.7	0.1	1.6	2.2
Closer to work/easier commute	6.2	5.8	7.1	3.2	Health reasons	2.3	2.2	2.8	–
Retired	1.0	0.6	1.6	0.7	Natural disaster	0.6	0.5	0.5	1.9
Other job–related reason [1]	1.2	0.9	1.3	4.3	Other reason [1]	5.4	4.9	4.6	21.1

– Represents or rounds to zero. [1] As of 2019, write-in responses for "other family," "other job-related," and "other housing" could potentially be recoded to more specific reasons for moving. Before 2019, only "other reason" responses could have been recoded.

Source: U.S. Census Bureau, "Geographical Mobility: 2018 to 2019," November 2019, <https://www.census.gov/topics/population/migration.html>.

Table 32. Geographic Mobility Status of Resident Population by State: 2018

[In percent, except as indicated (323,532 represents 323,532,000). Based on comparison of place of residence in 2018 vs. 2017. The American Community Survey universe includes the household population and the population living in institutions, college dormitories, and other group quarters. Based on a sample and subject to sampling variability. See text, this section and Appendix III]

State	Population 1 year old and over (1,000)	Same house in 2017	Different house in United States in 2017					Abroad in 2017
			Total	Same county	Different county			
					Total	Same state	Different state	
United States	**323,532**	**86.0**	**13.4**	**7.9**	**5.6**	**3.3**	**2.3**	**0.6**
Alabama	4,832	86.4	13.3	7.9	5.4	3.2	2.3	0.3
Alaska	727	83.7	15.6	8.8	6.8	2.4	4.4	0.7
Arizona	7,090	83.0	16.4	10.9	5.5	1.6	3.9	0.6
Arkansas	2,976	85.3	14.4	8.3	6.1	3.7	2.5	0.3
California	39,115	87.5	11.7	7.7	4.0	2.8	1.3	0.7
Colorado	5,633	82.1	17.2	7.9	9.3	5.1	4.2	0.7
Connecticut	3,538	87.7	11.4	7.0	4.5	2.1	2.4	0.9
Delaware	959	89.0	10.7	6.1	4.6	1.0	3.6	0.3
District of Columbia	694	81.9	16.7	9.9	6.9	0.0	6.9	1.4
Florida	21,093	84.7	14.3	8.3	5.9	3.2	2.8	1.1
Georgia	10,410	85.6	13.9	6.5	7.4	4.7	2.6	0.5
Hawaii	1,404	86.3	12.8	8.3	4.5	0.6	3.9	1.0
Idaho	1,735	82.9	16.7	8.7	8.0	3.4	4.6	0.4
Illinois	12,599	87.5	11.9	7.8	4.2	2.5	1.6	0.5
Indiana	6,613	84.9	14.6	8.6	6.0	3.8	2.2	0.5
Iowa	3,119	85.4	14.3	8.3	6.0	3.6	2.4	0.4
Kansas	2,874	83.3	16.2	9.3	7.0	3.7	3.3	0.5
Kentucky	4,415	84.8	14.9	8.7	6.2	3.7	2.5	0.3
Louisiana	4,603	87.6	12.1	7.3	4.8	3.1	1.8	0.3
Maine	1,324	86.4	13.4	8.0	5.4	2.8	2.6	0.3
Maryland	5,975	85.9	13.3	7.4	5.9	3.1	2.7	0.8
Massachusetts	6,834	87.4	11.7	6.8	4.9	2.8	2.1	1.0
Michigan	9,891	86.6	13.0	8.0	5.0	3.6	1.4	0.5
Minnesota	5,543	86.3	13.3	6.9	6.4	4.6	1.8	0.5
Mississippi	2,956	87.4	12.4	6.9	5.5	3.2	2.3	0.3
Missouri	6,053	85.3	14.4	7.8	6.6	4.1	2.5	0.3
Montana	1,052	84.8	14.9	7.5	7.4	3.3	4.1	0.3
Nebraska	1,906	84.1	15.4	8.7	6.7	3.8	2.9	0.5
Nevada	3,004	83.1	16.4	11.3	5.2	0.9	4.2	0.5
New Hampshire	1,345	87.0	12.5	6.4	6.2	2.6	3.6	0.4
New Jersey	8,816	89.3	10.0	5.5	4.5	2.7	1.8	0.7
New Mexico	2,073	86.7	12.7	7.5	5.2	2.3	2.9	0.5
New York	19,330	89.6	9.7	5.8	3.9	2.5	1.3	0.7
North Carolina	10,275	84.9	14.6	7.6	6.9	3.8	3.1	0.5
North Dakota	750	83.1	16.4	8.6	7.8	3.3	4.5	0.5
Ohio	11,555	85.6	14.1	9.0	5.1	3.4	1.7	0.3
Oklahoma	3,896	82.8	16.8	10.0	6.9	4.1	2.7	0.4
Oregon	4,153	82.8	16.7	9.6	7.1	3.7	3.4	0.5
Pennsylvania	12,675	87.7	11.8	6.9	4.9	2.9	2.0	0.5
Rhode Island	1,048	88.6	10.6	5.7	4.9	1.8	3.1	0.8
South Carolina	5,029	85.7	13.9	7.1	6.8	3.1	3.7	0.4
South Dakota	871	85.0	14.6	7.1	7.5	4.4	3.1	0.4
Tennessee	6,693	85.3	14.3	7.9	6.4	3.3	3.1	0.4
Texas	28,333	84.7	14.6	8.8	5.8	3.8	2.0	0.7
Utah	3,115	83.0	16.3	9.9	6.4	3.2	3.2	0.7
Vermont	622	87.2	12.4	6.1	6.3	2.1	4.2	0.4
Virginia	8,424	84.8	14.5	6.3	8.2	5.0	3.3	0.7
Washington	7,453	81.9	17.3	10.5	6.8	3.3	3.5	0.8
West Virginia	1,788	88.7	11.2	6.1	5.1	2.7	2.5	0.1
Wisconsin	5,752	86.2	13.5	7.9	5.6	3.6	2.0	0.3
Wyoming	571	84.0	15.5	8.3	7.3	2.8	4.5	0.5

Source: U.S. Census Bureau, 2018 American Community Survey, B07003, "Geographical Mobility in the Past Year by Sex for Current Residence in the United States," <http://data.census.gov/>, accessed December 2019.

Table 33. Geographic Mobility Status of Households by Household Income: 2019

[128,604 represents 128,604,000. As of March. Covers householders 15 years old and over. Based on comparison of place of residence in 2019 vs. 2018. Excludes members of the Armed Forces except those living off post or with their families on post. Based on Current Population Survey, Annual Social and Economic Supplement. See text, this section and Appendix III]

Household income in 2018	Total (1,000)	Percent distribution						Movers from abroad
		Non-movers	Movers (different house in United States)					
			Total	Same county	Different county			
					Total	Same state	Different state	
Householders, 15 years and over	**128,604**	**90.2**	**9.5**	**5.7**	**3.8**	**2.1**	**1.6**	**0.3**
Under $10,000 or loss	7,620	87.1	11.7	7.6	4.1	2.3	1.8	1.2
$10,000 to $19,999	11,283	89.0	10.9	7.1	3.8	2.2	1.6	0.1
$20,000 to $29,999	11,142	89.5	10.3	6.7	3.5	2.1	1.5	0.3
$30,000 to $39,999	11,225	89.3	10.5	6.7	3.7	2.6	1.1	0.3
$40,000 to $49,999	10,037	88.4	11.2	6.6	4.6	2.4	2.2	0.3
$50,000 to $59,999	9,723	89.5	10.2	6.0	4.2	2.4	1.8	0.3
$60,000 to $69,999	8,605	90.3	9.4	5.5	4.0	2.0	2.0	0.3
$70,000 to $84,999	11,104	89.6	10.2	6.0	4.3	2.3	1.9	0.1
$85,000 to $99,999	8,748	91.2	8.6	4.7	3.9	2.4	1.4	0.2
$100,000 and over	39,117	92.2	7.6	4.4	3.2	1.8	1.4	0.2

Source: U.S. Census Bureau, "Geographical Mobility: 2018 to 2019," November 2019, <https://www.census.gov/topics/population/migration/data/tables.html>.

Table 34. Persons 65 Years Old and Over—Characteristics by Sex: 2000 to 2019

[In percent except as noted (32.6 represents 32,600,000). As of March, except as noted. Covers civilian noninstitutional population. Excludes members of Armed Forces except those living off post or with their families on post. Data for 2000 data based on 1990 Census population controls; data for 2010 based on 2000 Census population controls; and data for 2015 and 2019 based on 2010 Census population controls. Beginning 2005, data based on an expanded sample of households. Based on Current Population Survey. See text, this section]

Characteristic	Total				Male				Female			
	2000	2010	2015	2019	2000	2010	2015	2019	2000	2010	2015	2019
Total (million).................	**32.6**	**38.6**	**46.0**	**52.7**	**13.9**	**16.8**	**20.4**	**23.9**	**18.7**	**21.8**	**25.5**	**28.8**
PERCENT DISTRIBUTION												
Marital status:												
Never married............................	3.9	4.3	4.8	5.7	4.2	4.1	4.9	6.0	3.6	4.5	4.8	5.4
Married......................................	57.2	57.6	58.6	59.7	75.2	74.5	72.4	72.3	43.8	44.5	47.6	49.4
Spouse present........................	54.6	55.2	56.2	57.1	72.6	71.7	70.0	69.3	41.3	42.4	45.2	47.0
Spouse absent [1].....................	2.6	2.4	2.4	2.6	2.6	2.8	2.4	3.0	2.5	2.1	2.4	2.4
Widowed....................................	32.1	28.1	24.4	21.8	14.4	12.7	11.9	10.8	45.3	39.9	34.3	30.8
Divorced....................................	6.7	10.0	12.2	12.8	6.1	8.7	10.8	10.8	7.2	11.1	13.3	14.4
Educational attainment:												
Less than 9th grade....................	16.7	10.2	7.5	5.7	17.8	10.2	7.5	5.6	15.9	10.1	7.4	5.8
Completed 9th to 12th grade, but no high school diploma............	13.8	10.3	8.2	6.5	12.7	9.7	7.0	6.1	14.7	10.8	9.2	6.9
High school graduate...................	35.9	36.4	34.6	31.3	30.4	32.0	30.8	28.0	39.9	39.8	37.6	34.1
Some college or associate's degree...................................	18.0	20.6	23.1	25.4	17.8	19.7	22.8	24.4	18.2	21.2	23.3	26.2
Bachelor's or advanced degree.........	15.6	22.5	26.7	31.1	21.4	28.4	31.8	35.9	11.4	18.0	22.5	27.0
Labor force status: [2]												
Employed...................................	12.4	16.2	18.2	19.6	16.9	20.5	22.5	24.0	9.1	12.9	14.7	15.9
Unemployed...............................	0.4	1.2	0.7	0.6	0.6	1.6	0.9	0.7	0.3	0.9	0.6	0.5
Not in labor force........................	87.2	82.6	81.1	79.8	82.5	77.9	76.6	75.3	90.6	86.2	84.7	83.6
Percent below poverty level [3]...........	9.7	8.9	10.0	9.7	6.9	6.6	7.4	8.1	11.8	10.7	12.1	11.1

[1] Includes separated. [2] Annual averages of monthly figures. Source: U.S. Bureau of Labor Statistics, "Labor Force Statistics from the Current Population Survey," <https://www.bls.gov/cps/tables.htm>. [3] Poverty status based on income in preceding year.

Source: Except as noted, U.S. Census Bureau, Current Population Reports, P20-546, and earlier reports; series P-23, No. 59; series P-60, No. 226; "The Older Population in the United States: March 2002 Detailed Tables (PPL-167)," May 2003; and "Educational Attainment," <https://www.census.gov/topics/education/educational-attainment.html>, "America's Families and Living Arrangements," <https://www.census.gov/topics/families/families-and-households/data/tables.html>, and "Poverty," <https://www.census.gov/data/tables/time-series/demo/income-poverty/cps-pov.html>, accessed April 2020.

Table 35. Persons 65 Years Old and Over by Living Arrangement: 2010 to 2018

[In thousands (40,434 represents 40,434,000), except as indicated. Based on the American Community Survey (ACS). Based on a sample and subject to sampling variability; see text, this section and Appendix III]

Relationship by household type	2010		2015		2017		2018	
	Number	Percent distribution	Number	Percent distribution	Number	Percent distribution	Number	Percent distribution
Total............................	**40,434**	**100.0**	**47,732**	**100.0**	**50,816**	**100.0**	**52,423**	**100.0**
In households.......................	38,869	96.1	46,232	96.9	49,274	97.0	50,905	97.1
In family households..............	26,809	66.3	32,232	67.5	34,560	68.0	35,597	67.9
Householder.......................	13,379	33.1	15,801	33.1	16,869	33.2	17,481	33.3
Spouse.............................	9,563	23.7	11,707	24.5	12,660	24.9	13,090	25.0
Parent..............................	2,208	5.5	2,637	5.5	2,755	5.4	2,704	5.2
Parent-in-law.....................	661	1.6	766	1.6	806	1.6	811	1.5
Other relatives....................	807	2.0	1,030	2.2	1,154	2.3	1,165	2.2
Nonrelatives.......................	191	0.5	291	0.6	315	0.6	345	0.7
In nonfamily households........	12,060	29.8	14,000	29.3	14,713	29.0	15,308	29.2
Householder.......................	11,495	28.4	13,199	27.7	13,823	27.2	14,362	27.4
Male...............................	3,417	8.5	4,244	8.9	4,570	9.0	4,789	9.1
Living alone....................	3,124	7.7	3,851	8.1	4,125	8.1	4,314	8.2
Female............................	8,078	20.0	8,955	18.8	9,253	18.2	9,572	18.3
Living alone....................	7,784	19.3	8,563	17.9	8,817	17.4	9,108	17.4
Nonrelatives.......................	565	1.4	801	1.7	890	1.8	946	1.8
In group quarters..................	1,565	3.9	1,500	3.1	1,542	3.0	1,518	2.9

Source: U.S. Census Bureau, American Community Survey, B09020, "Relationship by Household Type (Including Living Alone) for the Population 65 Years and Over," <https://data.census.gov>, accessed December 2019.

Table 36. Persons 65 Years Old and Over with a Disability by Type and Sex: 2018

[In thousands (17,330 represents 17,330,000). Based on data from the American Community Survey (ACS). Disability data limited to civilian noninstitutionalized population. Based on a sample and subject to sampling variability; see text in this section, and Appendix III]

Type of disability	Number					Percent				
	Total age 65 and over	Males		Females		Total age 65 and over	Males		Females	
		Age 65 to 74	Age 75 and over	Age 65 to 74	Age 75 and over		Age 65 to 74	Age 75 and over	Age 65 to 74	Age 75 and over
Persons with any disability...	**17,330**	**3,686**	**4,031**	**3,702**	**5,910**	**33.9**	**26.2**	**46.2**	**22.9**	**48.5**
With a hearing difficulty............	7,232	1,809	2,316	888	2,219	14.1	12.8	26.5	5.5	18.2
With a vision difficulty..............	3,151	605	711	656	1,179	6.2	4.3	8.1	4.1	9.7
With a cognitive difficulty..........	4,268	757	981	779	1,751	8.3	5.4	11.2	4.8	14.4
With an ambulatory difficulty.....	10,929	1,889	2,288	2,562	4,190	21.4	13.4	26.2	15.9	34.4
With a self-care difficulty..........	3,933	572	898	687	1,777	7.7	4.1	10.3	4.3	14.6
With an independent living difficulty............................	7,107	912	1,543	1,309	3,343	13.9	6.5	17.7	8.1	27.4

Source: U.S. Census Bureau, 2018 American Community Survey, Tables B18101, B18102, B18103, B18104, B18105, B18106, and B18107, <http://data.census.gov>, accessed December 2019.

Table 37. Selected Characteristics of Racial Groups and Hispanic or Latino Population: 2018

[In thousands (223,159 represents 223,159,000), except as indicated. The American Community Survey universe includes the household population and the population living in institutions, college dormitories, and other group quarters. Based on a sample and subject to sampling variability; see text, this section and Appendix III]

Characteristic	Total population	White alone	Black or African American alone	American Indian, Alaska Native alone	Asian alone	Native Hawaiian and Other Pacific Islander alone	Some other race alone	Two or more races	Hispanic or Latino origin [1]	White alone, not Hispanic or Latino [1]
EDUCATIONAL ATTAINMENT										
Persons 25 years old and over, total	**223,159**	**166,574**	**26,866**	**1,760**	**13,111**	**402**	**9,645**	**4,801**	**34,245**	**143,953**
Less than 9th grade	11,084	6,629	1,008	122	962	24	2,110	228	6,048	2,922
9th to 12th grade, no diploma	14,960	9,739	2,629	216	670	28	1,368	312	4,340	6,976
High school graduate (includes equivalency)	59,962	44,938	8,533	546	1,886	139	2,852	1,069	9,663	38,647
Some college, no degree	45,225	33,938	6,467	452	1,506	101	1,594	1,168	6,102	29,887
Associate's degree	19,178	14,807	2,320	157	883	36	529	446	2,282	13,216
Bachelor's degree	44,599	34,842	3,668	174	4,022	53	853	988	3,936	32,022
Graduate degree	28,151	21,681	2,242	94	3,183	21	340	589	1,875	20,283
OCCUPATION										
Employed civilian population, 16 years old and over, total	**156,783**	**115,316**	**18,479**	**1,130**	**9,591**	**301**	**7,837**	**4,129**	**27,376**	**97,448**
Management, business, science, and arts occupations	60,488	46,635	5,527	307	5,073	83	1,362	1,502	6,161	42,276
Management, business, and financial occupations	24,450	19,430	2,017	126	1,690	34	580	574	2,584	17,600
Computer, engineering, and science occupations	9,479	6,783	634	36	1,586	14	169	258	797	6,213
Education, legal, community service, arts, and media occupations	16,962	13,330	1,771	99	866	24	425	447	1,917	11,992
Healthcare practitioners and technical occupations	9,597	7,092	1,105	46	931	12	187	223	864	6,471
Service occupations	27,968	18,448	4,530	267	1,571	69	2,198	885	6,793	14,273
Sales and office occupations	33,556	25,075	4,083	235	1,724	67	1,431	940	5,467	21,412
Natural resources, construction, and maintenance occupations	13,843	10,833	934	141	263	25	1,361	286	4,242	8,123
Farming, fishing, and forestry occupations	1,066	806	42	13	16	3	167	20	529	461
Construction and extraction occupations	8,078	6,265	500	87	112	14	934	166	2,794	4,510
Installation, maintenance, and repair occupations	4,699	3,763	392	41	135	8	261	100	919	3,153
Production, transportation, and material moving occupations	20,928	14,325	3,406	179	960	57	1,485	515	4,712	11,363
Production occupations	8,867	6,251	1,181	70	508	20	644	192	2,000	4,998
Transportation occupations	6,132	4,197	1,120	52	235	17	365	146	1,204	3,428
Material moving occupations	5,929	3,876	1,104	57	217	20	477	178	1,509	2,938
FAMILY INCOME IN THE PAST 12 MONTHS										
Total families	**79,242**	**60,115**	**9,008**	**604**	**4,332**	**128**	**3,377**	**1,677**	**12,310**	**51,872**
Less than $10,000	2,901	1,718	719	48	130	6	198	83	671	1,286
$10,000 to $19,999	4,051	2,545	865	58	176	6	292	108	999	1,898
$20,000 to $29,999	5,575	3,723	1,006	68	231	12	401	134	1,345	2,850
$30,000 to $39,999	6,157	4,356	941	63	249	13	395	141	1,344	3,479
$40,000 to $49,999	6,070	4,451	820	55	247	9	351	136	1,207	3,661
$50,000 to $59,999	5,834	4,382	733	51	228	9	311	120	1,068	3,679
$60,000 to $74,999	8,260	6,355	918	70	346	15	390	166	1,367	5,453
$75,000 to $99,999	11,308	8,950	1,089	76	531	20	428	214	1,577	7,882
$100,000 to $124,999	8,693	6,991	714	44	492	14	259	179	1,014	6,297
$125,000 to $149,999	5,802	4,718	435	26	359	8	140	115	594	4,302
$150,000 to $199,999	6,705	5,452	433	27	524	10	128	132	614	5,007
$200,000 or more	7,884	6,474	335	19	818	7	83	148	510	6,079
Median family income in the past 12 months (in dollars) [2]	76,401	81,287	51,746	51,669	100,790	69,194	51,200	70,216	55,062	85,670
POVERTY STATUS IN THE PAST 12 MONTHS [3]										
Persons below poverty level	41,852	25,231	8,971	640	1,958	102	3,212	1,739	11,025	18,212
Families below poverty level	7,343	4,398	1,670	118	326	16	605	209	2,035	3,083
HOUSING TENURE										
Total householders	**121,520**	**92,353**	**15,098**	**903**	**5,926**	**170**	**4,416**	**2,654**	**16,352**	**81,415**
Owner-occupied	77,708	64,313	6,257	493	3,528	72	1,748	1,297	7,753	58,699
Renter-occupied	43,812	28,040	8,840	410	2,398	98	2,669	1,357	8,598	22,716

[1] Persons of Hispanic origin may be of any race. [2] For definition of median, see Guide to Tabular Presentation. [3] For explanation of poverty level, see text, Section 13.

Source: U.S. Census Bureau, 2018 American Community Survey, Tables B15002, B17001, B17010, B19101, B19113, B24010, and B25003, <https://data.census.gov>, accessed February 2020.

Table 38. Hispanic Population Social and Economic Characteristics: 2019

[60,095 represents 60,095,000, except as noted. As of March, except labor force status is annual average. Excludes members of the Armed Forces except those living off post or with their families on post. Based on Current Population Survey, Annual Social and Economic Supplement; see text, this section and Appendix III]

Characteristic	Number (1,000)						Percent distribution					
	Hispanic, total[1]	Mexican	Puerto Rican	Cuban	Central American[2]	South American	Hispanic, total[1]	Mexican	Puerto Rican	Cuban	Central American[2]	South American
Total persons	60,095	37,447	5,156	2,484	5,585	3,972	100.0	100.0	100.0	100.0	100.0	100.0
Under 5 years old	5,166	3,421	396	140	444	334	8.6	9.1	7.7	5.6	8.0	8.4
5 to 14 years old	10,583	7,126	796	293	868	551	17.6	19.0	15.5	11.8	15.6	13.9
15 to 44 years old	27,732	17,416	2,324	957	2,905	1,739	46.3	46.6	45.2	38.5	52.0	43.8
45 to 64 years old	12,070	7,142	1,107	638	1,087	964	20.0	19.0	21.5	25.7	19.5	24.3
65 years old and over	4,545	2,342	535	458	280	383	7.6	6.2	10.3	18.4	5.0	9.7
EDUCATIONAL ATTAINMENT												
Persons 25 years old and over	34,575	20,500	3,180	1,759	3,394	2,550	100.0	100.0	100.0	100.0	100.0	100.0
Less than high school graduate	9,761	6,776	489	234	1,408	194	28.2	33.1	15.4	13.3	41.5	7.6
High school graduate	10,848	6,643	1,020	584	981	658	31.4	32.4	32.1	33.2	28.9	25.8
Some college or associate degree	7,455	4,301	863	371	501	629	21.6	21.0	27.1	21.1	14.8	24.7
Bachelor's degree or more	6,512	2,780	808	570	505	1,069	18.8	13.6	25.4	32.4	14.9	41.9
NATIVITY AND CITIZENSHIP STATUS												
Total	60,095	37,447	5,156	2,484	5,585	3,972	100.0	100.0	100.0	100.0	100.0	100.0
Native	39,205	25,697	5,123	1,047	2,275	1,500	65.2	68.6	99.4	42.1	40.7	37.8
Foreign born	20,890	11,750	33	1,438	3,310	2,472	34.8	31.4	0.6	57.9	59.3	62.2
Naturalized citizen	7,890	3,862	24	797	1,080	1,182	13.1	10.3	0.5	32.1	19.3	29.8
Not a citizen	13,000	7,888	9	640	2,230	1,290	21.6	21.1	0.2	25.8	39.9	32.5
LABOR FORCE STATUS[3]												
Civilians 16 years old and over	43,507	26,251	3,941	2,043	(NA)	(NA)	100.0	100.0	100.0	100.0	(NA)	(NA)
Civilian labor force	29,053	17,611	2,448	1,304	(NA)	(NA)	66.8	67.1	62.1	63.8	(NA)	(NA)
Employed	27,805	16,836	2,325	1,265	(NA)	(NA)	63.9	64.1	59.0	62.0	(NA)	(NA)
Unemployed	1,248	775	124	39	(NA)	(NA)	2.9	3.0	3.1	1.9	(NA)	(NA)
Not in labor force	14,454	8,640	1,493	738	(NA)	(NA)	33.2	32.9	37.9	36.1	(NA)	(NA)
HOUSEHOLDS[4]												
Total	17,758	10,244	1,861	955	1,578	1,348	100.0	100.0	100.0	100.0	100.0	100.0
Family households	13,271	8,032	1,181	608	1,241	928	74.7	78.4	63.5	63.7	78.6	68.9
Married-couple families	8,444	5,098	672	428	798	670	47.5	49.8	36.1	44.9	50.5	49.7
Male householder, no spouse present	1,579	1,012	139	57	166	69	8.9	9.9	7.5	5.9	10.5	5.2
Female householder, no spouse present	3,249	1,922	370	123	278	189	18.3	18.8	19.9	12.9	17.6	14.0
Nonfamily households[5]	4,487	2,212	680	346	337	419	25.3	21.6	36.5	36.3	21.4	31.1
Male householder	2,323	1,221	326	157	175	226	13.1	11.9	17.5	16.5	11.1	16.8
Female householder	2,164	991	354	189	162	193	12.2	9.7	19.0	19.8	10.3	14.3
MONEY INCOME IN 2018												
Total families	13,271	8,032	1,181	608	1,241	928	100.0	100.0	100.0	100.0	100.0	100.0
Under $5,000	326	186	47	16	17	28	2.5	2.3	4.0	2.7	1.4	3.0
$5,000 to $9,999	233	141	36	13	13	10	1.8	1.8	3.0	2.1	1.0	1.0
$10,000 to $14,999	341	181	33	21	34	32	2.6	2.3	2.8	3.5	2.7	3.4
$15,000 to $19,999	529	304	52	27	53	32	4.0	3.8	4.4	4.4	4.3	3.5
$20,000 to $24,999	716	469	57	28	60	39	5.4	5.8	4.8	4.6	4.9	4.2
$25,000 to $34,999	1,395	833	107	73	137	101	10.5	10.4	9.1	12.0	11.1	10.9
$35,000 to $49,999	2,086	1,352	185	69	163	136	15.7	16.8	15.6	11.3	13.1	14.6
$50,000 to $74,999	2,677	1,680	200	117	274	159	20.2	20.9	16.9	19.2	22.1	17.2
$75,000 to $99,999	1,850	1,191	155	69	190	109	13.9	14.8	13.1	11.3	15.3	11.7
$100,000 and over	3,119	1,694	309	176	300	283	23.5	21.1	26.1	28.9	24.1	30.5
POVERTY STATUS IN 2018												
Total persons[6]	59,957	37,368	5,135	2,480	5,573	3,965	100.0	100.0	100.0	100.0	100.0	100.0
Below poverty level	10,526	6,903	970	342	934	511	17.6	18.5	18.9	13.8	16.8	12.9
At or above poverty level	49,431	30,465	4,165	2,137	4,640	3,455	82.4	81.5	81.1	86.2	83.2	87.1

NA Not available. [1] Includes other Hispanic groups not shown separately. [2] Central American totals exclude Mexican and Cuban. [3] Source: U.S. Bureau of Labor Statistics, "Labor Force Statistics from the Current Population Survey," <https://www.bls.gov/cps/tables.htm>. [4] Shown by the Hispanic origin of the householder. [5] Nonfamily households include a single householder living alone or sharing a home with unrelated individuals under 15 years old. [6] Persons for whom poverty level determined. Excludes unrelated individuals under 15 years old.

Source: U.S. Census Bureau, "The Hispanic Population in the United States: 2019," <https://www.census.gov/topics/population/hispanic-origin/data/tables.html>, accessed May 2020.

Table 39. Native and Foreign-Born Population by State: 2018

[282,439 represents 282,439,000. The term foreign-born refers to anyone who is not a U.S. citizen at birth. This includes naturalized U.S. citizens, legal permanent residents (immigrants), temporary migrants (such as foreign students), humanitarian migrants (such as refugees), and persons illegally present in the United States. The American Community Survey universe includes the household population and the population living in institutions, college dormitories, and other group quarters. Based on a sample and subject to sampling variability; see text, this section and Appendix III]

State	Native population (1,000)	Foreign-born population Number (1,000)	Foreign-born population Percent of total population	Foreign-born population Percent entered 2010 or later	State	Native population (1,000)	Foreign-born population Number (1,000)	Foreign-born population Percent of total population	Foreign-born population Percent entered 2010 or later
U.S.........	282,439	44,729	13.7	23.3	MO.........	5,868	258	4.2	33.5
AL..........	4,725	163	3.3	28.4	MT.........	1,039	23	2.2	(NA)
AK..........	677	61	8.2	25.1	NE.........	1,790	139	7.2	32.2
AZ..........	6,211	960	13.4	20.9	NV.........	2,447	588	19.4	17.9
AR..........	2,870	144	4.8	24.1	NH.........	1,273	83	6.1	25.4
CA..........	28,931	10,626	26.9	17.2	NJ.........	6,875	2,033	22.8	22.4
CO..........	5,146	549	9.6	23.7	NM.........	1,897	199	9.5	18.1
CT..........	3,052	520	14.6	25.0	NY.........	15,095	4,447	22.8	22.2
DE..........	876	91	9.4	24.9	NC.........	9,559	824	7.9	26.0
DC..........	605	98	13.9	32.8	ND.........	724	36	4.7	(NA)
FL..........	16,824	4,475	21.0	25.9	OH.........	11,134	556	4.8	33.2
GA..........	9,455	1,064	10.1	25.5	OK.........	3,706	237	6.0	26.5
HI..........	1,154	266	18.7	23.4	OR.........	3,758	432	10.3	23.8
ID..........	1,649	105	6.0	18.4	PA.........	11,884	923	7.2	30.3
IL..........	10,950	1,791	14.1	18.6	RI.........	918	139	13.2	24.4
IN..........	6,338	354	5.3	31.2	SC.........	4,827	257	5.1	28.9
IA..........	2,981	175	5.5	37.9	SD.........	847	35	4.0	(NA)
KS..........	2,702	209	7.2	28.7	TN.........	6,421	349	5.1	31.4
KY..........	4,299	169	3.8	38.3	TX.........	23,774	4,928	17.2	24.1
LA..........	4,465	195	4.2	34.2	UT.........	2,890	271	8.6	26.3
ME..........	1,291	47	3.5	29.1	VT.........	595	31	4.9	(NA)
MD..........	5,128	915	15.1	25.2	VA.........	7,453	1,065	12.5	26.7
MA..........	5,704	1,198	17.4	29.5	WA.........	6,431	1,105	14.7	26.8
MI..........	9,301	695	7.0	30.7	WV.........	1,778	28	1.5	(NA)
MN..........	5,127	484	8.6	30.0	WI.........	5,516	298	5.1	26.5
MS..........	2,916	71	2.4	38.5	WY.........	560	18	3.0	(NA)

NA Not available.

Source: U.S. Census Bureau, 2018 American Community Survey, B05002, "Place of Birth by Nativity and Citizenship Status"; and B05007, "Place of Birth by Year of Entry by Citizenship Status for the Foreign-Born Population"; <http://data.census.gov>, accessed December 2019.

Table 40. Nativity and Place of Birth of Resident Population—25 Largest Cities: 2018

[The American Community Survey universe includes the household population and the population living in institutions, college dormitories, and other group quarters. Based on a sample and subject to sampling variability; see text, this section and Appendix III. See headnote, Table 39]

City	Total population	Native population Total	Native population Born in United States	Native population Born outside United States [1]	Foreign born Total Number	Foreign born Total Percent of total population	Foreign born Entered 2010 or later Number	Foreign born Entered 2010 or later Percent of foreign-born population
Austin, TX..........	964,243	783,699	766,569	17,130	180,544	18.7	61,091	33.8
Boston, MA..........	695,926	501,557	477,369	24,188	194,369	27.9	61,733	31.8
Charlotte, NC..........	872,506	726,231	710,618	15,613	146,275	16.8	52,747	36.1
Chicago, IL..........	2,705,988	2,165,250	2,114,353	50,897	540,738	20.0	106,893	19.8
Columbus, OH..........	895,877	770,538	762,420	8,118	125,339	14.0	53,266	42.5
Dallas, TX..........	1,345,076	1,012,307	995,455	16,852	332,769	24.7	86,384	26.0
Denver, CO..........	716,492	614,546	601,997	12,549	101,946	14.2	23,253	22.8
Detroit, MI..........	672,681	628,161	620,013	8,148	44,520	6.6	15,349	34.5
El Paso, TX..........	682,686	520,698	502,326	18,372	161,988	23.7	28,639	17.7
Fort Worth, TX..........	898,919	739,974	726,746	13,228	158,945	17.7	32,118	20.2
Houston, TX..........	2,326,090	1,634,606	1,600,290	34,316	691,484	29.7	216,740	31.3
Indianapolis, IN [2]..........	864,131	782,367	772,227	10,140	81,764	9.5	32,040	39.2
Jacksonville, FL..........	903,896	792,098	762,559	29,539	111,798	12.4	38,431	34.4
Los Angeles, CA..........	3,990,469	2,504,061	2,458,249	45,812	1,486,408	37.2	236,970	15.9
Nashville–Davidson, TN [2]..........	665,498	570,458	563,374	7,084	95,040	14.3	36,090	38.0
New York, NY..........	8,398,748	5,305,662	4,993,403	312,259	3,093,086	36.8	703,611	22.7
Philadelphia, PA..........	1,584,138	1,350,933	1,282,814	68,119	233,205	14.7	74,948	32.1
Phoenix, AZ..........	1,660,272	1,337,303	1,317,217	20,086	322,969	19.5	64,258	19.9
Portland, OR..........	652,573	561,845	551,592	10,253	90,728	13.9	24,836	27.4
San Antonio, TX..........	1,532,212	1,302,993	1,267,602	35,391	229,219	15.0	53,738	23.4
San Diego, CA..........	1,425,999	1,045,901	1,015,896	30,005	380,098	26.7	87,318	23.0
San Francisco, CA..........	883,305	587,955	569,436	18,519	295,350	33.4	66,147	22.4
San Jose, CA..........	1,030,119	622,280	603,761	18,519	407,839	39.6	87,930	21.6
Seattle, WA..........	744,949	598,301	583,540	14,761	146,648	19.7	52,808	36.0
Washington, DC..........	702,455	604,609	587,702	16,907	97,846	13.9	32,107	32.8

[1] Includes persons born in Puerto Rico, Guam, the Northern Marianas, or the U.S. Virgin Islands, as well as those born abroad of at least one U.S. citizen parent. [2] Represents the portion of a consolidated city that is not within one or more separately incorporated places.

Source: U.S. Census Bureau, 2018 American Community Survey, C05002, "Place of Birth by Nativity"; and C05005, "Period of Entry by Nativity and Citizenship Status in the United States"; <http://data.census.gov>, accessed December 2019.

Table 41. Native and Foreign-Born Populations by Selected Characteristics: 2019

[In thousands (324,356 represents 324,356,000). As of March. The foreign-born population includes anyone who is not a U.S. citizen at birth. This includes legal permanent residents (immigrants), temporary migrants (such as foreign students), humanitarian migrants (such as refugees), and persons illegally present in the United States. Based on Current Population Survey, Annual Social and Economic Supplement, which includes the civilian noninstitutional population plus Armed Forces living in housing units on or off post with at least one other civilian adult; see text, this section, and Appendix III]

Characteristic	Total population	Native population	Foreign-born population			
			Total	Natural-ized citizen	Not a U.S. citizen	Year of entry: 2010 or later
Total	**324,356**	**278,536**	**45,820**	**22,296**	**23,524**	**11,619**
Under 5 years old	19,736	19,400	336	69	267	336
5 to 9 years old	20,212	19,487	725	112	613	721
10 to 14 years old	20,827	19,933	894	235	659	676
15 to 19 years old	20,849	19,530	1,319	411	907	698
20 to 24 years old	21,254	18,903	2,351	718	1,633	1,226
25 to 29 years old	23,277	19,760	3,516	1,120	2,396	1,776
30 to 34 years old	21,932	17,596	4,336	1,407	2,929	1,687
35 to 39 years old	21,443	16,687	4,756	1,777	2,978	1,315
40 to 44 years old	19,584	14,811	4,773	2,168	2,606	908
45 to 49 years old	20,345	15,512	4,833	2,431	2,402	697
50 to 54 years old	20,355	16,160	4,195	2,330	1,865	431
55 to 59 years old	21,163	17,496	3,667	2,280	1,387	388
60 to 64 years old	20,592	17,511	3,082	2,012	1,069	294
65 to 69 years old	17,356	15,047	2,309	1,607	702	185
70 to 74 years old	14,131	12,315	1,817	1,356	460	133
75 to 79 years old	9,357	8,089	1,268	961	307	77
80 to 84 years old	6,050	5,164	886	682	204	44
85 years and over	5,893	5,134	759	620	139	28
Median age (years)	38	36	45	52	39	31
MARITAL STATUS						
Persons 15 years old and over	**263,581**	**219,717**	**43,865**	**21,880**	**21,985**	**9,886**
Married	132,856	105,261	27,595	14,386	13,209	5,641
Widowed	14,908	12,882	2,025	1,394	631	201
Divorced	25,480	22,422	3,057	1,955	1,102	320
Separated	4,928	3,745	1,184	470	714	207
Never married	85,410	75,407	10,003	3,675	6,328	3,517
EDUCATIONAL ATTAINMENT						
Persons 25 years old and over	**221,478**	**181,283**	**40,195**	**20,751**	**19,444**	**7,963**
Not high school graduate	21,975	12,187	9,788	3,283	6,506	1,326
High school graduate	62,259	52,024	10,235	5,263	4,972	1,845
Some college or associate's degree	57,428	51,183	6,246	4,040	2,205	1,014
Bachelor's degree	49,937	41,686	8,250	5,036	3,214	2,145
Advanced degree	29,880	24,203	5,677	3,130	2,547	1,632
EMPLOYMENT STATUS						
Persons 16 years old and over	**162,709**	**133,896**	**28,813**	**13,983**	**14,830**	**6,383**
Employed	156,416	128,621	27,795	13,542	14,253	6,114
Unemployed	6,293	5,275	1,018	441	577	269
EARNINGS IN 2018 [1]						
Persons 15 years old and over with earnings	**118,000**	**96,579**	**21,421**	**10,792**	**10,628**	**4,411**
$1 to $14,999 or loss	3,698	2,908	790	266	524	190
$15,000 to $29,999	19,847	14,743	5,104	1,904	3,200	1,172
$30,000 to $39,999	18,351	14,669	3,681	1,672	2,010	737
$40,000 to $49,999	15,235	12,809	2,427	1,254	1,173	452
$50,000 to $74,999	28,148	23,969	4,180	2,470	1,710	785
$75,000 to $99,999	13,511	11,530	1,981	1,219	762	444
$100,000 and over	19,210	15,951	3,259	2,008	1,250	632
Median earnings (dollars)	50,653	51,323	42,317	51,122	36,825	41,208
HOUSEHOLD SIZE [2]						
Total households	**128,579**	**108,560**	**20,019**	**11,043**	**8,976**	**3,841**
One person	36,479	32,627	3,852	2,404	1,448	692
Two people	44,373	39,080	5,292	3,155	2,138	1,018
Three people	19,374	15,732	3,642	1,944	1,698	789
Four people	16,413	12,647	3,766	1,907	1,859	780
Five or more people	11,940	8,474	3,467	1,633	1,833	561
INCOME IN 2018 [2]						
Total family households	**83,482**	**68,388**	**15,094**	**8,287**	**6,808**	**2,702**
$1 to $14,999 or loss	4,400	3,459	941	381	559	231
$15,000 to $29,999	7,354	5,492	1,863	822	1,040	349
$30,000 to $39,999	6,307	4,899	1,408	670	738	285
$40,000 to $49,999	5,909	4,708	1,201	553	649	203
$50,000 to $74,999	14,587	11,870	2,717	1,429	1,288	492
$75,000 to $99,999	12,029	10,035	1,994	1,138	856	346
$100,000 and over	32,896	27,926	4,971	3,293	1,678	795
Median income (dollars)	80,663	83,368	68,182	79,762	56,002	61,025
POVERTY STATUS IN 2018 [3]						
Persons below poverty level	38,146	31,828	6,317	2,215	4,103	2,142
Persons at or above poverty level	285,702	246,223	39,479	20,080	19,399	9,455
HOUSEHOLD TENURE [2]						
Total households	**128,578**	**108,560**	**20,019**	**11,044**	**8,976**	**3,841**
Owner occupied unit	82,953	72,664	10,289	6,999	3,290	989
Renter occupied unit [4]	45,627	35,896	9,730	4,045	5,686	2,852

[1] Covers only year-round full-time workers. [2] Based on citizenship of householder. [3] Persons for whom poverty status is determined. Excludes unrelated individuals under 15 years old. [4] Includes occupiers who paid no cash rent.

Source: U.S. Census Bureau, "Foreign Born CPS Data Tables," <https://www.census.gov/topics/population/foreign-born/data/tables.html>, accessed May 2020.

Table 42. Foreign-Born Population—Selected Characteristics by Region of Origin: 2019

[In thousands (45,820 represents 45,820,000). As of March. The term foreign-born refers to anyone who is not a U.S. citizen at birth. This includes naturalized U.S. citizens, legal permanent residents (immigrants), temporary migrants (such as foreign students), humanitarian migrants (such as refugees), and persons illegally present in the United States. Based on Current Population Survey, Annual Social and Economic Supplement; see text, this section and Appendix III]

Characteristic	Total foreign-born	Asia	Europe	Latin America Total	Mexico	Other Latin America	Other areas [1]
Total...............................	**45,820**	**13,864**	**4,522**	**23,718**	**12,060**	**11,658**	**3,716**
Under 5 years old..........................	336	83	36	142	46	96	75
5 to 9 years old...........................	725	207	73	269	92	177	176
10 to 14 years old.........................	894	276	63	408	118	290	147
15 to 19 years old.........................	1,319	387	85	703	280	423	144
20 to 24 years old.........................	2,351	728	149	1,236	613	622	238
25 to 29 years old.........................	3,516	1,146	271	1,736	869	867	363
30 to 34 years old.........................	4,336	1,327	370	2,304	1,278	1,025	335
35 to 39 years old.........................	4,756	1,363	387	2,648	1,450	1,198	357
40 to 44 years old.........................	4,773	1,324	299	2,777	1,529	1,248	373
45 to 49 years old.........................	4,833	1,392	396	2,663	1,519	1,143	381
50 to 54 years old.........................	4,195	1,168	408	2,330	1,303	1,027	289
55 to 59 years old.........................	3,667	1,117	388	1,920	971	948	242
60 to 64 years old.........................	3,082	1,068	297	1,521	750	772	195
65 to 69 years old.........................	2,309	800	294	1,073	466	606	142
70 to 74 years old.........................	1,817	662	316	744	306	438	95
75 to 79 years old.........................	1,268	373	291	534	222	312	70
80 to 84 years old.........................	886	264	180	399	154	245	43
85 years old and over.....................	759	180	217	312	91	220	50
Median age (years) [2]..................	44.9	45.3	51.6	44.3	44.2	44.5	40.3
EDUCATIONAL ATTAINMENT							
Persons 25 years old and over...............	**40,195**	**12,184**	**4,115**	**20,960**	**10,910**	**10,050**	**2,936**
Not a high school graduate..........................	9,788	1,214	244	8,056	5,572	2,484	274
High school graduate.........................	10,235	2,338	956	6,313	3,264	3,049	627
Some college or associate's degree...........	6,246	1,709	843	3,066	1,107	1,960	627
Bachelor's degree.........................	8,250	3,822	1,079	2,491	735	1,756	857
Advanced degree.........................	5,677	3,100	992	1,034	232	802	551
INCOME IN 2018							
Total family households.........................	**15,094**	**4,554**	**1,449**	**7,960**	**4,180**	**3,780**	**1,132**
$1 to $14,999 or loss.........................	941	237	67	577	295	282	59
$15,000 to $29,999.........................	1,863	357	57	1,340	764	576	109
$30,000 to $39,999.........................	1,408	275	76	957	582	375	101
$40,000 to $49,999.........................	1,201	235	80	810	466	343	77
$50,000 to $74,999.........................	2,717	594	218	1,686	895	791	219
$75,000 to $99,999.........................	1,994	567	244	1,047	568	479	136
$100,000 and over.........................	4,971	2,289	707	1,544	610	934	432
Median income (dollars) [2].........................	68,182	100,258	97,941	52,539	49,420	57,899	75,124
POVERTY STATUS IN 2018 [3]							
Persons below poverty level.........................	6,317	1,525	355	3,947	2,184	1,763	491
Persons at or above poverty level.................	39,479	12,339	4,163	19,751	9,871	9,881	3,225

[1] Africa, Oceania, Northern America, and born at sea. [2] For definition of median, see Guide to Tabular Presentation. [3] Persons for whom poverty status is determined. Excludes unrelated individuals under age 15.

Source: U.S. Census Bureau, "Foreign Born CPS Data Tables," <https://www.census.gov/topics/population/foreign-born/data/tables.html>, accessed May 2020.

Table 43. Foreign-Born Population by Citizenship Status and Place of Birth: 2018

[The term foreign-born refers to anyone who is not a U.S. citizen at birth. This includes naturalized U.S. citizens, legal permanent residents (immigrants), temporary migrants (such as foreign students), humanitarian migrants (such as refugees), and persons illegally present in the United States. The American Community Survey universe includes the household population and the population living in institutions, college dormitories, and other group quarters. Based on a sample and subject to sampling variability; see text, this section and Appendix III]

Region and country	Foreign-born population, total	Naturalized citizens	Not a U.S. citizen Number	Percent of foreign-born
Total [1].....................................	**44,728,721**	**22,629,737**	**22,098,984**	**49.4**
Latin America...............................	22,517,787	9,382,390	13,135,397	58.3
Caribbean [2]...............................	4,461,065	2,741,900	1,719,165	38.5
Cuba..........................	1,343,960	(NA)	(NA)	(NA)
Central America...........................	14,753,640	4,855,586	9,898,054	67.1
Mexico..........................	11,171,893	3,594,306	7,577,587	67.8
Other Central America [2]............................	3,581,747	1,261,280	2,320,467	64.8
El Salvador..........................	1,419,330	(NA)	(NA)	(NA)
South America...........................	3,303,082	1,784,904	1,518,178	46.0
Asia [2].....................................	13,957,143	8,271,696	5,685,447	40.7
China, excluding Hong Kong and Taiwan.............	2,221,943	(NA)	(NA)	(NA)
India..........................	2,652,853	(NA)	(NA)	(NA)
Korea..........................	1,039,099	(NA)	(NA)	(NA)
Philippines..........................	2,013,756	(NA)	(NA)	(NA)
Vietnam..........................	1,345,753	(NA)	(NA)	(NA)
Europe..........................	4,747,145	3,115,878	1,631,267	34.4
Africa..........................	2,403,564	1,340,770	1,062,794	44.2
North America..........................	822,469	401,956	420,513	51.1
Oceania..........................	280,394	116,969	163,425	58.3

NA Not available. [1] Includes persons born at sea. [2] Includes other countries not shown separately.

Source: U.S. Census Bureau, 2018 American Community Survey, B05002, "Place of Birth by Nativity and Citizenship Status"; B05006, "Place of Birth for the Foreign-Born Population in the United States"; and B05007, "Place of Birth by Year of Entry by Citizenship Status for the Foreign-Born Population"; <http://data.census.gov/>, accessed December 2019.

Table 44. American Indian Reservations and Alaska Native Village Statistical Areas With Largest American Indian and Alaska Native Populations: 2010

[As of April. Rankings of the American Indian reservations and Alaska Native village statistical areas are based on the American Indian and Alaska Native alone-or-in-combination population]

Area	Total population	American Indian and Alaska Native			Not American Indian and Alaska Native alone or in combination [1]
		Alone or in combination [1]	Alone	In combination [1]	
AMERICAN INDIAN RESERVATION					
Navajo Nation Reservation and Off-Reservation Trust Land, AZ–NM–UT.	173,667	169,321	166,824	2,497	4,346
Pine Ridge Reservation, SD–NE.	18,834	16,906	16,580	326	1,928
Fort Apache Reservation, AZ.	13,409	13,014	12,870	144	395
Gila River Indian Reservation, AZ.	11,712	11,251	10,845	406	461
Osage Reservation, OK.	47,472	9,920	6,858	3,062	37,552
San Carlos Reservation, AZ.	10,068	9,901	9,835	66	167
Rosebud Indian Reservation and Off-Reservation Trust Land, SD.	10,869	9,809	9,617	192	1,060
Tohono O'odham Nation Reservation and Off-Reservation Trust Land, AZ.	10,201	9,278	9,139	139	923
Blackfeet Indian Reservation and Off-Reservation Trust Land, MT.	10,405	9,149	8,944	205	1,256
Flathead Reservation, MT.	28,359	9,138	7,042	2,096	19,221
ALASKA NATIVE VILLAGE STATISTICAL AREA					
Knik Alaska Native village statistical area.	65,768	6,582	3,529	3,053	59,186
Bethel Alaska Native village statistical area.	6,080	4,334	3,953	381	1,746
Kenaitze Alaska Native village statistical area.	32,902	3,417	2,001	1,416	29,485
Barrow Alaska Native village statistical area.	4,212	2,889	2,577	312	1,323
Ketchikan Alaska Native village statistical area.	12,742	2,605	1,692	913	10,137
Kotzebue Alaska Native village statistical area.	3,201	2,585	2,355	230	616
Nome Alaska Native village statistical area.	3,681	2,396	1,994	402	1,285
Chickaloon Alaska Native village statistical area.	23,087	2,373	1,369	1,004	20,714
Dillingham Alaska Native village statistical area.	2,378	1,583	1,333	250	795
Sitka Alaska Native village statistical area.	4,480	1,240	855	385	3,240

[1] In combination with one or more other race groups.

Source: U.S. Census Bureau, 2010 Census Briefs, *The American Indian and Alaska Native Population: 2010*, January 2012. See also <https://www.census.gov/about/partners/cic/resources/data-links/aian.html>.

Table 45. American Indian and Alaska Native Population by Selected Tribal Groupings: 2010

[As of April. Data shown for American Indian and Alaska Native tribes alone or in combination of tribes or races]

Tribal grouping	American Indian and Alaska Native tribal grouping alone or in any combination [1]	Tribal grouping	American Indian and Alaska Native tribal grouping alone or in any combination [1]
Total [2].	**5,220,579**	Navajo.	332,129
AMERICAN INDIAN TRIBES		Osage.	18,576
Apache.	111,810	Ottawa.	13,033
Arapaho.	10,861	Paiute.	13,767
Blackfeet.	105,304	Pima.	26,655
Canadian and French American Indian.	14,822	Potawatomi.	33,771
Central American Indian.	27,844	Pueblo.	62,540
Cherokee.	819,105	Puget Sound Salish.	20,260
Cheyenne.	19,051	Seminole.	31,971
Chickasaw.	52,278	Shoshone.	13,002
Chippewa.	170,742	Sioux.	170,110
Choctaw.	195,764	South American Indian.	47,233
Colville.	10,549	Spanish American Indian.	19,951
Comanche.	23,330	Tohono O'odham.	23,478
Cree.	7,983	Ute.	11,491
Creek.	88,332	Yakama.	11,527
Crow.	15,203	Yaqui.	32,595
Delaware.	18,264	Yuman.	10,089
Hopi.	18,327	**ALASKA NATIVE TRIBES**	
Houma.	10,768	Alaskan Athabascan.	22,484
Iroquois.	81,002	Aleut.	19,282
Kiowa.	13,787	Inupiat.	33,360
Lumbee.	73,691	Tlingit-Haida.	26,080
Menominee.	11,133	Tsimshian.	3,755
Mexican American Indian.	175,494	Yup'ik.	33,889

[1] The numbers by American Indian and Alaska Native tribal grouping do not add to the total American Indian and Alaska Native population. This is because the American Indian and Alaska Native tribal groupings are tallies of the number of American Indian and Alaska Native responses rather than the number of American Indian or Alaska Native respondents. Respondents reporting several American Indian or Alaska Native groups are counted several times. [2] Includes other tribal groupings not shown separately.

Source: U.S. Census Bureau, 2010 Census Briefs, *The American Indian and Alaska Native Population: 2010*, January 2012. See also <https://www.census.gov/about/partners/cic/resources/data-links/aian.html>.

Table 46. Refugee Arrivals and Individuals Granted Asylum by Country of Nationality: 2009 to 2018

[For year ending September 30. Data shown provide information on the number of persons admitted to the U.S. as refugees or granted asylum in the United States in the year shown. In cases with no country of nationality, the applicant's last country of residence is assigned. For definitions of refugee and asylee, see text, this section. The refugee data were derived from data on refugee admissions that are maintained in the Worldwide Refugee Admissions Processing System (WRAPS) of the Bureau of Population, Refugees, and Migration (PRM) of the U.S. Department of State. The asylee data were derived from data on applications for asylum maintained in the Refugee, Asylum, and Parole System (RAPS) of the U.S. Citizenship and Immigration Services (USCIS) of the U.S. Department of Homeland Security, and obtained from the Executive Office for Immigration Review (EOIR) of the U.S. Department of Justice]

Country of nationality	2009	2010	2011	2012	2013	2014	2015	2016	2017	2018
REFUGEE ARRIVALS										
Total	**74,602**	**73,293**	**56,384**	**58,179**	**69,909**	**69,975**	**69,920**	**84,988**	**53,691**	**22,405**
Congo, Democratic Republic	1,135	3,174	977	1,863	2,563	4,540	7,876	16,370	9,377	7,878
Burma	18,202	16,693	16,972	14,160	16,299	14,598	18,386	12,347	5,078	3,555
Ukraine	601	449	428	372	227	490	1,451	2,543	4,264	2,635
Bhutan	13,452	12,363	14,999	15,070	9,134	8,434	5,775	5,817	3,550	2,228
Eritrea	1,571	2,570	2,032	1,346	1,824	1,488	1,596	1,949	1,917	1,269
Afghanistan	349	515	428	481	661	753	910	2,737	1,311	805
El Salvador	0	0	0	0	0	0	0	364	1,124	725
Pakistan	67	59	54	274	158	240	159	545	346	441
Russia	495	326	165	197	125	139	281	462	377	437
Ethiopia	321	668	560	620	765	728	626	1,131	766	376
Iraq	18,838	18,016	9,388	12,163	19,488	19,769	12,676	9,880	6,886	140
Syria	25	25	29	31	36	105	1,682	12,587	6,557	62
Somalia	4,189	4,884	3,161	4,911	7,608	9,000	8,858	9,020	6,130	257
Iran	5,381	3,543	2,032	1,758	2,578	2,846	3,109	3,750	2,577	41
Sudan	683	558	334	1,077	2,160	1,315	1,578	1,458	980	76
Burundi	762	530	110	186	193	68	1,186	694	291	201
Cuba	4,800	4,818	2,920	1,948	4,205	4,062	1,527	354	177	0
Vietnam	1,486	873	79	41	69	67	22	52	21	10
All other countries [1]	2,245	3,229	1,716	1,681	1,816	1,333	2,222	2,928	1,962	1,269
ASYLEES										
Total	**22,314**	**19,772**	**23,572**	**27,951**	**25,014**	**23,371**	**26,015**	**20,362**	**26,509**	**38,687**
China, People's Republic	6,168	6,314	8,174	9,664	8,559	7,899	6,188	4,495	5,615	6,905
Venezuela	586	610	1,057	1,060	677	408	501	343	549	6,087
El Salvador	323	281	234	291	252	369	2,159	2,144	3,476	2,963
Guatemala	507	423	433	505	381	476	2,063	1,921	2,949	2,358
Honduras	86	106	117	211	200	240	1,401	1,474	2,045	2,029
Egypt	482	511	1,003	2,848	3,364	2,821	1,660	827	1,161	1,591
Mexico	255	170	264	420	357	574	859	904	1,042	1,361
India	411	308	307	344	405	481	478	479	685	1,327
Russia	494	525	634	699	537	333	409	284	344	906
Syria	26	23	52	355	794	914	968	724	758	714
Eritrea	436	355	620	456	320	315	383	406	587	606
Iraq	910	391	361	406	464	614	748	611	502	476
Ethiopia	1,112	1,044	1,010	1,072	878	832	868	488	443	539
Haiti	1,006	774	861	666	498	530	408	136	152	226
Colombia	1,006	546	500	432	245	312	302	96	111	370
All other countries [1]	8,506	7,391	7,945	8,522	7,083	6,253	6,620	5,030	6,090	10,229

[1] Includes unknown.

Source: U.S. Department of Homeland Security, Office of Immigration Statistics, *Annual Flow Report, Refugees and Asylees: 2018*, October 2019; and "2018 Yearbook of Immigration Statistics," <https://www.dhs.gov/immigration-statistics/yearbook>, accessed January 2020.

Table 47. Immigrant Orphans Adopted by U.S. Citizens by Sex, Age, Region, and Country of Birth: 2018

[For year ending September 30]

Region and country of birth	Total	Sex		Age		
		Male	Female	Under 1 year old	1 to 4 years old	5 years old and over
Total [1]	**4,033**	**1,931**	**2,102**	**107**	**2,106**	**1,820**
REGION						
Africa	584	278	306	13	267	304
Asia	2,325	1,111	1,214	62	1,589	674
Europe	515	260	255	7	105	403
North America	334	158	176	3	91	240
Oceania	12	8	4	8	(D)	(D)
South America	261	116	145	14	(D)	(D)
COUNTRY [2]						
China	1,484	735	749	5	1,039	440
India	303	83	220	18	215	70
Ukraine	234	128	106	7	25	202
Colombia	226	98	128	14	44	168
Korea, South	209	139	70	–	(D)	(D)
Haiti	201	107	94	–	70	131

– Represents zero. D Data withheld to limit disclosure. [1] Includes countries not shown separately. [2] Data ranked for countries with 200 or more immigrant orphans.

Source: U.S. Department of Homeland Security, Office of Immigration Statistics, "2018 Yearbook of Immigration Statistics," <https://www.dhs.gov/immigration-statistics/yearbook>, accessed January 2020.

Table 48. Immigrants Obtaining Legal Permanent Resident Status: 1901 to 2018

[8,795 represents 8,795,000. For fiscal years ending in year shown; see text, Section 8. Rates based on Census Bureau estimates as of July 1 for resident population through 1929 and for total population thereafter (excluding Alaska and Hawaii prior to 1959)]

Period/year	Number (1,000)	Rate [1]	Period/year	Number (1,000)	Rate [1]	Period/year	Number (1,000)	Rate [1]
1901 to 1910.....	8,795	10.4	2001 to 2010.....	10,501	3.5	2009...........	1,131	3.7
1911 to 1920.....	5,736	5.7	2011 to 2018.....	8,559	3.3	2010...........	1,043	3.4
1921 to 1930.....	4,107	3.5	1990............	1,536	6.1	2011...........	1,062	3.4
1931 to 1940.....	528	0.4	2000............	841	3.0	2012...........	1,032	3.3
1941 to 1950.....	1,035	0.7	2003............	704	2.4	2013...........	991	3.1
1951 to 1960.....	2,515	1.5	2004............	958	3.3	2014...........	1,017	3.2
1961 to 1970.....	3,322	1.7	2005............	1,122	3.8	2015...........	1,051	3.3
1971 to 1980.....	4,399	2.0	2006............	1,266	4.2	2016...........	1,184	3.7
1981 to 1990.....	7,256	3.0	2007............	1,052	3.5	2017...........	1,127	3.5
1991 to 2000.....	9,081	3.4	2008............	1,107	3.6	2018...........	1,097	3.4

[1] Annual rate per 1,000 U.S. population. Rate computed by dividing sum of annual immigration totals by sum of annual U.S. population totals for same number of years.

Source: U.S. Department of Homeland Security, Office of Immigration Statistics, "2018 Yearbook of Immigration Statistics," <https://www.dhs.gov/immigration-statistics/yearbook>, accessed January 2020.

Table 49. Petitions for Naturalization Filed, Persons Naturalized, and Petitions Denied: 1920 to 2018

[For years ending September 30. Naturalizations refer to immigrants aged 18 and over who become citizens of the United States]

Year	Petitions filed	Persons naturalized				Petitions denied
		Total	Civilian	Military	Not reported	
1920...........	218,732	177,683	125,711	51,972	–	15,586
1930...........	113,151	169,377	167,637	1,740	–	9,068
1940...........	278,028	235,260	232,500	2,760	–	6,549
1950...........	66,038	66,346	64,279	2,067	–	2,276
1960...........	127,543	119,442	117,848	1,594	–	2,277
1970...........	114,760	110,399	99,783	10,616	–	1,979
1980...........	192,230	156,627	152,073	4,554	–	4,370
1990...........	233,843	267,586	245,410	1,618	20,558	6,516
1995...........	959,963	485,720	472,518	3,855	9,347	46,067
2000...........	460,916	886,026	812,579	836	72,611	399,670
2005...........	602,972	604,280	589,269	4,614	10,397	108,247
2006...........	730,642	702,589	684,484	6,259	11,846	120,722
2007...........	1,382,993	660,477	648,005	3,808	8,664	89,683
2008...........	525,786	1,046,539	1,032,281	4,342	9,916	121,283
2009...........	570,442	743,715	726,043	7,100	10,572	109,832
2010...........	710,544	619,913	604,410	9,122	6,381	56,994
2011...........	756,008	694,193	677,385	8,373	8,435	57,065
2012...........	899,162	757,434	745,932	7,257	4,245	65,874
2013...........	772,623	779,929	769,073	6,652	4,204	83,112
2014...........	773,824	653,416	642,431	7,468	3,517	66,767
2015...........	783,062	730,259	720,645	7,234	2,380	75,810
2016...........	972,151	753,060	742,090	8,885	2,085	86,033
2017...........	986,851	707,265	695,718	6,883	4,664	83,176
2018...........	810,548	761,901	750,771	4,495	6,635	92,586

– Represents zero.

Source: U.S. Department of Homeland Security, Office of Immigration Statistics, "2018 Yearbook of Immigration Statistics," <https://www.dhs.gov/immigration-statistics/yearbook>, accessed January 2020.

Table 50. Estimated Unauthorized Immigrants (Illegal Aliens) by Selected Country of Birth and State: 2000 to 2015

[In thousands (8,460 represents 8,460,000). As of January. The unauthorized resident immigrant population is defined as all foreign-born non-citizens who are not legal U.S. residents; most entered the U.S. without inspection or were admitted temporarily and stayed past the date they were required to leave. Unauthorized immigrants applying for adjustment to legal permanent resident status under the Immigration and Nationality Act are unauthorized until they have been granted lawful permanent residence, though they may have been authorized to work. These estimates were calculated using a "residual method," whereby estimates of the legally resident foreign-born population were subtracted from the total foreign-born population. All of these component populations were resident in the United States on January 1 and entered during the period from 1980 to the year prior to the year shown. Persons who entered the U.S. prior to 1980 were assumed to be legally resident. Estimates of the legally resident foreign-born population were based primarily on administrative data of the Department of Homeland Security, while estimates of the total foreign-born population were obtained from the American Community Survey of the U.S. Census Bureau]

Country of birth	2000	2010 [1]	2015	State of residence	2000	2010 [1]	2015
Total..........................	8,460	11,590	11,960	Total..........................	8,460	11,590	11,960
Mexico.........................	4,680	6,830	6,580	California.......................	2,510	2,910	2,880
El Salvador.....................	430	670	750	Texas..........................	1,090	1,780	1,940
Guatemala......................	290	520	620	Florida.........................	800	730	810
India...........................	120	270	470	New York.......................	540	690	590
Honduras.......................	160	380	440	Illinois.........................	440	550	450
Philippines......................	200	290	370	New Jersey.....................	350	440	440
China..........................	190	300	320	Georgia........................	220	430	390
Korea..........................	180	220	230	North Carolina..................	260	390	390
Vietnam........................	160	190	170	Arizona........................	330	350	380
Ecuador........................	(NA)	210	150	Virginia........................	160	220	310
Other countries.................	1,940	1,720	1,870	Other states....................	1,760	3,080	3,390

NA Not available. [1] Revised to be consistent with estimates derived from the 2010 Census.

Source: U.S. Department of Homeland Security, Office of Immigration Statistics, *Illegal Alien Population Residing in the United States, January 2015*, December 2018. See also <https://www.dhs.gov/immigration-statistics>.

Table 51. Immigrants Obtaining Legal Permanent Resident Status by Class of Admission: 2000 to 2018

[For years ending September 30. For definition of immigrants, see text, this section]

Class of admission	2000	2005	2010	2015	2017	2018
Total	**841,002**	**1,122,257**	**1,042,625**	**1,051,031**	**1,127,167**	**1,096,611**
New arrivals	407,279	383,955	476,049	508,716	578,081	528,727
Adjustments	433,723	738,302	566,576	542,315	549,086	567,884
Family-sponsored preferences	235,092	212,970	214,589	213,910	232,238	216,563
Unmarried sons/daughters of U.S. citizens and their children	27,635	24,729	26,998	24,533	26,219	27,251
Spouses, children, and unmarried sons/daughters of alien residents	124,540	100,139	92,088	104,892	113,500	109,841
Married sons/daughters of U.S. citizens [1]	22,804	22,953	32,817	24,271	23,260	19,531
Brothers or sisters of U.S. citizens age 21 and older [1]	60,113	65,149	62,686	60,214	69,259	59,940
Immediate relatives of U.S. citizens	346,350	436,115	476,414	465,068	516,508	478,961
Spouses	196,405	259,144	271,909	265,367	292,909	268,149
Children [2]	82,638	94,858	88,297	66,740	74,989	66,794
Parents	67,307	82,113	116,208	132,961	148,610	144,018
Employment-based preferences	106,642	246,865	148,343	144,047	137,855	138,171
Priority workers [1]	27,566	64,731	41,055	41,688	41,060	39,514
Professionals with advanced degrees or aliens of exceptional ability [1]	20,255	42,597	53,946	44,344	39,331	40,095
Skilled workers, professionals, unskilled workers [1]	49,589	129,070	39,762	37,243	38,083	39,228
Special immigrants [1]	9,014	10,121	11,100	10,584	9,504	9,711
Employment creation (investors) [1]	218	346	2,480	10,188	9,877	9,623
Diversity (lottery) [3]	50,920	46,234	49,763	47,934	51,592	45,350
Refugees	56,091	112,676	92,741	118,431	120,356	155,734
Asylees	6,837	30,286	43,550	33,564	25,647	30,175
Parolees	3,162	7,715	1,592	23	26	14
Children born abroad to alien residents	(NA)	571	716	403	75	69
Nicaraguan Adjustment and Central American Relief Act	20,364	1,155	248	49	(NA)	(NA)
Haitian Refugee Immigration Fairness Act (HRIFA)	435	2,820	386	9	(NA)	(NA)
Certain Iraqis and Afghans employed by U.S. Government [1]	(NA)	(NA)	2,575	7,048	19,191	10,297
Cancellation of removal	12,154	20,785	8,180	4,713	3,539	4,421
Victims of human trafficking	(NA)	(NA)	511	970	1,317	1,208
Victims of crimes and their spouses and children	(NA)	(NA)	2,165	14,138	18,065	15,012
Other	2,955	4,065	852	724	758	636

NA Not available. [1] Includes spouses and children. [2] Includes orphans. [3] The Diversity Visa Program is a lottery available to nationals of countries with fewer than 50,000 persons granted legal permanent residency status during the preceding 5 years in the employment-based and family-sponsored preferences and immediate relative classes of admission. Includes categories of immigrants admitted under three laws intended to diversify immigration: P.L. 99-603, P.L. 100-658, and P.L. 101-649.

Source: U.S. Department of Homeland Security, Office of Immigration Statistics, "2018 Yearbook of Immigration Statistics," <https://www.dhs.gov/immigration-statistics/yearbook>, accessed January 2020.

Table 52. Immigrants Obtaining Legal Permanent Resident Status by Selected Country of Birth and Selected Characteristics: 2018

[For year ending September 30]

Age, marital status, occupation, class of admission	All countries [1]	Mexico	Cuba	China	India	Dominican Republic	Philippines	Vietnam	El Salvador
Total	**1,096,611**	**161,858**	**76,486**	**65,214**	**59,821**	**57,413**	**47,258**	**33,834**	**28,326**
AGE									
Under 18 years old	208,683	19,435	9,433	9,503	7,137	18,269	9,701	6,373	5,111
18 to 24 years old	125,852	19,502	7,325	4,611	4,770	7,572	5,161	4,562	5,028
25 to 34 years old	262,281	39,368	21,696	17,259	12,440	10,265	9,004	6,475	5,659
35 to 44 years old	210,160	37,008	14,975	12,442	15,177	8,593	8,550	4,435	5,917
45 to 54 years old	142,407	30,370	13,070	9,499	7,581	6,729	5,909	5,455	3,601
55 to 64 years old	87,007	10,749	5,520	6,344	6,469	3,832	5,385	4,688	1,798
65 years old and over	60,221	5,426	4,467	5,556	6,247	2,153	3,548	1,846	1,212
MARITAL STATUS									
Married	627,443	111,305	31,723	44,387	43,690	22,866	25,556	20,486	14,158
Single	400,196	40,678	35,200	16,935	12,684	31,721	19,169	11,283	12,235
Other	58,995	6,838	9,065	3,635	3,268	2,710	2,371	2,015	1,204
Unknown	9,977	3,037	498	257	179	116	162	50	729
OCCUPATION [2]									
Management, professional, and related	114,188	7,973	3,549	11,997	12,881	962	6,202	1,879	1,176
Service	42,652	8,344	6,417	4,113	500	508	1,308	476	1,663
Sales and office	44,871	5,731	2,519	5,388	2,476	862	1,864	3,771	867
Farming, fishing, and forestry	12,006	(D)	226	1,030	1,681	(D)	360	1,242	(D)
Construction, extraction, maintenance and repair	16,838	7,087	2,852	198	63	249	87	132	797
Production, transportation, and material moving	55,385	20,822	10,797	1,783	478	2,138	283	636	1,453
MAJOR CLASS OF ADMISSION									
Immediate relatives of U.S. citizens	478,961	105,539	3,024	24,022	20,652	26,731	23,018	15,866	15,410
Family-sponsored preferences	216,563	36,276	3,381	11,728	14,845	30,270	15,064	16,240	7,315
Employment-based preferences	138,171	5,600	13	18,843	22,672	223	8,655	1,560	1,475
Diversity programs	45,350	10	201	19	34	0	8	3	0
Refugees and asylees	185,909	1,270	69,860	10,420	1,228	97	23	58	2,480
Other	31,657	13,163	7	182	390	92	490	107	1,646

D Data withheld to avoid disclosure. [1] Includes other countries not shown separately. [2] Those in the military and without an occupation and unknown occupation are not shown.

Source: U.S. Department of Homeland Security, Office of Immigration Statistics, "Profiles on Lawful Permanent Residents: Fiscal Year 2018," <https://www.dhs.gov/profiles-lawful-permanent-residents>, accessed February 2020.

Table 53. Immigrants Obtaining Legal Permanent Resident Status by Country of Birth: 1991 to 2018

[In thousands (9,080.5 represents 9,080,500). For years ending September 30. Persons by country prior to 1996 are unrevised]

Region and country of birth	1991-2000	2001-2010	2011-2017	2018	Region and country of birth	1991-2000	2001-2010	2011-2017	2018
All countries [1]	**9,080.5**	**10,501.1**	**7,462.4**	**1,096.6**	**Africa [1]**	**382.5**	**860.4**	**738.0**	**115.7**
Europe [1]	**1,226.0**	**1,263.9**	**599.0**	**80.0**	Cameroon	5.8	23.2	30.4	4.2
Albania	26.2	50.5	30.1	5.0	Congo, Dem. Rep. of the...	2.5	7.9	34.1	9.9
France	27.4	39.6	30.9	4.3	Egypt	46.7	73.1	72.5	9.8
Germany	67.6	77.7	39.0	4.4	Ethiopia	49.3	109.7	93.0	12.4
Italy	22.5	26.5	22.7	3.3	Ghana	35.6	65.3	58.4	8.4
Poland	169.5	116.8	41.0	4.4	Kenya	14.0	59.7	45.6	7.2
Russia	[2]127.8	139.7	63.8	8.6	Liberia	16.0	45.2	27.0	3.1
Spain	13.7	15.8	19.0	2.8	Morocco	20.0	44.4	27.5	3.1
Ukraine	[2]141.0	149.3	60.4	11.9	Nigeria	67.2	111.2	91.5	14.0
United Kingdom	135.6	153.5	85.0	9.9	Somalia	20.1	64.2	39.8	7.6
Asia [1]	**2,973.2**	**3,784.6**	**3,018.6**	**397.2**	South Africa	22.6	32.9	19.6	3.0
Afghanistan	17.4	24.3	56.4	12.9	Sudan	12.6	32.9	19.7	3.7
Armenia	[2]26.6	29.9	21.2	3.2	Tanzania	4.2	10.4	7.6	3.2
Bangladesh	66.0	106.7	105.1	15.7	**Oceania [1]**	**47.9**	**58.1**	**36.2**	**4.7**
Burma	11.0	45.0	96.4	8.2	**North America [1]**	**3,910.1**	**3,605.1**	**2,508.8**	**419.0**
Cambodia	18.5	35.6	19.5	3.2	Canada	137.2	168.2	87.4	9.9
China	424.4	662.7	544.6	65.2	Cuba	178.7	318.4	334.1	76.5
India	383.0	662.5	471.0	59.8	Dominican Republic	340.8	329.1	343.9	57.4
Iran	112.5	125.9	92.4	10.1	El Salvador	217.3	252.8	140.5	28.3
Iraq	40.7	65.0	124.4	14.4	Guatemala	103.0	160.7	79.9	15.6
Israel	31.9	46.6	27.7	3.7	Haiti	181.7	213.8	142.9	21.4
Japan	61.4	76.1	38.9	4.3	Honduras	66.7	65.4	64.0	13.8
Jordan [3]	39.7	38.7	32.5	5.3	Jamaica	173.4	180.7	141.7	20.3
Korea, South [4]	171.1	221.5	145.4	17.7	Mexico	2,250.5	1,693.2	1,062.7	161.9
Malaysia	14.8	20.5	20.2	3.1	Nicaragua	94.6	60.9	22.3	3.1
Nepal	3.6	33.1	84.3	12.0	Trinidad and Tobago	63.2	61.8	28.7	2.8
Pakistan	124.5	157.0	116.9	15.8	**South America [1]**	**539.3**	**906.0**	**551.2**	**78.9**
Philippines	505.3	587.2	377.7	47.3	Argentina	24.3	50.5	28.4	3.1
Syria	26.1	25.9	27.2	14.7	Brazil	52.2	123.8	84.9	15.4
Taiwan	106.3	87.9	36.4	5.1	Colombia	130.8	251.3	136.8	17.5
Thailand	48.4	68.3	54.1	5.6	Ecuador	76.3	112.5	73.5	11.5
Turkey	26.3	41.1	30.1	5.6	Guyana	73.8	76.2	41.2	5.2
Uzbekistan	[2]22.9	36.0	31.8	4.6	Peru	105.6	145.7	81.0	9.9
Vietnam	420.8	306.1	230.4	33.8	Venezuela	29.9	84.4	68.3	11.8

[1] Includes other countries not shown separately. [2] Covers years 1992–2000. [3] Prior to 2003, includes Palestine; beginning in 2003, Palestine included in Unknown (not shown separately). [4] Prior to 2009, includes a small number of cases from North Korea.

Source: U.S. Department of Homeland Security, Office of Immigration Statistics, "2018 Yearbook of Immigration Statistics," <https://www.dhs.gov/immigration-statistics/yearbook>, accessed January 2020.

Table 54. Refugees and Asylees Obtaining Legal Permanent Resident Status by Country of Birth: 1991 to 2018

[For years ending September 30]

Country of birth	1991-2000	2001-2010	2011-2017	2018	Country of birth	1991-2000	2001-2010	2011-2017	2018
Total [1]	**1,016,820**	**1,325,365**	**1,028,369**	**185,909**	Burundi	148	3,387	2,769	597
Europe [1]	**425,047**	**296,794**	**28,509**	**6,335**	Cameroon	299	7,564	6,802	447
Albania	3,250	10,905	1,456	143	Congo, Dem. Rep. of the..	922	5,643	16,326	6,634
Belarus	[2]21,592	9,310	1,828	234	Congo, Rep. of the	25	5,243	2,960	378
Moldova	[2]10,150	10,813	2,980	624	Cote d' Ivoire	119	4,404	2,438	203
Russia	[2]54,488	32,819	4,933	684	Egypt	419	7,987	15,781	1,449
Soviet Union [3]	117,783	6,794	2,430	270	Eritrea	608	4,534	9,520	1,405
Spain	438	610	2,389	346	Ethiopia [4]	17,829	31,900	26,523	3,347
Ukraine	[2]96,974	57,186	6,086	3,277	Gambia, The	53	1,221	1,656	190
Asia [1]	**350,702**	**389,469**	**483,929**	**64,547**	Guinea	50	4,467	3,852	226
Afghanistan	9,711	13,533	4,442	1,929	Kenya	1,438	15,351	10,742	2,549
Armenia	1,794	12,408	2,619	173	Liberia	3,836	28,808	5,359	262
Bhutan	(D)	6,762	49,771	2,283	Rwanda	389	2,939	3,864	1,229
Burma	721	32,904	85,848	6,765	Somalia	16,737	59,069	29,991	6,798
China	7,577	111,632	103,008	10,420	Sudan	5,174	23,580	8,700	1,556
India	2,538	24,010	6,584	1,228	Tanzania	16	3,503	3,191	2,669
Indonesia	201	7,618	1,920	121	Uganda	439	2,482	3,320	1,463
Iran	24,251	45,515	24,341	4,441	Zimbabwe	32	1,563	1,525	131
Iraq	22,488	40,789	99,446	11,763	**Oceania [1]**	**291**	**1,453**	**304**	**28**
Jordan	331	1,013	2,625	1,327	**North America [1]**	**183,251**	**326,846**	**319,837**	**77,701**
Malaysia	383	1,125	9,594	1,753	Cuba	142,571	276,331	287,924	69,860
Nepal	32	6,000	35,696	3,346	El Salvador	4,072	4,061	(NA)	2,480
Pakistan	1,649	8,339	5,077	1,414	Guatemala	2,029	7,399	6,263	1,917
Sri Lanka	353	1,852	2,067	193	Haiti	9,354	29,824	10,719	476
Syria	2,119	2,223	6,617	13,035	Honduras	1,047	1,684	2,421	1,189
Thailand	22,716	22,405	23,854	1,646	Mexico	415	2,780	5,152	1,270
Uzbekistan	[2]17,991	14,047	2,373	226	**South America [1]**	**5,840**	**65,912**	**24,005**	**3,028**
Vietnam	206,530	36,990	3,028	58	Colombia	1,129	40,321	7,993	846
Africa [1]	**51,469**	**242,839**	**171,109**	**34,224**	Venezuela	1,390	10,726	8,679	1,168

NA Not available. [1] Includes other countries and unknown not shown separately. [2] Covers years 1992-2000. [3] Data are for unknown republics only. [4] Prior to 1993, data include Eritrea.

Source: U.S. Department of Homeland Security, Office of Immigration Statistics, "2018 Yearbook of Immigration Statistics," <https://www.dhs.gov/immigration-statistics/yearbook>, accessed January 2020.

Table 55. Population by Selected Ancestry Group and Region: 2018

[In thousands (327,167 represents 327,167,000), except percent. Covers single and multiple ancestries; includes all people who reported each ancestry. Ancestry refers to a person's ethnic origin, heritage, descent, or "roots," which may reflect their place of birth or that of previous generations of their family. The American Community Survey universe includes the household population and the population living in institutions, college dormitories, and other group quarters. Based on a sample and subject to sampling variability; see text, this section]

| Ancestry group | Total, (1,000) | Percent distribution by region | | | | Ancestry group | Total, (1,000) | Percent distribution by region | | | |
		North-east	Mid-west	South	West			North-east	Mid-west	South	West
Total population [1]	**327,167**	**17**	**21**	**38**	**24**	Irish	30,805	25	24	31	19
Afghan	139	12	7	29	52	Israeli	142	37	10	28	26
Albanian	199	57	22	16	5	Italian	16,412	42	17	24	17
American	19,613	13	18	56	14	Latvian	89	30	22	25	23
Arab [1]	2,111	23	24	30	23	Lithuanian	610	36	27	21	16
Egyptian	285	38	10	29	23	Northern European	546	12	18	28	42
Iraqi	149	11	39	20	30	Norwegian	4,360	6	48	14	33
Jordanian	96	14	23	37	27	Pennsylvania					
Lebanese	497	23	27	31	19	German	297	57	26	12	5
Moroccan	117	36	15	30	19	Polish	8,887	31	37	20	12
Palestinian	129	13	30	32	26	Portuguese	1,334	44	4	18	35
Syrian	192	31	20	26	23	Romanian	459	23	25	25	26
Arab	302	15	34	29	22	Russian	2,503	34	17	22	27
Armenian	447	21	8	10	61	Scandinavian	1,160	8	29	24	39
Assyrian [3]	107	3	66	2	29	Scotch-Irish	2,933	12	17	51	20
Australian	92	18	16	28	38	Scottish	5,212	16	20	39	26
Austrian	644	29	23	24	23	Serbian	200	19	41	19	21
Belgian	349	12	51	20	18	Slavic	124	25	25	24	26
Brazilian	478	41	5	38	16	Slovak	655	40	33	17	10
British	2,466	13	18	40	29	Slovene	176	15	51	16	18
Bulgarian	106	19	28	28	24	Sub-Saharan					
Cajun	115	5	2	85	8	African [1]	4,015	20	19	44	16
Canadian	655	25	17	29	30	Cape Verdean	103	88	2	7	3
Croatian	400	22	37	17	24	Ethiopian	331	8	17	42	33
Czech	1,299	11	45	27	17	Ghanaian	158	40	12	39	9
Czechoslovakian	296	20	34	26	20	Kenyan	87	15	27	36	23
Danish	1,221	8	31	16	45	Nigerian	463	22	16	47	14
Dutch	3,689	15	37	25	23	Somali	183	10	60	8	22
Eastern European	1,065	33	19	26	22	African	2,163	17	17	51	15
English	22,807	17	21	38	25	Swedish	3,615	13	38	17	32
European	6,404	11	20	36	34	Swiss	900	15	34	22	29
Finnish	650	12	45	15	29	Turkish	217	34	12	32	21
French						Ukrainian	997	38	18	20	24
(except Basque)	7,275	23	23	33	21	Welsh	1,805	18	22	33	27
French						West Indian [1,2]	2,949	42	4	49	5
Canadian	2,033	41	19	26	14	Haitian	1,036	38	3	56	2
German	41,222	16	39	26	19	Jamaican	1,111	43	4	48	5
Greek	1,284	33	22	25	20	Trinidadian and					
Guyanese	261	76	2	20	2	Tobagonian	208	51	3	42	4
Hungarian	1,352	31	30	21	18	West Indian	300	53	6	35	6
Iranian	467	12	8	28	52	Yugoslavian	242	17	35	22	26

[1] Includes other groups, not shown separately. [2] Excludes Hispanic-origin groups. [3] Assyrian, Chaldean, and Syriac.

Source: U.S. Census Bureau, 2018 American Community Survey, B04006, "People Reporting Ancestry," <http://data.census.gov/>, accessed December 2019.

Table 56. Language Spoken at Home and English Speaking Ability: 2018

[307,521 represents 307,521,000. See headnote, Table 55]

Language	Number of speakers of language at home (1,000)	Percent who speak English less than "very well"	Language	Number of speakers of language at home (1,000)	Percent who speak English less than "very well"
Total population 5 years old and over	**307,521**	(X)	Bengali	375	40.3
			Nepali, Marathi, or other Indic	424	35.9
Speak only English	240,252	(X)	Other Indo-European	574	29.1
Spanish	41,460	39.2	Telugu	400	17.5
French (including Cajun)	1,232	21.8	Tamil	309	15.7
Haitian	834	38.5	Malayalam, Kannada, or other Dravidian	280	20.0
Italian	554	24.3	Chinese (including Mandarin, Cantonese)	3,472	52.7
Portuguese	816	34.6	Japanese	459	41.1
German	890	14.7	Korean	1,086	52.9
Yiddish, Pennsylvania Dutch [1]	533	27.9	Hmong	235	40.3
Greek	260	21.8	Vietnamese	1,542	57.2
Russian	919	42.4	Khmer	184	50.3
Polish	509	37.5	Thai, Lao, or other Tai-Kadai	310	48.1
Serbo-Croatian	252	31.1	Tagalog (including Filipino)	1,760	29.5
Ukrainian or other Slavic languages	333	33.5	Ilocano, Samoan, Hawaiian [2]	486	34.6
Armenian	233	42.7	Arabic	1,259	35.1
Persian (including Farsi, Dari)	451	35.2	Hebrew	216	14.9
Gujarati	419	32.0	Amharic, Somali, or other Afro-Asiatic	582	41.0
Hindi	874	18.7	Yoruba, Twi, Igbo [3]	582	20.4
Urdu	485	28.7	Swahili and other African [4]	272	32.8
Punjabi	316	39.6	Navajo	171	22.5

X Not applicable. [1] Includes other West Germanic. [2] Includes other Austronesian. [3] Includes other West African. [4] Other languages of Central, Eastern, and Southern Africa.

Source: U.S. Census Bureau, 2018 American Community Survey, B16001, "Language Spoken at Home by Ability to Speak English for the Population 5 Years and Over," <data.census.gov/>, accessed December 2019.

Table 57. Language Spoken at Home by State: 2018

[In thousands (307,521 represents 307,521,000), except percent. The American Community Survey universe includes the household population and the population living in institutions, college dormitories, and other group quarters. Based on a sample and subject to sampling variability; see text, this section, and Appendix III]

State	Population 5 years old and over (1,000)	English only (1,000)	Language other than English Number (1,000)	Language other than English Percent of population 5 years and over	State	Population 5 years old and over (1,000)	English only (1,000)	Language other than English Number (1,000)	Language other than English Percent of population 5 years and over
U.S.	**307,521**	**240,252**	**67,269**	**21.9**	MO	5,756	5,392	364	6.3
AL	4,599	4,355	244	5.3	MT	1,001	956	44	4.4
AK	685	574	111	16.3	NE	1,798	1,597	202	11.2
AZ	6,738	4,882	1,855	27.5	NV	2,850	1,968	882	30.9
AR	2,826	2,609	217	7.7	NH	1,294	1,193	100	7.8
CA	37,129	20,574	16,554	44.6	NJ	8,391	5,735	2,656	31.7
CO	5,360	4,463	897	16.7	NM	1,977	1,303	674	34.1
CT	3,391	2,640	751	22.1	NY	18,402	12,757	5,645	30.7
DE	913	794	119	13.1	NC	9,786	8,608	1,178	12.0
DC	657	546	111	16.9	ND	708	656	52	7.4
FL	20,164	14,168	5,996	29.7	OH	10,996	10,189	807	7.3
GA	9,874	8,489	1,385	14.0	OK	3,685	3,292	393	10.7
HI	1,333	966	367	27.5	OR	3,960	3,329	631	15.9
ID	1,641	1,462	179	10.9	PA	12,107	10,660	1,446	11.9
IL	11,982	9,168	2,814	23.5	RI	1,003	785	218	21.7
IN	6,274	5,716	558	8.9	SC	4,797	4,443	353	7.4
IA	2,958	2,697	261	8.8	SD	822	766	56	6.8
KS	2,725	2,404	320	11.8	TN	6,366	5,900	466	7.3
KY	4,195	3,958	236	5.6	TX	26,691	17,132	9,559	35.8
LA	4,358	4,025	333	7.6	UT	2,911	2,450	461	15.8
ME	1,275	1,197	78	6.1	VT	597	564	33	5.6
MD	5,681	4,582	1,099	19.3	VA	8,016	6,703	1,312	16.4
MA	6,545	4,954	1,591	24.3	WA	7,077	5,660	1,418	20.0
MI	9,427	8,500	927	9.8	WV	1,712	1,669	42	2.5
MN	5,256	4,614	642	12.2	WI	5,483	4,999	484	8.8
MS	2,809	2,704	105	3.7	WY	542	504	38	7.0

Source: U.S. Census Bureau, 2018 American Community Survey, C16005, "Nativity by Language Spoken at Home by Ability to Speak English for the Population 5 Years and Over," <http://data.census.gov/>, accessed December 2019.

Table 58. Language Spoken at Home—25 Largest Cities: 2018

[In thousands (904 represents 904,000), except percent. Data shown for population aged 5 and over. The American Community Survey universe includes the household population and the population living in institutions, college dormitories, and other group quarters. Based on a sample and subject to sampling variability; see text, this section, and Appendix III]

City	Population 5 years old and over (1,000)	English only (1,000)	Language other than English, total [1] Number (1,000)	Language other than English, total [1] Percent	Speak English less than "very well" (1,000)	Spanish (1,000)	Other Indo-European languages (1,000) [2]	Asian and Pacific Island languages (1,000) [2]
Austin, TX	904	615	289	32.0	103	200	35	39
Boston, MA	661	418	242	36.7	111	109	73	46
Charlotte, NC	817	631	186	22.8	85	103	36	33
Chicago, IL	2,538	1,628	910	35.8	361	606	150	110
Columbus, OH	832	699	133	16.0	56	32	30	29
Dallas, TX	1,245	706	539	43.3	256	469	26	26
Denver, CO	674	505	169	25.1	64	128	15	14
Detroit, MI	627	551	76	12.1	32	45	10	3
El Paso, TX	633	199	434	68.6	200	420	5	6
Fort Worth, TX	830	548	282	34.0	118	226	18	23
Houston, TX	2,157	1,080	1,077	49.9	503	838	79	105
Indianapolis, IN [3]	803	698	104	13.0	43	61	12	19
Jacksonville, FL	841	700	141	16.8	57	65	33	31
Los Angeles, CA	3,762	1,535	2,227	59.2	953	1,601	254	318
Nashville–Davidson, TN [3]	622	505	117	18.8	58	57	25	16
New York, NY	7,864	4,044	3,820	48.6	1,762	1,880	1,010	695
Philadelphia, PA	1,480	1,126	354	23.9	154	166	81	80
Phoenix, AZ	1,543	957	586	38.0	201	486	42	32
Portland, OR	619	498	121	19.6	48	39	27	43
San Antonio, TX	1,426	802	625	43.8	204	566	19	33
San Diego, CA	1,340	785	555	41.4	205	308	64	160
San Francisco, CA	844	497	346	41.1	154	85	45	207
San Jose, CA	968	410	558	57.6	225	224	73	245
Seattle, WA	707	551	156	22.1	56	32	33	72
Washington, DC	657	546	111	16.9	37	55	26	15

[1] Includes other language groups, not shown separately. [2] Beginning 2016, data are not comparable with data from previous years due to changes in language classifications; for more information, see <https://www.census.gov/content/dam/Census/programs-surveys/acs/tech-doc/user-notes/2016_Language_User_Note.pdf>. [3] Represents the portion of a consolidated city that is not within one or more separately incorporated places.

Source: U.S. Census Bureau, 2018 American Community Survey, C16005, "Nativity by Language Spoken at Home by Ability to Speak English for the Population 5 Years and Over," <http://data.census.gov/>, accessed December 2019.

Table 59. Marital Status of the Population by Sex, Race, and Hispanic Origin: 2000 to 2019

[In millions, except percent (213.8 represents 213,800,000). As of March. Data are shown for persons aged 15 years and over. Excludes members of Armed Forces except those living off post or with their families on post. Beginning 2005 based on an expanded sample of households. Data for 2010 based on population controls from Census 2000. 2015 and 2019 data based on population controls from Census 2010. Based on Current Population Survey; see text, this section and Appendix III]

Marital status, race and Hispanic origin	Total				Male				Female			
	2000	2010	2015	2019	2000	2010	2015	2019	2000	2010	2015	2019
Total [1]	**213.8**	**242.0**	**255.0**	**263.5**	**103.1**	**117.7**	**123.6**	**127.9**	**110.7**	**124.4**	**131.4**	**135.6**
Never married	60.0	74.2	81.0	85.4	32.3	40.2	43.1	45.3	27.8	34.0	38.0	40.1
Married [2]	120.2	129.7	133.6	137.8	59.7	64.5	66.3	68.5	60.5	65.2	67.2	69.3
Widowed	13.7	14.3	14.6	14.9	2.6	3.0	3.3	3.5	11.1	11.4	11.3	11.4
Divorced	19.9	23.7	25.8	25.5	8.6	10.0	11.0	10.7	11.3	13.8	14.9	14.8
Percent of total	100.0	100.0	100.0	100.0	100.0	100.0	100.0	100.0	100.0	100.0	100.0	100.0
Never married	28.1	30.7	31.8	32.4	31.3	34.2	34.8	35.4	25.1	27.4	28.9	29.6
Married [2]	56.2	53.6	52.4	52.3	57.9	54.8	53.7	53.6	54.7	52.4	51.2	51.1
Widowed	6.4	5.9	5.7	5.6	2.5	2.5	2.6	2.7	10.0	9.1	8.6	8.4
Divorced	9.3	9.8	10.1	9.7	8.3	8.5	8.9	8.3	10.2	11.1	11.3	10.9
White, total [3]	**177.6**	**195.5**	**200.1**	**204.3**	**86.4**	**96.2**	**98.1**	**100.3**	**91.1**	**99.3**	**102.1**	**103.9**
Never married	45.3	54.7	57.3	59.5	25.1	30.6	31.4	32.3	20.2	24.1	25.9	27.1
Married [2]	104.2	109.6	110.1	112.4	51.9	54.7	55.0	56.4	52.3	54.8	55.1	56.1
Widowed	11.5	11.8	11.9	12.0	2.2	2.5	2.7	2.8	9.3	9.3	9.3	9.2
Divorced	16.5	19.4	20.8	20.3	7.2	8.3	9.0	8.8	9.3	11.1	11.8	11.6
Percent of total	100.0	100.0	100.0	100.0	100.0	100.0	100.0	100.0	100.0	100.0	100.0	100.0
Never married	25.5	28.0	28.6	29.1	29.1	31.8	32.0	32.2	22.1	24.3	25.4	26.1
Married [2]	58.7	56.1	55.0	55.0	60.0	56.9	56.1	56.2	57.4	55.2	54.0	53.9
Widowed	6.5	6.0	6.0	5.9	2.5	2.6	2.7	2.8	10.2	9.3	9.1	8.8
Divorced	9.3	9.9	10.4	9.9	8.4	8.7	9.2	8.7	10.2	11.2	11.6	11.1
Black, total [3]	**25.9**	**29.4**	**32.0**	**33.6**	**11.7**	**13.3**	**14.6**	**15.4**	**14.2**	**16.0**	**17.4**	**18.2**
Never married	11.3	13.7	15.5	16.5	5.2	6.5	7.3	7.9	6.0	7.2	8.2	8.6
Married [2]	10.1	10.6	11.1	11.7	5.0	5.2	5.5	5.8	5.1	5.4	5.6	6.0
Widowed	1.7	1.8	1.8	1.8	0.3	0.4	0.4	0.4	1.4	1.5	1.4	1.4
Divorced	2.8	3.2	3.6	3.6	1.1	1.2	1.4	1.3	1.7	2.0	2.2	2.3
Percent of total	100.0	100.0	100.0	100.0	100.0	100.0	100.0	100.0	100.0	100.0	100.0	100.0
Never married	43.5	46.8	48.5	48.9	44.9	48.8	49.9	51.1	42.4	45.2	47.4	47.1
Married [2]	39.2	36.1	34.7	34.9	42.8	39.4	37.8	37.5	36.2	33.4	32.0	32.7
Widowed	6.6	6.2	5.7	5.5	2.8	2.7	2.9	2.8	9.6	9.1	8.0	7.8
Divorced	10.7	10.9	11.2	10.6	9.5	9.1	9.4	8.6	11.8	12.4	12.6	12.4
Asian, total [3]	**8.4**	**11.2**	**14.6**	**16.5**	**4.0**	**5.3**	**6.9**	**7.8**	**4.4**	**5.9**	**7.7**	**8.7**
Never married	2.8	3.2	4.5	4.9	1.5	1.7	2.4	2.7	1.3	1.4	2.1	2.2
Married [2]	4.9	7.0	9.0	10.2	2.3	3.3	4.2	4.8	2.6	3.7	4.8	5.4
Widowed	0.3	0.5	0.6	0.7	0.0	0.1	0.1	0.1	0.3	0.5	0.5	0.6
Divorced	0.4	0.5	0.7	0.7	0.1	0.2	0.2	0.2	0.2	0.3	0.4	0.5
Percent of total	100.0	100.0	100.0	100.0	100.0	100.0	100.0	100.0	100.0	100.0	100.0	100.0
Never married	33.1	28.3	30.4	30.0	37.7	32.8	34.8	34.6	28.8	24.2	26.6	25.9
Married [2]	58.6	62.8	61.2	61.8	57.8	62.6	60.7	61.6	59.4	62.9	61.6	62.0
Widowed	4.0	4.7	3.9	4.0	1.2	1.3	1.5	1.2	6.6	7.7	6.1	6.6
Divorced	4.3	4.3	4.5	4.2	3.2	3.3	3.0	2.6	5.3	5.2	5.7	5.6
Hispanic, total [4]	**22.8**	**34.3**	**40.4**	**44.3**	**11.3**	**17.7**	**20.2**	**22.1**	**11.5**	**16.6**	**20.2**	**22.2**
Never married	7.5	13.3	16.1	18.3	4.2	7.7	8.8	10.0	3.3	5.6	7.3	8.3
Married [2]	12.7	17.2	19.8	21.3	6.2	8.6	9.7	10.4	6.5	8.6	10.1	10.9
Widowed	0.9	1.2	1.3	1.4	0.2	0.3	0.3	0.3	0.7	0.9	1.0	1.1
Divorced	1.6	2.6	3.1	3.3	0.7	1.1	1.3	1.3	1.0	1.5	1.8	2.0
Percent of total	100.0	100.0	100.0	100.0	100.0	100.0	100.0	100.0	100.0	100.0	100.0	100.0
Never married	33.1	38.7	39.9	41.3	37.5	43.4	43.7	45.3	28.9	33.7	36.1	37.3
Married [2]	55.9	50.1	49.1	48.1	55.1	48.7	48.1	47.2	56.6	51.7	50.1	49.0
Widowed	3.9	3.5	3.2	3.2	1.5	1.7	1.5	1.5	6.2	5.4	5.0	4.9
Divorced	7.1	7.7	7.8	7.4	5.9	6.2	6.6	6.0	8.3	9.2	8.9	8.8

[1] Includes persons of other races not shown separately. [2] Includes persons who are married with spouse present, married with spouse absent, and separated. Beginning 2019, estimates for married individuals include same-sex married couples. [3] Beginning 2003, data represent persons who selected this race group only and exclude persons reporting more than one race. Prior to 2003, the CPS allowed respondents to report only one race group. See also comments on race in the text for this section. [4] Hispanic persons may be of any race.

Source: U.S. Census Bureau, Families and Living Arrangements, Historical Marital Status Tables, "Table MS-1. Marital Status of the Population 15 Years Old and Over, by Sex, Race and Hispanic Origin: 1950 to Present," <https://census.gov/data/tables/time-series/demo/families/marital.html>, accessed December 2019.

Table 60. Marital Status of the Population by Sex and Age: 2019

[127,903 represents 127,903,000. As of March. Data are shown for population aged 15 and older. Excludes members of Armed Forces except those living off post or with their families on post. Population controls based on Census 2010. Based on Current Population Survey, see text, this section, and Appendix III]

Sex and age	Number of persons (1,000)					Percent distribution				
	Total	Never married	Married [1]	Widowed	Divorced	Total	Never married	Married [1]	Widowed	Divorced
MALE										
Total	**127,903**	**45,279**	**68,504**	**3,465**	**10,655**	**100.0**	**35.4**	**53.5**	**2.7**	**8.3**
15 to 17 years old	6,656	6,533	95	8	19	100.0	98.2	1.4	0.1	0.3
18 years old and over	121,247	38,746	68,408	3,457	10,636	100.0	32.0	56.5	2.9	8.8
18 to 19 years old	3,890	3,799	73	2	17	100.0	97.7	1.9	0.0	0.4
20 to 24 years old	10,715	9,708	933	14	60	100.0	90.6	8.7	0.1	0.6
25 to 29 years old	11,791	8,315	3,282	7	186	100.0	70.5	27.9	0.1	1.6
30 to 34 years old	10,925	4,856	5,559	19	491	100.0	44.4	50.9	0.2	4.5
35 to 39 years old	10,625	3,120	6,746	22	736	100.0	29.4	63.5	0.2	6.9
40 to 44 years old	9,627	2,103	6,557	41	926	100.0	21.8	68.1	0.4	9.6
45 to 49 years old	9,992	1,762	6,850	80	1,299	100.0	17.6	68.6	0.8	13.0
50 to 54 years old	9,923	1,481	6,913	166	1,364	100.0	14.9	69.7	1.7	13.7
55 to 64 years old	19,851	2,167	14,201	512	2,971	100.0	10.9	71.6	2.6	15.0
65 to 74 years old	14,877	1,071	11,048	853	1,905	100.0	7.2	74.3	5.7	12.8
75 to 84 years old	6,752	294	4,984	915	558	100.0	4.4	73.8	13.6	8.3
85 years old and over	2,278	71	1,259	825	123	100.0	3.1	55.2	36.2	5.4
FEMALE										
Total	**135,554**	**40,084**	**69,254**	**11,412**	**14,804**	**100.0**	**29.6**	**51.1**	**8.4**	**10.9**
15 to 17 years old	6,363	6,238	95	5	25	100.0	98.0	1.5	0.1	0.4
18 years old and over	129,191	33,846	69,159	11,407	14,780	100.0	26.2	53.5	8.8	11.4
18 to 19 years old	3,941	3,826	91	4	20	100.0	97.1	2.3	0.1	0.5
20 to 24 years old	10,537	8,957	1,452	23	105	100.0	85.0	13.7	0.2	1.0
25 to 29 years old	11,478	6,803	4,339	24	311	100.0	59.3	37.8	0.2	2.7
30 to 34 years old	10,987	3,822	6,513	53	599	100.0	34.8	59.3	0.5	5.5
35 to 39 years old	10,813	2,426	7,232	118	1,038	100.0	22.4	66.9	1.1	9.6
40 to 44 years old	9,949	1,718	6,914	120	1,197	100.0	17.3	69.5	1.2	12.0
45 to 49 years old	10,351	1,426	7,070	239	1,617	100.0	13.8	68.3	2.3	15.6
50 to 54 years old	10,421	1,177	7,038	362	1,844	100.0	11.3	67.6	3.5	17.7
55 to 64 years old	21,884	2,130	14,275	1,576	3,903	100.0	9.7	65.2	7.2	17.8
65 to 74 years old	16,586	1,054	9,817	2,922	2,792	100.0	6.4	59.2	17.6	16.8
75 to 84 years old	8,651	372	3,787	3,374	1,117	100.0	4.3	43.7	39.0	12.9
85 years old and over	3,593	135	630	2,591	237	100.0	3.8	17.5	72.1	6.6

[1] Includes persons who are married with spouse present, married with spouse absent, and separated.

Source: U.S. Census Bureau, America's Families and Living Arrangements, Adult (A table series), "Table A1. Marital Status of People 15 Years and Over, by Age, Sex, and Personal Earnings: 2019," <https://www.census.gov/data/tables/2019/demo/families/cps-2019.html>, accessed December 2019.

Table 61. Living Arrangements of Persons 18 Years Old and Over by Age and Sex: 2019

[In thousands (250,438 represents 250,438,000), except percent. As of March. Excludes members of Armed Forces except those living off post or with their families on post. Population controls based on Census 2010 and an expanded sample of households. Based on Current Population Survey (CPS); see text, this section, and Appendix III]

Living arrangement	Total	18 to 24 years old	25 to 34 years old	35 to 64 years old	65 to 74 years old	75 years old and over
NUMBER (1,000)						
Total	**250,438**	**29,083**	**45,181**	**123,437**	**31,463**	**21,274**
Male	121,247	14,605	22,717	60,018	14,877	9,030
Female	129,191	14,478	22,464	63,419	16,586	12,244
PERCENT DISTRIBUTION						
Male, total	**100.0**	**100.0**	**100.0**	**100.0**	**100.0**	**100.0**
Alone	(NA)	5.5	11.9	13.3	19.4	23.9
With spouse [1]	(NA)	5.5	35.6	64.8	71.2	66.2
Child of householder [2]	(NA)	55.6	19.4	4.8	(NA)	(NA)
Living with partner	(NA)	6.8	14.3	7.0	3.4	2.2
Other relatives	(NA)	15.4	9.7	7.1	[3] 4.6	[3] 6.1
Nonrelatives	(NA)	11.3	9.1	3.0	1.4	1.5
Female, total	**100.0**	**100.0**	**100.0**	**100.0**	**100.0**	**100.0**
Alone	(NA)	5.5	8.8	11.8	25.8	44.3
With spouse [1]	(NA)	9.0	44.8	62.4	56.6	34.0
Child of householder [2]	(NA)	52.2	12.3	2.7	(NA)	(NA)
Living with partner	(NA)	10.7	15.3	5.9	2.5	1.2
Other relatives	(NA)	14.4	13.9	15.6	[3] 13.6	[3] 19.4
Nonrelatives	(NA)	8.2	4.9	1.6	1.4	1.2

NA Not available. [1] Includes only adults who are married, spouse present in the household. This living arrangement supersedes the others shown in the table. For example, people living with their parents and a spouse are counted as living with a spouse, not as a child of the householder. [2] Children of the householder are not living with a spouse or unmarried partner, and are residing in the household of a parent. In CPS, unmarried college students living in dormitories are counted as living in the parental home. [3] Includes children of the householder who are not living with a spouse or unmarried partner, and are residing in the household of a parent.

Source: U.S. Census Bureau, America's Families and Living Arrangements, Historical Living Arrangements of Adults, "Table AD-3. Living Arrangements of Adults 18 and Over, 1967 to Present," <https://www.census.gov/data/tables/time-series/demo/families/adults.html>, accessed August 2020.

Table 62. Households, Families, Subfamilies, and Married Couples: 1990 to 2019

[In thousands (93,347 represents 93,347,000), except as indicated. As of March. Excludes members of the Armed Services except those living off post or with their families on post. Beginning 2001, based on an expanded sample of households. Population controls for 2010 based on Census 2000; beginning 2012, population controls based on Census 2010. Based on Current Population Survey (CPS), see text, this section and Appendix III. Minus sign (-) indicates decrease]

Type of unit	1990	2000	2010	2015	2018	2019	Percent change 1990 to 2000	2000 to 2010	2010 to 2019
Households	**93,347**	**104,705**	**117,538**	**124,587**	**127,586**	**128,579**	**12.2**	**12.3**	**9.4**
Persons per household	2.63	2.62	2.59	2.54	2.53	2.52	(X)	(X)	(X)
White [1]	80,163	87,671	95,489	98,679	100,065	100,528	9.4	8.9	5.3
Black [1]	10,486	12,849	14,730	16,437	16,997	17,167	22.5	14.6	16.5
Asian [1]	(NA)	(NA)	4,687	6,040	6,735	6,981	(NA)	(NA)	48.9
Hispanic [2]	5,933	9,319	13,298	16,239	17,318	17,758	57.1	42.7	33.5
Family households	66,090	72,025	78,833	81,716	83,088	83,482	9.0	9.5	5.9
Married couple	52,317	55,311	58,410	60,010	61,241	61,959	5.7	5.6	6.1
Male householder [3]	2,884	4,028	5,580	6,162	6,424	6,480	39.7	38.5	16.1
Female householder [3]	10,890	12,687	14,843	15,544	15,423	15,043	16.5	17.0	1.3
Nonfamily households	27,257	32,680	38,705	42,871	44,498	45,096	19.9	18.4	16.5
Male householder	11,606	14,641	18,263	20,143	21,017	21,582	26.2	24.7	18.2
Female householder	15,651	18,039	20,442	22,728	23,481	23,515	15.3	13.3	15.0
One person	22,999	26,724	31,399	34,866	35,740	36,479	16.2	17.5	16.2
Families	**66,090**	**72,025**	**78,833**	**81,716**	**83,088**	**83,482**	**9.0**	**9.5**	**5.9**
Persons per family	3.17	3.17	3.16	3.14	3.14	3.14	(X)	(X)	(X)
With own children under age 18	32,289	34,605	35,218	34,979	34,452	33,942	7.2	1.8	-3.6
Without own children under age 18	33,801	37,420	43,615	46,737	48,635	49,540	10.7	16.6	13.6
Married couple	52,317	55,311	58,410	60,010	61,241	61,959	5.7	5.6	6.1
With own children under age 18	24,537	25,248	24,575	24,040	23,812	23,735	2.9	-2.7	-3.4
Without own children under age 18	27,780	30,062	33,835	35,970	37,430	38,224	8.2	12.6	13.0
Male householder [3]	2,884	4,028	5,580	6,162	6,424	6,480	39.7	38.5	16.1
With own children under age 18	1,153	1,786	2,224	2,388	2,484	2,500	54.9	24.5	12.4
Without own children under age 18	1,731	2,242	3,356	3,774	3,939	3,980	29.5	49.7	18.6
Female householder [3]	10,890	12,687	14,843	15,544	15,423	15,043	16.5	17.0	1.3
With own children under age 18	6,599	7,571	8,419	8,551	8,156	7,707	14.7	11.2	-8.5
Without own children under age 18	4,290	5,116	6,424	6,993	7,267	7,337	19.3	25.6	14.2
Unrelated subfamilies [4]	**534**	**571**	**484**	**566**	**396**	**428**	**6.9**	**-15.2**	**-11.6**
Married couple	68	37	93	76	94	77	(B)	(B)	-17.2
Male reference persons [3]	45	57	44	63	52	78	(B)	(B)	(B)
Female reference persons [3]	421	477	347	428	250	274	13.3	-27.3	-21.0
Related subfamilies [4]	**2,403**	**2,984**	**4,300**	**4,508**	**4,619**	**4,730**	**24.2**	**44.1**	**10.0**
Married couple	871	1,149	1,881	2,144	2,404	2,411	31.9	63.7	28.2
Father-child [3]	153	201	313	308	430	482	31.4	55.7	54.0
Mother-child [3]	1,378	1,634	2,106	2,056	1,785	1,838	18.6	28.9	-12.7
Married couples	**53,256**	**56,497**	**60,384**	**62,230**	**63,739**	**64,447**	**6.1**	**6.9**	**6.7**
With own household	52,317	55,311	58,410	60,010	61,241	61,959	5.7	5.6	6.1
Without own household	939	1,186	1,974	2,220	2,498	2,488	26.3	66.4	26.0
Percent without own household	1.8	2.1	3.2	3.6	3.9	3.9	(X)	(X)	(X)

B Base less than 75,000. NA Not available. X Not applicable. [1] Beginning with the 2003 CPS, respondents could choose more than one race. Beginning in 2003, data represent persons who selected this race group only and exclude persons reporting more than one race. The CPS in prior years allowed respondents to report only one race group. See also comments on race in text for this section. [2] Persons of Hispanic origin may be of any race. [3] No spouse present. [4] A subfamily is a married couple or parent/child group that does not maintain its own household. A subfamily may be related to the householder, or unrelated to the householder.

Source: U.S. Census Bureau, America's Families and Living Arrangements, Tables F1, FG1, FG7, and H1, and Historical Households Tables, Table HH-6, <census.gov/topics/families/families-and-households/data/tables.html>, accessed December 2019, and earlier releases.

Table 63. Interracially Married Couples by Race and Hispanic Origin of Spouses: 1980 to 2019

[In thousands (49,714 represents 49,714,000), except percent. As of March. Persons 15 years old and over. Data shown for opposite-sex married couples only. Persons of Hispanic origin may be of any race. Population controls for 2010 based on Census 2000; beginning 2012, based on Census 2010. Based on Current Population Survey; see headnote, Table 62 and Appendix III]

Race and origin of spouses	1980	1990	2000	2010	2015	2017	2018	2019
Married couples, total [1]	**49,714**	**53,256**	**56,497**	**60,384**	**62,230**	**63,325**	**63,739**	**63,882**
Interracial married couples, total	**651**	**964**	**1,464**	**2,478**	**3,010**	**3,158**	**3,237**	**3,255**
Interracial married couples, percent	1.3	1.8	2.6	4.1	4.8	5.0	5.1	5.1
White [2] and Black [2]	167	211	363	558	562	695	665	697
Black husband and White wife	122	150	268	390	383	490	411	391
White husband and Black wife	45	61	95	168	179	205	254	306
White [2] and other race [3]	450	720	1,051	1,723	2,171	2,179	2,240	2,246
Black [2] and other race [3]	34	33	50	132	187	213	250	239
Other [4]	(NA)	(NA)	(NA)	65	90	71	82	73
HISPANIC ORIGIN								
Hispanic and Hispanic	1,906	3,085	4,739	6,166	7,176	7,624	7,662	7,726
Hispanic and other origin (not Hispanic)	891	1,193	1,743	2,289	2,830	3,154	3,300	3,284
All other couples (not of Hispanic origin)	46,917	48,979	50,015	51,928	52,224	52,546	52,778	52,872

NA Not available. [1] Includes other married couples not shown separately. [2] See footnote 1, Table 62. [3] "Other race," is any race other than White or Black, such as Asian; beginning 2003, "other race" includes Asian alone and other single race alone (excluding black and white) or any combination of races. [4] One spouse is Asian only and the other spouse is any other race (excluding black and white) or combination of races.

Source: U.S. Census Bureau, Families & Households, Historical Marital Status Tables, "Table MS-3. Interracial Married Couples: 1980 to 2002"; and America's Families and Living Arrangements, Family groups (FG table series), "Table FG3. Opposite-Sex Married Couple Family Groups, By Presence Of Own Children Under 18, And Age, Earnings, Education, And Race And Hispanic Origin Of Both Spouses," <https://www.census.gov/topics/families/families-and-households/data/tables.html>; accessed December 2019, and earlier releases.

Table 64. Households and Persons Per Household by Type of Household: 2000 to 2019

[104,705 represents 104,705,000. As of March. See headnote, Table 62]

Type of household	Households						Persons per household		
	Number (1,000)			Percent distribution					
	2000	2010	2019	2000	2010	2019	2000	2010	2019
Total households	**104,705**	**117,538**	**128,579**	**100.0**	**100.0**	**100.0**	**2.62**	**2.59**	**2.52**
Family households	72,025	78,833	83,482	68.8	67.1	64.9	3.24	3.24	3.21
Married couple family	55,311	58,410	61,959	52.8	49.7	48.2	3.26	3.24	3.19
Male householder, no spouse present	4,028	5,580	6,480	3.8	4.7	5.0	3.16	3.24	3.26
Female householder, no spouse present	12,687	14,843	15,043	12.1	12.6	11.7	3.17	3.23	3.26
Nonfamily households	32,680	38,705	45,096	31.2	32.9	35.1	1.25	1.26	1.25
Living alone	26,724	31,399	36,479	25.5	26.7	28.4	1.00	1.00	1.00
Male householder	14,641	18,263	21,582	14.0	15.5	16.8	1.34	1.35	1.32
Living alone	11,181	13,971	16,529	10.7	11.9	12.9	1.00	1.00	1.00
Female householder	18,039	20,442	23,515	17.2	17.4	18.3	1.17	1.18	1.19
Living alone	15,543	17,428	19,950	14.8	14.8	15.5	1.00	1.00	1.00

Source: U.S. Census Bureau, Current Population Reports, P20-537, 2001, and earlier reports; and America's Families and Living Arrangements, "Table AVG1" and "Table H1," <https://www.census.gov/data/tables/2019/demo/families/cps-2019.html>, accessed December 2019, and earlier releases.

Table 65. Households by Age of Householder and Size of Household: 1990 to 2019

[In millions (93.3 represents 93,300,000). As of March. Based on Current Population Survey; see headnote, Table 62]

Age of householder and size of household	1990	2000	2005	2010	2014	2015	2016	2017	2018	2019
Total	**93.3**	**104.7**	**113.3**	**117.5**	**123.2**	**124.6**	**125.8**	**126.2**	**127.6**	**128.6**
15 to 24 years old	5.1	5.9	6.7	6.2	6.4	6.4	6.4	6.2	6.2	6.2
25 to 29 years old	9.4	8.5	9.2	9.4	9.3	9.4	9.5	9.5	9.5	10.0
30 to 34 years old	11.0	10.1	10.1	9.8	10.7	10.7	10.6	10.6	10.7	10.6
35 to 44 years old	20.6	24.0	23.2	21.5	21.1	21.1	21.2	21.5	21.6	21.4
45 to 54 years old	14.5	20.9	23.4	24.9	23.7	23.6	23.3	22.8	22.5	22.1
55 to 64 years old	12.5	13.6	17.5	20.4	23.2	23.5	23.9	23.8	24.0	24.2
65 to 74 years old	11.7	11.3	11.5	13.2	16.0	16.9	17.6	18.2	19.0	19.7
75 years old and over	8.4	10.4	11.6	12.1	12.8	13.1	13.4	13.6	14.0	14.5
One person	23.0	26.7	30.1	31.4	34.2	34.9	35.4	35.3	35.7	36.5
Male	9.0	11.2	12.8	14.0	15.2	15.5	15.8	15.8	16.0	16.5
Female	14.0	15.5	17.3	17.4	19.0	19.4	19.6	19.5	19.7	20.0
Two persons	30.1	34.7	37.4	39.5	41.6	41.9	42.8	43.5	44.0	44.4
Three persons	16.1	17.2	18.3	18.6	19.4	19.3	19.4	19.5	19.3	19.4
Four persons	14.5	15.3	16.4	16.1	16.2	16.5	16.3	16.2	16.5	16.4
Five persons	6.2	7.0	7.2	7.4	7.5	7.5	7.5	7.3	7.4	7.4
Six persons	2.1	2.4	2.5	2.8	2.8	2.8	2.8	2.8	2.9	2.9
Seven persons or more	1.3	1.4	1.4	1.7	1.6	1.7	1.6	1.6	1.7	1.6

Source: U.S. Census Bureau, Current Population Reports, P20-537, and earlier reports; and America's Families and Living Arrangements, Households (H table series), <https://www.census.gov/data/tables/2019/demo/families/cps-2019.html>, accessed December 2019.

Table 66. Family Households With Own Children Under 18 Years of Age by Type of Family, 2000 to 2019, and by Age of Householder, 2019

[34,605 represents 34,605,000. As of March. See headnote, Table 67]

Age of householder	Family households with children		Married couple households with children		Male householder with children [1]		Female householder with children [1]	
	Number (1,000)	Percent of all family households	Number (1,000)	Percent of all married couple households	Number (1,000)	Percent of all male householder families [1]	Number (1,000)	Percent of all female householder families [1]
2000, total	34,605	48	25,248	46	1,786	44	7,571	60
2010, total	35,218	45	24,575	42	2,224	40	8,419	57
2015, total	34,979	43	24,040	40	2,388	39	8,551	55
2019, total	**33,942**	**41**	**23,735**	**38**	**2,500**	**39**	**7,707**	**51**
15 to 24 years old	1,124	37	465	52	99	11	559	47
25 to 34 years old	8,756	67	5,557	65	745	48	2,453	83
35 to 44 years old	13,566	80	9,811	80	875	69	2,880	84
45 to 54 years old	8,355	51	6,292	51	557	49	1,506	52
55 to 64 years old	1,738	11	1,313	10	184	22	241	12
65 years old and over	405	2	297	2	41	6	68	3

[1] No spouse present.

Source: U.S. Census Bureau, Current Population Reports, P20-537, 2001; and America's Families and Living Arrangements, Family households (F table series), "Table F1. Family Households, by Type, Age of Own Children, Age of Family Members, and Age of Householder," <https://www.census.gov/data/tables/2019/demo/families/cps-2019.html>, accessed December 2019, and earlier releases.

Table 67. Family Groups With Children Under 18 Years of Age by Race and Hispanic Origin: 2000 to 2019

[In thousands (37,496 represents 37,496,000). As of March. Family groups are family households, related subfamilies, and unrelated subfamilies; each married couple or parent/child group is counted separately, even if they reside in the same household. Excludes members of Armed Forces except those living off post or with their families on post. Beginning 2005, based on an expanded sample of households. Data for 2010 based on Census 2000 population controls. Data for 2015 and 2019 based on Census 2010 population controls. Based on Current Population Survey, Annual Social and Economic Supplement, see text, this section and Appendix III]

Race and Hispanic origin of householder or reference person	Number (1,000)				Percent distribution			
	2000	2010	2015	2019	2000	2010	2015	2019
All races, total [1]	**37,496**	**39,947**	**39,934**	**38,463**	**100**	**100**	**100**	**100**
Two-parent family groups [2]	25,771	27,082	26,862	26,285	69	68	67	68
One-parent family groups	11,725	11,686	11,780	11,008	31	29	29	29
Maintained by mother	9,681	9,924	9,891	8,880	26	25	25	23
Maintained by father	2,044	1,762	1,889	2,128	5	4	5	6
Grandparent householder with grandchild(ren) under 18	(NA)	1,179	1,292	1,170	(NA)	3	3	3
White, total [3]	**30,079**	**30,933**	**30,131**	**28,793**	**100**	**100**	**100**	**100**
Two-parent family groups [2]	22,241	22,457	21,664	20,928	74	73	72	73
One-parent family groups	7,838	7,729	7,639	7,116	26	25	25	25
Maintained by mother	6,216	6,396	6,177	5,544	21	21	21	19
Maintained by father	1,622	1,333	1,462	1,572	5	4	5	5
Grandparent householder with grandchild(ren) under 18	(NA)	747	828	749	(NA)	2	3	3
Black, total [3]	**5,530**	**5,903**	**5,837**	**5,501**	**100**	**100**	**100**	**100**
Two-parent family groups [2]	2,135	2,275	2,209	2,205	39	39	38	40
One-parent family groups	3,396	3,280	3,262	2,960	61	56	56	54
Maintained by mother	3,060	2,977	2,971	2,581	55	50	51	47
Maintained by father	335	303	291	379	6	5	5	7
Grandparent householder with grandchild(ren) under 18	(NA)	348	366	336	(NA)	6	6	6
Asian, total [3]	**1,469**	**2,025**	**2,443**	**2,663**	**100**	**100**	**100**	**100**
Two-parent family groups [2]	1,184	1,694	2,071	2,284	81	84	85	86
One-parent family groups	285	292	340	356	19	14	14	13
Maintained by mother	236	235	291	289	16	12	12	11
Maintained by father	49	57	49	67	3	3	2	3
Grandparent householder with grandchild(ren) under 18	(NA)	39	32	23	(NA)	2	1	1
Hispanic, total [4]	**5,503**	**7,572**	**8,345**	**8,468**	**100**	**100**	**100**	**100**
Two-parent family groups [2]	3,625	4,856	5,407	5,500	66	64	65	65
One-parent family groups	1,877	2,499	2,688	2,770	34	33	32	33
Maintained by mother	1,565	2,186	2,338	2,312	28	29	28	27
Maintained by father	313	313	350	458	6	4	4	5
Grandparent householder with grandchild(ren) under 18	(NA)	217	250	198	(NA)	3	3	2
Non-Hispanic White, total [3]	**24,847**	**23,911**	**22,657**	**21,240**	**100**	**100**	**100**	**100**
Two-parent family groups [2]	18,750	17,911	16,738	15,948	75	75	74	75
One-parent family groups	6,096	5,457	5,317	4,724	25	23	23	22
Maintained by mother	4,766	4,404	4,171	3,549	19	18	18	17
Maintained by father	1,331	1,053	1,146	1,175	5	4	5	6
Grandparent householder with grandchild(ren) under 18	(NA)	543	602	568	(NA)	2	3	3

NA Not available. [1] Includes other race/ethnicities, not shown separately. [2] Beginning 2007, includes children living with married and unmarried parents. [3] Beginning with the 2003 Current Population Survey (CPS), respondents could choose more than one race. Beginning 2003, data represent persons who selected this race group only and exclude persons reporting more than one race. The CPS prior to 2003 allowed respondents to report only one race group. See also comments on race in the text for this section. [4] Hispanic persons may be of any race.

Source: U.S. Census Bureau, Families and Living Arrangements, Current Population Reports, P20-537, 2001; and America's Families and Living Arrangements, Family groups (FG table series), "Table FG10. Family Groups: 2019," <https://www.census.gov/topics/families/families-and-households/data/tables.html>, accessed December 2019, and earlier releases.

Table 68. Parents and Children in Stay-At-Home Parent Family Groups: 1995 to 2019

[In thousands (22,973 represents 22,973,000), except percent. Family groups with children include those families that maintain their own household (family households with own children); those that live in the home of a relative (related subfamilies); and those that live in the home of a nonrelative (unrelated subfamilies). Stay-at-home family groups are opposite-sex married-couple family groups with children under age 15 where one parent is in the labor force all of the previous year and the other parent is out of the labor force for the entire year with the reason 'taking care of home and family.' Only opposite-sex married couples with children under age 15 are included. Based on Current Population Survey; see Appendix III]

Year	Married-couple family groups with children under 15 years old					Children under 15 years old in married-couple family groups				
	Number			Percent		Number			Percent	
	Total	With stay-at-home mothers	With stay-at-home fathers	With stay-at-home mothers	With stay-at-home fathers	Total	With stay-at-home mothers	With stay-at-home fathers	With stay-at-home mothers	With stay-at-home fathers
1995	22,973	4,440	64	19.3	0.3	41,008	9,106	125	22.2	0.3
2000	22,953	4,785	93	20.8	0.4	41,860	10,087	180	24.1	0.4
2005	23,305	5,584	142	24.0	0.6	41,111	11,224	247	27.3	0.6
2010	22,138	5,020	154	22.7	0.7	41,026	10,833	287	26.4	0.7
2014	21,549	5,203	211	24.1	1.0	39,424	10,791	420	27.4	1.1
2015	21,586	5,210	199	24.1	0.9	39,621	10,758	368	27.2	0.9
2016	21,531	5,031	209	23.4	1.0	39,693	10,360	392	26.1	1.0
2017	21,330	4,965	267	23.3	1.3	39,659	10,427	503	26.3	1.3
2018	21,361	5,061	190	23.7	0.9	39,813	10,574	336	26.6	0.8
2019	21,328	4,944	191	23.2	0.9	40,197	10,365	390	25.8	1.0

Source: U.S. Census Bureau, Families and Households, Historical Families Tables, "Table SHP-1. Parents and Children in Stay-At-Home Parent Family Groups: 1994 to Present," <census.gov/data/tables/time-series/demo/families/families.html>, accessed December 2019.

Table 69. Children Under 18 Years of Age by Presence of Parents: 2000 to 2019

[72,012 represents 72,012,000. As of March. Excludes persons under 18 years old who maintained households or family groups and their spouses. Based on Current Population Survey; see headnote, Table 67]

Race, Hispanic origin, and year	Number (1,000)	Both parents[1]	Mother only Total	Divorced	Married, spouse absent[2]	Never married	Widowed	Father only	Neither parent
ALL RACES[3]									
2000	72,012	69.1	22.4	7.9	4.5	9.2	1.0	4.2	4.2
2005	73,494	67.3	23.4	7.9	4.6	10.1	0.8	4.8	4.5
2010	74,718	69.4	23.1	7.1	5.1	10.1	0.8	3.4	4.1
2015	73,623	69.2	23.1	6.6	4.4	11.3	0.8	3.7	3.9
2019	73,525	70.1	21.4	6.2	3.9	10.6	0.8	4.4	4.0
WHITE[4]									
2000	56,455	75.3	17.3	(NA)	(NA)	(NA)	(NA)	4.3	3.1
2005	56,234	73.5	18.4	7.9	4.0	5.8	0.7	4.7	3.4
2010	56,416	74.9	18.3	6.9	4.5	6.1	0.8	3.5	3.4
2015	53,621	74.9	18.2	6.6	4.0	6.7	0.8	3.7	3.2
2019	52,956	75.5	16.8	6.0	3.5	6.4	0.8	4.4	3.4
BLACK[4]									
2000	11,412	37.6	49.0	(NA)	(NA)	(NA)	(NA)	4.2	9.2
2005	11,293	35.0	50.2	8.7	8.1	32.0	1.3	5.0	9.8
2010	11,272	39.2	49.7	8.6	8.4	31.5	1.2	3.6	7.5
2015	11,091	38.7	49.4	7.6	6.7	33.9	1.1	4.2	7.7
2019	11,101	42.2	45.7	7.4	6.1	31.5	0.7	5.1	7.0
ASIAN[4]									
2005	2,843	83.6	10.2	4.0	2.3	2.7	1.3	3.6	2.5
2010	3,300	85.5	10.1	3.8	3.7	2.1	0.6	2.2	2.1
2015	3,736	85.7	10.6	2.8	3.4	3.9	0.5	2.0	1.7
2019	3,993	85.8	9.8	3.9	3.0	2.2	0.8	2.5	2.0
HISPANIC[5]									
2000	11,613	65.1	25.1	(NA)	(NA)	(NA)	(NA)	4.4	5.4
2005	14,241	64.7	25.4	6.1	7.1	11.4	0.8	4.8	5.2
2010	16,941	67.0	26.3	5.8	8.1	11.7	0.7	2.7	4.0
2015	17,981	67.0	25.9	5.3	7.1	13.0	0.6	3.0	4.1
2019	18,757	68.0	24.3	5.5	5.7	12.2	0.8	4.2	3.6
NON-HISPANIC WHITE[4]									
2005	43,106	75.9	16.4	8.5	3.1	4.2	0.7	4.8	2.9
2010	41,089	77.5	15.5	7.5	3.1	4.2	0.8	3.8	3.1
2015	38,084	77.5	15.5	7.2	2.7	4.7	0.8	4.1	2.9
2019	36,800	78.2	14.0	6.3	2.6	4.4	0.8	4.5	3.3

NA Not available. [1] Beginning in 2007, includes children living with married and unmarried parents. [2] Includes separated. [3] Includes other races and non-Hispanic groups, not shown separately. [4] Beginning with the 2003 Current Population Survey (CPS), respondents could choose more than one race. Data represents persons who selected this race group only and exclude persons reporting more than one race. Prior to 2003, the CPS allowed respondents to report only one race group. See also comments on race in the text for this section. [5] Hispanic persons may be of any race.

Source: U.S. Census Bureau, America's Families and Living Arrangements, Children (C table series), "Table C3. Living Arrangements of Children Under 18 Years and Marital Status of Parents, by Age, Sex, Race, and Hispanic Origin and Selected Characteristics of the Child for All Children: 2019," <https://www.census.gov/data/tables/2019/demo/families/cps-2019.html>, accessed December 2019, and earlier releases.

Table 70. Grandparents Living With Grandchildren by Race, Hispanic Origin, and Sex: 2018

[In thousands (7,115 represents 7,115,000), except percent. Covers both grandparents living in own home with grandchildren present and grandparents living in grandchildren's home. The American Community Survey universe includes the household population and the population living in institutions, college dormitories, and other group quarters. Based on a sample and subject to sampling variability; see Appendix III]

Race, Hispanic origin, and sex	Grandparents living with own grandchildren, total	Grandparents responsible for grandchildren Total	30 to 59 years old	60 years old and over
Grandparents living with own grandchildren under 18 years old (1,000)	**7,115**	**2,401**	**1,307**	**1,094**
PERCENT DISTRIBUTION				
Total	100.0	100.0	100.0	100.0
One race	97.9	97.8	97.5	98.1
White alone	63.0	66.3	66.1	66.5
Black or African American alone	16.3	19.4	19.7	19.1
American Indian and Alaska Native alone	1.5	2.3	2.3	2.3
Asian alone	8.8	3.8	2.2	5.6
Native Hawaiian and Other Pacific Islander alone	0.4	0.4	0.4	0.4
Some other race alone	7.9	5.6	6.9	4.1
Two or more races	2.1	2.2	2.5	1.9
Hispanic origin[1]	26.2	19.6	23.1	15.4
White alone, not Hispanic	45.9	53.4	51.0	56.3
Male	36.2	36.9	33.8	40.6
Female	63.8	63.1	66.2	59.4

[1] Persons of Hispanic origin may be of any race.

Source: U.S. Census Bureau, 2018 American Community Survey, S1002, "Grandparents," <http://data.census.gov/>, accessed December 2019.

Table 71. Group Quarters Population by Type of Group Quarter and Selected Resident Characteristics: 2018

[In percent, except as indicated. The American Community Survey universe includes the household population and the population living in institutions, college dormitories, and other group quarters. Based on a sample and subject to sampling variability]

Characteristic	Total group quarters population [1]	Institutionalized group quarters population			Noninstitutionalized group quarters population	
		Total [1]	Adult correctional facilities	Nursing facilities/ skilled nursing facilities	Total [1]	College/ university housing
Total population.........................	**8,091,609**	**3,877,486**	**2,171,941**	**1,483,165**	**4,214,123**	**2,718,218**
PERCENT DISTRIBUTION						
Male..	60.9	69.4	90.8	37.7	53.1	45.6
Female.....................................	39.1	30.6	9.2	62.3	46.9	54.4
Under 15 years old.......................	0.9	1.0	(X)	(X)	0.8	(X)
15 to 17 years old........................	1.7	2.3	0.1	(X)	1.2	1.1
18 to 24 years old........................	41.4	8.0	12.2	0.2	72.1	96.5
25 to 34 years old........................	12.7	19.0	32.7	0.8	6.8	2.1
35 to 44 years old........................	9.6	15.6	26.6	1.2	4.2	0.2
45 to 54 years old........................	7.8	11.3	17.0	4.0	4.7	0.1
55 to 64 years old........................	7.1	9.7	8.8	11.5	4.6	–
65 to 74 years old........................	5.5	8.9	2.2	19.7	2.4	–
75 to 84 years old........................	5.7	10.3	0.4	26.1	1.6	(X)
85 years old and over....................	7.5	14.0	–	36.4	1.6	(X)
Median age (years).......................	29.4	48.5	36.6	80.3	20.5	19.7
One race...................................	100.0	100.0	100.0	100.0	100.0	100.0
White....................................	67.2	63.3	52.2	79.9	70.9	72.8
Black....................................	23.0	28.9	38.0	15.5	17.4	14.3
American Indian and Alaska Native........	1.2	1.7	2.3	0.6	0.9	0.5
Asian....................................	4.8	1.4	0.9	2.0	7.9	10.3
Native Hawaiian/Pacific Islander...........	0.2	0.2	0.3	0.1	0.3	0.2
Some other race.........................	3.5	4.5	6.3	1.8	2.7	1.9
Hispanic origin [2].........................	13.4	14.7	20.1	6.1	12.3	10.5
Not Hispanic..............................	86.6	85.3	79.9	93.9	87.7	89.5
White alone, not Hispanic.................	56.4	52.6	38.1	75.2	59.8	62.4

– Represents or rounds to zero. X Not applicable. [1] Includes other types of group quarters, not shown separately. [2] Persons of Hispanic origin may be of any race.

Source: U.S. Census Bureau, 2018 American Community Survey, S2601A, "Characteristics of the Group Quarters Population"; and S2602, "Characteristics of the Group Quarters Population by Group Quarters Type (3 Types)"; <http://data.census.gov/>, accessed December 2019.

Table 72. Population in Group Quarters by State: 2000 to 2019

[In thousands (7,780 represents 7,780,000). 2000 and 2010, as of April. 2018 and 2019, as of July. All persons not living in housing units are classified as living in group quarters. These individuals may be institutionalized, e.g., under care or custody in juvenile facilities, jails, correctional centers, hospitals, or nursing homes; or they may be residents in noninstitutional group quarters such as college dormitories, group homes, or military barracks]

State	2000 [1]	2010 [2]	2018	2019	State	2000 [1]	2010 [2]	2018	2019
United States........	**7,780**	**7,999**	**8,087**	**8,084**	Missouri.............	164	174	174	174
Alabama.................	115	116	117	117	Montana.............	25	29	29	29
Alaska...................	19	26	27	27	Nebraska.............	51	51	51	51
Arizona.................	110	140	160	162	Nevada.............	34	36	38	38
Arkansas................	74	79	84	84	New Hampshire....	36	40	41	41
California...............	820	820	826	827	New Jersey.........	195	187	182	180
Colorado................	103	116	119	119	New Mexico.........	36	43	43	43
Connecticut.............	108	118	111	111	New York.............	581	586	571	569
Delaware................	25	24	25	25	North Carolina......	254	257	281	281
District of Columbia....	36	40	39	39	North Dakota.......	24	25	25	24
Florida..................	389	425	432	430	Ohio.................	299	306	315	317
Georgia.................	234	254	262	267	Oklahoma.............	112	112	110	110
Hawaii..................	36	43	43	43	Oregon.............	77	87	89	89
Idaho...................	31	29	30	30	Pennsylvania.......	433	427	422	422
Illinois..................	322	302	297	297	Rhode Island.......	39	43	41	41
Indiana.................	178	187	190	190	South Carolina.....	135	139	135	134
Iowa....................	104	99	97	97	South Dakota.......	28	34	34	34
Kansas.................	82	79	81	81	Tennessee.........	148	154	161	158
Kentucky................	115	126	131	133	Texas.................	561	582	601	601
Louisiana...............	136	128	129	129	Utah.................	40	46	48	48
Maine...................	35	36	37	37	Vermont.............	21	25	26	26
Maryland................	134	139	140	140	Virginia.............	231	240	245	245
Massachusetts.........	221	239	246	246	Washington.........	136	139	146	148
Michigan................	250	230	226	223	West Virginia.......	43	49	47	47
Minnesota..............	136	135	131	131	Wisconsin.............	156	151	145	144
Mississippi..............	95	93	94	93	Wyoming.............	14	14	14	14

[1] The April 1, 2000, population estimates base reflects changes to the Census 2000 population from the Count Question Resolution program and geographic program revisions. [2] The April 1, 2010 population estimates base reflects changes to the Census 2010 population from the Count Question Resolution program and geographic program revisions.

Source: U.S. Census Bureau, "Annual Resident Population Estimates, Estimated Components of Resident Population Change, and Rates of the Components of Resident Population Change for States and Counties: April 1, 2000 to July 1, 2009"; and "Population, Population Change, and Estimated Components of Population Change: April 1, 2010 to July 1, 2019 (CO-EST2019-alldata)," <https://www.census.gov/data/tables/time-series/demo/popest/2010s-counties-total.html>, accessed June 2020.

Table 73. Opposite-Sex and Same-Sex Couple Households by Selected Characteristics: 2018

[In percent, except as indicated (57,582 represents 57,582,000). The American Community Survey universe includes the household population and the population living in institutions, college dormitories, and other group quarters. Based on a sample and subject to sampling variability. See text, this section and Appendix III]

| Characteristic | Married opposite-sex couples | Unmarried opposite-sex couples | Married and unmarried same-sex couples | | | Married same-sex couples |
			Total	Male-male couples	Female-female couples	
Total households (1,000)	**57,582**	**7,412**	**995**	**485**	**510**	**593**
Age of householder:						
15 to 24 years old	1.1	11.0	4.1	2.7	5.5	1.7
25 to 34 years old	12.7	35.1	21.0	18.6	23.3	15.6
35 to 44 years old	19.7	20.9	19.1	18.0	20.2	19.7
45 to 54 years old	20.9	15.3	21.0	23.8	18.4	22.6
55 to 64 years old	21.3	10.8	19.2	20.8	17.6	21.2
65 years old and over	24.2	6.9	15.5	16.1	14.9	19.1
Average age of householder (years)	52.6	39.7	47.8	49.0	46.6	50.6
Average age of spouse/partner (years)	51.9	39.0	46.0	46.5	45.5	49.3
Race of householder:						
White	80.8	76.2	81.1	82.7	79.6	82.1
Black or African American	7.0	11.3	8.2	5.9	10.5	7.3
American Indian or Alaska Native	0.6	1.1	0.9	0.9	0.8	0.8
Asian	6.1	2.6	3.3	4.1	2.6	3.7
Native Hawaiian or Pacific Islander	0.2	0.2	0.2	0.2	0.2	0.1
Some other race	3.5	5.4	3.0	3.2	2.9	3.2
Two or more races	1.8	3.3	3.2	3.1	3.4	2.9
Percent of couples interracial	7.7	14.6	16.7	19.9	13.7	14.6
Hispanic origin of householder:						
Hispanic [1]	13.4	18.3	12.9	13.0	12.8	12.1
White alone, not Hispanic	71.6	64.6	72.8	74.6	71.1	74.4
Children in the household:						
Children in the household [2]	38.6	37.6	16.3	9.3	23.0	19.2
Own children in the household	38.5	35.1	15.5	9.0	21.6	18.8
Household income:						
Less than $35,000	11.9	19.1	12.1	9.7	14.4	11.3
$35,000 to $49,999	9.8	13.8	9.6	8.1	10.9	8.7
$50,000 to $74,999	17.4	22.2	16.4	14.2	18.4	14.7
$75,000 to $99,999	15.7	16.1	15.3	14.6	15.9	14.9
$100,000 or more	45.3	28.8	46.7	53.4	40.3	50.3
Median household income (dollars)	91,678	68,501	93,549	105,451	83,579	100,489
Housing tenure:						
Owner occupied	80.1	44.7	65.0	67.4	62.7	72.6
Renter occupied	19.9	55.3	35.0	32.6	37.3	27.4

[1] Persons of Hispanic origin may be of any race. [2] Includes biological children, stepchildren, adopted children, and nonrelatives of the householder under 18 years old.

Source: U.S. Census Bureau, 2018 American Community Survey, "Characteristics of Same-Sex Couple Households: 2005 to Present," <https://www.census.gov/topics/families/same-sex-couples/data/tables.html>, accessed December 2019.

Table 74. Opposite Sex Unmarried Couples by Presence of Biological Children: 2019

[In thousands (8,741 represents 8,741,000), except percent. As of March. Excludes members of Armed Forces except those living off post or with their families on post. All opposite-sex unmarried couples are included, regardless of householder status. Unmarried couples of the opposite sex with children under 18 years old are included in the estimates if either partner had at least one never-married biological child living with them. Population controls based on Census 2010. Based on Current Population Survey; see text, this section and Appendix III]

| Sex and age of partner | Unmarried couples, total | Without children under 18 years old | With children under 18 years old | |
			Number	Percent of total
Total	**8,741**	**5,733**	**3,008**	**34.4**
Age of male partner:				
15 to 24 years old	955	712	243	25.4
25 to 29 years old	1,694	1,106	588	34.7
30 to 34 years old	1,428	809	619	43.3
35 to 39 years old	1,069	470	598	55.9
40 to 44 years old	751	357	394	52.5
45 to 49 years old	656	361	295	45.0
50 to 54 years old	574	434	140	24.4
55 to 64 years old	936	834	101	10.8
65 years old and over	678	650	28	4.1
Age of female partner:				
15 to 24 years old	1,466	1,042	424	28.9
25 to 29 years old	1,951	1,254	696	35.7
30 to 34 years old	1,312	651	661	50.4
35 to 39 years old	906	371	535	59.1
40 to 44 years old	640	293	347	54.2
45 to 49 years old	612	392	220	35.9
50 to 54 years old	537	456	81	15.1
55 to 64 years old	824	787	37	4.5
65 years old and over	494	486	8	1.6

Source: U.S. Census Bureau, America's Families and Living Arrangements, Unmarried couples (UC table series), "Table UC3. Opposite Sex Unmarried Couples by Presence of Biological Children under 18, and Age, Earnings, Education, and Race and Hispanic Origin of Both Partners," <https://www.census.gov/data/tables/2019/demo/families/cps-2019.html>, accessed December 2019.

Table 75. Opposite and Same-Sex Unmarried-Partner Households by Region: 2018

[121,520 represents 121,520,000. The American Community Survey universe includes the household population and the population living in institutions, college dormitories, and other group quarters. For composition of regions, see map inside front cover. Based on a sample and subject to sampling variability; see text, this section and Appendix III]

Item	Total (1,000s)					Percent distribution				
	Total	North-east	Midwest	South	West	Total	North-east	Midwest	South	West
Total households...............	**121,520**	**21,459**	**26,940**	**45,788**	**27,333**	**100.0**	**100.0**	**100.0**	**100.0**	**100.0**
Unmarried-partner households....	7,815	1,394	1,847	2,677	1,898	6.4	6.5	6.9	5.8	6.9
Male householder and male partner...........................	200	37	37	70	56	0.2	0.2	0.1	0.2	0.2
Male householder and female partner...........................	3,785	668	906	1,290	922	3.1	3.1	3.4	2.8	3.4
Female householder and female partner...........................	203	38	41	73	51	0.2	0.2	0.2	0.2	0.2
Female householder and male partner...........................	3,627	651	862	1,244	869	3.0	3.0	3.2	2.7	3.2
All other households...............	113,705	20,066	25,093	43,111	25,435	93.6	93.5	93.1	94.2	93.1

Source: U.S. Census Bureau, 2018 American Community Survey, B11009, "Unmarried-Partner Households by Sex of Partner," <http://data.census.gov/>, accessed December 2019.

Table 76. Young Adults Living in Parental Home by Sex and Age: 1990 to 2019

[In thousands (12,450 represents 12,450,000), except percent. As of March. Excludes members of Armed Forces except those living off post or with their families on post. Unmarried college students living in dormitories are counted as living in the home of their parent(s). Beginning 2005, based on an expanded sample of households. Population controls for 2005 to 2010 based on Census 2000; beginning 2012, population controls based on Census 2010. Based on Current Population Survey; see text, this section and Appendix III]

Year	Male young adults			Female young adults		
		Child of householder living at home			Child of householder living at home	
	Total	Number	Percent of total	Total	Number	Percent of total
18 TO 24 YEARS OLD						
1990............	12,450	7,232	58.1	12,860	6,135	47.7
1995............	12,545	7,328	58.4	12,613	5,896	46.7
2000............	13,291	7,593	57.1	13,242	6,232	47.1
2005............	14,060	7,448	53.0	13,933	6,413	46.0
2010............	14,824	8,501	57.3	14,469	7,123	49.2
2015............	15,123	8,808	58.2	14,893	7,714	51.8
2016............	15,023	8,875	59.1	14,646	7,664	52.3
2017............	14,777	8,518	57.6	14,488	7,518	51.9
2018............	14,837	8,573	57.8	14,510	7,534	51.9
2019............	14,605	8,222	56.3	14,478	7,649	52.8
25 TO 34 YEARS OLD						
1990............	21,462	3,213	15.0	21,779	1,774	8.1
1995............	20,589	3,166	15.4	20,800	1,759	8.5
2000............	18,563	2,387	12.9	19,222	1,602	8.3
2005............	19,656	2,660	13.5	19,632	1,597	8.1
2010............	20,685	3,387	16.4	20,383	2,133	10.5
2015............	21,417	3,896	18.2	21,574	2,613	12.1
2016............	21,839	4,284	19.6	21,912	2,736	12.5
2017............	22,105	4,333	19.6	22,123	2,775	12.5
2018............	22,477	4,669	20.8	22,355	2,868	12.8
2019............	22,716	4,635	20.4	22,465	2,945	13.1

Source: U.S. Census Bureau, Families and Households, Historical Living Arrangements of Adults, "Table AD-1. Young Adults, 18-34 Years Old, Living At Home: 1960 to Present," <https://www.census.gov/data/tables/time-series/demo/families/adults.html>, accessed December 2019.

Table 77. Children of Householders by Age and Whether Biological, Adopted, and Stepchildren: 2010

[88,820 represents 88,820,000. As of April. Includes children of the householder regardless of marital status and excludes persons under age 18 who are not children of the householder. Includes Puerto Rico. Based on 2010 Census of Population; see Appendix III]

Type of relationship		Under 18 years old					18 years old and over		
	Total	Total	Under 6 years old	6 to 11 years old	12 to 14 years old	15 to 17 years old	Total	18 to 24 years old	25 years old and over
NUMBER (1,000)									
Total children of householders..	**88,820**	**64,778**	**20,277**	**21,903**	**11,188**	**11,410**	**24,042**	**13,649**	**10,393**
Adopted children.....................	2,072	1,527	351	569	304	303	545	325	220
Stepchildren..........................	4,166	2,785	284	978	718	806	1,381	889	492
Biological children..................	82,582	60,467	19,643	20,356	10,166	10,301	22,115	12,435	9,681
PERCENT DISTRIBUTION									
Total children of householders.....	100.0	100.0	100.0	100.0	100.0	100.0	100.0	100.0	100.0
Adopted children.....................	2.3	2.4	1.7	2.6	2.7	2.7	2.3	2.4	2.1
Stepchildren..........................	4.7	4.3	1.4	4.5	6.4	7.1	5.7	6.5	4.7
Biological children..................	93.0	93.3	96.9	92.9	90.9	90.3	92.0	91.1	93.1

Source: U.S. Census Bureau, Adopted Children and Stepchildren: 2010, Current Population Reports, P20-572, April 2014. See also <https://www.census.gov/content/census/en/library/publications/2014/demo/p20-572.html>.

Table 78. Children in Households by Relationship to Householder: 2010 to 2018

[In thousands (73,904 represents 73,904,000). Data shown for population under age 18 in households, excluding householders, spouses, and unmarried partners. Based on a sample and subject to sampling variability; see text this section and Appendix III]

Type of relationship	2010	2012	2013	2014	2015	2016	2017	2018
NUMBER								
Total children in households..............	**73,904**	**73,462**	**73,336**	**73,325**	**73,386**	**73,399**	**73,403**	**73,106**
Own child............................	65,472	64,953	64,595	64,426	64,445	64,392	64,367	63,987
Biological child........................	61,540	61,139	60,766	60,628	60,632	60,564	60,518	60,180
Adopted child.........................	1,582	1,520	1,496	1,447	1,423	1,428	1,439	1,440
Stepchild.............................	2,351	2,293	2,332	2,351	2,391	2,400	2,410	2,367
Grandchild............................	5,397	5,603	5,712	5,830	5,887	5,964	5,957	6,038
Other relatives.......................	1,826	1,732	1,738	1,792	1,793	1,762	1,803	1,807
Foster child or other unrelated child......	1,209	1,175	1,292	1,277	1,261	1,280	1,276	1,274
PERCENT DISTRIBUTION								
Total children in households................	100.0	100.0	100.0	100.0	100.0	100.0	100.0	100.0
Own child............................	88.6	88.4	88.1	87.9	87.8	87.7	87.7	87.5
Biological child........................	83.3	83.2	82.9	82.7	82.6	82.5	82.4	82.3
Adopted child.........................	2.1	2.1	2.0	2.0	1.9	1.9	2.0	2.0
Stepchild.............................	3.2	3.1	3.2	3.2	3.3	3.3	3.3	3.2
Grandchild............................	7.3	7.6	7.8	8.0	8.0	8.1	8.1	8.3
Other relatives.......................	2.5	2.4	2.4	2.4	2.4	2.4	2.5	2.5
Foster child or other unrelated child......	1.6	1.6	1.8	1.7	1.7	1.7	1.7	1.7

Source: U.S. Census Bureau, American Community Survey, B09018, "Relationship to Householder for Children Under 18 in Households," <https://data.census.gov>, accessed December 2019.

Table 79. Living Arrangements of Young Adults by Selected Characteristics: 2015

[In thousands (15,795 represents 15,795,000), except as noted. Based on the American Community Survey; see Appendix III]

Characteristics	Young adults aged 18 to 24 Living in parents' home [1] Number	Young adults aged 18 to 24 Living in parents' home [1] Percent	Living independently [2]	Living with roommates [3]	Young adults aged 25 to 34 Living in parents' home [1] Number	Young adults aged 25 to 34 Living in parents' home [1] Percent	Living independently [2]	Living with roommates [3]
Total......................	**15,795**	**100.0**	**4,458**	**7,757**	**8,382**	**100.0**	**24,362**	**10,118**
By sex:								
Female..........................	7,317	46.3	2,587	3,851	3,679	43.9	12,662	5,252
Male............................	8,479	53.7	1,871	3,907	4,702	56.1	11,700	4,866
By race/ethnicity:								
White alone, non-Hispanic............	8,148	51.6	2,852	4,054	4,192	50.0	15,525	4,702
Black alone, non-Hispanic............	2,350	14.9	463	1,203	1,428	17.0	2,168	1,837
Asian alone, non-Hispanic............	769	4.9	137	534	571	6.8	1,554	750
Other race, non-Hispanic..............	665	4.2	179	338	326	3.9	746	365
Hispanic [4].......................	3,864	24.5	828	1,628	1,864	22.2	4,369	2,464
Has a disability [5].......................	1,044	6.6	224	413	904	10.8	1,019	630
Work status:								
Employed...........................	9,033	57.2	3,399	4,981	5,778	68.9	19,869	7,863
Worked full-time, year-round........	2,813	17.8	2,109	2,174	3,651	43.6	15,557	5,617
Mean hours worked per week.......	29.9	(X)	38.3	33.3	37.1	(X)	41.6	39.5
Unemployed........................	1,594	10.1	247	643	851	10.2	830	682
Not in labor force.....................	5,168	32.7	812	2,133	1,752	20.9	3,662	1,573
Educational attainment:								
High school diploma or less...........	7,850	49.7	1,681	3,209	3,474	41.4	6,834	4,044
Associate's degree or some college..	6,632	42.0	1,930	3,544	2,840	33.9	7,563	3,211
Bachelor's degree or higher..........	1,312	8.3	848	1,004	2,068	24.7	9,965	2,864
Enrolled in school...................	8,463	53.6	1,198	3,586	1,276	15.2	2,564	1,425
Personal income: [6]								
$0 to $29,999.....................	14,973	94.8	3,416	6,917	6,247	74.6	10,998	6,402
$30,000 to $59,999.................	736	4.7	885	715	1,730	20.7	8,292	2,706
$60,000 to $99,999.................	71	0.4	135	101	336	4.0	3,653	806
$100,000 or more..................	13	0.1	22	23	65	0.8	1,408	201
Housing type:								
Single-family home...................	12,512	79.2	1,628	3,975	6,687	79.8	14,531	5,478
Apartment or multifamily building.....	2,421	15.3	2,507	3,391	1,233	14.7	8,610	4,136
Other housing type...................	863	5.5	324	391	462	5.5	1,222	504
Lived at same address a year ago. ...	14,127	89.4	2,158	4,506	7,341	87.6	18,005	7,178
Tenure:								
Own home..........................	10,831	68.6	802	2,459	6,230	74.3	10,918	3,439
Rent home..........................	4,965	31.4	3,656	5,298	2,152	25.7	13,444	6,679

X Not applicable. [1] Child of the householder, regardless of the young adult's marital status. [2] The young adult lives alone, or is the householder living with a spouse or unmarried partner, or is the spouse or unmarried partner of the householder. [3] Living with other relatives or nonrelatives. [4] Persons of Hispanic origin may be of any race. [5] "Has a disability" means the young adult reported having at least one of the following six types of disabilities: hearing, vision, cognitive, ambulatory, self-care, or independent living difficulty. [6] Excludes young adults with incomes less than $0.

Source: U.S. Census Bureau, *The Changing Economics and Demographics of Young Adulthood: 1975-2016*, Current Population Reports, P20-579, April 2017. See also <https://www.census.gov/topics/families.html>.

Table 80. Self-Described Religious Identification of Adult Population: 1990, 2001, and 2008

[In thousands (175,440 represents 175,440,000). The methodology of the American Religious Identification Survey (ARIS) 2008 replicated that used in previous surveys. The three surveys are based on random-digit-dialing telephone surveys of residential households in the continental U.S. (48 states): 54,461 interviews in 2008, 50,281 in 2001, and 113,723 in 1990. Respondents were asked to describe themselves in terms of religion with an open-ended question. Interviewers did not prompt or offer a suggested list of potential answers. Moreover, the self-description of respondents was not based on whether established religious bodies, institutions, churches, mosques or synagogues considered them to be members. Instead, the surveys sought to determine whether the respondents regarded themselves as adherents of a religious community. Subjective rather than objective standards of religious identification were tapped by the surveys]

Religious group	1990	2001	2008
Adult population, total [1]	**175,440**	**207,983**	**228,182**
Christian, total [2]	151,225	159,514	173,402
Catholic	46,004	50,873	57,199
Baptist	33,964	33,820	36,148
Methodist	14,174	14,039	11,366
Lutheran	9,110	9,580	8,674
Presbyterian	4,985	5,596	4,723
Episcopalian/Anglican	3,043	3,451	2,405
Orthodox (Eastern)	502	645	824
United Church of Christ	438	1,378	736
Disciples of Christ	144	492	263
Reformed/Dutch Reform	161	289	206
Quaker	67	217	130
Christian unspecified	8,073	14,190	16,834
Nondenominational Christian [3]	194	2,489	8,032
Protestant unspecified [3]	17,214	4,647	5,187
Evangelical/Born Again [3]	546	1,088	2,154
Independent Christian Church	25	71	86
Pentecostal unspecified	3,116	4,407	5,416
Assemblies of God	617	1,105	810
Church of God	590	943	663
Holiness/Holy	610	569	352
Church of the Nazarene	549	544	358
Foursquare Gospel	28	70	116
Churches of Christ	1,769	2,593	1,921
Jehovah's Witness	1,381	1,331	1,914
Apostolic/New Apostolic	117	254	970
Seventh-day Adventist	668	724	938
Mennonite	235	346	438
Christian Reform	40	79	381
Christian Science	214	194	339
Church of the Brethren	206	358	231
Mormon/Latter-day Saints	2,487	2,697	3,158
Other Christian [4]	105	254	206
Other religions, total [2]	**5,853**	**7,740**	**8,796**
Jewish	3,137	2,837	2,680
Buddhist	404	1,082	1,189
Hindu	227	766	582
Sikh	13	57	78
Muslim	527	1,104	1,349
Unitarian/Universalist	502	629	586
Spiritualist	(NA)	116	426
Wiccan	8	134	342
Pagan	(NA)	140	340
Native American	47	103	186
Other unclassified [4]	991	774	1,030
No religion specified, total [2]	**14,331**	**29,481**	**34,169**
Agnostic	[5]1,186	991	1,985
Atheist	(5)	902	1,621
Humanist	29	49	90
No Religion	13,116	27,486	30,427
Other No Religion [4]	(NA)	57	45
Refused to reply to question	**4,031**	**11,246**	**11,815**

NA Not available. [1] Refers to the total number of adults in all fifty states. All other figures are based on projections from surveys conducted in the continental United States (48 states). [2] Includes other groups, not shown separately. [3] Because of the subjective nature of replies to open-ended questions, these categories are the most unstable as they do not refer to clearly identifiable denominations as much as underlying feelings about religion. Thus they may be the most subject to fluctuation over time. [4] Estimates for subpopulations smaller than 75,000 adults are aggregated to minimize sampling errors. [5] Atheist included in Agnostic.

Source: 1990 data, Barry A. Kosmin and Seymour P. Lachman, "One Nation Under God: Religion in Contemporary American Society, 1993"; 2001 data, Barry A. Kosmin and Ariela Keysar, *Religion in A Free Market: Religious and Non-Religious Americans, Who, What, Why, Where, 2006*; and 2008 data, Barry A. Kosmin & Ariela Keysar, *American Religious Identification Survey (ARIS 2008) Summary Report*, 2009, Institute for the Study of Secularism in Society and Culture, Trinity College, Hartford, CT <http://www.trincoll.edu/Academics/centers/ISSSC/Pages/ARIS-Data-Archive.aspx> and <www.AmericanReligionSurvey-ARIS.org> ©.

Table 81. Religious Adherents and Jewish Population—States: 2010 to 2011

[137,450 represents 137,450,000. Adherents were defined as "all members, including full members, their children and others who regularly attend services." The Jewish population includes Jews who define themselves as Jewish by religion as well as those who define themselves as Jewish in cultural or ethnic terms. Data on Jewish population are based on both scientific studies and informant estimates provided by local Jewish communities]

State	Number (1,000)			Percent of population [3]		
	Christian adherents, [1] 2010	Other religious adherents, [2] 2010	Jewish population, 2011	Christian adherents, [1] 2010	Other religious adherents, [2] 2010	Jewish population, 2011
United States.................	137,450	10,890	6,588	44.5	3.5	2.1
Alabama.........................	2,948	52	9	61.7	1.1	0.2
Alaska...........................	200	40	6	28.1	5.7	0.9
Arizona..........................	1,894	466	106	29.6	7.3	1.7
Arkansas........................	1,573	40	2	53.9	1.4	0.1
California........................	15,021	1,530	1,220	40.3	4.1	3.3
Colorado........................	1,684	199	91	33.5	4.0	1.8
Connecticut....................	1,735	48	116	48.6	1.3	3.2
Delaware........................	349	22	15	38.9	2.5	1.7
District of Columbia........	298	16	28	49.6	2.7	4.7
Florida...........................	6,829	400	639	36.3	2.1	3.4
Georgia..........................	4,702	186	128	48.5	1.9	1.3
Hawaii...........................	421	140	7	31.0	10.3	0.5
Idaho.............................	384	417	2	24.5	26.6	0.1
Illinois...........................	6,529	486	298	50.9	3.8	2.3
Indiana..........................	2,793	69	17	43.1	1.1	0.3
Iowa..............................	1,592	46	6	52.3	1.5	0.2
Kansas..........................	1,375	61	18	48.2	2.1	0.6
Kentucky........................	2,182	49	11	50.3	1.1	0.3
Louisiana.......................	2,688	50	11	59.3	1.1	0.2
Maine............................	345	19	14	26.0	1.4	1.0
Maryland........................	2,214	118	238	38.3	2.0	4.1
Massachusetts................	3,546	122	278	54.2	1.9	4.2
Michigan........................	3,910	211	82	39.6	2.1	0.8
Minnesota......................	2,894	69	46	54.6	1.3	0.9
Mississippi.....................	1,709	33	2	57.6	1.1	0.1
Missouri.........................	2,806	123	59	46.9	2.0	1.0
Montana.........................	326	50	1	33.0	5.0	0.1
Nebraska........................	974	38	6	53.3	2.1	0.3
Nevada..........................	725	196	74	26.8	7.3	2.8
New Hampshire...............	444	14	10	33.7	1.1	0.8
New Jersey.....................	4,321	272	504	49.1	3.1	5.7
New Mexico.....................	940	87	12	45.6	4.2	0.6
New York........................	8,529	611	1,635	44.0	3.2	8.4
North Carolina................	4,372	140	31	45.9	1.5	0.3
North Dakota..................	443	8	(Z)	65.9	1.2	0.1
Ohio..............................	4,861	146	148	42.1	1.3	1.3
Oklahoma.......................	2,148	75	5	57.3	2.0	0.1
Oregon..........................	998	187	41	26.1	4.9	1.1
Pennsylvania..................	6,530	206	295	51.4	1.6	2.3
Rhode Island..................	558	10	19	53.1	0.9	1.8
South Carolina................	2,337	70	13	50.5	1.5	0.3
South Dakota..................	464	13	(Z)	57.0	1.6	(Z)
Tennessee......................	3,425	82	20	54.0	1.3	0.3
Texas............................	13,062	872	140	51.9	3.5	0.6
Utah..............................	256	1,929	6	9.3	69.8	0.2
Vermont.........................	199	9	5	31.8	1.4	0.9
Virginia..........................	3,206	351	97	40.1	4.4	1.2
Washington....................	1,945	364	46	28.9	5.4	0.7
West Virginia..................	635	22	2	34.3	1.2	0.1
Wisconsin......................	2,973	62	28	52.3	1.1	0.5
Wyoming........................	158	65	1	28.0	11.5	0.2

Z Fewer than 500 or less than 0.05 percent. [1] Comprises evangelical Protestants, Black Protestants, mainline Protestants, Orthodox and Catholic groups. [2] Includes counts of Jain, Shinto, Sikh, Tao, National Spiritualist Association, Church of Jesus Christ of Latter Day Saints, Unitarian Universalist, Jehovah's Witnesses, Church of Christ Scientist, Bahá'í, three Buddhist groupings, four Hindu groupings, Muslims, and Zoroastrians. Excludes four Judaism groups. [3] Based on U.S. Census Bureau data for resident population enumerated as of April 1, 2010 and estimated as of July 2012.

Source: Religious adherents: Clifford Grammich, Kirk Hadaway, Richard Houseal, Dale E. Jones, Alexei Krindatch, Richie Stanley, and Richard H. Taylor, *2010 U.S. Religion Census: Religious Congregations & Membership Study* © 2012, Association of Statisticians of American Religious Bodies. See also <http://www.asarb.org>. Jewish population: Ira M. Sheskin and Arnold Dashefsky, University of Miami and University of Connecticut, *Jewish Population of the United States, 2011*, published by the Mandell L. Berman North American Jewish Data Bank in cooperation with the Association for the Social Scientific Study of Jewry and the Jewish Federations of North America, see also <http://www.jewishdatabank.org>

Table 82. Religious Adherents by Metropolitan Area Status and Religious Groups: 2010

[Groups shown have 500,000 adherents or more. Adherents were defined as all members, including full members, their children and the estimated number of other participants who are not considered members. Based on a study of 236 religious bodies sponsored by the Association of Statisticians of American Religious Bodies. Participants included 217 Christian denominations, associations, or communions (including Latter-day Saints, Messianic Jews, and Unitarian/Universalist groups); counts of Jain, Shinto, Sikh, Tao, and National Spiritualist Association congregations, and counts of congregations and individuals for Bahá'í, three Buddhist groupings, four Hindu groupings, four Jewish groupings, Muslims, and Zoroastrians. For definition of metropolitan and micropolitan areas, see Appendix II]

Religious group	Total adherents (1,000)	Percent		
		In metropolitan area	In micropolitan area	Outside metro/micro area
U.S. population, total............................	308,746	83.7	10.0	6.3
Total adherents.................................	**150,686**	**83.5**	**10.0**	**6.5**
Catholic..................................	58,929	90.5	6.2	3.3
Southern Baptist Convention......................	19,897	69.3	17.2	13.5
Non-denominational Christian Churches........	12,241	88.7	7.8	3.5
United Methodist Church..........................	9,948	73.6	15.3	11.1
Church of Jesus Christ of Latter-day Saints.....	6,145	82.8	11.6	5.6
Evangelical Lutheran Church in America........	4,181	70.4	16.0	13.6
Assemblies of God................................	2,945	82.7	11.0	6.3
Muslim, estimate...................................	2,600	97.4	2.0	0.6
Presbyterian Church (U.S.A.).....................	2,452	82.5	11.4	6.1
Lutheran Church—Missouri Synod..............	2,271	72.7	13.7	13.6
Episcopal...	1,952	88.2	8.1	3.7
National Baptist Convention, USA, Inc...........	1,881	90.3	7.0	2.7
Churches of Christ.................................	1,584	69.8	17.1	13.1
American Baptist Churches in the USA.........	1,561	83.8	9.8	6.4
Christian Churches and Churches of Christ.....	1,453	72.6	15.9	11.5
United Church of Christ...........................	1,284	79.3	13.5	7.2
Seventh-day Adventist Church....................	1,195	87.7	8.2	4.1
Church of God (Cleveland, Tennessee)..........	1,110	72.2	17.5	10.3
African Methodist Episcopal Church.............	1,010	77.7	12.3	10.0
Orthodox Judaism.................................	947	99.6	0.0	0.4
Church of the Nazarene..........................	894	76.2	15.6	8.2
Christian Church (Disciples of Christ)...........	786	70.3	17.7	12.0
Reform Judaism...................................	766	98.3	1.3	0.4
Mahayana Buddhism..............................	733	92.8	6.8	0.4
Church of God in Christ..........................	624	87.8	7.3	4.9
Conservative Judaism............................	502	99.5	0.4	0.1

Source: Clifford Grammich, Kirk Hadaway, Richard Houseal, Dale E. Jones, Alexei Krindatch, Richie Stanley, and Richard H. Taylor. *2010 U.S. Religion Census: Religious Congregations & Membership Study*, 2012 ©. Association of Statisticians of American Religious Bodies.

Births, Deaths, Marriages, and Divorces

This section presents vital statistics data on births, mortality, marriages, and divorces, as well as factors that help explain fertility, such as use of contraception, sexual activity, and prevalence of abortions and fetal deaths. Vital statistics are collected and disseminated for the nation through the National Vital Statistics System by the National Center for Health Statistics (NCHS) and published annually in *Vital Statistics of the United States, National Vital Statistics Reports (NVSR),* and other selected publications. Reports are also issued by various state bureaus participating in the National Vital Statistics System. Factors influencing fertility are collected in NCHS's National Survey of Family Growth and the U.S. Census Bureau's American Community Survey and Current Population Reports (published in *Fertility of American Women*).

Additionally, data on births, deaths, and other public health topics can be accessed via the Center for Disease Control's WONDER Online databases at <wonder.cdc.gov/>. Data on abortions are collected by CDC's Abortion Surveillance System and published in selected issues of *Morbidity and Mortality Weekly Report (MMWR) Surveillance Summaries*.

Registration of vital events—The registration of births, deaths, fetal deaths, and other vital events in the United States is primarily a state and local function. There are 57 vital registration jurisdictions in the United States: the 50 states, five territories (Puerto Rico, etc.), District of Columbia, and New York City. Each of the 57 jurisdictions has a direct statistical reporting relationship with NCHS. Vital events occurring to U.S. residents outside the United States are not included in the data.

Births and deaths—The live-birth, death, and fetal-death statistics prepared by NCHS are based on vital records filed in the registration offices of all states, New York City, and the District of Columbia. The annual collection of death statistics on a national basis began in 1900 with a national death-registration area of ten states and the District of Columbia; a similar annual collection of birth statistics for a national birth-registration area began in 1915, also with ten reporting states and the District of Columbia. Since 1933, the birth- and death-registration areas have comprised the entire United States, including Alaska (beginning 1959) and Hawaii (beginning 1960). National statistics on fetal deaths were first compiled for 1918 and annually since 1922. Prior to 1951, birth statistics came from a complete count of records received in the Public Health Service (now received in NCHS). From 1951 through 1971, they were based on a 50-percent sample of all registered births (except for a complete count in 1955 and a 20- to 50-percent sample in 1967). Since 1972, they have been based on a complete count for states participating in the Vital Statistics Cooperative Program (VSCP) (for details, see the technical appendix in *U.S. Vital Statistics System: Major Activities and Developments, 1950-95*) and on a 50-percent sample of all other areas. Beginning in 1986, all reporting areas participated in the VSCP. Mortality data have been based on a complete count of records for each area (except for a 50-percent sample in 1972). Beginning in 1970, births to and deaths of nonresident aliens of the United States and

U.S. citizens outside the United States have been excluded from the data. Fetal deaths and deaths among Armed Forces abroad are excluded. Data based on samples are subject to sampling error; for details, see annual issues of *National Vital Statistics Reports*.

Mortality statistics by cause of death are compiled in accordance with World Health Organization regulations according to the *International Classification of Diseases* (ICD). The ICD is revised approximately every 10 years. The tenth revision of the ICD was employed beginning in 1999. Deaths for prior years were classified according to the revision of the ICD in use at the time. Each revision of the ICD introduces a number of discontinuities in mortality statistics; for a discussion of those between the ninth and tenth revisions of the ICD, see *Deaths: Final Data for 2017, National Vital Statistics Report*, Vol. 68, No. 9. Information on tests of statistical significance, differences between death rates, and standard errors can also be found in the aforementioned report.

Some of the tables present age-adjusted death rates in addition to crude death rates. Age-adjusted death rates shown in this section were prepared using the direct method, in which age-specific death rates for a population of interest are applied to a standard population distributed by age. Age adjustment eliminates the differences in observed rates between points in time or among compared population groups that result from age differences in population composition.

Fertility and life expectancy—The total fertility rate, defined as the number of births that 1,000 women would have in their lifetime if at each year of age they experienced the birth rates occurring in the specified year, is compiled and published by NCHS. See *Births: Final Data for 2018, National Vital Statistics Reports*, Vol. 68, No. 13. Data on life expectancy, the average remaining lifetime in years for persons who attain a given age, are also computed and published by NCHS. See *Deaths: Final Data for 2017, National Vital Statistics Reports*, Vol. 68, No. 9 and <cdc.gov/nchs/nvss/deaths.htm> for details.

Marriage and divorce—In 1957 and 1958 respectively, the National Office of Vital Statistics established marriage- and divorce-registration areas consisting of an increasing number of States over time. Procedures for estimating the number of marriages and divorces in the registration States are discussed in *Vital Statistics of the United States, Vol. III—Marriage and Divorce*. Total counts of events for registration and nonregistration states are gathered by collecting already summarized data on marriages and divorces reported by state offices of vital statistics and by county offices of registration. The collection and publication of detailed marriage and divorce statistics was suspended beginning in January 1996. For additional information, visit the National Center for Health Statistics online at <cdc.gov/nchs/nvss/marriage-divorce.htm>.

With the suspension of detailed data collection by the NCHS, data on marriage and divorce can be found in the Census Bureau's American Community Survey data tables. See <census.gov/programs-surveys/acs/> for information and data access.

Vital statistics rates—Except as noted, vital statistics rates computed by NCHS are based on decennial census population figures as of April 1 for 1960, 1970, 1980, 1990, 2000, and 2010; and on midyear population figures for other years, as estimated by the Census Bureau (see text, Section 1).

Race—Data by race for births, deaths, marriages, and divorces from NCHS are based on information contained in the certificates of registration. The Census Bureau's Current Population Survey obtains information on race by asking respondents to classify their race as (1) White, (2) Black, (3) American Indian or Alaska Native, (4) Native Hawaiian or Other Pacific Islander, or (5) Asian. Beginning with the 1989 data year, NCHS has tabulated birth data primarily by race of the mother. In 1988 and prior years, births were tabulated by race of the child, which was determined from the race of the parents as entered on the birth certificate. Trend data by race shown in this section are by race of mother beginning with the 1980 data. Hispanic origin of the mother is reported and tabulated independently of race. Thus, persons of Hispanic origin may be of any race. The majority of women of Hispanic origin are reported as White.

Race categorizations found in the *National Vital Statistics Reports* are variously shown according to either 1977 or 1997 Office of Management and Budget (OMB) standards. States reporting multiple-race data according to new 1997 OMB standards has varied widely. In some cases, to provide a comparison of data by race between the 1977 and 1997 OMB standards, the responses of those reporting more than one race were "bridged" to a single race. See headnotes of individual tables and respective source reports for additional information.

Statistical reliability—For a discussion of statistical collection, estimation, and sampling procedures and measures of reliability applicable to data from NCHS and the Census Bureau, see Appendix III.

Table 83. Live Births, Deaths, Marriages, and Divorces: 1960 to 2018

[4,258 represents 4,258,000. Beginning 1970, excludes births to and deaths of nonresidents of the United States. See Appendix III]

Year	Number (1,000)					Rate per 1,000 population				
		Deaths		Mar-riages [2]	Divorces [3]		Deaths		Mar-riages [2]	Divorces [3]
	Births	Total	Infant [1]			Births	Total	Infant [1]		
1960.............	4,258	1,712	111	1,523	393	23.7	9.5	26.0	8.5	2.2
1965.............	3,760	1,828	93	1,800	479	19.4	9.4	24.7	9.3	2.5
1970.............	3,731	1,921	75	2,159	708	18.4	9.5	20.0	10.6	3.5
1971.............	3,556	1,928	68	2,190	773	17.2	9.3	19.1	10.6	3.7
1972.............	3,258	1,964	60	2,282	845	15.6	9.4	18.5	10.9	4.0
1973.............	3,137	1,973	56	2,284	915	14.8	9.3	17.7	10.8	4.3
1974.............	3,160	1,934	53	2,230	977	14.8	9.1	16.7	10.5	4.6
1975.............	3,144	1,893	51	2,153	1,036	14.6	8.8	16.1	10.0	4.8
1976.............	3,168	1,909	48	2,155	1,083	14.6	8.8	15.2	9.9	5.0
1977.............	3,327	1,900	47	2,178	1,091	15.1	8.6	14.1	9.9	5.0
1978.............	3,333	1,928	46	2,282	1,130	15.0	8.7	13.8	10.3	5.1
1979.............	3,494	1,914	46	2,331	1,181	15.6	8.5	13.1	10.4	5.3
1980.............	3,612	1,990	46	2,390	1,189	15.9	8.8	12.6	10.6	5.2
1981.............	3,629	1,978	43	2,422	1,213	15.8	8.6	11.9	10.6	5.3
1982.............	3,681	1,975	42	2,456	1,170	15.9	8.5	11.5	10.6	5.1
1983.............	3,639	2,019	41	2,446	1,158	15.6	8.6	11.2	10.5	5.0
1984.............	3,669	2,039	40	2,477	1,169	15.6	8.6	10.8	10.5	5.0
1985.............	3,761	2,086	40	2,413	1,190	15.8	8.8	10.6	10.1	5.0
1986.............	3,757	2,105	39	2,407	1,178	15.6	8.8	10.4	10.0	4.9
1987.............	3,809	2,123	38	2,403	1,166	15.7	8.8	10.1	9.9	4.8
1988.............	3,910	2,168	39	2,396	1,167	16.0	8.9	10.0	9.8	4.8
1989.............	4,041	2,150	40	2,403	1,157	16.4	8.7	9.8	9.7	4.7
1990.............	4,158	2,148	38	2,443	1,182	16.7	8.6	9.2	9.8	4.7
1991.............	4,111	2,170	37	2,371	1,187	16.2	8.6	8.9	9.4	4.7
1992.............	4,065	2,176	35	2,362	1,215	15.8	8.5	8.5	9.3	4.8
1993.............	4,000	2,269	33	2,334	1,187	15.4	8.7	8.4	9.0	4.6
1994.............	3,953	2,279	31	2,362	1,191	15.0	8.7	8.0	9.1	4.6
1995.............	3,900	2,312	30	2,336	1,169	14.6	8.7	7.6	8.9	4.4
1996.............	3,891	2,315	28	2,344	1,150	14.4	8.6	7.3	8.8	4.3
1997.............	3,881	2,314	28	2,384	1,163	14.2	8.5	7.2	8.9	4.3
1998.............	3,942	2,337	28	2,244	[4] 1,135	14.3	8.5	7.2	8.4	[4] 4.2
1999.............	3,959	2,391	28	2,358	(NA)	14.2	8.6	7.1	8.6	[4] 4.1
2000.............	4,059	2,403	28	2,315	[5] 944	14.4	8.5	6.9	8.2	[5] 4.0
2001.............	4,026	2,416	28	2,326	[5] 940	14.1	8.5	6.9	8.2	[5] 4.0
2002.............	4,022	2,443	28	2,290	[6] 955	14.0	8.5	7.0	8.0	[6] 3.9
2003.............	4,090	2,448	28	2,245	[7] 927	14.1	8.4	6.9	7.7	[7] 3.8
2004.............	4,112	2,398	28	2,279	[8] 879	14.0	8.2	6.8	7.8	[8] 3.7
2005.............	4,138	2,448	28	2,249	[9] 847	14.0	8.3	6.9	7.6	[9] 3.6
2006.............	4,266	2,426	29	[10] 2,193	[9] 872	14.3	8.1	6.7	[10] 7.5	[9] 3.7
2007.............	4,316	2,424	29	2,197	[9] 856	14.3	8.0	6.8	7.3	[9] 3.6
2008.............	4,248	2,472	28	2,157	[9] 844	14.0	8.1	6.6	7.1	[9] 3.5
2009.............	4,131	2,437	26	2,080	[9] 840	13.5	7.9	6.4	6.8	[9] 3.5
2010.............	3,999	2,468	25	2,096	[9] 872	13.0	8.0	6.2	6.8	[9] 3.6
2011.............	3,954	2,515	24	2,118	[9] 877	12.7	8.1	6.1	6.8	[9] 3.6
2012.............	3,953	2,543	24	2,131	[9] 851	12.6	8.1	6.0	6.8	[9] 3.4
2013.............	3,932	2,597	23	[11] 2,081	[12] 832	12.4	8.2	6.0	[11] 6.8	[12] 3.3
2014.............	3,988	2,626	23	[11] 2,140	[12] 814	12.5	8.2	5.8	[11] 6.9	[12] 3.2
2015.............	3,978	2,713	23	2,222	[12] 801	12.4	8.4	5.9	6.9	[12] 3.1
2016.............	3,946	2,744	23	2,251	[13] 776	12.2	8.5	5.9	7.0	[13] 3.0
2017.............	3,856	2,814	22	2,236	[14] 787	11.8	8.6	5.8	6.9	[14] 2.9
2018.............	3,792	2,839	21	2,133	[14] 782	11.6	8.7	5.7	6.5	[14] 2.9

NA Not available. [1] Infant mortality rate; infants under 1 year, excluding fetal deaths. [2] Marriages and marriage rates are by place of occurrence. Beginning 1991, data are provisional. Includes estimates for some States through 1965 and for 1976-1977, and marriage licenses for some states for all years except 1973 and 1975. Beginning 1978, includes nonlicensed marriages in California. [3] Divorces and divorce rates are by place of occurrence. Includes reported annulments and some estimated state figures for all years. Beginning 1991, data are provisional. [4] Excludes data for California, Colorado, Indiana, and Louisiana. [5] Excludes data for California, Indiana, Louisiana, and Oklahoma. [6] Excludes data for California, Indiana, New York City, and Oklahoma. [7] Excludes data for California, Hawaii, Indiana, and Oklahoma. [8] Excludes data for California, Georgia, Hawaii, Indiana, and Louisiana. [9] Excludes data for California, Georgia, Hawaii, Indiana, Louisiana, and Minnesota. [10] Excludes data for Louisiana. [11] Excludes data for Georgia. [12] Excludes data for California, Georgia, Hawaii, Indiana, and Minnesota. [13] Excludes data for California, Georgia, Hawaii, Indiana, Minnesota, and New Mexico. [14] Excludes data for California, Hawaii, Indiana, Minnesota, and New Mexico.

Source: U.S. National Center for Health Statistics, *Births: Final Data for 2018*, Vol. 68, No. 13, November 2019; and CDC WONDER Online Database, "Multiple Cause of Death, 1999-2018," <wonder.cdc.gov/>, and "National Marriage and Divorce Rate Trends," <cdc.gov/nchs/nvss/marriage-divorce.htm>; accessed July 2020.

Table 84. Births, Birth Rates, and Fertility Rates by Sex and Mother's Race and Age: 1980 to 2018

[Births in thousands (3,612 represents 3,612,000). Beginning 2016, all States and the District of Columbia reported race data according to 1997 OMB standards. To maintain comparability of 2016 data with earlier data, data for mothers reporting multiple-race were bridged to single-race categories; see Technical Notes in source for details. For population bases used to derive these data, see text this section, and Appendix III]

Item	1980	1990	2000	2005	2010	2013	2014	2015	2016	2017	2018
Live births [1]	**3,612**	**4,158**	**4,059**	**4,138**	**3,999**	**3,932**	**3,988**	**3,978**	**3,946**	**3,856**	**3,792**
Male	1,853	2,129	2,077	2,119	2,047	2,013	2,041	2,036	2,018	1,973	1,938
Female	1,760	2,029	1,982	2,019	1,952	1,919	1,947	1,942	1,928	1,883	1,854
Males per 100 females (sex ratio)	105	105	105	105	105	105	105	105	105	105	105
Race/ethnicity of mother:											
Non-Hispanic	(NA)	(NA)	(NA)	(NA)	3,027	3,004	3,044	3,022	2,991	2,924	2,872
White alone	(NA)	(NA)	(NA)	(NA)	(NA)	(NA)	(NA)	(NA)	2,056	1,992	1,956
Black or African American alone	(NA)	(NA)	(NA)	(NA)	(NA)	(NA)	(NA)	(NA)	559	561	552
American Indian or Alaska Native alone	(NA)	(NA)	(NA)	(NA)	(NA)	(NA)	(NA)	(NA)	31	30	29
Asian alone	(NA)	(NA)	(NA)	(NA)	(NA)	(NA)	(NA)	(NA)	254	249	241
Native Hawaiian or Other Pacific Islander alone	(NA)	(NA)	(NA)	(NA)	(NA)	(NA)	(NA)	(NA)	9	9	9
Hispanic	(NA)	595	816	986	945	901	914	924	918	899	886
Bridged race estimates: [2]											
White	2,936	3,290	3,194	3,229	3,069	2,986	3,020	3,013	2,946	2,858	2,835
Black	568	684	623	633	636	635	641	640	654	658	634
American Indian or Alaska Native	29	39	42	45	47	46	45	44	44	42	42
Asian or Pacific Islander	74	142	201	231	247	266	283	281	302	298	281
Age of mother:											
Under 20 years old	562	533	478	421	372	276	252	232	212	196	182
20 to 24 years old	1,226	1,094	1,018	1,040	952	897	883	851	804	765	726
25 to 29 years old	1,108	1,277	1,088	1,132	1,134	1,121	1,145	1,152	1,149	1,124	1,099
30 to 34 years old	550	886	929	951	962	1,037	1,081	1,095	1,111	1,092	1,091
35 to 39 years old	141	318	452	483	465	484	509	528	547	555	567
40 to 44 years old	(NA)	(NA)	90	105	107	109	110	112	113	115	117
45 to 54 years old	(NA)	(NA)	4	6	8	8	8	9	9	9	10
Mean age of mother at first birth (years)	22.7	24.2	24.9	25.2	25.4	26.0	26.3	26.4	26.6	26.8	26.9
Birth rate per 1,000 population	**15.9**	**16.7**	**14.4**	**14.0**	**13.0**	**12.4**	**12.5**	**12.4**	**12.2**	**11.8**	**11.6**
Race/ethnicity of mother:											
Non-Hispanic	(NA)	(NA)	(NA)	(NA)	11.7	11.5	11.6	11.4	11.3	11.0	10.7
White alone	(NA)	(NA)	(NA)	(NA)	(NA)	(NA)	(NA)	(NA)	10.4	10.1	9.9
Black or African American alone	(NA)	(NA)	(NA)	(NA)	(NA)	(NA)	(NA)	(NA)	13.9	13.8	13.5
American Indian or Alaska Native alone	(NA)	(NA)	(NA)	(NA)	(NA)	(NA)	(NA)	(NA)	13.2	12.5	12.0
Asian alone	(NA)	(NA)	(NA)	(NA)	(NA)	(NA)	(NA)	(NA)	14.3	13.6	12.9
Native Hawaiian or Other Pacific Islander alone	(NA)	(NA)	(NA)	(NA)	(NA)	(NA)	(NA)	(NA)	16.5	16.3	16.2
Hispanic	23.5	26.7	23.1	22.9	18.7	16.7	16.5	16.3	16.0	15.3	14.8
Bridged race estimates: [2]											
White	15.1	15.8	13.9	13.6	12.5	12.0	12.1	12.0	11.7	11.3	11.1
Black	21.3	22.4	17.0	16.1	15.1	14.5	14.5	14.3	14.4	14.3	13.7
American Indian or Alaska Native	20.7	18.9	14.0	12.6	11.0	10.3	9.9	9.7	9.4	8.9	8.9
Asian or Pacific Islander	19.9	19.0	17.1	15.9	14.5	14.3	14.6	14.0	14.8	14.0	13.0
Age of mother:											
10 to 14 years old	1.1	1.4	0.9	0.6	0.4	0.3	0.3	0.2	0.2	0.2	0.2
15 to 19 years old	53.0	59.9	47.7	39.7	34.2	26.5	24.2	22.3	20.3	18.8	17.4
20 to 24 years old	115.1	116.5	109.7	101.8	90.0	80.7	79.0	76.8	73.8	71.0	68.0
25 to 29 years old	112.9	120.2	113.5	116.5	108.3	105.5	105.8	104.3	102.1	98.0	95.3
30 to 34 years old	61.9	80.8	91.2	96.7	96.5	98.0	100.8	101.5	102.7	100.3	99.7
35 to 39 years old	19.8	31.7	39.7	46.4	45.9	49.3	51.0	51.8	52.7	52.3	52.6
40 to 44 years old	3.9	5.5	8.0	9.1	10.2	10.4	10.6	11.0	11.4	11.6	11.8
45 to 54 years old [3]	0.2	0.2	0.5	0.6	0.7	0.8	0.8	0.8	0.9	0.9	0.9
Fertility rate per 1,000 women [4]	**68.4**	**70.9**	**65.9**	**66.7**	**64.1**	**62.5**	**62.9**	**62.5**	**62.0**	**60.3**	**59.1**
Race/ethnicity of mother:											
Non-Hispanic	(NA)	(NA)	(NA)	(NA)	59.8	59.4	60.1	59.6	59.1	57.7	56.6
White alone	(NA)	(NA)	(NA)	(NA)	(NA)	(NA)	(NA)	(NA)	58.1	56.6	55.7
Black or African American alone	(NA)	(NA)	(NA)	(NA)	(NA)	(NA)	(NA)	(NA)	62.8	62.7	61.5
American Indian or Alaska Native alone	(NA)	(NA)	(NA)	(NA)	(NA)	(NA)	(NA)	(NA)	62.0	58.9	56.9
Asian alone	(NA)	(NA)	(NA)	(NA)	(NA)	(NA)	(NA)	(NA)	60.1	56.9	54.2
Native Hawaiian or Other Pacific Islander alone	(NA)	(NA)	(NA)	(NA)	(NA)	(NA)	(NA)	(NA)	71.6	71.4	71.1
Hispanic	95.4	107.7	95.9	96.4	80.2	72.9	72.1	71.7	70.6	67.6	65.9
Bridged race estimates: [2]											
White	65.6	68.3	65.3	66.8	64.4	62.7	63.2	63.1	61.8	59.8	59.2
Black	84.7	86.8	70.0	68.5	66.3	64.7	64.6	64.0	65.1	64.9	62.2
American Indian or Alaska Native	82.7	76.2	58.7	53.6	48.6	46.4	44.8	43.9	42.8	40.8	40.7
Asian or Pacific Islander	73.2	69.6	65.8	63.0	59.2	59.2	60.7	58.5	62.1	59.3	55.2

NA Not available. [1] Includes other races not shown separately. [2] Bridged race categories consistent with 1977 Office of Management and Budget standards. [3] Birth rates computed by relating births to women age 45 and over (includes mothers up to age 64) to women age 45-49. [4] Number of live births per 1,000 women, 15 to 44 years old in specified group.

Source: U.S. National Center for Health Statistics, National Vital Statistics Reports, *Births: Final Data for 2018*, Vol. 68, No. 13, November 2019, and earlier reports; and CDC WONDER Online Database, "Natality for 2007-2018," <https://wonder.cdc.gov/natality.html>, accessed January 2020.

Table 85. Births—Number and Rate by Race/Ethnicity and State and Island Area: 2018

[For registered births by place of residence. Excludes births to nonresidents of the United States. Based on race and Hispanic origin of mother. Race categories are consistent with 1997 Office of Management and Budget standards; see Technical Notes in source. Race alone is defined as only one race reported on the birth certificate. See Appendix III]

State and Island Area	All races [1]	White alone [2]	Black alone [2]	American Indian or Alaska Native alone [2]	Asian alone [2]	Native Hawaiian or Other Pacific Islander alone [2]	Hispanic [3]	Birth rate [4]	Fertility rate [5]
United States [6].............	**3,791,712**	**1,956,413**	**552,029**	**29,092**	**240,798**	**9,476**	**886,210**	**11.6**	**59.1**
Alabama........................	57,761	33,776	17,597	148	903	46	4,403	11.8	60.9
Alaska..........................	10,086	5,057	280	1,873	641	299	807	13.7	69.3
Arizona.........................	80,723	32,805	4,305	4,155	2,908	248	34,084	11.3	58.6
Arkansas.......................	37,018	23,609	6,966	220	775	498	4,099	12.3	64.0
California.......................	454,920	123,139	22,380	1,411	68,444	1,732	211,271	11.5	56.2
Colorado........................	62,885	36,466	3,032	352	2,496	155	17,817	11.0	54.1
Connecticut....................	34,725	18,488	4,423	38	2,232	5	8,762	9.7	51.8
Delaware.......................	10,621	5,171	2,773	10	634	4	1,710	11.0	59.1
District of Columbia...........	9,212	3,040	4,252	15	444	2	1,296	13.1	48.8
Florida..........................	221,542	95,868	48,174	261	6,996	152	67,201	10.4	57.2
Georgia.........................	126,172	55,676	43,746	102	5,768	104	17,432	12.0	58.3
Hawaii..........................	16,972	3,288	424	33	4,366	1,706	2,580	11.9	64.2
Idaho...........................	21,403	16,574	233	220	348	65	3,549	12.2	63.4
Illinois..........................	144,815	77,244	24,482	97	9,452	32	30,362	11.4	57.5
Indiana.........................	81,646	59,520	10,242	73	2,382	59	7,867	12.2	62.8
Iowa............................	37,785	29,327	2,615	152	1,176	149	3,694	12.0	63.5
Kansas.........................	36,261	25,323	2,575	151	1,228	66	5,977	12.5	64.7
Kentucky.......................	53,922	43,317	4,950	68	1,144	79	3,226	12.1	63.5
Louisiana.......................	59,615	30,458	22,119	299	1,156	32	4,717	12.8	64.3
Maine...........................	12,311	11,022	546	96	202	3	224	9.2	53.3
Maryland........................	71,080	29,585	21,893	83	4,928	31	12,470	11.8	59.9
Massachusetts..................	69,109	39,663	6,826	53	6,183	23	13,810	10.0	49.5
Michigan........................	110,032	74,777	20,558	412	4,395	34	7,139	11.0	58.5
Minnesota......................	67,344	46,014	8,207	983	5,298	57	4,991	12.0	62.7
Mississippi.....................	37,000	18,597	15,797	221	411	17	1,666	12.4	62.8
Missouri........................	73,269	53,697	10,589	140	1,698	199	4,409	12.0	62.4
Montana........................	11,513	9,224	58	1,162	112	15	558	10.8	59.6
Nebraska.......................	25,488	17,645	1,739	318	925	24	4,155	13.2	68.4
Nevada.........................	35,682	13,021	4,564	280	2,613	340	13,307	11.8	60.0
New Hampshire.................	11,995	10,317	241	7	472	6	745	8.8	49.1
New Jersey.....................	101,223	45,500	13,886	40	11,452	27	27,597	11.4	60.1
New Mexico.....................	23,039	6,450	387	2,590	409	13	12,783	11.0	58.0
New York........................	226,238	110,840	33,145	395	24,383	50	51,755	11.6	57.9
North Carolina..................	118,954	63,514	27,670	1,448	4,834	151	18,360	11.5	58.4
North Dakota....................	10,636	7,816	609	828	250	16	635	14.0	72.2
Ohio............................	135,134	97,423	22,201	96	4,285	73	7,432	11.6	61.1
Oklahoma.......................	49,800	28,444	4,136	4,557	1,306	214	7,545	12.6	64.6
Oregon..........................	42,188	28,265	959	388	2,260	309	7,993	10.1	51.4
Pennsylvania....................	135,673	90,862	17,779	74	6,207	54	15,826	10.6	56.9
Rhode Island....................	10,506	6,008	783	36	519	5	2,756	9.9	50.5
South Carolina..................	56,669	31,890	16,681	106	1,172	50	5,255	11.1	58.1
South Dakota...................	11,893	8,481	416	1,645	224	7	661	13.5	73.6
Tennessee......................	80,751	53,256	15,921	79	1,877	69	7,824	11.9	61.1
Texas...........................	378,624	125,549	48,144	721	19,850	487	179,142	13.2	63.4
Utah............................	47,209	34,303	521	418	1,131	468	8,133	14.9	68.4
Vermont.........................	5,432	4,934	118	11	152	1	121	8.7	47.2
Virginia.........................	99,843	54,798	20,860	157	7,625	103	14,397	11.7	59.1
Washington.....................	86,085	49,019	3,922	1,166	8,729	1,159	16,073	11.4	57.5
West Virginia...................	18,248	16,621	626	14	176	2	378	10.1	57.2
Wisconsin.......................	64,098	45,654	6,622	678	3,155	29	6,365	11.0	58.9
Wyoming........................	6,562	5,078	57	212	72	7	851	11.4	61.0
Puerto Rico.....................	21,424	480	49	3	30	–	20,837	6.7	34.8
Virgin Islands...................	(NA)	(NA)	(NA)	(NA)	(NA)	(NA)	(NA)	(NA)	(NA)
Guam...........................	3,165	170	23	6	719	2,096	25	18.9	96.1
American Samoa................	(NA)	(NA)	(NA)	(NA)	(NA)	(NA)	(NA)	(NA)	(NA)
Northern Marianas..............	566	13	–	–	162	377	–	10.9	63.0

– Represents zero. NA Not available. [1] Includes persons of other racial/ethnic groups, not shown separately. [2] Non-Hispanic. [3] Persons of Hispanic origin may be of any race. [4] Per 1,000 estimated population. [5] Number of births per 1,000 women aged 15 to 44 years. [6] Does not include data for the Island Areas.

Source: U.S. National Center for Health Statistics, National Vital Statistics Reports, *Births: Final Data for 2018*, Vol. 68, No. 13, November 2019. See also <https://www.cdc.gov/nchs/nvss/births.htm>.

Table 86. Births, Twin Births, and Triplet and Higher-order Births by Race and Hispanic Origin of Mother: 2010 to 2018

[Represents registered births. Excludes births to nonresidents of the United States. Data are based on Hispanic origin and race of mother. Persons of Hispanic origin may be of any race. Race categories are consistent with 1997 Office of Management and Budget standards; see source for details. See Appendix III]

Year and race and Hispanic origin	Number			Rate		
	Total births	Twin births	Triplet and higher-order births	Multiple births, total [1]	Twin births [2]	Triplet and higher-order births [3]
All races and origins: [4]						
2010	3,999,386	132,562	5,503	34.5	33.1	137.6
2011	3,953,590	131,269	5,417	34.6	33.2	137.0
2012	3,952,841	131,024	4,919	34.4	33.1	124.4
2013	3,932,181	132,324	4,700	34.8	33.7	119.5
2014	3,988,076	135,336	4,526	35.1	33.9	113.5
2015	3,978,497	133,155	4,123	34.5	33.5	103.6
2016	3,945,875	131,723	4,003	34.4	33.4	101.4
2017	3,855,500	128,310	3,917	34.3	33.3	101.6
2018	3,791,712	123,536	3,525	33.5	32.6	93.0
White alone, non-Hispanic						
2016	2,056,332	73,425	2,502	36.9	35.7	121.7
2017	1,992,461	70,704	2,324	36.7	35.5	116.6
2018	1,956,413	67,203	1,996	35.4	34.4	102.0
Black alone, non-Hispanic						
2016	558,622	22,267	628	41.0	39.9	112.4
2017	560,715	22,982	671	42.2	41.0	119.7
2018	552,029	22,502	658	42.0	40.8	119.2
Hispanic [5]						
2016	918,447	22,625	538	25.2	24.6	58.6
2017	898,764	22,041	614	25.2	24.5	68.3
2018	886,210	21,654	573	25.1	24.4	64.7

[1] Number of live births in all multiple deliveries per 1,000 live births. [2] Number of births in twin deliveries per 1,000 live births. [3] Number of births in greater than twin deliveries per 100,000 live births. [4] Includes other races not shown separately. [5] Persons of Hispanic origin may be of any race.

Source: U.S. National Center for Health Statistics, National Vital Statistics Reports, *Births: Final Data for 2018*, Vol. 68, No. 13, November 2019. See also <https://www.cdc.gov/nchs/nvss/births.htm>.

Table 87. Births by Method of Delivery and Race and Hispanic Origin: 2010 to 2018

[In thousands (3,999 represents 3,999,000), except rate. Race categories are consistent with 1997 Office of Management and Budget standards. Data are based on race and Hispanic origin of mother. Persons of Hispanic origin may be of any race. See Appendix III]

Method of delivery	2010	2013	2014	2015	2016	2017	2018			
							Total [1]	White alone, non-Hispanic	Black alone, non-Hispanic	Hispanic
Births, total	**3,999**	**3,932**	**3,988**	**3,978**	**3,946**	**3,856**	**3,792**	**1,956**	**552**	**886**
Vaginal	2,681	2,643	2,700	2,704	2,685	2,621	2,582	1,353	353	606
Cesarean	1,309	1,284	1,285	1,273	1,259	1,232	1,208	602	199	280
Not stated	9	5	4	2	2	2	2	1	(Z)	(Z)
Cesarean delivery rate [2]	32.8	32.7	32.2	32.0	31.9	32.0	31.9	30.8	36.1	31.6
Rate of vaginal birth after previous Cesarean [3]	(NA)	(NA)	(NA)	(NA)	12.4	12.8	13.3	13.5	13.0	12.7

Z Represents less than 500. NA Not available. [1] Includes other races, not shown separately. [2] Percent of all live births by cesarean delivery. [3] Number of births to women having a vaginal delivery per 100 births to women with a previous cesarean delivery.

Source: U.S. National Center for Health Statistics, National Vital Statistics Reports, *Births: Final Data for 2018*, Vol. 68, No. 13, November 2019, and earlier reports. See also <https://www.cdc.gov/nchs/nvss/births.htm>.

Table 88. Births Delivered by Physicians, Midwives, and Other Attendants by Place of Delivery: 2018

Place of delivery	Total births [1]	Physician			Midwife			Other
		Total	Doctor of medicine	Doctor of osteopathy	Total	Certified nurse midwife	Other midwife	
Total	**3,791,712**	**3,369,567**	**3,066,477**	**303,090**	**387,519**	**357,297**	**30,222**	**32,185**
In hospital [2]	3,729,199	3,366,916	3,064,153	302,763	341,657	336,267	5,390	19,364
Not in hospital	62,266	2,615	2,289	326	45,786	21,008	24,778	12,759
Freestanding birthing center	19,871	531	404	127	18,266	11,139	7,127	958
Clinic or doctor's office	596	140	125	15	426	305	121	23
Residence	38,512	1,416	1,296	120	26,222	9,399	16,823	10,089
Other	3,287	528	464	64	872	165	707	1,689
Not specified	247	36	35	1	76	22	54	62

[1] Includes those unspecified, not shown separately. [2] Includes births occurring en route to or upon arrival at hospital.

Source: U.S. National Center for Health Statistics, National Vital Statistics Reports, *Births: Final Data for 2018, Supplemental Tables*, Vol. 68, No. 13, November 2019. See also <https://www.cdc.gov/nchs/nvss/births.htm>.

Table 89. Total Fertility Rate by Race and Hispanic Origin: 2010 to 2018

[Based on race of mother. Excludes births to nonresidents of United States. The total fertility rate estimates the number of births that a hypothetical cohort of 1,000 women would have if they experienced throughout their childbearing years the same age-specific birth rates observed in a given year. The rate can be expressed as the average number of children that would be born per woman. A total fertility rate of 2,100 represents "replacement level" fertility for the total population under current mortality conditions (assuming no net immigration). Race categories are consistent with 1997 Office of Management and Budget standards. See Appendix III]

Race and Hispanic origin	2010	2012	2013	2014	2015	2016	2017	2018
Total	**1,931**	**1,881**	**1,858**	**1,863**	**1,844**	**1,821**	**1,766**	**1,730**
Non-Hispanic:								
White alone	(NA)	(NA)	(NA)	(NA)	(NA)	1,719	1,667	1,640
Black alone	(NA)	(NA)	(NA)	(NA)	(NA)	1,833	1,825	1,792
American Indian or Alaska Native alone	(NA)	(NA)	(NA)	(NA)	(NA)	1,795	1,702	1,651
Asian alone	(NA)	(NA)	(NA)	(NA)	(NA)	1,691	1,597	1,525
Native Hawaiian or other Pacific Islander alone	(NA)	(NA)	(NA)	(NA)	(NA)	2,077	2,086	2,107
Hispanic [1]	2,350	2,190	2,149	2,131	2,124	2,093	2,007	1,959

NA Not available. [1] Persons of Hispanic origin may be of any race.

Source: U.S. National Center for Health Statistics, National Vital Statistics Reports, *Births: Final Data for 2018, Supplemental Tables*, Vol. 68, No. 13, November 2019. See also <https://www.cdc.gov/nchs/nvss/births.htm>.

Table 90. Teenagers—Births and Birth Rates by Age, Race, and Hispanic Origin: 2010 to 2018

[Birth rates per 1,000 women in specified group. Based on race and Hispanic origin of mother. Race categories are consistent with 1997 Office of Management and Budget (OMB) standards. See source for details]

Item	Number of births				Birth rates			
	2010	2016	2017	2018	2010	2016	2017	2018
All races, 15 to 19 years [1]	**367,678**	**209,809**	**194,377**	**179,871**	**34.2**	**20.3**	**18.8**	**17.4**
15 to 17 years	109,173	54,741	48,547	44,291	17.3	8.8	7.9	7.2
18 to 19 years	258,505	155,068	145,830	135,580	58.2	37.5	35.1	32.3
Non-Hispanic:								
White alone	(NA)	78,133	71,854	64,917	(NA)	14.3	13.2	12.1
Black alone	(NA)	42,836	40,016	37,715	(NA)	29.3	27.5	26.3
American Indian or Alaska Native alone	(NA)	3,107	2,878	2,578	(NA)	35.1	32.9	29.7
Asian alone	(NA)	1,949	1,723	1,444	(NA)	3.9	3.3	2.8
Native Hawaiian or other Pacific Islander alone	(NA)	556	491	516	(NA)	28.6	25.5	26.5
Hispanic [2]	(NA)	74,822	69,354	65,122	(NA)	31.9	28.9	26.7

NA Not available. [1] Includes other racial/ethnic groups, not shown separately. [2] Persons of Hispanic origin may be of any race.

Source: U.S. National Center for Health Statistics, National Vital Statistics Reports, *Births: Final Data for 2018*, Vol. 68, No. 13, November 2019. See also <https://www.cdc.gov/nchs/nvss/births.htm>.

Table 91. Births to Unmarried Women by Age, Race, and Hispanic Origin: 2018

[Data are based on Hispanic origin and race of mother. Race categories are consistent with 1997 Office of Management and Budget standards; see source for details. See also Appendix III]

Race/ethnicity of mother	Total	Age of mother						
		Under 15 years old	15 to 19 years old	20 to 24 years old	25 to 29 years old	30 to 34 years old	35 to 39 years old	40 years and over
NUMBER								
Total	**1,503,361**	**1,733**	**161,547**	**479,425**	**437,867**	**261,055**	**128,958**	**32,776**
Non-Hispanic:								
White alone	551,217	336	55,719	182,007	160,778	94,865	46,157	11,355
Black alone	383,364	554	36,839	122,286	120,229	66,381	30,209	6,866
American Indian or Alaska Native alone	19,853	19	2,429	6,172	6,024	3,475	1,418	316
Asian alone	28,191	17	1,008	5,103	8,351	7,532	4,690	1,490
Native Hawaiian or other Pacific Islander alone	4,776	3	465	1,639	1,372	821	384	92
Hispanic [1]	459,242	729	58,055	142,699	125,361	79,267	41,704	11,427
PERCENT								
Total	**39.6**	**99.8**	**89.8**	**66.0**	**39.8**	**23.9**	**22.8**	**25.8**
Non-Hispanic:								
White alone	28.2	99.7	85.8	55.7	27.9	15.2	15.2	19.0
Black alone	69.4	100.0	97.7	88.6	72.1	53.4	44.9	39.2
American Indian or Alaska Native alone	68.2	(S)	94.2	78.7	65.9	56.9	50.9	51.3
Asian alone	11.7	(S)	69.8	34.3	14.4	7.8	8.2	11.3
Native Hawaiian or other Pacific Islander alone	50.4	(S)	90.1	66.0	47.5	37.5	35.0	30.5
Hispanic [1]	51.8	99.9	89.1	68.0	49.4	38.1	35.5	36.7

S Figure does not meet standards of reliability. [1] Persons of Hispanic origin may be of any race.

Source: U.S. National Center for Health Statistics, National Vital Statistics Reports, *Births: Final Data for 2018*, Vol. 68, No. 13, November 2019. See also <https://www.cdc.gov/nchs/nvss/births.htm>.

Table 92. Percent of Births to Teenage Mothers, Unmarried Women, and Births with Low Birth Weight by State: 2010 and 2018

[In percent. By place of residence. Excludes nonresidents of the United States]

State	Births to teenage mothers [1] 2010	2018	Births to unmarried women 2010	2018	Births with low birth weight [2] 2010	2018	State	Births to teenage mothers [1] 2010	2018	Births to unmarried women 2010	2018	Births with low birth weight [2] 2010	2018
U.S.	**9.2**	**4.7**	**40.8**	**39.6**	**8.1**	**8.3**	MO	10.0	5.6	40.2	40.3	8.2	8.7
AL	12.2	6.8	41.9	46.8	10.3	10.7	MT	9.4	4.6	36.4	34.9	7.5	7.4
AK	8.3	4.2	37.6	35.3	5.7	5.9	NE	7.6	4.2	33.6	32.5	7.1	7.6
AZ	10.7	5.8	44.9	44.9	7.1	7.6	NV	9.5	5.0	44.3	48.3	8.3	8.7
AR	13.6	7.9	45.3	45.4	8.8	9.4	NH	5.6	2.8	33.2	32.9	6.9	6.8
CA	8.5	3.7	40.5	37.1	6.8	7.0	NJ	5.4	2.8	35.4	33.8	8.2	7.9
CO	8.2	4.0	23.9	23.2	8.8	9.4	NM	13.9	7.5	52.3	51.2	8.7	9.0
CT	6.0	2.8	37.4	37.1	8.0	7.6	NY	6.2	3.0	41.7	37.5	8.2	8.1
DE	8.6	4.7	47.4	47.0	8.9	8.9	NC	10.1	5.3	42.0	40.9	9.1	9.2
DC	10.4	4.0	54.8	46.5	10.2	10.0	ND	7.2	3.5	32.7	31.9	6.7	6.6
FL	8.9	4.4	47.5	46.4	8.7	8.7	OH	9.9	5.2	43.8	43.2	8.6	8.5
GA	10.7	5.9	45.8	45.1	9.7	10.1	OK	12.2	7.0	41.8	42.2	8.4	8.3
HI	7.1	3.8	37.8	38.1	8.3	8.3	OR	7.7	3.8	35.7	36.3	6.3	6.7
ID	8.0	4.5	26.5	27.0	6.8	7.3	PA	8.3	4.1	41.5	40.8	8.3	8.3
IL	9.0	4.4	40.5	39.3	8.3	8.5	RI	8.0	3.9	45.0	43.6	7.7	7.6
IN	10.3	5.9	43.0	43.2	8.0	8.1	SC	11.7	6.1	47.6	46.2	9.9	9.6
IA	7.8	4.2	34.2	34.9	7.0	6.9	SD	8.3	4.8	37.6	36.1	6.8	6.6
KS	9.5	5.3	37.8	36.4	7.1	7.4	TN	11.6	6.5	44.1	43.5	9.0	9.3
KY	12.0	7.1	41.2	41.9	9.0	8.9	TX	12.4	6.6	42.4	40.8	8.4	8.5
LA	12.3	6.7	53.3	53.3	10.7	10.8	UT	5.8	3.4	19.2	19.2	7.0	7.2
ME	7.1	3.4	41.2	38.8	6.3	7.2	VT	6.4	3.4	39.2	38.5	6.1	7.0
MD	7.3	3.7	41.9	39.2	8.8	8.8	VA	7.2	3.8	35.5	34.7	8.2	8.2
MA	5.4	2.4	34.7	32.5	7.7	7.6	WA	6.9	3.2	33.0	31.1	6.3	6.6
MI	9.5	4.6	41.8	40.8	8.4	8.5	WV	12.7	7.2	43.9	45.7	9.2	9.4
MN	5.9	2.7	33.2	31.9	6.4	6.9	WI	7.4	3.8	36.7	37.4	7.0	7.7
MS	15.2	7.6	54.8	54.1	12.1	12.1	WY	9.6	5.5	34.0	33.3	9.0	9.4

[1] Defined as teenage mothers aged 15-19. [2] Less than 2,500 grams (5 pounds, 8 ounces).

Source: U.S. National Center for Health Statistics, National Vital Statistics Reports, *Births: Final Data for 2018, Supplemental Tables*, Vol. 68, No. 13, November 2019, and earlier reports; and CDC WONDER Online Database, "Natality for 2007-2018," <https://wonder.cdc.gov/natality.html>, accessed January 2020.

Table 93. Rate of Pregnancy Risk Factors, Labor and Delivery Characteristics, and Birth Defects by Age of Mother: 2018

[Rates are number of live births with specified risk factor, procedure, or characteristic per 1,000 live births in specified group, except as noted; birth defects are per 100,000 live births. In 2018, total number of births to residents of areas reporting risk factors, procedure, or defects was 3,791,712]

Factor/characteristic	Births with factor reported (number)	Rates by age — All ages	Under 20 years	20 to 24 years	25 to 29 years	30 to 34 years	35 to 39 years	40 to 54 years
RISK FACTORS IN CURRENT PREGNANCY								
Diabetes:								
Prepregnancy (diagnosis prior to pregnancy)	35,735	9.4	4.0	6.1	7.7	9.9	15.0	22.1
Gestational (diagnosis in current pregnancy)	252,522	66.6	21.8	36.6	56.1	76.9	104.3	137.9
Hypertension:								
Prepregnancy (chronic)	78,310	20.7	7.4	12.6	17.0	22.1	33.0	49.3
Gestational (pregnancy-induced, preeclampsia)	271,596	71.7	77.1	72.1	69.3	68.9	74.7	92.6
Eclampsia [1]	9,449	2.6	3.4	2.8	2.3	2.3	2.9	3.8
Previous preterm birth	134,038	35.4	8.3	26.3	35.7	38.3	46.1	51.1
Pregnancy resulted from infertility treatment	73,709	19.5	0.3	2.3	9.3	23.6	42.0	96.4
Mother had previous cesarean delivery [2]	591,618	226.7	102.4	165.4	210.5	240.4	276.5	291.7
LABOR AND DELIVERY CHARACTERISTICS								
Induction of labor	1,025,834	270.8	308.4	294.7	274.7	255.6	250.1	271.1
Breech presentation (rate per 100 live births)	150,057	4.0	2.6	2.9	3.6	4.4	5.1	6.5
BIRTH DEFECTS (CONGENITAL ANOMALIES)								
Anencephaly	354	9.4	10.5	11.7	9.8	8.2	7.6	7.9
Meningomyelocele or spina bifida	555	14.7	14.3	15.4	16.0	12.5	15.0	15.8
Cyanotic congenital heart disease	2,213	58.5	56.3	57.8	55.3	55.3	65.2	90.0
Gastroschisis	830	21.9	82.7	46.2	20.9	7.7	4.9	3.2
Cleft lip with or without cleft palate	2,050	54.2	54.6	59.7	54.9	48.8	53.5	63.1
Down syndrome	2,106	55.6	28.7	25.9	29.1	38.5	111.2	393.8

[1] Excludes data for South Carolina and Tennessee. [2] Excludes women who have not had a previous pregnancy and from whom total birth order is unknown.

Source: U.S. National Center for Health Statistics, National Vital Statistics Reports, *Births: Final Data for 2018, Supplemental Tables*, Vol. 68, No. 13, November 2019. See also <https://www.cdc.gov/nchs/nvss/births.htm>.

Table 94. Percent of Premature Births by Whether Early or Late Preterm and by Age, Race, and Hispanic Origin of Mother: 2018

[Preterm/premature births are those with less than 37 completed weeks of gestation based on obstetric estimates. Based on race and Hispanic origin of mother. Race categories are consistent with 1997 Office of Management and Budget standards. See source for details]

Characteristic	Total births (number)	Percent preterm Total under 37 weeks	Early preterm Under 28 weeks	Early preterm 28 to 31 weeks	Early preterm 32 to 33 weeks	Late preterm 34 to 36 weeks
Total [1]............................	**3,791,712**	**10.0**	**0.7**	**0.9**	**1.2**	**7.3**
Age of mother:						
Under 15 years..............................	1,736	15.4	1.3	1.7	1.5	10.8
15 to 19 years..............................	179,871	10.4	0.9	1.0	1.2	7.3
20 to 24 years..............................	726,175	9.7	0.7	0.9	1.1	7.0
25 to 29 years..............................	1,099,491	9.4	0.6	0.8	1.1	6.9
30 to 34 years..............................	1,090,697	9.6	0.6	0.9	1.2	7.0
35 to 39 years..............................	566,786	11.4	0.7	1.0	1.4	8.3
40 to 44 years..............................	117,381	13.8	0.8	1.3	1.7	10.0
45 to 54 years..............................	9,575	22.1	1.3	2.5	3.4	14.8
Race and Hispanic origin of mother:						
White alone, non-Hispanic..................	1,956,413	9.1	0.4	0.8	1.1	6.8
Black alone, non-Hispanic..................	552,029	14.1	1.5	1.6	1.8	9.2
Hispanic [2].................................	886,210	9.7	0.6	0.8	1.1	7.2

[1] Total includes those with gestational age not stated; and races other than White and Black, not shown separately. [2] Persons of Hispanic origin may be of any race.

Source: U.S. National Center for Health Statistics, *Births, Final Data for 2018*, Vol. 68, No. 13, November 2019. See also <https://www.cdc.gov/nchs/nvss/births.htm>.

Table 95. Women Who Had a Birth in the Past 12 Months by Selected Characteristics: 2018

[For women aged 15 to 50 years old. Based on the 2018 American Community Survey (ACS). The ACS sample includes the household population and the population living in institutions, dormitories, and other group quarters. Based on a sample and subject to sampling variability. See Appendix III for details]

Characteristic	Total women (number)	Women who had a birth in the past 12 months Number	Percent distribution	Rate per 1,000 women	Percent unmarried
Total, aged 15 to 50 years............................	**76,857,068**	**3,956,960**	**(X)**	**51**	**33.9**
Age:					
15 to 19 years.............................	10,472,771	122,217	3.1	12	86.4
20 to 34 years.............................	32,960,008	2,832,453	71.6	86	36.4
35 to 50 years.............................	33,424,289	1,002,290	25.3	30	20.5
Race/ethnicity:					
One race...................................	74,196,255	3,820,200	96.5	51	33.5
White.......................................	52,825,960	2,676,023	67.6	51	28.2
Black or African American...............	10,835,279	586,546	14.8	54	62.9
American Indian and Alaska Native......	700,940	41,092	1.0	59	59.3
Asian.......................................	5,269,281	263,152	6.7	50	9.9
Native Hawaiian and Other Pacific Islander...	171,834	11,442	0.3	67	39.1
Some other race..........................	4,392,961	241,945	6.1	55	42.1
Two or more races..........................	2,660,813	136,760	3.5	51	46.0
Hispanic origin:					
Hispanic or Latino origin (of any race)......	15,695,111	867,745	21.9	55	41.3
White alone, not Hispanic or Latino..............	42,562,402	2,111,164	53.4	50	25.0
Nativity:					
Native.......................................	63,909,910	3,170,229	80.1	50	37.0
Foreign born [1]............................	12,947,158	786,731	19.9	61	21.7
Education:					
Less than high school graduate............	12,519,966	449,060	11.3	36	53.5
High school graduate (includes equivalency)......	16,065,374	928,058	23.5	58	52.1
Some college or associate's degree............	24,111,302	1,201,310	30.4	50	39.5
Bachelor's degree..........................	15,692,255	851,894	21.5	54	12.7
Graduate or professional degree............	8,468,171	526,638	13.3	62	6.8
Poverty status in past 12 months:					
Women 15 to 50 years old with poverty status determined.......	75,087,522	3,945,566	(X)	53	33.8
Below 100 percent of poverty level............	11,484,450	883,722	22.4	77	67.1
100 to 199 percent of poverty level............	13,176,393	797,006	20.2	60	40.8
200 percent or more above poverty level..........	50,426,679	2,264,838	57.4	45	18.4
Labor force status:					
In labor force [2]............................	54,785,780	2,560,460	64.8	47	34.8
Public assistance income in past 12 months:					
Women 15 to 50 years old with public assistance status determined....	76,857,068	3,956,960	(X)	51	33.9
Received public assistance income............	1,454,772	171,706	4.3	118	68.0
Did not receive public assistance income......	75,402,296	3,785,254	95.7	50	32.4

X Not applicable. [1] Excludes persons born outside of the United States to a parent who is a U.S. citizen. [2] Data are shown for women aged 16 to 50 years old.

Source: U.S. Census Bureau, 2018 American Community Survey, S1301, "Fertility," <http://data.census.gov>, accessed December 2019.

Table 96. Women by Number of Children Ever Born by Age, Marital Status, and Race/Ethnicity: 2018

[76,414 represents 76,414,000. As of June. Data shown are for women aged 15 to 50. Based on the Current Population Survey; for more information, see <http://www.census.gov/cps/methodology>]

Age and marital status	Total women (1,000)	Percent distribution by number of children ever born						
		None	One	Two	Three	Four	Five and six	Seven or more
Total women: [1]............................	**76,414**	**44.2**	**16.8**	**21.7**	**10.7**	**4.3**	**1.9**	**0.4**
By age:								
15 to 19 years old...........................	10,294	96.9	2.1	0.8	0.1	–	0.1	–
20 to 24 years old...........................	10,607	78.6	14.0	6.0	1.0	0.3	0.2	–
25 to 29 years old...........................	11,476	54.2	20.4	16.2	6.5	2.1	0.5	0.1
30 to 34 years old...........................	10,889	33.6	22.3	24.6	12.8	4.4	1.9	0.3
35 to 39 years old...........................	10,727	20.0	19.2	32.6	17.4	7.3	3.2	0.4
40 to 44 years old...........................	9,896	15.0	18.7	34.6	18.6	8.7	3.8	0.7
45 to 50 years old...........................	12,524	15.4	19.8	35.4	17.3	7.4	3.6	1.2
By marital status:								
Women ever married........................	41,451	17.5	21.6	33.8	16.6	6.8	3.0	0.6
Women never married.......................	34,963	75.8	11.1	7.5	3.6	1.4	0.6	0.1
By race and Hispanic origin:								
White alone....................................	56,229	44.4	16.1	22.1	11.1	4.2	1.8	0.4
White alone, non-Hispanic.................	42,373	45.7	16.1	22.8	10.1	3.5	1.5	0.4
Black alone....................................	11,258	40.8	19.8	20.1	10.4	5.6	2.8	0.5
Asian alone...................................	5,519	45.5	18.1	25.0	7.7	2.4	1.0	0.4
Hispanic [2]....................................	15,674	40.2	16.7	19.9	13.7	6.3	2.7	0.5

– Represents or rounds to zero. [1] Includes women of other races, not shown separately. [2] Persons of Hispanic origin may be of any race.

Source: U.S. Census Bureau, "Fertility of Women in the United States: 2018," <https://www.census.gov/topics/health/fertility/data/tables.html>, accessed June 2019.

Table 97. Women's Relationship Status and Age at First Birth by Current Age and Race/Ethnicity: 2018

[In percent, except as noted (42,670 represents 42,670,000). As of June. Data are from the Current Population Survey; for more information, see <https://www.census.gov/programs-surveys/cps.html>.]

Current age and race/ethnicity	Total mothers, 1,000	Married at first birth			Not married at first birth					
					Living with unmarried partner			Neither married nor living with unmarried partner		
		Under age 20 at first birth	Age 20 to 25 at first birth	Over age 25 at first birth	Under age 20 at first birth	Age 20 to 25 at first birth	Over age 25 at first birth	Under age 20 at first birth	Age 20 to 25 at first birth	Over age 25 at first birth
TOTAL										
15 to 50 years old....	**42,670**	**5.9**	**21.9**	**34.7**	**6.7**	**9.9**	**4.6**	**6.4**	**7.3**	**2.5**
15 to 19 years old.......	321	6.7	(X)	(X)	52.3	(X)	(X)	41.0	(X)	(X)
20 to 24 years old.......	2,274	10.4	15.4	(X)	18.1	22.0	(X)	16.4	17.6	(X)
25 to 29 years old.......	5,258	6.6	22.1	10.9	12.7	19.5	3.3	9.8	12.7	2.4
30 to 34 years old.......	7,230	6.7	20.5	32.0	7.8	12.1	5.9	5.7	6.7	2.6
35 to 39 years old.......	8,583	6.0	21.6	38.3	5.6	8.9	5.6	6.1	5.4	2.5
40 to 44 years old.......	8,411	5.6	21.8	43.3	4.9	6.3	4.9	5.7	4.9	2.7
45 to 50 years old.......	10,593	4.1	25.1	47.0	1.6	5.2	4.5	3.0	6.5	3.0
WHITE ALONE										
15 to 50 years old.....	31,275	6.3	24.3	37.4	6.4	9.4	4.3	4.9	5.3	1.8
15 to 19 years old.......	252	8.2	(X)	(X)	51.9	(X)	(X)	39.9	(X)	(X)
20 to 24 years old.......	1,533	12.3	19.0	(X)	20.0	20.7	(X)	12.6	15.5	(X)
25 to 29 years old.......	3,644	8.2	26.1	12.3	12.3	18.9	2.7	7.7	9.8	2.0
30 to 34 years old.......	5,269	7.3	23.2	33.0	7.8	11.9	5.5	4.8	4.6	1.9
35 to 39 years old.......	6,315	5.7	23.0	41.4	5.3	8.4	5.6	4.7	3.9	2.1
40 to 44 years old.......	6,237	6.1	24.1	45.5	4.3	6.5	4.3	3.8	3.5	1.8
45 to 50 years old.......	8,025	4.2	27.0	50.3	1.5	4.6	4.1	2.1	4.5	1.8
BLACK ALONE										
15 to 50 years old.....	6,666	4.4	11.5	14.4	9.3	13.7	7.1	15.3	18.4	6.0
15 to 19 years old.......	42	–	(X)	(X)	45.1	(X)	(X)	54.9	(X)	(X)
20 to 24 years old.......	492	4.1	3.6	(X)	12.4	21.9	(X)	30.9	27.1	(X)
25 to 29 years old.......	1,078	2.2	7.7	3.1	16.3	21.2	5.2	17.8	23.1	3.5
30 to 34 years old.......	1,146	3.7	8.8	15.6	9.3	16.5	9.0	12.5	18.6	6.1
35 to 39 years old.......	1,286	6.5	13.3	15.1	8.9	13.7	7.3	14.8	14.3	6.1
40 to 44 years old.......	1,181	5.2	12.1	19.2	8.8	7.7	10.6	16.2	13.2	7.0
45 to 50 years old.......	1,439	4.2	17.4	22.5	2.5	8.3	6.7	8.9	20.2	9.3
HISPANIC [1]										
15 to 50 years old.....	9,376	9.8	25.5	21.4	10.2	11.9	5.4	6.9	6.7	2.2
15 to 19 years old.......	83	3.9	(X)	(X)	64.7	(X)	(X)	31.4	(X)	(X)
20 to 24 years old.......	663	12.7	13.2	(X)	25.4	16.1	(X)	17.5	15.2	(X)
25 to 29 years old.......	1,329	11.0	21.1	5.9	15.2	18.9	3.7	11.5	11.0	1.8
30 to 34 years old.......	1,660	11.7	21.5	17.8	13.8	15.6	5.6	6.9	5.1	2.0
35 to 39 years old.......	1,803	10.3	25.3	22.7	8.1	11.1	6.9	7.8	5.1	2.9
40 to 44 years old.......	1,794	9.0	28.9	29.9	6.3	10.0	6.0	4.3	3.8	1.9
45 to 50 years old.......	2,044	7.0	33.9	33.6	2.2	5.9	6.5	1.2	6.6	3.3

– Represents or rounds to zero. X Not applicable. [1] Persons of Hispanic origin may be of any race.

Source: U.S. Census Bureau, "Fertility of Women in the United States: 2018," <https://www.census.gov/topics/health/fertility/data/tables.html>, accessed June 2019.

Table 98. Women Who Had a Birth in the Past Year Who Are in the Labor Force by Educational Attainment: 2010 to 2017

[In thousands (2,562 represents 2,562,000), except percent. For women aged 16 to 50 years old. Based on the American Community Survey (ACS). The ACS universe includes the household population and population living in institutions, college dormitories, and other group quarters. Based on a sample and subject to sampling variability, see Appendix III]

Year	Number of women who had a birth in the past year who are in the labor force					Percent of women who had a birth in the past year who are in the labor force				
	Total	Less than high school diploma	High school diploma or GED	Some college	Bachelor's degree or higher	Total	Less than high school diploma	High school diploma or GED	Some college	Bachelor's degree or higher
2010.........	2,562	278	589	859	836	61.6	39.7	57.9	66.4	72.7
2013.........	2,418	221	513	805	879	61.7	38.8	56.4	64.4	73.8
2014.........	2,436	203	508	815	909	61.8	38.2	55.4	64.9	73.7
2015.........	2,447	196	508	816	927	62.4	38.2	56.0	65.1	74.2
2016.........	2,493	194	526	804	970	63.3	39.6	57.2	65.3	74.7
2017.........	2,534	182	532	794	1,027	63.5	39.6	56.7	64.3	75.4

Source: U.S. Census Bureau, "Fertility: Historical Time Series Tables," <https://www.census.gov/topics/health/fertility/data/tables.html>, accessed June 2019.

Table 99. Women Who Had a Birth in the Past 12 Months by Citizenship Status, Educational Attainment, and Poverty Status by State: 2018

[In percent, except for total. For women 15 to 50 years old. Based on 2018 American Community Survey (ACS). See headnote, Table 98]

State	Total (number)	Citizenship status		Educational attainment					Below poverty[3]
		Native born	Foreign born[1]	Less than high school graduate	High school graduate[2]	Some college or associate's degree	Bachelor's degree	Graduate or professional degree	
United States......	3,956,960	80.1	19.9	11.3	23.5	30.4	21.5	13.3	22.4
Alabama............	66,070	94.6	5.4	12.6	25.9	37.5	14.9	9.1	33.3
Alaska..............	10,747	88.0	12.0	11.1	35.7	23.5	18.2	11.5	23.4
Arizona.............	92,780	79.3	20.7	14.1	25.0	32.7	19.2	9.0	24.4
Arkansas............	39,677	91.5	8.5	10.0	34.3	32.4	15.7	7.7	29.8
California...........	454,027	67.3	32.7	12.2	21.8	30.0	22.8	13.1	19.3
Colorado............	71,267	82.8	17.2	11.1	18.0	28.0	25.6	17.3	14.3
Connecticut.........	35,625	74.2	25.8	9.4	13.6	25.8	28.7	22.4	15.4
Delaware............	10,138	77.7	22.3	13.2	28.7	23.8	17.5	16.8	22.0
District of Columbia...	8,651	87.0	13.0	5.5	18.0	28.0	14.3	34.2	16.0
Florida..............	230,832	71.8	28.2	10.2	26.7	31.2	21.0	10.9	22.5
Georgia.............	122,525	85.9	14.1	10.9	27.1	29.7	19.7	12.6	24.9
Hawaii..............	18,527	80.0	20.0	5.3	22.8	40.7	19.0	12.2	16.3
Idaho...............	23,502	87.4	12.6	9.1	29.9	33.8	22.2	5.1	21.7
Illinois..............	158,848	80.8	19.2	8.2	22.6	29.0	23.1	17.1	19.4
Indiana.............	89,630	90.5	9.5	12.1	26.2	34.9	18.3	8.4	25.0
Iowa................	40,916	89.8	10.2	8.3	20.9	35.5	25.3	10.0	17.1
Kansas.............	41,218	85.3	14.7	12.1	25.9	29.8	22.5	9.9	20.4
Kentucky...........	56,995	90.7	9.3	11.7	24.1	34.7	18.4	11.1	31.1
Louisiana...........	62,709	92.0	8.0	15.2	27.5	33.0	16.4	7.8	35.0
Maine...............	14,372	96.5	3.5	6.2	25.2	32.2	24.5	11.9	22.0
Maryland...........	72,172	69.8	30.2	11.9	18.1	22.6	23.1	24.3	13.9
Massachusetts.......	74,345	71.3	28.7	6.6	18.9	22.4	28.1	24.0	15.6
Michigan............	115,629	87.8	12.2	11.5	21.9	33.0	22.6	11.1	23.7
Minnesota..........	76,157	77.3	22.7	9.8	16.3	32.5	24.4	16.9	15.5
Mississippi..........	35,639	97.5	2.5	14.1	21.9	42.7	14.5	6.8	31.1
Missouri............	80,307	92.7	7.3	9.7	23.1	33.7	20.4	13.1	23.8
Montana............	11,388	99.0	1.0	8.8	25.2	34.0	23.7	8.4	25.8
Nebraska...........	25,692	84.9	15.1	9.4	16.7	33.1	26.5	14.4	18.8
Nevada.............	36,733	75.2	24.8	15.7	36.3	28.1	13.4	6.5	23.7
New Hampshire......	13,925	90.9	9.1	9.5	23.1	28.9	23.9	14.5	17.1
New Jersey..........	105,146	64.9	35.1	10.8	21.1	22.1	28.3	17.8	19.9
New Mexico.........	23,984	86.7	13.3	13.8	21.5	44.1	10.1	10.5	36.7
New York............	216,046	69.9	30.1	11.4	22.4	21.9	22.6	21.7	20.9
North Carolina.......	119,280	86.5	13.5	11.5	19.8	34.9	21.8	12.1	25.4
North Dakota........	11,264	90.3	9.7	6.7	16.1	30.6	37.0	9.6	16.8
Ohio................	146,391	90.2	9.8	11.1	26.9	32.0	18.5	11.6	28.1
Oklahoma...........	51,095	89.9	10.1	12.4	26.7	34.2	18.3	8.4	25.1
Oregon.............	45,820	75.6	24.4	12.1	17.4	31.7	24.5	14.3	20.7
Pennsylvania........	147,829	85.8	14.2	11.5	23.8	26.1	21.7	16.8	19.9
Rhode Island........	10,910	75.2	24.8	15.4	21.3	21.1	24.0	18.1	21.5
South Carolina.......	63,951	91.4	8.6	12.3	22.8	36.2	17.9	10.8	28.6
South Dakota........	11,346	95.5	4.5	10.0	25.0	33.1	19.2	12.6	26.3
Tennessee..........	83,897	90.9	9.1	8.3	27.8	31.9	20.5	11.5	29.2
Texas...............	383,580	75.5	24.5	15.5	26.0	28.0	20.0	10.5	24.9
Utah................	52,085	86.5	13.5	8.0	23.3	34.2	27.3	7.2	15.4
Vermont............	5,767	90.4	9.6	2.8	32.8	24.0	21.6	18.9	20.1
Virginia.............	99,351	81.7	18.3	8.5	21.1	32.4	21.7	16.3	19.4
Washington..........	92,209	74.8	25.2	11.1	17.8	35.8	21.9	13.4	17.8
West Virginia........	18,926	99.6	0.4	6.7	37.0	30.8	15.8	9.7	33.0
Wisconsin...........	68,743	90.1	9.9	7.6	21.5	33.0	26.0	11.8	17.1
Wyoming............	8,297	88.2	11.8	17.2	22.5	33.0	20.1	7.2	20.6

[1] Foreign born excludes people born outside the U.S. to a parent who is a U.S. citizen. [2] Includes equivalency. [3] The population universe used when determining poverty status excludes people institutionalized, in military group quarters, and in college dormitories, and unrelated individuals under 15 years old.

Source: U.S. Census Bureau, 2018 American Community Survey, Tables B13008, B13010, and B13014, <http://data.census.gov>, accessed December 2019.

Table 100. Women Who Had a Birth in the Past 12 Months by Household Income and Marital Status: 2017

[In thousands (3,412.3 represents 3,412,300), except percent. Data shown for women aged 15 to 50 years old; does not include women living in group quarters. Based on the American Community Survey (ACS). Based on a sample and subject to sampling variability]

Annual household income	Total women	Women with a birth in the past 12 months			Percent of total women	Percent of women with a birth in the past 12 months		
		Total	Married [1]	Unmarried [2]		Total	Married [1]	Unmarried [2]
Under $10,000.................	3,412.3	226.7	60.2	166.5	4.6	5.7	2.3	11.9
$10,000-$14,999.............	1,912.2	113.9	35.0	78.9	2.6	2.9	1.4	5.6
$15,000-$24,999.............	4,861.7	299.4	120.3	179.2	6.5	7.5	4.7	12.8
$25,000-$34,999.............	5,530.4	334.3	166.5	167.8	7.4	8.4	6.5	12.0
$35,000-$49,999.............	8,520.1	494.1	286.0	208.1	11.4	12.4	11.1	14.8
$50,000-$74,999.............	13,210.4	705.1	470.1	235.0	17.7	17.8	18.3	16.8
$75,000-$99,999.............	10,813.8	559.0	411.1	147.9	14.5	14.1	16.0	10.5
$100,000-$149,999...........	13,829.4	670.6	533.8	136.8	18.5	16.9	20.8	9.8
$150,000-$199,999...........	6,262.7	283.3	236.6	46.7	8.4	7.1	9.2	3.3
$200,000 or more.............	6,454.4	283.5	248.1	35.4	8.6	7.1	9.7	2.5

[1] Includes women who are married, spouse present. [2] Includes women who are widowed, divorced, separated, and never married.

Source: U.S. Census Bureau, "Fertility of Women in the United States: 2018," <https://www.census.gov/topics/health/fertility/data/tables.html>, accessed June 2019.

Table 101. Sexually Active High School Students and Birth Control Use by Sex, Race/Ethnicity, and Grade: 2019

[In percent. For public and private school students in grades 9 to 12. Current sexual activity defined as having had sexual intercourse with at least one person during the 3 months before the survey. Based on the Youth Risk Behavior Survey; see source for details]

Item	Total	Race/ethnicity			Grade level			
		White [1]	Black [1]	Hispanic	9th	10th	11th	12th
TOTAL								
Ever had sexual intercourse.................	38.4	38.0	42.3	41.8	19.2	33.6	46.5	56.7
Currently sexually active.....................	27.4	27.5	29.0	29.7	11.7	23.1	34.3	42.3
Condom use [2].............................	54.3	55.8	48.2	56.2	61.3	55.4	56.3	50.3
Birth control use [3]..........................	30.9	39.5	19.7	18.2	14.2	22.7	33.4	38.1
No pregnancy prevention method [2].......	11.9	8.4	23.0	13.3	15.3	12.0	11.2	11.4
MALE								
Ever had sexual intercourse.................	39.2	36.7	50.1	43.6	21.6	35.4	46.6	56.3
Currently sexually active.....................	26.3	25.2	32.4	29.2	12.5	22.0	32.7	40.6
Condom use [2].............................	60.0	60.9	51.8	62.3	69.0	64.2	60.7	53.4
Birth control use [3]..........................	25.9	33.0	18.7	16.7	11.2	16.5	29.4	33.7
No pregnancy prevention method [2].......	10.1	6.3	21.0	10.6	14.0	9.6	10.1	9.0
FEMALE								
Ever had sexual intercourse.................	37.6	39.2	34.0	40.3	16.7	31.8	46.6	56.8
Currently sexually active.....................	28.4	29.9	25.4	30.3	10.8	24.3	35.9	43.8
Condom use [2].............................	49.6	51.6	44.5	50.9	51.8	47.8	52.3	47.8
Birth control use [3]..........................	35.2	45.2	21.2	19.6	17.8	28.6	36.9	42.1
No pregnancy prevention method [2].......	13.4	10.1	24.1	15.6	16.9	14.2	12.1	13.3

[1] Non-Hispanic. [2] During last sexual intercourse. [3] Includes use of birth control pills, an IUD or implant, or a shot, patch, or birth control ring.

Source: U.S. Centers for Disease Control and Prevention, Youth Risk Behavior Surveillance System (YRBSS), "YRBS Explorer," <https://yrbs-explorer.services.cdc.gov/#/>, accessed August 2020. See also <https://www.cdc.gov/healthyyouth/data/yrbs/>.

Table 102. Adults Reporting Sexual Contact with Opposite- and Same-Sex Partners by Sex, Age, and Race/Ethnicity: 2011 to 2013

[In percent, except as indicated (55,271 represents 55,271,000). Data shown for persons aged 18 to 44 years old who have ever had specified types of sexual contact. Based on the 2011-2013 National Survey of Family Growth. See Appendix III]

Sex and selected characteristics	Number (1,000)	Percent reporting type of sexual contact [1]				
		Opposite-sex sexual contact [2]	Vaginal intercourse with opposite-sex partner	Oral sex with opposite-sex partner	Anal sex with opposite-sex partner	Same-sex sexual contact [3]
Women [1].................................	**55,271**	**95.3**	**94.2**	**86.2**	**35.9**	**17.4**
By age:						
18 to 24 years old.........................	14,269	85.6	81.7	77.3	28.4	19.4
25 to 44 years old.........................	41,002	98.7	98.5	89.3	38.5	16.7
By race/ethnicity:						
White alone, non-Hispanic.................	31,880	95.4	93.9	91.9	40.5	19.6
Black alone, non-Hispanic.................	7,581	96.3	95.6	82.7	27.5	19.4
Hispanic....................................	10,811	95.8	95.5	77.7	32.3	11.2
Men [1]....................................	**54,685**	**93.5**	**92.0**	**87.4**	**42.3**	**6.2**
By age:						
18 to 24 years old.........................	14,718	83.5	79.9	77.6	29.3	6.6
25 to 44 years old.........................	39,967	97.2	96.5	91.0	47.0	6.0
By race/ethnicity:						
White alone, non-Hispanic.................	31,423	93.7	92.0	91.0	44.1	6.9
Black alone, non-Hispanic.................	6,304	96.3	95.4	90.4	35.4	5.3
Hispanic....................................	11,292	93.3	92.4	78.6	40.4	6.2

[1] Includes other race/ethnicities not shown separately. [2] Includes vaginal, oral, or anal sex. [3] For women, any sexual contact with same-sex (female) partners includes oral sex or any sexual experience. For men, includes oral or anal sex with male partners.

Source: U.S. National Center for Health Statistics, National Health Statistics Reports, *Sexual Behavior, Sexual Attraction, and Sexual Orientation Among Adults Aged 18-44 in the United States: Data From the 2011-2013 National Survey of Family Growth*, No. 88, January 2016. See also <http://www.cdc.gov/nchs/nsfg/>.

Table 103. Sexual Attraction and Orientation by Sex, Age, and Race/Ethnicity: 2011 to 2013

[In percent, except as indicated (55,271 represents 55,271,000). Data shown for persons aged 18 to 44 years old. Based on the 2011-2013 National Survey of Family Growth. See Appendix III]

Sex and sexual attraction and orientation	Total [1]	Age 18 to 24 years old	25 to 44 years old Total	25 to 34 years old	35 to 44 years old	White, Non-His-panic	Black, Non-His-panic	His-panic
Women (1,000)	**55,271**	**14,269**	**41,002**	**20,790**	**20,212**	**31,880**	**7,581**	**10,811**
Percent distribution								
Sexual attraction:								
Total	100.0	100.0	100.0	100.0	100.0	100.0	100.0	100.0
Only opposite sex	81.0	75.9	82.8	79.1	86.6	79.6	84.2	84.7
Mostly opposite sex	12.9	14.4	12.4	15.4	9.2	15.2	9.1	9.3
Equally to both	3.2	5.3	2.5	3.3	1.7	2.9	3.7	3.5
Mostly same sex	0.8	1.7	0.5	0.3	0.7	0.8	0.6	1.1
Only same sex	0.8	1.0	0.8	0.9	0.6	0.9	0.8	0.8
Not sure	1.2	1.6	1.1	0.9	1.3	0.7	1.7	0.5
Sexual orientation:								
Total	100.0	100.0	100.0	100.0	100.0	100.0	100.0	100.0
Heterosexual or straight	92.3	89.5	93.3	92.5	94.2	93.1	93.1	92.6
Homosexual, gay, or lesbian	1.3	1.8	1.1	1.2	0.9	1.3	1.1	1.2
Bisexual	5.5	7.8	4.7	5.4	4.0	5.4	4.9	4.2
Not reported [2]	0.9	0.9	0.9	1.0	0.9	0.2	0.9	1.9
Men (1,000)	**54,685**	**14,718**	**39,967**	**20,453**	**19,514**	**31,423**	**6,304**	**11,292**
Percent distribution								
Sexual attraction:								
Total	100.0	100.0	100.0	100.0	100.0	100.0	100.0	100.0
Only opposite sex	92.1	88.6	93.4	92.7	94.1	92.5	93.5	91.5
Mostly opposite sex	4.1	5.9	3.4	3.4	3.5	3.9	2.8	3.9
Equally to both	0.9	1.0	0.7	0.9	0.6	0.9	0.4	1.1
Mostly same sex	0.8	0.7	0.8	1.2	0.3	0.6	1.1	0.8
Only same sex	1.5	2.5	1.2	1.0	1.4	1.7	0.9	1.8
Not sure	0.7	1.3	0.5	0.8	(S)	0.3	1.3	0.8
Sexual orientation:								
Total	100.0	100.0	100.0	100.0	100.0	100.0	100.0	100.0
Heterosexual or straight	95.1	94.0	95.4	95.4	95.5	95.4	96.5	93.2
Homosexual, gay, or lesbian	1.9	2.6	1.7	1.6	1.7	2.0	1.5	2.1
Bisexual	2.0	2.5	1.8	2.2	1.3	2.2	1.6	2.0
Not reported [2]	1.0	0.9	1.1	0.8	1.4	0.4	0.4	2.7

S Figure does not meet publication standards. [1] Includes other race/ethnicities not shown separately. [2] Includes "don't know" and "refused."

Source: U.S. National Center for Health Statistics, National Health Statistics Reports, *Sexual Behavior, Sexual Attraction, and Sexual Orientation Among Adults Aged 18-44 in the United States: Data From the 2011-2013 National Survey of Family Growth*, No. 88, January 2016. See also <http://www.cdc.gov/nchs/nsfg/>.

Table 104. Contraceptive Use Among Women by Race/Ethnicity, Age, and Method: 1995 to 2015

[In percent. Covers women who are sexually active. Based on National Survey of Family Growth interviews of women of childbearing age. Survey collects up to four methods of contraception used in the month of interview; percents may not add to total because more than one method could have been used in month of interview]

Year and race/ethnicity	By age [1, 2] 15 to 44 years, total	15 to 19 years	20 to 24 years	25 to 34 years	35 to 44 years	By method Female steril-ization	Inject-able	Pill [3]	Intra-uterine device	Con-dom	With-drawal
Total women: [4]											
1995	92.5	80.2	91.7	94.0	93.9	27.8	3.0	27.0	0.8	23.4	6.1
2002	89.3	82.0	87.9	90.2	90.7	27.0	5.5	31.0	2.1	23.8	8.8
2006 to 2010	89.0	82.0	87.0	89.8	90.6	26.6	3.9	28.4	5.6	23.1	10.1
2011 to 2015	89.7	84.9	89.1	89.9	90.9	23.2	4.2	26.6	11.5	22.2	14.0
White alone, non-Hispanic:											
1995	93.0	81.7	93.0	93.9	94.2	24.5	2.4	28.7	0.7	22.5	6.4
2002	90.9	84.4	90.9	91.5	91.7	23.9	4.3	34.9	1.7	21.7	9.5
2006 to 2010	90.5	85.7	89.1	91.6	91.2	23.6	2.5	33.1	5.6	20.8	10.3
2011 to 2015	91.2	89.4	90.0	91.3	92.2	20.7	2.8	30.9	11.4	20.9	13.8
Black alone, non-Hispanic:											
1995	90.0	80.0	91.3	91.6	90.9	39.9	5.4	23.7	(S)	24.9	3.3
2002	84.7	82.2	74.8	88.9	86.0	39.2	9.4	23.1	(S)	29.6	4.8
2006 to 2010	82.8	77.3	79.4	82.1	86.3	37.3	8.9	18.7	5.0	29.9	7.1
2011 to 2015	86.5	78.5	85.4	89.0	86.6	30.9	10.0	19.5	8.8	25.6	12.4
Hispanic or Latina: [5]											
1995	91.4	75.5	82.5	95.4	95.2	36.6	4.7	23.0	(S)	21.2	5.7
2002	88.4	76.4	87.5	87.4	92.3	33.8	7.8	22.0	5.3	24.1	6.3
2006 to 2010	89.6	75.5	87.0	89.7	93.4	31.7	6.0	20.2	6.8	22.2	10.4
2011 to 2015	87.1	72.0	87.5	87.1	90.4	28.2	5.0	18.3	14.3	21.3	13.9

S Figure does not meet standards of reliability or precision. [1] Includes women using contraception in the month of interview, or not using contraception in the month of interview but who had sexual intercourse in the 3 months prior to interview. [2] Any contraceptive use. Includes methods not shown separately. [3] For 2011-2015, includes the oral contraceptive pill only. Prior to 2011, also includes the emergency contraception/morning-after pill. [4] Includes women of other or multiple races, not shown separately. [5] Persons of Hispanic origin may be of any race.

Source: U.S. National Center for Health Statistics, *Health, United States, 2017*, September 2018. See also <https://www.cdc.gov/nchs/>.

Table 105. Abortions Reported and Rates by Age: 2007 to 2016

[Data on abortions are voluntarily provided to the CDC by the central health agencies of 48 reporting areas (New York City and 47 states, excluding California, the District of Columbia, Maryland, and New Hampshire). Data by age are from 44 reporting areas (excludes California, District of Columbia, Florida, Maine, Maryland, New Hampshire, Vermont, and Wyoming that did not report, did not report by age, or did not meet reporting standards for 1 year or more)]

Age	2007	2010	2011	2012	2013	2014	2015	2016	Percent change, 2007 to 2016
Total (number) [1]	825,240	762,755	727,554	696,587	661,874	649,849	636,902	623,471	-24.4
Rate per 1,000 women aged 15-44....	15.6	14.4	13.7	13.1	12.4	12.1	11.8	11.6	-25.6
BY AGE									
Total (number)	722,831	675,732	643,628	614,570	582,260	569,100	556,221	544,663	-24.6
Percent distribution:									
Under 15 years old	0.5	0.5	0.4	0.4	0.3	0.3	0.3	0.3	-40.0
15 to 19 years old	16.5	14.6	13.5	12.2	11.4	10.4	9.8	9.4	-43.0
20 to 24 years old	32.7	32.9	32.9	32.8	32.7	32.1	31.1	30.0	-8.3
25 to 29 years old	24.2	24.5	24.9	25.4	25.9	26.8	27.6	28.5	17.8
30 to 34 years old	14.1	15.3	15.8	16.4	16.8	17.2	17.7	18.0	27.7
35 to 39 years old	8.8	8.9	8.9	9.1	9.2	9.7	10.0	10.3	17.0
40 years old and over	3.2	3.4	3.6	3.7	3.6	3.6	3.6	3.6	12.5
Abortion rate: [2]									
Under 15 years old	1.2	1.0	0.9	0.8	0.6	0.5	0.5	0.4	-66.7
15 to 19 years old	14.1	11.7	10.5	9.2	8.2	7.3	6.7	6.2	-56.0
20 to 24 years old	29.2	26.8	25.0	23.3	21.9	20.9	19.9	19.1	-34.6
25 to 29 years old	21.8	20.2	19.4	18.9	18.2	18.1	17.9	17.8	-18.3
30 to 34 years old	13.6	13.2	12.7	12.4	11.8	11.7	11.7	11.6	-14.7
35 to 39 years old	7.8	7.6	7.5	7.3	7.0	7.1	7.0	6.9	-11.5
40 years old and over	2.6	2.8	2.8	2.8	2.5	2.5	2.5	2.5	-3.8

[1] Data shown for continuously reporting areas during the 2007-2016 period. [2] Number of abortions obtained by women in a given age group per 1,000 women in that same age group. Women aged 13–14 years were used as the denominator for the group of women aged under 15 years, and women aged 40–44 years were used as the denominator for the group of women aged 40 years or more. Women aged 15–44 years were used as the denominator for the overall rate. For each reporting area, abortions for women of unknown age were distributed according to the distribution of abortions among women of known age for that area.

Source: U.S. Centers for Disease Control and Prevention, *Morbidity and Mortality Weekly Report, Surveillance Summaries*, 68:11, November 29, 2019, "Abortion Surveillance—United States, 2017." See also <https://www.cdc.gov/mmwr/index.html>.

Table 106. Percent of Babies Breastfed by Selected Characteristics of Mother: 1986 to 2013

[In percent. Annual averages for 3-year period shown. Based on the National Survey of Family Growth. Data are from household interviews with a sample of women aged 15-44 years old]

Mother's characteristics	1986-1988	1989-1991	1992-1994	1995-1998	1999-2001	2002-2004	2005-2007	2008-2010	2011-2013
PERCENT OF BABIES EVER BREASTFED 3 MONTHS OR MORE									
Total	34.6	31.8	33.6	45.8	48.4	50.6	46.6	50.2	56.6
Age at baby's birth:									
Under 20 years	18.5	(S)	(S)	30.0	30.0	37.6	26.6	35.5	38.4
20-24 years	26.1	24.1	25.1	36.6	41.8	38.0	38.6	37.6	43.8
25-29 years	36.9	32.3	35.6	46.3	43.7	50.2	49.0	54.8	58.3
30-44 years	50.1	46.8	46.7	57.5	62.4	63.9	56.3	59.6	65.6
Race and Hispanic origin: [1]									
Not Hispanic or Latina									
White alone	37.7	35.2	36.6	47.8	49.7	54.5	49.5	48.4	57.8
Black or African American alone	11.6	11.5	13.3	29.6	33.7	29.2	26.3	35.7	37.0
Hispanic or Latina	38.2	33.9	35.0	49.7	54.3	55.9	49.4	55.6	58.8
Education: [2]									
No high school diploma or GED	21.8	17.6	25.2	33.9	37.0	39.9	41.3	42.8	50.8
High school diploma or GED	28.2	28.0	27.4	36.9	43.1	41.9	36.8	44.4	45.1
Some college, no bachelor's degree	38.7	33.1	38.7	49.6	52.8	43.2	48.7	46.7	52.3
Bachelor's degree or higher	55.0	56.1	59.3	64.5	64.1	75.9	65.8	63.7	73.9
Region:									
Northeast	29.9	37.2	36.4	48.2	48.8	59.9	51.5	46.9	57.7
Midwest	30.3	31.5	30.1	42.0	42.8	46.8	41.6	42.1	50.8
South	27.7	20.1	26.2	38.9	44.4	42.7	40.5	45.6	51.8
West	52.4	42.9	45.3	58.2	59.2	62.6	57.8	66.0	68.5

S Figure does not meet publication standards. [1] Starting with 1995 data, race-specific estimates are tabulated according to 1997 Revisions to the Standards for the Classification of Federal Data on Race and Ethnicity and are not strictly comparable with estimates for earlier years. Starting with 1995 data, race-specific estimates are for persons who reported only one racial group. Prior to data year 1995, data were tabulated according to the 1977 Standards. Estimates for single-race categories prior to 1995 included persons who reported one race or, if they reported more than one race, identified one race as best representing their race. [2] Educational attainment is presented only for women age 22 to 44 years old, as of day of interview.

Source: U.S. National Center for Health Statistics, *Health, United States, 2017*, September 2018. See also <http://www.cdc.gov/nchs/hus.htm>.

Table 107. Assisted Reproductive Technology (ART) Procedures and Outcomes: 2000 to 2018

[Covers ART procedures with the intent to transfer at least one embryo; excludes freezing/banking cycles. In 1996, Centers for Disease Control (CDC) initiated data collection regarding Assisted Reproductive Technology (ART) procedures performed in the United States, as mandated by the Fertility Clinic Success Rate and Certification Act. ARTs include those infertility treatments in which both eggs and sperm are handled in the laboratory for the purpose of establishing a pregnancy (i.e., in vitro fertilization and related procedures)]

Year	Procedures started [1]	Number of pregnancies [2]	Live birth deliveries [3]	Live born infants
2000........................	99,629	30,557	25,228	35,025
2005........................	134,260	47,651	38,910	52,041
2010........................	147,260	57,773	47,090	61,564
2015........................	186,157	72,870	60,778	72,913
2016........................	197,737	80,971	65,969	76,897
2017........................	196,850	(NA)	68,908	78,052
2018........................	203,119	(NA)	73,831	81,478

NA Not available. [1] Excludes procedures for which new treatments were being evaluated. [2] Beginning in 2012, excludes pregnancies from procedures performed in U.S. territories other than Puerto Rico; and, beginning in 2013, excludes pregnancies resulting from oocyte thaw procedures. [3] A live birth delivery is defined as the delivery of one or more live born infants.

Source: U.S. Centers for Disease Control and Prevention, *2016 Assisted Reproductive Technology, National Summary Report*, October 2018; *Assisted Reproductive Technology Surveillance - United States, 2016*, MMWR Surveillance Summaries, Vol. 68, No. 4, April 2019 and earlier reports; and "Assisted Reproductive Technology," <http://www.cdc.gov/art/artdata/index.html>, accessed July 2020.

Table 108. Life Expectancy at Birth, 1940 to 2017, and Projected, 2020 to 2060

[In years. Beginning 2001, life table data are based on revised life table methodology. Race and Hispanic-origin categories are consistent with 1977 Office of Management and Budget (OMB) standards. From 2003-2017, the number of states reporting multiple-race data according to new 1997 OMB standards varied widely. To provide a comparison of data by race between the 1977 and 1997 OMB standards, those reporting more than one race were "bridged" to single-race categories. For more information, see Technical notes, source]

Year	Total [1]			White, non-Hispanic			Black, non-Hispanic			Hispanic [2]		
	Total	Male	Female	Total	Male	Female	Total	Male	Female	Total	Male	Female
1940............	62.9	60.8	65.2	(NA)	(NA)	(NA)	(NA)	(NA)	(NA)	(NA)	(NA)	(NA)
1950............	68.2	65.6	71.1	(NA)	(NA)	(NA)	(NA)	(NA)	(NA)	(NA)	(NA)	(NA)
1960............	69.7	66.6	73.1	(NA)	(NA)	(NA)	(NA)	(NA)	(NA)	(NA)	(NA)	(NA)
1970............	70.8	67.1	74.7	(NA)	(NA)	(NA)	(NA)	(NA)	(NA)	(NA)	(NA)	(NA)
1980............	73.7	70.0	77.4	(NA)	(NA)	(NA)	(NA)	(NA)	(NA)	(NA)	(NA)	(NA)
1990............	75.4	71.8	78.8	(NA)	(NA)	(NA)	(NA)	(NA)	(NA)	(NA)	(NA)	(NA)
2000............	76.8	74.1	79.3	(NA)	(NA)	(NA)	(NA)	(NA)	(NA)	(NA)	(NA)	(NA)
2010 [3]........	78.7	76.2	81.0	78.8	76.4	81.1	74.7	71.5	77.7	81.7	78.8	84.3
2017 [3]........	78.6	76.1	81.1	78.5	76.1	81.0	74.9	71.5	78.1	81.8	79.1	84.3
Projections: [4]												
2020............	80.2	78.0	82.4	80.6	78.4	82.7	(NA)	(NA)	(NA)	82.1	79.9	84.2
2030............	81.7	79.6	83.7	82.1	80.2	84.0	(NA)	(NA)	(NA)	82.6	80.6	84.5
2040............	83.0	81.2	84.8	83.5	81.7	85.2	(NA)	(NA)	(NA)	83.5	81.7	85.2
2050............	84.4	82.7	86.0	84.8	83.2	86.4	(NA)	(NA)	(NA)	84.8	83.2	86.4
2060............	85.6	84.0	87.1	86.0	84.5	87.4	(NA)	(NA)	(NA)	86.0	84.5	87.4

NA Not available. [1] Includes races and origins not shown separately. [2] Based on death rates adjusted for misclassification; see Technical notes, source. [3] Life expectancies by Hispanic origin were revised using updated adjustment factors to correct for race and Hispanic-origin misclassification. [4] Based on mortality assumptions; for details, see source: U.S. Census Bureau, 2014 National Population Projections, "Table 17: Projected Life Expectancy at Birth by Sex, Race, and Hispanic Origin for the United States: 2015 to 2060 (NP2014-T17)," December 2014.

Source: Except as noted. U.S. National Center for Health Statistics, National Vital Statistics Reports (NVSR), *Deaths: Final Data for 2017*, Vol. 68, No. 9, June 2019. See also <https://www.cdc.gov/nchs/nvss/deaths.htm>.

Table 109. Life Expectancy by Sex, Age, and Race and Hispanic Origin: 2017

[Average number of years of life remaining. Excludes deaths of nonresidents of the United States. Race categories are consistent with 1977 Office of Management and Budget (OMB) standards; see source for details]

Age	Total [1]			White, Non-Hispanic [2]			Black, Non-Hispanic [2]			Hispanic [3]		
	Total	Male	Female	Total	Male	Female	Total	Male	Female	Total	Male	Female
0..................	78.6	76.1	81.1	78.5	76.1	81.0	74.9	71.5	78.1	81.8	79.1	84.3
1..................	78.1	75.6	80.5	77.9	75.5	80.3	74.7	71.4	77.9	81.2	78.5	83.7
5..................	74.1	71.7	76.6	74.0	71.6	76.4	70.8	67.5	74.0	77.3	74.6	79.8
10..................	69.2	66.7	71.6	69.0	66.6	71.4	65.9	62.5	69.0	72.3	69.6	74.8
15..................	64.2	61.8	66.7	64.0	61.7	66.4	61.0	57.6	64.1	67.4	64.7	69.8
20..................	59.4	57.0	61.8	59.2	56.9	61.5	56.2	53.0	59.2	62.5	59.9	64.9
25..................	54.7	52.4	56.9	54.5	52.2	56.7	51.6	48.5	54.4	57.7	55.2	60.1
30..................	50.0	47.8	52.1	49.8	47.7	51.9	47.0	44.1	49.6	53.0	50.5	55.2
35..................	45.3	43.2	47.3	45.2	43.2	47.2	42.5	39.7	44.9	48.2	45.8	50.3
40..................	40.7	38.7	42.6	40.6	38.6	42.5	38.0	35.3	40.3	43.5	41.2	45.5
45..................	36.1	34.2	37.9	36.0	34.2	37.8	33.6	31.0	35.8	38.8	36.6	40.7
50..................	31.6	29.8	33.4	31.6	29.8	33.3	29.3	26.9	31.4	34.2	32.1	36.0
55..................	27.4	25.6	28.9	27.3	25.6	28.8	25.2	23.0	27.2	29.8	27.7	31.4
60..................	23.3	21.7	24.7	23.2	21.7	24.6	21.5	19.4	23.3	25.5	23.6	27.0
65..................	19.4	18.0	20.6	19.3	18.0	20.5	18.1	16.2	19.5	21.4	19.7	22.7
70..................	15.7	14.5	16.7	15.6	14.5	16.6	14.9	13.3	16.0	17.5	16.0	18.6
75..................	12.3	11.3	13.0	12.2	11.2	12.9	11.9	10.6	12.7	13.8	12.6	14.7
80..................	9.2	8.4	9.8	9.1	8.3	9.7	9.2	8.1	9.8	10.5	9.4	11.1
85..................	6.6	5.9	7.0	6.5	5.9	6.9	6.9	6.1	7.3	7.6	6.7	8.0
90..................	4.5	4.1	4.8	4.5	4.0	4.7	5.0	4.5	5.2	5.3	4.6	5.5
95..................	3.1	2.8	3.2	3.0	2.7	3.2	3.6	3.3	3.7	3.6	3.2	3.7
100..................	2.2	2.0	2.2	2.1	1.9	2.2	2.7	2.5	2.7	2.6	2.2	2.6

[1] Includes other races and origins not shown separately. [2] Multiple-race data reported according to 1997 OMB standards were bridged to the single-race categories of 1977 OMB standards; see source for details. [3] Life expectancies by Hispanic origin are based on death rates adjusted for misclassification; see Technical Notes, source.

Source: U.S. National Center for Health Statistics, National Vital Statistics Reports (NVSR), *Deaths, Final Data for 2017*, Vol. 68, No. 9, June 2019. See also <https://www.cdc.gov/nchs/nvss/deaths.htm>.

Table 110. Selected Life Table Values—Life Expectancy and Percent Surviving by Age: 1959 to 2017

[Decennial life tables are based on population data from a decennial census and reported deaths of the 3-year period surrounding the census year; the census year is the middle year. The annual tables are based on deaths in a single year, and except for census years, on postcensal population estimates. Beginning in 1970, data exclude deaths of nonresidents of the United States. See Technical Notes, source]

Age and sex	All races						White						Black					
	1959-1961	1969-1971	1979-1981	1989-1991	1999-2001	2017	1959-1961	1969-1971	1979-1981	1989-1991	1999-2001	2017	1959-1961	1969-1971	1979-1981	1989-1991	1999-2001	2017
LIFE EXPECTANCY IN YEARS																		
Male by age:																		
At birth	66.8	67.0	70.1	71.8	74.1	76.1	67.6	67.9	70.8	72.7	74.8	76.4	61.5	60.0	64.1	64.5	68.2	71.9
Age 20	49.8	49.5	51.9	53.3	55.2	57.0	50.3	50.2	52.5	54.0	55.7	57.1	45.8	43.5	46.5	46.7	49.9	53.4
Age 30	40.6	40.5	42.8	44.1	45.9	47.8	41.0	41.1	43.3	44.7	46.3	47.9	37.1	35.4	37.8	38.1	41.0	44.5
Age 40	31.4	31.5	33.6	35.1	36.6	38.7	31.7	31.9	34.0	35.6	37.0	38.8	28.7	27.6	29.5	30.1	32.2	35.7
Age 50	23.0	23.1	25.0	26.4	27.8	29.8	23.2	23.3	25.3	26.7	28.1	29.9	21.3	20.7	22.0	22.5	24.1	27.1
Age 60	15.9	16.0	17.5	18.5	19.7	21.7	16.0	16.1	17.6	18.7	19.9	21.8	15.3	14.9	15.9	16.0	17.2	19.6
Age 65	13.0	13.0	14.2	15.1	16.1	18.0	13.0	13.0	14.3	15.2	16.2	18.1	12.8	12.5	13.3	13.3	14.1	16.4
Age 70	10.3	10.4	11.4	12.1	12.8	14.5	10.3	10.4	11.4	12.1	12.9	14.5	10.8	10.4	10.9	10.9	11.4	13.4
Age 80	6.0	6.3	6.8	7.1	7.4	8.4	5.9	6.2	6.8	7.1	7.4	8.3	6.9	7.4	7.0	7.0	7.1	8.2
Age 90	3.2	3.6	3.9	3.9	4.0	4.1	3.2	3.5	3.8	3.9	3.9	4.0	3.4	4.7	4.5	4.2	4.2	4.5
Female by age:																		
At birth	73.2	74.6	77.6	78.8	79.5	81.1	74.2	75.5	78.2	79.5	80.0	81.2	66.5	68.3	72.9	73.7	75.2	78.5
Age 20	55.6	56.6	59.0	59.9	60.3	61.8	56.3	57.2	59.4	60.4	60.7	61.8	50.1	51.2	54.9	55.5	56.5	59.5
Age 30	46.0	47.0	49.3	50.2	50.6	52.1	46.6	47.6	49.8	50.7	51.0	52.2	40.8	42.0	45.4	46.0	47.0	50.0
Age 40	36.6	37.6	39.8	40.7	41.0	42.6	37.1	38.1	40.2	41.0	41.3	42.7	32.2	33.3	36.3	37.0	37.7	40.6
Age 50	27.7	28.8	30.7	31.4	31.8	33.4	28.1	29.1	31.0	31.7	32.0	33.4	24.3	25.5	27.8	28.4	29.1	31.6
Age 60	19.5	20.6	22.3	22.9	23.1	24.7	19.7	20.8	22.5	23.1	23.3	24.7	17.8	18.7	20.4	20.7	21.2	23.4
Age 65	15.8	16.8	18.4	19.0	19.1	20.6	15.9	16.9	18.6	19.1	19.2	20.6	15.1	15.7	17.1	17.4	17.7	19.7
Age 70	12.4	13.4	14.8	15.4	15.4	16.7	12.4	13.4	14.9	15.5	15.5	16.6	12.5	13.0	14.1	14.3	14.4	16.1
Age 80	6.7	7.7	8.7	9.1	9.1	9.8	6.7	7.6	8.7	9.1	9.0	9.7	7.7	8.9	9.1	9.1	9.0	9.2
Age 90	3.3	4.1	4.7	4.7	4.7	4.8	3.2	4.1	4.6	4.7	4.7	4.7	3.5	5.4	5.5	5.2	5.2	5.2
PERCENT SURVIVING OUT OF 100,000 BORN ALIVE																		
Male by age:																		
At birth	100.0	100.0	100.0	100.0	100.0	100.0	100.0	100.0	100.0	100.0	100.0	100.0	100.0	100.0	100.0	100.0	100.0	100.0
Age 20	95.5	96.1	97.3	97.9	98.4	98.7	95.9	96.5	97.5	98.1	98.6	98.9	93.1	94.1	96.1	96.3	97.3	97.9
Age 30	93.8	94.1	95.4	96.2	97.1	97.2	94.4	94.7	95.8	96.7	97.4	97.4	90.3	89.6	93.1	93.1	94.9	95.7
Age 40	91.6	91.5	93.3	93.8	95.4	95.2	92.4	92.6	94.0	94.6	95.9	95.4	85.7	83.4	88.5	87.9	91.9	92.9
Age 50	86.2	86.1	89.0	89.9	91.8	92.1	87.4	87.7	90.1	91.1	92.6	92.4	77.2	73.3	80.1	80.0	85.7	88.6
Age 60	73.9	74.0	79.0	81.4	84.6	85.3	75.5	76.0	80.6	83.2	85.8	85.8	61.7	57.5	65.0	66.3	73.6	79.5
Age 65	64.2	64.3	70.6	74.0	78.2	79.8	65.8	66.3	72.4	76.0	79.7	80.4	51.4	47.5	55.1	56.8	65.0	71.9
Age 70	52.2	52.3	59.7	64.1	69.5	72.8	53.8	54.1	61.4	66.2	71.0	73.5	39.9	36.9	44.2	45.7	54.3	62.6
Age 80	25.3	24.9	31.8	36.7	42.8	51.1	26.0	25.9	32.8	38.2	44.1	51.7	20.0	16.6	22.0	22.5	28.5	39.5
Age 90	4.6	5.1	7.7	9.9	12.5	18.7	4.6	5.1	7.9	10.2	12.8	18.7	5.2	4.7	5.7	6.0	7.6	13.7
Female by age:																		
At birth	100.0	100.0	100.0	100.0	100.0	100.0	100.0	100.0	100.0	100.0	100.0	100.0	100.0	100.0	100.0	100.0	100.0	100.0
Age 20	96.8	97.3	98.2	98.6	98.9	99.1	97.1	97.6	98.4	98.8	99.0	99.2	94.7	95.7	97.2	97.6	98.1	98.6
Age 30	96.0	96.5	97.6	98.0	98.4	98.5	96.5	96.9	97.8	98.3	98.6	98.6	93.1	94.1	96.2	96.5	97.3	97.8
Age 40	94.6	95.1	96.5	97.0	97.5	97.5	95.3	95.8	96.9	97.5	97.8	97.6	89.7	90.8	94.1	94.4	95.6	96.5
Age 50	91.3	91.9	94.1	94.9	95.4	95.5	92.5	92.9	94.7	95.6	96.0	95.7	83.0	84.2	89.6	90.3	91.7	93.7
Age 60	84.4	85.1	88.4	89.7	90.8	91.2	86.3	86.7	89.5	90.8	91.6	91.4	69.9	72.8	80.3	81.9	84.0	87.6
Age 65	78.5	79.7	83.5	85.1	86.4	87.6	80.7	81.6	84.8	86.3	87.4	88.0	60.8	64.7	73.3	75.0	77.9	82.6
Age 70	70.1	72.0	76.7	78.5	80.2	82.6	72.5	74.1	78.1	80.0	81.4	83.1	51.3	54.9	64.7	66.3	69.8	76.1
Age 80	43.1	46.4	54.4	57.0	58.5	64.6	44.7	48.2	55.8	58.5	59.7	64.9	30.3	31.8	41.7	43.6	46.5	56.5
Age 90	10.1	14.2	20.6	23.7	23.9	30.2	10.2	14.4	21.0	24.3	24.5	30.1	9.7	12.2	16.3	17.5	18.3	26.1

Source: U.S. National Center for Health Statistics, National Vital Statistics Reports (NVSR), *United States Life Tables, 2017*, Vol. 68, No. 7, June 2019. See also <http://www.cdc.gov/nchs/products/life_tables.htm>.

Table 111. Life Expectancy at Birth by Sex, Race, and State: 1989 to 2001

[Average number of years of life remaining. Excludes deaths of nonresidents of the United States. Decennial life tables are based on population data from a decennial census and reported deaths of the 3-year period surrounding the census year; the census year is the middle year. The annual tables are based on deaths in a single year, and except for census years, on postcensal population estimates]

State	Total, 1989–1991	1999-2001						
		Total	Male			Female		
			Total	White	Black	Total	White	Black
United States	**75.37**	**76.83**	**74.10**	**74.74**	**68.08**	**79.45**	**79.97**	**75.12**
Alabama	73.64	74.80	71.32	72.85	66.42	78.34	79.14	74.94
Alaska	74.83	76.63	74.18	75.45	(B)	79.41	80.10	(B)
Arizona	76.10	78.15	75.25	75.51	70.95	81.16	81.64	77.70
Arkansas	74.33	75.43	72.05	73.17	67.30	78.99	79.59	73.58
California	75.86	78.80	76.02	76.11	69.97	81.63	81.36	76.67
Colorado	76.96	78.72	76.29	76.23	71.71	81.16	81.31	76.59
Connecticut	76.91	78.90	76.13	76.73	71.73	81.63	81.92	77.71
Delaware	74.76	77.04	74.24	75.05	70.27	79.78	80.55	75.21
District of Columbia	67.99	73.09	68.57	78.94	64.59	77.59	84.31	74.46
Florida	75.84	78.10	74.97	75.64	68.98	81.40	82.14	75.53
Georgia	73.61	75.27	72.28	73.88	68.29	78.22	79.53	76.16
Hawaii	78.21	80.23	77.17	78.40	(B)	83.65	83.31	(B)
Idaho	76.88	78.29	76.18	76.46	(B)	80.50	80.53	(B)
Illinois	74.90	77.06	73.91	75.33	66.81	80.26	80.78	74.20
Indiana	75.39	76.47	73.55	74.24	67.47	79.45	79.69	76.55
Iowa	77.29	78.76	76.11	76.19	70.81	81.39	81.35	75.16
Kansas	76.76	77.78	74.84	75.46	68.47	80.88	81.00	75.02
Kentucky	74.37	75.20	72.25	72.73	69.01	78.20	78.42	74.46
Louisiana	73.05	74.28	71.12	73.47	66.45	77.44	79.41	75.30
Maine	76.35	77.46	75.23	75.59	(B)	79.63	80.88	(B)
Maryland	74.79	76.36	73.55	75.58	68.41	79.08	80.66	75.78
Massachusetts	76.72	78.76	75.79	76.35	73.14	81.68	81.63	79.33
Michigan	75.04	76.90	73.98	75.26	67.38	79.83	80.59	75.95
Minnesota	77.76	79.26	76.74	77.03	71.59	81.80	82.61	76.60
Mississippi	73.03	73.88	70.30	72.25	66.72	77.62	79.13	73.68
Missouri	75.25	76.52	73.59	74.29	67.22	79.46	79.93	74.50
Montana	76.23	77.74	75.18	75.07	(B)	80.56	81.24	(B)
Nebraska	76.92	78.37	76.00	76.17	69.15	80.78	81.14	74.67
Nevada	74.18	76.05	73.34	73.49	70.56	79.24	78.97	74.75
New Hampshire	76.72	78.79	76.24	76.46	(B)	81.40	81.30	(B)
New Jersey	75.42	77.58	74.77	75.82	68.85	80.32	81.32	75.54
New Mexico	75.74	77.26	74.52	75.19	71.63	80.06	80.69	74.37
New York	74.68	78.20	75.13	75.78	70.13	81.16	81.49	77.84
North Carolina	74.48	76.27	73.05	74.27	66.33	79.56	80.34	76.68
North Dakota	77.62	79.06	75.96	76.65	(B)	82.61	82.67	(B)
Ohio	75.32	76.49	73.94	74.58	68.60	78.95	80.01	74.91
Oklahoma	75.10	75.61	72.75	73.00	68.97	78.59	78.75	74.34
Oregon	76.44	78.09	75.82	75.72	70.67	80.37	80.20	78.24
Pennsylvania	75.38	77.02	74.09	75.03	67.26	79.90	80.65	75.34
Rhode Island	76.54	78.65	75.83	76.06	72.18	81.42	81.60	77.39
South Carolina	73.51	75.04	71.68	73.76	67.34	78.49	79.77	75.41
South Dakota	76.91	78.34	75.19	76.35	(B)	81.79	82.61	(B)
Tennessee	74.32	75.29	71.98	73.31	66.86	78.66	79.28	74.16
Texas	75.14	77.04	74.12	74.74	69.18	80.05	80.35	74.76
Utah	77.70	78.89	76.84	76.95	(B)	80.95	80.93	(B)
Vermont	76.54	78.24	76.18	76.30	(B)	80.29	80.90	(B)
Virginia	75.22	76.95	74.48	75.62	69.37	79.34	80.69	76.20
Washington	76.82	78.64	76.18	76.10	71.90	81.14	80.98	77.11
West Virginia	74.26	75.28	72.75	72.75	69.87	77.84	78.36	72.65
Wisconsin	76.87	78.56	75.61	76.12	68.41	81.64	81.87	74.34
Wyoming	76.21	76.64	74.83	75.33	(B)	78.55	80.41	(B)

B Base figure too small to meet statistical standards for reliability.

Source: U.S. National Center for Health Statistics, National Vital Statistics Reports (NVSR), *U.S. Decennial Life Tables for 1999-2001: State Life Tables*, Vol. 60, No. 9, September 2012, and earlier reports. See also <http://www.cdc.gov/nchs/products/life_tables.htm>.

Table 112. Deaths and Death Rates by Sex, Race, and Hispanic Origin: 1970 to 2018

[Deaths in thousands (1,921 represents 1,921,000). Rates are per 100,000 population for specified groups. Excludes deaths of nonresidents of the United States and fetal deaths. Rates are based on population enumerated as of April 1 for census years and estimated as of July 1 for all other years. Data for Hispanic origin and specified races other than White and Black should be interpreted with caution because of inconsistent reporting of race and Hispanic origin on death certificates and censuses and surveys]

Sex and race	1970	1980	1990	2000	2010	2013	2014	2015	2016	2017	2018
Deaths [1]	**1,921**	**1,990**	**2,148**	**2,403**	**2,468**	**2,597**	**2,626**	**2,713**	**2,744**	**2,814**	**2,839**
Male [1]	1,078	1,075	1,113	1,178	1,232	1,306	1,328	1,373	1,400	1,439	1,458
Female [1]	843	915	1,035	1,226	1,236	1,291	1,298	1,339	1,344	1,374	1,381
White, non-Hispanic [2]	(NA)	(NA)	(NA)	1,960	1,970	2,053	2,067	2,124	2,133	2,180	2,188
Male	(NA)	(NA)	(NA)	945	972	1,021	1,035	1,064	1,077	1,103	1,112
Female	(NA)	(NA)	(NA)	1,015	998	1,032	1,032	1,060	1,056	1,077	1,077
Black, non-Hispanic [2]	(NA)	(NA)	(NA)	283	283	299	304	315	327	336	343
Male	(NA)	(NA)	(NA)	143	144	153	155	162	169	174	179
Female	(NA)	(NA)	(NA)	139	140	147	149	153	158	161	164
American Indian or Alaska Native, non-Hispanic [2]	(NA)	(NA)	(NA)	11	15	16	17	18	19	19	19
Male	(NA)	(NA)	(NA)	6	8	9	9	10	10	11	11
Female	(NA)	(NA)	(NA)	5	7	7	8	8	8	9	9
Asian or Pacific Islander, non-Hispanic [2]	(NA)	(NA)	(NA)	34	50	59	60	65	68	73	75
Male	(NA)	(NA)	(NA)	19	26	30	31	33	35	37	39
Female	(NA)	(NA)	(NA)	16	24	28	29	32	33	35	37
Hispanic origin [3]	(NA)	(NA)	(NA)	107	144	163	169	179	188	197	205
Male	(NA)	(NA)	(NA)	60	80	89	92	98	104	109	113
Female	(NA)	(NA)	(NA)	47	65	74	77	81	85	89	92
Death rates [1]	**945.3**	**878.3**	**863.8**	**854.0**	**799.5**	**821.5**	**823.7**	**844.0**	**849.3**	**863.8**	**867.8**
Male [1]	1,090.3	976.9	918.4	853.0	812.0	839.1	846.4	868.0	880.2	897.2	905.2
Female [1]	807.8	785.3	812.0	855.0	787.4	804.4	801.7	820.7	819.3	831.4	831.6
White, non-Hispanic [2]	(NA)	(NA)	(NA)	993.2	984.3	1,021.6	1,028.1	1,055.3	1,059.7	1,083.2	1,088.4
Male	(NA)	(NA)	(NA)	978.5	987.5	1,032.1	1,045.4	1,072.5	1,085.6	1,111.4	1,121.4
Female	(NA)	(NA)	(NA)	1,007.3	981.2	1,011.5	1,011.3	1,038.5	1,034.6	1,055.8	1,056.2
Black, non-Hispanic [2]	(NA)	(NA)	(NA)	805.5	718.7	733.4	735.4	754.6	775.5	787.5	799.8
Male	(NA)	(NA)	(NA)	859.5	764.5	782.5	783.3	809.4	836.2	854.2	869.6
Female	(NA)	(NA)	(NA)	756.7	676.9	688.4	691.4	704.3	719.7	726.1	735.6
American Indian or Alaska Native, non-Hispanic [2]	(NA)	(NA)	(NA)	470.3	577.8	613.7	642.5	670.7	685.9	703.4	709.8
Male	(NA)	(NA)	(NA)	517.0	640.1	681.4	713.4	747.4	772.8	784.4	807.7
Female	(NA)	(NA)	(NA)	425.0	517.7	548.3	574.2	596.7	602.2	625.5	615.6
Asian or Pacific Islander, non-Hispanic [2]	(NA)	(NA)	(NA)	301.4	310.0	331.8	327.7	341.5	350.3	359.8	366.3
Male	(NA)	(NA)	(NA)	338.3	336.7	359.2	352.7	364.9	374.9	386.2	394.4
Female	(NA)	(NA)	(NA)	266.5	285.6	306.7	305.0	320.1	327.8	335.6	340.5
Hispanic origin [3]	(NA)	(NA)	(NA)	303.8	286.2	301.9	305.8	317.1	327.6	334.6	341.9
Male	(NA)	(NA)	(NA)	331.3	310.8	323.7	330.1	343.2	356.8	364.6	373.9
Female	(NA)	(NA)	(NA)	274.6	260.9	279.4	281.0	290.4	297.7	304.0	309.3
Age-adjusted death rates [1, 4]	**1,222.6**	**1,039.1**	**938.7**	**869.0**	**747.0**	**731.9**	**724.6**	**733.1**	**728.8**	**731.9**	**723.6**
Male [1]	1,542.1	1,348.1	1,202.8	1,053.8	887.1	863.6	855.1	863.2	861.0	864.5	855.5
Female [1]	971.4	817.9	750.9	731.4	634.9	623.5	616.7	624.2	617.5	619.7	611.3
White, non-Hispanic [2]	(NA)	(NA)	(NA)	855.5	755.0	747.1	742.8	753.2	749.0	755.0	745.7
Male	(NA)	(NA)	(NA)	1,035.4	892.5	876.8	872.3	881.3	879.5	885.1	874.3
Female	(NA)	(NA)	(NA)	721.5	643.3	638.4	633.8	644.1	637.2	642.8	634.1
Black, non-Hispanic [2]	(NA)	(NA)	(NA)	1,137.0	920.4	885.2	870.7	876.1	882.8	881.0	879.5
Male	(NA)	(NA)	(NA)	1,422.0	1,131.7	1,083.3	1,060.3	1,070.1	1,081.2	1,083.3	1,085.2
Female	(NA)	(NA)	(NA)	941.2	770.8	740.6	731.2	731.0	734.1	728.0	724.2
American Indian or Alaska Native, non-Hispanic [2]	(NA)	(NA)	(NA)	800.5	818.8	787.5	796.9	805.7	800.3	800.2	780.8
Male	(NA)	(NA)	(NA)	955.6	965.8	930.6	935.0	950.2	954.0	943.9	937.4
Female	(NA)	(NA)	(NA)	679.1	696.8	666.4	677.4	679.5	668.0	674.0	641.7
Asian or Pacific Islander, non-Hispanic [2]	(NA)	(NA)	(NA)	507.0	425.6	407.5	390.5	396.2	394.4	395.3	392.2
Male	(NA)	(NA)	(NA)	624.9	513.0	490.2	464.2	468.9	466.6	470.1	467.6
Female	(NA)	(NA)	(NA)	417.3	360.6	344.8	333.3	339.6	337.4	336.4	332.4
Hispanic origin [3]	(NA)	(NA)	(NA)	665.7	558.6	535.4	523.3	525.3	525.8	524.7	524.1
Male	(NA)	(NA)	(NA)	818.1	677.7	639.8	626.8	628.9	631.8	631.8	633.1
Female	(NA)	(NA)	(NA)	546.0	463.4	448.6	437.5	438.3	436.4	434.2	431.7

NA Not available. [1] Includes other races not shown separately. [2] Multiple-race data reported according to 1997 OMB standards were bridged to single-race categories of 1977 OMB standards; see Technical Notes in source for details. [3] Persons of Hispanic origin may be of any race. [4] Age-adjusted death rates are better indicators than crude death rates for showing changes in the risk of death over time when the age distribution of the population is changing, and for comparing the mortality of population subgroups that have different age compositions. All age-adjusted death rates are standardized to the year 2000 population.

Source: U.S. National Center for Health Statistics, National Vital Statistics Reports (NVSR), *Deaths: Final Data*, annual; and CDC WONDER Online Database, "Multiple Cause of Death, 1999-2018," <https://wonder.cdc.gov/>, accessed September 2020. See also <http://www.cdc.gov/nchs/nvss/deaths.htm>.

Table 113. Death Rates by Age, Sex, and Race: 1960 to 2018

[Rates per 100,000 population]

Characteristic	All ages [1]	Under 1 year	1 to 4 years	5 to 14 years	15 to 24 years	25 to 34 years	35 to 44 years	45 to 54 years	55 to 64 years	65 to 74 years	75 to 84 years	85 years and over
MALE												
Total:												
1960	1,105	3,059	120	56	152	188	373	992	2,310	4,914	10,178	21,186
1970	1,090	2,410	93	51	189	215	403	959	2,283	4,874	10,010	17,822
1980	977	1,429	73	37	172	196	299	767	1,815	4,105	8,817	18,801
1990	918	1,083	52	29	147	204	310	610	1,553	3,492	7,889	18,057
2000	853	807	36	21	115	139	255	543	1,231	2,980	6,973	17,501
2010	812	680	30	15	98	142	213	506	1,076	2,275	5,694	15,414
2018	905	613	28	15	100	176	250	492	1,119	2,197	5,155	14,504
White:												
1990	931	896	46	26	131	176	268	549	1,467	3,398	7,845	18,268
2000	888	668	33	20	106	124	234	497	1,163	2,906	6,933	17,716
2010	866	584	27	14	92	136	207	492	1,033	2,232	5,704	15,640
2015	933	542	25	14	92	157	221	487	1,071	2,160	5,427	15,203
2017	963	515	25	14	99	181	245	487	1,079	2,153	5,304	15,150
2018	971	514	25	13	93	173	244	479	1,086	2,156	5,193	14,973
Black:												
1990	1,008	2,112	86	41	252	431	700	1,261	2,618	4,946	9,130	16,955
2000	834	1,568	55	28	181	261	453	1,018	2,080	4,254	8,486	16,791
2010	725	1,207	43	20	143	217	308	716	1,662	3,206	6,722	14,715
2015	765	1,150	46	21	151	229	326	678	1,613	3,042	6,205	13,066
2017	805	1,150	40	23	161	253	361	694	1,628	3,099	6,095	12,851
2018	820	1,128	44	22	154	246	366	705	1,622	3,131	6,107	12,829
Asian or Pacific Islander: [2]												
1990	334	605	45	21	76	80	131	287	789	2,041	5,009	12,446
2000	333	529	23	13	55	55	105	250	642	1,661	4,328	12,125
2010	327	434	19	8	43	53	84	214	519	1,226	3,439	10,825
2015	355	438	15	10	49	56	85	205	508	1,131	3,092	9,406
2017	375	451	19	9	49	60	92	217	504	1,148	3,076	9,190
2018	383	431	18	11	46	60	93	219	532	1,145	3,038	9,025
American Indian or Alaska Native: [2]												
1990	476	1,057	77	33	220	256	365	620	1,211	2,462	5,389	11,244
2000	416	700	45	20	136	179	295	520	1,090	2,478	5,351	10,726
2010	398	543	34	18	116	156	258	496	951	1,971	4,452	10,268
2015	455	486	35	15	101	191	281	544	994	1,841	4,171	8,277
2017	478	479	24	16	114	217	297	535	982	1,811	4,075	7,733
2018	490	478	32	14	115	231	307	522	1,004	1,852	3,894	7,268
FEMALE												
Total:												
1960	809	2,321	98	37	61	107	229	527	1,196	2,872	7,633	19,008
1970	808	1,864	75	32	68	102	231	517	1,099	2,580	6,678	15,518
1980	785	1,142	55	24	58	76	159	413	934	2,145	5,440	14,747
1990	812	856	41	19	49	74	138	343	879	1,991	4,883	14,274
2000	855	663	29	15	43	64	143	313	772	1,921	4,815	14,719
2010	787	564	23	11	36	64	129	311	644	1,528	4,138	13,219
2018	832	500	20	12	39	80	140	303	670	1,421	3,788	12,870
White:												
1990	847	690	36	18	46	62	117	309	823	1,924	4,839	14,401
2000	912	551	26	14	41	55	126	281	731	1,868	4,785	14,891
2010	857	488	22	11	36	61	123	295	618	1,505	4,165	13,419
2015	899	455	20	11	38	72	132	307	640	1,444	4,028	13,443
2017	910	426	19	11	40	82	139	301	654	1,434	3,923	13,385
2018	910	418	19	11	38	80	137	295	649	1,408	3,839	13,309
Black:												
1990	748	1,736	68	28	69	160	299	639	1,453	2,866	5,688	13,310
2000	733	1,280	45	20	58	122	272	588	1,227	2,690	5,697	13,941
2010	643	994	33	15	43	93	199	481	972	2,021	4,581	12,590
2015	666	970	32	15	46	93	192	447	970	1,864	4,310	11,741
2017	685	946	35	16	48	101	200	438	981	1,868	4,262	11,401
2018	694	915	32	18	48	105	204	435	974	1,884	4,183	11,351
Asian or Pacific Islander: [2]												
1990	234	518	32	13	29	38	70	183	483	1,089	3,128	10,254
2000	262	434	20	12	22	28	66	156	391	996	2,882	9,052
2010	277	342	16	8	17	27	49	128	299	789	2,446	8,590
2015	311	358	15	7	19	26	51	128	288	705	2,264	8,142
2017	326	390	11	8	22	27	50	129	290	689	2,197	8,125
2018	331	372	14	10	20	27	51	121	293	689	2,185	7,973
American Indian or Alaska Native: [2]												
1990	330	689	38	26	69	102	156	381	806	1,679	3,073	8,201
2000	346	492	40	18	59	85	172	285	772	1,900	3,850	9,118
2010	332	366	24	11	44	86	147	326	624	1,482	3,392	9,278
2015	376	431	27	14	47	105	171	354	622	1,360	3,193	7,637
2017	392	400	28	13	48	126	188	350	639	1,263	3,146	7,132
2018	386	371	15	15	41	120	179	334	623	1,279	2,927	6,734

[1] Figures for age not stated are included in "All ages" but not distributed among age groups. [2] The death rates for specified races other than White and Black should be interpreted with caution because of inconsistencies between reporting race on death certificates and censuses and surveys.

Source: U.S. National Center for Health Statistics, *Health, United States, 2017*, September 2018; and CDC WONDER Online Database, "Multiple Cause of Death, 1999-2018," <wonder.cdc.gov/>, accessed August 2020. See also <cdc.gov/nchs/nvss/deaths.htm>.

Table 114. Deaths and Death Rates by Age, Sex, Race, and Hispanic Origin: 2018

[Rates per 100,000 population in specified group; see Technical Notes. Race and Hispanic-origin categories are consistent with 1977 Office of Management and Budget (OMB) standards. Multiple-race data reported according to 1997 OMB standards were bridged to single-race categories of 1977 OMB standards. Data for specified race or Hispanic-origin groups other than non-Hispanic White and non-Hispanic Black should be interpreted with caution because of inconsistencies in reporting these items on death certificates and surveys; see Technical Notes, source]

Age	Total[1] Total	Total[1] Male	Total[1] Female	White, non-Hispanic Total	White, non-Hispanic Male	White, non-Hispanic Female	Black, non-Hispanic Total	Black, non-Hispanic Male	Black, non-Hispanic Female	American Indian or Alaska Native, non-Hispanic Total	AIAN Male	AIAN Female	Asian or Pacific Islander, non-Hispanic Total	API Male	API Female	Hispanic[2] Total	Hispanic[2] Male	Hispanic[2] Female
DEATHS																		
All ages	2,839,205	1,458,469	1,380,736	2,188,349	1,111,840	1,076,509	343,393	178,904	164,489	19,491	10,875	8,616	75,266	38,760	36,506	204,719	113,045	91,674
Under 1 year	21,467	12,068	9,399	9,244	5,197	4,047	6,356	3,580	2,776	270	156	114	891	498	393	4,487	2,502	1,985
1 to 4 years	3,830	2,243	1,587	1,825	1,067	758	975	574	401	66	44	22	156	93	63	794	455	339
5 to 9 years	2,330	1,286	1,044	1,074	604	470	622	343	279	43	27	16	120	64	56	461	241	220
10 to 14 years	3,120	1,795	1,325	1,563	933	630	699	397	302	63	23	40	132	71	61	656	366	290
15 to 19 years	10,380	7,380	3,000	5,372	3,688	1,684	2,456	1,887	569	189	138	51	313	217	96	2,033	1,442	591
20 to 24 years	19,774	14,628	5,146	10,557	7,548	3,009	4,549	3,493	1,056	337	251	86	575	404	171	3,707	2,891	816
25 to 29 years	27,461	19,629	7,832	15,747	11,060	4,687	6,104	4,406	1,698	566	385	181	716	510	206	4,266	3,230	1,036
30 to 34 years	31,383	21,235	10,148	19,289	12,913	6,376	6,206	4,185	2,021	645	433	212	811	522	289	4,345	3,126	1,219
35 to 39 years	37,617	24,523	13,094	23,172	15,026	8,146	7,412	4,675	2,737	674	437	237	1,052	672	380	5,225	3,658	1,567
40 to 44 years	42,763	26,853	15,910	25,965	16,234	9,731	8,751	5,301	3,450	749	475	274	1,253	752	501	5,905	4,002	1,903
45 to 49 years	64,873	39,969	24,904	41,349	25,392	15,957	12,456	7,339	5,117	925	571	354	1,986	1,211	775	7,915	5,281	2,634
50 to 54 years	99,964	61,061	38,903	66,297	40,472	25,825	18,593	10,877	7,716	1,305	792	513	2,636	1,621	1,015	10,742	7,030	3,712
55 to 59 years	160,963	98,261	62,702	112,226	68,727	43,499	28,482	16,663	11,819	1,760	1,067	693	3,858	2,322	1,536	13,920	8,969	4,951
60 to 64 years	213,873	130,012	83,861	153,066	93,581	59,485	36,718	21,391	15,327	1,895	1,121	774	5,130	3,090	2,040	16,087	10,114	5,973
65 to 69 years	251,246	148,548	102,698	185,889	110,575	75,314	38,919	22,260	16,659	2,002	1,156	846	6,356	3,708	2,648	17,054	10,123	6,931
70 to 74 years	292,532	164,363	128,169	228,314	129,158	99,156	35,790	19,214	16,576	1,985	1,069	916	7,084	3,931	3,153	18,379	10,331	8,048
75 to 79 years	321,745	171,972	149,773	257,093	138,475	118,618	34,187	17,240	16,947	1,848	948	900	8,319	4,567	3,752	19,433	10,188	9,245
80 to 84 years	353,460	175,216	178,244	286,272	143,519	142,753	32,950	14,907	18,043	1,683	829	854	9,889	4,904	4,985	21,971	10,685	11,286
85 years and over	880,280	337,318	542,962	743,988	287,637	456,351	61,155	20,161	40,994	2,486	953	1,533	23,985	9,599	14,386	47,327	18,403	28,924
DEATH RATES																		
All ages	867.8	905.2	831.6	1,088.4	1,121.4	1,056.2	799.8	869.6	735.6	709.8	807.7	615.6	366.3	394.4	340.5	341.9	373.9	309.3
Under 1 year	557.8	613.1	500.0	463.5	508.8	415.9	1,074.1	1,184.8	958.6	705.7	800.5	607.3	412.2	449.4	373.0	445.3	486.1	402.7
1 to 4 years	24.0	27.5	20.4	22.1	25.2	18.9	39.8	46.2	33.3	42.2	55.3	28.6	16.4	19.1	13.6	19.1	21.4	16.6
5 to 9 years	11.5	12.5	10.6	10.3	11.3	9.2	20.1	21.9	18.4	21.2	26.3	(S)	10.0	10.4	9.6	8.8	9.0	8.5
10 to 14 years	14.9	16.8	13.0	14.2	16.5	11.7	22.3	25.0	19.6	30.5	22.0	39.1	10.7	11.4	10.0	12.4	13.6	11.2
15 to 19 years	49.2	68.5	29.1	46.7	62.5	30.1	77.6	117.4	36.5	91.5	131.6	50.1	25.0	34.5	15.4	40.9	56.8	24.2
20 to 24 years	90.4	130.6	48.2	87.6	122.1	51.3	136.4	206.5	64.3	158.5	233.4	81.9	39.9	55.4	24.0	76.6	116.1	34.7
25 to 29 years	116.5	163.3	67.9	120.6	166.0	73.2	167.9	241.5	93.8	249.1	333.5	161.9	40.7	58.5	23.2	87.5	126.9	44.4
30 to 34 years	141.8	189.7	92.7	153.1	202.8	102.4	205.3	284.0	130.5	336.7	452.7	221.0	45.7	60.8	31.6	95.5	130.5	56.5
35 to 39 years	174.4	227.3	121.5	187.4	241.5	132.6	259.5	343.3	183.2	382.5	502.5	265.6	62.3	84.3	42.5	116.7	157.5	72.7
40 to 44 years	216.9	274.1	160.4	228.8	284.7	172.4	342.0	440.4	254.6	476.5	617.3	341.5	81.2	104.2	60.9	143.7	191.1	94.5
45 to 49 years	312.7	389.4	237.6	325.9	399.8	251.8	470.4	591.4	363.7	574.2	728.0	428.3	133.4	173.9	97.8	210.5	278.4	141.3
50 to 54 years	478.7	594.1	366.8	489.5	601.6	378.8	704.5	881.0	549.3	789.5	998.1	596.8	207.5	274.0	149.5	329.0	427.6	229.0
55 to 59 years	733.6	921.0	556.3	738.8	920.9	563.0	1,073.4	1,358.0	828.6	1,010.0	1,295.4	754.1	328.6	429.5	242.5	506.2	661.2	355.3
60 to 64 years	1,051.9	1,336.3	791.0	1,043.9	1,315.8	787.8	1,582.1	2,041.0	1,204.2	1,237.2	1,578.1	942.3	486.6	650.7	352.1	751.5	1,020.5	534.6
65 to 69 years	1,470.4	1,848.8	1,134.5	1,458.3	1,814.3	1,132.2	2,184.1	2,874.8	1,653.4	1,693.1	2,111.4	1,332.3	727.2	961.2	542.4	1,089.0	1,395.6	824.5
70 to 74 years	2,182.2	2,646.2	1,781.6	2,207.0	2,649.0	1,813.0	2,922.2	3,720.2	2,340.3	2,356.2	2,751.0	2,018.2	1,116.0	1,398.1	891.7	1,645.9	2,070.3	1,303.0
75 to 79 years	3,471.9	4,149.2	2,923.9	3,552.0	4,202.7	3,008.3	4,227.9	5,352.0	3,483.6	3,470.2	3,960.7	3,069.7	1,950.4	2,410.8	1,582.6	2,623.3	3,241.6	2,167.7
80 to 84 years	5,768.6	6,764.1	5,039.5	5,968.6	6,954.0	5,224.4	6,320.0	7,784.3	5,469.9	5,298.1	6,189.8	4,648.1	3,503.0	4,049.3	3,092.5	4,433.2	5,328.4	3,824.8
85 years and over	13,450.7	14,504.0	12,870.0	14,243.2	15,348.9	13,624.6	12,050.1	13,138.2	11,578.5	8,587.2	9,031.5	8,332.4	8,398.9	9,062.0	8,008.0	9,483.8	10,124.4	9,116.8

S Does not meet standards of reliability. [1] Includes deaths for origin not stated. [2] Persons of Hispanic origin may be of any race.

Source: U.S. National Center for Health Statistics, National Vital Statistics Reports (NVSR), Deaths: Final Data, annual; and CDC WONDER Online Database, "Multiple Cause of Death, 1999-2018." <https://wonder.cdc.gov/>, accessed September 2020. See also <http://www.cdc.gov/nchs/nvss/deaths.htm>.

Table 115. Deaths and Death Rates by State: 1990 to 2018

[2,148 represents 2,148,000. By state of residence. Excludes deaths of nonresidents of the United States. Caution should be used in comparing death rates by state; rates are affected by the population composition of the area. See also Appendix III]

State	Number of deaths (1,000)						Death rate per 1,000 population [1]						Age-adjusted rate, 2018 [1,2]
	1990	2000	2010	2015	2017	2018	1990	2000	2010	2015	2017	2018	
United States	**2,148**	**2,403**	**2,468**	**2,713**	**2,814**	**2,839**	**8.6**	**8.5**	**8.0**	**8.4**	**8.6**	**8.7**	**7.2**
Alabama	39	45	48	52	53	54	9.7	10.1	10.1	10.7	10.9	11.1	9.2
Alaska	2	3	4	4	4	4	4.0	4.6	5.2	5.8	6.0	6.0	7.0
Arizona	29	41	47	54	58	59	7.9	7.9	7.3	8.0	8.2	8.3	6.7
Arkansas	25	28	29	32	33	32	10.5	10.6	9.9	10.6	10.8	10.7	8.8
California	214	230	234	259	268	269	7.2	6.8	6.3	6.6	6.8	6.8	6.1
Colorado	22	27	31	36	38	39	6.6	6.3	6.3	6.7	6.8	6.8	6.5
Connecticut	28	30	29	31	31	31	8.4	8.8	8.0	8.5	8.7	8.7	6.4
Delaware	6	7	8	9	9	9	8.7	8.8	8.6	9.1	9.5	9.8	7.6
District of Columbia	7	6	5	5	5	5	12.0	10.5	7.8	7.2	7.2	7.1	7.2
Florida	134	164	174	192	204	205	10.4	10.3	9.2	9.5	9.7	9.6	6.6
Georgia	52	64	71	80	83	85	8.0	7.8	7.4	7.8	8.0	8.1	7.9
Hawaii	7	8	10	11	11	11	6.1	6.8	7.1	7.7	8.0	8.0	5.7
Idaho	7	10	11	13	14	14	7.4	7.4	7.3	7.9	8.2	8.1	7.3
Illinois	103	107	100	107	110	110	9.0	8.6	7.8	8.3	8.6	8.6	7.2
Indiana	50	55	57	63	66	66	8.9	9.1	8.8	9.5	9.8	9.8	8.3
Iowa	27	28	28	30	31	30	9.7	9.6	9.1	9.5	9.7	9.6	7.2
Kansas	22	25	25	27	27	28	9.0	9.2	8.6	9.2	9.3	9.5	7.7
Kentucky	35	40	42	47	48	49	9.5	9.8	9.7	10.5	10.8	10.9	9.2
Louisiana	38	41	41	44	46	46	8.9	9.2	9.0	9.4	9.8	9.9	8.7
Maine	11	12	13	14	15	15	9.0	9.7	9.6	10.9	11.0	11.0	7.5
Maryland	38	44	43	47	50	51	8.0	8.3	7.5	7.9	8.2	8.4	7.1
Massachusetts	53	57	53	58	59	59	8.8	8.9	8.0	8.5	8.6	8.6	6.7
Michigan	79	87	88	95	98	99	8.5	8.7	8.9	9.6	9.8	9.9	7.8
Minnesota	35	38	39	43	44	45	7.9	7.7	7.3	7.8	8.0	8.0	6.5
Mississippi	25	29	29	32	32	32	9.8	10.1	9.8	10.6	10.8	10.8	9.3
Missouri	50	55	55	60	62	63	9.8	9.8	9.2	9.8	10.1	10.3	8.2
Montana	7	8	9	10	10	10	8.6	9.0	8.9	9.6	9.7	9.4	7.2
Nebraska	15	15	15	17	17	17	9.4	8.8	8.3	8.8	8.8	8.8	7.2
Nevada	9	15	20	23	25	25	7.8	7.6	7.3	7.9	8.2	8.1	7.4
New Hampshire	8	10	10	12	13	13	7.7	7.8	7.7	9.0	9.3	9.4	7.1
New Jersey	70	75	69	72	75	76	9.1	8.9	7.9	8.1	8.3	8.5	6.7
New Mexico	11	13	16	18	19	19	7.0	7.4	7.7	8.5	8.9	9.1	7.5
New York	169	158	146	154	155	157	9.4	8.3	7.6	7.8	7.8	8.0	6.3
North Carolina	57	72	79	89	93	94	8.6	8.9	8.3	8.9	9.1	9.0	7.7
North Dakota	6	6	6	6	6	6	8.9	9.1	8.8	8.2	8.5	8.5	6.9
Ohio	99	108	109	118	124	124	9.1	9.5	9.4	10.2	10.6	10.6	8.4
Oklahoma	30	35	37	39	40	41	9.7	10.2	9.7	10.1	10.3	10.4	8.9
Oregon	25	30	32	36	37	36	8.8	8.6	8.3	8.9	8.8	8.6	6.9
Pennsylvania	122	131	125	133	136	135	10.3	10.7	9.8	10.4	10.6	10.5	7.6
Rhode Island	10	10	10	10	10	10	9.5	9.6	9.1	9.6	9.6	9.5	7.0
South Carolina	30	37	42	47	49	51	8.5	9.2	9.0	9.6	9.8	10.0	8.2
South Dakota	6	7	7	8	8	8	9.1	9.3	8.7	9.0	9.2	9.0	7.2
Tennessee	46	55	60	67	70	71	9.5	9.7	9.4	10.1	10.4	10.5	8.9
Texas	125	150	167	190	198	202	7.4	7.2	6.6	6.9	7.0	7.0	7.3
Utah	9	12	15	17	18	18	5.3	5.5	5.3	5.8	5.8	5.8	6.9
Vermont	5	5	5	6	6	6	8.2	8.4	8.6	9.5	9.6	9.6	7.1
Virginia	48	56	59	66	69	69	7.8	8.0	7.4	7.8	8.1	8.1	7.1
Washington	37	44	48	55	57	57	7.6	7.5	7.2	7.6	7.7	7.5	6.7
West Virginia	19	21	21	23	23	23	10.8	11.7	11.5	12.3	12.8	13.0	9.5
Wisconsin	43	46	47	51	53	54	8.7	8.7	8.3	8.9	9.1	9.2	7.2
Wyoming	3	4	4	5	5	5	7.1	7.9	7.9	8.2	8.2	8.8	7.5

[1] Rates based on enumerated resident population as of April 1 for 1990, 2000, and 2010; estimated resident population as of July 1 for all other years. [2] Age-adjusted death rates are better indicators than crude death rates for showing changes in the risk of death over time when the age distribution of the population is changing, and for comparing the mortality of population subgroups that have different age compositions. See text this section.

Source: U.S. National Center for Health Statistics, CDC WONDER Online Database, "Multiple Cause of Death, 1999-2018," <http://wonder.cdc.gov/>; and National Vital Statistics Reports (NVSR), *Deaths: Final Data*, annual report. See also <http://www.cdc.gov/nchs/nvss/deaths.htm>.

Table 116. Fetal and Infant Deaths: 1990 to 2017

[The term "fetal death," defined on an all inclusive basis to end confusion arising from the use of such terms as stillbirth, spontaneous abortion, and miscarriage, has been adopted by the National Center for Health Statistics (NCHS) as the nationally recommended standard. Fetal deaths do not include induced terminations of pregnancy. In 2014, the NCHS transitioned to the use of the obstetric estimate of gestational age (OE) rather than the last normal menses (LMP) estimate, introducing a discontinuity in perinatal measures for earlier years]

Year	Fetal deaths [1]			Infant deaths		Fetal mortality rate [2,6]			Perinatal mortality rate [6]	
	Total [1]	20 to 27 weeks [3]	28 weeks or more [3]	Less than 7 days	Less than 28 days	Total [1]	20 to 27 weeks [3]	28 weeks or more [3]	Defi- nition I [4]	Defi- nition II [5]
1990.....	31,386	13,427	17,959	19,439	23,591	7.5	3.2	4.3	9.0	13.1
1995.....	27,294	13,043	14,251	15,483	19,186	7.0	3.3	3.6	7.6	11.8
2000.....	27,003	13,497	13,506	14,893	18,733	6.6	3.3	3.3	7.0	11.2
2005.....	25,894	13,326	12,568	15,013	18,782	6.2	3.2	3.0	6.6	10.7
2006.....	25,972	13,269	12,703	15,148	19,041	6.1	3.1	3.0	6.5	10.5
2007.....	26,593	13,822	12,771	15,139	19,094	6.1	3.2	3.0	6.4	10.5
2008.....	26,335	13,347	12,988	14,648	18,238	6.2	3.1	3.0	6.5	10.4
2009.....	24,872	12,813	12,059	13,768	17,261	6.0	3.1	2.9	6.2	10.1
2010.....	24,258	12,388	11,870	12,900	16,193	6.0	3.1	3.0	6.2	10.1
2011.....	24,289	12,432	11,857	12,960	16,065	6.1	3.1	3.0	6.3	10.1
2012.....	24,073	12,334	11,739	12,911	15,887	6.1	3.1	3.0	6.2	10.1
2013.....	23,595	11,874	11,721	12,900	15,893	6.0	3.0	3.0	6.2	10.0
2014.....	23,980	(NA)	(NA)	12,772	15,737	6.0	(NA)	2.8	6.0	(NA)
2015.....	23,776	(NA)	(NA)	12,578	15,671	5.9	(NA)	2.9	6.0	(NA)
2016.....	23,880	(NA)	(NA)	12,353	15,302	(NA)	(NA)	2.9	6.0	(NA)
2017.....	22,827	(NA)	(NA)	11,971	14,844	(NA)	(NA)	(NA)	(NA)	(NA)

NA Not available. [1] Fetal deaths with stated or presumed gestation of 20 weeks or more. [2] Rate per 1,000 live births and fetal deaths in specified age group. [3] Not stated gestational age proportionally distributed. [4] Infant deaths of less than 7 days and fetal deaths with stated or presumed period of gestation of 28 weeks or more, per 1,000 live births and fetal deaths. [5] Infant deaths of less than 28 days and fetal deaths with stated or presumed period of gestation of 20 weeks or more per 1,000 live births and fetal deaths. [6] Prior to 2014, based on LMP (last normal menses) measure of gestational age. Beginning 2014, based on the OE (obstetric measure) of gestational age.

Source: U.S. National Center for Health Statistics, National Vital Statistics Reports (NVSR), *Fetal and Perinatal Mortality, United States, 2013*, Vol. 64. No. 8, July 2015; *Lack of change in Perinatal Mortality in the United States, 2014-2016*, NCHS Data Brief, August 2018; *Health, United States, 2017*, September 2018; and CDC WONDER Online Database, "Linked Birth / Infant Death Records, 2007-2017," and "Fetal Deaths, 2005-2017," <https://wonder.cdc.gov/>, accessed August 2019.

Table 117. Fetal, Infant, and Pregnancy-Related Mortality Rates by Race: 1980 to 2018

[Deaths per 1,000 live births, except as noted. Data based on death certificates, fetal death records, and birth certificates. Excludes deaths of nonresidents of the United States. See also Appendix III]

Race and year	Infant [1]	Neonatal [1]		Post- neonatal [1]	Pregnancy- related mortality rate [2]
		Under 28 days	Under 7 days		
ALL RACES					
1980.........................	12.6	8.5	7.1	4.1	(NA)
1990.........................	9.2	5.8	4.8	3.4	10.0
1995.........................	7.6	4.9	4.0	2.7	11.3
2000.........................	6.9	4.6	3.7	2.3	14.5
2005.........................	6.9	4.5	3.6	2.3	15.4
2010.........................	6.1	4.0	3.2	2.1	16.7
2015.........................	5.9	3.9	3.2	2.0	17.2
2016.........................	5.9	3.9	3.1	2.0	16.9
2017.........................	5.8	3.8	3.1	1.9	(NA)
2018.........................	5.7	3.8	3.0	1.9	(NA)
WHITE [3]					
1980.........................	10.9	7.4	6.1	3.5	(NA)
1990.........................	7.6	4.8	3.9	2.8	(NA)
1995.........................	6.3	4.1	3.3	2.2	(NA)
2000.........................	5.7	3.8	3.0	1.9	(NA)
2005.........................	5.7	3.8	3.0	1.9	(NA)
2010.........................	5.2	3.5	2.7	1.7	(NA)
2015.........................	4.9	3.3	2.7	1.6	(NA)
2016.........................	4.9	3.3	2.6	1.7	(NA)
2017.........................	4.9	3.3	2.6	1.6	(NA)
2018.........................	(NA)	(NA)	(NA)	(NA)	(NA)
BLACK [3]					
1980.........................	22.2	14.6	12.3	7.6	(NA)
1990.........................	18.0	11.6	9.7	6.4	(NA)
1995.........................	15.1	9.8	8.2	5.3	(NA)
2000.........................	14.1	9.4	7.6	4.7	(NA)
2005.........................	13.7	9.1	7.3	4.7	(NA)
2010.........................	11.6	7.5	6.0	4.1	(NA)
2015.........................	11.4	7.4	6.0	4.0	(NA)
2016.........................	11.1	7.2	5.8	3.9	(NA)
2017.........................	10.8	6.9	5.6	3.9	(NA)
2018.........................	(NA)	(NA)	(NA)	(NA)	(NA)

NA Not available. [1] Infant (under 1 year of age), neonatal (under 28 days), early neonatal (under 7 days), and postneonatal (28 days–11 months). [2] Number of pregnancy-related deaths per 100,000 live births. [3] Infant deaths are tabulated by race of decedent.

Source: U.S. National Center for Health Statistics, *Health, United States, 2018*, October 2019; and CDC WONDER Online database, "Multiple Cause of Death, 1999-2018," <wonder.cdc.gov/> and "Pregnancy Mortality Surveillance System," <https://www.cdc.gov/reproductivehealth/maternal-mortality/index.html>; accessed September 2020.

Table 118. Infant Deaths and Mortality Rates by Race, Hispanic Origin, and State: 2018

[Rates are for infant (under 1 year old) deaths per 1,000 live births in specified group. Infant deaths are based on race or Hispanic origin of decedent; live births are based on race or Hispanic origin of mother. Race and Hispanic-origin categories are consistent with 1977 Office of Management and Budget (OMB) standards. Multiple-race data reported according to 1997 OMB standards were bridged to the single-race categories of 1977 OMB standards. See Technical Notes in source for more detail]

State	Total [1]		White, non-Hispanic		Black, non-Hispanic		Hispanic	
	Number	Rate	Number	Rate	Number	Rate	Number	Rate
United States.........	**21,467**	**5.6**	**9,244**	**4.6**	**6,356**	**10.7**	**4,487**	**4.5**
Alabama................	405	7.1	182	5.7	196	10.6	13	(B)
Alaska.................	60	5.6	23	3.9	(D)	(D)	(D)	(D)
Arizona................	451	5.4	144	4.3	41	8.3	213	5.6
Arkansas..............	279	7.6	159	6.7	89	11.9	24	5.2
California.............	1,909	4.0	473	3.4	219	7.2	957	3.8
Colorado..............	298	4.5	152	3.9	24	6.5	111	5.4
Connecticut...........	147	4.2	63	3.4	34	7.1	47	4.9
Delaware..............	62	5.8	21	3.8	33	11.5	(D)	(D)
District of Columbia....	64	6.5	(D)	(D)	54	14.6	(D)	(D)
Florida................	1,332	6.0	423	4.4	536	11.6	345	4.8
Georgia...............	888	7.0	279	5.0	516	11.2	76	3.8
Hawaii................	116	6.7	15	(B)	12	(B)	25	8.2
Idaho.................	109	4.9	80	4.7	(D)	(D)	20	4.8
Illinois................	942	6.4	390	5.0	345	14.2	160	4.4
Indiana...............	556	6.9	350	5.9	139	13.1	48	5.5
Iowa..................	191	5.0	124	4.1	40	15.5	20	4.9
Kansas...............	236	6.5	134	5.4	34	10.2	55	8.1
Kentucky..............	315	5.9	244	5.7	50	8.4	15	(B)
Louisiana.............	454	7.6	172	5.6	253	11.5	25	4.7
Maine.................	67	5.4	59	5.2	(D)	(D)	(D)	(D)
Maryland..............	432	6.1	113	3.7	226	9.9	47	3.6
Massachusetts.........	290	4.1	145	3.3	63	9.9	63	4.1
Michigan..............	684	6.2	312	4.1	291	13.7	56	6.4
Minnesota.............	342	5.0	184	3.6	77	11.4	35	5.9
Mississippi............	306	8.5	119	6.9	176	10.9	(D)	(D)
Missouri...............	460	6.4	299	5.6	117	10.3	34	7.2
Montana...............	55	4.5	41	4.2	(D)	(D)	(D)	(D)
Nebraska..............	149	5.8	96	5.3	22	11.7	24	5.0
Nevada................	217	6.1	88	6.5	41	9.3	65	4.5
New Hampshire........	43	3.5	37	3.5	(D)	(D)	(D)	(D)
New Jersey............	390	3.9	124	2.8	124	8.3	121	3.8
New Mexico............	131	5.5	34	5.5	(D)	(D)	76	5.4
New York..............	974	4.3	404	3.8	275	6.8	182	2.9
North Carolina.........	797	6.7	327	5.2	345	11.6	88	4.2
North Dakota..........	59	5.5	43	5.1	(D)	(D)	(D)	(D)
Ohio..................	938	7.0	536	5.5	337	14.4	45	5.4
Oklahoma.............	353	7.0	164	5.6	65	10.6	55	6.8
Oregon...............	176	3.9	107	3.5	11	(B)	44	4.4
Pennsylvania..........	805	5.9	431	4.6	230	12.0	115	6.4
Rhode Island..........	53	5.0	25	4.0	10	(B)	14	(B)
South Carolina........	406	7.3	161	5.2	212	11.8	29	5.1
South Dakota..........	70	5.8	48	5.3	(D)	(D)	(D)	(D)
Tennessee.............	560	7.1	300	5.8	203	12.1	48	5.7
Texas.................	2,083	5.3	588	4.7	521	10.3	890	4.5
Utah..................	261	5.2	171	4.6	(D)	(D)	59	6.2
Vermont...............	35	6.2	33	6.5	(D)	(D)	(D)	(D)
Virginia...............	558	5.6	258	4.8	192	8.5	72	4.5
Washington............	401	4.4	210	3.8	52	8.7	78	4.1
West Virginia..........	130	7.3	111	6.8	16	(B)	(D)	(D)
Wisconsin.............	393	6.1	220	4.6	104	16.6	45	5.9
Wyoming..............	35	5.1	24	4.5	(D)	(D)	(D)	(D)

– Represents zero. D Figure withheld to avoid disclosure pertaining to a specific individual. B Base figure too small to meet statistical standards for reliability. [1] Includes other races, not shown separately.

Source: U.S. National Center for Health Statistics, National Vital Statistics Reports (NVSR), *Deaths: Final Data*, annual report; and CDC WONDER Online database, "Multiple Cause of Death, 1999-2018," <wonder.cdc.gov>, accessed August 2020. See also <http://www.cdc.gov/nchs/deaths.htm>.

Table 119. Maternal Mortality—Number and Rate by Race, Hispanic Origin, and Age: 2018

[Rates per 100,000 live births. Maternal mortality is deaths of women that occur while pregnant or within 42 days of being pregnant, from any cause related to or aggravated by the pregnancy or its management, but not from accidental or incidental causes. Late maternal deaths occur between 43 days and 1 year of being pregnant. Data are shown for maternal causes using the International Classification of Diseases, Tenth Revision (ICD-10) and the National Center for Health Statistics' 2018 coding method; see source for details]

Race/ethnicity and age	Maternal mortality		Late maternal mortality	
	Number	Rate	Number	Rate
Total [1]	**658**	**17.4**	**277**	**7.3**
Under 25 years old	96	10.6	51	5.6
25 to 39 years old	458	16.6	194	7.0
40 years and over	104	81.9	32	25.2
White alone, non-Hispanic	287	14.7	141	7.2
Under 25 years old	40	10.2	22	5.6
25 to 39 years old	206	13.7	102	6.8
40 years and over	41	68.7	17	(S)
Black alone, non-Hispanic	205	37.1	77	13.9
Under 25 years old	27	15.3	15	(S)
25 to 39 years old	136	38.0	52	14.5
40 years and over	42	239.9	10	(S)
Hispanic [2]	105	11.8	40	4.5
Under 25 years old	21	7.6	11	(S)
25 to 39 years old	72	12.4	26	4.5
40 years and over	12	(S)	3	(S)

S Data do not meet publication standards. [1] Includes race/ethnicities not shown separately. [2] Persons of Hispanic origin may be of any race.

Source: U.S. National Center for Health Statistics, National Vital Statistics Reports (NVSR), *Maternal Mortality in the United States: Changes in Coding, Publication, and Data Release, 2018*, Vol. 69, No. 2, January 2020. See also <https://www.cdc.gov/nchs/maternal-mortality/index.htm>.

Table 120. Coronavirus Disease 2019 (COVID-19) Deaths by Sex and State: Through July 11, 2020

[Data are provisional for the period Feb. 1 through July 11, 2020, reported as of July 22, 2020; counts are continually revised as more records are received and processed by the National Center for Health Statistics (NCHS). Number of deaths reported in this table are the total number of deaths received and coded as of the date of analysis and do not represent all deaths that occurred in that period. Data during this period are incomplete because of the lag in time between when the death occurred and when the death certificate is completed, submitted to NCHS, and processed for reporting purposes. This delay can range from 1 week to 8 weeks or more. COVID-19 deaths are identified using a new International Classification of Diseases, Tenth Revision (ICD–10) code. When COVID-19 is reported as a cause of death, or when it is listed as a "probable" or "presumed" cause, the death is coded as U07.1. This can include cases with or without laboratory confirmation]

State and jurisdiction	Total [1]	Female	Male	State and jurisdiction	Total [1]	Female	Male
United States	**130,250**	**60,570**	**69,675**	Montana	30	16	14
Alabama	1,265	614	651	Nebraska	286	133	153
Alaska	11	(D)	(D)	Nevada	577	229	348
Arizona	2,443	1,052	1,391	New Hampshire	383	191	192
Arkansas	362	170	192	New Jersey	13,811	6,462	7,348
California	7,100	3,034	4,066	New Mexico	516	249	267
Colorado	1,643	724	919	New York [2]	11,242	5,301	5,941
Connecticut	4,031	2,081	1,950	New York City	20,460	8,340	12,120
Delaware	517	275	242	North Carolina	1,222	570	652
District of Columbia	644	265	379	North Dakota	104	43	61
Florida	4,341	1,973	2,368	Ohio	2,703	1,284	1,419
Georgia	2,547	1,232	1,315	Oklahoma	421	195	226
Hawaii	20	(D)	12	Oregon	257	118	139
Idaho	114	58	56	Pennsylvania	7,227	3,710	3,517
Illinois	6,652	3,001	3,651	Rhode Island	940	516	422
Indiana	2,733	1,356	1,377	South Carolina	967	479	488
Iowa	794	370	424	South Dakota	116	59	57
Kansas	315	147	168	Tennessee	672	296	376
Kentucky	656	359	297	Texas	3,706	1,469	2,237
Louisiana	3,090	1,456	1,634	Utah	219	84	135
Maine	130	71	59	Vermont	57	24	33
Maryland	3,622	1,786	1,836	Virginia	2,068	1,033	1,035
Massachusetts	7,753	4,125	3,628	Washington	1,235	567	668
Michigan	5,596	2,678	2,917	West Virginia	103	50	53
Minnesota	1,484	765	719	Wisconsin	825	384	441
Mississippi	1,206	635	570	Wyoming	18	(D)	(D)
Missouri	1,016	518	498	Puerto Rico	29	(D)	20

D Data withheld to avoid individual disclosure. [1] Includes unknown sex. [2] Excludes New York City.

Source: U.S. National Center for Health Statistics, "COVID-19 Death Data and Resources," <https://www.cdc.gov/nchs/nvss/covid-19.htm>, and "Provisional COVID-19 Death Counts by Sex, Age, and State," <https://data.cdc.gov/NCHS/Provisional-COVID-19-Death-Counts-by-Sex-Age-and-S/9bhg-hcku/data>, accessed July 2020.

Table 121. Age-Adjusted Death Rates by Major Cause: 1960 to 2018

[Age-adjusted rates per 100,000 population. Age-adjusted death rates were prepared using the direct method, in which age specific death rates for a population of interest are applied to a standard population distributed by age. Age adjustment eliminates the differences in observed rates between points in time or among compared population groups that result from age differences in population composition. Beginning 1999, deaths classified according to International Classification of Diseases, Tenth Revision (ICD-10); for earlier years, causes of death were classified according to the revisions then in use. Changes in classification of causes of death due to these revisions may result in discontinuities in cause-of-death trends. See Appendix III]

Year	Dis-eases of the heart	Malignant neo-plasms (cancer)	Acci-dents [1]	Chronic lower res-piratory diseases	Cerebro-vascular diseases	Alz-heimer's disease	Dia-betes mellitus	Influenza and pneu-monia	Inten-tional self-harm (suicide)	Nephritis, nephrotic syndrome and nephrosis
1960......	559.0	193.9	63.1	12.5	177.9	(NA)	22.5	53.7	12.5	10.6
1970......	492.7	198.6	62.2	21.3	147.7	(NA)	24.3	41.7	13.1	5.5
1980......	412.1	207.9	46.4	28.3	96.4	(NA)	18.1	31.4	12.2	9.1
1990......	321.8	216.0	36.3	37.2	65.3	6.3	20.7	36.8	12.5	9.3
1995......	293.4	209.9	34.4	40.1	63.1	8.4	23.2	33.4	11.8	9.5
1996......	285.7	206.7	34.5	40.6	62.5	8.5	23.8	32.9	11.5	9.6
1997......	277.7	203.4	34.2	41.1	61.1	8.7	23.7	33.3	11.2	9.8
1998......	267.4	202.1	35.6	43.8	62.8	8.6	24.2	24.2	11.1	9.8
1999......	266.5	200.8	35.3	45.4	61.6	16.5	25.0	23.5	10.5	13.0
2000......	257.6	199.6	34.9	44.2	60.9	18.1	25.0	23.7	10.4	13.5
2001......	249.5	196.5	35.7	43.9	58.4	19.3	25.4	22.2	10.7	14.1
2002......	244.6	194.3	37.1	43.9	57.2	20.8	25.6	23.2	10.9	14.4
2003......	236.3	190.9	37.6	43.7	54.6	22.1	25.5	22.6	10.8	14.7
2004......	221.6	186.8	38.1	41.6	51.2	22.6	24.7	20.4	11.0	14.5
2005......	216.8	185.1	39.5	43.9	48.0	24.0	24.9	21.0	10.9	14.7
2006......	205.5	181.8	40.2	41.0	44.8	23.7	23.6	18.4	11.0	14.8
2007......	196.1	179.3	40.4	41.4	43.5	23.8	22.8	16.8	11.3	14.9
2008......	192.1	176.4	39.2	44.7	42.1	25.8	22.0	17.6	11.6	15.1
2009......	182.8	173.5	37.5	42.7	39.6	24.2	21.0	16.5	11.8	15.1
2010......	179.1	172.8	38.0	42.2	39.1	25.1	20.8	15.1	12.1	15.3
2011......	173.7	169.0	39.1	42.5	37.9	24.7	21.6	15.7	12.3	13.4
2012......	170.5	166.5	39.1	41.5	36.9	23.8	21.2	14.4	12.6	13.1
2013......	169.8	163.2	39.4	42.1	36.2	23.5	21.2	15.9	12.6	13.2
2014......	167.0	161.2	40.5	40.5	36.5	25.4	20.9	15.1	13.0	13.2
2015......	168.5	158.5	43.2	41.6	37.6	29.4	21.3	15.2	13.3	13.4
2016......	165.5	155.8	47.4	40.6	37.3	30.3	21.0	13.5	13.5	13.1
2017......	165.0	152.5	49.4	40.9	37.6	31.0	21.5	14.3	14.0	13.0
2018......	163.6	149.1	48.0	39.7	37.1	30.5	21.4	14.9	14.2	12.9

NA Not available. [1] Unintentional injuries.

Source: U.S. National Center for Health Statistics, National Vital Statistics Reports (NVSR), *Deaths: Final Data*, annual report; and CDC WONDER Online Database, "Multiple Cause of Death, 1999-2018," <wonder.cdc.gov>, accessed August 2020 . See also <http://www.cdc.gov/nchs/nvss/deaths.htm>.

Table 122. Deaths by Leading Cause, Race, and Hispanic Origin: 2018

[Rank based on number of deaths. Race and Hispanic origin are reported separately on death certificates. Persons of Hispanic origin may be of any race. Data for Hispanic persons are not tabulated by race; data for non-Hispanic persons are tabulated by race. Data for racial and ethnic groups other than non-Hispanic White and non-Hispanic Black should be interpreted with caution because of misreporting of Hispanic origin and race on the death certificate. Cause of death based on International Classification of Diseases, Tenth Revision (ICD-10). See Appendix III]

Cause of death	Non-Hispanic White Rank	Non-Hispanic White Deaths	Non-Hispanic Black Rank	Non-Hispanic Black Deaths	Non-Hispanic American Indian or Alaska Native Rank	Non-Hispanic American Indian or Alaska Native Deaths	Non-Hispanic Asian or Pacific Islander Rank	Non-Hispanic Asian or Pacific Islander Deaths	Hispanic Rank	Hispanic Deaths
All causes........................	(X)	2,188,349	(X)	343,393	(X)	19,491	(X)	75,266	(X)	204,719
Diseases of heart..................	1	512,039	1	80,781	1	3,573	2	16,171	2	40,537
Malignant neoplasms (cancer)....	2	463,971	2	70,014	2	3,305	1	18,643	1	42,066
Chronic lower respiratory diseases.............	3	138,516	6	11,696	6	878	8	2,125	8	5,801
Accidents (unintended injuries)..............	4	123,151	3	20,486	3	2,153	4	3,449	3	17,239
Cerebrovascular diseases.........	5	110,530	4	19,473	7	703	3	5,567	4	11,246
Alzheimer's disease...............	6	101,702	9	8,927	10	370	6	2,843	6	8,021
Diabetes mellitus..................	7	55,773	5	15,265	5	1,073	5	3,185	5	9,386
Influenza and pneumonia.........	8	45,728	12	6,105	9	441	7	2,392	11	4,254
Intentional self-harm (suicide).....	9	38,643	15	3,124	8	615	11	1,502	9	4,313
Nephritis, nephrotic syndrome and nephrosis........	10	35,342	7	9,745	11	350	9	1,580	10	4,274
Chronic liver disease and cirrhosis....................	11	30,887	14	3,287	4	1,148	14	742	7	6,628
Septicemia........................	12	29,831	10	6,654	13	261	13	846	13	3,029
Essential hypertension and hypertensive renal disease......	14	24,670	11	6,356	14	214	10	1,558	14	2,928
Assault (homicide).................	20	5,531	8	9,543	12	304	18	346	12	3,045

X Not applicable.

Source: U.S. National Center for Health Statistics, National Vital Statistics Reports (NVSR), *Deaths: Leading Causes*, annual; and CDC WONDER Online database, "Multiple Cause of Death, 1999-2018," <https://wonder.cdc.gov/>, accessed September 2020. See also <http://www.cdc.gov/nchs/nvss/deaths.htm>.

Table 123. Deaths and Death Rates by Selected Causes: 2017 and 2018

[Rates per 100,000 population. Figures are weighted data rounded to the nearest individual, so categories may not add to total or subtotal. Excludes deaths of nonresidents of the United States. Deaths classified according to the International Classification of Diseases, Tenth Revision (ICD-10). See also Appendix III]

Cause of death	2017			2018		
	Number	Rate	Age-adjusted rate [1]	Number	Rate	Age-adjusted rate [1]
All causes [2]	**2,813,503**	**863.8**	**731.9**	**2,839,205**	**867.8**	**723.6**
Major cardiovascular diseases [2]	854,390	262.3	218.1	863,834	264.0	215.8
Diseases of heart	647,457	198.8	165.0	655,381	200.3	163.6
Acute rheumatic fever and chronic rheumatic heart disease	3,320	1.0	0.9	3,560	1.1	0.9
Hypertensive heart disease	47,523	14.6	12.2	51,524	15.7	13.0
Hypertensive heart and renal disease	7,259	2.2	1.9	8,517	2.6	2.1
Ischemic heart disease	365,914	112.3	92.9	365,744	111.8	90.9
Acute myocardial infarction	110,346	33.9	28.1	108,610	33.2	27.0
Other heart diseases	223,441	68.6	57.3	226,036	69.1	56.8
Heart failure	80,480	24.7	20.4	83,616	25.6	20.8
Essential (primary) hypertension and hypertensive renal disease	35,316	10.8	9.0	35,835	11.0	8.9
Cerebrovascular diseases	146,383	44.9	37.6	147,810	45.2	37.1
Atherosclerosis	5,547	1.7	1.4	4,931	1.5	1.2
Malignant neoplasms (cancer) [2]	599,108	183.9	152.5	599,274	183.2	149.1
Malignant neoplasms of lip, oral cavity, and pharynx	10,126	3.1	2.5	10,158	3.1	2.5
Malignant neoplasms of esophagus	15,321	4.7	3.8	15,419	4.7	3.8
Malignant neoplasms of stomach	11,158	3.4	2.9	11,043	3.4	2.8
Malignant neoplasms of colon, rectum and anus	53,447	16.4	13.7	53,094	16.2	13.4
Malignant neoplasms of liver and intrahepatic bile ducts	27,106	8.3	6.7	27,686	8.5	6.7
Malignant neoplasms of pancreas	44,012	13.5	11.1	44,915	13.7	11.0
Malignant neoplasms of trachea, bronchus and lung	145,932	44.8	36.6	142,161	43.5	34.8
Malignant melanoma of skin	8,056	2.5	2.1	8,199	2.5	2.1
Malignant neoplasm of breast	42,510	13.1	11.0	42,950	13.1	10.9
Malignant neoplasm of ovary	14,193	4.4	3.6	13,748	4.2	3.4
Malignant neoplasm of prostate	30,488	9.4	7.8	31,489	9.6	7.8
Malignant neoplasms of kidney and renal pelvis	13,960	4.3	3.5	14,134	4.3	3.5
Malignant neoplasms of bladder	16,657	5.1	4.3	16,641	5.1	4.2
Malignant neoplasms of meninges, brain and other parts of central nervous system	16,804	5.2	4.4	17,127	5.2	4.4
Malignant neoplasms of lymphoid, hematopoietic and related tissue [2]	57,737	17.7	15.0	57,609	17.6	14.6
Non-Hodgkin's lymphoma	20,460	6.3	5.3	20,287	6.2	5.1
Leukemia	23,359	7.2	6.1	23,359	7.1	6.0
Accidents (unintentional injuries)	169,936	52.2	49.4	167,127	51.1	48.0
Transport accidents [2]	43,024	13.2	12.8	42,032	12.8	12.4
Motor vehicle accidents	40,231	12.4	12.0	39,404	12.0	11.7
Nontransport accidents [2]	126,912	39.0	36.6	125,095	38.2	35.6
Falls	36,338	11.2	9.4	37,455	11.4	9.4
Accidental discharge of firearms	486	0.1	0.2	458	0.1	0.1
Accidental drowning and submersion	3,709	1.1	1.1	3,710	1.1	1.1
Accidental exposure to smoke, fire and flames	2,812	0.9	0.8	2,972	0.9	0.8
Accidental poisoning and exposure to noxious substances	64,795	19.9	20.1	62,399	19.1	19.3
Chronic lower respiratory diseases [2]	160,201	49.2	40.9	159,486	48.7	39.7
Bronchitis, chronic and unspecified	502	0.2	0.1	492	0.2	0.1
Emphysema	7,085	2.2	1.8	7,560	2.3	1.9
Asthma	3,564	1.1	1.0	3,441	1.1	0.9
Pneumonitis due to solids and liquids	20,108	6.2	5.1	19,239	5.9	4.8
Influenza and pneumonia [2]	55,672	17.1	14.3	59,120	18.1	14.9
Influenza	6,515	2.0	1.7	11,164	3.4	2.8
Pneumonia	49,157	15.1	12.6	47,956	14.7	12.0
Septicemia (blood poisoning)	40,922	12.6	10.6	40,718	12.4	10.2
Viral hepatitis	5,611	1.7	1.4	4,842	1.5	1.2
Human immunodeficiency virus (HIV) disease	5,698	1.7	1.6	5,425	1.7	1.5
Anemias	5,382	1.7	1.4	5,262	1.6	1.3
Diabetes mellitus	83,564	25.7	21.5	84,946	26.0	21.4
Nutritional deficiencies	7,846	2.4	2.0	9,619	2.9	2.4
Malnutrition	7,592	2.3	1.9	9,335	2.9	2.3
Parkinson's disease	31,963	9.8	8.4	33,829	10.3	8.7
Alzheimer's disease	121,404	37.3	31.0	122,019	37.3	30.5
Chronic liver disease and cirrhosis	41,743	12.8	10.9	42,838	13.1	11.1
Alcoholic liver disease	22,246	6.8	5.9	23,172	7.1	6.1
Nephritis, nephrotic syndrome, and nephrosis [2]	50,633	15.5	13.0	51,386	15.7	12.9
Renal failure	49,709	15.3	12.8	50,404	15.4	12.7
Intentional self-harm (suicide)	47,173	14.5	14.0	48,344	14.8	14.2
Intentional self-harm (suicide) by discharge of firearms	23,854	7.3	6.9	24,432	7.5	7.0
Assault (homicide)	19,510	6.0	6.2	18,830	5.8	5.9
Assault (homicide) by discharge of firearms	14,542	4.5	4.6	13,958	4.3	4.4
Events of undetermined intent	5,799	1.8	1.8	5,653	1.7	1.7
Complications of medical and surgical care	4,459	1.4	1.2	4,604	1.4	1.2
Enterocolitis due to Clostridium difficile [3]	6,118	1.9	1.6	5,249	1.6	1.3
Drug-induced deaths [3]	73,990	22.7	22.8	71,147	21.7	21.8
Alcohol-induced deaths [3]	35,823	11.0	9.6	37,329	11.4	9.9
Injury by firearms [3]	39,773	12.2	12.0	39,740	12.1	11.9

[1] See text, this section. [2] Includes other causes, not shown separately. [3] Also included in selected other categories.

Source: U.S. National Center for Health Statistics, National Vital Statistics Reports, *Deaths: Final Data*, annual report; and CDC WONDER Online database, "Multiple Cause of Death, 1999-2018," <https://wonder.cdc.gov/>, accessed August 2020. See also <http://www.cdc.gov/nchs/nvss/deaths.htm>.

Table 124. Deaths by Age and Selected Cause: 2018

[Deaths are classified according to the International Classification of Diseases, Tenth Revision (ICD-10). See Appendix III]

Cause of death	All ages[1]	Under 1 year	1 to 4 years	5 to 14 years	15 to 24 years	25 to 34 years	35 to 44 years	45 to 54 years	55 to 64 years	65 to 74 years	75 to 84 years	85 years and over
All causes[2]	2,839,205	21,467	3,830	5,450	30,154	58,844	80,380	164,837	374,836	543,778	675,205	880,280
Septicemia	40,718	151	54	60	101	399	829	2,380	5,956	9,143	10,687	10,956
Human immunodeficiency virus (HIV) disease	5,425	–	1	–	62	482	753	1,490	1,653	737	214	33
Malignant neoplasms (cancer)[2]	599,274	51	326	843	1,371	3,684	10,640	37,301	113,947	169,056	158,794	103,252
Malignant neoplasm of esophagus	15,419	–	–	–	2	50	201	1,078	3,763	5,069	3,593	1,663
Malignant neoplasm of colon, rectum, and anus	53,094	–	–	3	32	372	1,451	4,971	10,256	12,988	12,513	10,508
Malignant neoplasm of liver and intrahepatic bile ducts	27,686	4	12	11	35	104	344	1,621	7,541	9,164	6,005	2,844
Malignant neoplasm of pancreas	44,915	–	–	2	9	57	432	2,460	8,737	13,982	12,409	6,826
Malignant neoplasms of trachea, bronchus, and lung	142,161	–	–	4	18	119	787	6,272	28,972	46,015	41,238	18,733
Malignant neoplasm of breast	42,950	–	–	–	13	397	1,812	4,671	8,945	10,527	9,088	7,496
Malignant neoplasm of ovary	13,748	–	–	1	24	84	290	1,221	2,983	4,015	3,367	1,761
Malignant neoplasm of prostate	31,489	–	–	–	–	–	24	412	2,916	7,420	10,461	10,254
Malignant neoplasms of kidney and renal pelvis	14,134	2	12	27	25	65	229	950	2,726	3,993	3,691	2,414
Malignant neoplasm of bladder	16,641	–	1	–	–	14	63	440	1,824	3,802	5,289	5,208
Malignant neoplasms of meninges, brain and other parts of central nervous system	17,127	14	69	326	229	444	849	1,754	4,007	4,796	3,339	1,299
Malignant neoplasms of lymphoid, hematopoietic and related tissue[2]	57,609	16	112	202	417	594	961	2,489	7,565	14,482	18,038	12,732
Non-Hodgkins lymphoma	20,287	1	5	23	74	160	318	842	2,726	4,952	6,444	4,742
Leukemia	23,359	15	106	176	323	371	524	1,039	2,779	5,679	7,123	5,223
Diabetes mellitus	84,946	2	3	33	246	837	2,282	6,414	14,941	21,971	21,171	17,040
Parkinson's disease	33,829	–	–	–	3	4	13	77	743	4,935	14,008	14,045
Alzheimer's disease	122,019	–	–	1	–	2	6	107	1,245	7,543	32,927	80,188
Major cardiovascular diseases[2]	863,834	405	161	265	1,118	4,439	13,194	39,963	100,934	154,091	209,425	339,794
Diseases of heart[2]	655,381	288	115	169	905	3,561	10,532	32,220	81,042	119,664	155,219	251,626
Hypertensive heart disease	51,524	10	3	13	64	526	1,747	4,345	8,339	8,534	9,330	18,637
Ischemic heart diseases	365,744	7	–	–	112	917	4,490	18,220	50,081	74,354	89,759	127,756
Acute myocardial infarction	108,610	19	–	7	48	367	1,734	6,701	17,500	25,051	26,960	30,229
Heart failure	83,616	19	13	8	41	161	479	1,588	4,847	10,500	20,385	45,573
Essential (primary) hypertension and hypertensive renal disease	35,835	1	–	–	13	120	476	1,557	4,110	6,164	8,375	15,016
Cerebrovascular diseases	147,810	98	13	88	148	567	1,704	5,128	12,789	23,414	39,415	64,415
Influenza and pneumonia	59,120	176	122	122	200	457	956	2,339	5,858	9,676	14,497	24,715
Influenza	11,164	19	52	71	65	117	266	606	1,287	1,704	2,476	4,501
Pneumonia	47,956	157	70	51	135	340	690	1,733	4,571	7,972	12,021	20,214
Chronic lower respiratory diseases[2]	159,486	15	50	132	165	300	648	3,807	18,804	39,221	51,677	44,662
Emphysema	7,560	–	–	–	–	4	28	229	1,063	1,950	2,463	1,823
Pneumonitis due to solids and liquids	19,239	4	7	12	45	86	204	542	1,555	3,007	4,999	8,778
Chronic liver disease and cirrhosis[2]	42,838	–	1	2	32	1,008	3,108	8,157	13,945	9,907	5,005	1,667
Alcoholic liver disease	23,172	–	–	–	21	832	2,404	5,617	8,526	4,382	1,182	207
Nephritis, nephrotic syndrome, and nephrosis[2]	51,386	78	11	17	52	260	753	2,240	5,740	10,841	14,514	16,880
Renal failure	50,404	69	9	11	50	249	725	2,187	5,634	10,651	14,240	16,576
Congenital malformations, deformations and chromosomal abnormalities	9,729	4,473	384	373	354	455	428	744	1,178	653	372	313
Accidents (unintentional injuries)[2]	167,127	1,168	1,226	1,426	12,044	24,614	22,667	23,056	23,693	15,957	17,134	24,122
Transport accidents	42,032	82	377	815	6,644	7,418	5,573	5,983	6,434	4,399	2,926	1,379
Motor vehicle accidents	39,404	81	362	765	6,434	7,062	5,219	5,522	5,846	3,996	2,779	1,336
Nontransport accidents	125,095	1,086	849	611	5,400	17,196	17,094	17,073	17,259	11,558	14,208	22,743
Falls	37,455	4	16	17	152	345	502	1,131	2,766	5,110	9,709	17,703
Accidental poisoning and exposure to noxious substances	62,399	8	22	36	4,245	15,353	14,978	13,620	10,854	2,620	460	189
Intentional self-harm (suicide)	48,344	–	–	605	6,211	8,020	7,521	8,345	8,540	4,974	2,880	1,248
Assault (homicide)	18,830	269	353	289	4,607	5,234	3,304	2,125	1,501	712	300	134
Assault (homicide) by discharge of firearms	13,958	6	54	191	4,107	4,348	2,569	1,382	802	347	114	37
Enterocolitis due to clostridium difficile	5,249	2	4	4	10	17	45	156	520	1,040	1,607	1,848

– Represents zero. [1] Includes persons with age not stated, not shown separately. [2] Includes other causes, not shown separately.

Source: U.S. National Center for Health Statistics, National Vital Statistics Reports (NVSR), Deaths: Final Data, annual report; and CDC WONDER Online Database, "Multiple Cause of Death, 1999–2018," <https://wonder.cdc.gov/>, accessed August 2020. See also <http://www.cdc.gov/nchs/nvss/deaths.htm>.

Table 125. Deaths and Death Rates by Leading Cause and Age: 2018

[Rates per 100,000 population in specified group. Data are based on the International Classification of Diseases, Tenth Revision (ICD-10)]

Age and cause of death	Number	Rate	Age and cause of death	Number	Rate
ALL AGES [1]			**25 TO 34 YEARS (continued)**		
All causes.....	**2,839,205**	**867.8**	Diseases of heart.....	3,561	7.8
Diseases of heart.....	655,381	200.3	Chronic liver disease and cirrhosis.....	1,008	2.2
Malignant neoplasms (cancer).....	599,274	183.2	Diabetes mellitus.....	837	1.8
Accidents (unintentional injuries).....	167,127	51.1	Cerebrovascular diseases.....	567	1.2
Chronic lower respiratory diseases.....	159,486	48.7	Human immunodeficiency virus (HIV).....	482	1.1
Cerebrovascular diseases.....	147,810	45.2	Influenza and pneumonia.....	457	1.0
Alzheimer's disease.....	122,019	37.3	**35 TO 44 YEARS**		
Diabetes mellitus.....	84,946	26.0	**All causes**.....	**80,380**	**194.7**
Influenza and pneumonia.....	59,120	18.1	Accidents (unintentional injuries).....	22,667	54.9
Nephritis, nephrotic syndrome and nephrosis...	51,386	15.7	Malignant neoplasms (cancer).....	10,640	25.8
Intentional self-harm (suicide).....	48,344	14.8	Diseases of heart.....	10,532	25.5
1 TO 4 YEARS			Intentional self-harm (suicide).....	7,521	18.2
All causes.....	**3,830**	**24.0**	Assault (homicide).....	3,304	8.0
Accidents (unintentional injuries).....	1,226	7.7	Chronic liver disease and cirrhosis.....	3,108	7.5
Congenital malformations [2].....	384	2.4	Diabetes mellitus.....	2,282	5.5
Assault (homicide).....	353	2.2	Cerebrovascular diseases.....	1,704	4.1
Malignant neoplasms (cancer).....	326	2.0	Influenza and pneumonia.....	956	2.3
Influenza and pneumonia.....	122	0.8	Septicemia.....	829	2.0
Diseases of heart.....	115	0.7	**45 TO 54 YEARS**		
Conditions originating in the perinatal period....	62	0.4	**All causes**.....	**164,837**	**395.9**
Septicemia.....	54	0.3	Malignant neoplasms (cancer).....	37,301	89.6
Chronic lower respiratory diseases.....	50	0.3	Diseases of heart.....	32,220	77.4
Cerebrovascular diseases.....	43	0.3	Accidents (unintentional injuries).....	23,056	55.4
5 TO 9 YEARS			Intentional self-harm (suicide).....	8,345	20.0
All causes.....	**2,330**	**11.5**	Chronic liver disease and cirrhosis.....	8,157	19.6
Accidents (unintentional injuries).....	734	3.6	Diabetes mellitus.....	6,414	15.4
Malignant neoplasms (cancer).....	393	1.9	Cerebrovascular diseases.....	5,128	12.3
Congenital malformations [2].....	201	1.0	Chronic lower respiratory diseases.....	3,807	9.1
Assault (homicide).....	121	0.6	Septicemia.....	2,380	5.7
Influenza and pneumonia.....	71	0.4	Influenza and pneumonia.....	2,339	5.6
Diseases of heart.....	68	0.3	**55 TO 64 YEARS**		
Chronic lower respiratory diseases.....	68	0.3	**All causes**.....	**374,836**	**886.7**
Cerebrovascular diseases.....	34	0.2	Malignant neoplasms (cancer).....	113,947	269.6
Septicemia.....	34	0.2	Diseases of heart.....	81,042	191.7
In situ and benign neoplasms and neoplasms			Accidents (unintentional injuries).....	23,693	56.0
of uncertain or unknown behavior.....	19	(B)	Chronic lower respiratory diseases.....	18,804	44.5
			Diabetes mellitus.....	14,941	35.3
10 TO 14 YEARS			Chronic liver disease and cirrhosis.....	13,945	33.0
All causes.....	**3,120**	**14.9**	Cerebrovascular diseases.....	12,789	30.3
Accidents (unintentional injuries).....	692	3.3	Intentional self-harm (suicide).....	8,540	20.2
Intentional self-harm (suicide).....	596	2.9	Septicemia.....	5,956	14.1
Malignant neoplasms (cancer).....	450	2.2	Influenza and pneumonia.....	5,858	13.9
Congenital malformations [2].....	172	0.8	**65 to 74 YEARS**		
Assault (homicide).....	168	0.8	**All causes**.....	**543,778**	**1,783.3**
Diseases of heart.....	101	0.5	Malignant neoplasms (cancer).....	169,056	554.4
Chronic lower respiratory diseases.....	64	0.3	Diseases of heart.....	119,664	392.4
Cerebrovascular diseases.....	54	0.3	Chronic lower respiratory diseases.....	39,221	128.6
Influenza and pneumonia.....	51	0.2	Cerebrovascular diseases.....	23,414	76.8
In situ and benign neoplasms and neoplasms			Diabetes mellitus.....	21,971	72.1
of uncertain or unknown behavior.....	30	0.1	Accidents (unintentional injuries).....	15,957	52.3
15 TO 19 YEARS			Nephritis, nephrotic syndrome and nephrosis...	10,841	35.6
All causes.....	**10,380**	**49.2**	Chronic liver disease and cirrhosis.....	9,907	32.5
Accidents (unintentional injuries).....	3,548	16.8	Influenza and pneumonia.....	9,676	31.7
Intentional self-harm (suicide).....	2,404	11.4	Septicemia.....	9,143	30.0
Assault (homicide).....	1,755	8.3	**75 TO 84 YEARS**		
Malignant neoplasms (cancer).....	621	2.9	**All causes**.....	**675,205**	**4,386.1**
Diseases of heart.....	276	1.3	Malignant neoplasms (cancer).....	158,794	1,031.5
Congenital malformations [2].....	172	0.8	Diseases of heart.....	155,219	1,008.3
Influenza and pneumonia.....	71	0.3	Chronic lower respiratory diseases.....	51,677	335.7
Diabetes mellitus.....	68	0.3	Cerebrovascular diseases.....	39,415	256.0
Chronic lower respiratory diseases.....	59	0.3	Alzheimer's disease.....	32,927	213.9
Cerebrovascular diseases.....	55	0.3	Diabetes mellitus.....	21,171	137.5
20 TO 24 YEARS			Accidents (unintentional injuries).....	17,134	111.3
All causes.....	**19,774**	**90.4**	Nephritis, nephrotic syndrome and nephrosis...	14,514	94.3
Accidents (unintentional injuries).....	8,496	38.8	Influenza and pneumonia.....	14,497	94.2
Intentional self-harm (suicide).....	3,807	17.4	Parkinson's disease.....	14,008	91.0
Assault (homicide).....	2,852	13.0			
Malignant neoplasms (cancer).....	750	3.4	**85 YEARS AND OVER**		
Diseases of heart.....	629	2.9	**All causes**.....	**880,280**	**13,450.7**
Congenital malformations [2].....	182	0.8	Diseases of heart.....	251,626	3,844.8
Diabetes mellitus.....	178	0.8	Malignant neoplasms (cancer).....	103,252	1,577.7
Influenza and pneumonia.....	129	0.6	Alzheimer's disease.....	80,188	1,225.3
Pregnancy, childbirth and the puerperium.....	121	0.6	Cerebrovascular diseases.....	64,415	984.3
Chronic lower respiratory diseases.....	106	0.5	Chronic lower respiratory diseases.....	44,662	682.4
25 TO 34 YEARS			Influenza and pneumonia.....	24,715	377.6
All causes.....	**58,844**	**128.8**	Accidents (unintentional injuries).....	24,122	368.6
Accidents (unintentional injuries).....	24,614	53.9	Diabetes mellitus.....	17,040	260.4
Intentional self-harm (suicide).....	8,020	17.6	Nephritis, nephrotic syndrome and nephrosis...	16,877	257.9
Assault (homicide).....	5,234	11.5	Essential hypertension and		
Malignant neoplasms (cancer).....	3,684	8.1	hypertensive renal disease.....	15,016	229.4

B Base figure too small to meet statistical standards for reliability of a derived figure. [1] Includes deaths under 1 year of age. [2] Congenital malformations, deformations and chromosomal abnormalities.

Source: U.S. National Center for Health Statistics, *Deaths: Leading Causes*, annual; and CDC WONDER Online database, "Multiple Cause of Death, 1999-2018," <https://wonder.cdc.gov/>, accessed September 2020. See also <http://www.cdc.gov/nchs/nvss/deaths.htm>.

Table 126. Age-Adjusted Death Rates for Major Causes of Death by State: 2018

[Age-adjusted rates per 100,000 resident population as of July 1. Excludes nonresidents of the United States. Causes of death classified according to the International Classification of Diseases, Tenth Revision (ICD-10)]

State	All causes of death	Diseases of heart	Malignant neoplasms (cancer)	Accidents Total	Accidents Motor vehicle accidents	Chronic lower respiratory disease	Cerebro-vascular diseases	Alz-heimer's disease	Diabetes mellitus	Influenza and pneumonia	Intentional self-harm (suicide)
U.S.	723.6	163.6	149.1	48.0	11.7	39.7	37.1	30.5	21.4	14.9	14.2
AL.	918.1	224.7	170.4	53.0	21.4	58.0	51.5	44.9	19.4	21.4	16.5
AK.	700.3	129.7	141.5	56.4	12.6	35.3	40.0	27.5	17.7	12.1	24.6
AZ.	669.2	136.4	131.9	55.4	14.0	41.2	31.0	33.0	22.4	12.4	19.2
AR.	876.6	217.4	168.8	48.6	17.9	61.7	41.5	38.9	32.3	18.0	18.3
CA.	609.0	139.7	135.0	33.7	10.1	30.9	37.0	37.1	21.4	15.6	10.9
CO.	651.4	124.3	127.6	52.3	11.5	44.0	34.7	29.6	16.1	9.7	21.9
CT.	644.2	142.1	134.1	53.1	8.2	28.9	27.2	18.5	14.6	14.8	10.6
DE.	757.2	159.1	159.4	67.1	11.9	40.4	46.4	32.7	18.8	13.1	11.4
DC.	718.8	187.0	155.6	55.5	5.8	22.7	35.4	14.3	21.0	11.2	7.5
FL.	657.9	143.1	141.7	53.1	14.6	37.0	39.6	19.2	19.8	9.6	15.2
GA.	790.2	175.8	152.4	41.7	14.2	45.7	43.4	46.5	22.1	14.5	14.6
HI.	572.5	125.6	123.5	37.6	7.9	19.6	37.4	20.2	16.1	24.5	11.9
ID.	726.6	157.9	149.5	49.5	14.3	44.1	36.4	35.0	20.3	11.9	23.9
IL.	716.9	163.9	153.5	44.3	9.1	36.2	37.3	25.3	18.6	16.3	11.3
IN.	832.7	180.7	165.7	55.2	12.8	57.2	39.3	33.4	26.0	14.0	16.0
IA.	723.9	165.1	155.3	40.8	10.9	43.8	33.0	31.7	21.9	15.7	15.5
KS.	771.3	158.9	156.4	46.5	13.9	50.4	35.9	23.6	22.6	17.1	19.3
KY.	920.0	198.3	181.6	66.8	16.9	62.1	41.5	32.5	27.9	18.3	17.5
LA.	870.9	212.2	169.0	58.8	17.2	43.1	46.7	42.2	26.9	15.6	15.1
ME.	753.9	147.0	162.1	65.0	11.0	45.6	33.7	28.4	23.4	15.3	18.5
MD.	714.1	161.9	149.9	35.0	8.4	31.0	40.3	15.8	19.6	13.6	10.2
MA.	670.6	131.5	142.8	53.0	5.4	30.9	27.1	19.5	15.8	15.8	9.9
MI.	782.3	195.0	161.1	52.0	9.8	44.1	40.0	34.3	21.9	14.5	15.0
MN.	648.0	119.0	143.1	43.8	8.3	34.0	32.2	33.7	18.8	10.0	13.1
MS.	934.8	222.1	179.7	54.4	23.3	59.9	51.8	46.0	30.6	26.1	13.8
MO.	823.2	188.4	165.3	61.6	15.2	50.2	38.5	32.9	20.8	18.7	19.5
MT.	720.2	163.2	140.7	51.0	16.8	47.0	30.1	21.7	19.1	10.7	24.9
NE.	717.4	145.7	150.5	38.5	13.1	47.7	31.5	27.4	26.0	16.1	13.4
NV.	741.1	190.7	146.5	48.4	11.7	49.3	36.6	23.6	19.2	16.0	20.8
NH.	712.7	151.0	143.7	66.0	10.2	40.9	27.2	26.4	17.3	14.3	19.4
NJ.	672.5	163.0	141.3	50.1	6.4	28.0	29.8	22.7	16.6	12.6	8.3
NM.	748.7	148.2	136.4	69.3	19.0	43.0	31.8	22.4	26.1	14.2	25.0
NY.	626.7	171.9	138.2	34.2	5.0	28.5	24.4	13.9	18.2	18.4	8.3
NC.	770.1	155.5	154.2	55.2	14.7	42.6	41.3	37.9	23.9	16.9	13.7
ND.	690.3	140.0	145.2	42.0	13.2	34.9	34.1	33.8	24.1	15.6	19.2
OH.	838.4	191.1	165.2	63.8	10.1	49.0	42.6	34.9	25.4	15.7	15.3
OK.	893.2	228.5	178.1	62.5	17.6	63.5	40.1	37.9	29.0	17.8	20.0
OR.	689.8	128.4	150.6	43.6	11.1	35.6	38.0	35.6	22.9	10.2	19.0
PA.	759.7	176.1	156.6	61.9	9.4	35.1	35.3	20.7	20.2	15.5	14.9
RI.	696.7	158.9	151.6	59.1	6.4	31.2	28.2	29.2	17.2	13.3	9.5
SC.	821.6	167.0	157.3	63.3	20.0	45.8	45.5	44.3	24.8	14.5	15.4
SD.	715.9	156.3	145.2	46.4	17.3	43.7	33.6	36.3	23.3	20.7	19.3
TN.	889.7	202.4	168.0	63.5	15.9	55.9	43.6	45.0	24.5	20.7	16.6
TX.	731.8	170.0	142.9	37.7	13.2	39.7	40.3	38.4	21.1	12.9	13.7
UT.	691.8	146.4	120.0	45.1	8.5	33.2	36.3	42.1	23.5	13.4	22.2
VT.	706.5	150.5	156.0	63.1	11.4	39.6	29.5	37.7	18.2	9.8	18.8
VA.	709.5	147.9	149.3	43.7	10.3	34.7	38.9	27.1	22.9	13.1	14.0
WA.	666.6	135.4	145.3	42.1	8.6	34.5	34.1	45.2	20.4	10.9	15.9
WV.	953.8	196.4	179.5	90.3	17.4	64.3	38.6	31.0	36.2	21.2	21.2
WI.	723.3	157.8	151.5	57.1	10.2	37.8	33.4	31.7	20.2	14.1	14.8
WY.	749.6	152.7	140.6	57.1	16.5	58.7	32.2	41.5	21.4	18.9	25.2

Source: U.S. National Center for Health Statistics, National Vital Statistics Reports (NVSR), *Deaths: Final Data*, annual; and CDC WONDER Online database, "Multiple Cause of Death, 1999-2018," <https://wonder.cdc.gov/>, accessed September 2020. See also <http://www.cdc.gov/nchs/nvss/deaths.htm>.

Table 127. Death Rates For Heart Disease by Selected Characteristics: 1980 to 2018

[Rates per 100,000 population. Excludes deaths of nonresidents of the United States. Beginning 1999, deaths classified according to the International Classification of Diseases, Tenth Revision (ICD-10); for earlier years, causes of death were classified according to the revisions then in use. Changes in classification of causes of death due to these revisions may result in discontinuities in cause-of-death trends. See Appendix III]

Characteristics	1980	1990	2000	2005	2010	2015	2016	2017	2018
All ages, age-adjusted [1]	**412.1**	**321.8**	**257.6**	**216.8**	**179.1**	**168.5**	**165.5**	**165.0**	**163.6**
All ages, crude rate	**336.0**	**289.5**	**252.6**	**220.7**	**193.6**	**197.2**	**196.6**	**198.8**	**200.3**
Under 1 year	22.8	20.1	13.0	8.9	8.3	7.3	7.4	7.7	7.5
1 to 4 years	2.6	1.9	1.2	0.9	1.0	0.9	0.7	0.8	0.7
5 to 14 years	0.9	0.9	0.7	0.6	0.5	0.5	0.5	0.4	0.4
15 to 24 years	2.9	2.5	2.6	2.6	2.4	2.3	2.2	2.1	2.1
25 to 34 years	8.3	7.6	7.4	8.3	7.8	8.0	7.7	8.1	7.8
35 to 44 years	44.6	31.4	29.2	29.2	25.8	25.6	25.9	25.4	25.5
45 to 54 years	180.2	120.5	94.2	89.7	81.6	79.3	79.5	77.1	77.4
55 to 64 years	494.1	367.3	261.2	212.8	186.6	188.1	189.6	190.7	191.7
65 to 74 years	1,218.6	894.3	665.6	512.3	409.2	389.5	392.5	392.9	392.4
75 to 84 years	2,993.1	2,295.7	1,780.3	1,458.5	1,172.0	1,071.6	1,037.1	1,028.4	1,008.3
85 years and over	7,777.1	6,739.9	5,926.1	5,188.3	4,285.2	3,986.5	3,873.4	3,882.9	3,844.8
MALE									
All ages, age-adjusted [1]	**538.9**	**412.4**	**320.0**	**268.2**	**225.1**	**211.8**	**209.1**	**209.0**	**207.5**
White	539.6	409.2	316.7	264.8	222.9	211.2	208.4	208.3	206.3
Black	561.4	485.4	392.5	338.8	280.6	258.6	258.1	257.5	259.5
American Indian, Alaska Native	320.5	264.1	222.2	191.7	158.7	148.0	147.7	148.0	141.0
Asian, Pacific Islander	286.9	220.7	185.5	149.4	127.2	109.7	106.6	108.0	110.2
Hispanic origin [2]	(NA)	270.0	238.2	210.5	165.1	146.4	144.6	143.9	143.0
Non-Hispanic, White [2]	(NA)	413.6	319.9	267.9	226.9	216.3	213.9	214.0	212.3
All ages, crude rate	**368.6**	**297.6**	**249.8**	**222.3**	**202.5**	**211.7**	**213.3**	**216.9**	**220.0**
Under 1 year	25.5	21.9	13.3	9.6	9.8	7.5	7.2	7.8	7.6
1 to 4 years	2.8	1.9	1.4	1.0	1.1	1.0	0.8	0.8	0.7
5 to 14 years	1.0	0.9	0.8	0.6	0.5	0.5	0.5	0.5	0.4
15 to 24 years	3.7	3.1	3.2	3.5	3.2	3.0	2.8	2.8	2.8
25 to 34 years	11.4	10.3	9.6	11.2	10.7	10.3	10.2	10.7	10.1
35 to 44 years	68.7	48.1	41.4	41.3	36.0	35.1	35.5	34.7	35.1
45 to 54 years	282.6	183.0	140.2	131.6	117.8	112.1	112.5	109.1	110.1
55 to 64 years	746.8	537.3	371.7	303.9	269.5	269.4	271.3	273.2	276.3
65 to 74 years	1,728.0	1,250.0	898.3	680.1	553.0	529.7	536.4	538.5	541.9
75 to 84 years	3,834.3	2,968.2	2,248.1	1,815.1	1,475.7	1,354.4	1,312.0	1,306.8	1,282.2
85 years and over	8,752.7	7,418.4	6,430.0	5,713.2	4,833.6	4,495.1	4,403.5	4,421.1	4,358.7
FEMALE									
All ages, age-adjusted [1]	**320.8**	**257.0**	**210.9**	**177.5**	**143.3**	**133.6**	**130.4**	**129.6**	**127.9**
White	315.9	250.9	205.6	173.2	140.4	132.4	128.7	128.4	126.6
Black	378.6	327.5	277.6	234.5	185.3	165.7	166.4	161.9	162.2
American Indian, Alaska Native	175.4	153.1	143.6	129.3	103.5	94.0	89.1	89.3	85.1
Asian, Pacific Islander	132.3	149.2	115.7	97.5	81.2	68.5	68.4	67.6	65.2
Hispanic origin [2]	(NA)	177.2	163.7	139.9	107.8	93.0	92.6	90.1	87.6
Non-Hispanic, White [2]	(NA)	252.6	206.8	174.8	142.5	135.6	131.7	131.9	130.3
All ages, crude rate	**305.1**	**281.8**	**255.3**	**219.0**	**184.9**	**183.1**	**180.4**	**181.2**	**181.3**
Under 1 year	20.0	18.3	12.5	8.2	6.8	7.2	7.6	7.6	7.4
1 to 4 years	2.5	1.9	1.0	0.9	0.9	0.9	0.7	0.8	0.7
5 to 14 years	0.9	0.8	0.5	0.6	0.4	0.5	0.4	0.4	0.4
15 to 24 years	2.1	1.8	2.1	1.7	1.5	1.5	1.5	1.4	1.4
25 to 34 years	5.3	5.0	5.2	5.3	4.9	5.6	5.2	5.5	5.4
35 to 44 years	21.4	15.1	17.2	17.2	15.6	16.2	16.4	16.2	16.0
45 to 54 years	84.5	61.0	49.8	49.1	46.5	47.4	47.4	45.9	45.5
55 to 64 years	272.1	215.7	159.3	128.0	109.3	112.3	113.5	113.9	112.8
65 to 74 years	828.6	616.8	474.0	369.5	284.2	266.2	266.0	265.1	261.4
75 to 84 years	2,497.0	1,893.8	1,475.1	1,213.8	952.7	855.9	826.4	813.5	795.2
85 years and over	7,350.5	6,478.1	5,720.9	4,955.1	4,020.3	3,717.6	3,589.7	3,589.9	3,561.6

NA Not available. [1] Age-adjusted death rates were prepared using the direct method, in which age-specific death rates for a population of interest are applied to a standard population distributed by age. Age adjustment eliminates the differences in observed rates between points in time or among compared population groups that result from age differences in population composition. [2] Persons of Hispanic origin may be of any race. Prior to 1997, excludes data from states lacking a Hispanic-origin item on their death certificates. See text, this section.

Source: U.S. National Center for Health Statistics, *Health, United States, 2017*, September 2018; and CDC WONDER Online database, "Multiple Cause of Death, 1999-2018," <https://wonder.cdc.gov/>, accessed May 2020. See also <http://www.cdc.gov/nchs/hus.htm>.

Table 128. Death Rates For Cerebrovascular Diseases (Stroke) by Sex and Age: 1990 to 2018

[Rates per 100,000 population. Excludes deaths of nonresidents of the United States. Beginning 1999, deaths classified according to the International Classification of Diseases, Tenth Revision (ICD-10); for earlier years, causes of death were classified according to the revisions then in use. Changes in classification of causes of death due to these revisions may result in discontinuities in cause-of-death trends. For explanation of age adjustment, see text, this section]

Characteristics	Total				Male				Female			
	1990	2000	2010	2018	1990	2000	2010	2018	1990	2000	2010	2018
All ages, age-adjusted [1]	65.3	60.9	39.1	37.1	68.5	62.4	39.3	37.6	62.6	59.1	38.3	36.1
All ages, crude rate	57.8	59.6	41.9	45.2	46.7	46.9	34.5	39.0	68.4	71.8	49.1	51.2
Under 1 year	3.8	3.3	3.3	2.5	4.4	3.8	3.2	2.8	3.1	2.7	3.4	2.3
1 to 4 years	0.3	0.3	0.3	0.3	0.3	(B)	0.3	0.3	0.3	0.4	0.3	0.3
5 to 14 years	0.2	0.2	0.2	0.2	0.2	0.2	0.3	0.2	0.2	0.2	0.2	0.2
15 to 24 years	0.6	0.5	0.4	0.3	0.7	0.5	0.5	0.4	0.6	0.5	0.4	0.3
25 to 34 years	2.2	1.5	1.3	1.2	2.1	1.5	1.3	1.4	2.2	1.5	1.2	1.1
35 to 44 years	6.4	5.8	4.6	4.1	6.8	5.8	5.0	4.7	6.1	5.7	4.2	3.6
45 to 54 years	18.7	16.0	13.1	12.3	20.5	17.5	14.9	14.3	17.0	14.5	11.4	10.4
55 to 64 years	47.9	41.0	29.3	30.3	54.3	47.2	34.7	36.0	42.2	35.3	24.3	24.9
65 to 74 years	144.2	128.6	81.7	76.8	166.6	145.0	92.0	88.7	126.7	115.1	72.8	66.3
75 to 84 years	498.0	461.3	288.3	256.0	551.1	490.8	295.2	266.5	466.2	442.1	283.4	247.9
85 years and over	1,628.9	1,589.2	993.8	984.3	1,528.5	1,484.3	892.0	879.8	1,667.6	1,632.0	1,043.0	1,041.9

B Figure too small to meet statistical standards for reliability. [1] See footnote 1, Table 127.

Source: U.S. National Center for Health Statistics, *Health, United States, 2017*, September 2018; and CDC WONDER Online database, "Multiple Cause of Death, 1999-2018," <https://wonder.cdc.gov/>, accessed May 2020. See also <http://www.cdc.gov/nchs/hus.htm>.

Table 129. Death Rates For All and Selected Types of Malignant Neoplasms (Cancer) by Age: 1990 to 2018

[Rates per 100,000 population. Excludes deaths of nonresidents of the United States. Beginning 1999, deaths classified according to the International Classification of Diseases, Tenth Revision (ICD-10); for earlier years, causes of death were classified according to the revisions then in use. Changes in classification of causes of death due to these revisions may result in discontinuities in cause-of-death trends. For explanation of age adjustment, see text, this section. See Appendix III]

Characteristic	1990	2000	2005	2010	2015	2016	2017	2018
All ages, age-adjusted [1]	216.0	199.6	185.1	172.8	158.5	155.8	152.5	149.1
All ages, crude rate	203.2	196.5	189.3	186.2	185.4	185.1	183.9	183.2
Under 1 year	2.3	2.4	1.9	1.6	1.3	1.7	1.4	1.3
1 to 4 years	3.5	2.7	2.4	2.1	2.2	2.4	2.0	2.0
5 to 14 years	3.1	2.5	2.5	2.2	2.1	2.1	2.1	2.1
15 to 24 years	4.9	4.4	4.0	3.7	3.4	3.3	3.2	3.2
25 to 34 years	12.6	9.8	9.2	8.8	8.4	8.5	8.0	8.1
35 to 44 years	43.3	36.6	33.5	28.8	26.9	26.9	26.7	25.8
45 to 54 years	158.9	127.5	118.6	111.6	99.7	96.5	92.7	89.6
55 to 64 years	449.6	366.7	323.9	300.1	284.1	280.6	273.4	269.6
65 to 74 years	872.3	816.3	733.2	666.1	594.3	578.3	567.5	554.4
75 to 84 years	1,348.5	1,335.6	1,272.8	1,202.2	1,100.8	1,081.7	1,060.2	1,031.5
85 years old and over	1,752.9	1,819.4	1,778.2	1,729.5	1,628.6	1,620.3	1,600.3	1,577.7
DEATH RATES FOR MALIGNANT NEOPLASM OF BREASTS FOR FEMALES								
All ages, age-adjusted [1]	33.3	26.8	24.2	22.1	20.3	20.1	19.9	19.7
All ages, crude rate	34.0	29.2	27.4	26.1	25.4	25.3	25.4	25.6
Under 25 years	(B)	(B)	(B)	(B)	(B)	(B)	(B)	(B)
25 to 34 years	2.9	2.3	1.8	1.6	1.8	2.0	1.7	1.8
35 to 44 years	17.8	12.4	11.4	9.8	9.0	9.4	9.1	8.7
45 to 54 years	45.4	33.0	28.7	25.7	23.7	23.5	23.0	21.9
55 to 64 years	78.6	59.3	54.0	47.7	43.3	41.3	41.0	40.5
65 to 74 years	111.7	88.3	78.5	73.9	66.7	64.9	64.0	63.9
75 to 84 years	146.3	128.9	119.6	109.1	101.7	102.6	100.8	103.4
85 years old and over	196.8	205.7	191.2	185.8	173.3	169.6	177.3	176.1
DEATH RATES FOR MALIGNANT NEOPLASM OF TRACHEA, BRONCHUS, AND LUNG								
All ages, age-adjusted [1]	59.3	56.1	52.7	47.6	40.5	38.4	36.6	34.8
All ages, crude rate	56.8	55.3	53.9	51.3	47.9	46.1	44.8	43.5
Under 25 years	(Z)	(Z)	(Z)	(Z)	(Z)	(Z)	(Z)	(Z)
25 to 34 years	0.7	0.5	0.3	0.4	0.3	0.3	0.2	0.3
35 to 44 years	6.8	6.1	5.3	3.3	2.5	2.2	2.1	1.9
45 to 54 years	46.8	31.6	29.7	26.9	20.5	18.6	16.5	15.1
55 to 64 years	160.6	122.4	102.4	85.4	76.8	73.2	70.3	68.5
65 to 74 years	288.4	284.2	256.3	223.9	181.0	167.9	160.5	150.9
75 to 84 years	333.3	370.8	375.0	357.2	306.4	295.4	283.6	267.9
85 years old and over	242.5	302.1	328.2	332.4	316.1	305.2	295.3	286.2

B Base figure too small to meet statistical standards for reliability of a derived figure. Z Less than 0.05. [1] Age-adjusted death rates were prepared using the direct method, in which age specific death rates for a population of interest are applied to a standard population distributed by age. Age adjustment eliminates the differences in observed rates between points in time or among compared population groups that result from age differences in population composition.

Source: U.S. National Center for Health Statistics, *Health, United States, 2017*, September 2018; and CDC WONDER Online database, "Multiple Cause of Death, 1999-2018," <https://wonder.cdc.gov/>, accessed May 2020. See also <http://www.cdc.gov/nchs/hus.htm>.

Table 130. Death Rates For Suicide by Selected Characteristics: 1990 to 2018

[Rates per 100,000 population. Excludes deaths of nonresidents of the United States. Beginning 1999, deaths classified according to the International Classification of Diseases, Tenth Revision (ICD-10). See Appendix III]

Characteristic	1990	2000	2005	2010	2014	2015	2016	2017	2018
All ages, age-adjusted [1]	**12.5**	**10.4**	**10.9**	**12.1**	**13.0**	**13.3**	**13.5**	**14.0**	**14.2**
All ages, crude rate	**12.4**	**10.4**	**11.0**	**12.4**	**13.4**	**13.7**	**13.9**	**14.5**	**14.8**
5 to 14 years	0.8	0.7	0.7	0.7	1.0	1.0	1.1	1.3	1.5
15 to 24 years	13.2	10.2	9.9	10.5	11.6	12.5	13.2	14.5	14.5
25 to 34 years	15.2	12.0	12.7	14.0	15.1	15.7	16.5	17.5	17.6
35 to 44 years	15.3	14.5	15.1	16.0	16.6	17.1	17.4	17.9	18.2
45 to 54 years	14.8	14.4	16.5	19.6	20.2	20.3	19.7	20.2	20.0
55 to 64 years	16.0	12.1	13.7	17.5	18.8	18.9	18.7	19.0	20.2
65 to 74 years	17.9	12.5	12.4	13.7	15.6	15.2	15.4	15.6	16.3
75 to 84 years	24.9	17.6	16.8	15.7	17.5	17.9	18.2	18.0	18.7
85 years and over	22.2	19.6	18.3	17.6	19.3	19.4	19.0	20.1	19.1
AGE-ADJUSTED RATES [1]									
Male	**21.5**	**17.7**	**18.1**	**19.8**	**20.7**	**21.1**	**21.4**	**22.4**	**22.8**
White	22.8	19.1	19.8	22.0	23.3	23.6	23.9	25.1	25.5
Black	12.8	10.0	9.2	9.1	9.5	9.6	10.2	11.0	11.6
Asian, Pacific Islander	9.6	8.6	7.3	9.5	8.9	9.1	10.1	9.7	10.4
American Indian, Alaska Native	20.1	16.0	17.3	15.5	16.4	18.8	20.7	20.4	20.9
Hispanic [2]	13.7	10.3	9.6	9.9	10.3	9.9	10.9	11.2	12.1
Non-Hispanic, White [2]	23.5	20.2	21.4	24.2	25.9	26.6	26.6	28.2	28.4
Female	**4.8**	**4.0**	**4.4**	**5.0**	**5.8**	**6.0**	**6.0**	**6.1**	**6.2**
White	5.2	4.3	4.9	5.6	6.6	6.9	6.9	6.9	7.0
Black	2.4	1.8	1.8	1.8	2.1	2.0	2.4	2.7	2.8
Asian, Pacific Islander	4.1	2.8	3.2	3.4	3.4	4.0	3.6	3.8	3.8
American Indian, Alaska Native	3.6	3.8	4.2	6.1	5.5	6.5	6.4	6.6	6.6
Hispanic [2]	2.3	1.7	1.8	2.1	2.5	2.6	2.6	2.6	2.8
Non-Hispanic, White [2]	5.4	4.7	5.3	6.2	7.5	7.8	7.9	7.9	8.0

[1] Age-adjusted death rates were prepared using the direct method, in which age-specific death rates for a population of interest are applied to a standard population distributed by age. Age adjustment eliminates the differences in observed rates between points in time or among compared population groups that result from age differences in population composition. [2] Persons of Hispanic origin may be of any race. Excludes data from states lacking a Hispanic-origin item on their death certificates.

Source: U.S. National Center for Health Statistics, *Health, United States, 2018*, October 2019; and CDC WONDER Online database, "Multiple Cause of Death, 1999-2018," <https://wonder.cdc.gov/>, accessed May 2020. See also <http://www.cdc.gov/nchs/hus.htm>.

Table 131. Suicide Deaths by Age, Sex, and Method: 2018

[It is generally accepted that children under 5 years of age cannot commit suicide. Deaths based on the International Classification of Diseases, Tenth Revision (ICD-10)]

Method	Total	Age								
		5-14 years	15-24 years	25-34 years	35-44 years	45-54 years	55-64 years	65-74 years	75-84 years	85+ years
Total [1]	**48,344**	**605**	**6,211**	**8,020**	**7,521**	**8,345**	**8,540**	**4,974**	**2,880**	**1,248**
MEN										
Total [1]	**37,761**	**394**	**4,989**	**6,350**	**5,779**	**6,202**	**6,471**	**3,963**	**2,516**	**1,097**
Knife or other sharp object	735	0	30	105	110	152	193	83	42	20
Drowning	327	1	42	64	60	50	50	31	20	9
Fall or jump from high place	841	2	161	172	143	130	106	64	40	23
Fire/flame	153	0	13	26	26	31	31	21	5	0
Firearm	21,101	159	2,650	2,930	2,703	3,103	3,739	2,863	2,074	880
Poisoning	3,137	4	248	441	493	697	716	347	125	66
Hanging, suffocation, strangulation	10,677	223	1,686	2,417	2,126	1,909	1,524	507	193	92
WOMEN										
Total [1]	**10,583**	**211**	**1,222**	**1,670**	**1,742**	**2,143**	**2,069**	**1,011**	**364**	**151**
Knife or other sharp object	162	0	2	19	24	38	46	24	6	3
Drowning	195	0	15	34	23	43	45	23	6	6
Fall or jump from high place	308	3	44	51	55	50	47	33	21	4
Fire/flame	61	0	3	8	13	17	15	4	1	0
Firearm	3,331	44	345	499	519	684	682	374	141	43
Poisoning	3,100	16	206	312	497	699	775	399	128	68
Hanging, suffocation, strangulation	3,163	146	551	700	562	572	410	142	53	27

[1] Includes other methods not shown separately and deaths with age not stated.

Source: U.S. National Center for Health Statistics, CDC WONDER Online database, "Multiple Cause of Death, 1999-2018," <https://wonder.cdc.gov/>, accessed May 2020.

Table 132. Firearm Deaths and Death Rates by Sex and Race/Ethnicity: 2010 to 2018

[Rates are age-adjusted, per 100,000 population, and based on populations enumerated as of April 1 for census years and as of July 1 for all other years. Deaths are those attributable to injury by firearms. Race and Hispanic-origin categories are consistent with 1977 Office of Management and Budget (OMB) standards. From 2003-2018, the number of states reporting multiple-race data according to new 1997 OMB standards varied widely. To provide a comparison of data by race between the 1977 and 1997 OMB standards, those reporting more than one race were "bridged" to single-race categories; see Technical notes, source]

Sex and race/ethnicity	Number of deaths					Age-adjusted rates				
	2010	2015	2016	2017	2018	2010	2015	2016	2017	2018
Total [1]	31,672	36,252	38,658	39,773	39,740	10.1	11.1	11.8	12.0	11.9
Male	27,356	31,032	32,994	34,062	33,955	17.9	19.4	20.5	20.9	20.7
Female	4,316	5,220	5,664	5,711	5,785	2.7	3.2	3.4	3.4	3.4
Non-Hispanic:										
White	20,513	23,026	23,857	24,690	24,789	9.5	10.6	11.0	11.4	11.3
Male	17,350	19,208	19,893	20,686	20,860	16.6	18.0	18.7	19.3	19.4
Female	3,163	3,818	3,964	4,004	3,929	3.0	3.6	3.8	3.8	3.7
Black	7,330	8,904	9,973	10,117	9,801	17.8	20.7	23.0	23.2	22.4
Male	6,607	8,068	8,906	9,107	8,640	33.4	38.6	42.2	42.8	40.5
Female	723	836	1,067	1,010	1,161	3.4	3.8	4.8	4.5	5.2
American Indian or Alaska Native	293	353	390	394	427	11.2	13.3	14.4	14.4	15.6
Male	246	301	323	333	356	18.7	23.0	24.4	24.9	26.4
Female	47	52	67	61	71	3.9	4.0	4.9	4.3	5.3
Asian or Pacific Islander	383	504	584	588	618	2.2	2.5	2.9	2.8	2.9
Male	329	426	480	479	503	4.1	4.4	4.9	4.7	4.9
Female	54	78	104	109	115	0.6	0.8	1.0	1.0	1.0
Hispanic [2]	3,008	3,332	3,771	3,884	4,018	5.9	5.8	6.4	6.5	6.6
Male	2,694	2,912	3,316	3,369	3,521	10.5	10.1	11.2	11.1	11.6
Female	314	420	455	515	497	1.3	1.5	1.6	1.8	1.7

[1] Includes deaths for other races and those not stated, not shown separately. [2] Persons of Hispanic origin may be of any race.

Source: U.S. National Center for Health Statistics, *Deaths: Final Data for 2017, Supplemental Tables*, Vol. 68, No. 9, June 2019; and CDC WONDER Online database "Multiple Cause of Death, 1999-2018," <https://wonder.cdc.gov/>, accessed September 2020. See also <http://www.cdc.gov/nchs/nvss/deaths.htm>.

Table 133. Drug Overdose/Poisoning Deaths and Those Involving Opioids: 1999 to 2018

[Rates are age-adjusted and per 100,000 population. Deaths may involve more than one drug and are classified according to the International Classification of Diseases, Tenth Revision (ICD-10). Opioids include opium, heroin, natural and semisynthetic opioids, methadone, synthetic opioids other than methadone, and other and unspecified narcotics]

Year	Total [1]		Opioids					
			Total [1]		Heroin		Synthetic opioids including fentanyl [2]	
	Number	Rate	Number	Rate	Number	Rate	Number	Rate
1999	16,849	6.1	8,050	2.9	1,960	0.7	730	0.3
2000	17,415	6.2	8,407	3.0	1,842	0.7	782	0.3
2001	19,394	6.8	9,496	3.3	1,779	0.6	957	0.3
2002	23,518	8.2	11,920	4.1	2,089	0.7	1,295	0.4
2003	25,785	8.9	12,940	4.5	2,080	0.7	1,400	0.5
2004	27,424	9.4	13,756	4.7	1,878	0.6	1,664	0.6
2005	29,813	10.1	14,918	5.1	2,009	0.7	1,742	0.6
2006	34,425	11.5	17,545	5.9	2,088	0.7	2,707	0.9
2007	36,010	11.9	18,516	6.1	2,399	0.8	2,213	0.7
2008	36,450	11.9	19,582	6.4	3,041	1.0	2,306	0.8
2009	37,004	11.9	20,422	6.6	3,278	1.1	2,946	1.0
2010	38,329	12.3	21,089	6.8	3,036	1.0	3,007	1.0
2011	41,340	13.2	22,784	7.3	4,397	1.4	2,666	0.8
2012	41,502	13.1	23,166	7.4	5,925	1.9	2,628	0.8
2013	43,982	13.8	25,052	7.9	8,257	2.7	3,105	1.0
2014	47,055	14.7	28,647	9.0	10,574	3.4	5,544	1.8
2015	52,404	16.3	33,091	10.4	12,989	4.1	9,580	3.1
2016	63,632	19.8	42,249	13.3	15,469	4.9	19,413	6.2
2017	70,237	21.7	47,600	14.9	15,482	4.9	28,466	9.0
2018	67,367	20.7	46,802	14.6	14,996	4.7	31,335	9.9

[1] Includes deaths due to other drug types not shown separately. [2] Synthetic opioids other than methadone include drugs such as fentanyl, fentanyl analogs, and tramadol.

Source: U.S. National Center for Health Statistics, CDC WONDER Online database, "Multiple Cause of Death, 1999-2018," <https://wonder.cdc.gov/>, accessed May 2020.

Table 134. Drug Overdose Death Rates by Sex, Age, and Race/Ethnicity: 2000 to 2017

[Rates per 100,000 resident population. Drug overdose deaths include those resulting from accidental or intentional overdose of a drug, being given the wrong drug, taking the wrong drug in error, taking a drug inadvertently, or other misuses of drugs. These deaths are from all manners and intents, including unintentional, suicide, homicide, legal intervention, operations of war, and undetermined intent. Deaths classified according to the International Classification of Diseases, Tenth Revision (ICD-10). See Appendix III]

Characteristic	2000	2005	2010	2012	2013	2014	2015	2016	2017
ALL PERSONS									
All ages, age-adjusted [1]	**6.2**	**10.1**	**12.3**	**13.1**	**13.8**	**14.7**	**16.3**	**19.8**	**21.7**
All ages, crude	**6.2**	**10.1**	**12.4**	**13.2**	**13.9**	**14.8**	**16.3**	**19.7**	**21.6**
Under 15 years old	0.1	0.2	0.2	0.2	0.2	0.2	0.2	0.2	0.2
15 to 24 years old	3.7	6.9	8.2	8.0	8.3	8.6	9.7	12.4	12.6
25 to 34 years old	7.9	13.6	18.4	20.1	20.9	23.1	26.9	34.6	38.4
35 to 44 years old	14.3	19.6	20.8	22.1	23.0	25.0	28.3	35.0	39.0
45 to 54 years old	11.6	21.1	25.1	26.9	27.5	28.2	30.0	34.5	37.7
55 to 64 years old	4.2	9.0	15.0	16.6	19.2	20.3	21.8	25.6	28.0
65 to 74 years old	2.0	3.2	4.7	5.8	6.4	6.9	7.2	8.2	9.2
75 to 84 years old	2.4	3.1	3.4	3.4	3.6	3.6	3.6	3.4	3.6
85 years old and over	4.4	4.1	4.7	4.3	4.3	4.1	4.4	4.0	4.0
AGE-ADJUSTED RATES [1] **MALE**									
Total	**8.3**	**12.8**	**15.0**	**16.1**	**17.0**	**18.3**	**20.8**	**26.2**	**29.1**
White	8.4	13.6	16.8	18.1	19.0	20.4	23.2	28.8	31.6
Black	10.8	12.8	10.1	11.3	12.9	13.8	16.8	24.0	29.7
American Indian, Alaska Native	6.1	10.8	11.8	12.8	12.9	15.9	16.0	17.7	19.7
Asian or Pacific Islander	1.4	2.2	2.5	3.1	3.2	3.3	4.1	4.7	5.2
Hispanic [2]	7.1	8.4	7.6	8.5	9.2	9.3	10.9	13.9	15.9
Non-Hispanic, White	8.6	14.7	19.0	20.4	21.4	23.2	26.2	32.7	35.8
Non-Hispanic, Black	10.9	13.0	10.5	11.6	13.3	14.2	17.3	24.7	30.8
FEMALE									
Total	**4.1**	**7.3**	**9.6**	**10.2**	**10.6**	**11.1**	**11.8**	**13.4**	**14.4**
White	4.3	8.0	10.9	11.6	12.1	12.7	13.6	15.2	16.3
Black	4.1	6.0	5.7	6.0	6.3	7.0	7.5	10.0	11.2
American Indian, Alaska Native	3.7	8.6	9.7	12.2	11.6	11.2	11.3	13.1	12.7
Asian or Pacific Islander	0.8	1.3	1.5	1.4	1.5	1.7	1.5	1.8	2.0
Hispanic [2]	2.0	3.0	3.6	4.0	4.1	4.1	4.4	5.0	5.1
Non-Hispanic, White	4.5	8.8	12.5	13.2	13.8	14.6	15.8	17.7	19.1
Non-Hispanic, Black	4.2	6.2	5.9	6.2	6.5	7.3	7.7	10.4	11.7

[1] Age-adjusted rates are calculated using the year 2000 standard population and were prepared using the direct method, in which age specific death rates for a population of interest are applied to a standard population distributed by age. Age adjustment eliminates the differences in observed rates between points in time or among compared population groups that result from age differences in population composition. [2] Persons of Hispanic origin may be of any race.

Source: U.S. National Center for Health Statistics, *Health, United States, 2018*, October 2019. See also <http://www.cdc.gov/nchs/hus.htm>.

Table 135. Drug Overdose Deaths and Age-adjusted Death Rates Involving Opioids, Benzodiazepines, and Stimulants by Drug: 2011 to 2016

[Age-adjusted rates per 100,000 population. Deaths may involve other drugs in addition to the referent drug and those involving more than one drug are counted in both totals. Deaths classified according to the International Classification of Diseases, Tenth Revision (ICD-10). See Appendix III]

Drug	Deaths						Age-adjusted death rates					
	2011	2012	2013	2014	2015	2016	2011	2012	2013	2014	2015	2016
Total	**41,340**	**41,502**	**43,982**	**47,055**	**52,404**	**63,632**	**13.2**	**13.1**	**13.8**	**14.7**	**16.3**	**19.8**
OPIOIDS												
Fentanyl	1,662	1,615	1,919	4,223	8,251	18,335	0.5	0.5	0.6	1.3	2.6	5.9
Heroin	4,571	6,155	8,418	10,882	13,318	15,961	1.5	2.0	2.7	3.5	4.3	5.1
Hydrocodone	3,206	3,037	3,113	3,299	3,051	3,199	1.0	1.0	1.0	1.0	0.9	1.0
Methadone	4,545	4,087	3,700	3,498	3,376	3,493	1.4	1.3	1.2	1.1	1.1	1.1
Morphine	3,290	3,513	3,772	4,024	4,226	5,014	1.0	1.1	1.2	1.2	1.3	1.5
Oxycodone	5,587	5,178	4,967	5,431	5,792	6,199	1.8	1.7	1.6	1.7	1.8	1.9
BENZODIAZEPINES												
Alprazolam	4,066	3,803	3,724	4,237	4,801	6,209	1.3	1.2	1.2	1.3	1.5	2.0
Diazepam	1,698	1,577	1,618	1,748	1,796	2,022	0.5	0.5	0.5	0.5	0.5	0.6
STIMULANTS												
Cocaine	5,070	4,780	5,319	5,892	7,324	11,316	1.6	1.5	1.7	1.8	2.3	3.6
Methamphetamine	1,887	2,267	3,194	3,747	5,092	6,762	0.6	0.7	1.0	1.2	1.6	2.1

Source: National Center for Health Statistics, National Vital Statistics Reports, "Drugs Most Frequently Involved in Drug Overdose Deaths: United States, 2011-2016," Vol. 67, No. 9, December 2018. See also <https://www.cdc.gov/nchs/products/nvsr.htm>.

Table 136. People Who Got Married and Divorced in the Past 12 Months by State: 2018

[For 12-month period prior to interview date, which occurred for each month in calendar year. For example, a person interviewed in January 2018 could report they got married between January 2017 and January 2018. Data shown for persons 15 years old and over. Vital event is counted in state in which respondent lived at the time of survey. Based on 2018 American Community Survey (ACS). The ACS universe includes the household population and the group quarters population. Based on a sample and subject to sampling variability. See Appendix III]

State	People who got married in the past 12 months				People who got divorced in the past 12 months			
	Males	Marriage rate per 1,000 men	Females	Marriage rate per 1,000 women	Males	Divorce rate per 1,000 men	Females	Divorce rate per 1,000 women
United States............	**2,293,282**	**17.6**	**2,268,129**	**16.6**	**945,533**	**7.3**	**1,052,151**	**7.7**
Alabama....................	33,795	17.8	35,583	17.1	19,260	10.1	20,527	9.8
Alaska.....................	6,321	20.8	5,799	20.8	2,356	7.7	2,105	7.6
Arizona....................	55,319	19.3	57,233	19.5	21,857	7.6	23,552	8.0
Arkansas..................	22,694	19.3	22,435	17.9	12,477	10.6	16,308	13.0
California.................	266,001	16.8	258,534	15.9	98,322	6.2	108,127	6.7
Colorado..................	43,284	18.6	45,244	19.5	21,389	9.2	20,064	8.7
Connecticut..............	20,383	14.2	20,252	13.2	8,607	6.0	10,423	6.8
Delaware.................	6,124	16.0	6,227	15.0	(NA)	(NA)	(NA)	(NA)
District of Columbia.......	7,175	25.9	7,009	22.3	1,322	4.8	1,808	5.8
Florida....................	148,381	17.2	143,698	15.7	64,018	7.4	73,225	8.0
Georgia...................	76,242	18.8	71,030	16.2	34,604	8.5	35,445	8.1
Hawaii....................	12,088	20.8	11,447	19.6	4,550	7.8	3,884	6.7
Idaho.....................	17,584	25.3	15,675	22.6	5,566	8.0	5,667	8.2
Illinois....................	91,940	18.2	88,628	16.7	30,851	6.1	35,231	6.6
Indiana...................	46,963	17.9	45,918	16.6	22,781	8.7	27,448	9.9
Iowa......................	23,797	19.0	22,584	17.5	7,272	5.8	9,214	7.1
Kansas....................	23,264	20.2	22,031	18.8	8,620	7.5	10,116	8.6
Kentucky..................	31,061	17.6	31,308	16.8	18,755	10.6	19,444	10.5
Louisiana.................	30,149	16.7	28,691	14.8	14,418	8.0	14,803	7.6
Maine.....................	6,765	12.3	7,722	13.2	4,818	8.7	4,818	8.3
Maryland..................	41,194	17.4	43,479	16.9	17,986	7.6	19,045	7.4
Massachusetts............	47,651	17.1	46,931	15.6	14,742	5.3	22,596	7.5
Michigan..................	64,531	16.1	66,312	15.8	30,112	7.5	28,985	6.9
Minnesota................	37,858	16.9	38,571	16.9	13,660	6.1	16,315	7.1
Mississippi...............	23,225	20.2	20,618	16.4	9,223	8.0	10,918	8.7
Missouri..................	46,612	19.3	49,442	19.3	21,238	8.8	23,500	9.2
Montana..................	7,117	16.3	6,775	15.6	3,187	7.3	3,975	9.1
Nebraska.................	13,275	17.5	12,452	16.1	5,228	6.9	5,405	7.0
Nevada...................	22,065	18.0	22,960	18.7	11,732	9.6	11,813	9.6
New Hampshire...........	8,051	14.3	9,060	15.5	4,460	7.9	4,878	8.4
New Jersey...............	56,183	15.9	54,029	14.3	17,768	5.0	21,328	5.7
New Mexico...............	12,288	14.7	14,131	16.4	5,581	6.7	5,671	6.6
New York.................	128,479	16.5	125,834	15.0	42,949	5.5	47,864	5.7
North Carolina............	74,132	18.2	69,067	15.7	30,149	7.4	38,011	8.6
North Dakota.............	6,078	19.5	6,397	21.5	2,314	7.4	1,407	4.7
Ohio......................	79,130	17.1	78,938	16.1	32,761	7.1	35,313	7.2
Oklahoma.................	32,359	21.0	32,545	20.3	16,176	10.5	17,258	10.8
Oregon...................	32,608	19.1	32,857	18.7	12,868	7.5	17,783	10.1
Pennsylvania.............	78,914	15.3	80,354	14.7	34,022	6.6	35,302	6.5
Rhode Island.............	6,333	14.7	6,521	14.1	2,215	5.2	2,253	4.9
South Carolina............	28,696	14.4	31,362	14.5	14,659	7.3	16,243	7.5
South Dakota.............	6,624	18.9	6,311	18.0	2,107	6.0	4,248	12.1
Tennessee................	47,886	18.0	49,833	17.4	23,223	8.7	25,881	9.1
Texas.....................	212,137	19.1	206,508	18.1	91,086	8.2	96,494	8.4
Utah......................	27,423	23.0	27,520	23.1	8,929	7.5	11,009	9.3
Vermont..................	4,245	16.3	5,161	19.0	1,182	4.6	1,724	6.3
Virginia...................	65,848	19.4	64,607	18.1	27,296	8.0	28,946	8.1
Washington..............	60,223	19.7	57,667	18.7	21,571	7.1	29,563	9.6
West Virginia.............	11,998	16.2	11,941	15.6	5,494	7.4	7,497	9.8
Wisconsin................	36,753	15.6	37,613	15.6	15,749	6.7	14,995	6.2
Wyoming.................	4,036	17.1	5,285	22.9	1,955	8.3	2,170	9.4

NA Not available.

Source: U.S. Census Bureau, 2018 American Community Survey, B12501, "Marriage in the Last Year by Sex by Marital Status for the Population 15 Years and Over," and B12503, "Divorces in the Last Year by Sex by Marital Status for the Population 15 Years and Over"; <http://data.census.gov>, accessed December 2019.

Table 137. Marriage and Divorce Rates by State: 1990 to 2018

[Rate per 1,000 population residing in area. Population enumerated as of April 1 for 1990, 2000, and 2010; estimated as of July 1 for all other years. Rates are based on provisional counts by state of occurrence. See Appendix III]

State	Marriage rates						Divorce rates [1]					
	1990	2000	2005	2010	2015	2018	1990	2000	2005	2010	2015	2018
United States [2]	**9.8**	**8.2**	**7.6**	**6.8**	**6.9**	**6.5**	**4.7**	**4.0**	**3.6**	**3.6**	**3.1**	**2.9**
Alabama	10.6	10.1	9.2	8.2	7.4	6.8	6.1	5.5	4.9	4.4	3.9	3.7
Alaska	10.2	8.9	8.2	8.0	7.4	6.7	5.5	3.9	4.3	4.7	4.1	3.7
Arizona	10.0	7.5	6.6	5.9	5.9	5.5	6.9	4.6	4.2	3.5	3.6	3.0
Arkansas	15.3	15.4	12.9	10.8	10.0	8.9	6.9	6.4	6.0	5.7	4.8	4.1
California [3]	7.9	5.8	6.4	5.8	6.2	6.0	4.3	(NA)	(NA)	(NA)	(NA)	(NA)
Colorado	9.8	8.3	7.6	6.9	6.8	7.6	5.5	4.7	4.4	4.3	3.7	3.3
Connecticut	7.9	5.7	5.8	5.6	5.3	5.3	3.2	3.3	3.0	2.9	3.1	2.9
Delaware	8.4	6.5	5.9	5.2	5.7	5.2	4.4	3.9	3.8	3.5	3.1	2.8
District of Columbia	8.2	4.9	4.1	7.6	8.2	7.8	4.5	3.2	2.0	2.8	2.8	2.5
Florida	10.9	8.9	8.9	7.3	8.2	7.3	6.3	5.1	4.6	4.4	4.0	3.6
Georgia	10.3	6.8	7.0	7.3	6.2	6.4	5.5	3.3	(NA)	(NA)	(NA)	2.5
Hawaii	16.4	20.6	22.6	17.6	15.9	15.3	4.6	3.9	(NA)	(NA)	(NA)	(NA)
Idaho	13.9	10.8	10.5	8.8	8.2	7.8	6.5	5.5	5.0	5.2	4.1	3.8
Illinois	8.8	6.9	5.9	5.7	5.9	5.5	3.8	3.2	2.6	2.6	2.2	1.5
Indiana	9.6	7.9	6.9	6.3	6.9	6.6	(NA)	(NA)	(NA)	(NA)	(NA)	(NA)
Iowa	9.0	6.9	6.9	6.9	6.3	5.7	3.9	3.3	2.7	2.4	1.2	2.2
Kansas	9.2	8.3	6.8	6.4	5.9	5.4	5.0	3.6	3.1	3.7	2.8	2.3
Kentucky	13.5	9.8	8.7	7.4	7.2	6.8	5.8	5.1	4.6	4.5	3.7	3.5
Louisiana	9.6	9.1	8.0	6.9	6.8	5.1	(NA)	(NA)	(NA)	(NA)	2.8	1.7
Maine	9.7	8.8	8.2	7.1	7.6	7.4	4.3	5.0	4.1	4.2	3.4	3.2
Maryland	9.7	7.5	6.9	5.7	6.2	5.9	3.4	3.3	3.1	2.8	2.6	2.4
Massachusetts	7.9	5.8	6.2	5.6	5.5	6.3	2.8	2.5	2.2	2.5	2.6	2.1
Michigan	8.2	6.7	6.1	5.5	6.0	5.7	4.3	3.9	3.4	3.5	3.0	2.8
Minnesota	7.7	6.8	6.0	5.3	5.6	5.3	3.5	3.2	(NA)	(NA)	(NA)	(NA)
Mississippi	9.4	6.9	5.8	4.9	7.0	6.3	5.5	5.0	4.4	4.3	3.4	2.7
Missouri	9.6	7.8	7.0	6.5	6.8	6.5	5.1	4.5	3.6	3.9	3.2	3.0
Montana	8.6	7.3	7.4	7.4	8.0	7.7	5.1	4.2	4.5	3.9	3.4	3.0
Nebraska	8.0	7.6	7.0	6.6	6.4	6.0	4.0	3.7	3.3	3.6	3.2	2.9
Nevada	99.0	72.2	57.4	38.3	31.0	26.7	11.4	9.9	7.4	5.9	4.6	4.4
New Hampshire	9.5	9.4	7.3	7.3	6.9	6.9	4.7	4.8	3.9	3.8	3.3	3.1
New Jersey	7.6	6.0	5.7	5.1	5.6	5.4	3.0	3.0	2.9	3.0	2.8	2.7
New Mexico	8.8	8.0	6.6	7.7	6.2	6.4	4.9	5.1	4.6	4.0	3.3	(NA)
New York	8.6	7.1	6.8	6.5	7.1	7.1	3.2	3.0	2.9	2.9	2.7	2.8
North Carolina	7.8	8.2	7.3	6.6	7.0	6.4	5.1	4.5	4.1	3.8	3.1	3.1
North Dakota	7.5	7.2	6.8	6.5	6.2	5.7	3.6	3.4	2.9	3.1	2.8	2.6
Ohio	9.0	7.8	6.5	5.8	5.9	5.6	4.7	4.2	3.5	3.4	3.1	2.9
Oklahoma	10.6	(NA)	7.3	7.2	7.4	6.4	7.7	(NA)	5.6	5.2	4.4	3.8
Oregon	8.9	7.6	7.3	6.5	6.9	6.3	5.5	4.8	4.2	4.0	3.4	3.4
Pennsylvania	7.1	6.0	5.8	5.3	5.7	5.5	3.3	3.1	2.3	2.7	2.6	2.6
Rhode Island	8.1	7.6	7.0	5.8	6.4	6.3	3.7	2.9	3.0	3.2	3.0	2.9
South Carolina	15.9	10.6	8.3	7.4	7.5	6.6	4.5	3.8	2.9	3.1	2.8	2.5
South Dakota	11.1	9.4	8.4	7.3	7.2	6.5	3.7	3.5	2.8	3.4	2.6	2.6
Tennessee	13.9	15.5	10.9	8.8	8.5	8.0	6.5	5.9	4.6	4.2	3.7	3.5
Texas	10.5	9.4	7.8	7.1	7.2	6.1	5.5	4.0	3.3	3.3	2.6	2.6
Utah	11.2	10.8	9.8	8.5	8.1	8.4	5.1	4.3	4.1	3.7	3.6	3.8
Vermont	10.9	10.0	8.9	9.3	8.1	7.9	4.5	4.1	3.6	3.8	3.1	3.1
Virginia	11.4	8.8	8.2	6.8	7.0	6.4	4.4	4.3	4.0	3.8	3.3	3.1
Washington	9.5	6.9	6.5	6.0	6.2	6.0	5.9	4.6	4.3	4.2	3.4	3.3
West Virginia	7.2	8.7	7.4	6.7	6.6	6.1	5.3	5.1	5.1	5.1	4.0	3.3
Wisconsin	7.9	6.7	6.1	5.3	5.6	5.4	3.6	3.2	2.9	3.0	2.6	2.5
Wyoming	10.7	10.0	9.3	7.6	7.3	7.1	6.6	5.8	5.2	5.1	4.1	3.8

NA Not available. [1] Includes annulments. Includes divorce petitions filed or legal separations for some counties or States. [2] Beginning 2000, rates based solely on the combined counts and populations for reporting states and the District of Columbia. [3] Marriage data includes nonlicensed marriages registered.

Source: U.S. National Center for Health Statistics, National Vital Statistics System, "Marriages and Divorces, Detailed State Tables," <https://www.cdc.gov/nchs/nvss/marriage-divorce.htm>, accessed February 2020.

Table 138. People Who Got Married or Divorced in the Past 12 Months by Selected Characteristics: 2018

[In units, as indicated (266,322 represents 266,322,000). For 12-month period prior to interview date, which occurred for each month in calendar year. For example, a person interviewed in January 2018 could report they got married between January 2017 and January 2018. Persons 15 years and over. Based on 2018 American Community Survey (ACS). The ACS universe includes the household population and the group quarters population. Based on a sample and subject to sampling variability. See Appendix III]

Characteristic	Total population	Married in the past 12 months		Divorced in the past 12 months	
		Males	Females	Males	Females
Population 15 years old and over (1,000).........................	**266,322**	**2,293**	**2,268**	**946**	**1,052**
AGE					
Median age...	45.8	32.3	30.5	45.7	43.8
EDUCATIONAL ATTAINMENT					
Population 18 years and over (1,000)................................	253,815	2,266	2,242	943	1,051
Bachelor's degree or higher (percent)............................	30.1	33.5	39.7	24.9	29.9
LABOR FORCE PARTICIPATION					
Population 16 years and over (1,000)................................	262,186	2,277	2,257	946	1,052
In labor force (percent)...	63.3	88.8	79.2	79.1	78.3
Not in labor force (percent)..	36.7	11.2	20.8	20.9	21.7
POVERTY STATUS IN PAST 12 MONTHS					
Population for whom poverty status is determined (1,000)..........	259,411	2,252	2,258	919	1,047
Below poverty (percent)...	11.9	6.9	8.0	11.1	19.3
PRESENCE OF OWN CHILD UNDER 18 YEARS					
Population in households (1,000)......................................	258,305	2,248	2,254	915	1,045
With own child under 18 years (percent)...........................	23.2	29.4	31.6	18.9	37.2
HOUSING TENURE					
Population 15 years and over in occupied housing units (1,000)...	258,305	2,248	2,254	915	1,045
Owner-occupied housing units (percent)...........................	67.4	52.3	52.3	55.6	52.0
Renter-occupied housing units (percent)...........................	32.6	47.7	47.7	44.4	48.0

Source: U.S. Census Bureau, 2018 American Community Survey, S1251, "Characteristics of People with a Marital Event in the Last 12 Months," <http://data.census.gov>, accessed December 2019.

Table 139. Marital Status of Population and Number of Times Married by Sex and Median Duration of Marriage: 2010 to 2018

[248,056 represents 248,056,000. Data shown are for the population age 15 years and over. Based on the American Community Survey (ACS). The ACS universe includes the household population and the group quarters population. Based on a sample and subject to sampling variability. See Appendix III]

Characteristic	2010	2012	2013	2014	2015	2016	2017	2018
NUMBER (1,000)								
Population aged 15 years and over......	**248,056**	**252,745**	**255,017**	**257,771**	**260,415**	**262,140**	**264,697**	**266,322**
Male...	120,743	123,175	124,380	125,665	127,013	127,864	129,186	129,974
Never married..................................	42,741	44,292	45,175	45,865	46,677	47,195	47,654	48,052
Ever married....................................	78,001	78,883	79,205	79,800	80,336	80,669	81,532	81,921
Once...	58,734	59,349	59,667	60,106	60,648	60,898	61,580	61,927
Two times....................................	15,183	15,382	15,284	15,406	15,381	15,438	15,592	15,635
Three or more times........................	4,085	4,152	4,253	4,287	4,307	4,333	4,359	4,359
Female...	127,313	129,571	130,637	132,106	133,402	134,277	135,511	136,349
Never married..................................	36,899	38,367	39,145	39,944	40,667	41,143	41,442	41,880
Ever married....................................	90,414	91,203	91,492	92,162	92,734	93,134	94,070	94,469
Once...	68,330	68,939	69,185	69,723	70,088	70,419	71,248	71,413
Two times....................................	17,449	17,620	17,533	17,642	17,776	17,838	17,945	18,110
Three or more times........................	4,636	4,644	4,774	4,796	4,871	4,876	4,876	4,945
PERCENT DISTRIBUTION								
Male:								
Never married..................................	35.4	36.0	36.3	36.5	36.7	36.9	36.9	37.0
Ever married....................................	64.6	64.0	63.7	63.5	63.3	63.1	63.1	63.0
Once...	48.6	48.2	48.0	47.8	47.7	47.6	47.7	47.6
Two times....................................	12.6	12.5	12.3	12.3	12.1	12.1	12.1	12.0
Three or more times........................	3.4	3.4	3.4	3.4	3.4	3.4	3.4	3.4
Female:								
Never married..................................	29.0	29.6	30.0	30.2	30.5	30.6	30.6	30.7
Ever married....................................	71.0	70.4	70.0	69.8	69.5	69.4	69.4	69.3
Once...	53.7	53.2	53.0	52.8	52.5	52.4	52.6	52.4
Two times....................................	13.7	13.6	13.4	13.4	13.3	13.3	13.2	13.3
Three or more times........................	3.6	3.6	3.7	3.6	3.7	3.6	3.6	3.6
Median duration of marriage (years) [1]........	19.0	19.3	19.5	19.5	19.6	19.7	19.7	19.7

[1] Data shown for current marriage.

Source: U.S. Census Bureau, American Community Survey, B12504, "Median Duration of Current Marriage in Years By Sex By Marital Status for the Married Population 15 years and Over," and B12505, "Number of Times Married by Sex By Marital Status for the Population 15 Years and Over"; <http://data.census.gov>, accessed December 2019.

Health and Nutrition

This section presents statistics on numerous indicators of the nation's health care system, the health care industry and its institutions, and the health of the population. Data in this section cover national and personal health expenditures, health insurance coverage, Medicare and Medicaid, medical personnel, hospitals, nursing homes and other health care facilities, injuries, diseases, vaccinations, disability status, substance use (including alcohol, tobacco, and illicit drug use), exercise, food consumption, and nutrition. This section also includes data on selected health conditions and indicators among children.

Also appearing in this section is a table showing weekly trends in cases of coronavirus infections and hospitalizations for the coronavirus disease, COVID-19, as available during the time of production of this *Abstract*. The data presented here are an illustration of the progression of the pandemic in the U.S.; please see the table source noted for revised and up-to-date data.

Data on national health expenditures, medical costs, and insurance coverage are compiled by the U.S. Centers for Medicare & Medicaid Services (CMS) and appear on the CMS website at <cms.gov/ NationalHealthExpendData/>. In the past, Medicare and Medicaid data came from the annual *Medicare and Medicaid Statistical Supplement,* but this report was discontinued after the 2013 release, and has been replaced with "CMS Program Statistics." Internet users can use the online CMS Program Statistics tool to obtain data on Medicare enrollment, utilization, and expenditures, and also data on Medicare-certified institutional and noninstitutional health care providers. Another key source of information on Medicare is the annual report to Congress from the Boards of Trustees for Medicare. The Trustees' report covers the financial operations and actuarial status of Medicare. Selected data on Medicaid and the Children's Health Insurance Program (CHIP) are available from the Medicaid.gov website, the U.S. National Center for Health Statistics (NCHS), and the Medicaid and CHIP Payment and Access Commission, a nonpartisan legislative branch agency that provides analysis to the states, Congress, and the Secretary of the Department of Health and Human Services.

Summary statistics showing recent trends in health care and health indicators of the population, and discussions of selected health issues are published annually by the NCHS in *Health, United States.* Statistics on health insurance are collected by surveys conducted by the Census Bureau. The NCHS also collects health insurance data and other detailed data on the population's health status annually in its National Health Interview Survey, the results of which are released in brief reports under the Early Release Program, and in online summary tables. After issuing reports covering the 2012 NHIS, the NCHS discontinued issuing NHIS data in *Vital and Health Statistics* Series 10 reports. NCHS also operates other programs to track various health indicators such as food and nutrition, exercise, body weight, and incidence of high blood cholesterol and blood pressure (hypertension).

Statistics on hospitals are published annually by the Health Forum, LLC, an affiliate of the American Hospital Association (AHA), in *AHA Hospital Statistics.* As a proxy for actual food consumption, the U.S. Dept of Agriculture's Economic Research Service provides data on food availability online at <ers.usda.gov/data- products/food-availability-per-capita-data-system/>. Available from the USDA's Agricultural Research Service are data compiled by the Food Surveys Research Group for the *What We Eat In America* program on nutrient and energy consumption.

National health expenditures—CMS compiles estimates of national health expenditures (NHE) to measure spending for health care in the United States. The NHE accounts are structured to show spending by type of expenditure: hospital care, physician and clinical care, dental care, and other professional care; home health care; retail sales of prescription drugs; other medical nondurable goods; nursing home care and other personal health expenditures; other health expenditures such as public health activities, administration, and the net cost of private health insurance; and medical sector investment, which is the sum of noncommercial medical research and capital formation in medical sector structures and equipment. The NHE also shows spending by source of funding (e.g., private health insurance, Medicare, Medicaid, out-of-pocket payments, and other third party payers and programs).

Data used to estimate health expenditures come from numerous public and private sources. The expenditure type estimates rely upon statistics produced by such groups as the AHA, the Census Bureau, and the U.S. Department of Health and Human Services (HHS). Funding source estimates are constructed using administrative and statistical records from the Medicare and Medicaid programs, the U.S. Department of Defense and Veterans Affairs medical programs, the Social Security Administration, the Census Bureau, state and local governments, other HHS agencies, and other nongovernment sources.

The Health Care Satellite Account (HCSA), developed by the Bureau of Economic Analysis, is a tool that measures health care spending as the cost to treat specific diseases and medical conditions (such as cancer, or diseases of the circulatory system), as opposed to spending on specific types of health care services (physician services, or prescription drugs). The HCSA can help answer questions regarding whether changes in medical expenditures are due to changes in costs of treatments or changes in number of persons receiving care, which medical conditions account for larger portions of spending, and which medical conditions experience the greatest changes in treatment costs. The BEA presents two versions of the HCSA. One version, the "MEPS Account," uses data from the Medical Expenditure Panel Survey; the other version, the "Blended Account," combines data from multiple sources, including large claims databases that cover millions of health insurance enrollees and billions of claims. The table in this section presents data from the Blended Account. See <bea.gov/data/special-topics/health-care> for detailed information about how the Health Care Satellite Account is constructed.

Medicare, Medicaid, and Children's Health Insurance Program (CHIP)—The Original Medicare program has two components. Hospital Insurance (HI), also known as Medicare Part A, helps pay for in-patient hospital stays, care in a skilled nursing facility, hospice care, and home health care after hospital stays. Supplementary Medical Insurance (SMI) consists of Medicare Part B and Part D. Part B coverage is optional, and helps pay for physician and outpatient hospital care services, durable medical equipment, and preventive services. Part D provides subsidized access to drug insurance coverage on a voluntary basis for all beneficiaries, and premium and cost-sharing subsidies for low-income enrollees. Participants in Parts B and D pay monthly premiums. In addition to covering persons age 65 and older, Medicare covers persons under age 65 with a disability and who have been receiving for the past 24 months disability benefits from Social Security or the Railroad Retirement Board; persons of any age with ALS (Amyotrophic Lateral Sclerosis, also known as Lou Gehrig's disease); and persons of any age with end-stage renal disease. Medicare's HI and SMI have separate trust funds, sources of revenue, and categories of expenditures.

Medicare also has an alternative option to Original Medicare coverage, the Medicare Advantage Plan (also known as Part C). Medicare Advantage plans are offered by private companies and organizations, are required to provide at least services covered by Medicare Parts A and B (except hospice services), and are financed from both Medicare's Hospital Insurance (HI) trust fund and the Part B account within the Supplementary Medical Insurance (SMI) trust fund in proportion to the relative weights of Part A and Part B benefits to the total benefits paid by the Medicare program.

Medicaid is a health insurance program for certain low-income people, families and children, pregnant women, the elderly, and people with disabilities. There are special rules for those who live in nursing homes and for disabled children living at home. Medicaid is funded and administered through a federal-state partnership. Although there are broad federal requirements for Medicaid, states have a wide degree of flexibility to design their programs.

The Children's Health Insurance Program Reauthorization Act of 2009 (CHIPRA or Public Law 111-3) reauthorized CHIP, which was originally signed into law in 1997. The program went into effect on April 1, 2009. CHIP replaced the State Children's Health Insurance Program (SCHIP). It preserves coverage for the millions of children who rely on CHIP, and provides the resources for states to reach millions of additional children who would otherwise be without health insurance coverage. CHIP is a federal-state partnership, similar to Medicaid, that expands health insurance to children whose families earn too much money to be eligible for Medicaid, but not enough money to purchase private health insurance. CHIPRA also gives states the option to provide prenatal, delivery, and postpartum care to low-income pregnant women without health insurance. Under CHIP, states can operate their programs as an expansion of Medicaid, a program entirely separate from Medicaid, or a combination of both approaches. Most states have either expanded Medicaid or run a combination of both types of programs. Only two states, Connecticut and Washington, run separate programs without Medicaid expansions.

Health care resources and utilization—Hospital statistics based on data from AHA's yearly survey are published annually in *AHA Hospital Statistics* and cover all hospitals accepted for registration by the Association. Up until fiscal year 2016, the AHA used its own detailed criteria for recognizing hospitals for registration. Beginning with fiscal year 2017, the AHA no longer uses its own methodology to classify hospitals as registered for inclusion in its database, and now uses the following definition: an institution is a hospital if it is licensed as a general or specialty hospital by the appropriate state agency and accredited by one of the following organizations: The Joint Commission, Healthcare Facilities Accreditation Program (HFAP), DNV Health Accreditation, Center for Improvement in Healthcare Quality Accreditation, or Medicare certified as a provider of acute services under Title 18 of the Social Security Act.

Ambulatory care data, including emergency room visits, are presented here from the National Hospital Ambulatory Medical Care Survey (NHAMCS). Data on physicians generally come from the professional organizations that collect data on medical school graduates and physicians. Statistics on patient visits to health care providers come from the National Health Interview Survey and the National Ambulatory Medical Care Survey.

Disability and illness, mental health, and substance use—General health statistics, including morbidity, disability, injuries, preventive care, and findings from physiological testing are collected by NCHS in its National Health Interview Survey and its National Health and Nutrition Examination Surveys. The Centers for Disease Control and Prevention in Atlanta, Georgia is responsible for collecting and publishing data on nationally notifiable diseases. Data are collected from State health departments and territories under the National Notifiable Diseases Surveillance System (NNDSS), which is operated by the CDC in collaboration with the Council of State and Territorial Epidemiologists. The list of diseases is revised annually. The Substance Abuse and Mental Health Services Administration, an agency within HHS, studies and provides data regarding mental health disorders and treatment (including mental health treatment facilities and clients), and substance use (including tobacco, alcohol, and prescription and illicit drugs).

Statistical reliability—For discussion of statistical collection, estimation, and sampling procedures and measures of reliability applicable to data from NCHS and CMS, see Appendix III.

Table 140. National Health Expenditures by Type of Service—Summary: 1960 to 2018

[In billions of dollars (27.2 represents $27,200,000,000). Excludes Puerto Rico and Island Areas. For definitions, methodology, and related information, see <https://www.cms.gov/files/document/definitions-sources-and-methods-2>]

Year	Total expenditures [1]	Health consumption expenditures, total [2]	Personal health care expenditures									
			Total [3]	Hospital care	Physician and clinical services	Dental services	Other professional services [4]	Home health care [5]	Nursing care facilities [6]	Prescription drugs	Durable medical equipment [7]	Nondurable medical equipment [8]
1960....	27.2	24.7	23.3	9.0	5.6	2.0	0.4	0.1	0.8	2.7	0.7	1.6
1961....	29.1	26.3	24.8	9.8	5.8	2.1	0.4	0.1	0.8	2.7	0.8	1.8
1962....	31.8	28.4	26.7	10.4	6.3	2.2	0.4	0.1	0.9	3.0	0.9	1.9
1963....	34.6	30.9	29.1	11.5	7.1	2.4	0.5	0.1	1.0	3.2	0.9	1.9
1964....	38.4	34.1	32.0	12.5	8.1	2.6	0.5	0.1	1.2	3.3	1.0	2.1
1965....	41.9	37.2	34.7	13.5	8.6	2.8	0.5	0.1	1.4	3.7	1.1	2.2
1966....	46.1	41.2	38.4	15.3	9.3	3.0	0.6	0.1	1.7	4.0	1.2	2.4
1967....	51.6	46.5	43.5	17.8	10.4	3.4	0.6	0.2	2.2	4.2	1.1	2.5
1968....	58.4	52.7	49.1	20.5	11.3	3.7	0.6	0.2	2.9	4.7	1.3	2.7
1969....	65.9	59.1	55.5	23.4	12.7	4.2	0.7	0.3	3.4	5.1	1.5	3.0
1970....	74.6	67.0	63.1	27.2	14.3	4.7	0.7	0.2	4.0	5.5	1.7	3.3
1971....	82.7	74.3	69.4	30.2	15.9	5.2	0.8	0.2	4.6	5.9	1.8	3.5
1972....	92.7	83.4	77.2	33.8	17.7	5.6	0.9	0.2	5.2	6.3	2.0	3.7
1973....	102.8	93.1	86.2	37.9	19.6	6.4	1.0	0.3	6.0	6.8	2.2	4.0
1974....	116.5	105.9	98.8	44.1	22.2	7.1	1.2	0.4	6.9	7.4	2.5	4.5
1975....	133.3	121.1	113.2	51.2	25.3	8.0	1.3	0.6	8.0	8.1	2.8	4.9
1976....	152.7	139.3	129.3	59.4	28.7	9.0	1.6	0.9	9.1	8.7	3.0	5.4
1977....	173.9	159.9	146.7	67.0	33.1	10.1	2.1	1.1	10.3	9.2	3.2	6.1
1978....	195.3	180.0	164.2	75.6	35.8	11.0	2.4	1.6	11.8	9.9	3.4	7.1
1979....	221.5	204.6	187.1	86.2	41.2	12.0	2.8	1.9	13.3	10.7	3.8	8.5
1980....	255.3	235.5	217.0	100.5	47.7	13.3	3.5	2.4	15.3	12.0	4.1	9.8
1981....	296.2	273.4	251.8	117.5	55.6	15.7	4.3	2.9	17.3	13.4	4.3	11.3
1982....	334.0	308.0	283.1	133.6	61.6	17.0	4.9	3.5	19.5	15.0	4.6	12.6
1983....	367.8	339.5	311.7	144.7	68.6	18.3	5.7	4.2	21.7	17.3	5.3	13.8
1984....	405.0	375.1	341.6	154.4	77.4	19.9	7.3	5.1	23.7	19.6	6.1	15.0
1985....	442.9	412.8	376.4	164.6	90.9	21.7	8.1	5.6	26.2	21.8	7.1	16.0
1986....	474.7	443.7	408.8	175.6	100.7	23.2	9.3	6.4	28.6	24.3	8.1	17.1
1987....	516.5	482.3	447.7	189.5	112.8	25.3	11.3	6.6	30.6	26.9	9.5	18.3
1988....	579.3	540.5	498.5	206.5	128.4	27.4	13.7	8.4	34.2	30.6	11.1	19.4
1989....	644.8	602.3	550.4	226.0	142.9	29.4	14.5	10.2	38.6	34.8	11.9	20.8
1990....	721.4	674.1	615.3	250.4	158.4	31.6	17.3	12.5	44.7	40.3	13.8	22.4
1991....	788.1	737.7	675.9	275.8	175.8	33.4	18.6	15.1	49.2	44.4	13.1	23.2
1992....	854.1	798.7	731.5	298.5	190.2	37.1	20.9	18.7	52.8	47.0	13.5	23.2
1993....	916.6	857.7	778.7	315.7	201.4	39.0	23.0	22.7	55.8	49.6	14.1	23.7
1994....	967.2	905.7	820.2	328.4	210.5	41.6	24.0	27.3	58.4	53.0	15.3	24.3
1995....	1,021.6	958.2	869.6	339.3	220.3	44.6	26.7	32.3	64.2	59.8	15.9	25.1
1996....	1,074.4	1,009.6	917.5	350.8	228.4	46.9	28.9	35.7	69.2	68.1	17.4	26.0
1997....	1,135.2	1,064.8	969.2	363.4	238.9	50.3	31.3	36.9	74.1	77.6	19.2	27.6
1998....	1,201.5	1,126.3	1,025.6	374.9	256.5	53.6	33.4	34.1	79.1	88.5	21.4	28.6
1999....	1,277.7	1,197.0	1,085.7	393.6	269.5	57.3	34.6	32.8	80.6	104.6	23.0	30.6
2000....	1,369.2	1,285.9	1,161.5	415.5	288.2	62.1	36.6	32.3	85.0	121.0	25.2	31.6
2001....	1,486.2	1,398.8	1,261.4	449.4	312.7	67.7	40.3	34.3	90.8	139.0	25.1	32.3
2002....	1,628.7	1,531.9	1,367.1	486.5	337.7	73.6	43.3	36.5	94.5	157.9	27.1	33.3
2003....	1,767.6	1,663.9	1,477.2	525.9	364.3	76.3	46.5	40.2	100.1	176.7	28.5	36.2
2004....	1,895.8	1,784.4	1,587.5	565.3	389.4	82.2	50.2	44.6	105.1	192.8	30.4	38.1
2005....	2,023.8	1,904.1	1,695.7	608.6	413.0	87.2	52.8	49.3	111.4	205.2	32.4	40.8
2006....	2,156.2	2,031.0	1,804.3	651.2	434.7	91.8	55.3	52.1	115.9	224.1	34.4	43.7
2007....	2,294.4	2,156.0	1,917.6	691.9	457.5	97.7	60.1	57.5	124.9	234.9	37.1	47.8
2008....	2,397.1	2,249.0	2,008.8	725.6	481.9	102.7	64.5	62.3	130.5	239.6	37.7	49.5
2009....	2,491.8	2,352.8	2,111.4	779.6	497.7	103.1	67.0	67.7	135.2	249.5	37.8	50.4
2010....	2,593.2	2,450.5	2,191.4	822.3	512.6	105.9	69.9	71.6	140.5	248.4	39.9	51.3
2011....	2,682.6	2,533.4	2,267.3	851.9	535.9	108.0	72.8	74.6	145.4	251.9	42.3	52.9
2012....	2,791.0	2,637.7	2,361.1	902.5	557.1	109.7	76.4	78.3	147.4	253.0	43.7	53.9
2013....	2,875.0	2,720.9	2,431.2	937.6	569.6	111.2	78.7	81.4	149.0	258.2	45.1	56.0
2014....	3,025.4	2,875.6	2,556.0	978.2	595.7	113.8	83.0	84.8	152.4	292.4	46.7	57.5
2015....	3,199.6	3,045.5	2,710.2	1,034.6	631.2	118.8	87.8	89.2	158.1	317.1	48.6	60.2
2016....	3,347.4	3,190.7	2,838.3	1,089.5	665.6	124.9	92.7	93.0	163.0	322.3	51.0	62.7
2017....	3,487.3	3,319.0	2,954.5	1,140.6	696.9	129.6	97.5	97.1	166.2	326.8	52.4	64.1
2018....	3,649.4	3,475.0	3,075.5	1,191.8	725.6	135.6	103.9	102.2	168.5	335.0	54.9	66.4

[1] Includes Health Consumption Expenditures plus, not shown here, expenditures for noncommercial medical research, and medical structures and equipment. [2] Includes Personal Health Expenditures plus, not shown, expenditures for government administration, net cost of health insurance, and government public health activities. [3] Includes items shown here, and also other health, residential, and personal services. [4] Includes health practitioners other than physicians and dentists, such as, but not limited to, chiropractors, optometrists, physical, occupational, and speech therapists, podiatrists, and private-duty nurses. [5] Services delivered by freestanding home health care facilities only. [6] Care provided in nursing care facilities (NAICS 6231), continuing care retirement communities (623311), state and local government nursing facilities, and nursing facilities operated by the Department of Veterans Affairs. [7] Retail sales of items such as contact lenses, eyeglasses and other ophthalmic products, surgical and orthopedic products, medical equipment rental, oxygen, and hearing aids. Durable products generally last over 3 years. [8] Non-prescription drugs and sundry medical items.

Source: U.S. Centers for Medicare and Medicaid Services, Office of the Actuary, National Health Statistics Group, "National Health Expenditure Data, Historical," <https://www.cms.gov/Research-Statistics-Data-and-Systems/Statistics-Trends-and-Reports/NationalHealthExpendData/index>, accessed December 2019.

Table 141. National Health Expenditures by Source of Funds: 1990 to 2018

[In billions of dollars (721.4 represents $721,400,000,000), except percent. Excludes Puerto Rico and Island Areas. For definitions and related information, see <https://www.cms.gov/files/document/definitions-sources-and-methods-2>]

Source of funds	1990	2000	2005	2010	2015	2016	2017	2018
National health expenditure, total	**721.4**	**1,369.2**	**2,023.8**	**2,593.2**	**3,199.6**	**3,347.4**	**3,487.3**	**3,649.4**
Annual percent change [1]	11.9	7.2	6.8	4.1	5.8	4.6	4.2	4.6
Percent of gross domestic product	12.1	13.4	15.5	17.3	17.6	17.9	17.9	17.7
Consumer out of pocket	137.9	198.9	263.8	300.2	341.7	357.2	365.2	375.6
Health insurance	439.1	919.0	1,414.0	1,871.2	2,373.4	2,487.5	2,592.3	2,729.0
Private health insurance	233.9	458.0	701.1	858.5	1,060.9	1,119.9	1,175.0	1,243.1
Medicare	110.2	224.8	339.8	519.8	648.8	676.8	705.1	750.2
Medicaid (Title XIX)	73.7	200.4	309.4	397.4	542.6	565.4	580.1	597.4
CHIP (Title XIX and Title XXI)	(X)	3.0	7.6	11.5	14.7	16.8	18.1	18.6
Department of Defense	10.4	13.7	26.5	38.3	41.6	41.2	41.9	41.7
Department of Veterans Affairs	10.9	19.1	29.8	45.7	64.7	67.4	72.1	78.0
Other third party payers and programs	77.1	124.9	169.0	203.4	244.6	257.3	270.1	276.9
Worksite health care	2.2	3.5	4.3	4.7	6.2	6.7	6.9	7.2
Other private revenues [2]	29.2	57.2	70.7	99.1	122.1	133.6	145.5	149.2
Indian health services	1.0	1.9	2.4	3.5	3.7	3.9	3.9	4.1
Workers' compensation	17.5	26.5	41.5	36.5	48.3	48.7	48.0	47.6
General assistance	5.0	3.9	6.3	7.1	6.7	6.2	5.9	6.1
Maternal and Child health	1.7	3.2	3.4	3.9	3.8	3.7	3.9	4.0
Vocational rehabilitation	0.3	0.4	0.5	0.6	0.5	0.5	0.5	0.6
Other federal programs [3]	1.6	4.5	6.4	7.7	12.6	12.4	12.2	12.8
Substance Abuse and Mental Health Services Administration	1.4	2.6	3.2	3.4	3.5	3.8	4.5	5.5
Other state and local programs [4]	15.9	18.7	26.9	32.6	32.3	32.9	33.4	34.4
School health	1.3	2.5	3.4	4.3	4.8	5.0	5.3	5.6
Public health activity [5]	20.0	43.1	57.3	75.7	85.8	88.7	91.4	93.5
Investment	**47.3**	**83.3**	**119.7**	**142.7**	**154.1**	**156.7**	**168.3**	**174.4**
Research [6]	12.7	25.5	40.3	49.1	46.4	47.4	50.1	52.6
Structures & equipment [7]	34.6	57.8	79.4	93.5	107.7	109.3	118.2	121.8

X Not applicable. [1] Average percent change from prior year. [2] Most common source is philanthropy; support can come from individuals or through philanthropic fund-raising organizations, and also from foundations or corporations. [3] Includes federal general hospital/medical, and pre-existing conditions insurance plans. [4] Includes temporary disability insurance, and state and local subsidies to providers. [5] Governments provide health services such as epidemiological surveillance, inoculations, immunization/vaccination services, disease prevention programs, and public health laboratories. In the National Health Expenditure Accounts, spending for these activities is reported in government public health activity. [6] Non-profit or government entities. Excludes R&D expenditures by drug and medical supply and equipment manufacturers. [7] Structures are defined as the value of new construction by the medical sector. Equipment includes the value of new capital equipment (including software). Includes establishments that provide health care, and excludes retail establishments that sell non-durable or durable medical goods. Excludes maintenance and repairs.

Source: U.S. Centers for Medicare and Medicaid Services, Office of the Actuary, National Health Statistics Group, "National Health Expenditure Data, Historical," <http://cms.gov/nationalhealthexpenddata>, accessed December 2019.

Table 142. National Health Expenditure Projections by Source of Funds and Type of Expenditure: 2019 to 2027

[In billions of dollars (3,823.1 represents $3,823,100,000,000). For calendar years. Projections are based on the 2016 version of the National Health Expenditures (NHE) released in December 2017; projections as of February 2018. Methodology available at <https://www.cms.gov/NationalHealthExpendData/Downloads/ProjectionsMethodology.pdf>. Excludes Puerto Rico and Island Areas]

Funding source and expenditure type	2019	2020	2021	2022	2023	2024	2025	2026	2027
Total	**3,823.1**	**4,031.1**	**4,255.2**	**4,501.5**	**4,767.1**	**5,048.7**	**5,344.8**	**5,650.8**	**5,963.2**
SOURCE OF FUNDS									
Consumer out-of-pocket	396.9	415.5	434.6	458.2	481.3	506.2	532.3	558.8	585.8
Health insurance	2,850.6	3,013.0	3,189.8	3,382.9	3,594.4	3,818.5	4,053.7	4,297.3	4,545.8
Private health insurance [1]	1,278.2	1,344.2	1,409.3	1,476.1	1,555.2	1,638.4	1,723.9	1,810.0	1,896.7
Medicare	800.1	857.7	926.1	1,000.9	1,080.4	1,165.7	1,254.5	1,341.2	1,436.8
Medicaid	623.4	654.6	689.8	732.7	777.1	823.9	875.6	936.6	992.1
Other health insurance programs [2]	148.8	156.5	164.6	173.2	181.7	190.4	199.6	209.5	220.2
Other third party payers and programs	575.5	602.6	630.8	660.5	691.4	724.1	758.8	794.7	831.7
TYPE OF EXPENDITURE									
Health consumption expenditures [3]	3,637.6	3,835.9	4,049.6	4,284.7	4,538.5	4,807.7	5,090.4	5,382.5	5,679.9
Personal health care	3,242.5	3,412.6	3,601.5	3,811.1	4,037.8	4,278.2	4,531.0	4,792.7	5,058.4
Hospital care	1,254.7	1,318.7	1,390.1	1,471.3	1,559.3	1,652.4	1,751.6	1,858.1	1,961.6
Physician and clinical services	767.6	808.8	853.7	900.0	950.3	1,004.4	1,061.3	1,115.8	1,172.0
Dental services	139.9	146.4	153.3	161.3	169.8	178.5	187.2	195.6	203.9
Other professional services [4]	106.2	112.0	118.5	125.6	133.1	141.2	149.0	156.8	165.3
Home health care [5]	108.8	116.1	124.2	133.0	142.4	152.6	163.4	174.7	186.8
Nursing care facilities and continuing care retirement communities [6]	178.0	186.3	195.5	206.2	217.8	230.2	243.2	256.7	270.7
Prescription drugs	360.3	378.9	400.4	425.2	452.4	481.2	511.1	542.9	576.7
Durable medical equipment	60.9	64.6	68.6	72.8	77.5	82.2	87.2	92.4	97.8
Nondurable medical products	69.3	73.0	76.9	81.2	85.6	90.2	95.0	99.9	105.0
Other health, residential, and personal care [7]	196.9	207.8	220.3	234.5	249.5	265.4	282.0	299.7	318.6
Government public health activity [8]	93.6	96.2	99.1	102.8	106.5	110.4	114.7	119.2	123.2
Research [9]	56.2	59.0	62.0	65.2	68.4	71.8	75.3	79.0	83.3
Structures & equipment [10]	129.3	136.1	143.6	151.7	160.2	169.3	179.0	189.3	200.0

[1] Includes employer sponsored insurance and other private insurance, which also includes marketplace plans. [2] Children's Health Insurance Program (Titles XIX and XXI), Department of Defense, and Department of Veterans' Affairs. [3] See footnote 2, Table 140. [4] See footnote 4, Table 140. [5] See footnote 5, Table 140. [6] See footnote 6, Table 140. [7] See footnote 4, Table 143. [8] See footnote 5, Table 141. [9] See footnote 6, Table 141. [10] See footnote 7, Table 141.

Source: U.S. Centers for Medicare and Medicaid Services, Office of the Actuary, National Health Statistics Group, "National Health Expenditure Data, Projected," <http://cms.gov/nationalhealthexpenddata>, accessed December 2019.

Table 143. Health Consumption Expenditures—Per Capita Spending by Type of Expenditure: 2000 to 2018

[In dollars, except percent. Based on U.S. Census Bureau estimates of total U.S. resident population. Health consumption expenditures include all personal health care spending, government administration and the net cost of private health insurance, and public health activities. Excludes investment in research, structures, and equipment. Excludes Puerto Rico and Island Areas]

Type of expenditure	2000	2005	2010	2013	2014	2015	2016	2017	2018
Total [1]	**4,560**	**6,448**	**7,932**	**8,624**	**9,047**	**9,514**	**9,893**	**10,224**	**10,638**
Annual percent change [2]	(NA)	5.7	3.3	2.4	4.9	5.2	4.0	3.3	4.0
Hospital care	1,474	2,061	2,662	2,972	3,078	3,232	3,378	3,513	3,649
Physician and clinical services	1,022	1,399	1,659	1,805	1,874	1,972	2,064	2,147	2,221
Dental services	220	295	343	353	358	371	387	399	415
Other professional services [3]	130	179	226	250	261	274	287	300	318
Other health, residential, and personal care [4]	227	322	418	457	477	514	538	564	587
Home health care	115	167	232	258	267	279	288	299	313
Nursing care facilities and continuing care retirement communities	302	377	455	472	479	494	505	512	516
Prescription drugs	429	695	804	818	920	990	999	1,007	1,026
Durable medical equipment [5]	89	110	129	143	147	152	158	161	168
Other nondurable medical products [6]	112	138	166	178	181	188	194	197	203
Public health activities [7]	153	194	245	250	258	268	275	281	286

NA Not available. [1] Includes other items, not shown separately. [2] Average annual growth from previous year. [3] See footnote 4, Table 140. [4] Includes expenditures for residential care facilities (NAICS 623210 and 623220), ambulance providers (NAICS 621910), medical care delivered in non-traditional settings (such as community centers, senior citizens centers, schools, and military field stations), and expenditures for Home and Community Waiver programs under Medicaid. [5] See footnote 7, Table 140. [6] See footnote 8, Table 140. [7] See footnote 5, Table 141.

Source: U.S. Centers for Medicare and Medicaid Services, Office of the Actuary, National Health Statistics Group, "National Health Expenditure Data, Historical," <https://cms.gov/nationalhealthexpenddata>, accessed December 2019.

Table 144. Health Consumption Expenditures by Type of Expenditure and Source of Funds: 2018

[In billions of dollars (3,475.0 represents $3,475,000,000,000). Excludes Puerto Rico and Island Areas. Excludes investment in research, structures, and equipment]

Type of expenditure	Total	Out-of-pocket	Health insurance Total	Private health insurance	Medicare	Medicaid	Other health insurance programs [1]	Other third party payers and programs [2]
Total	**3,475.0**	**375.6**	**2,729.0**	**1,243.0**	**750.2**	**597.4**	**138.3**	**276.9**
Personal health care [3]	3,075.5	375.6	2,440.6	1,078.7	697.2	532.8	131.9	259.3
Hospital care	1,191.8	34.8	1,046.9	481.1	297.0	196.6	72.2	110.1
Physician and clinical services	725.6	61.2	594.0	311.8	170.2	77.4	34.6	70.4
Dental services	135.6	54.9	80.2	62.2	1.2	12.8	4.0	0.6
Other health, residential, and personal care [4]	191.6	6.8	132.3	13.6	4.9	111.1	2.7	52.5
Home health care	102.2	10.2	89.2	12.2	40.3	35.9	0.8	2.8
Nursing care facilities and continuing care retirement communities	168.5	44.8	110.8	17.1	38.1	49.9	5.7	12.9
Prescription drugs	335.0	47.1	286.2	134.3	107.2	33.4	11.3	1.8
Durable medical equipment	54.9	25.5	28.4	11.3	8.9	8.1	0.2	1.0
Government administration [5]	47.5	(X)	44.6	(X)	12.0	27.5	5.0	2.9
Net cost of health insurance [5]	258.5	(X)	243.8	164.3	41.1	37.0	1.3	14.7
Public health activities [6]	93.5	(X)	(X)	(X)	(X)	(X)	(X)	(X)

X Not applicable. [1] Includes Children's Health Insurance Program (CHIP) Titles XIX and XXI, Department of Defense, and Department of Veterans Affairs. [2] Includes worksite health care, other private revenues, Indian Health Service, workers' compensation, general assistance, maternal and child health, vocational rehabilitation, other federal programs, Substance Abuse and Mental Health Services Administration, other state and local programs, and school health. [3] Comprises all medical goods and services that are rendered to treat or prevent a specific disease or condition in a specific person. Includes expenditures for other items, not shown separately. [4] See footnote 4, Table 143. [5] See source for definitions. [6] See footnote 5, Table 141.

Source: U.S. Centers for Medicare and Medicaid Services, Office of the Actuary, National Health Statistics Group, "National Health Expenditure Data, Historical," <https://cms.gov/nationalhealthexpenddata>, accessed December 2019.

Table 145. Personal Health Care Expenditures by Source of Funds: 2000 to 2018

[In billions of dollars (1,161.5 represents $1,161,500,000,000). Excludes Puerto Rico and Island Areas]

Source of funds	2000	2005	2010	2013	2014	2015	2016	2017	2018
Personal health care expenditures	**1,161.5**	**1,695.7**	**2,191.4**	**2,431.2**	**2,556.0**	**2,710.2**	**2,838.3**	**2,954.5**	**3,075.5**
Out-of-pocket	198.9	263.8	300.2	326.9	331.8	341.7	357.2	365.2	375.6
Health insurance	843.8	1,278.7	1,695.8	1,884.6	2,003.7	2,142.9	2,242.6	2,337.0	2,440.6
Private health insurance	405.6	604.3	750.8	824.2	869.5	936.5	989.7	1,032.4	1,078.7
Medicare	216.3	326.3	489.1	553.6	580.5	607.1	629.9	659.4	697.2
Medicaid	186.9	287.6	365.8	405.9	446.6	484.1	504.0	519.6	532.8
Other health insurance [1]	34.9	60.5	90.3	100.8	107.1	115.2	119.0	125.5	131.9
Other third party payers and programs [2]	118.9	153.3	195.3	219.8	220.6	225.6	238.5	252.3	259.3

[1] Includes Children's Health Insurance Program (Titles XIX and XXI), Department of Defense, and Department of Veterans Affairs. [2] See footnote 2, Table 144.

Source: U.S. Centers for Medicare and Medicaid Services, Office of the Actuary, National Health Statistics Group, "National Health Expenditure Data, Historical," <https://cms.gov/nationalhealthexpenddata>, accessed December 2019.

Table 146. National Health Expenditures by Sponsor: 2000 to 2018

[In billions of dollars (1,369.2 represents $1,369,200,000,000). Excludes Puerto Rico and Island Areas. Type of sponsor is defined as the entity that is ultimately responsible for financing the health care bill. These sponsors pay health insurance premiums and out-of-pocket costs, or finance health care through dedicated taxes and/or general revenues. See source for sponsor inclusion and exclusion details]

Type of sponsor	2000	2005	2010	2014	2015	2016	2017	2018
Total	1,369.2	2,023.8	2,593.2	3,025.4	3,199.6	3,347.4	3,487.3	3,649.4
Business, households and other private revenues	882.8	1,225.3	1,441.2	1,666.1	1,742.6	1,828.0	1,921.0	2,013.1
Private business [1]	335.3	469.4	516.1	599.0	622.7	652.8	684.2	726.8
Household [2]	443.3	618.7	750.1	862.5	908.1	950.5	992.5	1,035.7
Other private revenues	104.2	137.1	175.1	204.6	211.7	224.7	244.3	250.7
Governments	486.4	798.6	1,151.9	1,359.2	1,457.0	1,519.4	1,566.3	1,636.3
Federal government [3]	260.8	450.6	731.2	835.1	908.1	951.9	978.5	1,033.8
State and local government [4]	225.6	348.0	420.7	524.2	548.9	567.5	587.8	602.5

[1] Includes employer contributions to employer-sponsored health insurance premiums, employer Medicare Hospital Insurance (HI) Trust Fund payroll taxes, workers' compensation, temporary disability insurance, and worksite health care. [2] Includes employee contributions to employer-sponsored health insurance premiums, directly purchased health insurance, the medical portion of property and casualty insurance premiums, employee and self-employment payroll taxes and premiums paid to the Medicare HI Trust Fund, premiums paid to the Medicare Supplementary Medical Insurance (SMI) Trust Fund, premiums paid for the Pre-existing Condition Insurance Program (PCIP) for 2010-2014, and out-of-pocket health spending. [3] Includes employer contributions to employer-sponsored health insurance premiums, employer Medicare HI payroll taxes, federal general revenue and Medicare net Trust Fund expenditures, federal Medicaid expenditures, the federal portion of Medicaid buy-ins for the Medicare premiums of people eligible for both Medicaid and Medicare (dual eligibles), Medicare Retiree Drug Subsidy (RDS) payments to private business and state and local government employer plans beginning in 2006, Marketplace tax credits and subsidies, and other federal health programs. [4] Includes employer contributions to employer-sponsored health insurance premiums, employer Medicare HI payroll taxes, state and local Medicaid expenditures, the state and local portion of Medicaid buy-ins for the Medicare premiums of people eligible for both Medicaid and Medicare (dual eligibles), and other programs.

Source: U.S. Centers for Medicare and Medicaid Services, Office of the Actuary, National Health Statistics Group, "National Health Expenditure Data, Historical," <https://cms.gov/nationalhealthexpenddata>, accessed December 2019.

Table 147. Hospital Care, Physician and Clinical Services, Nursing Care Facilities and Continuing Care Retirement Communities, and Prescription Drug Expenditures by Source of Funds: 2000 to 2018

[In billions of dollars (415.5 represents $415,500,000,000). Excludes Puerto Rico and Island Areas]

Source of payment	2000	2005	2010	2014	2015	2016	2017	2018
Hospital care, total	415.5	608.6	822.3	978.2	1,034.6	1,089.5	1,140.6	1,191.8
Out-of-pocket	13.4	19.7	27.8	32.8	31.2	32.1	34.3	34.8
Health insurance	358.2	531.6	714.0	849.4	908.9	959.0	1,000.7	1,046.9
Private health insurance	141.0	215.9	300.6	366.2	400.5	431.0	454.1	481.1
Medicare	123.4	176.4	220.3	252.7	260.5	272.4	284.0	297.0
Medicaid	70.9	103.8	141.8	169.8	183.9	189.2	192.7	196.6
CHIP [1]	0.9	2.7	3.2	3.4	3.7	4.4	4.6	4.7
Dept. of Defense	7.6	12.0	16.5	16.6	15.8	16.2	16.7	16.0
Veterans Affairs	14.3	20.8	31.7	40.7	44.5	45.8	48.4	51.5
Other third party payers and programs [2]	43.9	57.3	80.5	95.9	94.5	98.5	105.7	110.1
Physician and clinical services, total	288.2	413.0	512.6	595.7	631.2	665.6	696.9	725.6
Out-of-pocket	31.9	41.7	48.7	54.4	56.5	58.8	60.1	61.2
Health insurance	220.1	325.6	411.1	484.3	513.4	538.5	565.3	594.0
Private health insurance	135.4	197.9	231.1	257.4	271.6	287.0	300.2	311.8
Medicare	58.7	85.6	115.8	137.9	144.4	149.2	157.9	170.2
Medicaid	19.3	30.1	43.3	63.4	69.1	72.2	75.2	77.4
CHIP [1]	0.7	1.7	3.1	3.2	3.5	3.9	4.3	4.4
Dept. of Defense	4.7	7.9	12.1	14.3	14.8	15.3	15.7	16.5
Veterans Affairs	1.3	2.5	5.8	7.9	9.9	10.9	12.0	13.6
Other third party payers and programs [2]	36.1	45.7	52.7	57.0	61.3	68.2	71.6	70.4
Nursing care facilities and continuing care retirement communities, total	85.0	111.4	140.5	152.4	158.1	163.0	166.2	168.5
Out-of-pocket	27.1	32.5	37.5	39.6	41.5	44.1	44.6	44.8
Health insurance	52.0	71.8	93.4	101.6	105.5	107.3	109.5	110.8
Private health insurance	7.5	7.1	10.7	12.2	14.0	15.3	16.6	17.1
Medicare	10.8	20.5	32.3	35.6	37.1	37.1	37.5	38.1
Medicaid	31.9	41.3	46.3	49.1	49.4	49.8	50.0	49.9
Veterans Affairs	1.9	2.8	4.0	4.7	5.0	5.0	5.4	5.6
Other third party payers and programs [2]	5.9	7.1	9.6	11.2	11.1	11.6	12.2	12.9
Prescription drugs, total	121.0	205.2	248.4	292.4	317.1	322.3	326.8	335.0
Out-of-pocket	33.6	51.3	45.6	45.6	46.3	47.8	46.8	47.1
Health insurance	85.1	149.9	199.4	244.9	268.9	272.7	278.2	286.2
Private health insurance	61.1	102.0	110.9	122.6	134.8	133.8	133.2	134.3
Medicare	2.1	3.9	58.9	84.8	92.4	96.6	101.3	107.2
Medicaid	19.8	36.5	20.4	27.3	30.5	32.0	32.9	33.4
CHIP [1]	0.3	1.1	1.4	1.4	1.6	1.8	2.0	2.0
Dept. of Defense	0.7	3.6	4.7	5.8	6.3	4.9	4.9	5.0
Veterans Affairs	1.1	2.7	3.0	3.0	3.3	3.6	3.9	4.3
Other third party payers and programs [2]	2.3	4.0	3.3	2.0	1.9	1.8	1.8	1.8

[1] Children's Health Insurance Program (Titles XIX and XXI), signed into law in 1997. [2] Includes worksite health care, other private revenues, Indian Health Service, workers' compensation, general assistance, maternal and child health, vocational rehabilitation, other federal programs, Substance Abuse and Mental Health Services Administration, other state and local programs, and school health.

Source: U.S. Centers for Medicare and Medicaid Services, Office of the Actuary, National Health Statistics Group, "National Health Expenditure Data, Historical," <https://cms.gov/nationalhealthexpenddata>, accessed December 2019.

Table 148. Medical Care Consumer Price Indexes: 1990 to 2019

[Indexes with base of 1982-1984=100. Indexes are annual averages of monthly data based on components of consumer price index for all urban consumers; for explanation, see text, Section 14 and Appendix III]

Year	Medical care, total	Medical care services				Hospital and related services	Medical care commodities		Annual percent change [3]		
			Professional services								
		Total [1]	Total [1]	Physicians	Dental		Total [2]	Prescription drugs	Medical care, total	Medical care services	Medical care commodities
1990........	162.8	162.7	156.1	160.8	155.8	178.0	163.4	181.7	9.0	9.3	8.4
1995........	220.5	224.2	201.0	208.8	206.8	257.8	204.5	235.0	4.5	5.1	1.9
2000........	260.8	266.0	237.7	244.7	258.5	317.3	238.1	285.4	4.1	4.3	3.2
2005........	323.2	336.7	281.7	287.5	324.0	439.9	276.0	349.0	4.2	4.8	2.5
2010........	388.4	411.2	328.2	331.3	398.8	607.7	314.7	407.8	3.4	3.5	3.1
2012........	414.9	440.3	342.0	347.3	417.5	672.1	333.6	440.1	3.7	3.9	2.9
2013........	425.1	454.0	349.5	354.2	431.8	701.3	335.1	442.6	2.5	3.1	0.4
2014........	435.3	464.8	355.2	359.1	441.0	733.8	343.4	458.3	2.4	2.4	2.5
2015........	446.8	476.2	361.5	366.1	452.2	761.9	354.6	479.3	2.6	2.4	3.3
2016........	463.7	494.8	371.5	378.1	465.0	795.1	366.8	502.5	3.8	3.9	3.4
2017........	475.3	506.8	375.1	380.1	472.6	831.7	377.0	519.6	2.5	2.4	2.8
2018........	484.7	517.8	378.4	380.5	485.5	866.9	381.4	528.0	2.0	2.2	1.2
2019........	498.4	536.1	382.6	383.2	496.2	885.2	381.3	526.8	2.8	3.5	–

– Represents or rounds to zero. [1] Includes other services not shown separately. [2] Includes other commodities not shown separately. [3] Percent change from the immediate prior year.

Source: U.S. Bureau of Labor Statistics, "Consumer Price Index Databases," <https://www.bls.gov/cpi/data.htm>, accessed January 2020.

Table 149. Consumer Expenditures per Consumer Unit for Health Care: 2018

[In dollars, except percent. Expenditures are direct out-of-pocket expenditures. Consumers units may be all members in a housing unit (families), a person living alone or sharing a household with others and financially independent, or 2 or more unrelated persons living together who share expenses. See also text for Section 13, and source. For composition of regions, see map, inside front cover]

Consumer characteristic	Health care, total					Percent distribution		
	Amount	Percent of total expenditures	Health insurance	Medical services	Drugs and medical supplies [1]	Health insurance	Medical services	Drugs and medical supplies [1]
Total............................	**4,968**	**8.1**	**3,405**	**909**	**655**	**68.5**	**18.3**	**13.2**
Age of reference person:								
Under 25 years old............................	1,206	3.8	700	314	192	58.0	26.0	15.9
25 to 34 years old............................	3,072	5.4	2,182	588	302	71.0	19.1	9.8
35 to 44 years old............................	4,317	6.1	2,888	946	484	66.9	21.9	11.2
45 to 54 years old............................	5,138	6.8	3,483	987	668	67.8	19.2	13.0
55 to 64 years old............................	5,743	8.7	3,848	1,144	751	67.0	19.9	13.1
65 years old and older............................	6,802	13.4	4,776	998	1,028	70.2	14.7	15.1
Race of reference person:								
White and other [2]............................	5,298	8.4	3,564	1,010	724	67.3	19.1	13.7
Asian............................	4,346	6.0	3,270	638	437	75.2	14.7	10.1
Black............................	3,123	7.0	2,449	368	306	78.4	11.8	9.8
Origin of reference person:								
Hispanic............................	3,173	5.9	2,223	575	374	70.1	18.1	11.8
Non-Hispanic............................	5,246	8.4	3,587	960	699	68.4	18.3	13.3
Region of residence:								
Northeast............................	4,992	7.6	3,574	831	588	71.6	16.6	11.8
Midwest............................	5,247	9.0	3,506	990	752	66.8	18.9	14.3
South............................	4,846	8.6	3,409	816	621	70.3	16.8	12.8
West............................	4,892	7.2	3,164	1,053	674	64.7	21.5	13.8
Size of consumer unit:								
One person............................	2,977	8.2	1,975	555	447	66.3	18.6	15.0
Two or more persons............................	5,799	8.1	4,002	1,056	741	69.0	18.2	12.8
Two persons............................	6,162	9.4	4,238	1,056	868	68.8	17.1	14.1
Three persons............................	5,515	7.6	3,883	979	653	70.4	17.8	11.8
Four persons............................	5,538	6.9	3,784	1,124	630	68.3	20.3	11.4
Five persons or more............................	5,286	6.6	3,632	1,086	568	68.7	20.5	10.7
Income before taxes, by quintile:								
Lowest 20 percent............................	2,475	9.4	1,745	348	382	70.5	14.1	15.4
Second 20 percent............................	3,997	10.0	2,776	628	593	69.5	15.7	14.8
Third 20 percent............................	4,637	9.0	3,167	801	669	68.3	17.3	14.4
Fourth 20 percent............................	5,866	8.5	4,102	1,046	719	69.9	17.8	12.3
Highest 20 percent............................	7,865	6.6	5,232	1,720	914	66.5	21.9	11.6
Education:								
Less than a high school graduate............	2,601	8.6	1,840	372	389	70.7	14.3	15.0
High school graduate............................	3,547	9.3	2,551	510	487	71.9	14.4	13.7
High school graduate with some college....	3,935	8.2	2,679	685	571	68.1	17.4	14.5
Associate's degree............................	5,024	8.5	3,428	952	644	68.2	18.9	12.8
Bachelor's degree............................	5,919	8.2	4,028	1,155	736	68.1	19.5	12.4
Master's, professional, or doctoral degree...	7,041	7.4	4,755	1,386	900	67.5	19.7	12.8

[1] Includes prescription and nonprescription drugs. [2] Other races includes Native Hawaiian or other Pacific Islander, American Indian or Alaska Native, and approximately 1 percent reporting more than one race.

Source: U.S. Bureau of Labor Statistics, "Consumer Expenditure Survey, Annual Calendar Year Tables, 2018," <http://www.bls.gov/cex/tables.htm>, accessed December 2019.

Table 150. Medical Expenditures by Health Condition in Current and Chained (2012) Dollars and Per Capita: 2000 to 2016

[In billions of dollars (1,109.59 represents $1,109,590,000,000), except as noted. Health conditions are classified according to the International Classification of Diseases, for the revisions noted below. Users should exercise caution when comparing trends across time. Based on Bureau of Economic Analysis' Health Care Satellite Account, Blended Account. The Blended Account blends data from multiple sources, including large claims databases. The BEA also has available health expenditure data based on the Medical Expenditure Panel Survey. See source for details]

Health expense item	Current dollars (billions)			Chained (2012) billion dollars			Per capita (dollars)		
	2000 [3]	2010 [3]	2016 [3]	2000 [3]	2010 [3]	2016 [3]	2000 [3]	2010 [3]	2016 [3]
Total health	**1,109.59**	**2,078.10**	**2,691.29**	**1,792.61**	**2,167.71**	**2,407.36**	**3,932.45**	**6,718.15**	**8,330.33**
Health services	1,052.23	1,973.87	2,555.25	1,733.41	2,063.00	2,271.04	3,729.16	6,381.19	7,909.24
Medical services by disease	900.75	1,714.32	2,252.97	1,498.13	1,792.61	1,992.40	3,192.31	5,542.11	6,973.60
Infectious and parasitic diseases	24.97	67.46	121.99	51.97	72.35	89.60	88.50	218.09	377.59
Neoplasms	60.66	111.64	135.83	106.34	117.46	119.21	214.98	360.91	420.43
Endocrine, nutritional, and metabolic diseases and immunity disorders	50.00	116.40	158.57	76.90	122.07	138.28	177.20	376.30	490.82
Mental illness	41.39	74.88	102.92	56.30	75.27	95.60	146.69	242.07	318.57
Diseases of the nervous system and sense organs	63.90	120.90	176.32	115.49	130.09	145.68	226.47	390.85	545.76
Diseases of the circulatory system	145.58	232.58	249.40	209.94	228.15	222.29	515.94	751.89	771.97
Diseases of the respiratory system	91.98	144.00	173.06	145.28	152.22	158.77	325.98	465.53	535.67
Diseases of the digestive system	56.94	94.36	121.02	98.64	101.28	106.56	201.80	305.05	374.59
Diseases of the genitourinary system	57.97	106.46	116.69	95.55	111.62	115.14	205.45	344.17	361.19
Complications of pregnancy, childbirth, and the puerperium	25.21	38.98	51.54	40.84	40.57	45.28	89.35	126.02	159.53
Diseases of the skin and subcutaneous organs	22.34	42.11	61.34	38.88	44.88	50.04	79.17	136.13	189.87
Diseases of the musculoskeletal system and connective tissue	76.64	169.84	228.13	132.39	173.20	193.76	271.62	549.06	706.13
Injury and poisoning	66.48	112.45	133.84	115.95	116.08	116.28	235.61	363.53	414.27
Symptoms, signs, and ill-defined conditions	83.78	212.75	334.06	147.04	224.92	304.48	296.92	687.79	1,034.01
Other diseases	32.91	69.52	88.28	66.69	82.72	91.68	116.63	224.75	273.25
Diseases of blood and blood-forming organs	9.40	20.28	24.79	27.69	31.34	36.28	33.31	65.56	76.73
Congenital anomalies	4.77	7.73	8.58	6.99	7.42	7.09	16.91	24.99	26.56
Conditions originating in perinatal period	4.84	6.79	9.13	8.61	8.71	8.19	17.15	21.95	28.26
Residual codes, unclassified, all E codes [1]	13.90	34.71	45.78	25.56	36.41	41.97	49.26	112.21	141.70
Medical services by provider	151.48	259.55	302.28	235.37	270.39	278.29	536.85	839.08	935.64
Dental services	63.57	104.46	122.35	102.63	109.35	109.82	225.30	337.70	378.71
Nursing homes	87.91	155.10	179.94	132.84	161.05	168.47	311.56	501.41	556.97
Proprietary and government nursing homes	56.85	102.36	122.47	85.91	106.29	114.66	201.48	330.91	379.08
Nonprofit nursing homes services to households	31.06	52.73	57.47	46.93	54.76	53.81	110.08	170.47	177.89
Medical products, appliances and equipment	57.36	104.22	136.04	63.51	104.85	136.92	203.29	336.93	421.08
Pharmaceutical and other medical products	25.19	51.82	72.06	27.16	51.59	74.00	89.27	167.53	223.05
Pharmaceutical products (excludes prescription drugs) [2]	23.24	47.82	66.40	25.12	47.54	68.26	82.36	154.59	205.53
Nonprescription drugs	23.24	47.82	66.40	25.12	47.54	68.26	82.36	154.59	205.53
Other medical products	1.95	4.00	5.66	2.05	4.06	5.73	6.91	12.93	17.52
Therapeutic appliances and equipment	32.17	52.40	63.98	36.46	53.28	62.96	114.01	169.40	198.04
Corrective eyeglasses and contact lenses	19.91	29.84	34.88	23.92	30.38	33.55	70.56	96.47	107.96
Therapeutic medical equipment	12.26	22.56	29.10	12.87	22.90	29.49	43.45	72.93	90.07

[1] E codes cover external causes of injury or poisoning. [2] Excludes prescription drugs; prescription drug expenses have been allocated by health condition. [3] Data for 2000 and 2010 are based on the International Classification of Diseases, 9th revision (ICD-9); 2016 data are based on ICD-10.

Source: U.S. Bureau of Economic Analysis, Health Care Satellite Account, "Blended Account, 2000-2016," <https://www.bea.gov/data/special-topics/health-care>, accessed December 2019.

Table 151. Medicare Enrollment by State: 2017 and 2018

[In thousands (58,457.2 represents 58,457,200). Covers Medicare beneficiaries enrolled in either Hospital Insurance and/or Supplementary Medical Insurance. Enrollment counts are determined by using a person-year methodology; for each calendar year, total person-year counts are determined by summing the total number of months that each beneficiary is enrolled during the year and dividing by 12 (see source for more information). Numbers may not add to totals because of rounding]

State	2017			2018		
	Total Medicare	Original Medicare [1]	Medicare Advantage [2]	Total Medicare	Original Medicare [1]	Medicare Advantage [2]
Total...............	**58,457.2**	**38,667.8**	**19,789.4**	**59,924.4**	**38,599.7**	**21,324.7**
United States [3]...............	**57,223.8**	**38,001.8**	**19,222.0**	**58,678.1**	**37,930.7**	**20,747.4**
Alabama........................	1,007.4	640.5	366.9	1,026.6	623.6	403.0
Alaska...........................	91.9	90.5	1.3	96.1	94.6	1.5
Arizona.........................	1,226.7	753.9	472.7	1,270.0	773.8	496.2
Arkansas.......................	616.2	480.2	136.0	627.1	475.7	151.4
California.......................	5,965.5	3,473.4	2,492.1	6,115.2	3,502.7	2,612.4
Colorado.......................	847.7	530.1	317.6	880.1	547.2	332.9
Connecticut...................	654.7	469.8	184.9	667.0	420.5	246.5
Delaware.......................	193.6	171.2	22.4	200.9	173.0	27.9
District of Columbia........	91.1	76.6	14.5	92.4	75.8	16.5
Florida..........................	4,295.2	2,468.0	1,827.2	4,408.7	2,455.5	1,953.2
Georgia.........................	1,624.1	1,051.5	572.6	1,674.2	1,044.9	629.3
Hawaii..........................	259.4	142.3	117.1	266.6	145.1	121.5
Idaho............................	306.4	210.4	96.0	320.0	216.7	103.4
Illinois..........................	2,149.6	1,632.4	517.3	2,191.5	1,633.2	558.3
Indiana.........................	1,204.9	883.8	321.1	1,232.3	869.2	363.1
Iowa.............................	598.2	490.2	108.0	611.9	490.4	121.5
Kansas..........................	509.9	429.8	80.1	522.8	433.9	88.9
Kentucky.......................	896.0	637.6	258.3	911.6	630.9	280.7
Louisiana......................	828.7	551.5	277.2	848.2	546.8	301.4
Maine...........................	322.2	231.1	91.0	331.0	226.2	104.8
Maryland.......................	984.0	872.7	111.3	1,010.3	886.7	123.6
Massachusetts...............	1,275.6	985.0	290.6	1,303.2	991.9	311.4
Michigan.......................	1,981.5	1,260.7	720.8	2,022.5	1,212.2	810.3
Minnesota.....................	967.3	412.9	554.4	995.2	417.2	577.9
Mississippi....................	580.0	481.2	98.8	590.6	479.7	110.9
Missouri........................	1,183.0	804.8	378.2	1,203.8	795.2	408.7
Montana........................	215.5	171.0	44.5	222.9	181.6	41.3
Nebraska.......................	329.5	286.4	43.0	337.7	288.0	49.7
Nevada..........................	492.3	319.2	173.1	511.1	325.9	185.2
New Hampshire..............	281.0	250.6	30.4	289.9	251.7	38.2
New Jersey....................	1,553.3	1,214.4	338.9	1,582.7	1,212.1	370.6
New Mexico...................	396.9	262.9	134.0	409.3	267.4	141.9
New York.......................	3,482.2	2,126.6	1,355.6	3,553.4	2,114.4	1,439.0
North Carolina...............	1,877.4	1,275.2	602.2	1,929.7	1,263.0	666.7
North Dakota..................	124.1	101.5	22.6	127.6	104.2	23.3
Ohio.............................	2,249.1	1,372.6	876.4	2,292.7	1,339.3	953.4
Oklahoma......................	706.3	578.3	128.0	721.7	581.3	140.4
Oregon..........................	807.6	447.5	360.1	836.1	458.4	377.7
Pennsylvania..................	2,629.8	1,552.5	1,077.2	2,680.7	1,565.7	1,115.1
Rhode Island..................	211.7	120.9	90.8	216.2	120.5	95.6
South Carolina...............	1,006.4	745.5	260.9	1,039.5	752.2	287.2
South Dakota.................	165.4	130.7	34.7	170.8	135.3	35.6
Tennessee.....................	1,294.9	820.0	474.9	1,323.9	816.8	507.1
Texas...........................	3,883.6	2,522.4	1,361.2	4,014.8	2,477.0	1,537.8
Utah.............................	371.9	240.6	131.4	385.8	245.8	139.9
Vermont........................	139.2	126.5	12.7	143.4	128.5	14.9
Virginia.........................	1,427.7	1,149.6	278.1	1,468.7	1,175.2	293.5
Washington....................	1,277.4	885.0	392.4	1,319.1	893.9	425.3
West Virginia..................	427.9	304.1	123.8	433.5	298.3	135.2
Wisconsin......................	1,110.3	667.6	442.7	1,141.3	669.9	471.4
Wyoming.......................	101.9	97.9	4.0	106.0	101.8	4.3
Guam...........................	16.2	16.1	0.1	16.7	16.7	0.1
Puerto Rico....................	734.1	171.9	562.2	740.8	167.7	573.1
U.S. Virgin Islands..........	19.7	19.4	0.3	19.6	19.3	0.4
Foreign and other outlying areas........................	447.2	444.3	2.9	461.6	458.2	3.4

[1] Original Medicare consists of Part A (Hospital Insurance) and Part B (Supplementary Medical Insurance). Enrollment in Original Medicare includes beneficiaries enrolled in either Part A and/or Part B. [2] Medicare Advantage and other health plans are also known as Medicare Part C. Medicare Part C includes both Part A and Part B coverage. Medicare Advantage and other health plan enrollees are Medicare beneficiaries who are enrolled in health plans offered by private companies approved by Medicare. [3] U.S. total excludes territories, possessions, foreign countries or outlying areas, and unknown.

Source: U.S. Centers for Medicare and Medicaid Services, CMS Program Statistics, "Medicare Enrollment Dashboard," <https://www.cms.gov/Research-Statistics-Data-and-Systems/Statistics-Trends-and-Reports/CMSProgramStatistics/index.html>, accessed April 2019.

Table 152. Medicare Enrollment by Type: 2012 to 2018

[In thousands (50,769 represents 50,769,000), except as noted. Based on person-year methodology; see source for details. Medicare Advantage is an alternative to traditional Medicare. Medicare Advantage plans are offered by private companies and organizations, are required to provide at least services covered by Medicare Parts A and B (except hospice services), and are financed from both Medicare's Hospital Insurance (HI) trust fund and the Part B account within the Supplementary Medical Insurance (SMI) trust fund in proportion to the relative weights of Part A and Part B benefits to the total benefits paid by the Medicare program. Numbers and percentages may not add to totals because of rounding]

Enrollment by type	2012	2013	2014	2015	2016	2017	2018
Total Medicare enrollment [1]	**50,769**	**52,426**	**54,013**	**55,496**	**56,981**	**58,457**	**59,990**
Aged	42,313	43,761	45,217	46,631	48,143	49,678	51,304
Disabled [2]	8,456	8,664	8,796	8,865	8,838	8,779	8,686
Part A, Hospital insurance	50,428	52,087	53,675	55,153	56,639	58,115	59,650
Aged	41,973	43,423	44,879	46,289	47,802	49,338	50,964
Disabled [2]	8,455	8,664	8,796	8,865	8,837	8,778	8,686
Part B, Medical insurance	46,493	47,959	49,412	50,758	52,086	53,350	54,690
Aged	38,937	40,175	41,475	42,741	44,074	45,394	46,813
Disabled [2]	7,556	7,784	7,937	8,017	8,012	7,956	7,877
Original Medicare enrollment [1]	**37,214**	**37,613**	**37,790**	**38,025**	**38,610**	**38,668**	**38,665**
Percent of total	73.3	71.8	70.0	68.5	67.8	66.2	64.5
Aged	30,440	30,847	31,110	31,479	32,204	32,471	32,745
Disabled [2]	6,773	6,766	6,681	6,547	6,406	6,197	5,920
Part A, Hospital insurance	36,895	37,298	37,477	37,708	38,288	38,348	38,352
Aged	30,122	30,533	30,796	31,162	31,883	32,152	32,432
Disabled [2]	6,773	6,765	6,680	6,546	6,406	6,196	5,919
Part B, Medical insurance	32,939	33,147	33,190	33,287	33,715	33,562	33,366
Aged	27,065	27,261	27,368	27,589	28,136	28,188	28,255
Disabled [2]	5,874	5,886	5,822	5,698	5,580	5,374	5,111
Medicare Advantage enrollment [1]	**13,555**	**14,813**	**16,223**	**17,471**	**18,371**	**19,789**	**21,325**
Percent of total	26.7	28.3	30.0	31.5	32.2	33.9	35.6
Part A, Hospital insurance	13,533	14,789	16,198	17,445	18,351	19,768	21,298
Aged	11,851	12,891	14,082	15,127	15,919	17,186	18,532
Disabled [2]	1,682	1,898	2,116	2,319	2,432	2,582	2,766
Part B, Medical insurance	13,555	14,812	16,222	17,471	18,370	19,788	21,324
Aged	11,872	12,914	14,107	15,152	15,939	17,206	18,558
Disabled [2]	1,682	1,898	2,116	2,318	2,432	2,582	2,766

[1] Enrollment in Medicare Part A and/or Part B. [2] Persons enrolled due to end stage renal disease-only are included in the disabled enrollee counts.

Source: U.S. Centers for Medicare & Medicaid Services, "CMS Program Statistics," <https://www.cms.gov/Research-Statistics-Data-and-Systems/Statistics-Trends-and-Reports/CMSProgramStatistics/index.html>, accessed February 2020.

Table 153. Medicare Utilization—Persons Utilizing Medicare, Program Payments, and Cost Sharing: 2013 to 2018

[37,613 represents 37,613,000. Covers all Original Medicare (also known as "fee-for-service"), which consists of Part A (Hospital Insurance), and Part B (Medical Insurance). Persons utilizing Medicare do not include beneficiaries who received services but for whom no program payments were reported. Amounts do not sum to totals because beneficiaries may have used more than one type of service during a year, and for payments and costs, due to rounding]

Item	2013	2014	2015	2016	2017	2018
ORIGINAL MEDICARE ENROLLEES (1,000)						
Total, Part A and/or Part B	**37,613**	**37,790**	**38,025**	**38,610**	**38,668**	**38,665**
Part A	37,298	37,477	37,708	38,288	38,348	38,352
Part B	33,147	33,190	33,287	33,715	33,562	33,366
UTILIZATION (1,000)						
Medicare Part A and/or Part B	**34,064**	**34,277**	**34,398**	**34,827**	**34,790**	**34,822**
Part A	7,750	7,603	7,656	7,680	7,719	7,627
Inpatient hospital services	6,797	6,628	6,630	6,619	6,609	6,460
Skilled nursing facility services	1,843	1,832	1,845	1,803	1,764	1,705
Hospice services [1]	1,319	1,333	1,395	1,441	1,505	1,564
Home health agency services	1,699	1,653	1,671	1,642	1,610	1,572
Part B	33,532	33,734	33,824	34,241	34,170	34,168
Physician and other medical services	33,104	33,264	33,311	33,713	33,609	33,601
Outpatient services	24,846	25,010	25,283	25,711	25,715	25,687
Home health agency services	1,921	1,931	1,954	1,982	1,953	1,964
PAYMENTS AND COSTS (mil. dol.)						
Medicare Part A and/or Part B	**345,657**	**350,424**	**360,096**	**368,728**	**376,979**	**389,526**
Part A	179,085	179,056	182,146	185,493	188,093	190,702
Inpatient hospital services	129,024	128,719	130,168	133,380	135,274	136,996
Skilled nursing facility services	28,218	28,637	29,152	28,409	28,064	27,652
Hospice services [1]	15,092	15,071	15,892	16,847	17,922	19,251
Home health agency services	6,750	6,628	6,934	6,857	6,833	6,802
Part B	166,572	171,368	177,950	183,235	188,886	198,824
Physician and other medical services	98,331	99,090	102,235	103,806	105,610	109,928
Outpatient services	57,066	61,169	64,445	68,169	72,278	77,764
Home health agency services	11,175	11,108	11,270	11,260	10,998	11,132
BENEFICIARY COST SHARING [2] (mil. dol.)						
Medicare Part A and/or Part B	**58,691**	**60,006**	**61,391**	**63,045**	**64,488**	**66,402**
Part A	15,826	15,923	16,302	16,210	16,171	15,908
Part B	42,865	44,083	45,089	46,835	48,317	50,493

[1] The total Medicare Part A enrollee counts are based on enrollees in Original Medicare and Medicare Advantage/Other Health Plans (also known as Part C), combined, because once a beneficiary enrolled in a Medicare Advantage/Other Health Plan elects the hospice benefit, his or her Medicare benefits revert to fee-for-service. [2] Includes costs for copayments, coinsurance, deductibles, and out-of-pocket payments for balanced billing (the difference between Medicare allowed charges and physicians' submitted charges). Excludes monthly premium for Part B coverage, Part D coverage, voluntary hospital insurance coverage, and supplemental insurance.

Source: U.S. Centers for Medicare and Medicaid Services, "CMS Program Statistics," <https://www.cms.gov/Research-Statistics-Data-and-Systems/Statistics-Trends-and-Reports/CMSProgramStatistics/index.html>, accessed February 2020.

Table 154. Medicare and Medicaid Dual Enrollment by Type of Eligibility: 2013 to 2018

[In thousands (9,586.4 represents 9,586,400). Covers Medicare beneficiaries who have low incomes and limited resources who also receive Medicaid program benefits. Services that are covered by Medicare are paid for by the Medicare program first before any payments are made by Medicaid. Based on person-year methodology; see source for details. See headnote, Table 152. Numbers may not sum to totals due to rounding]

| Year | Total Medicare-Medicaid dual enrollment | Type of eligibility | | | | | | | |
| | | Full benefit enrollment | | | | Partial benefit enrollment | | | |
		Total	Qualified Medicare beneficiary plus[1]	Specified low-income Medicare beneficiary plus[2]	Other full-benefit enrollees with Medicaid	Total	Qualified Medicare beneficiary[1]	Specified low-income Medicare beneficiary[2]	Qualified disabled & working individuals[3]
Total Medicare:									
2013	9,586.4	6,902.3	5,080.4	245.2	1,576.7	2,684.1	1,255.4	911.1	517.5
2014	9,913.8	7,131.2	5,188.1	251.1	1,691.9	2,782.6	1,329.1	922.7	530.7
2015	10,192.6	7,317.9	5,302.7	256.9	1,758.3	2,874.7	1,383.0	940.6	551.0
2016	10,415.7	7,464.6	5,394.7	263.1	1,806.8	2,951.1	1,447.9	961.8	541.4
2017	10,632.6	7,602.3	5,491.3	270.5	1,840.6	3,030.3	1,520.4	976.8	533.0
2018	10,822.7	7,709.7	5,612.8	286.3	1,810.6	3,112.9	1,552.5	1,002.5	558.0
Original Medicare:									
2013	7,219.8	5,494.4	4,002.0	200.5	1,292.0	1,725.4	875.1	555.1	295.1
2014	7,178.2	5,453.4	3,911.9	200.3	1,341.2	1,724.8	890.1	541.3	293.4
2015	7,025.4	5,312.3	3,777.7	196.6	1,338.0	1,713.1	889.6	529.7	293.9
2016	6,994.9	5,296.6	3,753.8	196.6	1,346.2	1,698.3	900.5	520.2	277.6
2017	6,889.5	5,222.5	3,689.1	195.4	1,338.0	1,667.0	898.4	506.4	262.3
2018	6,675.7	5,083.3	3,611.2	199.9	1,272.2	1,592.5	845.1	487.9	259.5
Medicare Advantage:									
2013	2,366.6	1,407.9	1,078.5	44.7	284.7	958.7	380.3	356.0	222.4
2014	2,735.6	1,677.8	1,276.2	50.9	350.8	1,057.8	439.0	381.4	237.3
2015	3,167.2	2,005.6	1,524.9	60.3	420.3	1,161.5	493.4	411.0	257.2
2016	3,420.8	2,168.0	1,640.8	66.5	460.6	1,252.8	547.5	441.6	263.8
2017	3,743.0	2,379.8	1,802.2	75.1	502.6	1,363.2	622.0	470.5	270.7
2018	4,146.9	2,626.5	2,001.7	86.4	538.3	1,520.5	707.4	514.6	298.5

[1] A qualified Medicare beneficiary (QMB) has Medicare Part A, income less than or equal to 100 percent of the Federal poverty level, and resources below twice the value allowed under supplemental security income (SSI). For those who qualify, the Medicaid program pays Medicare Part A premiums (if applicable), Part B premiums, and Medicare deductibles and coinsurance amounts for Medicare covered services depending on the Medicaid state plan. An individual qualifying for full Medicaid benefits is sometimes referred to as "QMB plus." [2] A specified low-income Medicare beneficiary (SLMB) has Medicare Part A, income above 100 percent but less than 120 percent of the Federal poverty level, and resources below twice the value allowed under SSI. For those who qualify, the Medicaid program pays only the Medicare Part B premium. An individual who qualifies for full Medicaid benefits is sometimes referred to as "SLMB plus". [3] Data are combined for qualified disabled and working individuals (QDWIs) and qualifying individuals; total counts for QDWIs are less than 100. For QDWIs, Medicaid pays Medicare Part A premiums for certain disabled individuals who lost Medicare coverage because they returned to work. These individuals have incomes below 200 percent of the Federal Poverty Level, resources not more than twice the value allowed under SSI, and are not otherwise eligible for Medicaid. Qualifying individuals are entitled to Medicare Part A, have income of at least 120% but less than 135% of the Federal Poverty Level, resources that do not exceed twice the limit for SSI eligibility, and are not otherwise eligible for Medicaid. Medicaid pays their Medicare Part B premiums only. There is an annual cap on the amount of money available, which may limit the number of individuals in the group.

Source: U.S. Centers for Medicare and Medicaid Services, "CMS Program Statistics," <https://www.cms.gov/Research-Statistics-Data-and-Systems/Statistics-Trends-and-Reports/CMSProgramStatistics/index.html>, accessed February 2020.

Table 155. Medicare Hospital Insurance and Supplementary Medical Insurance—Average Costs per Beneficiary: 1980 to 2021

[In dollars. See headnote, Table 156]

Year	Total	Hospital Insurance	SMI Part B	SMI Part D	Year	Total	Hospital Insurance	SMI Part B	SMI Part D
1980	1,352	929	423	(X)	2001	6,416	3,656	2,760	(X)
1981	1,583	1,093	490	(X)	2002	6,813	3,839	2,975	(X)
1982	1,819	1,249	570	(X)	2003	7,144	3,922	3,221	(X)
1983	2,025	1,367	658	(X)	2004	7,722	4,162	3,561	(X)
1984	2,236	1,512	724	(X)	2005	8,278	4,439	3,839	(X)
1985	2,373	1,579	795	(X)	2006	10,179	4,602	4,116	1,461
1986	2,504	1,596	907	(X)	2007	10,703	4,759	4,313	1,630
1987	2,661	1,636	1,024	(X)	2008	11,232	4,996	4,574	1,662
1988	2,781	1,646	1,135	(X)	2009	11,696	5,174	4,792	1,730
1989	3,097	1,860	1,237	(X)	2010	11,902	5,193	4,901	1,808
1990	3,334	1,979	1,355	(X)	2011	12,166	5,275	5,033	1,858
1991	3,569	2,125	1,443	(X)	2012	12,205	5,196	5,170	1,839
1992	3,941	2,411	1,530	(X)	2013	12,200	5,155	5,171	1,874
1993	4,259	2,648	1,611	(X)	2014	12,438	5,012	5,395	2,031
1994	4,678	2,948	1,730	(X)	2015	12,721	5,027	5,542	2,152
1995	5,061	3,194	1,867	(X)	2016	12,912	5,093	5,664	2,155
1996	5,378	3,424	1,954	(X)	2017	13,128	5,143	5,865	2,120
1997	5,649	3,616	2,033	(X)	2018	13,599	5,202	6,229	2,168
1998	5,602	3,468	2,134	(X)	2019	14,151	5,365	6,617	2,168
1999	5,561	3,306	2,255	(X)	2020 (P)	14,846	5,644	7,048	2,154
2000	5,879	3,383	2,496	(X)	2021 (P)	15,509	5,853	7,415	2,241

X Not applicable. P Projected.

Source: U.S. Centers for Medicare and Medicaid Services, Trustees Report & Trust Funds, "2020 Expanded and Supplementary Tables and Figures," <https://www.cms.gov/Research-Statistics-Data-and-Systems/Statistics-Trends-and-Reports/ReportsTrustFunds/index.html>, accessed May 2020.

Table 156. Medicare Insurance Trust Funds: 1990 to 2019

[In billions of dollars (126.3 represents $126,300,000,000), on cash basis, for calendar years. The Medicare program has two components: Medicare Part A Hospital Insurance (HI); and Supplementary Medical Insurance (SMI), consisting of Part B Medical Insurance, and Part D Prescription Drug Coverage. See text, this section, for details]

Type of trust fund	1990	2000	2005	2010	2015	2016	2017	2018	2019
TOTAL MEDICARE									
Total income [1]	126.3	257.1	357.5	486.1	644.4	710.2	705.1	755.7	794.8
Total expenditures	111.0	221.8	336.4	522.9	647.6	678.7	710.2	740.7	796.2
Net change in assets	15.3	35.3	21.0	-36.8	-3.2	31.5	-5.1	15.1	-1.4
Assets, end of year	114.4	221.5	309.8	344.0	263.2	294.7	289.6	304.7	303.3
HOSPITAL INSURANCE, PART A									
Net contribution income [2]	71.9	155.5	183.3	199.5	265.3	280.6	289.9	296.8	313.5
Interest and other income [3,4]	8.5	11.7	16.1	16.1	10.1	10.1	9.4	9.8	9.0
Benefit payments [4,5]	66.2	128.5	180.0	244.5	273.4	280.5	293.4	303.0	322.8
Trust fund balance, end of year	98.9	177.5	285.8	271.9	193.8	199.1	202.0	200.4	194.6
SMI, PART B									
Premiums from enrollees [1]	11.3	20.6	37.5	52.0	69.4	72.1	81.5	93.3	99.4
Government contributions [6]	33.0	65.9	118.1	153.5	203.9	235.6	217.3	253.2	268.2
Interest and other income [3,4]	1.6	3.5	1.4	3.3	5.7	5.5	6.8	7.1	5.9
Benefit payments [1,4,5]	42.5	88.9	149.2	209.7	275.8	289.5	308.6	333.0	365.7
Trust fund balance, end of year	15.5	44.0	24.0	71.4	68.2	88.0	79.9	96.3	99.6
SMI, PART D									
Premiums from enrollees [7]	(X)	(X)	–	6.5	12.8	13.8	15.5	15.9	15.8
Government contributions [8]	(X)	(X)	1.1	51.1	68.4	82.4	73.2	67.8	70.2
Interest and other income	(X)	(X)	–	(Z)	(Z)	(Z)	0.1	0.1	0.5
Benefit payments [9]	(X)	(X)	1.1	61.7	89.5	99.5	100.1	94.7	97.1
Trust fund balance, end of year	(X)	(X)	–	0.7	1.3	7.6	7.8	8.0	9.2

– Represents zero. X Not applicable. Z Less than $50 million. [1] Includes adjustments for benefit checks issued at the end of the year instead of the following January; see source for details on this and other adjustments. [2] Includes income from payroll taxes, taxation of benefits, railroad retirement account transfers, reimbursement for uninsured persons, premiums from voluntary enrollees, and payments for military wage credits. [3] Includes recoveries of amounts reimbursed from the trust fund, receipts from fraud and abuse control program, and other miscellaneous income. [4] Values after 2005 include additional premiums for Medicare Advantage (MA) plans that are deducted from beneficiaries' Social Security checks; see source for details. [5] Includes monies transferred to the SMI trust fund in 1998-2003 for home health agency costs. In 2008 benefit payments were $224 million and include a transfer of $8.5 million to the general fund of the Treasury for HI hospice costs that were misallocated to, and paid from, the Part B account of the SMI trust fund from May 2005 to September 2007. (The general fund, in turn, transferred $8.5 million to the Part B account.) [6] Matching payments from the general fund, plus certain interest-adjustment items. See also footnote 1. [7] Premiums include both amounts withheld from Social Security benefit checks (and other certain Federal benefit payments) and amounts paid directly to Part D plans. [8] Includes, net of transfers from States, all government transfers required to fund benefit payments, administrative expenses, and State expenses for making low-income eligibility determinations. [9] Includes payments to plans, subsidies to employer-sponsored retiree prescription drug plans, payments to States for making low-income eligibility determinations, Part D drug premiums collected from beneficiaries and transferred to Medicare Advantage plans and private drug plans, and premium amounts paid directly by enrollees to plans. Includes amounts for transitional assistance benefits in 2004-2007.

Source: U.S. Centers for Medicare and Medicaid Services, Trustees Report & Trust Funds, "2020 Expanded and Supplementary Tables and Figures," <https://www.cms.gov/Research-Statistics-Data-and-Systems/Statistics-Trends-and-Reports/ReportsTrustFunds/index.html>, accessed May 2020.

Table 157. Medicaid Enrollment by Race/Ethnicity, Age, and Poverty Status: 2017

[In thousands, except percent (62,032 represents 62,032,000). Based on the Current Population Survey, Annual Social and Economic Supplement (CPS ASEC). Represents number of persons who were enrolled at any time in year shown. Covers persons for whom poverty status was determined, and excludes unrelated individuals under age 15. Persons did not have to receive medical care paid for by Medicaid in order to be counted. For explanation of poverty level, see text, Section 13]

Poverty status	Total [1]	White alone [2]	Black alone [2]	Asian alone [2]	His-panic [3]	Under age 18	Age 18 to 24	Age 25 to 44	Age 45 to 64	Age 65 and over
Persons covered, total	**62,032**	**42,195**	**12,451**	**3,498**	**18,046**	**27,844**	**6,416**	**12,978**	**11,142**	**3,652**
Below poverty level	19,932	12,662	5,087	851	6,055	9,615	1,789	3,880	3,475	1,173
Above poverty level	42,100	29,533	7,364	2,646	11,991	18,229	4,627	9,097	7,667	2,479
Percent of population covered by Medicaid:										
All persons	**19.2**	**17.1**	**29.3**	**18.0**	**30.6**	**38.0**	**21.9**	**15.2**	**13.4**	**7.1**
Persons in poverty	50.2	47.9	56.6	43.6	56.1	75.1	37.8	40.8	43.6	25.1
Persons not in poverty	14.9	13.4	22.0	15.1	24.8	30.1	18.8	12.0	10.2	5.3

[1] Includes other races, not shown separately. [2] Refers to people who reported specified race and did not report any other race category. [3] Persons of Hispanic origin may be of any race.

Source: U.S. Census Bureau, 2018 Current Population Survey Annual Social and Economic Supplement, CPS Table Creator, <https://www.census.gov/cps/data/cpstablecreator.html>, accessed November 2018. See also *Health Insurance Coverage in the United States: 2017*, Current Population Reports, P60-P264, <https://www.census.gov/topics/health/health-insurance.html>.

Table 158. Medicaid Benefit Spending by Source of Funds and Per Enrollee by State and Island Area: 2018

[In units as indicated (588,212.6 represents $588,212,600,000). For the fiscal year 2018. Data exclude spending for program administration and Medicaid-expansion Children's Health Insurance Program enrollees. Data are based on analysis of administrative data submitted to the Centers for Medicare & Medicaid Services (CMS) via CMS-64 records, as of June or July 2019 for expenditures and as of October 2019 for enrollment. Not all states had certified their CMS-64 financial management report (FMR) submissions as of June 2019. Data may change if states revise their expenditure data after this date]

State and Island Area	Medicaid benefit spending (million dollars)			Medicaid full year enrollees (1,000) [1]	Total spending per enrollee (dollars)
	Total	Federal funds	State funds		
Total [2]	**588,212.6**	**368,933.9**	**219,278.7**	**76,488.9**	**7,690.2**
U.S. total [3]	**585,600.0**	**366,586.2**	**219,013.8**	**75,132.6**	**7,794.2**
Alabama	5,546.4	3,976.4	1,570.0	1,021.0	5,432.5
Alaska	2,033.4	1,467.5	565.9	200.5	10,143.4
Arizona	12,132.1	9,241.2	2,890.9	1,892.5	6,410.5
Arkansas	6,308.1	4,910.3	1,397.7	922.2	6,840.2
California [4]	83,157.9	51,225.9	31,932.0	13,009.7	6,392.0
Colorado	8,925.8	5,351.3	3,574.5	1,300.2	6,864.9
Connecticut	8,175.8	4,893.3	3,282.5	923.0	8,857.4
Delaware	2,237.9	1,443.9	794.0	210.8	10,615.9
District of Columbia	2,805.0	2,069.4	735.6	261.9	10,711.3
Florida	22,893.3	14,213.5	8,679.7	3,918.4	5,842.6
Georgia	10,839.4	7,445.9	3,393.5	1,962.1	5,524.5
Hawaii	2,213.1	1,469.4	743.7	327.3	6,762.7
Idaho	1,901.3	1,354.2	547.1	305.5	6,222.9
Illinois	22,194.8	12,890.9	9,304.0	2,868.9	7,736.4
Indiana	11,241.8	7,891.4	3,350.4	1,335.3	8,418.8
Iowa	4,828.4	3,171.2	1,657.2	598.7	8,064.9
Kansas	3,437.7	1,890.1	1,547.6	368.9	9,318.0
Kentucky	9,801.4	7,645.9	2,155.5	1,339.0	7,320.1
Louisiana	10,835.7	7,739.2	3,096.5	1,643.3	6,594.0
Maine	2,686.8	1,731.4	955.4	255.7	10,506.6
Maryland	11,417.3	6,934.3	4,483.0	1,224.2	9,326.5
Massachusetts	17,655.4	9,693.3	7,962.2	1,803.8	9,787.7
Michigan	16,286.6	11,612.8	4,673.8	2,430.1	6,702.0
Minnesota	12,324.5	7,035.0	5,289.6	1,093.2	11,274.0
Mississippi	5,278.7	3,998.5	1,280.2	691.4	7,635.3
Missouri	10,296.3	6,712.7	3,583.6	958.4	10,743.6
Montana	1,830.2	1,421.7	408.5	255.1	7,174.3
Nebraska	2,126.6	1,122.0	1,004.6	245.6	8,660.3
Nevada	3,922.5	2,941.0	981.5	598.7	6,551.7
New Hampshire	2,150.4	1,266.1	884.3	189.4	11,355.4
New Jersey	14,843.2	8,831.8	6,011.4	1,693.7	8,763.8
New Mexico	5,112.3	4,043.0	1,069.3	849.3	6,019.8
New York [5]	73,030.1	39,662.3	33,367.8	6,155.7	11,863.8
North Carolina	13,339.1	9,034.5	4,304.6	2,163.9	6,164.5
North Dakota	1,222.2	744.8	477.4	93.1	13,129.9
Ohio	21,743.9	14,940.8	6,803.1	2,987.9	7,277.3
Oklahoma	4,433.5	2,691.6	1,741.9	653.8	6,781.2
Oregon	8,877.4	6,504.0	2,373.4	959.6	9,250.9
Pennsylvania	29,863.6	17,612.5	12,251.0	2,769.2	10,784.1
Rhode Island	2,620.0	1,547.3	1,072.7	309.1	8,475.2
South Carolina	6,006.5	4,311.1	1,695.4	1,262.1	4,759.0
South Dakota	865.5	517.2	348.3	100.8	8,586.9
Tennessee	9,680.8	6,419.5	3,261.3	1,584.9	6,108.0
Texas	37,585.4	21,483.7	16,101.8	4,290.6	8,760.0
Utah	2,421.9	1,703.5	718.4	297.8	8,134.0
Vermont	1,596.0	933.6	662.3	177.4	8,998.9
Virginia	9,562.0	4,768.2	4,793.8	1,058.1	9,037.3
Washington	12,093.6	7,542.4	4,551.2	1,784.3	6,777.6
West Virginia	3,854.2	3,035.3	818.8	540.4	7,132.1
Wisconsin	8,768.7	5,185.9	3,582.8	1,187.6	7,383.6
Wyoming	595.4	313.4	282.0	58.9	10,113.3
American Samoa	33.6	18.7	14.9	27.9	1,206.1
Guam	82.1	53.7	28.4	36.0	2,282.8
Northern Mariana Islands	44.3	24.6	19.7	9.2	4,829.4
Puerto Rico	2,393.1	2,197.4	195.8	1,258.8	1,901.1
Virgin Islands	59.4	53.4	6.0	24.4	2,437.6

[1] Full year equivalent enrollment; may also be referred to as average monthly enrollment. [2] Total includes 50 states, DC, and Island Areas. [3] Includes 50 states and DC. [4] California's fourth quarter submissions were not certified. [5] New York's CMS-64 quarterly enrollment data was missing the first three quarters of FY2018. The count displayed here is the average monthly enrollment based on the last quarter of enrollment.

Source: Medicaid and CHIP Payment and Access Commission, "MACStats," <https://www.macpac.gov/macstats/>, accessed May 2020.

Table 159. Children's Health Insurance Program (CHIP) by State—Expenditures, 2018, and Enrollment, 2017 and 2018

[17,297.4 represents $17,297,400,000. For fiscal year. Expenditure data reported as of June 2019. Enrollment data reported as of May 2019, and subject to revision. Components may not add to total due to rounding. CHIP is a federal-state program that provides health benefits coverage to children without health insurance and living in families whose incomes are too high to qualify for Medicaid. States may create CHIP programs as an expansion of Medicaid, a program separate from Medicaid, or a combination of both approaches. Based on analysis of CHIP data from the Centers for Medicare & Medicaid Services; see source for details]

State	Expenditures, 2018 (million dollars)			Children enrolled (number)	
	Total	Federal	State	2017	2018
United States	**17,297.4**	**16,284.8**	**1,012.7**	**9,462,794**	**9,632,367**
Alabama [1,2]	376.3	376.3	–	220,980	222,072
Alaska	32.1	28.9	3.2	18,704	19,747
Arizona [1]	238.6	238.7	-(Z)	115,400	127,063
Arkansas [1,3]	159.3	159.3	-(Z)	143,618	98,127
California [4]	3,263.3	2,885.4	377.9	2,028,716	1,976,284
Colorado	322.0	283.4	38.6	176,426	182,199
Connecticut	49.3	96.3	-47.0	28,889	28,900
Delaware	38.7	36.0	2.7	13,890	13,958
District of Columbia	45.6	45.6	–	11,771	16,125
Florida	776.5	748.0	28.4	465,631	496,080
Georgia [1,5]	421.9	421.9	-0.1	237,011	262,135
Hawaii	65.9	60.0	5.9	27,589	29,375
Idaho [1]	73.6	73.6	–	36,658	39,657
Illinois	421.8	372.9	48.8	324,282	296,186
Indiana	251.1	248.4	2.7	126,317	135,308
Iowa	131.3	123.4	7.9	91,866	99,314
Kansas	123.9	113.1	10.7	64,601	63,850
Kentucky [1]	207.0	207.0	(Z)	96,379	103,244
Louisiana	363.2	354.5	8.8	158,298	172,934
Maine	35.9	35.2	0.7	23,318	25,219
Maryland	341.7	300.7	41.0	141,836	151,179
Massachusetts	782.4	688.1	94.4	220,128	227,819
Michigan [6]	264.3	260.0	4.4	79,737	81,391
Minnesota [1]	19.0	122.3	-103.4	4,051	4,043
Mississippi	244.2	244.2	–	90,904	88,491
Missouri [7]	269.4	264.9	4.5	93,800	109,169
Montana	87.4	86.3	1.1	32,121	31,284
Nebraska	91.9	82.5	9.4	56,197	59,608
Nevada	74.3	73.5	0.7	80,342	71,994
New Hampshire	33.1	42.6	-9.5	17,823	17,781
New Jersey	560.9	493.5	67.4	239,813	254,284
New Mexico [1]	96.4	96.2	0.1	13,709	13,224
New York	1,589.7	1,398.9	190.8	762,685	768,259
North Carolina	474.8	475.0	-0.2	273,850	296,759
North Dakota	28.5	25.2	3.3	7,883	8,689
Ohio	512.7	494.6	18.1	250,195	260,890
Oklahoma	236.0	221.9	14.2	201,006	206,350
Oregon	358.9	350.1	8.8	177,590	189,618
Pennsylvania	710.8	634.5	76.3	363,323	369,172
Rhode Island	99.2	88.3	10.9	27,433	35,920
South Carolina	174.7	174.7	–	87,624	111,051
South Dakota	32.1	29.5	2.7	20,308	20,129
Tennessee	224.8	222.4	2.4	103,293	107,140
Texas	1,535.9	1,425.4	110.6	1,137,899	1,136,587
Utah [1]	127.7	127.6	0.1	62,140	60,423
Vermont	12.7	26.8	-14.2	5,841	4,942
Virginia	408.3	359.3	49.0	202,974	207,725
Washington	174.5	222.4	-47.9	74,051	87,732
West Virginia [8]	73.5	73.5	–	37,464	39,419
Wisconsin	245.9	259.1	-13.1	179,342	196,416
Wyoming	14.4	12.7	1.7	7,088	7,102

– Represents zero. Z Less than $50,000. [1] State reports negative state CHIP spending for benefits or state program administration due to federal CHIP spending exceeding total CHIP spending. Federal CHIP spending exceeds total CHIP spending due to negative prior period adjustments and the 23 percent increase in the enhanced federal medical assistance percentage (E-FMAP) that went into effect in FY 2016. Because these prior period adjustments apply to periods before the 23 percent increase to the E-FMAP, these negative adjustments decrease total spending to a greater extent than federal spending. [2] The Alabama FY2017 enrollment totals are artificially high, as reports contain duplicate enrollees. [3] Due to system challenges and data limitations, the Arkansas FY2017 enrollment totals contain duplicates and are artificially high. [4] Due to reporting system updates, California's CHIP enrollment totals for FY2017 and FY2018 are estimates. [5] For Georgia, some Title XIX Medicaid children may be reported with the Title XXI CHIP children, and vice versa. [6] Michigan Title XXI funded Medicaid enrollees are included in Medicaid enrollment counts, rather than in CHIP for FY2017. [7] The Missouri FY2017 CHIP enrollment total is artificially low due to the inadvertent exclusion of certain CHIP members from reporting. [8] West Virginia CHIP annual numbers are artificially low in FY2017 due to de-duplication of data and other data quality improvement efforts.

Source: Medicaid and CHIP Payment and Access Commission, "MACStats: Program Enrollment and Spending, CHIP," <https://www.macpac.gov/macstats/>; and U.S. Centers for Medicare & Medicaid Services, CHIP Reports & Evaluations, "Annual Enrollment Reports," <https://www.medicaid.gov/chip/reports-and-evaluations/index.html>; accessed July 2020.

Table 160. Medicaid Managed Care Enrollment by State and Other Areas: 2000 to 2018

[In thousands except as noted (33,690 represents 33,690,000). Through 2010, for year ending June 30; beginning with 2013, as of July 1. Medicaid managed care provides Medicaid health benefits and additional services through contracted arrangements between state Medicaid agencies and managed care entities. The unduplicated Medicaid enrollment figures include dual Medicare-Medicaid enrollees. The unduplicated managed care enrollment figures include enrollees in any Medicaid managed care program, including comprehensive managed care organizations (MCOs), limited benefit plans such as prepaid inpatient and ambulatory health plans, primary care case management (PCCM) programs, and PCCM entities]

State and other areas	Total enroll-ment	Managed care enrollment		State and other areas	Total enroll-ment	Managed care enrollment		State and other areas	Total enroll-ment	Managed care enrollment	
		Number	Percent of total			Number	Percent of total			Number	Percent of total
2000.......	33,690	18,786	55.8	GA[4].......	2,074	1,485	71.6	NM........	842	666	79.1
2010.......	54,612	39,020	71.5	HI........	356	352	98.8	NY........	6,154	4,764	77.4
2012.......	(NA)	(NA)	(NA)	ID.........	300	273	90.9	NC.........	2,178	1,581	72.6
2013.......	62,507	45,923	73.5	IL..........	3,110	2,177	70.0	ND........	93	49	52.6
2014.......	72,050	55,459	77.0	IN..........	1,458	1,126	77.3	OH........	2,916	2,450	84.0
2015.......	77,847	62,373	80.1	IA..........	626	581	92.7	OK........	881	649	73.7
2016.......	80,185	65,006	81.1	KS.........	417	358	85.9	OR........	1,063	848	79.7
2017.......	80,243	65,796	82.0	KY.........	1,385	1,260	90.9	PA.........	2,897	2,628	90.7
2018				LA.........	1,640	1,505	91.7	RI.........	313	302	96.6
Total[1]...	**79,899**	**66,107**	**82.7**	ME........	270	234	86.7	SC.........	1,196	1,196	100.0
U.S......	78,393	64,602	82.4	MD........	1,402	1,170	83.4	SD.........	124	92	74.4
AL.........	1,019	638	62.6	MA........	1,866	1,211	64.9	TN.........	1,510	1,387	91.8
AK[2].......	198	–	–	MI.........	4,624	4,609	99.7	TX.........	3,982	3,846	96.6
AZ........	1,849	1,561	84.4	MN........	1,123	892	79.5	UT........	276	271	98.4
AR........	980	871	88.9	MS........	684	442	64.6	VT........	175	123	70.6
CA........	13,140	10,670	81.2	MO........	971	955	98.3	VA........	1,063	875	82.3
CO[3].......	1,303	1,171	89.9	MT........	292	215	73.8	WA........	1,781	1,781	100.0
CT[2].......	929	–	–	NE........	250	249	99.6	WV........	506	407	80.5
DE........	237	209	88.2	NV........	667	588	88.2	WI........	1,197	812	67.8
DC........	265	189	71.5	NH........	201	134	66.6	WY........	58	(Z)	0.6
FL.........	3,885	3,179	81.8	NJ........	1,668	1,569	94.1	PR[5].......	1,506	1,506	100.0

– Represents zero. NA Not available. Z Less than 500. [1] Includes enrollment for Puerto Rico. [2] Alaska and Connecticut did not provide total Medicaid enrollment as of July 1, 2018. This figure is from the July-September 2018 enrollment data collected through the Medicaid Budget and Expenditure System, updated December 2019, and accessed January 14, 2020. See <https://data.medicaid.gov/Enrollment/2018-4Q-Medicaid-MBES-Enrollment/qjmt-6zzy>. [3] Colorado reported plan level enrollment as 0 for plans that had less than 30 beneficiaries. [4] Georgia's total Medicaid enrollment in any type of managed care does not include 1,626,252 enrollees in Georgia's Non-Emergency Medical Transportation (NEMT) program; a portion of these enrollees are simultaneously enrolled in other managed care programs. [5] Puerto Rico provides expanded Medicaid to 421,577 low-income, childless adults under an authority other than ACA Section VIII.

Source: U.S. Centers for Medicare and Medicaid Services, "Medicaid Managed Care Enrollment Report: 2018 Medicaid Managed Care Enrollment Summary," <https://www.medicaid.gov/medicaid/managed-care/enrollment/index.html>, June 2020, and earlier releases and reports.

Table 161. Medicaid Benefit Spending by Service Category: 2014 to 2018

[In millions of dollars (469,683 represents $469,683,000,000). For fiscal years. Covers the 50 states, DC, and the territories. Includes federal and state funds. Service category definitions and spending amounts shown here may differ from other Centers for Medicare & Medicaid (CMS) sources. Data shown here are subject to revisions because States may have revised their expenditure data after an initial submission date]

Spending category	2014	2015	2016	2017	2018
Total benefit spending................................	**469,683**	**526,159**	**550,880**	**572,244**	**588,213**
Fee for service:					
Hospital services................................	85,537	92,745	88,607	77,790	78,862
Physician and surgical services....................	13,973	11,189	9,935	8,752	8,968
Dental services................................	3,960	4,218	3,929	3,951	3,420
Other practitioner services........................	1,913	2,150	2,599	1,892	1,784
Clinic and health centers........................	10,216	11,180	10,624	11,134	11,156
Other acute services [1]........................	38,294	38,905	36,541	45,622	45,430
Drugs [2]..	8,059	10,535	8,480	3,218	9,981
Institutional long-term services and supports (LTSS) [3]...........	65,692	59,552	60,070	58,001	56,652
Home and community LTSS [4]........................	55,796	58,107	62,052	63,987	71,485
Managed care and premium assistance............................	179,089	230,220	258,551	285,653	288,219
Medicare premiums and coinsurance..................................	15,094	15,428	17,159	19,209	19,884
Collections [5]..	-7,940	-8,070	-7,667	-6,966	-7,628

[1] Other acute services include laboratory or x-ray services; early periodic screening, diagnostic, and treatment (EPSDT) screenings; emergency services for unauthorized aliens; physical, occupational, speech, and hearing therapy; prosthetics, dentures, and eyeglasses; preventive services and vaccines; school-based services; rehabilitative services; hospice; and various other services not otherwise categorized. [2] Spending for drugs are net of rebates. [3] Institutional LTSS includes nursing facility, intermediate care facility for individuals with intellectual disabilities, and mental health facility. [4] Home- and community-based LTSS includes home health, waiver and state plan services, personal care, and certified community behavioral health clinic. [5] Collections includes third-party liability, estate, and other recoveries.

Source: Medicaid and CHIP Payment and Access Commission, *MACStats: Medicaid and CHIP Data Book*, December 2019, and previous editions. See also <https://www.macpac.gov/macstats/>.

Table 162. Medicare Hospital Insurance and Supplemental Medical Insurance Expenditures, Total and as a Percent of GDP: 1990 to 2040

[In millions of dollars (5,963,145 represents $5,963,145,000,000), except percent. Incurred amounts relate to expenditures for services performed in a given year, even if payment for those expenditures occurs in a later year. The Medicare program has two components: Medicare Part A Hospital Insurance (HI); and Supplementary Medical Insurance (SMI), consisting of Part B Medical Insurance, and Part D Prescription Drug Coverage. See text in this section for details]

Year	GDP	Medicare expenditures				Medicare expenditures as percent of GDP			
		Total	HI Part A	SMI Part B	SMI Part D	Total	HI Part A	SMI Part B	SMI Part D
ACTUAL									
1990.........	5,963,145	110,903	66,785	44,118	(X)	1.86	1.12	0.74	(X)
2000.........	10,252,347	225,983	132,803	93,180	(X)	2.20	1.30	0.91	(X)
2010.........	14,992,052	523,912	245,985	215,071	62,857	3.49	1.64	1.43	0.42
2011.........	15,542,582	548,532	256,104	226,049	66,379	3.53	1.65	1.45	0.43
2012.........	16,197,007	571,741	262,586	240,271	68,885	3.53	1.62	1.48	0.43
2013.........	16,784,851	590,166	268,930	247,942	73,294	3.52	1.60	1.48	0.44
2014.........	17,527,258	618,373	269,553	266,567	82,253	3.53	1.54	1.52	0.47
2015.........	18,224,780	648,971	277,717	281,303	89,952	3.56	1.52	1.54	0.49
2016.........	18,715,041	677,120	288,892	295,084	93,144	3.62	1.54	1.58	0.50
2017.........	19,519,424	707,822	300,063	313,481	94,278	3.63	1.54	1.61	0.48
2018.........	20,580,223	751,630	311,041	341,354	99,235	3.65	1.51	1.66	0.48
2019.........	21,426,410	800,173	326,509	371,325	102,339	3.73	1.52	1.73	0.48
PROJECTED [1]									
2020.........	22,340,837	860,506	351,398	403,941	105,168	3.85	1.57	1.81	0.47
2021.........	23,342,087	921,788	373,531	435,631	112,626	3.95	1.60	1.87	0.48
2022.........	24,343,839	987,963	397,943	468,958	121,062	4.06	1.63	1.93	0.50
2023.........	25,369,466	1,062,942	424,591	508,587	129,764	4.19	1.67	2.00	0.51
2024.........	26,441,359	1,141,188	451,200	551,157	138,831	4.32	1.71	2.08	0.53
2025.........	27,552,251	1,226,099	479,108	600,040	146,951	4.45	1.74	2.18	0.53
2030.........	33,806,194	1,748,552	649,499	896,733	202,319	5.17	1.92	2.65	0.60
2035.........	41,307,068	2,338,449	841,220	1,232,443	264,786	5.66	2.04	2.98	0.64
2040.........	50,291,151	2,987,424	1,062,854	1,589,413	335,156	5.94	2.11	3.16	0.67

X Not applicable. [1] Projections are a projected baseline, and are based on current law; that is, they assume that laws on the books will be implemented and adhered to with respect to scheduled taxes, premium revenues, and payments to providers and health plans. The one exception is that the projections disregard payment reductions that would result from the projected depletion of the Medicare Hospital Insurance trust fund (Part A), thus allowing the size of deficits to become apparent. To date, Congress has not allowed the assets of the Medicare Hospital Insurance trust fund to become depleted.

Source: U.S. Centers for Medicare and Medicaid Services, Trustees Report & Trust Funds, "2020 Expanded and Supplementary Tables and Figures," <https://www.cms.gov/Research-Statistics-Data-and-Systems/Statistics-Trends-and-Reports/ReportsTrustFunds/index.html>, accessed May 2020.

Table 163. Persons With and Without Health Insurance Coverage by State: 2018

[293,684 represents 293,684,000. Data are from the American Community Survey (ACS), and measures population without health insurance coverage at the time of the interview. See source for more information]

State	Total persons covered (1,000)	Total persons not covered		Children not covered [1]		State	Total persons covered (1,000)	Total persons not covered		Children not covered [1]	
		Number (1,000)	Percent of total	Number (1,000)	Percent of total			Number (1,000)	Percent of total	Number (1,000)	Percent of total
U.S.........	**293,684**	**28,566**	**8.9**	**4,055**	**5.2**	MO.........	5,448	566	9.4	83	5.7
AL..........	4,329	481	10.0	41	3.5	MT.........	961	86	8.2	15	6.1
AK..........	623	90	12.6	18	9.4	NE..........	1,743	158	8.3	26	5.2
AZ..........	6,315	750	10.6	146	8.4	NV..........	2,662	336	11.2	58	8.0
AR..........	2,717	244	8.2	34	4.5	NH..........	1,263	77	5.7	7	2.6
CA..........	36,237	2,826	7.2	299	3.1	NJ..........	8,149	655	7.4	80	3.9
CO..........	5,182	422	7.5	62	4.6	NM..........	1,864	196	9.5	27	5.3
CT..........	3,337	187	5.3	20	2.6	NY..........	18,261	1,041	5.4	107	2.5
DE..........	898	54	5.7	8	3.6	NC..........	9,092	1,092	10.7	130	5.3
DC..........	671	22	3.2	2	1.8	ND..........	690	54	7.3	11	6.0
FL..........	18,268	2,728	13.0	339	7.6	OH..........	10,773	744	6.5	133	4.8
GA..........	8,924	1,411	13.7	217	8.1	OK..........	3,313	548	14.2	83	8.2
HI..........	1,313	56	4.1	8	2.6	OR..........	3,858	293	7.1	33	3.6
ID..........	1,541	193	11.1	29	6.1	PA..........	11,905	699	5.5	124	4.4
IL..........	11,689	875	7.0	102	3.4	RI..........	999	42	4.1	5	2.2
IN..........	6,047	545	8.3	109	6.6	SC..........	4,468	522	10.5	56	4.7
IA..........	2,966	147	4.7	21	2.7	SD..........	780	85	9.8	13	5.9
KS..........	2,604	250	8.8	38	5.1	TN..........	5,993	675	10.1	83	5.2
KY..........	4,141	248	5.6	40	3.8	TX..........	23,240	5,003	17.7	873	11.2
LA..........	4,193	363	8.0	39	3.4	UT..........	2,840	295	9.4	72	7.4
ME..........	1,217	106	8.0	15	5.5	VT..........	595	25	4.0	2	2.0
MD..........	5,586	357	6.0	47	3.3	VA..........	7,570	731	8.8	102	5.1
MA..........	6,642	189	2.8	18	1.2	WA..........	6,950	477	6.4	47	2.7
MI..........	9,354	535	5.4	78	3.4	WV..........	1,663	114	6.4	13	3.4
MN..........	5,309	244	4.4	45	3.3	WI..........	5,428	313	5.5	51	3.8
MS..........	2,566	354	12.1	35	4.7	WY..........	508	59	10.5	10	7.1

[1] Children under age 19, who are eligible for health insurance coverage under Medicaid and the Children's Health Insurance Program.

Source: U.S. Census Bureau, 2018 American Community Survey, S2701 "Selected Characteristics of Health Insurance Coverage in the United States," <https://data.census.gov>, accessed November 2019.

Table 164. Health Insurance Coverage Status by Selected Characteristics: 2018

[323,668 represents 323,668,000. Data for coverage during all or part of 2018; people not covered had no health insurance for the entire year. Based on the Current Population Survey, Annual Social and Economic Supplement (CPS ASEC); see text, Section 1, and Appendix III. Private health insurance includes coverage provided through an employer or union, coverage purchased directly from an insurance company or through a federal or state marketplace, or TRICARE (formerly known as Civilian Health and Medical Program of the Uniformed Services). Public (government) health insurance coverage includes Medicaid, Medicare, CHAMPVA (Civilian Health and Medical Program of the Department of Veterans Affairs), and care provided by the Department of Veterans Affairs and the military. People covered only through the Indian Health Service are considered uninsured. Please note that data presented here reflect the implementation of an updated processing system that utilizes data from a redesigned questionnaire first used in the 2014 CPS ASEC. Comparisons to previous CPS ASEC health insurance data are not appropriate. See source for more information]

Characteristic	Number (1,000)							Percent			
	Total persons	Not covered by health insurance	Covered by private or public health insurance					Not covered by health insurance	Total covered [1]	Employer based coverage	Medicaid coverage
			Total [1]	Private		Public					
				Total	Employer based	Medicare	Medicaid				
Total..................	323,668	27,462	296,206	217,780	178,350	57,720	57,819	8.5	91.5	55.1	17.9
Sex:											
Male...................	158,689	14,915	143,774	107,726	88,629	26,089	26,778	9.4	90.6	55.9	16.9
Female...............	164,980	12,548	152,432	110,053	89,721	31,631	31,041	7.6	92.4	54.4	18.8
Race:											
White alone [2].........	247,472	20,345	227,127	171,563	139,718	47,783	38,703	8.2	91.8	56.5	15.6
Black alone [2].........	42,758	4,141	38,618	23,705	20,147	6,208	12,304	9.7	90.3	47.1	28.8
Asian alone [2].........	19,770	1,348	18,422	14,456	11,715	2,511	3,024	6.8	93.2	59.3	15.3
Hispanic origin [3]......	59,925	10,688	49,236	29,749	24,934	5,032	17,713	17.8	82.2	41.6	29.6
Age:											
Under 19 years.......	77,333	4,281	73,052	47,817	41,980	304	27,283	5.5	94.5	54.3	35.3
19 to 25 years........	29,297	4,192	25,105	20,492	17,278	463	4,921	14.3	85.7	59.0	16.8
26 to 34 years........	40,768	5,686	35,082	29,084	25,418	836	6,272	13.9	86.1	62.3	15.4
35 to 44 years........	41,027	5,112	35,915	30,252	26,707	1,082	5,663	12.5	87.5	65.1	13.8
45 to 64 years........	82,455	7,701	74,754	62,462	53,118	5,461	10,189	9.3	90.7	64.4	12.4
65 years and over....	52,788	491	52,296	27,671	13,849	49,573	3,491	0.9	99.1	26.2	6.6
Household income:											
Less than $25,000....	43,320	5,976	37,345	10,704	5,764	14,625	19,241	13.8	86.2	13.3	44.4
$25,000–$49,999.....	59,133	7,255	51,878	28,319	19,695	14,876	17,505	12.3	87.7	33.3	29.6
$50,000–$74,999.....	55,304	5,939	49,365	36,468	28,613	10,160	10,022	10.7	89.3	51.7	18.1
$75,000–$99,999.....	44,539	3,162	41,377	34,967	29,589	5,936	5,069	7.1	92.9	66.4	11.4
$100,000-$124,999...	34,142	1,924	32,217	28,748	25,042	3,809	2,655	5.6	94.4	73.3	7.8
$125,000-$149,999...	23,291	1,143	22,148	20,250	17,558	2,504	1,193	4.9	95.1	75.4	5.1
$150,000 or more....	63,939	2,063	61,876	58,324	52,089	5,810	2,134	3.2	96.8	81.5	3.3
Below poverty.........	38,056	6,212	31,844	8,357	5,182	6,984	20,556	16.3	83.7	13.6	54.0

[1] Includes other private and public insurance, not shown separately. Persons with coverage counted only once in total, even if covered by more than one type of policy. [2] Refers to people who reported specified race and no other race category. [3] Persons of Hispanic origin may be of any race.

Source: U.S. Census Bureau, *Health Insurance Coverage in the United States: 2018,* Current Population Reports, P60-267(RV), November 2019; and "Current Population Survey Tables for Health Insurance Coverage, Health Insurance: Tables 2018-forward," Table H-01, <https://www.census.gov/data/tables/time-series/demo/income-poverty/cps-hi.html>, accessed November 2019.

Table 165. People Without Health Insurance for the Entire Year by Age, Sex, Race/Ethnicity, and Marital Status: 2017 and 2018

[In thousands, except as noted (322,490 represents 322,490,000). Based on the Current Population Survey, Annual Social and Economic Supplement (CPS ASEC); see text, Section 1. Please note that data presented here reflect the implementation of an updated processing system that utilizes data from a redesigned questionnaire first used in the 2014 CPS ASEC. Comparisons to previous CPS ASEC health insurance data are not appropriate. See source for more information]

Characteristic	2017			2018		
	Total persons	Uninsured persons		Total persons	Uninsured persons	
		Number	Percent of total persons		Number	Percent of total persons
Total [1].....................................	322,490	25,600	7.9	323,668	27,462	8.5
Male..	158,063	13,836	8.8	158,689	14,915	9.4
Female.....................................	164,427	11,764	7.2	164,980	12,548	7.6
Under age 19 [2].............................	77,487	3,856	5.0	77,333	4,281	5.5
Age 19 to 25 [2].............................	29,811	4,070	13.7	29,297	4,192	14.3
Age 26 to 34 years........................	40,222	5,621	14.0	40,768	5,686	13.9
Age 35 to 44 years........................	40,662	4,649	11.4	41,027	5,112	12.5
Age 45 to 64 years........................	83,242	6,908	8.3	82,455	7,701	9.3
Age 65 and older..........................	51,066	496	1.0	52,788	491	0.9
White alone [3].............................	247,193	18,921	7.7	247,472	20,345	8.2
Black alone [3].............................	42,461	3,936	9.3	42,758	4,141	9.7
Asian alone [3].............................	19,498	1,241	6.4	19,770	1,348	6.8
Hispanic [4].................................	59,033	9,565	16.2	59,925	10,688	17.8
Married.....................................	102,487	7,841	7.7	101,805	8,463	8.3
Widowed....................................	3,331	415	12.5	3,385	464	13.7
Divorced....................................	19,241	2,364	12.3	18,683	2,428	13.0
Separated..................................	4,249	790	18.6	4,200	835	19.9
Never married..............................	64,629	9,838	15.2	65,475	10,500	16.0

[1] Includes other races not shown separately. [2] Children under age 19 may be eligible for Medicaid/CHIP (Children's Health Insurance Program). Individuals age 19-25 may be eligible to participate as a dependent on a parent's health insurance plan. [3] Refers to people who reported specified race and did not report any other race category. [4] Persons of Hispanic origin may be of any race.

Source: U.S. Census Bureau, *Health Insurance Coverage in the United States: 2018,* Current Population Reports, P60-267(RV), November 2019; and "Current Population Survey Tables for Health Insurance Coverage, Health Insurance: Tables 2018-forward," Table H-01, <https://www.census.gov/data/tables/time-series/demo/income-poverty/cps-hi.html>, accessed November 2019.

Table 166. Health Insurance Coverage—Public, Private, and Exchange-Based Coverage by Selected Characteristics: 2010 to 2019

[In percent, except as noted (10.2 represents 10,200,000). Covers persons age 18 to 64, except as noted. Based on the National Health Interview Survey. Data are estimates that have been released prior to final data editing and final weighting; see source for details. Data are based on a sample of the civilian noninstitutionalized population and are subject to sampling error]

Year and characteristics	No insurance [1]	Public health plan [2]	Private health insurance [3]	Exchange-based private health insurance [4] Total (millions)	Exchange-based private health insurance [4] Percent
Total age 64 and under:					
2010	18.2	22.0	61.2	(NA)	(NA)
2015	10.5	25.3	65.6	10.2	3.8
2018	11.1	25.5	65.1	10.0	3.7
2019	12.1	26.0	63.7	10.0	3.7
Age 17 and under:					
2010	7.8	39.8	53.8	(NA)	(NA)
2015	4.5	42.2	54.7	1.4	2.0
2018	5.2	41.8	54.7	1.7	2.3
2019	5.1	41.4	55.2	1.3	1.7
Age 18 to 64:					
2010	22.3	15.0	64.1	(NA)	(NA)
2015	12.8	18.9	69.7	8.8	4.5
2018	13.3	19.4	68.9	8.4	4.2
2019	14.7	20.4	66.8	8.7	4.4
Male:					
2010	25.3	12.5	63.4	(NA)	(NA)
2015	14.9	16.6	69.9	4.0	4.1
2018	15.0	17.3	69.4	3.9	4.0
2019	16.3	18.1	67.5	4.7	3.5
Female:					
2010	19.3	17.4	64.7	(NA)	(NA)
2015	10.8	21.2	69.6	4.8	4.8
2018	11.6	21.5	68.5	4.4	4.4
2019	13.1	22.6	66.1	5.3	3.9
White only, non-Hispanic:					
2010	16.4	12.8	72.2	(NA)	(NA)
2015	8.7	15.7	77.3	5.2	4.3
2018	9.0	16.2	76.7	4.7	3.9
2019	10.5	17.0	74.5	5.5	3.6
Black only, non-Hispanic:					
2010	27.2	25.3	49.3	(NA)	(NA)
2015	14.4	29.7	57.8	1.0	4.0
2018	15.2	29.0	57.9	1.0	3.9
2019	14.7	34.3	53.7	1.0	2.9
Hispanic or Latino: [5]					
2010	43.2	16.3	41.1	(NA)	(NA)
2015	27.7	23.0	50.0	1.7	5.1
2018	26.7	23.3	50.8	1.7	4.7
2019	29.7	22.5	48.8	2.1	3.8
Poor: [6]					
2010	42.2	38.8	19.6	(NA)	(NA)
2015	25.2	51.7	24.3	0.9	3.8
2018	27.4	52.7	21.4	0.6	2.7
2019	25.8	52.3	23.6	1.1	3.0
Near poor: [6]					
2010	43.0	23.7	34.7	(NA)	(NA)
2015	24.1	34.2	43.8	2.7	7.9
2018	25.1	37.8	39.3	2.3	7.2
2019	26.8	35.4	40.1	2.8	5.3
Not poor: [6]					
2010	12.6	8.1	80.8	(NA)	(NA)
2015	7.6	9.1	84.7	5.1	3.8
2018	8.3	10.1	83.1	5.6	3.8
2019	9.0	10.4	82.4	5.8	3.2
State Medicaid expansion [7]					
2019	11.0	23.4	67.6	5.7	3.3
State Medicaid non-expansion [7]					
2019	21.2	15.1	65.3	4.3	4.3

NA Not available. [1] Also includes persons who have only Indian Health Service coverage or only a private plan that covers one type of service, such as accidents or dental care. [2] Includes Medicaid, Children's Health Insurance Program (CHIP), state-sponsored or other government-sponsored health plan, Medicare, and military plans. A small number of persons covered by both public and private plans are included in both categories. [3] Includes plans obtained through an employer, purchased directly, purchased through local or community programs, or purchased through the Health Insurance Marketplace or a state-based exchange. Excludes plans that pay for only one type of service, such as accidents or dental care. A small number of persons covered by both public and private plans are included in both categories. [4] Covers persons who purchased a private health insurance plan through the Health Insurance Marketplace or state-based exchanges established under the Affordable Care Act of 2010 (P.L. 111-148, P.L. 111-152). These persons are also included under "private health insurance." [5] Persons of Hispanic or Latino origin may be of any race or combination of races. [6] Based on family size and income using the U.S. Census Bureau's poverty thresholds. "Poor" persons have incomes below the poverty threshold; "Near poor" persons have incomes of 100% to less than 200% of the poverty threshold; and "Not poor" persons have incomes of 200% of the poverty threshold or greater. Excludes persons with unknown poverty status. As of 2019, poverty categories are based the family's income in the previous calendar. [7] The Affordable Care Act gave states the option to expand Medicaid coverage to adults with incomes up to and including 138 percent of the federal poverty level. As of 2019, Medicaid has been expanded in 33 states and DC. States with no Medicaid expansion include Alabama, Florida, Georgia, Idaho, Kansas, Mississippi, Missouri, Nebraska, North Carolina, Oklahoma, South Carolina, South Dakota, Tennessee, Texas, Utah, Wisconsin, and Wyoming.

Source: U.S. National Center for Health Statistics, National Health Interview Survey Early Release Program, *Health Insurance Coverage: Early Release of Estimates From the National Health Interview Survey, 2019,* September 2020.

Table 167. Health Insurance Coverage Status and Plan Type: 1970 to 2018

[142.3 represents 142,300,000. Based on the National Health Interview Survey. Covers persons under age 65. Persons may report more than one type of health insurance coverage]

Year	Private insurance, any [1]	Private, employer based	Private, other [2]	Medicaid	Medicare	Other public	No health insurance [3]
NUMBER (mil.)							
1970.	142.3	124.1	18.0	(NA)	(NA)	(NA)	(NA)
1980.	154.1	138.5	15.6	13.8	2.7	3.9	23.3
1990.	162.7	146.3	16.3	15.4	3.0	6.1	33.4
1995.	159.8	146.2	13.5	25.6	3.1	6.4	40.6
2000.	174.2	163.4	10.5	21.9	4.1	5.2	38.5
2005.	174.7	162.9	11.1	33.2	4.5	6.4	42.1
2006.	171.2	158.8	11.8	36.2	5.4	6.5	43.9
2007.	174.1	160.7	12.7	36.2	5.4	7.0	43.3
2008.	171.9	158.6	12.6	38.4	5.9	7.0	44.1
2009.	166.7	152.8	13.1	42.4	6.2	7.7	46.2
2010.	163.9	150.2	12.7	44.8	6.0	8.1	48.3
2011.	164.5	150.1	12.7	47.4	6.4	7.9	45.8
2012.	164.9	151.8	11.8	48.1	6.5	8.1	45.2
2013.	165.3	151.5	12.5	48.5	7.1	8.1	44.6
2014.	170.7	151.3	17.2	52.6	6.7	8.4	35.7
2015.	176.6	154.7	20.8	55.4	7.0	8.1	28.7
2016.	177.7	155.5	21.2	57.0	7.5	7.6	27.9
2017.	177.7	157.5	19.2	54.6	7.3	8.5	28.9
2018.	177.5	157.8	18.9	54.7	7.8	10.2	30.0
PERCENT							
1970.	78.7	68.6	10.0	(NA)	(NA)	(NA)	(NA)
1980.	79.4	71.4	8.0	7.1	1.4	2.0	12.0
1990.	75.9	68.3	7.6	7.2	1.4	2.9	15.6
1995.	71.3	65.6	5.7	11.5	1.6	2.6	16.3
2000.	71.7	67.3	4.2	9.5	1.7	2.2	16.8
2005.	68.2	63.6	4.4	12.9	1.8	2.5	16.4
2006.	66.3	61.5	4.6	14.0	2.1	2.5	17.0
2007.	66.8	61.6	4.9	13.9	2.1	2.7	16.6
2008.	65.6	60.5	4.8	14.7	2.3	2.7	16.8
2009.	63.3	58.0	5.0	16.1	2.3	2.9	17.5
2010.	61.7	56.6	4.8	16.9	2.3	3.1	18.2
2011.	61.8	56.4	4.8	17.8	2.4	3.0	17.2
2012.	61.8	56.9	4.4	18.0	2.4	3.0	16.9
2013.	61.8	56.6	4.7	18.1	2.6	3.0	16.7
2014.	63.7	56.4	6.4	19.6	2.5	3.1	13.3
2015.	65.5	57.4	7.7	20.6	2.6	3.0	10.6
2016.	65.7	57.4	7.8	21.1	2.8	2.8	10.3
2017.	65.7	58.2	7.1	20.2	2.7	3.1	10.7
2018.	65.3	58.1	6.9	20.2	2.9	3.7	11.0

NA Not available. [1] Private health insurance coverage obtained through an employer, purchased directly, or obtained through any other means. Beginning in 2014, also includes plans purchased through the Health Insurance Marketplace or a state-based exchange under the Affordable Care Act of 2010. Excludes plans that cover only one type of service such as accidents or dental care. [2] Private insurance that is directly purchased as well as plans obtained through school or other means. Beginning 2014, also includes plans purchased through the Health Insurance Marketplace or a state-based exchange. [3] Includes persons who did not have any private or government-sponsored health plan, or military-related coverage, and persons with only Indian Health Service coverage or a private plan that covers only one type of service.

Source: U.S. National Center for Health Statistics, "Long-term Trends in Health Insurance: Estimates from the National Health Interview Survey, United States, 1968-2018," <https://www.cdc.gov/nchs/health_policy/coverage_and_access.htm>, accessed July 2019.

Table 168. Health Insurance Enrollment in High Deductible Health Plans (HDHP) and Health Savings Accounts: 2010 to 2018

[In percent. Covers persons under age 65 with private health insurance coverage. For 2018, an HDHP is a private health plan with an annual deductible of at least $1,350 for self-only coverage or $2,700 for family coverage. For 2015 to 2017, these amounts were $1,300 for self-only coverage and $2,600 for family coverage. The deductible is adjusted annually for inflation. For deductibles for earlier years, see Technical Notes in source. Components of HDHP may not sum due to rounding. The measures of HDHP enrollment and being in a family with a flexible spending account (FSA) for medical expenses are not mutually exclusive; a person may be counted in more than one measure. Based on the National Health Interview Survey. Data are based on a sample of the civilian noninstitutionalized population and are subject to sampling error]

Year	HDHP enrollment					In a family with a flexible spending account [5]
	Total	HDHP without health savings account [1]	HDHP with health savings account [2]	By source		
				Employment based [3]	Directly purchased [4]	
2010.	25.3	17.6	7.7	23.3	48.0	20.4
2011.	29.0	19.9	9.2	26.9	52.4	21.4
2012.	31.1	20.3	10.8	29.2	54.7	21.6
2013.	33.9	22.2	11.7	32.0	56.4	21.6
2014.	36.9	23.6	13.3	36.2	54.1	21.2
2015.	36.7	23.4	13.3	36.6	50.9	21.7
2016.	39.4	23.9	15.5	39.6	51.9	22.1
2017.	43.7	25.5	18.2	44.1	55.3	23.6
2018 (P).	45.8	25.4	20.4	46.6	52.2	23.9

P Preliminary. [1] Health savings accounts are tax-favored accounts available only to persons with an HDHP to pay for current and future medical expenses. Funds contributed are not subject to federal income tax at the time of deposit and may be used to cover qualified medical expenses without federal tax liability. HSA funds are rolled over annually and accumulate year to year. [2] An HDHP with a health savings account is also known as a consumer driven health plan. [3] Private insurance originally obtained through a current or former employer, union, or professional association. [4] Private insurance originally obtained through direct purchase or other means not related to employment. [5] A flexible spending account allows employees to set aside pretax dollars to cover out-of-pocket medical expenses. FSAs are typically available to persons who do not have an HDHP and thus are not eligible for an HSA. Any money not used during the year is lost to the employee.

Source: U.S. National Center for Health Statistics, *Health Insurance Coverage: Early Release of Estimates From the National Health Interview Survey, 2018*, May 2019. See also <https://www.cdc.gov/nchs/nhis/releases.htm>.

Table 169. Worker Participation in Employer-Sponsored Health Insurance and Benefit Programs, and Participant Contributions: 2019

[Based on the March 2019 National Compensation Survey; survey drew responses from approximately 6,470 private industry establishments of all sizes, representing about 120.4 million workers. Excludes federal government workers, the military, agricultural workers, private household workers, and the self-employed. For more information, see Appendix III, and the Bureau of Labor Statistics (BLS) Handbook of Methods, National Compensation Measures, at <https://www.bls.gov/opub/hom/ncs/home.htm>]

Characteristic	Percent of workers participating—				Single coverage medical plans		Family coverage medical plans	
	Medical care	Dental care	Vision care	Out-patient prescription drug coverage	Percent of employees required to contribute to premiums	Average monthly contri-bution[1] (dol.)	Percent of employees required to contribute to premiums	Average monthly contri-bution[1] (dol.)
Total	**49**	**33**	**20**	**48**	**86**	**137.43**	**93**	**577.44**
Management, professional, and related	65	48	30	64	88	133.23	95	562.61
Management, business, and financial	70	50	30	69	90	137.78	97	543.47
Professional and related	62	47	30	61	87	130.19	95	575.03
Service	26	17	10	25	86	145.17	92	685.26
Sales and office	47	30	18	46	89	136.26	96	576.32
Sales and related	35	20	11	34	91	137.91	97	563.01
Office and administrative support	54	37	22	54	88	135.51	96	582.25
Natural resources, construction, and maintenance	56	31	22	55	80	145.83	88	584.59
Production, transportation, and material moving	55	37	23	55	84	138.14	88	532.26
Production	60	40	24	59	85	132.85	89	502.31
Transportation, and material moving	51	35	23	50	84	144.38	87	566.99
Full-time[2]	61	41	26	60	87	137.25	94	573.28
Part-time[2]	12	8	5	11	80	140.44	84	649.39
Union[3]	76	61	46	75	65	133.62	68	427.60
Nonunion	46	30	18	46	90	137.87	97	594.23
Average hourly wage percentile:[4]								
Lowest 25 percent	21	11	6	21	88	144.67	95	665.36
Lowest 10 percent	13	7	4	13	87	148.43	94	621.83
Second 25 percent	48	30	19	47	88	137.43	95	598.54
Third 25 percent	65	43	27	63	86	139.33	92	571.59
Highest 25 percent	70	55	35	70	85	132.79	92	532.28
Highest 10 percent	72	59	38	72	87	132.43	94	512.68

[1] The average is for all workers with medical care benefits, and cover plans that have a flat monthly cost. [2] Employees are classified as working either a full-time or part-time schedule based on the definition used by each establishment. [3] Union workers are those whose wages are determined through collective bargaining. [4] Tenth percentile, $10.48; 25th, $13.25; 50th (median), $19.00; 75th, $30.61; and 90th, $48.28. See "Technical Note" in source, <https://www.bls.gov/ncs/ebs/benefits/2019/tech_note.htm>.

Source: U.S. Bureau of Labor Statistics, Annual Bulletin on Benefit Coverage, *National Compensation Survey: Employee Benefits in the United States, March 2019*, Bulletin 2791, September 2019. See also <https://www.bls.gov/ncs/ebs/benefits/2019/home.htm>.

Table 170. Employer-Sponsored Health Insurance Enrollment by Type of Plan and Employer Size: 2015

[In millions (177.5 represents 177,500,000). Based on the Current Population Survey, Annual and Social Economic Supplement, and Agency for Healthcare Research and Quality's Medical Expenditure Panel Surveys. For persons and their dependents covered by health insurance sponsored by a current or former employer. Abbreviations: HMO = health maintenance organization; PPO = preferred provider organization; POS = point-of-service plan; and HDED = high deductible health plan (including but not limited to IRS-qualified high deductible health plans)]

Employer sector and size	Total					Self-insured plans[1]					Fully insured plans[2]				
	Total	HMO	PPO	POS	HDED	Total	HMO	PPO	POS	HDED	Total	HMO	PPO	POS	HDED
TOTAL															
Total	**177.5**	**25.1**	**101.1**	**15.8**	**35.5**	**101.2**	**8.1**	**64.5**	**4.9**	**23.8**	**76.3**	**17.0**	**36.6**	**11.0**	**11.7**
Less than 50 employees	27.9	4.1	11.8	5.6	6.3	4.0	(Z)	2.6	0.5	1.0	23.9	4.1	9.3	5.2	5.3
50 to 99 employees	11.7	1.5	5.3	2.1	2.7	2.5	(Z)	1.6	0.2	0.6	9.2	1.5	3.6	1.9	2.1
100 to 499 employees	23.7	2.8	14.6	2.4	4.0	10.4	0.4	7.7	0.6	1.7	13.4	2.4	7.0	1.8	2.2
500 to 999 employees	12.9	1.4	8.3	1.1	2.1	6.5	0.3	4.9	0.3	1.0	6.4	1.2	3.4	0.8	1.1
1,000 or more employees	101.3	15.2	61.1	4.6	20.5	77.9	7.4	47.7	3.4	19.5	23.4	7.8	13.4	1.2	1.0
PRIVATE SECTOR[3]															
Total	**134.7**	**16.7**	**74.9**	**13.8**	**29.4**	**84.4**	**6.7**	**53.7**	**4.4**	**19.6**	**50.3**	**10.0**	**21.2**	**9.4**	**9.7**
Less than 50 employees	26.6	3.9	11.2	5.5	6.0	3.9	(Z)	2.5	0.4	1.0	22.7	3.9	8.8	5.0	5.0
50 to 99 employees	10.7	1.4	4.8	2.0	2.5	2.3	(Z)	1.5	0.2	0.6	8.4	1.4	3.3	1.8	1.9
100 to 499 employees	20.1	2.2	12.5	2.0	3.4	9.5	0.4	7.0	0.5	1.5	10.6	1.8	5.4	1.5	1.9
500 to 999 employees	10.0	1.1	6.5	0.8	1.5	5.6	0.2	4.4	0.3	0.8	4.4	0.8	2.2	0.6	0.8
1,000 or more employees	67.3	8.1	39.9	3.4	16.0	63.1	6.1	38.4	3.0	15.7	4.2	2.0	1.5	0.5	0.2

Z Less than 50,000 persons. [1] Self-insured plans are those in which the employer directly assumes some or all medical claim and administrative costs. [2] Fully insured plans are those in which the employer contracts with another organization to assume financial responsibility for the enrollees' medical claims and administrative costs. [3] Private sector includes self-employed.

Source: U.S. Department of Labor, Employee Benefits Security Administration, *Health Insurance Coverage Bulletin: Abstract of Auxiliary Data for the March 2016 Annual Social and Economic Supplement to the Current Population Survey*, July 2017. See also <https://www.dol.gov/agencies/ebsa/researchers/data/auxiliary-data>.

Table 171. Revenue for Health Care Industries: 2016 to 2018

[In millions of dollars (2,430,557 represents $2,430,557,000,000). For all employer firms, and taxable employer firms. Estimates have been adjusted to the results of the 2012 Economic Census. Based on the Service Annual Survey and administrative data; see Appendix III]

Kind of business	NAICS code [1]	Total, all firms [2]			Taxable employer firms		
		2016	2017	2018	2016	2017	2018
Health care and social assistance [3]...........	**62**	**2,430,557**	**2,545,317**	**2,652,544**	**1,199,010**	**1,251,386**	**1,301,666**
Ambulatory health care services [3]...........	**621**	**964,129**	**1,008,331**	**1,052,942**	**871,082**	**910,095**	**949,724**
Offices of physicians (except mental health specialists)......	621111	466,276	485,371	503,103	466,276	485,371	503,103
Offices of physicians, mental health specialists...............	621112	5,598	5,977	6,515	5,598	5,977	6,515
Offices of dentists.............................	6212	119,658	124,053	129,182	119,658	124,053	129,182
Offices of chiropractors........................	62131	12,728	13,202	13,897	12,728	13,202	13,897
Offices of optometrists........................	62132	14,703	15,249	15,853	14,703	15,249	15,853
Offices of mental health practitioners (except physicians)....	62133	10,282	11,092	12,151	10,282	11,092	12,151
Offices of PT/OT/speech therapists and audiologists [4].......	62134	30,007	31,466	33,792	30,007	31,466	33,792
Offices of podiatrists.........................	621391	4,442	4,584	4,883	4,442	4,584	4,883
Outpatient care centers........................	6214	128,242	135,938	143,778	67,537	71,019	74,913
Family planning centers........................	62141	2,638	2,856	3,076	1,235	1,308	1,475
Outpatient mental health and substance abuse centers......	62142	20,016	21,519	23,013	6,983	7,532	8,234
HMO medical centers [5]........................	621491	8,855	9,706	10,719	860	851	1,036
Kidney dialysis centers........................	621492	22,708	23,645	25,635	21,206	22,077	24,025
Freestanding ambulatory surgical and emergency centers...	621493	26,437	27,996	29,106	23,565	24,959	25,892
All other outpatient care centers.................	621498	47,588	50,216	52,229	13,688	14,292	14,251
Medical and diagnostic laboratories.............	6215	49,245	51,587	51,615	49,245	51,587	51,615
Home health care services.....................	6216	77,620	81,966	86,599	58,230	62,025	66,382
Ambulance services...........................	62191	15,877	16,273	15,992	12,526	12,913	12,506
Blood and organ banks........................	621991	10,802	10,997	11,898	2,677	3,007	3,431
Hospitals.................................	**622**	**1,059,406**	**1,108,935**	**1,154,989**	**126,260**	**130,141**	**131,574**
General medical and surgical hospitals, government.........	622118	185,098	198,610	207,780	(X)	(X)	(X)
General medical and surgical hospitals, private..............	622119	802,746	835,438	869,680	102,655	105,347	106,010
Psychiatric and substance abuse hospitals, government.....	622218	13,244	13,445	13,654	(X)	(X)	(X)
Psychiatric and substance abuse hospitals, private..........	622219	11,488	12,570	13,103	6,675	7,439	7,800
Specialty hospitals, government.................	622318	7,518	8,140	8,543	(X)	(X)	(X)
Specialty hospitals, private....................	622319	39,312	40,732	42,229	16,930	17,355	17,764
Nursing and residential care facilities [3]...........	**623**	**232,630**	**239,552**	**245,608**	**150,204**	**155,129**	**159,790**
Nursing care facilities (skilled nursing facilities)................	6231	122,256	123,308	123,864	98,503	99,848	101,093
Residential intellectual/developmental disability facilities.....	62321	25,140	26,487	27,582	7,226	7,721	8,187
Residential mental health and substance abuse facilities....	62322	15,080	16,204	17,413	6,673	7,303	7,755
Continuing care retirement communities.......................	623311	31,606	33,269	35,455	11,221	12,442	13,962
Assisted living facilities for the elderly..........................	623312	29,516	30,839	31,730	25,096	26,252	27,115

X Not applicable. [1] 2012 North American Industry Classification System (NAICS); see text, Section 15. [2] Includes taxable and tax-exempt employer firms. [3] Includes other kinds of business, not shown separately. See Table 608, for data on NAICS 624 Social assistance industries. [4] Offices of physical, occupational, and speech therapists, and audiologists. [5] HMO is health maintenance organization.

Source: U.S. Census Bureau, Service Annual Survey, "Service Annual Survey Latest Data (NAICS-basis): 2018," <https://www.census.gov/programs-surveys/sas/data.html>, accessed December 2019.

Table 172. Revenue for Selected Health Care Industries by Source: 2018

[In millions of dollars (509,618 represents $509,618,000,000). For all employer firms regardless of tax status. Estimates are adjusted to the results of the 2012 Economic Census, and are shown by industry classification based on the 2012 North American Industry Classification System (NAICS). Based on Service Annual Survey and administrative data; see Appendix III]

Source of revenue	Offices of physicians (NAICS 6211)	Offices of dentists (NAICS 6212)	Outpatient care centers (NAICS 6214)	Home health care services (NAICS 6216)	Hospitals (NAICS 622)	Nursing and residential care facilities (NAICS 623) [1]
Revenue, total...........................	**509,618**	**129,182**	**143,778**	**86,599**	**1,154,989**	**245,608**
Medicare [2].................................	81,447	820	21,011	35,730	275,406	37,517
Medicaid (fee for service only).............	18,887	7,218	16,713	14,161	91,635	76,317
Workers' compensation....................	4,832	(S)	2,346	512	7,214	(S)
All other government programs............	8,798	1,777	10,015	5,144	39,329	16,914
Revenue from health care providers for patient care...........................	37,003	3,216	3,247	2,524	8,290	(NA)
Private health insurance [3]..................	211,943	55,558	49,788	18,085	568,856	27,957
Property, auto, and casualty insurance. ..	2,495	(S)	(S)	(S)	3,212	220
Patient out-of-pocket from patients and their families.................	38,100	50,264	6,905	4,495	28,917	46,664
All other sources of revenue for patient care............................	71,839	9,072	12,732	3,811	51,566	17,505
Contributions, gifts, and grants received....................................	(NA)	(NA)	8,176	485	12,985	4,931
Investment and property income..........	(NA)	(NA)	542	123	10,968	1,253
Revenue from health care providers for non-patient care [4]......................	16,086	(S)	4,650	(S)	6,754	(NA)
All other non-patient care revenue........	15,508	(S)	6,531	(S)	49,677	12,845

NA Not available. S Figure does not meet publication standards. [1] Total revenue for NAICS 623 also includes $2,952 million in revenue from social security benefits—direct payments of social security on behalf of patients. [2] Fee for service, Medicare Part A hospital insurance, Part B medical insurance, and Part D prescription drug coverage. [3] Includes Medicare Part C (Medicare Advantage plans providing coverage from private insurance companies), and Medicaid managed care plans. [4] Includes revenue from medical administration and other administrative services, incentive payments, management fees, medical director fees, etc.

Source: U.S. Census Bureau, Service Annual Survey, "Service Annual Survey Latest Data (NAICS-basis): 2018," <https://www.census.gov/programs-surveys/sas/data.html>, accessed December 2019.

Table 173. Employment in the Health Service Industries: 2000 to 2019

[In thousands (12,861 represents 12,861,000). Covers persons on establishment payrolls who worked or received pay for any part of the pay period that includes the 12th day of the month. Excludes proprietors, the unincorporated self-employed, unpaid volunteer or family employees, farm employees, domestic employees, and military personnel. Based on the 2017 North American Industry Classification System (NAICS); see text, Section 15]

Industry	2017 NAICS code	2000	2005	2010	2015	2016	2017	2018	2019
Health care and social assistance [1]	**62**	**12,861**	**14,840**	**16,820**	**18,557**	**19,069**	**19,520**	**19,923**	**20,413**
Health care	**621,2,3**	**10,858**	**12,314**	**13,777**	**15,042**	**15,414**	**15,717**	**15,964**	**16,275**
Ambulatory health care services [1]	621	4,320	5,114	5,975	6,856	7,080	7,297	7,477	7,697
Offices of physicians	6211	1,801	2,049	2,264	2,471	2,527	2,581	2,616	2,672
Office of physicians, except mental health	621111	1,764	2,006	2,218	2,420	2,473	2,527	2,560	2,613
Office of mental health physicians	621112	37	43	46	51	53	55	56	59
Offices of dentists	6212	688	774	828	905	923	936	951	969
Offices of other health practitioners	6213	438	549	671	813	855	889	929	969
Outpatient care centers	6214	425	517	649	806	853	897	931	963
Medical and diagnostic laboratories	6215	162	198	228	260	266	269	275	283
Home health care services	6216	633	821	1,085	1,315	1,365	1,420	1,467	1,527
Hospitals	622	3,954	4,345	4,679	4,896	5,015	5,072	5,130	5,199
General medical and surgical hospitals	6221	3,745	4,096	4,357	4,498	4,608	4,669	4,713	4,780
Psychiatric and substance abuse hospitals	6222	86	93	109	138	142	140	150	148
Other hospitals	6223	123	156	213	260	265	263	267	271
Nursing and residential care facilities [1]	623	2,583	2,855	3,124	3,291	3,318	3,348	3,357	3,379
Nursing care facilities	6231	1,514	1,577	1,657	1,648	1,642	1,627	1,607	1,598

[1] Includes other industries, not shown separately.

Source: U.S. Bureau of Labor Statistics, Current Employment Statistics, "Employment, Hours, and Earnings—National," <https://stats.bls.gov/ces/data.htm>, accessed March 2020.

Table 174. Physicians by Sex, Osteopathic Physicians, and International Medical Graduates by Specialty: 2017

[Covers federal and nonfederal physicians working 20 or more hours per week in specialties in which there are over 2,500 active physicians. Active physicians include those working in direct patient care, administration, medical teaching, research, or other non-patient care activities. Physicians selected their specialties on the American Medical Association's Census of Physicians]

Specialty	Total [1]	By sex			By type		International medical graduates [2]
		Male	Female	Percent female	Patient care physicians	Osteopathic physicians	
Total	**892,856**	**577,962**	**313,808**	**35.2**	**782,585**	**69,581**	**218,540**
Allergy & immunology	4,774	2,939	1,833	38.4	4,132	166	1,093
Anatomic/clinical pathology	12,839	7,983	4,847	37.8	9,130	322	3,932
Anesthesiology	41,762	31,094	10,624	25.5	38,960	2,752	9,017
Cardiovascular disease	22,211	19,054	3,138	14.1	20,303	861	6,738
Child & adolescent psychiatry	9,204	4,350	4,849	52.7	8,181	507	2,794
Critical care medicine	11,559	8,529	3,013	26.1	9,932	617	4,741
Dermatology	12,051	6,151	5,889	48.9	11,338	691	591
Emergency medicine	42,348	30,657	11,658	27.6	38,964	4,789	2,765
Endocrinology [3]	7,495	3,815	3,668	49.0	6,045	216	2,969
Family medicine/general practice	113,514	68,004	45,342	40.0	104,937	18,762	25,860
Gastroenterology	14,747	12,135	2,593	17.6	13,488	594	4,270
General surgery	25,042	19,865	5,157	20.6	21,644	1,111	4,904
Geriatric medicine	5,598	2,653	2,939	52.6	4,733	308	2,844
Hematology & oncology	15,410	10,268	5,122	33.3	12,926	463	5,614
Infectious disease	9,136	5,369	3,753	41.1	7,012	310	3,136
Internal medicine	115,557	71,577	43,770	37.9	101,953	6,386	45,274
Internal medicine/pediatrics	5,122	2,416	2,704	52.8	4,581	275	551
Interventional cardiology	3,847	3,546	294	7.7	3,475	159	1,724
Neonatal-perinatal medicine	5,530	2,700	2,826	51.1	4,657	224	2,131
Nephrology	10,798	7,728	3,057	28.3	9,462	459	5,293
Neurological surgery	5,531	5,065	463	8.4	5,053	108	681
Neurology	13,717	9,674	4,029	29.4	11,674	703	4,289
Neuroradiology	3,682	2,958	718	19.5	3,160	162	532
Obstetrics & gynecology	41,656	17,879	23,740	57.0	38,850	2,813	5,943
Ophthalmology	18,817	14,041	4,767	25.3	17,488	462	1,327
Orthopedic surgery	19,001	17,981	1,016	5.3	18,069	1,053	988
Otolaryngology	9,526	7,890	1,630	17.1	8,932	385	603
Pain medicine & management	5,345	4,350	982	18.4	5,003	529	1,482
Pediatric cardiology	2,733	1,750	979	35.9	2,242	62	715
Pediatric hematology/oncology	2,794	1,302	1,489	53.4	2,041	79	711
Pediatrics	58,435	21,437	36,945	63.3	52,824	2,720	14,577
Physical medicine & rehabilitation	9,343	6,032	3,284	35.3	8,532	1,330	2,239
Plastic surgery	7,142	5,995	1,144	16.0	6,813	119	724
Preventive medicine	6,613	4,374	2,235	33.8	4,123	573	824
Psychiatry	38,205	23,244	14,941	39.1	33,364	1,705	11,615
Pulmonary disease	5,265	4,644	620	11.8	4,640	204	1,576
Radiation oncology	5,029	3,661	1,365	27.2	4,628	88	597
Radiology & diagnostic radiology	27,719	20,601	7,101	25.6	24,682	1,035	3,127
Rheumatology	5,881	3,246	2,622	44.7	5,029	315	1,973
Sports medicine (orthopedic surgery)	2,612	2,440	172	6.6	2,457	176	108
Thoracic surgery	4,411	4,102	309	7.0	4,052	98	875
Urology	9,921	9,051	866	8.7	9,374	251	1,087
Vascular & interventional radiology	3,416	3,090	325	9.5	3,011	112	457
Vascular surgery	3,688	3,204	482	13.1	3,384	149	642

[1] Includes active physicians with unknown sex and type of medical degree. [2] All physicians, including U.S. citizens, who completed their medical education in a school outside the U.S., Puerto Rico, and Canada. [3] Includes diabetes and metabolism specialties.

Source: Association of American Medical Colleges, *2018 Physician Specialty Data Report* ©. See also <https://www.aamc.org/data-reports/workforce-studies>.

Table 175. Physicians, Doctors of Osteopathy, and Female Physicians by State: 2018

[As of year end. Rates per 100,000 resident population, based on U.S. Census Bureau estimates as of July 1 of year shown. Covers active federal and nonfederal physicians who work at least 20 hours per week]

| State | Active physicians [1] | | | Active physicians in patient care | | | | | | |
| | Total (number) | Female | | Total [3] | | Osteopathic physicians | | Primary care physicians [4] | |
		Number	Percent [2]	Number	Rate	Number	Rate	Number	Rate
U.S. [5].......	**908,760**	**324,805**	**35.8**	**792,066**	**242.1**	**65,239**	**19.9**	**302,590**	**92.5**
AL............	10,614	3,025	28.5	9,614	196.7	527	10.8	3,772	77.2
AK............	2,042	775	38.0	1,893	256.7	240	32.5	832	112.8
AZ............	17,356	5,652	32.6	16,063	224.0	1,943	27.1	5,598	78.1
AR............	6,256	1,743	27.9	5,672	188.2	316	10.5	2,408	79.9
CA............	110,603	41,724	37.8	96,457	243.8	5,119	12.9	38,052	96.2
CO............	16,272	6,298	38.8	14,949	262.5	1,481	26.0	5,433	95.4
CT............	12,579	4,760	37.9	10,821	302.9	443	12.4	3,777	105.7
DE............	2,753	1,072	39.0	2,440	252.3	311	32.2	936	96.8
DC............	5,950	2,807	47.2	4,348	619.0	100	14.2	1,684	239.7
FL............	56,484	17,310	30.7	51,258	240.7	4,734	22.2	18,489	86.8
GA............	24,054	8,546	35.6	21,345	202.9	1,027	9.8	8,319	79.1
HI............	4,462	1,573	35.3	3,888	273.7	211	14.9	1,683	118.5
ID............	3,379	888	26.3	3,185	181.6	452	25.8	1,297	73.9
IL............	36,240	14,010	38.7	30,638	240.5	2,252	17.7	12,685	99.6
IN............	15,448	4,911	31.8	14,190	212.0	1,074	16.0	5,371	80.3
IA............	6,886	2,264	32.9	6,096	193.1	1,241	39.3	2,676	84.8
KS............	6,627	2,204	33.3	6,013	206.5	729	25.0	2,561	88.0
KY............	10,319	3,240	31.4	9,589	214.6	675	15.1	3,453	77.3
LA............	12,132	3,808	31.4	10,804	231.8	217	4.7	3,918	84.1
ME............	4,420	1,648	37.3	4,091	305.7	712	53.2	1,725	128.9
MD............	23,323	9,560	41.0	18,499	306.1	707	11.7	7,022	116.2
MA............	31,025	13,150	42.4	24,410	353.7	812	11.8	9,267	134.3
MI............	28,692	10,013	35.0	24,963	249.7	4,676	46.8	9,774	97.8
MN............	16,984	6,315	37.2	14,868	265.0	764	13.6	5,886	104.9
MS............	5,714	1,551	27.2	5,221	174.8	368	12.3	1,968	65.9
MO............	16,732	5,712	34.2	14,477	236.3	2,021	33.0	5,307	86.6
MT............	2,625	825	31.5	2,509	236.2	241	22.7	972	91.5
NE............	4,614	1,516	32.9	4,138	214.5	228	11.8	1,701	88.2
NV............	6,478	1,835	29.1	5,637	185.8	724	23.9	2,195	72.3
NH............	4,274	1,559	36.5	3,901	287.6	367	27.1	1,436	105.9
NJ............	27,305	10,026	36.8	24,146	271.0	2,769	31.1	8,705	97.7
NM............	5,129	1,966	38.4	4,481	213.8	273	13.0	1,909	91.1
NY............	73,299	28,489	38.9	59,420	304.1	3,325	17.0	22,064	112.9
NC............	26,481	9,410	35.6	23,209	223.5	1,304	12.6	8,948	86.2
ND............	1,806	547	30.3	1,650	217.1	97	12.8	661	87.0
OH............	34,217	11,928	34.9	29,056	248.6	3,877	33.2	10,957	93.7
OK............	8,151	2,433	29.9	7,455	189.1	1,595	40.5	2,915	73.9
OR............	12,714	4,989	39.3	11,378	271.5	897	21.4	4,585	109.4
PA............	41,041	14,591	35.6	35,002	273.3	5,208	40.7	12,910	100.8
RI............	3,912	1,607	41.1	3,439	325.3	238	22.5	1,242	117.5
SC............	11,666	3,643	31.3	10,423	205.0	667	13.1	4,072	80.1
SD............	2,121	674	31.8	1,933	219.1	161	18.2	819	92.8
TN............	17,133	5,188	30.3	15,284	225.8	773	11.4	5,764	85.1
TX............	64,533	22,705	35.2	57,384	199.9	4,380	15.3	20,922	72.9
UT............	6,833	1,676	24.6	6,318	199.9	593	18.8	2,065	65.3
VT............	2,299	958	41.7	2,021	322.7	81	12.9	816	130.3
VA............	22,419	8,445	37.7	19,741	231.8	1,187	13.9	7,691	90.3
WA............	21,007	8,131	38.8	18,561	246.3	1,253	16.6	7,582	100.6
WV............	4,757	1,411	29.7	4,182	231.6	710	39.3	1,808	100.1
WI............	15,399	5,382	35.0	13,853	238.3	1,009	17.4	5,497	94.6
WY............	1,201	312	26.0	1,153	199.6	130	22.5	461	79.8
PR............	9,787	3,658	37.5	8,031	251.3	2	0.1	3,857	120.7

[1] Active physicians work in direct patient care, administration, medical teaching, research, or other nonpatient care activities. [2] Excludes physicians whose sex was not reported. [3] Includes physicians with Doctor of Medicine degrees, and unknown degree type. [4] Primary care physicians include physicians in the following specialties: adolescent medicine (pediatrics), family medicine, general practice, geriatric medicine (family practice and internal medicine), internal medicine, and pediatrics. [5] U.S. totals exclude Puerto Rico (PR).

Source: Association of American Medical Colleges, *2019 State Physician Workforce Data Report*, November 2019 ©. See also <https://www.aamc.org/what-we-do/mission-areas/patient-care/workforce-studies>.

Table 176. Registered Nurses, Nurse Practitioners, and Licensed Practical and Vocational Nurses by State: 2019

[Covers nurses working in the health care and social assistance industry (North American Industry Classification System code 62), as of May. Rates per 100,000 resident population; based on U.S. Census Bureau estimates as of July 1 for year shown]

State	Registered nurses (RNs) Total	Registered nurses (RNs) Rate[2]	Nurse practitioners Total	Nurse practitioners Rate[2]	Licensed practical and vocational nurses (LPNs, VPNs) Total	Licensed practical and vocational nurses (LPNs, VPNs) Rate[2]
United States [1].........	2,604,270	793.4	182,420	55.6	607,450	185.1
Alabama..........	43,540	888.0	3,400	69.3	10,700	218.2
Alaska..........	5,290	723.1	440	60.1	200	27.3
Arizona..........	47,420	651.5	4,090	56.2	5,860	80.5
Arkansas..........	21,650	717.4	2,500	82.8	10,530	348.9
California..........	272,990	690.9	12,820	32.4	59,370	150.3
Colorado..........	46,490	807.3	2,690	46.7	4,720	82.0
Connecticut..........	29,910	838.9	2,450	68.7	7,880	221.0
Delaware..........	10,560	1,084.5	810	83.2	2,150	220.8
District of Columbia..........	9,320	1,320.6	800	113.4	1,700	240.9
Florida..........	163,240	760.0	11,350	52.8	41,870	194.9
Georgia..........	65,960	621.2	7,310	68.8	18,520	174.4
Hawaii..........	9,630	680.1	410	29.0	850	60.0
Idaho..........	12,410	694.4	710	39.7	2,370	132.6
Illinois..........	114,230	901.4	6,320	49.9	17,780	140.3
Indiana..........	62,240	924.5	5,180	76.9	14,260	211.8
Iowa..........	28,440	901.4	1,690	53.6	5,700	180.7
Kansas..........	26,800	919.9	2,530	86.8	6,630	227.6
Kentucky..........	38,830	869.1	3,480	77.9	8,730	195.4
Louisiana..........	35,560	764.9	2,990	64.3	17,660	379.9
Maine..........	12,710	945.5	1,340	99.7	920	68.4
Maryland..........	45,700	755.9	3,330	55.1	8,560	141.6
Massachusetts..........	70,250	1,019.2	6,080	88.2	13,720	199.1
Michigan..........	88,680	888.0	4,700	47.1	12,430	124.5
Minnesota..........	63,590	1,127.6	3,690	65.4	12,760	226.3
Mississippi..........	26,060	875.6	3,080	103.5	8,460	284.3
Missouri..........	60,040	978.3	4,380	71.4	13,120	213.8
Montana..........	9,060	847.7	560	52.4	1,860	174.0
Nebraska..........	19,570	1,011.7	1,050	54.3	4,700	243.0
Nevada..........	20,370	661.3	1,040	33.8	2,510	81.5
New Hampshire..........	12,440	914.9	1,050	77.2	1,670	122.8
New Jersey..........	68,700	773.5	6,000	67.6	15,280	172.0
New Mexico..........	14,110	672.9	1,020	48.6	1,860	88.7
New York..........	149,880	770.5	12,370	63.6	39,760	204.4
North Carolina..........	86,810	827.7	5,130	48.9	14,740	140.5
North Dakota..........	8,610	1,129.8	490	64.3	2,280	299.2
Ohio..........	110,310	943.7	8,260	70.7	36,980	316.4
Oklahoma..........	26,430	667.9	1,330	33.6	10,170	257.0
Oregon..........	29,020	688.0	1,970	46.7	3,050	72.3
Pennsylvania..........	130,670	1,020.7	7,030	54.9	32,340	252.6
Rhode Island..........	10,620	1,002.5	650	61.4	870	82.1
South Carolina..........	38,110	740.2	2,040	39.6	8,280	160.8
South Dakota..........	11,190	1,264.9	530	59.9	1,720	194.4
Tennessee..........	55,520	813.0	6,790	99.4	21,880	320.4
Texas..........	186,630	643.6	11,780	40.6	59,820	206.3
Utah..........	19,520	608.9	1,410	44.0	1,720	53.7
Vermont..........	5,760	923.1	410	65.7	1,040	166.7
Virginia..........	54,940	643.7	4,790	56.1	18,760	219.8
Washington..........	49,430	649.1	3,450	45.3	6,590	86.5
West Virginia..........	17,370	969.2	1,140	63.6	5,290	295.2
Wisconsin..........	53,590	920.4	3,280	56.3	6,400	109.9
Wyoming..........	4,070	703.2	280	48.4	430	74.3
Puerto Rico..........	15,090	472.5	(NA)	(NA)	2,950	92.4

NA Not available. [1] U.S. total excludes Puerto Rico. [2] Rates are calculated using data from the U.S. Census Bureau, "Annual Estimates of the Resident Population: April 1, 2010 to July 1, 2019," <https://www.census.gov/data/tables/time-series/demo/popest/2010s-state-total.html>, accessed May 2020.

Source: U.S. Bureau of Labor Statistics, Occupational Employment Statistics, "OES Data: Research Estimates by State and Industry," <https://www.bls.gov/oes/home.htm>, accessed May 2020.

Table 177. Physician Use of Electronic Medical or Health Record System by Physician Specialty: 2015 and 2017

[In percent. Data are from the National Electronic Health Records Survey of nonfederal office-based patient care physicians; survey excludes anesthesiologists, radiologists, and pathologists. Using any electronic health record/electronic medical record system was defined by physicians answering "yes" to use of an electronic health record system at the reporting location. Having a certified system was defined by physicians answering "yes" to having a current system that "meet meaningful use criteria defined by the Department of Health and Human Services." For more information on certified systems and meaningful use (renamed "promoting interoperability") criteria, see <https://www.cms.gov/ehrincentiveprograms>]

Physician specialty	2015		2017	
	Any electronic medical/health record system	Certified system	Any electronic medical/health record system	Certified system
All physicians	**86.9**	**77.9**	**85.9**	**79.7**
Primary care	89.6	80.9	88.5	83.5
Non-primary care	84.4	75.1	83.6	76.0
Surgical	84.5	77.0	84.2	77.3
Medical	84.4	74.0	83.1	75.1
BY SPECIALTY				
Cardiovascular disease	95.6	83.2	(S)	(S)
Dermatology	70.2	62.3	80.0	79.5
General surgery	93.8	77.6	95.8	94.2
General/family practice	92.7	84.0	86.1	81.5
Internal medicine	88.2	81.4	84.9	81.6
Neurology	94.5	89.9	(S)	(S)
Obstetrics/gynecology	89.2	80.6	95.7	90.7
Ophthalmology	72.7	70.0	(S)	(S)
Orthopedic surgery	93.2	86.6	96.7	(S)
Otolaryngology	89.4	82.7	94.6	(S)
Pediatrics	87.4	76.3	92.1	84.9
Psychiatry	61.3	40.8	(S)	(S)
Urology	94.0	92.6	88.7	86.7
Other	86.4	78.6	89.3	81.1

S Estimate does not meet standards of reliability.

Source: U.S. National Center for Health Statistics, Ambulatory Health Care Data, NAMCS and NHAMCS Web Tables, "NEHRS Specialty and Overall Physicians Electronic Health Record Adoption Summary Tables," <https://www.cdc.gov/nchs/ahcd/web_tables.htm>, accessed March 2019.

Table 178. Medical Record Confidentiality Breaches Reported—Incidents and Persons Affected by Type and Location of Breach: 2016 to 2019

[16,659 represents 16,659,000. Data for breaches by date of submission to the Secretary of Health and Human Services (HHS), affecting 500 or more individuals. As required by section 13402(e)(4) of the Health Information Technology for Economic and Clinical Health (HITECH) Act, the Secretary of HHS must post a list of breaches of unsecured protected health information affecting 500 or more individuals. The Privacy Rule of the Health Insurance Portability and Accountability Act of 1996 (HIPAA) provides federal protections for individually identifiable health information held by covered entities and their business associates. Covered entities include health care providers, health plans, and health care clearinghouses. Data are subject to revision]

Item	2016		2017		2018		2019	
	Incidents (number)	Individuals affected (1,000)	Incidents (number)	Individuals affected (1,000)	Incidents (number)	Individuals affected (1,000)	Incidents (number)	Individuals affected (1,000)
Total	**329**	**16,659**	**358**	**5,131**	**371**	**13,948**	**512**	**41,684**
TYPE OF BREACH								
Hacking/information technology incident	115	13,430	148	3,513	163	9,980	311	38,400
Improper disposal	7	126	11	31	10	342	6	26
Loss	16	558	16	39	13	30	15	74
Theft	61	899	55	304	42	697	38	364
Unauthorized access/disclosure	130	1,647	128	1,244	143	2,899	142	2,819
LOCATION OF INFORMATION BREACHED [1]								
Desktop computer	27	139	31	661	35	551	34	571
Electronic medical record	30	433	32	167	22	167	29	355
E-mail	47	998	86	673	113	3,652	207	3,609
Laptop computer	26	813	21	110	19	76	19	166
Network server	85	13,180	87	2,486	62	6,381	113	35,772
Other portable electronic device	14	24	20	821	15	43	11	142
Paper/films	74	898	60	135	77	1,199	54	166
Other [2]	26	174	21	77	28	1,880	45	904

[1] Locations of information breached can include a combination of other locations within the categories specified. For example, incidents involving desktop computers can also involve breaches of information via laptop computer, network server, email, and other locations. Incidents are categorized according to the first type as given in the source. [2] Other locations of information breaches can include incidents involving mailings (postal and electronic), computer systems and software (including cloud storage), computer hard drives and disks, the internet/websites, and other miscellaneous materials or locations.

Source: U.S. Department of Health and Human Services, Office for Civil Rights, HIPAA for Professionals—Breach Notification Rule, "Breaches Affecting 500 or More Individuals," <http://www.hhs.gov/hipaa/for-professionals/breach-notification/index.html>, accessed April 2020.

Table 179. Coronavirus Disease 2019 (COVID-19) Cases, Testing, and Hospitalizations by Week: 2020

[Counts of COVID-19 caused by SARS-CoV-2 (severe acute respiratory syndrome coronavirus 2) have been reported to the Centers for Disease Control and Prevention (CDC) since January 21, 2020. CDC data may differ from data from other sources due to differences in timing and reporting of data, and differences in processes for validating and confirming data. The CDC continually updates data. Data are presented here as an illustration of the progression of COVID-19 in the U.S.]

Week ending	Week number	New cases each week [1]	Testing [2]			Hospitalizations per 100,000 population [3]	
			Specimens tested	Number positive	Percent positive	Cumulative	Weekly
January 25, 2020............	4	2	(NA)	(NA)	(NA)	(NA)	(NA)
February 1, 2020............	5	6	(NA)	(NA)	(NA)	(NA)	(NA)
February 8, 2020............	6	3	(NA)	(NA)	(NA)	(NA)	(NA)
February 15, 2020...........	7	2	(NA)	(NA)	(NA)	(NA)	(NA)
February 22, 2020..........	8	2	(NA)	(NA)	(NA)	(NA)	(NA)
February 29, 2020..........	9	9	(NA)	(NA)	(NA)	(NA)	(NA)
March 7, 2020..............	10	251	8,298	973	11.7	0.1	0.1
March 14, 2020.............	11	1,959	38,888	3,693	9.5	0.8	0.7
March 21, 2020.............	12	22,349	92,538	8,215	8.9	3.8	3.0
March 28, 2020.............	13	98,070	113,035	14,617	12.9	11.5	7.7
April 4, 2020..............	14	182,173	662,660	144,032	21.7	21.0	9.6
April 11, 2020.............	15	220,878	645,725	137,779	21.3	30.4	9.3
April 18, 2020.............	16	194,926	653,594	120,845	18.5	40.4	10.1
April 25, 2020.............	17	207,989	834,236	127,689	15.3	50.1	9.7
May 2, 2020................	18	193,990	1,001,509	124,916	12.5	59.5	9.4
May 9, 2020................	19	178,087	1,174,236	112,986	9.6	67.7	8.2
May 16, 2020...............	20	166,369	1,438,964	108,403	7.5	75.5	7.7
May 23, 2020...............	21	155,049	1,746,301	111,693	6.4	82.9	7.4
May 30, 2020...............	22	139,389	1,736,886	99,449	5.7	89.0	6.1
June 6, 2020...............	23	159,401	1,948,496	107,354	5.5	93.8	4.9
June 13, 2020..............	24	142,908	2,147,617	130,871	6.1	97.9	4.1
June 20, 2020..............	25	184,217	2,434,964	194,437	8.0	101.9	4.0
June 27, 2020..............	26	256,146	2,888,221	273,737	9.5	106.6	4.7
July 4, 2020...............	27	336,318	2,838,205	274,892	9.7	112.8	6.2
July 11, 2020..............	28	395,637	3,131,443	307,275	9.8	120.6	7.8
July 18, 2020..............	29	462,031	3,098,576	277,584	9.0	128.7	8.2
July 25, 2020..............	30	465,731	2,785,379	234,801	8.4	136.5	7.8
August 1, 2020.............	31	437,634	2,578,609	191,205	7.4	143.5	7.0
August 8, 2020.............	32	373,433	2,478,970	165,066	6.7	149.9	6.4
August 15, 2020............	33	365,273	2,420,542	143,206	5.9	155.5	5.6
August 22, 2020............	34	303,580	2,401,286	129,976	5.4	160.6	5.1
August 29, 2020............	35	291,012	2,104,527	115,561	5.5	164.6	4.0
September 5, 2020.........	36	292,055	1,949,226	99,799	5.1	166.9	2.4

NA Not available. [1] Case reporting began January 21, 2020. Excludes cases among persons repatriated to the U.S. from Wuhan, China, and Japan. Cases are confirmed and probable, as reported by U.S. states, U.S. territories, New York City, and the District of Columbia from the previous day. Data were accessed September 11, 2020. [2] Data for Week 10 are from state and local public health laboratories only. Data for Weeks 11-13 are from clinical and state and local public health laboratories. Beginning Week 14, covers testing at commercial, clinical, and state and local public health laboratories. Data represent the number of specimens tested for SARS-CoV-2 and reported to the CDC. Commercial and clinical laboratory data represent select laboratories and do not capture all tests performed in the U.S. Data as of September 10, 2020. [3] Hospitalization data are preliminary and subject to change as more data become available. The Coronavirus Disease 2019 (COVID-19)-Associated Hospitalization Surveillance Network (COVID-NET) conducts population-based surveillance for laboratory-confirmed COVID-19-associated hospitalizations in children and adults. The current network covers nearly 100 counties in the 10 Emerging Infections Program (EIP) states (CA, CO, CT, GA, MD, MN, NM, NY, OR, and TN) and four additional states through the Influenza Hospitalization Surveillance Project (IA, MI, OH, and UT). The network represents approximately 10% of U.S. population (approximately 32 million people). For more information, see <https://www.cdc.gov/coronavirus/2019-ncov/covid-data/covidview/index.html>. Data accessed September 11, 2020.

Source: U.S. Centers for Disease Control and Prevention, "Coronavirus Disease 2019 (COVID-19)," <https://www.cdc.gov/coronavirus/2019-ncov/cases-updates/index.html>, accessed September 11, 2020.

Table 180. Long-Term Care Facilities, Staff, and Clients by Provider Type and Selected Characteristics: 2016

[Data for 2016 except as noted. Based on the National Study of Long-Term Care Providers. Long-term care services assist the needs of frail older people and other adults with limited capacity for self-care due to chronic illness, injury, disability, or other health-related conditions]

Item	Facilities by provider type				
	Adult day services center	Home health agency	Hospice	Nursing home	Residential care community
Number of providers	**4,600**	**12,200**	**4,300**	**15,600**	**28,900**
Number of beds or licensed maximum capacity [1]	298,400	(X)	(X)	1,660,400	996,100
Average capacity [1]	66	(X)	(X)	106	35
Average number of people served [2]	42	401	353	86	28
Provider ownership type (percent):					
For profit	44.7	80.6	63.0	69.3	81.0
Not for profit	50.8	14.8	22.8	23.5	17.7
Government and other	4.6	4.6	14.1	7.2	1.3
Services provided (percent):					
Social work	52.1	82.5	100.0	88.5	51.1
Mental health or counseling	33.8	(NA)	97.0	87.6	55.0
Therapy [3]	46.7	96.3	98.2	99.5	71.4
Skilled nursing or nursing	64.5	100.0	100.0	100.0	66.1
Pharmacy or pharmacist	30.0	4.9	(NA)	97.2	83.6
Hospice	20.8	5.7	(X)	80.7	67.7
Total nursing and social work employee FTEs [4]	**19,900**	**145,000**	**85,600**	**945,700**	**298,800**
Percent of total nursing employee FTEs:					
Registered nurse	20.6	53.0	48.0	11.9	6.1
Licensed practical nurse or licensed vocational nurse	11.3	19.5	8.8	22.4	9.9
Aide	56.8	25.1	31.8	63.9	83.3
Clients [2]	**286,300**	**4,455,700**	**1,426,000**	**1,347,600**	**811,500**
By age (percent):					
Under 65	37.4	18.1	5.5	16.5	6.6
65 and over	62.5	81.9	94.6	83.5	93.4
65 to 74	20.3	26.8	17.5	18.2	11.0
75 to 84	25.9	29.9	29.3	26.7	30.3
85 and over	16.3	25.2	47.8	38.6	52.1
By sex (percent):					
Men	41.8	39.1	41.3	35.4	29.4
Women	58.2	60.9	58.7	64.6	70.6
Selected conditions (percent):					
Diagnosed with Alzheimer's or other dementia	30.9	32.3	44.5	47.8	41.9
Diagnosed with depression	28.2	39.4	23.4	46.3	30.9

NA Not available. X Not applicable. [1] For adult day services, capacity is based on licensed maximum capacity. For nursing homes and residential care communities, capacity is based on number of licensed or certified beds. [2] For adult day services, nursing homes, and residential care communities, data are daily average or totals for 2016. For home health agencies, data are annual average or total discharges in 2015. For hospices, data are annual average or total patients served in 2015. [3] Physical, occupational, or speech therapy. [4] FTE is full-time equivalent.

Source: U.S. Centers for Disease Control and Prevention, National Center for Health Statistics, *Long-Term Care Providers and Services Users in the United States: Data From the National Study of Long-Term Care Providers, 2015-2016*, Series 3, No. 43, February 2019. See also <http://www.cdc.gov/nchs/nsltcp.htm>.

Table 181. Mental Health Treatment Facilities, Clients, and Beds by Service Setting and Facility Type: 2018

[Based on the National Mental Health Services Survey (N-MHSS), a census of all known facilities, public and private, that provide mental health treatment services in the 50 states, the District of Columbia, American Samoa, Guam, Puerto Rico, and the U.S. Virgin Islands. Facilities can offer treatment in more than one service setting. Client data are collected every other year and represent clients for an average day or month. Excludes: (1) Department of Defense (DoD) military treatment facilities, (2) individual private practitioners or small group practices not licensed as a mental health clinic or center, and (3) jails or prisons]

Facility type	24-hour hospital inpatient care			24-hour residential care			Outpatient, day treatment, or partial hospitalization	
	Facilities	Clients [1]	Beds [1]	Facilities	Clients [1]	Beds [1]	Facilities	Clients [2]
Total [3]	**1,920**	**129,115**	**109,241**	**1,932**	**58,762**	**62,253**	**9,379**	**3,937,407**
Psychiatric hospitals	688	83,425	69,112	126	6,696	8,338	323	80,050
Public	206	33,225	36,167	24	2,500	3,109	36	16,374
Private	482	50,200	32,945	102	4,196	5,229	287	63,676
General hospitals [4]	1,053	40,052	33,979	26	478	658	433	143,180
Residential treatment centers for children	6	154	314	575	18,569	21,277	106	6,166
Residential treatment centers for adults	7	249	289	834	14,605	14,795	73	3,029
Other types of residential facilities	1	51	59	66	3,217	3,461	18	1,124
Veterans Administration medical centers	101	2,662	2,872	82	4,330	5,185	459	399,993
Community mental health centers	34	1,549	1,348	25	1,580	1,666	2,549	1,330,342
Partial hospitalization or day treatment facilities	4	134	42	1	1	5	360	28,483
Outpatient mental health facilities	11	329	523	9	357	548	4,665	1,798,109
Multi-setting mental health facilities [5]	12	455	643	188	8,929	6,320	382	135,833

[1] On April 30, 2018. [2] For the month of April 2018, and enrolled on April 30, 2018. [3] Total includes data for other unspecified type of facilities not shown separately. [4] Nonfederal general hospitals with separate psychiatric units. [5] Includes non-hospital residential, plus either outpatient and/or partial hospitalization/day treatment.

Source: U.S. Substance Abuse and Mental Health Services Administration, *National Mental Health Services Survey (N-MHSS): 2018, Data on Mental Health Treatment Facilities*, October 2019. See also <http://www.samhsa.gov/data/data-we-collect/n-mhss-national-mental-health-services-survey>.

Table 182. Mental Health Treatment Facilities by Type: 2018

[Based on the National Mental Health Services Survey (N-MHSS), a census of all known facilities, public and private, that provide mental health treatment services in the 50 states, the District of Columbia, American Samoa, Guam, Puerto Rico, and the U.S. Virgin Islands. Excludes: (1) Department of Defense (DoD) military treatment facilities, (2) individual private practitioners or small group practices not licensed as a mental health clinic or center, and (3) jails or prisons]

Characteristic	Total [1]	Psychi- atric hos- pitals	General hos- pitals [2]	RTCs, total [3]	Veterans Affairs medical centers	Com- munity centers [4]	PHP/day treat- ment facilities [5]	Out- patient facilities [6]	Multi- setting facilities [7]
Total (number)........................	11,682	692	1,066	1,492	459	2,553	360	4,665	382
Percent.............................	100.0	5.9	9.1	12.8	3.9	21.9	3.1	39.9	3.3
SERVICE SETTING [8]									
24-hour hospital inpatient.............	1,920	688	1,053	14	101	34	4	11	12
24-hour residential.....................	1,932	126	26	1,475	82	25	1	9	188
Less than 24-hour day treatment or partial hospitalization................	1,745	247	247	96	61	284	349	254	206
Less than 24-hour outpatient.........	8,956	249	372	144	459	2,529	182	4,653	357
FACILITY CONTROL									
Private for-profit......................	2,137	313	197	337	2	144	101	961	81
Private non-profit......................	7,311	173	754	1,062	3	1,878	229	2,934	267
Public [9]...............................	2,234	206	115	93	454	531	30	770	34
AGE OF PATIENTS ACCEPTED [8]									
All ages...............................	5,018	187	149	9	–	1,811	17	2,678	161
Children age 12 and younger........	6,759	262	184	420	–	2,047	115	3,484	241
Children age 13 to 17.................	7,391	347	253	622	–	2,093	161	3,633	276
Young adults age 18 to 25............	10,202	590	858	851	455	2,458	263	4,350	364
Adults age 26 to 64..................	9,792	607	944	841	459	2,344	238	4,024	322
Senior adults age 65 and older......	9,387	593	987	743	458	2,285	228	3,794	286

– Represents zero. [1] Total includes other types of facilities not shown separately. [2] Nonfederal general hospitals with separate psychiatric units. [3] RTC is residential treatment center. [4] Community mental health centers provide outpatient services, 24-hour emergency care, day treatment or partial hospitalization or psychosocial rehabilitation services, or patient screening for admission to state facilities. [5] PHP (partial hospitalization program) and day treatment facilities provide services to ambulatory patients in 3/more hour sessions. [6] Outpatient mental health facilities provide services to clients, usually in under 3 hours per visit. [7] Includes non-hospital residential, plus either outpatient and/or partial hospitalization/day treatment. [8] Sums to more than the total because a facility could offer treatment in more than one service setting and to more than one age group. [9] Includes facilities operated by state mental health and other agencies, local/county/municipal governments, tribal governments, Indian Health Service, and Department of Veterans Affairs.

Source: U.S. Substance Abuse and Mental Health Services Administration, *National Mental Health Services Survey (N-MHSS): 2018, Data on Mental Health Treatment Facilities*, October 2019. See also <https://www.samhsa.gov/data/>.

Table 183. Mental Health Care Client Characteristics by Treatment Setting: 2018

[Data are for patients receiving inpatient or residential services on April 30, 2018, and for clients who were receiving outpatient services at least once during April 2018 and were enrolled in treatment on April 30, 2018. Not all facilities reported demographic data for all clients. See headnote, Table 181]

Client characteristic	24-hour hospital inpatient treatment		24-hour residential treatment		Outpatient, day treatment, or partial hospitalization [1]	
	Number	Percent	Number	Percent	Number	Percent
Total clients........................	129,115	100.0	58,762	100.0	3,937,407	100.0
SEX						
Male...................................	71,183	58.5	34,388	61.3	1,792,051	51.1
Female................................	50,594	41.5	21,733	38.7	1,714,789	48.9
AGE						
17 years old and under..............	16,657	13.7	25,269	45.2	902,665	25.8
18 to 64 years old...................	88,552	72.7	27,552	49.3	2,202,583	63.0
65 years old and over................	16,547	13.6	3,101	5.5	390,082	11.2
RACE						
American Indian or Alaska Native..................	764	0.7	1,010	1.8	44,503	1.3
Asian...................................	1,482	1.3	605	1.1	47,329	1.4
Black or African American............	17,326	14.9	10,421	19.1	511,483	15.1
Native Hawaiian or Other Pacific Islander........	463	0.4	146	0.3	15,526	0.5
White..................................	35,370	30.5	22,290	40.8	1,533,224	45.2
Two or more races....................	3,237	2.8	2,888	5.3	139,766	4.1
Unknown or not collected.............	57,399	49.5	17,299	31.6	1,096,992	32.4
HISPANIC ORIGIN [2]						
Hispanic or Latino....................	11,746	10.0	5,519	10.2	446,306	13.0
Not Hispanic or Latino...............	51,039	43.6	32,162	59.6	1,979,912	57.7
Unknown or not collected.............	54,346	46.4	16,260	30.1	1,005,421	29.3
LEGAL STATUS [3]						
Voluntary..............................	49,534	42.7	39,307	71.6	3,258,732	95.9
Involuntary, non-forensic.............	47,791	41.2	10,467	19.1	84,909	2.5
Involuntary, forensic.................	18,802	16.2	5,142	9.4	55,973	1.6

[1] Less than 24-hour care provided to ambulatory patients. Outpatient care typically involves care for less than 3 hours per visit. Day treatment and partial hospitalization programs typically involve care lasting more than 3 hours per visit, on a regular schedule. [2] Persons of Hispanic origin may be of any race. [3] Clients may voluntarily admit themselves to receive mental health treatment, or be admitted involuntarily with a forensic (criminal) or non-forensic (noncriminal) status.

Source: U.S. Substance Abuse and Mental Health Services Administration, *National Mental Health Services Survey (N-MHSS): 2018, Data on Mental Health Treatment Facilities*, October 2019. See also <http://www.samhsa.gov/data/data-we-collect/n-mhss-national-mental-health-services-survey>.

Table 184. Opioid Treatment and Medication-Assisted Therapy—Facilities: 2018

[As of the end of March. Based on the National Survey of Substance Abuse Treatment Services, a census of all known public and private facilities that provide substance abuse treatment in the United States and associated jurisdictions. Medication-assisted opioid therapy includes the use of methadone or buprenorphine for the treatment of opioid addiction or dependence, and the use of naltrexone for preventing a relapse in opioid addiction. Methadone is available only at opioid treatment programs (OTPs) certified by the Substance Abuse and Mental Health Services Administration (SAMHSA). Physicians or other authorized medical practitioners who receive Drug Addiction Treatment Act of 2000 (DATA 2000) specific training and a waiver may prescribe buprenorphine. All physicians or approved medical personnel can prescribe naltrexone. Data for 2018 are based on responses from 14,809 eligible facilities (90.5% of survey universe). Client data were omitted from the 2018 survey]

Facilities by type of therapy	Total	Private non-profit	Private for-profit	Local, county, or community govern- ment	State govern- ment	Federal govern- ment [1]	Tribal govern- ment
Substance abuse treatment facilities....................	14,809	7,642	5,584	690	304	327	262
Facilities offering detoxification from opioids.............	2,800	1,137	1,400	92	48	112	11
Facilities providing medication-assisted opioid therapy..	6,259	2,910	2,655	246	141	239	68
Buprenorphine..............................	4,951	2,292	2,128	169	106	212	44
Injectable naltrexone...........................	4,178	2,071	1,590	171	93	213	40
Opioid treatment program (OTP) [2]....................	**1,519**	**496**	**899**	**51**	**34**	**33**	**6**
Outpatient treatment.............................	1,411	431	869	45	28	32	6
Regular...................................	1,090	354	648	32	21	30	5
Intensive.................................	431	199	175	16	15	24	2
Day treatment or partial hospitalization.............	97	42	42	4	2	6	1
Detoxification.............................	661	175	436	15	10	23	2
Methadone/buprenorphine maintenance or injectable naltrexone treatment.......................	1,360	415	837	43	27	32	6
Residential, non-hospital............................	132	68	42	3	4	15	0
Hospital inpatient.................................	121	61	33	12	6	9	0

[1] Includes Department of Veteran's Affairs, Department of Defense, Indian Health Service, and other, not shown separately. [2] Facilities that have opioid treatment programs certified by SAMHSA. Methadone is available only at these facilities.

Source: U.S. Substance Abuse and Mental Health Services Administration, *National Survey of Substance Abuse Treatment Services (N-SSATS): 2018, Data on Substance Abuse Treatment Facilities*, September 2019. See also <http://www.samhsa.gov/data/data-we-collect/n-ssats-national-survey-substance-abuse-treatment-services>.

Table 185. Community Health Centers, Patients, and Medical Personnel: 2018

[Patient and patient visit data in thousands (28,380 represents 28,380,000). Community health centers are community-based and patient-directed organizations that provide primary health care services to underserved populations with limited access to health care. Populations served include low-income persons, the uninsured, those with limited English proficiency, migratory and seasonal agricultural workers and their families, people experiencing homelessness, and residents of public housing. Most health centers receive Health Center Program federal grant funding. Some health centers that meet all Health Center Program requirements do not receive Federal award funding; these are called health center program look-alikes]

Item	Health Center Program grantees	Health Center Program look-alikes	Item	Health Center Program grantees	Health Center Program look-alikes
Health centers, total (number)...........	**1,362**	**84**	Insurance source:		
PATIENTS (1,000s)			None/uninsured.........................	6,419	143
Total patients...............................	**28,380**	**885**	Regular Medicaid (Title XIX).................	13,579	504
Male...	12,018	367	CHIP Medicaid [2].........................	163	4
Female..	16,361	518	Dual eligible (Medicare and Medicaid).....	1,063	43
			Medicare [3]................................	2,741	94
Age 17 and under........................	8,737	274	Other public insurance [4].......................	269	6
Age 18 to 64...........................	17,042	524	Private insurance..........................	5,208	134
Age 65 and older..........................	2,602	88	PERSONNEL (FTEs) [5]		
			Total physicians [6].............................	13,394	505
Non-Hispanic, total [1]......................	17,409	478	Family, general practice, and internist.....	8,624	302
White..................................	9,929	225	Obstetrician/gynecologists.................	1,301	53
Black/African American.....................	5,118	151	Pediatricians...........................	2,950	127
American Indian/Alaska native............	254	2	Nurse practitioners..........................	9,658	265
Asian.................................	993	54	Physician assistants..........................	3,227	109
Native Hawaiian/Other Pacific Islander...	208	3	Certified nurse midwives..................	728	21
Multiracial.................................	346	6			
Hispanic.................................	9,906	337	PATIENT VISITS (1,000s)		
Unreported race and ethnicity..............	1,065	69	By type of practitioner seen:		
			Total physicians [6].............................	39,585	1,533
Income as percent of poverty level:			Family, general practice, and internist.....	24,923	947
100% and under..............................	13,900	426	Obstetrician/gynecologists.................	3,550	149
101 to 150%................................	3,166	79	Pediatricians...........................	9,268	380
151 to 200%................................	1,541	32	Nurse practitioners..........................	24,183	681
Over 200%.................................	1,765	49	Physician assistants..........................	9,006	279
Unknown.................................	8,007	298	Certified nurse midwives..................	1,555	51

[1] Includes unknown/unreported race, not shown separately. [2] CHIP, Children's Health Insurance Program. [3] Includes dual eligible and other Title XVIII beneficiaries. [4] CHIP and non-CHIP. [5] FTE, full-time equivalent. [6] Includes data for other specialty physicians, not shown separately.

Source: U.S. Health Resources & Services Administration, Bureau of Primary Health Care, "Health Center Program Data," <https://bphc.hrsa.gov/datareporting/index.html>, accessed March 2020.

Table 186. Health Care Sources Used Most Often—Percent Distribution of Persons Age 18 and Over by Selected Characteristics: 2018

[In percent, except as noted (249,456 represents 249,456,000). Data are age-adjusted, unless otherwise noted. Based on a survey question that asked, "Is there a place that you usually go to when you are sick or need advice about your health?" If there was at least one such place, a follow-up question was asked: "What kind of place [is it/do you go to most often]—a clinic, a doctor's office, an emergency room, or some other place?" From the National Health Interview Survey, a sample survey of the civilian noninstitutionalized population; see Appendix III]

Characteristic	Adults age 18 and over, number (1,000)	Without a usual place for health care	With a usual place for health care	Usual place of health care			
				Physician office or Health Maintenance Organization (HMO)	Clinic or health center	Hospital emergency room or outpatient department	Other place
Total [1]	249,456	14.6	85.4	69.7	26.1	2.9	1.3
SEX							
Male	120,442	18.6	81.4	67.1	27.5	3.7	1.7
Female	129,014	10.7	89.3	71.8	24.8	2.3	1.0
AGE [2]							
18 to 44 years	115,008	21.0	79.0	64.5	30.3	3.5	1.7
45 to 64 years	83,038	9.6	90.4	73.3	23.4	2.5	0.9
65 to 74 years	30,809	4.4	95.6	77.6	19.3	2.0	1.0
75 years and over	20,601	2.6	97.4	81.7	15.8	1.6	0.8
RACE							
Single race [3]	243,677	14.5	85.5	69.7	26.1	2.9	1.3
White	193,454	14.6	85.4	70.7	25.5	2.3	1.4
Black or African American	30,813	14.7	85.3	65.8	26.5	6.3	1.5
American Indian or Alaska Native	2,810	11.1	88.9	33.2	(B)	(NA)	(B)
Asian	15,960	14.0	86.0	72.3	24.8	2.3	0.6
Native Hawaiian or Other Pacific Islander	640	(B)	[9] 86.7	(B)	(B)	(NA)	(B)
Two or more races [4]	5,779	20.5	79.5	66.2	27.3	5.2	1.3
Black or African American, white	1,567	16.8	83.2	74.9	22.0	(NA)	(B)
American Indian or Alaska Native, white	1,879	24.7	75.3	54.5	33.3	(NA)	(B)
HISPANIC ORIGIN AND RACE [5]							
Hispanic or Latino	40,749	20.7	79.3	57.6	36.7	4.4	1.3
Not Hispanic or Latino	208,706	13.2	86.8	71.8	24.2	2.7	1.3
White, single race	157,289	12.8	87.2	73.5	23.2	2.0	1.4
Black or African American, single race	29,089	14.4	85.6	66.4	25.8	6.3	1.5
EDUCATION [6]							
Less than high school diploma	24,710	20.9	79.1	55.1	36.8	6.7	1.4
High school diploma or GED [7]	52,455	15.6	84.4	65.9	28.7	4.2	1.2
Some college	62,770	13.0	87.0	70.9	25.1	2.6	1.4
Bachelor's degree or higher	78,964	9.9	90.1	78.1	19.1	1.5	1.4
FAMILY INCOME							
Less than $35,000	58,573	20.8	79.2	55.2	37.4	5.9	1.6
$35,000 to $49,999	24,817	19.7	80.3	62.0	32.9	3.6	1.5
$50,000 to $74,999	38,139	15.0	85.0	69.2	27.3	2.3	1.1
$75,000 to $99,999	30,794	12.0	88.0	73.6	22.9	2.1	1.4
$100,000 or more	73,236	8.9	91.1	79.0	18.2	1.4	1.3
HEALTH INSURANCE COVERAGE [8]							
Under age 65:							
Private	136,568	12.3	87.7	73.9	23.0	1.8	1.4
Medicaid	24,908	11.1	88.9	54.7	39.4	4.6	1.3
Other	9,857	11.7	88.3	52.5	36.0	9.5	2.1
Uninsured	25,525	48.5	51.5	41.7	47.1	9.2	2.0
Age 65 and over:							
Private	21,274	2.5	97.5	83.8	14.7	0.8	0.7
Medicare and Medicaid	3,529	3.2	96.8	69.0	26.3	3.8	0.9
Medicare Advantage	13,113	3.0	97.0	83.1	15.3	1.0	0.6
Medicare only	7,945	7.0	93.0	78.6	18.8	2.2	0.3
Other	5,181	2.2	97.8	63.1	27.4	6.3	3.2
Uninsured	274	(B)	(B)	(B)	(B)	(NA)	(B)

B Estimate is considered unreliable. NA Not available. [1] Includes other races not shown separately, and persons with unknown education, family income, and health insurance characteristics. [2] Estimates for age groups are not age adjusted. [3] Persons who indicated only a single race group. [4] Persons who indicated more than one race group. [5] Persons of Hispanic or Latino origin may be of any race or combination of races. [6] Shown only for adults age 25 and over. [7] GED is General Educational Development high school equivalency diploma. [8] Based on a hierarchy of mutually exclusive categories. Persons with more than one type of health insurance were assigned to the first appropriate category in the hierarchy. "Uninsured" includes adults who had no coverage, had only Indian Health Service coverage, or had only a private plan that paid for one type of service such as accidents or dental care. [9] The estimate meets NCHS standards of reliability, but its complement does not.

Source: U.S. National Center for Health Statistics, 2018 National Health Interview Survey, "Tables of Summary Health Statistics," <https://www.cdc.gov/nchs/nhis/SHS.htm>, accessed December 2019.

Table 187. Health Care Visits—Percent Distribution by Selected Patient Characteristics: 2010 and 2017

[Covers visits to hospital emergency departments, home health care visits, and visits to doctor's offices, clinics, or some other place during a 12-month period. Excludes dental visits. Based on the National Health Interview Survey. See source, and Appendix III]

Characteristic	Percent distribution of health care visits							
	None		1–3 visits		4–9 visits		10 or more visits	
	2010	2017	2010	2017	2010	2017	2010	2017
All persons [1,2]............	**15.6**	**14.0**	**45.4**	**50.4**	**25.8**	**23.2**	**13.2**	**12.4**
SEX [2]								
Male............	20.4	17.6	46.4	51.9	22.7	20.9	10.5	9.7
Female............	10.9	10.5	44.4	49.0	28.8	25.6	15.9	15.0
AGE								
Under 18 years............	8.1	7.4	55.6	61.8	28.2	24.4	8.2	6.4
Under 6 years............	3.7	5.0	48.9	54.0	36.8	34.1	10.6	7.0
6 to 17 years............	10.4	8.5	59.1	65.5	23.6	19.9	6.9	6.2
18 to 44 years............	24.2	21.5	43.9	49.2	20.6	18.3	11.3	11.1
45 to 64 years............	14.8	12.7	42.8	46.7	26.1	24.9	16.4	15.7
65 years and over............	5.3	5.6	33.8	37.3	36.7	34.2	24.2	22.8
75 years and over............	4.1	4.4	31.0	32.6	38.0	35.3	27.0	27.6
RACE [2,3]								
White............	15.3	13.9	44.9	49.2	26.1	24.0	13.7	12.9
Black or African American............	15.7	13.9	47.2	53.5	24.7	21.4	12.4	11.3
American Indian or Alaska Native............	19.4	16.6	40.3	46.6	28.1	24.8	12.2	12.0
Asian............	20.4	14.9	49.9	59.2	22.1	18.5	7.6	7.4
Native Hawaiian or Other Pacific Islander only............	(B)	27.1	(B)	37.9	(B)	19.3	(B)	(B)
Two or more races............	13.9	13.1	42.3	48.6	25.2	20.3	18.6	18.1
HISPANIC ORIGIN AND RACE [2,3,4]								
Hispanic or Latino............	23.5	18.7	43.2	49.3	22.6	22.2	10.7	9.8
Not Hispanic or Latino............	14.0	12.9	45.8	50.5	26.5	23.7	13.7	13.0
White, non-Hispanic............	13.2	12.3	45.3	49.0	27.1	24.9	14.4	13.9
Black, non-Hispanic............	15.6	14.1	47.3	53.4	24.9	21.3	12.2	11.2
HEALTH INSURANCE STATUS [5,6]								
Insured............	12.3	12.2	48.5	53.5	26.1	22.8	13.1	11.6
Private............	12.4	12.2	51.0	55.8	25.5	22.3	11.1	9.6
Medicaid............	10.9	11.6	38.2	44.6	28.0	25.1	23.0	18.8
Uninsured............	37.2	38.9	42.2	44.5	15.2	11.4	5.4	5.2
Insured continuously 12 months prior to interview............	12.1	11.9	48.6	53.8	26.2	22.7	13.0	11.6
Uninsured for any period up to 12 months prior to interview............	18.5	20.9	47.8	48.8	22.0	20.3	11.6	10.1
Uninsured more than 12 months prior to interview............	43.8	47.9	39.7	40.1	12.6	8.5	3.9	3.5

B Base figure too small to meet standards for reliability of a derived figure. [1] Includes other categories not shown separately. [2] Age adjusted to the year 2000 standard population. [3] Race groups include persons of Hispanic and non-Hispanic origin. Race-specific estimates are for persons reporting one race only. [4] Persons of Hispanic or Latino origin may be of any race. [5] For persons under age 65, at time of interview. Estimates are age-adjusted to the year 2000 standard population. [6] Health insurance categories are mutually exclusive. Persons who reported both Medicaid and private coverage are classified as having private coverage. Medicaid coverage includes State-sponsored health plans and the Children's Health Insurance Program (CHIP). The insured category also includes military plans, other government-sponsored health plans, and Medicare, not shown separately. Persons not covered by private insurance, Medicaid, CHIP, state-sponsored or other government-sponsored health plans, Medicare, or military plans are considered to have no health insurance coverage. Persons with only Indian Health Service coverage are considered to have no health insurance coverage.

Source: U.S. National Center for Health Statistics, *Health, United States, 2018*, October 2019. See also <https://www.cdc.gov/nchs/hus/index.htm>.

Table 188. Physician Office Visits by Leading Reason for Visit by Patient Sex: 2016

[883,725 represents 883,725,000. Based on the 2016 National Ambulatory Medical Care Survey (NAMCS). NAMCS is an annual nationally representative sample survey of visits to nonfederal office-based patient care physicians, excluding anesthesiologists, radiologists, and pathologists. The sampling frame for the 2016 NAMCS was composed of all physicians contained in the master files maintained by the American Medical Association and the American Osteopathic Association. Data are subject to sampling and nonsampling errors]

Leading reason for visit	Number of visits (1,000)	Percent distribution Male [1]	Percent distribution Female [2]	Leading reason for visit	Number of visits (1,000)	Percent distribution Male [1]	Percent distribution Female [2]
All visits [3]............	**883,725**	**100.0**	**100.0**	Hypertension............	11,406	1.3	1.3
Progress visit [4]............	127,535	14.7	14.2	Knee symptoms............	10,581	1.4	1.0
General medical examination.......	72,132	10.1	6.7	Preoperative visit............	10,129	1.3	1.1
Prenatal examination, routine.......	22,477	(X)	4.4	Symptoms referable to throat.......	10,056	0.9	1.3
Postoperative visit............	18,636	2.2	2.0	For test results............	9,786	1.1	1.1
Medication............	17,283	2.6	1.5	Vision dysfunctions............	9,666	1.0	1.1
Cough............	16,417	2.2	1.6	Fever............	8,836	1.5	0.7
Well-baby examination............	15,865	1.8	1.8	Other special examination............	8,739	1.2	0.8
Medical counseling [4]............	13,485	1.4	1.6	Diabetes mellitus............	8,512	1.1	0.9
Skin rash............	13,374	1.7	1.4	Earache or ear infection............	8,507	1.0	0.9
Gynecological examination..........	11,743	(X)	2.3	All other reasons............	458,559	51.4	52.3

X Not applicable. [1] Based on 371,533,000 visits made by males. [2] Based on 512,192,000 visits made by females. [3] Numbers may not sum to totals due to rounding. [4] Not otherwise specified.

Source: U.S. National Center for Health Statistics, *National Ambulatory Medical Care Survey: 2016 State and National Summary Tables*, May 2019. See also <https://www.cdc.gov/nchs/ahcd/web_tables.htm>.

Table 189. Hospital Emergency Department (ER) Visits by Wait Time and Total Time Spent: 2015 to 2017

[136,943 represents 136,943,000. Based on the National Hospital Ambulatory Medical Care Survey (NHAMCS), an annual nationally representative sample survey of visits to hospital emergency departments and other outpatient departments and ambulatory surgical centers. Data presented here cover hospital emergency departments only]

Visit characteristic	Number of visits (1,000)			Percent distribution of visits		
	2015	2016	2017	2015	2016	2017
Total visits [1]	**136,943**	**145,591**	**138,977**	**100.0**	**100.0**	**100.0**
WAIT TIME TO SEE MEDICAL PROFESSIONAL [2]						
Fewer than 15 minutes	48,540	56,822	56,081	35.4	39.0	40.4
15 to 59 minutes	43,925	45,974	45,673	32.1	31.6	32.9
1 hour, but less than 2 hours	13,228	14,567	12,485	9.7	10.0	9.0
2 hours, but less than 3 hours	3,894	4,715	3,845	2.8	3.2	2.8
3 hours, but less than 4 hours	1,496	1,742	1,319	1.1	1.2	0.9
4 hours, but less than 6 hours	1,028	1,345	1,222	0.8	0.9	0.9
6 hours or more	870	750	731	0.6	0.5	0.5
TIME SPENT IN EMERGENCY DEPARTMENT						
Less than 1 hour	15,361	17,588	(NA)	11.2	12.1	(NA)
1 hour, but less than 2 hours	30,987	32,816	(NA)	22.6	22.5	(NA)
2 hours, but less than 4 hours	45,699	49,128	(NA)	33.4	33.8	(NA)
4 hours, but less than 6 hours	19,462	21,940	(NA)	14.2	15.1	(NA)
6 hours, but less than 10 hours	9,410	11,315	(NA)	6.9	7.8	(NA)
10 hours, but less than 14 hours	2,093	2,293	(NA)	1.5	1.6	(NA)
14 hours, but less than 24 hours	1,902	2,246	(NA)	1.4	1.5	(NA)
24 hours or more	1,093	1,546	(NA)	0.8	1.1	(NA)

NA Not available. [1] Totals include nonresponse and nonapplicable categories. [2] Medical professional may be a physician, physician assistant, or advanced nurse practitioner.

Source: U.S. National Center for Health Statistics, *National Hospital Ambulatory Medical Care Survey: 2017 Emergency Department Summary Tables*, January 2020, and earlier reports. See also <https://www.cdc.gov/nchs/ahcd/index.htm>.

Table 190. Hospital Emergency Department (ER) Visits by Patient Characteristics: 2017

[138,977 represents 138,977,000. Based on data collected in the National Hospital Ambulatory Medical Care Survey, and subject to sampling error; see sources for details]

Characteristic	Number (1,000)	Per 100 persons [1]	Characteristic	Number (1,000)	Per 100 persons [1]
Total	**138,977**	**43.3**	PATIENT RACE/ETHNICITY [2]		
			White	97,488	39.6
PATIENT AGE			Black or African American	36,276	86.1
Under 15 years old	28,369	46.5	Other	5,214	16.1
15 to 24 years old	20,194	47.8	Hispanic or Latino	22,077	37.9
25 to 44 years old	38,207	45.4			
45 to 64 years old	29,828	35.7	EXPECTED PAYMENT SOURCE [3]		
65 years and over	22,379	45.2	Private insurance	43,352	(X)
65 to 74 years old	10,316	35.0	Medicare	25,663	(X)
75 years old and over	12,063	60.0	Medicaid/CHIP/state-based program [4]	55,957	(X)
			No insurance [5]	11,119	(X)
			Self pay	10,782	(X)
PATIENT SEX			No charge/charity	[6] 671	(X)
Male	61,762	39.4	Worker's compensation	1,208	(X)
Female	77,215	47.1			

X Not applicable. [1] Visit rates are based on the Census Bureau's July 1, 2017 set of estimates of the civilian noninstitutional population. [2] Race groups White, Black or African American, and Other include persons of Hispanic origin. Persons of Hispanic origin may be of any race. See source for information on missing and imputed data. [3] Estimates include all expected sources of payment. Other and unknown not shown separately. [4] Children's Health Insurance Program (CHIP). [5] "No insurance" is self-pay, no charge, or charity as payment sources. [6] Figure does not meet standards of reliability.

Source: U.S. National Center for Health Statistics, *National Hospital Ambulatory Medical Care Survey: 2017 Emergency Department Summary Tables,* January 2020. See also <https://www.cdc.gov/nchs/ahcd/index.htm>.

Table 191. Medicare-Certified Hospitals, Institutions, and Physicians by Provider Type: 2010 to 2018

[Inpatient hospitals and other institutional providers are active and Medicare-certified in the reporting year. Physician provider counts originate from Medicare fee-for-service Part B claims, and reflect services provided by participating and non-participating physicians]

Providers by type	2010	2013	2014	2015	2016	2017	2018
INPATIENT HOSPITALS							
Total hospitals [1]	**6,169**	**6,164**	**6,142**	**6,140**	**6,146**	**6,123**	**6,072**
Beds (1,000)	927,535	934,874	931,057	931,951	933,209	934,197	931,555
Beds per 1,000 enrollees [2]	19.6	17.9	17.3	16.9	16.5	16.1	15.6
Short stay	3,566	3,506	3,466	3,436	3,419	3,392	3,334
Psychiatric units	1,180	1,128	1,114	1,118	1,113	1,092	1,063
Rehabilitation units	938	914	915	908	911	890	864
Swing bed hospitals	510	513	502	488	474	467	455
Psychiatric	511	541	551	560	570	586	598
Rehabilitation	235	245	255	266	277	282	296
Children's	77	98	98	100	99	97	96
Long term care	438	430	423	426	420	401	382
Critical access	1,325	1,329	1,334	1,336	1,343	1,347	1,351
SELECTED INSTITUTIONAL PROVIDERS							
Skilled nursing facilities	15,084	15,156	15,179	15,236	15,274	15,268	15,218
Beds (1,000)	1,572,511	1,588,797	1,594,927	1,600,752	1,607,056	1,605,515	1,602,222
Beds per 1,000 enrollees [2]	33.2	30.5	29.7	29.0	28.4	27.6	26.9
Home health agencies	10,914	12,459	12,268	12,149	11,956	11,593	11,317
Hospices	3,509	3,941	4,140	4,302	4,473	4,650	4,775
Independent and clinical labs	224,684	244,427	250,247	252,044	254,133	258,473	262,524
Outpatient physical therapy/speech pathology	2,536	2,172	2,102	2,130	2,080	2,043	2,016
End stage renal disease	5,631	6,145	6,374	6,558	6,843	7,082	7,429
Rural health clinics	3,845	4,026	4,062	4,104	4,153	4,233	4,402
Ambulatory surgical centers	5,316	5,368	5,444	5,470	5,529	5,598	5,718
Federally qualified health centers	4,308	5,882	6,451	7,022	7,723	8,289	8,836
PHYSICIAN PROVIDERS							
All physician specialties [1, 3]	**595,783**	**639,225**	**648,375**	**656,195**	**665,772**	**675,579**	**684,790**
Primary care	212,849	221,351	225,387	227,370	228,907	229,946	227,587
Family practice	84,982	89,917	91,570	92,830	93,893	94,703	95,031
General practice	13,401	10,724	10,470	9,985	9,492	9,225	8,849
Internal medicine	106,343	111,075	113,207	114,420	115,335	115,792	113,155
Pediatric medicine	8,123	9,635	10,140	10,135	10,187	10,226	10,552
Surgical specialties	108,093	110,485	111,213	111,272	111,439	112,390	112,839
Radiology	36,656	37,622	37,955	38,156	38,736	39,419	39,903
Obstetrics/gynecology	32,881	34,607	34,914	34,890	35,092	35,439	35,556
Psychiatry	27,550	28,162	28,258	28,139	28,150	28,224	28,200

[1] Includes other provider types not shown separately. [2] Beds per 1,000 enrollees based on Medicare Part A enrollee counts. [3] Physicians may be counted in more than one specialty.

Source: U.S. Centers for Medicare & Medicaid Services, "CMS Program Statistics," <https://www.cms.gov/Research-Statistics-Data-and-Systems/Statistics-Trends-and-Reports/CMSProgramStatistics/index.html>, accessed February 2020.

Table 192. Nursing Homes, Beds, Residents, and Occupancy Rate by State: 2016

[Based on a census of certified nursing facilities. Annual numbers of nursing homes, beds, and residents are based on the Centers for Medicare & Medicaid Services' reporting cycle. Starting with 2013 data, a new editing rule was used for number of beds. For the U.S., the number of beds decreased by less than 1%. For most states, this caused little or no change in the data. The change in the number of beds also caused a change in some occupancy rates. Because of the methodology change, interpret trends with caution]

State	Nursing homes	Beds	Residents	Occupancy rate [1]	State	Nursing homes	Beds	Residents	Occupancy rate [1]
U.S.	**15,647**	**1,690,304**	**1,346,941**	**79.7**	MO	513	55,120	38,279	69.4
AL	229	26,702	22,554	84.5	MT	78	6,614	4,385	66.3
AK	18	693	591	85.3	NE	214	15,750	11,718	74.4
AZ	147	16,535	11,480	69.4	NV	58	6,649	4,967	74.7
AR	229	24,649	17,707	71.8	NH	75	7,471	6,655	89.1
CA	1,205	118,666	101,744	85.7	NJ	366	52,784	44,598	84.5
CO	221	20,904	16,267	77.8	NM	75	7,198	5,713	79.4
CT	225	27,252	23,224	85.2	NY	624	115,542	104,187	90.2
DE	45	4,807	4,206	87.5	NC	425	45,537	36,654	80.5
DC	19	2,766	2,494	90.2	ND	81	6,169	5,562	90.2
FL	690	83,823	73,183	87.3	OH	963	90,547	74,844	82.7
GA	358	39,905	33,324	83.5	OK	304	28,517	18,729	65.7
HI	46	4,385	3,564	81.3	OR	137	11,419	7,462	65.3
ID	78	5,858	3,892	66.4	PA	701	88,263	78,042	88.4
IL	742	94,923	68,188	71.8	RI	84	8,720	7,829	89.8
IN	546	61,604	38,884	63.1	SC	189	19,948	16,932	84.9
IA	440	31,624	24,106	76.2	SD	110	6,867	6,234	90.8
KS	340	25,685	17,810	69.3	TN	320	36,902	27,486	74.5
KY	291	27,119	23,442	86.4	TX	1,216	137,028	92,737	67.7
LA	279	34,642	26,300	75.9	UT	98	8,479	5,443	64.2
ME	103	6,918	6,142	88.8	VT	37	3,174	2,603	82.0
MD	228	28,090	24,534	87.3	VA	288	32,783	27,713	84.5
MA	412	47,779	40,065	83.9	WA	221	21,109	16,652	78.9
MI	446	47,285	38,847	82.2	WV	126	10,866	9,446	86.9
MN	378	29,816	25,279	84.8	WI	386	33,079	25,766	77.9
MS	205	18,389	16,100	87.6	WY	38	2,950	2,378	80.6

[1] Percentage of beds occupied (number of nursing home residents per 100 nursing home beds).

Source: U.S. National Center for Health Statistics, *Health, United States, 2017*, September 2018. See also <https://www.cdc.gov/nchs/hus/index.htm>.

Table 193. Hospital Emergency Department Visits by Leading Reason for Visit by Patient Age and Sex: 2017

[138,977 represents 138,977,000. Based on the annual National Hospital Ambulatory Medical Care Survey and subject to sampling error; see source for details]

Principal reason for visit	Visits (1,000)	Percent of visits	Principal reason for visit	Visits (1,000)	Percent of visits
Total, all ages	**138,977**	**100.0**	**Patients age 15 to 64 years [2]**	**88,229**	**100.0**
			Female	50,846	57.6
Stomach & abdominal pain, cramps, spasms	12,248	8.8	Stomach & abdominal pain, cramps, spasms	6,548	7.4
Chest pain and related symptoms	6,523	4.7	Chest pain and related symptoms	2,990	3.4
Fever	5,491	4.0	Headache, pain in head	1,988	2.3
Cough	5,033	3.6	Pain [1]	1,493	1.7
Shortness of breath	3,988	2.9	Cough	1,461	1.7
Pain [1]	3,642	2.6	Male	37,384	42.4
Headache, pain in head	3,508	2.5	Stomach & abdominal pain, cramps, spasms	2,933	3.3
Back symptoms	3,290	2.4	Chest pain and related symptoms	1,957	2.2
Vomiting	2,964	2.1	Pain [1]	1,399	1.6
Symptoms referable to throat	2,787	2.0	Back symptoms	1,359	1.5
All other reasons	89,504	64.4	Shortness of breath	1,062	1.2
Patients under age 15 years [2]	**28,369**	**100.0**	**Patients age 65 years and over [2]**	**22,379**	**100.0**
Female	13,172	46.4	Female	13,198	59.0
Fever	2,031	7.2	Stomach & abdominal pain, cramps, spasms	913	4.1
Cough	987	3.5	Accident	756	3.4
Skin rash	602	2.1	Chest pain and related symptoms [1]	751	3.4
Stomach & abdominal pain, cramps, spasms	593	2.1	Shortness of breath	503	2.2
Vomiting	566	2.0	Vertigo—dizziness	428	1.9
Male	15,197	53.6	Male	9,181	41.0
Fever	2,198	7.7	Shortness of breath	661	3.0
Cough	1,219	4.3	Chest pain and related symptoms	540	2.4
Stomach & abdominal pain, cramps, spasms	752	2.7	Stomach & abdominal pain, cramps, spasms	510	2.3
Vomiting	721	2.5	General weakness	[4] 492	2.2
Injury, other [3]	688	2.4	Leg symptoms	[4] 313	1.4

[1] Not referable to a specific body system or body systems. [2] Totals for each age group and sex include all other reasons not shown separately, including unknown and blank responses. [3] Including unspecified injury of head, neck, and face. [4] Interpret with caution; the relative standard error of the estimate exceeds 30 percent.

Source: U.S. National Center for Health Statistics, *National Hospital Ambulatory Medical Care Survey, 2017 Emergency Department Summary Tables*, January 2020. See also <https://www.cdc.gov/nchs/ahcd/index.htm>.

Table 194. Hospital Overnight Stays by Selected Characteristics: 2018

[Numbers in thousands (322,904 represents 322,904,000). Covers overnight hospitals stays in the past 12 months. Hospital stays due to childbirth for both the mother and the child are included. Excludes overnight stays in hospital emergency rooms or departments. Based on the National Health Interview Survey, a sample survey of the civilian noninstitutionalized population; see Appendix III]

Selected characteristic	Total persons	Percent distribution by number of overnight hospital stays [1]			
		None	One	Two	Three or more
Total [2]	**322,904**	**92.6**	**5.4**	**1.1**	**0.9**
SEX					
Male	157,929	93.7	4.5	1.0	0.8
Female	164,975	91.5	6.4	1.2	1.0
AGE					
Under 12 years old	48,512	93.5	5.7	0.5	0.4
12 to 17 years old	24,940	98.2	1.3	0.3	0.2
18 to 44 years old	114,817	94.2	4.6	0.6	0.6
45 to 64 years old	83,391	92.3	5.0	1.6	1.1
65 years old and over	51,244	83.3	11.3	3.0	2.5
RACE AND ETHNICITY					
Single race [3]	313,706	92.6	5.4	1.1	0.9
White	246,914	92.7	5.4	1.0	0.8
Black or African American	41,706	91.1	5.9	1.6	1.4
American Indian or Alaska Native	3,971	92.4	4.3	1.6	1.7
Asian	20,145	94.5	4.3	0.6	0.6
Native Hawaiian or Other Pacific Islander	971	[6] 94.2	(B)	0.1	0.5
Two or more races [3]	9,197	91.1	5.9	1.6	1.3
Hispanic or Latino [4]	59,466	93.5	4.5	1.0	1.0
Not Hispanic or Latino	263,438	92.3	5.7	1.1	0.9
HEALTH INSURANCE COVERAGE [5]					
Private	175,253	94.7	4.4	0.5	0.4
Medicaid or other public insurance	52,116	89.3	6.6	2.0	2.1
Other coverage	11,329	91.1	5.9	1.6	1.5
Uninsured	29,581	96.0	2.9	0.7	0.5

B Figure considered unreliable. [1] May not sum to total due to rounding. Estimates are age-adjusted using the projected 2000 U.S. population. Estimates for age groups are not age-adjusted. [2] Includes other races not shown separately and persons with unknown health insurance coverage. [3] Includes persons of Hispanic and Latino origin. [4] Persons of Hispanic or Latino origin may be of any race. [5] For persons under age 65. Based on a hierarchy of mutually exclusive categories. Persons with more than one type of insurance were assigned to the first appropriate category in the hierarchy. "Uninsured" includes persons who had no coverage, had only Indian Health Service coverage, or had only a private plan with one type of service such as accidents or dental care. [6] The estimate meets NCHS standards of reliability but its complement does not.

Source: U.S. National Center for Health Statistics, 2018 National Health Interview Survey, "Tables of Summary Statistics," <https//:www.cdc.gov/nchs/nhis/SHS.htm>, accessed October 2019.

Table 195. Hospitals—Summary Characteristics: 2000 to 2018

[In units indicated (984 represents 984,000). Covers hospitals accepted for registration by the American Hospital Association; see text, this section. Short-term hospitals have an average patient stay of less than 30 days; long-term, an average stay of longer duration]

Item	2000	2005	2010	2013	2014	2015	2016	2017 [8]	2018
NUMBER									
All hospitals............................	5,810	5,756	5,754	5,686	5,627	5,564	5,534	6,210	6,146
With 100 beds or more...................	3,102	2,942	2,832	2,740	2,709	2,682	2,659	2,763	2,730
Nonfederal [1].............................	5,565	5,530	5,541	5,473	5,414	5,352	5,325	6,002	5,937
Community hospitals [2].................	4,915	4,936	4,985	4,974	4,926	4,862	4,840	5,262	5,198
Nongovernmental nonprofit...........	3,003	2,958	2,904	2,904	2,870	2,845	2,849	2,968	2,937
For profit..........................	749	868	1,013	1,060	1,053	1,034	1,035	1,322	1,296
State and local government............	1,163	1,110	1,068	1,010	1,003	983	956	972	965
Long term general and special..........	131	115	109	80	74	77	76	106	109
Psychiatric...........................	496	456	435	406	403	401	397	620	616
Tuberculosis..........................	4	3	2	1	1	2	2	2	2
Federal.................................	245	226	213	213	213	212	209	208	209
BEDS (1,000) [3]									
All hospitals............................	984	947	942	915	902	898	895	931	924
Rate per 1,000 population [4]............	3.5	3.2	3.0	2.9	2.8	2.8	2.8	2.9	2.8
Beds per hospital......................	169	165	164	161	160	160	162	150	150
Nonfederal [1].............................	931	901	897	876	863	859	857	893	887
Community hospitals [2].................	824	802	805	796	787	782	780	799	792
Rate per 1,000 population [4].........	2.9	2.7	2.6	2.5	2.5	2.4	2.4	2.5	2.4
Nongovernmental nonprofit...........	583	561	556	544	535	531	533	545	543
For profit..........................	110	114	125	135	136	135	134	142	140
State and local government............	131	128	125	117	116	117	113	111	110
Long term general and special..........	18	15	15	10	8	8	8	11	11
Psychiatric...........................	87	82	76	69	68	68	68	82	82
Federal.................................	53	46	45	39	39	39	38	38	38
AVERAGE DAILY CENSUS (1,000) [5]									
All hospitals............................	650	656	627	592	584	588	589	614	612
Community hospitals [2].................	526	540	520	500	494	497	499	510	508
Nongovernmental nonprofit...........	382	388	368	351	344	346	349	357	356
For profit..........................	61	68	71	76	77	77	78	81	81
State and local government............	83	85	80	74	73	74	72	72	71
EXPENSES (bil. dol.) [6]									
All hospitals............................	395.4	570.5	750.6	859.4	892.7	936.5	991.5	1,061.0	1,112.2
Nonfederal [1].............................	371.5	533.7	698.2	801.5	828.4	872.0	923.0	993.0	1,037.2
Community hospitals [2].................	356.6	515.7	678.0	782.0	808.9	851.5	902.9	966.0	1,010.0
Nongovernmental nonprofit...........	267.1	386.0	510.7	585.5	602.6	636.0	677.0	721.0	755.8
For profit..........................	35.0	51.8	67.2	81.6	85.4	88.8	94.0	105.0	108.0
State and local government............	54.5	77.9	100.1	115.0	120.9	126.7	132.1	140.0	146.0
Long term general and special..........	2.8	3.6	4.2	3.0	3.0	3.2	2.9	3.9	4.1
Psychiatric...........................	11.9	13.9	15.8	16.1	16.3	16.8	17.2	22.5	22.2
Federal.................................	23.9	36.8	52.4	57.9	64.3	64.5	68.1	67.6	75.0
PERSONNEL (1,000) [7]									
All hospitals............................	4,454	4,790	5,184	5,342	5,314	5,397	5,562	5,841	5,903
Nonfederal [1].............................	4,157	4,479	4,825	4,984	4,945	5,056	5,184	5,459	5,484
Community hospitals [2].................	3,911	4,260	4,600	4,786	4,755	4,859	4,992	5,216	5,239
Nongovernmental nonprofit...........	2,919	3,154	3,388	3,500	3,494	3,562	3,681	3,841	3,848
For profit..........................	378	421	474	553	522	534	551	591	594
State and local government............	614	681	738	734	739	762	759	783	797
Long term general and special..........	41	38	39	25	22	23	21	28	32
Psychiatric...........................	200	182	182	171	167	172	169	212	211
Federal.................................	297	311	359	358	369	341	379	382	419
OUTPATIENT VISITS (mil.)									
Total..................................	592.7	673.7	750.4	787.4	802.7	832.3	863.7	880.4	879.6
Emergency visits.......................	106.9	118.9	131.5	137.5	140.2	145.3	146.7	150.2	147.4

[1] Includes hospital units of institutions; and tuberculosis hospitals, not shown separately. [2] Short-term (average stay less than 30 days) general and special (e.g., obstetrics and gynecology, rehabilitation, etc. except psychiatric, tuberculosis, alcoholism, and chemical dependency). Excludes hospital units of institutions. [3] Number of beds at end of reporting period. [4] See footnote 2, Table 196. [5] The average number of people served on an inpatient basis on a single day during the reporting period. [6] Excludes new construction. [7] Includes full-time equivalents of part-time personnel. [8] Beginning with the 2019 edition of *AHA Hospital Statistics* presenting data from the 2017 annual survey, the AHA no longer employs its own methodology to classify hospitals as registered. As a result of the application of a new, broader hospital definition, the number of hospitals in 2017 increased significantly.

Source: Health Forum LLC, an affiliate of the American Hospital Association, Chicago, IL, *AHA Hospital Statistics 2020 Edition* ©, and previous editions. See also <http://www.ahadata.com/>.

Table 196. Hospital Utilization Rates by Type of Hospital: 1990 to 2018

[In units, as indicated (21.9 represents 21,900,000)]

Type of hospital	1990	2000	2005	2010	2015	2016	2017 [4]	2018
Community hospitals: [1]								
Admissions per 1,000 population [2].........................	125	117	119	114	104	103	105	105
Admissions per bed...........................	34	40	44	44	43	43	43	43
Average length of stay (days) [3]............................	7.2	5.8	5.6	5.4	5.5	5.5	5.5	5.4
Outpatient visits per admission....................	9.7	15.8	16.6	18.5	21.7	21.6	22.3	22.4
Outpatient visits per 1,000 population [2]..................	1,207	1,852	1,976	2,108	2,247	2,312	2,352	2,344
Surgical operations (million)...................	21.9	26.1	27.5	27.3	26.5	27.2	28.2	28.2
Number per admission.......................	0.7	0.8	0.8	0.8	0.8	0.8	0.8	0.8
Nonfederal psychiatric:								
Admissions per 1,000 population [2].........	2.9	2.4	2.5	2.5	2.6	2.5	3.7	3.7
Days in hospital per 1,000 population [2]..................	190	93	89	77	67	65	77	77

[1] See headnote, Table 197. [2] Based on Census Bureau estimated resident population as of July 1. Data for 1990, 2000, and 2010 based on enumerated resident population as of April 1. [3] Number of inpatient days divided by number of admissions. [4] See footnote 8, Table 195.

Source: Health Forum LLC, an affiliate of the American Hospital Association, Chicago, IL, *AHA Hospital Statistics 2020 Edition* ©, and previous editions. See also <http://www.ahadata.com/>.

Table 197. Community Hospital Summary Data by State: 2010 and 2018

[In units indicated (804.9 represents 804,900). Community hospitals are defined as all nonfederal, short-term general, and other special hospitals. Other special hospitals include obstetrics and gynecology; eye, ear, nose, and throat; rehabilitation; orthopedic; and other individually described specialty services. Community hospitals include academic medical centers or other teaching hospitals if they are nonfederal short-term hospitals. Excluded are hospitals not accessible by the general public, such as prison hospitals or college infirmaries]

State	Number of hospitals		Beds (1,000)		Patients admitted (1,000)		Average daily census [1] (1,000)		Outpatient visits (mil.)		Average cost per day (dol.)	
	2010	2018 [2]	2010	2018 [2]	2010	2018 [2]	2010	2018 [2]	2010	2018 [2]	2010	2018 [2]
United States..........	4,985	5,198	804.9	792.4	35,149	34,251	519.5	507.7	651.4	766.4	1,910	2,517
Alabama................	105	101	15.1	15.3	642	629	9.2	9.9	8.8	10.0	1,372	1,544
Alaska.................	22	21	1.5	1.6	57	53	0.9	1.1	1.8	2.0	2,020	2,196
Arizona................	73	83	13.4	13.8	712	652	8.7	8.5	8.1	8.4	2,173	2,687
Arkansas..............	85	88	9.5	9.5	370	358	5.2	5.0	5.0	6.4	1,477	1,880
California..............	343	359	70.4	73.0	3,424	3,401	47.8	47.9	51.7	55.7	2,566	3,532
Colorado..............	80	89	10.2	10.6	449	447	6.1	6.2	8.3	9.4	2,190	3,045
Connecticut...........	34	32	8.1	7.2	407	366	6.3	5.5	8.3	9.0	2,154	2,836
Delaware..............	7	7	2.2	2.1	102	102	1.6	1.5	1.8	2.2	2,227	3,038
District of Columbia......	11	10	3.5	3.1	132	116	2.5	2.3	2.3	2.6	2,434	3,473
Florida................	210	217	53.3	54.7	2,452	2,629	33.4	36.0	24.2	27.0	1,837	2,213
Georgia...............	154	145	25.5	25.1	961	1,016	16.8	17.6	14.3	19.6	1,338	1,845
Hawaii................	26	22	3.1	2.7	111	109	2.3	1.9	2.2	2.7	1,755	2,644
Idaho.................	41	45	3.4	3.4	131	140	1.7	1.7	3.2	6.3	1,748	3,192
Illinois................	189	187	33.3	32.0	1,543	1,358	20.7	18.7	32.6	37.6	1,983	2,636
Indiana................	125	132	17.8	18.2	718	729	10.3	10.2	18.7	21.5	1,964	2,591
Iowa..................	118	118	10.1	9.4	342	315	5.7	5.2	11.0	11.5	1,288	1,599
Kansas................	130	139	10.0	9.7	305	319	5.4	5.1	6.7	8.8	1,304	1,925
Kentucky..............	106	105	14.2	14.3	609	561	8.6	8.7	10.4	14.9	1,546	1,956
Louisiana.............	126	158	15.4	15.3	625	552	9.2	8.6	12.4	12.9	1,561	2,030
Maine.................	37	34	3.6	3.4	146	132	2.2	2.4	6.0	5.9	2,077	2,636
Maryland..............	47	50	11.7	11.5	708	567	8.7	8.1	8.4	9.8	2,383	2,815
Massachusetts.........	79	75	15.7	15.6	823	780	11.4	11.5	21.8	23.4	2,419	3,038
Michigan..............	156	144	25.6	24.9	1,208	1,134	17.0	15.7	30.3	39.0	1,959	2,400
Minnesota.............	133	127	15.3	14.0	592	572	9.9	9.1	11.1	13.4	1,731	2,379
Mississippi............	96	99	12.9	12.1	403	370	7.0	6.7	4.6	7.2	1,154	1,371
Missouri...............	122	122	18.7	18.7	821	780	11.5	11.4	19.8	25.2	1,981	2,361
Montana...............	48	56	3.7	3.5	97	98	2.3	2.1	3.5	4.4	1,190	1,594
Nebraska..............	88	93	7.2	6.8	209	210	4.0	3.8	4.6	5.7	1,516	2,073
Nevada................	36	44	5.2	6.5	241	306	3.6	4.6	2.7	3.7	1,885	1,991
New Hampshire........	28	28	2.9	2.8	120	124	1.7	1.8	4.8	5.4	2,164	2,623
New Jersey............	73	82	21.1	20.9	1,067	1,067	14.9	13.9	16.0	14.0	2,179	2,786
New Mexico............	36	41	4.0	3.8	186	189	2.3	2.3	4.6	5.8	2,058	2,842
New York..............	185	166	59.5	51.9	2,510	2,269	47.2	40.4	53.7	59.0	1,883	2,877
North Carolina.........	117	112	23.0	21.5	1,038	1,025	16.0	15.1	18.3	23.3	1,633	2,234
North Dakota..........	41	39	3.3	3.2	94	91	2.0	1.8	3.1	2.8	1,342	1,839
Ohio..................	183	194	34.3	33.2	1,517	1,430	20.8	19.7	35.8	43.3	2,138	2,829
Oklahoma..............	113	125	11.2	11.1	429	422	6.4	6.3	5.7	7.6	1,499	1,971
Oregon................	58	61	6.4	6.9	321	348	3.8	4.4	9.2	12.3	2,818	3,437
Pennsylvania..........	196	199	39.9	36.7	1,810	1,584	26.8	23.6	38.6	41.7	1,906	2,525
Rhode Island..........	11	11	2.5	2.2	123	115	1.7	1.5	2.7	2.2	2,325	2,809
South Carolina.........	67	69	12.5	12.1	523	533	8.2	7.8	6.4	9.6	1,788	2,085
South Dakota..........	53	57	4.1	4.2	101	107	2.6	2.6	2.0	3.2	1,113	1,543
Tennessee.............	134	115	20.8	19.4	833	818	12.5	12.2	11.4	14.1	1,462	2,147
Texas.................	426	523	61.4	65.7	2,580	2,779	36.5	39.8	38.3	46.2	1,943	2,604
Utah..................	44	54	5.1	5.8	224	274	2.7	3.3	5.5	4.7	2,233	2,935
Vermont...............	14	14	1.3	1.3	49	51	0.8	0.8	3.4	3.0	1,656	2,633
Virginia...............	89	96	17.7	18.1	777	801	11.8	12.5	13.8	18.3	1,736	2,081
Washington............	86	92	11.5	12.8	589	601	7.2	8.3	11.8	14.6	2,810	3,552
West Virginia..........	56	56	7.3	6.9	278	258	4.4	4.2	6.7	8.1	1,323	1,813
Wisconsin.............	124	133	13.5	12.1	589	522	8.1	7.2	14.6	19.5	1,953	2,528
Wyoming..............	24	29	2.0	2.0	50	42	1.1	1.1	1.0	1.3	1,103	1,433

[1] The average number of people served on an inpatient basis on a single day during the reporting period. [2] Beginning with the 2019 edition of *AHA Hospital Statistics* presenting data from the 2017 annual survey, the AHA no longer employs its own methodology to classify hospitals as registered. AHA included in the survey a greater number of hospitals that are appropriately licensed and accredited.

Source: Health Forum LLC, an affiliate of the American Hospital Association, Chicago, IL, *AHA Hospital Statistics 2020 Edition* ©, and previous editions. See also <http://www.ahadata.com/>.

Table 198. Average Cost to Community Hospitals Per Patient: 1990 to 2018

[In dollars, except percent. Covers non-federal short-term general or specialty hospitals (excluding psychiatric or tuberculosis hospitals and hospital units of institutions). Total cost per patient based on total hospital expenses (payroll, employee benefits, professional fees, supplies, etc.). Data have been adjusted for outpatient visits]

Type of expense and hospital	1990	2000	2005	2010	2013	2014	2015	2016	2017 [2]	2018
Average cost per day, total........	**687**	**1,149**	**1,522**	**1,910**	**2,157**	**2,212**	**2,271**	**2,338**	**2,424**	**2,517**
Annual percent change [1]...........	7.8	4.2	5.0	3.1	3.2	2.5	2.7	2.9	3.7	3.8
Nongovernmental nonprofit...........	692	1,182	1,585	2,025	2,289	2,346	2,413	2,488	2,574	2,653
For profit................................	752	1,057	1,412	1,629	1,791	1,798	1,831	1,889	1,996	2,093
State and local government..........	635	1,064	1,329	1,625	1,878	1,974	2,013	2,013	2,129	2,260
Average cost per stay, total.......	**4,947**	**6,649**	**8,793**	**10,313**	**11,651**	**12,015**	**12,359**	**12,777**	**13,126**	**13,542**
Nongovernmental nonprofit...........	5,001	6,717	8,670	10,652	12,000	12,385	12,755	13,182	13,504	13,883
For profit................................	4,727	5,642	7,351	8,336	9,296	9,414	9,510	9,698	10,273	10,684
State and local government..........	4,838	7,106	8,793	10,283	12,028	12,601	13,070	13,720	14,015	14,591

[1] Change from immediate prior year. [2] Beginning with the 2019 edition of *AHA Hospital Statistics* presenting data from the 2017 annual survey, the AHA no longer employs its own methodology to classify hospitals as registered. As a result of the application of a new, broader hospital definition, the number of hospitals in 2017 increased significantly.

Source: Health Forum LLC, an affiliate of the American Hospital Association, Chicago, IL, *AHA Hospital Statistics 2020 Edition* ©, and previous editions. See also <http://www.ahadata.com/>.

Table 199. Cosmetic Plastic Surgical and Nonsurgical Procedures: 2018 and 2019

[Data are projected to reflect nationwide statistics. Data cover procedures performed only by plastic surgeons who are certified by the American Board of Plastic Surgery. Previous surveys included procedures performed by physicians from specialties other than plastic surgery. For more information, see March 2018 press release, <https://www.surgery.org/media/news-releases/the-american-society-for-aesthetic-plastic-surgery-reports-that-modern-cosmetic-procedures-are-on-the-rise>]

Procedure	2018, Total	2019 Total	2019 Women	2019 Men
Total surgical procedures	**1,533,640**	**1,469,752**	**1,366,914**	**102,838**
Breast augmentation	329,914	280,692	280,692	0
Breast implant removal	49,834	66,982	66,982	(X)
Breast lift	158,964	146,711	146,711	(X)
Breast reduction, female	84,599	86,543	86,543	(X)
Brow lift	21,868	23,305	21,373	1,932
Buttock augmentation	26,774	35,880	35,800	80
Buttock lift	5,257	7,780	7,642	138
Chin augmentation	7,149	6,641	5,710	932
Ear surgery	10,724	11,989	7,814	4,175
Eyelid surgery	115,508	113,229	94,478	18,751
Facelift	73,174	68,983	64,912	4,071
Fat transfer: breast	23,340	24,892	24,892	0
Fat transfer: face	39,461	43,177	41,159	2,018
Labiaplasty (excluding vaginal rejuvenation)	12,756	12,903	12,903	(X)
Liposuction	289,261	270,670	237,843	32,827
Lower body lift	6,098	7,797	7,314	483
Male breast reduction (treats gynecomastia)	24,672	21,407	(X)	21,407
Neck lift	27,475	30,688	25,668	5,020
Nose surgery	41,213	39,692	34,655	5,037
Thigh lift	9,743	9,815	9,746	69
Tummy tuck	157,492	140,381	134,550	5,831
Upper arm lift	18,364	19,596	19,527	69
Total nonsurgical procedures	**3,315,888**	**3,121,439**	**2,818,219**	**303,221**
Total injectables	2,671,130	2,525,279	2,283,900	241,379
Botulinum toxin [1]	1,801,033	1,712,994	1,541,305	171,689
Calcium hydroxylapatite [2]	31,821	34,776	29,153	5,624
Hyaluronic acid [3]	810,240	749,409	687,102	62,307
Poly-L-Latic acid [4]	28,036	28,100	26,341	1,760
Total facial rejuvenation	341,619	276,017	248,642	27,376
Chemical peel	129,596	78,971	74,020	4,951
Full field ablative (laser skin resurfacing)	37,849	31,033	27,893	3,140
Micro-ablative resurfacing (fractional resurfacing)	38,550	66,275	57,029	9,246
Photorejuvenation (IPL, intense pulsed light)	135,624	99,740	89,700	10,040
Total other nonsurgical procedures	303,139	320,143	285,677	34,466
Hair removal (laser or pulsed light)	118,592	180,332	162,029	18,302
Nonsurgical fat reduction [5]	174,244	129,686	113,522	16,163
Sclerotherapy	10,303	10,126	10,126	0

X Not applicable. [1] Includes Botox, Dysport, and Xeomin. [2] Radiesse. [3] Includes Juvederm Ultra, Ultra Plus, Voluma, Restylane Lyft, Restylane, and Belotero. [4] Sculptra. [5] Includes CoolSculpting, Vaser Shape, and Liposonix.

Source: The American Society for Aesthetic Plastic Surgery, *2019 Aesthetic Plastic Surgery National Data Bank Statistics ©*. See also <https://www.surgery.org/media/statistics>.

Table 200. Cancer Survival Rates by Type/Body Site and Race and Year of Diagnosis: 1996 to 2016

[For invasive cancer, unless otherwise noted. For top 15 cancers ranked by incidence rates per 100,000 persons for 2013-2017 period. Based on follow-up of patients into 2017. The 5-year relative survival rate represents the proportion of patients alive 5 years after their cancer diagnosis, compared to similar persons among the general population without cancer. Based on information collected as part of the National Cancer Institute's Surveillance, Epidemiology and End Results (SEER) program, a collection of population-based registries in 9 areas]

Cancer type	5-year relative survival rates by year of diagnosis (percent) White 1996 to 1998	White 1999 to 2001	White 2002 to 2004	White 2005 to 2009	White 2010 to 2016	Black 1996 to 1998	Black 1999 to 2001	Black 2002 to 2004	Black 2005 to 2009	Black 2010 to 2016
All types [1]	**64.4**	**67.2**	**68.4**	**70.0**	**70.5**	**55.4**	**58.2**	**59.8**	**62.6**	**64.1**
Female breast	89.3	90.8	91.4	92.2	92.5	76.3	79.0	78.0	81.2	83.4
Lung and bronchus	14.8	15.5	16.5	18.8	21.9	12.3	12.7	13.3	15.5	20.4
Prostate	97.9	99.7	99.8	99.8	98.7	95.0	97.4	98.0	98.3	96.3
Colon and rectum	63.0	66.5	66.7	67.5	66.8	54.0	54.4	56.6	59.5	59.6
Melanoma of skin	90.9	92.3	93.2	93.4	94.9	[4] 73.9	[4] 73.9	[4] 72.2	73.0	[4] 69.5
Urinary bladder [2]	79.8	81.0	80.9	79.9	79.0	62.9	67.5	61.7	65.8	64.9
Non-Hodgkin's lymphoma [3]	59.4	65.0	71.0	73.3	75.9	54.8	55.7	63.7	62.9	71.5
Kidney and renal pelvis	62.1	64.9	69.4	74.8	75.7	67.1	64.1	65.7	74.6	77.9
Thyroid	95.9	96.8	97.4	98.4	98.8	95.1	92.1	95.9	97.0	96.7
Corpus and uterus	85.2	85.9	85.3	85.7	85.5	61.7	61.4	60.4	65.8	64.8
Leukemia [3]	49.8	52.1	59.1	63.9	67.3	38.6	43.9	53.9	56.0	62.5
Pancreas	4.1	5.0	5.7	7.8	10.4	3.4	5.6	4.5	6.4	10.3
Oral cavity and pharynx	59.9	62.3	65.7	67.7	71.2	36.3	44.6	48.4	44.8	51.3
Liver & intrahepatic bile duct	8.4	10.3	14.1	16.8	19.9	4.6	7.6	9.6	12.7	18.7
Stomach	20.3	22.3	26.0	29.0	31.8	22.6	23.1	29.1	29.3	33.9

[1] Includes other sites, not shown separately. [2] Invasive and in situ. [3] All types combined. [4] Standard error is 5 to 10 percent.

Source: U.S. National Institutes of Health, National Cancer Institute, Surveillance Epidemiology and End Results Program, "SEER Cancer Statistics Review (CSR), 1975-2017," <https://seer.cancer.gov/statistics/>, accessed April 2020.

Table 201. Top 15 Cancers Among Men and Women by Race/Ethnicity: 2013 to 2017

[Rates per 100,000 population, age-adjusted to the 2000 U.S. standard population. Cancer incidence measures the number of newly diagnosed cancers occurring during a year. Data are for 2013 to 2017 period, based on cancer registries in 21 areas monitored by the Surveillance, Epidemiology, and End Results (SEER) Program, covering 37 percent of the U.S. population. See source for more information]

Cancer by site, and sex	All race/ethnicities Rank	Rate	White Rank	Rate	Black Rank	Rate	Hispanic [1] Rank	Rate
TOTAL								
All Sites	(X)	**442.4**	(X)	**452.1**	(X)	**440.4**	(X)	**348.4**
Breast	1	68.9	1	69.5	2	71.3	1	53.2
Lung and bronchus	2	54.2	2	56.0	3	54.8	4	29.0
Prostate [2]	3	50.2	3	47.3	1	74.4	2	40.7
Colon and rectum	4	38.2	4	37.8	4	43.6	3	33.7
Melanoma of the skin	5	22.7	5	27.2	(X)	(X)	(X)	(X)
Urinary bladder	6	20.0	6	22.0	10	11.8	11	11.0
Non-Hodgkin lymphoma	7	19.6	7	20.6	8	14.7	5	18.1
Kidney and renal pelvis	8	16.3	8	16.8	5	17.5	6	16.1
Thyroid	9	15.7	9	16.4	14	9.5	7	14.2
Corpus and uterus, NOS [2,6]	10	14.8	11	14.9	6	15.9	9	13.1
Leukemia	11	14.1	10	15.0	11	10.8	12	10.9
Pancreas	12	13.1	12	13.1	7	15.3	10	11.6
Oral cavity and pharynx	13	11.4	13	12.0	15	8.5	14	6.8
Liver and IBD [3]	14	9.0	14	8.1	12	10.7	8	13.7
Stomach	15	7.3	(X)	(X)	13	10.1	13	10.5
Brain and ONS [4]	(X)	(X)	15	7.1	(X)	(X)	(X)	(X)
Myeloma	(X)	(X)	(X)	(X)	9	13.8	15	6.8
MEN								
All Sites	(X)	**480.3**	(X)	**485.5**	(X)	**515.1**	(X)	**370.4**
Prostate	1	109.8	1	102.3	1	175.2	1	92.0
Lung and bronchus	2	61.7	2	62.2	2	71.2	3	35.1
Colon and rectum	3	43.7	3	43.0	3	51.3	2	39.6
Urinary bladder	4	34.9	4	38.2	5	19.7	7	19.3
Melanoma of the skin	5	29.3	5	34.6	(X)	(X)	(X)	(X)
Non-Hodgkin lymphoma	6	23.8	6	25.0	7	17.7	5	20.9
Kidney and renal pelvis	7	22.4	7	23.0	4	24.5	4	21.4
Leukemia	8	18.1	8	19.2	11	13.6	8	13.2
Oral cavity and pharynx	9	17.2	9	18.1	12	13.3	11	10.0
Pancreas	10	14.9	10	15.0	8	16.9	10	12.5
Liver and IBD [3]	11	13.8	11	12.4	6	17.7	6	20.3
Stomach	12	9.9	12	8.9	10	13.8	9	13.1
Myeloma	13	8.8	15	8.2	9	16.5	12	8.2
Thyroid	14	8.1	13	8.6	(X)	(X)	13	5.9
Brain and ONS [4]	15	7.5	14	8.3	15	4.5	14	5.9
Esophagus	(X)	(X)	(X)	(X)	14	6.1	(X)	(X)
Larynx	(X)	(X)	(X)	(X)	13	7.3	(X)	(X)
Testis	(X)	(X)	(X)	(X)	(X)	(X)	15	5.4
WOMEN								
All Sites	(X)	**418.3**	(X)	**432.0**	(X)	**390.7**	(X)	**339.5**
Breast	1	128.5	1	131.3	1	124.8	1	99.1
Lung and bronchus	2	48.6	2	51.5	2	43.8	3	24.8
Colon and rectum	3	33.6	3	33.3	3	38.2	2	29.2
Corpus and uterus, NOS [6]	4	27.8	4	28.3	4	27.9	4	24.6
Thyroid	5	23.1	5	24.3	5	14.3	5	22.3
Melanoma of the skin	6	17.8	6	21.7	(X)	(X)	(X)	(X)
Non-Hodgkin lymphoma	7	16.2	7	17.0	7	12.5	6	15.9
Pancreas	8	11.6	10	11.6	6	14.1	8	10.8
Ovary [5]	9	11.2	8	11.7	10	9.1	9	10.4
Kidney and renal pelvis	10	11.1	11	11.4	8	12.2	7	11.7
Leukemia	11	11.0	9	11.6	11	8.9	11	9.1
Urinary bladder	12	8.6	12	9.4	14	6.5	15	5.0
Cervix uteri	13	7.4	13	7.2	12	8.7	10	9.2
Oral cavity and pharynx	14	6.4	14	6.6	(X)	(X)	(X)	(X)
Myeloma	15	5.7	(X)	(X)	9	12.0	14	5.7
Brain and ONS [4]	(X)	(X)	15	6.0	(X)	(X)	(X)	(X)
Liver & IBD [3]	(X)	(X)	(X)	(X)	15	5.4	13	8.1
Stomach	(X)	(X)	(X)	(X)	13	7.6	12	8.6

X Not applicable. [1] Persons of Hispanic origin may be of any race. [2] Rates for sex-specific cancer sites are calculated using the population for both sexes combined. [3] IBD, intrahepatic bile duct. [4] ONS, other nervous system. [5] Ovary excludes borderline cases or histologies 8442, 8451, 8462, 8472, and 8473. [6] NOS, not otherwise specified.

Source: National Institutes of Health, National Cancer Institute, Surveillance, Epidemiology, and End Results Program, "SEER Cancer Statistics Review, 1975-2017," <https://seer.cancer.gov/statistics/>, accessed April 2020.

Table 202. Cancer Incidence for Total and Top 5 Cancers by State: 2016

[For invasive cancer sites. Top five cancers are ranked by total number of cases. Data are produced by the Centers for Disease Control and Prevention (CDC) and the National Cancer Institute]

State	Total cancer cases (number	Rate per 100,000 population					
		All cancers	Breast	Lung and bronchus	Prostate	Colon and rectum	Melanoma of the skin
Total [1]	1,674,646	512.4	76.4	67.0	121.5	43.8	25.3
Alabama	27,195	559.5	79.5	82.0	152.8	52.8	28.4
Alaska	2,882	388.7	55.8	48.8	93.3	36.3	13.4
Arizona	31,443	455.1	71.5	56.2	89.1	36.7	30.0
Arkansas	17,053	570.7	75.7	96.5	138.4	50.2	25.6
California	164,887	419.6	67.9	41.2	91.1	36.5	24.3
Colorado	23,244	420.3	72.0	42.4	93.8	33.5	23.0
Connecticut	21,117	588.6	91.5	75.9	145.7	44.5	25.4
Delaware	6,001	629.9	88.7	90.5	163.3	49.9	37.8
District of Columbia	2,566	375.0	65.5	37.6	110.5	32.6	9.8
Florida	119,408	578.1	81.2	81.7	123.1	48.6	32.5
Georgia	52,056	504.7	74.7	65.8	142.6	44.3	27.3
Hawaii	7,395	517.6	84.8	57.4	116.9	50.9	31.3
Idaho	8,354	497.3	72.1	54.8	122.4	38.5	32.4
Illinois	68,954	537.2	81.7	73.0	123.1	49.9	25.0
Indiana	34,260	516.4	72.0	83.9	104.7	48.2	23.5
Iowa	18,146	579.6	80.6	74.8	132.3	51.7	32.2
Kansas	15,312	526.6	78.5	66.0	117.0	45.0	30.2
Kentucky	27,137	611.7	79.1	107.3	124.6	56.6	33.0
Louisiana	25,451	543.1	75.6	74.5	153.8	51.7	17.8
Maine	8,901	669.1	90.2	109.2	125.1	52.8	36.9
Maryland	30,942	513.6	80.8	63.1	142.1	40.6	27.4
Massachusetts	33,626	492.8	89.3	70.9	118.5	35.9	29.3
Michigan	53,911	542.7	79.3	77.3	136.8	44.6	24.1
Minnesota	29,619	536.1	78.0	66.1	122.3	43.7	35.1
Mississippi	16,265	544.8	74.8	89.9	148.1	53.8	19.9
Missouri	33,171	544.6	83.2	86.3	110.8	47.6	21.5
Montana	6,194	596.3	81.2	70.0	177.3	46.5	33.1
Nebraska	9,838	515.7	76.4	60.8	132.1	50.4	30.7
Nevada	13,054	444.1	66.3	58.7	94.2	40.7	20.7
New Hampshire	8,442	632.4	98.6	84.9	148.9	48.8	39.9
New Jersey	51,521	573.8	85.8	65.5	163.0	48.2	24.7
New Mexico	9,075	435.2	67.2	45.6	100.6	40.4	19.0
New York	113,026	569.8	81.7	69.9	147.2	45.3	20.8
North Carolina	55,394	545.4	85.1	79.7	135.4	42.0	30.0
North Dakota	3,765	498.3	74.6	60.8	128.6	43.9	24.1
Ohio	65,645	564.8	83.6	83.0	128.5	49.3	30.8
Oklahoma	20,167	514.3	75.4	75.4	108.3	48.3	27.9
Oregon	20,596	504.1	75.9	63.8	113.9	38.6	29.0
Pennsylvania	80,089	626.3	89.1	85.6	141.4	52.9	28.8
Rhode Island	5,972	564.7	88.3	88.6	118.1	38.3	26.4
South Carolina	27,313	550.7	84.5	77.7	145.3	46.5	29.3
South Dakota	4,612	535.3	66.5	72.0	141.6	47.1	26.7
Tennessee	36,598	550.4	75.8	88.7	138.1	47.9	22.3
Texas	109,083	390.9	57.7	47.3	86.4	35.9	12.4
Utah	10,494	344.7	51.6	21.4	96.1	24.0	36.4
Vermont	3,681	590.5	90.0	85.0	120.8	45.1	52.9
Virginia	40,322	479.2	77.3	67.0	114.9	39.5	21.8
Washington	37,378	513.4	79.8	61.4	114.2	40.6	28.7
West Virginia	11,698	639.7	81.0	109.0	134.1	59.5	28.3
Wisconsin	32,688	566.2	81.9	74.1	141.0	44.6	28.9
Wyoming	2,775	474.4	71.0	54.0	136.6	38.8	23.3
Puerto Rico	15,930	467.6	67.0	20.8	189.2	55.0	4.8

[1] Total includes States, District of Columbia, and Puerto Rico.

Source: U.S. Centers for Disease Control and Prevention, CDC WONDER Online Database, "Cancer Incidence 1999-2016," <https://wonder.cdc.gov/cancer.html>, accessed February 2020.

Table 203. Selected Notifiable Diseases—Cases Reported: 1990 to 2018

[In thousands only where indicated (690.2 represents 690,200). Interpret figures with caution. Although reporting of some of these diseases is incomplete, the figures are of value in indicating trends of disease incidence. Includes cases imported from outside the U.S.]

Disease	1990	2000	2005	2010	2014	2015	2016	2017	2018
Babesiosis	([1])	([1])	([1])	([1])	1,760	2,100	1,910	2,368	2,160
Botulism [3]	92	138	135	112	161	195	201	177	225
Campylobacteriosis	([1])	([1])	([1])	([1])	([1])	54,556	60,120	67,537	70,200
Chikungunya virus	([1])	([1])	([1])	([1])	([1])	896	247	156	117
Coccidoidomycosis	([1])	2,867	6,542	([1])	8,232	11,072	11,829	14,364	15,611
Cryptosporidiosis	([1])	3,128	5,659	8,944	8,682	9,735	13,453	11,414	12,533
Dengue virus infections [4]	([1])	([1])	([1])	700	680	951	953	437	424
Giardiasis	([1])	([1])	19,733	19,811	14,554	14,485	16,310	15,193	15,548
Haemophilus influenza	([1])	1,398	2,304	3,151	3,541	4,138	4,895	5,548	5,573
Hepatitis virus, acute: A	31,441	13,397	4,488	1,670	1,239	1,390	2,007	3,365	12,474
Hepatitis virus, acute: B	21,102	8,036	5,119	3,374	2,791	3,370	3,218	3,409	3,322
Hepatitis virus, acute: C	2,553	3,197	652	849	2,204	2,447	2,942	4,225	4,768
HIV diagnoses [2]	41,595	40,758	41,120	35,741	35,606	33,817	34,775	33,938	32,999
Invasive pneumococcal disease [5]	(X)	(X)	(X)	16,569	15,356	16,163	17,626	19,780	19,857
Legionellosis	1,370	1,127	2,301	3,346	5,166	6,079	6,141	7,458	9,933
Listeriosis	([1])	755	896	821	769	768	786	887	864
Lyme disease	([1])	17,730	23,305	30,158	33,461	38,069	36,429	42,743	33,666
Malaria	1,292	1,560	1,494	1,773	1,653	1,390	1,955	2,056	1,748
Measles	27,786	86	66	63	667	188	85	120	375
Meningococcal disease	2,451	2,256	1,245	833	433	372	375	353	327
Mumps	5,292	338	314	2,612	1,223	1,329	6,369	6,109	2,515
Pertussis (whooping cough)	4,570	7,867	25,616	27,550	32,971	20,762	17,972	18,975	15,609
Rabies, animal	4,826	6,934	5,915	4,331	5,988	5,491	4,609	4,423	4,984
Rubella [6]	1,125	176	11	5	6	5	1	7	4
Salmonellosis [7]	48,603	39,574	45,322	54,424	51,455	55,108	53,850	54,285	60,999
Shiga toxin-producing E. coli (STEC)	([1])	([1])	([1])	5,476	6,179	7,059	8,169	8,672	15,996
Shigellosis [8]	27,077	22,922	16,168	14,786	20,745	23,590	21,097	14,912	16,333
Spotted fever rickettsiosis (including Rocky Mountain spotted fever)	([1])	495	1,936	1,985	3,757	4,198	4,269	6,248	5,544
Streptococcal toxic-shock syndrome	([1])	83	129	142	259	335	283	372	371
Tetanus	64	35	27	26	25	29	34	33	23
Toxic-shock syndrome	322	135	90	82	59	64	40	30	33
Tuberculosis [9]	25,701	16,377	14,097	11,182	9,421	9,557	9,272	9,105	9,025
Typhoid fever	552	377	324	467	349	367	376	419	401
Varicella (chickenpox) morbidity [10]	173,099	27,382	32,242	15,427	10,172	9,789	8,953	8,775	8,201
West Nile virus, neuroinvasive [4]	([1])	([1])	1,309	629	1,347	1,455	1,308	1,425	1,657
West Nile virus, nonneuroinvasive [4]	([1])	([1])	1,691	392	858	720	841	672	989
Zika virus disease and infections [11]	([1])	([1])	([1])	([1])	([1])	([1])	6,118	1,177	334
Sexually transmitted diseases:									
Chlamydia (1,000)	([1])	702.1	976.4	1,307.9	1,441.8	1,526.7	1,598.4	1,708.6	1,758.7
Gonorrhea (1,000)	690.2	359.0	339.6	309.3	350.1	395.2	468.5	555.6	583.4
Syphilis (1,000)	134.3	31.6	33.3	45.8	63.5	74.7	88.0	101.6	115.0

X Not applicable. [1] Disease was not notifiable. [2] Human immunodeficiency virus diagnoses, including cases of AIDS (classified as HIV stage III). Cases reported to the Division of HIV/AIDS Prevention, National Center for HIV/AIDS, Viral Hepatitis, STD, and TB Prevention. In 2008, CDC revised the HIV case definition to cover HIV infection and AIDS into a single case definition. [3] Includes foodborne, infant, wound, and unspecified cases. [4] Totals reported to the Division of Vector-Borne Diseases (DVBD), National Center for Emerging and Zoonotic Infectious Diseases (NCEZID) (ArboNET Surveillance). [5] Data for 2010, 2011, and 2015 reported as Streptococcus pneumoniae invasive disease. [6] German measles excluding congenital syndrome. [7] Excludes typhoid fever. Beginning 2018, excludes paratyphoid fever. [8] Bacillary dysentery. [9] Totals reported to the Division of Tuberculosis Elimination, NCHHSTP. [10] Varicella (chickenpox) was removed from the nationally notifiable disease list in 1981; it became notifiable again in 2003. [11] Includes Zika virus diseases and infections, congenital and noncongenital.

Source: U.S. Centers for Disease Control and Prevention, National Notifiable Diseases Surveillance System, "Summary of Notifiable Infectious Diseases and Conditions—United States, 2015," *Morbidity and Mortality Weekly Report*, 64:53, August 11, 2017, and earlier reports; and "WONDER Annual Tables of Infectious Diseases and Conditions (2016 to present)," <cdc.gov/nndss/infectious-tables.html>, accessed February 2020.

Table 204. HIV Diagnoses and Chlamydia and Lyme Disease Cases Reported by State: 2018

[Finalized data are created within approximately 6 months after the end of the calendar year]

State	HIV [1]	Chlamydia [1]	Lyme disease	State	HIV [1]	Chlamydia [1]	Lyme disease	State	HIV [1]	Chlamydia [1]	Lyme disease
U.S. [2]	32,999	1,758,668	33,666	KS	149	14,231	30	ND	33	3,525	33
				KY	303	19,440	22	OH	888	63,220	293
AL	339	28,437	36	LA	1,006	36,293	4	OK	169	21,974	([4])
AK	22	6,159	11	ME	26	4,345	1,405	OR	223	19,224	70
AZ	677	40,807	7	MD	908	35,482	1,382	PA	929	59,340	10,208
AR	269	17,663	4	MA	583	30,460	16	RI	67	5,487	1,111
CA	3,799	231,415	104	MI	560	50,592	262	SC	714	33,910	39
CO	395	29,124	3	MN	262	23,569	1,541	SD	12	4,432	7
CT	208	16,732	1,859	MS	453	22,086	4	TN	635	38,212	29
DE	91	6,038	520	MO	422	34,728	11	TX	3,382	146,510	47
DC	175	9,014	79	MT	23	4,917	7	UT	122	10,541	27
FL	4,798	104,758	169	NE	72	8,026	15	VT	18	1,712	576
GA	1,991	65,936	19	NV	464	17,508	14	VA	819	42,965	1,139
HI	62	7,735	([3])	NH	36	3,734	1,428	WA	533	34,449	20
ID	29	6,572	9	NJ	842	36,514	4,000	WV	72	3,599	671
IL	1,169	77,325	276	NM	100	14,000	2	WI	207	28,027	1,869
IN	448	34,926	155	NY	2,167	119,571	3,638	WY	11	2,169	([4])
IA	117	14,682	283	NC	1,200	66,553	212	Island Areas	406	7,187	[1]

[1] Total diagnoses reported to the National Center for HIV/AIDS, Viral Hepatitis, STD, and TB Prevention. [2] Excludes Island areas. [3] Not reportable. [4] No cases reported.

Source: U.S. Centers for Disease Control and Prevention, National Notifiable Diseases Surveillance System, "WONDER Annual Tables of Infectious Diseases and Conditions (2016 to present)," <https://wwwn.cdc.gov/nndss/infectious-tables.html>, accessed March 2020.

Table 205. HIV (Human Immunodeficiency Virus) Infection Diagnoses and Persons Living With HIV by Selected Characteristics: 2015 to 2018

[For all HIV infections, regardless of stage of disease. Data reported to the Centers for Disease Control and Prevention's National HIV Surveillance System as of December 31, 2019. Covers the 50 states, the District of Columbia, and 6 U.S. dependent areas. As of April 2008, all jurisdictions had implemented confidential name-based HIV infection reporting. Data may not be representative of all persons with HIV. The completeness of HIV infection reporting is estimated to be at least 85% in all but 1 jurisdiction. See source for more information]

Characteristic	Diagnoses				Persons living with HIV			
	2015	2016	2017	2018	2015	2016	2017	2018 (P)
Total [1]	**40,538**	**40,252**	**38,919**	**37,968**	**970,627**	**995,233**	**1,018,765**	**1,042,270**
SEX AND GENDER IDENTITY [2]								
Male	32,413	31,970	30,902	30,166	727,563	747,652	766,842	785,983
Female	7,526	7,631	7,420	7,189	234,088	238,057	241,890	245,727
Transgender male-to-female	559	619	551	554	8,539	9,056	9,521	9,983
Transgender female-to-male	30	20	33	47	309	327	356	404
Additional gender identity	[11] 10	12	13	12	128	141	156	173
AGE AT DIAGNOSIS								
Under 13 years	142	129	105	87	2,357	2,240	2,081	1,918
13 to 14 years	26	26	27	20	729	678	674	672
15 to 19 years	1,765	1,727	1,780	1,719	5,015	4,670	4,550	4,363
20 to 24 years	7,367	6,994	6,543	6,152	31,168	30,140	28,683	27,184
25 to 29 years	7,689	8,033	7,792	7,768	65,941	69,112	71,124	71,544
30 to 34 years	5,512	5,714	5,712	5,723	76,826	80,172	83,795	88,720
35 to 39 years	4,325	4,303	4,336	4,250	88,470	91,100	93,231	95,007
40 to 44 years	3,470	3,322	3,021	3,025	103,274	99,252	97,854	98,506
45 to 49 years	3,376	3,156	2,994	2,861	145,330	138,984	132,713	125,890
50 to 54 years	3,056	2,920	2,703	2,528	169,712	170,064	166,422	161,131
55 to 59 years	1,915	1,944	1,911	1,877	130,405	138,713	147,471	156,237
60 to 64 years	1,014	1,106	1,103	1,058	80,916	89,517	98,212	106,641
65 years and over	881	878	892	900	70,484	80,591	91,955	104,457
RACE/ETHNICITY [3]								
American Indian/Alaska Native	180	220	208	186	2,646	2,821	2,989	3,136
Asian [4]	934	954	946	880	12,383	13,332	14,307	15,222
Black/African American	17,238	17,096	16,522	16,055	393,041	403,406	413,344	423,304
Native Hawaiian/other Pacific Islander	72	46	56	68	784	814	861	916
White	10,254	9,997	9,823	9,575	289,800	294,624	299,379	304,206
Multiple races	1,489	1,364	1,126	949	47,020	47,379	47,469	47,382
Hispanic/Latino	10,371	10,575	10,238	10,255	224,180	232,088	239,649	247,337
TRANSMISSION CATEGORY [5]								
Males age 13 and over, total [6]	32,906	32,534	31,419	30,691	735,111	755,772	775,511	795,198
Male-to-male sexual contact	26,704	26,430	25,693	24,933	518,787	538,710	557,914	576,787
Injection drug use	1,334	1,247	1,342	1,434	74,835	73,755	72,905	72,227
Male-to-male sexual contact and injection drug use	1,488	1,462	1,395	1,372	56,451	56,511	56,528	56,517
Heterosexual contact [7]	3,344	3,370	2,956	2,916	77,420	79,111	80,380	81,803
Perinatal [8]	15	[11] 7	11	14	4,742	4,827	4,915	5,005
Other [9]	20	18	22	21	2,876	2,857	2,869	2,858
Females age 13 and over, total [6]	7,490	7,589	7,395	7,190	233,159	237,221	241,173	245,154
Injection drug use	1,031	1,016	1,072	1,058	50,693	50,335	50,055	49,885
Heterosexual contact [7]	6,430	6,528	6,276	6,092	175,495	179,760	183,815	187,793
Perinatal [8]	23	39	40	33	5,305	5,436	5,602	5,761
Other [9]	[11] 6	[11] 7	[11] 7	[11] 7	1,667	1,690	1,701	1,715
Children under age 13 at diagnosis	142	129	105	87	2,357	2,240	2,081	1,918
Perinatal	110	103	88	65	1,930	1,832	1,703	1,544
Other [8]	32	26	17	22	427	408	378	374
REGION								
Northeast	6,479	6,221	5,997	5,582	227,551	231,643	233,669	235,944
Midwest	5,241	5,177	5,106	4,937	112,877	116,541	119,675	122,844
South	20,388	20,268	19,723	19,466	427,482	437,957	450,981	463,643
West	7,851	8,032	7,630	7,530	185,780	192,182	197,809	203,313
U.S. dependent areas [10]	579	554	463	453	16,937	16,910	16,631	16,526

P Preliminary [1] Total may include persons whose racial/ethnic category is unknown (not shown separately). [2] Sex as assigned at birth. Transgender male-to-female persons were assigned "male" sex at birth but have ever identified as "female" gender. Transgender female-to-male persons were assigned "female" sex at birth but have ever identified as "male" gender. Additional gender identity include "bi-gender," "gender queer," and "two-spirit." [3] Persons by race are not Hispanic or Latino, but may include persons whose Hispanic ethnicity was not reported. Persons of Hispanic/Latino ethnicity can be of race. [4] For persons living with HIV, the Asian category includes Asian/Pacific Islander legacy cases. See source for more information. [5] Data have been statistically adjusted to account for missing transmission category; therefore, values may not sum to total. [6] Data based on sex at birth and include transgender persons. [7] Heterosexual contact with a person known to have, or be at high risk for, HIV infection. [8] Persons were age 13 and over at the time of diagnosis of HIV infection. [9] Includes hemophilia, blood transfusion, and risk factor not reported or not identified. [10] American Samoa, Guam, Northern Mariana Islands, Puerto Rico, Republic of Palau, and the U.S. Virgin Islands. [11] Numbers less than 12 should be interpreted with caution.

Source: U.S. Centers for Disease Control and Prevention, *HIV Surveillance Report: Diagnoses of HIV Infection in the United States and Dependent Areas, 2018 (Updated)*, Vol. 31, May 2020. See also <https://www.cdc.gov/hiv/library/reports/hiv-surveillance.html>.

Table 206. AIDS Diagnoses and Persons Living with HIV Infection Ever Classified as Stage 3 (AIDS) by Selected Characteristics: 2015 to 2018

[Covers persons age 13 and over. Data reported to the Centers for Disease Control and Prevention's National HIV Surveillance System as of December 31, 2019. HIV infection is classified as stage 3 (AIDS) when the immune system of a person infected with human immunodeficiency virus becomes severely compromised (measured by CD4 lymphocyte count or percentage) and/or the person becomes ill with an AIDS-defining opportunistic illness. Data cover the 50 states, the District of Columbia, and 5 U.S. dependent areas (American Samoa, Guam, the Northern Mariana Islands, Puerto Rico, and the U.S. Virgin Islands). As of April 2008, all jurisdictions had implemented confidential name-based HIV infection reporting. Data may not be representative of all persons with HIV (not all persons are tested, and anonymous testing is excluded). The completeness of HIV infection reporting is estimated to be at more than 85%. See source for more information]

Characteristic	AIDS diagnoses				Persons living with HIV ever classified as stage 3			
	2015	2016	2017	2018	2015	2016	2017	2018 (P)
Total [1]......	18,590	18,375	17,749	17,113	513,356	518,917	524,083	529,197
SEX [2]								
Male......	14,077	14,064	13,472	13,008	391,430	395,764	399,641	403,559
Female......	4,513	4,311	4,277	4,105	121,926	123,153	124,442	125,638
RACE/ETHNICITY [3]								
American Indian/Alaska Native.............	88	92	72	65	1,356	1,412	1,450	1,483
Asian [4]......	316	326	335	338	5,925	6,170	6,451	6,728
Black/African American......	8,572	8,468	8,292	8,000	208,893	211,699	214,417	217,219
Native Hawaiian/Other Pacific Islander.....	22	14	24	19	381	385	400	411
White......	4,601	4,425	4,270	4,046	152,090	152,435	152,789	153,130
Multiple races......	917	848	772	687	27,447	27,437	27,316	27,128
Hispanic/Latino......	4,074	4,202	3,984	3,958	117,224	119,339	121,220	123,058
TRANSMISSION CATEGORY [5]								
Male transmission:								
Heterosexual contact......	2,042	2,125	1,899	1,760	45,746	46,541	47,133	47,712
Injection drug use......	958	915	943	896	47,596	46,669	45,879	45,122
Male-to-male sexual contact......	10,113	10,091	9,753	9,532	258,662	263,421	267,803	272,309
Male-to-male sexual contact and injection drug use......	870	857	808	735	34,948	34,648	34,334	33,922
Other [6]......	94	76	69	85	4,477	4,485	4,493	4,495
Female transmission:								
Heterosexual contact......	3,632	3,452	3,430	3,287	87,713	89,231	90,783	92,175
Injection drug use......	798	750	758	738	30,382	30,030	29,717	29,462
Other [6]......	83	109	90	80	3,830	3,892	3,943	4,001

P Preliminary. [1] HIV prevalence data may include persons whose racial/ethnic category is unknown (not shown separately). [2] Sex as assigned at birth. [3] Race categories are non-Hispanic. Persons of Hispanic/Latino origin may be of any race. [4] For persons living with HIV ever classified as stage 3 (AIDS), the Asian category includes Asian/Pacific Islander legacy cases. [5] Data have been statistically adjusted to account for missing transmission category; therefore, values may not sum to column subtotals and total. [6] All other transmission categories, including hemophilia, blood transfusion, perinatal exposure, and risk factor not reported or not identified.

Source: U.S. Centers for Disease Control and Prevention, National Center for HIV/AIDS, Viral Hepatitis, STD, and TB Prevention, "NCHHSTP AtlasPlus," updated 2019, <https://www.cdc.gov/nchhstp/atlas/index.htm>, accessed May 2020.

Table 207. Youth and Adult Vaccinations by Selected Type: 2010 to 2018

[In percent. Data for youth are from the National Immunization Survey-Teen, which monitors vaccines received by adolescents age 13-17 across the U.S. and its territories. Vaccination coverage estimates are based on provider-reported information, except for the influenza vaccination, which is parent-reported. Beginning in 2014, vaccination coverage estimates are not directly comparable to those for 2013 and previous years due to a change in the definition of adequate provider data. Data for adults are from the Behavioral Risk Factor Surveillance Survey, and excludes U.S. territories. Abbreviations: Td=tetanus diphtheria toxoid vaccine; Tdap=tetanus, diphtheria, and acellular pertussis vaccine; MenACWY=quadrivalent meningococcal conjugate vaccine; HPV=human papillomavirus]

Item	2010	2011	2012	2013	2014	2015	2016	2017	2018
YOUTH, AGE 13 to 17									
Tdap, ≥ 1 dose......	68.7	78.2	84.6	86.0	87.6	86.4	88.0	88.7	88.9
MenACWY, ≥ 1 dose......	62.7	70.5	74.0	77.8	79.3	81.3	82.2	85.1	86.6
HPV vaccine:									
Total, ≥ 1 dose......	(NA)	(NA)	(NA)	(NA)	(NA)	(NA)	60.4	65.5	68.1
Total, up-to-date [1]......	(NA)	(NA)	(NA)	(NA)	(NA)	(NA)	43.4	48.6	51.1
Males, ≥ 1 dose......	1.4	8.3	20.8	34.6	41.7	49.8	56.0	62.6	66.3
Males, ≥ 3 doses......	(NA)	1.3	6.8	13.9	21.6	28.1	31.5	34.8	32.1
Males, up-to-date [1]......	(NA)	(NA)	(NA)	(NA)	(NA)	(NA)	37.5	44.3	48.7
Females, ≥ 1 dose......	48.7	53.0	53.8	57.3	60.0	62.8	65.1	68.6	69.9
Females, ≥ 3 doses......	32.0	34.8	33.4	37.6	39.7	41.9	43.0	44.0	37.9
Females, up-to-date [1]......	(NA)	(NA)	(NA)	(NA)	(NA)	(NA)	49.5	53.1	53.7
Influenza [2]......	34.5	33.7	42.5	46.4	46.6	46.8	48.8	47.4	52.2
ADULTS									
Pneumococcal (pneumonia) vaccine:									
Age 18 to 64 at increased risk [3]......	27.0	29.9	28.8	31.2	31.2	33.5	33.3	36.1	(NA)
Age 65 and over......	68.0	69.6	68.3	68.4	69.3	71.9	72.4	74.7	(NA)
Tetanus (Td or Tdap) vaccine [4]									
Age 18 and over......	(NA)	(NA)	(NA)	57.5	(NA)	(NA)	60.3	(NA)	(NA)
Age 65 and over......	(NA)	(NA)	(NA)	48.9	(NA)	(NA)	48.7	(NA)	(NA)
Herpes zoster (shingles) vaccine [5]									
Age 60 and over......	(NA)	(NA)	(NA)	(NA)	31.8	(NA)	(NA)	39.4	(NA)
Age 65 and over......	(NA)	(NA)	(NA)	(NA)	35.9	(NA)	(NA)	44.4	(NA)
Influenza, age 18 and over [2]......	40.5	38.8	41.5	42.2	43.6	41.7	43.3	37.1	45.3

NA Not available. [1] HPV up-to-date measure assesses completion of the HPV vaccine series. Includes those with ≥3 doses, and those with 2 doses when the first HPV vaccine dose was initiated before age 15, and there was at least 5 months minus 4 days between the 1st and 2nd dose. [2] For the season beginning in the year shown. Excludes U.S. territories. [3] Self-reported. [4] Beginning 2013, vaccinated respondents include adults who received the Td or Tdap since 2005. [5] Recommended for all adults age 60 and over. Respondents were asked if they had ever received a shingles or zoster vaccine.

Source: U.S. Centers for Disease Control and Prevention, Vaccines & Immunizations, "TeenVaxView," "AdultVaxView," and "FluVaxView," <https://www.cdc.gov/vaccines/vaxview/index.html>, accessed April 2020.

Table 208. Organ Transplants: 2000 to 2019

[As of year end. Based on Organ Procurement and Transplantation Network data; data are from work supported in part by Health Resources and Services Administration contract 234-2005-37011C]

Procedure	Number of procedures					Number of people waiting				
	2000	2005	2010	2018	2019	2000	2005	2010	2018	2019
Total [1]	**23,274**	**28,119**	**28,668**	**36,529**	**39,719**	**74,078**	**90,526**	**110,375**	**114,155**	**113,226**
By transplant type: [2]										
Kidney	13,631	16,485	16,900	21,167	23,401	47,758	64,833	87,757	95,119	94,971
Liver	5,001	6,444	6,291	8,250	8,896	16,832	17,356	16,146	13,511	12,902
Pancreas	439	542	349	192	143	1,025	1,686	1,418	871	849
Kidney-pancreas	915	903	828	835	872	2,466	2,502	2,224	1,628	1,698
Heart	2,199	2,125	2,332	3,408	3,552	4,148	2,994	3,189	3,806	3,747
Lung	959	1,406	1,769	2,530	2,714	3,636	3,162	1,805	1,432	1,396
Heart-lung	48	35	42	32	45	207	141	70	48	48
Intestine	82	178	151	104	81	150	205	265	245	226
Multi-organ	222	522	560	1,017	1,074	(NA)	(NA)	(NA)	(NA)	(NA)

NA Not available. [1] Total may include other types of organ transplants not shown separately. [2] Kidney-pancreas and heart-lung transplants are each counted as one procedure. All other multiorgan transplants are included in the multi-organ row.

Source: U.S. Department of Health and Human Services, Health Resources and Services Administration, Organ Procurement and Transplantation Network (OPTN), <https://optn.transplant.hrsa.gov/data/view-data-reports/>, accessed June 2020; and unpublished data, based on OPTN data as of January 1, 2020.

Table 209. Disability Prevalence Among Adults Age 18 and Over by Type of Disability: 2014

[Numbers in thousands (240,054 represents 240,054,000). Covers civilian household population, and excludes persons living in institutions (including correctional facilities, nursing homes, and long-term care hospitals) and military barracks. Based on data from the Social Security Administration Supplement to the 2014 panel of the Survey of Income and Program Participation]

Type of disability	Adults age 18 and over		Adults age 18 to 64		Adults age 65 and over	
	Number	Percent	Number	Percent	Number	Percent
Total persons	240,054	100.0	194,788	100.0	45,266	100.0
Persons with any disability	**72,732**	**30.3**	**46,238**	**23.7**	**26,494**	**58.5**
Nonsevere	24,804	10.3	17,121	8.8	7,684	17.0
Severe [1]	47,928	20.0	29,117	14.9	18,810	41.6
Person needs assistance with ADLs or IADLs [2,3]	24,229	10.1	15,372	7.9	8,856	19.6
Serious difficulty seeing	12,316	5.1	8,044	4.1	4,272	9.4
Blind	1,561	0.7	1,051	0.5	510	1.1
Serious difficulty hearing	17,063	7.1	7,972	4.1	9,091	20.1
Deaf	3,442	1.4	1,700	0.9	1,742	3.8
Use of hearing aid	8,195	3.4	2,165	1.1	6,030	13.3
Difficulty with speech	4,937	2.1	3,337	1.7	1,601	3.5
Difficulty walking a quarter of a mile	32,251	13.4	17,530	9.0	14,721	32.5
Difficulty climbing a flight of stairs	29,032	12.1	16,268	8.4	12,764	28.2
Used a wheelchair	5,473	2.3	2,721	1.4	2,752	6.1
Used a cane/crutches/walker for 6 months or longer	15,372	6.4	6,940	3.6	8,432	18.6
Difficulty with physical tasks or movement [4]	29,729	12.4	17,921	9.2	11,809	26.1
Difficulty with activities of daily living (ADLs) (self-care)	17,701	7.4	10,705	5.5	6,996	15.5
Need assistance with at least one activity of daily living	9,621	4.0	5,851	3.0	3,770	8.3
Difficulty getting around	4,621	1.9	2,718	1.4	1,903	4.2
Difficulty getting into bed	11,467	4.8	7,341	3.8	4,126	9.1
Difficulty bathing	10,334	4.3	6,060	3.1	4,274	9.4
Difficulty dressing	7,668	3.2	4,773	2.5	2,894	6.4
Difficulty eating	2,546	1.1	1,755	0.9	791	1.7
Difficulty toileting	4,240	1.8	2,631	1.4	1,609	3.6
Difficulties with IADLs [3]	27,499	11.5	17,173	8.8	10,326	22.8
Need assistance with at least one IADL [3]	23,084	9.6	14,605	7.5	8,479	18.7
Mental disability	30,057	12.5	23,217	11.9	6,840	15.1
Learning disability	8,462	3.5	7,221	3.7	1,242	2.7
Alzheimer's, senility, or dementia	7,903	3.3	4,790	2.5	3,113	6.9
Intellectual disability	2,807	1.2	2,450	1.3	357	0.8
Developmental disability	1,458	0.6	1,350	0.7	108	0.2
Other mental/emotional condition	10,318	4.3	8,496	4.4	1,822	4.0
With one or more mental health symptoms or difficulties [5]	16,121	6.7	12,762	6.6	3,360	7.4

[1] Severe disability is indicated by the person's use of a wheelchair, cane, crutches, or walker; being blind or deaf; need for assistance with any of the activities of daily living; and presence of a mental disability (cognitive, developmental, or emotional) that interferes with everyday activities. See source for more information. [2] Activities of daily living (ADL) include getting around inside the home, getting in or out of bed or a chair, bathing, dressing, eating, and toileting. [3] Instrumental activities of daily living (IADL) include going out, managing money, preparing meals, housework, taking medication, and using the telephone. [4] Physical tasks or movement include lifting ten pounds, grasping, pushing/pulling, standing, sitting, crouching, and reaching. [5] Includes being depressed or anxious, trouble getting along with other people, trouble concentrating, and trouble coping with stress.

Source: U.S. Census Bureau, *Americans with Disabilities: 2014*, Current Population Reports P70-152, November 2018. See also <https://www.census.gov/topics/health/disability.html>.

Table 210. Population With a Disability by Age Group and State: 2010 and 2018

[In thousands (36,355 represents 36,355,000). Disability data limited to civilian noninstitutionalized population. Covers children under age 5 with a hearing or vision difficulty. Covers children age 5 to 14 with a hearing, vision, cognitive, ambulatory, or self-care difficulty. For people age 15 and older, also covers independent living difficulty. American Community Survey (ACS) disability data should not be compared with disability estimates from Census 2000, and more detailed measures of disability from sources such as the National Health Interview Survey and the Survey of Income and Program Participation. Based on a sample and subject to sampling variability; see Appendix III]

State	2010				2018			
	Total [1]	5 to 17 years	18 to 64 years	65 years and over	Total [1]	5 to 17 years	18 to 64 years	65 years and over
United States.........	**36,355**	**2,799**	**19,048**	**14,352**	**40,638**	**2,951**	**20,213**	**17,330**
Alabama.................	760	54	423	281	786	50	417	317
Alaska..................	75	6	48	20	89	6	51	32
Arizona.................	706	52	364	287	937	64	449	419
Arkansas...............	468	37	255	173	524	41	276	205
California..............	3,640	263	1,818	1,539	4,066	283	1,897	1,869
Colorado...............	499	38	273	185	601	41	311	247
Connecticut............	368	28	179	159	382	26	180	174
Delaware...............	108	8	60	39	126	9	62	55
District of Columbia.....	66	6	37	23	80	4	46	30
Florida.................	2,367	148	1,115	1,096	2,839	178	1,248	1,405
Georgia................	1,113	96	615	397	1,246	97	659	485
Hawaii.................	141	11	66	63	158	10	66	82
Idaho..................	196	17	103	74	233	18	118	97
Illinois.................	1,291	101	640	544	1,393	97	675	616
Indiana................	800	66	435	295	895	65	472	355
Iowa...................	337	25	172	138	366	29	175	160
Kansas................	341	26	178	136	390	32	194	162
Kentucky..............	711	51	423	233	762	61	418	282
Louisiana..............	672	58	378	232	701	60	374	266
Maine.................	198	15	104	78	220	15	114	90
Maryland..............	581	48	298	231	676	54	341	279
Massachusetts.........	699	57	354	285	791	60	384	344
Michigan..............	1,325	109	715	496	1,408	101	731	573
Minnesota.............	523	45	266	209	609	45	296	265
Mississippi............	473	36	267	168	481	34	263	183
Missouri...............	814	60	440	311	874	61	447	364
Montana...............	125	8	64	52	141	10	67	62
Nebraska..............	206	16	104	85	224	18	107	99
Nevada................	283	19	152	110	373	27	185	158
New Hampshire........	146	14	77	54	175	11	91	72
New Jersey............	845	69	398	375	901	61	417	420
New Mexico............	269	16	140	112	327	21	159	145
New York..............	2,020	142	1,012	858	2,201	152	1,061	983
North Carolina.........	1,235	95	673	460	1,351	99	681	566
North Dakota..........	69	4	32	32	81	6	38	37
Ohio...................	1,506	128	804	569	1,630	123	844	658
Oklahoma..............	577	39	323	212	629	43	327	256
Oregon................	525	37	287	198	581	39	295	245
Pennsylvania..........	1,638	132	824	677	1,775	136	885	748
Rhode Island..........	140	12	75	53	147	9	81	57
South Carolina........	629	37	352	237	717	46	366	303
South Dakota..........	90	6	43	40	105	7	54	44
Tennessee.............	947	66	530	348	1,029	70	553	403
Texas.................	2,864	273	1,549	1,029	3,221	285	1,640	1,280
Utah..................	234	22	124	85	300	30	155	114
Vermont...............	82	7	45	30	90	7	44	38
Virginia................	845	59	447	336	994	77	485	428
Washington............	792	56	425	307	934	64	479	389
West Virginia..........	345	21	197	126	339	19	175	145
Wisconsin.............	606	51	306	246	667	50	322	294
Wyoming..............	66	5	36	25	72	5	36	32
Puerto Rico...........	(NA)	(NA)	(NA)	(NA)	675	41	329	305

NA Not available. [1] Total population with a disability includes population under age 5, not shown separately.

Source: U.S. Census Bureau, 2018 American Community Survey, S1810, "Disability Characteristics," <https://data.census.gov>, accessed November 2019.

Table 211. Yoga, Meditation, and Chiropractor Use Among Children and Adults: 2017

[In percent. Covers use within the past 12 months. Data are from the National Health Interview Survey of the civilian noninstitutional population. Data are age-adjusted using the projected 2000 U.S. population as the standard population and age groups 4-11 and 12-17 for children, and age groups 18-44, 45-64, and 65 and over for adults. Data shown by age are not age-adjusted]

Characteristic	Children			Characteristic	Adults		
	Yoga	Medi-tation	Chiro-practor		Yoga	Medi-tation	Chiro-practor
Total....................	**8.4**	**5.4**	**3.4**	**Total**....................	**14.3**	**14.2**	**10.3**
				Men....................	8.6	11.8	9.4
Boys....................	5.6	4.9	3.0	Women....................	19.8	16.3	11.1
Girls....................	11.3	6.0	3.7	Age 18 to 44..............	17.9	13.4	9.9
Age 4 to 11..............	8.7	4.7	2.1	Age 45 to 64..............	12.2	15.9	11.4
Age 12 to 17..............	8.0	6.5	5.1	Age 65 and over..........	6.7	13.4	9.5
White, non-Hispanic	10.5	5.9	5.1	White, non-Hispanic	17.1	15.2	12.7
Black, non-Hispanic	4.6	4.7	1.0	Black, non-Hispanic	9.3	13.5	5.5
Hispanic....................	5.9	4.7	1.4	Hispanic....................	8.0	10.9	6.6

Source: U.S. National Center for Health Statistics, *Use of Yoga, Meditation, and Chiropractors Among U.S. Children Aged 4–17 Years*, NCHS Data Brief No. 324, November 2018; and *Use of Yoga, Meditation, and Chiropractors Among U.S. Adults Aged 18 and Over*, NCHS Data Brief No. 325, November 2018. See also <https://www.cdc.gov/nchs/nhis/nhis_db.htm>.

Table 212. Respiratory Diseases Among Persons Age 18 and Over by Selected Characteristics: 2018

[In thousands (249,456 represents 249,456,000). Respondents were asked in two separate questions if they had ever been told by a doctor or other health professional that they had emphysema or asthma. Respondents who had been told they had asthma were asked if they still had asthma. Respondents were asked in separate questions if they had been told by a doctor or other health professional in the past 12 months that they had hay fever, sinusitis, or chronic bronchitis. Based on the National Health Interview Survey, a sample survey of the civilian noninstitutionalized population; see Appendix III]

Selected characteristic	Total persons	Selected respiratory conditions [1]					
		Emphy-sema	Asthma		Hay fever	Sinusitis	Chronic bronchitis
			Ever	Still			
Total [2]....................	**249,456**	**3,780**	**33,401**	**19,223**	**19,174**	**28,949**	**9,003**
SEX							
Male....................	120,442	1,970	13,747	6,665	7,980	11,082	2,855
Female....................	129,014	1,810	19,654	12,559	11,193	17,867	6,148
AGE							
18 to 44 years....................	115,008	250	16,932	8,315	5,778	9,821	2,548
45 to 64 years....................	83,038	1,349	10,458	6,880	8,987	12,012	3,734
65 to 74 years....................	30,809	1,264	3,835	2,648	3,018	4,546	1,561
75 years and over....................	20,601	918	2,175	1,380	1,392	2,570	1,161
RACE							
Single race [3]....................	243,677	3,697	31,857	18,403	18,593	28,283	8,720
White....................	193,454	3,257	25,572	14,662	15,483	23,539	7,344
Black or African American..............	30,813	327	4,559	2,839	1,729	3,379	1,072
American Indian or Alaska Native......	2,810	12	440	278	238	294	(B)
Asian....................	15,960	101	1,211	572	1,116	1,037	174
Native Hawaiian or other Pacific Islander....................	640	(B)	(B)	(B)	(B)	(B)	(B)
Two or more races [4]....................	5,779	83	1,543	820	581	667	283
HISPANIC ORIGIN AND RACE [5]							
Hispanic or Latino....................	40,749	309	4,624	2,322	1,589	3,068	995
Not Hispanic or Latino....................	208,706	3,471	28,777	16,902	17,585	25,881	8,008
White....................	157,289	2,978	21,617	12,586	14,119	20,830	6,434
Black or African American..............	29,089	313	4,280	2,704	1,678	3,237	1,030

B Figure considered unreliable. [1] A person may be represented in more than one column. [2] Total includes other races not shown separately. [3] Refers to persons who indicated only a single race group, including those of Hispanic and Latino origin. [4] Refers to all persons who indicated more than one race group. [5] Persons of Hispanic or Latino origin may be of any race or combination of races.

Source: U.S. National Center for Health Statistics, 2018 National Health Interview Survey, "Tables of Summary Statistics," <https://www.cdc.gov/nchs/nhis/SHS.htm>, accessed December 2019.

Table 213. Selected Diseases and Conditions Among Persons Age 18 and Over by Selected Characteristics: 2018

[In thousands (249,456 represents 249,456,000). Persons with selected diseases and conditions may be represented in more than one column. Based on the National Health Interview Survey, a sample survey of the civilian noninstitutionalized population; see Appendix III]

Selected characteristic	Total persons	Persons with selected diseases and conditions					
		Diabe-tes [1]	Ulcers [1]	Kidney dis-ease [2]	Liver dis-ease [2]	Arthritis diag-nosis [3]	Chronic joint symp-toms [3]
Total [4]..........	249,456	25,158	14,795	5,986	4,509	59,042	75,472
SEX							
Male........	120,442	12,760	6,364	2,867	2,529	24,533	35,425
Female........	129,014	12,397	8,431	3,119	1,980	34,509	40,047
AGE							
18 to 44 years........	115,008	3,777	3,954	685	1,168	8,049	18,959
45 to 64 years........	83,038	10,320	5,719	1,985	2,141	25,105	31,163
65 to 74 years........	30,809	6,580	3,181	1,672	913	14,851	14,827
75 years and over........	20,601	4,481	1,941	1,645	288	11,037	10,523
RACE							
Single race [5]........	243,677	24,547	14,385	5,892	4,407	57,736	73,861
White........	193,454	18,473	12,002	4,436	3,683	48,683	62,206
Black or African American........	30,813	3,764	1,493	889	365	6,305	7,718
American Indian or Alaska Native........	2,810	583	229	(B)	64	832	1,102
Asian........	15,960	1,617	610	401	273	1,810	2,632
Native Hawaiian or other Pacific Islander........	640	(B)	(B)	(B)	(B)	106	202
Two or more races [6]........	5,779	611	410	94	102	1,306	1,611
HISPANIC ORIGIN [7]							
Hispanic or Latino........	40,749	4,303	1,581	760	1,029	5,705	8,293
Not Hispanic or Latino........	208,706	20,855	13,214	5,226	3,481	53,337	67,179

B Estimate is considered unreliable. [1] Respondents who had ever been told by a health professional that they had an ulcer or diabetes (excludes borderline and pregnancy-related diabetes). [2] Respondents who had been told in the last 12 months by a health professional that they had weak or failing kidneys, or any kind of liver condition. Excludes kidney stones, bladder infections, or incontinence. [3] Respondents with an arthritis diagnosis had ever been told by a health professional that they had some form of arthritis, rheumatoid arthritis, gout, lupus or fibromyalgia. Respondents with joint symptoms (excluding back and neck) that began more than 3 months prior to interview were classified as having chronic joint symptoms. [4] Total includes other races not shown separately. [5] Refers to persons who indicated only a single race group, including Hispanic or Latino origin. [6] Refers to all persons who indicated more than one race group. [7] Persons of Hispanic or Latino origin may be of any race or combination of races.

Source: U.S. National Center for Health Statistics, 2018 National Health Interview Survey, "Tables of Summary Health Statistics," <https://www.cdc.gov/nchs/nhis/SHS.htm>, accessed December 2019.

Table 214. Circulatory Diseases Among Persons Age 18 and Over by Selected Characteristics: 2018

[In thousands (249,456 represents 249,456,000). In separate questions, respondents were asked if they had ever been told by a doctor or other health professional that they have: hypertension (or high blood pressure), coronary heart disease, angina (or angina pectoris), heart attack (or myocardial infarction), any other heart condition or disease not already mentioned, or a stroke. A person may be represented in more than one column. Based on the National Health Interview Survey, a sample survey of the civilian noninstitutionalized population; see Appendix III]

Characteristic	Total adults	Selected circulatory diseases			
		Heart disease		Hyper-tension [3]	Stroke
		All types [1]	Coronary [2]		
Total [4]..........	249,456	30,252	15,780	67,856	7,801
SEX					
Male........	120,442	15,963	9,582	33,648	3,887
Female........	129,014	14,289	6,198	34,208	3,915
AGE					
18 to 44 years........	115,008	5,523	1,150	10,133	698
45 to 64 years........	83,038	9,792	4,967	28,520	2,552
65 to 74 years........	30,809	7,264	4,750	16,688	2,124
75 years and over........	20,601	7,674	4,913	12,516	2,428
RACE					
Single race [5]........	243,677	29,388	15,476	66,565	7,594
White........	193,454	24,874	13,018	52,497	5,968
Black or African American........	30,813	2,981	1,588	9,871	1,183
American Indian or Alaska Native........	2,810	377	208	721	74
Asian........	15,960	1,125	642	3,335	361
Native Hawaiian or Other Pacific Islander........	640	(B)	(B)	142	(B)
Two or more races [6]........	5,779	864	305	1,291	207
HISPANIC ORIGIN [7]					
Hispanic or Latino........	40,749	2,773	1,622	8,148	817
Not Hispanic or Latino........	208,706	27,480	14,159	59,708	6,985

B Estimate is considered unreliable. [1] Heart disease includes coronary heart disease, angina pectoris, heart attack, or any other heart condition or disease. [2] Coronary heart disease includes coronary heart disease, angina pectoris, or heart attack. [3] Persons told on two or more different visits that they have hypertension, or high blood pressure, are classified as hypertensive. [4] Includes other races not shown separately. [5] Refers to persons who indicated only a single race group, including Hispanic or Latino origin. [6] Refers to all persons who indicated more than one race group. [7] Persons of Hispanic or Latino origin may be of any race or combination of races.

Source: U.S. National Center for Health Statistics, 2018 National Health Interview Survey, "Tables of Summary Health Statistics," <https://www.cdc.gov/nchs/nhis/SHS.htm>, accessed December 2019.

Table 215. Migraine Headaches and Pain in the Neck, Lower Back, Face or Jaw Among Persons Age 18 and Over by Selected Characteristics: 2018

[In thousands (249,456 represents 249,456,000). Based on the National Health Interview Survey, a sample survey of the civilian noninstitutionalized population. See Appendix III]

Selected characteristic	Total persons	Migraine and pain [1]			
		Migraine or severe headache [2]	Pain in neck [2]	Pain in lower back [2]	Pain in face or jaw [2]
Total [3]	**249,456**	**38,619**	**40,136**	**74,416**	**12,914**
SEX					
Male	120,442	12,701	17,260	33,699	4,327
Female	129,014	25,918	22,876	40,717	8,588
AGE					
18 to 44 years	115,008	21,510	14,663	28,089	6,055
45 to 64 years	83,038	12,995	16,136	27,414	4,719
65 to 74 years	30,809	2,860	5,846	11,231	1,332
75 years and over	20,601	1,254	3,490	7,681	808
RACE					
Single race [4]	243,677	37,236	38,980	72,471	12,464
White	193,454	30,239	32,868	59,658	10,561
Black or African American	30,813	4,823	3,901	8,415	1,230
American Indian or Alaska Native	2,810	649	428	1,012	118
Asian	15,960	1,456	1,671	3,204	490
Native Hawaiian or Other Pacific Islander	640	(B)	113	181	(B)
Two or more races [5]	5,779	1,383	1,155	1,945	450
HISPANIC ORIGIN AND RACE [6]					
Hispanic or Latino	40,749	6,617	5,604	10,715	2,035
Not Hispanic or Latino	208,706	32,002	34,532	63,701	10,879
White, single race	157,289	24,380	27,802	50,157	8,639
Black or African American, single race	29,089	4,539	3,703	7,958	1,202

B Figure is considered unreliable. [1] A person may be represented in more than one column. [2] Respondents were asked, in separate questions, "During the past 3 months, did you have a severe headache or migraine [or neck pain; or low back pain; or facial ache or pain in the jaw muscles or the joint in front of the ear]?" Respondents were instructed to report pain that had lasted a whole day or more and, conversely, not to report fleeting or minor aches or pains. [3] Total includes other races not shown separately. [4] Refers to persons who indicated only a single race group. [5] Refers to all persons who indicated more than one race group. [6] Persons of Hispanic or Latino origin may be of any race or combination of races.

Source: U.S. National Center for Health Statistics, 2018 National Health Interview Survey, "Tables of Summary Health Statistics," <https://www.cdc.gov/nchs/nhis/SHS.htm>, accessed December 2019.

Table 216. Nonfatal Injury and Poisoning Episodes by Cause, Sex, and Age: 2018

[Data are from the National Electronic Injury Surveillance System–All Injury Program, which collects data on nonfatal injuries and poisonings treated in participating hospital emergency departments]

Cause of injury	Total		Male	Female	Under age 1	Age 1 to 14	Age 15 to 24	Age 25 to 64	Age 65 and over
	Number	Percent							
Total [1]	**28,028,762**	**100.0**	**15,127,138**	**12,900,542**	**197,898**	**4,161,119**	**4,264,556**	**14,674,162**	**4,723,690**
UNINTENTIONAL									
Fall	8,173,139	29.2	3,672,340	4,500,771	109,136	1,448,683	607,368	3,010,932	2,996,697
Struck by or against [2]	3,320,349	11.8	1,985,117	1,335,058	21,701	888,225	652,724	1,453,045	304,624
Overexertion	2,319,499	8.3	1,145,877	1,173,622	3,296	302,424	437,167	1,348,296	228,315
Motor vehicle occupant	2,275,835	8.1	1,027,608	1,248,214	3,002	121,427	527,745	1,410,924	212,217
Poisoning	1,703,618	6.1	1,122,952	580,371	4,106	58,156	219,942	1,286,786	132,510
Cut/pierce/stab	1,702,787	6.1	1,086,332	616,455	4,196	210,207	327,451	1,008,569	152,365
Bite or sting excl. dog bites [3]	1,005,587	3.6	493,852	511,734	10,372	254,724	120,623	505,645	114,222
Foreign object [4]	519,640	1.9	306,337	213,303	7,602	174,584	56,122	222,793	58,513
Dog bite	344,202	1.2	172,071	172,131	1,981	85,090	50,370	174,241	32,514
Fire/burn/smoke inhalation	334,532	1.2	172,474	162,057	7,483	64,537	51,926	185,500	24,909
VIOLENCE RELATED									
Assault (all)	1,540,007	5.5	915,364	624,544	3,859	100,796	384,826	1,011,516	37,458
Self-harm	495,348	1.8	205,024	290,324	(NA)	45,626	163,964	267,467	18,266
Legal intervention	85,075	0.3	71,173	13,780	(NA)	(NA)	18,179	64,352	(NA)

NA Not available. [1] Total includes injuries from various other causes not shown separately and for injuries with unknown age of victim. [2] Injury from being struck, hit, or crushed by, or hitting against, another person, object or force; excludes vehicles and machinery. [3] Include bites and stings from another person or any insect, animal, or plant; excludes dogs. [4] Injury resulting from the entrance of a foreign object into or through the eye or other natural body opening; excludes objects blocking an airway or causing suffocation.

Source: U.S. Centers for Disease Control and Prevention, National Center for Injury Prevention and Control, "WISQARS (Web-based Injury Statistics Query and Reporting System)," <https://www.cdc.gov/injury/wisqars/index.html>, accessed April 2020.

Table 217. Injuries Associated With Selected Consumer Products: 2018

[Estimates are based on a national probability sample of hospitals in the U.S. and its territories. Patient information is collected from each participating hospital for every emergency visit involving an injury associated with consumer products. From this sample, the total number of product-related injuries treated in hospital emergency rooms nationwide is estimated. A person's injury may be represented in up to two product groups]

Product type	Number	Product type	Number
Items for infants/children:		**Housewares:**	
All nursery equipment....................................	93,379	Cans, other containers.....................................	278,746
Baby strollers...	12,314	Drinking glasses..	60,426
High chairs..	11,837	Knives (not elsewhere classified).......................	321,417
Playground equipment (excluding swings).............	218,527	Soaps, detergents...	60,939
Swings or swings sets.....................................	43,553	Tableware and accessories................................	94,112
Toys...	224,704	**Tools & garden equipment:**	
Sports & recreational equipment:		Hand garden tools...	58,765
All terrain vehicles, mopeds, minibikes, etc............	201,170	Lawn and garden equipment..............................	86,805
Baseball, softball..	168,906	Lawn mowers...	91,825
Basketball...	435,452	Power home tools (excluding saws).....................	31,883
Bicycles & accessories....................................	424,346	Power home workshop saws...............................	76,490
Exercise, exercise equipment............................	498,498	Workshop manual tools....................................	116,873
Football..	296,944	**Household appliances:**	
Lacrosse, rugby, misc. ball games......................	76,840	Cooking ranges, ovens, etc...............................	52,380
Skateboards..	124,933	Heating stoves, space heaters...........................	25,256
Skating (excluding in-line)................................	67,736	Refrigerators, freezers.....................................	52,009
Soccer...	199,096	Small kitchen appliances..................................	52,492
Swimming, pools, equipment..............................	194,933	**Home furnishings & fixtures:**	
Trampolines...	116,191	Bathroom structures & fixtures...........................	548,890
Home entertainment equipment:		Beds, mattresses, pillows..................................	892,754
Computers (equipment and electronic games).........	29,756	Carpets, rugs...	209,908
Television sets & stands...................................	44,639	Chairs, sofas, sofa beds...................................	661,504
Personal use items:		Desks, cabinets, shelves, racks..........................	293,658
Grooming devices...	49,225	Glass doors, windows, panels.............................	127,721
Mobility carts, electric [1]................................	23,486	Ladders, stools...	240,733
Razors, shavers, razor blades...........................	46,006	Tables [2]...	343,002

[1] Motorized vehicles, not elsewhere classified (three or more wheels). [2] Excludes baby-changing tables, billiard or pool tables, and television tables or stands.

Source: Consumer Product Safety Commission, National Electronic Injury Surveillance System (NEISS), *2018 NEISS Data Highlights: Overview—All Products;* and "NEISS Estimates Query Builder," <https://www.cpsc.gov/cgibin/NEISSQuery/home.aspx>, accessed March 2020. See also <https://www.cpsc.gov/Research--Statistics/NEISS-Injury-Data/>.

Table 218. Food Security Status of Households and Households with Children: 2005 to 2018

[114,437 represents 114,437,000. Food security status of households is measured through a series of questions about experiences and behaviors that characterize households having difficulty meeting basic food needs. All questions refer to the previous 12 months and remind respondents to report only conditions resulting from inadequate financial resources; survey excludes voluntary fasting and dieting to lose weight. *Food-secure* households report 0-2 food-insecure conditions. *Food-insecure* households report 3 or more conditions. Low and very low food security differ in the extent and character of the adjustments the household makes to its eating patterns and food intake. Households classified as having *low food security* report multiple indications of food access problems, but typically report few, if any, indications of reduced food intake. Households classified as having *very low food security* report multiple indications of reduced food intake and disrupted eating patterns due to inadequate resources for food. Prior to 2006, households with very low food security were described as "food insecure with hunger." The omission of homeless persons biases the statistics downward. Data are from the Food Security Supplement to the Current Population Survey (CPS); for details about the CPS, see text, Section 1 and Appendix III]

Household status	Number (1,000)					Percent distribution				
	2005	2010	2015	2017	2018	2005	2010	2015	2017	2018
Households, total [1]..................	**114,437**	**118,756**	**125,164**	**127,272**	**129,245**	**100.0**	**100.0**	**100.0**	**100.0**	**100.0**
Food-secure...............................	101,851	101,527	109,315	112,254	114,934	89.0	85.5	87.3	88.2	88.9
Food-insecure.............................	12,586	17,229	15,849	15,018	14,311	11.0	14.5	12.7	11.8	11.1
With low food security..................	8,158	10,872	9,540	9,261	8,730	7.1	9.1	7.7	7.3	6.8
With very low food security............	4,428	6,357	6,309	5,757	5,581	3.9	5.4	5.0	4.5	4.3
Adult members [2]......................	**217,897**	**229,129**	**242,706**	**246,517**	**249,443**	**100.0**	**100.0**	**100.0**	**100.0**	**100.0**
In food-secure households..............	195,172	196,505	213,586	219,013	223,390	89.6	85.8	88.0	88.8	89.6
In food-insecure households............	22,725	32,624	29,120	27,504	26,053	10.4	14.2	12.0	11.2	10.4
With low food security..................	15,146	21,357	18,235	17,796	16,576	7.0	9.3	7.5	7.2	6.6
With very low food security............	7,579	11,267	10,885	9,708	9,477	3.5	4.9	4.5	3.9	3.8
Child members [2, 3]...................	**73,604**	**74,905**	**73,455**	**73,901**	**73,562**	**100.0**	**100.0**	**100.0**	**100.0**	**100.0**
In food-secure households..............	61,201	58,697	60,337	61,361	62,388	83.1	78.4	82.1	83.0	84.8
In food-insecure households............	12,403	16,208	13,118	12,540	11,174	16.9	21.6	17.9	17.0	15.2
With very low food security among children......................	606	976	541	540	540	0.8	1.3	0.7	0.7	0.7

[1] Total excludes households for which food security status is unknown. [2] The food security survey measures food security status at the household level. Not all individuals and children residing in food-insecure households were directly affected by the households' food insecurity. Similarly, not all individuals and children in households classified as having very low food security were subject to the reductions in food intake and disruptions in eating patterns that characterize this condition. Young children, in particular, are often protected from effects of the households' food insecurity. [3] Percents among only households with children.

Source: U.S. Department of Agriculture, Economic Research Service, *Household Food Security in the United States in 2018*, Economic Research Report Number 270, September 2019. See also <https://www.ers.usda.gov/topics/food-nutrition-assistance/food-security-in-the-us.aspx>.

Table 219. Mammography Use Among Women Age 40 and Over by Patient Characteristics: 2000 to 2015

[Percent of women having a mammogram within the past 2 years. Covers civilian noninstitutional population. Based on National Health Interview Survey; see Appendix III]

Characteristic	2000	2003	2005	2008	2010	2013	2015
Women age 40 and over, total [1]	**70.4**	**69.7**	**66.8**	**67.6**	**67.1**	**66.8**	**65.3**
AGE							
40 to 49 years	64.3	64.4	63.5	61.5	62.3	59.6	58.3
50 to 64 years	78.7	76.2	71.8	74.2	72.6	71.4	71.3
65 years and over	67.9	67.7	63.8	65.5	64.4	66.9	63.3
RACE AND ETHNICITY							
White, non-Hispanic	72.2	70.5	68.3	68.7	67.8	67.6	65.8
Black, non-Hispanic	67.9	70.5	65.2	68.3	67.4	67.2	69.7
Hispanic origin [2]	61.2	65.0	58.8	61.2	64.2	61.4	60.9
HEALTH INSURANCE STATUS [3]							
Insured	76.0	75.1	72.5	73.4	74.1	72.1	69.7
Private insurance	77.1	76.3	74.5	74.2	75.6	73.4	72.2
Medicaid	61.7	63.5	55.6	64.2	64.4	63.5	57.7
Uninsured	40.7	41.5	38.1	39.7	36.0	37.3	30.0
EDUCATION							
No high school diploma nor GED [4]	57.7	58.1	52.8	53.8	53.0	53.6	51.7
High school diploma or GED	69.7	67.8	64.9	65.2	64.4	63.4	60.1
Some college or more	76.2	75.1	72.7	73.4	72.1	71.6	70.5
POVERTY STATUS [5]							
Below 100% poverty	54.8	55.4	48.5	51.4	51.4	49.9	52.2
100% to 199% poverty	58.1	60.8	55.3	55.8	53.8	56.7	54.9
200% to 399% poverty	68.8	69.9	67.2	64.4	66.2	66.0	63.4
400% and over poverty	81.5	77.7	76.6	79.0	78.1	77.2	74.7

[1] Includes other races not shown separately and unknown education level and poverty status. [2] Persons of Hispanic origin may be of any race or combination of races. [3] Health insurance status at time of interview, only for women age 40 to 64. Health insurance categories are mutually exclusive. Persons who reported both Medicaid and private coverage are classified as having private coverage. Persons with only Indian Health Service coverage are considered to have no health insurance coverage. [4] GED is General Educational Development high school equivalency diploma. [5] Poverty as percent of Federal poverty level based on family income and family size and composition using U.S. Census Bureau poverty thresholds.

Source: U.S. National Center for Health Statistics, *Health, United States, 2018*, October 2019. See also <http://www.cdc.gov/nchs/hus.htm>.

Table 220. Current Cigarette Smoking Among Adults: 2000 to 2017

[In percent. A current smoker is a person who has smoked at least 100 cigarettes and who now smokes every day or some days. Excludes unknown smoking status. Race groups White and Black include persons of Hispanic and non-Hispanic origin. For definition of age adjustment, see text, Section 2. Based on National Health Interview Survey; for details, see Appendix III]

Sex, age, and race	2000	2005	2010	2017	Sex, age, and race	2000	2005	2010	2017
Total smokers, age-adjusted [1]	**23.1**	**20.8**	**19.3**	**14.1**	Black, total	26.2	26.5	24.3	18.4
Male	25.2	23.4	21.2	16.0	18 to 24 years	20.9	21.6	18.8	(B)
Female	21.1	18.3	17.5	12.3	25 to 34 years	23.2	29.8	25.7	25.1
					35 to 44 years	30.7	23.3	22.6	21.7
					45 to 64 years	32.2	32.4	31.8	17.1
White male	25.4	23.3	21.4	16.0	65 years and over	14.2	16.8	10.0	15.1
Black male	25.7	25.9	23.3	18.5	**Female, total**	**20.9**	**18.1**	**17.3**	**12.2**
					18 to 24 years	24.9	20.7	17.4	8.8
White female	22.0	19.1	18.3	13.0	25 to 34 years	22.3	21.5	20.6	13.0
Black female	20.7	17.1	16.6	11.5	35 to 44 years	26.2	21.3	19.0	12.9
					45 to 64 years	21.7	18.8	19.1	15.6
Total smokers [2]	**23.2**	**20.9**	**19.3**	**14.0**	65 years and over	9.3	8.3	9.3	7.5
Male, total	**25.6**	**23.9**	**21.5**	**15.8**	White, total	21.4	18.7	17.9	12.8
18 to 24 years	28.1	28.0	22.8	12.0	18 to 24 years	28.5	22.6	18.4	10.2
25 to 34 years	28.9	27.7	26.1	19.9	25 to 34 years	24.9	23.1	22.0	14.4
35 to 44 years	30.2	26.0	22.5	18.7	35 to 44 years	26.6	22.2	20.5	13.7
45 to 64 years	26.4	25.2	23.2	17.4	45 to 64 years	21.4	18.9	19.5	15.8
65 years and over	10.2	8.9	9.7	9.0	65 years and over	9.1	8.4	9.4	7.8
White, total	25.7	23.6	21.4	15.7	Black, total	20.8	17.3	17.0	11.7
18 to 24 years	30.4	29.7	23.8	12.7	18 to 24 years	14.2	14.2	14.2	(B)
25 to 34 years	29.7	27.7	26.6	19.9	25 to 34 years	15.5	16.9	19.3	10.4
35 to 44 years	30.6	26.3	23.1	18.2	35 to 44 years	30.2	19.0	17.2	12.3
45 to 64 years	25.8	24.5	22.5	17.7	45 to 64 years	25.6	21.0	19.8	16.7
65 years and over	9.8	7.9	9.6	8.4	65 years and over	10.2	10.0	9.4	7.1

B Estimates are considered unreliable. [1] Data are age-adjusted to the year 2000 standard population using five age groups: 18–24 years, 25–34 years, 35–44 years, 45–64 years, 65 years and over. [2] Crude, not age-adjusted.

Source: U.S. National Center for Health Statistics, *Health, United States, 2018,* October 2019. See also <https://www.cdc.gov/nchs/hus/index.htm>.

Table 221. Current Cigarette Smoking by Sex and State: 2018

[In percent. Current cigarette smoking is defined as persons age 18 and older who reported having smoked 100 or more cigarettes during their lifetime and who currently smoke every day or some days. Based on the Behavioral Risk Factor Surveillance System (BRFSS), a telephone survey of health behaviors of the civilian, noninstitutionalized U.S. population, age 18 and over. New methods, including surveying cellular telephone-only households, and a new weighting method, were implemented for the 2011 BRFSS and prior data cannot accurately be compared to current survey results; for details, see source]

State	Total	Male	Female	State	Total	Male	Female	State	Total	Male	Female
U.S. [1]...	**16.1**	**(NA)**	**(NA)**	KY......	23.4	23.4	23.3	OH......	20.5	22.1	19.0
AL.......	19.2	21.3	17.2	LA.......	20.5	22.9	18.3	OK......	19.7	22.2	17.2
AK.......	19.1	20.6	17.3	ME......	17.8	20.2	15.5	OR......	15.6	15.4	15.9
AZ......	14.0	15.5	12.6	MD......	12.6	14.0	11.3	PA......	17.0	17.3	16.8
AR......	22.7	23.9	21.6	MA......	13.4	15.3	11.7	RI.......	14.6	14.9	14.4
CA......	11.2	14.8	7.8	MI.......	18.9	21.1	16.9	SC.......	18.0	19.8	16.4
CO......	14.5	16.6	12.4	MN......	15.1	16.8	13.4	SD.......	19.0	21.7	16.3
CT......	12.2	13.6	10.8	MS......	20.5	23.2	18.1	TN......	20.7	21.5	19.9
DE......	16.5	18.3	14.9	MO......	19.4	20.5	18.4	TX......	14.4	17.5	11.4
DC......	13.8	15.1	12.6	MT......	18.0	18.7	17.3	UT......	9.0	10.5	7.5
FL......	14.5	16.2	12.8	NE......	16.0	17.5	14.5	VT......	13.7	14.7	12.6
GA......	16.1	17.7	14.6	NV......	15.7	17.3	14.1	VA......	15.0	17.3	12.7
HI.......	13.4	15.8	11.0	NH......	15.6	16.0	15.3	WA......	12.0	13.5	10.6
ID.......	14.7	15.9	13.6	NJ......	13.1	14.5	11.7	WV......	25.3	25.7	24.8
IL.......	15.5	19.0	12.1	NM......	15.2	17.3	13.2	WI.......	16.4	18.2	14.6
IN.......	21.1	23.4	19.0	NY......	12.8	14.9	10.9	WY [2].....	18.8	19.9	17.6
IA.......	16.6	17.9	15.3	NC......	17.4	20.2	14.9	GU [2].....	21.9	28.3	15.2
KS.......	17.3	18.3	16.3	ND......	19.1	21.1	17.1	PR [2].....	10.0	14.0	6.5

NA Not available. [1] Represents median value among the states and DC. For definition of median, see Guide to Tabular Presentation. [2] GU is Guam. PR is Puerto Rico.

Source: U.S. Centers for Disease Control and Prevention, Tobacco Use Data Portal: Tobacco Use, "Behavioral Risk Factor Data: Tobacco Use (2011 to present)," <https://chronicdata.cdc.gov/browse?category=Behavioral+Risk+Factors>, accessed March 2020.

Table 222. Substance Abuse Treatment Facilities and Clients: 2010 to 2018

[As of the end of March. Based on the National Survey of Substance Abuse Treatment Services, a census of all known public and private facilities that provide substance abuse treatment in the United States and associated jurisdictions. Selected missing data for responding facilities were imputed. Beginning 2013, the full survey on facilities and clients is administered in odd-numbered years; an alternate survey collecting facility data, and occasionally a limited amount of client data, is administered in even-numbered years. The 2018 survey did not collect client data]

Facility characteristic	Number of facilities				Number of clients		
	2010	2015	2017	2018	2010	2015	2017
Total............	**13,339**	**13,873**	**13,585**	**14,809**	**1,175,462**	**1,305,647**	**1,356,015**
FACILITY OPERATIONAL STRUCTURE							
Private non-profit............	7,683	7,577	7,163	7,642	625,321	670,593	658,896
Private for-profit............	3,985	4,659	4,931	5,584	372,525	475,531	550,992
Local, county, or community government............	751	702	640	690	70,963	67,060	66,577
State government............	380	350	304	304	47,203	30,675	28,529
Federal government............	348	321	289	327	47,676	46,721	34,435
Dept. of Veterans Affairs............	218	203	183	219	39,157	39,501	29,619
Dept. of Defense............	91	80	74	76	7,035	5,774	3,618
Indian Health Service............	36	31	27	23	1,431	1,218	1,103
Other............	3	7	5	9	53	228	95
Tribal government............	192	264	258	262	11,774	15,067	16,586
TYPE OF CARE OFFERED/RECEIVED [1]							
Outpatient............	10,753	11,336	11,184	12,243	1,056,532	1,161,456	1,238,654
Regular............	9,914	10,582	10,437	11,394	593,077	604,819	599,290
Intensive............	5,990	6,261	6,241	6,868	138,188	128,536	133,850
Detoxification............	1,227	1,350	1,366	1,505	13,216	14,457	11,839
Day treatment/partial hospitalization............	1,678	1,747	1,805	2,051	22,458	23,138	23,310
Medication-assisted treatment [2]............	1,137	2,673	3,395	4,087	289,593	390,506	470,365
Residential (non-hospital)............	3,452	3,383	3,125	3,500	103,692	119,900	99,881
Detoxification............	893	887	908	1,140	7,549	13,748	10,938
Short-term treatment (30 days or fewer)............	1,691	1,740	1,738	2,039	26,014	36,651	32,156
Long-term treatment (more than 30 days)............	2,801	2,769	2,513	2,770	70,129	69,501	56,787
Hospital inpatient............	748	724	715	785	15,238	24,291	17,480
Detoxification............	666	639	655	721	6,476	12,394	7,551
Treatment............	548	527	532	588	8,762	11,897	9,929
TREATMENT FOR SUBSTANCE ABUSE							
Both alcohol and drug............	(NA)	11,915	11,555	(NA)	498,671	520,866	500,948
Drug abuse only............	(NA)	10,692	10,571	(NA)	459,069	531,963	642,713
Alcohol abuse only............	(NA)	10,121	9,759	(NA)	215,101	200,187	211,460
Both substance abuse and mental health disorders............	(NA)	11,752	11,496	(NA)	479,699	614,789	683,810

NA Not available. [1] Number of facilities can sum to more than the total because a facility could provide more than one type of care. [2] Methadone/buprenorphine maintenance or injectable naltrexone treatment.

Source: U.S. Substance Abuse and Mental Health Services Administration, *National Survey of Substance Abuse Treatment Services (N-SSATS): 2018, Data on Substance Abuse Treatment Facilities,* September 2019, and earlier reports. See also <https://www.samhsa.gov/data/data-we-collect/n-ssats-national-survey-substance-abuse-treatment-services>.

Table 223. Drug Use by Type of Drug and Age Group: 2010 to 2018

[In percent. Data comes from the National Survey on Drug Use and Health (NSDUH). Based on a representative sample of the U.S. population age 12 and older, including persons living in households, in noninstitutional group quarters such as dormitories and homeless shelters, and civilians on military bases. Estimates are based on computer-assisted interviews of approximately 68,000 respondents. Please note that the NSDUH was redesigned in 2015, and therefore data from previous surveys for several survey items are not comparable to data from the 2015 NSDUH and subsequent surveys; see source for more information. Subject to sampling variability]

Age and type of drug	Lifetime (ever) use			Past year use			Past month use		
	2010	2017	2018	2010	2017	2018	2010	2017	2018
12 YEARS OLD AND OVER									
Any illicit drug [1]	(NA)	49.5	49.2	(NA)	19.0	19.4	(NA)	11.2	11.7
Marijuana	42.0	45.2	45.3	11.6	15.0	15.9	6.9	9.6	10.1
Cocaine	14.7	14.9	14.7	1.8	2.2	2.0	0.6	0.8	0.7
Crack	3.6	3.5	3.4	0.3	0.3	0.3	0.1	0.2	0.2
Heroin	1.6	1.9	1.9	0.2	0.3	0.3	0.1	0.2	0.1
Hallucinogens	(NA)	15.5	15.8	(NA)	1.9	2.0	(NA)	0.5	0.6
LSD	9.2	9.6	10.0	0.3	0.8	0.8	0.1	0.2	0.2
PCP	2.5	2.2	2.2	–	–	–	–	–	–
Ecstasy	(NA)	7.0	7.3	(NA)	0.9	0.9	(NA)	0.2	0.3
Inhalants	(NA)	9.3	9.1	(NA)	0.6	0.7	(NA)	0.2	0.2
Methamphetamine [2]	(NA)	5.4	5.4	(NA)	0.6	0.7	(NA)	0.3	0.4
Tobacco products [3]	68.8	62.7	61.5	(NA)	27.5	26.7	27.5	22.4	21.5
Cigarettes	64.2	57.1	55.7	(NA)	21.5	21.0	23.0	17.9	17.2
Smokeless tobacco	(NA)	16.1	15.6	(NA)	4.3	4.0	(NA)	3.2	2.9
Cigars	35.0	31.7	31.6	(NA)	8.6	8.4	5.2	4.6	4.5
Pipe tobacco	13.6	12.2	12.0	(NA)	(NA)	(NA)	0.8	0.9	0.8
Alcohol	82.5	80.9	80.8	(NA)	65.7	65.5	51.8	51.7	51.1
"Binge" alcohol use [4]	(NA)	(NA)	(NA)	(NA)	(NA)	(NA)	(NA)	24.5	24.5
12 TO 17 YEARS OLD									
Any illicit drug [1]	(NA)	23.9	23.9	(NA)	16.3	16.7	(NA)	7.9	8.0
Marijuana	17.1	15.3	15.4	14.0	12.4	12.5	7.4	6.5	6.7
Cocaine	1.5	0.7	0.7	1.0	0.5	0.4	0.2	0.1	–
Hallucinogens	(NA)	2.8	2.3	(NA)	2.1	1.5	(NA)	0.6	0.6
Inhalants	(NA)	8.6	8.5	(NA)	2.3	2.7	(NA)	0.6	0.7
Methamphetamine [2]	(NA)	0.3	0.3	(NA)	0.2	0.2	(NA)	0.1	0.1
Tobacco products [3]	25.1	14.9	13.4	(NA)	9.7	8.3	10.7	4.9	4.2
Cigarettes	20.5	10.8	9.6	(NA)	6.3	5.5	8.4	3.2	2.7
Smokeless tobacco	(NA)	5.0	4.4	(NA)	3.0	2.5	(NA)	1.3	1.1
Cigars	11.1	6.4	5.3	(NA)	4.6	3.7	3.2	1.9	1.7
Alcohol	35.4	27.1	26.3	(NA)	21.9	20.8	13.6	9.9	9.0
"Binge" alcohol use [4]	(NA)	(NA)	(NA)	(NA)	(NA)	(NA)	(NA)	5.3	4.7
18 TO 25 YEARS OLD									
Any illicit drug [1]	(NA)	57.0	55.6	(NA)	39.4	38.7	(NA)	24.2	23.9
Marijuana	51.4	52.7	51.5	30.0	34.9	34.8	18.5	22.1	22.1
Cocaine	13.4	12.0	11.4	4.7	6.2	5.8	1.5	1.9	1.5
Crack	2.6	1.3	1.0	0.5	0.3	0.3	0.2	0.1	0.1
Heroin	1.8	1.8	1.3	0.6	0.6	0.5	0.3	0.3	0.2
Hallucinogens	(NA)	17.1	16.4	(NA)	7.0	6.9	(NA)	1.7	1.7
Inhalants	(NA)	9.5	9.0	(NA)	1.6	1.5	(NA)	0.5	0.4
Methamphetamine [2]	(NA)	3.0	2.5	(NA)	1.1	0.8	(NA)	0.4	0.3
Tobacco products [3]	68.8	57.9	55.0	(NA)	39.8	36.7	40.9	29.1	25.8
Cigarettes	62.3	49.5	45.9	(NA)	31.0	27.9	34.3	22.3	19.1
Smokeless tobacco	(NA)	18.0	16.7	(NA)	7.7	7.1	(NA)	4.8	4.4
Cigars	41.1	33.4	32.6	(NA)	17.9	17.1	11.3	9.1	8.6
Alcohol	85.7	81.1	79.7	(NA)	74.0	73.1	61.4	56.3	55.1
"Binge" alcohol use [4]	(NA)	(NA)	(NA)	(NA)	(NA)	(NA)	(NA)	36.9	34.9
26 YEARS OLD AND OVER									
Any illicit drug [1]	(NA)	51.3	51.2	(NA)	16.1	16.7	(NA)	9.5	10.1
Marijuana	43.5	47.5	47.8	8.0	12.2	13.3	4.8	7.9	8.6
Cocaine	16.6	17.0	16.8	1.4	1.7	1.6	0.5	0.7	0.7
Crack	4.2	4.3	4.1	0.4	0.4	0.3	0.2	0.2	0.2
Heroin	1.8	2.2	2.2	0.2	0.3	0.3	0.1	0.2	0.1
Hallucinogens	(NA)	16.7	17.3	(NA)	1.0	1.3	(NA)	0.3	0.4
Inhalants	(NA)	9.3	9.1	(NA)	0.3	0.4	(NA)	0.1	0.1
Methamphetamine [2]	(NA)	6.4	6.5	(NA)	0.6	0.7	(NA)	0.3	0.4
Tobacco products [3]	74.2	69.0	68.1	(NA)	27.6	27.3	27.2	23.4	22.8
Cigarettes	70.0	63.8	62.6	(NA)	21.7	21.7	22.8	18.9	18.5
Smokeless tobacco	(NA)	17.1	16.7	(NA)	3.9	3.7	(NA)	3.1	2.9
Cigars	36.9	34.4	34.5	(NA)	7.6	7.5	4.4	4.2	4.1
Alcohol	87.8	87.1	87.3	(NA)	69.5	69.5	54.9	55.8	55.3
"Binge" alcohol use [4]	(NA)	(NA)	(NA)	(NA)	(NA)	(NA)	(NA)	24.7	25.1

– Represents or rounds to zero. NA Not available. [1] Illicit drugs include marijuana, cocaine (including crack), heroin, hallucinogens, inhalants, methamphetamine, and the misuse of prescription psychotherapeutic drugs. Prior to 2015, methamphetamine was included with prescription psychotherapeutic drugs. [2] Beginning with 2015, methamphetamine is included with illicit drugs. [3] Includes other products not shown separately. Tobacco product use in the past year excludes past year pipe tobacco use, but includes past month pipe tobacco use. [4] Binge alcohol use is defined as drinking five or more drinks (for males) or four or more drinks (for females) on the same occasion (i.e., at the same time or within a couple of hours of each other) on at least 1 day in the past 30 days. In 2015, the definition for females changed from five to four drinks.

Source: U.S. Substance Abuse and Mental Health Services Administration, *Results from the 2018 National Survey on Drug Use and Health: Detailed Tables,* August 2019, and earlier reports. See also <https://www.samhsa.gov/data/data-we-collect/nsduh-national-survey-drug-use-and-health>.

Table 224. Drug, Alcohol, and Cigarette Estimated Users by State: 2017 to 2018

[31,197 represents 31,197,000. Table presents annual averages for a 2-year period. Data are based on the National Survey on Drug Use and Health (NSDUH). Covers persons age 12 years and over who indicated use of a substance within the past month (during the 30 days prior to the interview). Based on a representative sample of the U.S. population, including persons living in households, noninstitutional group quarters such as dormitories and homeless shelters, and civilians living on military bases. Data were collected in 2017 and 2018 from 135,823 persons. For methodology information, see "2017-2018 NSDUH: Guide to State Tables and Summary of Small Area Estimation Methodology " at <https://www.samhsa.gov/data/nsduh/state-reports-NSDUH-2018>]

State	Estimated current users (1,000)					Current users as percent of population				
	Illicit drug use [1]	Mari-juana	Any illicit drug other than mari-juana [2]	Binge alcohol use [3]	Cigarette use	Illicit drug use [1]	Mari-juana	Any illicit drug other than mari-juana [2]	Binge alcohol use [3]	Cigarette use
United States	**31,197**	**26,832**	**9,007**	**66,848**	**47,823**	**11.4**	**9.8**	**3.3**	**24.5**	**17.5**
Northeast	5,694	4,915	1,564	12,484	7,779	11.9	10.3	3.3	26.0	16.2
Midwest	6,286	5,364	1,907	15,172	11,094	11.0	9.4	3.3	26.6	19.4
South	9,896	8,205	3,254	23,674	19,541	9.6	8.0	3.2	23.0	19.0
West	9,322	8,349	2,282	15,517	9,409	14.4	12.9	3.5	24.0	14.5
Alabama	439	339	143	937	987	10.7	8.3	3.5	22.9	24.2
Alaska	106	97	20	136	101	18.0	16.6	3.4	23.2	17.2
Arizona	736	646	183	1,360	1,006	12.5	10.9	3.1	23.0	17.0
Arkansas	266	214	90	496	603	10.7	8.6	3.6	19.9	24.2
California	4,443	3,955	1,163	8,084	3,990	13.4	12.0	3.5	24.5	12.1
Colorado	928	819	220	1,420	808	19.6	17.3	4.6	30.0	17.1
Connecticut	439	370	112	894	462	14.3	12.1	3.6	29.2	15.1
Delaware	107	91	28	191	155	13.1	11.2	3.5	23.5	19.0
District of Columbia	118	99	32	219	113	19.9	16.6	5.4	36.8	19.0
Florida	1,931	1,674	569	4,130	2,948	10.7	9.3	3.2	22.9	16.3
Georgia	821	710	264	1,864	1,534	9.5	8.2	3.1	21.6	17.8
Hawaii	119	102	33	264	152	10.3	8.8	2.8	22.8	13.1
Idaho	134	117	38	308	245	9.4	8.2	2.6	21.7	17.2
Illinois	1,179	1,033	348	2,989	1,786	11.0	9.6	3.2	27.9	16.7
Indiana	658	567	209	1,357	1,222	11.8	10.2	3.8	24.4	22.0
Iowa	247	185	91	749	529	9.4	7.0	3.5	28.5	20.1
Kansas	210	151	77	636	453	8.8	6.3	3.2	26.7	19.0
Kentucky	379	304	119	759	958	10.2	8.2	3.2	20.5	25.8
Louisiana	369	294	129	1,001	852	9.6	7.7	3.4	26.2	22.2
Maine	203	192	36	259	224	17.5	16.6	3.1	22.3	19.3
Maryland	584	501	164	1,249	753	11.6	9.9	3.2	24.7	14.9
Massachusetts	939	806	239	1,815	943	15.8	13.6	4.0	30.6	15.9
Michigan	1,218	1,068	306	2,214	1,652	14.4	12.6	3.6	26.1	19.5
Minnesota	498	443	161	1,223	799	10.7	9.5	3.4	26.2	17.1
Mississippi	214	171	78	525	613	8.7	7.0	3.2	21.4	25.0
Missouri	521	437	150	1,231	1,072	10.2	8.6	2.9	24.1	21.0
Montana	140	128	32	242	172	15.8	14.5	3.6	27.2	19.4
Nebraska	150	129	46	461	299	9.5	8.2	2.9	29.2	19.0
Nevada	412	379	88	579	505	16.3	15.1	3.5	23.0	20.0
New Hampshire	181	167	40	345	182	15.5	14.2	3.5	29.5	15.6
New Jersey	697	597	198	1,948	1,163	9.2	7.9	2.6	25.7	15.4
New Mexico	245	225	53	400	345	14.1	13.0	3.1	23.0	19.9
New York	1,901	1,634	554	3,979	2,450	11.4	9.8	3.3	23.8	14.6
North Carolina	797	671	257	1,862	1,676	9.2	7.8	3.0	21.6	19.5
North Dakota	54	47	18	195	125	8.7	7.6	3.0	31.6	20.3
Ohio	983	818	309	2,440	2,105	10.0	8.3	3.2	24.9	21.5
Oklahoma	305	242	113	754	737	9.5	7.5	3.5	23.4	22.9
Oregon	709	668	149	879	587	20.0	18.8	4.2	24.8	16.5
Pennsylvania	1,071	911	323	2,841	2,099	9.9	8.4	3.0	26.1	19.3
Rhode Island	152	133	37	251	152	16.7	14.6	4.1	27.5	16.7
South Carolina	416	352	152	1,129	915	9.8	8.3	3.6	26.7	21.6
South Dakota	60	51	21	211	139	8.5	7.1	2.9	29.6	19.5
Tennessee	564	482	181	1,124	1,205	10.0	8.5	3.2	19.9	21.4
Texas	1,814	1,402	682	5,514	3,974	7.8	6.1	2.9	23.9	17.2
Utah	189	151	72	374	304	7.6	6.1	2.9	15.0	12.2
Vermont	111	105	23	150	104	20.3	19.3	4.3	27.6	19.2
Virginia	609	512	205	1,606	1,093	8.6	7.3	2.9	22.8	15.5
Washington	1,118	1,024	221	1,358	1,098	17.9	16.4	3.5	21.7	17.6
West Virginia	163	145	47	313	428	10.6	9.4	3.0	20.3	27.7
Wisconsin	509	436	172	1,468	915	10.4	8.9	3.5	30.0	18.7
Wyoming	43	37	12	114	96	9.0	7.7	2.6	23.8	20.0

[1] "Illicit drug use" includes the misuse of prescription psychotherapeutics or the use of marijuana, cocaine (including crack), heroin, hallucinogens, inhalants, or methamphetamine. Misuse of prescription psychotherapeutics is defined as use in any way not directed by a doctor, including use without a prescription of one's own; use in greater amounts, more often, or longer than told; or use in any other way not directed by a doctor. Prescription psychotherapeutics do not include over-the-counter drugs. [2] "Illicit drug use other than marijuana" includes the misuse of prescription psychotherapeutics or the use of cocaine (including crack), heroin, hallucinogens, inhalants, or methamphetamine. [3] "Binge alcohol use" is defined as drinking 5/more drinks (for males) or 4/more drinks (for females) on the same occasion (i.e., at the same time or within a couple of hours of each other) on at least 1 day in the past 30 days. In 2015, the definition for females changed from five to four drinks.

Source: U.S. Substance Abuse and Mental Health Services Administration, National Survey on Drug Use and Health, "State Reports," <https://www.samhsa.gov/data/data-we-collect/nsduh-national-survey-drug-use-and-health>, accessed March 2020.

Table 225. Prescription Psychotherapeutic Drug Use and Misuse by Drug Type and User Characteristics: 2018

[In percent. Data are from the National Survey on Drug Use and Health, and cover persons age 12 and older. Misuse of prescription drugs is defined as use in any way not directed by a physician, including use without a prescription of one's own medication; use in greater amounts, more often, or longer than instructed to take a drug; or use in any other way not directed by a physician. Excludes over-the-counter drugs. See also headnote, Table 223]

User characteristics	Any use in past year				Misuse in past year			
	Pain relievers	Tranquil-izers	Stimu-lants	Seda-tives	Pain relievers	Tranquil-izers	Stimu-lants	Seda-tives
Total......	**31.6**	**13.7**	**6.6**	**6.1**	**3.6**	**2.1**	**1.9**	**0.4**
SEX								
Male......	29.5	10.6	6.5	5.0	3.9	2.2	2.1	0.5
Female......	33.6	16.7	6.7	7.2	3.4	2.0	1.6	0.3
AGE								
12 to 17 years......	16.6	4.0	7.0	2.0	2.8	1.7	1.5	0.3
18 years and over......	33.1	14.7	6.5	6.5	3.7	2.1	1.9	0.4
18 to 25 years......	26.2	10.8	13.1	3.1	5.5	4.6	6.5	0.6
26 years and over......	34.2	15.3	5.5	7.1	3.4	1.7	1.2	0.4
RACE AND ETHNICITY								
Not Hispanic......	32.7	14.5	6.9	6.7	3.7	2.1	2.0	0.4
White......	33.5	16.6	7.8	7.4	3.9	2.4	2.2	0.5
Black or African American......	33.6	8.5	4.2	4.6	3.3	1.0	0.9	0.1
American Indian or Alaska Native......	36.4	10.3	5.3	7.3	5.8	2.4	1.4	0.9
Native Hawaiian or Other Pacific Islander......	38.1	(S)	3.5	4.6	8.4	2.1	1.4	0.2
Asian......	19.5	5.5	3.3	3.6	1.4	0.7	1.6	0.1
Two or more races......	38.4	12.5	8.7	7.8	4.3	2.5	2.7	0.8
Hispanic or Latino......	26.4	9.8	4.9	3.2	3.5	2.0	1.4	0.4
REGION								
Northeast......	27.9	13.8	6.5	4.9	2.9	2.1	2.2	0.4
Midwest......	31.3	13.6	7.3	5.5	3.5	2.2	2.1	0.4
South......	33.7	14.1	6.8	6.7	3.9	2.1	1.6	0.3
West......	31.2	13.2	5.7	6.7	3.9	2.1	1.9	0.5
METRO STATUS								
Large metro [1]......	29.8	13.2	6.5	6.0	3.4	2.3	1.9	0.4
Small metro [2]......	33.7	14.8	7.3	6.5	4.0	2.0	2.0	0.3
Nonmetro......	34.2	13.8	5.5	6.0	3.7	1.7	1.3	0.5

S Figure does not meet standards of reliability or precision. [1] Over 1 million population. [2] Less than 1 million population.

Source: U.S. Substance Abuse and Mental Health Services Administration, *Results From the 2018 National Survey on Drug Use and Health: Detailed Tables,* August 2019. See also <http://www.samhsa.gov/data/data-we-collect/nsduh-national-survey-drug-use-and-health>.

Table 226. Prescription Drug Use in Past 30 Days by Sex, Race/Ethnicity, and Age: 1988 to 2016

[Data shown as percent of population using prescription drugs in past 30 days. Based on the National Health and Nutrition Examination Survey, covering a sample of the civilian noninstitutionalized population]

Sex, race/ethnicity, and age	Use of 1 or more prescription drugs			Use of 3 or more prescription drugs			Use of 5 or more prescription drugs		
	1988-1994	2007-2010	2013-2016	1988-1994	2007-2010	2013-2016	1988-1994	2007-2010	2013-2016
Both sexes, age adjusted [1,2]......	**39.1**	**47.5**	**45.8**	**11.8**	**20.8**	**21.8**	**4.0**	**10.1**	**11.2**
Male......	32.7	42.8	41.7	9.4	19.1	20.1	2.9	9.2	10.1
Female......	45.0	52.0	49.7	13.9	22.5	23.4	4.9	11.0	12.3
White alone [3]......	41.1	52.8	49.9	12.4	22.4	23.4	4.2	10.7	11.8
Male......	34.2	47.5	45.3	9.9	20.6	21.6	3.1	9.8	10.6
Female......	47.6	57.9	54.5	14.6	24.3	25.1	5.1	11.6	12.9
Black or African American alone [3]......	36.9	42.3	44.6	12.6	20.7	22.4	3.8	10.8	12.8
Male......	31.1	36.7	40.2	10.2	17.7	20.0	2.9	9.1	11.1
Female......	41.4	46.8	48.0	14.3	22.9	24.3	4.5	12.0	14.2
Asian alone [3]......	(NA)	(NA)	33.7	(NA)	(NA)	14.1	(NA)	(NA)	7.1
Male......	(NA)	(NA)	30.9	(NA)	(NA)	14.4	(NA)	(NA)	6.5
Female......	(NA)	(NA)	36.0	(NA)	(NA)	14.0	(NA)	(NA)	7.6
Hispanic or Latino [4]......	(NA)	35.2	36.7	(NA)	15.7	17.2	(NA)	8.4	8.9
Male......	(NA)	31.7	33.0	(NA)	14.0	16.1	(NA)	7.3	8.5
Female......	(NA)	38.8	40.5	(NA)	17.4	18.3	(NA)	9.5	9.4
Both sexes, crude......	**37.8**	**48.5**	**48.4**	**11.0**	**21.7**	**24.0**	**3.6**	**10.6**	**12.6**
Male......	30.6	43.0	43.5	8.3	19.0	21.4	2.5	9.1	10.8
Under 18 years......	20.4	24.5	22.4	2.6	4.4	4.3	(B)	0.8	0.8
18 to 44 years......	21.5	29.5	26.6	3.6	7.1	7.7	[5] 0.8	2.1	2.9
45 to 64 years......	47.2	61.3	64.3	15.1	30.4	34.0	4.8	14.4	17.1
65 years and over......	67.2	88.8	88.5	31.3	66.8	66.6	11.3	39.5	39.4
Female......	44.6	53.8	53.0	13.6	24.2	26.5	4.7	12.1	14.2
Under 18 years......	20.6	23.5	17.9	2.3	3.1	2.7	(B)	[5] 0.7	0.5
18 to 44 years......	40.7	47.6	44.9	7.6	12.2	12.9	1.7	4.0	4.9
45 to 64 years......	62.0	70.8	72.5	24.7	38.1	40.4	9.7	19.1	22.0
65 years and over......	78.3	90.4	89.5	38.2	66.4	68.3	15.6	39.8	42.0

NA Not available. B Estimate has a relative standard error greater than 30%. [1] Estimates are age-adjusted to the year 2000 standard population using four age groups: under 18 years, 18-44 years, 45-64 years, and 65 years and over. [2] Includes persons of other race/ethnicities, not shown separately. [3] Not Hispanic or Latino. [4] Persons of Hispanic or Latino origin may be of any race. [5] Estimate has a relative standard error (RSE) of 20% to 30% and is considered unreliable.

Source: U.S. National Center for Health Statistics, *Health, United States, 2018,* October 2019. See also <https://www.cdc.gov/nchs/hus/index.htm>.

Table 227. Height of Population Age 20 and Over by Sex, Age, and Race/Ethnicity: 2011 to 2014

[In inches. Data are for the 2011-2014 period. Based on National Health and Nutrition Examination Survey (NHANES), a sample of the civilian noninstitutional population. Data are collected through household interviews and health examinations. Height was measured without shoes. Survey oversampled persons age 80 and over, Hispanic persons, and non-Hispanic Black and Asian persons; see source for more information]

Age and race/ethnicity	Males, height in inches						Females, height in inches					
	Mean	Percentile					Mean	Percentile				
		10th	25th	50th	75th	90th		10th	25th	50th	75th	90th
Total: [1]												
20 years and over......	69.2	65.4	67.2	69.1	71.2	73.0	63.7	60.1	61.7	63.7	65.5	67.2
20-29 years.............	69.4	65.7	67.4	69.4	71.4	73.4	64.1	60.8	62.3	64.1	65.8	67.4
30-39 years.............	69.5	65.8	67.5	69.5	71.5	73.5	64.3	60.5	62.3	64.4	66.4	67.9
40-49 years.............	69.4	65.7	67.3	69.3	71.2	73.1	64.1	60.5	62.2	64.2	65.9	67.6
50-59 years.............	69.3	65.7	67.2	69.1	71.4	73.0	63.7	60.2	61.8	63.9	65.3	67.1
60-69 years.............	69.0	65.2	67.1	69.1	71.2	72.5	63.2	60.1	61.5	63.2	64.9	66.5
70-79 years.............	68.1	64.7	66.3	67.9	69.8	71.7	62.7	59.2	60.8	63.0	64.5	66.1
80 years and over......	67.6	64.2	65.9	67.7	69.4	71.0	61.3	57.7	59.6	61.3	63.1	64.3
White, non-Hispanic:												
20 years and over......	69.7	66.2	67.7	69.6	71.5	73.3	64.1	60.6	62.3	64.1	65.8	67.5
20-39 years.............	70.1	66.6	68.2	70.2	72.1	73.8	64.9	61.7	63.2	64.9	66.6	68.2
40-59 years.............	69.9	66.5	68.1	69.9	71.7	73.3	64.4	61.1	62.8	64.4	66.0	67.8
60 years and over......	69.0	65.3	67.0	69.0	70.9	72.4	63.0	59.7	61.1	63.0	64.7	66.3
Black, non-Hispanic:												
20 years and over......	69.5	66.0	67.4	69.3	71.4	73.3	64.2	60.7	62.5	64.2	65.9	67.4
20-39 years.............	69.8	66.3	67.6	69.7	71.9	73.6	64.4	60.9	62.9	64.4	66.0	67.5
40-59 years.............	69.5	66.1	67.6	69.3	71.4	72.8	64.5	61.1	62.9	64.6	66.1	67.7
60 years and over......	68.5	65.2	66.7	68.4	70.3	72.4	63.1	59.6	61.4	63.2	64.9	66.4
Hispanic:												
20 years and over......	67.4	63.8	65.5	67.3	69.3	71.1	62.0	58.7	60.3	61.9	63.7	65.3
20-39 years.............	67.9	64.4	65.9	67.8	69.8	71.5	62.6	59.2	60.8	62.6	64.2	65.5
40-59 years.............	67.2	63.6	65.3	67.2	69.1	70.9	61.9	58.7	60.1	61.6	63.5	65.4
60 years and over......	66.0	62.6	64.1	65.9	67.6	69.4	60.6	57.5	59.1	60.6	62.1	63.6

[1] Total includes persons of other race/ethnicities not shown separately.

Source: U.S. Centers for Disease Control and Prevention, National Health and Nutrition Examination Survey, *Anthropometric Reference Data For Children and Adults: United States, 2011-2014*, Series 3, No. 39, August 2016. See also <http://www.cdc.gov/nchs/nhanes.htm>.

Table 228. Weight of Population Age 20 and Over by Age, Sex, and Race/Ethnicity: 2011 to 2014

[In pounds. Data are for 2011-2014 period. Based on National Health and Nutrition Examination Survey (NHANES). Pregnant females are excluded from the tabulations on weight. See headnote, Table 227]

Age and race/ethnicity	Males, weight in pounds						Females, weight in pounds					
	Mean	Percentile					Mean	Percentile				
		10th	25th	50th	75th	90th		10th	25th	50th	75th	90th
Total: [1]												
20 years and over.......	195.7	146.2	165.1	189.3	218.8	249.9	168.5	119.8	136.0	159.1	191.1	229.3
20–29 years.............	186.8	137.6	152.9	177.8	208.5	247.2	161.8	113.9	128.8	149.8	184.6	228.7
30–39 years.............	198.8	150.2	168.1	190.8	221.2	259.6	172.9	124.0	137.7	160.5	195.9	237.7
40–49 years.............	201.7	156.3	171.7	196.4	222.5	249.0	173.1	124.8	138.8	164.0	196.8	237.2
50–59 years.............	199.5	152.0	170.2	195.9	222.3	250.4	174.4	124.9	141.0	167.4	197.2	239.4
60–69 years.............	199.7	147.0	168.0	195.3	223.1	255.3	168.8	122.5	140.3	164.4	191.2	224.8
70–79 years.............	189.3	146.2	166.6	183.6	212.0	236.3	165.8	120.2	138.6	158.5	188.5	216.5
80 years and over.......	174.6	132.6	154.2	171.1	194.5	216.1	141.9	103.8	121.7	141.0	160.6	180.4
White, non-Hispanic:												
20 years and over.......	198.8	151.6	169.1	192.9	221.4	250.5	168.4	122.2	137.4	158.7	190.3	226.5
20–39 years.............	193.8	144.9	161.7	183.5	218.5	255.0	167.9	119.8	134.0	155.9	189.0	230.8
40–59 years.............	204.6	161.2	175.7	199.3	225.5	250.4	173.4	127.0	140.9	166.1	195.4	237.5
60 years and over.......	196.5	149.0	168.9	190.2	219.3	249.2	162.9	117.0	136.2	157.0	183.4	215.3
Black, non-Hispanic:												
20 years and over.......	199.3	141.4	161.4	191.6	227.2	264.4	190.2	131.6	154.0	183.1	217.8	256.8
20–39 years.............	197.7	138.6	157.9	189.0	228.0	264.2	190.0	129.6	151.0	183.1	219.0	263.3
40–59 years.............	204.8	147.0	169.8	196.6	231.4	270.3	196.5	140.0	159.2	187.3	223.5	259.6
60 years and over.......	191.4	141.2	158.8	185.5	214.4	251.9	179.9	126.0	147.2	174.7	208.9	235.1
Hispanic:												
20 years and over.......	189.9	143.1	161.6	184.7	209.1	240.0	164.7	121.3	135.5	157.4	186.2	219.2
20–39 years.............	192.2	142.3	160.7	186.0	214.1	243.9	163.5	120.7	134.8	152.9	182.5	220.7
40–59 years.............	190.1	147.2	166.0	186.8	207.2	232.2	169.1	122.7	138.6	163.6	191.8	221.7
60 years and over.......	179.3	140.1	153.3	175.4	198.3	226.5	158.3	114.4	132.5	154.0	179.9	204.8

[1] Total includes persons of other race/ethnicities not shown separately.

Source: U.S. Centers for Disease Control and Prevention, National Health and Nutrition Examination Survey, *Anthropometric Reference Data For Children and Adults: United States, 2011-2014*, Series 3, No. 39, August 2016. See also <http://www.cdc.gov/nchs/nhanes.htm>.

Table 229. Body Mass Index of Population Age 20 and Over by Age, Sex, and Race/Ethnicity: 2011 to 2014

[Data are for 2011-2014 period. Body Mass Index (BMI) is a measure that adjusts body weight for height, and is calculated as weight in kilograms divided by the square of height in meters. For both men and women, BMI weight categories are: under 18.5 underweight, 18.5-24.9 normal, 25.0-29.9 overweight, and 30.0 and over obese. Data are based on National Health and Nutrition Examination Survey (NHANES), a sample of the civilian noninstitutional population. Data are collected through household interviews and health examinations. Excludes pregnant women. Survey oversampled persons age 80 and over, Hispanic persons, and non-Hispanic Black and Asian persons; see source for more information]

Age and race/ethnicity	Males, BMI						Females, BMI					
	Mean	Percentile					Mean	Percentile				
		10th	25th	50th	75th	90th		10th	25th	50th	75th	90th
Total: [1]												
20 years and over......	28.7	22.2	24.6	27.7	31.6	36.1	29.2	21.0	23.6	27.7	33.2	39.3
20–29 years...........	27.2	20.5	22.5	25.5	30.5	35.1	27.6	19.8	21.9	25.6	31.8	38.9
30–39 years...........	28.9	22.4	24.8	27.5	31.9	36.5	29.4	21.1	23.3	27.6	33.1	40.0
40–49 years...........	29.4	23.4	25.7	28.5	31.9	36.5	29.6	21.5	23.7	28.1	33.4	39.6
50–59 years...........	29.1	22.7	25.4	28.3	32.0	35.2	30.2	21.5	24.5	28.6	34.4	40.7
60–69 years...........	29.4	22.7	25.3	28.0	32.4	36.9	29.7	21.7	24.5	28.9	33.4	38.7
70–79 years...........	28.6	23.2	25.4	27.8	30.9	34.9	29.6	22.1	24.6	28.3	33.4	39.1
80 years and over......	26.7	21.5	24.1	26.3	29.0	32.3	26.6	20.4	23.3	26.1	29.7	32.8
White, non-Hispanic:												
20 years and over......	28.7	22.3	24.8	27.7	31.6	36.0	28.8	20.9	23.4	27.3	32.6	38.8
20–39 years...........	27.7	21.1	23.2	26.4	30.6	35.9	28.0	20.4	22.3	25.9	31.8	38.9
40–59 years...........	29.4	23.2	25.7	28.5	32.2	36.0	29.4	21.4	23.6	27.9	33.4	40.1
60 years and over......	29.0	22.8	25.3	27.9	31.6	36.0	28.9	21.4	24.2	27.9	32.4	37.5
Black, non-Hispanic:												
20 years and over......	28.9	21.1	24.0	27.9	32.2	37.7	32.5	22.8	26.6	31.3	36.8	43.5
20–39 years...........	28.4	20.5	23.3	26.4	32.5	37.2	32.1	21.8	25.9	31.0	36.9	43.4
40–59 years...........	29.7	21.9	25.1	28.7	32.4	39.2	33.3	23.5	27.1	31.9	37.2	44.8
60 years and over......	28.6	22.1	24.2	27.7	31.6	36.5	31.7	22.8	26.2	30.9	35.8	41.3
Hispanic:												
20 years and over......	29.3	22.9	25.5	28.6	32.0	36.4	30.0	22.1	25.1	28.9	33.9	38.8
20–39 years...........	29.3	22.1	24.9	28.6	32.4	37.3	29.3	21.7	24.4	27.9	32.9	38.6
40–59 years...........	29.5	23.8	26.4	28.8	31.7	35.3	31.0	22.7	26.1	30.2	34.9	39.5
60 years and over......	28.8	23.7	25.5	27.9	31.6	34.5	30.3	22.4	25.9	29.5	34.3	38.4

[1] Total includes persons of other race/ethnicities not shown separately.

Source: U.S. Centers for Disease Control and Prevention, National Health and Nutrition Examination Survey, *Anthropometric Reference Data For Children and Adults: United States, 2011-2014*, Series 3, No. 39, August 2016. See also <http://www.cdc.gov/nchs/nhanes.htm>.

Table 230. Leisure-Time Aerobic and Muscle-Strengthening Activity Among Adults Age 18 and Over by Selected Characteristics: 2018

[In percent. Percents are age-adjusted and allow for comparisons to results from earlier surveys and within demographic groups. Covers persons age 18 and over. Based on the National Health Interview Survey (NHIS), a sample survey of the civilian noninstitutionalized population. Measures of physical activity reflect the federal "2008 Physical Activity Guidelines for Americans"; see <https://health.gov/PAGuidelines/>. The guidelines include an aerobic component; the full physical activity guidelines include muscle-strengthening and aerobic activities. NHIS questions ask about frequency and duration of light-to moderate-intensity and vigorous-intensity leisure-time physical activities, and frequency of leisure-time muscle strengthening activities. Questions are phrased in terms of current behavior and lack a specific reference period. For definition of age adjustment, see text, Section 2]

Characteristic	Inactive/ insuffi- ciently active [1]	Suffi- ciently active [2]	Met muscle strength- ening and aerobic guide- lines [3]	Characteristic	Inactive/ insuffi- ciently active [1]	Suffi- ciently active [2]	Met muscle strength- ening and aerobic guide- lines [3]
Total....................	**45.8**	**54.2**	**24.1**	Asian............................	45.3	54.7	22.9
SEX				Native Hawaiian/			
Male............................	41.9	58.2	27.6	Pacific Islander.................	(NA)	44.5	21.9
Female........................	49.4	50.6	20.8	Two or more races..............	43.8	56.2	25.9
AGE [4]				HISPANIC ORIGIN AND RACE			
18 to 44 years.................	39.6	60.4	30.0	Hispanic or Latino [5].............	52.2	47.8	21.6
45 to 64 years.................	48.4	51.6	19.7	Not Hispanic or Latino...........	44.5	55.5	24.6
65 to 74 years.................	53.9	46.1	16.4	White, non-Hispanic...........	42.5	57.5	25.8
75 years and over.............	67.8	32.2	10.2	Black, non-Hispanic...........	54.3	45.8	20.0
RACE							
Single race.....................	45.8	54.1	24.0	EDUCATION [6]			
White..........................	44.5	55.5	24.9	Less than high school diploma...	65.4	34.6	9.8
Black or African American....	54.2	45.7	19.9	High school diploma or GED [7]. ...	56.8	43.2	14.8
American Indian/				Some college....................	48.3	51.6	21.8
Alaska Native...............	45.5	54.4	18.7	Bachelor's degree or higher......	34.7	65.3	32.1

NA Not available. [1] "Inactive" is having no leisure-time aerobic activity that lasted at least 10 minutes. "Insufficiently active" is having aerobic activity for 10 minutes or more but less than 150 minutes per week. [2] "Sufficiently active," which meets the aerobic component of the 2008 federal physical activity guidelines, is participating in moderate-intensity leisure-time physical activity 150 minutes or more per week, or in vigorous-intensity leisure-time physical activity 75 minutes or more per week, or an equivalent combination. [3] Persons who are sufficiently active, and who engage in muscle strengthening activities at least 2 times a week. [4] Age data are not age-adjusted. [5] Persons of Hispanic or Latino origin may be of any race. [6] For persons age 25 and over. [7] General educational development high school equivalency diploma.

Source: U.S. National Center for Health Statistics, 2018 National Health Interview Survey, "Tables of Summary Health Statistics," <http://www.cdc.gov/nchs/nhis/SHS.htm>, accessed December 2019.

Table 231. Overweight and Obesity Prevalence Among Adults Age 20 and Over by Sex, Age, and Race/Ethnicity: 1988 to 2016

[Shown as percent of population age 20 and over. Weight status is determined by body mass index (BMI), which is calculated as weight in kilograms divided by the square of height in meters. Excludes pregnant women. Data are based on the National Health and Nutrition Examination Survey (NHANES); measurements of height and weight of a sample of the civilian noninstitutionalized population were taken without shoes. Percents do not sum to 100 because data for persons with BMI under 18.5 are not shown, and percent of persons with obesity are included with the overweight]

Characteristics	Normal weight [1]			Overweight or obese [2]			Obese [3]		
	1988 to 1994	2001 to 2004	2013 to 2016	1988 to 1994	2001 to 2004	2013 to 2016	1988 to 1994	2001 to 2004	2013 to 2016
Total, age-adjusted [4].........	**41.6**	**32.3**	**27.7**	**56.0**	**66.0**	**70.9**	**22.9**	**31.4**	**38.8**
Male.........	37.9	28.3	24.2	60.9	70.5	74.6	20.2	29.5	36.8
Female.........	45.0	36.1	31.0	51.4	61.6	67.4	25.5	33.2	40.7
Total, crude.........	**42.6**	**32.2**	**27.4**	**54.9**	**66.1**	**71.1**	**22.3**	**31.5**	**38.9**
Male.........	39.4	28.4	24.4	59.4	70.4	74.3	19.5	29.5	36.6
Female.........	45.7	35.8	30.3	50.7	61.9	68.1	25.0	33.3	41.0
White, non-Hispanic.........	43.6	33.2	27.8	53.8	65.1	70.9	21.3	30.9	37.9
Male.........	38.2	27.4	23.2	60.6	71.6	75.6	19.8	30.5	36.9
Female.........	48.8	38.8	32.1	47.4	58.7	66.3	22.7	31.2	38.8
Black or African American, non-Hispanic....	35.9	24.8	22.8	61.8	73.3	75.7	29.5	41.9	47.6
Male.........	41.5	31.5	29.2	56.7	66.3	69.8	20.7	30.7	37.5
Female.........	31.2	19.3	17.6	66.0	79.1	80.5	36.7	51.1	56.1
Asian, non-Hispanic.........	(NA)	(NA)	53.7	(NA)	(NA)	42.6	(NA)	(NA)	12.7
Male.........	(NA)	(NA)	47.4	(NA)	(NA)	49.5	(NA)	(NA)	11.7
Female.........	(NA)	(NA)	59.2	(NA)	(NA)	36.5	(NA)	(NA)	13.6
Hispanic [5].........	(NA)	(NA)	19.6	(NA)	(NA)	79.6	(NA)	(NA)	44.8
Male.........	(NA)	(NA)	18.0	(NA)	(NA)	81.3	(NA)	(NA)	41.2
Female.........	(NA)	(NA)	21.3	(NA)	(NA)	77.8	(NA)	(NA)	48.4
Male by age:									
20 to 34 years.........	51.1	38.3	34.6	47.5	59.0	63.0	14.1	23.2	30.7
35 to 44 years.........	33.4	26.5	19.3	65.5	72.9	80.6	21.3	33.8	43.1
45 to 54 years.........	33.6	21.2	18.5	66.1	78.5	80.8	23.2	31.8	38.0
55 to 64 years.........	28.6	22.2	22.3	70.5	77.3	76.7	27.2	36.0	39.3
65 to 74 years.........	30.1	23.1	19.3	68.5	76.1	79.0	24.1	32.1	40.2
75 years and over.........	40.9	32.1	24.3	56.5	66.8	74.9	13.2	19.9	28.0
Female by age:									
20 to 34 years.........	57.9	44.2	37.5	37.0	51.6	59.6	18.5	28.6	34.8
35 to 44 years.........	47.1	38.3	31.3	49.6	60.1	67.7	25.5	33.3	43.4
45 to 54 years.........	37.2	31.0	29.3	60.3	67.4	69.5	32.4	38.0	42.9
55 to 64 years.........	31.5	29.2	23.8	66.3	69.9	74.5	33.7	39.0	48.2
65 to 74 years.........	37.0	27.0	23.9	60.3	71.5	75.6	26.9	37.9	43.5
75 years and over.........	43.0	34.6	31.0	52.3	63.7	67.4	19.2	23.2	32.7

NA Not available. [1] Normal weight status is a BMI of 18.5 to 24.9. [2] Overweight or obese is a BMI of 25.0 or more. [3] Obese is a BMI of 30.0 or more. [4] Estimates are age-adjusted to the year 2000 standard population using five age groups: 20–34 years, 35–44 years, 45–54 years, 55–64 years, and 65 years and over. [5] Persons of Hispanic origin may be of any race.

Source: U.S. National Center for Health Statistics, *Health, United States, 2018,* October 2019. See also <http://www.cdc.gov/nchs/hus/>.

Table 232. Dental Care Visit in the Past Year—Percent of Population by Age and Selected Characteristics: 2000 to 2017

[In percent. Covers civilian noninstitutionalized population who had a dental care visit in the past year. Based on the National Health Interview Survey; see Appendix III]

Characteristic	Age 2 years and over			Age 2 to 17 years			Age 18 to 64 years			Age 65 years and over		
	2000	2010	2017	2000	2010	2017	2000	2010	2017	2000	2010	2017
Total [1].........	**66.2**	**64.7**	**68.7**	**74.1**	**78.9**	**84.9**	**65.1**	**61.1**	**64.0**	**56.6**	**57.7**	**65.6**
Sex:												
Male.........	63.5	61.7	66.8	73.7	78.3	84.2	60.7	56.8	61.1	56.1	56.2	65.5
Female.........	68.8	67.5	70.4	74.6	79.6	85.6	69.4	65.4	66.8	56.9	58.9	65.7
Race/ethnicity: [2]												
White alone.........	67.9	65.6	69.7	75.8	79.2	85.8	67.2	62.4	65.0	58.4	59.3	67.8
Black or African American alone.....	59.5	58.8	64.8	70.0	79.0	83.2	57.1	53.1	60.0	38.2	40.6	53.0
American Indian/Alaska Native alone.........	58.6	57.4	70.1	71.3	73.2	86.3	55.0	49.8	64.7	(B)	72.2	(B)
Asian alone.........	67.1	66.5	66.1	72.8	74.8	83.2	65.6	64.6	63.5	60.6	61.9	53.1
Two or more races.........	65.1	65.2	65.3	71.4	77.9	78.8	60.5	54.7	56.0	57.4	48.1	59.7
Hispanic [3].........	52.3	56.5	63.1	60.6	74.8	84.9	48.6	48.5	54.0	44.5	42.1	54.7
Percent of poverty level: [4]												
Below 100%.........	50.4	50.6	57.1	62.4	73.2	81.9	46.8	41.0	48.2	33.3	32.8	42.1
100% to 199%.........	52.2	52.1	55.2	66.1	73.4	79.8	48.4	44.1	47.4	43.0	43.8	43.1
200% to 399%.........	65.6	63.5	65.9	75.5	79.0	83.8	62.2	59.6	59.9	62.8	57.9	65.4
400% or more.........	79.5	79.3	80.5	85.9	88.0	91.4	78.5	77.5	77.6	73.8	77.2	82.2

B Estimates are considered unreliable. [1] Includes persons of other race and ethnic groups, not shown separately. [2] Race groups include persons of Hispanic and non-Hispanic origin. [3] Persons of Hispanic origin may be of any race. [4] Poverty level is based on family income and family size and composition using Census Bureau poverty thresholds.

Source: U.S. National Center for Health Statistics, *Health, United States, 2018,* October 2019. See also <https://www.cdc.gov/nchs/hus/index.htm>.

Table 233. Sleep—Percent Distribution of Adults Age 18 and Over by Hours of Sleep by Selected Characteristics: 2011 to 2014

[235,845 represents 235,845,000. Data are annualized over 2011-2014 (4-year) period. Estimates are age-adjusted using the projected 2000 U.S. population as the standard population and using three age groups: 18–44 years, 45–64 years, and 65 years and over. All estimates are based on data from the Sample Adult files, which are derived from the Sample Adult component of the National Health Interview Survey. Survey respondents where asked, "On average, how many hours of sleep do you get in a 24 hour period?" Response options were 1-24 hours]

Characteristic	Adults age 18 and over (1,000)	Hours of sleep (percent distribution)		
		6 or less	7 to 8	9 or more
Total [1]...	235,845	29.7	61.6	8.7
SEX				
Male...	113,760	29.6	62.4	8.0
Female..	122,085	29.8	60.9	9.3
AGE [2]				
18 to 24 years old..............................	30,153	22.9	63.6	13.4
25 to 44 years old..............................	81,276	31.8	62.4	5.8
45 to 64 years old..............................	81,945	33.8	60.1	6.2
65 to 74 years old..............................	24,278	25.1	63.6	11.3
75 years old and over..........................	18,194	22.0	57.1	20.9
RACE				
Single race [3]...................................	232,068	29.6	61.7	8.6
White..	188,610	28.3	63.0	8.7
Black or African American....................	28,367	37.8	52.6	9.7
American Indian or Alaska Native............	1,954	35.0	55.3	9.6
Asian..	12,745	29.6	64.4	6.0
Native Hawaiian or Other Pacific Islander....	393	47.5	44.3	8.2
Two or more races [4]...........................	3,776	37.7	53.0	9.2
Black or African American, white..............	753	40.5	54.3	5.2
American Indian or Alaska Native, white.......	1,557	40.5	48.7	10.8
HISPANIC ORIGIN AND RACE [5]				
Hispanic or Latino..............................	34,996	28.8	62.2	8.9
Mexican or Mexican American.................	21,611	26.8	63.5	9.7
Not Hispanic or Latino..........................	200,849	30.1	61.4	8.6
White, single race............................	156,720	28.5	62.9	8.6
Black or African American, single race.......	27,201	38.0	52.4	9.6
EDUCATION [6]				
Less than high school graduate................	27,998	30.9	57.6	11.4
GED diploma [7].................................	6,018	37.3	53.2	9.5
High school graduate...........................	46,650	32.1	59.1	8.8
Some college, no degree.......................	35,745	35.2	57.3	7.5
Associate of arts degree.......................	23,771	33.3	59.2	7.5
Bachelor of arts, science degree..............	40,524	27.0	67.3	5.7
Masters, doctorate, medical degree...........	23,877	24.5	70.3	5.3
POVERTY STATUS [8]				
Below poverty level.............................	32,666	33.6	55.0	11.4
100% to less than 200% poverty level..........	45,025	32.2	57.2	10.6
200% to less than 400% poverty level..........	70,656	30.4	60.9	8.7
400% or more of poverty level.................	87,498	26.8	66.6	6.5
MARITAL STATUS				
Never married..................................	52,245	28.9	60.5	10.6
Married..	124,885	29.0	64.0	7.1
Cohabiting.....................................	17,226	32.4	58.6	9.0
Divorced or separated..........................	26,937	38.5	54.0	7.6
Widowed.......................................	14,165	38.4	54.0	7.7

[1] Includes persons of other races and unknown race and ethnicity, unknown education, unknown poverty status, and unknown marital status. [2] Estimates for age groups are not age adjusted. [3] Refers to persons who indicated only a single race group, including those of Hispanic or Latino origin. [4] Refers to all persons who indicated more than one race group, including those of Hispanic or Latino origin. [5] Persons of Hispanic or Latino origin may be of any race or combination of races. [6] Shown only for adults age 25 and over. Estimates are age adjusted to the projected 2000 U.S. population as the standard population using three age groups: 25–44, 45–64, and 65 and over. [7] General Educational Development high school equivalency diploma. [8] Based on family income and family size using the U.S. Census Bureau poverty thresholds for 2010, 2011, 2012, and 2013.

Source: U.S. National Center for Health Statistics, National Health Interview Survey, "Tables of Summary Health Statistics," <http://www.cdc.gov/nchs/nhis/SHS.htm>, accessed February 2017.

Table 234. Depression and Receipt of Mental Health Treatment in the Past Year Among Adults Age 18 and Over by Selected Characteristics: 2017 and 2018

[In thousands (17,297 represents 17,297,000), except percent. Based on the National Survey on Drug Use and Health. Covers adults who had a major depressive episode as defined in the 5th edition of the *Diagnostic and Statistical Manual of Mental Disorders* (DSM-5), which specifies a period of at least 2 weeks when a person experienced a depressed mood or loss of interest or pleasure in daily activities and had a majority of specified depression symptoms. Treatment is defined as seeing or talking to a professional or using prescription medication for depression in the past year; respondents with unknown treatment data were excluded]

Characteristic	Had major depressive episode (MDE)				Those with an MDE who received treatment for depression			
	2017		2018		2017		2018	
	Number (1,000)	Percent of population	Number (1,000)	Percent of population	Number (1,000)	Percent	Number (1,000)	Percent
Total......	**17,297**	**7.1**	**17,720**	**7.2**	**11,548**	**66.8**	**11,462**	**64.8**
AGE								
18 to 25 years old......	4,416	13.1	4,609	13.8	2,238	50.7	2,286	49.6
26 to 49 years old......	7,635	7.7	7,990	8.0	5,128	67.3	5,142	64.4
50 years old and older......	5,245	4.7	5,121	4.5	4,182	79.7	4,034	78.9
SEX AND AGE								
Male......	6,266	5.3	6,272	5.3	3,650	58.3	3,548	56.7
18 to 25 years old......	1,618	9.5	1,665	9.9	701	43.3	674	40.5
26 to 49 years old......	2,744	5.6	2,956	6.0	1,500	54.7	1,660	56.3
50 years old and older......	1,904	3.7	1,651	3.1	1,449	76.1	1,215	73.9
Female......	11,031	8.7	11,447	9.0	7,898	71.7	7,914	69.2
18 to 25 years old......	2,799	16.6	2,943	17.6	1,537	55.0	1,612	54.8
26 to 49 years old......	4,891	9.7	5,034	10.0	3,628	74.4	3,482	69.2
50 years old and older......	3,341	5.6	3,470	5.8	2,733	81.8	2,819	81.3
RACE AND HISPANIC ORIGIN								
Not Hispanic or Latino......	15,188	7.4	15,225	7.4	10,370	68.4	10,118	66.5
White......	12,398	7.9	12,224	7.8	8,737	70.5	8,366	68.5
Black or African American......	1,579	5.4	1,783	6.1	994	63.1	1,090	61.2
American Indian or Alaska Native......	102	8.0	125	8.5	(B)	(B)	(B)	(B)
Native Hawaiian or other Pacific Islander......	45	4.7	64	6.9	(B)	(B)	(B)	(B)
Asian......	600	4.4	593	4.3	251	41.9	261	43.9
Two or more races......	465	11.3	437	10.2	296	64.8	288	65.8
Hispanic or Latino......	2,109	5.4	2,495	6.2	1,178	55.9	1,344	53.9

B Low precision; does not meet statistical standards for reliability of a derived figure.

Source: U.S. Substance Abuse and Mental Health Services Administration, *Results from the 2018 National Survey on Drug Use and Health: Detailed Tables,* August 2019. See also <https://www.samhsa.gov/data/data-we-collect/nsduh-national-survey-drug-use-and-health>.

Table 235. Children With Allergies by Type and Selected Characteristics: 2018

[In percent, except as indicated (73,452 represents 73,452,000). Covers incidence of allergies in the past 12 months among children under age 18. A child may have multiple types of allergies. Based on household interviews of a sample of the civilian noninstitutionalized population, regarding the sample child, not all children in the family. Percent data are age-adjusted, except as indicated. Unknowns for the columns were not included in the denominators when calculating percentages]

Selected characteristic	Total (1,000)	Hay fever	Respiratory allergies	Food allergies	Skin allergies
Total [1]......	**73,452**	**7.2**	**9.6**	**6.5**	**12.6**
SEX					
Male......	37,489	7.9	11.0	6.4	12.2
Female......	35,963	6.4	8.1	6.5	12.9
AGE [2]					
4 years and under......	19,678	3.2	5.0	5.8	14.3
5 to 11 years......	29,220	7.0	10.4	5.8	12.3
12 to 17 years......	24,554	10.5	12.4	7.8	11.4
RACE					
Single race [3]......	69,541	7.0	9.3	6.1	12.3
White......	53,462	7.4	9.2	6.2	11.3
Black or African American......	10,618	5.7	10.8	6.4	18.2
American Indian or Alaska Native......	1,085	(B)	(B)	(B)	(B)
Asian......	4,148	6.9	8.1	5.1	11.6
Native Hawaiian or Other Pacific Islander......	228	(B)	(B)	(B)	(B)
Two or more races [3]......	3,912	9.2	15.9	12.7	17.2
HISPANIC ORIGIN AND RACE [4]					
Hispanic or Latino......	18,717	5.9	8.5	6.0	10.5
Not Hispanic or Latino......	54,736	7.6	10.0	6.6	13.2
White only......	37,234	8.3	9.6	6.6	12.0
Black or African American only......	9,692	5.2	11.0	6.0	17.9

B Estimate is considered unreliable. [1] Total includes children of other races not shown separately. [2] Estimates for age groups are not age-adjusted. [3] Includes children of Hispanic or Latino origin. [4] Children of Hispanic or Latino origin may be of any race or combination of races.

Source: U.S. National Center for Health Statistics, 2018 National Health Interview Survey, "Tables of Summary Health Statistics," <https://www.cdc.gov/nchs/nhis/shs.htm>, accessed December 2019.

Table 236. Learning Disability and Attention Deficit Hyperactivity Disorder Among Children Age 3 to 17 by Selected Characteristics: 2018

[In thousands (61,918 represents 61,918,000), except percent. Learning disability is based on the question, "Has a representative from a school or a health professional ever told you that (child's name) had a learning disability?" Attention deficit hyperactivity disorder is based on the question, "Has a doctor or other health professional ever told you that (child's name) had attention deficit hyperactivity disorder or attention deficit disorder?" Based on household interviews of a sample of the civilian noninstitutionalized population regarding the sample child, not all children in the family]

| Selected characteristic | Total | Ever told child had— | | | |
| | | Learning disability | | Attention deficit hyperactivity disorder | |
		Number [1]	Percent [2]	Number [1]	Percent [2]
Total [3]	**61,918**	**4,526**	**7.3**	**6,072**	**9.8**
SEX					
Male	31,421	2,969	9.5	4,038	13.0
Female	30,496	1,557	5.1	2,034	6.6
AGE [4]					
3 to 4 years	8,144	263	3.2	101	1.2
5 to 11 years	29,220	1,955	6.7	2,627	9.0
12 to 17 years	24,554	2,307	9.4	3,344	13.6
RACE					
Single race [5]	58,696	4,260	7.3	5,630	9.6
White	44,997	3,269	7.3	4,332	9.6
Black or African American	9,077	778	8.6	1,145	12.8
American Indian or Alaska Native	905	(B)	(B)	(B)	(B)
Asian	3,541	165	4.7	116	3.2
Native Hawaiian or other Pacific Islander	176	(B)	(B)	(B)	(B)
Two or more races [6]	3,222	265	8.3	442	14.0
Black or African American and White	1,398	(B)	(B)	209	15.5
American Indian or Alaska Native and White	602	(B)	(B)	148	26.4
HISPANIC ORIGIN AND RACE [7]					
Hispanic or Latino	15,729	1,301	8.4	1,070	6.9
Not Hispanic or Latino	46,189	3,225	7.0	5,002	10.8
White, single race	31,385	2,142	6.8	3,440	10.9
Black or African American, single race	8,248	710	8.7	1,064	13.1
CURRENT HEALTH STATUS					
Excellent or very good	52,849	3,082	5.9	4,625	8.8
Good	7,913	1,050	13.3	1,234	15.4
Fair or poor	1,150	394	32.3	213	16.2

B Estimate is considered unreliable. [1] Unknowns for the columns are not included in the frequencies, but they are included in the "Total" column. [2] Unknowns for the column variables are not included in the denominators when calculating percentages. Percents are age-adjusted to the projected 2000 U.S. standard population using age groups 3-4 years, 5-11 years, and 12-17 years, except for data shown by age group. [3] Includes other races not shown separately, and children with unknown health status. [4] Estimates for age groups are not age adjusted. [5] Refers to children of only a single race group, including those of Hispanic or Latino origin. [6] Refers to children of more than once race group, including those of Hispanic or Latino origin. [7] Persons of Hispanic or Latino origin may be of any race.

Source: U.S. National Center for Health Statistics, 2018 National Health Interview Survey, "Tables of Summary Health Statistics," <https://www.cdc.gov/nchs/nhis/shs.htm>, accessed December 2019.

Table 237. Autism and Other Developmental Disability Prevalence Among Children Age 3 to 17: 2014 to 2016

[As percent of all children age 3 to 17. Covers the 3-year period 2014 to 2016. Based on the National Health Interview Survey that asked the parent or guardian whether their child had been diagnosed with a developmental delay. Excludes conditions such as attention-deficit/hyperactivity disorder (ADHD), and learning disabilities. The NHIS is a nationally representative survey of the noninstitutionalized population. The Sample Child component of the NHIS collects information about one randomly selected child per family]

Characteristic	Any developmental disability [1]	Autism spectrum disorder [2]	Intellectual disability [3]	Other developmental delay [4]
Total	**6.27**	**2.47**	**1.19**	**3.89**
By sex:				
Male	8.15	3.63	1.48	4.77
Female	4.29	1.25	0.90	2.98
By age:				
3 to 7 years	6.18	2.23	0.73	4.37
8 to 12 years	6.87	2.88	1.45	4.24
13 to 17 years	5.76	2.30	1.40	3.08
By race/ethnicity:				
White, non-Hispanic	7.04	2.76	1.10	4.43
Black, non-Hispanic	6.20	2.49	1.53	3.67
Other, non-Hispanic	6.16	2.48	0.86	3.62
Hispanic [5]	4.69	1.82	1.33	2.98

[1] A composite measure of children with a diagnosis of autism spectrum disorder, intellectual disability, or any other developmental delay. [2] Based on positive responses to the question, "Has a doctor or health professional ever told you that [sample child] had Autism, Asperger's disorder, pervasive developmental disorder, or autism spectrum disorder?" [3] Based on positive responses to the question, "Has a doctor or health professional ever told you that [sample child] had an intellectual disability, also known as mental retardation?" [4] Based on positive responses to the question, "Has a doctor or health professional ever told you that [sample child] had any other developmental delay?" [5] Persons of Hispanic origin may be of any race.

Source: U.S. National Center for Health Statistics, *Estimated Prevalence of Children With Diagnosed Developmental Disabilities in the United States, 2014–2016*, Data Brief No. 291, November 2017. See also <https://www.cdc.gov/nchs/nhis/nhis_products.htm>.

Table 238. Children Under Age 18 Receiving Special Education or Early Intervention Services: 2017 and 2018

[In thousands (73,528 represents 73,528,000), except percent. Percents are age-adjusted. Receiving special education or early intervention services is based on the question, "Do any of these family members (under 18 years of age) receive special education or early intervention services?" Based on household interviews of a sample of the civilian noninstitutionalized population, and about all children in the family]

Selected characteristic	2017			2018		
		Children receiving special education or early intervention services			Children receiving special education or early intervention services	
	Total	Number [1]	Percent [2]	Total	Number [1]	Percent [2]
Total [3]........................	73,528	6,259	8.5	73,451	6,013	8.2
SEX						
Male.........................	37,520	4,114	11.0	37,488	4,022	10.8
Female.......................	36,009	2,145	6.0	35,963	1,992	5.5
AGE [4]						
4 years and under..........	19,852	992	5.0	19,795	946	4.8
5 to 11 years..............	28,844	2,882	10.0	28,717	2,619	9.1
12 to 17 years.............	24,832	2,385	9.6	24,940	2,449	9.8
RACE						
Single race [5].............	70,076	5,884	8.4	69,584	5,607	8.1
White......................	53,696	4,684	8.7	53,338	4,482	8.4
Black or African American....	10,920	974	8.9	10,685	824	7.8
American Indian or Alaska Native........	1,078	88	8.0	1,123	106	9.2
Asian......................	4,170	124	2.9	4,162	172	4.1
Native Hawaiian or other Pacific Islander..................	212	(B)	(B)	277	(B)	(B)
Two or more races [6].......	3,453	375	11.3	3,868	407	10.9
HISPANIC ORIGIN AND RACE [7]						
Hispanic or Latino...........	18,490	1,383	7.5	18,717	1,415	7.6
Not Hispanic or Latino.......	55,038	4,877	8.9	54,735	4,599	8.4
White, single race..........	37,805	3,558	9.4	37,170	3,225	8.7
Black or African American, single race. ..	9,883	855	8.6	9,738	770	8.0

B Estimate is considered unreliable. [1] Unknowns for the columns are not included in the frequencies, but they are included in the "Total" column. [2] Unknowns for the column variables are not included in the denominators when calculating percentages. Percents are age-adjusted to the 2000 projected U.S. standard population using the age groups shown; data by age group are not age-adjusted. [3] Includes other races not shown separately. [4] Estimates for the age groups are not age-adjusted. [5] Refers to persons who indicated only a single race group, including those of Hispanic or Latino origin. [6] Refers to all persons who indicated more than one race group, including those of Hispanic or Latino origin. [7] Persons of Hispanic or Latino origin may be of any race.

Source: U.S. National Center for Health Statistics, 2017 and 2018 National Health Interview Surveys, "Tables of Summary Health Statistics," <https://www.cdc.gov/nchs/nhis/shs.htm>, accessed December 2019.

Table 239. Children and Youth With Disabilities Receiving Special Education and Related Services by Type of Disability: 2000 to 2018

[In thousands (5,773.9 represents 5,773,900). As of Fall. For children and youth age 6 to 21 receiving special education and related services under the Individuals with Disabilities Education Act (IDEA) Part B. Includes outlying areas]

Disability	2000	2005	2010	2014	2015	2016	2017	2018
Total.....................	5,773.9	6,109.6	5,834.9	5,944.2	6,050.7	6,048.9	6,130.6	6,315.2
Autism...................	79.6	193.6	370.6	513.7	550.4	578.8	616.2	663.8
Deaf-blindness............	1.3	1.6	1.3	1.2	1.3	1.3	1.3	1.4
Developmental delay [1]...	28.6	79.1	109.4	141.9	149.3	154.0	159.5	167.7
Emotional disturbance.....	474.3	472.4	388.2	347.8	346.5	335.3	335.0	344.5
Hearing impairment.......	70.8	72.4	69.9	67.9	67.4	65.5	64.8	64.4
Intellectual disability......	613.4	545.5	445.8	415.3	418.5	416.2	418.4	423.2
Multiple disabilities.......	122.9	133.9	123.8	125.5	125.2	125.9	122.4	126.7
Orthopedic impairment.....	73.0	63.1	55.8	46.3	41.2	36.3	34.9	33.5
Other health impairment....	294.0	561.0	706.1	857.5	907.2	934.0	970.0	1,026.0
Specific learning disability..............	2,881.6	2,780.2	2,420.0	2,328.5	2,348.9	2,337.0	2,339.9	2,377.7
Speech or language impairment.......	1,093.4	1,157.2	1,093.7	1,047.6	1,044.3	1,014.8	1,018.5	1,036.8
Traumatic brain injury....	14.9	23.5	24.7	25.4	25.5	25.2	25.3	25.3
Visual impairment.........	26.0	26.0	25.7	25.6	24.9	24.7	24.4	24.2

[1] Beginning 1997, States could include children ages 3 to 9 with a developmental delay among children identified as having a disability. "Developmental delay" applies only to children ages 3 to 9.

Source: U.S. Department of Education, Office of Special Education Programs, "IDEA Section 618 Data Products: State Level Data Files," <https://www2.ed.gov/programs/osepidea/618-data/index.html>, accessed February 2020.

Table 240. Immunization of Children Born in 2015 and 2016 by Vaccine Type and State: 2018

[In percent. Data through 2018 covers civilian noninstitutionalized children born in 2015 and 2016 who received the recommended doses of each vaccine by age 24 months, except as noted. Based on estimates from the National Immunization Survey (NIS), which includes a survey of the parents or guardians of children age 19-35 months, and a survey of health care providers of the children to verify and/or complete vaccination information. Please note that previously the Centers for Disease Control and Prevention reported data by survey year; data are now reported by birth year of children. Data for the 2015 birth year are from survey years 2016, 2017, and 2018; data for the 2016 birth year are considered preliminary and come from survey years 2017 and 2018. Abbreviations: DTaP = diphtheria and tetanus toxoids, and pertussis vaccine; MMR = measles, mumps, and rubella vaccine; HepB = hepatitis B vaccine; HepA = hepatitis A vaccine; Hib = Haemophilus influenzae type b vaccine; PCV = pneumococcal conjugate vaccine]

State	DTaP, ≥3 doses [1]	DTaP, ≥4 doses [1]	Polio, ≥3 doses	MMR, ≥1 dose [2]	Hib, primary series [3]	Hib, full series [3]	HepB, birth dose [4]	HepB, ≥3 doses	Vari-cella, ≥1 dose	PCV, ≥3 doses	PCV, ≥4 doses	HepA, ≥2 doses [5]	Rota-virus [6]	Com-bined series [7]
U.S.....	93.8	80.3	92.7	90.4	92.7	79.6	75.0	91.0	90.0	92.0	81.0	76.6	73.6	68.5
AL......	94.5	84.2	93.8	93.6	94.1	77.7	78.3	93.6	94.1	95.2	85.4	77.7	73.2	71.0
AK......	89.5	76.1	88.9	85.8	91.3	80.0	69.7	89.8	82.9	89.4	78.6	72.3	71.0	68.2
AZ.....	93.0	76.2	90.1	88.0	91.6	74.8	79.6	86.2	89.5	88.9	71.7	77.0	70.1	62.6
AR.....	94.3	78.7	92.8	94.1	93.1	80.2	76.3	93.3	93.6	91.4	78.1	80.3	74.3	68.0
CA.....	92.7	80.7	91.6	88.7	89.6	79.8	68.9	89.2	88.6	88.8	78.7	80.5	68.1	67.2
CO.....	92.5	80.9	91.0	88.5	91.1	83.1	73.2	89.2	87.2	91.2	82.3	70.0	79.2	72.7
CT.....	97.3	84.0	96.0	90.7	97.9	84.7	80.2	94.5	92.6	96.2	85.7	86.7	84.0	76.3
DE.....	94.4	79.9	93.0	89.9	91.3	81.1	81.2	88.0	88.5	93.1	82.6	76.6	75.8	69.4
DC.....	93.6	84.7	92.0	88.2	92.9	79.3	75.2	91.0	89.5	91.8	84.7	83.2	72.8	68.9
FL......	92.3	77.2	91.3	91.1	91.5	75.0	66.2	89.2	90.8	90.5	74.9	67.0	68.5	65.4
GA.....	95.1	78.7	93.4	89.2	93.2	79.8	77.4	93.2	90.8	93.8	82.0	84.1	74.4	67.3
HI......	91.4	82.8	89.8	88.7	88.5	78.5	75.9	89.0	87.1	87.9	80.1	76.1	68.1	71.3
ID......	92.7	79.1	91.8	92.3	92.5	78.8	73.1	91.7	91.0	92.2	83.1	75.7	77.1	67.9
IL.......	96.2	82.6	95.0	92.6	96.4	83.0	75.0	92.6	93.2	94.2	84.0	76.5	73.5	72.4
IN......	92.3	73.8	90.6	85.8	88.9	70.1	78.6	89.5	84.7	89.9	72.3	75.7	70.4	60.1
IA......	94.9	84.9	94.3	89.7	96.0	84.0	82.3	96.4	89.4	93.5	85.9	77.4	78.3	73.2
KS.....	92.9	76.8	92.2	87.1	93.5	77.0	67.6	91.2	86.7	92.3	82.5	76.8	76.4	69.9
KY.....	97.7	86.2	97.7	91.8	97.7	85.2	83.9	94.4	92.3	95.4	88.6	72.1	82.4	75.5
LA......	95.9	79.6	94.9	92.5	95.2	81.3	79.8	94.9	92.1	95.2	79.0	79.8	71.1	70.4
ME.....	94.5	88.8	94.0	93.7	93.6	84.2	70.1	90.2	92.6	90.7	83.0	75.3	79.2	74.0
MD.....	93.7	79.7	93.9	91.6	93.7	82.3	75.1	90.9	90.9	93.4	81.0	72.2	75.4	71.0
MA.....	97.5	88.1	97.4	96.7	96.8	91.8	74.8	95.8	95.6	96.9	91.5	86.0	86.2	80.6
MI.....	94.4	82.7	94.1	90.4	93.9	82.6	77.7	92.7	91.3	93.3	82.7	81.1	77.8	70.0
MN.....	94.7	77.2	92.4	87.6	94.1	75.7	68.0	86.8	88.3	91.1	79.1	75.6	74.8	60.7
MS.....	93.9	75.6	92.1	90.5	92.9	76.9	75.5	92.5	91.2	93.7	78.1	53.8	68.2	66.7
MO.....	90.0	71.3	89.4	87.1	89.5	72.5	84.3	88.9	87.8	88.7	76.6	61.0	68.4	63.3
MT.....	90.4	73.0	89.5	85.3	90.2	74.7	75.4	89.9	84.9	89.2	78.0	65.0	71.6	61.7
NE.....	95.2	85.2	93.8	93.4	95.8	86.3	87.4	93.9	92.9	93.9	86.5	81.0	82.8	78.5
NV.....	88.5	73.8	88.7	88.0	88.5	73.2	76.4	89.2	88.4	87.1	73.9	75.6	71.1	61.8
NH.....	93.5	87.2	93.7	91.4	93.5	87.1	73.2	92.0	88.2	92.9	85.4	84.4	79.0	76.1
NJ......	95.7	83.3	94.4	90.3	94.2	80.6	68.0	91.8	88.8	94.0	82.8	76.0	71.3	71.5
NM.....	95.1	84.4	94.8	90.5	95.1	84.1	70.0	94.7	89.1	93.1	80.5	80.2	76.2	71.3
NY.....	95.0	80.1	94.8	91.0	93.7	80.4	72.0	91.2	91.3	92.4	80.9	69.6	73.9	64.6
NC.....	95.5	83.2	94.9	92.9	95.2	83.6	73.7	93.3	91.6	95.3	85.7	77.0	77.1	75.2
ND.....	95.2	85.0	94.6	93.2	95.3	86.4	88.2	94.8	91.9	95.0	87.4	87.2	80.8	77.3
OH.....	92.4	80.8	91.2	88.6	92.2	77.0	78.8	92.1	86.6	91.8	81.1	66.6	72.6	67.4
OK.....	92.2	78.1	91.7	89.3	92.5	78.2	78.5	89.4	88.5	91.1	78.1	75.2	70.0	65.3
OR.....	89.8	76.6	89.2	92.0	90.2	79.1	77.3	89.1	90.2	89.3	80.5	79.3	74.3	67.4
PA......	95.1	82.8	94.0	92.1	94.6	80.2	83.4	93.0	90.8	93.9	86.5	88.6	77.3	75.1
RI......	97.6	84.3	96.8	94.9	97.5	82.9	79.7	96.6	94.2	96.5	91.3	82.3	85.7	70.7
SC.....	94.4	81.9	93.7	88.4	94.6	76.3	71.3	93.9	88.4	91.4	82.1	75.4	73.8	65.7
SD.....	91.9	78.6	90.3	90.1	91.3	79.7	79.2	90.5	89.6	90.6	82.3	74.0	75.6	70.7
TN.....	92.9	80.7	93.3	89.9	93.5	76.8	71.2	92.5	90.6	93.4	77.7	75.5	70.0	68.5
TX.....	92.7	79.1	91.2	90.3	92.2	78.8	79.4	89.2	90.0	91.5	81.5	84.0	74.1	67.3
UT.....	92.3	79.2	91.6	88.4	91.5	78.8	85.2	91.6	88.6	91.6	82.7	75.4	76.6	69.8
VT.....	94.6	82.4	92.2	91.0	93.7	84.4	58.1	92.0	89.1	93.7	87.1	73.0	75.8	73.7
VA......	96.1	87.4	95.3	92.7	93.7	85.1	74.2	94.6	93.2	93.9	91.0	79.9	78.0	73.5
WA.....	91.5	75.8	87.0	89.4	86.7	75.5	72.0	86.7	85.1	87.4	75.7	66.7	74.7	61.3
WV.....	95.0	81.8	93.9	87.4	94.4	82.3	72.9	91.1	88.3	93.2	84.5	78.2	73.5	70.8
WI......	95.5	82.2	95.4	93.5	94.9	82.5	81.5	92.7	89.5	94.2	83.6	79.1	78.4	72.0
WY.....	93.3	72.9	92.1	88.5	92.1	79.9	62.5	91.5	88.8	90.6	80.5	52.9	72.5	66.2

[1] Includes children who might have received diphtheria and tetanus toxoids vaccine or diphtheria, tetanus toxoids, and pertussis vaccine. [2] Includes children who might have received measles, mumps, rubella, and varicella combination vaccine. [3] Hib primary series: receipt of ≥2 or ≥3 doses, depending on product type received. Full series: primary series and booster dose, which includes receipt of ≥3 or ≥4 doses, depending on product type received. [4] HepB administered from birth through age 3 days. [5] ≥2 doses of Hepatitis A vaccine administered by age 35 months. [6] ≥2 or ≥3 doses of Rotavirus vaccine, depending on product type received, administered through age 8 months. [7] The combined 7 vaccine series (4:3:1:3*:3:1:4) includes ≥4 doses of DTaP, ≥3 doses of poliovirus vaccine, ≥1 dose of measles-containing vaccine, full series of Hib vaccine (≥3 or ≥4 doses, depending on product type), ≥3 doses of HepB, ≥1 dose of varicella vaccine, and ≥4 doses of PCV.

Source: U.S. Centers for Disease Control and Prevention, Immunization Managers, *Morbidity and Mortality Weekly Report*, 68:41, October 18, 2019, "Vaccination Coverage by Age 24 Months Among Children Born in 2015 and 2016 — National Immunization Survey-Child, United States, 2016–2018"; and "ChildVaxView Interactive!," <https://www.cdc.gov/vaccines/imz-managers/coverage/childvaxview/index.html>, accessed April 2020.

Table 241. Child Immunization by Vaccine, Race/Ethnicity, Poverty Status, and Health Insurance Coverage: 2016 to 2018

[In percent. Data are from 2016-2018 surveys covering civilian noninstitutionalized children born in 2015 and 2016 who received the recommended doses of each vaccine by age 24 months, except as noted. Based on estimates from the National Immunization Survey (NIS), which includes a survey of the parents or guardians of children age 19-35 months, and a survey of health care providers of the children to verify and/or complete vaccination information. See headnote, Table 240. Abbreviations: DTaP = diphtheria and tetanus toxoids, and pertussis vaccine; MMR = measles, mumps, and rubella vaccine; HepB = hepatitis B vaccine; HepA = hepatitis A vaccine; Hib = Haemophilus influenzae type b vaccine; PCV = pneumococcal conjugate vaccine]

Vaccination	Total [1]	Race/ethnicity [2]				Poverty [3]		Health insurance		
		White	Black	His-panic	Asian	At or above poverty	Below poverty	Private only	Any Med-icaid	Unin-sured
DTaP, ≥3 doses [4]	93.8	94.3	92.7	93.5	95.5	95.2	90.5	96.9	91.8	80.6
DTaP, ≥4 doses [4]	80.3	81.6	75.0	79.7	86.0	83.6	72.5	87.1	75.8	59.8
Poliovirus, ≥3 doses	92.7	93.3	91.9	92.2	95.7	94.0	89.5	96.1	90.7	79.3
MMR, ≥1 dose [5]	90.4	89.5	89.4	91.4	94.7	91.4	87.5	93.7	88.6	73.2
Hib, Primary series [6]	92.7	93.3	92.0	92.4	92.8	94.2	89.3	95.7	90.7	78.4
Hib, Full series [6]	79.6	80.8	74.9	78.8	85.4	82.7	72.7	85.5	75.9	58.1
HepB, birth dose [7]	75.0	72.1	75.9	78.2	78.0	74.4	76.9	75.6	76.1	67.8
HepB, ≥ 3 doses	91.0	91.1	89.6	91.4	92.3	91.9	89.8	93.0	90.0	78.6
Varicella (chickenpox), ≥1 dose [5]	90.0	89.0	88.9	91.6	93.7	90.8	87.7	93.2	88.6	70.3
PCV, ≥3 doses	92.0	92.6	91.3	91.6	91.0	93.4	88.8	94.9	90.3	77.2
PCV, ≥4 doses	81.0	82.9	76.5	80.4	80.4	84.2	73.6	87.3	76.8	62.5
HepA, ≥1 dose	84.7	82.9	83.1	87.7	91.2	85.9	82.4	87.5	83.7	65.5
HepA, ≥2 doses by age 35 months...	76.6	75.6	73.6	78.8	86.1	77.0	75.8	80.5	75.2	48.2
Rotavirus [8]	73.6	77.9	64.9	71.1	70.5	78.3	62.7	83.5	65.9	59.8
Influenza, ≥ 2 doses	56.6	59.0	43.8	55.0	74.5	61.6	45.8	68.5	48.2	34.7
Combined series [9]	68.5	69.6	63.5	68.0	72.3	71.9	60.8	75.4	64.3	46.7
No vaccinations	1.3	1.6	(NA)	0.8	(NA)	1.3	1.1	0.8	1.2	7.4

NA Not available. [1] Includes other racial/ethnic and health insurance coverage categories not shown separately. [2] Children identified as White, Black, and Asian are Non-Hispanic. Children of Hispanic origin may be of any race. [3] Poverty level based on 2014 and 2015 U.S. Census Bureau poverty thresholds. [4] Includes diphtheria and tetanus toxoids vaccine; or diphtheria, tetanus toxoids, and pertussis vaccine. [5] May include measles, mumps, rubella, and varicella vaccine. [6] Hib primary series: receipt of ≥2 or ≥3 doses, depending on product type. Full series: primary series and booster dose, which includes receipt of ≥3 or ≥4 doses, depending on product type. [7] One dose given from birth through age 3 days. [8] Includes ≥2 doses of Rotarix monovalent rotavirus vaccine, or ≥3 doses of RotaTeq pentavalent rotavirus vaccine (RV5). Maximum age for the final dose is 8 months. [9] The combined 7 vaccine series (4:3:1:3*:3:1:4) includes ≥4 doses of DTaP, ≥3 doses of poliovirus vaccine, ≥1 dose of measles-containing vaccine, Hib full series vaccine (≥3 or ≥4 doses, depending on product type), ≥3 doses of HepB, ≥1 dose of varicella vaccine, and ≥4 doses of PCV.

Source: U.S. Centers for Disease Control and Prevention, Immunization Managers, Hill, Holly A. et al, "Vaccination Coverage by Age 24 Months Among Children Born in 2015 and 2016 — National Immunization Survey-Child, United States, 2016–2018," *Morbidity and Mortality Weekly Report*, 68:41, October 18, 2019, <https://www.cdc.gov/vaccines/imz-managers/coverage/childvaxview/pubs-presentations.html>.

Table 242. Asthma Incidence Among Children Under Age 18 by Selected Characteristics: 2018

[In thousands (73,452 represents 73,452,000), except percent. Based on the National Health Interview Survey, a sample survey of the civilian noninstitutionalized population; see Appendix III. Survey responses cover the sample child selected for the survey, not all children in the family]

Characteristic	Total (1,000)	Ever told had asthma		Still have asthma	
		Number (1,000) [1]	Percent [2]	Number (1,000) [1]	Percent [2]
Total [3]	**73,452**	**8,535**	**11.6**	**5,530**	**7.5**
SEX					
Male	37,489	4,880	13.1	3,122	8.4
Female	35,963	3,655	10.0	2,408	6.6
AGE [4]					
4 years and under	19,678	963	4.9	744	3.8
5 to 11 years	29,220	3,470	11.9	2,350	8.1
12 to 17 years	24,554	4,102	16.7	2,436	9.9
RACE					
Single race [5]	69,541	7,845	11.3	5,013	7.2
White	53,462	5,377	10.1	3,245	6.1
Black or African American	10,618	1,910	18.0	1,491	14.0
American Indian or Alaska Native	1,085	196	17.8	(B)	(B)
Asian	4,148	344	8.2	162	3.9
Native Hawaiian or Other Pacific Islander	228	(B)	(B)	(B)	(B)
Two or more races [6]	3,912	690	18.2	517	13.6
HISPANIC ORIGIN AND RACE [7]					
Hispanic or Latino	18,717	2,321	12.5	1,493	8.0
Not Hispanic or Latino	54,736	6,214	11.3	4,037	7.4
White, single race	37,234	3,526	9.4	2,077	5.6
Black or African American, single race	9,692	1,758	18.0	1,383	14.2

B Estimate is considered unreliable. [1] Unknowns for the columns are not included in the frequencies, but they are included in the "Total" column. [2] Unknowns for the column variables are not included in the denominators when calculating percentages. Percents are age-adjusted to the projected 2000 U.S. standard population using the age groups shown. [3] Includes other races, not shown separately. [4] Estimates for the age groups are not age-adjusted. [5] Refers to persons who indicated only a single race group, including those of Hispanic or Latino origin. [6] Refers to all persons who indicated more than one race group, including those of Hispanic or Latino origin. [7] Persons of Hispanic or Latino origin may be of any race or combination of races.

Source: U.S. National Center for Health Statistics, 2018 National Health Interview Survey, "Tables of Summary Health Statistics," <https://www.cdc.gov/nchs/nhis/shs.htm>, accessed December 2019.

Table 243. Child Obesity by Age, Sex, and Race/Ethnicity: 1976 to 2016

[In percent. For children age 6 to 17. Data are from U.S. National Center for Health Statistics, National Health and Nutrition Examination Surveys, a program of studies that combines interviews and physical examinations to assess the health and nutritional status of adults and children. Children classified as obese have a body mass index (BMI) at or above the 95th percentile]

Selected characteristic	1976 to 1980	1988 to 1994	1999 to 2002	2003 to 2006	2009 to 2012	2013 to 2016
Total [1]	**5.7**	**11.2**	**16.0**	**17.3**	**19.5**	**19.3**
RACE AND HISPANIC ORIGIN						
White, non-Hispanic	4.9	10.5	13.2	15.5	17.0	15.5
Black, non-Hispanic	8.2	14.0	20.7	21.5	22.7	23.5
Asian, non-Hispanic	(NA)	(NA)	(NA)	(NA)	9.7	11.0
Hispanic origin [2, 3]	(NA)	(NA)	(NA)	(NA)	25.1	25.5
Mexican-American [2, 3]	(NA)	15.4	23.0	22.7	26.6	26.4
SEX AND AGE						
Male	5.5	11.8	17.2	18.1	18.4	19.8
Female	5.8	10.6	14.7	16.3	20.6	18.8
Ages 6 to 11	6.5	11.3	15.8	17.0	17.7	17.9
Male	6.7	11.6	16.9	18.0	16.4	19.6
Female	6.4	11.0	14.7	15.8	19.1	16.1
Ages 12 to 17	4.9	11.1	16.1	17.5	21.1	20.7
Male	4.5	12.0	17.5	18.2	20.3	20.0
Female	5.4	10.2	14.7	16.8	21.9	21.4

NA Not available. [1] Includes other races not shown separately. [2] Persons of Hispanic and Mexican origin may be of any race. [3] From 1976 to 2006, the survey sample was designed to provide estimates specifically for persons of Mexican origin. Beginning in 2007, the survey allows for reporting of both total Hispanics and Mexican Americans.

Source: Federal Interagency Forum on Child and Family Statistics, "America's Children: Key National Indicators of Well-Being, 2018," <http://www.childstats.gov/index.asp>, accessed December 2018.

Table 244. High School Students Engaged in Physical Activity by Sex: 2019

[In percent. For students in grades 9 to 12. Based on the Youth Risk Behavior Survey, a biennial survey of students in grades 9-12 conducted in public and private schools, and subject to sampling error; see source for details]

Characteristic	No physical activity for 60+ min. on any day [1]	Physically active for 60+ min. on 5 of last 7 days [2]	Physically active for 60+ min. on all 7 days [2]	Played on at least one sports team [3]	Attended physical education class [4] Total	Attended daily	Used computers 3 or more hours/ day [5]	Watched TV 3 or more hours/ day [6]
All students	**17.0**	**44.1**	**23.2**	**57.4**	**52.2**	**25.9**	**46.1**	**19.8**
Male	**14.4**	**52.8**	**30.9**	**60.2**	**55.4**	**28.9**	**47.5**	**18.7**
Grade 9	12.6	55.8	34.7	62.3	69.7	36.5	48.5	18.8
Grade 10	14.4	53.9	30.4	61.2	55.8	30.3	48.6	19.5
Grade 11	14.3	50.6	29.5	62.6	48.6	24.4	45.2	17.6
Grade 12	16.3	50.5	28.7	54.3	46.0	23.7	47.7	18.7
Female	**19.6**	**35.3**	**15.4**	**54.6**	**48.6**	**22.8**	**44.6**	**20.8**
Grade 9	14.5	42.0	19.2	61.5	68.0	32.8	44.3	21.3
Grade 10	17.2	37.2	15.4	54.8	48.4	22.5	45.1	22.6
Grade 11	23.7	31.7	15.0	55.5	40.6	19.7	45.5	19.2
Grade 12	23.0	29.7	11.7	45.6	36.7	15.6	43.1	19.7

[1] Did not participate in 60 or more minutes in any physical activity that increased their heart rate and made them breathe hard some of the time for at least 1 day during the 7 days before the survey. [2] Did any kind of physical activity that increased their heart rate and made them breathe hard some of the time, during the 7 days before the survey. [3] Any team run by the school or community groups, during the 12 months before the survey. [4] In an average week when student was in school. [5] Includes time spent playing games, watching videos, texting, or using social media on their smartphone, computer, Xbox, PlayStation, iPad, or other device, for something unrelated to school, on an average school day. [6] On an average school day.

Source: U.S. Centers for Disease Control and Prevention, Youth Risk Behavior Surveillance System (YRBSS), "YRBS Explorer," <https://www.cdc.gov/healthyyouth/data/yrbs/index.htm>, accessed August 2020.

Table 245. High School Student Use of Tobacco and Nicotine Products by Sex and Race/Ethnicity: 2019

[In percent, except as noted (4,690 represents 4,690,000). Data represent current use of tobacco and nicotine products, defined as use within the past 30 days. Data are based on the National Youth Tobacco Survey, administered to students in middle school (grades 6-8) and high school (grades 9-12). Only high school data are shown here]

Tobacco and nicotine products	Total Number (1,000) [1]	Percent	Sex Male	Female	White, non-Hispanic	Black, non-Hispanic	Other race, non-Hispanic	Hispanic [2]
Use of any tobacco product [3]	**4,690**	**31.2**	**31.8**	**30.6**	**35.6**	**25.4**	**20.7**	**26.6**
Electronic cigarettes (vaping) [4]	4,110	27.5	27.6	27.4	32.4	17.7	18.6	23.2
Cigarettes	860	5.8	7.3	4.1	7.1	(B)	(B)	3.8
Cigars	1,140	7.6	9.0	6.2	7.6	12.3	(B)	6.2
Smokeless tobacco [5]	720	4.8	7.5	1.8	6.5	(B)	(B)	2.6
Hookah [6]	500	3.4	3.6	3.2	2.5	6.4	(B)	4.0
Pipe tobacco	160	1.1	1.5	(B)	1.3	(B)	(B)	(B)
Two or more tobacco products	1,620	10.8	13.4	8.0	12.0	11.5	(B)	8.5

B Statistically unreliable. Sample size less than 50 or relative standard error greater than 0.3. [1] Estimates are rounded down to nearest 10,000. [2] Persons of Hispanic origin may be of any race. [3] Includes use of bidis (small imported cigarettes wrapped in a leaf), not shown separately. [4] Electronic cigarettes (e-cigarettes) are battery-powered devices that vaporize a nicotine-based liquid for the user to inhale. [5] Includes chewing tobacco, snuff, dip, snus, and dissolvable tobacco. [6] Water pipes used to smoke tobacco, which is often flavored.

Source: U.S. Centers for Disease Control and Prevention, Wang, Teresa W. et al., "Tobacco Product Use and Associated Factors Among Middle and High School Students—United States, 2019, *Morbidity and Mortality Weekly Report,* Surveillance Summaries, 68:SS-12, December 6, 2019. See also <https://www.cdc.gov/tobacco/data_statistics/by_topic/youth_data/index.htm>.

Table 246. Depression and Receipt of Mental Health Treatment in the Past Year Among Youth Age 12 to 17 by Selected Characteristics: 2005 to 2018

[In percent. Data are from the National Survey on Drug Use and Health. Covers youth age 12 to 17 who had a major depressive episode (MDE) as defined in the 5th edition of the *Diagnostic and Statistical Manual of Mental Disorders* (DSM-5), which specifies a period of at least 2 weeks when a person experienced a depressed mood or loss of interest or pleasure in daily activities and had a majority of specified depression symptoms. Treatment is defined as seeing or talking to a medical doctor or other professional, or using prescription medication in the past year for depression. Respondents with unknown incidence of major depressive episode and unknown treatment data were excluded]

Characteristic	Youth with major depressive episode (MDE)				Youth with an MDE receiving treatment for depression			
	2005	2010	2017	2018	2005	2010	2017	2018
Total [1]	**8.8**	**8.0**	**13.3**	**14.4**	**37.8**	**37.8**	**41.5**	**41.4**
AGE								
12 to 13 years old	5.2	4.3	6.9	8.4	32.9	32.5	37.6	40.7
14 to 15 years old	9.5	9.0	14.5	15.3	41.1	38.4	37.9	41.2
16 to 17 years old	11.5	10.6	17.7	19.0	37.1	39.3	45.8	41.8
SEX								
Male	4.5	4.4	6.8	7.7	34.1	32.0	32.5	37.5
Female	13.3	11.9	20.0	21.5	39.0	40.1	44.8	42.9
RACE ETHNICITY								
White, non-Hispanic	9.1	8.6	14.0	15.1	39.3	41.1	47.5	46.1
Black, non-Hispanic	7.6	6.8	9.5	10.3	39.3	23.0	35.1	34.6
American Indian or Alaska Native	6.1	7.4	16.3	15.2	(NA)	(NA)	(NA)	(NA)
Asian	6.0	5.5	11.3	13.6	(NA)	(NA)	(NA)	(NA)
Two or more races	10.5	9.4	16.9	17.7	(NA)	(NA)	(NA)	(NA)
Hispanic [2]	9.1	7.8	13.8	15.1	31.8	38.4	32.7	37.9
POVERTY STATUS [3]								
Below 100% poverty	8.1	7.2	11.8	12.6	37.3	33.8	37.1	41.8
100-199% poverty	9.6	9.0	14.2	14.7	32.1	39.1	40.2	37.6
200% poverty and above	8.7	7.9	13.5	15.0	40.1	38.4	43.5	42.6

NA Not available. [1] Total includes persons of other races, not shown separately. [2] Persons of Hispanic origin may be of any race. [3] Estimates are based on a definition of poverty level that incorporates information on family income, size, and composition and is calculated as a percentage of the U.S. Census Bureau's poverty thresholds.

Source: Substance Abuse and Mental Health Services Administration, *Results From the 2018 National Survey on Drug Use and Health: Detailed Tables,* August 2019; see also <https://www.samhsa.gov/data/data-we-collect/nsduh-national-survey-drug-use-and-health>. Prior to 2016, Federal Interagency Forum on Child and Family Statistics, "America's Children: Key National Indicators of Well-Being, 2017," <http://www.childstats.gov/>, accessed July 2017, and previous editions.

Table 247. Foodborne Disease Outbreaks and Illnesses by Etiology, Food Category, and Location of Food Preparation: 2017

[Data reported as of February 6, 2019. Foodborne disease outbreaks are a nationally notifiable condition. An outbreak involves 2 or more cases of a similar illness resulting from consuming a common food. Public health agencies in all 50 States, D.C., and the U.S. territories voluntarily submit reports of foodborne disease outbreaks that their agencies investigate. Excludes outbreaks on cruise ships that dock in U.S. and international ports and those in which food was eaten outside the U.S. Not all outbreaks are identified, investigated, or reported. Data are subject to change. See source for other limitations]

Item	Out-breaks	Ill-nesses	Hospital-izations	Item	Out-breaks	Ill-nesses
Total [2]	**841**	**14,481**	**827**	**By food category:**		
By etiology (cause): [1]				Aquatic animals	86	468
Bacterial [2]	271	5,380	670	Land animals [2]	83	1,996
Salmonella	122	3,061	478	Dairy	14	85
Clostridium perfringens	41	843	1	Eggs	5	81
Campylobacter	23	147	14	Beef	19	329
Escherichia coli (E. coli) [3]	21	521	113	Pork	13	376
Vibrio parahaemolyticus	17	70	4	Chicken	23	487
Staphylococcus aureus	12	128	0	Turkey	4	609
Bacillus cereus	11	341	2	Plant products	45	1,339
Chemical and toxin [4]	40	156	6	Other [5]	627	10,921
Parasitic	13	155	5	**By location of food preparation:**		
Cyclospora	7	99	4	Restaurant	489	5,533
Cryptosporidium	3	35	1	Catering or banquet facility	104	3,584
Viral [2]	325	6,393	67	Private home	74	989
Norovirus	316	6,340	53	Institutional location	24	1,015
Hepatitis A	5	35	14	Grocery store	13	105
Other [5]	192	2,397	79	Hospital or nursing home	11	239

[1] Includes both confirmed and suspected etiologies. [2] Includes other categories not shown separately. [3] E. coli that produce shiga toxins, known as Shiga toxin-producing E. coli (STEC). These bacteria are also called verocytotoxic-producing E. coli and enterohemorrhagic E. coli. [4] Includes cases involving scombroid toxin/histamine, ciguatoxin, mycotoxins, paralytic and neurotoxic shellfish poison, and other not specified. [5] Other includes incidents that involved multiple categories and unknown or not reported categories.

Source: U.S. Centers for Disease Control and Prevention, *Surveillance for Foodborne Disease Outbreaks, United States, 2017: Annual Report,* 2019. See also <https://www.cdc.gov/fdoss/index.html>.

Table 248. Fruit and Vegetable Availability for Consumption Per Capita by Commodity: 1980 to 2017

[In pounds, farm weight. Available supply of fresh fruits and vegetables at the farm level or early stage of processing for domestic consumption after subtracting measurable uses, such as farm inputs (feed and seed), exports, ending stocks, and industrial uses. Food availability is a proxy for actual food consumption. Based on Census Bureau estimated resident population plus Armed Forces overseas for most commodities]

Commodity	1980	1990	2000	2005	2010	2014	2015	2016	2017
Fruits and vegetables, total [1]	**604.8**	**662.7**	**713.0**	**685.2**	**652.8**	**636.6**	**631.9**	**651.7**	**654.7**
Fruits, total	**266.1**	**271.0**	**288.1**	**270.8**	**256.0**	**250.1**	**252.7**	**256.4**	**252.4**
Fresh fruits	106.4	117.3	128.7	125.3	128.6	136.3	136.1	142.3	142.7
Noncitrus [2]	80.5	95.6	105.3	103.7	107.0	113.1	113.4	118.3	118.9
Apples	19.4	19.8	17.6	16.8	15.4	18.8	17.5	19.1	17.8
Avocados	2.1	1.4	2.2	3.5	4.0	7.0	7.2	6.9	7.5
Bananas	20.8	24.3	28.4	25.2	25.6	28.0	28.0	27.6	28.7
Blueberries	0.2	0.1	0.3	0.4	1.1	1.5	1.6	1.8	1.7
Cantaloupes	5.8	9.2	11.1	9.6	8.5	6.6	6.8	7.5	6.9
Cherries	0.7	0.4	0.6	0.9	1.3	1.2	1.1	1.2	1.5
Grapes	4.0	7.9	7.5	8.7	8.0	7.7	7.9	8.1	8.3
Honeydew melons	1.4	2.1	2.3	1.9	1.7	1.7	1.7	1.9	1.7
Mangoes	0.2	0.5	1.8	1.9	2.2	2.5	2.6	3.0	3.2
Papayas	0.2	0.2	0.7	0.9	1.2	1.1	1.3	1.4	1.4
Peaches and nectarines	7.1	5.5	5.3	4.8	4.7	3.3	3.0	2.9	2.7
Pears	2.6	3.3	3.4	2.9	2.9	2.9	2.7	2.8	2.7
Pineapples	1.5	2.0	3.2	4.9	5.7	7.2	7.0	7.3	7.8
Plums	1.5	1.5	1.2	1.1	0.8	0.6	0.6	0.8	0.8
Strawberries	2.0	3.2	4.9	5.8	7.2	8.0	7.7	8.1	8.4
Watermelons	10.7	13.3	13.8	13.5	15.7	13.9	14.9	16.5	16.1
Fresh citrus	25.9	21.7	23.4	21.6	21.6	23.3	22.7	24.0	23.8
Oranges and temples	14.2	12.6	11.6	11.4	9.7	9.4	8.7	9.2	8.0
Tangerines and tangelos	2.1	1.3	2.9	2.5	3.8	5.0	5.2	5.3	5.8
Grapefruit	7.3	4.6	5.1	2.6	2.8	2.4	2.2	2.0	1.9
Lemons	1.9	2.6	2.4	2.9	2.8	3.4	3.6	4.1	4.3
Limes	0.4	0.7	1.4	2.1	2.6	3.1	3.0	3.5	3.7
Processed fruit	159.7	153.6	159.4	145.5	127.4	113.8	116.6	114.1	109.7
Canned fruit [3]	24.6	21.1	17.6	16.7	15.0	13.7	14.4	13.7	13.5
Fruit juice [4]	119.7	115.8	126.5	112.9	97.2	84.1	85.4	84.6	80.9
Frozen fruit [5]	3.3	4.3	4.5	5.2	5.1	5.6	5.6	5.0	4.8
Dried fruit [6]	11.3	12.2	10.5	10.1	9.4	9.6	10.4	9.9	9.5
Vegetables, total	**338.7**	**391.8**	**424.9**	**414.4**	**396.8**	**386.5**	**379.2**	**395.3**	**402.3**
Fresh vegetables [7]	151.8	176.4	200.7	196.4	190.3	186.4	186.4	199.5	202.6
Asparagus	0.3	0.6	1.0	1.1	1.4	1.7	1.5	1.6	1.6
Bell peppers (all uses)	2.9	5.9	8.2	9.2	10.3	10.7	10.7	11.1	11.3
Broccoli	1.4	3.4	5.9	5.3	6.0	6.6	7.4	7.5	7.1
Cabbage	8.0	8.3	8.9	7.8	7.5	6.7	6.3	5.9	6.2
Carrots	6.2	8.3	9.2	8.7	7.8	8.5	8.8	7.8	7.4
Cauliflower	1.1	2.2	1.7	1.8	1.3	1.3	1.6	1.7	2.4
Celery (all uses)	7.4	7.2	6.3	5.9	6.1	5.5	5.1	5.0	4.7
Corn, sweet	6.5	6.7	9.0	8.7	9.2	7.6	8.6	7.1	7.2
Cucumbers	3.9	4.7	6.4	6.2	6.7	7.4	7.6	8.1	7.4
Garlic (all uses)	0.9	1.4	2.2	2.4	2.3	2.2	2.4	3.0	3.0
Kale	(NA)	(NA)	0.4	0.4	0.5	0.5	0.6	0.5	1.0
Lettuce, head	25.6	27.7	23.5	20.9	15.9	14.5	13.6	16.7	15.2
Lettuce, Romaine and leaf	(NA)	3.8	8.4	9.7	12.0	10.8	11.9	14.5	15.1
Mushrooms	1.2	2.0	2.6	2.6	2.6	2.9	3.0	3.0	3.0
Onions	11.4	15.1	18.9	20.9	19.6	18.4	18.3	22.7	25.1
Potatoes	51.1	46.7	47.1	41.3	36.8	33.6	34.1	33.6	34.4
Pumpkin (all uses)	(NA)	4.4	4.6	4.8	4.4	5.3	3.1	7.0	6.4
Snap beans	1.3	1.1	2.0	1.8	1.9	1.5	1.6	1.7	1.6
Spinach	0.4	0.8	1.4	2.3	1.7	1.7	1.7	2.0	1.9
Squash (all uses)	2.3	3.5	4.4	4.4	4.3	4.6	4.6	5.7	5.7
Sweet potatoes (all uses)	4.4	4.4	4.2	4.5	6.3	7.5	7.6	7.2	8.0
Tomatoes	12.8	15.5	19.0	20.2	20.6	20.6	20.6	20.3	20.5
Processed vegetables	187.0	215.3	224.2	218.0	206.5	200.1	192.9	195.8	199.7
Canned vegetables [8]	102.5	110.3	103.2	104.8	99.5	93.4	81.9	87.4	84.8
Frozen vegetables [9]	51.6	66.7	79.7	76.4	71.0	66.9	70.1	67.5	72.8
Dehydrated vegetables [10]	10.5	14.9	17.3	13.9	12.6	13.5	12.9	13.5	13.1
Chips, potato	16.5	16.3	15.6	16.0	15.0	20.0	19.6	16.6	17.8
Legumes [11]	5.9	7.2	8.5	6.8	8.4	6.4	8.3	10.8	11.2

NA Not available. [1] Excludes wine grapes. [2] Includes other fruits not shown separately. [3] Canned fruit include apples, apricots, cherries, olives, peaches, pears, pineapples, plums, and prunes. [4] Fruit juice includes apple, cranberry, grape, grapefruit, lemon, lime, orange, pineapple, and prune juice. [5] Frozen fruit include apples, apricots, blackberries, blueberries, boysenberries, cherries, loganberries, peaches, plums, prunes, raspberries, strawberries, and other miscellaneous fruit and berries. [6] Dried fruit include apples, apricots, dates, figs, peaches, pears, prunes, and raisins. [7] Includes other vegetables not shown separately. [8] Canned vegetables include asparagus, lima beans, snap beans, beets, cabbage, carrots, sweet corn, cucumbers, mushrooms, green peas, chile peppers, potatoes, spinach, tomatoes, and other miscellaneous vegetables. [9] Frozen vegetables include asparagus, lima beans, snap beans, broccoli, carrots, cauliflower, sweet corn, green peas, potatoes, spinach and other miscellaneous vegetables. [10] Onions and potatoes. [11] Dry peas, beans, and lentils.

Source: U.S. Department of Agriculture, Economic Research Service, "Food Availability (Per Capita) Data System," <https://www.ers.usda.gov/data-products/food-availability-per-capita-data-system/>, accessed February 2020.

Table 249. Food Availability for Consumption Per Capita by Major Food Commodity: 1980 to 2017

[In pounds, retail weight, except as indicated. Available supply for domestic consumption after subtracting measurable uses, such as farm inputs (feed and seed), exports, ending stocks, and industrial uses. Food availability is a proxy for actual food consumption. Based on Census Bureau estimated resident population plus Armed Forces overseas for most commodities. For commodities not shipped overseas in substantial amounts, such as fluid milk and cream, the resident population is used]

Commodity	Unit	1980	1990	2000	2005	2010	2016	2017
Red meat, total (boneless, trimmed weight) [1]	Pounds	126.4	112.2	113.7	110.2	102.0	100.5	102.0
Beef	Pounds	72.1	63.9	64.5	62.5	56.7	52.9	54.3
Veal	Pounds	1.3	0.9	0.5	0.4	0.3	0.2	0.2
Pork	Pounds	52.1	46.4	47.8	46.5	44.4	46.6	46.7
Lamb	Pounds	1.0	1.0	0.8	0.8	0.7	0.8	0.8
Poultry (boneless, trimmed weight)	Pounds	40.8	56.3	67.9	73.7	70.9	76.3	77.0
Chicken	Pounds	32.7	42.5	54.2	60.5	58.0	63.2	64.1
Turkey	Pounds	8.1	13.8	13.7	13.2	12.9	13.1	13.0
Fish and shellfish (boneless, trimmed weight)	Pounds	12.4	14.9	15.2	16.2	15.8	14.9	16.1
Eggs	Number	271.1	234.1	250.2	254.5	246.0	271.8	276.8
Shell	Number	236.2	186.2	178.0	176.9	172.1	189.4	198.1
Processed	Number	34.9	47.9	72.2	77.6	73.9	82.4	78.7
Dairy products, total [2]	Pounds	528.7	551.3	593.3	614.4	588.7	637.1	629.3
Fluid milk products [3]	Gallons	27.9	26.1	23.6	22.6	22.1	19.4	18.9
Beverage milks	Gallons	27.6	25.7	22.8	21.5	20.6	17.8	17.3
Plain whole milk	Gallons	16.5	10.2	7.8	6.8	5.5	5.6	5.7
Plain reduced-fat milk (2%)	Gallons	6.3	9.1	7.2	7.0	7.2	6.0	5.8
Plain reduced-fat milk (1%)	Gallons	1.8	2.3	2.6	2.5	2.8	2.6	2.5
Plain skim milk	Gallons	1.3	2.6	3.4	3.2	3.2	1.8	1.6
Flavored whole milk	Gallons	0.6	0.3	0.4	0.3	0.2	0.2	0.2
Flavored milk, low-fat and skim	Gallons	0.6	0.8	1.1	1.4	1.5	1.4	1.4
Buttermilk	Gallons	0.5	0.4	0.3	0.2	0.2	0.2	0.2
Yogurt (excl. frozen)	1/2 pints	4.6	7.2	12.0	19.1	24.9	25.4	25.4
Fluid cream products [4]	1/2 pints	10.5	14.3	13.6	7.5	8.3	8.8	8.9
Cream [5]	1/2 pints	6.3	8.7	6.7	(NA)	(NA)	(NA)	(NA)
Sour cream	1/2 pints	3.4	4.7	6.1	6.6	7.5	8.0	8.0
Condensed and evaporated milks	Pounds	7.0	7.9	5.8	6.1	7.2	7.6	7.1
Whole milk	Pounds	3.8	3.1	2.0	2.4	2.0	2.2	1.9
Skim milk	Pounds	3.3	4.8	3.8	3.7	5.2	5.4	5.1
Butter (product weight)	Pounds	4.5	4.3	4.5	4.5	4.9	5.7	5.7
Cheese [6]	Pounds	17.5	24.6	29.5	31.3	32.7	36.4	37.0
American [7]	Pounds	9.6	11.1	12.7	12.6	13.3	14.4	15.1
Cheddar	Pounds	6.8	9.1	9.9	10.2	10.1	10.4	11.1
Italian [7]	Pounds	4.4	8.9	11.4	12.7	13.5	15.2	15.1
Mozzarella	Pounds	3.0	6.9	9.1	9.9	10.6	11.7	11.6
Other [7]	Pounds	3.5	4.6	5.4	6.0	5.9	6.8	6.8
Swiss	Pounds	1.3	1.3	1.0	1.2	1.2	1.1	1.0
Cream and Neufchatel	Pounds	1.0	1.7	2.4	2.4	2.3	2.6	2.6
Cottage cheese, total	Pounds	4.4	3.3	2.6	2.6	2.3	2.2	2.1
Low-fat	Pounds	0.8	1.2	1.3	1.4	1.3	1.1	1.1
Frozen dairy products [8]	Pounds	26.0	28.4	27.5	25.2	23.9	22.9	23.1
Ice cream	Pounds	17.1	15.4	16.1	15.1	14.0	12.9	12.8
Low-fat ice cream	Pounds	6.1	6.6	6.6	6.0	6.5	6.4	6.7
Sherbet	Pounds	1.2	1.2	1.1	1.1	1.0	0.8	0.8
Frozen yogurt	Pounds	(NA)	2.8	2.0	1.3	1.0	1.2	1.2
Flour and cereal products [9]	Pounds	146.4	181.1	199.5	190.9	194.2	171.9	173.2
Wheat flour	Pounds	116.9	135.6	146.3	134.4	134.8	131.7	131.8
Rice, milled	Pounds	11.0	16.2	19.2	19.4	20.4	(NA)	(NA)
Corn products	Pounds	12.9	21.4	28.4	31.4	33.1	34.2	35.2
Oat products	Pounds	3.9	6.5	4.4	4.6	4.7	4.6	4.8
Caloric sweeteners, total [10]	Pounds	120.2	132.3	148.9	142.0	131.6	128.1	127.3
Sugar, refined cane and beet	Pounds	83.6	64.4	65.5	63.0	65.9	69.7	69.3
Corn sweeteners [11]	Pounds	35.3	66.8	81.6	77.3	63.9	56.5	55.9
High-fructose corn syrup	Pounds	19.0	49.6	62.5	58.8	48.3	41.4	39.8
Honey	Pounds	0.8	0.7	1.1	1.1	1.0	1.3	1.4
Other:								
Cocoa, bean equivalent	Pounds	3.4	5.4	5.9	6.5	5.5	(NA)	(NA)
Coffee, green bean equivalent	Pounds	10.3	10.3	10.3	9.5	9.2	(NA)	(NA)
Tea, dry leaf equivalent	Pounds	0.8	0.7	0.8	0.8	1.0	(NA)	(NA)
Peanuts, total	Pounds	5.1	6.1	5.9	6.7	7.0	7.2	7.4
Tree nuts, total	Pounds	1.8	2.5	2.6	2.7	3.9	4.9	5.0

NA Not available. [1] Excludes edible offal. [2] Milk-equivalent. Includes fluid milk and cream, butter, cheese, frozen and dry dairy products, and evaporated and condensed milk. [3] Fluid milk figures are aggregates of commercial sales and milk produced and consumed on farms. [4] Includes eggnog, not shown separately. [5] Heavy cream, light cream, and half-and-half. [6] Natural equivalent of cheese and cheese products. Excludes full-skim American, cottage, pot, and baker's cheese. [7] Includes other cheeses, not shown separately. [8] Includes mellorine until 1995, and other nonstandardized frozen dairy products. [9] Includes rye flour and barley products, not shown separately. Excludes wheat not ground into flour. [10] Dry weight. Includes edible syrups (maple, molasses, etc.), not shown separately. [11] Includes glucose and dextrose, not shown separately.

Source: U.S. Department of Agriculture, Economic Research Service, "Food Availability (Per Capita) Data System," <https://www.ers.usda.gov/data-products/food-availability-per-capita-data-system/>, accessed February 2020.

Table 250. Nutrient Consumption From Food and Beverages by Sex, Age, and Race and Hispanic Origin: 2017 to 2018

[In units as indicated. Covers population age 2 years and older. Data are mean amounts per person estimated from Day 1 dietary recall interviews conducted in the What We Eat in America, National Health and Nutrition Examination Survey (NHANES), 2017-2018. Data are based on consumption of food and beverages, including water, and exclude intake from dietary supplements and medications. What We Eat in America is a joint project of the USDA and the U.S. Department of Health and Human Services]

Nutrient	Unit	Total	Male	Female	Age 2 to 19	Age 20 and over	White, non-Hispanic	Black, non-Hispanic	Asian, non-Hispanic	Hispanic
Total energy intake......	kcal [1]	**2,093**	**2,378**	**1,821**	**1,894**	**2,155**	**2,110**	**2,061**	**1,922**	**2,071**
Protein.....................	g	78.3	90.1	67.0	66.8	81.9	78.8	72.9	78.5	79.5
Carbohydrate..............	g	247	277	219	243	248	244	245	241	254
Sugars, total............	g	108	119	97	110	107	108	111	87	106
Dietary fiber..............	g	16.2	17.5	15.0	14.1	16.9	15.7	13.8	19.5	18.4
Fats, total................	g	85.0	96.2	74.3	74.9	88.2	87.6	84.2	71.6	80.0
Saturated fat............	g	28.0	31.8	24.4	25.8	28.7	29.2	26.7	22.5	26.1
Monounsaturated fat....	g	28.8	32.8	25.1	24.6	30.2	29.7	28.8	24.9	26.9
Polyunsaturated fat......	g	19.9	22.3	17.6	17.1	20.8	20.2	20.8	17.0	18.9
Cholesterol................	mg	287	331	246	225	307	285	285	269	302
Vitamin A, RAE [2]..........	mcg	633	669	600	588	648	656	539	596	606
Vitamin B6................	mg	2.1	2.5	1.7	1.8	2.2	2.1	1.9	1.9	2.1
Folate [3]...................	mcg	198	215	182	150	213	195	174	235	211
Folic acid [3]...............	mcg	178	204	153	199	171	177	170	167	184
Vitamin B12................	mcg	4.7	5.7	3.8	4.4	4.8	4.9	4.2	4.0	4.8
Vitamin C.................	mg	75.4	79.0	72.1	72.7	76.3	70.1	76.6	91.8	87.8
Vitamin D.................	mcg	4.3	4.9	3.8	4.7	4.2	4.3	3.8	4.9	4.6
Vitamin E [4]...............	mg	9.1	9.9	8.3	7.7	9.5	9.3	8.3	8.1	8.6
Vitamin K.................	mcg	114.4	112.8	115.8	71.3	127.8	115.1	117.3	139.1	101.4
Thiamin...................	mg	1.6	1.8	1.4	1.5	1.6	1.6	1.5	1.6	1.6
Riboflavin.................	mg	2.0	2.3	1.8	1.8	2.1	2.2	1.7	1.8	2.0
Niacin....................	mg	25.1	29.7	20.8	21.7	26.2	25.6	23.9	23.1	24.8
Choline...................	mg	312	359	267	246	332	313	284	311	325
Calcium..................	mg	968	1,078	863	973	966	991	850	835	997
Copper...................	mg	1.1	1.2	1.0	0.9	1.2	1.1	1.0	1.3	1.1
Iron......................	mg	14.0	15.7	12.3	13.2	14.2	14.0	13.0	13.5	14.5
Magnesium...............	mg	289	320	259	234	306	292	250	304	295
Phosphorus...............	mg	1,357	1,543	1,181	1,249	1,391	1,380	1,225	1,282	1,377
Potassium................	mg	2,496	2,767	2,238	2,105	2,618	2,525	2,207	2,588	2,531
Selenium.................	mcg	109.6	127.5	92.6	93.1	114.8	109.0	106.1	112.6	111.4
Sodium...................	mg	3,389	3,895	2,908	2,934	3,531	3,406	3,299	3,451	3,350
Zinc......................	mg	10.7	12.4	9.1	9.4	11.1	10.9	9.6	9.9	10.8
Caffeine..................	mg	136.2	147.2	125.7	26.4	170.4	169.6	60.2	79.4	85.7

[1] A kilocalorie is equal to the amount of energy (heat) required to raise the temperature of 1 kilogram of water 1 degree centigrade. The "Calorie" commonly used to measure food energy is actually the kilocalorie. One kilocalorie is the same as one Calorie (upper case C), and represents 1,000 true calories of energy. [2] RAE, retinol activity equivalent. [3] Folate occurs naturally in foods, and covers several forms of vitamin B9. Folic acid is the synthetic form of folate and is added in the food manufacturing process. [4] Alpha-tocopherol.

Source: U.S. Department of Agriculture, Agricultural Research Service, Food Surveys Research Group: Beltsville, MD, "What We Eat in America," <https://www.ars.usda.gov/northeast-area/beltsville-md-bhnrc/beltsville-human-nutrition-research-center/food-surveys-research-group/>, accessed July 2020.

Table 251. Energy Consumption from Food and Beverages: 2003 to 2018

[In units as indicated. Data are shown for 2-year periods, and cover population age 2 years and older except as noted. Data are mean amounts per person estimated from Day 1 dietary recall interviews conducted in the What We Eat in America, National Health and Nutrition Examination Survey (NHANES). Data are based on consumption of food and beverages, including water, and exclude intake from dietary supplements and medications. What We Eat in America is a joint project of the USDA and the U.S. Department of Health and Human Services]

Energy and component	2003-2004	2005-2006	2007-2008	2009-2010	2011-2012	2013-2014	2015-2016	2017-2018
Energy (kcal) [1]....................	**2,195**	**2,157**	**2,070**	**2,081**	**2,139**	**2,079**	**2,048**	**2,093**
GRAMS								
Protein.............................	80.4	81.8	78.1	79.5	79.9	80.3	78.8	78.3
Carbohydrate......................	274.0	265.0	256.0	259.0	266.0	251.0	243.0	247.0
Sugar............................	(NA)	124.0	120.0	119.0	120.0	112.0	106.0	108.0
Fiber.............................	(NA)	15.1	15.2	16.2	17.2	16.3	16.5	16.2
Total fat...........................	82.7	81.9	78.3	76.8	80.0	80.0	81.4	85.0
Saturated fat......................	27.7	27.8	26.3	25.5	26.2	26.3	27.1	28.0
Monounsaturated fat...............	31.0	30.1	28.8	27.5	28.4	27.6	28.4	28.8
Polyunsaturated fat................	17.2	17.0	16.4	16.8	18.9	18.6	18.6	19.9
Alcohol [2]...........................	8.5	(NA)	(NA)	(NA)	12.1	11.0	9.9	10.0
PERCENT [3]								
Protein.............................	15	15	15	16	15	16	16	15
Carbohydrate......................	51	50	50	51	51	49	48	48
Total fat...........................	33	34	33	33	33	34	35	36
Saturated fat......................	11	11	11	11	11	11	12	12
Monounsaturated fat...............	13	12	12	12	12	12	12	12
Polyunsaturated fat................	7	7	7	7	8	8	8	8
Alcohol [2]...........................	2	(NA)	(NA)	(NA)	3	3	3	3

NA Not available. [1] A kilocalorie is equal to the amount of energy (heat) required to raise the temperature of 1 kilogram of water 1 degree centigrade. The "calorie" commonly used to measure food energy is actually the kilocalorie. One kilocalorie is the same as one Calorie (upper case C), and represents 1,000 true calories of energy. [2] Data for alcohol are shown for population age 20 and over. [3] Percents are estimated as a ratio of each person's energy intake of protein, carbohydrate, fat, and alcohol, divided by the individual's total food energy intake.

Source: U.S. Department of Agriculture, Agricultural Research Service, Food Surveys Research Group: Beltsville, MD, "What We Eat in America," <https://www.ars.usda.gov/northeast-area/beltsville-md-bhnrc/beltsville-human-nutrition-research-center/food-surveys-research-group/>, accessed July 2020.

Education

This section presents data primarily concerning formal education as a whole, at various levels, and for public and private schools. Data shown relate to the school-age population and school enrollment, educational attainment, education personnel, and financial aspects of education. In addition, data are shown for charter schools, homeschooling, post-secondary education, security measures used in schools, and academic libraries. The chief sources are the decennial census of population and the Current Population Survey (CPS), both conducted by the U.S. Census Bureau (see text, Section 1, Population); annual, biennial, and other periodic surveys conducted by the National Center for Education Statistics (NCES), a part of the U.S. Department of Education; and surveys conducted by the National Education Association.

The censuses of population have included data on school enrollment since 1840 and on educational attainment since 1940. The CPS has reported on school enrollment annually and on educational attainment periodically since 1947.

The NCES is continuing the pattern of statistical studies and surveys conducted by the U.S. Office of Education since 1870. The annual *Digest of Education Statistics*, found at <nces.ed.gov/programs/digest/>, provides summary data on pupils, staff, finances, including government expenditures, and organization at the elementary, secondary, and higher education levels. It is also a primary source for detailed information on federal funds for education, projections of enrollment, graduates, and teachers. The *Condition of Education*, issued annually and found at <nces.ed.gov/programs/coe/>, presents a summary of information on education of particular interest to policymakers. NCES also conducts special studies periodically.

The census of governments, conducted by the Census Bureau every 5 years (for the years ending in "2" and "7"), provides data on school district finances and state and local government expenditures for education. Reports published by the Bureau of Labor Statistics contain data relating civilian labor force experience to educational attainment (see also Tables 624, 653, and 660 in Section 12, Labor Force, Employment, and Earnings).

Types and sources of data—The statistics in this section are of two general types. One type, exemplified by data from the Census Bureau, is based on direct interviews with individuals to obtain information about their own and their family members' education. Data of this type relate to school enrollment and level of education attained, classified by age, sex, and other characteristics of the population. The school enrollment statistics reflect attendance or enrollment in any regular school within a given period; educational attainment statistics reflect the highest grade completed by an individual, or beginning 1992, the highest diploma or degree received.

Beginning in 2012, CPS estimates reflect population controls based on Census 2010. From 2000–2011, the CPS used Census 2000 population controls. From 1994 to 2000, the CPS used 1990 census population controls plus adjustment for undercount. Also beginning 1994, the survey is conducted through computer-assisted technology rather than by paper forms. For years 1981 through 1993, 1980 census population controls were used; 1971 through 1980, 1970 census population controls had been used. These changes had little impact on summary measures (e.g., medians) and proportional measures (e.g., enrollment rates); however, use of the controls may have significant impact on absolute numbers.

The second type of data, generally exemplified by data from the NCES and the National Education Association, is based on reports from administrators of educational institutions and of state and local agencies having jurisdiction over education. Data of this type relate to enrollment, attendance, staff, and finances for the nation, individual states, and local areas.

Unlike the NCES, the Census Bureau does not regularly include specialized vocational, trade, business, or correspondence schools in its surveys. The NCES includes nursery schools and kindergartens that are part of regular grade schools in their enrollment figures. The Census Bureau includes all nursery schools and kindergartens. At the higher education level, the statistics of both agencies are concerned with institutions granting degrees or offering work acceptable for degree-credit, such as junior colleges.

School attendance—All states require that children attend school. While state laws vary as to the ages and circumstances of compulsory attendance, generally they require that formal schooling begin by age 6 and continue to age 16.

Schools—The NCES defines a school as "a division of the school system consisting of students composing one or more grade groups or other identifiable groups, organized as one unit with one or more teachers to give instruction of a defined type, and housed in a school plant of one or more buildings. More than one school may be housed in one school plant, as is the case when the elementary and secondary programs are housed in the same school plant."

Regular schools are those which advance a person toward a diploma or degree. They include public and private nursery schools, kindergartens, graded schools, colleges, universities, and professional schools.

Public schools are schools controlled and supported by local, state, or federal governmental agencies.

Private schools are those controlled and supported mainly by religious organizations or by private persons or organizations.

The Census Bureau defines *elementary* schools as including grades 1 through 8; *high* schools as including grades 9 through 12; and *colleges* as including junior or community colleges, regular 4-year colleges, and universities and graduate or professional schools. Statistics reported by the NCES and the National Education Association by type of organization, such as elementary level and secondary level, may not be strictly comparable with those from the Census Bureau because the grades included at the two levels vary, depending on the level assigned to the middle or junior high school by the local school systems.

School year—Except as otherwise indicated in the tables, data refer to the school year which, for elementary and secondary schools, generally begins in August or September of the preceding year and ends in June of the year stated. For the most part, statistics concerning school finances are for a 12-month period, usually July 1 to June 30. Enrollment data generally refer to a specific point in time, such as Fall, as indicated in the tables.

Statistical reliability—For a discussion of statistical collection, estimation, and sampling procedures and measures of statistical reliability applicable to the Census Bureau and the NCES data, see Appendix III.

Table 252. Federal Funds for Education and Related Programs: 2010 to 2018

[In millions of dollars (170,511.5 represents $170,511,500,000), except percent. For fiscal years ending in September. Figures represent on-budget funds (appropriations or outlays). Excludes federal support for medical education benefits under Medicare in the U.S. Department of Health and Human Services]

Level, agency, and program	2010	2017	2018
Total, all programs	**170,511.5**	**227,166.8**	**199,765.5**
Percent of federal budget outlays	4.9	5.7	4.9
Elementary/secondary education programs	**75,187.1**	**81,833.2**	**85,042.6**
Department of Education [1]	39,646.5	37,568.3	39,133.6
Education for the disadvantaged	15,864.7	16,143.8	16,443.8
Impact aid program [2]	1,276.2	1,328.6	1,414.1
School improvement programs	6,999.9	4,408.6	5,158.5
Indian education	127.3	164.9	180.2
Special education	12,587.0	13,064.4	13,366.2
Vocational and adult education	2,016.4	1,720.7	1,830.7
Department of Agriculture [1]	18,336.1	23,947.4	25,284.0
Child nutrition programs	16,891.0	22,782.0	24,244.0
Agricultural Marketing Service—commodities [3]	1,053.0	842.0	840.0
Department of Defense [1]	1,981.3	2,111.0	2,154.8
Junior Reserve Officers' Training Corps (JROTC)	359.7	368.4	380.2
Overseas dependents schools	1,186.6	1,155.6	1,172.7
Domestic schools [4]	435.1	587.0	601.9
Department of Health and Human Services	7,234.0	9,150.7	9,190.3
Head Start	7,234.0	9,150.7	9,190.3
Department of Homeland Security [1]	0.5	0.4	(NA)
Department of the Interior [1]	781.1	879.9	912.2
Mineral Leasing Act and other funds [5]	73.0	55.5	69.0
Indian Education	707.1	824.4	843.2
Department of Justice	137.5	137.2	136.7
Department of Labor	4,845.7	5,018.4	5,020.6
Job Corps	1,017.2	1,685.9	1,692.6
Department of Veterans Affairs	760.5	1,522.5	1,752.2
Vocational rehab for disabled veterans	760.5	1,504.9	1,734.5
Social Security student benefits	1,313.0	1,362.7	1,332.7
Higher education programs [1]	**49,118.9**	**101,022.6**	**69,744.2**
Student financial assistance	35,518.2	82,309.5	51,025.7
Direct loan program [6]	24,596.6	31,199.1	31,754.7
Federal Family Education Loans [6]	3,481.9	37,028.3	13,619.8
Department of Agriculture	4,274.4	11,155.8	2,546.0
Department of Defense	80.7	84.5	84.1
Department of Defense	2,550.7	2,334.1	2,447.7
Tuition assistance for military personnel	669.9	540.1	572.6
Service academies [5]	402.6	234.9	242.2
Senior ROTC	885.5	850.9	896.1

Level, agency, and program	2010	2017	2018
Professional development education	592.6	708.2	736.2
Department of Health and Human Services [1]	1,292.6	1,492.4	1,613.5
Health professions training programs	406.0	538.7	641.7
National Health Service Corps scholarships [7]	41.0	33.7	38.0
National Institutes of Health training grants [7]	775.2	843.0	855.8
Department of Homeland Security	45.8	15.8	14.0
Department of the Interior	143.0	78.8	80.9
Shared revenues, Mineral Leasing Act and other receipts—estimated education share [5]	16.3	14.3	17.8
Indian programs	126.8	64.5	63.1
Department of State	657.7	589.8	646.1
Department of Transportation	90.0	118.4	111.7
Department of Veterans Affairs [1]	8,034.5	12,900.9	12,725.8
Post-Vietnam veterans	1.5	0.2	0.2
All-volunteer-force educational assistance	1,854.9	455.0	391.9
National Endowment for the Humanities	47.9	25.3	20.8
National Science Foundation	618.8	994.8	838.9
Other education programs [1]	**9,212.2**	**9,643.2**	**9,558.8**
Department of Education [1]	5,062.7	5,503.3	5,673.8
Administration	1,531.2	2,176.6	2,287.1
Rehabilitative services and disability research	3,506.9	3,301.1	3,359.2
Department of Agriculture	565.4	532.8	537.1
Department of Health and Human Services	339.7	394.7	406.9
Department of Homeland Security	341.1	244.0	240.9
Department of Justice	47.9	41.3	(NA)
Department of State	143.5	264.5	268.1
Agency for International Development	542.7	639.1	404.9
Library of Congress	510.9	500.9	510.4
National Archives and Records Administration	339.0	393.0	394.0
National Endowment for the Arts	2.9	4.0	3.7
National Endowment for the Humanities	94.6	74.4	69.9
Research programs at universities and related institutions [1,8]	**36,993.3**	**34,667.8**	**35,419.9**
Department of Agriculture	737.2	824.1	929.0
Department of Defense	3,154.3	2,785.7	2,938.3
Department of Energy	3,402.6	3,690.7	4,025.4
Department of Health and Human Services	21,796.2	18,454.7	18,313.2
National Aeronautics and Space Administration	1,585.5	2,683.0	3,317.3
National Science Foundation	4,914.7	4,961.3	4,611.3

NA Not available. [1] Includes other programs and agencies, not shown separately. [2] Includes funds used to support school districts with concentrations of children who reside on Indian lands, military bases, low-rent housing properties, and other federal properties, or who have parents in the uniformed services or employed on eligible federal properties. [3] Purchased under Section 32 of the Agricultural Adjustment Act of 1935 (Public Law 74-320) for use in child nutrition programs. [4] The DoD Domestic Dependent Elementary and Secondary Schools (DDESS) program supports students in military communities in the United States, Guam, and Puerto Rico. [5] Data for 2013 through 2018 are estimated. [6] The Education Department reestimated the subsidy costs of the Direct Loan Program and Federal Family Education Loan (FFEL) Program. In 2017, the majority of the net upward reestimates of $28.4 billion for the Direct Loan Program and $10.79 billion for the FFEL program reflect changes in collection and technical assumptions. The Direct Loan Program reestimate reflects an increase in loan discharges for student borrowers harmed by institutional misconduct, and the FFEL Program reflects reestimates for the Ensuring Continued Access to Student Loans Act (ECASLA) of 2008. The Federal Family Education Loan (FFEL) Program eliminated the authorization to originate new FFEL loans after June 30, 2010; all new loans are originated through the Direct Loan Program. [7] Includes alcohol, drug abuse, and mental health training programs. [8] Data for 2018 are estimated.

Source: U.S. National Center for Education Statistics, *Digest of Education Statistics*, "Advance Release of Selected 2019 Digest Tables," <http://www.nces.ed.gov/programs/digest/>, accessed July 2020.

Table 253. School Expenditures by Level of Instruction in Current and Constant (2018 to 2019) Dollars: 1980 to 2019

[In millions of dollars (160,075 represents $160,075,000,000). For school years ending in year shown. Data shown reflect historical revisions. Total expenditures for public elementary and secondary schools include current expenditures, interest on school debt, and capital outlay. Based on survey of state education agencies; see source for details]

Year	Current dollars			Constant 2018-2019 dollars [1]			
	Total	Elementary and secondary schools	Colleges and universities [2]	Total	Elementary and secondary schools		Colleges and universities [2]
					Total	Public	
1980	160,075	103,162	56,914	522,225	336,552	313,063	185,673
1990	365,825	231,170	134,656	729,685	461,097	424,396	268,588
2000	649,322	412,538	236,784	971,414	617,175	571,246	354,239
2005	875,988	540,969	335,019	1,157,376	714,741	660,042	442,635
2006	925,249	571,669	353,580	1,177,615	727,594	672,357	450,021
2007	984,048	608,495	375,553	1,220,879	754,942	697,499	465,938
2008	1,054,901	646,414	408,487	1,262,022	773,332	714,592	488,690
2009	1,089,683	658,926	430,757	1,285,682	777,445	720,104	508,237
2010	1,100,897	654,418	446,479	1,286,465	764,727	709,338	521,737
2011	1,124,352	652,356	471,997	1,288,011	747,312	692,325	540,699
2012	1,136,876	648,794	488,083	1,265,284	722,073	669,988	543,211
2013	1,153,874	655,013	498,861	1,263,180	717,063	664,297	546,118
2014	1,192,886	675,818	517,067	1,285,802	728,459	673,702	557,343
2015	1,241,626	706,135	535,491	1,328,664	755,635	696,780	573,028
2016	1,296,371	736,905	559,466	1,377,954	783,280	720,248	594,674
2017	1,352,976	769,401	583,574	1,412,145	803,049	738,547	609,096
2018 [3]	1,404,000	800,000	604,000	1,433,000	817,000	751,000	617,000
2019 [4]	1,453,000	832,000	620,000	1,453,000	832,000	765,000	620,000

[1] Constant dollars based on the Consumer Price Index, prepared by the Bureau of Labor Statistics, U.S. Department of Labor, adjusted to a school-year basis. [2] Postsecondary data through 1996 are for institutions of higher education; thereafter, data are for degree-granting institutions. See source for details. [3] Data for elementary and secondary education are estimated; data for degree-granting institutions are actual. [4] Estimated.

Source: U.S. National Center for Education Statistics, *Digest of Education Statistics*, "Advance Release of Selected 2019 Digest Tables," <http://www.nces.ed.gov/programs/digest/>, accessed August 2020.

Table 254. School Enrollment: 1990 to 2029

[In thousands (60,683 represents 60,683,000). As of Fall]

Year	All levels			Pre-kindergarten through grade 8		Grades 9 through 12		College [3]	
	Total	Public	Private	Public	Private [1,2]	Public	Private [1]	Public	Private
1990	60,683	52,061	8,622	29,876	4,512	11,341	1,136	10,845	2,974
1995	65,020	55,933	9,087	32,338	4,756	12,502	1,163	11,092	3,169
2000	68,685	58,956	9,729	33,686	4,906	13,517	1,264	11,753	3,560
2001	69,920	59,905	10,014	33,936	5,023	13,736	1,296	12,233	3,695
2002	71,015	60,935	10,080	34,114	4,915	14,069	1,306	12,752	3,860
2003	71,551	61,399	10,152	34,201	4,788	14,339	1,311	12,859	4,053
2004	72,154	61,776	10,379	34,178	4,756	14,618	1,331	12,980	4,292
2005	72,674	62,135	10,539	34,204	4,724	14,909	1,349	13,022	4,466
2006	73,061	62,491	10,570	34,235	4,631	15,081	1,360	13,175	4,579
2007	73,459	62,791	10,667	34,204	4,546	15,086	1,364	13,501	4,757
2008	74,055	63,236	10,818	34,286	4,365	14,980	1,342	13,971	5,111
2009	75,163	64,172	10,991	34,409	4,179	14,952	1,309	14,811	5,503
2010	75,886	64,626	11,260	34,625	4,084	14,860	1,299	15,142	5,877
2011	75,800	64,638	11,162	34,773	3,977	14,749	1,291	15,116	5,894
2012	75,748	64,656	11,092	35,018	4,031	14,753	1,302	14,885	5,760
2013	75,817	64,791	11,026	35,251	4,084	14,794	1,312	14,747	5,630
2014	76,097	64,967	11,130	35,370	4,202	14,943	1,373	14,655	5,554
2015	76,177	65,011	11,166	35,388	4,304	15,050	1,446	14,573	5,415
2016	76,216	65,201	11,015	35,477	4,272	15,138	1,482	14,586	5,261
2017	76,184	65,257	10,926	35,496	4,252	15,190	1,468	14,572	5,206
2018, projection [4]	76,013	65,179	10,834	35,443	4,213	15,206	1,504	14,529	5,117
2019, projection	76,070	65,220	10,850	35,402	4,203	15,232	1,512	14,586	5,135
2020, projection	76,112	65,260	10,852	35,293	4,183	15,361	1,531	14,605	5,139
2021, projection	76,122	65,276	10,845	35,094	4,161	15,549	1,539	14,633	5,145
2022, projection	76,247	65,382	10,865	35,019	4,171	15,703	1,542	14,661	5,152
2023, projection	76,342	65,466	10,875	35,022	4,174	15,746	1,538	14,698	5,163
2024, projection	76,386	65,505	10,881	35,123	4,187	15,635	1,515	14,747	5,179
2025, projection	76,397	65,500	10,897	35,267	4,204	15,438	1,496	14,796	5,197
2026, projection	76,441	65,525	10,915	35,452	4,224	15,220	1,474	14,854	5,217
2027, projection	76,538	65,611	10,927	35,641	4,245	15,093	1,460	14,877	5,222
2028, projection	76,714	65,772	10,943	35,818	4,263	15,067	1,456	14,887	5,223
2029, projection	76,921	65,961	10,960	35,987	4,281	15,081	1,457	14,893	5,222

[1] Since the biennial Private School Universe Survey (PSS) is collected in the fall of odd numbered years, data for even numbered years are estimated. [2] Excludes preprimary students in private schools that do not offer kindergarten or higher grades. [3] Data beginning 1996 based on new classification system. See headnote, Table 296. [4] Pre-K through 12 are projections; college data are actual.

Source: U.S. National Center for Education Statistics, *Digest of Education Statistics*, "Advance Release of Selected 2019 Digest Tables," <http://www.nces.ed.gov/programs/digest/>, accessed July 2020.

Table 255. School Enrollment, Faculty, Graduates, and Finances—Projections: 2019 to 2025

[In units as indicated (56,572 represents 56,572,000). As of the fall for the academic years indicated below, except as noted. Data for higher education are for degree-granting institutions that grant associate's or higher degrees and participate in Title IV federal financial aid programs]

Item	Unit	2019	2020	2021	2022	2023	2024	2025
ELEMENTARY AND SECONDARY SCHOOLS								
School enrollment, total	1,000	56,572	56,678	56,719	56,865	56,973	57,019	57,029
Pre-kindergarten through grade 8	1,000	39,765	39,700	39,541	39,526	39,591	39,750	39,911
Grades 9 through 12	1,000	16,807	16,978	17,178	17,338	17,383	17,269	17,119
Public	1,000	50,770	50,857	50,892	51,012	51,098	51,124	51,119
Pre-kindergarten through grade 8	1,000	35,457	35,384	35,231	35,189	35,235	35,376	35,519
Grades 9 through 12	1,000	15,313	15,473	15,661	15,823	15,863	15,748	15,601
Private	1,000	5,802	5,821	5,827	5,853	5,875	5,894	5,910
Pre-kindergarten through grade 8	1,000	4,308	4,316	4,310	4,337	4,356	4,374	4,392
Grades 9 through 12	1,000	1,494	1,505	1,517	1,515	1,520	1,521	1,518
Classroom teachers, total FTE [1]	1,000	3,691	3,708	3,724	3,750	3,771	3,795	3,820
Public	1,000	3,200	3,214	3,229	3,251	3,269	3,290	3,311
Private	1,000	491	493	495	499	502	505	509
High school graduates, total [2]	1,000	3,650	3,682	3,717	3,726	3,799	3,855	3,859
Public	1,000	3,304	3,331	3,354	3,373	3,442	3,493	3,498
Private	1,000	347	351	363	354	358	363	361
Public schools: [2]								
Constant (2017-2018) dollars: [3]								
Current school expenditure	Bil. dol.	650.2	657.3	663.5	668.8	673.1	676.8	681.3
Per pupil in fall enrollment	Dollar	12,850	12,970	13,090	13,180	13,260	13,340	13,440
HIGHER EDUCATION								
Enrollment, total	1,000	19,904	19,928	19,956	19,991	20,040	20,107	20,177
Full-time	1,000	12,135	12,133	12,129	12,131	12,145	12,178	12,220
Males	1,000	5,447	5,444	5,437	5,434	5,439	5,453	5,472
Females	1,000	6,689	6,689	6,691	6,696	6,706	6,725	6,748
Part-time	1,000	7,768	7,795	7,828	7,860	7,895	7,929	7,957
Males	1,000	3,181	3,193	3,207	3,222	3,237	3,250	3,261
Females	1,000	4,588	4,602	4,621	4,639	4,658	4,678	4,696
Public	1,000	14,665	14,685	14,708	14,736	14,774	14,824	14,876
Four-year institutions	1,000	8,910	8,918	8,926	8,938	8,957	8,986	9,017
Two-year institutions	1,000	5,755	5,767	5,782	5,798	5,817	5,839	5,859
Private	1,000	5,239	5,243	5,248	5,255	5,266	5,283	5,301
Four-year institutions	1,000	5,002	5,006	5,011	5,018	5,029	5,045	5,062
Two-year institutions	1,000	237	237	237	237	237	238	239
Undergraduate	1,000	16,877	16,897	16,920	16,949	16,990	17,047	17,106
Postbaccalaureate	1,000	3,027	3,031	3,036	3,042	3,050	3,060	3,071
Full-time equivalent	1,000	14,967	14,975	14,982	14,996	15,023	15,069	15,121
Public	1,000	10,629	10,635	10,641	10,652	10,672	10,705	10,742
2-year	1,000	3,279	3,283	3,287	3,293	3,301	3,312	3,323
4-year	1,000	7,350	7,352	7,354	7,359	7,371	7,393	7,419
Private	1,000	4,338	4,340	4,341	4,344	4,351	4,364	4,379
2-year	1,000	221	221	221	222	222	222	223
4-year	1,000	4,117	4,118	4,119	4,122	4,129	4,141	4,156
Degrees conferred, total [2]	1,000	3,968	3,973	3,979	3,985	3,996	4,008	4,022
Associate's	1,000	989	991	994	996	1,000	1,003	1,007
Bachelor's	1,000	1,975	1,976	1,978	1,980	1,984	1,990	1,997
Master's	1,000	820	821	822	824	826	829	831
Doctoral [4]	1,000	184	185	185	185	186	186	187

[1] Full-time equivalent. [2] For the academic year beginning in year shown. [3] Based on the Consumer Price Index (CPI) for all urban consumers, U.S. Bureau of Labor Statistics. CPI adjusted to a school year basis by NCES. [4] Doctoral degrees include Ph.D., Ed.D., and comparable degrees at the doctoral level. Includes most degrees formerly classified as first-professional, such as M.D., D.D.S., and law degrees.

Source: U.S. National Center for Education Statistics, *Projections of Education Statistics to 2028*, May 2020. See also <https://nces.ed.gov/surveys/annualreports/>.

Table 256. School Enrollment by Control and Level: 1980 to 2020

[In thousands (58,305 represents 58,305,000). As of Fall. Data below college level are for regular day schools and exclude subcollegiate departments of colleges, federal schools, and home-schooled children. Based on survey of state education agencies; see source for details. For more projections, see Table 254 and Table 255]

Control of school and level	1980	1990	2000	2005	2010	2015	2017	2018, proj.	2019, proj.	2020, proj.
Total	58,305	60,683	68,685	72,674	75,886	[5] 76,177	[5] 76,184	76,013	76,070	76,112
Public	50,335	52,061	58,956	62,135	64,626	65,011	65,257	65,179	65,220	65,260
Private	7,971	8,622	9,729	10,539	11,260	11,166	10,926	10,834	10,850	10,852
Pre-kindergarten through 8	31,639	34,388	38,592	38,928	38,708	4,304	39,748	39,656	39,605	39,476
Public	27,647	29,876	33,686	34,204	34,625	[5] 35,388	35,496	35,443	35,402	35,293
Private [1]	3,992	[4] 4,512	[4] 4,906	4,724	[4] 4,084	4,304	4,252	4,213	4,203	4,183
Grades 9 through 12	14,570	12,476	14,781	16,258	16,159	16,496	16,658	16,711	16,745	16,892
Public	13,231	11,341	13,517	14,909	14,860	15,050	15,190	15,206	15,232	15,361
Private [1]	1,339	[4] 1,136	[4] 1,264	1,349	[4] 1,299	1,446	1,468	1,504	1,512	1,531
College [2, 3]	12,097	13,819	15,312	17,487	21,019	19,988	19,778	19,646	19,720	19,744
Public	9,457	10,845	11,753	13,022	15,142	14,573	14,572	14,529	14,586	14,605
Private	2,640	2,974	3,560	4,466	5,877	5,415	5,206	5,117	5,135	5,139
Not-for-profit	2,528	2,760	3,109	3,455	3,854	4,066	4,108	4,134	(NA)	(NA)
For profit	112	214	450	1,011	2,023	1,349	1,098	982	(NA)	(NA)

NA Not available. [1] Beginning in fall 1985, data include estimates for an expanded universe of private schools; avoid direct comparisons with data for earlier years. [2] Beginning 2000, reflects new classification system. See both headnote and footnote 1, Table 296. [3] Data for 2018 are actual. [4] Estimated. [5] Data for public school prekindergarten enrollment includes imputations for California and Oregon.

Source: U.S. National Center for Education Statistics, *Digest of Education Statistics*, "Advance Release of Selected 2019 Digest Tables," <http://www.nces.ed.gov/programs/digest/>, accessed July 2020.

Table 257. School Enrollment by Age: 1970 to 2018

[Enrollment in thousands (60,357 represents 60,357,000); rate as percent of total population in each age group. As of October. Covers civilian noninstitutional population enrolled in nursery school and above. Based on Current Population Survey; see text, Section 1 and Appendix III]

Age	1970	1980	1990	1995	2000	2005	2010	2015	2017	2018
ENROLLMENT (1,000)										
Total, 3 to 34 years old	**60,357**	**57,348**	**60,588**	**66,939**	**69,560**	**72,768**	**75,148**	**77,066**	**73,883**	**74,247**
3 and 4 years old	1,461	2,280	3,292	4,042	4,097	4,383	4,706	4,203	4,319	4,393
5 and 6 years old	7,000	5,853	7,207	7,901	7,648	7,486	7,955	7,507	7,516	7,448
7 to 13 years old	28,943	23,751	25,016	27,003	28,296	27,936	27,984	28,250	28,152	28,262
14 and 15 years old	7,869	7,282	6,555	7,651	7,885	8,375	7,736	8,207	8,082	8,158
16 and 17 years old	6,927	7,129	6,098	6,997	7,341	8,472	7,963	7,923	7,933	7,761
18 and 19 years old	3,322	3,788	4,044	4,274	4,926	5,109	5,904	5,591	5,606	5,776
20 and 21 years old	1,949	2,515	2,852	3,025	3,314	4,069	4,552	4,641	4,570	4,563
22 to 24 years old	1,410	1,931	2,231	2,545	2,731	3,254	3,602	3,793	3,696	3,598
25 to 29 years old	1,011	1,714	2,013	2,216	2,030	2,340	3,088	2,880	2,758	2,916
30 to 34 years old	466	1,105	1,281	1,284	1,292	1,344	1,658	1,398	1,251	1,372
35 years old and over	(NA)	1,290	2,439	2,830	2,653	3,013	3,372	2,674	2,526	2,592
ENROLLMENT RATE										
Total, 3 to 34 years old	**56.4**	**49.7**	**50.2**	**53.7**	**55.9**	**56.5**	**56.5**	**55.2**	**54.6**	**54.6**
3 and 4 years old	20.5	36.7	44.4	48.7	52.1	53.6	53.2	52.7	53.8	54.0
5 and 6 years old	89.5	95.7	96.5	96.0	95.6	95.4	94.5	94.2	93.5	93.5
7 to 13 years old	99.2	99.3	99.6	98.9	98.2	98.6	98.0	97.7	97.5	97.7
14 and 15 years old	98.1	98.2	99.0	98.9	98.7	98.0	98.1	98.0	98.2	98.6
16 and 17 years old	90.0	89.0	92.5	93.6	92.8	95.1	96.1	93.7	92.9	92.3
18 and 19 years old	47.7	46.4	57.3	59.4	61.2	67.6	69.2	68.5	68.2	69.1
20 and 21 years old	31.9	31.0	39.7	44.9	44.1	48.7	52.4	53.3	55.0	54.6
22 to 24 years old	14.9	16.3	21.0	23.2	24.6	27.3	28.9	28.8	28.4	28.0
25 to 29 years old	7.5	9.3	9.7	11.6	11.4	11.9	14.6	13.2	12.1	12.7
30 to 34 years old	4.2	6.5	5.8	6.0	6.7	6.9	8.3	6.6	5.9	6.3
35 years old and over	(NA)	1.6	2.1	2.2	1.9	2.0	2.1	1.6	1.5	1.5

NA Not available.

Source: U.S. Census Bureau, Current Population Reports, P-20, and earlier reports; and "School Enrollment," <https://www.census.gov/topics/education/school-enrollment/data/tables.All.html>, accessed January 2020.

Table 258. School Enrollment by Race, Hispanic Origin, and Age: 2000 to 2018

[Enrollment in thousands (54,257 represents 54,257,000); rate as percent of total population in each age group. As of October. See headnote, Table 257]

Age	White [1]			Black [1]			Hispanic [2]		
	2000	2010	2018	2000	2010	2018	2000	2010	2018
ENROLLMENT (1,000)									
Total, 3 to 34 years old	**54,257**	**56,776**	**53,426**	**11,115**	**11,272**	**11,144**	**9,928**	**15,235**	**17,682**
3 and 4 years old	3,091	3,439	3,147	725	776	636	518	1,025	1,020
5 and 6 years old	5,959	5,956	5,365	1,219	1,207	1,086	1,390	1,961	1,932
7 to 13 years old	22,061	21,201	20,360	4,675	4,108	4,325	4,373	6,241	7,264
14 and 15 years old	6,176	5,907	5,983	1,260	1,157	1,176	1,093	1,555	1,992
16 and 17 years old	5,845	6,059	5,703	1,106	1,245	1,082	959	1,448	1,800
18 and 19 years old	3,924	4,566	4,271	716	837	832	617	1,171	1,273
20 and 21 years old	2,688	3,432	3,264	416	678	642	311	582	920
22 to 24 years old	2,101	2,720	2,536	393	514	543	309	559	683
25 to 29 years old	1,473	2,289	1,892	353	462	571	198	462	576
30 to 34 years old	939	1,207	905	252	288	251	160	231	222
35 years old and over	2,087	2,462	1,773	387	697	547	235	435	398
ENROLLMENT RATE									
Total, 3 to 34 years old	**55.1**	**55.8**	**53.9**	**59.0**	**58.4**	**55.3**	**51.3**	**55.1**	**55.7**
3 and 4 years old	50.2	52.1	54.7	59.9	56.2	54.5	35.9	44.2	47.9
5 and 6 years old	95.3	94.2	93.7	96.3	94.4	93.4	94.3	94.3	93.5
7 to 13 years old	98.2	97.9	97.7	98.0	98.0	97.9	97.5	97.8	97.4
14 and 15 years old	98.4	98.1	98.6	99.6	98.5	97.5	96.2	97.9	98.1
16 and 17 years old	92.8	96.2	93.3	91.4	95.5	87.9	87.0	96.0	91.7
18 and 19 years old	61.3	70.0	68.9	57.2	62.7	65.8	49.5	66.2	63.5
20 and 21 years old	44.9	51.6	53.9	36.6	50.2	52.7	26.1	37.0	46.0
22 to 24 years old	23.7	28.1	26.8	24.2	29.0	28.1	18.2	23.8	24.8
25 to 29 years old	10.4	13.9	11.3	14.3	16.0	16.1	7.4	11.4	12.0
30 to 34 years old	6.0	7.8	5.6	9.6	10.9	8.3	5.6	5.7	4.9
35 years old and over	1.8	1.9	1.3	2.6	4.0	2.6	2.0	2.3	1.6

[1] Beginning 2003, represents persons who selected this race group only. See footnote 4, Table 261. [2] Persons of Hispanic origin may be of any race.

Source: U.S. Census Bureau, Current Population Reports, P-20, and earlier reports; and "School Enrollment," <https://www.census.gov/topics/education/school-enrollment/data/tables.All.html>, accessed January 2020.

Table 259. Enrollment in Public and Private Schools: 1970 to 2018

[In millions (52.2 represents 52,200,000), except percent. As of October. For civilian noninstitutional population. Prior to 1995, total enrolled does not include the population age 35 and over. For enrollment of population age 35 and over, see Table 257. Based on Current Population Survey]

Year	Public						Private					
	Total	Nursery	Kinder-garten	Elemen-tary	High school	College	Total	Nursery	Kinder-garten	Elemen-tary	High school	College
1970.............	52.2	0.3	2.6	30.0	13.5	5.7	8.1	0.8	0.5	3.9	1.2	1.7
1980.............	(NA)	0.6	2.7	24.4	(NA)	(NA)	(NA)	1.4	0.5	3.1	(NA)	(NA)
1990 [1].........	51.8	1.2	3.3	26.6	11.8	8.9	8.7	2.2	0.6	2.7	0.9	2.4
1995.............	58.7	2.0	3.2	28.4	13.8	11.4	11.1	2.4	0.7	3.4	1.2	3.3
2000.............	61.2	2.2	3.2	29.4	14.4	12.0	11.0	2.2	0.7	3.5	1.3	3.3
2005.............	64.3	2.5	3.3	29.1	15.9	13.4	11.5	2.1	0.6	3.4	1.4	4.0
2006.............	64.1	2.5	3.6	29.0	15.6	13.5	11.1	2.2	0.5	3.1	1.5	3.8
2007.............	65.2	2.6	3.7	29.1	15.8	14.1	10.8	2.1	0.5	3.1	1.3	3.9
2008.............	65.5	2.6	3.6	29.2	15.4	14.7	10.8	2.0	0.5	3.2	1.3	3.9
2009.............	66.9	2.7	3.8	29.4	15.3	15.7	10.4	2.0	0.4	2.9	1.2	4.0
2010.............	67.9	2.8	3.8	29.8	15.3	16.2	10.6	2.1	0.4	2.8	1.2	4.1
2011.............	68.2	2.9	3.7	30.0	15.4	16.1	10.9	2.0	0.5	2.9	1.2	4.3
2012.............	67.8	2.7	3.7	29.9	15.7	15.8	10.7	1.9	0.5	2.8	1.3	4.2
2013.............	67.4	2.6	3.7	30.2	15.5	15.5	10.3	2.1	0.4	2.7	1.1	4.0
2014.............	66.8	2.7	3.6	29.8	15.4	15.3	10.4	2.0	0.5	2.8	1.3	3.9
2015.............	67.0	2.6	3.6	30.2	15.4	15.2	10.1	1.9	0.4	2.7	1.2	3.9
2016.............	66.7	2.8	3.7	30.0	15.3	15.0	10.5	1.9	0.4	2.6	1.3	4.2
2017.............	66.5	2.8	3.5	29.9	15.5	14.8	9.9	1.9	0.4	2.7	1.3	3.6
2018.............	66.7	2.8	3.5	29.7	15.5	15.2	10.5	2.1	0.4	2.8	1.2	3.7
Percent White:												
1970.............	84.5	59.5	84.4	83.1	85.6	90.7	93.4	91.1	88.2	94.1	96.1	92.8
1980.............	(NA)	68.2	80.7	80.9	(NA)	(NA)	(NA)	89.0	87.0	90.7	(NA)	(NA)
1990.............	79.6	71.7	78.3	78.9	79.3	83.4	87.5	89.6	83.2	88.2	89.4	85.1
2000.............	77.0	69.4	77.3	76.7	78.0	78.0	83.5	84.8	82.7	85.9	84.6	79.8
2005 [2]........	75.7	71.3	78.0	75.2	76.0	76.7	81.4	83.6	79.0	83.0	83.6	78.4
2010 [2]........	74.9	71.8	72.9	75.0	75.1	75.4	78.9	81.0	79.4	80.9	84.5	74.7
2014 [2]........	72.7	67.4	70.7	72.7	73.6	73.3	74.6	77.0	68.2	78.4	76.0	70.8
2015 [2]........	72.3	68.1	72.2	72.2	72.9	72.7	75.5	75.5	79.4	78.7	79.4	71.9
2016 [2]........	72.2	70.7	70.6	72.7	71.9	72.4	74.3	75.3	77.2	74.1	78.7	72.3
2017 [2]........	71.6	67.8	72.8	71.6	72.7	71.1	75.8	75.5	80.1	76.3	75.3	75.2
2018 [2]........	71.2	70.3	71.1	71.5	72.0	70.0	75.9	75.5	84.7	76.8	82.8	72.2

NA Not available. [1] Beginning 1990, based on a revised edit and tabulation package. [2] Beginning in 2003, represents persons who selected this race group only. See footnote 4, Table 261.

Source: U.S. Census Bureau, Current Population Reports, P-20, and earlier reports; and "School Enrollment," <https://www.census.gov/topics/education/school-enrollment/data/tables.All.html>, accessed January 2020.

Table 260. School Enrollment by Sex and Level: 1970 to 2018

[In millions (60.4 represents 60,400,000). As of October. For the civilian noninstitutional population. Prior to 1980, data cover persons age 3 to 34; beginning 1980, age 3 and over. Elementary includes kindergarten and grades 1–8; high school, grades 9–12; and college, 2-year and 4-year colleges, universities, and graduate and professional schools. Data for college represent degree-credit enrollment. See headnote, Table 257]

Year	All levels [1]			Elementary			High school			College		
	Total	Male	Female	Total	Male	Female	Total	Male	Female	Total	Male	Female
1970.............	60.4	31.4	28.9	37.1	19.0	18.1	14.7	7.4	7.3	7.4	4.4	3.0
1980.............	58.6	29.6	29.1	30.6	15.8	14.9	14.6	7.3	7.3	11.4	5.4	6.0
1990 [2]..........	63.0	31.5	31.5	33.2	17.1	16.0	12.8	6.5	6.4	13.6	6.2	7.4
1999.............	72.4	36.3	36.1	36.7	18.8	17.9	15.9	8.2	7.7	15.2	7.0	8.2
2000.............	72.2	35.8	36.4	36.7	18.9	17.9	15.8	8.1	7.7	15.3	6.7	8.6
2001.............	73.1	36.3	36.9	36.9	19.0	17.9	16.1	8.2	7.8	15.9	6.9	9.0
2002.............	74.0	36.8	37.3	36.7	18.9	17.8	16.4	8.3	8.0	16.5	7.2	9.3
2003.............	74.9	37.3	37.6	36.3	18.7	17.6	17.1	8.6	8.4	16.6	7.3	9.3
2004.............	75.5	37.4	38.0	36.5	19.0	17.6	16.8	8.4	8.4	17.4	7.6	9.8
2005.............	75.8	37.4	38.4	36.4	18.6	17.7	17.4	8.9	8.5	17.5	7.5	9.9
2006.............	75.2	37.2	38.0	36.1	18.5	17.6	17.1	8.8	8.4	17.2	7.5	9.7
2007.............	76.0	37.6	38.4	36.3	18.6	17.7	17.1	8.8	8.3	18.0	7.8	10.1
2008.............	76.4	37.8	38.6	36.4	18.7	17.7	16.7	8.5	8.2	18.6	8.3	10.3
2009.............	77.3	38.0	39.3	36.4	18.6	17.7	16.4	8.4	8.1	19.8	8.6	11.1
2010.............	78.5	38.7	39.8	36.8	18.8	18.1	16.6	8.5	8.1	20.3	9.0	11.3
2011.............	79.0	39.2	39.8	37.1	19.0	18.1	16.6	8.6	8.1	20.4	9.1	11.3
2012.............	78.4	38.5	39.9	36.8	19.0	17.9	17.0	8.6	8.5	19.9	8.6	11.3
2013.............	77.8	38.3	39.5	37.0	19.0	18.0	16.6	8.4	8.2	19.5	8.5	10.9
2014.............	77.2	38.2	39.0	36.7	18.8	17.9	16.7	8.4	8.2	19.2	8.6	10.5
2015.............	77.1	38.2	38.9	36.9	18.9	18.0	16.5	8.4	8.1	19.1	8.5	10.6
2016.............	77.2	38.4	38.9	36.6	18.7	17.9	16.7	8.5	8.1	19.2	8.6	10.6
2017.............	76.4	37.8	38.6	36.5	18.7	17.8	16.8	8.6	8.3	18.4	8.1	10.3
2018.............	76.8	38.0	38.8	36.4	18.6	17.8	16.7	8.6	8.1	18.9	8.4	10.5

[1] Includes nursery schools, not shown separately. [2] For data beginning 1990, based on a revised edit and tabulation package.

Source: U.S. Census Bureau, Current Population Reports, P-20, and earlier reports; and "School Enrollment," <https://www.census.gov/topics/education/school-enrollment/data/tables.All.html>, accessed January 2020.

Table 261. Educational Attainment by Race and Hispanic Origin: 1970 to 2019

[In percent. For persons 25 years old and over. 1970 and 1980 data as of April 1 and based on sample data from the censuses of population. Other years as of March and based on the Current Population Survey; see text, Section 1 and Appendix III. See Table 262 for data by sex]

Year	High school graduate or more [1]					College graduate or more [2]				
	Total [3]	White [4]	Black [4]	Asian and Pacific Islander [4, 5]	His-panic [6]	Total [3]	White [4]	Black [4]	Asian and Pacific Islander [4, 5]	His-panic [6]
1970.........	52.3	54.5	31.4	62.2	32.1	10.7	11.3	4.4	20.4	4.5
1975.........	62.5	64.5	42.5	(NA)	37.9	13.9	14.5	6.4	(NA)	6.3
1980.........	66.5	68.8	51.2	74.8	44.0	16.2	17.1	8.4	32.9	7.6
1985.........	73.9	75.5	59.8	(NA)	47.9	19.4	20.0	11.1	(NA)	8.5
1990.........	77.6	79.1	66.2	80.4	50.8	21.3	22.0	11.3	39.9	9.2
1995.........	81.7	83.0	73.8	(NA)	53.4	23.0	24.0	13.2	(NA)	9.3
2000.........	84.1	84.9	78.5	85.7	57.0	25.6	26.1	16.5	43.9	10.6
2005.........	85.2	85.8	81.1	87.6	58.5	27.7	28.1	17.6	50.2	12.0
2010.........	87.1	87.6	84.2	88.9	62.9	29.9	30.3	19.8	52.4	13.9
2011.........	87.6	88.1	84.5	88.6	64.3	30.4	31.0	19.9	50.3	14.1
2012.........	87.6	88.1	85.0	88.9	65.0	30.9	31.3	21.2	51.0	14.5
2013.........	88.2	88.6	85.1	90.1	66.2	31.7	32.0	21.8	53.2	15.1
2014.........	88.3	88.8	85.8	89.5	66.5	32.0	32.3	22.2	52.3	15.2
2015.........	88.4	88.8	87.0	89.1	66.7	32.5	32.8	22.5	53.9	15.5
2016.........	89.1	89.5	87.1	90.3	68.5	33.4	33.7	23.3	55.9	16.4
2017.........	89.6	90.1	87.3	90.9	70.5	34.2	34.5	23.9	54.8	17.2
2018.........	89.8	90.2	87.9	90.5	71.6	35.0	35.2	25.2	56.5	18.3
2019.........	90.1	90.5	87.9	91.2	71.8	36.0	36.3	26.1	58.1	18.8

NA Not available. [1] Through 1991, completed 4 years of high school or more. [2] Through 1991, completed 4 years of college or more. [3] Includes other races not shown separately. [4] The 2003 Current Population Survey (CPS) allowed respondents to choose more than one race. Beginning 2003, data represent persons who selected this race group only and exclude persons reporting more than one race. Before 2003, the CPS permitted respondents to report only one race group. See also comments on race in the text for Section 1, Population. [5] Starting in 2003, data are for Asians only; excludes Pacific Islanders. [6] Persons of Hispanic origin may be of any race.

Source: U.S. Census Bureau, U.S. Census of Population,1960, 1970, and 1980, Summary File 3; Current Population Reports, P20-550, and earlier reports; and "Educational Attainment in the United States: CPS Historical Time Series Tables," <https://www.census.gov/topics/education/educational-attainment.html>, accessed March 2020.

Table 262. Educational Attainment by Race, Hispanic Origin, and Sex: 1970 to 2019

[In percent. See Table 261 for headnote and totals for both sexes]

Year	All races [1]		White [2]		Black [2]		Asian and Pacific Islander [2, 5]		Hispanic [3]	
	Male	Female	Male	Female	Male	Female	Male	Female	Male	Female
HIGH SCHOOL GRADUATE OR MORE [4]										
1970..................	51.9	52.8	54.0	55.0	30.1	32.5	61.3	63.1	37.9	34.2
1980..................	67.3	65.8	69.6	68.1	50.8	51.5	78.8	71.4	45.4	42.7
1990..................	77.7	77.5	79.1	79.0	65.8	66.5	84.0	77.2	50.3	51.3
2000..................	84.2	84.0	84.8	85.0	78.7	78.3	88.2	83.4	56.6	57.5
2010..................	86.6	87.6	86.9	88.2	83.6	84.6	91.2	87.0	61.4	64.4
2011..................	87.1	88.0	87.4	88.6	83.8	85.0	90.4	87.1	63.6	65.1
2012..................	87.3	88.0	87.6	88.5	84.3	85.5	90.4	87.6	64.0	66.0
2013..................	87.6	88.6	88.0	89.2	84.1	86.0	91.5	89.0	64.6	67.9
2014..................	87.7	88.9	88.0	89.6	85.3	86.2	91.9	87.4	65.1	67.9
2015..................	88.0	88.8	88.3	89.3	86.4	87.6	91.0	87.4	65.5	67.8
2016..................	88.5	89.6	88.8	90.1	86.4	87.7	91.9	89.0	67.2	69.7
2017..................	89.1	90.0	89.5	90.6	86.5	87.9	92.6	89.4	69.5	71.6
2018..................	89.4	90.2	89.6	90.8	87.7	88.1	92.7	88.6	70.7	72.5
2019..................	89.6	90.5	89.9	91.0	87.1	88.6	92.8	89.8	70.8	72.8
COLLEGE GRADUATE OR MORE [4]										
1970..................	13.5	8.1	14.4	8.4	4.2	4.6	23.5	17.3	7.8	4.3
1980..................	20.1	12.8	21.3	13.3	8.4	8.3	39.8	27.0	9.4	6.0
1990..................	24.4	18.4	25.3	19.0	11.9	10.8	44.9	35.4	9.8	8.7
2000..................	27.8	23.6	28.5	23.9	16.3	16.7	47.6	40.7	10.7	10.6
2010..................	30.3	29.6	30.8	29.9	17.7	21.4	55.6	49.5	12.9	14.9
2011..................	30.8	30.1	31.5	30.5	18.0	21.4	53.4	47.7	13.1	15.2
2012..................	31.4	30.6	31.9	30.8	19.2	22.9	53.7	48.8	13.3	15.8
2013..................	32.0	31.4	32.4	31.6	19.8	23.3	56.1	50.8	13.9	16.2
2014..................	31.9	32.0	32.3	32.3	20.4	23.7	54.7	50.3	14.2	16.1
2015..................	32.3	32.7	32.6	32.9	20.6	24.0	56.8	51.5	14.3	16.6
2016..................	33.2	33.7	33.4	34.0	21.7	24.6	58.8	53.4	15.4	17.4
2017..................	33.7	34.6	34.0	35.0	22.1	25.4	56.6	53.2	15.8	18.6
2018..................	34.6	35.3	34.9	35.5	23.2	26.9	59.3	54.0	16.6	20.1
2019..................	35.4	36.6	35.7	36.8	24.1	27.7	60.4	56.1	16.9	20.8

[1] Includes other races not shown separately. [2] Beginning 2003, for persons who selected this race group only. See footnote 4, Table 261. [3] Persons of Hispanic origin may be of any race. [4] Through 1990, completed 4 years of high school or more and 4 years of college or more. [5] Starting in 2003, data are for Asians only; excludes Pacific Islanders.

Source: U.S. Census Bureau, U.S. Census of Population, 1960, 1970, and 1980, Summary File 3; Current Population Reports, P20-550, and earlier reports; and "Educational Attainment: CPS Historical Time Series Tables," <https://www.census.gov/topics/education/educational-attainment.html>, accessed March 2020.

Table 263. Educational Attainment by Selected Characteristics: 2019

[221,478 represents 221,478,000. For persons 25 years old and over. As of March. Based on the Current Population Survey; see text, Section 1 and Appendix III]

Characteristic	Population (1,000)	Percent of population—					
		Not a high school graduate	High school graduate	Some college, but no degree	Associate's degree [1]	Bachelor's degree	Advanced degree
Total persons	**221,478**	**9.9**	**28.1**	**15.7**	**10.3**	**22.5**	**13.5**
Age:							
25 to 34 years old	45,209	7.2	25.7	16.7	10.5	28.2	11.7
35 to 44 years old	41,027	9.8	24.8	13.9	10.5	24.8	16.1
45 to 54 years old	40,700	9.8	27.3	14.9	11.0	22.8	14.2
55 to 64 years old	41,755	10.2	30.6	15.8	11.0	20.1	12.3
65 to 74 years old	31,487	9.8	28.8	17.1	9.9	19.7	14.8
75 years old or over	21,301	15.8	35.0	16.0	7.1	14.8	11.3
Sex:							
Male	106,695	10.4	29.3	15.5	9.3	22.3	13.1
Female	114,783	9.5	27.0	15.8	11.2	22.8	13.8
Race:							
White [2]	173,452	9.5	28.1	15.6	10.5	22.9	13.4
Black [2]	27,428	12.1	32.6	18.7	10.6	16.6	9.5
Asian [2]	13,955	8.8	17.6	8.8	6.8	33.3	24.8
Hispanic origin:							
Hispanic	34,575	28.2	31.4	13.5	8.0	13.1	5.7
Non-Hispanic white	142,557	5.4	27.4	16.1	11.0	25.0	15.1
Marital status:							
Never married	46,348	10.6	29.9	17.0	9.2	23.0	10.4
Married, spouse present	126,768	8.3	25.6	14.5	10.6	24.7	16.3
Married, spouse absent [3]	3,633	17.4	29.3	12.9	8.1	19.0	13.3
Separated	4,643	20.0	34.8	16.3	9.8	13.3	5.8
Widowed	14,852	17.7	36.8	16.2	8.6	13.2	7.4
Divorced	25,235	9.3	30.9	19.1	12.0	18.7	10.1
Civilian labor force status:							
Employed	137,478	6.8	25.1	15.1	11.1	26.1	15.9
Unemployed	4,531	14.0	31.0	19.0	9.9	17.9	8.3
Not in the labor force	79,470	15.1	33.2	16.5	8.9	16.7	9.5

[1] Includes vocational degrees. [2] For persons who selected this race group only. See footnote 4, Table 261. [3] Excludes those separated.

Source: U.S. Census Bureau, "Educational Attainment in the United States: 2019," <https://www.census.gov/topics/education/educational-attainment.html>, accessed March 2020.

Table 264. Mean Earnings by Highest Level of Education or Degree and Selected Characteristics: 2018

[In dollars. Persons as of March 2019. For persons 18 years old and over with earnings. Based on Current Population Survey, Annual Social and Economic Supplement; see text, Section 1 and Appendix III. For definition of mean, see Guide to Tabular Presentation]

Characteristic	Mean earnings, total [1]	Mean earnings by highest level of education or degree (dollars)							
		Ninth to twelfth grade, non-graduate	High school graduate only	Some college, no degree	Asso-ciate's	Bach-elor's	Master's	Profes-sional	Doctorate
All persons [2]	**55,619**	**26,220**	**38,936**	**39,945**	**48,238**	**71,155**	**87,123**	**149,837**	**124,879**
Age:									
25 to 34 years old	48,277	27,365	35,327	36,622	41,062	60,178	71,419	91,781	85,347
35 to 44 years old	64,266	32,011	42,489	48,656	52,115	78,804	93,204	167,592	126,275
45 to 54 years old	68,674	31,265	45,482	54,110	57,468	86,467	101,957	183,826	151,761
55 to 64 years old	65,250	32,655	47,521	54,202	53,985	82,932	95,657	153,091	138,494
65 years old and over	50,105	28,319	33,995	40,717	39,177	56,604	58,253	143,675	115,061
Sex:									
Male	65,058	31,246	45,259	49,094	58,607	84,803	107,659	175,524	142,728
Female	45,136	18,472	30,103	30,301	39,079	57,551	70,789	114,211	101,817
White [3]	57,035	27,014	40,744	41,297	49,351	73,348	86,751	149,990	126,364
Male	66,977	32,106	47,199	51,179	60,396	87,842	109,298	173,104	146,076
Female	45,531	18,498	31,228	30,262	39,349	58,494	69,018	112,621	100,079
Black [3]	42,382	22,944	31,675	35,398	43,909	54,959	70,825	130,386	84,386
Male	46,402	26,797	36,716	41,783	50,925	58,970	79,022	(B)	71,871
Female	38,901	18,739	25,994	30,504	38,518	51,630	66,658	105,443	94,134
Asian [3]	71,116	24,000	34,610	38,090	47,099	72,857	103,187	170,425	141,654
Male	82,771	27,648	40,718	41,239	54,607	87,714	115,944	208,211	154,775
Female	57,945	19,867	27,444	34,134	39,966	58,117	86,087	135,628	122,353
Hispanic [4]	40,613	28,094	35,105	35,584	42,413	59,364	79,349	126,843	107,800
Male	44,851	33,158	40,028	41,501	49,072	64,478	95,345	172,284	133,911
Female	35,190	19,491	27,405	29,375	36,800	54,567	68,832	79,536	81,946

B Base figure too small to meet statistical standards for reliability of a derived figure. [1] Includes those with less than ninth grade education, not shown separately. [2] Includes other races not shown separately. [3] For persons who selected this race group only. See footnote 4, Table 261. [4] Persons of Hispanic origin may be of any race.

Source: U.S. Census Bureau, *Income and Poverty in the United States: 2018*, Current Population Reports, P60-266, September 2018; and "Current Population Survey Tables for Personal Income: Table PINC-04," <https://www.census.gov/data/tables/time-series/demo/income-poverty/cps-pinc/pinc-04.html>, accessed November 2019.

Table 265. Educational Attainment by State: 2000 to 2018

[In percent. 2000 as of April; 2010 and 2018 represents annual averages for calendar year. For persons 25 years old and over. Based on the 2000 Census of Population, and the American Community Survey, which includes the household population and the population living in institutions, college dormitories, and other group quarters. See text, Section 1 and Appendix III. For margin of error data, see source]

State	2000			2010			2018		
	High school graduate or more	Bachelor's degree or more	Advanced degree or more	High school graduate or more	Bachelor's degree or more	Advanced degree or more	High school graduate or more	Bachelor's degree or more	Advanced degree or more
United States.............	**80.4**	**24.4**	**8.9**	**85.6**	**28.2**	**10.4**	**88.3**	**32.6**	**12.6**
Alabama......................	75.3	19.0	6.9	82.1	21.9	8.0	86.6	25.5	9.5
Alaska........................	88.3	24.7	8.6	91.0	27.9	9.4	93.3	30.2	11.7
Arizona.......................	81.0	23.5	8.4	85.6	25.9	9.2	87.5	29.7	11.2
Arkansas.....................	75.3	16.7	5.7	82.9	19.5	6.3	87.2	23.3	8.6
California.....................	76.8	26.6	9.5	80.7	30.1	11.0	83.8	34.2	12.9
Colorado.....................	86.9	32.7	11.1	89.7	36.4	13.0	91.9	41.7	15.7
Connecticut..................	84.0	31.4	13.3	88.6	35.5	15.3	90.9	39.6	17.8
Delaware.....................	82.6	25.0	9.4	87.7	27.8	11.3	89.8	31.3	13.1
District of Columbia.........	77.8	39.1	21.0	87.4	50.1	26.9	92.1	60.4	34.5
Florida........................	79.9	22.3	8.1	85.5	25.8	9.2	88.5	30.4	11.3
Georgia.......................	78.6	24.3	8.3	84.3	27.3	9.8	87.6	31.9	12.3
Hawaii........................	84.6	26.2	8.4	89.9	29.5	9.6	92.0	33.5	11.5
Idaho.........................	84.7	21.7	6.8	88.3	24.4	7.7	90.9	27.7	9.0
Illinois........................	81.4	26.1	9.5	86.9	30.8	11.5	89.5	35.1	14.0
Indiana.......................	82.1	19.4	7.2	87.0	22.7	8.1	89.0	27.1	9.8
Iowa..........................	86.1	21.2	6.5	90.6	24.9	7.9	92.3	29.0	9.4
Kansas.......................	86.0	25.8	8.7	89.2	29.8	10.5	91.0	33.8	12.8
Kentucky.....................	74.1	17.1	6.9	81.9	20.5	8.1	86.8	24.8	10.3
Louisiana....................	74.8	18.7	6.5	81.9	21.4	7.0	85.8	24.3	8.4
Maine........................	85.4	22.9	7.9	90.3	26.8	9.5	93.0	31.5	11.4
Maryland.....................	83.8	31.4	13.4	88.1	36.1	16.4	90.5	40.8	18.9
Massachusetts...............	84.8	33.2	13.7	89.1	39.0	16.7	90.8	44.5	20.1
Michigan.....................	83.4	21.8	8.1	88.7	25.2	9.6	91.1	29.6	11.5
Minnesota....................	87.9	27.4	8.3	91.8	31.8	10.3	93.4	36.7	12.5
Mississippi...................	72.9	16.9	5.8	81.0	19.5	7.1	85.4	23.2	8.8
Missouri......................	81.3	21.6	7.6	86.9	25.6	9.5	90.5	29.5	11.5
Montana......................	87.2	24.4	7.2	91.7	28.8	9.0	93.9	31.7	11.0
Nebraska.....................	86.6	23.7	7.3	90.4	28.6	9.0	91.4	32.4	11.1
Nevada.......................	80.7	18.2	6.1	84.7	21.7	7.4	86.9	24.9	8.7
New Hampshire..............	87.4	28.7	10.0	91.5	32.8	12.4	93.1	36.8	14.5
New Jersey...................	82.1	29.8	11.0	88.0	35.4	13.3	90.2	40.8	16.0
New Mexico..................	78.9	23.5	9.8	83.3	25.0	10.8	85.4	27.7	12.0
New York.....................	79.1	27.4	11.8	84.9	32.5	14.0	87.1	37.2	16.4
North Carolina...............	78.1	22.5	7.2	84.7	26.5	8.7	88.2	31.9	11.4
North Dakota.................	83.9	22.0	5.5	90.3	27.6	7.9	92.3	29.7	7.6
Ohio..........................	83.0	21.1	7.4	88.1	24.6	8.9	90.7	29.0	11.1
Oklahoma....................	80.6	20.3	6.8	86.2	22.9	7.5	88.4	25.6	9.0
Oregon.......................	85.1	25.1	8.7	88.8	28.8	10.5	90.5	34.0	12.9
Pennsylvania.................	81.9	22.4	8.4	88.4	27.1	10.4	91.0	31.8	12.7
Rhode Island.................	78.0	25.6	9.7	83.5	30.2	12.2	89.1	34.4	14.5
South Carolina...............	76.3	20.4	6.9	84.1	24.5	8.8	88.4	28.3	10.4
South Dakota................	84.6	21.5	6.0	89.6	26.3	7.7	92.3	29.2	9.0
Tennessee...................	75.9	19.6	6.8	83.6	23.1	8.5	87.8	27.5	10.2
Texas.........................	75.7	23.2	7.6	80.7	25.9	8.6	84.0	30.3	10.7
Utah..........................	87.7	26.1	8.3	90.6	29.3	9.4	92.4	34.9	12.0
Vermont......................	86.4	29.4	11.1	91.0	33.6	13.3	93.5	38.7	15.6
Virginia.......................	81.5	29.5	11.6	86.5	34.2	14.2	89.9	39.3	17.1
Washington..................	87.1	27.7	9.3	89.8	31.1	11.1	91.6	36.7	13.9
West Virginia.................	75.2	14.8	5.9	83.2	17.5	6.6	87.8	21.3	8.5
Wisconsin....................	85.1	22.4	7.2	90.1	24.1	9.0	92.1	30.0	10.6
Wyoming.....................	87.9	21.9	7.0	92.3	22.3	8.4	93.3	26.9	10.0

Source: U.S. Census Bureau, 2000 Census of Population, P37, "Sex by Educational Attainment for the Population 25 Years and Over"; and American Community Survey, GCT1501, "Percent of People 25 Years and Over Who Have Completed High School (Includes Equivalency)," GCT1502, "Percent of People 25 Years and Over Who Have Completed a Bachelor's Degree," and GCT1503, "Percent of People 25 Years and Over Who Have Completed an Advanced Degree," <http://data.census.gov>, accessed November 2019.

Table 266. Children Who Speak a Language Other Than English at Home by Region: 2018

[In thousands (12,132 represents 12,132,000), except percent. For children 5 to 17 years old. For more on languages spoken at home, see Table 57 and Table 58. Based on the American Community Survey; see text Section 1, and Appendix III. For composition of regions, see map inside front cover]

Characteristic	U.S.	Northeast	Midwest	South	West
Children who speak another language at home...........................	**12,132**	**2,019**	**1,471**	**4,368**	**4,274**
Percent of children 5 to 17 years old.....................................	**22.6**	**23.8**	**13.0**	**20.9**	**32.8**
Speak Spanish..	8,662	1,096	851	3,457	3,258
Speak English "very well"...	7,068	880	713	2,711	2,763
Speak English less than "very well".............................	1,594	216	138	745	495
Speak other Indo-European languages................................	1,537	534	289	406	309
Speak English "very well"...	1,236	417	226	335	258
Speak English less than "very well".............................	301	117	63	71	50
Speak Asian and Pacific Island languages..........................	1,297	251	174	329	543
Speak English "very well"...	984	190	127	252	415
Speak English less than "very well".............................	312	60	47	76	129
Speak other languages..	636	139	156	177	164
Speak English "very well"...	518	115	125	145	133
Speak English less than "very well".............................	118	23	31	32	31
Have difficulty speaking English [1]....................................	2,325	417	279	925	705
Language spoken at home in linguistically isolated households [2].............	2,569	482	287	1,011	789
Speak only English...	203	47	26	72	58
Speak Spanish..	1,762	265	146	796	555
Speak other Indo-European languages..............................	211	85	38	51	37
Speak Asian and Pacific Island languages..........................	276	65	40	62	109
Speak other languages..	118	21	37	30	31

[1] Children age 5 to 17 who speak English less than "very well." [2] A household in which no person age 14 or over speaks English at least "very well."

Source: U.S. Census Bureau, 2018 American Community Survey, B16003, "Age by Language Spoken at Home for the Population 5 Years and Over" and B16004, "Age by Language Spoken at Home by Ability to Speak English for the Population 5 Years and Over," <http://data.census.gov>, accessed November 2019.

Table 267. Preprimary School Enrollment—Summary: 1970 to 2018

[10,949 represents 10,949,000. As of October. Civilian noninstitutional population. Includes public and private preschool (or nursery school) and kindergarten programs. Excludes 5-year-olds enrolled in elementary school. Based on Current Population Survey. See text, Section 1 and Appendix III]

Item	1970	1980	1990	2000	2010	2015	2016	2017	2018
NUMBER OF CHILDREN (1,000)									
Population, 3 to 5 years old..............	**10,949**	**9,284**	**11,207**	**11,858**	**12,949**	**11,958**	**12,032**	**12,001**	**12,109**
Total enrolled [1]............................	**4,104**	**4,878**	**6,659**	**7,592**	**8,493**	**7,683**	**7,777**	**7,717**	**7,747**
Preschool (or nursery school)..............	1,094	1,981	3,378	4,326	4,797	4,475	4,701	4,620	4,734
Public...	332	628	1,202	2,146	2,749	2,561	2,764	2,738	2,687
Private.......................................	762	1,353	2,177	2,180	2,048	1,914	1,937	1,882	2,047
Kindergarten...................................	3,010	2,897	3,281	3,266	3,449	3,207	3,075	3,097	3,013
Public...	2,498	2,438	2,767	2,701	3,079	2,864	2,822	2,763	2,711
Private.......................................	511	459	513	565	369	342	253	334	302
White [2].......................................	3,443	3,994	5,389	5,861	6,160	5,515	5,579	5,527	5,605
Black [2]..	586	725	964	1,265	1,301	1,193	1,133	1,151	1,094
Hispanic [3]....................................	(NA)	370	642	1,155	1,874	1,810	1,907	1,919	1,871
3 years old....................................	454	857	1,205	1,540	1,718	1,513	1,656	1,641	1,583
4 years old....................................	1,007	1,423	2,086	2,556	2,988	2,691	2,633	2,678	2,810
5 years old....................................	2,643	2,598	3,367	3,496	3,787	3,479	3,488	3,398	3,354
PERCENT ENROLLED									
Total enrolled [1]............................	**37.5**	**52.5**	**59.4**	**64.0**	**63.7**	**64.2**	**64.6**	**64.3**	**64.0**
White [2].......................................	37.8	52.7	59.7	63.2	63.4	63.9	65.0	64.4	65.1
Black [2]..	34.9	51.8	57.8	68.5	64.1	65.3	62.4	63.7	62.7
Hispanic [3]....................................	(NA)	43.3	49.0	52.6	56.0	58.7	61.9	60.9	59.4
3 years old....................................	12.9	27.3	32.6	39.2	38.2	38.4	41.6	40.2	39.7
4 years old....................................	27.8	46.3	56.0	64.9	68.6	66.7	65.9	67.9	67.7
5 years old....................................	69.3	84.7	88.8	87.6	88.1	87.3	85.9	85.5	84.5

NA Not available. [1] Includes races not shown separately. [2] Beginning 2003, for persons who selected this race group only. See footnote 4, Table 261. [3] Persons of Hispanic origin may be of any race. The method of identifying Hispanic children was changed in 1980 from allocation based on status of mother to status reported for each child. The number of Hispanic children using the new method is larger.

Source: U.S. Census Bureau, Current Population Reports, P-20, and unpublished data; and "School Enrollment," <https://www.census.gov/topics/education/school-enrollment.html>, accessed January 2020.

Table 268. Public Elementary and Secondary School Finances by Enrollment-Size Group: 2018

[In units, as indicated. 720,945 represents $720,945,000,000). School fiscal year ending in 2018. Enrollment as of Fall 2017. Data are based on the Annual Government Finance Survey. For details, see source. See also Appendix III]

Item	All school systems	School systems with enrollment of— 50,000 or more	25,000 to 49,999	15,000 to 24,999	7,500 to 14,999	5,000 to 7,499	3,000 to 4,999	Under 3,000
TOTAL (Millions of dollars)								
General revenue	**720,945**	**162,667**	**85,839**	**68,767**	**102,298**	**61,992**	**83,582**	**155,799**
From federal sources	55,213	13,581	7,083	5,302	7,440	3,928	5,465	12,414
Through state [1]	50,847	12,730	6,635	5,042	6,837	3,712	5,056	10,835
Child nutrition programs	16,369	4,372	2,263	1,750	2,289	1,247	1,578	2,869
Direct	4,367	851	448	260	603	216	409	1,579
From state sources [1]	336,994	67,752	42,142	36,151	51,433	28,089	37,819	73,609
General formula assistance	228,586	44,382	30,736	25,811	36,323	18,859	24,389	48,085
Compensatory programs	6,051	1,821	811	611	873	391	582	964
Special education	20,554	5,613	2,222	1,722	2,427	1,491	2,576	4,503
From local sources	328,737	81,335	36,614	27,315	43,424	29,975	40,298	69,776
Taxes [1]	222,482	40,785	25,386	20,411	31,933	22,526	29,964	51,477
Property taxes	212,441	38,540	23,480	19,508	30,476	21,823	28,735	49,877
Contributions from parent government	61,203	30,927	5,897	2,652	5,593	3,907	5,519	6,708
From other local governments	9,406	778	1,346	1,026	1,420	764	1,077	2,996
Current charges [1]	14,959	2,436	1,738	1,382	2,109	1,330	1,745	4,220
School lunch	5,499	754	610	557	890	559	738	1,391
Other	20,687	6,409	2,249	1,844	2,368	1,448	1,994	4,375
General expenditure	**720,892**	**162,985**	**86,246**	**69,447**	**102,598**	**62,270**	**82,293**	**155,052**
Current spending [2]	630,432	141,065	74,773	60,098	89,072	54,531	72,873	138,018
By function:								
Instruction	382,484	90,229	44,912	35,770	53,767	33,262	44,141	80,402
Support services	216,534	43,886	25,831	21,093	30,671	18,707	25,389	50,956
Other current spending [2]	31,414	6,950	4,030	3,235	4,633	2,562	3,344	6,660
By object:								
Total salaries and wages	350,931	77,155	43,695	34,634	50,440	30,348	40,205	74,453
Total employee benefits	153,071	32,585	16,946	14,484	22,084	13,747	18,572	34,654
Capital outlay	68,657	16,221	8,773	7,147	10,262	5,888	7,296	13,070
Interest on debt	18,906	4,727	2,500	2,151	2,821	1,604	1,953	3,150
Payments to other governments	2,897	971	201	51	443	247	170	814
Debt outstanding	477,891	115,331	62,005	55,256	70,720	39,965	50,815	83,799
Long-term	469,333	113,195	61,012	54,733	69,703	39,325	49,728	81,637
Short-term	8,558	2,136	993	523	1,017	640	1,087	2,163
Long-term debt issued	62,710	14,890	7,146	7,326	9,719	5,113	7,634	10,881
Long-term debt retired	43,770	10,240	4,841	4,944	6,245	3,555	5,146	8,798
Fall enrollment (1,000s)	48,582	10,863	6,534	5,151	7,278	4,144	5,299	9,314
PER PUPIL (Dollars)								
General revenue	**14,840**	**14,975**	**13,136**	**13,350**	**14,057**	**14,961**	**15,772**	**16,728**
From federal sources	1,136	1,250	1,084	1,029	1,022	948	1,031	1,333
From state sources [1]	6,937	6,237	6,449	7,018	7,067	6,779	7,136	7,903
General formula assistance	4,705	4,086	4,704	5,011	4,991	4,551	4,602	5,163
Special education	423	517	340	334	333	360	486	483
From local sources	6,767	7,488	5,603	5,303	5,967	7,234	7,604	7,492
Taxes [1]	4,579	3,755	3,885	3,962	4,388	5,436	5,654	5,527
Property taxes	4,373	3,548	3,593	3,787	4,188	5,267	5,422	5,355
Contributions from parent government	1,260	2,847	902	515	769	943	1,041	720
Current charges [1]	308	224	266	268	290	321	329	453
School lunch	113	69	93	108	122	135	139	149
General expenditure [1]	**14,474**	**14,489**	**12,885**	**13,235**	**13,789**	**14,643**	**15,154**	**16,329**
Current spending [2]	12,612	12,471	11,129	11,421	11,930	12,775	13,376	14,500
By function:								
Instruction	7,650	7,925	6,694	6,830	7,228	7,780	8,098	8,467
Support services	4,457	4,040	3,953	4,095	4,214	4,515	4,791	5,471
By object:								
Total salaries and wages	7,223	7,103	6,687	6,723	6,931	7,324	7,587	7,994
Total employee benefits	3,151	3,000	2,593	2,812	3,034	3,318	3,505	3,721
Capital outlay	1,413	1,493	1,343	1,387	1,410	1,421	1,377	1,403
Interest on debt	389	435	383	418	388	387	369	338
Debt outstanding	9,837	10,617	9,489	10,727	9,717	9,645	9,589	8,998
Long-term	9,661	10,421	9,337	10,625	9,578	9,491	9,384	8,765

[1] Includes other sources not shown separately. [2] Expenditures for adult education, community services, and other non-elementary/secondary programs are included in total "Current spending" and "Other current spending" but excluded under pupil amounts.

Source: U.S. Census Bureau, "Annual Survey of School System Finances Tables: 2018 Public Elementary-Secondary Education Finance Data," May 2020, <https://www.census.gov/programs-surveys/school-finances/data/tables.html>.

Table 269. Public Elementary and Secondary School Estimated Finances by State: 2018

[In millions of dollars (720,945 represents $720,945,000,000), except as noted. For the school fiscal year. Includes finances of charter schools whose charters are held directly by a government or government agency; excludes charters schools whose charters are held by nongovernmental entities]

State	Revenue receipts				Expenditures				
		Source				Per capita [2] (dol.)	Current expenditures		
							Total current spending [3]	Average per pupil [4]	
	Total	Federal	State	Local	Total [1]			Amount [5] (dol.)	Rank
Total....................	**720,945**	**55,213**	**336,994**	**328,737**	**720,892**	**2,218**	**630,432**	**12,612**	**(X)**
Alabama....................	8,069	844	4,431	2,793	8,156	1,673	7,328	9,696	40
Alaska....................	2,527	398	1,579	549	2,539	3,433	2,363	17,726	6
Arizona....................	8,862	1,170	3,580	4,111	8,656	1,229	7,714	8,239	49
Arkansas....................	5,562	589	4,229	745	5,626	1,874	4,900	10,139	38
California....................	92,048	7,986	51,600	32,462	91,054	2,313	79,024	12,498	21
Colorado....................	11,004	694	4,539	5,772	11,561	2,060	9,168	10,202	37
Connecticut....................	11,373	475	4,298	6,600	10,851	3,037	10,509	20,635	3
Delaware....................	2,181	141	1,383	658	2,098	2,193	1,955	15,639	13
District of Columbia..........	1,508	136	(X)	1,372	1,547	2,227	1,175	22,759	2
Florida....................	30,135	3,349	11,813	14,973	29,839	1,423	26,856	9,346	46
Georgia....................	21,326	1,806	9,765	9,755	20,988	2,016	18,783	10,810	35
Hawaii....................	3,272	270	2,941	61	3,071	2,156	2,774	15,242	14
Idaho....................	2,538	245	1,662	632	2,410	1,403	2,201	7,771	50
Illinois....................	37,066	2,306	15,570	19,190	35,033	2,741	31,764	15,741	12
Indiana....................	12,901	966	8,098	3,837	11,837	1,778	10,366	10,262	36
Iowa....................	7,050	490	3,753	2,807	6,959	2,215	6,040	11,732	27
Kansas....................	6,660	526	4,343	1,792	6,908	2,375	5,797	11,653	29
Kentucky....................	8,472	914	4,751	2,807	8,581	1,927	7,629	11,110	32
Louisiana....................	8,461	1,013	3,469	3,978	8,079	1,730	7,400	11,452	30
Maine....................	2,866	187	1,107	1,572	2,877	2,156	2,645	14,145	16
Maryland....................	15,894	862	6,663	8,369	14,921	2,477	13,214	14,762	15
Massachusetts..............	18,643	728	7,087	10,827	17,890	2,608	16,732	17,058	7
Michigan....................	19,539	1,567	11,405	6,567	18,976	1,903	16,656	12,345	23
Minnesota....................	12,799	659	8,339	3,801	13,875	2,493	11,199	12,975	20
Mississippi....................	4,768	657	2,404	1,707	4,774	1,597	4,275	8,935	47
Missouri....................	11,452	909	4,776	5,767	10,864	1,779	9,750	10,810	34
Montana....................	1,920	240	828	852	2,048	1,946	1,722	11,680	28
Nebraska....................	4,572	329	1,501	2,742	4,684	2,445	4,041	12,491	22
Nevada....................	4,914	420	3,115	1,378	5,045	1,699	4,236	9,417	44
New Hampshire..............	3,195	168	1,000	2,026	3,125	2,317	2,915	16,893	8
New Jersey....................	30,364	1,222	12,629	16,512	30,481	3,430	28,930	20,021	4
New Mexico....................	3,787	508	2,558	722	3,636	1,738	3,050	9,582	42
New York....................	72,905	3,100	28,895	40,910	73,368	3,745	66,173	24,040	1
North Carolina..............	14,422	1,561	8,863	3,998	15,153	1,476	13,683	9,377	45
North Dakota....................	1,820	171	1,016	633	1,842	2,440	1,551	13,758	17
Ohio....................	24,322	1,609	9,767	12,946	24,806	2,127	21,918	13,027	18
Oklahoma....................	6,357	668	2,930	2,759	6,268	1,594	5,513	8,239	48
Oregon....................	8,443	597	4,483	3,363	8,661	2,090	7,175	11,920	26
Pennsylvania....................	32,084	2,067	12,287	17,731	31,532	2,466	28,545	16,395	9
Rhode Island....................	2,483	168	1,014	1,301	2,502	2,370	2,338	16,121	11
South Carolina..............	10,079	854	4,797	4,427	10,028	1,997	8,265	10,856	33
South Dakota....................	1,645	223	565	856	1,655	1,896	1,407	10,073	39
Tennessee....................	10,557	1,165	4,902	4,491	10,811	1,612	9,640	9,544	43
Texas....................	61,925	6,308	20,893	34,723	65,202	2,304	49,424	9,606	41
Utah....................	5,427	415	2,841	2,171	5,556	1,792	4,590	7,628	51
Vermont....................	1,585	101	1,433	50	1,571	2,516	1,506	19,340	5
Virginia....................	17,005	1,101	6,795	9,109	17,367	2,052	15,853	12,216	25
Washington....................	17,005	1,053	10,903	5,050	18,042	2,430	14,453	12,995	19
West Virginia....................	3,443	366	1,899	1,178	3,345	1,841	3,128	11,334	31
Wisconsin....................	11,892	797	6,457	4,639	12,465	2,153	10,636	12,285	24
Wyoming....................	1,820	116	1,035	669	1,728	2,984	1,524	16,224	10

X Not applicable. [1] Includes interest on school debt and payments to state and local governments, not shown separately. [2] Based on U.S. Census Bureau estimated resident population, as of July 1, 2017. [3] Includes expenditures for adult education, community services, and other nonelementary-secondary programs. [4] Based on Fall 2017 enrollment, National Center for Education Statistics, Common Core of Data. [5] Per pupil amounts exclude expenditures for payments to other school systems, adult education, community services, and other nonelementary-secondary programs.

Source: U.S. Census Bureau, Annual Survey of School System Finances, "2018 Public Elementary-Secondary Education Finance Data," May 2020, <https://www.census.gov/programs-surveys/school-finances/data/tables.html>.

Table 270. Public Elementary and Secondary Schools—Summary: 1990 to 2020

[In units as indicated (44,949 represents 44,949,000). For school year ending in year shown, except as indicated. Data are estimates]

Item	Unit	1990	2000	2010	2015	2018	2019	2020
School districts, total	**Number**	**15,552**	**15,403**	**16,340**	**16,636**	**16,588**	**16,554**	**16,552**
ENROLLMENT								
Population 5-17 years old [1]	1,000	44,949	53,119	53,980	53,691	53,694	53,556	53,462
Percent of resident population	Percent	18.2	18.9	17.5	16.9	16.5	16.4	16.3
Fall enrollment [2]	**1,000**	**40,527**	**46,577**	**49,104**	**49,870**	**50,251**	**50,314**	**50,502**
Percent of population 5-17 years old	Percent	90.2	87.7	91.0	92.9	93.6	93.9	94.5
Elementary [3]	1,000	26,253	29,243	(NA)	(NA)	(NA)	(NA)	(NA)
Secondary [4]	1,000	14,274	17,334	(NA)	(NA)	(NA)	(NA)	(NA)
Average daily attendance	1,000	37,573	43,313	45,835	46,861	47,043	47,176	47,419
High school graduates	1,000	2,327	2,544	3,088	3,192	3,334	3,359	3,381
INSTRUCTIONAL STAFF								
Total [5]	**1,000**	**2,685**	**3,273**	**3,644**	3,694	3,772	3,793	3,836
Classroom teachers	1,000	2,362	2,891	3,182	3,153	3,181	3,196	3,211
Average salaries:								
Instructional staff	Dollar	32,638	43,837	56,995	59,751	62,956	64,545	66,126
Classroom teachers	Dollar	31,367	41,807	55,370	57,748	60,768	62,304	63,645
REVENUES								
Revenue receipts	**Mil. dol.**	**208,656**	**369,754**	**586,995**	**648,076**	**716,898**	**741,210**	**769,293**
Federal	Mil. dol.	13,184	26,346	75,592	53,927	54,792	55,885	56,760
State	Mil. dol.	100,787	183,986	258,396	302,835	334,990	348,189	365,690
Local	Mil. dol.	94,685	159,421	253,006	291,313	327,116	337,136	346,843
Percent of total:								
Federal	Percent	6.3	7.1	12.9	8.3	7.6	7.5	7.4
State	Percent	48.3	49.8	44.0	46.7	46.7	47.0	47.5
Local/other	Percent	45.4	43.1	43.1	45.0	45.6	45.5	45.1
EXPENDITURES								
Total	**Mil. dol.**	**209,698**	**374,782**	**615,210**	**656,044**	**734,998**	**757,339**	**784,221**
Current expenditures (day schools)	Mil. dol.	186,583	320,954	526,146	571,362	635,890	653,798	676,680
Other current expenditures [6]	Mil. dol.	3,341	6,618	10,621	13,508	12,742	14,174	13,527
Capital outlay	Mil. dol.	16,012	37,552	53,052	46,975	60,185	62,682	66,459
Interest on school debt	Mil. dol.	3,762	9,659	25,391	24,199	26,181	26,686	27,555
Current expenditures per pupil enrolled	Dollar	4,604	6,891	10,715	11,457	12,654	12,994	13,399

NA Not available. [1] Estimated resident population as of July 1 of the previous year, except 1990, 2000, and 2010 population enumerated as of April 1. Estimates reflect revisions based on the 2010 Census of Population. Source: U.S. Census Bureau, Population and Housing Estimates, "National Population Totals: 2010-2019," <https://www.census.gov/programs-surveys/popest/data/tables.html>, accessed August 2020. [2] Fall enrollment of the previous year. [3] Kindergarten through grades not higher than 8. [4] Starting from grade 7, 8, or 9, through grade 12. [5] Full-time equivalent. [6] Current expenses for summer schools, adult education, post-high school vocational education, personnel retraining, etc., when operated by local school districts and not part of regular public elementary and secondary day-school programs.

Source: National Education Association, Washington, DC. Data from *Rankings of the States 2019 and Estimates of School Statistics 2020*, used with permission of the National Education Association © 2020. All rights reserved.

Table 271. Public Elementary and Secondary School Enrollment by Grade: 1980 to 2017

[In thousands (40,877 represents 40,877,000). As of Fall of year shown. Covers the 50 states and DC. Based on survey of state education agencies; see source for details]

Grade	1980	1990	1995	2000	2005	2010	2013	2014	2015	2016	2017
Pupils enrolled [1]	**40,877**	**41,217**	**44,840**	**47,204**	**49,113**	**49,484**	**50,045**	**50,313**	**50,438**	**50,615**	**50,686**
Pre-kindergarten to 8 [1]	27,647	29,878	32,341	33,688	34,205	34,625	35,251	35,370	35,388	35,477	35,496
Pre-K and kindergarten	2,689	3,610	4,173	4,158	4,656	4,961	5,162	5,142	5,115	5,125	5,155
First	2,894	3,499	3,671	3,636	3,691	3,754	3,885	3,863	3,768	3,694	3,667
Second	2,800	3,327	3,507	3,634	3,606	3,701	3,791	3,857	3,842	3,761	3,684
Third	2,893	3,297	3,445	3,676	3,586	3,686	3,738	3,806	3,869	3,874	3,788
Fourth	3,107	3,248	3,431	3,711	3,578	3,711	3,708	3,719	3,793	3,858	3,859
Fifth	3,130	3,197	3,438	3,707	3,633	3,718	3,697	3,719	3,733	3,814	3,877
Sixth	3,038	3,110	3,395	3,663	3,670	3,682	3,684	3,710	3,731	3,754	3,827
Seventh	3,085	3,067	3,422	3,629	3,777	3,676	3,748	3,710	3,732	3,761	3,777
Eighth	3,086	2,979	3,356	3,538	3,802	3,659	3,753	3,757	3,719	3,749	3,772
Grades 9 to 12 [1]	13,231	11,338	12,500	13,515	14,909	14,860	14,794	14,943	15,050	15,138	15,190
Ninth	3,377	3,169	3,704	3,963	4,287	4,008	3,980	4,033	4,019	3,986	3,996
Tenth	3,368	2,896	3,237	3,491	3,866	3,800	3,761	3,794	3,846	3,860	3,834
Eleventh	3,195	2,612	2,826	3,083	3,455	3,538	3,526	3,568	3,598	3,669	3,677
Twelfth	2,925	2,381	2,487	2,803	3,180	3,472	3,476	3,496	3,537	3,571	3,631

[1] Includes unclassified students, not shown separately.

Source: U.S. National Center for Education Statistics, *Digest of Education Statistics*, "Advance Release of Selected 2019 Digest Tables," <http://www.nces.ed.gov/programs/digest/>, accessed August 2020.

Table 272. Selected Statistics for the Largest Public School Districts: 2017

[For the 50 largest districts by enrollment size. For school year ending in 2017. Data from the Common Core Data Program; see source for details. School district boundaries are not necessarily the same as city or county boundaries]

School district	City	County	Number of students [1]	Number of full-time equivalent (FTE) teachers [2]	Number of schools [3]	Total expend- itures per pupil
New York City Public Schools, NY......................	New York	(X)	984,462	63,791	1,542	31,212
Los Angeles Unified School District, CA................	Los Angeles	Los Angeles	633,621	28,088	1,012	15,506
City of Chicago School District, IL.....................	Chicago	Cook	378,199	19,016	585	15,409
Miami-Dade County Public School District, FL........	Miami	Miami-Dade	357,249	20,884	528	10,595
Clark County School District, NV......................	Las Vegas	Clark	326,953	16,269	364	10,528
Broward County School District, FL....................	Fort Lauderdale	Broward	271,852	16,391	353	10,134
Houston Independent School District, TX..............	Houston	Harris	216,106	11,546	287	13,833
Hillsborough County School District, FL...............	Tampa	Hillsborough	214,386	18,267	304	9,982
Orange County Public Schools, FL....................	Orlando	Orange	200,674	12,480	257	11,800
Palm Beach County School District, FL...............	West Palm Beach	Palm Beach	192,721	12,698	277	10,675
Fairfax County Public Schools, VA....................	Falls Church	Fairfax	187,467	12,488	222	16,186
Hawaii Department of Education, HI...................	Honolulu	Honolulu	181,550	11,782	290	15,305
Gwinnett County School District, GA..................	Lawrenceville	Gwinnett	178,214	11,125	137	10,413
Wake County Schools, NC.............................	Cary	Wake	160,467	9,991	177	11,149
Montgomery County Public Schools, MD..............	Rockville	Montgomery	159,010	10,709	206	18,250
Dallas Independent School District, TX................	Dallas	Dallas	157,886	10,508	240	12,273
Charlotte-Mecklenburg Schools, NC...................	Charlotte	Mecklenburg	147,428	9,124	170	10,674
Philadelphia City School District, PA..................	Philadelphia	Philadelphia	133,929	7,952	217	27,483
Prince George's County Public Schools, MD..........	Upper Marlboro	Prince George's	130,814	9,030	208	17,178
Duval County School District, FL......................	Jacksonville	Duval	129,479	7,293	209	9,698
San Diego City Unified School District, CA............	San Diego	San Diego	128,040	5,608	226	14,805
Cypress-Fairbanks Independent School District, TX..	Houston	Harris	114,868	6,972	87	12,484
Cobb County School District, GA......................	Marietta	Cobb	113,151	7,361	111	11,556
Baltimore County Public Schools, MD.................	Towson	Baltimore	112,139	7,184	173	16,528
Shelby County School District, TN.....................	Memphis	Shelby	111,403	6,771	196	11,732
Northside Independent School District, TX.............	San Antonio	Bexar	106,145	6,903	120	10,905
Pinellas County School District, FL....................	Largo	Pinellas	102,905	6,823	168	10,267
Polk County School District, FL.......................	Bartow	Polk	102,295	6,740	165	9,612
DeKalb County School District, GA....................	Stone Mountain	DeKalb	101,284	6,878	132	12,236
Jefferson County School District, KY..................	Louisville	Jefferson	99,813	6,097	174	13,657
Fulton County, GA....................................	Atlanta	Fulton	96,122	6,419	107	12,745
Lee County School District, FL........................	Fort Myers	Lee	92,686	5,750	125	10,605
Denver School District, CO...........................	Denver	Denver	91,138	5,980	204	15,273
Albuquerque Public Schools, NM......................	Albuquerque	Bernalillo	90,651	5,826	163	11,459
Prince William County Public Schools, VA.............	Manassas	Prince William	89,345	5,380	93	13,832
Fort Worth Independent School District, TX............	Fort Worth	Tarrant	87,428	5,689	145	11,570
Jefferson County School District, CO..................	Golden	Jefferson	86,371	4,735	164	10,949
Nashville Davidson County Schools, TN...............	Nashville	Davidson	85,163	4,951	162	13,495
Austin Independent School District, TX................	Austin	Travis	83,067	5,793	130	16,764
Baltimore City Public Schools, MD....................	Baltimore	Baltimore City	82,354	5,149	175	17,570
Anne Arundel County Public Schools, MD.............	Annapolis	Anne Arundel	81,379	5,524	122	15,665
Alpine School District, UT.............................	American Fork	Utah	78,957	(NA)	86	7,485
Loudoun County Public Schools, VA...................	Ashburn	Loudoun	78,348	5,229	92	17,344
Greenville County School District, SC.................	Greenville	Greenville	76,918	4,779	95	11,071
Long Beach Unified School District, CA................	Long Beach	Los Angeles	76,428	2,942	85	14,706
Milwaukee School District, WI........................	Milwaukee	Milwaukee	76,206	4,704	158	15,648
Katy Independent School District, TX..................	Katy	Fort Bend	75,428	4,996	67	14,084
Fort Bend Independent School District, TX.............	Sugar Land	Fort Bend	74,146	4,468	75	12,100
Brevard County School District, FL....................	Viera	Brevard	73,444	4,850	124	9,605
Fresno Unified School District, CA....................	Fresno	Fresno	73,356	3,166	107	13,156

NA Not available. [1] Number of students receiving educational services from the school district. [2] Full-time equivalent is the amount of time required to perform an assignment stated as a proportion of a full-time position. [3] Totals for number of schools may differ from published estimates since they exclude closed, inactive, and future schools.

Source: U.S. Department of Education, National Center for Education Statistics, "Elementary/Secondary Information System," <http://nces.ed.gov/ccd/elsi/>, accessed August 2020.

Table 273. Public Elementary and Secondary School Enrollment by State: 1990 to 2017

[In thousands (29,876 represents 29,876,000). As of Fall. Includes unclassified/ungraded students. Based on survey of state education agencies; see source for details]

State	Pre-kindergarten through grade 8					Grades 9 through 12				
	1990	2000	2010	2015	2017	1990	2000	2010	2015	2017
United States...............	**29,876**	**33,686**	**34,625**	**35,388**	**35,496**	**11,341**	**13,517**	**14,860**	**15,050**	**15,190**
Alabama........................	527	539	534	522	523	195	201	222	222	219
Alaska..........................	85	94	92	94	95	29	39	40	39	38
Arizona.........................	479	641	752	775	778	161	237	320	334	333
Arkansas.......................	314	318	346	350	353	123	132	136	142	144
California.......................	3,614	4,407	4,294	4,362	4,357	1,337	1,734	1,996	1,943	1,947
Colorado........................	420	517	601	638	640	154	208	242	261	270
Connecticut....................	347	406	387	371	366	122	156	173	167	166
Delaware.......................	73	81	90	95	95	27	34	39	40	41
District of Columbia...........	61	54	54	65	68	19	15	18	19	19
Florida..........................	1,370	1,760	1,858	1,952	1,981	492	675	785	840	851
Georgia.........................	849	1,060	1,202	1,243	1,247	303	385	475	514	522
Hawaii..........................	123	132	128	132	130	49	52	52	50	51
Idaho...........................	160	170	194	206	211	61	75	82	86	90
Illinois..........................	1,310	1,474	1,455	1,422	1,389	512	575	637	619	616
Indiana.........................	676	703	729	725	729	279	286	318	321	326
Iowa............................	345	334	348	361	364	139	161	148	147	148
Kansas.........................	320	323	343	353	353	117	147	141	143	144
Kentucky.......................	459	471	480	488	482	177	194	193	199	199
Louisiana.......................	586	547	512	520	514	199	197	184	199	201
Maine...........................	155	146	129	125	125	60	61	60	56	56
Maryland........................	527	609	588	627	634	188	244	264	253	260
Massachusetts.................	604	703	666	669	668	230	273	289	295	296
Michigan........................	1,145	1,222	1,076	1,052	1,038	440	498	511	484	479
Minnesota......................	546	578	570	599	614	211	277	268	266	270
Mississippi.....................	372	364	351	349	342	131	134	140	139	136
Missouri........................	588	645	643	650	649	228	268	276	269	267
Montana........................	111	105	98	103	106	42	50	43	42	43
Nebraska.......................	198	195	210	224	229	76	91	88	92	95
Nevada.........................	150	251	307	331	344	51	90	130	137	142
New Hampshire................	126	147	132	124	123	46	61	63	58	57
New Jersey.....................	783	968	981	989	988	306	346	421	420	420
New Mexico.....................	208	225	239	239	236	94	95	99	97	99
New York.......................	1,827	2,029	1,869	1,870	1,880	771	853	866	842	844
North Carolina..................	783	945	1,058	1,081	1,081	304	348	432	464	473
North Dakota...................	85	72	66	78	81	33	37	30	31	31
Ohio............................	1,258	1,294	1,223	1,195	1,187	514	541	531	522	517
Oklahoma.......................	425	445	483	505	504	154	178	176	188	191
Oregon..........................	340	379	393	427	428	132	167	178	182	180
Pennsylvania...................	1,172	1,258	1,210	1,177	1,183	496	556	584	541	544
Rhode Island...................	102	114	98	99	99	37	44	46	43	44
South Carolina.................	452	493	516	543	553	170	184	210	221	224
South Dakota...................	95	88	88	97	100	34	41	38	37	38
Tennessee......................	598	668	702	709	710	226	241	286	292	292
Texas...........................	2,511	2,943	3,587	3,809	3,853	872	1,117	1,349	1,492	1,548
Utah............................	325	333	425	464	475	122	148	161	184	193
Vermont.........................	71	70	68	62	63	25	32	29	26	25
Virginia.........................	728	816	871	897	900	270	329	380	387	391
Washington.....................	613	694	714	750	770	227	310	330	337	340
West Virginia...................	224	201	201	197	194	98	85	81	80	78
Wisconsin.......................	565	595	598	604	599	232	285	274	264	262
Wyoming........................	71	60	63	68	67	27	30	26	27	27

Source: U.S. National Center for Education Statistics, *Digest of Education Statistics*, "Advance Release of Selected 2019 Digest Tables," and earlier releases, <http://www.nces.ed.gov/programs/digest/>, accessed August 2020.

Table 274. Parent Participation in School-Related Activities by Selected School, Student, and Family Characteristics: 2019

[In percent, except as noted (51,498 represents 51,498,000). For school year ending in year shown. Covers parents with children in kindergarten through grade 12. Homeschooled students are excluded. Based on the Parent and Family Involvement in Education Survey, a component of the National Household Education Surveys Program]

Characteristic	Number of students in grades K through 12 (1,000)	Participation in school activities by parent or other household member				
		Attended a general school or PTO/PTA meeting [1]	Attended regularly scheduled parent-teacher conference	Attended a school or class event	Volunteered or served on school committee	Participated in school fundraising
Total	**51,498**	**89**	**75**	**79**	**43**	**57**
School type: [2]						
Public, assigned	39,830	88	73	78	39	54
Public, chosen	6,036	90	77	79	45	57
Private, religious	3,736	95	86	91	73	79
Private, nonreligious	916	95	91	92	74	75
Student's sex:						
Male	26,633	88	76	78	41	56
Female	24,865	89	74	81	45	57
Student's race/ethnicity:						
White, non-Hispanic	24,906	90	76	85	49	64
Black, non-Hispanic	7,032	88	77	76	35	49
Asian or Pacific Islander, non-Hispanic	3,166	83	73	70	41	55
Other, non-Hispanic [3]	3,268	90	79	83	45	58
Hispanic [4]	13,126	87	73	72	35	46
Student's grade level:						
Kindergarten to 2nd grade	12,229	94	90	83	57	66
3rd to 5th grade	12,173	93	88	86	49	61
6th to 8th grade	12,263	89	72	80	36	53
9th to 12th grade	14,833	80	54	70	32	48
Parents' highest education level:						
Less than high school	5,291	82	68	61	25	36
High school graduate or equivalent	9,745	82	71	69	28	44
Vocational/technical or some college	13,082	88	75	79	38	56
Bachelor's degree	13,609	92	78	86	54	66
Graduate or professional school	9,772	94	80	90	58	68
Parents' language at home:						
Both/only parent(s) speak(s) English	43,935	90	76	82	45	59
One of two parents speaks English	1,932	89	75	76	38	43
No parent speaks English	5,631	81	67	62	26	38

[1] Parent Teacher Organization (PTO) or Parent Teacher Association (PTA) meeting. [2] School type classifies the school currently attended as either public or private. Public schools are further classified according to whether the school was chosen or assigned. Private schools are classified as being religious or nonreligious. [3] Includes persons of all other races and multiple races, non-Hispanic. [4] Persons of Hispanic ethnicity may be of any race.

Source: U.S. Department of Education, National Center for Education Statistics, *Parent and Family Involvement in Education: 2019, First Look*, July 2020, NCES 2020-076. See also <http://nces.ed.gov/nhes/>.

Table 275. School Enrollment Below Postsecondary—Summary by Sex, Race, and Hispanic Origin: 2018

[In thousands (57,933 represents 57,933,000), except percent. As of October. Covers civilian noninstitutional population enrolled in nursery school through high school. Based on Current Population Survey, see text, Section 1 and Appendix III]

Characteristic	Total			Race and Hispanic origin				
				White [2]				
	Number [1]	Male	Female	Total	Non-Hispanic	Black [2]	Asian [2]	Hispanic [3]
All students	**57,933**	**29,663**	**28,269**	**41,876**	**29,431**	**8,681**	**3,089**	**14,506**
Nursery	4,836	2,458	2,378	3,509	2,550	680	263	1,149
Full day	2,647	(NA)	(NA)	1,831	1,229	457	156	709
Part day	2,189	(NA)	(NA)	1,677	1,321	223	107	441
Public schools	2,763	(NA)	(NA)	1,943	1,221	459	129	864
Full day	1,513	(NA)	(NA)	1018	555	296	84	537
Part day	1,250	(NA)	(NA)	926	666	163	45	328
Private schools	2,073	(NA)	(NA)	1,565	1,329	221	134	285
Full day	1,134	(NA)	(NA)	814	675	161	72	172
Part day	939	(NA)	(NA)	752	654	60	62	113
Kindergarten	3,908	2,034	1,874	2,831	1,972	555	220	970
Elementary	32,483	16,577	15,906	23,379	16,272	4,991	1,720	8,305
High school	16,706	8,593	8,112	12,157	8,637	2,456	886	4,082
Population 18 to 24 years old	29,553	14,845	14,708	21,716	15,789	4,416	1,842	6,762
Percent dropouts [4]	5.7	6.7	4.6	5.9	4.5	4.9	2.8	9.7
Percent high school graduates	88.1	86.3	89.9	88.1	89.8	87.2	93.4	83.7
Percent enrolled in college	40.9	37.6	44.3	40.4	42.3	37.8	58.6	36.0

NA Not available. [1] Includes other races not shown separately. [2] For persons who selected this race group only. See footnote 4, Table 261. [3] Persons of Hispanic origin may be of any race. [4] For persons not in regular school and who have not completed the 12th grade nor received a general equivalency degree.

Source: U.S. Census Bureau, "School Enrollment," <https://www.census.gov/topics/education/school-enrollment.html>, accessed January 2020.

Table 276. Elementary and Secondary Schools—Teachers, Enrollment, and Pupil-Teacher Ratio: 1970 to 2018

[In thousands (2,292 represents 2,292,000), except ratios. As of Fall. Data are for full-time equivalent teachers. Based on surveys of state education agencies and private schools; see source for details. Data may not sum due to rounding]

Year	Teachers			Enrollment			Pupil-teacher ratio		
	Total	Public	Private [1]	Total	Public	Private [1]	Total	Public	Private [1]
1970	2,292	2,059	233	51,257	45,894	5,363	22.4	22.3	23.0
1980	2,485	2,184	301	46,208	40,877	5,331	18.6	18.7	17.7
1990	2,759	2,398	361	46,864	41,217	5,648	17.0	17.2	15.6
2000	3,366	2,941	424	53,373	47,204	6,169	15.9	16.0	14.5
2003	3,490	3,049	441	54,639	48,540	6,099	15.7	15.9	13.8
2004	3,536	3,091	445	54,882	48,795	6,087	15.5	15.8	13.7
2005	3,593	3,143	450	55,187	49,113	6,073	15.4	15.6	13.5
2006	3,622	3,166	456	55,307	49,316	5,991	15.3	15.6	13.2
2007	3,656	3,200	456	55,201	49,291	5,910	15.1	15.4	13.0
2008	3,670	3,222	448	54,973	49,266	5,707	15.0	15.3	12.8
2009	3,647	3,210	437	54,849	49,361	5,488	15.0	15.4	12.5
2010	3,512	3,099	413	54,867	49,484	5,382	15.6	16.0	13.0
2011	3,508	3,103	405	54,790	49,522	5,268	15.6	16.0	13.0
2012	3,517	3,109	408	55,104	49,771	5,333	15.7	16.0	13.1
2013	3,555	3,114	441	55,440	50,045	5,396	15.6	16.1	12.2
2014	3,594	3,132	461	55,888	50,313	5,575	15.6	16.1	12.1
2015	3,633	3,151	482	56,189	50,438	5,751	15.5	16.0	11.9
2016	3,653	3,169	483	56,369	50,615	5,754	15.4	16.0	11.9
2017	3,652	3,170	482	56,406	50,686	5,720	15.4	16.0	11.9
2018 [2]	3,639	3,157	482	56,367	50,650	5,717	15.5	16.0	11.9

[1] Private school data are estimated based on the Private School Universe Survey, biennially 1990-2016. [2] Projected.

Source: U.S. National Center for Education Statistics, *Digest of Education Statistics*, "Advance Release of Selected 2019 Digest Tables," <http://www.nces.ed.gov/programs/digest/>, accessed September 2020.

Table 277. Private Schools—Number, Students, and Teachers by School Characteristics: 2018

[In thousands where indicated (4,898 represents 4,898,000). For school year ending in year shown. Based on the Private School Survey, conducted every 2 years; see source for details. For composition of regions, see map inside front cover]

Characteristic	Schools (number)	Students (1,000)	Teachers (1,000) [1]	Average enrollment by school level				Student to teacher ratio by school level			
				Total	Elementary	Secondary	Combined	Total	Elementary	Secondary	Combined
Total	32,461	4,898	482	150.9	108.0	284.2	201.5	10.2	10.8	11.0	9.2
School type:											
Catholic	7,047	1,962	153	278.4	218.6	509.7	397.8	12.8	13.3	12.6	10.9
Parochial	2,422	582	43	240.1	222.7	427.9	432.6	13.4	13.7	12.9	11.5
Diocesan	3,477	960	73	276.2	222.2	522.8	304.3	13.1	13.5	12.7	10.6
Private	1,148	420	36	365.7	176.3	509.2	439.6	11.6	10.5	12.6	10.8
Other religious	14,501	1,858	183	128.1	79.5	147.5	193.9	10.2	10.5	9.3	10.1
Conservative Christian	3,782	599	57	158.2	104.1	144.0	181.9	10.5	10.4	11.5	10.5
Affiliated	2,982	558	57	187.1	123.5	180.0	293.2	9.7	9.7	8.6	9.9
Unaffiliated	7,737	701	68	90.7	60.4	124.7	160.2	10.3	11.1	9.4	9.7
Nonsectarian	10,913	1,079	147	98.8	52.6	123.0	184.6	7.4	6.9	7.4	7.6
Regular	4,250	706	87	166.1	76.7	195.1	334.9	8.1	7.9	7.5	8.3
Special emphasis	4,889	262	39	53.6	37.1	87.6	121.7	6.8	6.1	8.3	7.6
Special education	1,774	111	21	62.6	45.5	39.7	70.7	5.3	4.7	5.2	5.4
Program emphasis:											
Regular	22,088	4,346	403	196.7	148.3	341.2	242.3	10.8	11.8	11.3	9.7
Montessori	3,053	120	19	39.5	32.9	(B)	92.9	6.2	5.5	7.3	9.5
Special program emphasis	1,042	165	20	158.0	106.5	177.1	214.3	8.4	7.8	8.5	8.8
Special education	1,979	122	23	61.5	46.1	40.8	68.6	5.4	4.7	5.3	5.5
Vocational/technical	22	3	(Z)	131.1	(B)	(B)	(B)	9.9	(B)	(B)	(B)
Alternative	2,245	107	13	47.6	28.6	82.7	98.6	8.5	8.5	10.2	7.8
Early childhood	2,031	36	5	17.7	17.3	(X)	[2] 25.8	7.2	7.1	(X)	[2] 8.3
Enrollment size:											
Less than 50	13,969	299	50	21.4	19.8	23.5	25.8	5.9	6.5	4.5	5.2
50 to 149	8,172	750	91	91.8	93.1	94.8	88.7	8.2	9.1	7.2	7.2
150 to 299	5,727	1,206	111	210.5	207.6	220.2	214.3	10.9	12.1	9.6	9.2
300 to 499	2,594	996	88	383.9	383.7	388.4	382.1	11.4	12.7	10.9	9.8
500 to 749	1,154	699	62	606.0	591.3	608.4	612.0	11.2	14.3	11.9	9.9
750 or more	845	949	80	1,122.3	1,053.9	1,058.3	1,167.7	11.9	14.1	13.7	10.9
Region:											
Northeast	7,007	1,076	117	153.6	103.8	279.1	215.5	9.2	10.5	9.9	7.8
Midwest	7,937	1,195	103	150.6	117.7	338.3	196.8	11.6	12.0	11.7	10.7
South	11,156	1,706	175	152.9	102.5	253.1	201.3	9.7	10.0	11.0	9.3
West	6,360	920	87	144.7	106.9	276.1	191.7	10.6	10.8	11.9	9.7
Urban/rural status:											
City	10,531	2,153	207	204.4	141.8	350.6	289.8	10.4	10.9	12.0	9.4
Suburban	12,152	1,906	185	156.9	115.2	318.5	208.4	10.3	10.9	11.1	9.3
Town	2,754	312	31	113.3	95.7	168.6	133.5	9.9	11.0	8.6	9.2
Rural	7,024	527	59	75.0	44.0	124.7	114.6	9.0	10.2	7.9	8.6

X Not applicable. Z Less than 500. B Base figure too small to meet statistical standards. [1] Full-time equivalents. [2] Interpret data with caution.

Source: U.S. National Center for Education Statistics, Private School Universe Survey, "Data Tables," <http://nces.ed.gov/surveys/pss/>, accessed August 2019.

Table 278. Public Elementary and Secondary Schools by Type and Size of School: 2018

[Enrollment in thousands (50,330 represents 50,330,000), except for average enrollment. For school year ending in 2018. Data reported by schools, rather than school districts. Based on the Common Core of Data Survey; see source for details]

Enrollment size of school	Number of schools					Enrollment [1]				
	Total	Elementary [2]	Secondary [3]	Combined [4]	Other [5]	Total	Elementary [2]	Secondary [3]	Combined [4]	Other [5]
Total..............	**98,469**	**67,408**	**23,882**	**6,278**	**901**	**50,330**	**32,346**	**15,811**	**2,165**	**8**
PERCENT										
Total..............	100.00	100.00	100.00	100.00	100.00	100.00	100.00	100.00	100.00	100.00
Under 100 students.......	9.86	5.04	17.40	34.98	85.25	0.85	0.53	1.07	3.84	53.41
100 to 199 students......	8.82	7.53	10.96	15.44	10.66	2.50	2.37	2.28	6.01	22.73
200 to 299 students......	11.01	11.71	9.17	10.15	3.28	5.26	6.16	3.21	6.70	10.74
300 to 399 students......	13.86	16.31	8.13	7.77	–	9.19	11.85	4.01	7.25	–
400 to 499 students......	14.26	17.28	7.29	6.41	–	12.10	16.07	4.60	7.76	–
500 to 599 students......	11.53	14.04	5.66	5.37	–	11.95	15.92	4.37	7.86	–
600 to 699 students......	8.56	10.20	4.73	4.45	–	10.48	13.67	4.32	7.76	–
700 to 799 students......	6.10	7.02	4.13	3.18	–	8.62	10.86	4.36	6.39	–
800 to 999 students.......	6.64	6.89	6.53	4.40	–	11.14	12.62	8.22	10.54	–
1,000 to 1,499 students. ..	5.49	3.61	11.42	4.59	0.82	12.41	8.67	19.75	14.79	13.13
1,500 to 1,999 students. ..	2.07	0.32	7.42	1.82	–	6.76	1.10	18.13	8.28	–
2,000 to 2,999 students. ..	1.50	0.04	6.04	0.93	–	6.66	0.16	20.10	5.66	–
3,000 or more students. ..	0.30	–	1.13	0.50	–	2.08	0.02	5.58	7.16	–
Average enrollment [1]....	(X)	(X)	(X)	(X)	(X)	528	483	709	372	64

– Represents or rounds to zero. X Not applicable. [1] Excludes data for schools not reporting enrollment. [2] Includes schools beginning with grade 6 or below and with no grade higher than 8. [3] Includes schools with no grade lower than 7. [4] Includes schools beginning with grade 6 or below and ending with grade 9 or above. [5] Includes special education, alternative, and other schools not classified by grade span.

Source: U.S. National Center for Education Statistics, *Digest of Education Statistics*, "Advance Release of Selected 2019 Digest Tables," <http://www.nces.ed.gov/programs/digest/>, accessed September 2020.

Table 279. Public Elementary and Secondary Schools—Number and Average Salary of Classroom Teachers: 1990 to 2018, and by State, 2019

[Estimates for school year ending in June of year shown]

Year and state	Teachers [1]	Average salary (dollars)	Year and state	Teachers [1]	Average salary (dollars)	Year and state	Teachers [1]	Average salary (dollars)
1990.........	2,361,588	31,367	HI.............	11,377	63,201	NM...........	21,089	47,826
2000.........	2,891,071	41,807	ID.............	16,572	50,757	NY............	211,029	85,889
2010.........	3,182,220	55,370	IL.............	129,178	67,049	NC............	93,411	53,940
2015.........	3,152,710	57,748	IN.............	61,775	51,119	ND............	8,692	53,434
2016.........	3,137,797	58,492	IA.............	37,514	57,489	OH............	112,719	59,713
2017.........	3,165,252	59,752	KS.............	35,278	51,082	OK............	42,461	52,397
2018.........	3,181,421	60,768	KY.............	39,747	53,434	OR............	29,946	65,125
2019			LA.............	47,937	50,288	PA............	120,834	68,930
U.S. total. ..	**3,195,571**	**62,304**	ME............	15,034	54,025	RI.............	10,808	67,040
AL........	46,684	52,009	MD............	61,247	70,463	SC............	51,266	50,882
AK..........	7,889	70,277	MA............	73,878	82,042	SD............	9,709	48,204
AZ..........	63,491	50,353	MI.............	81,944	62,170	TN............	61,710	51,349
AR..........	32,051	49,438	MN............	53,836	58,221	TX............	358,533	54,121
CA..........	288,715	83,059	MS............	31,657	45,105	UT............	29,944	51,858
CO..........	56,855	54,935	MO............	75,511	50,019	VT............	8,317	60,672
CT..........	41,756	76,465	MT............	10,596	50,721	VA............	104,457	53,267
DE..........	9,600	63,662	NE............	25,040	54,470	WA............	62,598	73,049
DC..........	7,067	78,477	NV............	21,992	55,950	WV............	18,777	47,681
FL..........	142,422	48,314	NH............	16,579	59,182	WI............	55,850	58,277
GA..........	116,175	57,095	NJ.............	116,826	74,760	WY............	7,198	58,861

[1] Full-time equivalent.

Source: National Education Association, Washington, DC. Data from *Rankings of the States 2019 and Estimates of School Statistics 2020*, July 2020, used with permission of the National Education Association © 2020, and earlier reports. All rights reserved.

Table 280. Public School Employment by Occupation, Sex, and Race/Ethnicity: 2018

[In thousands (5,311 represents 5,311,000). Covers all public elementary-secondary school districts with 100 or more full-time employees]

Occupation	Total [1]	Male	Female	White non-Hispanic	Black non-Hispanic	Hispanic [2]	Asian non-Hispanic
All occupations.....................	**5,311**	**1,324**	**3,986**	**3,781**	**649**	**682**	**105**
Officials, administrators....................	105	46	59	79	12	11	2
Principals and assistant principals........	146	61	85	102	24	15	2
Classroom teachers [3].....................	2,797	656	2,142	2,184	238	274	55
Elementary schools......................	1,287	145	1,141	1,004	101	137	24
Secondary schools......................	1,123	429	694	887	93	101	23
Other professional staff...................	505	87	419	361	65	58	11
Teachers' aides [4]........................	651	105	546	409	112	103	14
Clerical, secretarial staff.................	330	14	316	216	37	66	5
Service workers [5].......................	775	356	419	429	160	155	16

[1] Includes other races/ethnicities not shown separately. [2] Persons of Hispanic origin may be of any race. [3] Includes other classroom teachers not shown separately. [4] Includes technicians. [5] Includes craftworkers and laborers.

Source: U.S. Equal Employment Opportunity Commission, "Equal Employment Opportunity, EEO-5 Statistical File–2018, United States Summary," <eeoc.gov/statistics/job-patterns-minorities-and-women-elementary-secondary-public-schools-eeo-5>, accessed May 2020.

Table 281. Public School Teachers, Base Salary, and Additional Income by Selected Characteristics: 2018

[3,323 represents 3,323,000. Salary and income shown in current dollars. For school year ending in 2018. Data shown for regular full-time teachers only; excludes other staff even when they have full-time teaching duties. Based on the 2017-2018 National Teacher and Principal Survey and subject to sampling error; for details, see <https://nces.ed.gov/surveys/ntps/>]

Characteristic	Number of full-time teachers (1,000)	Base teacher salary (dollars)	Total income from school and nonschool sources [1,2] (dollars)	Teachers with additional income					
				Job outside the school system during the school year		Supplemental school system contract during summer [3]		Employed in a non-school job during the summer	
				Percent of teachers	Average income (dollars)	Percent of teachers	Average income (dollars)	Percent of teachers	Average income (dollars)
Total....................	**3,323**	**57,950**	**62,200**	**17.8**	**5,800**	**18.2**	**3,040**	**16.2**	**4,410**
Sex:									
Male.........................	794	59,360	66,560	25.1	7,320	21.6	3,880	23.8	5,730
Female.....................	2,529	57,500	60,840	15.5	5,030	17.1	2,710	13.9	3,700
Race/ethnicity:									
White........................	2,622	57,900	62,220	18.4	5,690	17.1	2,990	17.4	4,370
Black........................	228	56,480	60,540	17.5	6,020	23.5	3,090	12.4	4,330
Hispanic....................	317	58,310	62,320	13.7	7,030	21.9	3,210	11.0	4,970
Asian........................	71	65,200	68,610	12.2	5,480	20.6	3,230	9.8	5,150
Pacific Islander..........	8	62,980	66,900	15.0	(S)	24.6	(S)	[5] 11.6	(S)
American Indian or Alaska Native..............	17	48,980	54,220	14.9	6,110	26.2	(S)	13.1	5,850
Two or more races.........	60	56,850	61,330	23.8	5,230	20.5	2,610	17.9	3,910
Age:									
Under 30 years old........	507	45,590	49,790	20.8	4,490	20.2	2,470	25.6	3,510
30 to 39 years old..........	936	53,920	57,970	18.3	5,470	18.7	3,050	17.0	4,090
40 to 49 years old..........	967	61,440	65,540	17.3	6,520	17.9	3,010	14.2	5,350
50 years old or over........	913	65,240	69,900	16.3	6,290	16.9	3,460	12.4	4,760
Years of full- and part-time teaching experience:									
1 year or less................	231	44,150	48,110	17.7	5,470	16.4	2,860	26.4	4,840
2 to 4 years.................	485	46,870	51,100	20.3	5,310	20.4	2,670	20.2	3,910
5 to 9 years.................	598	50,750	54,780	18.5	5,560	19.6	2,900	17.0	4,030
10 to 14 years..............	647	57,860	61,710	17.4	5,620	18.6	3,140	14.8	4,270
15 to 19 years..............	557	64,980	69,180	17.2	6,360	17.1	3,130	13.8	4,950
20 to 24 years..............	385	68,440	72,680	17.3	6,240	17.0	3,300	14.2	4,350
25 to 29 years..............	238	69,170	73,530	16.3	6,180	15.9	3,250	12.9	5,110
30 years or more...........	184	70,450	77,430	15.7	6,130	17.2	3,550	11.5	5,090
Highest degree held:									
Less than bachelor's........	88	55,250	60,950	19.7	7,800	17.1	3,320	19.6	6,480
Bachelor's....................	1,327	49,890	53,780	16.7	5,550	17.4	2,820	17.5	4,410
Master's.....................	1,628	63,120	67,500	18.3	5,740	18.7	3,160	15.3	4,210
Education specialist........	243	66,510	71,100	18.7	5,910	19.0	3,120	14.9	4,490
Doctorate....................	37	69,520	76,070	24.6	9,310	17.3	4,610	14.7	6,650
Instructional level: [4]									
Elementary..................	1,639	56,640	59,690	14.5	5,130	16.8	2,710	13.9	3,920
Secondary...................	1,685	59,220	64,650	21.0	6,250	19.5	3,320	18.5	4,770
School locale:									
City..........................	970	59,430	63,630	17.3	5,900	19.9	3,140	14.5	4,370
Suburban....................	1,288	62,820	66,920	17.9	5,720	17.5	3,100	15.8	4,100
Town........................	387	50,590	55,130	18.5	5,980	19.6	2,720	17.0	5,040
Rural........................	679	50,770	55,240	18.0	5,710	16.3	2,980	19.0	4,620

S Figure does not meet publication standards. [1] Includes retirement pension funds paid during the school year. [2] Includes types of income not shown separately. [3] Includes teaching summer sessions and other non-teaching jobs at any school. [4] Teachers were classified as elementary or secondary on the basis of the grades they taught, rather than on the level of the school in which they taught. In general, elementary teachers include those teaching pre-kindergarten through grade 6 and those teaching multiple grades, with a preponderance of grades taught being kindergarten through grade 6. In general, secondary teachers include those teaching grades 7 through 12 and those teaching multiple grades, with a preponderance of grades taught being grades 7 through 12 and usually no grade taught being lower than grade 5. [5] Interpret data with caution, coefficient of variance is between 30 and 50 percent.

Source: U.S. National Center for Education Statistics, *Digest of Education Statistics*, "Advance Release of Selected 2019 Digest Tables," <http://www.nces.ed.gov/programs/digest/>, accessed May 2020.

Table 282. Education and Teaching Experience of Public Elementary and Secondary School Teachers by Selected Characteristics: 2018

[3,545 represents 3,545,000. For school year ending in 2018. Excludes prekindergarten teachers. Data are based on a head count of full-time and part-time teachers. Based on the National Teacher and Principal Survey (NTPS); see source for details]

Characteristic	Number of teachers (1,000s)	Percent of teachers by highest degree earned					Percent of teachers by years of teaching experience [1]			
		Less than bachelor's	Bach-elor's	Master's	Education specialist [2]	Doctor's	Less than 3	3 to 9	10 to 20	Over 20
Total	3,545	2.7	39.3	49.2	7.6	1.2	9.0	28.3	39.9	22.8
Sex:										
Male	834	4.0	39.0	49.6	5.7	1.7	8.9	44.0	40.6	23.2
Female	2,712	2.3	39.4	49.1	8.2	1.0	9.0	28.6	39.7	22.7
Race/ethnicity: [3]										
White	2,811	2.6	38.6	50.4	7.4	1.0	8.3	27.3	40.1	24.3
Black	239	3.0	32.9	50.7	11.3	2.1	10.8	30.3	38.7	20.2
Asian	75	1.7	29.0	55.1	11.3	2.8	12.0	31.1	42.1	14.8
Pacific Islander	8	(S)	44.2	38.6	[6] 8.7	(S)	[6] 6.7	24.0	44.2	25.1
American Indian/Alaska Native	18	[6] 5.3	51.6	36.2	6.2	(S)	9.0	20.9	42.5	27.6
Two or more races	63	3.2	40.8	47.0	7.8	[6] 1.2	12.5	35.5	34.6	17.4
Hispanic	331	3.6	51.1	37.9	6.1	1.3	11.8	34.0	39.6	14.6
Age:										
Under age 30	531	2.7	64.8	30.3	2.1	(S)	37.1	62.8	(S)	(S)
Age 30 to 39	991	2.2	37.9	52.9	6.5	0.6	6.7	42.9	50.3	(S)
Age 40 to 49	1,028	2.9	33.5	53.3	9.2	1.1	3.4	15.5	58.1	23.0
Age 50 to 59	732	2.9	33.4	52.1	9.5	2.1	2.0	9.2	33.5	55.2
Age 60 and over	263	3.6	32.1	49.2	12.0	3.1	1.7	6.5	28.2	63.6
Level of instruction: [4]										
Elementary	1,779	2.1	42.6	47.1	7.6	0.7	9.4	29.2	39.0	22.4
General	1,097	2.1	45.0	45.5	6.9	0.5	9.4	28.8	39.9	21.9
Arts/music	99	1.4	49.1	42.9	5.5	[6] 1.1	9.1	29.7	37.0	24.2
English	117	1.9	35.4	51.3	10.4	[6] 1.0	7.7	25.5	39.0	27.8
ESL/bilingual [5]	48	[6] 1.8	32.9	51.2	13.3	[6] 0.9	8.8	29.8	39.3	22.1
Health/physical education	65	5.1	50.2	41.5	3.0	(S)	7.6	24.1	38.9	29.4
Mathematics	36	[6] 2.7	43.1	48.0	6.2	(S)	7.5	31.2	41.4	19.8
Science	23	[6] 4.3	45.8	44.9	[6] 3.8	(S)	[6] 8.6	29.3	42.9	19.2
Special education	235	1.2	33.9	53.2	10.3	1.3	11.8	33.6	34.8	19.8
Other elementary	60	2.3	32.4	54.2	9.5	[6] 1.4	6.8	29.9	38.9	24.4
Secondary	1,766	3.4	36.0	51.3	7.7	1.6	8.6	27.4	40.9	23.2
Arts/music	130	3.3	44.8	44.6	5.8	1.4	9.7	28.6	35.9	25.9
English	294	1.5	34.1	54.2	8.4	1.8	8.4	27.6	41.2	22.7
ESL/bilingual [5]	24	(S)	24.0	58.1	14.7	[6] 1.7	6.8	25.8	43.7	23.6
Foreign language	85	0.8	31.3	57.5	7.5	2.9	8.7	26.0	43.8	21.5
Health/physical education	97	2.8	45.0	47.7	4.0	[6] 0.4	5.6	22.3	41.7	30.4
Mathematics	265	2.5	37.5	53.1	5.8	1.1	8.9	28.3	40.9	21.8
Science	220	2.9	33.7	54.5	6.4	2.5	9.1	27.1	42.5	21.3
Social studies	214	2.2	35.9	53.3	6.8	1.8	8.0	27.3	42.8	21.9
Special education	199	2.6	30.7	50.9	14.6	1.2	9.3	30.6	37.3	22.8
Vocational/technical	139	14.4	37.8	40.1	6.0	1.7	9.3	27.6	40.9	22.2
Other secondary	98	4.3	37.6	49.0	8.4	[6] 0.7	7.6	23.5	41.4	27.6

S Figure does not meet publication standards. [1] Includes full- and part-time teaching experience. [2] Education specialist degrees or certificates are generally awarded for 1 year of work beyond the master's degree level. Includes certificate of advanced graduate studies. [3] Data for race categories exclude persons of Hispanic origin. [4] Teachers were classified as elementary or secondary on the basis of the grades they taught, rather than on the level of the school in which they taught. Elementary teachers generally include those teaching prekindergarten through grade 5 and those teaching multiple grades, with a preponderance of grades taught being kindergarten through grade 6. Secondary teachers generally include those teaching any of grades 7 through 12 and those teaching multiple grades, with a preponderance of grades taught being grades 7 through 12. [5] ESL is English as a second language. [6] Interpret data with caution. The coefficient of variation (CV) for this estimate is between 30 and 50 percent.

Source: U.S. National Center for Education Statistics, *Digest of Education Statistics*, "Advance Release of Selected 2019 Digest Tables," <http://www.nces.ed.gov/programs/digest/>, accessed July 2020.

Table 283. Counselors, Psychologists, and Social Workers in Public Schools by Selected Characteristics: 2015 to 2016

[114 represents 114,000. Data are for academic year indicated. Detail may not sum to totals because of rounding and because some data are not shown. Based on the National Teacher and Principal Survey, "Public School Data File"]

Characteristic	Schools with at least one full- or part-time counselor			Schools with at least one full- or part-time psychologist			Schools with at least one full- or part-time social worker		
	Percent of schools	Number of FTE counselors (1,000) [1]	Number of students per FTE counselor [1]	Percent of schools	FTE psych-ologists (1,000) [1]	Number of students per FTE psych-ologists [1]	Percent of schools	Number FTE social workers (1,000) [1]	Number of students per FTE social worker [1]
Total.....................	80.7	114	380	66.5	44	820	41.5	33	700
School classification:									
Traditional public.........	82.3	108	380	68.1	42	820	42.2	31	720
Charter school...........	62.0	6	360	47.0	2	750	33.2	2	480
Community type:									
City......................	80.1	34	380	70.5	13	840	50.9	12	680
Suburban................	79.8	43	390	79.6	18	900	48.4	13	800
Town.....................	82.4	14	370	55.7	5	710	33.7	3	590
Rural.....................	81.6	24	340	52.3	8	670	27.5	5	600
School level: [2]									
Primary...................	75.3	39	480	71.7	25	720	42.3	17	610
Middle....................	91.9	22	370	71.7	7	880	46.6	6	760
High......................	90.6	45	310	59.1	9	1,120	42.8	8	990
Combined................	73.7	9	290	42.5	3	500	25.3	2	320
Student enrollment:									
Less than 100............	49.4	3	60	42.0	2	80	24.5	2	50
100 to 199................	70.2	5	170	46.1	2	240	27.5	2	180
200 to 499 students.....	80.2	30	340	64.1	15	540	40.4	11	450
500 to 749 students.....	83.6	26	450	73.5	12	830	44.8	9	720
750 to 999 students.....	90.9	17	430	77.7	6	1,100	46.7	4	860
1,000 students or more....................	96.7	34	380	81.5	7	1,530	56.1	5	1,480

[1] Full-time equivalent. [2] Primary schools are those with at least one grade lower than 5 and no grade higher than 8, middle schools have no grade lower than 5 and no grade higher than 8, high schools have no grade lower than 7 and at least one grade higher than 8, and all other schools are classified as combined.

Source: U.S. National Center for Education Statistics, *Mental Health Staff in Public Schools, by School Racial and Ethnic Composition*, Supplemental Tables, <https://nces.ed.gov/pubsearch/pubsinfo.asp?pubid=2019020>, accessed January 2019.

Table 284. Elementary and Secondary School Enrolled English Language Learner Students by Home Language and Grade: 2008 to 2017

[Data cover the academic year beginning with shown year. Data for 2013 and earlier years include all English Language Learner (ELL) students enrolled at any time during the school year; beginning 2014, data shown as of fall. Includes all students identified as English language learners (ELL), both those participating in ELL programs and those not participating in ELL programs. Data exclude Puerto Rico, Guam, the U.S. Virgin Islands, American Samoa, and the Bureau of Indian Education]

Selected student characteristic	2008 [1]	2009 [1]	2011 [1]	2012	2013	2014	2015	2016	2017
Total........................	4,685,746	4,647,016	4,635,185	4,850,293	4,929,989	4,813,693	4,854,285	4,949,423	5,010,505
HOME LANGUAGE									
Spanish, Castilian...................	3,617,597	3,577,649	3,562,860	3,718,047	3,770,816	3,709,828	3,741,066	3,790,949	3,749,314
Arabic..........................	65,278	71,228	86,162	97,971	109,170	109,165	114,371	129,386	136,531
Chinese.........................	77,240	80,124	96,509	104,799	107,825	104,279	101,347	104,147	106,516
English [2]......................	86,390	77,872	85,246	90,703	91,669	83,230	80,333	70,014	94,910
Vietnamese......................	91,607	93,204	89,536	92,560	89,705	85,289	81,157	78,732	77,765
Somali..........................	26,264	27,771	27,861	30,959	34,472	33,712	36,028	38,440	41,264
Russian.........................	34,085	33,349	32,225	33,678	33,821	32,493	33,057	34,843	36,809
Portuguese......................	18,055	15,229	15,725	17,085	19,142	19,839	23,673	28,214	33,252
Haitian, Haitian Creole............	37,074	39,736	39,883	38,768	37,371	31,428	30,231	31,608	32,655
Hmong..........................	52,990	49,697	43,845	41,368	39,860	37,412	34,813	33,059	32,174
GRADE									
Kindergarten......................	629,195	615,615	657,391	667,835	667,665	629,013	606,398	600,184	587,543
Grade 1.........................	621,541	617,599	646,362	665,327	665,612	640,017	621,106	603,824	588,515
Grade 2.........................	583,025	576,336	585,702	609,804	630,475	614,681	614,809	599,147	574,690
Grade 3.........................	495,814	511,545	500,032	540,396	558,925	567,131	564,811	576,051	551,257
Grade 4.........................	406,966	420,145	417,616	428,119	439,529	436,554	461,022	457,476	504,999
Grade 5.........................	333,975	336,194	338,174	367,088	361,651	364,178	372,817	389,304	400,053
Grade 6.........................	288,784	277,971	273,457	288,085	293,778	287,798	305,530	318,740	329,313
Grade 7.........................	263,483	254,830	239,156	255,395	267,416	260,507	267,094	286,261	291,873
Grade 8.........................	237,269	233,332	214,896	227,844	239,817	242,540	245,574	258,192	265,210
Grade 9.........................	268,927	258,728	244,266	255,008	261,564	263,081	269,704	286,168	280,408
Grade 10.........................	218,235	211,691	201,724	202,774	202,377	197,494	214,015	232,687	255,043
Grade 11.........................	172,084	175,544	162,804	170,847	168,437	157,395	162,269	183,982	202,429
Grade 12.........................	142,406	148,173	145,444	159,410	161,227	143,189	138,814	146,373	167,145
Ungraded [3].....................	23,489	8,672	8,118	11,783	11,422	10,114	10,218	11,019	11,803

[1] Includes data for California that reflect ELL students enrolled on a single date, rather than a cumulative count of all ELL students enrolled at any time during the school year. [2] Examples of situations in which English might be reported as an English learner's home language include students who live in multilingual households and students adopted from other countries who speak English at home but also have been raised speaking another language. [3] Includes students reported as being enrolled in grade 13.

Source: U.S. National Center for Education Statistics, *Digest of Education Statistics*, "Advance Release of Selected 2019 Digest Tables," <https://nces.ed.gov/programs/digest/>, accessed May 2020.

Table 285. Public and Private School Start Times by Selected Characteristics: 2018

[For academic year ending in 2018. Data are from the National Teacher and Principal Survey]

School characteristic	Average start time	Percent distribution of start times				
		Before 7:30 a.m.	7:30 a.m. to 7:59 a.m.	8:00 a.m. to 8:29 a.m.	8:30 a.m. to 8:59 a.m.	9:00 a.m. or later
All schools	**8:11**	**3.5**	**24.7**	**43.9**	**20.4**	**7.5**
Public schools	**8:10**	**4.3**	**27.5**	**40.3**	**19.8**	**8.2**
School classification:						
Traditional public	8:11	4.2	27.6	39.7	20.1	8.4
Charter school	8:05	4.6	26.1	46.9	16.4	5.9
School level:						
Primary	8:15	1.7	23.5	39.6	25.4	9.9
Middle	8:05	6.4	36.3	36.6	13.1	7.7
High	8:03	10.4	32.1	40.0	11.8	5.7
Combined	8:05	3.2	26.7	51.0	14.4	4.8
Private schools	**8:12**	**1.0**	**14.9**	**56.6**	**22.5**	**4.9**
School classification:						
Catholic	8:03	[1] 1.7	32.6	55.0	9.2	[1] 1.4
Other religious	8:13	[1] 0.8	9.9	61.4	24.1	3.9
Nonsectarian	8:19	[1] 0.9	6.2	49.9	33.0	10.1
School level:						
Elementary	8:11	[1] 1.0	15.1	55.0	25.7	3.2
Secondary	8:15	2.0	22.2	49.4	17.2	9.3
Combined	8:12	(S)	12.2	61.9	18.7	6.5

S Figure does not meet publication standards. [1] Interpret data with caution. The coefficient of variation (CV) for this estimate is between 30 percent and 50 percent.

Source: U.S. National Center for Education Statistics, National Teacher and Principal Survey, "2017–2018 NTPS Tables," <https://nces.ed.gov/surveys/ntps/tables_list.asp>, accessed May 2020.

Table 286. Homeschooled Students by Selected Characteristics: 2007 to 2016

[1,520 represents 1,520,000. As of Spring. For students age 5 to 17 with a grade equivalent of K–12. Homeschoolers are students whose parents reported them to be schooled at home instead of a public or private school. Excludes students who were enrolled in school for more than 25 hours a week or were homeschooled due to a temporary illness. Based on the Parent and Family Involvement in Education Survey of the National Household Education Surveys Program; see source and Appendix III for details]

Characteristic	2007		2012 [1]		2016	
	Home-schooled (1,000)	Percent home-schooled	Home-schooled (1,000)	Percent home-schooled	Home-schooled (1,000)	Percent home-schooled
Total	**1,520**	**3.0**	**1,773**	**3.4**	**1,690**	**3.3**
Grade equivalent: [2]						
Kindergarten to grade 5	717	3.0	833	3.2	767	3.0
Kindergarten	(S)	(S)	212	4.0	181	3.5
Grades 1 to 3	406	3.4	353	2.9	300	2.4
Grades 4 to 5	197	2.5	268	3.2	287	3.4
Grades 6 to 8	371	3.0	424	3.5	398	3.3
Grades 9 to 12	422	2.8	516	3.8	525	3.8
Sex:						
Male	639	2.4	875	3.3	807	3.0
Female	881	3.5	898	3.6	882	3.5
Race/ethnicity: [3]						
White, non-Hispanic	1,171	3.9	1,205	4.5	998	3.8
Black, non-Hispanic	[6] 61	[6] 0.8	140	2.0	132	1.9
Hispanic [4]	147	1.5	265	2.3	444	3.5
Asian/Pacific Islander	(S)	(S)	[6] 73	[6] 2.8	44	1.4
Other [5]	111	4.8	82	3.2	69	2.7
Number of children in the household:						
One child	197	2.3	418	3.4	338	2.7
Two children	414	2.0	493	2.5	475	2.3
Three or more children	909	4.1	862	4.5	877	4.7
Number of parents in the household:						
Two parents	1,357	3.6	1,354	3.8	1,358	3.7
One parent	118	1.0	342	2.5	293	2.3
Nonparental guardians	(S)	(S)	[6] 77	[6] 4.0	38	2.0
Parents' participation in the labor force:						
Two parents—both in labor force	518	2.0	588	2.5	427	1.7
Two parents—one in labor force	808	7.5	719	6.2	935	7.2
One parent in labor force	127	1.3	247	2.2	189	1.8
No parent in labor force	(S)	(S)	130	4.8	139	4.0
Household income:						
$20,000 or less	186	2.2	219	2.9	184	2.9
$20,001 to 50,000	420	3.1	528	3.8	483	3.7
$50,001 to 75,000	414	4.0	370	3.9	435	4.8
$75,001 to 100,000	264	3.8	288	4.2	268	3.8
$100,000 or more	236	2.0	367	2.7	319	1.9
Parents' highest educational attainment:						
High school diploma or less	208	1.5	560	3.4	510	3.3
Vocational/technical degree or some college	559	3.8	525	3.4	418	3.1
Bachelor's degree	444	3.9	434	3.7	501	3.6
Graduate/professional school	309	2.9	255	3.3	260	3.0

S Figure does not meet publication standards. [1] The NCES uses a statistical adjustment for estimates of total homeschoolers in 2012; therefore, data will not add to total. All other estimates about homeschoolers do not use a statistical adjustment. [2] Excludes those ungraded. [3] Includes other race/ethnicities not shown separately. [4] Persons of Hispanic origin may be of any race. [5] Includes two or more races and race/ethnicity not reported. [6] Interpret data with caution.

Source: U.S. National Center for Education Statistics, *Digest of Education Statistics,* "Advance Release of Selected 2017 Digest Tables," and earlier releases, <http://www.nces.ed.gov/programs/digest/>, accessed August 2018.

Table 287. Public Charter and Traditional Schools by Selected Characteristics: 2010 and 2017

[49,178 represents 49,178,000. As of Fall. A public charter school is a public school that, in accordance with an enabling state statute, has been granted a charter exempting it from selected state and local rules and regulations]

Characteristic	2010			2017		
	Total	Traditional	Public charter	Total	Traditional	Public charter
Enrollment (1,000)	**49,178**	**47,391**	**1,787**	**50,330**	**47,187**	**3,143**
PERCENT DISTRIBUTION OF STUDENTS						
Race/ethnicity	100.0	100.0	100.0	100.0	100.0	100.0
White, non-Hispanic	52.5	53.1	36.2	47.6	48.7	32.1
Black, non-Hispanic	16.0	15.5	28.9	15.2	14.5	25.8
Hispanic	23.1	22.9	27.3	26.7	26.3	33.1
Asian/Pacific Islander	5.0	5.0	3.7	5.6	5.6	4.4
American Indian/Alaska Native	1.1	1.1	0.9	1.0	1.0	0.7
Two or more races	2.4	2.3	2.9	3.9	3.9	3.9
Number of teachers (1,000)	3,002	2,911	91	3,080	2,923	157
Pupil/teacher ratio	16.4	16.4	18.0	16.1	16.0	17.7
Total number of schools	**98,817**	**93,543**	**5,274**	**98,469**	**91,276**	**7,193**
PERCENT DISTRIBUTION OF SCHOOLS						
School level	100.0	100.0	100.0	100.0	100.0	100.0
Elementary [1]	67.9	68.7	54.3	68.5	69.4	56.5
Secondary [2]	24.8	24.8	25.9	24.3	24.3	23.2
Combined [3]	6.2	5.5	19.5	6.4	5.3	20.3
Other	1.1	1.1	0.2	0.9	1.0	0.1
Size of enrollment	100.0	100.0	100.0	100.0	100.0	100.0
Less than 300 students	30.9	29.3	59.0	29.8	28.6	44.8
300 to 499 students	27.8	28.1	22.3	28.1	28.3	25.5
500 to 999 students	32.3	33.4	14.8	32.7	33.5	23.3
1,000 students or more	9.0	9.3	3.9	9.4	9.6	6.3
Region	100.0	100.0	100.0	100.0	100.0	100.0
Northeast	15.5	15.9	9.5	15.2	15.6	10.1
Midwest	26.4	26.6	23.1	26.0	26.5	20.6
South	34.7	35.0	29.5	34.8	35.0	32.6
West	23.4	22.5	37.9	23.9	22.9	36.7

[1] Includes schools beginning with grade 6 or below and no grade higher than 8. [2] Includes schools with no grade lower than 7. [3] Includes schools beginning with grade 6 or below and ending with grade 9 or above.

Source: U.S. National Center for Education Statistics, *Digest of Education Statistics,* "Advance Release of Selected 2019 Digest Tables," <http://www.nces.ed.gov/programs/digest/>, accessed July 2020.

Table 288. Public Charter Schools and Enrollment by State: 2017

[3,143.3 represents 3,143,300. As of Fall]

State	Number of charter schools	Number of students (1,000)	Charter schools as a percent of public schools	Charter school enrollment as a percent of public school enrollment	State	Number of charter schools	Number of students (1,000)	Charter schools as a percent of public schools	Charter school enrollment as a percent of public school enrollment
United States	**7,193**	**3,143.3**	**7.3**	**6.2**	Missouri	68	23.6	2.8	2.6
Alabama	1	0.2	0.1	–	Montana	–	–	–	–
Alaska	29	7.0	5.7	5.3	Nebraska	–	–	–	–
Arizona	557	189.7	23.9	17.2	Nevada	72	45.3	10.4	9.3
Arkansas	82	31.5	7.6	6.4	New Hampshire	31	3.5	6.3	2.0
California	1,268	627.0	12.3	10.1	New Jersey	89	49.4	3.4	3.6
Colorado	250	120.7	13.2	13.3	New Mexico	97	26.1	11.0	7.8
Connecticut	24	10.2	2.3	2.0	New York	279	139.4	5.8	5.2
Delaware	24	15.3	10.6	11.3	North Carolina	173	101.0	6.5	6.5
Dist. of Columbia	111	38.7	49.6	44.8	North Dakota	–	–	–	–
Florida	654	295.8	15.1	10.4	Ohio	340	113.2	9.4	6.6
Georgia	93	72.7	4.0	4.1	Oklahoma	58	29.0	3.2	4.2
Hawaii	36	11.2	12.3	6.2	Oregon	127	33.7	10.2	5.9
Idaho	59	21.1	8.0	7.0	Pennsylvania	179	137.7	6.0	8.1
Illinois	142	64.9	3.3	3.3	Rhode Island	31	8.9	9.8	6.3
Indiana	99	47.1	5.2	4.5	South Carolina	70	34.9	5.6	4.5
Iowa	3	0.4	0.2	0.1	South Dakota	–	–	–	–
Kansas	10	3.2	0.8	0.7	Tennessee	110	37.7	6.2	3.8
Kentucky	–	–	–	–	Texas	759	325.2	8.5	6.0
Louisiana	150	80.7	10.8	11.3	Utah	131	75.5	12.5	11.3
Maine	11	2.2	1.8	1.3	Vermont	–	–	–	–
Maryland	50	23.8	3.5	2.7	Virginia	8	1.2	0.4	0.1
Massachusetts	80	45.2	4.3	4.7	Washington	10	2.5	0.4	0.2
Michigan	366	145.9	9.8	9.9	West Virginia	–	–	–	–
Minnesota	221	56.8	8.8	6.4	Wisconsin	233	42.5	10.3	4.9
Mississippi	3	0.9	0.3	0.2	Wyoming	5	0.6	1.4	0.6

– Represents or rounds to zero.

Source: U.S. National Center for Education Statistics, *Digest of Education Statistics,* "Advance Release of Selected 2019 Digest Tables," <http://www.nces.ed.gov/programs/digest/>, accessed May 2020.

Table 289. Career and Technology Education (CTE) Programs in Public School Districts by District Characteristics: 2017

[In percent. For school year ending in year shown]

	Districts offering CTE programs to high school students [1]	Entities providing CTE Programs [2]			CTE program offerings [2]			
		Area CTE center or group/ consortium of school districts	District individually	2-year community or technical college	Student-run enterprises or services	Mentoring by local employers	On-the-job training, etc. [3]	Apprentice-ships or preappren-ticeship programs
All public school districts..................	**98**	**54**	**77**	**46**	**55**	**65**	**77**	**31**
District enrollment size:								
Less than 1,000..............	98	54	75	41	38	52	61	23
1,000 to 2,499...............	98	61	72	44	57	64	83	32
2,500 to 9,999...............	99	53	79	50	70	78	89	39
10,000 or more..............	100	38	95	61	86	86	96	42
Community type:								
City.........................	99	35	92	55	72	87	95	35
Suburban....................	97	66	69	44	74	77	90	38
Town........................	100	52	80	49	59	67	79	33
Rural.......................	98	53	78	43	43	55	68	26
Region:								
Northeast....................	97	78	50	24	75	75	92	33
Southeast....................	100	34	94	63	50	66	84	39
Central......................	98	62	76	49	56	66	75	36
West........................	99	37	89	46	42	55	66	17

[1] Respondents were asked to include all CTE programs that the district offered to high school students, including programs provided by the district or by other entities (such as an area/regional CTE center, a consortium of districts, or a community or technical college). [2] Based on the 98 percent of public school districts that offer CTE programs to students at the high school level. [3] Includes on-the-job training, internships, practicums, clinical experiences, or cooperative education (co-op).

Source: U.S. National Center for Education Statistics, *Career and Technical Education Programs in Public School Districts: 2016–17,* April 2018. See also <https://nces.ed.gov/pubsearch/pubsinfo.asp?pubid=2018028>.

Table 290. ACT Program Scores and Characteristics of College-Bound Students: 1990 to 2019

[For academic year ending in year shown. Except as indicated, test scores and characteristics of college-bound students. Data based on all ACT tested seniors graduating in year shown. Beginning 1990, not comparable with previous years because a new version of the ACT was introduced]

Type of test and characteristic	Unit	1990	1995	2000	2010	2014	2015	2016	2017	2018	2019
TEST SCORES [1]											
Composite..........................	**Point**	**20.6**	**20.8**	**21.0**	**21.0**	**21.0**	**21.0**	**20.8**	**21.0**	**20.8**	**20.7**
Male...............................	Point	21.0	21.0	21.2	21.2	21.1	21.1	20.9	21.0	20.8	20.6
Female............................	Point	20.3	20.7	20.9	20.9	20.9	21.0	20.9	21.1	20.9	20.8
English.............................	Point	20.5	20.2	20.5	20.5	20.3	20.4	20.1	20.3	20.2	20.1
Male...............................	Point	20.1	19.8	20.0	20.1	20.0	20.0	19.8	19.9	19.7	19.6
Female............................	Point	20.9	20.6	20.9	20.8	20.7	20.8	20.6	20.8	20.7	20.6
Math................................	Point	19.9	20.2	20.7	21.0	20.9	20.8	20.6	20.7	20.5	20.4
Male...............................	Point	20.7	20.9	21.4	21.6	21.1	21.3	21.0	21.2	20.9	20.8
Female............................	Point	19.3	19.7	20.2	20.5	20.5	20.4	20.3	20.4	20.2	20.0
Reading [2].........................	Point	(NA)	21.3	21.4	21.3	21.3	21.4	21.3	21.4	21.3	21.2
Male...............................	Point	(NA)	21.1	21.2	21.1	21.1	21.2	21.0	21.2	21.0	20.7
Female............................	Point	(NA)	21.4	21.5	21.4	21.5	21.6	21.6	21.8	21.7	21.7
Science reasoning [3]................	Point	(NA)	21.0	21.0	20.9	20.8	20.9	20.8	21.0	20.7	20.6
Male...............................	Point	(NA)	21.6	21.6	21.4	21.2	21.3	21.1	21.3	20.9	20.8
Female............................	Point	(NA)	20.5	20.6	20.5	20.5	20.6	20.6	20.8	20.6	20.5
PARTICIPANTS [4]											
Total [5]............................	**1,000**	**817**	**945**	**1,065**	**1,569**	**1,846**	**1,924**	**2,090**	**2,030**	**1,915**	**1,783**
Male...............................	Percent	46	44	43	45	46	47	46	46	47	46
White..............................	Percent	73	69	72	62	56	55	54	52	52	52
Black..............................	Percent	9	9	10	14	13	13	13	13	13	12
Obtaining composite scores of: [6]											
27 or above........................	Percent	12	13	14	16	17	18	14	15	15	15
18 or below........................	Percent	35	34	32	35	36	37	39	38	40	35

NA Not available. [1] Minimum score, 1; maximum score, 36. [2] Prior to 1990, social studies; data not comparable with previous years. [3] Prior to 1990, natural sciences; data not comparable with previous years. [4] Data by race are for those responding to the race question. [5] 817 represents 817,000. [6] Prior to 1990, 26 or above and 15 or below.

Source: ACT, Inc., Iowa City, IA. Most recent score reported in the *The ACT® Profile Report - National*, annual ©. Reproduced with permission.

Table 291. Proficiency Levels on Selected NAEP Tests for Students in Public Schools by State: 2019

[Represents percent of public school students scoring at or above basic and proficient levels. Basic denotes partial mastery of the knowledge and skills that are fundamental for proficient work at a given grade level. Proficient represents solid academic performance. Students reaching this level demonstrated competency over challenging subject matter. For more detail, see <http://nationsreportcard.gov/>. Based on the National Assessment of Educational Progress (NAEP) tests which are administered to a representative sample of students in public schools, private schools, and Department of Defense schools]

State	Grade 4 Math At or above Basic	Grade 4 Math At or above Proficient	Grade 8 Math At or above Basic	Grade 8 Math At or above Proficient	Grade 4 Reading At or above Basic	Grade 4 Reading At or above Proficient	Grade 8 Reading At or above Basic	Grade 8 Reading At or above Proficient
U.S. average	**80**	**40**	**68**	**33**	**65**	**34**	**72**	**32**
Alabama	71	28	57	21	58	28	64	24
Alaska	73	33	63	29	53	25	63	23
Arizona	77	37	68	31	61	31	70	28
Arkansas	75	33	63	27	62	31	68	30
California	75	34	61	29	63	32	68	30
Colorado	80	44	73	37	71	40	77	38
Connecticut	82	45	72	39	70	40	78	41
Delaware	79	39	65	29	62	33	69	31
District of Columbia	73	34	55	23	57	30	58	23
Florida	87	48	66	31	70	38	72	34
Georgia	77	36	67	31	63	32	72	32
Hawaii	78	40	65	28	63	34	68	29
Idaho	82	43	74	37	69	37	77	37
Illinois	77	38	69	34	64	34	74	35
Indiana	84	47	73	37	67	37	75	37
Iowa	81	42	72	33	68	35	73	33
Kansas	79	40	71	33	66	34	74	32
Kentucky	81	40	67	29	67	35	73	33
Louisiana	73	29	61	23	55	26	68	27
Maine	81	42	71	34	67	36	75	36
Maryland	76	39	65	33	64	35	73	36
Massachusetts	85	50	78	47	76	45	81	45
Michigan	76	36	68	31	64	32	73	31
Minnesota	85	53	77	44	69	38	74	34
Mississippi	84	39	62	24	65	32	67	25
Missouri	80	39	70	32	64	34	74	33
Montana	82	43	73	36	69	36	76	34
Nebraska	84	45	74	37	69	37	74	34
Nevada	77	34	62	26	64	31	69	29
New Hampshire	86	46	77	38	71	38	78	38
New Jersey	85	48	76	44	72	42	77	43
New Mexico	72	29	56	21	53	24	61	23
New York	76	37	66	34	66	34	70	32
North Carolina	82	41	71	37	67	36	72	33
North Dakota	84	44	75	37	69	34	75	32
Ohio	82	41	73	38	68	36	75	38
Oklahoma	80	35	66	26	63	29	71	26
Oregon	75	37	67	31	64	34	73	34
Pennsylvania	81	47	70	39	68	40	73	35
Rhode Island	81	40	64	29	66	35	71	35
South Carolina	77	36	64	29	61	32	69	29
South Dakota	83	43	76	39	69	36	74	32
Tennessee	79	40	68	31	66	35	73	32
Texas	84	44	68	30	61	30	67	25
Utah	82	46	72	37	72	40	77	38
Vermont	81	39	75	38	68	37	77	40
Virginia	87	48	75	38	69	38	71	33
Washington	79	39	72	40	65	35	74	38
West Virginia	74	30	62	24	60	30	67	25
Wisconsin	80	45	76	41	66	36	76	39
Wyoming	87	48	76	37	73	41	75	34

Source: U.S. National Center for Education Statistics, "NAEP Data Explorer," <https://www.nationsreportcard.gov/ndecore/xplore/nde>, accessed January 2020.

Table 292. School Enrollment Status by Race, Hispanic Origin, and Sex: 2010 and 2018

[17,210 represents 17,210,000. As of October. For persons 18 to 21 years old. For the civilian noninstitutional population. Based on the Current Population Survey; see text, Section 1 and Appendix III]

Characteristic	Total persons 18 to 21 years old (1,000)		Percent distribution							
			Enrolled in high school		High school graduates				Not high school graduates, not enrolled in high school	
					Total		In college			
	2010	2018	2010	2018	2010	2018	2010	2018	2010	2018
Total [1]	17,210	16,711	9.9	10.1	81.5	83.9	50.6	51.6	8.4	5.8
White	13,176	12,255	9.7	9.6	82.2	83.8	50.8	51.7	8.0	6.4
Black	2,538	2,482	13.9	13.7	73.0	82.3	41.5	45.5	13.0	3.9
Hispanic [2]	3,339	4,005	13.5	10.4	71.3	79.6	38.9	44.3	15.2	10.0
Male [1]	8,824	8,468	11.0	11.2	79.8	81.5	46.7	47.1	9.0	7.1
White	6,867	6,259	10.8	10.5	80.4	81.5	46.6	46.6	8.7	7.7
Black	1,277	1,209	15.5	16.0	69.1	79.2	36.2	42.7	15.4	4.5
Hispanic [2]	1,744	2,044	14.0	11.8	70.0	75.7	35.7	39.0	15.8	12.4
Female [1]	8,386	8,243	8.8	9.1	83.2	86.3	54.8	56.2	7.8	4.5
White	6,308	5,996	8.4	8.6	84.1	86.3	55.5	57.0	7.2	5.0
Black	1,261	1,272	12.3	11.6	76.9	85.3	46.9	48.3	10.5	3.1
Hispanic [2]	1,595	1,961	12.9	9.0	72.7	83.5	42.4	49.9	14.4	7.4

[1] Includes other races not shown separately. [2] Persons of Hispanic origin may be of any race.

Source: U.S. Census Bureau, Current Population Reports, P-20, and earlier reports; and "School Enrollment," <https://www.census.gov/topics/education/school-enrollment/data/tables.All.html>, accessed January 2020.

Table 293. Public High School Graduates by State: 1980 to 2019

[In thousands (2,747.7 represents 2,747,700). For school year ending in year shown. Data include regular diploma recipients, but exclude students receiving a certificate of attendance and persons receiving high school equivalency certificates]

State	1980	1990	2000	2010	2015 (P)	2017 (P)	2018 (P)	2019 (P)
United States	2,747.7	[1] 2,320.3	2,553.8	3,128.0	3,187.0	3,255.3	3,310.0	3,317.0
Alabama	45.2	40.5	37.8	43.2	45.4	47.6	48.0	47.6
Alaska	5.2	5.4	6.6	8.2	7.9	7.9	8.0	7.9
Arizona	28.6	32.1	38.3	61.1	67.2	68.8	66.7	66.4
Arkansas	29.1	26.5	27.3	28.3	30.4	30.8	30.9	31.3
California	249.2	236.3	309.9	405.0	422.8	411.7	415.9	411.3
Colorado	36.8	33.0	38.9	49.3	51.5	54.1	55.6	56.3
Connecticut	37.7	27.9	31.6	34.5	37.2	37.9	37.9	37.3
Delaware	7.6	5.6	6.1	8.1	8.4	8.7	8.8	8.9
District of Columbia [2]	5.0	3.6	2.7	3.6	4.0	4.4	4.8	4.7
Florida	87.3	88.9	106.7	156.1	163.7	170.8	175.1	177.2
Georgia	61.6	56.6	62.6	91.6	97.4	102.1	105.8	107.7
Hawaii	11.5	10.3	10.4	11.0	10.8	10.7	11.2	10.6
Idaho	13.2	12.0	16.2	17.8	18.1	19.1	19.5	19.8
Illinois	135.6	108.1	111.8	139.0	140.5	141.3	142.7	142.8
Indiana	73.1	60.0	57.0	64.6	66.8	69.0	71.6	74.3
Iowa	43.4	31.8	33.9	34.5	32.5	32.9	33.3	33.1
Kansas	30.9	25.4	29.1	31.6	31.9	32.9	33.5	33.3
Kentucky	41.2	38.0	36.8	42.7	42.5	43.3	44.2	44.2
Louisiana	46.3	36.1	38.4	36.6	37.7	39.4	41.9	41.7
Maine	15.4	13.8	12.2	14.1	12.6	12.6	12.7	12.6
Maryland	54.3	41.6	47.8	59.1	57.7	57.3	59.1	58.4
Massachusetts	73.8	55.9	53.0	64.5	65.8	68.6	69.3	69.6
Michigan	124.3	93.8	97.7	110.7	102.0	101.6	102.9	101.8
Minnesota	64.9	49.1	57.4	59.7	56.8	57.3	57.7	58.9
Mississippi	27.6	25.2	24.2	25.5	26.3	26.9	28.0	27.4
Missouri	62.3	49.0	52.8	64.0	60.6	60.9	61.4	61.0
Montana	12.1	9.4	10.9	10.1	9.4	9.4	9.5	9.9
Nebraska	22.4	17.7	20.1	19.4	20.7	21.1	21.8	21.9
Nevada	8.5	9.5	14.6	21.0	23.0	23.8	24.1	24.6
New Hampshire	11.7	10.8	11.8	15.0	13.5	13.2	13.1	12.9
New Jersey	94.6	69.8	74.4	96.2	95.3	98.0	98.3	97.9
New Mexico	18.4	14.9	18.0	18.6	19.5	19.8	19.9	19.7
New York	204.1	143.3	141.7	183.8	179.1	181.8	182.4	181.2
North Carolina	70.9	64.8	62.1	88.7	97.0	101.7	104.9	106.9
North Dakota	9.9	7.7	8.6	7.2	7.0	6.9	6.9	7.1
Ohio	144.2	114.5	111.7	123.4	120.9	126.6	126.9	125.3
Oklahoma	39.3	35.6	37.6	38.5	38.4	40.2	41.0	41.4
Oregon	29.9	25.5	30.2	34.7	34.8	34.7	34.5	34.9
Pennsylvania	146.5	110.5	114.0	131.2	123.6	124.0	124.8	123.1
Rhode Island	10.9	7.8	8.5	9.9	9.9	9.4	9.6	10.3
South Carolina	38.7	32.5	31.6	40.4	42.7	45.1	46.8	47.1
South Dakota	10.7	7.7	9.3	8.2	8.1	8.2	8.2	8.2
Tennessee	49.8	46.1	41.6	62.4	62.0	63.7	64.3	65.1
Texas	171.4	172.5	212.9	280.9	309.3	327.7	339.7	347.0
Utah	20.0	21.2	32.5	31.5	34.1	36.6	37.6	38.2
Vermont	6.7	6.1	6.7	7.2	6.2	6.0	5.7	5.7
Virginia	66.6	60.6	65.6	81.5	82.7	84.7	87.2	87.3
Washington	50.4	45.9	57.6	66.0	68.2	70.8	71.8	71.9
West Virginia	23.4	21.9	19.4	17.7	17.5	17.4	17.5	17.1
Wisconsin	69.3	52.0	58.5	64.7	60.5	60.7	61.4	60.7
Wyoming	6.1	5.8	6.5	5.7	5.6	5.7	5.8	5.8

P Projected. [1] U.S. total includes estimates for nonreporting states. [2] Beginning in 1985-86, graduates from adult programs are excluded.

Source: U.S. National Center for Education Statistics, *Digest of Education Statistics*, "Advance Release of Selected 2019 Digest Tables," and earlier releases, <http://www.nces.ed.gov/programs/digest/>, accessed August 2020.

Table 294. High School Dropouts by Selected Characteristics: 2010 to 2018

[3,294 represents 3,294,000. As of October. Data are for status dropouts which includes 16- to 24-year olds who are not enrolled in school and who have not completed a high school program, regardless of when they left school and whether they ever attended school in the United States. People who have received equivalency credentials, such as the GED, are counted as high school completers. Based on the American Community Survey, see Appendix III]

Characteristic	2010	2011	2012	2013	2014	2015	2016	2017	2018
Total (1,000)	**3,294**	**3,044**	**2,784**	**2,716**	**2,497**	**2,397**	**2,279**	**2,125**	**2,079**
PERCENT									
Total	**8.3**	**7.7**	**7.0**	**6.8**	**6.3**	**6.0**	**5.8**	**5.4**	**5.3**
Male	10.0	9.0	8.2	8.0	7.2	7.0	6.8	6.4	6.2
Female	6.6	6.2	5.7	5.6	5.2	5.0	4.7	4.4	4.4
Race/ethnicity:									
White	5.3	5.1	4.7	4.7	4.4	4.5	4.5	4.3	4.2
Black	10.3	9.6	9.0	9.0	7.9	7.2	7.0	6.5	6.4
Hispanic	16.7	14.5	12.8	11.8	10.7	9.9	9.1	8.2	8.0
Asian	2.8	2.7	2.6	2.5	2.5	2.4	2.0	2.1	1.9
Pacific Islander	4.8	8.8	9.1	5.0	10.6	5.4	6.9	3.9	8.1
American Indian/Alaska Native	15.4	13.1	12.8	12.8	11.5	13.2	11.0	10.1	9.5
Some other race [1]	9.2	7.9	5.9	5.1	5.6	7.5	5.1	5.2	4.5
Two or more races	6.1	6.0	5.6	5.2	5.0	4.7	4.8	4.5	5.2
Nativity:									
Native-born	7.0	6.6	6.1	6.1	5.6	5.5	5.3	5.0	4.9
Foreign-born	18.7	16.3	14.1	12.9	11.8	10.6	9.8	8.9	8.6
Disability status: [2]									
With a disability	17.4	15.8	15.4	15.2	13.9	12.6	12.4	12.1	11.7
Without a disability	7.8	7.2	6.5	6.3	5.8	5.6	5.3	5.0	4.9

[1] Respondents who wrote in some other race that was not included as an option on the questionnaire. [2] Individuals identified as having a disability reported difficulty in at least one of the following: walking, climbing stairs, dressing, bathing, learning, or remembering.

Source: U.S. National Center for Education Statistics, *Digest of Education Statistics*, "Advance Release of Selected 2019 Digest Tables," <http://www.nces.ed.gov/programs/digest/>, accessed May 2020.

Table 295. High School Dropouts by Age, Race, and Hispanic Origin: 1980 to 2018

[5,212 represents 5,212,000. As of October. For persons 14 to 24 years old. Dropouts are persons not in regular school and who have not completed the 12th grade nor received a general equivalency degree. Based on Current Population Survey; see text, Section 1 and Appendix III]

Age and race	Number of dropouts (1,000)					Percent of population				
	1980	1990	2000	2010	2018	1980	1990	2000	2010	2018
Total dropouts [1,2]	**5,212**	**3,854**	**3,883**	**2,952**	**2,281**	**12.0**	**10.1**	**9.1**	**6.4**	**4.9**
16 to 17 years	709	418	460	227	491	8.8	6.3	5.8	2.7	5.8
18 to 21 years	2,578	1,921	2,005	1,445	972	15.8	13.4	12.9	8.4	5.8
22 to 24 years	1,798	1,458	1,310	1,144	702	15.2	13.8	11.8	9.2	5.5
White [2,3]	4,169	3,127	3,065	2,232	1,669	11.3	10.1	9.1	6.3	4.9
16 to 17 years	619	334	366	181	303	9.2	6.4	5.8	2.9	5.0
18 to 21 years	2,032	1,516	1,558	1,048	779	14.7	13.1	12.6	8.0	6.4
22 to 24 years	1,416	1,235	1,040	893	505	14.0	14.0	11.7	9.2	5.3
Black [2,3]	934	611	705	498	368	16.0	10.9	10.9	7.2	5.4
16 to 17 years	80	73	84	30	122	6.9	6.9	7.0	2.3	9.9
18 to 21 years	486	345	383	283	96	23.0	16.0	16.0	10.5	3.9
22 to 24 years	346	185	232	167	120	24.0	13.5	14.3	9.4	6.2
Hispanic [2,4]	919	1,122	1,499	1,122	820	29.5	26.8	23.5	12.8	7.6
16 to 17 years	92	89	121	40	126	16.6	12.9	11.0	2.7	6.4
18 to 21 years	470	502	733	506	399	40.3	32.9	30.0	15.2	10.0
22 to 24 years	323	523	602	543	256	40.6	42.8	35.5	23.2	9.3

[1] Includes other racial/ethnic groups not shown separately. [2] Includes persons age 14 to 15, not shown separately. [3] Beginning 2003, for persons who selected this race only. See footnote 4, Table 261. [4] Persons of Hispanic origin may be of any race.

Source: U.S. Census Bureau, Current Population Reports, series PPL and P-20; and "School Enrollment," <https://www.census.gov/topics/education/school-enrollment/data/tables.All.html>, accessed January 2020.

Table 296. Higher Education—Institutions and Enrollment: 1990 to 2018

[13,819 represents 13,819,000. As of Fall. Covers universities, colleges, professional schools, and junior and teachers' colleges, both publicly and privately controlled, regular session. Includes estimates for institutions not reporting. Data for 1990 cover institutions of higher education; beginning 2000, data cover degree-granting institutions. Degree-granting institutions grant associate's or higher degrees and participate in Title IV federal financial aid programs. The degree-granting classification includes more 2-year colleges and excludes a few higher education institutions that did not grant degrees. Data are based on the Integrated Postsecondary Education Data System. See also Appendix III]

Item	Unit	1990	2000	2005	2010	2015	2017	2018
ALL INSTITUTIONS								
Number of institutions [1]	**Number**	**3,559**	**4,182**	**4,276**	**4,599**	**4,583**	**4,313**	**4,042**
4-year	Number	2,141	2,450	2,582	2,870	3,004	2,828	2,703
2-year	Number	1,418	1,732	1,694	1,729	1,579	1,485	1,339
Instructional staff—								
lecturer or above [2]	**1,000**	**(NA)**	**(NA)**	**1,290**	**(NA)**	**1,552**	**1,546**	**1,543**
Percent full-time	Percent	(NA)	(NA)	52	(NA)	52	53	54
Total enrollment [3]	**1,000**	**13,819**	**15,312**	**17,487**	**21,019**	**19,988**	**19,778**	**19,646**
Male	1,000	6,284	6,722	7,456	9,046	8,724	8,571	8,443
Female	1,000	7,535	8,591	10,032	11,974	11,264	11,207	11,203
4-year institutions	1,000	8,579	9,364	10,999	13,336	13,489	13,825	13,901
2-year institutions	1,000	5,240	5,948	6,488	7,684	6,499	5,953	5,745
Full-time	1,000	7,821	9,010	10,797	13,087	12,288	12,076	11,992
Part-time	1,000	5,998	6,303	6,690	7,932	7,701	7,702	7,654
Public	1,000	10,845	11,753	13,022	15,142	14,573	14,572	14,529
Private	1,000	2,974	3,560	4,466	5,877	5,415	5,206	5,117
Not-for-profit	1,000	2,760	3,109	3,455	3,854	4,066	4,108	4,134
For profit	1,000	214	450	1,011	2,023	1,349	1,098	982
Undergraduate	1,000	11,959	13,155	14,964	18,082	17,047	16,773	16,610
Men	1,000	5,380	5,778	6,409	7,836	7,502	7,351	7,226
Women	1,000	6,579	7,377	8,555	10,246	9,544	9,422	9,384
Full-time	1,000	6,976	7,923	9,446	11,457	10,603	10,372	10,267
Part-time	1,000	4,983	5,232	5,518	6,625	6,444	6,401	6,343
First-time freshmen [4]	1,000	2,257	2,428	2,657	3,157	2,883	2,883	2,886
Postbaccalaureate	1,000	1,860	2,157	2,524	2,937	2,942	3,005	3,036
Men	1,000	904	944	1,047	1,209	1,222	1,220	1,217
Women	1,000	955	1,213	1,476	1,728	1,720	1,785	1,819
2-YEAR INSTITUTIONS								
Number of institutions [1]	Number	1,418	1,732	1,694	1,729	1,579	1,485	1,339
Public	Number	972	1,076	1,053	978	910	876	868
Private	Number	446	656	641	751	669	609	471
Instructional staff—								
lecturer or above [2]	1,000	(NA)	(NA)	373	(NA)	372	337	326
Enrollment [3]	1,000	5,240	5,948	6,488	7,684	6,499	5,953	5,745
Public	1,000	4,996	5,697	6,184	7,218	6,224	5,717	5,547
Private	1,000	244	251	304	466	275	235	199
Male	1,000	2,233	2,559	2,680	3,266	2,818	2,567	2,452
Female	1,000	3,007	3,390	3,808	4,418	3,681	3,386	3,294
4-YEAR INSTITUTIONS								
Number of institutions [1]	Number	2,141	2,450	2,582	2,870	3,004	2,828	2,703
Public	Number	595	622	640	678	710	750	768
Private	Number	1,546	1,828	1,942	2,192	2,294	2,078	1,935
Instructional staff—								
lecturer or above [2]	1,000	(NA)	(NA)	917	(NA)	1,181	1,209	1,217
Enrollment [3]	1,000	8,579	9,364	10,999	13,336	13,489	13,825	13,901
Public	1,000	5,848	6,055	6,838	7,924	8,349	8,854	8,983
Private	1,000	2,730	3,308	4,162	5,412	5,140	4,971	4,918
Male	1,000	4,051	4,163	4,776	5,780	5,906	6,005	5,991
Female	1,000	4,527	5,201	6,224	7,556	7,583	7,821	7,910

NA Not available. [1] Number of institutions includes count of branch campuses. Includes schools accredited by the National Association of Trade and Technical Schools. [2] Beginning in 2007, includes institutions with fewer than 15 full-time employees; prior to 2007, these institutions did not report staff. [3] Branch campuses counted according to actual status, e.g., 2-year branch in 2-year category. May include unclassified students taking courses for credit but not towards a degree. [4] Students seeking certificates or degrees.

Source: U.S. National Center for Education Statistics, *Digest of Education Statistics*, "Advance Release of Selected 2019 Digest Tables," and earlier releases, <http://nces.ed.gov/Programs/digest/>, accessed July 2020.

Table 297. Degree-Granting Higher Education Institutions—Number and Enrollment by State and Selected Characteristics: 2018

[19,646 represents 19,646,000. Number of institutions beginning in academic year. Opening Fall enrollment of resident and extension students attending full-time or part-time. Based on data from the Integrated Postsecondary Education Data System (IPEDS)]

State	Num-ber of institu-tions [1]	Enrollment (1,000)							Minority			Non-resi-dent alien
		Total	Male	Female	Public	Private	Full-time	White [2]	Total [3]	Black [2]	His-panic	
United States........	**4,042**	**19,646**	**8,443**	**11,203**	**14,529**	**5,117**	**11,992**	**10,301**	**9,345**	**2,493**	**3,645**	**992**
Alabama...............	62	304	130	174	255	49	207	190	115	78	12	9
Alaska.................	8	26	10	16	25	1	11	15	11	1	2	1
Arizona................	71	582	231	351	367	215	324	283	299	71	146	20
Arkansas..............	53	160	66	94	142	17	101	109	50	24	11	5
California..............	420	2,712	1,211	1,501	2,250	462	1,493	738	1,974	166	1,112	148
Colorado..............	70	361	158	202	279	81	206	221	139	27	65	12
Connecticut...........	41	197	83	115	115	83	130	111	86	26	31	11
Delaware..............	8	61	24	37	43	18	37	33	27	13	5	5
District of Columbia....	18	98	39	59	5	93	65	42	55	24	9	11
Florida.................	181	1,068	442	626	800	268	616	456	612	189	298	46
Georgia...............	111	543	222	321	436	108	339	258	285	166	45	24
Hawaii.................	18	62	25	37	51	11	35	10	52	1	7	4
Idaho..................	15	123	53	71	77	46	61	92	31	1	12	9
Illinois.................	157	738	314	425	465	273	430	386	353	93	142	42
Indiana................	75	388	174	215	296	92	260	274	114	35	26	24
Iowa...................	61	254	113	141	199	55	151	185	69	21	20	11
Kansas................	64	213	96	117	180	33	122	142	70	17	22	13
Kentucky..............	59	263	113	150	200	63	160	200	63	22	10	17
Louisiana..............	56	241	95	147	211	31	163	131	110	74	14	7
Maine..................	31	72	29	43	48	23	43	60	12	3	2	2
Maryland..............	53	361	159	202	302	59	186	159	202	100	35	22
Massachusetts........	111	500	216	283	208	292	351	276	223	44	58	62
Michigan..............	94	541	244	297	467	74	328	373	168	62	30	30
Minnesota.............	88	409	157	252	245	164	218	266	143	61	25	15
Mississippi............	36	169	67	103	151	19	123	94	75	61	4	3
Missouri...............	101	374	160	215	232	142	226	265	109	43	21	17
Montana...............	23	49	23	27	45	4	34	39	10	(Z)	2	1
Nebraska..............	39	135	59	76	101	34	85	98	37	7	14	5
Nevada................	23	118	50	68	109	9	63	50	68	9	34	2
New Hampshire........	25	161	61	100	39	122	73	114	46	20	14	3
New Jersey............	83	414	189	226	329	85	274	193	221	57	91	21
New Mexico...........	39	123	51	73	120	3	60	40	84	4	60	3
New York..............	295	1,250	543	707	690	560	892	583	667	168	228	108
North Carolina.........	136	564	233	331	456	108	356	325	239	124	48	20
North Dakota..........	20	53	26	28	47	7	36	42	11	2	2	2
Ohio...................	169	645	281	364	496	149	407	465	180	74	30	32
Oklahoma.............	49	196	84	112	171	25	126	112	84	15	20	9
Oregon................	55	228	102	127	192	36	140	146	82	7	32	11
Pennsylvania..........	220	700	304	396	393	308	510	458	242	76	53	47
Rhode Island..........	13	81	35	46	40	41	62	52	29	6	11	5
South Carolina........	67	241	98	142	197	44	168	152	89	58	12	5
South Dakota..........	22	53	24	29	44	9	33	43	11	2	2	2
Tennessee............	88	322	133	189	225	97	228	218	104	59	16	9
Texas.................	242	1,644	704	940	1,469	175	852	584	1,060	203	632	67
Utah...................	30	360	154	206	184	176	268	268	92	18	38	7
Vermont...............	22	43	20	23	25	18	31	34	9	2	2	2
Virginia................	115	552	237	315	385	167	344	312	240	106	50	20
Washington...........	74	367	163	204	319	48	252	207	160	17	50	23
West Virginia..........	42	140	70	70	82	58	70	105	35	14	9	4
Wisconsin.............	75	336	147	189	277	59	207	254	82	18	25	12
Wyoming..............	9	33	15	18	32	(Z)	18	26	6	(Z)	3	1
U.S. military [4]...........	5	16	11	4	16	(X)	16	10	5	1	2	(Z)

X Not applicable. Z Fewer than 500. [1] Branch campuses counted as separate institutions. [2] Non-Hispanic. [3] Includes other races not shown separately. [4] Service academies.

Source: U.S. National Center for Education Statistics, *Digest of Education Statistics*, "Advance Release of Selected 2019 Digest Tables," <http://www.nces.ed.gov/programs/digest/>, accessed August 2020.

Table 298. College Enrollment of Recent High School Completers: 1970 to 2018

[2,758 represents 2,758,000. For persons 16 to 24 years old who graduated from high school in the preceding 12 months. Includes persons receiving GEDs. Based on sample surveys and subject to sampling error; data not comparable with that in other tables]

Year	Number of high school completers (1,000)						Percent enrolled in college [5]					
	Total [1]	Male	Female	White [2]	Black [2,3]	His-panic [3,4]	Total [1]	Male	Female	White [2]	Black [2,3]	His-panic [3,4]
1970	2,758	1,343	1,415	2,461	(NA)	(NA)	51.7	55.2	48.5	52.0	(NA)	(NA)
1975	3,185	1,513	1,672	2,701	302	132	50.7	52.6	49.0	51.1	41.7	58.0
1980	3,088	1,498	1,589	2,554	350	130	49.3	46.7	51.8	49.8	42.7	52.3
1985	2,668	1,287	1,381	2,104	332	141	57.7	58.6	56.8	60.1	42.2	51.0
1990	2,362	1,173	1,189	1,819	331	121	60.1	58.0	62.2	63.0	46.8	42.7
1991	2,276	1,140	1,136	1,727	310	154	62.5	57.9	67.1	65.4	46.4	57.2
1992	2,397	1,216	1,180	1,724	354	198	61.9	60.0	63.8	64.3	48.2	55.0
1993	2,342	1,120	1,223	1,719	304	201	62.6	59.9	65.2	62.9	55.6	62.2
1994	2,517	1,244	1,273	1,915	316	178	61.9	60.6	63.2	64.5	50.8	49.1
1995	2,599	1,238	1,361	1,861	349	288	61.9	62.6	61.3	64.3	51.2	53.7
1996	2,660	1,297	1,363	1,875	406	227	65.0	60.1	69.7	67.4	56.0	50.8
1997	2,769	1,354	1,415	1,909	384	336	67.0	63.6	70.3	68.2	58.5	65.6
1998	2,810	1,452	1,358	1,980	386	314	65.6	62.4	69.1	68.5	61.9	47.4
1999	2,897	1,474	1,423	1,978	436	329	62.9	61.4	64.4	66.3	58.9	42.3
2000	2,756	1,251	1,505	1,938	393	300	63.3	59.9	66.2	65.7	54.9	52.9
2001	2,549	1,277	1,273	1,834	381	241	61.8	60.1	63.5	64.3	55.0	51.7
2002	2,796	1,412	1,384	1,903	382	344	65.2	62.1	68.4	69.1	59.4	53.6
2003	2,677	1,306	1,372	1,832	327	314	63.9	61.2	66.5	66.2	57.5	58.6
2004	2,752	1,327	1,425	1,854	398	286	66.7	61.4	71.5	68.8	62.5	61.8
2005	2,675	1,262	1,414	1,799	345	390	68.6	66.5	70.4	73.2	55.7	54.0
2006	2,692	1,328	1,363	1,805	318	382	66.0	65.8	66.1	68.5	55.5	57.9
2007	2,955	1,511	1,444	2,043	416	355	67.2	66.1	68.3	69.5	55.7	64.0
2008	3,151	1,640	1,511	2,091	416	458	68.6	65.9	71.6	71.7	55.7	63.9
2009	2,937	1,407	1,531	1,863	415	459	70.1	66.0	73.8	71.3	69.5	59.3
2010	3,160	1,679	1,482	1,937	461	507	68.1	62.8	74.0	70.5	62.0	59.7
2011	3,079	1,611	1,468	1,747	464	623	68.2	64.7	72.2	68.3	67.1	66.6
2012	3,203	1,622	1,581	(NA)	(NA)	(NA)	66.2	61.3	71.3	65.7	56.4	70.3
2013	2,977	1,524	1,453	(NA)	(NA)	(NA)	65.9	63.5	68.4	68.8	56.7	59.8
2014	2,868	1,423	1,445	(NA)	(NA)	(NA)	68.4	64.0	72.6	67.7	70.2	65.2
2015	2,965	1,448	1,516	(NA)	(NA)	(NA)	69.2	65.8	72.5	71.3	55.6	68.9
2016	3,137	1,517	1,620	(NA)	(NA)	(NA)	69.8	67.5	71.9	69.7	57.3	72.0
2017	2,870	1,345	1,525	(NA)	(NA)	(NA)	66.7	61.1	71.7	69.1	59.4	61.0
2018	3,212	1,614	1,598	(NA)	(NA)	(NA)	69.1	66.9	71.4	70.9	64.5	65.4

NA Not available. [1] Includes persons of other racial/ethnic groups, not shown separately. [2] Beginning 2003, for persons of this race group only. See footnote 4, Table 261. [3] Due to small sample size, data are subject to relatively large sampling errors. [4] Persons of Hispanic origin may be of any race. [5] As of October.

Source: U.S. National Center for Education Statistics, *Digest of Education Statistics*, "2019 Digest Tables," <http://www.nces.ed.gov/programs/digest/>, accessed February 2020.

Table 299. College Enrollment by Sex and Attendance Status: 2000 to 2019

[In thousands (15,312 represents 15,312,000). As of Fall. Includes enrollment at branch campuses, some additional (primarily 2-year) colleges, and excludes a few institutions that did not award degrees. Includes enrollment at institutions that were eligible to participate in Title IV federal financial aid programs. Includes unclassified students (students taking courses for credit, but are not candidates for degrees)]

Sex and age	2000		2010		2015		2018		2019 (P)	
	Total	Part-time	Total	Part-time	Total	Part-time	Total	Part-time	Total	Part-time
Total	**15,312**	**6,303**	**21,019**	**7,932**	**19,988**	**7,701**	**19,646**	**7,654**	**19,720**	**7,695**
Male	**6,722**	**2,611**	**9,046**	**3,207**	**8,724**	**3,165**	**8,443**	**3,104**	**8,470**	**3,121**
14 to 17 years old	58	7	94	23	94	13	77	10	81	12
18 to 19 years old	1,464	212	1,820	245	1,684	270	1,654	247	1,815	357
20 to 21 years old	1,411	255	1,948	362	1,954	408	1,889	342	2,025	461
22 to 24 years old	1,222	388	1,723	508	1,746	538	1,653	554	1,613	581
25 to 29 years old	908	498	1,410	695	1,382	673	1,378	695	1,299	627
30 to 34 years old	581	395	731	430	655	405	662	418	623	373
35 years old and over	1,077	855	1,320	944	1,208	859	1,131	838	1,015	710
Female	**8,591**	**3,692**	**11,974**	**4,725**	**11,264**	**4,535**	**11,203**	**4,550**	**11,250**	**4,574**
14 to 17 years old	73	3	108	9	120	19	130	16	123	14
18 to 19 years old	1,794	223	2,237	316	2,049	275	2,115	284	2,276	343
20 to 21 years old	1,593	298	2,155	377	2,194	450	2,253	439	2,442	587
22 to 24 years old	1,378	497	2,036	666	2,038	679	2,014	738	1,937	725
25 to 29 years old	1,136	660	1,844	953	1,783	973	1,816	1,047	1,759	1,045
30 to 34 years old	752	520	1,074	630	945	595	899	581	943	629
35 years old and over	1,865	1,491	2,520	1,774	2,136	1,544	1,976	1,445	1,770	1,232

P Projection.

Source: U.S. National Center for Education Statistics, *Digest of Education Statistics*, "Advance Release of Selected 2019 Digest Tables," <https://nces.ed.gov/programs/digest/>, accessed August 2020.

Table 300. College Enrollment by Selected Characteristics: 1990 to 2018

[In thousands (13,818.6 represents 13,818,600). As of Fall. Nonresident alien students are not distributed among racial/ethnic groups. Beginning in 2000, data reflect a new classification of institutions; this includes some additional, primarily 2-year, colleges and excludes a few institutions that did not award degrees. Includes institutions that were eligible to participate in Title IV federal financial aid programs and schools accredited by the National Association of Trade and Technical Schools. Based on data from the Integrated Postsecondary Education Data System (IPEDS)]

Characteristic	1990	2000	2005	2010	2015	2017	2018
Total	**13,818.6**	**15,312.3**	**17,487.5**	**21,019.4**	**19,988.2**	**19,778.2**	**19,645.9**
Male	6,283.9	6,721.8	7,455.9	9,045.8	8,723.8	8,571.3	8,442.7
Female	7,534.7	8,590.5	10,031.6	11,973.7	11,264.4	11,206.8	11,203.3
Public	10,844.7	11,752.8	13,021.8	15,142.2	14,572.8	14,571.7	14,529.3
Private	2,973.9	3,559.5	4,465.6	5,877.3	5,415.4	5,206.4	5,116.7
2-year	5,240.1	5,948.4	6,488.1	7,683.6	6,499.5	5,952.8	5,745.2
4-year	8,578.6	9,363.9	10,999.4	13,335.8	13,488.7	13,825.4	13,900.7
Undergraduate	11,959.1	13,155.4	14,964.0	18,082.4	17,046.7	16,773.0	16,610.2
Postbaccalaureate	1,859.5	2,156.9	2,523.5	2,937.0	2,941.5	3,005.1	3,035.7
White [1]	**10,722.5**	**10,462.1**	**11,495.4**	**12,720.8**	**10,939.2**	**10,517.4**	**10,301.3**
Male	4,861.0	4,634.6	5,007.2	5,605.8	4,848.5	4,632.2	4,500.5
Female	5,861.5	5,827.5	6,488.2	7,115.0	6,090.7	5,885.2	5,800.8
Public	8,385.4	7,963.4	8,518.2	9,182.1	7,910.7	7,646.3	7,505.9
Private	2,337.0	2,498.7	2,977.3	3,538.7	3,028.5	2,871.1	2,795.4
2-year	3,954.3	3,804.1	3,998.6	4,321.3	3,225.8	2,879.5	2,726.5
4-year	6,768.1	6,658.0	7,496.9	8,399.5	7,713.4	7,637.9	7,574.8
Undergraduate	9,272.6	8,983.5	9,828.6	10,895.9	9,303.8	8,882.8	8,664.5
Postbaccalaureate	1,449.8	1,478.6	1,666.8	1,824.9	1,635.4	1,634.6	1,636.8
Black [1]	**1,247.0**	**1,730.3**	**2,214.6**	**3,039.0**	**2,681.0**	**2,549.5**	**2,493.3**
Male	484.7	635.3	774.1	1,089.0	998.9	942.0	909.7
Female	762.3	1,095.0	1,440.4	1,949.9	1,682.1	1,607.5	1,583.6
Public	976.4	1,319.2	1,580.4	1,988.8	1,775.1	1,725.3	1,711.8
Private	270.6	411.1	634.2	1,050.2	906.0	824.2	781.6
2-year	524.3	734.9	901.1	1,198.9	940.5	844.8	804.1
4-year	722.8	995.4	1,313.4	1,840.0	1,740.5	1,704.7	1,689.3
Undergraduate	1,147.2	1,548.9	1,955.4	2,677.1	2,316.5	2,184.0	2,127.9
Postbaccalaureate	99.8	181.4	259.2	361.9	364.5	365.5	365.4
Hispanic	**782.4**	**1,461.8**	**1,882.0**	**2,748.8**	**3,297.7**	**3,546.0**	**3,645.0**
Male	353.9	627.1	774.6	1,157.6	1,389.2	1,479.0	1,507.6
Female	428.5	834.7	1,107.3	1,591.2	1,908.5	2,067.0	2,137.4
Public	671.4	1,229.3	1,525.6	2,163.8	2,694.5	2,929.7	3,016.4
Private	111.0	232.5	356.4	585.0	603.2	616.3	628.7
2-year	424.2	843.9	981.5	1,393.0	1,555.6	1,510.2	1,499.9
4-year	358.2	617.9	900.5	1,355.9	1,742.1	2,035.7	2,145.1
Undergraduate	724.6	1,351.0	1,733.6	2,551.0	3,055.0	3,270.6	3,352.7
Postbaccalaureate	57.9	110.8	148.4	197.8	242.7	275.4	292.4
Asian/Pacific Islander [1]	**572.4**	**978.2**	**1,134.4**	**1,281.6**	**1,284.3**	**1,327.8**	**1,352.6**
Male	294.9	465.9	522.0	600.6	602.9	617.3	625.6
Female	277.5	512.3	612.4	681.0	681.5	710.5	727.0
Public	461.0	770.5	881.9	968.7	970.1	1,007.4	1,027.8
Private	111.5	207.7	252.4	312.8	314.2	320.4	324.8
2-year	215.2	401.9	434.4	463.1	401.9	369.0	366.1
4-year	357.2	576.3	700.0	818.5	882.5	958.8	986.5
Undergraduate	500.5	845.5	971.4	1,087.3	1,084.0	1,113.6	1,131.8
Postbaccalaureate	72.0	132.7	163.0	194.3	200.3	214.2	220.8
American Indian/Alaska Native [1]	**102.8**	**151.2**	**176.3**	**196.2**	**146.1**	**137.5**	**133.8**
Male	43.1	61.4	68.4	78.7	58.2	53.7	51.6
Female	59.7	89.7	107.9	117.5	88.0	83.7	82.2
Public	90.4	127.3	143.0	150.8	113.7	107.7	105.1
Private	12.4	23.9	33.3	45.5	32.5	29.7	28.6
2-year	54.9	74.7	80.7	87.2	62.8	55.7	53.0
4-year	47.9	76.5	95.6	109.0	83.4	81.7	80.7
Undergraduate	95.5	138.5	160.4	179.1	132.2	123.9	120.2
Postbaccalaureate	7.3	12.6	15.9	17.1	13.9	13.6	13.6
Nonresident alien	**391.5**	**528.7**	**584.8**	**707.7**	**982.3**	**1,000.0**	**992.1**
Male	246.3	297.3	309.5	379.6	548.6	551.6	543.0
Female	145.2	231.4	275.3	328.0	433.7	448.4	449.1
Public	260.0	343.1	372.8	453.0	626.8	623.6	611.1
Private	131.4	185.6	212.0	254.7	355.5	376.4	380.9
2-year	67.1	89.0	91.8	99.3	104.2	88.1	87.2
4-year	324.3	439.7	493.1	608.3	878.1	911.8	904.8
Undergraduate	218.7	288.0	314.7	398.4	565.1	574.1	566.6
Postbaccalaureate	172.7	240.7	270.1	309.3	417.2	425.9	425.4

[1] Non-Hispanic.

Source: U.S. National Center for Education Statistics, *Digest of Education Statistics*, "Advance Release of Selected 2019 Digest Tables," and earlier releases, <http://nces.ed.gov/programs/digest/>, accessed July 2020.

Table 301. College Enrollment by Sex, Age, and Race/Ethnicity: 1980 to 2018

[In thousands (11,387 represents 11,387,000). As of October for the civilian noninstitutional population, 14 years old and over. Based on the Current Population Survey; see text, Section 1 and Appendix III]

Characteristic	1980	1990 [1]	1995	2000	2005	2010	2014	2015	2016	2017	2018
Total [2]	**11,387**	**13,621**	**14,715**	**15,314**	**17,472**	**20,275**	**19,175**	**19,101**	**19,196**	**18,398**	**18,908**
Male [3]	5,430	6,192	6,703	6,682	7,539	9,007	8,629	8,484	8,644	8,112	8,373
18 to 24 years	3,604	3,922	4,089	4,342	4,972	5,698	5,677	5,694	5,800	5,459	5,587
25 to 34 years	1,325	1,412	1,561	1,361	1,486	2,055	1,792	1,803	1,838	1,714	1,842
35 years old and over	405	772	985	918	1,019	1,161	1,036	878	927	854	859
Female [3]	5,957	7,429	8,013	8,631	9,933	11,268	10,546	10,617	10,551	10,287	10,534
18 to 24 years	3,625	4,042	4,452	5,109	5,859	6,515	6,455	6,460	6,520	6,477	6,510
25 to 34 years	1,378	1,749	1,788	1,846	2,115	2,569	2,197	2,372	2,380	2,167	2,358
35 years old and over	802	1,546	1,684	1,589	1,838	2,049	1,784	1,672	1,491	1,492	1,541
White [3, 4]	9,925	11,488	12,021	11,999	13,467	15,258	13,953	13,859	13,901	13,224	13,323
18 to 24 years	6,334	6,635	7,011	7,566	8,499	9,324	9,077	8,969	9,106	8,690	8,770
25 to 34 years	2,328	2,698	2,686	2,339	2,647	3,414	2,830	2,966	2,966	2,706	2,737
35 years old and over	1,051	2,023	2,208	1,978	2,206	2,365	1,899	1,776	1,664	1,672	1,647
Male	4,804	5,235	5,535	5,311	5,844	6,883	6,398	6,253	6,222	5,864	5,980
Female	5,121	6,253	6,486	6,689	7,624	8,375	7,555	7,607	7,678	7,360	7,343
Black [3, 4]	1,163	1,393	1,772	2,164	2,297	3,083	2,934	2,826	2,885	2,812	3,009
18 to 24 years	688	894	988	1,216	1,229	1,692	1,529	1,637	1,644	1,595	1,670
25 to 34 years	289	258	426	567	520	715	656	627	652	674	807
35 years old and over	156	207	334	361	448	642	695	537	559	509	517
Male	476	587	710	815	864	1,185	1,132	1,147	1,217	1,175	1,183
Female	686	807	1,062	1,349	1,435	1,898	1,802	1,679	1,669	1,637	1,826
Asian [3, 4]	(NA)	(NA)	(NA)	(NA)	1,184	1,322	1,543	1,616	1,585	1,581	1,691
18 to 24 years	(NA)	(NA)	(NA)	(NA)	696	811	1,022	1,026	1,003	1,101	1,079
25 to 34 years	(NA)	(NA)	(NA)	(NA)	341	354	353	426	436	352	466
35 years old and over	(NA)	(NA)	(NA)	(NA)	130	125	148	143	127	95	127
Male	(NA)	(NA)	(NA)	(NA)	605	647	797	752	835	750	846
Female	(NA)	(NA)	(NA)	(NA)	579	676	746	864	749	831	844
Hispanic origin [3, 5]	443	748	1,207	1,426	1,942	2,879	3,295	3,374	3,661	3,574	3,574
18 to 24 years	315	435	745	899	1,216	1,814	2,282	2,369	2,564	2,410	2,431
25 to 34 years	118	168	250	309	438	652	630	648	682	717	780
35 years old and over	(NA)	130	193	195	257	372	332	315	326	368	305
Male	222	364	568	619	804	1,302	1,441	1,484	1,582	1,529	1,613
Female	221	384	639	807	1,139	1,576	1,855	1,890	2,079	2,045	1,960

NA Not available. [1] Beginning 1990, based on a revised edit and tabulation package. [2] Includes other races not shown separately. [3] Includes persons 14 to 17 years old not shown separately. [4] Beginning 2003, for persons who selected this race group only. See footnote 4, Table 261. [5] Persons of Hispanic origin may be of any race.

Source: U.S. Census Bureau, Current Population Reports, P-20, and earlier reports; and "School Enrollment," <https://www.census.gov/topics/education/school-enrollment/data/tables.All.html>, accessed January 2020.

Table 302. College Enrollment by Type of College, Sex, and Selected Characteristics: 2018

[In thousands (18,908 represents 18,908,000). As of October. Covers civilian noninstitutional population 15 years old and over enrolled in colleges and graduate schools. Based on Current Population Survey. See text, Section 1 and Appendix III]

Characteristic	Total				Male		Female	
	Total enrolled	Two-year college	Four-year college	Graduate school	Total enrolled [1]	Four-year college	Total enrolled [1]	Four-year college
Total enrollment [2]	**18,908**	**4,272**	**10,556**	**4,080**	**8,373**	**4,899**	**10,534**	**5,657**
Age:								
15 to 19 years old	4,432	1,487	2,906	38	1,997	1,315	2,435	1,591
20 to 24 years old	7,877	1,435	5,408	1,034	3,676	2,630	4,201	2,777
25 to 34 years old	4,200	818	1,504	1,878	1,843	684	2,357	820
35 years old and over	2,399	531	739	1,130	858	270	1,540	468
Race/ethnicity:								
White [3]	13,323	3,021	7,597	2,706	5,980	3,551	7,343	4,046
White non-Hispanic [3]	10,248	1,937	5,947	2,363	4,616	2,804	5,632	3,142
Black [3]	3,009	733	1,560	716	1,183	699	1,826	861
Asian [3]	1,691	260	882	548	846	463	844	418
Hispanic [4]	3,574	1,235	1,912	427	1,613	873	1,960	1,039
Control of school:								
Public	15,234	3,987	8,471	2,777	6,811	3,967	8,423	4,504
Private	3,674	285	2,085	1,304	1,562	933	2,111	1,152
Employment status:								
Employed full-time	4,958	1,036	1,914	2,008	2,088	853	2,870	1,061
Employed part-time	5,321	1,437	3,118	765	2,240	1,354	3,081	1,765
Not employed	8,629	1,799	5,524	1,307	4,046	2,693	4,583	2,830
Enrollment status:								
Full time students	14,204	2,758	8,967	2,479	6,542	4,247	7,663	4,719
15 to 19 years old	4,100	1,280	2,783	38	1,833	1,247	2,267	1,536
20 to 24 years old	6,587	929	4,841	818	3,143	2,353	3,444	2,487
25 to 34 years old	2,467	351	932	1,185	1,181	476	1,286	456
35 years old and over	1,050	198	412	439	385	171	665	240
Part time students	4,703	1,513	1,589	1,601	1,832	652	2,872	937
15 to 19 years old	332	208	123	–	164	67	168	55
20 to 24 years old	1,290	507	568	216	533	277	757	290
25 to 34 years old	1,733	467	572	693	662	208	1,071	364
35 years old and over	1,349	331	326	691	473	99	876	228

– Represents or rounds to zero. [1] Includes enrollment in two-year colleges and graduate school, not shown separately. [2] Includes other races not shown separately. [3] For persons who selected this race group only. [4] Persons of Hispanic origin may be of any race.

Source: U.S. Census Bureau, "School Enrollment," <https://www.census.gov/topics/education/school-enrollment/data/tables.All.html>, accessed January 2020.

Table 303. Foreign (Nonimmigrant) Student Enrollment in U.S. Colleges and Universities by World Region and Selected Country of Origin: 1980 to 2019

[In thousands (286 represents 286,000). For Fall of the previous year]

Region of origin	1980	1990	1995	2000	2005	2010	2011	2012	2013	2014	2015	2016	2017	2018	2019
All regions	**286**	**387**	**453**	**515**	**565**	**691**	**723**	**764**	**820**	**886**	**975**	**1,044**	**1,079**	**1,095**	**1,095**
Africa [1]	36	25	21	30	36	37	37	35	36	37	40	43	45	47	47
Nigeria	16	4	2	4	6	7	7	7	7	8	9	11	12	13	13
Asia [1,2,3]	165	245	292	315	356	469	504	547	597	655	724	790	827	842	842
China	1	33	39	54	63	128	158	194	236	274	304	329	351	363	370
Taiwan	18	31	36	29	26	27	25	23	22	21	21	21	22	22	23
Hong Kong	10	11	13	8	7	8	8	8	8	8	8	8	8	7	7
India	9	26	34	42	80	105	104	100	97	103	133	166	186	196	202
Indonesia	2	9	12	11	8	7	7	7	8	8	8	9	9	9	8
Iran	51	7	3	2	2	5	6	7	9	10	11	12	13	13	12
Japan	12	30	45	47	42	25	21	20	20	19	19	19	19	19	18
Malaysia	4	14	14	9	6	6	7	7	7	7	7	8	8	8	8
Saudi Arabia	10	4	4	5	3	16	23	34	45	54	60	61	53	44	37
South Korea	5	22	34	41	53	72	73	73	71	68	64	61	59	55	52
Thailand	7	7	11	11	9	9	8	8	7	7	7	7	7	7	7
Europe [4]	23	46	65	78	72	85	84	85	86	87	91	92	93	93	91
Latin America [1,5]	42	48	47	62	68	66	64	64	67	72	86	85	80	80	81
Mexico	6	7	9	11	13	13	14	14	14	15	17	17	17	15	15
Venezuela	10	3	4	5	5	5	5	6	6	7	8	8	9	8	8
North America [6]	16	19	23	24	29	29	28	27	27	28	27	27	27	26	26
Canada	15	18	23	24	28	28	28	27	27	28	27	27	27	26	26
Oceania	4	4	4	5	4	5	6	6	6	6	6	7	7	7	8

[1] Includes countries not shown separately. [2] Includes the Middle East. [3] Beginning 2006, excludes Cyprus and Turkey. [4] Beginning 2006, includes Cyprus and Turkey. [5] Includes Mexico, Central America, Caribbean, and South America. Prior to 2011, excludes Bermuda. [6] Prior to 2011, includes Bermuda.

Source: Institute of International Education, New York, NY, *Open Doors Report on International Educational Exchange* ©, annual (2019). See also <https://www.iie.org/opendoors>.

Table 304. Higher Education Enrollment in Languages Other Than English: 1970 to 2016

[1,153.2 represents 1,153,200. As of Fall. For credit enrollment]

Enrollment	1970	1980	1986	1990	1995	2006	2009	2013	2016
Registrations [1] (1,000)	**1,153.2**	**924.3**	**1,003.2**	**1,185.5**	**1,138.8**	**1,575.8**	**1,673.6**	**1,561.1**	**1,417.8**
By selected language (1,000):									
Spanish	386.6	379.0	411.4	534.1	606.3	822.1	861.0	789.9	712.2
French	358.5	248.3	275.1	273.1	205.4	206.0	215.2	197.7	175.7
American Sign Language	(NA)	(NA)	(NA)	1.6	4.3	79.7	92.1	109.6	107.1
German	201.8	127.0	120.9	133.6	96.3	94.1	95.6	86.8	80.6
Japanese	6.6	11.5	23.5	45.8	44.7	65.4	72.4	66.8	68.8
Italian	34.2	34.8	40.9	49.8	43.8	78.2	80.3	71.0	56.7
Chinese	6.1	11.4	16.9	19.4	26.5	51.4	59.9	61.1	53.1
Arabic	1.3	3.5	3.4	3.7	4.4	24.0	35.2	33.5	31.6
Latin	28.4	25.0	25.0	28.2	25.9	32.2	32.4	27.2	24.9
Russian	36.4	24.0	33.9	44.5	24.7	24.8	26.7	22.0	20.4
Korean	0.1	0.4	0.9	2.4	3.3	7.1	8.4	12.3	13.9
Ancient Greek	16.5	22.1	17.8	16.4	16.3	22.8	21.5	17.0	13.3
Hebrew	16.6	19.3	15.7	13.0	13.1	23.8	22.1	19.3	15.1
Portuguese	5.1	4.9	5.1	6.1	6.5	10.3	11.3	12.4	9.8
Index (1965=100)	111.5	89.3	97.0	114.6	110.1	152.3	161.8	150.9	137.0

NA Not available. [1] Includes other languages, not shown separately.

Source: Modern Language Association, Dennis Looney and Natalia Lusin. *Enrollments in Languages Other Than English in United States Institutions of Higher Education, Summer 2016 and Fall 2016: Final Report*, June 2019 ©. For 1970 to 2009, consult Association of Departments of Foreign Languages (ADFL) Bulletins. For 2002 to 2016 reports, go to: <https://www.mla.org/Resources/Research/Surveys-Reports-and-Other-Documents/Teaching-Enrollments-and-Programs/Enrollments-in-Languages-Other-Than-English-in-United-States-Institutions-of-Higher-Education>.

Table 305. Active Duty Military Personnel and Veterans Enrolled in Higher Education: 2012 and 2016

[23,055.4 represents 23,055,400. For school year ending in year shown. Based on the National Postsecondary Student-Aid Study]

Characteristic	Undergraduate				Graduate			
	2012		2016		2012		2016	
	Number (1,000)	Percent	Number (1,000)	Percent	Number (1,000)	Percent	Number (1,000)	Percent
Total students	23,055.4	100.0	19,532.3	100.0	3,682.2	100.0	3,572.9	100.0
Total military students	**1,132.9**	**4.9**	**1,192.7**	**6.1**	**159.7**	**4.3**	**241.0**	**6.7**
Veterans	855.9	3.7	870.5	4.5	109.7	3.0	181.8	5.1
Military service members	277.0	1.1	322.2	1.7	50.0	1.3	59.2	1.7
Active duty	170.8	0.7	293.0	1.5	26.3	0.7	49.4	1.4
Reserves or National Guard	106	0.4	29.2	0.2	24	0.6	9.8	0.3
Nonmilitary students	21,922.6	95.1	18,339.6	93.9	3,522.4	95.7	3,331.9	93.3

Source: U.S. National Center for Education Statistics, *After the Post-9/11 GI Bill: A Profile of Military Service Members and Veterans Enrolled in Undergraduate and Graduate Education*, August 2016; and *Veteran's Education Benefits: A Profile of Military Students Who Received Federal Veterans' Education Benefits in 2015-16*, March 2020.

Table 306. College Students Reporting Disability Status by Selected Characteristic: 2015 to 2016

[19,308 represents 19,308,000. Students with disabilities are those who reported having deafness or serious difficulty hearing; blindness or serious difficulty seeing; serious difficulty concentrating, remembering, or making decisions because of a physical, mental, or emotional condition; or serious difficulty walking or climbing stairs. For 2015-16, the question about difficulty concentrating, remembering, or making decisions was expanded to include examples of relevant conditions. Specifically, students were instructed to "consider conditions including, but not limited to, a serious learning disability, depression, ADD, or ADHD." Therefore, data for 2015-16 cannot be compared to estimates of the percentages in earlier years. Based on the 2015-2016 National Postsecondary Student-Aid Study; see source for details. See also Appendix III]

Student characteristic	Undergraduate			Graduate and first-professional		
	All students	Disabled students	Nondisabled students	All students	Disabled students	Nondisabled students
Total students (1,000)..........................	19,308	3,755	15,554	3,547	423	3,124
PERCENT DISTRIBUTION						
Total..	100.0	19.4	80.6	100.0	11.9	88.1
Age:						
15 to 23 years old...................	100.0	17.6	82.4	100.0	8.1	91.9
24 to 29 years old...................	100.0	21.6	78.4	100.0	11.3	88.7
30 years or older....................	100.0	22.6	77.4	100.0	13.5	86.5
Sex:						
Male..................................	100.0	19.2	80.8	100.0	9.9	90.1
Female...............................	100.0	19.6	80.4	100.0	13.3	86.7
Race/ethnicity of student:						
White non-Hispanic.................	100.0	20.8	79.2	100.0	13.0	87.0
Black non-Hispanic.................	100.0	17.2	82.8	100.0	10.3	89.7
Hispanic.............................	100.0	18.3	81.7	100.0	14.3	85.7
Asian.................................	100.0	15.2	84.8	100.0	6.2	93.8
Pacific Islander.....................	100.0	23.6	76.4	100.0	[1] 14.9	85.1
American Indian/Alaska Native....	100.0	27.8	72.2	100.0	[1] 11.8	88.2
Two or more races..................	100.0	22.1	77.9	100.0	19.7	80.3
Attendance status:						
Full-time, full-year..................	100.0	17.3	82.7	100.0	12.0	88.0
Part-time or part-year..............	100.0	20.8	79.2	100.0	11.9	88.1
Student housing status:						
On-campus..........................	100.0	15.8	84.2	(NA)	(NA)	(NA)
Off-campus..........................	100.0	20.6	79.4	(NA)	(NA)	(NA)
With parents or relatives...........	100.0	19.5	80.5	(NA)	(NA)	(NA)
Attended more than one institution..	100.0	18.7	81.3	(NA)	(NA)	(NA)
Dependency status:						
Dependent...........................	100.0	17.2	82.8	(NA)	(NA)	(NA)
Independent, unmarried............	100.0	23.9	76.1	100.0	11.5	88.5
Independent, married...............	100.0	20.5	79.5	100.0	10.3	89.7
Independent with dependents......	100.0	20.3	79.7	100.0	13.4	86.6

NA Not available. [1] Interpret data with caution.

Source: U.S. National Center for Education Statistics, *2017 Digest of Education Statistics*, January 2019. See also <http://www.nces.ed.gov/programs/digest/>.

Table 307. College Freshmen—Summary Characteristics: 1980 to 2019

[In percent. As of Fall for first-time full-time freshmen in 4-year colleges and universities. Based on sample survey and subject to sampling error; see source]

Characteristic	1980	1990	2000	2005	2010	2015	2017	2018	2019
Sex:									
Male..................................	48.8	46.9	45.2	45.0	44.3	43.8	44.8	44.6	45.5
Female...............................	51.2	53.1	54.8	55.0	55.7	56.2	55.2	55.4	54.5
Applied to more than three colleges....	31.5	42.9	50.5	55.4	64.1	71.9	71.0	69.6	71.9
Average grade in high school:									
A- to A+..............................	26.6	29.4	42.9	46.6	48.4	58.7	57.4	57.6	59.3
B- to B+..............................	58.2	57.0	50.5	48.0	47.5	38.5	39.6	39.3	38.2
C to C+...............................	14.9	13.4	6.5	5.4	4.1	2.8	3.1	3.1	2.5
D......................................	0.2	0.2	0.1	0.1	0.1	–	–	0.1	–
Political orientation:									
Liberal................................	21.0	24.6	24.8	27.1	27.3	29.6	32.2	30.5	32.2
Middle of the road...................	57.0	51.7	51.9	45.0	46.4	44.9	41.4	43.8	43.6
Conservative.........................	19.0	20.6	18.9	22.6	21.7	19.8	20.4	20.0	17.8
Probable field of study:									
Biological sciences..................	4.5	4.9	6.6	7.6	10.8	14.9	15.5	14.5	15.4
Business.............................	21.2	21.1	16.7	17.4	13.7	13.4	13.8	14.5	13.4
Education.............................	8.4	10.3	11.0	9.9	7.2	4.2	4.4	4.3	4.2
Engineering..........................	11.2	9.7	8.7	8.3	10.3	13.1	11.5	10.9	9.7
Physical science.....................	3.2	2.8	2.6	3.1	2.7	2.7	2.7	2.1	2.2
Social science.......................	8.2	11.0	10.0	10.7	8.9	10.8	11.0	11.1	11.7
Communications [1]..................	2.4	2.9	2.7	2.0	1.8	1.9	1.6	0.9	0.9
Computer science....................	2.6	1.7	3.7	1.1	1.0	3.8	4.2	3.8	4.3
Personal objectives—very important or essential:									
Being very well off financially........	62.5	72.3	73.4	74.5	77.4	81.9	82.5	82.9	84.3
Developing a meaningful philosophy of life..........	62.5	45.9	42.4	45.0	46.9	46.5	48.1	46.5	49.8
Keeping up to date with political affairs...............	45.2	46.6	28.1	36.4	33.2	40.4	48.1	43.5	45.2

– Represents or rounds to zero. [1] Beginning in 2012, the communications field includes journalism majors.

Source: The Higher Education Research Institute, University of California, Los Angeles, CA, *The American Freshman: National Norms Fall 2019* ©, 2020, and earlier editions. See also <https://heri.ucla.edu/publications-tfs/>.

Table 308. Residence and Migration of College Freshmen by State: 2018

[As of Fall. Includes first-time postsecondary students who had graduated from high school in the previous 12 months and were enrolled at public and private nonprofit 4-year degree-granting institutions that participated in Title IV federal financial aid programs. Excludes respondents for whom state residence and/or migration are unknown. Also excludes U.S. Service Academies (Air Force Academy, Coast Guard Academy, Merchant Marine Academy, Military Academy, and Naval Academy). Based on data from the Integrated Postsecondary Education Data System (IPEDS). See source for more information]

State	Total freshmen enrollment in institutions located in the state	Ratio of in-state students to freshmen enrollment	Ratio of in-state students to residents enrolled in any state[1]	State	Total freshmen enrollment in institutions located in the state	Ratio of in-state students to freshmen enrollment	Ratio of in-state students to residents enrolled in any state[1]
U.S.	1,664,346	0.72	0.74	MO	27,823	0.66	0.71
AL	26,723	0.57	0.81	MT	5,869	0.55	0.77
AK	1,858	0.92	0.56	NE	12,154	0.69	0.78
AZ	29,086	0.58	0.78	NV	12,934	0.85	0.79
AR	17,298	0.67	0.85	NH	8,821	0.36	0.42
CA	161,378	0.85	0.78	NJ	33,070	0.85	0.47
CO	30,521	0.70	0.71	NM	6,570	0.75	0.71
CT	21,195	0.54	0.45	NY	116,581	0.70	0.74
DE	8,181	0.56	0.67	NC	51,659	0.73	0.82
DC	8,461	0.06	0.20	ND	6,318	0.46	0.78
FL	114,005	0.85	0.86	OH	70,973	0.76	0.83
GA	59,654	0.80	0.79	OK	19,433	0.68	0.84
HI	4,129	0.62	0.42	OR	15,802	0.56	0.67
ID	9,371	0.50	0.68	PA	84,622	0.63	0.76
IL	46,485	0.72	0.51	RI	10,990	0.24	0.51
IN	47,845	0.66	0.85	SC	25,969	0.63	0.82
IA	20,112	0.54	0.79	SD	6,214	0.54	0.73
KS	15,561	0.66	0.76	TN	31,721	0.70	0.76
KY	23,573	0.72	0.82	TX	117,983	0.91	0.82
LA	25,916	0.78	0.85	UT	21,920	0.65	0.90
ME	7,537	0.52	0.61	VT	5,863	0.25	0.44
MD	19,679	0.65	0.46	VA	45,368	0.70	0.74
MA	51,505	0.50	0.57	WA	34,320	0.76	0.74
MI	53,212	0.82	0.85	WV	11,550	0.60	0.88
MN	25,443	0.71	0.58	WI	36,719	0.69	0.76
MS	12,608	0.54	0.81	WY	1,764	0.47	0.56

[1] Students residing in a particular state when admitted to an institution anywhere, either in their home state or another state.

Source: U.S. National Center for Education Statistics, *Digest of Education Statistics*, "Advance Release of Selected 2019 Digest Tables," <http://www.nces.ed.gov/programs/digest/>, accessed August 2020.

Table 309. Average Total Price of Attendance of Undergraduate Education: 2016

[In dollars. For school year ending in 2016. Excludes students attending more than one institution. Price of attendance includes tuition and fees, books and supplies, room and board, transportation, and personal and other expenses allowed for federal cost of attendance budgets. Based on the 2015–2016 National Postsecondary Student-Aid Study; see source for details. Includes Puerto Rico. See also Appendix III]

Student characteristic	All institutions[1]	Public 2-year	Public 4-year Non-doctorate granting	Public 4-year Doctorate granting	Private nonprofit 4-year Non-doctorate granting	Private nonprofit 4-year Doctorate granting	Private for-profit
Total	**18,288**	**9,400**	**14,806**	**23,238**	**31,343**	**39,225**	**20,963**
Age:[2]							
18 years or younger	23,318	10,870	17,812	26,127	42,967	51,969	23,058
19 to 23 years	21,799	9,712	16,104	24,748	38,557	47,102	22,073
24 to 29 years	13,313	9,112	12,961	18,441	20,061	24,912	21,333
30 to 39 years	11,959	8,958	12,609	17,351	15,725	17,906	20,326
40 years or older	10,632	8,283	11,210	16,023	14,395	16,174	18,674
Sex:							
Male	18,286	9,121	14,820	23,150	31,825	40,930	21,701
Female	18,289	9,626	14,795	23,317	30,985	37,963	20,561
Race:							
One race:							
White	19,129	9,162	15,308	23,104	33,192	39,217	20,769
Black or African American	16,714	9,667	14,951	22,611	25,514	32,691	20,110
Hispanic or Latino[3]	15,363	9,298	13,527	21,709	26,368	36,105	21,168
Asian	23,053	10,530	14,768	27,497	41,178	50,871	26,028
American Indian/Alaska Native	13,666	9,594	14,686	19,702	20,831	(S)	21,495
Native Hawaiian or other Pacific Islander	14,473	11,084	12,090	21,204	(S)	(S)	23,161
More than one race	19,522	9,938	15,767	23,965	33,818	44,272	22,175
Attendance pattern:							
Full-time, full-year	30,392	16,138	22,243	28,180	43,004	51,320	32,574
Full-time, part-year	12,719	8,145	11,543	15,063	18,949	22,914	17,346
Part-time, full-year	15,529	12,349	14,559	20,732	21,545	29,291	23,784
Part-time, part-year	6,250	4,959	6,685	10,145	9,780	10,027	12,451

S Data do not meet publication standards. [1] Includes public less-than-2-year and private nonprofit less-than-4-year. [2] As of December 31, 2015. [3] Persons of Hispanic origin may be of any race.

Source: U.S. Department of Education, National Center for Education Statistics, National Postsecondary Student Aid Study (NPSAS), "Datalab," <http://nces.ed.gov/datalab/>, accessed May 2018.

Table 310. Institutions of Higher Education—Average Charges: 1985 to 2019

[In current dollars. Estimated. For the entire academic year ending in year shown. Figures are average charges per full-time equivalent student. Room and board are based on full-time students]

Academic control and year	Tuition and required fees [1]			Dormitory room charges			Board rates [2]		
	All institutions	4-yr. institutions	2-yr. institutions	All institutions	4-yr. institutions	2-yr. institutions	All institutions	4-yr. institutions	2-yr. institutions
PUBLIC									
1985	971	1,228	584	1,196	1,217	921	1,241	1,237	1,302
1990	1,356	1,780	756	1,513	1,557	962	1,635	1,638	1,581
1995	2,057	2,681	1,192	1,959	2,023	1,232	1,949	1,967	1,712
2000	2,504	3,349	1,348	2,440	2,519	1,549	2,364	2,406	1,834
2005	3,629	5,027	1,849	3,304	3,418	2,174	2,931	2,981	2,353
2010	4,763	6,717	2,283	4,401	4,564	2,854	3,655	3,755	2,571
2012	5,563	7,713	2,651	4,849	5,031	3,100	3,946	4,042	2,866
2013	5,899	8,070	2,792	5,062	5,241	3,247	4,061	4,163	2,888
2014	6,120	8,312	2,881	5,304	5,479	3,448	4,205	4,308	2,955
2015	6,370	8,543	2,955	5,504	5,677	3,559	4,313	4,412	3,072
2016	6,612	8,778	3,038	5,686	5,850	3,759	4,469	4,576	3,118
2017	6,818	8,804	3,156	5,859	6,018	3,823	4,562	4,666	3,111
2018	7,051	9,036	3,242	6,060	6,227	3,834	4,682	4,785	3,204
2019	7,250	9,212	3,313	6,290	6,459	4,055	4,843	4,927	3,581
PRIVATE									
1985	5,315	5,556	3,485	1,426	1,426	1,424	1,462	1,469	1,294
1990	8,147	8,396	5,196	1,923	1,935	1,663	1,948	1,953	1,811
1995	11,111	11,481	6,914	2,587	2,601	2,233	2,509	2,520	2,023
2000	14,100	14,616	8,225	3,236	3,242	3,067	2,877	2,879	2,753
2005	18,154	18,604	12,122	4,178	4,173	4,475	3,485	3,483	3,700
2010	21,764	22,269	14,862	5,248	5,248	5,211	4,329	4,329	4,390
2012	22,850	23,464	13,961	5,622	5,627	5,169	4,586	4,586	4,475
2013	23,943	24,523	14,149	5,831	5,837	5,228	4,709	4,712	3,977
2014	25,110	25,707	14,170	6,021	6,026	5,489	4,864	4,866	4,211
2015	26,182	26,739	14,261	6,221	6,228	5,506	5,019	5,021	4,560
2016	27,436	27,942	14,528	6,457	6,464	5,666	5,123	5,128	4,181
2017	28,945	29,476	14,589	6,710	6,717	5,949	5,268	5,273	4,350
2018	30,274	30,723	14,894	6,961	6,968	6,057	5,437	5,440	4,645
2019	31,519	31,875	15,727	7,171	7,179	5,967	5,616	5,608	6,933

[1] For public institutions, data are for in-state students. [2] Beginning 1990, rates reflect 20 meals per week, rather than meals served 7 days a week.

Source: U.S. National Center for Education Statistics, *Digest of Education Statistics*, "Advance Release of Selected 2019 Digest Tables," <http://www.nces.ed.gov/programs/digest/>, accessed July 2020.

Table 311. Average Out-of-Pocket Net Price of Attendance for Undergraduates: 2016

[In dollars. For school year ending in 2016. Excludes students attending more than one institution. Net price of attendance is the price that students pay to receive postsecondary education after taking financial aid into account. Based on net tuition and net price for all students. Based on the 2015–2016 National Postsecondary Student-Aid Study; see source for details. Includes Puerto Rico. See also Appendix III]

Student characteristic	Type of institution						
	All institutions [1]	Public 2-year	Public 4-year		Private nonprofit 4-year		Private for-profit
			Non-doctorate granting	Doctorate granting	Non-doctorate granting	Doctorate granting	
Total	**9,842**	**6,695**	**8,630**	**11,995**	**12,744**	**17,442**	**10,487**
Age: [2]							
18 years or younger	11,641	7,670	9,514	12,942	15,920	21,535	10,164
19 to 23 years	11,517	7,137	9,102	13,153	15,320	20,940	11,623
24 to 29 years	7,549	6,263	8,177	8,684	9,312	11,265	10,432
30 to 39 years	6,903	6,103	7,752	8,191	6,947	8,549	9,742
40 years or older	6,615	5,939	7,209	7,884	7,217	8,352	9,674
Sex:							
Male	10,147	6,656	8,664	12,438	12,765	19,575	10,098
Female	9,594	6,726	8,604	11,595	12,729	15,863	10,699
Race:							
One race:							
White	10,337	6,586	8,967	12,476	13,729	17,620	10,219
Black or African American	7,173	6,176	7,791	7,834	8,121	8,988	9,645
Hispanic or Latino [3]	8,581	6,845	8,191	10,454	10,506	14,891	11,025
Asian	15,136	8,419	10,162	17,902	23,191	30,116	15,668
American Indian/Alaska Native	6,958	5,933	6,251	10,375	[4] 9,889	(S)	10,276
Native Hawaiian or other Pacific Islander	7,830	6,843	7,151	11,871	(S)	(S)	10,600
More than one race	9,684	6,398	8,125	11,007	12,407	20,539	10,160
Attendance pattern:							
Full-time, full-year	14,730	10,382	11,510	14,383	16,660	22,089	16,730
Full-time, part-year	6,974	5,572	6,929	7,166	8,253	12,191	8,987
Part-time, full-year	9,821	9,011	9,462	11,431	10,326	13,576	10,929
Part-time, part-year	4,370	3,893	4,817	5,787	5,028	5,593	5,705

S Data do not meet publication standards. [1] Includes public less-than-2-year and private nonprofit less-than-4-year. [2] As of December 31, 2015. [3] Persons of Hispanic origin may be of any race. [4] Interpret data with caution. Estimate is unstable because the standard error represents more than 30 percent of the estimate.

Source: U.S. Department of Education, National Center for Education Statistics, National Postsecondary Student Aid Study (NPSAS), "Datalab," <http://nces.ed.gov/datalab/>, accessed May 2018.

Table 312. Average Cost of Attendance for Undergraduate Education by Control of Institution and Type of Cost: 2016 and 2018

[In constant 2017-2018 dollars, except percent change. Data are preliminary. For school year ending in year shown. Data shown are for full-time, first-time degree/certificate-seeking undergraduates at Title IV institutions. Amounts are institutional averages as reported by the institution, not average amounts paid by students. Based on data from the Integrated Postsecondary Education Data System (IPEDS)]

Item	4-year			2-year			Less than 2-year		
	2016	2018	Percent change	2016	2018	Percent change	2016	2018	Percent change
Tuition and required fees:									
Public:									
In-district [1]	8,115	8,309	2.4	3,494	3,600	3.0	7,263	7,437	2.4
In-state	8,138	8,336	2.4	4,122	4,235	2.7	7,263	7,437	2.4
Out-of-state	18,304	18,674	2.0	8,015	8,186	2.1	8,322	8,578	3.1
Private nonprofit [2]	27,063	27,963	3.3	14,394	14,572	1.2	14,639	14,667	0.2
Private for-profit [2]	16,449	16,200	-1.5	15,010	14,749	-1.7	16,669	17,106	2.6
Books and supplies:									
Public	1,321	1,284	-2.8	1,456	1,447	-0.6	1,060	1,123	5.9
Private nonprofit	1,225	1,192	-2.7	1,423	1,380	-3.0	1,607	1,683	4.7
Private for-profit	1,414	1,293	-8.5	1,659	1,489	-10.3	1,141	1,055	-7.5
Room and board:									
Public:									
On campus	9,850	10,096	2.5	6,530	6,700	2.6	4,316	6,036	39.8
Off campus (not with family)	9,788	9,857	0.7	8,270	8,409	1.7	8,236	8,265	0.3
Private nonprofit:									
On campus	10,149	10,391	2.4	8,783	9,110	3.7	(X)	(X)	(X)
Off campus (not with family)	9,709	9,940	2.4	9,693	9,657	-0.4	7,437	7,289	-2.0
Private for-profit:									
On campus	10,168	10,550	3.8	9,312	9,241	-0.8	(X)	(X)	(X)
Off campus (not with family)	8,503	8,373	-1.5	8,647	8,428	-2.5	9,974	9,843	-1.3
Other expenses: [3]									
Public:									
On campus	3,407	3,360	-1.4	3,314	3,288	-0.8	1,275	1,200	-5.9
Off campus (not with family)	3,890	3,804	-2.2	4,074	4,001	-1.8	4,499	4,071	-9.5
Off campus (with family)	4,090	3,957	-3.3	4,072	4,030	-1.0	4,322	3,810	-11.8
Private nonprofit:									
On campus	2,927	2,887	-1.3	3,513	3,405	-3.1	(X)	(X)	(X)
Off campus (not with family)	3,662	3,597	-1.8	4,540	4,846	6.7	2,689	3,021	12.4
Off campus (with family)	3,887	3,811	-1.9	4,579	4,659	1.7	1,821	2,193	20.5
Private for-profit:									
On campus	4,148	4,494	8.3	2,875	3,654	27.1	(X)	(X)	(X)
Off campus (not with family)	4,551	4,371	-4.0	5,243	5,243	–	5,190	4,606	-11.2
Off campus (with family)	4,338	3,993	-8.0	4,609	4,523	-1.9	4,126	4,394	6.5

X Not applicable. – Rounds to zero. [1] For public institutions, "in-district" refers to the charges paid by a student who lives in the locality surrounding the institution, such as county. [2] For private institutions that reported varying tuitions by residency, out-of-state tuition and required fees were used in the averages displayed in this table. [3] Other expenses refers to the amount of money needed by a student to cover expenses such as laundry, transportation, and entertainment.

Source: U.S. National Center for Education Statistics, *Postsecondary Institutions and Cost of Attendance in 2017–18; Degrees and Other Awards Conferred, 2016–17; and 12-Month Enrollment, 2016–17,* November 2018.

Table 313. Bachelor's Degree Recipients with Loans and Amount Borrowed in Constant (2009) Dollars by Selected Characteristics: 2001 to 2017

[For first-time Bachelor's degree recipients 1 year after they complete their degrees. Estimates cover students who were enrolled in Title IV eligible postsecondary institutions in the 50 states, D.C., and Puerto Rico. Based on Baccalaureate and Beyond Longitudinal Studies]

Characteristic	Percent with loans			Average cumulative amount borrowed for undergraduate education (2009 dollars)		
	2001 [2]	2009	2017	2001 [2]	2009	2017
Total loans	**63.5**	**65.6**	**67.4**	**21,800**	**24,700**	**30,500**
Sex:						
Male	62.5	62.9	63.7	21,300	23,900	29,800
Female	64.3	67.6	70.3	22,100	25,200	31,000
Race/ethnicity: [1]						
White	62.2	64.6	66.8	21,700	24,500	30,500
Black	78.8	80.3	85.9	25,200	28,700	36,900
Hispanic	66.7	67.0	69.7	19,900	22,800	26,900
Asian	55.5	53.4	45.4	19,100	21,000	24,600
Other	62.8	68.8	70.4	21,500	25,600	30,300
Age at receipt of bachelor's degree:						
18 to 23	60.0	61.0	62.4	20,800	23,700	27,400
24 to 29	71.3	76.8	73.4	23,100	24,900	33,100
30 and older	65.7	72.5	82.0	23,000	28,300	37,700
Institution type:						
2-year or less:						
Public 2-year	67.8	67.5	71.1	21,500	24,500	30,600
Other 2-year or less	64.6	85.0	85.6	24,500	31,600	38,300
4-year:						
Public	59.5	62.1	64.1	20,100	21,900	28,600
Private nonprofit	69.0	69.4	66.4	24,100	27,900	31,200
For-profit	77.3	87.7	84.1	27,400	36,000	42,700

[1] Asian includes Pacific Islander and Native Hawaiian and other includes American Indian, Alaska Native, and graduates of two or more races or a race not listed. Excludes persons of Hispanic origin, unless specified. [2] Includes loans from family and friends.

Source: National Center for Education Statistics, *Trends in Debt for Bachelor's Degree Recipients a Year After Graduation: 1994, 2001, and 2009,* December 2012; and *Baccalaureate and Beyond (B&B:16/17): A First Look at the Employment and Educational Experiences of College Graduates, 1 Year Later,* June 2019. See also <https://nces.ed.gov/surveys/b&b/>.

Table 314. SAT Scores and Characteristics of High School Graduates: 2019

[Data reflect 2019 high school graduates who took the new SAT during high school. If a student took the SAT more than once, the most recent score and self-reported SAT questionnaire responses are summarized. Maximum total score is 1600. Data not comparable with prior years due to the new SAT test that was introduced in 2017]

Characteristic	Test takers		Mean score			Percent with benchmarks met			
	Number	Percent	Total	ERW [1]	Math	Both	ERW [1]	Math	None
Total	**2,220,087**	**(X)**	**1,059**	**531**	**528**	**45**	**68**	**48**	**30**
Took essay [2]	1,410,113	64	1,088	545	543	51	71	53	26
Race/ethnicity:									
White	947,842	43	1,114	562	553	57	80	59	18
Black	271,178	12	933	476	457	20	46	22	53
Hispanic/Latino	554,665	25	978	495	483	29	55	31	43
Asian	228,527	10	1,223	586	637	75	83	80	11
American Indian/Alaska Native	12,917	1	912	461	451	18	39	21	58
Native Hawaiian/Other Pacific Islander	5,430	(Z)	964	487	478	27	51	29	47
Two or more races	87,178	4	1,095	554	540	51	76	53	22
Sex:									
Male	1,061,599	48	1,066	529	537	48	66	51	31
Female	1,156,766	52	1,053	534	519	43	69	45	29
First language learned:									
English only	1,400,229	63	1,074	543	530	48	73	50	26
English and another language	439,931	20	1,047	521	526	42	63	45	34
Another language	269,381	12	1,057	515	543	44	60	50	34
Highest level of parental education:									
No High school diploma	198,564	9	926	464	462	19	40	23	56
High school diploma	608,174	27	989	500	490	31	58	33	40
Associate degree	159,521	7	1,027	519	508	38	67	41	30
Bachelor's degree	620,711	28	1,121	561	560	59	81	61	17
Graduate degree	461,235	21	1,194	596	598	71	87	73	11

X Not applicable. Z Represents less than .05%. [1] Evidence-based reading and writing. [2] Reflects test takers who completed the SAT essay at any point, not necessarily on the most recent test administration date.

Source: The College Board, *2019 SAT Suite of Assessments Annual Report*, © 2019. Reproduced with permission. See also <http://www.collegeboard.org>.

Table 315. Federal Student Financial Assistance: 1995 to 2017

[5,472 represents $5,472,000,000. For award years July 1 of year shown to the following June 30. Funds utilized exclude operating costs, and so forth, and represent funds given to students]

Type of assistance	1995	2000	2005	2010	2015	2016	2017
FUNDS UTILIZED (mil. dol.)							
Federal Pell Grants	5,472	7,956	12,693	35,677	28,559	26,894	28,672
TEACH Grants [1]	(X)	(X)	(X)	121	(NA)	(NA)	(NA)
Federal Supplemental Educational Opportunity Grant	764	908	1,084	1,013	993	987	1,008
Federal Work-Study	764	939	1,050	1,198	1,096	1,086	1,009
Federal Perkins Loan	1,029	1,144	1,594	857	1,045	886	631
Federal Direct Student Loan (FDSL)	8,296	10,348	12,930	84,704	(NA)	(NA)	(NA)
NUMBER OF AWARDS (1,000)							
Federal Pell Grants	3,612	3,899	5,168	9,308	7,660	7,195	7,112
TEACH Grants [1]	(X)	(X)	(X)	39	(NA)	(NA)	(NA)
Federal Supplemental Educational Opportunity Grant	1,083	1,174	1,419	1,633	1,530	1,484	1,499
Federal Work-Study	702	713	711	718	635	617	613
Federal Perkins Loan	688	639	728	461	422	356	256
Federal Direct Student Loan (FDSL)	2,339	2,739	2,971	16,647	(NA)	(NA)	(NA)
AVERAGE AWARD (dol.)							
Federal Pell Grants	1,515	2,040	2,456	3,833	3,728	3,738	4,031
TEACH Grants [1]	(X)	(X)	(X)	3	(NA)	(NA)	(NA)
Federal Supplemental Educational Opportunity Grant	706	773	764	620	649	665	672
Federal Work-Study	1,087	1,318	1,478	1,668	1,726	1,759	1,647
Federal Perkins Loan	1,496	1,790	2,190	1,860	2,479	2,491	2,461
Federal Direct Student Loan (FDSL)	3,547	3,778	4,352	5,088	(NA)	(NA)	(NA)

X Not applicable. NA Not available. [1] Teacher Education Assistance for College and Higher Education (TEACH) Grant Program.

Source: U.S. Department of Education, Office of Postsecondary Education, "OPE Program Data," <https://www2.ed.gov/finaid/prof/resources/data/ope.html>, accessed July 2020.

Table 316. Voluntary Financial Support of Higher Education: 1990 to 2019

[9,800 represents $9,800,000,000. For school years ending in years shown. Voluntary support, as defined in Gift Reporting Standards, excludes income from endowment and other invested funds as well as all support received from federal, state, and local governments and their agencies and contract research]

Item	Unit	1990	2000	2005	2010	2015	2017	2018	2019
Estimated support, total.....................	Mil. dol.	**9,800**	**23,200**	**25,600**	**28,000**	**40,300**	**43,600**	**46,730**	**49,600**
SOURCES OF SUPPORT									
Individuals, total.................................	Mil. dol.	4,770	12,220	12,100	12,020	18,850	19,230	20,721	19,500
Alumni.......................................	Mil. dol.	2,540	6,800	7,100	7,100	10,850	11,370	12,154	11,200
Nonalumni individuals.....................	Mil. dol.	2,230	5,420	5,000	4,920	8,000	7,860	8,567	8,300
Organizations, total.......................	Mil. dol.	5,030	10,980	13,500	15,675	21,450	24,370	26,008	30,100
Corporations.................................	Mil. dol.	2,170	4,150	4,400	4,730	5,750	6,600	6,732	6,800
Foundations.................................	Mil. dol.	1,920	5,080	7,000	8,400	11,600	13,130	14,010	17,000
Other organizations.........................	Mil. dol.	940	1,750	2,100	2,545	4,100	4640	5,266	6,300
PURPOSES OF SUPPORT									
Current operations, total.......................	Mil. dol.	5,440	11,270	14,200	17,000	24,650	25,800	27,400	28,500
Capital purposes.............................	Mil. dol.	4,360	11,930	11,400	11,000	15,650	17,800	19,330	21,100
Support for institutions reporting support only:									
Institutions reporting support..................	Number	1,056	945	997	996	983	933	929	913
Total support reported.......................	Mil. dol.	8,214	19,419	20,953	23,487	35,082	35,301	37,221	39,490
Private 4-year institutions...................	Mil. dol.	5,072	11,047	11,011	12,189	17,944	18,590	17,726	21,433
Public 4-year institutions...................	Mil. dol.	3,056	8,254	9,780	11,114	14,876	16,421	19,251	17,834
2-year colleges.............................	Mil. dol.	85	117	163	185	192	290	244	222

Source: Council for Advancement and Support of Education, Washington, DC, *Voluntary Support of Education* ©, annual. See also <http://www.case.org/>.

Table 317. Undergraduate Students Who Received a Pell Grant by Selected Characteristics: 2004 to 2016

[In units as indicated. For school year ending in year shown. Data shown for students enrolled in Title IV eligible postsecondary institutions in the 50 States, the District of Columbia, and Puerto Rico. Based on the National Postsecondary Student-Aid Study; see source for details]

Institutional and student characteristics	2004		2008		2012 [1]		2016	
	Percent	Average amount (dollars)	Percent	Average amount (dollars)	Percent	Average amount (dollars)	Percent	Average amount (dollars)
Total......................	**27.2**	**2,400**	**27.8**	**2,500**	**41.3**	**3,400**	**39.1**	**3,700**
AGE								
23 or younger..................	25.5	2,600	25.6	2,700	37.8	3,600	(NA)	(NA)
18 or younger.....................	(NA)	(NA)	(NA)	(NA)	(NA)	(NA)	39.7	4,100
19 to 23.............................	(NA)	(NA)	(NA)	(NA)	(NA)	(NA)	36.2	4,000
24 to 29.............................	36.6	2,400	36.1	2,400	48.9	3,200	47.3	3,500
30 or older..........................	24.8	2,300	26.9	2,300	43.5	3,200	(NA)	(NA)
30 to 39.............................	(NA)	(NA)	(NA)	(NA)	(NA)	(NA)	42.7	3,400
40 or older..........................	(NA)	(NA)	(NA)	(NA)	(NA)	(NA)	33.2	3,300
SEX								
Male.................................	22.3	2,500	21.9	2,600	36.5	3,400	34.0	3,700
Female...............................	30.8	2,400	32.2	2,500	44.8	3,400	43.1	3,700
RACE/ETHNICITY								
White................................	20.7	2,300	20.9	2,400	33.5	3,300	31.5	3,600
Black................................	47.9	2,500	46.0	2,600	61.9	3,400	57.7	3,700
Hispanic.............................	37.5	2,600	39.8	2,700	50.0	3,500	46.9	3,900
Asian/Pacific Islander.............	21.9	2,800	23.3	2,800	33.8	3,800	(NA)	(NA)
Asian................................	(NA)	(NA)	(NA)	(NA)	(NA)	(NA)	30.9	4,200
Pacific Islander.....................	(NA)	(NA)	(NA)	(NA)	(NA)	(NA)	35.6	4,100
American Indian.....................	31.9	2,400	36.0	2,500	54.0	3,400	51.1	3,500
Other or two or more races........	29.8	2,500	31.1	2,600	45.2	3,500	42.2	3,800
ATTENDANCE STATUS								
Full-time, full-year................	32.2	3,100	33.6	3,300	47.1	4,400	44.7	4,700
Part-time, full-year..................	(NA)	(NA)	(NA)	(NA)	(NA)	(NA)	44.0	3,500
Part-time or part-year...............	23.8	1,900	24.4	1,900	37.6	2,600	(NA)	(NA)
TYPE OF INSTITUTION								
Public 4-year........................	26.4	2,600	26.2	2,800	38.0	3,800	38.2	4,100
Private nonprofit 4-year...........	27.9	2,600	26.8	2,900	35.8	3,700	36.4	4,000
Public 2-year........................	22.3	2,200	21.1	2,300	37.7	3,000	33.5	3,300
EMPLOYMENT STATUS [2]								
Not employed.......................	28.8	2,600	31.0	2,700	44.7	3,500	41.7	3,900
Employed part-time................	28.1	2,500	29.2	2,600	41.4	3,500	38.3	3,800
Employed full-time.................	24.5	2,300	23.4	2,200	36.2	3,000	36.4	3,300

NA Not available. [1] 2012 excludes Puerto Rico. [2] Work-study, assistantships, and traineeships. Full-time work is defined as 35 or more hours per week, and part-time less than 35 hours.

Source: U.S. Department of Education, National Center for Education Statistics, *Trends in Pell Grant Receipt and the Characteristics of Pell Grant Recipients: Selected Years, 1999–2000 to 2011–12*, September 2015; and *Student Financing of Undergraduate Education in 2015-16: Financial Aid by Types and Source*, March 2019. See also <http://nces.ed.gov/surveys/npsas/>.

Table 318. Undergraduate Student Receipt of Financial Aid by Source and Type of Institution Attended: 2016

[In percent. For school year ending in 2016. Covers students enrolled in Title IV eligible postsecondary institutions in the 50 states, DC, and Puerto Rico. Based on the National Postsecondary Student-Aid Study; see source for details]

Type of institution	Total [1]	Source of aid				
		Federal [2]	Non-federal [3]	State [4]	Institutional [5]	Employer [6]
Total	**72.3**	**54.5**	**48.8**	**22.4**	**24.6**	**6.3**
Institution attended:						
Public 2-year	57.5	38.9	35.1	23.0	6.6	5.3
Public 4-year	77.1	58.9	57.1	27.6	30.4	6.3
Private nonprofit 4-year	86.3	63.3	71.0	18.1	57.2	9.9
Private for-profit 2-year or more	87.0	76.3	43.8	10.6	28.5	6.7
Private for-profit less-than-2-year	82.9	77.4	24.8	6.7	9.3	1.8

[1] Excludes aid from parents, friends, or relatives, and federal tax credits for education. Includes Direct PLUS Loans to parents and aid from Veterans' benefits and job training grants. [2] Includes federal grants, loans, work-study awards, and federal loans including Direct PLUS loans. Includes aid from programs in Title IV of the Higher Education Act, and aid from other federal sources such as Public Health Service Loans, Bureau of Indian Affairs Grants, and District of Columbia Tuition Assistance Grants. Excludes federal veterans' benefits and education tax credits and tax deduction benefits. [3] Includes grants from states, institutions, and private organizations, and loans from private sources. [4] Includes all grants and scholarships, loans, and work-study provided by state governments, including vocational rehabilitation and job training grants funded by the federal Workforce Investment Opportunity Act (WIA). [5] Includes all institution need- and merit-based grants, scholarships, tuition waivers, loans, and work-study assistance. [6] Excludes tuition waivers to students holding assistantships.

Source: U.S. Department of Education, National Center for Education Statistics, *Trends in Undergraduate Nonfederal Grant and Scholarship Aid by Demographic and Enrollment Characteristics, Selected Years: 2003–04 to 2015–16,* August 2019. See also <http://nces.ed.gov/surveys/npsas/>.

Table 319. Financial Aid for Graduate Students by Degree Type and Source of Aid: 2016

[For school year ending in 2016. Based on the National Postsecondary Student-Aid Study; see source for details. Excludes Puerto Rico]

Degree type	Percent receiving aid by source				Average aid received (dollars)	Tuition and fees (dollars)	Price of attendance [4] (dollars)	Out-of-pocket net price [5] (dollars)
	Total [1]	Federal [2]	Institutional [3]	Employer				
Total	**72.5**	**42.6**	**30.5**	**12.8**	**22,200**	**15,100**	**29,400**	**13,400**
Master's degree program:								
Business administration (M.B.A.)	71.0	35.0	24.0	21.9	18,700	14,700	27,600	14,600
Education (any master's)	66.9	44.4	20.9	13.3	14,100	8,400	19,300	9,900
M.A. (except in education)	71.1	43.4	29.1	9.9	16,900	11,200	24,100	12,300
M.S. (except in education)	68.7	35.4	28.5	13.4	17,100	12,200	25,300	13,800
Other master's [6]	74.4	47.2	27.4	14.4	19,500	14,000	27,900	13,600
Control of institution:								
Public	66.2	34.3	26.5	14.0	16,000	9,600	22,000	11,500
Private nonprofit	72.9	43.3	25.5	15.4	19,300	15,400	29,200	15,300
For-profit	74.7	52.9	24.5	14.6	14,900	9,400	19,500	8,700
Doctor's degree program - research/scholarship:								
Ph.D. (except in education)	84.8	23.4	66.5	6.9	28,000	19,000	36,900	13,200
Education (any doctorate)	73.6	44.0	33.4	16.3	16,200	9,500	22,300	10,800
Other doctorate	77.1	42.1	34.4	11.7	20,700	15,000	29,300	13,200
Control of institution:								
Public	80.4	18.0	64.3	8.4	21,500	12,800	28,900	11,800
Private nonprofit	82.8	27.2	59.3	9.9	33,700	25,000	44,800	16,900
For-profit	79.9	70.1	17.6	11.5	16,500	10,800	20,500	7,300
Doctor's degree program - professional practice:								
Medicine (M.D. or D.O.)	83.7	73.8	40.9	(S)	53,100	37,400	65,700	21,300
Other health science [7]	86.0	75.7	34.5	(S)	50,600	36,100	59,700	15,900
Law (LL.B. or J.D.)	89.7	71.1	57.8	[8] 1.6	45,700	35,700	58,300	18,400
Control of institution:								
Public	83.0	70.3	47.0	2.7	41,000	28,800	51,300	17,400
Private nonprofit	85.6	69.1	43.8	[8] 4.1	53,100	40,400	65,600	20,200
For-profit	91.8	82.3	37.5	[8] 9.9	43,300	30,300	49,700	10,300

S Figure does not meet publication standards. [1] Financial aid includes all types of financial aid from any source except parents, friends, or relatives. Types of aid such as employer aid, veterans benefits, and job-training grants are included, but federal tax credits for education are not included. [2] Consists of federal loans, federal grants, and federal work-study. Does not include military benefits. [3] Includes all institution need- and merit-based grants, scholarships, tuition waivers, graduate assistantships, loans, and work-study assistance funded by the institution attended. [4] Price of attendance is the total budget (attendance intensity-adjusted) at the institution for students who attended only one institution during the academic year. The budget includes tuition, fees, housing, meals, books, supplies, transportation, and personal expenses. Institutions typically use this value as a student's budget for the purpose of awarding federal financial aid. [5] Out-of-pocket net price is the total price of attendance minus all financial aid received, including Direct PLUS Loans. The total price of attendance includes tuition and fees, room and board, books and supplies, transportation, and personal or miscellaneous expenses. Federal education tax benefits are not included in the calculation. Averages include students who received no aid. [6] Includes M.S.W. (Master of Social Work), M.P.A. (Master of Public Administration), and M.F.A. (Master of Fine Arts). [7] Includes chiropractic (D.C. or D.C.M.), dentistry (D.D.S. or D.M.D.), optometry (O.D.), pharmacy (D.Pharm.), podiatry (Pod.D. or D.P.M.), and veterinary medicine (D.V.M.). [8] Underlying data has a standard error between 30-50%.

Source: U.S. Department of Education, National Center for Education Statistics, *Profile and Financial Aid Estimates of Graduate Students: 2015–16,* January 2019. See also <http://nces.ed.gov/surveys/npsas/>.

Table 320. State and Local Financial Support for Higher Education by State: 2019

[10,934.9 represents 10,934,900. For fiscal year ending in 2019. Educational appropriations include State and local appropriations for general operating expenses of public postsecondary education. Includes state-funded financial aid to students attending in-state public institutions. Excludes appropriations for independent institutions, financial aid for students attending independent institutions, research, hospitals, and medical education]

State	FTE enroll-ment [2] (1,000)	Educational appropri-ations (million dollars)	Educational appropri-ations per FTE enrollment (dollars)	State	FTE enroll-ment [2] (1,000)	Educational appropri-ations (million dollars)	Educational appropri-ations per FTE enrollment (dollars)
Total U.S. [1]	10,934.9	89,622.4	8,196	MO	182.5	1,320.9	7,238
AL	203.6	1,431.7	7,031	MT	36.4	233.8	6,427
AK	16.7	270.3	16,164	NE	75.9	768.2	10,116
AZ	292.9	1,536.6	5,247	NV	71.0	580.8	8,179
AR	112.7	943.3	8,368	NH	36.4	104.4	2,871
CA	1,556.0	14,125.3	9,078	NJ	262.2	1,717.7	6,550
CO	183.7	855.0	4,653	NM	80.0	953.5	11,922
CT	83.8	708.7	8,458	NY	537.1	4,908.7	9,139
DE [3]	36.4	197.7	5,431	NC	393.9	4,292.2	10,896
DC [3]	3.5	41.5	11,783	ND	33.7	292.3	8,679
FL	603.9	4,554.7	7,542	OH	390.9	2,447.8	6,262
GA	355.2	3,423.6	9,638	OK	128.8	852.6	6,617
HI	35.3	518.2	14,698	OR	137.9	924.6	6,703
ID	54.4	543.3	9,983	PA	346.3	1,550.2	4,477
IL	310.6	4,610.6	14,846	RI	30.2	189.9	6,286
IN	246.3	1,512.0	6,139	SC	162.1	1,047.7	6,465
IA	123.7	781.6	6,320	SD	32.8	209.9	6,397
KS	132.3	916.4	6,929	TN	185.9	1,727.3	9,291
KY	142.0	1,057.1	7,444	TX	1,066.7	8,414.2	7,888
LA	163.9	950.0	5,795	UT	128.1	985.1	7,688
ME	33.9	260.8	7,684	VT	20.5	59.6	2,914
MD	229.2	1,793.6	7,824	VA	305.0	1,770.5	5,805
MA	160.3	1,260.0	7,859	WA	235.3	1,746.8	7,424
MI	366.3	2,619.8	7,152	WV	66.6	350.3	5,261
MN	184.4	1,408.1	7,638	WI	209.4	1,433.6	6,846
MS	129.5	859.5	6,637	WY	22.2	420.8	18,960

[1] The U.S. total does not include data from the District of Columbia. [2] Full-time equivalent. Includes degree enrollment and enrollment in public postsecondary programs resulting in a certificate or other formal recognition. Includes summer sessions. Excludes medical education enrollments. [3] Adjustment factors to arrive at constant dollar figures include Cost of Living Index (COLI), Enrollment Mix Index (EMI), and Higher Education Cost Adjustment (HECA). The Cost of Living Index (COLI) is not a measure of inflation over time. The District of Columbia is not adjusted for COLI or EMI.

Source: State Higher Education Executive Officers, Boulder, CO, *State Higher Education Finance: FY2019* ©, 2020. See also <http://www.shef.sheeo.org>.

Table 321. Higher Education Price Indexes: 2010 to 2019 ©

[1983=100. For years ending June 30. The Higher Education Price Index (HEPI), calculated for the July-June academic fiscal year, reflects prices paid by colleges and universities for the following eight cost factors: faculty salaries, administrative salaries, clerical and service employees, fringe benefits, miscellaneous services, supplies and materials, and utilities. Minus sign (-) indicates decrease]

Item and year	Total	Personnel compensation					Contracted services, supplies, and equipment		
		Faculty salaries [1]	Admin-istrative salaries	Clerical salaries	Service employ-ees salaries	Fringe benefits [1]	Miscel-laneous services	Supplies and materials	Utilities
INDEXES									
2010	281.8	280.6	337.6	255.2	230.0	402.8	255.8	179.3	193.6
2011	288.4	284.5	343.2	260.2	233.2	417.6	260.3	193.9	201.5
2012	293.2	289.6	352.3	264.8	235.7	425.3	264.6	203.9	191.7
2013	297.8	294.6	362.4	269.8	239.4	437.5	269.4	180.0	195.6
2014	306.7	301.0	366.4	274.8	242.0	458.3	274.2	200.2	211.4
2015	312.9	306.4	381.9	280.4	248.4	484.0	279.8	190.7	183.5
2016	317.1	318.6	393.3	289.1	253.3	481.9	285.7	179.5	146.5
2017	327.8	326.4	405.2	297.3	262.7	503.6	290.7	180.1	167.8
2018	337.4	335.6	414.1	305.9	271.6	521.1	297.8	187.9	170.7
2019	345.9	342.2	424.1	316.6	282.5	533.3	304.8	195.6	172.3
ANNUAL PERCENT CHANGE [2]									
2010	0.9	1.2	2.0	1.4	1.4	2.1	1.1	-1.3	-9.5
2011	2.3	1.4	1.7	2.0	1.4	3.7	1.8	8.2	4.1
2012	1.7	1.8	2.7	1.7	1.1	1.8	1.7	5.2	-4.9
2013	1.6	1.7	2.9	1.9	1.6	2.9	1.8	-11.7	2.1
2014	3.0	2.2	1.1	1.9	1.1	4.8	1.8	11.2	8.1
2015	2.0	1.8	4.2	2.1	2.6	5.6	2.1	-4.8	-13.2
2016	1.4	4.0	3.0	3.1	2.0	-0.4	2.1	-5.8	-20.2
2017	3.4	2.5	3.0	2.8	3.7	4.5	1.7	0.3	14.5
2018	2.9	2.8	2.2	2.9	3.4	3.5	2.4	4.3	1.7
2019	2.5	2.0	2.4	3.5	4.0	2.4	2.4	4.1	0.9

[1] Data are derived from faculty compensation data published by the American Association of University Professors (AAUP), which in FY2016 began using a new methodology; data based on the new methodology are not comparable with prior year data. [2] Percent change from the immediate prior year.

Source: The Commonfund Institute, Wilton, CT ©. See also <http://www.commonfund.org>.

Table 322. Average Salaries for College Faculty Members: 2018 to 2020

[In thousands of dollars (85.1 represents $85,100). For academic year ending in year shown. Figures are for 9 months teaching for full-time faculty members in 2-year and 4-year institutions]

Type of control and academic rank	2018	2019	2020	Type of control and academic rank	2018	2019	2020
Public: All ranks	**85.1**	**93.4**	**96.1**	**Private:[1] All ranks**	**104.5**	**121.2**	**124.4**
Professor	125.8	128.2	131.9	Professor	167.5	172.0	176.9
Associate professor	89.4	91.2	93.6	Associate professor	102.9	106.0	108.0
Assistant professor	77.4	78.9	81.3	Assistant professor	89.8	91.7	93.9
Instructor	60.2	61.0	56.9	Instructor	74.6	77.1	75.9

[1] Excludes religiously-affiliated colleges and universities.

Source: American Association of University Professors, Washington, DC, *AAUP Annual Report on the Economic Status of the Profession* © 2020. See also <http://www.aaup.org/>.

Table 323. Employees in Higher Education Institutions by Employment Status, Sex, and Occupation: 2018

[In thousands (3,923.4 represents 3,923,400). As of Fall. Covers institutions that grant associate's or higher degrees and that participate in Title IV federal financial aid programs. Includes institutions with fewer than 15 full-time employees. Detail may not sum to totals because of rounding. Based on Integrated Postsecondary Education Data System data]

Primary occupation	Full-time and part-time		Female		Full-time		Part-time	
	Total	Male	Total	Percent	Male	Female	Male	Female
All institutions	**3,923.4**	**1,767.4**	**2,156.0**	**55.0**	**1,135.0**	**1,414.9**	**632.4**	**741.1**
Faculty	1,542.6	771.6	771.0	50.0	443.6	388.5	328.0	382.5
Instruction	1,422.8	705.7	717.0	50.4	387.1	344.4	318.6	372.6
Research	90.5	51.7	38.8	42.8	45.6	33.1	6.2	5.7
Public service	29.4	14.1	15.2	51.9	10.9	11.0	3.3	4.2
Graduate assistants[1]	382.7	196.8	185.9	48.6	(X)	(X)	196.8	185.9
Librarians, curators, and archivists	41.5	12.4	29.1	70.2	10.6	24.3	1.8	4.8
Student and academic affairs, and other education services	182.8	58.1	124.8	68.2	36.4	88.9	21.7	35.9
Management	262.9	113.5	149.4	56.8	110.7	145.2	2.8	4.2
Business and financial operations	219.8	59.6	160.2	72.9	56.0	150.4	3.6	9.9
Computer, engineering, and science	238.1	143.5	94.6	39.7	135.0	84.3	8.5	10.4
Community, social service, legal, arts, design, entertainment, sports, and media	185.8	83.1	102.7	55.3	66.1	84.9	17.0	17.8
Healthcare practitioners and technicians	111.1	32.6	78.5	70.7	28.0	65.4	4.5	13.1
Service occupations	242.2	139.3	102.9	42.5	118.0	84.9	21.3	18.0
Sales and related occupations	12.5	4.4	8.2	65.1	3.7	6.5	0.7	1.7
Office and administrative support	409.6	70.1	339.5	82.9	49.8	284.4	20.3	55.0
Natural resources, construction, and maintenance	73.1	67.3	5.8	8.0	64.5	4.7	2.8	1.1
Production, transportation, and material moving	18.7	15.3	3.4	18.0	12.7	2.5	2.6	0.9

X Not applicable. [1] By definition, all graduate assistants are part time.

Source: U.S. National Center for Education Statistics, *Digest of Education Statistics*, "Advance Release of Selected 2019 Digest Tables," and earlier releases, <http://nces.ed.gov/programs/digest/>, accessed July 2020.

Table 324. Faculty in Institutions of Higher Education: 1980 to 2018

[In thousands (686 represents 686,000), except percent. As of Fall. Beginning in 1997, data reflect a new classification of institutions; this classification includes some additional, primarily 2-year, colleges and excludes a few institutions that did not award degrees. Includes institutions that were eligible to participate in Title IV federal financial aid programs. Includes schools accredited by the National Association of Trade and Technical Schools. Based on complete census taken every other year; see source]

Year	Total	Employment status		Control		Level		Percent		
		Full-time	Part-time	Public	Private	4-year	2-year or less	Part-time	Public	2-year or less
1980[1]	686	450	236	495	191	494	192	34	72	28
1985[1]	715	459	256	503	212	504	211	36	70	30
1991[2]	826	536	291	581	245	591	235	35	70	28
1995	932	551	381	657	275	647	285	41	70	31
1999	1,038	593	444	719	319	719	318	43	69	31
2001	1,113	618	495	771	342	764	349	44	69	31
2003	1,174	630	544	792	382	814	359	46	67	31
2005	1,290	676	615	841	449	917	373	48	65	29
2007[3]	1,372	704	668	877	495	992	379	49	64	28
2009	1,439	729	710	914	525	1,038	401	49	63	28
2011	1,524	762	762	954	570	1,116	409	50	63	27
2013	1,545	791	754	969	577	1,152	394	49	63	25
2015	1,552	807	745	971	581	1,181	372	48	63	24
2016	1,546	814	732	974	572	1,197	349	47	63	23
2017	1,546	823	723	973	573	1,209	337	47	63	22
2018	1,543	832	710	981	562	1,217	326	46	64	21

[1] Estimated on the basis of enrollment. [2] Data beginning 1991 not comparable to prior years. [3] Beginning in 2007, data include institutions with fewer than 15 full-time employees; these institutions did not report staff data prior to 2007.

Source: U.S. National Center for Education Statistics, *Digest of Education Statistics,* "Advance Release of Selected 2019 Digest Tables," <http://www.nces.ed.gov/programs/digest/>, accessed July 2020.

Table 325. Starting Salaries for New College Graduates by Degree and Field of Study: 2017 to 2019

[In dollars. Data are actual starting base salaries. Data reported by representative colleges throughout the United States]

Field of study	Bachelors			Masters [1]			Doctorate		
	2017	2018	2019	2017	2018	2019	2017	2018	2019
Accounting....................	52,343	51,783	53,652	54,086	54,307	56,394	[3] 161,520	(NA)	(NA)
Business administration/ management [2]................	51,851	52,149	53,944	78,980	74,949	84,701	[3] 115,750	118,326	128,296
Marketing......................	45,842	45,539	47,777	72,732	56,921	59,025	(NA)	(NA)	(NA)
Engineering:									
Civil........................	57,495	57,965	60,250	62,172	66,012	69,740	[3] 71,477	67,097	73,898
Chemical...................	66,490	67,913	71,545	74,517	71,970	75,570	89,710	87,292	93,739
Computer...................	76,070	76,881	82,534	102,171	99,805	93,680	[3] 105,412	105,009	[3] 115,223
Electrical..................	72,930	72,619	78,048	93,543	86,398	91,765	118,871	105,975	112,289
Mechanical................	63,070	64,829	66,701	78,886	79,659	81,814	88,135	84,889	99,120
Nuclear [4].................	[3] 59,122	[3] 68,741	[3] 64,674	[3] 78,100	[3] 63,800	(NA)	[3] 107,769	[3] 89,389	(NA)
Petroleum..................	73,084	78,801	85,770	(NA)	[3] 82,411	[3] 76,500	(NA)	(NA)	(NA)
Chemistry....................	42,355	42,403	44,587	58,220	[3] 68,191	[3] 64,598	68,089	69,098	74,212
Mathematics................	59,846	59,681	64,914	56,861	50,195	[3] 58,908	74,091	65,979	77,511
Physics.......................	52,313	57,082	62,099	71,069	[3] 65,499	[3] 66,538	72,768	67,643	[3] 89,550
Humanities..................	42,763	48,961	51,943	58,033	56,017	62,921	63,746	69,774	66,899
Social sciences [5]..........	46,707	46,797	50,099	57,849	57,418	62,715	84,889	84,980	74,798
Computer science.............	78,803	77,564	84,010	95,603	96,852	97,897	114,373	125,168	119,601

NA Not available. [1] Candidates with 1 year or less of full-time nonmilitary employment. [2] For master's degree, starting salaries are after nontechnical undergraduate degree. [3] Fewer than 50 salaries reported. [4] Includes engineering physics. [5] Excludes economics.

Source: National Association of Colleges and Employers, Bethlehem, PA ©. Reprinted with permission from Spring 2015-2019, and Summer 2020 Salary Surveys. All rights reserved.

Table 326. Degrees Earned by Level and Sex: 1960 to 2018

[In thousands (477 represents 477,000), except percent. Based on data from the Integrated Postsecondary Education Data System (IPEDS)]

Year ending	All degrees		Associate's		Bachelor's		Master's		Doctoral [1]	
	Total	Percent male	Male	Female	Male	Female	Male	Female	Male	Female
1960..............	477	65.8	(NA)	(NA)	[2] 254	[2] 138	51	24	9	1
1970..............	1,271	59.2	117	89	451	341	131	83	54	6
1975..............	1,666	56.0	191	169	505	418	166	131	71	14
1980..............	1,732	51.1	184	217	474	456	157	148	70	26
1985..............	1,828	49.3	203	252	483	497	149	144	66	35
1986..............	1,830	49.0	196	250	486	502	149	146	65	35
1987..............	1,823	48.4	191	245	481	510	147	149	63	36
1988..............	1,835	48.0	190	245	477	518	150	156	63	36
1989..............	1,873	47.3	186	250	483	535	154	163	63	38
1990..............	1,940	46.6	191	264	492	560	158	172	64	40
1991..............	2,025	45.8	199	283	504	590	161	182	64	41
1992..............	2,108	45.6	207	297	521	616	166	192	67	43
1993..............	2,167	45.5	212	303	533	632	173	202	67	45
1994..............	2,206	45.1	215	315	532	637	181	212	67	46
1995..............	2,218	44.9	218	321	526	634	183	221	67	47
1996..............	2,248	44.2	220	336	522	642	183	229	67	48
1997..............	2,288	43.6	224	347	521	652	185	240	68	50
1998..............	2,298	43.2	218	341	520	664	189	247	67	52
1999..............	2,330	42.7	221	344	520	682	190	256	65	51
2000..............	2,385	42.6	225	340	530	708	196	267	65	54
2001..............	2,416	42.4	232	347	532	712	198	276	64	55
2002..............	2,494	42.2	238	357	550	742	203	285	63	57
2003..............	2,623	42.1	253	381	573	776	215	304	63	59
2004..............	2,755	41.8	260	405	595	804	233	331	64	62
2005..............	2,850	41.6	268	429	613	826	237	343	67	67
2006..............	2,936	41.3	270	443	631	855	242	358	69	69
2007..............	3,008	41.2	275	453	650	875	242	368	71	73
2008..............	3,094	41.2	283	467	668	896	250	381	73	76
2009..............	3,205	41.3	298	489	685	916	264	399	76	79
2010..............	3,351	41.2	323	526	707	943	275	418	77	82
2011..............	3,554	41.3	361	582	734	982	292	439	80	84
2012..............	3,740	41.3	393	628	766	1,026	302	453	83	88
2013..............	3,775	41.4	389	618	787	1,053	302	450	85	90
2014..............	3,807	41.5	391	614	802	1,068	303	452	86	92
2015..............	3,847	41.6	397	618	813	1,082	307	452	85	94
2016..............	3,893	41.6	392	616	822	1,099	321	465	84	94
2017..............	3,948	41.6	394	612	836	1,120	327	478	85	97
2018..............	3,996	41.4	399	613	845	1,136	327	493	86	99

NA Not available. [1] Includes Ph.D., Ed.D., and comparable degrees at the doctoral level. Includes most degrees formerly classified as first-professional, such as M.D., D.D.S., and law degrees. [2] Includes some degrees classified as master's or doctor's degrees in later years.

Source: U.S. National Center for Education Statistics, *Digest of Education Statistics*, "Advance Release of Selected 2019 Digest Tables," <https://nces.ed.gov/programs/digest/index.asp>, accessed April 2020.

Table 327. Degrees Earned by Level and Race/Ethnicity: 1990 to 2018

[For school year ending in year shown. Based on Integrated Postsecondary Education Data System surveys; see Appendix III]

Level of degree and race/ethnicity	Total					Percent distribution		
	1990	2000 [1]	2010	2017	2018	2000 [1]	2010	2018
Associate's degrees, total............	**455,102**	**564,933**	**848,856**	**1,005,687**	**1,011,487**	**100.0**	**100.0**	**100.0**
White, non-Hispanic...................	376,816	408,822	552,376	551,057	536,256	72.4	65.1	53.0
Black, non-Hispanic..................	34,326	60,208	113,867	129,880	125,517	10.7	13.4	12.4
Hispanic.............................	21,504	51,563	112,403	209,159	225,462	9.1	13.2	22.3
Asian or Pacific Islander.............	13,066	27,778	44,026	55,814	58,952	4.9	5.2	5.8
American Indian/Alaska Native.......	3,430	6,474	10,101	9,265	9,285	1.1	1.2	0.9
Two or more races...................	(NA)	(NA)	(NA)	29,603	32,971	(NA)	(NA)	3.3
Nonresident alien...................	5,960	10,088	16,083	20,909	23,044	1.8	1.9	2.3
Bachelor's degrees, total.............	**1,051,344**	**1,237,875**	**1,649,919**	**1,956,114**	**1,980,644**	**100.0**	**100.0**	**100.0**
White, non-Hispanic..................	887,151	929,102	1,167,322	1,195,977	1,189,619	75.1	70.8	60.1
Black, non-Hispanic..................	61,046	108,018	164,789	196,338	195,014	8.7	10.0	9.8
Hispanic.............................	32,829	75,063	140,426	252,203	267,065	6.1	8.5	13.5
Asian or Pacific Islander.............	39,230	77,909	117,391	144,093	150,999	6.3	7.1	7.6
American Indian/Alaska Native.......	4,390	8,717	12,405	9,589	9,157	0.7	0.8	0.5
Two or more races...................	(NA)	(NA)	(NA)	66,532	70,553	(NA)	(NA)	3.6
Nonresident alien...................	26,698	39,066	47,586	91,382	98,237	3.2	2.9	5.0
Master's degrees, total [2]............	**(NA)**	**463,185**	**693,313**	**804,542**	**820,102**	**100.0**	**100.0**	**100.0**
White, non-Hispanic..................	(NA)	324,990	445,158	433,638	439,051	70.2	64.2	53.5
Black, non-Hispanic..................	(NA)	36,606	76,472	89,577	91,273	7.9	11.0	11.1
Hispanic.............................	(NA)	19,379	43,603	67,026	72,470	4.2	6.3	8.8
Asian or Pacific Islander.............	(NA)	23,523	42,520	47,810	50,091	5.1	6.1	6.1
American Indian/Alaska Native.......	(NA)	2,263	3,965	3,397	3,318	0.5	0.6	0.4
Two or more races...................	(NA)	(NA)	(NA)	17,674	18,850	(NA)	(NA)	2.3
Nonresident alien...................	(NA)	56,424	81,595	145,420	145,049	12.2	11.8	17.7
Doctoral degrees, total [2,3]...........	**(NA)**	**118,736**	**158,590**	**181,357**	**184,074**	**100.0**	**100.0**	**100.0**
White, non-Hispanic..................	(NA)	82,984	104,419	107,444	107,415	69.9	65.8	58.4
Black, non-Hispanic..................	(NA)	7,078	10,413	14,070	14,241	6.0	6.6	7.7
Hispanic.............................	(NA)	5,042	8,085	12,493	13,253	4.2	5.1	7.2
Asian or Pacific Islander.............	(NA)	10,682	16,560	20,345	20,762	9.0	10.4	11.3
American Indian/Alaska Native.......	(NA)	708	952	747	707	0.6	0.6	0.4
Two or more races...................	(NA)	(NA)	(NA)	4,166	4,497	(NA)	(NA)	2.4
Nonresident alien...................	(NA)	12,242	18,161	22,092	23,199	10.3	11.5	12.6
First-professional degrees, total.....	**70,988**	**80,057**	**94,103**	**94,760**	**(NA)**	**100.0**	**100.0**	**100.0**
White, non-Hispanic..................	60,487	59,637	66,172	59,667	(NA)	74.5	70.3	(NA)
Black, non-Hispanic..................	3,409	5,555	6,850	7,253	(NA)	6.9	7.3	(NA)
Hispanic.............................	2,425	3,865	5,430	7,426	(NA)	4.8	5.8	(NA)
Asian or Pacific Islander.............	3,362	8,584	12,691	14,618	(NA)	10.7	13.5	(NA)
American Indian/Alaska Native.......	257	564	665	407	(NA)	0.7	0.7	(NA)
Two or more races...................	(NA)	(NA)	(NA)	2,466	(NA)	(NA)	(NA)	(NA)
Nonresident alien...................	1,048	1,852	2,295	2,923	(NA)	2.3	2.4	(NA)

NA Not available. [1] Beginning 2000, data reflect the new classification of institutions. See headnote, Table 296. [2] Data prior to 2009 have been revised. Revisions for 1990 not available. [3] Includes Ph.D., Ed.D., and comparable degrees at the doctoral level, as well as M.D., D.D.S., and law degrees that were formerly classified as first-professional degrees.

Source: U.S. National Center for Education Statistics, *Digest of Education Statistics*, "Advance Release of Selected 2019 Digest Tables," <http://www.nces.ed.gov/programs/digest/>, accessed May 2020.

Table 328. Bachelor's Degrees Earned by Field: 1980 to 2018

[For school year ending in year shown. A new Classification of Instructional Programs was introduced in 2009-2010; data for previous years has been reclassified where necessary. Based on Integrated Postsecondary Education Data System (IPEDS) surveys]

Field of study	1980	1990	2000	2010	2015	2017	2018
Total [1]...........................	**929,417**	**1,051,344**	**1,237,875**	**1,649,919**	**1,894,969**	**1,956,114**	**1,980,644**
Agriculture and natural resources.............................	22,802	12,900	24,238	26,343	36,278	37,734	39,314
Architecture and related services..............................	9,132	9,364	8,462	10,051	9,090	8,579	8,464
Area, ethnic, cultural, and gender studies....................	2,840	4,447	6,212	8,620	7,783	7,720	7,717
Biological and biomedical sciences...........................	46,190	37,204	63,005	86,391	109,904	116,768	118,663
Business...	186,264	248,568	256,070	358,119	363,741	381,109	386,201
Communication, journalism, and related programs...........	26,927	50,114	55,760	81,280	90,658	93,794	92,290
Communications technologies.............................	1,689	1,458	1,298	4,782	5,135	4,615	4,231
Computer and information sciences.........................	11,154	27,347	37,788	39,593	59,586	71,416	79,598
Education...	118,038	105,112	108,034	101,287	91,596	85,130	82,621
Engineering...	58,896	64,509	58,822	72,657	97,852	115,671	121,956
Engineering technologies.................................	10,491	17,971	14,597	16,078	17,253	18,119	18,727
English language and literature/letters.......................	32,187	46,803	50,106	53,229	45,851	41,314	40,002
Family and consumer sciences/human sciences..............	18,411	13,514	16,321	21,832	24,584	25,080	24,349
Foreign languages, literatures, and linguistics...............	12,480	13,133	15,886	21,507	19,493	17,643	16,958
Health professions and related clinical sciences..............	63,848	58,983	80,863	129,623	216,228	237,979	244,909
Homeland security, law enforcement, and firefighting........	15,015	15,354	24,877	43,613	62,723	59,553	58,114
Legal professions and studies.............................	683	1,632	1,969	3,886	4,420	4,272	4,239
Liberal arts/sciences, general studies, and humanities......	23,196	27,985	36,104	46,963	43,649	44,103	44,262
Mathematics and statistics................................	11,378	14,276	11,418	16,029	21,854	24,075	25,256
Multi/interdisciplinary studies.............................	11,457	16,557	28,561	37,717	47,556	49,631	51,909
Parks, recreation, leisure, and fitness studies................	5,753	4,582	17,571	33,332	49,008	53,292	53,883
Philosophy and religious studies..........................	7,069	7,034	8,535	12,503	11,071	9,711	9,603
Physical sciences and science technologies.................	23,407	16,056	18,331	23,381	30,042	31,272	31,542
Psychology...	42,093	53,952	74,194	97,215	117,573	116,859	116,432
Public administration and social services...................	16,644	13,908	20,185	25,421	34,364	35,461	35,629
Social sciences and history...............................	103,662	118,083	127,101	172,782	166,971	159,097	159,967
Theology and religious vocations..........................	6,170	5,185	6,789	8,719	9,713	9,518	9,521
Transportation and materials moving.......................	213	2,387	3,395	4,998	4,730	4,708	4,924
Visual and performing arts................................	40,892	39,934	58,791	91,798	95,840	91,291	88,582

[1] Includes other fields of study, not shown separately.

Source: U.S. National Center for Education Statistics, *Digest of Education Statistics*, "Advance Release of Selected 2019 Digest Tables," <https://nces.ed.gov/programs/digest/index.asp>, accessed April 2020.

Table 329. Associate's Degrees by Field of Study and Sex: 2010 to 2018

[For school year ending in year shown. Covers associate's degrees conferred by degree-granting institutions. Based on Integrated Postsecondary Education Data System (IPEDS) survey; see Appendix III]

Field of study	2010	2014	2015	2016	2017	2018 Total	2018 Male	2018 Female
Total [1]	**848,856**	**1,005,155**	**1,014,341**	**1,008,228**	**1,005,687**	**1,011,487**	**398,600**	**612,887**
Agriculture and natural resources, total	5,852	7,057	7,693	7,858	8,208	8,076	4,834	3,242
Architecture and related services	553	425	491	478	503	539	358	181
Area, ethnic, cultural, gender, and group studies	199	363	382	419	420	559	230	329
Biological and biomedical sciences	2,664	4,557	4,883	5,266	5,550	6,390	2,072	4,318
Business [1]	133,265	129,957	132,374	128,259	122,252	117,782	47,418	70,364
Business, management, marketing, and support services [1]	116,798	113,056	113,681	110,036	108,376	105,751	43,015	62,736
Accounting and related services	17,925	17,400	16,080	14,790	13,760	13,013	3,798	9,215
Business administration, management, and operations	46,086	50,121	52,668	52,758	53,930	55,382	25,198	30,184
Personal and culinary services	16,467	16,901	18,693	18,223	13,876	12,031	4,403	7,628
Communication, journalism, and related programs	2,841	4,970	6,034	6,759	7,379	7,785	3,269	4,516
Communications technologies	4,418	4,713	4,628	4,569	4,307	4,197	2,782	1,415
Computer and information sciences and support services	32,351	37,646	36,420	30,571	31,171	31,479	25,236	6,243
Construction trades	4,684	4,837	4,643	4,699	5,308	5,277	4,968	309
Education	17,346	17,605	17,178	17,032	16,603	16,182	1,843	14,339
Engineering	2,508	4,306	4,875	5,278	5,915	6,408	5,334	1,074
Engineering technologies and engineering-related fields	31,883	31,792	31,958	27,243	27,021	26,745	22,899	3,846
English language and literature/letters	1,658	2,082	2,324	2,551	2,870	3,133	1,049	2,084
Family and consumer sciences	9,515	8,669	8,750	8,930	8,871	8,854	400	8,454
Foreign languages, literatures, and linguistics	1,683	2,284	2,102	2,208	2,363	2,607	625	1,982
Health professions and related programs	177,321	208,885	200,018	191,442	186,312	181,056	29,483	151,573
Dental assisting	7,063	7,988	7,762	7,584	7,397	7,073	361	6,712
Emergency medical technician (EMT paramedic)	2,413	3,521	3,456	3,380	3,453	3,410	2,306	1,104
Clinical/medical lab science	2,621	3,517	3,143	3,186	3,062	3,051	722	2,329
Medical and other health assisting	29,776	39,126	36,813	34,749	32,297	28,723	4,611	24,112
Nursing and patient care assistant	1	38	50	52	56	100	11	89
Practical nursing	1,973	2,230	1,858	1,404	1,420	1,105	99	1,006
Nursing, R.N. and other	81,281	86,435	82,953	78,577	77,083	77,674	11,217	66,457
Health sciences, other	52,193	66,030	63,983	62,510	61,544	59,920	10,156	49,764
Homeland security, law enforcement, and firefighting	37,154	45,771	43,041	39,930	37,362	35,276	19,997	15,279
Legal professions and studies	9,999	10,502	9,095	8,017	6,904	6,237	1,011	5,226
Liberal arts and sciences, general studies, and humanities	284,954	353,946	367,852	381,202	386,746	397,926	151,028	246,898
Library science	112	194	170	146	158	156	21	135
Mathematics and statistics	1,051	2,148	2,697	3,027	3,454	4,135	2,880	1,255
Mechanic and repair technologies/technicians	16,326	20,100	19,984	20,543	20,821	21,295	19,846	1,449
Military technologies and applied sciences	668	1,084	1,229	1,047	1,093	1,226	946	280
Multi/interdisciplinary studies	17,279	28,167	29,139	30,482	30,780	31,068	13,002	18,066
Parks, recreation, leisure, and fitness studies	2,006	4,383	4,669	4,771	5,037	5,095	2,758	2,337
Philosophy and religious studies	256	435	697	814	1002	1,049	640	409
Physical sciences and science technologies	4,141	6,916	7,568	8,484	9,223	10,116	5,927	4,189
Precision production	2,794	3,903	4,382	4,794	5,251	5,333	4,967	366
Psychology	6,582	7,604	8,780	10,603	11,283	12,489	2,921	9,568
Public administration and social service professions	4,522	8,914	8,436	7,988	7,591	7,136	1,003	6,133
Social sciences and history	10,649	16,554	17,916	20,056	21,392	23,683	8,849	14,834
Theology and religious vocations	613	944	1135	1,089	1,546	1,435	786	649
Transportation and materials moving	1,444	2,102	1,810	1,497	1,547	1,610	1,394	216
Visual and performing arts	19,565	21,340	20,988	20,176	19,444	19,153	7,824	11,329

[1] Includes other fields of study, not shown separately.

Source: U.S. National Center for Education Statistics, *Digest of Education Statistics*, "Advance Release of Selected 2019 Digest Tables," <https://nces.ed.gov/programs/digest/index.asp>, accessed April 2020.

Table 330. Education Certificates Awarded by Field of Study and Sex: 2017

[For school year ending in 2017. Covers certificates below the associate's degree level based on postsecondary curriculums of less than 4 years in degree- and nondegree-granting institutions of higher education. Based on Integrated Postsecondary Education Data System (IPEDS) survey; see Appendix III]

Field of study	Less than 1-year awards			1- to less than 4-year awards		
	Total	Male	Female	Total	Male	Female
Total............................	**492,653**	**230,044**	**262,609**	**452,287**	**174,669**	**277,618**
Agriculture and natural resources, total....................	4,826	2,977	1,849	2,467	1,618	849
Agriculture, agriculture operations, and related sciences...........	3,788	2,349	1,439	2,261	1,480	781
Natural resources and conservation..................	1,038	628	410	206	138	68
Architecture and related services........................	171	91	80	103	61	42
Area, ethnic, cultural, gender, and group studies..................	471	103	368	119	27	92
Biological and biomedical sciences......................	673	212	461	229	82	147
Business, management, marketing, and support services...........	62,013	22,307	39,706	21,158	6,197	14,961
Accounting and related services.......................	11,315	3,381	7,934	5,130	1,200	3,930
Business/commerce, general........................	3,100	1,304	1,796	1,501	800	701
Business administration, management, and operations...........	18,233	7,381	10,852	4,449	1,589	2,860
Management information systems and services.............	539	377	162	109	75	34
Business operations support and assistant services..............	8,671	1,999	6,672	5,441	859	4,582
Business and management, other.....................	20,155	7,865	12,290	4,528	1,674	2,854
Communication, journalism, and related programs..............	3,110	1,530	1,580	1,378	789	589
Communications technologies...........................	2,572	1,488	1,084	2,937	2,163	774
Computer and information sciences and support services...........	29,309	21,327	7,982	8,951	6,907	2,044
Construction trades...................................	13,395	12,641	754	12,474	11,926	548
Education...	7,678	712	6,966	3,944	491	3,453
Engineering...	866	735	131	333	296	37
Engineering technologies and engineering-related fields...........	20,106	17,274	2,832	13,850	12,365	1,485
English language and literature/letters...................	1,189	419	770	442	168	274
Family and consumer sciences..........................	15,474	1,145	14,329	3,772	181	3,591
Foreign languages, literatures, and linguistics...............	1,560	340	1,220	695	143	552
Health professions and related programs.....................	148,840	29,080	119,760	154,259	20,891	133,368
Dental assisting......................................	6,124	541	5,583	12,552	1,032	11,520
Emergency medical technician (EMT paramedic).................	17,222	10,766	6,456	5,629	4,097	1,532
Clinical/medical lab science............................	10,129	1,399	8,730	1,836	473	1,363
Medical assisting....................................	11,044	780	10,264	45,899	3,939	41,960
Pharmacy assisting.................................	3,199	628	2,571	5,039	1,001	4,038
Other allied health assisting........................	6,918	2,143	4,775	2,099	240	1,859
Nursing and patient care assistant.....................	40,822	5,138	35,684	849	104	745
Practical nursing....................................	5,031	574	4,457	40,537	4,158	36,379
Nursing, R.N. and other...............................	1,369	145	1,224	2,585	365	2,220
Health sciences, other.............................	46,982	6,966	40,016	37,234	5,482	31,752
Homeland security, law enforcement, and firefighting...............	30,453	22,148	8,305	7,598	5,096	2,502
Criminal justice and corrections......................	22,941	15,660	7,281	6,369	3,998	2,371
Fire control and safety...............................	6,522	5,896	626	1,082	998	84
Homeland security and related protective services, other..........	990	592	398	147	100	47
Legal professions and studies...........................	1,821	339	1,482	2,470	388	2,082
[4] Liberal arts and sciences, general studies, & humanities....	3,795	1,450	2,345	63,806	24,910	38,896
Library science..	203	34	169	45	5	40
Mathematics and statistics.............................	195	156	39	26	21	5
Mechanic and repair technologies/technicians..............	36,097	33,970	2,127	47,122	44,940	2,182
Military technologies and applied sciences...................	15	13	2	2	2	0
Multi/interdisciplinary studies..........................	2,048	815	1,233	1,238	687	551
Parks, recreation, leisure, and fitness studies...............	1,677	846	831	670	380	290
Personal and culinary services........................	39,879	5,296	34,583	72,114	10,912	61,202
Philosophy and religious studies.........................	64	30	34	74	29	45
Physical sciences and science technologies................	1,793	847	946	1,240	793	447
Physical sciences....................................	192	105	87	27	18	9
Science technologies/technicians......................	1,601	742	859	1,213	775	438
Precision production...................................	29,106	27,000	2,106	18,744	17,570	1,174
Psychology..	136	20	116	85	21	64
Public administration and social service professions..............	2,321	455	1,866	836	145	691
Social sciences and history............................	1,137	623	514	460	239	221
Social sciences....................................	1,114	615	499	450	233	217
History..	23	8	15	10	6	4
Theology and religious vocations.....................	230	122	108	895	387	508
Transportation and materials moving..................	22,072	20,084	1,988	1,014	947	67
Visual and performing arts............................	7,358	3,415	3,943	6,737	2,892	3,845
Fine and studio arts.................................	895	326	569	2,068	742	1,326
Music and dance....................................	336	242	94	549	326	223
Visual and performing arts, other.....................	6,127	2,847	3,280	4,120	1,824	2,296

Source: U.S. National Center for Education Statistics, *2018 Digest of Education Statistics*, March 2019. See also <http://www.nces.ed.gov/programs/digest/>.

Table 331. Master's and Doctoral Degrees Earned by Field: 1971 to 2018

[For school years ending in years shown. The new Classification of Instructional Programs was introduced in 2009-2010. Data for previous years has been reclassified where necessary to conform to the new classifications. Based on data from the Integrated Postsecondary Education Data System (IPEDS)]

Field of study	1971	1981	1991	2001	2011	2017	2018
MASTER'S DEGREES							
Total [1]	**235,564**	**302,637**	**342,863**	**473,502**	**730,922**	**804,542**	**820,102**
Agriculture and natural resources	2,457	4,003	3,295	4,272	5,766	6,843	6,967
Architecture and related services	1,705	3,153	3,490	4,302	7,788	7,883	7,317
Area, ethnic, cultural, gender, and group studies	1,032	802	1,233	1,555	1,913	1,717	1,673
Biological and biomedical sciences	5,625	5,766	4,834	7,017	11,324	16,282	17,180
Business	26,490	57,888	78,255	115,602	187,178	187,412	192,184
Communication, journalism, and related programs	1,770	2,896	4,123	5,218	8,302	10,119	10,243
Communications technologies	86	209	204	427	502	539	529
Computer and information sciences	1,588	4,218	9,324	16,911	19,516	46,553	46,468
Education	87,666	96,713	87,352	127,829	185,127	145,624	146,367
Engineering	16,813	16,893	24,454	25,174	38,664	52,826	51,721
Engineering technologies	134	323	996	2,013	4,515	7,403	7,247
English language and literature/letters	10,441	5,742	6,784	6,763	9,475	8,244	8,300
Family and consumer sciences/human sciences	1,452	2,570	1,541	1,838	2,918	3,295	3,308
Foreign languages, literatures, and linguistics	5,480	2,934	3,049	3,035	3,727	3,271	3,261
Health professions and related programs	5,330	16,176	21,354	43,623	75,571	119,242	125,216
Homeland security, law enforcement, and firefighting	194	1,538	1,108	2,514	7,433	10,209	10,293
Legal professions and studies	955	1,832	2,057	3,829	6,475	8,674	9,177
Liberal arts and sciences, general studies, and humanities	885	2,375	2,213	3,193	3,997	2,485	2,473
Library science	7,001	4,859	4,763	4,727	7,729	4,843	4,953
Mathematics and statistics	5,191	2,567	3,549	3,209	5,866	9,082	10,443
Parks, recreation, leisure, and fitness studies	218	643	483	2,354	6,546	8,651	9,005
Philosophy and religious studies	1,326	1,231	1,471	1,386	1,839	1,704	1,692
Physical sciences and science technologies	6,336	5,246	5,281	5,134	6,386	7,136	7,196
Psychology	5,717	10,223	11,349	16,539	25,062	27,539	27,841
Public administration and social services	7,785	17,803	17,905	25,268	38,614	45,361	46,294
Social sciences and history	16,539	11,945	12,233	13,791	21,085	20,004	19,884
Theology and religious vocations	7,747	11,061	10,498	9,876	13,170	13,694	13,828
Transportation and materials moving	–	–	406	756	1,390	839	815
Visual and performing arts	6,675	8,629	8,657	11,404	16,277	17,516	17,686
DOCTORAL DEGREES							
Total [1]	**64,998**	**98,016**	**105,547**	**119,585**	**163,827**	**181,357**	**184,074**
Agriculture and natural resources	1,086	1,067	1,185	1,127	1,246	1,561	1,496
Architecture and related services	36	93	135	153	205	291	250
Area, ethnic, cultural, gender, and group studies	143	161	159	216	278	349	335
Biological and biomedical sciences	3,603	3,640	4,152	5,225	7,693	8,087	8,222
Business	774	808	1,185	1,180	2,286	3,328	3,338
Communication, journalism, and related programs	145	171	259	368	577	615	666
Computer and information sciences	128	252	676	768	1,588	1,982	2,017
Education	6,041	7,279	6,189	6,284	9,642	12,692	12,780
Engineering	3,687	2,598	5,316	5,485	8,369	10,371	10,817
English language and literature/letters	1,554	1,040	1,056	1,330	1,344	1,347	1,295
Foreign languages, literatures, and linguistics	1,084	931	889	1,078	1,158	1,168	1,213
Health professions and related programs	15,988	29,595	29,842	39,019	60,221	77,693	80,305
Legal professions and studies	17,441	36,391	38,035	38,190	44,853	35,123	34,544
Mathematics and statistics	1,199	728	978	997	1,586	1,925	2,010
Philosophy and religious studies	555	411	464	600	804	741	768
Physical sciences and science technologies	4,324	3,105	4,248	3,968	5,295	6,027	6,181
Psychology	2,144	3,576	3,932	5,091	5,851	6,702	6,275
Public administration and social services	174	362	430	574	851	1,116	1,157
Social sciences and history	3,660	3,122	3,012	3,930	4,390	4,706	4,676
Theology and religious vocations	312	1,273	1,076	1,461	2,374	1,792	2,023
Visual and performing arts	621	654	838	1,167	1,646	1,774	1,759

– Represents zero. [1] Includes other fields of study, not shown separately.

Source: U.S. National Center for Education Statistics, *Digest of Education Statistics*, "Advance Release of Selected 2019 Digest Tables," <http://www.nces.ed.gov/programs/digest/>, accessed April 2020.

Table 332. First Professional Degrees Earned in Selected Professions: 1970 to 2017

[First professional degrees include degrees which require at least 6 years of college work for completion (including at least 2 years of preprofessional training). Based on Integrated Postsecondary Education Data System surveys; see Appendix III]

Type of degree and sex of recipient	1970	1980	1990	1995	2000	2005	2010	2015	2016	2017
Medicine (M.D.):										
Institutions conferring degrees	86	112	124	119	118	120	120	127	128	131
Degrees conferred, total	8,314	14,902	15,075	15,537	15,286	15,461	16,356	18,302	18,409	18,698
Percent to women	8.4	23.4	34.2	38.8	42.7	47.3	48.2	47.8	46.5	47.4
Dentistry (D.D.S. or D.M.D.):										
Institutions conferring degrees	48	58	57	53	54	53	55	60	61	63
Degrees conferred, total	3,718	5,258	4,100	3,897	4,250	4,454	5,062	5,816	5,951	6,388
Percent to women	0.9	13.3	30.9	36.4	40.1	43.8	45.8	47.9	49.1	47.9
Law (LL.B. or J.D.):										
Institutions conferring degrees	145	179	182	183	190	198	205	212	214	214
Degrees conferred, total	14,916	35,647	36,485	39,349	38,152	43,423	44,346	40,024	36,798	34,894
Percent to women	5.4	30.2	42.2	42.6	45.9	48.7	47.3	48.0	48.5	49.6
Theological (B.D., M.Div., M.H.L.):										
Institutions conferring degrees	(NA)	(NA)	(NA)	192	198	(NA)	(NA)	(NA)	(NA)	(NA)
Degrees conferred, total	5,298	7,115	5,851	5,978	6,129	5,533	5,825	6,300	5,950	5,801
Percent to women	2.3	13.8	24.8	25.7	29.2	35.6	(NA)	31.4	32.4	31.8

NA Not available.

Source: U.S. National Center for Education Statistics, *Digest of Education Statistics*, "Advance Release of Selected 2018 Digest Tables," <http://www.nces.ed.gov/programs/digest/>, accessed May 2019.

Table 333. Graduate and Undergraduate Students Taking Online Classes and Degree Programs by Selected Characteristics: 2016

[In thousands (19,308 represents 19,308,000), except percent. For school year ending in 2016]

Student characteristics	Undergraduate students				Graduate students			
	Number of students		Percent of students taking—		Number of students		Percent of students taking—	
	Total enroll-ment	Students taking any online classes	Any online classes	Entire degree program is online[1]	Total enroll-ment	Students taking any online classes	Any online classes	Entire degree program is online[1]
Total............................	**19,308**	**8,319**	**43.1**	**10.8**	**3,547**	**1,617**	**45.6**	**27.3**
Sex:								
Male......................	8,406	3,340	39.7	9.2	1,446	591	40.8	24.6
Female....................	10,903	4,979	45.7	12.1	2,101	1,026	48.9	29.3
Race/ethnicity:								
White.....................	10,276	4,671	45.5	11.1	2,105	942	44.8	26.0
Black......................	3,006	1,278	42.5	14.9	504	315	62.5	45.3
Hispanic..................	3,723	1,431	38.4	7.7	326	161	49.5	31.2
Asian......................	1,399	544	38.9	7.8	500	138	27.5	10.8
Pacific Islander..........	83	35	42.2	12.0	8	5	64.1	[2] 33.4
American Indian or Alaska Native............	160	76	47.5	12.2	17	8	43.9	33.1
Two or more races........	661	283	42.8	10.4	88	49	55.6	33.8
Age:								
15 to 23 years old........	11,368	4,157	36.6	3.5	466	130	27.9	8.0
24 to 29 years old........	3,536	1,793	50.7	17.5	1,387	525	37.8	16.8
30 years old and over........	4,404	2,369	53.8	24.9	1,695	962	56.8	41.6
Attendance status:								
Exclusively full-time........	7,239	2,789	38.5	6.0	1,279	408	31.9	15.2
Exclusively part-time........	5,059	2,398	47.4	14.7	850	453	53.3	36.7
Mixed full-time and part-time.................	7,010	3,131	44.7	13.2	1,418	756	53.3	33.1
Field of study:								
Business/management........	2,973	1,525	51.3	17.0	592	320	54.1	36.7
Education.................	841	384	45.7	9.7	605	352	58.2	34.3
Engineering...............	1,140	380	33.3	5.1	(NA)	(NA)	(NA)	(NA)
Health....................	3,438	1,547	45.0	13.3	694	325	46.8	26.6
Humanities................	3,083	1,274	41.3	7.8	281	99	35.3	18.2
Law......................	(NA)	(NA)	(NA)	(NA)	132	21	15.9	8.0
Social/behavioral sciences.................	1,323	556	42.0	9.1	245	112	45.7	29.0
Vocational/technical........	594	188	31.7	6.0	(NA)	(NA)	(NA)	(NA)

NA Not available. [1] Excludes students not in a degree or certificate program. [2] Interpret data with caution. The coefficient of variation (CV) for this estimate is between 30 and 50 percent.

Source: U.S. National Center for Education Statistics, *Digest of Education Statistics*, "Advance Release of Selected 2018 Digest Tables," <http://www.nces.ed.gov/programs/digest/>, accessed May 2019.

Table 334. College and University Libraries by Selected Characteristics: 2014 to 2016

[As of Fall of year shown. In units as indicated (917,510 represents 917,510,000). Data shown for degree-granting postsecondary institution libraries. FTE is full-time equivalent. Based on data from the Integrated Postsecondary Education Data System (IPEDS)]

Collections, staff, and operating expenditures	Unit	2014	2015	2016			
				Total	Public	Private non-profit	Private for-profit
Number of libraries............................	Number	4,134	3,999	3,944	1,559	1,612	773
Percent of institutions with libraries........	Percent	90.2	91.7	91.4	95.9	95.4	77.5
Circulation transactions.......................	1,000	917,510	778,357	768,383	473,808	211,565	83,010
Physical transaction........................	1,000	81,182	67,796	58,244	34,691	22,855	699
Electronic transaction......................	1,000	836,328	710,561	710,139	439,117	188,710	82,311
Circulation transactions per FTE student........	Number	60	52	51	45	61	91
ENROLLMENT							
Total enrollment...............................	1,000	20,209	19,988	19,847	14,586	4,079	1,182
FTE enrollment................................	1,000	15,263	15,079	14,938	10,572	3,454	912
COLLECTIONS							
Total number of physical and electronic materials........	1,000	2,128,233	1,985,142	2,209,958	1,188,603	839,164	182,191
Number of books..........................	1,000	1,711,851	1,573,341	1,651,471	888,869	640,484	122,118
Physical books........................	1,000	1,036,223	824,767	799,263	485,998	309,346	3,918
Electronic books......................	1,000	675,629	748,575	852,208	402,871	331,138	118,200
Number of media (includes audiovisual materials)......	1,000	411,822	410,274	557,541	299,421	198,393	59,727
Number of databases......................	1,000	4,560	1,527	946	313	288	345
OPERATING EXPENDITURES (CURRENT DOLLARS)							
Total operating expenditures [1,2]........................	Mil. dol.	7,957	8,086	8,233	4,835	3,312	86
Salaries and wages [3]......................	Mil. dol.	3,422	3,456	3,500	2,168	1,296	36
Fringe benefits...........................	Mil. dol.	745	759	781	486	291	4
Information resources......................	Mil. dol.	3,016	3,084	3,126	1,767	1,322	37
Operating expenditures per FTE student..................	Dollars	521	536	551	457	959	94

NA Not available. [1] Excludes capital outlay. Expenditure data are reported only by degree-granting institutions with total expenditures over $100,000. [2] Includes other expenditures not shown separately. [3] Includes student hourly wages.

Source: U.S. National Center for Education Statistics, *Digest of Education Statistics*, "Advance Release of Selected 2019 Digest Tables," <http://www.nces.ed.gov/programs/digest/>, accessed April 2020.

Table 335. College Campus Crime—Incidents and Rates by Type of Crime and Institution: 2001 to 2017

[For school year ending in year shown. Data are from Department of Education's Campus Safety and Security Reporting System. Data are for degree-granting institutions, which are institutions that grant associate's or higher degrees and participate in Title IV federal financial aid programs. Some institutions that report data as mandated by the Clery Act, specifically, non-degree-granting institutions and institutions outside of the 50 states and the District of Columbia, are excluded from this table. Crimes, arrests, and referrals include incidents involving students, staff, and on-campus guests. Excludes off-campus crimes and arrests even if they involve college students or staff]

Control and level of institution and type of crime	Total, in residence halls and other locations						2017		
	2001	2006	2011	2014	2015	2016	Total	In residence halls	At other locations
NUMBER OF INCIDENTS									
Selected crimes against persons and property	**41,596**	**44,492**	**30,407**	**26,818**	**27,532**	**28,376**	**28,873**	**14,671**	**14,202**
Murder [1]	17	8	16	11	28	15	21	2	19
Negligent manslaughter [2]	2	–	1	2	2	2	3	1	2
Sex offenses, forcible [3]	2,201	2,670	3,375	6,751	8,022	8,931	10,398	7,517	2,881
Sex offenses, nonforcible [4]	461	43	46	53	63	60	80	57	23
Robbery	1,663	1,547	1,285	1,041	1,044	1,097	1,040	230	810
Aggravated assault	2,947	2,817	2,239	2,048	2,258	2,181	2,216	699	1,517
Burglary	26,904	31,260	19,472	13,419	12,320	11,965	11,053	5,810	5,243
Motor vehicle theft	6,221	5,231	3,334	2,890	3,218	3,528	3,450	26	3,424
Arson	1,180	916	639	603	577	597	612	329	283
Arrests [5]	**40,348**	**50,187**	**54,285**	**44,531**	**40,299**	**39,018**	**37,626**	**18,527**	**19,099**
Illegal weapons possession	1,073	1,316	1,023	990	1,183	1,200	1,245	317	928
Drug law violations	11,854	13,952	20,729	19,172	19,431	19,239	19,568	9,441	10,127
Liquor law violations	27,421	34,919	32,533	24,369	19,685	18,579	16,813	8,769	8,044
Referrals for disciplinary action [5]	**155,201**	**218,040**	**249,694**	**253,315**	**241,687**	**229,589**	**216,379**	**198,302**	**18,077**
Illegal weapons possession	1,277	1,871	1,282	1,425	1,425	1,405	1,309	923	386
Drug law violations	23,900	27,251	51,562	56,575	56,037	55,768	58,079	49,700	8,379
Liquor law violations	130,024	188,918	196,850	195,315	184,225	172,416	156,991	147,679	9,312
INCIDENTS PER 10,000 FTE STUDENTS [6,7]									
Selected crimes against persons and property	**35.6**	**33.4**	**20.0**	**18.1**	**18.7**	**19.3**	**19.6**	**25.1**	**6.2**
By type of crime:									
Murder [1]	(Z)	(Z)	(Z)	(Z)	(Z)	(Z)	(Z)	(Z)	(Z)
Negligent manslaughter [2]	(Z)	(Z)	(Z)	(Z)	(Z)	(Z)	(Z)	(Z)	(Z)
Sex offenses, forcible [3]	1.9	2.0	2.2	4.5	5.4	6.1	7.1	9.5	1.0
Sex offenses, nonforcible [4]	0.4	(Z)	(Z)	(Z)	(Z)	(Z)	0.1	0.1	(Z)
Robbery	1.4	1.2	0.8	0.7	0.7	0.7	0.7	0.8	0.4
Aggravated assault	2.5	2.1	1.5	1.4	1.5	1.5	1.5	1.8	0.8
Burglary	23.0	23.4	12.8	9.0	8.4	8.1	7.5	9.6	2.3
Motor vehicle theft	5.3	3.9	2.2	1.9	2.2	2.4	2.3	2.7	1.5
Arson	1.0	0.7	0.4	0.4	0.4	0.4	0.4	0.5	0.1
By type of institution:									
Public 4-year	36.2	35.5	22.0	19.5	19.7	19.8	20.4	21.9	7.0
Nonprofit 4-year	57.4	57.7	33.2	30.2	31.1	32.7	32.1	34.4	9.3
For-profit 4-year	19.1	9.6	6.0	5.8	4.4	4.5	5.3	19.4	2.6
Public 2-year	19.9	15.4	10.0	7.7	8.4	8.0	8.2	14.4	6.4
Nonprofit 2-year	64.0	81.9	45.5	27.4	20.0	21.9	14.4	37.8	8.4
For profit-2-year	25.4	18.2	7.5	6.1	6.9	6.7	5.0	7.4	4.9
Arrests [5]	**34.6**	**37.6**	**35.8**	**30.0**	**27.4**	**26.5**	**25.5**	**34.6**	**3.4**
Illegal weapons possession	0.9	1.0	0.7	0.7	0.8	0.8	0.8	1.0	0.5
Drug law violations	10.2	10.5	13.7	12.9	13.2	13.1	13.3	17.8	2.3
Liquor law violations	23.5	26.2	21.4	16.4	13.4	12.6	11.4	15.8	0.6
By type of institution:									
Public 4-year	60.1	68.7	67.2	53.1	47.3	44.1	41.4	45.4	5.3
Nonprofit 4-year	24.5	21.0	16.8	14.9	13.6	13.3	12.3	13.5	1.4
For-profit 4-year	0.4	0.8	2.0	1.5	1.5	1.8	2.2	11.8	0.3
Public 2-year	7.8	10.9	9.0	8.4	7.9	8.1	9.7	30.0	3.9
Nonprofit 2-year	27.9	22.0	16.0	16.7	12.1	21.5	11.3	37.8	4.5
For profit-2-year	8.8	1.8	0.7	2.7	1.5	2.0	1.4	3.7	1.2
Referrals for disciplinary action [5]	**132.9**	**163.4**	**164.5**	**170.7**	**164.1**	**155.8**	**146.9**	**205.7**	**2.7**
Illegal weapons possession	1.1	1.4	0.8	1.0	1.0	1.0	0.9	1.1	0.3
Drug law violations	20.5	20.4	34.0	38.1	38.0	37.8	39.4	55.0	1.4
Liquor law violations	111.3	141.6	129.7	131.6	125.1	117.0	106.6	149.6	1.1
By type of institution:									
Public 4-year	153.1	184.6	194.0	196.7	184.1	166.2	154.5	171.4	1.7
Nonprofit 4-year	275.5	353.9	341.4	332.3	314.4	302.5	280.6	308.6	10.3
For-profit 4-year	12.0	7.6	9.7	12.2	11.9	11.4	17.2	103.1	0.7
Public 2-year	10.3	16.1	19.7	19.5	20.4	20.6	21.0	85.4	2.6
Nonprofit 2-year	160.9	176.0	110.8	191.5	206.4	161.5	117.0	570.0	1.8
For profit-2-year	15.4	13.9	4.9	11.3	9.5	5.9	5.2	80.4	1.4

– Represents zero. Z Rounds to less than .05. [1] Excludes suicides, fetal deaths, traffic fatalities, accidental deaths, and justifiable homicide (such as the killing of a felon by a law enforcement officer in the line of duty). [2] Defined as the killing of another person through gross negligence (excludes traffic fatalities). [3] Any sexual act directed against another person forcibly and/or against that person's will. [4] Includes only statutory rape or incest. [5] If an individual is both arrested and referred to college officials for disciplinary action for a single offense, only the arrest is counted. [6] FTE is full-time equivalent. Although crimes, arrests, and referrals include incidents involving students, staff, and campus guests, they are expressed as a ratio to FTE students because comprehensive FTE counts of all these groups are not available. [7] Data on incidents per 10,000 FTE students are shown for institutions with and without residence halls.

Source: U.S. National Center for Education Statistics, *Digest of Education Statistics*, "Advance Release of Selected 2019 Digest Tables," <http://nces.ed.gov/programs/digest/index.asp>, accessed April 2020.

Table 336. Public Schools Reporting Incidents of Crime by Incident Type and Selected School Characteristics: 2018

[For school year ending in 2018. Includes incidents that happen in school buildings, on school grounds, on school buses, and at places that hold school-sponsored events or activities. Based on the School Survey on Crime and Safety (SSOCS). Based on sample; see source for details]

School characteristic	Total number of schools	Number of incidents		Percent of schools with—		Rate per 1,000 students	
		Violent incidents [1]	Serious violent incidents [2]	Violent incidents [1]	Serious violent incidents [2]	Violent incidents [1]	Serious violent incidents [2]
All public schools...............	**82,300**	**962,300**	**54,400**	**70.7**	**21.3**	**19.6**	**1.1**
Level: [3]							
Primary.............................	48,300	441,700	21,200	59.1	13.9	18.3	0.9
Middle................................	15,100	287,800	16,700	89.8	32.5	29.6	1.7
High school........................	12,600	205,200	14,300	90.4	35.5	16.0	1.1
Combined...........................	6,300	27,600	2,200	74.4	22.9	11.1	0.9
Enrollment size:							
Less than 300....................	16,800	74,000	4,500	53.1	13.7	20.3	1.2
300 to 499.........................	24,900	242,400	[4] 15,800	69.2	17.9	22.7	[4] 1.5
500 to 999.........................	31,700	430,300	18,200	75.0	22.0	19.9	0.8
1,000 or more....................	8,900	215,600	15,900	92.7	42.8	16.3	1.2
Percent minority enrollment:							
Zero to 25 percent..............	29,800	193,000	15,200	66.8	19.3	12.6	1.0
26 to 50 percent.................	18,000	203,200	[4] 13,200	69.5	20.9	18.3	[4] 1.2
51 to 75 percent.................	12,500	210,100	7,800	75.1	21.9	24.7	0.9
76 percent or more..............	22,000	356,000	18,200	74.4	24.0	25.1	1.3

[1] Violent incidents include rape, sexual battery other than rape, physical attack or fight with or without a weapon, threat of physical attack with or without a weapon, and robbery with or without a weapon. [2] Serious violent incidents include rape, sexual battery other than rape, physical attack or fight with a weapon, threat of physical attack with a weapon, and robbery with or without a weapon. [3] Primary schools are defined as schools in which the lowest grade is not higher than grade 3 and the highest grade is not higher than grade 8. Middle schools are defined as schools in which the lowest grade is not lower than grade 4 and the highest grade is not higher than grade 9. High schools are defined as schools in which the lowest grade is not lower than grade 9 and the highest grade is not higher than grade 12. Combined schools include all other combinations of grades, including K–12 schools. [4] Interpret data with caution.

Source: U.S. National Center for Education Statistics, *Digest of Education Statistics*, "Advance Release of Selected 2019 Digest Tables," <http://nces.ed.gov/programs/digest/index.asp>, accessed May 2020; and *Indicators of School Crime and Safety*, annual. See also <http://nces.ed.gov/surveys/ssocs/>.

Table 337. Disciplinary Problems Reported at Public Schools by Selected School Characteristics: 2018

[In percent. For school year ending in 2018. "At school" includes activities that happen in school buildings, on school grounds, on school buses, and at places that hold school-sponsored events or activities. Based on the School Survey on Crime and Safety (SSOCS). Respondents to the survey had the option of either completing the survey on paper and mailing it back, or completing the survey online. Based on sample; see source for details]

School characteristic	Happens at least once a week						Happens at all
	Student racial tensions	Student bullying	Student sexual harassment of other students [1]	Student verbal abuse of teachers	Widespread disorder in classrooms	Student acts of disrespect for teachers	Gang activities [2]
All public schools...........	**2.8**	**13.6**	**1.4**	**6.0**	**3.1**	**11.8**	**11.0**
Level: [3]							
Primary..........................	1.9	8.7	(S)	4.6	2.6	10.1	4.9
Middle............................	4.9	27.9	3.3	10.3	5.5	17.3	19.0
High school.....................	4.5	15.8	2.8	7.1	2.6	13.1	27.9
Combined........................	(S)	12.3	(S)	[4] 4.3	(S)	[4] 8.2	[4] 4.5
Enrollment size:							
Less than 300.................	(S)	9.6	(S)	[4] 3.0	[4] 1.5	4.9	3.3
300 to 499......................	3.4	11.3	[4] 1.2	5.9	4.3	14.4	6.6
500 to 999......................	2.3	15.6	0.9	6.8	2.7	12.1	12.3
1,000 or more.................	5.9	20.7	3.3	9.5	3.9	16.2	33.4
Percent minority enrollment:							
Zero to 25 percent...........	1.7	13.0	[4] 1.5	2.3	[4] 1.5	7.8	2.7
26 to 50 percent..............	2.4	11.7	1.3	5.2	3.6	10.1	9.8
51 to 75 percent..............	5.1	16.5	[4] 2.3	10.1	[4] 4.2	18.9	17.8
76 percent or more..........	3.3	14.3	0.8	9.5	4.1	14.5	19.3

S Figure does not meet publication standards. [1] Sexual harassment was defined as conduct that is unwelcome, sexual in nature, and denies or limits a student's ability to participate in or benefit from a school's education program. The conduct can be carried out by school employees, other students, and non-employee third parties. Both male and female students can be victims of sexual harassment, and the harasser and the victim can be of the same sex. The conduct can be verbal, nonverbal, or physical. [2] Gang includes an "ongoing loosely organized association of three or more persons, whether formal or informal, that has a common name, signs, symbols or colors, whose members engage, either individually or collectively, in violent or other forms of illegal behavior." [3] Primary schools are defined as schools in which the lowest grade is not higher than grade 3 and the highest grade is not higher than grade 8. Middle schools are defined as schools in which the lowest grade level is not lower than grade 4 and the highest grade is not higher than grade 9. High schools are defined as schools in which the lowest grade is not lower than grade 9 and the highest grade is not higher than grade 12. Combined schools include all other combinations of grades, including K–12 schools. [4] Interpret data with caution.

Source: U.S. National Center for Education Statistics, *Digest of Education Statistics*, "Advance Release of Selected 2019 Digest Tables," <http://nces.ed.gov/programs/digest/index.asp>, accessed May 2020; and *Indicators of School Crime and Safety*, annual. See also <http://nces.ed.gov/surveys/ssocs/>.

Table 338. Students Who Reported Being Threatened or Injured With a Weapon on School Property by Selected Student Characteristics: 2003 to 2017

[In percent. Based on the Centers for Disease Control and Prevention's Youth Risk Behavior Surveillance System, which surveys students in public and private schools, in grades 9 to 12. Data are for previous 12 months. "On school property" was not defined for survey respondents. "Weapon" was defined as a gun, knife, or club for survey respondents]

Characteristic	2003	2005	2007	2009	2011	2013	2015	2017
Total	**9.2**	**7.9**	**7.8**	**7.7**	**7.4**	**6.9**	**6.0**	**6.0**
Sex:								
Male	11.6	9.7	10.2	9.6	9.5	7.7	7.0	7.8
Female	6.5	6.1	5.4	5.5	5.2	6.1	4.6	4.1
Race/ethnicity: [1]								
White	7.8	7.2	6.9	6.4	6.1	5.8	4.9	5.0
Black	10.9	8.1	9.7	9.4	8.9	8.4	7.9	7.8
Hispanic	9.4	9.8	8.7	9.1	9.2	8.5	6.6	6.1
Asian	11.5	4.6	[2] 7.6	5.5	7.0	5.3	[2] 3.6	4.3
American Indian/Alaska Native	22.1	9.8	5.9	16.5	8.2	18.5	[2] 8.2	[2] 7.0
Pacific Islander/Native Hawaiian	16.3	[2] 14.5	[2] 8.1	12.5	11.3	[2] 8.7	[2] 20.5	13.7
More than one race	18.7	10.7	13.3	9.2	9.9	7.7	8.0	8.0
Grade:								
9th	12.1	10.5	9.2	8.7	8.3	8.5	7.2	7.2
10th	9.2	8.8	8.4	8.4	7.7	7.0	6.2	6.2
11th	7.3	5.5	6.8	7.9	7.3	6.8	5.5	5.5
12th	6.3	5.8	6.3	5.2	5.9	4.9	4.4	4.4
Sexual orientation: [3]								
Heterosexual	(NA)	(NA)	(NA)	(NA)	(NA)	(NA)	5.1	5.4
Gay, lesbian, or bisexual	(NA)	(NA)	(NA)	(NA)	(NA)	(NA)	10.0	9.4
Not sure	(NA)	(NA)	(NA)	(NA)	(NA)	(NA)	12.6	11.1

NA Not available. [1] Race categories exclude persons of Hispanic ethnicity. [2] Interpret data with caution. [3] Students were asked which sexual orientation, "heterosexual (straight)," "gay or lesbian," "bisexual," or "not sure," which best described them.

Source: U.S. National Center for Education Statistics, *Digest of Education Statistics,* "Advance Release of Selected 2018 Digest Tables," <https://nces.ed.gov/programs/digest/index.asp>, accessed January 2019; and *Indicators of School Crime and Safety,* annual. See also <https://nces.ed.gov/surveys/ssocs/>.

Table 339. Public Schools Using Selected Safety and Security Measures by Type: 2000 to 2018

[In percent. For school year ending in year shown. Based on the School Survey on Crime and Safety and subject to sampling error; see source for details]

Measure	2000	2008	2010	2014 [1]	2016	2018
Controlled access during school hours:						
Buildings (locked or monitored doors)	74.6	89.5	91.7	93.3	94.1	95.4
Grounds (locked or monitored gates)	33.7	42.6	46.0	42.7	49.9	50.8
Visitors required to sign or check in	96.6	98.7	99.3	98.6	93.5	94.6
Classrooms equipped with doors that lock from the inside	(NA)	(NA)	(NA)	(NA)	66.7	64.8
Student dress, IDs, and school supplies:						
Required students to wear uniforms	11.8	17.5	18.9	20.4	21.5	19.8
Enforced a strict dress code	47.4	54.8	56.9	58.5	53.1	48.8
Required students to wear badges or picture IDs	3.9	7.6	6.9	8.9	7.0	9.2
Required faculty and staff to wear badges or picture IDs	25.4	58.3	62.9	68.0	67.9	69.9
Required clear book bags or banned book bags on school grounds	5.9	6.0	5.5	6.3	3.9	3.5
Provided school lockers to students	46.5	48.9	52.1	49.9	50.4	49.0
Drug testing:						
Students participating in athletics or other extracurricular activities	(NA)	6.6	6.2	6.7	7.7	8.9
Athletes	(NA)	6.4	6.0	6.6	7.2	(NA)
Students in non-athletic extracurricular activities	(NA)	4.5	4.6	4.3	6.0	(NA)
Any other students	(NA)	3.0	3.0	3.5	(NA)	(NA)
Metal detectors and sweeps:						
Random metal detector checks on students	7.2	5.3	5.2	4.2	4.5	4.9
Students required to pass through metal detectors daily	0.9	1.3	1.4	2.0	1.8	2.2
Random sweeps for contraband [2]	25.3	26.3	27.7	28.2	28.2	27.4
Communications systems and technology:						
Provided telephones in most classrooms	44.6	71.6	74.0	78.7	79.3	(NA)
Provided electronic notification system for school wide emergencies	(NA)	43.2	63.1	81.6	73.0	71.6
Provided structured anonymous threat reporting system [3]	(NA)	31.2	35.9	46.5	43.9	49.3
Had silent alarms directly connected to law enforcement	(NA)	(NA)	(NA)	(NA)	27.1	29.1
Used security cameras to monitor the school	19.4	55.0	61.1	75.1	80.6	83.5
Provided two-way radios to any staff	(NA)	73.1	73.3	74.2	73.3	77.8
Limited access to social networking sites from school computers	(NA)	(NA)	93.4	91.9	89.1	(NA)
Prohibited non-academic use of cell phones or smartphones	(NA)	(NA)	90.9	75.9	65.8	70.3

NA Not available. [1] Data for 2013-14 were collected using the Fast Response Survey System. The 2013-14 survey was designed to allow comparisons with School Survey on Crime and Safety (SSOCS) data. However, respondents to the 2013-14 survey could choose either to complete the survey by mail or online, whereas respondents to SSOCS did not have the online option. The 2013-14 survey also relied on a smaller sample. These differences may have impacted 2013-14 results. [2] May include locker checks and/or random dog sniffs for items such as drugs and weapons. [3] For example, a system for reporting threats through online submission, telephone hotline, or written submission via drop box.

Source: U.S. National Center for Education Statistics, *Digest of Education Statistics,* "Advance Release of Selected 2019 Digest Tables," <http://nces.ed.gov/programs/digest/index.asp>, accessed May 2020; and *Indicators of School Crime and Safety,* annual. See also <http://nces.ed.gov/surveys/ssocs/>.

Table 340. Students Who Reported Being Bullied at School or Cyber-Bullied by Student Characteristics: 2017

[In percent. For school year ending in 2017. For students aged 12 through 18. "At school" includes the school building, on school property, on a school bus, or going to and from school. Based on the Bureau of Justice Statistics' School Crime Supplement to the National Crime Victimization Survey. For more information, see Appendix A of source]

| Characteristic | Bullied at school | | | | | | |
	Total bullying at school [1]	Made fun of, called names, or insulted	Subject of rumors	Threatened with harm	Purposefully excluded	Pushed, shoved, tripped, or spit on	Online or by text
Total	**20.2**	**13.0**	**13.4**	**3.9**	**5.2**	**5.3**	**15.3**
Sex:							
Male	16.7	10.3	9.3	4.2	3.5	6.1	6.8
Female	23.8	15.8	17.5	3.6	6.9	4.4	21.4
Race/ethnicity: [2]							
White	22.8	15.0	15.2	4.2	6.7	5.4	17.4
Black	22.9	16.0	14.5	5.4	3.9	6.5	12.1
Hispanic	15.7	8.9	10.6	2.6	3.3	4.6	12.8
Asian	7.3	5.3	4.7	(S)	(S)	[3] 1.7	(S)
Two or more races	23.2	12.9	15.7	7.6	7.5	6.9	[3] 11.0
Grade:							
6th	29.5	23.1	17.1	8.5	8.4	10.5	[3] 6.7
7th	24.4	17.7	14.2	4.9	7.6	8.2	13.1
8th	25.3	16.3	16.0	4.4	5.7	6.9	12.5
9th	19.3	12.5	12.3	3.7	4.3	5.4	19.7
10th	18.9	9.4	16.1	3.6	4.4	3.7	22.0
11th	14.7	9.5	9.6	3.2	3.2	3.3	22.3
12th	12.2	6.0	9.1	[3] 1.3	3.5	[3] 0.7	11.5

S Reporting standards not met. [1] In the total for students bullied at school, students who reported more than one type of bullying were counted only once. [2] Race categories exclude persons of Hispanic ethnicity. [3] Interpret data with caution.

Source: U.S. National Center for Education Statistics, *Digest of Education Statistics*, "Advance Release of Selected 2018 Digest Tables," <http://nces.ed.gov/programs/digest/>, accessed May 2019; and *Indicators of School Crime and Safety,* annual. See also <http://nces.ed.gov/surveys/ssocs/>.

Table 341. Cyberbullying Among Students in Grades 9 to 12 by Student Characteristics: 2011 to 2017

[In percent. Covers students in grades 9 to 12 who reported being electronically bullied during the previous 12 months. Data are based on the U.S. Centers for Disease Control and Prevention's Youth Risk Behavior Surveillance System. Electronic bullying, or cyberbullying, for 2011-2015 includes "being bullied through e-mail, chat rooms, instant messaging, websites, or texting," and for 2017 "being bullied through texting, Instagram, Facebook, or other social media"]

Student characteristic	2011	2013	2015	2017
Total	**16.2**	**14.8**	**15.5**	**14.9**
Sex:				
Male	10.8	8.5	9.7	9.9
Female	22.1	21.0	21.7	19.7
Race/ethnicity: [1]				
White	18.6	16.9	18.4	17.3
Black	8.9	8.7	8.6	10.9
Asian	14.4	12.9	13.9	10.0
Pacific Islander	19.6	15.7	[2] 11.8	15.0
American Indian/Alaska Native	16.2	18.0	18.7	13.2
Two or more races	21.0	18.9	20.4	16.0
Hispanic ethnicity	13.6	12.8	12.4	12.3
Sexual orientation:				
Heterosexual	(NA)	(NA)	14.2	13.3
Gay, lesbian, or bisexual	(NA)	(NA)	28.0	27.1
Not sure	(NA)	(NA)	22.5	22.0
Grade:				
9th	15.5	16.1	16.5	16.7
10th	18.1	14.5	16.6	14.8
11th	16.0	14.9	14.7	14.2
12th	15.0	13.5	14.3	13.5

NA Not available. [1] Race categories exclude persons of Hispanic ethnicity. [2] Interpret data with caution. The coefficient of variation (CV) for this estimate is between 30 and 50 percent.

Source: U.S. National Center for Education Statistics, *Digest of Education Statistics,* "Advance Release of Selected 2018 Tables," <https://nces.ed.gov/programs/digest/>, accessed May 2019. See also *Indicators of School Crime and Safety: 2018*, <https://nces.ed.gov/surveys/ssocs/>.

Table 342. Violent Deaths Occurring at Schools by Type; and Homicides and Suicides of Youth Aged 5 to 18, Total and School-Associated: 1993 to 2017

[For school year ending in year shown. A school-associated violent death is defined as a homicide, suicide, or legal intervention (involving a law enforcement officer) in which the fatal injury occurred on the campus of a functioning elementary or secondary school in the United States, including while the victim was on the way to or from regular sessions at school or while the victim was attending or traveling to or from an official school-sponsored event. Victims include students, staff members, and others who are not students. Data from school year 2000 onward are subject to change until interviews with school and law enforcement officials have been completed. The details learned during interviews can occasionally change the classification of a case. Based on data from U.S. Centers for Disease Control and Prevention, and Federal Bureau of Investigation and Bureau of Justice Statistics]

Year	School-associated violent deaths				Homicides of youth aged 5 to 18		Suicides of youth aged 5 to 18	
	Total [1]	Homicides	Suicides [2]	Legal inter-ventions	Total	At school	Total [2]	At school
1993.................	57	47	10	0	3,003	34	1,657	6
1994.................	48	38	10	0	3,253	29	1,779	7
1995.................	48	39	8	0	3,001	28	1,704	7
1996.................	53	46	6	1	2,791	32	1,691	6
1997.................	48	45	2	1	2,430	28	1,584	1
1998.................	57	47	9	1	2,231	34	1,681	6
1999.................	47	38	6	2	1,923	33	1,480	4
2000.................	37	26	11	0	1,694	14	1,420	8
2001.................	34	26	7	1	1,636	14	1,451	6
2002.................	36	27	8	1	1,593	16	1,343	5
2003.................	36	25	11	0	1,658	18	1,264	10
2004.................	45	37	7	1	1,620	23	1,411	5
2005.................	52	40	10	2	1,720	22	1,484	8
2006.................	44	37	6	1	1,859	21	1,311	3
2007.................	63	48	13	2	1,906	32	1,243	9
2008.................	48	39	7	2	1,858	21	1,256	5
2009.................	44	29	15	0	1,720	18	1,425	7
2010.................	35	27	5	3	1,551	19	1,441	2
2011.................	32	26	6	0	1,436	11	1,559	3
2012.................	45	26	14	5	1,360	15	1,541	5
2013.................	53	41	11	1	1,310	31	1,608	6
2014.................	48	26	20	1	1,160	12	1,638	8
2015.................	47	28	17	2	1,273	20	1,882	9
2016.................	38	30	7	1	1,478	18	1,941	3
2017.................	42	28	13	1	1,587	18	2,186	6

[1] Total includes unintentional firearm-related deaths, not shown separately. [2] Excludes self-inflicted deaths among children age 5 to 9. The number of self-inflicted deaths among children age 5 to 9 was generally less than 7 per year during the period covered by this table.

Source: U.S. National Center for Education Statistics, *Digest of Education Statistics,* "Advance Release of Selected 2019 Digest Tables," <http://nces.ed.gov/programs/digest/>, accessed July 2020; and *Indicators of School Crime and Safety,* annual. See also <http://nces.ed.gov/surveys/ssocs/>.

Law Enforcement, Courts, and Prisons

This section presents data on crimes committed, victims of crimes, arrests, and data related to criminal violations and the criminal justice system. The major sources of these data are the Bureau of Justice Statistics (BJS), the Federal Bureau of Investigation (FBI), and the Administrative Office of the U.S. Courts. BJS issues many reports—see our Guide to Sources for a complete listing. The Federal Bureau of Investigation's major annual reports are *Crime in the United States, Law Enforcement Officers Killed and Assaulted*, and *Hate Crimes*, which present data on reported crimes as gathered from state and local law enforcement agencies.

Legal jurisdiction and law enforcement—Law enforcement is, for the most part, a function of state and local officers and agencies. The U.S. Constitution reserves general police powers to the states. By act of Congress, federal offenses include only offenses against the U.S. government and against or by its employees while engaged in their official duties, and offenses which involve the crossing of state lines or an interference with interstate commerce. Excluding the military, there are 52 separate criminal law jurisdictions in the United States: one in each of the 50 states, one in the District of Columbia, and the federal jurisdiction. Each of these has its own criminal law and procedure and its own law enforcement agencies. While the systems of law enforcement are quite similar among the states, there are often substantial differences in the penalties for like offenses.

Law enforcement can be divided into three parts: Investigation of crimes and arrests of persons suspected of committing them; prosecution of those charged with crime; and the punishment or treatment of persons convicted of crime.

Crime—The U.S. Department of Justice administers two statistical programs to measure the magnitude, nature, and impact of crime in the nation: the Uniform Crime Reporting (UCR) Program and the National Crime Victimization Survey (NCVS). Each of these programs produces valuable information about aspects of the nation's crime problem. Because the UCR and NCVS programs are conducted for different purposes, use different methods, and focus on somewhat different aspects of crime, the information they produce together provides a more comprehensive panorama of the nation's crime problem than either could produce alone.

Uniform Crime Reports (UCR)—The FBI's UCR Program, which began in 1929, collects information on the following crimes reported to law enforcement authorities: Part 1 offenses, for which detailed data is reported—murder and nonnegligent manslaughter, rape, robbery, aggravated assault, burglary, larceny-theft, motor vehicle theft, and arson; and Part 2 offenses, 20 additional crime categories for which law enforcement agencies report only arrest data. UCR definitions of criminal offenses (including those listed) can be found at <ucr.fbi.gov/crime-in-the-u.s/2018/crime-in-the-u.s.-2018/topic-pages/offense-definitions>.

Beginning in 2013, the UCR program implemented a revised definition of rape. Not all state and local agencies have been able to effect the change in their records management systems and some agencies currently can report the offense based on only the legacy definition. Therefore, rape data collected under both definitions are used in the *Crime in the United States* report. In 2016, the FBI Director approved the recommendation to discontinue the reporting of rape data using the UCR legacy definition beginning in 2017. However, to maintain the availability of 20-year trend data, national estimates for rape under the legacy definition are provided along with estimates under the revised definition for 2017.

The UCR Program compiles data from monthly law enforcement reports or individual crime incident records transmitted directly to the FBI or to centralized state agencies that then report to the FBI. The Program thoroughly examines each report it receives for reasonableness, accuracy, and deviations that may indicate errors. Large variations in crime levels may indicate modified records procedures, incomplete reporting, or changes in a jurisdiction's boundaries. To identify any unusual fluctuations in an agency's crime counts, the Program compares monthly reports to previous submissions of the agency and with those for similar agencies.

The UCR Program presents crime counts for the nation as a whole, as well as for regions, states, counties, cities, towns, tribal law enforcement, and colleges and universities. This permits studies among neighboring jurisdictions and among those with similar populations and other common characteristics.

The UCR Program annually publishes its findings online in a preliminary release in the spring of the following calendar year, followed by a detailed report, *Crime in the United States*, issued in the fall. In addition to crime counts and trends, this report includes data on crimes cleared, persons arrested (age, sex, and race), law enforcement personnel (including the number of sworn officers killed or assaulted), and the characteristics of homicides (including age, sex, and race of victims and offenders; victim-offender relationships; weapons used; and circumstances surrounding the homicides). Other periodic reports are also available from the UCR Program.

National Crime Victimization Survey (NCVS)—A second perspective on crime is provided by this survey of the Bureau of Justice Statistics (BJS). The NCVS is an annual data collection (interviews of persons aged 12 or older), conducted by the U.S. Census Bureau for the BJS. As an ongoing survey of households, the NCVS measures crimes of violence and property both reported and not reported to police. It produces national rates and levels of personal and property victimization. No attempt is made to validate the information against police records or any other source.

The NCVS measures rape/sexual assault, robbery, assault, pocket-picking, purse snatching, burglary, and motor vehicle theft. Murder and kidnaping are not covered. The so-called victimless crimes, such as drunkenness, drug abuse, and prostitution, also are excluded, as are crimes for which it is difficult to identify knowledgeable respondents or to locate data records.

Crimes of which the victim may not be aware also cannot be measured effectively. Buying stolen property may fall into this category, as may some instances of embezzlement. Attempted crimes of many types probably are under-recorded for this reason. Events in which the victim has shown a willingness to participate in illegal activity also are excluded.

In any encounter involving a personal crime, more than one criminal act can be committed against an individual. For example, a rape may be associated with a robbery, or a household property offense, such as a burglary, can escalate into something more serious in the event of a personal confrontation. Each criminal incident has been counted only once, by the most serious act that took place during the incident, and ranked in accordance with the seriousness classification system used by the FBI. The order of seriousness for crimes against persons is as follows: rape, robbery, assault, and larceny. Personal crimes take precedence over household offenses.

A *victimization*, the basic measure of the occurrence of crime, is a specific criminal act as it affects a single victim. The number of victimizations is determined by the number of victims of such acts. Victimization counts serve as key elements in computing rates of victimization. For crimes against persons, the rates are based on the total number of individuals aged 12 and over or on a portion of that population sharing a particular characteristic or set of traits. As general indicators of the danger of having been victimized during the reference period, the rates are not sufficiently refined to represent true measures of risk for specific individuals or households.

An *incident* is a specific criminal act involving one or more victims; therefore the number of incidents of personal crimes is lower than that of victimizations.

Courts—Statistics on criminal offenses and the outcome of prosecutions are incomplete for the country as a whole, although data are available for many states individually.

State courts handle the majority of civil and criminal litigation in the country. Only when the U.S. Constitution and acts of Congress specifically confer jurisdiction upon the federal courts may civil or criminal litigation be heard and decided by them. Generally, the federal courts have jurisdiction over the following types of cases: suits or proceedings by or against the United States; civil actions between private parties arising under the Constitution, laws, or treaties of the United States; civil actions between private litigants who are citizens of different states; civil cases

involving admiralty, maritime, or private jurisdiction; and all matters in bankruptcy.

There are several types of courts with varying degrees of legal jurisdiction. These jurisdictions include original, appellate, general, and limited or special. A court of original jurisdiction is one having the authority initially to try a case and pass judgment on the law and the facts; a court of appellate jurisdiction is one with the legal authority to review cases and hear appeals; a court of general jurisdiction is a trial court of unlimited original jurisdiction in civil and/or criminal cases, also called a "major trial court"; a court of limited or special jurisdiction is a trial court with legal authority over only a particular class of cases, such as probate, juvenile, or traffic cases.

The 94 federal courts of original jurisdiction are known as the U.S. district courts. One or more of these courts is established in every state and one each in the District of Columbia, Puerto Rico, the Virgin Islands, the Northern Mariana Islands, and Guam. Appeals from the district courts are taken to intermediate appellate courts of which there are 13, known as U.S. courts of appeals and the United States Court of Appeals for the Federal Circuit. The Supreme Court of the United States is the final and highest appellate court in the federal system of courts.

Juvenile offenders—For statistical purposes, the FBI and most states classify as juvenile offenders persons under the age of 18 years who have committed a crime or crimes.

Delinquency cases are all cases of youths referred to a juvenile court for violation of a law or ordinance or for seriously "antisocial" conduct. Several types of facilities are available for those adjudicated delinquents, ranging from short-term physically unrestricted to long-term very restrictive supervision.

Prisoners and jail inmates—BJS started to collect annual data in 1979 on prisoners in federal and state prisons and reformatories. Adults convicted of criminal activity may be given a prison or jail sentence. A *prison* is a confinement facility having custodial authority over adults sentenced to confinement of more than 1 year. A *jail* is a facility, usually operated by a local law enforcement agency, holding persons detained pending adjudication and/or persons committed after adjudication for 1 year or less.

Data on inmates in local jails were collected by the BJS for the first time in 1970. Jail censuses are taken periodically. For details, see <bjs.gov/index.cfm?ty=tp&tid=12#data_collections>.

Statistical reliability—For discussion of statistical collection, estimation and sampling procedures, and measures of statistical reliability pertaining to the National Crime Victimization Survey and Uniform Crime Reporting Program, see Appendix III.

Table 343. Crimes and Crime Rates by Type of Offense: 1980 to 2018

[13,408 represents 13,408,000. Data include offenses reported to law enforcement, and offense estimations for nonreporting and partially reporting agencies within each state. Rates are based on Census Bureau estimated resident population as of July 1, except 1980, 1990, 2000, and 2010, which are enumerated as of April 1. See source for details]

Item and year	All crimes	Violent crime						Property crimes			
		Total	Murder [1]	Rape [2]	Rape legacy def. [2]	Robbery	Aggra-vated assault	Total	Burglary	Larceny/ theft	Motor vehicle theft
NUMBER OF OFFENSES (1,000)											
1980	13,408	1,345	23.0	(NA)	83.0	566	673	12,064	3,795	7,137	1,132
1990	14,476	1,820	23.4	(NA)	102.6	639	1,055	12,655	3,074	7,946	1,636
2000	11,608	1,425	15.6	(NA)	90.2	408	912	10,183	2,051	6,972	1,160
2001 [3]	11,877	1,439	16.0	(NA)	90.9	424	909	10,437	2,117	7,092	1,228
2002	11,879	1,424	16.2	(NA)	95.2	421	891	10,455	2,151	7,057	1,247
2003	11,827	1,384	16.5	(NA)	93.9	414	859	10,443	2,155	7,027	1,261
2004	11,679	1,360	16.1	(NA)	95.1	401	847	10,319	2,144	6,937	1,238
2005	11,565	1,391	16.7	(NA)	94.3	417	862	10,175	2,155	6,783	1,236
2006	11,455	1,435	17.3	(NA)	94.5	449	874	10,020	2,195	6,626	1,198
2007	11,305	1,423	17.1	(NA)	92.2	447	866	9,882	2,190	6,592	1,100
2008	11,169	1,394	16.5	(NA)	90.8	444	844	9,774	2,229	6,586	959
2009	10,663	1,326	15.4	(NA)	89.2	409	813	9,337	2,203	6,338	796
2010	10,364	1,251	14.7	(NA)	85.6	369	782	9,113	2,168	6,205	740
2011	10,259	1,206	14.7	(NA)	84.2	355	752	9,053	2,185	6,151	717
2012	10,219	1,217	14.9	(NA)	85.1	355	762	9,002	2,110	6,169	723
2013	9,820	1,168	14.3	113.7	82.1	345	727	8,652	1,932	6,019	700
2014	9,362	1,153	14.2	118.0	84.9	323	731	8,209	1,713	5,809	687
2015	9,223	1,199	15.9	126.1	91.3	328	764	8,024	1,588	5,723	713
2016	9,179	1,250	17.4	132.4	97.0	333	803	7,929	1,516	5,645	767
2017	8,931	1,248	17.3	135.7	99.7	321	810	7,683	1,397	5,513	773
2018	8,403	1,207	16.2	139.4	101.2	282	807	7,196	1,230	5,217	749
RATE PER 100,000 POPULATION											
1980	5,950	597	10.2	(NA)	36.8	251	299	5,353	1,684	3,167	502
1990	5,803	730	9.4	(NA)	41.1	256	423	5,073	1,232	3,185	656
2000	4,125	507	5.5	(NA)	32.0	145	324	3,618	729	2,477	412
2001 [3]	4,163	505	5.6	(NA)	31.8	149	319	3,658	742	2,486	431
2002	4,125	494	5.6	(NA)	33.1	146	310	3,631	747	2,451	433
2003	4,067	476	5.7	(NA)	32.3	143	295	3,591	741	2,417	434
2004	3,977	463	5.5	(NA)	32.4	137	289	3,514	730	2,362	422
2005	3,901	469	5.6	(NA)	31.8	141	291	3,432	727	2,288	417
2006	3,826	479	5.8	(NA)	31.6	150	292	3,347	733	2,213	400
2007	3,748	472	5.7	(NA)	30.6	148	287	3,276	726	2,185	365
2008	3,673	459	5.4	(NA)	29.8	146	278	3,215	733	2,166	315
2009	3,473	432	5.0	(NA)	29.1	133	265	3,041	718	2,065	259
2010	3,350	405	4.8	(NA)	27.7	119	253	2,946	701	2,006	239
2011	3,292	387	4.7	(NA)	27.0	114	242	2,905	701	1,974	230
2012	3,256	388	4.7	(NA)	27.1	113	243	2,868	672	1,965	230
2013	3,103	369	4.5	35.9	25.9	109	230	2,734	611	1,902	221
2014	2,936	362	4.4	37.0	26.6	101	229	2,574	537	1,822	215
2015	2,874	374	4.9	39.3	28.4	102	238	2,501	495	1,784	222
2016	2,838	387	5.4	40.9	30.0	103	248	2,452	469	1,745	237
2017	2,747	384	5.3	41.7	30.7	99	249	2,363	430	1,696	238
2018	2,568	369	5.0	42.6	30.9	86	247	2,200	376	1,595	229

NA Not available. [1] Includes nonnegligent manslaughter. [2] Beginning 2013, the FBI introduced a revised definition of rape. For more information, see <https://ucr.fbi.gov/crime-in-the-u.s/2018/crime-in-the-u.s.-2018/topic-pages/rape>. [3] The murder and non-negligent homicides that occurred as a result of the events of September 11, 2001, were not included in this table.

Source: U.S. Department of Justice, Federal Bureau of Investigation, "Crime in the United States 2018," <https://ucr.fbi.gov/>, accessed November 2019.

Table 344. Crimes and Crime Rates by Offense Type and Geographic Area: 2018

[In thousands (930.4 represents 930,400), except rate. Rate per 100,000 population. For area definitions, see <https://ucr.fbi.gov/crime-in-the-u.s/2018/crime-in-the-u.s.-2018/topic-pages/area-definitions>. See headnote, Table 343]

Type of crime	Cities		Metropolitan counties [1]		Nonmetropolitan counties [1]		Suburban areas [2]	
	Total	Rate	Total	Rate	Total	Rate	Total	Rate
Violent crime	930.4	451.5	173.3	253.9	43.2	204.6	305.0	241.0
Murder [3]	11.9	5.8	2.3	3.4	0.7	3.3	3.7	3.0
Rape [4]	96.8	48.0	22.8	34.4	8.3	40.7	41.3	33.5
Robbery	236.7	114.9	26.7	39.2	2.1	9.8	52.3	41.3
Aggravated assault	585.0	283.9	121.5	178.0	32.1	152.0	207.7	164.0
Property crime	5,316.3	2,579.9	1,005.0	1,473.0	226.8	1,072.9	2,108.4	1,665.6
Burglary	834.4	404.9	196.9	288.6	66.6	314.9	350.3	276.7
Larceny-theft	3,917.0	1,900.8	703.9	1,031.6	137.3	649.5	1,571.3	1,241.3
Motor vehicle theft	565.0	274.2	104.3	152.8	22.9	108.5	186.8	147.6

[1] Includes state police agencies that report aggregately for the entire state. [2] Suburban areas include law enforcement agencies in cities with less than 50,000 inhabitants and county law enforcement agencies within a Metropolitan Statistical Area. Excludes all metropolitan agencies associated with a principal city. Agencies associated with suburban areas also appear in other groups within this table. [3] Includes nonnegligent manslaughter. [4] Estimated using the revised FBI Uniform Crime Reporting (UCR) definition of rape. For more information, see <https://ucr.fbi.gov/crime-in-the-u.s/2018/crime-in-the-u.s.-2018/topic-pages/rape>.

Source: U.S. Department of Justice, Federal Bureau of Investigation, "Crime in the United States 2018," <https://ucr.fbi.gov/>, accessed November 2019.

Table 345. Crime Rates by State, 2017 and 2018, and by Type, 2018

[For year ending December 31. Rates per 100,000 population. Offenses reported to law enforcement. Based on Census Bureau estimated resident population as of July 1]

State	Violent crime 2017, total	Violent crime 2018 Total	Murder	Rape [1]	Robbery	Aggravated assault	Property crime 2017, total	Property crime 2018 Total	Burglary	Larceny/ theft	Motor vehicle theft
United States............	394.9	380.6	5.0	42.6	86.2	246.8	2,362.9	2,199.5	376.0	1,594.6	228.9
Alabama....................	522.4	519.6	7.8	40.8	83.4	387.6	2,949.1	2,817.2	590.1	1,958.9	268.3
Alaska.....................	856.7	885.0	6.4	161.6	121.5	595.4	3,542.0	3,300.5	539.6	2,219.0	541.9
Arizona....................	505.7	474.9	5.1	50.7	91.0	328.1	2,908.3	2,676.8	439.7	1,970.3	266.9
Arkansas...................	566.0	543.6	7.2	72.9	52.9	410.7	3,144.2	2,913.0	636.8	2,040.2	236.0
California..................	453.3	447.4	4.4	39.2	137.3	266.5	2,505.3	2,380.4	416.2	1,571.8	392.4
Colorado...................	372.2	397.2	3.7	71.5	66.7	255.4	2,707.2	2,671.6	375.2	1,915.9	380.5
Connecticut................	229.2	207.4	2.3	23.5	61.4	120.2	1,780.9	1,681.0	222.5	1,251.8	206.7
Delaware...................	457.3	423.6	5.0	34.9	89.5	294.2	2,448.1	2,324.4	326.5	1,845.3	152.6
District of Columbia [2]......	1,002.7	995.9	22.8	64.1	343.8	565.3	4,274.3	4,373.8	254.5	3,750.1	369.1
Florida.....................	408.1	384.9	5.2	39.6	79.3	260.8	2,512.9	2,281.8	337.7	1,750.8	193.3
Georgia....................	356.5	326.6	6.1	25.2	78.7	216.6	2,858.4	2,573.7	431.3	1,907.0	235.4
Hawaii.....................	251.2	248.6	2.5	44.0	66.6	135.5	2,836.1	2,870.3	396.4	2,076.2	397.7
Idaho......................	239.2	227.1	2.0	45.1	11.4	168.6	1,661.3	1,461.4	281.6	1,067.8	112.0
Illinois....................	436.2	404.1	6.9	46.0	111.5	239.7	1,995.2	1,932.8	306.7	1,472.3	153.8
Indiana....................	395.0	382.3	6.5	35.4	88.7	251.6	2,386.3	2,179.3	377.6	1,572.7	229.1
Iowa [3]...................	287.5	250.1	1.7	30.9	29.5	187.9	2,088.4	1,691.5	352.6	1,190.4	148.5
Kansas.....................	400.4	439.0	3.9	53.8	53.0	328.3	2,727.4	2,633.9	430.6	1,933.9	269.4
Kentucky...................	231.1	211.9	5.5	38.2	55.0	113.2	2,153.2	1,962.6	384.7	1,348.2	229.6
Louisiana..................	556.3	537.5	11.4	44.7	98.0	383.4	3,367.1	3,276.0	668.1	2,360.4	247.6
Maine......................	120.6	112.1	1.8	33.3	17.0	60.0	1,508.7	1,357.8	202.7	1,097.1	58.1
Maryland...................	503.3	468.7	8.1	32.8	160.8	267.0	2,235.8	2,033.3	312.6	1,519.8	200.9
Massachusetts..............	354.3	338.1	2.0	34.9	60.0	241.2	1,427.6	1,263.3	200.8	966.8	95.7
Michigan...................	449.9	449.4	5.5	76.9	56.6	310.3	1,802.6	1,653.5	316.6	1,162.3	174.6
Minnesota..................	239.7	220.4	1.9	43.9	52.5	122.2	2,198.8	1,993.8	288.4	1,524.8	180.5
Mississippi................	256.2	234.4	5.7	18.0	53.4	157.2	2,768.3	2,403.0	697.8	1,561.2	144.0
Missouri...................	531.2	502.1	9.9	47.5	84.8	359.8	2,838.3	2,647.1	444.9	1,878.8	323.4
Montana....................	373.9	374.1	3.2	51.9	25.3	293.7	2,591.8	2,496.3	306.6	1,926.5	263.2
Nebraska...................	311.8	284.8	2.3	63.9	39.2	179.4	2,287.1	2,079.9	271.9	1,555.3	252.6
Nevada.....................	560.6	541.1	6.7	76.8	127.3	330.4	2,634.9	2,438.2	584.7	1,461.2	392.3
New Hampshire.............	195.7	173.2	1.5	39.4	26.5	105.8	1,374.3	1,248.5	136.2	1,048.2	64.1
New Jersey.................	231.8	208.1	3.2	16.0	71.4	117.4	1,576.0	1,404.9	215.9	1,065.1	123.9
New Mexico.................	778.6	856.6	8.0	64.6	135.1	648.9	3,910.6	3,419.7	767.8	2,166.1	485.8
New York...................	361.1	350.5	2.9	33.6	93.1	220.9	1,497.6	1,440.5	159.3	1,214.0	67.2
North Carolina [4]..........	370.4	377.6	6.0	25.4	81.1	265.1	2,584.8	2,494.1	599.9	1,724.4	169.8
North Dakota...............	282.5	280.6	2.4	52.2	20.8	205.2	2,205.2	2,040.2	358.4	1,448.3	233.5
Ohio.......................	296.8	279.9	4.8	45.3	78.6	151.2	2,405.3	2,177.1	412.2	1,594.6	170.3
Oklahoma...................	457.4	466.1	5.2	58.3	70.8	331.8	2,888.9	2,875.0	681.1	1,856.8	337.0
Oregon.....................	280.4	285.5	2.0	47.1	60.8	175.6	2,954.8	2,894.0	389.1	2,109.9	395.1
Pennsylvania...............	313.0	306.0	6.1	35.0	76.9	188.0	1,644.3	1,489.9	211.6	1,175.9	102.4
Rhode Island...............	234.2	219.1	1.5	45.5	42.9	129.2	1,759.1	1,660.9	265.8	1,250.3	144.8
South Carolina.............	506.1	488.3	7.7	47.9	69.9	362.8	3,193.8	3,017.6	579.7	2,156.0	281.9
South Dakota...............	429.8	404.7	1.4	69.6	29.7	304.0	1,899.5	1,728.7	291.4	1,264.5	172.7
Tennessee..................	655.0	623.7	7.4	41.7	106.2	468.5	2,951.8	2,825.4	489.4	2,034.1	301.9
Texas......................	437.8	410.9	4.6	51.2	98.4	256.6	2,553.2	2,367.2	410.8	1,713.1	243.2
Utah.......................	242.2	233.1	1.9	55.5	39.1	136.6	2,777.9	2,377.5	315.3	1,817.7	244.5
Vermont....................	173.3	172.0	1.6	45.8	11.2	113.4	1,495.4	1,283.1	234.2	1,008.5	40.4
Virginia...................	210.4	200.0	4.6	34.3	42.3	118.7	1,801.7	1,665.8	182.8	1,356.4	126.5
Washington.................	302.8	311.5	3.1	45.3	73.9	189.1	3,167.6	2,946.2	533.5	2,045.4	367.3
West Virginia..............	361.2	289.9	3.7	36.1	31.7	218.5	1,791.9	1,485.6	296.5	1,049.6	139.5
Wisconsin..................	321.8	295.4	3.0	38.7	60.0	193.7	1,811.2	1,559.9	242.5	1,168.9	148.5
Wyoming....................	234.6	212.2	2.3	42.1	17.3	150.6	1,818.5	1,785.1	264.0	1,375.9	145.2
Puerto Rico................	233.4	200.8	20.0	6.2	71.1	103.6	937.6	777.8	171.7	490.1	116.0

[1] Beginning in 2013, the FBI has revised the definition of rape as used in Uniform Crime Reporting (UCR) Program. For more information, see <https://ucr.fbi.gov/crime-in-the-u.s/2018/crime-in-the-u.s.-2018/topic-pages/rape>. [2] Includes offenses reported by the Metro Transit Police and the District of Columbia Fire and Emergency Medical Services: Arson Investigation Unit. [3] Limited data available for 2018. [4] Submitted rape data according to the legacy UCR definition of rape.

Source: U.S. Department of Justice, Federal Bureau of Investigation, "Crime in the United States 2018," <https://ucr.fbi.gov/>, accessed November 2019.

Table 346. Crime Rates by Type—Selected Large Cities: 2018

[For year ending December 31. Rates per 100,000 population. Data for Iowa are not available. Offenses reported to law enforcement]

Cities ranked by population size, 2018	Violent crime					Property crime			
	Total	Murder	Rape [1]	Robbery	Aggra-vated assault	Total	Burglary	Larceny/ theft	Motor vehicle theft
New York, NY.................	541.0	3.5	33.0	152.1	352.5	1,502.4	127.1	1,310.3	64.9
Los Angeles, CA.................	747.6	6.4	62.7	256.3	422.2	2,513.0	396.8	1,686.5	429.7
Chicago, IL................	1,006.1	20.7	66.1	356.1	563.1	3,181.6	429.8	2,379.2	372.6
Houston, TX [2].................	1,026.1	11.8	53.8	373.6	587.0	4,010.0	695.8	2,804.6	509.6
Phoenix, AZ.................	732.6	8.0	65.7	188.3	470.6	3,492.4	633.9	2,385.7	472.8
Las Vegas, NV................	605.0	7.3	97.9	163.6	336.2	2,838.3	727.8	1,627.1	483.4
Philadelphia, PA.................	908.7	22.1	69.0	331.6	486.0	3,096.9	409.4	2,329.5	357.9
San Antonio, TX.................	626.7	7.0	87.4	114.8	417.5	3,993.8	592.3	3,005.9	395.6
San Diego, CA.................	373.1	2.4	42.1	100.2	228.4	1,908.5	261.2	1,286.6	360.7
Dallas, TX [2].................	764.9	11.4	60.8	292.6	400.2	3,249.0	665.3	1,874.6	709.0
San Jose, CA.................	424.3	2.7	58.7	152.1	210.8	2,459.0	433.4	1,290.0	735.6
Honolulu, HI [2].................	249.6	2.5	34.6	81.9	130.5	2,941.5	364.2	2,150.5	426.8
Austin, TX.................	382.2	3.3	80.9	104.9	193.1	3,457.7	467.4	2,729.6	260.8
Charlotte-Mecklenburg, NC [3]...	(NA)	6.3	(NA)	189.1	473.3	3,745.7	608.9	2,812.0	324.8
Jacksonville, FL.................	595.8	12.2	59.2	146.5	377.9	3,333.9	543.5	2,464.8	325.6
Fort Worth, TX.................	501.5	6.5	53.9	124.9	316.2	2,845.6	503.9	2,009.2	332.5
Columbus, OH.................	494.7	11.1	91.9	215.3	176.5	3,530.5	702.6	2,388.9	439.0
San Francisco, CA.................	690.9	5.2	39.8	355.9	290.0	5,534.1	598.5	4,461.5	474.2
Indianapolis, IN.................	1,272.8	18.5	77.1	351.1	826.1	4,129.2	893.6	2,671.9	563.7
Seattle, WA.................	680.2	4.3	39.3	222.0	414.5	5,149.2	1,075.0	3,529.9	544.2
Denver, CO.................	730.1	9.0	99.5	168.0	453.6	3,671.8	552.5	2,387.4	731.9
Washington, DC.................	941.4	22.8	63.3	307.1	548.2	4,269.7	254.3	3,652.6	362.9
Boston, MA.................	622.5	8.1	40.0	168.7	405.7	2,016.3	266.7	1,583.5	166.1
El Paso, TX.................	371.0	3.3	58.8	54.6	254.2	1,505.6	160.8	1,226.1	118.7
Nashville, TN.................	1,113.1	13.3	69.9	308.2	721.6	4,011.3	528.3	3,034.0	448.9
Detroit, MI.................	2,007.8	38.9	147.2	344.0	1,477.8	4,304.8	1,108.3	2,235.0	961.5
Portland, OR.................	520.0	3.8	66.6	160.7	288.9	5,459.6	676.1	3,728.8	1,054.7
Oklahoma City, OK.................	867.3	8.0	83.0	165.7	610.6	4,027.7	918.9	2,552.8	556.0
Memphis, TN.................	1,943.2	28.5	75.3	467.6	1,371.8	6,405.6	1,302.3	4,421.0	682.3
Baltimore, MD.................	1,833.4	51.0	59.6	836.8	886.0	4,495.4	998.9	2,773.9	722.6
Milwaukee, WI.................	1,413.0	16.6	82.1	382.6	931.6	2,971.5	715.1	1,486.0	770.5
Albuquerque, NM [2].................	1,364.8	12.3	85.5	353.2	913.7	6,179.4	1,138.5	3,860.0	1,180.9
Tucson, AZ.................	736.5	8.7	93.8	227.8	406.2	4,954.1	606.1	3,870.2	477.9
Fresno, CA.................	555.3	6.0	32.0	170.9	346.4	3,344.6	554.5	2,345.4	444.7
Sacramento, CA.................	656.6	7.1	20.1	207.5	421.9	3,040.6	542.6	1,929.4	568.6
Mesa, AZ.................	363.9	3.4	47.1	82.6	230.8	1,985.4	309.6	1,504.9	170.9
Atlanta, GA.................	768.8	17.7	49.4	221.5	480.1	4,654.4	621.2	3,366.4	666.8
Kansas City, MO.................	1,590.3	27.8	81.7	332.0	1,148.8	4,306.5	753.8	2,698.2	854.6
Miami, FL.................	629.5	9.7	27.7	175.0	417.1	3,559.3	434.8	2,776.9	347.5
Colorado Springs, CO..........	555.5	6.8	102.5	109.3	336.9	3,343.5	578.8	2,255.5	509.2
Long Beach, CA.................	698.1	6.4	46.6	208.1	437.0	2,534.2	494.9	1,554.9	484.4
Omaha, NE.................	559.9	4.7	85.9	97.2	372.2	3,475.9	393.7	2,416.7	665.4
Virginia Beach, VA.................	117.1	1.6	18.0	38.6	59.0	1,723.3	129.5	1,465.9	127.9
Oakland, CA.................	1,273.7	16.3	104.1	609.9	543.4	5,390.1	556.4	3,655.0	1,178.7
Minneapolis, MN.................	792.7	7.2	100.9	276.5	408.2	3,911.2	721.3	2,678.5	511.4
Tulsa, OK.................	1,065.1	14.9	104.7	205.9	739.7	5,430.5	1,190.6	3,431.5	808.4
Arlington, TX.................	445.0	1.7	50.6	89.8	302.8	2,938.2	376.4	2,253.1	308.8
New Orleans, LA.................	1,163.3	37.1	171.8	307.5	646.9	4,557.1	511.4	3,290.3	755.3
Tampa, FL.................	406.7	6.9	25.4	84.5	289.9	1,673.5	266.4	1,290.0	117.1
Wichita, KS.................	1,179.9	9.7	96.5	146.0	927.7	5,619.0	871.0	4,040.1	707.9
Bakersfield, CA.................	491.4	8.0	29.3	210.3	243.8	4,174.4	1,043.8	2,410.5	720.2
Cleveland, OH.................	1,449.6	22.4	119.8	460.7	846.7	4,411.6	1,210.9	2,428.6	772.1
Aurora, CO.................	728.5	4.6	103.8	169.2	450.9	2,983.2	462.1	1,928.3	592.8
Anaheim, CA.................	336.0	2.0	40.0	114.7	179.3	2,453.0	396.9	1,669.1	387.0
Santa Ana, CA.................	468.4	6.3	68.6	148.8	244.8	1,905.2	271.3	1,172.0	461.8
Riverside, CA.................	509.3	4.2	45.3	164.0	295.8	3,089.2	444.1	2,087.8	557.4
Corpus Christi, TX.................	757.1	7.3	89.8	156.7	503.3	3,644.1	653.0	2,712.3	278.7
Lexington, KY.................	301.6	6.8	74.6	129.6	90.6	3,172.5	467.8	2,381.9	322.8
Stockton, CA.................	1,399.6	10.5	61.6	384.8	942.7	3,768.1	743.7	2,368.5	655.9
St. Paul, MN.................	626.6	4.8	89.4	180.8	351.6	3,254.8	616.3	1,897.3	741.2
Henderson, NV.................	188.3	4.8	21.0	70.1	92.4	1,961.3	336.6	1,404.8	220.0
St. Louis, MO.................	1,800.4	60.9	100.7	473.2	1,165.6	5,911.9	970.8	4,045.0	896.1
Pittsburgh, PA.................	578.8	18.8	40.0	230.0	289.9	3,016.1	443.2	2,331.9	241.0
Cincinnati, OH.................	839.5	18.9	97.0	297.1	426.6	4,540.5	986.2	3,120.4	433.8
Greensboro, NC [3].................	(NA)	12.6	(NA)	182.7	411.5	3,351.9	721.8	2,398.6	231.5
Anchorage, AK.................	1,309.6	8.9	209.9	245.6	845.2	4,927.9	708.2	3,252.8	966.8
Plano, TX.................	138.7	1.7	26.6	38.6	71.7	1,709.2	231.5	1,349.1	128.7
Lincoln, NE.................	362.1	2.1	98.1	56.1	205.8	2,878.5	409.6	2,319.6	149.3
Irvine, CA.................	55.5	–	13.9	18.4	23.3	1,270.3	215.6	985.9	68.7
Orlando, FL.................	796.0	13.6	69.8	219.1	493.6	4,814.8	564.7	3,824.8	425.2
Newark, NJ.................	733.0	26.6	53.1	244.1	409.2	2,010.2	294.8	1,001.6	713.9
Toledo, OH.................	848.3	13.5	86.9	173.4	574.5	3,716.8	1,018.8	2,440.5	257.4
Chula Vista, CA.................	304.3	2.2	28.8	93.3	180.0	1,316.1	213.2	852.1	250.8
Durham, NC [3].................	(NA)	12.1	(NA)	264.1	410.9	3,563.4	817.5	2,443.0	302.8
Jersey City, NJ.................	456.4	6.3	32.9	169.5	247.6	1,769.6	365.7	1,180.7	223.2

NA Not available. – Represents or rounds to zero. [1] Beginning in 2013, the FBI has revised the definition of rape as used in Uniform Crime Reporting (UCR) Program. For more information, see <https://ucr.fbi.gov/crime-in-the-u.s/2018/crime-in-the-u.s.-2018/topic-pages/rape>. [2] Because of changes in the state/local agency's reporting practices, figures are not comparable to previous years' data. [3] This agency/state submits rape data classified according to the legacy UCR definition; therefore the rape offense and violent crime total, which rape is a part of, is not included in this table. See source for details.

Source: U.S. Department of Justice, Federal Bureau of Investigation, "Crime in the United States 2018," <https://ucr.fbi.gov/>, accessed November 2019.

Table 347. Homicide Trends: 1990 to 2018

[Based on Federal Bureau of Investigation's Uniform Crime Reports Supplementary Homicide Reports. Homicide includes murder and nonnegligent manslaughter, which is the willful killing of one human being by another. Excludes deaths caused by negligence, suicide, or accident; justifiable homicides; and attempts to murder. Justifiable homicides based on the reports of law enforcement agencies are analyzed separately. Deaths from the terrorist attacks of September 11, 2001 are not included. Data based on criminal homicides handled by state and local law enforcement, and as determined solely by police investigation, and not by the determination of a court, medical examiner, coroner, jury, or other non-law enforcement body. Excludes homicides handled by Federal law enforcement]

| Year | Number of victims | | | | | | | Rate [1] | | | | | | |
	Total [2]	Male	Female	White	Black	American Indian/ Alaskan Native	Asian [3]	Total [2]	Male	Female	White	Black	American Indian/ Alaska Native	Asian [3]
1990...	23,438	18,303	5,115	11,278	11,487	150	250	9.4	15.0	4.0	5.4	37.5	7.3	3.3
1995...	21,606	16,549	5,021	10,374	10,442	160	421	8.1	12.7	3.7	4.7	30.9	6.6	4.4
1996...	19,645	15,149	4,468	9,480	9,473	134	377	7.3	11.5	3.2	4.3	27.5	5.3	3.8
1997...	18,208	14,055	4,124	8,619	8,841	149	375	6.7	10.5	3.0	3.8	25.3	5.7	3.6
1998...	16,974	12,756	4,140	8,391	7,933	141	252	6.2	9.4	2.9	3.7	22.3	5.2	2.3
1999...	15,522	11,704	3,800	7,777	7,139	160	298	5.6	8.6	2.7	3.4	19.7	5.6	2.6
2000...	15,586	11,818	3,733	7,560	7,425	119	280	5.5	8.6	2.6	3.3	20.3	4.0	2.4
2001...	16,037	12,232	3,775	7,884	7,522	105	319	5.6	8.7	2.6	3.4	20.2	3.4	2.6
2002...	16,229	12,429	3,770	7,796	7,770	130	308	5.6	8.8	2.6	3.3	20.6	4.1	2.4
2003...	16,528	12,792	3,707	7,944	7,883	117	351	5.7	9.0	2.5	3.4	20.6	3.5	2.6
2004...	16,148	12,553	3,555	7,939	7,570	134	282	5.5	8.7	2.4	3.4	19.5	3.9	2.0
2005...	16,740	13,149	3,565	8,045	8,016	131	312	5.7	9.1	2.4	3.4	20.4	3.7	2.2
2006...	17,309	13,605	3,661	8,063	8,548	123	343	5.8	9.3	2.4	3.4	21.4	3.3	2.3
2007...	17,128	13,411	3,678	8,017	8,450	104	302	5.7	9.1	2.4	3.3	20.9	2.7	1.9
2008...	16,465	12,844	3,573	7,953	7,860	124	250	5.4	8.6	2.3	3.3	19.1	3.1	1.6
2009...	15,399	11,846	3,535	7,450	7,374	119	290	5.0	7.9	2.3	3.0	17.7	2.9	1.7
2010...	14,722	11,371	3,328	6,851	7,322	117	260	4.8	7.5	2.1	2.8	17.4	2.7	1.5
2011...	14,661	11,354	3,281	6,786	7,277	111	284	4.7	7.4	2.1	2.7	17.1	2.6	1.6
2012...	14,856	11,518	3,318	6,834	7,481	101	285	4.7	7.5	2.1	2.8	17.3	2.3	1.6
2013...	14,319	11,116	3,178	6,519	7,268	104	257	4.5	7.1	2.0	2.6	16.6	2.3	1.4
2014...	14,164	10,939	3,188	6,421	7,196	122	249	4.4	7.0	2.0	2.6	16.2	2.7	1.3
2015...	15,883	12,499	3,354	6,938	8,293	183	253	4.9	7.9	2.1	2.8	18.5	4.0	1.3
2016...	17,413	13,648	3,719	7,628	9,084	169	298	5.4	8.6	2.3	3.0	20.0	3.6	1.5
2017...	17,294	13,545	3,695	7,574	8,922	214	302	5.3	8.4	2.2	3.0	19.4	4.6	1.4
2018...	16,214	12,495	3,686	7,048	8,433	182	286	5.0	7.8	2.2	2.8	18.2	3.8	1.3

[1] Rate is per 100,000 inhabitants. [2] Includes unknown sex, race, or ethnicity. [3] Includes Native Hawaiian and Pacific Islanders.

Source: U.S. Department of Justice, Office of Justice Programs, "Easy Access to the FBI's Supplementary Homicide Reports (EZASHR)," <http://www.ojjdp.gov/ojstatbb/ezashr/>; and U.S. Centers for Disease Control and Prevention, WONDER Online Database, "Multiple Cause of Death, 1999-2018," <wonder.cdc.gov/>; accessed August 2020.

Table 348. Homicide Victims by Race and Sex: 1990 to 2018

[Excludes deaths to nonresidents of United States. Effective with data for 1999, causes of death are classified by the International Classification of Diseases, Tenth Revision (ICD-10), replacing the Ninth Revision (ICD-9) used for 1979–1998 data. In ICD-9, the category Homicide also includes death as a result of legal intervention. ICD-10 differentiates between homicides due to assault and deaths due to legal intervention. Some caution should be used in comparing data. See text, Section 2]

| Year | Homicide victims | | | | | Homicide rate [2] | | | | |
| | | White | | Black | | | White | | Black | |
	Total [1]	Male	Female	Male	Female	Total [1]	Male	Female	Male	Female
1990............	24,932	9,147	3,006	9,981	2,163	10.0	9.0	2.8	69.2	13.5
1995............	22,895	8,336	3,028	8,847	1,936	8.7	7.8	2.7	56.3	11.1
1996............	20,971	7,570	2,747	8,183	1,800	7.9	7.0	2.5	51.5	10.2
1997............	19,846	7,343	2,570	7,601	1,652	7.4	6.7	2.3	47.1	9.3
1998............	18,272	6,707	2,534	6,873	1,547	6.8	6.1	2.2	42.1	8.6
1999............	16,889	6,162	2,466	6,214	1,434	6.1	5.5	2.1	36.1	7.6
2000............	16,765	5,925	2,414	6,482	1,385	6.0	5.2	2.1	37.2	7.2
2001............	20,308	8,254	3,074	6,780	1,446	7.1	7.2	2.6	38.2	7.4
2002............	17,638	6,282	2,403	6,896	1,391	6.1	5.4	2.0	38.4	7.0
2003............	17,732	6,337	2,372	7,083	1,309	6.1	5.5	2.0	38.9	6.5
2004............	17,357	6,302	2,341	6,839	1,296	5.9	5.4	2.0	37.0	6.4
2005............	18,124	6,457	2,313	7,412	1,257	6.1	5.5	1.9	39.6	6.1
2006............	18,573	6,514	2,346	7,677	1,355	6.2	5.5	1.9	40.4	6.5
2007............	18,361	6,541	2,373	7,584	1,286	6.1	5.5	1.9	39.3	6.1
2008............	17,826	6,556	2,337	7,148	1,187	5.9	5.5	1.9	36.5	5.5
2009............	16,799	5,983	2,340	6,715	1,159	5.5	4.9	1.9	33.8	5.3
2010............	16,259	5,648	2,215	6,704	1,114	5.3	4.7	1.8	33.4	5.1
2011............	16,238	5,569	2,199	6,739	1,119	5.2	4.6	1.8	33.0	5.0
2012............	16,688	5,639	2,197	7,129	1,112	5.3	4.6	1.8	34.5	4.9
2013............	16,121	5,393	2,130	6,937	1,122	5.1	4.4	1.7	33.1	4.9
2014............	15,872	5,304	2,093	6,823	1,080	5.0	4.3	1.7	32.1	4.7
2015............	17,793	5,798	2,209	8,021	1,152	5.5	4.6	1.7	37.3	4.9
2016............	19,362	6,325	2,343	8,650	1,345	6.0	5.1	1.8	39.8	5.7
2017............	19,510	6,274	2,496	8,776	1,297	6.0	5.0	1.9	39.8	5.4
2018............	18,830	6,050	2,374	8,254	1,449	5.8	4.8	1.8	37.2	6.0

[1] Includes other races not shown separately. [2] Rates per 100,000 resident population in specified group. Based on enumerated population figures as of April 1 for 1990, 2000, and 2010; estimated resident population as of July 1 for other years.

Source: U.S. National Center for Health Statistics, through 2014, National Vital Statistics Reports (NVSR), *Deaths: Final Data for 2014*, Vol. 65, No. 4, June 2016 and earlier reports; thereafter, CDC WONDER Online Database, "Multiple Cause of Death, 1999-2018," <wonder.cdc.gov/>, accessed September 2020.

Table 349. Criminal Victimizations and Victimization Rates: 2010 to 2018

[20,348 represents 20,348,000. A victimization refers to a single victim or household that experienced a criminal incident. Includes victimizations reported and not reported to the police. Criminal incidents or crimes are distinguished from victimizations in that one criminal incident may have multiple victims or victimizations. Based on the National Crime Victimization Survey (NCVS). See source for more information]

Type of crime	Number of victimizations (1,000)				Victimization rates [1]			
	2010	2015	2017	2018	2010	2015	2017	2018
Total	20,348	19,618	18,953	19,888	(X)	(X)	(X)	(X)
Violent victimization [2]	4,936	5,007	5,613	6,386	19.3	18.6	20.6	23.2
Not injured	3,646	3,703	4,364	4,936	14.2	13.7	16.0	17.9
Injured	1,290	1,303	1,248	1,450	5.0	4.8	4.6	5.3
Serious violent victimization [3]	1,695	1,827	2,001	2,366	6.6	6.8	7.3	8.6
Rape/sexual assault	269	432	394	735	1.0	1.6	1.4	2.7
Robbery	569	579	614	573	2.2	2.1	2.3	2.1
Not injured	370	370	410	380	1.4	1.4	1.5	1.4
Injured	198	209	203	194	0.8	0.8	0.7	0.7
Aggravated assault	858	817	993	1,058	3.4	3.0	3.6	3.8
Not injured	538	526	669	705	2.1	1.9	2.5	2.6
Injured	320	291	325	353	1.2	1.1	1.2	1.3
Simple assault	3,241	3,179	3,612	4,020	12.7	11.8	13.3	14.6
Not injured	2,619	2,534	3,007	3,398	10.2	9.4	11.0	12.3
Injured	622	645	605	622	2.4	2.4	2.2	2.3
Personal theft/larceny [4]	138	89	101	139	0.5	0.3	0.4	0.5
Property crimes	15,412	14,611	13,340	13,503	125.4	110.7	108.4	108.2
Household burglary	3,176	2,905	2,538	2,640	25.8	22.0	20.6	21.1
Motor vehicle theft	607	564	517	534	4.9	4.3	4.2	4.3
Theft [5]	11,628	11,142	10,285	10,329	94.6	84.4	83.6	82.7

X Not applicable. [1] Per 1,000 persons age 12 or older for violent victimization and personal theft/larceny; per 1,000 households for property crime. [2] Excludes homicide because the NCVS is based on interviews with victims and therefore cannot measure murder. [3] Includes rape, sexual assault, personal robbery, and aggravated assault, attempted and completed crimes. [4] Includes pocket picking, completed purse snatching, and attempted purse snatching. [5] The taking or attempted unlawful taking of property or cash without personal contact with the victim. Incidents involving theft of property from within a household are classified as theft if the offender has a legal right to be in the house (such as a maid, delivery person, or guest).

Source: U.S. Department of Justice, Bureau of Justice Statistics, "NCVS Victimization Analysis Tool," <http://www.bjs.gov/index.cfm?ty=nvat>, accessed June 2020.

Table 350. Victimization Rates by Type of Crime and Characteristics of the Victim: 2018

[Rate per 1,000 persons age 12 years or older. Based on the National Crime Victimization Survey. See text, this section and Appendix III]

Victim characteristics	Violent victimization						Personal theft [2]
	Total	Serious violent victimization [1]	Rape/ sexual assault	Robbery	Aggravated assault	Simple assault	
Total	23.2	8.6	2.7	2.1	3.8	14.6	0.5
Male	22.1	7.5	0.6	2.4	4.5	14.6	0.5
Female	24.3	9.6	4.6	1.8	3.2	14.6	0.5
12 to 14 years old	44.2	9.3	[4] 2.0	[4] 3.2	4.2	34.8	[4] 0.6
15 to 17 years old	24.0	10.9	5.3	[4] 1.7	4.0	13.0	[4] 0.6
18 to 20 years old	41.9	19.0	10.1	4.1	4.8	22.8	[4] 1.5
21 to 24 years old	31.5	14.3	6.0	2.5	5.8	17.2	[4] 1.2
25 to 34 years old	31.8	11.3	3.5	2.3	5.5	20.5	[4] 0.6
35 to 49 years old	25.2	9.8	3.2	2.6	4.0	15.4	[4] 0.3
50 to 64 years old	18.3	6.4	0.7	1.8	3.9	12.0	0.3
65 years old and over	6.5	2.3	0.4	0.8	1.0	4.2	0.4
White	22.9	7.8	2.6	1.7	3.6	15.1	0.3
Black	21.4	10.9	1.7	3.8	5.4	10.5	1.4
Other [3]	27.6	11.9	4.4	3.2	4.2	15.8	[4] 0.8
White, non-Hispanic	24.7	8.2	2.8	1.6	3.8	16.5	0.3
Black, non-Hispanic	20.4	10.0	1.3	3.9	4.9	10.3	1.3
Hispanic	18.6	8.5	2.1	2.7	3.6	10.1	[4] 0.4
Household income:							
Less than $7,500	87.0	40.4	21.8	7.5	11.2	46.6	[4] 1.6
$7,500 to $14,999	66.2	33.9	10.7	9.5	13.7	32.3	[4] 1.4
$15,000 to $24,999	29.6	13.0	1.4	3.4	8.2	16.6	[4] 0.3
$25,000 to $34,999	29.7	13.9	6.2	4.1	3.6	15.8	[4] 0.4
$35,000 to $49,999	22.9	7.8	1.8	2.2	3.8	15.1	[4] 0.4
$50,000 to $74,999	18.7	5.8	2.2	0.9	2.7	12.9	[4] 0.4
$75,000 or more	19.9	5.0	1.3	1.1	2.6	14.8	0.5
Unknown	12.9	4.6	1.0	1.1	2.6	8.3	0.4

[1] Includes rape, sexual assault, personal robbery, and aggravated assault, attempted and completed crimes. [2] Includes pocket picking and purse snatching. [3] Includes American Indians and Alaska Natives, Asians, Native Hawaiians, other Pacific Islanders, and persons of two or more races. [4] Based on 10 or fewer sample cases or the coefficient of variation is greater than 50%.

Source: U.S. Department of Justice, Bureau of Justice Statistics, "NCVS Victimization Analysis Tool," <http://www.bjs.gov/index.cfm?ty=nvat>, accessed June 2020.

Table 351. Murder Victims—Circumstances and Weapons Used or Cause of Death: 2000 to 2018

[For year ending December 31. The FBI's Uniform Crime Reporting (UCR) Program defines murder and nonnegligent manslaughter as the willful (nonnegligent) killing of one human being by another. The classification of this offense is based solely on police investigation as opposed to the determination of a court, medical examiner, coroner, jury, or other judicial body. The UCR Program does not include the following situations in this offense classification: deaths caused by negligence, suicide, or accident; justifiable homicides; and attempts to murder, which are scored as aggravated assaults]

Characteristic	2000	2010	2014	2015	2016	2017	2018
Murders, total [1]	**13,230**	**13,164**	**12,278**	**13,780**	**15,318**	**15,195**	**14,123**
CIRCUMSTANCES							
Felonies, total [1]	2,229	1,974	1,730	1,924	2,130	2,260	2,108
Rape [2]	58	41	25	14	21	19	13
Robbery	1,077	803	563	596	691	691	548
Burglary	76	85	77	85	81	86	75
Larceny-theft	23	21	23	17	13	22	23
Motor vehicle theft	25	35	24	34	57	33	59
Arson	81	35	20	19	31	76	64
Prostitution and commercialized vice	6	5	19	7	15	15	13
Other sex offenses	10	14	3	15	4	8	5
Narcotic drug laws	589	474	363	449	472	546	560
Gambling	12	7	11	5	11	10	6
Suspected felony type	60	68	83	103	97	149	208
Other than felony type [1]	6,871	6,485	5,475	5,799	6,376	6,681	6,299
Domestic violence	122	90	83	103	111	111	131
Child killed by babysitter	30	36	38	42	37	32	29
Brawl due to influence of alcohol	188	122	73	116	97	85	65
Brawl due to influence of narcotics	99	60	68	72	130	65	59
Argument over money or property	206	187	146	180	196	202	199
Other arguments	3,589	3,280	2,741	2,916	3,114	3,191	3,196
Gangland killings	65	181	137	181	478	373	306
Juvenile gang killings	653	675	555	576	411	380	308
Institutional killings	10	17	18	24	17	27	23
Unknown	4,070	4,637	4,990	5,954	6,715	6,105	5,508
TYPE OF WEAPON OR CAUSE OF DEATH [1]							
Total firearms	8,661	8,874	7,803	9,103	10,372	11,006	10,265
Handguns	6,778	6,115	5,342	6,176	6,762	7,051	6,603
Rifles	411	367	235	215	300	390	297
Shotguns	485	366	238	247	247	264	235
Other guns	53	93	88	151	172	180	167
Firearms, type not stated	934	1,933	1,900	2,314	2,891	3,121	2,963
Knives or cutting instruments	1,782	1,732	1,545	1,525	1,558	1,609	1,515
Blunt objects (club, hammer, etc.)	617	549	431	436	464	472	443
Personal weapons (hands, fists, feet, pushed, etc.)	927	769	668	647	664	710	672
Fire	134	78	55	63	78	96	72
Narcotics	20	45	70	69	118	110	78
Drowning	15	10	12	12	9	8	9
Strangulation	166	122	84	96	97	89	70
Asphyxiation	92	98	93	105	92	111	90

[1] Includes items not shown separately. [2] Rape figures in this table are an aggregate total of data submitted using both the revised and legacy UCR definitions.

Source: U.S. Department of Justice, Federal Bureau of Investigation, "Crime in the United States 2018" and earlier releases, <https://ucr.fbi.gov/>, accessed April 2020.

Table 352. Murder Victims by Age, Sex, and Race/Ethnicity: 2018

[See headnote, Table 351]

Age	Total [1]	Sex		Race			Ethnicity [2]	
		Male	Female	White	Black	Other [3]	Hispanic or Latino	Not Hispanic or Latino
Murders, total	**14,123**	**10,914**	**3,180**	**6,088**	**7,407**	**395**	**2,173**	**9,066**
Percent of total [4]	100.0	77.3	22.5	43.1	52.4	2.8	16.6	69.3
Under 18 years old [1]	1,126	784	341	493	577	30	191	704
18 years old and over [1]	12,855	10,035	2,809	5,544	6,784	362	1,966	8,314
Infant (under 1 year old)	137	75	62	83	43	1	19	73
1 to 4 years old	255	153	101	129	113	4	33	168
5 to 8 years old	76	43	33	37	34	4	10	47
9 to 12 years old	60	34	26	28	26	5	8	33
13 to 16 years old	319	238	81	119	186	11	64	207
17 to 19 years old	1,107	948	159	364	712	21	199	709
20 to 24 years old	2,199	1,813	385	764	1,369	33	428	1,334
25 to 29 years old	2,239	1,855	382	760	1,402	57	337	1,460
30 to 34 years old	1,721	1,388	332	648	993	58	273	1,128
35 to 39 years old	1,441	1,116	325	630	757	40	245	926
40 to 44 years old	1,018	813	204	474	513	23	160	642
45 to 49 years old	820	600	219	431	344	33	124	519
50 to 54 years old	717	531	185	380	294	33	93	471
55 to 59 years old	651	476	172	360	259	18	62	455
60 to 64 years old	423	284	139	257	141	15	38	292
65 to 69 years old	316	200	116	212	87	10	33	209
70 to 74 years old	189	104	84	133	45	9	13	133
75 years old and over	293	148	145	228	43	17	18	212
Age unknown	142	95	30	51	46	3	16	48

[1] Includes unknown victim categories not shown separatley. [2] Not all agencies provide ethnicity data; therefore, data will not sum to total. [3] Includes American Indian or Alaska Native, Asian, and Native Hawaiian or Pacific Islander. [4] Percentages rounded, may not add to 100.

Source: U.S. Department of Justice, Federal Bureau of Investigation, "Crime in the United States 2018," <https://ucr.fbi.gov/>, accessed April 2020.

Table 353. Violent Crime Between Intimate Partners by Sex of Victims: 1993 to 2018

[Intimate partners are defined as current and former spouses, boyfriends, and girlfriends. Based on the National Crime Victimization Survey (NCVS); see text this section, and source]

Year	Female victims Total intimate partner violence	Female Rate per 1,000 [1] Overall intimate partner violence	Female Rate per 1,000 [1] Serious violence [3]	Female Rate per 1,000 [1] Simple assault [4]	Male victims Total intimate partner violence	Male Rate per 1,000 [1] Overall intimate partner violence	Male Rate per 1,000 [1] Serious violence [3]	Male Rate per 1,000 [1] Simple assault [4]
1993	1,689,687	15.5	5.7	9.9	347,924	3.4	1.5	1.9
1994	1,843,713	16.8	6.1	10.7	258,990	2.5	0.7	1.8
1995	1,727,462	15.5	3.7	11.8	285,907	2.8	1.0	1.8
1996	1,626,516	14.5	4.7	9.8	194,647	1.9	0.8	1.1
1997	1,661,683	14.7	4.8	9.8	176,651	1.7	0.5	1.2
1998	1,336,585	11.7	3.6	8.0	228,793	2.1	0.6	1.5
1999	1,164,554	10.0	3.5	6.5	230,230	2.1	0.5	1.6
2000	783,762	6.7	1.9	4.8	116,152	1.1	[5] 0.2	0.9
2001	981,671	8.3	2.9	5.4	108,740	1.0	0.5	0.5
2002	797,805	6.7	2.0	4.7	131,956	1.2	[5] 0.5	0.7
2003	906,628	7.4	3.6	3.8	133,657	1.2	0.5	0.7
2004	816,139	6.6	2.3	4.3	215,582	1.8	0.5	1.4
2005	621,041	4.9	1.6	3.4	194,966	1.6	[5] 0.9	0.7
2006 [2]	1,063,775	8.4	3.2	5.2	241,475	2.0	1.1	0.9
2007	780,979	6.1	2.1	4.0	124,831	1.0	[5] 0.4	0.7
2008	914,422	7.1	2.5	4.6	188,970	1.5	0.7	0.9
2009	914,529	7.0	1.6	5.4	125,121	1.0	0.3	0.7
2010	636,770	4.9	1.7	3.2	136,663	1.1	0.4	0.7
2011	604,645	4.6	1.6	3.0	246,127	2.0	[5] 0.4	1.6
2012	682,417	5.1	1.7	3.4	128,378	1.0	0.4	0.6
2013	619,357	4.6	2.1	2.5	129,438	1.0	0.6	0.4
2014	500,920	3.7	1.4	2.2	133,692	1.0	0.6	0.5
2015	741,645	5.4	2.2	3.1	64,403	0.5	[5] 0.2	0.3
2016	513,494	3.7	1.6	2.0	83,705	0.6	0.3	0.4
2017	602,902	4.3	1.7	2.6	63,407	0.5	0.2	0.2
2018	754,842	5.3	2.4	2.9	92,384	0.7	0.3	0.4

[1] Rates are per 1,000 persons age 12 and older. [2] Due to methodological changes, use caution when comparing 2006 National Crime Victimization Survey criminal victimization estimates to other years. See Criminal Victimization, 2007, NCJ 224390. [3] Rape or sexual assault, robbery, and aggravated assault. [4] Attack or attempted attack without a weapon that results in no injury, minor injury, or an undetermined injury requiring less than two days of hospitalization. [5] Interpret data with caution.

Source: U.S. Department of Justice, Bureau of Justice Statistics, "NCVS Victimization Analysis Tool," <https://www.bjs.gov/index.cfm?ty=nvat>, accessed June 2020.

Table 354. Nonfatal Firearm and Nonfirearm Violence by Victim-Offender Relationship and Location of Crime: 2007 to 2011

[Data are for victimizations. Covers period from 2007 to 2011. Detail may not sum to total due to rounding. Data from National Crime Victimization Survey]

Characteristic	Total nonfatal violence Number	Total nonfatal violence Percent [1]	Firearm violence Number	Firearm violence Percent [1]	Nonfirearm violence Number	Nonfirearm violence Percent [1]
RELATIONSHIP TO VICTIM						
Total	**29,611,300**	**(X)**	**2,218,500**	**7.5**	**27,392,800**	**92.5**
Nonstranger	15,715,900	(X)	738,000	4.7	14,977,900	95.3
Intimate [2]	4,673,600	(X)	195,700	4.2	4,477,900	95.8
Other relative	2,157,700	(X)	158,100	7.3	1,999,500	92.7
Friend/acquaintance	8,884,600	(X)	384,100	4.3	8,500,500	95.7
Stranger	10,983,100	(X)	1,177,900	10.7	9,805,200	89.3
Unknown [3]	2,912,300	(X)	302,600	10.4	2,609,600	89.6
LOCATION						
Total	**29,618,300**	**100.0**	**2,218,500**	**100.0**	**27,399,800**	**100.0**
Victim's home or lodging	6,491,400	21.9	427,600	19.3	6,063,800	22.1
Near victim's home	4,804,700	16.2	504,500	22.7	4,300,200	15.7
In, at, or near a friend, neighbor, or relative's home	2,175,900	7.3	132,600	6.0	2,043,300	7.5
Commercial place	2,878,600	9.7	195,400	8.8	2,683,200	9.8
Parking lot or garage	1,688,400	5.7	340,600	15.4	1,347,900	4.9
School [4]	3,931,100	13.3	[5] 12,600	[5] 0.6	3,918,500	14.3
Open area, on street, or public transportation	4,636,900	15.7	508,400	22.9	4,128,500	15.1
Other location	3,011,200	10.2	96,800	4.4	2,914,400	10.6

X Not applicable. [1] Percent of total violence is shown for data by relationship to victim. Percent distribution of specified type of violence is shown for data by location. [2] Includes current or former spouses, boyfriends, or girlfriends. [3] Includes relationships unknown and number of offenders unknown. [4] Includes inside a school building or on school property. [5] Interpret with caution. Estimate based on 10 or fewer sample cases, or coefficient of variation is greater than 50%.

Source: Department of Justice, Bureau of Justice Statistics, *Firearm Violence, 1993-2011*, NCJ 241730, May 2013. See also <http://www.bjs.gov/index.cfm?ty=pbdetail&iid=4616>.

Table 355. Hate Crimes—Number of Incidents, Offenses, Victims, and Known Offenders by Bias Motivation: 2000 to 2018

[2,026 law enforcement agencies submitted data on hate crimes. 16,039 law enforcement agencies covering over 306 million people participated in the Hate Crime Statistics Program in 2018. Hate crime offenses cover incidents motivated by race, ethnicity/national origin, religion, sexual orientation, gender identity, and disability. See source and Appendix III]

Bias motivation	Incidents reported	Offenses	Victims [1]	Known offenders [2]
2000...	8,213	9,619	10,117	7,690
2010...	6,628	7,699	8,208	6,008
2018, total [3]...........................	**7,120**	**8,496**	**8,819**	**6,266**
Race/ethnicity/ancestry, total........	**4,047**	**4,954**	**5,155**	**3,634**
Anti-White.............................	762	1,001	1,038	754
Anti-Black or African American........	1,943	2,325	2,426	1,707
Anti-American Indian/Alaska native.....	194	204	209	163
Anti-Asian.............................	148	171	177	125
Anti-Native Hawaiian or Other Pacific Islander.....	20	26	26	15
Anti-multiple races, group............	137	166	174	91
Anti-Arab..............................	82	100	100	80
Anti-Hispanic or Latino...............	485	644	671	495
Anti-Other race/ethnicity/ancestry....	276	317	334	204
Religion, total [3].....................	**1,419**	**1,550**	**1,617**	**917**
Anti-Jewish............................	835	896	920	484
Anti-Catholic..........................	53	59	63	36
Anti-Protestant........................	34	38	39	22
Anti-Islamic (Muslim).................	188	225	236	153
Anti-Sikh..............................	60	64	69	49
Sexual orientation, total..............	**1,196**	**1,404**	**1,445**	**1,268**
Anti-gay (male homosexual)............	726	839	863	841
Anti-lesbian (female homosexual)......	129	171	177	105
Anti-lesbian, gay, bisexual, or transgender....	303	353	360	294
Anti-heterosexual......................	17	20	24	13
Anti-bisexual..........................	21	21	21	15
Disability, total.......................	**159**	**177**	**179**	**151**
Anti-physical..........................	60	67	68	52
Anti-mental............................	99	110	111	99
Gender identity.........................	**168**	**184**	**189**	**180**
Anti-transgender.......................	142	157	160	156
Anti-gender non-conforming............	26	27	29	24
Multiple bias [4].......................	**84**	**169**	**173**	**78**

[1] "Victim" may refer to an individual, business/financial institution, government entity, religious organization, or society/public as a whole. [2] "Known offender" does not imply that the identity of the suspect is known, but only that an attribute of the suspect has been identified which distinguishes him/her from an unknown offender. [3] Includes other motivation types not shown separately. [4] Incident in which one or more offense types are motivated by two or more biases.

Source: U.S. Department of Justice, Federal Bureau of Investigation, "Hate Crime Statistics 2018," <https://www.fbi.gov/services/cjis/ucr>, accessed November 2019.

Table 356. Hate Crimes by Bias Motivation and Location of Incident: 2018

[See headnote, Table 355]

Location	Total incidents	Race/ ethnicity/ ancestry	Religion	Sexual orientation	Disability	Gender	Gender identity	Multiple-bias incidents [1]
Total [2]........................	**7,120**	**4,047**	**1,419**	**1,196**	**159**	**47**	**168**	**84**
Air/bus/train terminal..............	113	67	2	34	1	1	6	2
Bank/savings and loan...............	28	14	8	2	3	–	1	–
Bar/nightclub.......................	119	53	3	59	1	–	2	1
Church/synagogue/temple/mosque...	263	29	219	12	–	–	–	3
Commercial office building..........	145	97	22	16	1	3	4	2
Convenience store...................	141	100	13	19	4	–	5	–
Cyberspace..........................	23	15	4	2	1	–	–	1
Department/discount store...........	111	63	20	11	4	2	6	5
Drug store/doctor's office/hospital....	93	63	12	7	7	–	2	2
Field/woods.........................	47	31	5	7	2	–	1	1
Government/public building..........	163	116	22	12	4	2	2	5
Grocery/supermarket.................	98	75	5	10	3	–	5	–
Highway/road/alley/street/sidewalk...	1,328	846	143	259	23	4	42	11
Hotel/motel/etc.....................	67	41	6	17	2	–	1	–
Jail/prison/penitentiary/corrections facility...........................	69	45	3	19	1	–	1	–
Park/playground.....................	106	68	15	20	–	–	3	–
Parking/drop lot/garage.............	380	245	57	59	8	3	7	1
Residence/home......................	1,832	1,044	303	352	66	18	33	16
Restaurant..........................	189	136	15	30	–	1	6	1
School/college [3]..................	69	35	17	11	1	–	4	1
School—college/university...........	314	155	88	53	5	5	3	5
School—elementary/secondary........	273	153	59	33	6	–	5	17
Service/gas station.................	91	63	12	10	2	–	4	–
Specialty store (TV, fur, etc.).........	79	56	10	7	1	1	2	2
Other/unknown.......................	979	437	356	135	13	7	23	8

– Represents zero. [1] See footnote 4, Table 355. [2] Includes other locations not shown separately. [3] The location designation school/college has been retained for agencies that have not updated their records to include the new location designations of school, which allow for more specificity in reporting.

Source: U.S. Department of Justice, Federal Bureau of Investigation, "Hate Crime Statistics 2018," <https://www.fbi.gov/services/cjis/ucr>, accessed November 2019.

Table 357. Rape and Sexual Assault Rates Among College-Age Females: 1998 to 2013

[Estimated victimization rates per 1,000 females, based on 3-year rolling averages centered on the most recent year. Data from the National Crime Victimization Survey]

Year	Students 18 to 24 years old [1]	Nonstudents 18 to 24 years old [2]	Not college-age females [3]	Year	Students 18 to 24 years old [1]	Nonstudents 18 to 24 years old [2]	Not college-age females [3]
1998	7.8	8.9	3.1	2006	5.4	5.5	1.7
1999	6.0	11.2	3.5	2007	5.5	5.4	1.7
2000	7.1	12.2	2.8	2008	5.2	6.7	1.9
2001	8.8	11.2	3.0	2009	3.7	8.3	1.6
2002	8.9	10.0	2.2	2010	[4] 4.1	8.4	1.6
2003	7.6	8.8	2.2	2011	4.6	7.1	1.4
2004	6.5	7.0	1.8	2012	5.9	4.1	1.3
2005	4.7	5.6	1.6	2013	4.4	4.3	1.4

[1] Includes female victims age 18 to 24 enrolled part time or full time in a post-secondary institution (i.e., college or university, trade school, or vocational school). [2] Includes female victims age 18 to 24 not enrolled in a post-secondary institution. [3] Includes females age 12 to 17 and age 25 or older. [4] Interpret with caution, subject to sampling error.

Source: U.S. Bureau of Justice Statistics, *Rape and Sexual Assault Victimization Among College-Age Females, 1995–2013*, NCJ 248471, December 2014. See also <http://www.bjs.gov/index.cfm?ty=tp&tid=317>.

Table 358. Internet Crime Complaints—Victims and Value of Loss by Crime Type: 2017 to 2019

[Data shown are suspected criminal internet activities reported by victims to the FBI's Internet Crime Complaint Center (IC3). Victims are encouraged and often directed by law enforcement to file a complaint online at <www.ic3.gov> along with documentation and other information necessary to support the complaint. Complaints are reviewed by an IC3 analyst and categorized according to crime type. See source for full description of crime types and additional information]

Crime	2017 Victims (number)	2017 Loss (dollars)	2018 Victims (number)	2018 Loss (dollars)	2019 Victims (number)	2019 Loss (dollars)
Phishing/vishing/smishing/pharming	25,344	29,703,421	26,379	48,241,748	114,702	57,836,379
Non-payment/non-delivery	84,079	141,110,441	65,116	183,826,809	61,832	196,563,497
Extortion	14,938	15,302,792	51,146	83,357,901	43,101	107,498,956
Personal data breach	30,904	77,134,865	50,642	148,892,403	38,218	120,102,501
Spoofing	(NA)	(NA)	15,569	70,000,248	25,789	300,478,433
BEC/EAC [1]	15,690	676,151,185	20,373	1,297,803,489	23,775	1,776,549,688
Confidence/romance fraud	15,372	211,382,989	18,493	362,500,761	19,473	475,014,032
Identity theft	17,636	66,815,298	16,128	100,429,691	16,053	160,305,789
Harassment/threats of violence	16,194	12,569,185	18,415	21,903,829	15,502	19,866,654
Overpayment	23,135	53,450,830	15,512	53,225,507	15,395	55,820,212
Advanced fee	16,368	57,861,324	16,362	92,271,682	14,607	100,602,297
Employment	15,784	38,883,616	14,979	45,487,120	14,493	42,618,705
Credit card fraud	15,220	57,207,248	15,210	88,991,436	14,378	111,491,163
Government impersonation	9,149	12,467,380	10,978	64,211,765	13,873	124,292,606
Tech support	10,949	14,810,080	14,408	38,697,026	13,633	54,041,053
Real estate/rental property	9,645	56,231,333	11,300	149,458,114	11,677	221,365,911
Lottery/sweepstakes/inheritance	3,012	16,835,001	7,146	60,214,814	7,767	48,642,332
Misrepresentation	5,437	14,580,907	5,959	20,000,713	5,975	12,371,573
Investment	3,089	96,844,144	3,693	252,955,320	3,999	222,186,195
Intellectual property rights, copyright and counterfeit	2,644	5,536,912	2,249	15,802,011	3,892	10,293,307
Malware/scareware/virus	3,089	5,003,434	2,811	7,411,651	2,373	2,009,119
Ransomware [2]	1,783	2,344,365	1,493	3,621,857	2,047	8,965,847
Corporate data breach	3,785	60,942,306	2,480	117,711,989	1,795	53,398,278
Denial of service (DoS)/telephony DoS	1,201	1,466,195	1,799	2,052,340	1,353	7,598,198
Crimes against children	1,300	46,411	1,394	265,996	1,312	975,311
Re-shipping	1,025	809,746	907	1,684,179	929	1,772,692
Civil matter	1,057	5,766,550	768	15,172,692	908	20,242,867
Health care related	406	925,849	337	4,474,792	657	1,128,838
False charities	436	1,405,460	493	1,006,379	407	2,214,383
Gambling	203	598,853	181	926,953	262	1,458,118
Terrorism	177	18,926	120	10,193	61	49,589
Hacktivist	158	20,147	77	77,612	39	129,000
Other	14,023	23,853,704	10,826	63,126,929	10,842	66,223,160

NA Not available. [1] Business email compromise/email account compromise are scams carried out in order to conduct unauthorized transfer of funds. [2] Does not include estimates of lost business, time, wages, files, or equipment, or any third party remediation services acquired by a victim. In some cases victims do not report any loss amount to the FBI, thereby creating an artificially low overall ransomware loss rate. Represents what victims report to the FBI via the IC3 and does not account for victim direct reporting to FBI field offices and agents.

Source: U.S. Department of Justice, Federal Bureau of Investigation, *2019 Internet Crime Report*, and earlier reports. See also <www.ic3.gov/>.

Table 359. Property Crime by Selected Household Characteristics: 2018

[124,825 represents 124,825,000. For crimes against households (burglary, theft, and motor vehicle theft), each household affected by a crime is counted as a single victimization. Based on National Crime Victimization Survey (NCVS); see text, this section and Appendix III]

Characteristic	Number of house-holds (1,000)	Property crimes							
		Number of victimizations (1,000)				Victimization rate per 1,000 households			
		Total	Burglary	Motor vehicle theft	Theft	Total	Burglary	Motor vehicle theft	Theft
Total...................	**124,825**	**13,503**	**2,640**	**534**	**10,329**	**108.2**	**21.1**	**4.3**	**82.7**
Race:									
White....................	98,008	10,205	1,951	393	7,861	104.1	19.9	4.0	80.2
Black....................	16,449	1,980	464	102	1,414	120.4	28.2	6.2	86.0
Other [1].................	10,368	1,317	224	39	1,054	127.1	21.6	3.8	101.7
Ethnicity:									
Hispanic................	17,356	2,185	337	108	1,740	125.9	19.4	6.2	100.2
Non-Hispanic...........	107,469	11,318	2,303	426	8,589	105.3	21.4	4.0	79.9
Household income:									
Less than $7,500.......	4,334	826	248	23	555	190.7	57.2	5.4	128.1
$7,500 to $14,999.....	6,459	1,186	309	34	843	183.6	47.9	5.3	130.5
$15,000 to $24,999....	8,877	1,128	250	59	818	127.0	28.1	6.7	92.2
$25,000 to $34,999....	9,853	1,263	290	63	909	128.2	29.5	6.4	92.3
$35,000 to $49,999....	13,807	1,604	290	74	1,240	116.2	21.0	5.4	89.8
$50,000 to $74,999....	16,049	1,707	306	53	1,348	106.4	19.0	3.3	84.0
$75,000 or more.......	30,976	3,242	425	117	2,700	104.7	13.7	3.8	87.2
Unknown..............	34,470	2,547	520	110	1,916	73.9	15.1	3.2	55.6
Number of persons in household:									
1........................	41,129	3,931	1,008	137	2,786	95.6	24.5	3.3	67.7
2 or 3..................	60,455	6,115	1,049	244	4,822	101.2	17.3	4.0	79.8
4 or 5..................	19,995	2,842	458	125	2,259	142.1	22.9	6.3	113.0
6 or more..............	3,246	615	125	28	462	189.4	38.5	8.7	142.2

[1] Includes American Indians and Alaska Natives, Asians, Native Hawaiians and other Pacific Islanders, and persons of two or more races.

Source: U.S. Department of Justice, Bureau of Justice Statistics, "NCVS Victimization Analysis Tool," <http://www.bjs.gov/index.cfm?ty=nvat>, accessed June 2020.

Table 360. Robbery and Property Crimes by Type, Location, and Average Value Lost: 2010 to 2018

[300.3 represents 300,300. Data are from the FBI's Unified Crime Reporting (UCR) Program]

Characteristic of offense	Number of offenses (1,000)				Average value lost (dol.)			
	2010	2016	2017	2018	2010	2016	2017	2018
Robbery, total..........................	**300.3**	**280.4**	**280.5**	**230.6**	**1,239**	**1,400**	**1,373**	**2,119**
Location of crime:								
Street or highway.........................	129.6	109.0	104.3	83.8	908	1,191	1,202	1,739
Commercial house........................	39.7	42.8	43.4	37.0	1,858	1,689	1,284	1,546
Gas or service station...................	7.0	8.2	8.4	7.3	939	970	1,087	1,028
Convenience store.......................	15.7	17.4	18.4	16.1	782	732	957	961
Residence................................	51.9	46.4	44.9	37.2	1,491	1,758	1,732	4,600
Bank.....................................	6.5	5.0	4.8	3.7	4,410	3,531	3,483	4,303
Miscellaneous............................	49.9	51.6	56.4	45.6	1,115	1,367	1,474	1,662
Burglary, total..........................	**1,898.0**	**1,354.9**	**1,251.0**	**1,047.4**	**2,119**	**2,361**	**2,416**	**2,799**
Location and time of burglary:								
Residence (dwelling):....................	1,402.2	942.2	841.3	685.8	2,137	2,273	2,368	8,407
Night.................................	389.9	278.6	255.5	218.0	1,868	1,913	1,995	2,123
Day..................................	722.2	486.0	424.9	346.3	2,158	2,258	2,383	2,401
Unknown.............................	290.1	177.6	160.9	121.4	2,445	2,879	2,924	3,833
Nonresidence (store, office, etc.):......	495.7	412.7	409.7	361.6	2,070	2,562	2,514	10,183
Night.................................	204.6	178.5	179.9	161.8	1,765	2,585	2,337	2,833
Day..................................	168.9	142.6	140.9	128.1	2,010	2,182	2,211	3,199
Unknown.............................	122.2	91.6	88.9	71.7	2,662	3,109	3,353	4,151
Larceny-theft, total [1].................	**5,391.6**	**4,971.9**	**4,917.3**	**4,390.4**	**988**	**999**	**1,007**	**1,153**
Type of larceny:								
Pocket-picking...........................	21.1	24.4	27.7	22.9	526	646	648	1,169
Purse-snatching..........................	24.5	20.0	19.6	16.9	400	475	564	718
Shoplifting...............................	925.1	1,038.6	1,021.2	937.0	174	250	260	304
From motor vehicles (except accessories)......	1,423.9	1,301.4	1,318.0	1,183.6	704	869	879	994
Motor vehicle accessories................	477.8	366.0	363.0	272.1	681	541	505	648
Bicycles.................................	179.6	162.5	155.9	131.8	351	483	477	546
From buildings...........................	607.9	533.6	523.2	448.4	1,406	1,449	1,381	1,610
From coin-operated machines.............	17.6	10.9	10.7	9.7	365	607	538	851
All others................................	1,714.0	1,514.6	1,477.9	1,368.0	1,654	1,649	1,700	1,890
Larceny-theft by value:								
Over $200...............................	2,443.1	2,256.3	2,256.3	2,052.4	2,089	2,140	2,137	2,407
$50 to $200.............................	1,235.1	1,075.7	1,043.2	939.8	111	108	105	107
Under $50...............................	1,713.3	1,640.0	1,617.7	1,398.1	17	14	13	15
Motor vehicle theft, total...............	**641.9**	**700.1**	**705.3**	**660.3**	**6,152**	**7,680**	**7,708**	**8,407**

[1] Excludes motor vehicles.

Source: U.S. Department of Justice, Federal Bureau of Investigation, "Crime in the United States 2018," and earlier releases, <https://ucr.fbi.gov/>, accessed November 2019.

Table 361. Fraud and Identity Theft—Consumer Complaints by State: 2019

[Rate per 100,000 population. As of December 31. Rates based on U.S. Census Bureau's 2019 population estimates. The Consumer Sentinel Network is a secure online database of consumer complaints available only to law enforcement. Based on unverified complaints reported by consumers. Excludes complaints from state-specific data contributors]

State	Fraud and other complaints		Identity theft victims		State	Fraud and other complaints		Identity theft victims	
	Number	Rate	Number	Rate		Number	Rate	Number	Rate
U.S.	**2,063,030**	**629**	**607,101**	**185**	MO	39,843	650	7,406	121
AL	29,986	613	8,454	173	MT	6,064	571	707	67
AK	3,701	502	539	73	NE	9,179	476	1,320	68
AZ	50,964	711	10,744	150	NV	27,463	905	7,757	256
AR	15,351	509	4,525	150	NH	8,447	623	1,302	96
CA	243,620	616	101,639	257	NJ	56,880	638	18,220	205
CO	38,303	673	6,272	110	NM	11,948	570	2,088	100
CT	22,250	623	4,564	128	NY	128,208	656	36,337	186
DE	7,928	820	2,188	226	NC	67,350	649	18,584	179
DC	7,659	1,090	1,550	221	ND	2,867	377	448	59
FL	177,838	835	64,842	304	OH	72,903	624	13,788	118
GA	79,083	752	44,888	427	OK	18,738	475	3,706	94
HI	7,056	497	1,347	95	OR	28,711	685	4,005	96
ID	9,460	539	1,420	81	PA	81,284	635	20,899	163
IL	74,575	585	23,139	182	RI	5,779	547	1,146	108
IN	34,622	517	6,386	95	SC	33,675	662	10,851	213
IA	14,949	474	1,910	61	SD	3,227	366	411	47
KS	15,852	544	2,273	78	TN	43,087	636	10,664	158
KY	23,645	529	2,977	67	TX	171,242	597	73,553	256
LA	24,884	534	10,582	227	UT	17,228	545	4,702	149
ME	7,055	527	807	60	VT	3,102	495	338	54
MD	46,503	770	12,675	210	VA	57,202	672	10,284	121
MA	38,170	553	8,606	125	WA	49,601	658	7,110	94
MI	55,683	557	13,532	135	WV	10,190	564	1,061	59
MN	30,246	539	4,499	80	WI	31,610	544	5,023	86
MS	15,041	504	4,714	158	WY	2,778	481	319	55

Source: U.S. Federal Trade Commission, *Consumer Sentinel Network Data Book 2019,* January 2020. See also <https://www.ftc.gov/enforcement/consumer-sentinel-network/reports>.

Table 362. Victims of Identity Theft by Type of Account and Selected Victim Characteristics: 2016

[25,952.4 represents 25,952,400. Data shown are for persons age 16 or older who experienced at least one identity theft incident during the past 12 months. Estimates are based on the most recent identity theft incident. Includes successful and attempted identity theft, regardless of whether the victim experienced a loss. Details do not sum to totals because persons could experience more than one type of identity theft. Based on the National Crime Victimization Survey's Identity Theft Supplement]

Characteristic	Any identity theft		Misuse of existing credit card		Misuse of existing bank account		New account or personal information [1]	
	Number of victims	Percent of all persons	Number of victims	Percent of persons with credit card	Number of victims	Percent of persons with bank account	Number of victims	Percent of all persons
Total	**25,952.4**	**10.2**	**13,422.8**	**7.5**	**11,950.1**	**5.4**	**2,610.0**	**1.0**
By sex:								
Male	12,496.4	10.1	6,816.4	7.9	5,432.2	5.0	1,215.4	1.0
Female	13,456.0	10.3	6,606.4	7.1	6,517.9	5.7	1,394.6	1.1
By race/Hispanic origin:								
White [3]	19,425.2	11.8	10,661.5	8.4	8,476.0	5.6	1,639.7	1.0
Black [3]	2,314.8	7.4	756.1	4.5	1,424.0	5.9	398.9	1.3
Hispanic/Latino	2,538.3	6.3	1,026.2	4.5	1,427.5	4.7	354.6	0.9
Other race [3,4]	1,307.9	8.4	839.2	7.0	393.3	2.9	162.3	1.0
Two or more races [3]	366.2	12.0	139.7	8.1	229.3	8.8	54.5	1.8
By age:								
16 to 17 years old	81.4	1.0	[2] 13.7	[2] 2.5	50.5	1.6	[2] 2.0	[2] (Z)
18 to 24 years old	1,997.5	6.6	537.8	4.1	1,379.7	5.7	192.4	0.6
25 to 34 years old	4,781.7	10.8	2,030.1	6.5	2,521.0	6.6	463.3	1.1
35 to 49 years old	7,541.2	12.4	3,809.5	8.3	3,592.6	6.6	781.0	1.3
50 to 64 years old	7,480.0	11.8	4,235.0	8.4	3,115.9	5.4	800.3	1.3
65 years or older	4,070.6	8.5	2,796.7	7.3	1,290.5	2.9	371.0	0.8
By household income:								
$24,999 or less	3,273.3	6.2	1,053.6	4.2	1,831.2	4.6	548.0	1.0
$25,000-$49,999	5,315.6	8.0	2,349.0	5.4	2,800.4	4.9	588.6	0.9
$50,000-$74,999	4,623.3	10.2	2,212.9	6.4	2,285.7	5.6	374.7	0.8
$75,000 or more	12,740.3	14.1	7,807.3	10.2	5,032.9	6.0	1,098.7	1.2

Z Less than 1 or less than 0.05%. [1] Includes the misuse of personal information to open a new account or to commit other fraud. [2] Interpret with caution; estimates are based on 10 or fewer sample cases or coefficient of variation is greater than 50%. [3] Excludes persons of Hispanic or Latino origin. [4] Includes persons identifying as American Indian, Alaska Native, Asian, Hawaiian, or other Pacific Islander.

Source: U.S. Department of Justice, Bureau of Justice Statistics, *Victims of Identity Theft, 2016*, NCJ 251147, January 2019. See also <https://www.bjs.gov/index.cfm?ty=pbse&sid=60>.

Table 363. Firearm Violence Victimizations by Selected Characteristics: 2010 to 2018

[In units, as indicated. Includes violent crimes in which the offender possessed, showed, or used a firearm. Data are from the National Crime Victimization Survey]

Characteristic	2010	2012	2013	2014	2015	2016	2017	2018
Total violent victimizations (number)..........	4,935,983	6,842,593	6,126,423	5,359,570	5,006,615	5,353,816	5,612,667	6,385,515
Firearm victimizations (number) [1]...............	415,003	460,718	332,951	466,113	284,910	486,591	456,269	470,843
Rate of firearm victimization [2]....................	1.6	1.8	1.3	1.7	1.1	1.8	1.7	1.7
By race/ethnicity								
White, non-Hispanic...........................	1.1	1.2	1.0	1.4	0.7	1.6	1.4	1.4
Black, non-Hispanic...........................	3.2	3.8	3.0	2.9	2.8	3.1	2.0	2.6
Hispanic...	2.3	2.7	1.5	1.9	1.2	2.1	2.4	2.0
Firearm victimizations reported to police (number)..	211,383	305,875	250,580	381,659	217,850	314,502	254,913	310,306
Percent...	50.9	66.4	75.3	81.9	76.5	64.6	55.9	65.9

[1] Each victimization represents one person involved in an incident. [2] Rate is per 1,000 persons age 12 or older.

Source: U.S. Department of Justice, Bureau of Justice Statistics, "NCVS Victimization Analysis Tool," <http://www.bjs.gov/index.cfm?ty=nvat>, accessed May 2020.

Table 364. Active Shooter Incidents and Casualties: 2000 to 2019

[The Federal Bureau of Investigation (FBI) defines active shooters as "one or more individuals actively engaged in killing or attempting to kill people in a populated area." This definition encompasses shootings that happen in schools, workplaces, and other public spaces. A shooting can be categorized as an active shooter incident even if no one is killed or wounded. Excluded from this report are gang- and drug-related shootings and gun-related incidents that appeared not to have put other people in peril (e.g., the accidental discharge of a firearm in a bar)]

Year and location	Active shooter incidents	Casualties		
		Total	Fatal	Injury
2000..	1	7	7	0
2001..	6	43	12	31
2002..	4	29	11	18
2003..	11	51	29	22
2004..	4	20	14	6
2005..	9	51	24	27
2006..	10	46	23	23
2007..	14	126	69	57
2008..	8	63	29	34
2009..	19	143	65	78
2010..	26	86	37	49
2011..	10	84	32	52
2012..	21	208	90	118
2013..	17	86	44	42
2014..	20	97	36	61
2015..	20	134	56	78
2016..	20	214	83	129
2017..	30	729	138	591
2018..	27	213	85	128
2019..	28	247	97	150
BY LOCATION 2000-2019				
Place of commerce...............................	133	(NA)	(NA)	(NA)
Education facility..................................	60	(NA)	(NA)	(NA)
Open space..	42	(NA)	(NA)	(NA)
Government...	30	(NA)	(NA)	(NA)
Residence...	12	(NA)	(NA)	(NA)
Place of worship...................................	13	(NA)	(NA)	(NA)
Health care facility................................	14	(NA)	(NA)	(NA)
Other location.......................................	1	(NA)	(NA)	(NA)

NA Not available.

Source: U.S. Department of Justice, Federal Bureau of Investigation, Office of Partner Engagement, "Active Shooter Resources," <https://www.fbi.gov/about/partnerships/office-of-partner-engagement/active-shooter-resources#FBI-Resources>, accessed May 2020.

Table 365. Background Checks for Firearm Transfers: 2005 to 2015

[In thousands (8,324 represents 8,324,000), except as noted. The Brady Handgun Violence Prevention Act (Brady Act) P.L. 103–159, 1993 requires a background check on an applicant for a firearm purchase from a dealer who is a Federal Firearms Licensee. The period beginning November 30, 1998 is the effective date for the Brady Act. The National Instant Criminal Background Check System (NICS) began operations in 1998. Checks on handgun and long gun transfers are conducted by the FBI, and by state and local agencies. Totals combine Firearm Inquiry Statistics (FIST) estimates for state and local agencies with transactions and denials reported by the FBI]

Inquiries and rejections	2005	2006	2007	2008	2009	2010	2011	2012	2013	2014	2015
Applications received...............	8,324	8,772	8,836	10,131	11,071	10,643	12,135	15,718	17,602	14,993	16,610
Applications denied..................	132	135	136	147	150	153	160	192	193	193	226
Denied (percent)..................	_1.6_	_1.6_	_1.6_	_1.5_	_1.4_	_1.5_	_1.3_	_1.2_	_1.1_	_1.3_	_1.4_
Selected reasons for rejection: [1]											
Felony indictment/conviction......	(NA)	(NA)	(NA)	77	67	62	(NA)	82	(NA)	82	100
Other....................................	(NA)	(NA)	(NA)	70	83	91	(NA)	110	(NA)	111	126
Felony denials per 1,000 applications..............	(NA)	(NA)	(NA)	7.2	6.2	6.0	(NA)	5.2	(NA)	5.5	6.0

NA Not available. [1] Beginning in 2008, the FBI instituted a new classification system; therefore, data prior to 2008 aren't comparable to previously published estimates.

Source: U.S. Department of Justice, Bureau of Justice Statistics, _Background Checks for Firearm Transfers, 2015 Statistical Tables_, NCJ 250978, November 2017. See also <https://www.bjs.gov/index.cfm?ty=pbse&sid=13>.

Table 366. Denials of Firearm Transfer Applications by Reason and Agency Type: 2013 to 2015

[In percent. Reasons for denials are based on The Brady Handgun Violence Prevention Act, pursuant to 18 U.S.C. 922 and state laws. Denial occurs when an applicant is prohibited from receiving a firearm or a permit that can be used to receive a firearm because a disqualifying factor was found during a background check. Application for firearm transfer is information submitted by a person to a state or local checking agency to purchase a firearm or obtain a permit that can be used for a purchase. Information may be submitted directly to a checking agency or forwarded by a prospective seller. Totals were based on federal and state agencies that reported counts on reasons for denial. Reasons for denial for local agencies were estimated]

Reason for denial	2013 [1]		2014			2015		
	FBI	State	FBI	State	Local	FBI	State	Local
Felony indictment/conviction................	48.5	30.6	47.7	31.0	18.8	48.1	30.2	19.5
Felony indictment/information..............	5.6	3.5	5.5	8.7	2.7	5.3	1.6	3.1
Felony conviction.......................	42.9	27.1	42.2	22.3	16.1	42.8	28.6	16.4
Felony arrest with no disposition..............	(X)	7.7	(X)	4.4	2.5	(X)	11.9	3.2
Fugitive................................	18.2	12.9	19.1	10.8	3.2	18.7	7.0	3.9
Domestic violence......................	9.2	11.8	9.7	11.0	19.7	10.1	11.9	18.4
Misdemeanor conviction..............	6.1	6.3	6.8	6.1	15.0	7.3	6.8	14.4
Protection/restraining order...........	3.1	5.5	2.9	4.9	4.7	2.8	5.1	4.0
Drug user/addict.......................	10.4	3.7	10.4	5.3	4.6	9.6	5.2	5.0
Mental health commitment/adjudication...........	3.3	3.5	3.9	5.3	6.9	4.4	8.0	6.0
Illegal/unlawful alien..................	1.3	2.4	1.6	2.7	1.2	2.0	2.2	0.6
State law prohibition..................	8.8	23.9	7.3	25.7	19.9	6.8	20.1	25.0
Local law prohibition..................	(X)	(NA)	(X)	(NA)	2.3	(X)	(NA)	2.8
Other prohibitions [2]................	0.3	3.5	0.2	4.0	21.0	0.2	3.5	15.7

NA Not available. X Not applicable. [1] Data not available for local law prohibition; see source. [2] Includes juveniles, persons dishonorably discharged from the Armed Services, persons who have renounced their U.S. citizenship, and other unspecified persons.

Source: U.S. Department of Justice, Bureau of Justice Statistics, *Background Checks For Firearm Transfers, 2015 - Statistical Tables*, NCJ 250978, November 2017, and earlier reports. See also <https://www.bjs.gov/index.cfm?ty=pbse&sid=13>.

Table 367. Employment by State and Local Law Enforcement Agencies by Type of Agency and Employee: 2008

[As of September 30. Based on census of all state and local law enforcement agencies operating nationwide, conducted every 4 years]

Type of agency	Number of agencies	Full-time employees (number)			Part-time employees (number)		
		Total	Sworn	Civilian	Total	Sworn	Civilian
Total [1]............................	**17,985**	**1,133,905**	**765,237**	**368,668**	**100,340**	**44,062**	**56,278**
Local police..........................	12,501	593,003	461,054	131,949	58,129	27,810	30,319
Sheriffs' offices......................	3,063	353,461	182,979	170,482	26,052	11,334	14,718
Primary State.......................	50	93,148	60,772	32,376	947	54	893
Special jurisdiction..................	1,733	90,262	56,968	33,294	14,681	4,451	10,230
Constable/marshal..................	638	4,031	3,464	567	531	413	118

[1] Excludes agencies with less than one full-time officer or the equivalent in part-time officers.

Source: U.S. Bureau of Justice Statistics, *Census of State and Local Law Enforcement Agencies, 2008.* See also <https://www.bjs.gov/index.cfm?ty=pbse&sid=73>.

Table 368. State and Local Government Criminal Justice Expenditures Per Capita by State: 2017

[In dollars. Based on Census Bureau's Annual Survey of State and Local Government Finances]

State	Total justice system	Police protec-tion	Judicial and legal	Correc-tions	State	Total justice system	Police protec-tion	Judicial and legal	Correc-tions
Total....................	**743**	**354**	**147**	**242**	Missouri..................	546	290	92	164
Alabama.................	486	261	75	150	Montana.................	745	297	203	245
Alaska...................	1,255	493	326	436	Nebraska................	615	260	98	257
Arizona..................	737	355	147	235	Nevada..................	856	429	167	260
Arkansas................	500	229	73	198	New Hampshire.........	599	312	120	168
California................	1,087	487	229	371	New Jersey.............	793	392	171	230
Colorado................	717	335	140	243	New Mexico............	843	341	156	345
Connecticut.............	693	329	190	174	New York...............	1,088	529	219	340
Delaware................	942	394	210	339	North Carolina..........	595	332	78	185
District of Columbia.....	1,351	911	213	226	North Dakota...........	769	302	167	300
Florida..................	724	404	112	207	Ohio....................	665	328	157	181
Georgia.................	605	269	133	204	Oklahoma..............	557	279	93	185
Hawaii..................	725	338	227	161	Oregon.................	837	331	190	316
Idaho...................	628	271	122	235	Pennsylvania...........	746	301	156	290
Illinois..................	691	414	114	163	Rhode Island...........	785	425	151	210
Indiana.................	490	239	91	160	South Carolina.........	497	263	78	156
Iowa....................	517	260	118	139	South Dakota..........	558	241	109	208
Kansas.................	594	296	112	186	Tennessee.............	598	302	124	171
Kentucky...............	544	186	145	213	Texas..................	627	288	113	226
Louisiana...............	710	353	147	210	Utah...................	540	240	120	180
Maine...................	512	233	84	195	Vermont................	716	350	123	243
Maryland...............	922	442	162	318	Virginia................	729	298	120	310
Massachusetts.........	694	377	178	139	Washington.............	673	276	164	233
Michigan...............	624	255	120	249	West Virginia..........	558	217	147	195
Minnesota..............	694	358	136	200	Wisconsin..............	700	322	115	263
Mississippi.............	522	257	92	173	Wyoming...............	905	361	226	318

Source: U.S. Census Bureau, "2017 State and Local Government Finance Historical Datasets and Tables," <https://www.census.gov/programs-surveys/gov-finances.html>, accessed March 2020; and "Annual Estimates of the Resident Population for the United States, Regions, States, and Puerto Rico: April 1, 2010 to July 1, 2019 (NST-EST2019-01)," December 2019, <https://www.census.gov/programs-surveys/popest/data/tables.html>.

Table 369. Equal Employment Opportunity Commission (EEOC) Charges Filed by Type and Litigation: 2010 to 2019

[Number, except as noted (85.1 represents $85,100,000). For fiscal years ending in year shown. The EEOC enforces federal laws making it illegal to discriminate against a job applicant or employee for charges listed below. Most employers with at least 15 employees, labor unions, and employment agencies are covered by EEOC laws. If the EEOC does not resolve charges through conciliation or other informal methods, the Commission may pursue litigation against private sector employers, employment agencies, labor unions and, in cases alleging age discrimination or equal pay violations, against state and local governments. The number for total charges reflects the number of individual charge filings. Charge data do not sum to total because individuals often file charges claiming multiple types of discrimination. See <https://www.eeoc.gov/> for more information]

Charges and litigation	2010	2013	2014	2015	2016	2017	2018	2019
CHARGES FILED								
Total charges filed with EEOC.........	**99,922**	**93,727**	**88,778**	**89,385**	**91,503**	**84,254**	**76,418**	**72,675**
Race...	35,890	33,068	31,073	31,027	32,309	28,528	24,600	23,976
Sex..	29,029	27,687	26,027	26,396	26,934	25,605	24,655	23,532
National origin...............................	11,304	10,642	9,579	9,438	9,840	8,299	7,106	7,009
Religion..	3,790	3,721	3,549	3,502	3,825	3,436	2,859	2,725
Color...	2,780	3,146	2,756	2,833	3,102	3,240	3,166	3,415
Retaliation, all statutes....................	36,258	38,539	37,955	39,757	42,018	41,097	39,469	39,110
Retaliation, Title VII only [1].............	30,948	31,478	30,771	31,893	33,082	32,023	30,556	30,117
Age...	23,264	21,396	20,588	20,144	20,857	18,376	16,911	15,573
Disability (ADA) [2].........................	25,165	25,957	25,369	26,968	28,073	26,838	24,605	24,238
Equal Pay Act...............................	1,044	1,019	938	973	1,075	996	1,066	1,117
GINA [3].......................................	201	333	333	257	238	206	220	209
LITIGATION [4]								
Suits filed.....................................	271	148	167	174	114	201	217	157
Resolutions...................................	315	222	144	171	171	125	156	180
Monetary benefits (mil. dol.)..............	85.1	38.6	22.5	65.3	52.2	42.4	53.6	39.1

[1] Title VII of the Civil Rights Act of 1964. [2] Americans with Disabilities Act. [3] Genetic Information Non-Discrimination Act. [4] Suits filed and resolved in federal district courts.

Source: U.S. Equal Employment Opportunity Commission, "Enforcement and Litigation Statistics," <https://www.eeoc.gov/eeoc/statistics/enforcement/index.cfm>, accessed March 2020.

Table 370. Asset Forfeiture Fund—Net Deposits by State: 2017 to 2019

[In thousands of dollars (1,643,290 represents $1,643,290,000). For fiscal years ending September 30. Transactions to or from the Department of Justice Asset Forfeiture Fund (AFF), which encompasses the seizure and forfeiture of assets that represent the proceeds of or were used to facilitate federal crimes. They do not reflect total forfeiture activity for any jurisdiction. See source for more details. Minus sign indicates refunds]

State or territory	2017	2018	2019	State or territory	2017	2018	2019
Total...................	**1,643,290**	**1,379,047**	**2,227,068**	Montana....................	811	–	11
				Nebraska...................	2,757	3,951	4,432
Investment income [1]......	56,912	103,184	156,615	Nevada.....................	2,866	2,513	3,338
Alabama....................	2,583	12,256	8,019	New Hampshire..........	1,113	820	513
Alaska......................	1,181	1,260	795	New Jersey................	21,031	21,700	64,784
Arizona.....................	4,038	8,933	103,184	New Mexico..............	6,244	2,829	2,532
Arkansas...................	4,500	5,266	2,944	New York..................	306,497	157,328	305,404
California..................	395,190	437,560	283,079	North Carolina...........	22,727	30,925	16,270
Colorado...................	9,393	7,019	12,622	North Dakota.............	8	7	157
Connecticut...............	4,899	6,617	6,308	Ohio........................	17,943	42,594	16,610
Delaware...................	–	–	–	Oklahoma..................	2,429	4,258	3,384
District of Columbia.......	163,079	2,477	240,403	Oregon.....................	2,721	4,472	4,322
Florida.....................	95,600	121,747	83,486	Pennsylvania.............	15,367	25,868	24,349
Georgia....................	165,468	13,929	13,654	Rhode Island.............	502	–	–
Hawaii......................	1,772	810	–	South Carolina...........	2,623	4,088	7,092
Idaho.......................	1,982	49	–	South Dakota.............	17	58	–
Illinois.....................	41,586	25,201	58,331	Tennessee.................	4,255	12,747	5,597
Indiana.....................	4,875	7,064	5,255	Texas.......................	60,618	86,881	79,908
Iowa........................	1,177	954	500	Utah........................	2,535	2,501	2,581
Kansas.....................	2,668	9,313	7,107	Vermont....................	401	473	558
Kentucky...................	4,612	9,046	9,501	Virginia....................	12,752	22,170	664,453
Louisiana..................	6,392	5,591	2,090	Washington...............	4,888	36,107	8,749
Maine......................	216	6	–	West Virginia.............	2,447	1,717	1,590
Maryland...................	14,277	56,038	15,696	Wisconsin.................	3,052	3,785	8,727
Massachusetts............	110,510	19,922	30,519	Wyoming...................	1,012	425	–
Michigan...................	17,858	19,530	17,423	Guam.......................	1,615	353	1,413
Minnesota.................	6,103	13,209	27,274	Puerto Rico...............	5,688	7,624	5,157
Mississippi................	7,489	6,336	3,747	Virgin Islands.............	1,112	491	246
Missouri....................	24,647	27,419	15,980	Other [2]....................	-11,751	-18,373	-16,063

– Represents or rounds to zero. [1] Idle funds invested in U.S. Treasury Securities. [2] Comprised of transactions made to the AFF where a district has not been identified, where Federal reimbursements were made for services rendered, or summary estimates for financial reporting purposes where details by state were not available.

Source: U.S. Department of Justice, Asset Forfeiture Program, "Annual Reports to Congress," <https://www.justice.gov/afp>, accessed April 2020.

Table 371. Arrests by Type of Offense, Sex, and Age: 2018

[7,811.1 represents 7,811,100. For year ending December 31. Based on Uniform Crime Reporting Program. Arrests reported by 12,212 agencies with a total population of 247,752,415 as estimated by the FBI. Some persons may be arrested more than once during a year; therefore, in some cases, the data in this table could represent multiple arrests of the same person]

Offense charged	Total			Male			Female		
	Total	Under 18 years old	18 years and over	Total	Under 18 years old	18 years and over	Total	Under 18 years old	18 years and over
Total.....	**7,811.1**	**553.6**	**7,257.5**	**5,684.4**	**389.3**	**5,295.1**	**2,126.7**	**164.4**	**1,962.3**
Violent crime.....	**396.3**	**38.3**	**358.0**	**313.4**	**30.7**	**282.7**	**82.9**	**7.6**	**75.3**
Murder and nonnegligent manslaughter...	9.0	0.7	8.4	7.9	0.6	7.3	1.1	0.1	1.0
Rape [1].....	19.1	3.1	15.9	18.5	3.0	15.5	0.6	0.1	0.5
Robbery.....	67.4	13.2	54.2	57.2	11.7	45.5	10.2	1.5	8.7
Aggravated assault.....	300.7	21.2	279.5	229.8	15.4	214.4	71.0	5.9	65.1
Property crime.....	**895.0**	**100.7**	**794.2**	**564.4**	**68.4**	**496.1**	**330.6**	**32.4**	**298.2**
Burglary.....	135.9	16.9	119.0	109.3	14.8	94.5	26.7	2.2	24.5
Larceny-theft.....	682.5	71.2	611.3	396.1	43.3	352.7	286.5	27.9	258.6
Motor vehicle theft.....	69.5	11.2	58.3	53.7	9.1	44.5	15.8	2.1	13.8
Arson.....	7.1	1.4	5.7	5.5	1.1	4.3	1.6	0.2	1.4
Other assaults.....	809.1	95.1	713.9	575.4	59.9	515.5	233.7	35.2	198.5
Forgery and counterfeiting.....	38.1	0.8	37.3	25.2	0.6	24.6	12.9	0.2	12.7
Fraud.....	90.9	3.6	87.3	58.0	2.5	55.5	32.9	1.1	31.8
Embezzlement.....	11.3	0.4	10.8	5.7	0.3	5.4	5.6	0.2	5.4
Stolen property (buying, receiving, possessing).....	71.0	7.1	63.9	55.4	5.9	49.5	15.6	1.2	14.4
Vandalism.....	137.1	23.3	113.8	105.6	18.9	86.6	31.6	4.4	27.1
Weapons (carrying, possessing, etc.).....	127.6	13.0	114.6	115.7	11.6	104.1	11.9	1.4	10.5
Prostitution and commercialized vice.....	23.7	0.2	23.5	8.5	0.1	8.4	15.2	0.1	15.1
Sex offenses except rape & prostitution....	35.5	5.7	29.8	33.1	5.1	28.0	2.5	0.6	1.9
Drug abuse violations.....	1,251.9	68.6	1,183.2	942.7	51.2	891.5	309.1	17.4	291.8
Gambling.....	2.5	0.1	2.3	2.1	0.1	1.9	0.4	(Z)	0.4
Offenses against family and children.....	64.9	2.5	62.4	45.2	1.5	43.7	19.7	1.0	18.7
Driving under the influence.....	746.6	4.1	742.5	556.2	3.0	553.2	190.3	1.0	189.3
Liquor laws.....	130.9	19.9	111.0	91.0	11.5	79.5	39.9	8.4	31.5
Drunkenness.....	252.7	2.5	250.2	199.8	1.7	198.0	53.0	0.8	52.2
Disorderly conduct.....	251.2	44.1	207.1	176.9	28.2	148.7	74.3	15.9	58.4
Vagrancy.....	18.1	0.5	17.6	13.7	0.4	13.3	4.4	0.1	4.3
All other offenses (except traffic).....	2,439.5	106.1	2,333.4	1,784.4	75.7	1,708.7	655.1	30.4	624.7
Suspicion.....	0.4	(Z)	0.4	0.3	(Z)	0.3	0.1	(Z)	0.1
Curfew and loitering law violations.....	16.9	16.9	(X)	11.8	11.8	(X)	5.1	5.1	(X)

X Not applicable. Z Less than 50. [1] Data are an aggregate total of the data submitted using both the revised and legacy Uniform Crime Reporting definitions. For more information, see <https://ucr.fbi.gov/crime-in-the-u.s/2018/crime-in-the-u.s.-2018/topic-pages/rape>.

Source: U.S. Department of Justice, Federal Bureau of Investigation, "Crime in the United States 2018," <https://ucr.fbi.gov/>, accessed November 2019.

Table 372. Arrests by Offense and Race/Ethnicity: 2018

[Arrests reported by 12,212 agencies with an estimate total population of 247,752,415. See headnote, Table 371. Totals provided in this table reflect only those persons arrested by law enforcement agencies that provided race information to the UCR program]

Offense charged	Total	White	Black	Hispanic or Latino [1]	American Indian/ Alaska Native	Asian	Native Hawaiian/ other Pacific Islander
Total.....	**7,710,900**	**5,319,654**	**2,115,381**	**1,191,334**	**164,430**	**92,737**	**18,698**
Violent crime.....	**392,562**	**230,299**	**146,734**	**83,441**	**7,784**	**6,102**	**1,643**
Murder and nonnegligent manslaughter.....	8,957	3,953	4,778	1,472	105	94	27
Rape [2].....	18,776	12,794	5,376	4,090	267	289	50
Robbery.....	66,789	29,025	36,187	12,823	676	641	260
Aggravated assault.....	298,040	184,527	100,393	65,056	6,736	5,078	1,306
Property crime.....	**880,473**	**589,224**	**264,748**	**116,753**	**14,865**	**9,665**	**1,971**
Burglary.....	134,542	91,581	39,617	23,200	1,590	1,422	332
Larceny-theft.....	669,983	448,193	201,086	78,106	11,987	7,324	1,393
Motor vehicle theft.....	69,002	44,512	22,305	14,392	1,151	818	216
Arson.....	6,946	4,938	1,740	1,055	137	101	30
Other assaults.....	794,787	512,025	254,360	125,007	15,711	10,348	2,343
Forgery and counterfeiting.....	37,724	25,140	11,637	5,301	335	548	64
Fraud.....	89,610	58,572	28,387	9,636	1,419	1,088	144
Embezzlement.....	11,174	6,923	3,955	1,193	122	159	15
Stolen property (buying, receiving, possessing).....	69,874	44,179	23,661	11,278	881	819	334
Vandalism.....	134,794	91,176	38,887	21,479	2,949	1,552	230
Weapons (carrying, possessing, etc.).....	126,332	68,756	54,715	23,663	1,094	1,390	377
Prostitution and commercialized vice.....	23,502	12,928	9,109	4,379	95	1,309	61
Sex offenses except rape & prostitution.....	35,157	25,338	8,403	7,398	587	751	78
Drug abuse violations.....	1,234,178	871,295	333,113	211,692	14,148	13,345	2,277
Gambling.....	2,465	1,000	1,198	341	11	205	51
Offenses against the family and children.....	64,357	43,371	18,530	5,999	1,895	510	51
Driving under the influence.....	736,644	597,919	108,703	147,221	13,150	14,323	2,549
Liquor laws.....	128,453	100,687	18,743	15,979	6,973	1,876	174
Drunkenness.....	251,490	193,042	37,781	52,491	17,412	2,825	430
Disorderly conduct.....	248,716	158,533	78,192	24,553	9,770	1,926	295
Vagrancy.....	18,048	12,823	4,458	2,557	482	261	24
All other offenses (except traffic).....	2,413,408	1,666,825	663,086	317,928	54,410	23,550	5,537
Suspicion.....	432	237	129	15	65	1	0
Curfew and loitering law violations.....	16,720	9,362	6,852	3,030	272	184	50

[1] Persons of Hispanic origin may be of any race. [2] See footnote 1, Table 371.

Source: U.S. Department of Justice, Federal Bureau of Investigation, "Crime in the United States 2018," <https://ucr.fbi.gov/>, accessed November 2019.

Table 373. Law Enforcement Officers Killed and Assaulted: 1990 to 2018

[The statistics presented in this table are based on information collected by the staff of the FBI's Law Enforcement Officers Killed and Assaulted Program from law enforcement agencies throughout the U.S. and U.S. Territories. It contains statistics on line-of-duty felonious deaths, accidental deaths, and assaults of duly sworn local, state, tribal, and federal law enforcement officers]

Item	1990	2000	2010	2012	2013	2014	2015	2016	2017	2018
OFFICERS KILLED										
Total killed.......................	**132**	**134**	**127**	**97**	**76**	**96**	**86**	**118**	**94**	**106**
By region and area:										
Northeast..........................	13	13	11	15	7	16	9	9	9	9
Midwest.............................	20	32	24	9	8	12	11	25	20	23
South................................	68	67	61	50	46	36	48	54	51	53
West.................................	23	19	28	17	15	27	14	26	12	19
Puerto Rico......................	8	3	3	5	–	5	4	4	2	2
Island Areas.....................	–	–	–	1	–	–	–	–	–	–
Total feloniously killed...........	**65**	**51**	**55**	**49**	**27**	**51**	**41**	**66**	**46**	**55**
By type of weapon:										
Firearms..........................	56	47	54	44	26	46	38	62	42	51
Handgun........................	47	33	38	34	18	33	29	37	32	37
Rifle.............................	8	10	15	7	5	10	7	23	9	10
Shotgun.........................	1	4	1	3	3	3	1	1	1	2
Multiple firearms [1]..........	(NA)	(NA)	(NA)	–	–	–	–	1	–	–
Type of firearm unknown......	(NA)	(NA)	–	–	–	–	1	–	–	–
Firearm type not reported......	–	–	–	–	–	–	–	–	–	2
Knife/cutting instrument [2].......	3	1	–	1	–	–	–	–	1	–
Knife [2]............................	(NA)	(NA)	(NA)	1	–	–	–	–	1	–
Other cutting instrument [2].....	(NA)	(NA)	(NA)	–	–	–	–	–	–	–
Personal weapons [3]..............	2	–	–	2	–	1	–	–	–	–
Vehicle...........................	1	3	1	2	1	4	3	4	3	4
Other..............................	3	–	–	–	–	–	–	–	–	–
Total accidentally killed.........	**67**	**83**	**72**	**48**	**49**	**45**	**45**	**52**	**48**	**51**
OFFICERS ASSAULTED										
Population covered (1,000) [4].....	197,426	204,599	248,727	250,151	256,689	246,681	251,555	269,401	269,608	250,651
Number of—										
Reporting agencies...............	9,343	8,940	11,826	11,794	11,958	11,235	12,102	12,293	12,198	11,788
Officers employed................	410,131	452,531	557,884	525,217	551,893	543,331	547,398	593,097	596,604	546,247
Total assaulted.................	**72,091**	**58,398**	**56,491**	**53,867**	**50,802**	**48,988**	**50,991**	**58,011**	**60,211**	**58,866**
By type of weapon:										
Firearm............................	3,651	1,749	1,925	2,276	2,299	1,976	2,050	2,388	2,677	2,116
Knife/cutting instrument..........	1,647	1,015	918	909	901	966	921	1,107	1,083	1,163
Other dangerous weapon........	7,423	8,132	7,413	7,435	7,042	6,976	7,705	9,201	10,209	8,889
Personal weapons [1]..............	59,370	47,502	46,235	43,247	40,560	39,070	40,315	45,315	46,242	46,698

– Represents zero. NA Not available. [1] Beginning in 2011, a new option was added: "Multiple firearms used by offender(s), unable to determine which caused fatal injury." [2] Prior to 2011, the type of weapon categories "Knife" and "Other cutting instrument" were combined. [3] Includes hands, fists, feet, etc. [4] Represents the number of persons covered by reporting agencies.

Source: U.S. Department of Justice, Federal Bureau of Investigation, "Law Enforcement Officers Killed and Assaulted, 2018," and previous reports, <https://ucr.fbi.gov/>, accessed November 2019.

Table 374. Presidential Pardons and Commutations: 1961 to 2020

[For fiscal years shown. Not shown are petitions pending at the beginning of the fiscal year, or in the case of a change of administration, the number of cases pending at the time of the new President's inauguration]

Period	President	Petitions received	Petitions granted [1] Pardon	Petitions granted [1] Commutation	Petitions granted [1] Remission	Petitions denied or closed without Presidential Action
1961 to 2020 [2].........	**Total**	**82,154**	**4,500**	**2,251**	**17**	**62,383**
1961 to 1964...........	John F. Kennedy	1,749	472	100	3	831
1964 to 1969...........	Lyndon B. Johnson	4,537	960	226	1	2,830
1969 to 1975...........	Richard M. Nixon	2,591	863	60	3	2,614
1975 to 1977...........	Gerald R. Ford	1,527	382	22	5	900
1977 to 1981...........	Jimmy Carter	2,627	534	29	3	2,056
1981 to 1989...........	Ronald W. Reagan	3,404	393	13	–	2,804
1989 to 1993...........	George H.W. Bush	1,466	74	3	–	1,621
1993 to 2001...........	William J. Clinton	7,489	396	61	2	4,554
2001 to 2009...........	George W. Bush	11,074	189	11	–	11,914
2009 to 2017...........	Barack Obama	36,544	212	1,715	–	25,217
2017 to 2020 [2]........	Donald J. Trump	9,146	25	11	–	7,042

– Represents zero. [1] Petitions granted are taken from a count of clemency warrants maintained by the Office of the Pardon Attorney. Cases in which multiple forms of relief were granted are counted in only one category. Cases in which clemency was granted to a person who did not file an application with the Office of the Pardon Attorney are counted as "petitions granted" but have not been counted as "petitions pending" or "petitions received" since at least FY1990. Excludes individual members of a class of persons granted pardons by proclamation. [2] As of July 14, 2020.

Source: U.S. Department of Justice, Office of the Pardon Attorney, "Clemency Statistics," <https://www.justice.gov/pardon/clemency-statistics>, accessed September 2020.

Table 375. Forensic Services Requests and Backlog by Type of Request: 2014

[Numbers are rounded to the nearest hundred. Census of 409 laboratories, with a 88% return rate. Totals exclude requests outsourced to other laboratories. Request is classified as backlogged if it has been submitted to a crime lab, but has not yet been examined and reported to the submitting agency within 30 days. Estimates based on imputations for labs that did not report backlog data, see source for details]

Type of request	Received		Completed		Backlogged requests	
	Number	Percent	Number	Percent	Number	Percent
All requests.	**3,783,000**	**100**	**3,646,000**	**100**	**570,100**	**100**
Controlled substances	1,265,000	33	1,197,000	33	213,700	37
Crime scene	171,000	5	170,000	5	(X)	(X)
Digital evidence	25,000	1	24,000	1	7,800	1
Firearms/toolmarks	154,000	4	142,000	4	51,100	9
Forensic biology:						
Casework [1]	333,000	9	296,000	8	107,800	19
Convicted offender/arrestee samples [1]	908,000	24	904,000	25	64,800	11
Impressions	7,000	(Z)	7,000	(Z)	2,400	(Z)
Latent prints	295,000	8	301,000	8	69,400	12
Questioned documents	9,000	(Z)	9,000	(Z)	800	(Z)
Toxicology	566,000	15	554,000	15	40,000	7
Trace evidence	49,000	1	41,000	1	12,200	2

X Not applicable. Z Less than 0.5%. [1] Includes biology screening and DNA analysis.

Source: U.S. Bureau of Justice Statistics, *Publicly Funded Forensic Crime Laboratories: Resources and Services, 2014*, NCJ 250151, November 2016. See also <https://www.bjs.gov/index.cfm?ty=dcdetail&iid=244>.

Table 376. Freedom of Information Act (FOIA) Requests Received, Processed, Granted and Denied by Federal Department and Selected Agency: 2019

[For year ending September 30. Freedom of Information Act (FOIA) provides the public the right to request access to records from any executive federal agency. Agencies are required to disclose any information requested under the FOIA unless it falls under one of nine exemptions; see <https://www.foia.gov/faq.html#exemptions> for full listing. Each agency is required to file an annual report with the Department of Justice detailing their administration of the FOIA. Data are compiled from those reports]

Department or agency	Requests pending from prior year	Requests received	Requests processed	Requests pending at year end	Disposition		
					Requests granted in full	Requests granted in part	Full denials [2]
Total [1]	**199,544**	**858,952**	**877,964**	**180,532**	**221,912**	**351,481**	**304,571**
Department of Agriculture	6,593	26,458	26,094	6,957	20,903	2,863	2,328
Department of Commerce	890	2,391	2,017	1,264	437	412	1,168
Department of Defense	16,686	56,524	54,545	18,665	14,907	18,055	21,583
Department of Education	1,034	2,448	2,368	1,114	326	1,276	766
Department of Energy	666	1,855	1,883	638	483	368	1,032
Department of Health and Human Services	7,712	35,358	33,817	9,253	12,409	4,238	17,170
Department of Homeland Security	88,233	400,245	429,798	58,680	32,233	255,653	141,912
Department of Housing and Urban Development	1,052	2,140	2,018	1,174	446	489	1,083
Department of Interior	3,647	7,973	6,782	4,838	2,082	1,875	2,825
Department of Justice	26,322	95,119	88,668	32,773	37,770	10,427	40,471
Department of Labor	1,989	16,090	16,350	1,729	1,612	6,416	8,322
Department of State	11,324	8,589	6,545	13,368	138	2,459	3,948
Department of the Treasury	2,180	11,936	11,921	2,195	3,474	2,797	5,650
Department of Transportation	4,363	16,571	14,621	6,313	7,549	3,386	3,686
Department of Veterans Affairs	6,067	21,336	23,749	3,654	5,406	9,500	8,843
Board of Governors of the Federal Reserve System	34	562	561	35	318	72	171
Central Intelligence Agency	2,332	2,563	2,261	2,634	157	331	1,773
Consumer Financial Protection Bureau	169	484	435	218	82	175	178
Environmental Protection Agency	3,751	8,869	9,525	3,095	4,665	1,343	3,517
Equal Employment Opportunity Commission	3,698	17,794	19,794	1,698	763	13,977	5,054
Federal Communications Commission	62	700	703	59	81	299	323
Federal Deposit Insurance Corporation	14	345	341	18	66	46	229
Federal Housing Finance Agency	24	149	139	34	7	44	88
Federal Trade Commission	40	1,381	1,361	60	339	531	491
General Services Administration	382	1,461	1,355	488	256	576	523
National Aeronautics & Space Administration	64	812	800	76	124	190	486
National Archives & Records Administration	4,090	67,466	68,062	3,494	48,743	3,115	16,204
National Labor Relations Board	164	1,370	1,420	114	246	824	350
National Railroad Passenger Corporation (AMTRAK)	131	213	191	153	52	42	97
National Science Foundation	258	327	267	318	32	162	73
National Transportation Safety Board	899	435	761	573	120	65	576
Nuclear Regulatory Commission	232	369	510	91	106	111	293
Office of Management & Budget	520	374	293	601	34	34	225
Office of Personnel Management	259	10,495	10,493	261	7,494	2,704	295
Office of Special Counsel	130	149	183	96	14	107	62
Office of the Director of National Intelligence	549	503	464	588	40	236	188
Pension Benefit Guaranty Corporation	89	2,348	2,232	205	1,334	414	484
Securities & Exchange Commission	540	11,546	11,487	599	4,695	733	6,059
Small Business Administration	114	895	923	86	421	195	307
Social Security Administration	524	14,987	15,148	363	10,004	2,894	2,250
Tennessee Valley Authority	26	187	197	16	67	88	42
U.S. Agency for International Development	285	290	304	271	40	149	115
U.S. Consumer Product Safety Commission	374	505	316	563	46	121	149
U.S. Postal Service	194	2,972	2,960	206	477	566	1,917

[1] Includes other agencies not shown below. [2] Denials due to FOIA exemptions and other nonexemption reasons, including no records available, incorrect agency, duplicate, and not reasonably descriptive.

Source: U.S. Department of Justice, Office of Information Policy, "Annual FOIA Reports – FY 2019," <https://www.justice.gov/oip/annual-foia-reports-fy-2019>, accessed March 2020. See also <https://www.foia.gov/>

Table 377. Suspects Arrested by Drug Enforcement Administration by Type of Drug and Arrestee Characteristics: 2014

[For fiscal year ending in year shown. Data are from Drug Enforcement Administration's (DEA) Defendant Statistical System]

Arrestee characteristic	Total arrested	Percent arrested	Drug type					
			Cocaine powder	Crack cocaine	Marijuana	Metham-phetamine	Opiates	Other or non drug [2]
Total [1].................	**29,549**	**100.0**	**5,582**	**1,782**	**5,082**	**7,005**	**4,852**	**5,245**
SEX								
Male...................	23,968	81.3	4,871	1,521	4,380	5,394	3,960	3,842
Female................	5,521	18.7	695	260	695	1,595	882	1,393
RACE								
White..................	20,280	70.1	3,448	362	3,668	6,170	3,121	3,511
Black/African American...	7,799	27.0	1,947	1,394	1,080	408	1,563	1,406
American Indian/Alaska Native........	166	0.6	16	1	34	63	14	38
Asian/Pacific Islander..................	667	2.3	31	7	217	210	23	179
HISPANIC ORIGIN								
Hispanic/Latino...................	12,085	42.2	3,082	215	2,313	3,268	2,109	1,098
Non-Hispanic/Latino..................	16,549	57.8	2,309	1,501	2,639	3,572	2,582	3,946
AGE								
18 years old and under................	374	1.3	33	13	128	72	77	51
19 to 20 years old.......................	1,157	3.9	143	69	314	247	206	178
21 to 30 years old.....................	10,431	35.3	1,675	710	2,024	2,336	1,938	1,747
31 to 40 years old.....................	9,726	32.9	2,102	597	1,467	2,441	1,515	1,604
41 years old and older.................	7,861	26.6	1,629	393	1,149	1,909	1,116	1,665

[1] Details may not sum to the total number of arrestees due to missing data. [2] Includes pharmaceutical controlled substances, equipment used to manufacture controlled substances, and drug use paraphernalia.

Source: U.S. Department of Justice, Bureau of Justice Statistics, *Federal Justice Statistics 2014 - Statistical Tables*, NCJ 250183, March 2017. See also <https://www.bjs.gov/index.cfm?ty=pbse&sid=62>.

Table 378. Missing Person Reports by Selected Characteristics: 2017 to 2019

[Data shown are missing person records entered into the National Crime Information Center's (NCIC) Missing Person File during the year shown and does not include records removed (canceled, cleared, and located). The NCIC contained 87,438 active missing person records remaining in the database as of December 31, 2019; this figure includes entries from earlier years. For more information, see source]

Characteristic	2017			2018			2019		
	All ages	Under age 18	Age 18 and older	All ages	Under age 18	Age 18 and older	All ages	Under age 18	Age 18 and older
Total missing person entries............	**651,226**	**464,324**	**186,902**	**612,846**	**424,066**	**188,780**	**609,275**	**421,394**	**187,881**
By type:									
Juvenile (under age 21) [1]...	445,345	441,165	4,180	405,046	401,218	3,828	401,875	398,250	3,625
Endangered [2]................	45,967	9,518	36,449	45,673	9,482	36,191	44,840	9,580	35,260
Involuntary [3]..................	17,127	5,271	11,856	14,934	4,925	10,009	14,479	4,828	9,651
Disability [4]...................	33,896	4,978	28,918	33,014	4,770	28,244	32,058	4,988	27,070
Catastrophe [5]...............	327	85	242	379	88	291	280	59	221
Other (over age 21).........	108,564	3,307	105,257	113,800	3,583	110,217	115,743	3,689	112,054
By sex:									
Female....................	322,865	246,108	76,757	302,218	225,640	76,578	298,190	221,636	76,554
Male......................	328,270	218,143	110,127	310,517	198,327	112,190	311,008	199,701	111,307
Unknown....................	91	73	18	111	99	12	77	57	20
By race/ethnicity:									
White [6]......................	387,104	264,253	122,851	362,988	239,662	123,326	359,768	237,469	122,299
Black.......................	219,484	169,426	50,058	207,394	155,966	51,428	205,802	154,589	51,213
Asian.......................	13,177	7,479	5,698	12,994	7,060	5,934	12,671	6,700	5,971
American Indian.............	10,642	8,177	2,465	9,914	7,497	2,417	10,447	7,858	2,589
Unknown....................	20,819	14,989	5,830	19,556	13,881	5,675	20,587	14,778	5,809

[1] A person under the age of 21 who is missing and does not meet any of the entry criteria set forth in the other categories. [2] Indicating that physical safety may be in danger. [3] Disappearance may not have been voluntary, i.e. abduction or kidnapping. [4] Proven physical/mental disability or senile and subjecting themselves or others to personal and immediate danger. [5] Person missing after a catastrophe. [6] Includes Hispanic ethnicity or origin.

Source: U.S. Department of Justice, Federal Bureau of Investigation, "2019 NCIC Missing Person and Unidentified Person Statistics," and earlier releases, <https://www.fbi.gov/services/cjis/ncic>, accessed February 2020.

Table 379. Federal Prosecutions of Public Corruption by Prosecution Status: 2000 to 2018

[As of December 31. Prosecution of persons who have corrupted public office in violation of Federal Criminal Statutes]

Type of official	2000			2010			2017			2018		
	Charged	Con-victed	Await-ing trial	Charged	Con-victed	Await-ing trial	Charged	Con-victed	Await-ing trial	Charged	Con-victed	Await-ing trial
Total...................	**1,000**	**938**	**327**	**1,184**	**1,036**	**554**	**863**	**837**	**521**	**765**	**695**	**479**
Federal officials.........	441	422	92	422	397	103	383	334	169	275	250	165
State officials...........	92	91	37	168	108	105	63	68	53	85	72	59
Local officials...........	211	183	89	296	280	146	223	208	150	171	175	110
Others involved [1].......	256	242	109	298	251	200	194	227	149	234	198	145

[1] Includes individuals who are neither public officials nor employees, but were involved with public officials or employees in violating the law.

Source: U.S. Department of Justice, Criminal Division, *Report to Congress on the Activities and Operations of the Public Integrity Section for 2018*, and earlier reports. See also <http://www.justice.gov/criminal/pin/>.

Table 380. U.S. Supreme Court—Cases on Docket, Disposed of, and Remaining: 2000 to 2018

[Statutory term of court begins first Monday in October. Often the Court grants or denies cases after the Court recesses but before the next statutory term]

Action	2000	2005	2010	2013	2014	2015	2016	2017	2018
NUMBER OF CASES ON DOCKET									
Total	**8,965**	**9,608**	**9,066**	**8,580**	**8,066**	**7,535**	**7,334**	**7,390**	**7,622**
Original	9	8	4	5	6	8	7	8	9
Paid	2,305	2,025	1,895	1,869	1,845	1,839	1,850	2,062	1,910
In Forma Pauperis	6,651	7,575	7,167	6,706	6,215	5,688	5,477	5,320	5,703
CASES DISPOSED OF									
Total	**7,762**	**8,240**	**7,827**	**7,547**	**7,006**	**6,506**	**6,258**	**6,192**	**6,541**
Original	2	4	2	0	1	1	1	1	2
Paid	2,024	1,703	1,580	1,568	1,552	1,539	1,505	1,728	1,595
In Forma Pauperis	5,736	6,533	6,245	5,979	5,453	4,966	4,752	4,463	4,944
NUMBER REMAINING ON DOCKET									
Total	**1,203**	**1,368**	**1,239**	**1,033**	**1,060**	**1,029**	**1,076**	**1,198**	**1,081**
Original	7	4	2	5	5	7	6	7	7
Paid	281	322	315	301	293	300	345	334	315
In Forma Pauperis	915	1,042	922	727	762	722	725	857	759
Cases argued during term	86	90	86	79	75	82	71	69	73
Number disposed of by full opinions	83	82	83	77	75	70	68	63	69
Number disposed of by per curiam opinions	4	5	3	2	0	12	1	6	2
Number set for re-argument next term	0	3	0	0	1	0	2	0	2
Total cases granted plenary review	99	78	90	76	71	81	75	78	86
Cases reviewed and decided without oral argument	127	105	84	72	109	145	66	103	56
Total cases available for argument at start of next term	49	31	43	40	33	31	32	38	50

Source: Administrative Office of the U.S. Courts, "Judicial Business of the United States Courts, Table A-1–Supreme Court of the United States Judicial Business," September 2019, and earlier reports, <http://www.uscourts.gov/data-table-topics/us-supreme-court>. See also <http://www.supremecourt.gov/orders/journal.aspx>.

Table 381. Federal Judiciary Caseloads: 2000 to 2019

[For 12-month periods ending June 30]

Judicial caseload	2000	2010	2015	2016	2017	2018	2019
U.S. Courts of Appeals: [1]							
Cases filed	54,642	56,097	53,032	60,099	52,028	49,220	47,783
Cases terminated	56,509	59,343	53,934	56,244	56,709	50,804	47,832
Cases pending	40,815	46,816	40,913	44,739	40,040	38,481	38,432
U.S. District Courts Civil:							
Cases filed	263,049	289,630	280,037	290,430	271,721	281,202	293,520
Cases terminated	260,277	295,908	273,562	258,894	299,002	248,093	325,920
Cases pending	247,973	285,071	340,401	371,756	364,117	395,685	363,285
U.S. District Courts Criminal (includes transfers):							
Cases filed	62,523	78,213	60,866	61,021	58,121	67,257	72,926
Defendants filed	84,147	100,031	79,154	79,968	75,235	84,827	90,411
Cases terminated	57,543	77,633	61,299	60,521	57,610	61,287	66,307
Cases pending	46,796	80,506	72,094	72,041	72,454	78,869	84,687
U.S. Bankruptcy Courts:							
Cases filed	1,276,922	1,572,597	879,736	819,159	796,037	775,578	773,361
Cases terminated	1,271,300	1,441,419	1,024,504	931,085	869,448	825,364	791,523
Cases pending	1,396,916	1,659,399	1,316,672	1,194,843	1,100,309	1,050,476	1,032,306
Post-conviction supervision:							
Persons under supervision	99,577	126,642	133,428	137,882	135,947	131,036	128,649
Pretrial services:							
Total cases activated	86,067	110,666	95,538	93,220	87,517	97,144	106,019
Pretrial services cases activated	84,107	109,711	94,757	92,599	86,974	96,718	105,579
Pretrial diversion cases activated	1,960	955	781	621	543	426	440
Total released on supervision	31,607	29,748	24,429	24,027	22,960	23,474	25,392
Pretrial supervision	31,927	28,440	23,368	23,141	22,190	22,843	24,738
Diversion supervision	2,166	1,308	1,061	886	770	631	654

[1] Excludes the U.S. Court of Appeals for the Federal Circuit.

Source: Administrative Office of the United States Courts, "Statistical Tables for the Federal Judiciary," <http://www.uscourts.gov/statistics-reports/analysis-reports/statistical-tables-federal-judiciary>, accessed January 2020.

Table 382. U.S. District Courts—Civil Cases Filed by Basis of Jurisdiction and Nature of Suit: 2010 to 2019

[For 12-month periods ending June 30]

Type of case	Cases filed						
	2010	2014	2015	2016	2017	2018	2019
Total cases filed [1]................	**285,215**	**298,713**	**280,037**	**290,430**	**271,721**	**281,202**	**293,520**
BASIS OF JURISDICTION							
U.S. cases:							
U.S. plaintiff......................	8,427	6,833	6,182	5,007	5,014	4,705	4,237
U.S. defendant....................	34,306	39,926	35,651	52,943	41,677	38,235	37,135
Private cases:							
Federal question..................	137,776	149,380	151,330	149,294	149,577	149,243	151,513
Diversity of citizenship...........	104,703	102,568	86,865	83,170	75,449	89,018	100,629
Local jurisdiction.................	3	6	9	16	4	1	6
NATURE OF SUIT							
Contract actions [1].................	31,461	28,631	26,506	24,796	23,678	26,100	25,216
Insurance........................	9,236	11,728	9,923	8,894	8,774	10,374	10,749
Recovery of overpayments [2].......	3,079	2,357	2,307	1,670	1,515	1,114	1,043
Real property actions [1]............	6,809	8,454	8,963	9,147	8,202	7,018	6,966
Foreclosure......................	3,836	4,401	4,043	4,882	4,070	3,176	2,983
Tort actions........................	87,256	81,024	69,875	62,646	57,007	68,776	81,089
Personal injury...................	82,057	77,443	62,318	56,452	53,030	64,545	77,297
Personal injury product liability.............	66,958	63,245	41,607	41,019	35,340	47,335	53,456
Other personal injury [1].........	15,099	14,198	20,711	15,433	17,690	17,210	23,841
Medical malpractice...........	1,120	976	1,097	1,344	1,243	1,169	1,209
Personal property damage..........	5,199	3,581	7,557	6,194	3,977	4,231	3,792
Actions under statutes [1]............	159,683	180,604	174,693	193,841	182,834	179,308	180,249
Bankruptcy suits..................	2,615	2,708	2,688	2,492	2,141	2,132	2,233
Civil rights [1].....................	34,427	34,829	37,015	37,477	39,056	40,617	43,223
Employment....................	14,343	12,035	12,258	11,583	12,198	12,387	12,572
Environmental matters............	826	749	578	1,784	1,160	1,965	659
Prisoner petitions.................	52,450	62,402	52,844	70,863	61,031	53,626	54,445
Forfeiture and penalty.............	2,297	1,959	1,620	1,138	1,110	1,205	1,148
Labor laws.......................	18,878	18,702	19,047	19,235	17,887	17,816	16,840
Immigration......................	1,262	1,134	1,244	1,552	1,907	1,696	2,017
Protected property rights [3].......	8,519	13,195	14,145	12,415	11,060	11,845	13,185
Securities commodities and exchanges.....	1,442	1,000	1,012	1,069	1,353	1,527	1,655
Social security laws..............	13,725	19,530	19,102	18,407	18,953	19,115	17,903
Tax suits........................	1,171	969	1,005	973	993	948	773
Freedom of information............	315	432	481	516	602	859	819
Cases terminated.............	**295,909**	**260,352**	**273,562**	**258,894**	**299,002**	**248,093**	**325,920**
Cases pending.................	**285,071**	**334,261**	**340,401**	**371,756**	**364,117**	**395,685**	**363,285**

[1] Includes other types not shown separately. [2] Includes enforcement of judgments in student loan cases, and overpayments of veterans' benefits. [3] Includes copyright, patent, and trademark rights.

Source: Administrative Office of the United States Courts, "Statistical Tables for the Federal Judiciary," <http://www.uscourts.gov/statistics-reports/analysis-reports/statistical-tables-federal-judiciary>, accessed January 2020.

Table 383. U.S. District Courts—National Petit and Grand Juror Service: 2010 to 2019

[For years ending September 30. Includes data on jury selection days only. Data on juror service after the selection day are not included]

Juror service	2010	2013	2014	2015	2016	2017	2018	2019
PETIT JUROR SERVICE								
Jurors present for jury selection or orientation.............	262,376	237,251	218,203	195,206	194,211	184,019	189,504	192,595
Percent selected.................	22.7	22.2	22.4	22.6	22.5	22.8	22.0	22.0
Percent challenged..............	38.5	40.3	40.1	40.6	39.5	39.8	40.5	39.4
Percent not selected or challenged........	38.7	37.5	37.4	36.8	38.0	37.5	37.5	38.6
Voir Dire [1].....................	24.9	23.5	24.3	23.7	25.2	25.0	24.0	24.8
Non-Voir Dire [2].................	13.9	14.0	13.1	13.1	12.8	12.4	13.4	13.8
Total juries selected.............	5,332	4,656	4,278	4,149	3,887	3,708	3,660	3,718
GRAND JUROR SERVICE								
Juries serving....................	784	778	763	749	743	755	755	750
Sessions convened..............	9,277	8,531	8,230	8,087	8,249	8,124	8,258	8,369
Jurors in session................	186,020	171,038	164,856	161,493	164,733	161,759	163,859	167,210
Average per session.............	20.1	20.0	20.0	20.0	20.0	19.9	19.8	20.0
Hours in session.................	44,845	39,565	36,719	36,098	36,621	35,823	36,458	36,679
Average hours per session........	4.8	4.6	4.5	4.5	4.4	4.4	4.4	4.4
Proceedings filed by indictment:								
Cases..........................	49,654	(NA)	(NA)	(NA)	(NA)	(NA)	(NA)	(NA)
Defendants......................	70,433	64,015	55,890	56,164	55,227	55,818	63,877	70,078
Average defendants indicted per session...	7.6	7.5	6.8	6.9	6.7	6.9	7.7	8.4

NA Not available. [1] Jurors who completed pre-screening questionnaires or were in the courtroom during the conducting of voir dire. [2] Other jurors not selected or challenged who were not called to the courtroom or otherwise did not participate in the actual voir dire.

Source: Administrative Office of the United States Courts, "Judicial Business of the United States Courts 2019," <http://www.uscourts.gov/Statistics/JudicialBusiness.aspx>, accessed May 2020.

Table 384. U.S. Courts of Appeals—Nature of Suit or Offense in Cases Arising from the U.S. District Courts: 2010 to 2019

[For 12-month periods ending June 30. Excludes data for the U.S. Court of Appeals for the Federal Circuit. Includes appeals reopened, remanded, and reinstated (after being terminated due to procedural defaults) as well as original appeals]

Nature of suit and offense	2010	2014	2015	2016	2017	2018	2019
Total cases............................	**43,880**	**41,618**	**40,234**	**39,506**	**38,594**	**37,487**	**36,596**
Criminal cases.........................	12,863	11,340	10,902	11,945	10,216	9,614	9,895
Civil cases.............................	31,017	30,278	29,332	27,561	28,378	27,873	26,701
U.S cases.............................	7,772	7,668	7,471	6,586	7,609	7,660	6,778
U.S. plaintiff.........................	435	292	353	321	305	261	206
U.S. defendant......................	7,337	7,376	7,118	6,265	7,304	7,399	6,572
Private cases.........................	23,245	22,610	21,861	20,975	20,769	20,213	19,923
Federal question....................	20,599	19,012	18,821	18,005	17,918	17,423	17,133
Diversity of citizenship.............	2,646	3,598	3,040	2,969	2,851	2,790	2,789
General local jurisdiction............	–	–	–	1	–	–	1
Criminal cases.........................	12,863	11,340	10,902	11,945	10,216	9,614	9,895
Violent offenses.....................	621	563	483	477	570	512	523
Property offenses...................	1,624	1,606	1,420	1,403	1,271	1,212	1,241
Drug offenses.......................	5,066	3,766	3,843	4,844	3,578	3,207	3,371
Firearms and explosives offenses. ..	1,927	1,620	1,560	1,806	1,860	1,888	1,967
Sex offenses........................	651	733	786	736	769	762	765
Justice system offenses..............	142	138	169	129	147	134	133
Immigration offenses.................	1,787	1,473	1,491	1,342	957	897	929
General offenses.....................	411	348	289	261	253	235	279
Other [1]............................	634	1,093	861	947	811	767	687

– Represents or rounds to zero. [1] Other includes regulatory, traffic, and unclassified offenses.

Source: Administrative Office of the United States Courts, "Statistical Tables for the Federal Judiciary," <http://www.uscourts.gov/statistics-reports/analysis-reports/statistical-tables-federal-judiciary>, accessed January 2020.

Table 385. Total Incoming Caseloads in State Trial Courts by Case Category: 2018

[States reporting incomplete data or data not conforming to reporting guidelines are not shown. Represents new filings, plus reopened and reactivated cases when provided, as reported to the Court Statistics Project. Since state court caseload statistics should only be viewed in the context of each state's court structure, comparisons of the data reported here should not be made without additional information. See source for state court structures and characteristics]

State	Total	Civil [1]	Domestic relations [2]	Criminal [3]	Juvenile [4]	Traffic/other violations [5]
Alabama.....................	815,411	184,621	74,677	258,924	40,247	256,942
Alaska......................	119,479	23,427	11,438	30,871	3,416	50,327
Arizona.....................	1,948,936	319,621	88,948	522,532	13,268	1,004,567
California...................	6,418,134	950,113	361,230	1,205,325	75,854	3,825,612
Colorado....................	794,134	296,398	43,191	275,331	14,286	164,928
Connecticut.................	661,333	197,340	51,985	105,690	19,469	286,849
Delaware....................	400,059	66,425	33,112	82,777	4,918	212,827
District of Columbia.......	94,992	56,956	12,791	23,542	1,703	([6])
Florida......................	3,583,443	913,823	230,848	711,780	45,195	1,681,797
Hawaii......................	498,961	36,145	13,064	70,754	11,852	367,146
Idaho.......................	354,835	71,010	23,030	82,561	8,739	169,495
Illinois......................	2,447,778	433,326	123,031	268,939	17,726	1,604,756
Indiana.....................	1,330,852	406,088	91,059	316,627	51,811	465,267
Iowa........................	728,137	139,014	32,983	126,716	12,030	417,394
Kansas......................	763,422	152,679	33,476	46,104	14,101	517,062
Kentucky....................	885,612	234,997	65,415	314,568	37,252	233,380
Louisiana...................	1,240,574	197,936	58,698	248,113	35,339	700,488
Maine.......................	181,566	28,032	12,841	45,901	2,372	92,420
Maryland....................	1,939,883	1,040,942	101,336	255,975	12,459	529,171
Massachusetts..............	627,019	273,331	71,913	181,277	15,517	84,981
Michigan....................	3,312,477	678,999	112,759	865,874	34,287	1,620,558
Minnesota..................	1,261,590	178,685	52,913	178,771	28,508	822,713
Missouri....................	1,840,655	284,921	111,230	204,089	11,849	1,228,566
Nebraska...................	463,213	121,402	30,966	154,847	19,975	136,023
Nevada.....................	935,522	174,175	61,303	196,942	11,578	491,524
New Hampshire............	134,135	45,562	14,365	34,851	4,720	34,637
New Jersey.................	7,278,428	788,811	230,520	723,742	32,082	5,503,273
New Mexico.................	348,407	92,947	28,120	113,043	4,106	110,191
New York...................	3,134,541	1,451,855	537,155	518,618	56,251	570,662
Ohio........................	3,241,118	579,766	204,564	770,700	91,691	1,594,397
Pennsylvania...............	4,780,584	464,981	317,739	433,120	37,018	3,527,726
Rhode Island...............	176,832	51,111	10,608	31,094	5,660	78,359
Texas.......................	11,708,879	1,754,102	390,979	2,541,579	48,487	6,973,732
Utah........................	606,828	109,571	22,343	103,288	19,603	352,023
Vermont....................	118,630	17,579	17,752	15,123	2,572	65,604

[1] Includes tort, contract, real property, small claims, probate/estate, mental health, and civil appeals cases. [2] Includes divorce/dissolution, paternity, custody, support, visitation, adoption, and civil protection/restraining order cases. [3] Includes felony, misdemeanor, and appeals from limited jurisdiction courts. [4] Includes delinquency, dependency, and status offense petitions. [5] Includes non-criminal traffic violations (infractions), parking violations, and ordinance violations. [6] Data are not applicable because the reporting unit does not have jurisdiction over the case type or case category.

Source: National Center for State Courts, Court Statistics Project, DataViewer, "Statewide Incoming Caseloads," <http://www.courtstatistics.org>, accessed September 2020 ©.

Table 386. U.S. Sentencing Commission Summary—Cases Reviewed by Disposition and Primary Offense: 2019

[In numbers, except as noted. For fiscal year ending in year shown. Covers federal felony and Class A misdemeanor cases reported to the U.S. Sentencing Commission by federal courts as required under the Sentencing Reform Act. See source for details]

Characteristic	Total [1]	Immi-gration	Drug traffick-ing	Firearms	Fraud, theft, embezzle-ment	Robbery	Child porn-ography	Money launder-ing	All other
Total cases	**76,538**	**29,354**	**19,830**	**8,481**	**6,390**	**1,825**	**1,368**	**1,177**	**8,113**
CASES INVOLVING PRISON									
Total receiving prison	**70,231**	**27,991**	**19,099**	**7,994**	**4,738**	**1,800**	**1,354**	**1,040**	**6,215**
Prison only	68,138	27,715	18,458	7,700	4,384	1,727	1,325	985	5,844
Prison term ordered:									
Up to 12 months	24,869	19,835	1,252	487	1,357	36	27	152	1,723
13 to 60 months	27,136	7,730	8,088	5,048	2,566	502	404	466	2,332
61 to 120 months	9,799	144	5,599	1,736	382	601	553	198	586
Over 120 months	6,334	6	3,519	429	79	588	341	169	1,203
Prison & alternatives [2]	2,093	276	641	294	354	73	29	55	371
Mean sentence (in months) [3]	42	9	76	50	21	109	103	61	60
Median sentence (in months) [3]	18	6	60	39	12	92	84	33	12
CASES INVOLVING PROBATION PROBATION									
Total receiving probation	**5,888**	**1,361**	**729**	**487**	**1,573**	**25**	**13**	**137**	**1,563**
Probation only	4,558	1,168	521	306	1,192	17	10	89	1,255
Probation & alternatives [2]	1,330	193	208	181	381	8	3	48	308
CASES INVOLVING FINES & RESTITUTION									
Total receiving fines & restitution	[4] 12,269	278	1,371	713	4,838	1,221	590	357	2,901
Median amount (in dollars)	10,000	1,000	1,500	1,500	78,443	4,457	8,000	150,314	(NA)
Fine only	419	2	2	–	79	–	1	–	335

NA Not available. – Represents zero. [1] Details may not sum to total due to rounding. [2] Includes additional conditions of a term of community confinement, home detention, or intermittent confinement. [3] Life sentences are included in these calculations as 470 months. [4] 1,583 cases are excluded due to missing information.

Source: U.S. Sentencing Commission, "2019 Sourcebook of Federal Sentencing Statistics," <https://www.ussc.gov/research/sourcebook-2019>, accessed June 2020.

Table 387. Mandatory Minimum Sentencing Summary: 2015 to 2019

[For fiscal year ending in year shown for cases reported to the U.S. Sentencing Commission (USSC). Relief from mandatory minimum sentencing may be provided through a safety valve provision and/or by providing the government with substantial assistance; see source]

Item	2015	2016	2017	2018	2019
Cases reported to USSC (number)	71,003	67,742	66,873	69,425	76,538
Cases involving a mandatory minimum penalty (number)	14,138	13,604	13,577	16,228	18,819
Percent subject to mandatory minimum penalties	22.2	21.9	21.8	24.7	26.1
Percent receiving relief	39.2	38.7	37.3	40.6	44.3
Percent not receiving relief	60.8	61.3	62.7	59.4	55.7
Percent remaining subject to mandatory minimum at sentencing	13.5	13.4	13.7	14.2	14.1
Offenders convicted of an offence carrying a mandatory minimum sentence by race/ethnicity (percent distribution):					
White	27.2	27.2	26.9	27.3	27.6
Black	28.9	29.7	29.5	27.4	27.6
Hispanic	41.5	40.4	41.0	42.7	41.8
Other	2.4	2.7	2.6	2.6	3.0

Source: U.S. Sentencing Commission, *Quick Facts: Mandatory Minimum Penalties*, May 2020 and earlier reports. See also <https://www.ussc.gov/research/quick-facts>.

Table 388. Delinquency Cases Disposed by Juvenile Courts by Type of Offense: 1990 to 2018

[In thousands (1,304 represents 1,304,000), except rate. A delinquency offense is an act committed by a juvenile for which an adult could be prosecuted in a criminal court. Disposition of a case involves taking a definite action such as waiving the case to criminal court, dismissing the case, placing the youth on probation, placing the youth in a facility for delinquents, or actions such as fines, restitution, and community service. Data are developed and maintained by the National Center for Juvenile Justice]

Type of offense	1990	1995	2000	2005	2010	2012	2013	2014	2015	2016	2017	2018
All delinquency offenses......	**1,304**	**1,800**	**1,693**	**1,648**	**1,324**	**1,108**	**1,000**	**933**	**868**	**819**	**787**	**745**
Case rate [1].........	50.8	62.7	55.0	51.3	42.0	35.4	32.0	29.6	27.5	25.9	24.9	23.5
Person offenses [2].........	251	405	398	430	336	285	261	249	242	235	232	232
Criminal homicide.........	2	3	1	1	1	1	1	1	1	1	1	1
Rape.........	6	9	9	11	9	8	8	8	8	8	8	8
Robbery.........	25	37	22	26	25	20	20	19	18	19	20	19
Aggravated assault.........	44	63	48	48	34	27	24	24	25	25	26	26
Simple assault.........	135	233	257	278	220	189	173	164	159	153	147	147
Property offenses [2].........	767	909	703	606	490	398	347	322	297	273	257	226
Burglary.........	144	147	117	100	85	71	60	56	52	52	51	43
Larceny-theft.........	344	437	329	272	240	198	174	161	144	124	109	96
Motor vehicle theft.........	65	53	36	33	16	12	11	12	13	15	17	15
Arson.........	6	10	8	7	5	4	4	3	3	3	2	2
Drug law violations.........	68	164	184	183	160	145	134	124	111	105	105	101
Public order offenses [2].........	218	322	408	430	339	280	259	237	219	206	194	185
Obstruction of justice.........	85	131	206	193	161	135	126	118	110	104	98	91
Disorderly conduct.........	55	90	102	130	99	81	73	64	58	55	50	48
Weapons offenses.........	29	46	34	42	30	23	23	20	19	18	17	16
Liquor law violations.........	13	11	16	15	13	8	7	6	6	5	5	4
Nonviolent sex offenses.........	10	8	13	12	11	10	10	10	11	11	11	11

[1] Number of cases disposed per 1,000 juveniles ages 10 to upper age of juvenile court jurisdiction. The upper age of juvenile court jurisdiction is defined by statute in each state. [2] Total includes other offenses not shown.

Source: U.S. Department of Justice, Office of Juvenile Justice and Delinquency Prevention, "Delinquency Case Rates by Offense, Sex, and Race (1985-2018)," <https://www.ojjdp.gov/ojstatbb/court/data.html>; and "Easy Access to Juvenile Court Statistics, Detailed Offenses," <https://ojjdp.gov/ojstatbb/ezajcs/>; accessed May 2020.

Table 389. Delinquency Cases Disposed by Juvenile Courts by Type of Offense, Sex, and Race: 2005 to 2018

[See headnote, Table 388. Data are developed and maintained by the National Center for Juvenile Justice]

Item	Number of cases disposed				Case rate [1]			
	2005	2010	2017	2018	2005	2010	2017	2018
Male, total.........	**1,193,778**	**954,338**	**574,762**	**541,662**	**72.5**	**59.1**	**35.6**	**33.5**
Person.........	301,132	232,823	161,471	162,268	18.3	14.4	10.0	10.0
Property.........	438,440	344,739	194,555	169,581	26.6	21.4	12.0	10.5
Drugs.........	145,916	131,222	79,008	75,774	8.9	8.1	4.9	4.7
Public order.........	308,290	245,554	139,728	134,039	18.7	15.2	8.6	8.3
Female, total.........	**454,052**	**369,344**	**212,404**	**202,790**	**29.0**	**24.0**	**13.7**	**13.1**
Person.........	128,582	102,687	70,311	70,113	8.2	6.7	4.5	4.5
Property.........	167,630	145,080	62,585	56,354	10.7	9.4	4.0	3.6
Drugs.........	36,575	28,659	25,583	25,213	2.3	1.9	1.7	1.6
Public order.........	121,266	92,919	53,925	51,110	7.8	6.1	3.5	3.3
White, total [2].........	**792,413**	**595,998**	**345,696**	**326,939**	**40.9**	**33.1**	**20.2**	**19.3**
Person.........	189,396	140,911	94,540	96,062	9.8	7.8	5.5	5.7
Property.........	317,916	231,504	110,794	96,454	16.4	12.9	6.5	5.7
Drugs.........	103,309	88,646	58,612	55,588	5.3	4.9	3.4	3.3
Public order.........	181,793	134,938	81,749	78,835	9.4	7.5	4.8	4.7
Black, total [2].........	**547,266**	**443,576**	**275,405**	**258,531**	**108.6**	**92.8**	**59.3**	**55.5**
Person.........	172,873	134,257	90,955	88,777	34.3	28.1	19.6	19.1
Property.........	177,013	155,044	96,229	85,228	35.1	32.4	20.7	18.3
Drugs.........	43,478	32,625	19,120	18,735	8.6	6.8	4.1	4.0
Public order.........	153,902	121,649	69,101	65,792	30.5	25.4	14.9	14.1
Hispanic, total.........	**262,140**	**247,542**	**144,034**	**137,198**	**45.4**	**37.5**	**19.3**	**18.0**
Person.........	57,198	52,448	40,677	41,148	9.9	8.0	5.5	5.4
Property.........	91,477	87,912	41,887	37,068	15.8	13.3	5.6	4.9
Drugs.........	31,013	34,122	23,310	23,197	5.4	5.2	3.1	3.1
Public order.........	82,452	73,060	38,160	35,786	14.3	11.1	5.1	4.7
American Indian, total [3].........	**23,788**	**19,428**	**13,476**	**13,517**	**44.5**	**33.7**	**22.8**	**22.8**
Person.........	5,516	4,495	3,506	4,092	10.3	7.8	5.9	6.9
Property.........	9,712	7,577	5,045	4,455	18.2	13.1	8.6	7.5
Drugs.........	2,790	2,590	2,325	2,258	5.2	4.5	3.9	3.8
Public order.........	5,771	4,766	2,601	2,713	10.8	8.3	4.4	4.6
Asian/Native Hawaiian/Pacific Islander, total [2].........	**22,223**	**17,139**	**8,555**	**8,266**	**15.9**	**11.0**	**4.6**	**4.4**
Person.........	4,732	3,400	2,103	2,303	3.4	2.2	1.1	1.2
Property.........	9,952	7,782	3,185	2,729	7.1	5.0	1.7	1.5
Drugs.........	1,901	1,898	1,225	1,210	1.4	1.2	0.7	0.6
Public order.........	5,638	4,060	2,042	2,023	4.0	2.6	1.1	1.1

[1] Cases per 1,000 juveniles ages 10 to upper age of juvenile court jurisdiction. The upper age of juvenile court jurisdiction is defined by statute in each state. [2] Non-Hispanic. [3] Data do not always allow for identification of Hispanic ethnicity for cases involving American Indian youth. The American Indian group includes an unknown proportion of Hispanic youth.

Source: U.S. Department of Justice, Office of Juvenile Justice and Delinquency Prevention, "Delinquency Case Rates by Offense, Sex, and Race (1985-2018)," <http://www.ojjdp.gov/ojstatbb/court/data.html>; and "Easy Access to Juvenile Court Statistics, Analyze Delinquency Cases," <http://ojjdp.gov/ojstatbb/ezajcs/>; accessed May 2020.

Table 390. Child Victims of Abuse and Neglect—Total and First-Time Victims by State: 2017 and 2018

[For fiscal years ending in year shown. Data are unique counts, which count a child once, regardless of the number of reports concerning that child. Based on available State submissions to National Child Abuse and Neglect Data System (NCANDS) of alleged child abuse and neglect. States reporting 95 percent or more first-time victims are excluded due to potential issues with data quality. NCANDS collects case level data on children who received child protective services response in the form of an investigative or alternative response. Each state has its own definition of child abuse and neglect based on standards set by federal law. Child abuse is defined as any recent act or failure to act on the part of a parent or caretaker which results in death, serious physical or emotional harm, sexual abuse or exploitation; or an act or failure to act which presents an imminent risk or serious harm. See source for details]

State	2017		First-time victims		2018		First-time victims	
	Total child population	Victims	Number	Rate per 1,000 children	Total child population	Victims	Number	Rate per 1,000 children
Total................	74,234,537	673,756	470,444	6.8	73,993,353	677,529	469,126	6.8
Alabama...............	1,095,235	10,847	8,930	8.2	1,089,840	12,158	10,043	9.2
Alaska................	185,608	2,783	1,884	10.2	183,816	2,615	1,751	9.5
Arizona...............	1,639,058	9,909	7,780	4.7	1,642,657	15,504	12,469	7.6
Arkansas..............	705,584	9,334	7,790	11.0	703,180	8,538	7,115	10.1
California.............	9,044,860	65,342	55,585	6.1	8,989,955	63,795	50,619	5.6
Colorado..............	1,263,879	11,578	8,549	6.8	1,265,235	11,879	8,687	6.9
Connecticut...........	743,234	8,442	6,013	8.1	735,193	7,652	5,369	7.3
Delaware..............	203,576	1,542	1,255	6.2	203,616	1,251	993	4.9
District of Columbia.....	125,072	1,639	1,202	9.6	127,494	1,699	1,169	9.2
Florida................	4,201,122	40,103	18,773	4.5	4,229,081	36,795	16,937	4.0
Georgia...............	2,510,274	10,319	8,085	3.2	2,505,751	11,090	9,131	3.6
Hawaii................	305,575	1,280	1,105	3.6	303,414	1,265	1,042	3.4
Idaho.................	443,445	1,832	1,536	3.5	446,972	1,919	1,618	3.6
Illinois................	2,895,382	28,751	19,802	6.8	2,857,266	31,515	21,524	7.5
Indiana...............	1,572,675	29,198	21,064	13.4	1,568,130	25,731	18,458	11.8
Iowa..................	732,009	10,643	7,633	10.4	730,767	11,764	8,263	11.3
Kansas...............	712,035	4,153	3,782	5.3	705,961	3,188	2,824	4.0
Kentucky.............	1,011,179	22,410	15,230	15.1	1,008,829	23,752	15,886	15.7
Louisiana.............	1,106,369	10,356	7,920	7.2	1,095,916	9,380	7,155	6.5
Maine................	252,696	3,475	2,346	9.3	250,404	3,481	2,332	9.3
Maryland..............	1,343,582	7,578	5,565	4.1	1,340,148	7,743	5,661	4.2
Massachusetts..........	1,373,071	24,955	13,474	9.8	1,366,858	25,812	14,084	10.3
Michigan..............	2,181,147	38,062	25,874	11.9	2,164,668	37,703	25,185	11.6
Minnesota.............	1,298,811	8,709	7,310	5.6	1,302,615	7,785	6,448	5.0
Mississippi............	714,357	10,429	9,315	13.0	706,141	10,002	8,886	12.6
Missouri..............	1,382,519	4,585	3,972	2.9	1,376,830	5,662	4,867	3.5
Montana..............	229,243	3,534	2,926	12.8	229,434	3,763	3,093	13.5
Nebraska.............	475,750	3,246	2,421	5.1	476,841	2,635	1,977	4.1
Nevada...............	681,303	4,859	3,085	4.5	688,997	5,162	3,280	4.8
New Hampshire........	260,450	1,151	989	3.8	258,170	1,331	1,132	4.4
New Jersey............	1,962,020	6,614	5,138	2.6	1,953,643	6,008	4,718	2.4
New Mexico............	488,380	8,577	6,191	12.7	482,153	8,024	5,728	11.9
New York..............	4,109,166	71,226	43,061	10.5	4,068,102	68,785	41,116	10.1
North Carolina..........	2,299,976	7,392	5,955	2.6	2,300,645	6,502	5,328	2.3
North Dakota...........	176,374	1,981	1,432	8.1	178,698	2,097	1,552	8.7
Ohio..................	2,607,591	24,897	18,050	6.9	2,593,325	25,158	18,351	7.1
Oklahoma.............	959,232	14,457	11,254	11.7	956,486	15,355	12,073	12.6
Oregon...............	873,798	11,013	7,178	8.2	873,567	12,581	8,343	9.6
Pennsylvania...........	2,663,231	4,625	(NA)	(NA)	2,648,911	4,695	(NA)	(NA)
Rhode Island...........	206,899	3,095	2,168	10.5	205,213	3,644	2,496	12.2
South Carolina..........	1,103,430	17,071	12,974	11.8	1,105,945	19,130	13,969	12.6
South Dakota...........	216,151	1,339	1,045	4.8	217,606	1,426	1,080	5.0
Tennessee.............	1,506,198	9,354	4,509	3.0	1,506,220	9,186	4,770	3.2
Texas.................	7,365,879	61,506	49,535	6.7	7,398,099	63,271	51,063	6.9
Utah.................	927,441	9,947	7,227	7.8	932,462	10,122	6,984	7.5
Vermont...............	116,981	878	751	6.4	115,973	958	792	6.8
Virginia...............	1,870,958	6,277	(NA)	(NA)	1,869,792	6,132	(NA)	(NA)
Washington............	1,651,822	4,386	2,054	1.2	1,663,285	4,498	2,074	1.2
West Virginia...........	369,122	6,496	5,743	15.6	364,160	6,946	5,563	15.3
Wisconsin.............	1,283,019	4,902	4,185	3.3	1,276,103	5,017	4,272	3.3
Wyoming..............	136,247	950	799	5.9	134,775	1,044	856	6.4

NA Not available.

Source: U.S. Department of Health and Human Services, Administration for Children and Families, Statistics and Research, *Child Maltreatment 2018*, January 2020. See also <http://www.acf.hhs.gov/programs/cb/research-data-technology/statistics-research/child-maltreatment>.

Table 391. Child Abuse and Neglect Victims by Type of Maltreatment and Age and Sex of Victim: 2010 to 2018

[For fiscal years ending in year shown. Data are unique counts, which count a child once, regardless of the number of reports concerning that child. Based on available State submissions to National Child Abuse and Neglect Data System (NCANDS) of alleged child abuse and neglect. NCANDS collects case level data on children who received child protective services response in the form of an investigative or alternative response. Each state has its own definition of child abuse and neglect based on standards set by federal law. Child abuse is defined as any recent act or failure to act on the part of a parent or caretaker which results in death, serious physical or emotional harm, sexual abuse or exploitation; or an act or failure to act which presents an imminent risk or serious harm]

Item	2010	2013	2014	2015	2016	2017	2018
Victims, total [1]	688,251	678,932	702,208	683,487	671,622	673,830	677,529
SEX OF VICTIM							
Male	333,864	330,914	343,684	332,464	326,707	327,373	328,281
Female	352,174	345,633	355,928	348,087	342,203	343,949	346,957
Unknown	2,213	2,385	2,596	2,936	2,712	2,508	2,291
AGE OF VICTIM							
1 year and younger	136,910	139,360	146,300	144,354	145,976	147,300	149,828
2 to 5 years old	180,271	179,949	180,654	172,337	166,930	166,392	165,016
6 to 9 years old	145,354	147,888	156,232	153,019	149,514	146,435	143,389
10 to 13 years old	119,555	115,125	119,253	115,153	113,788	116,980	122,299
14 to 17 years old	103,764	93,459	96,428	95,134	92,921	93,955	94,361
18 years old and over [2]	490	(NA)	(NA)	(NA)	(NA)	(NA)	(NA)
Unknown [3]	979	3,151	3,341	3,490	2,493	2,768	2,636
TYPES OF MALTREATMENT [4,5]							
Neglect	499,691	539,576	526,744	514,500	502,615	504,545	411,969
Physical abuse	118,502	122,159	119,517	117,772	122,067	123,065	72,814
Sexual abuse	62,057	60,956	58,105	57,286	57,329	58,114	47,124
Psychological or emotional	53,426	59,236	42,290	42,549	37,859	38,635	15,605
Medical neglect	15,711	15,450	15,645	15,169	14,028	15,160	5,720
Sex trafficking	(NA)	(NA)	(NA)	(NA)	(NA)	(NA)	339
Multiple maltreatment types	(NA)	(NA)	(NA)	(NA)	(NA)	(NA)	105,322
Other and unknown	68,590	68,266	48,256	47,514	46,394	47,747	18,636

NA Not available. [1] Total victims is the sum for states contributing data to the Child File. The number of states not contributing data varies by year. [2] Beginning in 2011, data included in unknown. [3] Includes unborn, unknown age, and, beginning 2011, victims age 18–21. [4] Data for 2010-2017 are counts of the number of distinct victims of the specified types of maltreatment. A child may be a victim of more than one type of maltreatment; therefore, the sum of types is greater than the count of victims. Beginning 2018, if a victim is reported with two or more maltreatment types, the victim is counted in the multiple maltreatment category once. [5] Not all states use this taxonomy, nor do states define the categories in the same way.

Source: U.S. Department of Health and Human Services, Administration for Children and Families, Statistics and Research, *Child Maltreatment 2018*, January 2020; and earlier editions and unpublished data. See also <http://www.acf.hhs.gov/programs/cb/research-data-technology/statistics-research/child-maltreatment>.

Table 392. Prisoners Under Jurisdiction of Federal or State Correctional Authorities—Summary by State: 2000 to 2018

[For years ending December 31. Jurisdiction refers to the legal authority over a prisoner, regardless of where held. Occasionally, states do not submit data in a given year and estimates are imputed; see source for details]

State	2000	2010	2015	2017	2018	State	2000	2010	2015	2017	2018
U.S.	1,394,231	1,613,803	1,526,603	1,489,189	1,465,158	MS	20,241	21,067	18,911	19,103	19,275
Federal [1]	145,416	209,771	196,455	183,058	179,898	MO	27,543	30,623	32,330	32,601	30,369
State [2]	1,248,815	1,404,032	1,330,148	1,306,131	1,285,260	MT	3,105	3,716	3,685	3,698	3,765
AL	26,406	31,764	30,810	27,608	26,841	NE	3,895	4,587	5,372	5,313	5,491
AK [3]	4,173	5,391	5,338	4,399	4,380	NV	10,063	12,653	13,071	13,721	13,641
AZ	26,510	40,209	42,719	42,030	42,005	NH	2,257	2,761	2,897	2,750	2,745
AR	11,915	16,204	17,707	18,070	17,799	NJ	29,784	25,007	20,489	19,585	19,362
CA	163,001	165,062	129,593	131,039	128,625	NM	5,342	6,763	7,104	7,276	7,030
CO	16,833	22,815	20,041	19,946	20,372	NY	70,199	56,656	51,727	49,461	46,636
CT [3]	18,355	19,321	15,816	14,040	13,681	NC	31,266	40,382	36,617	36,394	34,899
DE [3]	6,921	6,615	6,654	6,443	6,067	ND	1,076	1,487	1,795	1,723	1,695
DC [4]	10,352	(NA)	(NA)	(NA)	(NA)	OH	45,833	51,712	52,233	51,478	50,431
FL	71,319	104,306	101,424	98,504	97,538	OK [5]	23,181	26,252	28,547	28,143	27,709
GA	44,232	56,432	52,193	53,667	53,647	OR	10,580	14,876	15,245	15,218	15,268
HI [3]	5,053	5,912	5,879	5,630	5,375	PA	36,847	51,264	49,858	48,333	47,239
ID	5,535	7,431	8,052	8,579	8,664	RI [3]	3,286	3,357	3,248	2,861	2,767
IL	45,281	48,418	46,240	41,427	39,965	SC	21,778	23,578	20,929	19,906	19,033
IN	20,125	28,028	27,355	26,024	26,877	SD	2,616	3,434	3,564	3,970	3,948
IA	7,955	9,455	8,849	9,024	9,419	TN	22,166	27,451	28,172	28,980	26,321
KS	8,344	9,051	9,857	10,015	10,218	TX	166,719	173,649	163,909	162,523	163,628
KY	14,919	20,544	21,701	23,543	23,431	UT [6]	5,637	6,807	6,495	6,219	6,648
LA	35,207	39,445	36,377	33,739	32,397	VT [3]	1,697	2,079	1,750	1,546	1,659
ME	1,679	2,154	2,279	2,404	2,425	VA	30,168	37,638	38,403	37,158	36,660
MD	23,538	22,645	20,764	19,367	18,856	WA	14,915	18,235	18,284	19,656	19,523
MA	10,722	11,313	9,922	9,133	8,692	WV	3,856	6,681	7,118	7,092	6,775
MI	47,718	44,165	42,628	39,666	38,761	WI	20,754	22,729	22,975	23,945	24,064
MN	6,238	9,796	10,798	10,708	10,101	WY	1,680	2,112	2,424	2,473	2,543

NA Not available. [1] Includes inmates held in nonsecure privately operated community corrections facilities and juveniles held in contract facilities. [2] Total and state estimates for 2018 include imputed counts for NH and OR, which did not submit data. Total and state estimates for 2017 include imputed data for NM and ND, which did not submit 2017 NPS data. See Methodology. [3] Data include both total jail and prison population. Prisons and jails form one integrated system. [4] As of December 31, 2001, sentenced felons from the District of Columbia are the responsibility of the Federal Bureau of Prisons. [5] 2016-2018 counts includes persons who were waiting in county jails to be moved to state prison. [6] Data for 2018 are not comparable to data for previous years. Total counts of the prisoner population from 2018 include an undetermined number of offenders excluded from counts in 2017 due to a change in legal-status requirements for a program for parole violators that was instituted in 2018.

Source: U.S. Department of Justice, Bureau of Justice Statistics, *Prisoners in 2018*, NCJ 253516, April 2020; and "Corrections Statistical Analysis Tool," <bjs.gov/index.cfm?ty=nps>, accessed June 2020.

Table 393. Jail Inmates by Sex, Race, and Hispanic Origin: 2010 to 2018

[Based on the number of inmates on the last weekday in June, except as noted. Data adjusted for nonresponse and rounded to the nearest 100. See source for methodology. Does not include offenders supervised outside of jail facilities. Based on the Annual Survey of Jails]

Characteristic	2010	2012	2013	2014	2015 [1]	2016 [1]	2017	2018
Total inmates................	748,700	744,500	731,200	744,600	727,400	740,700	745,200	738,400
Incarceration rate per 100,000 U.S. residents..................	242	237	231	233	226	229	229	226
Adults.....................................	741,200	739,100	726,600	740,400	723,800	736,800	741,600	735,000
Male...................................	649,300	640,900	624,700	631,600	620,300	629,700	628,200	620,500
Female...............................	91,900	98,100	101,900	108,800	103,500	107,100	113,400	114,500
Juveniles [2]............................	7,600	5,400	4,600	4,200	3,600	3,900	3,600	3,400
Held as adult [3]......................	5,600	4,600	3,500	3,700	3,200	3,200	3,200	2,700
Held as juvenile..................	1,900	900	1,100	500	400	700	300	700
White, non-Hispanic..................	331,600	341,100	344,900	352,800	351,600	356,100	370,100	368,500
Black, non-Hispanic..................	283,200	274,600	261,500	263,800	255,200	254,600	250,100	242,300
Hispanic/Latino [4]......................	118,100	112,700	107,900	110,600	103,900	112,700	108,400	109,300
American Indian or Alaska Native non-Hispanic...........	9,900	9,300	10,200	10,400	9,000	9,000	8,800	9,700
Asian or Pacific Islander.................	4,400	4,700	4,500	5,400	5,200	5,200	4,800	4,800
Other [5]..................................	1,500	2,200	2,200	1,700	2,500	2,900	2,900	3,900
Rated capacity [6].....................	857,900	877,400	872,900	890,500	901,400	915,400	915,100	907,000

[1] In 2015 and 2016, the Annual Survey of Jails collected demographic data on the inmate population at year-end instead of midyear. Jails typically hold fewer inmates at year-end than at midyear. The inmate populations were adjusted for seasonal variation and represent estimated midyear counts, see source for Methodology. [2] Juveniles age 17 or younger at midyear. [3] Includes juveniles who were tried or awaiting trial as adults. [4] Persons of Hispanic origin may be of any race. [5] Includes Native Hawaiians, Other Pacific Islanders, and persons of two or more races. [6] Maximum number of beds or inmates assigned by a rating official to a facility, excluding separate temporary holding areas.

Source: U.S. Department of Justice, Bureau of Justice Statistics, *Jail Inmates 2018*, NCJ 253044, March 2020. See also <https://www.bjs.gov/index.cfm?ty=pbse&sid=38>.

Table 394. Prisoners Under Federal and State Jurisdiction by Sex, Race, and Hispanic Origin: 1980 to 2018

[As of December 31. Represents prisoners sentenced to more than one year under jurisdiction of federal or state authorities rather than those in the custody of such authorities. Federal prisoners includes inmates held in nonsecure privately operated community corrections facilities and juveniles held in contract facilities. From the National Prisoner Statistics Program. See source for methodology]

Year	Total [1]		Sex		Race/ethnicity			Jurisdiction	
	Number [1]	Rate [2]	Male	Female	White [3,4]	Black [3,4]	Hispanic [3]	Federal	State
1980..........	315,974	139	303,643	12,331	(NA)	(NA)	(NA)	20,611	295,363
1981..........	353,673	154	339,375	14,298	(NA)	(NA)	(NA)	22,169	331,504
1982..........	395,516	171	379,075	16,441	(NA)	(NA)	(NA)	23,652	371,864
1983..........	419,346	179	401,870	17,476	(NA)	(NA)	(NA)	26,331	393,015
1984..........	443,398	188	424,193	19,205	(NA)	(NA)	(NA)	27,602	415,796
1985..........	480,568	202	459,223	21,345	(NA)	(NA)	(NA)	32,695	447,873
1986..........	522,084	217	497,540	24,544	(NA)	(NA)	(NA)	36,531	485,553
1987..........	560,812	231	533,990	26,822	(NA)	(NA)	(NA)	39,523	521,289
1988..........	603,732	247	573,587	30,145	(NA)	(NA)	(NA)	42,738	560,994
1989..........	680,907	276	643,643	37,264	(NA)	(NA)	(NA)	47,168	633,739
1990..........	739,980	297	699,416	40,564	(NA)	(NA)	(NA)	50,403	689,577
1991..........	789,610	313	745,808	43,802	(NA)	(NA)	(NA)	56,696	732,914
1992..........	846,277	332	799,776	46,501	(NA)	(NA)	(NA)	65,706	780,571
1993..........	932,074	359	878,037	54,037	(NA)	(NA)	(NA)	74,399	857,675
1994..........	1,016,691	389	956,566	60,125	(NA)	(NA)	(NA)	79,795	936,896
1995..........	1,085,022	411	1,021,059	63,963	(NA)	(NA)	(NA)	83,663	1,001,359
1996..........	1,137,722	427	1,068,123	69,599	(NA)	(NA)	(NA)	88,815	1,048,907
1997..........	1,195,498	445	1,121,663	73,835	(NA)	(NA)	(NA)	94,987	1,100,511
1998..........	1,245,402	461	1,167,802	77,600	(NA)	(NA)	(NA)	103,682	1,141,720
1999..........	1,304,074	476	1,221,611	82,463	(NA)	(NA)	(NA)	114,275	1,189,799
2000..........	1,334,174	[7] 470	1,249,130	85,044	(NA)	(NA)	(NA)	125,044	1,209,130
2001..........	1,345,217	470	1,260,033	85,184	(NA)	(NA)	(NA)	136,509	1,208,708
2002..........	1,380,516	477	1,291,450	89,066	(NA)	(NA)	(NA)	143,040	1,237,476
2003..........	1,408,361	483	1,315,790	92,571	(NA)	(NA)	(NA)	151,919	1,256,442
2004..........	1,433,728	487	1,337,730	95,998	(NA)	(NA)	(NA)	159,137	1,274,591
2005..........	1,462,866	492	1,364,178	98,688	(NA)	(NA)	(NA)	166,173	1,296,693
2006..........	1,504,598	501	1,401,261	103,337	507,100	590,300	313,600	173,533	1,331,065
2007..........	1,532,851	506	1,427,088	105,763	499,800	592,900	330,400	179,204	1,353,647
2008..........	1,547,742	506	1,441,384	106,358	499,900	592,800	329,800	182,333	1,365,409
2009..........	1,553,574	504	1,448,239	105,335	490,000	584,800	341,200	187,886	1,365,688
2010..........	1,552,669	500	1,447,766	104,903	484,400	572,700	345,800	190,641	1,362,028
2011..........	1,538,847	492	1,435,141	103,706	474,300	557,100	347,800	197,050	1,341,797
2012..........	1,512,430	480	1,411,076	101,354	466,600	537,800	340,300	196,574	1,315,856
2013..........	1,520,403	479	1,416,102	104,301	463,900	529,900	341,200	195,098	1,325,305
2014..........	1,507,781	472	1,401,685	106,096	461,500	518,700	338,900	191,374	1,316,407
2015..........	1,476,847	459	1,371,879	104,968	450,200	499,400	333,200	178,688	1,298,159
2016 [5].......	1,459,948	450	1,354,109	105,839	440,200	487,300	339,600	171,482	1,288,466
2017 [6].......	1,439,877	441	1,334,828	105,049	436,500	475,900	336,500	166,203	1,273,674
2018 [8]........	1,414,162	431	1,309,925	104,237	430,500	465,200	330,200	163,653	1,250,509

NA Not available. [1] Includes prisoners under the legal authority of state or federal correctional officials. [2] Rate per 100,000 estimated population. Based on U.S. Census Bureau estimated resident population. [3] Rounded to the nearest 100. [4] Excludes persons of Hispanic or Latino origin and persons of two or more races. [5] Total and state estimates include imputed counts for North Dakota, which did not submit data. [6] Total and state estimates include imputed counts for New Mexico and North Dakota, which did not submit 2017 NPS data. [7] Decrease in incarceration rate from 1999 to 2000 due to use of new Census numbers. [8] Total and state counts include imputed counts for New Hampshire and Oregon, which did not submit 2018 NPS data.

Source: U.S. Department of Justice, Bureau of Justice Statistics, *Prisoners in 2018*, NCJ 253516, April 2020, and earlier reports. See also <https://www.bjs.gov/index.cfm?ty=pbse&sid=40>.

Table 395. Prisoners Executed Under Civil Authority by State: 1977 to 2017

[Alaska, Connecticut, District of Columbia, Hawaii, Illinois, Iowa, Maine, Maryland, Massachusetts, Michigan, Minnesota, New Jersey, North Dakota, Rhode Island, Vermont, West Virginia, and Wisconsin are jurisdictions without a death penalty. New Mexico abolished the death penalty for offenses committed after July 1, 2009. As of December 31, 2016, two males in New Mexico were under previously imposed death sentences. In Delaware, capital cases are no longer pursued due to a 2016 court ruling; however, one prisoner remained under a previously imposed death sentence]

State	1977 to 2017	2000	2010	2015	2016	2017	State	1977 to 2017	2000	2010	2015	2016	2017
United States[1]	1,465	85	46	28	20	23	Missouri	88	5	–	6	1	1
							Montana	3	–	–	–	–	–
Alabama	61	4	5	–	2	3	Nebraska	3	–	–	–	–	–
Arizona	37	3	1	–	–	–	Nevada	12	–	–	–	–	–
Arkansas	31	2	–	–	–	4	New Mexico	1	–	–	–	–	–
California	13	1	–	–	–	–	North Carolina	43	1	–	–	–	–
Colorado	1	–	–	–	–	–	Ohio	55	–	8	–	–	2
Connecticut	1	–	–	–	–	–	Oklahoma	112	11	3	1	–	–
Delaware	16	1	–	–	–	–	Oregon	2	–	–	–	–	–
Florida	95	6	1	2	1	3	Pennsylvania	3	–	–	–	–	–
Georgia	70	–	2	5	9	1	South Carolina	43	1	–	–	–	–
Idaho	3	–	–	–	–	–	South Dakota	3	–	–	–	–	–
Illinois	12	–	–	–	–	–	Tennessee	6	1	–	–	–	–
Indiana	20	–	–	–	–	–	Texas	545	40	17	13	7	7
Kentucky	3	–	–	–	–	–	Utah	7	–	1	–	–	–
Louisiana	28	1	1	–	–	–	Virginia	113	8	3	1	–	2
Maryland	5	–	–	–	–	–	Washington	5	–	1	–	–	–
Mississippi	21	–	3	–	–	–	Wyoming	1	–	–	–	–	–

– Represents zero. [1] Includes persons executed within the Federal system.

Source: Through 1978, U.S. Law Enforcement Assistance Administration; thereafter, U.S. Department of Justice, Bureau of Justice Statistics, *Capital Punishment, 2017: Selected Findings*, NCJ 253060, July 2019, and earlier reports. See also <https://www.bjs.gov/index.cfm?ty=pbse&sid=1>.

Table 396. Prisoners Executed Under Civil Authority by Sex and Race: 1930 to 2017

[Excludes executions by military authorities. See source for more information]

Period or year	Total[1]	Male	Female	White[2]	Black[2]	Hispanic	Period or year	Total[1]	Male	Female	White[2]	Black[2]	Hispanic
1930 to 1939	1,667	1,656	11	827	816	(NA)	1995	56	56	–	31	22	2
1940 to 1949	1,284	1,272	12	490	781	(NA)	1996	45	45	–	29	14	2
1950 to 1959	717	709	8	336	376	(NA)	1997	74	74	–	41	26	5
1960 to 1967	191	190	1	98	93	(NA)	1998	68	66	2	40	18	8
1968 to 1976[3]	–	–	–	–	–	–	1999	98	98	–	53	33	9
1977	1	1	–	1	–	–	2000	85	83	2	43	35	6
1978	–	–	–	–	–	–	2001	66	63	3	45	17	3
1979	2	2	–	2	–	–	2002	71	69	2	47	18	6
1980	–	–	–	–	–	–	2003	65	65	–	41	20	3
1981	1	1	–	1	–	–	2004	59	59	–	36	19	3
1982	2	2	–	1	1	–	2005	60	59	1	38	19	3
1983	5	5	–	4	1	–	2006	53	53	–	25	20	8
1984	21	20	1	13	8	–	2007	42	42	–	22	14	6
1985	18	18	–	9	7	2	2008	37	37	–	17	17	3
1986	18	18	–	9	7	2	2009	52	52	–	24	21	7
1987	25	25	–	11	11	3	2010	46	45	1	28	13	5
1988	11	11	–	6	5	–	2011	43	43	–	22	16	5
1989	16	16	–	6	8	2	2012	43	43	–	25	11	7
1990	23	23	–	16	7	–	2013	39	38	1	23	13	3
1991	14	14	–	6	7	1	2014	35	33	2	(NA)	(NA)	(NA)
1992	31	31	–	17	11	2	2015	28	(NA)	(NA)	(NA)	(NA)	(NA)
1993	38	38	–	19	14	4	2016	20	(NA)	(NA)	16	2	2
1994	31	31	–	19	11	1	2017	23	(NA)	(NA)	13	8	2

– Represents zero. NA Not available. [1] Includes American Indians, Alaska Natives, Asians, Native Hawaiians, and other Pacific Islanders, not shown separately. [2] Excludes persons of Hispanic or Latino origin. In 2017, two of the white prisoners executed in Texas were of Hispanic or Latino origin. [3] In 1972, the U.S. Supreme Court invalidated capital punishment statutes in several states, effecting a moratorium on executions. Executions resumed in 1977 when the Supreme Court found revisions to several state statutes had effectively addressed the issues previously held as unconstitutional.

Source: Through 1978, U.S. Law Enforcement Assistance Administration; thereafter, U.S. Department of Justice, Bureau of Justice Statistics, *Capital Punishment, 2017: Selected Findings*, NCJ 253060, July 2019. See also <https://www.bjs.gov/index.cfm?ty=pbse&sid=1>.

Table 397. Prisoners Under Death Sentence by Race: 1980 to 2017

[As of December 31. Excludes prisoners under sentence of death who remained within local correctional systems pending exhaustion of appellate process or who had not been committed to prison. Data from the National Prisoner Statistics Program]

Year	Total	White	Black	Other	Year	Total	White	Black	Other
1980	692	424	264	4	1999	3,540	1,960	1,515	65
1981	860	499	353	8	2000	3,601	1,989	1,541	71
1982	1,066	613	441	12	2001	3,577	1,968	1,538	71
1983	1,209	692	505	12	2002	3,562	1,939	1,551	72
1984	1,420	806	598	16	2003	3,377	1,882	1,417	78
1985	1,575	896	664	15	2004	3,320	1,856	1,390	74
1986	1,800	1,013	762	25	2005	3,245	1,802	1,366	77
1987	1,967	1,128	813	26	2006	3,233	1,806	1,353	74
1988	2,117	1,235	848	34	2007	3,215	1,806	1,338	71
1989	2,243	1,308	898	37	2008	3,210	1,795	1,343	72
1990	2,346	1,368	940	38	2009	3,173	1,779	1,318	76
1991	2,465	1,449	979	37	2010	3,139	1,743	1,309	87
1992	2,580	1,511	1,031	38	2011	3,065	1,721	1,274	70
1993	2,727	1,575	1,111	41	2012	3,011	1,684	1,258	69
1994	2,905	1,653	1,203	49	2013	2,983	1,670	1,251	62
1995	3,064	1,732	1,284	48	2014	2,942	1,647	1,233	62
1996	3,242	1,833	1,358	51	2015	2,872	1,606	1,202	64
1997	3,328	1,864	1,408	56	2016	2,797	1,553	1,179	65
1998	3,465	1,917	1,489	59	2017	2,703	1,508	1,129	66

Source: U.S. Department of Justice, Bureau of Justice Statistics, *Capital Punishment, 2017: Selected Findings*, NCJ 253060, July 2019, and earlier reports. See also <http://www.bjs.gov/index.cfm?ty=pbse&sid=1>.

Table 398. Prisoners—Firearm Possession and Use During Offense That Led to Imprisonment by Type of Controlling Offense: 2016

[Controlling offense for sentenced prisoners and those awaiting sentencing with one offense is that one offense. For sentenced prisoners with multiple offenses and sentences, the controlling offense is the one with the longest sentence. For sentenced prisoners with multiple offenses and one sentence and those awaiting sentencing with multiple offenses, the controlling offense is the most serious offense. Data are from the Survey of Prison Inmates]

Controlling offense	State prisoners			Federal prisoners		
		Percent who—			Percent who—	
	Number [1]	Possessed a firearm [1]	Used a firearm [2]	Number [1]	Possessed a firearm [1]	Used a firearm [2]
Total	**1,211,200**	**20.9**	**13.9**	**170,400**	**20.0**	**5.0**
Violent	667,300	29.1	23.0	20,900	36.2	25.3
Homicide [3]	191,400	43.6	37.2	3,800	35.9	28.4
Rape/sexual assault	144,800	2.0	0.8	2,400	(B)	(B)
Robbery	149,600	43.3	31.5	10,700	46.3	32.1
Assault	149,400	25.0	20.6	2,900	29.0	18.1
Other violent [4]	32,200	17.0	12.6	1,200	34.1	(B)
Property	186,100	[9] 4.9	[9] 2.0	12,000	[9] 2.6	(B)
Burglary	88,100	6.7	3.2	300	(B)	(B)
Other property [5]	98,000	3.3	1.0	11,800	2.4	(B)
Drug	180,800	[9] 8.4	[9] 0.8	80,500	[9] 12.3	[9] 0.6
Trafficking [6]	130,500	9.4	0.9	72,300	12.9	0.7
Possession	45,900	6.1	(B)	3,500	(B)	(B)
Other/unspecified drug	4,300	(B)	(B)	4,700	(B)	(B)
Public order	158,300	[9] 21.5	[9] 5.6	52,900	30.2	[9] 5.3
Weapons [7]	43,800	67.2	15.7	22,200	66.9	11.3
Other public order [8]	114,400	4.0	1.7	30,700	3.6	(B)
Other	3,900	(B)	(B)	1,800	(B)	(B)
Unknown	14,900	[9] 4.3	(B)	2,200	(B)	(B)

B Not calculated. Too few cases to provide a reliable estimate, or coefficient of variation is greater than 50%. [1] Data are estimates. Excludes prisoners who were missing responses on firearm possession; includes prisoners who were missing responses on firearm use. [2] Excludes prisoners who were missing responses on firearm use. [3] Includes murder and negligent and non-negligent manslaughter. [4] Includes kidnapping, blackmail, extortion, hit-and-run driving with bodily injury, child abuse, and criminal endangerment. [5] Includes larceny, theft, motor vehicle theft, arson, fraud, stolen property, destruction of property, vandalism, hit-and-run driving with no bodily injury, criminal tampering, trespassing, entering without breaking, and possession of burglary tools. [6] Includes possession with intent to distribute. [7] Includes being armed while committing a crime; possession of ammunition, concealed weapons, firearms and explosive devices; selling or trafficking weapons; and other weapons offenses. [8] Includes commercialized vice, immigration crimes, DUI, violations of probation/parole, and other public-order offenses. [9] Difference with comparison group (total violent offenders) is significant at the 95% confidence level across main categories, and no testing was done on subcategories (e.g., homicide).

Source: U.S. Department of Justice, Bureau of Justice Statistics, *Source and Use of Firearms Involved in Crimes: Survey of Prison Inmates, 2016*, NCJ 251776, January 2019. See also <https://www.bjs.gov/index.cfm?ty=pbdetail&iid=6486>.

Table 399. Rate of Adults Under Community Supervision, Probation, and Parole: 2000 to 2018

[From the Annual Survey of Probation and Parole. Probation is a court-ordered period of correctional supervision in the community, generally as an alternative to incarceration. Probation can be a combined sentence of incarceration followed by a period of community supervision. Parole is a period of conditional supervised release in the community following a prison term. Including parolees released through discretionary or mandatory supervised release from prison, those released through other types of post-custody conditional supervision, and those sentenced to a term of supervised release]

Year	Rate per 100,000 population			U.S. residents on—		
	Community supervision [1, 2]	Probation	Parole	Community supervision [1]	Probation	Parole
2000...............	2,162	1,818	344	1 in 46	1 in 53	1 in 285
2010...............	2,067	1,715	356	1 in 48	1 in 58	1 in 281
2017...............	1,784	1,443	346	1 in 56	1 in 69	1 in 289
2018...............	1,726	1,389	344	1 in 58	1 in 72	1 in 290

[1] Adults on probation, parole or other post-prison supervision. [2] Beginning 2008, detail does not sum to total because the community supervision rate was adjusted to exclude parolees who were also on probation.

Source: U.S. Department of Justice, Bureau of Justice Statistics, *Probation and Parole in the United States, 2017-2018*, NCJ 252072, August 2020, and earlier reports. See also <https://www.bjs.gov/index.cfm?ty=pbse&sid=42>.

Table 400. Adults Under Community Supervision, Probation, and Parole by State: 2018

[As of December 31, 2018. Counts are rounded to nearest hundred. Rates computed using the estimated U.S. adult resident population in each jurisdiction on January 1, 2019. Counts may not be actual as reporting agencies may provide estimates on some or all detailed data; see source. From Annual Survey of Probation and Parole]

Area	Community supervision [1]		Probation		Parole	
	Number	Rate per 100,0000	Number	Rate per 100,0000	Number	Rate per 100,0000
United States, total.........	**4,399,000**	**1,726**	**3,539,950**	**1,389**	**877,953**	**344**
Federal.........................	122,800	48	14,943	6	107,872	42
States.........................	4,276,200	1,678	3,525,007	1,383	770,081	302
Alabama.......................	60,900	1,599	50,997	1,339	10,266	270
Alaska [3]......................	3,400	618	2,074	375	1,348	244
Arizona........................	84,300	1,509	76,844	1,375	7,536	135
Arkansas.......................	53,800	2,323	36,719	1,584	24,698	1,066
California [3]...................	312,400	1,018	209,765	684	[2] 102,586	334
Colorado.......................	91,300	2,042	80,537	1,801	10,759	241
Connecticut....................	43,100	1,518	38,668	1,362	4,452	157
Delaware.......................	14,500	1,890	14,176	1,844	350	46
District of Columbia...........	8,600	1,483	5,564	964	3,164	548
Florida [3].....................	209,400	1,216	205,033	1,191	4,345	25
Georgia [3]....................	433,200	5,369	416,771	5,166	20,426	253
Hawaii.........................	21,900	1,958	20,196	1,808	1,673	150
Idaho..........................	39,700	2,996	34,392	2,598	5,267	398
Illinois........................	116,100	1,175	88,927	900	27,185	275
Indiana........................	118,400	2,303	111,986	2,178	6,399	124
Iowa...........................	35,600	1,462	29,137	1,198	6,652	274
Kansas.........................	21,900	991	16,455	745	5,438	246
Kentucky.......................	62,800	1,812	46,967	1,354	15,881	458
Louisiana......................	62,300	1,749	35,025	983	29,321	823
Maine..........................	6,800	620	6,742	618	20	2
Maryland.......................	80,600	1,710	70,248	1,490	10,338	219
Massachusetts [3]..............	53,700	966	52,228	940	1,441	26
Michigan [3]...................	164,800	2,099	150,338	1,915	14,479	184
Minnesota......................	107,500	2,482	100,076	2,312	7,381	171
Mississippi....................	37,200	1,628	27,294	1,196	9,866	432
Missouri [3]...................	63,100	1,326	43,871	921	19,251	404
Montana [3]....................	11,400	1,358	9,917	1,184	1,461	174
Nebraska.......................	15,900	1,087	14,894	1,021	958	66
Nevada.........................	19,800	832	13,260	559	6,492	273
New Hampshire..................	6,300	570	3,916	355	2,367	215
New Jersey.....................	146,300	2,099	131,347	1,885	14,967	215
New Mexico [3].................	13,700	850	12,090	747	2,805	173
New York.......................	139,700	903	94,542	611	45,192	292
North Carolina.................	94,100	1,155	80,068	983	14,215	175
North Dakota...................	7,000	1,201	6,096	1,046	906	155
Ohio [3].......................	253,900	2,785	232,741	2,553	21,113	232
Oklahoma.......................	43,300	1,448	41,562	1,388	1,780	59
Oregon.........................	59,900	1,794	35,732	1,070	24,183	724
Pennsylvania [3]...............	288,000	2,831	178,730	1,757	109,247	1074
Rhode Island...................	20,900	2,453	20,402	2,390	535	63
South Carolina.................	36,700	916	31,975	797	4,980	124
South Dakota...................	9,200	1,375	5,989	896	3,201	479
Tennessee......................	72,100	1,362	61,253	1,157	10,842	205
Texas..........................	474,600	2,209	368,167	1,714	109,213	508
Utah...........................	16,600	736	12,692	563	3,914	174
Vermont........................	4,800	940	3,936	770	870	170
Virginia.......................	65,000	973	63,111	945	1,860	28
Washington [3].................	88,900	1,501	76,672	1,295	12,222	206
West Virginia..................	10,900	756	6,593	458	4,287	298
Wisconsin [3]..................	63,900	1,404	42,909	943	21,015	462
Wyoming........................	6,300	1,426	5,383	1,215	934	211

NA Not available. [1] December 31, 2018 population excludes 18,878 offenders under community supervision who were on both probation and parole. [2] In California, includes post-release community supervision and mandatory supervision parolees. [3] Includes estimates for nonreporting agencies; see source for explanatory notes.

Source: U.S. Department of Justice, Bureau of Justice Statistics, *Probation and Parole in the United States, 2017-18*, NCJ 252072, August 2020. See also <https://www.bjs.gov/index.cfm?ty=pbse&sid=42>.

Table 401. Prisoner Recidivism by Selected Characteristics: 2005 to 2010

[In percent. Prisoners released on community supervision in 2005 who were arrested for a new crime/returned to prison 2005 through 2010. See source for details]

Characteristic	Federal prisoners		State prisoners	
	Arrested	Returned to prison [1]	Arrested [2]	Returned to prison [1,3]
Total, released prisoners...................	**47.2**	**31.6**	**76.5**	**59.4**
SEX				
Male........................	49.6	33.4	77.5	56.4
Female......................	35.4	22.1	68.1	44.9
RACE/HISPANIC ORIGIN				
White alone, non-Hispanic..............	39.7	26.2	73.1	53.2
Black alone, non-Hispanic..............	55.1	35.7	80.6	55.6
Hispanic/Latino.....................	48.3	33.1	75.7	57.8
Other [4]...........................	48.5	38.5	74.2	58.8
AGE AT RELEASE				
24 years old and under..............	64.7	45.8	84.2	62.2
25 to 29 years old..................	59.3	40.7	80.6	57.3
30 to 34 years old..................	52.9	34.7	77.0	54.8
35 to 39 years old..................	48.6	31.9	78.1	56.0
40 to 44 years old..................	44.5	29.4	74.2	55.0
45 to 49 years old..................	37.7	24.7	69.0	48.8
50 years old and over...............	23.5	14.7	58.8	41.9
MOST SERIOUS COMMITMENT OFFENSE				
Violent [5].........................	58.1	44.3	73.8	51.0
Property...........................	39.5	26.1	82.2	62.5
Drug...............................	44.0	27.1	76.7	53.2
Other public order [6]...............	57.0	40.2	73.0	54.2
Sex offense [7]......................	36.7	33.9	61.0	45.4
NUMBER OF PRIOR ARRESTS [8]				
1-2................................	27.0	16.3	52.4	31.1
3-4................................	46.4	29.6	67.3	44.3
5-9................................	59.9	40.8	75.6	53.8
10 or more.........................	72.2	52.4	86.3	65.8

[1] Includes returns to a federal or state prison. [2] Based on prisoners released conditionally in 30 states. [3] Based on prisoners released conditionally in 23 states that provided the necessary prison admission data. [4] Includes American Indian, Alaska Native, Asian, Native Hawaiian, Other Pacific Islander, and persons of two or more races. [5] Excludes rape and sexual assault. [6] Excludes sex offenses. [7] Includes rape, sexual assault, and sexual abuse; possession, distribution, and production of child pornography; and transportation for illegal sexual purposes. [8] Number of times prisoner arrested before release in 2005, including the arrest that led to the 2005 release.

Source: U.S. Department of Justice, Bureau of Justice Statistics, *Recidivism of Offenders Placed on Federal Community Supervision in 2005: Patterns from 2005 to 2010*, NCJ 249743, June 2016. See also <http://www.bjs.gov/index.cfm?ty=pbdetail&iid=5642>.

Table 402. Fires—Number and Loss by Type and Property Use: 2015 to 2018

[Number of fires in thousands (1,346 represents 1,346,000); property loss in millions of dollars (14,298 represents $14,298,000,000). Based on annual sample survey of fire departments. No adjustments were made for unreported fires and losses]

Type and property use	Number (1,000)				Direct property loss (mil. dol.) [1]			
	2015	2016	2017	2018	2015 [7]	2016 [8]	2017 [9]	2018 [10]
Fires, total.................	**1,346**	**1,342**	**1,320**	**1,319**	**14,298**	**10,628**	**23,000**	**25,600**
Structure.......................	502	476	499	499	10,280	7,898	10,700	11,066
Outside of structure [2].........	76	88	74	71	151	333	137	139
Brush and rubbish..............	460	471	458	439	–	–	–	–
Vehicle [3]......................	205	204	198	213	1,816	1,356	2,044	1,876
Other..........................	104	104	91	98	101	130	136	176
Structure fires by property use:								
Public assembly................	17	14	15	16	323	308	285	384
Educational....................	5	4	6	5	40	34	51	109
Institutional...................	7	6	7	7	51	37	40	44
Stores and offices.............	17	16	18	18	635	436	763	778
Residential....................	388	372	379	387	7,210	5,804	7,900	8,286
1-2 family homes [4]...........	271	257	263	277	5,799	4,943	6,141	6,493
Apartments..................	95	95	95	87	1,161	711	1,600	1,529
Other residential [5]...........	23	20	23	24	250	150	162	264
Storage.......................	31	27	28	27	1,032	665	834	833
Industry, utility, defense [6].....	9	9	9	11	924	419	503	508
Special structures.............	29	29	39	30	65	195	331	124

– Represents zero. [1] Direct property damage figures do not include indirect losses (such as business interruption and temporary shelter costs) and adjustments for inflation. [2] Includes outside storage, crops, timber, etc. [3] Includes highway and other vehicles (trains, boats, ships, aircraft, and farm and construction vehicles). [4] Includes manufactured homes. [5] Includes hotels and motels, college dormitories, boarding houses, etc. [6] Data underreported as some incidents were handled by private fire brigades or fixed suppression systems which do not report. [7] Includes $1,950 million, total property loss for the Valley and Butte Wildfires in California. Loss by specific property type was not available for these fires. [8] Includes $911 million, total property loss estimate for the Gatlinburg, Tennessee Wildfires. Loss by specific property type was not available for these fires. [9] Includes $10 billion estimated property loss for Northern California Wildfires. [10] Includes $12.4 billion in losses from major California Wildfires.

Source: National Fire Protection Association, Quincy, MA, *Fire Loss in the United States During 2018* ©, October 2019, and earlier reports. See also <http://www.nfpa.org/News-and-Research>.

Table 403. The U.S. Fire Service: Departments, Personnel, and Responses by Type: 1990 to 2018

[In thousands (1,025.7 represents 1,025,700), except where noted. A fire department is a public or private organization that provides fire prevention, fire suppression, and associated emergency and non-emergency services to a jurisdiction such as a county, municipality, or organized fire district]

Items	1990	2000	2005	2010	2014	2015	2016	2017	2018
FIRE DEPARTMENTS (NUMBER)									
Total departments	**30,391**	**30,339**	**30,300**	**30,125**	**29,980**	**29,727**	**29,710**	**29,819**	**29,705**
All career	1,949	2,178	2,087	2,495	2,440	2,651	2,775	2,785	3,009
Mostly career	1,338	1,667	1,766	1,860	2,045	1,893	2,048	2,316	2,368
Mostly volunteer	4,000	4,523	4,902	5,290	5,580	5,421	5,451	5,405	5,206
All volunteer	23,104	21,971	21,575	20,480	19,915	19,762	19,436	19,313	19,122
By whether Emergency Medical Service (EMS) provided:									
Provide EMS service only	(NA)	(NA)	12,900	13,440	13,665	13,500	(NA)	13,631	(NA)
Provide EMS service and advance life support	(NA)	(NA)	4,260	4,515	4,635	4,617	(NA)	4,629	(NA)
No EMS service	(NA)	(NA)	13,170	12,170	11,680	11,610	(NA)	11,559	(NA)
FIRE DEPARTMENT PERSONNEL (1,000)									
Total personnel	**1,025.7**	**1,064.2**	**1,136.7**	**1,103.3**	**1,134.4**	**1,160.5**	**1,090.1**	**1,056.2**	**1,115.0**
Career [1]	253.0	286.8	313.3	335.2	346.2	345.6	361.1	373.6	370.0
Volunteer [2]	772.7	777.4	823.7	768.2	788.3	814.9	729.0	682.6	745.0
RESPONSES BY TYPE (1,000)									
Total responses	**13,708**	**20,520**	**23,252**	**28,205**	**31,645**	**33,636**	**35,320**	**34,684**	**36,747**
Fires	2,019	1,708	1,602	1,332	1,298	1,346	1,342	1,320	1,319
Medical aid	7,650	12,251	14,375	18,522	20,178	21,500	22,751	22,341	23,552
False alarms	1,476	2,127	2,134	2,187	2,488	2,567	2,622	2,547	2,889
Malicious mischievous	442	300	241	163	162	166	173	141	172
System malfunctions	593	884	746	709	820	828	837	752	889
Unintentional calls	318	714	838	992	1,166	1,200	1,226	1,286	1,379
Other [3]	124	230	310	324	342	374	387	369	451
Mutual aid/assistance	487	864	1,091	1,190	1,447	1,493	1,515	1,353	1,513
Hazardous material	210	319	375	402	405	442	425	424	426
Other hazardous [4]	423	544	667	660	615	643	685	693	707
All other [5]	1,443	2,708	3,009	3,913	5,214	5,646	5,981	6,006	6,343

NA Not available. [1] Includes full-time uniform firefighters regardless of assignment (i.e., suppression, administrative, prevention/inspection, etc.). Does not include firefighters who work for the state or federal government or in private fire brigades. [2] Volunteer firefighters include any active part-time (call or volunteer) firefighters. [3] Bomb scares, etc. [4] Arcing wires, bomb removal, power line down, biological hazard, etc. [5] Smoke scares, lock-outs, animal rescue, unauthorized burning, severe weather, etc.

Source: National Fire Protection Association, Quincy, MA, *U.S. Fire Department Profile 2018* ©, and *Fire Loss in the United States During 2018* ©, and earlier reports. See also <http://www.nfpa.org/News-and-Research>.

Table 404. Firefighter On-Duty Fatalities and Injuries: 2010 to 2018

[Number, unless otherwise noted. On-duty refers to involvement in operations at the scene of an emergency, whether it is a fire or nonfire incident; responding to or returning from an incident; performing other officially assigned duties including training; and being on call]

Item	2010	2011	2012	2013	2014	2015	2016	2017	2018
Total fatalities [1]	**90**	**87**	**85**	**109**	**97**	**90**	**91**	**88**	**82**
Fatalities per 100,000 fires (rate)	2.33	2.52	2.33	4.84	2.39	2.45	2.01	(NA)	(NA)
Emergency duty deaths (percent)	55.6	51.7	52.9	70.6	45.3	48.9	40.7	45.4	51.2
By incident characteristic:									
Wildland related fatalities	12	10	16	31	11	12	15	10	10
Incidents with multiple fatalities	4	3	4	4	2	3	3	1	2
Training fatalities	12	8	8	7	10	7	9	12	9
Cause of fatal injury:									
Stress/overexertion [2]	56	54	49	39	65	60	44	53	37
Vehicle collision	12	5	18	9	11	5	19	10	12
Total nonfatal Injuries [3]	**71,875**	**70,090**	**69,400**	**65,880**	**63,350**	**68,085**	**62,085**	**58,835**	**58,250**
Fireground injuries	32,675	30,505	31,490	29,760	27,015	29,130	24,325	24,495	22,975
Injuries at nonfire emergencies	13,355	14,905	12,760	12,535	14,595	14,320	12,780	12,240	11,625
Nature of injury:									
Burns (fire or chemical)	2,585	2,385	2,220	1,975	1,810	2,020	1,900	1,310	1,550
Smoke or gas inhalation	1,500	1,760	1,685	1,895	1,980	1,645	2,355	2,135	3,150
Other respiratory distress	940	1,060	910	915	855	1,060	800	850	975
Burns and smoke inhalation	635	695	320	195	585	535	880	1,525	1,450
Wound, cut, bleeding, bruise	11,110	10,210	9,905	10,530	9,705	10,205	9,450	9,470	8,075
Dislocation, fracture	1,820	1,885	1,695	1,900	1,995	1,685	1,850	1,330	1,300
Heart attack or stroke	810	860	780	620	905	920	575	550	825
Strain, sprain, muscular pain	40,385	39,960	39,535	37,565	35,015	37,945	32,650	30,970	29,550
Thermal stress (frostbite, heat exhaustion)	3,195	2,945	2,465	2,080	2,245	2,860	2,475	2,095	2,875
Other	8,895	8,660	9,885	8,205	8,255	9,210	9,150	8,600	8,500
Fire department vehicle collisions	14,200	14,850	14,300	12,350	14,910	16,600	15,430	15,425	14,425
Injuries	775	970	725	730	550	1,150	700	1,005	575
Personal vehicle collisions	1,000	790	750	830	620	700	850	795	700
Injuries	75	190	70	185	90	50	175	75	50

NA Not available. [1] Includes causes not shown, such as struck by object, caught/trapped, structural collapse, fall, violence, lost/disoriented, and unknown. [2] Stress/overexertion include all firefighter deaths that are cardiac or cerebrovascular in nature such as heart attacks, strokes, and other events such as extreme climatic thermal exposure (heat exhaustion). [3] Includes other types of nonfatal injuries not shown separately.

Source: Fatalities: U.S. Department of Homeland Security, Federal Emergency Management Agency, *U.S. Fire Administration, Firefighter Fatalities in the United States in 2018*, September 2019, and earlier reports. See also <https://apps.usfa.fema.gov/firefighter-fatalities/>. Nonfatal Injuries: National Fire Protection Association, *United States Firefighter Injury Report 2018* ©, December 2019, and earlier reports. See also <https://www.nfpa.org/News-and-Research>.

Table 405. Fires and Property Loss for Incendiary and Suspicious Fires and Civilian Fire Deaths and Injuries by Selected Property Type: 2010 to 2018

[In thousands (482 represents 482,000), except as indicated. Based on sample survey of fire departments]

Characteristic	2010	2012	2013	2014	2015	2016	2017	2018
NUMBER (1,000)								
Structure fires, total	**482**	**481**	**488**	**494**	**502**	**476**	**499**	**499**
Structure fires that were intentionally set	28	26	23	19	23	20	23	26
PROPERTY LOSS (mil. dol.) [1]								
Structure fires, total	**9,716**	**9,776**	**9,526**	**9,846**	**10,280**	**7,898**	**10,700**	**11,066**
Structure fires that were intentionally set	585	581	577	613	460	473	582	593
CIVILIAN FIRE DEATHS								
Deaths, total [2]	**3,120**	**2,855**	**3,240**	**3,275**	**3,280**	**3,390**	**3,400**	**3,655**
Residential property	2,665	2,405	2,785	2,795	2,605	2,800	2,710	2,820
One- and two-family dwellings	2,200	2,000	2,430	2,345	2,155	2,410	2,290	2,360
Apartments	440	380	325	400	405	325	340	360
Vehicles [3]	310	325	320	345	500	355	430	560
CIVILIAN FIRE INJURIES								
Injuries, total [2]	**17,720**	**16,500**	**15,925**	**15,775**	**15,700**	**14,650**	**14,670**	**15,200**
Residential property	13,800	13,175	12,575	12,175	11,575	11,125	10,910	11,600
One- and two-family dwellings	9,400	8,825	8,300	8,025	8,050	7,375	7,470	7,800
Apartments	3,950	4,050	3,900	3,800	3,025	3,375	3,130	3,400
Vehicles [3]	1,590	975	1,050	1,450	1,875	1,225	1,610	1,500

[1] Direct property loss only. [2] Includes deaths or injuries from other types of fires, not shown separately. [3] Includes highway vehicles, and trains, boats, ships, farm vehicles, and construction vehicles.

Source: National Fire Protection Association, Quincy, MA, *Fire Loss in the United States During 2018* ©, October 2019, and earlier reports. See also <http://www.nfpa.org/News-and-Research>.

Section 6
Geography and Environment

This section presents a variety of information on the physical environment of the United States, starting with basic area measurement data and ending with climatic data for selected weather stations around the country. The subjects covered between those points are mostly concerned with environmental trends but include related subjects such as land use, water consumption, air pollutant emissions, toxic releases, oil spills, hazardous waste sites, municipal waste and recycling, threatened and endangered wildlife, and the environmental industry.

The information in this section is selected from a wide range of federal agencies that compile the data for various administrative or regulatory purposes, such as the Environmental Protection Agency (EPA), U.S. Geological Survey (USGS), National Oceanic and Atmospheric Administration (NOAA), and the Natural Resources Conservation Service (NRCS).

Area—2018 area measurements are the latest available. These measurements were calculated by computer based on the information contained in a single, consistent geographic database, the Topologically Integrated Geographic Encoding & Referencing system (TIGER®) database, a national geographic and cartographic database prepared by the Census Bureau. The 2018 area measurements may be found in Table 406.

Geography—The USGS conducts investigations, surveys, and research in the fields of geography, geology, topography, geographic information systems, mineralogy, hydrology, and geothermal energy resources as well as natural hazards. The USGS provides United States cartographic data through the Earth Sciences Information Center and water resources data through the *Water Resources of the United States* at <water.usgs.gov/>. In a joint project with the U.S. Census Bureau, during the 1980s, the USGS provided the basic information on geographic features for input into the TIGER® database. Since then, using a variety of sources, the Census Bureau has updated these features and their related attributes (names, descriptions, etc.) and inserted current information on the boundaries, names, and codes of legal and statistical geographic entities. The 2018 measures of land and water area, including their classifications, reflect base feature updates made in the Master Address File (MAF)/TIGER® database through May 2018. The boundaries of the states and equivalent areas are as of January 1, 2018. Maps prepared by the Census Bureau using the TIGER® database show the names and boundaries of entities and are available on a current basis.

An inventory of the nation's land resources by type of use/cover was conducted by the NRCS every 5 years from 1977 through 1997. Since 2000, data have been gathered annually, though major releases of these data continue to be reported at 5-year intervals. The most recent survey results, covered all nonfederal land for the contiguous 48 states. Details are available at <nrcs.usda.gov/wps/portal/nrcs/main/national/technical/nra/nri/>.

Environment—The principal federal agency responsible for pollution abatement and control activities is the EPA. It is responsible for establishing and monitoring national air quality standards, water quality activities, solid and hazardous waste disposal, and control of toxic substances. Many of these series now appear in the "Envirofacts" portion of the EPA website at <enviro.epa.gov/>.

The Clean Air Act, which was last amended in 1990, requires the EPA to set National Ambient Air Quality Standards (NAAQS) (40 CFR part 50) for pollutants considered harmful to public health and the environment. The Clean Air Act established two types of national air quality standards. *Primary standards* set limits to protect public health, including the health of "sensitive" populations such as asthmatics, children, and the elderly. *Secondary standards* set limits to protect public welfare, including protection against decreased visibility and damage to animals, crops vegetation, and buildings. See <epa.gov/criteria-air-pollutants/naaqs-table> for more information. The EPA Office of Air Quality Planning and Standards (OAQPS) has set National Ambient Air Quality Standards for six principal pollutants, which are called "criteria" pollutants. These pollutants are: carbon monoxide, lead, nitrogen dioxide, particulate matter, ozone, and sulfur dioxide. NAAQS are periodically reviewed and revised to include any additional or new health or welfare data. Table 420 gives some of the health-related standards for the six air pollutants having NAAQS. Data gathered from state networks are periodically submitted to EPA's National Aerometric Information Retrieval System (AIRS) for summarization in annual reports on the nationwide status and trends in air quality. For details, see "Air Trends" on the EPA website at <epa.gov/airtrends/>.

The Toxics Release Inventory (TRI), a database published by the EPA, is a valuable source of information on approximately 767 chemicals that are being used, manufactured, treated, transported, or released into the environment. Sections 313 of the Emergency Planning and Community Right-to-Know Act (EPCRA) and 6607 of the Pollution Prevention Act (PPA) mandate that a publicly-accessible toxic chemical database be developed and maintained by the EPA. The TRI database contains information concerning waste management activities and the release of toxic chemicals by facilities that manufacture, process, or otherwise use said materials. Data on the release of these chemicals are collected from about 21,000 facilities that have the equivalent of 10 or more full time employees and meet the established thresholds for manufacturing, processing, or "other use" of listed chemicals. Facilities must report their releases and other waste management quantities. Since 1994 federal facilities have been required to report their data regardless of industry classification. More current information on this program can be found at <epa.gov/toxics-release-inventory-tri-program>.

Climate—NOAA, through the National Weather Service and the National Environmental Satellite, Data, and Information Service, is responsible for collecting climate data. NOAA maintains about 8,000 weather stations, of which a portion produce precipitation measurement records, some take hourly readings of a series of weather elements, and the remainder record data once a day. These data are reported using the Storm Events Database (see <ncdc.noaa.gov/stormevents/>, and published monthly and annually in the *Local Climatological Data* (published by location for major cities). Data can be found in tables 440–444.

Table 406. Land and Water Area of States and Other Entities: 2018

[One square mile = 2.59 square kilometers. The area measurements were derived from the Census Bureau's Master Address File/Topologically Integrated Geographic Encoding and Referencing (MAF/TIGER®) database. The boundaries of the states and equivalent areas are as of January 1, 2018. The land and water areas, including their classifications, reflect base feature updates made in the MAF/TIGER® database through May 2018. For more details, see <census.gov/geo/maps-data/data/tiger-line.html>]

State and other areas [2]	Total area		Land area [1]		Water area [1]					
					Total		Inland (sq. mi.)	Coastal (sq. mi.)	Great Lakes (sq. mi.)	Territo-rial (sq. mi.)
	Sq. mi.	Sq. km.	Sq. mi.	Sq. km.	Sq. mi.	Sq. km.				
Total [3]	**3,806,358**	**9,858,422**	**3,536,641**	**9,159,859**	**269,717**	**698,563**	**85,076**	**42,390**	**60,093**	**82,157**
United States [4]	**3,797,173**	**9,834,633**	**3,532,614**	**9,149,429**	**264,559**	**685,204**	**84,961**	**42,355**	**60,093**	**77,150**
Alabama	52,420	135,767	50,647	131,174	1,773	4,593	1,057	517	–	200
Alaska	665,764	1,724,321	570,983	1,478,840	94,781	245,482	18,983	26,139	–	49,658
Arizona	113,987	295,226	113,591	294,199	397	1,027	397	–	–	–
Arkansas	53,179	137,732	52,035	134,769	1,144	2,963	1,144	–	–	–
California	163,695	423,968	155,794	403,504	7,901	20,464	2,818	245	–	4,838
Colorado	104,095	269,605	103,639	268,423	456	1,182	456	–	–	–
Connecticut	5,544	14,358	4,843	12,542	701	1,816	171	530	–	–
Delaware	2,489	6,446	1,948	5,046	541	1,400	92	355	–	94
District of Columbia	68	177	61	158	7	19	7	–	–	–
Florida	65,757	170,310	53,649	138,949	12,109	31,361	5,002	1,349	–	5,757
Georgia	59,423	153,905	57,715	149,482	1,708	4,423	1,211	47	–	450
Hawaii	10,970	28,412	6,422	16,634	4,547	11,778	42	9	–	4,496
Idaho	83,569	216,442	82,645	214,050	923	2,392	923	–	–	–
Illinois	57,914	149,995	55,514	143,781	2,400	6,215	826	–	1,574	–
Indiana	36,420	94,327	35,826	92,789	594	1,538	361	–	232	–
Iowa	56,273	145,745	55,854	144,661	419	1,084	419	–	–	–
Kansas	82,278	213,099	81,759	211,755	519	1,344	519	–	–	–
Kentucky	40,407	104,655	39,490	102,279	917	2,375	917	–	–	–
Louisiana	52,375	135,651	43,204	111,898	9,171	23,754	4,562	2,876	–	1,733
Maine	35,380	91,634	30,845	79,887	4,535	11,747	2,312	591	–	1,633
Maryland	12,406	32,131	9,711	25,151	2,695	6,980	765	1,820	–	111
Massachusetts	10,554	27,335	7,801	20,205	2,753	7,130	483	1,176	–	1,093
Michigan	96,713	250,487	56,603	146,601	40,111	103,886	1,937	–	38,174	–
Minnesota	86,940	225,174	79,625	206,229	7,315	18,945	4,769	–	2,546	–
Mississippi	48,441	125,460	46,924	121,534	1,516	3,927	768	620	–	129
Missouri	69,707	180,540	68,746	178,051	961	2,489	961	–	–	–
Montana	147,040	380,832	145,546	376,963	1,494	3,869	1,494	–	–	–
Nebraska	77,347	200,328	76,818	198,957	530	1,372	530	–	–	–
Nevada	110,571	286,377	109,780	284,330	790	2,047	790	–	–	–
New Hampshire	9,350	24,216	8,953	23,189	396	1,027	328	–	–	69
New Jersey	8,723	22,593	7,354	19,048	1,369	3,545	437	427	–	505
New Mexico	121,593	314,925	121,312	314,196	281	729	281	–	–	–
New York	54,555	141,296	47,123	122,049	7,431	19,247	1,992	976	3,986	478
North Carolina	53,819	139,390	48,619	125,924	5,199	13,466	4,050	–	–	1,149
North Dakota	70,699	183,111	68,999	178,708	1,700	4,403	1,700	–	–	–
Ohio	44,826	116,098	40,861	105,829	3,965	10,269	474	–	3,491	–
Oklahoma	69,899	181,038	68,596	177,663	1,303	3,375	1,303	–	–	–
Oregon	98,379	254,799	95,988	248,607	2,391	6,192	1,068	72	–	1,251
Pennsylvania	46,054	119,279	44,743	115,884	1,311	3,395	562	–	748	–
Rhode Island	1,545	4,001	1,034	2,678	511	1,324	182	64	–	266
South Carolina	32,023	82,940	30,064	77,865	1,960	5,075	1,061	109	–	790
South Dakota	77,116	199,730	75,810	196,347	1,306	3,383	1,306	–	–	–
Tennessee	42,144	109,153	41,237	106,803	907	2,350	907	–	–	–
Texas	268,596	695,659	261,257	676,653	7,338	19,006	5,590	401	–	1,347
Utah	84,898	219,885	82,196	212,886	2,702	6,999	2,702	–	–	–
Vermont	9,616	24,905	9,218	23,874	398	1,030	398	–	–	–
Virginia	42,775	110,786	39,482	102,258	3,293	8,529	1,289	1,565	–	438
Washington	71,302	184,672	66,453	172,113	4,849	12,559	1,715	2,467	–	668
West Virginia	24,230	62,756	24,041	62,266	189	489	189	–	–	–
Wisconsin	65,496	169,635	54,166	140,290	11,330	29,345	1,989	–	9,341	–
Wyoming	97,810	253,326	97,089	251,459	721	1,868	721	–	–	–
Puerto Rico	5,325	13,791	3,424	8,869	1,901	4,922	76	13	–	1,812
Island Areas:	3,860	9,998	603	1,562	3,257	8,436	39	22	–	3,196
American Samoa	581	1,505	76	198	505	1,307	8	–	–	497
Guam	571	1,478	210	544	361	934	8	1	–	352
Northern Mariana Islands	1,976	5,117	182	472	1,793	4,644	6	5	–	1,782
U.S. Virgin Islands	733	1,898	134	348	599	1,550	17	16	–	565

– Represents or rounds to zero. [1] Water area calculations in this table include only perennial water. All other water (intermittent, glacier, and marsh/swamp) is included in this table as part of land area calculations. [2] This table does not include area calculations for the U.S. Minor Outlying Islands. [3] Includes all 50 states, the District of Columbia, Puerto Rico, and the Island Areas. [4] Includes all 50 states and the District of Columbia.

Source: U.S. Census Bureau, unpublished data from the MAF/TIGER® database. See <census.gov/geo/maps-data/data/tiger.html>.

Table 407. Great Lakes Profile

[The Great Lakes contain the largest supply of freshwater in the world, holding about 21% of the world's total freshwater and about 84% of the United States' total freshwater. The Lakes are a series of five interconnecting large lakes, one small lake, four connecting channels, and the St. Lawrence Seaway. Combined, the lakes cover an area of over 94,000 square miles (245,000 square kilometers) and contain over 5,400 cubic miles (23,000 cubic kilometers) of water]

Characteristics	Unit	Lake Superior	Lake Michigan	Lake Huron	Lake Erie	Lake Ontario
Length	Miles	350	307	206	241	193
Breadth	Miles	160	118	183	57	53
Depth:						
Average	Feet	489	279	195	62	283
Maximum	Feet	1,333	923	750	210	802
Volume	Cubic miles	2,935	1,180	849	116	393
Water surface area [1]	Square miles	31,700	22,300	23,000	9,910	7,340
Surface area in U.S. [2]	Square miles	20,598	22,300	9,111	4,977	3,560
Retention/replacement time [2]	Years	173	62	21	3	6

[1] Includes surface area in both U.S. and Canada. [2] The amount of time it takes for lakes to get rid of pollutants.

Source: U.S. National Oceanic and Atmospheric Administration, Great Lakes Environmental Research Laboratory, "About Our Great Lakes, Lake by Lake Profiles," <https://www.glerl.noaa.gov/education/ourlakes/>, accessed April 2019.

Table 408. Great Lakes Length of Shoreline in Separate Basin

[In statute miles]

Shorelines	Total	Canada	U.S.	MI	MN	WI	IL	IN	OH	PA	NY
Total	**10,368**	**5,127**	**5,241**	**3,288**	**189**	**820**	**63**	**45**	**312**	**51**	**473**
Lake Superior	2,980	1,549	1,431	917	189	325	–	–	–	–	–
St. Marys River	297	206	91	91	–	–	–	–	–	–	–
Lake Michigan	1,661	–	1,661	1,058	–	495	63	45	–	–	–
Lake Huron	3,350	2,416	934	934	–	–	–	–	–	–	–
St. Clair River	128	47	81	81	–	–	–	–	–	–	–
Lake St. Clair	160	71	89	89	–	–	–	–	–	–	–
Detroit River	107	43	64	64	–	–	–	–	–	–	–
Lake Erie	860	366	494	54	–	–	–	–	312	51	77
Niagara River	99	34	65	–	–	–	–	–	–	–	65
Lake Ontario	726	395	331	–	–	–	–	–	–	–	331

– Represents zero.

Source: State of Michigan, Department of Environment Quality, "Great Lakes, Shorelines of the Great Lakes," and U.S. Lake Survey, File no. 3-3284 corrected to 1952, <https://www.michigan.gov/ogl>.

Table 409. Largest Lakes in the United States

[The list of lakes include manmade lakes and those that are only partially within the United States]

Lake	Location	Area in sq. mi.	Lake	Location	Area in sq. mi.
Lake Superior	MI-MN-WI-Ontario	31,700	Lake Pontchartrain	Louisiana	631
Lake Huron	MI-Ontario	23,000	Lake Sakakawea [1]	North Dakota	520
Lake Michigan	IL-IN-MI-WI	22,300	Lake Champlain	NY-VT-Quebec	490
Lake Erie	MI-NY-OH-PA-Ontario	9,910	Becharof Lake	Alaska	453
Lake Ontario	NY-Ontario	7,340	Lake St. Clair	MI-Ontario	430
Great Salt Lake	Utah	2,117	Red Lake	Minnesota	427
Lake of the Woods	MN-Manitoba-Ontario	1,485	Selawik Lake	Alaska	404
Iliamna Lake	Alaska	1,014	Fort Peck Lake [1]	Montana	393
Lake Oahe [1]	ND-SD	685	Salton Sea	California	347
Lake Okeechobee	Florida	662	Rainy Lake	MN-Ontario	345

[1] Manmade lakes.

Source: U.S. Geological Survey, 2003, and National Oceanic and Atmospheric Administration, "Great Lakes, 2002" and The National Atlas of the United States of America, *Lakes*, <http://nationalmap.gov/small_scale/#ten>.

Table 410. Coastline Counties Most Frequently Hit by Hurricanes: 1960 to 2008

[Hurricane is a type of tropical cyclone, an intense tropical weather system of strong thunderstorms with a well-defined surface circulation and maximum sustained winds of 74 miles per hour or higher. See <https://coast.noaa.gov/digitalcoast/> for more info]

County and State	Coastline region	Number of hurricanes	Percent change in population 1960 to 2008	Percent change in population 2000 to 2008	Percent change in housing units 1960 to 2008	Percent change in housing units 2000 to 2008
Monroe County, FL	Gulf of Mexico	15	50.8	-9.2	221.8	4.3
Lafourche Parish, LA	Gulf of Mexico	14	67.2	2.9	151.5	8.9
Carteret County, NC	Atlantic	14	104.3	6.4	366.4	12.4
Dare County, NC	Atlantic	13	465.9	12.1	709.6	22.8
Hyde County, NC	Atlantic	13	-10.1	-11.1	83.7	5.8
Jefferson Parish, LA	Gulf of Mexico	12	108.9	-4.2	201.4	-3.5
Palm Beach County, FL	Atlantic	12	454.7	11.9	616.9	15.2
Miami-Dade County, FL	Atlantic	11	156.5	6.4	180.6	14.9
St. Bernard Parish, LA	Gulf of Mexico	11	17.2	-43.9	-2.6	-67.9
Cameron Parish, LA	Gulf of Mexico	11	4.8	-27.6	87.7	-8.1
Terrebonne Parish, LA	Gulf of Mexico	11	78.7	3.9	179.4	11.0

Source: U.S. National Oceanic and Atmospheric Administration (NOAA), Coastal Services Center, Historical Hurricane Tracks: 1851 to 2008; U.S. Census Bureau, Current Population Reports, P25-1139, Population Estimates and Projections, "Coastline Population Trends in the United States: 1960 to 2008," May 2010. See also <https://www.census.gov/topics/preparedness/about/coastal-areas.html>.

Table 411. U.S.–Canada and U.S.–Mexico Border Lengths

[In statute miles. Each statute mile equals one mile]

State	Length of international border	State	Length of international border
United States–Canada total	**5,525**	Ohio	146
Alaska	1,538	Pennsylvania	42
Idaho	45	Vermont	90
Maine	611	Washington	427
Michigan	721		
Minnesota	547	**United States–Mexico total**	**1,933**
Montana	545	Arizona	373
New Hampshire	58	California	140
New York	445	New Mexico	180
North Dakota	310	Texas	1,241

Source: U.S.–Canada lengths: International Boundary Commission, 2003; U.S. Mexico lengths: U.S. Geological Survey; and The National Atlas of the United States, 1976, "Borders," <https://www.usgs.gov/core-science-systems/national-geospatial-program>.

Table 412. Coastline and Shoreline of the United States by State

[In statute miles. Each statute mile equals one mile. The term coastline is used to describe the general outline of the seacoast. For the table below, United States coastline measurements were made from small-scale maps, and the coastline was generalized. The coastlines of large sounds and bays were included. Measurements were made in 1948. Shoreline is the term used to describe a more detailed measure of the seacoast. The tidal shoreline figures in the table below were obtained in 1939-1940 from the largest-scale charts and maps then available. Shoreline of the outer coast, offshore islands, sounds, and bays was included, as well as the tidal portion of rivers and creeks. Only States with coastline or shoreline are included in the following table]

State	General coastline	Tidal shoreline	State	General coastline	Tidal shoreline
United States	**12,383**	**88,633**	Mississippi	44	359
Alabama	53	607	New Hampshire	13	131
Alaska	6,640	33,904	New Jersey	130	1,792
California	840	3,427	New York	127	1,850
Connecticut	–	618	North Carolina	301	3,375
Delaware	28	381	Oregon	296	1,410
Florida	1,350	8,426	Pennsylvania	–	89
Georgia	100	2,344	Rhode Island	40	384
Hawaii	750	1,052	South Carolina	187	2,876
Louisiana	397	7,721	Texas	367	3,359
Maine	228	3,478	Virginia	112	3,315
Maryland	31	3,190	Washington	157	3,026
Massachusetts	192	1,519			

– Represents zero.

Source: National Oceanic Atmospheric Administration, 1975 and The National Atlas of the United States, "Coastline and Shoreline," <http://nationalmap.gov/small_scale/>. See also <http://shoreline.noaa.gov/>.

Table 413. Flows of Largest U.S. Rivers—Length, Discharge, and Drainage Area

[A flow of 1,000 cubic ft. per second is equal to 646 million gallons per day, 724,000 acre-feet per year, or 28.3 cubic meters per second. One acre-foot is the volume of water that would cover 1 acre to a depth of 1 foot]

River	Location of mouth	Source stream (name and location)	Length (miles) [1]	Average discharge at mouth (1,000 cubic feet per second)	Drainage area (1,000 sq. miles)
Missouri	Missouri	Red Rock Creek, MT	[2] 2,540	76.2	[3] 529
Mississippi	Louisiana	Mississippi River, MN	2,340	[4] 593	[3,5] 1,150
Yukon	Alaska	McNeil River, Canada	1,980	225	[3] 328
St. Lawrence	Canada	North River, MN	1,900	348	[3] 396
Rio Grande	Mexico-Texas	Rio Grande, CO	1,900	([6])	336
Arkansas	Arkansas	East Fork Arkansas River, CO	1,460	41	161
Colorado	Mexico	Colorado River, CO	1,450	([6])	246
Atchafalaya [7]	Louisiana	Tierra Blanca Creek, NM	1,420	58	95
Ohio	Illinois-Kentucky	Allegheny River, PA	1,310	281	203
Red [7]	Louisiana	Tierra Blanca Creek, NM	1,290	56	93
Brazos	Texas	Blackwater Draw, NM	1,280	([6])	46
Columbia	Oregon-Washington	Columbia River, Canada	1,240	265	[3] 258
Snake	Washington	Snake River, WY	1,040	56.9	108
Platte	Nebraska	Grizzly Creek, CO	990	([6])	85
Pecos	Texas	Pecos River, NM	926	([6])	44
Canadian	Oklahoma	Canadian River, CO	906	([6])	47
Tennessee	Kentucky	Courthouse Creek, NC	886	68	41

[1] From source to mouth. [2] The length from the source of the Missouri River to the Mississippi River and thence to the Gulf of Mexico is about 3,710 miles. [3] Drainage area includes both the United States and Canada. [4] Includes about 167,000 cubic feet per second diverted from the Mississippi into the Atchafalaya River but excludes the flow of the Red River. [5] Excludes the drainage areas of the Red and Atchafalaya Rivers. [6] Less than 15,000 cubic feet per second. [7] In east-central Louisiana, the Red River flows into the Atchafalaya River, a distributary of the Mississippi River. Data on average discharge, length, and drainage area include the Red River, but exclude all water diverted into the Atchafalaya from the Mississippi River.

Source: U.S. Geological Survey, *Largest Rivers in the United States*, September 2005, <http://pubs.usgs.gov/of/1987/ofr87-242/>.

Table 414. Extreme and Mean Elevations by State and Other Areas

[One foot = .305 meter. There are 2,130 square miles of the United States below sea level (Death Valley is the lowest point). There are 20,230 square miles above 10,000 feet (Mount McKinley is the highest point in the United States). Minus sign (-) indicates below sea level]

State and other areas	Highest point Name	Elevation Feet	Elevation Meters	Lowest point Name	Elevation Feet	Elevation Meters	Approximate mean elevation Feet	Approximate mean elevation Meters
U.S.......	**Mount McKinley (AK)**	**20,310**	**6,190**	**Death Valley (CA)**	**-282**	**-86**	**2,500**	**763**
AL...........	Cheaha Mountain	2,407	734	Gulf of Mexico	([1])	([1])	500	153
AK.........	Mount McKinley	20,310	6,190	Pacific Ocean	([1])	([1])	1,900	580
AZ.........	Humphreys Peak	12,633	3,853	Colorado River	70	21	4,100	1,251
AR.........	Magazine Mountain	2,753	840	Ouachita River	55	17	650	198
CA.........	Mount Whitney	14,494	4,419	Death Valley	-282	-86	2,900	885
CO.........	Mount Elbert	14,433	4,402	Arikaree River	3,315	1,011	6,800	2,074
CT.........	Mount Frissell on south slope	2,380	726	Long Island Sound	([1])	([1])	500	153
DE.........	Ebright Road [2]	448	137	Atlantic Ocean	([1])	([1])	60	18
DC.........	Tenleytown at Reno Reservoir	410	125	Potomac River	1	(Z)	150	46
FL.........	Britton Hill	345	105	Atlantic Ocean	([1])	([1])	100	31
GA.........	Brasstown Bald	4,784	1,459	Atlantic Ocean	([1])	([1])	600	183
HI.........	Pu'u Wekiu, Mauna Kea	13,796	4,208	Pacific Ocean	([1])	([1])	3,030	924
ID.........	Borah Peak	12,662	3,862	Snake River	710	217	5,000	1,525
IL.........	Charles Mound	1,235	377	Mississippi River	279	85	600	183
IN.........	Hoosier Hill	1,257	383	Ohio River	320	98	700	214
IA.........	Hawkeye Point	1,670	509	Mississippi River	480	146	1,100	336
KS.........	Mount Sunflower	4,039	1,232	Verdigris River	679	207	2,000	610
KY.........	Black Mountain	4,145	1,264	Mississippi River	257	78	750	229
LA.........	Driskill Mountain	535	163	New Orleans	-8	-2	100	31
ME.........	Mount Katahdin	5,268	1,607	Atlantic Ocean	([1])	([1])	600	183
MD.........	Hoye Crest	3,360	1,025	Atlantic Ocean	([1])	([1])	350	107
MA.........	Mount Greylock	3,491	1,065	Atlantic Ocean	([1])	([1])	500	153
MI.........	Mount Arvon	1,979	604	Lake Erie	571	174	900	275
MN.........	Eagle Mountain	2,301	702	Lake Superior	601	183	1,200	366
MS.........	Woodall Mountain	806	246	Gulf of Mexico	([1])	([1])	300	92
MO.........	Taum Sauk Mountain	1,772	540	St. Francis River	230	70	800	244
MT.........	Granite Peak	12,799	3,904	Kootenai River	1,800	549	3,400	1,037
NE.........	Panorama Point	5,424	1,654	Missouri River	840	256	2,600	793
NV.........	Boundary Peak	13,140	4,007	Colorado River	479	146	5,500	1,678
NH.........	Mount Washington	6,288	1,918	Atlantic Ocean	([1])	([1])	1,000	305
NJ.........	High Point	1,803	550	Atlantic Ocean	([1])	([1])	250	76
NM.........	Wheeler Peak	13,161	4,014	Red Bluff Reservoir	2,842	867	5,700	1,739
NY.........	Mount Marcy	5,344	1,630	Atlantic Ocean	([1])	([1])	1,000	305
NC.........	Mount Mitchell	6,684	2,039	Atlantic Ocean	([1])	([1])	700	214
ND.........	White Butte	3,506	1,069	Red River of the North	750	229	1,900	580
OH.........	Campbell Hill	1,550	473	Ohio River	455	139	850	259
OK.........	Black Mesa	4,973	1,517	Little River	289	88	1,300	397
OR.........	Mount Hood	11,239	3,428	Pacific Ocean	([1])	([1])	3,300	1,007
PA.........	Mount Davis	3,213	980	Delaware River	([1])	([1])	1,100	336
RI.........	Jerimoth Hill	812	248	Atlantic Ocean	([1])	([1])	200	61
SC.........	Sassafras Mountain	3,560	1,086	Atlantic Ocean	([1])	([1])	350	107
SD.........	Harney Peak	7,242	2,209	Big Stone Lake	966	295	2,200	671
TN.........	Clingmans Dome	6,643	2,026	Mississippi River	178	54	900	275
TX.........	Guadalupe Peak	8,749	2,668	Gulf of Mexico	([1])	([1])	1,700	519
UT.........	Kings Peak	13,528	4,126	Beaverdam Wash	2,000	610	6,100	1,861
VT.........	Mount Mansfield	4,393	1,340	Lake Champlain	95	29	1,000	305
VA.........	Mount Rogers	5,729	1,747	Atlantic Ocean	([1])	([1])	950	290
WA.........	Mount Rainier	14,411	4,395	Pacific Ocean	([1])	([1])	1,700	519
WV.........	Spruce Knob	4,863	1,483	Potomac River	240	73	1,500	458
WI.........	Timms Hill	1,951	595	Lake Michigan	579	177	1,050	320
WY.........	Gannett Peak	13,804	4,210	Belle Fourche River	3,099	945	6,700	2,044
Other areas:								
Puerto Rico.......	Cerro de Punta	4,390	1,339	Atlantic Ocean	([1])	([1])	1,800	549
American Samoa....	Lata Mountain	3,160	964	Pacific Ocean	([1])	([1])	1,300	397
Guam.......	Mount Lamlam	1,332	406	Pacific Ocean	([1])	([1])	330	101
U.S. Virgin Islands....	Crown Mountain	1,556	475	Atlantic Ocean	([1])	([1])	750	229

Z Less than .5 meter. [1] Sea level. [2] At DE–PA state line.

Source: For highest and lowest points, see U.S. Geological Survey, "Elevations and Distances in the United States," <https://www.usgs.gov/products/publications/official-usgs-publications>, released April 2005. For mean elevations, see *Elevations and Distances in the United States*, 1983 edition.

Table 415. Acres of Land Cover by Type and Use: 1997 to 2015

[In millions of acres (1,944 represents 1,944,000,000), except percent. Excludes Alaska and District of Columbia. For inventory-specific glossary of key terms, see <http://www.nrcs.usda.gov/wps/portal/nrcs/main/national/technical/nra/nri/>]

Year	Total surface area [1]	Nonfederal rural land							Developed land	Water areas	Federal land
		Rural land total	Cropland	CRP land [2]	Pastureland	Rangeland	Forest land	Other rural land			
Land											
1997	1,944	1,395	376	33	120	408	414	43	96	51	403
2002	1,944	1,384	368	31	119	408	415	43	105	51	404
2007	1,944	1,377	359	33	120	407	414	44	111	52	405
2012	1,944	1,373	362	24	122	405	415	45	114	52	405
2015	1,944	1,372	367	18	122	404	416	45	115	52	405
Percent of total land											
1997	100.0	71.7	19.4	1.7	6.2	21.0	21.3	2.2	4.9	2.6	20.7
2002	100.0	71.2	18.9	1.6	6.1	21.0	21.3	2.2	5.4	2.6	20.8
2007	100.0	70.8	18.5	1.7	6.2	20.9	21.3	2.3	5.7	2.7	20.8
2012	100.0	70.6	18.6	1.2	6.3	20.8	21.3	2.3	5.8	2.7	20.8
2015	100.0	70.6	18.9	0.9	6.3	20.8	21.4	2.3	5.9	2.7	20.8

[1] Includes Puerto Rico and Virgin Islands. [2] Conservation Reserve Program (CRP) land. CRP is a federal program established under the Food Security Act of 1985 to assist private landowners to convert highly erodible cropland to vegetative cover for 10 years.

Source: U.S. Department of Agriculture, Natural Resources Conservation Service, *Summary Report: 2015 National Resources Inventory*, September 2018. See also <http://www.nrcs.usda.gov/technical/NRI/>.

Table 416. Wetlands on Nonfederal Land and Water Areas by Land Cover Type and Farm Production Region: 2015

[In thousands of acres (110,639 represents 110,639,000). Covers both palustrine (nontidal) and estuarine (tidal) wetlands; see source]

Farm production region [1]	Total	Cropland [3]	Forest land	Rangeland	Other rural land	Developed land	Water area
Wetlands, total [2]	**110,639**	**17,262**	**65,848**	**7,816**	**14,648**	**1,476**	**3,588**
Southeast	22,725	897	16,737	945	3,164	380	603
Lake states	22,170	3,110	14,980	–	3,714	164	202
Delta states	17,405	2,881	11,277	152	2,501	179	416
Northeast	13,513	1,101	10,466	–	1,481	233	232
Northern plains	7,873	3,226	226	2,822	1,141	80	379
Appalachian	7,437	381	6,087	–	544	117	309
Southern plains	5,660	1,021	2,622	833	389	164	630
Mountain	5,020	1,692	250	2,343	601	15	119
Corn belt	4,720	1,350	2,406	–	389	104	471
Pacific	3,982	1,582	733	719	694	40	214

– Represents zero. [1] Ten regions established by USDA, Economic Research Service, that group states according to differences in soils, slope of land, climate, distance to market, and storage and marketing facilities. [2] Total includes Hawaii and Caribbean territories, which are not included in the regions. [3] Cultivated and non-cultivated. Includes pastureland and Conservation Reserve Program (CRP) lands.

Source: U.S. Department of Agriculture, Natural Resources Conservation Service, *Summary Report: 2015 National Resources Inventory*, September 2018. See also <http://www.nrcs.usda.gov/technical/NRI/>.

Table 417. Acres of Federal and Non-Federal Land Cover by Type and State: 2015

[In thousands of acres (1,944,143 represents 1,944,143,000), except percent. Excludes Alaska and District of Columbia]

State	Total surface area [1]	Selected nonfederal rural land, percent of total			State	Total surface area [1]	Selected nonfederal rural land, percent of total		
		Cropland	Rangeland	Forest land			Cropland	Rangeland	Forest land
United States [2]	**1,944,143**	**18.9**	**20.8**	**21.4**	Montana	94,110	16.4	39.2	6.2
Alabama	33,424	6.8	0.2	65.5	Nebraska	49,510	40.7	46.1	1.7
Arizona	72,964	1.2	45.7	5.7	Nevada	70,763	0.8	12.4	0.5
Arkansas	34,037	21.0	0.1	44.3	New Hampshire	5,941	1.9	–	63.7
California	101,510	9.2	18.7	13.9	New Jersey	5,216	9.2	–	31.1
Colorado	66,625	12.1	36.8	5.3	New Mexico	77,823	1.8	52.7	7.2
Connecticut	3,195	5.2	–	49.9	New York	31,409	15.9	–	56.0
Delaware	1,534	26.0	–	22.6	North Carolina	33,709	15.1	–	46.5
Florida	37,534	7.5	6.6	35.2	North Dakota	45,251	55.8	23.6	1.0
Georgia	37,741	11.7	–	57.8	Ohio	26,445	42.2	–	27.1
Hawaii	4,123	2.1	27.1	36.1	Oklahoma	44,738	19.5	30.2	17.9
Idaho	53,488	10.1	12.7	7.5	Oregon	62,161	5.8	14.4	19.9
Illinois	36,059	66.4	–	11.3	Pennsylvania	28,995	17.0	–	54.2
Indiana	23,158	57.5	–	16.9	Rhode Island	813	2.1	–	44.1
Iowa	36,017	72.3	–	6.6	South Carolina	19,939	10.7	–	56.4
Kansas	52,661	49.8	29.8	3.4	South Dakota	49,358	36.5	44.9	1.1
Kentucky	25,863	21.9	–	41.8	Tennessee	26,974	16.9	–	44.3
Louisiana	31,377	15.7	0.6	41.6	Texas	171,052	13.8	54.0	8.7
Maine	20,966	1.8	–	83.5	Utah	54,339	2.9	19.8	4.1
Maryland	7,870	18.1	–	29.4	Vermont	6,154	8.5	–	65.9
Massachusetts	5,339	4.1	–	47.7	Virginia	27,087	10.4	–	48.9
Michigan	37,349	21.4	–	44.6	Washington	44,035	13.8	13.6	28.0
Minnesota	54,010	39.5	–	30.4	West Virginia	15,508	4.2	–	67.8
Mississippi	30,527	15.6	–	56.8	Wisconsin	35,920	28.8	–	41.2
Missouri	44,614	33.2	0.1	28.3	Wyoming	62,603	3.4	43.3	1.7

– Represents or rounds to zero. [1] Total surface area includes both Federal and non-Federal land. [2] Includes Puerto Rico and U.S. Virgin Islands, not shown separately.

Source: U.S. Department of Agriculture, Natural Resources Conservation Service, *Summary Report, 2015 National Resources Inventory*, September 2018. See also <http://www.nrcs.usda.gov/technical/NRI/>.

Table 418. U.S. Wetland Resources and Deepwater Habitats by Type: 2004 and 2009

[In thousands of acres (153,121.4 represents 153,121,400). Wetlands and deepwater habitats are defined separately because the term wetland does not include permanent water bodies. Deepwater habitats are permanently flooded land lying below the deepwater boundary of wetlands. Deepwater habitats include environments where surface water is permanent and often deep, so that water, rather than air, is the principal medium within which the dominant organisms live, whether or not they are attached to the substrate. As in wetlands, the dominant plants are hydrophytes; however, the substrates are considered nonsoil because the water is too deep to support emergent vegetation. In general terms, wetlands are lands where saturation with water is the dominant factor determining the nature of soil development and the types of plant and animal communities living in the soil and on its surface. The single feature that most wetlands share is soil or substrate that is at least periodically saturated with or covered by water. Wetlands are lands transitional between terrestrial and aquatic systems where the water table is usually at or near the surface or the land is covered by shallow water. For more information on wetlands, see the "Classification of Wetlands and Deepwater Habitats of the United States" at <https://www.fws.gov/wetlands/documents/classwet/index.html>]

Wetland or deepwater category	Estimated area, 2004	Estimated area, 2009	Change, 2004 to 2009
All wetlands and deepwater habitats, total.............	**153,121.4**	**153,206.4**	**85.0**
All deepwater habitats, total......................................	42,999.4	43,146.6	147.2
Lacustrine [1]...	16,786.0	16,859.6	73.6
Riverine [2]...	7,517.9	7,510.5	-7.4
Estuarine Subtidal [3]...	18,695.4	18,776.5	81.1
All wetlands, total..	110,122.1	110,059.8	-62.3
Intertidal wetlands [4]...	5,869.3	5,785.2	-84.1
Marine intertidal..	219.2	227.8	8.5
Estuarine intertidal nonvegetated......................	999.4	1,017.7	18.3
Estuarine intertidal vegetated............................	4,650.7	4,539.7	-110.9
Freshwater wetlands..	104,252.7	104,274.6	21.9
Freshwater nonvegetated...................................	6,502.1	6,709.3	207.2
Freshwater vegetated...	97,750.6	97,565.3	-185.3
Freshwater emergent [5]......................................	27,162.7	27,430.5	267.8
Freshwater forested [6]...	52,256.5	51,623.3	-633.1
Freshwater shrub [7]..	18,331.4	18,511.5	180.1

[1] The lacustrine system includes deepwater habitats with all of the following characteristics: (1) situated in a topographic depression or a dammed river channel; (2) lacking trees, shrubs, persistent emergents, emergent mosses or lichens with greater than 30 percent coverage; and (3) total area exceeds 20 acres (8 hectares). [2] The riverine system includes deepwater habitats contained within a channel, with the exception of habitats with water containing ocean derived salts in excess of 0.5 parts per thousand. [3] The estuarine system consists of deepwater tidal habitats and adjacent tidal wetlands that are usually semi-enclosed by land but have open, partly obstructed, or sporadic access to the open ocean, and in which ocean water is at least occasionally diluted by freshwater runoff from the land. Subtidal is where the substrate is continuously submerged by marine or estuarine waters. [4] Intertidal is where the substrate is exposed and flooded by tides. Intertidal includes the splash zone of coastal waters. [5] Emergent wetlands are characterized by erect, rooted, herbaceous hydrophytes, excluding mosses and lichens. This vegetation is present for most of the growing season in most years. These wetlands are usually dominated by perennial plants. [6] Forested wetlands are characterized by woody vegetation that is 20 feet tall or taller. [7] Shrub wetlands include areas dominated by woody vegetation less than 20 feet tall. The species include true shrubs, young trees, and trees or shrubs that are small or stunted because of environmental conditions.

Source: U.S. Fish and Wildlife Service, *Status and Trends of Wetlands in the Conterminous United States, 2004 to 2009*, September 2011. See also <http://www.fws.gov/wetlands/Status-And-Trends-2009/index.html>.

Table 419. U.S. Water Withdrawals Per Day by End Use: 1950 to 2015

[In billions of gallons of water per day (180 represents 180,000,000,000). Includes the District of Columbia, Puerto Rico and U.S. Virgin Islands, as noted. Withdrawal signifies water physically withdrawn from a source. Includes fresh and saline water; excludes water used for hydroelectric power. For information on changes in data collection and presentation methods, see source report]

Year	Total with-drawals	Public supply	Rural domestic and livestock — Self supplied domestic	Rural domestic and livestock — Live-stock	Irri-gation	Thermo-electric power	Other — Self supplied industrial	Other — Mining	Other — Com-mercial	Other — Aqua-culture
1950 [1].........	180	14	2.1	1.5	89	40	37.0	[5]	[5]	[5]
1955 [2].........	240	17	2.1	1.5	110	72	39.0	[5]	[5]	[5]
1960 [3].........	270	21	2.0	1.6	110	100	38.0	[5]	[5]	[5]
1965 [4].........	310	24	2.3	1.7	120	130	46.0	[5]	[5]	[5]
1970 [4].........	370	27	2.6	1.9	130	170	47.0	[5]	[5]	[5]
1975 [3].........	420	29	2.8	2.1	140	200	45.0	[5]	[5]	[5]
1980 [3].........	430	33	3.4	2.2	150	210	45.0	[5]	[5]	[5]
1985 [3].........	397	37	3.3	2.2	135	187	25.8	3.4	1.2	2.2
1990 [3].........	404	39	3.4	2.3	134	194	22.4	4.9	2.4	2.2
1995 [3].........	398	40	3.4	2.3	130	190	21.6	3.6	2.9	3.3
2000 [3].........	413	43	3.6	2.4	139	195	19.5	4.1	(NA)	5.8
2005 [3].........	410	44	3.7	2.2	127	201	18.1	3.8	(NA)	8.8
2010 [3].........	354	42	3.5	2.0	116	162	16.2	4.0	(NA)	9.0
2015 [3].........	322	39	3.3	2.0	118	133	14.8	4.0	(NA)	7.6

NA Not available. [1] Population covered: 48 states, District of Columbia (D.C.), and Hawaii. [2] Population covered: 48 states and D.C. [3] Population covered: 50 states, D.C., Puerto Rico, and the Virgin Islands. [4] Population covered: 50 states, D.C., and Puerto Rico. [5] Included in "self-supplied industrial."

Source: U.S. Geological Survey, *Estimated Use of Water in the United States in 2015*, circular 1441, 2018. See also <https://pubs.er.usgs.gov/publication/cir1441>.

Table 420. National Ambient Air Pollutant Concentrations by Type of Pollutant: 2010 to 2018

[Data represent composite averages across monitoring stations meeting minimum data completeness requirements for the trend period. Carbon monoxide is based on the second-highest, nonoverlapping, 8-hour average; ozone, the fourth-highest maximum 8-hour value; particulates (PM-10) on the second highest daily 24-hour average; fine particulates (PM2.5) annual average on the weighted annual mean of daily 24-hour averages; and lead on the maximum rolling three-month average. Based on data from the Air Quality System. µg/m^3 = micrograms of pollutant per cubic meter of air; ppm = parts per million; ppb = parts per billion]

Pollutant	Unit	Moni-toring stations, number	Air quality stan-dard [1]	2010	2012	2013	2014	2015	2016	2017	2018
Carbon monoxide..............	ppm	213	[2] 9	1.4	1.3	1.3	1.2	1.2	1.2	1.2	1.2
Ozone............................	ppm	1,151	[3] 0.070	0.071	0.073	0.066	0.066	0.067	0.067	0.067	0.068
Sulfur dioxide..................	ppb	287	[4] 75	43	35	29	27	23	18	14	14
Particulates (PM-10)..........	µg/m^3	556	[5] 150	77.0	81.3	74.6	72.3	70.9	68.7	79.6	75.1
Fine particulates (PM2.5) annual average...............	µg/m^3	649	[6] 12	9.7	9.0	8.8	8.7	8.4	7.6	8.0	8.1
Nitrogen dioxide...............	ppb	221	[7] 100	41	39	38	38	37	35	35	35
Lead............................	µg/m^3	117	[8] 0.15	0.16	0.14	0.08	0.05	0.04	0.03	0.03	0.03

[1] Refers to the primary National Ambient Air Quality Standard. [2] Based on 8-hour standard of 9 ppm. [3] Based on 8-hour standard of 0.070 ppm. On December 28, 2015, EPA revised the level of the primary and secondary 8-hour ozone standards to 0.070 ppm. [4] Based on a 1-hour daily maximum concentration of 75 ppb. [5] Based on 24-hour (daily) standard of 150 µg/m^3. The particulates (PM-10) standard replaced the previous standard for total suspended particulates in 1987. In 2006, EPA revoked the annual PM-10 standard. [6] Based on annual standard of 12 µg/m^3. The PM-2.5 national monitoring network was deployed in 1999. [7] Based on a 1-hour daily maximum concentration of 100 ppb. [8] Based on 3-month rolling average of 0.15 µg/m^3.

Source: U.S. Environmental Protection Agency, "Air Trends," <https://www.epa.gov/air-trends>, accessed April 2020.

Table 421. Selected Air Pollutant Emissions: 1990 to 2019

[In thousands of tons (4,320 represents 4,320,000). For documentation regarding the data, see <https://www.epa.gov/air-emissions-inventories/national-emissions-inventory-nei>]

Year	Ammonia	Carbon monoxide	Nitrogen oxide	PM-10 [1]	PM-2.5 [1]	Sulfur dioxide	VOCs [2]
1990..............	4,320	154,188	25,527	27,753	7,560	23,077	24,108
2000..............	4,907	114,467	22,598	23,747	7,288	16,347	17,512
2010..............	4,271	73,771	14,846	20,823	5,964	7,732	17,835
2011..............	4,032	73,762	14,519	20,723	6,100	6,479	18,154
2012..............	3,823	71,758	13,879	19,970	5,940	5,079	17,872
2013..............	3,813	69,755	13,239	19,217	5,780	4,873	17,590
2014..............	3,571	65,537	12,589	18,183	5,381	4,674	16,883
2015..............	3,764	63,516	11,682	17,526	5,229	3,945	16,330
2016..............	3,955	58,904	10,304	16,830	5,060	3,204	15,459
2017..............	4,297	66,805	9,907	17,103	5,699	2,550	17,218
2018..............	4,291	65,115	9,381	17,116	5,693	2,462	16,980
2019..............	4,289	64,188	8,950	17,110	5,686	2,168	16,864

[1] PM = Particular Matter; PM-10 is equal to or less than ten microns in diameter; PM-2.5 to or less than 2.5 microns effective diameter. [2] Volatile organic compounds.

Source: U.S. Environmental Protection Agency, "National Emissions Inventory (NEI) Air Pollutant Emissions Trends Data, 1970-2019," <https://www.epa.gov/air-emissions-inventories/air-pollutant-emissions-trends-data>, accessed May 2020.

Table 422. Air Pollutant Emissions by Selected Pollutant and Source: 2019

[In thousands of tons (4,289 represents 4,289,000). See headnote, Table 421]

Source	Ammonia	Carbon monoxide	Nitrogen oxide	PM-10 [1]	PM-2.5 [1]	Sulfur dioxide	VOCs [2]
Total emissions...................	**4,289**	**64,188**	**8,950**	**17,110**	**5,686**	**2,168**	**16,864**
Fuel combustion, stationary sources.................	90	4,071	2,522	748	657	1,438	505
Electric utilities.....................	20	588	996	132	107	1,017	32
Industrial............................	16	812	1,032	246	185	377	112
Other fuel combustion................	54	2,671	494	370	364	44	362
Industrial and other processes................	79	2,995	1,139	1,132	590	463	6,784
Chemical and allied product manufacturing........	24	118	41	19	15	111	75
Metals processing.................	1	468	66	51	35	85	22
Petroleum and related industries....................	2	652	623	27	23	95	2,493
Other................................	27	447	321	767	297	146	346
Solvent utilization.................	–	2	1	5	4	–	2,972
Storage and transport.............	4	7	5	36	13	1	697
Waste disposal and recycling........	21	1,301	81	227	203	25	177
Highway vehicles...................	93	16,866	2,775	253	107	11	1,496
Off highway [3]......................	2	11,579	2,105	135	127	38	1,190
Miscellaneous [4]...................	4,026	28,676	409	14,843	4,205	218	6,888

– Rounds to zero. [1] See footnote 1, Table 421. [2] Volatile organic compounds. [3] Includes emissions from farm tractors and other farm machinery, construction equipment, industrial machinery, recreational marine vessels, and small general utility engines such as lawn mowers. [4] Includes emissions from forest fires and other kinds of burning, various agricultural activities, fugitive dust from paved and unpaved roads, other construction and mining activities, and natural sources.

Source: U.S. Environmental Protection Agency, "National Emissions Inventory (NEI) Air Pollutant Emissions Trends Data, 1970-2019," <https://www.epa.gov/air-emissions-inventories/air-pollutant-emissions-trends-data>, accessed June 2020.

Table 423. Greenhouse Gas Emissions by Type and Source: 1990 to 2018

[In millions of metric tons of carbon dioxide equivalent (MMT CO2 Eq.). 6,437.0 represents 6,437,000,000. MMT CO2 Eq. weights each gas by its global warming potential (GWP) value. GWP is a quantified measure of the globally averaged relative radiative forcing impacts of a particular greenhouse gas. The reference gas used is CO2; therefore, GWP-weighted emissions are measured in MMT CO2 Eq. See source for details]

Type and/or source	1990	2000	2010	2014	2015	2016	2017	2018
Total emissions	**6,437.0**	**7,275.4**	**6,981.6**	**6,829.0**	**6,676.4**	**6,524.1**	**6,488.2**	**6,676.6**
BY SOURCE								
Energy	5,338.1	6,160.4	5,875.5	5,704.0	5,550.1	5,421.6	5,383.8	5,547.2
Industrial processes and product use [1]	345.6	394.7	364.1	380.8	377.1	370.4	370.7	376.5
Sulfur hexafluoride (SF6)	28.8	16.6	7.3	6.5	5.5	6.1	5.9	5.9
Hydrofluorocarbons (HFCs)	46.5	118.3	157.4	166.3	170.5	170.5	172.5	171.6
Perfluorocarbons (PFCs)	24.3	15.9	4.6	5.6	5.1	4.3	4.0	4.6
Agriculture	554.4	556.0	595.0	608.6	614.6	600.5	602.3	618.5
Land use, land-use change, and forestry	7.4	10.7	11.4	16.6	27.4	12.8	26.1	26.1
Waste	199.0	164.4	147.0	135.6	134.7	131.6	131.4	134.4
Net CO2 flux from land use, land use change, and forestry [2]	*-853.4*	*-811.6*	*-740.5*	*-723.0*	*-775.5*	*-788.9*	*-763.9*	*-773.5*
Net emissions (sources and sinks) [2]	5,583.6	6,463.8	6,241.1	6,106.0	5,900.8	5,735.1	5,724.3	5,903.2
BY TYPE AND SOURCE								
Carbon dioxide (CO2), total	**5,128.3**	**5,998.1**	**5,698.1**	**5,561.7**	**5,412.4**	**5,292.3**	**5,253.6**	**5,424.9**
Energy	4,909.3	5,772.9	5,518.0	5,375.4	5,231.5	5,119.8	5,081.3	5,249.3
Fossil fuel combustion	4,740.0	5,585.1	5,351.0	5,184.8	5,031.8	4,942.4	4,892.2	5,031.8
Electricity	1,820.0	2,296.0	2,258.6	2,037.1	1,900.6	1,808.9	1,732.0	1,752.8
Transportation	1,469.1	1,779.4	1,695.5	1,713.7	1,725.3	1,765.3	1,787.3	1,820.7
Industrial	857.0	867.3	794.7	812.9	801.3	801.4	805.0	833.3
Residential	338.2	370.7	334.9	346.8	317.8	293.1	293.8	337.3
Commercial	228.2	236.2	224.9	232.8	245.4	232.3	232.8	246.5
Biomass (wood) [3]	219.4	227.4	290.6	323.2	317.7	317.2	322.2	328.9
Industrial processes and product use	212.3	217.9	171.9	178.8	173.1	165.3	164.7	167.8
Agriculture	6.7	7.3	8.1	7.5	7.8	7.1	7.6	7.7
Land use, land-use change, and forestry (sink)	*-860.7*	*-822.3*	*-752.0*	*-739.6*	*-802.9*	*-801.7*	*-790.0*	*-799.6*
Methane (CH4), total	**774.4**	**703.0**	**682.3**	**639.0**	**638.5**	**624.2**	**630.3**	**634.5**
Energy	361.2	305.8	295.8	275.6	269.3	253.9	257.3	253.9
Industrial processes and product use	0.3	0.3	0.1	0.2	0.2	0.3	0.3	0.3
Agriculture	217.6	237.9	245.6	234.3	241.0	245.3	248.4	253.0
Land use, land-use change, and forestry	4.4	5.7	6.5	9.5	16.1	7.3	15.2	15.2
Waste management	195.3	159.0	140.9	129.0	128.0	124.7	124.3	127.2
Nitrous oxide (N2O), total	**434.6**	**423.3**	**431.4**	**449.3**	**443.8**	**426.1**	**421.3**	**434.5**
Energy	67.6	81.6	61.6	53.1	49.2	47.8	45.2	44.0
Industrial processes and product use	33.3	25.4	22.4	22.8	22.2	23.3	22.7	25.5
Agriculture	330.1	310.8	341.3	366.7	365.8	348.1	346.2	357.8
Land use, land-use change, and forestry	3.0	5.0	4.9	7.0	11.2	5.5	10.8	10.9
Waste management	3.7	5.5	6.2	6.6	6.7	6.9	7.2	7.2

[1] Total includes items not shown separately. [2] The net CO2 flux total includes both emissions and sequestration, and constitutes a sink in the United States. Sinks are only included in net emissions total. [3] Emissions from wood biomass and ethanol consumption are not included specifically in summing energy sector totals. Net carbon fluxes from changes in biogenic carbon reservoirs are accounted for in the estimates for land use, land-use change, and forestry.

Source: U.S. Environmental Protection Agency, *Inventory of U.S. Greenhouse Gas Emissions and Sinks, 1990-2018*, April 2020. See also <https://www.epa.gov/ghgemissions/inventory-us-greenhouse-gas-emissions-and-sinks>.

Table 424. Carbon Dioxide Emissions from Fossil Fuel Combustion by Fuel Type and Sector: 1990 to 2018

[In millions of metric tons of carbon dioxide equivalent (MMT CO2 Eq.); 4,740.0 represents 4,740,000,000. See source for details on methodology]

Fuel and sector	1990	2000	2005	2010	2015	2016	2017	2018
Total [1]	**4,740.0**	**5,585.1**	**5,740.7**	**5,351.0**	**5,031.8**	**4,942.5**	**4,892.3**	**5,031.8**
Coal	**1,717.3**	**2,064.4**	**2,111.2**	**1,927.5**	**1,424.7**	**1,307.5**	**1,267.5**	**1,208.5**
Residential	3.0	1.1	0.8	–	–	–	–	–
Commercial	12.0	8.8	9.3	6.6	3.0	2.3	2.0	1.8
Industrial	155.2	127.3	115.3	90.2	66.3	59.2	54.4	49.8
Electricity generation	1,546.5	1,926.4	1,982.8	1,827.3	1,351.4	1,242.0	1,207.1	1,152.9
Natural gas	**999.7**	**1,219.7**	**1,167.0**	**1,274.0**	**1,460.2**	**1,471.8**	**1,451.4**	**1,611.6**
Residential	237.8	270.8	262.2	258.9	252.7	238.4	241.5	273.7
Commercial	142.0	172.5	162.9	168.0	175.4	170.5	173.2	192.6
Industrial	408.5	459.2	388.6	407.9	464.4	474.8	485.8	514.8
Transportation	36.0	35.7	33.1	38.2	39.4	40.1	42.3	50.2
Electricity generation	175.4	280.8	318.9	399.5	525.2	545.0	505.6	577.4
Petroleum	**2,022.4**	**2,300.5**	**2,462.1**	**2,149.2**	**2,146.5**	**2,162.7**	**2,172.9**	**2,211.3**
Residential	97.4	98.8	94.9	76.0	65.1	54.8	52.3	63.5
Commercial	74.2	54.9	54.7	50.3	67.1	59.5	57.6	52.1
Industrial	293.3	280.8	346.2	296.5	270.5	267.4	264.8	268.6
Transportation	1,433.1	1,743.7	1,823.0	1,657.3	1,685.9	1,725.2	1,745.0	1,770.5
Electricity generation	97.5	88.4	97.9	31.4	23.7	21.4	18.9	22.2

– Represents zero. [1] Includes data for geothermal energy-related carbon dioxide emissions and U.S. territories, not shown separately.

Source: U.S. Environmental Protection Agency, *Inventory of U.S. Greenhouse Gas Emissions and Sinks, 1990-2018*, April 2020. See also <https://www.epa.gov/ghgemissions/inventory-us-greenhouse-gas-emissions-and-sinks>.

Table 425. Municipal Solid Waste Generation, Materials Recovery, Recycling, Combustion With Energy Recovery, and Discards: 1980 to 2017

[In millions of tons (151.6 represents 151,600,000), except as indicated. Covers post-consumer residential, commercial, and institutional solid wastes that comprise the major portion of typical municipal collections. Excludes mining, agricultural and industrial processing, demolition and construction wastes, sewage sludge, junked autos, and obsolete equipment wastes. Based on material-flows estimating procedure and wet weight as generated]

Item and material	1980	1990	2000	2010	2015	2016	2017
Waste generated...............................	**151.6**	**208.3**	**243.5**	**251.1**	**262.1**	**266.8**	**267.8**
Per person per day (lb.).......................	3.7	4.6	4.7	4.5	4.5	4.5	4.5
Total materials recovery...................	**14.5**	**33.2**	**69.5**	**85.4**	**91.0**	**93.7**	**94.2**
Per person per day (lb.).......................	0.4	0.7	1.4	1.5	1.6	1.6	1.6
Recovery for recycling.........................	14.5	29.0	53.0	65.3	67.6	68.6	67.2
Per person per day (lb.).......................	0.4	0.6	1.0	1.2	1.2	1.2	1.1
Recovery for composting [1].................	(Z)	4.2	16.5	20.2	23.4	25.1	27.0
Per person per day (lb.).......................	(Z)	0.1	0.3	0.4	0.4	0.4	0.5
Combustion with energy recovery..........	2.8	29.8	33.7	29.3	33.6	33.9	34.0
Per person per day (lb.).......................	0.1	0.7	0.7	0.5	0.6	0.6	0.6
Discards to landfill, other disposal..........	134.4	145.3	140.3	136.3	137.6	139.2	139.6
Per person per day (lb.).......................	3.2	3.2	2.7	2.4	2.4	2.4	2.4
PERCENT DISTRIBUTION OF GENERATION							
Materials in products.......................	**71.8**	**70.3**	**73.4**	**70.9**	**70.1**	**70.3**	**70.2**
Paper and paperboard.........................	36.4	34.9	36.0	28.4	26.0	25.3	25.0
Glass...	10.0	6.3	5.2	4.6	4.4	4.3	4.2
Metals...	10.2	7.9	7.8	8.9	9.1	9.2	9.4
Plastics..	4.5	8.2	10.5	12.5	13.2	13.1	13.2
Rubber and leather..............................	2.8	2.8	2.7	3.1	3.3	3.4	3.4
Textiles..	1.7	2.8	3.9	5.3	6.1	6.3	6.3
Wood...	4.6	5.9	5.6	6.3	6.2	6.8	6.7
Other...	1.7	1.5	1.6	1.9	1.8	1.9	2.0
Other waste....................................	**28.2**	**29.7**	**26.6**	**29.1**	**29.9**	**29.7**	**29.8**
Food waste...	8.6	11.5	12.6	14.2	15.2	15.1	15.2
Yard trimmings....................................	18.1	16.8	12.5	13.3	13.2	13.1	13.1
Miscellaneous inorganic wastes............	1.5	1.4	1.4	1.5	1.5	1.5	1.5

Z Less than 5,000 tons or 0.05 percent. [1] Composting of yard trimmings, food scraps, and other municipal solid waste organic material. Does not include backyard composting.

Source: U.S. Environmental Protection Agency, *Advancing Sustainable Materials Management: 2016 and 2017 Tables and Figures*, November 2019. See also <https://www.epa.gov/smm>.

Table 426. Generation and Recovery of Selected Materials in Municipal Solid Waste: 1980 to 2017

[In millions of tons (151.6 represents 151,600,000), except as indicated. Covers post-consumer residential, commercial, and institutional solid wastes that comprise the major portion of typical municipal collections. Excludes mining, agricultural and industrial processing, demolition and construction wastes, sewage sludge, and junked autos and obsolete equipment wastes. Based on material-flows estimating procedure and wet weight as generated. Material recovered includes material recycled and composted]

Item and material	1980	1990	2000	2010	2015	2016	2017
Waste generated, total [1].................	**151.6**	**208.3**	**243.5**	**251.1**	**262.1**	**266.8**	**267.8**
Paper and paperboard.........................	55.2	72.7	87.7	71.3	68.1	67.5	67.0
Glass...	15.1	13.1	12.8	11.5	11.5	11.5	11.4
Ferrous metals....................................	12.6	12.6	14.2	16.9	18.2	18.7	18.9
Aluminum...	1.7	2.8	3.2	3.5	3.7	3.8	3.8
Other nonferrous metals.......................	1.2	1.1	1.6	2.0	2.0	2.1	2.3
Plastics..	6.8	17.1	25.6	31.4	34.5	34.9	35.4
Food waste...	13.0	23.9	30.7	35.7	39.7	40.3	40.7
Yard trimmings....................................	27.5	35.0	30.5	33.4	34.7	35.0	35.2
Materials recovered, total [1]..............	**14.5**	**33.2**	**69.5**	**85.4**	**91.0**	**93.7**	**94.2**
Paper and paperboard.........................	11.7	20.2	37.6	44.6	45.3	45.5	44.2
Glass...	0.8	2.6	2.9	3.1	3.2	3.2	3.0
Ferrous metals....................................	0.4	2.2	4.7	5.8	6.1	6.2	6.2
Aluminum...	0.3	1.0	0.9	0.7	0.7	0.6	0.6
Other nonferrous metals.......................	0.5	0.7	1.1	1.4	1.3	1.4	1.5
Plastics..	(Z)	0.4	1.5	2.5	3.1	3.2	3.0
Food waste [2]....................................	(Z)	(Z)	0.7	1.0	2.1	2.2	2.6
Yard trimmings....................................	(Z)	4.2	15.8	19.2	21.3	23.0	24.4
Percent of generation recovered, total [1]...........	**9.6**	**16.0**	**28.5**	**34.0**	**34.7**	**35.1**	**35.2**
Paper and paperboard.........................	21.3	27.8	42.8	62.5	66.6	67.5	65.9
Glass...	5.0	20.1	22.6	27.2	27.8	27.5	26.6
Ferrous metals....................................	2.9	17.6	33.1	34.3	33.4	33.0	32.7
Aluminum...	17.9	35.9	27.0	19.4	18.3	16.4	16.2
Other nonferrous metals.......................	46.6	66.4	66.3	71.3	64.2	65.0	66.1
Plastics..	0.3	2.2	5.8	8.0	9.0	9.3	8.4
Food waste [2]....................................	(Z)	(Z)	2.2	2.7	5.3	5.3	6.3
Yard trimmings....................................	(Z)	12.0	51.7	57.5	61.3	65.7	69.4

Z Less than 5,000 tons or 0.05 percent. [1] Includes other types of materials not shown separately. [2] Includes collection of other municipal solid waste organic materials for composting.

Source: U.S. Environmental Protection Agency, *Advancing Sustainable Materials Management: 2016 and 2017 Tables and Figures*, November 2019. See also <https://www.epa.gov/smm>.

Table 427. Municipal Solid Waste—Generation, Recycling, and Landfill Disposal by Selected Type of Product: 2017

[67,010 represents 67,010,000. See headnote, Table 426]

Type of product	Generation (1,000 tons)	Recycling Volume recycled (1,000 tons)	Recycling Percent of generation	Landfill disposal (1,000 tons)
Paper and paperboard products [1]	**67,010**	**44,170**	**65.9**	**18,350**
Nondurable goods	25,950	14,090	54.3	9,530
Newspapers/mechanical papers	5,440	4,180	76.8	1,010
Other paper nondurable goods	20,510	9,910	48.3	8,520
Containers and packaging	41,060	30,080	73.3	8,820
Corrugated boxes	32,540	28,780	88.4	3,020
Other paper and paperboard packaging	8,520	1,300	15.3	5,800
Glass products [1]	**11,380**	**3,030**	**26.6**	**6,870**
Containers and packaging	8,930	3,030	33.9	4,740
Beer and soft drink bottles	5,270	2,060	39.1	2,580
Wine and liquor bottles	1,740	680	39.1	850
Other bottles and jars	1,920	290	15.1	1,310
Metal products [1]	**25,050**	**8,330**	**33.3**	**13,800**
Metals in durable goods	20,930	6,240	29.8	12,170
Ferrous	16,880	4,700	27.8	9,990
Aluminum	1,720	(NA)	(NA)	1,460
Other nonferrous	780	(Z)	(Z)	710
Metals in containers and packaging	3,900	2,090	53.6	1,450
Plastics [1]	**35,370**	**2,960**	**8.4**	**26,820**
Plastics in durable goods	13,460	850	6.3	10,890
Plastics in nondurable goods	7,420	220	3.0	5,800
Plastics in containers and packaging	14,490	1,890	13.0	10,130
Rubber and leather [1]	**9,110**	**1,670**	**18.3**	**4,950**
Durable goods	7,940	1,670	21.0	4,000
Rubber in tires	4,190	1,670	39.9	780
Other durables	3,750	(Z)	(Z)	3,220
Nondurable goods	1,170	(Z)	(Z)	950
Clothing and footwear	890	(Z)	(Z)	720
Other nondurables	280	(Z)	(Z)	230

NA Not available. Z Less than 5,000 tons or .05 percent. [1] Includes products not shown separately.

Source: U.S. Environmental Protection Agency, *Advancing Sustainable Materials Management: 2016 and 2017 Tables and Figures,* November 2019. See also <https://www.epa.gov/smm>.

Table 428. Environmental Industry—Revenues and Employment by Industry Segment: 2000 to 2019

[210.1 represents $210,100,000,000. Covers approximately 30,000 private and public companies engaged in revenue-generating environmental activities]

Industry segment	Revenue (billion dollars) 2000	2010	2018	2019	Employment 2000	2010	2018	2019
Industry total	**210.1**	**303.3**	**394.5**	**408.9**	**1,264,600**	**1,595,400**	**1,721,000**	**1,732,500**
SERVICES								
Analytical services [1]	1.8	1.9	2.1	2.1	17,900	17,000	16,400	16,500
Wastewater treatment works [2]	28.7	45.5	63.1	65.3	118,800	170,100	198,500	199,900
Solid waste management [3]	39.4	53.4	64.6	66.4	221,400	278,000	289,800	290,100
Hazardous waste management [4]	8.8	10.0	11.0	11.0	48,300	48,500	47,700	47,300
Remediation/industrial services	9.9	12.4	14.2	14.4	98,400	105,000	97,300	98,100
Consulting and engineering	17.4	26.8	32.7	33.8	170,400	240,400	230,600	231,500
EQUIPMENT								
Water equipment and chemicals	19.8	26.9	32.8	33.8	130,500	160,100	167,900	167,700
Instrument manufacturing	3.8	5.4	7.9	8.3	30,200	37,100	48,300	50,300
Air pollution control equipment [5]	19.0	14.9	17.3	17.2	129,600	96,400	95,900	93,100
Waste management equipment [6]	11.1	12.7	15.8	16.0	84,300	86,600	95,400	94,700
RESOURCES								
Water utilities [7]	29.9	43.5	61.8	64.4	130,000	172,100	214,600	217,700
Resource recovery [8]	16.0	28.5	23.0	21.6	61,900	102,600	72,800	68,000
Clean energy systems and power [9]	4.4	21.4	48.5	54.8	22,900	81,500	145,800	157,600

[1] Covers environmental laboratory testing and services. [2] Mostly revenues collected by municipal entities for sewage or wastewater plants. [3] Covers public & private sector collection, transportation, transfer stations, disposal, landfill ownership and management for solid waste and recyclables. [4] Transportation and disposal of hazardous, medical, and nuclear waste. [5] Includes stationary and mobile sources. [6] Equipment for handling, storing or transporting solid, liquid or hazardous waste. Includes recycling/remediation equipment. [7] Revenues generated from the sale of water, majority in public sector. [8] Revenues generated from the sale of recovered metals, paper, plastic, etc. [9] Revenues generated from the sale of equipment and systems and electricity.

Source: Environmental Business International, Inc., San Diego, CA, publisher of *Environmental Business Journal;* © 2020 EBI Inc. See also <http://www.ebionline.org>.

Table 429. Toxic Chemical Releases and Transfers by Media: 2011 to 2018

[In millions of pounds (4,117.8 represents 4,117,800,000), except as indicated. Based on reports filed to the Toxic Release Inventory (TRI) Program, as required by Section 313 of the Emergency Planning and Community Right-to-Know Act (EPCRA). The Pollution Prevention Act (PPA) of 1990 mandates collection of data on toxic chemicals that are treated on-site, recycled, and combusted for energy recovery. Owners and operators of facilities within specific North American Industry Classification System industries that have 10 or more full-time employees, and that manufacture, process, or otherwise use any listed toxic chemical in quantities greater than the established threshold in the course of a calendar year are covered and required to report. For trend analysis, a 2011 core list of must-be-reported chemicals is used. Includes carcinogens; persistent, bioaccumulative, toxic (PBT) chemicals; and dioxin and dioxin-like compounds. Does not include off-site disposal or other releases transferred to other TRI program facilities that reported the amounts as on-site disposal or other releases]

Media	2011	2012	2013	2014	2015	2016	2017	2018
Total facilities reporting (number)...............	**21,921**	**22,090**	**22,281**	**22,355**	**22,300**	**21,993**	**21,752**	**21,595**
Total on- and off-site disposal or other releases.......	**4,117.8**	**3,622.4**	**4,133.9**	**3,974.3**	**3,419.5**	**3,506.0**	**3,900.3**	**3,766.4**
On-site releases.............................	3,701.7	3,206.0	3,701.4	3,519.5	2,946.3	3,105.8	3,512.5	3,337.1
Air emissions [1].............................	808.5	753.6	753.9	742.8	676.4	598.7	588.3	586.0
Surface water discharges....................	222.9	218.4	213.8	218.7	198.9	192.2	190.9	194.9
Underground injection class I...............	197.8	203.9	200.3	202.0	209.2	198.4	197.5	209.9
Underground injection class II-V...........	0.2	0.2	2.1	0.9	0.8	0.6	0.5	0.6
RCRA subtitle C landfills [2]...................	69.4	94.3	68.3	58.0	78.4	90.7	83.7	87.6
Other landfills.............................	273.6	269.9	297.6	298.1	290.3	279.3	306.1	287.8
Land treatment/application farming........	15.0	16.0	14.0	13.3	14.1	12.2	14.5	15.2
Surface impoundments....................	884.8	724.3	738.7	758.8	793.1	840.6	909.1	901.3
Other land disposal........................	1,229.5	925.3	1,412.6	1,227.0	685.0	893.3	1,221.9	1,053.8
Off-site releases...........................	416.1	416.4	432.5	454.8	473.2	400.2	387.8	429.3
Total transfers offsite for further waste management..........	**3,723.1**	**3,918.6**	**3,621.4**	**3,656.6**	**3,597.8**	**3,540.8**	**3,641.0**	**3,829.9**
Transfers to recycling.....................	2,370.4	2,485.7	2,201.1	2,240.9	2,178.0	2,197.2	2,326.9	2,460.5
Transfers to energy recovery...............	354.7	388.3	407.8	422.4	413.0	424.7	403.6	415.5
Transfers to treatment....................	550.2	594.8	540.8	526.6	524.4	514.5	509.7	542.1
Transfers to POTWs (treatment) [3].........	242.0	248.4	239.2	216.7	212.8	212.7	227.0	205.2
Transfers to POTWs (releases to class I UI wells & landfills) [3]...........................	–	–	–	0.5	0.4	0.5	0.6	2.0
Transfers to POTWs (other releases) [3].....	0.8	0.9	0.7	26.5	29.6	31.3	31.9	61.0
Transfers off-site for disposal or other releases...	447.8	449.9	471.7	466.8	482.5	404.4	400.8	411.7
Total production-related waste managed..............	**22,714.0**	**22,513.9**	**25,420.7**	**28,703.7**	**27,700.1**	**27,649.0**	**28,326.8**	**30,914.0**
Recycled on-site...........................	6,295.0	6,640.2	8,796.2	11,822.5	11,477.4	11,661.8	11,884.1	14,379.5
Recycled off-site...........................	2,367.0	2,181.5	2,200.6	2,239.1	2,177.1	2,194.0	2,325.1	2,459.0
Energy recovery on-site....................	2,110.7	2,146.6	2,195.1	2,560.0	2,455.3	2,426.0	2,442.5	2,539.8
Energy recovery off-site....................	354.9	387.4	407.4	421.3	412.0	422.7	402.0	414.8
Treated on-site............................	6,899.7	6,923.5	7,310.0	7,133.1	7,210.1	6,895.8	6,827.1	6,772.3
Treated off-site............................	523.9	570.0	518.7	524.7	523.5	511.8	508.6	541.2
Quantity disposed or otherwise release of on-/off-site. ..	4,162.7	3,664.8	3,992.7	4,003.0	3,444.7	3,536.8	3,937.4	3,807.3
Non-production-related waste managed..................	14.6	14.3	203.8	14.0	17.2	14.1	13.5	7.3

– Represents or rounds zero. [1] Air emissions include both fugitive and point source. [2] RCRA=Resource Conservation and Recovery Act. [3] POTW (Publicly Owned Treatment Work) is a wastewater treatment facility that is owned by a state or municipality.

Source: U.S. Environmental Protection Agency, Toxic Release Inventory (TRI) Program, "TRI Explorer, 2018 Updated Dataset (released April 2020)," <enviro.epa.gov/triexplorer/tri_release.chemical>, accessed September 2020.

Table 430. Industrial Pollution—Toxic Chemical Releases by Industry: 2018

[In millions of pounds (3,766.4 represents 3,766,400,000). Based on 21,595 facilities. See headnote, Table 429]

Industry	NAICS [1] code	Total on- and off-site releases	On-site releases Total [2]	On-site releases Air emissions	On-site releases Other surface impoundments	Off-site releases/ transfers to disposal [3]
Total [4].............................	**(X)**	**3,766.4**	**3,337.1**	**586.0**	**896.2**	**429.3**
Coal mining..............................	2121	3.8	3.8	(Z)	0.2	(Z)
Metal mining.............................	2122	1,797.7	1,796.5	1.8	795.6	1.2
Electric utilities..........................	2211	332.0	283.6	81.2	34.9	48.4
Food/beverages/tobacco..............	311/312	155.6	128.6	44.5	0.3	27.0
Textiles..................................	313/314	2.8	2.5	1.0	(Z)	0.3
Apparel..................................	315	(Z)	(Z)	(Z)	–	(Z)
Leather..................................	316	1.8	0.2	0.1	–	1.6
Wood products..........................	321	9.6	9.2	9.0	(Z)	0.4
Paper....................................	322	151.1	144.5	112.9	1.7	6.6
Printing and publishing..................	323/511	3.4	3.0	3.0	–	0.5
Petroleum...............................	324	75.9	71.1	38.2	(Z)	4.8
Chemicals...............................	325	527.0	443.4	153.4	23.0	83.6
Plastics and rubber......................	326	38.4	31.6	31.4	(Z)	6.8
Stone/clay/glass.........................	327	29.3	24.0	19.8	0.1	5.3
Primary metals..........................	331	325.9	180.9	28.8	39.1	144.9
Fabricated metals.......................	332	44.2	19.0	18.2	(Z)	25.2
Machinery...............................	333	6.5	2.2	1.9	(Z)	4.3
Computers/electronic products........	334	5.2	2.1	1.0	(Z)	3.1
Electrical equipment.....................	335	6.0	1.4	1.4	(Z)	4.5
Transportation equipment..............	336	34.7	27.1	26.9	0.1	7.6
Furniture.................................	337	4.5	4.1	4.1	–	0.3
Miscellaneous manufacturing.........	339	2.8	1.6	1.6	–	1.2
Chemical wholesalers..................	4246	1.9	1.2	1.2	–	0.7
Petroleum bulk terminals..............	4247	1.6	1.3	1.3	(Z)	0.2
Hazardous waste.......................	562	170.6	126.6	0.3	(Z)	44.0

– Represents zero. X Not applicable. Z less than 50,000 lbs. [1] North American Industry Classification System, see text, Section 12. [2] Includes other on-site releases, not shown separately. [3] Includes off-site disposal to underground injection for Class I wells, Class II to V wells, other surface impoundments, land releases, and other releases, not shown separately. [4] Includes industries with no specific industry identified, and uses a double counting algorithm.

Source: U.S. Environmental Protection Agency, Toxic Release Inventory (TRI) Program, "TRI Explorer, 2018 Updated Dataset (released April 2020)," <enviro.epa.gov/triexplorer/tri_release.chemical>, accessed September 2020.

Table 431. Pollution—Toxic Chemical Releases by State and Outlying Area: 2018

[In millions of pounds (3,766.4 represents 3,766,400,000). Based on reports filed as required by Section 313 of the EPCRA. See headnote, Table 429]

State and outlying area	Total on- and off-site releases	On-site releases or other disposal Total[2]	Total air emissions	Other surface impoundments	Off-site releases/transfers to disposal	State and outlying area	Total on- and off-site releases	On-site releases or other disposal Total[2]	Total air emissions	Other surface impoundments	Off-site releases/transfers to disposal
Total[1]	3,766.4	3,337.1	586.0	896.2	429.3	MO	60.2	55.4	9.5	33.1	4.8
U.S. total	3,759.7	3,331.1	584.3	896.2	428.6	MT	51.3	50.6	2.0	33.1	0.7
AL	76.8	61.7	26.5	3.3	15.1	NE	18.5	14.6	5.8	(Z)	3.8
AK	972.0	971.5	0.3	372.6	0.5	NV	339.1	335.4	0.8	217.2	3.7
AZ	170.5	169.3	2.3	43.7	1.2	NH	0.4	0.2	0.2	(Z)	0.2
AR	34.9	28.4	13.7	0.1	6.5	NJ	12.7	6.0	2.1	(Z)	6.7
CA	34.4	23.8	7.3	0.2	10.6	NM	7.6	6.4	0.8	1.0	1.1
CO	24.4	22.9	2.1	3.7	1.5	NY	19.5	14.1	4.3	1.8	5.4
CT	2.1	0.8	0.7	(Z)	1.4	NC	51.9	36.9	19.3	2.5	15.1
DE	6.4	6.2	0.7	(Z)	0.3	ND	30.1	25.4	7.0	3.0	4.7
DC	(Z)	(Z)	(Z)	(Z)	(Z)	OH	113.1	87.1	36.7	3.7	26.1
FL	60.6	56.9	17.6	(Z)	3.7	OK	31.1	28.6	17.0	0.5	2.5
GA	48.3	43.9	30.5	3.0	4.4	OR	20.5	18.0	10.8	(Z)	2.6
HI	2.9	2.7	1.8	(Z)	0.2	PA	54.5	34.2	14.5	(Z)	20.3
ID	34.2	33.1	5.0	5.7	1.2	RI	0.4	0.1	0.1	–	0.3
IL	121.5	69.4	23.2	3.6	52.1	SC	36.5	26.5	20.2	0.4	10.0
IN	128.7	87.8	27.2	1.1	40.9	SD	7.5	7.4	1.7	(Z)	0.2
IA	39.6	30.0	18.9	0.8	9.6	TN	87.6	74.0	22.9	21.7	13.6
KS	23.4	17.0	9.2	0.5	6.4	TX	214.9	182.1	53.1	2.0	32.8
KY	50.8	37.5	18.9	2.1	13.3	UT	291.3	288.7	7.4	87.1	2.6
LA	144.5	135.6	52.0	2.2	9.0	VT	0.4	0.2	(Z)	–	0.2
ME	11.0	8.8	2.6	–	2.2	VA	34.0	27.8	16.0	(Z)	6.2
MD	6.2	4.5	3.0	(Z)	1.6	WA	29.8	24.3	6.7	13.4	5.5
MA	3.4	0.8	0.8	(Z)	2.6	WV	30.8	23.0	12.6	1.0	7.8
MI	78.4	40.3	11.4	8.3	38.1	WI	31.4	16.1	9.1	0.1	15.3
MN	27.1	21.0	9.6	5.3	6.1	WY	21.4	19.3	2.4	3.1	2.1
MS	60.9	54.9	15.7	14.9	6.0	PR	6.0	5.4	1.4	–	0.7

– Represents zero. Z Less than 50,000 lbs. [1] Total includes all states, Puerto Rico, and other outlying areas not shown separately. [2] Includes other types of release, not shown separately.

Source: U.S. Environmental Protection Agency, Toxic Release Inventory (TRI) Program, "TRI Explorer, 2018 Updated Dataset (released April 2020)," <enviro.epa.gov/triexplorer/tri_release.geography>, accessed September 2020.

Table 432. Hazardous Waste Sites on the Superfund National Priority List by State and Outlying Area: 2019

[As of June 2020. Includes both proposed and final sites listed on the National Priorities List for the Superfund program as authorized by the Comprehensive Environmental Response, Compensation, and Liability Act (CERCLA) of 1980 and the Superfund Amendments and Reauthorization Act (SARA) of 1986. For information on CERCLA and SARA, see <https://www.epa.gov/superfund/superfund-cercla-overview> and <https://www.epa.gov/superfund/superfund-amendments-and-reauthorization-act-sara>]

State and outlying area	Total sites	Rank	Percent distribution	Federal	Non-federal	State and outlying area	Total sites	Rank	Percent distribution	Federal	Non-federal
Total[1]	1,386	(X)	(X)	160	1,226	Missouri	34	14	2.5	3	31
United States	1,364	(X)	(X)	158	1,206	Montana	18	22	1.3	–	18
Alabama	14	30	1.0	3	11	Nebraska	17	24	1.2	1	16
Alaska	6	45	0.4	5	1	Nevada	2	47	0.1	–	2
Arizona	9	42	0.7	2	7	New Hampshire	21	19	1.5	1	20
Arkansas	9	42	0.7	–	9	New Jersey	115	1	8.4	6	109
California	99	2	7.3	24	75	New Mexico	16	27	1.2	1	15
Colorado	21	19	1.5	3	18	New York	86	4	6.3	4	82
Connecticut	14	30	1.0	1	13	North Carolina	38	12	2.8	2	36
Delaware	17	24	1.2	1	16	North Dakota	–	51	–	–	–
Dist. of Columbia	1	49	0.1	1	–	Ohio	43	10	3.2	4	39
Florida	54	7	4.0	6	48	Oklahoma	10	39	0.7	1	9
Georgia	17	24	1.2	2	15	Oregon	14	30	1.0	2	12
Hawaii	3	46	0.2	2	1	Pennsylvania	93	3	6.8	6	87
Idaho	9	42	0.7	2	7	Rhode Island	12	35	0.9	2	10
Illinois	50	8	3.7	5	45	South Carolina	27	17	2.0	2	25
Indiana	42	11	3.1	–	42	South Dakota	2	47	0.1	1	1
Iowa	12	35	0.9	1	11	Tennessee	18	22	1.3	3	15
Kansas	14	30	1.0	1	13	Texas	56	6	4.1	4	52
Kentucky	13	34	1.0	1	12	Utah	15	29	1.1	5	10
Louisiana	16	27	1.2	1	15	Vermont	12	35	0.9	–	12
Maine	12	35	0.9	3	9	Virginia	31	16	2.3	11	20
Maryland	21	19	1.5	10	11	Washington	48	9	3.5	13	35
Massachusetts	32	15	2.3	6	26	West Virginia	10	39	0.7	2	8
Michigan	67	5	4.9	1	66	Wisconsin	37	13	2.7	–	37
Minnesota	26	18	1.9	2	24	Wyoming	1	49	0.1	1	–
Mississippi	10	39	0.7	–	10	Puerto Rico	19	(X)	(X)	1	18

– Represents zero. X Not applicable. [1] Total includes areas not shown separately.

Source: U.S. Environmental Protection Agency, "Superfund National Priorities List," <http://www.epa.gov/superfund>, accessed June 2020.

Table 433. Hazardous Waste Generated, Shipped, and Received by State and Other Areas: 2017

[In thousands of tons (35,155.7 represents 33,155,700). Covers hazardous waste regulated under the Resource Conservation and Recovery Act (RCRA) of 1976 as amended. See source for data exclusions]

State and other area	Hazardous waste quantity			State and other area	Hazardous waste quantity		
	Generated	Shipped	Received		Generated	Shipped	Received
Total	**35,155.7**	**6,493.8**	**6,354.5**	Montana	36.8	36.8	–
United States	**35,133.8**	**6,474.3**	**6,354.1**	Nebraska	29.7	43.0	56.5
Alabama	706.3	204.7	448.0	Nevada	21.9	27.2	95.2
Alaska	2.2	2.1	0.2	New Hampshire	4.9	4.9	–
Arizona	190.9	33.6	9.3	New Jersey	243.3	239.9	145.6
Arkansas	334.9	243.9	275.0	New Mexico	4.3	6.1	2.3
California	345.4	659.3	198.1	New York	157.1	141.6	56.3
Colorado	28.9	35.7	29.1	North Carolina	80.2	93.7	22.2
Connecticut	47.5	47.5	19.0	North Dakota	421.8	2.1	0.1
Delaware	11.1	11.0	0.1	Ohio	1,580.6	547.3	638.8
District of Columbia	0.8	0.8	–	Oklahoma	103.0	79.1	181.7
Florida	141.1	47.2	13.7	Oregon	52.5	46.7	67.2
Georgia	86.3	61.4	0.5	Pennsylvania	308.2	257.6	380.3
Hawaii	499.2	0.7	(Z)	Rhode Island	8.0	15.3	8.0
Idaho	10.6	8.8	24.0	South Carolina	164.5	192.3	337.3
Illinois	676.5	228.4	262.8	South Dakota	2.0	2.1	0.1
Indiana	951.8	444.2	576.5	Tennessee	162.3	91.7	97.7
Iowa	56.4	55.8	0.2	Texas	17,761.3	704.0	625.7
Kansas	1,210.6	92.5	122.6	Utah	34.4	76.6	169.9
Kentucky	111.8	160.0	78.5	Vermont	2.1	3.4	148.4
Louisiana	5,015.9	444.3	339.0	Virginia	61.1	61.4	0.4
Maine	2.1	2.2	0.6	Washington	107.0	72.5	24.6
Maryland	42.8	43.3	34.5	West Virginia	65.3	50.6	12.9
Massachusetts	31.8	38.9	10.7	Wisconsin	215.0	231.7	100.7
Michigan	368.8	349.0	481.9	Wyoming	4.7	4.7	–
Minnesota	84.7	52.2	27.3	Guam	0.2	0.2	0.1
Mississippi	2,259.1	101.1	23.8	Puerto Rico	19.1	16.7	0.3
Missouri	284.5	73.7	206.9	Virgin Islands	2.6	2.6	–

– Represents zero. Z Less than 50.

Source: U.S. Environmental Protection Agency, Office of Resource Conservation and Recovery, RCRAInfo Web, "Biennial Report," <https://rcrainfo.epa.gov/rcrainfoweb/>, accessed March 2019.

Table 434. Oil Spills in U.S. Water—Number and Volume: 2000 to 2018

[Based on reported discharges of oil and petroleum based products into U.S. navigable waters, including territorial waters (extending 3 to 12 miles from the coastline), tributaries, the contiguous zone, onto shoreline, or into other waters that threaten the marine environment. Data from the U.S. Coast Guard; see also *Polluting Incidents In and Around U.S. Waters, A Spill/Release Compendium: 1969–2011*]

Spill source	Number of spills					Spill volume (gallons)				
	2000	2010	2016	2017	2018	2000	2010	2016	2017	2018
Total	**8,354**	**3,008**	**2,663**	**2,472**	**2,834**	**1,431,370**	**207,712,793**	**301,723**	**241,204**	**549,914**
Vessel sources, total	5,560	1,508	1,500	1,390	1,977	1,033,643	894,934	238,651	214,153	342,454
Tankship	111	23	73	10	18	608,176	421,583	32,165	100	1,520
Tank barge	229	73	17	50	58	133,540	965	87,416	84,319	41,360
Other vessels [1]	5,220	1,412	1,410	1,330	1,901	291,927	472,386	119,070	129,734	299,574
Nonvessel sources, total	1,645	1,008	943	887	687	373,761	206,809,141	59,318	22,183	206,173
Offshore pipelines	4	34	22	16	26	17	4,627	9,139	83	17,306
Onshore pipelines	21	–	–	–	–	17,004	–	–	–	–
Other [2]	1,620	974	921	871	491	356,740	206,804,514	50,179	22,101	187,579
Unknown source	1,149	492	220	195	170	23,966	8,718	3,754	4,868	1,288

– Represents zero. [1] Commercial vessels, fishing boats, freight barges, freight ships, industrial vessels, oil recovery vessels, passenger vessels, unclassified public vessels, recreational boats, research vessels, school ships, tow and tug boats, mobile offshore drilling units, offshore supply vessels, publicly owned tank and freight ships, and vessels not fitting any particular class (unclassified). [2] Deepwater ports, designated waterfront facilities, nonmarine land facilities, fixed offshore and inshore platforms, mobile facility, municipal facility, aircraft, land vehicles, railroad equipment, bridges, factories, fleeting areas, industrial facilities, intakes, locks, marinas, MARPOL reception facilities, nonvessel common carrier facilities, outfalls, sewers, drains, permanently moored facilities, shipyards, and ship repair facilities.

Source: U.S. Bureau of Transportation Statistics, "National Transportation Statistics," <https://www.bts.gov/topics/national-transportation-statistics>, accessed April 2020.

Table 435. Petroleum and Hazardous Waste Underground Storage Tanks, Releases, and Corrective Actions: 2010 to 2019

[For year ending September 30. EPA collects data from states and territories regarding Underground Storage Tank (UST) systems storing either petroleum or certain hazardous substances. Approximately 1,200 substances (excluding radionuclides) are identified as hazardous under the Comprehensive Environmental Response, Compensation, and Liability Act (CERCLA). See <https://www.epa.gov/ust>]

Year	Active tanks	Closed tanks	Confirmed releases		Cleanups initiated [1]	Cleanups completed		Cleanups remaining
			Current year actions	Cumulative		Current year actions	Cumulative	
2010	597,333	1,748,204	6,328	494,997	470,460	11,591	401,874	93,123
2015	565,956	1,823,543	6,830	528,521	505,468	9,869	456,660	71,861
2016	560,872	1,840,070	5,582	532,420	510,426	8,977	461,441	70,979
2017	555,079	1,856,451	5,678	538,193	516,882	8,775	469,898	68,295
2018	550,379	1,871,148	5,654	543,812	522,801	8,128	478,366	65,446
2019	546,192	1,885,633	5,375	550,897	536,957	8,358	493,589	57,308

[1] Cleanups initiated are cumulative. Even as a cleanup progresses and is completed, it is still counted in the cleanups initiated category.

Source: Environmental Protection Agency, "Underground Storage Tanks (USTs), UST Performance Measures," <https://www.epa.gov/ust/ust-performance-measures>, accessed April 2020.

Table 436. Tornadoes, Floods, Tropical Storms, and Lightning: 2000 to 2019

[424 represents $424,000,000]

Weather type	2000	2005	2010	2013	2014	2015	2016	2017	2018	2019
Tornadoes: [1]										
Number	1,072	1,262	1,282	906	886	1,177	976	1,429	1,126	1,520
Lives lost	41	38	45	55	47	36	18	35	10	42
Injuries	882	537	699	756	641	924	325	516	199	537
Property loss (mil. dol.)	424	422	1,107	3,642	622	317	181	632	670	3,102
Floods and flash floods:										
Lives lost	38	43	103	82	40	187	126	116	80	92
Injuries	47	38	310	33	20	50	31	19	21	45
Property loss (mil. dol.)	1,255	1,538	3,927	2,173	2,626	2,277	10,708	60,576	1,188	2,418
North Atlantic tropical cyclones and hurricanes: [2]	15	27	21	15	9	12	16	18	15	18
Hurricanes	8	15	12	2	6	4	7	10	8	6
Lives lost	–	1,016	–	1	–	14	11	43	7	–
Property loss (mil. dol.)	8	93,064	15	10	3	41	3,054	22,383	12,145	24
Pacific Basin tropical cyclones [2]	19	15	12	19	21	19	22	20	22	18
Hurricanes	6	7	3	9	14	13	13	9	12	7
Extreme temperature										
Lives lost	184	182	142	116	63	98	125	133	144	98
Injuries	469	299	593	1,521	107	643	417	179	506	166
Property and crop loss (mil. dol.)	9.2	142.3	779.0	621.4	8.3	2.8	0.4	954.1	150.0	1.7
Cold:										
Lives lost	26	24	34	24	43	53	31	26	36	35
Injuries	–	1	1	2	–	3	6	3	3	1
Property and crop loss (mil. dol.)	9.2	139.3	775.2	619.3	8.3	2.8	0.4	954.1	150.0	0.2
Heat:										
Lives lost	158	158	138	92	20	45	94	107	108	63
Injuries	469	298	592	1,519	107	640	411	176	503	165
Property and crop loss (mil. dol.)	–	3.0	4.3	2.1	–	–	–	(Z)	(Z)	1.5
Lightning:										
Deaths	51	38	29	23	26	27	38	16	20	20
Injuries	364	309	182	145	154	130	120	86	82	100

– Represents zero. Z Less than $500,000. [1] Source: U.S. National Weather Service, <http://www.spc.noaa.gov/climo/online/monthly/newm.html>. A violent, rotating column of air descending from a cumulonimbus cloud in the form of a tubular- or funnel-shaped cloud, usually characterized by movements along a narrow path and wind speeds from 100 to over 300 miles per hour. Also known as a "twister" or "waterspout." [2] Tropical cyclones include depressions, storms and hurricanes. Fatalities are assumed to be caused by wind-driven debris or structural failure due to winds. For data on individual hurricanes, see National Hurricane Center (NHC) at <http://www.nhc.noaa.gov/>.

Source: Except as noted, U.S. National Oceanic and Atmospheric Administration (NOAA), National Weather Service (NWS), Office of Climate, Water, and Weather Services, "Summary of Natural Hazard Statistics," <https://www.weather.gov/hazstat/>, accessed August 2020.

Table 437. Number of Earthquakes in the United States: 2000 to 2012

[For information by region, see <https://earthquake.usgs.gov/earthquakes/byregion>]

Magnitude (Richter seismic scale)	2000	2004	2005	2006	2007	2008	2009	2010	2011	2012	State earthquakes	1974–2003 [1]
Total	2,342	3,550	3,685	2,783	2,791	3,618	4,262	8,496	5,237	3,365	Total	21,080
8.0 to 9.9	–	–	–	–	–	–	–	–	–	–	AK	[2] 12,053
7.0 to 7.9	–	–	1	–	1	–	–	1	1	–	CA	4,895
6.0 to 6.9	6	2	4	7	9	9	4	8	3	4	HI	1,533
5.0 to 5.9	63	25	47	51	72	85	58	89	51	25	NV	778
4.0 to 4.9	281	284	345	346	366	432	288	631	347	250	WA	424
3.0 to 3.9	917	1,362	1,475	1,213	1,137	1,486	1,492	3,584	1,838	1,096	ID	404
2.0 to 2.9	660	1,336	1,738	1,145	1,173	1,573	2,379	4,132	2,941	1,951	WY	217
1.0 to 1.9	–	1	2	7	11	13	26	39	47	34	MT	186
0.1 to 0.9	–	–	–	1	–	–	1	–	1	–	UT	139
No magnitude	415	540	73	13	22	20	14	12	8	5	OR	73

– Represents zero. [1] The total number represents earthquakes of a magnitude range of 3.5 and greater. [2] Number of earthquakes is underreported since events with magnitude from 3.5 to 4.0 in the in the Aleutian Islands are not recorded on enough seismograph stations to be located.

Source: U.S. Geological Survey, *Earthquake Facts and Statistics*, <http://earthquake.usgs.gov/earthquakes>, accessed August 2016.

Table 438. Wildland Fires, Number, and Acres: 1970 to 2019

[Acres in thousands (3,278.6 represents 3,278,600). As of December 31. Wildland fire is any nonstructural fire that occurs in the wildland. Includes those that are unplanned and unwanted, and include unauthorized human-caused fires, and escaped prescribed fire projects)]

Year	Total [1] Fires	Total [1] Acres (1,000)	Year	Total [1] Fires	Total [1] Acres (1,000)	State	Top states ranked by wildland acres burned in 2019 [1] Fires	Top states ranked by wildland acres burned in 2019 [1] Acres (1,000)
1970	121,736	3,278.6	2009	78,792	5,921.8	Total	50,477	4,664.4
1975	134,872	1,791.3	2010	71,971	3,422.7	AK	720	2,498.2
1980	234,892	5,260.8	2011	74,126	8,711.4	AZ	1,869	384.9
1985	82,591	2,896.1	2012	67,774	9,326.2	ID	960	284.0
1990	66,481	4,621.6	2013	47,579	4,319.5	CA	8,194	259.1
1995	82,234	1,840.5	2014	63,612	3,595.6	TX	6,892	215.5
2000	92,250	7,393.5	2015	68,151	10,125.1	WA	1,394	169.7
2005	66,753	8,689.4	2016	67,743	5,510.0	FL	2,121	122.5
2007	85,705	9,328.0	2017	71,499	10,026.1	UT	1,025	92.4
2008	78,949	5,292.5	2018	58,083	8,767.5	NV	562	82.3

[1] Data are for wildland fires only. Data do not include prescribed fires.

Source: National Interagency Coordination Center, *Wildland Fire Summary and Statistics Annual Report, 2019*, and earlier reports. See also <http://www.predictiveservices.nifc.gov/intelligence/intelligence.htm>.

Table 439. Major U.S. Weather and Climate Disasters: 2019

[4.5 represents $4,500,000,000. Cost in CPI-adjusted dollars. Covers only weather and climate related disasters costing $1 billion or more. See source for more information]

Event	Description	Time period	Estimated cost (bil. dol.)	Deaths (number)
California and Alaska Wildfires	California experienced a damaging wildfire season in 2019, largely resulting from the Kincade and Saddle Ridge wildfires. In addition, a key CA electrical utility provider turned off power to millions of homes and businesses several times during days with forecasted high winds and extremely dry conditions. This step was designed to minimize wildfires, with some success, but it also caused billions of dollars in losses to those affected. AK also suffered a near-historic wildfire season with more than 2.5 million acres burned. These wildfire conditions were primed due to AK's record-breaking heat and dry conditions during the summer months.	June 1 to Nov. 30, 2019	4.5	3
Texas Tornadoes and Central Severe Weather	Numerous tornadoes caused widespread damage across northern Dallas damaging thousands of homes, vehicles, businesses, and other public infrastructure. Tornadoes up to EF-3 intensity with maximum winds of 140 mph tracked across a large section of highly developed northern Dallas. Additionally high winds and hail damage also caused damage in other states including OK, MO, AR, LA and TN.	Oct. 20, 2019	1.7	2
Tropical Storm Imelda	Tropical storm and its remnants cause 24 to 36 inches of rainfall over a 3-day period across a large area between Houston and Beaumont, TX. The largest storm total, 43.39 inches, was reported at North Fork Taylors Bayou, Texas. Many thousands of homes, cars, and businesses were impacted by flood water due to this extraordinarily heavy rainfall.	Sept. 17-21, 2019	5.1	5
Hurricane Dorian	Category 1 hurricane makes landfall on the Outer Banks of North Carolina, after devastating the northern Bahama Islands as a historically-powerful and slow-moving category 5 hurricane. Dorian tracked offshore parallel to the FL, GA, and SC coastline before making a NC landfall, bringing a destructive sound-side surge that inundated many coastal properties and isolated residents who did not evacuate. Significant flood, severe storm, and tornado damage to many homes and businesses occurred on the Outer Banks of NC.	Aug. 28 to Sept. 6, 2019	1.6	10
Mississippi River, Midwest and Southern Flooding	Additional major flooding impacted many Southern Plains states significantly affecting agriculture, roads, bridges, levees, dams and other assets across many cities and towns. The states most affected were OK, NE, MO, IL, KS, AR, KY, TN, TX, MS, and LA. Very high water levels also disrupted barge traffic along the Mississippi River, which negatively impacted a variety of dependent industries. IN and OH were also affected by persistent heavy rainfall that flooded farmland and prevented and reduced crop planting by millions of acres.	Mar. 15 to July 31, 2019	6.3	4
Colorado Hail Storms	CO hail storms across the Denver and Fort Collins areas that damaged many homes and vehicles.	July 4-5, 2019	1.0	–
Arkansas River Flooding	Historic flooding impacts the Arkansas River Basin with damage to homes, agriculture, roads, bridges and levees focused across eastern OK and western AR. Thousands of homes, cars, and businesses were flooded due to a combination of high rivers, levee failure, and persistently heavy rainfall.	May 20 to June 14, 2019	3.1	5
Rockies, Central and Northeast Tornadoes and Severe Weather	A four-day tornado outbreak impacts many states across the Rockies, Central and Northeast (CO, WY, NE, KS, OK, MO, IA, IL, IN, OH, PA, and NJ). This outbreak produced 190 tornadoes in addition to hundreds of reports of damaging hail and straight-line thunderstorm winds. Of particular note was an EF-4 tornado that produced heavy damage near the city of Dayton, OH on May 27.	May 26-29, 2019	4.5	3
Central Severe Weather	Central severe storms across Illinois, Indiana, Iowa, and Texas damaged many homes, businesses, and vehicles.	May 16-18, 2019	1.0	–
South and Southeast Severe Weather	Persistent severe storms impacted numerous states from TX to NC (TX, OK, KS, AR, LA, MS, AL, NC). Tornadoes and damaging hail particularly affected TX, LA, and NC focused across the Raleigh metro region.	May 7-13, 2019	1.5	–
Southern and Eastern Tornadoes and Severe Weather	Tornado outbreak and severe storms impacted many states (TX, LA, MS, AL, GA, NC, OH, and PA). More than 50 tornadoes occurred across central MS and AL causing damage to vehicles, homes, and businesses. More than 25 additional tornadoes caused damage across several eastern states from GA to PA. These severe storms also delivered widespread damaging hail and high wind.	Apr. 13-14, 2019	1.3	7
Missouri River and North Central Flooding	Historic Midwest flooding inundated millions of acres of agriculture, numerous cities, and towns, and caused widespread damage to roads, bridges, levees, and dams. The states most affected were NE, IA, MO, SD, MN, ND, WI, and MI. This flood was triggered by a powerful storm with heavy precipitation that intensified snow melt and flooding. Of note, the Offutt Air Force Base in NE was also severely flooded - the third U.S. military base to be damaged by a billion-dollar disaster event over a 6-month period (Sept 2018-Feb 2019).	Mar. 14-31, 2019	10.9	3
Texas Hail Storm	TX hail storm over the Dallas metroplex damaged many homes, businesses, and vehicles. OK also received hail damage resulting from the same severe weather system.	Mar. 22-24, 2019	1.6	–
Southeast, Ohio Valley and Northeast Severe Weather	Tornadoes, severe weather, and flooding in the south (MS, AL, TN) and high-wind damage across many Ohio Valley (IL, IN, OH) and Northeastern states (CT, MD, MA, NJ, NY, PA, VA, WV). This storm system produced heavy rain that caused major flooding along parts of the Ohio, Mississippi, and Tennessee rivers.	Feb. 23-25, 2019	1.3	2

– Represents zero.

Source: U.S. National Oceanic and Atmospheric Administration, National Centers for Environmental Information, "Billion-Dollar Weather and Climate Disasters, 1980-2020," <http://www.ncdc.noaa.gov/billions/events>, accessed June 2020.

Table 440. Highest and Lowest Temperatures by State Through 2019

[Data have been evaluated by the National Oceanic and Atmospheric Administration National Climatic Data Center, and/or by the State Climate Extremes Committee and determined to be valid. The data may come from sources other than official NOAA-supervised weather stations, but are archived, officially recognized observations]

State	Highest temperatures			Lowest temperatures		
	Station	Temperature (°F)	Date	Station	Temperature (°F)	Date
U.S.	**Greenland Ranch, CA**	**134**	**July 10, 1913**	**Prospect Creek Camp, AK**	**-80**	**Jan. 23, 1971**
AL	Centreville	112	Sept. 6, 1925	New Market	-27	Jan. 30, 1966
AK	Fort Yukon	100	June 27, 1915	Prospect Creek Camp	-80	Jan. 23, 1971
AZ	Lake Havasu City	128	June 29, 1994	Hawley Lake	-40	Jan. 7, 1971
AR	Ozark	120	Aug. 10, 1936	Gravette	-29	Feb. 13, 1905
CA	Greenland Ranch	134	July 10, 1913	Boca	-45	Jan. 20, 1937
CO	John Martin Dam	115	July 20, 2019	Maybell	-61	Feb. 1, 1985
CT	Danbury	106	[1] July 15, 1995	Coventry	-32	[1] Jan. 22, 1961
DE	Millsboro	110	July 21, 1930	Millsboro	-17	Jan. 17, 1893
FL	Monticello	109	June 29, 1931	Tallahassee	-2	Feb. 13, 1899
GA	Greenville	112	[1] Aug. 20, 1983	CCC Camp F-16	-17	Jan. 27, 1940
HI	Pahala	100	Apr. 27, 1931	Mauna Kea Obs. 111.2	12	May 17, 1979
ID	Orofino	118	July 28, 1934	Island Park Dam	-60	Jan. 18, 1943
IL	East St. Louis	117	July 14, 1954	Mount Carroll	-38	Jan. 31, 2019
IN	Collegeville	116	July 14, 1936	New Whiteland	-36	Jan. 19, 1994
IA	Keokuk	118	July 20, 1934	Elkader	-47	[1] Feb. 3, 1996
KS	Alton	121	[1] July 24, 1936	Lebanon	-40	Feb. 13, 1905
KY	Greensburg	114	July 28, 1930	Shelbyville	-37	Jan. 19, 1994
LA	Plain Dealing	114	Aug. 10, 1936	Minden	-16	Feb. 13, 1899
ME	North Bridgton	105	[1] July 10, 1911	Big Black River	-50	Jan. 16, 2009
MD	Frederick Police Barracks	109	[1] July 10, 1936	Oakland	-40	Jan. 13, 1912
MA	Chester	107	[1] Aug. 2, 1975	Chester	-35	[1] Jan. 12, 1981
MI	Stanwood	112	July 13, 1936	Vanderbilt	-51	Feb. 9, 1934
MN	Beardsley	115	July 29, 1917	Tower	-60	Feb. 2, 1996
MS	Holly Springs	115	July 29, 1930	Corinth	-19	Jan. 30, 1966
MO	Warsaw	118	July 14, 1954	Warsaw	-40	Feb. 13, 1905
MT	Medicine Lake	117	[1] July 5, 1937	Rogers Pass	-70	Jan. 20, 1954
NE	Minden	118	[1] July 24, 1936	Oshkosh	-47	[1] Dec. 22, 1989
NV	Laughlin	125	June 29, 1994	San Jacinto	-50	Jan. 8, 1937
NH	Nashua	106	July 4, 1911	Mt. Washington	-50	Jan. 22, 1885
NJ	Runyon	110	July 10, 1936	River Vale	-34	Jan. 5, 1904
NM	Waste Isolation Pilot Plant	122	June 27, 1994	Gavilan	-50	Feb. 1, 1951
NY	Troy	108	July 22, 1926	Old Forge	-52	Feb. 18, 1979
NC	Fayetteville	110	Aug. 21, 1983	Mt. Mitchell	-34	Jan. 21, 1985
ND	Steele	121	July 6, 1936	Parshall	-60	Feb. 15, 1936
OH	Gallipolis (near)	113	July 21, 1934	Milligan	-39	Feb. 10, 1899
OK	Altus Irig Res	120	[1] Aug. 12, 1936	Nowata	-31	Feb. 10, 2011
OR	Pendleton	119	[1] Aug. 10, 1898	Seneca	-54	[1] Feb. 10, 1933
PA	Phoenixville	111	[1] July 10, 1936	Smethport	-42	Jan. 5, 1904
RI	Providence	104	Aug. 2, 1975	Wood River Junction	-28	Jan. 11, 1942
SC	Columbia Univ. of SC	113	June 29, 2012	Caesars Head	-19	Jan. 21, 1985
SD	Fort Pierre	120	[1] July 15, 2006	McIntosh	-58	Feb. 17, 1936
TN	Perryville	113	[1] Aug. 9, 1930	Mountain City	-32	Dec. 30, 1917
TX	Monahans	120	[1] June 28, 1994	Seminole	-23	Feb. 8, 1933
UT	Saint George	117	July 5, 1985	East Portal	-50	Jan. 5, 1913
VT	Vernon	107	July 7, 1912	Bloomfield	-50	Dec. 30, 1933
VA	Balcony Falls	110	[1] July 15, 1954	Mtn. Lake Bio. Stn.	-30	Jan. 21, 1985
WA	Ice Harbor Dam	118	[1] Aug. 5, 1961	Winthrop	-48	[1] Dec. 30, 1968
WV	Martinsburg	112	[1] July 10, 1936	Lewisburg	-37	Dec. 30, 1917
WI	Wisconsin Dells	114	July 13, 1936	Couderay	-55	[1] Feb. 4, 1996
WY	Diversion Dam	115	[1] July 15, 1988	Riverside R.S.	-66	Feb. 9, 1933

[1] Also on earlier dates at the same or other places.

Source: U.S. National Oceanic and Atmospheric Administration, National Climatic Data Center, State Climate Extremes Committee, "Maximum and Minimum Temperature Records," <http://www.ncdc.noaa.gov/extremes/scec/records>, accessed June 2020.

Table 441. Highest Temperature of Record—Selected Cities

[In degrees Fahrenheit. Airport data, except as noted. Data for each city are shown for varying periods of record; see source for date ranges for each location]

State	Station	Jan.	Feb.	Mar.	Apr.	May	June	July	Aug.	Sept.	Oct.	Nov.	Dec.	Annual [1]
AL.....	Mobile	84	84	89	94	100	103	104	105	99	93	88	81	105
AK.....	Juneau	60	57	61	74	80	86	90	84	78	63	56	54	90
AZ.....	Phoenix	88	92	100	105	113	122	121	117	118	107	96	88	122
AK.....	Little Rock	83	85	91	95	98	107	112	114	106	98	86	81	114
CA....	Los Angeles	95	95	98	106	102	112	108	105	113	108	100	92	113
CA....	Sacramento	76	78	88	95	105	115	114	110	109	104	87	73	115
CA....	San Diego	88	90	93	98	97	101	99	98	111	107	100	88	111
CA....	San Francisco	79	81	87	94	93	103	95	98	106	102	86	76	106
CO.....	Denver	74	83	84	90	96	104	104	102	98	89	81	75	104
CT.....	Hartford	72	77	89	96	99	101	103	102	101	91	83	76	103
DE.....	Wilmington	75	78	86	94	96	100	103	101	100	91	85	75	103
DC....	Washington	79	82	89	95	99	104	105	105	101	94	86	79	105
FL.....	Jacksonville	85	88	91	95	102	103	105	102	100	96	89	85	105
FL.....	Miami	88	89	93	96	98	98	98	98	97	95	91	89	98
GA....	Atlanta	79	80	89	93	97	106	105	104	99	95	84	79	106
HI.....	Honolulu	88	88	89	91	93	92	94	93	95	94	93	89	95
ID.....	Boise	63	71	81	92	99	110	111	110	102	94	78	65	111
IL.....	Chicago	65	72	88	91	97	104	104	101	99	91	78	71	104
IL......	Peoria	70	74	86	92	97	105	104	103	100	93	81	71	105
IN.....	Indianapolis	71	77	85	89	95	104	105	102	100	91	81	74	105
IA......	Des Moines	67	75	91	93	99	103	106	108	101	95	81	69	108
KS.....	Wichita	75	87	89	96	102	110	113	111	108	97	86	83	113
KY.....	Louisville	77	82	86	91	95	105	106	105	104	93	85	76	106
LA.....	New Orleans	83	85	89	92	97	101	101	102	101	94	88	85	102
ME....	Portland	67	68	88	92	94	98	100	103	95	88	74	71	103
MD....	Baltimore	75	79	89	94	100	103	106	105	100	99	86	77	106
MA....	Boston	72	73	89	94	96	100	103	102	100	90	83	76	103
MI.....	Detroit	64	70	86	89	95	104	102	100	98	91	78	69	104
MI.....	Sault Ste. Marie	47	49	83	85	89	93	97	98	95	81	74	62	98
MN....	Duluth	48	55	75	88	92	94	97	95	95	86	71	55	97
MN....	Minneapolis-St. Paul	58	63	83	95	100	103	105	102	98	90	77	68	105
MS....	Jackson	83	86	89	94	99	105	106	107	104	96	88	84	107
MO....	Kansas City	74	79	87	93	95	105	107	109	106	95	82	74	109
MO....	St. Louis	77	85	89	93	98	108	115	107	104	94	85	76	115
MT....	Great Falls	67	70	78	89	93	101	105	106	98	91	76	69	106
NE....	Omaha	69	78	91	97	101	105	110	107	103	95	83	69	110
NV....	Reno	71	75	83	90	97	104	108	105	101	93	77	71	108
NH....	Concord	69	74	89	95	97	98	102	101	98	90	80	73	102
NJ.....	Atlantic City	78	76	87	94	99	106	105	103	99	90	81	77	106
NM....	Albuquerque	69	76	85	89	98	107	105	101	100	91	77	72	107
NY....	Albany	71	74	89	93	94	99	100	99	100	91	82	72	100
NY....	Buffalo	72	71	82	94	91	96	97	99	98	87	80	74	99
NY....	New York City Central Park	72	78	86	96	99	101	106	104	102	94	84	75	106
NC....	Charlotte	79	82	90	93	100	104	104	104	104	98	85	80	104
NC....	Raleigh	80	84	92	95	97	105	105	105	104	98	88	81	105
ND....	Bismarck	63	73	81	93	96	111	112	107	105	95	79	65	112
OH....	Cincinnati	74	79	84	89	93	102	104	102	102	91	82	75	104
OH....	Cleveland	73	77	83	88	93	104	103	102	101	90	82	77	104
OH....	Columbus	74	78	85	89	93	101	104	101	100	91	80	76	104
OK....	Oklahoma City	80	92	93	100	104	105	110	113	108	96	87	86	113
OR....	Portland	66	71	80	90	100	102	107	107	105	92	73	65	107
PA.....	Philadelphia	74	77	86	95	97	100	104	101	100	89	84	73	104
PA.....	Pittsburgh	75	78	83	89	91	98	103	100	97	89	82	74	103
RI.....	Providence	69	72	85	98	96	97	102	104	100	88	81	77	104
SC....	Columbia	84	84	91	94	101	109	107	107	101	101	90	83	109
SD....	Sioux Falls	66	70	88	94	104	110	110	109	104	94	81	63	110
TN.....	Memphis	79	81	86	94	99	104	108	107	103	95	86	81	108
TN.....	Nashville	78	84	87	91	95	109	107	106	105	94	88	79	109
TX.....	Dallas	88	95	97	100	103	112	112	111	110	100	92	89	112
TX.....	El Paso	80	85	93	98	105	114	112	108	104	96	87	80	114
TX.....	Houston	84	91	91	95	99	107	104	109	109	96	89	85	109
UT.....	Salt Lake City	63	69	80	89	99	105	107	106	100	89	75	69	107
VT.....	Burlington	66	72	84	91	93	100	100	101	98	85	75	68	101
VA.....	Norfolk	80	82	88	97	100	101	105	104	99	95	86	82	105
VA.....	Richmond	81	82	91	96	100	104	105	104	103	99	86	81	105
WA....	Seattle	64	70	78	89	93	96	103	99	98	89	74	66	103
WA....	Spokane	62	63	72	90	97	105	108	108	98	87	70	60	108
WV....	Charleston	79	81	89	94	94	103	104	104	102	93	85	80	104
WI....	Milwaukee	63	71	84	91	95	101	103	103	98	89	77	68	103
WY....	Cheyenne	70	71	76	83	91	100	100	98	95	84	75	69	100
PR....	San Juan	92	96	96	97	96	97	95	97	97	98	96	94	98

[1] Represents the highest observed temperature in any month.

Source: U.S. National Oceanic and Atmospheric Administration, *Comparative Climatic Data for the United States Through 2018.* See also <https://www.ncdc.noaa.gov/ghcn/comparative-climatic-data>.

Table 442. Lowest Temperature of Record—Selected Cities

[In degrees Fahrenheit. Airport data, except as noted. Data for each city are shown for varying periods of record; see source for date ranges for each location]

State	Station	Jan.	Feb.	Mar.	Apr.	May	June	July	Aug.	Sept.	Oct.	Nov.	Dec.	Annual[1]
AL.....	Mobile	3	11	21	32	43	49	62	59	42	30	22	8	3
AK.....	Juneau	-22	-22	-15	6	25	31	36	27	23	11	-5	-21	-22
AZ.....	Phoenix	17	22	25	34	40	50	61	60	47	34	25	22	17
AR.....	Little Rock	-4	-5	11	28	38	46	54	52	37	28	17	-1	-5
CA.....	Los Angeles	28	29	35	39	43	49	53	51	50	41	38	30	28
CA.....	Sacramento	20	23	26	31	34	41	48	48	42	35	26	18	18
CA.....	San Diego	29	36	39	41	48	50	55	57	51	43	38	34	29
CA.....	San Francisco	30	31	35	40	43	47	47	48	48	43	39	27	27
CO.....	Denver	-25	-25	-10	-2	22	30	43	41	17	3	-10	-25	-25
CT.....	Hartford	-26	-21	-8	9	28	37	44	36	27	17	1	-14	-26
DE.....	Wilmington	-14	-6	2	18	30	41	48	43	36	24	14	-7	-14
DC.....	Washington Nat'l (VA)	-5	4	14	24	34	47	54	49	39	29	16	3	-5
FL.....	Jacksonville	7	19	23	31	45	47	61	63	48	33	21	11	7
FL.....	Miami	30	35	32	42	55	60	69	68	68	53	39	30	30
GA.....	Atlanta	-8	5	10	26	37	46	53	55	36	28	3	0	-8
HI.....	Honolulu	52	53	55	56	60	65	66	65	66	61	57	54	52
ID.....	Boise	-17	-15	6	19	22	31	35	34	23	11	-3	-25	-25
IL.....	Chicago	-27	-19	-8	7	24	36	40	41	28	17	1	-25	-27
IL.....	Peoria	-25	-19	-10	14	25	39	47	41	29	19	-2	-23	-25
IN.....	Indianapolis	-27	-21	-7	18	28	37	48	41	32	20	-2	-23	-27
IA.....	Des Moines	-24	-26	-22	9	28	41	47	40	28	14	-4	-22	-26
KS.....	Wichita	-12	-21	-2	15	31	43	51	48	31	18	1	-16	-21
KY.....	Louisville	-22	-19	-1	22	31	42	50	46	33	23	-1	-15	-22
LA.....	New Orleans	14	16	25	32	41	50	60	60	42	35	24	11	11
ME.....	Portland	-26	-39	-21	8	23	33	40	33	23	15	3	-21	-39
MD.....	Baltimore	-7	-3	4	20	32	40	50	45	35	25	13	0	-7
MA.....	Boston	-12	-14	1	16	34	41	50	46	37	25	12	-11	-14
MI.....	Detroit	-21	-15	-4	10	25	36	41	38	29	17	9	-10	-21
MI.....	Sault Ste. Marie	-36	-37	-28	-2	18	26	36	29	25	16	-10	-31	-37
MN.....	Duluth	-39	-39	-29	-5	17	27	35	32	23	8	-23	-34	-39
MN.....	Minneapolis-St. Paul	-34	-32	-32	2	18	34	43	39	26	13	-17	-29	-34
MS.....	Jackson	2	10	15	27	36	47	51	54	35	26	17	4	2
MO.....	Kansas City	-17	-19	-10	12	30	42	51	43	31	17	1	-23	-23
MO.....	St. Louis	-18	-12	-5	22	31	43	51	47	32	22	1	-16	-18
MT.....	Great Falls	-37	-35	-29	-8	12	31	36	30	16	-11	-25	-43	-43
NE.....	Omaha	-23	-21	-16	5	27	38	44	43	25	13	-9	-23	-23
NV.....	Reno	-16	-16	0	13	18	25	33	24	20	8	1	-16	-16
NH.....	Concord	-33	-37	-16	4	21	26	33	29	20	10	-5	-22	-37
NJ.....	Atlantic City	-10	-11	2	12	25	37	42	40	32	20	10	-2	-11
NM.....	Albuquerque	-17	-7	8	18	28	40	52	50	35	21	-7	-7	-17
NY.....	Albany	-28	-22	-21	10	26	35	40	34	24	16	-11	-22	-28
NY.....	Buffalo	-16	-20	-7	12	26	35	43	38	31	20	7	-10	-20
NY.....	Central Park	-6	-15	3	12	32	44	52	50	39	28	5	-13	-15
NC.....	Charlotte	-5	5	4	21	32	45	53	50	39	24	11	2	-5
NC.....	Raleigh	-9	0	11	23	29	38	48	46	37	19	11	4	-9
ND.....	Bismarck	-44	-43	-31	-12	15	30	35	33	11	-10	-30	-43	-44
OH.....	Cincinnati	-25	-15	-11	15	27	39	47	43	31	16	0	-20	-25
OH.....	Cleveland	-20	-17	-5	10	25	31	41	38	32	19	3	-15	-20
OH.....	Columbus	-22	-13	-6	14	25	35	43	39	31	17	-4	-17	-22
OK.....	Oklahoma City	-4	-5	1	20	32	47	53	50	36	16	11	-8	-8
OR.....	Portland	-2	-3	19	29	29	39	43	44	34	26	13	6	-3
PA.....	Philadelphia	-7	-4	7	19	28	44	51	44	35	25	15	1	-7
PA.....	Pittsburgh	-22	-12	-5	14	26	34	42	39	31	16	-1	-12	-22
RI.....	Providence	-13	-9	1	14	29	41	48	40	32	20	6	-10	-13
SC.....	Columbia	-1	5	4	26	34	44	54	53	40	23	12	4	-1
SD.....	Sioux Falls	-36	-31	-23	4	17	33	38	34	22	9	-17	-28	-36
TN.....	Memphis	-4	-11	12	28	36	48	52	48	36	25	9	-13	-13
TN.....	Nashville	-17	-13	2	23	34	42	54	49	36	26	-1	-10	-17
TX.....	Dallas	0	7	11	31	39	53	60	56	36	27	17	1	0
TX.....	El Paso	-8	1	14	21	31	46	57	56	41	25	1	5	-8
TX.....	Houston	12	20	22	31	42	52	62	60	48	29	19	7	7
UT.....	Salt Lake City	-22	-14	2	15	25	35	40	37	27	16	-14	-15	-22
VT.....	Burlington	-30	-30	-20	2	24	33	39	35	25	15	-2	-26	-30
VA.....	Norfolk	-3	8	18	28	36	45	54	49	45	27	20	7	-3
VA.....	Richmond	-12	-8	10	23	31	40	51	47	35	21	14	1	-12
WA.....	Seattle	0	1	11	29	28	38	43	44	35	28	6	6	0
WA.....	Spokane	-24	-24	-10	14	24	33	37	35	22	7	-21	-25	-25
WV.....	Charleston	-16	-12	0	19	26	33	46	41	34	17	6	-12	-16
WI.....	Milwaukee	-26	-26	-10	12	21	33	40	44	28	18	-5	-20	-26
WY.....	Cheyenne	-30	-34	-21	-8	9	25	33	36	8	-1	-21	-28	-34
PR.....	San Juan	61	62	60	64	66	69	69	70	69	67	66	63	60

[1] Represents the lowest observed temperature in any month.

Source: U.S. National Oceanic and Atmospheric Administration, *Comparative Climatic Data for the United States Through 2018*. See also <https://www.ncdc.noaa.gov/ghcn/comparative-climatic-data>.

Table 443. Average Snow, Hail, Ice Pellets, and Sleet—Selected Cities

[Average in inches. Data for each city are shown for varying periods of record; see source for date ranges for each location. T denotes trace. Stations may show snowfall (hail) during the warm months]

State	Station	Jan.	Feb.	Mar.	Apr.	May	June	July	Aug.	Sept.	Oct.	Nov.	Dec.	Annual
AL.....	Mobile	0.1	0.1	0.1	–	–	–	–	–	–	–	–	0.1	0.4
AK.....	Juneau	25.3	18.1	13.9	2.5	–	–	–	–	–	1.0	12.5	21.0	94.3
AZ.....	Phoenix	–	–	–	–	–	–	–	–	–	–	–	–	–
AR.....	Little Rock	2.0	1.5	0.5	–	–	–	–	–	–	–	0.1	0.6	4.7
CA.....	Los Angeles	–	–	–	–	–	–	–	–	–	–	–	–	–
CA.....	Sacramento	–	–	–	–	–	–	–	–	–	–	–	–	–
CA.....	San Diego	–	–	–	–	–	–	–	–	–	–	–	–	–
CA.....	San Francisco	–	–	–	–	–	–	–	–	–	–	–	–	–
CO.....	Denver	7.4	7.5	11.8	7.9	1.6	–	–	–	1.3	3.9	8.0	7.6	57.0
CT.....	Hartford	13.2	12.9	9.0	1.3	–	–	–	–	–	0.3	1.8	9.8	48.3
DE.....	Wilmington	6.6	6.8	3.2	0.2	–	–	–	–	–	–	0.7	3.3	20.8
DC....	Washington Nat'l (VA)	5.3	5.4	2.2	–	–	–	–	–	–	–	0.6	2.7	16.2
FL.....	Jacksonville	–	–	–	–	–	–	–	–	–	–	–	–	–
FL.....	Miami	–	–	–	–	–	–	–	–	–	–	–	–	–
GA....	Atlanta	0.9	0.5	0.4	–	–	–	–	–	–	–	–	0.2	2.0
HI......	Honolulu	–	–	–	–	–	–	–	–	–	–	–	–	–
ID.....	Boise	6.3	3.4	1.6	0.5	0.1	–	–	–	–	0.1	2.1	5.9	20.0
IL......	Chicago	11.2	9.2	6.3	1.4	–	–	–	–	–	0.3	1.9	8.4	38.7
IL......	Peoria	6.8	6.0	3.9	0.7	T	–	–	–	–	–	1.8	6.1	25.3
IN.....	Indianapolis	7.9	6.2	3.6	0.4	–	–	–	–	–	0.2	1.4	5.8	25.5
IA......	Des Moines	8.3	8.3	5.7	1.7	0.1	–	–	–	–	0.3	2.7	7.2	34.3
KS.....	Wichita	3.8	4.1	2.4	0.3	–	–	–	–	–	–	1.1	3.3	15.0
KY.....	Louisville	5.1	4.4	2.9	0.1	–	–	–	–	–	0.1	0.8	2.3	15.7
LA.....	New Orleans	–	–	–	–	–	–	–	–	–	–	–	0.1	0.1
ME....	Portland	19.2	17.6	13.0	2.8	0.1	–	–	–	–	0.2	2.9	14.5	70.3
MD....	Baltimore	5.9	6.8	3.4	–	–	–	–	–	–	–	0.6	3.1	19.8
MA....	Boston	13.2	12.6	8.0	1.2	–	–	–	–	–	–	1.1	7.9	44.0
MI....	Detroit	11.9	10.7	6.7	1.6	–	–	–	–	–	0.1	2.4	9.8	43.2
MI....	Sault Ste. Marie	30.1	19.8	14.2	6.3	0.4	–	–	–	0.1	2.0	15.4	30.4	118.7
MN....	Duluth	17.2	12.7	14.0	7.7	0.6	–	–	–	0.1	1.8	11.9	17.0	83.0
MN....	Minneapolis-St. Paul	10.3	8.4	10.1	3.0	0.1	–	–	–	–	0.5	6.8	10.1	49.3
MS....	Jackson	0.4	0.3	0.1	–	–	–	–	–	–	–	–	0.2	1.0
MO....	Kansas City	5.1	5.5	2.2	0.6	–	–	–	–	–	0.2	1.2	4.2	19.0
MO....	St. Louis	5.4	4.4	3.7	0.3	–	–	–	–	–	–	1.2	3.6	18.6
MT....	Great Falls	9.6	8.8	10.4	8.0	1.8	0.3	–	0.1	1.1	3.4	7.7	9.3	60.5
NE.....	Omaha	6.9	6.8	5.5	0.8	0.1	–	–	–	–	0.3	2.4	5.8	28.6
NV.....	Reno	5.4	4.9	3.8	1.0	0.6	–	–	–	–	0.3	1.9	4.6	22.5
NH.....	Concord	17.9	15.6	11.8	2.4	0.1	–	–	–	–	0.4	3.4	13.7	65.3
NJ.....	Atlantic City	6.0	6.3	2.3	0.4	–	–	–	–	–	–	0.3	2.9	18.2
NM....	Albuquerque	2.1	1.9	1.5	0.5	–	–	–	–	–	0.1	1.0	2.5	9.6
NY.....	Albany	16.3	13.9	11.4	2.4	0.1	–	–	–	–	0.2	3.8	13.6	61.7
NY.....	Buffalo	24.6	18.2	12.4	2.9	0.2	–	–	–	–	0.5	10.0	23.1	91.9
NY.....	New York Central Park	7.9	8.9	4.9	0.8	–	–	–	–	–	–	0.8	5.4	28.7
NC....	Charlotte	2.0	1.6	0.9	T	–	–	–	–	–	–	0.1	0.5	5.1
NC....	Raleigh	2.5	2.3	1.0	–	–	–	–	–	–	–	0.1	0.8	6.7
ND....	Bismarck	8.3	7.2	8.5	4.0	0.7	–	–	–	0.1	1.4	6.7	8.5	45.4
OH....	Cincinnati	7.3	6.0	4.1	0.5	–	–	–	–	–	0.2	1.6	4.1	23.8
OH....	Cleveland	14.7	13.1	10.5	2.5	–	–	–	–	–	0.4	4.9	11.9	58.0
OH....	Columbus	8.9	6.7	4.4	0.8	–	–	–	–	–	0.1	1.9	5.5	28.3
OK....	Oklahoma City	2.6	2.3	1.2	–	–	–	–	–	–	T	0.6	1.9	8.6
OR....	Portland	3.0	1.3	0.4	–	–	–	–	–	–	–	0.4	1.3	6.4
PA.....	Philadelphia	7.1	7.4	3.7	0.3	–	–	–	–	–	–	0.5	3.6	22.6
PA.....	Pittsburgh	12.1	10.1	8.0	1.5	0.1	–	–	–	–	0.3	3.5	8.2	43.8
RI.....	Providence	10.4	10.2	6.8	0.7	0.1	–	–	–	–	0.1	1.0	7.0	36.3
SC.....	Columbia	0.6	0.7	0.2	–	–	–	–	–	–	–	–	0.2	1.7
SD.....	Sioux Falls	7.0	8.4	8.7	3.2	0.1	–	–	–	–	0.7	5.1	7.8	41.0
TN....	Memphis	1.9	1.2	0.6	–	–	–	–	–	–	–	0.1	0.5	4.3
TN....	Nashville	3.6	2.6	1.2	–	–	–	–	–	–	–	0.4	1.1	8.9
TX.....	Dallas	0.9	0.7	0.2	–	–	–	–	–	–	–	0.1	0.2	2.1
TX.....	El Paso	1.2	0.7	0.3	0.3	–	–	–	–	–	–	0.9	1.6	5.0
TX.....	Houston	0.1	0.1	–	–	–	–	–	–	–	–	–	0.1	0.3
UT.....	Salt Lake City	13.1	10.1	8.9	4.9	0.6	–	–	–	0.1	1.3	6.6	13.0	58.6
VT.....	Burlington	19.5	17.4	14.1	3.9	0.1	–	–	–	T	0.3	6.4	18.7	80.4
VA.....	Norfolk	3.1	2.7	0.9	–	–	–	–	–	–	–	–	1.0	7.7
VA.....	Richmond	5.0	3.9	2.1	0.1	–	–	–	–	–	–	0.3	1.9	13.3
WA....	Seattle	4.5	1.7	1.2	0.1	–	–	–	–	–	–	0.8	2.4	10.7
WA....	Spokane	13.0	7.6	3.6	0.6	0.1	–	–	–	–	0.2	5.6	11.8	42.5
WV....	Charleston	10.7	8.7	5.2	0.8	–	–	–	–	–	0.3	2.0	5.0	32.7
WI.....	Milwaukee	13.7	10.6	8.2	1.8	0.1	–	–	–	–	0.2	2.9	10.4	47.9
WY....	Cheyenne	6.0	7.4	11.0	10.4	3.3	0.2	–	–	0.7	4.2	7.1	7.1	57.4
PR.....	San Juan	–	–	–	–	–	–	–	–	–	–	–	–	–

– Represents zero.

Source: U.S. National Oceanic and Atmospheric Administration, *Comparative Climatic Data for the United States Through 2018*. See also <https://www.ncdc.noaa.gov/ghcn/comparative-climatic-data>.

Table 444. Cloudiness, Average Wind Speed, and Average Relative Humidity—Selected Cities

[Airport data, except as noted. Data shown for varying periods of record; see source for date ranges for each location. M = morning. A = afternoon]

State	Station	Cloudiness- average percent of days annually [1]	Average wind speed (miles per hour, m.p.h.) Annual	Average wind speed Jan- uary	Average wind speed July	Average relative humidity (percent) Annual M	Annual A	Jan. M	Jan. A	July M	July A
AL........	Mobile	72.1	7.5	8.6	5.7	87	57	83	60	90	61
AK........	Juneau	87.9	7.4	7.3	6.6	84	74	84	80	84	72
AZ........	Phoenix	42.5	6.1	5.0	7.3	46	23	60	33	42	21
AR........	Little Rock	67.7	7.0	7.7	6.0	84	57	80	61	87	56
CA........	Los Angeles	49.0	1.9	1.4	2.2	58	54	52	49	65	59
CA........	Sacramento	48.5	6.3	5.0	7.6	78	45	87	69	71	29
CA........	San Diego	60.0	6.4	5.2	7.0	74	63	69	58	80	67
CA........	San Francisco	56.2	10.5	6.8	13.1	87	69	87	66	91	71
CO........	Denver	68.5	8.0	7.8	7.9	50	43	53	54	46	35
CT........	Hartford	77.5	7.8	8.3	6.7	76	53	73	57	78	51
DE........	Wilmington	73.4	8.5	9.2	7.4	78	55	75	59	78	54
DC........	Washington Nat'l (VA)	74.0	8.9	9.5	8.1	74	53	71	55	76	53
FL........	Jacksonville	74.2	6.7	7.0	5.9	88	56	87	57	89	59
FL........	Miami	79.5	8.4	8.6	7.3	82	61	84	59	81	63
GA........	Atlanta	70.1	8.3	9.3	7.1	81	55	79	58	86	58
HI........	Honolulu	75.3	10.3	8.4	11.9	74	56	79	61	70	53
ID........	Boise	67.1	7.6	6.5	7.5	64	42	79	70	49	20
IL........	Chicago	77.0	9.9	11.2	8.2	80	60	78	68	81	55
IL........	Peoria	73.7	8.3	9.5	6.4	83	61	80	70	86	58
IN........	Indianapolis	76.2	9.5	10.9	7.6	82	60	81	70	83	58
IA........	Des Moines	71.5	9.8	10.6	8.3	81	60	78	68	84	58
KS........	Wichita	64.9	11.5	11.1	10.8	80	55	79	61	80	50
KY........	Louisville	74.8	7.8	9.0	6.6	79	56	78	64	81	56
LA........	New Orleans	72.3	8.0	9.1	5.9	87	62	84	65	90	65
ME........	Portland	72.3	7.9	8.2	6.9	78	59	75	59	79	60
MD........	Baltimore	71.2	7.2	7.9	6.3	77	53	73	56	78	52
MA........	Boston	73.2	11.5	12.6	10.2	72	57	69	58	72	56
MI........	Detroit	79.5	9.4	11.1	7.9	80	59	80	69	80	53
MI........	Sault Ste. Marie	81.9	7.7	7.9	6.7	84	65	80	73	87	61
MN........	Duluth	79.2	10.0	10.6	8.5	82	63	78	70	86	60
MN........	Minneapolis-St. Paul	74.0	9.7	9.6	8.7	79	59	77	68	81	54
MS........	Jackson	69.6	6.1	7.2	4.6	90	57	85	62	93	58
MO........	Kansas City	67.1	10.4	11.0	8.9	81	60	78	64	85	59
MO........	St. Louis	72.6	9.0	10.1	7.6	81	58	79	65	82	55
MT........	Great Falls	78.4	11.4	13.9	9.1	63	46	65	61	60	30
NE........	Omaha	69.6	10.0	10.2	8.5	81	59	79	66	85	57
NV........	Reno	56.7	6.4	4.5	7.2	63	31	75	51	54	18
NH........	Concord	75.3	6.0	6.6	5.1	80	53	76	58	81	51
NJ........	Atlantic City	74.2	8.7	9.5	7.4	80	56	77	58	81	57
NM........	Albuquerque	54.2	8.2	7.3	8.2	53	29	62	40	54	28
NY........	Albany	81.1	7.9	8.7	6.6	79	57	77	63	79	54
NY........	Buffalo	85.2	10.3	12.5	9.0	79	62	79	72	78	55
NY........	Central Park	71.0	6.2	7.6	4.8	70	54	67	56	73	54
NC........	Charlotte	70.4	6.4	6.6	5.7	81	52	78	54	84	55
NC........	Raleigh	69.9	6.5	6.9	6.1	83	53	79	53	86	56
ND........	Bismarck	74.5	9.4	9.2	8.6	81	58	77	71	85	49
OH........	Cincinnati	77.8	8.3	9.7	6.6	81	59	80	68	84	57
OH........	Cleveland	81.9	9.6	11.4	7.8	79	61	79	70	80	56
OH........	Colurnbus	80.3	7.6	9.1	6.1	80	58	78	68	82	55
OK........	Oklahoma City	61.9	11.3	11.6	9.9	80	55	78	59	82	51
OR........	Portland	81.1	7.4	9.2	7.1	82	59	84	76	77	44
PA........	Philadelphia	74.5	9.3	9.9	8.3	76	54	73	58	77	52
PA........	Pittsburgh	83.8	7.8	9.2	6.3	79	57	77	66	82	54
RI........	Providence	73.2	9.2	9.7	8.5	75	55	71	57	76	56
SC........	Columbia	68.5	6.1	6.6	5.7	84	50	82	52	86	52
SD........	Sioux Falls	71.2	10.2	10.3	9.1	82	60	77	69	85	55
TN........	Memphis	67.7	8.1	9.0	6.9	80	56	77	62	84	57
TN........	Nashville	71.8	7.1	8.1	5.9	84	56	80	64	87	56
TX........	Dallas	63.0	9.5	8.9	8.9	78	54	76	58	77	49
TX........	El Paso	47.1	8.1	7.4	7.7	50	27	58	34	56	29
TX........	Houston	75.3	7.5	7.9	6.1	89	59	85	62	93	57
UT........	Salt Lake City	65.8	8.4	6.5	9.1	63	43	78	70	47	21
VT........	Burlington	84.1	8.3	9.2	7.1	76	58	74	64	77	53
VA........	Norfolk	71.2	9.6	10.0	8.5	78	57	74	58	80	59
VA........	Richmond	72.9	7.7	8.3	6.9	81	53	78	55	83	55
WA........	Seattle	80.5	7.9	8.4	7.4	82	63	83	76	79	48
WA........	Spokane	76.4	8.7	8.1	8.6	74	52	86	80	59	26
WV........	Charleston	82.2	4.6	5.7	3.5	83	56	78	62	89	58
WI........	Milwaukee	75.3	10.1	11.0	8.9	79	63	76	68	81	60
WY........	Cheyenne	71.2	12.3	14.4	9.9	61	45	55	51	63	38
PR........	San Juan	80.0	7.9	7.7	9.5	78	66	81	65	78	67

[1] Percent of days that are either partly cloudy or cloudy.

Source: U.S. National Oceanic and Atmospheric Administration, *Comparative Climatic Data For the United States Through 2018*. See also <https://www.ncdc.noaa.gov/ghcn/comparative-climatic-data>.

Table 445. Drought Conditions—Area and Population Impacted by Level of Drought: 2019

[In percent. For continental United States. Data shown for the last week of each month, as of Tuesday. Drought classifications are measured in four intensity levels—D0: Abnormally dry, D1: Moderate drought, D2: Severe drought, D3: Extreme drought, and D4: Exceptional drought. Data are categorical statistics showing percent of the area or population that is in a certain drought category. See source for details, <http://droughtmonitor.unl.edu/AboutUSDM.aspx>. The U.S. Drought Monitor is jointly produced by the National Drought Mitigation Center at the University of Nebraska-Lincoln, the United States Department of Agriculture, and the National Oceanic and Atmospheric Administration]

Week	Area (percent of continental U.S. square miles)						Population (percent of continental U.S. population)					
	None	D0	D1	D2	D3	D4	None	D0	D1	D2	D3	D4
1/29/2019....	70.20	13.27	9.78	4.84	1.76	0.15	79.70	10.14	8.59	1.31	0.25	0.02
2/26/2019....	73.33	14.76	8.06	3.30	0.52	0.04	88.51	8.95	2.10	0.36	0.07	0.01
3/26/2019....	81.65	13.50	3.99	0.86	–	–	85.55	13.17	1.14	0.14	–	–
4/30/2019....	88.88	8.79	2.06	0.27	–	–	91.62	7.42	0.92	0.05	–	–
5/28/2019....	87.90	8.79	3.31	0.00	–	–	87.38	9.79	2.83	0.00	–	–
6/25/2019....	89.90	6.81	2.65	0.65	–	–	91.69	4.89	2.77	0.65	–	–
7/30/2019....	86.35	10.18	3.05	0.42	–	–	89.17	7.52	2.91	0.39	–	–
8/27/2019....	72.16	18.77	7.64	1.26	0.17	–	76.04	17.38	5.79	0.69	0.10	–
9/24/2019....	60.99	21.64	13.45	3.60	0.31	–	51.90	30.80	12.52	4.56	0.22	–
10/29/2019...	66.24	15.90	10.47	6.87	0.51	–	65.09	21.27	8.76	4.36	0.53	–
11/26/2019...	67.06	18.84	8.38	5.54	0.19	–	70.08	23.33	5.35	1.19	0.04	–
12/31/2019...	75.80	13.00	7.37	3.76	0.06	–	87.56	6.47	5.28	0.69	0.01	–

– Represents zero.

Source: National Drought Mitigation Center, "United States Drought Monitor," <http://droughtmonitor.unl.edu/>, accessed January 2020.

Table 446. Top 20 Significant Flood Event Losses Covered by the National Flood Insurance Program, as of January 30, 2019

[In nominal dollars. Covers period beginning in 1978. A significant event is one with 1,500 or more paid losses, or occasionally one added for other reasons]

Event	Date	Number of paid losses	Amount paid ($)	Average paid loss ($)
Hurricane Katrina.............	Aug. 2005	166,790	16,257,744,061	97,474
Hurricane Harvey.............	Sept. 2017	76,257	8,908,547,689	116,823
Superstorm Sandy.............	Oct. 2012	132,360	8,804,242,152	66,517
Hurricane Ike.................	Sept. 2008	46,701	2,702,388,727	57,866
Louisiana severe storms and flooding...............	Aug. 2016	26,976	2,468,493,541	91,507
Hurricane Ivan.............	Sept. 2004	28,154	1,607,512,533	57,097
Hurricane Irene.............	Aug. 2011	44,314	1,345,775,273	30,369
Tropical Storm Allison.............	June 2001	30,671	1,105,003,344	36,028
Hurricane Irma.............	Sept. 2017	21,920	1,054,248,877	48,095
Hurricane Matthew.............	Oct. 2016	16,586	654,394,214	39,455
Hurricane Florence.............	Sept. 2018	13,754	648,333,990	47,138
Louisiana flood.............	May 1995	31,343	585,071,593	18,667
Hurricane Isaac.............	Aug. 2012	12,084	561,527,299	46,469
Hurricane Isabel.............	Sept. 2003	19,938	500,270,118	25,091
Texas torrential rain.............	Apr. 2016	7,437	471,517,374	63,402
Texas flooding.............	May 2015	6,774	468,799,696	69,206
Hurricane Rita.............	Sept. 2005	9,354	466,223,897	49,842
Tropical Storm Lee.............	Sept. 2011	9,905	462,459,225	46,689
Hurricane Floyd.............	Sept. 1999	20,439	462,326,389	22,620
Hurricane Opal.............	Oct. 1995	10,343	405,527,543	39,208

Source: U.S. Department of Homeland Security, Federal Emergency Management Agency, National Flood Insurance Program Statistics, "Significant Flood Events [since 1978], as of January 31, 2019," <http://www.fema.gov/significant-flood-events>, accessed September 2019.

Table 447. Threatened and Endangered Wildlife and Plant Species: 2020

[As of June 2020. Endangered species: one in danger of becoming extinct throughout all or a significant part of its natural range. Threatened species: one likely to become endangered in the foreseeable future]

Item	Total [1]	Mammals	Birds	Reptiles	Amphibians	Fishes	Snails	Clams	Crustaceans	Insects	Arachnids	Plants
Total listings..........	2,361	379	337	140	45	205	54	93	28	92	17	946
Endangered species, total...............	1,873	328	294	87	29	120	41	78	24	79	17	773
United States [2].........	1,275	68	77	16	21	94	40	76	24	75	12	772
Foreign..................	598	260	217	71	8	26	1	2	–	4	5	1
Threatened species, total.............	488	51	43	53	16	85	13	15	4	13	–	173
United States [2].........	391	28	22	29	15	75	12	15	4	13	–	171
Foreign..................	97	23	21	24	1	10	1	–	–	–	–	2

– Represents zero. [1] Includes other categories not shown separately. Twenty-two animal species (14 in the U.S. and 8 Foreign) are counted more than once, primarily because these animals have distinct population segments (each with its own individual listing status). [2] United States listings include those populations in which the U.S. shares jurisdiction with another nation.

Source: U.S. Fish and Wildlife Service, Environmental Conservation Online System, Threatened & Endangered Species, "Listed Species Summary," <http://ecos.fws.gov/ecp/>, accessed June 2020.

Section 7
Elections

This section relates primarily to presidential, congressional, and gubernatorial elections. Also presented are summary tables on congressional legislation; state legislatures; minority and female officeholders; population of voting age; voter participation; and campaign finances.

Official statistics on federal elections, collected by the Clerk of the House, are published biennially in *Statistics of the Presidential and Congressional Election* and *Statistics of the Congressional Election*. Federal elections data also appear in the *Congressional Directory* and in official state documents. Data on reported registration and voting for social and economic groups are obtained by the U.S. Census Bureau as part of the Current Population Survey (CPS) and are published in *Current Population Reports*, Series P20 (see text, Section 1).

Almost all federal, state, and local governmental units in the United States conduct elections for political offices and other purposes. The conduct of elections is regulated by state laws or, in some cities and counties, by local charter. An exception is that the U.S. Constitution prescribes the basis of representation in Congress and the manner of electing the president and grants to Congress the right to regulate the times, places, and manner of electing federal officers. Amendments to the Constitution have prescribed national criteria for voting eligibility. The 15th Amendment, adopted in 1870, gave all male citizens the right to vote regardless of race, color, or previous condition of servitude. The 19th Amendment, adopted in 1920, further extended the right to vote to all citizens regardless of sex. The payment of poll taxes as a prerequisite to voting in federal elections was banned by the 24th Amendment in 1964. In 1971, as a result of the 26th Amendment, eligibility to vote in national elections was extended to all citizens, 18 years old and over.

Presidential election—The Constitution specifies how the president and vice president are selected. Each state elects, by popular vote, a group of electors equal in number to its total of members of Congress. The 23rd Amendment, adopted in 1961, grants the District of Columbia three presidential electors, a number equal to that of the least populous state. Subsequent to the election, the electors meet in their respective states to vote for president and vice president. Usually, each elector votes for the candidate receiving the most popular votes in his or her state. A majority vote of all electors is necessary to elect the president and vice president. If no candidate receives a majority, the House of Representatives, with each state having one vote, is empowered to elect the president and vice president, again, with a majority of votes required.

The 22nd Amendment to the Constitution, adopted in 1951, limits presidential tenure to two elective terms of 4 years each or to one elective term for any person who, upon succession to the presidency, has held the office or acted as President for more than 2 years.

Congressional election—The Constitution provides that representatives be apportioned among the states according to their population, that a census of population be taken every 10 years as a basis for apportionment, and that each state have at least one representative. At the time of each apportionment, Congress decides what the total number of representatives will be. Since 1912, the total has been 435, except during 1960 to 1962 when it increased to 437, adding one representative each for Alaska and Hawaii. The total reverted to 435 after reapportionment following the 1960 census. Members are elected for 2-year terms, all terms covering the same period. The District of Columbia, American Samoa, Guam, and the Virgin Islands each elect one nonvoting delegate, and Puerto Rico elects a nonvoting resident commissioner.

The Senate is composed of 100 members, two from each state, who are elected to serve for a term of 6 years. One-third of the Senate is elected every 2 years. Senators were originally chosen by the state legislatures. The 17th Amendment to the Constitution, adopted in 1913, prescribed that senators be elected by popular vote.

Voter eligibility and participation—The Census Bureau publishes estimates of the population of voting age and the percent casting votes in each state for presidential and congressional election years. These voting-age estimates include a number of persons who meet the age requirement but are not eligible to vote, (e.g. aliens and some institutionalized persons). In addition, since 1964, voter participation and voter characteristics data have been collected during November of election years as part of the CPS. Survey data on voting age population estimates includes non-citizens but excludes members of the Armed Forces and institutionalized populations. Data on percent casting votes excludes institutionalized populations, members of the Armed forces and citizens residing outside the U.S. casting absentee ballots.

Statistical reliability—For a discussion of statistical collection and estimation, sampling procedures, and measures of statistical reliability applicable to Census Bureau data, see Appendix III.

Table 448. Participation in Elections for President and U.S. Representatives: 1934 to 2018

[77,997 represents 77,997,000. As of November, except as noted. Estimated resident population 21 years old and over, 1934 to 1970, except as noted, and 18 years old and over thereafter. Includes Armed Forces stationed in the U.S. Prior to 1958, excludes Alaska and prior to 1960, excludes Hawaii. District of Columbia is included in votes cast for President beginning 1964]

Year	Resident population (includes aliens) of voting age [1] (1,000)	Votes cast			
		For President (1,000)	Percent of voting-age population	For U.S. Representatives (1,000)	Percent of voting-age population
1934	77,997	(X)	(X)	32,804	42.1
1936	80,174	45,647	56.9	(NA)	(NA)
1938	82,354	(X)	(X)	(NA)	(NA)
1940	84,728	49,815	58.8	(NA)	(NA)
1942	86,465	(X)	(X)	28,074	32.5
1944	85,654	48,026	56.1	45,110	52.7
1946	92,659	(X)	(X)	34,410	37.1
1948	95,573	48,834	51.1	46,220	48.4
1950	98,134	(X)	(X)	40,430	41.2
1952	99,929	61,552	61.6	57,571	57.6
1954	102,075	(X)	(X)	42,583	41.7
1956	104,515	62,027	59.3	58,886	56.3
1958	106,447	(X)	(X)	45,719	43.0
1960	109,672	68,836	62.8	64,124	58.5
1962	112,952	(X)	(X)	51,242	45.4
1964	114,090	70,098	61.4	65,879	57.7
1966	116,638	(X)	(X)	52,902	45.4
1968	120,285	73,027	60.7	66,109	55.0
1970	124,498	(X)	(X)	54,259	43.6
1972	140,777	77,625	55.1	71,188	50.6
1974	146,338	(X)	(X)	52,313	35.7
1976	152,308	81,603	53.6	74,259	48.8
1978	158,369	(X)	(X)	54,584	34.5
1980	163,945	86,497	52.8	77,874	47.5
1982	169,643	(X)	(X)	63,881	37.7
1984	173,995	92,655	53.3	82,422	47.4
1986	177,922	(X)	(X)	59,758	33.6
1988	181,956	91,587	50.3	81,682	44.9
1990	185,812	(X)	(X)	62,355	33.6
1992	189,493	104,600	55.2	97,198	51.3
1994	193,010	(X)	(X)	70,494	36.5
1996	196,789	96,390	49.0	90,233	45.9
1998	201,270	(X)	(X)	66,605	33.1
2000	[2] 209,130	105,594	50.5	98,800	47.2
2002	[2] 214,689	(X)	(X)	74,707	34.8
2004	[2] 219,508	122,349	55.7	113,192	51.6
2006	[2] 224,622	(X)	(X)	80,976	36.0
2008	[2] 229,989	131,407	57.1	122,586	53.3
2010	[2] 234,576	(X)	(X)	86,785	37.0
2012	[2] 240,177	129,140	53.8	122,346	50.9
2014	[2] 244,821	(X)	(X)	78,813	32.2
2016	[2] 249,422	136,787	54.8	129,833	52.1
2018	[2] 253,768	(X)	(X)	114,017	44.9

X Not applicable. NA Not available. [1] Population 18 and over in Georgia, 1944-70, and in Kentucky, 1956–70; and 20 and over in Alaska and Hawaii, 1960–70. Source: Through 1990, U.S. Census Bureau, "Table 4. Participation in Elections for President and U.S. Representatives: 1930 to 1992," May 1994, <http://www.census.gov/population/socdemo/voting/p25-1117/tab03-04.pdf>. For 1992–1998, "Estimates and Projections of the Voting-Age Population, 1992 to 2000, and Percent Casting Votes for President, by State: November 1992 and 1996," July 2000, <http://www.census.gov/population/socdemo/voting/proj00/tab03.txt>. For 2000-2009, "Annual Estimates of the Resident Population for Selected Age Groups by Sex for the United States, States, Counties, and Puerto Rico Commonwealth and Municipios: April 1, 2000 to July 1, 2009," <https://www.census.gov/topics/population.html>, accessed June 2015. Starting 2010, "Annual estimates of the resident population by single year of age and sex for the United States: April 1, 2010 to July 1, 2018," <https://www.census.gov/programs-surveys/popest.html>, accessed July 2019. [2] 2000 and 2010, as of April 1, population estimates base. All other years as of July 1.

Source: Except as noted, U.S. House of Representatives, Office of the Clerk, *Statistics of the Presidential and Congressional Election*, February 2019, and earlier reports. See also <http://clerk.house.gov/member_info/election.aspx>.

Table 449. Voters by Whether Voting on Election Day or Utilizing Alternative Early Voting: 1996 to 2016

[Percent distribution of persons voting. As of November. Data are from November Voting and Registration Supplements to the Current Population Survey (see text, Section 1, and Appendix III)]

Election Year	Total	On election day [1]	Alternative early voting methods		
			Total	Before election day [1]	By mail
1996 [2]	100.0	89.5	10.5	2.7	7.8
1998	100.0	89.2	10.8	2.4	8.4
2000 [2]	100.0	86.0	14.0	3.8	10.2
2002	100.0	85.9	14.1	3.4	10.7
2004 [2]	100.0	79.3	20.7	7.8	12.9
2006	100.0	80.4	19.6	5.8	13.7
2008 [2]	100.0	69.3	30.7	14.3	16.4
2010	100.0	73.5	26.5	8.4	18.1
2012 [2]	100.0	67.2	32.8	14.3	18.5
2014	100.0	68.9	31.2	10.3	20.9
2016 [2]	100.0	59.9	40.1	19.1	21.0

[1] Voted in person. [2] Presidential election year.

Source: U.S. Census Bureau, *Characteristics of Voters in the Presidential Election of 2016*, September 2018. See also <https://www.census.gov/library/publications/2018/demo/p20-582.html>.

Table 450. Resident Population of Voting-Age, Total Votes Cast, and Percent Casting Votes—States: 2016 to 2018

[249,422 represents 249,422,000. Votes cast as of November. Estimated population, 18 years old and over. Includes Armed Forces stationed in each state, aliens, and institutional population]

State	Voting-age population (1,000) [1]		Total votes cast (1,000)			Percent casting votes for–		
			Presidential electors	U.S. Representatives		Presidential electors	U.S. Representatives	
	2016	2018	2016	2016	2018	2016	2016	2018
U.S.	**249,422**	**253,768**	**136,787**	**129,833**	**114,017**	**54.8**	**52.1**	**44.9**
AL.	3,765	3,798	2,123	1,890	1,660	56.4	50.2	43.7
AK.	555	554	319	308	282	57.4	55.6	51.0
AZ.	5,309	5,529	2,573	2,412	2,341	48.5	45.4	42.3
AR.	2,284	2,311	1,131	1,069	889	49.5	46.8	38.5
CA.	30,122	30,567	14,182	13,414	12,185	47.1	44.5	39.9
CO.	4,278	4,430	2,780	2,701	2,514	65.0	63.1	56.7
CT.	2,827	2,837	1,645	1,575	1,380	58.2	55.7	48.6
DE.	746	764	442	421	354	59.2	56.4	46.3
DC.	565	575	313	(X)	(X)	55.3	(X)	(X)
FL.	16,471	17,070	9,420	8,837	7,021	57.2	53.7	41.1
GA.	7,797	8,014	4,115	3,773	3,802	52.8	48.4	47.4
HI.	1,121	1,117	438	438	399	39.1	39.1	35.7
ID.	1,245	1,307	690	682	596	55.5	54.8	45.6
IL.	9,897	9,884	5,536	5,242	4,540	55.9	53.0	45.9
IN.	5,058	5,124	2,735	2,658	2,256	54.1	52.6	44.0
IA.	2,401	2,425	1,566	1,516	1,316	65.2	63.1	54.3
KS.	2,194	2,206	1,184	1,174	1,050	54.0	53.5	47.6
KY.	3,426	3,460	1,924	1,765	1,570	56.2	51.5	45.4
LA.	3,564	3,564	2,029	1,749	1,461	56.9	49.1	41.0
ME.	1,077	1,088	772	772	631	71.7	71.7	58.0
MD.	4,659	4,703	2,781	2,708	2,286	59.7	58.1	48.6
MA.	5,448	5,535	3,379	3,379	2,753	62.0	62.0	49.7
MI.	7,757	7,831	4,799	4,671	4,155	61.9	60.2	53.1
MN.	4,232	4,309	2,945	2,860	2,577	69.6	67.6	59.8
MS.	2,267	2,280	1,209	1,182	939	53.3	52.1	41.2
MO.	4,701	4,750	2,809	2,750	2,418	59.7	58.5	50.9
MT.	813	833	495	508	504	60.8	62.5	60.6
NE.	1,432	1,452	844	788	697	58.9	55.0	48.0
NV.	2,245	2,345	1,125	1,078	961	50.1	48.0	41.0
NH.	1,080	1,098	744	716	571	68.9	66.4	52.0
NJ.	6,904	6,955	3,874	3,463	3,099	56.1	50.2	44.6
NM.	1,598	1,613	798	780	693	50.0	48.8	43.0
NY.	15,493	15,474	7,802	7,800	6,251	50.4	50.3	40.4
NC.	7,863	8,083	4,742	4,598	3,381	60.3	58.5	41.8
ND.	579	581	344	338	322	59.5	58.5	55.3
OH.	9,017	9,096	5,496	5,218	4,406	61.0	57.9	48.4
OK.	2,964	2,987	1,453	1,133	1,179	49.0	38.2	39.5
OR.	3,221	3,317	2,001	1,912	1,848	62.1	59.4	55.7
PA.	10,109	10,158	6,115	5,744	4,930	60.5	56.8	48.5
RI.	848	852	464	432	373	54.7	50.9	43.8
SC.	3,860	3,978	2,103	2,012	1,709	54.5	52.1	43.0
SD.	649	665	370	370	336	57.0	57.0	50.5
TN.	5,142	5,264	2,508	2,391	2,160	48.8	46.5	41.0
TX.	20,621	21,304	8,969	8,529	8,203	43.5	41.4	38.5
UT.	2,122	2,229	1,131	1,114	1,053	53.3	52.5	47.2
VT.	505	510	320	320	278	63.4	63.4	54.5
VA.	6,542	6,648	3,983	3,782	3,313	60.9	57.8	49.8
WA.	5,662	5,872	3,317	3,141	3,022	58.6	55.5	51.5
WV.	1,457	1,442	713	686	578	49.0	47.1	40.1
WI.	4,485	4,537	2,976	2,774	2,572	66.4	61.8	56.7
WY.	446	443	259	259	205	58.1	58.1	46.3

X Not applicable. [1] As of July 1. Source: U.S. Census Bureau, "Annual Estimates of the Resident Population for Selected Age Groups by Sex for the United States, States, Counties, and Puerto Rico Commonwealth and Municipios: April 1, 2010 to July 1, 2018," <data.census.gov>, accessed July 2019.

Source: Except as noted, U.S. House of Representatives, Office of the Clerk, *Statistics of the Presidential and Congressional Election*, November 2018, and earlier reports. See also <http://history.house.gov/Institution/Election-Statistics/Election-Statistics/>.

Table 451. Voting-Age Population—Reported Registration and Voting by Selected Characteristics: 2004 to 2018

[220.6 represents 220,600,000. As of November. Covers civilian noninstitutional population 18 years old and over. Includes aliens. Figures are based on Current Population Survey (see text, Section 1 and Appendix III) and differ from those in Table 448 based on population estimates and official vote counts]

Characteristic	Voting-age population (mil.) 2006	2008	2010	2012	2014	2016	2018	Registered – Presidential 2004	2008	2012	2016	Registered – Congressional 2010	2014	2018	Voted – Presidential 2004	2008	2012	2016	Voted – Congressional 2010	2014	2018
Total [1]	**220.6**	**225.5**	**229.7**	**235.2**	**239.9**	**245.5**	**249.7**	**65.9**	**64.9**	**65.1**	**64.2**	**59.8**	**59.3**	**61.3**	**58.3**	**58.2**	**56.5**	**56.0**	**41.8**	**38.5**	**49.0**
AGE																					
18 to 20 years old	11.6	11.7	12.2	12.3	11.9	11.7	12.0	50.7	49.3	44.2	46.7	34.4	32.6	40.8	41.0	41.0	35.1	36.4	16.4	14.1	27.2
21 to 24 years old	16.2	16.6	16.7	17.6	17.8	13.2	17.0	52.1	56.2	53.1	71.4	47.2	43.6	49.1	42.5	46.6	40.0	55.2	22.0	17.1	32.1
25 to 34 years old	39.4	40.2	41.2	41.1	42.3	43.8	44.8	55.6	56.5	57.0	56.4	49.8	49.4	52.1	46.9	48.5	46.1	46.4	26.9	24.2	37.0
35 to 44 years old	42.6	41.5	39.9	39.6	39.6	39.9	40.8	64.2	61.4	61.7	60.0	57.3	56.3	57.3	56.9	55.2	52.9	51.8	37.7	32.8	44.2
45 to 64 years old	75.0	78.1	80.7	82.1	82.8	83.8	83.3	72.7	70.4	70.4	68.5	66.3	65.4	66.1	66.6	65.0	63.4	61.7	51.1	46.0	55.0
65 years old and over	35.8	37.5	39.0	42.5	45.6	48.7	51.9	76.9	75.0	76.9	75.3	72.5	73.0	73.3	68.9	68.1	69.7	68.4	58.9	57.5	63.8
SEX																					
Male	106.5	109.0	111.1	113.2	115.6	118.5	120.6	64.0	62.6	63.1	62.3	57.9	57.2	59.5	56.3	55.7	54.4	53.8	40.9	37.2	47.2
Female	114.1	116.5	118.6	122.0	124.2	127.0	129.2	67.6	67.0	67.0	66.0	61.5	61.2	63.0	60.1	60.4	58.5	58.1	42.7	39.6	50.6
RACE/ETHNICITY																					
White [2]	179.9	183.2	185.8	187.1	189.3	192.1	194.1	67.9	66.6	66.7	66.3	61.6	61.3	63.7	60.3	59.6	57.6	58.2	43.4	40.3	51.1
Black [2]	25.7	26.5	27.4	28.7	29.7	30.6	31.6	64.4	65.5	68.5	65.3	58.8	59.7	60.2	56.3	60.8	62.0	55.9	40.7	37.3	48.0
Asian [2,3]	9.9	10.5	11.0	12.5	13.5	14.9	15.7	34.9	37.3	37.2	38.9	34.1	34.4	37.7	29.8	32.1	31.3	33.9	21.3	19.1	28.9
Hispanic [4]	29.0	30.9	32.5	35.2	36.8	39.0	41.0	34.3	37.6	38.9	39.2	33.8	34.9	37.9	28.0	31.6	31.8	32.5	20.5	18.4	28.5
REGION [5]																					
Northeast	41.2	41.5	42.3	42.9	43.5	43.9	44.2	65.3	63.7	65.2	64.0	59.7	58.3	60.7	58.6	57.4	56.6	56.2	41.6	36.3	48.4
Midwest	49.1	49.4	50.1	50.6	51.0	51.6	51.8	72.8	70.6	71.4	70.2	65.0	65.0	67.5	65.0	63.4	62.3	61.4	45.1	42.3	53.5
South	80.0	82.4	84.2	87.1	89.2	92.0	94.5	65.5	65.5	65.3	64.0	59.4	60.0	60.8	56.4	57.7	55.7	54.9	39.3	38.4	47.3
West	50.4	52.2	53.2	54.6	56.1	58.0	59.3	60.1	59.4	58.9	59.3	55.5	53.7	57.0	54.4	54.6	52.3	52.9	42.7	36.8	48.0
EDUCATIONAL ATTAINMENT																					
8 years or less	12.1	11.1	11.1	10.5	9.9	9.8	8.9	32.5	30.1	28.7	24.5	27.0	24.5	22.9	23.6	23.4	21.6	18.3	15.8	13.2	14.4
High school: Less than high school graduate	20.2	19.1	18.8	18.7	18.6	17.7	16.7	45.8	43.2	42.6	39.0	37.8	37.5	36.6	34.6	33.7	32.2	29.3	20.8	18.2	23.2
High school graduate or GED [6]	70.0	70.4	71.0	70.6	70.6	71.3	71.6	61.5	59.5	59.0	57.5	54.0	53.5	53.1	52.4	50.9	48.7	47.4	35.2	31.5	38.8
College: Some college or Associate's degree	60.2	63.8	65.3	67.7	68.8	69.9	69.5	73.7	72.0	71.2	69.8	65.5	64.0	67.0	66.1	65.0	61.5	60.5	44.4	40.0	52.2
Bachelor's or advanced degree	58.2	61.1	63.5	67.8	72.0	76.8	83.1	78.1	76.8	77.2	76.2	72.5	70.8	72.7	74.2	73.3	71.7	71.0	57.1	52.5	63.9
EMPLOYMENT STATUS																					
Employed	143.8	143.2	138.3	142.6	146.2	150.9	156.0	67.1	66.4	67.1	65.9	61.5	60.4	62.4	60.0	60.1	58.6	57.8	42.5	38.2	49.6
Unemployed	6.2	9.5	13.9	11.1	8.4	6.9	5.5	56.3	57.2	56.9	57.0	52.3	50.7	56.5	46.4	48.8	46.1	44.8	31.6	26.9	40.2
Not in labor force	70.5	72.8	77.5	81.6	85.2	87.8	88.2	64.4	62.9	62.8	61.8	58.0	58.2	59.6	56.2	55.5	54.3	55.5	42.3	40.1	48.4

[1] Includes other races, not shown separately. [2] Beginning with the 2003 Current Population Survey (CPS), respondents could choose more than one race. As of 2004, data represent persons who selected this race group only and exclude persons reporting more than one race. The CPS in prior years allowed respondents to report only one race group. See also comment on race in the text for Section 1. [3] Prior to 2004, this category was "Asian and Pacific Islanders," therefore rates are not comparable with prior years. [4] Persons of Hispanic origin may be of any race. [5] For composition of regions, see map, inside cover. [6] The General Educational Development (GED) Test measures how well a non-high school graduate has mastered the skills and general knowledge that are acquired in a 4-year high school education. Successfully passing the exam is a credential generally considered to be equivalent to a high school diploma.

Source: U.S. Census Bureau, "Voting and Registration in the Election of November 2018 - Detailed Tables," <https://www.census.gov/topics/public-sector/voting.html>, accessed April 2019, and earlier releases.

Table 452. Persons Reporting Voter Registration and Whether Voted by State: 2018

[249,748 represents 249,748,000. As of November. See headnote, Table 451]

State	Voting-age population (1,000)	Percent of voting-age population Registered	Percent of voting-age population Voted	State	Voting-age population (1,000)	Percent of voting-age population Registered	Percent of voting-age population Voted
United States	**249,748**	**61.3**	**49.0**	Missouri	4,676	70.6	53.7
Alabama	3,753	66.4	48.8	Montana	822	70.4	63.0
Alaska	523	64.4	50.2	Nebraska	1,428	61.9	47.3
Arizona	5,361	60.8	52.2	Nevada	2,324	55.0	43.3
Arkansas	2,261	55.8	40.6	New Hampshire	1,080	67.2	53.3
California	30,243	51.9	43.8	New Jersey	7,009	61.3	48.3
Colorado	4,353	60.8	53.8	New Mexico	1,576	58.1	45.3
Connecticut	2,834	60.9	48.3	New York	15,478	55.3	43.8
Delaware	756	62.4	48.8	North Carolina	7,911	65.2	49.3
District of Columbia	567	70.0	55.2	North Dakota	560	70.9	59.8
Florida	16,845	56.0	47.0	Ohio	8,873	68.3	51.1
Georgia	7,850	61.7	52.0	Oklahoma	2,868	62.0	47.1
Hawaii	1,057	49.5	40.4	Oregon	3,293	69.1	58.2
Idaho	1,299	57.2	45.2	Pennsylvania	9,928	65.2	52.1
Illinois	9,732	62.4	48.7	Rhode Island	828	64.2	48.7
Indiana	5,006	62.5	47.2	South Carolina	3,914	62.1	46.9
Iowa	2,376	69.8	56.2	South Dakota	648	66.2	51.0
Kansas	2,149	67.4	53.6	Tennessee	5,202	61.2	47.8
Kentucky	3,370	70.9	51.8	Texas	21,064	55.2	42.2
Louisiana	3,458	65.4	47.9	Utah	2,247	64.2	54.0
Maine	1,074	77.1	64.5	Vermont	503	68.1	54.2
Maryland	4,666	66.3	49.7	Virginia	6,386	65.1	52.0
Massachusetts	5,460	61.3	50.0	Washington	5,775	66.7	56.0
Michigan	7,657	71.2	57.7	West Virginia	1,406	63.4	43.4
Minnesota	4,238	70.8	59.5	Wisconsin	4,436	70.5	62.6
Mississippi	2,194	72.9	53.8	Wyoming	430	62.4	51.2

Source: U.S. Census Bureau, "Voting and Registration in the Election of November 2018 - Detailed Tables," <https://www.census.gov/data/tables/time-series/demo/voting-and-registration/p20-583.html>, accessed April 2019.

Table 453. Reported Voting and Registration Among Native and Naturalized Citizens by Race and Hispanic Origin: 2018

[In thousands, except percent, (228,832 represents 228,832,000). Data shown for population aged 18 years and over. As of November]

Nativity status, race, and Hispanic origin	Total citizen population (1,000)	U.S. citizen Reported registered Number (1,000)	U.S. citizen Reported registered Percent	U.S. citizen Not registered Number (1,000)	U.S. citizen Not registered Percent	U.S. citizen Reported voted Number (1,000)	U.S. citizen Reported voted Percent	U.S. citizen Did not vote Number (1,000)	U.S. citizen Did not vote Percent
TOTAL									
All races [1]	228,832	153,066	66.9	33,791	14.8	122,281	53.4	66,109	28.9
White alone [2]	180,522	123,727	68.5	25,850	14.3	99,255	55.0	51,597	28.6
White alone, non-Hispanic	154,982	110,054	71.0	19,640	12.7	89,075	57.5	41,671	26.9
Black alone [2]	29,758	19,023	63.9	4,041	13.6	15,194	51.1	7,928	26.6
Asian alone [2]	11,128	5,898	53.0	2,245	20.2	4,519	40.6	3,764	33.8
Hispanic [3]	28,955	15,558	53.7	6,994	24.2	11,695	40.4	11,091	38.3
NATIVE CITIZEN									
All races [1]	207,022	140,377	67.8	28,947	14.0	112,303	54.2	58,321	28.2
White alone [2]	168,406	116,762	69.3	23,200	13.8	93,680	55.6	47,453	28.2
White alone, non-Hispanic	149,884	106,939	71.3	18,759	12.5	86,591	57.8	40,122	26.8
Black alone [2]	26,974	17,234	63.9	3,551	13.2	13,742	50.9	7,076	26.2
Asian alone [2]	4,795	2,278	47.5	700	14.6	1,798	37.5	1,222	25.5
Hispanic [3]	21,193	11,298	53.3	5,053	23.8	8,261	39.0	8,258	39.0
White alone or in combination [4]	172,046	119,099	69.2	23,856	13.9	95,450	55.5	48,710	28.3
Black alone or in combination [4]	28,544	18,170	63.7	3,836	13.4	14,392	50.4	7,675	26.9
Asian alone or in combination [4]	5,791	2,945	50.9	860	14.9	2,344	40.5	1,514	26.1
NATURALIZED CITIZEN									
All races [1]	21,810	12,689	58.2	4,844	22.2	9,978	45.7	7,787	35.7
White alone [2]	12,116	6,965	57.5	2,650	21.9	5,575	46.0	4,144	34.2
White alone, non-Hispanic	5,098	3,115	61.1	881	17.3	2,485	48.7	1,549	30.4
Black alone [2]	2,785	1,789	64.2	490	17.6	1,453	52.2	852	30.6
Asian alone [2]	6,333	3,620	57.2	1,546	24.4	2,721	43.0	2,542	40.1
Hispanic [3]	7,763	4,260	54.9	1,941	25.0	3,433	44.2	2,833	36.5
White alone or in combination [4]	12,348	7,094	57.5	2,710	21.9	5,666	45.9	4,248	34.4
Black alone or in combination [4]	2,878	1,845	64.1	517	18.0	1,495	52.0	899	31.2
Asian alone or in combination [4]	6,379	3,650	57.2	1,553	24.3	2,736	42.9	2,564	40.2

[1] Includes other races, not shown separately. [2] Beginning with the 2003 Current Population Survey (CPS), respondents could choose more than one race. Data shown represent persons who selected this race group only and exclude persons reporting more than one race. [3] Persons of Hispanic origin may be of any race. [4] In combination with one or more races.

Source: U.S. Census Bureau, "Voting and Registration in the Election of November 2018 - Detailed Tables," <https://www.census.gov/data/tables/time-series/demo/voting-and-registration/p20-583.html>, accessed April 2019.

Table 454. Vote Cast for President by Major Political Party: 1948 to 2016

[In thousands (48,834 represents 48,834,000), except percent and electoral vote. Prior to 1960, excludes Alaska and Hawaii; prior to 1964, excludes DC. Vote cast for major party candidates includes the votes of minor parties cast for those candidates]

Year	Candidates for President — Democratic	Candidates for President — Republican	Total popular vote [1] (1,000)	Democratic — Popular vote Number (1,000)	Democratic — Popular vote Percent	Democratic — Electoral vote	Republican — Popular vote Number (1,000)	Republican — Popular vote Percent	Republican — Electoral vote
1948..........	Truman	Dewey	48,834	24,106	49.4	303	21,969	45.0	189
1952..........	Stevenson	Eisenhower	61,552	27,315	44.4	89	33,779	54.9	442
1956..........	Stevenson	Eisenhower	62,027	26,739	43.1	73	35,581	57.4	457
1960..........	Kennedy	Nixon	68,836	34,227	49.7	303	34,108	49.5	219
1964..........	Johnson	Goldwater	70,098	42,825	61.1	486	27,147	38.7	52
1968..........	Humphrey	Nixon	73,027	30,989	42.4	191	31,710	43.4	301
1972..........	McGovern	Nixon	77,625	28,902	37.2	17	46,740	60.2	520
1976..........	Carter	Ford	81,603	40,826	50.0	297	39,148	48.0	240
1980..........	Carter	Reagan	86,497	35,481	41.0	49	43,643	50.5	489
1984..........	Mondale	Reagan	92,655	37,450	40.4	13	54,167	58.5	525
1988..........	Dukakis	Bush	91,587	41,717	45.5	111	48,643	53.1	426
1992..........	Clinton	Bush	104,600	44,858	42.9	370	38,799	37.1	168
1996..........	Clinton	Dole	96,390	47,402	49.2	379	39,198	40.7	159
2000..........	Gore	Bush	105,594	50,996	48.3	266	50,465	47.8	271
2004..........	Kerry	Bush	122,349	58,895	48.1	251	61,873	50.6	286
2008..........	Obama	McCain	131,407	69,498	52.9	365	59,948	45.6	173
2012..........	Obama	Romney	129,140	65,752	50.9	332	60,670	47.0	206
2016..........	Clinton	Trump	136,787	65,677	48.0	227	62,692	45.8	304

[1] Include votes for minor party candidates, independents, unpledged electors, and scattered write-in votes.

Source: U.S. House of Representatives, Office of the Clerk, *Statistics of the Presidential and Congressional Election*, February 2017, and earlier reports. See also <http://clerk.house.gov/member_info/election.aspx>.

Table 455. Vote Cast for Leading Minority Party Candidates for President: 1948 to 2016

[In thousands (1,169 represents 1,169,000). See headnote, Table 454. Data do not include write-ins, scatterings, or votes for candidates who ran on party tickets not shown, unless otherwise noted]

Year	Candidate	Party	Popular vote (1,000)	Candidate	Party	Popular vote (1,000)
1948..........	Strom Thurmond	States' Rights	1,169	Henry Wallace	Progressive	1,156
1952..........	Vincent Hallinan	Progressive	135	Stuart Hamblen	Prohibition	73
1956 [1]........	T. Coleman Andrews	States' Rights	91	Eric Hass	Socialist Labor	41
1960..........	Eric Hass	Socialist Labor	46	Rutherford Decker	Prohibition	46
1964..........	Eric Hass	Socialist Labor	43	Clifton DeBerry	Socialist Workers	22
1968..........	George Wallace	American Independent	9,446	Henning Blomen	Socialist Labor	52
1972 [1]........	John Schmitz	American	993	Benjamin Spock	People's	9
1976..........	Eugene McCarthy	Independent	680	Roger McBride	Libertarian	172
1980..........	John Anderson	Independent	5,251	Ed Clark	Libertarian	920
1984..........	David Bergland	Libertarian	227	Lyndon H. LaRouche	Independent	79
1988..........	Ron Paul	Libertarian	410	Lenora B. Fulani	New Alliance	129
1992..........	H. Ross Perot	Independent	19,722	Andre Marrou	Libertarian	281
1996..........	H. Ross Perot	Reform	7,137	Ralph Nader	Green	527
2000..........	Ralph Nader	Green	2,530	Pat Buchanan	Reform	324
2004..........	Michael Badnarik	Libertarian	369	Ralph Nader	Independent	156
2008..........	Ralph Nader	Independent	739	Bob Barr	Libertarian	515
2012..........	Gary Johnson	Libertarian	1,216	Jill Stein	Green	401
2016..........	Gary Johnson	Libertarian	4,081	Jill Stein	Green	1,351

[1] Data include write-ins, scatterings, and/or votes for candidates who ran on party tickets not shown.

Source: U.S. House of Representatives, Office of the Clerk, *Statistics of the Presidential and Congressional Election*, February 2017, and earlier reports. See also <http://clerk.house.gov/member_info/election.aspx>.

Table 456. Electoral Vote Cast for President by Major Political Party—States: 1976 to 2016

[D = Democratic, R = Republican. For composition of regions, see map, inside front cover]

State	1976 [1]	1980	1984	1988 [2]	1992	1996	2000 [3]	2004 [4]	2008 [5]	2012	2016 [6]
Democratic.........	**297**	**49**	**13**	**111**	**370**	**379**	**266**	**251**	**365**	**332**	**227**
Republican.........	**240**	**489**	**525**	**426**	**168**	**159**	**271**	**286**	**173**	**206**	**304**
Northeast:											
Democratic..........	86	4	–	53	106	106	102	101	101	96	75
Republican..........	36	118	113	60	–	–	4	–	–	–	21
Midwest:											
Democratic..........	58	10	10	29	100	100	68	57	97	80	30
Republican..........	87	135	127	108	29	29	61	66	27	38	88
South:											
Democratic..........	149	31	3	8	68	80	15	16	71	58	29
Republican..........	20	138	174	168	116	104	168	173	118	138	165
West:											
Democratic..........	4	4	–	21	96	93	81	77	96	98	93
Republican..........	97	98	111	90	23	26	38	47	28	30	30
Alabama.............	D-9	R-9	R-9	R-9	R-9	R-9	R-9	R-9	R-9	R-9	R-9
Alaska..............	R-3	R-3	R-3	R-3	R-3	R-3	R-3	R-3	R-3	R-3	R-3
Arizona.............	R-6	R-6	R-7	R-7	R-8	D-8	R-8	R-10	R-10	R-11	R-11
Arkansas............	D-6	R-6	R-6	R-6	D-6	D-6	R-6	R-6	R-6	R-6	R-6
California..........	R-45	R-45	R-47	R-47	D-54	D-54	D-54	D-55	D-55	D-55	D-55
Colorado............	R-7	R-7	R-8	R-8	D-8	R-8	R-8	R-9	D-9	D-9	D-9
Connecticut.........	R-8	R-8	R-8	R-8	D-8	D-8	D-8	D-7	D-7	D-7	D-7
Delaware............	D-3	R-3	R-3	R-3	D-3	D-3	D-3	D-3	D-3	D-3	D-3
District of Columbia...	D-3	D-3	D-3	D-3	D-3	D-3	D-2	D-3	D-3	D-3	D-3
Florida.............	D-17	R-17	R-21	R-21	R-25	D-25	R-25	R-27	D-27	D-29	R-29
Georgia.............	D-12	D-12	R-12	R-12	D-13	R-13	R-13	R-15	R-15	R-16	R-16
Hawaii..............	D-4	D-4	R-4	D-4	D-4	D-4	D-4	D-4	D-4	D-4	D-3
Idaho...............	R-4	R-4	R-4	R-4	R-4	R-4	R-4	R-4	R-4	R-4	R-4
Illinois............	R-26	R-26	R-24	R-24	D-22	D-22	D-22	D-21	D-21	D-20	D-20
Indiana.............	R-13	R-13	R-12	R-12	R-12	R-12	R-12	R-11	D-11	R-11	R-11
Iowa................	R-8	R-8	R-8	D-8	D-7	D-7	D-7	R-7	D-7	D-6	R-6
Kansas..............	R-7	R-7	R-7	R-7	R-6	R-6	R-6	R-6	R-6	R-6	R-6
Kentucky............	D-9	R-9	R-9	R-9	D-8	D-8	R-8	R-8	R-8	R-8	R-8
Louisiana...........	D-10	R-10	R-10	R-10	D-9	D-9	R-9	R-9	R-9	R-8	R-8
Maine...............	R-4	R-4	R-4	R-4	D-4	D-4	D-4	D-4	D-4	D-4	D-3
Maryland............	D-10	D-10	R-10	R-10	D-10	D-10	D-10	D-10	D-10	D-10	D-10
Massachusetts.......	D-14	R-14	R-13	D-13	D-12	D-12	D-12	D-12	D-12	D-11	D-11
Michigan............	R-21	R-21	R-20	R-20	D-18	D-18	D-18	D-17	D-17	D-16	R-16
Minnesota...........	D-10	D-10	D-10	D-10	D-10	D-10	D-10	D-9	D-10	D-10	D-10
Mississippi.........	D-7	R-7	R-7	R-7	R-7	R-7	R-7	R-6	R-6	R-6	R-6
Missouri............	D-12	R-12	R-11	R-11	D-11	D-11	R-11	R-11	R-11	R-10	R-10
Montana.............	R-4	R-4	R-4	R-4	D-3	R-3	R-3	R-3	R-3	R-3	R-3
Nebraska............	R-5	R-5	R-5	R-5	R-5	R-5	R-5	R-5	R-4	R-5	R-5
Nevada..............	R-3	R-3	R-4	R-4	D-4	D-4	R-4	R-5	D-5	D-6	D-6
New Hampshire.......	R-4	R-4	R-4	R-4	D-4	D-4	R-4	D-4	D-4	D-4	D-4
New Jersey..........	R-17	R-17	R-16	R-16	D-15	D-15	D-15	D-15	D-15	D-14	D-14
New Mexico..........	R-4	R-4	R-5	R-5	D-5	D-5	D-5	R-5	D-5	D-5	D-5
New York............	D-41	R-41	R-36	D-36	D-33	D-33	D-33	D-31	D-31	D-29	D-29
North Carolina......	D-13	R-13	R-13	R-13	R-14	R-14	R-14	R-15	D-15	R-15	R-15
North Dakota........	R-3	R-3	R-3	R-3	R-3	R-3	R-3	R-3	R-3	R-3	R-3
Ohio................	D-25	R-25	R-23	R-23	D-21	D-21	R-21	R-20	D-20	D-18	R-18
Oklahoma............	R-8	R-8	R-8	R-8	R-8	R-8	R-8	R-7	R-7	R-7	R-7
Oregon..............	R-6	R-6	R-7	D-7	D-7	D-7	D-7	D-7	D-7	D-7	D-7
Pennsylvania........	D-27	R-27	R-25	R-25	D-23	D-23	D-23	D-21	D-21	D-20	R-20
Rhode Island........	D-4	D-4	R-4	D-4	D-4	D-4	D-4	D-4	D-4	D-4	D-4
South Carolina......	D-8	R-8	R-8	R-8	R-8	R-8	R-8	R-8	R-8	R-9	R-9
South Dakota........	R-4	R-4	R-3	R-3	R-3	R-3	R-3	R-3	R-3	R-3	R-3
Tennessee...........	D-10	R-10	R-11	R-11	D-11	D-11	R-11	R-11	R-11	R-11	R-11
Texas...............	D-26	R-26	R-29	R-29	R-32	R-32	R-32	R-34	R-34	R-38	R-36
Utah................	R-4	R-4	R-5	R-5	R-5	R-5	R-5	R-5	R-5	R-6	R-6
Vermont.............	R-3	R-3	R-3	R-3	D-3	D-3	D-3	D-3	D-3	D-3	D-3
Virginia............	R-12	R-12	R-12	R-12	R-13	R-13	R-13	R-13	D-13	D-13	D-13
Washington..........	R-8	R-9	R-10	D-10	D-11	D-11	D-11	D-11	D-11	D-12	D-8
West Virginia.......	D-6	D-6	R-6	D-5	D-5	D-5	R-5	R-5	R-5	R-5	R-5
Wisconsin...........	D-11	R-11	R-11	D-11	D-11	D-11	D-11	D-10	D-10	D-10	R-10
Wyoming.............	R-3	R-3	R-3	R-3	R-3	R-3	R-3	R-3	R-3	R-3	R-3

– Represents zero. [1] Excludes one electoral vote cast for Ronald Reagan in Washington. [2] Excludes one electoral vote cast for Lloyd Bentsen for President in West Virginia. [3] Excludes one electoral vote left blank by a Democratic elector in the District of Columbia. [4] Excludes one electoral vote cast for Democratic vice presidential nominee John Edwards in Minnesota. [5] Excludes one electoral vote for Barack Obama in Nebraska. [6] Excludes one electoral vote cast for Bernie Sanders in Hawaii, one electoral vote cast for Donald J. Trump in Maine, one electoral vote each cast for John Kasich and Ron Paul in Texas, and three electoral votes for Colin Powell and one electoral vote for Faith Spotted Eagle in Washington.

Source: U.S. House of Representatives, Office of the Clerk, *Statistics of the Presidential and Congressional Election*, February 2017, and earlier reports. See also <http://clerk.house.gov/member_info/election.aspx>.

Table 457. Popular Vote Cast for President by Political Party—States: 2012 and 2016

[In thousands (129,140 represents 129,140,000), except percent]

State	2012			2012 Percent of total vote		2016			2016 Percent of total vote	
	Total [1]	Demo-cratic party	Republi-can party	Demo-cratic party	Republi-can party	Total [1]	Demo-cratic party	Republi-can party	Demo-cratic party	Republi-can party
United States.........	**129,140**	**65,752**	**60,670**	**50.9**	**47.0**	**136,787**	**65,677**	**62,692**	**48.0**	**45.8**
Alabama.................	2,074	796	1,256	38.4	60.5	2,123	730	1,318	34.4	62.1
Alaska.................	300	123	165	40.8	54.8	319	116	163	36.6	51.3
Arizona.................	2,299	1,025	1,234	44.6	53.7	2,573	1,161	1,252	45.1	48.7
Arkansas.................	1,069	394	648	36.9	60.6	1,131	380	685	33.7	60.6
California.................	13,039	7,854	4,840	60.2	37.1	14,182	8,754	4,484	61.7	31.6
Colorado.................	2,570	1,323	1,185	51.5	46.1	2,780	1,339	1,202	48.2	43.3
Connecticut.................	1,558	905	635	58.1	40.7	1,645	898	673	54.6	40.9
Delaware.................	414	243	165	58.6	40.0	442	236	185	53.4	41.9
District of Columbia.....	294	267	21	90.9	7.3	313	283	13	90.5	4.1
Florida.................	8,474	4,238	4,163	50.0	49.1	9,420	4,505	4,618	47.8	49.0
Georgia.................	3,898	1,774	2,079	45.5	53.3	4,115	1,878	2,089	45.6	50.8
Hawaii.................	437	307	121	70.1	27.7	438	267	129	61.0	29.4
Idaho.................	652	213	421	32.6	64.5	690	190	409	27.5	59.3
Illinois.................	5,242	3,020	2,135	57.6	40.7	5,536	3,091	2,146	55.8	38.8
Indiana.................	2,625	1,153	1,421	43.9	54.1	2,735	1,033	1,557	37.8	56.9
Iowa.................	1,582	823	731	52.0	46.2	1,566	654	801	41.8	51.2
Kansas.................	1,160	441	693	38.0	59.7	1,184	427	671	36.1	56.7
Kentucky.................	1,797	679	1,087	37.8	60.5	1,924	629	1,203	32.7	62.5
Louisiana.................	1,994	809	1,152	40.6	57.8	2,029	780	1,179	38.4	58.1
Maine.................	725	401	292	55.4	40.3	772	358	336	46.3	43.5
Maryland.................	2,707	1,678	972	62.0	35.9	2,781	1,678	943	60.3	33.9
Massachusetts.................	3,184	1,921	1,188	60.3	37.3	3,379	1,995	1,091	59.1	32.3
Michigan.................	4,731	2,565	2,115	54.2	44.7	4,799	2,269	2,280	47.3	47.5
Minnesota.................	2,937	1,546	1,320	52.7	45.0	2,945	1,368	1,323	46.4	44.9
Mississippi.................	1,286	563	711	43.8	55.3	1,209	485	701	40.1	57.9
Missouri.................	2,757	1,224	1,482	44.4	53.8	2,809	1,071	1,595	38.1	56.8
Montana.................	484	202	268	41.7	55.4	495	178	279	35.9	56.5
Nebraska.................	794	302	475	38.0	59.8	844	284	496	33.7	58.7
Nevada.................	1,015	531	464	52.4	45.7	1,125	539	512	47.9	45.5
New Hampshire..........	711	370	330	52.0	46.4	744	349	346	46.8	46.5
New Jersey..............	3,638	2,123	1,478	58.3	40.6	3,874	2,148	1,602	55.5	41.4
New Mexico..........	784	415	336	53.0	42.8	798	385	320	48.3	40.0
New York.................	7,117	4,324	2,223	60.8	31.2	7,802	4,380	2,527	56.1	32.4
North Carolina............	4,505	2,178	2,270	48.4	50.4	4,742	2,189	2,363	46.2	49.8
North Dakota............	323	125	188	38.7	58.3	344	94	217	27.2	63.0
Ohio.................	5,581	2,828	2,661	50.7	47.7	5,496	2,394	2,841	43.6	51.7
Oklahoma.................	1,335	444	891	33.2	66.8	1,453	420	949	28.9	65.3
Oregon.................	1,789	970	754	54.2	42.1	2,001	1,002	782	50.1	39.1
Pennsylvania.............	5,742	2,990	2,680	52.1	46.7	6,115	2,926	2,971	47.9	48.6
Rhode Island.............	446	280	157	62.7	35.2	464	253	181	54.4	38.9
South Carolina..........	1,964	866	1,072	44.1	54.6	2,103	855	1,155	40.7	54.9
South Dakota............	364	145	211	39.9	57.9	370	117	228	31.7	61.5
Tennessee.................	2,459	961	1,462	39.1	59.5	2,508	871	1,523	34.7	60.7
Texas.................	7,994	3,308	4,570	41.4	57.2	8,969	3,878	4,685	43.2	52.2
Utah.................	1,017	252	741	24.7	72.8	1,131	311	515	27.5	45.5
Vermont.................	299	199	93	66.6	31.0	320	179	95	55.7	29.8
Virginia.................	3,854	1,972	1,823	51.2	47.3	3,983	1,981	1,769	49.8	44.4
Washington.................	3,126	1,755	1,291	56.2	41.3	3,317	1,743	1,222	52.5	36.8
West Virginia.............	670	238	418	35.5	62.3	713	189	489	26.5	68.6
Wisconsin.................	3,071	1,621	1,411	52.8	45.9	2,976	1,383	1,405	46.5	47.2
Wyoming.................	251	69	171	27.6	68.2	259	56	174	21.6	67.4

[1] Includes other parties.

Source: U.S. House of Representatives, Office of the Clerk, *Statistics of the Presidential and Congressional Election*, February 2017, and earlier reports. See also <http://clerk.house.gov/member_info/election.aspx>.

Table 458. Vote Cast for U.S. Senators, 2016 and 2018, and Incumbent Senators, 2019—States

[2,087 represents 2,087,000. D = Democrat, R = Republican, I = Independent]

State	2016 Total [2] (1,000)	2016 Percent for leading party	2018 Total [2] (1,000)	2018 Percent for leading party	Incumbent senators and year term expires [1] Name, party, and year	Name, party, and year
Alabama.............	2,087	R-64.0	(X)	(X)	Doug Jones [3] (D) 2021	Richard C. Shelby (R) 2023
Alaska...............	311	R-44.4	(X)	(X)	Lisa Murkowski (R) 2023	Dan Sullivan (R) 2021
Arizona..............	2,531	R-53.7	2,384	D-50.0	Kyrsten Sinema (D) 2025	Martha McSally [4] (R) 2023
Arkansas............	1,108	R-59.8	(X)	(X)	John Boozman (R) 2023	Tom Cotton (R) 2021
California............	12,244	[5] D-100.0	11,113	[5] D-100.0	Kamala D. Harris (D) 2023	Dianne Feinstein (D) 2025
Colorado............	2,743	D-50.0	(X)	(X)	Cory Gardner (R) 2021	Michael F. Bennet (D) 2023
Connecticut.........	1,596	D-57.7	1,387	D-56.8	Richard Blumenthal (D) 2023	Christopher Murphy (D) 2025
Delaware............	(X)	(X)	363	D-60.0	Christopher Coons (D) 2021	Thomas R. Carper (D) 2025
Florida..............	9,302	R-52.0	8,190	R-50.1	Marco Rubio (R) 2023	Rick Scott (R) 2025
Georgia.............	3,899	R-54.8	(X)	(X)	David A. Perdue (R) 2021	Johnny Isakson (R) 2023
Hawaii..............	438	D-70.1	399	D-69.3	Brian Schatz (D) 2023	Mazie Hirono (D) 2025
Idaho...............	679	R-66.1	(X)	(X)	James E. Risch (R) 2021	Mike Crapo (R) 2023
Illinois..............	5,492	D-54.9	(X)	(X)	Richard J. Durbin (D) 2021	Tammy Duckworth (D) 2023
Indiana.............	2,733	R-52.1	2,283	R-50.7	Todd C. Young (R) 2023	Mike Braun (R) 2025
Iowa................	1,541	R-60.1	(X)	(X)	Chuck Grassley (R) 2023	Joni Ernst (R) 2021
Kansas.............	1,178	R-62.2	(X)	(X)	Jerry Moran (R) 2023	Pat Roberts (R) 2021
Kentucky...........	1,903	R-57.3	(X)	(X)	Rand Paul (R) 2023	Mitch McConnell (R) 2021
Louisiana [6]........	820	R-58.8	(X)	(X)	Bill Cassidy (R) 2021	John Kennedy (R) 2023
Maine..............	(X)	(X)	646	I-53.3	Susan M. Collins (R) 2021	Angus King (I) 2025
Maryland...........	2,726	D-60.9	2,300	D-64.9	Chris Van Hollen (D) 2023	Benjamin L. Cardin (D) 2025
Massachusetts......	(X)	(X)	2,753	D-59.3	Elizabeth Warren (D) 2025	Ed Markey (D) 2021
Michigan...........	(X)	(X)	4,237	D-52.3	Gary C. Peters (D) 2021	Debbie Stabenow (D) 2025
Minnesota..........	(X)	(X)	2,597	D-60.3	Tina Smith [7] (D) 2021	Amy Klobuchar (D) 2025
Mississippi.........	(X)	(X)	936	R-58.5	Cindy Hyde-Smith [8] (R) 2021	Roger F. Wicker (R) 2025
Missouri............	2,803	R-49.2	2,442	R-51.4	Roy Blunt (R) 2023	Josh Hawley (R) 2025
Montana............	(X)	(X)	504	D-50.3	Steve Daines (R) 2021	John Tester (D) 2025
Nebraska...........	(X)	(X)	699	R-57.7	Ben Sasse (R) 2021	Deb Fischer (R) 2025
Nevada.............	1,108	D-47.1	972	D-50.4	Jacky Rosen (D) 2025	Catherine Cortez Masto (D) 2023
New Hampshire.....	739	D-48.0	(X)	(X)	Maggie Hassan (D) 2023	Jeanne Shaheen (D) 2021
New Jersey..........	(X)	(X)	3,169	D-54.0	Robert Menendez (D) 2025	Cory A. Booker (D) 2021
New Mexico.........	(X)	(X)	697	D-54.1	Martin Heinrich (D) 2025	Tom Udall (D) 2021
New York...........	7,801	D-61.3	6,251	D-60.1	Kirsten E. Gillibrand (D) 2025	Charles E. Schumer (D) 2023
North Carolina.......	4,691	R-51.1	(X)	(X)	Richard Burr (R) 2023	Thom Tillis (R) 2021
North Dakota.......	343	R-78.5	326	R-55.1	Kevin Cramer (R) 2025	John Hoeven (R) 2023
Ohio................	5,374	R-58.0	4,411	D-53.4	Sherrod Brown (D) 2025	Rob Portman (R) 2023
Oklahoma...........	1,448	R-67.7	(X)	(X)	James Lankford (R) 2023	James M. Inhofe (R) 2021
Oregon.............	1,952	D-56.6	(X)	(X)	Jeff Merkley (D) 2021	Ron Wyden (D) 2023
Pennsylvania........	6,052	R-48.8	5,009	D-55.7	Robert P. Casey Jr. (D) 2025	Patrick J. Toomey (R) 2023
Rhode Island........	(X)	(X)	377	D-61.4	Sheldon Whitehouse (D) 2025	Jack Reed (D) 2021
South Carolina......	2,050	R-60.6	(X)	(X)	Tim Scott (R) 2023	Lindsey Graham (R) 2021
South Dakota.......	370	R-71.8	(X)	(X)	Mike Rounds (R) 2021	John Thune (R) 2023
Tennessee..........	(X)	(X)	2,244	R-54.7	Lamar Alexander (R) 2021	Marsha Blackburn (R) 2025
Texas...............	(X)	(X)	8,372	R-50.9	John Cornyn (R) 2021	Ted Cruz (R) 2025
Utah................	1,116	R-68.1	1,063	R-62.6	Mike Lee (R) 2023	Mitt Romney (R) 2025
Vermont............	320	D-60.0	278	I-70.6	Bernard Sanders (I) 2025	Patrick J. Leahy (D) 2023
Virginia.............	(X)	(X)	3,351	D-57.0	Tim Kaine (D) 2025	Mark R. Warner (D) 2021
Washington.........	3,243	D-59.0	3,086	D-58.4	Maria Cantwell (D) 2025	Patty Murray (D) 2023
West Virginia........	(X)	(X)	586	D-49.6	Joe Manchin III (D) 2025	Shelley Moore Capito (R) 2021
Wisconsin...........	2,949	R-50.2	2,661	D-55.4	Ronald H. Johnson (R) 2023	Tammy Baldwin (D) 2025
Wyoming............	(X)	(X)	205	R-66.4	Michael B. Enzi (R) 2021	John Barrasso (R) 2025

X Not applicable. [1] As of March 14, 2019; see <http://www.senate.gov/pagelayout/reference/three_column_table/Senators.htm>. [2] Includes vote cast for minor parties. [3] Elected in a special election on December 12, 2017 to fill the vacancy caused by the resignation of Jeff Sessions. [4] Appointed December 18, 2018 to fill the vacancy caused by the resignation of Jon Kyl. [5] Two Democrats ran for Senate; no Republican challenger. [6] Louisiana holds an open-primary election with candidates from all parties running on the same ballot. Any candidate who receives a majority is elected. No candidate received a majority in the 2016 open-primary and a runoff election was held on Dec. 10, 2016. Data shown are runoff election totals. [7] Appointed December 13, 2017 to fill the vacancy caused by the resignation of Al Franken, and elected in a special election on November 6, 2018 to serve the remainder of the term. [8] Elected in a runoff election on November 27, 2018 to fill the vacancy caused by the resignation of Thad Cochran.

Source: U.S. House of Representatives, Office of the Clerk, *Statistics of the Congressional Election of November 6, 2018*, February 2019, and earlier reports; and ProQuest research. See also <http://clerk.house.gov/member_info/election.aspx>.

Table 459. Vote Cast for U.S. House of Representatives by Major Political Party—States: 2014 to 2018

[In thousands (78,813 represents 78,813,000), except percent. R = Republican, D = Democrat, and I = Independent. In each state, totals represent the sum of votes cast in each Congressional District or votes cast for Representative-at-Large in states where only one member is elected. In all years there are numerous districts within the state where either the Republican or Democratic party had no candidate. In some states the Republican and Democratic vote includes votes cast for the party candidate by endorsing parties]

State	2014 Total [1]	2014 Democratic	2014 Republican	2014 Percent for leading party	2016 Total [1]	2016 Democratic	2016 Republican	2016 Percent for leading party	2018 Total [1]	2018 Democratic	2018 Republican	2018 Percent for leading party
U.S..........	78,813	35,369	39,927	R-50.7	129,833	61,417	62,772	R-48.3	114,017	60,320	50,467	D-52.9
AL..........	1,081	332	705	R-65.2	1,890	622	1,222	R-64.7	1,660	679	976	R-58.8
AK..........	280	115	143	R-51.0	308	111	155	R-50.3	282	131	150	R-53.1
AZ..........	1,468	578	817	R-55.7	2,412	1,035	1,264	R-52.4	2,341	1,179	1,139	D-50.4
AR..........	831	255	510	R-61.4	1,069	111	760	R-71.2	889	313	556	R-62.6
CA..........	7,132	4,068	2,951	D-57.0	13,414	8,624	4,682	D-64.3	12,185	8,010	3,973	D-65.7
CO..........	2,001	936	1,000	R-50.0	2,701	1,264	1,289	R-47.7	2,514	1,343	1,080	D-53.4
CT..........	1,068	596	410	D-55.8	1,575	917	558	D-58.2	1,380	809	512	D-58.6
DE..........	232	137	85	D-59.3	421	234	172	D-55.5	354	227	125	D-64.3
FL [2]......	4,999	2,131	2,713	R-54.3	8,837	3,985	4,734	R-53.6	7,021	3,307	3,675	R-52.3
GA..........	2,306	956	1,349	R-58.5	3,773	1,498	2,272	R-60.2	3,802	1,814	1,987	R-52.3
HI..........	370	235	120	D-63.7	438	316	86	D-72.3	399	288	87	D-72.2
ID..........	435	160	275	R-63.2	682	209	448	R-65.7	596	207	368	R-61.8
IL..........	3,568	1,823	1,722	D-51.1	5,242	2,811	2,397	D-53.6	4,540	2,758	1,754	D-60.7
IN..........	1,342	502	789	R-58.8	2,658	1,053	1,443	R-54.3	2,256	1,000	1,248	R-55.3
IA..........	1,120	509	596	R-53.2	1,516	674	813	R-53.7	1,316	665	612	D-50.5
KS..........	862	312	541	R-62.7	1,174	318	694	R-59.1	1,050	464	563	R-53.6
KY [2]......	1,398	508	887	R-63.5	1,765	517	1,248	R-70.7	1,570	613	935	R-59.6
LA [2]......	1,569	406	1,031	R-65.7	1,749	530	1,178	R-67.3	1,461	553	836	R-57.2
ME..........	617	305	228	D-49.5	772	387	357	D-50.1	631	344	250	D-54.4
MD..........	1,703	978	704	D-57.4	2,708	1,636	962	D-60.4	2,286	1,493	738	D-65.3
MA..........	2,187	1,475	309	D-67.5	3,379	2,345	451	D-69.4	2,753	1,944	498	D-70.6
MI..........	3,089	1,519	1,467	D-49.2	4,671	2,194	2,243	R-48.0	4,155	2,175	1,853	D-52.4
MN..........	1,964	986	914	D-50.2	2,860	1,435	1,335	D-50.2	2,577	1,421	1,126	D-55.1
MS..........	626	230	329	R-52.6	1,182	450	681	R-57.6	939	399	471	R-50.2
MO..........	1,426	514	838	R-58.8	2,750	1,041	1,601	R-58.2	2,418	1,028	1,331	R-55.0
MT..........	368	149	204	R-55.4	508	206	285	R-56.2	504	233	257	R-50.9
NE..........	536	185	341	R-63.6	788	221	558	R-70.7	697	264	432	R-62.0
NV..........	543	210	305	R-56.1	1,078	508	498	D-47.1	961	491	440	D-51.1
NH..........	481	247	232	D-51.5	716	336	316	D-47.0	571	311	249	D-54.5
NJ..........	1,821	914	877	D-50.2	3,463	1,822	1,542	D-52.6	3,099	1,857	1,199	D-59.9
NM..........	512	271	241	D-53.0	780	437	343	D-56.0	693	404	265	D-58.3
NY..........	3,935	1,788	1,257	D-45.4	7,800	4,202	2,141	D-53.9	6,251	3,761	1,640	D-60.2
NC..........	2,808	1,234	1,555	R-55.4	4,598	2,143	2,447	R-53.2	3,381	1,633	1,707	R-50.5
ND..........	249	96	138	R-55.5	338	80	234	R-69.1	322	114	194	R-60.2
OH..........	3,000	1,180	1,771	R-59.0	5,218	2,155	2,996	R-57.4	4,406	2,083	2,291	R-52.0
OK [2]......	653	174	458	R-70.0	1,133	305	782	R-69.0	1,179	428	731	R-62.0
OR..........	1,451	778	583	D-53.6	1,912	1,027	731	D-53.7	1,848	1,061	703	D-57.4
PA..........	3,324	1,468	1,833	R-55.2	5,744	2,625	3,097	R-53.9	4,930	2,713	2,206	D-55.0
RI..........	316	193	123	D-61.0	432	264	141	D-61.1	373	243	130	D-65.0
SC..........	1,156	377	734	R-63.5	2,012	768	1,177	R-58.5	1,709	758	927	R-54.3
SD..........	276	92	184	R-66.5	370	133	237	R-64.1	336	121	203	R-60.3
TN..........	1,371	448	849	R-61.9	2,391	814	1,494	R-62.5	2,160	846	1,280	R-59.2
TX..........	4,453	1,474	2,685	R-60.3	8,529	3,161	4,878	R-57.2	8,203	3,853	4,135	R-50.4
UT..........	566	183	351	R-62.0	1,114	356	711	R-63.8	1,053	374	617	R-58.7
VT..........	192	123	59	D-64.4	320	264	(X)	D-82.5	278	189	71	D-67.8
VA..........	2,135	846	1,144	R-53.6	3,782	1,859	1,843	D-49.2	3,313	1,867	1,409	D-56.4
WA..........	2,030	1,048	982	D-51.6	3,141	1,736	1,405	D-55.3	3,022	1,889	900	D-62.5
WV..........	439	182	243	R-55.3	686	224	445	R-64.8	578	235	337	R-58.3
WI..........	2,356	1,103	1,233	R-52.4	2,774	1,380	1,270	D-49.8	2,572	1,367	1,173	D-53.2
WY..........	171	38	113	R-66.0	259	75	156	R-60.3	205	60	128	R-62.3

X Not applicable. [1] Includes votes cast for minor parties. [2] State law does not require tabulation of votes for unopposed candidates.

Source: U.S. House of Representatives, Office of the Clerk, *Statistics of the Congressional Election of November 6, 2018*, February 2019, and earlier reports. See also <http://clerk.house.gov/member_info/election.aspx>.

[As of February 2019. Does not include special elections or votes received from endorsing parties. If multiple candidates from the same party ran in the general election, only the candidate with the leading number of votes is shown]

State and district	Democrat Name	Percent of total	Republican Name	Percent of total
AL......	(X)	(X)	(X)	(X)
1st. ...	Kennedy Jr.	36.8	Byrne	63.2
2d.....	Isner	38.4	Roby	61.4
3d.....	Hagan	36.2	Rogers	63.7
4th....	Auman	20.1	Aderholt	79.8
5th....	Joffrion	38.9	Brooks	61.0
6th....	Kline	30.8	Palmer	69.2
7th....	Sewell	97.8	(1)	(1)
AK....	Galvin	46.5	Young	53.1
AZ.....	(X)	(X)	(X)	(X)
1st. ...	O'Halleran	53.8	Rogers	46.1
2d.....	Kirkpatrick	54.7	Marquez Peterson	45.2
3d.....	Grijalva	63.9	Pierson	36.1
4th....	Brill	30.5	Gosar	68.2
5th....	Greene	40.6	Biggs	59.4
6th....	Malik	44.8	Schweikert	55.2
7th....	Gallego	85.6	(1)	(1)
8th....	Tipirneni	44.5	Lesko	55.5
9th....	Stanton	61.1	Ferrara	38.9
AR.....	(X)	(X)	(X)	(X)
1st. ...	Desai	28.8	Crawford	68.9
2d.....	Tucker	45.8	Hill	52.1
3d.....	Mahony	32.6	Womack	64.8
4th....	Shamel	31.2	Westerman	66.7
CA.....	(X)	(X)	(X)	(X)
1st. ...	Denney	45.1	LaMalfa	54.9
2d.....	Huffman	77.0	Mensing	23.0
3d.....	Garamendi	58.1	Schaupp	41.9
4th....	Morse	45.9	McClintock	54.1
5th....	Thompson	78.9	(1)	(1)
6th....	Matsui	80.4	(1)	(1)
7th....	Bera	55.0	Grant	45.0
8th....	(1)	(1)	Cook	60.0
9th....	McNerney	56.5	Livengood	43.5
10th...	Harder	52.3	Denham	47.7
11th...	DeSaulnier	74.1	Fitzgerald	25.9
12th...	Pelosi	86.8	Remmer	13.2
13th...	Lee	88.4	(1)	(1)
14th...	Speier	79.2	Osmeña	20.8
15th...	Swalwell	73.0	Peters Jr.	27.0
16th...	Costa	57.5	Heng	42.5
17th...	Khanna	75.3	Cohen	24.7
18th...	Eshoo	74.5	Russell	25.5
19th...	Lofgren	73.8	Aguilera	26.2
20th...	Panetta	81.4	(1)	(1)
21st...	Cox	50.4	Valadao	49.6
22d...	Janz	47.3	Nunes	52.7
23d...	Matta	36.3	McCarthy	63.7
24th...	Carbajal	58.6	Fareed	41.4
25th...	Hill	54.4	Knight	45.6
26th...	Brownley	61.9	Sabato Jr.	38.1
27th...	Chu	79.2	(1)	(1)
28th...	Schiff	78.4	Nalbandian	21.6
29th...	Cárdenas	80.6	Bernal	19.4
30th...	Sherman	73.4	Reed	26.6
31st...	Aguilar	58.7	Flynn	41.3
32d...	Napolitano	68.8	Scott	31.2
33d...	Lieu	70.0	Wright	30.0
34th...	Gomez	72.5	(1)	(1)
35th...	Torres	69.4	Valiente	30.6
36th...	Ruiz	59.0	Pelzer	41.0
37th...	Bass	89.1	Bassilian	10.9
38th...	Sánchez	68.9	Downing	31.1
39th...	Cisneros	51.6	Kim	48.4
40th...	Roybal-Allard	77.3	(1)	(1)
41st...	Takano	65.1	Smith	34.9
42d...	Peacock	43.5	Calvert	56.5
43d...	Waters	77.7	Navarro	22.3
44th...	Barragán	68.3	(1)	(1)
45th...	Porter	52.1	Walters	47.9
46th...	Correa	69.1	Lambert	30.9
47th...	Lowenthal	64.9	Briscoe	35.1
48th...	Rouda	53.6	Rohrabacher	46.4
49th...	Levin	56.4	Harkey	43.6
50th...	Campa-Najjar	48.3	Hunter	51.7
51st...	Vargas	71.2	Hidalgo Jr.	28.8
52d...	Peterson	63.8	Qudrat	36.2
53d...	Davis	69.1	Murtaugh	30.9
CO.....	(X)	(X)	(X)	(X)
1st. ...	DeGette	73.8	Stockham	23.0
2d.....	Neguse	60.3	Yu	33.6

State and district	Democrat Name	Percent of total	Republican Name	Percent of total
3d.....	Bush	43.6	Tipton	51.5
4th....	McCormick	39.4	Buck	60.6
5th....	Spaulding	39.3	Lamborn	57.0
6th....	Crow	54.1	Coffman	42.9
7th....	Perlmutter	60.4	Barrington	35.4
CT......	(X)	(X)	(X)	(X)
1st. ...	Larson	60.6	Nye	35.0
2d.....	Courtney	58.0	Postemski Jr.	35.4
3d.....	DeLauro	60.4	Cadena	35.4
4th....	Himes	61.2	Arora	37.4
5th....	Hayes	52.8	Santos	42.5
DE.....	Rochester	64.3	Walker	35.4
DC.....	(X)	(X)	(X)	(X)
FL......	(X)	(X)	(X)	(X)
1st. ...	Zimmerman	32.9	Gaetz	67.1
2d.....	Rackleff	32.6	Dunn	67.4
3d.....	Hinson	42.4	Yoho	57.6
4th....	Selmont	32.4	Rutherford	65.2
5th....	Lawson Jr.	66.8	Fuller	33.2
6th....	Soderberg	43.7	Waltz	56.3
7th....	Murphy	57.7	Miller	42.3
8th....	Patel	39.5	Posey	60.5
9th....	Soto	58.0	Liebnitzky	42.0
10th...	Demings	(2)	(1)	(1)
11th...	Cottrell	34.8	Webster	65.1
12th...	Hunter	39.7	Bilirakis	58.1
13th...	Crist	57.6	Buck	42.4
14th...	Castor	(2)	(1)	(1)
15th...	Carlson	47.0	Spano	53.0
16th...	Shapiro	45.4	Buchanan	54.6
17th...	Ellison	37.7	Steube	62.3
18th...	Baer	45.7	Mast	54.3
19th...	Holden	37.7	Rooney	62.3
20th...	Hastings	99.9	(1)	(1)
21st...	Frankel	(2)	(1)	(1)
22d...	Deutch	62.0	Kimaz	38.0
23d...	Wasserman Schultz	58.5	Kaufman	36.0
24th...	Wilson	(2)	(1)	(1)
25th...	Flores	39.5	Diaz-Balart	60.5
26th...	Mucarsel-Powell	50.9	Curbelo	49.1
27th...	Shalala	51.8	Salazar	45.8
GA.....	(X)	(X)	(X)	(X)
1st. ...	Ring	42.3	Carter	57.7
2d.....	Bishop Jr.	59.6	West Jr.	40.4
3d.....	Enderlin	34.5	Ferguson IV	65.5
4th....	Johnson Jr.	78.8	Profit	21.2
5th....	Lewis	100.0	(1)	(1)
6th....	McBath	50.5	Handel	49.5
7th....	Bourdeaux	49.9	Woodall	50.1
8th....	(1)	(1)	Scott	99.7
9th....	McCall	20.5	Collins	79.5
10th...	Johnson-Green	37.1	Hice	62.9
11th...	Broady Jr.	38.2	Loudermilk	61.8
12th...	Johnson	40.5	Allen	59.5
13th...	Scott	76.2	Callahan	23.8
14th...	Foster	23.5	Graves	76.5
HI......	(X)	(X)	(X)	(X)
1st. ...	Case	70.3	Cavasso	22.2
2d.....	Gabbard	74.0	Evans	21.7
ID......	(X)	(X)	(X)	(X)
1st. ...	McNeil	30.8	Fulcher	62.8
2d.....	Swisher	39.3	Simpson	60.7
IL......	(X)	(X)	(X)	(X)
1st. ...	Rush	73.5	Tillman II	19.8
2d.....	Kelly	81.1	Merkle	18.9
3d.....	Lipinski	73.0	Jones	25.9
4th....	Garcia	86.6	Lorch	13.4
5th....	Quigley	76.7	Hanson	23.3
6th....	Casten	53.6	Roskam	46.4
7th....	Davis	87.6	Cameron	12.4
8th....	Krishnamoorthi	66.0	Diganvker	34.0
9th....	Schakowsky	73.5	Elleson	26.5
10th...	Schneider	65.6	Bennett	34.4
11th...	Foster	63.8	Stella	36.2
12th...	Kelly	45.4	Bost	51.6
13th...	Londrigan	49.6	Davis	50.4
14th...	Underwood	52.5	Hultgren	47.5
15th...	Gaither	29.1	Shimkus	70.9
16th...	Dady	40.9	Kinzinger	59.1
17th...	Bustos	62.1	Fawell	37.9
18th...	Rodriguez	32.8	LaHood	67.2

See footnotes at end of table.

Table 460. Vote Cast for U.S. House of Representatives by Major Political Party—Congressional Districts: 2018-Continued.

See headnote on page 289.

State and district	Democrat Name	Percent of total	Republican Name	Percent of total
IN......	(X)	(X)	(X)	(X)
1st....	Visclosky	65.1	Leyva	34.9
2d....	Hall	45.2	Walorski	54.8
3d.....	Tritch	35.3	Banks	64.7
4th....	Beck	35.9	Baird	64.1
5th....	Thornton	43.2	Brooks	56.8
6th....	Lake	32.9	Pence	63.8
7th....	Carson	64.9	Harmon	35.1
8th....	Tanoos	35.6	Bucshon	64.4
9th....	Watson	43.5	Hollingsworth	56.5
IA......	(X)	(X)	(X)	(X)
1st....	Finkenauer	51.0	Blum	45.9
2d....	Loebsack	54.8	Peters	42.6
3d.....	Axne	49.3	Young	47.1
4th....	Scholten	47.0	King	50.4
KS.....	(X)	(X)	(X)	(X)
1st....	LaPolice	31.9	Marshall	68.1
2d....	Davis	46.8	Watkins	47.6
3d.....	Davids	53.6	Yoder	43.9
4th....	Thompson	40.6	Estes	59.4
KY.....	(X)	(X)	(X)	(X)
1st....	Walker	31.4	Comer	68.6
2d.....	Linderman	31.1	Guthrie	66.7
3d.....	Yarmuth	62.1	Glisson	36.6
4th....	Hall	34.6	Massie	62.2
5th....	Stepp	21.0	Rogers	78.9
6th....	McGrath	47.8	Barr	51.0
LA.....	(X)	(X)	(X)	(X)
1st....	Savoie	16.4	Scalise	71.5
2d.....	Richmond	80.6	(1)	(1)
3d.....	Methvin	17.8	Higgins	55.7
4th....	Trundle	33.6	Johnson	64.2
5th....	Fleenor	30.0	Abraham	66.5
6th....	Dewitt	20.5	Graves	69.5
ME.....	(X)	(X)	(X)	(X)
1st....	Pingree	57.5	Holbrook	31.8
2d....	Golden	50.6	Poliquin	49.4
MD.....	(X)	(X)	(X)	(X)
1st....	Colvin	38.1	Harris	60.0
2d....	Ruppersberger	66.0	Matory	30.7
3d.....	Sarbanes	69.1	Anthony	28.3
4th....	Brown	78.1	McDermott	19.9
5th....	Hoyer	70.3	Devine III	27.1
6th....	Trone	59.0	Hoeber	38.0
7th....	Cummings	76.4	Davis	21.3
8th....	Raskin	68.2	Walsh	30.2
MA.....	(X)	(X)	(X)	(X)
1st....	Neal	77.0	(1)	(1)
2d....	McGovern	65.3	Lovvorn	31.9
3d.....	Trahan	60.4	Green	32.6
4th....	Kennedy III	76.1	(1)	(1)
5th....	Clark	73.0	Hugo	23.1
6th....	Moulton	63.3	Schneider	30.5
7th....	Pressley	86.8	(1)	(1)
8th....	Lynch	79.2	(1)	(1)
9th....	Keating	58.0	Tedeschi	39.7
MI......	(X)	(X)	(X)	(X)
1st....	Morgan	43.7	Bergman	56.3
2d.....	Davidson	43.0	Huizenga	55.3
3d.....	Albro	43.2	Amash	54.4
4th....	Hilliard	37.4	Moolenaar	62.6
5th....	Kildee	59.5	Wines	35.9
6th....	Longjohn	45.7	Upton	50.2
7th....	Driskell	46.2	Walberg	53.8
8th....	Slotkin	50.6	Bishop	46.8
9th....	Levin	59.7	Stearns	36.8
10th...	Bizon	35.0	Mitchell	60.3
11th...	Stevens	51.8	Epstein	45.2
12th...	Dingell	68.1	Jones	28.9
13th...	Tlaib	84.2	(1)	(1)
14th...	Lawrence	80.9	Herschfus	17.3
MN.....	(X)	(X)	(X)	(X)
1st....	Feehan	49.7	Hagedorn	50.1
2d.....	Craig	52.7	Lewis	47.1
3d.....	Phillips	55.6	Paulsen	44.2
4th....	McCollum	66.0	Ryan	29.7
5th....	Omar	78.0	Zielinski	21.7
6th....	Todd	38.7	Emmer	61.1
7th....	Peterson	52.1	Hughes	47.8
8th....	Radinovich	45.2	Stauber	50.7
MS.....	(X)	(X)	(X)	(X)
1st....	Wadkins	32.4	Kelly	66.9
2d.....	Thompson	71.8	(1)	(1)
3d.....	Evans	36.7	Guest	62.3
4th....	Anderson	30.7	Palazzo	68.2
MO.....	(X)	(X)	(X)	(X)
1st....	Clay	80.1	Vroman	16.7
2d.....	VanOstran	47.2	Wagner	51.2
3d.....	Geppert	32.8	Luetkemeyer	65.1
4th....	Hoagenson	32.7	Hartzler	64.8
5th....	Cleaver	61.7	Turk	35.6
6th....	Martin	32.0	Graves	65.4
7th....	Schoolcraft	30.1	Long	66.2
8th....	Ellis	25.0	Smith	73.4
MT.....	Williams	46.2	Gianforte	50.9
NE.....	(X)	(X)	(X)	(X)
1st....	McClure	39.6	Fortenberry	60.4
2d.....	Eastman	49.0	Bacon	51.0
3d.....	Theobald	23.3	Smith	76.7
NV.....	(X)	(X)	(X)	(X)
1st....	Titus	66.2	Bentley	30.9
2d.....	Koble	41.8	Amodei	58.2
3d.....	Lee	51.9	Tarkanian	42.8
4th....	Horsford	51.9	Hardy	43.7
NH.....	(X)	(X)	(X)	(X)
1st....	Pappas	53.6	Edwards	45.0
2d.....	Kuster	55.5	Negron	42.2
NJ......	(X)	(X)	(X)	(X)
1st....	Norcross	64.4	Dilks	33.3
2d.....	Van Drew	52.9	Grossman	45.2
3d.....	Kim	50.0	MacArthur	48.7
4th....	Welle	43.1	Smith	55.4
5th....	Gottheimer	56.2	McCann Jr.	42.5
6th....	Pallone Jr.	63.6	Pezzullo	36.4
7th....	Malinowski	51.7	Lance	46.7
8th....	Sires	78.1	Muniz	18.7
9th....	Pascrell Jr.	70.3	Fisher	28.9
10th...	Payne Jr.	87.6	Khan	10.1
11th...	Sherrill	56.8	Webber	42.1
12th...	Coleman	68.7	Kipnis	31.3
NM.....	(X)	(X)	(X)	(X)
1st....	Haaland	59.1	Arnold-Jones	36.3
2d.....	Small	50.9	Herrell	49.1
3d.....	Luján	63.4	McFall	31.2
NY.....	(X)	(X)	(X)	(X)
1st....	Gershon	45.3	Zeldin	44.3
2d.....	Shirley	44.2	King	45.8
3d.....	Suozzi	54.9	DeBono	36.1
4th....	Rice	58.7	Benno	33.8
5th....	Meeks	86.1	(1)	(1)
6th....	Meng	69.7	(1)	(1)
7th....	Velázquez	81.4	(1)	(1)
8th....	Jeffries	83.4	(1)	(1)
9th....	Clarke	80.5	Gayot	9.0
10th...	Nadler	75.0	Levin	15.6
11th...	Rose	49.6	Donovan Jr.	41.2
12th...	Maloney	80.3	Rabin	11.9
13th...	Espaillat	86.9	Butler	4.8
14th...	Ocasio-Cortez	75.4	Pappas	13.1
15th...	Serrano	91.1	Gonzalez	3.4
16th...	Engel	76.4	(1)	(1)
17th...	Lowey	62.2	(1)	(1)
18th...	Maloney	48.4	O'Donnell	36.9
19th...	Delgado	46.2	Faso	38.3
20th...	Tonko	58.2	Vitollo	32.1
21st...	Cobb	39.1	Stefanik	48.7
22d...	Brindisi	45.5	Tenney	43.2
23d...	Mitrano	41.0	Reed	46.7
24th...	Balter	43.7	Katko	42.8
25th...	Morelle	53.7	Maxwell	33.1
26th...	Higgins	64.8	Zeno	25.4
27th...	McMurray	43.7	Collins	39.1
NC.....	(X)	(X)	(X)	(X)
1st....	Butterfield	69.8	Allison	30.2
2d.....	Coleman	45.8	Holding	51.3
3d.....	(1)	(1)	Jones	100.0
4th....	Price	72.4	Von Loor	24.0
5th....	Adams	43.0	Foxx	57.0
6th....	Watts	43.5	Walker	56.5
7th....	Horton	42.8	Rouzer	55.5
8th....	McNeill	44.7	Hudson	55.3
9th....	(3)	(3)	(3)	(3)
10th...	Brown	40.7	McHenry	59.3
11th...	Price	38.7	Meadows	59.2
12th...	Adams	73.1	Wright	26.9
13th...	Manning	45.5	Budd	51.5

See footnotes at end of table.

Table 460. Vote Cast for U.S. House of Representatives by Major Political Party—Congressional Districts: 2018-Continued.

See headnote on page 289.

State and district	Democrat Name	Percent of total	Republican Name	Percent of total	State and district	Democrat Name	Percent of total	Republican Name	Percent of total
ND.....	Schneider	35.6	Armstrong	60.2	5th....	Wood	37.5	Gooden	62.3
OH.....	(X)	(X)	(X)	(X)	6th....	Sanchez	45.4	Wright	53.1
1st....	Pureval	46.9	Chabot	51.3	7th....	Fletcher	52.5	Culberson	47.5
2d.....	Schiller	41.2	Wenstrup	57.6	8th....	David	24.9	Brady	73.4
3d.....	Beatty	73.6	Burgess	26.4	9th....	Green	89.1	(1)	(1)
4th....	Garrett	34.7	Jordan	65.3	10th...	Siegel	46.8	McCaul	51.1
5th....	Galbraith	35.1	Latta	62.3	11th...	Leeder	18.4	Conaway	80.1
6th....	Roberts	30.7	Johnson	69.3	12th...	Adia	33.9	Granger	64.3
7th....	Harbaugh	41.3	Gibbs	58.7	13th...	Sagan	16.9	Thornberry	81.5
8th....	Enoch	33.4	Davidson	66.6	14th...	Bell	39.3	Weber Sr.	59.2
9th....	Kaptur	67.8	Kraus	32.2	15th...	Gonzalez	59.7	Westley	38.8
10th...	Gasper	42.2	Turner	55.9	16th...	Escobar	68.5	Seeberger	27.0
11th...	Fudge	82.2	Goldstein	17.7	17th...	Kennedy	41.3	Flores	56.8
12th...	O'Connor	47.2	Balderson	51.4	18th...	Lee	75.2	Pate	20.8
13th...	Ryan	61.0	DePizzo	39.0	19th...	Levario	24.8	Arrington	75.2
14th...	Rader	44.8	Joyce	55.2	20th...	Castro	80.9	(1)	(1)
15th...	Neal	39.7	Stivers	58.3	21st...	Kopser	47.6	Roy	50.2
16th...	Palmer	43.3	Gonzalez	56.7	22d....	Kulkarni	46.5	Olson	51.4
OK.....	(X)	(X)	(X)	(X)	23d....	Ortiz Jones	48.7	Hurd	49.2
1st....	Gilpin	40.7	Hern	59.3	24th...	McDowell	47.5	Marchant	50.6
2d.....	Nichols	30.1	Mullin	65.0	25th...	Oliver	44.8	Williams	53.5
3d.....	Robbins	26.1	Lucas	73.9	26th...	Fagan	39.0	Burgess	59.4
4th....	Brannon	33.0	Cole	63.1	27th...	Holguin	36.6	Cloud	60.3
5th....	Horn	50.7	Russell	49.3	28th...	Cuellar	84.4	(1)	(1)
OR.....	(X)	(X)	(X)	(X)	29th...	Garcia	75.1	Aronoff	23.9
1st....	Bonamici	63.6	Verbeek	32.1	30th...	Johnson	91.1	(1)	(1)
2d.....	McLeod-Skinner	39.4	Walden	56.3	31st...	Hegar	47.7	Carter	50.6
3d.....	Blumenauer	72.6	Harrison	19.8	32d....	Allred	52.3	Sessions	45.8
4th....	DeFazio	56.0	Robinson	40.9	33d....	Veasey	76.2	Billups	21.9
5th....	Schrader	55.0	Callahan	41.8	34th...	Vela	60.0	Gonzalez	40.0
PA......	(X)	(X)	(X)	(X)	35th...	Doggett	71.3	Smalling	26.0
1st....	Wallace	48.7	Fitzpatrick	51.3	36th...	Steele	27.4	Babin	72.6
2d.....	Boyle	79.0	Torres	21.0	**UT......**	(X)	(X)	(X)	(X)
3d.....	Evans	93.4	Leib	6.6	1st....	Castillo	24.9	Bishop	61.6
4th....	Dean	63.5	David	36.5	2d.....	Ghorbani	38.9	Stewart	56.1
5th....	Scanlon	65.2	Kim	34.8	3d.....	Singer	27.3	Curtis	67.5
6th....	Houlahan	58.9	McCauley	41.1	4th....	McAdams	50.1	Love	49.9
7th....	Wild	53.5	Nothstein	43.5	**VT......**	Welch	67.8	Tynio	25.4
8th....	Cartwright	54.6	Chrin	45.4	**VA......**	(X)	(X)	(X)	(X)
9th....	Wolff	40.3	Meuser	59.7	1st....	Williams	44.7	Wittman	55.2
10th...	Scott	48.7	Perry	51.3	2d.....	Luria	51.1	Taylor	48.8
11th...	King	41.0	Smucker	59.0	3d.....	Scott	91.2	(1)	(1)
12th...	Friedenberg	34.0	Marino	66.0	4th....	McEachin	62.6	McAdams	35.9
13th...	Ottaway	29.5	Joyce	70.5	5th....	Cockburn	46.6	Riggleman III	53.2
14th...	Boerio	42.1	Reschenthaler	57.9	6th....	Lewis	40.2	Cline	59.7
15th...	Boser	32.2	Thompson	67.8	7th....	Spanberger	50.3	Brat	48.4
16th...	DiNicola	47.3	Kelly	51.6	8th....	Beyer Jr.	76.1	Oh	23.7
17th...	Lamb	56.3	Rothfus	43.7	9th....	Flaccavento	34.8	Griffith	65.2
18th...	Doyle	100.0	(1)	(1)	10th...	Wexton	56.1	Comstock	43.7
RI......	(X)	(X)	(X)	(X)	11th...	Connolly	71.1	Dove Jr.	26.9
1st....	Cicilline	66.7	Donovan	33.1	**WA.....**	(X)	(X)	(X)	(X)
2d.....	Langevin	63.5	Caiozzo	36.3	1st....	DelBene	59.3	Beeler	40.7
SC.....	(X)	(X)	(X)	(X)	2d.....	Larsen	71.3	(1)	(1)
1st....	Cunningham	50.6	Arrington	49.2	3d.....	Long	47.3	Beutler	52.7
2d.....	Carrigan	42.5	Wilson	56.3	4th....	Brown	37.2	Newhouse	62.8
3d.....	Geren	31.0	Duncan	67.8	5th....	Brown	45.2	McMorris Rodgers	54.8
4th....	Brown	36.6	Timmons	59.6	6th....	Kilmer	63.9	Dightman	36.1
5th....	Parnell	41.5	Norman	57.0	7th....	Jayapal	83.6	Keller	16.4
6th....	Clyburn	70.1	Gressman	28.2	8th....	Schrier	52.4	Rossi	47.6
7th....	Williams	40.3	Rice	59.6	9th....	Smith	67.9	(1)	(1)
SD.....	Bjorkman	36.0	Johnson	60.3	10th...	Heck	61.5	Brumbles	38.5
TN......	(X)	(X)	(X)	(X)	**WV.....**	(X)	(X)	(X)	(X)
1st....	Olsen	21.0	Roe	77.1	1st....	Fershee	35.4	McKinley	64.6
2d.....	Hoyos	33.1	Burchett	65.9	2d.....	Sergent	43.0	Mooney	54.0
3d.....	Mitchell	34.5	Fleischmann	63.7	3d.....	Ojeda II	43.6	Miller	56.4
4th....	Phillips	33.6	DesJarlais	63.4	**WI......**	(X)	(X)	(X)	(X)
5th....	Cooper	67.8	Ball	32.2	1st....	Bryce	42.3	Steil	54.6
6th....	Barlow	28.3	Rose	69.5	2d.....	Pocan	97.4	(1)	(1)
7th....	Kanew	32.1	Green	66.9	3d.....	Kind	59.6	Toft	40.3
8th....	Pearson	30.1	Kustoff	67.7	4th....	Moore	74.3	Rogers	21.2
9th....	Cohen	80.0	Bergman	19.2	5th....	Palzewicz	38.0	Sensenbrenner Jr.	61.9
TX......	(X)	(X)	(X)	(X)	6th....	Kohl	44.5	Grothman	55.5
1st....	McKellar	26.3	Gohmert	72.3	7th....	Engebretson	38.5	Duffy	60.1
2d.....	Litton	45.6	Crenshaw	52.8	8th....	Liegeois	36.3	Gallagher	63.7
3d.....	Burch	44.3	Taylor	54.3	**WY.....**	Hunter	29.2	Cheney	62.3
4th....	Krantz	23.0	Ratcliffe	75.7					

X Not applicable. [1] No candidate. [2] According to Florida law, the names of those with no opposition are not printed on the ballot. [3] On February 21, 2019, the North Carolina State Board of Elections ordered a new election in this Congressional District.

Source: U.S. House of Representatives, Office of the Clerk, *Statistics of the Congressional Election of November 6, 2018* February 2019, and earlier reports. See also <http://clerk.house.gov/member_info/election.aspx>.

Table 461. Apportionment of Membership in House of Representatives by State: 1800 to 2010

[Total membership includes Representatives assigned to newly admitted States after the apportionment acts. Population figures used for apportionment purposes are those determined for States by each decennial census. No reapportionment based on 1920 population census. For method of calculating apportionment and a short history of apportionment, see House Report 91-1314, 91st Congress, 2d session, The Decennial Population Census and Congressional Apportionment]

State	___ Membership based on Census of—																				
	1800	1820	1830	1840	1850	1860	1870	1880	1890	1900	1910	1920	1930	1940	1950	1960	1970	1980	1990	2000	2010
U.S.	142	213	242	232	237	243	293	332	357	391	435	435	435	435	437	435	435	435	435	435	435
AL	X	3	5	7	7	6	8	8	9	9	10	10	9	9	9	8	7	7	7	7	7
AK	X	X	X	X	X	X	X	X	X	X	X	X	X	X	1[1]	1	1	1	1	1	1
AZ	X	X	X	X	X	X	X	X	X	X	1[2]	1	1	2	2	3	4	5	6	8	9
AR	X	X	X	1	2	3	4	5	6	7	7	7	7	7	6	4	4	4	4	4	4
CA	X	X	X	X	2	3	4	6	7	8	11	11	20	23	30	38	43	45	52	53	53
CO	X	X	X	X	X	X	X	1	2	3	4	4	4	4	4	4	5	6	6	7	7
CT	7	6	6	4	4	4	4	4	4	5	5	5	6	6	6	6	6	6	6	5	5
DE	1	1	1	1	1	1	1	1	1	1	1	1	1	1	1	1	1	1	1	1	1
FL	X	X	X	X	1	1	2	2	2	3	4	4	5	6	8	12	15	19	23	25	27
GA	4	7	9	8	8	7	9	10	11	11	12	12	10	10	10	10	10	10	11	13	14
HI	X	X	X	X	X	X	X	X	X	X	X	X	X	X	1[1]	2	2	2	2	2	2
ID	X	X	X	X	X	X	X	X	1[1]	1	2	2	2	2	2	2	2	2	2	2	2
IL	X	1	3	7	9	14	19	20	22	25	27	27	27	26	25	24	24	22	20	19	18
IN	X	3	7	10	11	11	13	13	13	13	13	13	12	11	11	11	11	10	10	9	9
IA	X	X	X	X	2	6	9	11	11	11	11	11	9	8	8	7	6	6	5	5	4
KS	X	X	X	X	X	1	3	7	8	8	8	8	7	6	6	5	5	5	4	4	4
KY	6	12	13	10	10	9	10	11	11	11	11	11	9	9	8	7	7	7	6	6	6
LA	X	3	3	4	4	5	6	6	6	7	8	8	8	8	8	8	8	8	7	7	6
ME	X	7	8	7	6	5	5	4	4	4	4	4	3	3	3	2	2	2	2	2	2
MD	9	9	8	6	6	5	6	6	6	6	6	6	6	6	7	8	8	8	8	8	8
MA	17	13	12	10	11	10	11	12	13	14	16	16	15	14	14	12	12	11	10	10	9
MI	X	X	X	3	4	6	9	11	12	12	13	13	17	17	18	19	19	18	16	15	14
MN	X	X	X	X	X	2	3	5	7	9	10	10	9	9	9	8	8	8	8	8	8
MS	X	1	2	4	5	5	6	7	7	8	8	8	7	7	6	5	5	5	5	4	4
MO	X	1	2	5	7	9	13	14	15	16	16	16	13	13	11	10	10	9	9	9	8
MT	X	X	X	X	X	X	X	X	1	1	2	2	2	2	2	2	2	2	1	1	1
NE	X	X	X	X	X	X	1	3	6	6	6	6	5	4	4	3	3	3	3	3	3
NV	X	X	X	X	X	X	1	1	1	1	1	1	1	1	1	1	1	2	2	3	4
NH	5	6	5	4	3	3	3	2	2	2	2	2	2	2	2	2	2	2	2	2	2
NJ	6	6	6	5	5	5	7	7	8	10	12	12	14	14	14	15	15	14	13	13	12
NM	X	X	X	X	X	X	X	X	X	X	1[2]	1	1	2	2	2	2	3	3	3	3
NY	17	34	40	34	33	31	33	34	34	37	43	43	45	45	43	41	39	34	31	29	27
NC	12	13	13	9	8	7	8	9	9	10	10	10	11	12	12	11	11	11	12	13	13
ND	X	X	X	X	X	X	X	X	1	2	3	3	2	2	2	2	1	1	1	1	1
OH	1[1]	14	19	21	21	19	20	21	21	21	22	22	24	23	23	24	23	21	19	18	16
OK	X	X	X	X	X	X	X	X	X	5[2]	8	8	9	8	6	6	6	6	6	5	5
OR	X	X	X	X	X	1	1	1	2	2	3	3	3	4	4	4	4	5	5	5	5
PA	18	26	28	24	25	24	27	28	30	32	36	36	34	33	30	27	25	23	21	19	18
RI	2	2	2	2	2	2	2	2	2	2	3	3	2	2	2	2	2	2	2	2	2
SC	8	9	9	7	6	4	5	7	7	7	7	7	6	6	6	6	6	6	6	6	7
SD	X	X	X	X	X	X	X	X	2	2	3	3	2	2	2	2	2	1	1	1	1
TN	3	9	13	11	10	8	10	10	10	10	10	10	9	10	9	9	8	9	9	9	9
TX	X	X	X	X	2	4	6	11	13	16	18	18	21	21	22	23	24	27	30	32	36
UT	X	X	X	X	X	X	X	X	X	1	2	2	2	2	2	2	2	3	3	3	4
VT	4	5	5	4	3	3	3	2	2	2	2	2	1	1	1	1	1	1	1	1	1
VA	22	22	21	15	13	11	9	10	10	10	10	10	9	9	10	10	10	10	11	11	11
WA	X	X	X	X	X	X	X	X	2	3	5	5	6	6	7	7	7	8	9	9	10
WV	X	X	X	X	X	X	3	4	4	5	6	6	6	6	6	5	4	4	3	3	3
WI	X	X	X	X	3	6	8	9	10	11	11	11	10	10	10	10	9	9	9	8	8
WY	X	X	X	X	X	X	X	X	1	1	1	1	1	1	1	1	1	1	1	1	1

X Not applicable. [1] Assigned after apportionment. [2] Included in apportionment in anticipation of statehood.

Source: U.S. Census Bureau, Congressional Apportionment, Census 2010, <https://www.census.gov/topics/public-sector/congressional-apportionment.html>.

Table 462. Composition of Congress by Political Party Affiliation—States: 2013 to 2019

[Figures are for the beginning of the first session, except as noted. Dem. = Democratic; Rep. = Republican]

State	Representatives								Senators							
	113th Cong.,[1] 2013		114th Cong.,[2] 2015		115th Cong., 2017		116th Cong.,[3] 2019		113th Cong.,[4] 2013		114th Cong.,[4] 2015		115th Cong.,[4] 2017		116th Cong.,[4] 2019	
	Dem.	Rep.	Dem.	Rep.	Dem.	Rep.	Dem.	Rep.	Dem.	Rep.	Dem.	Rep.	Dem.	Rep.	Dem.	Rep.
U.S.......	201	232	188	245	194	241	235	197	53	45	44	54	46	52	45	53
AL.........	1	6	1	6	1	6	1	6	–	2	–	2	–	2	1	1
AK.........	–	1	–	1	–	1	–	1	1	1	–	2	–	2	–	2
AZ.........	5	4	4	5	4	5	5	4	–	2	–	2	–	2	1	1
AR.........	–	4	–	4	–	4	–	4	1	1	–	2	–	2	–	2
CA.........	38	15	39	14	39	14	46	7	2	–	2	–	2	–	2	–
CO.........	3	4	3	4	3	4	4	3	2	–	1	1	1	1	1	1
CT.........	5	–	5	–	5	–	5	–	2	–	2	–	2	–	2	–
DE.........	1	–	1	–	1	–	1	–	2	–	2	–	2	–	2	–
FL.........	10	17	10	17	11	16	13	14	1	1	1	1	1	1	–	2
GA.........	5	9	4	10	4	10	5	9	–	2	–	2	–	2	–	2
HI.........	2	–	2	–	2	–	2	–	2	–	2	–	2	–	2	–
ID.........	–	2	–	2	–	2	–	2	–	2	–	2	–	2	–	2
IL.........	12	6	10	8	11	7	13	5	1	1	1	1	2	–	2	–
IN.........	2	7	2	7	2	7	2	7	1	1	1	1	1	1	–	2
IA.........	2	2	1	3	1	3	3	1	1	1	–	2	–	2	–	2
KS.........	–	4	–	4	–	4	1	3	–	2	–	2	–	2	–	2
KY.........	1	5	1	5	1	5	1	5	–	2	–	2	–	2	–	2
LA.........	1	5	1	5	1	5	1	5	1	1	–	2	–	2	–	2
ME.........	2	–	1	1	1	1	2	–	–	1	–	1	–	1	–	1
MD.........	7	1	7	1	7	1	7	1	2	–	2	–	2	–	2	–
MA.........	9	–	9	–	9	–	9	–	2	–	2	–	2	–	2	–
MI.........	5	9	5	9	5	9	7	7	2	–	2	–	2	–	2	–
MN.........	5	3	5	3	5	3	5	3	2	–	2	–	2	–	2	–
MS.........	1	3	1	2	1	3	1	3	–	2	–	2	–	2	–	2
MO.........	2	5	2	6	2	6	2	6	1	1	1	1	1	1	–	2
MT.........	–	1	–	1	–	1	–	1	2	–	1	1	1	1	1	1
NE.........	–	3	1	2	–	3	–	3	–	2	–	2	–	2	–	2
NV.........	2	2	1	3	3	1	3	1	1	1	1	1	1	1	2	–
NH.........	2	–	1	1	2	–	2	–	1	1	1	1	2	–	2	–
NJ.........	6	6	6	6	7	5	11	1	2	–	2	–	2	–	2	–
NM.........	2	1	2	1	2	1	3	–	2	–	2	–	2	–	2	–
NY.........	21	6	18	8	18	9	21	6	2	–	2	–	2	–	2	–
NC.........	4	9	3	10	3	10	3	8	1	1	–	2	–	2	–	2
ND.........	–	1	–	1	–	1	–	1	1	1	1	1	1	1	–	2
OH.........	4	12	4	12	4	12	4	12	1	1	1	1	1	1	1	1
OK.........	–	5	–	5	–	5	1	4	–	2	–	2	–	2	–	2
OR.........	4	1	4	1	4	1	4	1	2	–	2	–	2	–	2	–
PA.........	5	13	5	13	5	13	9	8	1	1	1	1	1	1	1	1
RI.........	2	–	2	–	2	–	2	–	2	–	2	–	2	–	2	–
SC.........	1	5	1	6	1	6	2	5	–	2	–	2	–	2	–	2
SD.........	–	1	–	1	–	1	–	1	1	1	–	2	–	2	–	2
TN.........	2	7	2	7	2	7	2	7	–	2	–	2	–	2	–	2
TX.........	12	24	11	25	11	25	13	23	–	2	–	2	–	2	–	2
UT.........	1	3	–	4	–	4	1	3	–	2	–	2	–	2	–	2
VT.........	1	–	1	–	1	–	1	–	1	–	1	–	1	–	1	–
VA.........	3	8	3	8	4	7	7	4	2	–	2	–	2	–	2	–
WA.........	6	4	6	4	6	4	7	3	2	–	2	–	2	–	2	–
WV.........	1	2	–	3	–	3	–	3	2	–	1	1	1	1	1	1
WI.........	3	5	3	5	3	5	3	5	1	1	1	1	1	1	1	1
WY.........	–	1	–	1	–	1	–	1	–	2	–	2	–	2	–	2

– Represents zero. [1] Two vacancies—one in Missouri due to the resignation of Jo Ann Emerson, January 22, 2013, and one in South Carolina due to the resignation of Tim Scott, January 2, 2013. [2] Two vacancies—one in Mississippi due to the death of Alan Nunnelee, February 6, 2015, and one in New York due to the resignation of Michael G. Grimm, January 5, 2015. [3] Three vacancies—one in Pennsylvania due the resignation of Tom Marino on January 23, 2019; and two in North Carolina, one due to the death of Walter Jones on February 10, 2019, and one due to North Carolina's State Board of Elections and Ethics Reform's refusal to certify the results of the NC-09 election due to irregularities involving absentee ballots. [4] Vermont and Maine had one Independent senator each.

Source: U.S. House of Representatives, Office of the Clerk, *Official List of Members*, February 2019, and earlier editions. See also <http://clerk.house.gov/member_info/>.

Table 463. Members of Congress—Seniority of Senators and Representatives: 1963 to 2019

[Represents the makeup of Congress on the 1st day of the session]

Congress	Senators — Number by length of service — 6 years or less [1]	7-12 years	13-18 years	19 or more years	Mean years of service	Representatives — Number by terms served — 1-3 terms	4-6 terms	7-9 terms	10+ terms	Mean terms of service
88th (1963)	42 (12)	26	18	14	9.9	182	106	78	68	5.5
89th (1965)	29 (8)	36	16	19	11.1	198	97	73	67	5.1
90th (1967)	28 (7)	34	19	19	11.6	183	108	69	73	5.3
91st (1969)	32 (14)	32	17	19	11.2	171	126	65	73	5.6
92nd (1971)	25 (10)	24	29	22	11.5	162	122	68	83	5.8
93rd (1973)	40 (13)	20	20	20	11.2	162	128	66	76	5.5
94th (1975)	[2] 36 (12)	22	23	19	11.5	196	100	78	61	5.2
95th (1977)	42 (17)	25	13	20	10.6	219	87	70	59	4.9
96th (1979)	48 (20)	24	10	18	9.6	219	95	65	54	4.8
97th (1981)	55 (18)	20	10	15	8.5	209	121	56	49	4.7
98th (1983)	43 (5)	28	16	13	9.6	210	125	45	54	4.7
99th (1985)	32 (7)	38	18	12	10.1	184	138	58	54	5.1
100th (1987)	26 (13)	44	16	14	9.6	163	143	64	65	5.5
101st (1989)	31 (10)	26	29	14	9.8	120	167	86	60	5.8
102nd (1991)	30 (5)	23	28	19	11.1	133	137	91	74	6.1
103rd (1993)	30 (13)	17	32	21	11.3	192	109	69	65	5.2
104th (1995)	29 (11)	26	20	25	12.3	220	78	78	59	4.9
105th (1997)	40 (15)	24	13	23	11.2	243	71	65	56	4.8
106th (1999)	35 (8)	24	16	25	11.2	185	127	58	65	4.8
107th (2001)	37 (11)	21	19	23	11.5	149	155	54	76	5.6
108th (2003)	30 (10)	29	16	25	12.7	149	158	60	68	5.5
109th (2005)	29 (9)	27	15	29	12.5	137	128	97	72	5.9
110th (2007)	29 (10)	26	14	31	13.1	149	116	99	71	6.0
111th (2009)	[3] 32 (11)	19	20	29	14.0	147	102	106	79	6.2
112th (2011)	42 (13)	17	14	27	12.3	170	97	69	97	6.0
113th (2013)	43 (13)	23	15	19	10.2	196	91	72	74	5.7
114th (2015)	45 (13)	24	11	20	9.4	205	91	51	88	5.5
115th (2017)	36 (7)	34	11	19	10.2	177	118	55	85	5.8
116th (2019)	32 (9)	33	17	18	10.1	184	121	56	73	5.4

[1] Numbers in parentheses are number of freshman senators. Senators who are currently in their first full term are listed under "6 years or less." [2] Total includes John Durkin (D-NH). After a contested election in 1974, the Senate declared the seat vacant as of August 8, 1975. Durkin was then elected by special election, September 16, 1975, to fill the vacancy. [3] Total includes Al Franken (D-MN), who was declared elected after a challenge in court to the vote count by his Republican challenger on June 30, 2009; and Roland Burris (D-IL) who was appointed to fill the seat vacated by Barack Obama on December 31, 2008. Total also includes Joe Biden (D-DE), who resigned his seat on January 15, 2009, but was present on the first day of the session.

Source: The Brookings Institution, "Vital Statistics on Congress" ©, March 2019, <https://www.brookings.edu/multi-chapter-report/vital-statistics-on-congress/>.

Table 464. Women, Black, Asian, and Hispanic Members of Congress by Party Affiliation: 1999 to 2019

[As of beginning of first session of each Congress. Data do not include delegates or commissioners]

Characteristic	106th (1999)	107th (2001)	108th (2003)	109th (2005)	110th (2007)	111th (2009) [1]	112th (2011)	113th (2013) [2]	114th (2015)	115th (2017)	116th (2019)
Women, total	65	72	73	79	87	91	93	96	104	104	127
Representatives	56	59	59	65	71	74	76	76	84	83	102
Democrat	40	41	38	42	50	57	52	56	62	62	89
Republican	16	18	21	23	21	17	24	20	22	21	13
Senators	9	13	14	14	16	17	17	20	20	21	25
Democrat	6	10	9	9	11	13	12	16	14	16	17
Republican	3	3	5	5	5	4	5	4	6	5	8
Black, total	37	36	37	41	41	39	42	42	46	50	56
Representatives	37	36	37	40	40	39	42	41	44	47	53
Democrat	36	35	37	40	40	39	40	41	42	45	52
Republican	1	1	0	0	0	0	2	0	2	2	1
Senators	0	0	0	1	1	0	0	1	2	3	3
Democrat	0	0	0	1	1	0	0	0	1	2	2
Republican	0	0	0	0	0	0	0	1	1	1	1
Asian, total	6	7	6	7	8	7	10	11	12	15	15
Representatives	4	5	4	5	6	5	8	10	11	12	12
Democrat	4	5	4	4	5	4	7	10	11	12	12
Republican	0	0	0	1	1	1	1	0	0	0	0
Senators	2	2	2	2	2	2	2	1	1	3	3
Democrat	2	2	2	2	2	2	2	1	1	3	3
Republican	0	0	0	0	0	0	0	0	0	0	0
Hispanic, total	19	19	22	25	26	26	29	31	35	42	43
Representatives	19	19	22	23	23	24	27	28	32	38	39
Democrat	16	16	18	19	20	21	19	23	23	28	32
Republican	3	3	4	4	3	3	8	5	9	10	7
Senators	0	0	0	2	3	2	2	3	3	4	4
Democrat	0	0	0	1	2	1	1	1	1	2	2
Republican	0	0	0	1	1	1	1	2	2	2	2

[1] Roland Burris was not seated on the first day of the 111th session. [2] Tim Scott, who was appointed on December 17th to replace outgoing Senator Jim DeMint, is included in the Senate totals.

Source: The Brookings Institution, "Vital Statistics on Congress" ©, March 2019, <https://www.brookings.edu/multi-chapter-report/vital-statistics-on-congress/>.

Table 465. Composition of Congress by Political Party: 1977 to 2019

[D = Democratic, R = Republican. As of beginning of first session of each Congress unless otherwise noted. Data reflect immediate result of elections. Vacancies and third party candidates are noted]

Year	Party and president	Congress	House Majority party	House Minority party	House Other	Senate Majority party	Senate Minority party	Senate Other
1977[1]	D (Carter)	95th	D-292	R-143	–	D-61	R-38	1
1979[1]	D (Carter)	96th	D-277	R-158	–	D-58	R-41	1
1981[2]	R (Reagan)	97th	D-242	R-192	1	R-53	D-46	1
1983	R (Reagan)	98th	D-269	R-166	–	R-54	D-46	–
1985	R (Reagan)	99th	D-253	R-182	–	R-53	D-47	–
1987	R (Reagan)	100th	D-258	R-177	–	D-55	R-45	–
1989	R (Bush)	101st	D-260	R-175	–	D-55	R-45	–
1991[3]	R (Bush)	102nd	D-267	R-167	1	D-56	R-44	–
1993[3]	D (Clinton)	103rd	D-258	R-176	1	D-57	R-43	–
1995[3]	D (Clinton)	104th	R-230	D-204	1	R-52	D-48	–
1997[4]	D (Clinton)	105th	R-226	D-207	2	R-55	D-45	–
1999[3]	D (Clinton)	106th	R-223	D-211	1	R-55	D-45	–
2001[4]	R (Bush)	107th	R-221	D-212	2	D-50	R-50	–
2003[2,5]	R (Bush)	108th	R-229	D-204	1	R-51	D-48	1
2005[2]	R (Bush)	109th	R-232	D-202	1	R-55	D-44	1
2007[6]	R (Bush)	110th	D-233	R-202	–	D-49	R-49	2
2009[5,6,7]	D (Obama)	111th	D-256	R-178	–	D-55	R-41	2
2011[6]	D (Obama)	112th	R-242	D-193	–	D-51	R-47	2
2013[5,6]	D (Obama)	113th	R-234	D-200	–	D-53	R-45	2
2015[6]	D (Obama)	114th	R-247	D-188	–	R-54	D-44	2
2017[6]	R (Trump)	115th	R-241	D-194	–	R-52	D-46	2
2019[6,8]	R (Trump)	116th	D-235	R-197	–	R-53	D-45	2

– Represents zero. [1] Senate had one Independent. [2] House and Senate each had one Independent. [3] House had one Independent-Socialist. [4] House had one Independent-Socialist and one Independent. [5] House had one vacancy. [6] Senate had two Independents. [7] Senate had two vacancies. [8] House had three vacancies.

Source: U.S. House of Representatives, Office of the Clerk, *Official List of Members*, February 2019, and earlier editions. See also <http://clerk.house.gov/member_info/>.

Table 466. U.S. Congress—Measures Introduced and Enacted and Time in Session: 2003 to 2020

[Excludes simple and concurrent resolutions]

Item	108th Cong., 2003–04	109th Cong., 2005–06	110th Cong., 2007–08	111th Cong., 2009–10	112th Cong., 2011–12	113th Cong., 2013–14	114th Cong., 2015–16	115th Cong., 2017–18	116th Cong., 2019–20 [3]
Measures introduced	8,625	10,703	11,228	10,778	10,612	9,097	10,223	13,558	14,369
Bills	8,468	10,560	11,081	10,629	10,439	8,919	10,074	11,201	12,309
Joint resolutions	157	143	147	149	173	178	149	215	166
Measures enacted	504	590	460	385	239	296	329	339	150
Public [1]	498	589	460	383	238	296	329	338	150
Private [2]	6	1	0	2	1	0	0	1	0
HOUSE OF REPRESENTATIVES									
Number of days	243	241	283	286	327	295	288	366	291
Number of hours	1,894	1,917	2,138	2,126	1,718	1,471	1,438	1,515	1,107
Number of hours per day	7.8	8.0	7.6	7.4	5.3	5.0	5.0	4.1	3.8
SENATE									
Number of days	300	297	374	349	323	292	333	386	298
Number of hours	2,486	2,250	2,364	2,495	2,032	2,003	1,855	2,181	1,535
Number of hours per day	8.3	7.6	6.3	7.1	6.3	6.9	5.6	5.7	5.2

[1] Laws on public matters that apply to all persons. [2] Laws designed to provide legal relief to specified persons or entities adversely affected by laws of general applicability. [3] Current session. Data for January 3, 2019 through July 31, 2020.

Source: U.S. Congress, *Résumé of Congressional Activity*, August 2020, and earlier reports. See also <https://www.senate.gov/legislative/ResumesofCongressionalActivity1947present.htm>.

Table 467. Congressional Bills Vetoed: 1961 to 2020

Period	President	Total vetoes	Regular vetoes	Pocket vetoes	Vetoes sustained	Bills passed over veto
1961 to 1963	John F. Kennedy	21	12	9	21	0
1963 to 1969	Lyndon B. Johnson	30	16	14	30	0
1969 to 1974	Richard M. Nixon	43	26	17	36	7
1974 to 1977	Gerald R. Ford	66	48	18	54	12
1977 to 1981	Jimmy Carter	31	13	18	29	2
1981 to 1989	Ronald W. Reagan	78	39	39	69	9
1989 to 1993	George Bush	44	29	15	43	1
1993 to 2001	William J. Clinton	37	36	1	35	2
2001 to 2009	George W. Bush	12	12	0	8	4
2009 to 2017	Barack Obama	12	12	0	11	1
2017 to 2020 [1]	Donald J. Trump	8	8	0	8	0

[1] For the period January 20, 2017 through July 27, 2020.

Source: Congressional Research Service, *Regular Vetoes and Pocket Vetoes: In Brief,* July 2019; and U.S. Senate, "Summary of Bills Vetoed," <https://www.senate.gov/reference/reference_index_subjects/Vetoes_vrd.htm>, and "Vetoes by President Donald J. Trump," <https://www.senate.gov/legislative/vetoes/TrumpDJ.htm>, accessed July 2020.

Table 468. Number of Governors by Political Party Affiliation: 1975 to 2020

[Reflects figures after inaugurations for each year. State governors only]

Year	Democratic	Republican	Independent/other	Year	Democratic	Republican	Independent/other	Year	Democratic	Republican	Independent/other
1975........	36	13	1	2005........	22	28	–	2015........	18	31	1
1980........	31	19	–	2010........	26	24	–	2016........	18	31	1
1985........	34	16	–	2011........	20	29	1	2017........	16	33	1
1990........	29	21	–	2012........	20	29	1	2018........	16	33	1
1995........	19	30	1	2013........	20	30	–	2019........	23	27	–
2000........	18	30	2	2014........	21	29	–	2020........	24	26	–

– Represents zero.

Source: ProQuest research.

Table 469. Vote Cast for and Governor Elected by State: 2015 to 2018

[D = Democratic, R = Republican, I = Independent]

State	Current governor [1]	Year of election	Total vote [2]	Republican	Democratic	Percent leading party
Alabama............	Kay Ivey	2018	1,713,843	1,019,558	691,671	R-59.5
Alaska..............	Mike Dunleavy	2018	283,134	145,631	125,739	R-51.4
Arizona.............	Doug Ducey	2018	2,376,441	1,330,863	994,341	R-56.0
Arkansas...........	Asa Hutchinson	2018	891,509	582,406	283,218	R-65.3
California...........	Gavin Christopher Newsom	2018	12,464,235	4,742,825	7,721,410	D-61.9
Colorado...........	Jared Schutz Polis	2018	2,525,062	1,080,801	1,348,888	D-53.4
Connecticut........	Ned Lamont	2018	1,406,803	650,138	694,510	D-50.7
Delaware...........	John Carney Jr.	2016	425,784	166,852	248,404	D-58.3
Florida.............	Ronald Dion DeSantis	2018	8,220,561	4,076,186	4,043,723	R-49.6
Georgia.............	Brian P. Kemp	2018	3,939,328	1,978,408	1,923,685	R-50.2
Hawaii..............	David Ige	2018	390,843	131,719	244,934	D-62.7
Idaho...............	Brad Little	2018	605,131	361,661	231,081	R-59.8
Illinois..............	J.B. Pritzker	2018	4,547,657	1,765,751	2,479,746	D-54.5
Indiana.............	Eric Holcomb	2016	2,719,968	1,397,396	1,235,503	R-51.4
Iowa................	Kim Reynolds	2018	1,327,638	667,275	630,986	R-50.3
Kansas.............	Laura Kelly	2018	1,055,566	453,645	506,727	D-48.0
Kentucky...........	Matt Bevin	2015	973,692	511,374	426,620	R-52.5
Louisiana..........	John Bel Edwards	2015	1,152,864	505,940	646,924	D-56.1
Maine..............	Janet Trafton Mills	2018	630,667	272,311	320,962	D-50.9
Maryland...........	Larry Hogan	2018	1,482,029	855,539	608,810	R-57.7
Massachusetts.....	Charlie Baker	2018	2,674,615	1,781,341	885,770	R-66.6
Michigan...........	Gretchen Esther Whitmer	2018	4,250,585	1,859,534	2,266,193	D-53.3
Minnesota..........	Timothy James Walz	2018	2,587,287	1,097,705	1,393,096	D-53.8
Mississippi.........	Phil Bryant	2015	718,185	476,697	231,643	R-66.4
Missouri............	Mark Parson [3]	2016	2,777,854	1,424,730	1,261,110	R-51.3
Montana............	Steve Bullock	2016	509,360	236,115	255,933	D-50.2
Nebraska...........	Pete Ricketts	2018	697,981	411,812	286,169	R-59.0
Nevada.............	Steve Sisolak	2018	971,799	440,320	480,007	D-49.4
New Hampshire....	Chris Sununu	2018	573,602	302,764	262,359	R-52.8
New Jersey.........	Phil Murphy	2017	2,147,415	899,583	1,203,110	D-56.0
New Mexico........	Michelle Lujan Grisham	2018	696,459	298,091	398,368	D-57.2
New York...........	Andrew Cuomo	2018	6,097,362	2,207,602	3,635,340	D-59.6
North Carolina......	Roy Cooper	2016	4,711,014	2,298,880	2,309,157	D-49.0
North Dakota.......	Doug Burgum	2016	339,601	259,863	65,855	R-76.5
Ohio................	Mike DeWine	2018	4,429,582	2,231,917	2,067,847	R-50.4
Oklahoma..........	Kevin Stitt	2018	1,186,385	644,579	500,973	R-54.3
Oregon.............	Kate Brown	2016	1,561,819	684,321	796,006	D-51.0
Pennsylvania.......	Tom Wolf	2018	5,012,555	2,039,882	2,895,652	D-57.8
Rhode Island.......	Gina Raimondo	2018	376,401	139,932	198,122	D-52.6
South Carolina.....	Henry McMaster	2018	1,707,569	921,342	784,182	R-54.0
South Dakota.......	Kristi Noem	2018	338,715	172,706	161,171	R-51.0
Tennessee.........	Bill Lee	2018	2,243,294	1,336,106	864,863	R-59.6
Texas..............	Greg Abbot	2018	8,343,443	4,656,196	3,546,615	R-55.8
Utah...............	Gary Hebert	2016	1,124,913	750,828	322,462	R-66.7
Vermont............	Phil Scott	2018	274,087	151,261	110,335	R-55.2
Virginia.............	Ralph Northam	2017	2,614,282	1,175,731	1,409,175	D-53.9
Washington.........	Jay Inslee	2016	3,236,866	1,476,346	1,760,520	D-54.4
West Virginia.......	Jim Justice [4]	2016	713,858	301,987	350,408	D-49.1
Wisconsin..........	Anthony Steven Evers	2018	2,672,342	1,295,080	1,324,307	D-49.6
Wyoming...........	Matt Mead	2018	203,238	136,412	55,965	R-67.1

[1] As of June 2019. [2] Includes minor party and scattered votes. [3] Lt. Gov. Mark Parson was sworn in as governor in June 2018 after Eric Greitens resigned. [4] In August 2017, Gov. Jim Justice switched from the Democratic party to the Republican party.

Source: The Council of State Governments, Lexington, KY, *The Book of the States 2019*, and earlier reports ©. See also <http://www.csg.org/>.

Table 470. Political Party Control of State Legislatures by Party: 1990 to 2020

[As of beginning of year. Nebraska has a nonpartisan legislature]

Year	Demo-cratic control	Split control or tie	Repub-lican control	Year	Demo-cratic control	Split control or tie	Repub-lican control	Year	Demo-cratic control	Split control or tie	Repub-lican control
1990	29	11	9	2007	22	12	15	2014	19	3	27
1995	18	12	19	2008	23	14	12	2015	11	8	30
2000	16	15	18	2009	27	8	14	2016	11	8	30
2003	16	12	21	2010	27	8	14	2017	14	3	32
2004	17	11	21	2011	15	8	26	2018	13	4	32
2005	19	10	20	2012	15	8	26	2019	18	1	30
2006	19	10	20	2013	19	4	26	2020	19	1	29

Source: National Conference of State Legislatures, Denver, CO, *Post Election 2019 State & Legislative Partisan Composition*, January 2020 ©. See also <ncsl.org>.

Table 471. Composition of State Legislatures by Political Party Affiliation: 2018 and 2019

[Data as of January. Figures reflect immediate results of elections, including holdover members in state houses which do not have all of their members running for reelection. Dem. = Democrat, Rep. = Republican, Vac. = Vacancies. In general, Lower House refers to body consisting of state representatives and Upper House of state senators]

State	Lower House 2018 Dem.	Rep.	Other	Vac.	Lower House 2019 Dem.	Rep.	Other	Vac.	Upper House 2018 Dem.	Rep.	Other	Vac.	Upper House 2019 Dem.	Rep.	Other	Vac.
U.S.	2,339	3,002	32	37	2,580	2,779	25	27	791	1,112	6	15	857	1,049	4	13
AL[1]	32	70	–	3	28	77	–	–	7	26	1	1	8	27	–	–
AK[2]	17	21	2	–	16	22	1	1	6	14	–	–	7	13	–	–
AZ[3]	25	35	–	–	29	31	–	–	13	17	–	–	13	17	–	–
AR[2]	24	75	–	1	24	76	–	–	9	23	–	3	9	26	–	–
CA[2]	52	25	–	3	60	20	–	–	27	13	–	–	28	10	–	2
CO[2]	36	29	–	–	41	24	–	–	16	18	1	–	19	16	–	–
CT[3]	80	71	–	–	90	59	–	2	18	18	–	–	20	13	–	3
DE[2]	25	16	–	–	26	15	–	–	11	10	–	–	12	9	–	–
FL[2]	40	75	–	5	46	72	–	2	16	23	–	1	17	23	–	–
GA[3]	64	116	–	–	75	103	–	2	19	37	–	–	21	35	–	–
HI[2]	46	5	–	–	46	5	–	–	25	–	–	–	24	1	–	–
ID[3]	11	59	–	–	14	56	–	–	6	29	–	–	7	28	–	–
IL[4]	67	51	–	–	72	44	–	2	37	22	–	–	40	19	–	–
IN[2]	30	70	–	–	33	67	–	–	9	41	–	–	10	40	–	–
IA[2]	41	59	–	–	46	54	–	–	20	29	1	–	18	32	–	–
KS[2]	40	85	–	–	40	85	–	–	9	31	–	–	11	28	1	–
KY[2]	37	63	–	–	39	61	–	–	11	27	–	–	9	28	–	1
LA[1]	41	61	3	–	36	59	3	7	14	25	–	–	14	25	–	–
ME[3]	74	70	7	–	88	57	6	–	17	18	–	–	21	14	–	–
MD[1]	91	50	–	–	99	42	–	–	32	14	–	1	32	15	–	–
MA[3]	121	34	2	3	127	32	1	–	32	7	–	1	34	6	–	–
MI[2]	46	63	–	1	52	58	–	–	11	27	–	–	16	22	–	–
MN[2]	57	77	–	–	75	59	–	–	33	34	–	–	32	34	–	1
MS[1]	48	73	–	1	47	74	–	–	19	33	–	–	19	33	–	–
MO[2]	47	115	–	1	47	115	–	1	9	24	–	1	10	24	–	–
MT[2]	41	59	–	–	42	58	–	–	18	32	–	–	20	30	–	–
NE[5]	(5)	(5)	(5)	(5)	(5)	(5)	(5)	(5)	(5)	(5)	(5)	(5)	(5)	(5)	(5)	(5)
NV[2]	27	14	–	1	29	13	–	–	10	8	1	2	13	8	–	–
NH[3]	175	218	3	4	233	167	–	–	10	14	–	–	14	10	–	–
NJ[2]	54	26	–	–	53	26	–	1	25	15	–	–	25	15	–	–
NM[2]	38	32	–	–	46	24	–	–	26	16	–	–	26	16	–	–
NY[3]	103	37	1	9	106	43	1	–	30	31	–	2	40	23	–	–
NC[3]	45	75	–	–	55	65	–	–	15	35	–	–	21	28	–	1
ND[1]	13	81	–	–	15	79	–	–	9	38	–	–	10	37	–	–
OH[2]	33	66	–	–	38	60	–	1	9	24	–	–	9	23	–	1
OK[2]	28	72	–	1	24	77	–	–	8	40	–	1	9	39	–	–
OR[2]	35	25	–	–	38	22	–	–	17	13	–	–	18	12	–	–
PA[2]	81	120	–	1	91	110	–	2	16	34	–	–	21	28	–	1
RI[3]	64	11	–	–	66	8	1	–	33	4	–	1	33	5	–	–
SC[2]	44	79	–	1	44	79	–	1	18	28	–	–	19	26	–	1
SD[3]	10	60	–	–	11	59	–	–	6	29	–	–	5	30	–	–
TN[2]	25	74	–	–	26	73	–	–	5	28	–	–	5	26	1	1
TX[2]	56	93	–	1	67	83	–	–	11	20	–	–	12	19	–	–
UT[2]	13	62	–	–	16	59	–	–	5	24	–	–	6	23	–	–
VT[3]	83	53	14	–	94	42	12	2	21	7	2	–	22	6	2	–
VA[2]	49	51	–	–	48	51	–	1	19	21	–	–	19	21	–	–
WA[2]	50	48	–	–	57	41	–	–	26	23	–	–	28	20	–	1
WV[2]	36	64	–	–	41	59	–	–	12	22	–	–	14	20	–	–
WI[2]	35	63	–	1	35	63	–	1	13	19	–	1	14	19	–	–
WY[2]	9	51	–	–	9	51	–	–	3	27	–	–	3	27	–	–

– Represents zero. [1] Members of both houses serve 4-year terms. [2] Upper House members serve 4-year terms and Lower House members serve 2-year terms. [3] Members of both houses serve 2-year terms. [4] Illinois– 4- and 2-year term depending on district. [5] Nebraska– 4-year term and only state to have a nonpartisan unicameral legislature. For 2018 and 2019, Nebraska legislature has 49 members.

Source: The Council of State Governments, Lexington, KY, *The Book of the States 2019*, and earlier reports ©. See also <http://www.csg.org/>.

Table 472. Women Holding State Public Offices by Office and State: 2020

[As of July]

State	Total	Statewide elective executive office [1]	State legislature Total	State legislature Percent	State	Total	Statewide elective executive office [1]	State legislature Total	State legislature Percent
U.S.	**2,246**	**90**	**2,156**	**29**	MO.	49	1	48	24
					MT.	47	1	46	31
AL.	24	2	22	16	NE.	14	–	14	29
AK.	22	–	22	37	NV.	36	3	33	52
AZ.	40	5	35	39	NH.	145	–	145	34
AR.	36	2	34	25	NJ.	38	1	37	31
CA.	41	3	38	32	NM.	43	3	40	36
CO.	46	2	44	44	NY.	69	2	67	31
CT.	62	2	60	32	NC.	46	3	43	25
DE.	19	4	15	24	ND.	34	3	31	22
FL.	50	3	47	29	OH.	36	–	36	27
GA.	73	1	72	31	OK.	36	4	32	21
HI.	24	–	24	32	OR.	43	4	39	43
ID.	36	3	33	31	PA.	68	–	68	27
IL.	66	2	64	36	RI.	44	2	42	37
IN.	43	5	38	25	SC.	30	2	28	16
IA.	45	1	44	29	SD.	28	2	26	25
KS.	49	2	47	28	TN.	20	–	20	15
KY.	36	2	34	25	TX.	45	1	44	24
LA.	26	–	26	18	UT.	27	–	27	29
ME.	71	1	70	38	VT.	74	1	73	41
MD.	75	–	75	40	VA.	41	–	41	29
MA.	62	4	58	29	WA.	63	3	60	41
MI.	57	3	54	36	WV.	19	–	19	14
MN.	66	2	64	32	WI.	37	2	35	27
MS.	29	1	28	16	WY.	16	2	14	16

– Represents zero. [1] Excludes women elected to the judiciary, women appointed to state cabinet-level positions, women elected to executive posts by the legislature, and elected members of university Boards of Trustees or Boards of Education.

Source: Center for American Women and Politics, Eagleton Institute of Politics, Rutgers University, New Brunswick, NJ, "Women in Elective Office," <http://www.cawp.rutgers.edu/> ©, accessed July 2020.

Table 473. Hispanic Public Elected Officials by Office, 2010 to 2019, and by State, 2019

[As of January or November of year shown. For states not shown, no Hispanic public officials had been identified]

State	Total [1]	State executives and legislators [2]	County and municipal officials	Judicial and law enforcement	Education and school boards	State	Total [1]	State executives and legislators [2]	County and municipal officials	Judicial and law enforcement	Education and school boards
2010	5,763	275	2,270	874	2,072	MD	11	3	8	0	0
2013	6,042	320	2,285	878	2,287	MA	52	8	25	1	18
2014	6,115	334	2,313	878	2,322	MI	21	5	6	4	6
2015	6,124	349	2,334	860	2,342	MN	22	6	6	8	2
2016	6,176	347	2,388	859	2,344	MO	2	1	1	0	0
2017	6,600	377	2,638	879	2,473	MT	0	0	0	0	0
2018	6,749	378	2,733	890	2,496	NE	4	1	0	0	3
						NV	29	10	7	6	6
2019	**6,832**	**389**	**2,775**	**882**	**2,535**	NH	4	2	1	1	0
AK	0	0	0	0	0	NJ	164	12	87	1	64
AZ	381	26	136	37	176	NM	685	51	335	112	144
AR	1	0	0	0	1	NY	169	28	62	49	30
CA	1,640	48	546	102	817	NC	4	0	2	1	1
CO	167	15	91	17	38	OH	25	3	15	3	4
CT	76	13	45	0	18	OK	3	3	0	0	0
DE	3	3	0	0	0	OR	40	3	5	9	20
FL	208	28	107	59	12	PA	26	2	13	4	7
GA	12	2	6	2	2	RI	25	9	13	0	3
HI	4	4	0	0	0	TN	6	1	3	1	1
ID	5	0	5	0	0	TX	2,739	53	1,087	447	1,096
IL	125	16	74	8	19	UT	7	4	3	0	0
IN	26	2	14	2	8	VT	3	1	1	0	1
IA	22	0	12	0	10	VA	13	5	5	0	3
KS	9	5	4	0	0	WA	62	8	39	0	15
KY	1	1	0	0	0	WI	14	3	3	5	3
LA	5	0	2	2	1	WV	4	3	0	1	0
ME	5	0	2	0	3	WY	8	1	4	0	3

[1] Includes special district officials, not shown separately. [2] Includes U.S. Senators and Representatives, not shown separately.

Source: National Association of Latino Elected and Appointed Officials (NALEO) Educational Fund, Washington, DC, *National Directory of Latino Elected Officials* ©, and earlier reports. See also <http://www.naleo.org/>.

Table 474. Political Action Committees—Financial Activity Summary by Committee Type: 2013 to 2018

[In millions of dollars (2,368.6 represents $2,368,600,000). Covers financial activity during 2-year calendar period indicated]

Committee type	Receipts			Disbursements [1]			Contributions to candidates		
	2013 to 2014	2015 to 2016	2017 to 2018	2013 to 2014	2015 to 2016	2017 to 2018	2013 to 2014	2015 to 2016	2017 to 2018
Total	2,368.6	4,046.3	4,674.2	2,304.8	3,973.3	4,554.1	435.9	444.0	465.6
Corporate	384.8	405.5	417.2	370.7	385.7	404.8	178.1	182.8	178.1
Labor	305.7	342.4	365.8	289.2	331.5	342.2	50.6	46.7	53.8
Trade	146.3	159.9	174.3	140.4	148.2	164.1	79.2	82.8	87.3
Membership	156.4	159.8	100.4	150.1	152.0	97.6	40.1	40.3	33.0
Cooperative	7.7	8.0	9.1	7.0	7.0	8.4	4.9	4.7	5.1
Corporation without stock	19.7	15.7	14.3	19.4	14.5	14.4	7.0	7.5	7.4
Nonconnected	1,347.9	2,954.9	3,593.0	1,327.9	2,934.3	3,522.5	76.0	79.2	100.8

[1] Comprises contributions to candidates, independent expenditures, and other disbursements.

Source: U.S. Federal Election Commission, Campaign Finance Statistics, "Public Action Committee (PAC) Data Summary Tables," <http://www.fec.gov/press/campaign_finance_statistics.shtml>, accessed March 2019.

Table 475. Congressional Campaign Finances—Receipts and Disbursements: 2009 to 2018

[In millions of dollars (1,103.2 represents $1,103,200,000). Covers all campaign finance activity during 2-year calendar period indicated for primary, general, run-off, and special elections. Data have been adjusted to eliminate transfers between all committees within a campaign. For further information on legal limits of contributions, see Federal Election Campaign Act of 1971, as amended]

Item	House of Representatives					Senate				
	2009 to 2010	2011 to 2012	2013 to 2014	2015 to 2016	2017 to 2018	2009 to 2010	2011 to 2012	2013 to 2014	2015 to 2016	2017 to 2018
Total receipts [1]	1,103.2	1,136.5	1,033.9	1,049.8	1,740.8	757.2	742.3	635.4	594.5	1,033.3
Individual contributions	640.6	637.0	557.0	546.4	1,063.0	468.0	466.1	439.4	424.2	691.4
Other committees	326.2	351.0	341.9	354.5	406.1	87.6	80.9	98.4	92.8	84.8
Candidate contributions & loans	109.6	108.2	96.4	107.0	165.5	149.6	167.3	51.2	31.6	188.4
Democrats	510.3	486.8	446.4	476.4	1,034.5	314.7	307.9	299.6	313.4	571.5
Incumbents	393.0	249.1	286.1	249.9	299.3	139.5	172.1	204.1	67.0	399.2
Challengers	64.4	174.8	82.9	126.7	446.7	38.8	71.4	41.3	176.2	119.5
Open seats [2]	52.9	62.9	77.3	99.7	288.6	136.5	64.4	54.1	70.1	52.8
Republicans	587.5	632.7	583.7	559.4	693.1	427.4	416.1	327.9	278.8	430.8
Incumbents	231.7	436.2	355.5	406.7	494.5	109.5	77.8	90.2	201.3	80.4
Challengers	266.0	125.7	119.7	51.5	61.6	148.9	143.1	144.1	29.1	295.0
Open seats [2]	89.8	70.7	108.5	101.2	137.0	169.1	195.3	93.5	48.5	55.5
Others	5.4	17.0	3.9	14.0	13.1	15.0	18.3	8.0	2.3	30.9
Incumbents	1.7	2.2	0.1	4.4	0.9	–	6.3	–	–	15.6
Challengers	3.2	13.5	1.3	5.0	8.0	0.5	8.7	6.4	2.1	15.2
Open seats [2]	0.5	1.3	2.5	4.6	4.2	14.5	3.3	1.5	0.2	0.2
Total disbursements	1,096.3	1,099.3	960.8	971.7	1,698.9	737.3	747.9	654.2	625.3	1,019.5
Democrats	534.7	479.1	422.5	425.1	983.5	319.3	315.7	311.5	316.0	557.8
Republicans	556.6	604.3	534.5	533.5	703.0	403.2	417.7	334.8	306.8	436.4
Others	5.1	15.9	3.9	13.1	12.4	14.9	14.5	8.0	2.5	25.3

– Represents or rounds to zero. [1] Includes other types of receipts, not shown separately. [2] Elections in which an incumbent did not seek reelection.

Source: U.S. Federal Election Commission, Campaign Finance Statistics, "Congressional Candidate Data Summary Tables," <http://www.fec.gov/press/campaign_finance_statistics.shtml>, accessed March 2019.

Table 476. Contributions to Congressional Campaigns by Political Action Committees (PAC) by Type of Committee: 2015 to 2018

[In millions of dollars (351.5 represents $351,500,000). Covers amounts given to candidates in primary, general, run-off, and special elections during the 2-year calendar period indicated]

Type of committee	Total [1]	Democrats	Republicans	Incumbents	Challengers	Open seats [2]
HOUSE OF REPRESENTATIVES						
2015–2016	351.5	145.1	203.6	313.8	17.7	20.0
2017–2018, total [3]	**383.9**	**167.7**	**215.1**	**328.9**	**24.5**	**30.5**
Corporate	148.2	52.3	95.6	142.4	0.8	5.0
Trade association [4]	101.4	37.5	63.7	92.6	2.4	6.4
Labor	47.2	39.8	7.3	33.3	7.5	6.4
Nonconnected [5]	76.0	33.6	41.9	50.1	13.7	12.2
Cooperative	4.5	1.9	2.6	4.2	0.1	0.3
Corporation without stock	6.5	2.6	4.0	6.3	0.1	0.2
SENATE						
2015–2016	89.8	29.4	60.4	68.4	9.4	12.0
2017–2018, total [3]	**81.5**	**47.8**	**32.4**	**60.5**	**12.1**	**8.9**
Corporate	29.8	16.6	12.8	23.8	3.2	2.8
Trade association [4]	18.8	10.1	8.4	13.9	2.9	2.0
Labor	6.6	5.9	0.5	5.3	0.6	0.7
Nonconnected [5]	24.8	14.3	10.2	16.2	5.2	3.3
Cooperative	0.6	0.4	0.2	0.5	0.1	(Z)
Corporation without stock	0.9	0.6	0.3	0.7	0.1	0.1

Z represents less than $50,000. [1] Includes other parties, not shown separately. [2] Elections in which an incumbent did not seek reelection. [3] Includes other types of political action committees, not shown separately. [4] Includes membership organizations and health organizations. [5] Represents "ideological" groups as well as other issue groups not necessarily ideological in nature.

Source: U.S. Federal Election Commission, Campaign Finance Statistics, "Political Action Committees (PAC) Data Summary Tables," <http://www.fec.gov/press/campaign_finance_statistics.shtml>, accessed March 2019.

Section 8
State and Local Government Finances and Employment

This section presents data on revenues, expenditures, debt, and employment of state and local governments. Nationwide statistics relating to state and local governments, their numbers, finances, and employment are compiled primarily by the U.S. Census Bureau through a program of censuses and surveys. Every fifth year (for years ending in "2" and "7"), the Census Bureau conducts a census of governments involving collection of data for all governmental units in the United States. In addition, the Census Bureau conducts annual surveys which cover all the state governments and a sample of local governments.

Annually, the Census Bureau releases information on financial data for the federal government, nationwide totals for state and local governments, and state-local data by states. Also released annually is a series on state, city, county, and school finances and on state and local public employment. There is also a series of quarterly data releases covering tax revenue and finances of major public employee retirement systems.

Basic information for Census Bureau statistics on governments is obtained by mail canvass from state and local officials; however, financial data for each state government and for many of the large local governments are compiled from their official records and reports by Census Bureau personnel. In over two-thirds of the states, all or part of local government financial data are obtained through central collection arrangements with state governments. Financial data on the federal government's aid to state and local areas are primarily based on the *Budget of the United States Government* published by the Office of Management and Budget.

Governmental units—The governmental structure of the United States includes, in addition to the federal government and the states, thousands of local governments—counties, municipalities, townships, school districts, and many "special districts." In 2017, 90,075 local governments were identified by the census of governments (see table 477 and table 478). As defined by the census, governmental units include all agencies or bodies having an organized existence, governmental character, and substantial autonomy. While most of these governments can impose taxes, many of the special districts—such as independent public housing authorities and numerous local irrigation, power, and other types of districts—are financed from rentals, charges for services, benefit assessments, grants from other governments, and other non-tax sources. The count of governments excludes semi-autonomous agencies through which states, cities, and counties sometimes provide for certain functions—for example, "dependent" school systems, state institutions of higher education, and certain other "authorities" and special agencies which are under the administrative or fiscal control of an established governmental unit.

Finances—The financial statistics relate to government fiscal years ending June 30 or at some date within the 12 previous months. The following governments are exceptions and are included as though they were part of the June 30 group: the state governments of Alabama and Michigan, and the city government of The District of Columbia, with fiscal years ending September 30; the state government of Texas ending August 31; and New York State ending its fiscal year on March 31. The federal government ended the fiscal year June 30 until 1976 when its fiscal year, by an act of Congress, was revised to extend from October 1 to September 30. A 3-month quarter (July 1 to September 30, 1976) bridged the transition.

Nationwide government finance statistics have been classified and presented in terms of uniform concepts and categories, rather than according to the highly diverse terminology, organization, and fund structure utilized by individual governments.

Statistics on governmental finances distinguish among general government, utilities, liquor stores, and insurance trusts. *General government* comprises all activities except utilities, liquor stores, and insurance trusts. *Utilities* include government water supply, electric light and power, gas supply, and transit systems. *Liquor stores* are operated by 17 states and by local governments in 6 states. *Insurance trusts* relate to employee retirement, unemployment compensation, and other social insurance systems administered by the federal, state, and local governments.

Data for cities or counties relate only to municipal or county and their dependent agencies and do not include amounts for other local governments in the same geographic location. Therefore, expenditure figures for "education" do not include spending by the separate school districts which administer public schools within most municipal or county areas. Variations in the assignment of governmental responsibility for public assistance, health, hospitals, public housing, and other functions to a lesser degree also have an important effect upon reported amounts of city or county expenditure, revenue, and debt.

Employment and payrolls—These data are based mainly on mail canvassing of state and local governments. Payroll includes all salaries, wages, and individual fee payments for the month specified. Employment relates to all persons on governmental payrolls during a pay period of the month covered, including paid officials, temporary help, and (unless otherwise specified) part-time as well as full-time personnel. Effective with the 1997 Census of Governments, the reference period for measuring government employment was changed from October of the calendar year to March of the calendar year. As a result, there was no annual survey of government employment covering the October 1996 period. The prior reference month of October was used from 1958 to 1995. Figures shown for individual governments cover major dependent agencies such as institutions of higher education, as well as the basic central departments and agencies of the government.

Statistical reliability—For a discussion of statistical collection and estimation, sampling procedures, and measures of statistical reliability applicable to Census Bureau data, see Appendix III.

Table 477. Number of Governmental Units by Type: 1972 to 2017

Type of government	1972	1977	1982	1987	1992	1997	2002	2007	2012	2017
Total units	**78,269**	**79,913**	**81,831**	**83,237**	**85,006**	**87,504**	**87,576**	**89,527**	**90,107**	**90,126**
U.S. government	1	1	1	1	1	1	1	1	1	1
State governments	50	50	50	50	50	50	50	50	50	50
Local governments	78,218	79,862	81,780	83,186	84,955	87,453	87,525	89,476	90,056	90,075
County	3,044	3,042	3,041	3,042	3,043	3,043	3,034	3,033	3,031	3,031
Municipal	18,517	18,862	19,076	19,200	19,279	19,372	19,429	19,492	19,519	19,495
Township and town	16,991	16,822	16,734	16,691	16,656	16,629	16,504	16,519	16,360	16,253
School district	15,781	15,174	14,851	14,721	14,422	13,726	13,506	13,051	12,880	12,754
Special district	23,885	25,962	28,078	29,532	31,555	34,683	35,052	37,381	38,266	38,542

Source: U.S. Census Bureau, Census of Governments, "2017 Census of Governments Organization Tables," <https://www.census.gov/programs-surveys/cog.html>, accessed May 2019.

Table 478. Number of Local Governments by Type—States: 2017

[Governments in existence in January. Excludes a few counties and numerous townships and incorporated places existing as areas for which statistics can be presented as to population and other subjects, but lacking any separate organized county, township, or municipal government. See Appendix III]

State	All govern-mental units [1]	County	Municipal	Township [1]	School district	Special district Total [2]	Special district Natural resources	Special district Fire protection	Special district Housing [3]
United States	**90,075**	**3,031**	**19,495**	**16,253**	**12,754**	**38,542**	**7,253**	**5,975**	**3,344**
Alabama	1,195	67	461	–	137	530	68	13	147
Alaska	179	15	149	–	–	15	–	–	14
Arizona	658	15	91	–	242	310	84	151	–
Arkansas	1,541	75	501	–	235	730	258	73	117
California	4,444	57	482	–	1,011	2,894	484	357	64
Colorado	3,141	62	271	–	180	2,628	168	261	91
Connecticut	625	–	30	149	17	429	1	65	113
Delaware	334	3	57	–	19	255	233	–	4
District of Columbia	2	–	1	–	–	1	–	–	–
Florida	1,712	66	412	–	95	1,139	119	54	92
Georgia	1,380	152	537	–	180	511	37	–	191
Hawaii	21	3	1	–	–	17	16	–	–
Idaho	1,170	44	200	–	118	808	177	156	11
Illinois	6,918	102	1,297	1,429	886	3,204	1,014	838	113
Indiana	2,638	91	567	1,004	289	687	142	2	64
Iowa	1,941	99	943	–	348	551	238	60	27
Kansas	3,792	103	625	1,265	306	1,493	256	1	177
Kentucky	1,322	118	417	–	173	614	126	151	19
Louisiana	516	60	304	–	69	83	8	2	–
Maine	834	16	23	465	98	232	17	–	30
Maryland	344	23	157	–	–	164	128	–	20
Massachusetts	858	5	53	298	85	417	17	11	250
Michigan	2,863	83	533	1,240	571	436	77	24	–
Minnesota	3,643	87	853	1,780	333	590	144	9	153
Mississippi	969	82	298	–	157	432	233	30	52
Missouri	3,768	114	944	283	530	1,897	323	401	135
Montana	1,226	54	129	–	313	730	132	214	13
Nebraska	2,538	93	529	366	269	1,281	87	413	163
Nevada	189	16	19	–	17	137	34	15	3
New Hampshire	541	10	13	221	168	129	11	14	21
New Jersey	1,338	21	324	241	519	233	15	183	–
New Mexico	1013	33	105	–	96	779	561	–	–
New York	3,450	57	601	929	678	1,185	1	885	–
North Carolina	970	100	552	–	–	318	136	–	93
North Dakota	2,664	53	357	1,308	179	767	74	275	38
Ohio	3,897	88	931	1,308	666	904	103	116	81
Oklahoma	1,830	77	590	–	542	621	104	27	128
Oregon	1,510	36	240	–	230	1,004	186	265	19
Pennsylvania	4,830	66	1,013	1,546	514	1,691	5	–	90
Rhode Island	129	–	8	31	4	86	5	31	26
South Carolina	671	46	270	–	81	274	45	64	42
South Dakota	1,916	66	311	902	150	487	105	80	1
Tennessee	906	92	345	–	14	455	105	1	93
Texas	5,343	254	1,218	–	1,073	2,798	435	267	384
Utah	619	29	250	–	41	299	79	12	19
Vermont	729	14	42	237	277	159	14	16	8
Virginia	517	95	228	–	1	193	47	–	–
Washington	1,900	39	281	–	295	1,285	181	368	43
West Virginia	651	55	232	–	55	309	14	–	35
Wisconsin	3,096	72	601	1,251	438	734	272	1	160
Wyoming	794	23	99	–	55	617	134	69	–

– Represents zero. [1] Includes town governments in the six New England States and in Minnesota, New York, and Wisconsin. [2] Includes other special districts not shown separately. [3] Includes community development.

Source: U.S. Census Bureau, Census of Governments, "2017 Census of Governments Organization Tables," <https://www.census.gov/programs-surveys/cog.html>, accessed May 2019.

Table 479. State and Local Government Current Receipts and Expenditures in the National Income and Product Accounts: 1990 to 2019

[In billions of dollars (730.1 represents $730,100,000,000). For explanation of national income, see text, Section 13. Minus sign (-) indicates net loss]

Item	1990	2000	2005	2010	2015	2016	2017	2018	2019
Current receipts............................	**730.1**	**1,304.1**	**1,718.5**	**1,994.4**	**2,375.3**	**2,431.9**	**2,515.1**	**2,623.0**	**2,736.4**
Current tax receipts............................	519.1	893.2	1,173.2	1,306.4	1,600.1	1,639.4	1,722.9	1,796.8	1,875.4
Personal current taxes....................	122.6	236.7	275.2	294.1	407.1	409.5	432.7	457.4	482.9
Income taxes............................	109.6	217.4	249.1	265.8	374.3	375.9	397.9	420.9	445.3
Other....................................	13.0	19.4	26.2	28.3	32.8	33.6	34.8	36.5	37.6
Taxes on production and imports..........	374.1	621.3	843.0	966.3	1,136.8	1,176.3	1,235.8	1,281.0	1,325.7
Sales taxes............................	125.6	221.4	272.8	295.1	375.5	382.7	394.7	411.9	431.5
Excise taxes............................	58.7	95.5	127.4	154.8	180.9	188.9	198.6	204.4	207.8
Property taxes.........................	161.5	254.7	351.2	438.6	490.3	513.5	545.8	562.0	581.4
Other....................................	28.2	49.8	91.7	77.8	90.1	91.3	96.6	102.7	105.0
Taxes on corporate income..............	22.5	35.2	54.9	46.1	56.2	53.5	54.5	58.4	66.8
Contributions for government social insurance....................................	10.0	10.8	24.6	17.8	19.2	20.1	20.8	22.2	22.7
Income receipts on assets................	68.5	94.2	89.6	83.5	84.5	86.1	89.3	91.4	94.0
Interest receipts........................	64.1	86.6	77.3	69.0	67.3	69.3	72.0	73.6	75.1
Dividends...............................	0.2	1.4	2.5	3.0	5.6	5.6	5.9	6.1	7.0
Rents and royalties......................	4.2	6.3	9.8	11.4	11.6	11.1	11.4	11.7	11.9
Current transfer receipts................	126.4	299.7	436.6	604.4	673.6	687.4	685.6	716.6	748.8
Federal grants-in-aid....................	104.4	233.1	343.5	505.2	533.2	556.9	559.8	582.9	611.4
From business (net)......................	7.1	28.6	36.5	40.3	65.0	54.5	48.8	52.3	53.3
From persons...........................	14.9	38.0	56.5	58.8	75.0	76.0	77.0	80.0	82.9
From the rest of the world...............	(NA)	–	–	–	0.5	–	–	1.3	1.2
Current surplus of government enterprises....................................	6.1	6.1	-5.5	-17.7	-2.0	-1.0	-3.4	-4.0	-4.5
Current expenditures....................	**766.3**	**1,344.8**	**1,821.3**	**2,301.8**	**2,595.7**	**2,678.7**	**2,763.2**	**2,862.1**	**2,950.4**
Consumption expenditures................	544.0	961.7	1,237.3	1,509.5	1,660.0	1,702.8	1,764.6	1,847.4	1,904.5
Government social benefit payments to persons....................................	127.7	271.4	406.5	523.9	665.5	693.6	712.2	736.6	775.4
Interest payments........................	94.3	111.1	177.1	266.9	269.7	281.7	285.8	277.5	269.9
Subsidies................................	0.4	0.5	0.4	1.6	0.5	0.5	0.6	0.6	0.6
Net state and local government saving....................................	**-36.2**	**-40.6**	**-102.8**	**-307.5**	**-220.3**	**-246.8**	**-248.1**	**-239.2**	**-213.9**
Social insurance funds....................	2.0	2.0	7.2	0.9	3.4	4.3	5.0	5.6	5.5
Other....................................	-38.2	-42.6	-110.0	-308.4	-223.7	-251.1	-253.1	-244.7	-219.5

– Represents zero. NA Not available.

Source: U.S. Bureau of Economic Analysis, National Income and Product Accounts Tables, "Table 3.3. State and Local Government Current Receipts and Expenditures," <http://www.bea.gov/itable/>, accessed June 2020.

Table 480. Federal Grants–in–Aid to State and Local Governments: 1990 to 2020

[135,325 represents $135,325,000,000, except as indicated. For fiscal year ending September 30. Minus sign (-) indicates decrease]

Year	Current dollars						Constant (2012) dollars	
			Grants to individuals		Grants as percent of—			
	Total grants (mil. dol.)	Annual percent change [1]	Total (mil. dol.)	Percent of total grants	Federal outlays	Gross domestic product	Total grants (bil. dol.)	Annual percent change [1]
1990...............	135,325	11.0	77,431	57.2	10.8	2.3	238.9	5.9
1995...............	224,991	6.8	145,652	64.7	14.8	3.0	338.7	3.9
2000...............	285,874	6.7	186,534	65.3	16.0	2.8	389.1	3.8
2001...............	318,542	11.4	208,008	65.3	17.1	3.0	422.5	8.6
2002...............	352,895	10.8	231,854	65.7	17.5	3.3	460.9	9.1
2003...............	388,542	10.1	251,235	64.7	18.0	3.4	496.7	7.8
2004...............	407,512	4.9	267,046	65.5	17.8	3.4	506.2	1.9
2005...............	428,018	5.0	278,764	65.1	17.3	3.3	511.6	1.1
2006...............	434,099	1.4	277,559	63.9	16.3	3.2	500.1	-2.2
2007...............	443,797	2.2	289,460	65.2	16.3	3.1	494.2	-1.2
2008...............	461,317	3.9	306,123	66.4	15.5	3.1	493.7	-0.1
2009...............	537,991	16.6	362,031	67.3	15.3	3.7	573.0	16.1
2010...............	608,390	13.1	391,427	64.3	17.6	4.1	637.6	11.3
2011...............	606,770	-0.3	392,713	64.7	16.8	3.9	620.9	-2.6
2012...............	544,573	-10.3	364,095	66.9	15.4	3.4	544.6	-12.3
2013...............	546,178	0.3	379,008	69.4	15.8	3.3	536.4	-1.5
2014...............	576,978	5.6	412,466	71.5	16.5	3.3	556.9	3.8
2015...............	624,357	8.2	463,392	74.2	16.9	3.4	599.6	7.7
2016...............	660,833	5.8	495,711	75.0	17.2	3.6	630.9	5.2
2017...............	674,712	2.1	507,976	75.3	16.9	3.5	633.1	0.3
2018...............	696,507	3.2	525,813	75.5	17.0	3.4	638.6	0.9
2019...............	721,140	3.5	549,313	76.2	16.2	3.4	649.3	1.7
2020, estimate.....	790,732	9.7	597,345	75.5	16.5	3.6	695.6	7.1

NA Not available. [1] Average annual percent change from previous year.

Source: U.S. Office of Management and Budget, *Budget of the U.S. Government, Fiscal Year 2021: Historical Tables*, February 2020. See also <http://www.whitehouse.gov/omb/budget>.

Table 481. Federal Outlays for Grants to State and Local Governments—Selected Agencies and Programs: 1990 to 2021

[In millions of dollars (135,325 represents $135,325,000,000). For fiscal year ending September 30. Includes trust funds]

Agency and program	1990	2000	2005	2010	2015	2016	2017	2018	2019	2020 est.	2021 est.
Total outlays for grants	**135,325**	**285,874**	**428,018**	**608,390**	**624,357**	**660,833**	**674,712**	**696,507**	**721,140**	**790,732**	**810,076**
Energy	461	433	636	2,656	577	764	774	771	819	913	896
Natural resources and environment	3,745	4,595	5,858	9,132	7,043	6,702	6,155	6,394	6,698	6,627	6,789
Environmental Protection Agency [1]	2,874	3,490	3,734	6,883	4,570	4,270	3,750	3,862	4,103	3,155	3,723
Agriculture	1,118	724	933	843	707	806	763	815	828	1,105	968
Transportation [1]	19,174	32,222	43,370	60,981	60,835	63,876	64,795	64,836	65,637	68,314	71,002
Grants for airports [1]	1,220	1,624	3,530	3,156	2,988	2,963	3,129	3,036	3,303	3,309	3,382
Federal-aid highways [2]	13,854	24,711	30,915	30,385	41,205	43,035	43,236	43,305	43,768	44,571	46,329
Urban mass transportation [1]	3,728	5,262	8,114	12,939	11,784	12,271	12,124	12,608	13,109	14,078	14,950
Community and regional development	4,965	8,665	20,167	18,908	14,357	15,298	14,797	19,089	15,565	23,217	26,893
Rural Community Advancement Program	139	479	814	—	—	—	—	—	—	—	—
Community Development Fund	2,818	4,955	4,985	7,043	6,548	6,013	5,616	5,889	5,178	7,427	9,573
Homeland Security	1,184	2,439	13,541	8,483	5,924	7,951	7,758	12,038	8,988	13,400	14,648
State and local programs	—	—	2,116	3,337	2,918	2,683	2,119	1,704	903	209	222
Firefighter assistance grants	—	—	1,185	—	—	—	—	—	—	—	—
Federal assistance, FEMA	11	192	132	—	—	—	84	516	—	—	2,128
Operations and support, FEMA	—	13	39	—	—	—	—	—	—	—	—
Natural predisaster mitigation grants	—	—	—	—	—	—	—	—	—	—	—
Disaster relief fund	1,173	2,234	10,069	5,141	2,919	5,155	5,348	9,715	6,735	10,953	12,298
Education, training, employment, social services	21,780	36,672	57,247	97,586	60,527	60,867	61,553	60,591	63,106	68,768	65,985
Education for the disadvantaged [3]	4,437	8,511	14,539	19,515	15,199	15,570	16,186	15,277	16,203	17,637	16,521
School improvement programs	1,080	2,394	6,569	5,184	4,138	4,224	4,295	4,060	4,616	5,146	5,200
Special education	1,485	4,696	10,661	17,075	12,077	12,357	12,479	12,753	12,978	13,562	13,644
Social Services block grant	2,749	1,827	1,822	2,035	1,832	1,780	1,661	1,587	1,646	1,715	352
Children and family services programs	2,618	5,843	8,490	10,473	9,608	10,026	10,232	10,651	11,240	11,730	12,183
Training and employment services	3,042	2,957	3,372	4,592	2,639	2,673	2,783	2,724	2,684	3,020	3,071
Health	43,890	124,843	197,848	290,168	368,026	396,666	406,946	421,117	442,324	485,678	498,994
Substance abuse and mental health services [4]	1,241	1,931	3,203	2,846	2,671	2,927	2,903	3,258	3,679	5,506	5,055
Grants to states for Medicaid [4]	41,103	117,921	181,720	272,771	349,762	368,280	374,682	389,157	409,421	447,241	448,145
State children's health insurance fund [4]	—	1,220	5,129	7,887	9,233	14,305	16,224	17,282	17,689	17,654	15,778
Income security	36,935	68,653	90,885	115,156	101,082	104,769	107,400	110,649	112,566	116,981	116,873
Supplemental Nutrition Assistance Program (SNAP) (formerly Food Stamp Program) [4]	2,130	3,508	4,385	5,739	5,100	6,406	6,954	7,485	7,100	6,975	7,121
Child nutrition programs [4]	4,871	9,060	11,726	16,259	20,999	21,952	22,445	22,803	23,247	22,797	25,872
Temporary Assistance for Needy Families (TANF) [4]	—	15,464	17,357	17,513	15,940	15,620	15,972	16,414	15,493	16,103	15,712
Veterans benefits and services [4]	134	434	552	836	1,821	1,829	1,992	2,061	2,050	2,579	2,713
Administration of justice	574	5,263	4,784	5,086	3,664	3,536	3,973	4,195	5,161	9,291	7,950

– Represents zero. [1] Grants include trust funds. [2] Trust funds. [3] Formerly Accelerating Achievement and Ensuring Equity. [4] Includes grants for payments to individuals.

Source: U.S. Office of Management and Budget, *Budget of the U.S. Government, Fiscal Year 2021: Historical Tables*, February 2020. See also <http://www.whitehouse.gov/omb/budget>.

Table 482. State and Local Governments—Summary of Finances: 2000 to 2017

[In millions of dollars (1,942,328 represents $1,942,328,000,000). For fiscal year ending in year shown; see text, this section. Local government amounts are estimates subject to sampling variation; see Appendix III and source]

Item	2000	2005	2010	2015	2016	2017
Revenue [1]	**1,942,328**	**2,528,546**	**3,180,023**	**3,416,065**	**3,408,695**	**3,918,843**
From federal government	**291,950**	**438,558**	**623,801**	**658,012**	**693,989**	**710,076**
From state and local sources	**1,650,379**	**2,089,988**	**2,556,222**	**2,758,053**	**2,714,706**	**3,208,767**
General, net intergovernmental	1,249,373	1,587,476	1,887,045	2,262,308	2,324,383	2,408,610
Taxes	872,351	1,098,513	1,278,847	1,563,701	1,602,018	1,652,829
Property	249,178	335,779	443,947	484,251	504,593	525,920
Sales and gross receipts	309,290	384,266	435,571	544,359	559,625	580,355
Individual income	211,661	242,273	261,510	368,862	375,310	384,578
Corporation net income	36,059	43,256	44,108	57,130	53,581	52,739
Other	66,164	92,939	93,710	109,100	108,909	109,237
Charges and miscellaneous	377,022	488,963	608,198	698,607	722,365	755,781
Utility and liquor stores	89,546	119,608	154,758	175,655	173,720	178,031
Water supply system	30,515	37,378	49,327	61,157	62,205	65,678
Electric power system	42,436	59,157	76,492	81,250	78,971	79,936
Gas supply system	3,954	6,937	8,219	7,478	6,559	6,058
Transit system	8,049	10,146	13,003	16,359	16,744	16,788
Liquor stores	4,592	5,990	7,716	9,412	9,241	9,570
Insurance trust revenue [2]	311,460	382,904	514,420	320,090	216,603	622,126
Employee retirement	273,881	316,576	416,536	247,486	149,386	556,877
Unemployment compensation	23,366	35,367	75,191	49,303	43,111	40,547
Direct expenditure	**1,742,914**	**2,363,696**	**3,110,833**	**3,405,439**	**3,532,825**	**3,663,342**
By function:						
Direct general expenditure [2]	1,502,768	2,007,490	2,537,892	2,841,079	2,961,032	3,071,187
Education [2]	521,612	688,314	860,118	934,353	973,025	1,010,131
Elementary and secondary	365,181	473,843	573,641	609,926	633,561	660,443
Higher education	134,352	182,003	243,515	273,935	288,119	296,452
Public welfare	233,350	360,730	456,200	613,502	652,514	678,238
Hospitals	75,976	103,555	145,902	170,198	181,437	191,135
Health	51,366	66,637	81,383	91,810	95,887	99,827
Highways	101,336	126,350	155,912	171,084	177,982	181,990
Police protection	56,798	74,131	95,772	104,807	109,116	114,503
Fire protection	23,102	30,830	41,335	45,967	47,982	50,457
Natural resources	20,235	23,519	28,433	28,560	30,614	31,773
Parks and recreation	25,038	31,925	40,247	39,678	41,939	45,264
Housing and community development	26,590	40,014	53,923	49,754	49,871	52,401
Sanitation and sewerage	45,261	57,940	75,620	75,830	80,213	81,746
Financial administration	29,300	36,695	40,241	43,117	44,187	45,508
Interest on general debt [3]	69,814	81,122	105,715	105,613	105,221	106,323
Utility and liquor stores [3]	114,916	160,470	213,914	236,041	231,267	239,954
Water supply system	35,789	45,695	60,655	66,905	68,866	70,823
Electric power system	39,719	58,612	78,478	79,045	75,543	76,150
Gas supply system	3,724	7,075	8,273	7,457	6,992	6,427
Transit system	31,883	44,203	60,149	74,947	72,124	78,429
Liquor stores	3,801	4,885	6,359	7,687	7,742	8,127
Insurance trust expenditure [2]	125,230	195,735	359,027	325,109	337,320	348,942
Employee retirement	95,679	145,796	204,803	275,406	289,474	302,560
Unemployment compensation	18,648	29,849	135,367	33,352	32,533	31,069
By character and object:						
Current operation	1,288,746	1,760,283	2,228,794	2,561,396	2,659,156	2,764,306
Capital outlay	217,063	278,063	355,437	336,088	352,195	364,614
Construction	161,694	218,691	284,213	271,190	283,864	291,616
Equipment, land, and existing structures	55,369	59,372	71,224	64,898	68,331	72,999
Assistance and subsidies	31,375	37,755	47,636	57,332	59,570	59,758
Interest on debt (general and utility)	80,499	91,859	119,939	122,305	121,378	122,463
Insurance benefits and repayments	125,230	195,735	359,027	325,109	337,320	348,942
Expenditure for salaries and wages [4]	548,796	694,583	844,650	900,861	927,896	965,035
Debt outstanding, year end	**1,451,815**	**2,085,026**	**2,844,190**	**2,988,463**	**3,022,488**	**3,068,056**
Short-term	24,291	30,758	45,088	34,621	34,371	36,119
Long-term	1,427,524	2,054,268	2,799,101	2,953,842	2,988,117	3,031,937
Long-term debt:						
Issued	184,831	323,739	398,962	362,594	383,431	407,700
Retired	121,897	224,639	275,810	370,232	370,597	391,128

[1] Aggregates exclude duplicative transactions between state and local governments; see source. [2] Includes amounts for other items not shown separately. [3] Interest on utility debt included in "utility and liquor stores expenditure." For total interest on debt, see "Interest on debt (general and utility)." [4] Included in items above.

Source: U.S. Census Bureau, Federal, State, and Local Governments, Government Finance Statistics, "Annual Surveys of State and Local Government Finances," <census.gov/programs-surveys/gov-finances.html>, accessed June 2020.

Table 483. State and Local Governments—Revenue and Expenditures by Function: 2010 and 2017

[In millions of dollars (3,180,023 represents $3,180,023,000,000). For fiscal year ending in year shown; see text, this section. Local government amounts are estimates subject to sampling variation; see Appendix III and source]

Item	2010			2017		
	Total	State	Local	Total	State	Local
Revenue [1]	**3,180,023**	**2,039,927**	**1,635,634**	**3,918,843**	**2,531,103**	**1,938,485**
Intergovernmental revenue [1]	623,801	575,372	543,967	710,076	658,792	602,030
Total revenue from own sources [1]	2,556,222	1,464,555	1,091,667	3,208,767	1,872,312	1,336,456
General revenue from own sources	1,887,045	991,835	895,210	2,408,610	1,317,020	1,091,390
Taxes [2]	1,278,847	705,929	572,917	1,652,829	946,077	706,753
Property	443,947	14,454	429,494	525,920	16,494	509,426
Individual income	261,510	236,987	24,524	384,578	351,526	33,051
Corporation income	44,108	38,006	6,102	52,739	44,657	8,082
Sales and gross receipts	435,571	344,522	91,048	580,355	456,695	123,660
General sales	288,499	224,314	64,185	389,019	299,574	89,445
Selective sales [2]	147,072	120,208	26,864	191,337	157,121	34,215
Motor fuel	37,922	36,632	1,291	46,621	45,036	1,585
Alcoholic beverages	6,021	5,511	511	7,297	6,620	677
Tobacco products	17,303	16,858	444	19,032	18,644	388
Public utilities	28,487	14,653	13,834	27,057	12,248	14,809
Motor vehicle and operators' licenses	22,459	20,861	1,598	28,240	26,101	2,139
Charges and miscellaneous [2]	608,198	285,906	322,293	755,781	371,144	384,637
Current charges [2]	411,200	169,855	241,345	525,936	225,944	299,992
Education [2]	121,138	94,530	26,608	134,574	110,254	24,320
School lunch sales	6,600	34	6,567	5,603	34	5,569
Higher education	105,515	93,081	12,434	118,598	109,216	9,381
Hospitals	113,339	42,938	70,401	160,050	69,511	90,539
Highways	12,001	6,885	5,116	20,551	11,430	9,121
Airports	18,067	1,327	16,740	24,093	1,771	22,323
Sea and inland port facilities	3,881	1,038	2,843	5,763	1,757	4,005
Natural resources	4,633	2,788	1,845	5,171	2,981	2,190
Parks and recreation	9,329	1,516	7,813	11,438	1,707	9,731
Housing and community development	5,789	622	5,167	7,104	827	6,277
Sewerage	43,472	612	42,860	58,065	1,014	57,051
Solid waste management	15,738	420	15,317	18,396	260	18,136
Interest earnings	59,828	34,523	25,305	51,472	37,001	14,470
Special assessments	7,001	165	6,836	9,885	19	9,866
Sale of property	2,829	692	2,137	4,464	1,344	3,120
Utility and liquor store revenue	154,758	21,617	133,141	178,031	21,766	156,265
Insurance trust revenue	514,420	451,103	63,316	622,126	533,325	88,801
Expenditures [1]	**3,115,172**	**1,943,523**	**1,666,796**	**3,663,342**	**2,316,929**	**1,913,388**
Intergovernmental expenditure [1]	4,339	485,557	13,929	3,259	553,351	16,882
Direct expenditure [1]	3,110,833	1,457,965	1,652,867	3,660,083	1,763,578	1,896,505
General expenditure [2]	2,537,892	1,108,137	1,429,755	3,071,187	1,433,369	1,637,819
Education [1]	860,118	253,758	606,360	1,010,131	313,313	696,819
Elementary and secondary education	573,641	7,832	565,809	660,443	6,984	653,460
Higher education	243,515	202,964	40,551	296,452	253,093	43,359
Public welfare	456,200	403,572	52,627	678,238	620,660	57,578
Hospitals	145,902	58,752	87,150	191,135	84,005	107,131
Health	81,383	39,971	41,412	99,827	43,276	56,551
Highways	155,912	93,127	62,786	181,990	109,832	72,158
Police protection	95,772	12,376	83,395	114,503	15,426	99,078
Fire protection	41,335	–	41,335	50,457	–	50,457
Corrections	73,100	46,095	27,005	78,733	48,851	29,882
Natural resources	28,433	19,336	9,097	31,773	21,385	10,388
Parks and recreation	40,247	4,912	35,335	45,264	5,687	39,577
Housing and community development	53,923	11,487	42,437	52,401	8,771	43,630
Sewerage	51,991	1,118	50,873	56,555	1,309	55,246
Solid waste management	23,629	2,281	21,348	25,191	1,114	24,078
Governmental administration	126,719	52,147	74,572	144,245	61,252	82,993
Interest on general debt	105,715	45,260	60,455	106,323	43,752	62,571
Utility	207,555	23,864	183,691	231,828	28,350	203,477
Liquor store expenditure	6,359	5,244	1,115	8,127	6,874	1,253
Insurance trust expenditure	359,027	320,721	38,306	348,942	294,985	53,957
By character and object:						
Current operation	2,228,794	934,322	1,294,473	2,764,306	1,241,555	1,522,751
Capital outlay	355,437	118,011	237,426	364,614	131,635	232,979
Construction	284,213	100,962	183,251	291,616	112,129	179,486
Equipment, land, and existing structures	71,224	17,048	54,175	72,999	19,506	53,493
Assistance and subsidies	47,636	37,562	10,074	59,758	49,175	10,583
Interest on debt (general and utility)	119,939	47,351	72,588	122,463	46,227	76,236
Insurance benefits and repayments	359,027	320,721	38,306	348,942	294,985	53,957
Expenditure for salaries and wages [3]	844,650	244,952	599,698	965,035	276,286	688,749

– Represents or rounds to zero. [1] Aggregates exclude duplicative transactions between levels of government; see source. [2] Includes data for other items not shown separately. [3] Included in items shown above.

Source: U.S. Census Bureau, Federal, State, and Local Governments, Government Finance Statistics, "Annual Surveys of State and Local Government Finances," <census.gov/programs-surveys/gov-finances.html>, accessed June 2020.

Table 484. State and Local Governments—Capital Outlays: 2000 to 2017

[In millions of dollars (217,063 represents $217,063,000,000), except percent. For fiscal year ending in year shown; see text, this section. Local government amounts are subject to sampling variation; see Appendix III and source]

Level and function	2000	2005	2010	2012	2013	2014	2015	2016	2017
State & local governments, total	**217,063**	**278,063**	**355,437**	**329,450**	**324,274**	**319,063**	**336,088**	**352,195**	**364,614**
Percent of direct expenditure	12.5	11.8	11.4	10.4	10.2	9.7	9.9	10.0	10.0
By function:									
Education [1]	60,968	77,780	93,562	84,709	80,455	79,493	84,148	92,857	98,067
Elementary and secondary	45,150	54,563	60,240	51,087	47,827	48,559	52,892	58,371	63,671
Higher education	15,257	22,735	31,644	32,333	31,501	29,910	30,641	34,024	33,975
Highways	56,439	70,689	89,895	88,803	89,394	88,639	93,810	99,262	101,898
Hospitals [2]	5,502	6,100	8,553	9,597	9,396	10,010	8,782	9,074	8,969
Natural resources	4,347	4,541	5,214	5,258	4,702	4,208	4,697	6,120	5,376
Parks and recreation	6,916	8,136	10,711	8,438	7,969	7,780	8,342	9,261	10,342
Sewerage	10,093	14,081	21,915	20,667	18,412	18,196	17,847	20,042	19,276
Utilities	24,847	34,790	49,258	46,279	52,706	47,688	54,829	50,708	53,143
State governments, total	**76,233**	**95,155**	**118,011**	**117,981**	**120,268**	**116,228**	**128,925**	**130,229**	**131,635**
Percent of direct expenditure	10.1	8.9	8.1	7.8	7.9	7.4	7.9	7.6	7.5
By function:									
Education [1]	14,077	20,585	28,643	28,711	28,625	27,280	28,126	30,915	30,497
Elementary and secondary	521	447	1,066	486	581	605	757	923	806
Higher education	12,995	19,656	25,899	26,936	26,917	25,651	26,753	29,530	29,270
Highways	41,651	52,607	64,755	65,286	64,787	65,179	68,979	72,518	74,606
Hospitals [2]	2,228	2,363	2,654	3,341	3,104	3,392	3,562	3,717	3,497
Natural resources	2,758	2,667	2,337	2,099	2,051	1,912	2,565	3,652	2,634
Parks and recreation	1,044	915	910	701	667	650	851	837	976
Sewerage	403	486	488	192	139	122	60	95	147
Utilities	4,232	4,319	5,318	4,656	9,922	5,299	12,747	7,211	8,130
Local governments, total	**140,830**	**182,908**	**237,426**	**211,469**	**204,005**	**202,834**	**207,163**	**221,967**	**232,979**
Percent of direct expenditure	14.3	14.1	14.4	12.8	12.3	11.8	11.7	12.2	12.3
By function:									
Education [1]	46,890	57,195	64,919	55,998	51,829	52,213	56,022	61,942	67,570
Elementary and secondary	44,629	54,116	59,174	50,601	47,246	47,954	52,134	57,448	62,865
Higher education	2,261	3,079	5,745	5,397	4,583	4,259	3,888	4,494	4,705
Highways	14,789	18,083	25,140	23,516	24,607	23,460	24,832	26,744	27,292
Hospitals [2]	3,274	3,737	5,899	6,256	6,292	6,618	5,219	5,357	5,472
Natural resources	1,589	1,873	2,878	3,159	2,651	2,296	2,131	2,468	2,742
Parks and recreation	5,872	7,221	9,802	7,737	7,301	7,130	7,490	8,424	9,365
Sewerage	9,690	13,595	21,426	20,476	18,273	18,073	17,788	19,946	19,130
Utilities	20,615	30,471	43,940	41,623	42,784	42,389	42,083	43,496	45,014

[1] Includes other education, not shown separately. [2] For 2000 only, data include outlays for both health and hospitals.

Source: U.S. Census Bureau, Federal, State, and Local Governments, Government Finance Statistics, "Annual Surveys of State and Local Government Finances," <census.gov/programs-surveys/gov-finances.html>, accessed June 2020.

Table 485. State and Local Governments—Expenditures for Public Works: 2000 to 2017

[In millions of dollars (230,569 represents $230,569,000,000), except percent. Represents direct expenditures excluding intergovernmental grants]

Item	Total	Highways	Air trans- portation	Sea and inland port facilities	Sewerage	Solid waste manage- ment	Water supply	Mass transit
2000, total	230,569	101,336	13,160	3,141	28,052	17,208	35,789	31,883
State	74,974	61,942	1,106	863	955	2,347	354	7,407
Local	155,595	39,394	12,054	2,277	27,098	14,861	35,435	24,476
Capital expenditures (percent)	41.9	55.7	51.0	51.5	36.0	8.9	29.5	30.5
2010, total	381,808	155,912	24,209	5,263	51,991	23,629	60,655	60,149
State	111,280	93,127	1,724	1,245	1,118	2,281	378	11,407
Local	270,529	62,786	22,485	4,019	50,873	21,348	60,277	48,742
Capital expenditures (percent)	(NA)	57.7	(NA)	(NA)	42.2	8.9	(NA)	(NA)
2014, total	399,979	165,051	21,840	6,243	51,789	23,076	65,538	66,442
State	119,521	99,275	1,972	1,613	1,054	1,090	451	14,066
Local	280,457	65,776	19,868	4,630	50,735	21,986	65,087	52,377
Capital expenditures (percent)	(NA)	53.7	(NA)	(NA)	35.1	7.4	(NA)	(NA)
2015, total	417,753	171,084	22,675	6,312	51,888	23,942	66,905	74,947
State	131,651	102,754	2,388	1,743	1,040	1,173	447	22,106
Local	286,102	68,330	20,287	4,569	50,849	22,768	66,459	52,840
Capital expenditures (percent)	(NA)	54.8	(NA)	(NA)	34.4	9.0	(NA)	(NA)
2016, total	429,235	177,982	24,009	6,042	55,546	24,666	68,866	72,124
State	131,478	107,278	2,165	1,888	1,248	1,356	461	17,082
Local	297,757	70,704	21,845	4,154	54,298	23,311	68,405	55,042
Capital expenditures (percent)	(NA)	55.8	(NA)	(NA)	36.1	9.1	(NA)	(NA)
2017, total	445,361	181,990	25,968	6,405	56,555	25,191	70,823	78,429
State	136,000	109,832	2,335	2,146	1,309	1,114	500	18,765
Local	309,360	72,158	23,634	4,259	55,246	24,078	70,323	59,664
Capital expenditures (percent)	(NA)	56.0	(NA)	(NA)	34.1	8.8	(NA)	(NA)

NA Not available.

Source: U.S. Census Bureau, Federal, State, and Local Governments, Government Finance Statistics, "Annual Surveys of State and Local Government Finances," <census.gov/programs-surveys/gov-finances.html>, accessed June 2020, and unpublished data.

Table 486. State and Local Governments—Indebtedness: 1990 to 2017

[In billions of dollars (858.0 represents $858,000,000,000). For fiscal year ending in year shown; see text, this section. Local government amounts are estimates subject to sampling variation; see Appendix III and source]

Item	Debt outstanding						Long-term	
	Total	Cash and security holdings	Short-term	Long-term			Debt issued	Debt retired
				Total	Public debt for private purposes	All other		
1990, total.........	858.0	1,490.8	19.3	838.7	294.1	544.6	108.5	64.8
State..............	318.3	963.3	2.8	315.5	154.4	161.1	43.5	22.9
Local..............	539.8	527.5	16.5	523.2	139.7	383.5	65.0	42.0
2000, total.........	1,451.8	3,503.7	24.3	1,427.5	372.6	1,054.9	184.8	121.9
State..............	547.9	2,518.9	6.4	541.5	227.3	314.2	75.0	44.4
Local..............	903.9	984.8	17.9	886.0	145.3	740.7	109.8	77.5
2005, total.........	2,085.0	4,439.2	30.8	2,054.3	483.3	1,571.0	323.7	224.6
State..............	810.9	3,153.8	5.6	805.3	297.4	507.9	131.6	93.6
Local..............	1,274.2	1,285.4	25.2	1,249.0	185.9	1,063.0	192.2	131.1
2009, total.........	2,713.2	4,537.4	36.9	2,676.3	627.8	2,048.6	371.3	256.5
State..............	1,048.7	3,082.5	7.3	1,041.3	395.1	646.2	154.2	109.0
Local..............	1,664.6	1,454.9	29.6	1,635.0	232.7	1,402.3	217.1	147.6
2010, total.........	2,844.2	4,826.0	45.1	2,799.1	625.9	2,173.2	399.0	275.8
State..............	1,115.5	3,323.0	14.7	1,100.8	397.1	703.6	183.7	125.1
Local..............	1,728.7	1,503.0	30.4	1,698.3	228.8	1,469.6	215.2	150.7
2011, total.........	2,923.1	5,265.1	34.7	2,888.4	616.1	2,272.3	364.6	275.1
State..............	1,139.7	3,681.4	5.4	1,134.2	389.1	745.1	138.1	112.4
Local..............	1,783.5	1,583.7	29.3	1,754.2	227.0	1,527.2	226.5	162.7
2012, total.........	2,950.5	5,305.6	43.6	2,906.8	599.4	2,307.4	341.8	333.0
State..............	1,146.7	3,700.9	15.5	1,131.3	373.6	757.7	137.1	138.6
Local..............	1,803.7	1,604.7	28.2	1,775.6	225.8	1,549.7	204.7	194.5
2013, total.........	2,970.0	5,640.4	31.9	2,938.0	600.5	2,337.6	369.5	355.7
State..............	1,138.6	3,952.1	5.7	1,133.0	366.2	766.7	148.5	147.0
Local..............	1,831.3	1,688.4	26.3	1,805.1	234.2	1,570.8	221.0	208.8
2014, total.........	2,980.0	6,095.2	33.7	2,946.3	578.9	2,367.4	303.9	305.8
State..............	1,152.3	4,330.8	8.7	1,143.6	355.6	788.0	130.1	123.7
Local..............	1,827.7	1,764.5	25.0	1,802.7	223.3	1,579.4	173.8	182.1
2015, total.........	2,988.5	6,277.8	34.6	2,953.8	566.1	2,387.8	362.6	370.2
State..............	1,155.1	4,415.6	8.6	1,146.5	354.4	792.1	143.3	144.0
Local..............	1,833.3	1,862.3	26.1	1,807.3	211.7	1,595.6	219.3	226.2
2016, total.........	3,022.5	6,326.4	34.4	2,988.1	555.2	2,432.9	383.4	370.6
State..............	1,170.6	4,416.3	9.0	1,161.6	353.9	807.7	142.4	132.1
Local..............	1,851.9	1,910.0	25.4	1,826.5	201.4	1,625.1	241.1	238.5
2017, total.........	3,068.1	6,806.0	36.1	3,031.9	560.3	2,471.7	407.7	391.1
State..............	1,159.8	4,764.5	7.9	1,151.9	354.9	797.1	154.5	153.7
Local..............	1,908.3	2,041.5	28.3	1,880.0	205.4	1,674.6	253.2	237.4

Source: U.S. Census Bureau, Federal, State, and Local Governments, Government Finance Statistics, "Annual Surveys of State and Local Government Finances," <census.gov/programs-surveys/gov-finances.html>, accessed June 2020.

Table 487. New Security Issues—State and Local Governments: 1990 to 2019

[In billions of dollars (122.9 represents $122,900,000,000)]

Type of issue, issuer, or use	1990	1995	2000	2005	2010	2015	2016	2017	2018	2019
All issues, new and refunding [1]......	122.9	145.7	180.4	409.6	460.8	399.6	431.0	425.6	351.2	434.1
By type of issue:										
General obligation.........................	39.5	57.0	64.5	145.8	137.5	161.1	161.4	152.4	107.6	137.7
Revenue......................	83.3	88.7	115.9	263.8	323.2	238.7	269.9	273.3	243.6	296.3
By type of issuer:										
State........................	15.0	14.7	19.9	31.6	55.2	(NA)	(NA)	(NA)	(NA)	(NA)
Special district or statutory authority [2]....	75.9	93.5	121.2	298.6	294.9	(NA)	(NA)	(NA)	(NA)	(NA)
Municipality, county, or township..........	32.0	37.5	39.3	79.4	86.6	(NA)	(NA)	(NA)	(NA)	(NA)
Issues for new capital...................	97.9	102.4	154.3	223.8	278.5	169.5	168.4	197.5	230.9	233.9
By use of proceeds:										
Education.....................................	17.1	24.0	38.7	71.0	60.4	46.5	50.4	57.6	59.1	63.9
Transportation............................	11.8	11.9	19.7	25.4	32.3	13.9	19.6	20.2	25.7	30.2
Utilities and conservation..................	10.0	9.6	11.9	9.9	22.3	8.5	3.9	7.4	10.9	15.2
Industrial aid................................	6.6	6.6	7.1	18.6	35.7	14.7	14.1	17.7	32.6	27.2
Other purposes.............................	31.7	30.8	47.3	60.6	92.4	56.0	56.7	60.5	64.0	55.6

NA Not available. [1] Par amounts of long-term issues based on date of sale. [2] Includes school districts.

Source: Board of Governors of the Federal Reserve System, Business Finance, "New Security Issues, State and Local Governments," <https://www.federalreserve.gov/data.htm>, accessed June 2020.

Table 488. State and Local Governments—Total Revenue and Expenditures by State: 2000 to 2017

[In millions of dollars (1,942,328 represents $1,942,328,000,000). For fiscal year ending in year shown; see text, this section. These data cannot be used to compute the deficit or surplus for any single government, as these are estimates for all state and local governments within a state area. For further information, see the *2006 Government Finance and Employment Classification Manual* at <http://www.census.gov/govs/classification/>]

State	Revenue				Expenditures			
	2000	2010	2016	2017	2000	2010	2016	2017
United States............	**1,942,328**	**3,180,023**	**3,408,695**	**3,918,843**	**1,746,943**	**3,115,172**	**3,532,825**	**3,663,342**
Alabama................	25,726	42,189	46,651	49,900	25,319	42,255	47,286	48,700
Alaska.................	10,525	15,643	11,497	14,287	8,628	14,450	15,839	14,931
Arizona................	27,778	54,099	59,058	67,173	27,293	53,432	56,102	58,536
Arkansas...............	13,833	24,539	26,683	31,281	12,245	22,798	26,783	27,714
California.............	270,380	453,354	511,974	615,808	236,645	432,363	550,056	566,781
Colorado...............	29,603	49,260	55,106	62,002	26,173	48,630	57,852	60,836
Connecticut............	25,828	39,427	42,802	49,519	24,011	39,311	41,773	40,974
Delaware...............	6,224	9,831	10,285	11,971	5,153	9,745	11,269	12,015
District of Columbia........	6,383	11,644	14,628	15,031	6,527	13,682	16,594	18,555
Florida................	92,402	166,817	164,755	192,144	84,301	163,536	167,777	177,052
Georgia................	49,310	76,370	78,330	91,081	43,517	78,158	82,044	85,131
Hawaii.................	8,488	14,666	17,454	20,330	8,254	14,340	16,354	16,783
Idaho..................	7,590	12,490	13,189	15,535	6,404	12,054	12,476	13,178
Illinois...............	80,695	126,384	128,361	148,648	74,727	129,518	140,192	146,853
Indiana................	32,716	54,803	60,406	62,854	31,250	53,247	57,690	58,656
Iowa...................	17,220	31,055	36,751	41,261	17,275	29,537	34,587	35,148
Kansas.................	16,235	26,330	28,166	32,015	14,419	26,536	28,812	30,554
Kentucky...............	25,200	37,560	40,310	45,191	21,473	38,595	45,494	46,103
Louisiana..............	27,109	47,078	42,675	52,285	25,018	48,755	46,766	48,980
Maine..................	8,554	12,557	12,568	14,432	7,652	12,286	12,566	12,826
Maryland...............	33,949	57,493	65,195	73,282	30,598	57,485	67,446	69,639
Massachusetts..........	46,103	76,100	85,616	95,392	44,362	76,679	90,082	92,836
Michigan...............	70,112	93,819	98,855	106,961	61,506	90,935	96,460	98,798
Minnesota..............	38,785	57,410	63,851	73,381	35,424	55,975	65,182	68,335
Mississippi............	16,672	28,690	29,457	32,785	15,379	27,216	29,656	30,035
Missouri...............	31,635	51,592	52,638	61,103	27,953	50,040	54,097	55,536
Montana................	5,643	9,784	9,628	11,839	4,983	9,296	9,931	10,828
Nebraska...............	11,650	20,121	22,686	24,563	10,831	19,315	22,800	23,148
Nevada.................	11,885	22,838	26,302	31,493	11,230	23,856	24,327	26,098
New Hampshire..........	6,948	11,581	12,703	14,111	6,222	11,439	12,251	12,650
New Jersey.............	62,331	99,751	103,802	116,473	54,590	102,667	109,939	110,723
New Mexico.............	13,073	21,998	23,439	26,067	11,195	22,372	25,011	24,619
New York...............	188,907	313,781	326,701	379,650	171,858	295,467	331,888	347,869
North Carolina.........	50,542	86,699	92,594	103,562	46,135	79,955	90,475	92,403
North Dakota...........	4,495	7,890	9,950	10,695	4,041	6,746	10,703	10,848
Ohio...................	80,074	123,289	117,027	139,066	68,418	113,844	125,103	129,596
Oklahoma...............	18,760	32,939	32,752	37,451	15,962	31,338	34,391	34,675
Oregon.................	28,644	41,031	47,936	58,101	24,086	39,506	51,888	53,489
Pennsylvania...........	80,546	124,379	134,707	149,030	75,624	130,085	143,821	151,256
Rhode Island...........	7,427	11,726	12,297	13,182	6,432	11,303	12,530	12,842
South Carolina.........	23,467	42,509	46,702	52,864	23,436	42,800	47,428	50,420
South Dakota...........	4,277	6,941	7,345	9,092	3,760	6,845	7,968	8,027
Tennessee..............	33,625	54,297	56,601	62,818	32,010	53,554	57,765	59,367
Texas..................	120,666	209,930	247,566	276,479	109,634	218,807	251,602	263,778
Utah...................	14,954	24,149	27,789	32,102	13,044	24,552	28,056	30,344
Vermont................	4,019	7,016	7,809	8,222	3,766	6,781	7,979	8,116
Virginia...............	44,175	71,093	79,075	91,759	38,092	67,673	80,899	84,056
Washington.............	46,372	71,623	85,279	100,498	41,794	75,167	86,684	91,739
West Virginia..........	10,760	16,993	16,985	19,813	9,990	15,685	18,367	18,458
Wisconsin..............	43,003	66,291	53,991	64,159	34,559	55,839	59,453	62,325
Wyoming................	7,030	10,176	9,767	10,102	3,743	8,720	10,332	10,183

Source: U.S. Census Bureau, Federal, State, and Local Governments, Government Finance Statistics, "Annual Surveys of State and Local Government Finances," <census.gov/programs-surveys/gov-finances.html>, accessed June 2020.

Table 489. State and Local Governments—Revenue by State: 2017

[In millions of dollars (3,918,843 represents $3,918,843,000,000). For fiscal year ending in year shown; see text, this section]

State	Total revenue	General revenue: Total	Intergovernmental from federal government: Total	General revenue from own sources	Select taxes: Total¹	Property	Sales and gross receipt	Individual income	Corporation income	Current charges and miscellaneous revenue: Total	Current charges: Total¹	Education	Hospitals	Sewerage	Miscellaneous revenue: Total¹	Interest earnings	Special assessments	Utility and liquor stores	Insurance trust revenue
U.S.	3,918,843	3,118,686	710,076	2,408,610	1,652,829	525,920	580,355	384,578	52,739	755,781	525,936	134,574	160,050	58,065	229,845	51,472	9,885	178,031	622,126
AL	49,900	40,007	10,970	29,038	16,428	2,837	8,060	3,749	520	12,610	10,386	2,997	5,502	563	2,225	334	27	3,454	6,438
AK	14,287	11,630	3,518	8,112	3,029	1,568	615	–	88	5,083	1,632	227	397	108	3,451	1,036	7	428	2,229
AZ	67,173	52,634	15,822	36,812	25,832	7,748	12,612	4,132	368	10,979	6,988	3,119	693	934	3,991	1,133	48	5,023	9,516
AR	31,281	25,596	8,149	17,447	12,027	2,228	6,080	2,768	397	5,420	3,768	1,188	1,374	331	1,652	275	28	999	4,686
CA	615,808	453,986	100,799	353,187	243,142	63,306	71,605	84,197	10,113	110,045	85,527	13,327	27,250	8,398	24,518	4,494	2,481	29,569	132,253
CO	62,002	51,879	9,866	42,013	27,529	8,669	10,259	6,792	529	14,484	10,213	3,538	2,226	1,040	4,272	994	385	3,047	7,076
CT	49,519	41,244	8,098	33,146	27,638	10,792	6,991	7,959	897	5,508	3,417	1,484	429	420	2,091	697	33	823	7,452
DE	11,971	10,179	2,455	7,725	4,676	883	573	1,181	246	3,048	1,507	676	6	171	1,542	111	26	490	1,301
DC	15,031	13,023	4,007	9,016	7,456	2,432	1,814	1,958	554	1,560	838	43	135	322	722	72	–	969	1,039
FL	192,144	156,410	29,987	126,424	77,736	27,898	40,368	–	2,384	48,688	32,176	4,811	8,392	3,583	16,511	1,892	2,827	9,594	26,140
GA	91,081	72,739	16,327	56,411	38,941	12,090	13,693	10,978	972	17,470	13,012	3,114	4,093	1,933	4,459	526	81	4,779	13,564
HI	20,330	17,232	3,099	14,133	9,457	1,760	4,790	2,096	185	4,676	2,697	443	686	528	1,978	135	41	431	2,667
ID	15,535	12,209	2,775	9,434	6,366	1,749	2,283	1,660	217	3,068	2,260	516	501	253	808	166	30	406	2,920
IL	148,648	119,096	23,182	95,915	73,702	28,625	24,840	13,257	2,877	22,213	14,059	4,457	1,811	1,424	8,154	2,042	519	5,343	24,209
IN	62,854	55,568	15,104	40,464	26,048	6,935	11,140	6,056	1,026	14,415	10,859	3,788	4,208	1,836	3,556	1,003	68	2,794	4,493
IA	41,261	34,397	6,149	28,249	15,693	5,132	5,214	3,759	432	12,555	7,451	2,082	3,796	591	5,104	2,785	22	1,499	5,365
KS	32,015	26,727	4,413	22,315	13,485	4,482	5,669	2,329	387	8,830	6,543	1,636	3,323	479	2,286	489	126	1,629	3,659
KY	45,191	37,456	12,171	25,286	17,343	3,702	6,368	5,849	639	7,943	6,355	1,743	2,585	671	1,588	289	18	1,820	5,914
LA	52,285	42,128	13,009	29,118	19,979	4,211	11,548	2,950	291	9,139	6,125	1,679	2,271	481	3,014	596	11	1,195	8,962
ME	14,432	12,234	3,057	9,177	7,079	2,855	2,172	1,535	175	2,098	1,508	379	135	197	590	164	7	157	2,041
MD	73,282	63,163	14,041	49,121	37,964	9,778	10,201	14,402	1,002	11,157	7,527	2,678	181	1,342	3,630	605	86	1,440	8,680
MA	95,392	77,468	17,187	60,281	45,061	16,714	9,229	14,724	2,196	15,220	8,936	3,130	357	1,733	6,284	1,198	10	3,948	13,976
MI	106,961	88,569	22,840	65,729	41,757	14,069	13,968	10,030	1,195	23,972	17,380	6,219	5,001	1,872	6,591	1,443	178	3,759	14,634
MN	73,381	58,576	11,762	46,814	34,391	8,902	11,044	10,956	1,227	12,423	8,379	2,536	1,868	1,068	4,044	797	349	2,710	12,095
MS	32,785	26,650	8,536	18,114	10,937	3,039	5,063	1,799	408	7,177	5,916	1,355	3,589	295	1,261	163	8	1,176	4,960
MO	61,103	47,601	11,982	35,619	23,340	6,348	8,822	6,554	383	12,280	8,313	2,592	2,999	1,103	3,967	968	101	2,768	10,734
MT	11,839	9,238	3,277	5,962	4,105	1,672	590	1,178	125	1,857	1,176	515	85	128	681	232	78	250	2,351
NE	24,563	17,712	3,456	14,256	9,817	3,754	2,901	2,228	264	4,440	3,137	1,047	808	306	1,303	265	32	4,360	2,491
NV	31,493	23,790	5,577	18,213	13,434	3,007	8,614	–	–	4,779	3,370	572	710	500	1,409	229	71	1,294	6,409
NH	14,111	11,636	2,434	9,202	6,703	4,464	962	65	574	2,500	1,497	667	7	155	1,003	380	5	823	1,652
NJ	116,473	100,039	18,159	81,880	62,801	29,118	14,339	13,958	2,110	19,079	11,571	3,952	1,232	1,719	7,508	1,315	6	2,258	14,175
NM	26,067	21,145	7,413	13,732	8,482	1,658	4,275	1,339	92	5,249	2,761	695	1,191	205	2,489	801	15	628	4,295
NY	379,650	296,667	66,871	229,796	177,751	56,853	44,119	56,372	10,586	52,045	32,516	4,367	10,492	2,911	19,529	4,861	141	15,570	67,412

See footnotes at end of table.

Table 489. State and Local Governments—Revenue by State: 2017 -Continued.

See headnote on page 310.

State	Total revenue	Intergovern- mental from federal govern- ment — Total	General revenue from own sources	General revenue from own sources — Select taxes — Total [1]	Property	Sales and gross receipt	Indi- vidual income	Corpo- ration income	Current charges and miscellaneous revenue — Total	Current charges — Total [1]	Educa- tion	Hospi- tals	Sewer- age	Miscellaneous revenue — Total [1]	Interest earnings	Special assess- ments	Utility and liquor stores	Insur- ance trust revenue
NC...	103,562	20,517	64,558	40,686	10,005	15,029	12,086	757	23,872	18,663	4,091	9,936	1,486	5,209	899	21	5,178	13,309
ND...	10,695	1,945	7,148	5,033	1,249	1,616	320	61	2,115	1,211	513	5	71	903	357	126	253	1,349
OH...	139,066	25,985	80,650	54,009	15,346	21,452	14,082	217	26,641	17,965	6,372	5,370	2,423	8,676	1,628	308	4,223	28,208
OK...	37,451	7,654	22,510	13,889	2,872	6,113	3,123	158	8,621	5,540	2,371	1,253	446	3,081	440	43	2,011	5,276
OR...	58,101	10,772	32,850	19,543	6,166	2,102	8,379	717	13,307	9,470	2,150	2,483	1,191	3,836	745	97	2,256	12,224
PA...	149,030	32,136	93,275	66,521	19,544	21,594	17,124	2,762	26,754	19,641	6,712	3,967	2,815	7,113	1,714	112	4,975	18,644
RI...	13,182	2,890	8,350	5,879	2,543	1,722	1,239	130	2,471	1,425	496	7	234	1,047	370	5	244	1,699
SC...	52,864	9,899	32,918	17,685	6,032	5,485	4,142	376	15,233	12,000	2,639	6,724	673	3,233	527	64	3,929	6,118
SD...	9,092	1,663	5,303	3,720	1,415	1,923	–	31	1,582	937	405	88	108	645	245	17	372	1,754
TN...	62,818	11,917	34,501	22,873	5,881	12,766	250	1,726	11,628	8,186	2,166	3,049	947	3,443	496	159	9,046	7,354
TX...	276,479	45,876	176,679	117,852	53,017	57,021	–	–	58,827	38,520	10,333	13,043	3,876	20,307	6,792	456	14,479	39,446
UT...	32,102	5,026	21,087	12,609	3,220	4,947	3,621	330	8,478	6,550	2,015	2,530	408	1,928	485	43	2,508	3,480
VT...	8,222	2,044	5,082	3,805	1,667	1,084	744	111	1,277	911	599	–	81	366	110	4	312	785
VA...	91,759	11,793	62,154	40,600	13,987	9,936	13,053	827	21,554	15,849	4,918	5,119	1,715	5,706	1,113	57	2,816	14,997
WA...	100,498	15,684	61,393	39,663	11,122	24,586	–	–	21,730	16,456	3,395	4,775	2,604	5,273	1,103	416	7,044	16,377
WV...	19,813	5,124	11,179	7,186	1,722	2,797	1,814	116	3,993	2,655	940	400	315	1,338	359	15	367	3,144
WI...	64,159	9,939	40,982	28,329	9,586	8,477	7,793	960	12,653	8,447	2,695	1,860	991	4,206	872	69	2,218	11,021
WY...	10,102	2,725	5,853	2,817	1,267	884	–	–	3,036	1,711	192	1,112	79	1,324	726	10	369	1,155

– Represents or rounds to zero. [1] Includes items not shown separately.

Source: U.S. Census Bureau, Federal, State, and Local Governments, Government Finance Statistics, "Annual Surveys of State and Local Government Finances," <census.gov/programs-surveys/gov-finances.html>, accessed June 2020.

Table 490. State and Local Governments—Expenditures and Debt by State: 2017

[In millions of dollars (3,663,342 represents $3,663,342,000,000). For fiscal year ending in year shown; see text, this section]

State	Total expenditures	General expenditures Total [1]	Direct general expenditures Total [1]	Education	Public welfare	Health	Hospitals	Highways	Police protection	Corrections	Natural resources	Parks and recreation	Housing and community development	Sewerage	Solid waste	Governmental administration	Interest on general debt	Utility and liquor store expenditures	Insurance trust expenditures	Total debt outstanding
U.S...	3,663,342	3,074,446	3,071,187	1,010,131	678,238	99,827	191,135	181,990	114,503	78,733	31,773	45,264	52,401	56,555	25,191	144,245	106,323	239,954	348,942	3,068,056
AL.....	48,700	41,515	41,515	14,067	8,484	841	6,311	2,533	1,274	730	289	528	566	420	292	1,556	1,011	3,460	3,725	29,986
AK.....	14,931	12,723	12,723	3,279	2,577	224	456	1,413	365	323	369	129	298	125	116	931	306	802	1,406	9,470
AZ.....	58,536	48,201	48,201	15,107	14,505	802	789	2,517	2,502	1,657	477	747	453	779	459	2,465	1,528	5,553	4,782	47,064
AR.....	27,714	24,703	24,703	8,310	7,438	248	1,284	2,075	671	511	354	276	201	314	230	1,131	502	980	2,031	18,558
CA.....	566,781	458,355	455,469	131,236	111,893	22,985	29,617	15,532	19,170	14,614	6,926	6,467	8,671	9,144	3,343	22,042	17,431	43,780	64,646	463,442
CO.....	60,836	50,317	50,315	17,409	8,352	844	2,789	3,269	1,855	1,359	550	1,525	1,108	1,021	135	3,104	2,037	4,512	6,007	57,355
CT.....	40,974	33,914	33,914	13,481	3,817	1,062	1,437	2,276	1,178	622	215	252	788	639	263	2,052	1,933	1,421	5,639	49,993
DE.....	12,015	10,689	10,688	3,984	2,509	490	83	840	379	328	88	85	160	193	85	677	288	540	787	7,563
DC.....	18,555	13,255	13,255	2,907	3,930	397	264	455	633	157	83	259	767	554	127	729	588	4,731	569	14,901
FL.....	177,052	154,092	154,092	42,787	28,081	5,511	9,759	11,271	8,509	4,556	3,887	3,301	2,315	3,788	2,607	7,052	3,979	10,982	11,979	136,280
GA.....	85,131	71,554	71,554	28,063	12,158	2,286	4,776	4,353	2,729	2,120	573	1,384	1,132	1,255	672	3,775	1,496	6,053	7,524	57,807
HI.....	16,783	14,006	14,006	3,410	3,086	593	618	603	482	229	157	362	264	399	266	916	349	1,288	1,489	15,999
ID.....	13,178	11,630	11,630	3,563	2,522	263	670	884	454	416	330	196	157	228	173	754	236	393	1,154	6,052
IL.....	146,853	117,235	117,229	37,803	22,676	2,046	3,209	9,347	5,283	2,107	683	3,116	2,105	1,648	623	6,181	6,961	8,440	21,178	154,921
IN.....	58,656	53,024	53,022	17,820	13,944	808	4,479	2,444	1,333	1,061	510	475	816	822	236	2,112	1,845	2,650	2,983	46,701
IA.....	35,148	31,010	31,010	11,067	5,650	444	3,890	2,749	813	436	479	352	257	538	278	1,179	607	1,503	2,634	19,379
KS.....	30,554	26,928	26,928	9,811	4,139	652	3,587	1,923	862	542	285	380	268	436	162	1,184	844	1,598	2,027	27,172
KY.....	46,103	39,402	39,402	12,876	11,446	908	2,498	2,355	829	949	427	375	459	684	233	1,828	1,352	2,059	4,641	43,918
LA.....	48,980	42,713	42,713	12,351	11,309	636	2,624	2,405	1,645	987	1,075	762	658	654	363	2,090	1,447	1,375	4,892	36,259
ME.....	12,826	11,619	11,619	3,549	3,196	245	212	988	310	260	147	96	287	218	116	600	271	180	1,028	7,856
MD.....	69,639	60,525	60,525	20,807	13,202	1,573	592	3,371	2,669	1,936	576	1,312	1,527	1,300	931	2,962	1,908	3,272	5,841	54,514
MA.....	92,836	77,591	77,578	23,162	22,249	1,572	1,578	3,829	2,585	953	248	504	2,721	1,426	400	3,672	3,071	6,323	8,922	96,817
MI.....	98,798	85,086	85,081	30,736	17,089	4,145	5,293	4,281	2,547	2,484	427	1,398	1,063	2,493	516	3,345	2,814	3,864	9,847	72,318
MN.....	68,335	59,022	59,022	19,717	14,917	1,266	1,995	4,810	1,980	1,059	871	1,303	1,099	1,032	376	2,667	1,651	3,617	5,696	53,009
MS.....	30,035	26,154	26,154	8,180	6,369	391	3,971	1,729	767	517	305	228	302	283	185	1,047	552	1,135	2,746	14,562
MO.....	55,536	47,193	47,162	15,328	9,415	2,395	4,170	2,368	1,809	946	435	735	703	1,217	152	1,990	1,604	2,815	5,528	47,104
MT.....	10,828	9,443	9,443	2,942	2,234	364	157	845	315	258	332	109	89	142	88	650	179	306	1,079	5,324
NE.....	23,148	17,649	17,597	7,325	2,828	330	1,021	1,574	498	493	326	246	232	255	100	759	368	4,381	1,119	15,888
NV.....	26,098	21,949	21,947	6,676	3,915	410	1,062	2,030	1,269	771	306	591	288	465	31	1,368	772	1,542	2,606	27,357
NH.....	12,650	11,098	11,098	4,160	2,437	116	62	757	420	226	65	109	217	162	127	620	431	740	812	10,410
NJ.....	110,723	93,185	93,169	36,871	17,694	3,140	2,319	4,990	3,562	2,138	493	736	1,465	1,723	925	3,851	3,326	3,958	13,580	96,990
NM.....	24,619	21,367	21,367	6,814	6,042	456	1,371	904	706	718	348	329	132	235	232	1,074	531	857	2,396	15,806
NY.....	347,869	281,743	281,743	85,161	70,353	6,996	17,077	12,220	10,381	6,523	664	3,095	6,571	3,571	3,009	10,792	13,971	30,747	35,379	356,836

See footnotes at end of table.

Table 490. State and Local Governments—Expenditures and Debt by State: 2017-Continued.

See headnote on page 312.

State	Total expenditures	General expenditures Total[1]	Direct general expenditures Total[1]	Education	Public welfare	Health	Hospitals	Highways	Police protection	Corrections	Natural resources	Parks and recreation	Housing and community development	Sewerage	Solid waste	Governmental administration	Interest on general debt	Utility and liquor store expenditures	Insurance trust expenditures	Total debt outstanding
NC....	92,403	80,603	80,603	27,126	15,124	3,841	10,004	4,867	3,212	1,947	633	1,108	1,597	977	750	3,496	1,903	5,581	6,219	47,296
ND....	10,848	9,698	9,698	3,044	1,536	219	54	1,734	232	224	276	366	83	102	71	407	185	450	700	7,993
OH....	129,596	107,335	107,318	35,724	28,696	3,538	5,079	6,065	3,812	2,025	417	1,519	1,995	2,332	494	5,696	2,924	4,769	17,491	87,814
OK....	34,675	29,389	29,331	10,474	6,774	1,030	1,257	2,596	1,046	746	181	514	513	331	230	1,344	531	2,516	2,771	18,715
OR....	53,489	44,814	44,814	13,631	10,494	1,663	2,687	2,122	1,372	1,309	579	735	707	941	161	2,674	1,163	2,959	5,716	36,681
PA....	151,256	129,331	129,206	43,396	34,281	5,584	4,426	9,786	3,868	3,744	797	1,051	2,092	2,545	952	6,329	4,200	6,801	15,124	122,532
RI.....	12,842	10,903	10,884	3,451	3,100	236	62	473	454	210	80	84	267	178	103	687	543	359	1,581	11,512
SC....	50,420	43,253	43,253	15,061	7,983	1,401	6,739	2,293	1,313	734	273	584	485	689	389	1,809	880	3,473	3,694	38,656
SD....	8,027	7,066	7,066	2,424	1,159	199	132	1,003	210	187	206	171	105	118	51	396	183	358	603	6,247
TN....	59,367	46,413	46,413	14,513	11,710	1,042	3,774	2,239	1,979	1,095	418	657	827	818	432	2,649	980	9,532	3,422	42,564
TX....	263,778	226,090	226,090	89,473	38,160	6,239	18,620	15,696	8,195	6,383	1,463	2,680	1,995	3,999	1,489	8,559	9,115	17,166	20,522	289,687
UT....	30,344	26,000	26,000	9,949	3,915	618	2,262	1,829	743	558	291	500	374	304	177	1,738	493	2,458	1,886	20,967
VT....	8,116	7,353	7,353	2,839	1,847	375	24	623	219	152	114	63	160	74	36	316	131	342	420	4,754
VA....	84,056	73,689	73,689	26,959	12,028	2,284	5,281	4,927	2,522	2,621	456	1,119	1,082	1,589	643	3,735	2,292	4,258	6,108	65,941
WA....	91,739	74,531	74,531	24,596	12,389	3,802	6,679	4,392	2,056	1,731	1,202	1,305	1,471	1,937	765	3,131	2,883	9,717	7,491	88,557
WV....	18,458	16,375	16,375	5,394	5,021	292	476	1,228	395	354	238	208	129	314	86	890	297	453	1,630	12,235
WI....	62,325	53,799	53,799	18,251	12,700	1,576	2,433	5,496	1,862	1,525	656	695	363	1,060	406	2,522	1,383	2,469	6,058	46,318
WY....	10,183	8,912	8,889	3,066	864	447	1,130	679	224	204	194	143	19	83	108	709	51	434	838	1,978

[1] Includes items not shown separately.

Source: U.S. Census Bureau, Federal, State, and Local Governments, Government Finance Statistics, "Annual Surveys of State and Local Government Finances," <https://www.census.gov/programs-surveys/gov-finances.html>, accessed June 2020.

Table 491. Estimated State and Local Taxes Paid by a Family of Three for Largest City in Selected States: 2018

[Data based on average family of three (two wage earners and one school age child) owning their own home and living in a city where taxes apply. Comprises state and local sales, income, auto, and real estate taxes. Negative number indicates the family would receive a net refund. For definition of median, see Guide to Tabular Presentation]

City	Total taxes paid by gross family income level (dollars)					Total taxes paid as percent of income				
	$25,000	$50,000	$75,000	$100,000	$150,000	$25,000	$50,000	$75,000	$100,000	$150,000
Albuquerque, NM.......	1,923	4,236	7,040	9,616	14,750	7.7	8.5	9.4	6.4	9.8
Atlanta, GA.............	3,480	5,121	8,386	11,316	16,033	13.9	10.2	11.2	7.5	10.7
Baltimore, MD.........	2,188	7,046	11,138	13,645	20,462	8.8	14.1	14.9	9.1	13.6
Boston, MA.............	3,250	4,764	7,432	9,809	15,398	13.0	9.5	9.9	6.5	10.3
Charlotte, NC...........	3,072	4,460	7,245	9,574	14,332	12.3	8.9	9.7	6.4	9.6
Chicago, IL.............	3,621	5,638	8,831	11,604	16,877	14.5	11.3	11.8	7.7	11.3
Columbus, OH.........	2,898	5,376	8,310	11,047	16,862	11.6	10.8	11.1	7.4	11.2
Denver, CO.............	2,829	3,805	6,141	8,195	12,825	11.3	7.6	8.2	5.5	8.5
Detroit, MI..............	3,101	6,114	10,727	14,135	21,099	12.4	12.2	14.3	9.4	14.1
Honolulu, HI............	3,779	3,476	5,861	8,022	12,221	15.1	7.0	7.8	5.3	8.1
Houston, TX............	2,589	3,297	4,889	6,256	8,918	10.4	6.6	6.5	4.2	5.9
Indianapolis, IN.........	3,369	4,774	8,113	10,752	16,307	13.5	9.5	10.8	7.2	10.9
Jacksonville, FL........	2,259	2,665	4,421	5,917	8,757	9.0	5.3	5.9	3.9	5.8
Kansas City, MO.......	3,174	5,284	8,703	11,408	17,657	12.7	10.6	11.6	7.6	11.8
Las Vegas, NV.........	2,584	3,554	5,301	6,648	9,694	10.3	7.1	7.1	4.4	6.5
Los Angeles, CA.......	3,691	5,124	8,229	11,208	18,093	14.8	10.2	11.0	7.5	12.1
Louisville, KY..........	3,316	5,775	8,689	11,326	16,707	13.3	11.6	11.6	7.6	11.1
Milwaukee, WI.........	2,052	5,784	9,790	13,244	19,788	8.2	11.6	13.1	8.8	13.2
Minneapolis, MN.......	-311	3,761	6,783	9,589	14,816	-1.2	7.5	9.0	6.4	9.9
Nashville, TN..........	3,067	3,133	4,453	5,447	7,358	12.3	6.3	5.9	3.6	4.9
New Orleans, LA.......	3,123	3,848	6,280	8,480	13,155	12.5	7.7	8.4	5.7	8.8
New York, NY..........	3,260	4,922	8,785	11,981	19,052	13.0	9.8	11.7	8.0	12.7
Oklahoma City, OK.....	2,525	4,027	6,535	8,686	13,134	10.1	8.1	8.7	5.8	8.8
Philadelphia, PA.......	4,533	6,129	9,341	12,180	17,660	18.1	12.3	12.5	8.1	11.8
Phoenix, AZ............	2,736	4,432	6,660	8,715	13,147	10.9	8.9	8.9	5.8	8.8
Portland, OR............	2,995	5,039	8,138	11,090	17,360	12.0	10.1	10.9	7.4	11.6
Seattle, WA............	4,330	3,814	5,654	6,970	9,758	17.3	7.6	7.5	4.6	6.5
Virginia Beach, VA.....	2,952	4,721	7,588	9,916	13,957	11.8	9.4	10.1	6.6	9.3
Washington, DC........	1,711	3,303	6,062	8,962	14,981	6.8	6.6	8.1	6.0	10.0
Wichita, KS.............	2,436	4,168	6,998	9,334	14,467	9.7	8.3	9.3	6.2	9.6
Average [1]...........	**2,626**	**4,459**	**7,238**	**9,654**	**14,817**	**10.5**	**8.9**	**9.7**	**6.4**	**9.9**
Median [1].............	**2,712**	**4,432**	**7,026**	**9,625**	**15,015**	**10.8**	**8.9**	**9.4**	**6.4**	**10.0**

[1] Based on selected cities and District of Columbia. For complete list of cities, see Table 492.

Source: Government of the District of Columbia, Office of the Chief Financial Officer, *Tax Rates and Tax Burdens in the District of Columbia – A Nationwide Comparison 2018*, March 2020, and earlier reports. See also <http://cfo.dc.gov/>.

Table 492. Residential Property Tax Rates for Largest City in Each State: 2018

[The real property tax is a function of housing values, real estate tax rates, assessment levels, and homeowner exemptions and credits. Effective rate is the amount each jurisdiction considers based upon assessment level used. Assessment level is ratio of assessed value to assumed market value. Nominal rates represent the "announced" rates levied by the jurisdiction]

City	Effective tax rate per $100		Assessment level (percent)	Nominal rate per $100	City	Effective tax rate per $100		Assessment level (percent)	Nominal rate per $100
	Rank	Rate				Rank	Rate		
Detroit, MI..............	1	3.58	50.0	7.17	Sioux Falls, SD..........	28	1.29	78.5	1.65
Bridgeport, CT.........	2	3.24	59.5	5.44	Louisville, KY..........	29	1.26	100.0	1.26
Indianapolis, IN........	3	3.11	100.0	3.11	Oklahoma City, OK......	30	1.25	11.0	11.34
Newark, NJ.............	4	2.97	80.4	3.69	Minneapolis, MN.........	31	1.24	94.2	1.32
Milwaukee, WI.........	5	2.95	100.0	[1] 2.95	Wichita, KS.............	32	1.22	10.4	11.72
Des Moines, IA.........	6	2.53	52.8	4.78	Los Angeles, CA.........	33	1.20	100.0	1.20
Houston, TX............	7	2.50	99.0	2.53	Fargo, ND.............	34	1.18	4.1	28.86
Baltimore, MD..........	8	2.23	94.4	2.36	Charleston, SC..........	35	1.18	4.0	29.46
Burlington, VT..........	9	2.15	79.9	2.68	Las Vegas, NV..........	36	1.14	34.8	3.28
Manchester, NH........	10	2.10	90.2	2.33	Portland, OR............	37	1.10	49.0	2.25
Omaha, NE.............	11	2.08	93.0	2.24	Charlotte, NC...........	38	1.01	74.7	1.35
Portland, ME...........	12	2.04	94.0	2.17	Cheyenne, WY..........	39	0.97	9.5	10.25
Chicago, IL.............	13	1.98	[2] 10.0	6.79	Billings, MT..............	40	0.96	1.4	71.43
Columbus, OH.........	14	1.92	28.1	6.82	Boston, MA..............	41	0.96	91.0	1.05
Jackson, MS...........	15	1.89	10.0	18.93	Seattle, WA.............	42	0.94	92.1	1.02
Providence, RI..........	16	1.88	100.0	1.88	Virginia Beach, VA.......	43	0.90	89.8	1.00
Jacksonville, FL........	17	1.81	100.0	1.81	Nashville, TN............	44	0.86	21.2	4.05
Atlanta, GA............	18	1.76	39.4	4.46	Charleston, WV..........	45	0.86	60.0	1.43
Wilmington, DE.........	19	1.66	29.6	5.60	Washington, DC.........	46	0.83	97.4	0.85
Albuquerque, NM.......	20	1.59	33.3	4.77	New York City, NY.......	47	0.79	3.9	20.31
New Orleans, LA.......	21	1.51	10.0	15.10	Salt Lake City, UT.......	48	0.73	55.0	1.33
Anchorage, AK.........	22	1.46	89.0	1.64	Birmingham, AL.........	49	0.86	10.0	6.61
Boise, ID...............	23	1.44	94.0	1.53	Denver, CO.............	50	0.59	7.2	8.22
Phoenix, AZ............	24	1.42	10.0	14.16	Honolulu, HI..............	51	0.35	100.0	0.35
Little Rock, AR.........	25	1.40	20.0	7.00					
Kansas City, MO.......	26	1.38	16.9	8.13	**Unweighted average...**	**(X)**	**1.56**	**56.1**	**7.12**
Philadelphia, PA........	27	1.31	93.6	1.40	**Median.................**	**(X)**	**1.38**	**57.3**	**3.11**

X Not applicable. [1] For Milwaukee, WI, the nominal tax rate takes the assessment sales ratio statistic into account. [2] For Chicago, IL, the state equalizer of 2.9 percent was applied to the assessment level of 10 percent to reflect the equalizer's impact on the final rate.

Source: Government of the District of Columbia, Office of the Chief Financial Officer, *Tax Rates and Tax Burdens in the District of Columbia—A Nationwide Comparison 2018*, March 2020. See also <https://cfo.dc.gov/>.

Table 493. Gross Revenue From Parimutuel and Amusement Taxes and Lotteries by State: 2016 to 2018

[In millions of dollars (79,965.8 represents $79,965,800,000). For fiscal years; see text, this section]

State	2016, total gross revenue	2017, total gross revenue	2018 Total gross revenue	2018 Amuse-ment taxes [1]	2018 Pari-mutuel taxes [2]	Lottery revenue Total [3]	Apportionment of funds Prizes	Apportionment of funds Adminis-tration	Apportionment of funds Proceeds available from ticket sales
United States..........	79,965.8	79,774.4	84,659.0	8,169.0	127.4	76,362.6	49,303.4	3,444.6	23,614.6
Alabama.................	1.2	1.2	1.1	–	1.1	(X)	(X)	(X)	(X)
Alaska...................	10.3	10.7	11.0	11.0	(X)	(X)	(X)	(X)	(X)
Arizona..................	815.8	799.0	918.3	3.6	0.2	914.5	647.7	51.2	215.7
Arkansas................	488.5	486.7	538.4	64.6	2.3	471.5	341.9	39.1	90.5
California...............	6,290.1	6,248.2	6,981.7	(X)	15.9	6,965.8	4,476.6	370.9	2,118.3
Colorado................	667.5	632.5	691.1	124.7	0.5	565.9	383.5	42.1	140.3
Connecticut............	1,473.2	1,451.1	1,503.1	300.7	5.6	1,196.8	792.6	57.2	347.0
Delaware...............	400.7	460.2	444.0	(X)	0.1	443.9	136.5	89.6	217.8
Florida..................	5,941.3	6,034.4	6,549.9	207.5	8.4	6,334.1	4,394.4	175.6	1,764.0
Georgia.................	4,028.4	4,016.4	4,089.8	(X)	(X)	4,089.8	2,768.5	176.2	1,145.1
Hawaii..................	–	–	–	(X)	(X)	(X)	(X)	(X)	(X)
Idaho...................	221.6	222.1	225.2	(X)	0.9	224.3	176.2	13.6	34.6
Illinois..................	3,649.5	3,685.5	3,821.0	888.3	6.4	2,926.4	1,910.9	363.3	652.2
Indiana.................	1,732.2	1,730.3	1,787.6	602.4	1.8	1,183.4	797.3	67.8	318.4
Iowa....................	668.6	655.9	678.1	303.4	3.8	371.0	227.5	57.8	85.7
Kansas..................	256.3	243.0	253.4	0.3	(X)	253.1	157.9	26.7	68.5
Kentucky................	926.5	932.1	982.0	0.2	7.7	974.1	657.4	48.4	268.3
Louisiana...............	1,185.8	1,132.4	1,177.1	708.5	5.2	463.5	263.6	27.7	172.1
Maine...................	309.2	304.2	334.9	56.3	1.4	277.2	194.1	33.2	49.9
Maryland................	2,557.0	2,780.2	3,066.3	1,022.4	1.2	2,042.8	1,248.7	91.3	702.8
Massachusetts..........	5,302.1	5,153.6	5,350.3	70.5	0.9	5,279.0	3,891.6	100.3	1,287.1
Michigan...............	2,935.2	3,135.5	3,362.2	115.4	2.9	3,243.9	2,237.0	101.0	905.9
Minnesota..............	614.1	594.4	637.4	75.6	1.2	560.6	387.0	31.8	141.7
Mississippi.............	133.8	132.9	129.9	129.9	(X)	(X)	(X)	(X)	(X)
Missouri................	1,660.1	1,631.0	1,710.9	369.4	(X)	1,341.5	862.1	62.1	417.3
Montana................	115.9	123.4	120.2	60.3	–	59.7	32.6	10.0	17.1
Nebraska...............	174.0	168.6	201.2	5.8	0.1	195.2	106.6	20.0	68.6
Nevada.................	930.0	919.6	915.5	915.5	–	(X)	(X)	(X)	(X)
New Hampshire.........	291.6	288.2	338.9	0.5	0.5	337.8	211.5	19.0	107.3
New Jersey..............	3,313.3	3,223.7	3,329.1	217.7	(X)	3,111.3	1,939.2	73.2	1,098.9
New Mexico.............	228.6	187.5	198.0	63.1	0.8	134.0	73.1	20.1	40.8
New York...............	8,365.0	8,349.5	8,609.4	2.8	21.3	8,585.2	4,815.9	384.9	3,384.4
North Carolina..........	2,217.2	2,258.6	2,423.8	0.1	(X)	2,423.7	1,647.5	64.2	712.1
North Dakota...........	38.9	31.3	27.7	3.1	1.5	23.1	17.3	4.7	1.1
Ohio....................	3,145.9	3,083.4	3,229.7	270.5	5.2	2,954.0	1,998.7	81.3	874.1
Oklahoma...............	211.7	173.3	248.6	26.4	1.1	221.1	129.6	31.0	60.5
Oregon..................	957.2	1,009.3	1,059.1	(X)	1.9	1,057.2	231.7	102.5	723.0
Pennsylvania............	5,271.8	5,138.2	5,338.4	1,429.6	10.2	3,898.6	2,733.8	85.6	1,079.1
Rhode Island............	543.3	531.9	539.7	(X)	1.1	538.6	162.1	11.5	364.9
South Carolina..........	1,524.1	1,559.1	1,666.5	39.8	(X)	1,626.7	1,149.8	42.4	434.5
South Dakota...........	165.7	161.8	174.7	9.1	0.2	165.4	33.7	8.2	123.5
Tennessee..............	1,375.7	1,360.9	1,471.2	(X)	(X)	1,471.2	1,023.9	30.2	417.1
Texas...................	4,830.9	4,837.2	5,357.7	30.0	6.5	5,321.1	3,666.1	189.9	1,465.1
Utah....................	–	–	–	(X)	(X)	(X)	(X)	(X)	(X)
Vermont................	116.5	114.9	124.3	(X)	(X)	124.3	87.4	10.0	26.9
Virginia.................	1,894.3	1,878.0	2,018.6	0.1	(X)	2,018.5	1,307.7	102.2	608.7
Washington.............	660.7	677.9	703.2	4.4	1.7	697.0	457.9	44.0	195.1
West Virginia...........	667.9	626.8	657.6	35.2	2.7	619.8	105.2	31.8	482.8
Wisconsin..............	627.4	569.2	632.1	0.2	0.2	631.6	404.4	47.5	179.7
Wyoming................	29.0	28.5	29.2	(X)	4.7	24.5	14.8	3.5	6.3

– Represents or rounds to zero. X Not applicable. [1] Represents nonlicense taxes. [2] Represents legalized gambling taxes. [3] Excludes commissions.

Source: U.S. Census Bureau, "Annual Survey of State Government Finances," and "Annual Survey of State Government Tax Collections," <https://www.census.gov/govs/>, accessed June 2020.

Table 494. Lottery Sales—Type of Game and Proceeds: 1990 to 2019

[In millions of dollars (20,137 represents $20,137,000,000). For fiscal years]

Game	1990	2000	2005	2010	2015	2017	2018	2019
Total ticket sales......................	20,137	37,201	47,425	54,200	66,715	73,519	77,351	82,289
Instant [1]............................	5,204	15,387	26,006	30,665	41,653	46,495	48,921	51,109
Three-digit [2]........................	4,572	5,780	5,858	5,861	5,925	5,566	6,119	6,282
Four-digit [2].........................	1,302	2,273	2,869	3,419	3,865	4,601	4,175	4,376
Lotto [3].............................	8,563	9,339	9,828	10,894	10,820	11,178	12,158	14,227
Other [4].............................	497	4,423	2,864	3,362	4,452	5,678	5,979	6,295
State proceeds (net income) [5]..........	7,703	11,871	15,792	17,957	21,154	22,563	23,695	25,330

[1] Player scratches a latex section on ticket that reveals instantly whether ticket is a winner. [2] Players choose and bet on three or four digits, depending on game, with various payoffs for different straight order or mixed combination bets. [3] Players typically select six digits out of a large field of numbers. Varying prizes are offered for matching three through six numbers drawn by lottery. [4] Includes break-open tickets, spiel, keno, video lottery, etc. [5] Sales minus prizes and expenses equal net government income.

Source: TLF Publications, Inc. © 2020. All Rights Reserved.

Table 495. State Financial Resources, Expenditures, and Balances: 2018 and 2019

[In millions of dollars (2,004,219 represents $2,004,219,000,000). For fiscal year ending in year shown; see text, this section. General funds exclude special funds earmarked for particular purposes, such as highway trust funds and federal funds; they support most on-going broad-based state services, and are available for appropriation to support any governmental activity. Minus sign (-) indicates deficit]

State	Expenditures by fund source			State general fund					
	Total, 2018 actual	2019 estimated		Resources [2,3]		Expenditures [3]		Balance [4]	
		Total [1]	General fund	Federal fund	2018	2019 (P)	2018	2019 (P)	2018	2019 (P)
United States......	2,004,219	2,119,109	864,177	650,435	898,087	953,526	823,178	871,019	49,426	57,637
Alabama.............	27,262	26,697	8,481	10,165	8,900	9,910	8,307	8,775	593	798
Alaska...............	10,302	11,704	5,943	3,973	3,158	5,468	4,489	4,889	-2,151	-472
Arizona..............	37,494	38,006	10,389	15,544	10,258	11,681	9,808	10,414	450	996
Arkansas............	25,637	25,771	5,504	7,829	5,495	5,921	5,495	5,626	–	295
California.............	269,668	311,325	142,693	100,007	135,767	149,465	124,756	142,693	11,419	6,772
Colorado.............	39,814	41,638	12,533	9,781	12,437	13,967	11,215	12,828	1,366	1,140
Connecticut.........	33,152	34,061	19,244	6,318	18,199	19,650	18,685	19,279	-483	371
Delaware............	10,847	11,325	4,394	2,403	4,868	5,342	4,118	4,394	750	947
Florida..............	78,523	89,314	32,849	29,809	33,476	35,698	31,830	33,494	1,646	2,204
Georgia..............	51,394	53,537	25,401	14,426	26,863	28,376	24,134	25,404	2,729	2,972
Hawaii...............	15,199	15,619	7,915	2,528	8,554	8,667	7,804	7,915	750	752
Idaho................	7,963	9,291	3,702	3,260	3,845	3,917	3,466	3,691	239	102
Illinois..............	72,783	72,218	35,678	17,055	42,624	40,320	35,409	36,335	125	466
Indiana..............	33,621	34,279	16,208	13,777	16,289	17,116	15,736	16,280	366	835
Iowa.................	23,382	23,563	7,644	6,513	7,384	7,930	7,224	7,528	127	289
Kansas..............	15,934	17,205	7,123	4,166	7,411	8,137	6,649	7,033	762	1,104
Kentucky............	34,052	34,837	11,556	12,667	11,527	12,014	11,330	11,661	29	130
Louisiana............	31,253	34,881	9,898	14,263	10,051	10,073	9,605	9,765	308	–
Maine...............	8,411	8,812	3,658	2,797	3,595	3,936	3,515	3,708	75	139
Maryland............	43,796	46,235	17,911	13,166	17,666	18,807	17,287	17,912	590	974
Massachusetts.......	57,125	59,832	29,136	14,494	46,484	50,345	31,503	33,495	2,387	3,839
Michigan............	56,614	57,171	10,571	22,849	11,136	11,177	10,082	10,432	788	645
Minnesota...........	39,819	42,167	23,144	12,050	25,630	26,224	22,347	23,144	3,283	3,080
Mississippi..........	19,653	22,024	5,548	9,372	5,699	5,786	5,576	5,544	5	5
Missouri.............	26,038	26,402	9,536	8,490	9,762	10,195	9,267	9,541	495	654
Montana.............	6,952	7,173	2,304	2,983	2,455	2,760	2,287	2,415	187	358
Nebraska............	12,141	12,109	4,367	2,791	4,803	5,103	4,350	4,367	454	737
Nevada..............	14,263	14,758	4,404	4,888	4,554	4,870	4,018	4,426	425	336
New Hampshire......	6,131	6,234	1,505	2,313	1,596	1,696	1,504	1,505	74	192
New Jersey..........	60,775	64,811	37,349	16,695	36,723	39,361	35,733	37,721	991	1,640
New Mexico.........	20,460	20,534	6,364	8,474	7,430	9,308	6,191	7,565	1,185	1,707
New York............	163,744	170,875	72,783	60,416	79,169	79,989	69,724	72,783	9,445	7,206
North Carolina.......	49,832	51,513	23,666	14,438	24,037	25,822	22,746	23,666	995	1,709
North Dakota........	5,889	6,591	2,159	1,639	2,414	2,818	2,160	2,206	253	65
Ohio................	69,683	71,004	32,678	15,417	33,028	34,989	31,807	33,451	1,221	1,538
Oklahoma............	22,669	23,833	6,180	8,153	6,416	7,679	6,034	7,015	–	310
Oregon..............	40,619	42,641	9,613	10,835	11,245	12,895	9,773	10,172	1,471	2,532
Pennsylvania........	84,909	89,513	35,522	30,640	31,993	33,718	31,949	33,401	22	–
Rhode Island........	9,262	10,103	3,934	3,334	3,861	3,961	3,799	3,922	53	29
South Carolina.......	25,257	25,658	8,294	8,058	9,221	9,996	7,895	8,142	1,187	1,709
South Dakota........	4,457	4,491	1,638	1,449	1,616	1,674	1,591	1,638	17	19
Tennessee...........	34,190	36,909	15,693	14,164	16,044	16,087	13,828	14,939	1,140	866
Texas...............	115,208	111,756	52,054	38,331	58,966	60,332	56,050	52,281	148	4,721
Utah................	14,789	16,828	7,493	4,664	7,164	7,902	6,739	7,578	317]	291
Vermont.............	5,675	5,836	1,650	1,887	1,641	1,693	1,564	1,596	–	–
Virginia.............	52,076	55,264	21,774	11,447	20,662	21,674	20,450	21,445	212	230
Washington..........	46,021	49,530	23,643	12,111	22,464	23,709	20,448	22,908	2,016	801
West Virginia........	16,857	18,280	3,792	4,975	4,648	5,139	4,232	4,604	378	518
Wisconsin...........	48,199	50,243	17,152	11,787	17,332	18,699	17,139	17,964	589	1,087
Wyoming............	4,425	4,708	1,507	844	1,530	1,530	1,530	1,530	–	–

P Preliminary. – Represents zero. [1] Includes bonds and other state funds, not shown separately. [2] Includes funds budgeted, adjustments, and balances from previous year. [3] May or may not include budget stabilization fund transfers, depending on state accounting practices. [4] Resources less expenditures, minus adjustments.

Source: National Association of State Budget Officers, Washington, DC, *2019 State Expenditure Report: Fiscal Years 2017-2019* ©, 2019; and *Fiscal Survey of States, Fall 2019* ©, 2019. See also <nasbo.org>.

Table 496. State Governments—Summary of Finances: 2000 to 2018

[In millions of dollars (1,260,829 represents $1,260,829,000,000). For fiscal year ending in year shown; see text, this section]

Item	2000	2005	2010	2012	2013	2014	2015	2016	2017	2018
Total revenue	**1,260,829**	**1,642,468**	**2,039,927**	**1,861,834**	**2,222,646**	**2,357,406**	**2,164,784**	**2,141,692**	**2,531,288**	**2,630,991**
General revenue	984,783	1,286,899	1,567,207	1,626,072	1,695,053	1,748,172	1,860,023	1,917,520	1,975,973	2,097,939
Intergovernmental revenue	274,382	407,792	575,372	524,296	527,227	550,390	605,936	641,557	658,792	688,138
Total taxes	539,655	650,612	705,929	798,518	850,862	870,437	911,430	923,259	946,077	1,022,783
General sales and gross receipts taxes	174,461	212,921	224,314	250,756	261,709	273,899	286,023	291,902	299,574	315,930
Selective sales and gross receipts taxes	77,685	99,663	120,208	132,401	139,650	141,007	144,686	149,255	157,121	164,533
License taxes	32,598	42,584	50,429	50,111	51,035	51,318	52,053	53,909	51,489	57,176
Individual income taxes	194,573	221,597	236,987	280,590	309,881	311,562	336,558	342,376	351,526	390,003
Corporation net income taxes	32,522	38,691	38,006	41,716	44,871	46,492	48,612	45,575	44,657	47,648
All other taxes	27,815	35,155	35,985	42,943	43,716	46,159	43,498	40,241	41,709	47,494
Current charges	86,467	123,129	169,855	177,477	186,149	193,781	201,657	215,373	225,944	235,936
Miscellaneous general revenue	84,279	105,367	116,051	125,781	130,816	133,564	140,999	137,330	145,160	151,082
Utility revenue	4,513	14,628	15,122	13,636	13,582	14,317	14,721	13,828	13,608	14,019
Liquor stores revenue	3,895	5,118	6,495	7,542	7,328	7,615	8,020	7,818	8,159	8,499
Insurance trust revenue [1]	267,639	335,822	451,103	214,584	506,683	587,302	282,020	202,526	533,549	510,534
Total expenditure	**1,084,097**	**1,472,542**	**1,943,523**	**1,991,289**	**2,023,358**	**2,078,644**	**2,161,620**	**2,244,467**	**2,315,997**	**2,410,706**
Intergovernmental expenditure	**327,070**	**405,925**	**485,557**	**490,077**	**499,645**	**507,163**	**525,656**	**542,753**	**553,520**	**562,588**
Direct expenditure	757,027	1,066,617	1,457,965	1,501,212	1,523,713	1,571,481	1,635,964	1,701,714	1,762,476	1,848,118
Current operations	523,114	738,886	934,322	987,449	1,020,683	1,067,552	1,140,270	1,192,437	1,240,597	1,307,733
Capital outlay	76,233	95,155	118,011	117,740	120,029	115,874	128,561	130,532	131,635	135,313
Insurance benefits and repayments	105,456	168,000	320,721	304,902	291,295	296,189	275,454	284,865	294,845	304,533
Assistance and subsidies	22,136	28,403	37,562	42,586	44,460	45,307	45,847	47,966	49,172	52,021
Interest on debt	30,089	35,974	47,351	48,535	47,245	46,559	45,832	45,913	46,227	48,518
Exhibit: salaries and wages	154,504	194,907	244,952	237,472	241,051	248,674	253,951	260,783	271,106	279,061
General expenditure	964,723	1,278,434	1,593,694	1,656,710	1,698,088	1,751,941	1,847,037	1,926,373	1,985,929	2,067,955
Intergovernmental general expenditure	327,070	405,925	485,557	490,077	499,645	507,163	525,656	542,753	553,520	562,588
Direct general expenditure	637,653	872,508	1,108,137	1,166,633	1,198,444	1,244,778	1,321,381	1,383,619	1,432,409	1,505,367
General expenditure, by function:										
Education	346,465	454,348	571,147	591,408	604,036	613,568	644,358	669,623	686,936	705,090
Public welfare	238,890	368,765	462,431	493,117	521,763	547,809	613,061	654,770	680,404	716,795
Hospitals	32,578	43,623	64,509	68,163	66,396	71,787	73,645	79,029	85,700	90,476
Health	42,066	48,634	58,245	58,226	59,929	60,010	56,423	58,300	58,645	60,251
Highways	74,415	92,816	111,170	114,484	115,084	119,629	122,417	127,452	129,943	132,040
Police protection	9,788	11,395	13,828	13,927	14,603	15,029	15,267	15,798	16,621	17,343
Correction	35,129	40,562	48,550	48,470	48,225	49,941	51,171	51,481	51,477	53,380
Natural resources	15,967	18,822	21,515	21,101	20,679	20,777	21,572	23,714	23,656	24,336
Parks and recreation	4,676	5,334	5,720	5,592	5,353	5,496	6,060	6,276	6,613	6,658
Governmental administration	35,527	46,464	53,976	57,913	58,152	67,426	60,366	61,591	63,093	65,023
Interest on general debt	29,187	34,242	45,260	45,976	44,828	44,122	43,336	43,404	43,752	45,901
Other and unallocable	100,034	113,427	137,344	92,399	90,705	90,416	91,670	86,940	89,413	100,500
Utility expenditure	10,723	21,827	23,864	34,636	39,487	35,462	44,043	37,737	39,955	42,272
Liquor store expenditure	3,195	4,082	5,244	5,917	5,547	6,092	6,480	6,506	6,873	7,067
Insurance trust expenditure [1]	105,456	168,200	320,721	304,902	291,295	296,189	275,454	284,865	294,845	304,533
Debt outstanding, long term and short term [2]	**547,876**	**810,852**	**1,115,463**	**1,146,720**	**1,138,643**	**1,152,282**	**1,155,113**	**1,170,612**	**1,159,804**	**1,173,607**
Cash and security holdings	**2,518,936**	**3,153,795**	**3,323,047**	**2,615,089**	**2,721,689**	**2,915,718**	**2,996,239**	**3,009,115**	**3,155,565**	**3,442,075**

[1] Within insurance trust revenue, net earnings of state-administered pension systems is a calculated statistic, and thus can be positive or negative. Net earnings is the sum of earnings on investments plus gains on investments minus losses on investments. [2] As of fiscal year 2005, the Census Bureau no longer collects government debt information by the character of long-term debt. For further information, see the 2006 Government Finance and Employment Classification Manual at <census.gov/gov/pubs/>.

Source: U.S. Census Bureau, "Annual Survey of State Government Finances," <census.gov/programs-surveys/state.html>, accessed August 2020.

Table 497. State Governments—Revenue by State: 2017

[In millions of dollars (2,531,103 represents $2,531,103,000,000). For fiscal year ending in year shown. See text, this section. Includes local shares of state imposed taxes]

State	Total revenue [1,2]	General revenue							Utilities and liquor store revenue	Insurance trust revenue
		Total	Intergovernmental revenue		General revenue from own sources					
			Total [1]	From federal government	Total	Total taxes	Current charges	Miscellaneous general revenue		
United States......	2,531,103	1,976,012	658,792	641,715	1,317,220	946,077	225,944	145,200	21,766	533,325
Alabama.............	33,248	26,771	9,949	9,857	16,822	10,417	5,041	1,364	335	6,142
Alaska...............	10,563	8,345	3,287	3,279	5,058	1,189	749	3,120	19	2,200
Arizona.............	45,049	36,117	15,159	14,897	20,958	15,249	3,094	2,614	29	8,903
Arkansas...........	25,712	21,088	7,903	7,853	13,185	9,516	2,547	1,122	–	4,624
California...........	392,868	288,644	93,014	88,470	195,630	155,692	30,604	9,334	1,004	103,220
Colorado...........	34,830	28,237	8,807	8,743	19,430	13,346	4,131	1,953	–	6,593
Connecticut.........	34,379	28,258	7,642	7,518	20,615	16,687	2,248	1,681	41	6,080
Delaware...........	9,649	8,438	2,429	2,359	6,009	3,589	1,088	1,332	22	1,189
Florida.............	106,908	84,794	26,519	26,209	58,275	41,334	8,447	8,494	25	22,090
Georgia.............	56,288	43,915	15,184	15,121	28,731	22,421	3,758	2,552	10	12,363
Hawaii..............	16,118	13,452	2,787	2,780	10,664	7,029	1,897	1,738	–	2,667
Idaho...............	11,619	8,537	2,642	2,625	5,895	4,498	867	530	164	2,918
Illinois.............	87,434	68,454	20,070	19,669	48,384	37,979	5,344	5,061	–	18,981
Indiana.............	43,082	38,748	14,713	14,630	24,035	18,171	3,551	2,313	–	4,334
Iowa................	29,082	23,417	5,722	5,691	17,695	9,755	3,619	4,321	306	5,359
Kansas.............	21,205	17,686	4,161	4,113	13,525	8,174	4,119	1,232	–	3,519
Kentucky...........	34,459	28,662	11,684	11,642	16,979	11,908	3,908	1,163	–	5,796
Louisiana...........	36,284	27,555	12,637	12,147	14,918	10,861	2,070	1,987	9	8,721
Maine..............	10,631	8,579	3,021	2,943	5,559	4,233	860	467	10	2,041
Maryland...........	47,773	41,240	13,036	12,796	28,204	21,600	3,894	2,711	146	6,387
Massachusetts.......	66,796	54,718	16,349	15,759	38,369	27,509	5,738	5,121	926	11,152
Michigan...........	77,155	64,022	21,351	21,176	42,671	28,652	9,502	4,518	1,082	12,051
Minnesota..........	53,459	41,456	10,985	10,809	30,471	25,595	2,823	2,054	104	11,899
Mississippi.........	24,310	19,001	8,211	8,096	10,789	7,725	2,241	823	350	4,960
Missouri............	39,317	29,582	11,349	11,148	18,233	12,496	3,129	2,608	–	9,735
Montana............	9,086	6,643	3,055	3,049	3,589	2,654	501	433	97	2,346
Nebraska...........	12,202	10,054	3,180	3,102	6,874	5,103	997	775	–	2,148
Nevada.............	21,727	15,275	5,235	4,999	10,041	8,625	825	591	43	6,409
New Hampshire......	9,398	7,081	2,720	2,330	4,361	2,592	958	810	686	1,630
New Jersey..........	78,295	63,010	17,887	17,254	45,123	33,101	6,699	5,323	1,123	14,163
New Mexico.........	21,014	16,719	7,230	7,001	9,489	5,639	1,743	2,106	–	4,295
New York...........	214,236	162,712	60,888	59,694	101,823	79,678	10,357	11,788	7,717	43,808
North Carolina.......	68,162	54,949	18,492	18,309	36,456	26,864	6,083	3,509	(Z)	13,214
North Dakota........	7,767	6,468	1,737	1,694	4,732	3,465	728	538	–	1,299
Ohio................	97,791	68,716	24,239	23,666	44,476	29,476	9,313	5,687	1,102	27,973
Oklahoma...........	26,759	21,051	7,298	7,134	13,753	8,523	2,889	2,341	621	5,087
Oregon.............	42,989	30,269	9,981	9,951	20,288	11,840	5,712	2,737	595	12,124
Pennsylvania........	102,214	84,114	29,453	29,225	54,661	38,397	11,575	4,689	2,013	16,087
Rhode Island........	9,502	8,002	2,806	2,730	5,196	3,267	992	938	23	1,477
South Carolina.......	34,721	26,888	9,827	9,463	17,061	9,829	5,186	2,046	1,729	6,104
South Dakota........	5,979	4,271	1,534	1,496	2,737	1,828	387	522	2	1,706
Tennessee..........	35,484	29,444	11,323	11,212	18,121	13,894	2,158	2,070	–	6,040
Texas..............	163,801	128,176	44,658	41,963	83,518	53,613	15,932	13,973	–	35,625
Utah...............	21,774	17,922	4,535	4,532	13,387	7,833	4,366	1,189	381	3,471
Vermont............	6,881	6,076	1,977	1,974	4,099	3,157	661	281	64	741
Virginia............	61,192	47,234	10,700	9,966	36,534	22,202	10,193	4,139	779	13,178
Washington.........	63,289	47,362	14,237	13,773	33,125	23,998	5,975	3,153	(Z)	15,926
West Virginia........	15,919	12,752	5,016	4,930	7,736	5,093	1,584	1,058	96	3,072
Wisconsin...........	45,883	35,560	9,583	9,361	25,977	18,133	4,643	3,200	–	10,324
Wyoming............	6,819	5,553	2,592	2,574	2,961	1,650	220	1,091	112	1,155

– Represents zero. Z Less than $500,000. [1] Includes amounts for categories not shown separately. [2] Duplicate intergovernmental transactions are excluded.

Source: U.S. Census Bureau, Federal, State, and Local Governments, Government Finance Statistics, "Annual Surveys of State and Local Government Finances," <census.gov/programs-surveys/gov-finances.html>, accessed June 2020.

Table 498. State Government Tax Collections by State: 2019

[In millions of dollars (1,090,242 represents $1,090,242,000,000)]

State	All taxes	Total property taxes	Sales and gross receipts: Total	Total general sales and gross receipts	Selective sales tax: Total[1]	Alcoholic beverage sales	Insurance premiums	Motor fuels sales	Public utilities	Tobacco products	License taxes: Total[1]	Corporation	Motor vehicle	Occupation and business n.e.c.[2]	Income taxes: Total	Individual income	Corporation net income	Other taxes: Total[1]	Death and gift	Severance
U.S.	1,090,242	21,123	505,225	335,686	169,540	6,994	23,556	50,682	12,186	18,690	59,138	6,694	28,170	15,371	470,575	412,393	58,182	34,181	5,051	14,910
AL	11,577	422	5,619	2,913	2,707	202	414	606	700	174	556	161	241	73	4,879	4,195	684	100	(X)	52
AK	1,781	122	279	(X)	279	41	80	46	5	60	160	(X)	37	69	333	(X)	333	888	(X)	888
AZ	18,164	1,091	10,444	8,358	2,086	78	591	885	22	309	580	40	265	190	5,872	5,357	514	177	(X)	17
AR	10,218	1,209	4,920	3,573	1,347	60	241	496	(X)	219	404	30	168	139	3,546	3,012	534	139	–	56
CA	188,235	2,977	60,234	41,539	18,694	353	2,723	7,558	713	1,979	11,041	81	4,869	4,818	113,872	100,080	13,793	110	(Z)	110
CO	15,870	(X)	5,989	3,375	2,613	48	315	677	(X)	190	697	22	458	51	8,966	8,172	795	218	(X)	218
CT	17,994	(X)	7,788	4,589	3,199	64	170	498	273	358	411	32	243	78	9,358	8,457	900	437	225	(X)
DE	4,596	(X)	603	(X)	603	27	113	143	52	123	1,785	1,561	59	141	2,031	1,741	290	177	2	(X)
DC	8,679	2,789	2,098	1,597	501	7	121	28	198	29	208	45	39	52	2,942	2,299	643	643	22	(X)
FL	44,800	(X)	36,492	28,006	8,486	309	1,178	2,925	1,748	1,137	2,124	242	1,474	170	3,115	(X)	3,115	3,069	(Z)	34
GA	24,713	865	9,509	6,250	3,259	199	511	1,838	(X)	223	711	67	387	80	13,448	12,177	1,271	180	(Z)	(X)
HI	8,208	(X)	5,062	3,809	1,253	52	180	88	127	112	280	2	196	54	2,759	2,568	190	106	19	(X)
ID	4,884	(X)	2,534	1,909	625	10	106	377	2	50	387	3	206	53	1,954	1,669	285	9	(X)	6
IL	42,501	61	19,534	12,014	7,521	297	424	1,351	1,444	769	2,780	355	1,739	445	19,632	16,541	3,091	494	413	(X)
IN	20,171	13	12,579	8,087	4,492	52	256	1,475	223	405	768	10	348	34	6,809	6,057	752	1	(Z)	1
IA	10,584	2	4,858	3,405	1,453	22	153	666	56	202	991	53	686	137	4,634	4,098	536	99	77	(X)
KS	10,030	753	4,524	3,335	1,189	147	406	460	(Z)	126	433	28	230	95	4,265	3,778	486	55	–	55
KY	12,896	649	6,311	3,985	2,326	148	173	720	56	370	530	118	223	129	5,209	4,629	580	196	43	150
LA	11,749	76	6,400	3,740	2,661	76	901	665	9	161	438	196	79	107	4,329	3,833	495	505	(X)	505
ME	4,674	41	2,328	1,613	715	20	94	257	20	126	291	11	117	117	1,962	1,709	253	53	16	(X)
MD	23,606	836	9,896	4,889	5,007	32	556	1,140	146	357	913	118	517	224	11,368	10,067	1,301	593	180	(X)
MA	31,805	7	9,558	6,834	2,724	87	445	775	(X)	553	1,200	28	449	311	20,098	17,151	2,947	943	601	(X)
MI	30,270	2,194	14,347	9,614	4,734	169	435	1,476	38	887	2,031	28	1,375	230	11,293	10,150	1,143	405	(Z)	24
MN	28,176	812	11,170	6,206	4,964	93	525	936	(Z)	627	1,496	9	847	457	14,112	12,400	1,712	586	222	60
MS	8,289	28	5,233	3,732	1,501	41	354	445	2	139	513	156	171	78	2,463	1,968	495	52	–	52
MO	13,181	34	5,549	3,732	1,817	40	446	726	(X)	95	629	3	306	163	6,957	6,588	369	13	(Z)	(Z)
MT	3,169	312	663	(X)	663	38	108	261	43	77	389	5	172	117	1,598	1,413	185	206	202	3
NE	5,755	(Z)	2,580	1,966	613	31	61	392	43	53	184	6	110	36	2,969	2,546	424	21	(X)	(X)
NV	9,745	335	7,836	5,500	2,335	46	424	354	54	182	701	80	210	264	(X)	(X)	(X)	873	(X)	124
NH	2,969	408	994	(X)	994	13	114	186	45	201	465	72	84	241	954	123	832	148	(X)	3
NJ	38,844	5	16,043	10,847	5,196	146	520	517	1,037	632	1,709	372	669	509	19,955	15,903	4,051	1,132	518	(X)
NM	7,428	87	3,684	2,863	821	21	210	240	33	91	332	35	205	47	1,793	1,590	202	1,531	–	1,492
NY	91,621	(X)	27,231	15,373	11,858	263	1,866	1,722	886	1,071	1,809	1	1,416	125	58,636	54,297	4,339	3,946	1,067	(X)

See footnotes at end of table.

Table 498. State Government Tax Collections by State: 2019-Continued.

See headnote on page 319.

State	All taxes	Total property taxes	Total general sales and gross receipts: Total	Selective sales and gross receipts — Selective sales tax: Total[1]	Alcoholic beverage sales	Insurance premiums	Motor fuels sales	Public utilities	Tobacco products	License taxes — Selected license taxes: Total[1]	Corporation	Motor vehicle	Occupation and business n.e.c.[2]	Income taxes: Total	Individual income	Corporation net income	Other taxes — Selected other taxes: Total[1]	Death and gift	Severance
NC.....	29,316	(X)	12,804	4,343	438	578	2,099	(Z)	293	2,327	843	894	352	14,095	13,259	836	90	(Z)	2
ND.....	4,970	5	1,564	510	9	69	199	52	27	229	(X)	120	84	562	415	147	2,611	(X)	2,611
OH.....	30,147	(X)	18,529	5,837	107	607	1,980	794	920	2,228	316	792	840	9,321	9,313	7	69	(Z)	69
OK.....	10,732	(X)	4,644	1,572	139	336	574	48	421	1,045	58	754	1	3,868	3,565	303	1,175	–	1,153
OR.....	13,960	21	1,865	1,865	20	81	586	9	250	1,135	43	568	395	10,758	9,847	911	180	162	16
PA.....	43,132	37	22,140	10,393	431	845	3,348	1,255	1,304	2,774	4	1,154	1,098	16,479	13,517	2,962	1,702	1,017	(X)
RI.....	3,724	3	1,831	710	21	117	76	103	137	116	5	30	66	1,553	1,376	176	222	148	(X)
SC.....	11,221	42	5,241	1,777	185	244	726	29	28	649	112	307	157	5,155	4,759	396	134	(X)	(X)
SD.....	1,940	(X)	1,615	470	18	91	190	3	46	273	6	85	118	46	(X)	46	6	(X)	6
TN.....	14,827	(X)	10,729	2,884	222	995	1,167	8	246	1,910	1,031	372	393	1,899	202	1,697	288	2	1
TX.....	63,330	(X)	53,905	15,782	1,373	2,599	3,743	649	1,410	3,659	155	2,228	760	(X)	(X)	(X)	5,766	(X)	5,766
UT.....	9,968	(X)	4,057	1,225	54	156	571	56	112	363	(Z)	234	57	5,501	4,979	522	46	(X)	46
VT.....	3,429	1,112	1,123	711	29	58	85	9	68	126	4	69	26	1,010	861	150	57	13	(X)
VA.....	26,286	33	8,596	3,138	245	554	1,084	112	151	897	65	502	239	15,796	14,872	924	965	(Z)	3
WA.....	27,992	3,359	21,374	4,727	390	640	1,698	590	397	1,747	43	836	363	(X)	(X)	(X)	1,513	300	47
WV.....	5,938	7	2,919	1,424	18	129	443	127	171	241	1	5	31	2,296	2,097	199	475	(X)	462
WI.....	20,039	100	8,446	2,751	62	217	1,065	364	600	1,265	25	525	511	10,124	8,760	1,365	103	(Z)	12
WY.....	2,111	274	954	184	2	26	121	4	22	209	15	99	50	(X)	(X)	(X)	675	–	668

X Not applicable. Z Less than $500,000. – Represents zero. [1] Includes other items not shown separately. [2] N.e.c. means not elsewhere classified.

Source: U.S. Census Bureau, Census of Governments, "2019 State Government Tax Tables," <census.gov/programs-surveys/stc.html>, accessed August 2020.

Table 499. State Governments—Expenditures and Debt by State: 2017

[In millions of dollars (2,316,929 represents $2,316,929,000,000) except as indicated. For fiscal year ending in year shown; see text, this section]

State	Total expenditures	Inter- govern- mental	Direct expenditures Total	Direct general expenditures Total [1]	Educa- tion	Public welfare	Health	Hospi- tals	High- ways	Police protec- tion	Correc- tions	Parks and recre- ation	Hous- ing and com- munity devel- opment	Sewer- age	Solid waste man- age- ment	Gov- ern- men- tal admin- istra- tion	Inter- est on gen- eral debt	Utility and liquor store	Insur- ance trust	Cash and security holdings	Total debt out- stand- ing
U.S...	2,316,929	553,351	1,763,578	1,433,369	313,313	620,660	43,276	84,005	109,832	15,426	48,851	5,687	8,771	1,309	1,114	61,252	43,752	35,224	294,985	4,764,484	1,159,804
AL....	32,500	6,932	25,569	21,749	6,213	8,442	415	2,220	1,648	167	515	18	38	-	-	568	390	329	3,491	48,857	8,793
AK...	11,296	1,830	9,467	7,949	1,393	2,567	146	29	1,143	117	316	15	123	-	-	657	198	144	1,374	90,326	5,922
AZ...	39,530	10,030	29,500	25,157	5,657	14,387	497	5	1,416	251	1,041	81	81	-	1	678	550	27	4,315	64,494	14,291
AR...	22,699	5,427	17,273	15,293	3,177	7,416	173	1,075	1,500	106	334	66	16	(Z)	9	693	159	-	1,980	37,579	6,969
CA...	349,898	107,877	242,021	188,848	35,945	93,560	1,325	13,427	7,653	1,883	8,376	510	286	445	314	8,587	6,899	1,743	51,430	743,019	147,215
CO...	35,172	7,462	27,711	22,084	7,196	7,523	381	1,036	1,495	193	892	88	202	4	10	1,112	716	15	5,612	75,169	16,981
CT...	27,853	5,557	22,296	17,028	4,123	3,718	906	1,437	1,594	223	622	29	179	-	75	1,399	1,540	515	4,753	48,775	38,756
DE...	9,938	1,606	8,332	7,469	1,932	2,508	450	83	651	147	328	49	86	15	57	517	222	159	704	16,008	5,058
FL....	90,302	18,243	72,059	62,404	11,302	26,990	3,949	1,215	8,082	606	2,593	205	239	-	184	2,413	1,016	340	9,315	226,178	28,828
GA...	49,605	12,325	37,279	30,663	8,195	12,039	1,249	1,164	2,671	416	1,290	263	294	9	17	983	593	72	6,544	105,474	13,050
HI....	12,682	328	12,354	10,866	3,410	2,985	550	618	312	45	229	81	153	(Z)	-	585	114	-	1,489	25,137	9,656
ID....	9,578	2,409	7,169	5,889	1,219	2,492	146	52	521	64	273	34	102	-	-	380	142	127	1,152	25,640	3,369
IL....	87,665	21,279	66,386	51,088	8,488	22,082	1,099	913	6,038	409	1,380	77	223	(Z)	8	2,019	3,495	5	15,293	164,293	61,821
IN....	40,817	9,989	30,828	27,946	7,601	13,923	549	141	1,637	223	632	52	410	1	5	778	906	-	2,882	61,703	20,837
IA....	22,778	5,363	17,416	14,573	3,424	5,569	110	1,860	1,610	96	287	22	109	1	3	580	207	213	2,630	46,599	6,150
KS...	19,598	4,860	14,738	12,825	3,037	4,096	342	2,682	983	108	309	37	84	-	-	472	180	-	1,913	24,708	7,538
KY...	35,468	4,875	30,593	25,994	6,250	11,406	366	1,886	1,857	242	644	125	276	-	3	1,147	645	37	4,562	43,339	13,555
LA...	33,768	6,415	27,353	22,705	4,272	11,227	422	357	1,420	243	506	298	48	-	-	889	819	8	4,640	65,240	18,033
ME...	9,024	1,307	7,717	6,668	1,007	3,147	202	100	671	90	163	7	177	-	-	371	168	21	1,028	20,176	4,750
MD...	45,442	9,687	35,756	30,131	5,724	13,043	1,055	538	2,379	547	1,498	199	388	190	25	1,537	1,197	1,257	4,367	73,933	28,027
MA...	65,326	9,168	56,158	46,081	7,134	22,155	1,412	717	2,688	856	953	195	1,141	303	1	2,359	2,531	3,262	6,815	101,005	78,184
MI...	72,138	21,279	50,859	41,912	11,698	15,740	1,488	4,385	1,471	474	1,866	132	623	-	5	937	1,548	873	8,074	109,236	33,675
MN...	47,192	13,728	33,464	27,447	6,713	13,428	406	314	1,751	357	509	226	142	161	18	1,210	629	477	5,539	87,175	16,362
MS...	21,861	4,837	17,023	13,990	2,803	6,342	296	1,495	1,062	136	331	36	36	-	-	406	316	287	2,746	35,381	7,470
MO...	34,147	6,343	27,804	23,033	4,199	9,224	1,955	2,274	1,187	274	733	63	215	-	2	885	773	7	4,764	86,125	18,420
MT...	7,727	1,142	6,585	5,409	1,022	2,170	205	65	597	38	212	17	29	-	-	406	109	99	1,077	19,700	2,796
NE...	10,611	2,457	8,154	7,393	2,203	2,719	266	190	809	83	350	52	2	-	5	299	58	-	761	21,583	2,015
NV...	16,220	4,790	11,431	8,780	2,060	3,532	269	269	907	88	305	23	13	-	5	432	138	44	2,606	44,643	3,249
NH...	8,815	1,739	7,076	5,724	1,188	2,194	98	62	463	71	146	26	113	21	31	299	319	561	791	15,516	7,739
NJ....	76,870	15,050	61,820	45,301	11,004	16,687	2,756	2,045	3,367	620	1,432	199	574	69	10	2,045	2,203	2,951	13,568	118,490	65,874
NM...	20,661	4,904	15,758	13,361	2,746	5,923	377	1,144	624	125	481	49	55	-	(Z)	504	388	1	2,396	57,506	7,058
NY...	201,926	63,219	138,706	102,405	12,763	58,041	3,218	5,436	4,914	865	3,120	617	450	(Z)	18	5,737	4,085	13,770	22,532	418,187	145,205
NC...	58,445	14,262	44,182	37,861	10,546	13,363	966	2,136	4,207	533	1,388	175	316	1	10	1,901	677	153	6,168	131,758	16,310

See footnotes at end of table.

State	Total expend-itures	Inter-govern-mental	Direct expenditures		Direct general expenditures													Utility and liquor store	Insur-ance trust	Cash and security holdings	Total debt out-stand-ing
			Total	Total¹	Educa-tion	Public welfare	Health	Hospi-tals	High-ways	Police protec-tion	Correc-tions	Parks and recre-ation	Hous-ing and com-munity devel-opment	Sewer-age	Solid waste man-age-ment	Gov-ern-men-tal admin-istra-tion	Inter-est on gen-eral debt				
ND...	7,803	2,202	5,601	4,855	1,237	1,452	141	54	834	35	103	32	22	—	—	202	80	79	667	29,249	2,886
OH...	87,473	18,585	68,888	50,661	10,555	25,836	1,107	3,294	3,401	333	1,520	137	73	—	28	2,025	1,329	904	17,324	238,573	33,490
OK...	25,164	4,508	20,656	16,953	4,720	6,749	787	287	1,797	177	593	54	156	—	(Z)	660	334	1,035	2,667	45,186	8,457
OR...	36,849	5,669	31,180	25,178	5,002	10,263	846	2,332	1,182	200	766	86	99	3	9	1,565	353	487	5,516	103,805	13,815
PA...	103,965	22,499	81,466	66,811	12,704	29,995	2,437	4,424	7,381	1,082	2,171	307	144	17	46	2,585	1,502	1,921	12,734	133,174	47,520
RI...	9,142	1,244	7,897	6,487	992	3,092	216	62	339	93	210	36	84	54	45	515	449	121	1,289	16,934	8,932
SC...	33,564	6,523	27,040	21,738	6,042	7,952	1,157	1,826	1,756	181	470	128	159	1	—	635	252	1,617	3,686	45,909	15,323
SD...	5,137	863	4,274	3,702	828	1,143	155	24	594	45	125	42	43	—	—	209	109	—	572	17,165	3,528
TN...	32,514	7,457	25,057	22,402	4,844	11,541	622	332	1,319	223	657	91	267	1	32	1,161	272	(Z)	2,654	65,368	6,127
TX...	146,994	30,733	116,262	98,029	28,176	37,415	2,872	7,241	9,823	1,230	3,814	230	43	6	66	2,178	1,305	4	18,229	376,025	50,963
UT...	20,581	3,766	16,815	14,669	4,826	3,750	308	1,945	1,165	150	373	53	90	—	6	976	236	275	1,871	37,268	7,459
VT...	7,009	1,801	5,208	4,751	1,189	1,845	365	24	374	104	152	21	94	2	3	194	101	61	396	8,987	3,503
VA...	53,448	11,939	41,509	35,726	9,119	10,437	1,001	4,943	3,591	407	1,431	157	179	(Z)	2	1,467	1,114	774	5,009	104,613	27,826
WA...	55,822	13,407	42,416	34,980	8,848	12,181	2,242	3,413	2,290	305	999	150	38	—	11	1,207	1,505	245	7,191	117,221	33,428
WV...	15,194	2,699	12,494	10,835	2,267	5,010	235	150	1,137	81	301	53	18	3	10	456	207	86	1,574	23,224	8,568
WI...	42,358	11,250	31,108	25,628	5,452	10,518	348	2,283	3,033	45	981	21	29	2	6	1,048	653	21	5,459	117,073	23,252
WY...	6,359	1,487	4,872	3,937	867	845	395	4	489	39	134	24	11	—	5	385	22	97	838	31,761	770

— Represents zero. Z Less than $500,000. ¹ Includes other direct general expenditures not shown separately.

Source: U.S. Census Bureau, Federal, State, and Local Governments, Government Finance Statistics, "Annual Surveys of State and Local Government Finances," <census.gov/programs-surveys/gov-finances.html>, accessed June 2020.

Table 500. Local Governments—Revenue by State: 2017

[In millions of dollars (1,938,485 represents $1,938,485,000,000). For fiscal year ending in year shown; see text, this section. Minus sign (-) indicates decrease]

State	Total revenue	General revenue, total	Intergovernmental revenue	General revenue from own sources — Total	Taxes — Total	Taxes — Property	Taxes — Sales and gross receipt	Taxes — Individual income	Current charges and miscellaneous general revenue	Current charges — Total	Current charges — Education	Current charges — Hospitals	Current charges — Sewerage	Miscellaneous general revenue — Total	Miscellaneous general revenue — Interest earnings	Miscellaneous general revenue — Special assessment	Utility revenue	Liquor store revenue	Insurance trust revenue
U.S...	1,938,485	1,693,420	602,030	1,091,390	706,753	509,426	123,660	33,051	384,637	299,992	24,320	90,539	57,051	84,645	14,470	9,866	154,854	1,411	88,801
AL....	22,815	19,401	7,184	12,216	6,011	2,441	2,812	124	6,206	5,345	333	3,398	563	861	119	27	3,119	–	296
AK....	5,476	5,038	1,983	3,054	1,840	1,448	352	–	1,214	884	25	391	108	330	123	7	400	10	29
AZ. ..	30,657	25,050	9,196	15,854	10,583	6,754	3,397	–	5,271	3,894	474	693	934	1,377	418	48	4,994	–	613
AR. ..	10,634	9,573	5,311	4,262	2,511	1,090	1,378	–	1,751	1,221	160	175	331	530	159	28	999	–	62
CA. ..	335,477	277,879	120,321	157,558	87,450	60,624	20,074	–	70,107	54,923	2,373	16,001	8,398	15,184	2,207	2,481	28,565	–	29,034
CO...	34,211	30,681	8,098	22,583	14,183	8,669	4,982	–	8,400	6,082	527	1,346	1,040	2,318	343	385	3,047	–	483
CT....	20,184	18,030	5,499	12,531	10,952	10,792	–	–	1,579	1,169	119	–	420	410	61	33	782	–	1,372
DE. ..	3,897	3,317	1,601	1,716	1,087	883	17	–	628	419	13	–	171	210	18	26	468	–	113
DC. ..	15,254	13,246	4,231	9,016	7,456	2,432	1,814	1,958	1,560	838	43	135	322	722	72	–	969	–	1,039
FL....	106,675	93,056	24,907	68,149	36,402	27,898	6,278	–	31,747	23,729	1,948	7,415	3,583	8,018	1,221	2,827	9,570	–	4,050
GA. ..	46,830	40,861	13,181	27,680	16,520	11,101	4,884	–	11,160	9,253	525	3,847	1,933	1,907	289	81	4,769	–	1,201
HI. ..	4,522	4,091	622	3,469	2,428	1,760	424	–	1,041	801	–	–	528	240	27	24	431	–	–
ID. ..	6,288	6,045	2,505	3,539	1,869	1,749	51	–	1,671	1,393	79	496	253	278	42	30	242	–	2
IL....	80,938	70,367	22,836	47,531	35,723	28,561	6,210	–	11,808	8,715	1,328	996	1,424	3,093	373	519	5,343	–	5,228
IN....	30,299	27,346	10,917	16,429	7,878	6,922	126	621	8,551	7,308	359	4,208	1,836	1,243	106	68	2,794	–	159
IA.....	17,832	16,634	6,080	10,554	5,938	5,130	601	103	4,616	3,832	544	1,948	591	784	108	22	1,193	6	6
KS....	15,893	14,124	5,335	8,790	5,311	3,798	1,368	1	3,479	2,425	424	854	479	1,054	259	126	1,629	–	140
KY....	15,427	13,489	5,182	8,307	5,435	2,992	719	1,454	2,872	2,446	101	734	671	426	68	18	1,820	–	118
LA....	22,079	20,651	6,450	14,201	9,118	4,141	4,777	–	5,083	4,055	48	2,212	481	1,027	230	11	1,186	–	242
ME...	5,226	5,080	1,461	3,619	2,847	2,816	7	–	772	648	40	108	197	124	21	7	147	–	–
MD...	33,808	30,221	9,304	20,917	16,365	9,001	959	5,336	4,552	3,633	490	58	1,172	919	95	86	995	298	2,293
MA...	38,153	32,307	10,394	21,913	17,552	16,707	420	–	4,361	3,198	411	357	1,265	1,163	86	10	3,022	–	2,824
MI....	49,048	43,789	20,732	23,058	13,106	11,945	265	544	9,952	7,879	1,139	797	1,872	2,073	251	178	2,676	263	2,583
MN...	32,199	29,397	13,054	16,342	8,796	8,047	436	–	7,546	5,556	552	1,676	814	1,990	412	349	2,343	–	196
MS. ..	13,056	12,230	4,906	7,325	3,212	3,012	113	–	4,112	3,675	338	2,513	295	438	72	8	826	–	–
MO...	28,526	24,759	7,373	17,386	10,844	6,317	3,418	404	6,543	5,184	637	2,040	1,103	1,359	237	101	2,768	–	999
MT...	4,086	3,928	1,555	2,373	1,450	1,397	14	–	923	675	75	83	128	247	39	78	153	–	5
NE....	14,866	10,163	2,782	7,382	4,713	3,754	493	–	2,668	2,140	252	774	306	528	112	32	4,360	–	343
NV....	15,318	14,067	5,895	8,172	4,809	2,707	1,691	–	3,363	2,545	30	710	500	818	90	69	1,251	–	–
NH...	6,534	6,376	1,535	4,841	4,111	4,059	3	–	731	539	49	–	153	192	26	5	137	–	22
NJ....	50,430	49,282	12,525	36,757	29,701	29,113	176	–	7,056	4,872	1,081	270	1,712	2,185	176	6	1,136	–	12
NM...	9,124	8,496	4,253	4,243	2,843	1,576	1,205	–	1,400	1,018	98	186	205	382	103	15	628	–	–
NY...	223,729	192,271	64,298	127,973	98,073	56,853	18,757	11,740	29,900	22,159	1,262	5,580	2,911	7,741	1,334	141	7,854	–	23,605

See footnotes at end of table.

Table 500. Local Governments—Revenue by State: 2017-Continued.

See headnote on page 323.

State	Total revenue	General revenue, total	Intergovernmental revenue	General revenue from own sources — Taxes: Total	Taxes: Total¹	Taxes: Property	Taxes: Sales and gross receipt	Taxes: Individual income	Current charges and miscellaneous general revenue	Current charges: Total¹	Current charges: Education	Current charges: Hospitals	Current charges: Sewerage	Miscellaneous general revenue: Total¹	Miscellaneous general revenue: Interest earnings	Miscellaneous general revenue: Special assessment	Utility revenue	Liquor store revenue	Insurance trust revenue
NC..	49,756	44,482	16,381	28,101	13,822	10,005	3,330	–	14,280	12,580	551	8,158	1,486	1,700	139	21	4,356	822	96
ND...	5,004	4,702	2,286	2,416	1,568	1,245	267	–	849	484	70	–	71	365	27	126	253	–	50
OH...	58,706	55,350	19,176	36,174	24,533	15,346	2,709	5,704	11,641	8,651	1,274	1,648	2,423	2,989	604	308	3,120	–	235
OK...	14,666	13,087	4,330	8,757	5,366	2,872	2,348	–	3,391	2,651	313	996	446	740	60	43	1,390	–	189
OR...	21,902	20,141	7,580	12,561	7,703	6,146	579	–	4,858	3,759	505	328	1,191	1,100	323	97	1,661	–	100
PA....	70,225	64,707	26,092	38,614	28,124	19,501	1,420	5,060	10,490	8,066	874	27	2,815	2,424	839	112	2,962	–	2,557
RI....	5,002	4,560	1,406	3,154	2,612	2,540	31	–	542	433	42	–	135	109	16	5	220	–	222
SC....	24,402	22,188	6,331	15,857	7,856	5,994	847	–	8,000	6,814	245	4,864	673	1,187	210	64	2,200	–	14
SD....	3,988	3,570	1,005	2,565	1,892	1,415	405	–	673	550	97	87	108	123	15	17	352	18	48
TN....	34,848	24,488	8,108	16,380	8,979	5,881	2,755	–	7,401	6,028	488	3,021	947	1,373	254	159	9,046	–	1,314
TX....	147,680	129,381	36,220	93,160	64,239	53,017	10,124	–	28,922	22,588	2,314	6,293	3,876	6,334	1,835	456	14,479	–	3,821
UT....	13,789	11,652	3,952	7,700	4,776	3,220	1,416	–	2,924	2,185	188	336	408	739	98	43	2,128	–	9
VT....	3,106	2,815	1,833	982	647	611	25	–	335	250	30	–	81	86	9	4	247	–	44
VA....	43,512	39,657	14,037	25,620	18,397	13,956	3,020	–	7,222	5,655	483	345	1,715	1,567	284	57	2,037	–	1,818
WA....	51,367	43,873	15,605	28,268	15,666	9,025	5,415	–	12,602	10,481	341	2,905	2,604	2,121	263	416	7,044	–	450
WV....	5,695	5,352	1,909	3,443	2,093	1,715	124	–	1,350	1,070	30	337	303	280	41	15	271	–	72
WI....	30,124	27,210	12,205	15,005	10,195	9,454	504	–	4,810	3,804	526	81	991	1,006	126	69	2,218	–	697
WY....	5,219	4,961	2,069	2,892	1,167	993	121	–	1,725	1,491	74	1,111	79	233	31	10	258	–	–

– Represents or rounds to zero. ¹ Includes corporation income, not shown separately.

Source: U.S. Census Bureau, Federal, State, and Local Governments, Government Finance Statistics, "Annual Surveys of State and Local Government Finances," <census.gov/programs-surveys/gov-finances.html>, accessed June 2020.

Table 501. Local Governments—Expenditures and Debt by State: 2017

[In millions of dollars (1,913,388 represents $1,913,388,000,000). For fiscal year ending in year shown; see text, this section]

State	Total expenditures [1]	Total [1]	Direct expenditures / Direct general expenditures — Total	Education	Public welfare	Hospitals	Health	Highways	Police protection	Corrections	Parks and recreation	Housing and community development	Sewerage	Solid waste management	Governmental administration	Interest on general debt	Other	Utility expenditures	Insurance trust expenditures	Debt outstanding
U.S...	1,913,388	1,896,505	1,637,819	696,819	57,578	107,131	56,551	72,158	99,078	29,882	39,577	43,630	55,246	24,078	82,993	62,571	101,807	203,477	53,957	1,908,252
AL....	23,167	23,132	19,766	7,854	42	4,091	426	885	1,107	214	509	529	420	292	988	621	981	3,131	234	21,192
AK....	5,464	5,464	4,774	1,886	10	427	77	269	249	6	114	175	125	116	274	107	439	651	32	3,549
AZ....	29,436	29,037	23,044	9,450	118	785	305	1,101	2,251	616	666	372	779	458	1,787	978	1,212	5,525	468	32,772
AR....	10,461	10,441	9,410	5,132	22	209	75	575	566	177	210	184	314	221	438	343	337	980	51	11,589
CA....	322,768	321,874	266,621	95,291	18,333	16,190	21,660	7,879	17,287	6,238	5,957	8,385	8,698	3,029	13,456	10,531	13,448	42,037	13,216	316,227
CO....	33,157	33,123	28,231	10,213	829	1,754	463	1,774	1,662	467	1,437	906	1,018	125	1,991	1,321	1,795	4,497	395	40,374
CT....	18,682	18,678	16,886	9,358	99	—	157	682	955	—	223	610	639	188	652	393	2,051	907	886	11,237
DE....	3,684	3,682	3,219	2,052	1	—	40	189	232	—	35	74	179	28	160	67	35	381	82	2,505
DC....	18,555	18,555	13,255	2,907	3,930	264	397	455	633	157	259	767	554	127	729	588	852	4,731	569	14,901
FL....	105,284	104,993	91,688	31,485	1,092	8,543	1,562	3,189	7,903	1,963	3,096	2,076	3,788	2,422	4,639	2,963	5,729	10,641	2,664	107,452
GA....	47,873	47,852	40,890	19,869	119	3,613	1,037	1,683	2,313	831	1,121	838	1,246	655	2,793	903	1,590	5,981	980	44,756
HI....	4,428	4,428	3,140	—	101	—	43	290	437	—	281	111	399	266	331	235	378	1,288	—	6,343
ID....	6,012	6,009	5,741	2,344	30	618	117	363	390	143	162	55	228	173	373	95	189	266	2	2,683
IL....	80,461	80,461	66,141	29,316	593	2,296	947	3,309	4,873	727	3,040	1,882	1,648	616	4,161	3,466	3,685	8,435	5,885	93,099
IN....	27,841	27,826	25,076	10,220	21	4,338	259	807	1,110	429	424	407	820	230	1,334	938	1,985	2,650	101	25,864
IA....	17,760	17,732	16,437	7,643	81	2,030	334	1,139	718	148	330	148	538	275	599	400	1,286	1,290	4	13,229
KS....	15,821	15,816	14,103	6,774	43	905	311	940	754	233	343	184	436	162	712	664	959	1,598	114	19,633
KY....	15,518	15,510	13,408	6,626	41	612	543	499	587	305	251	183	684	205	681	707	596	2,022	79	30,363
LA....	21,653	21,627	20,008	8,078	82	2,267	214	985	1,403	481	464	610	654	363	1,201	628	780	1,367	253	18,226
ME....	5,112	5,109	4,951	2,542	50	112	43	317	220	98	89	110	218	116	229	103	415	159	—	3,105
MD....	33,884	33,883	30,394	15,083	159	53	518	992	2,123	438	1,113	1,138	1,110	907	1,425	712	2,936	1,745	1,474	26,486
MA....	37,089	36,665	31,497	16,027	94	861	160	1,141	1,729	—	309	1,580	1,123	399	1,314	540	4,326	3,061	2,107	18,633
MI....	48,233	47,934	43,169	19,038	1,349	907	2,658	2,810	2,073	618	1,266	440	2,493	511	2,408	1,265	3,089	2,991	1,773	38,644
MN....	34,959	34,871	31,575	13,005	1,489	1,681	860	3,059	1,623	550	1,077	957	871	357	1,458	1,022	1,814	2,878	157	36,647
MS....	13,013	13,012	12,164	5,376	28	2,476	95	668	631	186	192	266	283	185	641	236	400	848	—	7,092
MO....	27,704	27,702	24,129	11,129	191	1,896	440	1,182	1,535	213	672	488	1,217	150	1,106	831	1,459	2,808	764	28,685
MT....	4,244	4,243	4,034	1,920	64	91	159	248	277	46	92	60	142	88	245	70	226	208	1	2,528
NE....	14,947	14,942	10,204	5,121	109	830	64	765	415	143	194	231	255	95	461	310	608	4,381	358	13,873
NV....	14,699	14,665	13,167	4,616	383	793	141	1,123	1,180	466	568	276	465	26	936	633	328	1,498	—	24,108
NH....	5,643	5,574	5,374	2,972	243	—	18	294	349	80	83	103	141	96	321	113	181	179	21	2,671
NJ....	49,357	48,886	47,868	25,867	1,008	274	384	1,623	2,942	706	537	891	1,654	915	1,806	1,123	6,415	1,007	11	31,116
NM....	8,865	8,862	8,006	4,067	119	227	80	280	581	237	280	78	235	232	571	143	302	856	—	8,749
NY....	220,023	209,162	179,338	72,398	12,312	11,641	3,779	7,306	9,516	3,403	2,478	6,121	3,571	2,991	5,055	9,886	20,393	16,977	12,847	211,631

See footnotes at end of table.

Table 501. Local Governments—Expenditures and Debt by State: 2017-Continued.
See headnote on page 325.

State	Total expenditures [1]	Total [1]	Direct general expenditures															Utility expenditures	Insurance trust expenditures	Debt outstanding
			Total	Education	Public welfare	Hospitals	Health	Highways	Police protection	Corrections	Parks and recreation	Housing and community development	Sewerage	Solid waste management	Governmental administration	Interest on general debt	Other			
NC...	48,337	48,221	42,742	16,580	1,762	7,868	2,875	660	2,679	558	933	1,281	976	740	1,595	1,226	886	4,729	51	30,986
ND...	5,261	5,247	4,843	1,807	84	–	78	900	196	122	335	61	102	71	205	104	403	371	33	5,107
OH...	61,190	60,691	56,657	25,169	2,860	1,785	2,431	2,664	3,479	505	1,382	1,922	2,332	466	3,671	1,595	3,071	3,866	167	54,325
OK...	13,964	13,962	12,378	5,754	25	970	244	798	869	153	460	357	331	230	683	197	400	1,481	103	10,258
OR...	22,313	22,308	19,636	8,629	232	355	817	940	1,172	543	649	608	938	152	1,109	810	844	2,472	200	22,866
PA...	69,680	69,665	62,395	30,692	4,286	2	3,147	2,405	2,786	1,574	744	1,948	2,528	906	3,744	2,698	2,735	4,880	2,390	75,012
RI...	4,926	4,926	4,397	2,459	8	–	21	134	361	–	47	183	124	57	172	94	337	237	292	2,579
SC...	23,425	23,380	21,516	9,018	31	4,914	244	537	1,132	264	456	326	688	389	1,175	628	672	1,857	8	23,332
SD...	3,754	3,753	3,364	1,596	16	108	45	409	165	62	129	62	118	51	187	74	158	344	30	2,719
TN...	34,313	34,310	24,011	9,669	168	3,442	420	920	1,756	438	566	560	818	401	1,488	708	1,207	9,532	767	36,437
TX...	149,323	147,516	128,061	61,297	745	11,378	3,367	5,872	6,965	2,570	2,450	1,952	3,993	1,423	6,381	7,810	4,028	17,162	2,293	238,723
UT...	13,536	13,528	11,331	5,123	165	317	310	664	593	186	447	284	304	171	762	256	829	2,183	15	13,508
VT...	2,909	2,907	2,602	1,651	2	–	10	249	114	–	41	66	72	33	122	30	84	281	24	1,251
VA...	42,581	42,546	37,963	17,840	1,590	338	1,283	1,336	2,115	1,190	962	903	1,589	641	2,268	1,178	2,001	3,484	1,100	38,115
WA...	49,549	49,323	39,551	15,749	208	3,265	1,560	2,103	1,751	732	1,155	1,433	1,937	753	1,924	1,378	1,827	9,473	300	55,130
WV...	5,968	5,964	5,540	3,127	11	326	56	91	314	53	155	110	311	76	434	90	170	367	56	3,667
WI...	31,273	31,217	28,171	12,799	2,182	150	1,228	2,463	1,818	544	674	334	1,058	400	1,473	729	728	2,447	599	23,065
WY...	5,289	5,289	4,952	2,199	19	1,127	52	191	185	70	119	8	83	103	324	29	209	337	–	1,208

– Represents or rounds to zero. [1] Includes other items not shown separately.

Source: U.S. Census Bureau, Federal, State, and Local Governments, Government Finance Statistics, "Annual Surveys of State and Local Government Finances," <census.gov/programs-surveys/gov-finances.html>, accessed June 2020.

Table 502. Government Employment and Payrolls by Level of Government: 1982 to 2019

[Employees in thousands (15,841 represents 15,841,000); payroll in millions of dollars (23,173 represents $23,173,000,000). Data through 1992 are for the month of October. Beginning with the 1997 survey, data are for the month of March. Covers both full-time and part-time employees. Local government data are estimates subject to sampling variation; see Appendix III and source]

Type of government	1982	1987	1992	1997	2000	2005	2010	2015	2018	2019
EMPLOYEES (1,000)										
Total	**15,841**	**17,212**	**18,745**	**19,540**	**20,876**	**21,725**	**22,607**	**(NA)**	**(NA)**	**(NA)**
Federal (civilian) [1]	2,848	3,091	3,047	2,807	2,899	2,720	3,008	(NA)	(NA)	(NA)
State and local	12,993	14,121	15,698	16,733	17,976	19,004	19,599	19,293	19,619	19,688
Percent of total	82	82	84	86	86	87	87	(NA)	(NA)	(NA)
State	3,744	4,116	4,595	4,733	4,877	5,078	5,326	5,344	5,436	5,478
Local	9,249	10,005	11,103	12,000	13,099	13,926	14,274	13,949	14,183	14,210
PAYROLLS (mil. dol.)										
Total	**23,173**	**32,669**	**43,120**	**49,156**	**58,166**	**71,599**	**86,643**	**(NA)**	**(NA)**	**(NA)**
Federal (civilian) [1]	5,959	7,924	9,937	9,744	11,485	13,475	16,238	(NA)	(NA)	(NA)
State and local	17,214	24,745	33,183	39,412	46,681	58,123	70,404	75,072	82,885	85,762
Percent of total	74	76	77	80	80	81	81	(NA)	(NA)	(NA)
State	5,022	7,263	9,828	11,413	13,279	16,062	19,579	21,568	23,836	24,709
Local	12,192	17,482	23,355	27,999	33,402	42,062	50,825	53,503	59,049	61,053

NA Not available. [1] Includes employees outside the United States.

Source: U.S. Census Bureau, Census of Governments, "Annual Survey of Public Employment and Payroll Datasets and Tables," <census.gov/programs-surveys/apes.html>, accessed July 2020.

Table 503. State and Local Government Employment and Payrolls by Function: 2019

[Employees in thousands (19,688 represents 19,688,000); payroll in millions of dollars (85,762.2 represents $85,762,200,000). Data are for the month of March. See headnote, Table 502]

Function	Employees (1,000)			Payrolls (mil. dol.)		
	Total	State	Local	Total	State	Local
Total	**19,688**	**5,478**	**14,210**	**85,762.2**	**24,709.4**	**61,052.8**
Financial administration	455	175	280	2,241.5	929.8	1,311.7
Other government administration	418	57	361	1,456.0	285.9	1,170.1
Judicial & legal	443	182	262	2,444.9	1,090.3	1,354.5
Police protection	1,000	107	893	5,977.3	706.9	5,270.5
Fire protection	450	–	450	2,551.0	–	2,551.0
Corrections	717	443	274	3,614.6	2,231.8	1,382.8
Streets & highways	506	214	292	2,486.4	1,141.4	1,345.0
Air transportation	54	3	51	315.3	20.2	295.1
Water transport/terminals	14	5	9	93.8	32.7	61.1
Public welfare	544	252	292	2,397.4	1,088.7	1,308.8
Health	487	200	288	2,318.0	993.4	1,324.6
Hospitals	1,101	434	666	5,913.5	2,301.5	3,612.0
Social insurance administration	66	66	1	333.0	328.7	4.2
Solid waste management	114	2	111	483.1	13.4	469.7
Sewerage	131	2	129	663.8	12.2	651.6
Parks and recreation	432	40	392	1,085.1	135.3	949.7
Housing and community development	111	1	110	535.8	7.4	528.4
Natural resources	190	143	47	856.7	658.9	197.8
Water supply	188	1	187	972.4	4.8	967.6
Electric power	78	4	74	632.4	35.3	597.0
Gas supply	12	–	12	60.6	–	60.6
Transit	268	40	228	1,720.1	293.4	1,426.7
Elementary and secondary education	7,795	59	7,736	30,750.6	256.1	30,494.5
Higher education	3,342	2,772	571	12,626.1	10,765.9	1,860.2
Other education	86	86	–	404.4	404.4	–
Libraries	183	1	182	498.9	2.4	496.5
State liquor stores	13	13	–	32.9	32.9	–
Other and unallocable	489	177	313	2,296.5	935.6	1,360.9

– Represents or rounds to zero.

Source: U.S. Census Bureau, Census of Governments, "Annual Survey of Public Employment and Payroll Datasets and Tables," <census.gov/programs-surveys/apes.html>, accessed July 2020.

Table 504. State and Local Government—Employer Costs Per Hour Worked: 2020

[In dollars. As of March. Based on a sample; see source for details]

Occupation and industry	Total compen-sation	Wages and salaries	Benefit cost Total	Paid leave	Supple-mental pay	Insur-ance	Retire-ment and savings	Legally required benefits
Total workers	**52.45**	**32.62**	**19.82**	**3.89**	**0.52**	**6.15**	**6.39**	**2.88**
OCCUPATIONAL GROUP								
Management, professional, and related	62.88	40.48	22.40	4.38	0.41	6.72	7.66	3.24
Professional and related	61.06	39.60	21.45	3.89	0.38	6.69	7.38	3.12
Teachers [1]	69.06	46.03	23.03	3.42	0.25	7.22	8.82	3.32
Primary, secondary, and special education school teachers	68.85	45.29	23.56	3.11	0.24	7.72	9.35	3.15
Sales and office	36.29	20.88	15.42	3.15	0.33	5.77	4.00	2.16
Office and administrative support	36.46	20.92	15.54	3.17	0.34	5.85	4.03	2.16
Service	38.25	21.90	16.35	3.20	0.82	4.86	5.12	2.34
INDUSTRY GROUP								
Education and health services	54.79	35.30	19.49	3.57	0.35	6.31	6.46	2.80
Educational services	56.15	36.40	19.75	3.42	0.26	6.42	6.84	2.80
Elementary and secondary schools	54.59	35.43	19.16	2.83	0.22	6.48	6.97	2.66
Junior colleges, colleges, and universities	60.71	39.25	21.46	5.24	0.35	6.20	6.43	3.24
Health care and social assistance	46.54	28.60	17.94	4.47	0.92	5.63	4.10	2.81
Hospitals	49.15	30.79	18.36	4.74	1.07	5.59	4.00	2.96
Public administration	50.58	29.20	21.38	4.67	0.80	6.11	6.74	3.06

[1] Includes postsecondary teachers; primary, secondary, and special education teachers; and other teachers and instructors.

Source: U.S. Bureau of Labor Statistics, National Compensation Survey, *Employer Costs for Employee Compensation–March 2020*, June 2020. See also <bls.gov/ncs/ect/>.

Table 505. State and Local Government—Full-Time Employment and Salary by Sex and Race/Ethnicity: 1980 to 2017

[2,350 represents 2,350,000. As of June 30. Excludes school systems and educational institutions. Based on reports from state governments (42 in 1980; 49 in 1984 through 1987; and 50 in 1989 through 1991) and a sample of county, municipal, township, and special district jurisdictions employing 15 or more nonelected, nonappointed full-time employees. Beginning 1993, only for state and local governments with 100 or more employees. For definition of median, see Guide to Tabular Presentation]

Year and occupation	Employment (1,000) Male	Female	White [1]	Minority Total [2]	Black [1]	His-panic [3]	Median annual salary ($1,000) Male	Female	White [1]	Minority Black [1]	His-panic [3]
1980	2,350	1,637	3,146	842	619	163	15.2	11.4	13.8	11.5	12.3
1985	2,789	1,952	3,563	1,179	835	248	22.3	17.3	20.6	17.5	19.2
1986	2,797	1,982	3,549	1,230	865	259	23.4	18.1	21.5	18.7	20.2
1987	2,818	2,031	3,600	1,249	872	268	24.2	18.9	22.4	19.3	21.1
1989	3,030	2,227	3,863	1,394	961	308	26.1	20.6	24.1	20.7	22.7
1990	3,071	2,302	3,918	1,456	994	327	27.3	21.8	25.2	22.0	23.8
1991	3,110	2,349	3,965	1,494	1,011	340	28.4	22.7	26.4	22.7	24.5
1993	2,820	2,204	3,588	1,436	948	341	30.6	24.3	28.5	24.2	26.8
1995	2,960	2,355	3,781	1,534	993	379	33.5	27.0	31.4	26.8	28.6
1997	2,898	2,307	3,676	1,529	973	392	34.6	27.9	32.2	27.4	29.5
1999	2,939	2,393	3,723	1,609	1,012	417	37.0	29.9	34.8	29.6	31.2
2001	3,080	2,554	3,888	1,746	1,077	471	39.8	32.1	37.5	31.5	33.8
2003	3,134	2,610	3,919	1,826	1,097	508	42.2	34.7	40.0	33.6	36.6
2005	3,185	2,644	3,973	1,856	1,100	532	44.1	36.4	41.5	35.3	38.9
2007	3,383	2,823	4,156	(NA)	(NA)	(NA)	(NA)	(NA)	(NA)	(NA)	(NA)
2009	3,239	2,742	3,976	2,004	1,145	601	50.3	41.5	47.6	40.3	44.8
2011	2,924	2,477	3,561	1,839	1,015	570	51.8	43.1	49.1	41.7	47.0
2013	3,055	2,568	3,671	1,952	1,057	634	52.5	43.8	49.9	42.0	46.8
2015	2,969	2,492	3,536	1,926	1,011	634	54.9	46.5	52.2	44.1	49.8
2017, total	**3,031**	**2,536**	**3,511**	**2,056**	**1,025**	**698**	**(NA)**	**(NA)**	**54.0**	**46.2**	**52.3**
Officials/administrators	222	187	295	114	49	37	(NA)	(NA)	72.4	71.9	71.8
Professionals	637	901	1,009	529	254	144	(NA)	(NA)	64.1	55.8	65.5
Technicians	240	170	267	143	65	50	(NA)	(NA)	52.1	44.1	50.8
Protective service	951	235	785	401	198	163	(NA)	(NA)	56.8	47.7	61.3
Paraprofessionals	98	252	184	166	97	51	(NA)	(NA)	(NA)	(NA)	(NA)
Administrative support	129	652	458	323	150	126	(NA)	(NA)	39.4	39.0	41.3
Skilled craft	372	20	271	122	58	47	(NA)	(NA)	39.3	49.0	53.5
Service/maintenance	381	118	242	257	154	81	(NA)	(NA)	32.2	41.0	42.1

NA Not available. [1] Non-Hispanic. [2] Includes other minority groups, not shown separately. [3] Persons of Hispanic origin may be of any race.

Source: U.S. Equal Employment Opportunity Commission, "Job Patterns for Minorities and Women in State and Local Government," <https://www.eeoc.gov/eeo-4/job-patterns-minorities-and-women-state-and-local-government-eeo-4>, accessed August 2019.

Table 506. State and Local Government Full-Time Equivalent Employment by Selected Function and State: 2019

[In thousands (1,990.3 represents 1,990,300). For March. Local government amounts are estimates subject to sampling variation; see Appendix III and source]

State	Education Total [1] State	Education Total [1] Local	Elementary/ secondary State	Elementary/ secondary Local	Higher education State	Higher education Local	Public welfare State	Public welfare Local	Health State	Health Local	Hospitals State	Hospitals Local	Highways State	Highways Local	Police protection State	Police protection Local	Fire protection State	Fire protection Local	Corrections State	Corrections Local	Parks and recreation State	Parks and recreation Local
U.S.	1,990.3	7,081.9	48.5	6,748.2	1,862.6	333.7	249.1	275.5	191.8	261.4	401.3	610.3	211.0	278.0	105.5	837.9	(X)	370.6	438.9	267.2	35.4	245.0
AL	47.1	95.9	-	95.9	44.2	0.1	4.2	1.1	7.2	6.4	13.3	26.3	4.3	6.4	1.5	13.2	(X)	6.3	4.3	3.7	0.5	4.1
AK	8.3	16.5	3.2	16.4	4.7	-	1.8	0.1	0.7	0.4	0.2	0.9	2.9	0.7	0.6	1.3	(X)	0.9	2.2	0.1	0.2	0.6
AZ	39.3	119.9	-	107.7	36.9	12.2	6.3	1.2	2.4	3.8	0.6	3.0	2.4	4.0	2.0	18.0	(X)	9.6	9.0	5.1	0.3	4.7
AR	26.9	69.5	-	69.5	25.6	-	4.4	0.1	3.1	0.7	6.6	1.2	3.6	3.8	1.4	7.8	(X)	3.2	5.7	2.5	1.3	1.7
CA	182.1	752.6	-	679.6	177.8	73.0	8.8	83.2	16.3	55.1	47.6	71.6	20.7	23.1	10.9	91.9	(X)	35.2	61.5	34.2	3.5	32.4
CO	60.6	111.4	-	110.2	59.7	1.2	2.3	7.4	1.5	5.4	4.2	10.2	3.1	5.3	1.4	15.3	(X)	7.5	7.4	4.3	1.2	8.7
CT	22.6	88.0	-	88.0	19.3	-	5.3	1.4	3.1	1.2	3.1	-	3.5	3.2	1.7	8.2	(X)	4.4	6.3	-	0.4	1.9
DE	8.3	18.4	-	18.4	8.0	-	1.6	-	2.0	0.3	1.2	-	1.5	0.5	1.1	1.7	(X)	0.2	2.9	-	0.3	0.3
DC	(X)	10.3	(X)	9.4	(X)	0.9	(X)	2.5	(X)	2.3	(X)	1.5	(X)	1.0	(X)	4.6	(X)	2.0	(X)	1.7	(X)	0.9
FL	72.0	391.7	-	363.7	69.2	28.0	9.4	4.2	16.4	5.9	4.1	54.3	6.0	12.3	4.3	58.8	(X)	30.7	23.5	17.2	1.3	19.3
GA	70.4	243.5	-	243.5	67.2	-	6.8	1.5	3.6	7.6	7.8	21.1	3.8	7.1	2.7	25.2	(X)	14.7	15.2	10.0	3.4	6.1
HI	36.5	-	26.7	-	9.6	-	0.4	0.2	2.0	0.4	3.1	-	0.8	0.9	-	3.9	(X)	2.1	2.4	-	0.2	2.1
ID	10.0	36.3	-	34.4	9.6	2.0	1.8	0.1	1.9	0.8	0.6	4.2	1.4	1.9	0.5	3.8	(X)	1.6	2.4	1.8	0.2	1.2
IL	57.1	294.7	-	272.9	54.9	21.9	9.3	4.5	2.1	6.0	10.5	11.5	6.7	10.9	3.1	38.5	(X)	17.3	13.4	10.3	0.6	17.9
IN	65.1	134.5	-	134.5	64.1	-	6.3	1.1	1.6	3.1	1.5	24.0	3.5	5.8	1.9	14.0	(X)	8.5	6.0	6.7	0.1	3.6
IA	25.4	87.3	-	80.4	24.4	6.9	2.3	1.2	0.4	1.7	8.8	12.5	2.2	5.3	0.9	6.3	(X)	2.1	2.7	1.7	0.1	2.1
KS	24.7	93.6	-	86.2	24.2	7.4	2.4	0.6	1.2	2.9	11.7	8.8	2.5	4.6	1.1	8.1	(X)	3.7	3.1	2.7	0.6	2.8
KY	38.5	106.5	-	106.5	36.3	-	6.9	0.4	3.5	4.6	8.2	5.3	4.0	3.0	2.1	7.9	(X)	4.6	4.0	4.1	0.8	1.9
LA	30.2	98.1	0.1	98.1	26.8	-	5.4	1.2	3.8	1.4	10.3	17.9	4.4	1.7	1.8	15.3	(X)	5.2	5.8	6.2	1.0	3.6
ME	7.5	34.3	-	34.3	7.2	-	2.1	0.2	0.9	0.2	0.5	1.0	2.0	4.6	0.6	2.5	(X)	1.7	1.3	0.7	0.4	0.7
MD	30.6	145.1	-	133.5	28.6	11.6	6.1	2.7	6.2	4.8	3.3	0.5	4.4	6.1	2.2	15.6	(X)	7.1	10.2	3.4	0.5	6.6
MA	36.7	149.7	2.4	149.4	33.2	0.3	8.1	2.2	7.1	3.1	5.8	3.4	2.8	7.7	3.1	18.0	(X)	13.4	12.4	-	0.9	2.8
MI	79.6	168.2	-	156.0	79.0	12.2	11.4	3.6	6.1	9.2	18.9	7.6	2.7	6.6	3.0	18.3	(X)	7.4	11.9	5.2	0.2	3.6
MN	39.9	132.6	-	132.6	38.2	-	3.2	12.0	3.6	3.4	5.3	4.8	4.9	4.3	1.0	11.8	(X)	3.2	4.3	5.9	0.6	4.9
MS	20.9	76.1	-	69.9	19.6	6.2	4.1	0.4	3.3	0.7	10.9	19.3	3.1	8.2	1.2	8.2	(X)	3.6	2.2	2.3	0.2	1.4
MO	30.9	140.3	-	134.9	29.3	5.4	6.4	3.0	2.7	3.7	10.9	11.9	5.5	6.4	2.4	16.2	(X)	7.5	11.1	3.8	0.5	4.6
MT	12.4	22.7	-	22.6	12.0	0.1	1.4	0.5	0.8	1.3	0.7	0.3	2.0	1.3	0.5	2.2	(X)	0.7	1.2	0.8	0.1	0.7
NE	19.8	54.3	-	50.5	19.1	3.7	2.6	1.3	0.5	0.8	2.0	4.8	2.0	3.2	0.7	4.4	(X)	1.6	2.8	1.6	0.3	1.1
NV	11.1	49.4	-	49.4	10.9	-	2.5	1.5	1.5	0.9	1.4	4.4	1.7	1.1	0.8	7.9	(X)	2.7	3.6	2.5	0.3	3.0
NH	7.3	33.8	-	33.8	7.1	-	2.0	2.3	0.8	0.2	0.6	-	1.6	1.6	0.5	3.5	(X)	2.1	1.0	0.7	0.3	5.8
NJ	59.6	216.8	15.6	206.2	41.6	10.6	9.0	8.2	3.8	4.2	14.2	1.4	6.0	8.8	4.2	31.8	(X)	8.4	8.7	6.1	0.8	2.5
NM	18.2	47.1	-	43.9	17.3	3.2	1.7	0.5	3.3	0.7	7.9	1.2	2.0	1.4	0.7	5.5	(X)	2.6	3.6	2.2	0.6	13.0
NY	65.0	503.0	-	477.5	61.3	25.6	4.9	42.3	7.7	16.3	41.5	51.5	10.6	26.3	6.3	82.6	(X)	25.7	33.2	26.2	2.9	6.1
NC	67.9	215.1	-	194.4	65.0	20.6	1.1	16.6	2.0	16.7	23.1	52.3	8.4	3.8	6.0	25.8	(X)	10.6	17.8	5.4	1.0	6.1
ND	8.4	17.3	-	17.3	8.1	-	0.7	1.1	1.9	0.7	0.8	-	0.9	1.4	0.2	1.8	(X)	0.6	0.9	0.6	0.2	1.2
OH	74.9	241.2	-	236.8	72.8	4.3	2.8	20.2	2.7	14.1	14.6	11.4	6.1	11.1	2.7	28.4	(X)	17.8	13.4	9.2	0.5	9.5
OK	30.4	88.6	-	88.6	28.8	-	6.9	0.2	4.8	1.8	1.0	11.2	2.9	4.9	1.9	9.7	(X)	4.7	4.9	2.0	0.7	1.6
OR	28.3	74.8	-	66.6	27.3	8.2	8.8	1.4	1.8	5.3	8.8	2.6	3.9	3.5	1.5	7.6	(X)	4.3	5.3	3.6	0.5	4.2
PA	65.0	242.5	-	232.7	60.4	9.9	11.4	14.5	5.0	5.5	8.0	-	12.7	10.9	6.4	26.1	(X)	6.4	17.2	13.5	1.1	3.3
RI	6.7	18.9	0.5	18.9	5.8	-	1.5	0.2	0.9	0.1	0.7	-	0.8	0.9	0.3	2.7	(X)	2.4	1.5	-	0.5	0.5
SC	40.2	105.5	-	105.5	37.1	-	5.6	0.4	5.2	2.6	6.8	26.1	4.3	2.6	2.1	12.7	(X)	6.5	7.3	3.4	0.9	4.1
SD	5.8	21.4	-	20.9	5.4	0.5	1.6	0.3	0.8	0.4	0.3	0.7	1.0	1.5	0.4	1.8	(X)	0.5	0.7	0.7	0.1	0.7
TN	38.0	135.3	-	135.3	35.8	-	7.4	1.4	4.1	4.7	2.9	24.7	4.1	6.2	1.7	20.3	(X)	8.4	5.9	5.8	1.0	4.5
TX	146.5	787.2	-	742.4	144.2	44.7	24.6	3.9	20.6	30.0	23.9	60.3	12.6	21.0	7.4	71.1	(X)	30.0	39.4	27.0	1.4	18.8
UT	32.5	57.0	-	57.0	30.7	-	2.9	0.7	2.1	3.2	10.7	1.0	1.6	1.8	0.6	5.7	(X)	2.8	3.1	2.1	0.3	4.1
VT	5.0	17.7	-	17.7	4.7	-	1.5	-	0.5	0.1	0.2	-	1.0	1.1	0.6	0.9	(X)	0.3	1.0	-	0.1	0.3
VA	59.7	198.5	-	197.3	57.8	1.2	3.2	9.0	6.9	6.7	11.1	2.3	7.8	4.2	3.2	18.8	(X)	11.8	13.2	10.9	1.2	7.9
WA	58.3	197.6	-	127.6	56.4	-	11.7	1.3	7.9	3.7	13.4	20.3	6.7	7.0	2.0	12.7	(X)	9.6	8.8	4.7	0.6	6.3
WV	14.9	41.6	-	41.6	13.7	-	3.3	-	0.7	1.2	1.4	2.2	5.1	1.0	1.0	3.0	(X)	1.0	3.3	0.2	0.6	0.9
WI	39.3	128.9	-	119.2	38.3	9.7	2.3	11.7	1.7	5.4	3.6	0.8	5.1	8.6	0.8	15.2	(X)	5.0	9.1	3.9	0.2	3.0
WY	3.9	21.0	-	18.7	3.7	2.3	0.5	0.1	0.9	0.3	0.6	7.6	1.7	0.7	0.3	1.7	(X)	0.5	1.2	0.7	0.2	0.9

– Represents or rounds to zero. X Not applicable. [1] Includes other categories, not shown separately.

Source: U.S. Census Bureau, Census of Governments, "Annual Survey of Public Employment and Payroll Datasets and Tables," <census.gov/programs-surveys/apes.html>, accessed July 2020.

Table 507. State and Local Government Employment and Average Monthly Earnings by State: 2010 to 2019

[4,378 represents 4,378,000. As of March. Full-time equivalent is a computed statistic representing the number of full-time employees that could have been employed if the reported number of hours worked by part-time employees had been worked by full-time employees. This statistic is calculated separately for each function of a government by dividing the "part-time hours paid" by the standard number of hours for full-time employees in the particular government and then adding the resulting quotient to the number of full-time employees]

State	Full-time equivalent employment (1,000)						Average monthly earnings [2] (dol.)					
	State			Local [1]			State			Local [1]		
	2010	2018	2019	2010	2018	2019	2010	2018	2019	2010	2018	2019
United States......	**4,378**	**4,428**	**4,459**	**12,171**	**12,261**	**12,255**	**4,620**	**5,593**	**5,753**	**4,310**	**5,018**	**5,168**
Alabama..............	90	92	95	198	192	193	4,099	4,853	5,045	3,240	3,860	4,012
Alaska................	27	24	24	28	28	27	5,176	6,083	6,206	4,935	5,714	5,865
Arizona..............	67	73	74	225	206	210	4,365	5,288	5,292	4,163	4,761	4,929
Arkansas............	63	62	62	106	108	108	3,795	4,325	4,450	3,208	3,374	3,472
California............	411	451	439	1,381	1,447	1,450	5,740	7,532	7,889	5,787	6,980	7,087
Colorado............	71	87	94	199	211	217	5,033	6,059	6,340	4,230	5,017	5,144
Connecticut.........	63	59	61	123	125	122	5,632	6,785	6,752	5,063	5,836	5,945
Delaware............	26	27	25	23	24	25	4,113	5,092	5,117	4,484	5,115	5,205
District of Columbia...........	(X)	(X)	(X)	44	53	56	(X)	(X)	(X)	5,900	7,170	7,328
Florida..............	184	181	182	727	719	723	3,861	4,661	4,745	3,986	4,402	4,533
Georgia.............	124	133	131	392	393	398	3,795	4,569	4,715	3,439	4,140	4,215
Hawaii...............	58	58	57	15	17	17	3,943	4,991	5,272	5,040	5,652	5,849
Idaho................	22	25	25	55	61	61	4,280	5,592	5,770	3,341	3,801	3,978
Illinois..............	131	122	124	513	499	493	5,324	5,857	6,310	4,716	5,462	5,641
Indiana..............	90	97	97	254	234	239	4,023	4,526	4,627	3,547	3,959	4,145
Iowa.................	51	51	51	124	135	137	5,326	6,709	6,803	3,831	4,596	4,642
Kansas..............	44	54	54	156	148	147	4,178	4,831	4,970	3,361	3,858	3,983
Kentucky............	81	84	82	161	159	159	3,940	4,675	4,861	3,101	3,701	3,812
Louisiana............	89	74	77	187	183	182	4,282	5,027	4,884	3,397	3,723	3,786
Maine................	21	20	21	51	50	50	4,063	4,728	4,818	3,545	4,032	4,160
Maryland............	88	84	84	215	219	220	4,650	5,465	5,642	5,190	5,894	6,071
Massachusetts.......	95	104	106	233	237	230	4,973	6,311	6,535	4,800	5,685	5,838
Michigan.............	146	148	150	329	289	283	5,208	6,132	6,262	4,618	4,768	4,965
Minnesota...........	80	85	84	201	218	216	5,338	6,256	6,356	4,447	5,190	5,406
Mississippi..........	57	55	54	136	133	130	3,537	4,312	4,463	2,985	3,368	3,429
Missouri..............	89	85	85	234	233	231	3,518	4,079	4,204	3,502	3,928	4,074
Montana.............	20	24	25	38	37	37	4,016	4,147	4,308	3,476	4,159	4,339
Nebraska............	33	32	35	88	90	91	4,013	4,926	5,016	3,785	4,696	4,840
Nevada..............	28	30	30	86	87	89	4,891	5,374	5,714	5,149	5,537	5,588
New Hampshire......	19	19	19	53	59	51	4,584	5,559	5,817	3,813	4,648	4,776
New Jersey..........	152	146	146	356	336	338	5,767	6,155	6,360	5,449	6,311	6,396
New Mexico.........	48	45	47	80	78	77	3,978	4,791	4,958	3,440	3,835	4,024
New York............	251	248	252	975	947	962	5,484	6,554	6,533	5,315	6,284	6,493
North Carolina.......	146	140	149	402	419	406	3,886	5,105	5,166	3,690	4,249	4,407
North Dakota........	18	18	18	26	29	29	4,103	5,144	5,213	3,550	4,536	4,646
Ohio.................	140	135	136	466	453	446	4,995	5,714	5,830	4,101	4,572	4,805
Oklahoma............	71	65	64	146	146	143	3,864	4,570	4,632	3,119	3,582	3,879
Oregon..............	65	73	74	133	134	133	4,452	5,629	5,818	4,348	5,385	5,615
Pennsylvania........	168	154	155	429	400	402	4,564	5,825	5,979	4,290	5,182	5,217
Rhode Island........	19	18	19	31	30	29	5,298	6,283	6,279	4,953	5,689	5,892
South Carolina.......	77	85	85	171	189	192	3,810	4,327	4,482	3,557	3,987	4,107
South Dakota........	14	14	14	31	34	33	3,938	4,786	4,740	3,149	3,890	4,049
Tennessee...........	83	80	80	247	259	256	3,822	4,649	4,885	3,358	3,918	4,062
Texas................	318	308	315	1,134	1,204	1,204	4,280	5,350	5,500	3,604	4,243	4,355
Utah.................	51	62	63	90	91	96	4,409	5,352	5,588	3,706	4,533	4,717
Vermont..............	14	14	14	26	26	23	4,645	5,738	5,849	3,589	4,645	4,947
Virginia.............	125	126	126	319	327	324	4,384	5,412	5,510	3,905	4,518	4,617
Washington..........	123	135	130	226	253	259	4,913	5,942	6,102	5,416	6,639	7,011
West Virginia........	39	40	39	62	63	62	3,554	4,107	4,366	3,219	3,398	3,554
Wisconsin............	72	71	72	211	212	211	4,901	5,487	5,730	4,239	4,781	4,977
Wyoming.............	14	13	13	37	37	38	4,240	4,671	4,705	4,068	4,708	4,800

X Not applicable. [1] Estimates subject to sampling variation; see Appendix III and source. [2] For full-time employees.

Source: U.S. Census Bureau, Census of Governments, "Annual Survey of Public Employment and Payroll Datasets and Tables," <census.gov/programs-surveys/apes.html>, accessed July 2020.

Section 9
Federal Government Finances and Employment

This section presents statistics relating to the financial structure and civilian employment of the federal government. The fiscal data cover taxes, other receipts, outlays, and debt. The principal sources of fiscal data are the *Budget of the United States Government* and related documents, published annually by the Office of Management and Budget (OMB), and the U.S. Department of the Treasury's *Combined Statement of Receipts, Outlays, and Balances of the United States Government*. Detailed data on tax returns and collections are published annually by the Internal Revenue Service. Data on government staffing, payrolls, and retirements are published by the Office of Personnel Management (OPM). Data on federally owned land and real property are collected by the General Services Administration and presented in its annual *Federal Real Property Report*.

Budget concept—Under the unified budget concept, all federal monies are included in one comprehensive budget. These monies comprise both federal funds and trust funds. Federal funds are derived mainly from taxes and borrowing and are not restricted by law to any specific government purpose. Trust funds, such as the Unemployment Trust Fund, collect certain taxes and other receipts for use in carrying out specific purposes or programs in accordance with the terms of the trust agreement or statute. Fund balances include both cash balances with the Treasury and investments in U.S. securities. Part of the balance is obligated, part unobligated. Prior to 1985, the budget totals, under provisions of law, excluded some federal activities—including the Federal Financing Bank, the Postal Service, the Synthetic Fuels Corporation, and the lending activities of the Rural Electrification Administration. The Balanced Budget and Emergency Deficit Control Act of 1985 (P.L.99-177) repealed the off-budget status of these entities and placed Social Security (Federal Old-Age and Survivors Insurance and the Federal Disability Insurance Trust Funds) off-budget. Though Social Security is now off-budget and, by law excluded from coverage of the congressional budget resolutions, it continues to be a federal program.

Receipts arising from the government's sovereign powers are reported as governmental receipts and all other receipts, i.e., from business or market-oriented activities, are offset against outlays. Outlays are reported on a checks-issued (net) basis (i.e., outlays are recorded at the time the checks to pay bills are issued).

Debt concept—For most of U.S. history, the total debt consisted of debt borrowed by the Treasury (i.e., public debt). The present debt series includes both public debt and agency debt. The *gross federal debt* includes money borrowed by the Treasury and by various federal agencies; it is the broadest generally used measure of the federal debt. *Total public debt* is covered by a statutory debt limitation and includes only borrowing by the Treasury.

Treasury receipts and outlays—All receipts of the government, with a few exceptions, are deposited to the credit of the U.S. Treasury regardless of ultimate disposition. Under the Constitution, no money may be withdrawn from the Treasury unless appropriated by the Congress.

The day-to-day cash operations of the federal government clearing through the accounts of the U.S. Treasury are reported in the *Daily Treasury Statement*. Extensive detail on the public debt is published in the *Monthly Statement of the Public Debt of the United States*.

Budget receipts such as taxes, customs duties, and miscellaneous receipts, which are collected by government agencies, and outlays represented by checks issued and cash payments made by disbursing officers as well as government agencies, are reported in the *Monthly Treasury Statement of Receipts and Outlays of the United States Government* and in the Treasury's *Combined Statement of Receipts, Outlays, and Balances of the United States Government*. These deposits in and payments from accounts maintained by government agencies are on the same basis as the unified budget.

The quarterly *Treasury Bulletin* contains data on fiscal operations and related Treasury activities, including financial statements of government corporations and other business-type activities.

Income tax returns and tax collections—Tax data are compiled by the Internal Revenue Service of the Treasury Department. The annual *Internal Revenue Service Data Book* gives a detailed account of tax collections by kind of tax. The agency's annual *Statistics of Income* reports present detailed data from individual income tax returns and corporation income tax returns as well as historical tax data. The quarterly *Statistics of Income Bulletin* presents data on such diverse subjects as tax-exempt organizations, unincorporated businesses, fiduciary income tax and estate tax returns, sales of capital assets by individuals, international income and taxes reported by corporations and individuals, and estate tax wealth.

Employment and payrolls—The Office of Personnel Management collects employment, payroll, and retirement data from all departments and agencies of the federal government, except the Central Intelligence Agency, the National Security Agency, the National Geospatial-Intelligence Agency, and the Defense Intelligence Agency. Employment figures represent the number of persons who occupied civilian positions at the end of the report month shown and who are paid for services rendered to the federal government, regardless of the nature of appointment or method of payment. Federal payrolls include all payments for personnel services rendered during the report month and payments for accumulated annual leave of employees who separate from the service. Since most federal employees are paid on a biweekly basis, the calendar month earnings are partially estimated on the basis of the number of work days in each month where payroll periods overlap.

Federal employment and payroll figures are published by the Office of Personnel Management in its *Federal Civilian Workforce Statistics—Employment and Trends* and the FedScope database system. OPM also publishes employment data on minority groups, white- and blue-collar workers, employment by geographic area, and salary and wage distribution of federal employees. General schedule is primarily white-collar; wage system primarily blue-collar. Data on federal employment are also issued by the Bureau of Labor Statistics in its *Monthly Labor Review* and *Employment and Earnings Online* and by the U.S. Census Bureau in its annual report series *Federal, State, and Local Governments: Public Employment and Payroll Data.*

Table 508. Federal Budget—Receipts and Outlays: 1960 to 2020

[92.5 represents $92,500,000,000. For fiscal years ending in year shown; See text, Section 8. See also headnote, Table 510]

Fiscal year	In current dollars (bil. dol.)			In constant (2012) dollars (bil. dol.)			As percentage of GDP [1]		
	Receipts	Outlays	Surplus or deficit (-)	Receipts	Outlays	Surplus or deficit (-)	Receipts	Outlays	Surplus or deficit (-)
1960...............	92.5	92.2	0.3	696.5	694.2	2.3	17.3	17.3	0.1
1970...............	192.8	195.6	-2.8	1,080.2	1,096.1	-15.9	18.4	18.7	-0.3
1980...............	517.1	590.9	-73.8	1,393.5	1,592.4	-198.9	18.5	21.2	-2.6
1990...............	1,032.0	1,253.0	-221.0	1,755.0	2,130.9	-375.9	17.5	21.2	-3.7
2000...............	2,025.2	1,789.0	236.2	2,691.3	2,377.3	313.9	20.0	17.7	2.3
2001...............	1,991.1	1,862.8	128.2	2,578.5	2,412.4	166.1	18.9	17.7	1.2
2002...............	1,853.1	2,010.9	-157.8	2,363.4	2,564.6	-201.2	17.1	18.6	-1.5
2003...............	1,782.3	2,159.9	-377.6	2,210.2	2,678.4	-468.2	15.8	19.1	-3.3
2004...............	1,880.1	2,292.8	-412.7	2,272.3	2,771.1	-498.8	15.6	19.1	-3.4
2005...............	2,153.6	2,472.0	-318.3	2,516.5	2,888.5	-372.0	16.8	19.3	-2.5
2006...............	2,406.9	2,655.0	-248.2	2,718.4	2,998.7	-280.3	17.6	19.5	-1.8
2007...............	2,568.0	2,728.7	-160.7	2,822.3	2,998.9	-176.6	18.0	19.1	-1.1
2008...............	2,524.0	2,982.5	-458.6	2,681.1	3,168.2	-487.1	17.1	20.2	-3.1
2009...............	2,105.0	3,517.7	-1,412.7	2,236.3	3,737.0	-1,500.8	14.6	24.4	-9.8
2010...............	2,162.7	3,457.1	-1,294.4	2,257.3	3,608.3	-1,351.0	14.6	23.3	-8.7
2011...............	2,303.5	3,603.1	-1,299.6	2,349.3	3,674.7	-1,325.4	15.0	23.4	-8.4
2012...............	2,450.0	3,526.6	-1,076.6	2,450.0	3,526.6	-1,076.6	15.3	22.0	-6.7
2013...............	2,775.1	3,454.9	-679.8	2,736.3	3,406.5	-670.3	16.7	20.8	-4.1
2014...............	3,021.5	3,506.3	-484.8	2,932.9	3,403.5	-470.6	17.4	20.2	-2.8
2015...............	3,249.9	3,691.8	-442.0	3,138.5	3,565.3	-426.8	18.0	20.4	-2.4
2016...............	3,268.0	3,852.6	-584.7	3,135.0	3,695.9	-560.9	17.6	20.8	-3.2
2017...............	3,316.2	3,981.6	-665.4	3,129.4	3,757.3	-628.0	17.2	20.6	-3.5
2018...............	3,329.9	4,109.0	-779.1	3,072.2	3,791.0	-718.8	16.4	20.2	-3.8
2019...............	3,464.2	4,448.3	-984.2	3,141.0	4,033.3	-892.3	16.3	21.0	-4.6
2020, estimate......	3,706.3	4,789.7	-1,083.4	3,288.7	4,250.0	-961.3	16.7	21.6	-4.9

[1] Gross domestic product; see text, Section 13.

Source: U.S. Office of Management and Budget, *Budget of the U.S. Government, Fiscal Year 2021: Historical Tables*, February 2020. See also <http://www.whitehouse.gov/omb/budget>.

Table 509. Federal Budget Debt: 1960 to 2020

[290.5 represents $290,500,000,000. As of the end of the fiscal year. See text, Section 8]

Fiscal year	Total (billion dollars)					As percent of GDP [1]				
	Gross federal debt	Federal govern- ment accounts	Held by the public			Gross federal debt	Federal govern- ment accounts	Held by the public		
			Total	Federal Reserve System	Other			Total	Federal Reserve System	Other
1960...............	290.5	53.7	236.8	26.5	210.3	54.4	10.0	44.3	5.0	39.4
1970...............	380.9	97.7	283.2	57.7	225.5	36.4	9.3	27.1	5.5	21.5
1980...............	909.0	197.1	711.9	120.8	591.1	32.6	7.1	25.5	4.3	21.2
1990...............	3,206.3	794.7	2,411.6	234.4	2,177.1	54.4	13.5	40.9	4.0	36.9
1991...............	3,598.2	909.2	2,689.0	258.6	2,430.4	59.1	14.9	44.1	4.2	39.9
1992...............	4,001.8	1,002.1	2,999.7	296.4	2,703.3	62.4	15.6	46.8	4.6	42.1
1993...............	4,351.0	1,102.6	3,248.4	325.7	2,922.7	64.2	16.3	47.9	4.8	43.1
1994...............	4,643.3	1,210.2	3,433.1	355.2	3,077.9	64.7	16.9	47.8	4.9	42.9
1995...............	4,920.6	1,316.2	3,604.4	374.1	3,230.3	65.1	17.4	47.7	4.9	42.7
1996...............	5,181.5	1,447.4	3,734.1	390.9	3,343.1	65.2	18.2	47.0	4.9	42.0
1997...............	5,369.2	1,596.9	3,772.3	424.5	3,347.8	63.5	18.9	44.6	5.0	39.6
1998...............	5,478.2	1,757.1	3,721.1	458.2	3,262.9	61.3	19.7	41.7	5.1	36.5
1999...............	5,605.5	1,973.2	3,632.4	496.6	3,135.7	59.1	20.8	38.3	5.2	33.1
2000...............	5,628.7	2,218.9	3,409.8	511.4	2,898.4	55.6	21.9	33.7	5.1	28.6
2001...............	5,769.9	2,450.3	3,319.6	534.1	2,785.5	54.8	23.3	31.5	5.1	26.5
2002...............	6,198.4	2,658.0	3,540.4	604.2	2,936.2	57.2	24.5	32.7	5.6	27.1
2003...............	6,760.0	2,846.6	3,913.4	656.1	3,257.3	59.9	25.2	34.7	5.8	28.9
2004...............	7,354.7	3,059.1	4,295.5	700.3	3,595.2	61.2	25.4	35.7	5.8	29.9
2005...............	7,905.3	3,313.1	4,592.2	736.4	3,855.9	61.6	25.8	35.8	5.7	30.0
2006...............	8,451.4	3,622.4	4,829.0	768.9	4,060.0	62.0	26.6	35.4	5.6	29.8
2007...............	8,950.7	3,915.6	5,035.1	779.6	4,255.5	62.6	27.4	35.2	5.5	29.8
2008...............	9,986.1	4,183.0	5,803.1	491.1	5,311.9	67.7	28.4	39.4	3.3	36.0
2009...............	11,875.9	4,331.1	7,544.7	769.2	6,775.5	82.3	30.0	52.3	5.3	46.9
2010...............	13,528.8	4,509.9	9,018.9	811.7	8,207.2	91.2	30.4	60.8	5.5	55.3
2011...............	14,764.2	4,636.0	10,128.2	1,664.7	8,463.5	95.8	30.1	65.8	10.8	54.9
2012...............	16,050.9	4,769.8	11,281.1	1,645.3	9,635.8	100.0	29.7	70.3	10.2	60.0
2013...............	16,719.4	4,736.7	11,982.7	2,072.3	9,910.4	100.7	28.5	72.2	12.5	59.7
2014...............	17,794.5	5,014.6	12,779.9	2,451.7	10,328.2	102.6	28.9	73.7	14.1	59.6
2015...............	18,120.1	5,003.4	13,116.7	2,461.9	10,654.7	100.1	27.6	72.5	13.6	58.9
2016...............	19,539.5	5,371.8	14,167.6	2,463.5	11,704.2	105.3	29.0	76.4	13.3	63.1
2017...............	20,205.7	5,540.3	14,665.4	2,465.4	12,200.0	104.8	28.7	76.0	12.8	63.3
2018...............	21,462.3	5,712.7	15,749.6	2,313.2	13,436.4	105.5	28.1	77.4	11.4	66.1
2019...............	22,669.5	5,868.7	16,800.7	2,113.3	14,687.4	106.9	27.7	79.2	10.0	69.2
2020, estimate...	23,900.2	6,019.1	17,881.2	(NA)	(NA)	107.6	27.1	80.5	(NA)	(NA)

NA Not available. [1] Gross domestic product; see text, Section 13.

Source: U.S. Office of Management and Budget, *Budget of the U.S. Government, Fiscal Year 2021: Historical Tables*, February 2020. See also <http://www.whitehouse.gov/omb/budget>.

Table 510. Federal Budget Outlays by Type: 1990 to 2020

[1,253.0 represents $1,253,000,000,000. For fiscal years ending September 30. Given the inherent imprecision in adjusting outlays for inflation, the data shown in constant dollars present a reasonable perspective, not precision. The deflators and the categories that are deflated are as comparable over time as feasible. Minus sign (-) indicates offset]

Type	Unit	1990	2000	2010	2015	2018	2019	2020, estimate
Current dollar outlays...........	**Bil. dol.**	**1,253.0**	**1,789.0**	**3,457.1**	**3,691.9**	**4,109.0**	**4,448.3**	**4,789.7**
National defense [1]...........................	Bil. dol.	299.3	294.4	693.5	589.7	631.1	686.0	724.5
Nondefense, total........................	Bil. dol.	953.7	1,494.6	2,763.6	3,102.2	3,477.9	3,762.3	4,065.3
Payments for individuals.................	Bil. dol.	592.4	1,067.4	2,305.9	2,653.8	2,893.1	3,114.7	3,367.4
Direct payments [2]........................	Bil. dol.	513.5	876.6	1,906.7	2,186.3	2,363.6	2,561.5	2,765.5
Grants to state and local governments....	Bil. dol.	78.9	190.7	399.2	467.5	529.4	553.2	601.9
All other grants............................	Bil. dol.	56.2	95.1	209.2	156.9	167.1	168.0	188.9
Net interest [2].............................	Bil. dol.	184.3	222.9	196.2	223.2	325.0	375.2	376.2
All other [2]................................	Bil. dol.	157.4	151.7	134.4	184.1	190.7	202.7	242.1
Undistributed offsetting receipts [2].........	Bil. dol.	-36.6	-42.6	-82.1	-115.8	-97.9	-98.2	-109.2
Constant (2012) dollar outlays.........	**Bil. dol.**	**2,130.9**	**2,377.3**	**3,608.3**	**3,565.3**	**3,791.0**	**4,033.3**	**4,250.0**
National defense [1]...........................	Bil. dol.	542.7	431.6	723.7	573.3	586.4	625.5	647.9
Nondefense, total........................	Bil. dol.	1,588.4	1,945.8	2,884.5	2,991.8	3,204.6	3,407.9	3,602.4
Payments for individuals.................	Bil. dol.	942.4	1,367.2	2,406.3	2,565.5	2,675.9	2,834.5	2,997.6
Direct payments [2]........................	Bil. dol.	816.6	1,122.2	1,989.7	2,113.6	2,186.3	2,331.2	2,461.9
Grants to state and local governments....	Bil. dol.	125.7	245.0	416.7	451.9	489.6	503.3	535.7
All other grants............................	Bil. dol.	112.1	143.2	220.8	147.9	149.1	146.1	160.1
Net interest [2].............................	Bil. dol.	290.8	285.8	203.9	212.6	294.6	333.6	328.0
All other [2]................................	Bil. dol.	325.5	214.4	139.6	175.4	170.7	177.9	208.4
Undistributed offsetting receipts [2].........	Bil. dol.	-82.4	-64.8	-86.0	-109.5	-85.6	-84.3	-92.0
Outlays as percent of GDP [3].............	**Percent**	**21.2**	**17.7**	**23.3**	**20.4**	**20.2**	**21.0**	**21.6**
National defense [1]...........................	Percent	5.1	2.9	4.7	3.3	3.1	3.2	3.3
Nondefense, total........................	Percent	16.2	14.8	18.6	17.1	17.1	17.7	18.3
Payments for individuals.................	Percent	10.0	10.5	15.5	14.7	14.2	14.7	15.2
Direct payments [2]........................	Percent	8.7	8.7	12.8	12.1	11.6	12.1	12.5
Grants to state and local governments....	Percent	1.3	1.9	2.7	2.6	2.6	2.6	2.7
All other grants............................	Percent	1.0	0.9	1.4	0.9	0.8	0.8	0.9
Net interest [2].............................	Percent	3.1	2.2	1.3	1.2	1.6	1.8	1.7
All other [2]................................	Percent	2.7	1.5	0.9	1.0	0.9	1.0	1.1
Undistributed offsetting receipts [2].........	Percent	-0.6	-0.4	-0.6	-0.6	-0.5	-0.5	-0.5

[1] Includes a small amount of grants to state and local governments and direct payments for individuals. [2] Includes some off-budget amounts; most of the off-budget amounts are direct payments for individuals (social security benefits). [3] Gross domestic product; see text, Section 13.

Source: U.S. Office of Management and Budget, *Budget of the U.S. Government, Fiscal Year 2021: Historical Tables*, February 2020. See also <http://www.whitehouse.gov/omb/budget>.

Table 511. Federal Budget Outlays by Agency: 1990 to 2020

[In billions of dollars (1,253.0 represents $1,253,000,000,000). For fiscal years ending September 30]

Department or other unit	1990	2000	2005	2010	2015	2018	2019	2020 est.
Outlays, total........................	**1,253.0**	**1,789.0**	**2,472.0**	**3,457.1**	**3,691.9**	**4,109.0**	**4,448.3**	**4,789.7**
Legislative branch........................	2.2	2.9	4.0	5.8	4.3	4.7	5.0	6.0
Judicial branch...........................	1.6	4.1	5.5	7.2	7.1	7.8	8.0	8.6
Agriculture...............................	45.9	75.1	85.3	129.5	139.1	136.7	150.1	154.6
Commerce................................	3.7	7.8	6.1	13.2	9.0	8.6	11.3	17.1
Defense—Military........................	289.7	281.0	474.4	666.7	562.5	600.7	654.0	689.6
Education................................	23.0	33.5	72.9	93.7	90.0	63.7	104.4	159.3
Energy....................................	12.1	15.0	21.3	30.8	25.4	26.5	28.9	34.4
Health and Human Services...............	175.5	382.3	581.4	854.1	1,027.5	1,120.5	1,213.8	1,322.1
Homeland Security........................	7.2	13.2	38.7	44.5	42.6	68.4	57.7	62.2
Housing and Urban Development...........	20.2	30.8	42.5	60.1	35.5	54.7	29.2	36.0
Interior..................................	5.8	8.0	9.3	13.2	12.3	13.2	13.9	17.5
Justice...................................	5.9	16.8	22.4	29.6	26.9	34.5	35.1	45.3
Labor....................................	26.1	31.9	46.9	173.1	45.2	39.6	35.8	36.4
State....................................	4.8	6.7	12.7	23.8	26.5	26.4	28.0	32.2
Transportation...........................	25.6	41.6	56.6	77.8	75.4	78.5	80.7	84.7
Treasury.................................	253.9	390.5	410.2	444.3	485.6	629.5	689.5	701.0
Veterans Affairs..........................	29.0	47.0	69.8	108.3	159.2	178.5	199.6	214.3
Corps of Engineers—Civil Works...........	3.3	4.2	4.7	9.9	6.7	5.1	6.5	5.5
Other Defense—Civil Programs............	21.7	32.8	43.5	54.0	63.0	55.4	60.9	64.5
Environmental Protection Agency..........	5.1	7.2	7.9	11.0	7.0	8.1	8.1	7.5
Executive Office of the President...........	0.2	0.3	7.7	0.6	0.4	0.4	0.4	0.4
General Services Administration..........	-0.2	0.1	(Z)	0.9	-0.9	-0.6	-1.1	1.2
International Assistance Programs.........	10.1	12.1	15.0	20.0	24.4	21.6	23.6	25.7
National Aeronautics and Space Administration....	12.4	13.4	15.6	18.9	18.3	19.8	20.2	21.5
National Science Foundation..............	1.8	3.4	5.4	6.7	6.8	7.2	7.3	7.5
Office of Personnel Management...........	31.9	48.7	59.5	69.9	91.7	98.8	103.1	106.4
Small Business Administration............	0.7	-0.4	2.5	6.1	-0.7	(Z)	0.5	-0.2
Social Security Administration (on-budget).........	17.3	45.1	54.6	70.8	87.4	87.9	93.6	97.3
Social Security Administration (off-budget).........	245.0	396.2	506.8	683.4	856.8	952.0	1,008.3	1,057.9
Other independent agencies (on-budget)..........	68.7	8.8	16.8	-7.5	16.0	10.5	21.0	27.4
Other independent agencies (off-budget)..........	1.6	2.0	-1.8	4.7	-1.7	-1.5	-1.1	0.1
Undistributed offsetting receipts [1]..........	-98.9	-173.0	-226.2	-267.9	-257.6	-248.0	-247.8	-254.8

Z Less than $50,000,000. [1] Includes some off-budget amounts; most of the off-budget amounts are direct payments to individuals (social security benefits).

Source: U.S. Office of Management and Budget, *Budget of the U.S. Government, Fiscal Year 2021: Historical Tables*, February 2020. See also <http://www.whitehouse.gov/omb/budget>.

Table 512. Federal Budget Outlays by Detailed Function: 1990 to 2020

[In billions of dollars (1,253.0 represents $1,253,000,000,000). For fiscal years ending September 30. Minus sign (-) indicates decrease]

Superfunction and function	1990	2000	2005	2010	2015	2017	2018	2019	2020, est.
Total outlays	**1,253.0**	**1,789.0**	**2,472.0**	**3,457.1**	**3,691.9**	**3,981.6**	**4,109.0**	**4,448.3**	**4,789.7**
National defense [1]	299.3	294.4	495.3	693.5	589.7	598.7	631.1	686.0	724.5
Department of Defense—Military	289.7	281.0	474.1	666.7	562.5	568.9	600.7	654.0	689.6
Military personnel	75.6	76.0	127.5	155.7	145.2	144.7	145.8	156.3	162.1
Operation and maintenance	88.3	105.8	188.1	276.0	247.2	245.2	256.7	271.7	283.7
Procurement	81.0	51.7	82.3	133.6	101.3	104.1	112.7	124.7	135.1
Research, development, test, and evaluation	37.5	37.6	65.7	77.0	64.1	68.1	77.0	89.3	97.5
Military construction	5.1	5.1	5.3	21.2	8.1	6.7	6.7	7.4	8.1
Atomic energy defense activities	9.0	12.1	18.0	19.3	18.7	20.5	20.9	22.8	25.5
International affairs [1]	13.8	17.2	34.6	45.2	52.0	46.3	49.0	52.7	58.3
International development and humanitarian assistance	5.5	6.5	17.7	19.0	24.1	24.5	25.1	26.3	28.3
International security assistance	8.7	6.4	7.9	11.4	12.9	12.2	11.4	11.2	14.8
Conduct of foreign affairs	3.0	4.7	9.1	13.6	13.2	12.9	12.0	12.6	14.9
General science, space, and technology	14.4	18.6	23.6	30.1	29.4	30.4	31.5	32.4	35.0
General science and basic research	2.8	6.2	8.8	11.7	11.7	12.3	12.4	12.9	14.2
Space flight, research, and supporting activities	11.6	12.4	14.8	18.4	17.7	18.1	19.1	19.5	20.8
Energy [1]	3.3	-0.8	0.4	11.6	6.8	3.9	2.2	5.0	4.6
Energy supply	2.0	-1.8	-0.9	5.8	4.7	2.8	1.4	4.1	2.6
Natural resources and environment [1]	17.1	25.0	28.0	43.7	36.0	37.9	39.1	37.8	42.8
Water resources	4.4	5.1	5.7	11.7	7.8	7.5	6.0	7.8	7.8
Conservation and land management	4.0	6.8	6.2	10.8	10.5	12.2	13.4	11.1	14.7
Recreational resources	1.4	2.5	3.0	3.9	3.5	3.9	4.0	3.9	4.8
Pollution control and abatement	5.2	7.4	8.1	10.8	7.2	8.1	8.0	8.2	7.6
Agriculture	11.6	36.5	26.6	21.4	18.5	18.9	21.8	38.3	38.3
Farm income stabilization	9.6	33.4	22.0	16.5	13.4	14.2	16.7	32.9	31.0
Agricultural research and services	2.1	3.0	4.5	4.9	5.1	4.7	5.1	5.4	7.3
Commerce and housing credit [1]	67.6	3.2	7.6	-82.3	-37.9	-26.7	-9.5	-25.7	0.7
Mortgage credit	3.8	-3.3	-0.9	35.8	-35.7	-30.1	-7.4	-43.5	-24.4
Postal service	2.1	2.1	-1.2	-0.7	-1.6	-2.2	-1.4	-1.0	0.1
Deposit insurance	57.9	-3.1	-1.4	-32.0	-12.8	-12.1	-15.9	-8.0	-5.5
Transportation [1]	29.5	46.9	67.9	92.0	89.5	93.6	92.8	97.1	101.6
Ground transportation	19.0	31.7	42.3	60.8	59.1	62.9	61.9	63.1	65.5
Air transportation	7.2	10.6	18.8	21.4	20.0	20.3	20.2	22.6	22.7
Water transportation	3.2	4.4	6.4	9.4	10.0	10.1	10.2	11.0	12.8
Community and regional development [1]	8.5	10.6	26.3	23.9	20.7	24.9	42.2	26.9	30.3
Community development	3.5	5.5	5.9	9.9	7.8	6.7	7.1	6.3	9.5
Disaster relief and insurance	2.1	2.6	17.7	10.7	9.0	15.1	32.3	17.2	16.3
Education, training, employment, and social services [1]	37.2	53.8	97.6	128.6	122.0	144.0	95.5	136.8	195.5
Elementary, secondary, and vocational education	9.9	20.6	38.3	73.3	40.0	40.6	39.5	41.4	44.7
Higher education	11.1	10.1	31.4	20.9	51.3	71.8	24.6	63.1	115.2
Research and general education aids	1.6	2.5	3.1	3.6	3.5	3.7	3.6	3.7	4.0
Training and employment	5.6	6.8	6.9	9.9	7.1	7.0	6.8	6.7	7.4
Social services	8.1	12.6	16.3	19.2	18.3	18.9	19.1	19.9	22.2
Health	57.7	154.5	250.6	369.1	482.3	533.2	551.2	584.8	640.9
Health care services	47.6	136.2	219.6	330.7	446.4	492.8	511.6	542.2	595.1
Health research and training	8.6	16.0	28.1	34.2	31.4	34.9	35.5	37.7	40.3
Consumer and occupational health and safety	1.5	2.3	2.9	4.1	4.5	5.4	4.2	4.9	5.5
Medicare	98.1	197.1	298.6	451.6	546.2	597.3	588.7	651.0	699.3
Income security [1]	148.8	253.7	345.8	622.1	508.8	503.4	495.3	514.8	529.3
General retirement and disability insurance (excluding social security)	5.1	5.2	7.0	6.6	7.8	4.5	6.3	3.7	5.8
Federal employee retirement and disability	52.0	77.1	93.3	119.8	139.1	142.2	140.7	149.6	155.0
Unemployment compensation	18.9	23.0	35.4	160.1	35.0	33.3	30.9	29.9	29.9
Housing assistance	15.9	28.9	37.9	58.7	47.8	50.0	49.5	50.6	51.2
Food and nutrition assistance	24.1	32.5	50.8	95.1	104.8	99.7	98.1	93.6	95.1
Social security	248.6	409.4	523.3	706.7	887.8	944.9	987.8	1,044.4	1,097.2
Veterans' benefits and services [1]	29.1	47.0	70.1	108.5	159.8	176.6	178.9	199.8	215.1
Income security for veterans	15.3	25.0	35.8	49.3	76.4	86.1	85.6	101.1	111.4
Veterans education, training, and rehabilitation	0.2	1.3	2.8	8.1	13.4	13.3	12.4	13.1	14.4
Hospital and medical care for veterans	12.1	19.5	28.8	45.7	61.9	69.7	73.9	80.3	82.2
Veterans housing	0.5	0.4	0.9	0.5	0.7	-0.5	-1.3	-3.1	-2.8
Administration of justice	10.2	28.5	40.0	54.4	51.9	57.9	60.4	65.7	79.6
Federal law enforcement activities	4.8	12.1	19.9	28.7	26.9	29.8	31.3	34.2	39.6
Federal litigative and judicial activities	3.6	7.8	10.7	14.5	14.7	15.1	17.0	17.3	19.9
Federal correctional activities	1.3	3.7	4.8	6.3	7.0	7.0	6.8	7.1	7.4
Criminal justice assistance	0.5	4.9	4.6	4.8	3.2	6.0	5.3	7.2	12.7
General government	10.5	13.0	17.0	23.0	21.0	23.8	23.9	23.4	29.5
Net interest [1]	184.3	222.9	184.0	196.2	223.2	262.6	325.0	375.2	376.2
Interest on Treasury debt securities (gross)	264.7	361.9	352.3	413.9	402.4	456.9	521.6	572.9	576.5
Interest received by on-budget trust funds	-46.3	-69.3	-69.2	-67.3	-45.8	-60.5	-66.3	-67.1	-66.5
Interest received by off-budget trust funds	-16.0	-59.8	-91.8	-118.5	-96.0	-86.5	-83.8	82.6	-79.0
Allowances	–	–	–	–	–	–	–	–	0.4
Undistributed offsetting receipts [2]	-36.6	-42.6	-65.2	-82.1	-115.8	-89.8	-97.9	-98.2	-109.2

– Represents or rounds to zero. [1] Includes functions not shown separately. [2] Includes some off-budget amounts; most of the off-budget amounts are direct payments for individuals (social security benefits).

Source: U.S. Office of Management and Budget, *Budget of the U.S. Government, Fiscal Year 2021: Historical Tables*, February 2020. See also <http://www.whitehouse.gov/omb/budget>.

Table 513. Federal Budget Outlays for Payments for Individuals by Category and Major Program: 1990 to 2020

[In billions of dollars (592.4 represents $592,400,000,000). For fiscal years ending September 30]

Category and program	1990	2000	2005	2010	2015	2017	2018	2019	2020, est
Total, payments for individuals	**592.4**	**1,067.4**	**1,512.6**	**2,307.0**	**2,654.9**	**2,873.0**	**2,894.5**	**3,116.2**	**3,368.8**
Social security and railroad retirement	253.3	410.7	523.5	706.6	890.2	948.6	991.2	1,048.0	1,102.0
Social security:									
Old age and survivors insurance	221.9	351.4	434.0	576.6	738.0	795.5	837.6	892.9	944.4
Disability insurance	24.4	54.4	84.2	123.5	143.4	143.2	143.9	145.1	146.8
Railroad retirement (excl. social security)	7.0	4.8	5.4	6.5	8.9	9.9	9.7	10.0	10.9
Federal employees' retirement and insurance	64.1	100.4	127.0	166.7	211.9	224.9	224.0	249.1	265.4
Military retirement	21.5	32.8	39.0	50.6	56.7	57.7	54.5	60.7	63.1
Civil service retirement	31.0	45.1	54.7	69.5	81.8	83.7	85.9	88.8	91.8
Veterans service-connected compensation	10.7	20.8	30.9	43.5	69.7	79.8	80.0	95.6	106.1
Other	0.8	1.7	2.4	3.2	3.7	3.7	3.6	4.0	4.3
Unemployment assistance	17.5	21.1	33.1	158.3	32.7	30.9	28.5	27.4	27.8
Medical care [1]	167.4	368.6	575.4	876.8	1,111.0	1,233.5	1,264.1	1,366.7	1,482.5
Medicare:									
Hospital insurance	65.9	127.9	181.3	245.6	273.5	290.3	292.1	318.4	341.9
Supplementary medical insurance	41.5	87.2	150.0	264.9	348.6	399.8	400.1	444.3	482.1
State children's health insurance	–	1.2	5.1	7.9	9.2	16.3	17.3	17.7	18.0
Medicaid	41.1	117.9	181.7	272.8	349.8	374.7	389.2	409.4	447.2
Indian health	1.1	2.4	3.1	4.4	4.6	4.1	4.2	4.6	5.7
Hospital and medical care for veterans	12.3	20.1	30.7	48.5	63.7	67.9	72.9	79.7	82.9
Health resources and services	1.4	3.9	5.9	7.1	7.7	9.3	9.5	9.9	9.9
Substance abuse and mental health services	1.2	2.5	3.2	3.3	3.1	3.4	3.8	4.3	6.4
Uniformed Services retiree health care fund	–	–	6.3	8.4	10.0	9.9	10.1	10.5	11.3
Other	2.9	5.4	8.2	14.0	12.7	14.0	14.3	14.6	15.5
Assistance to students	11.2	10.9	32.1	55.5	74.7	102.0	60.9	84.6	139.9
Veterans' education benefits	0.8	1.6	3.3	8.8	13.6	13.5	12.7	13.4	14.6
Student assistance, Department of Education and other	10.4	9.2	28.9	46.8	61.1	88.5	48.2	71.1	125.3
Housing assistance	15.9	28.6	37.5	57.6	46.7	48.9	48.4	49.4	50.4
Food and nutrition assistance	24.0	32.4	50.7	95.0	104.6	99.6	97.9	93.3	94.7
SNAP (including Puerto Rico) [2]	15.9	18.3	32.6	70.5	76.1	70.1	68.5	63.5	65.6
Child nutrition and special milk programs	5.0	9.2	11.9	16.4	21.0	22.5	22.8	23.3	22.8
Supplemental feeding programs (WIC and CSFP [3])	2.1	4.0	5.0	6.5	6.3	5.7	5.4	5.3	5.0
Commodity donations and other	1.0	0.9	1.2	1.6	1.1	1.2	1.1	1.3	1.3
Public assistance and related programs [1]	34.9	88.5	123.4	183.2	175.3	174.2	169.7	186.5	191.3
Supplemental security income program	11.5	29.7	35.4	44.0	52.3	51.9	47.9	53.1	53.8
Family support payments to states and TANF [4]	12.2	18.4	21.3	21.9	20.0	20.0	20.6	19.6	20.4
Low income home energy assistance	1.3	1.5	2.1	4.6	3.4	3.2	3.4	3.7	3.8
Earned income tax credit	4.4	26.1	34.6	54.7	60.1	59.7	58.6	59.2	60.3
Payments to states for daycare assistance	–	3.3	4.9	5.9	5.1	5.7	5.9	7.2	8.3
Veterans' non-service-connected pensions	3.6	3.0	3.7	4.4	5.3	5.5	4.8	4.9	4.8
Payments to states for foster care/adoption assistance	1.6	5.5	6.4	7.0	7.3	7.7	8.6	8.6	9.4
Payment where child credit exceeds tax liability	–	0.8	14.6	22.7	20.6	19.4	18.6	28.9	29.6
Other public assistance	0.3	0.3	0.4	18.1	1.2	0.9	1.4	1.3	1.0
All other payments for individuals	4.0	6.3	9.8	7.3	7.8	10.5	9.7	11.2	14.8
Coal miners and black lung benefits	1.5	1.5	1.4	0.5	0.4	0.5	0.5	0.4	0.4
Veterans' insurance and burial benefits	1.4	1.4	1.4	1.3	1.2	0.6	0.6	0.6	1.0
Aging services programs	–	0.9	1.4	1.5	1.7	1.9	1.9	2.0	2.5
Energy employees compensation fund	–	–	0.6	1.1	1.0	1.2	1.4	1.4	1.5
September 11th victim compensation	–	–	(Z)	–	0.1	1.0	1.2	1.3	2.2
Refugee assistance and other	1.1	2.5	5.0	2.9	3.3	5.3	4.1	5.4	7.2

– Represents zero. Z Less than $50,000,000. [1] Includes other items not shown separately. [2] Supplemental Nutrition Assistance Program, formerly known as food stamps. [3] WIC is Women, Infants, and Children. CSFP is Commodity Supplemental Food Program. [4] TANF is Temporary Assistance for Needy Families.

Source: U.S. Office of Management and Budget, *Budget of the U.S. Government, Fiscal Year 2021: Historical Tables*, February 2020. See also <http://www.whitehouse.gov/omb/budget>.

Table 514. Federal Budget Receipts by Source: 1990 to 2020

[In billions of dollars (1,032.0 represents $1,032,000,000,000). For fiscal years ending September 30. Receipts reflect collections. Covers both federal funds and trust funds; see text, this section. Minus sign (-) indicates decrease]

Source	1990	2000	2005	2010	2015	2017	2018	2019	2020, est.
Total federal receipts	**1,032.0**	**2,025.2**	**2,153.6**	**2,162.7**	**3,249.9**	**3,316.2**	**3,329.9**	**3,464.2**	**3,706.3**
(On-budget)	750.3	1,544.6	1,576.1	1,531.0	2,479.5	2,465.6	2,475.2	2,549.9	2,739.3
(Off-budget)	281.7	480.6	577.5	631.7	770.4	850.6	854.7	914.3	967.1
Individual income taxes	466.9	1,004.5	927.2	898.5	1,540.8	1,587.1	1,683.5	1,717.9	1,812.0
Corporation income taxes	93.5	207.3	278.3	191.4	343.8	297.0	204.7	230.2	263.6
Social insurance and retirement receipts	380.0	652.9	794.1	864.8	1,065.3	1,161.9	1,170.7	1,243.4	1,312.0
Excise taxes	35.3	68.9	73.1	66.9	98.3	83.8	95.0	99.5	94.6
Other	56.2	91.7	80.9	141.0	201.8	186.3	175.9	173.2	224.0
Social insurance and retirement receipts	**380.0**	**652.9**	**794.1**	**864.8**	**1,065.3**	**1,161.9**	**1,170.7**	**1,243.4**	**1,312.0**
Employment and general retirement, total	353.9	620.5	747.7	815.9	1,010.4	1,111.9	1,121.2	1,197.4	1,264.8
Old–age and survivors insurance (off–budget)	255.0	411.7	493.6	540.0	658.5	688.0	691.2	770.3	826.6
Disability insurance (off–budget)	26.6	68.9	83.8	91.7	111.8	162.6	163.5	144.0	140.5
Hospital insurance	68.6	135.5	166.1	180.1	234.2	255.9	260.7	277.6	292.1
Railroad retirement/pension fund	2.3	2.7	2.3	2.3	3.3	3.1	3.4	3.3	3.2
Unemployment insurance funds	21.6	27.6	42.0	44.8	51.2	45.8	45.0	41.2	42.0
Other retirement	4.5	4.8	4.5	4.1	3.7	4.2	4.5	4.8	5.2
Federal employees retirement—employee share	4.4	4.7	4.4	4.1	3.6	4.2	4.5	4.8	5.2
Excise taxes, total	**35.3**	**68.9**	**73.1**	**66.9**	**98.3**	**83.8**	**95.0**	**99.5**	**94.6**
Federal funds [1]	15.6	22.7	22.5	18.3	37.8	21.2	30.1	34.9	30.0
Alcohol	5.7	8.1	8.1	9.2	9.6	9.9	10.1	10.0	9.7
Tobacco	4.1	7.2	7.9	17.2	14.5	13.8	12.9	12.5	12.3
Telephone	3.0	5.7	6.0	1.0	0.6	0.6	0.5	0.4	0.4
Ozone–depleting chemicals/products	0.4	0.1	–	–	–	–	–	–	–
Transportation fuels	–	0.8	-0.8	-11.0	-3.4	-3.4	-1.5	-3.6	-11.0
Health insurance providers	–	–	–	–	11.3	0.1	4.7	9.6	15.4
Indoor tanning services	–	–	–	–	0.1	0.1	0.1	0.1	0.1
Trust funds [1]	19.8	46.2	50.5	48.7	60.5	62.6	64.9	64.5	64.6
Transportation	13.9	35.0	37.9	35.0	40.8	41.0	42.6	44.1	42.4
Airport and airway	3.7	9.7	10.3	10.6	14.3	15.1	15.8	16.0	17.0
Black lung disability	0.7	0.5	0.6	0.6	0.6	0.4	0.4	0.2	0.3
Inland waterway	0.1	0.1	0.1	0.1	0.1	0.1	0.1	0.1	0.1
Hazardous substance superfund	0.8	(Z)	–	–	–	–	–	–	–
Oil spill liability	0.1	0.2	–	0.5	0.5	0.5	0.5	0.2	0.5
Aquatic resources	0.2	0.3	0.4	0.6	0.6	0.6	0.6	0.6	0.6
Leaking underground storage tank	0.1	0.2	0.2	0.2	0.2	0.2	0.2	0.2	0.2
Tobacco assessments	–	–	0.9	0.9	(Z)	(Z)	(Z)	–	–
Vaccine injury compensation	0.2	0.1	0.1	0.2	0.3	0.3	0.3	0.3	0.3
Supplementary medical insurance	–	–	–	–	3.0	4.1	4.1	2.4	2.8

– Represents zero. Z less than $50,000,000. [1] Includes other funds, not shown separately.

Source: U.S. Office of Management and Budget, *Budget of the U.S. Government, Fiscal Year 2021: Historical Tables*, February 2020. See also <http://www.whitehouse.gov/omb/budget>.

Table 515. Federal Trust Fund Income, Outlays, and Balances: 2019 to 2021

[In billions of dollars (16.9 represents $16,900,000,000). For fiscal years ending September 30. Income reflects receipts deposited. Outlays are on a checks-issued basis less refunds collected. Balances reflect funds that have not been spent. See text, this section, for discussion of the budget concept and trust funds]

Fund type	Income			Outlays			Balances [1]		
	2019	2020, estimate	2021, estimate	2019	2020, estimate	2021, estimate	2019	2020, estimate	2021, estimate
Airport and airway trust fund	16.9	18.0	18.5	-16.0	-18.2	-18.3	17.9	17.7	17.8
Civil service retirement and disability fund	105.6	111.3	116.1	-88.9	-91.9	-93.9	939.7	959.1	981.3
Federal employees' health benefits fund	55.6	58.5	60.6	-55.3	-57.5	-59.3	27.5	28.5	29.8
Employee life insurance fund	4.5	4.8	4.9	-3.3	-3.4	-3.4	47.7	49.2	50.6
Foreign military sales trust fund	33.0	47.8	44.3	-34.0	-47.2	-51.8	32.5	33.1	25.7
Foreign service retirement and disability fund	1.1	1.4	1.4	-1.0	-1.0	-1.0	19.3	19.7	20.2
Highway trust fund	45.2	43.1	43.2	-56.4	-57.9	-59.9	32.9	18.1	1.4
Medicare:									
Hospital insurance (HI) trust fund	325.6	343.0	361.4	-329.8	-352.3	-360.3	198.9	189.7	190.7
Supplemental medical insurance trust fund	459.8	498.0	519.8	-452.7	-492.8	-523.1	104.1	109.3	105.9
Military retirement fund	143.9	151.3	159.2	-60.7	-63.1	-64.8	818.5	906.6	1,001.0
Railroad retirement trust funds	12.0	12.2	12.3	-13.4	-14.6	-13.8	23.3	20.9	19.4
Social security:									
Disability insurance trust fund	151.1	147.8	154.3	-147.8	-149.5	-151.2	96.4	94.8	98.0
Old-age and survivors trust fund	900.1	956.8	995.5	-896.8	-948.3	-1,005.3	2,804.3	2,813.0	2,803.3
Unemployment trust funds	43.3	44.5	45.9	-31.3	-31.2	-34.3	84.8	98.1	109.7
Other trust funds	27.0	28.0	26.4	-24.6	-25.7	-24.8	52.2	54.6	56.2

[1] Balances available on a cash basis (rather than an authorization basis) at the end of the year. Balances are primarily invested in federal debt securities.

Source: U.S. Office of Management and Budget, *Budget of the U.S. Government, Fiscal Year 2021: Analytical Perspectives*, February 2020. See also <http://www.whitehouse.gov/omb/budget>.

Table 516. Tax Expenditure Estimates Relating to Individual and Corporate Income Taxes by Selected Function: 2019 to 2022

[In millions of dollars (12,460 represents $12,460,000,000). For fiscal years ending September 30. Tax expenditures are defined as revenue losses attributable to provisions of the federal tax laws which allow a special exclusion, exemption, or deduction from gross income or which provide a special credit, a preferential rate of tax, or a deferral of liability. Minus sign (-) indicates decrease]

Function and provision	2019	2020	2021	2022
National defense:				
Exclusion of benefits and allowances to armed forces personnel.	12,460	12,910	11,660	11,700
International affairs:				
Exclusion of income earned abroad by U.S. citizens.	6,930	7,280	7,640	8,020
Exclusion of certain allowances for Federal employees abroad.	240	250	260	280
Reduced tax rate on active income of controlled foreign corporations.	35,470	40,000	42,980	44,660
General science, space, and technology:				
Expensing of research and experimentation expenditures (normal tax method).	5,520	5,740	6,330	-19,090
Credit for increasing research activities.	15,300	16,810	18,380	19,890
Energy:				
Energy production credit.	4,230	4,310	4,290	4,250
Energy investment credit.	3,710	4,510	4,820	4,490
Credit for residential energy efficient property.	1,980	1,740	1,410	360
Commerce and housing:				
Financial institutions and insurance:				
Exclusion of life insurance death benefits.	13,210	13,760	14,340	14,870
Housing:				
Deductibility of mortgage interest on owner–occupied homes.	25,130	27,090	29,580	32,290
Deductibility of state and local property tax on owner–occupied homes.	6,010	6,270	6,650	7,030
Capital gains exclusion on home sales.	43,610	45,750	48,040	50,330
Exclusion of net imputed rental income.	121,320	125,990	130,430	134,570
Exception from passive loss rules for $25,000 of rental loss.	6,070	6,430	6,780	7,110
Credit for low–income housing investments.	8,760	9,110	9,360	9,580
Commerce:				
Capital gains (except agriculture, timber, iron ore, and coal).	111,470	104,920	103,790	104,580
Step–up basis of capital gains at death.	49,980	51,750	53,640	56,200
Accelerated depreciation of machinery and equipment (normal tax method).	49,280	43,460	40,610	38,030
Allow 20-percent deduction to certain pass-through income.	34,923	53132	54698	56499
Transportation:				
Exclusion of reimbursed employee parking expenses.	2,250	2,270	2,400	2,510
Education, training, employment, and social services:				
Education:				
Exclusion of scholarship and fellowship income (normal tax method).	3,040	3,220	3,390	3,580
Tax credits and deductions for postsecondary education expenses.	17,380	16,390	16,310	16,290
Exclusion of interest on bonds for private nonprofit educational facilities.	1,850	1,950	1,940	1,990
Deductibility of charitable contributions (education).	4,140	4,450	4,790	5,100
Training, employment, and social services:				
Exclusion of employee meals and lodging (other than military).	5,100	5,240	5,420	5,620
Credit for child and dependent care expenses.	4,260	4,360	4,440	4,540
Deductibility of charitable contributions, other than education and health.	36,660	39,540	42,760	45,510
Health:				
Exclusion of employer contributions for medical insurance premiums and medical care.	202,290	214,420	227,880	242,230
Self–employed medical insurance premiums.	7,050	7,320	7,780	8,320
Medical Savings Accounts/Health Savings Accounts.	7,880	8,510	9,110	9,800
Deductibility of medical expenses.	6,500	6,640	7,310	8,140
Exclusion of interest on hospital construction bonds.	2,660	2,820	2,790	2,870
Refundable Premium Assistance Tax Credit.	7,040	3,910	4,110	3,690
Deductibility of charitable contributions (health).	7,540	8,080	8,650	9,180
Income security:				
Child credit.	74,880	75,770	76,530	77,100
Exclusion of workers' compensation benefits.	9,680	9,770	9,870	9,970
Net exclusion of pension contributions and earnings:				
Defined benefit employer plans.	71,653	73,831	75,807	78,012
Defined contribution employer plans.	75,680	83,520	90,680	100,410
Individual Retirement Accounts (IRAs).	20,520	21,650	22,760	23,990
Self-employed plans.	24,150	26,580	29,250	32,070
Exclusion of other employee benefits:				
Premiums on group term life insurance.	2,960	3,080	3,200	3,320
Earned income tax credit.	2,700	2,660	2,700	2,770
Social security:				
Exclusion of social security benefits:				
Social security benefits for retired and disabled workers, spouses, dependents, and survivors.	29,100	30,900	32,490	33,990
Veterans' benefits and services:				
Exclusion of veterans' death benefits and disability compensation.	7,590	8,340	8,910	9,200
General purpose fiscal assistance:				
Exclusion of interest on public purpose state and local bonds.	23,210	24,580	24,340	25,010
Deductibility of nonbusiness state and local tax, other than owner-occupied homes.	4,430	7,110	7,510	7,920
Interest:				
Deferral of interest on U.S. savings bonds.	850	840	840	830
Addendum: Aid to state and local governments:				
Deductibility of:				
Property taxes on owner–occupied homes.	6,010	6,270	6,650	7,030
Nonbusiness state and local taxes other than on owner–occupied homes.	4,430	7,110	7,510	7,920
Exclusion of interest on state and local bonds for:				
Public purposes.	23,210	24,580	24,340	25,010
Private nonprofit educational facilities.	1,850	1,950	1,940	1,990
Hospital construction.	2,660	2,820	2,790	2,870

Source: U.S. Office of Management and Budget, *Fiscal Year 2021 Budget of the U.S. Government: Analytical Perspectives*, February 2020. See also <http://www.whitehouse.gov/omb/budget/>.

Table 517. Internal Revenue Gross Collections by Type of Tax: 2005 to 2019

[2,269 represents $2,269,000,000,000, except percent. For fiscal years ending September 30. See text, this section, for information on taxes]

Type of tax	Gross collections (bil. dol.)						Percent of total					
	2005	2010	2015	2017	2018	2019	2005	2010	2015	2017	2018	2019
United States, total............	**2,269**	**2,345**	**3,303**	**3,417**	**3,465**	**3,565**	**100.0**	**100.0**	**100.0**	**100.0**	**100.0**	**100.0**
Individual income taxes............	1,108	1,164	1,760	1,838	1,933	1,942	48.8	49.7	53.3	53.8	55.8	54.5
Withheld by employers...........	787	900	1,241	1,331	1,349	1,351	34.7	38.4	37.6	39.0	38.9	37.9
Tax payments [1]................	321	264	519	507	585	591	14.1	11.3	15.7	14.8	16.9	16.6
Estate and trust income tax.......	(NA)	12	33	29	38	39	(NA)	0.5	1.0	0.8	1.1	1.1
Employment taxes.................	771	824	1,022	1,123	1,133	1,208	34.0	35.1	31.0	32.9	32.7	33.9
Old-age and disability insurance.....................	760	813	1,007	1,109	1,118	1,195	33.5	34.7	30.5	32.5	32.3	33.5
Unemployment insurance........	7	7	9	8	9	6	0.3	0.3	0.3	0.2	0.3	0.2
Railroad retirement............	5	5	6	6	6	6	0.2	0.2	0.2	0.2	0.2	0.2
Business income taxes [2].........	307	278	390	339	263	277	13.5	11.9	11.8	9.9	7.6	7.8
Estate and gift taxes............	26	20	20	24	24	18	1.1	0.8	0.6	0.7	0.7	0.5
Excise taxes....................	57	47	77	64	74	81	2.5	2.0	2.3	1.9	2.1	2.3

NA Not available. [1] Includes collections of estimated income tax and payments made in conjunction with individual income tax return filings. Also includes estate and trust income tax for 2005. [2] Includes corporate income tax and tax-exempt organization unrelated business income tax.

Source: U.S. Internal Revenue Service, *IRS Data Book 2019*, June 2020, and earlier editions. See also <https://www.irs.gov/statistics/soi-tax-stats-irs-data-book>.

Table 518. Individual Income Tax Returns Filed—Audits Coverage: 1995 to 2019

[In units as indicated (114,683 represents 114,683,000). An IRS audit is a review/examination of an organization's or individual's tax return to determine if income, expenses, and credits are being reported accurately. Includes audits based on an earned income tax credit claim, and the resulting recommended additional taxes]

Year	Returns filed [1] (1,000)	Returns examined		Total recommended additional tax [3] ($1,000)	Average recommended additional tax per return [3] (dollars)
		Total [2] (1,000)	Percent coverage		
1995...................	114,683	1,919	1.7	7,756,954	4,041
1996...................	116,060	1,942	1.7	7,600,191	3,915
1997...................	118,363	1,519	1.3	8,363,918	5,505
1998...................	120,342	1,193	1.0	6,095,698	5,110
1999...................	122,547	1,100	0.9	4,458,474	4,052
2000...................	124,887	618	0.5	3,388,905	5,486
2001...................	127,097	732	0.6	3,301,860	4,512
2002...................	129,445	744	0.6	3,636,486	4,889
2003...................	130,341	849	0.7	4,559,902	5,369
2004...................	130,134	997	0.8	6,201,693	6,220
2005...................	130,577	1,199	0.9	13,355,087	11,138
2006...................	132,276	1,284	1.0	13,045,221	10,160
2007...................	134,543	1,385	1.0	15,705,155	11,343
2008...................	137,850	1,392	1.0	12,462,770	8,956
2009 [4]...............	138,950	1,426	1.0	14,940,892	10,478
2010...................	142,823	1,581	1.1	15,066,486	9,527
2011...................	140,837	1,565	1.1	14,652,239	9,364
2012...................	143,400	1,482	1.0	15,310,908	10,331
2013...................	145,819	1,405	1.0	14,049,657	10,000
2014...................	145,236	1,242	0.9	11,885,411	9,566
2015...................	146,861	1,228	0.8	12,308,319	10,022
2016...................	147,967	1,035	0.7	9,864,674	9,532
2017...................	149,919	934	0.6	9,028,417	9,669
2018...................	150,043	892	0.6	9,050,651	10,144
2019...................	152,625	681	0.4	6,897,890	10,136

[1] Returns generally filed in previous calendar year. [2] Includes examinations conducted in person and by correspondence (mail). [3] For 1995, amount includes associated penalties. [4] Excludes returns filed by individuals only to receive an economic stimulus payment and who had no other reason to file.

Source: U.S. Internal Revenue Service, *IRS Data Book, 2019*, June 2020, and earlier editions. See also <https://www.irs.gov/statistics/soi-tax-stats-irs-data-book>.

Table 519. Federal Individual Income Tax Returns—Adjusted Gross Income, Taxable Income, and Total Income Tax: 2010 to 2017

[142,892 represents 142,892,000. For tax years. Based on a sample of returns; see source and Appendix III]

Year	2010		2015		2017		Percent change in amount, 2015-17
	Number of returns (1,000)	Amount (mil. dol.)	Number of returns (1,000)	Amount (mil. dol.)	Number of returns (1,000)	Amount (mil. dol.)	
Adjusted gross income (less deficit).....	**142,892**	**8,089,142**	**150,493**	**10,210,310**	**152,903**	**11,009,900**	**7.8**
Exemptions [1].....................	287,679	1,049,272	291,939	1,140,740	292,661	1,155,506	1.3
Taxable income....................	107,304	5,502,001	114,872	7,350,295	119,045	8,008,418	9.0
Total income tax..................	84,476	951,674	99,041	1,457,891	103,747	1,605,282	10.1
Alternative minimum tax..................	4,020	27,461	4,468	31,166	5,075	36,404	16.8

[1] The number of returns represent the number of exemptions.

Source: U.S. Internal Revenue Service, *Statistics of Income, Individual Income Tax Returns Complete Report 2017*, September 2019. See also <https://www.irs.gov/statistics/soi-tax-stats-individual-income-tax-return-form-1040-statistics>.

Table 520. Federal Individual Income Tax Returns—Adjusted Gross Income (AGI) by Selected Source of Income and Income Class: 2017

[In millions of dollars ($10,395,142 represents $10,395,142,000,000), except as indicated. For the tax year. Minus sign (-) indicates net loss was greater than net income. Based on a sample of returns; see source and Appendix III]

Item	Total [1]	Under $10,000 [1]	$10,000 to $19,999	$20,000 to $29,999	$30,000 to $39,999	$40,000 to $49,999	$50,000 to $99,999	$100,000 and over
Number of taxable returns (1,000)	**103,747**	**2,114**	**9,491**	**11,019**	**10,905**	**9,955**	**32,770**	**27,493**
Adjusted gross income (AGI) [2]	**10,395,142**	**4,121**	**146,248**	**275,722**	**381,751**	**446,596**	**2,349,600**	**6,791,104**
Salaries and wages	6,896,585	14,758	118,594	222,104	310,125	363,196	1,789,884	4,077,924
Percent of AGI	66.3	358.1	81.1	80.6	81.2	81.3	76.2	60.0
Interest received	148,126	857	814	1,723	2,163	2,149	14,577	125,843
Dividends in AGI	459,740	1,306	1,144	2,447	3,831	4,370	40,695	405,946
Business, profession, net profit less loss	283,167	237	5,950	8,542	8,715	10,370	56,573	192,781
Sales of property, net gain less loss [3]	830,828	3,543	357	539	953	2,316	22,318	800,803
Pensions and annuities in AGI	681,436	219	14,178	27,645	35,057	37,774	230,766	335,797
Rents and royalties, net income less loss [4]	59,265	126	622	697	480	853	3,660	52,827
Number of all returns (1,000)	**152,903**	**22,572**	**22,260**	**18,808**	**15,209**	**11,916**	**34,467**	**27,672**
Adjusted gross income [2]	**11,009,900**	**-125,561**	**331,099**	**466,669**	**529,630**	**533,338**	**2,457,203**	**6,817,523**
Salaries and wages	7,577,564	107,376	247,512	382,789	441,282	437,486	1,870,907	4,090,212
Interest received	166,114	9,505	2,570	3,030	2,968	2,884	17,083	128,075
Dividends in AGI	499,183	12,678	6,053	6,314	6,843	6,614	48,655	412,026
Business, profession, net profit less loss	346,372	947	37,568	20,931	15,919	15,545	61,524	193,938
Sales of property, net gain less loss [3]	855,852	11,581	1,544	2,244	3,063	4,084	27,934	805,402
Pensions and annuities in AGI	729,187	12,258	29,370	36,795	38,155	40,253	234,998	337,359
Rents and royalties, net income less loss [4]	55,529	-3,867	1,645	897	45	635	3,295	52,879

[1] Includes a small number of returns with no adjusted gross income. [2] Includes other sources, not shown separately. [3] Includes sales of capital assets and other property. [4] Excludes rental passive losses disallowed in the computation of AGI.

Source: U.S. Internal Revenue Service, *Statistics of Income—Individual Income Tax Returns 2017*, Publication 1304, September 2019. See also <https://www.irs.gov/statistics/soi-tax-stats-individual-income-tax-return-form-1040-statistics>.

Table 521. Federal Individual Income Tax Returns—Total and Selected Sources of Adjusted Gross Income: 2016 and 2017

[In units as indicated (150,272 represents 150,272,000). For tax years. Based on a sample of returns; see source and Appendix III. Minus sign (-) indicates decrease]

Item	2016 Number of returns (1,000)	2016 Amount (mil. dol.)	2017 Number of returns (1,000)	2017 Amount (mil. dol.)	Change in amount, 2016-2017 Net change (mil. dol.)	Change in amount, 2016-2017 Percent change
Adjusted gross income (less deficit) [1]	**150,272**	**10,225,938**	**152,903**	**11,009,900**	**783,962**	**7.7**
Salaries and wages	124,472	7,217,426	126,264	7,577,564	360,138	5.0
Taxable interest	42,583	96,640	44,193	106,055	9,415	9.7
Ordinary dividends	27,470	254,065	28,171	282,336	28,271	11.1
Qualified dividends	25,630	202,034	26,216	216,847	14,813	7.3
Business or profession net income (less loss)	25,064	328,082	25,899	346,372	18,290	5.6
Net capital gain	24,043	620,975	25,400	854,487	233,512	37.6
Capital gain distributions [2]	13,233	42,534	14,173	73,274	30,740	72.3
Sales of property other than capital assets, net gain (less loss)	2,082	6,293	2,110	12,737	6,444	102.4
Sales of property other than capital assets, net gain	978	27,611	996	34,607	6,996	25.3
Taxable social security benefits	19,967	285,939	20,929	309,540	23,601	8.3
Total rental and royalty net income (less net loss) [3]	10,986	51,250	10,839	55,529	4,279	8.3
Partnership and S corporation net income (less loss)	8,711	628,666	9,113	680,280	51,614	8.2
Estate and trust net income (less loss)	652	26,571	663	31,128	4,556	17.1
Farm net income (less loss)	1,751	-17,666	1,789	-19,166	-1,500	8.5
Farm net income	481	11,506	481	11,222	-284	-2.5
Unemployment compensation	5,567	25,420	5,204	23,946	-1,474	-5.8
Taxable pensions and annuities	27,861	693,627	28,265	729,187	35,561	5.1
Taxable Individual Retirement Account (IRA) distributions	14,387	257,508	15,117	286,497	28,989	11.3
Other net income (less loss) [4]	6,228	38,245	6,435	40,012	1,767	4.6
Gambling earnings	1,975	31,574	2,094	32,580	1,006	3.2

[1] Includes other sources of income, not shown separately. [2] Includes both Schedule D and Form 1040 or 1040A capital gain distributions. [3] Includes farm rental net income (less loss). [4] Other net income (less loss) represents data reported on Form 1040, line 21, except net operating losses, foreign-earned income exclusions, cancellation of debt, taxable health savings account distributions, and gambling earnings.

Source: U.S. Internal Revenue Service, *Statistics of Income—Individual Income Tax Returns 2017*, Publication 1304, September 2019. See also <https://www.irs.gov/statistics/soi-tax-stats-individual-income-tax-return-form-1040-statistics>.

Table 522. Federal Individual Income Tax Returns—Net Capital Gains, with Capital Gain Distributions from Mutual Funds: 1990 to 2017

[14,288 represents 14,288,000. For tax years. Based on a sample of returns; see source and Appendix III. Minus sign (-) indicates decrease]

| Tax year | Net capital gain (less loss) | | | | Capital gain distributions [2] | | | |
| | Number of returns (1,000) | Current dollars (mil. dol.) | Constant (1982–1984) dollars [1] | | Number of returns (1,000) | Current dollars (mil. dol.) | Constant (1982–1984) dollars [1] | |
			Amount (mil. dol.)	Percent change			Amount (mil. dol.)	Percent change
1990	14,288	114,231	87,399	-25.6	5,069	3,905	2,988	-32.4
1991	15,009	102,776	75,460	-13.7	5,796	4,665	3,425	14.6
1992	16,491	118,230	84,269	11.7	5,917	7,426	5,293	54.5
1993	18,409	144,172	99,773	18.4	9,998	11,995	8,301	56.8
1994	18,823	142,288	96,011	-3.8	9,803	11,322	7,640	-8.0
1995	19,963	170,415	111,821	16.5	10,744	14,391	9,443	23.6
1996	22,065	251,817	160,495	43.5	12,778	24,722	15,757	66.9
1997	24,240	356,083	221,859	38.2	14,969	45,132	28,120	78.5
1998	25,690	446,084	273,671	23.4	16,070	46,147	28,311	0.7
1999	27,701	542,758	325,785	19.0	17,012	59,473	35,698	26.1
2000	29,521	630,542	366,168	12.4	17,546	79,079	45,923	28.6
2001	25,956	326,527	184,374	-49.6	12,216	13,609	7,684	-83.3
2002	24,189	238,789	132,734	-28.0	7,567	5,343	2,970	-61.4
2003	22,985	294,354	159,975	20.5	7,265	4,695	2,552	-14.1
2004	25,267	473,662	250,747	56.7	10,733	15,336	8,119	218.2
2005	26,196	668,015	342,046	36.4	13,393	35,581	18,219	124.4
2006	26,668	779,462	386,638	13.0	14,511	59,417	29,473	61.8
2007	27,156	907,656	437,758	13.2	15,714	86,397	41,669	41.4
2008	23,731	469,273	217,959	-50.2	11,544	21,954	10,197	-75.5
2009	20,291	231,548	107,929	-50.5	4,191	2,411	1,124	-89.0
2010	21,315	364,410	167,118	54.8	6,567	6,270	2,875	155.9
2011	22,154	377,037	167,617	0.3	8,859	14,171	6,300	119.1
2012	22,721	622,887	271,299	61.9	10,412	17,829	7,766	23.3
2013	23,993	489,621	210,176	-22.5	12,845	44,774	19,220	147.5
2014	24,268	698,649	295,117	40.4	13,665	79,059	33,396	73.8
2015	24,278	706,515	298,086	1.0	14,056	74,060	31,247	-6.4
2016	24,043	620,975	258,732	-13.2	13,233	42,534	17,722	-43.3
2017	25,400	854,487	348,599	34.7	14,173	73,274	29,893	68.7

[1] Constant dollars were calculated using the U.S. Bureau of Labor Statistics consumer price index for urban consumers (CPI-U, 1982-1984=100). See Table 761. [2] Capital gain distributions are included in net capital gain (less loss). For 1991–1996, and 1999 and later years, capital gain distributions from mutual funds are the sum of the amounts reported on the Form 1040 and Schedule D. For 1997 and 1998, capital gain distributions were reported entirely on the Schedule D.

Source: U.S. Internal Revenue Service, Statistics of Income, "SOI Tax Stats - Individual Statistical Tables by Size of Adjusted Gross Income," <https://www.irs.gov/statistics/soi-tax-stats-individual-statistical-tables-by-size-of-adjusted-gross-income>, accessed November 2019.

Table 523. Alternative Minimum Tax: 1986 to 2017

[609 represents 609,000. For tax years. Based on a sample of returns; see source and Appendix III]

| Tax year | Highest statutory alternative minimum tax rate (percent) [1] | Alternative minimum tax | | Tax year | Highest statutory alternative minimum tax rate (percent) [1] | Alternative minimum tax | |
		Number of returns (1,000)	Amount (mil. dol.)			Number of returns (1,000)	Amount (mil. dol.)
1986	20	609	6,713	2002	28	1,911	6,854
1987	21	140	1,675	2003	28	2,358	9,470
1988	21	114	1,028	2004	28	3,096	13,029
1989	21	117	831	2005	28	4,005	17,421
1990	21	132	830	2006	28	3,967	21,565
1991	24	244	1,213	2007	28	4,109	24,110
1992	24	287	1,357	2008	28	3,935	25,649
1993	28	335	2,053	2009	28	3,828	22,580
1994	28	369	2,212	2010	28	4,020	27,461
1995	28	414	2,291	2011	28	4,248	30,479
1996	28	478	2,813	2012	28	4,225	32,770
1997	28	618	4,005	2013	28	3,940	27,426
1998	28	853	5,015	2014	28	4,278	28,646
1999	28	1,018	6,478	2015	28	4,468	31,166
2000	28	1,304	9,601	2016	28	4,634	31,016
2001	28	1,120	6,757	2017	28	5,075	36,404

[1] Beginning 1997, the top rate on most long-term capital gains was 20 percent; beginning 2003, the rate was 15 percent.

Source: U.S. Internal Revenue Service, Statistics of Income, "SOI Tax Stats - Individual Statistical Tables by Size of Adjusted Gross Income," <https://www.irs.gov/statistics/soi-tax-stats-individual-statistical-tables-by-size-of-adjusted-gross-income>, accessed November 2019.

Table 524. Federal Individual Income Tax Returns—Sources of Net Losses Included in Adjusted Gross Income: 2016 and 2017

[26,002 represents 26,002,000. For tax years. Based on a sample of returns; see source and Appendix III]

Item	2016 Number of returns (1,000)	2016 Amount (mil. dol.)	2017 Number of returns (1,000)	2017 Amount (mil. dol.)	Percent change in amount, 2016–2017
Total net losses..	**26,002**	**500,834**	**24,968**	**564,989**	**12.8**
Business or profession net loss................................	6,103	60,997	6,463	69,638	14.2
Net capital loss [1]...	9,054	20,126	7,471	16,779	-16.6
Net loss, sales of property other than capital assets.......	1,105	21,319	1,114	21,870	2.6
Total rental and royalty net loss [2]...........................	4,308	46,943	4,202	49,241	4.9
Partnership and S corporation net loss......................	2,673	125,646	2,873	153,150	21.9
Estate and trust net loss..	49	3,857	58	3,978	3.1
Farm net loss...	1,270	29,172	1,308	30,388	4.2
Net operating loss [3]..	1,110	185,805	1,163	213,364	14.8
Other net loss [4]...	330	6,969	316	6,579	-5.6

[1] As reported on Form 1040, Schedule D. Includes only the portion of capital losses allowable in the calculation of adjusted gross income. Only $3,000 of net capital loss per return ($1,500 for married filing separately) are allowed to be included in negative total income. Any excess is carried forward to future years. [2] Includes farm rental net loss. [3] Net operating loss is a carryover of the loss from a business when taxable income from a prior year was less than zero. [4] Other net loss represents losses reported on Form 1040, line 21, except net operating loss and the foreign-earned income exclusion.

Source: U.S. Internal Revenue Service, Statistics of Income, "SOI Tax Stats - Individual Statistical Tables by Size of Adjusted Gross Income," <https://www.irs.gov/statistics/soi-tax-stats-individual-statistical-tables-by-size-of-adjusted-gross-income>, accessed November 2019.

Table 525. Federal Individual Income Tax Returns—Number, Income Tax, and Average Tax by Size of Adjusted Gross Income: 2015 and 2016

[150,493 represents 150,493,000. Based on sample of returns; see Appendix III. Minus sign (-) indicates net loss was greater than net income]

Size of adjusted gross income	Number of returns (1,000) 2015	2016	Adjusted gross income (AGI) (bil. dol.) 2015	2016	Income tax total [1] (bil. dol.) 2015	2016	Taxes as percent of AGI (for taxable returns only) 2015	2016	Average tax (for taxable returns only) (dol.) 2015	2016
Total..............................	**150,493**	**150,272**	**10,210**	**10,226**	**1,458**	**1,446**	**15.3**	**15.1**	**14,720**	**14,453**
No AGI [2]...........................	2,072	2,093	-203.8	-201.5	0.2	0.1	(X)	(X)	36,515	21,134
$1 to $4,999.......................	10,135	9,989	26.2	25.8	–	–	6.6	5.4	205	171
$5,000 to $9,999..................	11,399	10,999	86.4	83.5	0.4	0.3	2.4	2.4	191	192
$10,000 to $14,999...............	12,219	11,835	152.8	147.8	1.4	1.4	2.5	2.5	319	323
$15,000 to $19,999...............	11,228	10,910	195.9	190.2	3.5	3.5	3.9	3.8	678	671
$20,000 to $24,999...............	9,981	9,847	224.2	221.0	6.2	6.1	5.1	5.0	1,145	1,131
$25,000 to $29,999...............	8,833	8,888	242.6	243.9	8.8	9.0	6.0	6.0	1,645	1,646
$30,000 to $39,999...............	14,914	15,088	519.5	525.1	25.2	25.7	6.8	6.8	2,382	2,378
$40,000 to $49,999...............	11,625	11,665	520.8	522.3	32.5	32.5	7.5	7.5	3,353	3,346
$50,000 to $74,999...............	19,980	20,224	1,228.3	1,241.8	99.8	101.5	8.7	8.7	5,341	5,385
$75,000 to $99,999...............	12,822	12,975	1,111.2	1,125.7	105.9	108.3	9.7	9.8	8,430	8,517
$100,000 to $199,999.............	18,533	18,858	2,506.5	2,552.5	316.3	321.6	12.7	12.7	17,191	17,186
$200,000 to $499,999.............	5,428	5,583	1,546.5	1,588.3	299.8	308.2	19.4	19.4	55,334	55,319
$500,000 to $999,999.............	884	893	597.7	599.6	154.4	154.7	25.9	25.8	174,789	173,327
$1,000,000 to $1,499,999........	196	193	236.5	232.6	66.3	65.2	28.1	28.0	338,945	338,234
$1,500,000 to $1,999,999........	80	78	137.7	133.6	39.7	38.6	28.8	28.9	496,618	497,142
$2,000,000 to $4,999,999........	117	111	346.9	329.9	101.5	96.0	29.3	29.1	870,364	864,605
$5,000,000 to $9,999,999........	29	27	195.7	181.7	56.3	52.0	28.8	28.6	1,965,939	1,952,541
$10,000,000 or more.............	18	16	538.8	482.1	139.6	121.4	25.9	25.2	7,731,699	7,548,877

X Not applicable. – Represents or rounds to zero [1] Consists of income tax after credits (including alternative minimum tax). [2] In addition to low-income taxpayers, this size class (and others) includes taxpayers with "tax preferences," not reflected in "adjusted gross income" or "taxable income," which are subject to the "alternative minimum tax" (included in "total income tax").

Source: U.S. Internal Revenue Service, Statistics of Income Bulletin, "Historical Data Tables," <https://www.irs.gov/statistics>, accessed May 2019.

Table 526. Federal Individual Income Tax Returns—Selected Itemized Deductions and the Standard Deduction: 2016 and 2017

[45,153 represents 45,153,000. For tax years. Based on a sample of returns; see source and Appendix III. Minus sign (-) indicates decrease]

Item	2016 Number of returns [1] (1,000)	2016 Amount (mil. dol.)	2017 Number of returns [1] (1,000)	2017 Amount (mil. dol.)	Percent change, 2016–2017 Number of returns [1] (1,000)	Percent change, 2016–2017 Amount (percent)
Total itemized deductions	**45,153**	**1,293,399**	**46,853**	**1,402,092**	**3.8**	**8.4**
Medical and dental expenses after Adjusted Gross Income (AGI) limitation	8,934	90,195	10,171	102,533	13.8	13.7
Taxes paid [2]	44,803	566,098	45,107	389,389	0.7	-31.2
State and local income taxes	33,423	337,680	34,175	368,655	2.2	9.2
State and local general sales taxes	9,746	18,328	10,932	20,735	12.2	13.1
Interest paid [3]	33,485	304,997	34,327	313,944	2.5	2.9
Home mortgage interest	32,933	282,953	33,746	292,558	2.5	3.4
Charitable contributions	36,937	233,867	37,979	256,065	2.8	9.5
Other than cash contributions	22,969	79,569	23,184	88,062	0.9	10.7
Casualty and theft losses	154	5,187	113	2,765	-26.5	-46.7
Total limited miscellaneous deductions after 2% AGI limitation	13,014	115,544	13,300	121,291	2.2	5.0
Total unlimited miscellaneous deductions	1,238	23,245	1,723	35,210	39.1	51.5
Itemized deductions in excess of limitation	2,981	45,734	3,310	54,537	11.0	19.2
Basic standard deduction	**103,013**	**865,094**	**104,013**	**876,178**	**1.0**	**1.3**
Additional standard deduction	**15,316**	**28,572**	**15,749**	**29,365**	**2.8**	**2.8**

[1] Returns with no adjusted gross income are excluded from the deduction counts. For this reason, the sum of the number of returns with total itemized deductions and the number of returns with total standard deduction is less than the total number of returns for all filers. [2] Includes real estate taxes, personal property taxes, and other taxes, not shown separately. [3] Includes investment interest, deductible mortgage "points," and qualified mortgage interest premiums, not shown separately.

Source: U.S. Internal Revenue Service, Statistics of Income, "SOI Tax Stats - Individual Statistical Tables by Size of Adjusted Gross Income," <https://www.irs.gov/statistics/soi-tax-stats-individual-statistical-tables-by-size-of-adjusted-gross-income>, accessed November 2019.

Table 527. Federal Individual Income Tax Returns—Statutory Adjustments: 2016 and 2017

[38,858 represents 38,858,000. For tax years. Based on a sample of returns; see source and Appendix III. Minus sign (-) indicates decrease]

Item	2016 Number of returns (1,000)	2016 Amount (mil. dol.)	2017 Number of returns (1,000)	2017 Amount (mil. dol.)	Percent change in amount, 2016-2017
Total statutory adjustments	**38,858**	**153,414**	**39,090**	**160,181**	**4.4**
Payments to an Individual Retirement Account (IRA)	2,667	13,387	2,638	13,427	0.3
Educator expenses deduction	3,853	983	3,612	931	-5.3
Certain business expenses of reservists, performing artists, etc.	157	605	147	766	26.5
Moving expenses adjustment	1,115	3,487	1,082	3,467	-0.6
Student loan interest deduction	12,396	13,446	12,564	13,687	1.8
Tuition and fees deduction	1,687	3,910	1,109	2,585	-33.9
Health savings account deduction	1,721	4,967	1,858	5,351	7.7
Self-employment tax deduction	19,583	29,866	20,064	31,915	6.9
Self-employment health insurance deduction	4,057	30,112	4,110	31,709	5.3
Payments to a self-employed retirement (Keogh) plan	989	24,683	1,012	25,821	4.6
Early withdrawal of savings penalty	416	108	411	124	14.8
Alimony paid	586	12,639	586	13,436	6.3
Domestic production activities deduction	720	13,377	790	15,126	13.1
Other adjustments [1]	138	1,844	127	1,746	-5.3

[1] Includes foreign housing adjustment, medical savings accounts deduction, and other adjustments.

Source: U.S. Internal Revenue Service, Statistics of Income, "SOI Tax Stats - Individual Statistical Tables by Size of Adjusted Gross Income," <https://www.irs.gov/statistics/soi-tax-stats-individual-statistical-tables-by-size-of-adjusted-gross-income>, accessed November 2019.

Table 528. Federal Individual Income Tax Returns—Itemized Deductions and Statutory Adjustments by Size of Adjusted Gross Income: 2017

[46,853 represents 46,853,000. Based on a sample of returns; see Appendix III]

Item	Unit	Total [1]	Under $10,000 [1]	$10,000 to $19,999	$20,000 to $29,999	$30,000 to $39,999	$40,000 to $49,999	$50,000 to $99,999	$100,000 and over
Returns with itemized deductions:									
Number of returns [2]	1,000	46,853	685	1,424	2,026	2,496	2,996	14,903	22,323
Amount [2,3]	Mil. dol.	1,402,092	11,005	22,003	33,621	41,892	50,145	294,481	948,943
Medical and dental expenses: [4]									
Returns	1,000	10,171	519	896	1,055	1,015	931	3,663	2,093
Amount	Mil. dol.	102,533	4,824	7,877	10,175	8,598	7,854	35,267	27,939
Taxes paid:									
Returns	1,000	46,431	645	1,359	1,969	2,430	2,946	14,800	22,283
Amount	Mil. dol.	624,821	2,567	4,838	6,961	9,996	13,372	97,524	489,562
State and local taxes: [5]									
Returns	1,000	45,107	535	1,214	1,834	2,327	2,832	14,403	21,961
Amount	Mil. dol.	389,389	474	1,048	2,026	3,500	5,482	45,523	331,336
Real estate taxes:									
Returns	1,000	39,102	489	969	1,256	1,668	2,182	12,300	20,238
Amount	Mil. dol.	222,238	1,946	3,557	4,465	5,913	7,212	48,374	150,770
Interest paid:									
Returns	1,000	34,327	349	726	979	1,420	1,919	10,952	17,982
Amount	Mil. dol.	313,944	2,273	4,792	6,444	8,955	12,319	78,956	200,207
Home mortgage interest:									
Returns	1,000	33,746	329	714	968	1,398	1,898	10,857	17,582
Amount	Mil. dol.	292,558	2,143	4,601	6,245	8,622	11,906	75,924	183,117
Charitable contributions:									
Returns	1,000	37,979	424	930	1,384	1,798	2,177	11,730	19,536
Amount	Mil. dol.	256,065	531	1,918	3,553	5,153	6,389	40,462	198,059
Unreimbursed employee business expenses:									
Returns	1,000	14,806	66	278	651	910	1,111	5,377	6,413
Amount	Mil. dol.	101,153	277	1,874	4,987	7,319	8,254	36,068	42,374
Returns with statutory adjustments:									
Number of returns [1]	1,000	39,090	3,817	4,999	3,502	3,342	3,125	10,160	10,144
Amount of adjustments [3]	Mil. dol.	160,181	6,055	6,093	6,076	6,859	6,963	29,422	98,714
Payments to IRAs: [6]									
Returns	1,000	2,638	55	125	211	231	241	895	878
Amount	Mil. dol.	13,427	199	390	744	970	1,043	4,425	5,656
Deduction for self-employment tax:									
Returns	1,000	20,064	3,071	3,914	1,869	1,331	1,201	3,913	4,765
Amount	Mil. dol.	31,915	1,435	3,212	2,040	1,682	1,542	6,109	15,895
Self-employment health insurance:									
Returns	1,000	4,110	291	266	295	272	244	932	1,809
Amount	Mil. dol.	31,709	1,166	852	1,074	1,188	1,289	5,926	20,215
Payments to Keogh plans:									
Returns	1,000	1,012	[7] 8	[7] 14	[7] 11	22	26	145	786
Amount	Mil. dol.	25,821	[7] 179	[7] 54	[7] 86	189	221	1,678	23,415

[1] For returns with statutory adjustments, includes a small number of taxable returns with no adjusted gross income. [2] After limitations. [3] Includes other deductions and adjustments, not shown separately. [4] After AGI limitation. [5] State and local taxes include income taxes and sales taxes. [6] Individual retirement accounts. [7] Includes estimates that should be used with caution due to the small number of sample returns on which they are based.

Source: U.S. Internal Revenue Service, Statistics of Income, "SOI Tax Stats - Individual Statistical Tables by Size of Adjusted Gross Income," <https://www.irs.gov/statistics/soi-tax-stats-individual-statistical-tables-by-size-of-adjusted-gross-income>, accessed November 2019.

Table 529. Federal Individual Income Tax Returns—Selected Tax Credits: 2016 and 2017

[48,478 represents 48,478,000. For tax years. Based on a sample of returns; see source and Appendix III]

Item	2016 Number of returns (1,000)	2016 Amount (mil. dol.)	2017 Number of returns (1,000)	2017 Amount (mil. dol.)	Percent change, 2016-2017 Number of returns (1,000)	Percent change, 2016-2017 Amount (mil. dol.)
Total tax credits [1]	**48,478**	**75,381**	**48,849**	**77,829**	**0.8**	**3.2**
Child care credit	6,469	3,635	6,469	3,719	–	2.3
Earned income credit [2]	4,437	1,403	4,654	1,516	4.9	8.1
Foreign tax credit	7,798	20,090	8,652	21,757	10.9	8.3
General business credit	352	4,131	410	4,803	16.3	16.3
Minimum tax credit	321	907	293	1,046	-8.7	15.4
Child tax credit	22,097	26,800	22,075	26,877	-0.1	0.3
Education credit [3]	8,998	9,653	8,751	9,353	-2.7	-3.1
Retirement savings contribution credit	8,458	1,536	8,712	1,564	3.0	1.8
Residential energy credit	2,613	2,336	1,578	2,125	-39.6	-9.1

– Represents or rounds to zero. [1] Includes credits not shown separately. [2] Represents portion of credit used to offset income tax before credits. [3] Excludes refundable portion.

Source: U.S. Internal Revenue Service, Statistics of Income, "SOI Tax Stats - Individual Statistical Tables by Size of Adjusted Gross Income," <https://www.irs.gov/statistics/soi-tax-stats-individual-statistical-tables-by-size-of-adjusted-gross-income>, accessed November 2019.

Table 530. Federal Individual Income Tax Returns by State: 2017

[In units as indicated (152,456 represents 152,456,000). For tax year. Data may not agree with data in other tables due to differing survey methodology used to derive state data]

State	Total number of returns (1,000)	Adjusted gross income (mil. dol.)			Itemized deductions (mil. dol.)				Income tax (mil. dol.)
		Total [1]	Salaries and wages	Net capital gain [2]	Total [1]	State and local income tax	Real estate taxes	Home mortgage interest paid	
United States......	152,456	10,991,387	7,557,396	855,728	1,403,313	368,945	219,757	287,022	1,589,761
Alabama..............	2,060	118,876	84,007	5,599	13,039	2,438	684	2,758	14,449
Alaska................	349	23,851	16,790	960	1,720	31	350	625	3,284
Arizona..............	3,023	193,797	132,702	13,751	22,963	4,077	2,368	6,018	25,595
Arkansas.............	1,233	73,645	48,570	6,513	8,288	2,057	481	1,272	8,911
California.............	18,099	1,521,053	1,039,470	142,449	252,954	91,787	35,179	54,755	234,500
Colorado.............	2,714	209,871	143,021	18,086	24,590	6,038	2,560	7,233	30,583
Connecticut..........	1,766	174,258	114,532	16,194	26,350	9,291	5,590	4,496	29,409
Delaware............	464	31,276	21,257	1,417	3,769	1,061	415	1,030	4,072
District of Columbia..	348	34,162	23,950	2,710	5,105	1,976	519	1,031	6,050
Florida...............	10,181	726,990	426,690	91,373	78,752	4,666	11,349	15,252	116,971
Georgia..............	4,543	298,099	212,663	19,041	43,384	10,256	4,259	8,414	40,049
Hawaii................	693	45,428	31,009	2,975	5,800	1,722	429	1,863	5,688
Idaho................	764	45,121	30,859	2,989	5,700	1,546	579	1,308	5,274
Illinois...............	6,129	455,607	316,820	33,590	54,969	12,297	13,766	10,939	67,180
Indiana..............	3,135	185,559	135,210	8,014	16,819	4,776	1,659	3,490	23,073
Iowa.................	1,458	92,282	65,158	4,386	10,520	2,992	1,642	1,821	11,251
Kansas..............	1,333	85,640	60,027	4,931	9,001	2,091	1,260	1,621	11,102
Kentucky............	1,920	107,719	77,759	4,749	11,755	3,897	1,167	2,359	12,661
Louisiana............	1,970	114,167	81,713	5,172	12,313	2,255	891	2,408	14,877
Maine................	660	38,804	26,730	2,289	4,387	1,286	808	948	4,581
Maryland............	2,986	235,433	169,181	11,379	40,983	13,327	5,237	9,426	32,942
Massachusetts.......	3,457	327,916	218,869	34,587	41,575	13,118	8,100	8,933	54,205
Michigan.............	4,763	299,669	208,649	15,911	30,754	7,687	5,177	6,287	39,851
Minnesota............	2,772	205,975	146,891	12,588	27,051	9,509	3,783	5,735	28,235
Mississippi...........	1,235	60,763	44,585	2,087	7,174	1,191	507	1,193	6,575
Missouri..............	2,812	171,470	120,735	9,297	19,079	5,082	2,216	3,652	21,868
Montana..............	506	29,912	18,919	2,373	3,632	990	435	818	3,661
Nebraska.............	906	57,728	41,089	3,506	6,614	1,756	1,103	1,093	7,196
Nevada..............	1,418	94,289	61,295	10,052	10,906	721	994	2,598	13,802
New Hampshire......	707	54,638	38,428	4,226	5,427	589	1,651	1,422	7,890
New Jersey..........	4,438	393,192	279,914	23,101	62,045	18,390	16,794	11,262	62,813
New Mexico..........	922	49,150	33,048	2,871	4,943	987	525	1,202	5,770
New York............	9,695	836,755	549,679	85,440	132,916	56,723	23,622	17,181	140,510
North Carolina.......	4,578	286,383	203,716	16,219	33,993	8,957	3,745	7,654	36,903
North Dakota.........	363	24,152	17,026	1,502	1,773	207	239	391	3,372
Ohio.................	5,621	340,322	241,635	15,563	33,895	9,334	6,218	6,629	43,285
Oklahoma............	1,630	97,446	67,690	5,922	10,842	2,090	948	1,793	12,018
Oregon..............	1,939	132,370	87,930	9,500	20,507	6,864	2,882	4,581	16,949
Pennsylvania.........	6,237	426,878	297,936	26,590	45,728	12,105	8,928	9,580	59,451
Rhode Island........	537	35,968	25,549	2,221	4,503	1,255	944	1,033	4,850
South Carolina.......	2,241	132,262	90,321	7,173	15,790	4,085	1,342	3,551	16,233
South Dakota........	419	26,394	17,074	1,887	2,065	93	286	387	3,477
Tennessee...........	3,036	183,899	131,332	11,264	15,186	710	1,626	3,640	24,585
Texas...............	12,521	886,241	625,941	77,864	95,704	1,947	19,040	17,438	133,417
Utah.................	1,326	89,567	64,453	7,036	13,283	3,132	1,133	3,161	10,946
Vermont..............	328	20,318	13,649	1,600	2,334	629	536	476	2,474
Virginia..............	3,961	309,804	220,152	17,313	42,810	11,384	5,705	11,457	44,246
Washington..........	3,568	298,356	204,003	27,365	29,934	1,058	5,265	9,247	45,091
West Virginia........	767	40,036	28,953	1,050	3,064	1,003	214	660	4,467
Wisconsin............	2,867	184,819	130,567	9,681	21,705	6,606	4,154	4,139	23,717
Wyoming.............	271	21,037	12,309	3,319	1,926	145	168	399	3,084
Other [3].............	786	62,039	56,939	8,051	2,995	732	282	364	6,319

[1] Includes other items, not shown separately. [2] Less loss. [3] Includes returns filed from Army Post Office and Fleet Post Office addresses by members of the armed forces stationed overseas; returns filed by other U.S. citizens abroad; and returns filed by residents of Puerto Rico with income from sources outside of Puerto Rico or with income earned as U.S. government employees.

Source: U.S. Internal Revenue Service, Statistics of Income Bulletin, "Historical Data Tables," <https://www.irs.gov/statistics/soi-tax-stats-historical-data-tables>, accessed November 2019.

Table 531. Individuals Due an Unclaimed Income Tax Refund by State: 2016

[1,518,155 represents $1,518,155,000. Data are estimates, and are for unclaimed income tax refunds for taxpayers who did not file a 2016 Form 1040 federal income tax return. Taxpayers have a 3-year window in which to claim a tax refund, after which the money becomes the property of the U.S. Treasury]

State	Total persons (number)	Value of potential refunds ($1,000) [1]	Median potential refund (dol.)	State	Total persons (number)	Value of potential refunds ($1,000) [1]	Median potential refund (dol.)
Total U.S.	1,418,300	1,518,155	861	Missouri	32,400	33,522	828
Alabama	23,300	24,614	859	Montana	4,600	4,582	781
Alaska	5,500	6,755	979	Nebraska	7,800	8,082	845
Arizona	32,400	32,282	762	Nevada	15,900	16,922	859
Arkansas	13,400	13,799	822	New Hampshire	6,500	7,474	965
California	130,600	135,981	816	New Jersey	36,200	41,269	936
Colorado	27,500	28,277	809	New Mexico	9,600	10,220	833
Connecticut	14,300	16,213	930	New York	70,300	80,830	958
Delaware	5,600	6,115	878	North Carolina	44,900	46,045	833
District of Columbia	3,700	4,225	904	North Dakota	4,000	4,540	949
Florida	99,000	105,706	874	Ohio	52,900	54,543	841
Georgia	48,600	49,683	792	Oklahoma	21,000	22,600	866
Hawaii	7,700	8,786	932	Oregon	21,400	21,237	762
Idaho	6,200	5,876	727	Pennsylvania	55,200	60,505	919
Illinois	51,700	57,312	909	Rhode Island	3,900	4,410	926
Indiana	32,700	35,130	887	South Carolina	17,200	17,324	769
Iowa	14,700	15,736	908	South Dakota	3,800	3,976	899
Kansas	14,600	15,707	877	Tennessee	29,000	29,835	840
Kentucky	18,700	19,517	869	Texas	143,400	159,810	898
Louisiana	24,400	26,410	849	Utah	11,100	11,038	766
Maine	5,600	5,482	802	Vermont	2,800	2,897	892
Maryland	28,200	31,620	873	Virginia	37,900	39,978	827
Massachusetts	29,900	34,262	956	Washington	37,200	42,273	918
Michigan	46,600	49,591	853	West Virginia	7,200	7,830	921
Minnesota	21,000	21,155	803	Wisconsin	19,900	19,483	781
Mississippi	12,900	12,932	777	Wyoming	3,400	3,766	920

[1] Excluding credits.

Source: U.S. Internal Revenue Service, News Release, "IRS unclaimed refunds of $1.5 billion waiting for tax year 2016; taxpayers face July 15 deadline," IR-2020-135, July 2020. See also <https://www.irs.gov/newsroom>.

Table 532. Federal Employees—Summary Characteristics: 1990 to 2017

[In percent, except as indicated. As of September 30. For civilian employees of executive branch agencies participating in Office of Personnel Management's Central Personnel Data File (CPDF)]

Characteristics	1990	1995	2000	2005	2010	2015	2016	2017
Average age (years) [1]	42.3	44.3	46.3	46.9	46.8	47.4	47.4	47.5
Average length of service (years)	13.4	15.5	17.1	16.4	14.3	13.7	13.5	13.5
Retirement eligible: [2]								
Civil Service Retirement System	8.0	10.0	17.0	33.0	57.0	81.1	85.7	89.5
Bachelor's degree or higher	35.0	39.0	41.0	43.0	46.0	51.0	51.2	51.7
Sex: Male	57.0	56.0	55.0	56.0	55.9	56.8	56.7	56.6
Female	43.0	44.0	45.0	44.0	44.1	43.2	43.3	43.4
Race and national origin:								
Total minorities	27.4	28.9	30.4	31.7	33.3	35.3	35.9	36.7
Black	16.7	16.8	17.1	17.0	17.5	17.7	17.9	18.2
Hispanic	5.4	5.9	6.6	7.4	7.7	8.4	8.5	8.8
Asian/Pacific Islander	3.5	4.2	4.5	5.1	5.6	6.2	6.4	6.5
American Indian/Alaska Native	1.8	2.0	2.2	2.1	2.1	1.7	1.7	1.7
Disabled	7.0	7.0	7.0	7.0	7.0	12.5	9.5	9.9
Veterans preference	30.0	26.0	24.0	22.0	23.1	25.9	26.2	26.3
Vietnam era veterans	17.0	17.0	14.0	11.0	8.0	3.2	2.7	2.2
Retired military	4.9	4.2	3.9	5.4	7.0	8.3	8.3	8.3
Retired officers	0.5	0.5	0.5	1.0	1.6	1.9	1.9	1.9
Average base salary (dollar) [1]	32,026	41,557	51,618	64,175	76,231	81,249	82.709	84,913

[1] For full-time permanent employees. [2] Represents full-time permanent employees under the Civil Service Retirement System (excluding hires since January 1984), and the Federal Employees Retirement System (since January 1984).

Source: U.S. Office of Personnel Management, Office of Workforce Information, *The Fact Book, Federal Civilian Workforce Statistics*, annual. Beginning 2008, Central Personnel Data File, "Profile of Federal Civilian Non-Postal Full-Time Employees," <http://www.opm.gov/policy-data-oversight/data-analysis-documentation/federal-employment-reports/reports-publications/profile-of-federal-civilian-non-postal-employees/>, accessed April 2018.

Table 533. Full-Time Federal Civilian Employment—Employees and Average Pay by Pay System: 2010 to 2019

[1,950 represents 1,950,000. As of September 30. Data are shown for all full-time nonseasonal employees. Includes employees in U.S., U.S. territories, foreign countries, and unspecified locations. Excludes postal employees and other selected agencies; see <http://www.fedscope.opm.gov/datadefn/aboutehri_sdm.asp> for details. See text, this section, for explanation of general schedule and wage system]

Pay system	Employees (1,000)				Average annual pay (dol.)			
	2010	2015	2018	2019	2010	2015	2018	2019
Total, excluding postal	1,950	1,940	1,965	1,999	75,707	70,453	74,035	75,415
General schedule and equivalently graded	1,410	1,430	1,414	1,433	73,656	66,920	70,690	71,913
Prevailing rate pay plans (blue collar)	195	185	183	185	52,056	53,279	56,727	57,783
Other white collar pay plans	344	325	368	382	97,480	95,892	95,562	97,161

Source: U.S. Office of Personnel Management, "FedScope," <http://www.fedscope.opm.gov/>, accessed September 2020.

Table 534. Federal Government Civilian Employment by State: 2010 to 2019

[As of September 30. For agencies excluded from total, see <http://www.fedscope.opm.gov/datadefn/aboutehri_sdm.asp>]

State	2010	2015	2018	2019	State	2010	2015	2018	2019
U.S. [1]....	2,061,320	2,029,342	2,055,904	2,087,064	MO.........	38,351	33,812	34,854	35,422
AL..........	42,267	38,004	38,196	38,868	MT.........	12,010	10,345	10,212	10,329
AK........	14,072	11,604	11,010	10,979	NE.........	10,686	9,626	9,742	9,775
AZ........	42,409	31,284	31,480	32,376	NV.........	11,475	10,964	11,496	11,841
AR........	14,741	13,203	13,095	13,203	NH.........	4,436	4,352	4,421	4,513
CA........	172,547	140,357	141,954	144,710	NJ.........	30,101	20,438	20,205	20,486
CO........	40,744	37,504	37,191	37,638	NM.........	27,682	22,057	21,441	21,902
CT........	8,671	8,027	7,945	8,087	NY.........	68,202	51,489	51,210	51,548
DE........	3,425	3,084	3,085	3,117	NC.........	43,678	42,989	44,493	45,527
DC........	167,893	147,300	142,417	142,027	ND.........	6,723	5,423	5,463	5,497
FL........	88,933	76,233	79,666	82,301	OH.........	53,014	48,196	49,860	50,675
GA........	80,229	70,201	72,067	73,494	OK.........	39,463	36,860	38,952	39,192
HI........	25,354	21,907	22,545	23,272	OR.........	22,470	20,114	20,183	20,260
ID........	10,496	9,695	9,831	9,759	PA.........	69,792	59,424	60,538	61,885
IL........	51,136	41,197	40,618	41,013	RI.........	7,135	7,227	7,459	7,756
IN........	24,734	22,152	23,074	24,054	SC.........	21,675	20,594	21,314	22,126
IA........	9,245	8,642	8,790	8,643	SD.........	8,849	8,229	8,369	8,306
KS........	17,792	15,998	16,177	16,414	TN.........	28,822	26,169	26,083	26,602
KY........	26,523	22,501	22,208	21,324	TX.........	140,292	109,531	113,080	115,276
LA........	21,075	17,833	18,752	19,013	UT.........	31,051	27,556	28,733	30,241
ME........	11,132	10,274	11,037	11,226	VT.........	4,495	3,073	3,204	3,294
MD........	128,281	128,961	128,907	128,525	VA.........	145,449	133,044	134,796	136,785
MA........	29,223	25,065	24,298	24,805	WA.........	57,894	54,082	54,567	55,150
MI........	30,023	25,396	25,490	25,977	WV.........	16,287	15,030	14,956	15,456
MN........	18,561	16,066	16,423	16,670	WI.........	15,809	15,272	15,723	15,863
MS........	19,353	17,993	17,822	18,214	WY.........	6,640	6,327	6,348	6,362

[1] Total does not include employees based in U.S. Territories or foreign countries and includes data that has been suppressed for security purposes; see source for details.

Source: U.S. Office of Personnel Management, "FedScope," <http://www.fedscope.opm.gov/>, accessed September 2020.

Table 535. Federal Executive Branch Retirements: 2005 to 2017

[For fiscal years ending September 30. Covers non-postal, executive branch federal civilian employees with personnel records in the Enterprise Human Resources Integration-Statistical Data Mart (EHRI-SDM) and Central Personnel Data File (CPDF). Retiring employees must satisfy the minimum years of service requirement; for more information, see source]

Characteristic	2005	2010	2012	2013	2014	2015	2016	2017
Total retirements.................	61,860	52,660	69,320	65,264	68,746	65,375	64,051	62,155
Sex:								
Male.....................................	37,241	30,481	38,493	36,787	38,115	36,115	35,650	34,916
Female..................................	24,619	22,179	30,827	28,477	30,631	29,260	28,401	27,238
Race:								
White.....................................	46,687	38,947	50,259	46,816	49,454	46,243	45,472	43,779
Black.....................................	8,970	7,547	10,621	9,664	10,582	10,248	9,880	9,907
Hispanic.................................	3,438	3,008	4,149	3,953	4,262	4,225	4,183	4,113
Other.....................................	2,757	3,070	4,259	4,805	4,440	4,640	4,505	4,340
Retirement type:								
Mandatory.............................	557	755	941	965	1,024	960	984	1,034
Disability................................	5,606	3,925	3,743	3,254	3,669	4,279	2,964	1,734
Voluntary...............................	47,155	45,758	59,812	58,295	61,017	58,294	58,666	57,947
Early out...............................	7,511	1,456	4,124	2,184	2,468	1,298	954	771
Other.....................................	1,031	766	700	566	568	544	483	669
Occupational category:								
Administrative........................	24,711	21,673	29,460	27,153	28,633	26,995	26,130	26,842
Professional...........................	12,434	10,906	14,322	14,410	16,090	15,198	15,179	15,086
Technical...............................	11,514	9,539	12,237	11,416	11,825	11,794	10,914	10,182
Blue collar.............................	8,232	6,489	8,097	7,296	7,066	6,529	6,027	5,556
Other.....................................	4,934	4,033	5,194	4,982	5,122	4,845	4,638	4,480
Veteran status:								
Veteran...................................	23,828	18,686	22,738	21,276	21,752	20,507	20,117	18,906
Exempt..................................	1,770	1,130	923	611	548	534	548	544
Non-veteran...........................	36,262	32,844	45,659	43,377	46,446	44,334	43,386	42,705
Average retirement age (years).....	58.9	60.3	60.8	61.3	61.4	61.5	61.8	62.0
Average length of service (years)...	27.9	27.7	27.9	27.5	26.9	26.3	25.6	25.3

Source: U.S. Office of Personnel Management, *Executive Branch Retirement Statistics: Fiscal Years 2007-2018*, April 2018 and earlier reports. See also <http://www.opm.gov/policy-data-oversight/data-analysis-documentation/federal-employment-reports/>.

Table 536. Area of Federally Owned Buildings, Excluding Department of Defense, by State: 2018

[1,141.2 represents 1,141,200,000. As of September 30. For executive branch departments and agencies subject to the Chief Financial Officers Act of 1990. Department of Defense Data is under review and is not included in FY 2018 totals]

State	Total building area (mil. sq. ft.) [2]	Owned building area (mil. sq. ft.)	Leased building area (mil. sq. ft.)	State	Total building area (mil. sq. ft.) [2]	Owned building area (mil. sq. ft.)	Leased building area (mil. sq. ft.)
United States [1]...	**1,141.2**	**884.7**	**254.3**	Missouri...........	25.7	15.0	10.6
Alabama............	17.3	13.7	3.6	Montana...........	10.7	8.5	2.2
Alaska..............	11.5	10.1	1.3	Nebraska..........	5.7	4.3	1.4
Arizona.............	30.3	26.1	4.1	Nevada............	10.3	8.2	2.1
Arkansas...........	10.1	8.8	1.3	New Hampshire...	3.0	2.4	0.5
California...........	99.7	81.6	17.9	New Jersey.......	18.2	13.8	4.4
Colorado............	23.5	17.3	6.3	New Mexico.......	32.1	29.0	3.1
Connecticut.........	6.0	5.1	0.9	New York..........	51.2	43.2	7.9
Delaware...........	1.3	0.9	0.4	North Carolina....	18.3	13.0	5.3
Dist. of Columbia. ..	75.5	52.5	23.0	North Dakota......	6.4	5.7	0.7
Florida..............	41.8	30.9	10.8	Ohio...............	34.3	29.2	5.0
Georgia.............	31.2	21.4	9.8	Oklahoma..........	11.7	6.7	5.0
Hawaii..............	4.4	3.4	0.7	Oregon............	17.4	14.6	2.7
Idaho...............	12.4	10.8	1.6	Pennsylvania......	32.9	25.1	7.7
Illinois..............	34.7	29.3	5.4	Rhode Island......	1.8	1.1	0.6
Indiana.............	13.1	10.5	2.6	South Carolina....	19.6	17.8	1.8
Iowa................	7.4	5.9	1.4	South Dakota.....	10.2	9.4	0.8
Kansas.............	9.0	6.2	2.8	Tennessee........	26.3	23.1	3.1
Kentucky...........	20.6	17.9	2.7	Texas..............	61.9	44.4	17.4
Louisiana...........	17.3	14.3	3.1	Utah...............	9.8	7.3	2.5
Maine...............	4.3	3.6	0.7	Vermont...........	2.6	1.5	1.2
Maryland............	71.5	52.7	18.7	Virginia............	52.3	26.5	25.7
Massachusetts......	18.7	15.5	2.6	Washington.......	32.6	27.4	5.1
Michigan............	16.6	12.2	4.2	West Virginia......	17.2	14.9	2.3
Minnesota..........	10.8	8.7	2.0	Wisconsin.........	9.9	7.6	2.2
Mississippi..........	13.0	11.1	1.9	Wyoming..........	9.2	8.5	0.7

[1] Includes property in U.S. territories, not shown separately. [2] Includes museum trust and state government owned. Non-federal government entities hold title to the real property asset but rights for use have been granted to the Federal Government in a method other than a leasehold arrangement; in the case of a museum trust, the trust holds title but Federal funds may be received to cover operational and maintenance costs.

Source: U.S. General Services Administration, "Federal Real Property Profile (FRPP) Summary Report Library," <https://www.gsa.gov/policy-regulations/policy/real-property-policy/data-collection-and-reports/frpp-summary-report-library>, accessed November 2019.

Section 10
National Security and Veterans Affairs

This section displays data for national security (national defense and homeland security) and benefits for veterans. Data are presented on national defense and its human and financial costs; active and reserve military personnel; federally sponsored programs and benefits for veterans; and funding, budget and selected agencies for homeland security. The principal sources of these data are the *Veterans Benefits Administration Annual Benefits Report*, U.S. Department of Veterans Affairs; *Budget in Brief*, U.S. Department of Homeland Security; and *The Budget of the United States Government*, Office of Management and Budget.

Department of Defense (DoD)—The U.S. Department of Defense is responsible for providing the military forces of the United States. It includes the Office of the Secretary of Defense, the Joint Chiefs of Staff, the Army, the Navy, the Air Force, and the defense agencies. The President serves as Commander-in-Chief of the Armed Forces; from him, the authority flows to the Secretary of Defense and through the Joint Chiefs of Staff to the commanders of unified and specified commands (e.g., U.S. Strategic Command).

Reserve components—The Reserve components of the Armed Forces consist of the Army National Guard of the United States, Army Reserve, Naval Reserve, Marine Corps Reserve, Air National Guard, Air Force Reserve, and Coast Guard Reserve. They provide trained personnel and units available for active duty in the Armed Forces during times of war or national emergency, and at such other times as national security may require. The National Guard has dual federal/state responsibilities and uses jointly provided equipment, facilities, and budget support. The President is empowered to mobilize the National Guard and to use the Armed Forces as he considers necessary to enforce federal authority in any state. There is in each Armed Force a ready reserve, a standby reserve, and a retired reserve. The Ready Reserve includes the Selected Reserve, which provides trained and ready units and individuals to augment the active forces during times of war or national emergency, or at other times when required; and the Individual Ready Reserve, which is a manpower pool that can be called to active duty during times of war or national emergency and would normally be used as individual fillers for active, guard, and reserve units, and as a source of combat replacements. Most of the Ready Reserve serves in an active status.

Department of Veterans Affairs (VA)—A veteran is someone 18 years and older (there are a few 17-year-old veterans) who is not currently on active duty, but who once served on active duty in the United States Army, Navy, Air Force, Marine Corps, or Coast Guard, or who served in the Merchant Marine during World War II. There are many groups whose active service makes them veterans including: those who incurred a service-connected disability during active duty for training in the Reserves or National Guard even though that service would not otherwise have counted for veteran status, and members of a national guard or reserve component who have been ordered to active duty by order of the President or those who have a full-time military job. The latter are called AGRs (Active Guard and Reserve). No one who has received a dishonorable discharge is a veteran.

The VA administers laws authorizing benefits for eligible former and present members of the Armed Forces and for the beneficiaries of deceased members. Veterans' benefits available under various acts of Congress include compensation for service-connected disability or death; pensions for non-service-connected disability or death; vocational rehabilitation, education and training; home loan insurance; life insurance; health care; special housing and automobiles or other conveyances for certain disabled veterans; burial and plot allowances; and educational assistance to families of deceased or totally disabled veterans, servicemen missing in action, or prisoners of war. Since these benefits are legislated by Congress, the dates they were enacted and the dates they apply to veterans may be different from the actual dates the conflicts occurred. VA estimates of veterans cover all persons discharged from active U.S. military service under conditions other than dishonorable.

Department of Homeland Security (DHS)—The creation of DHS, which began operations in March 2003, represents a fusion of 22 federal agencies from different legacy agencies (the Coast Guard and Secret Service remained intact) to coordinate and centralize the leadership of many homeland security activities under a single department. The largest organizations under DHS include: Customs and Border Protection (CBP), Immigration and Customs Enforcement (ICE), Transportation Security Administration (TSA), Federal Emergency Management Agency (FEMA), and the Coast Guard.

Coast Guard—With more than 218 years of service to the Nation, the Coast Guard is a military, multi-mission, maritime organization that promotes safety and safeguards U.S. economic and security interests throughout the maritime environment. As one of the five Armed Services of the United States, it is the only military organization within the DHS. Unlike its sister services in the Department of Defense (DoD), the Coast Guard is also a law enforcement and regulatory agency with broad domestic authorities.

Federal Emergency Management Agency (FEMA)—FEMA manages and coordinates the federal response to and recovery from major domestic disasters and emergencies of all types in accordance with the Robert T. Stafford Disaster Relief and Emergency Assistance Act. The agency ensures the effectiveness of emergency response providers at all levels of government in responding to terrorist attacks, major disasters, and other emergencies. Through the Disaster Relief Fund, FEMA provides individual and public assistance to help families and communities impacted by declared disasters rebuild and recover. FEMA is also the principal component for preparing state and local governments to prevent or respond to threats or incidents of terrorism and other catastrophic events, through their state and local programs.

The Customs and Border Protection (CBP)—CBP is responsible for managing, securing, and controlling U.S. borders. This includes carrying out traditional border-related responsibilities, such as stemming the tide of illegal drugs and illegal aliens; securing and facilitating legitimate global trade and travel; and protecting the food supply and agriculture industry from pests and disease. CBP is composed of the Border Patrol and Inspections (both moved from Immigration and Naturalization Service) along with Customs (absorbed from the U.S. Department of Treasury) and Animal and Plant Health Inspections Services (absorbed from the U.S. Department of Agriculture).

The Immigration and Customs Enforcement (ICE)—ICE's mission is to protect America and uphold public safety by targeting the people, money, and materials crossing the nation's borders that support terrorist and criminal activities. ICE is the largest investigation arm of DHS. ICE is composed of five law enforcement divisions: Investigations, Intelligence, Federal Protective Service, International Affairs, and Detention and Removal Operations. ICE investigates a wide range of national security, financial, and smuggling violations including drug smuggling, human trafficking, illegal arms exports, financial crimes, commercial fraud, human smuggling, document fraud, money laundering, child pornography/exploitation, and immigration fraud.

The Transportation Security Administration (TSA)—TSA was created as part of the Aviation and Transportation Security Act on November 19, 2001. TSA was originally part of the U.S. Department of Transportation, but was moved to DHS. TSA's mission is to provide security to our nation's transportation systems with a primary focus on aviation security.

Table 537. National Defense Outlays and Veterans' Benefits: 1965 to 2021

[In billions of dollars (56.3 represents $56,300,000,000), except percent. For fiscal year ending in year shown; see text, Section 8. Includes outlays of Department of Defense, Department of Veterans Affairs, and other agencies for activities primarily related to national defense and veterans programs. For explanation of average annual percent change, see Guide to Tabular Presentation. Minus sign (-) indicates decrease]

| Year | National defense and veterans' outlays | | | | Annual percent change [1] | | | Defense outlays, percent of— | |
| | | Defense outlays | | | | | | | |
	Total outlays	Current dollars	Constant (2012) dollars	Veterans' outlays	Total outlays	Defense outlays	Veterans' outlays	Federal outlays	Gross domestic product [2]
1965	56.3	50.6	388.5	5.7	-6.78	-7.56	0.72	42.8	7.1
1970	90.4	81.7	498.2	8.7	0.26	-0.98	13.57	41.8	7.8
1980	155.2	134.0	384.5	21.2	13.87	15.17	6.29	22.7	4.8
1990	328.4	299.3	542.7	29.1	-1.55	-1.39	-3.16	23.9	5.1
2000	341.4	294.4	431.5	47.0	7.36	7.13	8.85	16.5	2.9
2001	349.8	304.7	432.0	45.0	2.45	3.52	-4.29	16.4	2.9
2002	399.4	348.5	478.4	51.0	14.20	14.35	13.23	17.3	3.2
2003	461.6	404.7	521.9	56.8	15.55	16.15	11.48	18.7	3.6
2004	515.5	455.8	566.5	59.7	11.69	12.62	5.10	19.9	3.8
2005	565.4	495.3	587.5	70.1	9.67	8.66	17.38	20.0	3.9
2006	591.7	521.8	593.5	69.8	4.64	5.36	-0.40	19.7	3.8
2007	624.1	551.3	607.0	72.8	5.48	5.64	4.29	20.2	3.9
2008	700.8	616.1	653.3	84.7	12.29	11.76	16.32	20.7	4.2
2009	756.6	661.0	702.4	95.5	7.96	7.30	12.79	18.8	4.6
2010	802.0	693.5	723.6	108.5	6.00	4.91	13.54	20.1	4.7
2011	832.8	705.6	715.2	127.3	3.85	1.74	17.32	19.6	4.6
2012	802.5	677.9	677.8	124.7	-3.64	-3.93	-2.04	19.2	4.2
2013	772.5	633.4	629.0	139.0	-3.74	-6.55	11.52	18.3	3.8
2014	753.1	603.5	589.6	149.6	-2.51	-4.73	7.61	17.2	3.5
2015	749.4	589.7	573.3	159.8	-0.48	-2.29	6.79	16.0	3.3
2016	767.9	593.4	574.6	174.6	2.47	0.63	9.25	15.4	3.2
2017	775.3	598.7	571.7	176.6	0.96	0.90	1.16	15.0	3.1
2018	810.0	631.1	586.4	178.9	4.48	5.41	1.31	15.4	3.1
2019	**885.8**	**686.0**	**625.5**	**199.8**	**9.36**	**8.69**	**11.71**	**15.4**	**3.2**
2020 estimate	939.6	724.5	647.9	215.1	6.06	5.61	7.62	15.1	3.3
2021 estimate	1,002.9	767.1	672.8	235.8	6.74	5.88	9.62	15.9	3.3

NA Not available. [1] Change from immediate prior year. [2] Represents fiscal year GDP; for definition, see text, Section 13.

Source: U.S. Office of Management and Budget, *Budget of the U.S. Government, Fiscal Year 2021: Historical Tables*, February 2020. See also <http://www.whitehouse.gov/omb/budget/>.

Table 538. National Defense Budget Authority and Outlays for Defense Functions: 2000 to 2021

[In billions of dollars (304.0 represents $304,000,000,000). For year ending September 30. Data includes defense budget authority and outlays by other departments. Minus sign (-) indicates decrease]

Function	2000	2010	2013	2014	2015	2016	2017	2018	2019	2020 est.	2021 est.
Total budget authority	**304.0**	**721.2**	**610.2**	**622.3**	**598.4**	**624.1**	**656.3**	**726.8**	**745.7**	**757.2**	**753.5**
Department of Defense—Military	290.3	695.6	585.2	595.7	570.8	595.7	626.2	694.5	712.6	721.5	716.2
Military personnel	73.8	157.1	153.5	150.2	145.9	145.4	146.1	150.9	157.3	163.3	174.1
Operation and maintenance	108.7	293.6	258.3	262.5	246.6	245.1	258.7	274.1	283.1	290.6	290.3
Procurement	55.0	135.8	97.8	100.4	102.1	118.9	124.3	147.5	146.8	144.0	137.2
Research, development, test, and evaluation	38.7	80.2	63.3	63.5	63.9	69.5	74.1	92.0	95.5	104.7	106.7
Military construction	5.1	22.6	8.1	8.4	5.7	6.9	6.9	10.4	11.3	16.7	6.8
Family housing	3.5	2.3	1.5	1.4	1.1	1.3	1.3	1.4	1.6	1.5	1.4
Other	5.4	4.0	2.8	9.4	5.6	8.5	14.7	18.3	16.9	0.7	-0.3
Atomic energy defense activities	12.4	18.2	17.5	18.4	19.0	20.1	21.4	23.3	24.0	25.9	27.6
Defense-related activities	1.3	7.3	7.4	8.2	8.5	8.3	8.7	9.0	9.1	9.7	9.7
Total outlays	**294.4**	**693.5**	**633.4**	**603.5**	**589.7**	**593.4**	**598.7**	**631.1**	**686.0**	**724.5**	**767.1**
Department of Defense—Military	281.0	666.7	607.8	577.9	562.5	565.4	568.9	600.7	654.0	689.6	729.3
Military personnel	76.0	155.7	150.8	148.9	145.2	147.9	144.7	145.8	156.3	162.1	173.9
Operation and maintenance	105.8	276.0	259.7	244.5	247.2	243.2	245.2	256.7	271.7	283.7	295.1
Procurement	51.7	133.6	114.9	107.5	101.3	102.7	104.1	112.7	124.7	135.1	142.0
Research, development, test, and evaluation	37.6	77.0	66.9	64.9	64.1	64.9	68.1	77.0	89.3	97.5	104.6
Military construction	5.1	21.2	12.3	9.8	8.1	6.7	6.7	6.7	7.4	8.1	11.4
Family housing	3.4	3.2	1.8	1.4	1.2	1.3	1.2	1.2	1.2	1.4	1.6
Other	1.4	0.1	1.4	0.9	-4.7	-1.2	-1.1	0.7	3.5	1.7	0.7
Atomic energy defense activities	12.1	19.3	17.6	17.4	18.7	19.4	20.5	20.9	22.8	25.5	28.0
Defense-related activities	1.2	7.5	8.0	8.1	8.5	8.6	9.3	9.5	9.3	9.4	9.8

Source: U.S. Office of Management and Budget, *Budget of the U.S. Government, Fiscal Year 2021: Historical Tables*, February 2020. See also <http://www.whitehouse.gov/omb/budget/>.

Table 539. Department of Defense Property—Sites, Land, and Assets: 2017

[In units, as indicated (1,173.2 represents $1,173,200,000,000). Data collected as of September 30, 2017. A site is a physical location owned by, leased to, or otherwise possessed by a DoD component]

Asset type	Unit	Total	Army	Navy	Air Force	Marine Corps	WHS [1]
DoD sites, total	**Number**	**4,775**	**1,807**	**970**	**1,710**	**213**	**75**
United States	Number	4,150	1,565	785	1,535	190	75
Territories	Number	111	40	62	9	–	–
Overseas	Number	514	202	123	166	23	–
Acres of land, total	**Number**	**26,882,845**	**13,699,399**	**2,213,278**	**8,479,371**	**2,489,833**	**963**
Owned	Number	8,921,349	5,693,971	639,550	1,528,280	1,058,584	963
Leased	Number	901,879	726,370	72,488	102,533	488	–
Other [2]	Number	17,059,616	7,279,058	1,501,240	6,848,558	1,430,760	–
Facility assets, total [3]	**Number**	**585,816**	**288,388**	**116,675**	**128,166**	**51,674**	**913**
Buildings	Number	279,240	138,639	63,768	49,223	27,438	172
Structures	Number	184,508	85,468	33,891	46,679	17,958	512
Linear structures	Number	122,068	64,281	19,016	32,264	6,278	229
Plant replacement value of assets, total [4]	**Bil. dol.**	**1,173.2**	**451.6**	**267.9**	**351.3**	**94.7**	**7.6**
Buildings	Bil. dol.	748.9	293.5	162.8	216.3	69.1	7.2
Structures	Bil. dol.	238.8	88.4	70.0	67.9	12.2	0.3
Linear structures	Bil. dol.	185.5	69.7	35.2	67.1	13.4	0.1

– Represents zero. [1] Washington Headquarters Service. [2] Includes buildings that have been privatized or are operated by private entities in direct support of the DoD mission. [3] Buildings (roofed and floored facilities enclosed by exterior walls); structures (facilities other than buildings or linear structures, constructed on or in the land, such as towers, storage tanks, wharfs, and piers); and linear structures (facilities that traverse land such as runways, roads, rail lines, pipelines, fences, pavements, and electrical distribution line and are reported by a linear unit of measure). [4] Calculated cost to replace the current physical plant (facilities and supporting infrastructure) using today's construction costs (labor and materials) and standards (methodologies and codes).

Source: U.S. Department of Defense, Office of the Deputy Assistant Secretary of Defense (OASD) for Infrastructure, *Base Structure Report Fiscal Year 2018 Baseline, A Summary of the Real Property Inventory*, 2019. See also <http://www.acq.osd.mil/eie/Library.html#BSR>.

Table 540. Military Personnel and Families by Selected Characteristics: 2005 to 2018

[In units, as indicated. Reserve and National Guard includes Selected Reserve only, unless otherwise noted. Personnel data primarily from Defense Manpower Data Center (DMDC). Family member data is from the Defense Enrollment and Eligibility Reporting System]

Characteristic	2005 Active Duty	2005 Reserve and Guard	2010 Active Duty	2010 Reserve and Guard	2017 Active Duty	2017 Reserve and Guard	2018 Active Duty	2018 Reserve and Guard
MILITARY PERSONNEL								
Total (number)	**1,373,534**	**829,005**	**1,417,370**	**857,261**	**1,294,520**	**815,116**	**1,304,418**	**802,842**
Ratio of officers to enlisted members	1 to 5.1	1 to 5.6	1 to 5.0	1 to 5.7	1 to 4.6	1 to 5.2	1 to 4.6	1 to 5.1
Separations from duty (number)	217,598	160,882	176,248	133,223	174,403	119,841	182,876	121,303
Retired personnel (number) [1]	1,522,532	627,424	1,540,830	716,228	1,585,220	775,598	1,589,881	779,316
PERCENT								
Male	85.4	82.8	85.6	82.1	83.8	80.4	83.5	80.0
Female	14.6	17.2	14.4	17.9	16.2	19.6	16.5	20.0
Minority race/ethnicity [2]	35.9	30.4	30.0	24.1	31.3	26.1	31.0	26.1
Duty location in the U.S. & territories	85.3	96.9	86.4	99.1	87.5	98.9	87.3	99.1
25 years old and under	46.6	31.2	44.2	33.3	45.0	32.5	45.6	32.3
With bachelor's degree or higher	17.7	19.7	17.7	19.4	21.8	23.0	21.9	24.5
Married	54.6	51.4	56.4	48.2	52.6	44.4	51.5	44.3
In dual-military marriages	6.9	2.6	6.7	2.6	6.6	2.7	6.7	2.6
MILITARY FAMILIES								
Family members (number)	**1,865,058**	**1,141,735**	**1,983,236**	**1,161,631**	**1,623,305**	**1,054,783**	**1,596,169**	**1,042,071**
Spouses (number)	679,738	415,548	725,877	413,295	612,127	369,653	605,677	364,796
Adult dependents (number)	8,130	1,762	9,485	1,961	8,988	1,605	8,621	1,545
PERCENT								
With children	43.2	43.0	44.1	43.2	38.3	41.5	37.3	41.5
With children age 5 & under	39.8	24.8	42.3	27.9	42.2	31.3	42.1	31.5
Single parents	5.4	8.2	5.4	9.3	4.0	9.1	4.0	9.1
Average age at birth of first child (years)	24.8	27.3	24.9	26.6	25.9	28.2	25.8	28.2

[1] Retired Reserve and Guard includes ready reserve. [2] Black or African American, Asian, American Indian or Alaska Native, Native Hawaiian or Other Pacific Islander, multi-racial, or other/unknown.

Source: U.S. Department of Defense, Office of the Deputy Assistant Secretary of Defense, Military Community and Family Policy, *2018 Demographics Profile of the Military Community*, and earlier reports. See also <https://www.militaryonesource.mil/reports-and-surveys>.

Table 541. Department of Defense Personnel by Service Branch and Sex: 1960 to 2019

[In thousands (2,475 represents 2,475,000). As of end of fiscal year; see text, Section 8. Includes National Guard, Reserve, and retired regular personnel on extended or continuous active duty. Excludes Coast Guard. Other officer candidates are included under enlisted personnel]

Year	Total[1,2]	Army Total[1]	Army Male Officers	Army Male Enlisted	Army Female Officers	Army Female Enlisted	Navy[2] Total[1]	Navy Male Officers	Navy Male Enlisted	Navy Female Officers	Navy Female Enlisted	Marine Corps Total[1]	Marine Male Officers	Marine Male Enlisted	Marine Female Officers	Marine Female Enlisted	Air Force Total[1]	Air Force Male Officers	Air Force Male Enlisted	Air Force Female Officers	Air Force Female Enlisted
1960	2,475	873	97	762	4.3	8.3	617	67	540	2.7	5.4	171	16	153	0.1	1.5	815	126	677	3.7	5.7
1965	2,654	969	108	846	3.8	8.5	670	75	583	2.6	5.3	190	17	172	0.1	1.4	825	128	685	4.1	4.7
1970	3,065	1,323	162	1,142	5.2	11.5	691	78	600	2.9	5.8	260	25	233	0.3	2.1	791	125	648	4.7	9.0
1975	2,128	784	98	640	4.6	37.7	535	62	449	3.7	17.5	196	19	174	0.3	2.8	613	100	478	5.0	25.2
1980	2,051	777	91	612	7.6	61.7	527	58	430	4.9	30.1	189	18	164	0.5	6.2	558	90	404	8.5	51.9
1985	2,151	781	99	599	10.8	68.4	571	64	449	6.9	45.7	198	19	169	0.7	9.0	602	96	431	11.9	58.1
1986	2,169	781	99	597	11.3	69.7	581	65	457	7.3	47.2	200	19	170	0.6	9.2	608	97	434	12.4	61.2
1987	2,174	781	96	596	11.6	71.6	587	65	462	7.2	47.7	200	19	170	0.6	9.1	607	94	432	12.6	63.2
1988	2,138	772	95	588	11.8	72.0	593	65	466	7.3	49.7	197	19	168	0.7	9.0	576	92	405	12.9	61.5
1989	2,130	770	95	584	12.2	74.3	593	65	464	7.5	52.1	197	19	168	0.7	9.0	571	91	399	13.4	63.7
1990	2,044	732	92	553	12.4	71.2	579	64	451	7.8	52.1	197	19	168	0.7	8.7	535	87	370	13.3	60.8
1991	1,986	711	91	535	12.5	67.8	570	63	444	8.0	51.4	194	19	166	0.7	8.3	510	84	350	13.3	59.1
1992	1,807	610	83	449	11.7	61.7	542	61	417	8.3	51.0	185	18	157	0.6	7.9	470	77	320	12.7	56.1
1993	1,705	572	77	420	11.1	60.2	510	58	390	8.3	49.3	178	17	153	0.6	7.2	444	72	302	12.3	54.5
1994	1,610	541	74	394	10.9	59.0	469	54	355	8.0	47.9	174	17	149	0.6	7.0	426	69	287	12.3	54.0
1995	1,518	509	72	365	10.8	57.3	435	51	324	7.9	47.9	175	17	150	0.7	7.4	400	66	266	12.1	52.1
1996	1,472	491	70	347	10.6	59.0	417	50	308	7.8	46.9	175	17	149	0.8	7.8	389	64	256	12.0	52.8
1997	1,439	492	69	346	10.4	62.4	396	48	290	7.8	44.8	174	17	148	0.8	8.5	377	62	246	12.0	53.8
1998	1,407	484	68	340	10.4	61.4	382	47	280	7.8	42.9	173	18	146	0.9	8.9	368	60	237	12.0	54.2
1999	1,386	479	67	337	10.5	61.5	373	46	271	7.7	43.9	173	17	145	0.9	9.3	361	58	232	11.8	54.6
2000	1,384	482	66	339	10.8	62.9	373	46	272	7.8	43.8	173	17	146	0.9	9.5	356	57	227	11.8	55.0
2001	1,385	481	65	337	11.0	63.4	378	46	273	8.0	46.6	173	17	145	1.0	9.6	354	57	224	12.0	55.6
2002	1,414	487	66	341	11.5	63.2	385	47	279	8.2	47.3	174	17	146	1.0	9.5	368	59	233	12.9	58.6
2003	1,434	499	68	352	12.0	63.5	382	47	276	8.2	47.3	178	18	149	1.1	9.6	375	61	237	13.5	60.0
2004	1,427	500	69	358	12.3	61.0	373	46	273	8.1	46.1	178	18	149	1.1	9.7	377	61	242	13.6	60.2
2005	1,389	493	69	353	12.4	57.9	363	45	266	7.8	44.5	180	18	151	1.0	9.8	354	60	225	13.4	55.6
2006	1,385	505	69	365	12.5	58.5	350	44	255	7.6	43.2	180	18	151	1.1	10.0	349	58	223	12.8	55.8
2007	1,380	522	71	379	13.0	58.8	338	44	244	7.6	42.2	186	18	156	1.1	10.5	333	54	214	11.8	53.4
2008	1,402	544	74	392	13.5	59.7	332	44	235	7.7	41.4	199	19	167	1.2	11.1	327	53	207	11.9	51.4
2009	1,419	553	76	399	14.3	59.4	329	44	231	7.9	42.2	203	19	170	1.2	11.7	333	53	211	12.1	52.0
2010	1,431	566	79	407	15.1	60.3	328	44	228	8.2	43.4	202	18	169	1.3	12.2	334	54	212	12.4	50.9
2011	1,425	565	82	403	15.7	60.2	325	44	224	8.5	44.0	201	21	167	1.3	12.4	333	53	213	12.3	50.3
2012	1,400	550	82	390	16.0	57.4	318	44	217	8.6	44.3	198	20	164	1.3	12.6	333	53	214	12.5	49.8
2013	1,383	532	82	373	16.2	55.7	324	45	219	9.0	47.0	196	20	162	1.4	12.8	330	52	213	12.7	49.1
2014	1,338	508	81	353	16.2	53.8	326	45	219	9.2	48.1	188	19	154	1.4	12.8	316	50	203	12.4	46.7
2015	1,314	491	79	339	15.9	53.4	328	45	219	9.4	49.9	183	19	150	1.5	12.6	311	49	200	12.4	46.3
2016	1,301	475	76	326	15.7	53.2	325	45	216	9.8	50.2	184	19	149	1.5	13.3	318	48	204	12.6	48.3
2017	1,307	476	76	325	15.9	54.4	324	44	214	10.1	51.4	184	20	149	1.6	13.9	323	49	207	12.9	50.1
2018	1,317	476	76	325	16.1	54.6	330	44	217	10.4	53.6	185	20	150	1.7	14.3	326	49	207	13.3	51.8
2019	1,339	484	76	330	16.5	56.8	337	44	221	10.7	55.9	186	20	150	1.8	14.9	332	50	210	13.9	54.2

[1] Includes cadets, midshipmen, and others, not shown separately. [2] Beginning 1980, excludes Navy Reserve personnel on active duty for Training and Administration of Reserves (TARS).

Source: U.S. Department of Defense, Statistical Information Analysis Division, *Selected Manpower Statistics*, discontinued; and Defense Manpower Data Center, "Active Duty Military Personnel by Service by Rank/Grade," <https://www.dmdc.osd.mil/appj/dwp/dwp_reports.jsp>, accessed May 2020.

Table 542. Military Personnel on Active Duty by Rank or Grade: 2000 to 2019

[As of September 30]

Rank/grade	2000	2010	2015	2016	2017	2018	2019
Total.	1,384,338	1,430,985	1,313,940	1,301,308	1,307,364	1,317,325	1,339,036
Total officers.	217,178	234,000	230,468	228,148	228,972	230,708	232,889
General – Admiral.	34	39	38	39	37	40	37
Lieutenant General – Vice Admiral.	119	150	141	137	147	147	142
Major General – Rear Admiral (U).	282	310	310	307	301	296	295
Brigadier General – Rear Admiral (L).	436	482	420	420	418	438	409
Colonel – Captain.	11,304	12,160	11,240	11,253	11,222	10,999	11,080
Lieutenant Colonel – Commander.	27,461	28,773	27,221	27,079	27,028	27,126	27,152
Major – LT Commander.	43,229	45,295	43,609	42,958	42,630	43,145	43,908
Captain – Lieutenant.	68,106	74,997	75,525	74,633	74,838	74,120	73,820
1st Lieutenant – Lieutenant (JG).	24,713	25,523	29,484	28,303	27,642	28,250	29,228
2nd Lieutenant – Ensign.	26,405	27,128	23,724	24,745	26,607	28,002	28,590
Chief Warrant Officer W-5.	473	746	797	769	739	783	774
Chief Warrant Officer W-4.	2,029	3,233	2,782	2,631	2,756	2,761	2,647
Chief Warrant Officer W-3.	3,824	4,795	5,424	5,348	5,327	5,225	5,153
Chief Warrant Officer W-2.	6,674	7,489	7,694	7,393	6,875	6,737	6,768
Warrant Officer W-1.	2,089	2,880	2,059	2,133	2,405	2,639	2,886
Total enlisted.	1,154,624	1,183,200	1,070,546	1,060,084	1,065,163	1,073,324	1,092,937
E-9.	10,240	10,192	9,991	9,979	10,071	10,369	10,472
E-8.	26,035	27,331	26,443	25,965	26,137	26,195	27,477
E-7.	97,717	97,070	89,580	89,428	88,408	91,086	92,617
E-6.	164,857	170,856	156,786	154,408	154,681	157,265	160,725
E-5.	229,492	249,981	219,613	214,296	218,278	221,114	226,193
E-4.	250,999	279,315	277,371	262,254	251,734	245,602	253,718
E-3.	196,276	228,152	174,695	183,762	186,496	191,054	189,579
E-2.	98,983	75,177	66,744	67,996	71,613	70,960	71,703
E-1.	80,025	45,126	49,323	51,996	57,745	59,679	60,453
Cadets and Midshipmen.	12,536	13,785	12,926	13,076	13,229	13,293	13,210

Source: U.S. Department of Defense, Statistical Information Analysis Division, *Atlas/Data Abstract for the United States and Selected Areas*, annual, discontinued; and "Active Duty Military Personnel by Rank/Grade," <https://www.dmdc.osd.mil/appj/dwp/dwp_reports.jsp>, accessed January 2020.

Table 543. Military Retirement System—Disabled and Non-Disabled Personnel and Payments: 2019

[Payment in thousands of dollars (4,742,352 represents $4,742,352,000). As of September 30. The data published in the source report are produced from files maintained by the Defense Manpower Data Center. This report compiles data primarily from the "Retiree Pay and Survivor Pay" files. Any grouping of members by address reflects mailing, not necessarily residence, address. Only those members in plans administered by the Department of Defense (DoD) are included in this table. The data are preliminary because of reporting delays about members who retired or died within one month of the September 30 reporting date. These data were not processed in time to be included in this report. For more information, see Introduction and Overview, source]

State	Retired military personnel [1]			Monthly payment ($1,000)	State	Retired military personnel [1]			Monthly payment ($1,000)
	Total	Disabled [2]	Non-disabled			Total	Disabled [2]	Non-disabled	
Total [3].	2,174,409	283,762	1,890,647	4,742,352	MS.	27,873	3,159	24,714	52,652
					MO.	39,038	5,841	33,197	73,992
U.S.	2,133,256	278,660	1,854,596	4,660,758	MT.	9,726	1,246	8,480	19,945
AL.	62,233	7,233	55,000	135,845	NE.	14,641	1,525	13,116	32,727
AK.	11,045	1,577	9,468	23,961	NV.	30,021	3,002	27,019	66,106
AZ.	58,052	6,710	51,342	128,012	NH.	9,533	1,141	8,392	20,699
AR.	25,300	3,442	21,858	47,881	NJ.	19,081	3,222	15,859	32,889
CA.	151,880	19,113	132,767	331,169	NM.	20,946	2,365	18,581	47,263
CO.	54,048	7,445	46,603	135,427	NY.	40,215	7,963	32,252	64,390
CT.	10,146	1,564	8,582	19,516	NC.	100,325	13,891	86,434	225,830
DE.	9,186	845	8,341	18,411	ND.	5,521	542	4,979	10,170
DC.	2,354	348	2,006	6,329	OH.	47,998	7,789	40,209	93,077
FL.	204,864	22,611	182,253	482,722	OK.	36,318	4,870	31,448	72,078
GA.	100,389	14,425	85,964	211,756	OR.	20,852	3,396	17,456	40,250
HI.	18,081	1,831	16,250	43,880	PA.	51,880	7,352	44,528	98,173
ID.	14,912	1,854	13,058	30,941	RI.	5,252	681	4,571	11,270
IL.	36,607	5,863	30,744	72,792	SC.	61,800	7,014	54,786	131,926
IN.	26,645	4,833	21,812	44,941	SD.	8,812	841	7,971	17,871
IA.	13,428	2,055	11,373	23,244	TN.	57,702	7,955	49,747	118,556
KS.	22,509	3,140	19,369	48,223	TX.	218,279	33,132	185,147	491,464
KY.	28,972	4,663	24,309	56,687	UT.	17,771	2,006	15,765	37,170
LA.	26,514	4,174	22,340	52,109	VT.	3,904	565	3,339	6,808
ME.	11,894	1,481	10,413	22,911	VA.	157,914	12,347	145,567	464,992
MD.	55,884	5,581	50,303	137,180	WA.	74,878	8,611	66,267	168,361
MA.	18,265	2,967	15,298	32,843	WV.	10,994	1,630	9,364	19,855
MI.	31,050	6,087	24,963	51,950	WI.	22,441	3,323	19,118	38,951
MN.	19,523	2,767	16,756	32,780	WY.	5,760	642	5,118	11,783

[1] Represents military personnel (officers and enlisted) receiving and not receiving pay from DoD. [2] A disabled military member is entitled to disability retired pay if the disability is not the result of the member's intentional misconduct or willful neglect, was not incurred during a period of unauthorized absence, and either: (1) the member has at least 20 years of service; or (2) at the time of determination, the disability is at least 30 percent (under a standard schedule of rating disabilities by the Veterans Administration) and one of four additional conditions are met. For details on these conditions and additional information, see Overview, source. [3] Includes states, U.S. territories, and retirees living in foreign countries.

Source: U.S. Department of Defense, Office of the Actuary, *Statistical Report on the Military Retirement System, Fiscal Year Ended September 30, 2019*, August 2020. See also <http://actuary.defense.gov>.

Table 544. U.S. Active Duty Military Deaths and Personnel Wounded in Action by Conflict and Manner of Death: 2001 to 2020

[As of September 14, 2020. See source for details]

Item	Operation Enduring Freedom (OEF) [1]	Operation Iraqi Freedom (OIF) [2]	Operation New Dawn (OND) [3]	Operation Inherent Resolve (OIR) [4]	Operation Freedom's Sentinel (OFS) [5]
Deaths, total...................	**2,349**	**4,418**	**74**	**98**	**93**
Total hostile deaths.......	**1,845**	**3,481**	**38**	**21**	**64**
Killed in action................	1,370	2,675	22	13	39
Died of wounds...............	472	799	16	8	25
Died while missing in action..	(NA)	1	–	–	–
Died while captured...........	(NA)	5	–	–	–
Died while detained...........	(NA)	1	–	–	–
Died of terrorist activities.....	2	–	–	–	–
Total non-hostile deaths.......................	**504**	**937**	**36**	**77**	**29**
Accident.......................	304	570	7	30	18
Illness or injury................	62	97	10	16	2
Homicide.......................	14	37	3	2	1
Undetermined..................	10	11	3	1	–
Self-inflicted...................	112	222	13	27	8
Pending........................	2	–	–	1	–
Wounded in action..........	**20,149**	**31,994**	**298**	**235**	**572**

– Represents zero. NA Not available. [1] OEF October 2001-December 2014 combat operations in Afghanistan and against al Qaeda. [2] OIF March 2003-September 2010 combat operations in Iraq. [3] OND September 2010-December 2011 advise and train Iraqi security forces in Iraq. [4] OIR August 2014-present to support Iraqi Security Force operations against the Islamic State of Iraq and the Levant (ISIL). [5] OFS 2015-present to train, advise, and assist Afghan National Defense and Security Forces in Afghanistan and conduct counterterrorism operations against the remnants of al Qaeda.

Source: U.S. Department of Defense, Defense Manpower Data Center, "Defense Casualty Analysis System," <https://dcas.dmdc.osd.mil/>, accessed September 2020.

Table 545. U.S. Military Personnel on Active Duty Overseas by Selected Country: 2010 to 2019

[As of September 30. Data from Defense Manpower Data Center (DMDC). This data catalogues the history of personnel in the military and their family for purposes of healthcare, retirement funding, and other administrative needs, and may not accurately reflect current force totals]

Country	2010	2011	2012	2013	2014	2015	2016	2017	2018 [1]	2019 [1]
Total overseas [2]........	**339,360**	**336,645**	**272,623**	**251,737**	**232,790**	**213,067**	**198,557**	**215,249**	**172,370**	**174,253**
Afghanistan.................	81,875	82,177	63,243	48,807	24,170	9,392	9,027	13,329	[4] (NA)	[4] (NA)
Australia....................	163	176	344	229	1,147	1,201	187	1,239	1,496	2,858
Bahrain.....................	4,626	4,623	5,310	6,308	5,502	5,160	5,370	8,610	4,214	4,202
Belgium.....................	1,157	1,176	1,159	1,155	1,202	1,202	852	867	1,049	1,046
Canada.....................	131	130	149	149	145	146	139	129	144	144
Cuba (Guantanamo)......	870	843	996	978	892	782	797	753	831	776
Diego Garcia [3].............	484	468	522	451	521	486	294	264	299	325
Djibouti.....................	990	1,417	1,837	2,084	1,984	1,970	1,702	3,132	954	88
Egypt.......................	262	230	280	266	304	350	356	375	280	276
Germany....................	43,911	43,393	42,891	35,849	36,855	35,216	34,612	34,516	35,116	35,275
Greece......................	380	378	364	393	380	371	360	433	410	389
Honduras...................	391	356	408	376	374	660	397	505	467	474
Hungary....................	50	57	63	65	66	70	207	215	202	194
Iraq.........................	38,591	28,675	164	138	498	4,231	4,626	7,402	[4] (NA)	[4] (NA)
Italy........................	8,836	10,451	9,074	10,686	11,373	11,614	12,090	11,756	12,703	12,902
Japan.......................	46,313	48,235	49,350	52,972	52,518	55,744	38,834	44,562	54,281	55,245
Jordan......................	42	195	422	1,140	1,386	1,861	1,556	1,862	59	95
Kenya.......................	23	62	98	120	104	96	40	208	46	44
Korea, South...............	27,869	28,271	27,724	30,252	29,074	24,934	24,190	23,635	25,813	26,525
Kosovo.....................	52	68	58	514	496	87	366	384	(NA)	(NA)
Kuwait......................	17,584	16,881	10,006	8,109	11,377	8,809	5,818	9,241	1,863	1,798
Kyrgyzstan.................	5,483	10,194	6,857	3,222	121	83	67	65	5	2
Netherlands................	433	407	398	378	411	399	382	407	404	393
Niger.......................	2	3	16	97	119	139	8	510	8	13
Norway.....................	68	80	88	84	81	83	77	344	474	556
Pakistan....................	268	121	92	87	94	116	121	111	35	27
Philippines.................	546	551	416	398	251	234	36	101	145	170
Poland......................	18	33	40	47	51	61	53	173	150	163
Portugal....................	699	709	733	698	653	464	197	192	233	232
Qatar.......................	12,036	11,812	6,865	5,919	5,589	5,219	3,216	4,666	783	545
Romania....................	7	11	76	166	675	611	682	451	294	108
Saudi Arabia...............	325	524	471	654	553	515	371	402	323	314
Singapore..................	216	206	163	214	217	252	176	206	205	200
Somalia.....................	2	178	173	310	53	232	106	285	60	85
Spain.......................	1,396	1,591	1,719	1,915	3,095	3,393	3,272	3,940	3,602	3,658
Syria........................	3	3	1	1	(NA)	(NA)	(NA)	1,547	[4] (NA)	[4] (NA)
Thailand....................	201	233	117	106	110	108	296	309	316	303
Turkey......................	1,721	1,651	1,566	1,514	1,595	2,081	2,139	1,950	1,695	1,659
United Arab Emirates.....	1,427	1,851	2,424	3,384	2,045	2,620	1,510	3,455	414	352
United Kingdom............	8,764	8,673	8,516	9,045	8,495	8,062	8,404	8,341	9,137	9,254
Yemen......................	104	30	115	248	161	8	7	14	4	7
Guam.......................	5,423	5,470	5,494	5,467	6,337	6,531	3,977	4,590	6,199	5,560
Puerto Rico.................	654	680	704	667	657	725	142	176	158	161

NA Not available. [1] Starting in December 2017, the table no longer includes personnel on temporary duty, or deployed in support of contingency operations. [2] Includes items not shown separately, and also personnel in unknown and classified locations. [3] British Indian Ocean Territory. [4] Data are not shown for Afghanistan, Iraq, and Syria. With ongoing operations, any questions concerning DoD personnel strength numbers are deferred to OSD Public Affairs/Joint Chiefs of Staff.

Source: U.S. Department of Defense, DoD Personnel, Workforce Reports & Publications, "Military and Civilian Personnel by Service/Agency by State/Country," <https://www.dmdc.osd.mil/appj/dwp/stats_reports.jsp>, accessed May 2020.

Table 546. Suicides of Military Personnel by Selected Characteristics: 2013 to 2018

[Data are shown for suicides reported in Department of Defense Suicide Event Report (DoDSER). Beginning 2013, covers service members in the active component of the military only. DoDSER standardizes suicide surveillance efforts across the military services to support the DoD's suicide prevention mission. Confirmed suicides are those that have been confirmed by the Armed Forces Medical Examiner System (AFMES)]

Characteristics	Suicides					
	2013	2014	2015	2016	2017	2018
Suicides confirmed/pending confirmation [1]	**256**	**276**	**266**	**280**	**285**	**325**
By sex:						
Male	241	256	252	260	269	304
Female	15	20	14	20	16	21
By race/ethnicity:						
White	192	199	186	215	220	234
Black or African American	32	42	44	33	28	42
Asian or Pacific Islander	8	8	12	9	13	23
American Indian or Alaska Native	8	3	4	6	2	2
By Hispanic origin:						
Hispanic or Latino	21	34	29	29	41	50
Non-Hispanic or Latino	232	240	231	245	236	265
Unknown	3	2	6	6	8	10
By age:						
Under 25 years old	108	102	107	127	121	144
25-29 years old	72	72	62	68	75	74
30-39 years old	57	83	77	62	60	83
40 years old and over	19	19	20	23	29	24
By marital status:						
Never married	106	105	116	120	115	133
Married	126	145	132	135	141	179
Legally separated	2	–	–	2	–	–
Divorced	22	25	17	22	28	13
Widowed	–	1	1	1	1	–

– Represents zero. [1] Includes other or unknown race/ethnicity, age, and marital status, not shown separately.

Source: U.S. Department of Defense, Psychological Health Center for Excellence, *Department of Defense Suicide Event Report, Calendar Year 2018 Annual Report*, 2020, and earlier reports. See also <http:/www.dspo.mil>.

Table 547. Sexual Assault in the Military—Incident Reports and Victims by Type of Report and Selected Characteristics: 2016 to 2019

[Data are for fiscal years. Reports of sexual assault (rape, aggravated sexual assault, sexual assault, aggravated sexual contact, abusive sexual contact, wrongful sexual contact, non-consensual sodomy, and attempts to commit these offenses) by or against Service Members. Restricted Reporting allows victim confidential access to medical care and advocacy services. When a victim makes an Unrestricted Report, the report is also referred to a Military Criminal Investigation Organization for investigation and command is notified]

Item	Unrestricted				Restricted			
	2016	2017	2018	2019	2016	2017	2018	2019
REPORTS [1]								
Total	**4,499**	**5,032**	**5,685**	**5,578**	**1,581**	**1,659**	**1,818**	**2,126**
Service member on service member	2,232	2,450	2,853	2,830	720	851	1,006	1,153
Service member on non-service member	739	822	900	870	39	43	40	50
Non-service member on service member	157	199	178	174	407	419	413	497
Unidentified subject on service member	785	843	913	738	345	343	359	424
Unknown	586	718	841	966	70	3	–	2
VICTIMS IN COMPLETED INVESTIGATIONS [2]								
Total	**4,409**	**4,606**	**5,053**	**5,245**	**(X)**	**(X)**	**(X)**	**(X)**
Service member victims	3,551	3,735	4,162	4,320	(X)	(X)	(X)	(X)
Non-service member victims	858	871	891	925	(X)	(X)	(X)	(X)
VICTIMS [3]								
By sex:								
Male	824	832	905	980	312	300	366	440
Female	3,558	3,744	4,143	4,256	1,266	1,357	1,452	1,685
By age:								
0-15 years old	45	66	67	44	182	149	150	141
16-19 years old	1,028	1,083	1,263	1,350	359	440	434	567
20-24 years old	1,858	1,966	2,157	2,240	616	670	783	870
25-34 years old	842	869	956	938	307	310	360	412
35-49 years old	193	205	205	210	68	65	64	89
50-64 years old	17	16	5	16	4	3	3	7
65 years and older	21	35	86	68	–	–	–	–
SERVICE MEMBER VICTIMS								
By service branch:								
Army	1,567	1,599	1,849	1,940	485	513	569	644
Navy	951	1,016	1,064	1,005	355	406	423	553
Marines	424	444	524	522	303	315	347	369
Air Force	607	674	725	849	392	380	438	508
Coast Guard	1	1	–	–	1	–	1	–

– Represents zero. X Not applicable. [1] Reports of sexual assault during the fiscal year. [2] Victims in investigations completed during the fiscal year. Includes victims of unknown sex, age, and service branch, not shown separately. [3] For unrestricted reports, data shown for victims in investigations completed during the fiscal year.

Source: U.S. Department of Defense, *Annual Report on Sexual Assault in the Military, Fiscal Year 2019*, April 2020, and earlier reports. See also <https://www.sapr.mil/reports>.

Table 548. U.S. Military Sales and Assistance to Foreign Governments: 1990 to 2017

[In millions of dollars (14,600 represents $14,600,000,000). For year ending September 30. Department of Defense (DoD) sales deliveries cover deliveries against sales orders authorized under Arms Export Control Act, as well as earlier and applicable legislation. For details regarding individual programs, see source]

Item	1990	2000	2010	2012	2013	2014	2015	2016	2017
Military sales agreements...............	14,600	10,829	22,158	63,505	23,823	32,824	45,322	27,617	51,025
Military construction sales agreements.............................	628	284	955	790	340	1,444	441	102	1,655
Military sales deliveries [1]...............	8,360	10,938	13,440	14,250	15,669	15,250	16,913	16,709	27,963
Military construction sales deliveries...	348	183	459	488	497	389	493	423	491
Military financing program............	4,354	4,333	5,016	5,929	4,874	4,601	5,212	5,616	5,144
Commercial exports licensed under Arms Export Control Act [2].............	6,216	478	–	–	–	–	–	–	–
Military assistance program delivery [3]..............................	125	5	–	–	60	111	101	35	–
IMET program/deliveries [4]..............	43	50	108	105	99	103	104	111	139

– Represents or rounds to zero. [1] Includes military construction sales deliveries. [2] The total dollar value of deliveries made for purchases of munitions-controlled items by foreign governments directly from U.S. manufacturers. [3] Includes Military Assistance Service Funded (MASF) program data and Section 506(a) drawdown authority. [4] International Military Education and Training. Includes military assistance services and emergency drawdowns.

Source: U.S. Department of Defense, Defense Security Cooperation Agency, DSCA Historical Facts Book & Fiscal Year Series, *DSCA Fiscal Year Series, as of September 30, 2017.* See also <http://dsca.mil/resources/dsca-historical-facts-book-fiscal-year-series>.

Table 549. U.S. Military Sales Deliveries by Selected Country: 2000 to 2017

[In millions of dollars (10,938 represents $10,938,000,000). For year ending September 30. Represents Department of Defense military sales]

Country	2000	2010	2011	2012	2013	2014	2015	2016	2017
Total [1]..	10,938	13,440	13,726	14,250	15,669	15,250	16,913	16,709	27,963
International organizations...............	61	86	147	116	165	167	124	125	140
Afghanistan..............................	–	18	17	4	8	34	87	55	98
Argentina................................	10	26	12	14	13	16	84	43	31
Australia.................................	332	891	726	631	628	804	2,301	1,158	1,224
Bahrain..................................	55	111	51	94	69	56	35	30	65
Belgium..................................	61	26	27	57	22	49	67	30	76
Brazil....................................	61	29	36	133	54	52	73	59	39
Canada..................................	84	381	395	287	289	239	179	284	217
Chile....................................	1	23	23	81	56	46	74	48	54
Colombia................................	14	425	149	122	146	91	76	74	55
Denmark.................................	43	43	67	45	91	51	85	147	137
Ecuador.................................	1	3	1	1	2	1	–	–	9
Egypt....................................	1,186	956	908	846	1,540	980	448	1,242	503
El Salvador..............................	14	6	5	6	4	2	2	2	1
Finland..................................	690	127	94	82	103	62	135	74	99
France...................................	217	112	132	125	184	143	295	120	217
Georgia..................................	3	10	28	18	36	14	9	14	15
Germany.................................	136	296	160	141	148	163	139	153	106
Greece...................................	389	265	149	163	61	94	112	83	132
India....................................	–	31	57	167	194	370	656	212	244
Indonesia................................	–	16	17	35	39	122	165	68	218
Iraq.....................................	–	400	765	610	520	1,098	1,722	2,216	1,755
Israel....................................	550	938	789	925	937	897	661	666	547
Italy.....................................	51	179	101	87	69	78	85	70	65
Japan....................................	432	779	435	498	352	523	1,317	863	1,014
Jordan...................................	52	173	211	376	337	281	193	173	166
Kenya....................................	2	2	16	29	3	4	3	4	18
Korea, South.............................	1,399	594	712	723	603	600	453	596	10,238
Kuwait...................................	321	242	434	262	303	553	368	474	615
Lebanon.................................	5	69	19	25	60	89	97	66	57
Malaysia.................................	411	45	29	35	41	46	93	63	40
Mexico..................................	9	59	38	8	19	195	19	100	118
Morocco.................................	8	28	976	381	213	79	42	79	108
Netherlands.............................	278	200	184	177	134	145	198	195	226
Nigeria..................................	–	5	13	8	14	10	34	5	6
Norway..................................	64	127	147	94	166	143	136	193	127
Oman....................................	1	34	36	49	58	413	178	141	71
Pakistan.................................	–	1,129	549	382	275	338	176	255	138
Philippines...............................	10	37	27	26	23	20	76	57	46
Poland...................................	13	74	190	162	154	87	126	164	203
Portugal.................................	20	29	36	46	16	18	21	21	21
Saudi Arabia.............................	1,988	1,683	1,493	1,619	3,308	2,264	2,796	3,215	5,572
Singapore...............................	131	296	250	240	210	222	141	241	186
Spain....................................	141	152	98	67	98	113	89	87	89
Switzerland..............................	69	80	82	87	82	66	53	62	43
Taiwan..................................	784	863	767	975	784	1,681	1,090	1,063	1,022
Thailand.................................	114	41	89	62	82	100	80	95	106
Tunisia..................................	4	12	14	12	12	10	20	22	109
Turkey...................................	216	251	876	1,240	644	194	420	231	342
Ukraine..................................	1	21	8	4	4	10	19	18	17
United Arab Emirates.....................	40	594	634	1,367	769	797	452	555	376
United Kingdom..........................	347	261	343	311	1,295	403	305	283	275
Yemen...................................	–	6	5	4	7	6	3	1	1

– Represents or rounds to zero. [1] Includes countries, programs, and classified totals not shown.

Source: U.S. Department of Defense, Defense Security Cooperation Agency, DSCA Historical Facts Book & Fiscal Year Series, *DSCA Fiscal Year Series, as of September 30, 2017.* See also <https://dsca.mil/resources/dsca-historical-facts-book-fiscal-year-series>.

Table 550. Veterans by Selected Period of Service, State, and Island Area: 2018

[In thousands (19,929 represents 19,929,000). As of September 30. The Veteran Population Projection Model 2018 (VetPop2018) is the Department of Veterans Affairs (VA) latest official estimate and projection of the veteran population. It is based on tabulations prepared for the VA Office of the Actuary; recent American Community Survey, Internal Revenue Service, and Social Security Administration data; administrative data and projections of service member separations from active duty provided by the Department of Defense, Defense Manpower Data Center and the Office of the Actuary; and VA data on veterans benefits. Data may not sum due to rounding]

State and Island Area	Total [1,2]	Gulf War era [3]	Vietnam era [4]	State and Island Area	Total [1,2]	Gulf War era [3]	Vietnam era [4]
United States	**19,929**	**7,883**	**6,453**	Montana	91	33	33
Alabama	368	163	117	Nebraska	130	54	41
Alaska	71	39	19	Nevada	225	91	75
Arizona	516	193	183	New Hampshire	101	35	35
Arkansas	209	86	72	New Jersey	351	108	115
California	1,705	669	541	New Mexico	154	62	55
Colorado	396	180	122	New York	763	243	243
Connecticut	177	55	60	North Carolina	708	309	225
Delaware	72	25	26	North Dakota	55	25	16
District of Columbia	30	14	6	Ohio	758	260	251
Florida	1,543	561	511	Oklahoma	300	132	99
Georgia	703	336	206	Oregon	301	97	111
Hawaii	116	56	35	Pennsylvania	814	257	277
Idaho	126	48	46	Rhode Island	64	22	23
Illinois	621	217	206	South Carolina	401	171	136
Indiana	420	147	137	South Dakota	66	28	21
Iowa	204	70	68	Tennessee	463	187	151
Kansas	201	89	64	Texas	1,585	752	478
Kentucky	293	117	95	Utah	136	64	42
Louisiana	293	131	89	Vermont	43	14	14
Maine	112	36	41	Virginia	730	396	198
Maryland	392	174	114	Washington	562	243	183
Massachusetts	324	99	105	West Virginia	141	52	50
Michigan	582	182	202	Wisconsin	361	114	126
Minnesota	322	100	110	Wyoming	48	18	18
Mississippi	188	85	54	Puerto Rico	73	21	26
Missouri	429	159	147	Island Areas & Foreign	91	60	35

[1] Veterans serving in more than one period of service are counted only once in the total. [2] Current civilians discharged from active duty, other than for training only without service-connected disability. [3] Service from August 2, 1990 to the present. [4] Service from August 5, 1964 to May 7, 1975.

Source: U.S. Department of Veterans Affairs, National Center for Veterans Analysis and Statistics, "The Veteran Population Projection Model 2018 (VetPop2018)," <va.gov/vetdata/veteran_population.asp>, accessed July 2020.

Table 551. Veterans Living by Period of Service, Age, and Sex: 2019

[19,929 represents 19,929,000. As of September 30. Includes veterans living outside the United States. Based on the Department of Veterans Affairs' (VA) latest official estimate and projection of the veteran population, the Veteran Population Projection Model 2018 (VetPop2018)]

Period of service and age	Total	Male	Female	Period of service and age	Total	Male	Female
Total	**19,929**	**17,914**	**2,015**	30 to 34 years old	960	782	178
PERIOD OF SERVICE				35 to 39 years old	1,098	887	211
Wartime vets [1]	15,453	13,871	1,582	40 to 44 years old	1,057	863	194
Gulf War Era [2]	7,883	6,591	1,292	45 to 49 years old	1,313	1,114	198
Vietnam Era [3]	6,453	6,189	263	50 to 54 years old	1,626	1,412	214
Korean conflict [4]	1,244	1,210	34	55 to 59 years old	1,887	1,643	244
World War II	434	412	22	60 to 64 years old	1,878	1,667	211
Peacetime	4,476	4,043	433	65 to 69 years old	1,853	1,707	147
AGE				70 to 74 years old	2,767	2,679	89
Under 20 years old	10	7	3	75 to 79 years old	1,754	1,700	54
20 to 24 years old	266	210	56	80 to 84 years old	1,202	1,162	40
25 to 29 years old	654	531	123	85 years old and over	1,604	1,550	53

[1] Veterans who served in more than one wartime period are counted only once in the total. [2] Service from August 2, 1990 to the present. [3] Service from August 5, 1964 to May 7, 1975. [4] Service during period June 27, 1950 to January 31, 1955.

Source: U.S. Department of Veterans Affairs, National Center for Veterans Analysis and Statistics, "The Veteran Population Projection Model 2018 (VetPop2018)," <va.gov/vetdata/Veteran_Population.asp>, accessed June 2020.

Table 552. Veterans Benefits—Expenditures by Program and Compensation for Service-Connected Disabilities: 2000 to 2019

[In millions of dollars (47,086 represents $47,086,000,000). For years ending September 30]

Program	2000	2005	2010	2012	2013	2014	2015	2016	2017	2018	2019
Total expenditures.......	47,086	69,667	108,635	120,405	142,822	161,229	167,210	173,686	180,591	180,604	202,405
Medical programs........	19,637	29,433	42,372	45,521	55,994	59,424	65,561	63,473	69,710	71,303	77,803
Construction..............	466	483	1,618	1,538	1,330	1,536	1,828	1,708	1,467	1,177	1,238
General operating expenses...............	1,016	1,294	6,101	6,445	6,890	7,602	8,056	7,898	9,223	9,513	10,117
Compensation and pension............	22,012	34,694	47,785	53,243	63,575	75,265	75,787	84,028	84,138	82,776	97,638
Vocational rehabilitation and education...	1,610	2,937	8,260	10,425	11,949	13,681	13,408	13,838	13,182	13,178	13,811
All other [1].................	2,345	826	2,499	3,233	3,085	3,721	2,570	2,740	2,871	2,656	1,798
Compensation for service-connected disabilities..............	15,511	24,515	36,486	44,359	49,152	54,229	60,213	64,714	69,991	76,709	84,915

[1] Includes insurance, indemnities, and miscellaneous funds and expenditures and offsets from public receipts. Excludes expenditures from personal funds of patients.

Source: U.S. Department of Veterans Affairs, "Summary of Expenditures By State," <http://www.va.gov/vetdata/Expenditures.asp>, accessed April 2020; and *Annual Benefits Report*, July 2020, and earlier reports. See also <https://www.benefits.va.gov/REPORTS/abr/>.

Table 553. Veterans Compensation and Pension Benefits—Number on Rolls by Period of Service and Status: 1990 to 2019

[In thousands (3,584 represents 3,584,000). As of September 30. Living veterans refers to veterans receiving compensation for disability incurred or aggravated while on active duty, and war veterans receiving pension benefits for non-service connected disabilities and/or who are age 65 and older. Survivors include veterans' spouses, dependent children, and (based on need) dependent parents of veterans]

Period of service and veteran status	1990	2000	2010	2011	2012	2013	2014	2015	2016	2017	2018	2019
Total......................	3,584	3,236	4,070	4,226	4,425	4,639	4,848	5,061	5,247	5,442	5,619	5,787
Living veterans.............	2,746	2,672	3,524	3,668	3,852	4,051	4,254	4,464	4,645	4,829	5,003	5,183
Compensation [1]..........	2,184	2,308	3,210	3,355	3,537	3,743	3,949	4,169	4,356	4,553	4,743	4,944
Pension [2].................	562	364	314	314	315	308	305	295	289	277	260	239
Survivors of veterans................	838	564	546	557	574	587	594	597	602	613	616	604
Compensation [1]..........	320	307	347	355	366	377	382	390	399	411	423	434
Pension [2].................	518	257	199	202	207	210	212	206	203	201	193	170
World War I and earlier......................	198	34	6	5	5	4	4	3	3	2	2	2
Living veterans............	18	(Z)	(Z)	(Z)	(Z)	(Z)	(Z)	(Z)	(Z)	(Z)	(Z)	(Z)
World War II..............	1,723	968	529	498	469	434	399	357	320	286	249	205
Living veterans............	1,294	676	298	271	245	215	189	160	135	112	89	69
Korean conflict [3].........	390	323	275	275	274	271	268	262	256	249	238	221
Living veterans............	305	255	209	207	204	199	194	186	178	169	158	145
Vietnam era [4].............	774	969	1,447	1,524	1,594	1,660	1,716	1,765	1,803	1,840	1,868	1,890
Living veterans............	685	848	1,261	1,326	1,381	1,433	1,477	1,514	1,538	1,560	1,572	1,581
Gulf War era [5]............	(X)	334	1,140	1,239	1,383	1,561	1,723	1,915	2,090	2,267	2,441	2,622
Living veterans............	(X)	326	1,117	1,215	1,357	1,523	1,694	1,883	2,057	2,231	2,403	2,581
Peacetime..................	495	607	673	685	701	709	738	759	775	797	821	848
Living veterans............	444	567	638	650	665	683	700	720	737	758	781	806

X Not applicable. Z Fewer than 500. [1] Compensation is based on military service-connected disability and death. [2] Pension is based on need and includes coverage for veterans with disabilities not connected to military service. [3] Service during period June 27, 1950 to January 31, 1955. [4] Service from August 5, 1964 to May 7, 1975. [5] Service from August 2, 1990 to the present.

Source: U.S. Department of Veterans Affairs, 1990 to 1995, *Annual Report of the Secretary of Veterans Affairs*; 1996 to 2010, *Annual Accountability Report* and unpublished data; and beginning 2011, *Annual Benefits Report, Fiscal Year 2019*, April 2020 and earlier reports. See also <https://www.benefits.va.gov/REPORTS/abr/>.

Table 554. Veteran Income, Education, Poverty, and Disability Status Compared to Nonveteran Population: 2017 and 2018

[251,048 represents 251,048,000. Data are based on American Community Survey (ACS). The ACS universe includes the civilian household and group quarters population. Based on a sample and subject to sampling variability]

Characteristic	2017 Total	2017 Veterans	2017 Nonveterans	2018 Total	2018 Veterans	2018 Nonveterans
Population 18 years old and over (1,000).......	**251,048**	**18,205**	**232,843**	**252,806**	**17,964**	**234,842**
INCOME						
Median income in past 12 months (dollars) [1].......	30,696	40,577	30,098	31,476	41,555	30,883
Male.................................	(NA)	40,995	36,573	(NA)	42,064	37,736
Female................................	(NA)	35,517	24,653	(NA)	35,991	25,501
EDUCATIONAL ATTAINMENT						
Population 25 years old and over...................	220,624	17,953	202,670	222,557	17,714	204,844
Less than high school graduate (percent).........	12.0	5.8	12.6	11.7	5.5	12.2
High school graduate or equivalency (percent)...	27.2	28.2	27.1	26.9	27.7	26.8
Some college or associate's degree (percent)....	28.8	37.2	28.1	28.8	37.5	28.1
Bachelor's degree or higher (percent)............	32.0	28.8	32.2	32.6	29.4	32.9
POVERTY AND DISABILITY STATUS						
Population for whom poverty status is determined..	244,592	17,884	226,708	246,337	17,656	228,681
Below poverty in the past 12 months (percent)...	11.9	6.9	12.3	11.7	6.7	12.1
With any disability (percent).......................	15.3	29.5	14.2	15.2	29.3	14.1

NA Not available. [1] For population with income.

Source: U.S. Census Bureau, American Community Survey, S2101, "Veteran Status," <data.census.gov>, accessed May 2020.

Table 555. Veterans by Sex, Race, and Hispanic Origin: 2017 and 2018

[See headnote, Table 554]

Characteristic	2017 Total veterans	2017 18 to 64 years	2017 65 years and over	2018 Total veterans	2018 18 to 64 years	2018 65 years and over
Total......................	**18,204,605**	**9,117,616**	**9,086,989**	**17,964,242**	**8,973,535**	**8,990,707**
Male..........................	16,584,495	7,807,552	8,776,943	16,311,444	7,656,867	8,654,577
Female........................	1,620,110	1,310,064	310,046	1,652,798	1,316,668	336,130
White alone...................	14,971,878	6,897,994	8,073,884	14,698,804	6,744,091	7,954,713
Male..........................	13,809,369	5,992,812	7,816,557	13,527,706	5,853,178	7,674,528
Female........................	1,162,509	905,182	257,327	1,171,098	890,913	280,185
Black or African American alone........	2,139,651	1,474,012	665,639	2,150,689	1,465,798	684,891
Male..........................	1,826,298	1,194,900	631,398	1,825,182	1,177,069	648,113
Female........................	313,353	279,112	34,241	325,507	288,729	36,778
American Indian/Alaska Native alone...	141,494	88,423	53,071	141,438	85,654	55,784
Male..........................	125,750	75,555	50,195	125,355	72,475	52,880
Female........................	15,744	12,868	2,876	16,083	13,179	2,904
Asian alone...................	297,891	181,567	116,324	308,983	185,975	123,008
Male..........................	262,186	150,237	111,949	269,031	152,473	116,558
Female........................	35,705	31,330	4,375	39,952	33,502	6,450
Native Hawaiian and other Pacific Islander alone........................	33,981	21,530	12,451	41,271	31,247	10,024
Male..........................	28,820	17,725	11,095	33,327	24,317	9,010
Female........................	5,161	3,805	1,356	7,944	6,930	1,014
Some other race alone.................	251,899	186,355	65,544	244,340	179,827	64,513
Male..........................	222,528	159,914	62,614	213,175	151,878	61,297
Female........................	29,371	26,441	2,930	31,165	27,949	3,216
Two or more races....................	367,811	267,735	100,076	378,717	280,943	97,774
Male..........................	309,544	216,409	93,135	317,668	225,477	92,191
Female........................	58,267	51,326	6,941	61,049	55,466	5,583
Hispanic or Latino origin [1]...............	1,264,460	892,464	371,996	1,284,854	898,180	386,674
Male..........................	1,113,263	756,128	357,135	1,132,008	762,843	369,165
Female........................	151,197	136,336	14,861	152,846	135,337	17,509

[1] Persons of Hispanic or Latino origin may be of any race.

Source: U.S. Census Bureau, American Community Survey, Tables B21001, C21001A, C21001B, C21001C, C21001D, C21001E, C21001F, C21001G, and C21001I, <data.census.gov>, accessed May 2020.

Table 556. Deferred Action for Childhood Arrivals (DACA) Recipients by Selected Characteristics and Top Country of Birth: 2020

[As of March 31, 2020. The active DACA population are individuals who have an approved I-821D Consideration of DACA form with validity as of March 31, 2020. Data are estimates. Individuals who have obtained Lawful Permanent Resident Status or U.S. Citizenship are excluded]

Characteristic	Number	Top 20 countries of birth	Number
Total	**643,560**	Mexico	517,460
		El Salvador	24,830
		Guatemala	16,840
SEX		Honduras	15,450
Female	342,680	Peru	6,250
Male	300,820	Korea, South	6,210
Not available	60	Brazil	5,060
AGE		Ecuador	4,780
Under 16 years old	70	Colombia	4,240
16 to 20 years old	74,570	Argentina	3,360
21 to 25 years old	240,890	Philippines	3,270
26 to 30 years old	191,840	Jamaica	2,250
31 to 35 years old	108,390	India	2,220
36 to 38 years old	27,800	Venezuela	2,100
Median age	26	Dominican Republic	1,990
MARITAL STATUS		Uruguay	1,700
Single	482,100	Trinidad And Tobago	1,500
Married	148,190	Bolivia	1,430
Divorced	10,640	Costa Rica	1,340
Widowed	360	Nicaragua	1,270
Not available	2,270		

Source: Department of Homeland Security, U.S. Citizenship and Immigration Services, "Immigration and Citizenship Data," <https://www.uscis.gov/tools/reports-studies/immigration-forms-data>, accessed September 2020.

Table 557. Department of Homeland Security Total Budget Authority and Personnel by Organization: 2019 and 2020

[81,045,464 represents $81,045,464,000. For the fiscal year ending September 30. Not all activities carried out by the Department of Homeland Security (DHS) constitute homeland security funding (e.g., Coast Guard search and rescue activities)]

Organization or activity	Budget authority (thousand dollars)		Full-time employees (number)	
	2019 [1]	2020 [1]	2019 [1]	2020 [1]
Total	**81,045,464**	**88,407,203**	**231,134**	**236,558**
Departmental management and operations [2]	2,981,793	3,292,178	4,137	4,227
Analysis and operations	253,253	284,141	841	852
Office of the Inspector General	168,000	190,186	760	756
U.S. Customs & Border Protection	17,257,250	17,372,298	60,855	61,644
U.S. Immigration & Customs Enforcement	7,905,712	8,399,871	20,080	20,912
Transportation Security Administration	8,090,347	8,300,481	55,607	56,425
U.S. Coast Guard	12,237,046	12,188,870	48,810	49,412
U.S. Secret Service	2,513,159	2,680,845	7,359	7,647
Cybersecurity and Infrastructure Security Agency [3]	1,681,757	2,015,622	1,976	2,158
Federal Emergency Management Agency (FEMA)	21,643,469	27,310,748	10,438	11,333
FEMA Grants [4]	2,858,531	2,949,000	([5])	([5])
U.S. Citizenship & Immigration Services	4,730,177	4,851,219	18,498	19,380
Federal Law Enforcement Training Center	328,819	351,170	1,068	1,081
Science & Technology Directorate (S&T)	819,785	737,275	473	499
Countering Weapons of Mass Destruction	434,897	432,299	232	232

[1] Revised enacted. [2] Comprised of the Office of the Secretary & Executive Management, and the Management Directorate, which includes the Under Secretary for Management and its team of chief officers. [3] The Cybersecurity and Infrastructure Security Agency Act of 2018 elevated the mission of the former National Protection and Programs Directorate within DHS and established the Cybersecurity and Infrastructure Security Agency. [4] Includes State and Local Programs, Emergency Management Performance Grants, and Assistance to Firefighters Grants. [5] Employee data are included among FEMA full-time employees.

Source: U.S. Department of Homeland Security, *Budget-in-Brief, Fiscal Year 2021*, February 2020. See also <http://www.dhs.gov/dhs-budget>.

Table 558. Homeland Security Grants by State and Outlying Area: 2019 and 2020

[In thousands of dollars (1,095,000 represents $1,095,000,000). For years ending September 30. The Homeland Security Grant Program consists of the following: State Homeland Security Program (SHSP), Urban Areas Security Initiative (UASI), and Operation Stonegarden]

State/territory	2019	2020	State/territory	2019	2020	State/territory	2019	2020
Total.........	**1,095,000**	**1,116,500**	KS..............	4,078	4,288	OK..............	4,078	4,288
			KY..............	4,078	4,288	OR..............	7,328	7,788
U.S.............	**1,084,333**	**1,105,541**	LA..............	4,807	5,041	PA..............	29,525	29,426
			ME..............	5,948	6,203	RI..............	4,078	4,288
AL.............	4,474	4,655	MD..............	12,000	11,942	SC..............	4,078	4,288
AK.............	4,078	4,288	MA..............	23,900	23,631	SD..............	4,078	4,288
AZ.............	23,863	25,332	MI..............	13,468	13,632	TN..............	4,078	4,288
AR.............	4,078	4,288	MN..............	10,246	10,738	TX..............	98,437	98,320
CA.............	197,911	208,671	MS..............	4,389	4,609	UT..............	4,078	4,288
CO.............	7,328	7,788	MO..............	7,328	7,788	VT..............	4,851	5,193
CT.............	4,078	4,288	MT..............	5,956	6,148	VA..............	12,450	12,346
DE.............	4,078	4,288	NE..............	4,078	4,288	WA..............	15,581	15,656
DC.............	58,500	57,279	NV..............	9,078	9,538	WV..............	4,078	4,288
FL.............	27,149	34,918	NH..............	4,344	4,591	WI..............	4,078	4,288
GA.............	11,750	12,000	NJ..............	28,050	26,742	WY..............	4,078	4,288
HI.............	7,328	7,788	NM..............	7,587	7,125	AS [1].........	1,000	1,000
ID.............	4,430	4,655	NY..............	258,937	255,894	GU [1].........	1,000	1,000
IL.............	83,712	83,107	NC..............	5,750	5,529	MP [1].........	1,000	1,000
IN.............	4,078	4,288	ND..............	5,787	5,930	PR [1].........	5,929	6,159
IA.............	4,078	4,288	OH..............	8,751	8,365	VI [1].........	1,739	1,800

[1] AS—American Samoa, GU—Guam, MP—Northern Mariana Islands, PR—Puerto Rico, VI—Virgin Islands.

Source: U.S. Department of Homeland Security, Federal Emergency Management Agency, *Grant Programs Directorate Information Bulletin*, No. 451, June 2020, and earlier reports. See also <https://www.fema.gov/grant-programs-directorate>.

Table 559. Urban Areas Security Initiative (UASI) Grant Program: 2020

[In thousands of dollars (615,000 represents $615,000,000). For year ending September 30. The UASI Program provides financial assistance to address the unique multi-disciplinary planning, operations, equipment, training, and exercise needs of high-threat, high-density urban areas]

State	Urban area	Amount	State	Urban area	Amount
Total........	(X)	**615,000**	LA............	New Orleans	3,500
			MD...........	Baltimore	4,250
AZ............	Phoenix	5,250	MA...........	Boston	16,900
CA............	Anaheim/Santa Ana	5,250	MI............	Detroit	5,250
CA............	San Francisco Bay Area	37,500	MN...........	Minneapolis-Saint Paul (Twin Cities)	5,250
CA............	Los Angeles/Long Beach	68,000	MO...........	St. Louis	3,500
CA............	Riverside	3,500	NV............	Las Vegas	5,250
CA............	Sacramento	3,500	NJ............	Jersey City/Newark	19,050
CA............	San Diego	16,900	NY............	New York City	178,750
CO............	Denver	3,500	OR............	Portland	3,500
DC............	National Capital Region	51,750	PA............	Philadelphia	16,900
FL............	Miami/Fort Lauderdale	14,750	PA............	Pittsburgh	3,500
FL............	Orlando	3,500	TX............	Dallas/Fort Worth/Arlington	16,900
FL............	Tampa	3,500	TX............	Houston	24,600
GA............	Atlanta	6,250	TX............	San Antonio Area	3,500
HI............	Honolulu	3,500	VA............	Hampton Roads Area	3,500
IL............	Chicago	68,000	WA...........	Seattle	6,250

X Not applicable.

Source: U.S. Department of Homeland Security, Federal Emergency Management Agency, *Grant Programs Directorate Information Bulletin*, No. 451, June 2020. See also <https://www.fema.gov/grant-programs-directorate>.

Table 560. Preparedness Grant Programs: 2010 to 2020

[In millions of dollars (2,968 represents $2,968,000,000. For years ending September 30]

Program	2010	2011	2012	2013	2014	2015	2016	2017	2018	2019	2020
Total [1]........................	**2,968**	**2,191**	**1,381**	**1,507**	**1,616**	**1,617**	**1,617**	**1,622**	**1,687**	**1,715**	**1,780**
Homeland Security Grant Program [1].....	1,786	1,289	831	968	1,043	1,044	1,037	1,037	1,067	1,095	1,120
State Homeland Security Program......	842	527	294	355	401	402	402	402	402	415	415
Urban Areas Security Initiative...........	833	663	490	559	587	587	580	580	580	590	615
Operation Stonegarden...................	60	55	47	55	55	55	55	55	85	90	90
Emergency Management Performance Grants Program............	330	329	340	332	350	350	350	350	350	350	355
Tribal Homeland Security Grant Program........................	10	10	6	10	10	10	10	10	10	10	15
Nonprofit Security Grant Program........	19	19	10	10	13	13	20	25	60	60	90
Transit Security Grant Program [1].........	253	200	88	84	90	87	87	88	88	88	88
Port Security Grant Program...........	288	235	98	93	100	100	100	100	100	100	100
Intercity Bus Security Grant Program....	12	5	(NA)	(NA)	(NA)	3	3	2	2	2	2

NA Not available. [1] Includes grant programs not listed separately.

Source: U.S. Department of Homeland Security, Federal Emergency Management Agency, *Grant Programs Directorate Information Bulletin*, No. 451, June 2020, and earlier reports. See also <https://www.fema.gov/grant-programs-directorate>.

Table 561. Aliens Returned or Removed by Leading Crime Category and Country of Nationality: 2010 to 2018

[For year ending September 30. For definitions of immigration enforcement terms, see source. "Crime categories" and "Countries of nationality" are ranked by data for most recent year]

Crime category and country of nationality	2010	2012	2013	2014	2015	2016	2017	2018
Total aliens returned or removed	**854,261**	**646,745**	**611,259**	**569,092**	**455,334**	**438,691**	**388,801**	**446,370**
Returns [1]	471,800	231,109	178,978	163,853	129,666	106,464	100,708	109,083
Removals [2]	382,461	415,636	432,281	405,239	325,668	332,227	288,093	337,287
Noncriminal	211,431	215,597	233,793	235,780	204,822	216,926	178,101	187,847
Criminal [3]	171,030	200,039	198,488	169,459	120,846	115,301	109,992	149,440
Leading crime category:								
Immigration	31,944	47,559	62,033	53,810	37,047	36,728	28,997	42,563
Dangerous drugs	43,463	42,738	30,692	27,728	22,216	21,491	19,937	18,194
Criminal traffic offenses	31,112	46,141	29,966	24,019	15,532	14,795	15,818	17,554
Assault	12,291	12,993	20,192	17,391	13,213	12,035	12,461	12,337
Weapon offenses	2,839	2,510	5,277	4,561	3,501	3,441	3,268	3,217
Burglary	4,275	3,557	5,504	4,667	3,404	3,063	3,087	2,825
Fraudulent activities	3,903	3,870	5,186	3,916	2,620	2,158	2,956	2,718
Larceny	5,468	5,419	5,329	4,314	2,818	2,460	2,591	2,585
Sexual assault	3,333	3,363	3,168	2,937	2,506	2,481	2,481	2,416
Obstructing police	2,486	2,063	2,594	2,404	1,954	1,960	2,136	2,084
All other categories	29,916	29,826	28,547	24,118	16,456	14,866	16,260	42,945
Leading country of nationality of criminals removed:								
Mexico	129,661	151,337	146,170	123,202	86,771	81,751	74,497	91,509
Guatemala	9,422	13,497	15,426	13,722	10,509	10,601	11,110	19,827
Honduras	10,416	13,824	16,598	14,064	8,556	8,592	9,282	12,735
El Salvador	8,412	8,670	9,472	8,952	7,221	6,719	6,489	7,003
Colombia	1,249	1,057	929	876	795	763	640	2,275
Dominican Republic	2,292	2,187	1,821	1,642	1,521	1,485	1,515	1,500
Venezuela	136	123	87	79	61	55	81	1,280
Brazil	497	426	375	281	288	330	407	1,186
Jamaica	1,168	1,157	999	834	641	620	678	1,001
Ecuador	693	708	579	571	488	465	507	887
Nigeria	187	159	135	126	108	111	112	609
China	160	198	180	136	122	106	120	581
Nicaragua	805	729	692	643	440	392	379	568

[1] Returns are the confirmed movement of an inadmissible or deportable alien out of the U.S., not based on an order of removal. Most voluntary departures are of Mexican nationals who have been apprehended by the U.S. Border Patrol and are returned to Mexico. [2] Removals are the compulsory and confirmed movement of an inadmissible or deportable alien out of the U.S., based on an order of removal. An alien who is removed has administrative or criminal consequences placed on subsequent reentry. [3] Persons removed based on a criminal charge or those with a criminal conviction.

Source: U.S. Department of Homeland Security, Office of Immigration Statistics, "2018 Yearbook of Immigration Statistics," <https://www.dhs.gov/immigration-statistics>, accessed March 2020; and *Immigration Enforcement Actions: 2018*, and previous editions.

Table 562. Deportable Aliens Apprehended or Arrested by Program and Border Patrol Sector: 2000 to 2018

[As of the end of September. Deportable aliens located refer to Border Patrol apprehensions and Immigration and Customs Enforcement (ICE) administrative arrests]

Program and sector	2000	2010	2015	2016	2017	2018
Total	**1,814,729**	**796,587**	**462,388**	**530,250**	**461,540**	**572,566**
Investigations	138,291	18,290	7,288	4,330	7,539	9,843
Enforcement and Removal Operations (ERO) [1]	(X)	314,915	117,983	110,104	143,470	158,581
Border Patrol (apprehensions)	**1,676,438**	**463,382**	**337,117**	**415,816**	**310,531**	**404,142**
All southwest sectors	**1,643,679**	**447,731**	**331,333**	**408,870**	**303,916**	**396,579**
Rio Grande Valley, Texas	133,243	59,766	147,257	186,830	137,562	162,262
Tucson, Arizona	616,346	212,202	63,397	64,891	38,657	52,172
San Diego, California	151,681	68,565	26,290	31,891	26,086	38,591
Laredo, Texas	108,973	35,287	35,888	36,562	25,460	32,641
El Paso, Texas	115,696	12,251	14,495	25,634	25,193	31,561
El Centro, California	238,126	32,562	12,820	19,448	18,633	29,230
Yuma, Arizona	108,747	7,116	7,142	14,170	12,847	26,244
Del Rio, Texas	157,178	14,694	19,013	23,078	13,476	15,833
Big Bend, Texas [2]	13,689	5,288	5,031	6,366	6,002	8,045
All other sectors	**32,759**	**15,651**	**5,784**	**6,946**	**6,615**	**7,563**
Miami, Florida	6,237	4,651	1,752	3,205	2,280	2,169
Detroit, Michigan	2,057	1,669	637	716	1,070	1,930
New Orleans, Louisiana	6,478	3,171	849	764	920	798
Swanton, Vermont	1,957	1,422	341	291	449	736
Grand Forks, North Dakota	562	543	789	505	496	461
Buffalo, New York	1,570	2,422	291	226	447	384
Blaine, Washington	2,581	673	282	271	288	359
Spokane, Washington	1,324	356	190	206	208	347
Ramey, Puerto Rico	1,731	398	557	694	388	280
Houlton, Maine	489	56	32	25	30	52
Havre, Montana	1,568	290	64	43	39	47
Livermore, California [3]	6,205	(X)	(X)	(X)	(X)	(X)

X Not applicable. [1] Includes arrests of fugitive and nonfugitive aliens under the Office of Detention and Removal Operations (DRO), National Fugitive Operations Program. Beginning in 2008, includes all administrative arrests conducted by ICE ERO. [2] Formerly known as Marfa, TX. [3] Livermore sector closed August 31, 2004.

Source: U.S. Department of Homeland Security, Office of Immigration Statistics, "2018 Yearbook of Immigration Statistics," and earlier reports, <https://www.dhs.gov/immigration-statistics/yearbook>, accessed March 2020.

Table 563. Deportable Aliens Apprehended or Arrested: 1925 to 2018

[As of the end of September. Prior to 1952, data refer to Border Patrol Apprehensions. Detention and Removal Operations data are included beginning in 2006. Beginning in 2008, includes all administrative arrests conducted by the ICE, Office of Enforcement and Removal Operations. Beginning in 2009, data also include administrative arrests conducted under the 287(g) program (Delegation of Immigration Authority)]

Year	Number	Year	Number	Year	Number	Year	Number
1925..........	22,199	1975..........	766,600	1999..........	1,714,035	2009..........	889,212
1930..........	20,880	1980..........	910,361	2000..........	1,814,729	2010..........	796,587
1935..........	11,016	1985..........	1,348,749	2001..........	1,387,486	2011..........	678,606
1940..........	10,492	1990..........	1,169,939	2002..........	1,062,270	2012..........	671,327
1945..........	69,164	1993..........	1,327,261	2003..........	1,046,422	2013..........	662,483
1950..........	468,339	1994..........	1,094,719	2004..........	1,264,232	2014..........	679,996
1955..........	254,096	1995..........	1,394,554	2005..........	1,291,065	2015..........	462,388
1960..........	70,684	1996..........	1,649,986	2006..........	1,206,408	2016 [1]..........	530,250
1965..........	110,371	1997..........	1,536,520	2007..........	960,673	2017..........	461,540
1970..........	345,353	1998..........	1,679,439	2008..........	1,043,759	2018..........	572,566

[1] The counting methodology for administrative arrests by ICE ERO was revised to align with ICE ERO reporting for 2016; prior to 2016, only one administrative arrest could be counted for the same person on the same day.

Source: U.S. Department of Homeland Security, Office of Immigration Statistics, "2018 Yearbook of Immigration Statistics," <https://www.dhs.gov/immigration-statistics/yearbook>, accessed March 2020.

Table 564. Federal Arrests for Immigration Offenses by Sex, Age, Citizenship Status, and Country and World Region of Citizenship: 1998 to 2018

[For fiscal years ending in year shown. Suspects with more than one arrest are counted separately. Immigration violations subject to federal arrest and prosecution include smuggling, transporting, and harboring aliens; illegal entry and re-entry; and misuse of visas and other violations. Excludes D.C. Superior Court arrests. Based on data from the U.S. Marshals Service's Justice Detainee Information System]

Suspect characteristics	Number				Percent			
	1998	2008	2017	2018	1998	2008	2017	2018
Total........................	20,942	78,033	58,031	108,667	100.0	100.0	100.0	100.0
SEX								
Male........................	19,100	70,236	53,343	97,473	91.2	90.0	91.9	89.7
Female......................	1,841	7,797	4,684	11,191	8.8	10.0	8.1	10.3
AGE								
17 years old or under...........	60	63	25	49	0.3	0.1	(Z)	0.1
18 to 19 years.................	1,508	6,211	3,530	8,889	7.2	8.0	6.1	8.2
20 to 24 years.................	5,464	17,607	10,417	24,034	26.1	22.6	18.0	22.1
25 to 29 years.................	5,208	17,164	11,162	21,854	24.9	22.0	19.2	20.1
30 to 34 years.................	3,819	14,456	10,955	18,639	18.2	18.5	18.9	17.2
35 to 39 years.................	2,470	10,177	9,046	14,793	11.8	13.0	15.6	13.6
40 to 44 years.................	1,347	6,178	6,325	10,215	6.4	7.9	10.9	9.4
45 to 49 years.................	622	3,440	3,592	5,746	3.0	4.4	6.2	5.3
50 to 54 years.................	262	1,733	1,790	2,697	1.3	2.2	3.1	2.5
55 years and over..............	172	1,003	1,185	1,747	0.8	1.3	2.0	1.6
Mean age (in years)............	29	30	32	31	(X)	(X)	(X)	(X)
CITIZENSHIP STATUS								
U.S. citizen [1]................	1,072	2,433	2,356	2,913	5.2	3.2	4.1	2.7
Non-U.S. citizen..............	19,556	74,000	55,454	105,748	94.8	96.8	95.9	97.3
COUNTRY AND WORLD REGION								
North America.................	19,400	75,137	56,954	106,100	94.0	98.3	98.5	97.6
United States..............	1,072	2,433	2,356	2,913	5.2	3.2	4.1	2.7
Mexico....................	17,143	61,924	40,884	65,491	83.1	81.0	70.7	60.3
Canada....................	47	64	26	27	0.2	0.1	(Z)	(Z)
Caribbean Islands...........	416	790	506	553	2.0	1.0	0.9	0.5
Central America............	722	9,926	13,182	37,116	3.5	13.0	22.8	34.2
South America.................	166	472	566	1,227	0.8	0.6	1.0	1.1
Asia and Oceania.............	736	476	118	928	3.6	0.6	0.2	0.9
Europe.......................	262	261	150	359	1.3	0.3	0.3	0.3
Africa.......................	64	87	22	47	0.3	0.1	(Z)	(Z)

X Not applicable. Z Less than 0.1 percent. [1] Citizenship is defined as the country of citizenship indicated at the time of federal booking.

Source: U.S. Department of Justice, Bureau of Justice Statistics, *Immigration, Citizenship, and the Federal Justice System, 1998-2018*, NCJ 253116, August 2019. See also <https://www.bjs.gov/index.cfm?ty=pbdetail&iid=6666>

Table 565. Foreign Visitor Overstays by Country of Citizenship: 2019

[Data shown for foreign nationals entering the U.S. as nonimmigrant visitors for business or pleasure through an air or sea point of entry. For fiscal year ending Sept. 30. An overstay is a nonimmigrant who was lawfully admitted to the U.S. for an authorized period but stayed or remains in the U.S. beyond the lawful admission period. The Visa Waiver Program (VWP) allows citizens of specific countries to travel to the U.S. for tourism, business, or while in transit for up to 90 days without obtaining a visa. Data are generated from Department of Homeland Security's Arrival and Departure Information System (ADIS)]

Country of citizenship	Expected departures	Overstays (number)			Overstays (percent)	
		Total	Out-of-country [1]	Suspected in-country [2]	Total	Suspected in-country [2]
Total...............................	**55,928,990**	**676,422**	**101,682**	**574,740**	**1.21**	**1.03**
North American, total..................	**13,265,226**	**132,600**	**13,510**	**119,090**	**1.00**	**0.90**
Canada...............................	10,080,680	83,674	8,276	75,398	0.83	0.75
Mexico...............................	3,184,546	48,926	5,234	43,692	1.54	1.37
VISA WAIVER PROGRAM						
Total...............................	**23,248,729**	**102,505**	**12,674**	**89,831**	**0.44**	**0.39**
United Kingdom.......................	4,951,991	16,234	1,771	14,463	0.33	0.29
Japan...............................	3,137,270	4,803	271	4,532	0.15	0.14
Germany.............................	2,112,076	8,141	825	7,316	0.39	0.35
France...............................	2,027,550	11,074	920	10,154	0.55	0.50
Korea, South.........................	1,424,211	3,835	961	2,874	0.27	0.20
Australia.............................	1,367,307	5,061	821	4,240	0.37	0.31
Italy.................................	1,353,613	8,559	1,061	7,498	0.63	0.55
Spain................................	1,126,636	14,784	1,628	13,156	1.31	1.17
Netherlands..........................	818,371	2,818	281	2,537	0.34	0.31
Ireland...............................	593,373	1,722	181	1,541	0.29	0.26
Sweden..............................	486,556	1,389	198	1,191	0.29	0.24
Chile................................	439,414	5,868	790	5,078	1.34	1.16
Taiwan...............................	425,442	2,226	633	1,593	0.52	0.37
Switzerland..........................	399,535	1,778	154	1,624	0.45	0.41
New Zealand.........................	343,673	1,243	260	983	0.36	0.29
Denmark.............................	331,189	964	91	873	0.29	0.26
Belgium..............................	302,680	1,084	114	970	0.36	0.32
Norway..............................	273,182	686	104	582	0.25	0.21
Austria...............................	214,480	815	82	733	0.38	0.34
Portugal..............................	206,758	3,725	434	3,291	1.80	1.59
Finland...............................	151,596	526	47	479	0.35	0.32
Singapore............................	144,793	427	62	365	0.29	0.25
Czechia..............................	129,682	655	140	515	0.51	0.40
Hungary..............................	111,247	1,151	230	921	1.03	0.83
NON-VISA WAIVER PROGRAM						
Total...............................	**15,501,970**	**320,086**	**25,140**	**294,946**	**2.06**	**1.90**
Brazil................................	2,322,284	43,741	2,254	41,487	1.88	1.79
China................................	2,306,250	19,120	2,765	16,355	0.83	0.71
India................................	1,226,989	13,203	2,371	10,832	1.08	0.88
Colombia.............................	1,000,279	29,806	1,147	28,659	2.98	2.87
Argentina............................	941,326	6,473	284	6,189	0.69	0.66
Venezuela............................	475,953	39,270	1,356	37,914	8.25	7.97
Dominican Republic....................	463,309	14,009	471	13,538	3.02	2.92
Ecuador..............................	461,990	8,206	427	7,779	1.78	1.68
Israel................................	398,420	2,805	419	2,386	0.70	0.60
Costa Rica...........................	330,387	3,585	192	3,393	1.09	1.03
Jamaica..............................	326,075	10,344	458	9,886	3.17	3.03
Peru.................................	321,068	5,284	338	4,946	1.65	1.54
Philippines...........................	310,920	5,152	716	4,436	1.66	1.43
Guatemala............................	288,678	5,664	289	5,375	1.96	1.86
Bahamas, The........................	268,870	2,478	186	2,292	0.92	0.85
Russia...............................	242,710	5,545	624	4,921	2.28	2.03
Poland...............................	226,110	1,574	254	1,320	0.70	0.58
El Salvador...........................	220,416	3,462	261	3,201	1.57	1.45
Honduras.............................	214,563	4,745	275	4,470	2.21	2.08
Trinidad and Tobago...................	182,286	956	127	829	0.52	0.45
Nigeria...............................	177,835	17,566	764	16,802	9.88	9.45
Panama..............................	159,096	895	88	807	0.56	0.51

[1] Individuals whose departure was recorded after their lawful admission period expired. [2] Individuals for whom no departure has been recorded.

Source: Department of Homeland Security, *Fiscal Year 2019 Entry/Exit Overstay Report*, March 2020. See also <https://www.dhs.gov/publication/entryexit-overstay-report>.

Table 566. Terrorism Related Deaths, Injuries, and Kidnappings of Private U.S. Citizens by Selected Country: 2012 to 2018

[Private U.S. citizen refers to any U.S. citizen overseas not acting in an official capacity on behalf of the U.S. government. Includes U.S. government employees' households and U.S. citizens working for contractors hired by the U.S. government. Excludes U.S. military personnel while on active duty or employees of the Department of State and other federal agencies while overseas on U.S. government orders]

Incident type and location	2012	2013	2014	2015	2016	2017	2018
DEATHS							
Total	**10**	**16**	**24**	**20**	**16**	**7**	**6**
Afghanistan	10	12	20	8	1	–	4
Algeria	–	3	–	–	–	–	–
Bangladesh	–	–	–	1	1	–	–
Belgium	–	–	–	–	4	–	–
Burkina Faso	–	–	–	–	1	–	–
Egypt	–	–	1	–	–	1	–
France	–	–	–	1	3	–	–
Israel, Jerusalem, West Bank, Gaza	–	–	5	3	3	–	–
Jordan	–	–	–	2	–	–	–
Lebanon	–	1	–	–	–	–	–
Libya	–	–	–	1	–	–	–
Mali	–	–	–	1	–	–	–
Pakistan	–	–	–	1	1	1	–
Somalia	–	–	3	1	–	3	–
Spain	–	–	–	–	–	1	–
Syria	–	–	4	1	–	–	–
Tajikistan	–	–	–	–	–	–	2
Turkey	–	–	–	–	2	–	–
United Arab Emirates	–	–	1	–	–	–	–
United Kingdom	–	–	–	–	–	1	–
INJURIES							
Total	**2**	**¹7**	**8**	**22**	**34**	**8**	**6**
Afghanistan	1	1	2	2	5	1	2
Bangladesh	–	–	–	1	–	–	–
Belgium	–	–	–	–	17	–	–
Burkina Faso	–	–	–	–	1	–	–
France	–	–	–	6	3	–	–
Germany	–	–	–	–	2	–	–
Iraq	1	–	–	1	–	–	–
Israel, Jerusalem, West Bank, Gaza	–	–	5	6	6	1	2
Jordan	–	–	–	2	–	–	–
Kenya	–	6	–	–	–	–	–
Netherlands	–	–	–	–	–	–	2
Pakistan	–	–	–	1	–	–	–
Saudi Arabia	–	–	1	2	–	–	–
Somalia	–	–	–	1	–	–	–
Spain	–	–	–	–	–	1	–
Turkey	–	–	–	–	–	1	–
United Kingdom	–	–	–	–	–	4	–
KIDNAPPINGS							
Total	**3**	**13**	**3**	**–**	**6**	**3**	**–**
Afghanistan	–	–	2	–	1	–	–
Colombia	–	1	–	–	–	3	–
Iraq	–	–	–	–	3	–	–
Libya	–	1	–	–	–	–	–
Niger	–	–	–	–	1	–	–
Nigeria	1	3	1	–	–	–	–
Somalia	1	–	–	–	–	–	–
Syria	–	7	–	–	1	–	–
Yemen	1	1	–	–	–	–	–

– Represents zero. ¹ Excludes 2 citizens held hostage in Algeria; and 48 citizens present, but not medically injured, at Westgate Mall in Kenya.

Source: U.S. State Department, Bureau of Counterterrorism, "Country Reports on Terrorism," <https://www.state.gov/country-reports-on-terrorism/>, accessed November 2019.

Table 567. Customs and Border Protection (CBP)—Processed and Cleared Passengers, Planes, Vehicles, and Containers: 2008 to 2015

[In thousands (93,768 represents 93,768,000). For year ending September 30]

Item	2008	2009	2010	2011	2012	2013	2014	2015
AIR								
Passengers	93,768	87,749	91,488	94,605	98,367	10,221	107,049	112,505
Commercial aircraft ¹	696	638	657	662	675	870	900	941
Private aircraft	138	109	115	121	116	116	117	116
LAND								
Passengers ²,³	290,146	257,476	244,322	227,965	234,898	242,064	247,813	250,449
Privately owned vehicles ²	109,548	99,017	93,966	92,673	94,952	98,460	100,909	103,022
Truck containers ⁴	11,013	9,238	10,003	10,117	10,419	10,473	10,851	10,937
Rail containers	2,747	2,179	2,431	2,634	2,936	3,061	3,272	3,290
SEA								
Passengers ⁵	16,636	15,967	17,170	17,796	18,335	17,883	19,713	19,796
Vessels ⁶	148	146	152	141	139	133	133	136
Vessel containers	10,886	9,300	10,282	10,721	10,975	11,044	11,549	12,119

¹ Aircraft transporting passengers and/or cargo for some payment or other consideration, including money or services rendered. ² See Table 1290 for more details. ³ Includes pedestrians. ⁴ Number of trucks entering the U.S. ⁵ Excludes passengers on ferries. ⁶ Includes every description of water craft or other contrivance used or capable of being used as a means of kidnapping transportation on water; does not include aircraft.

Source: U.S. Department of Homeland Security, Customs and Border Protection, ProQuest Freedom of Information Act request, received March 2016. See also <http://www.cbp.gov>.

Table 568. Passengers Screened and Firearms Discovered at TSA Checkpoints: 2015 to 2019

[Number, unless otherwise noted (708,316 represents 708,316,000). Firearms are those found in carry-on bags]

Item	2015	2016	2017	2018	2019	Top 5 airports in firearm discoveries	Firearms found in 2019
Passengers and crew screened (1,000s)...........................	708,316	738,318	771,557	813,791	848,096	Atlanta (ATL).................	323
Firearms found..........................	2,653	3,391	3,957	4,239	4,432	Dallas-Fort Worth (DFW)....	217
Firearms loaded.........................	2,198	2,815	3,324	3,656	3,863	Denver (DEN)................	140
Percentage loaded......................	83	83	84	86	87	Houston (IAH)................	138
Airports with firearms discovered........	236	238	239	249	278	Phoenix (PHX)................	132

Source: U.S. Department of Homeland Security, Transportation Security Administration, "TSA Year in Review: 2019," <https://www.tsa.gov/blog>, and earlier releases.

Table 569. Value of Counterfeit Goods Seized for Intellectual Property Rights Violations by Commodity and Country of Origin: 2018 and 2019

[In thousands of dollars (1,399,874 represents $1,399,874,000), except as indicated. Customs and Border Protection enforces Intellectual Property Rights (IPR), most visibly by seizing products that infringe IPR such as trademarks, copyrights, and patents. Value of goods seized represent Manufacturer's Suggested Retail Price (MSRP), which is the price at which merchandise is sold at retail to the consumer or what the value of the counterfeit goods would have been at retail had they been genuine]

Commodity	2018	2019	Country of origin	2018	2019
Number of IPR seizures..........................	**33,810**	**27,599**			
Total MSRP value of IPR seizures.............	**1,399,874**	**1,555,269**	China...........................	761,115	1,030,182
Jewelry, watches, and parts.....................	618,167	687,167	Hong Kong.....................	440,345	397,277
Wearing apparel/accessories...................	115,164	343,732	Turkey.........................	5,759	14,241
Handbags/wallets/backpacks..................	226,506	212,782	Vietnam........................	5,192	13,556
Consumer electronics/parts....................	89,593	105,957	Pakistan........................	2,779	12,157
Pharmaceuticals/personal care................	131,458	48,772	Singapore......................	(NA)	10,453
Footwear......................................	77,501	37,994	Dominican Republic...................	(NA)	9,542
Consumer products............................	40,846	27,908	India...........................	19,952	9,540
Computers/technology components............	29,940	13,217	Korea, South...................	10,136	5,633
Automotive/aerospace.........................	14,862	12,143	Netherlands....................	(NA)	4,970
Labels/tags...................................	(NA)	10,379	Canada.........................	7,799	(NA)
Toys..	10,590	(NA)			
All other commodities.........................	45,248	55,219	All other countries................	146,797	47,718

NA Not available.

Source: U.S. Department of Homeland Security, Customs and Border Protection, *Intellectual Property Rights Seizure Statistics FY2019*, May 2020, and earlier reports. See also <http://www.cbp.gov/trade/priority-issues/ipr/statistics>.

Section 11

Social Insurance and Human Services

This section presents data related to government expenditures for social insurance and human services; the population receiving government assistance; government programs for Old-Age, Survivors, and Disability Insurance (OASDI), commonly known as Social Security; state and local government employee retirement; private retirement savings plans; government unemployment and disability insurance; federal supplemental security income payments and aid to the needy; child and other welfare services; and federal food programs. Also included here are selected data on workers' compensation, child support, child care, homelessness, social assistance organizations, charitable contributions, and philanthropic foundations.

A principal source for these data is the Social Security Administration's *Annual Statistical Supplement to the Social Security Bulletin* which presents current data on many of the programs. Additional sources of data include the Census Bureau's Annual Social and Economic Supplement of the Current Population Survey, and the Survey of Income and Program Participation (conducted as a series of surveys over a period of time spanning several years); and the Department of Health and Human Services' Administration for Children and Families.

Social insurance under the Social Security Act—Programs established by the Social Security Act provide protection against wage loss resulting from retirement, prolonged disability, death, or unemployment, and protection against the cost of medical care during old age and disability. The federal OASDI program provides monthly benefits to retired or disabled insured workers and their dependents, and to survivors of insured workers. To be eligible, a worker must have had a specified period of employment in which OASDI taxes were paid. The age of eligibility for full retirement benefits had been 65 for many years. For persons born in 1938 or later, that age gradually increases until it reaches age 67 for those born in 1960 and later. Reduced benefits may be obtained as early as age 62. The worker's spouse is under the same limitations. Survivor benefits are payable to dependents of deceased insured workers. Disability benefits are payable to an insured worker under full retirement age with a prolonged disability, and to the disabled worker's dependents on the same basis as dependents of retired workers. Disability benefits are provided at age 50 to the disabled widow or widower of a deceased worker who was fully insured at the time of death. Disabled children, age 18 or older, of retired, disabled, or deceased workers are also eligible for benefits. A special lump sum benefit may be payable on the death of an insured worker to a spouse or minor children. For information on the Medicare program, see Section 3, Health and Nutrition.

Retirement, survivors, and disability insurance benefits are funded by a payroll tax on annual earnings (up to a maximum share of earnings set by law) of workers, employers, and the self-employed. The maximum taxable earnings are adjusted annually to reflect increasing wage levels (see Table 575). Tax receipts and benefit payments are administered through federal trust funds. Special benefits for

uninsured persons; hospital benefits for persons age 65 and over with specified amounts of social security coverage less than that required for cash benefit eligibility; and that part of the cost of supplementary medical insurance not financed by contributions from participants are all financed from federal general revenues.

Retirement—Social security benefits are a component of retirement income. This section also includes data on the use of individual retirement savings plans and accounts, including benefits sponsored by employers. The Bureau of Labor Statistics collects detailed data for the National Compensation Survey on the availability of and participation in employer-sponsored defined benefit and defined contribution retirement savings plans. Defined benefit plans are funded by the employer; defined contribution plans require the employee to save for retirement. Additional data on individual retirement savings also come from surveys conducted by the Investment Company Institute.

Unemployment insurance—Unemployment insurance is administered by the U.S. Employment and Training Administration and each state's employment security agency. By agreement with the U.S. Secretary of Labor, state agencies also administer unemployment compensation for eligible former military personnel and federal employees. Under state unemployment insurance laws, benefits related to an individual's past earnings are paid to eligible unemployed workers. State laws vary concerning the length of time benefits are paid and their amount. In most states, benefits are payable for 26 weeks and, during periods of high unemployment, extended benefits are payable under a federal-state program to those who have exhausted their regular state benefits. Some states also supplement the basic benefit with allowances for dependents. Unemployment insurance is financed through Federal and state employer payroll taxes. Generally, employers pay both Federal and state unemployment taxes for workers paid $1,500 or more during any quarter of a calendar year, or if they had at least 1 employee during any day of the week during 20 weeks in a calendar year (weeks need not be consecutive).

Workers' compensation—All states provide protection against work-connected injuries and deaths, although some states exclude certain workers (e.g., domestic workers). Federal laws cover federal employees, private employees in the District of Columbia, and longshoremen and harbor workers. In addition, the Department of Labor administers "black lung" benefit programs for coal miners disabled by pneumoconiosis and for specified dependents and survivors. Specified occupational diseases are compensable to some extent. In most states, benefits are related to the worker's salary. The benefits may or may not be augmented by dependents' allowances or automatically adjusted to prevailing wage levels.

Income support—Income support programs are designed to provide benefits that assist persons with limited income and resources. The Supplemental Security Income (SSI) program and Temporary Assistance for Needy Families (TANF) program are the major programs providing monthly payments. In addition, a number of programs provide money payments or in-kind benefits for special needs or purposes. Several programs offer food and nutritional services. Also, various federal-state programs provide energy assistance, public housing, and subsidized housing to individuals and families with low incomes. General assistance may also be available at the state or local level.

The SSI program, administered by the Social Security Administration, provides income support to persons with low income and few resources who are age 65 and older, or blind or disabled, and children who have limited income and resources. Unlike social security, SSI benefits are not based on a person's work history, and the program is financed by general funds of the U.S. Treasury. Eligibility requirements and federal payment standards are nationally uniform. Most states supplement the basic SSI payment for all or selected categories of persons.

The Personal Responsibility and Work Opportunity Reconciliation Act of 1996 contains provisions that replaced the Aid to Families With Dependent Children (AFDC), Job Opportunities and Basic Skills (JOBS), and Emergency Assistance programs with the TANF block grant program. This law contains strong work requirements, comprehensive child support enforcement, support for families moving from welfare to work, and other features. The TANF program became effective as soon as each state submitted a complete implementation plan, but no later than July 1, 1997. The older AFDC program provided cash assistance based on need, income, resources, and family size.

Federal nutrition assistance—Under the Supplemental Nutrition Assistance Program (SNAP), formerly known as the food stamp program, single persons and those living in households meeting nationwide standards for income and assets may receive benefits to assist in purchasing food. Benefits come on an electronic benefits transfer card that recipients use much like a bank debit card for purchasing eligible food items in retail food stores. The monthly amount of benefits, also known as allotments, is determined by household size and income. Households without income receive the

determined monthly cost of a nutritionally adequate diet for their household size. This amount is regularly updated to account for food price increases. Households are expected to spend about 30 percent of their own resources on food, thus for households with income, the program provides a benefit that equals the maximum monthly allotment according to household size minus 30 percent of the household's net monthly income.

The USDA website has detailed information regarding eligibility for SNAP, including income limits and maximum monthly SNAP allotments by household size, at <fns.usda.gov/snap/recipient/eligibility>. All households in which all members receive TANF or SSI are categorically eligible for SNAP without meeting these income or resource criteria. Households are certified for varying lengths of time, depending on their income sources and individual circumstances.

Health and welfare services—Programs providing health and welfare services are aided through federal grants to states for child welfare services, vocational rehabilitation, activities for the elderly, maternal and child health services, maternity and infant care projects, comprehensive health services, and a variety of public health activities. For information about the Medicaid program, see Section 3, Health and Nutrition.

Noncash benefits—The U.S. Census Bureau annually collects data on the characteristics of recipients of noncash (in-kind) benefits to supplement the collection of annual money income data in the Current Population Survey (see text, Section 1, Population, and Section 13, Income, Expenditures, Poverty, and Wealth). Noncash benefits are those benefits received in a form other than money which serve to enhance or improve the economic well-being of the recipient. As for money income, the data for noncash benefits are for the calendar year prior to the date of the interview. The major categories of noncash benefits covered are public transfers (e.g., SNAP, school lunch, public housing, and Medicaid) and employer or union-provided benefits to employees.

Statistical reliability—For discussion of statistical collection, estimation, and sampling procedures and measures of statistical reliability applicable to Census Bureau data, see Appendix III.

Table 570. Government Transfer Payments to Individuals—Summary: 1990 to 2018

[In billions of current dollars (568.1 represents $568,100,000,000)]

Year	Government transfer payments to individuals, total	Retirement and disability insurance benefits	Medical payments	Income maintenance benefits	Unemployment insurance benefits	Veterans benefits	Education and training assistance payments [1]	Other [2]
1990	568.1	263.9	188.8	65.4	18.2	17.7	12.3	1.7
2000	1,032.4	424.5	427.2	110.6	21.0	25.0	21.9	2.3
2002	1,235.4	474.5	522.4	125.0	53.7	29.5	27.8	2.4
2003	1,304.2	493.4	556.5	137.6	53.6	31.8	28.3	3.0
2004	1,387.1	517.0	611.4	149.1	37.1	34.1	30.8	7.7
2005	1,473.5	545.5	655.6	165.9	32.3	36.4	33.0	4.9
2006	1,575.4	576.9	720.4	170.4	30.9	38.9	34.8	3.1
2007	1,679.8	608.8	775.9	180.6	33.4	41.7	36.8	2.6
2008	1,900.5	639.0	825.5	196.0	52.0	45.0	42.5	100.4
2009	2,087.4	698.5	890.4	230.8	132.0	51.5	53.5	30.6
2010	2,260.4	724.9	938.4	256.0	139.7	58.0	64.5	78.8
2011	2,288.7	747.4	970.1	264.1	107.9	63.3	65.0	70.9
2012	2,300.2	796.2	1,001.6	267.6	84.4	70.1	63.7	16.5
2013	2,363.2	832.8	1,040.5	271.2	63.0	79.1	63.8	12.8
2014	2,475.6	870.3	1,117.7	271.0	35.8	84.2	64.7	31.9
2015	2,610.3	908.3	1,196.1	272.7	32.5	92.6	64.4	43.8
2016	2,691.4	930.9	1,248.5	270.0	31.9	95.9	64.9	49.3
2017	2,777.0	960.0	1,292.9	268.2	30.2	104.0	65.6	56.0
2018	2,894.9	1,007.3	1,355.7	259.9	27.6	109.9	69.1	65.4

[1] See footnote 9, Table 571. [2] See footnote 10, Table 571.

Source: U.S. Bureau of Economic Analysis, Regional Economic Accounts, Annual Personal Income and Employment by State, "Personal Current Transfer Receipts (SAINC35)," <http://www.bea.gov/regional/index.htm>, accessed January 2020.

Table 571. Government Transfer Payments to Individuals by Payment Type: 1990 to 2018

[In millions of current dollars (568,060 represents $568,060,000,000)]

Payment type	1990	2000	2005	2010	2016	2017	2018
Total	**568,060**	**1,032,404**	**1,473,518**	**2,260,351**	**2,691,422**	**2,777,003**	**2,894,854**
Retirement & disability insurance benefits	263,888	424,461	545,484	724,895	930,941	959,967	1,007,322
Social security	244,135	401,393	512,728	690,174	896,472	926,072	972,412
Railroad retirement & disability	7,221	8,267	9,194	10,779	12,352	12,475	12,731
Workers' compensation (federal & state)	8,618	10,898	15,863	15,505	13,659	13,297	13,199
Other government disability insurance & retirement [1]	3,914	3,903	7,699	8,437	8,458	8,123	8,980
Medical payments	188,808	427,194	655,571	938,402	1,248,524	1,292,919	1,355,734
Medicare	107,638	219,117	332,127	513,390	660,209	689,273	730,858
Public assistance medical care [2]	78,176	205,021	315,189	410,957	574,149	589,049	610,068
Military medical insurance [3]	2,994	3,056	8,255	14,055	14,166	14,597	14,808
Income maintenance benefits	65,441	110,582	165,905	256,034	270,027	268,224	259,860
Supplemental Security Income (SSI)	16,670	31,675	38,261	49,158	56,449	56,414	56,857
Earned income tax credit	6,313	30,423	39,237	59,778	70,405	69,547	68,439
Supplemental Nutrition Assistance Program	14,741	14,565	29,492	66,515	65,513	64,251	57,139
Family assistance [4]	19,187	18,440	18,355	22,421	20,223	20,152	20,430
Other, excluding family assistance [5]	8,530	15,479	40,560	58,162	57,437	57,860	56,995
Unemployment insurance compensation	18,208	20,989	32,277	139,715	31,891	30,216	27,569
State unemployment insurance compensation	17,644	20,223	31,001	137,016	31,039	29,227	26,696
Unemployment compensation for federal civilian employees	215	226	225	535	171	181	162
Unemployment compensation for railroad employees	89	81	72	116	132	103	89
Unemployment compensation for veterans	144	181	446	1,155	281	217	160
Other unemployment compensation [6]	116	278	533	893	268	488	462
Veterans' benefits	17,687	25,004	36,389	57,962	95,892	104,041	109,886
Veterans pension & disability	15,550	21,966	32,511	48,455	82,890	90,906	97,387
Veterans readjustment [7]	257	1,322	2,256	7,976	11,819	12,056	11,424
Veterans life insurance benefits	1,868	1,706	1,597	1,442	1,096	992	989
Other assistance to veterans [8]	12	10	25	89	87	87	86
Federal education & training assistance payments [9]	12,286	21,851	33,015	64,511	64,879	65,624	69,053
Other payments to individuals [10]	1,742	2,323	4,877	78,832	49,268	56,012	65,430

[1] Mostly temporary disability, pension benefit guaranty, black lung, and Panama Canal construction annuity payments. [2] Medicaid and other medical vendor payments. [3] Payments made under TRICARE Program (formerly called CHAMPUS) for medical care of dependents of active duty and retired military personnel and their dependents at nonmilitary medical facilities. [4] Through 1995, consists of Emergency Assistance and Aid to Families with Dependent Children. Beginning 1998, consists of Temporary Assistance for Needy Families benefits. [5] Mostly general assistance; food expenditures under Special Supplemental Nutrition Program for Women, Infants, and Children (WIC); other needs assistance; refugee assistance; foster home care and adoption assistance; Additional Child Tax Credits; and energy assistance. [6] Trade readjustment allowance, Redwood Park benefit, public service employment benefit, and transitional benefit. [7] Mostly veterans' readjustment benefit payments, educational assistance to spouses and children of disabled or deceased veterans, and payments to paraplegics and for autos and conveyances for disabled veterans. [8] Mostly state and local government payments to veterans. [9] Mostly federal fellowship payments (National Science Foundation fellowships and traineeships, subsistence payments to state maritime academy cadets, and other fellowships), interest subsidy on higher education loans, Pell Grants, Job Corps payments, education exchange payments, and state education assistance payments. [10] Mostly other refundable tax credits; Bureau of Indian Affairs payments; Alaska Permanent Fund dividend payments; compensation of survivors of public safety officers; compensation of crime victims; disaster relief payments; compensation for Japanese internment; ARRA funded Federal Additional Compensation for unemployment, COBRA premium reduction, and Economic Recovery lump sum payment; Affordable Care Act cost sharing reductions; and other special payments to individuals.

Source: U.S. Bureau of Economic Analysis, Regional Economic Accounts, Annual State Personal Income and Employment, "Personal Current Transfer Receipts (SAINC35)," <http://www.bea.gov/regional/index.htm>, accessed January 2020.

Table 572. Government Transfer Payments to Individuals by State: 2010 to 2018

[In millions of current dollars not adjusted for inflation (2,260,351 represents $2,260,351,000,000)]

State	2010, total	2017, total	2018 Total	Retirement and disability insurance benefits	Medical payments	Income maintenance benefits	Unemployment insurance benefits	Veterans benefits	Education and training assistance [1]	Other [2]
United States.........	2,260,351	2,777,003	2,894,854	1,007,322	1,355,734	259,860	27,569	109,886	69,053	65,430
Alabama................	36,885	44,509	46,076	17,881	18,414	4,453	168	2,640	1,356	1,163
Alaska..................	5,189	6,691	6,871	1,538	3,152	787	76	402	79	838
Arizona................	46,551	59,181	61,818	21,954	27,905	4,610	290	2,511	3,479	1,070
Arkansas..............	23,007	28,265	29,152	10,640	13,470	2,475	131	1,345	805	286
California..............	259,129	320,701	336,848	101,523	170,722	32,340	4,924	10,201	9,773	7,366
Colorado...............	28,542	38,279	41,593	14,583	19,631	2,875	378	2,373	1,006	747
Connecticut...........	28,329	32,444	34,622	11,973	17,548	2,481	607	672	634	708
Delaware..............	6,972	9,775	10,238	3,705	4,946	663	68	315	383	158
District of Columbia....	5,301	6,517	6,655	1,277	4,071	904	65	136	170	32
Florida.................	147,547	190,057	199,087	73,749	86,729	16,458	443	8,494	3,934	9,280
Georgia................	59,961	75,583	79,389	28,862	31,935	8,763	335	4,785	2,163	2,547
Hawaii.................	9,006	11,541	11,759	4,311	5,078	1,219	146	684	202	118
Idaho..................	9,921	12,677	13,469	5,586	5,434	986	90	616	292	465
Illinois.................	90,583	100,479	103,663	37,391	46,996	10,601	1,640	2,464	2,634	1,937
Indiana................	45,972	56,233	58,545	22,605	27,021	4,805	260	1,682	1,630	543
Iowa...................	21,092	24,659	26,845	10,529	12,010	1,913	370	786	761	475
Kansas................	18,598	21,860	22,896	9,336	9,792	1,755	161	898	415	539
Kentucky..............	34,555	42,815	44,119	15,493	21,134	3,763	326	1,595	1,394	412
Louisiana.............	33,352	43,197	44,928	13,661	23,053	4,670	186	1,637	1,087	634
Maine.................	11,056	13,236	13,953	5,156	6,383	920	93	680	238	481
Maryland..............	37,990	48,787	51,232	17,192	25,425	4,200	513	2,020	953	929
Massachusetts........	54,798	64,852	67,842	20,780	36,081	6,117	1,361	1,645	1,047	812
Michigan..............	80,630	91,374	95,431	37,247	43,344	8,066	769	2,646	2,098	1,262
Minnesota............	37,924	46,607	49,502	17,264	24,267	4,044	753	1,483	1,230	459
Mississippi...........	23,427	27,634	28,582	9,995	13,127	2,958	88	1,088	740	586
Missouri...............	44,332	52,978	55,014	20,706	25,284	4,039	299	2,159	1,147	1,381
Montana...............	6,854	9,155	9,479	3,818	4,096	590	106	436	167	265
Nebraska..............	11,489	14,285	15,057	5,882	6,177	1,134	77	716	333	737
Nevada................	16,258	22,436	23,750	8,486	10,538	2,121	302	1,264	625	414
New Hampshire........	8,864	11,454	12,061	5,119	5,315	578	66	458	297	228
New Jersey............	68,883	79,116	81,713	29,615	37,911	7,224	1,876	1,520	1,696	1,872
New Mexico...........	15,448	19,072	20,190	6,579	9,573	2,134	133	1,011	435	325
New York..............	178,462	220,777	217,817	61,179	122,661	21,485	2,021	3,453	4,254	2,763
North Carolina........	68,663	86,390	90,261	33,368	37,346	8,227	206	5,201	2,250	3,663
North Dakota...........	4,405	5,529	5,900	2,256	2,622	489	91	230	104	107
Ohio...................	88,300	104,047	106,807	38,431	52,085	9,053	871	3,121	2,269	977
Oklahoma.............	26,910	32,514	33,544	12,505	13,479	3,084	221	2,415	833	1,005
Oregon................	28,483	36,878	39,020	14,393	18,288	2,938	487	1,728	583	604
Pennsylvania..........	108,365	127,320	136,341	47,438	67,219	11,692	1,814	3,333	2,255	2,590
Rhode Island..........	9,319	10,872	11,143	3,818	5,377	1,095	147	304	274	127
South Carolina........	35,399	44,533	46,943	18,380	19,007	3,794	179	2,798	1,506	1,278
South Dakota..........	5,212	6,469	6,770	2,750	2,798	518	30	313	137	223
Tennessee.............	49,089	58,196	61,136	22,942	26,124	5,687	226	2,952	1,409	1,796
Texas..................	153,344	198,324	207,306	66,200	95,713	22,069	2,057	11,529	4,348	5,390
Utah...................	13,185	16,679	17,714	6,840	6,718	1,674	150	687	749	897
Vermont...............	5,220	6,409	6,679	2,383	3,187	573	62	184	189	101
Virginia................	47,926	62,826	66,024	25,287	26,899	5,073	300	4,530	1,710	2,225
Washington...........	48,772	61,097	64,074	24,592	26,957	6,099	1,030	3,104	1,562	730
West Virginia..........	16,457	19,922	20,396	7,786	9,148	1,712	142	909	505	194
Wisconsin.............	40,869	47,366	49,959	20,251	21,803	3,723	388	1,514	827	1,453
Wyoming..............	3,525	4,405	4,641	2,086	1,742	225	47	219	85	237

[1] Mostly federal fellowship payments (National Science Foundation fellowships and traineeships, subsistence payments to state maritime academy cadets, and other federal fellowships), interest subsidy on higher education loans, Pell Grants, Job Corps payments, education exchange payments, and state education assistance payments. [2] Mostly other refundable tax credits; Bureau of Indian Affairs payments; Alaska Permanent Fund dividend payments; compensation of survivors of public safety officers; compensation of crime victims; disaster relief payments; compensation for Japanese internment; the American Recovery and Reinvestment Act of 2009 funded Federal Additional Compensation for unemployment, COBRA premium reduction, and the Economic Recovery lump sum payment; Affordable Care Act cost sharing reductions; and other special payments to individuals.

Source: U.S. Bureau of Economic Analysis, Regional Economic Accounts, Annual Personal Income and Employment by State, "Personal Current Transfer Receipts (SAINC35)," <https://www.bea.gov/regional/index.htm>, accessed January 2020.

Table 573. Number of Persons With Income by Source of Income: 2018

[In thousands (232,139 represents 232,139,000). Persons age 15 and over as of March of following year. Based on Current Population Survey, Annual Social and Economic Supplement (CPS ASEC); see text, Sections 1 and 13, and Appendix III. Data for 2018 reflect an updated CPS ASEC processing system. See source for more information]

Source of income	Total persons with income	Under 65 years	65 years and over	Men	Women	White[1]	Black[1]	Hispanic origin[2]
Total	**232,139**	**181,210**	**50,929**	**115,219**	**116,920**	**182,597**	**28,311**	**35,649**
Earnings	167,555	155,143	12,412	88,115	79,440	130,591	20,691	28,942
Wages and salary	158,938	147,933	11,005	82,784	76,154	123,348	20,043	27,369
Nonfarm self-employment	11,960	10,395	1,565	7,046	4,915	9,855	1,064	1,948
Farm self-employment	1,982	1,692	290	1,167	815	1,652	188	184
Unemployment compensation	3,200	2,953	248	1,870	1,330	2,516	470	535
State or local only	2,933	2,708	225	1,728	1,205	2,331	401	504
Combinations	270	247	23	142	128	187	70	31
Workers' compensation	1,313	1,162	151	689	624	1,041	179	213
State payments	244	224	20	135	109	170	51	57
Employment insurance	585	523	63	333	253	478	71	99
Own insurance	10	10	–	2	8	10	–	–
Other	704	615	89	338	366	569	91	91
Social Security	53,871	11,202	42,669	24,287	29,583	44,986	5,767	4,523
SSI (Supplemental Security Income)	6,004	4,550	1,454	2,546	3,459	3,801	1,633	1,053
Public assistance, total	1,506	1,380	126	394	1,112	883	470	353
TANF only[3]	969	918	50	222	747	517	351	249
Other assistance only	511	447	64	169	342	352	114	101
Both	26	15	11	3	23	15	5	3
Veterans' benefits	4,296	2,204	2,092	3,574	722	3,423	636	343
Disability only	2,795	1,570	1,224	2,487	307	2,238	396	240
Survivors only	267	56	212	19	248	216	35	13
Pension only	732	219	513	671	61	598	93	40
Education only	118	118	–	76	43	81	25	22
Other only	151	75	76	129	21	120	28	3
Combinations	234	166	68	191	42	170	59	24
Means-tested	602	321	281	495	107	497	80	56
Nonmeans-tested	3,694	1,883	1,811	3,078	615	2,926	555	287
Survivors benefits[4]	3,132	969	2,163	735	2,397	2,783	190	152
Company or union	1,314	205	1,109	172	1,141	1,174	81	65
Federal government	276	73	203	49	227	239	29	17
Military retirement	225	51	175	24	202	198	10	9
State or local government	298	72	227	65	234	274	16	21
Estates or trusts	333	221	112	167	166	308	11	8
Annuities	235	89	145	64	170	206	8	6
Disability benefits[4]	2,498	2,124	374	1,203	1,294	1,908	430	332
Workers' compensation	349	310	39	193	156	276	48	50
Company or union	516	455	61	225	291	423	73	47
Federal government	184	154	30	87	97	142	30	12
Military retirement	203	135	67	157	46	156	41	25
State or local government	414	370	44	179	235	280	104	98
Accident insurance	263	230	33	118	145	219	35	29
Retirement income[4]	29,237	7,221	22,017	14,977	14,260	25,573	2,247	1,499
Pension income	17,691	3,613	14,078	10,098	7,592	15,461	1,457	861
Company or union retirement	11,716	2,358	9,358	6,590	5,126	10,257	947	575
Federal government retirement	1,910	547	1,363	1,074	836	1,599	229	98
Military retirement	1,135	523	612	788	347	933	134	69
State or local government retirement	5,897	1,598	4,299	2,541	3,356	5,124	510	395
Annuities	4,263	691	3,572	1,987	2,277	3,802	271	160
Retirement accounts[5]	10,591	1,340	9,250	5,472	5,119	9,685	415	339
Property income	138,228	105,184	33,044	68,460	69,768	114,525	11,615	14,044
Interest	135,517	103,498	32,018	67,101	68,416	112,363	11,363	13,728
Dividends	31,154	21,331	9,823	16,821	14,333	27,056	1,451	1,599
Rents, royalties, estates or trusts[6]	11,783	7,616	4,167	6,258	5,525	10,051	695	898
Educational assistance[4]	7,654	7,629	25	3,329	4,325	5,617	1,133	1,415
Pell grant only	1,960	1,951	9	758	1,202	1,401	370	488
Other government only	950	942	8	465	485	724	147	206
Scholarships only	2,575	2,573	2	1,163	1,412	1,926	260	434
Child support	3,932	3,885	46	370	3,562	2,852	797	707
Financial assistance from outside the household	2,945	2,639	306	1,252	1,693	2,009	370	347
Other income, not elsewhere classified	2,397	1,938	458	1,217	1,179	1,950	193	230

– Represents or rounds to zero. [1] Refers to people who reported specified race only and no other race category. [2] Persons of Hispanic origin may be of any race. [3] TANF is Temporary Assistance for Needy Families Program. [4] Includes other sources not shown separately. [5] Includes individual retirement account, tax-deferred retirement plan for self-employed and unincorporated businesses, employer-sponsored retirement plan, and other plan types. [6] Includes estates and trusts.

Source: U.S. Census Bureau, *Income and Poverty in the United States: 2018,* Current Population Reports, P60-266, September 2019; and "Current Population Survey Tables for Personal Income: Table PINC-09," <https://www.census.gov/topics/income-poverty/income/data/tables.html>, accessed January 2020.

Table 574. Persons Living in Households Receiving Selected Benefits by Selected Characteristics: 2018

[323,847 represents 323,847,000, except percent. Based on Current Population Survey, Annual Social and Economic Supplement (CPS ASEC); see text of Section 1 and Appendix III. Persons who lived with someone (a nonrelative or a relative) who received aid. Not every person tallied here received the aid themselves. Persons living in households receiving more than one type of aid are counted only once. Excludes members of the Armed Forces except those living off post or with their families on post. Population controls are based on Census 2010. SNAP = Supplemental Nutrition Assistance Program. Data reflect an updated CPS ASEC processing system. See source for more information]

Characteristic	Total (1,000)	In household receiving means-tested assistance [1] (1,000)	Percent	In household receiving means-tested cash assistance (1,000)	Percent	In household receiving food stamps (SNAP) (1,000)	Percent	In household in which one or more persons are covered by Medicaid (1,000)	Percent	Living in public or authorized housing (1,000)	Percent
Total.	323,847	91,342	28.2	18,658	5.8	34,909	10.8	32,007	9.9	12,286	3.8
Under 18 years.	73,284	32,853	44.8	4,276	5.8	12,480	17.0	11,830	16.1	3,785	5.2
18 to 24 years.	29,085	8,389	28.8	1,602	5.5	3,145	10.8	2,756	9.5	1,174	4.0
25 to 34 years.	45,208	11,693	25.9	2,197	4.9	4,704	10.4	4,051	9.0	1,627	3.6
35 to 44 years.	41,027	12,270	29.9	2,112	5.1	4,051	9.9	4,092	10.0	1,229	3.0
45 to 54 years.	40,700	9,493	23.3	2,366	5.8	3,298	8.1	3,214	7.9	1,043	2.6
55 to 59 years.	21,163	4,351	20.6	1,645	7.8	1,834	8.7	1,802	8.5	614	2.9
60 to 64 years.	20,592	4,004	19.4	1,473	7.2	1,717	8.3	1,743	8.5	646	3.1
65 years and over.	52,788	8,287	15.7	2,987	5.7	3,680	7.0	2,519	4.8	2,167	4.1
Male.	158,741	42,836	27.0	8,811	5.6	15,618	9.8	14,418	9.1	5,162	3.3
Female.	165,106	48,506	29.4	9,847	6.0	19,290	11.7	17,589	10.7	7,125	4.3
White alone [2].	247,634	61,445	24.8	11,800	4.8	21,434	8.7	20,816	8.4	6,046	2.4
Black alone [2].	42,773	19,697	46.0	4,817	11.3	9,796	22.9	7,368	17.2	4,882	11.4
Asian alone [2].	19,768	4,409	22.3	895	4.5	1,178	6.0	1,821	9.2	471	2.4
Hispanic [3].	59,957	28,610	47.7	4,070	6.8	9,564	16.0	8,946	14.9	2,925	4.9
In married couple families.	196,418	43,863	22.3	7,550	3.8	11,626	5.9	14,437	7.4	2,303	1.2
In families with male householder, no spouse present. . . .	18,932	7,875	41.6	1,579	8.3	3,292	17.4	1,885	10.0	861	4.5
In families with female householder, no spouse present. . . .	46,660	26,220	56.2	5,975	12.8	13,583	29.1	9,787	21.0	4,953	10.6

[1] Means-tested assistance includes means-tested cash assistance, supplemental nutrition assistance program benefits, Medicaid, and public or authorized housing. [2] Refers to people who reported specific race and did not report any other race category. [3] People of Hispanic origin may be of any race.

Source: U.S. Census Bureau, *Income and Poverty in the United States: 2018*, Current Population Reports, P60-266, September 2019; and "Current Population Survey Detailed Tables for Poverty: Table POV-26," <https://www.census.gov/topics/income-poverty/poverty/data/tables.html>, accessed January 2020.

Table 575. Social Security—Covered Employment, Earnings, and Contribution Rates: 1990 to 2019

[164.3 represents 164,300,000. Includes the Island Areas of the U.S. Represents all reported employment. Data are estimated. OASDI is Old-age, survivors, and disability insurance; SMI is Supplementary medical insurance. All data are subject to revision by source]

Item	Unit	1990	2000	2010	2014	2015	2016	2017	2018	2019
Workers with insured status [1].	**Million**	**164.3**	**185.3**	**204.3**	**212.1**	**214.8**	**217.5**	**220.0**	**222.1**	**224.2**
Male.	Million	86.8	95.5	103.5	107.0	108.2	109.4	110.5	111.5	112.4
Female.	Million	77.5	89.8	100.8	105.1	106.6	108.0	109.4	110.6	111.8
Under 20 years old.	Million	4.8	4.9	2.5	2.2	2.3	2.6	2.7	2.6	2.5
Age 20 to 24.	Million	16.6	16.0	16.0	15.7	15.8	15.9	16.0	16.2	16.4
Age 25 to 29.	Million	20.6	17.5	19.3	19.9	20.2	20.6	20.9	21.0	21.0
Age 30 to 34.	Million	21.3	19.2	18.7	19.7	19.8	19.9	20.0	20.3	20.6
Age 35 to 39.	Million	19.3	21.2	18.2	18.3	18.8	19.2	19.5	19.8	19.9
Age 40 to 44.	Million	17.0	21.4	19.6	18.8	18.2	17.9	17.9	18.1	18.4
Age 45 to 49.	Million	12.8	19.2	21.2	19.4	19.4	19.4	19.3	19.0	18.7
Age 50 to 54.	Million	10.1	16.6	20.9	21.1	20.8	20.3	19.8	19.4	19.1
Age 55 to 59.	Million	8.8	12.2	18.3	19.9	20.2	20.4	20.5	20.5	20.5
Age 60 to 64.	Million	8.6	9.3	15.5	17.1	17.6	18.1	18.5	18.9	19.1
Age 65 to 69.	Million	8.0	7.9	11.2	14.0	14.8	15.2	15.5	15.8	16.3
Age 70 to 74.	Million	6.4	7.1	8.1	9.9	10.2	10.9	11.7	12.3	12.9
Age 75 and older.	Million	9.9	12.8	14.9	16.0	16.4	16.9	17.6	18.3	18.9
Workers reported with—										
Taxable earnings [2].	Million	133.0	154.7	157.1	165.4	168.2	170.9	173.0	175.6	177.9
Maximum earnings [2].	Million	7.6	9.6	9.0	9.9	10.5	11.0	10.2	10.6	10.7
Earnings in covered employment [2]. . . .	Bil. dol.	2,716	4,832	6,294	7,436	7,803	8,020	8,392	8,810	9,217
Reported taxable [2].	Bil. dol.	2,359	4,008	5,307	6,181	6,471	6,664	7,004	7,343	7,674
Percent of total.	Percent	86.9	82.9	84.3	83.1	82.9	83.1	83.5	83.4	83.3
Average per worker:										
Total earnings [2].	Dollars	20,422	31,236	40,075	44,948	46,395	46,938	48,505	50,174	51,822
Taxable earnings [2].	Dollars	17,737	25,908	33,788	37,363	38,475	39,006	40,482	41,821	43,143
Annual maximum taxable earnings [3].	Dollars	51,300	76,200	106,800	117,000	118,500	118,500	127,200	128,400	132,900
Contribution rates for OASDI: [4]										
Each employer and employee.	Percent	7.65	7.65	7.65	7.65	7.65	7.65	7.65	7.65	7.65
Self-employed [5].	Percent	15.30	15.30	15.30	15.30	15.30	15.30	15.30	15.30	15.30
SMI, monthly premium (as of Jan. 1). . .	Dollars	28.60	45.50	110.50	104.90	104.90	121.80	134.00	134.00	135.50

[1] Estimated number fully insured for retirement and/or survivor benefits as of end of year. [2] Includes self-employment. Averages per worker computed with unrounded earnings and worker amounts, and may not agree with rounded table amounts. [3] Beginning in 1994, the upper limit on earnings subject to HI taxes was removed. [4] OASDI tax rates for employees and self-employed workers were reduced by 2 percent for 2011 and 2012. This reduction is being made up by transfers from the General Fund of the Treasury to the OASI and DI trust funds. [5] Half of self-employment tax is deductible for income tax purposes and for computing self-employment income subject to social security tax.

Source: U.S. Social Security Administration, *Annual Statistical Supplement to the Social Security Bulletin, 2020* and unpublished data. See also <https://www.ssa.gov/policy/docs/statcomps/supplement/index.html>.

Table 576. Social Security (OASDI)—Benefits by Type of Beneficiary: 1990 to 2019

[39,832 represents 39,832,000. A person eligible to receive more than one type of benefit is generally classified or counted only once as a retired-worker beneficiary. OASDI = Old-age, survivors, and disability insurance. See also headnote, Table 577]

Type of beneficiary	1990	2000	2010	2013	2014	2015	2016	2017	2018	2019 (P)
Number of benefits [1] (1,000)	**39,832**	**45,415**	**54,032**	**57,979**	**59,007**	**59,963**	**60,907**	**61,903**	**62,906**	**64,064**
Retired workers [2]	24,838	28,499	34,593	37,893	39,009	40,089	41,233	42,447	43,721	45,094
Disabled workers [3]	3,011	5,042	8,204	8,941	8,955	8,909	8,809	8,695	8,537	8,378
Wives and husbands [2,4]	3,367	2,963	2,477	2,442	2,452	2,478	2,506	2,502	2,510	2,544
Children	3,187	3,803	4,313	4,413	4,355	4,297	4,222	4,169	4,108	4,051
Under age 18	2,497	2,976	3,209	3,237	3,166	3,096	3,007	2,938	2,858	2,798
Disabled children [5]	600	729	949	1,030	1,049	1,068	1,085	1,105	1,127	1,141
Students [6]	89	98	155	146	140	133	129	125	122	113
Of retired workers	422	459	580	625	635	649	662	675	690	702
Of deceased workers	1,776	1,878	1,913	1,899	1,892	1,893	1,893	1,904	1,911	1,916
Of disabled workers	989	1,466	1,820	1,888	1,828	1,755	1,667	1,590	1,507	1,434
Widowed mothers and fathers [7]	304	203	158	150	143	140	133	128	121	117
Widows and widowers [2,8]	5,111	4,901	4,286	4,139	4,092	4,050	4,004	3,961	3,908	3,878
Parents [2]	6	3	2	1	1	1	1	1	1	1
Special benefits [9]	7	(Z)	(Z)	(NA)	(NA)	(NA)	(NA)	(NA)	(NA)	(NA)
AVERAGE MONTHLY BENEFIT, CURRENT DOLLARS										
Retired workers [2]	603	844	1,176	1,294	1,329	1,342	1,360	1,404	1,461	1,503
Retired worker and wife [2]	1,027	1,420	1,930	2,140	2,209	2,249	2,296	2,383	2,494	2,583
Disabled workers [3]	587	786	1,068	1,146	1,165	1,166	1,171	1,197	1,234	1,258
Wives and husbands [2,4]	298	416	561	626	651	669	687	712	744	767
Children of retired workers	259	395	577	632	647	651	657	675	697	713
Children of deceased workers	406	550	752	814	831	832	837	858	885	902
Children of disabled workers	164	228	318	341	349	351	355	366	381	391
Widowed mothers and fathers [7]	409	595	849	918	935	940	947	975	1,007	1,034
Widows and widowers, nondisabled [2]	556	810	1,134	1,244	1,276	1,286	1,301	1,338	1,388	1,423
Parents [2]	482	704	998	1,094	1,121	1,133	1,154	1,186	1,232	1,271
Special benefits [9]	167	217	276	(NA)	(NA)	(NA)	(NA)	(NA)	(NA)	(NA)
AVERAGE MONTHLY BENEFIT, CONSTANT (2019) DOLLARS [10]										
Retired workers [2]	1,158	1,247	1,378	1,427	1,454	1,458	1,448	1,464	1,495	1,503
Retired worker and wife [2]	1,972	2,097	2,263	2,361	2,418	2,444	2,443	2,484	2,551	2,583
Disabled workers [3]	1,127	1,161	1,252	1,265	1,275	1,267	1,247	1,248	1,262	1,258
Wives and husbands [2,4]	572	615	658	691	713	727	731	742	761	767
Children of deceased workers	780	812	881	898	909	904	891	894	905	902
Widowed mothers and fathers [7]	786	879	995	1,012	1,023	1,021	1,008	1,017	1,030	1,034
Widows and widowers, nondisabled [2]	1,068	1,197	1,329	1,372	1,396	1,397	1,385	1,395	1,420	1,423
Number of benefits awarded (1,000)	**3,717**	**4,290**	**5,697**	**5,533**	**5,361**	**5,440**	**5,456**	**5,520**	**5,597**	**5,700**
Retired workers [2]	1,665	1,961	2,634	2,794	2,772	2,839	2,911	2,975	3,082	3,175
Disabled workers [3]	468	622	1,027	869	779	741	706	716	687	679
Wives and husbands [2,4]	379	385	409	420	428	463	476	452	476	523
Children	695	777	1,045	877	810	798	776	777	754	721
Widowed mothers and fathers [7]	58	40	32	27	25	25	24	23	22	21
Widows and widowers [2,8]	452	505	550	546	547	573	563	577	577	581
Parents [2]	(Z)	(Z)	(Z)	(Z)	(Z)	(Z)	(Z)	(Z)	(Z)	(Z)
Special benefits [9]	(Z)	(Z)	(Z)	(NA)	(NA)	(NA)	(NA)	(NA)	(NA)	(NA)
BENEFIT PAYMENTS DURING YEAR (bil. dol.)										
Total [11]	**247.8**	**407.6**	**701.6**	**812.2**	**848.4**	**886.2**	**911.3**	**941.5**	**988.6**	**1,047.9**
Monthly benefits [12]	247.6	407.4	701.4	812.0	848.2	886.0	911.1	941.3	988.4	1,047.7
Retired workers [2]	156.8	253.5	443.4	528.9	560.1	592.4	616.0	644.0	686.0	738.0
Disabled workers [3]	22.1	49.8	115.1	130.4	132.2	133.9	143.0	134.0	144.0	137.0
Wives and husbands [2,4]	14.5	19.4	24.6	26.9	28.1	29.3	30.0	31.0	32.0	34.0
Children	12.0	19.3	30.7	32.7	33.0	33.5	33.5	33.9	34.6	35.4
Under age 18	9.0	14.1	21.4	22.2	22.2	22.3	22.1	22.1	22.3	22.6
Disabled children [5]	2.5	4.6	8.0	9.2	9.6	10.0	10.3	10.6	11.1	11.6
Students [6]	0.5	0.7	1.3	1.3	1.3	1.2	1.2	1.2	1.2	1.2
Of retired workers	1.3	2.1	4.1	4.8	5.0	5.2	5.4	5.6	5.8	6.1
Of deceased workers	8.6	12.5	18.0	18.9	19.2	19.6	19.8	20.0	20.7	21.3
Of disabled workers	2.2	4.7	8.5	9.0	8.9	8.7	8.5	8.3	8.2	8.0
Widowed mothers and fathers [7]	1.4	1.4	1.6	1.7	1.6	1.6	1.6	1.5	1.5	1.5
Widows and widowers [2,8]	40.7	63.9	86.0	91.4	93.2	95.1	95.8	96.7	99.0	102.6
Parents [2]	(Z)	(Z)	(Z)	(Z)	(Z)	(Z)	(Z)	(Z)	(Z)	(Z)
Special benefits [9]	(Z)	(Z)	(Z)	(NA)	(NA)	(NA)	(NA)	(NA)	(NA)	(NA)
Lump sum	0.2	0.2	0.2	0.2	0.2	0.2	0.2	0.2	0.2	0.2

NA Not available. P Preliminary. Z Fewer than 500 or less than $50 million. [1] Number of benefit payments in current-payment status, i.e., actually being made at a specified time with no deductions or with deductions amounting to less than a month's benefit. [2] Age 62 and over. [3] Disabled workers under full retirement age. [4] Includes spouse beneficiaries with entitled children in their care and entitled divorced spouses. [5] Age 18 and over. Disability began before age 22. [6] Full-time students age 18 and 19. [7] Includes surviving divorced mothers and fathers with entitled children in their care. [8] Includes widows and widowers and surviving divorced widows and widowers age 60 and over, and disabled widows and widowers age 50 and over. [9] Benefits for persons age 72 and over not insured under regular or transitional provisions of Social Security Act. [10] Constant dollar figures are based on the consumer price index (CPI-U) for December as published by the U.S. Bureau of Labor Statistics. [11] Represents total disbursements of benefit checks by the U.S. Department of the Treasury during the years specified. [12] Distribution by type estimated.

Source: U.S. Social Security Administration, *Annual Statistical Supplement to the Social Security Bulletin, 2020*, and earlier editions. See also <http://www.ssa.gov/policy/index.html>.

Table 577. Social Security—Beneficiaries, Annual Payments, and Average Monthly Benefit, 2000 to 2018, and by State and Other Areas, 2019

[45,417 represents 45,417,000. Number of beneficiaries in current-payment status, and annual and average monthly benefit as of December. Data for 2000 are based on 10-percent sample of administrative records. All other years are 100 percent data. See also headnote, Table 576]

Year, state, and other area	Number of beneficiaries (1,000)				Annual payments [2] (mil. dol.)				Average monthly benefit (dol.)		
	Total	Retired workers and dependents [1]	Survivors	Disabled workers and dependents	Total	Retired workers and dependents [1]	Survivors	Disabled workers and dependents	Retired workers [3]	Disabled workers	Widows and widowers [4]
2000	45,417	31,761	6,981	6,675	407,431	274,645	77,848	54,938	845	787	810
2010	54,032	37,489	6,358	10,184	701,436	471,505	105,740	124,191	1,176	1,068	1,134
2012	56,758	39,613	6,256	10,889	774,626	527,402	110,346	136,878	1,262	1,130	1,215
2013	57,979	40,804	6,189	10,988	812,050	559,946	112,032	140,072	1,294	1,146	1,244
2014	59,007	41,918	6,790	10,931	848,228	592,616	114,037	141,620	1,329	1,165	1,276
2015	59,963	43,073	6,084	10,806	886,012	626,378	116,352	143,282	1,342	1,166	1,286
2016	60,907	44,266	6,031	10,610	911,132	651,280	117,149	142,703	1,360	1,171	1,301
2017	61,903	45,498	5,994	10,411	941,252	680,233	118,279	142,740	1,404	1,197	1,338
2018	62,906	46,803	5,940	10,162	988,373	723,542	121,175	143,656	1,461	1,234	1,388
Total, 2019 [5, 6]	64,064	48,227	5,912	9,925	1,047,676	777,258	125,369	145,049	1,503	1,258	1,423
United States	62,503	47,078	5,696	9,729	1,031,672	766,866	122,294	142,512	(NA)	(NA)	(NA)
Alabama	1,159	775	122	263	18,494	12,333	2,417	3,744	1,474	1,236	1,390
Alaska	105	81	10	14	1,634	1,238	197	199	1,442	1,240	1,395
Arizona	1,399	1,107	116	176	23,298	18,124	2,502	2,672	1,535	1,307	1,469
Arkansas	704	474	70	160	10,867	7,329	1,346	2,192	1,424	1,198	1,351
California	6,070	4,831	517	722	97,899	75,629	11,193	11,077	1,473	1,292	1,400
Colorado	898	711	75	113	14,911	11,556	1,651	1,704	1,521	1,276	1,473
Connecticut	690	543	55	92	12,492	9,760	1,312	1,420	1,659	1,308	1,596
Delaware	219	171	18	31	3,896	3,005	402	489	1,633	1,348	1,561
District of Columbia	84	62	7	15	1,318	984	131	203	1,468	1,117	1,296
Florida	4,747	3,725	382	640	77,516	59,754	8,233	9,529	1,494	1,281	1,443
Georgia	1,872	1,360	181	331	30,064	21,639	3,633	4,792	1,476	1,260	1,408
Hawaii	277	232	21	25	4,546	3,729	449	368	1,497	1,293	1,395
Idaho	359	276	30	53	5,721	4,344	641	736	1,474	1,232	1,469
Illinois	2,267	1,736	214	316	38,279	28,724	4,817	4,738	1,532	1,275	1,503
Indiana	1,370	1,000	134	236	23,325	16,931	2,960	3,434	1,562	1,258	1,542
Iowa	657	509	59	89	10,889	8,340	1,303	1,246	1,511	1,198	1,478
Kansas	562	427	51	84	9,499	7,174	1,133	1,192	1,557	1,228	1,522
Kentucky	1,002	661	112	229	15,612	10,160	2,206	3,246	1,431	1,226	1,355
Louisiana	922	612	125	185	14,102	9,108	2,454	2,540	1,399	1,205	1,328
Maine	350	257	28	65	5,388	3,913	584	891	1,414	1,179	1,380
Maryland	1,020	786	89	145	17,764	13,554	1,976	2,234	1,599	1,308	1,505
Massachusetts	1,288	960	102	226	21,714	16,116	2,271	3,327	1,557	1,265	1,487
Michigan	2,237	1,636	208	393	38,728	28,124	4,754	5,850	1,591	1,290	1,556
Minnesota	1,053	832	81	140	17,948	14,070	1,853	2,025	1,569	1,248	1,511
Mississippi	677	454	76	147	10,334	6,890	1,414	2,030	1,405	1,201	1,318
Missouri	1,313	946	125	242	21,195	15,166	2,577	3,452	1,478	1,223	1,452
Montana	239	188	21	30	3,753	2,895	434	424	1,427	1,190	1,424
Nebraska	353	273	32	48	5,807	4,458	696	653	1,514	1,182	1,476
Nevada	552	435	44	73	8,947	6,870	934	1,143	1,467	1,321	1,448
New Hampshire	312	233	22	57	5,414	4,068	509	837	1,619	1,298	1,571
New Jersey	1,647	1,289	136	221	29,946	23,103	3,247	3,596	1,663	1,388	1,575
New Mexico	446	329	42	74	6,840	5,000	812	1,028	1,418	1,190	1,329
New York	3,667	2,797	303	567	62,076	46,738	6,794	8,544	1,554	1,297	1,474
North Carolina	2,145	1,597	182	366	35,101	26,046	3,708	5,347	1,504	1,257	1,428
North Dakota	137	106	14	16	2,177	1,649	303	225	1,449	1,176	1,388
Ohio	2,386	1,733	258	396	38,755	27,621	5,531	5,603	1,477	1,210	1,453
Oklahoma	802	571	85	146	12,801	9,026	1,734	2,041	1,465	1,208	1,417
Oregon	892	703	69	119	14,739	11,418	1,565	1,756	1,508	1,245	1,492
Pennsylvania	2,861	2,137	264	460	48,732	36,035	5,949	6,748	1,558	1,262	1,503
Rhode Island	228	169	17	42	3,802	2,820	374	608	1,540	1,236	1,500
South Carolina	1,174	868	104	202	19,344	14,237	2,109	2,998	1,519	1,282	1,418
South Dakota	183	145	16	22	2,878	2,251	332	295	1,440	1,168	1,373
Tennessee	1,478	1,052	146	281	23,854	16,939	2,920	3,995	1,491	1,227	1,417
Texas	4,338	3,211	466	660	69,001	50,036	9,620	9,345	1,472	1,241	1,378
Utah	419	323	40	56	6,976	5,307	879	790	1,549	1,257	1,554
Vermont	153	116	12	25	2,511	1,911	251	349	1,527	1,186	1,461
Virginia	1,560	1,181	138	241	26,300	19,759	2,974	3,567	1,553	1,270	1,454
Washington	1,376	1,075	107	194	23,642	18,227	2,491	2,924	1,583	1,278	1,535
West Virginia	478	320	58	100	7,710	5,028	1,217	1,465	1,473	1,255	1,402
Wisconsin	1,258	971	101	186	21,196	16,247	2,274	2,675	1,545	1,246	1,521
Wyoming	115	90	10	15	1,937	1,483	228	226	1,531	1,265	1,517
American Samoa	6	3	1	2	61	29	15	17	935	917	848
Guam	19	14	3	2	211	145	40	26	1,018	1,146	964
Northern Mariana Islands	3	2	1	(Z)	28	18	7	3	772	889	754
Puerto Rico	828	553	98	178	9,339	5,677	1,373	2,289	992	1,112	875
U.S. Virgin Islands	22	18	2	2	314	254	34	26	1,298	1,289	1,140
Abroad	683	559	111	13	6,034	4,261	1,601	172	786	1,231	823

NA Not available. Z Less than 500. [1] Data for 1990-2006 include special benefits for persons age 72 years and over not insured under regular or transitional provisions of Social Security Act. [2] Unnegotiated checks not deducted. [3] Excludes persons with special benefits. [4] Nondisabled only. [5] Includes those with state or area unknown. [6] 2019 data are preliminary.

Source: U.S. Social Security Administration, *Annual Statistical Supplement to the Social Security Bulletin, 2020*, and earlier reports. See also <http://www.ssa.gov/policy/index.html>.

Table 578. Social Security Trust Funds: 1990 to 2019

[In billions of dollars (286.7 represents $286,700,000,000). Trust fund operations and asset reserves reflect the 12 months of benefits scheduled for payment in each year]

Type of trust fund	1990	2000	2010	2014	2015	2016	2017	2018	2019
OLD-AGE AND SURVIVORS INSURANCE (OASI)									
Total income [1]	286.7	490.5	677.1	769.4	801.6	797.5	825.6	831.0	917.9
Net payroll tax contributions	266.1	421.4	544.8	646.2	679.5	678.8	706.5	715.9	805.1
Taxation of benefits	4.8	11.6	22.1	28.0	30.6	31.6	35.9	34.5	34.9
Interest received [2]	16.4	57.5	108.2	94.8	91.2	87.0	83.2	80.7	77.9
Total expenditures [1]	227.5	358.3	584.9	714.2	750.5	776.4	806.7	853.5	911.4
Benefit payments [3]	223.0	352.7	577.4	706.8	742.9	768.6	798.7	844.9	902.8
Assets, end of year	214.2	931.0	2,429.0	2,729.2	2,780.3	2,801.3	2,820.3	2,797.9	2,804.3
DISABILITY INSURANCE (DI)									
Total income [1]	28.8	77.9	104.0	114.9	118.6	160.0	171.0	172.3	143.9
Net payroll tax contributions	28.4	71.1	92.5	109.7	115.4	157.4	167.1	169.2	139.4
Taxation of benefits	0.1	0.7	1.9	1.7	1.1	1.2	2.0	0.5	1.6
Interest received [2]	0.9	6.9	9.3	3.4	2.1	1.4	1.9	2.6	2.9
Total expenditures [1]	25.6	56.8	127.7	145.1	146.6	145.9	145.8	146.8	147.9
Benefit payments [3]	24.8	55.0	124.2	141.7	143.4	142.8	142.8	143.7	145.1
Assets, end of year	11.1	118.5	179.9	60.2	32.3	46.3	71.5	97.1	93.1

[1] Includes other income or expenses not shown separately. [2] Includes relatively small amounts of gifts to the fund. [3] Includes payments for vocational rehabilitation services furnished to disabled persons receiving benefits because of their disabilities. Amounts reflect deductions for unnegotiated benefit checks.

Source: U.S. Social Security Administration, Office of the Chief Actuary, "Statistical Tables," <https://www.ssa.gov/oact/STATS/index.html>, accessed May 2020.

Table 579. Retirement Employee Benefit Participation by Worker Characteristics: 2010 to 2019

[In percent. Based on National Compensation Survey (NCS). The March 2019 NCS obtained data from approximately 6,470 private industry establishments, representing about 120.4 million workers; see Appendix III. Defined benefit plans provide retirement benefits based on employer benefit formulas that may take into account salary, years of service, and age. Defined contribution plans provide benefits based on employer and employee contributions to individual employee accounts and the rate of return on money invested; the retirement benefit depends on the account balance at retirement. See source for more information]

Characteristic	Total [1]				Defined benefit				Defined contribution			
	2010	2017	2018	2019	2010	2017	2018	2019	2010	2017	2018	2019
All workers	**50**	**50**	**51**	**52**	**19**	**15**	**13**	**12**	**41**	**44**	**47**	**47**
Management, professional, and related	68	70	72	72	25	20	19	18	60	64	67	69
Service	23	22	24	25	7	6	5	6	18	19	22	21
Sales and office	53	51	52	54	16	11	10	9	46	47	49	51
Natural resources, construction, and maintenance	51	48	47	47	26	21	19	16	40	41	39	40
Production, transportation, and material moving	51	53	54	55	24	19	17	15	38	44	47	48
Full-time	59	60	61	61	22	18	16	15	50	54	56	57
Part-time	21	21	22	22	8	5	5	5	15	17	18	19
Union	82	82	82	82	67	66	61	57	44	44	46	48
Nonunion	46	47	48	49	13	9	8	8	41	45	47	47

[1] Total is less than the sum of the individual retirement items because many employees participate in both types of plans.

Source: U.S. Bureau of Labor Statistics, *National Compensation Survey: Employee Benefits in the United States, March 2019*, Bulletin 2791, September 2019, and previous editions. See also <https://www.bls.gov/ncs/ebs/benefits/2019/home.htm>.

Table 580. Households Owning Individual Retirement Accounts (IRAs): 2000 to 2019

[In percent. Prior to 2014, incidence of individual retirement account (IRA) ownership is based on an annual tracking survey of approximately 4,000 randomly selected, representative U.S. households conducted via landline telephones only. Beginning in 2014, the survey was expanded and is based on a dual frame sample of landline and cell phone numbers, for a total of approximately 4,000 to 5,000 U.S. households. See source for details]

Year and characteristic	Any type of IRA [1]	Tradi-tional IRA	Roth IRA	Employer-spon-sored IRA [2]	Year and characteristic	Any type of IRA [1]	Tradi-tional IRA	Roth IRA	Employer-spon-sored IRA [2]
2000	35.7	28.7	9.2	6.8	2017 [3]	34.8	27.8	19.7	6.0
2005	37.9	30.0	12.8	7.4	2018 [3]	33.4	26.0	17.6	5.9
2010	41.4	32.8	16.6	8.0	**2019, total [3, 4]**	**36.1**	**28.1**	**19.4**	**6.1**
2012	40.4	32.5	16.8	7.6	Under 35 years	31.0	19.0	16.0	6.0
2013	37.6	29.4	15.6	7.5	35 to 44 years	37.0	28.0	25.0	6.0
2014 [3]	33.7	25.3	15.6	6.0	45 to 54 years	38.0	30.0	24.0	6.0
2015 [3]	32.3	24.4	16.3	5.4	55 to 64 years	40.0	32.0	21.0	7.0
2016 [3]	33.8	25.5	17.4	5.7	65 years and over	36.0	31.0	14.0	5.0

[1] Excludes ownership of Coverdell Education Savings Accounts, which were referred to as Education IRAs before July 2001. [2] Employer-sponsored IRAs include SEP IRAs, SAR-SEP IRAs, and SIMPLE IRAs. [3] Beginning 2014, lower incidence likely results in part from a revised sampling methodology. See source for details. [4] Age is based on the age of the sole or co-decision maker for household saving and investing.

Source: Investment Company Institute, Washington, DC, Holden, Sarah, and Daniel Schrass, "Appendix: The Role of IRAs in US Households' Saving for Retirement, 2019," ICI Research Perspective 25, No. 10, December 2019 ©. See also <https://www.ici.org/research/retirement>.

Table 581. State and Local Government Retirement Systems—Beneficiaries and Finances: 2015 to 2019

[In billions of dollars (179.9 represents $179,900,000,000), except as indicated. For fiscal years closed during the 12 months ending June 30. Based on the Annual Survey of Public Pensions. Beginning 2015: 1) the universe of local pension systems was enhanced compared to prior survey years, and 2) for state-administered pension plans, each pension fund is treated as a separate unit of analysis rather than as part of a larger system]

Year and level of government	Number of bene- ficiaries (1,000)	Receipts				Benefits and withdrawals			Cash and investment holdings
		Contributions			Earnings on invest- ments	Total benefits paid	Admin- istrative costs	With- drawals	
		Total	Employee	Govern- ment					
2015: All systems.........	9,993	179.9	47.9	132.1	155.8	269.1	(NA)	6.3	3,802.1
State-administered......	8,502	141.1	40.5	100.6	125.9	220.8	(NA)	5.1	3,112.1
Locally administered....	1,491	38.9	7.4	31.5	29.9	48.3	(NA)	1.2	690.0
2017: All systems.........	10,704	201.5	54.6	146.9	81.6	295.1	17.3	7.6	4,032.4
State-administered......	9,141	159.1	46.3	112.8	64.7	242.6	13.3	6.2	3,299.7
Locally administered....	1,563	42.4	8.3	34.1	16.9	52.5	4.1	1.4	732.8
2018: All systems.........	11,043	221.1	55.9	165.2	99.7	310.4	19.3	7.6	4,354.2
State-administered......	9,415	173.6	46.8	126.8	79.9	254.5	14.8	6.3	3,541.4
Locally administered....	1,628	47.6	9.1	38.5	19.8	55.9	4.5	1.4	812.8
2019: All systems......	**11,239**	**226.0**	**58.0**	**168.0**	**94.3**	**323.0**	**20.0**	**7.2**	**4,412.5**
State-administered......	9,633	179.3	49.1	130.2	76.0	264.6	15.6	5.8	3,625.3
Locally administered....	1,606	46.7	8.9	37.8	18.3	58.4	4.4	1.5	787.2

NA Not available.

Source: U.S. Census Bureau, "Federal, State, and Local Governments—Annual Survey of Public Pensions," <https://www.census.gov/programs-surveys/aspp.html>, accessed July 2020.

Table 582. Defined Benefit Retirement Plan Participation Among Workers by Plan Status: 2019

[In percent. All workers participating in defined benefit plans = 100 percent. Based on the March 2019 National Compensation Survey; survey drew responses from 6,470 private industry establishments of all sizes, representing about 120.4 million workers. Excludes farm and private households, the self-employed, Federal government, and establishments with no workers in the survey scope. For more information, see Appendix III, and source <https://www.bls.gov/ncs/ebs/benefits/2019/home.htm>]

Characteristic	Open plans [1]	Frozen plans [2]			Workers in plans frozen over 5 years
		No participants accrue benefits [3]	All participants accrue benefits	Some participants accrue benefits	
All workers.........	**62**	**14**	**21**	**3**	**88**
OCCUPATION					
Management, professional, and related.........	55	17	24	4	90
Management, business, and financial.........	59	20	19	2	91
Professional and related.........	53	15	28	4	89
Service.........	81	7	(S)	(S)	64
Sales and office.........	57	17	23	3	91
Sales and related.........	59	22	18	1	96
Office and administrative support.........	56	16	24	4	90
Natural resources, construction, and maintenance.........	78	6	14	2	87
Construction, extraction, farming, fishing, and forestry.........	89	(S)	7	(S)	96
Installation, maintenance, and repair.........	64	9	23	3	84
Production, transportation, and material moving.........	60	11	24	5	87
Production.........	41	19	33	7	86
Transportation and material moving.........	75	(S)	17	(S)	88
WORK STATUS					
Full time.........	61	15	21	3	89
Part time.........	72	(S)	22	(S)	78
UNION STATUS					
Union.........	79	5	15	1	89
Nonunion.........	50	19	26	5	88
AVERAGE WAGE PERCENTILE [4]					
Lowest 25 percent.........	65	(S)	22	(S)	74
Lowest 10 percent.........	55	(S)	(S)	(S)	(NA)
Second 25 percent.........	65	13	17	5	89
Third 25 percent.........	59	13	24	3	87
Highest 25 percent.........	62	14	21	3	90
Highest 10 percent.........	59	15	22	3	93
INDUSTRY					
Goods-producing industries.........	51	16	26	7	91
Manufacturing.........	31	21	38	11	91
Service-providing industries.........	65	13	20	2	87
Trade, transportation, and utilities.........	69	5	24	2	91
Information.........	34	(S)	47	(S)	95
Financial activities.........	50	25	22	3	87
Professional and business services.........	72	17	(S)	(S)	94
Education and health services.........	64	(S)	22	(S)	75

NA Not available. S No workers in this category or data do not meet publication standards. [1] Plans open to new participants. [2] New employees are not allowed in the plan. Benefit accruals may continue for existing participants. [3] Participants in these plans stopped accruing benefits on the date the plan was frozen. The benefit the employee receives is calculated as of the day the plan was frozen. [4] Based on the average wage for the occupation, which may include workers with earnings both above and below the threshold. For values, see "Technical Note" in source.

Source: U.S. Bureau of Labor Statistics, *National Compensation Survey: Employee Benefits in the United States, March 2019*, Bulletin 2791, September 2019. See also <https://www.bls.gov/ncs/ebs/benefits/2019/home.htm>.

Table 583. Private Pension Plans—Summary by Type of Plan: 2000 to 2017

[In units as indicated (735.7 represents 735,700). Pension plans include defined benefit plans, and defined contribution plans. A defined benefit plan, funded by the employer, promises a specific monthly benefit at retirement, often determined by a formula that includes factors such as salary, age, and job tenure. A defined contribution plan requires the employee to make contributions to an individual account; employers may add contributions to accounts for each employee. The retirement benefit is dependent upon the account balance at retirement, which will reflect contributions, investment gains or losses, and fees charged to the account. Employee Stock Ownership Plans (ESOP) and 401(k) plans are included among defined contribution plans. Data are based on Form 5500 series reports filed with the Department of Labor and exclude (1) selected pension plans qualified under sections 403(b), 457(b) and 457(f) of the Internal Revenue Code, (2) most SARSEP, SEP and SIMPLE IRA plans, (3) unfunded excess benefit plans, (4) selected church plans, (5) unfunded pension plan for select group of management or highly compensated employees, (6) individual retirement accounts (IRAs), and (7) governmental plans]

Item	Unit	Total				Defined contribution plan				Defined benefit plan			
		2000	2005	2010	2017	2000	2005	2010	2017	2000	2005	2010	2017
Number of plans [1]	1,000	735.7	679.1	701.0	709.5	686.9	631.5	654.5	662.8	48.8	47.6	46.5	46.7
Total participants [2]	Million	103.3	117.4	129.7	137.4	61.7	75.5	88.3	102.4	41.6	41.9	41.4	35.0
Active participants [3]	Million	73.1	82.7	90.6	94.6	50.9	62.4	73.4	81.2	22.2	20.3	17.2	13.5
Assets [4]	Bil. dol.	4,203	5,062	6,282	9,759	2,216	2,808	3,833	6,550	1,986	2,254	2,448	3,209
Contributions [5]	Bil. dol.	231.9	341.4	445.3	651.7	198.5	248.8	314.3	492.7	33.4	92.7	131.1	159.0
Benefits [6]	Bil. dol.	341.0	354.5	456.9	737.4	213.5	218.0	287.3	494.0	127.5	136.6	169.6	243.4

[1] Excludes all plans covering only one participant. [2] Includes active, retired, and separated vested participants not yet in pay status. Also includes double counting of workers in more than one plan. [3] Active participants includes individuals who are eligible to elect to have the employer make payments to a 401(k) type plan (even if individuals are not contributing) and nonvested individuals who are earning or retaining credited service under the plan. [4] Asset amounts shown exclude funds held by life insurance companies under allocated group insurance contracts for payment of retirement benefits. [5] Includes both employer and employee contributions. [6] Includes benefits paid directly from trust funds and premium payments made from plans to insurance carriers. Excludes benefits paid directly by insurance carriers.

Source: U.S. Department of Labor, Employee Benefits Security Administration, Retirement Bulletins, *Private Pension Plan Bulletin Historical Tables and Graphs, 1975-2017,* September 2019. See also <https://www.dol.gov/agencies/ebsa/researchers/statistics/retirement-bulletins/private-pension-plan>.

Table 584. Characteristics of U.S. Households Owning Individual Retirement Accounts (IRAs): 2019

[Data are based on a 2019 mutual fund shareholder tracking survey of 1,800 households conducted via landline telephone and of 2,200 households conducted via cell phone; and a 2019 IRA owners survey of 3,228 U.S. households owning traditional or Roth IRAs, conducted via a self-administered survey online. See source for details and changes in methodology]

Characteristic	Unit	Households owning IRAs				House-holds not own-ing IRAs
		Total	Tradi-tional IRA	Roth IRA	Employer-spon-sored [1]	
MEDIAN PER HOUSEHOLD						
Age of household sole or co-decision maker for saving & investing	Years	54	56	51	53	51
Household income [2]	Dollars	99,100	112,500	112,500	97,000	45,000
Household financial assets [3]	Dollars	300,000	350,000	350,000	250,000	30,000
Household financial assets in traditional or Roth IRAs	Dollars	87,500	120,000	87,500	(NA)	(X)
Share of household financial assets in type of IRA indicated	Percent	37	29	12	(NA)	(X)
PERCENT OF HOUSEHOLDS						
Household has defined contribution account or defined benefit plan coverage (total) [4]	Percent	82	83	85	86	43
Defined contribution retirement plan account	Percent	75	73	78	79	34
Defined benefit plan coverage	Percent	37	44	44	36	20
Types of IRAs owned: [4]						
Traditional IRA	Percent	78	100	69	58	(X)
Roth IRA	Percent	54	47	100	43	(X)
Employer-sponsored IRA [1]	Percent	17	13	14	100	(X)

X Not applicable. NA Not available. [1] Employer-sponsored IRAs include SEP IRAs, SAR-SEP IRAs, and SIMPLE IRAs. [2] Total reported is household income before taxes in 2018. [3] Household financial assets include assets in employer-sponsored retirement plans but exclude the household's primary residence. [4] Multiple responses are included.

Source: Investment Company Institute, Washington, DC. Holden, Sarah, and Daniel Schrass, "Appendix: The Role of IRAs in US Households' Saving for Retirement, 2019," *ICI Research Perspective* 25, No. 10, December 2019 ©. See also <https://www.ici.org/pubs/research>.

Table 585. Households with Assets in Individual Retirement Accounts (IRAs) by Type of IRA: 2018 and 2019

[Shown as percent of households with assets in IRAs, by household asset size group. Data are based on an annual survey of approximately 3,200 U.S. households owning traditional IRAs and Roth IRAs, conducted via a self-administered survey online. The IRA Owners Survey excludes households owning only employer-sponsored IRAs (SEP, SAR-SEP, and SIMPLE IRAs) or Coverdell Education Savings Accounts (education IRAs). See source for details]

Size of assets	Unit	2018			2019		
		Total assets in IRAs	Type of IRA owned		Total assets in IRAs	Type of IRA owned	
			Traditional IRAs	Roth IRAs		Traditional IRAs	Roth IRAs
PERCENT DISTRIBUTION OF HOUSEHOLDS							
Less than $10,000.............................	Percent	17	16	27	13	15	22
$10,000 to $24,999............................	Percent	14	15	21	12	14	21
$25,000 to $49,999............................	Percent	13	12	15	12	12	16
$50,000 to $99,999............................	Percent	13	15	14	15	14	18
$100,000 to $249,999........................	Percent	18	19	15	18	20	15
$250,000 or more..............................	Percent	25	23	8	30	25	8
TOTAL ASSETS IN IRAs							
Mean...	Dollars	191,200	178,600	77,400	218,900	194,800	80,700
Median..	Dollars	65,000	62,500	25,000	87,500	70,000	30,000

Source: Investment Company Institute, Washington, DC. Holden, Sarah, and Daniel Schrass, "Appendix: The Role of IRAs in US Households' Saving for Retirement, 2019," *ICI Research Perspective,* 25, No. 10, December 2019 ©, and previous edition. See also <https://www.ici.org/pubs/research>.

Table 586. Defined Contribution 401(k) Type Plans, Active Participants, Assets, Contributions, Benefits, and Return Rates: 1990 to 2017

[Participants in thousands (19,466 represents 19,466,000); values in millions of dollars (384,854 represents $384,854,000,000). Excludes "one-participant plans." Based on Form 5500 filings with Department of Labor. See source for methodology]

Year	Number of 401(k) type plans	Active participants [1] (1,000)	Total assets [2] (mil. dol.)	Total contributions [3] (mil. dol.)	Total benefits [4] (mil. dol.)	Investment rates of return [5]
1990.................	97,614	19,466	384,854	48,998	32,028	(NA)
2000.................	348,053	39,847	1,724,549	169,238	172,211	-3.8
2005.................	436,207	54,623	2,395,792	223,533	189,822	6.3
2006.................	465,653	58,351	2,768,242	251,233	229,217	12.4
2007.................	490,917	59,566	2,981,522	273,235	262,108	7.6
2008.................	511,583	59,976	2,230,188	285,773	233,452	-24.9
2009.................	512,464	60,285	2,734,064	258,357	208,467	18.8
2010.................	518,675	60,510	3,142,141	267,584	245,474	12.0
2011.................	513,496	61,371	3,146,851	285,679	252,692	0.1
2012.................	516,293	63,088	3,530,122	306,092	284,677	11.2
2013.................	527,047	64,495	4,179,351	327,886	328,680	18.3
2014.................	533,769	62,651	4,399,891	349,216	365,657	6.7
2015.................	546,896	65,307	4,382,033	377,743	385,907	0.1
2016.................	560,373	67,121	4,738,481	398,920	391,540	7.6
2017.................	571,841	68,187	5,476,365	429,440	425,013	15.8

NA Not available. [1] Since 2005, includes individuals who are eligible to elect to have the employer make payments to a 401(k) type plan (even if individuals are not contributing), and nonvested individuals who are earning or retaining credited service under the plan. Prior to 2005, active participants were adjusted to exclude individuals who were not contributing to the retirement plan and not entitled to receive benefits. Between 2009 and 2013, all participants reported on the Form 5500-SF were assumed to be active. Since 2014, active participants are separately reported on the Form 5500-SF. [2] Excludes funds held by life insurance companies under allocated group insurance contracts for payment of retirement benefits. [3] Includes both employer and employee contributions. [4] Includes both benefits paid directly from trust funds and premium payments made by plans to insurance carriers. Amounts exclude benefits paid directly by insurance carriers. [5] For plans with 100 or more participants.

Source: U.S. Department of Labor, Employee Benefits Security Administration, Retirement Bulletins, *Private Pension Plan Bulletin Historical Tables and Graphs, 1975-2017,* September 2019. See also <https://www.dol.gov/agencies/ebsa/researchers/statistics/retirement-bulletins/private-pension-plan>.

Table 587. State Unemployment Insurance—Summary: 2000 to 2018

[In units as indicated (2,110 represents 2,110,000). Includes unemployment compensation for state and local government employees where covered by state law]

Item	Unit	2000	2005	2010	2013	2014	2015	2016	2017	2018
Insured unemployment, average weekly.........	1,000	2,110	2,661	4,487	2,947	2,574	2,237	2,099	1,948	1,755
Percent of covered employment [1]...............	Percent	1.7	2.1	3.6	2.2	1.9	1.6	1.5	1.4	1.2
Percent of civilian unemployed.................	Percent	37.1	35.1	30.3	25.7	26.8	27.0	27.1	27.9	27.8
Unemployment benefits, average weekly........	Dollars	221	267	299	309	315	329	344	351	356
Percent of weekly wage.........................	Percent	32.9	34.6	33.7	32.6	32.2	32.6	33.7	33.3	32.7
Weeks compensated...............................	Million	96.0	121.2	203.1	132.2	115.1	100.7	94.8	87.6	79.3
Beneficiaries, first payments.....................	1,000	7,033	7,917	10,727	7,819	7,043	6,506	6,097	5,696	5,166
Average duration of benefits [2]..................	Weeks	13.7	15.3	18.9	16.9	16.3	15.5	15.5	15.4	15.3
Claimants exhausting benefits...................	1,000	2,144	2,856	6,365	3,689	3,029	2,510	2,324	2,120	1,928
Exhaustion rate (percent of first payments) [3]...	Percent	31.8	35.9	53.4	44.6	40.3	37.6	36.7	36.4	35.5
Contributions collected [4]..........................	Bil. dol.	19.9	34.8	35.9	47.2	43.9	41.8	38.9	36.8	34.9
Benefits paid......................................	Bil. dol.	19.4	29.3	53.9	36.3	32.4	29.8	29.5	27.8	25.6
Unemployment trust fund reserves [5].............	Bil. dol.	54.1	29.0	9.5	23.0	30.4	38.8	47.0	55.2	66.6
Average employer tax rate [6].....................	Percent	1.8	2.9	3.0	3.3	2.9	2.7	2.4	2.2	2.0

[1] Insured unemployment as percent of average covered employment. [2] Weeks compensated during the year divided by the number of first payments. May include more than one period of continuous unemployment. [3] Percent of claimants who started receiving unemployment insurance benefits who also received the maximum benefits they were entitled to before the end of their benefit year. Based on first payments for 12-month period ending June 30. [4] Contributions collected through unemployment taxes paid by employers and by employees in states that tax workers. [5] Reserves as of December 31 are the funds on deposit in a State's account, as reported by the U.S. Treasury. Trust fund balances are the major portion of reserves. The reserves for all States have been adjusted to contain amounts loaned or advanced from the Federal Unemployment Account. These advances, which can be used only for the payment of unemployment benefits, must be repaid. [6] As percent of taxable wages.

Source: U.S. Department of Labor, Employment and Training Administration, Unemployment Insurance Data, "Benefits and Claims: Annual Program and Financial Data (Handbook 394)," <https://oui.doleta.gov/unemploy/DataDashboard.asp>, accessed February 2020.

Table 588. State Unemployment Insurance by State and Island Area: 2018

[In units, as indicated (5,166 represents 5,166,000). See headnote, Table 587. For state data on insured unemployment, see Table 662]

State and Island Areas	Bene-ficiaries, first payments (1,000)	Benefits paid (mil. dol.)	Avg. weekly unemploy-ment benefits (dol.)	Average duration of benefits (weeks)	State and Island Areas	Bene-ficiaries, first payments (1,000)	Benefits paid (mil. dol.)	Avg. weekly unemploy-ment benefits (dol.)	Average duration of benefits (weeks)
Total [1].....	5,166	25,642	356	15.3	MT...........	21	94	345	15.4
AL...........	51	146	223	13.3	NE...........	17	67	336	12.0
AK...........	20	92	265	17.9	NV...........	56	277	350	15.1
AZ...........	64	217	231	15.3	NH...........	12	49	334	12.5
AR...........	36	93	266	11.2	NJ...........	251	1,751	451	18.1
CA...........	886	4,855	329	17.6	NM...........	23	114	332	17.4
CO...........	65	376	430	13.9	NY...........	385	1,941	344	16.9
CT...........	105	585	392	16.8	NC...........	75	161	258	8.9
DE...........	14	62	261	17.2	ND...........	15	91	463	13.4
DC...........	19	111	352	18.6	OH...........	157	796	373	14.9
FL...........	154	349	248	9.2	OK...........	35	195	364	16.5
GA...........	134	293	291	8.0	OR...........	79	464	397	15.1
HI...........	21	145	508	15.1	PA...........	315	1,639	379	15.6
ID...........	27	76	322	9.8	RI...........	28	145	357	14.8
IL...........	274	1,549	382	16.5	SC...........	49	157	257	12.5
IN...........	68	239	294	12.5	SD...........	5	26	337	14.6
IA...........	74	362	399	12.8	TN...........	57	198	238	15.1
KS...........	33	98	378	11.6	TX...........	340	1,826	401	15.6
KY...........	46	274	341	18.8	UT...........	30	135	410	12.3
LA...........	41	168	212	16.1	VT...........	14	58	364	13.5
ME...........	20	84	335	13.1	VA...........	63	275	310	14.9
MD...........	73	421	348	18.4	WA...........	127	848	467	16.0
MA...........	168	1,320	520	17.4	WV...........	33	126	291	14.2
MI...........	202	738	309	12.1	WI...........	107	370	321	12.7
MN...........	106	700	457	16.5	WY...........	9	43	373	14.0
MS...........	24	59	208	13.5	PR...........	48	107	118	19.3
MO...........	84	257	265	12.3	VI...........	2	19	313	27.2

[1] Includes all States, District of Columbia, Puerto Rico, and Virgin Islands.

Source: U.S. Department of Labor, Employment and Training Administration, Unemployment Insurance Data, "Benefits and Claims: Annual Program and Financial Data (Handbook 394)," <https://oui.doleta.gov/unemploy/DataDashboard.asp>, accessed February 2020.

Table 589. Workers' Compensation Costs and Payments: 2000 to 2017

[In units as indicated (127.1 represents 127,100,000). See headnote, Table 590]

Item	2000	2005	2009	2010	2011	2012	2013	2014	2015	2016	2017
Workers covered (mil.)...................	127.1	128.2	124.9	124.6	125.9	127.9	130.6	133.1	136.0	138.5	140.4
Covered wages (bil. dol.)..................	4,495	5,213	5,675	5,834	6,058	6,335	6,509	6,840	7,206	7,432	7,785
Employer costs [1] (bil. dol.).............	**60.7**	**89.8**	**73.9**	**72.8**	**78.9**	**84.7**	**89.2**	**93.5**	**96.1**	**97.0**	**97.4**
Private carriers [1].......................	36.0	51.0	43.0	42.8	46.6	51.3	55.0	57.3	59.2	60.2	60.7
State funds............................	8.9	18.2	10.6	9.6	10.4	11.0	12.1	13.3	13.3	13.1	12.2
Federal programs [2].....................	3.6	4.1	4.1	4.2	4.4	4.5	4.6	4.9	5.4	5.7	6.1
Self-insured employers...................	12.1	16.5	16.3	16.2	17.5	17.9	17.5	18.0	18.1	18.1	18.3
Benefits paid [3] (bil. dol.)...............	**47.7**	**57.1**	**58.4**	**58.5**	**61.4**	**62.7**	**63.4**	**63.1**	**62.3**	**62.1**	**62.0**
By private carriers......................	26.9	29.0	30.9	31.1	33.0	33.9	35.2	35.0	34.5	34.6	34.4
From state funds......	7.4	11.1	10.0	9.8	9.8	10.0	9.5	9.2	9.0	8.9	8.8
Federal programs [2].....................	3.0	3.3	3.5	3.7	3.8	3.8	3.7	3.7	3.7	3.6	3.5
Self-insured employers...................	10.5	13.7	14.0	13.9	14.8	15.0	15.0	15.2	15.0	15.0	15.3
Type of benefit:											
Medical.............................	20.9	26.4	28.2	28.7	30.8	31.3	32.1	32.1	31.4	31.2	30.9
Cash................................	26.8	30.7	30.3	29.8	30.6	31.4	31.3	31.0	30.9	30.9	31.1
Per $100 of covered wages: (dol.)											
Employer costs.......................	1.35	1.72	1.30	1.25	1.30	1.34	1.37	1.37	1.33	1.31	1.25
Benefits paid........................	1.06	1.09	1.03	1.00	1.01	0.99	0.97	0.92	0.86	0.84	0.80

[1] Costs are employer expenditures in the calendar year for workers' compensation benefits, administrative costs, and/or insurance premiums; for private carriers, includes benefit payments made under deductible provisions. [2] Federal costs and benefits include costs to the federal government and benefits paid, under the Federal Employees' Compensation Act, and costs associated with and benefits paid via the Federal Black Lung Disability Trust Fund. Beginning 1997, data also account for the Longshore and Harbor Workers' Compensation Act. [3] Benefits are payments in the calendar year to injured workers and to providers of their medical care, including benefits paid by employers under deductible provisions in their workers' compensation insurance.

Source: National Academy of Social Insurance, Washington, DC, *Workers' Compensation: Benefits, Costs, and Coverage, 2017,* October 2019, and earlier reports ©. See also <http://www.nasi.org>.

Table 590. Workers' Compensation Payments by State: 2000 to 2017

[In millions of dollars (47,699 represents $47,699,000,000). Calendar-year data. Workers' compensation provides medical care, rehabilitation, and cash benefits for workers who are injured on the job or who contract work-related illnesses. It also pays benefits to families of workers who die of work-related causes. Workers' compensation benefits are paid by private insurance carriers, by state or federal workers' compensation funds, or by self-insured employers. See source for data estimation methodology]

State	2000	2010	2015	2016	2017	State	2000	2010	2015	2016	2017
Total...................	**47,699**	**58,939**	**62,266**	**62,108**	**62,016**	Missouri..................	780	801	1,002	1,026	1,071
						Montana.................	155	266	253	261	254
Alabama................	529	629	617	601	600	Nebraska................	230	316	301	314	310
Alaska..................	139	222	241	226	226	Nevada..................	347	430	340	353	353
Arizona.................	498	702	736	752	744	New Hampshire.........	177	252	214	206	207
Arkansas................	214	214	199	197	215	New Jersey.............	1,378	2,067	2,344	2,357	2,387
California...............	9,449	10,099	12,018	12,142	12,134	New Mexico.............	144	276	327	309	297
Colorado................	810	800	829	800	811	New York................	2,761	4,617	5,866	5,957	6,191
Connecticut.............	638	795	982	895	911	North Carolina..........	865	1,357	1,217	1,204	1,115
Delaware...............	118	212	228	225	222	North Dakota...........	70	120	181	166	157
District of Columbia.....	78	105	120	120	130	Ohio....................	2,099	2,209	1,931	1,841	1,757
Florida..................	2,577	2,777	3,315	3,312	3,432	Oklahoma...............	485	843	708	604	567
Georgia.................	965	1,459	1,314	1,377	1,372	Oregon.................	425	681	632	630	689
Hawaii..................	231	242	298	306	325	Pennsylvania...........	2,379	2,935	2,975	3,124	2,818
Idaho...................	114	240	263	268	283	Rhode Island...........	127	160	162	157	156
Illinois..................	1,944	3,003	2,401	2,356	2,314	South Carolina..........	515	891	890	905	926
Indiana.................	545	599	566	576	595	South Dakota...........	63	100	107	105	100
Iowa....................	343	564	618	664	658	Tennessee..............	774	781	723	688	662
Kansas.................	323	405	424	424	425	Texas..................	2,160	1,491	1,537	1,468	1,424
Kentucky...............	584	663	671	640	599	Utah....................	172	275	269	275	274
Louisiana...............	547	802	775	796	799	Vermont.................	101	137	150	140	144
Maine..................	245	252	232	241	255	Virginia..................	597	786	919	946	968
Maryland...............	641	954	965	908	933	Washington.............	1,527	2,309	2,412	2,437	2,465
Massachusetts..........	801	1,016	1,089	1,139	1,205	West Virginia...........	661	543	414	429	413
Michigan...............	1,474	1,272	1,078	957	920	Wisconsin..............	765	1,072	1,167	1,172	1,170
Minnesota..............	798	1,035	1,033	1,029	1,057	Wyoming................	89	154	178	175	176
Mississippi..............	293	338	332	306	318	**Federal, total [1]**.........	**2,957**	**3,672**	**3,706**	**3,603**	**3,483**

[1] Federal benefits include: those paid under the Federal Employees' Compensation Act for civilian employees; the portion of the black lung benefit program that is financed by employers; and a portion of benefits under the Longshore and Harbor Workers' Compensation Act (LHWCA) that are not reflected in state data, namely, benefits paid by self-insured employers and by special funds under the LHWCA. See Appendix B in source for more information about federal programs.

Source: National Academy of Social Insurance, Washington, DC, *Workers' Compensation: Benefits, Costs, and Coverage, 2017*, October 2019, and earlier reports ©. See also <http://www.nasi.org>.

Table 591. Supplemental Security Income (SSI)—Recipients and Payments: 1990 to 2018

[In units as indicated (4,817 represents 4,817,000). Recipients and monthly payment as of December. Payments are federally administered, for the calendar year. Includes persons with a federal SSI payment and/or state supplementation]

Program	Unit	1990	2000	2005	2010	2014	2015	2016	2017	2018
Recipients, total.............	**1,000**	**4,817**	**6,602**	**7,114**	**7,912**	**8,336**	**8,310**	**8,251**	**8,228**	**8,129**
Aged.............................	1,000	1,454	1,289	1,214	1,184	1,152	1,157	1,165	1,176	1,169
Blind.............................	1,000	84	79	75	69	67	68	68	69	69
Disabled.......................	1,000	3,279	5,234	5,825	6,659	7,116	7,084	7,018	6,982	6,891
Payments, total [1].............	**Mil. dol.**	**16,133**	**30,672**	**37,236**	**48,195**	**54,693**	**54,966**	**54,799**	**54,516**	**54,847**
Aged.............................	Mil. dol.	3,559	4,540	4,965	5,454	5,688	5,729	5,797	5,838	5,924
Blind.............................	Mil. dol.	329	386	414	423	440	448	455	458	463
Disabled.......................	Mil. dol.	12,245	25,746	31,857	42,317	48,565	48,788	48,547	48,220	48,460
Average monthly payment....	**Dollars**	**276**	**379**	**439**	**501**	**532**	**541**	**542**	**542**	**551**
Aged.............................	Dollars	208	300	360	400	420	428	429	429	437
Blind.............................	Dollars	319	413	475	522	548	558	560	560	569
Disabled.......................	Dollars	303	398	455	518	550	560	561	561	570

[1] Totals for Aged, Blind, and Disabled are derived. The derivation creates slight discrepancies between the sum of the group totals and total payments.

Source: U.S. Social Security Administration, *Annual Statistical Supplement to the Social Security Bulletin, 2019,* November 2019. See also <https://www.ssa.gov/policy/docs/statcomps/supplement/index.html>.

Table 592. Supplemental Security Income (SSI)—Recipients and Payments by State and Other Area: 2010 to 2018

[In units as indicated (7,912 represents 7,912,000). Recipients as of December; payments for calendar year. Data cover federal SSI payments and/or federally administered state supplementation]

State and other area	Recipients (1,000)		Payments for the year (mil. dol.)			State and other area	Recipients (1,000)		Payments for the year (mil. dol.)		
	2010	2018	2010	2017	2018		2010	2018	2010	2017	2018
Total [1]....	**7,912**	**8,129**	**48,195**	**54,516**	**54,847**	MO.........	134	136	785	875	886
U.S.........	7,911	8,128	48,189	54,509	54,840	MT.........	18	18	98	110	112
AL..........	172	162	996	1,049	1,046	NE.........	26	28	144	175	180
AK..........	12	13	70	78	79	NV.........	41	56	241	374	382
AZ..........	110	119	644	781	787	NH.........	18	19	103	120	118
AR..........	107	105	603	695	691	NJ.........	169	180	1,001	1,158	1,172
CA..........	1,269	1,240	8,870	9,442	9,384	NM.........	60	63	340	402	401
CO..........	66	73	377	470	478	NY.........	681	629	4,445	4,123	4,146
CT..........	58	66	340	429	442	NC.........	219	229	1,243	1,497	1,503
DE..........	16	17	91	111	115	ND.........	8	8	43	50	52
DC..........	24	26	153	187	184	OH.........	286	308	1,784	2,072	2,097
FL..........	484	576	2,760	3,688	3,747	OK.........	94	96	541	624	633
GA..........	228	259	1,317	1,692	1,714	OR.........	75	88	439	580	590
HI..........	25	23	157	162	163	PA.........	358	356	2,229	2,459	2,457
ID..........	27	31	155	196	199	RI.........	33	33	201	213	214
IL..........	273	267	1,662	1,805	1,808	SC.........	112	115	635	743	751
IN..........	118	127	716	863	871	SD.........	14	15	75	91	92
IA..........	48	51	266	317	326	TN.........	175	176	1,023	1,164	1,171
KS..........	46	48	269	309	315	TX.........	617	650	3,316	4,026	4,063
KY..........	192	174	1,116	1,128	1,127	UT.........	28	31	160	207	210
LA..........	175	175	989	1,136	1,150	VT.........	15	15	87	98	99
ME..........	35	37	196	233	235	VA.........	148	156	832	1,007	1,021
MD..........	107	121	658	840	843	WA.........	137	149	881	1,016	1,027
MA..........	193	184	1,211	1,186	1,186	WV.........	80	72	472	478	481
MI..........	254	272	1,581	1,861	1,882	WI.........	107	117	625	779	783
MN..........	86	93	516	623	636	WY [2].........	6	7	35	41	42
MS..........	126	117	699	746	747	MP [2]........	1	1	6	7	7

[1] Includes Northern Mariana Islands and recipients whose residence was "unknown." Total may not equal sum due to rounding. [2] Northern Marianas.

Source: U.S. Social Security Administration, *Annual Statistical Supplement to the Social Security Bulletin, 2019*, November 2019, and previous editions, <https://www.ssa.gov/policy/docs/statcomps/supplement/index.html>.

Table 593. Temporary Assistance for Needy Families (TANF)—Families and Recipients: 1980 to 2019

[In thousands (3,712 represents 3,712,000). Average monthly families and recipients for the calendar year through 2018; beginning with 2019, data are shown for the fiscal year ending in September. Prior to TANF, the cash assistance program to families was called Aid to Families with Dependent Children (1980–1996). Under the Personal Responsibility and Work Opportunity Reconciliation Act of 1996, the program became TANF. See text, this section. Includes Puerto Rico, Guam, and Virgin Islands]

Year	Families	Recipients	Year	Families	Recipients	Year	Families	Recipients
1980.........	3,712	10,774	2004.........	1,979	4,748	2012.........	1,723	4,017
1990.........	4,057	11,695	2005.........	1,894	4,469	2013.........	1,612	3,713
1998.........	3,050	8,347	2006.........	1,777	4,148	2014.........	1,476	3,407
1999.........	2,554	6,824	2007.........	1,674	3,897	2015.........	1,300	3,010
2000.........	2,215	5,778	2008.........	1,633	3,795	2016.........	1,174	2,678
2001.........	2,104	5,359	2009.........	1,769	4,154	2017.........	1,075	2,486
2002.........	2,048	5,069	2010.........	1,858	4,403	2018.........	984	2,197
2003.........	2,024	4,929	2011.........	1,846	4,363	2019 [1].........	920	2,045

[1] Data are for the fiscal year ending in September of the year shown.

Source: U.S. Department of Health and Human Services, Administration for Children and Families, "Temporary Assistance for Needy Families, Caseload Data," <https://www.acf.hhs.gov/ofa/programs/tanf>, accessed May 2020.

Table 594. Temporary Assistance for Needy Families (TANF)—Recipients by State and Island Area: 2010 to 2019

[In thousands (1,858.2 represents 1,858,200). Average monthly families and recipients for the calendar year through 2018; beginning with 2019, data are shown for the fiscal year ending in September. See headnote, Table 593]

State and Island Area	Families 2010	Families 2018	Families 2019 [1]	Recipients 2010	Recipients 2018	Recipients 2019 [1]	State and Island Area	Families 2010	Families 2018	Families 2019 [1]	Recipients 2010	Recipients 2018	Recipients 2019 [1]
Total [2]......	1,858.2	983.8	920.0	4,402.9	2,197.5	2,044.8	MT............	3.7	3.9	3.4	9.4	9.7	8.3
U.S...........	1,842.9	977.5	914.7	4,361.3	2,180.6	2,030.3	NE............	7.6	4.2	3.9	18.3	10.0	9.1
AL...........	22.0	8.2	7.6	53.5	18.4	17.1	NV............	10.5	9.3	8.3	27.1	23.6	20.9
AK...........	3.4	2.7	2.4	9.3	7.2	6.5	NH............	5.3	3.3	3.5	11.0	6.8	7.2
AZ...........	27.7	7.3	7.0	60.3	14.9	14.0	NJ............	33.9	10.9	9.3	80.7	24.8	21.0
AR...........	8.5	2.9	2.5	19.3	6.2	5.6	NM............	20.3	10.4	10.0	53.5	25.9	24.8
CA...........	583.9	316.6	290.3	1,437.4	767.1	700.6	NY............	121.8	89.8	84.1	272.3	203.0	189.4
CO...........	11.4	14.4	14.2	29.3	36.1	35.1	NC............	23.9	14.9	13.6	45.8	25.5	22.8
CT...........	17.1	9.6	8.2	34.0	23.0	16.9	ND............	2.0	1.0	0.9	5.1	2.5	2.3
DE...........	5.4	3.7	3.5	15.4	10.3	9.7	OH............	103.5	49.9	51.2	238.4	90.7	92.5
DC...........	8.1	5.0	6.9	18.5	13.7	19.4	OK............	9.3	6.3	6.0	21.0	13.9	13.3
FL...........	57.6	41.9	39.7	105.5	66.3	62.1	OR............	28.0	15.0	14.6	72.2	33.3	32.9
GA...........	20.4	10.7	9.5	37.8	20.7	17.8	PA............	53.6	45.7	41.5	130.4	113.0	102.0
HI...........	9.1	4.5	4.2	25.9	12.2	11.5	RI............	7.2	4.2	4.0	16.8	10.0	9.7
ID...........	1.8	2.0	2.0	2.7	3.0	3.0	SC............	18.6	8.1	8.1	43.8	17.6	17.8
IL...........	23.4	11.3	10.8	66.2	22.2	21.5	SD............	3.2	3.0	2.9	6.8	6.0	5.8
IN...........	35.1	6.1	5.4	86.2	12.1	10.7	TN............	61.5	21.8	19.6	157.2	47.3	41.8
IA...........	17.9	8.4	7.6	45.7	20.0	17.9	TX............	51.2	25.7	23.5	116.7	55.3	50.1
KS...........	14.8	4.2	3.8	38.3	4.2	3.8	UT............	6.5	3.5	3.2	17.6	8.3	7.5
KY...........	30.5	19.2	17.4	62.0	37.9	34.8	VT............	2.9	2.4	2.2	6.3	4.9	4.6
LA...........	10.6	5.6	4.9	23.7	13.8	11.9	VA............	35.2	20.1	19.2	79.3	33.9	32.5
ME...........	11.1	3.3	3.1	26.2	7.5	7.3	WA............	66.7	25.4	25.1	161.7	55.1	54.3
MD...........	24.7	17.5	16.5	59.6	43.1	40.6	WV............	10.0	6.6	6.4	22.5	12.9	12.5
MA...........	49.7	27.9	28.0	97.5	52.3	57.0	WI............	22.9	15.1	14.4	53.2	31.9	29.6
MI...........	68.1	12.5	11.4	178.5	30.4	27.9	WY............	0.3	0.5	0.5	0.7	1.2	1.2
MN...........	23.1	17.2	16.0	49.5	40.8	37.7	GU............	1.3	0.5	0.5	3.0	1.1	1.0
MS...........	12.0	4.2	3.4	25.3	8.3	6.6	PR............	13.5	5.6	4.8	37.1	15.2	13.1
MO...........	35.8	9.6	8.7	86.2	21.5	19.5	VI............	0.5	0.2	0.1	1.5	0.5	0.4

[1] Data are for the fiscal year ending in September of the year shown. [2] Includes Puerto Rico (PR), Guam (GU), and the Virgin Islands (VI).

Source: U.S. Department of Health and Human Services, Administration for Children and Families, Temporary Assistance for Needy Families, "Caseload Data," <https://www.acf.hhs.gov/ofa/programs/tanf>, accessed May 2020.

Table 595. Household Use of Food Pantries and Emergency (Soup) Kitchens: 2018

[In thousands (128,879 represents 128,879,000), except percent. Based on the 2018 Current Population Survey Food Security Supplement that asked questions about use of food pantries and emergency kitchens among households with incomes below 185 percent of the Federal poverty level, and households above this level that indicated difficulty in meeting food needs. Covers the use of food pantries and emergency kitchens at least once during the 12-month period ended December 2018, for persons occupying housing units; survey excludes homeless persons, and may also miss persons in tenuous housing arrangements (such as temporarily living with another family)]

Category	Food pantries Total households [1]	Food pantries Number of users	Food pantries Percent using	Emergency (soup) kitchens Total households [1]	Emergency (soup) kitchens Number of users	Emergency (soup) kitchens Percent using
All households......................	**128,879**	**5,687**	**4.4**	**128,870**	**657**	**0.5**
All persons in households........................	321,970	14,600	4.5	321,897	1,230	0.4
Adults in households............................	248,718	10,118	4.1	248,664	986	0.4
Children in households...........................	73,252	4,482	6.1	73,233	244	0.3
Households by food security status: [2]						
Food-secure households........................	114,688	1,949	1.7	114,670	162	0.1
Food-insecure households........................	14,129	3,737	26.4	14,150	494	3.5
Households with low food security.............	8,637	1,852	21.4	8,657	147	1.7
Households with very low food security........	5,492	1,886	34.3	5,492	347	6.3

[1] Totals exclude households that did not answer questions about using food pantries and emergency kitchens, and also households that did not answer questions about food security. [2] Food secure households report zero or 1-2 indications, typically anxiety over food sufficiency or supply, with little or no indication of changes in diets or food intake. Households with low food security report reduced quality, variety, or desirability of diet, with little or no indication of reduced food intake. Households with very low food security report multiple indications of disrupted eating patterns and reduced food intake. See also headnote, Table 218.

Source: U.S. Department of Agriculture, Economic Research Service, *Statistical Supplement to Household Food Security in the United States in 2018*, No. 081, September 2019. See also <https://www.ers.usda.gov/topics/food-nutrition-assistance/food-security-in-the-us.aspx>.

Table 596. Temporary Assistance for Needy Families (TANF)—Expenditures by State: Fiscal Years 2000 to 2018

[In millions of dollars (24,781 represents $24,781,000,000). Represents federal and state funds expended in fiscal year. Negative values occur when contracted obligations are fulfilled or terminated and the actual cost for the service is less than the obligated amount. Expenditures on basic assistance includes cash, payments, vouchers, and other forms of benefits designed to meet a family's ongoing basic needs (food, clothing, shelter, utilities, household goods, personal care items, and general incidental expenses)]

State	2000, Total	2010, Total	2018 Total [1]	2018 Expenditures on basic assistance	State	2000, Total	2010, Total	2018 Total [1]	2018 Expenditures on basic assistance
U.S.	24,781	33,255	28,720	6,711	MO	321	405	399	36
AL	96	191	174	20	MT	44	47	49	25
AK	93	62	81	42	NE	79	98	88	26
AZ	261	350	314	42	NV	69	108	103	38
AR	139	233	165	4	NH	73	86	83	31
CA	6,481	7,239	6,231	2,330	NJ	321	1,446	1,280	82
CO	205	323	369	56	NM	149	237	215	55
CT	436	500	472	50	NY	3,512	5,347	4,734	1,490
DE	55	75	117	14	NC	440	563	513	37
DC	157	251	286	114	ND	33	37	43	4
FL	781	901	775	160	OH	995	1,331	1,068	237
GA	386	563	489	96	OK	130	179	108	29
HI	162	378	189	29	OR	169	392	276	83
ID	43	35	41	8	PA	1,327	964	940	167
IL	879	1,255	1,142	32	RI	172	149	141	25
IN	342	344	353	15	SC	245	180	165	53
IA	163	194	172	34	SD	21	31	31	15
KS	151	207	155	13	TN	293	338	138	18
KY	203	281	262	172	TX	727	908	831	53
LA	118	264	209	20	UT	100	132	96	19
ME	108	141	105	30	VT	62	78	79	14
MD	336	564	478	112	VA	418	299	248	68
MA	690	1,022	958	197	WA	535	1,494	946	136
MI	1,264	1,703	1,318	169	WV	134	199	116	26
MN	381	475	520	86	WI	382	524	504	82
MS	62	106	126	7	WY	34	29	24	9

[1] In addition to basic assistance, TANF provides funding for numerous additional activities covering work, education and training, work supports (including assistance for transportation, and work-related supplies and fees), financial education, supportive counseling services, child care and early education, child welfare services, prevention of out-of-wedlock pregnancies, and other services, as well as funding for program management.

Source: U.S. Department of Health and Human Services, Administration for Children and Families, "Temporary Assistance for Needy Families, Expenditure Data," <http://www.acf.hhs.gov/programs/ofa/programs/tanf/data-reports>, accessed May 2020.

Table 597. Federal Food Programs: Fiscal Years 1990 to 2019

[20.0 represents 20,000,000, except as noted. For fiscal years ending September 30. Program data include Puerto Rico, Virgin Islands, Guam, American Samoa, Northern Marianas, and the former Trust Territory when a federal food program was operated in these areas. Participation data are average monthly figures except as noted. Participants are not reported for The Emergency Food Assistance Program (TEFAP)]

Program	Unit	1990	2000	2005	2010	2016	2017	2018	2019 (P)
Supplemental nutrition assistance program: [1]									
Participants	Million	20.0	17.2	25.6	40.3	44.2	42.2	40.0	35.7
Value of benefits	Mil. dol.	14,143	14,983	28,568	64,702	66,539	63,711	60,408	55,084
Average monthly benefit value per recipient	Dollars	59	73	93	134	125	126	126	129
Nutrition assistance program for Puerto Rico: [2]									
Federal grant	Mil. dol.	937	1,268	1,495	2,001	1,959	1,949	1,920	1,924
National school lunch program (NSLP):									
Children participating [3]	Million	24.1	27.3	29.6	31.8	30.4	30.0	29.6	29.5
Free lunches served	Million	1,662	2,205	2,477	2,948	3,366	3,282	3,331	3,320
Reduced-price lunches served	Million	273	409	479	498	336	315	287	279
Federal cost (cash payments)	Mil. dol.	3,214	5,493	7,055	9,752	12,259	12,251	12,580	12,834
School breakfast (SB):									
Children participating [3]	Million	4.1	7.6	9.4	11.7	14.6	14.7	14.7	14.7
Federal cash payments	Mil. dol.	599	1,393	1,927	2,859	4,212	4,252	4,396	4,527
Special supplemental food program for Women, Infants, and Children (WIC): [4]									
Participants	Million	4.5	7.2	8.0	9.2	7.7	7.3	6.9	6.4
Federal cost for food	Mil. dol.	1,637	2,853	3,603	4,562	3,950	3,606	3,377	3,142
Child and adult care (CACFP): [5]									
Participants [6]	Million	1.5	2.7	3.1	3.4	4.4	4.5	4.6	4.7
Federal cash payments	Mil. dol.	719	1,500	1,904	2,398	3,217	3,240	3,322	3,424
Federal cost of food commodities for: [7]									
School food programs [8]	Mil. dol.	617	655	975	1,128	1,311	1,393	1,243	1,330
The Emergency Food Assistance Program (TEFAP) [9]	Mil. dol.	282	182	314	566	586	578	540	621

P Preliminary. [1] The program name was changed from Food Stamp to Supplemental Nutrition Assistance (SNAP) in October 2008. [2] Puerto Rico receives a grant in lieu of SNAP benefits. [3] Average participation per day are 9-month averages (excludes summer months). Includes children in public and nonprofit private elementary and secondary schools and in residential child care institutions. [4] WIC serves pregnant and postpartum women, infants, and children up to age 5. [5] CACFP provides year-round subsidies to feed preschool children and elderly and disabled adults in day care centers, and children and youth in emergency shelters for the homeless and eligible afterschool care programs. [6] Average quarterly daily attendance at participating institutions. [7] Includes the federal cost of commodity entitlements, cash-in-lieu of commodities, and bonus foods. [8] National school lunch and breakfast programs, and special milk program. [9] Emergency food assistance is food made available to hunger relief organizations such as food banks and soup kitchens. It is not disaster relief.

Source: U.S. Department of Agriculture, Food and Nutrition Service, "Program Data, Overview," <https://www.fns.usda.gov/pd/overview>, accessed January 2020.

Table 598. Supplemental Nutrition Assistance Program (SNAP) by State: 2000 to 2019

[17,194 represents 17,194,000; 14,983 represents $14,983,000,000. Participation data are average monthly number participating in fiscal year ending September 30. The Food Stamp Program was renamed the Supplemental Nutrition Assistance Program (SNAP) in October 2008]

State	Persons (1,000) 2000	2010	2019	Benefits (mil. dol.) 2000	2010	2019	State	Persons (1,000) 2000	2010	2019	Benefits (mil. dol.) 2000	2010	2019
Total [1]	17,194	40,302	34,474	14,983	64,702	53,761	MS	276	576	421	226	847	606
							MO	423	901	639	358	1,361	998
U.S.	17,156	40,245	34,412	14,927	64,562	53,616	MT	59	114	99	51	177	147
AL	396	805	667	344	1,226	1,032	NE	82	163	149	61	238	222
AK	38	76	79	46	159	171	NV	61	278	392	57	415	588
AZ	259	1,018	737	240	1,588	1,147	NH	36	104	70	28	152	93
AR	247	467	355	206	686	460	NJ	345	622	649	304	1,030	954
CA	1,831	3,239	3,529	1,639	5,692	5,977	NM	169	357	415	140	542	633
CO	156	405	415	127	688	639	NY	1,439	2,758	2,662	1,361	4,985	4,340
CT	165	336	340	138	570	585	NC	488	1,346	(NA)	403	2,072	(NA)
DE	32	113	120	31	171	178	ND	32	60	45	25	95	69
DC	81	118	101	77	196	172	OH	610	1,607	1,273	520	2,734	2,020
FL	882	2,603	2,650	771	4,417	4,035	OK	253	582	532	208	900	820
GA	559	1,591	1,333	489	2,565	2,115	OR	234	705	555	198	1,067	884
HI	118	138	145	166	358	449	PA	777	1,575	1,628	656	2,333	2,514
ID	58	194	136	46	300	193	RI	74	139	141	59	238	244
IL	817	1,646	1,639	777	2,784	2,646	SC	295	797	559	249	1,256	855
IN	300	813	530	268	1,291	820	SD	43	95	75	37	153	122
IA	123	340	296	100	526	429	TN	496	1,224	832	415	1,966	1,307
KS	117	270	185	83	403	265	TX	1,333	3,552	3,187	1,215	5,447	4,767
KY	403	778	502	337	1,186	739	UT	82	247	161	68	367	235
LA	500	826	750	448	1,286	1,215	VT	41	86	68	32	124	100
ME	102	230	144	81	356	204	VA	336	786	655	263	1,213	1,002
MD	219	561	570	199	878	879	WA	295	956	833	241	1,387	1,192
MA	232	749	704	182	1,166	1,131	WV	227	341	283	185	487	398
MI	603	1,776	1,182	457	2,809	1,701	WI	193	715	572	129	1,000	779
MN	196	430	382	165	625	510	WY	22	35	24	19	52	36

NA Not available. [1] Includes Guam and the Virgin Islands. Puerto Rico, American Samoa, and the Northern Marianas, which receive nutrition assistance grants in lieu of SNAP.

Source: U.S. Department of Agriculture, Food and Nutrition Service, Supplemental Nutrition Assistance Program (SNAP), "National and/or State Level Monthly and/or Annual Data," <https://www.fns.usda.gov/pd/supplemental-nutrition-assistance-program-snap>, accessed January 2020.

Table 599. Supplemental Nutrition Assistance Program (SNAP) Households and Participants by Type: 1990 to 2018

[7,811 represents 7,811,000. For fiscal years ending September 30. Data for 1990 exclude Guam and the Virgin Islands. The Food Stamp Program was renamed Supplemental Nutrition Assistance Program (SNAP) in October 2008. Based on a sample of households from the SNAP Quality Control System]

Fiscal year	Households Total [1] (1,000)	Percent of total Children	Elderly [2]	Disabled [3]	Participants Total (1,000)	Percent of total Children	Elderly [2]
1990	7,811	60.3	18.1	8.9	20,440	49.6	7.7
1995	10,883	59.7	16.0	18.9	26,955	51.5	7.1
1996	10,552	59.5	16.2	20.2	25,926	51.0	7.3
1997	9,452	58.3	17.6	22.3	23,117	51.4	7.9
1998	8,246	58.3	18.2	24.4	19,969	52.8	8.2
1999	7,670	55.7	20.1	26.4	18,149	51.5	9.4
2000	7,252	54.6	20.4	26.7	16,916	51.6	9.6
2001	7,276	54.2	19.7	26.6	16,850	51.3	9.3
2002	8,010	55.1	17.9	25.7	18,608	51.4	8.5
2003	8,971	55.1	17.1	22.1	20,764	50.8	8.1
2004	10,069	54.3	17.3	22.7	23,279	50.0	8.2
2005	10,852	53.7	17.1	23.0	24,794	49.9	8.3
2006	11,313	52.0	17.9	23.1	25,472	49.1	8.7
2007	11,561	51.0	17.8	23.8	25,775	48.9	8.8
2008	12,464	50.6	18.5	22.6	27,607	48.4	9.1
2009	14,981	49.9	16.6	21.2	32,889	47.5	8.3
2010	18,369	48.7	15.5	19.8	39,759	46.6	7.9
2011	20,803	47.1	16.5	20.2	44,148	45.1	8.5
2012	22,046	45.3	17.2	20.0	46,022	44.5	9.0
2013	22,802	44.8	17.4	20.3	47,098	44.4	9.3
2014	22,445	43.6	19.0	20.4	45,874	44.2	10.1
2015	22,293	42.7	19.6	20.2	45,184	44.0	10.6
2016	21,511	42.9	21.8	20.3	43,539	44.1	11.8
2017	20,597	41.7	24.1	20.8	41,491	43.5	13.1
2018	19,699	40.9	25.9	20.7	39,271	43.6	14.2

[1] Total excludes those who are ineligible and those receiving disaster benefits. [2] Persons age 60 and over. [3] Non-elderly individuals with disabilities. The fluctuations in 1995 and 2003 are in part due to changes in the definition of a household with an individual with a disability. Changes involve primarily raising and lowering the age to be considered "nonelderly," and the inclusion of households receiving supplemental security income and/or other government benefits due to a disability. Additional changes in definitions were made in 2015 and 2016. See source, appendix A, for details.

Source: U.S. Department of Agriculture, Food and Nutrition Service, *Characteristics of Supplemental Nutrition Assistance Program Households: Fiscal Year 2018*, Report No. SNAP-19-CHAR, November 2019. See also <https://www.fns.usda.gov/research-analysis>.

Table 600. Supplemental Nutrition Assistance Program (SNAP) Households and Participants—Summary: 2018

[19,699 represents 19,699,000. For fiscal year ending September 30. Based on a sample of households from the SNAP Quality Control System. Figures are lower than official participation counts because they do not include ineligible participants or those receiving disaster food stamp assistance]

Household type and income source	Households Number (1,000)	Percent	Age, sex, race, and ethnicity	Participants Number (1,000)	Percent
Total............................	**19,699**	**100.0**	**Total**............................	**39,271**	**100.0**
With children........................	8,064	40.9	Children............................	17,103	43.6
Single-parent households...........	4,925	25.0	Under age 5.......................	5,030	12.8
Married-couple households..........	1,316	6.7	Age 5 to 17.......................	12,074	30.7
Other [1]............................	1,823	9.3	Nonelderly adults.................	16,609	42.3
With elderly.........................	5,105	25.9	Age 18 to 35......................	7,738	19.7
Living alone........................	4,268	21.7	Age 36 to 59......................	8,871	22.6
Not living alone....................	837	4.2	Elderly, age 60 and over..........	5,559	14.2
Disabled nonelderly..................	4,073	20.7			
Living alone........................	2,627	13.3	Male..............................	16,725	42.6
Not living alone....................	1,445	7.3	Female............................	22,546	57.4
With earned income..................	5,897	29.9	White, non-Hispanic...............	14,006	35.7
Wages and salaries.................	5,036	25.6	Black, non-Hispanic...............	9,864	25.1
Unearned income.....................	11,862	60.2	Hispanic..........................	6,541	16.7
TANF [2]............................	877	4.5	Asian, non-Hispanic...............	1,177	3.0
Supplemental security income.......	4,506	22.9	Native American, non-Hispanic.....	570	1.5
Social security.....................	5,847	29.7	Multiracial, non-Hispanic.........	296	0.8
No gross income.....................	3,796	19.3	Race unknown......................	6,817	17.4

[1] Other households with children include other multiple-adult households and children-only households. [2] Temporary Assistance for Needy Families (TANF) program.

Source: U.S. Department of Agriculture, Food and Nutrition Service, *Characteristics of Supplemental Nutrition Assistance Program Households: Fiscal Year 2018*, Report No. SNAP-19-CHAR, November 2019. See also <https://www.fns.usda.gov/research-analysis>.

Table 601. Children Under Age 6 in Child Care by Type of Child Care Arrangement by Child and Family Characteristics: 2019

[In percent, except as indicated (21,195 represents 21,195,000). Covers children under age 6 (from birth through age 5) not enrolled in kindergarten who are in a nonparental care arrangement on a weekly basis. Children may have multiple weekly care arrangements, thus a single child may be represented in multiple columns. Based on the Early Childhood Program Participation Survey, a component of the National Household Education Surveys (NHES) Program. The NHES methodology changes over time and users should use caution when comparing results here to previous surveys. Detail may not sum to totals because of rounding]

Selected child or family characteristic	Number of children (1,000)	Children in weekly nonparental care arrangement [1] At least one nonparental care arrangement	Relative	Nonrelative care	Center-based care [2]	Children with no weekly nonparental care
Total children under age 6...........	**21,195**	**59**	**37**	**18**	**62**	**41**
Age of child:						
Under 1 year old........................	4,621	42	58	22	31	58
1 to 2 years old........................	8,425	55	45	23	46	45
3 to 5 years old........................	8,149	74	25	13	83	26
Non-Hispanic race of child:						
White..................................	10,420	61	33	22	65	39
Black..................................	2,706	63	43	9	59	37
Asian or Pacific Islander..............	1,181	55	34	10	66	45
Other [3]..............................	1,463	59	32	21	62	41
Hispanic, any race......................	5,424	56	45	14	56	44
Number of parents in household:						
Two parents............................	17,105	58	34	19	63	42
One parent.............................	4,089	65	51	13	58	35
Highest education of parents/guardians:						
Less than high school..................	1,884	43	46	13	58	57
High school/GED [4]....................	4,001	49	49	12	54	51
Vocational/technical/some college......	5,061	56	43	16	57	44
Bachelor's degree......................	5,988	64	33	20	64	36
Graduate/professional degree...........	4,261	75	28	22	70	25
Household income:						
$20,000 or less........................	2,401	51	43	11	61	49
$20,001 to $50,000.....................	5,063	46	44	12	59	54
$50,001 to $75,000.....................	3,659	55	45	20	50	45
$75,001 to $100,000....................	2,849	58	41	18	59	42
Over $100,000..........................	5,376	72	32	19	66	28
Assistance to pay for primary child care arrangement: [5]						
Parents received assistance............	1,577	100	26	19	80	(X)
Parents did not receive assistance.....	7,013	100	24	25	71	(X)
No fee for care........................	4,004	100	64	4	40	(X)

[1] Estimates represent about 12,594,000 children who have at least one weekly nonparental care arrangement. Eleven percent of children's parents reported having more than one type of regularly scheduled weekly nonparental care arrangement. [2] Includes day care centers, Head Start programs, preschools, prekindergartens, and other early childhood programs. [3] Includes children of all other races or multiple races, non-Hispanic. [4] GED, General Educational Development diploma. [5] Assistance could be from a state welfare or family assistance program, a relative, an employer, another social service, or someone else.

Source: U.S. National Center for Education Statistics, *Early Childhood Program Participation: 2019, First Look,* August 2020, NCES2020-075. See also <https://nces.ed.gov/pubsearch/pubsinfo.asp?pubid=2020075>.

Table 602. Child Support—Award and Recipient Status of Custodial Parents: 2017

[In thousands (12,918 represents 12,918,000), except as noted. Income and support received in 2017 dollars. Based on the Child Support Supplement to the April 2018 Current Population Survey (CPS). Custodial parents are 15 years and older with own children under 21 years of age living with them who receive support from noncustodial parents living outside the household. Covers civilian noninstitutional population]

Award and recipient status	All custodial parents				Custodial parents below poverty level			
	Total				Total			
	Number	Percent distribution	Mothers	Fathers	Number	Percent distribution	Mothers	Fathers
Total	**12,918**	(X)	**10,319**	**2,598**	**3,110**	(X)	**2,817**	**292**
With child support agreement or award [1]	6,376	(X)	5,301	1,075	1,452	(X)	1,328	124
Supposed to receive payments in 2017	5,429	100.0	4,600	828	1,207	100.0	1,121	86
Actually received payments in 2017	3,792	69.8	3,282	510	829	68.7	781	48
Received full amount	2,491	45.9	2,133	357	483	40.0	456	27
Received partial payments	1,301	24.0	1,149	153	346	28.7	325	21
Did not receive payments in 2017	1,637	30.2	1,318	318	377	31.2	340	38
Child support not awarded	6,542	(X)	5,018	1,524	1,658	(X)	1,489	169
MEAN INCOME AND CHILD SUPPORT								
Received child support payments in 2017: [2]								
Mean total money income (dol.)	40,795	(X)	36,947	65,557	9,954	(X)	9,856	11,551
Mean child support received (dol.)	4,912	(X)	4,913	4,908	4,173	(X)	4,205	3,650
Received the full amount due:								
Mean total money income (dol.)	44,936	(X)	41,241	67,002	9,775	(X)	9,761	10,023
Mean child support received (dol.)	6,295	(X)	6,315	6,173	5,581	(X)	5,553	6,067
Received partial payments:								
Mean total money income (dol.)	32,870	(X)	28,972	62,178	10,203	(X)	9,989	13,469
Mean child support received (dol.)	2,266	(X)	2,309	1,948	2,210	(X)	2,315	615
Received no payments in 2017: [2]								
Mean total money income (dol.)	35,189	(X)	31,908	48,777	9,024	(X)	9,600	3,842
Without child support agreement or award:								
Mean total money income (dol.)	36,172	(X)	30,546	54,702	8,727	(X)	8,344	12,105

X Not applicable. [1] Child support award status as of April 2018. [2] For parents who were supposed to receive child support.

Source: U.S. Census Bureau, *Custodial Mothers and Fathers and Their Child Support: 2017*, Current Population Report P60-269, May 2020; and "2017 Child Support Detailed Tables," <https://www.census.gov/topics/families/child-support.Tables.html>, accessed June 2020. See also <https://www.census.gov/topics/families/child-support.html>.

Table 603. Child Support Enforcement Program—Caseload and Finances: 2010 to 2019

[In units as indicated (15,859 represents 15,859,000). For fiscal years ending September 30. Includes Puerto Rico, Guam, and the Virgin Islands. The Child Support Program is a federal/state/tribal/local partnership that operates under Title IV-D of the Social Security Act. The Office of Child Support (OCSE) locates absent parents, establishes paternity of children, and establishes and enforces support orders. The OCSE does not assist families directly but rather helps child support agencies in the states and tribes to develop, manage and operate their programs. Case types include IV-A cases in which children are eligible for Temporary Assistance for Needy Families (TANF); and IV-E cases in which children are entitled to foster care maintenance; case types reflect Social Security Act Titles IV-A and IV-E. Child support collected for families not receiving TANF goes to the family to help it remain self-sufficient. Most child support collected on behalf of TANF and foster care families goes to Federal and State governments to offset program payments. Some States pass-through a portion of their collections to help families become self-sufficient. Based on data reported by state agencies. Minus sign (-) indicates net outlay]

Item	Unit	2010	2015	2016	2017	2018	2019 (P)
Total cases	**1,000**	**15,859**	**14,745**	**14,522**	**14,229**	**13,924**	**13,605**
Number of children	1,000	17,509	15,899	15,562	15,147	14,728	14,271
Paternities established or acknowledged, total	1,000	1,734	1,484	1,479	1,435	1,413	1,401
Support orders established, total	1,000	1,297	1,016	981	936	872	838
FINANCES							
Total distributed collections	**Mil. dol.**	**26,556**	**28,559**	**28,834**	**28,625**	**28,584**	**28,767**
Total payments to families or foster care	Mil. dol.	24,474	26,592	26,880	26,725	26,703	26,890
Total medical support	Mil. dol.	303	511	540	559	593	625
Total passed through	Mil. dol.	135	112	105	102	98	93
Total fees withheld by state	Mil. dol.	37	53	53	54	53	59
Total assistance reimbursement [1]	Mil. dol.	1,607	1,292	1,256	1,185	1,137	1,100
State share	Mil. dol.	704	574	559	526	504	487
Federal share	Mil. dol.	903	717	697	658	633	613
Current Assistance Collections [2]	Mil. dol.	1,015	808	771	711	681	653
Former Assistance Collections [3]	Mil. dol.	8,971	8,959	8,868	8,615	8,445	8,322
Medicaid Never Assistance Collections [4]	Mil. dol.	4,729	7,368	7,904	8,368	8,724	9,080
Never Assistance Collections [5]	Mil. dol.	11,840	11,425	11,291	10,932	10,734	10,712
Total administrative expenditures	Mil. dol.	5,776	5,749	5,728	5,880	5,877	6,012
Federal share	Mil. dol.	3,811	3,474	3,444	3,560	3,551	3,618
State share	Mil. dol.	1,964	2,275	2,284	2,320	2,326	2,394
Cost effectiveness ratio	Dol.	4.88	5.26	5.33	5.15	5.14	5.06

P Preliminary. [1] Equals collections that will be divided between State and Federal governments to reimburse their respective shares of either Title IV-A (TANF) payments or Title IV-E (foster care) maintenance payments. [2] Made on behalf of families currently receiving Title IV-A (TANF) or Title IV-E (foster care) assistance. [3] Made on behalf of families formerly receiving Title IV-A (TANF) or Title IV-E (foster care) assistance. [4] Collections received and distributed on behalf of children who are receiving Child Support Enforcement services under Title IV-D of the Social Security Act, and who either currently receive or formerly received Medicaid payments, but who do not and never did receive assistance under either Title IV-A (TANF or AFDC) or Title IV-E (Foster Care) of the Social Security Act. [5] Made on behalf of families never receiving public assistance under Medicaid, TANF, or Foster Care.

Source: U.S. Department of Health and Human Services, Administration for Children & Families, Office of Child Support Enforcement, *Preliminary Report FY2019*, June 2020, and earlier editions. See also <https://www.acf.hhs.gov/css/data>.

Table 604. Children in Foster Care and Awaiting Adoption: 2018

[Data cover fiscal year ending September 30 of year shown, and are current as of August 2019. Data are preliminary. States may resubmit data, and therefore estimates may change. Due to missing data for some characteristics, data may not sum to totals]

Characteristic	In foster care [1]	Entered foster care	Exited foster care	Waiting to be adopted [1,2]	Adopted [3]
Total	**437,283**	**262,956**	**250,103**	**125,422**	**63,123**
SEX					
Male	226,156	(NA)	(NA)	65,694	31,183
Female	211,083	(NA)	(NA)	59,721	31,935
AGE					
Under 1 year	31,693	49,765	11,512	4,638	2,924
1 to 5 years	151,140	80,137	92,819	51,018	33,446
6 to 10 years	101,506	56,278	59,534	33,487	16,212
11 to 15 years	93,470	53,786	45,847	27,759	8,494
16 to 17 years	46,844	20,946	20,451	8,520	1,853
18 to 20 years	12,450	2,018	18,759	(X)	103
Mean age, years	8.3	7.1	8.5	7.7	6.1
Median age, years	7.6	6.1	7.5	6.9	4.9
RACE/ETHNICITY [4]					
American Indian/Alaska Native	10,449	5,856	5,557	2,369	1,059
Asian	2,112	1,567	1,473	509	270
Black	99,025	55,608	52,194	27,397	10,795
White	193,117	121,747	115,616	55,278	30,924
Hispanic origin [5]	90,688	52,783	51,565	27,765	13,327
Two or more races	32,882	18,373	18,344	10,122	5,614
TIME IN CARE					
Mean months	19.7	(X)	19.2	30.8	(NA)
Median months	13.2	(X)	14.7	25.1	(NA)

NA Not available. X Not applicable. [1] As of September 30. [2] Includes children whose goal is adoption and/or whose parents' parental rights have been terminated. Excludes children age 16 and older whose parents' parental rights have been terminated and whose goal is emancipation. [3] Children adopted with public agency involvement. Data are from the Adoption and Foster Care Analysis and Reporting System (AFCARS) Adoption file; the number of adoptions reported here may not equal the number reported as discharges to adoption from foster care. [4] Race groups exclude children of Hispanic origin. [5] Children of Hispanic origin may be of any race.

Source: U.S. Department of Health and Human Services, Administration for Children and Families, *The Adoption and Foster Care Analysis and Reporting System Report, Preliminary FY2018 Estimates as of August 22, 2019,* No. 26. See also <https://www.acf.hhs.gov/cb/focus-areas/foster-care>.

Table 605. Child Care Mean Hourly Cost by Type of Child Care Arrangement and Child and Family Characteristics: 2019

[In dollars. Covers children from birth through age 5. Estimates represent 8,101,000 children who are not in kindergarten, and who have at least one regularly scheduled weekly nonparental care arrangement with an out-of-pocket expense. Excludes children for whom no fee was charged, or for whom another source paid the entire fee. Data cover the primary care arrangement where the child spends the most time. Some children have multiple primary care arrangements; a single child may be represented in multiple columns of this table. Based on the Early Childhood Program Participation Survey, a component of the National Household Education Surveys (NHES) Program. The NHES methodology changes over time and users should use caution when comparing results here to previous surveys. Detail may not sum to totals because of rounding]

Selected child and family characteristics	Hourly cost by type of primary care			Selected child and family characteristics	Hourly cost by type of primary care		
	Relative care	Non-relative care	Center-based care [1]		Relative care	Non-relative care	Center-based care [1]
Total children under 6 years old	**6.05**	**7.75**	**8.22**	Region:			
Age of child:				Northeast	7.90	10.55	10.20
Under 1 year old	6.63	8.85	7.91	South	5.80	7.35	6.71
1 to 2 years old	5.43	8.03	8.92	Midwest	4.09	5.29	7.05
3 to 5 years old	6.64	6.72	7.88	West	6.54	8.80	10.16
Non-Hispanic race of child:							
White	6.76	6.48	7.51	Household income:			
Black	4.29	6.66	6.97	$20,000 or less	7.85	(B)	[6] 8.26
Asian or Pacific Islander	6.45	[6] 16.45	11.87	$20,001 to $50,000	3.91	6.02	6.73
Other or multiple races	[6] 7.95	9.58	9.54	$50,001 to $75,000	5.87	5.27	5.60
Hispanic, any race	6.34	10.04	9.59	$75,001 to $100,000	7.10	5.40	7.85
Family type:				Over $100,000	6.18	7.97	8.23
Two parents or guardians	6.49	7.78	8.35				
One parent or guardian	5.10	7.60	7.55	Poverty status of household: [4]			
Parents' highest education: [2]				At or above poverty threshold	6.07	7.50	8.26
Less than high school	6.79	[6] 7.91	3.47	Below poverty threshold	5.97	[6] 10.00	7.71
High school/GED [3]	5.40	[6] 8.96	7.20				
Vocational/technical or some college	5.53	5.51	6.23	Assistance to pay for primary child care arrangement: [5]			
Bachelor's degree	6.38	6.83	8.37	Parents received assistance	6.16	[6] 8.88	6.82
				Parents did not receive assistance	6.02	7.58	8.43
Graduate/professional degree	7.20	9.50	9.53				

B Reporting standards not met. There are too few cases for a reliable estimate. [1] Includes day care centers, Head Start programs, preschools, and prekindergartens. [2] Parents or guardians. [3] GED, General Educational Development diploma. [4] Children are considered poor if living in households with incomes below the poverty threshold, which is a dollar amount determined by the federal government, given household size and composition. Income is reported in categories rather than in exact amounts, and therefore the poverty measures are approximations. [5] Assistance could be from a state welfare or family assistance program, a relative, an employer, another social service, or someone else. Parents were asked about assistance only for the primary arrangement within each type of care. [6] Interpret data with caution. The coefficient of variation for this estimate is 30 percent or greater.

Source: U.S. National Center for Education Statistics, *Early Childhood Program Participation: 2019, First Look,* August 2020, NCES2020-075. See also <https://nces.ed.gov/pubsearch/pubsinfo.asp?pubid=2020075>.

Table 606. Head Start—Summary: 2010 to 2019

[Funding data in millions of dollars (7,234.8 represents $7,234,800,000); all other data in thousands (904.1 represents 904,100). For fiscal years. The Head Start program serves children, families, and pregnant women in all 50 states, DC, and six territories. Data on cumulative enrollment, staff, and volunteers are submitted by Head Start grantees and delegates. Federal funding covers all Head Start programs, including Early Head Start, American Indian and Alaska Native programs, and Migrant and Seasonal Head Start Programs]

Item	2010	2014	2015	2016	2017	2018	2019
Federal funding (million dollars)...............	7,234.8	[3] 8,598.1	8,285.5	8,438.9	8,877.4	9,127.2	9,967.1
Funded enrollment slots [1]........................	904.1	927.3	944.6	915.6	899.4	887.1	873.0
Cumulative enrollment [2]......................	**1,117.7**	**1,076.1**	**1,100.4**	**1,097.4**	**1,074.2**	**1,054.7**	**1,047.4**
Children age 2 and under.....................	146.3	173.2	193.2	230.3	243.4	258.0	266.1
Children age 3.................................	386.7	375.9	399.4	383.9	374.0	364.1	363.7
Children age 4.................................	548.0	497.1	480.1	455.9	427.6	404.8	391.6
Children age 5 and older.....................	23.2	15.3	12.2	11.9	13.9	12.4	10.3
Hispanic/Latino................................	405.4	406.6	414.0	411.4	400.4	385.7	387.7
Non-Hispanic/non-Latino.....................	712.3	669.5	686.3	686.0	673.7	669.0	659.7
American Indian/Alaska Native...............	41.7	45.2	45.4	42.1	42.1	41.3	40.6
Asian...	19.0	19.8	21.8	22.6	22.6	22.8	22.5
Black/African American.......................	326.5	309.9	318.3	319.9	313.5	312.7	310.7
Native Hawaiian/Pacific Islander.............	6.9	7.0	9.8	7.4	7.7	7.1	7.1
White..	450.3	458.0	473.5	477.8	469.6	461.2	462.1
Biracial/multiracial............................	83.9	102.2	107.2	107.5	106.2	103.3	102.2
Other/unspecified.............................	189.4	134.1	124.3	120.1	112.5	106.2	102.2
Total staff......................................	228.3	226.0	230.0	241.5	240.0	246.1	254.4
Total volunteers................................	1,335.9	1,167.1	1,141.5	1,118.8	1,086.4	1,046.4	1,060.9
Parent volunteers..........................	881.1	800.2	782.2	783.6	769.6	738.7	749.5

[1] Funded enrollment is the number of children and pregnant women supported by federal Head Start funds at any one time during the year. Data are derived from the annual Administration for Children and Families budget and congressional documents, and do not reflect changes made during the year. [2] Cumulative enrollment refers to actual number of children and pregnant women served, including enrollees who left during the year and enrollees who filled those empty slots. More children and families may receive Head Start services cumulatively throughout the year than indicated by funded enrollment numbers. [3] Represents funding available after Congress restored funds in the amount of the previous year's fiscal sequestration.

Source: U.S. Department of Health and Human Services, Administration for Children and Families, Early Childhood Learning & Knowledge Center, "Head Start Program Facts Sheets," <https://eclkc.ohs.acf.hhs.gov/about-us/article/office-head-start-ohs>; and "Office of Head Start Enterprise System," <https://hses.ohs.acf.hhs.gov/pir/home>; accessed May 2020.

Table 607. Social Assistance Services—Nonemployer Establishments and Receipts: 2010 to 2018

[Receipts in millions of dollars (12,753 represents $12,753,000,000). Includes only firms subject to federal income tax. Nonemployers are businesses with no paid employees. Nonemployer firm receipts may include commissions or earnings]

Kind of business	NAICS code [1]	2010	2013	2014	2015	2016	2017	2018
ESTABLISHMENTS								
Social assistance, total.............................	**624**	**912,247**	**861,579**	**850,786**	**822,350**	**782,320**	**729,150**	**784,922**
Individual and family services.........................	6241	141,971	154,024	160,562	163,337	164,218	170,672	176,958
Community/emergency and other relief services....	6242	6,080	6,058	6,399	6,355	6,384	6,512	6,296
Vocational rehabilitation services......................	6243	11,984	12,769	12,938	12,916	12,700	12,510	12,355
Child day care services...............................	6244	752,212	688,728	670,887	639,742	599,018	539,456	589,313
RECEIPTS (mil. dol)								
Social assistance, total.............................	**624**	**12,753**	**12,813**	**13,114**	**13,238**	**13,099**	**12,992**	**14,100**
Individual and family services.........................	6241	2,599	3,016	3,275	3,492	3,641	3,881	4,176
Community/emergency and other relief services....	6242	96	98	106	111	114	114	122
Vocational rehabilitation services......................	6243	287	312	318	341	345	343	351
Child day care services...............................	6244	9,772	9,387	9,415	9,294	8,999	8,653	9,451

[1] North American Industry Classification System; see text, Section 15. Data for 2010 based on NAICS 2007; data for 2013-2016 based on NAICS 2012; and beginning 2017, data based on 2017 NAICS.

Source: U.S. Census Bureau, Nonemployer Statistics, "All Sectors: Nonemployer Statistics for the U.S., States, Counties, Metropolitan Areas, and Combined Statistical Areas; and by Legal Form of Organization and Sales, Value of Shipments, or Revenue Size for Selected Geographies: 2018," <data.census.gov/>, accessed May 2020.

Table 608. Social Assistance Services—Revenue for Employer Firms: 2017 and 2018

[In millions of dollars (188,499 represents $188,499,000,000). Based on Census Bureau's Service Annual Survey and administrative data. Estimates have been adjusted to the results of the 2012 Economic Census. See Appendix III]

Kind of business	NAICS code [1]	2017 Total	2017 Taxable firms	2017 Tax-exempt firms	2018 Total	2018 Taxable firms	2018 Tax-exempt firms
Social assistance, total...........................	624	**188,499**	**56,021**	**132,478**	**199,005**	**60,578**	**138,427**
Child and youth services..............................	62411	14,656	1,358	13,298	14,948	1,541	13,407
Services for elderly and disabled persons.........	62412	48,245	19,885	28,360	51,212	21,532	29,680
Other individual and family services................	62419	34,146	4,650	29,496	36,426	4,794	31,632
Community food services.............................	62421	11,554	57	11,497	11,886	63	11,823
Community housing services.........................	62422	12,741	114	12,627	13,842	136	13,706
Emergency and other relief services...............	62423	11,542	209	11,333	11,098	243	10,855
Vocational rehabilitation services..................	6243	14,027	2,289	11,738	14,578	2,265	12,313
Child day care services..............................	6244	41,588	27,459	14,129	45,015	30,004	15,011

[1] 2012 North American Industry Classification System.

Source: U.S. Census Bureau, Service Annual Survey, "Service Annual Survey Latest Data (NAICS-basis): 2018," <https://www.census.gov/programs-surveys/sas/data.html>, accessed January 2020.

Table 609. Emergency and Transitional Beds in Homeless Assistance Systems: 2019

[Data cover all States, DC, Guam, Northern Marianas, Puerto Rico, and the Virgin Islands. Data were reported by approximately 400 Continuums of Care, and were collected for a point-in-time during the last week of January 2019. Data were not independently verified by Department of Housing and Urban Development (HUD)]

Homeless program	Total year-round beds	Dedicated units/beds [1] Family units	Dedicated units/beds [1] Family beds	Dedicated units/beds [1] Adult-only beds	Dedicated units/beds [1] Child-only beds	Other beds Seasonal beds [2]	Other beds Overflow/ voucher [3]
Total........................	**911,657**	**135,468**	**418,859**	**489,164**	**3,634**	**21,746**	**16,311**
Shelter for homeless people..............	389,549	58,332	186,849	199,276	3,424	21,746	16,311
Emergency shelters......................	291,837	43,203	141,686	147,350	2,801	21,746	16,311
Safe haven [4]............................	2,266	(X)	(X)	2,266	(X)	(X)	(X)
Transitional housing [5]...................	95,446	15,129	45,163	49,660	623	(X)	(X)
Permanent housing........................	522,108	77,136	232,010	289,888	210	(X)	(X)
Permanent supportive housing [6]........	369,293	43,199	125,676	243,528	89	(X)	(X)
Rapid re-housing.........................	112,961	26,147	82,652	30,229	80	(X)	(X)
Other permanent housing [7]..............	39,854	7,790	23,682	16,131	41	(X)	(X)

X Not applicable. [1] Dedicated beds are available for use throughout the year and are considered part of the stable inventory of beds for homeless persons. [2] Seasonal beds are typically available during particularly high-demand seasons of the year (e.g. winter months in the North or summer months in the South) to accommodate increased need for emergency shelters to prevent illness or death due to the weather. [3] Overflow beds are typically used during unanticipated emergencies (e.g., precipitous temperature drops or a natural disaster that displaces residents). Voucher beds are made available in a hotel or motel, and often function like overflow beds. [4] A safe haven provides temporary shelter and services for hard-to-reach homeless persons with severe mental illness who come primarily from the streets and have been unable or unwilling to participate in housing or supportive services. Accommodations are private or semi-private. [5] Provides a place to stay with supportive services for up to 24 months. [6] Provides long-term housing with supportive services for formerly homeless people with disabilities, and often also those with chronic homelessness. [7] May or may not include services, and does not require people to have a disability.

Source: U.S. Department of Housing and Urban Development, *2019 Continuum of Care Homeless Assistance Programs: Housing Inventory Count Report,* October 2019. See also <https://www.hudexchange.info/manage-a-program/coc-housing-inventory-count-reports/>.

Table 610. Homeless Population by Type and Shelter Status: 2010 to 2019

[Data are point-in-time (PIT) counts made on a single night in January by Continuums of Care (CoCs) in all States, DC, and U.S. territories. Data are not independently verified by the Department of Housing and Urban Development (HUD). CoCs are required to provide an unduplicated count of homeless persons according to HUD standards. See HUD's Point-in-Time Count Methodology Guide at <https://www.hudexchange.info/programs/hdx/guides/pit-hic/#general-pit-guides-and-tools>. Sheltered homeless people may be staying in emergency shelters, hotels/motels paid for by charities or government programs, transitional housing programs, or safe havens (temporary shelter for hard-to-serve individuals). People staying in places not designed for use as regular accommodations, including cars, abandoned buildings, transit stations, and campgrounds, are considered unsheltered]

Homeless population by type	2010	2014	2015	2016	2017	2018	2019
Total	**637,077**	**576,450**	**564,708**	**549,928**	**550,996**	**552,830**	**567,715**
Male	(NA)	(NA)	339,075	330,890	333,049	332,925	343,187
Female	(NA)	(NA)	224,344	217,268	214,975	216,211	219,911
Sheltered	403,543	401,051	391,440	373,571	360,867	358,363	356,422
Unsheltered	233,534	175,399	173,268	176,357	190,129	194,467	211,293
Individuals [1]	395,140	360,189	358,422	355,212	366,585	372,417	396,045
Sheltered	212,218	209,148	205,616	198,008	193,144	194,340	199,531
Unsheltered	182,922	151,041	152,806	157,204	173,441	178,077	196,514
Persons in families with children	241,937	216,261	206,286	194,716	184,411	180,413	171,670
Sheltered	191,325	191,903	185,824	175,563	167,723	164,023	156,891
Unsheltered	50,612	24,358	20,462	19,153	16,688	16,390	14,779
Children under age 18, total	(NA)	135,701	127,787	120,819	114,529	111,592	107,069
Sheltered	(NA)	119,291	114,477	108,866	103,289	101,086	97,153
Unsheltered	(NA)	16,410	13,310	11,953	11,240	10,506	9,916
Children under age 18, unaccompanied	8,153	(NA)	4,667	3,824	4,635	4,093	3,976
Sheltered	4,349	(NA)	2,287	2,218	2,122	2,014	1,874
Unsheltered	3,804	(NA)	2,380	1,606	2,513	2,079	2,102
Chronically homeless individuals [2]	106,062	83,989	83,170	77,486	86,705	88,640	96,141
Sheltered	43,329	31,203	28,355	24,596	26,629	30,754	35,200
Unsheltered	62,733	52,786	54,815	52,890	60,076	57,886	60,941
Chronically homeless people in families [2]	(NA)	15,143	13,105	8,646	8,387	8,273	9,442
Sheltered	(NA)	9,362	8,412	5,512	5,980	5,821	7,407
Unsheltered	(NA)	5,781	4,693	3,134	2,407	2,452	2,035
Veterans	74,087	49,689	47,725	39,471	40,020	37,878	37,085
Sheltered	43,437	32,119	31,505	26,404	24,690	23,312	22,740
Unsheltered	30,650	17,570	16,220	13,067	15,330	14,566	14,345
Severely mentally ill	107,539	116,363	104,083	107,801	(NA)	111,122	116,179
Sheltered	71,989	70,253	59,394	61,846	(NA)	58,942	63,936
Unsheltered	35,550	46,110	44,689	45,955	(NA)	52,180	52,243
Chronic substance abuse	139,853	116,516	103,888	94,496	(NA)	86,647	88,873
Sheltered	95,049	70,500	60,071	52,290	(NA)	45,372	45,804
Unsheltered	44,804	46,016	43,817	42,206	(NA)	41,275	43,069
Persons with HIV/AIDS	14,498	12,223	9,294	9,240	(NA)	10,064	10,945
Sheltered	10,590	9,638	6,532	6,860	(NA)	7,244	7,733
Unsheltered	3,908	2,585	2,762	2,380	(NA)	2,820	3,212
Domestic violence victims	66,878	59,352	67,690	68,464	(NA)	48,666	44,752
Sheltered	49,709	42,893	41,015	41,779	(NA)	30,607	31,509
Unsheltered	17,169	16,459	26,675	26,685	(NA)	18,059	13,243

NA Not available. [1] People who are not part of a family with children. Includes homeless single adults, unaccompanied youth, or individuals in multiple-adult or multiple-child households. [2] An individual or household head of a family with a disability, and continuously homeless for a year or more, or with at least four episodes of homelessness in the last 3 years.

Source: U.S. Department of Housing and Urban Development, HUD Exchange, "PIT and HIC Data Since 2007: 2007 - 2019 PIT Counts by State," January 2020, <https://www.hudexchange.info/resource/3031/pit-and-hic-data-since-2007/>, accessed January 2020; and *2019 CoC (Continuum of Care) Homeless Populations and Subpopulations Report,* September 2019 and earlier reports.

Table 611. Volunteers by Selected Characteristics: 2017

[In percent. Covers adults age 16 and over who performed unpaid volunteer activities for an organization at any time during the 12-month period from September 1 to the week of the survey. Data were collected by the September 2017 Volunteering and Civic Life Supplement to the Current Population Survey (CPS)]

Volunteer characteristics	Percent volunteering	Percent of volunteers by main organization type [1]							
		Civic and political [2]	Educational or youth service	Environ-mental or animal care	Hospital or other health	Public safety	Religious	Sport, hobby, cultural, or arts	Other
Total [3]	**30.3**	**6.2**	**19.2**	**5.0**	**6.0**	**6.0**	**32.0**	**25.7**	**3.6**
Men	26.5	7.8	16.2	4.7	4.3	3.1	30.3	29.6	4.0
Women	33.8	5.1	21.4	5.1	7.2	1.7	33.3	22.8	3.3
Age 16 to 19	28.3	3.7	24.1	4.5	4.7	1.5	22.9	35.5	3.0
Age 20 to 24	22.7	8.7	19.9	9.5	10.1	2.4	25.6	20.6	3.2
Age 25 to 34	27.8	6.8	24.6	7.2	7.3	2.7	25.5	22.7	3.3
Age 35 to 44	36.9	5.1	27.1	3.7	4.3	2.7	24.2	29.7	3.2
Age 45 to 54	34.0	4.9	19.7	4.2	5.5	2.0	30.7	29.8	3.3
Age 55 to 64	30.2	7.3	12.7	5.3	6.0	2.5	40.0	22.1	4.2
Age 65 and older	28.0	7.5	9.4	3.5	6.2	1.9	45.7	21.5	4.4
Less than high school	10.1	4.0	25.3	2.8	3.2	1.7	32.6	26.7	3.7
High school [4]	18.8	4.6	19.4	4.6	5.4	2.4	39.1	19.8	4.5
Some college [5]	32.1	6.3	17.8	5.0	6.1	3.4	34.0	23.7	3.8
College graduate	45.7	7.0	19.1	5.4	6.5	1.7	28.6	28.6	3.2

[1] Main organization is the organization for which the volunteer worked the most hours. [2] Includes organizations involved in professional and/or international activities. [3] Data by education cover persons age 25 and over. [4] Includes high school diploma or equivalent. [5] Includes "some college, no degree" and "associate degree."

Source: Corporation for National and Community Service, "Volunteering in America," <https://www.nationalservice.gov/serve/via>, accessed April 2019.

Table 612. Charitable Giving by Source and Type of Recipient Organization: 1990 to 2019

[In billions of dollars (98.5 represents $98,500,000,000). Individual giving is estimated using Internal Revenue Service information from individual tax returns, and from a study of households participating in the Philanthropy Panel Study conducted by Indiana University Lilly Family School of Philanthropy. Data on foundation giving are provided by Candid (formerly the Foundation Center). Corporate giving data are based on itemized contributions claimed on federal tax returns, and also from Candid. Data on contributions by bequest are primarily based on data from the Council for Advancement and Support of Education, with additional calculations performed by Giving USA using IRS tax data on charitable bequest deductions. Giving to recipient organizations are from various research organizations, including the Evangelical Council for Financial Accountability and other nonprofit research organizations]

Source and allocation	1990	2000	2005	2010	2012	2013	2014	2015	2016	2017	2018	2019
Total charitable giving	**98.5**	**229.7**	**292.4**	**288.2**	**332.6**	**332.5**	**357.6**	**376.7**	**397.2**	**432.1**	**431.4**	**449.6**
Individuals	79.0	174.1	220.8	208.0	244.4	242.4	252.3	264.7	279.4	302.8	295.9	309.7
Foundations [1]	7.2	24.6	32.4	41.0	46.4	49.9	54.9	57.3	63.1	70.7	73.9	75.7
Corporations	5.5	10.7	15.2	15.8	17.2	15.9	18.3	19.1	20.0	19.3	18.6	21.1
Charitable bequests	6.8	20.3	24.0	23.4	24.6	24.4	32.2	35.6	34.6	39.3	43.1	43.2
Giving by recipient organization:												
Religion	49.8	77.0	90.9	97.5	105.8	110.4	116.0	119.2	123.8	125.0	125.3	128.2
Education	11.8	28.8	35.0	42.2	46.9	44.5	49.4	53.2	53.6	56.1	57.2	64.1
Human services	6.7	20.8	30.4	36.8	41.1	41.1	43.7	46.9	49.0	52.3	53.3	56.0
Health	7.8	15.3	20.3	27.7	26.2	32.3	33.1	34.3	38.1	38.3	38.8	41.5
Public/societal benefit	6.6	15.0	20.8	19.2	22.9	24.3	25.8	27.3	30.9	34.1	32.9	37.2
Arts, culture, and humanities	3.7	10.6	12.4	13.4	13.9	14.6	15.9	17.7	17.2	18.1	19.2	21.6
International affairs	2.1	6.3	12.7	13.9	16.0	19.4	20.2	23.5	21.6	25.5	29.0	28.9
Environment/animals	1.3	4.9	6.5	7.9	8.9	8.6	9.6	10.7	11.3	12.0	12.7	14.2
Gifts to foundations [1]	3.8	24.7	24.5	26.1	40.1	40.8	44.6	39.3	40.8	52.4	52.2	53.5
Gifts to individuals	(NA)	(NA)	3.1	4.9	5.8	7.2	6.7	6.7	9.5	10.9	9.9	10.1
Unallocated [2]	5.0	26.4	36.0	-1.4	5.0	-10.7	-7.5	-2.2	1.3	7.5	0.9	-5.5

NA Not available. [1] Data are from Candid, formerly the Foundation Center. [2] Money deducted as a charitable contribution by donors but not allocated to sources. May include gifts to governmental entities, in-kind giving, or gifts to new charities.

Source: Giving USA Foundation, Chicago, IL, *Giving USA 2020: The Annual Report on Philanthropy for the Year 2019* ©, researched and written at the Indiana University Lilly Family School of Philanthropy. See also <https://givingusa.org/>.

Table 613. Domestic Private Foundations—Financial Information: 2000 to 2016

[Financial data in billions of dollars (409.5 represents $409,500,000,000). Minus sign (-) indicates loss]

Item	2000	2005	2008	2009	2010	2011	2012	2013	2014	2015	2016
Number of tax returns	66,738	79,535	90,850	92,624	93,436	92,990	93,542	95,121	97,484	99,683	100,488
Nonoperating foundations [1]	61,501	72,800	83,024	84,660	86,254	85,500	85,447	86,584	88,878	90,699	91,396
Operating foundations [2]	5,238	6,734	7,826	7,964	7,181	7,490	8,095	8,537	8,606	8,984	9,092
Total assets, book value [3]	409.5	481.8	531.4	550.9	584.2	594.3	633.1	693.3	738.4	754.3	796.5
Total assets, fair market value [3]	471.6	545.9	526.5	588.5	641.0	641.3	698.6	791.0	830.3	829.4	889.4
Investments in securities	361.4	373.1	287.6	324.7	353.3	344.8	373.3	430.9	459.3	451.7	476.7
Total revenue	72.8	76.4	49.7	52.2	72.5	79.4	95.3	106.1	119.5	107.0	114.1
Total expenses	37.4	42.8	60.3	56.2	60.1	64.3	64.8	73.7	79.2	81.0	88.1
Contributions, gifts, and grants paid	27.6	31.9	42.8	40.9	44.7	46.9	48.6	54.2	57.6	58.7	65.8
Excess of revenue over expenses (net)	35.3	33.5	-10.6	-4.0	12.3	15.1	30.5	32.4	40.3	26.0	26.0
Net investment income [4]	48.8	44.3	23.1	17.6	29.8	34.2	38.4	50.4	59.9	48.8	44.2

[1] Generally provide charitable support through grants and other financial means to charitable organizations; the majority of foundations are nonoperating. [2] Generally conduct their own charitable activities, e.g., museums. [3] Data for book and fair market value of assets were reduced to avoid overstating the joint assets of the Bill and Melinda Gates Foundation and the Bill and Melinda Gates Foundation Trust, by tax year as follows: 2008, $29.6 billion; 2009, $33.4 billion; 2010, $36.7 billion; 2011, $33.8 billion; 2012, $36.4 billion; 2013, $40.5 billion; 2014, $43.4 billion; 2015, $39.3 billion; and 2016, $40.3 billion. [4] This equals gross investment income less allowable deductions. Represents income not considered related to a foundation's charitable purpose, e.g., interest, dividends, and capital gains. Foundations could be subject to an excise tax on such income.

Source: Internal Revenue Service, *Statistics of Income Bulletin*, "SOI Tax Stats – Domestic Private Foundation and Charitable Trust Statistics," <https://www.irs.gov/statistics>, accessed February 2020.

Table 614. Foundations—Number and Finances by Foundation Type: 2000 to 2018

[In millions of dollars (24,563 represents $24,563,000,000), except number of foundations. Figures are for fiscal years, and cover only grantmaking foundations. Covers nongovernmental nonprofit organizations with funds and programs managed by their own trustees or directors, whose goals were to maintain or aid social, educational, religious, or other activities deemed to serve the common good. Excludes organizations that make general appeals to the public for funds, act as trade associations for industrial or other special groups, or do not currently award grants]

Year	Number	Total giving [1] (million dollars)	Assets (million dollars)	Gifts received (million dollars)
2000	56,582	24,563	486,085	27,614
2010	76,610	45,858	643,974	37,961
2015	86,203	62,794	890,061	53,157
2016	85,987	68,948	907,625	57,500
2017	86,124	77,183	1,013,523	72,993
Total, 2018	**86,310**	**80,664**	**1,017,899**	**72,526**
Independent	79,558	53,179	833,758	40,345
Corporate	2,649	6,809	33,460	7,809
Community	759	9,159	97,129	11,772
Operating	3,344	11,517	53,552	12,600

[1] Includes grants, scholarships, and employee matching gifts; excludes set-asides, loans, program-related investments (PRIs), and program and other administrative expenses.

Source: Candid, New York, NY ©, all rights reserved, "Foundation Stats," <http://data.foundationcenter.org/>, and unpublished data.

Table 615. Nonprofit Charitable Organizations—Financial Information: 2000 to 2016

[In billions of dollars (1,562.5 represents $1,562,500,000,000), except as indicated. Includes data reported by organizations described in Internal Revenue Code, Section 501(c)(3), excluding private foundations and most religious organizations. Prior to 2010, organizations with receipts under $25,000 were not required to file. Beginning with 2010, organizations with receipts under $50,000 were not required to file]

Year	Number of tax returns (1,000)	Total assets	Net assets	Revenue Total [1]	Revenue Program service revenue [2]	Revenue Contributions, gifts, and grants	Total expenses	Excess of revenue over expenses (net)
2000...............	230.2	1,562.5	1,023.2	866.2	579.1	199.1	796.4	69.8
2001...............	240.6	1,631.7	1,020.3	897.0	630.8	212.4	862.7	34.3
2002...............	251.7	1,733.9	1,040.3	955.3	691.8	214.5	934.7	20.6
2003...............	263.4	1,899.9	1,164.3	1,072.2	754.6	230.0	1,009.7	62.5
2004...............	276.2	2,058.6	1,276.1	1,153.0	801.2	248.6	1,058.5	94.5
2005...............	286.6	2,241.9	1,411.3	1,252.9	852.6	276.3	1,137.9	115.0
2006...............	301.2	2,549.7	1,617.7	1,370.9	920.2	303.2	1,230.4	140.5
2007...............	313.1	2,683.4	1,674.4	1,445.9	980.3	324.5	1,317.2	128.7
2008...............	315.2	2,521.2	1,434.7	1,378.3	1,038.0	322.0	1,396.4	-18.1
2009...............	320.8	2,697.1	1,564.2	1,481.1	1,085.9	327.4	1,433.9	47.2
2010...............	269.5	2,946.5	1,772.4	1,593.0	1,147.3	344.9	1,497.2	95.8
2011...............	274.3	3,030.1	1,781.9	1,647.9	1,194.2	357.4	1,558.4	89.5
2012...............	279.4	3,274.0	1,970.4	1,734.2	1,248.2	371.1	1,624.1	110.1
2013...............	285.9	3,507.6	2,184.0	1,828.2	1,296.1	394.1	1,700.4	127.8
2014...............	293.0	3,711.1	2,288.0	1,949.9	1,384.1	422.5	1,801.3	148.6
2015...............	298.4	3,801.4	2,303.6	2,013.0	1,468.0	430.6	1,908.2	104.8
2016...............	302.1	4,027.9	2,519.0	2,124.4	1,530.5	465.3	2,013.3	111.2

[1] Includes other sources of revenue not shown separately. [2] Represents fees collected by organizations in support of their tax-exempt purposes, such as tuition and fees at educational institutions, hospital patient charges, and admission and activity fees collected by museums and other nonprofit organizations or institutions.

Source: U.S. Internal Revenue Service, Statistics of Income, "SOI Tax Stats – Charities & Other Tax-Exempt Organizations Statistics," September 2019, <https://www.irs.gov/statistics>, accessed March 2020.

Table 616. Individual Charitable Contributions by State: 2017

[In units, as indicated (256,341 represents $256,341,000,000). Covers returns primarily for 2017 tax year that were filed during 2018, but may also include a limited number of returns for earlier tax years that were also received during 2018. Data will not agree with data in other tables due to differing survey methodology used to derive state data]

State	Charitable contributions Number of returns (1,000)	Charitable contributions Amount (mil. dol.)	State	Charitable contributions Number of returns (1,000)	Charitable contributions Amount (mil. dol.)	State	Charitable contributions Number of returns (1,000)	Charitable contributions Amount (mil. dol.)	State	Charitable contributions Number of returns (1,000)	Charitable contributions Amount (mil. dol.)
Total [1].....	37,972	256,341	ID.........	181	1,243	MO.......	598	4,073	PA.......	1,456	7,740
AL...........	478	3,879	IL.........	1,627	9,268	MT.......	115	669	RI........	146	514
AK..........	57	345	IN........	572	3,631	NE.......	210	1,355	SC.......	530	3,604
AZ..........	756	4,088	IA........	358	1,841	NV.......	305	2,032	SD.......	59	680
AR..........	227	2,913	KS........	284	2,073	NH.......	171	699	TN.......	508	4,583
CA..........	5,279	34,940	KY.......	411	2,236	NJ........	1,571	7,336	TX.......	2,457	22,139
CO..........	728	4,471	LA.......	371	2,595	NM.......	160	915	UT.......	413	4,306
CT..........	608	3,875	ME.......	135	533	NY.......	2,817	21,674	VT.......	65	327
DE..........	124	612	MD.......	1,155	6,417	NC.......	1,123	7,272	VA.......	1,228	7,296
DC..........	116	961	MA.......	1,065	6,756	ND.......	52	419	WA.......	881	6,215
FL..........	2,041	17,958	MI.......	1,075	5,864	OH.......	1,146	6,104	WV.......	94	530
GA..........	1,302	11,988	MN.......	817	4,273	OK.......	307	2,739	WI.......	718	3,353
HI..........	167	777	MS.......	254	1,884	OR.......	569	2,973	WY.......	42	662

[1] Includes returns filed by members of the armed forces stationed overseas, other U.S. citizens abroad, and residents of Puerto Rico with income from sources outside Puerto Rico or with income earned as U.S. government employees.

Source: U.S. Internal Revenue Service, Statistics of Income, Individual Income Tax Return (Form 1040) Statistics: State Data, "SOI Tax Stats - Historic Table 2," <https://www.irs.gov/uac/soi-tax-stats-individual-income-tax-return-form-1040-statistics>, accessed February 2020.

Labor Force, Employment, and Earnings

This section presents statistics on the labor force; its distribution by occupation and industry affiliation; and the supply of, demand for, and conditions of labor. The chief source of these data is the Current Population Survey (CPS) conducted by the U.S. Census Bureau for the Bureau of Labor Statistics (BLS). Comprehensive historical and current data are available from the BLS internet site at <bls.gov/cps/>. These data are published on a current basis in the BLS monthly publication *Employment and Earnings Online*. Detailed data on the labor force are also available from the Census Bureau's decennial census of population.

Types of data—Most statistics in this section are obtained by two methods: household interviews or questionnaires and reports of establishment payroll records. Each method provides data that the other cannot suitably supply. Population characteristics, for example, are readily obtainable only from the household survey, while detailed industrial classifications can be readily derived only from establishment records.

CPS data are obtained from a monthly sample survey of the population. The CPS is used to gather data for the calendar week, generally the week including the 12th of the month, and provides current comprehensive data on the labor force (see text, Section 1, Population). The CPS provides information on the work status of the population without duplication since each person is classified as employed, unemployed, or not in the labor force. Employed persons holding more than one job are counted only once, according to the job at which they worked the most hours during the survey week.

Employment and Earnings Online presents data including national totals of the number of persons in the civilian labor force by sex, disability status, race, Hispanic origin, and age; the number employed; hours of work; industry and occupational groups; usual weekly earnings; and the number unemployed, as well as reasons for and duration of unemployment. Annual data shown in this section are averages of monthly figures for each calendar year, unless otherwise specified.

The CPS also produces annual estimates of employment and unemployment for each state, 50 large metropolitan statistical areas, and selected cities. These estimates are published annually in *Geographic Profile of Employment and Unemployment* available at <bls.gov/opub/geographic-profile/home.htm>.

Data based on establishment records are compiled by the BLS and cooperating state agencies as part of an ongoing Current Employment Statistics (CES) program. The BLS collects survey data monthly from a probability-based sample of nonfarm, business establishments. Data collection centers perform initial enrollment of each firm via telephone, collect the data for several months via Computer Assisted Telephone Interviewing (CATI), and where possible transfer respondents to a self-reporting mode such as touch-tone data entry, fax, or web collection. Very large, multi-establishment firms' ongoing reporting is established via Electronic Data Interchange (EDI). CES data are adjusted annually to data from government unemployment insurance administrative records, which are supplemented by data from other government agencies. The estimates exclude self-employed persons, private household workers, unpaid family workers, agricultural workers, and members of the Armed Forces.

The CES counts workers each time they appear on a payroll during the reference period (the payroll period that includes the 12th of the month). Thus, unlike the CPS, a person with two jobs is counted twice. The establishment survey is designed to provide estimates of nonfarm wage and salary employment, average weekly hours, and average hourly and weekly earnings by detailed industry for the nation, states, and selected metropolitan areas. Establishment survey data also are published in *Employment and Earnings Online*. Historical national data are available at <bls.gov/ces/>. Historical data for states and metropolitan areas are available at <bls.gov/sae/>. CES estimates are currently classified by the 2017 North American Industry Classification System (NAICS). All published series for the nation have a NAICS-based history extending back to at least 1990. Employment series for total nonfarm and other high-level aggregates start in 1939.

For more information on data concepts, sample design, and estimating methods for the CES Survey, see the BLS Handbook of Methods, Chapter 2 <bls.gov/opub/hom/>. For information regarding revisions and collection rates, see <bls.gov/web/empsit/cesbmart.htm>.

Labor force—According to the CPS definitions, the civilian labor force comprises all civilians in the noninstitutionalized population aged 16 years and over classified as "employed" or "unemployed" according to specific criteria. *Employed* civilians comprise (a) all civilians, who, during the reference week, did any work for pay or profit (minimum of an hour's work) or worked 15 hours or more as unpaid workers in a family enterprise and (b) all civilians who were not working but who had jobs or businesses from which they were temporarily absent for noneconomic reasons (illness, weather conditions, vacation, labor-management dispute, etc.) whether they were paid for the time off or were seeking other jobs. *Unemployed* persons comprise all civilians who had no employment during the reference week, who made specific efforts to find a job within the previous 4 weeks (such as applying directly to an employer or to a public employment service or checking with friends) and who were available for work during that week, except for temporary illness. Persons on layoff from a job and expecting recall also are classified as unemployed. All other civilian persons, 16 years old and over, are classified as "not in the labor force."

Various breaks in the CPS data series have occurred over time due to the introduction of population adjustments and other changes. For details on these breaks in series and the effect that they had on the CPS data, see the BLS website at <bls.gov/cps/documentation.htm#concepts>.

Beginning in January of each year, the CPS data reflect the introduction of revised population controls. For additional information on the effects of revised population controls on estimates from the CPS, see <bls.gov/cps/documentation.htm#pop>.

Hours and earnings—Average hourly earnings, based on establishment data from the CES, are gross earnings (i.e., earnings before payroll deductions) and include overtime premiums; they exclude irregular bonuses and value of payments in kind. Hours are those for which pay was received. Annual wages and salaries, as presented by the CPS, consist of total monies received for work performed by an employee during the income year. It includes wages, salaries, commissions, tips, piece-rate payments, and cash bonuses earned before deductions were made for taxes, bonds, union dues, etc. Persons who worked 35 hours or more are classified as working full-time.

Industry and occupational groups—Industry data derived from the CPS for 1983-91 utilize the 1980 census industrial classification developed from the 1972 Standard Industrial Classification (SIC). CPS data from 1971 to 1982 were based on the 1970 census classification system, which was developed from the 1967 SIC. Most of the industry categories were not affected by the change in classification.

The occupational classification system used in the 1980 census and in the CPS for 1983-91, evolved from the 1980 Standard Occupational Classification (SOC) system, first introduced in 1977. Occupational categories used in the 1980 census classification system are so radically different from the 1970 census system used in the CPS through 1982 that their implementation represented a break in historical data series.

Beginning in January 1992, the occupational and industrial classification systems used in the 1990 census were introduced into the CPS. (These systems were largely based on the 1980 SOC and the 1987 SIC systems, respectively.)

Beginning in 2003, the 2002 occupational and industrial classification systems were introduced into the CPS. These systems were derived from the 2000 SOC and the 2002 NAICS. The composition of detailed occupational and industrial classifications in the new classification systems was substantially changed from the previous systems in use, as was the structure for aggregating them into broad groups. Consequently, the use of the new classification systems created breaks in existing data series at all levels of aggregation. CPS data using the new classification systems are available for data from 2000. Additional information on the occupational and industrial classifications systems used in the CPS, including changes over time, appear on the BLS website at <bls.gov/cps/documentation.htm#oi>. Establishments responding to the establishment survey are classified according to the 2017 NAICS. Previously they were classified according to the SIC manual. See text, Section 15, Business Enterprise, for information about the SIC manual and NAICS.

Productivity—BLS publishes data on output per hour (labor productivity), output per combined unit of labor and capital input (multifactor productivity), and, for industry groups and industries, output per combined unit of capital, labor, energy, materials, and purchased service inputs. Labor productivity and related indexes are published for the business sector as a whole and its major subsectors: nonfarm business, manufacturing, and nonfinancial corporations, and for over 200 detailed industries. Productivity indexes that take into account capital, labor, energy, materials, and service inputs are published for 18 major manufacturing industry groups, 86 detailed manufacturing industries, utility services, and air and railroad transportation. The major sector data are published in the BLS quarterly news release *Productivity and Costs* and in the annual *Multifactor Productivity Trends* release. Industry productivity measures are updated and published annually in the news releases *Productivity and Costs by Industry* and *Multifactor Productivity Trends by Industry*. The latest data are available at the Labor Productivity and Costs website at <bls.gov/lpc/> and the Multifactor Productivity website at <bls.gov/mfp>. Detailed information on methods, limitations, and data sources appears in the BLS *Handbook of Methods*, Chapters 10 and 11 at <bls.gov/opub/hom/home.htm> and <bls.gov/lpc/lpcmethods.htm>.

Unions—As defined here, unions include traditional labor unions and employee associations similar to labor unions. Data on union membership status provided by BLS are for employed wage and salary workers and relate to their principal job. Earnings by union membership status are usual weekly earnings of full-time wage and salary workers. The information is collected through the Current Population Survey.

Work stoppages—Work stoppages include all strikes and lockouts known to BLS that last for at least 1 full day or shift and involve 1,000 or more workers. All stoppages, whether or not authorized by a union, legal or illegal, are counted. Excluded are work slowdowns and instances where employees report to work late or leave early to attend meetings or rallies.

Seasonal adjustment—Many economic statistics reflect a regularly recurring seasonal movement that can be estimated on the basis of past experience. By eliminating that part of the change which can be ascribed to usual seasonal variation (e.g., climate or school openings and closings), it is possible to observe the cyclical and other nonseasonal movements in the series. However, in evaluating deviations from the seasonal pattern—that is, changes in a seasonally adjusted series—it is important to note that seasonal adjustment is merely an approximation based on past experience. Seasonally adjusted estimates have a broader margin of possible error than the original data on which they are based, since they are subject not only to sampling and other errors, but also are affected by the uncertainties of the adjustment process itself. Consistent with BLS practices, annual estimates will be published only for not seasonally-adjusted data.

Statistical reliability—For discussion of statistical collection, estimation, sampling procedures, and measures of statistical reliability applicable to Census Bureau and BLS data, see Appendix III.

Table 617. Civilian Population—Employment Status: 1970 to June 2020

[In thousands (137,085 represents 137,085,000), except as indicated. Annual averages of monthly figures, except monthly data. Civilian noninstitutionalized population 16 years old and over. Data not strictly comparable with data for earlier years; see BLS Handbook of Methods, <http://www.bls.gov/opub/hom/>. Based on Current Population Survey; see text, Section 1 and Appendix III]

Year	Civilian noninsti- tutional population	Civilian labor force				Unemployed		Not in labor force	
		Total	Percent of population	Employed	Employ- ment/ population ratio [1]	Number	Percent of labor force	Number	Percent of population
1970.............	137,085	82,771	60.4	78,678	57.4	4,093	4.9	54,315	39.6
1980.............	167,745	106,940	63.8	99,303	59.2	7,637	7.1	60,806	36.2
1990.............	189,164	125,840	66.5	118,793	62.8	7,047	5.6	63,324	33.5
2000.............	212,577	142,583	67.1	136,891	64.4	5,692	4.0	69,994	32.9
2005.............	226,082	149,320	66.0	141,730	62.7	7,591	5.1	76,762	34.0
2006.............	228,815	151,428	66.2	144,427	63.1	7,001	4.6	77,387	33.8
2007.............	231,867	153,124	66.0	146,047	63.0	7,078	4.6	78,743	34.0
2008.............	233,788	154,287	66.0	145,362	62.2	8,924	5.8	79,501	34.0
2009.............	235,801	154,142	65.4	139,877	59.3	14,265	9.3	81,659	34.6
2010.............	237,830	153,889	64.7	139,064	58.5	14,825	9.6	83,941	35.3
2011.............	239,618	153,617	64.1	139,869	58.4	13,747	8.9	86,001	35.9
2012.............	243,284	154,975	63.7	142,469	58.6	12,506	8.1	88,310	36.3
2013.............	245,679	155,389	63.2	143,929	58.6	11,460	7.4	90,290	36.8
2014.............	247,947	155,922	62.9	146,305	59.0	9,617	6.2	92,025	37.1
2015.............	250,801	157,130	62.7	148,834	59.3	8,296	5.3	93,671	37.3
2016.............	253,538	159,187	62.8	151,436	59.7	7,751	4.9	94,351	37.2
2017.............	255,079	160,320	62.9	153,337	60.1	6,982	4.4	94,759	37.1
2018.............	257,791	162,075	62.9	155,761	60.4	6,314	3.9	95,716	37.1
2019.............	259,175	163,539	63.1	157,538	60.8	6,001	3.7	95,636	36.9
2020 Monthly [2]									
January...........	259,502	164,606	63.4	158,714	61.2	5,892	3.6	94,896	36.6
February..........	259,628	164,546	63.4	158,759	61.1	5,787	3.5	95,082	36.6
March.............	259,758	162,913	62.7	155,772	60.0	7,140	4.4	96,845	37.3
April..............	259,896	156,481	60.2	133,403	51.3	23,078	14.7	103,415	39.8
May...............	260,047	158,227	60.8	137,242	52.8	20,985	13.3	101,820	39.2
June..............	260,204	159,932	61.5	142,182	54.6	17,750	11.1	100,273	38.5

[1] Civilian employed as a percent of the civilian noninstitutional population. [2] Seasonally adjusted, except for population figures.

Source: U.S. Bureau of Labor Statistics, "Labor Force Statistics from the Current Population Survey," <https://www.bls.gov/cps/tables. htm#empstat>, accessed July 2020.

Table 618. Civilian Labor Force and Participation Rates Projections: 2019 to 2028

[163.0 represents 163,000,000. Civilian noninstitutionalized population 16 years old and over. Based on Current Population Survey; see text, Section 1 and Appendix III]

Race, Hispanic origin, sex, and age	Civilian labor force (mil.)						Participation rate (percent) [1]					
	2019 [2]	2024	2025	2026	2027	2028	2019 [2]	2024	2025	2026	2027	2028
Total [3].................	163.0	167.4	168.3	169.2	170.1	171.0	62.7	61.7	61.6	61.4	61.3	61.2
White....................	126.2	127.7	128.0	128.3	128.6	128.9	62.6	61.5	61.4	61.2	61.1	61.0
Male....................	68.2	68.6	68.6	68.7	68.8	68.8	69.2	67.4	67.1	66.9	66.6	66.4
Female..................	58.0	59.1	59.4	59.6	59.8	60.1	56.3	55.9	55.8	55.8	55.7	55.7
Black....................	20.7	21.5	21.7	21.9	22.0	22.2	62.3	61.2	61.0	60.9	60.7	60.6
Male....................	9.8	10.2	10.2	10.3	10.4	10.4	64.8	63.0	62.6	62.3	62.0	61.8
Female..................	10.8	11.4	11.5	11.6	11.7	11.8	60.2	59.8	59.7	59.7	59.6	59.6
Asian....................	10.4	11.6	11.8	12.1	12.3	12.5	63.5	63.2	63.2	63.2	63.2	63.2
Male....................	5.5	6.1	6.2	6.3	6.4	6.6	71.5	71.0	71.0	70.9	70.9	70.8
Female..................	4.9	5.5	5.6	5.7	5.9	6.0	56.4	56.4	56.4	56.5	56.6	56.6
All others [4].............	5.9	6.6	6.8	7.0	7.2	7.3	64.4	63.8	63.8	63.7	63.7	63.7
Male....................	3.0	3.4	3.5	3.6	3.7	3.7	68.8	67.2	67.0	66.7	66.6	66.4
Female..................	2.8	3.2	3.3	3.4	3.5	3.6	60.4	60.6	60.7	60.8	61.0	61.2
Hispanic [5]...............	29.0	32.7	33.4	34.2	35.0	35.7	66.3	65.8	65.8	65.8	65.8	65.8
Male....................	16.5	18.4	18.8	19.2	19.6	20.0	75.5	74.3	74.1	73.9	73.7	73.6
Female..................	12.6	14.3	14.6	15.0	15.4	15.7	57.1	57.4	57.5	57.7	57.8	58.0
Male....................	86.5	88.2	88.6	88.9	89.3	89.6	68.8	67.1	66.8	66.6	66.3	66.1
16 to 19 years...........	2.9	2.7	2.6	2.6	2.5	2.4	33.8	30.9	30.6	30.2	29.5	29.0
20 to 24 years...........	7.7	7.4	7.4	7.3	7.3	7.3	73.1	70.3	69.6	69.0	68.4	67.8
25 to 34 years...........	20.0	20.2	20.1	20.0	19.8	19.6	88.9	87.8	87.5	87.3	87.0	86.8
35 to 44 years...........	18.3	19.7	20.0	20.3	20.6	20.8	90.8	90.1	90.0	89.8	89.6	89.5
45 to 54 years...........	17.2	16.7	16.7	16.7	16.8	17.0	86.8	85.9	85.8	85.7	85.5	85.3
55 to 64 years...........	14.5	14.2	14.1	14.1	14.0	13.8	71.2	71.2	71.3	71.5	71.6	71.8
65 years and over......	5.8	7.4	7.7	8.0	8.3	8.6	24.4	26.2	26.6	26.9	27.2	27.4
Female..................	76.5	79.2	79.7	80.3	80.8	81.4	57.0	56.6	56.6	56.6	56.5	56.6
16 to 19 years...........	3.0	2.8	2.8	2.8	2.7	2.7	35.7	34.0	33.8	33.6	33.3	32.9
20 to 24 years...........	7.3	7.3	7.2	7.2	7.3	7.3	68.8	68.2	68.1	67.9	67.8	67.7
25 to 34 years...........	17.2	17.5	17.4	17.4	17.3	17.3	76.0	76.3	76.3	76.4	76.5	76.5
35 to 44 years...........	15.7	16.7	16.9	17.1	17.3	17.5	75.1	75.1	75.1	75.1	75.1	75.1
45 to 54 years...........	15.6	15.4	15.5	15.5	15.7	15.9	75.0	75.9	76.1	76.3	76.5	76.7
55 to 64 years...........	13.1	13.2	13.2	13.3	13.2	13.2	59.6	62.0	62.6	63.2	63.7	64.3
65 years and over......	4.8	6.3	6.6	6.9	7.2	7.5	16.4	18.5	18.9	19.3	19.6	19.9

[1] Civilian labor force as a percent of the civilian noninstitutional population projections. [2] Data for 2019 are actual. [3] Includes other races, not shown separately. [4] Includes persons classified as multi-racial, American Indian and Alaska Native, or Native Hawaiian and Other Pacific Islander. [5] Persons of Hispanic origin may be of any race.

Source: U.S. Bureau of Labor Statistics, "Employment Projections Program," <bls.gov/emp/data/labor-force.htm>, accessed June 2020.

Table 619. Civilian Population—Employment Status by Sex, Race, and Ethnicity: 1980 to 2019

[In thousands (79,398 represents 79,398,000), except as indicated. Annual averages of monthly figures. Data not strictly comparable with data for earlier years; see BLS Handbook of Methods, <https://www.bls.gov/opub/hom/>. For U.S. totals see Table 617]

Year, sex, race, and Hispanic origin	Civilian noninstitu- tionalized population	Civilian labor force				Unemployed		Not in labor force	
		Total	Percent of population	Employed	Employ- ment/ population ratio [1]	Number	Percent of labor force	Number	Percent of population
Male:									
1980.........	79,398	61,453	77.4	57,186	72.0	4,267	6.9	17,945	22.6
1990.........	90,377	69,011	76.4	65,104	72.0	3,906	5.7	21,367	23.6
2000.........	101,964	76,280	74.8	73,305	71.9	2,975	3.9	25,684	25.2
2010.........	115,174	81,985	71.2	73,359	63.7	8,626	10.5	33,189	28.8
2017.........	123,275	85,145	69.1	81,402	66.0	3,743	4.4	38,130	30.9
2018.........	124,678	86,096	69.1	82,698	66.3	3,398	3.9	38,582	30.9
2019.........	125,353	86,687	69.2	83,460	66.6	3,227	3.7	38,667	30.8
Female:									
1980.........	88,348	45,487	51.5	42,117	47.7	3,370	7.4	42,861	48.5
1990.........	98,787	56,829	57.5	53,689	54.3	3,140	5.5	41,957	42.5
2000.........	110,613	66,303	59.9	63,586	57.5	2,717	4.1	44,310	40.1
2010.........	122,656	71,904	58.6	65,705	53.6	6,199	8.6	50,752	41.4
2017.........	131,804	75,175	57.0	71,936	54.6	3,239	4.3	56,629	43.0
2018.........	133,112	75,978	57.1	73,063	54.9	2,916	3.8	57,134	42.9
2019.........	133,822	76,852	57.4	74,078	55.4	2,774	3.6	56,970	42.6
White: [2]									
1980.........	146,122	93,600	64.1	87,715	60.0	5,884	6.3	52,523	35.9
1990.........	160,625	107,447	66.9	102,261	63.7	5,186	4.8	53,178	33.1
2000.........	176,220	118,545	67.3	114,424	64.9	4,121	3.5	57,675	32.7
2010.........	192,075	125,084	65.1	114,168	59.4	10,916	8.7	66,991	34.9
2017.........	198,942	124,941	62.8	120,176	60.4	4,765	3.8	74,001	37.2
2018.........	200,221	125,815	62.8	121,461	60.7	4,354	3.5	74,407	37.2
2019.........	200,827	126,600	63.0	122,441	61.0	4,159	3.3	74,227	37.0
Black: [2]									
1980.........	17,824	10,865	61.0	9,313	52.2	1,553	14.3	6,959	39.0
1990.........	21,477	13,740	64.0	12,175	56.7	1,565	11.4	7,737	36.0
2000.........	24,902	16,397	65.8	15,156	60.9	1,241	7.6	8,505	34.2
2010.........	28,708	17,862	62.2	15,010	52.3	2,852	16.0	10,846	37.8
2017.........	32,247	20,088	62.3	18,587	57.6	1,501	7.5	12,159	37.7
2018.........	32,761	20,414	62.3	19,091	58.3	1,322	6.5	12,347	37.7
2019.........	33,036	20,632	62.5	19,381	58.7	1,251	6.1	12,404	37.5
Asian: [2,3]									
2000.........	9,330	6,270	67.2	6,043	64.8	227	3.6	3,060	32.8
2010.........	11,199	7,248	64.7	6,705	59.9	543	7.5	3,951	35.3
2017.........	15,368	9,781	63.6	9,448	61.5	333	3.4	5,587	36.4
2018.........	15,961	10,137	63.5	9,832	61.6	304	3.0	5,825	36.5
2019.........	16,351	10,460	64.0	10,179	62.3	280	2.7	5,891	36.0
Hispanic: [4]									
1980.........	9,598	6,146	64.0	5,527	57.6	620	10.1	3,451	36.0
1990.........	15,904	10,720	67.4	9,845	61.9	876	8.2	5,184	32.6
2000.........	23,938	16,689	69.7	15,735	65.7	954	5.7	7,249	30.3
2010.........	33,713	22,748	67.5	19,906	59.0	2,843	12.5	10,964	32.5
2017.........	41,371	27,339	66.1	25,938	62.7	1,401	5.1	14,032	33.9
2018.........	42,734	28,336	66.3	27,012	63.2	1,323	4.7	14,398	33.7
2019.........	43,507	29,053	66.8	27,805	63.9	1,248	4.3	14,454	33.2
Mexican:									
1990.........	9,752	6,707	68.8	6,146	63.0	561	8.4	3,045	31.2
2000.........	15,333	10,783	70.3	10,144	66.2	639	5.9	4,550	29.7
2010.........	21,267	14,403	67.7	12,622	59.4	1,781	12.4	6,864	32.3
2017.........	25,455	16,808	66.0	15,958	62.7	849	5.1	8,647	34.0
2018.........	26,031	17,312	66.5	16,497	63.4	815	4.7	8,718	33.5
2019.........	26,251	17,611	67.1	16,836	64.1	775	4.4	8,640	32.9
Puerto Rican:									
1990.........	1,718	960	55.9	870	50.6	91	9.5	758	44.1
2000.........	2,193	1,411	64.3	1,318	60.1	92	6.6	783	35.7
2010.........	3,110	1,906	61.3	1,612	51.8	293	15.4	1,204	38.7
2017.........	3,902	2,409	61.7	2,265	58.1	144	6.0	1,493	38.3
2018.........	3,938	2,408	61.2	2,272	57.7	136	5.7	1,529	38.8
2019.........	3,941	2,448	62.1	2,325	59.0	124	5.0	1,493	37.9
Cuban:									
1990.........	918	603	65.7	559	60.9	44	7.2	315	34.3
2000.........	1,174	740	63.1	707	60.3	33	4.5	434	37.0
2010.........	1,549	970	62.6	850	54.9	120	12.4	579	37.4
2017.........	1,723	1,063	61.7	1,019	59.2	43	4.1	660	38.3
2018.........	1,905	1,181	62.0	1,139	59.8	41	3.5	725	38.1
2019.........	2,043	1,304	63.8	1,265	62.0	39	3.0	738	36.1

[1] Civilian employed as a percent of the civilian noninstitutional population. [2] Beginning with the 2003 CPS, respondents could choose more than one race. Beginning in 2003, data represent persons who selected this race group only and exclude persons reporting more than one race. The CPS in prior years allowed respondents to report only one race group. See also comments on race in text for section 1. [3] Prior to 2003, Asian includes Pacific Islanders. [4] Persons of Hispanic origin may be of any race. Includes persons of other Hispanic or Latino ethnicity, not shown separately.

Source: U.S. Bureau of Labor Statistics, CPS Tables, "Employment status of the civilian noninstitutional population by age, sex, and race" and "Employment status of the Hispanic or Latino population by sex, age, and detailed ethnic group," February 2020, and earlier releases, <https://www.bls.gov/cps/tables.htm>.

Table 620. Foreign-Born and Native-Born Populations—Employment Status by Selected Characteristics: 2019

[259,175 represents 259,175,000. For civilian noninstitutional population 16 years old and over, except as indicated. The foreign born are persons who reside in the United States but who were born outside the country or in one of its outlying areas to parents who were not U.S. citizens. The foreign born include legally admitted immigrants, refugees, temporary residents such as students and temporary workers, and undocumented immigrants. Annual averages of monthly figures. Based on Current Population Survey; see text, Section 1 and Appendix III]

Characteristic	Civilian noninstitu-tionalized population (1,000)	Civilian labor force					Not in the labor force (1,000)
		Total (1,000)	Participa-tion rate [1]	Employed (1,000)	Unemployed		
					Number (1,000)	Unemploy-ment rate	
Total........	259,175	163,539	63.1	157,538	6,001	3.7	95,636
Male........	125,353	86,687	69.2	83,460	3,227	3.7	38,666
Female........	133,822	76,852	57.4	74,078	2,774	3.6	56,970
FOREIGN BORN							
Total [2]........	42,990	28,390	66.0	27,502	888	3.1	14,600
Male........	20,814	16,234	78.0	15,791	443	2.7	4,580
Female........	22,176	12,156	54.8	11,711	446	3.7	10,020
Age:							
16 to 24 years old........	3,330	1,735	52.1	1,619	116	6.7	1,595
25 to 34 years old........	7,665	5,917	77.2	5,726	191	3.2	1,748
35 to 44 years old........	9,361	7,459	79.7	7,273	187	2.5	1,902
45 to 54 years old........	8,878	7,219	81.3	7,018	201	2.8	1,659
55 to 64 years old........	6,699	4,585	68.5	4,450	135	3.0	2,114
65 years old and over........	7,057	1,475	20.9	1,416	59	4.0	5,582
Race and Hispanic ethnicity:							
White, non-Hispanic........	7,710	4,651	60.3	4,515	136	2.9	3,059
Black, non-Hispanic........	3,837	2,716	70.8	2,606	110	4.1	1,121
Asian, non-Hispanic........	11,180	7,187	64.3	7,013	174	2.4	3,993
Hispanic [3]........	19,753	13,506	68.4	13,046	460	3.4	6,247
Educational attainment:							
Total, 25 years old and over........	39,660	26,655	67.2	25,883	773	2.9	13,005
Less than a high school diploma........	9,494	5,432	57.2	5,217	214	3.9	4,062
High school graduates, no college [4]........	9,983	6,632	66.4	6,454	178	2.7	3,351
Some college or associate's degree........	6,233	4,312	69.2	4,196	116	2.7	1,921
Bachelor's degree and higher [5]........	13,950	10,280	73.7	10,015	264	2.6	3,670
NATIVE BORN							
Total [2]........	216,185	135,148	62.5	130,036	5,112	3.8	81,037
Male........	104,540	70,453	67.4	67,669	2,784	4.0	34,087
Female........	111,645	64,696	57.9	62,367	2,328	3.6	46,949
Age:							
16 to 24 years old........	34,418	19,358	56.2	17,703	1,654	8.5	15,060
25 to 34 years old........	37,211	31,274	84.0	30,081	1,193	3.8	5,937
35 to 44 years old........	31,599	26,598	84.2	25,854	743	2.8	5,001
45 to 54 years old........	31,566	25,713	81.5	25,024	689	2.7	5,853
55 to 64 years old........	35,542	23,018	64.8	22,443	575	2.5	12,524
65 years old and over........	45,848	9,188	20.0	8,931	257	2.8	36,660
Race and Hispanic ethnicity:							
White, non-Hispanic........	154,457	96,132	62.2	93,210	2,922	3.0	58,325
Black, non-Hispanic........	27,105	16,566	61.1	15,497	1,069	6.5	10,539
Asian, non-Hispanic........	4,720	2,973	63.0	2,874	99	3.3	1,747
Hispanic [3]........	23,754	15,547	65.4	14,759	788	5.1	8,207
Educational attainment:							
Total, 25 years and over........	181,767	115,791	63.7	112,333	3,458	3.0	65,976
Less than a high school diploma........	12,132	4,544	37.5	4,224	320	7.0	7,588
High school graduates, no college [4]........	52,476	29,530	56.3	28,383	1,146	3.9	22,946
Some college or associate's degree........	51,280	33,108	64.6	32,086	1,022	3.1	18,172
Bachelor's degree and higher [5]........	65,878	48,609	73.8	47,640	969	2.0	17,269

[1] Civilian labor force as a percent of the civilian noninstitutionalized population. [2] Includes other races, not shown separately. [3] Persons of Hispanic origin may be of any race. [4] Includes persons with a high school diploma or equivalent. [5] Includes persons with bachelor's, master's, professional, and doctoral degrees.

Source: U.S. Bureau of Labor Statistics, *Foreign-Born Workers: Labor Force Characteristics—2019*, USDL 20-0922, May 2020. See also <http://www.bls.gov/news.release/forbrn.toc.htm>.

Table 621. Employment Status of Veterans by Period of Service and Sex: 2019

[In thousands (250,377 represents 250,377,000). For civilian noninstitutional population 18 years old and over. Veterans are defined as men and women who have previously served on active duty in the U.S. Armed Forces and who were civilians at the time they were surveyed. Veterans are counted in only one period of service, their most recent wartime period; veterans who served in both a wartime period and any other service period are classified in the wartime period. See text, Section 10. Annual averages of monthly figures. Beginning with 2014, estimates for veterans incorporate updated weighting procedures. The primary impact of the change was an increase in the "Gulf War-era I" veteran population and a decrease in the number of veterans in the "Other service periods" category. For more information, see <http://www.bls.gov/cps/vetsweights2014.pdf>. Based on Current Population Survey; see text, Section 1 and Appendix III]

Veteran status, period of service, and sex	Civilian non-institu-tionalized popula-tion	Civilian labor force						Not in labor force
		Total	Percent of popula-tion	Employed		Unemployed		
				Total	Percent of popula-tion	Total	Percent of labor force	
Total, 18 years and over....................	250,377	161,458	64.5	155,749	62.2	5,709	3.5	88,919
Veterans..................................	**18,822**	**9,270**	**49.2**	**8,986**	**47.7**	**284**	**3.1**	**9,552**
Gulf War era, total............................	7,399	5,808	78.5	5,624	76.0	183	3.2	1,591
Gulf War era II [1]...........................	4,328	3,468	80.1	3,345	77.3	123	3.5	860
Gulf War era I [2]...........................	3,070	2,339	76.2	2,279	74.2	60	2.6	731
WWII, Korean War, and Vietnam era [3]......	7,213	1,479	20.5	1,437	19.9	42	2.8	5,735
Other service periods [4]....................	4,210	1,983	47.1	1,925	45.7	59	3.0	2,227
Nonveterans [5]................................	231,555	152,188	65.7	146,763	63.4	5,425	3.6	79,367
Male, 18 years and over..................	120,898	85,660	70.9	82,582	68.3	3,078	3.6	35,238
Veterans..................................	**16,938**	**8,169**	**48.2**	**7,926**	**46.8**	**243**	**3.0**	**8,769**
Gulf War era, total............................	6,170	4,968	80.5	4,815	78.0	153	3.1	1,202
Gulf War era II [1]...........................	3,602	2,974	82.6	2,874	79.8	100	3.4	628
Gulf War era I [2]...........................	2,568	1,994	77.6	1,941	75.6	53	2.7	574
WWII, Korean War, and Vietnam era [3]......	6,964	1,425	20.5	1,386	19.9	39	2.7	5,539
Other service periods [4]....................	3,803	1,776	46.7	1,726	45.4	51	2.8	2,027
Nonveterans [5]................................	103,960	77,491	74.5	74,655	71.8	2,835	3.7	26,469
Female, 18 years and over................	129,479	75,798	58.5	73,167	56.5	2,631	3.5	53,681
Veterans..................................	**1,884**	**1,101**	**58.4**	**1,060**	**56.2**	**41**	**3.7**	**784**
Gulf War era, total............................	1,228	840	68.4	810	65.9	30	3.6	389
Gulf War era II [1]...........................	726	495	68.1	471	64.9	23	4.7	232
Gulf War era I [2]...........................	502	345	68.7	338	67.4	7	2.0	157
WWII, Korean War, and Vietnam era [3]......	249	54	21.6	51	20.4	3	5.4	195
Other service periods [4]....................	407	207	50.9	199	49.0	8	3.9	200
Nonveterans [5]................................	127,595	74,697	58.5	72,107	56.5	2,590	3.5	52,898

[1] Gulf War era II: September 2001–present. [2] Gulf War era I: August 1990–August 2001. [3] World War II: December 1941–December 1946. Korean War: July 1950–January 1955. Vietnam era: August 1964–April 1975. [4] Other service periods: all other time periods. [5] Nonveterans are men and women who never served on active duty in the U.S. Armed Forces.

Source: U.S. Bureau of Labor Statistics, *Employment Situation of Veterans—2019*, USDL 20-0452, March 2020. See also <http://www.bls.gov/news.release/vet.nr0.htm>.

Table 622. Labor Force Status of Persons With and Without a Disability: 2019

[30,392 represents 30,392,000. For civilian noninstitutionalized population 16 years old and over. Persons with a disability are those who have a physical, mental, or emotional condition that causes serious difficulty with their daily activities. Annual averages of monthly figures. Based on the Current Population Survey; see text, Section 1 and Appendix III]

Characteristic	Civilian non-institutional-ized popula-tion (1,000)	Civilian labor force					Not in the labor force (1,000)
		Total (1,000)	Participation rate [1]	Employed (1,000)	Unemployed		
					Number (1,000)	Unemploy-ment rate	
WITH DISABILITY							
Total.........................	**30,392**	**6,321**	**20.8**	**5,858**	**463**	**7.3**	**24,070**
Sex:							
Male................................	14,184	3,442	24.3	3,189	254	7.4	10,741
Female.............................	16,208	2,879	17.8	2,669	210	7.3	13,329
Age:							
16 to 64 years.....................	15,231	5,117	33.6	4,706	411	8.0	10,113
16 to 19 years.....................	667	157	23.5	123	34	21.7	510
20 to 24 years.....................	909	412	45.4	365	47	11.4	497
25 to 34 years.....................	1,992	973	48.8	866	107	11.0	1,019
35 to 44 years.....................	2,168	899	41.5	836	63	7.0	1,269
45 to 54 years.....................	3,393	1,154	34.0	1,069	86	7.4	2,238
55 to 64 years.....................	6,103	1,522	24.9	1,448	74	4.9	4,580
65 years and over..................	15,161	1,204	7.9	1,152	52	4.3	13,957
WITHOUT DISABILITY							
Total.........................	**228,783**	**157,218**	**68.7**	**151,680**	**5,537**	**3.5**	**71,566**
Sex:							
Male................................	111,170	83,244	74.9	80,272	2,973	3.6	27,925
Female.............................	117,614	73,973	62.9	71,409	2,564	3.5	43,641
Age:							
16 to 64 years.....................	191,039	147,758	77.3	142,485	5,273	3.6	43,282
16 to 19 years.....................	16,026	5,739	35.8	5,027	712	12.4	10,286
20 to 24 years.....................	20,147	14,784	73.4	13,807	977	6.6	5,363
25 to 34 years.....................	42,885	36,218	84.5	34,942	1,277	3.5	6,667
35 to 44 years.....................	38,792	33,159	85.5	32,292	867	2.6	5,634
45 to 54 years.....................	37,052	31,777	85.8	30,973	804	2.5	5,275
55 to 64 years.....................	36,138	26,081	72.2	25,445	636	2.4	10,057
65 years and over..................	37,744	9,460	25.1	9,195	265	2.8	28,284

[1] Civilian labor force as a percent of the civilian noninstitutional population.

Source: U.S. Bureau of Labor Statistics, "Persons with A Disability: Labor Force Characteristics—2019," USDL 20-0339, <http://www.bls.gov/cps/demographics.htm#disability>, accessed February 2020.

Table 623. Civilian Labor Force—Percent Distribution by Sex and Age: 1980 to 2019

[106,940 represents 106,940,000. Civilian noninstitutionalized population 16 years old and over. Annual averages of monthly figures. Data not strictly comparable with data for earlier years; see BLS Handbook of Methods, <https://www.bls.gov/opub/hom/>. Based on Current Population Survey; see text, Section 1 and Appendix III]

Year and sex	Civilian labor force (1,000)	Percent distribution						
		16 to 19 years	20 to 24 years	25 to 34 years	35 to 44 years	45 to 54 years	55 to 64 years	65 years and over
Total:								
1980....................	106,940	8.8	14.9	27.3	19.1	15.8	11.2	2.9
1990....................	125,840	6.2	11.7	28.6	25.5	16.1	9.2	2.7
2000....................	142,583	5.8	10.0	23.0	26.3	21.8	10.1	3.0
2010....................	153,889	3.8	9.8	21.8	21.7	23.4	15.1	4.4
2019....................	163,539	3.6	9.3	22.7	20.8	20.1	16.9	6.5
Male:								
1980....................	61,453	8.1	14.0	27.6	19.3	16.1	11.8	3.1
1990....................	69,011	5.9	11.4	28.8	25.3	16.1	9.6	2.9
2000....................	76,280	5.6	9.9	23.4	26.3	21.3	10.2	3.3
2010....................	81,985	3.6	9.6	22.4	22.1	23.0	14.8	4.5
2019....................	86,687	3.4	9.0	23.0	21.1	19.9	16.8	6.8
Female:								
1980....................	45,487	9.6	16.1	26.9	19.0	15.4	10.4	2.6
1990....................	56,829	6.5	12.0	28.3	25.8	16.1	8.7	2.6
2000....................	66,303	6.0	10.2	22.5	26.4	22.3	9.9	2.7
2010....................	71,904	4.1	10.0	21.2	21.2	23.8	15.6	4.2
2019....................	76,852	3.8	9.6	22.4	20.5	20.4	17.0	6.2

Source: U.S. Bureau of Labor Statistics, CPS Tables, "Employment status of the civilian noninstitutional population by age, sex, and race," February 2020, and earlier releases, <https://www.bls.gov/cps/tables.htm>.

Table 624. Civilian Labor Force and Participation Rates by Educational Attainment, Sex, Race, and Hispanic Origin: 2005 to 2019

[127,030 represents 127,030,000. Civilian noninstitutional population 25 years old and over. Annual averages of monthly figures. Revisions to population controls and other changes can affect the comparability of data over time; see BLS Handbook of Methods, <https://www.bls.gov/opub/hom/>. See Table 660 for unemployment data. Rates are based on annual average civilian noninstitutional population of each specified group and represent proportion of each specified group in the civilian labor force]

Year, sex, and race/ethnicity	Civilian labor force					Participation rate (percent) [1]				
		Percent distribution								
	Total (1,000)	Less than a high school diploma	High school graduate, no college	Less than a bachelor's degree	College graduate	Total	Less than a high school diploma	High school graduate, no college	Less than a bachelor's degree	College graduate
Total: [2]										
2005..............	127,030	10.0	30.1	27.5	32.4	67.1	45.5	63.2	72.5	77.9
2010..............	132,955	8.9	28.8	27.7	34.6	66.5	46.3	61.6	70.5	76.7
2015..............	135,907	8.1	26.0	27.6	38.4	64.0	45.4	57.2	66.6	74.4
2019..............	142,447	7.0	25.4	26.3	41.3	64.3	46.1	57.9	65.1	73.8
Male:										
2005..............	68,389	11.7	30.9	25.4	32.1	75.4	58.6	73.6	79.3	82.9
2010..............	71,129	10.6	30.4	25.6	33.4	74.1	59.1	71.4	76.7	81.3
2015..............	72,698	9.7	28.1	25.8	36.4	71.5	58.3	67.2	73.1	79.0
2019..............	75,947	8.4	28.0	25.1	38.5	71.4	58.7	67.7	71.9	77.8
Female:										
2005..............	58,641	8.0	29.2	30.0	32.8	59.4	32.9	53.8	66.8	72.9
2010..............	61,825	7.0	26.9	30.1	36.0	59.5	33.5	52.4	65.4	72.4
2015..............	63,209	6.2	23.6	29.6	40.7	57.2	32.3	47.6	61.1	70.2
2019..............	66,498	5.4	22.4	27.5	44.6	57.8	33.5	48.0	59.2	70.2
White: [3]										
2005..............	104,240	9.8	29.9	27.6	32.7	66.9	46.4	62.5	72.0	77.5
2010..............	108,274	8.9	28.7	27.5	34.9	66.5	47.7	61.2	70.1	76.5
2015..............	107,366	8.1	25.9	27.5	38.5	63.8	46.7	56.7	65.9	74.0
2019..............	110,610	7.1	25.4	26.2	41.3	63.9	48.1	57.4	64.0	73.0
Black: [3]										
2005..............	14,252	11.2	36.4	30.2	22.2	67.2	39.8	67.9	75.6	82.0
2010..............	15,114	9.4	33.3	32.8	24.5	65.8	38.8	63.8	73.5	79.5
2015..............	16,279	7.5	30.9	33.3	28.3	63.9	37.5	58.8	70.2	77.7
2019..............	17,705	6.5	30.1	31.4	32.0	64.5	37.3	58.9	69.0	77.6
Asian: [3]										
2005..............	5,805	8.0	17.7	17.3	57.0	69.4	45.3	61.8	71.6	77.5
2010..............	6,601	7.3	18.8	17.1	56.7	68.7	44.1	62.8	70.6	75.9
2015..............	8,200	6.1	17.1	16.0	60.9	66.7	40.8	58.8	68.1	73.7
2019..............	9,520	5.1	14.8	15.0	65.1	67.9	38.4	58.3	67.8	75.2
Hispanic: [4]										
2005..............	16,135	35.5	29.4	20.9	14.2	70.8	61.4	74.3	78.8	81.7
2010..............	18,987	31.4	30.8	21.7	16.0	71.4	61.9	73.9	77.8	81.7
2015..............	21,618	27.7	29.8	23.6	18.9	69.3	59.3	69.6	75.5	80.1
2019..............	24,298	23.3	31.4	23.5	21.8	69.9	58.6	70.5	75.2	79.2

[1] Civilian labor force as a percent of the civilian noninstitutional population. [2] Includes other races, not shown separately. [3] Beginning in 2003, data represent persons who selected this race group only and exclude persons reporting more than one race. See footnote 2, Table 619. [4] Persons of Hispanic origin may be of any race.

Source: U.S. Bureau of Labor Statistics, CPS Tables, "Employment status of the civilian noninstitutional population 25 years and over by educational attainment, sex, race, and Hispanic or Latino ethnicity," February 2020, and earlier releases, <https://www.bls.gov/cps/tables.htm>.

Table 625. Civilian Labor Force by Employment Status and Sex by State: 2019

[In thousands (163,539 represents 163,539,000), except ratio and rate. Preliminary data. Civilian noninstitutionalized population 16 years old and over. Annual averages of monthly figures. Data for states may not sum to national totals due to rounding]

State	Labor force Total	Labor force Female	Employed Total	Employed Female	Employ-ment/ population ratio [1]	Unemployed Number Total	Unemployed Number Female	Unemployed Rate [2] Total	Unemployed Rate [2] Male	Unemployed Rate [2] Female	Participation rate [3] Male	Participation rate [3] Female
United States	**163,539**	**76,852**	**157,538**	**74,078**	**60.8**	**6,001**	**2,774**	**3.7**	**3.7**	**3.6**	**69.2**	**57.4**
Alabama	2,263	1,069	2,196	1,034	56.9	67	35	3.0	2.7	3.3	65.3	52.6
Alaska	345	159	324	152	59.3	21	7	6.1	7.4	4.6	66.7	59.5
Arizona	3,544	1,659	3,374	1,573	59.0	171	87	4.8	4.5	5.2	67.5	56.7
Arkansas	1,370	649	1,321	625	56.3	49	24	3.5	3.5	3.6	63.9	53.1
California	19,435	8,826	18,642	8,463	59.6	794	364	4.1	4.1	4.1	69.5	55.2
Colorado	3,144	1,443	3,063	1,401	67.2	81	42	2.6	2.3	2.9	75.1	62.9
Connecticut	1,915	924	1,842	893	63.8	73	31	3.8	4.2	3.4	71.3	61.8
Delaware	490	239	471	231	60.2	20	9	4.0	4.3	3.6	67.6	58.3
District of Columbia	412	211	388	200	67.1	24	12	5.7	5.9	5.5	74.6	68.1
Florida	10,357	4,879	10,032	4,720	57.3	325	160	3.1	3.0	3.3	65.2	53.5
Georgia	5,084	2,446	4,910	2,359	59.9	174	87	3.4	3.3	3.6	68.1	56.5
Hawaii	661	323	643	316	58.9	19	7	2.8	3.6	2.0	64.5	57.0
Idaho	883	396	857	385	62.6	26	11	2.9	3.1	2.8	71.8	57.3
Illinois	6,464	3,072	6,209	2,954	62.0	255	118	3.9	4.0	3.8	70.0	59.4
Indiana	3,384	1,580	3,268	1,529	62.4	116	51	3.4	3.6	3.2	70.9	58.6
Iowa	1,759	832	1,709	812	69.0	49	20	2.8	3.2	2.4	75.6	66.4
Kansas	1,481	703	1,435	683	64.4	46	20	3.1	3.3	2.8	71.4	61.7
Kentucky	2,069	959	1,980	924	56.5	89	34	4.3	4.9	3.6	65.6	52.8
Louisiana	2,098	1,015	1,997	961	55.8	100	53	4.8	4.4	5.2	63.9	53.9
Maine	689	332	668	324	60.2	21	9	3.1	3.5	2.6	66.3	58.2
Maryland	3,309	1,647	3,191	1,590	66.8	118	58	3.6	3.6	3.5	73.6	65.5
Massachusetts	3,841	1,889	3,728	1,840	65.7	113	49	2.9	3.3	2.6	71.8	64.0
Michigan	4,965	2,366	4,767	2,275	59.5	199	91	4.0	4.1	3.9	66.8	57.4
Minnesota	3,107	1,496	3,006	1,457	67.8	101	39	3.3	3.9	2.6	73.5	66.7
Mississippi	1,277	624	1,205	588	52.5	72	36	5.6	5.4	5.8	60.5	51.3
Missouri	3,080	1,495	2,981	1,445	61.9	99	50	3.2	3.0	3.4	68.3	59.9
Montana	536	252	518	243	60.7	19	9	3.5	3.4	3.7	66.9	59.1
Nebraska	1,047	492	1,013	477	68.2	34	15	3.3	3.5	3.0	75.7	65.4
Nevada	1,565	724	1,502	697	61.6	63	27	4.0	4.3	3.7	69.8	58.7
New Hampshire	777	364	757	355	67.4	20	9	2.6	2.7	2.5	74.8	63.9
New Jersey	4,541	2,178	4,381	2,103	61.7	160	74	3.5	3.6	3.4	69.0	59.1
New Mexico	953	446	906	425	55.2	47	21	4.9	5.1	4.7	63.7	52.8
New York	9,492	4,510	9,115	4,344	58.1	377	166	4.0	4.2	3.7	66.5	55.1
North Carolina	5,092	2,428	4,892	2,331	59.3	200	97	3.9	3.9	4.0	68.2	55.9
North Dakota	405	187	396	183	67.7	10	4	2.3	2.5	2.2	73.1	65.3
Ohio	5,855	2,766	5,623	2,664	60.7	232	102	4.0	4.2	3.7	69.1	57.7
Oklahoma	1,839	837	1,777	806	58.8	63	31	3.4	3.1	3.7	68.5	53.6
Oregon	2,109	993	2,029	957	59.3	80	36	3.8	3.9	3.6	66.7	56.9
Pennsylvania	6,508	3,120	6,232	2,996	60.6	276	124	4.2	4.5	4.0	68.2	58.6
Rhode Island	554	263	535	252	61.9	19	11	3.5	3.0	4.0	70.4	58.4
South Carolina	2,398	1,143	2,330	1,113	57.3	69	29	2.9	3.1	2.6	65.4	53.3
South Dakota	471	222	454	214	67.1	16	8	3.5	3.3	3.6	73.5	65.5
Tennessee	3,363	1,573	3,250	1,518	60.3	113	55	3.4	3.3	3.5	69.4	56.0
Texas	14,078	6,337	13,588	6,112	61.8	490	225	3.5	3.4	3.6	72.3	56.2
Utah	1,612	718	1,571	699	66.6	42	20	2.6	2.5	2.7	76.1	60.6
Vermont	344	166	336	162	64.6	8	4	2.3	2.4	2.2	69.9	62.5
Virginia	4,434	2,090	4,309	2,028	64.4	125	61	2.8	2.7	2.9	73.2	59.8
Washington	3,959	1,825	3,792	1,753	62.8	168	72	4.2	4.5	4.0	71.7	59.6
West Virginia	801	374	763	358	52.6	39	17	4.8	5.2	4.4	60.4	50.5
Wisconsin	3,089	1480	2,985	1,429	64.3	104	51	3.4	3.3	3.5	70.5	62.8
Wyoming	292	132	282	128	62.9	10	5	3.5	3.6	3.4	70.8	59.6

[1] Civilian employment as a percent of civilian noninstitutionalized population. [2] Percent unemployed of the civilian labor force. [3] Percent of civilian noninstitutionalized population of each specified group in the civilian labor force.

Source: U.S. Bureau of Labor Statistics, Labor Force Statistics from the Current Population Survey, "Employment status of the civilian noninstitutional population by sex, age, and race," <http://www.bls.gov/cps/tables.htm>; and Local Area Unemployment Statistics, "Expanded State Employment Status Demographic Data," <https://www.bls.gov/lau/#tables>; accessed July 2020.

Table 626. Civilian Labor Force Status by Selected Metropolitan Area: 2019

[163,539 represents 163,539,000. Civilian noninstitutional population 16 years old and over. Annual averages of monthly figures. Data are derived from the Local Area Unemployment Statistics program, a Federal-State cooperative effort in which monthly estimates of total employment and unemployment are prepared for approximately 7,500 areas. For definitions of metropolitan areas, see Appendix II]

Metropolitan area ranked by 2010 population	Civilian labor force (1,000)	Unemployment rate [1]	Metropolitan area ranked by 2010 population	Civilian labor force (1,000)	Unemployment rate [1]
United States, total	**163,539**	**3.0**	San Antonio-New Braunfels, TX	1,205	3.1
New York-Newark-Jersey City, NY-NJ-PA	9,941	3.7	Orlando-Kissimmee-Sanford, FL	1,362	3.0
Los Angeles-Long Beach-Anaheim, CA	6,745	4.0	Cincinnati, OH-KY-IN	1,127	3.7
Chicago-Naperville-Elgin, IL-IN-WI	4,860	3.8	Cleveland-Elyria, OH	1,043	4.0
Dallas-Fort Worth-Arlington, TX	3,972	3.3	Kansas City, MO-KS	1,139	3.3
Philadelphia-Camden-Wilmington, PA-NJ-DE-MD	3,126	4.1	Las Vegas-Henderson-Paradise, NV	1,132	4.0
Houston-The Woodlands-Sugar Land, TX	3,429	3.8	Columbus, OH	1,099	3.6
Washington-Arlington-Alexandria, DC-VA-MD-WV	3,469	3.1	Indianapolis-Carmel-Anderson, IN	1,072	3.0
Miami-Fort Lauderdale-West Palm Beach, FL	3,158	2.8	San Jose-Sunnyvale-Santa Clara, CA	1,085	2.6
Atlanta-Sandy Springs-Roswell, GA	3,090	3.2	Austin-Round Rock, TX	1,237	2.7
Boston-Cambridge-Nashua, MA-NH NECTA [2]	2,831	2.6	Virginia Beach-Norfolk-Newport News, VA-NC	860	3.1
San Francisco-Oakland-Hayward, CA	2,589	2.6	Nashville-Davidson-Murfreesboro-Franklin, TN	1,091	2.6
Detroit-Warren-Dearborn, MI	2,162	4.3	Providence-Warwick, RI-MA NECTA [2]	691	3.6
Riverside-San Bernardino-Ontario, CA	2,072	4.0	Milwaukee-Waukesha-West Allis, WI	818	3.5
Phoenix-Mesa-Scottsdale, AZ	2,498	4.1	Jacksonville, FL	785	3.1
Seattle-Tacoma-Bellevue, WA	2,172	3.3	Memphis, TN-MS-AR	645	4.2
Minneapolis-St. Paul-Bloomington, MN-WI	2,031	3.0	Oklahoma City, OK	686	3.0
San Diego-Carlsbad, CA	1,591	3.2	Louisville-Jefferson County, KY-IN	676	3.8
St. Louis, MO-IL	1,477	3.3	Hartford-W. Hartford-E. Hartford, CT NECTA [2]	630	3.8
Tampa-St. Petersburg-Clearwater, FL	1,554	3.2	Richmond, VA	689	2.9
Baltimore-Columbia-Towson, MD	1,522	3.6	New Orleans-Metairie, LA	596	4.5
Denver-Aurora-Lakewood, CO	1,677	2.7	Buffalo-Cheektowaga-Niagara Falls, NY	540	4.4
Pittsburgh, PA	1,212	4.3	Raleigh, NC	732	3.4
Portland-Vancouver-Hillsboro, OR-WA	1,326	3.5	Birmingham-Hoover, AL	554	2.7
Charlotte-Concord-Gastonia, NC-SC	1,370	3.5	Salt Lake City, UT	669	2.5
Sacramento-Roseville-Arden-Arcade, CA	1,101	3.6	Rochester, NY	521	4.1

[1] Percent of the civilian labor force unemployed. [2] New England City and Town Areas. See Appendix II.

Source: U.S. Bureau of Labor Statistics, "Local Area Unemployment Statistics," <http://www.bls.gov/lau/>, accessed May 2020.

Table 627. School Enrollment and Labor Force Status of Teenagers and Young Adults: 2019

[In thousands (37,734 represents 37,734,000), except percent rate. As of October. Covers civilian noninstitutional population age 16 to 24. Based on Current Population Survey; see text, Section 1 and Appendix III]

Characteristic	Population	Civilian labor force	Employed	Unemployed Total	Unemployed Rate [1]	Not in labor force
Total, 16 to 24 years [2]	**37,734**	**21,331**	**19,702**	**1,628**	**7.6**	**16,403**
Enrolled in school [2]	**21,542**	**8,189**	**7,691**	**498**	**6.1**	**13,353**
Enrolled in high school	9,392	2,096	1,859	237	11.3	7,296
Male	4,922	1,036	904	132	12.7	3,886
Female	4,470	1,060	955	105	9.9	3,410
Enrolled in college	12,150	6,093	5,833	261	4.3	6,057
Male	5,530	2,548	2,405	143	5.6	2,982
Female	6,620	3,545	3,427	118	3.3	3,075
Enrolled in two-year college	3,072	1,838	1,728	110	6.0	1,233
Enrolled in four-year college	9,078	4,255	4,104	151	3.5	4,823
White:						
Enrolled in high school	6,840	1,658	1,483	175	10.6	5,182
Enrolled in college	8,737	4,557	4,379	179	3.9	4,180
Black or African American:						
Enrolled in high school	1,356	206	176	30	14.8	1,150
Enrolled in college	1,621	754	715	39	5.2	867
Asian:						
Enrolled in high school	512	68	62	6	(NA)	444
Enrolled in college	1,164	422	412	10	2.4	741
Hispanic: [3]						
Enrolled in high school	2,269	393	338	54	13.9	1,877
Enrolled in college	2,505	1,390	1,341	50	3.6	1,114
Not enrolled in school [2]	**16,192**	**13,142**	**12,011**	**1,131**	**8.6**	**3,050**
White	12,075	9,898	9,209	690	7.0	2,176
Black	2,570	2,040	1,720	320	15.7	530
Asian	640	505	462	44	8.6	134
Hispanic [3]	4,024	3,229	2,920	309	9.6	795

NA Not available. [1] Percent unemployed of civilian labor force in each category. [2] Includes other races, not shown separately. [3] Persons of Hispanic origin may be of any race.

Source: U.S. Bureau of Labor Statistics, *College Enrollment and Work Activity of Recent High School and College Graduates—2019*, USDL 20-0715, April 2020. See also <http://www.bls.gov/news.release/hsgec.toc.htm>.

Table 628. Labor Force Participation Rates by Marital Status, Sex, and Age: 1970 to 2019

[In percent. For the civilian noninstitutional population 16 years old and over. Annual averages of monthly figures. Participation rate is the civilian labor force as a percent of the civilian noninstitutional population. Based on Current Population Survey; see text, Section 1 and Appendix III]

Marital status and year	Male participation rate							Female participation rate						
	Total	16–19 years	20–24 years	25–34 years	35–44 years	45–64 years	65 years and over	Total	16–19 years	20–24 years	25–34 years	35–44 years	45–64 years	65 years and over
Single: [1]														
1970	65.5	54.6	73.8	87.9	86.2	75.7	25.2	56.8	44.7	73.0	81.4	78.6	73.0	19.7
1980	72.6	59.9	81.3	89.2	82.2	66.9	16.8	64.4	53.6	75.2	83.3	76.9	65.6	13.9
1990	74.8	55.1	81.6	89.9	84.5	67.3	15.7	66.7	51.7	74.5	80.9	80.8	66.2	12.1
2000	73.6	52.5	80.5	89.4	82.9	69.7	17.3	68.9	51.1	76.1	83.9	80.9	69.9	10.8
2010	67.3	34.6	73.1	85.8	83.7	67.6	25.0	63.3	34.9	69.8	81.3	78.2	69.4	20.1
2012	66.8	33.7	72.9	85.8	81.7	67.1	23.6	62.8	34.5	68.5	79.8	78.1	68.2	20.5
2013	66.9	34.0	72.5	85.4	82.2	66.9	24.5	63.0	34.5	69.2	79.2	77.5	67.3	22.7
2014	66.7	33.3	72.5	85.1	82.4	64.4	25.9	62.9	34.4	69.1	79.9	77.6	65.5	21.3
2015	66.8	33.9	71.7	85.6	81.2	64.6	26.6	62.9	34.1	69.3	79.7	77.6	65.8	20.9
2016	67.3	35.1	71.8	85.5	82.5	65.2	26.1	63.4	35.0	69.2	80.9	77.3	65.4	22.6
2017	67.4	34.4	72.9	85.6	82.8	64.2	26.3	64.3	35.7	69.8	81.7	78.9	66.0	23.7
2018	67.7	34.0	72.1	85.9	83.4	66.4	25.9	64.5	35.9	70.2	81.4	78.4	66.3	25.2
2019	68.1	34.7	72.9	86.0	82.6	67.0	26.5	65.0	35.7	71.5	81.9	77.9	67.0	24.4
Married: [2]														
1970	86.1	92.3	94.7	98.0	98.1	91.2	29.9	40.5	37.8	47.9	38.8	46.8	44.0	7.3
1980	80.9	91.3	96.9	97.5	97.2	84.3	20.5	49.8	49.3	61.4	58.8	61.8	46.9	7.3
1990	78.6	92.1	95.6	96.9	96.7	82.6	17.5	58.4	49.5	66.1	69.6	74.0	56.5	8.5
2000	77.3	79.5	94.1	96.7	95.8	83.0	19.2	61.1	53.2	63.8	70.3	74.8	65.4	10.1
2010	75.8	78.2	89.3	94.3	94.5	83.6	23.5	61.0	40.2	60.9	68.8	72.8	68.8	15.2
2012	74.6	83.7	91.3	94.2	94.3	83.0	25.6	59.5	42.1	60.5	68.5	72.3	67.3	15.9
2013	74.2	81.7	90.1	94.0	94.1	83.0	25.7	58.9	46.3	58.4	67.8	71.3	67.1	16.5
2014	73.5	76.8	92.0	93.4	94.0	82.9	24.9	58.4	45.1	58.9	67.7	71.3	66.6	16.8
2015	73.4	75.9	89.7	93.5	94.2	83.1	25.2	58.1	47.1	61.6	67.1	71.9	66.0	16.8
2016	73.1	71.5	89.3	93.7	94.2	83.2	25.5	57.9	43.8	59.9	67.9	71.8	66.3	16.6
2017	72.9	80.1	89.1	93.4	94.1	83.5	25.4	58.2	50.6	61.0	68.4	72.3	67.0	17.0
2018	73.1	89.5	88.9	94.4	94.4	83.9	25.7	58.2	48.7	61.7	69.4	72.4	67.2	17.1
2019	73.0	89.9	90.6	94.4	94.6	84.3	26.4	58.6	48.4	62.4	70.5	73.5	67.6	17.9
Other: [3]														
1970	60.7	(B)	90.4	93.7	91.1	78.5	19.3	40.3	48.6	60.3	64.6	68.8	61.9	10.0
1980	67.5	(B)	92.6	94.1	91.9	73.3	13.7	43.6	50.0	68.4	76.5	77.1	60.2	8.2
1990	68.9	(B)	93.1	93.0	90.7	74.9	12.0	47.2	53.9	65.4	77.0	82.1	65.0	8.4
2000	66.8	60.5	88.1	93.2	89.9	73.9	12.9	49.0	46.0	74.0	83.1	82.9	69.8	8.7
2010	63.0	37.6	78.8	89.0	88.5	71.8	17.2	48.8	35.2	66.3	77.7	80.7	68.8	12.1
2012	61.7	35.1	78.3	88.5	87.4	70.9	17.6	48.3	34.9	68.4	77.4	79.8	67.6	12.6
2013	60.2	29.2	74.1	89.4	88.3	69.4	16.8	47.3	36.6	63.8	76.4	79.7	66.6	12.8
2014	59.6	31.2	80.3	88.8	87.1	70.4	16.9	47.3	38.2	66.3	77.2	80.1	66.8	13.0
2015	58.8	36.6	73.0	87.0	86.8	70.3	17.7	46.7	42.9	67.0	75.4	79.0	66.4	13.4
2016	59.6	37.7	71.0	88.2	87.1	71.0	19.1	46.9	40.4	67.5	76.1	80.6	66.4	13.8
2017	59.0	34.7	77.5	88.7	87.9	71.1	19.0	46.0	31.8	63.5	79.0	79.7	66.0	13.5
2018	58.3	33.3	75.3	87.0	87.6	71.7	19.1	45.9	31.9	64.3	79.8	80.6	66.4	13.8
2019	58.2	39.0	71.3	86.9	88.0	72.0	19.6	45.9	31.7	66.9	79.3	81.0	67.2	14.2

B Percentage not shown where base is less than 50,000. [1] Never married. [2] Spouse present. [3] Widowed, divorced, and separated (married, spouse absent).

Source: U.S. Bureau of Labor Statistics, Current Population Survey, unpublished data. See also <http://www.bls.gov/cps/home.htm>.

Table 629. Marital Status of Women in the Civilian Labor Force: 1970 to 2019

[31,543 represents 31,543,000. For civilian noninstitutional population 16 years and over. Annual averages of monthly figures. Based on the Current Population Survey; see text, Section 1 and Appendix III]

Year	Female civilian labor force (1,000)				Female participation rate (percent) [3]			
	Total	Never married	Married [1]	Other [2]	Total	Never married	Married [1]	Other [2]
1970	31,543	7,265	18,475	5,804	43.3	56.8	40.5	40.3
1980	45,487	11,865	24,980	8,643	51.5	64.4	49.8	43.6
1990	56,829	14,612	30,901	11,315	57.5	66.7	58.4	47.2
2000	66,303	17,849	35,146	13,308	59.9	68.9	61.1	49.0
2005	69,288	19,183	35,941	14,163	59.3	66.0	60.7	49.4
2010	71,904	20,592	36,742	14,570	58.6	63.3	61.0	48.8
2011	71,642	20,878	36,141	14,623	58.1	62.8	60.2	48.8
2012	72,648	21,506	36,436	14,706	57.7	62.8	59.5	48.3
2013	72,722	22,070	36,137	14,515	57.2	63.0	58.9	47.3
2014	73,039	22,320	36,082	14,637	57.0	62.9	58.4	47.3
2015	73,510	22,738	36,135	14,637	56.7	62.9	58.1	46.7
2016	74,433	23,321	36,387	14,725	56.8	63.4	57.9	46.9
2017	75,174	23,993	36,776	14,405	57.0	64.3	58.2	46.0
2018	75,979	24,556	36,885	14,538	57.1	64.5	58.2	45.9
2019	76,852	25,023	37,214	14,615	57.4	65.0	58.6	45.9

[1] Spouse present. [2] Widowed, divorced, and separated (married, spouse absent). [3] Civilian labor force as a percent of the civilian noninstitutional population.

Source: U.S. Bureau of Labor Statistics, Current Population Survey, unpublished data. See also <http://www.bls.gov/cps/home.htm>.

Table 630. Employment Status of Women by Marital Status and Presence and Age of Children: 1970 to 2018

[7.0 represents 7,000,000. As of March. Data are from the Current Population Survey, Annual Social and Economic Supplement (ASEC), which includes civilian noninstitutionalized population, age 16 years old and over. For more information; see text, Section 1 and Appendix III]

| Item | Total | | | With any children under age 18 | | | | | | | | |
| | | | | Total | | | Children 6 to 17 years | | | Children under 6 years | | |
	Single [1]	Married [2]	Other [3]	Single [1]	Married [2]	Other [3]	Single [1]	Married [2]	Other [3]	Single [1]	Married [2]	Other [3]
IN LABOR FORCE (millions)												
1970	7.0	18.4	5.9	(NA)	10.2	1.9	(NA)	6.3	1.3	(NA)	3.9	0.6
1980	11.2	24.9	8.8	0.6	13.7	3.6	0.2	8.4	2.6	0.3	5.2	1.0
1990	14.0	31.0	11.2	1.5	16.5	4.2	0.6	9.3	3.0	0.9	7.2	1.2
2000	17.8	35.0	13.2	3.1	18.2	4.5	1.2	10.8	3.4	1.8	7.3	1.1
2010	20.0	37.2	14.7	3.6	17.6	4.5	1.6	10.4	3.3	2.1	7.2	1.2
2016	23.2	36.9	14.7	4.1	16.9	4.1	1.9	10.2	3.0	2.2	6.7	1.1
2017	23.7	37.4	14.4	4.0	16.9	3.9	2.0	10.2	2.9	2.1	6.7	1.0
2018	24.4	37.1	14.5	4.0	16.9	3.9	2.0	10.1	3.0	2.1	6.8	0.9
PARTICIPATION RATE [4]												
1970	53.0	40.8	39.1	(NA)	39.7	60.7	(NA)	49.2	66.9	(NA)	30.3	52.2
1980	61.5	50.1	44.0	52.0	54.1	69.4	67.6	61.7	74.6	44.1	45.1	60.3
1990	66.4	58.2	46.8	55.2	66.3	74.2	69.7	73.6	79.7	48.7	58.9	63.6
2000	68.6	62.0	50.2	73.9	70.6	82.7	79.7	77.2	84.9	70.5	62.8	76.6
2010	62.3	61.7	49.2	70.1	69.7	79.2	77.0	75.9	81.8	65.6	62.5	73.1
2016	62.7	58.9	47.2	72.8	68.6	79.3	78.3	73.0	80.6	68.6	62.9	75.5
2017	63.9	59.1	46.4	73.4	69.3	79.0	78.9	74.3	80.8	68.9	62.9	74.1
2018	64.5	58.3	46.3	75.0	69.0	79.7	79.5	74.7	81.2	71.3	61.8	75.1
EMPLOYMENT (millions)												
1970	6.5	17.5	5.6	(NA)	9.6	1.8	(NA)	6.0	1.2	(NA)	3.6	0.6
1980	10.1	23.6	8.2	0.4	12.8	3.3	0.2	8.1	2.4	0.2	4.8	0.9
1990	12.9	29.9	10.5	1.2	15.8	3.8	0.5	8.9	2.7	0.7	6.9	1.1
2000	16.4	34.0	12.7	2.7	17.6	4.3	1.1	10.6	3.2	1.6	7.1	1.1
2010	17.5	35.0	13.3	3.0	16.5	4.0	1.3	9.8	2.9	1.6	6.7	1.1
2016	21.4	35.7	14.0	3.7	16.3	3.9	1.8	9.9	2.9	1.9	6.5	1.0
2017	22.3	36.4	13.6	3.7	16.4	3.7	1.8	9.9	2.8	1.9	6.5	0.9
2018	23.0	36.2	13.9	3.7	16.5	3.7	1.8	9.9	2.8	1.9	6.6	0.8
UNEMPLOYMENT RATE [5]												
1970	7.1	4.8	4.8	(NA)	6.0	7.2	(NA)	4.8	5.9	(NA)	7.9	9.8
1980	10.3	5.3	6.4	23.2	5.9	9.2	15.6	4.4	7.9	29.2	8.3	12.8
1990	8.2	3.5	5.7	18.4	4.2	8.5	14.5	3.8	7.7	20.8	4.8	10.2
2000	7.3	2.7	4.3	11.0	2.9	5.1	8.7	2.6	4.8	12.6	3.5	5.9
2010	12.3	6.0	9.7	18.1	6.3	11.1	14.4	6.0	10.3	20.9	6.7	13.4
2016	8.0	3.1	4.7	10.4	3.2	5.5	8.7	3.1	4.5	11.9	3.4	8.2
2017	6.3	2.8	5.1	9.4	3.1	5.4	7.3	3.1	4.8	11.3	3.1	7.3
2018	5.6	2.6	4.2	8.0	2.5	5.2	6.6	2.3	4.7	9.3	2.8	6.6

NA Not available. [1] Never married. [2] Spouse present. [3] Widowed, divorced, or separated (married, spouse absent). [4] Percent of women in each specific category in the labor force. [5] Unemployed as a percent of civilian labor force in specified group.

Source: U.S. Bureau of Labor Statistics, unpublished data. See also <http://www.bls.gov/cps/home.htm>.

Table 631. Labor Force Participation Rates for Wives, Spouse Present, by Age of Own Youngest Child: 1990 to 2018

[In percent. As of March. Based on Current Population Survey, Annual Social and Economic Supplement (ASEC), which includes civilian noninstitutionalized population, 16 years old and over, and military personnel who live in households with at least one other civilian adult. Armed Forces includes only those Armed Forces members living on or off post with their families; all other members of the Armed Forces are excluded. Data refer to persons in primary families. For more information; see text, Section 1 and Appendix III]

| Presence and age of child | 1990 | 2000 | 2010 | 2016 | 2017 | 2018 | | | | |
						Total	White [1]	Black [1]	Asian [1, 2]	Hispanic [3]
Wives, total	**58.3**	**62.2**	**61.9**	**59.1**	**59.3**	**58.5**	**58.2**	**62.7**	**56.9**	**55.0**
No children under 18 years	51.1	54.8	56.0	52.7	52.8	51.8	51.3	54.6	52.9	52.1
With children under 18 years	66.5	70.9	70.1	68.9	69.5	69.2	69.9	75.0	60.4	57.2
Under 6 years, total	59.1	63.1	62.9	63.1	63.1	62.1	63.5	68.3	50.0	47.2
Under 3 years	55.9	59.4	59.5	62.3	62.1	60.0	61.7	62.1	46.6	43.3
Under 1 year	53.9	58.4	59.0	60.0	60.4	59.2	60.6	64.1	46.6	30.4
1 year	(NA)	(NA)	57.6	62.3	62.3	59.7	62.5	54.6	43.1	47.9
2 years	60.9	61.9	62.4	64.9	63.7	61.3	62.0	69.3	49.3	51.1
3 to 5 years	64.1	68.6	67.7	64.2	64.5	64.9	66.0	76.3	53.7	51.6
3 years	63.0	66.0	66.4	61.2	62.2	64.3	67.0	70.1	44.4	49.4
4 years	65.0	69.6	68.9	65.7	65.4	65.0	65.3	76.6	57.5	57.2
5 years	64.4	70.7	68.1	66.2	66.5	65.7	65.4	83.7	59.9	48.2
6 to 13 years	73.1	76.0	74.8	72.2	73.5	74.1	74.0	81.4	69.3	63.5
14 to 17 years	75.0	80.8	79.0	75.8	76.8	76.6	77.1	77.4	71.8	68.8

NA Not available. [1] Persons in this race group only. See footnote 2, Table 619. [2] Excludes Pacific Islanders. [3] Persons of Hispanic origin may be of any race.

Source: U.S. Bureau of Labor Statistics, unpublished data. See also <http://www.bls.gov/cps/home.htm>.

Table 632. Married Couples by Labor Force Status of Spouses: 1990 to 2019

[52,317 represents 52,317,000. As of March. For opposite-sex married family groups only. Based on the Annual Social and Economic Supplement (ASEC) to the Current Population Survey; for details see source and Appendix III]

Year	All married couples	In labor force — Husband & wife	In labor force — Husband only	In labor force — Wife only	Husband & wife not in labor force	All married couples	In labor force — Husband & wife	In labor force — Husband only	In labor force — Wife only	Husband & wife not in labor force
	Number (1,000)					Percent distribution				
TOTAL										
1990	52,317	28,056	13,013	2,453	8,794	100.0	53.6	24.9	4.7	16.8
2000	55,311	31,095	11,815	3,301	9,098	100.0	56.2	21.4	6.0	16.4
2010	60,384	32,731	13,074	4,526	10,053	100.0	54.2	21.7	7.5	16.6
2013	61,295	31,673	13,901	4,656	11,065	100.0	51.7	22.7	7.6	18.1
2014	61,850	31,666	13,913	4,708	11,563	100.0	51.2	22.5	7.6	18.7
2015	62,230	31,688	14,164	4,757	11,622	100.0	50.9	22.8	7.6	18.7
2016	62,628	32,120	13,885	4,790	11,833	100.0	51.3	22.2	7.6	18.9
2017	63,325	32,658	13,803	4,797	12,068	100.0	51.6	21.8	7.6	19.1
2018	63,739	32,373	14,202	4,826	12,339	100.0	50.8	22.3	7.6	19.4
2019	63,882	32,773	13,614	4,976	12,519	100.0	51.3	21.3	7.8	19.6
WITH CHILDREN UNDER AGE 18										
1990	24,537	15,768	7,667	558	544	100.0	64.3	31.2	2.3	2.2
2000	25,248	17,116	6,950	795	387	100.0	67.8	27.5	3.1	1.5
2010	25,317	16,710	7,220	962	425	100.0	66.0	28.5	3.8	1.7
2013	24,677	15,755	7,408	1,051	462	100.0	63.8	30.0	4.3	1.9
2014	24,775	15,945	7,336	949	545	100.0	64.4	29.6	3.8	2.2
2015	24,857	15,828	7,454	987	589	100.0	63.7	30.0	4.0	2.4
2016	24,638	15,873	7,176	1,042	546	100.0	64.4	29.1	4.2	2.2
2017	24,465	15,895	7,029	1,058	483	100.0	65.0	28.7	4.3	2.0
2018	24,555	15,903	7,132	1,043	476	100.0	64.8	29.0	4.2	1.9
2019	24,421	16,175	6,868	921	458	100.0	66.2	28.1	3.8	1.9
WITH CHILDREN UNDER AGE 6										
1990	12,051	6,932	4,692	192	235	100.0	57.5	38.9	1.6	2.0
2000	11,393	6,984	4,077	211	121	100.0	61.3	35.8	1.9	1.1
2010	11,599	6,924	4,181	335	159	100.0	59.7	36.0	2.9	1.4
2013	10,867	6,347	3,951	403	166	100.0	58.4	36.4	3.7	1.5
2014	10,887	6,378	3,965	340	204	100.0	58.6	36.4	3.1	1.9
2015	10,862	6,351	3,969	320	222	100.0	58.5	36.5	2.9	2.0
2016	10,688	6,349	3,759	383	197	100.0	59.4	35.2	3.6	1.8
2017	10,727	6,410	3,811	339	166	100.0	59.8	35.5	3.2	1.5
2018	11,001	6,464	4,025	356	157	100.0	58.8	36.6	3.2	1.4
2019	10,903	6,697	3,770	290	147	100.0	61.4	34.6	2.7	1.3

Source: U.S. Census Bureau, Families and Living Arrangements, Detailed Table MC-1, "Married Couples by Labor Force Status of Spouses: 1986 to Present," <https://www.census.gov/data/tables/time-series/demo/families/families.html>, accessed January 2020.

Table 633. Employed Civilians and Weekly Hours: 1990 to 2019

[In thousands (118,793 represents 118,793,000), except as indicated. Annual averages of monthly figures. Civilian noninstitutionalized population 16 years old and over. Based on Current Population Survey; see text, Section 1 and Appendix III]

Item	1990	2000	2010	2015	2016	2017	2018	2019
Total employed	**118,793**	**136,891**	**139,064**	**148,834**	**151,436**	**153,337**	**155,761**	**157,538**
Age:								
16 to 19 years old	6,581	7,189	4,378	4,734	4,965	5,074	5,126	5,150
20 to 24 years old	13,401	13,229	12,699	14,022	14,027	14,132	14,051	14,172
25 to 34 years old	33,935	31,549	30,229	32,742	33,722	34,439	35,324	35,807
35 to 44 years old	30,817	36,433	30,663	31,252	31,562	31,892	32,616	33,127
45 to 54 years old	19,525	30,310	33,191	32,643	32,720	32,503	32,373	32,042
55 to 64 years old	11,189	14,002	21,636	24,975	25,524	26,064	26,565	26,893
65 years old and over	3,346	4,179	6,268	8,465	8,916	9,234	9,705	10,347
Sex:								
Male	65,104	73,305	73,359	79,131	80,568	81,402	82,698	83,460
Female	53,689	63,586	65,705	69,703	70,868	71,936	73,063	74,078
Marital status:								
Single (never married)	30,741	36,967	38,800	45,148	46,823	47,995	49,566	50,855
Married, spouse present	70,543	78,287	77,874	79,935	80,621	81,487	81,920	82,315
Widowed, divorced, separated	17,510	21,636	22,390	23,751	23,993	23,856	24,276	24,369
Class of worker:								
Nonagricultural industries	115,570	134,427	136,858	146,411	148,976	150,883	153,336	155,113
Wage and salary worker [1]	106,598	125,114	127,914	137,678	140,161	142,096	144,326	146,262
Self-employed	8,719	9,205	8,860	8,665	8,751	8,736	8,941	8,799
Unpaid family workers	253	108	84	68	65	52	69	53
Agriculture and related industries	3,223	2,464	2,206	2,422	2,460	2,454	2,425	2,425
Wage and salary worker [1]	1,740	1,421	1,353	1,547	1,583	1,640	1,632	1,658
Self-employed	1,378	1,010	821	844	853	790	766	741
Unpaid family workers	105	33	33	32	23	24	27	26
Weekly hours:								
Nonagricultural industries:								
Wage and salary workers [1]	39.2	39.6	38.3	38.7	38.8	38.6	38.9	38.9
Self-employed	40.8	39.7	35.6	36.1	36.1	36.0	36.4	36.1
Unpaid family workers	34.0	32.5	33.3	28.9	30.6	31.0	32.4	32.3

[1] Includes the incorporated self-employed.

Source: U.S. Bureau of Labor Statistics, "Labor Force Statistics from the Current Population Survey," <http://www.bls.gov/cps>, accessed June 2020.

Table 634. Persons at Work by Hours Worked: 2019

[In thousands (152,240 represents 152,240,000), except as indicated. Annual averages of monthly figures. Persons "at work" are a subgroup of employed persons. This subgroup excludes those absent from their jobs during reference period for reasons such as vacation, illness, or industrial dispute. Civilian noninstitutionalized population 16 years old and over. Based on Current Population Survey; see text, Section 1, and Appendix III]

Hours of work	Persons at work (1,000)			Percent distribution		
	Total	Agriculture and related industries	Non-agricultural industries	Total	Agriculture and related industries	Non-agricultural industries
Total...............................	**152,240**	**2,333**	**149,907**	**100.0**	**100.0**	**100.0**
1 to 34 hours............................	33,693	569	33,124	22.1	24.4	22.1
1 to 4 hours.............................	1,489	49	1,440	1.0	2.1	1.0
5 to 14 hours...........................	5,274	126	5,148	3.5	5.4	3.4
15 to 29 hours..........................	16,887	258	16,629	11.1	11.0	11.1
30 to 34 hours..........................	10,043	136	9,907	6.6	5.8	6.6
35 hours and over......................	118,547	1,765	116,783	77.9	75.6	77.9
35 to 39 hours..........................	9,418	100	9,319	6.2	4.3	6.2
40 hours................................	71,010	747	70,263	46.6	32.0	46.9
41 hours and over......................	38,119	918	37,202	25.0	39.3	24.8
41 to 48 hours..........................	13,324	179	13,145	8.8	7.7	8.8
49 to 59 hours..........................	14,787	289	14,498	9.7	12.4	9.7
60 hours and over......................	10,008	450	9,558	6.6	19.3	6.4
Average weekly hours of:						
Total persons at work..................	39.0	42.4	38.9	(X)	(X)	(X)
Persons usually working full-time [1].......	42.5	47.6	42.5	(X)	(X)	(X)

X Not applicable. [1] Full-time workers are those who usually worked 35 hours or more (at all jobs).

Source: U.S. Bureau of Labor Statistics, CPS Tables, "Persons at Work in Agriculture and Nonagricultural Industries by Hours of Work," <http://www.bls.gov/cps/tables.htm>, accessed February 2020.

Table 635. Persons With a Job, But Not at Work by Reason: 1990 to 2019

[In thousands (6,160 represents 6,160,000), except percent. For civilian noninstitutionalized population 16 years old and over. Annual averages of monthly figures. Based on Current Population Survey; see text, Section 1 and Appendix III]

Reason for not working	1990	2000	2010	2012	2013	2014	2015	2016	2017	2018	2019
Total not at work....................	**6,160**	**5,681**	**5,060**	**5,132**	**5,003**	**5,029**	**5,066**	**5,284**	**5,607**	**5,367**	**5,298**
Percent of employed................	5.2	4.2	3.6	3.6	3.5	3.4	3.4	3.5	3.7	3.4	3.4
Reason for not working:											
Vacation..............................	3,529	3,109	2,487	2,633	2,501	2,512	2,563	2,671	2,893	2,724	2,702
Illness................................	1,341	1,156	942	906	940	953	907	1,001	951	981	960
Child care problems.................	(NA)	(NA)	(NA)	20	22	28	32	29	30	33	33
Other family/personal obligations..	(NA)	(NA)	(NA)	253	245	258	259	284	266	269	271
Labor/industrial dispute.............	24	14	8	6	6	3	5	5	5	6	11
Bad weather..........................	90	89	172	107	112	138	119	130	241	179	125
Maternity or paternity leave........	(NA)	(NA)	(NA)	286	279	288	322	303	315	331	344
School/training.......................	(NA)	(NA)	(NA)	119	113	120	134	125	135	131	140
Civic/military duty....................	(NA)	(NA)	(NA)	11	9	7	8	7	9	6	7
All other..............................	1,177	1,313	1,451	792	775	721	718	729	762	707	706

NA Not available.

Source: U.S. Bureau of Labor Statistics, Current Population Survey, unpublished data. See also <http://www.bls.gov/cps/>.

Table 636. Class of Worker by Sex and Selected Characteristics: 2016

[In percent, except as indicated (9,604 represents 9,604,000). Civilian noninstitutionalized population 16 years old and over. Annual averages of monthly figures. Based on Current Population Survey; see text, Section 1 and Appendix III]

Characteristic	Unincorporated self-employed			Incorporated self-employed			Wage and salary workers [1]		
	Total	Male	Female	Total	Male	Female	Total	Male	Female
Total (1,000)......................	**9,604**	**5,980**	**3,624**	**5,643**	**3,963**	**1,680**	**136,111**	**70,600**	**65,511**
PERCENT DISTRIBUTION........	100.0	100.0	100.0	100.0	100.0	100.0	100.0	100.0	100.0
Age:									
16 to 19 years old.................	0.8	0.8	0.9	0.2	0.1	0.3	3.6	3.4	3.7
20 to 24 years old.................	2.8	2.9	2.5	1.0	1.1	1.0	10.1	9.9	10.2
25 to 34 years old.................	14.2	14.1	14.4	10.6	10.3	11.1	23.3	24.0	22.6
35 to 44 years old.................	19.8	19.5	20.4	20.1	19.6	21.5	21.0	21.4	20.5
45 to 54 years old.................	23.6	23.1	24.3	29.0	28.5	30.1	21.2	20.9	21.4
55 to 64 years old.................	23.6	23.7	23.5	26.0	26.0	25.9	16.0	15.5	16.5
65 years old and over.............	15.2	16.0	14.0	13.2	14.5	10.2	4.9	4.8	5.0
Race/ethnicity:									
White [2].............................	85.4	85.4	85.3	85.1	86.4	82.0	78.1	79.4	76.6
Black [2].............................	6.8	6.8	6.7	5.5	5.3	6.1	12.5	11.1	14.0
Asian [2].............................	5.1	5.0	5.4	7.3	6.4	9.4	6.1	6.2	6.0
Hispanic [3].........................	16.3	17.7	14.0	9.5	9.6	9.3	17.0	18.6	15.3
Country of birth:									
U.S. born...........................	80.1	78.7	82.3	82.1	82.4	81.4	83.2	81.6	85.0
Foreign-born........................	19.9	21.3	17.7	17.9	17.6	18.6	16.8	18.4	15.0

[1] Excludes the incorporated self-employed. [2] For persons in this race group only. [3] Persons of Hispanic origin may be of any race.

Source: U.S. Bureau of Labor Statistics, Current Population Survey, unpublished data. See also <http://www.bls.gov/cps>.

Table 637. Self-Employed Workers by Industry and Occupation: 2000 to 2019

[In thousands (10,214 represents 10,214,000). Civilian noninstitutionalized population 16 years old and over. Annual averages of monthly figures. Data represent the unincorporated self-employed. Excludes the incorporated self-employed who are considered wage and salary workers. Based on the occupational and industrial classification derived from those used in the 2000 census. See text, this section. Based on the Current Population Survey (CPS); see text, Section 1 and Appendix III]

Item	2000	2010	2014	2015	2016	2017	2018	2019
Total self-employed................	**10,214**	**9,681**	**9,358**	**9,509**	**9,604**	**9,526**	**9,707**	**9,539**
INDUSTRY								
Agriculture and related industries............................	1,010	821	756	844	853	790	766	741
Mining........................	12	20	20	21	17	11	10	14
Construction........................	1,728	1,699	1,595	1,603	1,628	1,567	1,650	1,671
Manufacturing........................	334	304	278	288	267	280	258	264
Wholesale and retail trade........................	1,221	962	851	870	888	842	812	762
Transportation and utilities........................	348	360	368	397	417	453	443	550
Information........................	139	139	132	161	120	143	144	139
Financial activities........................	735	641	628	625	687	666	724	678
Professional and business services........................	1,927	1,999	1,984	1,944	2,073	2,102	2,054	1,982
Education and health services........................	1,107	1,100	1,074	1,069	1,037	985	1,072	1,034
Leisure and hospitality........................	660	610	658	698	668	682	701	683
Other services........................	993	1,028	1,014	988	949	1,005	1,075	1,022
OCCUPATION								
Management, professional, and related occupations........	4,169	3,928	3,878	3,958	3,953	3,985	4,109	4,051
Service occupations........................	1,775	1,885	1,969	1,948	1,943	1,984	2,023	1,904
Sales and office occupations........................	1,982	1,586	1,438	1,470	1,463	1,448	1,432	1,432
Natural resources, construction, and maintenance occupations........................	1,591	1,635	1,462	1,482	1,548	1,418	1,463	1,405
Production, transportation, and material moving occupations........................	698	647	610	650	697	691	679	748

Source: U.S. Bureau of Labor Statistics, "Labor Force Statistics from the Current Population Survey," <http://www.bls.gov/cps/tables.htm>, accessed July 2020; and unpublished CPS data.

Table 638. Type of Work Flexibility Provided to Employees: 2016

[In percent. The National Study of Employers does not ask employers to report on whether they have "written policies," but rather whether their organization "allows employees to" or "provides the following benefits or programs." The wording is used for two reasons. First, employers may have written policies, but not allow employees to use them. Second, smaller employers are less likely to have written policies than larger ones. For methodology, see source]

Type of work flexibility provided to employees	Organizations allowing flexibility to all or most employees		
	Total employers	Employers with 50 to 99 employees	Employers with 1,000 or more employees
FLEX TIME AND PLACE			
Periodically change starting and quitting times within some range of hours......................	32	36	17
Change starting and quitting times on a daily basis...	11	12	4
Compress workweek by working longer hours on fewer days for at least part of the year......	9	10	4
Work some regular paid hours at home occasionally...	8	9	1
Work some regular paid hours at home on regular basis..	2	2	3
CHOICES IN MANAGING TIME			
Have control over when to take breaks..	59	63	47
Have choices about and control over which shifts to work...	10	10	14
Have control over paid and unpaid overtime hours...	21	22	11
REDUCED TIME			
Move from full time to part time and back again while remaining in same position or level...................................	8	8	10
Work part year (work reduced time on annual basis).................................	2	2	3
CAREGIVING LEAVE			
Return to work gradually after childbirth or adoption.................................	52	57	42
TIME OFF			
Family or personal time off without loss of pay.................................	47	51	33
Do volunteer work during regular work hours.................................	23	26	21
FLEX CAREERS			
Phase into retirement by working reduced hours over time prior to full retirement...............	21	25	17
Take sabbaticals (paid or unpaid for six months or more).........................	11	12	10
Take extended career breaks for caregiving or other personal or family reasons................	35	42	27
Receive special consideration when returning to the organization after an extended career break..................................	13	18	10

Source: Society for Human Resource Management, Families and Work Institute, *2016 National Study of Employers* ©. See also <http://www.whenworkworks.org/be-effective/guides-tools/2016-national-study-of-employers>.

Table 639. Multiple Jobholders: 2019

[8,050 represents 8,050,000. Annual average of monthly figures. Civilian noninstitutionalized population 16 years old and over. Multiple jobholders are employed persons who either had jobs as wage or salary workers with two employers or more; were self-employed and also held a wage and salary job; or were unpaid family workers and also held a wage and salary job. Based on the Current Population Survey; see text, Section 1 and Appendix III]

Characteristic	Total		Male		Female	
	Number (1,000)	Percent of employed	Number (1,000)	Percent of employed	Number (1,000)	Percent of employed
Total [1,2]	**8,050**	**5.1**	**3,908**	**4.7**	**4,141**	**5.6**
Age:						
16 to 19 years old	201	3.9	82	3.2	119	4.5
20 to 24 years old	769	5.4	297	4.1	472	6.8
25 to 54 years old	5,365	5.3	2,634	4.9	2,731	5.8
55 to 64 years old	1,275	4.7	646	4.6	628	4.9
65 years old and over	440	4.2	249	4.4	191	4.1
Race and ethnicity:						
White	6,304	5.1	3,086	4.7	3,218	5.7
Black	1,074	5.5	488	5.3	586	5.7
Asian	338	3.3	174	3.3	164	3.4
Hispanic [3]	1,027	3.7	550	3.5	478	4.0
Marital status:						
Married, spouse present [4]	3,971	4.8	2,233	4.9	1,738	4.8
Widowed, divorced, or separated	1,388	5.7	472	4.6	916	6.5
Single, never married	2,690	5.3	1,203	4.4	1,487	6.3
Full- or part-time status: [5]						
Primary job full-time, secondary job part-time	4,499	(S)	2,381	(S)	2,118	(S)
Both jobs part-time	2,062	(S)	720	(S)	1,342	(S)
Both jobs full-time	307	(S)	203	(S)	104	(S)
Hours vary on primary or secondary job	1,127	(S)	580	(S)	547	(S)

S No data or data do not meet publication criteria. [1] Includes a small number of persons who work part-time on their primary job and full-time on their secondary job(s), not shown separately. [2] Includes other races, not shown separately. [3] Persons of Hispanic origin may be of any race. [4] Opposite-sex married couples only. [5] Full-time work is 35 or more hours per week; part-time work is less than 35 hours per week.

Source: U.S. Bureau of Labor Statistics, CPS Tables, "Multiple Jobholders by Selected Characteristics," <http://www.bls.gov/cps/tables.htm>, accessed February 2020.

Table 640. Average Number of Jobs Held From Ages 18 to 52 during 1978 to 2016

[For persons ages 51 to 60 in 2016-17 (and who were ages 14 to 22 when first interviewed in 1979). A job is an uninterrupted period of work with a particular employer. Educational attainment as of 2016-2017 survey. Based on the National Longitudinal Survey of Youth 1979; see source for details]

Sex, race, ethnicity and educational attainment	Average jobs held [1]	Average number of jobs held by age			
		18 to 24 years	25 to 34 years	35 to 44 years	45 to 52 years
Total [2]	**12.3**	**5.7**	**4.5**	**2.9**	**1.9**
Less than a high school diploma	11.9	5.1	4.6	2.8	1.5
High school graduate, no college	12.0	5.3	4.5	3.0	1.9
Some college or associate's degree	12.8	5.7	4.6	3.0	2.1
Bachelor's degree or more	12.4	6.3	4.4	2.8	2.1
Male	12.5	5.9	4.7	2.9	1.9
Less than a high school diploma	13.3	6.0	5.5	3.1	1.6
High school graduate, no college	12.6	5.8	4.8	2.9	1.9
Some college or associate's degree	13.0	6.0	4.7	2.9	2.0
Bachelor's degree or more	11.6	5.9	4.3	2.8	2.0
Female	12.1	5.4	4.3	2.9	2.0
Less than a high school diploma	9.9	3.8	3.5	2.5	1.3
High school graduate, no college	11.4	4.8	4.0	3.0	1.8
Some college or associate's degree	12.6	5.6	4.5	3.0	2.1
Bachelor's degree or more	13.1	6.6	4.5	2.8	2.1
White, non-Hispanic	12.4	5.9	4.5	2.9	1.9
Less than a high school diploma	12.6	5.6	5.0	3.0	1.5
High school graduate, no college	12.2	5.5	4.5	2.9	1.8
Some college or associate's degree	12.8	5.9	4.5	2.9	2.1
Bachelor's degree or more	12.3	6.4	4.4	2.8	2.0
Black, non-Hispanic	11.8	4.8	4.6	3.1	1.9
Less than a high school diploma	10.3	3.9	4.0	2.5	1.3
High school graduate, no college	11.4	4.5	4.6	3.1	1.9
Some college or associate's degree	12.5	5.0	4.8	3.4	2.1
Bachelor's degree or more	12.8	5.6	4.7	3.2	2.4
Hispanic [3]	12.1	5.1	4.3	3.0	1.9
Less than a high school diploma	11.4	4.5	4.1	2.8	1.6
High school graduate, no college	11.7	5.1	4.2	3.0	1.9
Some college or associate's degree	13.3	5.4	4.5	3.2	2.1
Bachelor's degree or more	11.7	5.3	4.5	2.8	1.9

[1] Jobs held in more than one age category were counted in each category, but only once in the total. [2] Includes other races, not shown separately. [3] Persons of Hispanic origin may be of any race.

Source: U.S. Bureau of Labor Statistics, *Number of Jobs Held, Labor Market Experience, and Earnings Growth: Results from a National Longitudinal Survey*, USDL 19-1520, August 2019. See also <http://www.bls.gov/news.release/nlsoy.nr0.htm>.

Table 641. Distribution of Workers by Tenure With Current Employer by Selected Characteristics: 2018

[137,442 represents 137,442,000. As of January. From the 2018 Displaced Worker Supplement to the Current Population Survey. For employed wage and salary workers 16 years old and over. Data exclude the incorporated and unincorporated self-employed; see source and Appendix III]

Characteristic	Number employed (1,000)	Percent distribution by tenure with current employer								Median years [1]
		12 months or less	13-23 months	2 years	3-4 years	5-9 years	10-14 years	15-19 years	20 years or more	
Total [2]	**137,442**	**22.3**	**6.9**	**5.6**	**17.6**	**18.8**	**11.6**	**6.9**	**10.3**	**4.2**
AGE AND SEX										
16 to 19 years old	4,597	74.0	11.9	7.4	6.2	0.4	–	–	–	(NA)
20 years old and over	132,845	20.5	6.7	5.5	18.0	19.5	12.1	7.2	10.6	(NA)
20 to 24 years old	13,455	53.6	12.6	11.0	18.3	4.5	0.1	–	–	1.2
25 to 34 years old	32,512	27.7	9.5	7.9	26.2	21.8	6.3	0.7	–	2.8
35 to 44 years old	29,110	17.1	6.0	4.8	18.5	23.8	17.3	8.8	3.8	4.9
45 to 54 years old	28,528	11.9	4.7	3.5	14.5	20.5	15.9	11.9	17.2	7.6
55 to 64 years old	22,367	9.2	3.5	3.2	11.5	18.5	14.9	11.9	27.4	10.1
65 years old and over	6,872	8.4	4.0	2.9	11.5	18.8	15.4	10.4	28.6	10.2
Male	**71,178**	**21.8**	**6.6**	**5.5**	**17.5**	**19.1**	**11.8**	**6.9**	**10.9**	**4.3**
16 to 19 years old	2,217	72.9	12.2	6.5	8.0	0.4	–	–	–	(NA)
20 years old and over	68,960	20.2	6.4	5.5	17.8	19.7	12.1	7.1	11.2	(NA)
20 to 24 years old	6,838	52.2	12.0	11.3	19.9	4.5	0.2	–	–	1.3
25 to 34 years old	17,374	27.2	9.1	7.6	25.0	23.6	6.9	0.6	–	2.9
35 to 44 years old	15,334	16.2	6.0	4.8	18.2	23.4	17.8	9.3	4.3	5.0
45 to 54 years old	14,673	12.2	4.0	3.4	14.2	19.4	16.0	12.2	18.6	8.1
55 to 64 years old	11,202	9.5	3.5	3.0	11.4	18.8	13.3	10.9	29.7	10.2
65 years old and over	3,539	7.9	3.7	3.3	11.5	18.2	16.6	9.7	29.1	10.2
Female	**66,264**	**22.8**	**7.1**	**5.7**	**17.7**	**18.6**	**11.5**	**7.0**	**9.6**	**4.0**
16 to 19 years old	2,380	75.1	11.6	8.3	4.6	0.3	–	–	–	(NA)
20 years old and over	63,884	20.9	7.0	5.6	18.2	19.3	12.0	7.2	9.9	(NA)
20 to 24 years old	6,617	55.0	13.1	10.8	16.6	4.5	–	–	–	1.2
25 to 34 years old	15,138	28.4	9.9	8.2	27.6	19.7	5.5	0.7	–	2.7
35 to 44 years old	13,776	18.1	5.9	4.7	18.9	24.3	16.8	8.1	3.2	4.7
45 to 54 years old	13,856	11.6	5.4	3.7	14.8	21.7	15.7	11.5	15.7	7.1
55 to 64 years old	11,165	8.9	3.4	3.4	11.6	18.2	16.5	12.9	25.1	10.1
65 years old and over	3,333	8.9	4.4	2.4	11.6	19.3	14.2	11.1	28.1	10.1
RACE AND HISPANIC ORIGIN										
White [3]	106,391	21.6	6.7	5.3	17.0	19.1	11.9	7.3	11.2	(NA)
Male	56,112	20.9	6.4	5.2	17.0	19.4	12.0	7.2	11.9	(NA)
Female	50,280	22.3	7.0	5.4	17.0	18.7	11.8	7.4	10.4	(NA)
Black [3]	16,978	25.6	6.7	6.7	18.7	17.6	10.5	6.4	7.7	(NA)
Male	7,764	26.8	6.8	7.0	17.5	17.4	10.5	6.6	7.3	(NA)
Female	9,214	24.6	6.6	6.5	19.8	17.8	10.5	6.3	8.0	(NA)
Asian [3]	8,941	20.4	7.7	6.1	20.6	20.3	12.6	5.7	6.6	(NA)
Male	4,725	19.8	7.3	6.1	21.5	20.2	12.6	5.6	6.7	(NA)
Female	4,216	21.1	8.1	6.1	19.6	20.4	12.6	5.7	6.5	(NA)
Hispanic [4]	23,720	25.6	5.9	7.5	19.1	19.4	10.4	5.7	6.5	(NA)
Male	13,206	23.7	5.4	7.9	19.9	20.1	10.9	5.2	6.9	(NA)
Female	10,514	28.0	6.5	6.9	18.0	18.5	9.8	6.2	6.0	(NA)

– Represents or rounds to zero. NA Not available. [1] Median definition, see Guide to Tabular Presentation. [2] Includes other races, not shown separately. [3] For persons in this race group only. See footnote 2, Table 619. [4] Persons of Hispanic origin may be of any race.

Source: U.S. Bureau of Labor Statistics, "Employee Tenure in 2018," USDL 18-1500, September 2018, <http://www.bls.gov/news.release/tenure.toc.htm>.

Table 642. Part-Time Workers by Reason: 2019

[33,693 represents 33,693,000, except hours. For persons working 1 to 34 hours during the reference week of the survey. For civilian noninstitutionalized population 16 years old and over. Annual average of monthly figures. Based on the Current Population Survey; see text, Section 1 and Appendix III]

Reason	All industries			Nonagricultural industries		
		Usually work—			Usually work—	
	Total	Full-time	Part-time	Total	Full-time	Part-time
Total working fewer than 35 hours	**33,693**	**9,233**	**24,459**	**33,124**	**9,072**	**24,052**
Economic reasons	4,407	1,378	3,029	4,330	1,336	2,994
Slack work or business conditions	2,759	1,137	1,622	2,707	1,107	1,600
Could find only part time work	1,333	(S)	1,333	1,324	(S)	1,324
Seasonal work	210	137	74	195	125	69
Job started or ended during the week	104	104	(S)	103	103	(S)
Non-economic reasons	29,286	7,856	21,430	28,794	7,736	21,058
Child-care problems	1,072	89	983	1,062	87	975
Other family or personal obligations	5,135	689	4,446	5,053	679	4,374
Health or medical limitations	1,125	(S)	1,125	1,104	(S)	1,104
In school or training	6,152	78	6,074	6,095	78	6,017
Retired or social security limit on earnings	2,824	(S)	2,824	2,701	(S)	2,701
Vacation or personal day	3,845	3,845	(S)	3,801	3,801	(S)
Holiday, legal, or religious	283	283	(S)	279	279	(S)
Weather-related curtailment	486	486	(S)	454	454	(S)
Other	8,365	2,385	5,980	8,244	2,357	5,887
Average hours per week:						
Economic reasons	23.2	23.9	22.9	23.2	24.0	22.9
Noneconomic reasons	21.2	24.6	20.0	21.3	24.6	20.0

S No data or data do not meet publication standards.

Source: U.S. Bureau of Labor Statistics, CPS Tables, "Persons at work 1 to 34 hours in all and in nonagricultural industries by reason for working less than 35 hours and usual full- or part-time status," <http://www.bls.gov/cps/tables.htm>, accessed February 2020.

Table 643. Displaced Workers by Selected Characteristics: 2020

[In percent, except total (2,672 represents 2,672,000). As of January 2020. For persons 20 years old and over with job tenure of 3 years or more who lost or left a job between January 2017 and December 2019 because of plant closings or moves, insufficient work for workers to do, or the abolishment of their positions. Based on Current Population Survey; see source and Appendix III]

Characteristic	Total (1,000)	Employment status in January 2020			Reason for job loss, 2017-2019		
		Employed	Unemployed	Not in the labor force	Plant or company closed down or moved	Insufficient work	Position or shift abolished
Total [1]	**2,672**	**70.1**	**12.4**	**17.5**	**40.6**	**23.2**	**36.2**
20 to 24 years old	63	([2])	([2])	([2])	([2])	([2])	([2])
25 to 54 years old	1,676	75.1	13.9	11.0	42.6	23.2	34.2
55 to 64 years old	702	66.5	10.7	22.8	33.2	24.7	42.1
65 years old and over	232	44.1	7.4	48.5	43.8	19.5	36.7
Males	1,466	71.9	12.3	15.7	40.2	25.7	34.2
20 to 24 years old	20	([2])	([2])	([2])	([2])	([2])	([2])
25 to 54 years old	947	74.5	14.6	10.9	40.0	27.5	32.5
55 to 64 years old	382	71.7	8.3	20.0	36.6	22.1	41.3
65 years old and over	117	52.6	9.3	38.2	48.8	21.2	30.0
Females	1,206	67.8	12.5	19.7	41.0	20.3	38.7
20 to 24 years old	42	([2])	([2])	([2])	([2])	([2])	([2])
25 to 54 years old	729	75.9	12.9	11.2	46.0	17.7	36.3
55 to 64 years old	321	60.3	13.4	26.3	29.1	27.7	43.1
65 years old and over	115	35.4	5.6	59.1	38.7	17.7	43.6
White only	2,162	70.9	10.5	18.6	40.7	23.0	36.3
Male	1,211	73.5	11.0	15.5	40.8	25.1	34.1
Female	951	67.7	9.7	22.6	40.6	20.3	39.1
Black only	335	61.8	22.2	16.0	47.3	21.4	31.3
Male	152	58.5	21.8	19.7	46.1	26.0	27.9
Female	183	64.6	22.6	12.9	48.3	17.6	34.1
Asian only	110	73.5	25.6	0.9	13.8	24.4	61.8
Male	62	([2])	([2])	([2])	([2])	([2])	([2])
Female	48	([2])	([2])	([2])	([2])	([2])	([2])
Hispanic [3]	461	67.6	8.5	23.9	50.6	27.5	22.0
Male	262	72.6	7.0	20.5	50.2	29.6	20.2
Female	199	61.2	10.5	28.3	51.0	24.7	24.3

[1] Includes other races, not shown separately. [2] Data not shown where base is less than 75,000. [3] Persons of Hispanic or Latino origin may be of any race.

Source: U.S. Bureau of Labor Statistics, *Worker Displacement: 2017-2019,* USDL 20-1620, August 2020. See also <http://www.bls.gov/news.release/disp.toc.htm>.

Table 644. Persons Not in the Labor Force By Age, Sex, and Reason: 2019

[In thousands (95,636 represents 95,636,000). For civilian noninstitutional population 16 years old and over. Persons who are neither employed nor unemployed are not in the labor force. This includes retired persons, students, those taking care of children or other family members, and others who are neither working nor seeking work. Annual average of monthly figures. Based on the Current Population Survey; see text, Section 1, and Appendix III]

Status and reason	Total	Age			Sex	
		16 to 24 years old	25 to 54 years old	55 years old and over	Male	Female
Total not in the labor force	**95,636**	**16,656**	**22,102**	**56,879**	**38,667**	**56,970**
Do not want a job now [1]	90,593	15,153	20,023	55,417	36,252	54,341
Want a job now [1]	5,043	1,503	2,078	1,462	2,415	2,629
In the previous year:						
Did not search for a job	3,084	883	1,157	1,045	1,430	1,654
Did search for a job, but not in past 4 weeks [2]	1,959	620	921	418	984	975
Not available for work now	556	229	252	75	242	314
Available for work now, but not looking for work [3]	1,403	391	669	343	742	661
Reason for not currently looking for work:						
Discouraged over job prospects [4]	382	86	193	103	239	143
Family responsibilities	156	21	103	32	44	112
In school or training	146	116	27	4	76	70
Ill health or disability	135	14	63	58	73	63
Other [5]	584	155	283	147	310	274

[1] Includes some persons who are not asked if they want a job. [2] Persons who had a job in previous 12 months must have searched since the end of that job. [3] Persons who want a job, have searched for work during the previous 12 months, and were available to take a job during the reference week, but had not looked for work in the past 4 weeks; persons are referred to as "marginally attached to the labor force." [4] Includes such things as believes no work available, could not find work, lacks necessary schooling or training, employer thinks too young or old, and other types of discrimination. [5] Includes such things as child care and transportation problems.

Source: U.S. Bureau of Labor Statistics, CPS Tables, "Persons not in the labor force by desire and availability for work, age, and sex," <http://www.bls.gov/cps/tables.htm>, accessed February 2020.

Table 645. Employment Status of Parents by Age of Youngest Child and Family Type: 2016 to 2019

[In thousands (34,206 represents 34,206,000), except percent distribution. Annual average of monthly figures. For families with own children (sons, daughters, step-children, and adopted children). Based on the Current Population Survey, see text, Section 1, and Appendix III]

Characteristic	Number				Percent distribution			
	2016	2017	2018	2019	2016	2017	2018	2019
WITH OWN CHILDREN UNDER 18 YEARS OLD								
Total families	**34,206**	**33,615**	**33,632**	**33,399**	**100.0**	**100.0**	**100.0**	**100.0**
Parent(s) employed	30,671	30,318	30,522	30,484	89.7	90.2	90.8	91.3
No parent employed	3,534	3,297	3,109	2,915	10.3	9.8	9.2	8.7
Married-couple families	23,125	22,855	22,883	22,854	100.0	100.0	100.0	100.0
Parent(s) employed	22,379	22,158	22,296	22,275	96.8	96.9	97.4	97.5
Mother employed	15,377	15,389	15,545	15,736	66.5	67.3	67.9	68.9
Both parents employed	14,123	14,151	14,407	14,661	61.1	61.9	63.0	64.2
Mother employed, not father	1,254	1,238	1,138	1,075	5.4	5.4	5.0	4.7
Father employed, not mother	7,001	6,769	6,751	6,539	30.3	29.6	29.5	28.6
Neither parent employed	746	697	586	579	3.2	3.1	2.6	2.5
Families maintained by women [1]	8,538	8,259	8,125	7,914	100.0	100.0	100.0	100.0
Mother employed	6,191	6,043	6,018	5,966	72.5	73.2	74.1	75.4
Mother not employed	2,347	2,216	2,108	1,948	27.5	26.8	25.9	24.6
Families maintained by men [1]	2,544	2,500	2,624	2,631	100.0	100.0	100.0	100.0
Father employed	2,102	2,117	2,209	2,243	82.6	84.7	84.2	85.2
Father not employed	442	383	416	389	17.4	15.3	15.8	14.8
WITH OWN CHILDREN 6 to 17 YEARS OLD								
Total families	**19,774**	**19,621**	**19,377**	**19,297**	**100.0**	**100.0**	**100.0**	**100.0**
Parent(s) employed	17,814	17,742	17,627	17,630	90.1	90.4	91.0	91.4
No parent employed	1,960	1,879	1,751	1,667	9.9	9.6	9.0	8.6
Married-couple families	13,105	13,032	12,859	12,846	100.0	100.0	100.0	100.0
Parent(s) employed	12,649	12,595	12,488	12,463	96.5	96.6	97.1	97.0
Mother employed	9,284	9,362	9,384	9,406	70.8	71.8	73.0	73.2
Both parents employed	8,483	8,553	8,643	8,680	64.7	65.6	67.2	67.6
Mother employed, not father	801	810	741	725	6.1	6.2	5.8	5.6
Father employed, not mother	3,365	3,233	3,104	3,058	25.7	24.8	24.1	23.8
Neither parent employed	456	437	370	382	3.5	3.4	2.9	3.0
Families maintained by women [1]	5,189	5,093	5,028	4,868	100.0	100.0	100.0	100.0
Mother employed	3,955	3,890	3,887	3,845	76.2	76.4	77.3	79.0
Mother not employed	1,234	1,204	1,141	1,023	23.8	23.6	22.7	21.0
Families maintained by men [1]	1,481	1,496	1,491	1,583	100.0	100.0	100.0	100.0
Father employed	1,211	1,257	1,251	1,321	81.8	84.1	83.9	83.5
Father not employed	270	239	240	262	18.2	15.9	16.1	16.5
WITH OWN CHILDREN UNDER 6 YEARS OLD								
Total families	**14,432**	**13,994**	**14,254**	**14,102**	**100.0**	**100.0**	**100.0**	**100.0**
Parent(s) employed	12,857	12,576	12,896	12,855	89.1	89.9	90.5	91.2
No parent employed	1,575	1,418	1,359	1,248	10.9	10.1	9.5	8.8
Married-couple families	10,020	9,823	10,024	10,008	100.0	100.0	100.0	100.0
Parent(s) employed	9,730	9,562	9,808	9,812	97.1	97.3	97.8	98.0
Mother employed	6,093	6,027	6,161	6,330	60.8	61.4	61.5	63.3
Both parents employed	5,640	5,598	5,764	5,981	56.3	57.0	57.5	59.8
Mother employed, not father	453	428	396	350	4.5	4.4	4.0	3.5
Father employed, not mother	3,637	3,536	3,647	3,482	36.3	36.0	36.4	34.8
Neither parent employed	290	261	216	196	2.9	2.7	2.2	2.0
Families maintained by women [1]	3,349	3,166	3,097	3,046	100.0	100.0	100.0	100.0
Mother employed	2,236	2,154	2,130	2,121	66.8	68.0	68.8	69.6
Mother not employed	1,113	1,013	967	925	33.2	32.0	31.2	30.4
Families maintained by men [1]	1,063	1,005	1,133	1,048	100.0	100.0	100.0	100.0
Father employed	891	860	957	921	83.8	85.6	84.5	87.9
Father not employed	172	145	176	127	16.2	14.4	15.5	12.1

[1] No spouse present.

Source: U.S. Bureau of Labor Statistics, *Employment Characteristics of Families—2019,* USDL 20-0670, April 2020, and earlier releases. See also <http://www.bls.gov/news.release/famee.toc.htm>.

Table 646. Working Poor and People and Families in the Labor Force by Poverty Status: 2009 to 2018

[In thousands (147,902 represents 147,902,000), except rate. The labor force includes people working or looking for work for at least 27 weeks during the year. The working poor rate is the number of individuals in the labor force (working or looking for work) whose incomes are below the official poverty level, as a percent of all people in the labor force. Based on the Current Population Survey, Annual Social and Economic Supplement]

Characteristic	2009	2010	2011	2012	2013	2014	2015	2016	2017	2018
Total in the labor force [1]	**147,902**	**146,859**	**147,475**	**148,735**	**149,483**	**150,319**	**152,230**	**153,364**	**154,762**	**156,454**
In poverty	10,391	10,512	10,382	10,612	10,450	9,487	8,560	7,572	6,946	6,964
Working poor rate	7.0	7.2	7.0	7.1	7.0	6.3	5.6	4.9	4.5	4.5
Unrelated individuals	33,798	34,099	33,731	34,810	35,061	35,018	35,953	35,789	36,959	37,082
In poverty	3,947	3,947	3,621	3,851	4,141	3,395	3,137	2,792	2,524	2,684
Working poor rate	11.7	11.6	10.7	11.1	11.8	9.7	8.7	7.8	6.8	7.2
Primary families [2]	65,467	64,931	66,225	66,541	66,462	66,732	67,193	67,628	67,588	68,099
In poverty	5,193	5,269	5,469	5,478	5,137	5,108	4,607	4,082	3,854	3,628
Working poor rate	7.9	8.1	8.3	8.2	7.7	7.7	6.9	6.0	5.7	5.3

[1] Includes individuals in families, not shown separately. [2] Primary families with at least one member in the labor force for more than half the year.

Source: U.S. Bureau of Labor Statistics, "A Profile of the Working Poor, 2018," <https://www.bls.gov/opub/reports/working-poor/2018/home.htm>, accessed July 2020.

Table 647. Employed Civilians by Occupation, Sex, Race, and Hispanic Origin: 2019

[157,538 represents 157,538,000. Civilian noninstitutionalized population 16 years old and over. Annual average of monthly figures. Based on Current Population Survey; see text, Section 1 and Appendix III. Occupational classifications are those used in the 2010 Census]

Occupation	Total employed	Percent of total			
		Female	Black [1]	Asian [1]	Hispanic [2]
Total, 16 years and over................................	**157,538**	**47.0**	**12.3**	**6.5**	**17.6**
Management, professional and related occupations........................	**64,218**	**51.8**	**9.6**	**8.7**	**10.1**
Management, business, and financial operations occupations................	26,981	44.1	8.4	7.0	10.4
Management occupations [3]..............................	18,985	40.0	7.8	6.1	10.7
Chief executives.................................	1,602	27.6	4.1	5.8	6.2
General and operations managers...................	1,058	30.6	6.6	3.5	12.5
Marketing and sales managers....................	1,184	48.5	6.1	5.6	8.9
Administrative services managers.................	184	42.0	10.5	3.2	10.9
Computer and information systems managers.........	654	28.7	9.6	15.8	4.7
Financial managers..............................	1,194	53.5	8.5	9.4	11.4
Human resources managers......................	321	74.7	11.1	7.1	10.1
Industrial production managers....................	274	22.4	5.4	5.5	10.9
Purchasing managers............................	227	42.8	14.4	5.9	10.0
Transportation, storage, and distribution managers....	281	17.3	9.6	2.4	17.3
Farmers, ranchers, and other agricultural managers...	962	24.5	0.9	1.0	5.7
Construction managers...........................	994	10.0	3.5	2.5	13.9
Education administrators.........................	958	67.7	15.3	3.3	11.8
Architectural and engineering managers............	154	11.7	6.0	11.8	6.7
Food service managers..........................	1,249	46.5	9.8	9.6	19.8
Lodging managers..............................	162	49.5	7.0	9.3	14.6
Medical and health services managers.............	677	69.7	12.7	5.7	11.8
Property, real estate, and community association managers.	780	47.3	8.9	4.5	12.8
Social and community service managers............	470	68.2	12.3	3.2	10.6
Business and financial operations occupations [3]......	7,996	54.0	9.9	9.0	9.5
Wholesale and retail buyers, except farm products....	226	47.8	6.9	3.5	14.6
Purchasing agents, except wholesale, retail, and farm products...........	279	48.5	9.9	4.2	10.3
Claims adjusters, appraisers, examiners, and investigators.......	318	62.1	19.5	4.4	9.5
Compliance officers............................	298	59.5	10.2	6.1	10.5
Cost estimators................................	127	14.3	3.1	5.8	8.1
Human resources workers........................	770	73.5	13.8	7.1	13.8
Management analysts............................	950	42.1	7.5	13.7	8.6
Market research analysts and marketing specialists....	369	56.6	5.9	11.4	7.2
Accountants and auditors........................	1,964	61.7	8.5	12.0	8.9
Financial analysts..............................	345	34.2	8.6	11.7	8.3
Personal financial advisors......................	551	32.1	6.9	8.6	6.3
Insurance underwriters..........................	105	51.1	5.9	5.4	6.2
Credit counselors and loan officers................	403	53.9	12.2	4.2	11.6
Tax preparers..................................	97	62.3	16.6	5.6	15.2
Professional and related occupations...............	37,237	57.4	10.5	10.0	9.9
Computer and mathematical occupations [3].........	5,352	25.8	8.7	23.1	7.8
Computer systems analysts......................	663	40.1	9.7	20.3	8.3
Computer programmers..........................	454	20.3	8.5	21.8	8.7
Software developers, applications and systems software.........	1,815	18.7	5.8	37.7	5.1
Web developers................................	193	41.4	6.7	12.0	4.6
Computer support specialists....................	547	26.4	10.5	12.7	11.3
Network and computer systems administrators.......	199	26.1	9.7	11.7	8.5
Operations research analysts....................	152	42.7	6.8	8.3	9.7
Architecture and engineering occupations [3]........	3,305	15.7	6.8	13.3	9.2
Architects, except naval........................	208	24.5	6.3	8.8	8.5
Aerospace engineers...........................	134	13.8	6.5	14.5	7.3
Civil engineers................................	475	13.9	5.9	12.2	8.4
Computer hardware engineers...................	77	22.8	5.7	38.4	10.2
Electrical and electronics engineers...............	285	11.6	7.3	19.9	8.7
Industrial engineers, including health and safety......	245	24.3	7.9	9.4	5.9
Mechanical engineers..........................	351	6.6	5.1	11.6	8.4
Drafters......................................	113	23.3	3.5	2.7	14.7
Engineering technicians, except drafters...........	496	19.8	12.1	8.3	12.7
Life, physical, and social science occupations [3].....	1,485	49.4	6.3	14.4	9.5
Biological scientists............................	104	47.7	3.4	14.4	8.7
Medical scientists..............................	170	51.8	7.3	27.8	8.8
Chemists and materials scientists.................	97	42.5	7.0	13.7	8.2
Environmental scientists and geoscientists.........	119	33.0	4.8	7.4	12.4
Psychologists.................................	234	79.7	5.8	3.5	10.3
Community and social services occupations [3]......	2,717	67.5	20.1	3.6	13.0
Counselors...................................	927	75.7	21.2	2.7	12.7
Social workers................................	823	81.9	23.0	3.7	14.3
Social and human service assistants..............	238	79.0	25.5	4.3	16.4
Clergy.......................................	413	20.7	12.2	5.9	7.7
Legal occupations..............................	1,955	52.7	8.3	6.1	9.5
Lawyers......................................	1,240	36.4	5.9	5.7	5.8
Judges, magistrates, and other judicial workers.....	70	52.5	13.4	4.8	8.6
Paralegals and legal assistants..................	444	89.6	11.8	6.7	17.7
Miscellaneous legal support workers..............	193	72.5	13.2	8.0	13.9
Education, training, and library occupations [3]......	9,455	73.6	10.2	5.3	11.0
Postsecondary teachers........................	1,386	47.4	7.0	15.1	8.3
Preschool and kindergarten teachers.............	655	98.7	15.7	5.2	14.9
Elementary and middle school teachers...........	3,604	80.5	10.2	2.6	10.2
Secondary school teachers......................	1,015	56.5	7.3	3.3	8.8
Special education teachers......................	331	86.7	9.2	3.5	6.5
Other teachers and instructors..................	1,017	64.6	11.7	6.1	11.6
Librarians....................................	179	79.9	6.0	3.2	9.8
Teacher assistants............................	999	89.7	13.4	4.1	18.0

See footnotes at end of table.

Labor Force, Employment, and Earnings 413

Table 647. Employed Civilians by Occupation, Sex, Race, and Hispanic Origin: 2019-Continued.

See headnote on page 413.

Occupation	Total employed	Percent of total			
		Female	Black [1]	Asian [1]	Hispanic [2]
Arts, design, entertainment, sports, and media occupations [3]	3,285	49.0	7.7	5.9	11.6
Artists and related workers	248	54.0	4.5	3.8	11.1
Designers	983	54.0	5.7	9.0	11.0
Producers and directors	186	42.5	6.4	3.5	8.0
Athletes, coaches, umpires, and related workers	345	35.3	9.3	4.3	10.8
Musicians, singers, and related workers	202	36.7	12.4	3.9	9.7
News analysts, reporters and correspondents	93	45.1	6.9	9.7	9.3
Public relations specialists	137	63.6	9.9	5.8	13.6
Editors	147	63.3	3.0	2.4	10.6
Writers and authors	225	63.5	5.9	3.4	4.8
Miscellaneous media and communication workers	118	66.4	14.6	11.2	35.3
Broadcast and sound engineering technicians and radio operators	119	12.0	9.1	7.9	14.0
Photographers	188	49.3	8.6	3.5	12.3
Healthcare practitioner and technical occupations [3]	9,684	75.4	12.5	9.6	9.0
Dentists	162	33.9	0.8	23.6	7.2
Dietitians and nutritionists	128	92.1	15.2	5.9	9.0
Pharmacists	341	60.4	10.5	22.0	2.7
Physicians and surgeons	1,098	40.8	8.2	18.0	7.6
Physician assistants	131	70.8	4.5	6.8	8.6
Occupational therapists	136	88.0	10.2	12.4	10.2
Physical therapists	304	67.9	5.9	14.1	4.0
Speech-language pathologists	180	95.8	3.9	2.2	6.7
Veterinarians	104	68.3	–	6.1	1.6
Registered nurses	3,242	88.9	12.4	9.2	7.2
Clinical laboratory technologists and technicians	323	73.8	15.3	10.0	13.0
Dental hygienists	208	96.0	5.1	5.0	11.3
Diagnostic-related technologists and technicians	398	70.0	12.8	5.8	9.7
Emergency medical technicians and paramedics	206	33.5	10.5	0.8	11.5
Health practitioner support technologists and technicians	710	79.0	15.6	5.4	16.5
Licensed practical and licensed vocational nurses	687	90.8	27.0	3.3	13.8
Medical records and health information technicians	185	93.3	17.5	6.0	14.4
Service occupations	**26,978**	**57.6**	**17.1**	**5.9**	**25.0**
Healthcare support occupations [3]	3,758	86.9	26.7	5.1	19.1
Nursing, psychiatric, and home health aides	2,086	88.3	37.2	4.4	17.6
Massage therapists	183	83.6	8.8	13.1	11.1
Dental assistants	284	94.9	6.7	3.1	28.9
Medical assistants	596	92.7	15.3	4.8	29.0
Protective service occupations [3]	3,128	22.1	20.3	2.2	15.3
First-line supervisors of police and detectives	83	9.9	7.6	0.4	5.6
Firefighters	318	3.3	8.5	1.3	11.6
Bailiffs, correctional officers, and jailers	372	30.1	34.2	1.7	12.3
Detectives and criminal investigators	164	23.0	12.7	1.9	8.4
Police and sheriff's patrol officers	716	17.6	12.6	1.5	17.0
Private detectives and investigators	97	47.6	23.5	3.0	17.7
Security guards and gaming surveillance officers	937	21.5	29.6	3.5	18.8
Lifeguards and other protective service workers	139	49.4	6.4	0.7	14.7
Food preparation and serving related occupations	8,378	54.5	13.9	6.9	27.0
Chefs and head cooks	474	22.0	14.3	16.4	26.0
First-line supervisors of food preparation and serving workers	597	57.4	14.9	4.8	22.6
Cooks	2,031	41.7	18.1	6.2	36.7
Food-preparation workers	1,079	59.3	13.2	8.3	28.1
Bartenders	464	53.1	6.3	2.8	16.5
Combined food preparation and serving workers, including fast food	372	62.4	19.6	5.4	19.9
Counter attendants, cafeteria, food concession, and coffee shop	200	59.2	11.3	5.2	18.6
Waiters and waitresses	2,038	71.3	11.1	7.6	23.4
Food servers, nonrestaurant	191	66.1	19.2	6.6	21.6
Dining room and cafeteria attendants and bartender helpers	338	40.5	12.6	6.2	34.2
Dishwashers	264	21.0	16.1	4.2	28.9
Hosts and hostesses, restaurant, lounge, and coffee shop	322	82.1	8.6	4.0	17.7
Building and grounds cleaning and maintenance occupations	5,746	42.0	14.9	2.9	38.2
First-line supervisors of housekeeping and janitorial workers	352	41.6	15.0	3.2	27.5
First-line supervisors of landscaping, lawn service, and groundskeeping workers	285	9.3	7.5	1.1	28.1
Janitors and building cleaners	2,265	37.2	18.2	3.4	31.6
Maids and housekeeping cleaners	1,475	89.0	17.4	4.1	49.2
Pest control workers	96	6.7	8.5	1.6	18.5
Grounds maintenance workers	1,273	6.3	8.2	0.9	43.6
Personal care and service occupations [3]	5,968	76.9	16.1	10.1	18.2
First-line supervisors of gaming workers	211	43.2	9.1	4.1	10.3
First-line supervisors of personal service workers	213	68.5	4.5	19.8	13.0
Nonfarm animal caretakers	296	75.1	5.0	2.1	12.5
Gaming services workers	93	45.1	19.6	27.3	12.2
Barbers	137	23.0	31.1	4.5	29.0
Hairdressers, hairstylists, and cosmetologists	803	92.3	13.9	6.1	17.0
Miscellaneous personal appearance workers	409	85.5	7.7	59.2	11.6
Baggage porters, bellhops, and concierges	92	24.3	26.2	12.4	30.6
Child care workers	1,193	93.4	17.4	3.3	24.6
Personal care aides	1,458	85.6	25.1	8.4	21.6
Recreation and fitness workers	440	63.3	10.8	3.4	10.2
Sales and office occupations	**33,370**	**60.6**	**13.0**	**5.2**	**17.1**
Sales and related occupations [3]	15,582	48.8	11.2	5.4	16.7

See footnotes at end of table.

Table 647. **Employed Civilians by Occupation, Sex, Race, and Hispanic Origin:** 2019-Continued.

See headnote on page 413.

Occupation	Total employed	Percent of total			
		Female	Black [1]	Asian [1]	Hispanic [2]
First-line supervisors of retail sales workers.............	3,232	45.5	9.5	5.5	14.7
First-line supervisors of non-retail sales workers...........	1,247	27.1	6.5	5.7	14.4
Cashiers..	3,164	71.2	17.9	7.3	24.1
Counter and rental clerks...............................	97	42.6	18.3	6.6	15.8
Parts salespersons......................................	142	12.0	10.4	1.3	19.8
Retail salespersons.....................................	3,105	48.5	12.4	4.5	18.7
Advertising sales agents................................	190	49.7	10.8	3.7	13.7
Insurance sales agents..................................	595	50.6	10.1	5.6	13.4
Securities, commodities, and financial services sales agents..............	231	30.0	5.4	7.5	11.9
Travel agents...	82	86.0	9.5	7.1	6.7
Sales representatives, services, all other...............	557	30.4	7.7	5.0	12.3
Sales representatives, wholesale and manufacturing.........	1,281	27.2	5.9	3.9	10.9
Real estate brokers and sales agents....................	1,095	58.9	7.9	5.2	10.7
Telemarketers...	49	–	–	–	–
Door-to-door sales, news and street vendors, and related workers........	135	59.5	9.4	1.2	24.9
Office and administrative support occupations [3]...................	17,789	70.9	14.5	5.0	17.5
First-line supervisors of office and administrative support workers........	1,306	68.5	13.4	3.7	13.3
Bill and account collectors.............................	116	80.8	30.2	1.3	17.8
Billing and posting clerks..............................	459	89.5	10.3	4.7	15.7
Bookkeeping, accounting, and auditing clerks..............	1,015	88.5	6.9	5.4	13.0
Payroll and timekeeping clerks..........................	155	85.2	8.4	6.9	17.9
Tellers...	294	84.7	9.9	4.8	20.0
Court, municipal, and license clerks....................	95	75.3	14.5	1.2	17.3
Customer service representatives........................	2,552	64.2	17.7	5.3	19.6
File clerks...	175	83.1	16.8	4.1	14.2
Hotel, motel, and resort desk clerks....................	116	74.6	21.6	7.4	22.3
Interviewers, except eligibility and loan...............	131	85.5	18.1	4.7	18.3
Library assistants, clerical............................	88	81.4	12.0	8.9	12.6
Loan interviewers and clerks............................	116	76.8	16.3	4.3	13.3
Order clerks..	112	53.3	18.2	9.9	18.3
Receptionists and information clerks....................	1,288	89.3	15.4	4.6	21.8
Reservation and transportation ticket agents and travel clerks...........	119	58.9	27.9	9.1	13.5
Couriers and messengers................................	402	20.7	17.4	4.4	21.4
Dispatchers...	261	53.1	14.2	2.5	15.2
Postal service clerks...................................	96	55.1	35.8	13.0	6.7
Postal service mail carriers............................	331	36.6	19.6	5.5	14.4
Postal service mail sorters, processors, and processing machine operators..........	76	53.3	42.3	17.8	5.8
Production, planning, and expediting clerks..............	297	57.7	14.0	3.3	12.5
Shipping, receiving, and traffic clerks.................	563	34.9	15.5	4.2	25.1
Stock clerks and order fillers..........................	1,512	37.5	18.2	5.0	23.1
Weighers, measurers, checkers, and samplers, recordkeeping...........	66	47.3	10.6	8.5	21.1
Secretaries and administrative assistants...............	2,688	93.2	8.7	3.5	13.4
Computer operators.....................................	72	47.5	11.9	9.1	19.4
Data entry keyers.......................................	250	73.4	14.7	6.5	20.3
Word processors and typists............................	57	86.0	12.6	3.3	16.1
Insurance claims and policy processing clerks...........	269	81.7	21.8	2.4	15.5
Mail clerks and mail machine operators, except postal service............	68	49.8	24.0	4.1	14.2
Office clerks, general..................................	1,355	82.7	13.6	8.6	20.9
Natural resources, construction, and maintenance occupations........	**14,343**	**5.4**	**7.7**	**2.2**	**31.9**
Farming, fishing, and forestry occupations [3]............	1,156	25.2	4.4	1.8	47.6
Construction and extraction occupations [3].............	8,325	3.5	7.3	1.6	36.4
First-line supervisors of construction trades and extraction workers.........	682	3.4	7.5	1.2	24.8
Brickmasons, blockmasons, and stonemasons..............	152	0.7	5.2	1.2	37.7
Carpenters..	1,292	2.8	5.1	1.5	37.3
Carpet, floor, and tile installers and finishers.......	170	1.9	5.1	0.5	59.7
Cement masons, concrete finishers, and terrazzo workers.......	65	3.0	4.4	1.1	53.5
Construction laborers...................................	2,051	3.5	8.6	1.6	46.7
Operating engineers and other construction equipment operators........	375	1.7	8.9	0.9	14.9
Drywall installers, ceiling tile installers, and tapers......	178	0.7	2.5	1.7	67.7
Electricians..	914	2.2	6.8	2.6	21.1
Painters, construction and maintenance..................	599	8.9	8.1	0.6	55.5
Pipelayers, plumbers, pipefitters, and steamfitters.....	637	2.7	8.4	0.9	27.1
Roofers...	222	1.9	5.2	0.7	50.7
Sheet metal workers.....................................	140	6.8	6.7	2.3	28.9
Construction and building inspectors....................	105	10.4	8.3	6.8	12.8
Highway maintenance workers............................	113	3.6	12.7	0.4	13.3
Installation, maintenance, and repair occupations [3]......	4,862	3.9	9.1	3.3	20.3
First-line supervisors of mechanics, installers, and repairers...........	272	8.2	9.9	1.5	16.1
Computer, automated teller, and office machine repairers.....	184	14.0	11.7	9.3	15.9
Radio and telecommunications equipment installers and repairers.......	131	7.6	15.8	4.9	15.0
Aircraft mechanics and service technicians..............	152	4.8	10.5	4.8	12.4
Automotive body and related repairers..................	125	2.2	3.4	1.8	29.6
Automotive service technicians and mechanics...........	880	1.9	8.7	3.2	27.7
Bus and truck mechanics and diesel engine specialists.....	347	1.5	6.5	3.7	14.1
Heavy vehicle and mobile equip. service technicians and mechanics.....	211	1.5	6.0	2.6	15.8
Heating, air conditioning, and refrigeration mechanics and installers...........	466	1.5	9.1	3.0	20.2
Industrial and refractory machinery mechanics..........	408	4.1	8.7	2.5	18.1
Maintenance and repair workers, general................	579	3.8	9.4	3.2	20.1
Electrical power-line installers and repairers.........	133	1.6	3.0	0.6	15.4
Telecommunications line installers and repairers.......	184	4.5	12.5	2.3	24.7

See footnotes at end of table.

Table 647. Employed Civilians by Occupation, Sex, Race, and Hispanic Origin: 2019-Continued.

See headnote on page 413.

Occupation	Total employed	Percent of total			
		Female	Black [1]	Asian [1]	Hispanic [2]
Production, transportation, and material moving occupations............	**18,628**	**23.0**	**16.9**	**5.0**	**23.0**
Production occupations [3]...	8,565	28.6	13.3	6.0	23.1
First-line supervisors of production and operating workers..................	844	21.3	12.2	3.8	17.2
Electrical, electronics, and electromechanical assemblers..................	101	50.4	8.0	20.2	20.1
Bakers...	228	60.4	11.7	9.6	30.7
Butchers and other meat, poultry, and fish processing workers............	297	26.9	17.1	6.2	37.3
Food batchmakers...	82	62.7	7.3	1.6	36.2
Computer control programmers and operators...........................	108	3.7	6.6	5.0	11.4
Machinists..	375	5.6	7.0	4.9	11.5
Welding, soldering, and brazing workers................................	592	5.3	8.8	2.3	22.8
Metal workers and plastic workers, all other............................	392	19.5	14.5	8.2	26.0
Printing press operators..	133	22.1	7.2	4.0	23.1
Laundry and dry-cleaning workers......................................	134	75.4	25.1	12.2	37.9
Sewing machine operators...	179	72.4	11.0	15.3	35.4
Tailors, dressmakers, and sewers.......................................	86	75.4	9.5	23.7	20.9
Water and wastewater treatment plant and system operators.............	110	8.0	8.4	3.5	9.7
Crushing, grinding, polishing, mixing, and blending workers..............	90	7.5	11.4	1.9	26.1
Inspectors, testers, sorters, samplers, and weighers....................	802	35.6	11.5	5.4	17.5
Medical, dental, and ophthalmic laboratory technicians...................	91	60.0	4.6	10.5	17.7
Packaging and filling machine operators and tenders.....................	262	54.6	20.4	6.3	37.3
Painting workers..	171	10.6	13.0	1.8	41.8
Transportation and material-moving occupations [3].......................	10,063	18.2	20.0	4.1	22.9
Supervisors, transportation and material-moving workers.................	206	21.5	19.4	6.7	20.3
Aircraft pilots and flight engineers......................................	141	7.5	2.6	3.4	2.2
Bus drivers...	546	45.3	27.0	3.1	15.0
Driver/sales workers and truck drivers..................................	3,608	6.7	18.1	2.9	20.5
Taxi drivers and chauffeurs..	790	16.8	29.5	13.1	23.6
Parking lot attendants...	83	14.8	19.3	5.7	31.0
Automotive and water craft service attendants..........................	88	18.4	12.1	13.7	14.5
Industrial truck and tractor operators..................................	571	8.7	25.8	1.7	31.4
Cleaners of vehicles and equipment....................................	344	16.0	19.4	1.4	34.8
Laborers and freight, stock, and material movers, hand..................	2,235	21.5	19.8	2.7	23.1
Packers and packagers, hand...	628	54.8	19.0	7.7	41.5
Refuse and recyclable material collectors...............................	99	7.6	18.2	3.6	29.7

– Represents or rounds to zero. [1] Data represent persons who selected this race group only and exclude persons reporting more than one race. See also comments on race in the text for Section 1. [2] Persons of Hispanic origin may be of any race. [3] Includes other occupations, not shown separately.

Source: U.S. Bureau of Labor Statistics, CPS Tables, "Employed persons by detailed occupation, sex, race, and Hispanic or Latino ethnicity," <http://www.bls.gov/cps/tables.htm>, accessed February 2020.

Table 648. Employed Workers With Contract, On-Call, Temporary, and Traditional Work Arrangements: 2017

[In thousands (153,331 represents 153,331,000). As of February. For employed workers 16 years old and over. Based on the Current Population Survey; see text, Section 1 and Appendix III]

Characteristic	Total employed [1]	Workers with alternative arrangements				Workers with traditional arrangements
		Independent contractors	On-call workers	Temporary help agency workers	Workers provided by contract firms	
Total employed......................	**153,331**	**10,614**	**2,579**	**1,356**	**933**	**137,853**
16 to 19 years old....................	4,842	43	107	25	14	4,647
20 to 24 years old....................	14,212	330	263	195	53	13,370
25 to 34 years old....................	33,991	1,593	516	303	224	31,361
35 to 44 years old....................	32,065	2,160	565	283	207	28,849
45 to 54 years old....................	32,745	2,562	446	276	206	29,263
55 to 64 years old....................	26,236	2,426	399	170	124	23,110
65 years old and over................	9,240	1,500	283	105	106	7,253
Male.................................	81,545	6,820	1,355	709	625	72,035
16 to 19 years old....................	2,365	42	53	20	9	2,235
20 to 24 years old....................	7,412	187	169	100	28	6,931
25 to 34 years old....................	18,169	1,016	271	170	157	16,554
35 to 44 years old....................	17,585	1,430	329	122	144	15,557
45 to 54 years old....................	17,099	1,611	208	166	146	14,971
55 to 64 years old....................	13,840	1,547	209	81	81	11,914
65 years old and over................	5,076	986	117	50	60	3,873
Female...............................	71,785	3,794	1,224	647	308	65,818
16 to 19 years old....................	2,477	1	55	5	5	2,412
20 to 24 years old....................	6,800	143	94	95	25	6,439
25 to 34 years old....................	15,823	577	245	133	67	14,807
35 to 44 years old....................	14,480	730	237	161	63	13,292
45 to 54 years old....................	15,646	951	238	110	60	14,292
55 to 64 years old....................	12,396	878	190	88	44	11,196
65 years old and over................	4,164	514	166	55	45	3,380
Full-time workers.....................	125,240	7,485	1,428	1,042	785	114,496
Part-time workers.....................	28,091	3,129	1,151	314	148	23,357

[1] Includes day laborers (an alternative arrangement) and a small number of workers who were both "on call" and "provided by contract firms," not shown separately.

Source: U.S. Bureau of Labor Statistics, *Contingent and Alternative Employment Arrangements, May 2017*, USDL 18–0942, June 2018. See also <https://www.bls.gov/cps/lfcharacteristics.htm#contingent>.

Table 649. Employment and Annual and Hourly Wages by Occupation: 2019

[In dollars, except employment. As of May. Data shown for occupations with over 1,500,000 employees. Data from the Occupational Employment Statistics survey. For definition of mean and median, see Guide to Tabular Presentation]

Occupation	Employment (number)	Mean hourly wage	Annual wages [1]	Median hourly wage
All occupations [2]	146,875,480	25.72	53,490	19.14
Management occupations	8,054,120	58.88	122,480	50.80
Top executives	2,658,440	61.09	127,070	49.63
General and operations managers	2,400,280	59.15	123,030	48.45
Operations specialties managers	1,996,160	64.69	134,550	58.15
Other management occupations	2,628,970	49.31	102,560	43.90
Business and financial operations occupations	8,183,750	37.56	78,130	33.57
Business operations specialists	5,427,140	36.31	75,530	33.04
Financial specialists	2,756,610	40.03	83,260	34.59
Computer and mathematical occupations	4,552,880	45.08	93,760	42.47
Computer occupations	4,358,410	45.01	93,620	42.43
Software and web developers, programmers, and testers	1,754,750	51.44	106,980	49.20
Architecture and engineering occupations	2,592,680	42.69	88,800	39.15
Engineers	1,730,720	48.45	100,770	45.43
Community and social service occupations	2,244,310	24.27	50,480	22.16
Counselors, social workers, and other community and social service specialists	2,159,870	24.23	50,410	22.15
Educational instruction and library occupations	8,886,600	27.75	57,710	24.42
Postsecondary teachers	1,407,110	(3)	90,830	(3)
Preschool, elementary, middle, secondary, and special education teachers	4,211,470	(3)	61,420	(3)
Elementary and middle school teachers	2,064,680	(3)	63,820	(3)
Arts, design, entertainment, sports, and media occupations	2,017,810	29.79	61,960	24.59
Healthcare practitioners and technical occupations	8,673,140	40.21	83,640	32.78
Healthcare diagnosing or treating practitioners	5,685,500	49.26	102,470	39.61
Registered nurses	2,982,280	37.24	77,460	35.24
Health technologists and technicians	2,902,300	22.86	47,540	21.34
Healthcare support occupations	6,521,790	14.91	31,010	13.69
Nursing, psychiatric, and home health aides	4,683,430	13.39	27,860	12.68
Protective service occupations	3,498,800	23.98	49,880	19.99
Food preparation and serving related occupations	13,494,590	12.82	26,670	11.65
Cooks and food preparation workers	3,367,740	13.03	27,100	12.45
Cooks	2,504,000	13.24	27,550	12.67
Food and beverage serving workers	7,500,280	12.01	24,990	11.02
Fast food and counter workers	3,996,820	11.18	23,250	10.93
Waiters and waitresses	2,579,020	12.88	26,800	11.00
Building and grounds cleaning and maintenance occupations	4,429,100	15.03	31,250	13.62
Building cleaning and pest control workers	3,170,010	14.11	29,350	12.78
Building cleaning workers	3,090,570	13.98	29,080	12.68
Janitors and cleaners, except maids and housekeeping cleaners	2,145,450	14.43	30,010	13.19
Personal care and service occupations	3,303,200	15.03	31,260	12.61
Sales and related occupations	14,371,410	20.70	43,060	14.24
Retail sales workers	8,603,590	13.27	27,600	11.84
Cashiers	3,617,910	11.73	24,400	11.38
Retail salespersons	4,317,950	14.12	29,360	12.14
Sales representatives, services	2,084,000	34.45	71,660	26.62
Sales representatives, wholesale and manufacturing	1,651,500	36.14	75,180	30.29
Office and administrative support occupations	19,528,250	19.73	41,040	18.07
Financial clerks	2,910,660	19.60	40,770	18.52
Bookkeeping, accounting, and auditing clerks	1,512,660	20.65	42,960	19.82
Information and record clerks	5,780,040	17.59	36,580	16.37
Customer service representatives	2,919,230	17.94	37,320	16.69
Material recording, scheduling, dispatching, and distributing workers	2,155,080	21.13	43,950	19.39
Secretaries and administrative assistants	3,353,950	20.87	43,410	19.16
Secretaries and administrative assistants, except legal, medical, and executive	2,038,340	18.84	39,180	18.12
Other office and administrative support workers	3,764,620	17.75	36,920	16.67
Office clerks, general	2,956,060	17.48	36,360	16.37
Construction and extraction occupations	6,194,140	25.28	52,580	22.80
Construction trades workers	4,617,440	24.68	51,330	22.28
Installation, maintenance, and repair occupations	5,713,450	24.10	50,130	22.42
Vehicle and mobile equipment mechanics, installers, and repairers	1,638,920	22.81	47,440	21.44
Other installation, maintenance, and repair occupations	3,031,220	22.83	47,480	21.20
Production occupations	9,158,980	19.30	40,140	17.31
Assemblers and fabricators	1,856,870	17.46	36,310	16.21
Metal workers and plastic workers	1,825,170	20.22	42,050	18.96
Other production occupations	2,669,650	18.64	38,770	17.11
Transportation and material moving occupations	12,532,030	18.23	37,920	15.60
Motor vehicle operators	4,174,700	19.57	40,710	18.53
Driver/sales workers and truck drivers	3,223,840	20.27	42,170	19.38
Heavy and tractor-trailer truck drivers	1,856,130	22.52	46,850	21.76
Material moving workers	7,061,370	15.28	31,790	13.97
Laborers and material movers	6,168,600	14.70	30,570	13.53
Laborers and freight, stock, and material movers, hand	2,953,170	15.45	32,130	14.19

[1] Annual wages have been calculated by multiplying the hourly mean wage by a "year-round, full-time" hours figure of 2,080 hours; for those occupations where there is not an hourly mean wage published, the annual wage has been directly calculated from the reported survey data. [2] Includes occupations not shown separately. [3] Wages for some occupations that do not generally work year-round full-time are reported as either hourly wages or as annual salaries, depending on how they are typically paid.

Source: U.S. Bureau of Labor Statistics, Occupational Employment Statistics, *Occupational Employment and Wages—May 2019*, USDL 20-0520, March 2020. See also <http://www.bls.gov/oes/>.

Table 650. Employed Civilians by Occupation—States: 2018

[In thousands (155,761 represents 155,761,000). Excludes persons with no previous work experience. Based on the Current Population Survey see text, Section 1 and Appendix III]

State	Total employed	Management, professional, and related occupations		Service occupations	Sales and office occupations		Natural resources, construction, and maintenance occupations			Production, transportation, and material-moving occupations	
		Management, business, and financial	Professional and related		Sales and related	Office and administrative	Farming, fishing, and forestry	Construction and extraction occupations	Installation, maintenance, and repair	Production	Transportation and material-moving
Total U.S....	155,761	25,850	36,586	26,854	15,806	17,655	1,121	8,338	5,012	8,621	9,918
AL..............	2,121	285	484	327	202	244	(S)	110	95	194	167
AK..............	332	55	68	62	30	45	(S)	17	17	(S)	23
AZ..............	3,272	550	724	626	311	440	(S)	167	104	127	205
AR..............	1,289	172	279	200	147	148	(S)	89	46	108	83
CA..............	18,561	3,101	4,485	3,302	1,837	2,085	269	941	525	916	1,101
CO..............	2,994	631	744	432	298	315	(S)	218	(S)	(S)	153
CT..............	1,819	325	492	335	161	182	(S)	(S)	(S)	99	85
DE..............	467	74	109	83	46	63	(S)	27	(S)	(S)	28
DC..............	382	117	142	52	19	31	(S)	(S)	(S)	(S)	10
FL..............	9,871	1,536	2,058	1,886	1,257	1,224	(S)	599	363	289	604
GA..............	4,916	791	1,097	755	570	584	(S)	256	179	290	366
HI..............	661	111	146	146	65	82	(S)	38	(S)	(S)	(S)
ID..............	832	140	168	123	84	106	(S)	50	(S)	44	57
IL..............	6,196	1,067	1,458	1,001	617	759	(S)	260	192	363	462
IN..............	3,289	490	684	548	340	365	(S)	124	123	343	256
IA..............	1,646	290	343	254	174	207	(S)	(S)	(S)	120	114
KS..............	1,431	238	325	220	140	167	(S)	85	(S)	115	86
KY..............	1,975	309	417	291	197	253	(S)	101	(S)	162	155
LA..............	2,000	259	419	420	208	225	(S)	146	73	108	135
ME..............	672	110	164	120	60	72	(S)	(S)	(S)	42	(S)
MD..............	3,051	606	891	516	264	301	(S)	170	(S)	(S)	143
MA..............	3,693	684	1,103	628	322	366	(S)	183	(S)	150	171
MI..............	4,702	740	1,162	779	440	536	(S)	190	128	407	296
MN..............	2,975	611	662	487	287	310	(S)	132	(S)	215	165
MS..............	1,215	138	248	206	131	135	(S)	85	50	108	101
MO..............	2,960	514	673	470	302	362	(S)	151	(S)	191	199
MT..............	506	89	107	101	48	57	(S)	31	(S)	(S)	26
NE..............	1,001	180	208	165	93	114	(S)	(S)	(S)	80	(S)
NV..............	1,442	187	212	365	158	190	(S)	92	63	61	110
NH..............	745	135	188	119	76	76	(S)	42	(S)	52	34
NJ..............	4,232	841	1,096	666	447	477	(S)	172	115	133	277
NM..............	905	123	221	184	93	100	(S)	60	33	(S)	52
NY..............	9,147	1,452	2,433	1,862	898	939	(S)	450	224	301	554
NC..............	4,800	766	1,165	807	464	493	(S)	286	180	335	280
ND..............	388	66	79	66	41	45	(S)	24	(S)	20	27
OH..............	5,495	900	1,254	940	544	600	(S)	213	182	444	401
OK..............	1,782	269	386	282	188	216	(S)	132	83	107	105
OR..............	1,999	360	506	348	190	211	(S)	82	(S)	97	124
PA..............	6,156	1,035	1,484	1,032	598	695	(S)	264	208	365	446
RI..............	534	91	145	91	57	55	(S)	(S)	(S)	35	28
SC..............	2,235	321	512	337	236	272	(S)	130	102	176	136
SD..............	447	79	87	76	45	49	(S)	(S)	(S)	(S)	(S)
TN..............	3,127	473	687	530	334	356	(S)	158	111	235	234
TX..............	13,353	2,143	2,873	2,240	1,446	1,550	(S)	1,004	504	678	882
UT..............	1,504	253	350	211	145	210	(S)	96	(S)	92	86
VT..............	338	54	92	54	34	36	(S)	21	(S)	19	(S)
VA..............	4,224	767	1,126	717	389	407	(S)	252	(S)	(S)	254
WA..............	3,613	610	873	639	350	380	82	171	100	175	233
WV..............	743	91	160	137	75	88	(S)	42	35	49	60
WI..............	3,029	504	639	490	287	356	(S)	134	(S)	279	186
WY..............	277	45	52	51	25	31	(S)	25	13	12	21

S Data are not shown when the labor force base does not meet publication standard of reliability for the particular area, as determined by the sample size.

Source: U.S. Bureau of Labor Statistics, "Geographic Profile of Employment and Unemployment, 2018," October 2019. See also <https://www.bls.gov/opub/geographic-profile/>.

Table 651. Fastest Growing and Largest Occupations Projected with Education Needed and Median Wages: 2018 to 2028

[In thousands (9.7 represents 9,700), except percent and wage. Estimates based on the Current Employment Statistics Program, the Occupational Employment Statistics Survey, and the Current Population Survey. See source for methodological assumptions. Occupations based on the 2010 Standard Occupational Classification system. Additional occupation information in the Occupational Outlook Handbook <http://www.bls.gov/ooh>]

Occupation	Employment (1,000)		Change, 2018–2028		Median annual wage (in dollars), 2018	Typical education needed for entry [1]
	2018	2028	Number (1,000)	Percent		
FASTEST GROWING						
Solar photovoltaic installers	9.7	15.8	6.1	63.3	42,680	High school diploma or equivalent
Wind turbine service technicians	6.6	10.3	3.8	56.9	54,370	Postsecondary nondegree award
Home health aides	831.8	1,136.6	304.8	36.6	24,200	High school diploma or equivalent
Personal care aides	2,421.2	3,302.1	881.0	36.4	24,020	High school diploma or equivalent
Occupational therapy assistants	43.8	58.3	14.5	33.1	60,220	Associate's degree
Information security analysts	112.3	147.7	35.5	31.6	98,350	Bachelor's degree
Physician assistants	118.8	155.7	37.0	31.1	108,610	Master's degree
Statisticians	44.4	58.0	13.6	30.7	87,780	Master's degree
Nurse practitioners	189.1	242.4	53.3	28.2	107,030	Master's degree
Speech-language pathologists	153.7	195.6	41.9	27.3	77,510	Master's degree
Physical therapist assistants	98.4	125.0	26.7	27.1	58,040	Associate's degree
Genetic counselors	3.0	3.8	0.8	27.0	80,370	Master's degree
Mathematicians	2.9	3.6	0.8	26.0	101,900	Master's degree
Operations research analysts	109.7	137.9	28.1	25.6	83,390	Bachelor's degree
Software developers, applications	944.2	1,185.7	241.5	25.6	103,620	Bachelor's degree
Forest fire inspectors and prevention specialists	2.2	2.8	0.5	24.1	39,600	High school diploma or equivalent
Health specialties teachers, postsecondary	254.8	313.9	59.1	23.2	97,370	Doctoral or professional degree
Phlebotomists	128.3	157.8	29.5	23.0	34,480	Postsecondary nondegree award
Physical therapist aides	49.8	61.2	11.3	22.8	26,240	High school diploma or equivalent
Medical assistants	686.6	841.5	154.9	22.6	33,610	Postsecondary nondegree award
Substance abuse, behavioral disorder, and mental health counselors	304.5	373.1	68.5	22.5	44,630	Bachelor's degree
Marriage and family therapists	55.3	67.7	12.3	22.3	50,090	Master's degree
Massage therapists	159.8	195.2	35.4	22.2	41,420	Postsecondary nondegree award
Cooks, restaurant	1,362.3	1,661.3	299.0	21.9	26,530	No formal educational credential
Physical therapists	247.7	301.9	54.2	21.9	87,930	Doctoral or professional degree
Respiratory therapists	134.0	162.0	27.9	20.8	60,280	Associate's degree
Market research analysts and marketing specialists	681.9	821.1	139.2	20.4	63,120	Bachelor's degree
Actuaries	25.0	30.0	5.0	20.1	102,880	Bachelor's degree
Computer numerically controlled machine tool programmers, metal and plastic	24.3	29.2	4.9	20.0	53,190	Postsecondary nondegree award
Nursing instructors and teachers, postsecondary	69.0	82.8	13.8	20.0	73,490	Doctoral or professional degree
LARGEST JOB GROWTH						
Personal care aides	2,421.2	3,302.1	881.0	36.4	24,020	High school diploma or equivalent
Combined food preparation and serving workers, including fast food	3,704.2	4,344.3	640.1	17.3	21,250	No formal educational credential
Registered nurses	3,059.8	3,431.3	371.5	12.1	71,730	Bachelor's degree
Home health aides	831.8	1,136.6	304.8	36.6	24,200	High school diploma or equivalent
Cooks, restaurant	1,362.3	1,661.3	299.0	21.9	26,530	No formal educational credential
Software developers, applications	944.2	1,185.7	241.5	25.6	103,620	Bachelor's degree
Waiters and waitresses	2,634.6	2,804.8	170.2	6.5	21,780	No formal educational credential
General and operations managers	2,376.4	2,541.4	165.0	6.9	100,930	Bachelor's degree
Janitors and cleaners, except maids and housekeeping cleaners	2,404.4	2,564.2	159.8	6.6	26,110	No formal educational credential
Medical assistants	686.6	841.5	154.9	22.6	33,610	Postsecondary nondegree award
Construction laborers	1,405.0	1,553.1	148.1	10.5	35,800	No formal educational credential
Laborers and freight, stock, and material movers, hand	2,953.8	3,097.9	144.0	4.9	28,260	No formal educational credential
Market research analysts and marketing specialists	681.9	821.1	139.2	20.4	63,120	Bachelor's degree
Nursing assistants	1,513.2	1,648.6	135.4	8.9	28,540	Postsecondary nondegree award
Management analysts	876.3	994.6	118.3	13.5	83,610	Bachelor's degree
First-line supervisors of food preparation and serving workers	988.9	1,096.1	107.2	10.8	32,450	High school diploma or equivalent
Landscaping and groundskeeping workers	1,205.2	1,311.6	106.4	8.8	29,000	No formal educational credential
Financial managers	653.6	758.3	104.7	16.0	127,990	Bachelor's degree
Heavy and tractor-trailer truck drivers	1,958.8	2,058.5	99.7	5.1	43,680	Postsecondary nondegree award
Medical secretaries	601.7	698.1	96.4	16.0	35,760	High school diploma or equivalent
Accountants and auditors	1,424.0	1,514.7	90.7	6.4	70,500	Bachelor's degree
Maintenance and repair workers, general	1,488.0	1,573.4	85.4	5.7	38,300	High school diploma or equivalent
Carpenters	1,006.5	1,086.6	80.1	8.0	46,590	High school diploma or equivalent
Licensed practical and licensed vocational nurses	728.9	807.0	78.1	10.7	46,240	Postsecondary nondegree award
Sales representatives, services, all other	1,060.6	1,137.0	76.4	7.2	54,550	High school diploma or equivalent
Electricians	715.4	789.5	74.1	10.4	55,190	High school diploma or equivalent
Taxi drivers and chauffeurs	370.4	442.8	72.4	19.5	25,980	No formal educational credential
Medical and health services managers	406.1	477.6	71.6	17.6	99,730	Bachelor's degree
Business operations specialists, all other	1,135.7	1,207.0	71.3	6.3	70,530	Bachelor's degree
Computer user support specialists	671.8	742.7	70.9	10.6	50,980	Some college, no degree

[1] An occupation is placed into 1 of 8 categories that best describes the typical education needed by most workers to enter that occupation. For more information, see "Measures of Education and Training" at <https://www.bls.gov/emp/documentation/education/tech.htm>.

Source: U.S. Bureau of Labor Statistics, Employment Projections, "EP Tables—Occupations," <https://www.bls.gov/emp/tables.htm>, accessed January 2020.

Table 652. Employment Projections by Industry: 2018 to 2028

[11,926.3 represents 11,926,300. Estimates based on the Current Employment Statistics program. See source for methodological assumptions. Minus sign (-) indicates decline]

Industry	2017 NAICS code [1]	Employment (1,000) 2018	Employment (1,000) 2028	Change, 2018–2028 (1,000)	Average annual rate of change 2018–2028
LARGEST GROWTH					
Food services and drinking places...	722	11,926.3	13,315.8	1,389.5	1.1
Construction...	23	7,289.3	8,096.8	807.5	1.1
Individual and family services..	6241	2,464.2	3,255.7	791.5	2.8
Home health care services..	6216	1,472.7	2,186.4	713.7	4.0
Computer systems design and related services............................	5415	2,121.6	2,642.3	520.7	2.2
Offices of physicians...	6211	2,620.6	2,970.5	349.9	1.3
Nursing and residential care facilities..................................	623	3,362.2	3,698.7	336.5	1.0
Outpatient care centers...	6214	934.4	1,265.4	331.0	3.1
Hospitals...	622	5,145.1	5,467.8	322.7	0.6
Management, scientific, and technical consulting services.................	5416	1,483.2	1,776.0	292.8	1.8
Offices of other health practitioners....................................	6213	930.2	1,184.8	254.6	2.4
Junior colleges, colleges, universities, and professional schools........	6112, 6113	1,863.6	2,085.2	221.6	1.1
Services to buildings and dwellings......................................	5617	2,153.2	2,350.8	197.6	0.9
Warehousing and storage..	493	1,139.6	1,309.0	169.4	1.4
Elementary and secondary schools..	6111	1,083.3	1,220.4	137.1	1.2
Other amusement and recreation industries................................	7139	1,386.1	1,508.8	122.7	0.9
Local government, other compensation.....................................	(X)	4,214.3	4,335.7	121.4	0.3
Other educational services...	6114-7	780.6	895.4	114.8	1.4
Management of companies and enterprises..................................	55	2,371.8	2,481.8	110.0	0.5
Agencies, brokerages, and other insurance related activities.............	5242	1,168.9	1,278.4	109.5	0.9
FASTEST GROWTH					
Home health care services..	6216	1,472.7	2,186.4	713.7	4.0
Outpatient care centers...	6214	934.4	1,265.4	331.0	3.1
Individual and family services..	6241	2,464.2	3,255.7	791.5	2.8
Other information services..	519	307.8	393.5	85.7	2.5
Offices of other health practitioners....................................	6213	930.2	1,184.8	254.6	2.4
Medical and diagnostic laboratories......................................	6215	277.9	350.3	72.4	2.3
Computer systems design and related services............................	5415	2,121.6	2,642.3	520.7	2.2
Forestry..	1131, 1132	5.7	7.0	1.3	2.1
Other ambulatory health care services....................................	6219	307.6	372.3	64.7	1.9
Software publishers...	5112	407.9	489.1	81.2	1.8
Management, scientific, and technical consulting services.................	5416	1,483.2	1,776.0	292.8	1.8
Data processing, hosting, and related services...........................	518	329.8	391.4	61.6	1.7
Office administrative services..	5611	515.2	607.9	92.7	1.7
Support activities for mining...	213	346.1	408.2	62.1	1.7
Warehousing and storage..	493	1,139.6	1,309.0	169.4	1.4
Other educational services...	6114-7	780.6	895.4	114.8	1.4
Other professional, scientific, and technical services....................	5419	738.5	845.0	106.5	1.4
Offices of physicians...	6211	2,620.6	2,970.5	349.9	1.3
Elementary and secondary schools..	6111	1,083.3	1,220.4	137.1	1.2
Junior colleges, colleges, universities, and professional schools........	6112, 6113	1,863.6	2,085.2	221.6	1.1
MOST RAPIDLY DECLINING					
Tobacco manufacturing..	3122	11.7	7.3	-4.4	-4.6
Federal electric utilities..	(X)	14.9	10.4	-4.5	-3.5
Apparel, leather and allied product manufacturing........................	315, 316	139.6	99.5	-40.1	-3.3
Communications equipment manufacturing...................................	3342	85.7	62.2	-23.5	-3.2
Manufacturing and reproducing magnetic and optical media.................	3346	14.2	10.6	-3.6	-2.8
Newspaper, periodical, book, and directory publishers....................	5111	324.7	247.9	-76.8	-2.7
Wired telecommunications carriers..	517311	547.3	420.1	-127.2	-2.6
Satellite, telecommunications resellers, and all other telecommunications................	5174, 5179	89.5	70.6	-18.9	-2.4
Postal Service..	491	608.6	482.1	-126.5	-2.3
Pulp, paper, and paperboard mills..	3221	95.1	76.4	-18.7	-2.2
Printing and related support activities..................................	323	430.9	346.4	-84.5	-2.2
Cable and other subscription programming.................................	5152	53.6	43.5	-10.1	-2.1
Textile mills and textile product mills..................................	313314	228.9	188.6	-40.3	-1.9
Logging...	1133	48.6	40.3	-8.3	-1.9
Gambling industries (except casino hotels)...............................	7132	120.4	100.8	-19.6	-1.8
Foundries...	3315	119.7	101.0	-18.7	-1.7
Iron and steel mills and ferroalloy manufacturing........................	3311	82.8	70.1	-12.7	-1.6
Household appliance manufacturing..	3352	63.1	53.5	-9.6	-1.6
Natural gas distribution..	2212	110.0	95.6	-14.4	-1.4
Coal mining..	2121	51.8	45.3	-6.5	-1.3

X Not applicable. [1] Based on the North American Industry Classification System, 2017; see text, Section 15.

Source: U.S. Bureau of Labor Statistics, Employment Projections, "EP Data Tables—Industries," <https://www.bls.gov/emp/tables.htm>, accessed July 2020.

Table 653. Occupations of the Employed by Race/Ethnicity and Educational Attainment: 2019

[In thousands (138,216 represents 138,216,000). Annual averages of monthly figures. Civilian noninstitutional population 25 years old and over. Based on Current Population Survey; see text, Section 1 and Appendix III]

Race/ethnicity and educational attainment	Total employed	Managerial, professional, and related	Service	Sales and office	Natural resources, construction, and maintenance	Production, transpor- tation, and material- moving
Total [1]	**138,216**	**60,388**	**21,037**	**27,818**	**12,695**	**16,278**
Less than a high school diploma	9,441	747	2,992	1,083	2,342	2,276
High school graduate, no college	34,837	5,805	7,767	8,182	5,490	7,594
Some college or associate degree	36,282	12,048	6,623	9,598	3,607	4,406
Bachelor's degree or higher	57,655	41,788	3,655	8,955	1,256	2,002
White	107,636	47,736	14,954	21,997	10,940	12,009
Less than a high school diploma	7,519	629	2,216	826	2,090	1,759
High school graduate, no college	27,183	4,875	5,295	6,613	4,758	5,642
Some college or associate degree	28,182	9,762	4,734	7,473	3,041	3,171
Bachelor's degree or higher	44,752	32,470	2,709	7,084	1,051	1,437
Black	16,858	5,816	3,817	3,433	991	2,802
Less than a high school diploma	1,029	60	434	136	123	276
High school graduate, no college	5,007	602	1,649	983	421	1,352
Some college or associate degree	5,315	1,462	1,261	1,384	337	870
Bachelor's degree or higher	5,506	3,691	473	929	110	304
Asian	9,298	5,297	1,373	1,459	293	876
Less than a high school diploma	468	27	201	64	34	142
High school graduate, no college	1,384	158	498	287	91	349
Some college or associate degree	1,387	413	316	385	99	173
Bachelor's degree or higher	6,059	4,699	357	722	69	211
Hispanic [2]	23,477	5,882	5,423	4,355	4,104	3,712
Less than a high school diploma	5,411	280	1,791	466	1,665	1,209
High school graduate, no college	7,394	890	1,923	1,488	1,551	1,541
Some college or associate degree	5,509	1,539	1,180	1,497	633	660
Bachelor's degree or higher	5,164	3,173	528	904	256	302

[1] Includes other races, not shown separately. [2] Persons of Hispanic origin may be of any race.

Source: U.S. Bureau of Labor Statistics, Current Population Survey, unpublished data. See also <http://www.bls.gov/cps/>.

Table 654. Employment by Industry, Sex, Race, and Hispanic Origin: 2000 to 2019

[In thousands (136,891 represents 136,891,000), except percent. Civilian noninstitutional population 16 years old and over. Annual average of monthly figures. Based on Current Population Survey; see text, Section 1, Population, and Appendix III]

Industry	Total				2019, percent of total			
	2000	2005	2010	2019	Female	Black [1]	Asian [1]	Hispanic [2]
Total employed	**136,891**	**141,730**	**139,064**	**157,538**	**47.0**	**12.3**	**6.5**	**17.6**
Agriculture and related industries	2,464	2,197	2,206	2,425	26.2	2.2	1.7	27.5
Mining and related industries	475	624	731	750	15.8	5.1	3.7	20.1
Construction	9,931	11,197	9,077	11,373	10.3	6.4	1.9	30.4
Manufacturing	19,644	16,253	14,081	15,741	29.4	10.4	6.8	16.8
Durable goods	12,519	10,333	8,789	9,970	25.1	9.5	7.3	14.8
Nondurable goods	7,125	5,919	5,293	5,771	36.8	11.9	5.9	20.2
Wholesale trade	4,216	4,579	3,805	3,525	28.6	9.1	5.3	17.2
Retail trade	15,763	16,825	15,934	16,217	47.6	12.3	5.7	18.3
Transportation and utilities	7,380	7,360	7,134	8,991	24.1	20.1	5.6	18.8
Transportation and warehousing	6,096	6,184	5,880	7,614	24.8	22.0	5.8	20.1
Utilities	1,284	1,176	1,253	1,377	19.9	9.7	4.3	11.9
Information	4,059	3,402	3,149	2,766	40.5	11.3	8.5	12.5
Financial activities	9,374	10,203	9,350	10,765	52.6	10.5	7.5	12.9
Finance and insurance	6,641	7,035	6,605	7,464	54.7	10.5	8.5	11.7
Real estate and rental and leasing	2,734	3,168	2,745	3,301	47.7	10.4	5.1	15.5
Professional and business services	13,649	14,294	15,253	19,606	41.3	10.0	9.6	16.0
Professional and technical services	8,266	8,584	9,115	12,808	42.6	7.4	13.0	9.2
Management, administrative, and waste services	5,383	5,709	6,138	6,799	39.0	14.8	3.2	28.8
Education and health services	26,188	29,174	32,062	35,894	74.8	15.1	6.4	13.5
Educational services	11,255	12,264	13,155	14,193	69.6	11.1	5.7	12.3
Health care and social assistance	14,933	16,910	18,907	21,701	78.1	17.7	6.9	14.2
Hospitals	5,202	5,719	6,249	7,425	74.9	16.0	8.9	10.8
Health services, except hospitals	7,009	8,332	9,406	10,846	78.6	18.1	6.2	14.9
Social assistance	2,722	2,860	3,252	3,430	83.8	20.1	4.6	19.4
Leisure and hospitality	11,186	12,071	12,530	14,643	51.2	13.1	6.9	24.0
Arts, entertainment, and recreation	2,539	2,765	2,966	3,444	46.0	10.5	4.2	14.2
Accommodation and food services	8,647	9,306	9,564	11,200	52.8	13.9	7.7	27.0
Other services	6,450	7,020	6,769	7,617	53.9	10.6	8.4	19.9
Other services, except private households	5,731	6,208	6,102	6,796	49.4	10.4	9.0	17.3
Private households	718	812	667	821	91.0	12.6	3.7	41.3
Public administration	6,113	6,530	6,983	7,225	45.7	17.5	4.7	12.5

[1] Persons in this race group only. See footnote 2, Table 619. [2] Persons of Hispanic origin may be of any race.

Source: U.S. Bureau of Labor Statistics, CPS Tables, "Employed persons by detailed industry, sex, race, and Hispanic or Latino ethnicity," February 2020, and earlier releases, <http://www.bls.gov/cps/tables.htm>.

Table 655. Unemployed Workers—Summary: 1990 to 2019

[In thousands (7,047 represents 7,047,000), except as indicated. For civilian noninstitutionalized population 16 years old and over. Annual averages of monthly figures. Revisions to population controls and other changes can affect the comparability of data over time. Based on the Current Population Survey; see text, Section 1 and Appendix III]

Item	1990	2000	2010	2013	2014	2015	2016	2017	2018	2019
UNEMPLOYED										
Total [1]	**7,047**	**5,692**	**14,825**	**11,460**	**9,617**	**8,296**	**7,751**	**6,982**	**6,314**	**6,001**
16 to 19 years old	1,212	1,081	1,528	1,327	1,106	966	925	827	759	746
20 to 24 years old	1,299	1,022	2,329	1,997	1,747	1,501	1,286	1,127	1,048	1,024
25 to 34 years old	1,995	1,207	3,386	2,504	2,224	1,905	1,797	1,647	1,450	1,384
35 to 44 years old	1,328	1,133	2,703	1,913	1,539	1,351	1,258	1,143	1,003	930
45 to 54 years old	723	762	2,769	1,945	1,507	1,259	1,189	1,060	938	890
55 to 64 years old	386	355	1,660	1,340	1,107	978	941	835	789	710
65 years and over	105	132	449	435	387	337	355	343	327	317
Male	3,906	2,975	8,626	6,314	5,190	4,490	4,187	3,743	3,398	3,227
16 to 19 years old	667	599	863	746	605	531	512	457	422	408
20 to 24 years old	715	547	1,398	1,143	996	865	742	667	596	602
25 to 34 years old	1,092	602	1,993	1,381	1,185	1,030	966	884	763	741
35 to 44 years old	711	557	1,534	1,015	813	695	644	575	515	475
45 to 54 years old	413	398	1,614	1,039	782	649	602	537	490	471
55 to 64 years old	249	189	962	741	600	536	528	445	435	361
65 years and over	59	83	262	250	210	184	193	179	177	170
Female	3,140	2,717	6,199	5,146	4,426	3,807	3,564	3,239	2,916	2,774
16 to 19 years old	544	483	665	581	501	435	413	371	338	339
20 to 24 years old	584	475	931	854	751	636	545	460	452	421
25 to 34 years old	902	604	1,392	1,123	1,039	874	832	763	687	643
35 to 44 years old	617	577	1,169	898	726	656	614	568	488	455
45 to 54 years old	310	364	1,156	906	725	610	586	523	448	419
55 to 64 years old	137	165	698	600	507	442	413	389	354	350
65 years and over	46	50	187	185	177	153	162	164	150	147
White [2]	5,186	4,121	10,916	8,033	6,540	5,662	5,345	4,765	4,354	4,159
Black [2]	1,565	1,241	2,852	2,429	2,141	1,846	1,655	1,501	1,322	1,251
Asian [2,3]	(NA)	227	543	448	436	347	349	333	304	280
Hispanic [4]	876	954	2,843	2,257	1,878	1,726	1,548	1,401	1,323	1,248
UNEMPLOYMENT RATE [5] (percent)										
Total [1]	**5.6**	**4.0**	**9.6**	**7.4**	**6.2**	**5.3**	**4.9**	**4.4**	**3.9**	**3.7**
16 to 19 years old	15.5	13.1	25.9	22.9	19.6	16.9	15.7	14.0	12.9	12.7
20 to 24 years old	8.8	7.2	15.5	12.8	11.2	9.7	8.4	7.4	6.9	6.7
25 to 34 years old	5.6	3.7	10.1	7.4	6.5	5.5	5.1	4.6	3.9	3.7
35 to 44 years old	4.1	3.0	8.1	5.9	4.7	4.1	3.8	3.5	3.0	2.7
45 to 54 years old	3.6	2.5	7.7	5.6	4.4	3.7	3.5	3.2	2.8	2.7
55 to 64 years old	3.3	2.5	7.1	5.3	4.3	3.8	3.6	3.1	2.9	2.6
65 years and over	3.0	3.1	6.7	5.4	4.6	3.8	3.8	3.6	3.3	3.0
Male	5.7	3.9	10.5	7.6	6.3	5.4	4.9	4.4	3.9	3.7
16 to 19 years old	16.3	14.0	28.8	25.5	21.4	18.4	17.1	15.5	14.5	13.8
20 to 24 years old	9.1	7.3	17.8	14.0	12.2	10.8	9.3	8.4	7.7	7.7
25 to 34 years old	5.5	3.4	10.9	7.6	6.4	5.5	5.0	4.6	3.9	3.7
35 to 44 years old	4.1	2.8	8.5	5.8	4.6	4.0	3.6	3.2	2.8	2.6
45 to 54 years old	3.7	2.4	8.6	5.7	4.4	3.6	3.4	3.0	2.8	2.7
55 to 64 years old	3.8	2.4	8.0	5.6	4.5	3.9	3.8	3.1	3.0	2.5
65 years and over	3.0	3.3	7.1	5.5	4.6	3.8	3.8	3.4	3.2	2.9
Female	5.5	4.1	8.6	7.1	6.1	5.2	4.8	4.3	3.8	3.6
16 to 19 years old	14.7	12.1	22.8	20.3	17.7	15.5	14.3	12.5	11.3	11.5
20 to 24 years old	8.5	7.1	13.0	11.5	10.1	8.5	7.4	6.3	6.2	5.7
25 to 34 years old	5.6	4.1	9.1	7.3	6.6	5.5	5.1	4.6	4.0	3.7
35 to 44 years old	4.2	3.3	7.7	6.0	4.9	4.4	4.1	3.7	3.2	2.9
45 to 54 years old	3.4	2.5	6.8	5.5	4.5	3.8	3.7	3.3	2.8	2.7
55 to 64 years old	2.8	2.5	6.2	5.0	4.2	3.6	3.3	3.1	2.7	2.7
65 years and over	3.1	2.7	6.2	5.1	4.7	3.9	3.9	3.8	3.3	3.1
White [2]	4.8	3.5	8.7	6.5	5.3	4.6	4.3	3.8	3.5	3.3
Black [2]	11.4	7.6	16.0	13.1	11.3	9.6	8.4	7.5	6.5	6.1
Asian [2,3]	(NA)	3.6	7.5	5.2	5.0	3.8	3.6	3.4	3.0	2.7
Hispanic [4]	8.2	5.7	12.5	9.1	7.4	6.6	5.8	5.1	4.7	4.3
PERCENT WITHOUT WORK FOR—										
Fewer than 5 weeks	46.3	44.9	18.7	22.5	25.7	28.9	30.5	32.5	34.4	34.8
5 to 14 weeks	32.0	31.9	22.0	24.1	25.3	27.7	28.7	28.8	29.7	29.8
15 weeks and over	21.6	23.2	59.3	53.4	49.0	43.3	40.8	38.7	35.9	35.4
15 to 26 weeks	11.7	11.8	16.0	15.8	15.6	15.3	14.9	14.6	14.5	14.3
27 weeks and over	10.0	11.4	43.3	37.6	33.5	28.1	25.9	24.2	21.4	21.1
Unemployment duration, average (weeks) [6]	12.0	12.6	33.0	36.5	33.7	29.2	27.5	25.0	22.7	21.6

NA Not available. [1] Includes other races not shown separately. [2] For persons reporting this race group only. [3] Prior to 2003, includes Pacific Islanders. [4] Persons of Hispanic or Latino origin may be of any race. [5] Unemployed as percent of civilian labor force in specified group. [6] Beginning 2011, the CPS increased the maximum duration of unemployment that respondents could report from 2 years to 5 years. For more information, see <http://www.bls.gov/cps/duration.htm>.

Source: U.S. Bureau of Labor Statistics, "Labor Force Statistics from the Current Population Survey," <http://www.bls.gov/cps>, accessed March 2020.

Table 656. Unemployed Jobseekers' Job Search Methods: 2019

[6,001 represents 6,001,000. For the civilian noninstitutionalized population 16 years old and over. Annual averages of monthly data. Based on the Current Population Survey; see text, Section 1 and Appendix III]

Characteristic	Population (1,000)		Jobseekers' job search methods (percent)							Average number of methods used
	Total unemployed	Total jobseekers [1]	Contact employer directly	Sent out a resume or filled out applications	Placed or answered ads	Friends or relatives	Public employment agency	Private employment agency	Other activities	
Total, 16 years and over [2]...	**6,001**	**5,177**	**51.1**	**56.0**	**13.1**	**23.3**	**13.6**	**7.7**	**13.5**	**1.8**
AGE										
16 to 19 years old..............	746	704	48.3	60.8	9.6	16.8	6.3	2.9	9.9	1.5
20 to 24 years old..............	1,024	942	53.2	56.1	11.6	20.5	11.7	5.8	12.2	1.7
25 to 34 years old..............	1,384	1,222	52.6	57.5	13.8	23.1	14.1	7.8	13.3	1.8
35 to 44 years old..............	930	777	51.3	56.5	14.2	27.1	16.1	9.5	13.9	1.9
45 to 54 years old..............	890	734	51.0	54.9	15.4	27.0	18.9	10.2	15.6	1.9
55 to 64 years old..............	710	565	51.2	52.2	15.0	26.0	15.7	10.4	16.2	1.9
65 years old and over..........	317	233	43.3	44.6	11.5	23.8	11.0	7.8	16.2	1.6
SEX										
Male, total.......................	3,227	2,749	51.9	53.8	12.9	24.2	13.9	7.6	14.0	1.8
16 to 19 years old.............	408	386	47.4	58.9	9.3	17.7	7.0	2.7	10.5	1.5
20 to 24 years old.............	602	548	55.1	52.9	10.5	22.1	12.2	6.4	13.0	1.7
25 to 34 years old.............	741	639	52.7	54.7	13.6	23.8	14.9	7.6	13.9	1.8
35 to 44 years old.............	475	390	51.7	55.1	14.5	29.6	16.3	8.7	14.3	1.9
45 to 54 years old.............	471	383	53.5	51.3	15.8	28.9	18.0	10.4	15.6	1.9
55 to 64 years old.............	361	281	52.4	52.3	15.6	25.0	16.4	11.1	17.1	1.9
65 years old and over.........	170	122	42.6	43.3	11.2	22.9	12.0	8.6	17.7	1.6
Female, total....................	2,774	2,429	50.2	58.6	13.4	22.3	13.3	7.7	12.9	1.8
16 to 19 years old.............	339	318	49.4	63.2	9.9	15.7	5.4	3.2	9.3	1.6
20 to 24 years old.............	421	394	50.4	60.7	13.1	18.3	11.0	4.9	11.1	1.7
25 to 34 years old.............	643	583	52.4	60.7	14.1	22.4	13.2	8.0	12.6	1.8
35 to 44 years old.............	455	387	50.8	57.9	14.0	24.6	15.8	10.3	13.5	1.9
45 to 54 years old.............	419	351	48.3	58.8	14.9	25.1	20.0	10.0	15.5	1.9
55 to 64 years old.............	350	285	50.0	52.1	14.4	27.0	15.1	9.8	15.2	1.8
65 years old and over.........	147	110	44.1	46.0	11.7	24.8	10.0	6.9	14.6	1.6
RACE/ETHNICITY										
White [3].........................	4,159	3,492	51.0	56.1	12.7	23.6	12.5	7.4	14.1	1.8
Male............................	2,266	1,871	52.2	54.0	12.6	24.7	13.1	7.4	14.4	1.8
Female.........................	1,893	1,621	49.6	58.5	12.8	22.3	11.9	7.3	13.7	1.8
Black [3].........................	1,251	1,155	50.4	56.0	14.1	22.9	17.0	8.1	10.8	1.8
Male............................	645	597	50.5	51.9	14.0	23.1	16.7	7.5	11.4	1.8
Female.........................	607	558	50.3	60.3	14.2	22.8	17.4	8.7	10.2	1.8
Asian [3].........................	280	256	51.5	55.2	15.1	22.9	11.2	10.4	18.0	1.9
Male............................	149	136	51.1	55.9	15.0	23.2	9.6	10.6	19.3	1.9
Female.........................	132	120	52.1	54.4	15.3	22.6	12.9	10.1	16.5	1.9
Hispanic [4]......................	1,248	1,038	49.8	54.0	10.7	28.1	13.2	7.9	11.6	1.8
Male............................	657	526	51.4	50.3	10.4	28.8	12.9	8.1	12.7	1.8
Female.........................	591	512	48.2	57.8	11.0	27.5	13.5	7.8	10.4	1.8

[1] Excludes persons on temporary layoff. [2] Includes other races not shown separately. [3] Data for this race group only. [4] Persons of Hispanic or Latino origin may be of any race.

Source: U.S. Bureau of Labor Statistics, CPS Tables, "Unemployed jobseekers by sex, age, race, Hispanic or Latino ethnicity, and active jobsearch methods used," February 2020, <http://www.bls.gov/cps/tables.htm>.

Table 657. Unemployed Persons by Sex and Reason: 2000 to 2019

[In thousands (2,975 represents 2,975,000). For civilian noninstitutionalized population 16 years old and over. Annual averages of monthly figures. Revisions to population controls and other changes affect comparability of data over time. Based on Current Population Survey; see text, Section 1 and Appendix III]

Sex and reason	2000	2009	2010	2011	2012	2013	2014	2015	2016	2017	2018	2019
Male, total...............	**2,975**	**8,453**	**8,626**	**7,684**	**6,771**	**6,314**	**5,190**	**4,490**	**4,187**	**3,743**	**3,398**	**3,227**
Job losers [1]...............	1,516	5,967	5,919	4,968	4,103	3,690	2,926	2,441	2,232	2,038	1,772	1,611
Job leavers................	387	438	457	494	487	465	416	397	414	382	413	444
Reentrants................	854	1504	1,608	1,545	1,481	1491	1,279	1,178	1,108	961	896	851
New entrants.............	217	545	641	678	699	668	569	474	433	362	317	321
Female, total...........	**2,717**	**5,811**	**6,199**	**6,063**	**5,734**	**5,146**	**4,426**	**3,807**	**3,564**	**3,239**	**2,916**	**2,774**
Job losers [1]...............	1,001	3,193	3,331	3,139	2,774	2,383	1,952	1,622	1,508	1,397	1,218	1,175
Job leavers................	393	444	432	463	480	467	408	423	444	396	381	370
Reentrants................	1,107	1,683	1,858	1,857	1,864	1,716	1,550	1,357	1,222	1,118	1,032	959
New entrants.............	217	491	579	605	617	579	517	405	390	328	285	270

[1] Includes persons who completed temporary jobs.

Source: U.S. Bureau of Labor Statistics, CPS Tables, "Unemployed jobseekers by sex, reason for unemployment, and active jobsearch methods used," February 2020, and earlier releases, <http://www.bls.gov/cps/tables.htm>.

Table 658. Unemployment Rates by Industry and by Sex: 2010 to June 2020

[In percent. Civilian noninstitutionalized population 16 years old and over. Annual averages of monthly figures, except June 2020. Rate represents unemployment as a percent of labor force in each specified group. Based on Current Population Survey; see text, Section 1 and Appendix III. See also headnote, Table 637, regarding industries]

Industry	Total				Male		Female	
	2010	2018	2019	June, 2020	2019	June, 2020	2019	June, 2020
All employed [1]	**9.6**	**3.9**	**3.7**	**11.2**	**3.7**	**10.5**	**3.6**	**12.0**
Wage and salary workers:								
Agriculture and related industries	13.9	7.2	7.4	5.4	6.3	4.5	10.5	8.0
Mining, quarrying, and oil and gas extraction	9.4	3.4	3.2	17.8	3.4	19.0	2.0	8.9
Construction	20.6	5.1	4.5	10.1	4.5	10.4	3.8	7.9
Manufacturing	10.6	3.3	3.0	9.1	2.7	8.4	3.5	10.9
Wholesale trade	7.3	3.1	2.8	7.3	2.5	7.4	3.3	7.0
Retail trade	10.0	4.6	4.4	12.0	4.1	11.1	4.7	13.1
Transportation and utilities	8.4	3.4	3.5	12.9	3.3	11.3	3.9	18.6
Transportation and warehousing	9.4	3.6	3.8	14.6	3.6	12.8	4.2	20.9
Utilities	3.4	1.8	1.8	3.6	1.7	3.2	2.1	5.2
Information	9.7	3.7	3.5	12.0	3.5	13.3	3.5	10.0
Telecommunications	9.2	2.7	2.1	7.2	1.6	7.5	3.1	6.7
Financial activities	6.9	2.2	2.1	5.1	2.3	4.8	2.0	5.3
Finance and insurance	6.6	1.9	2.0	3.8	2.1	3.7	1.9	3.9
Real estate and rental and leasing	7.6	2.8	2.5	8.8	2.7	7.9	2.3	9.9
Professional and business services	10.8	3.9	3.6	8.6	3.5	7.1	3.8	10.6
Professional and technical services	6.5	2.3	2.3	5.8	2.1	4.4	2.7	7.8
Management, administrative, and waste services	16.8	6.7	6.1	14.0	6.1	12.2	6.1	16.7
Education and health services	5.8	2.6	2.5	8.6	2.6	8.0	2.5	8.8
Educational services	6.4	3.4	3.5	14.2	3.7	13.6	3.4	14.5
Health care and social assistance	5.6	2.4	2.2	7.2	2.1	5.7	2.3	7.6
Leisure and hospitality	12.2	5.7	5.2	28.9	5.3	30.5	5.2	27.4
Arts, entertainment, and recreation	11.6	5.6	5.1	37.3	5.0	37.4	5.2	37.2
Accommodation and food services	12.3	5.7	5.3	26.6	5.4	28.4	5.1	24.8
Other services	8.5	3.3	3.2	14.5	2.9	11.0	3.4	17.6
Government workers	4.4	2.3	2.3	7.3	2.2	5.6	2.4	8.5

[1] Includes a small amount of persons whose last job was in the Armed Forces.

Source: U.S. Bureau of Labor Statistics, CPS Tables, "Unemployed persons by industry, class of worker, and sex," <http://www.bls.gov/cps/tables.htm>, accessed July 2020.

Table 659. Unemployment by Occupation: 2010 to June 2020

[14,825 represents 14,825,000. Civilian noninstitutionalized population 16 years old and over. Annual averages of monthly data, except June 2020. Rate represents unemployment as a percent of the labor force for each specified group. Based on Current Population Survey; see text, Section 1 and Appendix III. See also headnote, Table 637, regarding occupations]

Occupation	Number unemployed (1,000)				Unemployment rate				
							June, 2020		
	2010	2018	2019	June, 2020	2010	2019	Total	Male	Female
Total [1]	**14,825**	**6,314**	**6,001**	**18,072**	**9.6**	**3.7**	**11.2**	**10.5**	**12.0**
Management, professional, and related occupations	2,566	1,346	1,310	4,390	4.7	2.0	6.5	5.6	7.3
Management, business, and financial operations	1,117	523	499	1,367	5.1	1.8	4.8	4.4	5.4
Management	762	328	314	929	4.8	1.6	4.7	4.5	4.9
Business and financial operations	355	196	185	438	5.6	2.3	5.2	3.9	6.3
Professional and related occupations	1,449	822	811	3,022	4.5	2.1	7.7	6.8	8.3
Computer and mathematical	195	113	107	270	5.2	2.0	4.3	4.4	4.2
Architecture and engineering	173	59	58	194	6.2	1.7	6.1	5.8	7.1
Life, physical, and social science	69	31	27	115	4.6	1.8	6.3	7.9	4.6
Community and social services	114	62	56	156	4.6	2.0	5.2	4.5	5.5
Legal	48	31	27	82	2.7	1.4	4.1	4.1	4.1
Education, training, and library	379	286	279	1,070	4.2	2.9	11.2	8.5	12.1
Arts, design, entertainment, sports, and media	269	107	121	717	8.9	3.5	19.6	21.7	17.9
Healthcare practitioner and technical	203	133	136	419	2.5	1.4	4.2	2.3	4.9
Service occupations	2,819	1,353	1,255	4,887	10.3	4.4	18.8	17.9	19.4
Healthcare support	276	129	122	473	7.6	3.1	9.5	12.4	8.9
Protective service	207	89	93	239	5.9	2.9	7.3	4.8	14.9
Food preparation and serving-related	1,079	530	491	2,247	12.4	5.5	28.6	30.6	26.8
Building and grounds cleaning and maintenance	780	338	310	720	12.8	5.1	12.7	11.2	15.0
Personal care and service	477	266	239	1,209	8.7	3.9	28.4	30.2	27.8
Sales and office occupations	3,315	1,337	1,274	3,819	9.0	3.7	11.8	11.8	11.8
Sales and related	1,596	669	614	2,059	9.4	3.8	13.3	11.7	14.9
Office and administrative support	1,719	668	659	1,759	8.7	3.6	10.5	12.1	9.9
Natural resources, construction, and maintenance	2,504	780	703	1,513	16.1	4.7	10.6	10.3	15.0
Farming, fishing, and forestry	193	114	123	76	16.3	9.6	7.4	5.8	13.0
Construction and extraction	1,809	530	452	961	20.1	5.2	11.5	11.2	17.7
Installation, maintenance, and repair	503	136	129	475	9.3	2.6	9.6	9.5	12.7
Production, transportation, and material moving	2,365	881	847	2,593	12.8	4.3	13.2	12.4	15.6
Production	1,206	361	350	889	13.1	3.9	11.0	9.7	14.4
Transportation and material moving	1,159	520	497	1,704	12.4	4.7	14.7	14.2	16.8

[1] Includes a small amount of persons whose last job was in the Armed Forces.

Source: U.S. Bureau of Labor Statistics, CPS Tables, "Unemployed persons by occupation and sex," July 2020, and earlier releases, <http://www.bls.gov/cps/tables.htm>.

Table 660. Unemployed and Unemployment Rates by Educational Attainment, Sex, Race, and Hispanic Origin: 2000 to 2019

[3,589 represents 3,589,000. Annual averages of monthly figures. Civilian noninstitutionalized population 25 years old and over. See Table 624 for civilian labor force and participation rate data. Revisions to population controls and other changes can affect the comparability of data over time. Based on Current Population Survey; see text, Section 1 and Appendix III]

Year, sex, and race/ethnicity	Unemployed (1,000)					Unemployment rate [1]				
	Total	Less than a high school diploma	High school graduate, no college	Some college or associate's degree	Bachelor's degree or higher	Total	Less than a high school diploma	High school graduate, no college	Some college or associate's degree	Bachelor's degree or higher
Total: [2]										
2000	3,589	791	1,298	890	610	3.0	6.3	3.4	2.7	1.7
2010	10,968	1,765	3,943	3,093	2,167	8.2	14.9	10.3	8.4	4.7
2019	4,231	535	1,324	1,138	1,234	3.0	5.4	3.7	3.0	2.1
Male:										
2000	1,829	411	682	427	309	2.8	5.4	3.4	2.6	1.5
2010	6,365	1,137	2,452	1,646	1,130	8.9	15.0	11.3	9.0	4.8
2019	2,216	309	765	533	609	2.9	4.9	3.6	2.8	2.1
Female:										
2000	1,760	380	616	463	301	3.2	7.8	3.5	2.8	1.8
2010	4,603	628	1,492	1,447	1,037	7.4	14.6	9.0	7.8	4.7
2019	2,015	226	559	605	625	3.0	6.2	3.8	3.3	2.1
White: [3]										
2000	2,644	564	924	667	489	2.6	5.6	2.9	2.4	1.6
2010	8,174	1,337	2,937	2,278	1,622	7.5	13.9	9.5	7.6	4.3
2019	2,974	387	898	792	897	2.7	4.9	3.2	2.7	2.0
Black: [3]										
2000	731	179	315	169	68	5.4	10.7	6.4	4.0	2.5
2010	2,022	321	795	614	292	13.4	22.5	15.8	12.4	7.9
2019	847	113	330	243	161	4.8	9.9	6.2	4.4	2.8
Asian: [3,4]										
2000	146	28	34	35	49	2.7	5.7	3.0	3.2	1.8
2010	446	54	95	92	205	6.8	11.1	7.6	8.1	5.5
2019	221	15	27	37	142	2.3	3.0	1.9	2.6	2.3
Hispanic: [5]										
2000	569	297	150	85	38	4.4	6.2	3.9	3.2	2.2
2010	2,041	787	674	399	182	10.8	13.2	11.5	9.7	6.0
2019	819	248	245	191	135	3.4	4.4	3.2	3.4	2.6

[1] Unemployed as percent of the civilian labor force. [2] Includes other races, not shown separately. [3] Beginning 2003, data are for persons in this race group only; 2000 data reflect the primary race persons identified with. [4] 2000 data include Pacific Islanders. [5] Persons of Hispanic origin may be of any race.

Source: U.S. Bureau of Labor Statistics, CPS Tables, "Employment status of the civilian noninstitutional population 25 years and over by educational attainment, sex, race, and Hispanic or Latino ethnicity," February 2020, and earlier releases, <http://www.bls.gov/cps/tables.htm>.

Table 661. Unemployed Persons by Reason for Unemployment and Duration: 2019

[6,001 represents 6,001,000. Annual averages of monthly data. Based on Current Population Survey; see text, Section 1 and Appendix III]

Age, sex, and reason	Total unemployed (1,000)	Percent distribution by duration				
		Less than 5 weeks	5 to 14 weeks	15 weeks and over		
				Total	15 to 26 weeks	27 weeks or longer
Total 16 years old and over	**6,001**	**34.8**	**29.8**	**35.4**	**14.3**	**21.1**
16 to 19 years old	746	46.1	32.6	21.4	11.2	10.2
Males, 20 years old and over	**2,819**	**32.1**	**29.0**	**38.9**	**14.8**	**24.1**
Job losers and persons who completed temporary jobs	1,548	36.7	29.8	33.5	14.5	19.1
On temporary layoff	457	55.0	31.0	13.9	10.0	3.9
Not on temporary layoff	1,091	29.0	29.3	41.7	16.3	25.4
Permanent job losers	736	27.2	29.2	43.7	16.4	27.2
Persons who completed temporary jobs	355	32.7	29.6	37.6	16.0	21.6
Job leavers	418	32.3	29.8	37.9	15.0	22.9
Reentrants	708	24.2	26.9	48.9	15.7	33.2
New entrants	144	21.5	27.4	51.1	13.6	37.6
Females, 20 years old and over	**2,435**	**34.4**	**30.0**	**35.7**	**14.7**	**20.9**
Job losers and persons who completed temporary jobs	1,132	38.0	30.4	31.5	14.8	16.7
On temporary layoff	324	59.7	31.8	8.5	5.7	2.8
Not on temporary layoff	807	29.3	29.9	40.8	18.4	22.3
Permanent job losers	569	26.5	29.0	44.5	19.9	24.6
Persons who completed temporary jobs	238	36.1	32.1	31.8	15.1	16.8
Job leavers	344	37.0	31.3	31.7	14.4	17.2
Reentrants	836	29.9	29.4	40.7	14.5	26.2
New entrants	123	23.8	25.4	50.8	16.7	34.1

Source: U.S. Bureau of Labor Statistics, CPS Tables, "Unemployed persons by reason for unemployment, sex, age, and duration of unemployment," <http://www.bls.gov/cps/tables.htm>, accessed February 2020.

Table 662. Total Unemployed and Insured Unemployed by State: 2000 to 2019

[5,692 represents 5,692,000. Civilian noninstitutionalized population 16 years old and over. Annual averages of monthly figures, except as noted. State total unemployment estimates come from the Local Area Unemployment Statistics program, while U.S. totals come from the Current Population Survey; see text, Section 1 and Appendix III. U.S. totals derived by independent population controls; therefore, state data may not add to U.S. totals. Unemployment data are based on population controls from Census 2010]

State	Total unemployed								Insured unemployed [2,4]			
	Number (1,000)				Percent [1]				Number (1,000)		Percent [3]	
	2000	2010	2018	2019	2000	2010	2018	2019	2010	2019	2010	2019
United States..........	5,692	14,825	6,314	6,001	4.0	9.6	3.9	3.7	4,487	1,684	3.6	1.2
Alabama.................	98	231	86	67	4.6	10.5	3.9	3.0	53	16	3.0	0.8
Alaska..................	20	28	23	21	6.4	7.9	6.5	6.1	14	6	4.6	2.0
Arizona.................	99	320	162	167	4.0	10.4	4.7	4.7	79	23	3.5	0.8
Arkansas...............	54	111	49	48	4.3	8.2	3.6	3.5	44	12	4.0	1.0
California..............	835	2,244	820	784	4.9	12.2	4.3	4.0	655	323	4.6	1.9
Colorado...............	65	238	97	87	2.8	8.7	3.2	2.8	64	19	3.0	0.7
Connecticut............	42	174	79	71	2.4	9.1	4.1	3.7	67	32	4.3	2.0
Delaware...............	15	37	18	18	3.7	8.4	3.8	3.8	13	5	3.4	1.1
District of Columbia.....	17	33	23	22	5.6	9.4	5.7	5.5	5	6	1.1	1.0
Florida.................	291	1,018	365	321	3.7	11.1	3.6	3.1	225	36	3.2	0.4
Georgia................	151	495	200	175	3.6	10.5	3.9	3.4	117	26	3.2	0.6
Hawaii.................	26	45	17	18	4.2	6.9	2.5	2.7	17	7	3.1	1.1
Idaho..................	31	68	25	26	4.7	9.0	2.9	2.9	26	6	4.5	0.8
Illinois.................	282	688	279	256	4.3	10.4	4.3	4.0	220	95	4.1	1.6
Indiana................	97	330	118	112	3.1	10.4	3.5	3.3	79	20	3.0	0.7
Iowa...................	42	101	44	48	2.6	6.0	2.6	2.7	40	19	2.9	1.3
Kansas................	50	106	49	47	3.6	7.1	3.3	3.2	37	9	2.9	0.6
Kentucky..............	82	210	89	89	4.2	10.2	4.3	4.3	50	17	3.0	0.9
Louisiana..............	108	166	103	101	5.3	8.0	4.9	4.8	55	12	3.1	0.6
Maine..................	23	57	23	21	3.4	8.1	3.2	3.0	18	5	3.2	0.9
Maryland...............	100	235	127	117	3.6	7.7	3.9	3.6	73	27	3.1	1.0
Massachusetts.........	90	289	127	111	2.7	8.3	3.4	2.9	116	57	3.7	1.6
Michigan...............	186	605	203	201	3.6	12.6	4.1	4.1	160	54	4.3	1.3
Minnesota..............	89	218	90	100	3.2	7.4	2.9	3.2	81	40	3.2	1.4
Mississippi.............	71	136	61	69	5.4	10.4	4.8	5.4	36	8	3.4	0.8
Missouri...............	106	293	96	102	3.6	9.6	3.2	3.3	75	21	3.0	0.8
Montana...............	23	37	19	19	5.0	7.3	3.6	3.5	17	7	4.2	1.5
Nebraska..............	27	46	30	32	2.8	4.6	2.9	3.0	19	4	2.1	0.4
Nevada................	45	184	67	60	4.2	13.5	4.4	3.9	54	18	4.9	1.3
New Hampshire.........	18	43	20	20	2.7	5.8	2.6	2.5	18	3	3.1	0.5
New Jersey............	158	434	182	160	3.7	9.5	4.1	3.6	166	91	4.5	2.3
New Mexico............	42	76	46	46	4.9	8.1	4.9	4.9	25	9	3.4	1.1
New York..............	415	826	394	377	4.5	8.6	4.1	4.0	290	133	3.5	1.4
North Carolina..........	152	501	198	197	3.7	10.9	4.0	3.9	156	18	4.2	0.4
North Dakota...........	10	14	10	10	3.0	3.8	2.6	2.4	5	3	1.5	0.8
Ohio...................	231	600	259	239	4.0	10.3	4.5	4.1	144	50	3.0	0.9
Oklahoma..............	50	120	63	61	3.0	6.8	3.4	3.3	34	14	2.4	0.9
Oregon................	93	211	85	79	5.1	10.6	4.1	3.7	83	27	5.3	1.4
Pennsylvania...........	252	540	273	284	4.1	8.5	4.2	4.4	265	109	4.9	1.9
Rhode Island...........	22	63	22	20	4.1	11.2	4.0	3.6	18	8	4.1	1.8
South Carolina.........	75	241	81	68	3.8	11.2	3.5	2.8	71	15	4.1	0.7
South Dakota...........	10	22	14	15	2.5	5.0	3.1	3.3	4	2	1.2	0.4
Tennessee.............	110	299	114	113	3.9	9.7	3.5	3.4	68	16	2.7	0.5
Texas.................	445	997	532	494	4.3	8.1	3.8	3.5	216	119	2.2	1.0
Utah..................	38	106	48	42	3.3	7.8	3.0	2.6	28	8	2.5	0.6
Vermont...............	9	22	9	8	2.8	6.1	2.5	2.4	10	4	3.6	1.2
Virginia................	83	297	132	123	2.3	7.1	3.0	2.8	62	19	1.8	0.5
Washington............	158	351	169	166	5.2	10.0	4.5	4.3	109	46	4.0	1.4
West Virginia..........	44	70	41	39	5.5	8.7	5.2	4.9	21	11	3.2	1.6
Wisconsin..............	105	267	94	104	3.5	8.7	3.0	3.3	122	31	4.7	1.1
Wyoming...............	10	20	11	11	3.9	6.4	3.9	3.6	7	2	2.6	0.8

[1] Total unemployment as percent of civilian labor force. [2] Number of average weekly jobless workers who are receiving state unemployment benefits. Source: U.S. Employment and Training Administration, "Unemployment Insurance, Financial Data Handbook 394," <https://workforcesecurity.doleta.gov/unemploy/hb394.asp>, accessed August 2020. [3] Those currently collecting unemployment insurance as a percent of the total number of eligible workers. [4] U.S. totals include Puerto Rico and the Virgin Islands.

Source: Except as noted, U.S. Bureau of Labor Statistics, "Local Area Unemployment Statistics," <http://www.bls.gov/lau/>, accessed August 2020.

[109,526 represents 109,526,000. Annual averages of monthly data. Based on data from establishment reports. Includes all full- and part-time employees who worked during, or received pay for, any part of the pay period including the 12th of the month. Excludes proprietors, the self-employed, farm workers, unpaid family workers, private household workers, and Armed Forces. Establishment data shown here conform to industry definitions in the 2017 North American Industry Classification System (NAICS) and are adjusted to March employment benchmarks. Based on the Current Employment Statistics Program; see source and Appendix III]

Item and year	Total nonfarm	Private industry Total[1]	Construction	Manufacturing	Wholesale trade	Retail trade	Transportation and warehousing	Utilities	Information	Finance and insurance	Real estate and rental and leasing	Professional and technical services	Administrative and waste services	Educational services	Health care and social assistance	Arts entertainment and recreation	Accommodations and food services	Government
EMPLOYEES (1,000)																		
1990	109,526	91,112	5,263	17,695	5,230	13,186	3,478	740	2,688	4,976	1,637	4,565	4,646	1,688	9,336	1,132	8,156	18,415
2000	132,011	111,221	6,787	17,263	5,888	15,284	4,401	601	3,630	5,773	2,011	6,732	8,172	2,390	12,861	1,788	10,074	20,790
2005	134,034	112,230	7,336	14,227	5,706	15,285	4,348	554	3,061	6,063	2,134	7,065	8,175	2,836	14,840	1,892	10,923	21,804
2010	130,345	107,855	5,518	11,528	5,387	14,446	4,179	553	2,707	5,761	1,934	7,486	7,419	3,155	16,820	1,913	11,135	22,490
2015	141,825	119,796	6,461	12,336	5,780	15,611	4,859	556	2,750	6,035	2,088	8,658	8,823	3,472	18,557	2,166	12,994	22,029
2016	144,336	122,112	6,728	12,354	5,787	15,832	5,004	556	2,794	6,148	2,139	8,881	8,981	3,570	19,069	2,252	13,408	22,224
2017	146,608	124,258	6,969	12,439	5,814	15,846	5,178	555	2,814	6,262	2,189	9,058	9,142	3,668	19,520	2,333	13,718	22,350
2018	148,908	126,454	7,288	12,688	5,841	15,786	5,426	553	2,839	6,337	2,253	9,282	9,294	3,715	19,923	2,383	13,913	22,455
2019	150,939	128,346	7,492	12,840	5,903	15,644	5,618	549	2,860	6,425	2,321	9,543	9,343	3,765	20,413	2,433	14,143	22,594
WEEKLY EARNINGS[2] (dol.)																		
1990	(NA)	349.63	513.43	436.13	443.61	235.72	471.70	670.80	479.50	(NA)	(NA)	505.10	273.81	(NA)	319.26	219.02	147.92	(NA)
2000	(NA)	480.90	685.78	590.89	630.09	333.48	559.63	955.09	700.92	(NA)	(NA)	746.12	387.72	(NA)	447.45	273.79	207.44	(NA)
2005	(NA)	543.94	750.37	673.30	683.99	377.58	615.26	1,095.91	805.11	(NA)	(NA)	862.36	432.08	(NA)	555.82	330.31	226.48	(NA)
2010	(NA)	636.02	891.83	765.18	814.04	400.38	707.93	1,262.89	939.85	(NA)	(NA)	1,073.43	536.08	(NA)	652.07	363.91	266.78	(NA)
2015	(NA)	708.70	998.02	832.25	907.72	446.01	800.14	1,444.03	1,038.10	(NA)	(NA)	1,201.23	569.06	(NA)	722.49	379.22	300.17	(NA)
2016	(NA)	723.20	1031.88	855.77	929.09	447.69	807.25	1,502.09	1,068.23	(NA)	(NA)	1,223.94	585.46	(NA)	737.17	380.57	310.02	(NA)
2017	(NA)	742.48	1061.98	876.10	957.95	463.10	813.69	1,540.27	1,100.03	(NA)	(NA)	1,254.18	605.86	(NA)	755.48	387.40	323.66	(NA)
2018	(NA)	766.99	1,108.59	908.01	979.82	483.03	835.39	1,569.38	1,139.52	(NA)	(NA)	1,294.63	622.68	(NA)	776.46	389.91	338.00	(NA)
2019	(NA)	790.67	1,135.17	921.66	1,007.57	503.07	849.29	1,566.66	1,196.36	(NA)	(NA)	1,321.52	655.91	(NA)	799.03	395.42	351.57	(NA)
WEEKLY HOURS[2]																		
1990	(NA)	34.3	38.3	40.5	38.4	30.6	37.7	41.6	35.8	(NA)	(NA)	36.1	32.3	(NA)	31.8	26.1	25.9	(NA)
2000	(NA)	34.3	39.2	41.3	38.8	30.7	37.3	42.0	36.8	(NA)	(NA)	36.2	33.1	(NA)	32.1	25.6	26.2	(NA)
2005	(NA)	33.8	38.6	40.7	37.7	30.6	37.0	41.1	36.5	(NA)	(NA)	35.7	32.8	(NA)	32.8	25.7	25.7	(NA)
2010	(NA)	33.4	38.4	41.1	37.9	30.2	37.1	42.0	36.3	(NA)	(NA)	35.9	33.9	(NA)	32.2	23.8	25.0	(NA)
2015	(NA)	33.7	39.6	41.8	38.6	30.1	38.7	42.4	35.7	(NA)	(NA)	36.4	34.0	(NA)	32.2	23.7	25.3	(NA)
2016	(NA)	33.6	39.7	41.9	38.6	29.7	38.8	42.5	35.5	(NA)	(NA)	36.3	33.9	(NA)	32.3	23.2	25.2	(NA)
2017	(NA)	33.7	39.7	41.9	39.0	30.2	38.4	42.5	35.8	(NA)	(NA)	36.5	34.0	(NA)	32.4	22.9	25.2	(NA)
2018	(NA)	33.8	40.0	42.2	38.9	30.4	38.4	42.7	35.6	(NA)	(NA)	36.6	34.0	(NA)	32.4	22.5	25.3	(NA)
2019	(NA)	33.6	39.8	41.6	38.7	30.3	37.9	42.4	35.3	(NA)	(NA)	36.4	34.1	(NA)	32.4	21.6	25.2	(NA)
HOURLY EARNINGS[2] (dol.)																		
1990	(NA)	10.20	13.42	10.78	11.55	7.71	12.50	16.14	13.40	(NA)	(NA)	13.99	8.48	(NA)	10.03	8.41	5.70	(NA)
2000	(NA)	14.01	17.48	14.32	16.24	10.87	15.00	22.75	19.07	(NA)	(NA)	20.62	11.70	(NA)	13.93	10.68	7.92	(NA)
2005	(NA)	16.12	19.46	16.56	18.13	12.36	16.65	26.68	22.06	(NA)	(NA)	24.13	13.17	(NA)	16.94	12.85	8.80	(NA)
2010	(NA)	19.04	23.22	18.61	21.46	13.25	19.10	30.04	25.87	(NA)	(NA)	29.93	15.81	(NA)	20.23	15.27	10.68	(NA)
2015	(NA)	21.03	25.20	19.91	23.52	14.83	20.66	34.02	29.05	(NA)	(NA)	32.96	16.73	(NA)	22.41	15.97	11.87	(NA)
2016	(NA)	21.53	25.97	20.44	24.07	15.05	20.83	35.33	30.05	(NA)	(NA)	33.72	17.26	(NA)	22.83	16.38	12.32	(NA)
2017	(NA)	22.05	26.74	20.90	24.58	15.33	21.22	36.22	30.74	(NA)	(NA)	34.41	17.82	(NA)	23.35	16.94	12.85	(NA)
2018	(NA)	22.71	27.75	21.54	25.17	15.91	21.75	36.76	31.97	(NA)	(NA)	35.42	18.32	(NA)	23.96	17.31	13.37	(NA)
2019	(NA)	23.51	28.51	22.15	26.06	16.62	22.40	36.91	33.89	(NA)	(NA)	36.27	19.25	(NA)	24.68	18.29	13.95	(NA)

NA Not available. [1] Includes other industries not shown separately. [2] Average hours and earnings of production and nonsupervisory employees.

Source: U.S. Bureau of Labor Statistics, Current Employment Statistics, "Employment, Hours, and Earnings—National," <https://www.bls.gov/ces/data.htm>, accessed August 2020.

Table 664. Employees in Nonfarm Establishments by State and Industry: 2019

[In thousands (150,753.6 represents 150,753,600). Includes all full- and part-time employees who worked during, or received pay for, any part of the pay period reported. Excludes proprietors, the self-employed, farm workers, unpaid family workers, private household workers, and Armed Forces. Compiled from data supplied by cooperating state agencies. Based on North American Industry Classification System, 2017; see text, section 15]

State	Total [1]	Con-struction	Manu-facturing	Trade, transpor-tation and utilities	Infor-mation	Fin-ancial activi-ties [2]	Profes-sional and business ser-vices [3]	Educa-tion and health ser-vices [4]	Leisure and hospi-tality [5]	Other ser-vices [6]	Govern-ment
U.S.........	150,753.6	7,464.5	12,792.8	27,724.5	2,867.2	8,619.0	21,241.4	24,100.1	16,466.1	5,831.2	22,923.4
AL..........	2,072.6	93.5	268.6	383.2	21.2	96.3	250.5	249.6	208.6	99.3	391.7
AK..........	329.4	16.4	12.8	64.7	5.3	11.7	27.5	50.8	36.1	11.0	79.8
AZ..........	2,937.4	170.7	177.3	542.8	48.8	229.9	444.6	461.8	330.7	94.9	422.5
AR..........	1,276.4	52.4	162.4	252.1	11.3	62.5	145.4	193.6	119.9	59.7	211.2
CA..........	17,425.1	882.6	1,322.5	3,051.9	562.6	841.2	2,721.1	2,803.4	2,033.2	576.1	2,608.0
CO..........	2,785.6	178.8	150.1	477.3	76.0	173.9	440.0	347.6	344.6	113.1	455.3
CT..........	1,686.7	59.8	162.0	291.7	31.5	123.8	219.5	339.2	157.3	65.0	236.4
DE..........	465.7	22.9	27.3	81.0	3.9	47.7	63.3	81.1	52.9	18.7	66.9
DC..........	798.3	14.9	1.4	33.2	20.1	29.8	171.1	130.2	81.7	77.5	238.5
FL..........	8,952.6	565.5	384.5	1,803.4	138.9	590.9	1,392.2	1,340.0	1,255.2	353.1	1,123.2
GA..........	4,613.8	203.4	406.1	944.0	117.0	250.2	716.0	610.3	502.1	165.0	690.4
HI..........	655.7	37.2	14.0	123.5	8.7	29.9	74.1	87.2	126.5	28.3	126.3
ID..........	759.2	52.8	68.6	144.6	9.0	36.8	96.6	110.7	82.7	26.7	127.1
IL..........	6,118.0	226.7	585.5	1,204.9	95.4	411.1	944.8	939.4	621.1	255.4	825.4
IN..........	3,166.2	146.2	541.8	599.1	28.8	141.5	344.0	482.0	313.3	134.3	429.3
IA..........	1,585.7	78.1	226.1	310.3	21.3	109.7	139.3	235.2	144.4	58.3	260.5
KS..........	1,423.0	63.5	167.1	267.0	18.1	77.3	179.0	202.0	130.5	51.7	260.0
KY..........	1,938.7	80.3	252.1	402.9	21.6	93.4	216.5	283.2	201.7	65.9	311.4
LA..........	1,988.8	141.7	137.5	378.8	22.2	92.2	215.8	320.3	238.3	74.0	331.2
ME..........	635.5	29.8	53.3	118.5	7.2	32.9	69.4	129.3	69.2	22.4	101.2
MD..........	2,768.9	166.1	112.9	469.1	35.3	143.8	463.3	473.5	281.7	115.1	506.7
MA..........	3,689.8	162.1	243.8	578.7	92.6	224.1	601.6	812.1	377.3	139.1	457.3
MI..........	4,432.6	173.4	627.2	795.9	55.2	224.5	654.0	681.6	434.2	166.0	613.3
MN..........	2,977.6	127.1	323.8	530.1	46.8	192.6	383.0	551.3	275.6	114.3	426.5
MS..........	1,158.4	44.4	147.1	231.0	10.7	44.5	108.0	147.0	136.4	40.6	241.9
MO..........	2,901.6	126.4	277.0	542.9	47.8	174.9	382.1	484.5	308.5	116.8	436.4
MT..........	483.8	30.1	20.9	94.4	6.2	25.9	43.4	78.9	66.8	19.1	90.8
NE..........	1,027.1	53.5	99.7	198.5	17.2	75.2	119.8	157.2	94.1	37.3	173.6
NV..........	1,417.8	96.2	59.4	261.2	15.8	69.0	195.5	144.0	355.3	41.5	165.2
NH..........	684.2	27.9	71.5	139.1	12.4	34.8	83.7	124.8	72.9	25.7	90.4
NJ..........	4,194.9	159.8	251.5	886.8	67.4	252.3	683.9	717.9	394.2	173.7	605.9
NM..........	856.9	50.0	28.5	136.9	11.2	35.6	110.9	141.3	98.8	29.0	188.7
NY..........	9,785.5	404.7	439.2	1,551.6	278.3	728.0	1,374.9	2,140.0	959.9	415.1	1,488.6
NC..........	4,574.2	231.5	478.5	846.5	76.2	252.6	648.6	626.3	516.3	159.8	732.5
ND..........	439.2	28.1	26.4	93.7	6.1	24.8	32.8	67.2	40.5	15.4	83.0
OH..........	5,586.8	226.0	701.4	1,025.4	69.5	309.5	735.1	940.3	568.6	213.1	786.1
OK..........	1,703.4	82.6	140.8	301.3	19.6	79.4	193.8	238.8	174.7	70.6	353.1
OR..........	1,940.5	108.9	197.7	356.3	35.1	103.3	253.6	301.0	214.0	65.0	298.9
PA..........	6,063.7	260.6	575.4	1,125.1	86.9	329.7	815.0	1,296.1	577.4	261.9	706.5
RI..........	503.6	19.9	39.7	77.3	5.9	35.3	68.2	108.8	60.0	23.0	65.3
SC..........	2,189.4	107.3	258.2	408.2	27.1	104.6	298.4	258.2	271.5	79.5	372.1
SD..........	440.6	23.6	44.8	86.0	5.5	29.0	33.2	73.5	47.3	16.9	79.9
TN..........	3,122.1	129.8	355.1	638.7	45.5	172.2	426.6	442.2	349.1	121.2	437.2
TX..........	12,801.3	776.3	906.6	2,514.2	208.6	801.0	1,792.0	1,741.2	1,394.1	445.6	1,971.8
UT..........	1,561.0	110.0	136.6	290.9	39.9	89.9	223.8	210.1	154.4	42.4	253.7
VT..........	316.1	15.3	30.0	53.9	4.3	12.2	29.4	65.9	37.4	10.3	56.7
VA..........	4,058.5	202.8	243.4	658.8	68.3	212.0	766.5	555.2	410.7	202.1	730.8
WA..........	3,469.2	220.2	293.5	643.6	144.4	160.7	434.9	502.2	348.4	127.9	587.5
WV..........	719.5	36.0	47.0	127.4	8.1	29.2	69.2	129.2	74.9	24.3	151.8
WI..........	2,981.4	124.0	484.3	534.1	47.0	154.5	326.3	464.3	284.5	152.3	406.0
WY..........	289.6	22.7	10.1	52.0	3.4	11.2	19.2	28.6	36.6	16.2	68.9

[1] Includes mining and logging, not shown separately. [2] Finance and insurance; and real estate and rental and leasing. [3] Professional, scientific, and technical services; management of companies and enterprises; and administrative and support, and waste management and remediation services. [4] Education services; and health care and social assistance. [5] Arts, entertainment, and recreation; and accommodations and food services. [6] Includes repair and maintenance; personal and laundry services; and membership associations and organizations.

Source: U.S. Bureau of Labor Statistics, State and Metro Area Employment, Hours, and Earnings, "Employees on nonfarm payrolls in States and selected areas by major industry," <http://www.bls.gov/sae/tables.htm>, accessed August 2020.

Table 665. Nonfarm Industries—Employees and Earnings: 1990 to 2019

[Annual averages of monthly figures (109,526 represents 109,526,000). Covers all full- and part-time employees who worked during, or received pay for, any part of the pay period including the 12th of the month. See also headnote, Table 663]

Industry	2017 NAICS code [1]	All employees (1,000)					Average hourly earnings [2] (dol.)		
		1990	2000	2010	2018	2019	2000	2010	2019
Total nonfarm	(X)	**109,526**	**132,011**	**130,345**	**148,908**	**150,939**	**(NA)**	**(NA)**	**(NA)**
Goods-producing [3]	(X)	23,723	24,649	17,751	20,704	21,067	15.27	20.28	24.74
Service-providing [4]	(X)	85,803	107,362	112,594	128,205	129,872	(NA)	(NA)	(NA)
Total private	(X)	**91,112**	**111,221**	**107,855**	**126,454**	**128,346**	**14.01**	**19.04**	**23.51**
Mining and logging	(X)	**765**	**599**	**705**	**727**	**735**	**16.55**	**23.82**	**29.95**
Logging	1133	85	79	50	50	51	13.70	18.85	22.70
Mining	21	**680**	**520**	**655**	**678**	**685**	**16.94**	**24.24**	**30.53**
Oil and gas extraction	211	190	125	159	142	150	19.43	27.36	37.28
Mining, except oil and gas	212	302	225	205	191	191	18.07	24.63	28.09
Support activities for mining	213	188	171	292	344	343	14.55	22.95	29.83
Construction	23	**5,263**	**6,787**	**5,518**	**7,288**	**7,492**	**17.48**	**23.22**	**28.51**
Construction of buildings	236	1,413	1,633	1,230	1,625	1,660	16.74	22.73	28.46
Residential building	2361	673	823	572	798	821	15.18	19.80	25.72
Nonresidential building	2362	741	809	658	827	839	18.18	25.13	30.80
Heavy and civil engineering construction	237	813	937	825	1,051	1,078	16.80	23.76	30.14
Highway, street, and bridge construction	2373	289	340	287	341	351	18.17	23.76	29.28
Specialty trade contractors	238	3,037	4,217	3,463	4,613	4,755	17.91	23.22	28.10
Building foundation and exterior contractors	2381	703	919	680	915	940	16.93	21.20	26.24
Building equipment contractors	2382	1,282	1,897	1,634	2,180	2,267	19.52	24.89	29.86
Building finishing contractors	2383	665	857	634	836	844	16.44	22.06	26.88
Manufacturing	31-33	**17,695**	**17,263**	**11,528**	**12,688**	**12,840**	**14.32**	**18.61**	**22.15**
Durable goods	(X)	**10,737**	**10,877**	**7,064**	**7,946**	**8,059**	**14.93**	**19.81**	**23.08**
Wood products	321	543	615	342	406	409	11.63	14.85	18.51
Nonmetallic mineral products	327	528	554	371	417	422	14.53	17.48	22.12
Cement and concrete products	3273	195	234	170	194	199	14.64	17.84	23.50
Primary metals	331	689	622	362	380	385	16.64	20.13	23.44
Iron and steel mills and ferroalloy production	3311	187	135	87	84	86	(NA)	(NA)	(NA)
Foundries	3315	214	217	112	120	119	14.72	18.22	21.96
Fabricated metal products	332	1,610	1,753	1,282	1,470	1,492	13.77	17.94	21.29
Architectural and structural metals	3323	357	428	321	392	401	13.43	17.47	21.60
Machine shops and threaded products	3327	309	365	313	363	365	14.53	18.68	22.59
Machinery	333	1,410	1,457	996	1,117	1,126	15.21	18.96	23.82
Agricultural, construction, and mining machinery	3331	229	222	208	218	221	14.21	18.95	22.90
Heating, ventilation and air conditioning, and commercial refrigeration equipment	3334	165	194	125	133	138	13.10	16.16	20.32
Metalworking machinery	3335	267	274	155	182	180	16.66	20.00	24.11
Computer and electronic products	334	1,903	1,820	1,095	1,054	1,081	14.73	22.78	25.20
Computer and peripheral equipment	3341	367	302	158	157	163	(NA)	(NA)	(NA)
Communications equipment	3342	223	239	117	85	84	14.39	23.88	21.47
Semiconductors and electronic components	3344	574	676	369	369	377	13.46	20.35	22.30
Electronic instruments	3345	635	488	406	410	424	15.80	24.82	29.52
Electrical equipment and appliances	335	633	591	360	400	405	13.23	16.87	20.42
Household appliances	3352	114	106	60	64	62	(NA)	(NA)	(NA)
Electrical equipment	3353	244	210	136	141	147	13.28	16.51	20.10
Transportation equipment	336	2,135	2,057	1,333	1,702	1,734	18.89	25.23	27.14
Motor vehicles	3361	271	291	153	234	237	24.45	29.05	29.64
Motor vehicle parts	3363	653	840	419	600	596	17.95	20.66	21.68
Aerospace products and parts	3364	841	517	478	508	534	20.52	33.65	37.85
Ship and boat building	3366	174	154	125	139	142	(NA)	(NA)	(NA)
Furniture and related products	337	602	680	357	393	388	11.73	15.06	18.34
Household and institutional furniture	3371	398	441	223	247	243	11.39	14.75	17.99
Miscellaneous durable goods manufacturing	339	686	728	567	608	618	11.93	16.56	19.62
Medical equipment and supplies	3391	283	305	303	318	325	12.70	17.56	20.59
Nondurable goods	(X)	**6,958**	**6,386**	**4,464**	**4,742**	**4,781**	**13.31**	**16.80**	**20.61**
Food manufacturing	311	1,507	1,553	1,451	1,621	1,643	11.77	14.41	18.19
Fruit and vegetable preserving	3114	218	197	173	175	173	11.90	14.56	18.02
Dairy products	3115	145	136	130	151	156	14.85	18.92	22.91
Animal slaughtering and processing	3116	427	507	489	522	531	10.27	12.69	15.92
Bakeries and tortilla manufacturing	3118	292	306	277	312	316	11.45	14.44	17.43
Textile mills	313	492	378	119	112	109	11.23	13.56	16.59
Textile product mills	314	236	230	119	116	113	10.31	11.79	15.52
Apparel	315	903	484	157	114	110	8.61	11.43	15.92
Cut and sew apparel	3152	750	380	124	91	87	(NA)	(NA)	(NA)
Leather and allied products	316								
Paper and paper products	322	647	605	395	366	365	15.91	20.04	22.47
Pulp, paper, and paperboard mills	3221	238	191	112	95	96	(NA)	(NA)	(NA)
Converted paper products	3222	409	413	282	270	269	(NA)	(NA)	(NA)
Printing and related support activities	323	809	807	488	432	425	14.09	16.91	18.98
Petroleum and coal products	324	153	123	114	115	115	22.80	31.31	41.37
Chemicals	325	1,036	980	787	835	850	17.09	21.07	25.46
Basic chemicals	3251	249	188	142	151	153	21.06	24.93	28.95
Resin, rubber, and artificial fibers	3252	158	136	89	94	95	(NA)	(NA)	(NA)
Pharmaceuticals and medicines	3254	207	274	277	297	306	17.27	21.95	25.57
Plastics and rubber products	326	825	951	625	730	737	12.70	15.71	19.38
Plastics products	3261	618	737	502	593	599	12.04	15.47	19.28
Rubber products	3262	207	214	123	137	138	14.83	16.64	19.81
Trade, transportation, and utilities	(X)	**22,633**	**26,174**	**24,565**	**27,607**	**27,715**	**13.28**	**16.78**	**20.64**
Wholesale trade	42	**5,230**	**5,888**	**5,387**	**5,841**	**5,903**	**16.24**	**21.46**	**26.06**
Durable goods	423	2,913	3,342	2,848	3,149	3,203	16.83	21.30	26.60
Motor vehicles and parts	4231	314	361	317	352	360	14.37	17.86	22.22
Lumber and construction supplies	4233	186	233	196	241	245	13.79	18.87	24.07
Commercial equipment	4234	628	758	657	676	686	20.35	25.29	31.69

See footnotes at end of table.

Table 665. Nonfarm Industries—Employees and Earnings: 1990 to 2019-Continued.

See headnote on page 429.

Industry	2017 NAICS code [1]	All employees (1,000)					Average hourly earnings [2] (dol.)		
		1990	2000	2010	2018	2019	2000	2010	2019
Electric goods........................	4236	369	438	328	352	359	19.51	23.42	28.97
Hardware and plumbing................	4237	221	253	227	276	284	15.21	20.14	25.55
Machinery and supplies................	4238	703	739	629	700	717	16.57	21.27	27.43
Nondurable goods.......................	424	1,958	2,131	2,026	2,151	2,169	14.54	20.03	23.80
Paper and paper products............	4241	168	184	135	129	128	15.87	22.96	25.56
Druggists' goods......................	4242	154	212	219	234	239	19.22	24.08	31.25
Apparel and piece goods.............	4243	154	166	141	152	153	14.70	21.54	23.05
Grocery and related products.........	4244	636	704	726	790	796	13.73	19.33	21.66
Alcoholic beverages..................	4248	117	130	166	201	204	15.80	20.14	24.09
Electronic markets and agents and brokers..	425	359	415	513	541	531	20.38	28.21	32.47
Retail trade........................	**44, 45**	**13,186**	**15,284**	**14,446**	**15,786**	**15,644**	**10.87**	**13.25**	**16.62**
Motor vehicle and parts dealers..........	441	1,494	1,847	1,629	2,015	2,035	14.94	17.06	21.02
Automobile dealers....................	4411	983	1,217	1,012	1,297	1,300	16.95	18.22	22.85
Auto parts, accessories, and tire stores.....	4413	418	499	489	559	571	11.04	14.54	16.88
Furniture and home furnishings stores........	442	432	544	438	477	473	12.33	15.25	18.86
Furniture stores......................	4421	244	289	217	225	222	13.37	16.17	19.62
Home furnishings stores..............	4422	188	254	221	252	251	11.06	14.03	17.98
Electronics and appliance stores..............	443	451	648	523	491	477	13.17	16.84	23.12
Building material and garden supply stores...	444	891	1,143	1,133	1,303	1,296	11.26	14.12	17.72
Building material and supplies dealers....	4441	753	983	1,006	1,145	1,141	11.31	14.14	17.87
Food and beverage stores.....................	445	2,779	2,993	2,808	3,073	3,078	9.76	12.03	13.77
Grocery stores........................	4451	2,406	2,582	2,461	2,688	2,688	9.71	12.12	13.75
Specialty food stores.................	4452	232	270	211	225	227	9.97	11.13	14.25
Beer, wine, and liquor stores.........	4453	141	141	136	161	163	10.40	11.89	13.46
Health and personal care stores..........	446	792	928	981	1,063	1,052	11.68	16.99	19.47
Gasoline stations........................	447	910	936	819	932	945	8.05	10.25	12.11
Clothing & clothing accessories stores........	448	1,313	1,322	1,353	1,359	1,299	9.96	11.59	15.92
Clothing stores.......................	4481	930	954	1,040	1,022	974	9.88	10.91	15.28
Shoe stores..........................	4482	216	193	182	202	196	8.96	11.80	15.88
Jewelry, luggage, and leather goods stores..	4483	167	175	131	135	130	11.48	15.56	19.55
Sporting goods, hobby, book, and music stores.................	451	464	603	579	573	550	9.38	11.69	14.80
Sporting goods and musical instrument stores..................	4511	352	437	459	496	471	9.55	11.82	14.89
Book stores and news dealers..............	4512	111	166	120	77	79	8.91	11.10	14.03
General merchandise stores..................	452	2,500	2,820	2,998	3,098	3,043	9.22	10.98	14.69
Department stores....................	4522	1,481	1,740	1,485	1,138	1,083	(NA)	(NA)	(NA)
Miscellaneous store retailers.................	453	738	1,007	762	835	834	10.20	12.50	14.49
Florists..............................	4531	121	130	69	59	58	8.95	11.05	13.61
Office supplies, stationery, and gift stores....	4532	358	471	303	250	240	10.46	13.06	14.59
Used merchandise stores..............	4533	56	107	125	175	178	8.07	10.72	12.73
Nonstore retailers........................	454	422	495	425	569	563	13.27	17.83	20.79
Electronic shopping and mail-order houses..	4541	159	258	250	395	387	13.43	18.34	20.58
Transportation and warehousing............	**48,49**	**3,478**	**4,401**	**4,179**	**5,426**	**5,618**	**15.00**	**19.10**	**22.40**
Air transportation........................	481	529	614	458	497	503	13.57	24.56	33.56
Scheduled air transportation................	4811	503	570	417	452	457	(NA)	(NA)	(NA)
Rail transportation........................	482	270	206	183	182	175	(NA)	(NA)	(NA)
Water transportation......................	483	57	56	62	65	66	(NA)	(NA)	(NA)
Truck transportation......................	484	1,123	1,406	1,251	1,496	1,531	15.86	18.62	23.29
General freight trucking..................	4841	807	1,013	868	1,034	1,059	16.37	18.51	23.11
Specialized freight trucking.............	4842	315	393	383	463	472	14.52	18.89	23.71
Transit and ground passenger transport.......	485	272	376	436	495	499	11.88	14.98	18.38
Urban, interurban, rural, and charter bus transportation...................	4851, 2,5	70	101	100	109	108	(NA)	(NA)	(NA)
Taxi and limousine service..............	4853	57	72	68	75	72	(NA)	(NA)	(NA)
School and employee bus transportation....	4854	114	152	186	201	206	11.42	14.90	18.93
Pipeline transportation.................	486	60	46	42	50	51	(NA)	(NA)	(NA)
Scenic and sightseeing transportation........	487	16	28	27	35	36	(NA)	(NA)	(NA)
Support activities for transportation..........	488	367	546	553	729	754	14.54	21.01	22.87
Support activities for air transportation.....	4881	96	141	154	222	233	13.42	17.04	20.31
Support activities for water transportation....	4883	91	97	91	95	96	19.57	35.16	35.78
Support activities for road transportation.....	4884	35	66	80	104	105	13.98	15.68	18.44
Freight transportation arrangement........	4885	111	178	169	229	240	13.46	21.24	22.95
Couriers and messengers..................	492	375	605	528	740	816	13.51	17.67	18.66
Couriers and express delivery services......	4921	340	546	480	647	707	(NA)	(NA)	(NA)
Warehousing and storage..................	493	409	518	638	1,139	1,188	14.49	15.57	18.55
Utilities.................................	**22**	**740**	**601**	**553**	**553**	**549**	**22.75**	**30.04**	**36.91**
Power generation and supply..................	2211	550	434	398	391	386	23.13	31.25	38.12
Natural gas distribution....................	2212	155	121	108	110	110	23.41	28.36	38.30
Water, sewage and other systems..............	2213	35	46	47	52	53	16.93	23.73	23.97
Information.................................	**51**	**2,688**	**3,630**	**2,707**	**2,839**	**2,860**	**19.07**	**25.87**	**33.89**
Publishing industries, except internet.........	511	871	1,035	759	739	760	(NA)	26.78	37.17
Newspaper, book, and directory publishers...	5111	773	774	498	322	299	(NA)	20.98	25.03
Software publishers....................	5112	98	261	261	416	461	28.48	36.41	44.24
Motion picture and sound recording............	512	255	383	370	441	444	21.25	22.11	27.26
Broadcasting, except internet..............	515	284	344	290	270	267	16.74	24.01	31.30
Radio and television broadcasting.............	5151	232	253	210	216	214	(NA)	(NA)	(NA)
Cable and other subscription programming...	5152	52	91	80	53	53	(NA)	(NA)	(NA)
Telecommunications.......................	517	1,009	1,397	903	750	713	18.59	26.24	31.87
Wired telecommunications carriers...........	517311	760	922	603	548	520	(NA)	(NA)	(NA)
Wireless telecommunications carriers (except satellite).....................	517312	36	186	170	112	106	(NA)	(NA)	(NA)
Data processing, hosting and related services.................	518	211	316	243	331	339	16.97	27.03	37.39
Financial activities......................	**(X)**	**6,614**	**7,783**	**7,695**	**8,590**	**8,746**	**15.04**	**21.55**	**27.67**

See footnotes at end of table.

Industry	2017 NAICS code [1]	All employees (1,000)					Average hourly earnings [2] (dol.)		
		1990	2000	2010	2018	2019	2000	2010	2019
Finance and insurance	**52**	**4,976**	**5,773**	**5,761**	**6,337**	**6,425**	**(NA)**	**(NA)**	**(NA)**
Monetary authorities—central bank	521	24	23	20	20	20	(NA)	(NA)	(NA)
Credit intermediation and related activities	522	2,425	2,548	2,550	2,651	2,652	13.14	18.25	24.43
Depository credit intermediation	5221	1,938	1,723	1,763	1,759	1,776	12.01	17.65	23.25
Commercial banking	52211	1,448	1,325	1,366	1,381	1,391	11.92	17.70	23.52
Nondepository credit intermediation	5222	371	606	532	589	574	15.41	20.00	28.28
Activities related to credit intermediation	5223	117	219	255	303	301	15.42	18.27	23.47
Securities, commodity contracts, and investments, and funds and trusts	523, 5	489	851	850	954	964	20.04	31.21	41.47
Securities and commodity contracts brokerage and exchanges	5231,2	341	569	471	458	456	20.05	31.72	40.72
Other financial investment activities, incl. funds trusts	5239, 525	148	282	379	495	508	20.03	30.51	42.18
Insurance carriers and related activities	524	2,039	2,351	2,341	2,713	2,790	17.47	24.58	30.25
Insurance carriers	5241	1,349	1,544	1,445	1,541	1,599	18.03	25.95	31.42
Insurance agencies, brokerages, and related services	5242	690	807	896	1,172	1,192	16.32	22.18	28.54
Real estate and rental and leasing	**53**	**1,637**	**2,011**	**1,934**	**2,253**	**2,321**	**(NA)**	**(NA)**	**(NA)**
Real estate	531	1,109	1,316	1,396	1,663	1,718	12.26	17.37	22.46
Lessors of real estate	5311	566	610	565	606	619	11.19	16.52	21.42
Offices of real estate agents and brokers	5312	217	281	286	343	363	12.57	17.10	22.49
Activities related to real estate	5313	327	424	544	714	736	13.60	18.37	23.35
Rental and leasing services	532	514	667	514	567	579	11.69	15.96	21.49
Automotive equipment rental and leasing	5321	163	208	161	218	227	(NA)	(NA)	(NA)
Consumer goods rental	5322	220	292	198	149	143	(NA)	(NA)	(NA)
Machinery/equipment rental and leasing	5324	84	103	114	165	176	14.95	19.83	27.62
Lessors of nonfinancial intangible assets	533	14	28	25	23	23	(NA)	(NA)	(NA)
Professional and business services	**(X)**	**10,881**	**16,704**	**16,783**	**20,950**	**21,313**	**15.53**	**22.80**	**27.78**
Professional and technical services	**54**	**4,565**	**6,732**	**7,486**	**9,282**	**9,543**	**20.62**	**29.93**	**36.27**
Legal services	5411	944	1,066	1,114	1,142	1,150	21.38	31.04	36.90
Accounting and bookkeeping services	5412	665	867	887	1,004	1,026	14.42	21.03	26.92
Architectural and engineering services	5413	942	1,239	1,276	1,474	1,513	20.49	30.22	35.01
Specialized design services	5414	82	132	113	142	144	15.32	22.36	29.57
Computer systems design and related	5415	414	1,259	1,456	2,118	2,202	27.11	37.12	43.70
Management and technical consulting	5416	324	694	1,031	1,482	1,531	20.87	28.54	35.72
Scientific research and development	5417	495	517	623	693	729	21.39	35.63	42.20
Advertising and related services	5418	383	498	410	490	493	17.01	24.64	29.88
Management of companies and enterprises	**55**	**1,671**	**1,800**	**1,878**	**2,374**	**2,427**	**15.30**	**23.81**	**29.85**
Administrative and waste services	**56**	**4,646**	**8,172**	**7,419**	**9,294**	**9,343**	**11.70**	**15.81**	**19.25**
Administrative and support services	561	4,416	7,859	7,062	8,858	8,888	11.53	15.60	18.97
Office administrative services	5611	211	264	407	514	526	14.68	23.56	28.30
Facilities support services	5612	58	97	133	156	164	16.73	20.97	20.62
Employment services	5613	1,513	3,850	2,724	3,657	3,637	11.90	16.19	19.29
Temporary help services	56132	1,156	2,636	2,094	2,989	2,948	11.79	14.23	18.72
Business support services	5614	506	788	811	895	878	11.10	14.53	18.56
Travel arrangement and reservation	5615	250	299	186	220	220	12.72	17.10	22.99
Investigation and security services	5616	508	690	782	946	956	9.79	14.15	17.30
Services to buildings and dwellings	5617	1,175	1,571	1,745	2,145	2,168	10.02	12.97	16.22
Waste management and remediation services	562	229	313	357	436	454	15.29	19.32	23.85
Waste collection	5621	82	100	141	182	190	12.97	17.50	20.77
Waste treatment and disposal	5622	77	119	96	99	101	15.02	20.29	27.40
Education and health services	**(X)**	**11,024**	**15,252**	**19,975**	**23,638**	**24,177**	**13.91**	**19.95**	**24.35**
Educational services	**61**	**1,688**	**2,390**	**3,155**	**3,715**	**3,765**	**(NA)**	**(NA)**	**(NA)**
Elementary and secondary schools	6111	461	716	849	1,080	1,107	(NA)	(NA)	(NA)
Junior colleges	6112	44	79	99	54	51	(NA)	(NA)	(NA)
Colleges and universities	6113	939	1,196	1,591	1,797	1,790	(NA)	(NA)	(NA)
Business, computer, and management training	6114	60	86	78	74	77	(NA)	(NA)	(NA)
Technical and trade schools	6115	72	91	126	114	115	(NA)	(NA)	(NA)
Other schools and instruction	6116	96	184	309	444	467	(NA)	(NA)	(NA)
Educational support services	6117	17	39	103	152	158	(NA)	(NA)	(NA)
Health care and social assistance	**62**	**9,336**	**12,861**	**16,820**	**19,923**	**20,413**	**13.93**	**20.23**	**24.68**
Health care	621,2,3	8,211	10,858	13,777	15,964	16,275	14.63	21.71	26.75
Ambulatory health care services	621	2,842	4,320	5,975	7,477	7,697	15.00	21.68	26.63
Offices of physicians	6211	1,251	1,801	2,264	2,616	2,672	15.65	24.03	31.93
Offices of dentists	6212	513	688	828	951	969	15.96	22.65	26.62
Offices of other health practitioners	6213	276	438	671	929	969	14.24	20.48	23.88
Outpatient care centers	6214	287	425	649	931	963	15.36	22.81	26.72
Medical and diagnostic laboratories	6215	129	162	228	275	283	15.74	23.48	26.30
Home health care services	6216	288	633	1,085	1,467	1,527	12.86	16.64	18.93
Hospitals	622	3,513	3,954	4,679	5,130	5,199	16.71	26.11	32.30
General medical and surgical hospitals	6221	3,305	3,745	4,357	4,713	4,780	16.75	26.33	32.56
Psychiatric and substance abuse hospitals	6222	113	86	109	150	148	(NA)	(NA)	(NA)
Nursing and residential care facilities	623	1,856	2,583	3,124	3,357	3,379	10.67	14.21	17.11
Nursing care facilities	6231	1,170	1,514	1,657	1,607	1,598	11.08	15.26	18.14
Residential mental health facilities	6232	269	437	565	642	648	9.96	13.06	16.28
Community care facilities for the elderly	6233	330	478	741	944	968	9.83	12.89	15.94
Social assistance	624	1,125	2,003	3,043	3,958	4,137	9.72	12.75	15.31
Individual and family services	6241	429	821	1,664	2,480	2,611	10.30	13.07	15.65
Emergency and other relief services	6242	67	117	143	177	184	10.95	14.41	18.11
Vocational rehabilitation services	6243	242	370	388	329	324	9.57	12.47	14.85
Child day care services	6244	388	696	848	973	1,018	8.88	11.99	14.16
Leisure and hospitality	**(X)**	**9,288**	**11,862**	**13,049**	**16,295**	**16,576**	**8.32**	**11.31**	**14.49**
Arts, entertainment, and recreation	**71**	**1,132**	**1,788**	**1,913**	**2,383**	**2,433**	**10.68**	**15.27**	**18.29**

See footnotes at end of table.

Table 665. Nonfarm Industries—Employees and Earnings: 1990 to 2019-Continued.

See headnote on page 429.

Industry	2017 NAICS code [1]	All employees (1,000)					Average hourly earnings [2] (dol.)		
		1990	2000	2010	2018	2019	2000	2010	2019
Performing arts and spectator sports...........	711	273	382	406	506	516	13.11	21.01	26.64
Museums, historical sites, zoos, and parks....	712	68	110	128	170	173	12.20	15.60	18.58
Amusements, gambling, and recreation........	713	791	1,296	1,379	1,707	1,744	9.86	13.38	15.46
Accommodation and food services...........	**72**	**8,156**	**10,074**	**11,135**	**13,913**	**14,143**	**7.92**	**10.68**	**13.95**
Accommodation.................................	721	1,616	1,884	1,760	2,035	2,078	9.48	13.02	15.43
Traveler accommodation..................	7211	1,582	1,837	1,703	1,964	2,007	9.49	13.07	15.48
Food services and drinking places........	722	6,540	8,189	9,376	11,878	12,065	7.49	10.15	13.65
Full-service restaurants..................	722511	3,070	3,845	4,482	5,502	5,535	7.78	10.93	14.99
Limited-service restaurants..................	722513	2,429	3,042	3,418	4,434	4,525	6.80	8.86	11.63
Special food services..................	7223	392	491	543	719	731	9.45	11.83	15.24
Drinking places, alcoholic beverages.........	7224	312	391	341	398	397	7.24	10.15	16.06
Other services.................................	**81**	**4,261**	**5,168**	**5,331**	**5,831**	**5,893**	**12.73**	**17.06**	**21.41**
Repair and maintenance..................	811	1,009	1,242	1,139	1,327	1,352	13.28	16.82	21.45
Automotive repair and maintenance.....	8111	659	888	801	934	949	12.45	15.55	20.02
Electronic equipment repair and maintenance..................	8112	100	107	98	103	105	16.31	19.41	24.36
Commercial machinery repair and maintenance..................	8113	161	161	172	211	220	15.53	21.03	26.09
Personal and laundry services..................	812	1,120	1,243	1,265	1,507	1,525	10.18	13.42	16.46
Personal care services..................	8121	430	490	601	724	738	10.18	13.97	17.40
Death care services..................	8122	123	136	131	137	137	13.04	17.46	20.81
Dry-cleaning and laundry services............	8123	371	388	302	297	294	9.17	11.80	13.83
Dry-cleaning and laundry services, except coin-operated..................	81232	215	211	146	128	123	8.14	10.56	12.79
Other personal services..................	8129	196	229	232	348	357	10.52	12.43	15.98
Pet care services, except veterinary.........	81291	23	31	63	124	134	12.12	12.83	14.99
Parking lots and garages..................	81293	68	93	111	146	143	8.81	11.18	14.36
Membership associations & organizations.....	813	2,132	2,683	2,926	2,998	3,016	13.66	18.76	23.77
Grantmaking and giving services..............	8132	113	116	178	181	183	14.65	23.51	32.92
Social advocacy organizations..................	8133	126	143	202	231	236	12.08	17.36	23.96
Civic and social organizations..................	8134	377	404	392	389	392	9.85	12.16	16.50
Professional and similar organizations........	8139	379	473	477	474	476	15.98	22.67	29.30
Government.................................	**(X)**	**18,415**	**20,790**	**22,490**	**22,455**	**22,594**	**(NA)**	**(NA)**	**(NA)**
Federal....................................	(X)	3,196	2,865	2,977	2,800	2,834	(NA)	(NA)	(NA)
Federal, except U.S. Postal Service.............	(X)	2,371	1,985	2,318	2,192	2,227	(NA)	(NA)	(NA)
U.S. Postal Service..................	(X)	825	880	659	609	607	(NA)	(NA)	(NA)
State....................................	(X)	4,305	4,786	5,137	5,173	5,177	(NA)	(NA)	(NA)
Local....................................	(X)	10,914	13,139	14,376	14,481	14,583	(NA)	(NA)	(NA)

NA Not available. X Not applicable. [1] Based on the North American Industry Classification System, 2017. See text, Section 15. [2] Production employees in the goods-producing industries and nonsupervisory employees in service-providing industries. [3] Mining and logging, construction, and manufacturing. [4] Trade, transportation and utilities, information, financial activities, professional and business services, education and health services, leisure and hospitality, other services, and government.

Source: U.S. Bureau of Labor Statistics, Current Employment Statistics, "Employment, Hours, and Earnings—National," <http://www.bls.gov/ces/data.htm>, accessed June 2020.

Table 666. Women Employed by Nonfarm Industry: 1990 to 2019

[51,619 represents 51,619,000. Annual averages of monthly data. For coverage, see headnote, Table 663]

Industry	Women employees (1,000)				Percent of total employees			
	1990	2000	2010	2019 (P)	1990	2000	2010	2019 (P)
Total nonfarm.................................	**51,619**	**63,398**	**65,089**	**75,308**	**47.1**	**48.0**	**49.9**	**49.9**
Total private.................................	**41,764**	**51,627**	**52,260**	**62,263**	**45.8**	**46.4**	**48.5**	**48.5**
Construction.................................	656	846	723	971	12.5	12.5	13.1	13.0
Manufacturing.................................	5,702	5,359	3,268	3,645	32.2	31.0	28.3	28.4
Trade, transportation, and utilities..................	9,352	10,845	9,992	11,095	41.3	41.4	40.7	40.0
Wholesale trade..................	1,598	1,812	1,619	1,776	30.6	30.8	30.1	30.1
Retail trade..................	6,697	7,681	7,228	7,757	50.8	50.3	50.0	49.6
Transportation and warehousing..................	880	1,202	1,006	1,430	25.3	27.3	24.1	25.5
Utilities..................	177	151	139	132	24.0	25.1	25.1	24.0
Information.................................	1,324	1,697	1,104	1,136	49.3	46.7	40.8	39.7
Financial activities..................	4,055	4,697	4,530	4,954	61.3	60.3	58.9	56.6
Professional and business services..................	5,116	7,693	7,472	9,718	47.0	46.1	44.5	45.6
Professional and technical services..................	2,217	3,156	3,537	4,453	48.6	46.9	47.2	46.7
Management of companies and enterprises......	850	925	940	1,203	50.9	51.4	50.1	49.6
Administrative and waste services..................	2,049	3,612	2,995	4,062	44.1	44.2	40.4	43.5
Education and health services..................	8,455	11,703	15,435	18,693	76.7	76.7	77.3	77.3
Educational services..................	958	1,417	1,929	2,352	56.8	59.3	61.2	62.5
Health care and social assistance..................	7,496	10,286	13,505	16,342	80.3	80.0	80.3	80.1
Leisure and hospitality..................	4,829	6,082	6,819	8,809	52.0	51.3	52.3	53.1
Arts, entertainment, and recreation..................	516	815	886	1,195	45.6	45.6	46.3	49.1
Accommodation and food services..................	4,312	5,267	5,933	7,614	52.9	52.3	53.3	53.8
Other services..................	2,164	2,614	2,820	3,146	50.8	50.6	52.9	53.4
Government.................................	**9,855**	**11,771**	**12,829**	**13,045**	**53.5**	**56.6**	**57.0**	**57.7**
Federal....................................	1,378	1,231	1,326	1,274	43.1	43.0	44.5	45.0
State government..................	2,137	2,464	2,639	2,805	49.6	51.5	51.4	54.2
Local government..................	6,340	8,076	8,864	8,966	58.1	61.5	61.7	61.5

P Preliminary.

Source: U.S. Bureau of Labor Statistics, Current Employment Statistics, "Employment, Hours, and Earnings—National," <http://www.bls.gov/ces/data.htm>, accessed February 2020.

Table 667. Job Gains and Job Losses of Private Sector Establishments by Industry Sector: 2000 to 2019

[In thousands (16,145 represents 16,145,000). For year ending in March. Based on the Quarterly Census of Employment and Wages (QCEW). Excludes self-employed and certain nonprofit organizations. Minus sign (-) indicates a decrease in employment and comes from either closing establishments or contracting establishments. For more information, see source]

Year and industry	Gross job gains			Gross job losses			Net change [1]
	Total	Expanding establishments	Opening establishments	Total	Contracting establishments	Closing establishments	
2000	16,145	10,620	5,525	13,160	8,291	4,869	2,985
2005	13,829	9,406	4,423	11,826	7,675	4,151	2,003
2006	14,096	9,629	4,467	11,494	7,715	3,779	2,602
2007	13,517	9,243	4,274	12,002	8,249	3,753	1,515
2008	12,786	8,718	4,068	12,674	8,776	3,898	112
2009	10,149	6,668	3,481	15,969	11,706	4,263	-5,820
2010	10,075	6,839	3,236	12,760	9,142	3,618	-2,685
2011	11,629	8,295	3,334	9,721	6,623	3,098	1,908
2012	12,216	8,662	3,554	9,546	6,508	3,038	2,670
2013	12,045	8,553	3,492	9,924	6,829	3,095	2,121
2014	12,282	8,700	3,582	10,008	6,945	3,063	2,274
2015	12,834	9,143	3,691	10,115	6,940	3,175	2,719
2016	13,168	9,394	3,774	10,656	7,426	3,230	2,512
2017	12,953	9,156	3,797	10,921	7,638	3,283	2,032
2018	13,116	9,359	3,757	10,948	7,635	3,313	2,168
2019, Total private	**13,134**	**9,359**	**3,775**	**11,259**	**7,854**	**3,405**	**1,875**
Goods producing	2,354	1,874	480	1,916	1,440	476	438
Natural resources and mining	245	188	57	225	171	54	20
Construction	1,192	883	309	969	693	276	223
Manufacturing	917	803	114	722	576	146	195
Service providing	10,777	7,483	3,294	9,343	6,414	2,929	1,434
Wholesale trade	574	436	138	494	333	161	80
Retail trade	1,264	887	377	1,407	971	436	-143
Transportation and warehousing	596	448	148	386	279	107	210
Utilities	27	22	5	31	27	4	-4
Information	324	235	89	306	227	79	18
Financial activities	804	581	223	728	497	231	76
Professional and business services	2,660	1,980	680	2,324	1,671	653	336
Education and health services	1,973	1,429	544	1,519	1,024	495	454
Leisure and hospitality	1,907	1,115	792	1,658	1,087	571	249
Other services	517	341	176	456	292	164	61

[1] Net change is the difference between total gross job gains and total gross job losses.

Source: U.S. Bureau of Labor Statistics, Business Employment Dynamics, "Annual Business Employment Dynamics Data," <http://www.bls.gov/bdm/bdmann.htm#TOTAL>, accessed February 2020.

Table 668. Private Sector Gross Job Gains and Job Losses by State: 2019

[In thousands (13,134 represents 13,134,000). For year ending in March. Based on the Quarterly Census of Employment and Wages (QCEW). Excludes self-employed and certain nonprofit organizations. Minus sign (-) indicates a decrease in employment and comes from either closing establishments or contracting establishments. For more information, see source]

State	Gross job gains			Gross job losses			Net change [1]	State	Gross job gains			Gross job losses			Net change [1]
	Total	Expanding establishments	Opening establishments	Total	Contracting establishments	Closing establishments			Total	Expanding establishments	Opening establishments	Total	Contracting establishments	Closing establishments	
U.S.	**13,134**	**9,359**	**3,775**	**11,259**	**7,854**	**3,405**	**1,875**	MO	224	154	69	209	145	64	15
AL	179	127	52	152	109	43	27	MT	40	27	13	37	24	12	3
AK	24	18	6	23	16	6	2	NE	75	51	24	73	52	21	2
AZ	276	202	74	209	143	66	67	NV	145	103	42	107	76	31	38
AR	97	68	29	88	64	24	9	NH	55	40	15	48	33	14	7
CA	1,760	1,214	546	1,496	1,000	496	264	NJ	365	262	102	316	228	88	48
CO	260	180	81	217	148	70	43	NM	74	53	21	62	43	19	12
CT	125	94	32	124	84	40	1	NY	837	606	231	714	475	239	123
DE	39	27	12	35	23	12	5	NC	411	300	110	323	223	99	88
DC	57	39	18	52	36	16	5	ND	36	26	10	30	22	8	6
FL	948	615	332	777	490	287	171	OH	410	312	98	385	286	99	25
GA	467	319	148	388	258	130	80	OK	149	98	50	135	90	45	14
HI	49	34	15	51	36	15	-2	OR	166	122	45	143	102	41	24
ID	72	48	24	53	38	15	19	PA	447	344	103	385	281	104	62
IL	458	334	124	453	319	134	5	RI	39	28	11	35	25	10	4
IN	249	190	59	213	158	55	36	SC	227	158	69	181	131	50	46
IA	109	82	27	108	81	27	1	SD	29	22	7	28	21	7	1
KS	111	81	29	103	73	30	7	TN	260	192	68	206	152	54	54
KY	157	113	44	144	107	37	13	TX	1,213	880	333	942	672	271	270
LA	174	124	50	172	125	47	2	UT	162	110	52	123	86	37	40
ME	49	34	15	41	28	13	8	VT	23	16	7	21	15	7	2
MD	232	161	70	211	143	68	20	VA	349	241	107	303	209	95	45
MA	297	214	83	257	177	80	40	WA	313	222	91	248	193	55	65
MI	320	239	81	299	215	84	20	WV	58	42	16	56	40	16	2
MN	207	159	48	190	141	49	17	WI	197	150	47	188	142	47	8
MS	88	63	25	84	62	22	5	WY	26	18	8	21	15	6	5

[1] Net change is the difference between total gross job gains and total gross job losses.

Source: U.S. Bureau of Labor Statistics, Business Employment Dynamics, "Annual Business Employment Dynamics Data," <http://www.bls.gov/bdm/bdmann.htm>, accessed August 2020.

Table 669. Hires and Separations Affecting Establishment Payrolls By Industry: 2016 to 2019

[63,731 represents 63,731,000. Hires represent any additions to payrolls, including new and rehired employees, full- and part-time workers, short-term and seasonal workers, and other hires. Separations represent terminations of employment, including quits, layoffs, and discharges, and other separations. Based on a monthly survey of private nonfarm establishments and governmental entities]

Industry	Annual hires (1,000)				Annual separations (1,000)			
	2016	2017	2018	2019	2016	2017	2018	2019
Total	**63,731**	**65,638**	**68,594**	**69,943**	**61,512**	**63,497**	**66,199**	**67,856**
Total private industry	59,502	61,502	64,286	65,567	57,440	59,429	62,058	63,640
Mining and logging	294	374	449	319	393	327	393	346
Construction	4,059	4,585	4,524	4,981	3,920	4,278	4,215	4,855
Manufacturing	3,353	3,985	4,390	4,081	3,363	3,813	4,123	4,021
Durable goods	1,923	2,238	2,512	2,297	1,981	2,116	2,291	2,277
Nondurable goods	1,427	1,748	1,879	1,783	1,382	1,695	1,830	1,744
Trade, transportation, and utilities	12,856	12,642	13,682	13,870	12,486	12,512	13,501	13,685
Wholesale trade	1,643	1,656	1,756	1,806	1,617	1,625	1,714	1,741
Retail trade	8,784	8,479	9,032	9,088	8,631	8,540	9,154	9,106
Transportation, warehousing, and utilities	2,429	2,507	2,895	2,976	2,239	2,352	2,630	2,840
Information	980	1,018	1,088	1,123	929	1,014	1,057	1,100
Financial activities	2,407	2,530	2,501	2,649	2,217	2,381	2,334	2,508
Finance and insurance	1,600	1,657	1,636	1,672	1,471	1,576	1,530	1,597
Real estate and rental and leasing	804	874	864	977	747	806	804	912
Professional and business services	13,337	13,430	13,747	13,860	13,013	13,024	13,294	13,488
Education and health services	7,687	8,007	8,509	8,689	7,107	7,558	8,034	8,046
Educational services	1,109	1,141	1,159	1,209	1,038	1,068	1,129	1,101
Health care and social assistance	6,577	6,867	7,350	7,480	6,071	6,487	6,906	6,945
Leisure and hospitality	12,222	12,236	12,797	13,388	11,764	11,910	12,547	13,064
Arts, entertainment, and recreation	1,910	2,048	2,211	1,979	1,829	1,969	2,108	1,943
Accommodation and food services	10,314	10,188	10,587	11,408	9,936	9,941	10,438	11,120
Other services	2,313	2,687	2,598	2,603	2,246	2,609	2,561	2,525
Government workers	4,229	4,138	4,310	4,376	4,073	4,068	4,138	4,216
Federal	411	380	420	506	371	401	400	465
State and local	3,816	3,757	3,889	3,868	3,702	3,666	3,739	3,748

Source: U.S. Bureau of Labor Statistics, *Job Openings and Labor Turnover—April 2020*, USDL 20-1185, June 2020. See also <http://www.bls.gov/jlt/news.htm>.

Table 670. Type of Separations Affecting Establishment Payrolls: 2019

[42,113 represents 42,113,000. Covers all private nonfarm establishments. Separations are the total number of terminations of employment occurring at any time during the reference month, and are reported by type of separation—quits, layoffs and discharges, and other separations. Annual rate estimates are computed by dividing annual levels by the Current Employment Statistics (CES) annual average employment level and multiplying that quotient by 100]

Industry	Number (1,000)			Rate (percent) [1]		
	Annual quits [2]	Annual layoffs and discharges [3]	Annual other separations [4]	Annual quits [2]	Annual layoffs and discharges [3]	Annual other separations [4]
Total	**42,113**	**21,739**	**4,002**	**27.9**	**14.4**	**2.7**
Total private industry	39,878	20,492	3,269	31.1	16.0	2.5
Mining and logging	177	152	17	24.0	20.7	2.3
Construction	2,082	2,571	202	27.8	34.3	2.7
Manufacturing	2,475	1,305	240	19.3	10.2	1.9
Durable goods	1,380	747	151	17.1	9.3	1.9
Nondurable goods	1,093	559	89	22.9	11.7	1.9
Trade, transportation, and utilities	8,897	4,022	765	32.1	14.5	2.8
Wholesale trade	1,022	604	113	17.3	10.2	1.9
Retail trade	6,238	2,400	470	39.9	15.3	3.0
Transportation, warehousing, and utilities	1,639	1,019	182	26.6	16.5	3.0
Information	563	449	91	19.7	15.7	3.2
Financial activities	1,560	644	304	17.8	7.4	3.5
Finance and insurance	1,014	323	260	15.8	5.0	4.0
Real estate and rental and leasing	546	319	44	23.5	13.7	1.9
Professional and business services	7,782	5,012	692	36.5	23.5	3.2
Education and health services	5,543	2,008	497	22.9	8.3	2.1
Educational services	640	399	64	17.0	10.6	1.7
Health care and social assistance	4,901	1,611	432	24.0	7.9	2.1
Leisure and hospitality	9,181	3,560	323	55.4	21.5	1.9
Arts, entertainment, and recreation	942	965	37	38.7	39.7	1.5
Accommodation and food services	8,239	2,594	284	58.3	18.3	2.0
Other services	1,621	763	142	27.5	12.9	2.4
Government workers	2,236	1,248	735	9.9	5.5	3.3
Federal	206	120	140	7.3	4.2	4.9
State and local	2,028	1,127	593	10.3	5.7	3.0

[1] As a percent of total employment. [2] Quits are voluntary separations by employees (except for retirements, which are reported as other separations). [3] Layoffs and discharges are involuntary separations initiated by the employer and include layoffs with no intent to rehire; formal layoffs lasting or expected to last more than seven days; discharges resulting from mergers, downsizing, or closings, firings or other discharges for cause; terminations of permanent or short term employees; and terminations of seasonal employees. [4] Other separations include retirements, transfers to other locations, deaths, and separations due to disability.

Source: U.S. Bureau of Labor Statistics, *Job Openings and Labor Turnover—April 2020*, USDL 20-1185, June 2020. See also <https://www.bls.gov/jlt/news.htm>.

Table 671. Private Nonprofit Establishments, Employees, and Average Annual Wages by Selected Industry: 2017

[In units, as indicated. 122,387 represents 122,387,000. Data from Bureau of Labor Statistics' Quarterly Census of Employment and Wages and IRS Exempt Organization Business Master File]

Industry	NAICS code	All establishments			501(c)(3) nonprofit establishments			501(c)(3) percent of total employ- ment
		Establish- ments (number)	Annual average employ- ment (1,000s)	Annual wages per employee (dollars)	Establish- ments (number)	Annual average employ- ment (1,000s)	Annual wages per employee (dollars)	
Total private..........................	(X)	**9,536,831**	**122,387**	**55,338**	**299,457**	**12,489**	**53,667**	**10.2**
Agriculture, forestry, fishing and hunting..........	11	104,445	1,261	34,464	338	3	34,981	0.2
Construction..	23	784,852	6,919	60,735	930	9	46,364	0.1
Manufacturing......................................	31-33	346,723	12,407	66,840	267	7	38,240	0.1
Wholesale trade...................................	42	612,359	5,899	75,904	732	4	57,227	0.1
Retail trade...	44-45	1,042,096	15,854	31,217	5,750	93	22,467	0.6
Transportation and warehousing..................	48-49	242,932	4,947	51,726	893	21	34,523	0.4
Information...	51	162,702	2,793	105,722	4,705	68	52,650	2.4
Finance and insurance............................	52	484,801	5,909	106,185	1,301	44	95,789	0.7
Real estate and rental and leasing...............	53	385,826	2,180	56,970	3,916	36	38,779	1.7
Professional, scientific, and technical services...	54	1,183,104	8,996	93,687	11,944	270	80,686	3.0
Management of companies and enterprises.....	55	64,772	2,278	119,885	4,633	281	69,142	12.3
Administrative and support and waste management and remediation services.........	56	534,038	9,065	39,621	5,098	101	53,689	1.1
Educational services...............................	61	117,479	2,824	50,053	32,832	2,004	55,389	70.9
Elementary and secondary schools..............	6111	17,969	811	41,234	12,879	684	41,766	84.3
Colleges, universities, and professional schools...	6113	8,934	1,242	64,605	5,331	1,138	66,097	91.6
Health care and social assistance.................	62	1,532,134	19,322	49,076	138,319	8,307	54,742	43.0
Hospitals...	622	10,024	5,018	62,595	5,171	4,207	63,923	83.8
Other residential care facilities..................	6239	6,585	165	31,853	3,680	112	33,615	67.8
Community food and housing, and emergency and other relief services...........	6242	11,389	169	37,870	9,871	154	37,301	91.2
Vocational rehabilitation services...............	6243	9,574	335	26,599	6,940	289	25,542	86.1
Arts, entertainment, and recreation..............	71	141,502	2,294	37,759	15,261	356	29,810	15.5
Performing arts companies......................	7111	10,026	123	49,541	3,498	70	38,353	57.0
Museums, historical sites, and similar institutions......................................	712	6,475	163	34,795	4,960	141	35,759	86.5
Accommodation and food services...............	72	697,728	13,607	20,731	1,909	38	20,838	0.3
Other services (except public administration)....	81	839,795	4,435	37,320	66,719	838	39,198	18.9
Religious, grantmaking, civic, professional, and similar organizations......................	813	146,264	1,370	43,941	64,730	819	39,353	59.8
Religious organizations..........................	8131	23,174	192	28,976	18,324	163	29,495	84.9
Grantmaking and giving services...............	8132	16,042	143	66,667	14,118	131	66,139	91.5
Social advocacy organizations..................	8133	22,277	212	48,115	18,070	185	47,191	87.6
Civic and social organizations..................	8134	25,771	392	19,976	8,992	280	18,957	71.3

Source: U.S. Bureau of Labor Statistics, Business Employment Dynamics, "Research Data on the Nonprofit Sector," <https://www.bls.gov/bdm/nonprofits/nonprofits.htm>, accessed May 2019.

Table 672. Indexes of Multifactor Productivity and Related Measures: 1990 to 2019

[2012=100. Data shown for private nonfarm business. Multifactor productivity (MFP) is a measure of economic performance comparing the amount of goods and services produced (output) to the amount of combined inputs used to produce those goods and services. Measured using output and compensation data published by the Bureau of Economic Analysis (BEA), hours data published by other BLS programs, and capital data supplied by BEA and U.S. Department of Agriculture. See source for details]

Year	Labor productivity (output per hour worked)	Output per unit of capital services	Multifactor produc- tivity [1]	Value added output [2]	Labor [3]	Capital services [4]	Combined units of labor and capital services	Capital intensity (capital services per hour)
1990....................	60.6	116.4	80.8	53.4	79.6	45.9	66.1	52.0
1995....................	65.7	113.4	83.0	61.7	87.3	54.4	74.4	58.0
2000....................	75.6	109.4	89.0	79.1	99.1	72.3	88.9	69.1
2005....................	88.7	106.0	96.8	90.9	98.8	85.8	93.8	83.7
2010....................	99.2	98.6	99.4	95.0	95.0	96.4	95.6	100.7
2015....................	102.8	100.6	101.5	109.3	107.1	108.6	107.7	102.1
2018....................	105.8	100.2	102.6	118.3	113.7	118.2	115.4	105.6
2019....................	107.8	100.0	103.5	121.5	114.9	121.6	117.4	107.8
ANNUAL PERCENT CHANGE								
1990....................	1.7	-1.9	0.1	1.5	0.4	3.4	1.4	3.7
1995....................	1.2	-0.9	0.2	3.5	2.7	4.5	3.3	2.1
2000....................	3.3	-1.6	1.5	4.7	1.7	6.5	3.2	5.0
2005....................	2.2	0.5	1.5	4.0	1.9	3.4	2.4	1.7
2010....................	3.4	2.5	2.7	3.3	0.5	0.8	0.6	0.8
2015....................	1.4	0.5	0.9	3.6	2.4	3.0	2.6	0.9
2018....................	1.4	0.7	0.9	3.5	2.4	2.8	2.6	0.8
2019....................	1.9	-0.2	0.9	2.7	1.1	2.9	1.8	2.1

[1] Output per combined units of labor input and capital services. [2] Gross domestic product originating in the sector. [3] Index of hours worked of all persons including employees, proprietors, and unpaid family workers, classified by age, education, and gender. [4] Measures the services derived from the stock of physical assets and intellectual property products.

Source: U.S. Bureau of Labor Statistics, Multifactor Productivity, "Multifactor Productivity Trends, 2019," March 2020. See also <https://www.bls.gov/mfp/home.htm>

Table 673. Productivity and Related Measures for Selected NAICS Industries: 1987 to 2019

[For a discussion of productivity measures and methodology, see text, this section and BLS Handbook of Methods, Chapter 11, <http://www.bls.gov/opub/hom/homch11.htm>. Minus sign (-) indicates decrease]

Industry	2017 NAICS code [1]	Average annual percent change [2] 1987-2019 [3]				2018-2019			
		Labor productivity	Unit labor costs	Output	Hours	Labor productivity	Unit labor costs	Output	Hours
Mining............................	21	1.5	2.3	1.7	0.2	5.4	-1.7	8.2	2.6
Oil and gas extraction..............	211	2.9	2.0	2.0	-0.9	-2.3	-3.4	11.0	13.6
Mining, except oil and gas..........	212	1.3	1.6	0.1	-1.2	-3.8	5.6	-1.7	2.1
Coal mining.....................	2121	1.5	1.1	-1.5	-2.9	-6.6	7.0	-6.4	0.1
Utilities............................	22	2.2	1.4	1.5	-0.7	-0.1	5.0	-1.8	-1.8
Power generation and supply........	2211	2.9	0.7	2.1	-0.9	1.1	5.2	-2.6	-3.7
Natural gas distribution............	2212	1.2	3.1	0.1	-1.1	-2.2	3.2	1.7	4.0
Water, sewage and other systems....	2213	-1.7	4.6	0.8	2.5	-3.7	8.1	-2.5	1.2
Manufacturing:									
Food............................	311	0.7	1.8	1.2	0.5	0.6	2.3	0.1	-0.4
Fruit and vegetable preserving and specialty. . .	3114	0.8	1.9	0.9	–	0.3	5.1	-0.9	-1.2
Dairy products..................	3115	1.0	2.1	1.2	0.2	-6.8	5.7	-0.4	6.9
Animal slaughtering and processing..	3116	0.6	1.7	1.8	1.1	3.4	2.3	2.4	-1.0
Bakeries and tortilla manufacturing..	3118	–	1.8	0.2	0.3	-0.4	1.5	-1.0	-0.6
Beverages and tobacco products......	312	-0.6	2.8	-0.3	0.3	-1.4	7.9	-3.5	-2.2
Textile mills.......................	313	2.5	-0.1	-2.2	-4.6	-2.3	-0.8	-0.3	2.1
Apparel...........................	315	-0.3	1.9	-6.5	-6.2	-0.7	6.8	-6.9	-6.3
Leather and allied products.........	316	0.6	2.2	-4.0	-4.6	-9.8	7.5	-5.1	5.1
Paper and paper products...........	322	1.5	1.5	-0.3	-1.8	–	5.0	-2.8	-2.8
Converted paper products........	3222	1.4	1.8	0.1	-1.3	2.4	5.1	-2.5	-4.8
Printing and related support activities.	323	1.1	1.2	-0.7	-1.8	-2.6	4.4	-4.1	-1.5
Petroleum and coal products.........	324	1.9	2.5	1.2	-0.7	-4.2	4.7	-1.2	3.2
Chemicals.........................	325	1.0	2.2	0.7	-0.4	-3.4	7.2	-1.4	2.1
Pharmaceuticals and medicines....	3254	-0.8	3.8	1.0	1.8	-6.7	9.1	-1.1	5.9
Plastics and rubber products.........	326	1.4	1.4	1.2	-0.2	-1.9	4.7	-2.6	-0.7
Plastics products................	3261	1.2	1.5	1.4	0.1	-2.6	4.5	-2.4	0.1
Wood products....................	321	0.8	2.1	-0.1	-0.9	-3.5	5.1	-1.5	2.1
Nonmetallic mineral products........	327	0.7	1.9	0.1	-0.5	-1.0	2.7	-0.5	0.5
Primary metals....................	331	2.0	0.8	0.3	-1.7	-0.8	5.9	-1.9	-1.1
Fabricated metal products...........	332	0.9	1.7	0.8	-0.1	-0.1	3.4	–	0.1
Forging and stamping............	3321	2.1	0.7	1.1	-1.0	-1.4	5.9	-3.0	-1.6
Cutlery and hand tools...........	3322	1.1	1.6	-1.1	-2.2	0.9	6.2	-4.7	-5.6
Architectural and structural metals..	3323	0.6	2.2	1.0	0.4	0.5	1.6	2.1	1.6
Machine shops and threaded products..........	3327	1.6	1.3	2.3	0.6	-1.7	5.2	-2.2	-0.6
Other fabricated metal products....	3329	0.4	2.0	–	-0.5	1.3	3.0	1.0	-0.2
Machinery.........................	333	1.7	1.1	1.1	-0.6	-1.2	3.4	-1.1	0.1
Agriculture, construction, and mining machinery................	3331	1.8	1.0	1.8	–	3.1	0.9	1.9	-1.2
Industrial machinery.............	3332	1.5	1.3	0.8	-0.7	-2.9	4.1	-5.0	-2.2
Computer and electronic products....	334	8.4	-4.8	6.3	-1.9	-0.8	1.8	1.3	2.1
Semiconductors and electronic components....	3344	12.0	-7.9	10.4	-1.5	-0.1	0.9	-0.2	–
Electronic instruments...........	3345	3.0	0.5	1.6	-1.4	-2.3	3.9	1.0	3.4
Electrical equipment and appliances..	335	1.7	1.4	–	-1.6	0.2	6.2	-1.5	-1.8
Transportation equipment...........	336	2.4	0.1	1.7	-0.6	-1.5	5.7	-2.2	-0.7
Motor vehicles..................	3361	2.5	0.1	1.9	-0.6	-2.1	4.0	-1.7	0.4
Motor vehicle parts..............	3363	2.7	-0.9	2.5	-0.2	-0.6	4.9	-4.7	-4.1
Aerospace products and parts.....	3364	2.1	0.7	0.7	-1.3	-2.2	6.8	0.2	2.4
Ship and boat building...........	3366	1.5	1.8	0.8	-0.7	-6.7	5.1	-0.8	6.4
Furniture and related products.......	337	1.3	1.6	-0.1	-1.4	-0.3	2.3	-1.9	-1.6
Household and institutional furniture............	3371	1.1	1.6	-0.5	-1.6	3.0	-0.6	-0.4	-3.3
Miscellaneous manufacturing........	339	1.7	1.4	1.5	-0.1	-0.5	3.8	0.5	1.0
Medical equipment and supplies....	3391	2.2	1.2	3.1	0.9	0.9	3.7	1.8	0.9
Wholesale trade....................	42	2.7	1.0	3.0	0.3	0.4	2.5	1.0	0.6
Durable goods.....................	423	4.1	-0.3	4.4	0.2	-1.1	3.6	0.3	1.4
Nondurable goods..................	424	1.1	2.7	1.3	0.2	1.3	1.5	1.7	0.4
Electronic markets and agents and brokers.......	425	1.5	0.8	3.0	1.5	5.6	0.2	1.4	-4.0
Retail trade........................	44-45	2.9	–	3.3	0.4	5.3	-1.1	3.7	-1.5
Motor vehicle and parts dealers.....	441	2.2	0.6	3.0	0.8	1.4	1.2	3.0	1.6
Automobile dealers..............	4411	2.3	0.6	3.1	0.8	2.4	1.3	2.9	0.4
Other motor vehicle dealers......	4412	2.5	0.8	3.9	1.4	0.5	-2.0	6.6	6.2
Auto parts, accessories, and tire stores..........	4413	1.0	1.4	1.7	0.7	-1.4	2.5	1.7	3.1
Furniture and home furnishings stores............	442	3.8	-1.0	3.6	-0.2	4.9	-3.7	-0.3	-5.0
Furniture stores.................	4421	3.2	-0.6	3.0	-0.2	1.9	0.4	-2.2	-4.0
Home furnishings stores..........	4422	4.6	-1.5	4.4	-0.2	8.3	-8.1	1.8	-6.0
Electronics and appliance stores.....	443	10.7	-7.2	10.9	0.2	11.7	-6.2	3.3	-7.5
Building material and garden supply stores.......	444	2.5	–	3.2	0.7	-2.3	2.8	-0.2	2.2
Building material and supplies dealers..........	4441	2.4	0.1	3.2	0.9	-3.0	1.9	0.3	3.4
Lawn and garden equipment and supplies stores.................	4442	3.2	-0.5	3.0	-0.3	2.2	9.0	-3.4	-5.5
Food and beverage stores...........	445	0.7	2.1	0.7	–	1.8	1.5	1.7	-0.1
Grocery stores..................	4451	0.5	2.4	0.6	0.1	1.1	2.1	1.9	0.7
Specialty food stores............	4452	0.5	1.8	-0.3	-0.8	11.5	-4.1	-1.6	-11.7
Beer, wine and liquor stores......	4453	2.0	0.7	1.5	-0.5	-2.9	2.5	1.4	4.4
Health and personal care stores.....	446	1.8	1.4	2.8	1.0	4.5	-1.9	3.2	-1.3
Gasoline stations..................	447	1.4	1.6	1.1	-0.2	2.0	2.8	1.8	-0.2
Clothing and clothing accessories stores..........	448	4.0	-1.0	3.6	-0.4	5.5	0.6	1.3	-4.0
Clothing stores.................	4481	4.3	-1.2	4.0	-0.3	6.8	–	0.8	-5.6
Shoe stores....................	4482	2.9	-0.7	2.6	-0.3	0.9	2.9	2.7	1.8
Jewelry, luggage, and leather goods stores.....	4483	3.3	-0.1	2.6	-0.7	5.7	1.0	2.5	-3.0
Sporting goods, hobby, book, and music stores...	451	3.6	-0.6	3.6	–	6.2	0.9	-0.2	-6.0

See footnotes at end of table.

Table 673. Productivity and Related Measures for Selected NAICS Industries: 1987 to 2019-Continued.

See headnote on page 436.

Industry	2017 NAICS code [1]	Average annual percent change [2]							
		1987-2019 [3]				2018-2019			
		Labor produc-tivity	Unit labor costs	Output	Hours	Labor produc-tivity	Unit labor costs	Output	Hours
Sporting goods and musical instrument stores..	4511	4.1	-1.1	4.4	0.3	6.7	0.6	-0.1	-6.4
Book, periodical, and music stores...............	4512	1.8	1.2	0.2	-1.6	2.2	2.7	-0.8	-2.9
General merchandise stores.........................	452	3.0	-0.7	4.1	1.1	7.0	-0.9	1.2	-5.4
Department stores..............................	4522	0.7	0.9	0.3	-0.4	5.1	1.1	-3.6	-8.3
Other general merchandise stores...............	4523	4.9	-1.7	7.2	2.1	6.7	-0.7	2.4	-4.0
Miscellaneous store retailers.......................	453	3.3	-0.8	3.1	-0.2	1.9	0.8	2.1	0.2
Florists...	4531	3.1	–	–	-3.1	6.0	-7.3	5.8	-0.2
Office supplies, stationery and gift stores........	4532	5.6	-2.4	3.7	-1.8	5.8	–	1.4	-4.1
Used merchandise stores......................	4533	4.4	-1.8	5.7	1.2	-6.8	5.3	-1.9	5.2
Other miscellaneous store retailers..............	4539	1.0	0.6	2.5	1.5	2.8	1.2	3.1	0.3
Nonstore retailers....................................	454	8.4	-3.8	9.2	0.8	14.0	-7.2	15.6	1.5
Electronic shopping and mail-order houses.....	4541	10.1	-4.7	14.2	3.7	13.2	-5.4	16.9	3.2
Vending machine operators.....................	4542	0.3	3.1	-1.8	-2.1	-3.8	8.7	2.4	6.4
Direct selling establishments.......................	4543	2.7	-0.1	1.3	-1.4	10.9	-10.8	7.2	-3.4
Transportation and warehousing:									
Air transportation....................................	481	3.1	0.9	2.8	-0.3	2.5	3.5	4.0	1.5
Line-haul railroads..................................	482111	3.5	-0.4	1.8	-1.6	5.3	-1.9	-0.1	-5.1
Truck transportation................................	484	0.6	1.1	2.0	1.1	-6.4	11.0	-4.2	2.3
General freight trucking..........................	4841	1.1	1.2	2.4	0.9	-6.6	11.3	-4.3	2.5
Used household and office goods moving.......	48421	-0.6	2.6	-0.1	0.5	(NA)	(NA)	(NA)	(NA)
Postal service..	491	0.4	2.9	-0.6	-1.0	-2.7	11.4	-2.4	0.3
Couriers and messengers..........................	492	-2.0	3.3	0.7	2.7	-10.8	13.2	1.1	13.4
Warehousing and storage.........................	493	1.0	0.6	5.4	3.8	5.6	2.6	6.7	1.0
General warehousing and storage..............	49311	2.0	-0.1	6.7	4.0	(NA)	(NA)	(NA)	(NA)
Refrigerated warehousing and storage..........	49312	-0.3	1.7	2.8	2.9	(NA)	(NA)	(NA)	(NA)
Information:									
Publishing..	511	3.8	1.7	3.5	-0.4	6.6	-0.5	8.2	1.4
Newspaper, book, and directory publishers.....	5111	0.2	4.0	-2.6	-2.8	2.6	0.3	-5.3	-7.7
Software publishers...............................	5112	10.4	-5.0	17.1	6.0	4.8	-1.1	13.5	8.3
Motion picture and video exhibition..............	51213	1.2	2.3	1.7	0.5	(NA)	(NA)	(NA)	(NA)
Broadcasting, except internet......................	515	3.0	1.5	2.9	-0.1	-0.9	5.2	-0.3	0.6
Radio and television broadcasting...............	5151	2.2	1.5	1.9	-0.4	0.6	4.4	1.4	0.8
Cable and other subscription programming.....	5152	5.0	2.6	6.3	1.2	-2.4	5.4	-2.4	-0.1
Wired telecommunications carriers...............	517311	3.6	-0.5	2.4	-1.2	5.5	2.1	-2.1	-7.2
Wireless telecommunications carriers............	517312	12.1	-7.0	18.2	5.5	13.2	-0.5	2.3	-9.6
Finance and insurance:									
Commercial banking................................	52211	3.0	2.0	2.9	-0.1	2.5	0.8	1.9	-0.6
Real estate and rental and leasing:									
Passenger car rental...............................	532111	2.2	1.6	3.1	0.9	(NA)	(NA)	(NA)	(NA)
Truck, trailer and RV rental and leasing..........	53212	2.2	1.1	3.0	0.8	-5.7	10.4	1.9	8.1
Video tape and disc rental.........................	532282	5.1	-0.8	-2.7	-7.5	(NA)	(NA)	(NA)	(NA)
Professional and technical services:									
Accounting and bookkeeping services..........	5412	2.4	1.4	3.0	1.0	-1.8	4.5	0.1	2.0
Architectural services..............................	54131	1.6	1.7	2.7	1.1	(NA)	(NA)	(NA)	(NA)
Engineering services...............................	54133	1.1	2.8	2.7	1.6	-2.3	3.4	1.4	3.8
Advertising agencies...............................	54181	2.2	1.6	2.9	0.7	(NA)	(NA)	(NA)	(NA)
Photography studios, portrait......................	541921	0.7	1.3	1.3	0.6	(NA)	(NA)	(NA)	(NA)
Administrative and waste services:									
Employment placement agencies.................	56131	4.7	-0.5	5.8	1.6	(NA)	(NA)	(NA)	(NA)
Travel arrangement and reservation services....	5615	6.3	-1.3	4.3	-0.3	–	6.4	-0.6	-0.6
Janitorial services..................................	56172	2.0	1.4	3.7	1.6	(NA)	(NA)	(NA)	(NA)
Health care and social assistance:									
Medical and diagnostic laboratories..............	6215	1.9	0.6	4.9	3.2	-1.2	6.9	2.0	3.3
Arts, entertainment, and recreation:									
Amusement parks and arcades....................	7131	0.4	5.0	-0.1	1.8	-0.7	4.6	1.9	2.6
Fitness and recreational sports centers..........	71394	3.3	-0.3	4.1	2.6	(NA)	(NA)	(NA)	(NA)
Accommodation and food services:									
Food services and drinking places................	722	0.5	3.0	2.2	1.7	0.5	3.9	1.6	1.1
Special food services..............................	7223	0.9	1.7	2.3	1.4	(NA)	(NA)	(NA)	(NA)
Drinking places, alcoholic beverages............	7224	-0.3	3.0	–	0.3	(NA)	(NA)	(NA)	(NA)
Restaurants and other eating places.............	72251	0.5	3.2	2.4	1.9	0.3	3.9	1.5	1.2
Other services:									
Automotive repair and maintenance..............	8111	1.0	2.3	1.5	0.5	3.7	0.6	0.7	-2.9
Reupholstery and furniture repair..................	81142	-0.8	3.6	-2.8	-2.0	(NA)	(NA)	(NA)	(NA)
Personal care services.............................	8121	2.2	1.7	3.5	1.3	(NA)	(NA)	(NA)	(NA)
Funeral homes and funeral services..............	81221	-0.4	4.0	-0.4	0.1	(NA)	(NA)	(NA)	(NA)
Dry cleaning and laundry services................	8123	2.2	1.4	1.2	-1.0	-3.4	3.4	0.2	3.7
Coin-operated laundries and drycleaners.........	81231	2.9	1.9	0.5	-2.3	(NA)	(NA)	(NA)	(NA)
Dry cleaning and laundry services................	81232	0.8	2.2	-1.2	-2.0	(NA)	(NA)	(NA)	(NA)
Photofinishing.......................................	81292	3.0	1.7	-3.9	-6.7	(NA)	(NA)	(NA)	(NA)

NA Not available. – Represents zero or rounds to less than half the unit of measurement shown. [1] North American Industry Classification System, 2017 (NAICS); see text, Section 15. [2] Average annual percent changes based on compound rate formula. Rates of change are calculated using index numbers to three decimal places. [3] For NAICS industries 22, 48-71, and 81, average annual percent changes are for 1987-2018. For NAICS industries 484, 4841, 493, 49311, and 49312, annual percent changes are for 1992-2018. For NAICS industries 48421, 71391 and 71394, average annual percent changes are for 2002-2018. For NAICS industries 5412, and 5615, average annual percent changes are for 1997-2017. For NAICS industries 56131, and 6215, average annual percent changes are for 1994-2017. For NAICS industry 7131, average annual percent change is for 2007-2018.

Source: U.S. Bureau of Labor Statistics, Labor Productivity and Costs, "Productivity and Costs by Industry," <http://www.bls.gov/lpc/data.htm>, accessed September 2020.

Table 674. Productivity and Related Measures: 1980 to 2019

[See text, this section. Minus sign (-) indicates decrease]

Item	1980	1990	2000	2010	2015	2016	2017	2018	2019
INDEXES (2012=100)									
Output per hour, business sector..................	50.7	60.7	76.1	99.3	102.9	103.2	104.6	106.1	108.2
Nonfarm business............................	51.9	61.1	76.1	99.2	102.7	103.0	104.4	105.8	107.9
Manufacturing............................	(NA)	47.7	69.5	100.2	98.9	98.7	98.2	98.6	98.7
Output [1], business sector........................	38.1	54.0	79.8	95.2	109.4	111.3	114.4	118.3	121.6
Nonfarm business............................	38.2	53.9	79.7	95.0	109.1	111.0	114.2	118.1	121.3
Manufacturing............................	(NA)	68.3	99.1	96.1	102.2	102.0	102.6	104.9	104.9
Hours [2], business sector........................	75.2	88.9	104.9	95.9	106.3	107.9	109.4	111.5	112.3
Nonfarm business............................	73.7	88.3	104.7	95.9	106.2	107.8	109.4	111.6	112.4
Manufacturing............................	(NA)	143.4	142.7	95.8	103.4	103.4	104.5	106.4	106.4
Compensation per hour [3], business sector.......	27.3	46.5	69.1	95.3	107.1	108.3	112.1	115.9	120.3
Nonfarm business............................	27.6	46.7	69.3	95.3	107.4	108.5	112.3	115.9	120.3
Manufacturing............................	(NA)	48.2	69.9	96.6	105.9	106.4	110.2	112.6	116.4
Real hourly compensation [3], business sector....	72.4	79.2	92.3	100.4	103.6	103.4	104.8	105.7	107.8
Nonfarm business............................	73.2	79.6	92.4	100.4	103.8	103.6	105.0	105.8	107.9
Manufacturing............................	(NA)	82.3	93.3	101.7	102.4	101.7	103.1	102.8	104.4
Unit labor costs [4], business sector...............	53.8	76.5	90.9	95.9	104.1	105.0	107.2	109.2	111.2
Nonfarm business............................	53.1	76.3	91.0	96.1	104.5	105.4	107.6	109.5	111.5
Manufacturing............................	(NA)	101.2	100.6	96.3	107.1	107.9	112.2	114.3	118.0
ANNUAL PERCENT CHANGE [5]									
Output per hour, business sector..................	–	2.0	3.4	3.3	1.2	0.3	1.4	1.5	2.0
Nonfarm business............................	–	1.7	3.3	3.4	1.3	0.3	1.3	1.4	1.9
Manufacturing............................	(NA)	3.3	3.4	6.4	-1.8	-0.2	-0.4	0.4	0.1
Output [1], business sector........................	-0.9	1.6	4.9	3.2	3.5	1.8	2.8	3.4	2.7
Nonfarm business............................	-0.9	1.5	4.7	3.3	3.5	1.7	2.9	3.5	2.7
Manufacturing............................	(NA)	–	2.6	6.4	-0.9	-0.2	0.6	2.3	–
Hours [2], business sector........................	-0.9	-0.4	1.4	-0.1	2.3	1.5	1.4	1.9	0.7
Nonfarm business............................	-0.8	-0.2	1.4	-0.1	2.1	1.5	1.5	2.0	0.7
Manufacturing............................	(NA)	-3.1	-0.8	–	1.0	–	1.0	1.9	-0.1
Compensation per hour [3], business sector.......	10.7	6.3	6.9	1.8	2.9	1.1	3.5	3.4	3.8
Nonfarm business............................	10.8	6.0	7.0	1.9	3.1	1.1	3.5	3.3	3.8
Manufacturing............................	(NA)	5.4	6.5	1.3	2.5	0.5	3.6	2.2	3.4
Real hourly compensation [3], business sector....	-0.4	1.3	3.4	0.1	2.7	-0.2	1.3	0.9	2.0
Nonfarm business............................	-0.4	1.0	3.5	0.2	2.9	-0.2	1.3	0.8	1.9
Manufacturing............................	(NA)	0.5	3.0	-0.4	2.3	-0.8	1.4	-0.3	1.5
Unit labor costs [4], business sector...............	10.7	4.2	3.4	-1.5	1.6	0.8	2.1	1.9	1.8
Nonfarm business............................	10.8	4.2	3.6	-1.5	1.7	0.8	2.1	1.8	1.8
Manufacturing............................	(NA)	2.1	3.0	-4.8	4.4	0.7	4.0	1.8	3.3

– Represents or rounds to zero. NA Not available. [1] Refers to gross sectoral product, a chain–type, current–weighted index. [2] Hours at work of all persons engaged in the business and nonfarm business sectors (employees, proprietors, and unpaid family workers), and employees' and proprietors' hours in manufacturing. [3] Wages and salaries of employees plus employers' contributions for social insurance and private benefit plans. Also includes an estimate of same for self-employed. Real compensation deflated by the Consumer Price Index research series; see text, Section 14. [4] Hourly compensation divided by output per hour. [5] All changes are from the immediate prior year.

Source: U.S. Bureau of Labor Statistics, Labor Productivity and Costs, "Major Sector Productivity and Costs," <http://www.bls.gov/lpc/home.htm>, accessed June 2020.

Table 675. Employed Persons and Average Hours Worked Per Day at Workplace and at Home: 2019

[166,302 represents 166,302,000. Civilian noninstitutionalized population 15 years old and over, except as indicated. Includes work at main job and any other jobs. Excludes travel related to work. Based on the American Time Use Survey]

Characteristic	Total employed (1,000)	Employed persons who worked on an average day [1]								
		Total			Worked at workplace			Worked at home [2]		
		Number (1,000)	Percent of employed	Hours of work	Number (1,000)	Percent of those who worked	Hours of work	Number (1,000)	Percent of those who worked	Hours of work
Total.....................	**166,302**	**112,700**	**67.8**	**7.62**	**92,274**	**81.9**	**7.86**	**26,730**	**23.7**	**3.27**
Work status: [3]										
Full-time workers [4]........	129,758	92,422	71.2	8.08	76,840	83.1	8.28	21,996	23.8	3.40
Part-time workers [4].......	36,544	20,278	55.5	5.48	15,434	76.1	5.80	4,734	23.3	2.64
Male [3]....................	88,481	62,714	70.9	7.97	53,215	84.9	8.20	13,657	21.8	3.01
Full-time workers [4].......	75,124	55,194	73.5	8.32	47,265	85.6	8.50	12,120	22.0	3.08
Part-time workers [4].......	13,357	7,520	56.3	5.38	5,950	79.1	5.80	1,537	20.4	2.51
Female [3]....................	77,821	49,987	64.2	7.17	39,058	78.1	7.40	13,073	26.2	3.53
Full-time workers [4].......	54,634	37,228	68.1	7.73	29,575	79.4	7.92	9,876	26.5	3.80
Part-time workers [4].......	23,187	12,759	55.0	5.54	9,483	74.3	5.80	3,197	25.1	2.70
Jobholding status:										
Single jobholders.........	149,821	99,423	66.4	7.59	82,444	82.9	7.89	21,753	21.9	3.30
Multiple jobholders........	16,481	13,277	80.6	7.84	9,829	74.0	7.64	4,976	37.5	3.14
Educational attainment: [5]										
Less than high school. ...	10,339	6,832	66.1	8.07	6,105	89.4	8.04	687	10.1	(S)
High school diploma [6]. ...	36,458	24,095	66.1	8.11	21,490	89.2	8.18	3,744	15.5	2.65
Some college............	34,223	22,597	66.0	7.82	18,481	81.8	8.14	4,393	19.4	3.90
Bachelor's degree or higher..................	63,210	45,069	71.3	7.36	33,249	73.8	7.82	16,761	37.2	3.29

S Estimate is suppressed because it does not meet publication standards. [1] Individuals may have worked at more than one location. [2] "Working at home" includes any time persons did work at home and is not restricted to persons whose usual workplace is their home. [3] Includes workers whose hours vary. [4] Full-time workers usually worked 35 or more hours per week at all jobs combined; part-time workers worked fewer than 35 hours per week. [5] For persons 25 years old and over. [6] Includes persons with a high school diploma or equivalent.

Source: U.S. Bureau of Labor Statistics, *American Time Use Survey—2019 Results*, USDL 20-1275, June 2020. See also <http://www.bls.gov/tus/home.htm#news>.

Table 676. Annual Total Compensation and Wages and Salary Accruals Per Full-Time Equivalent Employee by Industry: 2000 to 2019

[In dollars. Compensation averages are equal to the sum of wages and salaries and of supplements to wages and salaries; supplements are made on behalf of employees but are not included in regular wage payments to employees, such as contributions for employee pension and insurance funds, and employer contributions for government social insurance. Wages and salaries consist of cash remuneration of labor, including sick or vacation pay, severance pay, commissions, tips, and bonuses. Based on the 2012 North American Industry Classification System (NAICS); see text, Section 15]

Industry	Total annual compensation (average)				Annual salary and wages			
	2000	2010	2018	2019	2000	2010	2018	2019
Compensation of employees................	47,550	66,208	79,675	82,008	39,238	53,235	64,716	66,778
Domestic industries...........................	47,450	65,823	78,913	81,214	39,166	52,939	64,111	66,148
Private industries............................	46,136	62,441	75,500	77,731	38,862	51,913	63,327	65,374
Agriculture, forestry, fishing, and hunting........	25,814	37,634	44,242	45,990	22,146	30,610	35,853	36,663
Mining..	70,434	107,738	127,294	130,591	58,134	91,837	106,310	110,582
Utilities..	84,821	123,905	154,394	162,154	64,772	89,603	113,758	117,030
Construction..................................	46,201	63,648	77,699	79,929	38,551	52,757	65,484	67,503
Manufacturing................................	54,167	75,485	88,891	90,398	43,957	59,997	71,316	72,735
Wholesale trade.............................	59,068	78,065	95,567	97,624	50,896	67,167	81,544	84,161
Retail trade..................................	31,224	38,464	45,497	47,459	26,589	32,028	38,196	39,457
Transportation and warehousing..................	48,462	62,458	73,766	75,563	39,055	49,744	59,509	60,875
Information....................................	72,135	98,952	143,144	151,095	62,571	81,295	123,569	130,574
Finance and insurance........................	76,234	104,130	132,620	135,194	64,574	88,165	112,307	115,557
Real estate and rental and leasing..............	43,235	58,043	75,463	77,635	37,150	49,209	65,360	67,561
Professional, scientific, and technical services..	71,592	95,391	118,353	122,039	62,472	82,570	102,680	105,907
Management of companies and enterprises [1]...	90,766	126,701	152,812	159,514	74,253	103,873	130,903	137,088
Administrative and waste management services.....	28,921	44,896	53,832	55,780	25,035	37,374	45,270	47,470
Educational services.........................	34,164	50,711	60,248	62,358	29,244	41,367	49,031	50,040
Health care and social assistance..............	42,009	59,618	68,351	70,103	35,249	48,977	56,044	57,719
Arts, entertainment, and recreation..............	37,384	49,745	60,272	61,435	32,482	42,672	51,313	52,956
Accommodation and food services..............	20,819	27,965	35,220	36,233	18,045	24,138	30,732	31,679
Other services, except government.............	30,412	41,739	52,220	53,259	25,990	35,876	45,105	46,030
Government....................................	54,624	82,264	98,705	101,650	40,824	57,925	68,655	70,691
Federal..	61,449	104,416	122,705	124,627	46,749	74,664	85,758	86,414
State and local...............................	52,718	76,234	92,558	95,686	39,169	53,369	64,274	66,611

[1] Consists of offices of bank and other holding companies and of corporate, subsidiary, and regional managing offices.

Source: U.S. Bureau of Economic Analysis, National Income and Product Accounts Tables, "Table 6.2D. Compensation of Employees by Industry," "Table 6.5D. Full-Time Equivalent Employees by Industry," and "Table 6.6D. Wages and Salaries Per Full-Time Equivalent Employee by Industry," <http://www.bea.gov/itable/>, accessed August 2020.

Table 677. Average Hourly and Weekly Earnings of Employees by Private Industry Group: 2000 to 2019

[In dollars. Average earnings include overtime. Data are for production and nonsupervisory employees. See headnote, Table 663]

Private industry group	Current dollars					Constant (1982–84) dollars [1]				
	2000	2010	2017	2018	2019	2000	2010	2017	2018	2019
AVERAGE HOURLY EARNINGS										
Total private.................................	14.01	19.04	22.05	22.71	23.51	8.29	8.90	9.22	9.26	9.43
Mining and logging...........................	16.55	23.82	27.44	28.27	29.95	9.80	11.13	11.48	11.53	12.02
Construction.................................	17.48	23.22	26.74	27.75	28.51	10.35	10.85	11.19	11.32	11.44
Manufacturing................................	14.32	18.61	20.90	21.54	22.15	8.48	8.70	8.74	8.79	8.89
Trade, transportation, and utilities [2]........	13.28	16.78	19.29	19.88	20.64	7.86	7.84	8.07	8.11	8.28
Information...................................	19.07	25.87	30.74	31.97	33.89	11.29	12.09	12.86	13.04	13.60
Financial activities [2]........................	15.04	21.55	26.57	26.93	27.67	8.90	10.07	11.11	10.99	11.10
Professional and business services [2].....	15.53	22.80	26.05	26.82	27.78	9.19	10.66	10.90	10.94	11.15
Education and health services [2]..........	13.91	19.95	23.03	23.64	24.35	8.24	9.32	9.63	9.64	9.77
Leisure and hospitality [2]....................	8.32	11.31	13.38	13.87	14.49	4.93	5.29	5.60	5.66	5.81
Other services...............................	12.73	17.06	20.10	20.78	21.41	7.54	7.97	8.41	8.48	8.59
AVERAGE WEEKLY EARNINGS										
Total private.................................	481	636	742	767	791	285	297	311	313	317
Mining and logging...........................	735	1,063	1,266	1,322	1,403	435	497	530	539	563
Construction.................................	686	892	1,062	1,109	1,135	406	417	444	452	455
Manufacturing................................	591	765	876	908	922	350	358	366	370	370
Trade, transportation, and utilities........	449	558	652	675	698	266	261	273	275	280
Information...................................	701	940	1,100	1,140	1,196	415	439	460	465	480
Financial activities [2]........................	540	780	982	997	1,020	320	365	411	407	409
Professional and business services [2].....	536	799	923	949	984	317	374	386	387	395
Education and health services [2]..........	448	639	742	762	784	265	299	310	311	315
Leisure and hospitality [2]....................	217	281	333	345	358	129	131	139	141	144
Other services...............................	413	524	618	641	660	245	245	258	261	265

[1] Earnings in current dollars divided by the Consumer Price Index (CPI-W) on a 1982–84 base; see text, Section 14. [2] For composition of industries, see Table 665.

Source: U.S. Bureau of Labor Statistics, Current Employment Statistics, "Employment, Hours, and Earnings—National," <http://www.bls.gov/ces/data.htm>, accessed August 2020.

Table 678. Employment and Wages of Private Sector and Government Employees: 2000 to 2019

[7,879 represents 7,879,000. Based on federal-state cooperative program, The Quarterly Census of Employment and Wages (QCEW), also referenced as ES-202. Includes workers covered by state unemployment insurance laws and federal civilian workers covered by unemployment compensation for federal employees. Excludes most agricultural workers on small farms, all Armed Forces, elected officials in most states, railroad employees, most domestic workers, most student workers at school, value of meals and lodging, and tips and other gratuities]

Employment and wages	Unit	2000	2010	2015	2016	2017	2018	2019
Establishments:								
Total	1,000	**7,879**	**8,993**	**9,523**	**9,717**	**9,835**	**10,011**	**10,234**
Excluding federal	1,000	7,829	8,926	9,462	9,656	9,775	9,952	10,173
Private	1,000	7,622	8,696	9,224	9,418	9,537	9,712	9,932
State government	1,000	65	67	69	69	69	70	70
Local governments	1,000	141	164	169	169	169	170	171
Federal government	1,000	50	67	61	60	60	59	60
Average annual employment:								
Total	1,000	**129,877**	**127,820**	**139,492**	**141,870**	**143,860**	**146,132**	**148,105**
Excluding federal	1,000	127,006	124,840	136,735	139,077	141,057	143,337	145,281
Private	1,000	110,015	106,201	118,308	120,505	122,387	124,552	126,359
State government	1,000	4,370	4,606	4,567	4,570	4,629	4,625	4,666
Local governments	1,000	12,620	14,032	13,861	14,003	14,042	14,160	14,256
Federal government	1,000	2,871	2,981	2,756	2,793	2,803	2,795	2,824
Annual wages:								
Total	Bil. dol.	**4,588**	**5,976**	**7,385**	**7,607**	**7,968**	**8,368**	**8,769**
Excluding federal	Bil. dol.	4,455	5,769	7,170	7,388	7,743	8,135	8,531
Private	Bil. dol.	3,888	4,934	6,256	6,449	6,773	7,124	7,481
State government	Bil. dol.	159	226	255	261	272	281	293
Local governments	Bil. dol.	409	610	659	678	698	729	757
Federal government	Bil. dol.	133	206	215	219	225	234	238
Average annual wage per employee:								
Total	Dol.	**35,323**	**46,751**	**52,942**	**53,621**	**55,390**	**57,266**	**59,209**
Excluding federal	Dol.	35,077	46,215	52,439	53,124	54,892	56,752	58,721
Private	Dol.	35,337	46,455	52,876	53,515	55,338	57,198	59,202
State government	Dol.	36,296	48,960	55,878	57,168	58,802	60,751	62,830
Local governments	Dol.	32,387	43,493	47,573	48,440	49,720	51,515	53,112
Federal government	Dol.	46,228	69,198	77,900	78,379	80,432	83,657	84,310
Average weekly wage per employee:								
Total	Dol.	**679**	**899**	**1,018**	**1,031**	**1,065**	**1,101**	**1,139**
Excluding federal	Dol.	675	889	1,008	1,022	1,056	1,091	1,129
Private	Dol.	680	893	1,017	1,029	1,064	1,100	1,138
State government	Dol.	698	942	1,075	1,099	1,131	1,168	1,208
Local governments	Dol.	623	836	915	932	956	991	1,021
Federal government	Dol.	889	1,331	1,498	1,507	1,547	1,609	1,621

Source: U.S. Bureau of Labor Statistics, Quarterly Census of Employment and Wages, "QCEW Data Viewer," and earlier releases, <http://www.bls.gov/cew/>, accessed September 2020.

Table 679. Average Annual Wage by State: 2018 and 2019

[In dollars, except percent change. See headnote, Table 678]

State/area	Average wage per employee 2018	Average wage per employee 2019	Percent change, 2018-19	State/area	Average wage per employee 2018	Average wage per employee 2019	Percent change, 2018-19
United States	**57,266**	**59,209**	**3.4**	Montana	43,407	44,883	3.4
Alabama	47,414	48,839	3.0	Nebraska	46,262	47,854	3.4
Alaska	55,668	57,518	3.3	Nevada	50,041	51,422	2.8
Arizona	51,865	53,807	3.7	New Hampshire	56,782	58,671	3.3
Arkansas	43,950	45,448	3.4	New Jersey	65,727	67,364	2.5
California	68,478	71,351	4.2	New Mexico	45,167	47,043	4.2
Colorado	58,941	61,820	4.9	New York	72,900	75,365	3.4
Connecticut	67,742	69,771	3.0	North Carolina	50,756	52,379	3.2
Delaware	56,814	58,479	2.9	North Dakota	52,356	54,102	3.3
District of Columbia	95,909	98,051	2.2	Ohio	50,573	52,125	3.1
Florida	50,094	51,741	3.3	Oklahoma	46,727	48,023	2.8
Georgia	53,496	55,263	3.3	Oregon	53,053	55,023	3.7
Hawaii	50,977	52,686	3.4	Pennsylvania	55,628	57,497	3.4
Idaho	42,882	44,264	3.2	Rhode Island	53,736	54,918	2.2
Illinois	59,941	61,572	2.7	South Carolina	44,729	46,383	3.7
Indiana	47,590	48,793	2.5	South Dakota	43,694	45,150	3.3
Iowa	47,511	48,672	2.4	Tennessee	50,450	51,702	2.5
Kansas	46,607	48,060	3.1	Texas	57,747	59,794	3.5
Kentucky	46,302	47,723	3.1	Utah	48,513	50,766	4.6
Louisiana	48,116	49,286	2.4	Vermont	47,640	49,337	3.6
Maine	45,370	47,188	4.0	Virginia	58,239	60,200	3.4
Maryland	61,151	62,976	3.0	Washington	66,119	69,593	5.3
Massachusetts	72,606	75,404	3.9	West Virginia	46,120	46,618	1.1
Michigan	53,803	54,972	2.2	Wisconsin	48,872	50,413	3.2
Minnesota	58,007	59,630	2.8	Wyoming	48,059	49,880	3.8
Mississippi	39,762	40,687	2.3	Puerto Rico	28,784	28,433	-1.2
Missouri	49,053	50,536	3.0	Virgin Islands	47,535	52,421	10.3

Source: U.S. Bureau of Labor Statistics, Quarterly Census of Employment and Wages, "Employment and Wages Online Annual Averages, 2019," and earlier editions, <http://www.bls.gov/cew/home.htm>, accessed September 2020.

Table 680. Full-Time Wage and Salary Workers—Number and Earnings: 2010 to 2019

[99,531 represents 99,531,000. Earnings shown in current dollars; data represent annual averages of usual weekly earnings. Full time workers are those who usually worked 35 hours or more per week at all jobs combined. Based on the Current Population Survey; see text, Section 1 and Appendix III. For definition of median, see Guide to Tabular Presentation]

Characteristic	Number of workers (1,000)			Median weekly earnings (dollars)		
	2010	2018	2019	2010	2018	2019
All workers [1]	**99,531**	**115,567**	**117,584**	**747**	**886**	**917**
Male	55,059	64,142	65,007	824	973	1,007
Female	44,472	51,425	52,577	669	789	821
White [2]	80,656	88,953	90,194	765	916	945
Black [2]	11,658	15,041	15,460	611	694	735
Asian [2]	4,946	7,643	7,898	855	1,095	1,174
Hispanic [3]	14,837	20,297	21,227	535	680	706
OCCUPATION						
Management, professional and related occupations	39,145	48,808	50,119	1,063	1,246	1,309
Management, business, and financial operations	15,648	19,863	20,696	1,155	1,355	1,415
Professional and related occupations	23,497	28,945	29,423	1,008	1,176	1,237
Computer and mathematical occupations	3,202	4,755	4,947	1,289	1,539	1,579
Architecture and engineering occupations	2,366	2,994	3,011	1,255	1,484	1,550
Life, physical, and social science occupations	1,127	1,308	1,233	1,062	1,270	1,334
Community and social services occupations	1,909	2,223	2,240	802	913	968
Legal occupations	1,248	1,466	1,478	1,213	1,467	1,562
Education, training, and library occupations	6,535	7,166	7,238	913	1,002	1,057
Arts, design, entertainment, sports, and media	1,431	1,880	1,762	920	1,086	1,151
Healthcare practitioner and technical occupations	5,678	7,154	7,514	986	1,140	1,180
Service occupations	14,424	16,288	16,558	479	569	592
Healthcare support occupations	2,219	2,595	2,700	471	561	591
Protective service occupations	2,872	2,836	2,725	747	848	900
Food preparation and serving-related occupations	3,823	4,394	4,689	406	501	522
Building and grounds cleaning and maintenance	3,310	3,695	3,679	446	551	580
Personal care and service occupations	2,199	2,768	2,764	455	544	565
Sales and office occupations	23,060	23,714	23,883	631	742	758
Sales and related occupations	9,121	10,077	9,929	666	798	830
Office and administrative support occupations	13,939	13,637	13,954	619	717	732
Natural resources, construction, and maintenance	9,869	11,546	11,671	719	824	869
Farming, fishing, and forestry occupations	729	850	900	416	581	574
Construction and extraction occupations	5,020	6,414	6,467	709	808	866
Installation, maintenance, and repair occupations	4,120	4,282	4,304	794	934	939
Production, transportation, and material-moving	13,034	15,210	15,353	599	707	727
Production occupations	6,861	7,668	7,741	599	723	745
Transportation and material-moving occupations	6,172	7,542	7,612	599	689	711

[1] Includes other races, not shown separately. [2] For persons in this race group only. [3] Persons of Hispanic origin may be of any race.

Source: U.S. Bureau of Labor Statistics, CPS Tables, "Median weekly earnings of full-time wage and salary workers by selected characteristics," and "Median weekly earnings of full-time wage and salary workers by detailed occupation and sex," February 2020, and earlier releases, <http://www.bls.gov/cps/tables.htm>.

Table 681. Median Usual Weekly Earnings of Full-Time Wage and Salary Workers by Sex and Education: 1980 to 2019

[In current dollars. For wage and salary workers 25 years old and over. Based on Current Population Survey; see text, Section 1 and Appendix III. Wages and salaries are collected before taxes and other deductions and include overtime pay, commissions, or tips usually received at principal job. Earnings reported on basis other than weekly are converted to a weekly equivalent. Excludes all incorporated and unincorporated self employed. Data not strictly comparable to data for earlier years. See text this section and <http://www.bls.gov/cps/eetech_methods.pdf>]

Year and sex	Total	Less than a high school diploma	High school, no college [1]	Some college or associate's degree	Bachelor's degree and higher [2]
CURRENT DOLLARS					
Male:					
1980	339	267	327	358	427
1990	512	349	459	542	741
2000	693	406	591	691	1,020
2010	874	486	710	845	1,330
2018	1,026	607	819	951	1,524
2019	1,070	644	844	991	1,573
Female:					
1980	213	164	201	231	290
1990	369	240	315	395	535
2000	516	304	420	505	756
2010	704	388	543	638	986
2018	830	469	616	717	1,145
2019	865	494	633	737	1,195
WOMEN'S EARNINGS AS PERCENT OF MEN'S					
1980	62.8	61.4	61.5	64.5	67.9
1990	72.1	68.8	68.6	72.9	72.2
2000	74.5	74.9	71.1	73.1	74.1
2010	80.5	79.8	76.5	75.5	74.1
2018	80.9	77.3	75.2	75.4	75.1
2019	80.8	76.7	75.0	74.4	76.0

[1] Includes persons with a high school diploma or equivalent. [2] Includes bachelor's, master's, professional, or doctoral degree.

Source: U.S. Bureau of Labor Statistics, "Labor Force Statistics from the Current Population Survey," <http://www.bls.gov/cps/data.htm>, accessed August 2020.

Table 682. Workers With Earnings by Occupation of Longest Held Job and Sex: 2018

[79,440 represents 79,440,000. As of March. For definition of median, see Guide to Tabular Presentation. Based on the Current Population Survey, Annual Social and Economic Supplement (CPS ASEC); includes civilian noninstitutional population 15 years old and over, and military personnel who live in households with at least one other civilian adult. See text, Section 1, and Appendix III]

Major occupation group of longest job held in 2018	All workers				Full-time, year-round			
	Female		Male		Female		Male	
	Number (1,000)	Median earnings (dol.)	Number (1,000)	Median earnings (dol.)	Number (1,000)	Median earnings (dol.)	Number (1,000)	Median earnings (dol.)
Total........................	**79,440**	**32,654**	**88,115**	**46,741**	**50,795**	**45,097**	**67,205**	**55,291**
Management, business, and financial occupations........................	12,376	57,292	15,083	77,499	10,064	62,400	12,986	82,083
Professional and related occupations..............................	22,454	47,797	16,365	71,245	14,995	55,704	12,983	80,252
Service occupations.........................	17,187	20,028	12,586	26,773	8,554	28,196	7,840	36,144
Sales and office occupations...............	21,917	30,321	13,935	40,415	13,669	38,544	10,206	50,853
Natural resources, construction, and maintenance.........................	868	26,210	14,122	40,487	501	33,438	10,834	45,941
Production, transportation, and material-moving occupations..............	4,590	25,647	15,368	38,018	2,983	31,449	11,761	43,270
Armed Forces................................	48	(B)	655	51,308	29	(B)	596	52,345

B Base less than 75,000.

Source: U.S. Census Bureau, *Income and Poverty in the United States: 2018*, September 2019, Current Population Reports, P60-266; and "Detailed Tables: Person Table PINC-06," <https://www.census.gov/data/tables/time-series/demo/income-poverty/cps-pinc.html>, accessed August 2020.

Table 683. Employment Cost Index (ECI) for Total Compensation by Occupation and Industry: 2010 to 2019

[As of December (2005 = 100). The ECI is a measure of the rate of change in compensation (wages, salaries, and employer costs for employee benefits). Data are not seasonally adjusted. Industry classifications based on North American Industry Classification System (NAICS); occupation classifications based on the 2010 Standard Occupational Classification (SOC)]

Occupational group and industry	Indexes (December 2005 = 100)				Annual percent change from immediate prior year			
	2010	2017	2018	2019	2010	2017	2018	2019
Civilian workers [1]........................	**113.2**	**131.2**	**135.0**	**138.7**	**2.0**	**2.6**	**2.9**	**2.7**
State and local government.................	**116.2**	**134.2**	**137.7**	**141.7**	**1.8**	**2.5**	**2.6**	**2.9**
Workers, by occupational group:								
Management, professional and related occupations. . .	115.5	133.0	136.4	140.3	1.5	2.5	2.6	2.9
Sales and office occupations.............................	116.6	135.7	140.0	144.0	1.9	2.5	3.2	2.9
Service occupations.....................................	118.0	137.0	140.8	145.1	2.3	2.6	2.8	3.1
Workers, by industry division:								
Service-providing industries: [2]								
Education and health services [2]..........................	115.6	132.9	136.5	140.3	1.5	2.4	2.7	2.8
Schools...	115.3	132.4	136.0	139.8	1.4	2.3	2.7	2.8
Health care and social assistance [2].....................	117.9	135.8	139.3	143.5	2.2	2.3	2.6	3.0
Hospitals..	117.0	133.4	136.5	140.8	2.4	2.2	2.3	3.2
Public administration..................................	116.8	135.7	139.2	143.4	1.9	2.8	2.6	3.0
Private industry workers [3]....................	**112.5**	**130.5**	**134.4**	**138.0**	**2.1**	**2.6**	**3.0**	**2.7**
Workers, by occupational group:								
Management, professional, and related occupations...	113.0	130.5	133.8	136.8	2.1	2.4	2.5	2.2
Sales and office occupations.............................	111.6	130.1	135.0	138.8	2.2	2.6	3.8	2.8
Natural resources, construction, and maintenance occupations...........................	113.3	131.2	134.5	137.9	1.9	2.7	2.5	2.5
Production, transportation, and material moving occupations...........................	111.5	131.0	134.7	139.2	2.4	3.1	2.8	3.3
Service occupations.....................................	113.5	130.9	135.6	140.6	1.5	2.9	3.6	3.7
Workers, by industry division:								
Goods-producing industries [2]...........................	111.1	128.9	131.9	135.8	2.3	2.5	2.3	3.0
Construction.......................................	112.7	128.8	132.4	137.0	0.9	2.4	2.8	3.5
Manufacturing.....................................	110.0	128.9	131.6	135.3	2.8	2.7	2.1	2.8
Service-providing industries [2]...........................	113.0	131.0	135.2	138.7	2.0	2.6	3.2	2.6
Trade, transportation, and utilities......................	111.4	132.3	136.8	140.7	2.4	3.0	3.4	2.9
Information.......................................	110.0	128.4	134.3	135.7	1.6	2.4	4.6	1.0
Financial activities.................................	111.4	129.9	134.2	138.2	2.6	2.0	3.3	3.0
Professional and business services....................	114.6	131.9	135.2	138.7	2.0	3.0	2.5	2.6
Education and health services........................	114.7	130.4	134.1	137.2	1.7	2.0	2.8	2.3
Leisure and hospitality..............................	114.1	130.3	135.7	140.0	1.2	3.6	4.1	3.2
Bargaining status:								
Union...	114.8	134.5	138.8	142.3	3.3	3.0	3.2	2.5
Nonunion..	112.1	129.9	133.7	137.3	1.8	2.6	2.9	2.7

[1] Includes workers in the private nonfarm economy except those in private households, and workers in the public sector except those in the federal government. [2] Includes all other items not shown separately. [3] Excludes farm and household workers.

Source: U.S. Bureau of Labor Statistics, Employment Cost Trends, "Employment Cost Index," <http://www.bls.gov/ncs/ect/home.htm#data>, accessed March 2020.

Table 684. Federal and State Minimum Wage Rates: 1940 to 2020

[In current dollars. Wage rates are as of January 1, except as noted. Where an employee is subject to both the state and federal minimum wage laws, the employee is entitled to the higher minimum wage rate]

Year	Federal minimum wage rates per hour	State	2020 minimum wage rates per hour	State	2020 minimum wage rates per hour	State	2020 minimum wage rates per hour
1940...................	0.30	AL.........	(X)	KY.........	7.25	ND.........	7.25
1945 (as of Oct. 24).....	0.40	AK.........	10.19	LA.........	(X)	OH.........	[7] 7.25/8.70
1950 (as of Jan. 25).....	0.75	AZ.........	12.00	ME.........	12.00	OK.........	[8] 2.00/7.25
1960...................	1.00	AR.........	[2] 10.00	MD.........	11.00	OR.........	12.00
1965 (as of Sept. 3).....	1.25	CA.........	[9] 12.00/13.00	MA.........	12.75	PA.........	7.25
1970 (as of Feb. 1)......	1.45	CO.........	12.00	MI.........	[1] 9.65	RI.........	10.50
1975...................	2.10	CT.........	11.00	MN.........	[4] 8.15/10.00	SC.........	(X)
1980...................	3.10	DE.........	9.25	MS.........	(X)	SD.........	9.30
1985...................	3.35	DC.........	15.00	MO.........	9.45	TN.........	(X)
1990 (as of Apr. 1)......	3.80	FL.........	8.56	MT.........	[5] 4.00/8.65	TX.........	7.25
1995...................	4.25	GA.........	[3] 5.15	NE.........	[2] 9.00	UT.........	7.25
2000...................	5.15	HI.........	10.10	NV.........	[6] 8.00/9.00	VT.........	[1] 10.96
2005...................	5.15	ID.........	7.25	NH.........	7.25	VA.........	[2] 7.25
2007 (as of Jul. 24).....	5.85	IL.........	[2] 10.00	NJ.........	11.00	WA.........	13.50
2008 (as of Jul. 24).....	6.55	IN.........	[1] 7.25	NM.........	9.00	WV.........	[3] 8.75
2009 (as of Jul. 24).....	7.25	IA.........	7.25	NY.........	[10] 11.80	WI.........	7.25
2020 (as of July 1).....	**7.25**	KS.........	7.25	NC.........	7.25	WY.........	5.15

X Not applicable. [1] Employers of 2 or more. [2] Employers of 4 or more. [3] Employers of 6 or more. [4] Large employer (receipts of $500,000 or more) and small employer (with annual receipts of less than $500,000). [5] Lower rate for businesses with gross annual sales of $110,000 or less. [6] Nevada: $9.00 with no health insurance benefits provided by employer. $8.00 with health insurance provided by employer and received by employee. [7] Ohio: $7.25 for those employers grossing $305,000 or less. [8] Oklahoma: employers of 10 or more full time employees at any one location, and employers with gross sales over $100,000 regardless of number of full-time employees. All other employers $2.00. [9] California: $12.00 minimum wage for employers with 25 or fewer employees, and $13.00 minimum wage for employers with 26 or more employees. [10] Basic minimum rate: $11.80; $13.00 (Long Island & Westchester); $15.00 (NYC).

Source: U.S. Department of Labor, Wage and Hour Division, "Changes in Basic Minimum Wages in Non-Farm Employment Under State Law: Selected Years 1968 to 2019," and "State Minimum Wage Laws," <https://www.dol.gov/agencies/whd/minimum-wage/state>, accessed August 2020.

Table 685. Workers Paid Hourly Rates At or Below Federal Minimum Wage by Selected Characteristics: 2019

[82,289 represents 82,289,000. Data are annual averages. For employed wage and salary workers, excluding all self-employed. Based on the Current Population Survey; see text, Section 1 and Appendix III]

Characteristic	Number of workers paid hourly rates (1,000)				Percent of workers paid hourly rates at or below federal minimum wage		
		At or below federal minimum wage					
	Total	Total	At prevailing federal minimum wage	Below prevailing federal minimum wage	Total	At prevailing federal minimum wage	Below prevailing federal minimum wage
Total, 16 years and over [1]..........	**82,289**	**1,603**	**392**	**1,211**	**1.9**	**0.5**	**1.5**
16 to 24 years......................	16,021	691	229	462	4.3	1.4	2.9
25 years and over..................	66,269	912	163	749	1.4	0.2	1.1
Male, 16 years old and over...........	40,918	536	125	411	1.3	0.3	1.0
16 to 24 years......................	7,978	226	84	142	2.8	1.1	1.8
25 years and over..................	32,940	310	40	270	0.9	0.1	0.8
Female, 16 years old and over.........	41,372	1,067	268	800	2.6	0.6	1.9
16 to 24 years......................	8,043	465	145	320	5.8	1.8	4.0
25 years and over..................	33,329	602	123	479	1.8	0.4	1.4
White [2].............................	62,461	1,164	260	904	1.9	0.4	1.4
Men...............................	31,681	379	89	290	1.2	0.3	0.9
Women............................	30,780	785	171	614	2.6	0.6	2.0
Black [2].............................	12,063	287	101	186	2.4	0.8	1.5
Men...............................	5,492	104	26	79	1.9	0.5	1.4
Women............................	6,571	183	76	107	2.8	1.2	1.6
Asian [2].............................	4,159	70	12	58	1.7	0.3	1.4
Men...............................	1,930	23	5	18	1.2	0.3	0.9
Women............................	2,230	47	7	40	2.1	0.3	1.8
Hispanic [3]..........................	17,941	292	77	215	1.6	0.4	1.2
Men...............................	9,717	97	24	72	1.0	0.3	0.7
Women............................	8,223	195	52	143	2.4	0.6	1.7
Full-time workers....................	62,450	717	98	618	1.1	0.2	1.0
Men...............................	34,090	256	21	236	0.8	0.1	0.7
Women............................	28,360	460	78	383	1.6	0.3	1.3
Part-time workers [4].................	19,730	886	294	592	4.5	1.5	3.0
Men...............................	6,778	279	104	175	4.1	1.5	2.6
Women............................	12,952	607	190	417	4.7	1.5	3.2
Private sector industries...............	72,601	1,516	362	1,154	2.1	0.5	1.6
Public sector industries...............	9,689	88	30	58	0.9	0.3	0.6

[1] Includes other races, not shown separately. Also includes a small number of multiple jobholders whose full- or part-time status cannot be determined for their principal job. [2] For persons in this race group only. [3] Persons of Hispanic or Latino origin may be of any race. [4] Working fewer than 35 hours per week.

Source: U.S. Bureau of Labor Statistics, *Characteristics of Minimum Wage Workers: 2019*, April 2020. See also <https://www.bls.gov/cps/earnings.htm#minwage>.

Table 686. Earnings by Sex and Women's Earnings as a Percent of Men's Earnings by Occupation: 2017 and 2018

[Median earnings in inflation-adjusted dollars for the full-time, year round civilian employed population age 16 years and over. Estimates subject to sampling variability. Based on the American Community Survey]

Occupation	2017 Median earnings 2017 inflation-adjusted Female	2017 Median earnings 2017 inflation-adjusted Male	Women's earnings as a percent of men's earnings	2018 Median earnings 2018 inflation-adjusted Female	2018 Median earnings 2018 inflation-adjusted Male	Women's earnings as a percent of men's earnings
Total:..	**41,512**	**51,421**	**80.7**	**42,295**	**52,144**	**81.1**
Management, business, science, and arts...............	56,743	77,953	72.8	58,498	80,405	72.8
Management, business, and financial...................	61,683	81,395	75.8	62,477	82,285	75.9
Management..	64,266	83,387	77.1	64,685	85,289	75.8
Business and financial operations.....................	59,584	75,902	78.5	61,601	79,998	77.0
Computer, engineering, and science...................	71,502	84,802	84.3	72,103	85,843	84.0
Computer and mathematical.............................	75,555	87,012	86.8	75,914	89,396	84.9
Architecture and engineering..........................	72,047	83,593	86.2	73,701	85,119	86.6
Life, physical, and social science...................	62,345	71,799	86.8	63,226	71,923	87.9
Education, legal, community service, arts, and media........	48,245	60,609	79.6	49,995	61,666	81.1
Community and social service..........................	44,800	47,178	95.0	45,904	48,773	94.1
Legal...	67,050	122,231	54.9	69,361	126,800	54.7
Education, training, and library......................	47,033	57,802	81.4	48,123	60,158	80.0
Arts, design, entertainment, sports, and media........	50,300	57,128	88.0	51,939	60,227	86.2
Healthcare practitioners and technical................	60,334	80,092	75.3	60,940	81,376	74.9
Health diagnosing and treating practitioners and other technical.......	70,039	102,039	68.6	71,232	106,777	66.7
Health technologists and technicians.................	41,031	46,933	87.4	41,030	50,212	81.7
Service...	25,558	33,232	76.9	26,372	35,028	75.3
Healthcare support.....................................	29,262	32,119	91.1	29,172	32,025	91.1
Protective service.....................................	41,728	55,080	75.8	42,186	55,696	75.7
Fire fighting and prevention, and other protective service workers including supervisors........	35,044	45,068	77.8	36,261	45,951	78.9
Law enforcement workers including supervisors.........	49,793	62,220	80.0	50,133	63,451	79.0
Food preparation and serving related..................	21,710	26,046	83.4	22,344	26,893	83.1
Building and grounds cleaning and maintenance.........	22,449	31,124	72.1	23,483	31,697	74.1
Personal care and service.............................	24,682	31,141	79.3	26,103	34,453	75.8
Sales and office.......................................	36,103	47,360	76.2	37,068	50,679	73.1
Sales and related......................................	35,512	52,335	67.9	36,519	54,754	66.7
Office and administrative support.....................	36,261	40,709	89.1	37,220	44,296	84.0
Natural resources, construction, and maintenance......	31,725	42,203	75.2	33,877	43,592	77.7
Farming, fishing, and forestry........................	21,200	30,115	70.4	22,783	31,411	72.5
Construction and extraction...........................	35,760	41,422	86.3	37,272	42,023	88.7
Installation, maintenance, and repair.................	41,113	47,168	87.2	42,132	48,691	86.5
Production, transportation, and material moving........	28,993	40,690	71.3	30,009	41,004	73.2
Production...	29,317	41,565	70.5	30,617	42,766	71.6
Transportation...	31,941	44,173	72.3	32,858	46,008	71.4
Material moving..	25,935	31,790	81.6	26,535	31,792	83.5

Source: U.S. Census Bureau, 2017 and 2018 American Community Survey, B24022, "Sex by Occupation and Median Earnings in the Past 12 Months (in 2017 and 2018 Inflation-Adjusted Dollars) for the Full-time, Year-Round Civilian Employed Population 16 Years and Over," <https://data.census.gov/>, accessed April 2020.

Table 687. Workers' Earnings by Certification and License Status and Selected Characteristics: 2019

[In dollars, unless otherwise noted (117,584 represents 117,584,000). Data shown for wage and salary workers aged 16 years old and over, unless otherwise noted. Excludes self-employed workers. Certifications are issued by a non-governmental certification body and convey that an individual has the knowledge or skill to perform a specific job. A license is awarded by a government agency and conveys a legal authority to work in an occupation. For definition of median, see Guide to Tabular Presentation]

Characteristic	Full-time wage and salary workers (1,000)	Median weekly earnings Total	With a certification or license [1] Total	With a certification or license [1] Certification only	With a certification or license [1] With a license [2]	Without a certification or license
Total workers, 16 years old and over....	**117,584**	**917**	**1,135**	**1,226**	**1,129**	**852**
AGE						
16 to 24 years old..............................	10,766	581	679	693	677	567
25 to 54 years old..............................	81,748	958	1,144	1,263	1,136	895
55 years old and over...........................	25,070	1,001	1,237	1,301	1,233	935
SEX						
Men...	65,007	1,007	1,254	1,374	1,243	945
Women...	52,577	821	1,029	1,016	1,029	749
RACE/ETHNICITY						
White...	90,194	945	1,156	1,232	1,151	877
Black or African American.......................	15,460	735	903	971	896	701
Asian...	7,898	1,174	1,430	1,713	1,396	1,131
Hispanic or Latino..............................	21,227	706	960	950	960	678
EDUCATIONAL ATTAINMENT						
Workers, 25 years old and over..................	106,818	969	1,160	1,267	1,152	904
Less than a high school diploma.................	7,011	592	712	751	709	585
High school graduates, no college [3]...........	26,756	746	853	898	846	733
Some college or associate degree................	27,279	856	927	977	921	830
Bachelor's degree and higher....................	45,772	1,367	1,393	1,663	1,370	1,354

[1] A person may have more than one certification or license. [2] Persons with a license may also have a certification. [3] Includes persons with a high school diploma or equivalent.

Source: U.S. Bureau of Labor Statistics, "Labor Force Statistics from the Current Population Survey," <http://www.bls.gov/cps/certifications-and-licenses.htm>, accessed August 2020.

Table 688. Average Hours Spent Per Day on Primary Activities by Married Mothers and Fathers by Employment Status: 2015 to 2019

[Data are shown for households with own children under age 18. Data are averages for the 2015-2019 period and cover an individual's main activity. Does not include secondary activities done simultaneously]

Activity	Both spouses work full time		Mother employed part time and father employed full time		Mother not employed and father employed full time	
	Mothers	Fathers	Mothers	Fathers	Mothers	Fathers
Total, all activities........................	24.00	24.00	24.00	24.00	24.00	24.00
Personal care activities......................	9.20	8.63	9.21	8.60	9.59	8.90
Sleeping...................................	8.37	8.04	8.49	7.99	8.93	8.27
Household activities........................	1.88	1.37	2.71	1.30	3.82	1.00
Housework..............................	0.73	0.27	1.05	0.22	1.60	0.16
Food preparation and cleanup.............	0.83	0.42	1.22	0.41	1.75	0.30
Lawn and garden care....................	0.05	0.24	0.08	0.23	0.11	0.19
Purchasing goods and services..............	0.49	0.34	0.56	0.29	0.64	0.35
Grocery shopping........................	0.14	0.07	0.17	0.05	0.22	0.07
Consumer goods purchases, except grocery shopping........	0.27	0.21	0.30	0.20	0.34	0.22
Caring for and helping household members..............	1.43	0.94	1.97	0.89	2.73	0.88
Caring for and helping household children......	1.41	0.91	1.95	0.88	2.71	0.86
Physical care...........................	0.61	0.31	0.71	0.29	1.01	0.23
Education-related activities...............	0.10	0.07	0.23	0.04	0.28	0.06
Reading to/with children.................	0.05	0.03	0.08	0.04	0.09	0.03
Playing/doing hobbies with children.......	0.28	0.27	0.39	0.28	0.63	0.33
Working and work-related activities [1].......	5.10	6.14	2.92	6.33	0.05	6.37
Working [1]...............................	5.08	6.11	2.88	6.31	0.02	6.35
Leisure and sports........................	2.86	3.60	3.19	3.45	3.71	3.31
Socializing and communicating.............	0.57	0.57	0.65	0.61	0.81	0.71
Watching television......................	1.45	1.98	1.45	1.81	1.84	1.68
Participating in sports, exercise, and recreation........	0.19	0.28	0.25	0.33	0.25	0.25
Travel....................................	1.40	1.41	1.40	1.45	1.17	1.45
Travel related to caring for/helping household children........	0.26	0.16	0.33	0.14	0.32	0.09
Other activities, not elsewhere classified........	1.63	1.57	2.04	1.70	2.28	1.74

[1] Estimates include a small amount of work time done by persons who do not meet the American Time Use Survey definition of employed.

Source: U.S. Bureau of Labor Statistics, "American Time Use Survey," <http://www.bls.gov/tus/#tables>, accessed August 2020.

Table 689. Workers With Access to Unmarried Domestic Partner Benefits for Partners of Same and Opposite Sex by Selected Characteristics: 2011 to 2019

[In percent. All workers = 100 percent. As of March. For employees in private industry. Based on National Compensation Survey (NCS). See headnote, Table 692, and Appendix III. See Table 169 for data on health benefit program participation]

Characteristic	Defined benefit retirement survivor benefits for partners						Healthcare benefits for partners					
	Same sex			Opposite sex			Same sex			Opposite sex		
	2011	2018	2019	2011	2018	2019	2011	2018	2019	2011	2018	2019
Total........................	**7**	**11**	**10**	**7**	**10**	**10**	**29**	**40**	**41**	**25**	**36**	**38**
WORKER CHARACTERISTICS												
Management, professional, and related........................	11	17	16	10	17	16	46	58	60	38	54	55
Service..............................	3	4	4	3	4	4	17	22	23	14	21	23
Sales and office.......................	8	10	10	7	10	9	30	41	43	26	38	40
Natural resources, construction, and maintenance........................	8	10	9	7	8	7	22	32	33	18	29	31
Production, transportation, and material moving.......................	8	12	11	7	11	10	25	35	37	21	31	34
Full-time [1]...........................	9	13	12	8	12	11	36	48	49	31	44	46
Part-time [1]...........................	4	5	5	4	5	5	9	16	17	8	16	17
Union [2]..............................	25	36	37	22	30	31	46	60	62	31	46	52
Nonunion [2]..........................	6	8	8	5	8	8	28	38	39	24	35	37
AVERAGE HOURLY WAGE [3]												
Lowest 25 percent (under $13.25)........	2	3	3	2	3	3	11	19	19	9	18	19
Lowest 10 percent (under $10.48)......	1	1	1	1	1	1	6	10	11	4	10	11
Second 25 percent ($13.25 to $19.00)....	5	8	7	5	8	7	26	38	39	23	36	37
Third 25 percent ($19.00 to $30.61)......	9	13	11	8	12	11	35	47	49	30	42	44
Highest 25 percent ($30.61 and over).....	15	22	21	14	21	21	50	62	65	41	56	59
Highest 10 percent ($48.28 and over)...	16	24	23	15	23	23	59	69	72	49	61	64
ESTABLISHMENT CHARACTERISTICS												
1 to 99 workers.......................	3	5	5	3	5	5	18	27	29	16	26	28
100 or more workers...................	12	18	17	12	17	16	42	55	56	34	48	51
Goods producing [4]...................	6	10	10	6	9	9	27	37	39	24	35	37
Service producing [4]...................	8	11	10	7	11	10	30	41	42	25	37	39

[1] Employees are classified as working either a full-time or part-time schedule based on the definition used by each establishment. [2] See footnote 6, Table 692. [3] The National Compensation Survey—Benefits program presents wage data in percentiles rather than dollar amounts; 2019 average wages shown here; for calculation detail, see "Technical Note" in source. [4] See Table 665 for composition of goods- and service-producing industries.

Source: U.S. Bureau of Labor Statistics, *National Compensation Survey: Employee Benefits in the United States, March 2019*, Bulletin 2791, September 2019, and earlier reports. See also <https://www.bls.gov/ncs/ebs/benefits/2019/home.htm>.

Table 690. Employer Costs for Employee Compensation Per Hour Worked: 2019

[In dollars. As of December. Based on the National Compensation Survey (NCS). See Appendix III]

Compensation component	Total civilian workers	State and local govern- ment workers	Private industry workers						
			Total	Goods produc- ing [1]	Service provid- ing [2]	Union workers	Non- union workers	1–99 workers	100 workers or more
Total compensation.....................	**37.10**	**52.14**	**34.72**	**39.91**	**33.68**	**48.15**	**33.53**	**28.77**	**41.75**
Wages and salaries............................	25.47	32.50	24.36	26.80	23.87	28.62	23.98	21.27	28.01
Total benefits................................	11.63	19.63	10.37	13.11	9.81	19.53	9.55	7.50	13.75
Paid leave [3]................................	2.72	3.89	2.53	2.57	2.52	3.42	2.45	1.78	3.42
Vacation...................................	1.33	1.47	1.30	1.31	1.30	1.74	1.26	0.89	1.79
Holiday....................................	0.80	1.11	0.75	0.88	0.73	1.01	0.73	0.56	0.97
Sick.......................................	0.43	1.01	0.34	0.30	0.35	0.50	0.33	0.23	0.47
Supplemental pay [3]........................	1.09	0.51	1.19	1.74	1.07	1.72	1.14	0.74	1.71
Overtime [4]................................	0.30	0.22	0.31	0.70	0.24	0.89	0.26	0.24	0.40
Insurance [3]................................	3.22	6.08	2.76	3.68	2.58	6.78	2.41	1.89	3.79
Health insurance...........................	3.06	5.93	2.61	3.47	2.44	6.45	2.27	1.80	3.57
Retirement and savings.....................	1.92	6.30	1.22	1.77	1.11	3.97	0.98	0.70	1.85
Defined benefit............................	1.17	5.85	0.42	0.78	0.35	2.68	0.22	0.21	0.68
Defined contributions......................	0.75	0.45	0.80	0.99	0.76	1.29	0.76	0.49	1.16
Legally required............................	2.69	2.86	2.66	3.35	2.52	3.65	2.57	2.39	2.98
Social Security and Medicare..............	2.07	2.24	2.05	2.31	1.99	2.51	2.01	1.78	2.36
Social Security [5].........................	1.65	1.71	1.64	1.86	1.60	2.02	1.61	1.43	1.89
Medicare..................................	0.42	0.53	0.41	0.45	0.40	0.49	0.40	0.35	0.48
Federal unemployment.....................	0.02	([6])	0.03	0.02	0.03	0.03	0.03	0.03	0.02
State unemployment.......................	0.13	0.06	0.14	0.18	0.13	0.18	0.14	0.14	0.14
Workers' compensation...................	0.46	0.56	0.45	0.84	0.37	0.93	0.40	0.45	0.45

[1] Based on the 2012 North American Industry Classification System (NAICS). See text, this section. Includes mining, construction, and manufacturing. Excludes the agriculture, forestry, farming, and hunting sector. [2] Based on the 2012 NAICS. Includes utilities; wholesale and retail trade; transportation and warehousing; information; finance and insurance; real estate and rental and leasing; professional and technical services; management of companies and enterprises, administrative and waste services; education services; health care and social assistance; arts, entertainment, and recreation; accommodations and food services; and other services, except public administration. [3] Includes costs for other items not shown separately. [4] Includes premium pay for work in addition to regular work schedule, such as, overtime, weekends, and holidays. [5] Comprises the Old-Age, Survivors, and Disability Insurance Program (OASDI). [6] Cost per hour worked is $0.01 or less.

Source: U.S. Bureau of Labor Statistics, *Employer Costs for Employee Compensation—December 2019*, USDL 20-0451, March 2020. See also <http://www.bls.gov/ncs/ect/home.htm>.

Table 691. Workers With Access to Retirement and Health Care Benefits by Selected Characteristics: 2019

[In percent. All workers = 100 percent. As of March. For employees in private industry. Based on National Compensation Survey (NCS). See headnote, Table 692, and Appendix III. See Table 169 for data on health benefit program participation]

Characteristic	Retirement benefits			Healthcare benefits			
	All plans [1]	Defined benefit [2]	Defined contribu- tion [2]	Medical care	Dental care	Vision care	Outpatient prescription drug coverage
Total.........................	**67**	**16**	**64**	**69**	**43**	**26**	**67**
WORKER CHARACTERISTICS							
Management, professional, and related................	84	23	81	86	62	37	85
Service..	43	7	39	43	24	14	42
Sales and office...............................	72	14	69	67	39	22	66
Natural resources, construction, and maintenance................................	61	18	56	72	36	26	71
Production, transportation, and material moving......	72	20	65	76	46	29	75
Full-time [3].....................................	77	19	73	84	53	32	83
Part-time [3]....................................	39	8	35	21	12	8	21
Union [4].......................................	91	66	58	94	72	56	92
Nonunion [4]..................................	65	11	64	66	40	23	65
AVERAGE HOURLY WAGE [5]							
Lowest 25 percent (under $13.25).....................	43	5	40	36	16	9	35
Lowest 10 percent (under $10.48)..................	31	2	30	24	10	6	23
Second 25 percent ($13.25 to $19.00).................	67	12	63	70	39	23	69
Third 25 percent ($19.00 to $30.61)...................	80	20	75	86	55	34	84
Highest 25 percent ($30.61 and over)................	87	32	82	91	67	42	90
Highest 10 percent ($48.28 and over)...............	88	33	85	94	73	46	93
ESTABLISHMENT CHARACTERISTICS							
1 to 99 workers..	54	7	52	55	30	18	54
100 or more workers.....................................	84	27	78	85	58	35	84
Goods producing [6]...................................	76	21	73	85	52	33	84
Service producing [6].................................	66	15	62	65	41	24	64

[1] Employees may have access to defined benefit and/or defined contribution plans. Total excludes duplication. [2] A defined benefit plan is a retirement plan that uses a specific, predetermined formula to calculate the amount of an employee's guaranteed future benefit. A defined contribution plan provides benefits based on employer and employee contributions to individual employee accounts and the rate of return on money invested; the retirement benefit depends on the account balance at retirement. [3] Employees are classified as working either a full-time or part-time schedule based on the definition used by each establishment. [4] See footnote 6, Table 692. [5] The National Compensation Survey—Benefits program presents wage data in percentiles rather than dollar amounts; for calculation detail, see "Technical Note" in source. [6] See Table 665 for composition of goods- and service-producing industries.

Source: U.S. Bureau of Labor Statistics, *National Compensation Survey: Employee Benefits in the United States, March 2019*, Bulletin 2791, March 2019. See also <http://www.bls.gov/ncs/ebs/benefits/2019/home.htm>.

Table 692. Workers With Access to Selected Employee Benefits: 2019

[In percent. All workers = 100 percent. As of March. For employees in private industry. Based on National Compensation Survey (NCS). The NCS benefits survey obtained data from 6,470 private industry establishments of all sizes, representing approximately 120.4 million workers. Excludes agricultural establishments, private households, and the self-employed. An employee has access to a benefit plan if the plan is made available by the employer, regardless of whether the employee participates in the plan. See Appendix III. See also <https://www.bls.gov/ncs/ebs/national-compensation-survey-glossary-of-employee-benefit-terms.htm> for glossary of terms]

Characteristic	Leave benefits						Quality of life benefits			Nonproduction bonuses	
	Paid holidays	Paid sick leave	Paid vacation	Paid jury duty leave	Family leave [1] Paid	Family leave [1] Unpaid	Employer assistance for child care [2]	Flexible work-place [3]	Subsidized commuting	All non-production bonuses [4]	End of year bonus
Total	**79**	**73**	**79**	**56**	**18**	**88**	**10**	**7**	**7**	**40**	**11**
WORKER CHARACTERISTIC											
Management, professional, and related occupations	91	90	90	76	30	93	18	18	14	48	15
Service occupations	56	58	60	34	12	82	8	1	5	25	7
Sales and office occupations	83	75	80	57	18	89	8	7	6	43	11
Natural resources, construction, and maintenance occupations	79	66	77	42	11	83	7	1	3	42	15
Production, transportation, and material moving occupations	86	69	84	58	9	89	5	2	3	40	9
Full-time [5]	90	83	91	66	21	90	12	9	9	45	13
Part-time [5]	47	43	42	25	8	81	5	2	3	23	6
Union [6]	91	86	89	77	17	93	17	2	9	31	4
Nonunion [6]	78	72	78	54	18	87	9	8	7	40	12
AVERAGE HOURLY WAGE [7]											
Lowest 25 percent (under $13.25)	56	47	55	30	8	81	4	1	3	26	6
Lowest 10 percent (under $10.48)	41	30	42	24	5	79	4	(S)	3	22	7
Second 25 percent ($13.25 to $19.00)	82	77	82	55	17	88	6	4	5	39	11
Third 25 percent ($19.00 to $30.61)	91	86	91	68	20	90	10	8	8	47	14
Highest 25 percent ($30.61 and over)	93	90	92	77	30	94	21	19	14	50	15
Highest 10 percent ($48.28 and over)	94	93	94	80	35	95	25	25	19	51	16
ESTABLISHMENT CHARACTERISTICS											
1 to 99 workers	72	65	71	43	14	82	5	6	5	37	13
100 or more workers	88	84	88	70	23	95	16	9	10	43	8
Goods producing [8]	89	72	88	58	12	87	9	6	4	49	16
Service producing [8]	77	73	77	55	19	88	10	7	8	38	10
GEOGRAPHIC AREA [9]											
New England	77	81	76	64	23	90	17	11	12	40	18
Middle Atlantic	80	75	77	67	26	87	13	7	10	38	11
South Atlantic	78	68	78	56	14	85	11	8	8	44	13
East South Central	80	62	78	59	13	86	6	6	2	44	9
West South Central	80	71	79	56	17	87	9	7	6	43	15
East North Central	76	65	77	54	16	88	8	7	4	42	10
West North Central	78	70	77	56	13	92	7	6	5	37	9
Mountain	82	75	83	54	21	91	8	8	7	37	9
Pacific	81	91	81	44	20	89	10	6	11	31	7

S Indicates no workers in this category or data did not meet publication criteria. [1] Some workers may have access to both types of plans. [2] A workplace program that provides for either the full or partial cost of caring for an employee's children in a nursery, day care center, or a babysitter in facilities either on or off the employer's premises. [3] Permits employees to work an agreed-upon portion of their work schedule at home or at some other approved location. [4] Includes cash profit-sharing, employee recognition, end-of-year, holiday, payment in lieu of benefits, longevity, referral, and all other bonuses. [5] Employees are classified as working either a full-time or part-time schedule based on the definition used by each establishment. [6] Union workers are those whose wages are determined through collective bargaining. [7] The National Compensation Survey—Benefits program presents wage data in percentiles rather than dollar amounts; see "Technical Note" in source. [8] See Table 665, for composition of goods- and service-producing industries. [9] For composition of census divisions, see inside front cover.

Source: U.S. Bureau of Labor Statistics, *National Compensation Survey: Employee Benefits in the United States, March 2019*, Bulletin 2791, September 2019. See also <http://www.bls.gov/ncs/ebs/benefits/2019/home.htm>.

Labor Force, Employment, and Earnings

Table 693. Industries With the Highest Total Case Incidence Rates for Nonfatal Injuries and Illnesses: 2018

[Rates per 100 full-time employees. Private industry unless otherwise noted. Incidence rates refer to any Occupational Safety & Health Administration (OSHA)-recordable occupational injury or illness, whether or not it resulted in days away from work, job transfer, or restriction. Incidence rates were calculated as: number of injuries and illnesses divided by total hours worked by all employees during the year multiplied by 200,000 as base for 100 full-time equivalent workers (working 40 hours per week, 50 weeks per year)]

Industry	2012 NAICS code [1]	Inci- dence rate	Industry	2012 NAICS code [1]	Inci- dence rate
All industries, including State and local government [2]	(X)	3.1	Consumer electronics and appliances rental...........	53221	8.2
Nursing and residential care facilities [3].........	623	11.9	Hospitals [3]..	622	8.1
Pet care (except veterinary) services............	81291	11.4	All other misc. wood product manufacturing............	321999	7.8
Veterinary services...............................	54194	10.4	Hog and pig farming...................................	1122	7.7
Steel foundries (except investment).............	331513	10.2	Interurban and rural bus transportation.................	4852	7.7
Skiing facilities..................................	71392	10.0	Concrete block and brick manufacturing...............	327331	7.5
Manufactured home (mobile home) manufacturing..................................	321991	9.7	Ambulance services..................................	62191	7.5
Travel trailer and camper manufacturing........	336214	9.3	Psychiatric and substance abuse hospitals...........	6222	7.4
Motor home manufacturing......................	336213	9.2	Pet and pet supplies stores...........................	45391	7.3
Other animal production..........................	1129	8.9	Nursing and residential care facilities [4].................	623	7.3
Beef cattle ranching and farming, including feedlots......................................	11211	8.5	Correctional institutions [3]............................	92214	7.3
Aluminum foundries (except die-casting).......	331524	8.5	Ice cream and frozen dessert manufacturing...........	31152	7.2
Couriers and express delivery services.........	4921	8.2	Truss manufacturing..................................	321214	7.1
			Truck trailer manufacturing.............................	336212	7.1

X Not applicable. [1] Based on the North American Industry Classification System, 2012 (NAICS). See text, this section. [2] Excludes farms with fewer than 11 employees. [3] State government. [4] Local government.

Source: U.S. Bureau of Labor Statistics, Industry Injury and Illness Data, "Supplemental News Release Tables," <http://www.bls.gov/iif/oshsum.htm>, accessed December 2019.

Table 694. Nonfatal Occupational Injuries and Illnesses by Industry: 2017 and 2018

[3,475.9 represents 3,475,900. Rates per 100 full-time employees. Except as noted, data refer to any Occupational Safety and Health Administration (OSHA) recordable occupational injury or illness, whether or not it resulted in days away from work, job transfer, or restriction. Incidence rates were calculated as: number of injuries and illnesses divided by total hours worked by all employees during the year multiplied by 200,000 as base for 100 full-time equivalent workers (working 40 hours, per week, 50 weeks per year)]

Industry	2012 NAICS code [1]	Number of cases (1,000)		Incidence rate of cases	
		2017	2018	2017	2018
Total...................	(X)	**3,475.9**	**3,544.4**	**3.1**	**3.1**
Private industry [2]...................	(X)	**2,811.5**	**2,834.5**	**2.8**	**2.8**
Agriculture, forestry, fishing, hunting [2]...............	11	50.2	54.4	5.0	5.3
Mining [3]...............................	21	10.2	9.8	1.5	1.4
Construction............................	23	198.1	199.1	3.1	3.0
Manufacturing..........................	31–33	428.9	430.3	3.5	3.4
Wholesale trade........................	42	157.9	160.8	2.8	2.9
Retail trade.............................	44–45	395.7	409.9	3.3	3.5
Transportation and warehousing [4]...............	48–49	215.7	221.4	4.6	4.5
Utilities.................................	22	11.2	10.6	2.0	1.9
Information.............................	51	33.7	33.3	1.3	1.3
Finance and insurance..................	52	27.5	28.5	0.5	0.5
Real estate and rental and leasing......	53	46.6	46.1	2.4	2.3
Professional, scientific, and technical services...............	54	69.6	70.5	0.8	0.8
Management of companies and enterprises.................	55	20.6	17.5	0.9	0.8
Administrative and support & waste management and remediation services.............	56	116.9	118.6	2.2	2.3
Educational services....................	61	38.5	36.9	1.9	1.9
Health care and social assistance............	62	582.8	577.4	4.1	3.9
Arts, entertainment, and recreation............	71	58.9	57.9	4.2	4.1
Accommodation and food services............	72	282.6	278.5	3.2	3.1
Other services, except public administration..........	81	66.0	72.8	2.1	2.2
State and local government [2]...............	(X)	**664.3**	**709.9**	**4.6**	**4.8**
State government........................	(X)	143.9	141.3	3.6	3.6
Local government.......................	(X)	520.4	568.6	5.0	5.3

X Not applicable. [1] North American Industry Classification System, 2012; see text, this section. [2] Excludes farms with fewer than 11 employees. [3] Data for Mining (2012 NAICS Sector 21) include establishments not governed by the Mine Safety and Health Administration rules and reporting, such as those in Oil and Gas Extraction and related support activities. Data for mining operators in coal, metal, and nonmetal mining are provided to BLS by the Mine Safety and Health Administration, U.S. Department of Labor. Independent mining contractors are excluded from the coal, metal, and nonmetal mining industries. These data do not reflect the changes the Occupational Safety and Health Administration made to its recordkeeping requirements effective January 1, 2002; therefore, estimates for these industries are not comparable to estimates in other industries. [4] Data for employers in railroad transportation are provided to BLS by the Federal Railroad Administration, U.S. Department of Transportation.

Source: U.S. Bureau of Labor Statistics, "Employer-Reported Workplace Injuries and Illnesses – 2018, Supplemental Files, Summary Tables," <https://www.bls.gov/news.release/osh.toc.htm>, accessed April 2020.

Table 695. Fatal Work Injuries by Event or Exposure: 2018

[For the 50 states and the District of Columbia. Based on the Census of Fatal Occupational Injuries. For details, see source]

Event or exposure	Number of fatalities	Percent distribution	Event or exposure	Number of fatalities	Percent distribution
Total [1]	**5,250**	**100**	Contacts with objects and equipment [1]	786	15
Transportation incidents [1]	2,080	40	Struck by object or equipment [1]	566	11
Roadway incident [1]	1,276	24	Struck by falling object or equipment	278	5
Collision between motor vehicles [2]	677	13	Struck by flying object	32	1
Noncollision incidents	222	4	Caught in or compressed by equipment		
Nonroadway incident	225	4	or objects	137	3
Aircraft accidents	133	3	Caught in or crushed in collapsing materials	73	1
Pedestrians struck by a vehicle [2]	325	6	Falls	791	15
Water vehicle accidents	58	1	Exposure to harmful substances or		
Railway accidents	48	1	environments [1]	621	12
Assaults and violent acts [1]	828	16	Contact with electric current	160	3
Homicides [1]	453	9	Exposure to caustic, noxious or allergenic		
Shooting	351	7	substances	355	7
Stabbing	44	1	Oxygen deficiency	46	1
Self-inflicted injury	304	6	Fires and explosions	115	2

[1] Includes other causes, not shown separately. [2] Including mobile equipment.

Source: U.S. Bureau of Labor Statistics, "Census of Fatal Occupational Injuries—Current and Revised Data," <http://www.bls.gov/iif/oshcfoi1.htm>, accessed April 2020.

Table 696. Worker Fatalities on the Job by Industry and Occupation: 2018

[Excludes homicides and suicides]

Industry group	Deaths Number	Deaths Rate [1]	Occupations with highest fatal work injury rates	Deaths Number	Deaths Rate [1]
Total	**5,250**	**3.5**	Logging workers	56	97.6
			Fishers & related fishing workers	30	77.4
			Aircraft pilots & flight engineers	70	58.9
Agriculture [2]	574	23.4	Roofers	96	51.5
Mining [3]	130	14.1	Refuse & recyclable material collectors	37	44.3
Construction	1,008	9.5	Driver/sales workers & truck drivers	966	26.0
Manufacturing	343	2.2	Farmers, ranchers, & other agricultural managers	257	24.7
Wholesale trade	202	5.3	Structural iron & steel workers	15	23.6
Retail trade	274	1.9	First-line supervisors of construction trades &		
Transportation & warehousing	874	14.0	extraction workers	144	21.0
Utilities	29	2.6	First-line supervisors of landscaping, lawn service, &		
Information	31	1.2	groundskeeping workers	48	20.2
Financial activities [4]	108	1.1	Electrical power-line installers & repairers	29	19.3
Professional & business services [4]	585	3.3	Grounds maintenance workers	225	18.6
Educational & health services	168	0.7	Miscellaneous agricultural workers	157	18.0
Leisure & hospitality [4]	253	2.2	Helpers, construction trades	11	15.8
Other services [5]	195	2.6	First-line supervisors of mechanics, installers, & repairers	46	15.1
Government	471	1.8	Transportation & material moving occupations	1,443	15.0

[1] The rate represents the number of fatal occupational injuries per 100,000 full-time equivalent workers. [2] Includes forestry, fishing, and hunting. [3] Includes oil and gas extraction. [4] For composition of industry, see Table 665. [5] Excludes public service administration.

Source: U.S. Bureau of Labor Statistics, Census of Fatal Occupational Injuries, "Fatal Injury Rates," <http://stats.bls.gov/iif/oshcfoi1.htm#rates>, accessed April 2020.

Table 697. Nonfatal Occupational Injury and Illness Cases in Private Industry by Type of Injury or Illness and Days Away from Work: 2018

[900.4 represents 900,400. Covers work-related injuries and illnesses involving one or more days of missed work]

Type of work-related injury or illness	Number of injury or illness cases (1,000)								Median number of days away from work
	All cases	1 day	2 days	3-5 days	6-10 days	11-20 days	21-30 days	31 days or more	
Total [1]	**900.4**	**124.0**	**97.4**	**158.5**	**107.6**	**95.4**	**54.4**	**263.1**	**8**
Traumatic injuries and disorders	875.6	120.4	94.9	154.7	105.2	92.4	52.9	255.1	8
Fractures	79.5	3.6	3.8	7.1	7.9	8.5	6.2	42.4	35
Sprains, strains, tears	308.6	31.2	28.8	55.0	39.4	34.2	19.7	100.3	10
Hernia	10.3	0.2	0.3	0.6	1.0	1.9	1.9	4.4	26
Concussions	16.2	2.1	1.5	3.7	2.6	1.7	1.0	3.7	7
Soreness, pain, hurt-nonspecified injury	159.6	22.9	18.9	28.5	18.4	15.3	9.6	46.1	8
Disease and disorders of body systems	13.9	1.3	1.1	1.8	1.5	2.0	1.0	5.3	16
Carpal tunnel syndrome	5.1	0.2	0.3	0.5	0.3	0.8	0.5	2.5	30
Disorders of the eye, adnexa, vision	0.7	0.2	0.1	0.2	0.1	(Z)	(S)	0.1	3
Infectious and parasitic diseases	1.7	0.3	0.5	0.4	0.3	0.1	(Z)	(Z)	3
Mental disorders or syndromes	2.6	0.1	0.1	0.1	0.2	0.3	0.3	1.5	50

Z Less than 50 cases. S Data do not meet publication guidelines. [1] Total includes unclassified and ill-defined conditions.

Source: U.S. Bureau of Labor Statistics, Survey of Occupational Injuries and Illnesses, 2018 Resource Tables, "R.67. Detailed nature by number of days away from work," <https://stats.bls.gov/iif/oshcdnew2018.htm>, accessed December 2019.

Table 698. Labor Union Membership by Sector: 1990 to 2019

[16,740 represents 16,740,000. Annual averages of monthly figures. For wage and salary workers in agriculture and nonagricultural industries. Data represent union members by place of residence. Based on the Current Population Survey and subject to sampling error. For methodological details, see source]

Sector	1990	2000	2010	2013	2014	2015	2016	2017	2018	2019
TOTAL (1,000)										
Wage and salary workers:										
Union members..............	16,740	16,258	14,715	14,516	14,570	14,786	14,550	14,812	14,740	14,567
Covered by unions..............	19,058	17,944	16,290	16,016	16,142	16,433	16,265	16,436	16,374	16,375
Public sector workers:										
Union members..............	6,485	7,111	7,623	7,203	7,214	7,234	7,113	7,211	7,162	7,862
Covered by unions..............	7,691	7,976	8,406	7,894	7,923	8,023	7,827	7,945	7,059	7,813
Private sector workers:										
Union members..............	10,255	9,148	7,092	7,313	7,356	7,552	7,436	7,600	7,578	7,508
Covered by unions..............	11,366	9,969	7,884	8,122	8,219	8,410	8,438	8,491	8,512	8,562
PERCENT										
Wage and salary workers:										
Union members..............	16.1	13.5	11.9	11.2	11.1	11.1	10.7	10.7	10.5	10.3
Covered by unions..............	18.3	14.9	13.1	12.4	12.3	12.3	11.9	11.9	11.7	11.6
Public sector workers:										
Union members..............	36.5	37.5	36.2	35.3	35.7	35.2	34.4	34.4	33.9	33.6
Covered by unions..............	43.3	42.0	40.0	38.7	39.2	39.0	37.9	37.9	37.2	37.2
Private sector workers:										
Union members..............	11.9	9.0	6.9	6.7	6.6	6.7	6.4	6.5	6.4	6.2
Covered by unions..............	13.2	9.8	7.7	7.5	7.4	7.4	7.3	7.3	7.2	7.1

Source: *Union Membership and Coverage Database from the Current Population Survey*, accessed at <http://unionstats.com>, authored by Barry Hirsch of Georgia State University and David Macpherson of Trinity University. Copyright 2020.

Table 699. Labor Union Members by Selected Characteristics: 2019

[In units as indicated (141,737 represents 141,737,000). Annual averages of monthly data. Covers employed wage and salary workers 16 years old and over. Excludes self-employed workers whose businesses are incorporated and not incorporated. Based on Current Population Survey; see text, Section 1 and Appendix III]

Characteristic	Employed wage and salary workers			Median usual weekly earnings [3] (dollars)			
		Percent					
	Total (1,000)	Union members [1]	Repre-sented by union [2]	Total	Union members [1]	Repre-sented by union [2]	Not repre-sented by union
Total [4].............	**141,737**	**10.3**	**11.6**	**917**	**1,095**	**1,082**	**892**
SEX							
Men.............	73,349	10.8	12.1	1,007	1,147	1,139	986
Women.............	68,388	9.7	11.0	821	1,018	1,004	792
AGE							
16 to 24 years old.............	18,869	4.4	5.2	581	692	684	575
25 to 34 years old.............	33,718	8.8	10.3	846	980	970	827
35 to 44 years old.............	29,898	11.8	13.1	1,035	1,203	1,196	1,007
45 to 54 years old.............	28,191	12.6	13.9	1,033	1,174	1,160	1,008
55 to 64 years old.............	23,207	12.7	14.1	1,017	1,136	1,132	999
65 years and over.............	7,854	9.7	10.9	936	1,006	1,016	920
RACE/ETHNICITY							
White [5].............	109,132	10.3	11.5	945	1,127	1,115	917
Men.............	57,537	10.9	12.1	1,036	1,181	1,173	1,012
Women.............	51,594	9.6	10.9	840	1,044	1,023	810
Black [5].............	18,231	11.2	12.7	735	905	901	711
Men.............	8,440	11.9	13.4	769	948	930	746
Women.............	9,791	10.6	12.0	704	874	875	683
Asian [5].............	9,291	8.8	10.0	1,174	1,173	1,158	1,179
Men.............	4,795	8.0	9.1	1,336	1,151	1,135	1,357
Women.............	4,496	9.6	11.0	1,025	1,216	1,180	995
Hispanic [6].............	25,417	8.9	10.2	706	954	926	686
Men.............	14,100	9.3	10.6	747	1,009	992	722
Women.............	11,317	8.4	9.7	642	875	845	622
INDUSTRY [7]							
Private sector.............	120,714	6.2	7.1	893	1,025	1,013	881
Mining.............	710	4.0	4.7	1,423	(B)	(B)	1,410
Construction.............	8,352	12.6	13.6	909	1,257	1,240	868
Manufacturing.............	15,070	8.6	9.4	936	962	962	933
Wholesale and retail trade.............	18,113	4.1	4.8	748	790	779	746
Transportation and utilities.............	6,745	17.3	18.7	906	1,184	1,151	862
Information.............	2,352	10.3	11.2	1,182	1,265	1,214	1,174
Financial activities.............	9,364	1.9	2.5	1,125	950	980	1,128
Professional and business services.......	15,720	2.2	3.0	1,149	903	918	1,155
Education and health services.............	23,690	8.0	9.2	896	1,059	1,051	879
Leisure and hospitality.............	13,097	2.9	3.5	601	722	698	597
Other services.............	6,150	2.8	3.3	762	1,091	1,098	752
Public sector.............	21,023	33.6	37.2	1,043	1,147	1,141	973

B Base is less than 50,000. [1] Members of a labor union or an employee association similar to a labor union. [2] Members of a labor union or an employee association similar to a union as well as workers who report no union affiliation but whose jobs are covered by a union or an employee association contract. [3] For full-time employed wage and salary workers. [4] Includes other races not shown separately. Also includes a small number of multiple jobholders whose full- and part-time status cannot be determined for their principal job. [5] For persons in this race group only. [6] Persons of Hispanic origin may be of any race. [7] For composition of industries, see Table 665.

Source: U.S. Bureau of Labor Statistics, *Union Members—2019*, USDL 20-0108, January 2020. See also <http://www.bls.gov/news.release/union2.toc.htm>.

Table 700. Labor Union Membership by State: 2010 and 2019

[Annual averages of monthly figures (14,715.1 represents 14,715,100). For wage and salary workers in agriculture and nonagricultural industries. Data represent union members by place of residence. Based on the Current Population Survey and subject to sampling error. For methodological details, see source]

State	Union members (1,000)		Workers covered by unions (1,000)		Percent of workers					
					Union members		Covered by unions		Private sector union members	
	2010	2019	2010	2019	2010	2019	2010	2019	2010	2019
United States......	**14,715.1**	**14,566.7**	**16,289.5**	**16,374.9**	**11.9**	**10.3**	**13.1**	**11.6**	**6.9**	**6.2**
Alabama [1]............	183.3	173.8	202.8	200.2	10.1	8.5	11.2	9.8	5.7	6.5
Alaska..............	67.6	48.4	73.0	52.8	22.9	17.1	24.8	18.7	11.2	8.4
Arizona [1]............	161.0	173.8	203.0	214.3	6.4	5.7	8.1	7.1	3.6	3.4
Arkansas [1]...........	43.6	61.7	58.6	70.8	4.0	5.1	5.4	5.9	2.7	4.3
California.............	2,431.3	2,499.5	2,577.8	2,721.6	17.5	15.1	18.6	16.5	9.3	8.8
Colorado.............	140.4	238.5	170.9	260.1	6.6	9.1	8.0	9.9	3.8	6.0
Connecticut..........	258.3	243.8	269.7	268.3	16.7	14.5	17.4	16.0	8.3	7.1
Delaware.............	40.2	37.7	43.9	42.9	11.4	8.7	12.5	9.9	5.8	4.4
District of Columbia..	25.9	33.6	30.0	36.9	9.0	9.3	10.5	10.2	5.9	5.3
Florida [1]..............	391.8	551.0	488.0	666.6	5.6	6.2	6.9	7.5	2.3	3.0
Georgia [1]............	153.3	179.5	191.3	222.2	4.0	4.1	5.0	5.0	2.5	3.2
Hawaii...............	111.3	134.5	120.3	146.4	21.8	23.4	23.5	25.4	14.6	14.6
Idaho [1]..............	41.5	37.6	50.1	46.3	7.1	4.9	8.6	6.1	3.6	3.0
Illinois...............	843.8	771.5	891.2	833.1	15.5	13.6	16.4	14.7	9.5	8.9
Indiana [3]............	278.6	248.8	312.8	295.1	10.9	8.3	12.2	9.8	8.2	6.7
Iowa [1]..............	158.2	96.9	191.8	121.5	11.4	6.3	13.8	7.9	7.1	4.0
Kansas [1]............	83.7	111.1	111.0	129.3	6.8	8.7	9.1	10.1	4.5	5.6
Kentucky [6]..........	146.5	143.1	166.1	168.6	8.9	8.0	10.1	9.4	7.2	6.7
Louisiana [1]..........	75.6	94.1	96.0	107.5	4.3	5.3	5.5	6.0	3.2	3.4
Maine................	62.9	69.4	70.7	80.9	11.6	11.8	13.0	13.7	5.1	5.5
Maryland.............	296.1	328.8	328.8	370.5	11.6	11.3	12.9	12.7	6.1	4.6
Massachusetts.......	414.8	406.3	446.4	448.9	14.5	12.0	15.6	13.2	7.0	6.6
Michigan [3]..........	627.3	591.1	658.7	649.7	16.5	13.7	17.3	15.0	11.1	9.8
Minnesota...........	384.6	363.4	397.3	379.7	15.6	13.7	16.1	14.3	8.4	7.4
Mississippi [1].........	46.3	69.6	58.3	93.2	4.5	6.3	5.6	8.4	3.7	4.1
Missouri [7]............	244.3	296.3	274.4	332.3	9.9	11.1	11.1	12.5	8.5	8.2
Montana.............	46.1	46.0	52.2	52.2	12.7	10.5	14.4	12.0	5.6	5.3
Nebraska [1]...........	75.3	74.4	95.6	85.4	9.3	8.3	11.8	9.5	4.8	4.6
Nevada [1]............	151.3	200.7	169.9	221.3	15.0	14.6	16.8	16.1	10.8	11.6
New Hampshire......	63.2	69.5	72.6	78.6	10.2	10.3	11.7	11.6	4.4	5.2
New Jersey..........	636.9	642.2	660.0	711.8	17.1	15.7	17.7	17.4	9.0	8.0
New Mexico..........	54.8	57.6	72.4	71.8	7.3	7.1	9.7	8.8	2.6	3.6
New York.............	1,958.7	1,732.6	2,098.6	1,876.9	24.2	21.0	26.0	22.7	13.7	12.7
North Carolina [1]......	116.7	102.4	179.6	150.5	3.2	2.3	4.9	3.4	1.8	1.2
North Dakota [1].......	23.0	21.3	28.4	26.6	7.4	6.0	9.1	7.5	4.6	3.3
Ohio.................	654.9	610.3	701.9	672.9	13.7	11.9	14.7	13.1	8.4	6.9
Oklahoma [2]..........	77.4	96.6	98.5	123.4	5.5	6.2	6.9	7.9	3.5	3.1
Oregon..............	245.1	255.0	267.9	277.0	16.2	14.4	17.7	15.6	9.1	7.3
Pennsylvania.........	770.2	676.5	831.4	740.5	14.7	12.0	15.9	13.1	9.3	7.1
Rhode Island.........	74.9	82.5	79.4	90.1	16.4	17.4	17.4	19.0	8.4	10.0
South Carolina [1].....	79.6	47.1	106.8	58.6	4.6	2.2	6.2	2.7	2.7	1.3
South Dakota [1].......	20.0	22.0	23.5	26.4	5.6	5.6	6.6	6.7	3.0	2.6
Tennessee [1]..........	115.5	134.0	142.5	161.5	4.7	4.5	5.8	5.5	2.2	2.9
Texas [1]..............	545.4	496.9	676.7	642.1	5.4	4.0	6.7	5.2	3.2	2.5
Utah [1]...............	74.6	61.5	95.6	83.2	6.5	4.4	8.4	5.9	3.9	3.1
Vermont..............	34.2	32.6	39.5	34.8	11.8	11.3	13.6	12.0	5.3	5.3
Virginia [1]............	160.6	156.2	196.4	201.1	4.6	4.0	5.7	5.2	2.9	2.5
Washington...........	551.8	637.9	605.2	684.2	19.4	18.8	21.3	20.2	10.7	12.0
West Virginia [5].......	99.9	71.5	111.4	78.4	14.8	10.2	16.5	11.1	11.2	7.8
Wisconsin [4]..........	354.9	217.9	379.8	245.0	14.2	8.1	15.1	9.1	8.4	5.1
Wyoming [1]...........	18.1	17.6	20.7	21.1	7.4	7.3	8.4	8.7	4.9	5.1

[1] Right to work state as of 2000. [2] Passed right to work law in 2001. [3] Passed right to work law in 2012. [4] Passed right to work law in 2015. [5] Passed right to work law in 2016. [6] Passed right to work law in 2017. [7] Passed right to work law in 2017; rejected by voters 2018

Source: *Union Membership and Coverage Database from the Current Population Survey*, accessed at <http://unionstats.com>, authored by Barry Hirsch of Georgia State University and David Macpherson of Trinity University. Copyright 2020.

Table 701. Work Stoppages: 1960 to 2019

[896 represents 896,000. Excludes work stoppages involving fewer than 1,000 workers and lasting less than 1 day. The term "major work stoppage" includes both worker-initiated strikes and employer-initiated lockouts that involve 1,000 or more workers. Information is based on reports of labor disputes appearing in daily newspapers, trade journals, and other public sources]

Year	Number of work stop-pages [1]	Workers involved [2] (1,000)	Days idle total Number [3] (1,000)	Days idle total Percent estimated working time [4]	Year	Number of work stop-pages [1]	Workers involved [2] (1,000)	Days idle total Number [3] (1,000)	Days idle total Percent estimated working time [4]
1960........	222	896	13,260	0.09	2000........	39	394	20,419	0.06
1970........	381	2,468	52,761	0.29	2001........	29	99	1,151	(Z)
1980........	187	795	20,844	0.09	2002........	19	46	660	(Z)
1983........	81	909	17,461	0.08	2003........	14	129	4,091	0.01
1984........	62	376	8,499	0.04	2004........	17	171	3,344	0.01
1985........	54	324	7,079	0.03	2005........	22	100	1,736	0.01
1986........	69	533	11,861	0.05	2006........	20	70	2,688	0.01
1987........	46	174	4,481	0.02	2007........	21	189	1,265	(Z)
1988........	40	118	4,381	0.02	2008........	15	72	1,954	0.01
1989........	51	452	16,996	0.07	2009........	5	13	124	(Z)
1990........	44	185	5,926	0.02	2010........	11	45	302	(Z)
1991........	40	392	4,584	0.02	2011........	19	113	1,020	(Z)
1992........	35	364	3,989	0.01	2012........	19	148	1,131	(Z)
1993........	35	182	3,981	0.01	2013........	15	55	290	(Z)
1994........	45	322	5,021	0.02	2014........	11	34	200	(Z)
1995........	31	192	5,771	0.02	2015........	12	47	740	(Z)
1996........	37	273	4,889	0.02	2016........	15	99	1,543	(Z)
1997........	29	339	4,497	0.01	2017........	7	25	440	(Z)
1998........	34	387	5,116	0.02	2018........	20	485	2,815	0.01
1999........	17	73	1,996	0.01	2019........	25	426	3,244	0.01

Z Less than 0.005 percent. [1] Beginning in year indicated. [2] Workers counted more than once if involved in more than one stoppage during the year. [3] Resulting from all stoppages in effect in a year, including those that began in an earlier year. The number of total days of idleness is computed by multiplying the number of workers idled by the number of lost workdays during the reference period. [4] Agricultural and government employees are included in the total working time; private household and forestry and fishery employees are excluded.

Source: U.S. Bureau of Labor Statistics, *Major Work Stoppages in 2019*, USDL 20-0244, February 2020. See also <bls.gov/wsp>.

Section 13
Income, Expenditures, Poverty, and Wealth

This section presents data on gross domestic product (GDP), gross national product (GNP), national and personal income, savings and investment, money income, poverty, and national and personal wealth. The data on income and expenditures measure two aspects of the U.S. economy. One aspect relates to the National Income and Product Accounts (NIPA), a summation reflecting the entire complex of the nation's economic income and output and the interaction of its major components; the other relates to personal and household income and wealth, and consumer expenditures.

The primary source for data on GDP, GNP, national and personal income, gross saving and investment, and fixed assets and consumer durables is the *Survey of Current Business*, issued monthly by the Bureau of Economic Analysis (BEA). These data are also available in tables accessible through an interactive tool on the BEA's website, <bea.gov/iTable/>. Revisions occur annually. The BEA conducts a comprehensive revision using data from the Census Bureau's Economic Census approximately every 5 years. The most recent comprehensive revision to the NIPA was released beginning in July 2018. Discussions of the revision are available at the BEA's website.

Sources of income distribution data are the decennial censuses of population, the Annual Social and Economic Supplement of the Current Population Survey (CPS), and the American Community Survey, all products of the U.S. Census Bureau (see text, Section 1). Annual data on income of families, individuals, and households are presented in *Current Population Reports, Income and Poverty in the United States,* in print and online. Detailed statistics and historical data are available on the Census Bureau's website at <census.gov/topics/income-poverty.html>.

Data on the household sector's savings and assets are published by the Board of Governors of the Federal Reserve System in the quarterly statistical release, *Financial Accounts of the United States.* The Federal Reserve Board also periodically conducts the *Survey of Consumer Finances,* which presents financial information on family assets and net worth. The most recent survey is available online at <federalreserve.gov/econresdata/scf/scfindex.htm>. Detailed information on personal wealth is published periodically by the Internal Revenue Service (IRS) in the *SOI (Statistics of Income) Bulletin.*

National income and product—*GDP,* or value added, is the value of the goods and services produced by the nation's economy less the value of the goods and services used up in production. GDP is equal to the sum of personal consumption expenditures, gross private domestic investment, net exports of goods and services, and government consumption expenditures and gross investment. The goods and services included are largely those bought for final use (excluding illegal transactions) in the market economy. A number of inclusions, however, represent imputed values, the most important of which is the rental value of owner-occupied housing. GDP, in this broad context, measures the output attributable to the factors of production located in the United States. GDP by state is the gross market value of the goods and

services attributable to labor and property located in a state. It is the state counterpart of the nation's GDP.

The BEA releases GDP and related data in current dollar estimates, which reflect the value when transactions occurred, and in real values that are inflation-adjusted estimates that exclude the effects of price changes. Quantities, or "real" volume measures, and prices are expressed as index numbers with a specified reference year equal to 100 (currently 2012). Quantity and price indexes are calculated using a Fisher-chained weighted formula that incorporates weights from two adjacent periods (years for annual data). Chained-dollar values are calculated by multiplying the quantity index by the current dollar value in the reference year (2012) and then dividing by 100. Percent changes calculated from real quantity indexes and chained-dollar levels are conceptually the same; any differences are due to rounding. Chained-dollar values are not additive because the relative weights for a given period differ from those of the reference year. In tables that display chained-dollar values, a "residual" line shows the difference between the sum of detailed chained-dollar series and its corresponding aggregate.

Gross national product measures the output attributable to all labor and property supplied by United States residents, including residents working abroad. The GNP takes into account net income payments to the rest of the world. In brief, the GNP is the result of subtracting net income payments to the rest of the world from GDP.

National income includes all net incomes, net of consumption of fixed capital (CFC), earned in production. National income is also the sum of compensation of employees, proprietors' income with inventory valuation adjustment (IVA) and capital consumption adjustment (CCAdj), rental income of persons with CCAdj, corporate profits with IVA and CCAdj, net interest and miscellaneous payments, taxes on production and imports less subsidies, business current transfer payments (net), and current surplus of government enterprises, less subsidies.

Capital consumption adjustment for corporations and for nonfarm sole proprietorships and partnerships is the difference between capital consumption based on income tax returns and capital consumption measured using empirical evidence on prices of used equipment and structures in resale markets, which have shown that depreciation for most types of assets approximates a geometric pattern. The tax return data are valued at historical costs and reflect changes over time in service lives and depreciation patterns as permitted by tax regulations. Inventory valuation adjustment represents the difference between the book value of inventories used up in production and the cost of replacing them.

Personal income is the current income that persons receive in return for their provision of labor, land, and capital used in current production, plus current transfer receipts less contributions for government social insurance (domestic). Classified as "persons" are individuals (including owners of unincorporated firms), nonprofit institutions that primarily serve individuals, private trust funds, and private noninsured welfare funds. Personal income includes personal current transfer receipts (payments not resulting from current production) from government and business such as social security benefits, public assistance, etc., but excludes transfers among persons. Also included are certain nonmonetary types of income—chiefly, estimated net rental value to owner-occupants of their homes and the value of services furnished without payment by financial intermediaries. Capital gains (and losses) are excluded.

Disposable personal income is personal income less personal current taxes. It is the income available to persons for spending or saving. Personal current taxes are tax payments (net of refunds) by persons (except personal contributions for government social insurance) that are not chargeable to business expense. Personal taxes include income taxes, personal property taxes, motor vehicle licenses, and other miscellaneous taxes.

Gross domestic product by industry—The BEA also prepares estimates of value added by industry. *Value added* is a measure of the contribution of each private industry and of government to the nation's GDP. It is defined as an industry's gross output (which consists of sales or receipts and other operating income, commodity taxes, and inventory change) minus its intermediate inputs (which consist of energy, raw materials, semi-finished goods, and purchased services). Data are available by industry, for private industries and for Federal and state and local government. Industries are classified according to the North American Industry Classification System.

The estimates by industry are available in current dollars and are derived from the estimates of gross domestic income, which consists of three components—the compensation of employees, gross operating surplus, and taxes on production and imports, less subsidies. Real, or inflation-adjusted, estimates are also available.

Regional Economic Accounts—These accounts consist of estimates of state and local area personal income and of gross domestic product by state and are consistent with estimates of personal income and gross domestic product in the BEA's national economic accounts. BEA's estimates of state and local area personal income provide a framework for analyzing individual state and local economies, and they show how the economies compare with each other. The *personal income* of a state and/or local area is the income received by, or on behalf of, the residents of that state or area. Estimates of labor and proprietors' earnings by place of work indicate the economic activity of business and government within that area, and estimates of personal income by place of residence indicate the income within the area that is available for spending. BEA prepares estimates for states, counties, metropolitan areas, and BEA economic areas.

Gross domestic product by state estimates measure the value added to the nation's production by the labor and property in each state. GDP by state is often considered the state counterpart of the nation's GDP. The GDP by state estimates provide the basis for analyzing the regional impacts of national economic trends. GDP by state is measured as the sum of the distributions by industry and state of the components of gross domestic income; that is, the sum of the

costs incurred and incomes earned in the production of GDP by state. GDP estimates are available in current dollars and in real (chained dollars) by industry.

Consumer Expenditure Survey—The Consumer Expenditure Survey program began in 1980. The principal objective of the survey is to collect current consumer expenditure data, which provide a continuous flow of data on the buying habits of American consumers. The data are necessary for revisions of the Consumer Price Index.

The survey conducted by the Census Bureau for the Bureau of Labor Statistics consists of two components: (1) an interview panel survey in which the expenditures of consumer units are obtained over 4 quarters, and (2) a diary or recordkeeping survey completed by participating households for two consecutive 1-week periods. See Appendix III for more information.

Money income of households, families, and individuals—Money income statistics are based on data collected in various field surveys of income conducted since 1936. Since 1947, the Census Bureau has collected the data on an annual basis and published them in *Current Population Reports*, P60 Series. In each of the surveys, field representatives interview samples of the population with respect to income received during the previous year. *Money income* as defined by the Census Bureau differs from the BEA concept of "personal income." Data on consumer income collected in the CPS by the Census Bureau cover money income received (exclusive of certain money receipts such as capital gains) before payments for personal income taxes, social security, union dues, Medicare deductions, etc. Money income does not reflect the fact that some families receive part of their income in the form of noncash benefits (see Section 11) such as food stamps, health benefits, and subsidized housing; that some farm families receive noncash benefits in the form of goods produced and consumed on the farm; or that noncash benefits are also received by some nonfarm residents, which often take the form of the use of business transportation and facilities, full or partial payments by business for retirement programs, medical and educational expenses, etc. These elements should be considered when comparing income levels. None of the aggregate income concepts (GDP, national income, or personal income) is exactly comparable with money income, although personal income is the closest. For a definition of families and households, see text, Section 1.

Poverty—Families and unrelated individuals are classified as being above or below poverty following the Office of Management and Budget's Statistical Policy Directive 14. The Census Bureau uses a set of thresholds that vary by family size and composition.

The official poverty thresholds do not vary geographically, but they are updated every year to reflect changes in the consumer price index (CPI-U). The official poverty definition uses money income before taxes and does not include capital gains or noncash benefits (such as public housing, Medicaid, and food stamps).

The original thresholds were based on the U.S. Department of Agriculture's 1961 Economy Food Plan and reflected the different consumption requirements of families. The following technical changes to the thresholds were made in 1981: (1) distinctions based on sex of householder were eliminated, (2) separate thresholds for farm families were dropped, and (3) the matrix was expanded to families of nine or more persons from the previous cutoff of seven or more persons. These changes were incorporated in the calculation of poverty data beginning with data for 1981. Besides the Census Bureau website at <http://www.census.gov/topics/income-poverty/poverty.html>, information on poverty guidelines and research may be found at the U.S. Department of Human Services website at <https://aspe.hhs.gov/poverty-guidelines>.

Statistical reliability—For a discussion of statistical collection and estimation, sampling procedures, and measures of statistical reliability pertaining to Census Bureau data, see Appendix III.

Table 702. Gross Domestic Product in Current and Chained (2012) Dollars: 1990 to 2019

[In billions of dollars (5,963 represents $5,963,000,000,000). For explanation of gross domestic product and chained dollars, see text, this section. Minus sign (-) indicates decline in inventories or net imports]

Item	1990	2000	2005	2007	2008	2009	2010	2011	2012	2013	2014	2015	2016	2017	2018	2019
CURRENT DOLLARS																
Gross domestic product	**5,963**	**10,252**	**13,037**	**14,452**	**14,713**	**14,449**	**14,992**	**15,543**	**16,197**	**16,785**	**17,527**	**18,238**	**18,745**	**19,543**	**20,612**	**21,433**
Personal consumption expenditures	3,809	6,762	8,747	9,706	9,976	9,842	10,186	10,641	11,007	11,317	11,823	12,297	12,770	13,340	13,993	14,545
Durable goods	497	913	1,129	1,188	1,099	1,012	1,049	1,093	1,144	1,189	1,242	1,308	1,350	1,411	1,482	1,534
Nondurable goods	994	1,541	1,954	2,179	2,264	2,168	2,269	2,425	2,494	2,541	2,621	2,615	2,648	2,762	2,890	2,978
Services	2,318	4,309	5,664	6,339	6,613	6,662	6,868	7,123	7,369	7,587	7,960	8,374	8,772	9,168	9,621	10,032
Gross private domestic investment	993	2,038	2,535	2,673	2,478	1,930	2,165	2,333	2,622	2,826	3,044	3,237	3,188	3,351	3,633	3,751
Fixed investment	979	1,984	2,477	2,639	2,507	2,080	2,112	2,286	2,551	2,721	2,960	3,100	3,160	3,335	3,575	3,702
Nonresidential	739	1,498	1,621	1,949	1,991	1,690	1,735	1,907	2,119	2,211	2,400	2,467	2,460	2,574	2,777	2,895
Residential	240	485	856	690	516	390	377	379	432	510	560	634	699	760	798	807
Change in private inventories	15	55	58	34	-29	-151	54	46	71	105	84	137	28	16	58	49
Net exports of goods and services	-78	-375	-721	-718	-723	-396	-514	-579	-569	-491	-508	-527	-513	-556	-609	-610
Exports	552	1,096	1,305	1,661	1,837	1,582	1,846	2,103	2,191	2,273	2,372	2,266	2,227	2,375	2,529	2,515
Imports	630	1,471	2,026	2,379	2,560	1,978	2,360	2,682	2,760	2,764	2,879	2,792	2,740	2,930	3,138	3,125
Government consumption expenditures and gross investment	1,239	1,827	2,476	2,791	2,982	3,074	3,155	3,148	3,137	3,132	3,168	3,230	3,299	3,407	3,595	3,748
Federal	562	634	947	1,051	1,151	1,218	1,298	1,299	1,287	1,227	1,215	1,221	1,235	1,264	1,339	1,419
National defense	405	393	609	679	750	788	828	834	814	764	743	730	729	747	794	852
Nondefense	157	241	338	371	400	431	470	465	472	462	472	491	506	517	545	567
State and local	676	1,193	1,529	1,740	1,831	1,855	1,857	1,849	1,850	1,906	1,953	2,009	2,065	2,143	2,256	2,329
CHAINED (2012) DOLLARS [1]																
Gross domestic product	**9,365**	**13,131**	**14,913**	**15,626**	**15,605**	**15,209**	**15,599**	**15,841**	**16,197**	**16,495**	**16,912**	**17,432**	**17,731**	**18,144**	**18,688**	**19,092**
Personal consumption expenditures	6,012	8,643	10,076	10,615	10,593	10,460	10,643	10,844	11,007	11,167	11,497	11,934	12,265	12,587	12,928	13,240
Durable goods	(NA)	(NA)	1,005	1,100	1,036	973	1,027	1,080	1,144	1,214	1,302	1,401	1,482	1,585	1,693	1,775
Nondurable goods	(NA)	(NA)	2,383	2,503	2,464	2,423	2,461	2,483	2,494	2,538	2,605	2,694	2,762	2,834	2,910	3,001
Services	1,223	2,347	6,689	7,004	7,093	7,070	7,157	7,282	7,369	7,415	7,595	7,849	8,036	8,195	8,367	8,521
Gross private domestic investment	(NA)	2,294	2,671	2,684	2,463	1,942	2,216	2,362	2,622	2,801	2,959	3,122	3,075	3,183	3,385	3,443
Fixed investment	(NA)	1,616	2,619	2,653	2,499	2,100	2,164	2,318	2,551	2,692	2,869	2,979	3,032	3,147	3,310	3,372
Nonresidential	(NA)	647	1,716	1,982	1,994	1,704	1,781	1,935	2,119	2,206	2,365	2,420	2,433	2,524	2,699	2,777
Residential	(NA)	79	885	666	505	395	383	382	432	485	504	555	592	616	612	602
Change in private inventories	(NA)	(NA)	64	41	-33	-177	57	47	71	109	86	138	25	16	53	49
Net exports of goods and services	(NA)	(NA)	-888	-824	-662	-485	-566	-568	-569	-533	-577	-720	-764	-817	-878	-918
Exports	693	1,380	1,533	1,822	1,925	1,764	1,978	2,119	2,191	2,270	2,365	2,375	2,382	2,476	2,550	2,547
Imports	795	1,930	2,421	2,646	2,587	2,249	2,544	2,687	2,760	2,802	2,942	3,095	3,146	3,292	3,427	3,464
Government consumption expenditures and gross investment	2,377	2,663	3,015	3,119	3,196	3,307	3,307	3,203	3,137	3,061	3,033	3,088	3,144	3,172	3,230	3,304
Federal	(NA)	(NA)	1,099	1,147	1,219	1,293	1,346	1,311	1,287	1,215	1,184	1,184	1,191	1,194	1,228	1,277
National defense	(NA)	(NA)	709	740	791	837	861	843	814	760	728	713	710	715	739	780
Nondefense	(NA)	(NA)	391	407	427	456	485	468	472	456	455	470	480	478	488	497
State and local	(NA)	(NA)	1,920	1,975	1,979	2,016	1,961	1,892	1,850	1,845	1,849	1,903	1,952	1,976	2,000	2,026
Residual	-166	-50	35	26	-2	-15	-11	-4	–	(Z)	(Z)	11	22	21	1	-25

– Represents zero. NA Not available. Z Less than $500 million. [1] Chained (2012) dollar series are calculated as the product of the chain-type quantity index and the 2012 current-dollar value of the corresponding series, divided by 100. Because the formula for the chain-type quantity indexes uses weights of more than one period, the corresponding chained-dollar estimates are usually not additive. The residual line is the difference between the first line and the sum of the most detailed lines.

Source: U.S. Bureau of Economic Analysis, National Income and Product Accounts Tables, "Table 1.1.5. Gross Domestic Product," and "Table 1.1.6. Real Gross Domestic Product, Chained Dollars," <http://www.bea.gov/iTable/>, accessed July 2020.

Table 703. Real Gross Domestic Product, Chained (2012) Dollars—Annual Percent Change: 1990 to 2019

[Percent change from immediate previous year; for example, 1990, change from 1989. Minus sign (-) indicates decrease]

Component	1990	2000	2010	2013	2014	2015	2016	2017	2018	2019
Gross domestic product (GDP)	**1.9**	**4.1**	**2.6**	**1.8**	**2.5**	**3.1**	**1.7**	**2.3**	**3.0**	**2.2**
Personal consumption expenditures	2.0	5.1	1.7	1.5	3.0	3.8	2.8	2.6	2.7	2.4
Durable goods	-0.4	8.6	5.6	6.1	7.2	7.6	5.8	6.9	6.8	4.8
Nondurable goods	1.2	3.2	1.6	1.8	2.6	3.4	2.5	2.6	2.7	3.1
Services	2.9	5.0	1.2	0.6	2.4	3.3	2.4	2.0	2.1	1.8
Gross private domestic investment	-2.6	6.7	14.1	6.9	5.6	5.5	-1.5	3.5	6.3	1.7
Fixed investment	-1.4	7.1	3.1	5.6	6.6	3.8	1.8	3.8	5.2	1.9
Nonresidential	1.1	9.3	4.5	4.1	7.2	2.3	0.5	3.7	6.9	2.9
Structures	1.5	8.1	-16.1	1.3	11.0	-0.9	-4.4	4.2	3.7	-0.6
Equipment	-2.1	9.7	20.2	4.7	7.0	3.0	-1.7	3.2	8.0	2.1
Intellectual property products	8.4	9.5	2.7	5.4	4.8	3.8	7.6	4.2	7.8	6.4
Residential	-8.5	0.7	-3.1	12.4	3.8	10.2	6.6	4.0	-0.6	-1.7
Exports	8.8	8.3	12.1	3.6	4.2	0.4	0.3	3.9	3.0	-0.1
Goods	8.6	9.9	15.0	3.2	4.6	-0.4	0.5	4.1	4.2	-0.1
Services	9.5	4.3	6.3	4.5	3.3	2.0	-0.2	3.7	0.8	-0.1
Imports	3.6	12.9	13.1	1.5	5.0	5.2	1.7	4.7	4.1	1.1
Goods	2.9	13.0	15.4	1.8	5.6	5.7	1.4	4.7	5.0	0.5
Services	6.5	12.5	3.6	0.5	2.3	3.0	2.9	4.5	0.4	3.7
Government consumption expenditures and gross investment	3.2	1.8	–	-2.4	-0.9	1.8	1.8	0.9	1.8	2.3
Federal	2.1	0.3	4.1	-5.5	-2.6	–	0.6	0.3	2.8	4.0
National defense	0.3	-0.9	2.9	-6.7	-4.1	-2.1	-0.5	0.8	3.3	5.6
Nondefense	7.3	2.3	6.2	-3.5	-0.1	3.3	2.2	-0.5	2.1	1.8
State and local	4.1	2.7	-2.7	-0.3	0.2	2.9	2.6	1.2	1.2	1.3

– Represents or rounds to zero.

Source: U.S. Bureau of Economic Analysis, National Income and Product Accounts Tables, "Table 1.1.1. Percent Change From Preceding Period in Real Gross Domestic Product," <http://www.bea.gov/iTable/index_nipa.cfm>, accessed July 2020.

Table 704. Gross Domestic Product in Current and Chained (2012) Dollars by Type of Product and Sector: 1990 to 2019

[In billions of dollars (5,963 represents $5,963,000,000,000). For explanation of chained dollars, see text, this section]

Type of product and sector	1990	2000	2010	2014	2015	2016	2017	2018	2019
CURRENT DOLLARS									
Gross domestic product	**5,963**	**10,252**	**14,992**	**17,527**	**18,238**	**18,745**	**19,543**	**20,612**	**21,433**
Product:									
Goods	2,121	3,439	4,396	5,323	5,484	5,491	5,688	6,053	6,322
Durable goods	1,176	2,084	2,478	2,991	3,032	3,064	3,166	3,416	3,563
Nondurable goods	946	1,355	1,918	2,332	2,451	2,427	2,523	2,637	2,759
Services [1]	3,293	5,826	9,537	10,794	11,249	11,697	12,190	12,805	13,306
Structures	549	987	1,060	1,410	1,505	1,557	1,664	1,754	1,805
Sector:									
Business [2]	4,542	7,876	11,140	13,281	13,841	14,212	14,854	15,709	16,330
Nonfarm [3]	4,464	7,800	11,023	13,112	13,694	14,081	14,714	15,569	16,194
Farm	78	76	118	168	147	131	140	140	136
Households and institutions	636	1,192	1,905	2,159	2,256	2,349	2,447	2,570	2,686
General government [4]	785	1,184	1,946	2,088	2,141	2,184	2,241	2,333	2,417
Federal	307	360	640	667	674	685	700	727	751
State and local	478	824	1,306	1,421	1,467	1,499	1,541	1,607	1,666
CHAINED (2012) DOLLARS									
Gross domestic product	**9,365**	**13,131**	**15,599**	**16,912**	**17,432**	**17,731**	**18,144**	**18,688**	**19,092**
Product:									
Goods	2,228	3,468	4,510	5,317	5,485	5,546	5,741	6,070	6,319
Durable goods	(NA)	(NA)	2,491	3,000	3,036	3,096	3,213	3,468	3,582
Nondurable goods	(NA)	(NA)	2,022	2,317	2,449	2,449	2,527	2,603	2,737
Services [1]	6,133	8,137	9,969	10,296	10,589	10,805	10,985	11,200	11,380
Structures	1,154	1,543	1,122	1,301	1,359	1,380	1,424	1,443	1,437
Sector:									
Business [2]	6,584	9,729	11,607	12,877	13,362	13,609	13,980	14,469	14,820
Nonfarm [3]	6,494	9,594	11,444	12,695	13,167	13,406	13,779	14,258	14,609
Farm	92	138	165	182	196	207	202	211	209
Households and institutions	1,232	1,641	1,975	2,065	2,098	2,131	2,161	2,203	2,234
General government [4]	1,660	1,770	2,016	1,972	1,977	1,996	2,011	2,028	2,053
Federal	613	532	658	647	642	645	646	649	656
State and local	1,042	1,240	1,358	1,325	1,334	1,350	1,364	1,379	1,397

NA Not available. [1] Includes government consumption expenditures, which are for services (such as education and national defense) produced by government. In current dollars, these services are valued at their cost of production. [2] Equals gross domestic product excluding gross value added of households and institutions and of general government. [3] Equals gross domestic business value added excluding gross farm value added. [4] Equals compensation of general government employees plus general government consumption of fixed capital.

Source: U.S. Bureau of Economic Analysis, "National Income and Product Accounts Tables," <http://www.bea.gov/iTable/index_nipa.cfm>, accessed July 2020.

Table 705. Gross Domestic Product in Current and Chained (2012) Dollars by Industry: 2000 to 2019

[In billions of dollars (10,252 represents $10,252,000,000,000). Based on 2012 North American Industry Classification System (NAICS); see text, Section 15. GDP by industry is the contribution of each private industry and of government to the nation's output, or GDP. An industry's GDP, or its "value added," is equal to its gross output (sales or receipts and other operating income, commodity taxes, and inventory change) minus its intermediate inputs (energy, raw materials, semifinished goods, and services that are purchased from domestic industries or from foreign sources). Detail may not add to total due to rounding]

Industry	Current dollars				Chained (2012) dollars [1]			
	2000	2010	2018	2019	2000	2010	2018	2019
Gross domestic product.............................	**10,252**	**14,992**	**20,580**	**21,428**	**13,131**	**15,599**	**18,638**	**19,073**
Private industries.................................	8,929	12,884	18,036	18,797	11,384	13,467	16,345	16,766
Agriculture, forestry, fishing, and hunting......................	98	146	166	169	162	194	230	240
Farms..................................	76	118	130	131	138	165	196	206
Forestry, fishing, and related activities....................	22	29	37	38	25	29	33	34
Mining..............................	111	306	347	320	236	309	468	536
Oil and gas extraction........................	68	189	237	211	138	182	389	480
Mining, except oil and gas........................	29	69	61	60	94	75	67	66
Mining support activities.......................	14	48	49	49	19	52	49	48
Utilities..............................	180	279	326	335	261	266	283	289
Construction..............................	461	525	839	887	783	547	654	654
Manufacturing..............................	1,550	1,797	2,321	2,360	1,679	1,933	2,161	2,177
Durable goods..........................	925	964	1,296	1,343	753	968	1,217	1,239
Wood products..........................	28	23	41	41	25	23	29	31
Nonmetallic mineral products..................	43	38	62	64	49	39	48	48
Primary metals..........................	47	51	64	65	62	51	68	77
Fabricated metal products..................	121	120	160	166	156	126	145	143
Machinery..........................	113	127	156	160	130	132	136	132
Computer and electronic products..............	225	240	297	314	68	227	330	348
Electrical equipment, appliances, and components........	46	51	66	68	54	53	62	62
Motor vehicles, bodies & trailers, & parts.............	138	89	162	166	100	87	140	142
Other transportation equipment..................	71	121	162	167	95	124	147	149
Furniture and related products..................	34	22	30	31	40	23	28	26
Miscellaneous manufacturing..................	59	83	97	100	61	84	91	90
Nondurable goods..........................	625	833	1,025	1,017	967	972	943	937
Food & beverage & tobacco..................	163	223	269	272	225	233	245	244
Textile mills and textile product mills..................	28	16	19	19	31	17	18	17
Apparel and leather and allied products..................	22	10	9	9	20	11	8	8
Paper products..........................	62	56	57	58	71	56	49	48
Printing and related support activities..................	44	39	40	41	38	38	38	37
Petroleum and coal products..................	53	123	172	143	185	213	202	190
Chemical products..........................	188	303	378	393	289	347	313	320
Plastics and rubber products..................	66	62	80	82	77	68	75	74
Wholesale trade..........................	623	889	1,212	1,278	809	948	1,128	1,137
Retail trade..........................	686	852	1,127	1,173	820	900	1,093	1,131
Transportation and warehousing..................	308	433	658	685	425	461	562	561
Air transportation..........................	58	84	143	149	77	92	126	125
Rail transportation..........................	23	34	44	43	42	38	40	36
Water transportation..........................	8	15	15	16	5	12	10	11
Truck transportation..........................	98	113	169	173	129	121	136	134
Transit & ground passenger transport..................	18	31	47	49	31	33	42	44
Pipeline transportation..........................	9	20	46	49	16	22	38	38
Other transportation & support..................	66	90	124	131	106	101	103	102
Warehousing and storage..................	27	45	70	75	27	41	68	74
Information..........................	471	753	1,068	1,120	422	750	1,157	1,210
Publishing industries (except internet, includes software)...	116	187	273	292	126	189	266	283
Motion picture and sound recording..................	54	91	100	103	45	92	100	106
Broadcasting and telecommunications..................	277	375	438	446	225	369	513	519
Data processing, internet publishing, & related services....	24	101	256	278	24	100	277	300
Finance and insurance..........................	743	1,004	1,567	1,628	905	1,078	1,165	1,204
Real estate and rental and leasing..................	1,232	1,939	2,734	2,864	1,546	1,987	2,374	2,412
Professional, scientific, and technical services..................	652	1,064	1,546	1,649	845	1,093	1,443	1,522
Legal services..........................	129	204	266	279	237	222	214	215
Computer systems design, related services..................	114	203	351	387	86	199	381	424
Miscellaneous services..................	409	657	929	983	545	673	858	899
Management of companies & enterprises..................	171	265	395	418	277	270	402	434
Administrative and waste management services..............	282	438	638	675	338	445	563	580
Educational services..........................	95	199	256	264	153	212	217	219
Health care and social assistance..................	600	1,112	1,537	1,618	836	1,149	1,404	1,448
Ambulatory health care services..................	288	532	752	792	375	545	733	764
Hospitals..........................	190	370	498	522	279	385	432	440
Nursing and residential care facilities..................	69	121	153	160	108	125	132	132
Social assistance..........................	53	90	134	145	76	94	111	116
Arts, entertainment, and recreation..................	99	152	227	236	138	159	197	199
Performing arts, spectator sports, museums, & related.....	49	88	136	141	72	90	117	119
Amusements, gambling, & recreation..................	50	65	91	95	66	69	80	80
Accommodation and food services..................	288	404	633	663	425	427	518	522
Accommodation..........................	93	112	175	181	127	119	144	145
Food services and drinking places..................	194	291	459	481	298	308	374	377
Other services, except government..................	280	328	437	457	431	346	368	369
Government..........................	1,323	2,108	2,545	2,631	1,978	2,182	2,200	2,211
Federal..........................	424	697	791	813	624	716	706	708
State and local..........................	899	1,411	1,754	1,818	1,355	1,466	1,494	1,503

[1] Chained (2012) dollar series are calculated as the product of the chain-type quantity index and the 2012 current-dollar value of the corresponding series, divided by 100. Because the formula for the chain-type quantity indexes uses weights of more than one period, the corresponding chained-dollar estimates are usually not additive.

Source: U.S. Bureau of Economic Analysis, Industry Economic Accounts, "GDP by Industry Data," <http://www.bea.gov/industry/index.htm>, accessed April 2020.

Table 706. Relation of GDP, GNP, Net National Product, National Income, Personal Income, Disposable Personal Income, and Personal Saving: 2000 to 2019

[In billions of dollars (10,252 represents $10,252,000,000,000). For definitions, see text, this section. Minus sign (-) indicates deficit or net disbursement]

Item	2000	2010	2014	2015	2016	2017	2018	2019
Gross domestic product (GDP).................	**10,252**	**14,992**	**17,527**	**18,238**	**18,745**	**19,543**	**20,612**	**21,433**
Plus: Income receipts from the rest of the world..	381	715	854	861	894	1,033	1,143	1,170
Less: Income payments to the rest of the world...	346	519	612	640	661	740	858	900
Equals: Gross national product (GNP).........	**10,287**	**15,188**	**17,768**	**18,459**	**18,977**	**19,835**	**20,897**	**21,703**
Less: Consumption of fixed capital................	1,511	2,391	2,815	2,911	2,987	3,113	3,265	3,421
Equals: Net national product....................	**8,776**	**12,797**	**14,953**	**15,547**	**15,991**	**16,722**	**17,632**	**18,282**
Less: Statistical discrepancy....................	-96	60	-287	-237	-92	-131	-58	13
Equals: National income........................	**8,872**	**12,737**	**15,240**	**15,785**	**16,083**	**16,854**	**17,690**	**18,269**
Less: Corporate profits [1]......................	787	1,729	2,120	2,060	2,024	2,115	2,243	2,251
Taxes on production and imports less subsidies.................................	663	1,007	1,183	1,218	1,250	1,304	1,381	1,418
Contributions for government social insurance..	706	984	1,154	1,205	1,239	1,298	1,360	1,419
Net interest and miscellaneous payments on assets.................................	541	465	516	586	577	636	619	573
Business current transfer payments (net).......	85	128	130	154	165	151	157	158
Current surplus of government enterprises......	11	-20	-11	-5	-4	-5	-6	-8
Plus: Personal income receipts on assets.........	1,486	1,782	2,302	2,472	2,552	2,738	2,947	2,968
Personal current transfer receipts................	1,087	2,325	2,542	2,685	2,777	2,855	2,970	3,125
Equals: Personal income.......................	**8,653**	**12,552**	**14,992**	**15,724**	**16,161**	**16,949**	**17,852**	**18,552**
Less: Personal current taxes.....................	1,236	1,238	1,785	1,940	1,958	2,047	2,085	2,203
Equals: Disposable personal income...........	**7,416**	**11,314**	**13,207**	**13,784**	**14,203**	**14,902**	**15,767**	**16,349**
Less: Personal outlays..........................	7,060	10,574	12,236	12,746	13,228	13,831	14,529	15,117
Equals: Personal saving........................	**356**	**740**	**971**	**1,039**	**975**	**1,071**	**1,237**	**1,231**

[1] Corporate profits with inventory valuation and capital consumption adjustments.

Source: U.S. Bureau of Economic Analysis, National Income and Product Accounts Tables, "Table 1.7.5. Relation of Gross Domestic Product, Gross National Product, Net National Product, National Income, and Personal Income," and "Table 2.1. Personal Income and Its Disposition," <http://www.bea.gov/iTable/index_nipa.cfm>, accessed July 2020.

Table 707. Gross Saving and Investment: 2000 to 2019

[In billions of dollars (2,129 represents $2,129,000,000,000), except as noted. Minus (-) sign indicates deficit]

Item	2000	2010	2014	2015	2016	2017	2018	2019
Gross saving..............................	**2,129**	**2,319**	**3,568**	**3,673**	**3,512**	**3,755**	**3,927**	**3,988**
Net saving..................................	618	-72	753	762	525	643	662	567
Net private saving...........................	499	1,554	1,588	1,538	1,433	1,604	1,807	1,822
Domestic business............................	143	813	617	499	458	533	570	591
Undistributed corporate profits.................	103	919	761	567	559	601	514	578
Inventory valuation adjustment, corporate.......	-17	-48	2	56	-1	-53	-55	-5
Capital consumption adjustment, corporate.....	57	-58	-146	-124	-101	-16	111	19
Households and institutions....................	356	740	971	1,039	975	1,071	1,237	1,231
Personal saving............................	356	740	971	1,039	975	1,071	1,237	1,231
Net government saving.........................	119	-1,626	-835	-776	-908	-961	-1,145	-1,255
Federal...................................	160	-1,318	-597	-560	-669	-722	-932	-1,047
State and local.............................	-41	-307	-238	-216	-239	-239	-214	-208
Consumption of fixed capital...................	1,511	2,391	2,815	2,911	2,987	3,113	3,265	3,421
Private....................................	1,232	1,934	2,298	2,388	2,458	2,570	2,699	2,833
Domestic business..........................	1,005	1,537	1,831	1,903	1,949	2,032	2,125	2,234
Households and institutions...................	227	397	467	485	509	538	574	599
Government................................	280	457	517	523	528	543	566	588
Federal...................................	163	244	270	271	272	277	286	295
State and local.............................	117	213	246	251	256	266	280	293
Gross domestic investment, capital account transactions, and net lending.......	**2,033**	**2,379**	**3,281**	**3,436**	**3,419**	**3,624**	**3,869**	**4,001**
Gross domestic investment.....................	2,427	2,810	3,647	3,860	3,827	4,015	4,337	4,504
Gross private domestic investment...............	2,038	2,165	3,044	3,237	3,188	3,351	3,633	3,751
Gross government investment....................	389	645	603	623	638	664	704	753
Capital account transactions (net) [1].................	5	7	7	8	7	16	5	7
Net lending or net borrowing....................	-399	-439	-372	-432	-414	-408	-472	-509
Statistical discrepancy........................	-96	60	-287	-237	-92	-131	-58	13
Addenda:								
Gross private saving...........................	1,730	3,487	3,886	3,926	3,892	4,173	4,506	4,655
Gross government saving.......................	399	-1,169	-319	-253	-380	-418	-579	-666
Federal...................................	323	-1,075	-327	-289	-397	-445	-646	-752
State and local.............................	76	-94	8	36	17	27	67	86
Net domestic investment.......................	916	419	832	948	840	903	1,072	1,083
Gross saving as a percent of gross national income.........................	20.5	15.3	19.8	19.6	18.4	18.8	18.7	18.4
Net saving as a percent of gross national income.........................	6.0	-0.5	4.2	4.1	2.8	3.2	3.2	2.6
Disaster losses [2]................................	–	–	–	–	–	104	51	–

– Represents zero. [1] Consists of capital transfers and the acquisition and disposal of nonproduced nonfinancial assets. [2] Consists of damages to fixed assets.

Source: U.S. Bureau of Economic Analysis, National Income and Product Accounts Tables, "Table 5.1 Saving and Investment by Sector," <http://www.bea.gov/iTable/index_nipa.cfm>, accessed July 2020.

Table 708. Gross Domestic Product by State in Current and Chained (2012) Dollars: 2000 to 2019

[In billions of dollars (10,252.3 represents $10,252,300,000,000). For definition of gross domestic product by state or chained dollars, see text, this section]

State	Current dollars					Chained (2012) dollars [2]				
	2000	2010	2017	2018	2019	2000	2010	2017	2018	2019
United States [1]	10,252.3	14,992.1	19,519.4	20,580.2	21,427.7	13,131.0	15,598.8	18,108.1	18,638.2	19,073.1
Alabama	119.2	174.8	210.4	221.7	231.0	156.6	182.3	193.0	198.4	202.9
Alaska	26.8	52.9	51.8	54.7	55.4	39.5	54.2	52.7	53.1	54.4
Arizona	164.6	248.2	327.5	348.3	366.2	207.8	257.5	299.4	311.7	321.4
Arkansas	68.8	101.7	123.4	128.4	133.2	90.2	105.9	115.3	117.3	119.4
California	1,366.6	1,974.6	2,819.1	2,997.7	3,137.5	1,709.9	2,058.1	2,610.7	2,721.7	2,792.0
Colorado	180.6	255.1	350.0	371.7	390.3	232.8	264.8	329.6	341.1	353.1
Connecticut	165.9	237.7	268.3	275.7	285.6	216.4	247.5	243.7	244.9	248.8
Delaware	43.4	57.4	70.8	73.5	75.4	56.1	60.0	62.7	62.8	63.3
District of Columbia	61.1	106.1	134.0	140.7	146.2	85.3	110.0	121.0	124.0	125.9
Florida	489.5	737.8	985.7	1,039.2	1,093.4	642.7	766.2	896.1	924.9	950.8
Georgia	307.6	416.9	566.5	592.2	616.3	393.2	433.0	516.6	529.0	539.5
Hawaii	41.5	68.2	89.4	93.8	97.3	56.4	71.0	80.7	82.7	83.5
Idaho	38.0	55.2	72.7	77.1	80.9	47.3	57.9	67.8	70.5	72.5
Illinois	487.2	662.6	826.8	865.3	897.1	641.7	695.0	753.6	769.8	782.0
Indiana	203.1	280.1	351.1	366.8	377.1	263.7	295.1	322.7	329.3	332.0
Iowa	93.0	141.5	181.8	189.7	194.8	122.2	149.5	168.4	172.1	173.7
Kansas	85.9	127.7	161.2	168.3	173.1	114.0	134.9	151.5	154.6	155.9
Kentucky	114.3	164.6	200.7	208.1	214.7	152.1	172.0	184.5	187.2	189.4
Louisiana	132.8	225.7	239.2	257.3	263.9	206.7	247.4	231.4	237.4	240.5
Maine	36.8	51.7	62.0	64.9	67.5	48.5	53.8	56.2	57.5	58.5
Maryland	192.1	316.5	394.3	412.6	428.3	251.0	327.2	360.0	368.9	374.4
Massachusetts	289.9	409.8	540.8	569.5	595.6	359.5	424.6	490.8	506.1	518.7
Michigan	351.6	386.6	505.6	527.1	541.6	438.3	400.9	459.1	470.5	473.9
Minnesota	190.0	271.8	351.4	368.9	380.9	246.0	284.9	325.3	333.9	338.8
Mississippi	65.6	95.2	110.2	114.8	118.8	88.1	100.0	101.5	102.8	104.2
Missouri	187.3	258.5	304.9	318.9	332.1	246.0	269.7	278.2	284.9	291.0
Montana	21.9	38.1	47.6	50.3	52.2	31.4	40.5	45.0	46.2	47.2
Nebraska	56.5	91.8	120.5	124.0	127.0	76.6	97.9	113.1	114.2	114.9
Nevada	76.6	123.6	158.8	169.3	177.6	105.3	128.8	143.7	149.8	154.1
New Hampshire	45.2	64.2	80.9	84.5	88.6	56.7	66.4	74.1	75.8	77.9
New Jersey	362.0	495.1	595.3	622.0	644.8	473.0	516.6	543.5	555.8	563.9
New Mexico	55.2	84.0	94.3	100.3	104.0	72.0	87.0	91.3	93.6	97.1
New York	838.7	1,213.9	1,604.1	1,668.9	1,731.9	1,088.0	1,269.5	1,418.9	1,435.6	1,461.6
North Carolina	275.7	415.2	538.4	563.7	587.7	354.8	433.4	485.5	497.3	508.6
North Dakota	18.0	35.4	52.5	56.1	57.0	24.6	37.7	51.0	52.9	54.1
Ohio	391.1	497.2	645.3	675.9	698.5	509.0	521.1	594.3	605.4	615.6
Oklahoma	90.8	152.9	188.4	202.6	206.1	124.1	159.2	191.5	196.5	201.3
Oregon	117.3	163.8	226.6	239.8	251.6	137.8	169.0	208.6	216.6	222.4
Pennsylvania	407.7	599.3	744.3	783.2	813.5	537.2	622.5	693.7	711.8	728.0
Rhode Island	34.5	49.6	58.5	60.6	63.5	45.2	51.5	53.0	53.6	55.0
South Carolina	115.2	163.9	223.1	233.9	246.3	150.5	170.2	201.9	207.2	213.5
South Dakota	22.7	37.5	49.7	52.0	53.3	29.4	40.1	45.6	46.5	46.8
Tennessee	181.6	255.9	345.9	364.1	380.1	233.2	266.7	313.8	323.7	330.8
Texas	738.9	1,237.2	1,665.6	1,802.5	1,887.0	998.3	1,301.7	1,646.3	1,712.8	1,788.5
Utah	70.3	118.0	167.3	178.1	188.5	92.5	123.3	153.1	158.8	164.8
Vermont	18.3	27.1	32.2	33.3	34.8	23.0	28.1	29.4	29.8	30.5
Virginia	266.9	422.9	509.4	532.9	554.2	346.2	437.3	464.8	477.0	486.0
Washington	237.8	365.6	524.8	565.8	599.6	312.2	381.3	483.8	511.7	531.2
West Virginia	42.6	65.3	73.2	77.4	78.2	62.1	68.4	69.9	71.5	72.2
Wisconsin	180.5	254.4	322.0	336.3	347.3	233.1	264.8	294.7	301.6	305.9
Wyoming	17.2	37.4	37.5	39.1	39.6	27.7	39.8	38.0	38.0	39.3

[1] The difference between the United States and sum-of-states reflects federal military and civilian activity located overseas, as well as the differences in source data used to estimate GDP by industry and the expenditures measure of real GDP. [2] Chained (2012) dollar series are calculated as the product of the chain-type quantity index and the 2012 current-dollar value of the corresponding series, divided by 100. Because the formula for the chain-type quantity indexes uses weights of more than one period, the corresponding chained-dollar estimates are usually not additive.

Source: U.S. Bureau of Economic Analysis, Regional Economic Accounts, "Gross Domestic Product by State," <https://www.bea.gov/data/economic-accounts/regional>, accessed April 2020.

Table 709. Gross Domestic Product by Selected Industry and State: 2019

[In billions of dollars (21,427.7 represents $21,427,700,000,000). Data are subject to revision. For definition of gross domestic product by state, see text, this section. Industries based on 2012 North American Industry Classification System; see text, Section 15]

State	Total [1]	Manu- facturing	Whole- sale trade	Retail trade	Infor- mation	Finance and insur- ance	Real estate, rental, and leasing	Profes- sional and technical services	Health care and social assist- ance	Govern- ment [2]
United States [3]	21,427.7	2,359.9	1,278.1	1,172.9	1,120.3	1,627.9	2,863.8	1,649.1	1,617.9	2,630.9
Alabama	231.0	38.6	12.9	16.2	5.2	13.6	24.6	14.6	17.2	37.6
Alaska	55.4	1.8	1.5	2.4	1.4	1.3	5.4	2.0	4.5	11.1
Arizona	366.2	30.8	20.3	25.1	13.0	26.4	57.0	21.5	31.9	45.5
Arkansas	133.2	19.5	10.3	9.2	4.1	6.9	13.9	5.0	11.8	16.8
California	3,137.5	322.4	167.1	159.9	298.5	160.8	530.1	288.0	198.2	350.5
Colorado	390.3	26.3	22.1	20.0	21.7	22.6	58.1	38.5	24.6	46.5
Connecticut	285.6	30.6	18.4	14.4	15.0	37.7	41.3	20.4	23.3	28.3
Delaware	75.4	4.9	2.1	2.9	1.1	22.2	11.0	4.8	5.8	7.4
District of Columbia	146.2	0.3	1.4	1.7	8.1	6.1	13.1	31.1	6.9	47.5
Florida	1,093.4	59.2	75.9	76.0	44.8	69.8	181.6	81.4	94.3	117.9
Georgia	616.3	64.7	47.4	33.2	48.2	49.0	77.8	42.4	41.4	71.6
Hawaii	97.3	1.9	3.0	6.2	2.1	3.5	19.8	3.9	6.6	19.1
Idaho	80.9	8.5	4.9	6.2	1.7	3.6	11.2	4.6	6.9	10.6
Illinois	897.1	108.6	72.7	43.0	31.3	92.1	113.8	75.5	64.7	85.4
Indiana	377.1	101.5	21.5	20.8	6.2	21.5	37.8	16.8	32.8	35.0
Iowa	194.8	33.9	11.6	10.1	4.8	27.0	20.4	6.7	13.0	22.4
Kansas	173.1	27.7	11.3	10.3	6.7	9.3	21.1	9.7	13.1	22.6
Kentucky	214.7	38.3	14.9	12.6	4.8	12.4	22.6	9.1	19.3	28.7
Louisiana	263.9	53.4	13.9	16.6	5.3	12.1	27.0	13.2	20.1	29.4
Maine	67.5	6.3	3.7	5.4	1.3	4.3	9.7	3.9	8.1	9.2
Maryland	428.3	24.4	18.5	20.8	18.8	23.2	71.9	43.3	32.4	86.2
Massachusetts	595.6	52.5	29.1	23.7	33.1	55.4	84.6	77.4	55.2	57.3
Michigan	541.6	100.0	36.0	33.1	13.7	27.9	66.1	42.7	46.9	57.4
Minnesota	380.9	52.7	26.1	20.2	12.4	34.3	42.3	26.8	36.6	37.6
Mississippi	118.8	18.9	6.6	9.4	2.3	5.9	12.5	3.8	9.4	20.2
Missouri	332.1	39.8	22.2	19.1	13.6	27.2	37.4	23.6	30.7	38.6
Montana	52.2	3.4	2.8	3.4	1.2	2.8	7.4	2.7	5.4	7.6
Nebraska	127.0	13.5	7.9	6.8	3.7	12.7	12.9	5.6	10.1	16.1
Nevada	177.6	8.7	7.1	12.3	5.9	9.9	26.7	8.8	11.0	19.0
New Hampshire	88.6	10.1	5.7	5.8	3.4	7.2	12.7	7.2	8.4	9.0
New Jersey	644.8	53.9	53.8	37.1	27.4	43.0	103.8	60.3	52.3	66.5
New Mexico	104.0	4.4	3.4	5.7	2.9	3.6	13.7	7.6	7.9	24.0
New York	1,731.9	71.3	78.7	74.3	136.8	320.3	247.6	152.7	130.5	181.5
North Carolina	587.7	100.2	35.0	30.7	20.1	52.2	67.3	39.7	39.8	76.2
North Dakota	57.0	4.0	4.8	3.0	1.4	2.8	6.8	1.9	4.7	6.4
Ohio	698.5	112.9	43.5	39.9	18.1	63.8	76.9	37.2	61.9	75.3
Oklahoma	206.1	18.6	11.7	11.4	4.9	7.8	19.7	9.2	14.9	32.3
Oregon	251.6	35.2	13.4	12.4	9.4	11.6	40.8	14.9	21.7	31.5
Pennsylvania	813.5	93.8	46.9	38.6	51.8	55.1	99.3	61.2	80.5	77.8
Rhode Island	63.5	5.1	3.9	3.4	1.6	6.4	9.1	4.0	6.4	8.1
South Carolina	246.3	40.4	14.3	16.2	6.9	11.3	30.7	14.0	16.2	37.1
South Dakota	53.3	5.2	4.0	3.6	1.3	8.4	5.0	1.7	5.3	6.1
Tennessee	380.1	55.9	26.4	25.2	11.4	22.6	42.1	21.8	38.0	41.8
Texas	1,887.0	246.4	148.0	105.2	69.6	109.5	184.4	137.8	116.2	194.1
Utah	188.5	20.6	9.7	12.8	9.3	16.2	25.7	13.1	11.0	22.9
Vermont	34.8	3.2	1.7	2.6	0.9	1.9	4.9	2.4	3.9	5.0
Virginia	554.2	45.3	23.6	27.6	19.3	28.8	78.7	73.8	36.0	100.7
Washington	599.6	65.5	29.8	49.6	79.2	23.2	81.9	39.6	37.9	75.3
West Virginia	78.2	7.9	3.7	5.2	1.4	2.8	8.0	3.6	8.6	12.5
Wisconsin	347.3	64.6	21.1	19.2	12.2	27.0	40.9	16.2	31.7	36.6
Wyoming	39.6	2.3	1.6	2.2	0.6	1.1	4.5	1.3	1.8	6.5

[1] Includes industries not shown separately. [2] Includes federal civilian and military, and state and local government. [3] The difference between the United States and sum-of-states reflects overseas activity, economic activity taking place outside the borders of the United States by the military and associated federal civilian support staff.

Source: U.S. Bureau of Economic Analysis, Regional Economic Accounts, "Gross Domestic Product by State," <https://www.bea.gov/data/economic-accounts/regional>, accessed April 2020.

Table 710. Household Production Value: 1965 to 2017

[In billions of dollars (277.4 represents $277,400,000,000). Measures the value of time spent on the unpaid work of household production tasks. Household production hours are aggregated across seven categories: housework, cooking, odd jobs, gardening, shopping, child care, and domestic travel related to these tasks. The value of these nonmarket services is the product of the wage rate of general purpose domestic workers and the number of hours worked]

Year	Household production value (bil. dol.)	Year	Household production value (bil. dol.)	Year	Household production value (bil. dol.)
1965	277.4	1996	2,465.1	2007	3,630.4
1970	428.0	1997	2,488.7	2008	3,828.1
1975	707.4	1998	2,701.4	2009	3,691.7
1980	1,106.9	1999	2,601.5	2010	3,643.1
1985	1,467.0	2000	2,921.2	2011	3,706.0
1990	1,902.6	2001	2,799.3	2012	3,781.5
1991	1,908.1	2002	2,780.1	2013	4,097.2
1992	1,984.7	2003	3,043.3	2014	4,228.4
1993	2,119.3	2004	3,183.3	2015	4,405.0
1994	2,272.5	2005	3,208.3	2016	4,594.6
1995	2,395.9	2006	3,405.5	2017	4,516.1

Source: U.S. Bureau of Economic Analysis, Special Topics, "Household Production Satellite Account," <https://www.bea.gov/data/special-topics/household-production>, accessed August 2019.

Table 711. Financial Accounts of the United States—Composition of Individuals' Savings: 1990 to 2019

[In billions of dollars (662.3 represents $662,300,000,000). Combined statement for households, nonprofit organizations, and nonfinancial noncorporate business. Minus sign (-) indicates decrease]

Composition of savings	1990	2000	2010	2015	2016	2017	2018	2019
Net acquisition of financial assets	**662.3**	**875.1**	**983.0**	**1,605.3**	**1,590.5**	**1,787.8**	**2,369.6**	**2,442.7**
Foreign deposits	1.4	7.6	4.5	-13.8	-5.6	12.6	0.8	-5.9
Checkable deposits and currency	1.7	-95.9	-35.1	96.9	-40.0	195.3	96.4	-103.1
Time and savings deposits	43.8	355.1	221.7	518.0	723.3	282.1	482.7	607.9
Money market fund shares	43.1	184.1	-301.6	-14.3	9.9	68.1	189.3	355.8
Debt securities	211.6	-49.1	189.4	245.9	-69.4	-48.8	807.1	249.7
Treasury securities	97.0	-192.5	284.1	331.4	102.6	-36.3	618.9	327.4
Agency and GSE-backed securities [1]	36.4	30.5	23.9	192.1	-96.5	54.0	201.5	88.8
Municipal securities	35.9	17.6	77.4	-39.8	12.6	-37.9	-8.3	-50.1
Corporate and foreign bonds	42.2	95.4	-196.0	-237.8	-88.1	-28.6	-5.0	-116.4
Loans	16.4	111.4	21.3	-63.7	-14.0	-66.8	-16.0	11.5
Corporate equities [2]	-67.4	-400.8	-202.1	-123.0	-7.3	133.3	-89.7	233.6
Mutual fund shares	29.8	82.1	260.0	92.4	54.1	309.1	-25.1	244.9
Trade receivables	5.9	10.1	6.3	0.2	6.3	6.3	4.3	4.8
Life insurance reserves	27.0	43.7	15.0	47.2	41.8	19.0	49.4	42.4
Pension entitlements	331.6	444.1	662.9	410.7	350.7	475.0	399.1	417.8
Miscellaneous and other assets	17.5	182.7	140.6	408.9	543.6	402.5	471.2	383.4
Gross investment in nonfinancial assets	**829.7**	**1,592.6**	**1,675.2**	**2,289.7**	**2,388.9**	**2,521.9**	**2,650.5**	**2,718.3**
Minus: Consumption of fixed capital	617.7	1,010.5	1,568.4	1,792.8	1,852.6	1,929.0	2,023.7	2,080.5
Equals: Net investment in nonfinancial assets	**212.0**	**582.1**	**106.8**	**496.9**	**536.3**	**593.0**	**626.9**	**637.7**
Net increase in liabilities	**238.7**	**923.5**	**-153.6**	**613.2**	**1,135.0**	**1,025.2**	**1,029.7**	**1,045.1**
Home mortgages	206.9	423.0	-129.4	152.5	231.2	329.9	302.4	321.8
Other mortgages	-4.4	106.3	-33.2	177.2	266.9	208.2	217.0	243.0
Consumer credit	15.1	176.5	-28.2	233.8	233.1	184.0	181.8	181.0
Other loans and advances	4.7	16.0	80.5	-70.6	-7.5	64.5	-16.7	45.5
Other liabilities	16.4	201.6	-43.3	120.3	411.3	238.6	345.2	253.8
Personal saving, FOF concept (FOF) [3]	651.3	569.4	1,215.3	1,510.4	1,006.6	1,331.1	1,973.5	2,053.7
Personal saving, NIPA concept (FOF) [3]	574.5	326.1	1,159.2	1,308.9	789.0	1,093.6	1,714.2	1,759.7
Personal saving, NIPA concept (NIPA) [4]	361.1	358.3	740.9	1,048.8	958.8	1,030.9	1,210.4	1,298.8

[1] GSE = government-sponsored enterprises. [2] Only directly held and those in closed-end and exchange-traded funds. Other equities are included in mutual funds, life insurance reserves, and pension entitlements. [3] Flow of Funds measure. [4] National Income and Product Accounts measure.

Source: Board of Governors of the Federal Reserve System, "Z.1 Financial Accounts of the United States: Summary Table F.6 Derivation of Measures of Personal Saving," March 2020, <https://www.federalreserve.gov/releases/Z1/current/default.htm>, accessed March 2020.

Table 712. Government Consumption Expenditures and Gross Investment by Level of Government and Type: 2002 to 2019

[In billions of dollars (2,089 represents $2,089,000,000,000). Government consumption expenditures are services (such as education and national defense) produced by government that are valued at their cost of production; excludes government sales to other sectors and government own-account investment (construction, software, and research and development). Gross government investment consists of general government and government enterprise expenditures for fixed assets; inventory investment is included in government consumption expenditures. For explanation of national income and chained dollars, see text, Section 13]

Level of government and type	Current dollars				Chained (2012) dollars			
	2002	2010	2018	2019	2002	2010	2018	2019
Government consumption expenditures and gross investment, total	**2,089**	**3,155**	**3,595**	**3,748**	**2,885**	**3,307**	**3,230**	**3,304**
Consumption expenditures	1,645	2,510	2,891	2,995	2,300	2,633	2,585	2,631
Gross investment	444	645	704	753	585	675	645	673
Structures	220	312	337	361	358	335	293	302
Equipment	96	148	153	164	95	150	151	161
Intellectual property products	127	184	214	228	147	190	202	212
Federal	**743**	**1,298**	**1,339**	**1,419**	**970**	**1,346**	**1,228**	**1,277**
Consumption expenditures	561	1,001	1,044	1,097	761	1,040	947	977
Gross investment	182	297	296	322	210	306	281	301
Structures	16	33	18	22	24	35	16	18
Equipment	58	108	104	114	61	111	103	112
Intellectual property products	108	156	174	186	127	161	163	171
National defense	**459**	**828**	**794**	**852**	**606**	**861**	**739**	**780**
Consumption expenditures	359	652	636	677	491	679	587	614
Gross investment	100	176	158	176	116	182	152	167
Structures	6	17	6	7	9	18	5	6
Equipment	46	89	84	93	50	91	84	93
Intellectual property products	48	70	68	75	57	73	63	68
Nondefense	**284**	**470**	**545**	**567**	**363**	**485**	**488**	**497**
Consumption expenditures	202	349	407	421	269	361	359	363
Gross investment	82	121	138	146	94	124	129	135
Structures	10	16	12	15	15	17	11	12
Equipment	12	19	20	20	11	19	19	19
Intellectual property products	60	86	106	111	70	88	100	103
State and local	**1,346**	**1,857**	**2,256**	**2,329**	**1,928**	**1,961**	**2,000**	**2,026**
Consumption expenditures	1,084	1,509	1,848	1,898	1,545	1,593	1,637	1,653
Gross investment	262	347	408	431	383	368	364	372
Structures	204	280	319	339	334	301	277	284
Equipment	38	40	49	50	34	40	48	49
Intellectual property products	19	28	40	42	21	28	39	40

Source: U.S. Bureau of Economic Analysis, National Income and Product Accounts Tables, "Table 3.9.5. Government Consumption Expenditures and Gross Investment" and "Table 3.9.6. Real Government Consumption Expenditures and Gross Investment, Chained Dollars," <http://www.bea.gov/iTable/index_nipa.cfm>, accessed July 2020.

Table 713. Personal Consumption Expenditures by Function: 2002 to 2019

[In billions of dollars (7,343 represents $7,343,000,000,000). In current and chained (2012) dollars. For definition of chained dollars, see text, this section. Minus sign (-) indicates decrease]

Function	Current dollars				Chained (2012) dollars			
	2002	2010	2018	2019	2002	2010	2018	2019
Personal consumption expenditures [1]	**7,343**	**10,186**	**13,993**	**14,545**	**9,089**	**10,643**	**12,928**	**13,240**
Food and nonalcoholic beverages purchased for off-premises consumption	490	679	856	878	645	728	829	843
Alcoholic beverages purchased for off-premises consumption	84	108	142	147	99	109	136	138
Clothing, footwear, and related services	295	332	411	420	298	349	411	426
Clothing (garments, cleaning, repair, and rental)	249	269	326	332	248	285	329	341
Footwear [2]	46	62	85	88	50	64	82	85
Housing [1]	1,133	1,604	2,224	2,331	1,415	1,662	1,859	1,883
Rental of tenant-occupied nonfarm housing [3]	250	373	593	622	324	389	487	492
Imputed rental of owner-occupied nonfarm housing [4]	869	1,214	1,611	1,687	1,072	1,253	1,353	1,372
Household utilities and fuels	215	324	367	370	334	336	335	336
Water supply and sanitation	55	78	104	108	92	87	84	84
Electricity, gas, and other fuels	160	246	262	262	243	249	252	252
Furnishings, household equipment, and routine household maintenance [1]	366	411	575	600	351	409	620	639
Furniture, furnishings, and floor coverings [5]	122	128	193	202	104	125	221	229
Household appliances [6]	42	50	65	66	45	52	74	74
Tools and equipment for house and garden	18	20	32	32	18	20	32	32
Medical products, appliances, and equipment [1]	234	379	581	621	305	401	507	542
Pharmaceutical and other medical products [7]	200	326	512	549	267	347	440	473
Outpatient services	515	775	1,067	1,104	639	795	1,018	1,042
Physician services [8]	269	411	559	572	324	422	553	561
Dental services	76	104	132	135	112	109	113	113
Paramedical services [9]	170	260	376	397	205	264	353	369
Hospital and nursing home services	568	925	1,278	1,347	804	967	1,157	1,191
Transportation	807	962	1,319	1,322	1,162	1,085	1,407	1,411
Motor vehicles	360	288	448	443	359	300	461	456
New motor vehicles	244	182	287	285	250	191	281	277
Net purchases of used motor vehicles	116	106	161	159	109	109	184	183
Motor vehicle operation [1]	371	570	702	701	688	671	778	782
Motor vehicle fuels, lubricants, and fluids	154	312	329	316	411	406	421	420
Motor vehicle maintenance and repair	121	137	188	192	164	142	169	167
Public transportation	76	104	168	177	110	115	162	167
Telephone and related communication equipment	6	18	31	30	2	15	87	100
Postal and delivery services	9	15	13	13	14	16	11	11
Telecommunication services	131	148	157	161	130	145	207	223
Internet access	14	40	72	75	11	40	72	75
Recreation [1]	669	884	1,210	1,278	590	863	1,274	1,352
Video and audio equipment	86	83	85	93	28	66	150	179
Information processing equipment	44	95	143	157	16	81	197	231
Services related to video/audio goods and computers	61	97	134	136	78	103	115	115
Sports and recreational goods and related services	156	177	257	272	134	171	302	327
Magazines, newspapers, books, and stationery	81	75	95	103	89	76	89	93
Gambling	74	109	142	147	95	115	130	132
Pets, pet products, and related services	45	76	115	118	64	80	108	108
Education [1]	150	240	299	311	269	263	251	255
Higher education	87	155	186	192	164	171	155	156
Food services	383	537	810	843	514	567	700	709
Accommodations [10]	53	99	151	156	67	104	132	133
Financial services	319	465	704	733	407	507	488	491
Insurance [1]	215	289	415	443	294	304	359	374
Life insurance	59	78	94	100	74	80	81	84
Net health insurance	107	143	233	246	155	151	208	215
Net motor vehicle and other transportation insurance	46	60	78	87	60	65	62	67
Personal care [11]	143	207	288	301	169	211	272	280
Personal items [12]	63	85	105	107	73	90	108	112
Social services and religious activities [13]	93	139	203	212	120	145	175	177
Professional and other services [1]	127	159	198	204	181	167	166	169
Legal services	74	87	108	111	106	92	91	93
Accounting and other business services	20	28	39	41	29	30	31	32
Funeral and burial services	17	24	27	26	25	25	24	23
Tobacco	70	98	99	100	130	104	79	76
Net foreign travel and expenditures abroad by: U.S. residents [1]	-12	-29	-21	-3	-4	-35	-6	15
Foreign travel by U.S. residents	67	103	167	182	105	108	169	183
Less: Expenditures in the United States by nonresidents	83	140	199	196	117	151	185	178
Final consumption expenditures of nonprofit institutions serving households (NPISHs) [14]	198	294	439	439	194	299	365	354

[1] Includes other expenditures not shown separately. [2] Also includes repair and hire of footwear. [3] Rent for space (see footnote 4), and for appliances, furnishings, and furniture. [4] Rent for space and for heating and plumbing facilities, water heaters, lighting fixtures, kitchen cabinets, linoleum, storm windows and doors, window screens, and screen doors; excludes rent for appliances and furniture and purchases of fuel and electricity. [5] Includes clocks, lamps, lighting fixtures, other household decorative items, and repair of furniture, furnishings, and floor coverings. [6] Includes appliance repair. [7] Excludes drug preparations and related products dispensed by physicians, hospitals, and other medical services. [8] Offices of physicians, HMO medical centers, and freestanding ambulatory surgical and emergency centers. [9] Includes home health care, medical laboratories, and other health professionals (except physicians) and services. [10] Hotels, motels, other traveler accommodations, clubs, and housing at schools. [11] Cosmetics, toiletries, and personal care appliances and services. [12] Jewelry, watches, luggage, and similar items. [13] Household purchases from business, government, and nonprofit institutions providing social services and religious activities. Purchases from nonprofit establishments exclude unrelated sales, secondary sales, and sales to businesses, government, and the rest of the world, but include membership dues and fees. [14] Net expenses of NPISHs, defined as their gross operating expenses less primary sales to households.

Source: U.S. Bureau of Economic Analysis, National Income and Product Accounts Tables, "2.5.5 Personal Consumption Expenditures by Function," and "2.5.6 Real Personal Consumption Expenditures by Function, Chained Dollars," <bea.gov/iTable/index_nipa.cfm>, accessed July 2020.

Table 714. Personal Income By Source and Disposition: 2000 to 2019

[In billions of dollars (8,653 represents $8,653,000,000,000), except as indicated. For definition of personal income and chained dollars, see text, this section]

Item	2000	2010	2014	2015	2016	2017	2018	2019
Personal income..........	**8,653**	**12,552**	**14,992**	**15,724**	**16,161**	**16,949**	**17,852**	**18,552**
Compensation of employees, received........	5,848	7,925	9,249	9,699	9,964	10,423	10,950	11,432
Wages and salaries.................	4,826	6,372	7,475	7,859	8,089	8,471	8,894	9,309
Supplements to wages and salaries...........	1,022	1,553	1,774	1,840	1,875	1,951	2,056	2,123
Proprietors' income [1]..........	754	1,109	1,448	1,423	1,425	1,509	1,586	1,658
Farm.......................	31	39	70	56	36	42	43	50
Nonfarm.....................	722	1,070	1,378	1,367	1,389	1,467	1,543	1,608
Rental income of persons [2]...........	183	394	605	649	683	722	759	787
Personal income receipts on assets........	1,486	1,782	2,302	2,472	2,552	2,738	2,947	2,968
Personal interest income............	1,102	1,238	1,349	1,439	1,474	1,578	1,642	1,677
Personal dividend income............	384	544	953	1,033	1,077	1,161	1,305	1,290
Personal current transfer receipts............	1,087	2,325	2,542	2,685	2,777	2,855	2,970	3,125
Government social benefits to persons [3].......	1,045	2,281	2,499	2,635	2,717	2,806	2,923	3,078
Social security [4]..........	401	690	835	872	896	926	972	1,031
Unemployment insurance............	21	139	35	33	32	30	28	28
Veterans' benefits............	25	58	84	93	97	111	120	131
Other current transfer receipts, from business (net).......	42	44	43	50	60	49	47	47
Less: Contributions for government social insurance.......	706	984	1,154	1,205	1,239	1,298	1,360	1,419
Less: Personal current taxes...........	1,236	1,238	1,785	1,940	1,958	2,047	2,085	2,203
Equals: Disposable personal income........	**7,416**	**11,314**	**13,207**	**13,784**	**14,203**	**14,902**	**15,767**	**16,349**
Less: Personal outlays...........	7,060	10,574	12,236	12,746	13,228	13,831	14,529	15,117
Personal consumption expenditures........	6,762	10,186	11,823	12,297	12,770	13,340	13,993	14,545
Personal interest payments [5]............	215	243	244	265	273	297	333	362
Personal current transfer payments............	83	145	170	183	185	193	203	210
Equals: Personal saving...........	**356**	**740**	**971**	**1,039**	**975**	**1,071**	**1,237**	**1,231**
Personal saving as a percentage of disposable personal income........	4.8	6.5	7.4	7.5	6.9	7.2	7.8	7.5
Addenda:								
Disposable personal income:								
Total, billions of chained (2012) dollars [6]............	9,479	11,822	12,844	13,377	13,641	14,061	14,566	14,882
Per capita:								
Current dollars............	26,262	36,523	41,450	42,953	43,946	45,821	48,223	49,763
Chained (2012) dollars............	33,568	38,162	40,309	41,684	42,207	43,234	44,553	45,301

[1] With inventory valuation and capital consumption adjustments. [2] Includes capital consumption adjustment. [3] Includes other benefits not shown separately. [4] Social security benefits include benefits distributed from the Old-Age and Survivors Insurance Trust Fund and the Disability Insurance Trust Fund. [5] Consists of nonmortgage interest paid by households. [6] The current-dollar measure is deflated by the implicit price deflator for personal consumption expenditures.

Source: U.S. Bureau of Economic Analysis, National Income and Product Accounts Tables, "Table 2.1 Personal Income and Its Disposition," <http://www.bea.gov/iTable/index_nipa.cfm>, accessed July 2020.

Table 715. Selected Per Capita Income and Product Measures in Current and Chained (2012) Dollars: 1970 to 2019

[In dollars. Based on U.S. Census Bureau estimated population including Armed Forces abroad, and institutionalized population; based on monthly averages. For explanation of chained dollars, see text, this section]

Year	Current dollars					Chained (2012) dollars				
	Gross domestic product	Gross national product	Personal income	Disposable personal income	Personal consumption expenditures	Gross domestic product	Gross national product	Disposable personal income	Personal consumption expenditures
1970............	5,233	5,265	4,218	3,715	3,153	24,142	24,329	17,734	15,051
1980............	12,547	12,697	10,204	8,888	7,688	29,681	30,079	21,542	18,631
1990............	23,835	23,974	19,641	17,264	15,225	37,435	37,673	27,250	24,031
2000............	36,305	36,429	30,640	26,262	23,945	46,498	46,672	33,568	30,607
2001............	37,100	37,271	31,574	27,230	24,772	46,497	46,726	34,149	31,067
2002............	37,980	38,137	31,807	28,153	25,499	46,858	47,067	34,847	31,563
2003............	39,426	39,627	32,645	29,192	26,574	47,756	48,013	35,446	32,267
2004............	41,648	41,914	34,219	30,643	28,004	49,125	49,454	36,302	33,176
2005............	44,044	44,307	35,806	31,710	29,552	50,381	50,697	36,526	34,041
2006............	46,231	46,400	38,089	33,548	30,990	51,330	51,532	37,621	34,752
2007............	47,902	48,263	39,801	34,854	32,173	51,794	52,199	38,118	35,186
2008............	48,311	48,819	40,855	35,905	32,758	51,240	51,788	38,124	34,783
2009............	47,028	47,490	39,250	35,499	32,034	49,501	49,991	37,727	34,045
2010............	48,397	49,028	40,518	36,523	32,881	50,355	51,017	38,162	34,357
2011............	49,814	50,572	42,713	38,054	34,105	50,770	51,542	38,778	34,755
2012............	51,548	52,287	44,588	39,784	35,030	51,548	52,287	39,784	35,030
2013............	53,057	53,786	44,826	39,527	35,774	52,142	52,859	39,002	35,298
2014............	55,008	55,765	47,050	41,450	37,105	53,077	53,813	40,309	36,084
2015............	56,832	57,518	48,998	42,953	38,320	54,320	54,991	41,684	37,188
2016............	58,001	58,719	50,004	43,946	39,513	54,862	55,558	42,207	37,949
2017............	60,091	60,990	52,114	45,821	41,019	55,790	56,642	43,234	38,703
2018............	63,043	63,914	54,601	48,223	42,800	57,158	57,966	44,553	39,542
2019............	65,240	66,061	56,469	49,763	44,272	58,113	58,864	45,301	40,302

Source: U.S. Bureau of Economic Analysis, National Income and Product Accounts Tables, "Table 7.1. Selected Per Capita Product and Income Series in Current and Chained Dollars," <http://www.bea.gov/iTable/index_nipa.cfm>, accessed July 2020.

Table 716. Personal Income in Current and Constant (2012) Dollars by State: 2000 to 2019

[In billions of dollars (8,650.3 represents $8,650,300,000,000). Represents income that all persons who are state residents receive from all sources. Data exclude income of foreign nationals employed in the U.S. by their home governments, and income earned by U.S. citizens while living abroad. Data also exclude the earnings of federal civilian and military personnel stationed abroad. Totals may differ from those in Table 706, Table 714, and Table 715]

State	Current dollars					Constant (2012) dollars [1]				
	2000	2005	2010	2018	2019 (P)	2000	2005	2010	2018	2019 (P)
United States............	8,650.3	10,593.9	12,542.0	17,813.0	18,599.1	11,056.8	12,203.3	13,104.8	16,471.7	16,961.6
Alabama....................	108.4	136.3	161.5	206.5	215.1	138.5	157.0	168.8	190.9	196.2
Alaska.....................	20.1	26.0	35.3	43.8	45.4	25.7	29.9	36.9	40.5	41.4
Arizona....................	135.4	188.1	215.5	317.9	336.5	173.1	216.7	225.2	294.0	306.9
Arkansas..................	61.0	78.0	93.3	130.3	135.3	77.9	89.8	97.5	120.5	123.4
California..................	1,134.0	1,407.3	1,628.5	2,514.1	2,633.9	1,449.4	1,621.1	1,701.5	2,324.8	2,402.0
Colorado..................	147.9	175.3	205.4	332.9	353.3	189.1	201.9	214.6	307.9	322.2
Connecticut...............	147.1	175.5	222.2	273.2	282.0	188.0	202.1	232.2	252.6	257.1
Delaware..................	26.7	33.3	36.7	50.8	52.8	34.1	38.4	38.4	47.0	48.2
District of Columbia.......	24.8	30.2	38.5	57.6	59.7	31.7	34.7	40.2	53.3	54.4
Florida....................	472.2	642.5	725.1	1,066.4	1,116.6	603.6	740.1	757.6	986.1	1,018.3
Georgia...................	237.4	297.5	335.3	489.0	511.7	303.5	342.7	350.3	452.1	466.7
Hawaii....................	35.7	47.3	57.2	78.7	81.3	45.6	54.5	59.7	72.8	74.2
Idaho.....................	32.8	41.8	50.2	77.0	81.6	41.9	48.2	52.4	71.2	74.4
Illinois....................	412.4	476.6	540.5	724.2	746.8	527.2	549.0	564.7	669.7	681.1
Indiana...................	172.0	197.7	230.1	315.5	327.6	219.8	227.7	240.4	291.8	298.7
Iowa......................	80.4	96.6	116.2	158.2	166.1	102.8	111.2	121.5	146.3	151.4
Kansas...................	76.1	88.7	113.1	149.9	155.7	97.2	102.2	118.2	138.6	142.0
Kentucky..................	100.8	121.8	144.1	189.7	196.7	128.8	140.3	150.6	175.4	179.3
Louisiana..................	107.1	135.9	171.1	215.5	223.2	136.9	156.6	178.8	199.3	203.5
Maine.....................	35.2	43.4	50.3	65.5	68.5	45.0	50.0	52.6	60.5	62.5
Maryland..................	189.5	245.2	289.5	382.8	397.1	242.2	282.4	302.5	354.0	362.1
Massachusetts.............	245.3	285.6	348.4	494.8	516.7	313.5	329.0	364.1	457.5	471.2
Michigan..................	302.6	330.5	349.6	484.0	502.5	386.8	380.7	365.3	447.6	458.3
Minnesota.................	160.1	195.1	226.3	322.7	336.6	204.6	224.8	236.4	298.4	307.0
Mississippi................	61.6	77.6	91.8	113.0	117.2	78.8	89.4	95.9	104.5	106.9
Missouri...................	157.0	187.5	220.8	292.5	304.3	200.7	216.0	230.7	270.5	277.6
Montana..................	20.9	28.0	35.6	50.5	52.4	26.7	32.3	37.2	46.7	47.8
Nebraska..................	49.7	60.8	74.9	102.8	106.1	63.6	70.0	78.2	95.0	96.8
Nevada....................	64.3	92.7	100.6	149.2	156.7	82.2	106.7	105.1	138.0	142.9
New Hampshire............	43.9	52.9	61.6	83.1	86.9	56.1	60.9	64.4	76.9	79.2
New Jersey................	331.0	387.4	452.5	607.9	630.4	423.0	446.2	472.8	562.1	574.9
New Mexico...............	42.3	55.8	69.3	87.2	92.2	54.1	64.3	72.4	80.6	84.1
New York..................	684.6	782.6	950.1	1,341.9	1,389.8	875.0	901.5	992.7	1,240.9	1,267.4
North Carolina.............	222.6	281.0	341.6	478.9	501.4	284.5	323.7	357.0	442.8	457.2
North Dakota..............	16.7	20.4	29.3	42.1	43.8	21.3	23.5	30.7	39.0	40.0
Ohio......................	325.8	373.4	422.0	569.7	590.8	416.4	430.2	441.0	526.8	538.8
Oklahoma.................	83.2	111.1	137.4	182.3	189.7	106.4	128.0	143.6	168.6	173.0
Oregon...................	98.0	117.4	138.6	213.1	223.3	125.2	135.3	144.8	197.0	203.6
Pennsylvania..............	373.4	452.0	534.5	720.1	752.4	477.2	520.6	558.5	665.9	686.2
Rhode Island..............	32.0	39.7	45.3	58.0	59.9	41.0	45.8	47.3	53.6	54.6
South Carolina.............	101.2	124.6	150.5	222.2	233.3	129.4	143.5	157.2	205.5	212.8
South Dakota..............	20.3	26.1	33.6	46.1	47.7	25.9	30.1	35.1	42.6	43.5
Tennessee.................	154.4	187.9	226.6	317.5	333.0	197.4	216.5	236.8	293.6	303.7
Texas.....................	589.3	745.9	966.1	1,445.3	1,522.4	753.2	859.2	1,009.5	1,336.4	1,388.4
Utah......................	54.5	70.9	89.2	146.4	155.2	69.6	81.6	93.2	135.4	141.5
Vermont...................	17.7	21.7	25.9	33.9	35.4	22.7	25.0	27.1	31.4	32.3
Virginia...................	232.3	305.0	365.0	492.3	513.1	296.9	351.4	381.4	455.2	467.9
Washington................	194.5	235.8	287.8	467.4	494.2	248.6	271.7	300.7	432.2	450.7
West Virginia..............	40.4	48.9	59.9	73.8	75.9	51.6	56.3	62.6	68.3	69.2
Wisconsin.................	159.3	191.0	221.9	299.9	312.0	203.7	220.0	231.9	277.3	284.5
Wyoming..................	14.6	19.7	25.8	34.9	36.6	18.7	22.6	27.0	32.2	33.4

P Preliminary. [1] Constant dollar estimates are computed by ProQuest using the national implicit price deflator for personal consumption expenditures from the Bureau of Economic Analysis' National Income and Product Accounts Tables. Any regional differences in the rate of inflation are not reflected in these constant dollar estimates.

Source: Except as noted, U.S. Bureau of Economic Analysis, Regional Economic Accounts, Personal Income by State, Interactive Data, "Table SAINC1 Personal Income Summary," <https://www.bea.gov/data/economic-accounts/regional>, accessed March 2020.

Table 717. Personal Income Per Capita in Current and Constant (2012) Dollars by State: 2000 to 2019

[In dollars, except as indicated. Represents income that all persons who are state residents receive from all sources. Data exclude income of foreign nationals employed in the U.S. by their home governments, and income earned by U.S. citizens while living abroad. Data also exclude the earnings of federal civilian and military personnel stationed abroad. Totals may differ from those in Table 706, Table 714, and Table 715]

State	Current dollars				Constant (2012) dollars [1]				Income rank [2]	
	2000	2010	2018	2019 (P)	2000	2010	2018	2019 (P)	2010	2019 (P)
United States..................	**30,657**	**40,547**	**54,526**	**56,663**	**39,186**	**42,367**	**50,420**	**51,674**	**(X)**	**(X)**
Alabama.........................	24,338	33,752	42,240	43,880	31,109	35,267	39,059	40,017	42	49
Alaska...........................	31,974	49,437	59,605	62,102	40,869	51,656	55,117	56,635	6	11
Arizona..........................	26,235	33,638	44,414	46,233	33,534	35,148	41,070	42,163	43	43
Arkansas........................	22,762	31,927	43,292	44,845	29,094	33,360	40,032	40,897	50	46
California........................	33,364	43,636	63,711	66,661	42,646	45,594	58,914	60,792	11	6
Colorado........................	34,187	40,689	58,500	61,348	43,698	42,515	54,095	55,947	23	12
Connecticut.....................	43,102	62,090	76,481	79,087	55,093	64,876	70,722	72,124	2	2
Delaware........................	33,907	40,825	52,599	54,264	43,340	42,657	48,638	49,487	22	22
District of Columbia.............	43,344	63,582	82,111	84,538	55,402	66,435	75,928	77,095	1	1
Florida..........................	29,428	38,475	50,199	51,989	37,615	40,202	46,419	47,412	26	29
Georgia.........................	28,861	34,521	46,519	48,199	36,890	36,070	43,016	43,956	41	39
Hawaii...........................	29,404	41,921	55,414	57,450	37,584	43,802	51,241	52,392	18	18
Idaho............................	25,235	31,957	43,994	45,642	32,255	33,391	40,681	41,624	49	44
Illinois...........................	33,169	42,093	56,919	58,935	42,397	43,982	52,633	53,746	16	15
Indiana..........................	28,233	35,454	47,124	48,657	36,087	37,045	43,576	44,373	39	37
Iowa.............................	27,463	38,105	50,243	52,636	35,103	39,815	46,460	48,002	28	27
Kansas..........................	28,244	39,563	51,474	53,453	36,101	41,338	47,598	48,747	24	25
Kentucky........................	24,894	33,141	42,527	44,017	31,820	34,628	39,325	40,142	45	47
Louisiana........................	23,943	37,649	46,245	48,008	30,604	39,339	42,763	43,781	30	40
Maine............................	27,584	37,910	48,881	50,950	35,258	39,611	45,200	46,464	29	30
Maryland........................	35,681	50,007	63,426	65,683	45,607	52,251	58,650	59,900	5	7
Massachusetts..................	38,555	53,062	71,886	74,967	49,281	55,443	66,473	68,367	3	3
Michigan.........................	30,409	35,391	48,480	50,320	38,869	36,979	44,830	45,890	40	33
Minnesota.......................	32,447	42,606	57,566	59,683	41,474	44,518	53,231	54,428	15	14
Mississippi......................	21,640	30,902	37,904	39,368	27,660	32,289	35,050	35,902	51	51
Missouri.........................	28,001	36,823	47,784	49,589	35,791	38,476	44,186	45,223	32	34
Montana.........................	23,094	35,896	47,611	49,074	29,519	37,507	44,026	44,753	36	35
Nebraska........................	29,020	40,920	53,364	54,871	37,093	42,756	49,346	50,040	21	21
Nevada..........................	31,871	37,228	49,290	50,883	40,738	38,899	45,579	46,403	31	31
New Hampshire..................	35,380	46,785	61,429	63,880	45,223	48,885	56,803	58,256	8	9
New Jersey......................	39,257	51,420	68,409	70,979	50,178	53,728	63,258	64,730	4	5
New Mexico.....................	23,237	33,542	41,663	43,984	29,702	35,047	38,526	40,112	44	48
New York........................	36,028	48,973	68,710	71,440	46,051	51,171	63,536	65,150	7	4
North Carolina...................	27,540	35,682	46,126	47,803	35,202	37,283	42,653	43,594	37	42
North Dakota....................	25,955	43,492	55,598	57,501	33,176	45,444	51,412	52,439	12	17
Ohio.............................	28,671	36,575	48,793	50,546	36,647	38,216	45,119	46,096	33	32
Oklahoma.......................	24,096	36,541	46,267	47,951	30,800	38,181	42,783	43,729	34	41
Oregon..........................	28,561	36,122	50,951	52,937	36,507	37,743	47,114	48,276	35	26
Pennsylvania....................	30,393	42,047	56,252	58,775	38,848	43,934	52,016	53,600	17	16
Rhode Island....................	30,515	42,944	54,800	56,542	39,004	44,871	50,674	51,564	13	20
South Carolina..................	25,152	32,458	43,702	45,314	32,149	33,915	40,411	41,325	46	45
South Dakota...................	26,832	41,163	52,426	53,925	34,297	43,010	48,478	49,177	20	23
Tennessee......................	27,073	35,653	46,889	48,761	34,605	37,253	43,358	44,468	38	36
Texas...........................	28,135	38,276	50,483	52,504	35,962	39,994	46,682	47,882	27	28
Utah............................	24,266	32,156	46,431	48,395	31,017	33,599	42,935	44,134	48	38
Vermont.........................	29,109	41,444	54,342	56,691	37,207	43,304	50,250	51,700	19	19
Virginia..........................	32,693	45,495	57,910	60,116	41,788	47,537	53,549	54,823	10	13
Washington......................	32,909	42,676	62,122	64,898	42,064	44,591	57,444	59,184	14	8
West Virginia....................	22,331	32,319	40,907	42,336	28,543	33,769	37,827	38,609	47	50
Wisconsin.......................	29,648	38,997	51,647	53,583	37,896	40,747	47,758	48,866	25	24
Wyoming........................	29,519	45,714	60,375	63,316	37,731	47,766	55,829	57,742	9	10

P Preliminary. X Not applicable. [1] Constant dollar estimates are computed by ProQuest using the national implicit price deflator for personal consumption expenditures from the Bureau of Economic Analysis' National Income and Product Accounts tables. Any regional differences in the rate of inflation are not reflected in these constant dollar estimates. [2] Ranking based on current dollar income.

Source: Except as noted, U.S. Bureau of Economic Analysis, Regional Economic Accounts, Personal Income by State, Interactive Data, "Table SAINC1 Personal Income Summary," <https://www.bea.gov/data/economic-accounts/regional>, accessed March 2020.

Table 718. Disposable Personal Income Per Capita in Current and Constant (2012) Dollars by State: 2000 to 2019

[In dollars, except as indicated. Per capita disposable personal income is total disposable personal income divided by total midyear population. Disposable personal income is total personal income minus personal current taxes. It is the portion of personal income that is available for saving and spending. The estimate of personal income in the United States is derived as the sum of the state estimates and the estimate for the District of Columbia; it differs from the estimate of personal income in the national income and product accounts (NIPAs) because of differences in coverage, in the methodologies used to prepare the estimates, and in the timing of the availability of source data. See text, Section 13]

State	Current dollars				Constant (2012) dollars [1]				Index, compared to U.S. average [2]	
	2000	2010	2018	2019 (P)	2000	2010	2018	2019 (P)	2010	2019 (P)
United States..........	26,279	36,551	48,172	50,023	33,590	38,191	44,545	45,619	100.0	100.0
Alabama.................	21,606	30,992	38,217	39,671	27,617	32,383	35,339	36,178	84.8	79.3
Alaska...................	28,536	45,697	54,601	56,874	36,475	47,748	50,490	51,867	125.0	113.7
Arizona..................	22,895	30,921	40,031	41,630	29,264	32,309	37,017	37,965	84.6	83.2
Arkansas................	20,199	29,278	39,224	40,604	25,818	30,592	36,270	37,029	80.1	81.2
California...............	27,613	38,861	54,932	57,393	35,295	40,605	50,796	52,340	106.3	114.7
Colorado................	29,054	36,384	51,444	53,848	37,137	38,017	47,570	49,107	99.5	107.6
Connecticut.............	35,012	54,308	65,084	67,322	44,752	56,745	60,183	61,395	148.6	134.6
Delaware................	29,315	36,869	46,487	47,901	37,470	38,524	42,987	43,684	100.9	95.8
District of Columbia......	36,307	55,842	70,258	72,295	46,408	58,348	64,968	65,930	152.8	144.5
Florida..................	25,721	35,369	45,390	46,977	32,877	36,956	41,972	42,841	96.8	93.9
Georgia.................	24,916	31,317	41,611	43,073	31,848	32,722	38,478	39,281	85.7	86.1
Hawaii..................	25,823	38,424	49,483	51,279	33,007	40,148	45,757	46,764	105.1	102.5
Idaho...................	22,111	29,412	39,670	41,133	28,262	30,732	36,683	37,512	80.5	82.2
Illinois..................	28,396	37,801	49,960	51,691	36,296	39,497	46,198	47,140	103.4	103.3
Indiana.................	24,745	32,291	42,360	43,743	31,629	33,740	39,170	39,892	88.3	87.4
Iowa....................	24,296	34,725	45,073	47,298	31,055	36,283	41,679	43,134	95.0	94.6
Kansas..................	24,597	35,875	46,060	47,816	31,440	37,485	42,592	43,606	98.2	95.6
Kentucky................	21,818	30,161	38,137	39,446	27,888	31,515	35,265	35,973	82.5	78.9
Louisiana...............	21,428	34,703	42,058	43,675	27,389	36,260	38,891	39,830	94.9	87.3
Maine...................	24,098	34,626	43,887	45,725	30,802	36,180	40,582	41,699	94.7	91.4
Maryland................	30,221	44,321	55,191	57,120	38,628	46,310	51,035	52,091	121.3	114.2
Massachusetts..........	31,120	46,564	61,320	63,829	39,778	48,654	56,703	58,209	127.4	127.6
Michigan................	26,290	32,253	43,030	44,701	33,604	33,700	39,790	40,765	88.2	89.4
Minnesota...............	27,619	37,952	49,946	51,817	35,303	39,655	46,185	47,255	103.8	103.6
Mississippi..............	19,552	28,591	34,817	36,179	24,991	29,874	32,195	32,994	78.2	72.3
Missouri.................	24,432	33,558	42,681	44,288	31,229	35,064	39,467	40,389	91.8	88.5
Montana................	20,389	32,842	42,693	43,946	26,061	34,316	39,478	40,077	89.9	87.9
Nebraska...............	25,481	37,353	48,022	49,341	32,570	39,029	44,406	44,997	102.2	98.6
Nevada.................	27,756	34,134	44,148	45,563	35,478	35,666	40,824	41,552	93.4	91.1
New Hampshire..........	30,554	42,940	55,112	57,295	39,054	44,867	50,962	52,251	117.5	114.5
New Jersey..............	32,913	45,545	59,330	61,563	42,069	47,589	54,863	56,143	124.6	123.1
New Mexico.............	20,753	31,017	38,117	40,222	26,526	32,409	35,247	36,681	84.9	80.4
New York...............	30,003	42,251	58,040	60,185	38,350	44,147	53,670	54,886	115.6	120.3
North Carolina...........	23,864	32,444	41,057	42,506	30,503	33,900	37,965	38,764	88.8	85.0
North Dakota............	23,442	39,669	50,169	51,833	29,964	41,449	46,391	47,270	108.5	103.6
Ohio....................	24,721	33,036	43,628	45,180	31,598	34,519	40,343	41,202	90.4	90.3
Oklahoma...............	21,196	33,595	42,038	43,562	27,093	35,103	38,873	39,727	91.9	87.1
Oregon..................	24,364	32,433	44,490	46,197	31,142	33,889	41,140	42,130	88.7	92.4
Pennsylvania............	26,271	37,863	49,893	52,117	33,580	39,562	46,136	47,529	103.6	104.2
Rhode Island............	26,358	38,960	48,697	50,258	33,691	40,708	45,030	45,833	106.6	100.5
South Carolina...........	22,219	29,842	39,401	40,834	28,400	31,181	36,434	37,239	81.6	81.6
South Dakota............	24,273	38,423	47,947	49,291	31,026	40,147	44,337	44,951	105.1	98.5
Tennessee..............	24,375	33,300	42,912	44,615	31,156	34,794	39,681	40,687	91.1	89.2
Texas...................	24,776	35,195	46,021	47,821	31,669	36,774	42,556	43,611	96.3	95.6
Utah....................	21,193	29,337	41,377	43,054	27,089	30,654	38,261	39,264	80.3	86.1
Vermont.................	25,433	37,993	48,771	50,880	32,508	39,698	45,099	46,400	103.9	101.7
Virginia.................	27,822	40,612	50,725	52,624	35,562	42,435	46,905	47,991	111.1	105.2
Washington.............	28,443	39,235	55,538	57,930	36,356	40,996	51,356	52,830	107.3	115.8
West Virginia............	19,959	29,568	37,092	38,426	25,512	30,895	34,299	35,043	80.9	76.8
Wisconsin...............	25,576	35,234	45,781	47,515	32,691	36,815	42,334	43,332	96.4	95.0
Wyoming................	25,558	41,573	54,726	57,362	32,668	43,439	50,605	52,312	113.7	114.7

P Preliminary. [1] Constant dollar estimates are computed by ProQuest using the national implicit price deflator for personal consumption expenditures from the Bureau of Economic Analysis' National Income and Product Accounts Tables. Any regional differences in the rate of inflation are not reflected in these constant dollar estimates. [2] Indexes calculated using disposable personal income per capita in current dollars.

Source: Except as noted, U.S. Bureau of Economic Analysis, Regional Economic Accounts, Personal Income by State, Interactive Data, "Table SAINC51 Disposable Personal Income Summary," <https://www.bea.gov/data/economic-accounts/regional>, accessed March 2020.

Table 719. Personal Income by Selected Large Metropolitan Area: 2000 to 2018

[7,647,166 represents $7,647,166,000,000. MSA=Metropolitan Statistical Area. The MSAs used by the Bureau of Economic Analysis are defined in the Office of Management and Budget Bulletin No. 18-04 issued September 14, 2018. Per capita personal income was computed using Census Bureau midyear population estimates. Estimates for 2010-2018 reflect county population estimates available as of March 2019]

Metropolitan statistical areas ranked by 2018 population	Personal income			Personal income per capita			Index (U.S.= 100), 2018
	2000 (mil. dol.)	2010 (mil. dol.)	2018 (mil. dol.)	2000 (dol.)	2010 (dol.)	2018 (dol.)	
United States, metropolitan portion.............	**7,647,166**	**11,074,966**	**15,924,514**	**32,138**	**42,004**	**56,527**	**100.0**
New York-Newark-Jersey City, NY-NJ-PA MSA.....	752,632	1,033,821	1,480,233	41,002	54,631	76,681	135.7
Los Angeles-Long Beach-Anaheim, CA MSA........	394,920	578,373	849,493	31,867	45,048	63,913	113.1
Chicago-Naperville-Elgin, IL-IN-WI MSA.............	328,421	418,681	580,270	36,038	44,207	61,089	108.1
Dallas-Fort Worth-Arlington, TX MSA................	174,789	262,043	417,481	33,697	40,994	55,886	98.9
Houston-The Woodlands-Sugar Land, TX MSA.....	156,256	267,613	392,394	33,122	44,997	56,077	99.2
Washington-Arlington-Alexandria, DC-VA-MD-WV MSA............................	207,538	331,671	453,978	42,564	58,410	72,483	128.2
Miami-Fort Lauderdale-Pompano Beach, FL MSA................................	162,832	239,474	354,746	32,399	42,889	57,228	101.2
Philadelphia-Camden-Wilmington, PA-NJ-DE-MD MSA........................	200,465	287,527	392,847	35,219	48,154	64,440	114.0
Atlanta-Sandy Springs-Alpharetta, GA MSA.........	145,805	203,514	312,213	33,960	38,379	52,473	92.8
Boston-Cambridge-Newton, MA-NH MSA...........	187,074	265,132	383,665	42,505	58,061	78,694	139.2
Phoenix-Mesa-Chandler, AZ MSA...................	94,374	146,976	224,072	28,830	34,955	46,125	81.6
San Francisco-Oakland-Berkeley, CA MSA..........	204,406	266,002	470,222	49,423	61,237	99,424	175.9
Riverside-San Bernardino-Ontario, CA MSA.........	77,216	127,927	187,142	23,563	30,153	40,486	71.6
Detroit-Warren-Dearborn, MI MSA...................	154,608	163,055	229,674	34,700	37,994	53,086	93.9
Seattle-Tacoma-Bellevue, WA MSA.................	119,257	168,310	293,954	39,073	48,796	74,620	132.0
Minneapolis-St. Paul-Bloomington, MN-WI MSA....	112,229	154,354	227,292	37,051	46,214	62,889	111.3
San Diego-Chula Vista-Carlsbad, CA MSA.........	95,625	136,970	205,236	33,821	44,137	61,386	108.6
Tampa-St. Petersburg-Clearwater, FL MSA........	70,269	107,124	148,460	29,230	38,418	47,240	83.6
Denver-Aurora-Lakewood, CO MSA...............	82,930	111,542	188,515	38,199	43,660	64,287	113.7
St. Louis, MO-IL MSA...........................	85,716	118,384	156,779	31,998	42,432	55,883	98.9
Baltimore-Columbia-Towson, MD MSA.............	88,618	132,299	174,901	34,644	48,716	62,402	110.4
Charlotte-Concord-Gastonia, NC-SC MSA..........	53,631	87,058	135,350	30,577	38,691	52,176	92.3
Orlando-Kissimmee-Sanford, FL MSA..............	45,783	71,145	111,901	27,632	33,258	43,491	76.9
San Antonio-New Braunfels, TX MSA..............	46,089	77,234	118,335	26,796	35,872	46,995	83.1
Portland-Vancouver-Hillsboro, OR-WA MSA.........	63,038	89,154	141,270	32,581	39,940	56,991	100.8
Sacramento-Roseville-Folsom, CA MSA............	56,969	88,581	131,984	31,510	41,131	56,278	99.6
Pittsburgh, PA MSA............................	74,565	101,017	135,003	30,707	42,857	58,072	102.7
Las Vegas-Henderson-Paradise, NV MSA..........	43,189	69,602	105,088	30,984	35,645	47,090	83.3
Cincinnati, OH-KY-IN MSA.......................	62,811	86,412	119,888	31,067	40,366	54,176	95.8
Austin-Round Rock-Georgetown, TX MSA..........	41,785	70,355	127,439	33,033	40,726	58,773	104.0
Kansas City, MO-KS MSA.......................	58,394	82,755	115,303	32,121	41,103	53,788	95.2
Columbus, OH MSA............................	52,184	73,475	107,781	31,024	38,542	51,165	90.5
Cleveland-Elyria, OH MSA.......................	68,638	82,196	110,539	31,961	39,604	53,738	95.1
Indianapolis-Carmel-Anderson, IN MSA............	54,697	78,249	110,997	32,871	41,344	54,179	95.8
San Jose-Sunnyvale-Santa Clara, CA MSA.........	93,724	111,534	212,332	53,904	60,564	106,213	187.9
Nashville-Davidson–Murfreesboro–Franklin, TN MSA.............................	43,730	68,943	110,453	32,038	41,763	57,953	102.5
Virginia Beach-Norfolk-Newport News, VA-NC MSA..............................	45,209	69,482	89,345	27,950	40,467	50,619	89.5
Providence-Warwick, RI-MA MSA.................	47,484	67,625	88,501	29,938	42,184	54,585	96.6
Milwaukee-Waukesha, WI MSA...................	50,729	67,896	89,846	33,765	43,616	57,005	100.8
Jacksonville, FL MSA...........................	34,189	52,231	76,357	30,356	38,721	49,754	88.0
Oklahoma City, OK MSA........................	29,154	48,692	67,827	26,548	38,712	48,571	85.9
Raleigh-Cary, NC MSA..........................	27,639	48,714	75,001	34,370	42,830	55,045	97.4
Memphis, TN-MS-AR MSA.......................	35,660	48,627	62,580	29,514	36,909	46,620	82.5
Richmond, VA MSA.............................	33,703	51,017	73,485	32,299	42,935	57,301	101.4
New Orleans-Metairie, LA MSA...................	36,373	50,931	66,609	27,158	42,609	52,431	92.8
Louisville/Jefferson County, KY-IN MSA...........	33,163	45,592	63,373	30,347	37,846	50,101	88.6
Salt Lake City, UT MSA..........................	26,025	39,345	63,249	27,611	36,047	51,736	91.5
Hartford-East Hartford-Middletown, CT MSA........	43,736	61,473	77,610	38,003	50,634	64,337	113.8
Buffalo-Cheektowaga, NY MSA...................	32,827	43,978	56,976	28,080	38,726	50,414	89.2
Birmingham-Hoover, AL MSA.....................	29,065	41,703	55,469	29,577	39,279	50,979	90.2
Grand Rapids-Kentwood, MI MSA.................	27,868	35,984	54,120	29,680	36,191	50,463	89.3
Rochester, NY MSA............................	31,947	42,758	54,804	29,955	39,592	51,167	90.5
Tucson, AZ MSA...............................	21,063	33,444	45,748	24,838	34,069	44,028	77.9
Fresno, CA MSA...............................	18,496	29,568	42,843	23,083	31,723	43,084	76.2
Tulsa, OK MSA................................	23,685	38,856	54,526	27,501	41,344	54,866	97.1
Urban Honolulu, HI MSA........................	27,571	43,398	58,421	31,452	45,381	59,608	105.5
Worcester, MA-CT MSA.........................	27,875	39,446	52,892	32,349	42,926	55,801	98.7
Bridgeport-Stamford-Norwalk, CT MSA............	55,098	95,360	113,853	62,303	103,728	120,630	213.4
Omaha-Council Bluffs, NE-IA MSA................	25,257	38,969	54,682	32,831	44,912	58,037	102.7
Albuquerque, NM MSA..........................	19,627	30,635	38,960	26,805	34,438	42,536	75.2
Greenville-Anderson, SC MSA...................	19,363	27,099	40,085	26,607	32,822	44,213	78.2
Bakersfield, CA MSA...........................	14,244	26,097	35,604	21,459	31,028	39,703	70.2
Albany-Schenectady-Troy, NY MSA...............	26,801	38,694	51,315	32,392	44,421	58,104	102.8
McAllen-Edinburg-Mission, TX MSA...............	8,106	17,084	22,869	14,141	21,925	26,410	46.7
Knoxville, TN MSA.............................	19,457	28,329	39,343	26,682	34,718	45,739	80.9

Source: U.S. Bureau of Economic Analysis, Regional Economic Accounts, Personal Income by County, Metro, and Other Areas, "CAINC1 Personal Income Summary: Personal Income, Population, Per Capita Personal Income," <https://www.bea.gov/data/economic-accounts/regional>, accessed February 2020.

Table 720. Households by Income Level and Median Income by State: 2018

[In thousands (121,520 represents 121,520,000), except as indicated. The American Community Survey universe includes the household population and the population living in institutions, college dormitories, and other group quarters. Based on a sample and subject to sampling variability; see text, Section 1 and Appendix III. For definition of median, see Guide to Tabular Presentation]

State	Number of households (1,000)								Median income (dollars)
	Total	Under $25,000	$25,000 to $49,999	$50,000 to $74,999	$75,000 to $99,999	$100,000 to $149,999	$150,000 to $199,999	$200,000 or more	
United States........	**121,520**	**23,803**	**25,816**	**21,098**	**15,255**	**18,235**	**8,033**	**9,280**	**61,937**
Alabama..............	1,855	500	430	322	222	225	82	74	49,861
Alaska................	255	36	43	49	34	48	21	22	74,346
Arizona...............	2,614	501	597	500	342	372	149	153	59,246
Arkansas.............	1,156	306	306	206	122	131	44	42	47,062
California.............	13,072	2,163	2,306	2,045	1,602	2,176	1,166	1,614	75,277
Colorado..............	2,177	333	416	381	297	381	180	189	71,953
Connecticut...........	1,378	226	238	214	169	232	128	171	76,348
Delaware..............	368	67	77	67	50	58	24	24	64,805
District of Columbia. ..	287	56	39	35	31	47	26	53	85,203
Florida...............	7,809	1,654	1,870	1,437	948	1,031	403	467	55,462
Georgia...............	3,803	789	848	677	468	541	224	255	58,756
Hawaii................	455	62	81	71	60	91	44	46	80,212
Idaho.................	640	128	158	135	79	84	29	27	55,583
Illinois...............	4,865	924	978	837	608	764	352	402	65,030
Indiana...............	2,599	534	627	502	355	358	121	101	55,746
Iowa..................	1,268	238	291	244	182	190	62	59	59,955
Kansas...............	1,133	222	269	212	150	158	64	58	58,218
Kentucky..............	1,733	431	431	310	205	217	70	69	50,247
Louisiana.............	1,737	486	409	276	192	214	84	77	47,905
Maine.................	570	124	133	103	77	81	28	25	55,602
Maryland..............	2,216	302	353	347	293	417	226	278	83,242
Massachusetts........	2,624	447	420	384	311	459	258	345	79,835
Michigan..............	3,957	826	926	727	505	551	219	204	56,697
Minnesota............	2,194	342	440	383	303	392	168	167	70,315
Mississippi...........	1,109	329	277	189	131	109	40	34	44,717
Missouri..............	2,435	517	602	452	303	322	117	121	54,478
Montana..............	431	92	104	86	57	55	20	17	55,328
Nebraska.............	765	143	177	148	103	119	40	36	59,566
Nevada...............	1,130	214	267	208	150	164	66	61	58,646
New Hampshire.......	531	81	99	86	73	99	45	48	74,991
New Jersey...........	3,250	496	521	482	398	570	330	453	81,740
New Mexico...........	794	220	195	138	86	91	34	31	47,169
New York.............	7,367	1,498	1,344	1,122	879	1,152	586	785	67,844
North Carolina........	4,011	869	984	730	488	522	193	226	53,855
North Dakota..........	319	57	68	58	44	56	20	16	63,837
Ohio..................	4,685	1,009	1,091	856	603	662	239	226	56,111
Oklahoma.............	1,485	341	371	280	183	184	64	63	51,924
Oregon...............	1,640	293	357	298	222	254	107	109	63,426
Pennsylvania..........	5,071	1,018	1,092	905	648	764	314	330	60,905
Rhode Island..........	407	83	76	71	49	70	29	29	64,340
South Carolina........	1,928	449	468	358	241	235	89	88	52,306
South Dakota.........	345	64	90	65	51	47	15	13	56,274
Tennessee............	2,603	600	634	478	322	333	115	120	52,375
Texas................	9,776	1,931	2,133	1,730	1,198	1,445	632	706	60,629
Utah.................	999	129	201	195	153	189	69	64	71,414
Vermont..............	261	50	56	49	38	42	14	13	60,782
Virginia..............	3,176	518	594	517	406	531	268	341	72,577
Washington...........	2,896	421	537	506	390	512	248	282	74,073
West Virginia.........	735	211	195	129	72	83	23	21	44,097
Wisconsin............	2,372	432	545	457	328	370	127	113	60,773
Wyoming.............	230	41	53	42	32	37	14	11	61,584
Puerto Rico...........	1,180	684	285	114	44	32	8	12	20,296

Source: U.S. Census Bureau, 2018 American Community Survey, B19001, "Household Income in the Past 12 Months (In 2018 Inflation-Adjusted Dollars)"; and B19013, "Median Household Income in the Past 12 Months (In 2018 Inflation-Adjusted Dollars)"; <https://data.census.gov/>, accessed November 2019.

Table 721. Families by Income Level and Median Income by State: 2018

[In thousands (79,242 represents 79,242,000), except as indicated. The American Community Survey universe includes the household population and the population living in institutions, college dormitories, and other group quarters. Based on a sample and subject to sampling variability; see text, Section 1 and Appendix III. For definition of median, see Guide to Tabular Presentation]

State	Number of families (1,000)								Median income (dollars)
	Total	Less than $25,000	$25,000 to $49,999	$50,000 to $74,999	$75,000 to $99,999	$100,000 to $149,999	$150,000 to $199,999	$200,000 and over	
United States.......	**79,242**	**9,711**	**15,044**	**14,095**	**11,308**	**14,495**	**6,705**	**7,884**	**76,401**
Alabama................	1,215	206	266	230	181	193	74	66	63,837
Alaska.................	168	15	24	31	24	38	17	18	89,847
Arizona................	1,713	221	352	344	253	291	124	127	69,981
Arkansas..............	769	134	193	151	100	115	39	37	58,080
California.............	8,935	1,024	1,505	1,391	1,142	1,645	920	1,308	86,165
Colorado..............	1,373	116	218	230	211	288	148	163	88,955
Connecticut...........	892	82	128	130	113	180	109	150	98,100
Delaware..............	238	25	42	46	38	47	20	20	79,386
District of Columbia. ..	122	18	14	14	10	16	13	37	117,713
Florida................	5,027	681	1,125	984	709	811	332	386	66,995
Georgia...............	2,537	359	514	452	354	443	191	224	71,457
Hawaii................	317	24	47	48	46	74	38	39	95,448
Idaho.................	438	52	99	101	65	72	26	23	65,987
Illinois................	3,119	354	547	538	435	601	300	345	81,313
Indiana...............	1,683	208	349	350	279	300	107	90	70,150
Iowa..................	800	81	152	161	141	158	55	52	76,068
Kansas................	727	79	146	143	117	133	57	51	74,042
Kentucky..............	1,139	190	262	219	162	184	62	59	62,228
Louisiana.............	1,105	207	246	191	144	176	74	67	61,847
Maine.................	343	37	73	67	58	64	23	20	72,390
Maryland..............	1,472	118	191	212	200	317	185	248	101,437
Massachusetts........	1,644	146	223	230	205	339	206	294	101,548
Michigan..............	2,520	313	505	495	382	455	192	179	72,036
Minnesota............	1,397	107	224	238	222	314	143	148	89,039
Mississippi...........	728	147	172	138	108	96	36	29	57,380
Missouri..............	1,551	193	343	306	234	266	102	107	69,188
Montana..............	266	29	59	57	43	45	18	15	68,940
Nebraska.............	486	49	94	96	80	98	36	33	75,990
Nevada...............	707	84	150	134	113	124	53	49	71,864
New Hampshire.......	342	23	51	56	53	79	38	42	93,930
New Jersey...........	2,232	205	303	304	286	450	279	405	101,404
New Mexico...........	495	97	114	96	64	71	27	26	58,760
New York.............	4,633	603	770	718	603	864	452	623	83,311
North Carolina........	2,622	363	579	501	377	432	170	201	67,816
North Dakota..........	188	15	32	32	31	45	18	15	86,205
Ohio..................	2,924	372	588	561	449	548	209	198	72,028
Oklahoma.............	983	147	226	197	146	156	56	55	64,082
Oregon...............	1,028	110	193	192	156	195	90	92	77,655
Pennsylvania.........	3,235	359	604	596	489	628	272	287	77,491
Rhode Island.........	247	29	39	41	37	52	24	25	84,212
South Carolina........	1,258	185	286	246	188	200	77	77	65,742
South Dakota.........	220	23	46	45	40	41	13	11	72,183
Tennessee............	1,708	257	380	334	257	275	101	104	65,656
Texas.................	6,730	945	1,353	1,194	905	1,171	546	617	71,868
Utah..................	744	59	127	149	126	165	61	57	81,599
Vermont..............	156	15	27	29	29	33	12	11	80,452
Virginia...............	2,094	200	338	335	298	408	219	297	88,929
Washington...........	1,880	162	298	327	274	389	197	233	87,652
West Virginia.........	462	82	116	94	60	70	21	18	57,718
Wisconsin.............	1,487	146	281	297	247	307	111	99	76,814
Wyoming..............	145	14	28	26	24	31	12	9	78,352
Puerto Rico...........	791	403	217	92	35	27	7	10	24,482

Source: U.S. Census Bureau, 2018 American Community Survey, B19101, "Family Income in the Past 12 Months (In 2018 Inflation-Adjusted Dollars)"; and B19113, "Median Family Income in the Past 12 Months (In 2018 Inflation-Adjusted Dollars)"; <https://data.census.gov/>, accessed November 2019.

Table 722. Consumer Unit Expenditures—Annual Averages by Major Type of Expenditure: 1990 to 2018

[Consumer units in thousands (96,968 represents 96,968,000); expenditures in dollars. Based on Consumer Expenditure Survey. Data are averages for the noninstitutional population. Expenditures are direct out-of-pocket expenditures. Consumers units may be all members in a housing unit (families), a person living alone or sharing a household with others and financially independent, or 2 or more unrelated persons living together who share expenses]

Type of expenditure	1990	2000	2005	2010	2015	2016	2017	2018
Number of consumer units (1,000).............	96,968	109,367	117,356	121,107	128,437	129,549	130,001	131,439
Expenditures [1], avg. (dol.)..................	**28,381**	**38,045**	**46,409**	**48,109**	**55,978**	**57,311**	**60,060**	**61,224**
Food.........	4,296	5,158	5,931	6,129	7,023	7,203	7,729	7,923
Food at home [1].....................	2,485	3,021	3,297	3,624	4,015	4,049	4,363	4,464
Cereals and bakery products...............	368	453	445	502	518	524	564	569
Meats, poultry, fish, and eggs................	668	795	764	784	896	890	944	961
Dairy products.....................	295	325	378	380	413	410	450	449
Fruits and vegetables.....................	408	521	552	679	769	783	837	858
Other food at home.....................	746	927	1,158	1,278	1,419	1,442	1,568	1,627
Food away from home.....................	1,811	2,137	2,634	2,505	3,008	3,154	3,365	3,459
Alcoholic beverages.....................	293	372	426	412	515	484	558	583
Housing [1].....................	8,703	12,319	15,167	16,557	18,409	18,886	19,884	20,091
Shelter.....................	4,836	7,114	8,805	9,812	10,742	11,128	11,895	11,747
Utilities, fuels, and public services............	1,890	2,489	3,183	3,660	3,885	3,884	3,836	4,049
Apparel and services.....................	1,618	1,856	1,886	1,700	1,846	1,803	1,833	1,866
Transportation [1].....................	5,120	7,417	8,344	7,677	9,503	9,049	9,576	9,761
Vehicle purchases.....................	2,129	3,418	3,544	2,588	3,997	3,634	4,054	3,975
Gasoline and motor oil.....................	1,047	1,291	2,013	2,132	2,090	1,909	1,968	2,109
Other vehicle expenses.....................	1,642	2,281	2,339	2,464	2,756	2,884	2,842	2,859
Public transportation.....................	302	427	448	493	661	623	712	818
Health care [2].....................	1,480	2,066	2,664	3,157	4,342	4,612	4,928	4,968
Entertainment.....................	1,422	1,863	2,388	2,504	2,842	2,913	3,203	3,226
Personal care products and services...........	364	564	541	582	683	707	762	768
Reading.....................	153	146	126	100	114	118	110	108
Education.....................	406	632	940	1,074	1,315	1,329	1,491	1,407
Tobacco products, smoking supplies...........	274	319	319	362	349	337	332	347
Personal insurance and pensions...............	2,592	3,365	5,204	5,373	6,349	6,831	6,771	7,296
Life and other personal insurance............	345	399	381	318	333	322	418	465
Pensions and Social Security.................	2,248	2,966	4,823	5,054	6,016	6,509	6,353	6,831

[1] Includes expenditures not shown separately. [2] Due to changes implemented with the 2014 questionnaire on health insurance, 2014 and subsequent data are not directly comparable to data from previous years.

Source: U.S. Bureau of Labor Statistics, Consumer Expenditure Survey program, "Annual Calendar Year Tables, 2018," <http://www.bls.gov/cex/tables.htm>, accessed November 2019; and previous releases.

Table 723. Consumer Expenditures—Annual Averages by Metropolitan Statistical Area: 2017 to 2018

[In dollars. Annual averages all consumer units, for 2-year period 2017-2018. MSA = Metropolitan Statistical Area. See text, Section 1 and Appendix II. See headnote, Table 722]

Metropolitan statistical area	Total expendi-tures [1]	Food	Housing Total [1]	Housing Shelter	Housing Utility, fuels [2]	Transportation Total [1]	Transportation Vehicle pur-chases	Transportation Gasoline and motor oil	Health care
Anchorage, Alaska............................	71,855	9,031	22,619	13,688	4,744	11,290	5,025	2,366	5,233
Atlanta, Georgia............................	64,719	7,475	21,208	12,019	4,559	10,557	4,015	2,585	5,189
Baltimore, Maryland........................	74,174	8,813	23,957	14,959	3,905	11,741	6,325	2,081	5,425
Boston, Massachusetts.....................	79,747	9,667	29,871	18,805	4,354	9,571	3,538	1,820	5,703
Chicago, Illinois............................	63,726	8,481	22,501	14,426	3,892	8,443	3,438	1,819	5,476
Dallas-Fort Worth, Texas....................	66,282	7,330	24,339	15,292	4,395	11,140	4,655	2,211	4,954
Denver, Colorado...........................	73,670	9,106	25,164	15,149	4,126	11,218	4,591	2,026	5,820
Detroit, Michigan...........................	64,998	7,998	19,587	10,670	4,052	12,541	4,432	2,039	4,930
Honolulu, Hawaii...........................	60,710	10,985	23,045	14,710	4,416	6,611	[3] 1,595	1,800	4,134
Houston, Texas............................	69,153	8,182	23,550	13,630	4,324	10,984	4,316	2,371	4,909
Los Angeles, California.....................	68,129	8,974	24,326	16,613	3,787	9,273	2,966	2,706	3,890
Miami, Florida.............................	57,555	6,763	21,450	13,960	3,857	8,820	2,843	2,284	4,554
Minneapolis-St. Paul, Minnesota...........	72,382	8,403	24,335	14,685	3,559	9,318	3,132	2,104	5,517
New York City.............................	70,875	8,706	27,626	19,298	4,109	8,494	2,015	1,514	4,787
Philadelphia, Pennsylvania.................	70,813	8,919	23,225	13,592	4,403	11,065	4,034	1,972	5,669
Phoenix, Arizona...........................	66,908	7,817	20,730	10,767	4,337	12,720	6,531	2,041	6,038
San Diego, California.......................	79,672	10,613	28,591	19,562	3,689	11,363	3,737	2,487	5,174
San Francisco, California...................	80,733	10,146	31,786	21,578	4,385	9,138	[3] 2,860	1,977	4,602
Seattle, Washington........................	84,864	11,412	29,269	18,966	4,004	11,999	4,412	2,175	5,355
St. Louis, Missouri.........................	64,318	7,511	21,181	11,285	4,477	9,687	4,146	2,107	4,846
Tampa, Florida.............................	50,386	7,218	17,871	10,695	3,377	7,694	3,461	1,545	3,810
Washington, DC............................	91,118	11,211	30,872	20,502	4,164	13,095	5,703	2,040	6,301

[1] Includes expenditures not shown separately. [2] Includes public services. [3] Data are likely to have large sampling errors.

Source: U.S. Bureau of Labor Statistics, Consumer Expenditure Survey program, "Metropolitan Statistical Area Tables," <http://www.bls.gov/cex/tables.htm>, accessed December 2019.

Table 724. Personal Consumption Expenditures—Total and Per Capita by State: 2000 to 2018

[Total in millions of current dollars (6,758,606 represents $6,758,606,000,000); per capita amounts in current dollars. Per capita data reflect Census Bureau midyear population estimates for years 2010-2018, available as of December 2018]

State	Total personal consumption expenditures (million dollars)					Per capita personal consumption expenditures (dollars)				
	2000	2010	2016	2017	2018	2000	2010	2016	2017	2018
United States......	**6,758,606**	**10,177,465**	**12,741,883**	**13,305,559**	**13,988,762**	**23,953**	**32,902**	**39,440**	**40,922**	**42,757**
Alabama.............	87,080	130,834	153,224	158,574	165,717	19,559	27,340	31,497	32,527	33,904
Alaska..............	16,578	27,841	34,261	35,549	37,053	26,400	38,998	46,205	48,053	50,246
Arizona.............	116,522	186,603	229,608	242,980	257,506	22,579	29,121	33,059	34,471	35,906
Arkansas............	49,704	77,005	94,581	98,838	102,755	18,556	26,354	31,628	32,913	34,095
California............	853,510	1,279,143	1,668,316	1,753,358	1,858,421	25,112	34,274	42,549	44,502	46,981
Colorado............	117,009	172,803	224,694	237,076	251,595	27,042	34,230	40,552	42,215	44,174
Connecticut.........	102,017	149,077	176,126	181,887	189,141	29,902	41,652	49,215	50,893	52,941
Delaware............	19,864	32,002	39,313	40,711	42,655	25,260	35,573	41,416	42,536	44,103
Dist. of Columbia....	20,447	31,247	40,367	42,069	44,361	35,744	51,640	58,795	60,471	63,151
Florida..............	386,622	609,693	793,162	829,401	876,422	24,092	32,352	38,447	39,539	41,148
Georgia.............	181,590	276,668	348,182	364,092	383,834	22,072	28,488	33,788	34,965	36,488
Hawaii..............	29,315	48,197	62,839	65,911	69,262	24,157	35,336	44,001	46,279	48,759
Idaho...............	26,034	42,495	56,817	60,716	64,514	20,035	27,053	33,761	35,322	36,777
Illinois..............	313,177	440,902	528,632	549,540	574,429	25,187	34,336	41,213	42,979	45,085
Indiana.............	132,488	190,954	231,053	242,122	252,150	21,748	29,421	34,832	36,354	37,680
Iowa................	63,727	93,260	113,876	118,533	122,914	21,757	30,569	36,361	37,706	38,944
Kansas..............	58,190	85,462	102,838	106,176	110,339	21,603	29,900	35,324	36,478	37,897
Kentucky............	81,301	119,806	145,217	150,668	157,066	20,079	27,553	32,720	33,828	35,150
Louisiana............	86,643	131,421	157,719	162,059	168,245	19,375	28,919	33,713	34,696	36,104
Maine...............	31,242	48,019	55,700	57,990	60,894	24,464	36,169	41,836	43,436	45,497
Maryland............	137,125	214,790	261,760	272,369	282,921	25,819	37,105	43,593	45,207	46,820
Massachusetts......	195,220	282,701	350,117	365,714	380,277	30,690	43,052	51,292	53,286	55,095
Michigan............	238,774	313,221	376,137	390,263	407,475	23,991	31,710	37,795	39,118	40,764
Minnesota...........	135,428	191,103	239,698	253,012	266,161	27,450	35,984	43,397	45,439	47,434
Mississippi..........	48,686	74,667	86,987	89,518	92,831	17,093	25,136	29,109	29,942	31,083
Missouri............	131,533	190,110	226,997	235,905	245,425	23,457	31,706	37,291	38,618	40,060
Montana............	18,848	31,759	40,840	43,106	45,359	20,855	32,057	39,236	40,933	42,698
Nebraska............	38,744	59,503	74,009	77,068	80,432	22,607	32,524	38,831	40,190	41,690
Nevada.............	48,155	89,587	114,088	118,886	125,801	23,854	33,150	39,074	39,997	41,458
New Hampshire.....	34,807	54,545	64,884	67,534	70,699	28,073	41,423	48,335	50,034	52,120
New Jersey.........	242,214	363,204	435,270	449,237	469,735	28,730	41,275	49,047	50,541	52,729
New Mexico.........	36,477	58,724	70,646	72,613	75,977	20,029	28,443	33,757	34,687	36,258
New York...........	502,799	739,393	936,268	976,732	1,029,888	26,461	38,113	47,668	49,857	52,701
North Carolina......	171,052	263,160	333,703	351,043	370,883	21,166	27,486	32,856	34,179	35,718
North Dakota........	13,954	24,090	34,603	35,353	36,863	21,734	35,704	45,871	46,814	48,499
Ohio................	262,645	365,848	442,596	458,883	477,536	23,113	31,704	38,040	39,341	40,852
Oklahoma...........	65,057	102,404	126,312	129,642	136,037	18,833	27,238	32,167	32,966	34,500
Oregon.............	83,046	123,275	160,221	169,473	179,015	24,214	32,123	39,160	40,870	42,717
Pennsylvania........	299,506	448,280	528,162	546,921	573,815	24,381	35,267	41,316	42,760	44,805
Rhode Island........	25,120	37,393	44,283	45,710	47,731	23,918	35,479	41,893	43,266	45,144
South Carolina......	81,492	129,331	162,263	168,899	176,365	20,250	27,899	32,726	33,637	34,689
South Dakota........	15,992	27,043	35,345	37,107	38,950	21,157	33,134	40,961	42,491	44,149
Tennessee..........	123,295	179,916	222,868	234,042	246,025	21,617	28,310	33,539	34,886	36,340
Texas..............	474,925	756,111	1,009,482	1,059,158	1,120,665	22,675	29,954	36,134	37,396	39,045
Utah................	46,452	77,743	104,919	111,096	119,240	20,696	28,012	34,483	35,801	37,721
Vermont............	15,405	23,755	28,955	29,904	31,284	25,269	37,954	46,429	47,882	49,950
Virginia.............	174,097	288,202	353,976	367,872	384,479	24,501	35,919	42,085	43,457	45,139
Washington.........	153,764	235,508	309,494	328,464	350,959	26,015	34,927	42,427	44,235	46,574
West Virginia........	33,653	51,738	61,317	62,878	65,138	18,624	27,903	33,489	34,604	36,071
Wisconsin...........	126,171	187,741	226,021	235,220	246,818	23,478	32,992	39,152	40,611	42,456
Wyoming............	11,111	19,190	23,140	23,691	24,707	22,479	33,996	39,604	40,921	42,766

Source: U.S. Bureau of Economic Analysis, Regional Economic Accounts, "Personal Consumption Expenditures (PCE) by State," <http://bea.gov/regional/index.htm>, accessed February 2020.

Table 725. Consumer Expenditures—Average for All Consumer Units by Race, Hispanic Origin, and Age of Householder: 2018

[In dollars. See headnote, Table 722. See source for definitions, standard errors, and other information]

Expenditure type	All consumer units [1]	White and other races [2]	Asian	Black or African American	Hispanic [3]	Age of householder Under 25 years	Age of householder 65 years old and over
Expenditures, total............................	**61,224**	**63,188**	**72,971**	**44,752**	**53,762**	**32,039**	**50,860**
Food..	7,923	8,220	10,257	5,228	7,906	4,748	6,607
Food at home...................................	4,464	4,635	5,626	2,982	4,304	2,412	4,009
Cereals and bakery products.............	569	593	707	374	526	307	532
Cereals and cereal products.............	178	178	292	134	178	109	139
Bakery products...........................	392	415	414	240	348	198	393
Meats, poultry, fish, and eggs [4].......	961	967	1,362	772	1,003	495	830
Beef...	253	262	302	183	248	112	215
Pork...	180	184	211	142	201	95	171
Poultry.......................................	180	174	291	176	204	125	130
Fish and seafood.........................	154	143	350	146	154	71	142
Eggs..	64	65	102	45	81	41	54
Dairy products [4]..........................	449	487	407	233	411	245	419
Fresh milk and cream....................	147	156	168	78	155	79	128
Fruits and vegetables [4].................	858	872	1,444	549	885	459	790
Fresh fruits.................................	318	324	559	189	344	175	302
Fresh vegetables.........................	283	284	609	151	284	143	247
Processed vegetables..................	144	148	141	115	140	71	128
Other food at home [4]....................	1,627	1,716	1,705	1,054	1,479	906	1,438
Sugar and other sweets................	151	161	139	88	122	70	151
Nonalcoholic beverages................	438	461	377	320	462	212	399
Food away from home.......................	3,459	3,585	4,631	2,246	3,601	2,336	2,598
Alcoholic beverages...........................	583	647	435	243	374	271	446
Housing..	20,091	20,403	24,963	16,413	19,409	11,410	16,940
Shelter...	11,747	11,759	16,978	9,803	11,771	7,706	9,357
Owned dwellings...........................	6,678	6,978	9,723	3,703	4,998	1,006	5,910
Mortgage interest and charges.......	2,775	2,850	4,431	1,712	2,489	508	1,333
Property taxes.............................	2,200	2,290	3,882	1,034	1,404	329	2,283
Maintenance, repair, insurance, other expenses........	1,703	1,838	1,409	957	1,105	169	2,294
Rented dwellings...........................	4,249	3,895	6,322	5,730	6,348	6,421	2,585
Other lodging...............................	821	886	934	369	424	279	861
Utilities, fuels, and public services.........	4,049	4,090	3,857	3,860	3,882	1,896	3,806
Natural gas..................................	410	405	463	420	344	135	421
Electricity....................................	1,496	1,512	1,273	1,474	1,394	722	1,470
Fuel oil and other fuels..................	121	134	87	53	39	19	183
Telephone (includes mobile service)...	1,407	1,416	1,336	1,381	1,491	778	1,108
Water and other public services.......	614	622	699	532	615	242	625
Household operations........................	1,522	1,581	1,831	1,040	1,130	490	1,361
Personal services.........................	472	483	675	331	380	122	172
Other household expenses.............	1,050	1,098	1,157	709	750	368	1,189
Housekeeping supplies [4]..................	747	803	621	455	704	324	759
Laundry and cleaning supplies........	184	196	160	118	245	84	162
Postage and stationery..................	132	141	137	72	106	60	158
Household furnishings and equipment [4]...	2,025	2,170	1,677	1,255	1,922	994	1,657
Household textiles.........................	111	121	72	67	112	67	114
Furniture.....................................	518	540	419	421	544	235	344
Major appliances..........................	304	324	242	199	326	154	255
Miscellaneous household equipment...	948	1,032	808	481	842	445	794
Apparel and services [4]......................	1,866	1,849	3,123	1,511	2,043	1,128	1,207
Men and boys...............................	420	418	787	297	491	253	246
Women and girls...........................	755	756	1,174	590	696	438	514
Footwear.....................................	392	383	642	350	524	249	270
Other apparel products and services...	222	211	425	213	200	92	158
Transportation.................................	9,761	10,116	9,964	7,473	9,188	5,526	7,270
Vehicle purchases (net outlay) [4].........	3,975	4,154	3,519	3,011	3,599	2,085	2,667
Cars and trucks, new.....................	1,825	1,923	2,504	972	1,550	465	1,530
Cars and trucks, used....................	2,084	2,167	894	1,986	1,995	1,519	1,099
Gasoline and motor oil....................	2,109	2,164	2,107	1,765	2,360	1,416	1,442
Other vehicle expenses..................	2,859	2,982	2,704	2,158	2,596	1,565	2,450
Vehicle finance charges...............	222	227	143	216	235	139	114
Maintenance and repair................	890	938	703	654	734	471	815
Vehicle insurance.......................	976	1,034	890	657	948	647	937
Vehicle rental, leases, licenses, other charges...	772	783	968	631	679	307	584
Public transportation......................	818	816	1,632	539	632	460	711
Health care.....................................	4,968	5,298	4,346	3,123	3,173	1,206	6,802
Entertainment [5]..............................	3,226	3,531	2,519	1,585	2,282	1,409	2,958
Personal care products and services.......	768	778	783	699	656	475	682
Reading..	108	119	75	52	56	35	165
Education..	1,407	1,361	3,209	1,054	946	2,270	375
Tobacco products and smoking supplies...	347	373	112	265	155	228	196
Miscellaneous..................................	993	987	1,309	915	671	308	1,032
Cash contributions...........................	1,888	2,009	1,516	1,258	855	353	2,625
Personal insurance and pensions..........	7,296	7,497	10,360	4,932	6,050	2,671	3,556
Life and other personal insurance........	465	468	534	420	270	41	512
Pensions and social security.............	6,831	7,029	9,826	4,512	5,780	2,630	3,044
Personal taxes............................	**11,394**	**11,580**	**23,961**	**5,731**	**6,470**	**2,475**	**4,634**

[1] Includes other races not shown separately. [2] Other races includes Native Hawaiian/Pacific Islander, Native American/Alaskan, and about 1 percent reporting more than one race. [3] People of Hispanic origin may be of any race. [4] Includes other types, not shown separately. [5] For additional recreation expenditures, see Section 26.

Source: U.S. Bureau of Labor Statistics, Consumer Expenditure Survey Program, "Annual Calendar Year Tables, 2018," <http://www.bls.gov/cex/tables.htm>, accessed December 2019.

Table 726. Consumer Expenditures—Averages for All Consumer Units by Region and Size of Unit: 2018

[In dollars. For composition of regions, see map, inside front cover. See headnote, Table 722. See source for definitions, standard errors, and other information]

Expenditure type	Region				Size of consumer unit				
	North-east	Mid-west	South	West	One person	Two persons	Three persons	Four persons	Five or more
Expenditures, total	**66,076**	**58,241**	**56,667**	**68,113**	**36,087**	**65,535**	**72,696**	**80,795**	**79,693**
Food	8,401	7,511	7,351	8,913	4,436	8,226	8,964	10,899	11,731
Food at home	4,845	4,255	4,127	4,938	2,421	4,583	5,057	6,128	7,048
Cereals and bakery products	662	534	523	609	295	554	639	816	1,013
Cereals and cereal products	197	166	163	199	84	161	209	267	353
Bakery products	465	368	360	411	211	394	431	549	660
Meats, poultry, fish, and eggs [1]	1,063	892	926	1,004	478	983	1,114	1,363	1,559
Beef	245	254	251	264	116	254	317	373	405
Pork	161	179	186	186	83	193	222	232	293
Poultry	212	149	177	191	95	173	202	272	308
Fish and seafood	226	128	133	156	86	163	153	213	247
Dairy products	509	450	385	512	254	461	518	601	684
Fresh milk and cream	164	143	126	171	85	137	174	205	247
Other dairy products	345	307	259	341	169	324	344	396	437
Fruits and vegetables [1]	987	772	769	988	457	906	968	1,176	1,287
Fresh fruits	376	291	274	372	167	343	355	430	472
Fresh vegetables	338	246	247	334	150	305	318	385	403
Processed vegetables	148	139	142	148	72	145	175	197	232
Other food at home [1]	1,624	1,607	1,524	1,825	937	1,678	1,818	2,172	2,505
Sugar and other sweets	171	148	133	167	85	157	157	205	240
Nonalcoholic beverages	420	415	442	466	261	460	479	574	642
Food away from home	3,557	3,255	3,224	3,975	2,015	3,643	3,906	4,771	4,683
Alcoholic beverages	647	606	500	653	395	804	511	577	463
Housing	23,646	17,850	18,116	22,840	13,797	20,640	23,217	25,550	25,606
Shelter	14,531	9,935	10,058	14,204	8,968	11,891	13,156	14,578	13,949
Owned dwellings	8,510	6,206	5,822	7,152	3,566	7,181	8,042	9,627	8,543
Mortgage interest and charges	2,850	2,318	2,571	3,512	1,169	2,602	3,782	4,915	4,009
Property taxes	3,836	2,177	1,559	2,024	1,222	2,483	2,506	3,087	2,582
Maintenance, repair, insurance, other expenses	1,824	1,711	1,692	1,617	1,175	2,097	1,755	1,625	1,952
Rented dwellings	5,020	2,965	3,513	6,151	5,004	3,616	4,216	3,940	4,619
Other lodging	1,001	764	723	901	398	1,094	898	1,011	787
Utilities, fuels, and public services	4,258	3,936	4,069	3,955	2,475	4,229	4,808	5,146	5,663
Natural gas	612	580	264	337	273	413	500	530	530
Electricity	1,378	1,366	1,722	1,325	990	1,569	1,724	1,813	2,033
Fuel oil and other fuels	406	92	55	38	81	154	107	123	150
Telephone services (includes mobile)	1,437	1,347	1,402	1,451	771	1,463	1,758	1,869	2,032
Water and other public services	425	551	626	804	359	630	719	813	918
Household operations	1,732	1,349	1,403	1,728	799	1,326	2,169	2,747	1,861
Personal services	588	473	385	529	100	80	1,084	1,457	798
Other household expenses	1,144	875	1,018	1,200	700	1,247	1,086	1,289	1,063
Housekeeping supplies [1]	762	699	750	777	515	772	835	818	1,146
Laundry and cleaning supplies	190	172	188	183	109	172	217	234	335
Postage and stationery	127	112	124	168	111	149	130	115	165
Household furnishings and equipment [1]	2,364	1,931	1,836	2,175	1,040	2,422	2,248	2,262	2,986
Household textiles	122	94	119	104	70	142	95	95	174
Furniture	565	501	484	559	243	650	645	551	665
Major appliances	343	272	294	319	133	322	363	405	548
Miscellaneous household equipment	1,172	924	802	1,047	512	1,136	954	1,061	1,451
Apparel and services [1]	2,137	1,872	1,664	1,998	974	1,817	2,210	2,885	2,810
Men and boys	478	403	362	491	246	376	544	594	683
Women and girls	827	794	705	748	361	789	815	1,194	1,119
Footwear	468	400	347	400	195	371	487	658	539
Other apparel products and services	287	202	176	267	154	242	231	291	245
Transportation	9,324	9,279	9,789	10,530	4,892	10,175	13,121	13,507	13,271
Vehicle purchases (net outlay) [1]	3,199	3,673	4,376	4,193	1,669	4,076	6,223	5,639	5,145
Cars and trucks, new	1,404	1,555	2,150	1,862	769	2,143	2,911	2,321	1,675
Cars and trucks, used	1,752	2,076	2,142	2,257	869	1,877	3,223	3,157	3,431
Gasoline and motor oil	1,855	2,051	2,115	2,357	1,084	2,118	2,582	2,979	3,369
Other vehicle expenses	3,144	2,819	2,670	2,998	1,672	3,028	3,452	3,811	3,738
Vehicle finance charges	164	225	259	201	88	237	307	320	321
Maintenance and repair	847	922	854	956	537	999	974	1,140	1,127
Vehicle insurance	992	913	1,023	942	646	922	1,198	1,252	1,461
Vehicle rental, leases, licenses, other charges	1,140	759	535	898	401	870	974	1,099	829
Public transportation	1,125	737	629	981	467	954	863	1,078	1,019
Health care [2]	4,992	5,247	4,846	4,892	2,977	6,162	5,515	5,538	5,286
Entertainment [3]	3,117	3,630	2,778	3,696	1,822	3,897	3,519	3,793	3,969
Personal care products and services	776	739	734	848	490	835	850	1,014	923
Reading	139	126	81	114	94	127	92	114	98
Education	2,103	1,189	1,176	1,462	756	1,134	2,015	2,278	2,319
Tobacco products/smoking supplies	345	416	355	267	252	341	421	389	493
Miscellaneous	1,086	926	926	1,099	732	1,125	868	1,276	1,133
Cash contributions	1,587	1,830	1,693	2,520	1,290	2,539	1,717	1,651	1,981
Personal insurance and pensions	7,775	7,019	6,660	8,281	3,181	7,713	9,676	11,322	9,609
Life and other personal insurance	526	495	458	399	224	552	513	675	548
Pensions and social security	7,248	6,524	6,202	7,882	2,957	7,160	9,163	10,647	9,061
Personal taxes	**16,031**	**10,081**	**9,471**	**12,290**	**5,388**	**12,719**	**14,101**	**17,177**	**13,522**

[1] Includes other types not shown separately. [2] For additional health care expenditures, see Table 149. [3] For additional recreation expenditures, see Section 26.

Source: U.S. Bureau of Labor Statistics, Consumer Expenditure Survey Program, "Annual Calendar Year Tables, 2018," <http://www.bls.gov/cex/tables.htm>, accessed December 2019.

Table 727. Consumer Unit Expenditures—Averages by Income Level: 2018

[In dollars. See headnote, Table 722. See source for definitions, standard errors, and other information]

Income level	Total expenditures [1]	Food	Housing Total [1]	Housing Shelter	Housing Utilities, fuels [2]	Transportation Total [1]	Transportation Vehicle purchases	Transportation Gasoline and motor oil	Health care	Pensions and social security
All consumer units..........	**61,224**	**7,923**	**20,091**	**11,747**	**4,049**	**9,761**	**3,975**	**2,109**	**4,968**	**6,831**
BY INCOME										
Less than $15,000.............	25,346	4,130	10,083	6,089	2,205	3,411	1,110	952	2,134	509
$15,000 to $29,999............	32,386	4,628	12,664	7,584	3,005	5,177	1,881	1,217	3,438	955
$30,000 to $39,999............	42,611	6,077	14,744	8,229	3,599	7,301	3,104	1,720	4,293	2,074
$40,000 to $49,999............	46,850	6,286	16,552	9,485	3,808	7,250	2,489	1,922	4,334	3,812
$50,000 to $69,999............	53,104	7,168	18,274	10,538	4,002	9,158	3,613	2,151	4,739	4,846
$70,000 to $99,999............	65,814	8,753	21,281	12,460	4,539	11,303	4,799	2,520	5,519	7,449
$100,000 to $149,999........	85,730	10,854	25,957	14,959	5,107	14,167	6,158	3,036	6,836	11,884
$150,000 to $199,999........	108,909	13,195	32,737	18,687	5,684	16,523	6,227	3,293	7,664	16,978
$200,000 and over............	158,738	16,392	47,553	29,025	6,553	22,698	10,271	3,402	9,031	27,378

[1] Includes expenditures not shown separately. [2] Includes public services.

Source: U.S. Bureau of Labor Statistics, Consumer Expenditure Survey, "Annual Calendar Year Tables, 2018," <http://stats.bls.gov/cex/tables.htm>, accessed December 2019.

Table 728. Annual Expenditures Per Child by Married-Couple Families by Family Income and Expenditure Type: 2015

[In dollars. Excludes expenses for college. Estimates are based on 2011-2015 Consumer Expenditure Survey data updated to 2015 dollars by using the Consumer Price Index. Data are for the younger child in a two-child family. Estimates are about the same for the older child, so to calculate expenses for two children, figures should be summed for the appropriate age categories. To estimate expenses for an only child, multiply the total expense for the appropriate age category by 1.27. To estimate expenses for each child in a family with three or more children, multiply the total expense for each appropriate age category by 0.76; for expenses on all children in a family, these totals should be summed. Please note that estimates for 2015 are not directly comparable to estimates published for 2013 due to the change in using base data from the 2005-2006 vs. 2011-2015 Consumer Expenditure surveys. For methodology, see source]

Family income and age of child	Total	Expenditure type Housing	Expenditure type Food	Expenditure type Transportation	Expenditure type Clothing	Expenditure type Health care	Expenditure type Child care and education [1]	Expenditure type Miscellaneous [2]
INCOME: LESS THAN $59,200 (Average = $36,300)								
Less than 2 years old........................	9,690	3,160	1,310	1,200	670	820	2,080	450
3 to 5 years old.............................	9,700	3,160	1,350	1,250	540	760	2,080	560
6 to 8 years old.............................	9,330	3,160	1,930	1,310	540	790	920	680
9 to 11 years old............................	9,960	3,160	2,200	1,350	690	900	920	740
12 to 14 years old...........................	9,570	3,160	2,290	1,500	740	860	440	580
15 to 17 years old...........................	9,980	3,160	2,300	1,690	720	910	640	560
INCOME: $59,200 to $107,400 (Average = $81,700)								
Less than 2 years old........................	12,680	3,680	1,580	1,790	750	1,180	2,870	830
3 to 5 years old.............................	12,730	3,680	1,690	1,840	600	1,110	2,870	940
6 to 8 years old.............................	12,350	3,680	2,280	1,900	600	1,130	1,710	1,050
9 to 11 years old............................	13,180	3,680	2,680	1,940	780	1,280	1,710	1,110
12 to 14 years old...........................	13,030	3,680	2,780	2,090	860	1,240	1,430	950
15 to 17 years old...........................	13,900	3,680	2,790	2,270	830	1,300	2,090	940
INCOME: MORE THAN $107,400 (Average = $185,400)								
Less than 2 years old........................	19,770	5,460	2,210	2,590	1,110	1,580	5,170	1,650
3 to 5 years old.............................	19,790	5,460	2,320	2,640	940	1,490	5,170	1,770
6 to 8 years old.............................	19,380	5,460	2,960	2,690	940	1,440	4,010	1,880
9 to 11 years old............................	20,700	5,460	3,570	2,740	1,180	1,800	4,010	1,940
12 to 14 years old...........................	21,050	5,460	3,560	2,890	1,310	1,740	4,310	1,780
15 to 17 years old...........................	23,380	5,460	3,720	3,070	1,280	1,820	6,270	1,760

[1] Includes only families with child care and education expenses. [2] Expenses include personal care items, entertainment, and reading materials.

Source: U.S. Department of Agriculture, Center for Nutrition Policy and Promotion, *Expenditures on Children by Families, 2015*, March 2017 (revised). See also <https://www.fns.usda.gov/cnpp>.

Table 729. Money Income of Households—Percent Distribution by Income Level, Race, and Hispanic Origin, in Constant (2018) Dollars: 2000 to 2018

[In percent except as noted (108,209 represents 108,209,000). Households as of March of following year. Constant dollars based on CPI-U-RS deflator. Based on Current Population Survey, Annual Social and Economic Supplement (CPS ASEC); see text, this section and Section 1, and Appendix III. For definition of median, see Guide to Tabular Presentation. A household consists of all the persons who occupy a housing unit. Household count excludes persons living in group quarters and institutions. For 2001 data and earlier, the CPS allowed respondents to report only one race group. Beginning with the 2003 CPS covering data for 2002, refers to respondents reporting only one race. Two basic ways of defining a race group are possible: a group such as Asian may be defined as 1) those who reported Asian and no other race (the race-alone concept), or 2) those who reported Asian regardless of whether they also reported another race (the race-alone-or-in-combination concept). Data users should exercise caution when comparing trends over time due to changes in CPS ASEC methodology and data processing. Changes are noted below as appropriate. See source for more information]

Year and race/ethnicity	Number of house-holds (1,000)	Percent distribution							Median income (dollars)
		Under $15,000	$15,000 to $24,999	$25,000 to $34,999	$35,000 to $49,999	$50,000 to $74,999	$75,000 to $99,999	$100,000 and over	
ALL HOUSEHOLDS [1]									
2000 [4]	108,209	9.6	9.5	8.8	13.3	18.0	13.1	27.7	61,399
2010 [5]	119,927	11.4	11.0	10.1	12.7	16.9	12.4	25.5	56,873
2017 [6]	127,669	10.3	9.4	9.1	12.2	16.6	12.2	30.2	62,626
2018 [6]	128,579	10.2	8.9	8.8	12.0	17.2	12.5	30.4	63,179
WHITE [2]									
2000 [4]	90,030	8.4	9.2	8.6	13.2	18.1	13.5	29.1	64,216
2010 [5]	96,306	9.6	10.6	9.9	12.7	17.2	12.8	27.2	59,682
2017 [6]	100,113	8.8	8.9	8.8	12.0	16.7	12.8	32.0	66,413
2018 [6]	100,528	8.7	8.4	8.5	11.9	17.5	13.0	32.0	66,943
BLACK [2]									
2000 [4]	13,174	18.1	12.1	11.1	14.9	17.9	10.8	15.1	43,380
2010 [5]	15,265	22.3	13.8	12.3	13.9	15.2	9.9	12.6	37,077
2017 [6]	17,019	19.4	13.0	12.0	13.7	15.9	9.4	16.6	40,325
2018 [6]	17,167	19.2	12.6	11.6	13.7	16.4	9.6	16.7	41,361
ASIAN AND PACIFIC ISLANDER [2]									
2000 [4]	3,963	7.8	6.3	6.0	10.7	16.1	13.4	39.8	81,530
2010 [5]	5,212	9.8	7.8	7.6	8.9	16.4	11.9	37.6	74,167
2017 [6]	6,750	8.1	6.5	5.8	9.8	14.9	12.1	42.7	83,376
2018 [6]	6,981	8.4	6.1	6.0	8.5	14.2	12.0	44.7	87,194
HISPANIC [3]									
2000 [4]	10,034	11.5	12.5	11.1	16.4	20.1	11.7	16.7	48,500
2010 [5]	14,435	14.8	13.1	13.3	14.8	17.7	11.0	15.2	43,433
2017 [6]	17,336	12.1	11.0	11.2	14.6	19.1	11.7	20.5	51,390
2018 [6]	17,758	11.4	11.0	10.8	15.0	18.8	12.7	20.2	51,450

[1] Includes other races not shown separately. [2] Beginning 2002, data represent White alone, Black alone, or Asian alone. [3] People of Hispanic origin may be of any race. Data for Hispanics overlap with data for racial groups. [4] Data reflect implementation of Census 2000-based population controls and a 28,000 household sample expansion to 78,000 households. [5] Beginning with 2009 income data, the Census Bureau expanded the upper income intervals used to calculate medians to $250,000 or more. Medians falling in the upper open-ended interval are plugged with "$250,000." Before 2009, the upper open-ended interval was $100,000 and a plug of "$100,000" was used. Data reflect implementation of Census 2010-based population controls. [6] Beginning 2013, data are based on redesigned questions on income. Beginning 2017, data reflect implementation of an updated processing system.

Source: U.S. Census Bureau, *Income and Poverty in the United States: 2018,* Current Population Reports, P60-266, September 2019; and "Historical Income Tables: Households, Table H-17," <http://www.census.gov/topics/income-poverty/income/data/tables.html>, accessed November 2019.

Table 730. Money Income of Households—Median Income by Race and Hispanic Origin, in Current and Constant (2018) Dollars: 1990 to 2018

[In dollars. See headnote, Table 729. Beginning 2013, data are based on redesigned questions on income]

Year	Median income in current dollars					Median income in constant (2018) dollars				
	All house-holds [1]	White [2]	Black [2]	Asian, Pacific Islander [2]	His-panic [3]	All house-holds [1]	White [2]	Black [2]	Asian, Pacific Islander [2]	His-panic [3]
1990	29,943	31,231	18,676	38,450	22,330	55,952	58,359	34,898	71,848	41,726
2000 [4,5]	41,990	43,916	29,667	55,757	33,168	61,399	64,216	43,380	81,530	48,500
2010 [6]	49,276	51,709	32,124	64,259	37,631	56,873	59,682	37,077	74,167	43,433
2011 [7]	50,054	52,214	32,229	65,129	38,624	56,006	58,423	36,061	72,874	43,217
2012	51,017	53,706	33,321	68,636	39,005	55,900	58,846	36,510	75,205	42,738
2013	53,585	56,745	35,324	72,383	39,687	57,856	61,268	38,140	78,153	42,850
2014	53,657	56,866	35,398	74,297	42,491	56,969	60,376	37,583	78,883	45,114
2015	56,516	60,109	36,898	77,166	45,148	59,901	63,710	39,108	81,788	47,852
2016	59,039	61,858	39,490	81,431	47,675	61,779	64,729	41,323	85,210	49,887
2017 [8]	61,136	64,833	39,365	81,392	50,167	62,626	66,413	40,325	83,376	51,390
2018 [8]	63,179	66,943	41,361	87,194	51,450	63,179	66,943	41,361	87,194	51,450

[1] Includes other races, not shown separately. [2] Beginning 2002, data represent White alone, Black alone, or Asian alone. [3] People of Hispanic origin may be of any race. [4] Implementation of Census 2000-based population controls. [5] Implementation of a 28,000 household sample expansion. [6] Median income is calculated using $2,500 income intervals. Beginning with 2009 income data, the Census Bureau expanded the upper income intervals used to calculate medians to $250,000 or more. Before 2009, the upper open-ended interval was $100,000 and a plug of "$100,000" was used. [7] Implementation of Census 2010-based population controls. [8] Implementation of an updated processing system.

Source: U.S. Census Bureau, *Income and Poverty in the United States: 2018,* Current Population Reports, P60-266, September 2019; and "Historical Income Tables: Households, Table H-5," <http://www.census.gov/topics/income-poverty/income/data/tables.html>, accessed November 2019.

Table 731. Money Income of Households—Households by Income Level and Selected Characteristics: 2018

[128,579 represents 128,579,000. Households as of March of the following year. Based on Current Population Survey, Annual Social and Economic Supplement (CPS ASEC); see text, this section and Section 1, and Appendix III. For definition of median, see Guide to Tabular Presentation. See headnote, Table 729]

Characteristic	Total house-holds	Under $15,000	$15,000 to $24,999	$25,000 to $34,999	$35,000 to $49,999	$50,000 to $74,999	$75,000 to $99,999	$100,000 and over	Median house-hold income [1] (dollars)
Total....................	**128,579**	**13,130**	**11,444**	**11,291**	**15,438**	**22,115**	**16,046**	**39,116**	**63,179**
Region: [2]									
Northeast......................	22,054	2,166	1,765	1,856	2,341	3,522	2,673	7,730	70,113
Midwest.......................	27,686	2,574	2,408	2,434	3,388	4,963	3,648	8,269	64,069
South..........................	49,743	5,797	4,950	4,742	6,280	8,723	5,929	13,321	57,299
West...........................	29,096	2,593	2,321	2,259	3,428	4,906	3,794	9,795	69,520
Age of householder:									
15 to 24 years.................	6,199	877	781	826	992	1,202	640	881	43,531
25 to 34 years.................	20,611	1,603	1,301	1,658	2,839	4,279	3,222	5,708	65,890
35 to 44 years.................	21,370	1,405	1,252	1,463	2,289	3,491	3,033	8,438	80,743
45 to 54 years.................	22,071	1,597	1,207	1,375	2,054	3,496	2,919	9,422	84,464
55 to 64 years.................	24,172	2,757	1,891	1,807	2,473	3,992	2,968	8,285	68,951
65 years and over............	34,156	4,889	5,012	4,162	4,789	5,652	3,265	6,386	43,696
Type of household:									
Family household.............	83,482	4,400	4,572	5,895	9,103	14,586	12,029	32,897	80,663
Married-couple.............	61,959	1,763	2,221	3,429	5,883	10,328	9,455	28,879	93,654
Male householder, spouse absent............	6,480	478	465	591	948	1,473	903	1,621	61,518
Female householder, spouse absent............	15,043	2,160	1,887	1,875	2,272	2,784	1,671	2,396	45,128
Nonfamily household.........	45,096	8,730	6,871	5,396	6,334	7,528	4,018	6,222	38,122
Male householder...........	21,582	3,440	2,628	2,426	3,056	4,002	2,283	3,746	45,754
Female householder........	23,515	5,290	4,242	2,970	3,278	3,527	1,734	2,472	32,007
Size of household:									
One person...................	36,479	8,269	6,404	4,795	5,330	5,742	2,666	3,270	31,954
Two people...................	44,373	2,760	2,918	3,707	5,470	8,564	6,313	14,645	70,870
Three people.................	19,374	1,054	993	1,293	2,046	3,365	2,875	7,748	82,139
Four people..................	16,413	627	610	791	1,434	2,463	2,458	8,029	97,522
Five people..................	7,429	271	303	428	712	1,154	1,078	3,483	93,297
Six people...................	2,909	87	133	190	280	524	452	1,245	86,820
Seven or more people.......	1,602	64	81	87	168	304	204	697	84,702
Number of earners:									
No earners...................	30,736	9,876	6,043	4,017	3,795	3,489	1,488	2,029	23,875
One earner...................	46,467	2,959	4,707	5,908	8,101	10,104	5,627	9,059	51,971
Two earners and more.......	51,376	294	692	1,365	3,542	8,524	8,931	28,029	106,818
Two earners................	40,981	273	644	1,252	3,242	7,392	7,348	20,829	101,091
Three earners..............	7,734	21	47	105	264	970	1,279	5,046	124,824
Four earners or more.......	2,661	–	2	8	37	161	303	2,152	153,486
Work experience of householder:									
Total........................	**128,579**	**13,130**	**11,444**	**11,291**	**15,438**	**22,115**	**16,046**	**39,116**	**63,179**
Worked.......................	84,315	2,799	4,579	5,958	9,644	15,709	12,494	33,134	80,762
Worked at full-time jobs....	71,083	1,359	2,982	4,598	7,955	13,548	11,005	29,634	85,355
50 weeks or more..........	62,551	656	2,155	3,789	6,853	11,885	9,894	27,319	88,920
27 to 49 weeks.............	5,612	214	522	502	747	1,156	784	1,693	66,436
26 weeks or less...........	2,920	490	304	308	356	509	327	624	50,048
Worked at part-time jobs...	13,232	1,440	1,597	1,360	1,690	2,161	1,489	3,498	55,025
50 weeks or more..........	7,663	591	916	810	942	1,286	929	2,190	61,134
27 to 49 weeks.............	2,837	282	345	283	415	464	282	767	53,146
26 weeks or less...........	2,732	568	337	266	333	410	278	540	43,765
Did not work..................	44,264	10,331	6,865	5,332	5,794	6,406	3,552	5,983	34,127
Educational attainment of householder: [3]									
Total........................	**122,380**	**12,252**	**10,663**	**10,465**	**14,446**	**20,912**	**15,407**	**38,237**	**64,761**
Less than 9th grade...........	4,100	1,116	800	523	524	600	281	260	26,875
9th to 12th grade (no diploma)..................	7,132	1,943	1,223	943	1,033	974	492	527	29,204
High school graduate.........	31,806	4,388	3,936	3,823	4,812	5,900	3,531	5,417	46,073
Some college, no degree.....	20,741	2,052	2,052	1,970	2,853	4,011	2,868	4,936	57,807
Associate's degree............	13,195	835	1,038	1,215	1,792	2,591	1,950	3,773	65,647
Bachelor's degree or more....	45,405	1,918	1,613	1,992	3,431	6,838	6,285	23,326	101,822
Bachelor's degree............	27,948	1,395	1,148	1,410	2,362	4,524	3,982	13,127	93,533
Master's degree..............	13,048	398	346	462	871	1,887	1,798	7,287	110,252
Professional degree..........	1,746	48	41	43	72	160	183	1,196	160,007
Doctoral degree..............	2,663	77	77	77	126	268	323	1,713	135,196
Housing tenure:									
Owner occupied...............	82,952	5,453	5,739	5,975	8,767	13,950	11,221	31,850	77,690
Renter occupied..............	44,101	7,276	5,490	5,156	6,457	7,944	4,694	7,086	43,837
Occupier paid no cash rent..	1,526	402	215	159	213	220	134	182	33,762

– Represents or rounds to zero. [1] Median income calculated using $2,500 income intervals. Medians falling in the upper open-ended interval are plugged with "$250,000." [2] For composition of regions, see map, inside front cover. [3] Data shown for householders age 25 and over.

Source: U.S. Census Bureau, *Income and Poverty in the United States: 2018*, Current Population Reports, P60-266, September 2019; and "Current Population Survey Tables for Household Income: Table HINC-01," <http://www.census.gov/topics/income-poverty/income/data/tables.html>, accessed November 2019.

Table 732. Money Income of Households—Households by Income Level, Race, and Hispanic Origin: 2018

[128,579 represents 128,579,000. Households as of March of the following year. Based on Current Population Survey, Annual Social and Economic Supplement (ASEC); see text, this section and Section 1, and Appendix III. Data for 2018 reflect an updated CPS ASEC processing system]

Income interval	Number of households (1,000)					Percent distribution				
	All races [1]	White alone	Black alone	Asian alone	His-panic [2]	All races [1]	White alone	Black alone	Asian alone	His-panic [2]
All households...............	**128,579**	**100,528**	**17,167**	**6,981**	**17,758**	**100.0**	**100.0**	**100.0**	**100.0**	**100.0**
Under $10,000................	7,620	4,899	2,025	388	1,171	5.9	4.9	11.8	5.6	6.6
$10,000 to $14,999............	5,510	3,821	1,278	197	846	4.3	3.8	7.4	2.8	4.8
$15,000 to $19,999............	5,772	4,173	1,181	203	918	4.5	4.2	6.9	2.9	5.2
$20,000 to $24,999............	5,672	4,244	982	226	1,039	4.4	4.2	5.7	3.2	5.9
$25,000 to $29,999............	5,469	4,132	936	214	948	4.3	4.1	5.5	3.1	5.3
$30,000 to $34,999............	5,822	4,367	1,064	207	966	4.5	4.3	6.2	3.0	5.4
$35,000 to $39,999............	5,404	4,178	840	192	990	4.2	4.2	4.9	2.8	5.6
$40,000 to $44,999............	5,195	3,949	832	244	876	4.0	3.9	4.8	3.5	4.9
$45,000 to $49,999............	4,839	3,830	683	161	801	3.8	3.8	4.0	2.3	4.5
$50,000 to $59,999............	9,717	7,648	1,334	429	1,536	7.6	7.6	7.8	6.1	8.6
$60,000 to $74,999............	12,398	9,956	1,483	561	1,810	9.6	9.9	8.6	8.0	10.2
$75,000 to $84,999............	7,299	5,880	845	374	1,116	5.7	5.8	4.9	5.4	6.3
$85,000 to $99,999............	8,747	7,233	809	465	1,145	6.8	7.2	4.7	6.7	6.4
$100,000 to $149,999.........	19,222	15,807	1,639	1,262	2,032	14.9	15.7	9.5	18.1	11.4
$150,000 to $199,999.........	8,948	7,335	692	714	805	7.0	7.3	4.0	10.2	4.5
$200,000 to $249,999.........	4,572	3,719	310	449	355	3.6	3.7	1.8	6.4	2.0
$250,000 and above...........	6,375	5,356	237	693	405	5.0	5.3	1.4	9.9	2.3

[1] Includes other races, not shown separately. [2] Persons of Hispanic origin may be of any race.

Source: U.S. Census Bureau, *Income and Poverty in the United States: 2018*, Current Population Reports, P60-266, September 2019; and "Current Population Survey Tables for Household Income: Table HINC-06," <http://www.census.gov/topics/income-poverty/income/data/tables.html>, accessed November 2019.

Table 733. Share of Aggregate Income Received by Each Fifth and Top 5 Percent of Households: 1990 to 2018

[In units as indicated (94,312 represents 94,312,000). Households as of March of the following year. Income in constant 2018 CPI-U-RS-adjusted dollars. The shares method ranks households from highest to lowest on the basis of income and then divides them into groups of equal population size, typically quintiles. The aggregate income of each group is then divided by the overall aggregate income to derive shares. Based on the Current Population Survey, Annual Social and Economic Supplement (CPS ASEC); see text, this section and Section 1, and Appendix III. For data collection changes over time, see source. See also headnote, Table 729]

Year	Number of house-holds (1,000)	Income at selected positions in constant (2018) dollars					Percent distribution of aggregate income					
		Upper limit of each fifth				Top 5 percent, lower limit	Lowest 5th	Second 5th	Third 5th	Fourth 5th	Highest 5th	Top 5 percent
		Lowest	Second	Third	Fourth							
1990............	94,312	23,358	44,215	67,644	103,157	177,048	3.8	9.6	15.9	24.0	46.6	18.5
1995 [1].........	99,627	23,636	44,176	68,941	106,892	185,474	3.7	9.1	15.2	23.3	48.7	21.0
2000 [2, 3]........	108,209	26,203	48,254	76,291	119,561	212,346	3.6	8.9	14.8	23.0	49.8	22.1
2005............	114,384	24,719	46,402	74,321	118,203	213,966	3.4	8.6	14.6	23.0	50.4	22.2
2006............	116,011	25,013	47,160	74,909	121,143	217,251	3.4	8.6	14.5	22.9	50.5	22.3
2007............	116,783	24,634	47,469	75,271	121,405	214,887	3.4	8.7	14.8	23.4	49.7	21.2
2008............	117,181	24,215	45,597	73,335	117,195	210,446	3.4	8.6	14.7	23.3	50.0	21.5
2009 [4]..........	117,538	23,996	45,228	72,506	117,322	211,181	3.4	8.6	14.6	23.2	50.3	21.7
2010 [5]..........	119,927	23,084	43,859	70,982	115,452	208,313	3.3	8.5	14.6	23.4	50.3	21.3
2011............	121,084	22,671	43,100	69,858	113,661	208,117	3.2	8.4	14.3	23.0	51.1	22.3
2012............	122,459	22,570	43,570	70,763	114,058	209,450	3.2	8.3	14.4	23.0	51.0	22.3
2013 [6]..........	123,931	22,674	44,306	72,556	119,018	221,478	3.1	8.2	14.3	23.0	51.4	22.2
2014 [6]..........	124,587	22,755	43,728	72,423	119,192	219,319	3.1	8.2	14.3	23.2	51.2	21.9
2015 [6]..........	125,819	24,166	46,117	76,314	124,011	227,309	3.1	8.2	14.3	23.2	51.1	22.1
2016 [6]..........	126,224	25,116	47,716	78,343	126,634	235,704	3.1	8.3	14.2	22.9	51.5	22.6
2017 [6]..........	127,669	25,432	48,369	79,039	129,691	250,038	3.0	8.1	14.0	22.6	52.3	23.2
2018 [6]..........	128,579	25,600	50,000	79,542	130,000	248,728	3.1	8.3	14.1	22.6	52.0	23.1

[1] Data reflect full implementation of the 1990 Census-based sample design and metropolitan definitions, 7,000 household sample reduction, and revised race edits. [2] Implementation of Census 2000-based population controls. [3] Implementation of a 28,000 household sample expansion. [4] Beginning with 2009 income data, the Census Bureau expanded the upper income interval used to calculate medians and Gini indexes to $250,000 or more. Medians falling in the upper open-ended interval are plugged with "$250,000." [5] Implementation of Census 2010-based population controls. [6] Beginning 2013, data are based on redesigned questions on income. Beginning 2017, data reflect implementation of an updated processing system. See source for more information.

Source: U.S. Census Bureau, *Income and Poverty in the United States: 2018*, Current Population Reports, P60-266, September 2019; and "Historical Income Tables: Households, Tables H1 and H2," <http://www.census.gov/topics/income-poverty/income/data/tables.html>, accessed November 2019.

Table 734. Money Income of Families—Families by Income Level, Race, and Hispanic Origin: 2018

[83,508 represents 83,508,000. Families as of March of the following year. Based on Current Population Survey, Annual Social and Economic Supplement (CPS ASEC); see text, this section, Section 1, and Appendix III. A family is a group of persons residing together and related by birth, marriage, or adoption. See also headnote in Table 729 regarding changes in the CPS ASEC. Data for 2018 reflect an updated processing system]

Income interval	Number of families (1,000)					Percent distribution				
	All races	White alone	Black alone	Asian alone	His-panic [1]	All races	White alone	Black alone	Asian alone	His-panic [1]
All families...............	83,508	66,132	9,772	5,099	13,279	100.0	100.0	100.0	100.0	100.0
Under $10,000................	3,153	2,112	757	148	715	3.8	3.2	7.7	2.9	5.4
$10,000 to $14,999.............	1,816	1,153	463	99	374	2.2	1.7	4.7	1.9	2.8
$15,000 to $19,999.............	2,055	1,377	437	102	555	2.5	2.1	4.5	2.0	4.2
$20,000 to $24,999.............	2,753	2,038	462	149	764	3.3	3.1	4.7	2.9	5.8
$25,000 to $29,999.............	2,915	2,175	509	148	733	3.5	3.3	5.2	2.9	5.5
$30,000 to $34,999.............	3,242	2,402	608	147	735	3.9	3.6	6.2	2.9	5.5
$35,000 to $39,999.............	3,280	2,560	463	129	783	3.9	3.9	4.7	2.5	5.9
$40,000 to $44,999.............	3,055	2,295	487	163	652	3.7	3.5	5.0	3.2	4.9
$45,000 to $49,999.............	2,922	2,346	376	103	638	3.5	3.5	3.8	2.0	4.8
$50,000 to $59,999.............	6,189	4,853	834	295	1,207	7.4	7.3	8.5	5.8	9.1
$60,000 to $74,999.............	8,225	6,638	938	370	1,412	9.8	10.0	9.6	7.3	10.6
$75,000 to $84,999.............	5,194	4,197	580	274	897	6.2	6.3	5.9	5.4	6.8
$85,000 to $99,999.............	6,592	5,491	556	359	896	7.9	8.3	5.7	7.0	6.7
$100,000 to $149,999.............	15,226	12,536	1,267	1,029	1,627	18.2	19.0	13.0	20.2	12.3
$150,000 to $199,999.............	7,498	6,168	574	587	648	9.0	9.3	5.9	11.5	4.9
$200,000 to $249,999.............	3,946	3,221	258	391	304	4.7	4.9	2.6	7.7	2.3
$250,000 and above..............	5,447	4,571	200	606	340	6.5	6.9	2.0	11.9	2.6

[1] Persons of Hispanic origin may be of any race.

Source: U.S. Census Bureau, *Income and Poverty in the United States: 2018,* Current Population Reports, P60-266, September 2019; and "Current Population Survey Tables for Family Income: Table FINC-07," <https://www.census.gov/topics/income-poverty/income/data/tables.html>, accessed November 2019.

Table 735. Money Income of Families—Percent Distribution of Families by Income Level in Constant (2018) Dollars: 2000 to 2018

[73,778 represents 73,778,000. Income in 2018 Consumer Price Index Research Series Using Current Methods (CPI-U-RS) adjusted dollars. Families as of March of the following year. Based on Current Population Survey, Annual Social and Economic Supplement (CPS ASEC); see text, this section and Section 1, and Appendix III. For definition of median, see Guide to Tabular Presentation. For comments on race, see headnote, Table 729, and also text for Section 1, Population. Data users should exercise caution when comparing trends over time due to changes in CPS ASEC methodology. See source for more information]

Year and race/ethnicity	Number of families (1,000)	Percent distribution							Median income (dollars)
		Under $15,000	$15,000 to $24,999	$25,000 to $34,999	$35,000 to $49,999	$50,000 to $74,999	$75,000 to $99,999	$100,000 and over	
ALL FAMILIES [1]									
2000 [4]................	73,778	5.5	6.7	7.6	12.6	18.5	14.9	34.2	74,182
2010 [5]................	79,559	7.5	7.5	8.9	12.2	17.5	14.0	32.2	69,523
2017 [6]................	83,539	6.2	6.3	7.9	11.1	16.8	13.7	38.1	77,991
2018 [6]................	83,508	6.0	5.8	7.4	11.1	17.3	14.1	38.4	78,646
WHITE [2]									
2000 [4]................	61,330	4.4	6.0	7.2	12.3	18.7	15.3	36.1	77,541
2010 [5]................	63,976	6.1	6.8	8.5	12.1	17.7	14.5	34.2	72,614
2017 [6]................	66,064	5.2	5.5	7.5	10.8	16.9	14.2	40.1	82,093
2018 [6]................	66,132	4.9	5.2	6.9	10.9	17.4	14.6	40.1	81,976
BLACK [2]									
2000 [4]................	8,731	13.1	11.2	11.1	15.5	18.4	12.2	18.6	49,242
2010 [5]................	9,571	16.5	12.1	12.6	14.3	16.5	11.6	16.4	44,545
2017 [6]................	10,034	13.2	10.9	11.1	13.5	17.5	11.5	22.4	51,884
2018 [6]................	9,772	12.5	9.2	11.4	13.6	18.1	11.6	23.6	53,105
ASIAN AND PACIFIC ISLANDER [2]									
2000 [4]................	2,982	4.6	5.4	5.4	9.6	15.6	14.2	45.2	91,561
2010 [5]................	3,879	6.0	6.5	6.4	8.9	15.8	12.6	43.8	86,814
2017 [6]................	4,944	4.5	5.8	5.0	9.2	14.4	12.6	48.4	97,015
2018 [6]................	5,099	4.9	4.9	5.8	7.8	13.0	12.4	51.2	101,244
HISPANIC ORIGIN [3]									
2000 [4]................	8,017	9.6	12.0	11.6	16.7	20.4	12.0	17.5	50,362
2010 [5]................	11,284	13.4	12.5	13.7	15.0	18.2	11.2	16.1	45,359
2017 [6]................	13,266	9.2	10.1	11.4	14.7	20.2	12.2	22.1	54,901
2018 [6]................	13,279	8.2	9.9	11.1	15.6	19.7	13.5	22.0	55,093

[1] Includes other races not shown separately. [2] Beginning with data for 2002, represents White alone, Black alone, or Asian alone. [3] People of Hispanic origin may be of any race. [4] Data reflect implementation of Census 2000-based population controls and a 28,000 household sample expansion to 78,000 households. [5] Median income is calculated using $2,500 income intervals. Beginning with 2009 income data, the Census Bureau expanded the upper income intervals used to calculate medians to $250,000 or more. Medians falling in the upper open-ended interval are plugged with "$250,000." Before 2009, the upper open-ended interval was $100,000 and a plug of "$100,000" was used. Implementation of Census 2010-based population controls. [6] Data are based on redesigned questions on income, and reflect an updated CPS ASEC processing system. See source for more information.

Source: U.S. Census Bureau, *Income and Poverty in the United States: 2018,* Current Population Reports, P60-266, September 2019; and "Historical Income Tables: Families, Table F-23," <https://www.census.gov/topics/income-poverty/income/data/tables.html>, accessed November 2019.

Table 736. Money Income of Families—Median Income by Race and Hispanic Origin in Current and Constant (2018) Dollars: 1990 to 2018

[In dollars. For 2001 and earlier data, the CPS allowed respondents to report only one race group. Beginning with the 2003 CPS covering data for 2002, respondents could choose more than one race. The CPS uses two basic ways to define a race group. A group such as Asian may be defined as those who reported Asian and no other race (the race-alone or single-race concept), or as those who reported Asian regardless of whether they also reported another race (the race-alone-or-in-combination concept). See also comments on race in the text for Section 1, Population. See also headnote, Table 735]

Year	Median income in current dollars					Median income in constant (2018) dollars				
	All races [1]	White [2]	Black [2]	Asian, Pacific Islander [2]	His-panic [3]	All races [1]	White [2]	Black [2]	Asian, Pacific Islander [2]	His-panic [3]
1990............	35,353	36,915	21,423	42,246	23,431	66,061	68,980	40,031	78,942	43,784
2000 [4]............	50,732	53,029	33,676	62,617	34,442	74,182	77,541	49,242	91,561	50,362
2010 [5]............	60,236	62,914	38,594	75,217	39,300	69,523	72,614	44,545	86,814	45,359
2011............	60,974	64,081	40,495	72,996	40,061	68,224	71,701	45,310	81,676	44,825
2012............	62,241	65,880	40,517	77,864	40,764	68,198	72,185	44,395	85,316	44,665
2013 [6]............	65,471	68,802	41,890	82,793	40,939	70,690	74,286	45,229	89,392	44,202
2014 [6]............	66,632	70,609	43,151	82,732	45,114	70,745	74,968	45,815	87,839	47,899
2015 [6]............	70,697	74,291	45,781	90,847	47,328	74,932	78,741	48,523	96,289	50,163
2016 [6]............	72,707	76,264	49,365	93,498	51,105	76,081	79,803	51,656	97,837	53,477
2017 [6]............	76,135	80,139	50,649	94,706	53,595	77,991	82,093	51,884	97,015	54,901
2018 [6]............	78,646	81,976	53,105	101,244	55,093	78,646	81,976	53,105	101,244	55,093

[1] Includes other races not shown separately. [2] Beginning 2002, data represent White alone, Black alone, or Asian alone. [3] Persons of Hispanic origin may be of any race. [4] Implementation of Census 2000-based population controls and 28,000 household sample expansion. [5] Beginning 2009, Census Bureau expanded upper income intervals used to calculate medians to $250,000 or more. Medians falling in the upper open-ended interval are plugged with "$250,000." Before 2009, the upper open-ended interval was $100,000 and a plug of "$100,000" was used. Implementation of Census 2010-based population controls. [6] Beginning 2013, based on redesigned questions on income. Beginning 2017, reflects updated processing system.

Source: U.S. Census Bureau, *Income and Poverty in the United States: 2018*, Current Population Reports, P60-266, September 2019; and "Historical Income Tables: Families, Table F-05," <https://www.census.gov/topics/income-poverty/income/data/tables.html>, accessed November 2019.

Table 737. Money Income of Families—Distribution of Families by Income Level and Selected Characteristics: 2018

[83,508 represents 83,508,000. See headnote, Table 735. Median income is calculated using $2,500 income intervals. Medians falling in the upper open-ended interval are plugged with "$250,000." For composition of regions, see map inside front cover]

Characteristic	Number of families (1,000)								Median income (dollars)
	Total	Under $15,000	$15,000 to $24,999	$25,000 to $34,999	$35,000 to $49,999	$50,000 to $74,999	$75,000 to $99,999	$100,000 and over	
All families..................	**83,508**	**4,969**	**4,808**	**6,157**	**9,257**	**14,414**	**11,787**	**32,117**	**78,646**
Region:									
Northeast....................	14,035	747	653	954	1,384	2,241	1,780	6,278	88,486
Midwest......................	17,556	830	885	1,184	1,888	3,095	2,681	6,990	82,926
South........................	32,518	2,357	2,233	2,681	3,902	5,797	4,504	11,041	71,136
West.........................	19,398	1,035	1,036	1,337	2,082	3,280	2,822	7,808	81,677
Type of family:									
Married-couple families..........	61,971	1,768	2,234	3,452	5,898	10,369	9,471	28,780	93,329
Male householder, no spouse present.............	6,485	585	561	715	1,071	1,401	826	1,327	54,336
Female householder, no spouse present.............	15,052	2,617	2,013	1,990	2,289	2,643	1,491	2,010	40,233
Unrelated subfamilies............	467	119	85	72	85	68	17	21	30,010
Age of householder:									
15 to 24 years old................	3,006	356	353	362	476	612	359	486	48,356
25 to 34 years old................	12,994	1,146	844	1,061	1,682	2,506	1,975	3,779	66,728
35 to 44 years old................	16,986	955	941	1,134	1,677	2,601	2,386	7,291	86,400
45 to 54 years old................	16,414	705	661	844	1,331	2,383	2,260	8,230	100,175
55 to 64 years old...............	15,667	790	677	864	1,401	2,576	2,262	7,098	91,196
65 years old and over...........	18,441	1,017	1,330	1,894	2,689	3,734	2,543	5,237	64,023
Number of earners:									
No earners.......................	13,459	3,073	1,696	1,792	2,086	2,171	1,079	1,561	36,026
One earner......................	26,741	1,665	2,529	3,299	4,418	5,452	3,298	6,081	54,898
Two earners or more............	43,308	232	582	1,066	2,753	6,791	7,410	24,473	110,282
Educational attainment of householder:									
Persons age 25 and over, total..	**80,502**	**4,614**	**4,455**	**5,795**	**8,781**	**13,802**	**11,425**	**31,628**	**80,305**
Less than 9th grade...............	2,608	334	485	396	439	481	243	231	37,116
9th to 12th grade (no diploma). ..	4,497	822	650	633	764	776	414	439	37,202
High school graduate (includes equivalency).................	20,288	1,665	1,574	2,210	3,159	4,273	2,769	4,637	57,627
Some college, no degree.........	13,436	747	738	1,049	1,758	2,761	2,234	4,148	71,027
Associate's degree................	8,923	358	387	678	1,021	1,724	1,534	3,224	78,502
Bachelor's degree or more........	30,750	690	621	829	1,638	3,784	4,234	18,952	121,062
Bachelor's degree..............	18,642	495	475	578	1,186	2,620	2,615	10,673	111,415
Master's degree................	9,004	139	102	191	366	947	1,304	5,957	131,172
Professional degree.............	1,232	15	21	26	31	86	97	958	186,902
Doctoral degree.................	1,872	40	24	34	54	132	219	1,368	158,342

Source: U.S. Census Bureau, *Income and Poverty in the United States: 2018*, Current Population Reports, P60-266, September 2019; and "Current Population Survey Tables for Family Income: Table FINC-01," <https://www.census.gov/topics/income-poverty/income/data/tables.html>, accessed November 2019.

Table 738. Median Income of Families by Type of Family in Current and Constant (2018) Dollars: 1990 to 2018

[In dollars. See headnote, Table 735. For definition of median, see Guide to Tabular Presentation]

Year	Current dollars						Constant (2018) dollars			
	Married-couple families				Male house-holder, no spouse present	Female house-holder, no spouse present	All families	Married-couple families	Male house-holder, no spouse present	Female house-holder, no spouse present
	All families	Total	Wife in paid labor force	Wife not in paid labor force						
1990	35,353	39,895	46,777	30,265	29,046	16,932	66,061	74,549	54,276	31,639
1991	35,939	40,995	48,169	30,075	28,351	16,692	64,799	73,915	51,118	30,096
1992 [1]	36,573	41,890	49,775	30,174	27,576	17,025	64,342	73,696	48,514	29,952
1993 [2]	36,959	43,005	51,204	30,218	26,467	17,443	63,422	73,797	45,418	29,932
1994 [3]	38,782	44,959	53,309	31,176	27,751	18,236	65,189	75,572	46,647	30,653
1995 [4]	40,611	47,062	55,823	32,375	30,358	19,691	66,658	77,246	49,829	32,320
1996	42,300	49,707	58,381	33,748	31,600	19,911	67,629	79,471	50,522	31,833
1997	44,568	51,591	60,669	36,027	32,960	21,023	69,747	80,738	51,581	32,900
1998	46,737	54,180	63,751	37,161	35,681	22,163	72,164	83,657	55,093	34,221
1999 [5]	48,831	56,501	66,478	38,480	37,339	23,762	73,825	85,421	56,451	35,925
2000 [6]	50,732	59,099	69,235	39,982	37,727	25,716	74,182	86,417	55,166	37,603
2001	51,407	60,335	70,834	40,782	36,590	25,745	73,088	85,782	52,022	36,603
2002	51680	61130	72806	40102	37739	26423	72336	85563	52823	36984
2003	52,680	62,281	75,170	41,122	38,032	26,550	72,099	85,239	52,051	36,337
2004	54,061	63,626	76,854	42,215	40,361	26,969	72,042	84,789	53,786	35,939
2005	56,194	65,906	78,755	44,457	41,111	27,244	72,431	84,950	52,990	35,116
2006	58,407	69,404	82,788	45,757	41,844	28,829	72,920	86,650	52,241	35,992
2007	61,355	72,589	86,435	47,329	44,358	30,296	74,488	88,127	53,853	36,781
2008	61,521	72,743	86,621	48,502	43,571	30,129	71,927	85,047	50,941	35,225
2009 [7]	60,088	71,627	85,948	47,649	41,501	29,770	70,497	84,034	48,690	34,927
2010 [8]	60,236	72,241	87,397	48,733	43,206	29,155	69,523	83,379	49,868	33,650
2011	60,974	73,790	89,017	50,414	43,069	30,259	68,224	82,564	48,190	33,857
2012	62,241	75,535	91,779	50,881	42,358	30,686	68,198	82,764	46,412	33,623
2013 [9]	63,815	76,339	94,299	51,839	44,475	31,408	68,902	82,424	48,020	33,911
2013 [10]	65,471	78,614	96,062	54,231	47,191	31,131	70,690	84,880	50,953	33,612
2014 [11]	66,632	80,814	99,983	54,779	47,597	31,770	70,745	85,803	50,535	33,731
2015 [11]	70,697	84,324	103,699	56,010	49,772	34,126	74,932	89,375	52,753	36,170
2016	72,707	86,811	106,082	58,694	51,568	36,658	76,081	90,840	53,961	38,359
2017	75,938	90,148	110,893	61,901	52,950	37,098	77,789	92,346	54,241	38,002
2017 [12]	76,135	91,105	(NA)	(NA)	51,695	36,816	77,991	93,326	52,955	37,713
2018	78,646	93,329	(NA)	(NA)	54,336	40,233	78,646	93,329	54,336	40,233

[1] Data reflect implementation of 1990 census population controls. [2] Data collection method changed from paper and pencil to computer-assisted interviewing. [3] Data reflect introduction of 1990 census-based sample design. [4] Data reflect full implementation of the 1990 census-based sample design and metropolitan definitions, 7,000 household sample reduction, and revised race edits. [5] Implementation of Census 2000-based population controls. [6] Implementation of 28,000 household sample expansion. [7] Median income is calculated using $2,500 income intervals. Beginning with 2009 income data, the Census Bureau expanded the upper income intervals used to calculate medians to $250,000 or more. Medians falling in the upper open-ended interval are plugged with "$250,000." Before 2009, the upper open-ended interval was $100,000 and a plug of "$100,000" was used. [8] Implementation of Census 2010-based population controls. [9] The 2014 CPS ASEC included redesigned questions for income and health insurance coverage. All of the approximately 98,000 addresses were eligible to receive the redesigned set of health insurance coverage questions. The redesigned income questions were implemented to a subsample of the 98,000 addresses using a probability split panel design. Approximately 68,000 addresses were eligible to receive a set of income questions similar to those used in the 2013 CPS ASEC and the remaining 30,000 addresses were eligible to receive the redesigned income questions. The source of these 2013 estimates is the portion of the CPS ASEC sample which received the income questions consistent with the 2013 CPS ASEC, approximately 68,000 addresses. [10] The source of these 2013 estimates is the portion of the CPS ASEC sample which received the redesigned income questions, approximately 30,000 addresses. [11] Implementation of redesigned questionnaire for the full CPS ASEC survey sample. [12] Implementation of an updated CPS ASEC processing system.

Source: U.S. Census Bureau, *Income and Poverty in the United States: 2018*, Current Population Reports, P60-266, September 2019; and "Historical Income Tables: Families, Table F-7," <https://www.census.gov/topics/income-poverty/income/data/tables.html>, accessed November 2019.

Table 739. Median Income of People in Constant (2018) Dollars by Sex, Race, and Hispanic Origin: 2000 to 2018

[In dollars. People as of March of following year. People age 15 and over. Constant dollars based on CPI-U-RS deflator. Based on the Current Population Survey, Annual Social and Economic Supplement (CPS ASEC); see text, this section and Section 1 and Appendix III. For 2001 and earlier data, the CPS allowed respondents to report only one race group. Beginning with the 2003 CPS covering data for 2002, respondents could choose more than one race. The CPS uses two basic ways of defining a race group. A group such as Asian may be defined as 1) those who reported Asian and no other race (the race-alone or single-race concept), or 2) those who reported Asian regardless of whether they also reported another race (the race-alone-or-in-combination concept). See also headnote, Table 735]

Race and Hispanic origin	Male					Female				
	2000 [1]	2010 [2]	2015 [3]	2017 [3]	2018 [3]	2000 [1]	2010 [2]	2015 [3]	2017 [3]	2018 [3]
All races [4]	**41,444**	**37,170**	**39,363**	**41,380**	**41,615**	**23,488**	**23,978**	**25,193**	**26,528**	**27,079**
White [5]	43,570	39,674	41,857	42,822	43,413	23,511	24,118	25,732	26,930	27,344
Black [5]	31,209	26,888	29,046	30,092	31,122	23,222	22,675	22,908	24,510	25,462
Asian [5]	45,085	41,346	46,323	50,385	51,788	25,379	27,196	28,121	28,275	31,187
Hispanic [6]	28,511	25,877	29,794	31,235	31,417	17,909	18,804	20,037	21,011	21,687
White non-Hispanic	46,072	42,882	44,735	47,318	47,817	24,368	25,063	27,164	28,489	29,468

[1] Implementation of Census 2000-based population controls and sample expanded by 28,000 households. [2] See footnote 2, Table 738. [3] Based on redesigned questions on income. As of 2017, data reflect an updated processing system. [4] Includes other races not shown separately. [5] Data for 2002 and later refer to people reporting White alone, Black alone, or Asian alone ("Asian alone" replaced "Asian and Pacific Islander"). [6] People of Hispanic origin may be of any race.

Source: U.S. Census Bureau, *Income and Poverty in the United States: 2018*, Current Population Reports, P60-266, September 2019; and "Historical Income Tables: People, Tables P-2 and P-5," <https://www.census.gov/topics/income-poverty/income/data/tables.html>, accessed November 2019.

Table 740. Money Income of People—People by Income Level and by Sex and Selected Characteristics: 2018

[127,956 represents 127,956,000. People age 15 and over as of March of following year. Based on the Current Population Survey, Annual Social and Economic Supplement (CPS ASEC), see text, this section and Section 1, and Appendix III. Median income is calculated using $2,500 income intervals. Medians falling in the upper open-ended interval are plugged with "$250,000." For definition of median, see Guide to Tabular Presentation. Data reflect an updated CPS ASEC processing system]

Characteristic	All persons (1,000)	People with income (1,000)								Median income (current dollars)
		Total	Under $5,000 or loss	$5,000 to $9,999	$10,000 to $14,999	$15,000 to $24,999	$25,000 to $34,999	$35,000 to $49,999	$50,000 to $74,999	$75,000 and over	
MALE										
Total..................	127,956	115,219	6,711	5,380	7,022	14,903	14,353	17,425	20,655	28,770	41,615
15 to 24 years old.............	21,261	13,343	3,325	1,804	1,476	2,529	1,797	1,274	810	328	15,224
25 to 34 years old.............	22,726	21,308	728	792	932	2,541	3,297	4,266	4,509	4,243	41,646
35 to 44 years old.............	20,257	19,315	495	509	687	1,715	2,058	3,182	4,131	6,538	53,957
45 to 54 years old.............	19,923	19,029	506	534	754	1,508	1,986	2,681	4,203	6,858	56,712
55 to 64 years old.............	19,865	18,943	706	692	1,107	2,116	1,927	2,600	3,618	6,175	50,962
65 years old and over........	23,923	23,281	950	1,048	2,067	4,494	3,289	3,422	3,384	4,628	34,267
Educational attainment:											
Total [1]......................	106,695	101,876	3,386	3,576	5,546	12,374	12,556	16,151	19,845	28,442	46,680
Less than 9th grade...........	4,313	3,935	190	366	591	989	717	574	359	149	22,678
9th to 12th grade [2].........	6,792	6,080	409	577	799	1,400	997	954	597	346	23,649
High school graduate [3].......	31,257	29,311	1,090	1,288	2,079	4,666	4,691	5,936	5,556	4,005	36,476
Some college, no degree.....	16,591	16,034	540	551	838	2,173	2,268	2,899	3,470	3,294	42,379
Associate's degree............	9,936	9,647	276	197	404	1,057	1,209	1,674	2,462	2,369	50,034
Bachelor's degree or more...	37,807	36,869	880	596	834	2,090	2,675	4,115	7,402	18,279	74,161
Bachelor's degree............	23,785	23,087	631	412	587	1,471	1,991	2,924	5,031	10,039	65,981
Master's degree.............	9,621	9,430	183	147	163	432	498	917	1,736	5,355	85,600
Professional degree.........	1,820	1,796	18	13	49	71	72	98	253	1,222	120,030
Doctoral degree..............	2,580	2,556	.47	24	35	116	114	176	382	1,663	100,658
Housing tenure:											
Owner-occupied..............	87,515	79,384	4,610	3,167	4,250	9,168	8,768	11,142	14,896	23,383	47,249
Renter-occupied..............	39,084	34,650	2,004	2,100	2,679	5,553	5,397	6,063	5,611	5,243	33,237
Occupier paid no cash rent..................	1,358	1,186	97	113	94	181	189	220	148	144	30,888
Region:											
Northeast......................	22,009	19,965	1,250	912	1,114	2,412	2,276	2,722	3,578	5,700	45,135
Midwest.......................	26,857	24,705	1,567	1,110	1,484	2,886	2,950	3,949	4,735	6,025	42,383
South..........................	48,071	42,752	2,396	2,105	2,686	5,978	5,778	6,533	7,521	9,754	40,151
West...........................	31,019	27,798	1,499	1,253	1,738	3,626	3,350	4,221	4,821	7,291	41,946
FEMALE										
Total....................	135,625	116,920	12,456	9,729	12,131	19,876	15,854	16,343	15,919	14,613	27,079
15 to 24 years old.............	20,842	13,187	3,703	1,736	1,669	2,641	1,634	1,031	515	258	12,971
25 to 34 years old.............	22,482	19,474	1,863	1,142	1,210	2,877	3,326	3,732	3,257	2,067	32,098
35 to 44 years old.............	20,770	18,209	1,707	1,039	1,041	2,412	2,360	2,936	3,232	3,482	36,946
45 to 54 years old.............	20,776	18,604	1,551	1,026	1,312	2,445	2,391	2,892	3,350	3,637	36,894
55 to 64 years old.............	21,890	19,798	2,028	1,489	1,992	2,886	2,542	2,729	3,060	3,072	30,616
65 years old and over........	28,865	27,648	1,605	3,296	4,907	6,615	3,600	3,023	2,505	2,097	20,431
Educational attainment:											
Total [1]......................	114,783	103,733	8,753	7,993	10,462	17,235	14,220	15,312	15,404	14,355	30,137
Less than 9th grade...........	4,290	3,082	364	715	720	717	328	144	65	29	12,735
9th to 12th grade [2].........	6,580	5,201	607	1,043	1,074	1,303	600	383	153	38	14,176
High school graduate [3].......	31,002	27,264	2,523	2,987	4,035	6,225	4,630	3,717	2,104	1,043	21,133
Some college, no degree.....	18,099	16,616	1,406	1,246	1,876	3,285	2,849	2,702	2,202	1,050	26,498
Associate's degree............	12,802	11,924	905	650	982	2,122	2,123	2,151	1,981	1,011	30,957
Bachelor's degree or more...	42,010	39,645	2,948	1,351	1,775	3,584	3,690	6,215	8,898	11,185	50,385
Bachelor's degree............	26,151	24,458	2,127	959	1,314	2,538	2,617	4,191	5,061	5,651	43,951
Master's degree.............	12,593	12,023	692	311	372	864	924	1,730	3,247	3,884	56,545
Professional degree.........	1,317	1,275	49	36	38	76	58	115	235	669	77,868
Doctoral degree..............	1,948	1,889	80	46	51	106	91	179	355	982	77,412
Housing tenure:											
Owner-occupied..............	91,952	80,757	8,811	6,069	7,802	12,844	10,137	11,369	11,904	11,823	29,640
Renter-occupied..............	42,309	35,056	3,506	3,514	4,164	6,806	5,576	4,849	3,906	2,735	24,004
Occupier paid no cash rent..................	1,364	1,107	140	146	165	226	141	125	109	55	20,033
Region:											
Northeast......................	23,818	20,956	2,271	1,734	2,010	3,154	2,791	2,656	2,988	3,353	29,264
Midwest.......................	28,039	25,234	2,521	2,013	2,471	4,446	3,616	3,889	3,479	2,799	27,389
South..........................	51,942	43,882	4,725	3,722	4,905	7,875	6,085	6,007	5,878	4,685	25,926
West...........................	31,826	26,848	2,939	2,259	2,745	4,402	3,362	3,790	3,574	3,777	27,623

[1] Population age 25 and over. [2] No diploma attained. [3] Includes high school equivalency.

Source: U.S. Census Bureau, *Income and Poverty in the United States: 2018*, Current Population Reports, P60-266, September 2019; and "Current Population Survey Tables for Personal Income: Table PINC-01," <https://www.census.gov/topics/income-poverty/income/data/tables.html>, accessed November 2019.

Table 741. Average Earnings of Year-Round, Full-Time Workers by Educational Attainment: 2018

[In dollars. For people 18 years old and over, as of March of the following year. Based on the Current Population Survey, Annual Social and Economic Supplement (ASEC); see text, this section and Section 1, and Appendix III. Data reflect an updated CPS ASEC processing system]

| Sex and age | All workers | Less than 9th grade | High school | | College | | |
			9th to 12th grade (no diploma)	High school graduate [1]	Some college, no degree	Associate degree	Bachelor's degree or more
Male, total	**75,440**	**36,804**	**40,794**	**51,998**	**61,748**	**65,158**	**108,474**
18 to 24 years old	37,922	(B)	29,294	33,962	33,597	52,066	52,442
25 to 34 years old	59,939	35,430	38,837	45,946	49,232	53,596	78,935
35 to 44 years old	78,804	38,363	43,532	53,291	63,580	67,564	110,761
45 to 54 years old	87,147	37,904	40,335	57,277	71,015	70,907	130,083
55 to 64 years old	87,937	36,595	43,721	60,672	79,853	75,116	126,387
65 years old and over	87,168	31,070	47,385	58,427	78,147	58,862	116,127
Female, total	**57,368**	**26,113**	**27,771**	**37,616**	**41,861**	**48,157**	**77,673**
18 to 24 years old	31,905	(B)	24,424	25,198	28,617	35,203	44,402
25 to 34 years old	49,561	(B)	25,107	31,962	35,457	39,102	63,549
35 to 44 years old	63,901	26,106	27,251	37,667	43,973	48,491	84,663
45 to 54 years old	64,246	26,578	28,933	40,133	48,783	56,794	87,363
55 to 64 years old	60,612	26,635	30,939	44,860	48,204	51,360	83,931
65 years old and over	58,934	(B)	28,570	41,490	44,532	49,423	81,905

B Base figure too small to meet statistical standards for reliability of derived figure. [1] Includes general educational development equivalency.

Source: U.S. Census Bureau, *Income and Poverty in the United States: 2018,* Current Population Reports, P60-266, September 2019; and "Current Population Survey Tables for Personal Income: Table PINC-04," <https://www.census.gov/topics/income-poverty/income/data/tables.html>, accessed November 2019.

Table 742. Per Capita Money Income in Current and Constant (2018) Dollars by Race and Hispanic Origin: 1990 to 2018

[In dollars. Constant dollars based on 2018 CPI-U-RS deflator. People as of March of following year. Based on the Current Population Survey, Annual Social and Economic Supplement (ASEC); see text, this section, Section 1, and Appendix III. See headnote, Table 735]

| Year | Current dollars | | | | | Constant (2018) dollars | | | | |
	All races [1]	White [2]	Black [2]	Asian [2]	His-panic [3]	All races [1]	White [2]	Black [2]	Asian [2]	His-panic [3]
1990	14,387	15,265	9,017	(NA)	8,424	26,884	28,524	16,849	(NA)	15,741
2000 [4]	22,346	23,582	14,796	23,350	12,651	32,675	34,482	21,635	34,143	18,499
2005 [5]	25,036	26,496	16,874	27,331	14,483	32,270	34,152	21,750	35,228	18,668
2010 [6]	26,558	28,356	18,019	28,673	15,044	30,653	32,728	20,797	33,094	17,364
2014 [7]	30,176	32,089	21,066	34,096	17,699	32,039	34,070	22,366	36,201	18,792
2015 [7]	31,653	33,564	22,452	36,280	19,457	33,549	35,575	23,797	38,453	20,623
2016 [7]	33,205	35,168	23,622	38,156	20,430	34,746	36,800	24,718	39,927	21,378
2017 [7]	35,048	37,303	24,148	40,517	20,746	35,902	38,212	24,737	41,505	21,252
2018 [7]	36,080	38,323	24,731	43,193	21,975	36,080	38,323	24,731	43,193	21,975

NA Not available. [1] Includes other races, not shown separately. [2] As of 2002, data refer to people reporting specified race alone ("Asian alone" replaces "Asian and Pacific Islander"). [3] People of Hispanic origin may be of any race. [4] Implementation of Census 2000-based population controls, and of a 28,000 household sample expansion. [5] Data have been revised to reflect a correction to the weights in the 2005 ASEC. [6] Implementation of Census 2010-based population controls. [7] As of 2013, data based on redesigned income questions. As of 2017, data reflect an updated processing system.

Source: U.S. Census Bureau, *Income and Poverty in the United States: 2018*, Current Population Reports, P60-266, September 2019; and "Historical Income Tables: People, Table P-1," <https://www.census.gov/topics/income-poverty/income/data/tables.html>, accessed November 2019.

Table 743. Money Income of People—People by Income Level and by Sex, Race, and Hispanic Origin: 2018

[In thousands (127,956 represents 127,956,000). People age 15 years and over as of March of the following year. Based on Current Population Survey, Annual Social and Economic Supplement (ASEC); see text, this section, Section 1, and Appendix III. Data reflect an updated CPS ASEC processing system]

| Income interval | Male | | | | | Female | | | | |
	All races [1]	White alone	Black alone	Asian alone	His-panic [2]	All races [1]	White alone	Black alone	Asian alone	His-panic [2]
Total	**127,956**	**100,349**	**15,451**	**7,814**	**22,149**	**135,625**	**103,991**	**18,196**	**8,686**	**22,197**
Under $10,000 [3]	24,828	17,422	4,454	1,656	5,379	40,890	30,185	5,613	3,232	9,372
$10,000 to $19,999	14,268	10,838	2,209	660	2,988	22,430	17,239	3,372	1,006	3,697
$20,000 to $29,999	14,608	11,291	1,996	756	3,530	17,648	13,715	2,510	844	3,156
$30,000 to $39,999	13,803	10,893	1,760	641	3,072	13,967	10,773	2,088	660	1,957
$40,000 to $49,999	11,024	8,890	1,294	508	1,949	10,159	8,037	1,295	509	1,291
$50,000 to $59,999	9,810	8,053	982	488	1,608	7,996	6,329	1,022	447	910
$60,000 to $74,999	10,845	8,919	1,000	649	1,413	7,921	6,241	903	569	725
$75,000 to $84,999	5,430	4,439	481	380	554	3,531	2,737	383	326	293
$85,000 to $99,999	5,380	4,492	390	389	497	3,178	2,538	303	265	250
$100,000 to $149,999	9,817	8,094	625	915	663	4,994	3,849	513	522	339
$150,000 to $199,999	3,914	3,325	143	403	247	1,307	1,034	124	119	103
$200,000 to $249,999	1,642	1,450	59	118	103	672	551	25	82	40
$250,000 and above	2,587	2,242	58	255	147	931	761	47	106	62

[1] Includes other races not shown separately. [2] Persons of Hispanic origin may be of any race. [3] Includes persons without income.

Source: U.S. Census Bureau, *Income and Poverty in the United States: 2018*, Current Population Reports, P60-266, September 2019; and "Current Population Survey Tables for Personal Income: Table PINC-11," <https://www.census.gov/topics/income-poverty/income/data/tables.html>, accessed November 2019.

Table 744. Household, Family, and Per Capita Income, and Individuals and Families Below Poverty Level, by City: 2018

[The American Community Survey universe includes the household population and the population living in institutions, college dormitories, and other group quarters. Based on a sample and subject to sampling variability; see text, Section 1 and Appendix III. For definition of median, see Guide to Tabular Presentation. CDP is Census designated place]

City	Median household income (dol.)	Median family income (dol.)	Per capita income (dol.)	Number below poverty level [1]		Percent below poverty level	
				Individuals [1]	Families	Individuals [1]	Families
Albuquerque, NM.	51,099	64,835	30,328	93,230	15,721	16.8	12.1
Anaheim, CA.	76,154	83,621	29,188	50,365	7,743	14.5	10.2
Anchorage, AK.	83,648	99,797	39,291	26,386	4,479	9.2	6.4
Arlington, TX.	63,091	71,516	28,744	52,975	9,718	13.5	10.4
Atlanta, GA.	65,345	81,207	48,869	93,612	13,444	20.2	14.9
Aurora, CO.	63,128	75,864	30,792	35,970	6,265	9.7	7.2
Austin, TX.	71,543	93,491	43,923	125,720	19,299	13.3	9.4
Bakersfield, CA.	60,002	65,433	26,630	69,143	14,131	18.2	15.5
Baltimore, MD.	51,000	65,702	31,433	107,073	16,365	18.4	13.9
Boston, MA.	71,834	85,934	43,367	118,946	15,613	18.2	12.1
Charlotte, NC.	60,764	76,201	37,913	109,800	18,083	12.8	9.1
Chicago, IL.	57,238	67,206	37,160	461,399	78,434	17.4	13.8
Cincinnati, OH.	43,585	58,549	31,874	73,460	12,405	25.2	18.9
Cleveland, OH.	29,953	37,509	22,525	123,640	21,719	33.1	27.5
Colorado Springs, CO.	65,331	75,589	33,194	51,057	8,830	11.0	7.6
Columbus, OH.	52,971	63,443	28,989	173,394	26,574	19.9	13.7
Corpus Christi, TX.	56,602	69,004	27,729	50,818	10,745	15.9	13.7
Dallas, TX.	52,210	58,835	34,016	239,889	40,481	18.0	13.8
Denver, CO.	68,377	90,020	44,556	79,859	11,715	11.3	8.1
Detroit, MI.	31,283	36,842	18,427	220,431	39,036	33.4	28.3
El Paso, TX.	45,031	50,245	22,777	135,037	26,588	20.1	17.0
Fort Worth, TX.	58,448	66,765	29,010	138,120	26,089	15.6	12.5
Fresno, CA.	49,813	56,951	23,222	125,545	22,659	24.1	19.8
Greensboro, NC.	45,787	60,233	28,947	52,172	9,895	18.6	14.1
Henderson, NV.	72,884	85,539	39,020	25,620	4,190	8.3	5.3
Honolulu CDP, HI.	71,247	92,833	37,284	32,557	4,735	9.7	6.4
Houston, TX.	51,203	56,693	31,162	466,418	89,115	20.4	16.9
Indianapolis, IN.	47,678	61,771	27,860	139,574	22,312	16.5	12.0
Jacksonville, FL.	54,269	63,851	30,632	132,478	25,602	15.0	11.8
Kansas City, MO.	54,372	71,542	32,108	72,665	11,587	15.0	10.5
Las Vegas, NV.	53,575	69,526	30,895	103,948	16,804	16.3	11.5
Lexington-Fayette, KY.	54,896	73,455	34,190	45,230	6,890	14.5	9.1
Long Beach, CA.	61,610	69,164	32,233	70,449	10,594	15.3	10.8
Los Angeles, CA.	62,474	70,932	35,089	646,765	99,695	16.5	12.2
Louisville/Jefferson County, KY [2].	52,303	63,388	30,353	104,213	19,539	17.3	13.2
Memphis, TN.	37,199	48,627	24,187	176,932	30,078	27.8	21.6
Mesa, AZ.	58,247	65,916	28,709	70,407	12,711	13.9	10.2
Miami, FL.	41,818	46,701	30,651	100,683	18,278	21.7	18.4
Milwaukee, WI.	42,087	48,972	23,439	143,029	25,055	24.9	19.7
Minneapolis, MN.	63,590	85,303	39,047	74,151	8,162	18.0	10.3
Nashville-Davidson, TN [2].	60,324	71,507	35,834	100,253	20,092	15.6	13.1
New Orleans, LA.	38,423	60,826	29,048	89,130	11,220	23.8	16.5
New York, NY.	63,799	72,268	39,589	1,426,628	267,728	17.3	14.1
Oakland, CA.	76,469	83,718	46,921	58,604	8,600	13.8	10.0
Oklahoma City, OK.	53,973	65,588	30,429	104,037	19,534	16.3	13.1
Omaha, NE.	59,266	77,640	33,507	59,519	9,159	13.0	8.4
Philadelphia, PA.	46,116	55,109	28,379	377,116	62,475	24.5	19.2
Phoenix, AZ.	57,957	67,557	29,310	255,923	44,351	15.6	12.2
Pittsburgh, PA.	47,417	72,654	34,636	57,333	6,716	20.5	11.7
Plano, TX.	93,012	110,032	46,659	19,870	3,451	6.9	4.7
Portland, OR.	73,097	97,385	42,814	73,582	8,093	11.5	5.9
Raleigh, NC.	65,695	87,214	38,804	55,698	7,679	12.3	7.4
Riverside, CA.	67,850	75,360	25,441	46,014	6,462	14.7	10.4
Sacramento, CA.	65,046	75,604	31,816	76,556	10,986	15.3	10.0
San Antonio, TX.	49,024	60,689	24,684	301,024	48,806	20.0	15.6
San Diego, CA.	79,646	92,773	40,760	179,296	26,303	12.9	8.4
San Francisco, CA.	112,376	131,253	71,606	87,087	9,114	10.0	5.1
San Jose, CA.	113,036	126,462	48,264	84,442	11,972	8.3	5.0
San Juan, Puerto Rico.	22,729	29,035	18,386	123,640	30,178	40.6	37.4
Santa Ana, CA.	65,313	65,117	21,552	43,479	7,117	13.3	11.3
Seattle, WA.	93,481	130,656	60,625	79,805	8,188	11.0	5.3
St. Louis, MO.	43,889	60,075	31,537	65,085	10,832	22.1	17.0
St. Paul, MN.	59,033	79,666	33,489	57,979	8,975	19.4	15.0
Stockton, CA.	54,297	60,430	22,591	56,917	11,641	18.7	16.6
Tampa, FL.	54,599	70,538	35,694	69,014	11,649	18.1	13.4
Tucson, AZ.	43,676	54,924	23,553	114,326	17,518	21.9	15.3
Tulsa, OK.	47,583	61,482	30,709	70,484	13,132	17.9	14.1
Virginia Beach, VA.	77,059	88,366	38,424	30,243	5,293	6.9	4.5
Washington, DC.	85,203	117,713	55,328	108,055	13,761	16.2	11.3
Wichita, KS.	51,051	65,261	28,729	58,059	9,825	15.1	10.7

[1] Poverty status was determined for all people except institutionalized people, people in military group quarters, people in college dormitories, and unrelated individuals under 15 years old. [2] Represents metropolitan government (balance) of locality.

Source: U.S. Census Bureau, 2018 American Community Survey, Tables DP03, B01003, B17001, and B17019, <https://data.census.gov/>, accessed November 2019. See also <https://www.census.gov/topics/income-poverty/poverty.html>.

Table 745. Persons and Families Below Poverty Level—Number and Rate by State: 2008 and 2018

[In thousands (39,108 represents 39,108,000), except as indicated. Represents number and percent below poverty in the past 12 months. Poverty status was determined for all people except institutionalized people, people in military group quarters, people in college dormitories, and unrelated individuals under 15 years old. These groups were excluded from the numerator and denominator when calculating poverty rates. Based on a sample and subject to sampling variability; see Appendix III]

| State | Number below poverty (1,000) | | | | Percent below poverty | | | |
| | Persons | | Families | | Persons | | Families | |
	2008	2018	2008	2018	2008	2018	2008	2018
United States..........	39,108	41,852	7,252	7,343	13.2	13.1	9.7	9.3
Alabama................	713	800	146	149	15.7	16.8	12.0	12.2
Alaska.................	56	79	9	13	8.4	10.9	5.7	7.5
Arizona................	939	983	154	170	14.7	14.0	10.3	9.9
Arkansas...............	481	505	98	97	17.3	17.2	13.0	12.7
California.............	4,778	4,969	825	812	13.3	12.8	10.0	9.1
Colorado...............	553	537	95	86	11.4	9.6	7.8	6.2
Connecticut............	315	361	59	63	9.3	10.4	6.7	7.1
Delaware...............	85	117	15	20	10.0	12.5	6.9	8.4
District of Columbia.....	97	108	15	14	17.2	16.2	13.7	11.3
Florida................	2,371	2,841	433	488	13.2	13.6	9.5	9.7
Georgia................	1,381	1,469	263	275	14.7	14.3	11.1	10.8
Hawaii.................	115	122	18	18	9.1	8.8	6.0	5.7
Idaho..................	188	203	37	36	12.6	11.8	9.4	8.2
Illinois...............	1,532	1,509	283	265	12.2	12.1	9.0	8.5
Indiana................	808	853	158	157	13.1	13.1	9.6	9.3
Iowa...................	335	344	58	57	11.5	11.2	7.3	7.2
Kansas.................	307	338	57	58	11.3	12.0	7.7	8.0
Kentucky...............	721	730	147	143	17.3	16.9	13.1	12.6
Louisiana..............	744	844	146	151	17.3	18.6	13.4	13.6
Maine..................	158	152	29	25	12.3	11.6	8.6	7.3
Maryland...............	443	528	75	89	8.1	9.0	5.4	6.0
Massachusetts..........	627	664	112	107	10.0	10.0	7.1	6.5
Michigan...............	1,410	1,373	265	238	14.4	14.1	10.5	9.5
Minnesota..............	491	529	83	80	9.6	9.6	6.2	5.7
Mississippi............	602	568	128	109	21.2	19.7	17.0	15.0
Missouri...............	768	786	148	140	13.4	13.2	9.7	9.0
Montana................	140	135	23	20	14.8	13.0	9.7	7.7
Nebraska...............	187	206	31	35	10.8	11.0	6.8	7.1
Nevada.................	290	387	49	64	11.3	12.9	7.9	9.1
New Hampshire.........	97	100	17	16	7.6	7.6	5.0	4.7
New Jersey.............	741	832	135	155	8.7	9.5	6.2	6.9
New Mexico.............	333	399	61	75	17.1	19.5	12.6	15.1
New York...............	2,581	2,591	472	465	13.6	13.6	10.3	10.0
North Carolina..........	1,302	1,418	260	266	14.6	14.0	10.9	10.2
North Dakota...........	74	79	13	11	12.0	10.7	7.9	5.7
Ohio...................	1,492	1,579	289	284	13.4	13.9	9.8	9.7
Oklahoma...............	562	597	110	113	15.9	15.6	11.8	11.4
Oregon.................	506	517	90	83	13.6	12.6	9.6	8.0
Pennsylvania...........	1,458	1,518	271	263	12.1	12.2	8.5	8.1
Rhode Island...........	119	131	19	23	11.7	12.9	7.7	9.1
South Carolina..........	680	755	132	136	15.7	15.3	11.6	10.8
South Dakota...........	96	112	17	18	12.5	13.1	8.2	8.0
Tennessee..............	938	1,011	187	193	15.5	15.3	11.6	11.3
Texas..................	3,760	4,181	726	768	15.8	14.9	12.4	11.4
Utah...................	258	281	42	46	9.6	9.0	6.6	6.1
Vermont................	63	66	10	10	10.6	11.0	6.5	6.2
Virginia...............	768	885	147	149	10.2	10.7	7.3	7.1
Washington.............	728	759	126	119	11.3	10.3	7.7	6.3
West Virginia..........	301	312	61	60	17.0	17.8	12.4	13.0
Wisconsin..............	569	626	98	104	10.4	11.0	6.7	7.0
Wyoming................	49	62	8	10	9.4	11.1	5.7	7.1
Puerto Rico............	(NA)	1,364	(NA)	314	(NA)	43.1	(NA)	39.7

NA Not available.

Source: U.S. Census Bureau, 2008 and 2018 American Community Survey: B17001, "Poverty Status in the Past 12 Months by Sex By Age," and B17019, "Poverty Status in the Past 12 Months of Families by Household Type by Tenure"; <https://data.census.gov/>, accessed November 2019. See also <http://www.census.gov/programs-surveys/acs/>.

Table 746. Poverty Thresholds by Size of Family Unit: 1980 to 2018

[In dollars per year. The official poverty definition uses money income before taxes and does not include capital gains and noncash benefits (such as public housing and food stamps). For information on the official poverty thresholds, see text, this section. For more on poverty, see <http://www.census.gov/topics/income-poverty/poverty.html>. See also headnote, Table 747]

Size of family unit	1980	1990	1995	2000 [2]	2005	2010 [3]	2016 [4]	2017 [4]	2018 [4]
One person (unrelated individual) [1]......	4,190	6,652	7,763	8,791	9,973	11,137	12,228	12,485	12,784
Under 65 years old........................	4,290	6,800	7,929	8,959	10,160	11,344	12,486	12,752	13,064
65 years old and over...................	3,949	6,268	7,309	8,259	9,367	10,458	11,511	11,756	12,043
Two persons...............................	5,363	8,509	9,933	11,235	12,755	14,216	15,569	15,880	16,247
Householder under 65 years old........	5,537	8,794	10,259	11,589	13,145	14,676	16,151	16,491	16,889
Householder 65 years old and over.....	4,983	7,905	9,219	10,418	11,815	13,194	14,522	14,829	15,193
Three persons.............................	6,565	10,419	12,158	13,740	15,577	17,373	19,105	19,515	19,985
Four persons..............................	8,414	13,359	15,569	17,604	19,971	22,315	24,563	25,093	25,701
Five persons..............................	9,966	15,792	18,408	20,815	23,613	26,442	29,111	29,716	30,459
Six persons...............................	11,269	17,839	20,804	23,533	26,683	29,904	32,928	33,610	34,533
Seven persons............................	12,761	20,241	23,552	26,750	30,249	34,019	37,458	38,170	39,194
Eight persons............................	14,199	22,582	26,237	29,701	33,610	37,953	41,781	42,642	43,602
Nine or more persons.....................	16,896	26,848	31,280	35,150	40,288	45,224	49,721	50,723	51,393

[1] A person living alone or with non-relatives. [2] Implementation of Census 2000-based population controls and sample expanded by 28,000 households. [3] Implementation of Census 2010-based population controls. [4] Based on redesigned questions on income. As of 2017, data reflect an updated processing system. See source for more information.

Source: U.S. Census Bureau, *Income and Poverty in the United States: 2018,* Current Population Reports, P60-266, September 2019; and "Poverty Thresholds," <https://www.census.gov/topics/income-poverty/poverty/data/tables.html>, accessed November 2019.

Table 747. People Below Poverty Level by Race and Hispanic Origin, and Below 125 Percent of Poverty Level: 1990 to 2018

[33,585 represents 33,585,000. People as of March of the following year. Based on Current Population Survey, Annual Social and Economic Supplement (ASEC); see text, this section, Section 1, and Appendix III. Beginning with 2003 CPS ASEC covering data for 2002, refers to persons of specified race only and who did not report any other race category; "Asian" replaced "Asian Pacific Islander." For information on measuring poverty, see <http://www.census.gov/topics/income-poverty/poverty/guidance/poverty-measures.html>. Data users should exercise caution when comparing trends over time due to changes in CPS ASEC methodology and data processing. Changes are noted below for the years as appropriate. See source for more information]

Year	Number of persons below poverty (1,000)					Percent of persons below poverty					Below 125 percent of poverty level [1]	
	All races [2]	White	Black	Asian	His-panic [3]	All races [2]	White	Black	Asian	His-panic [3]	Number (1,000)	Percent of total pop-ulation
1990.........	33,585	22,326	9,837	858	6,006	13.5	10.7	31.9	12.2	28.1	44,837	18.0
1991.........	35,708	23,747	10,242	996	6,339	14.2	11.3	32.7	13.8	28.7	47,527	18.9
1992 [4].......	38,014	25,259	10,827	985	7,592	14.8	11.9	33.4	12.7	29.6	50,592	19.7
1993 [5].......	39,265	26,226	10,877	1,134	8,126	15.1	12.2	33.1	15.3	30.6	51,801	20.0
1994.........	38,059	25,379	10,196	974	8,416	14.5	11.7	30.6	14.6	30.7	50,401	19.3
1995.........	36,425	24,423	9,872	1,411	8,574	13.8	11.2	29.3	14.6	30.3	48,761	18.5
1996.........	36,529	24,650	9,694	1,454	8,697	13.7	11.2	28.4	14.5	29.4	49,310	18.5
1997.........	35,574	24,396	9,116	1,468	8,308	13.3	11.0	26.5	14.0	27.1	47,853	17.8
1998.........	34,476	23,454	9,091	1,360	8,070	12.7	10.5	26.1	12.5	25.6	46,036	17.0
1999 [6].......	32,791	22,169	8,441	1,285	7,876	11.9	9.8	23.6	10.7	22.7	45,030	16.3
2000 [7].......	31,581	21,645	7,982	1,258	7,747	11.3	9.5	22.5	9.9	21.5	43,612	15.6
2001.........	32,907	22,739	8,136	1,275	7,997	11.7	9.9	22.7	10.2	21.4	45,320	16.1
2002.........	34,570	23,466	8,602	1,161	8,555	12.1	10.2	24.1	10.1	21.8	47,084	16.5
2003.........	35,861	24,272	8,781	1,401	9,051	12.5	10.5	24.4	11.8	22.5	48,687	16.9
2004 [8].......	37,040	25,327	9,014	1,201	9,122	12.7	10.8	24.7	9.8	21.9	49,693	17.1
2005.........	36,950	24,872	9,168	1,402	9,368	12.6	10.6	24.9	11.1	21.8	49,327	16.8
2006.........	36,460	24,416	9,048	1,353	9,243	12.3	10.3	24.3	10.3	20.6	49,688	16.8
2007.........	37,276	25,120	9,237	1,349	9,890	12.5	10.5	24.5	10.2	21.5	50,876	17.0
2008.........	39,829	26,990	9,379	1,576	10,987	13.2	11.2	24.7	11.8	23.2	53,805	17.9
2009.........	43,569	29,830	9,944	1,746	12,350	14.3	12.3	25.8	12.5	25.3	56,840	18.7
2010 [9].......	46,343	31,083	10,746	1,899	13,522	15.1	13.0	27.4	12.2	26.5	60,669	19.8
2011.........	46,247	30,849	10,929	1,973	13,244	15.0	12.8	27.6	12.3	25.3	60,949	19.8
2012.........	46,496	30,816	10,911	1,921	13,616	15.0	12.7	27.2	11.7	25.6	61,202	19.7
2013 [10]......	46,269	31,287	10,186	2,255	13,356	14.8	12.9	25.2	13.1	24.7	60,396	19.3
2014 [10]......	46,657	31,089	10,755	2,137	13,104	14.8	12.7	26.2	12.0	23.6	61,339	19.4
2015 [10]......	43,123	28,566	10,020	2,078	12,133	13.5	11.6	24.1	11.4	21.4	56,912	17.9
2016 [10]......	40,616	27,113	9,234	1,908	11,137	12.7	11.0	22.0	10.1	19.4	54,430	17.0
2017 [10]......	39,564	26,026	9,224	1,891	10,816	12.3	10.5	21.7	9.7	18.3	53,512	16.6
2018 [10]......	38,146	24,945	8,884	1,996	10,526	11.8	10.1	20.8	10.1	17.6	51,706	16.0

[1] People with incomes below 125 percent of poverty level. [2] Includes other races, not shown separately. [3] People of Hispanic origin may be of any race. [4] Implementation of 1990 Census population controls. [5] The March 1994 income supplement was revised to allow for the coding of different income amounts on selected questionnaire items. Limits either increased or decreased in the following categories: earnings increased to $999,999; Social Security increased to $49,999; Supplemental Security Income and public assistance increased to $24,999; veterans' benefits increased to $99,999; child support and alimony decreased to $49,999. [6] Implementation of Census-2000-based population controls. [7] Implementation of sample expansion by 28,000 households. [8] Data have been revised to reflect a correction to the weights in the 2005 ASEC. [9] Implementation of Census 2010-based population controls. [10] Data based on redesigned income questions. Beginning 2017, data reflect an updated processing system. See source for more information.

Source: U.S. Census Bureau, *Income and Poverty in the United States: 2018,* Current Population Reports, P60-266, September 2019; and "Historical Poverty Tables: People and Families, Tables 2 and 6," <https://www.census.gov/topics/income-poverty/poverty/data/tables.html>, accessed November 2019.

Table 748. Children Below Poverty Level by Race and Hispanic Origin: 1990 to 2018

[12,715 represents 12,715,000. Persons as of March of the following year. Covers only related children under age 18, in families. Based on Current Population Survey, Annual Social and Economic Supplement (CPS ASEC); see text, this section, Section 1, and Appendix III. See headnote, Table 747]

Year	Number of children below poverty level (1,000)					Percent of children below poverty level				
	All races [1]	White	Black	Asian	His-panic [2]	All races [1]	White	Black	Asian	His-panic [2]
1990............	12,715	7,696	4,412	356	2,750	19.9	15.1	44.2	17.0	37.7
1995 [3]...........	13,999	8,474	4,644	532	3,938	20.2	15.5	41.5	18.6	39.3
1996............	13,764	8,488	4,411	553	4,090	19.8	15.5	39.5	19.1	39.9
1997............	13,422	8,441	4,116	608	3,865	19.2	15.4	36.8	19.9	36.4
1998............	12,845	7,935	4,073	542	3,670	18.3	14.4	36.4	17.5	33.6
1999 [4]..........	11,678	7,194	3,698	367	3,561	16.6	13.1	32.8	11.5	29.9
2000 [5]..........	11,005	6,834	3,495	407	3,342	15.6	12.4	30.9	12.5	27.6
2001............	11,175	7,086	3,423	353	3,433	15.8	12.8	30.0	11.1	27.4
2002............	11,646	7,203	3,570	302	3,653	16.3	13.1	32.1	11.4	28.2
2003............	12,340	7,624	3,750	331	3,982	17.2	13.9	33.6	12.1	29.5
2004 [6]..........	12,473	7,876	3,702	265	3,985	17.3	14.3	33.4	9.4	28.6
2005............	12,335	7,652	3,743	312	3,977	17.1	13.9	34.2	11.0	27.7
2006............	12,299	7,522	3,690	351	3,959	16.9	13.6	33.0	12.0	26.6
2007............	12,802	8,002	3,838	345	4,348	17.6	14.4	34.3	11.8	28.3
2008............	13,507	8,441	3,781	430	4,888	18.5	15.3	34.4	14.2	30.3
2009............	14,774	9,440	3,919	444	5,419	20.1	17.0	35.3	13.6	32.5
2010 [7]..........	15,598	9,590	4,271	477	5,815	21.5	17.9	39.0	14.0	34.3
2011............	15,539	9,643	4,247	466	5,820	21.4	18.1	38.6	13.0	33.7
2012............	15,437	9,547	4,097	470	5,773	21.3	17.9	37.5	13.3	33.3
2013 [8]..........	15,116	9,702	3,678	538	5,638	20.9	18.4	33.8	14.4	32.2
2014 [8]..........	14,987	9,172	4,036	492	5,522	20.7	17.4	37.1	13.4	31.3
2015 [8]..........	13,962	8,838	3,571	420	5,139	19.2	16.7	32.7	11.4	28.6
2016 [8]..........	12,803	7,963	3,382	412	4,764	17.6	15.1	30.6	10.7	26.3
2017 [8]..........	12,358	7,520	3,280	405	4,525	17.0	14.3	30.2	10.1	24.7
2018 [8]..........	11,491	6,783	3,212	426	4,316	15.9	13.0	29.4	10.8	23.4

[1] Includes other races, not shown separately. [2] People of Hispanic origin may be of any race. [3] See Table 747, footnote 5. [4] Implementation of Census 2000-based population controls. [5] Sample expanded by 28,000 households. [6] Data have been revised to reflect a correction to the weights in the 2005 ASEC. [7] Implementation of Census 2010-based population controls. [8] Data based on redesigned income questions. As of 2017, data reflect an updated processing system. See source for more information.

Source: U.S. Census Bureau, *Income and Poverty in the United States: 2018*, Current Population Reports, P60-266, September 2019; and "Historical Poverty Tables: People and Families, Table 3," <https://www.census.gov/topics/income-poverty/poverty/data/tables.html>, accessed November 2019.

Table 749. People Below Poverty Level by Selected Characteristics: 2018

[38,146 represents 38,146,000. People as of March of the following year. Based on the Current Population Survey, Annual Social and Economic and Supplement (CPS ASEC). Data by education cover people age 25 and over, based on the highest grade completed]

Characteristic	Number below poverty level (1,000)					Percent below poverty level				
	All races [1]	White alone	Black alone	Asian alone	His-panic [2]	All races [1]	White alone	Black alone	Asian alone	His-panic [2]
Total....................	**38,146**	**24,945**	**8,884**	**1,996**	**10,526**	**11.8**	**10.1**	**20.8**	**10.1**	**17.6**
Male........................	16,782	10,961	3,839	959	4,737	10.6	8.9	19.1	10.1	15.7
Female......................	21,363	13,984	5,045	1,036	5,789	12.9	11.2	22.2	10.1	19.4
AGE										
Under 18 years old..............	11,869	7,049	3,273	453	4,436	16.2	13.4	29.5	11.3	23.7
18 to 24 years old..............	4,360	2,888	818	392	1,091	15.0	13.5	19.2	21.6	16.4
25 to 34 years old..............	4,926	3,090	1,256	321	1,325	10.9	9.3	18.9	9.5	14.1
35 to 44 years old..............	4,133	2,804	874	241	1,313	10.1	9.1	16.0	7.6	15.3
45 to 54 years old..............	3,429	2,392	737	150	858	8.4	7.6	14.0	5.5	12.2
55 to 59 years old..............	2,059	1,432	465	70	309	9.7	8.5	17.5	6.6	11.2
60 to 64 years old..............	2,223	1,526	510	81	309	10.8	9.2	21.8	7.2	13.8
65 years old and over..........	5,146	3,762	951	289	884	9.7	8.5	18.9	11.7	19.5
65 to 74 years old.............	2,733	1,897	589	157	485	8.7	7.3	18.1	10.1	17.2
75 years old and over........	2,413	1,866	362	132	400	11.3	10.2	20.2	14.2	23.1
EDUCATION [3]										
No high school diploma........	5,693	3,975	1,209	255	2,301	25.9	24.1	36.4	20.8	23.6
High school, no college........	7,925	5,257	2,046	281	1,548	12.7	10.8	22.9	11.5	14.3
Some college, less than 4-year degree.................	4,812	3,230	1,125	177	738	8.4	7.1	14.0	8.2	9.9
College, 4-year degree or higher.....................	3,486	2,546	413	438	413	4.4	4.0	5.8	5.4	6.3
NATIVITY [4]										
Native......................	31,828	20,823	8,131	735	6,873	11.4	9.4	21.7	9.5	17.6
Foreign born................	6,317	4,122	753	1,261	3,653	13.8	15.2	14.3	10.5	17.5
Naturalized citizen.............	2,215	1,418	247	483	1,044	9.9	11.5	9.0	7.2	13.2
Not a citizen.................	4,103	2,704	506	778	2,609	17.5	18.2	20.1	14.6	20.1
REGION										
Northeast....................	5,682	3,634	1,299	464	1,526	10.3	8.6	17.6	11.2	19.6
Midwest.....................	7,005	4,554	1,800	260	889	10.4	8.2	25.3	11.1	15.7
South.......................	16,757	10,426	5,041	474	4,304	13.6	11.6	20.7	10.1	18.4
West........................	8,701	6,330	745	797	3,807	11.2	10.6	19.1	9.3	16.5

[1] Includes other races, not shown separately. [2] Persons of Hispanic origin may be of any race. [3] Highest grade completed for persons age 25 and over. [4] For persons age 15 and over.

Source: U.S. Census Bureau, *Income and Poverty in the United States: 2018*, Current Population Reports, P60-266, September 2019; and "Current Population Survey Detailed Tables for Poverty: Tables POV01, POV29, and POV41," <https://www.census.gov/topics/income-poverty/poverty/data/tables.html>, accessed November 2019.

Table 750. Work Experience of People During Year by Poverty Status by Sex and Age: 2018

[117,957 represents 117,957,000. Covers persons age 16 and over. Based on the Current Population Survey, Annual Social and Economic Supplement (ASEC); see text, this section, Section 1, and Appendix III. Data reflect an updated processing system; see source for more information]

Sex and age	Worked full-time year-round			Did not work full-time year-round			Did not work		
	Number (1,000)	Below poverty level Number (1,000)	Percent	Number (1,000)	Below poverty level Number (1,000)	Percent	Number (1,000)	Below poverty level Number (1,000)	Percent
BOTH SEXES									
Total..................	**117,957**	**2,591**	**2.2**	**49,304**	**5,621**	**11.4**	**92,188**	**19,283**	**20.9**
16 to 17 years old........	177	5	2.9	1,811	153	8.4	6,897	1,062	15.4
18 to 64 years old........	111,702	2,544	2.3	41,133	5,237	12.7	44,940	13,349	29.7
18 to 24 years old.......	8,216	328	4.0	11,208	1,476	13.2	9,661	2,557	26.5
25 to 34 years old......	28,356	746	2.6	9,281	1,509	16.3	7,571	2,670	35.3
35 to 54 years old......	53,802	1,233	2.3	13,517	1,678	12.4	14,408	4,651	32.3
55 to 64 years old......	21,328	238	1.1	7,127	574	8.0	13,300	3,471	26.1
65 years old and over....	6,078	42	0.7	6,360	232	3.7	40,350	4,872	12.1
MALE									
Total..................	**67,185**	**1,276**	**1.9**	**20,771**	**2,313**	**11.1**	**37,920**	**7,735**	**20.4**
16 to 17 years old........	96	3	3.1	903	88	9.7	3,577	526	14.7
18 to 64 years old........	63,523	1,250	2.0	16,747	2,134	12.7	17,107	5,387	31.5
18 to 24 years old.......	4,482	131	2.9	5,208	617	11.8	4,915	1,190	24.2
25 to 34 years old......	16,319	322	2.0	3,865	562	14.5	2,542	966	38.0
35 to 54 years old......	30,708	681	2.2	4,947	689	13.9	4,525	1,771	39.1
55 to 64 years old......	12,014	116	1.0	2,727	267	9.8	5,125	1,460	28.5
65 years old and over....	3,565	24	0.7	3,121	92	2.9	17,237	1,822	10.6
FEMALE									
Total..................	**50,771**	**1,315**	**2.6**	**28,533**	**3,308**	**11.6**	**54,267**	**11,547**	**21.3**
16 to 17 years old........	81	2	2.7	908	65	7.1	3,321	536	16.1
18 to 64 years old........	48,179	1,295	2.7	24,386	3,103	12.7	27,833	7,962	28.6
18 to 24 years old.......	3,734	196	5.3	6,000	859	14.3	4,746	1,367	28.8
25 to 34 years old......	12,037	424	3.5	5,416	948	17.5	5,029	1,705	33.9
35 to 54 years old......	23,094	552	2.4	8,570	989	11.5	9,882	2,880	29.1
55 to 64 years old......	9,314	122	1.3	4,401	307	7.0	8,175	2,010	24.6
65 years old and over....	2,512	18	0.7	3,239	141	4.3	23,114	3,050	13.2

Source: U.S. Census Bureau, *Income and Poverty in the United States: 2018*, Current Population Reports, P60-266, September 2019; "Current Population Survey Detailed Tables for Poverty: Table POV22," <https://www.census.gov/topics/income-poverty/poverty/data/tables. html>, accessed November 2019.

Table 751. Families Below Poverty Level by Race and Hispanic Origin, and Below 125 Percent of Poverty Level: 1990 to 2018

[7,098 represents 7,098,000. Families as of March of the following year. Based on Current Population Survey, Annual Social and Economic Supplement (ASEC); see text, this section and Section 1, and Appendix III. For data collection changes over time, see "Changes in Methodology for the March Current Population Survey" at <https://www.census.gov/topics/income-poverty/income/guidance/cps-methodology-changes.html>. Beginning with the 2003 CPS covering data for 2002, respondents were allowed to choose more than one race. Two basic ways of defining a race group are possible: a group such as Asian may be defined as those who reported Asian and no other race (the race-alone concept), or as those who reported Asian regardless of whether they also reported another race (the race-alone-or-in-combination concept). For 2001 data and earlier, the CPS allowed respondents to report only one race group. See also comments on race in the text for Section 1, Population. See comments on changes to the CPS ASEC in headnote, Table 747]

Year	Number of families below poverty (1,000)					Percent of families below poverty					Below 125 percent of poverty level	
	All races [1]	White [2]	Black [2]	Asian [2]	His-panic [3]	All races [1]	White [2]	Black [2]	Asian [2]	His-panic [3]	Number (1,000)	Percent
1990.........	7,098	4,622	2,193	169	1,244	10.7	8.1	29.3	11.0	25.0	9,564	14.4
1995.........	7,532	4,994	2,127	264	1,695	10.8	8.5	26.4	12.4	27.0	10,223	14.7
2000 [4]......	6,400	4,333	1,686	233	1,540	8.7	7.1	19.3	7.8	19.2	9,032	12.2
2005.........	7,657	5,068	1,997	289	1,948	9.9	8.0	22.1	9.0	19.7	10,442	13.5
2006.........	7,668	5,118	2,007	260	1,922	9.8	8.0	21.6	7.8	18.9	10,531	13.4
2007.........	7,623	5,046	2,045	261	2,045	9.8	7.9	22.1	7.9	19.7	10,551	13.5
2008.........	8,147	5,414	2,055	341	2,239	10.3	8.4	22.0	9.8	21.3	11,164	14.2
2009.........	8,792	5,994	2,125	337	2,369	11.1	9.3	22.7	9.4	22.7	11,620	14.7
2010 [5]......	9,400	6,305	2,311	362	2,739	11.8	9.9	24.1	9.3	24.3	12,448	15.6
2011.........	9,497	6,334	2,334	401	2,651	11.8	9.8	24.2	9.7	22.9	12,500	15.5
2012.........	9,520	6,299	2,327	387	2,807	11.8	9.7	23.7	9.4	23.5	12,669	15.7
2013 [6]......	9,645	6,526	2,204	448	2,865	11.7	9.9	22.4	10.2	23.1	12,605	15.3
2014 [6]......	9,467	6,310	2,265	401	2,684	11.6	9.7	22.9	8.9	21.5	12,635	15.5
2015 [6]......	8,589	5,743	2,082	374	2,502	10.4	8.8	21.1	8.0	19.6	11,603	14.1
2016 [6]......	8,081	5,433	1,893	340	2,253	9.8	8.3	19.0	7.2	17.3	11,083	13.4
2017 [6]......	7,790	5,135	1,898	367	2,178	9.3	7.8	18.9	7.4	16.4	10,696	12.8
2018 [6]......	7,504	5,004	1,730	387	2,057	9.0	7.6	17.7	7.6	15.5	10,241	12.3

[1] Includes other races, not shown separately. [2] Beginning 2002, data refer to persons who reported specified race only and no other race category; prior to 2002, Asian included Pacific Islander. [3] People of Hispanic origin may be of any race. [4] Implementation of Census 2000 based population controls and sample expanded by 28,000 households. [5] Implementation of Census 2010-based population controls. [6] Data are based on redesigned income questions. As of 2017, data reflect updated processing system. See source for more information.

Source: U.S. Census Bureau, *Income and Poverty in the United States: 2018*, Current Population Reports, P60-266, September 2019; and "Historical Poverty Tables: People and Families, Table 4," and "Current Population Survey Detailed Tables for Poverty: Table POV04," <https://www.census.gov/topics/income-poverty/poverty/data/tables.html>, accessed November 2019.

Table 752. Families Below Poverty Level by Selected Characteristics: 2018

[In thousands (7,504 represents 7,504,000), except as noted. All families as of March of the following year. Based on the Current Population Survey, Annual Social and Economic Supplement (CPS ASEC); see text, this section and Section 1, and Appendix III. Data below represent persons who selected each race group only and exclude persons reporting more than one race. See also comments on race in the text for Section 1. For composition of regions, see map, inside front cover. Data reflect an updated CPS ASEC processing system; see source for more information]

Characteristic	Number below poverty level (1,000)					Percent below poverty level				
	All races [1]	White alone	Black alone	Asian alone	His-panic [2]	All races [1]	White alone	Black alone	Asian alone	His-panic [2]
Total families...................	**7,504**	**5,004**	**1,730**	**387**	**2,057**	**9.0**	**7.6**	**17.7**	**7.6**	**15.5**
Age of householder:										
18 to 24 years old..............	539	346	111	35	156	19.0	16.7	25.2	19.6	16.9
25 to 34 years old..............	1,836	1,101	576	59	565	14.1	11.3	30.7	7.1	19.8
35 to 44 years old..............	1,793	1,181	408	109	590	10.6	9.2	18.8	8.1	17.6
45 to 54 years old..............	1,088	754	229	52	353	6.6	5.9	11.4	4.7	12.7
55 to 64 years old..............	1,026	731	197	49	163	6.5	5.7	12.3	6.1	8.7
65 years old and over.........	1,185	868	205	78	216	6.4	5.5	12.4	9.8	15.3
Region:										
Northeast.....................	1,084	697	255	91	288	7.7	6.3	14.9	8.8	17.1
Midwest......................	1,286	854	333	44	150	7.3	5.7	21.3	7.3	12.8
South.........................	3,539	2,290	1,000	104	889	10.9	9.3	17.6	8.3	16.4
West..........................	1,596	1,163	142	149	730	8.2	7.6	17.1	6.7	14.6
Type of family:										
Married couple..................	2,938	2,258	332	239	855	4.7	4.4	7.1	5.7	10.1
Male householder, no spouse present............	824	492	212	31	200	12.7	10.4	19.8	9.2	12.6
Female householder, no spouse present............	3,742	2,253	1,187	117	1,002	24.9	23.1	29.4	19.6	30.8
Families with children [3]........	5,091	3,246	1,316	243	1,646	13.6	11.5	25.0	9.2	20.5

[1] Includes other races, not shown separately. [2] Hispanic persons may be of any race. [3] Children under age 18 related to the householder.

Source: U.S. Census Bureau, *Income and Poverty in the United States: 2018*, Current Population Reports, P60-266, September 2019; and "Current Population Survey Detailed Tables for Poverty: Tables POV04 and POV44," <https://www.census.gov/topics/income-poverty/poverty/data/tables.html>, accessed November 2019.

Table 753. Top Wealth Holders With Gross Assets of $5 Million or More—Debts, Mortgages, and Net Worth: 2013

[7,289,626 represents $7,289,626,000,000. Figures are estimates from the Personal Wealth Study, based on a sample of Federal estate tax returns (Form 706). Covers the segment of the population for whom personal wealth is at least equal to the estate tax filing threshold in effect for the estimation period. Based on the estate multiplier technique; for more information on this methodology, see source]

Sex and net worth	Total assets [1]		Debts and mortgages		Net worth [2]	
	Number of top wealth holders	Amount (mil. dol.)	Number of top wealth holders	Amount (mil. dol.)	Number of top wealth holders	Amount (mil. dol.)
Both sexes, total................	**584,194**	**7,289,626**	**442,290**	**432,333**	**584,194**	**6,857,292**
Size of net worth:						
Under $5 million [3]...............	102,954	437,172	88,466	122,350	102,954	314,823
$5 million to under $10 million..............	325,371	2,358,888	232,032	115,554	325,371	2,243,334
$10 million to under $20 million............	103,903	1,458,237	80,269	69,199	103,903	1,389,038
$20 million to under $50 million............	37,596	1,163,133	28,766	59,877	37,596	1,103,255
$50 million or more..........................	14,369	1,872,193	12,756	65,352	14,369	1,806,841
Males, total.............................	**356,549**	**4,540,744**	**268,058**	**327,470**	**356,549**	**4,213,273**
Size of net worth:						
Under $5 million [3]...............	73,415	321,029	61,536	104,926	73,415	216,102
$5 million to under $10 million..............	189,343	1,359,306	132,853	78,395	189,343	1,280,911
$10 million to under $20 million............	60,875	851,278	47,186	47,931	60,875	803,346
$20 million to under $50 million............	24,132	756,426	18,744	49,080	24,132	707,345
$50 million or more..........................	8,784	1,252,704	7,739	47,136	8,784	1,205,567
Females, total..........................	**227,645**	**2,748,882**	**174,232**	**104,865**	**227,645**	**2,644,019**
Size of net worth:						
Under $5 million [3]...............	29,540	116,144	26,930	17,424	29,540	98,720
$5 million to under $10 million..............	136,028	999,582	99,178	37,159	136,028	962,423
$10 million to under $20 million............	43,029	606,959	33,084	21,267	43,029	585,692
$20 million to under $50 million............	13,463	406,708	10,022	10,800	13,463	395,910
$50 million or more..........................	5,586	619,489	5,017	18,216	5,586	601,274

[1] Total assets is the sum of all assets owned by the individual before subtracting debts, mortgages, and liens owed to others. It differs from gross assets, which is a Federal estate tax concept of wealth, in that it includes the cash value of life insurance instead of the full face value of life insurance minus indebtedness. [2] Net worth is defined as total assets minus debts and mortgages. [3] Includes individuals with zero net worth.

Source: U.S. Internal Revenue Service, Statistics of Income Division, "SOI Tax Stats - Personal Wealth Statistics," August 2017. See also <https://www.irs.gov/uac/soi-tax-stats-personal-wealth-statistics>.

Table 754. Top Wealth Holders With Gross Assets of $5 Million or More by Type of Property, Sex, and Size of Net Worth: 2013

[7,289,626 represents $7,289,626,000,000. Figures are estimates from the Personal Wealth Study, based on a sample of Federal estate tax returns (Form 706). Covers the segment of the population for whom personal wealth is at least equal to the estate tax filing threshold in effect for the estimation period. Based on the estate multiplier technique; for more information on this methodology, see source]

Sex and net worth	Number of top wealth holders	Assets (mil. dol.)				
		Total [1]	Personal residences	Other real estate	Closely held stock	Publicly traded stock
Both sexes, total.....................	**584,194**	**7,289,626**	**458,121**	**618,807**	**888,688**	**1,348,302**
Size of net worth:						
Under $5 million [2].....................	102,954	437,172	55,285	51,141	27,611	46,999
$5 million to under $10 million..........	325,371	2,358,888	215,480	255,585	173,468	389,202
$10 million to under $20 million.........	103,903	1,458,237	94,574	138,159	169,026	267,517
$20 million to under $50 million.........	37,596	1,163,133	54,624	88,287	184,229	235,082
$50 million or more....................	14,369	1,872,193	38,156	85,633	334,353	409,499
Males, total.........................	**356,549**	**4,540,744**	**238,165**	**369,694**	**659,317**	**742,460**
Size of net worth:						
Under $5 million [2].....................	73,415	321,029	33,892	39,347	20,802	31,674
$5 million to under $10 million..........	189,343	1,359,306	97,826	136,043	121,452	202,227
$10 million to under $20 million.........	60,875	851,278	50,755	77,898	120,811	137,956
$20 million to under $50 million.........	24,132	756,426	33,883	57,061	146,894	133,897
$50 million or more....................	8,784	1,252,704	21,809	59,343	249,356	236,705
Females, total.......................	**227,645**	**2,748,882**	**219,956**	**249,113**	**229,371**	**605,842**
Size of net worth:						
Under $5 million [2].....................	29,540	116,144	21,393	11,794	6,809	15,325
$5 million to under $10 million..........	136,028	999,582	117,655	119,542	52,015	186,976
$10 million to under $20 million.........	43,029	606,959	43,819	60,261	48,214	129,562
$20 million to under $50 million.........	13,463	406,708	20,742	31,226	37,335	101,185
$50 million or more....................	5,586	619,489	16,347	26,290	84,997	172,794

[1] Total assets is the sum of all assets owned by the individual before subtracting debts, mortgages, and liens owed to others. Includes other types of assets, not shown separately. [2] Includes individuals with zero or negative net worth.

Source: U.S. Internal Revenue Service, Statistics of Income Division, "SOI Tax Stats - Personal Wealth Statistics," August 2017. See also <https://www.irs.gov/uac/soi-tax-stats-personal-wealth-statistics>.

Table 755. Top Wealth Holders With Net Worth of $5 Million or More—Number and Net Worth by State: 2013

[6,542,469 represents $6,542,469,000,000. Estimates based on a sample of federal estate tax returns (Form 706). Estimates of wealth by state can be subject to significant year-to-year fluctuations, especially for individuals at the extreme tail of the net worth distribution and for states with relatively small decedent populations. Based on the estate multiplier technique; for more information on this methodology, see source]

State	Number of top wealth holders	Net worth (mil. dol.)	State	Number of top wealth holders	Net worth (mil. dol.)
Total [1].....................	**481,239**	**6,542,469**	Missouri..........................	3,899	113,689
			Montana..........................	1,073	45,527
Alabama.........................	4,115	55,864	Nebraska.........................	3,299	59,527
Alaska...........................	2,648	19,056	Nevada...........................	3,383	78,822
Arizona..........................	5,345	65,383	New Hampshire...................	1,684	20,798
Arkansas........................	1,342	19,783	New Jersey.......................	13,957	200,859
California........................	78,413	1,123,895	New Mexico......................	4,763	34,411
Colorado.........................	4,962	92,484	New York.........................	53,038	712,276
Connecticut......................	12,316	207,003	North Carolina....................	11,931	113,321
Delaware........................	350	3,571	North Dakota.....................	2,877	22,144
District of Columbia..............	4,993	46,716	Ohio.............................	10,861	116,394
Florida...........................	36,703	617,817	Oklahoma........................	9,960	80,432
Georgia..........................	10,149	108,776	Oregon...........................	3,115	33,312
Hawaii...........................	826	13,066	Pennsylvania.....................	13,428	194,665
Idaho............................	2,660	28,187	Rhode Island.....................	2,322	21,151
Illinois...........................	17,597	240,630	South Carolina....................	7,889	91,076
Indiana..........................	5,416	66,877	South Dakota.....................	1,165	14,388
Iowa............................	4,448	75,025	Tennessee........................	4,716	48,567
Kansas...........................	5,643	61,054	Texas............................	41,736	530,581
Kentucky.........................	3,288	55,828	Utah.............................	1,701	27,181
Louisiana........................	3,611	40,627	Vermont..........................	2,287	26,514
Maine............................	4,335	37,156	Virginia...........................	11,208	137,868
Maryland.........................	7,792	118,316	Washington.......................	10,303	128,356
Massachusetts...................	12,383	158,892	West Virginia.....................	613	6,653
Michigan.........................	8,535	98,191	Wisconsin........................	4,722	63,550
Minnesota........................	11,323	145,541	Wyoming..........................	1,412	21,746
Mississippi.......................	2,340	32,678	Other areas [1]....................	2,365	66,245

[1] Includes U.S. territories and possessions.

Source: U.S. Internal Revenue Service, Statistics of Income Division, "SOI Tax Stats - Personal Wealth Statistics," August 2017, <https://www.irs.gov/uac/soi-tax-stats-personal-wealth-statistics>.

Table 756. Nonfinancial Assets Held by Families by Type of Asset: 2016

[Value of assets in thousands of constant (2016) dollars (189.9 represents $189,900). Families include one-person units and, as used in this table, are comparable to the U.S. Census Bureau's household concept. Based on internal data from the Survey of Consumer Finances; see Appendix III. All dollar amounts are adjusted to 2016 dollars using the "current methods" version of the consumer price index (CPI) for all urban consumers. For definition of median, see Guide to Tabular Presentation. For data on financial assets, see Table 1198]

Family characteristic	Any financial or non-financial asset	Any non-financial asset	Vehicles	Primary residence	Other resi-dential property	Equity in nonresi-dential property	Bus-iness equity	Other asset
PERCENT OF FAMILIES HOLDING ASSET								
All families, total	**99.4**	**90.8**	**85.2**	**63.7**	**13.8**	**6.2**	**13.0**	**6.5**
Age of family head:								
Under 35 years old	99.1	84.2	80.2	33.1	4.0	2.3	5.6	5.2
35 to 44 years old	98.7	91.3	86.7	57.8	12.0	3.8	15.0	3.9
45 to 54 years old	99.9	93.6	89.1	68.8	13.2	5.5	17.3	6.4
55 to 64 years old	99.5	91.4	86.1	73.7	19.2	9.3	17.3	7.2
65 to 74 years old	99.9	93.6	86.8	79.1	21.4	8.7	13.3	9.9
75 years old and over	99.4	93.2	82.2	83.1	16.3	9.9	8.5	7.8
Race or ethnicity of respondent:								
White, non-Hispanic	99.7	94.6	89.6	72.5	16.3	7.5	15.5	8.5
Black/African-American, non-Hispanic	99.1	81.2	73.1	44.7	8.3	4.1	6.6	1.8
Hispanic or Latino	98.1	84.4	80.0	45.5	6.3	2.3	5.8	2.2
Other or multiple race	99.1	87.5	80.4	53.6	13.3	5.2	13.4	5.2
Tenure:								
Owner occupied	100.0	100.0	92.9	100.0	18.5	8.4	17.0	8.0
Renter occupied or other	98.3	74.7	71.8	(B)	5.6	2.3	6.0	4.0
MEDIAN VALUE [1] ($1,000)								
All families, total	**189.9**	**158.9**	**17.3**	**185.0**	**145.7**	**70.0**	**79.9**	**13.0**
Age of family head:								
Under 35 years old	31.7	24.0	14.0	160.0	85.0	13.0	20.0	7.5
35 to 44 years old	159.1	144.6	19.5	200.0	115.0	32.0	40.0	6.0
45 to 54 years old	239.3	182.7	19.3	200.0	150.0	100.0	100.0	12.0
55 to 64 years old	286.7	210.0	19.8	200.0	200.0	121.0	100.0	25.0
65 to 74 years old	291.8	200.3	17.7	180.0	130.0	45.0	57.4	20.0
75 years old and over	304.1	201.1	13.6	175.0	170.8	125.0	235.8	15.0
Race or ethnicity of respondent:								
White, non-Hispanic	264.7	193.5	18.4	200.0	180.0	89.6	100.0	15.0
Black/African-American, non-Hispanic	46.6	62.4	13.0	124.0	50.0	12.0	27.2	6.8
Hispanic or Latino	54.0	68.0	15.2	158.0	100.0	50.0	30.0	10.0
Other or multiple race	134.2	145.6	17.9	240.0	141.3	50.0	67.5	10.3
Tenure:								
Owner occupied	341.7	237.4	21.4	185.0	150.0	90.0	100.0	20.0
Renter occupied or other	14.5	11.7	10.1	(B)	115.0	12.0	30.0	6.8

B Base too small to meet statistical standards for reliability of derived figure. [1] Median value of asset for families holding such assets.

Source: Board of Governors of the Federal Reserve System, 2016 Survey of Consumer Finances, *Changes in U.S. Family Finances From 2013 to 2016: Evidence from the Survey of Consumer Finances,* Federal Reserve Bulletin, Vol. 103, No. 3, September 2017. See also <http://www.federalreserve.gov/econresdata/scf/scfindex.htm>.

Table 757. Family Net Worth—Median and Mean Net Worth in Constant (2016) Dollars by Selected Family Characteristics: 2007 to 2016

[Net worth in thousands of constant (2016) dollars (139.7 represents $139,700). Constant dollar figures are based on Consumer Price Index for all urban consumers published by U.S. Bureau of Labor Statistics. Families include one-person units and as used in this table are comparable to the U.S. Census Bureau's household concept. Based on internal data from the Survey of Consumer Finances; see Appendix III. For definition of mean and median, see Guide to Tabular Presentation]

Family characteristic	2007 Median	2007 Mean	2010 Median	2010 Mean	2013 Median	2013 Mean	2016 Median	2016 Mean
All families	**139.7**	**645.9**	**85.4**	**551.3**	**83.7**	**551.3**	**97.3**	**692.0**
Age of family head:								
Under 35 years old	13.7	122.8	10.3	72.2	10.7	77.8	11.0	76.1
35 to 44 years old	102.2	377.9	46.6	240.3	48.2	358.0	59.8	288.6
45 to 54 years old	214.1	766.9	130.3	633.4	108.6	546.6	124.2	727.5
55 to 64 years old	294.3	1,090.7	198.3	973.2	171.1	823.3	187.3	1,167.4
65 to 74 years old	277.3	1,176.2	228.4	937.7	239.3	1,089.8	223.4	1,066.0
75 years old and over	247.3	739.2	239.6	749.3	200.8	665.3	264.8	1,066.9
Race or ethnicity of respondent:								
White, non-Hispanic	198.3	803.7	144.3	723.5	146.4	727.8	171.0	933.7
Black or African-American, non-Hispanic	24.4	155.7	17.6	109.8	13.6	102.1	17.1	138.0
Hispanic or Latino	24.4	215.6	17.9	127.8	14.2	111.0	20.6	191.2
Other or multiple race	70.3	457.0	47.1	370.7	42.5	383.6	64.7	457.7
Tenure:								
Owner occupied	271.9	903.4	192.8	788.6	201.5	807.3	231.4	1,034.2
Renter occupied or other	5.9	82.5	5.6	63.3	5.5	72.5	5.0	91.0

Source: Board of Governors of the Federal Reserve System, 2016 Survey of Consumer Finances, *Changes in U.S. Family Finances From 2013 to 2016: Evidence from the Survey of Consumer Finances,* Federal Reserve Bulletin, Vol. 103, No. 3, September 2017. See also <https://www.federalreserve.gov/econres/scfindex.htm>.

Table 758. Household and Nonprofit Organization Sector Balance Sheet: 1990 to 2019

[In billions of dollars (26,295 represents $26,295,000,000,000), unless otherwise noted. As of December 31. Sector includes domestic hedge funds, private equity funds, and personal trusts. For details of financial assets and liabilities, see Table 1197 and Table 1199]

Item	1990	2000	2005	2010	2016	2017	2018	2019
Assets	**26,295**	**52,057**	**76,825**	**81,164**	**112,064**	**121,548**	**123,247**	**134,944**
Nonfinancial assets [1]	10,108	17,567	29,816	25,552	33,670	35,960	37,867	39,335
Real estate [2]	7,964	14,175	25,430	20,614	27,941	30,056	31,712	32,909
Households [3]	7,171	12,860	23,357	18,764	24,947	26,806	28,383	29,326
Consumer durable goods [4]	2,039	3,202	4,106	4,535	5,155	5,303	5,519	5,752
Financial assets [1]	16,187	34,489	47,009	55,611	78,394	85,587	85,380	95,610
Time and savings deposits	2,666	3,067	4,880	6,405	9,078	9,261	9,664	10,163
Money market fund shares	421	1,296	1,262	1,658	1,558	1,619	1,800	2,148
Debt securities [1]	1,529	2,041	3,161	5,183	4,470	4,517	5,179	5,514
Treasury securities	505	548	263	1,043	1,107	1,145	1,716	1,961
Municipal securities	660	476	1,701	1,913	1,877	1,887	1,859	1,894
Corporate and foreign bonds	249	441	828	2,002	1,083	1,025	956	938
Corporate equities [2]	1,702	7,074	8,088	8,565	15,235	18,110	16,656	21,076
Mutual fund shares	471	2,558	3,409	4,702	7,306	8,655	7,961	9,683
Life insurance reserves	392	839	1,136	1,273	1,568	1,627	1,659	1,766
Pension entitlements [5]	4,957	11,030	14,521	18,293	24,351	25,919	25,904	27,996
Equity in noncorporate business [6]	3,065	5,020	8,473	6,906	11,314	12,169	12,732	13,542
Liabilities [1]	**3,714**	**7,407**	**12,259**	**14,035**	**14,975**	**15,545**	**16,029**	**16,576**
Loans [1]	3,538	7,102	11,816	13,465	14,377	14,929	15,399	15,936
Home mortgages [7]	2,489	4,817	8,940	9,992	9,761	10,049	10,316	10,610
Consumer credit	824	1,741	2,321	2,647	3,644	3,828	4,010	4,191
Net worth	**22,581**	**44,650**	**64,566**	**67,129**	**97,089**	**106,003**	**107,219**	**118,368**
Replacement cost value of structures:								
Residential [1]	4,287	7,732	12,245	12,732	16,440	17,199	18,193	18,905
Households	4,184	7,596	12,053	12,529	16,175	16,919	17,896	18,597
Nonresidential (nonprofits)	469	808	1,181	1,415	1,722	1,798	1,900	1,961
Disposable personal income	4,319	7,416	9,386	11,314	14,165	14,833	15,742	16,420
Owners' equity in real estate	4,682	8,043	14,417	8,772	15,186	16,757	18,067	18,716
Owners' equity as percent of real estate	65.3	62.5	61.7	46.7	60.9	62.5	63.7	63.8

[1] Includes other types of assets and/or liabilities not shown separately. [2] At market value. [3] Includes all types of owner-occupied housing, including farm houses, mobile homes, second homes that are not rented, vacant homes for sale, and vacant land. [4] At replacement (current) cost. [5] Includes public and private defined benefit and defined contribution pension plans and annuities, including those in IRAs (individual retirement accounts) and at life insurance companies. Excludes social security. [6] Net worth of nonfinancial noncorporate business and owners' equity in unincorporated security brokers and dealers. [7] Includes loans made under home equity lines of credit and home equity loans secured by junior liens.

Source: Board of Governors of the Federal Reserve System, "Z.1 Financial Accounts of the United States: B.101 Balance Sheet of Households and Nonprofit Organizations," March 2020, <https://www.federalreserve.gov/releases/Z1/Current/>, accessed March 2020.

Table 759. Net Stock of Fixed Assets and Consumer Durable Goods in Current and Chained (2012) Dollars: 1990 to 2018

[In billions of dollars (18,925 represents $18,925,000,000,000)]

Item	1990	2000	2005	2010	2015	2016	2017	2018
CURRENT DOLLARS								
Net stock, total	**18,925**	**31,025**	**43,481**	**50,635**	**60,045**	**62,451**	**65,109**	**68,409**
Fixed assets	16,886	27,824	39,375	46,099	55,039	57,296	59,807	62,889
Private	12,803	21,483	30,662	34,582	41,606	43,475	45,443	47,832
Nonresidential	7,101	11,672	15,512	18,799	22,646	23,255	24,284	25,475
Equipment	2,424	3,805	4,423	5,224	6,305	6,452	6,691	7,008
Structures	4,055	6,468	9,311	11,286	13,448	13,740	14,323	15,024
Intellectual property products	621	1,399	1,777	2,289	2,893	3,063	3,270	3,443
Residential [1]	5,702	9,810	15,150	15,783	18,960	20,220	21,160	22,357
Government	4,083	6,341	8,713	11,517	13,433	13,821	14,363	15,058
Nonresidential	3,941	6,111	8,381	11,185	13,041	13,407	13,937	14,614
Equipment	535	655	735	923	993	1,006	1,023	1,060
Structures	2,908	4,800	6,842	9,249	10,928	11,254	11,726	12,335
Intellectual property products	498	656	803	1,012	1,120	1,147	1,188	1,220
Residential	142	230	332	333	392	414	427	444
Consumer durable goods	2,039	3,202	4,106	4,535	5,006	5,155	5,303	5,519
Motor vehicles and parts	650	1,051	1,313	1,288	1,500	1,553	1,587	1,649
Furnishings and durable household equipment	649	977	1,259	1,396	1,498	1,534	1,578	1,690
Recreational goods and vehicles	419	724	964	1,061	1,116	1,134	1,180	1,226
Other	322	449	570	792	892	934	957	955
CHAINED (2012) DOLLARS								
Net stock, total	**(NA)**	**41,512**	**47,828**	**52,140**	**55,853**	**56,759**	**57,641**	**58,643**
Fixed assets	(NA)	39,037	43,998	47,606	50,575	51,264	51,915	52,667
Private	(NA)	29,071	32,935	35,477	37,900	38,487	39,031	39,677
Nonresidential	(NA)	15,942	17,728	19,458	21,468	21,861	22,265	22,762
Equipment	(NA)	3,970	4,668	5,311	6,420	6,615	6,827	7,087
Structures	(NA)	10,669	11,271	11,927	12,394	12,485	12,583	12,712
Intellectual property products	(NA)	1,482	1,830	2,228	2,671	2,787	2,894	3,019
Residential	(NA)	13,142	15,190	16,017	16,452	16,651	16,804	16,972
Government	(NA)	9,994	11,063	12,129	12,669	12,769	12,873	12,976
Nonresidential	(NA)	9,689	10,742	11,793	12,329	12,429	12,533	12,637
Equipment	(NA)	740	800	944	975	980	990	1,006
Structures	(NA)	8,159	9,041	9,819	10,269	10,358	10,444	10,524
Intellectual property products	(NA)	794	907	1,030	1,084	1,091	1,099	1,107
Residential	(NA)	300	319	336	341	341	341	340
Consumer durable goods	(NA)	2,757	3,863	4,535	5,309	5,550	5,816	6,110

NA Not available.

Source: U.S. Bureau of Economic Analysis, National Data, "Fixed Assets Accounts Tables," <https://www.bea.gov/iTable/index_FA.cfm>, accessed August 2020.

Prices

The Prices section contains producer and consumer price indexes and actual prices for selected commodities. The primary sources of the data are monthly publications of the U.S. Department of Labor, Bureau of Labor Statistics (BLS), which include *Consumer Price Index Detailed Report, Producer Price Index Detailed Report*, and *U.S. Import and Export Price Indexes*. Additionally, BLS provides comprehensive databases for the respective price indexes at <bls.gov/data/>. The Bureau of Economic Analysis (BEA) is the source for gross domestic product measures. Table 764 on housing price indexes contains data from the Federal Housing Finance Agency's Housing Price Index. Other commodity, housing, and energy prices may be found in the Energy and Utilities; Forestry, Fishing and Mining; and Construction and Housing sections.

Most price data is measured by an index. An index is a tool that simplifies the measurement of movements in a numerical series. An index allows you to properly compare two or more values in different time periods or places by comparing both to a base year. An index of 110, for example, means there has been a 10-percent increase in price since the reference period; similarly, an index of 90 means a 10-percent decrease. Movements of the index from one date to another can be expressed as changes in index points (simply, the difference between index levels), but it is more useful to express the movements as percent changes. This is because index points are affected by the level of the index in relation to its reference period, while percent changes are not.

Consumer price indexes (CPI)—The CPI is a measure of the average change in prices over time in a "market basket" of goods and services purchased either by urban wage earners and clerical workers or by all urban consumers. The all urban consumer group represents approximately 93 percent of the total U.S. population and is based on the expenditures of residents of urban or metropolitan areas, including wage earners and clerical workers; professional, managerial, and technical workers; the self-employed; short-term workers; the unemployed; and retirees and others not in the labor force. Not included in the CPI are the spending patterns of people living in rural nonmetropolitan areas, farm families, people in the Armed Forces, and those in institutions, such as prisons and mental hospitals. Consumer inflation for all urban consumers is measured by two indexes, the Consumer Price Index for All Urban Consumers (CPI-U) and the Chained Consumer Price Index for All Urban Consumers (C-CPI-U). The broadest and most comprehensive CPI is called the All Items Consumer Price Index for All Urban Consumers (CPI-U) for the U.S. City Average. CPIs in this section generally have a base of 1982–84 = 100.

The CPI is a product of a series of interrelated samples. Data from the 2010 Decennial Census determines the urban areas from which data on prices are collected and the housing units within each area that are eligible for use in the shelter component of the CPI. The Census of Population also provides data on the number of consumers represented by each area selected as a CPI price collection area. A sample of about 14,500 families each year serves as the basis

for a Telephone Point-of-Purchase Survey that identifies the places where households purchase various types of goods and services. The CPI market basket is developed from detailed expenditure information provided by families and individuals on what they actually bought. There is a time lag between the expenditure survey and its use in the CPI. For example, CPI data in 2016 and 2017 was based on data collected from the Consumer Expenditure Surveys for 2013 and 2014. In each of those years, about 24,000 consumers from around the country provided information each quarter on their spending habits in the interview survey. To collect information on frequently purchased items, such as food and personal care products, another 12,000 consumers in each of these years kept diaries listing everything they bought during a 2-week period. Over that period, expenditure information came from approximately 24,000 weekly diaries and 48,000 quarterly interviews used to determine the importance, or weight, of the item categories in the CPI index structure.

The CPI represents all goods and services purchased for consumption by the reference population. BLS has classified all expenditure items into more than 200 categories, arranged into eight major groups which are food and beverages, housing, apparel, transportation, medical care, recreation, education and communication, and other goods and services. The CPI does not include investment items, such as stocks, bonds, real estate, and life insurance, as these items relate to savings and not to day-to-day consumption expenses.

Producer price index (PPI)—Dating from 1890, the PPI is the oldest continuous statistical series published by BLS. The PPI is a family of indexes that measures the average change over time in the selling prices received by domestic producers of goods and services. Imports are excluded. The target set of goods and services included in the PPI is the entire marketed output of U.S. producers. The set includes both goods and services purchased by other producers as inputs to their operations or as capital investment, as well as goods and services purchased by consumers either directly from the service producer or indirectly from a retailer. About 10,000 PPIs for individual products and groups of products are released each month.

PPIs are published for the output of almost all industries in the goods-producing sectors of the U.S. economy, and, while more indexes are gradually being introduced, are currently available for approximately 72 percent of the service sector. For any given industry, producers are usually selected for the PPI survey using a systematic sampling from a listing of all firms that file with the Unemployment Insurance System. Establishments are asked to report their prices as of Tuesday of the week containing the 13th of the month. Each month over 100,000 prices are solicited from roughly 25,000 reporters. Currently, some PPIs have an index base set at 1982 = 100, while the remainder have an index base that corresponds with the month prior to the month that the index was introduced. For further detail regarding the PPI, see the BLS Handbook of Methods, Chapter 14, <bls.gov/opub/hom/pdf/ppi-20111028.pdf>.

In January 2014, PPI transitioned from the Stage of Processing (SOP) system to the Final Demand–Intermediate Demand (FD-ID) system as its primary index aggregation structure. The transition to the FD-ID system is the culmination of a long-standing PPI objective to improve the SOP system (domestically produced goods for domestic, nongovernment consumption) by incorporating PPIs for services, construction, government purchases, and exports. The FD portion of the FD-ID system expands coverage relative to the finished goods stage of the SOP system by including indexes that examine inflation from the producer perspective for goods, services, and construction sold as personal consumption, capital investment, government purchase, and export. The ID portion of the system allows data users to examine inflation from the producer perspective for goods, services, and construction sold to businesses as inputs to production, excluding capital investment.

BEA price indexes—BEA chain-weighted price indexes are weighted averages of the detailed price indexes used in the deflation of the goods and services that make up the gross domestic product (GDP) and its major components. Growth rates are constructed for years and quarters using quantity weights for the current and preceding year or quarter; these growth rates are used to move the index for the preceding period forward a year or quarter at a time. All chain-weighted price indexes are expressed in terms of the reference year value 2012 = 100.

Personal consumption expenditures (PCE) price and quantity indexes are based on market transactions for which there are corresponding price measures. The price index provides a measure of the prices paid by persons for domestic purchases of goods and services. PCEs are defined as market value of spending by individuals and not-for-profit institutions on all goods and services. Personal consumption expenditures also include the value of certain imputed goods and services—such as the rental value of owner-occupied homes and compensation paid in kind—such as employer-paid health and life insurance premiums. The PCE price index is known for capturing inflation (or deflation) across a wide range of consumer expenses and for reflecting changes in consumer behavior. More information on this index may be found at <bea.gov/data/personal-consumption-expenditures-price-index>.

Measures of inflation—Inflation is a period of rising price levels for goods and factors of production. Inflation results in a decline in the purchasing power of the dollar. It is suggested that changes in price levels be compared from the same month of the prior year and not as a change from the prior month. The BLS offers several indexes that measure different aspects of inflation, three of which are included in this section. The CPI measures inflation as experienced by consumers in their day-to-day living expenses. The PPI measures prices at the producer level only. The International Price Program measures change in the prices of imports and exports of nonmilitary goods between the United States and other countries.

Whereas the CPI and PPI measure a benchmark approach to price levels, the BEA's Personal Consumption Expenditures uses a chain-weight approach which links weighted averages from adjoining years.

Other measures of inflation include spot market price indexes from the Commodity Research Bureau and the employment cost, hourly compensation, and unit labor cost indexes from the BLS. Found in Section 12, Labor Force, Employment, and Earnings, these BLS indexes are used as a measure of the change in cost of the labor factor of production and changes in long-term interest rates that are often used to measure changes in the cost of the capital factor of production.

International price indexes—The BLS International Price Program produces Import/Export Price Indexes (MXP) for nonmilitary goods traded between the United States and the rest of the world.

The U.S. Import and U.S. Export Price Indexes measure the change over time in the prices of goods or services purchased from abroad by U.S. residents (imports) or sold to foreign buyers by U.S. residents (exports). The reference period for the indexes is 2000 = 100, unless otherwise indicated. The product universe for both the import and export indexes includes raw materials, agricultural products, semifinished manufactures, and finished manufactures, including both capital and consumer goods. Price data for these items are collected primarily via a secure internet address.

To the extent possible, the data gathered refer to prices at the U.S. border for exports and at either the foreign border or the U.S. border for imports. For nearly all products, the prices refer to transactions completed during the first week of the month. Survey respondents are asked to indicate all discounts, allowances, and rebates applicable to the reported prices, so that the price used in the calculation of the indexes is the actual price for which the product was bought or sold.

Table 760. Purchasing Power of the Dollar: 1950 to 2019

[Indexes: PPI, 1982=$1.00; CPI, 1982-84=$1.00. Producer prices prior to 1961 and consumer prices prior to 1964 exclude Alaska and Hawaii. Producer prices based on final demand, finished goods index. Data is obtained by dividing the average price index for the 1982=100, PPI and the 1982-84=100, CPI base periods (100.0) by the price index for a given period and expressing the result in dollars and cents. Annual figures are based on average of monthly data]

Year	Annual average as measured by— Producer prices	Annual average as measured by— Consumer prices	Year	Annual average as measured by— Producer prices	Annual average as measured by— Consumer prices
1950	3.546	4.149	1990	0.839	0.765
1955	3.279	3.731	1991	0.822	0.734
1960	2.994	3.378	1992	0.812	0.713
1963	2.994	3.268	1993	0.802	0.692
1964	2.985	3.226	1994	0.797	0.675
1965	2.933	3.175	1995	0.782	0.656
1966	2.841	3.086	1996	0.762	0.637
1967	2.809	2.994	1997	0.759	0.623
1968	2.732	2.874	1998	0.765	0.613
1969	2.632	2.725	1999	0.752	0.600
1970	2.545	2.577	2000	0.725	0.581
1971	2.469	2.469	2001	0.711	0.565
1972	2.392	2.392	2002	0.720	0.556
1973	2.193	2.252	2003	0.698	0.543
1974	1.901	2.028	2004	0.673	0.529
1975	1.718	1.859	2005	0.642	0.512
1976	1.645	1.757	2006	0.623	0.496
1977	1.546	1.650	2007	0.600	0.482
1978	1.433	1.534	2008	0.565	0.464
1979	1.289	1.377	2009	0.580	0.466
1980	1.136	1.214	2010	0.556	0.459
1981	1.041	1.100	2011	0.524	0.445
1982	1.000	1.036	2012	0.515	0.436
1983	0.984	1.004	2013	0.508	0.429
1984	0.964	0.962	2014	0.499	0.422
1985	0.955	0.929	2015	0.516	0.422
1986	0.969	0.912	2016	0.521	0.417
1987	0.949	0.880	2017	0.505	0.408
1988	0.926	0.845	2018	0.490	0.398
1989	0.880	0.806	2019	0.486	0.391

Source: U.S. Bureau of Labor Statistics, "CPI Databases," <http://www.bls.gov/cpi/#data>; and "PPI Databases," <http://www.bls.gov/ppi/#data>; accessed May 2020.

Table 761. Consumer Price Indexes (CPI-U) by Major Group: 1990 to 2019

[1982-84=100, except as indicated. Represents annual averages of monthly figures. Reflects buying patterns of all urban consumers. Minus sign (-) indicates decrease. See text, this section]

Year	All items	Com-modities	Ser-vices	Food	Food and bever-ages	Energy	All items less food and energy	Hous-ing	Apparel	Trans-porta-tion	Medical care	Educa-tion and com-munica-tion [1]
1990	130.7	122.8	139.2	132.4	132.1	102.1	135.5	128.5	124.1	120.5	162.8	(NA)
1995	152.4	136.4	168.7	148.4	148.9	105.2	161.2	148.5	132.0	139.1	220.5	92.2
2000	172.2	149.2	195.3	167.8	168.4	124.6	181.3	169.6	129.6	153.3	260.8	102.5
2005	195.3	160.2	230.1	190.7	191.2	177.1	200.9	195.7	119.5	173.9	323.2	113.7
2008	215.3	174.8	255.5	214.1	214.2	236.7	215.6	216.3	118.9	195.5	364.1	123.6
2009	214.5	169.7	259.2	218.0	218.2	193.1	219.2	217.1	120.1	179.3	375.6	127.4
2010	218.1	174.6	261.3	219.6	220.0	211.4	221.3	216.3	119.5	193.4	388.4	129.9
2011	224.9	183.9	265.8	227.8	227.9	243.9	225.0	219.1	122.1	212.4	400.3	131.5
2012	229.6	187.6	271.4	233.8	233.7	246.1	229.8	222.7	126.3	217.3	414.9	133.8
2013	233.0	187.7	277.9	237.0	237.0	244.4	233.8	227.4	127.4	217.4	425.1	135.9
2014	236.7	187.9	285.1	242.7	242.4	243.6	237.9	233.2	127.5	215.9	435.3	137.5
2015	237.0	181.7	291.7	247.2	246.8	202.9	242.2	238.1	125.9	199.1	446.8	138.2
2016	240.0	179.2	299.9	247.9	247.7	189.5	247.6	244.0	126.0	194.9	463.7	139.1
2017	245.1	181.2	308.1	250.1	249.8	204.5	252.2	251.2	125.6	201.6	475.3	136.5
2018	251.1	184.6	316.6	253.6	253.3	219.9	257.6	258.5	125.7	210.7	484.7	136.8
2019	255.7	185.3	325.1	258.3	258.0	215.3	263.2	266.0	124.1	210.1	498.4	137.8
PERCENT CHANGE [2]												
1990	5.4	5.2	5.5	5.8	5.8	8.3	5.0	4.5	4.6	5.6	9.0	(NA)
1995	2.8	1.9	3.4	2.8	2.8	0.6	3.0	2.6	-1.0	3.6	4.5	3.8
2000	3.4	3.3	3.4	2.3	2.3	16.9	2.4	3.5	-1.3	6.2	4.1	1.3
2005	3.4	3.6	3.3	2.4	2.5	17.0	2.2	3.3	-0.7	6.6	4.2	1.9
2008	3.8	4.3	3.5	5.5	5.4	13.9	2.3	3.2	-0.1	5.9	3.7	3.4
2009	-0.4	-2.9	1.4	1.8	1.9	-18.4	1.7	0.4	1.0	-8.3	3.2	3.0
2010	1.6	2.9	0.8	0.8	0.8	9.5	1.0	-0.4	-0.5	7.9	3.4	2.0
2011	3.2	5.3	1.7	3.7	3.6	15.4	1.7	1.3	2.2	9.8	3.0	1.2
2012	2.1	2.0	2.1	2.6	2.5	0.9	2.1	1.6	3.4	2.3	3.7	1.8
2013	1.5	–	2.4	1.4	1.4	-0.7	1.8	2.1	0.9	–	2.5	1.5
2014	1.6	0.1	2.6	2.4	2.3	-0.3	1.7	2.6	0.1	-0.7	2.4	1.2
2015	0.1	-3.3	2.3	1.9	1.8	-16.7	1.8	2.1	-1.3	-7.8	2.6	0.5
2016	1.3	-1.4	2.8	0.3	0.3	-6.6	2.2	2.5	0.1	-2.1	3.8	0.7
2017	2.1	1.1	2.7	0.9	0.9	7.9	1.8	3.0	-0.3	3.4	2.5	-1.9
2018	2.4	1.9	2.8	1.4	1.4	7.5	2.1	2.9	–	4.5	2.0	0.2
2019	1.8	0.4	2.7	1.9	1.8	-2.1	2.2	2.9	-1.3	-0.3	2.8	0.7

– Represents or rounds to zero. NA Not available. [1] Dec. 1997=100. [2] Change from immediate prior year. 1990 change from 1989.

Source: U.S. Bureau of Labor Statistics, "CPI Databases," <https://www.bls.gov/cpi/data.htm>, accessed April 2020.

Table 762. Consumer Price Indexes (CPI-U) and Annual Percent Change for Selected Urban Areas: 2019

[1982–84=100. Percent changes computed from annual averages of monthly figures published by source. In January 2018, BLS introduced a new geographic area sample for the Consumer Price Index (CPI) that utilizes the 2010 Decennial Census and incorporates an updated area sample design; see source for more information. Local area CPI indexes are by-products of the national CPI program. Each local index has a smaller sample size than the national index and is therefore subject to substantially more sampling and other measurement error. As a result, local area indexes show greater volatility than the national index, although their long-term trends are similar. Minus sign (–) indicates decrease. See also text, this section and Appendix III]

Urban area	Consumer Price Index							
	All items	Food and beverage	Food	Housing	Apparel	Transportation	Medical care	Fuel and other utilities
U.S. city average	255.7	258.0	258.3	266.0	124.1	210.1	498.4	242.6
Atlanta-Sandy Springs-Roswell, GA	243.7	258.0	268.5	252.7	143.6	206.3	459.3	301.4
Baltimore-Columbia-Towson, MD	256.9	263.0	262.5	261.2	124.5	201.4	461.9	223.4
Boston-Cambridge-Newton, MA-NH	281.1	267.7	269.4	293.2	137.7	193.1	678.6	293.6
Chicago-Naperville-Elgin, IL-IN-WI	241.2	252.9	252.4	253.4	86.2	187.1	509.7	206.8
Dallas-Fort Worth-Arlington, TX	237.7	257.8	252.0	231.2	112.1	207.9	453.3	244.6
Denver-Aurora-Lakewood, CO	267.0	238.2	242.3	268.9	95.6	259.8	615.6	239.0
Detroit-Warren-Dearborn, MI	235.3	226.2	225.4	223.8	115.4	245.3	446.4	251.0
Houston-The Woodlands-Sugar Land, TX	228.8	233.0	233.5	225.4	183.8	184.2	511.0	179.3
Los Angeles-Long Beach-Anaheim, CA	274.1	266.2	267.1	315.4	108.5	217.3	483.5	330.2
Miami-Fort Lauderdale-West Palm Beach, FL	269.8	264.9	267.1	285.1	138.7	222.6	560.5	179.9
Minneapolis-St. Paul-Bloomington, MN-WI	250.1	284.2	273.2	236.6	138.2	201.0	560.0	209.7
New York-Newark-Jersey City, NY-NJ-PA	278.2	271.1	271.1	303.2	121.9	220.9	511.0	195.2
Philadelphia-Camden-Wilmington, PA-NJ-DE-MD	256.6	237.8	238.4	267.1	106.6	212.5	542.4	212.1
Phoenix-Mesa-Scottsdale, AZ	142.9	148.9	150.1	148.0	135.5	129.3	185.1	163.6
San Diego-Carlsbad, CA	299.4	261.0	259.0	355.9	158.0	233.3	491.0	340.0
San Francisco-Oakland-Hayward, CA	295.0	289.8	287.6	347.5	114.8	208.5	541.2	415.5
Seattle-Tacoma-Bellevue, WA	278.0	276.4	278.9	329.4	128.4	224.4	407.3	270.3
St. Louis, MO-IL	231.2	257.7	257.7	225.9	142.5	191.0	463.3	218.4
Tampa-St. Petersburg-Clearwater, FL	228.1	230.9	231.3	232.6	144.0	200.8	396.5	211.1
Urban Alaska	228.7	215.2	220.9	209.3	153.2	227.2	617.5	359.6
Urban Hawaii	281.6	287.6	288.5	307.9	114.8	223.7	(NA)	368.1
Washington-Arlington-Alexandria, DC-VA-MD-WV	264.8	252.9	258.2	277.6	165.2	216.1	458.8	238.5

PERCENT CHANGE, 2018-2019

Urban area	All items	Food and beverage	Food	Housing	Apparel	Transportation	Medical care	Fuel and other utilities
U.S. city average	1.8	1.8	1.9	2.9	-1.3	-0.3	2.8	0.4
Atlanta-Sandy Springs-Roswell, GA	2.2	1.8	1.8	4.4	2.6	-2.1	2.3	3.3
Baltimore-Columbia-Towson, MD	1.4	1.5	1.4	1.2	-7.6	-1.1	8.7	-2.8
Boston-Cambridge-Newton, MA-NH	1.9	1.2	1.3	3.0	-1.2	-1.5	4.2	-0.3
Chicago-Naperville-Elgin, IL-IN-WI	1.5	1.9	2.0	2.3	-1.8	0.1	1.3	0.7
Dallas-Fort Worth-Arlington, TX	2.1	2.3	2.3	3.0	1.7	-0.8	3.8	3.3
Denver-Aurora-Lakewood, CO	1.9	1.2	1.3	2.7	-3.9	1.0	3.4	-2.5
Detroit-Warren-Dearborn, MI	1.3	1.2	1.1	2.6	-3.8	1.1	1.3	1.5
Houston-The Woodlands-Sugar Land, TX	1.3	1.7	2.0	2.5	-2.4	-1.3	3.3	-0.8
Los Angeles-Long Beach-Anaheim, CA	3.1	2.6	2.8	4.6	-0.6	2.0	1.6	2.8
Miami-Fort Lauderdale-West Palm Beach, FL	1.8	0.6	0.6	3.7	-1.6	-1.7	1.0	1.1
Minneapolis-St. Paul-Bloomington, MN-WI	2.1	1.6	1.6	3.4	6.1	-1.2	4.6	-3.3
New York-Newark-Jersey City, NY-NJ-PA	1.7	1.7	1.7	1.8	-3.0	-0.4	4.7	-1.2
Philadelphia-Camden-Wilmington, PA-NJ-DE-MD	2.0	1.8	2.0	2.9	-3.4	-0.6	4.0	2.7
Phoenix-Mesa-Scottsdale, AZ	2.9	2.9	3.1	4.6	-4.9	1.1	(NA)	-1.2
San Diego-Carlsbad, CA	2.4	1.5	1.7	3.6	-4.3	2.5	(NA)	1.5
San Francisco-Oakland-Hayward, CA	3.3	4.3	4.3	3.1	1.8	2.3	6.4	4.9
Seattle-Tacoma-Bellevue, WA	2.5	2.3	2.2	4.0	0.7	-1.3	2.1	0.4
St. Louis, MO-IL	1.0	1.6	1.8	1.6	-9.4	-0.5	2.0	-0.9
Tampa-St. Petersburg-Clearwater, FL	1.7	2.1	2.0	4.1	-3.9	-0.4	1.9	-0.3
Urban Alaska	1.4	2.7	2.7	1.2	-8.3	0.2	6.6	7.9
Urban Hawaii	1.6	2.1	2.1	2.4	4.1	-1.8	(NA)	1.6
Washington-Arlington-Alexandria, DC-VA-MD-WV	1.3	2.0	2.2	2.0	–	-0.4	2.0	4.3

– Represents or rounds to zero. NA Not available.

Source: U.S. Bureau of Labor Statistics, CPI Databases, "All Urban Consumers (Current Series)," <https://www.bls.gov/cpi/data.htm>, accessed April 2020.

Table 763. Consumer Price Indexes for All Urban Consumers (CPI-U) for Selected Items and Groups: 2000 to 2019

[1982-1984=100, unless otherwise noted. Annual averages of monthly figures. Reflects buying patterns of all urban consumers. For information about the CPI methodology, see the U.S. Bureau of Labor Statistics Handbook of Methods, Chapter 17, Consumer Price Index at <https://www.bls.gov/opub/hom/pdf/cpi-20180214.pdf>]

Item	2000	2010	2014	2015	2016	2017	2018	2019
All items....................	**172.2**	**218.1**	**236.7**	**237.0**	**240.0**	**245.1**	**251.1**	**255.7**
Food and beverages.................	**168.4**	**220.0**	**242.4**	**246.8**	**247.7**	**249.8**	**253.3**	**258.0**
Food........................	167.8	219.6	242.7	247.2	247.9	250.1	253.6	258.3
Food at home.................	167.9	215.8	239.5	242.3	239.1	238.6	239.7	241.8
Cereals and bakery products..........	188.3	250.4	271.1	274.1	273.1	271.7	272.8	276.6
Cereals and cereal products.........	175.9	217.6	232.9	234.1	231.2	227.7	226.6	227.6
Rice, pasta, and cornmeal.........	150.7	224.4	238.1	241.6	239.1	234.3	236.2	238.0
Rice [1, 2]................	99.3	156.9	170.7	167.2	163.1	160.0	161.7	162.6
Bakery products................	194.1	268.0	292.5	296.6	296.9	296.8	299.3	304.8
Bread [2]...................	107.4	159.8	176.4	178.7	178.5	178.3	179.4	184.1
Cakes, cupcakes, and cookies.........	187.9	251.7	273.5	278.8	281.6	282.7	287.5	291.2
Other bakery products............	191.5	247.1	264.8	266.4	265.4	264.9	264.7	269.9
Meats, poultry, fish and eggs........	154.5	207.7	253.0	260.3	247.7	245.8	248.9	249.8
Meats, poultry, and fish...........	155.5	208.6	253.7	258.5	249.4	249.0	250.7	253.3
Meats...................	150.7	206.2	256.5	264.2	252.5	251.0	252.1	255.3
Beef and veal.............	148.1	224.5	300.7	322.5	302.1	298.4	302.6	307.4
Uncooked ground beef............	125.2	203.6	276.0	295.3	268.2	266.6	268.2	269.3
Uncooked beef steaks [2].........	109.1	153.3	199.9	214.6	206.2	201.1	203.7	207.4
Pork...................	156.5	190.0	227.6	218.7	209.9	211.1	210.2	212.7
Poultry..................	159.8	204.0	236.3	237.3	230.9	231.3	232.1	231.5
Chicken [2]...............	102.5	131.8	151.7	152.1	147.5	148.6	150.3	149.9
Fish and seafood..............	190.4	243.2	289.0	286.3	284.2	287.7	293.8	298.5
Eggs....................	131.9	192.8	243.0	286.2	226.0	204.5	226.6	203.9
Dairy products................	160.7	199.2	225.3	222.4	217.3	217.5	216.5	218.7
Milk [2]...................	107.8	133.6	156.6	147.5	140.7	139.7	137.0	140.7
Cheese and related products.........	162.8	204.8	234.1	233.6	228.0	228.5	229.2	228.7
Ice cream and related products.........	164.4	195.0	215.4	219.2	219.4	219.9	220.6	221.8
Fruits and vegetables.............	204.6	273.5	294.4	293.8	296.3	295.7	297.8	300.9
Fresh fruits and vegetables..........	238.8	314.8	339.2	337.7	341.7	342.4	346.1	349.5
Fresh fruits................	258.3	322.3	359.7	352.0	359.8	361.4	365.2	360.1
Fresh vegetables.............	219.4	305.5	316.3	321.4	321.5	321.1	324.7	337.1
Processed fruits and vegetables [2]......	105.6	146.6	157.3	158.5	157.9	155.4	154.5	156.2
Nonalcoholic beverages and beverage materials. ..	137.8	161.6	166.0	167.9	167.3	167.6	167.6	170.8
Juices and nonalcoholic drinks [2]......	105.6	124.5	127.1	128.5	128.6	129.0	129.7	133.4
Carbonated drinks............	123.4	154.7	158.8	159.6	161.1	161.6	163.7	169.5
Nonfrozen noncarbonated juices and drinks [2]....	104.2	114.8	116.2	117.9	117.4	117.7	117.7	120.4
Beverage materials including coffee and tea [2].....	97.9	114.0	118.9	120.4	118.3	118.3	116.7	116.6
Coffee..................	154.0	186.4	201.0	205.5	199.3	199.2	194.9	193.2
Other food at home..............	155.6	191.1	206.2	209.3	209.5	209.9	210.2	211.1
Sugar and sweets.............	154.0	201.2	209.3	216.1	215.3	215.1	215.9	220.2
Candy and chewing gum [2].........	103.8	132.5	139.7	145.4	145.1	144.3	145.7	150.0
Fats and oils...............	147.4	200.6	229.7	227.3	225.9	227.7	228.0	226.4
Other foods................	172.2	204.6	219.9	223.4	224.1	224.4	224.7	225.3
Frozen and freeze dried prepared food..........	148.5	165.3	168.7	170.9	169.7	167.9	166.8	166.7
Snacks..................	166.3	216.6	244.3	250.6	252.2	251.8	253.4	251.8
Spices, seasonings, condiments, sauces........	175.6	214.4	229.7	235.6	237.7	239.6	241.7	242.9
Other miscellaneous food [2]..........	107.5	121.7	130.4	131.8	131.6	131.9	131.5	132.1
Food away from home..............	169.0	226.1	249.0	256.1	262.7	268.8	275.9	284.4
Full service meals and snacks [2].......	106.8	141.1	155.3	159.4	163.1	167.1	171.0	176.4
Limited service meals and snacks [2]......	106.3	143.9	158.4	163.3	167.7	171.8	176.6	182.1
At employee sites and schools [2].......	104.4	141.0	158.2	161.7	170.0	172.1	178.1	181.2
From vending machines and mobile vendors [2].......	102.4	133.1	143.1	146.3	150.8	154.8	159.5	166.5
Other food away from home [2].........	109.0	159.3	173.8	179.6	182.7	184.5	191.8	196.4
Alcoholic beverages.............	174.7	223.3	237.3	239.5	242.5	245.4	249.1	252.5
Alcoholic beverages at home..........	158.1	191.0	197.0	197.3	199.0	200.3	202.5	205.5
Beer, ale, and other malt beverages at home.......	156.8	201.0	213.8	215.0	218.9	222.9	226.0	230.1
Distilled spirits at home...........	162.3	188.8	192.4	192.6	193.3	192.5	192.0	194.8
Wine at home..............	151.6	169.7	169.0	168.5	168.4	167.9	170.0	171.8
Alcoholic beverages away from home..............	207.1	291.9	323.8	330.5	336.6	343.5	350.9	355.2
Housing..................................	**169.6**	**216.3**	**233.2**	**238.1**	**244.0**	**251.2**	**258.5**	**266.0**
Shelter.....................	193.4	248.4	270.5	278.8	288.2	297.8	307.7	318.1
Rent of primary residence...........	183.9	249.4	276.2	286.0	296.8	308.1	319.3	331.1
Lodging away from home [2]..........	117.5	133.7	148.5	153.0	158.1	159.4	161.1	165.9
Other lodging away from home including hotels and motels..........	252.4	280.4	307.8	317.4	325.3	327.1	329.4	339.5
Owners' equivalent rent of primary residence [3]........	198.7	256.6	277.8	285.9	295.3	305.1	315.2	325.7
Tenants' and household insurance [2]......	103.7	125.7	141.9	146.4	147.7	148.8	150.7	151.8
Fuels and utilities...............	137.9	214.2	234.6	230.1	228.9	237.3	241.6	242.6
Household energy...............	122.8	189.3	202.2	194.7	191.1	198.3	200.8	200.0
Fuel oil and other fuels...........	129.7	275.1	338.9	256.2	226.3	254.4	293.0	280.8
Fuel oil.................	130.3	282.9	365.0	254.3	209.2	241.7	296.1	284.2
Propane, kerosene, and firewood [4]........	155.5	320.6	358.4	305.9	295.5	322.1	340.9	329.1
Energy services..............	128.0	192.9	203.4	198.7	196.1	202.7	203.8	203.5
Electricity................	128.5	193.1	208.0	209.2	207.0	211.4	212.9	213.4
Utility (piped) gas service..........	132.0	189.7	186.8	164.6	160.6	173.4	173.6	171.0
Water and sewer and trash collection services [2].......	106.5	170.9	204.9	214.0	221.7	229.1	237.1	244.7
Water and sewerage maintenance............	227.5	380.7	468.1	492.9	513.7	532.8	550.7	568.1
Garbage and trash collection [5].........	269.8	384.4	425.8	432.0	439.4	449.1	466.9	481.9
Household furnishings and operations.................	**128.2**	**125.5**	**123.1**	**122.6**	**121.6**	**120.7**	**121.6**	**123.8**
Furniture and bedding.............	134.4	119.7	115.5	114.7	112.1	111.0	111.1	113.6
Living room, kitchen, and dining room furniture [2]......	102.4	88.9	87.1	86.8	85.3	84.6	85.2	88.0
Appliances [2].................	96.3	86.9	82.5	79.3	76.6	74.7	75.8	77.5
Other household equipment and furnishings [2].........	98.0	70.8	60.7	59.1	57.1	54.4	51.5	50.7
Clocks, lamps, and decorator items..............	111.7	62.9	49.4	47.1	44.8	41.0	37.7	37.1

See footnotes at end of table.

Table 763. Consumer Price Indexes for All Urban Consumers (CPI-U) for Selected Items and Groups: 2000 to 2019-Continued.

See headnote on page 497.

Item	2000	2010	2014	2015	2016	2017	2018	2019
Nonelectric cookware and tableware [2]	98.4	96.6	93.3	90.4	88.7	86.3	83.9	81.2
Tools, hardware, outdoor equipment and supplies [2]	97.0	91.6	91.3	91.1	90.1	89.6	89.5	90.9
Tools, hardware, and supplies [2]	97.3	96.5	100.2	100.1	98.3	97.9	98.5	99.7
Outdoor equipment and supplies [2]	96.8	88.9	87.0	86.8	86.2	85.7	85.3	86.7
Housekeeping supplies	153.4	183.3	187.6	186.8	186.3	184.9	186.4	189.9
Household cleaning products [2]	105.1	120.6	119.1	118.9	119.4	118.2	118.7	120.8
Household paper products [2]	113.8	158.0	170.3	169.2	169.2	168.7	169.6	175.5
Miscellaneous household products [2]	104.3	116.9	119.8	119.0	117.5	116.4	118.3	119.2
Household operations [2]	110.5	150.3	161.6	166.9	171.6	176.3	186.0	194.5
Domestic services [2]	109.7	144.4	153.7	155.6	157.2	160.9	165.8	169.6
Gardening and lawncare services [2]	111.4	155.3	165.0	171.8	174.4	179.3	193.1	205.3
Apparel	**129.6**	**119.5**	**127.5**	**125.9**	**126.0**	**125.6**	**125.7**	**124.1**
Men's and boy's apparel	129.7	111.9	120.6	119.6	118.8	117.2	118.1	118.5
Men's apparel	133.1	117.5	125.0	124.0	122.6	121.5	120.7	120.2
Men's shirts and sweaters [2]	98.3	78.6	81.0	79.5	79.5	78.6	78.2	76.3
Boys' apparel	116.2	91.5	103.9	103.0	103.8	100.8	106.7	110.0
Women's and girl's apparel	121.5	107.1	114.4	111.2	111.2	111.0	110.4	106.7
Women's apparel	121.9	109.5	117.6	114.4	114.6	114.2	113.5	109.2
Women's suits and separates [2]	98.2	83.9	85.3	81.8	81.5	80.1	79.1	75.5
Women's underwear, nightwear, swimwear, and accessories [2]	101.8	96.0	106.3	105.2	106.4	107.1	105.6	104.2
Girls' apparel	119.7	95.4	99.0	96.0	95.6	95.8	95.0	94.3
Footwear	123.8	128.0	135.5	136.8	137.3	136.7	136.1	136.7
Men's footwear	129.5	127.6	138.0	137.9	138.8	138.6	139.7	140.2
Women's footwear	119.6	125.3	128.0	128.9	128.6	127.1	124.9	124.2
Jewelry and watches [4]	137.0	152.4	163.6	160.0	169.1	174.2	172.7	171.5
Jewelry [4]	141.2	161.2	170.6	165.5	175.8	179.4	175.0	172.5
Transportation	**153.3**	**193.4**	**215.9**	**199.1**	**194.9**	**201.6**	**210.7**	**210.1**
Private transportation	149.1	188.7	211.0	193.7	189.5	196.6	206.4	205.8
New and used motor vehicles [2]	100.8	97.1	100.8	100.8	100.2	98.9	99.1	99.5
New vehicles	142.8	138.0	146.3	147.1	147.4	147.0	146.3	146.8
Used cars and trucks	155.8	143.1	149.1	147.1	143.5	138.3	138.4	139.8
Leased cars and trucks [6]	(NA)	97.0	84.8	84.2	84.5	84.8	89.2	86.9
Motor fuel	129.3	239.2	292.4	213.1	188.4	212.7	241.9	233.2
Gasoline (all types)	128.6	238.6	290.9	212.0	187.6	211.8	240.6	232.0
Motor vehicle parts and equipment	101.5	137.0	144.8	144.2	143.6	143.0	143.7	146.4
Motor vehicle maintenance and repair	177.3	248.0	266.0	270.7	275.4	280.8	286.4	296.0
Motor vehicle insurance	256.7	375.2	437.2	460.6	489.1	526.9	566.0	571.0
Motor vehicle fees [2]	107.3	165.5	176.5	178.9	182.6	185.0	188.7	192.9
Public transportation	209.6	251.4	276.4	268.7	265.4	263.1	258.8	259.5
Airline fare	239.4	278.2	307.7	292.2	282.6	275.8	264.9	265.4
Medical care	**260.8**	**388.4**	**435.3**	**446.8**	**463.7**	**475.3**	**484.7**	**498.4**
Medical care commodities	238.1	314.7	343.4	354.6	366.8	377.0	381.4	381.3
Prescription drugs	285.4	407.8	458.3	479.3	502.5	519.6	528.0	526.8
Nonprescription drugs [10]	(NA)	100.0	98.5	97.8	96.6	97.4	96.9	97.3
Medical care services	266.0	411.2	464.8	476.2	494.8	506.8	517.8	536.1
Professional medical services	237.7	328.2	355.2	361.5	371.5	375.1	378.4	382.6
Physicians' services	244.7	331.3	359.1	366.1	378.1	380.1	380.5	383.2
Dental services	258.5	398.8	441.0	452.2	465.0	472.6	485.5	496.2
Eyeglasses and eye care [4]	149.7	176.7	183.9	184.0	187.0	187.3	189.6	191.4
Services by other medical professionals [4]	161.9	214.4	226.4	228.2	231.0	236.6	237.4	239.2
Hospital and related services	317.3	607.7	733.8	761.9	795.1	831.7	866.9	885.2
Hospital services [7]	115.9	227.2	278.8	290.1	303.3	318.2	332.2	338.8
Nursing homes and adult day services [7]	117.0	177.0	200.1	206.4	213.7	220.3	227.8	235.3
Health insurance [9]	(NA)	106.6	122.1	123.6	131.8	133.9	135.5	155.2
Recreation [2]	**103.3**	**113.3**	**115.5**	**115.9**	**117.0**	**118.5**	**119.1**	**120.6**
Video and audio [2]	101.0	99.1	99.8	99.6	100.9	104.2	104.2	104.7
Cable and satellite television and radio service [5]	266.8	372.4	416.1	422.8	438.3	462.2	470.5	479.4
Pets, pet products and services [2]	106.1	154.4	165.7	167.3	169.6	170.3	172.4	178.0
Sporting goods	119.0	118.8	116.5	114.6	113.1	111.0	111.0	112.3
Other recreational goods [2]	87.8	57.8	49.4	47.0	43.9	40.6	37.4	35.2
Other recreation services [2]	111.7	145.1	152.7	156.2	159.9	164.1	167.9	171.8
Club membership for shopping clubs, fraternal or other organizations & participant sports fees [2]	108.9	123.5	129.3	130.1	132.2	135.3	139.2	142.9
Admissions	230.5	322.8	341.9	354.1	365.8	374.8	381.6	389.2
Recreational reading materials	188.3	220.7	236.7	240.7	240.7	241.5	246.3	255.6
Education and communication [2]	**102.5**	**129.9**	**137.5**	**138.2**	**139.1**	**136.5**	**136.8**	**137.8**
Education [2]	112.5	199.3	231.9	240.5	247.5	253.2	258.8	265.8
Educational books and supplies	279.9	505.6	615.4	648.2	678.8	689.5	696.1	685.4
Tuition, other school fees, and childcare	324.0	573.2	664.8	688.8	708.1	724.7	741.3	762.7
College tuition and fees	331.9	638.2	759.5	785.9	807.0	823.1	841.3	865.4
Day care and preschool [11]	156.3	240.4	264.9	275.4	283.1	290.4	295.0	303.3
Communication [2]	93.6	84.7	82.1	80.2	79.2	75.0	73.9	73.2
Postage and delivery services [2]	103.2	145.9	174.2	174.6	175.6	180.3	184.9	194.8
Information and information processing [2]	92.8	81.5	78.2	76.4	75.4	71.1	70.0	69.2
Telephone services [2]	98.5	102.4	101.1	99.3	98.8	91.8	90.4	89.4
Wireless telephone services [2]	76.0	62.4	57.4	55.2	54.7	48.8	47.6	46.4
Land-line telephone services [10]	(NA)	101.6	111.1	113.4	114.5	116.1	117.2	120.8
Information technology, hardware, and services [8]	25.9	9.4	8.4	8.1	7.8	7.6	7.5	7.4
Other goods and services	**271.1**	**381.3**	**408.1**	**414.9**	**423.1**	**432.6**	**442.3**	**451.3**
Tobacco and smoking products	394.9	807.3	903.3	930.8	963.4	1,022.8	1,063.5	1,115.9
Cigarettes [2]	159.9	329.0	368.4	380.0	393.5	418.3	434.9	457.0
Personal care	165.6	206.6	218.0	220.8	224.3	227.0	231.1	234.0
Personal care products	153.7	161.1	163.4	163.3	163.1	161.7	161.5	160.7
Hair, dental, shaving, and miscellaneous personal care products [2]	103.3	104.3	103.4	103.7	103.1	102.3	102.3	103.0

See footnotes at end of table.

Table 763. Consumer Price Indexes for All Urban Consumers (CPI-U) for Selected Items and Groups: 2000 to 2019-Continued.

See headnote on page 497.

Item	2000	2010	2014	2015	2016	2017	2018	2019
Cosmetics, perfume, bath, nail preparations and implements..........	166.8	182.2	189.3	188.2	188.8	187.0	186.3	182.8
Personal care services..........................	178.1	229.6	242.0	247.2	252.9	257.4	264.2	271.4
Haircuts and other personal care services [2]..........	108.7	140.1	147.7	150.8	154.3	157.0	161.2	165.6
Miscellaneous personal services........................	252.3	354.1	389.7	399.3	411.8	424.0	439.8	448.9
Legal services [4]..........................	189.3	288.1	318.5	323.6	334.5	346.4	361.2	364.8
Funeral expenses [4]..........................	187.8	282.0	307.1	313.7	319.4	325.6	331.7	337.9
SPECIAL AGGREGATE INDEXES								
Commodities...........................	149.2	174.6	187.9	181.7	179.2	181.2	184.6	185.3
Commodities less food and beverages..................	137.7	150.4	159.6	149.2	145.4	147.2	150.3	149.5
Nondurables less food and beverages..................	147.4	189.9	210.0	189.4	183.8	190.6	199.0	196.5
Nondurables less food, beverages, and apparel.......	162.5	238.1	266.2	233.3	223.9	235.3	249.0	245.9
Durables...........................	125.4	111.3	110.3	109.1	107.3	105.3	104.4	104.8
Services...........................	195.3	261.3	285.1	291.7	299.9	308.1	316.6	325.1
Rent of shelter [3]...........................	201.3	258.8	281.8	290.4	300.3	310.3	320.7	331.6
Transportation services........................	196.1	259.8	285.3	291.0	299.4	309.9	321.8	325.0
Other services...........................	229.9	309.6	334.4	339.4	346.0	347.8	352.7	358.9
All items less food........................	173.0	217.8	235.8	235.4	238.8	244.3	250.7	255.2
All items less shelter........................	165.7	208.6	226.2	223.3	223.8	227.2	231.8	234.2
All items less medical care....................	167.3	209.7	227.1	226.9	229.3	234.1	239.9	244.0
Commodities less food........................	139.2	153.0	162.3	152.2	148.6	150.5	153.6	152.9
Nondurables less food........................	149.1	191.9	211.7	192.3	187.2	193.8	201.9	199.7
Nondurables less food and apparel...............	162.9	235.6	262.3	232.7	224.5	235.0	247.8	245.3
Nondurables...........................	158.2	205.3	226.7	217.6	215.0	219.6	225.8	226.6
Apparel less footwear........................	126.2	113.3	121.1	118.8	118.9	118.5	118.7	116.6
Services less rent of shelter [3]..................	202.9	284.4	311.2	315.8	322.8	329.3	336.4	342.8
Services less medical care services..................	188.9	249.6	271.5	277.7	285.2	293.0	301.3	309.1
Energy...........................	124.6	211.4	243.6	202.9	189.5	204.5	219.9	215.3
All items less energy........................	178.6	220.5	238.0	242.3	247.0	251.2	256.3	261.8
All items less food and energy..................	181.3	221.3	237.9	242.2	247.6	252.2	257.6	263.2
Commodities less food and energy commodities.......	144.9	143.6	146.8	146.1	145.4	144.4	144.1	144.4
Energy commodities........................	129.5	242.6	296.9	216.7	191.6	216.3	246.2	237.4
Services less energy services..................	202.1	268.3	293.5	301.1	310.4	318.7	328.0	337.3
Domestically produced farm food..................	170.1	221.6	247.9	251.0	247.3	246.6	247.7	249.5
Utilities and public transportation..................	152.6	203.1	216.7	214.8	215.2	216.4	217.2	218.0

NA Not available. [1] Special indexes based on a substantially smaller sample. [2] December 1997=100. [3] December 1982=100. [4] December 1986=100. [5] December 1983=100. [6] December 2001=100. [7] December 1996=100. [8] December 1988=100. [9] December 2005=100. [10] December 2009=100. [11] December 1990=100.

Source: U.S. Bureau of Labor Statistics, CPI Databases, "All Urban Consumers (Current Series)," <https://www.bls.gov/cpi/data.htm>, accessed April 2020.

Table 764. Single-Family Housing Price Indexes by State: 2000 to 2019

[Data are for the fourth quarter of the year shown. Index 1991, 1st quarter = 100. Purchase only indexes. Data are seasonally adjusted. The index reflects average price changes in repeat sales or refinancings on the same properties. The information is obtained by reviewing repeat mortgage transactions on single-family properties whose mortgages have been purchased or securitized by either Fannie Mae or Freddie Mac; for more information on methodology, see source]

State	2000	2005	2010	2015	2019	State	2000	2005	2010	2015	2019
U.S.........	**143.9**	**216.4**	**182.3**	**220.7**	**277.8**	MO.........	150.3	197.4	178.0	203.0	255.8
AL.........	143.0	183.0	176.1	192.7	236.9	MT.........	179.4	275.8	281.4	339.6	422.5
AK.........	137.2	208.3	220.3	247.9	269.3	NE.........	162.0	193.6	187.2	223.8	278.5
AZ.........	155.6	303.8	172.5	257.2	347.1	NV.........	128.3	269.7	124.7	194.2	274.2
AR.........	141.2	185.3	175.9	197.3	230.6	NH.........	146.3	237.9	194.0	215.3	269.9
CA.........	123.5	283.8	159.7	232.4	295.5	NJ.........	133.3	253.7	213.6	215.7	251.8
CO.........	217.1	269.9	257.1	359.2	495.1	NM.........	145.3	214.4	209.2	214.0	257.3
CT.........	117.7	194.3	165.9	163.9	177.7	NY.........	128.5	212.6	202.6	211.6	257.4
DE.........	121.4	208.6	187.4	188.7	219.6	NC.........	146.1	182.6	181.5	202.7	262.1
DC.........	132.1	320.9	316.8	460.0	589.0	ND.........	138.1	191.2	223.3	300.4	324.5
FL.........	139.7	300.6	173.3	244.0	330.3	OH.........	148.1	174.2	150.6	171.2	216.1
GA.........	151.7	191.1	152.9	197.2	260.4	OK.........	144.2	177.7	191.7	220.7	255.6
HI.........	92.3	203.6	175.9	222.2	270.1	OR.........	184.0	296.3	252.6	341.2	452.0
ID.........	154.0	228.2	189.3	251.2	377.4	PA.........	121.1	189.3	184.8	198.7	239.9
IL.........	145.5	203.0	172.5	182.3	208.5	RI.........	119.8	235.8	182.1	194.9	248.4
IN.........	142.4	165.3	155.8	176.8	227.0	SC.........	145.0	185.7	179.0	205.8	262.5
IA.........	157.4	190.6	193.7	218.9	254.0	SD.........	160.0	207.4	215.1	255.9	316.0
KS.........	154.2	188.2	189.0	211.0	259.4	TN.........	146.9	185.1	180.5	214.6	284.7
KY.........	150.7	184.4	186.8	207.6	253.9	TX.........	143.0	172.3	184.5	241.1	305.3
LA.........	157.2	213.3	225.1	255.8	287.9	UT.........	193.9	255.5	249.2	320.2	451.4
ME.........	133.0	220.0	200.4	213.3	267.8	VT.........	127.3	207.5	202.8	213.8	250.1
MD.........	121.9	254.7	206.3	223.0	260.5	VA.........	131.1	234.4	206.4	229.6	274.9
MA.........	156.5	251.6	212.5	243.0	303.2	WA.........	154.4	242.3	219.3	276.0	394.7
MI.........	173.2	200.0	143.0	187.3	244.1	WV.........	137.6	180.2	186.4	208.7	226.1
MN.........	172.0	252.2	204.6	242.7	305.6	WI.........	166.4	222.3	203.8	220.0	280.5
MS.........	143.0	178.5	173.3	190.8	215.5	WY.........	168.9	257.8	277.8	321.1	365.1

Source: Federal Housing Finance Agency, "House Price Index Datasets, Quarterly Data, Purchase-Only Indexes," <https://www.fhfa.gov/DataTools/Downloads/Pages/House-Price-Index-Datasets.aspx#qpo>, accessed March 2020.

Table 765. Average Prices of Selected Fuels and Electricity: 1990 to 2019

[Fuels in dollars per unit; electricity in cents per kWh. Represents price to end-users, except as noted]

Item	Unit	1990	2000	2010	2014	2015	2016	2017	2018	2019
Crude oil, composite [1]	Barrel	22.22	28.26	76.69	92.02	48.39	40.66	50.68	64.38	59.33
Motor gasoline: [2]										
Unleaded regular	Gallon	1.16	1.51	2.79	3.37	2.45	2.14	2.41	2.74	2.64
Unleaded premium	Gallon	1.35	1.69	3.05	3.71	2.87	2.61	2.91	3.27	3.21
No. 2 fuel oil (heating oil)	Gallon	0.73	0.93	2.46	3.33	2.02	1.72	2.01	2.38	2.27
No. 2 diesel fuel	Gallon	0.73	0.94	2.31	2.92	1.82	1.51	1.81	2.26	2.11
Propane, consumer grade	Gallon	0.75	0.60	1.48	1.10	0.48	0.50	0.77	0.93	0.60
Residual fuel oil	Gallon	0.44	0.60	1.71	2.33	1.29	0.95	1.29	1.66	1.58
Natural gas, residential	1,000 cu/ft	5.80	7.76	11.39	10.97	10.38	10.05	10.91	10.50	10.60
Electricity, residential	kWh	7.83	8.24	11.54	12.52	12.65	12.55	12.89	12.87	13.04

[1] Refiner acquisition cost. [2] Average, all service.

Source: U.S. Energy Information Administration, *Monthly Energy Review*, April 2020. See also <http://www.eia.gov/totalenergy/data/monthly/>.

Table 766. Retail Gasoline Prices—U.S. Total and Selected Cities: 2016 to 2019

[In dollars per gallon. Prices are annual averages. Gasoline is classified by octane rating: regular, 85 or less; midgrade, 88-90; and premium, greater than 90. Octane requirements may vary by altitude]

Area	Regular				Midgrade				Premium			
	2016	2017	2018	2019	2016	2017	2018	2019	2016	2017	2018	2019
U.S. total	**2.14**	**2.42**	**2.72**	**2.60**	**2.40**	**2.68**	**3.06**	**3.00**	**2.62**	**2.92**	**3.29**	**3.25**
Boston, MA	2.11	2.40	2.73	2.59	2.36	2.66	3.01	2.89	2.57	2.86	3.20	3.09
Chicago, IL	2.24	2.49	2.78	2.75	2.57	2.82	3.16	3.15	2.91	3.20	3.55	3.53
Cleveland, OH	2.07	2.28	2.56	2.51	2.36	2.58	2.88	2.85	2.65	2.87	3.20	3.20
Denver, CO	2.02	2.31	2.60	2.50	2.30	2.61	2.92	2.83	2.56	2.89	3.21	3.13
Houston, TX	1.87	2.12	2.42	2.29	2.16	2.43	2.78	2.68	2.44	2.71	3.02	2.90
Los Angeles, CA	2.80	3.05	3.51	3.59	2.91	3.17	3.68	3.81	3.01	3.29	3.78	3.88
Miami, FL	2.31	2.70	2.73	2.47	2.62	3.00	3.03	2.82	2.90	3.25	3.30	3.08
New York, NY	2.12	2.47	2.77	2.62	2.43	2.76	3.05	2.92	2.62	2.96	3.22	3.10
San Francisco, CA	2.75	3.08	3.54	3.65	2.89	3.24	3.72	3.86	3.01	3.35	3.85	4.02
Seattle, WA	2.50	2.87	3.27	3.29	2.66	3.05	3.53	3.63	2.77	3.16	3.61	3.66

Source: U.S. Energy Information Administration, "Weekly Retail Gasoline and Diesel Prices," <https://www.eia.gov/petroleum/data.php#prices>, accessed January 2020.

Table 767. Weekly Food Cost of a Nutritious Diet by Type of Family and Individual: 2010 and 2019

[In dollars. As of December. Suggested plans assume that food for all meals and snacks is purchased at the store and prepared at home. All four Food Plans are based on 2001-02 data and updated to current dollars by using the Consumer Price Index for specific food items. See source for details]

Family and individual type	Thrifty plan		Low-cost plan		Moderate plan		Liberal plan	
	2010	2019	2010	2019	2010	2019	2010	2019
FAMILIES								
Family of two (male & female):								
19 to 50 years old	81.10	89.10	103.40	114.10	128.40	141.50	160.80	177.00
51 to 70 years old	76.90	84.50	99.20	109.50	122.60	136.30	148.00	164.80
Family of four:								
Couple (male & female),								
19 to 50 years old and children aged—								
2 to 3 and 4 to 5 years old	118.10	130.10	150.20	166.30	185.50	205.30	229.90	253.80
6 to 8 and 9 to 11 years old	135.60	149.30	176.60	196.10	221.00	245.10	268.50	297.10
INDIVIDUALS [1]								
Child:								
1 year old	20.10	21.80	26.80	29.40	30.60	33.40	37.10	40.50
2 to 3 years old	21.70	23.90	27.50	30.90	33.30	37.00	40.50	45.00
4 to 5 years old	22.70	25.20	28.70	31.70	35.50	39.60	43.30	47.90
6 to 8 years old	28.80	32.00	39.20	44.60	48.20	53.90	56.90	63.50
9 to 11 years old	33.00	36.30	43.40	47.80	56.10	62.50	65.50	72.80
Male:								
12 to 13 years old	35.10	38.80	49.50	55.20	61.70	69.00	72.70	81.20
14 to 18 years old	36.20	40.00	50.80	56.00	63.80	70.90	73.40	81.90
19 to 50 years old	39.00	42.90	50.30	55.50	62.90	69.60	77.10	85.20
51 to 70 years old	35.60	39.10	47.60	52.50	58.60	65.50	71.10	79.10
71 years old and over	35.80	39.30	47.00	51.50	58.50	64.30	71.90	79.20
Female:								
12 to 13 years old	35.30	38.60	42.90	47.40	51.90	57.60	63.00	70.30
14 to 18 years old	34.80	38.00	43.10	47.40	52.00	56.70	63.90	70.20
19 to 50 years old	34.70	38.10	43.70	48.20	53.80	59.10	69.00	75.70
51 to 70 years old	34.30	37.80	42.50	47.00	52.90	58.50	63.50	70.70
71 years old and over	33.80	36.90	42.10	46.30	52.50	57.80	63.40	69.70

[1] The costs given are for individuals in 4-person families. For individuals in other size families, the following adjustments are suggested: 1-person, add 20 percent; 2-person, add 10 percent; 3-person, add 5 percent; 5- or 6-person, subtract 5 percent; and 7-or-more person, subtract 10 percent.

Source: U.S. Department of Agriculture, Center for Nutrition Policy and Promotion, *Official USDA Food Plans: Cost of Food at Home at Four Levels, U.S. Average, December 2019*, January 2020, and earlier reports. See also <https://www.fns.usda.gov/cnpp/usda-food-plans-cost-food-reports-monthly-reports>.

Table 768. Food—Retail Prices of Selected Items: 1990 to 2019

[In dollars per pound, except as indicated. As of December. See Appendix III]

Food	1990	2000	2005	2010	2015	2016	2017	2018	2019
Cereals and bakery products:									
Flour, white, all purpose......................	0.24	0.28	0.30	0.44	0.50	0.50	0.46	0.44	0.43
Rice, white, long grain, raw....................	0.49	(NA)	0.52	0.73	0.71	0.69	0.71	0.71	0.71
Spaghetti and macaroni.................	0.85	0.88	0.87	1.19	1.29	1.29	1.24	1.16	1.19
Bread, white, pan...........................	0.70	0.99	1.05	1.39	1.43	1.36	1.32	1.29	1.36
Bread, whole wheat......................	(NA)	1.36	1.29	1.88	1.95	1.96	1.97	1.92	1.96
Beef:									
Ground beef, 100% beef.................	1.63	1.63	2.30	2.38	4.06	3.56	3.71	3.73	3.86
Ground chuck, 100% beef..............	2.02	1.98	2.61	2.93	4.03	3.62	3.73	3.71	4.07
Ground beef, lean and extra lean.............	(NA)	2.33	2.91	3.49	5.89	5.54	5.52	5.26	5.52
Beef roasts (all, uncooked).............	(NA)	2.93	3.73	4.15	5.48	5.16	5.21	5.20	5.54
Beef steaks (all, uncooked).................	(NA)	4.09	5.03	5.60	7.51	7.12	7.36	7.58	7.71
Round steak, USDA Choice.............	3.42	3.28	4.12	4.30	5.93	5.56	5.83	5.69	5.98
Sirloin steak, boneless.....................	4.24	4.81	5.93	6.07	8.29	7.91	7.93	8.31	8.48
Pork:									
Bacon, sliced............................	2.28	3.03	3.33	4.16	5.73	5.10	5.63	5.50	5.47
Chops, center cut, bone-in...............	3.32	3.46	3.28	3.58	4.09	3.63	3.81	3.95	3.77
Ham, boneless, excluding canned...........	(NA)	2.75	3.09	3.47	4.03	3.93	3.87	3.88	4.07
Poultry, fish, and eggs:									
Chicken, fresh, whole.....................	0.86	1.08	1.06	1.28	1.44	1.46	1.47	1.47	1.45
Chicken breast, boneless................	(NA)	(NA)	(NA)	3.32	3.28	3.20	3.19	3.11	3.11
Chicken legs, bone-in......................	1.17	1.26	1.33	1.48	1.57	1.43	1.46	1.40	1.51
Turkey, frozen, whole......................	0.96	0.99	1.07	1.38	1.45	1.50	1.50	1.41	1.39
Tuna, light, chunk, canned...............	2.11	1.92	(NA)	(NA)	3.26	3.15	(NA)	(NA)	(NA)
Eggs, grade A large (dozen).................	1.00	0.96	1.35	1.79	2.75	1.38	1.82	1.60	1.54
Dairy products:									
Milk, fresh, whole, fortified (per gal.)..........	(NA)	2.79	3.24	3.32	3.31	3.29	3.16	2.85	3.19
Milk, low-fat, reduced fat, skim, per gallon...	(NA)	(NA)	(NA)	(NA)	(NA)	(NA)	(NA)	2.63	2.87
Yogurt, per 8 ounce.....................	(NA)	(NA)	(NA)	(NA)	(NA)	(NA)	(NA)	1.08	1.15
Butter, in sticks........................	(NA)	(NA)	(NA)	(NA)	(NA)	(NA)	(NA)	3.93	3.62
American processed cheese.................	(NA)	3.69	3.92	3.80	4.35	4.21	4.13	3.94	3.91
Cheddar cheese, natural.................	(NA)	3.76	4.43	4.93	5.33	4.90	4.95	5.36	5.30
Ice cream, prepack., bulk, reg. (1/2 gal.).....	2.54	3.66	3.69	4.58	4.73	4.68	4.76	4.81	4.74
Fresh fruits and vegetables:									
Apples, Red Delicious......................	0.77	0.82	0.97	1.20	1.40	1.31	(NA)	(NA)	(NA)
Bananas................................	0.43	0.49	0.48	0.59	0.58	0.58	0.56	0.58	0.57
Oranges, navel...........................	0.56	0.62	0.89	1.02	1.23	1.17	1.32	1.39	1.33
Grapefruit...............................	0.56	0.58	1.10	0.99	1.09	1.25	1.33	1.35	1.25
Grapes, Thompson seedless................	(NA)	2.36	2.76	2.87	2.83	2.88	2.61	2.28	2.39
Lemons..................................	0.97	1.11	1.51	1.60	1.98	1.99	1.99	2.39	2.00
Pears, Anjou.............................	0.79	(NA)	1.00	1.42	(NA)	1.63	1.55	1.57	(NA)
Strawberries, dry pint, per 12 ounces........	(NA)	(NA)	2.67	3.07	3.50	3.28	3.09	3.17	3.10
Lettuce, iceberg..........................	0.58	0.85	0.85	0.99	1.48	1.02	1.01	1.25	1.30
Tomatoes, field grown.....................	0.86	1.57	1.85	1.59	1.93	1.97	2.24	2.18	1.95
Peppers, sweet...........................	(NA)	(NA)	(NA)	2.40	(NA)	2.20	2.42	2.65	2.50
Potatoes, white..........................	0.32	0.35	0.50	0.58	0.64	0.69	0.73	0.72	0.78
Sugar and fats and oils:									
Sugar, white, all sizes.....................	0.43	0.41	0.45	0.64	0.64	0.61	0.65	0.57	0.59
Margarine, tubs, soft......................	(NA)	0.84	0.91	1.62	1.86	1.78	1.70	1.57	(NA)
Peanut butter, creamy, all sizes..............	2.07	1.96	1.70	1.99	2.68	2.62	2.48	(NA)	(NA)
Nonalcoholic beverages:									
All soft drinks, 2 liter......................	(NA)	(NA)	(NA)	(NA)	(NA)	(NA)	(NA)	1.47	1.48
All soft drinks, per 12 oz can in 12-pack.....	(NA)	(NA)	(NA)	(NA)	(NA)	(NA)	(NA)	0.33	0.35
Coffee, 100% ground roast, all sizes.........	2.94	3.21	3.24	4.15	4.49	4.28	4.29	(NA)	4.05
Prepared foods:									
Potato chips, per 16 ounces.................	2.97	3.44	3.46	4.74	4.41	4.35	4.43	4.45	4.53

NA Not available.

Source: U.S. Bureau of Labor Statistics, CPI Databases, "Average Price Indexes," <http://www.bls.gov/cpi/data.htm>, accessed February 2020.

Table 769. Employment Cost Index for Total Compensation, Wages and Salaries, and Benefits: 2009 to 2019

[As of December (2005=100). Data are not seasonally adjusted. For data by industry, see Table 683]

Compensation type and occupation	2009	2010	2011	2012	2013	2014	2015	2016	2017	2018	2019
Total compensation:											
All civilian workers [1]......................	111.0	113.2	115.5	117.7	120.0	122.7	125.1	127.9	131.2	135.0	138.7
Private industry workers................	110.2	112.5	115.0	117.1	119.4	122.2	124.5	127.2	130.5	134.4	138.0
State and local government workers...	114.2	116.2	117.7	119.9	122.2	124.7	127.8	130.9	134.2	137.7	141.7
Wages and salaries:											
All civilian workers [1]......................	111.2	113.0	114.6	116.5	118.7	121.2	123.7	126.6	129.8	133.8	137.7
Private industry workers................	110.8	112.8	114.6	116.6	119.0	121.6	124.2	127.1	130.6	134.7	138.7
State and local government workers...	112.5	113.8	114.9	116.2	117.5	119.4	121.6	124.1	126.7	129.7	133.0
Benefits:											
All civilian workers [1]......................	110.7	113.9	117.5	120.3	123.0	126.2	128.4	131.1	134.4	138.1	141.2
Private industry workers................	108.7	111.9	115.9	118.2	120.5	123.5	125.1	127.3	130.2	133.6	136.2
State and local government workers...	117.7	121.1	123.6	127.8	132.0	135.8	140.6	145.0	149.7	154.4	159.5

[1] Includes workers in the private nonfarm economy except those in private households and workers in the public sector except the federal government.

Source: U.S. Bureau of Labor Statistics, Employment Cost Trends, "Employment Cost Index," <http://www.bls.gov/ncs/ect/#data>, accessed February 2020.

Table 770. Indexes of Spot Primary Market Prices: 1990 to 2019

[1967=100. Represents unweighted geometric average of price quotations of 23 commodities. The indexes are computed daily and therefore much more sensitive to changes in market conditions than a monthly producer price index]

Items and number	1990	1995	2000	2005	2010	2013	2014	2015	2016	2017	2018	2019
All commodities (23).....	258.1	289.1	224.0	303.3	520.3	456.2	438.0	374.8	423.1	432.5	409.2	401.6
Foodstuffs (10)..............	206.4	236.4	184.7	241.7	440.3	364.7	369.4	335.0	338.8	336.0	324.2	338.5
Raw industrials (13).........	301.2	332.2	255.8	354.7	583.8	532.4	492.6	404.9	493.2	514.7	480.4	451.8
Livestock and products (5)..	292.7	307.4	265.5	326.6	528.0	547.8	556.2	392.2	446.2	437.3	396.4	386.8
Metals (5).....................	283.2	300.6	214.0	440.9	1,006.2	935.2	824.4	556.0	803.9	911.6	829.9	752.1
Textiles and fibers (4).......	257.6	274.3	245.7	252.5	342.1	278.2	257.7	271.9	287.3	304.5	286.9	280.9
Fats and oils (4)..............	188.7	226.7	163.6	223.4	478.3	387.3	364.0	315.2	393.3	380.8	357.4	366.5

Source: cmdty by Barchart, Chicago, IL, *CRB Commodity Index Report*, weekly ©. See also <http://www.barchart.com/cmdty>.

Table 771. Producer Price Indexes—Final and Intermediate Demand: 2010 to 2019

[November 2009=100, except as noted. Minus sign (-) indicates decrease. For information on producer prices, see Bureau of Labor Statistics, <http://www.bls.gov/ppi/>]

Commodity type	Index						
	2010	2014	2015	2016	2017	2018	2019
FINAL DEMAND							
Total......	**101.8**	**110.9**	**109.9**	**110.4**	**113.0**	**116.2**	**118.2**
Final demand goods............................	102.8	114.0	109.1	107.6	111.2	115.0	115.5
Final demand foods........................	103.7	121.6	118.4	115.1	116.5	116.7	118.9
Final demand energy.......................	107.2	124.2	98.6	90.4	99.8	110.0	105.0
Final demand goods less foods and energy...................	101.4	109.5	109.9	110.7	113.2	116.0	117.6
Final demand services.........................	101.3	109.0	110.0	111.5	113.5	116.5	119.1
Final demand trade services...............	101.7	110.2	111.6	113.1	114.8	116.9	119.7
Final demand transportation and warehousing services...........	103.2	117.7	115.3	113.5	115.9	122.0	125.5
Final demand services less trade, transportation, and warehousing...................	100.9	107.5	108.7	110.6	112.8	115.8	118.2
INTERMEDIATE DEMAND							
Processed goods for intermediate demand [1].....................	183.4	201.9	188.0	182.2	190.7	200.9	198.1
Processed foods and feeds [1]................	171.7	210.8	197.7	188.4	190.3	191.6	192.5
Processed energy goods [1].................	187.8	211.5	168.9	152.6	171.0	190.8	179.2
Processed materials less foods and energy [1]........	180.8	195.2	189.4	186.9	193.3	201.8	201.1
Unprocessed goods for intermediate demand [1]............	212.2	249.3	189.1	173.4	190.8	200.1	185.9
Unprocessed foodstuffs and feedstuffs [1]........	152.4	210.1	181.4	162.4	167.1	163.9	165.3
Unprocessed energy materials [1]..............	216.7	233.1	141.1	128.1	150.7	168.7	143.4
Unprocessed nonfood materials less energy [1]............	329.1	345.7	296.0	288.0	324.1	340.7	323.4
Services for intermediate demand................	101.1	108.9	110.2	112.1	115.0	118.6	121.4
Trade services for intermediate demand................	100.8	110.4	113.1	112.1	115.3	120.0	125.0
Transportation and warehousing services for intermediate demand...............	103.3	119.4	119.1	118.2	120.6	125.4	129.0
Services less trade, transportation, and warehousing for intermediate demand................	100.7	106.5	107.8	110.9	113.8	117.0	119.1
PERCENT CHANGE [2]							
FINAL DEMAND							
Total.......	**(NA)**	**1.6**	**-0.9**	**0.5**	**2.4**	**2.8**	**1.7**
Final demand goods............................	(NA)	1.2	-4.3	-1.4	3.3	3.4	0.4
Final demand foods........................	(NA)	3.2	-2.6	-2.8	1.2	0.2	1.9
Final demand energy.......................	(NA)	-0.9	-20.6	-8.3	10.4	10.2	-4.5
Final demand goods less foods and energy...................	(NA)	1.5	0.4	0.7	2.3	2.5	1.4
Final demand services.........................	(NA)	1.8	0.9	1.4	1.8	2.6	2.2
Final demand trade services...............	(NA)	1.8	1.3	1.3	1.5	1.8	2.4
Final demand transportation and warehousing services...........	(NA)	2.1	-2.0	-1.6	2.1	5.3	2.9
Final demand services less trade, transportation, and warehousing...................	(NA)	1.6	1.1	1.7	2.0	2.7	2.1
INTERMEDIATE DEMAND							
Processed goods for intermediate demand.....................	6.3	0.5	-6.9	-3.1	4.7	5.3	-1.4
Processed foods and feeds................	3.4	3.2	-6.2	-4.7	1.0	0.7	0.5
Processed energy goods.................	15.6	-1.0	-20.1	-9.7	12.1	11.6	-6.1
Processed materials less foods and energy........	4.3	0.7	-3.0	-1.3	3.4	4.4	-0.3
Unprocessed goods for intermediate demand............	21.1	1.1	-24.1	-8.3	10.0	4.9	-7.1
Unprocessed foodstuffs and feedstuffs........	13.3	4.9	-13.7	-10.5	2.9	-1.9	0.9
Unprocessed energy materials..............	22.6	-0.7	-39.5	-9.2	17.6	11.9	-15.0
Unprocessed nonfood materials less energy............	32.5	-1.6	-14.4	-2.7	12.5	5.1	-5.1
Services for intermediate demand................	(NA)	1.6	1.2	1.7	2.6	3.1	2.4
Trade services for intermediate demand................	(NA)	1.1	2.4	-0.9	2.9	4.1	4.2
Transportation and warehousing services for intermediate demand...............	(NA)	2.8	-0.3	-0.8	2.0	4.0	2.9
Services less trade, transportation, and warehousing for intermediate demand................	(NA)	1.4	1.2	2.9	2.6	2.8	1.8

NA Not available. [1] 1982=100. [2] Change from immediate prior year. 2010, change from 2009.

Source: U.S. Bureau of Labor Statistics, PPI Databases, "Commodity Data including "headline" FD-ID Indexes," <http://www.bls.gov/ppi/data.htm>, accessed May 2020.

Table 772. Producer Price Indexes—Final and Intermediate Demand by Commodity: 2000 to 2019

[1982=100, unless otherwise noted. For information on producer prices, see Bureau of Labor Statistics, <http://www.bls.gov/ppi/>]

Item	2000	2005	2010	2015	2017	2018	2019
Final demand (Nov. 2009=100)	**(NA)**	**(NA)**	**101.8**	**109.9**	**113.0**	**116.2**	**118.2**
Final demand goods (Nov. 2009=100)	**(NA)**	**(NA)**	**102.8**	**109.1**	**111.2**	**115.0**	**115.5**
Final demand foods (Nov. 2009=100)	**(NA)**	**(NA)**	**103.7**	**118.4**	**116.5**	**116.7**	**118.9**
Fresh fruits & melons	91.4	102.8	123.8	124.2	147.9	145.1	136.3
Fresh & dry vegetables	126.7	142.6	178.5	200.2	215.2	211.6	239.2
Grains	78.3	83.4	160.2	151.9	135.6	144.9	149.6
Eggs for fresh use (Dec. 1991=100)	84.9	79.6	123.4	219.3	123.8	162.9	116.1
Oilseeds	93.8	113.4	191.0	176.6	176.6	168.3	160.1
Bakery products	182.3	201.1	244.8	275.0	279.6	286.5	291.9
Milled rice	101.2	120.1	183.6	199.0	184.0	204.0	205.9
Dry macaroni, spaghetti, and egg noodle products (June 1985=100)	121.6	127.9	170.7	216.2	201.2	202.9	202.5
Beef & veal	113.7	147.4	157.1	243.6	201.5	204.9	209.0
Pork	113.4	131.9	142.6	145.6	147.1	137.8	144.1
Processed young chickens	110.4	136.2	149.0	174.0	174.6	160.1	162.6
Processed turkeys	98.7	105.1	132.1	164.3	137.2	139.9	146.0
Unprocessed and prepared seafood	198.1	222.6	272.4	322.0	337.9	344.5	349.9
Dairy products	133.7	154.5	174.0	193.6	196.9	192.3	201.3
Processed fruits & vegetables	128.6	140.4	176.6	197.7	202.8	207.6	208.9
Confectionery end products	170.6	205.1	236.4	282.8	275.3	278.5	283.1
Soft drinks	144.1	159.1	183.9	196.7	203.3	205.6	213.5
Coffee (whole bean, ground, & instant)	133.5	151.1	190.2	204.7	193.9	194.1	194.2
Shortening, cooking oil, and margarine	132.4	176.7	233.6	243.3	256.9	250.7	239.0
Frozen specialty food	143.5	152.7	176.4	189.5	186.5	186.1	185.6
Final demand energy (Nov. 2009=100)	**(NA)**	**(NA)**	**107.2**	**98.6**	**99.8**	**110.0**	**105.0**
Liquefied petroleum gas	127.1	244.7	301.8	109.8	154.3	196.0	123.8
Residential electric power (Dec. 1990=100)	110.8	126.4	154.7	172.2	177.1	179.4	181.9
Residential natural gas (Dec. 1990=100)	135.5	216.8	201.7	184.4	198.0	198.2	200.8
Gasoline	94.6	168.6	225.3	177.2	171.5	202.5	183.3
Home heating oil & distillates	93.5	178.4	207.5	160.9	155.9	203.7	186.4
No. 2 diesel fuel	93.3	189.1	232.9	181.4	185.6	247.3	221.3
Other final demand goods (Nov. 2009=100)	**(NA)**	**(NA)**	**101.4**	**109.9**	**113.2**	**116.0**	**117.6**
Alcoholic beverages	140.6	158.5	175.1	192.6	195.6	199.6	199.8
Women's, girls', and infants' apparel (December 2003=100)	(NA)	100.3	101.6	105.2	107.7	109.0	108.3
Men's and boys' apparel (December 2003=100)	(NA)	98.7	101.5	113.0	114.2	115.6	117.4
Textile house furnishings	122.0	122.9	131.7	162.8	167.5	167.9	169.2
Footwear	144.9	148.1	162.4	196.0	201.9	203.5	208.8
Industrial chemicals	129.1	188.5	269.2	242.2	254.0	274.0	252.6
Pharmaceutical preparations (June 2001=100)	(NA)	117.9	155.1	212.8	246.5	259.2	268.4
Soaps and detergents	128.2	134.6	161.2	175.7	177.9	183.1	182.1
Cosmetics and other toilet preparations	137.4	143.0	149.9	161.4	162.8	165.1	167.0
Tires, tubes, tread, & repair materials	93.0	108.1	138.1	149.3	148.7	150.5	152.1
Agricultural machinery and equipment	153.7	174.7	203.5	222.2	226.6	230.4	237.3
Construction machinery and equipment	148.6	168.3	191.4	217.0	220.9	223.1	232.6
Industrial material handling equipment	134.7	150.6	183.1	207.0	212.7	219.2	225.4
Electronic computers (December 2004=100)	261.6	85.5	30.3	20.4	18.4	17.8	16.6
Textile machinery and equipment	156.2	160.5	165.9	176.1	171.3	171.7	172.2
Paper industries machinery (June 1982=100)	164.7	178.1	197.2	216.2	219.5	222.3	227.8
Printing trades machinery and equipment	142.1	144.3	155.4	162.3	163.0	164.0	164.6
Transformers and power regulators	135.8	150.3	223.1	212.8	214.6	225.9	232.0
Oil field and gas field machinery	128.2	155.9	200.7	216.5	214.3	216.7	219.6
Mining machinery and equipment	146.1	175.9	221.5	260.6	266.3	277.4	298.0
Office and store machines and equipment	112.7	115.1	121.0	122.7	122.5	121.1	121.5
Household furniture	152.7	166.5	187.4	203.9	209.1	215.2	219.9
Household appliances	107.3	103.3	110.5	116.8	116.0	119.0	123.6
Home electronic equipment	71.8	62.6	52.9	51.3	51.6	51.3	52.0
Lawn and garden equipment	132.0	134.5	141.7	143.7	144.4	146.9	149.7
Passenger cars	132.8	131.8	129.0	133.4	134.1	134.0	134.9
Light motor trucks	157.6	148.4	153.3	171.4	176.1	178.0	177.8
Heavy motor trucks	148.0	162.4	195.7	218.1	227.1	229.9	232.3
Truck trailers	139.4	157.1	181.5	201.0	202.7	213.1	225.2
Aircraft	184.2	223.5	263.0	290.8	296.2	301.3	307.0
Ships (December 1985=100)	146.9	176.6	215.1	225.2	223.8	224.2	227.7
Railroad equipment	135.7	160.4	184.4	201.9	203.2	202.1	203.7
Final demand services (Nov. 2009=100)	**(NA)**	**(NA)**	**101.3**	**110.0**	**113.3**	**116.5**	**119.1**
Final demand trade services (Nov. 2009=100)	**(NA)**	**(NA)**	**101.7**	**111.6**	**114.8**	**116.9**	**119.7**
Furnishings wholesaling (Mar. 2009=100)	(NA)	(NA)	78.5	89.1	95.2	96.8	98.5
Apparel wholesaling (Mar. 2009=100)	(NA)	(NA)	97.3	117.9	117.5	119.1	121.6
Food & alcohol wholesaling (June 2009=100)	(NA)	(NA)	105.7	105.2	107.3	110.0	114.6
Food & alcohol retailing (Mar. 2009=100)	(NA)	(NA)	98.9	126.4	129.9	131.9	134.7
Health, beauty, & optical goods retailing (Mar. 2009=100)	(NA)	(NA)	107.8	118.9	117.4	119.5	123.6
Apparel, jewelry, footwear, & accessories retailing (June 2009=100)	(NA)	(NA)	104.2	113.9	113.5	112.2	112.8
Automobiles & automobile parts retailing (June 2009=100)	(NA)	(NA)	105.9	101.2	94.4	94.7	95.4
Sporting goods, including boats, retailing (Mar. 2009=100)	(NA)	(NA)	96.6	108.9	112.6	113.2	114.2
Furniture retailing (Mar. 2009=100)	(NA)	(NA)	99.7	102.2	106.5	103.5	104.9
Major household appliances retailing (Mar. 2009=100)	(NA)	(NA)	97.3	80.5	84.7	91.2	96.8
Book retailing (Mar. 2009=100)	(NA)	(NA)	104.8	110.3	107.1	109.5	120.2
Final demand transportation & warehousing services (Nov. 2009=100)	**(NA)**	**(NA)**	**103.2**	**115.3**	**115.9**	**122.0**	**125.5**
Rail transportation of freight & mail (Dec. 2008=100)	(NA)	(NA)	101.6	116.5	117.8	124.6	128.4
Truck transportation of freight (June 2009=100)	(NA)	(NA)	102.0	113.4	114.9	122.6	125.4
Air transportation of freight (Dec. 2008=100)	(NA)	(NA)	100.1	112.5	109.7	112.1	111.8
Courier, messenger, & U.S. postal services (June 2009=100)	(NA)	(NA)	105.5	131.5	134.3	139.9	145.8

See footnotes at end of table.

Table 772. Producer Price Indexes—Final and Intermediate Demand by Commodity: 2000 to 2019-Continued.

See headnote on page 503.

Item	2000	2005	2010	2015	2017	2018	2019
Rail transportation of passengers (Dec. 2008=100)	(NA)	(NA)	100.7	115.2	119.8	122.1	125.4
Airline passenger services (Dec. 2008=100)	(NA)	(NA)	102.8	112.3	110.7	113.6	117.7
Other final demand services (Nov. 2009=100)	**(NA)**	**(NA)**	**100.9**	**108.7**	**112.8**	**115.8**	**118.2**
Sales of books	218.2	264.0	317.1	363.9	376.3	384.7	392.6
Cellphone & other wireless telecom services (Mar. 2009=100)	(NA)	(NA)	94.4	77.6	66.2	63.7	63.7
Cable & satellite subscriber services (Dec. 2008=100)	(NA)	(NA)	103.7	112.7	122.3	129.9	135.3
Internet access services (Mar. 2009=100)	(NA)	(NA)	98.3	98.2	96.0	93.8	93.4
Processed goods for intermediate demand	**129.2**	**154.0**	**183.4**	**188.0**	**190.7**	**200.9**	**198.1**
Processed materials less foods & feeds	**130.1**	**155.1**	**184.4**	**187.2**	**190.9**	**201.9**	**198.8**
Synthetic fibers	107.2	112.3	111.6	121.3	121.9	130.2	131.9
Processed yarns & threads	107.9	111.7	130.0	135.6	136.4	143.2	141.2
Finished fabrics	122.5	124.1	137.1	154.0	154.1	157.4	161.4
Commercial electric power	131.5	149.8	182.5	195.8	199.4	199.9	199.6
Industrial electric power	131.5	156.2	193.1	223.7	240.6	247.0	243.3
Commercial natural gas (Dec. 1990=100)	134.7	232.5	208.0	176.6	189.0	190.7	191.5
Industrial natural gas (Dec. 1990=100)	139.0	249.4	202.0	158.6	159.5	157.8	149.2
Natural gas to electric power (Dec. 1990=100)	120.7	204.0	174.8	159.6	168.1	169.6	152.2
Jet fuels	88.5	169.6	225.5	171.3	167.9	221.3	202.4
Prepared paint	160.8	187.9	237.1	273.0	274.6	285.6	299.1
Medicinal and botanical chemicals, drugs, and other products	146.2	136.0	175.2	177.1	174.6	181.1	181.3
Biological products, including diagnostics	172.2	195.1	223.7	256.4	262.6	265.9	275.6
Fats & oils, inedible	70.1	146.9	244.3	204.9	225.2	198.6	193.4
Plastic resins & materials	141.6	193.0	210.1	228.0	232.7	243.9	225.5
Synthetic rubber	119.1	151.3	215.5	197.6	210.4	215.9	207.0
Plastic construction products	135.8	158.8	190.9	213.1	217.3	226.1	229.4
Softwood lumber	178.6	203.6	160.8	192.7	223.7	241.9	215.4
Hardwood lumber	185.9	196.6	187.3	221.1	219.6	230.1	215.1
Millwork	176.4	197.2	207.0	237.2	247.6	259.5	263.5
Plywood	157.6	186.8	176.7	198.9	204.2	230.2	202.9
Paper	149.8	159.6	182.1	189.8	186.4	197.6	200.6
Paperboard	176.7	175.5	224.9	243.1	257.5	273.5	268.1
Paper boxes & containers	172.6	183.7	219.4	247.3	259.5	264.8	269.5
Foundry & forge shop products	136.5	156.2	191.2	209.2	206.4	210.3	211.9
Steel mill products	108.4	159.7	191.7	177.1	187.4	211.1	204.0
Primary nonferrous metals	113.6	158.2	210.3	170.7	186.5	193.7	184.3
Aluminum mill shapes	149.0	161.1	171.9	172.4	180.8	202.8	197.5
Copper & brass mill shapes	162.3	235.8	421.3	356.9	393.0	408.8	392.8
Nonferrous wire & cable	143.7	169.4	258.1	238.2	235.6	248.6	247.4
Hardware	151.2	168.0	194.0	209.7	213.8	218.1	223.8
Plumbing fixtures & fittings	180.4	197.6	231.4	257.1	262.4	270.2	281.6
Heating equipment	155.6	179.9	221.5	248.2	255.9	266.5	279.2
Fabricated structural metal products	144.9	175.1	201.1	215.6	218.9	234.2	239.8
Air conditioning & refrigeration equipment	135.3	146.2	163.8	179.2	184.6	192.6	200.2
Motors, generators, motor generator sets	146.2	157.8	190.6	211.6	211.1	216.8	221.3
Electronic components & accessories	97.1	87.0	73.5	68.2	66.8	65.9	65.3
Internal combustion engines	143.8	147.7	161.7	168.4	166.0	168.1	169.5
Machine shop products	138.0	151.0	174.7	184.0	184.9	189.9	194.3
Cement	150.1	176.4	193.5	223.4	246.0	252.1	258.1
Concrete products	147.8	177.2	210.6	239.4	254.1	263.7	271.7
Motor vehicle parts	113.6	113.1	121.8	125.9	125.2	126.9	127.1
Aircraft engines & engine parts (Dec. 1985=100)	141.0	165.9	197.4	221.2	224.3	226.7	229.7
Aircraft parts & auxiliary equipment (June 1985=100)	145.7	155.3	167.7	183.3	185.0	186.4	188.5
Medical/surgical/personal aid devices	146.0	159.2	169.0	176.2	178.5	180.5	182.8
Unprocessed goods for intermediate demand	**120.6**	**182.2**	**212.2**	**189.1**	**190.8**	**200.1**	**185.9**
Unprocessed foodstuffs & feedstuffs	**100.2**	**122.7**	**152.4**	**181.4**	**167.1**	**163.9**	**165.3**
Wheat	80.3	102.7	157.2	153.3	131.6	150.3	138.3
Corn	76.4	75.9	160.8	149.6	136.1	141.0	151.4
Slaughter cattle	104.1	131.5	139.8	225.6	178.8	172.4	171.1
Slaughter hogs	72.7	82.7	92.6	80.6	88.5	80.1	83.8
Broilers and other meat type chickens	127.6	181.0	221.3	246.8	257.2	270.1	242.3
Slaughter turkeys	120.7	131.1	173.0	234.3	201.7	170.5	186.3
Raw milk	92.0	113.5	121.9	127.7	134.5	123.4	141.9
Hay and hayseeds	156.3	190.1	214.3	309.2	274.7	327.8	338.2
Raw cane sugar & byproducts	100.2	124.9	179.9	149.4	161.9	151.9	155.5
Unprocessed nonfood materials	**130.4**	**223.4**	**249.3**	**183.7**	**198.3**	**217.0**	**192.0**
Raw cotton	95.2	78.9	117.9	101.6	114.4	124.1	100.5
Hides & skins	174.0	189.9	224.9	258.8	204.3	171.0	128.7
Coal	87.9	116.8	189.5	194.0	195.8	199.6	199.9
Natural gas	155.5	335.4	185.8	105.4	118.7	112.1	85.5
Crude petroleum	85.2	150.1	218.6	129.5	138.3	182.0	157.7
Logs, bolts, timber, pulpwood and wood chips	196.4	197.4	213.4	241.9	239.8	248.7	239.9
Wastepaper	282.5	230.9	421.5	291.8	399.9	276.9	181.2
Iron ore	94.8	116.9	147.1	132.0	131.9	136.8	145.5
Iron & steel scrap	142.1	289.8	541.1	342.8	440.4	523.5	413.3
Nonferrous metal ores (Dec. 1983=100)	68.0	150.0	298.6	272.6	309.4	330.6	360.1
Copper base scrap	123.7	258.6	548.2	427.6	428.9	460.7	410.3
Aluminum base scrap	177.0	210.1	241.6	208.7	210.2	215.6	178.0
Construction sand, gravel, & crushed stone	163.1	195.8	262.2	299.9	323.2	334.7	348.7

NA Not available.

Source: U.S. Bureau of Labor Statistics, PPI Databases, "Commodity Data including "headline" FD-ID Indexes," <http://www.bls.gov/ppi/data.htm>, accessed May 2020.

Table 773. Chain-Type Price Indexes for Personal Consumption Expenditures by Type of Expenditure: 1990 to 2019

[2012=100. For explanation of "chain-type," see text, Section 13. See also Table 713]

Type of Expenditure	1990	2000	2005	2010	2015	2017	2018	2019
Personal consumption expenditures...........................	**63.4**	**78.2**	**86.8**	**95.7**	**103.0**	**106.0**	**108.2**	**109.9**
Household consumption expenditures [1]........................	62.7	77.8	86.5	95.6	102.8	105.6	107.9	109.4
Food and beverages purchased for off-premises consumption.......	61.1	73.9	82.6	93.9	104.1	102.9	103.4	104.4
Food and nonalcoholic beverages purchased for off-premises consumption....................	60.5	72.8	81.6	93.2	104.4	102.7	103.2	104.1
Alcoholic beverages purchased for off-premises consumption.......	64.6	81.7	89.3	98.7	102.1	103.7	104.7	106.3
Food produced and consumed on farms..............................	76.5	64.1	75.6	81.7	101.9	93.0	92.0	89.9
Clothing, footwear, and related services............................	109.2	103.0	95.9	95.0	100.3	99.7	99.8	98.7
Clothing...	111.8	105.0	96.6	94.5	99.5	98.7	99.0	97.5
Garments...	117.3	108.0	97.7	94.4	99.1	98.1	98.3	96.4
Women's and girls' clothing....................	122.9	107.5	98.0	94.8	98.5	98.3	97.8	94.5
Men's and boys' clothing........................	109.9	108.5	97.1	93.6	100.1	98.1	98.8	99.2
Children's and infants' clothing...................	111.2	109.0	97.5	95.4	100.0	96.0	100.5	99.7
Footwear [2].............................	96.8	93.6	92.9	97.1	103.8	103.8	103.3	103.8
Housing, utilities, and fuels............................	54.5	71.8	85.3	96.5	107.6	114.4	118.1	121.7
Housing...	55.4	74.1	86.4	96.5	108.2	115.7	119.6	123.8
Rental of tenant-occupied nonfarm housing [3]....................	53.7	71.2	83.7	95.8	109.4	117.6	121.8	126.3
Imputed rental of owner-occupied nonfarm housing [4]...............	56.1	75.0	86.9	96.9	108.0	115.2	119.0	123.0
Household utilities and fuels............................	49.9	61.9	80.5	96.6	103.9	106.9	109.5	110.1
Water supply and sanitation............................	37.1	56.2	68.9	90.5	112.8	120.7	124.9	128.9
Electricity, gas, and other fuels............................	54.3	63.9	84.7	98.8	100.8	102.2	104.2	103.7
Electricity...	59.8	65.3	76.7	98.2	106.4	107.5	108.3	108.5
Natural gas...	58.4	80.1	128.9	113.9	99.2	104.3	104.3	102.8
Fuel oil and other fuels............................	27.1	35.8	58.7	77.5	69.9	66.8	80.8	77.2
Furnishings, household equipment, and routine household maintenance....................	97.4	105.3	102.2	100.3	95.4	92.6	92.7	93.8
Furniture, furnishings, and floor coverings [5].................	114.3	121.8	112.9	102.5	92.8	88.2	87.0	88.2
Household textiles......................	179.3	161.9	134.5	106.4	89.4	83.9	82.6	80.2
Household appliances [6]............................	95.8	93.2	91.4	96.3	90.2	83.9	87.1	89.3
Glassware, tableware, and household utensils [7]....................	126.5	126.6	113.1	106.3	92.8	88.3	83.6	81.8
Health...	48.8	70.9	83.4	96.1	103.8	107.3	109.1	110.7
Medical products, appliances, and equipment.......................	51.9	71.0	83.1	94.5	106.4	113.0	114.4	114.5
Pharmaceutical and other medical products [8].................	49.1	68.5	81.5	93.9	107.2	114.7	116.2	116.0
Pharmaceutical products....................	48.8	68.2	81.3	93.8	107.3	114.9	116.4	116.2
Other medical products....................	76.4	95.2	96.6	98.5	99.2	99.0	99.6	101.6
Therapeutic appliances and equipment....................	70.0	88.2	93.4	98.3	100.9	101.9	102.8	104.3
Outpatient services...	54.3	77.0	86.4	97.4	101.7	103.6	104.7	105.9
Physician services [9]...	57.5	80.8	87.4	97.4	99.6	100.2	101.0	101.9
Dental services...	37.5	61.9	77.6	95.5	108.3	113.2	116.3	118.9
Paramedical services...	58.3	78.3	88.6	98.3	102.6	105.6	106.4	107.8
Hospital and nursing home services....................	43.8	65.9	81.1	95.7	104.4	107.8	110.5	113.0
Hospitals [10]...	44.2	65.8	81.0	95.5	104.4	107.5	110.1	112.3
Nursing homes...	42.5	66.2	81.5	96.3	104.1	109.5	113.2	117.4
Transportation...	57.8	70.8	78.9	88.6	90.6	90.4	93.7	93.7
Motor vehicles...	80.7	100.7	97.2	96.0	100.7	97.9	97.3	97.3
New motor vehicles...	83.8	99.5	95.8	95.6	102.6	102.8	102.3	102.7
Net purchases of used motor vehicles....................	74.3	103.9	100.6	97.0	96.2	88.2	87.5	86.8
Motor vehicle operation....................	44.4	54.5	70.4	84.9	83.2	84.2	90.2	89.7
Motor vehicle parts and accessories....................	73.7	72.3	78.3	94.0	99.8	99.7	100.7	102.7
Motor vehicle fuels, lubricants, and fluids....................	32.3	41.3	62.3	76.9	68.7	68.9	78.0	75.3
Public transportation....................	67.5	77.5	76.1	90.4	101.9	102.3	103.9	106.3
Ground transportation [11]...	49.7	63.3	77.2	93.7	104.9	108.9	110.2	110.6
Air transportation...	75.8	82.9	74.5	88.5	100.5	98.9	100.7	104.2
Water transportation...	130.4	145.3	115.3	103.2	100.4	105.0	105.3	104.6
Communication...	111.9	111.8	105.2	102.6	88.6	78.5	76.7	73.6
Telecommunication services....................	106.4	102.9	97.9	101.9	89.7	78.1	75.9	72.1
Internet access...	180.7	125.9	125.1	100.7	101.3	100.1	99.3	100.8
Recreation...	120.6	116.7	109.4	102.4	97.1	95.7	95.0	94.5
Video and audio equipment, computers, and related services.......	398.7	216.5	156.1	110.7	89.6	84.6	81.8	78.6
Video and audio equipment....................	508.7	343.5	241.3	126.1	76.7	63.1	56.4	52.1
Sports and recreational goods and related services....................	124.4	120.8	110.5	104.1	92.9	87.6	85.0	83.3
Sports and recreational vehicles....................	78.0	90.4	92.4	96.3	100.3	101.4	103.0	106.0
Other sporting and recreational goods....................	145.1	133.3	117.0	106.4	90.7	83.6	79.7	76.8
Magazines, newspapers, books, and stationery....................	65.7	87.8	91.9	98.6	104.7	105.4	106.7	110.7
Education...	27.8	49.4	69.3	91.3	110.9	116.6	119.3	122.3
Higher education...	24.9	47.2	67.6	90.8	111.8	117.1	119.7	123.1
Net foreign travel and expenditures abroad by U.S. residents:								
Foreign travel by U.S. residents....................	48.8	60.1	78.7	94.6	98.2	96.1	98.7	99.1
Less: Expenditures in the United States by nonresidents............	54.2	70.5	80.4	92.4	102.5	105.3	107.7	109.7

[1] Consists of household purchases of goods and services from business, government, nonprofit institutions, and the rest of the world. [2] Consists of shoes and other footwear, and of repair and hire of footwear. [3] Consists of rent for space (see footnote 4) and rent for appliances, furnishings, and furniture. [4] Consists of rent for space and for heating and plumbing facilities, water heaters, lighting fixtures, kitchen cabinets, linoleum, storm windows and doors, window screens, and screen doors, but excludes rent for appliances and furniture and purchases of fuel and electricity. [5] Includes clocks, lamps, lighting fixtures, and other household decorative items; also includes repair of furniture, furnishings, and floor coverings. [6] Consists of major household appliances, small electric household appliances, and repair of household appliances. [7] Consists of dishes, flatware, and non-electric cookware and tableware. [8] Excludes drug preparations and related products dispensed by physicians, hospitals, and other medical services. [9] Consists of offices of physicians, health maintenance organization medical centers, and freestanding ambulatory surgical and emergency centers. [10] Consists of nonprofit hospitals, proprietary hospitals, and government hospitals. Consists of primary sales of these hospitals for personal consumption. [11] Includes railway transportation, taxicab services, school and employee services, limousine services, and airport bus fares.

Source: U.S. Bureau of Economic Analysis, National Income and Product Accounts Tables, "Table 2.5.4. Price Indexes for Personal Consumption Expenditures by Function," <https://apps.bea.gov/iTable/index_nipa.cfm>, accessed July 2020.

Table 774. Chain-Type Price Indexes for Gross Domestic Product: 1990 to 2019

[2012=100. For explanation of "chain-type," see text, Section 13]

Component	1990	2000	2005	2010	2014	2015	2016	2017	2018	2019
Gross domestic product	**63.7**	**78.1**	**87.4**	**96.1**	**103.6**	**104.6**	**105.7**	**107.8**	**110.3**	**112.3**
Personal consumption expenditures	**63.4**	**78.2**	**86.8**	**95.7**	**102.8**	**103.0**	**104.1**	**106.0**	**108.2**	**109.9**
Goods	81.9	89.1	91.1	95.2	98.9	95.9	94.3	94.6	95.2	94.8
Durable goods	131.9	125.7	112.3	102.1	95.4	93.4	91.1	89.0	87.5	86.5
Nondurable goods	63.1	74.0	82.0	92.2	100.6	97.1	95.9	97.4	99.3	99.2
Services	54.8	72.9	84.7	96.0	104.8	106.7	109.2	111.9	115.0	117.7
Gross private domestic investment	**81.3**	**86.8**	**94.8**	**97.7**	**102.9**	**103.5**	**103.5**	**105.2**	**107.2**	**109.0**
Fixed investment	80.3	86.5	94.6	97.6	103.2	104.1	104.2	106.0	108.0	109.8
Nonresidential	92.5	92.7	94.4	97.4	101.5	101.9	101.1	102.0	102.9	104.3
Structures	40.9	55.3	75.7	92.0	107.2	109.4	109.8	112.7	114.6	118.7
Equipment	135.0	114.2	104.6	99.5	99.2	98.7	97.6	97.6	97.7	97.9
Intellectual property products	88.1	97.8	96.0	98.3	100.8	101.4	100.2	101.1	102.4	103.7
Residential	56.3	75.0	96.7	98.3	111.0	114.1	118.1	123.5	130.5	134.2
Net exports of goods and services:										
Exports	79.7	79.5	85.1	93.3	100.3	95.4	93.5	95.9	99.2	98.8
Goods	85.7	80.0	84.9	93.0	98.3	91.3	87.7	90.0	93.3	91.8
Services	65.7	78.2	85.6	94.2	104.7	104.6	106.4	109.2	112.5	114.4
Imports	79.2	76.2	83.7	92.8	97.9	90.0	86.9	88.8	91.3	90.0
Goods	83.1	76.6	83.2	92.1	96.7	87.6	83.9	85.7	88.2	86.4
Services	63.7	74.3	86.7	96.4	103.6	102.5	102.4	104.5	107.7	108.8
Government consumption expenditures and gross investment	**52.1**	**68.6**	**82.1**	**95.4**	**104.4**	**104.6**	**104.9**	**107.4**	**111.3**	**113.4**
Federal	57.3	72.9	86.2	96.4	102.6	103.1	103.7	105.8	109.1	111.1
National defense	57.2	71.9	86.0	96.1	102.1	102.3	102.7	104.4	107.5	109.3
Nondefense	57.1	74.6	86.5	96.9	103.6	104.4	105.3	108.0	111.6	114.0
State and local	49.2	66.0	79.6	94.7	105.6	105.6	105.8	108.5	112.8	115.0

Source: U.S. Bureau of Economic Analysis, National Income and Product Accounts Tables, "Table 1.1.4. Price Indexes for Gross Domestic Product," <https://apps.bea.gov/iTable/index_nipa.cfm>, accessed July 2020.

Table 775. Import and Export Price Indexes by End-Use Category: 1990 to 2020

[As of June. Import indexes are weighted by the 2000 Tariff Schedule of the United States Annotated, a scheme for describing and reporting product composition and value of U.S. imports. Import prices are based on U.S. dollar prices paid by importer. Export indexes are weighted by 2000 export values according to the Schedule B classification system of the U.S. Census Bureau. Prices used in these indexes were collected from a sample of U.S. manufacturers of exports and are factory transaction prices, except as noted. Minus sign (-) indicates decrease]

	Index (2000 = 100)						Percent change [1]					
	Imports			Exports			Imports			Exports		
Year	Total	Petroleum imports	Non–petroleum imports	Total	Agricultural exports	Non–agricultural exports	Total	Petroleum imports	Non–petroleum imports	Total	Agricultural exports	Non–agricultural exports
1990	90.8	55.4	96.4	95.1	107.7	93.5	-0.8	-13.4	0.5	-0.1	-4.0	0.5
1991	93.4	63.2	98.3	96.1	104.3	95.3	2.9	14.1	2.0	1.1	-3.2	1.9
1992	94.8	66.0	99.5	96.5	104.0	95.8	1.5	4.4	1.2	0.4	-0.3	0.5
1993	95.0	60.4	100.5	96.9	100.3	96.7	0.2	-8.5	1.0	0.4	-3.6	0.9
1994	96.3	57.6	102.6	98.5	109.3	97.5	1.4	-4.6	2.1	1.7	9.0	0.8
1995	101.4	62.9	107.6	104.5	117.0	103.3	5.3	9.2	4.9	6.1	7.0	5.9
1996	100.7	66.4	106.2	105.4	140.8	101.7	-0.7	5.6	-1.3	0.9	20.3	-1.5
1997	98.8	62.5	104.3	103.2	120.5	101.5	-1.9	-5.9	-1.8	-2.1	-14.4	-0.2
1998	93.1	44.3	100.5	99.9	110.8	98.8	-5.8	-29.1	-3.6	-3.2	-8.0	-2.7
1999	92.9	54.5	98.8	98.2	101.1	97.9	-0.2	23.0	-1.7	-1.7	-8.8	-0.9
2000 [2]	100.2	101.9	99.9	100.1	100.5	100.0	7.9	87.0	1.1	1.9	-0.6	2.1
2001	97.6	89.4	98.9	99.4	100.9	99.3	-2.6	-12.3	-1.0	-0.7	0.4	-0.7
2002	94.1	85.3	96.2	98.0	100.7	97.8	-3.6	-4.6	-2.7	-1.4	-0.2	-1.5
2003	96.2	96.4	97.3	99.5	110.0	98.7	2.2	13.0	1.1	1.5	9.2	0.9
2004	101.7	129.7	99.7	103.4	127.4	101.5	5.7	34.5	2.5	3.9	15.8	2.8
2005	109.2	181.5	102.0	106.7	123.9	105.4	7.4	39.9	2.3	3.2	-2.7	3.8
2006	117.3	242.6	104.2	111.2	124.1	110.3	7.4	33.7	2.2	4.2	0.2	4.6
2007	120.0	245.6	107.1	116.0	146.7	113.8	2.3	1.2	2.8	4.3	18.2	3.2
2008	145.5	450.3	114.9	126.1	195.2	121.2	21.3	83.3	7.3	8.7	33.1	6.5
2009	120.0	241.5	107.4	117.8	169.7	114.1	-17.5	-46.4	-6.5	-6.6	-13.1	-5.9
2010	125.2	267.4	110.7	122.2	165.3	119.1	4.3	10.7	3.1	3.7	-2.6	4.4
2011	142.2	397.8	116.4	134.5	217.2	128.6	13.6	48.8	5.1	10.1	31.4	8.0
2012	138.7	357.2	116.3	131.7	204.5	126.5	-2.5	-10.2	-0.1	-2.1	-5.8	-1.6
2013	138.8	364.9	115.7	132.8	224.2	126.2	0.1	2.2	-0.5	0.8	9.6	-0.2
2014	140.5	387.9	115.8	133.0	221.4	126.6	1.2	6.3	0.1	0.2	-1.2	0.3
2015	126.6	229.7	112.8	125.3	184.3	120.9	-9.9	-40.8	-2.6	-5.8	-16.8	-4.5
2016	120.7	173.1	110.5	120.9	181.9	116.3	-4.7	-24.6	-2.0	-3.5	-1.3	-3.8
2017	122.4	178.7	112.0	121.6	174.9	117.5	1.4	3.2	1.4	0.6	-3.8	1.0
2018	128.2	255.4	113.5	128.0	184.2	123.7	4.7	42.9	1.3	5.3	5.3	5.3
2019	125.6	236.6	112.0	126.0	180.5	121.8	-2.0	-7.4	-1.3	-1.6	-2.0	-1.5
2020	120.8	145.3	112.0	120.5	172.3	116.5	-3.8	-38.6	0.0	-4.4	-4.5	-4.4

[1] Percent change from immediate prior year. [2] June 2000 may not equal 100 because indexes were reweighted to an "average" trade value in 2000.

Source: U.S. Bureau of Labor Statistics, U.S. Import and Export Price Indexes, "History Tables: Complete Historical Index Information," <http://www.bls.gov/mxp/>, accessed July 2020.

Table 776. Export Price Indexes—Selected Commodities: 2000 to 2020

[2000=100. As of June. Indexes are weighted by 2000 export values according to the Schedule B commodity classification system of the U.S. Census Bureau. Prices used in these indexes were collected from a sample of U.S. manufacturers of exports and are factory transaction prices; see source]

Commodity	2000 [1]	2005	2010	2015	2017	2018	2019	2020
All commodities	**100.1**	**106.7**	**122.2**	**125.3**	**121.6**	**128.0**	**126.0**	**120.5**
Live animals and animal products	102.2	130.9	172.2	193.5	207.2	208.0	217.8	209.7
Vegetable products	100.0	130.3	177.5	206.1	187.1	203.5	199.1	184.4
Fruit and nuts	94.8	126.5	131.0	175.1	133.2	142.6	139.9	122.2
Cereals	100.0	118.1	171.4	194.4	177.4	203.0	205.7	182.4
Wheat and meslin	99.4	130.0	151.6	198.3	169.9	206.1	197.0	196.6
Corn (maize)	101.0	111.8	174.3	181.1	175.6	192.0	204.7	164.3
Oilseeds	102.8	136.2	196.2	204.7	190.4	212.3	186.9	184.9
Prepared foodstuffs, beverages, and tobacco	100.0	110.3	139.3	153.2	147.7	153.3	153.5	151.3
Mineral products	97.8	182.3	247.9	211.3	190.8	245.8	217.0	150.0
Fuels	97.4	172.8	239.2	205.0	182.4	237.0	208.5	141.5
Petroleum oils	97.4	184.8	231.5	228.8	181.2	244.4	217.2	142.5
Chemicals and related products	100.3	115.3	144.5	143.9	132.7	139.2	138.6	134.2
Plastics and rubber products	101.5	118.4	136.8	143.0	137.1	145.0	143.9	136.6
Woodpulp and paper products	101.6	101.9	117.6	123.7	128.0	133.8	124.5	123.1
Textiles	100.2	100.8	115.7	122.2	120.2	126.0	121.4	117.4
Stone and glass products	100.7	103.5	115.9	122.4	122.7	124.2	127.5	126.2
Gems and precious metals	98.1	106.5	211.0	233.8	233.4	238.7	245.3	275.2
Base metals	100.5	131.8	160.4	153.1	151.3	165.1	158.5	151.4
Iron and steel	101.7	164.0	194.3	165.5	153.6	(NA)	(NA)	(NA)
Copper	98.7	143.1	217.0	191.3	167.6	205.5	178.6	165.3
Aluminum	98.4	113.2	117.8	115.5	111.3	123.8	104.1	91.1
Machinery	99.9	94.9	95.5	97.1	96.1	97.6	98.0	97.9
Nonelectrical machinery	100.0	100.5	106.8	113.5	113.8	115.1	116.3	115.8
Computer equipment	99.9	76.6	53.1	43.8	37.7	36.8	35.5	33.7
Electrical machinery	99.8	88.6	83.2	79.3	77.0	78.7	78.3	78.7
Transportation equipment	100.0	108.8	121.4	130.8	132.7	135.2	137.2	137.9
Motor vehicles and their parts	100.0	103.2	108.5	115.0	115.1	116.3	116.7	116.5
Instruments	100.0	101.3	106.2	107.8	106.3	109.5	110.0	110.3
Miscellaneous manufactured articles	100.4	100.6	108.1	111.3	112.4	112.1	112.9	114.1

NA Not available. [1] June 2000 may not equal 100 because indexes were reweighted to an "average" trade value in 2000.

Source: U.S. Bureau of Labor Statistics, U.S. Import and Export Price Indexes, "History Tables: Complete Historical Index Information," <http://www.bls.gov/mxp/>, accessed July 2020.

Table 777. Import Price Indexes—Selected Commodities: 2000 to 2020

[2000=100. As of June. Indexes are weighted by the 2000 Tariff Schedule of the United States Annotated, a scheme for describing and reporting product composition and value of U.S. imports. Import prices are based on U.S. dollar prices paid by importer]

Commodity	2000 [1]	2005	2010	2015	2017	2018	2019	2020
All commodities	**100.2**	**109.2**	**125.2**	**126.6**	**122.4**	**128.2**	**125.6**	**120.8**
Live animals and animal products	99.9	112.7	143.0	185.2	198.2	192.4	195.7	198.5
Meat	100.5	138.7	183.2	234.5	254.9	248.3	265.8	323.3
Fish	100.2	88.3	107.1	127.3	143.9	138.5	139.6	128.0
Vegetable products	97.1	116.9	169.5	201.8	222.6	201.4	215.1	213.5
Vegetables	93.9	136.8	326.2	459.9	467.6	357.4	506.8	482.7
Fruit and nuts	96.9	89.7	106.8	95.5	134.7	124.0	124.5	114.2
Prepared foodstuffs, beverages and tobacco	100.0	114.0	141.2	160.7	160.7	167.1	165.3	167.4
Mineral products	101.3	178.1	248.5	210.9	166.6	230.5	215.4	140.3
Fuels	101.3	177.5	244.9	208.1	163.8	228.6	212.7	135.7
Chemicals and related products	99.8	111.3	139.3	148.3	152.0	158.2	156.1	153.5
Organic chemicals	100.6	109.6	133.8	123.7	123.6	133.6	127.5	119.8
Pharmaceutical products	99.8	111.0	117.9	136.7	149.2	151.6	152.3	154.5
Plastics and rubber products	99.9	113.5	136.7	142.1	139.4	141.4	140.9	138.2
Hides, skins, and leather products	100.2	104.0	114.5	128.1	123.6	125.8	124.6	126.6
Wood products	100.5	124.2	134.3	138.6	154.3	180.3	143.5	152.8
Woodpulp and paper products	100.0	102.3	112.5	111.9	110.5	117.9	120.2	112.8
Textiles	99.7	100.4	103.1	114.5	113.1	114.3	114.2	114.3
Footwear	99.6	100.3	106.1	122.3	121.4	121.1	121.3	122.6
Stone and glass products	99.5	105.4	123.8	132.8	130.0	132.3	132.1	131.8
Gems and precious metals	99.3	98.3	161.5	170.8	170.6	174.2	177.6	200.0
Gold	98.3	150.7	430.5	424.4	458.8	464.3	476.6	613.4
Base metals	101.5	132.1	180.2	168.1	166.9	185.3	174.3	164.1
Iron and steel	104.1	170.6	238.8	181.6	196.5	231.5	216.9	187.9
Articles of iron and steel	100.6	122.7	149.9	148.2	144.0	153.1	149.8	145.9
Copper	97.2	142.7	313.8	299.8	266.1	316.2	271.5	263.2
Aluminum	97.9	113.2	132.8	131.5	128.4	144.0	130.6	120.3
Machinery	100.2	89.7	86.5	82.5	80.4	80.5	79.3	79.1
Nonelectrical machinery	99.8	90.1	87.9	87.7	85.8	86.9	85.5	84.8
Electrical machinery	100.5	89.4	85.2	77.6	75.3	74.6	73.5	73.6
Transportation equipment	100.0	104.4	109.7	114.6	114.1	114.3	113.5	114.3
Motor vehicles and their parts	100.1	103.8	108.8	113.2	113.1	113.3	112.6	113.5
Instruments	99.8	100.1	100.8	103.7	101.4	102.5	101.6	102.1
Miscellaneous manufactured articles	99.7	99.4	106.5	112.8	110.9	112.3	112.2	110.9
Furniture	99.5	103.4	109.4	117.3	116.4	118.1	118.3	116.5

[1] June 2000 may not equal 100 because indexes were reweighted to an "average" trade value in 2000.

Source: U.S. Bureau of Labor Statistics, U.S. Import and Export Price Indexes, "History Tables: Complete Historical Index Information," <http://www.bls.gov/mxp/>, accessed July 2020.

Section 15
Business Enterprise

This section relates to the place and behavior of the business firm and to business initiative in the American economy. It includes data on the number, type, and size of businesses; financial data of domestic and multinational U.S. corporations; business investments, expenditures, and profits; and sales and inventories.

The principal sources of these data are the *Survey of Current Business*, published online by the Bureau of Economic Analysis (BEA); the web site of the Board of Governors of the Federal Reserve System at <federalreserve.gov/data.htm>; the annual *Statistics of Income (SOI)* reports of the Internal Revenue Service (IRS); and the U.S. Census Bureau's Economic Census, *County Business Patterns, Quarterly Financial Report for Manufacturing, Mining, and Trade Corporations (QFR), the Annual Capital Expenditures Survey*, and beginning in 2019, the *Annual Business Survey*. See also BEA Interactive Tables <bea.gov/iTable/index.cfm>.

Business firms—A firm is generally defined as a business organization or entity consisting of one or more domestic establishment locations under common ownership or control. The terms firm, business, company, and enterprise are used interchangeably throughout this section. A firm doing business in more than one industry is classified by industry according to the major activity of the firm as a whole.

The IRS concept of a business firm relates primarily to the legal entity used for tax reporting purposes. A sole proprietorship is an unincorporated business owned by one person and may include large enterprises with many employees and hired managers and part-time operators. A partnership is an unincorporated business owned by two or more persons, each of whom has a financial interest in the business. A corporation is a business that is legally incorporated under state laws. While many corporations file consolidated tax returns, most corporate tax returns represent individual corporations, some of which are affiliated through common ownership or control with other corporations filing separate returns.

Economic Census—The Economic Census is the major source of facts about the structure and functioning of the nation's economy. It provides essential information for government, business, industry, and the general public. It establishes benchmarks for economic indicators such as the gross domestic product estimates, production and price indexes, business sales, and other statistical series that measure short-term changes in economic conditions. The Census Bureau takes the Economic Census every 5 years, covering years ending in "2" and "7."

The Economic Census is collected on an establishment basis. A company operating at more than one location is required to file a separate report for each store, factory, shop, or other location. Companies engaged in distinctly different lines of activity at one location are requested to submit separate reports, if the business records permit such a separation, and if the activities are substantial in size. Each establishment is assigned a separate industry classification based on

its primary activity and not that of its parent company. Establishments responding to the establishment survey are classified into industries on the basis of their principal product or activity (determined by self-reporting, annual sales volume, or products manufactured by a plant). The statistics issued by industry in the 2017 Economic Census are classified primarily on the 2017 North American Industry Classification System (NAICS).

Data from the 2017 Economic Census are being released on a flow basis between September 2019 and December 2021 via the Census Bureau's dissemination platform at <data.census.gov>. The American FactFinder® service was discontinued in 2020. More detailed information about the scope, coverage, methodology, classification system, data items, and publications for the Economic Censuses and related surveys is available at <census.gov/programs-surveys/economic-census.html>.

Annual Business Survey—The Annual Business Survey replaces the five-year *Survey of Business Owners (SBO)* for employer businesses, the *Annual Survey of Entrepreneurs (ASE)*, the *Business R&D and Innovation for Microbusinesses survey (BRDI-M)*, and the innovation section of the *Business R&D and Innovation Survey (BRDI-S)*. It is collected on an company or firm basis, not an establishment basis, and provides information on selected economic and demographic characteristics for businesses and business owners by sex, ethnicity, race, and veteran status. Data are published in a series of releases: *Characteristics of Businesses, Characteristics of Business Owners, Company Summary*, and a variable module designed to capture information on relevant business components.

North American Industry Classification System (NAICS)—NAICS is the standard used by federal statistical agencies in classifying business establishments for the purpose of collecting, analyzing, and publishing statistical data related to the U.S. business economy. NAICS was developed under the auspices of the Office of Management and Budget (OMB), and adopted in 1997 to replace the Standard Industrial Classification (SIC) system. The official *2017 NAICS Manual* includes definitions for each industry, background information, tables showing changes between the 2012 and 2017 revisions, and a comprehensive index. Noticeable changes were made to six of the twenty NAICS sectors during the 2012 revision of NAICS. Those sectors are 22 (utilities), 23 (construction), 31-33 (manufacturing), 42 (wholesale trade), 44-45 (retail trade) and 72 (accommodation and food services). The 2017 revision impacted 28 of the 2012 NAICS 6-digit industries. For more information, see <census.gov/eos/www/naics/>.

Quarterly Financial Report—The Quarterly Financial Report (QFR) program publishes quarterly aggregate statistics on the financial conditions of U.S. corporations. The QFR requests companies to report estimates from their statements of income and retained earnings, and balance sheets. The statistical data are classified and aggregated by type of industry and asset size. The QFR sample includes corporations that have a plurality of business activity in manufacturing industries with domestic assets of $250,000 and above, and mining, wholesale, retail, and selected service industries with assets of $50 million and above. The data are available in the *Quarterly Financial Report for Manufacturing, Mining, Trade, and Selected Service Industries* at <census.gov/econ/qfr/>.

Multinational enterprises—BEA collects financial and operating data on U.S. multinational enterprises. These data provide a picture of the overall activities of foreign affiliates and U.S. parent enterprises, using a variety of indicators of their financial structure and operations. The data on foreign affiliates cover the entire operations of the affiliate, irrespective of the percentage of U.S. ownership. These data cover items such as sales, value added, employment and compensation of employees, capital expenditures, exports and imports, and research and development expenditures. Separate tabulations are available for all affiliates and for affiliates that are majority-owned by their U.S. parent(s). More information is available at <bea.gov/international/index.htm#omc>.

Statistical reliability—For a discussion of statistical collection, estimation, and sampling procedures and measures of reliability applicable to data from the Census Bureau and the Internal Revenue Service, see Appendix III.

Table 778. Number of Tax Returns, Receipts, and Net Income by Type of Business: 1990 to 2017

[14,783 represents 14,783,000. Covers active enterprises only. Nonfarm sole proprietorship and partnership data are for tax year shown, which covers returns processed by the IRS during the following calendar year. Corporation data are for tax year shown, which covers (a) corporate returns with accounting periods for the calendar year ending December of year shown and (b) those returns with accounting periods for the noncalendar year ending between July of year shown and June of the following year. Figures are estimates based on sample of unaudited tax returns]

Year	Number of returns (1,000)			Business receipts [2] (bil. dol.)			Net income (less loss) [3] (bil. dol.)		
	Nonfarm proprietor- ships [1]	Partner- ships	Corpora- tions	Nonfarm proprietor- ships [1]	Partner- ships	Corpora- tions	Nonfarm proprietor- ships [1]	Partner- ships	Corpora- tions
1990...........	14,783	1,554	3,717	731	483	9,860	141	17	383
1991...........	15,181	1,515	3,803	713	483	9,966	142	21	361
1992...........	15,495	1,485	3,869	737	515	10,360	154	43	414
1993...........	15,848	1,468	3,965	757	561	10,866	156	67	510
1994...........	16,154	1,494	4,342	791	656	11,884	167	82	595
1995...........	16,424	1,581	4,474	807	761	12,786	169	107	736
1996...........	16,955	1,654	4,631	843	916	13,659	177	145	839
1997...........	17,176	1,759	4,710	870	1,142	14,461	187	168	957
1998...........	17,409	1,855	4,849	918	1,357	15,010	202	187	895
1999...........	17,576	1,937	4,936	969	1,616	16,314	208	228	985
2000...........	17,903	2,058	5,045	1,021	2,062	17,637	215	269	987
2001...........	18,338	2,132	5,136	1,017	2,278	17,504	217	276	649
2002...........	18,926	2,242	5,267	1,030	2,414	17,297	221	271	597
2003...........	19,710	2,375	5,401	1,050	2,546	18,264	230	301	822
2004...........	20,591	2,547	5,558	1,140	2,819	19,976	248	385	1,170
2005...........	21,468	2,764	5,671	1,223	3,280	21,800	270	546	2,027
2006...........	22,075	2,947	5,841	1,278	3,571	23,310	278	667	2,024
2007...........	23,123	3,096	5,869	1,324	3,847	24,217	281	683	1,950
2008...........	22,614	3,146	5,847	1,317	4,344	24,718	265	458	1,061
2009...........	22,660	3,169	5,825	1,178	3,562	21,585	245	410	971
2010...........	23,004	3,248	5,814	1,196	3,946	23,058	268	594	1,422
2011...........	23,427	3,285	5,823	1,266	4,455	25,198	283	581	1,406
2012...........	23,554	3,389	5,841	1,302	4,690	26,029	305	778	1,872
2013...........	24,075	3,461	5,888	1,342	5,069	26,850	302	769	1,994
2014...........	24,632	3,611	6,001	1,394	5,186	28,075	317	837	2,145
2015...........	25,226	3,715	6,120	1,444	4,877	27,492	332	781	2,034
2016...........	25,526	3,763	6,189	1,422	4,919	27,575	328	792	1,913
2017...........	26,426	3,905	(NA)	1,531	5,460	(NA)	346	810	(NA)

NA Not available. [1] Number of returns represents returns with nonfarm business net income or deficit. [2] Excludes investment income for S corporations; for definition, see footnote 1, Table 787. [3] Net income (less loss) is defined differently by form of organization, basically as follows: (a) Proprietorships: Total taxable receipts less total business deductions, including cost of sales and operations, depletion, and certain capital expensing, excluding charitable contributions and owners' salaries; (b) Partnerships: Total taxable receipts (including investment income except capital gains) less deductions, including cost of sales and operations and certain payments to partners, excluding charitable contributions, oil and gas depletion, and certain capital expensing; and (c) Corporations: Includes "Total net income (less deficit)" from S Corporations; net income is before income tax.

Source: U.S. Internal Revenue Service, "Tax Statistics," <https://www.irs.gov/statistics>, accessed September 2020.

Table 779. Number of Business Tax Returns by Size of Receipts: 2000 to 2017

[In thousands (5,045 represents 5,045,000). Covers active enterprises only. Figures are estimates based on sample of unaudited tax returns]

Size-class of receipts	2000	2005	2010	2011	2012	2013	2014	2015	2016	2017
Corporations, total...............	**5,045**	**5,671**	**5,814**	**5,823**	**5,841**	**5,888**	**6,001**	**6,120**	**6,189**	**(NA)**
Under $25,000 [1].....................	1,220	1,300	1,484	1,449	1,409	1,419	1,419	1,442	1,437	(NA)
$25,000 to $100,000...............	783	884	977	961	952	922	953	974	969	(NA)
$25,000 to $49,999...............	305	340	385	379	396	(NA)	(NA)	(NA)	(NA)	(NA)
$50,000 to $99,999...............	477	544	592	582	556	(NA)	(NA)	(NA)	(NA)	(NA)
$100,000 to $499,999...............	1,515	1,755	1,731	1,743	1,761	1,800	1,810	1,821	1,856	(NA)
$500,000 to $999,999...............	582	644	618	624	646	644	670	707	719	(NA)
$1,000,000 or more.................	946	1,088	1,005	1,047	1,073	1,103	1,151	1,176	1,207	(NA)
Partnerships, total...............	**2,058**	**2,764**	**3,249**	**3,285**	**3,389**	**3,461**	**3,611**	**3,715**	**3,763**	**3,905**
Under $25,000 [1].....................	1,105	1,465	1,788	1,774	1,815	1,845	1,951	2,031	1,993	(NA)
$25,000 to $49,999...............	183	218	238	254	272	297	267	275	345	(NA)
$50,000 to $99,999...............	187	233	289	289	293	274	316	293	278	(NA)
$100,000 to $499,999...............	353	489	531	556	565	580	590	621	645	(NA)
$500,000 to $999,999...............	92	131	151	150	164	171	175	171	171	(NA)
$1,000,000 or more.................	137	227	252	262	280	294	312	325	331	1,047
Nonfarm proprietorships, total..................................	**17,903**	**21,468**	**23,004**	**23,427**	**23,554**	**24,075**	**24,632**	**25,226**	**25,526**	**26,426**
Under $25,000 [1].....................	11,997	14,456	16,258	16,468	16,450	16,843	17,181	17,528	17,718	18,066
$25,000 to $49,999...............	2,247	2,587	2,652	2,740	2,838	2,816	2,886	2,991	3,080	3,306
$50,000 to $99,999...............	1,645	1,981	1,892	1,869	1,899	1,969	2,034	2,107	2,215	2,333
$100,000 to $499,999...............	1,733	2,091	1,869	2,002	1,999	2,067	2,130	2,181	2,087	2,273
$500,000 to $999,999...............	190	235	219	222	234	239	251	265	271	279
$1,000,000 or more.................	92	117	114	126	134	140	150	154	155	170

NA Not available. [1] Includes firms with no receipts.

Source: U.S. Internal Revenue Service, Statistics of Income (SOI), "SOI Tax Stats - Historical Data Tables," <https://www.irs.gov/statistics/soi-tax-stats-historical-data-tables>; "SOI Tax Stats - Corporation Complete Report," <https://www.irs.gov/statistics/soi-tax-stats-corporation-complete-report>; and SOI Bulletin: Spring 2020, <https://www.irs.gov/statistics/soi-tax-stats-soi-bulletins>; accessed September 2020.

Table 780. Number of Tax Returns, Receipts, and Net Income by Type of Business and Industry: 2017

[Tax returns in thousands (26,426 represents 26,426,000); receipts and income in billions of dollars (1,531 represents $1,531,000,000,000). Covers active enterprises only. Nonfarm sole proprietorship and partnership data are for tax year shown, which covers returns processed by the IRS during 2018. Figures are estimates based on sample of unaudited tax returns. Based on the North American Industry Classification System (NAICS); see text, this section. Minus sign (-) indicates net loss]

Industry	NAICS code	Number of returns (1,000)		Business receipts [1] (bil. dol.)		Net income (less loss) [2] (bil. dol.)	
		Non-farm propri-etor-ships	Part-ner-ships	Non-farm propri-etor-ships	Part-ner-ships	Non-farm propri-etor-ships	Part-ner-ships
Total..........	(X)	**26,426**	**3,905**	**1,531**	**5,460**	**346**	**810**
Agriculture, forestry, fishing, and hunting...............	11	309	145	23	37	2	-2
Mining..........	21	113	53	10	161	1	37
Utilities..........	22	13	5	1	187	(Z)	-23
Construction..........	23	2,832	176	266	364	44	18
Special trade contractors..........	238	2,207	(NA)	183	(NA)	33	(NA)
Manufacturing..........	31–33	402	73	35	896	4	35
Wholesale trade..........	42	334	63	50	697	5	14
Retail trade [3]..........	44–45	2,434	192	181	589	10	10
Motor vehicle and parts dealers..........	441	144	(NA)	39	(NA)	1	(NA)
Food and beverage stores..........	445	95	(NA)	24	(NA)	1	(NA)
Gasoline stations..........	447	11	(NA)	17	(NA)	(Z)	(NA)
Transportation and warehousing..........	48–49	2,354	39	119	240	17	4
Information..........	51	385	50	14	399	3	46
Finance and insurance..........	52	660	379	84	296	23	422
Real estate and rental and leasing..........	53	1,352	1,934	93	209	33	89
Professional, scientific, and technical services [3]......	54	3,536	266	200	521	83	98
Legal services..........	5411	372	(NA)	44	(NA)	18	(NA)
Management, scientific, and technical consulting services..........	5416	1,001	(NA)	56	(NA)	29	(NA)
Management of companies and enterprises..........	55	6	26	(Z)	23	(Z)	15
Administrative and support and waste management and remediation services..........	56	2,602	72	84	126	24	7
Educational services..........	61	857	122	14	53	5	3
Health care and social assistance..........	62	2,131	86	122	320	47	36
Arts, entertainment, and recreation..........	71	1,696	58	49	92	11	(Z)
Accommodation and food services..........	72	553	164	69	251	3	(Z)
Other services [3]..........	81	3,430	(NA)	113	(NA)	30	(NA)
Auto repair and maintenance..........	8111	403	(NA)	27	(NA)	3	(NA)
Personal and laundry services..........	812	2,375	(NA)	65	(NA)	21	(NA)
Religious, grantmaking, civic, professional, and similar organizations..........	813	263	(NA)	4	(NA)	2	(NA)
Unclassified..........	(X)	434	–	4	–	1	–

– Represents zero. NA Not available. X Not applicable. Z Less than 500 or $500 million. [1] Excludes investment income for S corporations; for definition, see footnote 1, Table 787. [2] Net income (less loss) is defined differently by form of organization, basically as follows: (a) Proprietorships: Total taxable receipts less total business deductions, including cost of sales and operations, depletion, and certain capital expensing, excluding charitable contributions and owners' salaries; (b) Partnerships: Total taxable receipts (including investment income except capital gains) less deductions, including cost of sales and operations and certain payments to partners, excluding charitable contributions, oil and gas depletion, and certain capital expensing; and (c) Corporations: Total taxable receipts (including investment income, capital gains, and income from foreign subsidiaries deemed received for tax purposes, except for S corporations) less business deductions, including cost of sales and operations, depletion, certain capital expensing, and officers' compensation excluding S corporation charitable contributions and investment expenses; net income is before income tax. [3] Includes other industries, not shown separately.

Source: U.S. Internal Revenue Service, "SOI Tax Stats - Business Tax Statistics," <http://www.irs.gov/uac/SOI-Tax-Stats-Business-Tax-Statistics>, accessed September 2020.

Table 781. Nonfarm Sole Proprietorships—Selected Income and Deduction Items: 2000 to 2017

[In billions of dollars (1,021 represents $1,021,000,000,000), except as indicated. Data are for tax year shown which covers returns processed by the IRS during the following calendar year. All figures are estimates based on samples. Tax law changes have affected the comparability of the data over time; see Statistics of Income reports for a description]

Item	2000	2005	2010	2012	2013	2014	2015	2016	2017
Number of returns (1,000)	17,905	21,468	23,004	23,554	24,075	24,632	25,226	25,526	26,426
Returns with net income (1,000)	13,308	15,750	17,007	17,571	17,972	18,294	18,785	18,959	19,434
Business receipts	1,021	1,223	1,196	1,302	1,342	1,394	1,444	1,422	1,531
Income from sales and operations	1,008	1,205	1,176	1,281	1,323	1,375	1,423	1,404	1,511
Business deductions [1]	806	953	929	998	1,040	1,078	1,113	1,095	1,187
Cost of sales and operations [1]	387	397	367	390	406	417	432	411	432
Purchases	269	253	240	251	260	256	265	239	255
Labor costs	29	32	27	31	33	33	37	36	42
Materials and supplies	43	56	45	50	52	57	61	64	65
Advertising	10	14	13	14	15	15	16	16	17
Car and truck expenses	46	71	73	86	89	92	90	89	97
Commissions	12	15	12	14	14	14	17	16	19
Contract labor	(NA)	28	34	42	48	54	54	57	65
Depreciation	32	39	35	34	35	37	38	38	42
Insurance	14	19	16	17	18	19	20	20	21
Interest paid [2]	12	12	11	9	9	9	9	9	10
Legal and professional services	7	10	10	11	12	12	13	13	15
Office expenses	10	13	12	12	12	13	13	13	15
Rent paid [3]	33	39	42	43	45	47	48	48	51
Repairs	12	15	15	17	18	18	19	18	21
Salaries and wages (net)	63	75	74	80	83	87	89	91	97
Supplies	22	29	30	34	35	37	38	39	44
Taxes paid	14	17	18	18	19	19	20	20	21
Travel	8	11	12	13	14	15	17	17	18
Utilities	19	23	24	28	31	32	31	32	33
Net income (less loss) [4]	215	270	268	305	302	317	332	328	346
Net income [4]	245	315	323	357	357	375	392	389	416
Constant (2012) Dollars [5]									
Business receipts	1,247	1,329	1,181	1,237	1,255	1,281	1,312	1,276	1,421
Business deductions	985	1,036	918	948	973	991	1,012	983	1,101
Net income (less loss)	262	293	265	290	283	291	302	295	321
Net income	300	342	319	339	334	344	357	349	386

NA Not available. [1] Includes other amounts not shown separately. [2] Interest paid includes "mortgage interest" and "other interest paid on business indebtedness." [3] Rent paid includes "Rent on machinery and equipment" and "Rent on other business property." [4] After adjustment for the passive loss carryover from prior years. Therefore, "business receipts" minus "total deductions" do not equal "net income." [5] Based on the overall implicit price deflator for gross domestic product.

Source: U.S. Internal Revenue Service, "SOI Tax Stats - Nonfarm Sole Proprietorship Statistics," <http://www.irs.gov/uac/SOI-Tax-Stats-Nonfarm-Sole-Proprietorship-Statistics>, accessed July 2020.

Table 782. Partnerships—Selected Income and Balance Sheet Items: 2000 to 2017

[In billions of dollars (6,694 represents $6,694,000,000,000), except as indicated. Covers active partnerships only. Data are for tax year shown, which covers returns processed by the IRS during the following calendar year. All figures are estimates based on samples]

Item	2000	2005	2010	2012	2013	2014	2015	2016	2017
Number of returns (1,000)	2,058	2,764	3,248	3,389	3,461	3,611	3,715	3,763	3,905
Returns with net income (1,000)	1,261	1,580	1,635	1,869	1,944	2,019	2,152	2,196	2,200
Number of partners (1,000)	13,660	16,212	22,428	25,334	27,491	27,714	27,093	28,164	27,501
Assets [1, 2]	6,694	13,734	19,820	22,015	24,163	26,129	27,366	28,950	32,404
Depreciable assets (net)	1,487	2,176	3,263	3,570	3,798	4,093	4,423	4,751	5,185
Inventories, end of year	150	315	277	304	313	331	343	367	378
Land	359	607	913	957	1,001	1,069	1,143	1,200	1,307
Liabilities [1, 2]	3,696	7,483	8,994	9,277	9,841	10,625	11,019	12,022	13,125
Accounts payable	230	400	492	509	533	537	529	583	618
Short-term debt [3]	252	373	481	326	306	328	351	407	433
Long-term debt [4]	1,132	1,772	2,693	2,706	2,717	2,993	3,222	3,477	3,844
Nonrecourse loans	639	914	1,225	1,212	1,225	1,254	1,270	1,318	1,378
Partners' capital accounts [2]	2,999	6,251	10,826	12,738	14,322	15,504	16,347	16,928	19,279
Total receipts [1]	2,405	3,863	4,721	5,557	5,921	6,100	5,798	5,886	5,950
Business receipts	2,062	3,280	3,946	4,690	5,069	5,186	4,877	4,919	5,460
Deductions from a trade or business [1]	2,136	3,317	4,128	4,779	5,152	5,263	5,018	5,094	5,591
Cost of goods sold/operations	1,226	1,976	2,336	2,828	3,087	3,066	2,696	2,660	3,012
Salaries and wages	201	293	405	463	502	541	578	607	657
Taxes paid	31	47	63	73	79	83	87	89	95
Interest paid	93	103	86	81	78	83	85	97	111
Depreciation [5]	116	140	247	261	288	304	325	352	227
Net income (less loss)	269	546	594	778	769	837	781	792	810
Net income	410	724	904	1,068	1,080	1,156	1,137	1,173	1,278

[1] Includes items not shown separately. [2] Assets, liabilities, and partners' capital accounts are understated because not all partnerships file complete balance sheets. [3] Mortgages, notes, and bonds payable in less than 1 year. [4] Mortgages, notes, and bonds payable in 1 year or more. [5] Represents the more complete amounts reported in depreciation computation schedules, rather than the amounts reported as the depreciation deduction.

Source: U.S. Internal Revenue Service, "SOI Tax Stats - Partnership Statistics," <http://www.irs.gov/uac/SOI-Tax-Stats-Partnership-Statistics>, accessed September 2020.

Table 783. Partnerships—Selected Items by Industry: 2017

[In billions of dollars (32,404 represents $32,404,000,000,000), except as indicated. Covers active partnerships only. Data are for tax year shown, which covers returns processed by the IRS during 2018. Figures are estimates based on samples. Based on the North American Industry Classification System (NAICS), 2012; see text, this section. Minus sign (-) indicates net loss.]

Industry	NAICS code	Partnerships (1,000)			Total assets [1]	Business receipts	Total deduc- tions	Net income less loss	Net income	Net loss
		Total	With net income	With net loss						
Total [2]	(X)	**3,905**	**2,200**	**1,705**	**32,404**	**5,460**	**5,591**	**810**	**1,278**	**468**
Agriculture, forestry, fishing, and hunting	11	145	70	75	256	37	51	-2	11	13
Mining	21	53	29	24	831	161	158	37	56	18
Utilities	22	5	1	4	493	187	219	-23	9	32
Construction	23	176	107	68	270	364	355	18	27	8
Manufacturing	31–33	73	36	38	896	896	893	35	61	26
Wholesale trade	42	63	38	25	389	697	691	14	24	10
Retail trade	44–45	192	89	103	249	589	596	10	19	9
Transportation and warehousing	48–49	39	21	18	857	240	255	4	26	21
Information	51	50	23	27	988	399	381	46	68	22
Finance and insurance	52	379	241	139	17,721	296	409	422	497	75
Real estate and rental and leasing	53	1,934	1,093	841	7,262	209	240	89	236	147
Professional, scientific, and technical services	54	266	159	107	369	521	446	98	118	19
Management of companies and enterprises	55	26	14	13	900	23	47	15	34	20
Administrative and support & waste management and remediation services	56	72	44	28	146	126	134	7	12	5
Educational and other services [3]	61/81	122	75	47	46	320	51	3	6	3
Health care and social assistance	62	86	50	36	224	92	304	36	46	10
Arts, entertainment, and recreation	71	58	24	34	173	251	103	(Z)	11	11
Accommodation and food services	72	164	86	79	334	53	259	(Z)	19	18

X Not applicable. Z Less than $500 million. [1] Total assets are understated because not all partnerships file complete balance sheets. [2] Includes businesses not allocable to individual industries. [3] The educational and other services sectors were combined due to disclosure concerns.

Source: U.S. Internal Revenue Service, "SOI Tax Stats - Partnership Statistics," <http://www.irs.gov/uac/SOI-Tax-Stats-Partnership-Statistics-by-Sector-or-Industry>, accessed July 2020.

Table 784. Nonfinancial Noncorporate Business-Sector Balance Sheet: 2000 to 2019

[In billions of dollars (7,804 represents $7,804,000,000,000), except as noted. Represents year-end (4th quarter) outstandings]

Item	2000	2005	2010	2014	2015	2016	2017	2018	2019
Assets	**7,804**	**12,636**	**12,551**	**16,387**	**17,440**	**18,626**	**19,913**	**20,990**	**22,281**
Nonfinancial assets	6,332	10,039	8,822	11,413	12,068	12,709	13,570	14,119	14,900
Real estate [1]	5,575	9,092	7,680	10,088	10,762	11,424	12,232	12,673	13,209
Residential	3,271	5,738	4,337	5,604	5,999	6,407	6,878	7,270	7,665
Nonresidential	2,310	3,360	3,359	4,496	4,764	4,984	5,325	5,427	5,749
Equipment [2]	447	562	682	788	800	809	834	876	940
Residential [3]	35	42	43	47	48	48	50	56	57
Nonresidential	412	521	639	741	752	761	784	820	883
Intellectual property products [2]	119	160	200	234	244	259	273	285	296
Inventories [2]	185	218	244	291	261	250	260	261	250
Financial assets	1,473	2,597	3,728	4,974	5,372	5,917	6,344	6,871	7,381
Checkable deposits and currency	181	224	182	247	254	279	280	298	334
Time and savings deposits	248	474	706	850	861	909	973	1,053	1,162
Money market fund shares	49	69	77	86	88	91	98	107	114
Debt securities [4]	43	61	54	61	66	68	73	80	86
U.S. government securities	40	56	48	57	62	63	68	74	79
Municipal securities	2	4	6	4	4	5	6	6	6
Loans	23	36	42	34	42	40	43	46	50
Mortgages	23	36	42	34	42	40	43	46	50
Trade receivables	342	431	533	669	663	738	795	866	927
Miscellaneous assets	587	1,302	2,135	3,027	3,398	3,793	4,082	4,421	4,708
Insurance receivables	77	99	132	129	119	116	120	119	129
Equity in Farm Credit System	3	4	7	9	9	10	12	12	13
Other	506	1,198	1,996	2,889	3,270	3,666	3,950	4,289	4,566
Liabilities	**2,799**	**4,182**	**5,674**	**6,454**	**6,713**	**7,379**	**7,813**	**8,336**	**8,822**
Loans	1,912	2,898	3,951	4,446	4,692	5,078	5,339	5,664	5,941
Depository institution loans n.e.c. [5]	402	671	928	1,078	1,142	1,258	1,303	1,400	1,426
Other loans and advances	129	135	171	196	200	203	206	215	224
Mortgages	1,381	2,093	2,853	3,172	3,350	3,618	3,829	4,049	4,292
Trade payables	267	335	428	537	521	587	660	745	822
Taxes payable	65	87	99	117	123	133	140	150	158
U.S. real estate owned by foreigners	6	5	6	14	17	20	28	28	34
Miscellaneous liabilities	549	858	1,189	1,339	1,360	1,561	1,645	1,749	1,867
Net worth	**5,005**	**8,454**	**6,877**	**9,934**	**10,727**	**11,247**	**12,101**	**12,654**	**13,458**
Debt/net worth (percent)	38.2	34.3	57.5	44.8	43.7	45.2	44.1	44.8	44.1

[1] At market value. [2] At replacement (current) cost. [3] Durable goods in rental properties. [4] Includes other items not shown separately. [5] Not elsewhere classified.

Source: Board of Governors of the Federal Reserve System, "Z.1, Financial Accounts of the United States," March 2020, <http://www.federalreserve.gov/releases/z1/>, accessed April 2020.

Table 785. Nonfinancial Corporate Business-Sector Balance Sheet: 2000 to 2019

[In billions of dollars (20,603 represents $20,603,000,000,000). Represents year-end outstandings]

Item	2000	2005	2010	2014	2015	2016	2017	2018	2019
Assets	**20,603**	**26,269**	**27,008**	**34,103**	**36,370**	**38,406**	**40,734**	**42,042**	**45,120**
Nonfinancial assets	10,811	14,317	14,853	19,245	20,394	21,321	22,736	23,468	24,873
Real estate [1]	5,445	8,005	7,316	10,295	11,246	11,875	12,840	13,083	14,069
Equipment [2]	2,889	3,258	3,835	4,486	4,594	4,694	4,872	5,104	5,273
Intellectual property products [2]	1,138	1,435	1,841	2,231	2,305	2,435	2,600	2,733	2,935
Inventories [2]	1,340	1,619	1,860	2,233	2,249	2,316	2,423	2,548	2,596
Financial assets [3]	9,792	11,953	12,155	14,858	15,976	17,086	17,998	18,575	20,246
Checkable deposits and currency	224	327	470	764	814	968	976	1,030	1,231
Money market fund shares	214	359	555	558	577	464	476	466	577
Debt securities	123	213	211	208	212	207	236	239	300
Corporate equities	1,718	1,059	917	1,552	1,498	1,711	1,948	1,784	2,249
Mutual fund shares [1]	118	134	186	242	248	258	303	271	312
Trade receivables	1,939	2,108	2,203	2,720	2,753	2,952	3,114	3,257	3,330
U.S. direct investment abroad	2,378	3,060	3,855	5,290	5,175	5,468	6,684	5,503	6,165
Liabilities [3]	**11,661**	**13,191**	**15,583**	**20,560**	**22,061**	**23,694**	**25,309**	**25,546**	**28,217**
Debt securities	2,698	2,985	3,961	5,138	5,551	5,838	6,159	6,299	6,558
Commercial paper	278	90	83	182	179	181	207	196	195
Municipal securities [4]	154	243	503	523	537	554	567	563	578
Corporate bonds	2,265	2,652	3,375	4,432	4,835	5,104	5,385	5,539	5,785
Loans	1,958	2,263	2,104	2,389	2,530	2,531	2,892	3,355	3,559
Depository institution loans n.e.c. [5]	901	591	482	861	965	969	1,005	1,081	1,103
Other loans and advances	701	904	947	1,126	1,090	1,102	1,388	1,726	1,855
Mortgages	356	768	674	402	475	460	500	549	601
Trade payables	1,541	1,699	1,739	2,080	2,104	2,288	2,370	2,507	2,586
Taxes payable	78	86	78	95	74	66	277	263	237
Foreign direct investment in U.S.	2,329	2,321	2,830	4,546	4,785	5,493	6,553	6,302	7,503
Net worth (market value)	**8,942**	**13,078**	**11,425**	**13,543**	**14,309**	**14,712**	**15,425**	**16,496**	**16,903**
Debt/net worth (percent)	42.4	34.7	43.8	42.7	43.5	42.7	42.3	43.4	42.5

[1] At market value. [2] At replacement (current) cost. [3] Includes items not shown separately. [4] Industrial revenue bonds. Issued by state and local governments to finance private investment and secured in interest and principal by the industrial user of the funds. [5] Not elsewhere classified.

Source: Board of Governors of the Federal Reserve System, "Z.1, Financial Accounts of the United States," March 2020 <http://www.federalreserve.gov/releases/z1/>, accessed May 2020.

Table 786. Corporate Funds—Sources and Uses: 2000 to 2019

[In billions of dollars (451 represents $451,000,000,000)]

Item	2000	2005	2010	2014	2015	2016	2017	2018	2019
Profits before tax	451	1,030	1,042	1,377	1,286	1,249	1,265	1,157	1,103
- Taxes on corporate income	165	263	204	291	283	263	232	156	155
- Net dividends	251	171	375	598	641	691	681	197	491
+ Inventory valuation adjustment (IVA)	-17	-36	-48	2	53	-1	-49	-52	5
+ Capital consumption allowance [1]	786	805	1,087	1,239	1,317	1,360	1,440	1,640	1,679
+ Foreign earnings retained abroad	103	-29	212	206	201	205	216	-293	27
- Net capital transfers	(Z)	-16	21	-7	-3	3	192	-6	-1
=Gross saving less net capital transfers paid	907	1,352	1,693	1,942	1,937	1,856	1,767	2,105	2,168
Gross investment	1,302	1,532	1,657	1,603	1,934	1,969	1,955	2,071	1,915
Capital expenditures [2]	1,147	1,206	1,300	1,822	1,925	1,780	1,887	2,051	2,131
Fixed investment [3]	1,098	1,154	1,247	1,746	1,783	1,746	1,859	2,001	2,067
Inventory change + IVA	50	51	54	74	113	27	28	51	63
Nonproduced nonfinancial assets	-1	1	-1	2	29	7	(Z)	-1	1
Net lending (+) or net borrowing (-)	155	326	357	-219	9	189	67	20	-216
Net acquisition of financial assets [2]	1,483	928	555	674	1,137	951	549	319	706
Foreign deposits	-7	10	13	-9	-19	4	119	-128	2
Checkable deposits and currency	35	100	130	117	49	154	8	55	201
Time and savings deposits	35	10	6	-88	11	17	-8	-7	5
Money market fund shares	17	53	-170	22	19	-113	12	-9	111
Debt securities [2]	19	40	-6	26	4	-4	29	5	57
Commercial paper	10	16	-12	25	8	-7	-9	32	87
Treasury securities	-1	18	7	2	-4	4	30	-20	-22
Loans	8	2	-4	2	23	-22	1	1	1
Mortgages	2	2	-2	2	24	-23	2	1	1
Mutual fund shares	(Z)	1	7	24	12	-3	8	-10	-10
Trade receivables	282	278	142	107	33	199	162	143	73
U.S. direct investment abroad	136	15	299	317	264	260	282	-69	123
Miscellaneous assets [2]	1,119	596	189	91	768	366	76	409	193
Net increase in liabilities and equity [2]	1,328	601	198	892	1,128	762	482	299	922
Debt securities [2]	186	0	243	327	413	287	321	140	259
Commercial paper	48	-8	25	38	-3	2	26	-10	-2
Corporate bonds	136	-36	186	290	403	268	281	155	246
Loans	157	270	-299	123	163	5	223	137	200
Depository institution loans n.e.c. [4]	55	-27	-85	98	102	4	36	76	22
Other loans and advances [5]	78	110	-108	63	-6	12	148	4	129
Mortgages	24	187	-106	-38	67	-11	40	57	49
Corporate equities	-118	-300	-251	-394	-550	-577	-321	-530	-409
Trade payables	313	199	157	149	24	184	81	138	79
Foreign direct investment in U.S.	249	103	162	185	413	409	249	232	203
Miscellaneous liabilities [2]	534	331	143	491	685	461	-282	196	617
Claims of pension fund on sponsor	118	93	-21	42	59	56	-79	-77	-51

Z Less than $500 million. [1] Consumption of fixed capital plus capital consumption adjustment. [2] Includes other items not shown separately. [3] Nonresidential fixed investment plus residential fixed investment. [4] Not elsewhere classified. [5] Loans from rest of the world, U.S. government, and nonbank financial institutions.

Source: Board of Governors of the Federal Reserve System, "Z.1, Financial Accounts of the United States," March 2020, <http://www.federalreserve.gov/releases/z1/>, accessed May 2020.

Table 787. Corporations—Selected Financial Items: 2000 to 2016

[In billions of dollars (47,027 represents $47,027,000,000,000), except as noted. Covers active corporations only. Corporation data are for tax year shown, which covers (a) corporate returns with accounting periods for the calendar year ending December of year shown and (b) those returns with accounting periods for the noncalendar year ending between July of year shown and June of the following year. All corporations are required to file returns except those specifically exempt. See source for changes in law affecting comparability of historical data. Based on samples; see Appendix III]

Item	2000	2005	2010	2011	2012	2013	2014	2015	2016
Number of returns (1,000)	5,045	5,671	5,814	5,823	5,841	5,888	6,001	6,120	6,189
Number with net income (1,000)	2,819	3,324	3,265	3,385	3,549	3,581	3,725	3,801	3,881
S Corporation returns [1] (1,000)	2,860	3,684	4,128	4,159	4,205	4,258	4,380	4,487	4,592
Assets [2]	47,027	66,445	79,905	81,280	84,952	88,214	95,864	97,048	101,991
Cash	1,820	2,823	3,893	4,196	4,404	4,871	5,578	5,305	5,374
Notes and accounts receivable	8,754	11,962	12,718	13,089	13,016	12,714	14,090	13,753	15,102
Inventories	1,272	1,505	1,544	1,653	1,750	1,836	1,945	1,991	2,000
Investments in government obligations	1,236	1,613	2,730	2,859	3,002	2,958	3,237	3,450	4,107
Mortgage and real estate	2,822	4,777	7,914	7,615	7,579	7,533	7,506	8,151	8,192
Other investments	17,874	25,162	29,389	29,745	32,158	34,758	37,093	37,164	39,315
Depreciable assets	7,292	8,416	9,875	10,226	10,672	11,210	11,852	12,350	12,680
Depletable assets	191	310	661.36	757	855	922	1,031	1,038	923
Land	303	407	548.41	567	584	601	633	669	691
Liabilities [2]	47,027	66,445	79,905	81,280	84,952	88,214	95,864	97,048	101,991
Accounts payable	3,758	6,029	5,768	5,343	5,288	5,063	6,337	6,111	6,433
Short-term debt [3]	4,020	4,192	3,752	3,839	3,557	3,682	3,757	3,643	3,404
Long-term debt [4]	6,184	8,332	14,680	14,489	14,473	13,579	14,304	14,998	15,753
Net worth [5]	17,349	23,525	28,938	29,250	31,804	35,079	37,998	38,072	40,834
Capital stock	3,966	2,482	3,064	2,983	3,067	2,982	3,118	3,472	3,588
Paid-in or capital surplus [6]	12,265	17,828	24,283	24,859	26,243	27,642	30,068	31,327	33,175
Retained earnings [6]	3,627	4,331	3534.4	3,586	4,804	6,969	7,623	6,341	7,364
Receipts [2, 7]	20,606	25,505	26,199	28,336	29,404	30,192	31,563	31,030	31,208
Business receipts [7, 8]	17,637	21,800	23,058	25,198	26,029	26,850	28,075	27,492	27,575
Interest [9]	1,628	1,773	1,366	1,344	1,209	1,109	1,100	1,107	1,190
Rents and royalties	254	290	307.19	315	332	355	369	376	402
Deductions [2, 7]	19,692	23,613	24,944	27,093	27,713	28,357	29,522	29,102	29,395
Cost of goods sold [8]	11,135	13,816	14,502	16,180	16,579	17,141	17,850	17,044	16,948
Compensation of officers	401	445	435.41	454	479	479	488	501	498
Rent paid on business property	380	439	467.08	471	484	495	513	529	540
Taxes paid	390	473	493.25	519	546	564	581	580	590
Interest paid	1,272	1,287	888	860	814	711	706	728	793
Depreciation	614	531	727.8	874	709	730	769	822	857
Advertising	234	253	255.67	264	275	285	295	316	325
Net income (less loss) [7, 10]	928	1,949	1356.5	1,323	1,774	1,929	2,145	2,034	1,913
Net income	1,337	2,235	1,836	1,829	2,175	2,329	2,561	2,531	2,458
Deficit	409	286	479.88	506	401	401	416	498	545
Income subject to tax	760	1,201	1022.2	994	1,150	1,258	1,401	1,375	1,271
Income tax before credits [11]	266	419	358.41	349	403	442	491	481	446
Income tax after credits [12]	204	312	222.97	221	268	293	336	330	316

[1] Represents certain small corporations with a limit on the number of shareholders, mostly individuals, electing to be taxed at the shareholder level. [2] Includes items not shown separately. [3] Payable in less than 1 year. [4] Payable in 1 year or more. [5] Net worth is the sum of capital stock, additional paid-in capital, retained earnings, appropriated, retained earnings, unappropriated, adjustments to shareholders' equity, minus cost of treasury stock. [6] Appropriated and unappropriated and adjustments to shareholders' equity. [7] Receipts, deductions, and net income of S corporations are limited to those from trade or business. Those from investments are excluded. [8] Includes gross sales and cost of sales of securities, commodities, and real estate by exchanges, brokers, or dealers selling on their own accounts. Excludes investment income. [9] Includes tax-exempt interest in state and local government obligations. [10] Excludes regulated investment companies. [11] Consists of regular (and alternative tax) only. [12] Includes minimum tax, alternative minimum tax, adjustments for prior year credits, and other income-related taxes.

Source: U.S. Internal Revenue Service, "SOI Tax Stats - Corporation Complete Report," <https://www.irs.gov/statistics/soi-tax-stats-corporation-complete-report>, accessed August 2020.

Table 788. Economic Census Summary: 2017

[25 represents 25,000. Covers establishments with payroll. Data are based on the 2017 Economic Census and subject to nonsampling error. Data for the construction sector are also subject to sampling errors. For details on survey methodology and nonsampling and sampling errors, see Appendix III]

Kind of business	NAICS code [1]	Establish- ments (1,000)	Sales, receipts, or shipments (bil. dol.)	Annual payroll (bil. dol.)	Paid employees [2] (1,000)
Mining, quarrying, and oil and gas extraction..............	21	25	400	48	599
Oil & gas extraction........................	211	6	230	13	125
Mining (except oil & gas)...................	212	6	84	12	170
Support activities for mining...................	213	13	87	23	303
Utilities..........................	22	19	577	68	658
Construction.............................	23	715	1,994	399	6,647
Construction of buildings...................	236	214	800	85	1,346
Heavy and civil engineering construction..........	237	38	318	72	1,008
Specialty trade contractors....................	238	463	876	241	4,293
Manufacturing...........................	31-33	292	5,549	671	11,522
Wholesale trade.........................	42	408	8,735	427	6,242
Merchant wholesalers, durable goods............	423	241	3,688	252	3,547
Merchant wholesalers, nondurable goods.........	424	130	4,344	160	2,397
Wholesale electronic markets and agents and brokers..........................	425	38	703	14	298
Retail trade............................	44–45	1,064	4,950	442	15,939
Motor vehicle & parts dealers..................	441	119	1,168	91	2,003
Furniture & home furnishings stores.............	442	51	113	14	466
Electronics & appliance stores.................	443	30	91	10	332
Building material & garden equipment & supplies dealers.......................	444	75	347	39	1,285
Food & beverage stores.....................	445	150	721	72	3,176
Health & personal care stores.................	446	95	319	34	1,039
Gasoline stations.........................	447	115	475	19	943
Clothing & clothing accessories stores............	448	144	255	32	1,791
Sporting goods, hobby, musical instrument, and book stores.....................	451	45	81	10	539
General merchandise stores...................	452	54	690	68	2,793
Miscellaneous store retailers.................	453	109	110	17	774
Nonstore retailers.........................	454	77	579	35	797
Transportation & warehousing [3]...............	48-49	237	895	242	4,955
Truck transportation.......................	484	127	291	71	1,480
Information............................	51	154	1,582	361	3,565
Publishing industries (except internet)............	511	30	368	125	1,016
Motion picture & sound recording industries........	512	26	102	18	341
Broadcasting (except internet).................	515	8	166	23	262
Telecommunications......................	517	60	617	82	1,085
Data processing, hosting, and related services.........	518	18	157	54	553
Other information services...................	519	12	172	58	309
Finance & insurance [4]......................	52	476	4,340	639	6,500
Credit intermediation & related activities...........	522	193	1,287	231	2,944
Insurance carriers & related activities............	524	180	2,340	211	2,583
Real estate & rental & leasing [4]................	53	411	674	113	2,195
Professional, scientific, & technical services...........	54	914	1,845	729	9,015
Management of companies & enterprises...........	55	59	122	368	3,571
Admin/support waste management/remediation services.........................	56	417	951	470	11,889
Administrative & support services...............	561	392	851	447	11,461
Waste management & remediation services.........	562	25	100	23	428
Educational services.......................	61	77	66	22	723
Health care and social assistance...............	62	892	2,528	990	20,507
Ambulatory health care services...............	621	624	1,031	431	7,563
Hospitals..............................	622	7	1,071	383	6,174
Nursing & residential care facilities..............	623	89	236	101	3,502
Social assistance.........................	624	172	191	76	3,267
Arts, entertainment, & recreation...............	71	143	266	82	2,390
Performing arts, spectator sports, & related industries...................	711	54	120	41	489
Museums, historical sites, & like institutions.........	712	8	20	5	158
Amusement, gambling, & recreation industries........	713	82	126	36	1,743
Accommodation & food services...............	72	726	938	265	14,003
Accommodation..........................	721	68	260	62	2,121
Food services & drinking places................	722	658	678	203	11,881
Other services (except public administration).........	81	561	544	134	3,697
Repair & maintenance......................	811	218	181	51	1,286
Personal and laundry services.................	812	236	111	36	1,474
Religious, grantmaking, civic, professional, and similar organizations..........	813	107	252	47	937

[1] Based on North American Industry Classification System, 2017; see text, this section. [2] For pay period including March 12. [3] For detailed industries, see Table 1087. [4] For detailed industries, see Table 1190.

Source: U.S. Census Bureau, 2017 Economic Census, Table EC1700BASIC, "All Sectors: Summary Statistics for the U.S., States, and Selected Geographies: 2017," <data.census.gov>, accessed August 2020.

Table 789. Nonemployer Establishments and Receipts by Industry: 2010 to 2018

[22,111 represents 22,111,000. Includes only firms subject to federal income tax. Nonemployers are businesses with no paid employees. Data originate chiefly from administrative records of the Internal Revenue Service; see Appendix III. Data for 2010 based on the North American Industry Classification System (NAICS), 2007; data for 2015 based on NAICS 2012; and data for 2018 based on NAICS 2017]

Industry	NAICS code	Establishments (1,000)			Receipts (mil. dol.)		
		2010	2015	2018	2010	2015	2018
All industries...............	(X)	**22,111**	**24,331**	**26,486**	**950,814**	**1,148,716**	**1,292,867**
Agriculture, forestry, fishing and hunting.................	11	237	236	256	10,115	11,014	12,051
Mining, quarrying, and oil and gas extraction............	21	106	98	83	6,923	6,111	5,723
Utilities......................................	22	17	20	14	698	981	904
Construction...............................	23	2,424	2,430	2,635	120,151	146,341	169,733
Manufacturing.............................	31–33	318	355	354	14,572	17,473	18,641
Wholesale trade...........................	42	393	417	399	34,082	37,946	37,978
Retail trade................................	44–45	1,822	1,986	2,103	75,720	87,352	92,223
Transportation & warehousing.............	48–49	1,021	1,528	2,572	60,746	83,890	117,316
Information................................	51	311	329	359	10,739	12,762	14,019
Finance & insurance.......................	52	717	718	755	50,626	55,329	63,410
Real estate & rental & leasing.............	53	2,343	2,636	2,876	209,549	259,768	289,866
Professional, scientific, & technical services............	54	3,121	3,411	3,727	130,613	157,584	178,373
Admin/support waste mgmt/remediation services......	56	1,937	2,069	2,522	39,111	46,393	59,169
Educational services.......................	61	567	710	806	7,703	9,893	11,875
Health care & social assistance............	62	1,935	1,979	2,071	57,686	64,702	71,676
Arts, entertainment, & recreation..........	71	1,154	1,342	1,514	26,756	34,549	40,346
Accommodation & food services...........	72	329	371	460	14,355	17,658	18,744
Other services (except public administration)...........	81	3,358	3,695	2,978	80,669	98,971	90,820

X Not applicable.

Source: U.S. Census Bureau, Nonemployer Statistics, "Geographic Area Series: Nonemployer Statistics for the U.S., States, Metropolitan Areas, and Counties," <data.census.gov>, accessed May 2020. See also <https://www.census.gov/programs-surveys/nonemployer-statistics.html>.

Table 790. Establishments, Employees, and Payroll by Employment-Size Class: 1990 to 2018

[In units as noted (6,176 represents 6,176,000). Excludes self-employed individuals, employees of private households, railroad employees, agricultural production employees, and most government employees. Employees are for the pay period including March 12. Covers establishments with payroll. An establishment is a single physical location where business is conducted or where services or industrial operations are performed. For statement on methodology, see Appendix III]

Employment-size class	Unit	1990	2000	2005	2010	2015	2016	2017	2018
Establishments, total...........	1,000	**6,176**	**7,070**	**7,500**	**7,397**	**7,664**	**7,758**	**7,861**	**7,912**
Under 20 employees................	1,000	5,354	6,069	6,468	6,408	6,559	6,627	6,713	6,746
20 to 99 employees................	1,000	684	826	856	824	919	941	956	971
100 to 499 employees..............	1,000	122	157	157	148	166	169	171	174
500 to 999 employees..............	1,000	10	12	12	11	13	13	13	13
1,000 or more employees..........	1,000	6	7	7	7	7	8	8	8
Employees, total.................	1,000	**93,476**	**114,065**	**116,317**	**111,970**	**124,086**	**126,752**	**128,592**	**130,881**
Under 20 employees................	1,000	24,373	27,569	28,874	28,958	29,406	29,815	30,196	30,277
20 to 99 employees................	1,000	27,414	33,147	34,302	32,730	36,640	37,545	38,019	38,544
100 to 499 employees..............	1,000	22,926	29,736	29,591	27,718	31,416	32,050	32,294	32,933
500 to 999 employees..............	1,000	6,551	8,291	8,053	7,331	8,550	8,647	8,883	9,128
1,000 or more employees..........	1,000	12,212	15,322	15,497	15,233	18,074	18,695	19,199	19,999
Annual payroll, total..............	Bil. dol.	**2,104**	**3,879**	**4,483**	**4,941**	**6,253**	**6,435**	**6,725**	**7,097**
Under 20 employees................	Bil. dol.	485	818	970	1,057	1,235	1,262	1,318	1,350
20 to 99 employees................	Bil. dol.	547	1,006	1,177	1,281	1,584	1,630	1,691	1,764
100 to 499 employees..............	Bil. dol.	518	1,031	1,176	1,280	1,651	1,697	1,767	1,874
500 to 999 employees..............	Bil. dol.	174	336	376	410	550	563	591	637
1,000 or more employees..........	Bil. dol.	381	690	784	913	1,235	1,283	1,359	1,472

Source: U.S. Census Bureau, County Business Patterns, "County Business Patterns by Legal Form of Organization and Employment Size Class for U.S., States, and Selected Geographies," <data.census.gov>, accessed July 2020. See also <https://www.census.gov/programs-surveys/cbp.html>.

Table 791. Establishments, Employees, and Payroll by Employment-Size Class and Industry: 2000 to 2018

[Establishments and employees in thousands (7,070.0 represents 7,070,000); payroll in billions of dollars (3,879.4 represents $3,879,400,000,000). See headnote, Table 790. Data for 2000 based on the North American Industry Classification System (NAICS), 1997; 2010 data based on NAICS 2007; and 2018 data based on NAICS 2017. See text, this section]

Industry	NAICS code	2000, total	2010, total	2018 Total	2018 Under 20 employees	2018 20 to 99 employees	2018 100 to 499 employees	2018 500 to 999 employees	2018 1,000 more employees
ESTABLISHMENTS (1,000s)									
Total [1]	(X)	7,070.0	7,396.6	7,912.4	6,746.4	970.9	173.5	13.4	8.2
Agriculture, forestry, fishing & hunting.........	113–115	26.1	21.7	23.4	21.9	1.3	0.2	(Z)	(Z)
Mining, quarrying, & oil and gas extraction....	21	23.7	27.1	25.6	20.2	4.3	1.0	0.1	(Z)
Utilities........	22	17.3	17.6	19.0	13.5	4.2	1.1	0.1	0.1
Construction........	23	709.6	682.7	733.7	666.7	58.3	8.1	0.4	0.2
Manufacturing........	31–33	354.5	300.0	290.1	200.3	64.3	22.4	2.2	1.0
Wholesale trade........	42	446.2	414.6	403.6	340.8	53.5	8.6	0.6	0.2
Retail trade........	44–45	1,113.6	1,068.0	1,050.2	885.0	135.7	29.1	0.3	0.1
Transportation and warehousing........	48–49	190.0	208.5	244.8	204.8	31.1	7.6	0.9	0.4
Information........	51	133.6	135.4	157.8	130.3	21.2	5.3	0.7	0.3
Finance and insurance........	52	423.7	473.5	477.6	438.3	30.6	6.9	1.0	0.7
Real estate and rental and leasing........	53	300.2	347.3	418.0	400.7	15.4	1.8	0.1	(Z)
Professional, scientific, & technical services...	54	722.7	851.5	921.5	848.3	60.7	11.1	0.9	0.5
Management of companies and enterprises...	55	47.4	50.9	54.7	35.4	12.8	5.3	0.8	0.5
Administrative/support waste management/ remediation services........	56	351.5	381.8	418.9	352.3	48.0	15.5	1.8	1.2
Educational services........	61	68.0	90.1	106.9	83.3	19.0	3.8	0.4	0.5
Health care and social assistance........	62	658.6	812.9	907.4	752.8	123.7	26.7	2.1	2.1
Arts, entertainment, and recreation........	71	103.8	123.2	147.1	123.8	19.1	3.9	0.3	0.1
Accommodation and food services........	72	542.4	644.0	733.1	499.9	221.1	11.4	0.5	0.2
Other services [2]........	81	723.3	725.5	766.8	716.0	46.7	3.8	0.2	0.1
Unclassified establishments........	99	99.0	20.5	12.2	12.1	(Z)	–	–	–
EMPLOYEES (1,000s)									
Total [1]	(X)	114,065	111,970	130,881	30,277	38,544	32,933	9,128	19,999
Agriculture, forestry, fishing & hunting.........	113–115	184	156	164	73	50	30	5	6
Mining, quarrying, & oil and gas extraction....	21	456	582	606	95	177	191	61	82
Utilities........	22	655	638	647	72	186	223	89	77
Construction........	23	6,573	5,389	6,815	2,442	2,272	1,474	296	331
Manufacturing........	31–33	16,474	10,863	11,913	1,136	2,828	4,517	1,471	1,960
Wholesale trade........	42	6,112	5,599	6,164	1,648	2,117	1,636	386	377
Retail trade........	44–45	14,841	14,497	15,683	4,918	5,242	5,219	155	149
Transportation and warehousing........	48–49	3,790	4,012	5,032	795	1,290	1,498	586	862
Information........	51	3,546	3,124	3,601	571	894	1,085	457	594
Finance and insurance........	52	5,963	5,929	6,499	1,837	1,203	1,428	720	1,312
Real estate and rental and leasing........	53	1,942	1,946	2,210	1,181	574	338	58	58
Professional, scientific, & technical services...	54	6,816	7,822	9,112	2,770	2,410	2,134	641	1,157
Management of companies and enterprises...	55	2,874	2,833	3,529	188	579	1,102	540	1,120
Administrative/support waste management/ remediation services........	56	9,138	8,977	12,288	1,345	2,073	3,159	1,242	4,469
Educational services........	61	2,532	3,274	3,731	406	801	727	313	1,484
Health care and social assistance........	62	14,109	17,788	20,499	3,942	4,990	4,993	1,477	5,096
Arts, entertainment, and recreation........	71	1,741	2,004	2,436	451	812	725	172	275
Accommodation and food services........	72	9,881	11,312	14,345	3,408	8,356	1,807	334	439
Other services [2]........	81	5,293	5,204	5,596	2,984	1,689	646	125	152
Unclassified establishments........	99	144	([3])	14	13	1	–	–	–
ANNUAL PAYROLL (BIL. DOLLARS)									
Total [1]	(X)	3,879.4	4,941.0	7,097.3	1,350.2	1,764.3	1,873.7	637.4	1,471.7
Agriculture, forestry, fishing & hunting.........	113–115	4.7	5.3	7.4	3.4	2.4	1.2	0.2	0.1
Mining, quarrying, & oil and gas extraction....	21	22.1	46.1	57.2	7.2	15.2	19.8	6.0	9.0
Utilities........	22	40.7	55.4	70.0	6.3	18.4	24.3	11.3	9.8
Construction........	23	239.9	261.0	428.7	122.3	148.1	110.7	23.2	24.4
Manufacturing........	31–33	644.0	550.4	717.9	52.5	151.1	265.7	95.1	153.6
Wholesale trade........	42	270.1	339.1	450.5	101.8	142.9	122.5	36.2	47.0
Retail trade........	44–45	302.6	359.4	457.4	134.3	150.7	158.2	7.0	7.2
Transportation and warehousing........	48–49	125.6	166.8	262.5	38.6	64.6	73.2	29.8	56.1
Information........	51	209.4	224.0	385.2	39.4	68.7	118.8	55.0	103.3
Finance and insurance........	52	346.8	472.4	673.5	131.8	137.4	166.9	78.5	158.8
Real estate and rental and leasing........	53	59.2	80.5	122.9	58.3	34.6	21.9	3.6	4.5
Professional, scientific, & technical services...	54	362.0	543.1	801.7	185.6	210.1	216.9	70.2	118.9
Management of companies and enterprises...	55	211.4	281.8	393.6	22.8	58.4	118.0	61.1	133.3
Administrative/support waste management/ remediation services........	56	210.3	304.1	512.1	61.5	89.1	112.9	41.8	206.8
Educational services........	61	61.9	110.4	148.5	11.3	26.4	30.9	10.1	69.7
Health care and social assistance........	62	431.4	752.9	1,039.4	194.8	216.7	209.7	80.0	338.2
Arts, entertainment, and recreation........	71	43.2	62.3	88.2	20.6	19.6	27.4	10.9	9.7
Accommodation and food services........	72	125.6	185.6	291.4	67.4	151.9	45.9	10.8	15.5
Other services [2]........	81	109.9	140.3	189.0	90.0	57.9	28.7	6.6	5.8
Unclassified establishments........	99	3.9	0.3	0.4	0.4	(Z)	–	–	–

– Represents zero. X Not applicable. Z Less than 50 establishments, 500 employees, or $500 million. [1] Totals for 2000 include auxiliaries. Beginning 2003, cases previously classified under NAICS code 95 (auxiliaries) are coded in the operating NAICS sector of the establishment. [2] Except public administration. [3] 10,000 to 24,999 employees.

Source: U.S. Census Bureau, County Business Patterns, "County Business Patterns by Legal Form of Organization and Employment Size Class for U.S., States, and Selected Geographies," <http://data.census.gov>, accessed July 2020. See also <https://www.census.gov/programs-surveys/cbp.html>.

Table 792. Employer Firms by Industry and Owner's Education and Age: 2017

[In thousands (4,730 represents 4,730,000). Includes all U.S. firms with paid employees operating during the survey reference year with receipts of $1,000 or more and classified in the 2017 North American Industry Classification System (NAICS). Based on the 2018 Annual Business Survey that collected data for 2017; see <census.gov/programs-surveys/abs/technical-documentation/methodology.html>]

Industry	NAICS code	Owner's highest level of education						Age of owner			
		Total [1]	High school or less	Some college, no degree	Associate's or technical degree	Bachelor's degree	Advanced degree [2]	Total [1]	Under 35	35 to 64	65 or over
All industries [3]	(X)	**4,730**	**1,046**	**679**	**526**	**1,422**	**1,055**	**4,729**	**269**	**3,509**	**952**
Forestry, fishing & hunting, and agricultural support services	113-115	26	10	4	3	7	2	26	2	19	6
Mining, quarrying, and oil & gas extraction	21	18	6	3	1	6	2	18	1	12	5
Utilities	22	2	1	(Z)	(Z)	1	(Z)	2	(Z)	1	1
Construction	23	595	221	112	114	122	26	595	34	470	91
Manufacturing	31-33	255	65	43	34	83	30	255	12	176	67
Wholesale trade	42	265	56	43	25	109	31	265	11	186	69
Retail trade	44-45	558	165	99	65	173	56	558	36	401	121
Transportation & warehousing [4]	48-49	138	57	24	19	30	8	138	9	103	26
Information	51	65	6	9	4	32	14	65	5	48	13
Finance & insurance [5]	52	203	21	30	14	102	36	203	9	146	48
Real estate & rental & leasing	53	269	42	44	24	111	47	269	13	176	80
Professional, scientific, & technical services	54	749	37	61	39	274	338	749	34	561	154
Management of companies & enterprises	55	21	3	2	1	10	5	21	1	13	7
Administrative & support and waste management & remediation services	56	280	78	54	34	84	29	280	19	214	47
Educational services	61	54	5	7	4	22	16	54	4	40	9
Health care & social assistance	62	465	18	19	19	58	352	465	21	360	85
Arts, entertainment, & recreation	71	86	15	13	7	37	14	86	7	61	17
Accommodation & food services	72	411	140	66	42	124	39	411	33	314	64
Other services (except public administration) [6]	81	301	101	50	76	58	17	301	20	231	51

X Not applicable. Z Less than 500. [1] Total firms that reported either education or age of owner in survey response. [2] Master's, doctorate, or professional degree. [3] Firms with more than one domestic establishment are counted in each industry in which they operate, but only once in the total. [4] Excludes rail transportation (NAICS 482) and the postal service (NAICS 491). [5] Excludes monetary authorities-central banks (NAICS 521) and funds, trusts, and other financial vehicles (NAICS 525). [6] Excludes religious, grantmaking, civic, professional, and similar organizations (NAICS 813) and private households (NAICS 814).

Source: U.S. Census Bureau, Annual Business Survey, "Owner Characteristics of Respondent Employer Firms by Sector, Sex, Ethnicity, Race, and Veteran Status for the U.S., States, Metro Areas, Counties, and Places: 2017," <data.census.gov/>, accessed June 2020.

Table 793. Employer Firms by Industry and Source of Start Up Capital: 2017

[Includes all U.S. firms with paid employees operating during the survey reference year with receipts of $1,000 or more and classified in the 2017 North American Industry Classification System (NAICS). Based on the 2018 Annual Business Survey that collected data for 2017; see <https://www.census.gov/programs-surveys/abs/technical-documentation/methodology.html>]

Industry	NAICS code	Total firms [2]	Source of capital to start or acquire business [1]					
			Personal savings or assets	Personal home equity loan	Credit cards [3]	Business loans [4]	Grants	Investment by venture capitalists
All industries	(X)	**5,744,643**	**2,307,708**	**171,550**	**449,402**	**706,551**	**6,403**	**17,337**
Forestry, fishing & hunting, and agricultural support services	113-115	28,556	11,796	870	1,729	5,589	3	35
Mining, quarrying, and oil & gas extraction	21	19,382	6,387	226	667	2,737	(S)	264
Utilities	22	6,088	877	71	137	367	34	(S)
Construction	23	706,354	299,437	20,903	68,953	61,020	S	969
Manufacturing	31-33	251,707	104,533	10,921	21,586	43,553	709	1,920
Wholesale trade	42	303,607	115,804	9,035	19,502	33,422	172	1,285
Retail trade	44-45	648,335	265,314	26,796	53,277	103,288	588	1,325
Transportation & warehousing	48-49	188,227	63,238	5,193	14,326	25,236	71	360
Information	51	79,322	29,134	1,739	6,154	6,492	193	1,445
Finance & insurance	52	239,154	106,292	6,879	18,769	(S)	87	790
Real estate & rental & leasing	53	311,301	122,836	6,510	15,650	30,140	212	1,061
Professional, scientific, & technical services	54	817,377	397,237	18,495	71,853	66,204	1,578	3,568
Management of companies and enterprises	55	29,783	6,154	363	(S)	3,493	40	487
Administrative & support and waste management remediation services	56	350,537	143,478	9,110	32,043	31,608	201	806
Educational services	61	92,814	29,460	2,062	5,925	6,097	362	270
Health care & social assistance	62	659,399	229,269	15,452	43,705	122,101	1,276	1,095
Arts, entertainment, & recreation	71	129,066	40,742	2,556	7,106	12,743	124	449
Accommodation & food services	72	533,176	187,666	19,944	35,330	81,009	500	1,755
Other services (except public administration)	81	395,072	154,165	14,880	32,619	53,402	198	451

X Not applicable. S Data does not meet publication standards. [1] Not all sources of capital are shown separately. [2] Includes firms that did not respond to survey questions regarding source of capital. [3] Includes personal and business credit cards carrying balances. [4] Includes loans from federal/state/local government, banks/financial institutions, and loans/investments from family and friends.

Source: U.S. Census Bureau, Annual Business Survey, "Business Characteristics of Respondent Employer Firms by Sector, Sex, Ethnicity, Race, and Veteran Status for the U.S., States, Metro Areas, Counties, and Places: 2017," <data.census.gov/>, accessed June 2020.

Table 794. Franchised Businesses by Type of Business: 2012

[129,242 represents $129,242,000,000. Data shown for franchisor- and franchisee-owned establishments with paid employees. Covers franchised businesses with over 5,000 establishments. Data are based on the 2012 Economic Census; for details see Appendix III]

Kind of business	NAICS code [1]	Establishments (number)	Revenue (mil. dol.)	Annual payroll (mil. dol.)	Paid employees (number)
Limited-service restaurants	722513	122,042	129,242	31,726	2,630,074
Gasoline stations with convenience stores	447110	32,845	158,109	4,267	251,960
Full-service restaurants	722511	28,940	36,070	11,828	879,771
Hotels (except casino hotels) and motels	721110	23,305	51,556	11,645	601,424
New car dealers	441110	21,292	672,550	47,524	973,745
Snack and nonalcoholic beverage bars	722515	16,494	9,614	2,275	195,342
Offices of real estate agents and brokers	531210	14,588	16,241	1,406	41,156
Fitness and recreational sports centers	713940	7,340	2,584	729	60,957
Beauty salons	812112	6,326	1,873	839	49,174
Janitorial services	561720	6,194	3,987	1,457	81,833
Optical goods stores	446130	5,982	5,492	928	40,343
Tax preparation services	541213	5,702	1,331	395	55,215
Other gasoline stations	447190	5,212	32,855	918	45,866

[1] Based on the 2012 North American Industry Classification System (NAICS); see text, this section.

Source: U.S. Census Bureau, 2012 Economic Census, Table "EC1200CFRA1," <data.census.gov>, accessed February 2016.

Table 795. Employer Firms, Employment, and Payroll by Employment Size of Firm and State: 2016 and 2017

[5,955 represents 5,955,000. A firm is an aggregation of all establishments owned by a parent company (within a state) with some annual payroll. A firm may have an establishment in a single location or multiple establishments in more than one location]

State	Employer firms (1,000) 2016 Total	Less than 20 employees	Less than 500 employees	Employer firms (1,000) 2017 Total	Less than 20 employees	Less than 500 employees	Employment (1,000), 2017 Total	Less than 20 employees	Less than 500 employees	Annual payroll (bil. dol.), 2017 Total	Less than 20 employees	Less than 500 employees
U.S.	5,955	5,306	5,935	5,997	5,340	5,977	128,592	21,096	60,556	6,725	869	2,712
AL	74	62	71	74	62	72	1,690	273	803	72	10	31
AK	17	15	16	17	15	17	262	57	137	15	3	7
AZ	107	91	104	110	93	107	2,449	356	1,066	113	14	43
AR	51	43	49	51	43	49	1,031	177	491	42	6	17
CA	752	667	746	764	677	757	14,897	2,605	7,225	955	126	376
CO	136	119	133	140	122	136	2,372	434	1,141	127	19	53
CT	72	60	69	71	60	69	1,537	253	745	96	12	38
DE	20	16	19	20	16	19	401	64	187	22	3	9
DC	18	13	17	18	13	17	527	59	250	41	4	18
FL	445	403	440	453	410	448	8,386	1,375	3,494	378	54	142
GA	177	153	173	181	156	176	3,889	584	1,678	192	23	70
HI	25	21	24	26	21	25	544	90	276	24	4	11
ID	38	33	37	40	34	38	578	130	325	24	4	12
IL	257	222	252	256	222	252	5,498	827	2,477	301	36	120
IN	109	91	105	110	91	106	2,779	397	1,233	123	14	48
IA	63	53	61	63	54	61	1,354	218	650	59	8	25
KS	58	49	56	58	48	56	1,199	199	605	53	7	24
KY	69	58	66	67	56	65	1,625	241	712	68	8	26
LA	81	68	79	81	68	79	1,689	297	905	75	11	36
ME	34	30	33	34	30	33	514	111	294	22	4	11
MD	110	93	107	110	93	107	2,335	380	1,156	127	17	57
MA	143	122	140	144	123	141	3,317	502	1,508	217	25	84
MI	173	149	170	174	149	171	3,860	629	1,892	187	25	82
MN	119	101	116	119	101	116	2,685	391	1,259	142	16	55
MS	44	37	43	45	37	43	939	162	437	35	5	15
MO	126	109	123	115	98	112	2,517	389	1,164	117	14	46
MT	32	29	32	33	29	32	377	107	246	15	4	9
NE	43	37	42	44	37	42	833	146	413	36	5	16
NV	52	43	49	53	44	50	1,192	170	503	51	7	20
NH	31	25	29	31	26	29	604	108	301	31	5	14
NJ	194	170	191	195	170	191	3,679	664	1,836	220	30	91
NM	34	28	33	35	29	33	626	121	340	26	4	13
NY	465	416	460	466	417	461	8,261	1,515	4,110	547	69	220
NC	174	150	171	178	153	174	3,774	608	1,711	176	22	66
ND	20	17	19	20	16	19	341	68	195	16	3	8
OH	185	155	181	184	154	180	4,816	690	2,180	225	25	88
OK	73	62	70	73	62	71	1,361	247	710	60	9	28
OR	94	81	91	95	82	93	1,597	335	871	79	12	36
PA	230	197	226	230	196	226	5,434	839	2,513	271	32	108
RI	24	20	23	24	20	23	436	82	229	21	3	10
SC	81	69	78	83	70	80	1,866	290	817	77	10	30
SD	22	19	21	22	19	21	360	76	209	15	3	8
TN	98	81	95	99	82	96	2,650	364	1,117	120	14	46
TX	434	374	428	443	381	437	10,580	1,578	4,769	545	66	212
UT	65	56	62	67	57	64	1,282	206	590	58	8	24
VT	18	16	17	18	15	17	259	61	157	11	2	6
VA	152	130	148	153	131	150	3,311	534	1,558	177	22	73
WA	152	133	149	156	136	152	2,769	533	1,404	170	23	67
WV	27	22	26	27	22	25	549	98	270	22	3	9
WI	109	91	106	109	91	106	2,561	398	1,267	121	14	50
WY	18	15	17	18	16	17	202	58	129	9	2	5

Source: U.S. Census Bureau, Statistics of U.S. Businesses (SUSB), "2017 SUSB Annual Data Tables by Establishment Industry," and earlier releases, <https://www.census.gov/programs-surveys/susb/data/tables.html>, accessed May 2020.

Table 796. Employer Firms, Employment, and Annual Payroll by Employment Size of Firm and Industry: 2017

[5,997 represents 5,997,000. A firm is an aggregation of all establishments owned by a parent company (within a geographic location and/or industry) with some annual payroll. A firm may have an establishment in a single location or multiple establishments in more than one location. Employment is measured in March and payroll is annual; some firms may have zero employment in March but with paid employees at some time during the year. Numbers in parentheses represent 2017 North American Industry Classification System codes; see text, this section]

Industry and data type	Unit	Total	All industries—employment size of firm						
			0 to 4	5 to 9	10 to 19	20 to 99	100 to 499	Less than 500	500 or more
Total, all industries [1]:									
Firms.........	1,000	5,997	3,698	1,010	632	544	92	5,977	20
Employment.........	1,000	128,592	5,937	6,656	8,503	21,348	18,112	60,556	68,036
Annual payroll.........	Bil. dol.	6,725	277	255	338	928	914	2,712	4,014
Construction (23):									
Firms.........	1,000	701	468	111	65	50	7	700	1
Employment.........	1,000	6,533	725	725	865	1,919	1,140	5,374	1,159
Annual payroll.........	Bil. dol.	399	34	33	45	118	80	310	90
Manufacturing (31–33):									
Firms.........	1,000	248	102	46	38	46	12	244	4
Employment.........	1,000	11,722	188	306	511	1,872	2,162	5,040	6,682
Annual payroll.........	Bil. dol.	683	8	12	22	92	113	249	434
Wholesale trade (42):									
Firms.........	1,000	298	171	49	34	33	8	295	3
Employment.........	1,000	6,115	283	321	454	1,246	1,109	3,413	2,702
Annual payroll.........	Bil. dol.	434	16	18	26	77	72	209	226
Retail trade (44–45):									
Firms.........	1,000	648	387	132	70	48	8	646	2
Employment.........	1,000	15,706	714	866	925	1,812	1,210	5,526	10,180
Annual payroll.........	Bil. dol.	444	20	23	27	65	49	185	259
Transportation & warehousing (48–49):									
Firms.........	1,000	185	122	24	17	16	4	183	2
Employment.........	1,000	4,866	173	161	230	579	543	1,685	3,181
Annual payroll.........	Bil. dol.	245	7	6	9	26	25	74	172
Information (51):									
Firms.........	1,000	80	49	11	8	8	2	78	1
Employment.........	1,000	3,508	69	73	105	319	418	984	2,524
Annual payroll.........	Bil. dol.	357	6	4	6	23	36	75	282
Finance & insurance (52):									
Firms.........	1,000	238	172	35	13	12	4	237	2
Employment.........	1,000	6,408	296	221	174	507	712	1,910	4,498
Annual payroll.........	Bil. dol.	644	16	13	14	46	70	161	483
Professional, scientific and technical services (54):									
Firms.........	1,000	811	598	102	57	42	8	808	3
Employment.........	1,000	8,906	858	671	757	1,589	1,316	5,191	3,715
Annual payroll.........	Bil. dol.	747	53	40	50	126	117	386	361
Management of companies and enterprises (55):									
Firms.........	1,000	27	3	1	1	6	9	19	8
Employment.........	1,000	3,462	3	3	7	77	333	423	3,039
Annual payroll.........	Bil. dol.	371	1	(Z)	1	6	26	33	338
Administrative & support and waste management & remediation services (56):									
Firms.........	1,000	348	222	51	32	30	8	344	4
Employment.........	1,000	11,897	327	337	424	1,182	1,485	3,754	8,143
Annual payroll.........	Bil. dol.	482	15	13	17	47	52	144	338
Educational services (61):									
Firms.........	1,000	94	46	15	12	15	4	92	1
Employment.........	1,000	3,689	71	99	166	639	671	1,646	2,043
Annual payroll.........	Bil. dol.	143	3	2	4	20	27	56	87
Health care and social assistance (62):									
Firms.........	1,000	655	338	138	86	70	18	651	4
Employment.........	1,000	20,241	586	921	1,146	2,824	3,508	8,984	11,257
Annual payroll.........	Bil. dol.	996	33	39	50	114	133	368	627
Accommodation and food services (72):									
Firms.........	1,000	540	203	104	107	114	10	537	2
Employment.........	1,000	14,088	330	701	1,464	4,215	1,833	8,543	5,546
Annual payroll.........	Bil. dol.	275	11	11	24	77	34	158	117
Other services (except public administration) (81):									
Firms.........	1,000	697	448	136	65	41	5	695	1
Employment.........	1,000	5,535	816	886	860	1,469	666	4,698	837
Annual payroll.........	Bil. dol.	181	23	24	26	46	26	146	35

Z Less than $500 million. [1] Includes other industries, not shown separately.

Source: U.S. Census Bureau, Statistics of U.S. Businesses (SUSB), "2017 SUSB Annual Data Tables by Establishment Industry," <https://www.census.gov/data/tables/2017/econ/susb/2017-susb-annual.html>, accessed May 2020.

Table 797. Employer Firms, Establishments, Employment, and Annual Payroll by Firm Size: 1990 to 2017

[5,074 represents 5,074,000. Firms are an aggregation of all establishments owned by a parent company with some annual payroll. Establishments are locations with active payroll in any quarter. This table illustrates the changing importance of enterprise sizes over time, not job growth, as enterprises can grow or decline and change enterprise size cells over time]

Item	Total	Employment size of firm						
		0 to 4 [1]	5 to 9	10 to 19	20 to 99	100 to 499	Less than 500	500 or more
Firms (1,000):								
1990................	5,074	3,021	952	563	454	70	5,060	14
2000................	5,653	3,397	1,021	617	516	84	5,635	17
2005................	5,984	3,678	1,050	630	521	87	5,966	17
2010................	5,735	3,575	968	617	475	82	5,717	17
2015................	5,901	3,644	1,005	617	526	89	5,881	19
2017................	5,997	3,698	1,010	632	544	92	5,977	20
Establishments (1,000):								
1990................	6,176	3,032	971	600	590	255	5,448	728
2000................	7,070	3,406	1,035	652	674	312	6,080	990
2005................	7,500	3,684	1,063	662	679	332	6,421	1,079
2010................	7,397	3,583	982	653	648	354	6,220	1,176
2015................	7,664	3,650	1,016	649	698	367	6,380	1,284
2017................	7,861	3,704	1,022	667	739	382	6,513	1,348
Employment (1,000):								
1990................	93,469	5,117	6,252	7,543	17,710	13,545	50,167	43,302
2000................	114,065	5,593	6,709	8,286	20,277	16,260	57,124	56,941
2005................	116,317	5,937	6,898	8,454	20,444	16,911	58,645	57,672
2010................	111,970	5,926	6,359	8,288	18,554	15,869	54,997	56,973
2015................	124,086	5,877	6,614	8,298	20,645	17,503	58,938	65,148
2017................	128,592	5,937	6,656	8,503	21,348	18,112	60,556	68,036
Annual payroll (bil. dol.):								
1990................	2,104	117	114	144	352	279	1,007	1,097
2000................	3,879	186	174	231	608	528	1,727	2,152
2005................	4,483	220	206	269	700	617	2,013	2,470
2010................	4,941	227	212	283	719	666	2,107	2,834
2015................	6,253	263	244	322	876	846	2,551	3,702
2017................	6,725	277	255	338	928	914	2,712	4,014

[1] Employment is measured in March, thus some firms (start-ups after March, closures before March, and seasonal firms) will have zero employment and some annual payroll.

Source: U.S. Census Bureau, Statistics of U.S. Businesses (SUSB), "SUSB Historical Data," <https://www.census.gov/data/tables/time-series/econ/susb/susb-historical.html>, accessed May 2020.

Table 798. Job Creation and Job Destruction of Active Establishments by Firm Age: 2016

[6,886 represents 6,886,000. An establishment is a single physical location where business is conducted or where services or industrial operations are performed. A firm is a business organization consisting of one or more domestic establishments that are under common ownership or control. Firms may have one or more establishments. The firm and the establishment are the same for single-establishment firms. Data cover nonfarm private establishments with paid employees; exclusions include self–employed individuals, employees of private households, and railroad, agricultural production, and most government employees. Data are from the Business Dynamics Statistics (BDS) program and compiled from the Longitudinal Business Database. The BDS program is based on the same basic source data as the Census Bureau's County Business Patterns and Statistics of U.S. Business programs, but differences in how the source data are processed lead to differences in published statistics. For more information about concepts and methodology, see <https://www.census.gov/programs-surveys/bds/documentation/methodology.html>]

Firm age [1]	Establish-ments	Employ-ees	Percent of employ-ment	Job creation [2]		Job destruction [3]		Net job creation		Percent of net job creation
				Total	Rate	Total	Rate	Total	Rate	
Total....................	**6,886**	**124,231**	**100.0**	**16,453**	**13.4**	**13,528**	**11.0**	**2,925**	**2.4**	**100.0**
Startups....................	439	2,573	2.1	2,573	200.0	–	–	2,573	200.0	88.0
1 year....................	328	2,370	1.9	591	24.5	672	27.9	-81	-3.4	-2.8
2 years....................	286	2,337	1.9	476	20.2	519	22.0	-43	-1.8	-1.5
3 years....................	251	2,084	1.7	377	17.9	416	19.8	-38	-1.9	-1.3
4 years....................	231	2,085	1.7	363	17.2	408	19.4	-46	-2.2	-1.6
5 years....................	210	2,077	1.7	329	15.7	361	17.2	-32	-1.5	-1.1
6 to 10 years..............	937	9,777	7.9	1,360	13.8	1,465	14.9	-105	-1.1	-3.6
11 to 15 years.............	742	9,051	7.3	1,095	12.1	1,156	12.7	-60	-0.6	-2.1
16 to 20 years.............	584	8,285	6.7	920	11.1	956	11.5	-36	-0.4	-1.2
21 to 25 years.............	432	6,863	5.5	782	11.4	808	11.8	-27	-0.4	-0.9
26 years and older........	1,096	25,501	20.5	2,662	10.5	2,460	9.7	201	0.8	6.9
Unknown\left censored [4]..............	1,351	51,229	41.2	4,926	9.7	4,308	8.5	618	1.2	21.1

– Represents zero. [1] Establishment age is computed by taking the difference between the current year of operation and the birth year. Firm age is computed from the age of the establishments belonging to that particular firm. [2] Job creation is employment gains from expanding establishments, including establishment startups. [3] Job destruction is all employment losses from contracting establishments, including establishments shutting down. [4] Within the BDS, all firms/establishments born prior to 1976 have an unknown birth year and are therefore of an unknown age and are grouped into the age category "left censored."

Source: U.S. Census Bureau, Center for Economic Studies, "Business Dynamics Statistics (BDS)," <https://www.census.gov/programs-surveys/bds.html>, accessed July 2019.

Table 799. Establishments and Employment Changes from Births, Deaths, Expansions, and Contractions by Employment Size of Enterprise: 2015 to 2016

[In thousands (6,872 represents 6,872,000), except percent. Data represent activity from March of the beginning year to March of the ending year. This table provides the number of births and deaths of initial establishments (based on Census ID) as an approximation of firm births and deaths. An establishment is a single physical location at which business is conducted or where services or industrial operations are performed. An enterprise is a business organization consisting of one or more domestic establishments under common ownership or control. Minus sign (-) indicates decrease]

Employment size of firm	Establishments			Employment		Percent change in employment due to—			
	Number in initial year	Births [1]	Deaths [2]	Number in initial year	Change in employ-ment	Births [1]	Deaths [2]	Births and expan-sions [3]	Deaths and con-tractions [4]
Total....................	6,872	705	598	124,067	2,685	4.4	-3.6	13.2	-11.0
1 to 4......................	2,896	453	396	5,873	830	13.5	-11.6	32.0	-17.9
5 to 9......................	1,016	66	59	6,610	192	6.5	-5.7	18.4	-15.5
10 to 19....................	648	33	32	8,294	179	5.2	-4.8	15.3	-13.2
20 to 99...................	697	30	29	20,641	311	4.3	-4.0	12.7	-11.2
100 to 499................	364	20	15	17,502	260	3.4	-3.0	11.5	-10.0
Less than 500............	5,621	603	531	58,920	1,772	5.3	-4.8	15.3	-12.3
500 or more.............	1,252	102	67	65,147	913	3.5	-2.5	11.3	-9.9

[1] Births are establishments that have zero employment in the first quarter of the initial year and positive employment in the first quarter of the subsequent year. [2] Deaths are establishments that have positive employment in the first quarter of the initial year and zero employment in the first quarter of the subsequent year. [3] Expansions are establishments that have positive first quarter employment in both the initial and subsequent years and increase employment during the time period between the first quarter of the initial year and the first quarter of the subsequent year. [4] Contractions are establishments that have positive first quarter employment in both the initial and subsequent years and decrease employment during the time period between the first quarter of the initial year and the first quarter of the subsequent year.

Source: U.S. Census Bureau, "Statistics of U.S. Businesses," <https://www.census.gov/programs-surveys/susb.html>, accessed March 2019.

Table 800. Small Business Administration Loans to Minority-Owned Small Businesses: 1980 to 2019

[381 represents $381,000,000. For year ending September 30. A small business must be independently owned and operated, must not be dominant in its particular industry, and must meet standards set by the Small Business Administration as to its annual receipts or number of employees]

Year	Number of loans					Amount (mil. dol.)				
	Total minority loans [1]	Black	Asian or Pacific Islander	Hispanic (incl. Puerto Rican)	Amer-ican Indian	Total minority loans [1]	Black	Asian or Pacific Islander	Hispanic (incl. Puerto Rican)	Amer-ican Indian
1980..............	4,276	1,732	659	1,715	170	381	146	70	149	15
1985..............	2,028	608	657	689	74	291	64	115	102	10
1990..............	2,368	515	1,074	694	85	576	97	316	149	14
1995..............	10,879	2,775	3,768	3,936	400	1,839	294	946	539	61
1996..............	9,963	2,337	3,829	3,355	442	2,088	301	1,174	529	83
1997..............	10,247	1,929	4,533	3,378	407	2,507	299	1,501	626	81
1998..............	10,890	1,955	5,194	3,279	462	2,718	315	1,693	633	77
1999..............	12,081	2,217	5,578	3,749	537	3,389	402	2,149	754	84
2000..............	12,041	2,183	5,827	3,491	540	3,675	415	2,390	767	102
2001..............	11,926	2,025	5,711	3,619	571	3,510	409	2,257	740	103
2002..............	14,417	2,298	7,226	4,259	634	4,287	458	2,808	893	128
2003..............	20,483	4,138	9,469	6,089	787	4,307	462	2,770	957	119
2004..............	25,906	5,451	12,007	7,656	792	5,271	582	3,408	1,167	115
2005..............	30,226	7,302	13,353	8,748	823	6,294	756	4,072	1,341	125
2006..............	34,374	8,056	14,336	11,116	866	6,803	862	4,249	1,576	116
2007..............	36,962	9,812	15,312	10,918	920	7,020	1,072	4,331	1,490	127
2008..............	24,995	7,475	10,732	6,130	658	5,730	1,081	3,510	1,027	112
2009..............	11,072	3,067	5,142	2,537	293	3,371	612	2,100	600	47
2010..............	11,235	1,707	5,942	3,192	387	3,982	345	2,743	806	86
2011..............	13,151	1,643	7,119	3,915	470	6,000	446	4,369	1,053	131
2012..............	11,883	1,308	6,490	3,665	420	5,385	349	3,920	1,032	85
2013..............	12,777	1,415	7,178	3,831	353	6,336	491	4,679	1,072	94
2014..............	13,738	1,787	7,321	4,249	381	6,629	500	4,779	1,245	105
2015..............	17,112	2,325	8,792	5,533	462	8,038	648	5,613	1,628	149
2016..............	18,131	2,589	9,133	5,985	424	8,746	703	6,258	1,649	136
2017..............	17,992	2,638	9,180	5,713	459	9,596	738	6,989	1,721	144
2018..............	17,572	2,857	8,634	5,638	442	9,682	857	6,808	1,830	186
2019..............	15,716	2,572	7,494	5,262	387	8,796	828	5,974	1,840	153

[1] Beginning 2010, includes other minority loans not shown separately.

Source: U.S. Small Business Administration, "SBA Lending Statistics for Major Programs (as of 9/30/2019)," <https://www.sba.gov/about-sba/sba-newsroom/weekly-lending-report/archive>, accessed September 2020.

Table 801. Employer Firm Ownership by Industry and Sex, Race/Ethnicity, and Veteran Status: 2017

[In thousands (3,480.4 represents 3,480,400). Includes all U.S. firms with paid employees operating during the survey reference year with receipts of $1,000 or more and classified in the 2017 North American Industry Classification System (NAICS). Each owner had the option of selecting more than one race and is therefore included in each race selected. Based on the 2018 Annual Business Survey that collected data for 2017; see <https://www.census.gov/programs-surveys/abs/technical-documentation/methodology.html>]

| Industry | NAICS code | Sex | | Race/ethnicity | | | | | | Veteran owned |
		Male	Fe-male	White	Black	American Indian and Alaska Native	Asian	Native Hawaiian and other Pacific Islander	His-panic [1]	
All industries [2]	(X)	**3,480.4**	**1,134.5**	**4,769.8**	**124.0**	**24.5**	**555.6**	**6.8**	**322.1**	**351.2**
Forestry, fishing & hunting, and agricultural support services	113-115	17.3	3.4	27.0	0.2	0.2	0.2	(Z)	1.4	1.7
Mining, quarrying, and oil & gas extraction	21	12.6	1.9	17.4	(Z)	0.1	0.1	(S)	0.5	1.4
Utilities	22	2.0	0.3	2.5	(Z)	(Z)	0.1	(Z)	0.1	(S)
Construction	23	542.4	59.6	675.9	8.2	4.8	14.2	1.1	50.2	50.2
Manufacturing	31-33	164.7	36.2	224.0	1.6	1.0	11.6	0.3	10.5	19.1
Wholesale trade	42	202.9	42.0	248.1	2.0	0.8	36.0	0.1	15.8	20.4
Retail trade	44-45	378.0	132.9	519.6	8.8	2.3	105.0	0.8	31.1	32.5
Transportation & warehousing [3]	48-49	127.6	24.0	164.5	7.2	0.8	9.8	0.4	18.8	13.7
Information	51	49.5	11.1	62.8	1.2	0.3	5.5	0.1	2.6	3.5
Finance & insurance [4]	52	161.1	38.1	207.9	4.6	0.9	9.2	0.2	10.6	20.1
Real estate & rental & leasing	53	166.2	70.5	274.6	3.5	0.8	15.2	(S)	11.8	19.5
Professional, scientific, & technical services	54	521.4	185.6	714.3	16.4	4.1	60.9	1.0	34.3	60.4
Management of companies and enterprises	55	13.4	2.4	16.9	0.2	0.1	0.7	(Z)	0.4	1.5
Administrative & support and waste management & remediation services	56	216.4	69.4	313.8	10.1	1.8	12.1	0.6	30.5	23.1
Educational services	61	25.3	25.7	54.2	1.8	0.3	6.9	(S)	2.6	3.0
Health care & social assistance	62	327.7	192.2	467.4	39.7	2.6	75.3	0.6	31.2	40.6
Arts, entertainment, & recreation	71	59.6	22.2	94.5	2.5	0.5	3.1	0.1	3.0	4.6
Accommodation & food services	72	300.1	111.3	376.8	7.5	1.8	132.7	0.6	41.8	16.2
Other services (except public administration) [5]	81	211.3	107.1	320.9	8.3	1.3	57.9	0.4	25.2	21.1
Industries not classified	99	9.9	2.9	21.9	0.3	(Z)	0.4	(Z)	0.3	1.4

X Not applicable. S Data does not meet publication standards. Z Less than 50. [1] A Hispanic firm may be of any race and therefore may be included in more than one race group. [2] Firms with more than one domestic establishment are counted in each industry in which they operate, but only once in the total. [3] Excludes rail transportation (NAICS 482) and the postal service (NAICS 491). [4] Excludes monetary authorities-central banks (NAICS 521) and funds, trusts, and other financial vehicles (NAICS 525). [5] Excludes religious, grantmaking, civic, professional, and similar organizations (NAICS 813) and private households (NAICS 814).

Source: U.S. Census Bureau, Annual Business Survey, Table AB1700CSA01, "Statistics for Employer Firms by Industry, Sex, Ethnicity, Race, and Veteran Status for the U.S., States, Metro Areas, Counties, and Places: 2017," <data.census.gov/>, accessed June 2020.

Table 802. Women-Owned Employer Firms by Kind of Business: 2017

[1,490,299,620 represents $1,490,299,620,000. Data are shown for U.S. firms with paid employees, operating during the survey reference year, and with receipts of $1,000 or more. Based on the 2018 Annual Business Survey that collected data for 2017; see <https://www.census.gov/programs-surveys/abs/technical-documentation/methodology.html>]

Kind of business	NAICS code [1]	Firms (number)	Sales, value of shipments, or revenue ($1,000)	Employees (number) [2]	Annual payroll ($1,000)
Total [3]	(X)	**1,134,549**	**1,490,299,620**	**10,105,165**	**359,411,080**
Forestry, fishing & hunting, and agricultural support services	113–115	3,400	2,335,672	34,776	1,113,600
Mining, quarrying, and oil & gas extraction	21	1,937	6,899,963	23,953	1,607,588
Utilities	22	340	952,673	2,503	164,520
Construction	23	59,580	125,119,882	578,975	30,114,969
Manufacturing	31–33	36,202	142,686,256	609,016	28,893,285
Wholesale trade	42	42,022	256,404,889	407,204	21,640,629
Retail trade	44–45	132,894	246,599,026	918,413	24,859,390
Transportation and warehousing [4]	48–49	23,968	44,728,784	273,863	10,794,266
Information	51	11,072	22,389,845	115,532	7,039,135
Finance and insurance [5]	52	38,133	42,532,538	197,909	13,798,521
Real estate and rental and leasing	53	70,496	56,591,879	232,488	10,179,452
Professional, scientific, and technical services	54	185,649	145,621,200	941,424	53,838,786
Management of companies and enterprises	55	2,427	7,719,818	66,879	4,880,987
Administrative & support and waste management & remediation services	56	69,437	93,379,203	1,366,936	42,355,002
Educational services	61	25,746	12,498,643	208,819	4,975,053
Health care and social assistance	62	192,159	137,498,771	1,922,240	58,086,198
Arts, entertainment, and recreation	71	22,219	17,524,564	147,719	5,571,367
Accommodation and food services	72	111,319	90,787,507	1,511,913	26,216,843
Other services (except public administration) [6]	81	107,105	38,026,744	537,273	13,151,304
Industries not classified	99	2,922	1,765	7,331	130,185

[1] Based on the 2017 North American Industry Classification System (NAICS); see text, this section. [2] Paid employees for pay period including March 12. [3] Firms with more than one domestic establishment are counted in each industry in which they operate, but only once in the total. [4] Excludes rail transportation (NAICS 482) and the postal service (NAICS 491). [5] Excludes monetary authorities-central banks (NAICS 521) and funds, trusts, and other financial vehicles (NAICS 525). [6] Excludes religious, grantmaking, civic, professional, and similar organizations (NAICS 813) and private households (NAICS 814).

Source: U.S. Census Bureau, Annual Business Survey, Table AB1700CSA01, "Statistics for Employer Firms by Industry, Sex, Ethnicity, Race, and Veteran Status for the U.S., States, Metro Areas, Counties, and Places: 2017," <data.census.gov/>, accessed June 2020.

Table 803. Minority-Owned Employer Firms by Kind of Business: 2017

[1,401,793,981 represents $1,401,793,981,000. Data are shown for U.S. firms with paid employees, operating during the survey reference year, and with receipts of $1,000 or more. Based on the 2018 Annual Business Survey that collected data for 2017; see <https://www.census.gov/programs-surveys/abs/technical-documentation/methodology.html>]

Kind of business	NAICS code [1]	Firms (number)	Sales, value of shipments, or revenue ($1,000)	Employees (number) [2]	Annual payroll ($1,000)
Total [3]........................	(X)	1,014,958	1,401,793,981	8,922,965	294,898,962
Forestry, fishing & hunting, and agricultural support services........................	113–115	1,915	3,454,732	97,653	2,154,921
Mining, quarrying, and oil & gas extraction........................	21	799	1,468,268	8,147	484,161
Utilities........................	22	183	552,352	1,065	61,155
Construction........................	23	76,329	103,682,745	499,112	22,199,333
Manufacturing........................	31–33	24,415	86,438,218	341,176	15,629,870
Wholesale trade........................	42	54,260	292,094,252	400,569	19,317,359
Retail trade........................	44–45	145,097	272,707,002	866,964	21,406,427
Transportation and warehousing [4]........................	48–49	36,143	42,090,734	225,314	8,093,119
Information........................	51	9,571	25,058,473	105,915	7,876,683
Finance and insurance [5]........................	52	24,883	24,300,689	115,734	6,910,992
Real estate and rental and leasing........................	53	31,131	21,481,678	101,982	3,875,250
Professional, scientific, and technical services........................	54	114,308	131,523,553	745,841	50,910,902
Management of companies and enterprises........................	55	1,248	5,194,036	42,070	2,580,710
Administrative & support and waste management & remediation services........................	56	53,353	63,577,198	962,986	28,976,992
Educational services........................	61	11,708	6,250,231	94,430	2,165,822
Health care and social assistance........................	62	147,729	119,742,536	1,406,622	47,570,019
Arts, entertainment, and recreation........................	71	8,993	7,429,085	58,688	2,330,937
Accommodation and food services........................	72	182,604	162,667,445	2,458,803	43,355,612
Other services (except public administration) [6]........................	81	91,532	32,079,791	386,345	8,949,249
Industries not classified........................	99	950	962	3,551	49,449

[1] Based on the 2017 North American Industry Classification System (NAICS); see text, this section. [2] Paid employees for pay period including March 12. [3] Firms with more than one domestic establishment are counted in each industry in which they operate, but only once in the total. [4] Excludes rail transportation (NAICS 482) and the postal service (NAICS 491). [5] Excludes monetary authorities-central banks (NAICS 521) and funds, trusts, and other financial vehicles (NAICS 525). [6] Excludes religious, grantmaking, civic, professional, and similar organizations (NAICS 813) and private households (NAICS 814).

Source: U.S. Census Bureau, Annual Business Survey (ABS), Table AB1700CSA01, "Statistics for Employer Firms by Industry, Sex, Ethnicity, Race, and Veteran Status for the U.S., States, Metro Areas, Counties, and Places: 2017," <https://data.census.gov/>, accessed June 2020.

Table 804. Hispanic-Owned Employer Firms by Kind of Business: 2017

[422,573,589 represents $422,573,589,000. Data are shown for U.S. firms with paid employees, operating during the survey reference year, and with receipts of $1,000 or more. Based on the 2018 Annual Business Survey that collected data for 2017; see <https://www.census.gov/programs-surveys/abs/technical-documentation/methodology.html>]

Kind of business	NAICS code [1]	Firms (number)	Sales, value of shipments, or revenue ($1,000)	Employees (number) [2]	Annual payroll ($1,000)
Total [3]........................	(X)	322,076	422,573,589	2,872,550	90,985,526
Forestry, fishing & hunting, and agricultural support services........................	113–115	1,362	2,644,024	90,699	1,842,578
Mining, quarrying, and oil & gas extraction........................	21	547	910,457	6,024	341,330
Utilities........................	22	101	128,184	697	39,867
Construction........................	23	50,187	63,362,420	327,799	13,728,565
Manufacturing........................	31–33	10,504	25,186,540	116,591	5,164,210
Wholesale trade........................	42	15,781	82,684,049	119,019	5,359,708
Retail trade........................	44–45	31,090	69,886,335	230,526	6,397,549
Transportation and warehousing [4]........................	48–49	18,817	19,846,391	105,971	3,796,068
Information........................	51	2,583	6,092,124	27,170	1,589,811
Finance and insurance [5]........................	52	10,610	9,623,436	48,236	2,416,247
Real estate and rental and leasing........................	53	11,779	7,174,743	37,788	1,434,283
Professional, scientific, and technical services........................	54	34,292	29,514,634	185,395	10,487,211
Management of companies and enterprises........................	55	371	1,787,740	11,638	682,728
Administrative & support and waste management & remediation services........................	56	30,479	28,057,579	455,675	12,297,243
Educational services........................	61	2,600	1,793,713	24,196	644,398
Health care and social assistance........................	62	31,230	23,603,620	316,697	9,719,193
Arts, entertainment, and recreation........................	71	3,034	1,975,725	18,758	515,791
Accommodation and food services........................	72	41,817	37,996,309	644,051	11,631,487
Other services (except public administration) [6]........................	81	25,217	10,305,566	104,133	2,875,084
Industries not classified........................	99	290	–	1,487	22,176

X Not applicable. – Represents or rounds to zero. [1] Based on the 2017 North American Industry Classification System (NAICS); see text, this section. [2] Paid employees for pay period including March 12. [3] Firms with more than one domestic establishment are counted in each industry in which they operate, but only once in the total. [4] Excludes rail transportation (NAICS 482) and the postal service (NAICS 491). [5] Excludes monetary authorities-central banks (NAICS 521) and funds, trusts, and other financial vehicles (NAICS 525). [6] Excludes religious, grantmaking, civic, professional, and similar organizations (NAICS 813) and private households (NAICS 814).

Source: U.S. Census Bureau, Annual Business Survey, Table AB1700CSA01, "Statistics for Employer Firms by Industry, Sex, Ethnicity, Race, and Veteran Status for the U.S., States, Metro Areas, Counties, and Places: 2017," <data.census.gov/>, accessed June 2020.

Table 805. Black-Owned Employer Firms by Kind of Business: 2017

[127,850,815 represents $127,850,815,000. Data are shown for U.S. firms with paid employees, operating during the survey reference year, and with receipts of $1,000 or more. Based on the 2018 Annual Business Survey that collected data for 2017; see <https://www.census.gov/programs-surveys/abs/technical-documentation/methodology.html>]

Kind of business	NAICS code [1]	Firms (number)	Sales, value of shipments, or revenue ($1,000)	Employees (number) [2]	Annual payroll ($1,000)
Total [3]	**(X)**	**124,004**	**127,850,815**	**1,208,270**	**36,105,467**
Forestry, fishing & hunting, and agricultural support services	113–115	165	148,959	1,082	51,779
Mining, quarrying, and oil & gas extraction	21	21	17,993	53	3,468
Utilities	22	18	84,824	49	3,198
Construction	23	8,218	11,062,034	54,093	2,481,191
Manufacturing	31–33	1,608	9,408,794	23,999	1,125,880
Wholesale trade	42	1,986	11,809,954	14,898	797,585
Retail trade	44–45	8,753	16,894,627	50,539	1,472,858
Transportation and warehousing [4]	48–49	7,201	4,882,146	45,069	1,295,686
Information	51	1,242	2,450,300	12,946	904,335
Finance and insurance [5]	52	4,645	2,909,211	18,746	884,007
Real estate and rental and leasing	53	3,547	2,280,332	11,800	418,961
Professional, scientific, and technical services	54	16,392	14,787,229	96,267	5,682,935
Management of companies and enterprises	55	186	397,780	6,017	263,976
Administrative & support and waste management & remediation services	56	10,136	10,992,530	208,408	5,568,770
Educational services	61	1,830	712,173	12,392	314,649
Health care and social assistance	62	39,714	24,471,738	446,594	10,856,283
Arts, entertainment, and recreation	71	2,538	2,350,899	10,341	737,335
Accommodation and food services	72	7,492	9,231,711	159,930	2,460,623
Other services (except public administration) [6]	81	8,313	2,957,582	33,637	771,592
Industries not classified	99	305	–	1,411	10,359

– Represents or rounds to zero. [1] Based on the 2017 North American Industry Classification System (NAICS); see text, this section. [2] Paid employees for pay period including March 12. [3] Firms with more than one domestic establishment are counted in each industry in which they operate, but only once in the total. [4] Excludes rail transportation (NAICS 482) and the postal service (NAICS 491). [5] Excludes monetary authorities-central banks (NAICS 521) and funds, trusts, and other financial vehicles (NAICS 525). [6] Excludes religious, grantmaking, civic, professional, and similar organizations (NAICS 813) and private households (NAICS 814).

Source: U.S. Census Bureau, Annual Business Survey, Table AB1700CSA01, "Statistics for Employer Firms by Industry, Sex, Ethnicity, Race, and Veteran Status for the U.S., States, Metro Areas, Counties, and Places: 2017," <data.census.gov/>, accessed June 2020.

Table 806. Asian-Owned Employer Firms by Kind of Business: 2017

[814,806,324 represents $814,806,324,000. Data are shown for U.S. firms with paid employees, operating during the survey reference year, and with receipts of $1,000 or more. Based on the 2018 Annual Business Survey that collected data for 2017; see <https://www.census.gov/programs-surveys/abs/technical-documentation/methodology.html>]

Kind of business	NAICS code [1]	Firms (number)	Sales, value of shipments, or revenue ($1,000)	Employees (number) [2]	Annual payroll ($1,000)
Total [3]	**(X)**	**555,638**	**814,806,324**	**4,649,688**	**158,725,110**
Forestry, fishing & hunting, and agricultural support services	113–115	193	494,701	3,211	185,903
Mining, quarrying, and oil & gas extraction	21	117	286,109	1,070	72,773
Utilities	22	56	72,882	202	9,810
Construction	23	14,169	21,160,223	82,746	4,162,689
Manufacturing	31–33	11,632	48,361,943	187,235	8,628,711
Wholesale trade	42	36,043	193,020,098	262,886	12,928,043
Retail trade	44–45	104,957	182,012,250	575,103	13,177,556
Transportation and warehousing [4]	48–49	9,757	15,928,705	66,528	2,657,197
Information	51	5,529	16,066,120	63,355	5,249,202
Finance and insurance [5]	52	9,247	10,967,081	46,815	3,337,683
Real estate and rental and leasing	53	15,248	11,478,909	49,666	1,910,703
Professional, scientific, and technical services	54	60,907	81,592,941	432,567	32,520,040
Management of companies and enterprises	55	653	2,645,966	23,363	1,574,445
Administrative & support and waste management & remediation services	56	12,135	23,074,141	282,344	10,390,117
Educational services	61	6,887	3,533,265	53,902	1,116,981
Health care and social assistance	62	75,336	69,137,320	619,608	25,993,617
Arts, entertainment, and recreation	71	3,055	2,502,401	26,303	817,220
Accommodation and food services	72	132,698	114,284,365	1,630,669	28,884,124
Other services (except public administration) [6]	81	57,850	18,185,942	241,454	5,090,787
Industries not classified	99	353	962	661	17,508

[1] Based on the 2017 North American Industry Classification System (NAICS); see text, this section. [2] Paid employees for pay period including March 12. [3] Firms with more than one domestic establishment are counted in each industry in which they operate, but only once in the total. [4] Excludes rail transportation (NAICS 482) and the postal service (NAICS 491). [5] Excludes monetary authorities-central banks (NAICS 521) and funds, trusts, and other financial vehicles (NAICS 525). [6] Excludes religious, grantmaking, civic, professional, and similar organizations (NAICS 813) and private households (NAICS 814).

Source: U.S. Census Bureau, Annual Business Survey, Table AB1700CSA01, "Statistics for Employer Firms by Industry, Sex, Ethnicity, Race, and Veteran Status for the U.S., States, Metro Areas, Counties, and Places: 2017," <data.census.gov/>, accessed June 2020.

Table 807. Native Hawaiian and Other Pacific Islander-Owned Employer Firms by Kind of Business: 2017

[8,426,209 represents $8,426,209,000. Data are shown for U.S. firms with paid employees, operating during the survey reference year, and with receipts of $1,000 or more. Based on the 2018 Annual Business Survey that collected data for 2017; see <https://www.census.gov/programs-surveys/abs/technical-documentation/methodology.html>]

Kind of business	NAICS code [1]	Firms (number)	Sales, value of shipments, or revenue ($1,000)	Employees (number) [2]	Annual payroll ($1,000)
Total [3]	(X)	6,847	8,426,209	55,413	1,960,819
Forestry, fishing & hunting, and agricultural support services	113–115	6	1,410	5	268
Mining, quarrying, and oil & gas extraction	21	(S)	(S)	([7])	(S)
Utilities	22	5	293	2	77
Construction	23	1,093	1,517,730	7,795	359,508
Manufacturing	31–33	253	1,066,895	3,595	168,717
Wholesale trade	42	138	264,150	1,174	29,492
Retail trade	44–45	806	1,904,725	6,757	173,756
Transportation and warehousing [4]	48–49	351	368,123	2,426	92,954
Information	51	76	63,085	345	19,771
Finance and insurance [5]	52	203	165,058	929	56,569
Real estate and rental and leasing	53	(S)	(S)	([8])	(S)
Professional, scientific, and technical services	54	971	957,403	6,118	385,489
Management of companies and enterprises	55	23	30,982	295	23,863
Administrative & support and waste management & remediation services	56	609	470,858	6,107	194,735
Educational services	61	(S)	(S)	([8])	(S)
Health care and social assistance	62	628	312,315	3,929	118,610
Arts, entertainment, and recreation	71	129	154,718	1,009	26,750
Accommodation and food services	72	592	573,016	10,021	165,086
Other services (except public administration) [6]	81	420	166,935	1,703	49,451
Industries not classified	99	6	–	9	185

– Represents or rounds to zero. S Figure does not meet publication standards. [1] Based on the 2017 North American Industry Classification System (NAICS); see text, this section. [2] Paid employees for pay period including March 12. [3] Firms with more than one domestic establishment are counted in each industry in which they operate, but only once in the total. [4] Excludes rail transportation (NAICS 482) and the postal service (NAICS 491). [5] Excludes monetary authorities-central banks (NAICS 521) and funds, trusts, and other financial vehicles (NAICS 525). [6] Excludes religious, grantmaking, civic, professional, and similar organizations (NAICS 813) and private households (NAICS 814). [7] 100 to 249 employees. [8] 1,000 to 2,499 employees.

Source: U.S. Census Bureau, Annual Business Survey, Table AB1700CSA01, "Statistics for Employer Firms by Industry, Sex, Ethnicity, Race, and Veteran Status for the U.S., States, Metro Areas, Counties, and Places: 2017," <data.census.gov/>, accessed June 2020.

Table 808. American Indian and Alaska Native-Owned Employer Firms by Kind of Business: 2017

[37,992,217 represents $37,992,217,000. Data are shown for U.S. firms with paid employees, operating during the survey reference year, and with receipts of $1,000 or more. Based on the 2018 Annual Business Survey that collected data for 2017; see <https://www.census.gov/programs-surveys/abs/technical-documentation/methodology.html>]

Kind of business	NAICS code [1]	Firms (number)	Sales, value of shipments, or revenue ($1,000)	Employees (number) [2]	Annual payroll ($1,000)
Total [3]	(X)	24,503	37,992,217	221,193	8,793,842
Forestry, fishing & hunting, and agricultural support services	113–115	231	202,224	3,155	104,534
Mining, quarrying, and oil & gas extraction	21	117	252,496	1,000	66,795
Utilities	22	15	267,008	120	8,357
Construction	23	4,821	8,095,145	35,355	1,828,684
Manufacturing	31–33	968	2,969,635	12,705	627,861
Wholesale trade	42	781	5,537,974	8,403	424,405
Retail trade	44–45	2,347	5,565,181	18,232	532,874
Transportation and warehousing [4]	48–49	820	1,802,633	9,214	399,330
Information	51	262	461,502	2,633	120,180
Finance and insurance [5]	52	870	449,652	3,174	145,142
Real estate and rental and leasing	53	833	486,200	2,603	104,571
Professional, scientific, and technical services	54	4,142	4,800,227	29,953	1,823,661
Management of companies and enterprises	55	50	462,017	1,141	67,015
Administrative & support and waste management & remediation services	56	1,762	1,764,432	24,715	785,345
Educational services	61	328	90,968	1,955	37,907
Health care and social assistance	62	2,603	1,610,792	22,531	686,972
Arts, entertainment, and recreation	71	475	650,566	3,658	273,181
Accommodation and food services	72	1,798	1,836,455	33,235	542,587
Other services (except public administration) [6]	81	1,335	687,109	7,301	213,330
Industries not classified	99	23	–	111	1,110

– Represents or rounds to zero. [1] Based on the 2017 North American Industry Classification System (NAICS); see text, this section. [2] Paid employees for pay period including March 12. [3] Firms with more than one domestic establishment are counted in each industry in which they operate, but only once in the total. [4] Excludes rail transportation (NAICS 482) and the postal service (NAICS 491). [5] Excludes monetary authorities-central banks (NAICS 521) and funds, trusts, and other financial vehicles (NAICS 525). [6] Excludes religious, grantmaking, civic, professional, and similar organizations (NAICS 813) and private households (NAICS 814).

Source: U.S. Census Bureau, Annual Business Survey, Table AB1700CSA01, "Statistics for Employer Firms by Industry, Sex, Ethnicity, Race, and Veteran Status for the U.S., States, Metro Areas, Counties, and Places: 2017," <data.census.gov/>, accessed June 2020.

Table 809. Bankruptcy Petitions by Type and Chapter: 2000 to 2019

[For years ending June 30. Covers only bankruptcy cases filed under the Bankruptcy Reform Act of 1978. Bankruptcy: legal recognition that a company or individual is insolvent and must restructure or liquidate assets. Section 101 of the U.S. Bankruptcy Code defines consumer (nonbusiness) debt as that incurred by an individual primarily for a personal, family, or household purpose. If the debtor is a corporation or partnership, or if debt related to operation of a business predominates, the nature of the debt is business]

Item	2000	2005	2010	2014	2015	2016	2017	2018	2019
Total filed...................	**1,276,922**	**1,637,254**	**1,572,597**	**1,000,083**	**879,736**	**819,159**	**796,037**	**775,578**	**773,361**
Chapter 7 [1]...................	885,447	1,196,212	1,133,320	669,976	568,679	509,769	489,011	479,151	479,043
Chapter 9 [2]...................	8	6	12	13	7	5	9	6	3
Chapter 11 [3].................	9,947	6,703	14,272	8,347	6,672	7,928	6,999	7,141	7,007
Chapter 12 [4].................	732	290	660	394	357	459	482	475	535
Chapter 13 [5].................	380,770	433,945	424,242	321,278	303,945	300,858	299,398	288,741	286,635
Section 304 [6]...............	18	98	(X)	(X)	(X)	(X)	(X)	(X)	(X)
Chapter 15 [7].................	(X)	(X)	91	74	76	140	138	64	138
Business [8]..................	**36,910**	**32,406**	**59,608**	**30,113**	**25,046**	**25,227**	**23,443**	**22,245**	**22,483**
Nonbusiness [9].............	**1,240,012**	**1,604,848**	**1,512,989**	**969,970**	**854,690**	**793,932**	**772,594**	**753,333**	**750,878**
Chapter 7 [1]...................	864,183	1,174,681	1,091,322	649,975	551,808	494,218	474,258	465,472	464,978
Chapter 11 [3].................	722	847	1,827	1,211	1,078	1,146	1,099	1,071	1,039
Chapter 13 [5].................	375,107	429,315	419,836	318,781	301,802	298,566	297,237	286,790	284,861
Total pending...............	**1,400,416**	**1,750,562**	**1,659,399**	**1,461,132**	**1,316,672**	**1,194,843**	**1,100,309**	**1,050,476**	**1,032,306**

X Not applicable. [1] Chapter 7, liquidation of nonexempt assets of businesses or individuals. [2] Chapter 9, adjustment of debts of a municipality. [3] Chapter 11, individual or business reorganization. [4] Chapter 12, adjustment of debts of a family farmer with regular income, effective November 26, 1986. [5] Chapter 13, adjustment of debts of an individual with regular income. [6] Chapter 11, U.S.C., Section 304, cases ancillary to foreign proceedings. [7] Chapter 15 was added and Section 304 was terminated by changes in Bankruptcy Laws effective October 2005. [8] Business bankruptcies include those filed under Chapters 7, 9, 11, 12, 13, or 15. [9] Includes other petitions, not shown separately.

Source: Administrative Office of the United States Courts, "Caseload Statistics Data Tables," <http://www.uscourts.gov/statistics-reports/caseload-statistics-data-tables>, accessed March 2020.

Table 810. Bankruptcy Cases Filed by State: 2000 to 2019

[In thousands (1,276.9 represents 1,276,900). For years ending June 30. See headnote, Table 809]

State	2000	2005	2010	2013	2014	2015	2016	2017	2018	2019
Total [1]....................	**1,276.9**	**1,637.3**	**1,572.6**	**1,138.0**	**1,000.1**	**879.7**	**819.2**	**796.0**	**775.6**	**773.4**
Alabama..................	31.4	42.6	34.9	27.7	26.1	25.2	26.1	27.2	26.7	26.6
Alaska....................	1.4	1.6	1.1	0.7	0.5	0.4	0.5	0.5	0.4	0.5
Arizona...................	21.7	32.4	40.7	25.1	21.9	18.0	16.5	15.4	16.1	16.7
Arkansas.................	16.3	25.5	16.9	12.6	11.8	10.4	10.4	10.7	10.5	10.6
California.................	160.6	122.6	242.0	161.2	116.7	91.9	77.8	73.4	69.5	69.0
Colorado..................	15.6	30.2	31.9	24.3	20.3	16.0	13.8	12.5	11.8	11.4
Connecticut..............	11.4	11.8	11.3	7.5	7.1	6.6	6.1	5.7	5.9	6.2
Delaware.................	4.9	3.6	4.5	3.5	3.4	2.7	2.9	2.8	3.2	2.9
District of Columbia......	2.6	1.9	1.3	0.8	0.8	0.8	0.7	0.7	0.8	0.8
Florida...................	74.0	85.8	107.4	78.5	73.3	62.4	50.3	44.7	41.3	45.8
Georgia..................	57.9	77.3	77.8	61.6	55.2	51.1	49.4	48.1	45.7	44.5
Hawaii...................	5.0	3.2	3.7	2.4	1.9	1.6	1.5	1.4	1.5	1.6
Idaho....................	7.3	9.7	8.3	5.9	5.1	4.4	3.9	3.8	3.7	3.7
Illinois...................	62.3	83.6	80.8	69.1	62.9	58.8	55.8	52.3	49.7	47.9
Indiana..................	37.5	55.9	49.3	35.1	31.2	28.0	25.1	24.0	23.0	23.0
Iowa.....................	8.2	14.3	10.4	5.9	5.5	4.7	4.4	4.2	4.6	4.7
Kansas..................	11.4	17.3	11.4	8.7	8.0	7.2	6.5	6.8	6.8	6.8
Kentucky.................	20.8	29.2	26.0	18.9	17.9	15.8	15.4	15.5	15.4	15.1
Louisiana................	23.1	31.1	19.5	15.9	15.6	14.3	14.0	13.4	13.5	13.3
Maine....................	4.1	4.7	4.1	2.7	2.2	2.0	1.7	1.4	1.5	1.4
Maryland.................	31.1	28.5	29.1	23.2	21.9	19.0	17.9	17.5	17.5	17.4
Massachusetts...........	16.7	19.6	22.9	14.0	11.4	9.6	8.9	8.6	8.5	8.1
Michigan.................	36.4	68.5	71.0	45.4	38.6	33.6	32.1	30.6	30.2	30.0
Minnesota................	15.4	19.4	22.6	15.4	13.4	11.3	10.1	9.6	9.9	9.8
Mississippi...............	17.9	21.8	14.8	12.4	12.4	10.9	11.1	11.9	12.6	12.6
Missouri..................	26.3	39.2	32.9	27.1	22.3	19.9	18.8	18.4	17.8	17.0
Montana.................	3.3	4.4	3.1	2.0	1.7	1.4	1.4	1.3	1.3	1.3
Nebraska................	5.6	9.6	7.9	5.6	4.9	4.3	4.2	4.0	4.0	4.1
Nevada..................	14.3	16.3	31.0	15.7	12.3	10.2	9.2	8.9	9.0	9.8
New Hampshire..........	3.9	4.9	5.7	3.6	2.9	2.3	2.0	1.8	1.8	1.8
New Jersey..............	38.7	40.7	39.7	29.3	28.4	26.1	25.7	26.5	26.7	25.9
New Mexico..............	7.1	10.1	6.6	4.6	4.0	3.6	3.3	3.4	3.3	3.2
New York.................	61.7	81.7	58.2	38.3	34.6	30.9	30.2	31.6	34.2	35.5
North Carolina...........	25.8	37.5	27.7	20.0	17.6	16.2	15.4	14.7	14.3	13.4
North Dakota.............	2.0	2.5	1.6	0.9	0.7	0.6	0.6	0.8	0.8	0.8
Ohio.....................	53.6	95.8	72.9	49.8	43.6	39.9	37.7	37.4	37.9	37.2
Oklahoma................	19.3	28.2	15.1	11.3	10.2	9.4	9.1	9.5	9.6	9.5
Oregon..................	18.1	25.3	20.1	14.0	13.1	11.5	9.9	9.1	9.0	8.9
Pennsylvania.............	43.8	62.3	38.8	27.5	25.9	22.7	22.2	22.4	21.7	21.4
Rhode Island.............	4.8	4.4	5.4	3.6	3.3	2.7	2.4	2.2	2.3	2.0
South Carolina...........	11.7	15.2	9.7	7.7	7.6	7.1	6.7	6.6	6.6	6.8
South Dakota............	2.1	2.9	2.0	1.4	1.3	1.2	1.1	1.0	1.1	1.0
Tennessee...............	47.1	60.8	52.5	43.3	40.7	37.3	36.5	35.8	34.5	34.0
Texas....................	62.9	97.5	57.8	44.0	38.9	34.7	33.7	35.6	33.5	35.2
Utah.....................	14.4	20.5	17.0	15.2	14.0	13.0	11.8	11.7	10.3	9.6
Vermont..................	1.6	1.7	1.7	0.9	0.8	0.7	0.6	0.5	0.6	0.6
Virginia..................	37.1	38.8	37.8	27.2	25.1	23.2	23.3	22.8	22.8	22.9
Washington..............	31.2	37.7	33.5	26.5	22.9	19.7	17.4	15.5	13.9	13.0
West Virginia............	8.2	12.6	6.6	3.8	3.5	3.3	3.3	3.4	3.1	2.9
Wisconsin................	18.0	29.0	30.0	23.9	22.0	19.9	17.7	17.1	16.9	16.4
Wyoming.................	2.0	2.5	1.5	1.3	1.1	0.9	0.9	1.0	1.0	0.9

[1] Includes Island Areas, not shown separately.

Source: Administrative Office of the United States Courts, "Caseload Statistics Data Tables," <http://www.uscourts.gov/statistics-reports/caseload-statistics-data-tables>, accessed March 2020.

Table 811. Patents and Trademarks: 2000 to 2018

[In thousands (176.0 represents 176,000), unless otherwise noted. Calendar year data. Covers U.S. patents issued to citizens of the United States and residents of foreign countries. For data on foreign countries, see Table 1402]

Type	2000	2005	2010	2013	2014	2015	2016	2017	2018
Patents issued..................	**176.0**	**157.7**	**244.3**	**302.9**	**326.0**	**326.0**	**333.6**	**351.4**	**340.0**
Inventions.....................	157.5	143.8	219.6	277.8	300.7	298.4	303.0	318.8	307.8
Individuals.................	22.4	14.7	16.6	18.7	19.3	18.9	18.7	19.3	18.7
Corporations:									
United States............	70.9	65.2	97.8	124.7	136.4	133.4	136.8	145.3	140.0
Foreign [1]...............	63.3	63.2	104.3	133.4	144.0	145.1	146.7	153.3	148.1
U.S. government.............	0.9	0.7	0.9	1.0	1.0	1.0	0.9	1.0	0.9
Designs.......................	17.4	13.0	22.8	23.5	23.7	26.0	28.9	30.9	30.5
Botanical plants...............	0.5	0.7	1.0	0.8	1.1	1.1	1.2	1.3	1.2
Reissues......................	0.5	0.2	0.9	0.8	0.6	0.5	0.4	0.4	0.5
U.S. residents.................	96.9	82.6	121.2	147.7	158.7	156.0	160.5	169.2	161.8
Foreign country residents.........	79.1	75.2	123.2	155.3	167.3	170.0	173.0	182.2	178.2
Percent of total.............	44.9	47.6	50.4	51.3	51.3	52.1	51.9	51.8	52.4
Trademarks:									
Applications filed..............	361.8	334.7	368.9	433.7	455.0	503.9	530.3	594.1	638.8

[1] Includes patents to foreign governments.

Source: U.S. Patent and Trademark Office, "General Patent Statistics Reports Available for Viewing," <http://www.uspto.gov/web/offices/ac/ido/oeip/taf/reports_stco.htm>, accessed December 2019; and unpublished data.

Table 812. Patents by State and Island Areas: 2018

[Includes only U.S. patents granted to residents of the United States and U.S. territories]

State	Total	Inven-tions	De-signs	Botani-cal plants	Reis-sues	State	Total	Inven-tions	De-signs	Botani-cal plants	Reis-sues
Total [1]..................	**161,809**	**144,413**	**16,644**	**493**	**259**	Missouri............	1,406	1,270	135	0	1
						Montana............	172	145	27	0	0
Alabama.................	510	456	53	1	0	Nebraska............	314	279	33	0	2
Alaska..................	57	46	11	0	0	Nevada.............	745	646	96	0	3
Arizona.................	2,812	2,551	249	3	9	New Hampshire. ..	998	890	102	1	5
Arkansas...............	403	335	67	1	0	New Jersey.........	4,682	4,071	597	4	10
California...............	43,960	39,814	3,909	171	66	New Mexico........	535	483	49	3	0
Colorado...............	3,259	2,899	356	1	3	New York..........	9,780	8,475	1,289	4	12
Connecticut............	2,977	2,781	192	2	2	North Carolina.....	3,781	3,465	291	19	6
Delaware...............	285	267	17	0	1	North Dakota.......	123	117	5	1	0
District of Columbia. ..	228	183	44	0	1	Ohio...............	4,608	3,898	700	5	5
Florida.................	4,893	4,163	675	42	13	Oklahoma..........	614	556	57	0	1
Georgia................	3,064	2,646	402	13	3	Oregon............	3,522	2,771	704	39	8
Hawaii.................	136	108	26	2	0	Pennsylvania......	4,456	3,950	482	18	6
Idaho..................	843	794	49	0	0	Rhode Island.......	415	335	80	0	0
Illinois.................	5,655	4,812	830	6	7	South Carolina.....	1,142	1,017	122	3	0
Indiana................	2,265	2,044	220	0	1	South Dakota.....	157	134	23	0	0
Iowa...................	1,056	988	67	0	1	Tennessee.........	1,289	1,071	213	3	2
Kansas................	894	768	123	2	1	Texas.............	11,359	10,469	859	11	20
Kentucky..............	745	665	79	0	1	Utah..............	1,795	1,527	268	0	0
Louisiana..............	490	429	43	16	2	Vermont...........	388	357	30	0	1
Maine.................	228	208	19	0	1	Virginia............	2,542	2,370	164	1	7
Maryland..............	2,042	1,861	167	3	11	Washington........	7,445	6,933	488	12	12
Massachusetts........	7,687	7,207	461	7	12	West Virginia.......	152	143	9	0	0
Michigan...............	7,293	6,460	752	73	8	Wisconsin.........	2,702	2,200	478	19	5
Minnesota.............	4,513	4,043	457	3	10	Wyoming..........	118	109	9	0	0
Mississippi............	208	160	45	3	0	Island areas........	66	44	21	1	0

[1] Includes unspecified areas.

Source: U.S. Patent and Trademark Office, "General Patent Statistics Reports Available for Viewing," <http://www.uspto.gov/web/offices/ac/ido/oeip/taf/reports_stco.htm>, accessed December 2019.

Table 813. Copyright Registration by Subject Matter: 1990 to 2018

[In thousands (590.7 represents 590,700). For years ending September 30. Comprises claims to copyrights registered for both U.S. and foreign works. Semiconductor chips and renewals are not considered copyright registration claims]

Subject matter	1990	2000	2005	2010	2013	2014	2015	2016	2017	2018
Total copyright basic registrations.	**590.7**	**497.6**	**515.2**	**636.0**	**496.2**	**476.0**	**443.0**	**414.1**	**452.1**	**559.5**
Monographs [1]............................	179.7	169.7	191.4	245.8	180.6	175.4	175.5	168.8	153.0	197.3
Serials................................	111.5	69.0	57.7	90.5	44.2	43.2	55.1	41.9	49.5	54.9
Sound recordings........................	37.5	34.2	49.9	77.9	72.4	65.5	43.0	42.4	59.2	77.2
Performing arts [2].......................	185.3	138.9	133.7	124.5	116.1	103.3	80.1	75.3	103.5	136.4
Works of the visual arts [3]................	76.7	85.8	82.5	97.2	82.9	88.7	89.2	85.6	86.5	93.7
Renewals.............................	51.8	16.8	15.8	0.1	0.2	0.1	0.8	0.2	0.4	0.4
Mask work (semiconductor chip products)...........................	1.0	0.7	0.5	0.3	0.3	0.1	0.1	(Z)	(Z)	0.2

Z Less than 50. [1] Includes computer software and machine readable works. [2] Includes musical works, dramatic works, choreography, pantomimes, motion pictures, and filmstrips. [3] Two-dimensional works of fine and graphic art, including prints and art reproductions; sculptural works; technical drawings and models; photographs; commercial prints and labels; and works of applied arts, cartographic works, and multimedia works.

Source: The Library of Congress, *Annual Report of the Librarian of Congress, For the Fiscal Year Ending September 30, 2018*, 2019. See also <http://www.loc.gov/about/reports-and-budgets/annual-reports/>.

Table 814. Net Stock of Private Fixed Assets by Industry: 2000 to 2018

[In billions of dollars (21,483 represents $21,483,000,000,000). Estimates as of Dec. 31. Fixed assets are assets that are used repeatedly, or continuously, in processes of production for more than a year. Net stock estimates are presented in terms of current-cost, and cover equipment, structures, and intellectual property products. (pt) = part]

Industry	NAICS code [1]	2000	2010	2016	2017	2018
Private fixed assets..................	(X)	**21,483**	**34,582**	**43,475**	**45,443**	**47,832**
Agriculture, forestry, fishing, and hunting..........................	11	338	487	658	679	712
Farms [2].................................	111, 112	311	438	593	610	637
Forestry, fishing, and related activities.................	113-115	27	49	65	69	75
Mining............................	21	576	1,575	2,154	2,213	2,229
Oil and gas extraction...............	211	442	1,328	1,811	1,865	1,874
Mining, except oil and gas..........	212	90	138	201	207	215
Support activities for mining.......	213	44	109	142	141	140
Utilities..................................	22	1,039	1,859	2,349	2,447	2,593
Construction............................	23	174	264	323	337	359
Manufacturing...........................	31-33	2,315	3,215	3,832	3,995	4,150
Durable goods..........................	(X)	1,289	1,664	1,940	2,008	2,081
Wood products.....................	321	32	38	43	45	48
Nonmetallic mineral products.....	327	67	90	97	101	105
Primary metals.....................	331	134	162	174	177	182
Fabricated metal products.........	332	124	162	192	199	209
Machinery..........................	333	166	203	238	244	251
Computer and electronic products.....	334	360	482	560	578	595
Electrical equipment, appliances, and components...........	335	58	68	77	80	83
Motor vehicles, bodies and trailers, and parts..............	3361-3363	156	190	249	261	273
Other transportation equipment.....	3364, 3365, 3369	112	158	182	192	201
Furniture and related products......	337	17	22	23	23	24
Miscellaneous manufacturing.......	339	64	91	105	108	112
Nondurable goods......................	(X)	1,026	1,551	1,893	1,987	2,069
Food and beverage and tobacco products...................	311, 312	201	287	337	351	367
Textile mills and textile product mills.....	313, 314	45	42	40	40	41
Apparel and leather and allied products..........	315, 316	18	18	18	18	18
Paper products....................	322	105	110	120	123	127
Printing and related support activities.....	323	42	50	47	47	48
Petroleum and coal products......	324	117	198	244	254	264
Chemical products.................	325	422	755	980	1,042	1,088
Plastics and rubber products......	326	75	92	107	112	117
Wholesale trade.........................	42	348	491	617	649	688
Retail trade.............................	44-45	656	1,132	1,326	1,382	1,440
Transportation and warehousing [3].....	48-49	821	1,095	1,366	1,423	1,498
Air transportation..................	481	184	219	259	273	290
Railroad transportation............	482	288	359	420	426	432
Water transportation...............	483	37	43	58	59	62
Truck transportation...............	484	71	106	148	154	166
Transit and ground passenger transportation........	485	37	42	45	46	47
Pipeline transportation............	486	73	161	250	270	295
Warehousing and storage..........	493	21	40	52	55	59
Information..............................	51	1,201	1,830	2,210	2,342	2,479
Publishing industries (includes software).....	511, 516 (pt)	118	258	339	355	373
Motion picture and sound recording industries.............	512	186	258	284	295	303
Broadcasting and telecommunications........	515, 517	858	1,215	1,346	1,402	1,467
Information and data processing services...................	516 (pt), 518, 519	40	99	242	291	336
Finance and insurance..................	52	782	1,154	1,391	1,442	1,513
Federal Reserve banks.............	521	9	10	10	10	11
Credit intermediation and related activities..........	522	487	717	898	926	968
Securities, commodity contracts, and investments..............	523	92	152	172	184	197
Insurance carriers and related activities.................	524	177	236	272	281	296
Funds, trusts, and other financial vehicles.............	525	18	40	40	40	41
Real estate and rental and leasing.....	53	10,739	17,227	22,033	23,069	24,386
Real estate........................	531	10,512	16,880	21,527	22,545	23,836
Rental and leasing services and lessors of intangible assets [4].........	532, 533	227	347	506	524	550
Professional, scientific, and technical services [3]........	54	313	576	696	738	786
Legal services.....................	5411	23	43	45	47	49
Computer systems design and related services........	5415	52	96	99	99	101
Management of companies and enterprises [5].................	55	266	355	388	402	421
Administrative and support and waste management..............	56	151	245	315	325	340
Administrative and support services.....	561	85	153	211	218	229
Waste management and remediation services...........	562	67	92	103	106	111
Educational services....................	61	217	469	584	614	652
Health care and social assistance......	62	694	1,221	1,491	1,556	1,649
Ambulatory health care services....	621	208	317	375	393	420
Hospitals..........................	622	428	773	949	987	1,043
Nursing and residential care facilities.....	623	33	77	100	106	113
Social assistance...................	624	26	53	68	70	74
Arts, entertainment, and recreation......	71	164	289	391	420	454
Performing arts, spectator sports, museums, and related activities....	711, 712	84	142	184	194	205
Amusements, gambling, and recreation industries...........	713	80	147	206	226	249
Accommodation and food services.......	72	342	542	683	723	769
Accommodation.....................	721	188	327	433	461	495
Food services and drinking places.....	722	154	215	250	262	274
Other services, except government......	81	347	557	668	688	713

X Not applicable. [1] Based on North American Industry Classification System; see text this section. [2] NAICS crop and animal production. [3] Includes other activities, not shown separately. [4] Intangible assets include patents, trademarks, and franchise agreements, but not copyrights. [5] Consists of bank and other holding companies.

Source: U.S. Bureau of Economic Analysis, National Economic Accounts, "Table 3.1ESI. Current-Cost Net Stock of Private Fixed Assets by Industry," <http://www.bea.gov/itable/>, accessed January 2020.

Table 815. Capital Expenditures: 2000 to 2018

[In billions of dollars (1,161 represents $1,161,000,000,000). Based on the Annual Capital Expenditure Survey, which is a sample survey and subject to sampling error; see source for details]

Item	All companies				Companies with employees				Companies without employees			
	2000	2010	2017	2018 [1]	2000	2010	2017	2018	2000	2010	2017	2018 [1]
Capital expenditures, total.........	**1,161**	**1,106**	**1,679**	**1,698**	**1,090**	**1,036**	**1,578**	**1,698**	**71**	**70**	**101**	**(NA)**
Structures..........................	364	430	666	644	338	396	612	644	26	33	54	(NA)
New..........................	329	395	617	608	309	368	576	608	20	28	40	(NA)
Used..........................	35	34	49	36	29	29	36	36	6	6	13	(NA)
Equipment..........................	797	676	1,013	1,053	752	640	966	1,053	45	36	47	(NA)
New..........................	751	638	957	1,000	718	612	921	1,000	32	27	36	(NA)
Used..........................	46	38	57	53	34	28	45	53	12	10	12	(NA)
Capitalized computer software [2].........	(NA)	(NA)	(NA)	(NA)	(NA)	(NA)	102	107	(NA)	(NA)	(NA)	(NA)
Capital leases [2]..........................	20	16	37	35	19	15	36	35	(Z)	1	1	(NA)

NA Not available. Z Less than $500 million. [1] Data for companies without employment was not collected in 2018. [2] Included in structures and equipment data shown above.

Source: U.S. Census Bureau, "Annual Capital Expenditures: 2018," and earlier reports, <http://www.census.gov/programs-surveys/aces.html>, accessed March 2020.

Table 816. Capital Expenditures by Industry: 2000 to 2018

[In billions of dollars (1,090 represents $1,090,000,000,000). Covers only companies with employees. Data from 2000 based on the North American Industry Classification System (NAICS), 1997; 2005 data based on NAICS 2002; 2010 through 2013 based on NAICS 2007; 2014 through 2017 data based on NAICS 2012; and, beginning 2018, data based on NAICS 2017, see text this section. Based on the Annual Capital Expenditure Survey, which is a sample survey and subject to sampling error; see source for details]

Industry	NAICS code	2000	2005	2010	2014	2015	2016	2017	2018
Total expenditures..........................	(X)	**1,090**	**1,063**	**1,036**	**1,507**	**1,548**	**1,479**	**1,578**	**1,698**
Forestry, fishing, and agricultural services......	113–115	1	3	3	4	3	5	4	5
Mining..........................	21	43	67	116	231	174	93	134	153
Utilities..........................	22	61	58	94	119	131	133	134	146
Construction..........................	23	25	30	18	30	33	36	35	39
Manufacturing..........................	31–33	215	166	161	231	245	244	247	259
Durable goods..........................	321, 327, 33	134	92	87	125	128	123	129	138
Nondurable goods..........................	31, 322–326	81	73	74	106	117	121	118	121
Wholesale trade..........................	42	34	41	31	45	42	44	44	42
Retail trade..........................	44–45	70	74	65	82	86	87	90	89
Transportation and warehousing..............	48–49	60	57	59	111	117	110	109	122
Information..........................	51	160	91	97	132	133	143	159	176
Finance and insurance..........................	52	134	161	103	153	165	162	163	182
Real estate and rental and leasing.............	53	92	103	81	122	152	151	161	174
Professional, scientific, & technical services...	54	34	33	28	30	33	32	37	42
Management of companies and enterprises...	55	5	3	5	5	5	6	7	7
Administrative & support and waste management & remediation services..........	56	18	18	17	23	26	28	27	29
Educational services..........................	61	18	17	23	26	33	30	37	36
Health care and social assistance..............	62	52	74	78	89	94	94	105	108
Arts, entertainment, and recreation.............	71	19	14	12	20	16	23	22	25
Accommodation and food services..........	72	26	31	20	30	33	30	36	36
Other services (except public administration)...	81	21	20	21	20	23	27	22	22
Structure and equipment expenditures serving multiple industry categories...........	(X)	2	2	2	3	4	4	5	4

X Not applicable.

Source: U.S. Census Bureau, "Annual Capital Expenditures: 2018," and earlier reports, <http://www.census.gov/programs-surveys/aces.html>, accessed March 2020.

Table 817. Private Domestic Investment in Current and Chained (2012) Dollars: 2000 to 2019

[In billions of dollars (2,038 represents $2,038,000,000,000). Covers equipment, structures, and intellectual property products. For explanation of chained dollars; see text, Section 13]

Item	2000	2005	2010	2015	2016	2017	2018	2019
CURRENT DOLLARS								
Gross private domestic investment...........	**2,038**	**2,535**	**2,166**	**3,237**	**3,188**	**3,351**	**3,633**	**3,751**
Less: Consumption of fixed capital..............	1,232	1,623	1,934	2,389	2,458	2,570	2,699	2,833
Equals: Net private domestic investment........	807	912	232	849	730	782	934	919
Fixed investment..........................	1,984	2,477	2,112	3,100	3,160	3,335	3,575	3,702
Less: Consumption of fixed capital..............	1,232	1,623	1,934	2,389	2,458	2,570	2,699	2,833
Equals: Net fixed investment....................	752	855	178	712	702	765	876	870
Nonresidential..........................	1,498	1,621	1,735	2,467	2,461	2,575	2,777	2,895
Residential..........................	485	856	377	634	700	760	799	807
Change in private inventories...................	55	58	54	137	28	16	58	49
CHAINED (2012) DOLLARS								
Gross private domestic investment...........	**2,347**	**2,671**	**2,217**	**3,122**	**3,075**	**3,183**	**3,385**	**3,443**
Less: Consumption of fixed capital..............	1,414	1,732	1,986	2,296	2,366	2,434	2,509	2,595
Equals: Net private domestic investment........	933	938	230	826	709	750	876	848
Fixed investment..........................	2,294	2,619	2,164	2,979	3,032	3,147	3,310	3,372
Nonresidential..........................	1,616	1,716	1,781	2,420	2,433	2,524	2,699	2,777
Residential..........................	647	885	383	555	592	616	612	602
Change in private inventories...................	79	64	57	138	25	16	53	49

Source: U.S. Bureau of Economic Analysis, National Economic Accounts, "Table 5.2.5. Gross and Net Domestic Investment by Major Type" and "Table 5.2.6. Real Gross and Net Domestic Investment by Major Type, Chained Dollars," <bea.gov/itable/>, accessed July 2020.

Table 818. Business Cycle Expansions and Contractions—Months of Duration: 1945 to 2020

[A trough is the low point of a business cycle; a peak is the high point. Contraction, or recession, is the period from peak to subsequent trough; expansion is the period from trough to subsequent peak. Business cycle reference dates are determined by the National Bureau of Economic Research, Inc]

Business cycle reference date				Contraction (Peak to trough)	Expansion (Previous trough to peak)	Length of cycle	
Peak		Trough				Trough from previous trough	Peak from previous peak
Month	Year	Month	Year				
February......................	1945	October	1945	8	[1] 80	[1] 88	[2] 93
November....................	1948	October	1949	11	37	48	45
July...........................	1953	May	1954	10	45	55	56
August.......................	1957	April	1958	8	39	47	49
April.........................	1960	February	1961	10	24	34	32
December...................	1969	November	1970	11	106	117	116
November....................	1973	March	1975	16	36	52	47
January......................	1980	July	1980	6	58	64	74
July...........................	1981	November	1982	16	12	28	18
July...........................	1990	March	1991	8	92	100	108
March........................	2001	November	2001	8	120	128	128
December...................	2007	June	2009	18	73	91	81
February......................	2020	(X)	(X)	(X)	128	(X)	146
Average, all cycles: 1945 to 2009 (11 cycles)...	(X)	(X)	(X)	11.1	59.4	69.5	68.5

X Not applicable. [1] Previous trough: June 1938. [2] Previous peak: May 1937.

Source: National Bureau of Economic Research, Inc., Cambridge, MA, "US Business Cycle Expansions and Contractions," <http://www.nber.org/cycles.html>, accessed August 2020 ©.

Table 819. The Conference Board Leading, Coincident, and Lagging Economic Indexes®: 2000 to 2019

[299.4 represents 299,400]

Item	Unit	2000	2005	2010	2015	2019
The Conference Board Leading Economic Index®						
(LEI) for the U.S., composite.......................	2016=100	91.9	101.5	82.3	99.1	111.5
Average weekly hours, manufacturing...........................	Hours	41.2	40.6	41.1	41.8	41.6
Average weekly initial claims for unemployment insurance.....................................	1,000	299.4	330.6	458.5	277.1	218.1
Manufacturers' new orders, consumer goods and materials (1982 dollars).....................................	Mil. dol.	152,070	150,555	122,223	134,702	136,669
Building permits, new private housing units....................	1,000	1,598	2,160	604	1,178	1,350
Manufacturers' new orders, nondefense capital goods excluding aircraft (1982 dollars).......................	Mil. dol.	45,991	40,545	36,351	37,595	38,917
Leading Credit Index™ (standard deviation from the mean)..	Std. dev.	1.5	-0.6	-1.0	-0.6	-1.0
Interest rate spread, 10-year Treasury bonds less federal funds.....................................	Percent	-0.21	1.08	3.04	2.00	-0.01
The Conference Board Coincident Economic Index®						
(CEI) for the U.S., composite.......................	2016=100	86.7	90.5	88.5	98.9	106.5
Employees on nonagricultural payrolls...........................	1,000	132,018	134,022	130,337	141,804	150,935
Index of industrial production.......................	2012=100	95.2	99.6	94.1	104.1	109.5
Personal income less transfer payments (2012 dollars).......	Bil. dol.	9,669	10,460	10,685	12,649	14,071
Manufacturing and trade sales (2012 dollars).................	Mil. dol.	1,127,075	1,248,214	1,198,692	1,389,010	1,516,485
Composite index of 7 lagging indicators	2016=100	75.3	78.9	82.7	97.2	107.9
Inventories to sales ratio, manufacturing and trade............	Ratio	1.4	1.3	1.4	1.4	1.5
Average duration of unemployment...........................	Weeks	12.7	18.4	33.1	29.1	21.7
Consumer installment credit to personal income ratio.........	Percent	18.7	21.2	20.2	21.8	22.1
Commercial and industrial loans outstanding (2012 dollars).......................................	Mil. dol.	1,131,602	786,673	800,353	1,253,837	1,466,087
Change in labor cost per unit of output, manufacturing........	Percent	2.3	-1.8	-2.4	4.1	3.5
Change in consumer price index for services..................	Percent	3.8	3.5	0.9	2.4	2.8
Average prime rate...	Percent	9.2	6.2	3.3	3.3	5.3

Source: The Conference Board, New York, NY 10022-6601, *Business Cycle Indicators*, monthly. Reproduced with permission from The Conference Board, Inc. © 2020, The Conference Board, Inc. For more information, see <http://www.conference-board.org/data/>.

Table 820. Manufacturing and Trade—Sales and Inventories: 1993 to 2019

[In billions of dollars (567 represents $567,000,000,000), except ratios. Based on North American Industry Classification System (NAICS); see text, this section]

Year	Sales, average monthly [1]				Inventories [2]				Inventory-sales ratio [3]			
	Total	Manufac-turing	Retail trade	Merchant whole-salers	Total	Manufac-turing	Retail trade	Merchant whole-salers	Total	Manufac-turing	Retail trade	Merchant whole-salers
1993......	567	252	161	154	863	380	278	205	1.50	1.50	1.68	1.30
1994......	610	270	175	165	926	400	304	222	1.46	1.44	1.66	1.29
1995......	655	290	185	180	985	425	322	238	1.48	1.44	1.72	1.29
1996......	687	300	197	190	1,005	430	333	241	1.45	1.44	1.67	1.27
1997......	723	320	206	198	1,045	443	344	258	1.42	1.37	1.64	1.26
1998......	742	325	215	202	1,077	448	357	272	1.44	1.39	1.62	1.32
1999......	786	336	234	217	1,137	463	384	290	1.40	1.35	1.59	1.30
2000......	834	351	249	235	1,196	481	406	309	1.41	1.35	1.59	1.29
2001......	818	331	255	232	1,119	427	394	298	1.42	1.38	1.58	1.32
2002......	823	326	261	236	1,140	423	415	301	1.36	1.29	1.55	1.26
2003......	855	335	272	248	1,148	408	431	308	1.34	1.25	1.56	1.22
2004......	926	359	289	278	1,242	441	460	340	1.30	1.19	1.56	1.17
2005......	1,006	395	307	303	1,314	475	472	368	1.27	1.17	1.51	1.17
2006......	1,069	418	323	328	1,409	523	486	399	1.28	1.20	1.49	1.17
2007......	1,128	443	333	352	1,488	563	501	424	1.28	1.22	1.49	1.17
2008......	1,161	456	328	377	1,466	544	477	445	1.31	1.26	1.52	1.20
2009......	989	369	301	319	1,332	505	429	397	1.38	1.39	1.47	1.29
2010......	1,089	409	318	361	1,450	554	455	442	1.27	1.28	1.39	1.15
2011......	1,207	458	342	407	1,566	607	471	487	1.26	1.29	1.35	1.15
2012......	1,267	475	359	434	1,655	625	506	523	1.28	1.30	1.38	1.17
2013......	1,303	484	372	448	1,719	630	545	544	1.29	1.29	1.41	1.19
2014......	1,341	491	387	464	1,779	640	562	576	1.31	1.31	1.44	1.22
2015......	1,295	460	394	441	1,810	636	590	584	1.39	1.39	1.46	1.33
2016......	1,286	446	404	435	1,839	630	613	595	1.42	1.41	1.50	1.35
2017......	1,349	466	421	462	1,898	657	628	613	1.38	1.38	1.48	1.30
2018......	1,431	497	439	495	1,991	681	657	653	1.36	1.35	1.46	1.28
2019......	1,453	501	454	498	2,028	700	664	664	1.39	1.38	1.46	1.34

[1] Averages of monthly not-seasonally-adjusted figures. [2] Seasonally adjusted end-of-year data. [3] Averages of seasonally adjusted monthly ratios.

Source: U.S. Census Bureau, "Manufacturing & Trade Inventories & Sales," <https://www.census.gov/mtis/index.html>, accessed July 2020.

Table 821. Industrial Production Indexes by Industry: 2000 to 2019

[2012 = 100]

Industry	NAICS code [1]	2000	2005	2010	2015	2016	2017	2018	2019
Total index.............................	([2])	**95.2**	**99.6**	**94.1**	**104.1**	**102.1**	**104.4**	**108.6**	**109.4**
Manufacturing (SIC) [3]	([4])	98.2	103.4	94.7	101.5	100.7	102.7	105.0	104.8
Manufacturing (NAICS)........................	31–33	95.1	101.2	94.2	101.9	101.1	103.2	106.0	105.9
Durable goods............................	([5])	85.0	93.4	89.2	103.9	101.7	104.0	107.5	108.2
Wood products................................	321	138.3	147.7	94.1	112.7	116.9	124.1	127.1	126.7
Nonmetallic mineral products.................	327	132.8	138.6	95.9	109.8	111.3	115.3	119.6	119.4
Primary metals................................	331	105.0	99.1	95.1	96.8	92.5	93.7	97.6	96.9
Fabricated metal products....................	332	110.7	104.4	90.7	100.2	96.5	97.9	102.5	103.5
Machinery....................................	333	94.8	88.9	82.1	89.0	82.2	87.9	92.6	92.2
Computers and electronic products..........	334	37.6	59.7	85.6	108.1	110.4	115.2	120.9	127.2
Electrical equipment, appliances, and components.........................	335	134.9	112.9	93.1	101.3	101.0	101.8	103.7	103.3
Motor vehicles and parts.....................	3361–3363	103.3	108.8	82.7	123.2	124.8	124.7	129.9	127.0
Aerospace and other misc. transportation equipment....................	3364–3369	73.2	77.3	90.6	106.8	99.5	99.9	100.1	101.9
Furniture and related products...............	337	147.2	149.8	91.9	106.3	106.6	106.3	106.3	105.7
Miscellaneous products.......................	339	91.6	105.3	103.4	100.4	100.7	99.5	99.4	101.7
Nondurable goods............................	([6])	107.8	110.5	99.8	99.6	100.4	102.3	104.3	103.5
Food, beverage, and tobacco products......	311–312	98.1	102.7	99.8	103.8	105.0	107.6	109.7	109.5
Textile and product mills.....................	313–314	204.1	176.6	105.4	100.9	99.0	99.7	100.9	98.3
Apparel and leather...........................	315–316	408.0	225.7	107.8	84.7	80.9	74.6	72.5	64.7
Paper..	322	120.1	112.4	97.4	98.6	97.7	97.0	96.0	93.0
Printing and related support.................	323	144.2	131.0	103.5	97.5	99.2	99.8	97.6	93.7
Petroleum and coal products.................	324	89.2	100.1	97.9	98.1	104.4	107.1	106.9	105.8
Chemical.....................................	325	96.2	109.3	101.3	95.2	94.7	96.6	100.4	100.5
Plastics and rubber products.................	326	116.7	116.6	94.2	105.8	107.1	109.3	110.2	108.3
Other manufacturing (non-NAICS) [7]	1133, 5111	192.5	169.2	111.3	90.4	88.0	87.5	78.9	73.2
Mining.......................................	**21**	**88.8**	**84.0**	**87.2**	**113.9**	**102.6**	**110.1**	**123.8**	**132.7**
Electric and gas utilities......................	**2211–2212**	**92.0**	**99.5**	**102.8**	**102.7**	**102.3**	**101.5**	**105.9**	**104.8**
Electric power generation, transmission, and distribution....................	2211	90.4	99.2	102.3	101.9	101.8	100.8	104.0	102.7
Natural gas distribution.........................	2212	103.6	102.0	106.2	109.6	105.9	106.7	118.9	120.4

[1] Except as noted, based on North American Industry Classification System, 2012; see text, this section. [2] Includes NAICS codes 31–33, 1133, 5111, 21, 2211, and 2212. [3] Standard Industrial Classification (SIC); see text, this section. [4] Includes NAICS codes 31–33, 1133, and 5111. [5] Includes NAICS codes 321, 327, and 331–339. [6] Includes NAICS codes 311–316, and 322–326. [7] Those industries—logging and newspaper, periodical, book, and directory publishing—that have traditionally been considered to be manufacturing.

Source: Board of Governors of the Federal Reserve System, "Industrial Production and Capacity Utilization, G.17," <https://www.federalreserve.gov/econres.htm>, accessed July 2020.

Table 822. Index of Industrial Capacity and Utilization Rate: 1990 to 2019

[2012 output = 100. Annual figures are averages of monthly data. The capacity index is an indicator of the maximum sustainable output a plant can maintain under realistic circumstances; capacity here is expressed as a proportion of 2012 actual output. Capacity utilization rate is a measure of output as a proportion of capacity; this is the output index divided by the capacity index]

| Year | Index of capacity | | Utilization rate | | | | |
| | Total industry | Manufacturing [1] | Total industry | Stage of process | | | Manufacturing [1] |
				Crude [2]	Primary and semifinished [3]	Finished [4]	
1990..........	77.9	77.4	82.4	87.9	82.6	80.5	81.5
1995..........	88.2	89.0	83.9	89.0	86.4	79.7	83.1
2000..........	116.9	123.2	81.5	88.5	84.0	76.9	79.7
2005..........	124.3	131.8	80.1	86.7	81.9	75.7	78.5
2010..........	128.0	134.1	73.5	83.2	71.8	71.2	70.7
2012..........	130.0	134.1	76.9	85.5	74.7	74.8	74.5
2013..........	132.2	135.6	77.2	86.0	75.5	73.8	74.4
2014..........	133.8	135.6	78.6	88.4	76.7	74.6	75.2
2015..........	135.4	134.8	76.9	82.7	76.3	75.1	75.3
2016..........	136.0	135.7	75.0	78.4	75.2	73.6	74.2
2017..........	136.6	136.6	76.5	83.7	75.7	74.2	75.1
2018..........	137.9	137.2	78.7	88.8	77.5	75.4	76.6
2019..........	140.8	138.8	77.8	88.6	75.9	74.7	75.6

[1] Manufacturing consists of those industries included in the North American Industry Classification System (NAICS) definition of manufacturing plus those industries—logging and newspaper, periodical, book, and directory publishing—that have traditionally been considered to be a part of manufacturing and are included in the industrial sector under the Standard Industrial Classification (SIC) system. [2] Crude processing covers a relatively small portion of total industrial capacity and consists of logging (NAICS 1133), much of mining (excluding stone, sand, and gravel mining, and oil and gas drilling, NAICS 21231, 21221–2, and 213111) and some basic manufacturing industries, including basic chemicals (NAICS 3251); fertilizers, pesticides, and other agricultural chemicals (NAICS 32531, 2); pulp, paper, and paperboard mills (NAICS 3221); and alumina, aluminum, and other nonferrous production and processing mills (NAICS 3313, 4). [3] Primary and semifinished processing loosely corresponds to the previously published aggregate, primary processing. Includes utilities and portions of several 2-digit SIC industries included in the former advanced processing group. These include printing and related support activities (NAICS 3231); paints and adhesives (NAICS 3255); and newspaper, periodical, book, and directory publishers (NAICS 5111). [4] Finished processing generally corresponds to the previously published aggregate, advanced processing. Includes oil and gas well drilling and carpet and rug mills.

Source: Board of Governors of the Federal Reserve System, "Industrial Production and Capacity Utilization, G.17," <https://www.federalreserve.gov/data.htm>, accessed July 2020.

Table 823. Corporate Profits, Taxes, and Dividends: 2000 to 2019

[In billions of dollars (786.6 represents $786,600,000,000). Covers corporations organized for profit and other entities treated as corporations. Represents profits to U.S. residents, without deduction of depletion charges and exclusive of capital gains and losses; intercorporate dividends from profits of domestic corporations are eliminated; and net receipts of dividends, reinvested earnings of incorporated foreign affiliates, and earnings of unincorporated foreign affiliates are added. Minus (-) sign indicates loss]

Item	2000	2005	2010	2014	2015	2016	2017	2018	2019
Corporate profits with IVA and CCAdj [1]..................	786.6	1,488.6	1,728.7	2,120.2	2,060.5	2,023.7	2,114.5	2,243.0	2,250.5
Taxes on corporate income...................	233.4	379.7	272.3	407.1	396.3	376.2	311.3	282.9	298.7
Profits after tax with IVA and CCAdj [1]..................	553.1	1,108.9	1,456.5	1,713.1	1,664.2	1,647.6	1,803.2	1,960.1	1,951.8
Net dividends...................	410.2	602.0	643.2	1,096.1	1,164.9	1,189.4	1,270.4	1,390.1	1,360.8
Undistributed profits with IVA and CCAdj [1]...........	142.9	506.9	813.3	617.1	499.3	458.2	532.8	570.0	591.0
Addenda for corporate cash flow:									
Net cash flow with IVA and CCAdj [1]..................	981.5	1,536.7	2,105.0	2,141.3	2,090.7	2,079.8	1,934.4	2,332.9	2,460.0
Undistributed profits with IVA and CCAdj [1]...........	142.9	506.9	813.3	617.1	499.3	458.2	532.8	570.0	591.0
Consumption of fixed capital..........................	838.6	1,042.0	1,271.2	1,527.5	1,588.2	1,626.1	1,695.8	1,773.6	1,867.9
Less: Capital transfers paid (net).....................	–	12.2	-20.6	3.3	-3.2	4.4	294.2	10.7	-1.1

– Represents or rounds to zero. [1] Inventory valuation adjustment (IVA) and capital consumption adjustment (CCAdj).

Source: U.S. Bureau of Economic Analysis, National Income and Product Accounts Tables, "Table 1.12. National Income by Type of Income," <http://www.bea.gov/itable/>, accessed July 2020.

Table 824. Corporate Profits With Inventory Valuation and Capital Consumption Adjustments—Financial and Nonfinancial Industries: 2000 to 2019

[In billions of dollars (787 represents $787,000,000,000). Based on the North American Industry Classification System, 2012; see text, this section. Minus sign (-) indicates loss. See headnote, Table 823]

Industry group	2000	2005	2010	2015	2016	2017	2018	2019
Corporate profits with IVA/CCAdj [1]...........	**787**	**1,489**	**1,729**	**2,061**	**2,024**	**2,115**	**2,243**	**2,251**
Domestic industries......................................	641	1,263	1,343	1,665	1,604	1,617	1,730	1,745
Rest of the world..	146	226	386	395	420	497	513	505
Corporate profits with IVA [1]....................	**730**	**1,629**	**1,786**	**2,185**	**2,124**	**2,131**	**2,132**	**2,232**
Domestic industries......................................	584	1,403	1,401	1,789	1,704	1,633	1,620	1,727
Financial [2]...	150	410	406	447	456	436	418	471
Nonfinancial...	434	994	995	1,342	1,249	1,198	1,201	1,256
Utilities..	24	32	31	20	9	14	22	27
Manufacturing..	176	280	282	427	333	305	338	337
Wholesale trade......................................	60	96	99	152	127	122	106	111
Retail trade..	51	123	116	169	171	149	147	168
Transportation and warehousing...............	10	28	45	61	64	59	53	56
Information..	-12	101	102	136	157	138	139	131
Other nonfinancial [3]..............................	126	334	320	376	388	411	398	426
Rest of the world..	146	226	386	395	420	497	513	505

[1] Inventory valuation adjustment (IVA) and capital consumption adjustment (CCAdj). [2] Consists of finance and insurance and bank and other holding companies. [3] Consists of agriculture, forestry, fishing, and hunting; mining; construction; real estate and rental and leasing; professional, scientific, and technical services; administrative and waste management services; educational services; health care and social assistance; arts, entertainment, and recreation; accommodation and food services; and other services, except government.

Source: U.S. Bureau of Economic Analysis, National Income and Product Accounts Tables, "Table 6.16D. Corporate Profits by Industry," <http://www.bea.gov/itable/>, accessed July 2020.

Table 825. Corporate Profits Before Taxes by Industry: 2000 to 2019

[In billions of dollars (747 represents $747,000,000,000). Profits are without inventory valuation and capital consumption adjustments. Minus sign (-) indicates loss. See headnote, Table 823]

Industry	2012 NAICS code [1]	2000	2010	2015	2016	2017	2018	2019
Corporate profits before tax	(X)	**747**	**1,834**	**2,128**	**2,125**	**2,183**	**2,187**	**2,237**
Domestic industries	(X)	601	1,448	1,733	1,705	1,686	1,674	1,732
Agriculture, forestry, fishing, and hunting	11	1	8	12	8	8	5	6
Mining	21	15	33	-9	-25	-2	5	-4
Utilities	221	25	31	19	10	14	22	27
Construction	23	36	27	76	94	100	106	112
Manufacturing	31-33	186	299	393	333	337	368	336
Wholesale trade	42	63	117	136	126	135	117	112
Retail trade	44–45	53	126	167	171	153	153	172
Transportation and warehousing	48–49	10	45	60	64	60	53	56
Information	51	-12	102	136	158	138	140	131
Finance and insurance	52	46	220	289	302	313	302	332
Real estate and rental and leasing	53	9	14	20	24	20	-11	0
Professional, scientific, and technical services	54	9	82	75	75	68	77	80
Management of companies and enterprises [2]	551111, 2	103	186	158	153	122	116	138
Administrative and waste management services	56	9	28	34	37	40	39	43
Educational services	61	2	11	5	5	5	6	6
Health care and social assistance	62	23	78	86	96	99	95	101
Arts, entertainment, and recreation	71	3	8	11	14	16	16	16
Accommodation and food services	72	14	18	44	41	40	40	40
Other services, except public administration	81	6	15	21	21	21	25	26
Rest of the world [3]	(X)	146	386	395	420	497	513	505

X Not applicable. [1] Based on North American Industry Classification System, 2012; see text, this section. [2] Consists of bank and other holding companies. [3] Consists of receipts by all U.S. residents, including both corporations and persons, of dividends from foreign corporations, and, for U.S. corporations, their share of reinvested earnings of their incorporated foreign affiliates, and earnings of unincorporated foreign affiliates, net of corresponding payments.

Source: U.S. Bureau of Economic Analysis, National Income and Product Accounts Tables, "Table 6.17D. Corporate Profits Before Tax by Industry," <http://www.bea.gov/itable/>, accessed July 2020.

Table 826. U.S. Majority-Owned Foreign Affiliates—Value Added by Industry of Affiliate and Country: 2017

[In millions of dollars (1,418,362 represents $1,418,362,000,000). Data are preliminary. See headnote, Table 828. Numbers in parentheses represent North American Industry Classification System codes; see text, this section]

Country	All industries [1]	Mining (21)	Manufacturing (31-33) Total [1]	Chemicals (325)	Wholesale trade (42)	Finance and insurance (52)	Professional, scientific, and technical services (54)
All countries [2]	**1,418,362**	**104,421**	**600,694**	**127,480**	**160,338**	**100,951**	**146,708**
United Kingdom	179,738	3,845	59,200	6,659	12,506	30,775	21,023
Canada	131,276	9,317	52,538	7,028	13,043	4,372	8,274
Ireland	97,478	(D)	43,703	16,594	4,120	554	14,088
Germany	85,514	933	41,963	8,367	11,834	2,710	8,082
China	71,515	1,231	43,037	9,322	8,998	1,697	4,718
Netherlands	69,606	497	31,891	7,823	6,800	7,451	6,467
Switzerland	52,780	181	18,006	8,055	17,384	1,410	3,835
France	52,053	72	25,265	5,773	7,104	1,988	5,042
Mexico	50,956	3,258	26,953	3,660	2,978	2,733	1,654
Singapore	49,775	351	25,040	6,358	7,890	2,791	3,012
Australia	48,329	7,910	16,124	1,882	7,284	1,928	5,854
Japan	46,574	–	16,144	5,844	8,263	5,206	6,785
Brazil	37,602	1,056	22,971	5,460	2,127	2,968	2,875
India	34,747	27	6,716	2,319	2,679	3,218	15,444
Italy	32,005	131	13,160	3,249	3,003	623	2,322
Belgium	27,066	30	13,218	6,288	5,887	2,680	1,649
Hong Kong	19,024	5	3,860	739	4,311	5,277	2,642
Spain	17,408	16	10,169	3,200	2,278	159	1,682
Argentina	17,203	3,820	7,694	1,866	786	1,027	330
Korea, South	16,250	(D)	10,522	1,727	1,839	960	814
Thailand	15,165	(D)	9,168	942	1,356	424	284

– Represents or rounds to zero. D Data withheld to avoid disclosure. [1] Includes other industries, not shown separately. [2] Includes other countries, not shown separately.

Source: U.S. Bureau of Economic Analysis, International Economic Accounts, "Activities of U.S. Multinational Enterprises, Majority-owned Foreign Affiliates, Value Added by Country and Industry 2009-2017," <http://www.bea.gov/international/di1usdop.htm>, accessed February 2020.

Table 827. U.S. Multinational Enterprises—Value Added, Employment, and Capital Expenditures: 1989 to 2017

[Value added and capital expenditures in billions of dollars (1,401 represents $1,401,000,000,000); employees in thousands. For the years shown prior to 2007, the data items needed to calculate value added and capital expenditures for individual U.S. parents and foreign affiliates were collected for nonbank businesses only. The value added and capital expenditures statistics for bank parents and affiliates for those years are estimates. See headnote, Table 828. MNE = Multinational enterprise. MOFA = Majority-owned foreign affiliate]

Item	1989	1994	1999	2004	2009	2010	2015	2016	2017 (P)
VALUE ADDED									
MNEs worldwide:									
Parents and MOFAs	1,401	1,773	2,645	3,221	3,741	4,191	5,308	5,218	5,321
Parents	1,077	1,362	2,064	2,366	2,596	2,949	3,949	3,916	3,903
MOFAs	324	411	580	854	1,145	1,242	1,359	1,302	1,418
EMPLOYEES									
MNEs worldwide:									
Parents and all affiliates	26,370	26,571	33,398	32,892	35,962	36,287	44,685	44,733	45,094
Parents and MOFAs	24,826	25,142	31,913	31,466	33,727	34,105	42,127	42,288	42,471
Parents	19,617	19,330	23,985	22,446	22,933	22,791	28,046	28,023	28,071
Affiliates, total	6,753	7,241	9,412	10,445	13,029	13,496	16,639	16,710	17,023
MOFAs	5,209	5,812	7,928	9,020	10,794	11,313	14,081	14,265	14,400
Other	1,544	1,429	1,484	1,426	2,235	2,182	2,558	2,445	2,623
CAPITAL EXPENDITURES									
MNEs worldwide:									
Parents and all affiliates	279	331	563	500	653	(NA)	(NA)	(NA)	(NA)
Parents and MOFAs	263	306	531	476	599	607	927	837	853
Parents	204	235	417	351	432	441	713	641	654
Affiliates, total	75	96	146	149	221	(NA)	(NA)	(NA)	(NA)
MOFAs	59	72	115	125	167	166	215	195	200
Other	16	25	31	24	54	(NA)	(NA)	(NA)	(NA)

P Preliminary. NA Not available.

Source: U.S. Bureau of Economic Analysis, "Activities of U.S. Multinational Enterprises in 2017," *Survey of Current Business*, Vol. 99, No. 9, September 2019. See also <https://apps.bea.gov/scb/issues.htm>.

Table 828. U.S. Multinational Enterprises—Selected Characteristics: 2017

[In billions of dollars (42,144 represents $42,144,000,000,000), except as indicated. Data for 2017 are preliminary. Consists of U.S. parent enterprises and their foreign affiliates. U.S. parent comprises the domestic operations of a multinational and is a U.S. person that owns or controls, directly or indirectly, 10 percent or more of the voting securities of an incorporated foreign business enterprise, or an equivalent interest in an unincorporated foreign business enterprise. A U.S. person can be an incorporated business enterprise. A majority-owned foreign affiliate (MOFA) is a foreign business enterprise in which a U.S. parent enterprise owns or controls more than 50 percent of the voting securities]

Industry	NAICS code [1]	U.S. parents [2]				Majority-owned foreign affiliates [3]		
		Total assets	Capital expenditures	Value added	Employment (1,000)	Capital expenditures	Value added	Employment (1,000)
All industries	(X)	**42,144**	**654**	**3,903**	**28,071**	**200**	**1,418**	**14,400**
Mining [4]	21	552	45	88	272	41	104	243
Oil and gas extraction	211	282	32	43	48	33	69	52
Manufacturing [4]	31-33	8,626	193	1,347	7,351	69	601	5,441
Food	311	726	14	112	830	6	42	461
Beverages and tobacco products	312	325	4	55	126	3	53	242
Petroleum and coal products	324	1,145	29	144	326	2	39	15
Chemicals [4]	325	1,944	30	236	914	14	127	661
Pharmaceuticals and medicines	3254	1,296	13	124	424	4	63	269
Machinery	333	500	8	73	516	3	59	522
Computers and electronic products [4]	334	1,233	27	240	949	14	100	874
Computers and peripheral equipment	3341	394	7	88	226	1	39	238
Transportation equipment [4]	336	1,427	49	214	1,465	11	62	1,112
Motor vehicles, bodies and trailers, & parts	3361-3363	720	38	104	674	10	55	1,018
Wholesale trade	42	1,744	42	228	1,739	10	160	983
Retail trade [4]	44, 45	1,008	48	383	5,812	7	82	1,629
General merchandise stores	452	296	13	143	2,494	3	33	970
Information [4]	51	2,881	99	484	2,222	14	89	613
Publishing industries	511	522	8	91	462	2	38	187
Broadcasting (except internet)	515	315	4	57	260	1	6	28
Telecommunications	517	1,356	63	210	805	7	15	93
Finance and insurance [4]	52	23,676	66	491	2,844	7	101	732
Insurance carriers and related activities	524	7,227	14	132	1,113	1	22	217
Professional, scientific, & technical services [4]	54	795	12	241	1,619	7	147	1,493
Computer systems design & related services	5415	352	5	66	435	4	63	822
Other industries [4]	(X)	2,862	147	639	6,212	45	134	3,266
Utilities	22	731	49	74	172	8	13	35
Transportation and warehousing	48-49	568	38	194	1,414	5	25	326
Real estate & rental and leasing	53	495	32	65	359	21	52	182
Administration, support, and waste management	56	209	6	72	1,120	2	42	1,169

X Not applicable. [1] Based on North American Industry Classification System; see text, this section. [2] Data are by industry of U.S. parent. [3] Data are by industry of foreign affiliate. [4] Includes other industries, not shown separately.

Source: U.S. Bureau of Economic Analysis, International Economic Accounts, "Direct Investment and Multinational Enterprises," <http://www.bea.gov/iTable/index_MNC.cfm>, accessed March 2020.

Table 829. U.S. Multinational Enterprises—Value Added: 2010 and 2017

[In billions of dollars (4,191 represents $4,191,000,000,000). See headnote, Table 828. Data are by industry of U.S. parent]

Industry	NAICS [1] code	U.S. multinationals		U.S. parents		Majority-owned foreign affiliates	
		2010	2017	2010	2017	2010	2017
All industries...........................	(X)	**4,191**	**5,321**	**2,949**	**3,903**	**1,242**	**1,418**
Mining [2]................................	21	118	118	75	88	43	31
Oil and gas extraction......................	211	58	54	41	43	18	10
Manufacturing [2]........................	31-33	1,900	2,087	1,147	1,347	753	739
Food....................................	311	145	159	96	112	49	47
Beverages and tobacco products..........	312	67	69	49	55	18	14
Petroleum and coal products.............	324	383	277	135	144	248	134
Chemicals [2]...........................	325	337	387	197	236	140	150
Pharmaceuticals and medicines.........	3254	187	209	113	124	74	85
Machinery..............................	333	104	110	69	73	35	37
Computers and electronic products [2].....	334	235	385	155	240	80	144
Computers and peripheral equipment....	3341	68	146	38	88	31	58
Semiconductors and other electronic components.....	3344	79	105	51	68	28	37
Transportation equipment [2].............	336	314	320	229	214	85	106
Motor vehicles, bodies and trailers, and parts..........	3361-3363	133	166	83	104	49	62
Wholesale trade...........................	42	174	281	143	228	32	53
Retail trade [2]...........................	44, 45	303	445	257	383	46	62
General merchandise stores..............	452	(NA)	(NA)	122	143	(D)	(D)
Information [2]...........................	51	392	585	333	484	58	101
Publishing industries.....................	511	100	120	72	91	27	29
Broadcasting (except internet).............	515	49	66	41	57	8	10
Telecommunications.....................	517	172	226	162	210	10	16
Finance and insurance [2]..................	52	480	666	357	491	123	175
Depository credit intermediation (banking)................	5221	157	206	139	184	18	22
Insurance carriers and related activities....	524	101	156	84	132	17	24
Professional, scientific, and technical services [2]..........	54	275	339	196	241	79	98
Computer systems design and related services..........	5415	133	128	80	66	53	62
Other industries [2].......................	(X)	548	799	440	639	108	160
Utilities.................................	22	66	82	61	74	5	8
Transportation and warehousing...........	48-49	132	211	116	194	17	17
Real estate and rental and leasing.........	53	44	83	35	65	9	18
Administration, support, and waste management........	56	99	102	73	72	26	30
Accommodation and food services......................	72	75	86	54	64	22	22

X Not applicable. NA Not available. D Data withheld to avoid disclosure. [1] Based on North American Industry Classification System; see text, this section. [2] Includes other industries, not shown separately.

Source: U.S. Bureau of Economic Analysis, International Economic Accounts, "Direct Investment and Multinational Enterprises," <http://www.bea.gov/iTable/index_MNC.cfm>, accessed February 2020.

Section 16
Science and Technology

This section presents statistics on scientific, engineering, and technological resources, with emphasis on patterns of research and development (R&D) funding and on scientific, engineering, and technical personnel; education; and employment.

The National Science Foundation (NSF) gathers data chiefly through recurring surveys and reports the data via detailed statistical tables; information briefs; and annual, biennial, and special reports; see <nsf.gov/statistics>. Areas of coverage include R&D expenditures; Federal R&D funding; scientific employment; graduate enrollment and support in academic science and engineering; characteristics of doctoral scientists and engineers; and of recent graduates in the United States. Report titles include: *Science and Engineering Indicators; National Patterns of R&D Resources; Federal Funds for Research and Development; Federal R&D Funding by Budget Function; Federal Support for S&E to Universities, Colleges, and Selected Nonprofit Institutions*; and *Business Research and Development and Innovation.* Statistical surveys in these areas pose problems of concept and definition and the data should therefore be regarded as broad estimates rather than precise, quantitative statements. See sources for methodological and technical details.

The National Science Board's biennial *Science and Engineering Indicators* at <nsf.gov/statistics/seind/> contains data and analysis of international and domestic science and technology, including education and workforce statistics.

Research and development outlays—NSF defines research as "systematic study directed toward fuller scientific knowledge of the subject studied" and development as "the systematic use of scientific knowledge directed toward the production of useful materials, devices, systems, or methods, including design and development of prototypes and processes."

National coverage of R&D expenditures is developed primarily from periodic surveys in four principal economic sectors: (1) *government,* made up primarily of federal executive agencies; (2) *industry,* consisting of manufacturing and nonmanufacturing firms and the federally funded research and development centers (FFRDCs) they administer; (3) *universities and colleges,* composed of universities, colleges, and their affiliated institutions, agricultural experiment stations, and associated schools of agriculture and of medicine, and FFRDCs administered by educational institutions; and (4) *other nonprofit institutions,* consisting of such organizations as private philanthropic foundations, nonprofit research institutes, voluntary health agencies, and FFRDCs administered by nonprofit organizations.

The R&D funds reported consist of current operating costs, including planning and administration costs, except as otherwise noted. They exclude funds for routine testing, mapping and surveying, collection of general purpose data, dissemination of scientific information, and training of scientific personnel.

Scientists, engineers, and technicians—Scientists and engineers are defined as persons engaged in scientific and engineering work at a level requiring a knowledge of sciences equivalent at least to that acquired through completion of a 4-year college course. Technicians are defined as persons engaged in technical work at a level requiring knowledge acquired through a technical institute, junior college, or other type of training less extensive than 4-year college training. Craftsmen and skilled workers are excluded.

Table 830. Research and Development (R&D) Expenditures by Source of Funding: 1960 to 2018

[In millions of dollars (13,711 represents $13,711,000,000), except percent]

Year		Sources of funds					Percent of total				
	Total	Federal government	Industry	Universities/colleges [1]	Non-profit	Non-federal government [2]	Federal government	Industry	Universities/colleges [1]	Non-profit	Non-federal government [2]
1960.....	13,711	8,915	4,516	67	123	90	65.0	32.9	0.5	0.9	0.7
1970.....	26,271	14,984	10,449	259	343	237	57.0	39.8	1.0	1.3	0.9
1980.....	63,224	29,986	30,929	920	871	519	47.4	48.9	1.5	1.4	0.8
1985.....	114,671	52,641	57,962	1,743	1,491	834	45.9	50.5	1.5	1.3	0.7
1986.....	120,249	54,622	60,991	2,019	1,647	969	45.4	50.7	1.7	1.4	0.8
1987.....	126,360	58,609	62,576	2,262	1,849	1,065	46.4	49.5	1.8	1.5	0.8
1988.....	133,881	60,131	67,977	2,527	2,081	1,165	44.9	50.8	1.9	1.6	0.9
1989.....	141,891	60,465	74,966	2,852	2,333	1,274	42.6	52.8	2.0	1.6	0.9
1990.....	151,993	61,610	83,208	3,187	2,589	1,399	40.5	54.7	2.1	1.7	0.9
1991.....	160,876	60,783	92,300	3,458	2,852	1,483	37.8	57.4	2.1	1.8	0.9
1992.....	165,350	60,915	96,229	3,569	3,113	1,525	36.8	58.2	2.2	1.9	0.9
1993.....	165,730	60,528	96,549	3,709	3,388	1,557	36.5	58.3	2.2	2.0	0.9
1994.....	169,207	60,777	99,204	3,938	3,665	1,623	35.9	58.6	2.3	2.2	1.0
1995.....	183,625	62,969	110,871	4,110	3,925	1,751	34.3	60.4	2.2	2.1	1.0
1996.....	197,346	63,394	123,417	4,436	4,239	1,861	32.1	62.5	2.2	2.1	0.9
1997.....	211,894	64,362	136,208	4,852	4,571	1,902	30.4	64.3	2.3	2.2	0.9
1998.....	225,759	65,908	147,774	5,193	4,963	1,920	29.2	65.5	2.3	2.2	0.9
1999.....	244,451	66,817	164,545	5,654	5,399	2,036	27.3	67.3	2.3	2.2	0.8
2000.....	267,950	67,238	185,975	6,270	6,285	2,182	25.1	69.4	2.3	2.3	0.8
2001.....	278,539	73,793	188,408	6,874	7,122	2,341	26.5	67.6	2.5	2.6	0.8
2002.....	277,911	78,873	180,704	7,673	8,109	2,553	28.4	65.0	2.8	2.9	0.9
2003.....	291,365	85,133	186,171	8,286	8,988	2,788	29.2	63.9	2.8	3.1	1.0
2004.....	302,731	90,795	191,346	8,637	9,028	2,926	30.0	63.2	2.9	3.0	1.0
2005.....	325,288	95,413	207,775	9,353	9,771	2,977	29.3	63.9	2.9	3.0	0.9
2006.....	350,908	99,938	227,182	10,176	10,320	3,293	28.5	64.7	2.9	2.9	0.9
2007.....	377,890	105,128	246,815	10,933	11,420	3,594	27.8	65.3	2.9	3.0	1.0
2008.....	404,773	117,615	258,016	11,738	13,184	4,221	29.1	63.7	2.9	3.3	1.0
2009.....	402,931	125,765	246,610	12,057	14,205	4,295	31.2	61.2	3.0	3.5	1.1
2010.....	406,579	126,616	248,124	12,262	15,275	4,303	31.1	61.0	3.0	3.8	1.1
2011.....	426,160	127,014	266,422	13,103	15,235	4,386	29.8	62.5	3.1	3.6	1.0
2012.....	433,619	123,837	275,718	14,300	15,607	4,158	28.6	63.6	3.3	3.6	1.0
2013.....	453,966	120,130	297,168	15,378	17,046	4,244	26.5	65.5	3.4	3.8	0.9
2014.....	475,425	118,365	318,383	16,210	18,254	4,214	24.9	67.0	3.4	3.8	0.9
2015.....	493,684	119,524	333,208	17,299	19,386	4,267	24.2	67.5	3.5	3.9	0.9
2016.....	515,641	116,492	355,545	18,484	20,640	4,481	22.6	69.0	3.6	4.0	0.9
2017 [3]....	547,886	120,961	381,137	19,723	21,482	4,582	22.1	69.6	3.6	3.9	0.8
2018 [4]....	579,985	127,246	404,231	21,120	22,662	4,726	21.9	69.7	3.6	3.9	0.8

[1] Figures for university and college (U&C) R&D prior to 2003 cover only science and engineering (S&E) fields; in 2003 and later years, R&D in non-S&E fields is also included. Also, adjustments have been made to U&C R&D for 1998 and later years to eliminate double counting of funds passed through from one academic institution to another. [2] Nonfederal R&D expenditures to university and college performers. [3] Some data for 2017 are preliminary. [4] Estimated.

Source: U.S. National Science Foundation, *National Patterns of R&D Resources, 2017-18 Data Update*, NSF 20-307, January 2020. See also <http://www.nsf.gov/statistics/natlpatterns/>.

Table 831. National Research and Development (R&D) Expenditures as a Percent of Gross Domestic Product by Country: 1990 to 2018

Year	United States	Japan [1]	Germany [2]	France	United Kingdom	Italy	Canada	South Korea	OECD total [3]	Russia	China
1990....	[4] 2.56	[7] 2.71	[7] 2.61	2.27	1.95	[8] 1.20	1.48	(NA)	[7] 2.16	1.89	(NA)
1995....	[4] 2.41	[7] 2.61	2.14	2.24	1.65	0.93	1.65	[9] 2.15	[5,7] 1.95	0.79	[10] 0.57
2000....	[4] 2.63	2.91	2.41	[5] 2.09	1.62	1.00	1.86	[9] 2.13	[7] 2.10	0.98	[5] 0.89
2005....	[4] 2.52	3.18	2.44	2.05	1.55	1.04	1.97	[9] 2.52	[7] 2.12	0.99	1.31
2007....	[4] 2.63	3.34	2.46	2.02	1.61	1.13	1.90	[5] 2.87	[7] 2.18	1.04	1.37
2008....	[4] 2.77	[5] 3.34	2.62	2.06	[7] 1.61	1.16	1.86	2.99	[7] 2.25	0.97	1.45
2009....	[4] 2.81	3.23	2.74	2.21	[7] 1.67	1.22	1.92	3.15	[7] 2.29	1.17	[5] 1.66
2010....	[4] 2.74	3.14	2.73	[5] 2.18	[7] 1.65	1.22	1.83	3.32	[7] 2.25	1.05	1.71
2011....	[4] 2.77	3.24	2.81	2.19	1.65	1.20	1.79	3.59	[7] 2.28	1.02	1.78
2012....	[4] 2.68	3.21	2.88	2.23	[7] 1.58	1.26	[5] 1.77	3.85	[7] 2.28	1.03	1.91
2013....	[4] 2.71	[5] 3.31	2.84	2.24	1.62	1.30	1.71	3.95	[7] 2.30	1.03	2.00
2014....	[4] 2.72	3.40	2.88	[5] 2.28	[7] 1.64	[7] 1.34	[5] 1.71	4.08	[7] 2.32	1.07	2.02
2015....	[4] 2.72	3.28	2.93	2.27	1.65	1.34	1.69	3.98	[7] 2.31	1.10	2.06
2016....	[4] 2.76	3.16	2.94	2.22	[7] 1.66	[5] 1.37	1.73	3.99	[7] 2.30	1.10	2.10
2017....	[4,6] 2.81	3.21	3.07	[6] 2.20	1.68	1.37	1.67	4.29	[7] 2.34	1.11	2.12
2018....	[4,7] 2.83	[5] 3.28	3.13	[7] 2.19	1.73	1.43	[6] 1.56	4.53	[7] 2.38	0.98	2.14

NA Not available. [1] Data on Japanese research and development after 1996 may not be consistent with data in earlier years because of changes in methodology. [2] Data for 1990 are for West Germany only. [3] Organisation for Economic Cooperation and Development. [4] Excludes most or all capital expenditure. [5] Time series break. [6] Provisional. [7] Estimated value. [8] Excluding extramural R&D expenditure. [9] Excluding R&D in the social sciences and humanities. [10] Underestimated or based on underestimated data.

Source: Organisation for Economic Co-operation and Development (OECD), 2020, "Main Science and Technology Indicators," OECD Science, Technology and R&D Statistics (database) ©, <dx.doi.org/10.1787/data-00182-en>, accessed August 2020.

Table 832. Research and Development (R&D) Expenditures By Performing Sector and Source of Funds: 1990 to 2018

[In millions of dollars (151,993 represents $151,993,000,000). For calendar year. FFRDCs are federally funded research and development centers]

Year	Total	All federal research	Federal intra-mural[1]	FFRDCs[2]	Non-federal govern-ment	Industry Total[3]	Industry Funded by Federal govern-ment	Industry Funded by Indus-try[4]	Universities and colleges Total	Univ. Funded by Federal govern-ment	Univ. Funded by Non-federal govern-ment	Univ. Funded by Indus-try	Univ. Funded by Universi-ties & colleges	Univ. Funded by Non-profits	Other nonprofit Total	Other nonprofit Funded by Federal govern-ment	Other nonprofit Funded by Indus-try	Other nonprofit Funded by Non-profits
R&D TOTAL																		
1990	151,993	23,524	15,671	7,853	(NA)	107,404	25,802	81,602	16,939	9,939	1,399	1,166	3,187	1,249	4,126	2,346	440	1,340
2000	267,950	28,516	19,247	9,269	(NA)	199,961	17,117	182,844	29,916	17,095	2,182	2,112	6,270	2,258	9,557	4,510	1,020	4,027
2010	406,579	50,798	31,970	18,828	691	278,977	34,199	218,187	58,083	34,681	3,674	2,953	12,262	4,515	18,030	7,093	1,265	9,672
2013	453,966	51,086	33,406	17,680	620	322,528	29,362	259,908	61,547	33,839	3,643	3,376	15,378	5,313	18,185	5,970	1,444	10,770
2014	475,425	52,687	34,783	17,903	583	340,722	26,554	277,272	62,349	33,122	3,714	3,602	16,210	5,702	19,078	6,135	1,520	11,423
2015	493,684	52,847	34,199	18,649	595	355,821	26,990	289,892	64,623	33,555	3,773	3,843	17,299	6,154	19,798	6,247	1,572	11,979
2016	515,641	51,187	31,762	19,424	622	374,685	23,772	306,611	67,800	34,674	3,919	4,042	18,484	6,682	21,347	6,971	1,649	12,728
2017[5]	547,886	52,553	32,231	20,322	641	400,101	24,277	319,796	71,251	36,034	4,046	4,276	19,723	7,173	23,340	8,218	1,734	13,389
2018[6]	579,985	58,240	36,856	21,383	641	422,070	23,397	336,950	74,722	37,202	4,159	4,551	21,120	7,690	24,312	8,558	1,811	13,944
BASIC RESEARCH																		
1990	23,029	5,352	2,319	3,033	(NA)	4,629	869	3,760	11,126	6,889	847	705	1,929	756	1,922	947	245	730
2000	42,033	7,801	3,765	4,037	(NA)	7,040	925	6,115	22,290	13,469	1,501	1,453	4,314	1,553	4,902	2,099	566	2,236
2010	75,985	11,748	5,111	6,637	103	16,371	1,406	13,239	38,277	23,471	2,252	1,754	7,887	2,913	9,487	3,414	702	5,370
2013	78,572	9,519	5,330	4,188	92	19,508	1,196	14,986	39,640	22,372	2,189	1,943	9,779	3,358	9,813	3,031	802	5,980
2014	82,138	9,875	5,705	4,170	99	21,936	2,044	15,805	39,951	21,868	2,229	2,061	10,228	3,566	10,276	3,090	844	6,342
2015	83,538	10,017	5,890	4,127	100	21,792	2,038	15,933	41,071	21,960	2,279	2,181	10,886	3,766	10,558	3,034	873	6,651
2016	88,642	10,315	6,119	4,196	94	24,644	2,005	18,473	42,383	22,315	2,329	2,257	11,525	3,958	11,207	3,224	915	7,067
2017[5]	91,453	10,388	6,259	4,128	104	24,829	1,783	17,669	44,302	23,082	2,357	2,376	12,231	4,257	11,830	3,434	963	7,434
2018[6]	96,490	11,129	6,907	4,222	110	26,212	1,718	18,617	46,585	23,849	2,405	2,549	13,140	4,642	12,454	3,706	1,005	7,742
APPLIED RESEARCH																		
1990	34,897	4,808	3,652	1,156	(NA)	24,399	5,967	18,432	4,406	2,140	453	377	1,031	404	1,284	780	120	384
2000	56,503	7,856	6,105	1,750	(NA)	39,176	2,682	36,494	6,361	3,081	558	540	1,604	578	3,110	1,831	258	1,021
2010	79,181	13,203	8,016	5,187	572	44,906	4,705	34,912	14,687	8,712	1,013	773	3,132	1,058	5,813	3,041	321	2,451
2013	88,249	15,132	8,309	6,823	513	51,013	6,028	37,385	16,030	8,828	1,061	929	3,922	1,291	5,561	2,465	366	2,730
2014	91,810	15,727	8,775	6,952	471	53,415	6,445	38,281	16,342	8,662	1,083	991	4,192	1,415	5,854	2,574	385	2,895
2015	97,234	16,698	9,347	7,351	481	56,472	6,102	43,330	17,359	9,046	1,091	1,100	4,523	1,599	6,225	2,791	398	3,036
2016	104,840	17,433	9,805	7,628	511	61,019	5,181	47,098	18,937	9,752	1,167	1,216	4,957	1,846	6,940	3,297	418	3,226
2017[5]	108,810	18,170	10,124	8,046	514	62,133	5,037	46,360	20,009	10,232	1,234	1,267	5,328	1,948	7,984	4,152	439	3,393
2018[6]	114,958	20,045	11,570	8,475	508	65,574	4,854	48,847	20,827	10,540	1,276	1,314	5,671	2,026	8,004	4,011	459	3,534
DEVELOPMENT																		
1990	94,067	13,363	9,700	3,663	(NA)	78,376	18,966	59,410	1,407	910	99	83	226	89	920	619	75	226
2000	169,414	12,859	9,377	3,482	(NA)	153,745	13,510	140,235	1,265	545	123	119	352	127	1,545	580	195	771
2010	251,413	25,847	18,844	7,004	16	217,700	28,089	170,036	5,120	2,498	409	427	1,243	544	2,730	638	242	1,850
2013	287,145	26,436	19,767	6,668	14	252,007	22,137	207,537	5,878	2,639	394	504	1,678	664	2,811	474	276	2,061
2014	301,478	27,084	20,303	6,781	13	265,377	18,065	223,186	6,056	2,592	403	551	1,790	722	2,948	471	291	2,185
2015	312,911	26,132	18,961	7,171	14	277,557	18,850	230,629	6,194	2,549	404	562	1,890	789	3,015	422	301	2,292
2016	322,158	23,439	15,838	7,601	18	289,021	16,586	241,040	6,481	2,608	423	570	2,002	879	3,200	450	315	2,435
2017[5]	347,622	23,995	15,848	8,147	22	313,139	17,457	255,767	6,941	2,721	455	633	2,164	969	3,526	632	332	2,562
2018[6]	368,537	27,065	18,379	8,686	23	330,285	16,824	269,487	7,310	2,812	478	688	2,310	1,023	3,855	841	346	2,668

NA Not available. [1] Federal intramural performers are agencies of the federal government, with work carried on directly by agency personnel. Intramural expenditures include those for federal intramural R&D as well as cost associated with administering extramural R&D. Extramural R&D is performed outside the federal sector with federal funds under contract, grant, or cooperative agreement. [2] R&D expenditures of FFRDC's are chiefly federally funded; the remainder reflects funding from state or local government, businesses, other nonprofit organizations, and other sources. [3] Beginning 2008, total funding for industry R&D includes other sources of funding not shown separately, including funding from other nonfederal U.S. sources and sources outside the U.S. [4] Through 2007, includes all other nonfederal sources. Beginning 2008, excludes funding from parent or unaffiliated businesses outside the U.S. and foreign subsidiaries of U.S. businesses. [5] Some data for 2017 are preliminary. [6] Estimates.

Source: National Science Foundation, National Center for Science and Engineering Statistics, *National Patterns of R&D Resources: 2017-18 Data Update*, NSF 20-307, January 2020. See also <http://www.nsf.gov/statistics/natlpatterns/>.

Table 833. Federal Obligations for Research by Field of Science: 2010 to 2019

[In millions of dollars (63,728 represents $63,728,000,000). For years ending September 30. Excludes research and development (R&D) plant (facilities and fixed equipment)]

Field of science	2010	2013	2014	2015	2016	2017	2018	2019 (P)
Research, total	**63,728**	**59,533**	**63,191**	**63,825**	**67,105**	**69,871**	**74,588**	**83,443**
Basic	31,795	29,779	31,588	31,527	32,293	33,271	36,195	39,685
Applied	31,933	29,753	31,604	32,298	34,812	36,600	38,392	43,758
Computer sciences and mathematics	3,412	3,427	3,883	3,863	4,223	3,894	4,207	4,546
Engineering	11,081	10,948	11,888	11,984	12,972	13,207	13,759	17,132
Environmental sciences	3,339	4,041	4,366	4,414	4,450	4,470	4,568	6,014
Life sciences	33,909	29,663	30,951	30,625	32,045	34,090	36,994	38,985
Physical sciences	5,871	6,282	6,483	6,510	6,706	6,582	7,881	9,064
Psychology	2,156	1,935	1,968	1,995	2,021	2,081	2,327	2,485
Social sciences	1,197	1,237	1,435	1,136	1,227	1,027	1,039	1,170
Other sciences, n.e.c. [1]	2,763	1,999	2,218	3,299	3,461	4,521	3,812	4,048

P Data are preliminary. [1] Not elsewhere classified.

Source: U.S. National Science Foundation, *Federal Funds for Research and Development, Fiscal Years 2018-19; Data Tables*, January 2020, and earlier reports. See also <http://www.nsf.gov/statistics/fedfunds/>.

Table 834. Federal Budget Authority for Research and Development (R&D) by Selected Budget Function: 2000 to 2019

[In millions of current dollars (78,664 represents $78,664,000,000). For year ending September 30. Excludes R&D plant]

Function	2000	2010	2014	2015	2016	2017	2018	2019 (P)
Total [1]	**78,664**	**146,596**	**133,547**	**136,090**	**147,813**	**124,710**	**140,701**	**144,074**
National defense	42,580	86,517	70,611	72,560	79,828	57,055	68,325	69,899
Health	17,869	31,488	30,927	30,331	32,365	34,255	37,151	38,894
General science and basic research	4,977	9,280	9,482	10,068	10,042	9,947	10,692	10,791
Space flight, research, and supporting activities	5,363	8,232	11,055	10,875	12,789	10,134	10,455	10,011
Energy	996	2,455	2,387	3,153	3,473	3,519	4,212	4,435
Natural resources and environment	1,999	2,237	2,172	2,161	2,294	2,378	2,383	2,347
Agriculture	1,426	2,043	1,967	1,989	2,030	2,090	2,074	2,135
Transportation	1,636	1,496	1,261	1,363	1,326	1,444	1,551	1,600
Veterans benefits and services	645	1,034	1,101	1,178	1,222	1,346	1,286	1,342

P Preliminary [1] Includes other functions, not shown separately.

Source: U.S. National Science Foundation, *Federal R&D Funding by Budget Function: Fiscal Years 2018-20*, NSF 20-305, December 2019, and earlier reports. See also <http://www.nsf.gov/statistics/fedbudget/>.

Table 835. Federal Research and Development (R&D) Budget by Federal Agency: 2019 to 2021

[In millions of dollars (140,134 represents $140,134,000,000). For fiscal years ending September 30. R&D refers to actual research and development activities as well as R&D facilities. R&D facilities (also known as R&D plants) includes construction, repair, or alteration of physical plant used in the conduct of R&D]

Federal agency	2019	2020, estimated	2021, proposed
Total research and development	**140,134**	**155,973**	**142,185**
Agriculture [1]	3,026	2,941	2,769
Agriculture Research Service	1,702	1,625	1,435
Economic Research Service	88	85	62
Forest Service	306	309	255
National Institute of Food and Agriculture	882	873	968
Commerce [1]	1,959	1,948	1,506
Bureau of the Census	122	155	163
National Institute of Standards and Technology	763	807	653
National Oceanic and Atmospheric Administration	1,066	978	678
Defense	54,691	64,544	59,831
Education	248	259	230
Institute of Education Sciences	230	241	213
Energy [1]	18,271	19,219	16,051
National Nuclear Security Administration	7,280	7,723	7,885
Environmental Protection Agency	489	492	318
Health and Human Services [1]	38,511	40,818	37,875
Centers for Disease Control and Prevention	466	435	435
Food and Drug Administration	491	410	410
National Institutes of Health	37,499	39,907	36,965
Homeland Security [1]	668	532	450
Countering Weapons of Mass Destruction Office	47	61	47
Interior [1]	958	973	725
Bureau of Reclamation	129	115	76
United States Geological Survey	640	660	460
Bureau of Ocean Energy Management	86	100	93
National Aeronautics and Space Administration	10,698	14,057	13,334
National Science Foundation	6,586	6,752	6,328
Transportation [1]	1,071	1,134	594
Federal Aviation Administration	501	533	447
Federal Highway Administration	375	404	–
Federal Transit Administration	28	36	33
National Highway Traffic Safety Administration	76	68	19
Smithsonian Institution	339	330	328
Veterans Affairs	1,370	1,313	1,351

– Represents or rounds to zero. [1] Total includes R&D funds allocated to programs or agency accounts not shown separately.

Source: U.S. Office of Management and Budget, *Budget of the U.S. Government, Fiscal Year 2021: Analytical Perspectives*, February 2020. See also <whitehouse.gov/omb/budget>.

Table 836. Funds for Domestic Business Research and Development (R&D) Performed by Companies by Industry: 2017

[In millions of dollars (400,100 represents $400,100,000,000), except percent. For the calendar year. The data represent for-profit companies that have ten or more paid employees in the United States, have at least one establishment that is in business during the survey year, and is located in the United States. Covers basic research, applied research, and development performed by the company and others. Based on the Business R&D Survey. For information, see <https://nsf.gov/statistics/srvyberd/>]

Industry	NAICS[1] code	Domestic R&D paid for by the company and others		Domestic R&D paid for by the company	
		Value (million dollars)	As a percent of domestic sales[2]	Value (million dollars)	As a percent of domestic sales[2]
All industries, total [3]....................	(X)	**400,100**	**4.1**	**339,036**	**3.5**
All manufacturing industries, total [3].............	31–33	**257,227**	**4.7**	**216,155**	**4.0**
Chemicals.................................	325	74,977	8.3	63,285	7.0
Pharmaceuticals and medicines.................	3254	66,202	14.2	55,229	11.8
Machinery.................................	333	13,197	4.1	12,257	3.8
Semiconductor machinery....................	333242	3,694	18.4	3,228	16.1
Computer and electronic products.................	334	78,575	11.3	69,942	10.0
Electrical equipment, appliances, and components.............	335	4,291	3.8	4,110	3.6
Transportation equipment....................	336	53,292	4.5	34,629	3.0
Aerospace products and parts.................	3364	26,383	7.5	11,903	3.4
All nonmanufacturing industries, total [3].............	(X)	**142,874**	**3.4**	**122,881**	**2.9**
Mining, extraction, and support activities.............	21	3,150	1.3	2,841	1.1
Information...............................	51	80,252	6.7	78,898	6.6
Software publishers.......................	5112	34,264	14.9	33,201	14.4
Professional, scientific, and technical services.........	54	36,922	9.2	18,972	4.7
Computer systems design and related services........	5415	13,327	8.8	11,669	7.7
Scientific research and development services.........	5417	17,321	25.1	2,817	4.1

X Not applicable. [1] 2012 North American Industry Classification System (NAICS); see text, Section 15. [2] Includes companies located in the United States that performed or funded R&D. [3] Includes industries not shown separately.

Source: U.S. National Science Foundation, *Business Research and Development: 2017*, NSF 20-311, February 2020. See also <nsf.gov/statistics/industry/>.

Table 837. Academic and Industrial Research and Development (R&D) Expenditures by State: 2017

[In millions of dollars (71,251 represents $71,251,000,000). Industry R&D data refer to calendar years; other R&D data refer to fiscal years but are used here as approximations to calendar year data. For definition of research and development see text this section]

State	Academic R&D [2] (mil. dol.)	Academic R&D per $1,000 of state GDP	Industry-performed R&D (mil. dol.)	Industry R&D per $1,000 of state GDP	State	Academic R&D [2] (mil. dol.)	Academic R&D per $1,000 of state GDP	Industry-performed R&D (mil. dol.)	Industry R&D per $1,000 of state GDP
U.S. [1]...	**71,251**	**3.65**	**400,101**	**20.50**	MO.......	1,149	3.78	5,299	17.43
AL........	1,005	4.75	1,896	8.96	MT.......	229	4.86	133	2.83
AK........	176	3.41	912	17.64	NE........	514	4.34	592	4.99
AZ........	1,213	3.71	6,338	19.41	NV........	206	1.31	624	3.97
AR........	313	2.53	466	3.77	NH.......	456	5.62	1,361	16.77
CA........	9,226	3.28	132,473	47.14	NJ........	1,253	2.09	16,405	27.37
CO.......	1,462	4.21	4,703	13.55	NM.......	374	3.97	802	8.51
CT........	1,254	4.72	8,694	32.74	NY.......	6,360	3.98	15,671	9.80
DE........	204	2.83	2,048	28.38	NC.......	3,082	5.73	10,246	19.05
DC.......	602	4.46	406	3.01	ND.......	256	4.96	304	5.89
FL........	2,618	2.67	6,463	6.60	OH.......	2,299	3.56	9,769	15.13
GA.......	2,340	4.16	6,450	11.47	OK.......	506	2.70	833	4.45
HI........	301	3.38	169	1.90	OR.......	781	3.45	7,691	34.02
ID........	163	2.25	1,747	24.12	PA.......	4,180	5.56	10,986	14.60
IL........	2,503	3.03	14,399	17.44	RI........	331	5.59	730	12.32
IN........	1,462	4.16	6,283	17.90	SC.......	699	3.15	1,370	6.17
IA........	831	4.54	2,938	16.06	SD.......	113	2.28	199	4.01
KS........	578	3.61	2,212	13.82	TN.......	1,184	3.40	1,407	4.05
KY........	582	2.90	983	4.89	TX.......	5,495	3.32	21,002	12.69
LA........	692	2.91	297	1.25	UT.......	611	3.69	2,846	17.18
ME.......	123	1.99	292	4.73	VT........	123	3.77	253	7.76
MD.......	4,020	10.09	5,595	14.04	VA.......	1,551	3.04	4,332	8.49
MA.......	3,928	7.26	23,655	43.73	WA.......	1,741	3.33	21,462	41.08
MI........	2,662	5.26	21,042	41.60	WV.......	210	2.87	212	2.90
MN.......	969	2.75	7,146	20.29	WI........	1,504	4.68	5,436	16.90
MS.......	479	4.36	266	2.42	WY.......	125	3.32	87	2.31

[1] States will not sum to U.S. totals because the U.S. totals include data for outlying areas (Puerto Rico, Guam, American Samoa, and Virgin Islands), R&D expenditures that cannot be allocated to specific states, and double counting of U&C (universities and colleges) data (see footnote 2). [2] State level university R&D data have not been adjusted to eliminate double counting of funds passed through from one academic institution to another. See source for more information.

Source: National Science Foundation, *National Patterns of R&D Resources: 2017-18 Data Update*, NSF 20-307, January 2020. See also <http://www.nsf.gov/statistics/natlpatterns/>.

Table 838. Higher Education Research and Development (R&D) Expenditures, Total and in Science and Engineering: 2010 to 2018

[In millions of dollars (61,287 represents $61,287,000,000). Data include R&D expenditures for both science and engineering (S&E) as well as non S&E fields, except for data by field. Beginning with FY2012, includes institutions reporting $1 million or more in total R&D expenditures; prior to FY2012 includes all institutions. Totals may not add due to rounding. Reference period is the fiscal year of the surveyed institutions. Data are based on the Higher Education R&D (HERD) Survey, which in 2010 succeeded the Survey of Research and Development Expenditures at Colleges and Universities; see source for details]

Characteristic	2010	2013	2014	2015	2016	2017	2018
Expenditures, total	**61,287**	**67,013**	**67,199**	**68,551**	**71,751**	**75,184**	**79,286**
Basic research	40,486	43,402	43,075	43,939	45,194	46,597	49,391
Applied research & development (R&D)	20,801	23,611	24,124	24,612	26,557	28,588	29,895
SOURCE OF FUNDS							
Federal government	37,478	39,446	37,962	37,849	38,778	40,237	41,945
State and local government	3,887	3,696	3,903	3,855	4,024	4,160	4,308
Institutions' own funds	11,943	14,936	15,735	16,592	17,921	18,971	20,395
Industry	3,202	3,511	3,728	4,002	4,210	4,424	4,719
Nonprofit organizations	3,730	3,889	3,964	4,220	4,615	5,118	5,439
Other	1,048	1,535	1,908	2,033	2,203	2,274	2,480
FIELD							
Total science and engineering	**58,388**	**63,354**	**63,767**	**64,940**	**67,626**	**70,887**	**74,667**
Computer and information sciences	1,638	2,068	1,928	1,963	2,079	2,193	2,401
Geosciences	2,992	3,195	3,228	3,247	3,086	3,151	3,162
Life sciences	34,984	37,565	37,958	38,782	40,864	43,129	45,844
Mathematics and statistics	592	671	658	641	680	701	753
Physical sciences	4,622	4,647	4,616	4,659	4,885	5,049	5,238
Psychology	1,078	1,128	1,142	1,182	1,218	1,241	1,263
Social sciences	2,000	2,173	2,216	2,317	2,362	2,557	2,747
Other sciences	1,156	1,172	1,044	1,078	1,077	946	887
Engineering	9,326	10,734	10,977	11,071	11,375	11,919	12,374

Source: U.S. National Science Foundation, "Higher Education Research and Development: Fiscal Year 2018, Data Tables," and earlier editions, <http://www.nsf.gov/statistics/herd/>, accessed January 2020.

Table 839. Federal Research and Development (R&D) Obligations to Selected Universities and Colleges: 1990 to 2018

[In millions of dollars (9,031.4 represents $9,031,400,000). Year ending September 30. Top 40 institutions receiving Federal Research & Development (R&D) funds in FY2018. From the Survey of Federal Science and Engineering Support to Universities, Colleges, and Nonprofit Institutions. Included are colleges of liberal arts; schools of arts and sciences; professional schools, as in engineering and medicine, including affiliate hospitals and associated research institutes; and agricultural experiment stations. Does not cover academic Federally Funded Research and Development Centers (FFRDC) administered by higher education institutions. Includes administrative expenses for R&D and excludes investments in physical assets, routine testing, quality control, and monitoring, and training of scientific and technical personnel; see <ncsesdata.nsf.gov/datatables/fedsupport/2018/fss18-tech-notes.pdf>]

Major institution ranked by 2018 obligations	1990	2000	2010 [2]	2015	2017	2018
Total, all institutions [1]	**9,031.4**	**17,271.7**	**30,748.2**	**26,772.3**	**29,471.8**	**31,882.9**
Johns Hopkins University	469.5	795.5	1,515.8	1,340.7	1,658.3	1,753.5
University of Michigan, all campuses	176.4	346.7	686.6	606.1	656.7	703.8
University of Washington, all campuses	217.2	396.1	736.6	611.9	612.7	665.7
University of California—San Diego	164.8	314.4	613.2	536.6	586.7	636.4
University of California—San Francisco	167.3	289.2	531.3	528.5	573.5	617.0
Columbia University in the City of New York	154.1	284.6	497.6	476.1	534.7	601.8
Stanford University	248.0	355.0	516.8	504.0	550.2	576.3
University of Pittsburgh, all campuses	116.6	246.2	497.1	450.0	503.6	558.2
Duke University	116.1	232.2	496.8	428.5	490.3	543.7
University of Pennsylvania	142.5	348.5	609.0	494.6	509.3	540.9
University of Colorado—Boulder	116.4	272.3	427.0	416.7	442.2	517.2
University of California—Los Angeles	176.7	372.4	548.8	481.8	492.4	509.9
Georgia Institute of Technology—Atlanta	54.3	58.4	234.9	295.2	465.7	485.3
Washington University	117.9	287.3	445.5	391.6	447.8	484.6
University of North Carolina at Chapel Hill	100.2	232.7	429.7	416.8	430.3	475.6
Yale University	142.5	260.0	470.5	370.8	431.6	466.9
Harvard University	148.1	299.9	548.7	425.5	447.5	463.8
Pennsylvania State University, all campuses	136.4	230.1	413.1	362.9	428.9	459.0
University of Wisconsin—Madison	155.2	263.4	461.9	386.6	453.8	451.4
Northwestern University	61.1	151.5	282.0	337.0	357.8	421.5
University of Southern California	122.7	203.9	378.9	289.2	405.8	411.1
Vanderbilt University	70.6	138.4	399.1	329.3	368.6	405.4
University of Minnesota, all campuses	137.5	276.8	420.3	359.5	355.1	397.6
Cornell University, all campuses	144.7	240.1	359.8	296.4	369.1	378.1
Emory University	49.6	145.6	303.1	324.2	340.0	366.5
New York University	80.0	130.0	257.1	263.8	328.5	356.2
Massachusetts Institute of Technology	218.3	248.9	340.2	350.5	319.5	332.2
University of California—Davis	68.9	148.5	313.2	315.4	315.3	331.2
Mount Sinai School of Medicine	44.0	119.5	216.5	262.4	303.7	331.1
University of Alabama at Birmingham	74.5	182.9	236.0	254.2	249.2	306.7
Case Western Reserve University	71.3	179.4	287.0	273.3	287.4	299.1
University of Texas at Austin	91.8	135.0	192.9	203.4	299.2	284.1
University of Florida	55.5	129.2	228.2	239.0	254.7	275.4
Ohio State University, all campuses	80.1	140.8	313.6	232.5	261.8	272.2
Baylor College of Medicine	72.3	172.3	251.3	227.5	254.5	266.0
University of Rochester	102.5	153.2	293.8	232.2	243.1	265.2
University of Utah	65.3	125.0	230.2	201.4	211.9	261.3
Carnegie Mellon University	50.0	88.3	132.1	104.3	263.3	259.9
Oregon Health & Science University	25.3	113.2	225.3	198.9	219.3	243.5
University of California—Berkeley	121.7	196.2	306.0	295.0	254.6	238.4

[1] Includes other institutions, not shown separately. [2] Includes American Recovery and Reinvestment Act of 2009 obligations.

Source: U.S. National Science Foundation, National Center for Science and Engineering Statistics, "NCES Interactive Tool," <ncsesdata.nsf.gov/ids/>, accessed June 2020. See also <http://www.nsf.gov/statistics/fedsupport/>.

Table 840. Research and Development (R&D) Spending and Employment by Company Size: 2017

[Expenditures in millions of dollars (400,100 represents $400,100,000,000); employment in thousands (19,893 represents 19,893,000). Data are from the Business R&D and Innovation Survey. Data represent all for-profit, nonfarm companies that are publicly or privately held and have ten or more employees in the United States]

Company size	Domestic R&D expenditures[1] (mil. dollars)	R&D as a percent of domestic sales of R&D performers or funders	R&D as a percent of domestic sales of R&D performers	Domestic employment of R&D performing companies		
				Total employment (1,000s)	R&D employment[2] (1,000s)	R&D employment as a percent of total employment
All companies.................	**400,100**	**4.1**	**4.3**	**19,893**	**1,609**	**8.1**
Small companies:						
10–19 employees................	3,311	13.7	15.4	73	26	35.6
20–49 employees................	9,435	11.0	11.7	285	78	27.4
Medium companies:						
50–99 employees................	10,141	8.7	9.0	366	74	20.2
100–249 employees.............	17,216	6.7	6.9	669	111	16.6
Large companies:						
250–499 employees.............	14,103	5.0	5.2	686	87	12.7
500–999 employees.............	17,871	4.8	5.0	849	90	10.6
1,000–4,999 employees.........	65,112	5.2	5.3	2,668	275	10.3
5,000–9,999 employees.........	40,198	4.3	4.4	1,710	185	10.8
10,000–24,999 employees......	73,485	4.0	4.1	3,007	248	8.2
25,000 or more employees......	149,227	3.3	3.5	9,581	437	4.6

[1] Domestic R&D paid for by the company and others and performed by the company. [2] Includes researchers, R&D technicians, and other supporting staff.

Source: U.S. National Science Foundation, *Business Research & Development 2017*, Data Tables, NSF 20-311, February 2020. See also <ncses.nsf.gov/pubs/nsf20311>.

Table 841. Graduate Science and Engineering Students in Doctorate-Granting Colleges by Characteristic and Field: 2010 to 2018

[In thousands (575.8 represents 575,800). As of Fall. Includes outlying areas. Based on the Survey of Graduate Students and Postdoctorates in Science and Engineering (GSS). In 2017, the GSS underwent a redesign, which included a reorganization of the taxonomy of academic disciplines; therefore, data from 2017 and after are not fully comparable to earlier data. See source for more information]

Field of science or engineering	Total			Characteristic								
				Female			Foreign[1]			Part-time		
	2010	2017[2]	2018[2]	2010	2017[2]	2018[2]	2010	2017[2]	2018[2]	2010	2017[2]	2018[2]
Total, all surveyed fields....	**575.8**	**577.1**	**602.3**	**265.0**	**253.0**	**270.9**	**165.9**	**217.3**	**219.7**	**142.5**	**135.1**	**144.8**
Science/engineering..........	508.1	521.9	541.4	215.3	212.2	225.5	158.3	210.1	211.9	121.7	118.4	126.1
Engineering, total............	141.8	157.6	156.5	32.9	38.8	39.6	64.2	86.3	83.5	35.4	38.7	39.4
Sciences, total[3]............	366.3	364.3	384.9	182.4	173.3	185.9	94.1	123.8	128.3	86.4	79.7	86.7
Agricultural sciences[4].....	14.6	8.9	9.1	7.2	4.7	4.9	3.2	2.8	2.9	4.1	2.4	2.4
Biological sciences.........	69.5	78.3	81.6	39.3	44.2	46.9	16.9	17.0	17.6	9.5	10.4	11.1
Computer sciences.........	45.9	73.4	80.3	11.2	21.6	24.0	22.6	45.3	46.5	15.8	24.8	27.8
Geosciences[5]..............	14.8	11.8	11.6	6.7	5.3	5.2	2.9	2.7	2.7	2.9	2.3	2.2
Math sciences..............	21.3	26.6	29.0	7.4	9.6	10.7	8.4	14.0	15.6	4.4	4.6	5.0
Multidisciplinary and interdisciplinary studies...	6.7	8.6	9.0	3.7	4.5	4.8	1.2	2.4	2.5	2.3	2.8	2.9
Natural resources and conservation................	(NA)	9.5	10.1	(NA)	5.2	5.5	(NA)	1.5	1.6	(NA)	2.6	2.8
Physical sciences..........	37.9	40.7	41.1	12.4	13.5	13.8	15.0	16.2	16.3	3.6	4.1	3.9
Psychology.................	45.2	37.2	41.7	33.8	27.6	31.6	2.9	2.8	3.0	11.7	9.1	11.3
Social sciences............	95.9	69.2	71.3	51.0	37.1	38.4	18.8	19.0	19.7	28.1	16.6	17.3
Health fields, total............	67.7	55.3	60.9	49.7	40.8	45.4	7.6	7.2	7.8	20.8	16.7	18.7

NA Not available. [1] Temporary residents. [2] The list of GSS-eligible disciplinary fields was updated in 2017 to align with the National Center for Science and Engineering Statistics Taxonomy of Disciplines. Natural resources and conservation was split from agricultural sciences; neurosciences are included in biological and biomedical sciences; physical sciences adds materials sciences; social sciences no longer includes public administration; and multidisciplinary and interdisciplinary studies no longer includes nanoscience. See source for more information. [3] For 2010, sciences includes communication, family and consumer/human science, multidisciplinary/interdisciplinary studies, and neuroscience, not shown separately. Starting 2017, communication and family and consumer/human science became ineligible. [4] Through 2016, agricultural sciences includes data for natural resources and conservation. [5] Earth or geosciences, atmospheric, and ocean sciences.

Source: U.S. National Science Foundation, National Center for Science and Engineering Statistics, "NCSES Interactive Data Tool," <ncsesdata.nsf.gov/ids/>, accessed June 2020. See also <nsf.gov/statistics/gradpostdoc/>.

Table 842. Temporary Visa Holders Awarded Doctorates in Science and Engineering For Top 10 Countries of Origin: 2008 to 2018

[Based on the Survey of Earned Doctorates; for information, see <http://www.nsf.gov/statistics/srvydoctorates/>]

Country of origin	2008	2009	2010	2011	2012	2013	2014	2015	2016	2017	2018
All temporary visa holders [1]	**15,261**	**14,736**	**13,636**	**14,235**	**14,784**	**15,674**	**15,839**	**16,129**	**16,474**	**16,290**	**17,604**
Science	8,553	8,349	7,809	8,021	8,374	8,676	8,764	8,902	9,469	9,086	9,640
Engineering	4,492	4,221	3,866	4,164	4,355	4,759	4,961	5,108	4,842	5,038	5,583
COUNTRY											
China [2]	4,148	3,753	3,457	3,652	3,906	4,443	4,650	4,970	5,140	5,149	5,689
India	2,158	2,112	1,994	2,036	2,142	2,074	2,208	2,119	2,085	1,883	1,919
South Korea	1,153	1,179	1,076	1,085	1,132	1,012	928	920	891	814	725
Taiwan	462	544	501	570	581	571	558	514	499	435	444
Turkey	467	445	405	422	352	391	360	386	380	392	362
Iran	132	(D)	(D)	193	278	380	463	608	664	728	869
Canada	370	387	339	307	299	332	321	318	272	288	301
Thailand	291	220	182	235	240	227	200	193	168	153	155
Mexico	161	171	169	159	185	146	161	155	191	145	156
Japan	209	193	173	179	179	166	129	120	129	92	93

D Data is suppressed to avoid disclosure of confidential information. [1] Total includes doctorates awarded in fields other than science and engineering and to temporary visa holders from other countries, not shown separately. [2] Includes Hong Kong.

Source: U.S. National Science Foundation, National Center for Science and Engineering Statistics, "Doctorate Recipients from U.S. Universities: 2018, Data Tables," <https://ncses.nsf.gov/pubs/nsf20301/data-tables/>, and earlier reports, accessed January 2020.

Table 843. Science and Engineering (S&E) Degrees Awarded by Degree Level and Sex of Recipient: 2000 to 2017

[Aggregated for degrees in the following science and engineering (S&E) fields: astronomy, chemistry, physics, atmospheric sciences, earth sciences, ocean sciences, mathematics and statistics, computer sciences, agricultural sciences, biological sciences, psychology, social sciences, and engineering. For doctoral degrees, medical and health sciences are included under S&E because these data correspond to the doctor's research/scholarship degree level which are research focused degrees]

Academic year ending	Bachelor's degree				Master's degree				Doctoral degree [1]			
	Total S&E	Men	Women	Percent women	Total S&E	Men	Women	Percent women	Total S&E	Men	Women	Percent women
2000	398,602	197,650	200,952	50.4	96,230	54,560	41,670	43.3	27,862	17,024	10,838	38.9
2001	400,435	197,771	202,664	50.6	99,528	55,884	43,644	43.9	28,096	16,873	11,223	39.9
2002	415,983	204,675	211,308	50.8	99,650	55,939	43,711	43.9	27,588	16,164	11,424	41.4
2003	442,755	219,815	222,940	50.4	108,355	61,183	47,172	43.5	28,746	16,569	12,177	42.4
2004	458,658	227,861	230,797	50.3	119,296	67,215	52,081	43.7	30,979	17,532	13,447	43.4
2005	470,214	233,924	236,290	50.3	120,870	67,244	53,626	44.4	34,468	18,970	15,498	45.0
2006	478,858	238,029	240,829	50.3	120,999	66,249	54,750	45.2	37,541	20,254	17,287	46.0
2007	485,772	241,697	244,075	50.2	120,278	65,353	54,925	45.7	40,980	21,653	19,327	47.2
2008	496,168	246,719	249,449	50.3	126,404	68,810	57,594	45.6	41,480	21,995	19,485	47.0
2009	505,435	250,742	254,693	50.4	134,517	73,489	61,028	45.4	41,111	21,743	19,368	47.1
2010	525,374	261,091	264,283	50.3	139,926	76,266	63,660	45.5	36,711	20,361	16,350	44.5
2011	554,365	275,258	279,107	50.3	150,653	82,451	68,202	45.3	38,470	21,377	17,093	44.4
2012	589,567	291,890	297,677	50.5	161,372	87,859	73,513	45.6	39,864	22,107	17,757	44.5
2013	615,475	305,777	309,698	50.3	166,397	90,046	76,351	45.9	41,563	23,021	18,542	44.6
2014	635,915	318,015	317,900	50.0	171,228	92,457	78,771	46.0	43,995	24,072	19,923	45.3
2015	650,057	327,122	322,935	49.7	180,955	99,282	81,673	45.1	44,521	24,371	20,150	45.3
2016	666,157	335,274	330,883	49.7	198,292	110,442	87,850	44.3	44,845	24,699	20,146	44.9
2017	684,557	346,087	338,470	49.4	206,172	116,326	89,846	43.6	45,729	25,048	20,681	45.2

[1] Prior to 2008, the National Center for Education Statistics (NCES) used two doctoral degree categories (doctor's and first professional). Data in this table for those years include only the doctor's category. In 2008 and 2009, NCES allowed optional reporting in three new doctoral degree categories (doctor's research/scholarship, doctor's professional practice, and doctor's other) in addition to the doctor's category. For those 2 years, data in this table include only doctorates reported in the doctor's category plus those reported in doctor's research/scholarship. In 2010, NCES required institutions to use only the three new doctoral degree categories, and data in this table for 2010 and later include only doctorates reported in the category doctor's research/scholarship.

Source: U.S. National Science Foundation, Science and Engineering Indicators 2020, *Higher Education in Science and Engineering, Supplemental Tables*, NSB-2019-7, September 2019. See also <http://www.nsf.gov/statistics/seind/>.

Table 844. Science and Engineering (S&E) Degrees as Percent of Higher Education Degrees Conferred by State: 2017

[Includes bachelor's, master's, and doctorate degrees. S&E degrees include degrees in physical, life, earth, ocean, atmospheric, computer, and social sciences; mathematics; engineering; and psychology. They do not include medical fields or technologies]

State	S&E degrees con- ferred	All higher educa- tion degrees	S&E higher education degrees (percent)	State	S&E degrees con- ferred	All higher educa- tion degrees	S&E higher education degrees (percent)	State	S&E degrees con- ferred	All higher educa- tion degrees	S&E higher education degrees (percent)
U.S. [1]......	**930,257**	**2,854,362**	**32.6**	KS.........	6,979	28,356	24.6	ND........	2,296	8,294	27.7
				KY.........	8,769	34,102	25.7	OH........	29,772	98,727	30.2
AL............	11,412	45,487	25.1	LA.........	8,693	30,628	28.4	OK........	8,189	28,384	28.9
AK............	962	2,695	35.7	ME........	3,282	10,045	32.7	OR........	12,017	33,176	36.2
AZ............	21,852	84,527	25.9	MD........	23,121	56,160	41.2	PA........	44,509	134,027	33.2
AR............	6,098	22,547	27.0	MA........	37,711	103,927	36.3	RI........	5,058	15,447	32.7
CA............	119,341	299,449	39.9	MI.........	28,880	85,530	33.8	SC........	10,230	32,773	31.2
CO............	19,690	51,649	38.1	MN........	19,088	64,658	29.5	SD........	2,530	7,757	32.6
CT............	12,890	35,754	36.1	MS........	5,347	21,025	25.4	TN........	12,827	49,645	25.8
DE............	3,283	11,173	29.4	MO........	18,735	65,639	28.5	TX........	59,372	188,813	31.4
DC............	9,228	22,290	41.4	MT........	2,788	7,327	38.1	UT........	12,091	50,769	23.8
FL............	42,022	142,098	29.6	NE........	5,529	20,796	26.6	VT........	3,361	8,990	37.4
GA............	23,724	72,946	32.5	NV........	3,502	11,403	30.7	VA........	28,195	85,612	32.9
HI............	3,078	8,757	35.1	NH........	6,753	22,692	29.8	WA........	18,326	45,319	40.4
ID............	4,065	13,812	29.4	NJ........	22,753	62,241	36.6	WV........	6,695	22,933	29.2
IL............	36,249	122,960	29.5	NM........	4,131	12,823	32.2	WI........	16,235	47,509	34.2
IN............	20,093	65,368	30.7	NY........	74,272	218,713	34.0	WY........	1,223	2,788	43.9
IA............	11,151	36,847	30.3	NC........	25,998	76,140	34.1	PR........	5,611	21,944	25.6

[1] Total higher education degrees and S&E degrees include U.S. territories.

Source: National Science Foundation, Science and Engineering Indicators 2020, "State Indicators," <https://ncses.nsf.gov/indicators/states>, accessed February 2020.

Table 845. Doctorates Conferred in Science and Engineering by Field, Sex, Citizenship Status, Race, and Hispanic Origin: 2018

[In percent, except as indicated. Based on the Survey of Earned Doctorates. For description of methodology, see <https://www.nsf.gov/statistics/srvydoctorates/>]

Characteristic	Total	Life sciences		Physical sciences			Mathematics and computer science		Social sciences		Engi- neering
		Total [1]	Biolog- ical	Total [1]	Chem- istry	Phys- ics [2]	Total [1]	Mathe- matics	Total [1]	Psycho- logy	
Total conferred (number)...............	**42,227**	**12,780**	**8,801**	**6,335**	**2,810**	**2,340**	**4,030**	**2,026**	**8,899**	**3,837**	**10,183**
SEX											
Male..........................	57.5	44.3	46.5	66.5	62.0	77.4	75.5	72.8	40.9	28.6	75.9
Female........................	42.4	55.7	53.5	33.4	38.0	22.4	24.4	27.0	59.1	71.4	24.1
CITIZENSHIP											
U.S. citizen or permanent resident.........	60.3	70.7	72.8	59.5	60.9	55.6	43.2	49.2	75.3	86.6	41.4
Temporary visa holders.......	36.1	26.3	24.5	37.5	36.4	41.1	52.9	47.6	19.9	7.4	54.8
RACE/ETHNICITY [3]											
Total conferred (number)...............	**25,473**	**9,041**	**6,406**	**3,771**	**1,711**	**1,300**	**1,739**	**996**	**6,704**	**3,321**	**4,218**
Non-Hispanic (number):											
White..........................	70.3	69.4	69.6	77.1	74.1	78.5	70.9	74.0	69.4	70.5	67.1
Asian [4]......................	10.7	11.0	12.1	9.4	10.3	10.6	13.3	11.9	7.1	6.0	16.1
Black..........................	5.7	6.5	4.8	2.7	4.5	1.2	3.7	2.5	7.8	7.3	4.0
American Indian/Alaska Native......................	0.3	0.2	0.2	0.2	0.2	0.2	0.2	0.2	0.5	0.4	0.2
Two or more races...........	3.2	3.2	3.3	2.7	2.5	2.5	3.3	3.7	3.8	3.4	3.1
Hispanic [5]...................	7.3	7.3	7.8	5.9	6.2	5.1	5.4	5.1	8.8	9.9	6.6
Other/unknown [6]............	2.5	2.3	2.2	2.0	2.2	2.0	3.2	2.5	2.6	2.4	3.0

[1] Includes other fields, not shown separately. [2] Includes astronomy. [3] Covers U.S. citizens and permanent residents only. [4] Excludes Native Hawaiians or Other Pacific Islanders. [5] Persons reporting Hispanic ethnicity may be of any race or combination of races. [6] Includes other non-Hispanic race, and individuals who did not report race nor ethnicity.

Source: U.S. National Science Foundation, National Center for Science and Engineering Statistics, "Doctorate Recipients from U.S. Universities: 2018, Data Tables," <https://ncses.nsf.gov/pubs/nsf20301/data-tables/>, accessed January 2020.

Table 846. Doctorates Awarded by Field of Study and Year of Doctorate: 2010 to 2018

[Based on the Survey of Earned Doctorates. For description of methodology, see <http://www.nsf.gov/statistics/srvydoctorates/>]

Field of study	2010	2012	2013	2014	2015	2016	2017	2018
Total, all fields	48,028	50,943	52,703	53,989	54,889	54,798	54,559	55,195
Science and engineering, total	34,997	37,846	39,031	40,633	41,178	41,234	41,294	42,227
Science, total	27,419	29,377	30,031	31,007	31,303	31,776	31,517	32,044
Life sciences	11,319	11,964	12,207	12,484	12,493	12,536	12,555	12,780
Agricultural sciences & natural resources	1,100	1,255	1,324	1,338	1,434	1,378	1,494	1,445
Biological/biomedical sciences	8,046	8,322	8,354	8,868	8,783	8,861	8,566	8,801
Health sciences	2,173	2,387	2,529	2,278	2,276	2,297	2,495	2,534
Physical and earth sciences	4,995	5,419	5,584	5,910	5,917	6,251	6,084	6,335
Chemistry	2,304	2,416	2,484	2,673	2,667	2,703	2,701	2,810
Geosciences, atmospheric & ocean sciences	862	941	989	1,098	1,057	1,227	1,169	1,185
Physics and astronomy	1,829	2,062	2,111	2,139	2,193	2,321	2,214	2,340
Mathematics and computer sciences	3,223	3,496	3,660	3,862	3,818	3,954	3,842	4,030
Computer and information sciences	1,633	1,793	1,843	1,988	2,003	2,082	1,998	2,004
Mathematics & statistics	1,590	1,703	1,817	1,874	1,815	1,872	1,844	2,026
Psychology & social sciences	7,882	8,498	8,580	8,751	9,075	9,035	9,036	8,899
Psychology	3,420	3,599	3,592	3,724	3,775	3,910	3,926	3,837
Anthropology	507	547	550	523	492	460	446	424
Economics	1,073	1,243	1,183	1,196	1,255	1,235	1,239	1,247
Political science & government	728	724	803	777	859	745	743	734
Sociology	639	633	636	679	742	613	683	669
Other social sciences	1,515	1,752	1,816	1,852	1,952	2,072	1,999	1,988
Engineering, total	7,578	8,469	9,000	9,626	9,875	9,458	9,777	10,183
Aerospace, aeronautical & astronautical	252	307	348	386	361	370	379	383
Bioengineering & biomedical	824	943	1,039	1,046	1,125	1,089	1,032	1134
Chemical	822	840	824	973	1,002	921	931	981
Civil	643	495	542	617	632	564	713	677
Electrical, electronics & communications	1,778	1,938	1,897	1,952	1,997	1,822	1,880	1,951
Industrial & manufacturing	215	226	241	298	243	256	249	272
Materials science	670	743	815	832	871	984	937	995
Mechanical	983	1,220	1,277	1,331	1,466	1,297	1,399	1,504
Other	1,391	1,757	2,017	2,191	2,178	2,155	2,257	2,286
Non-science and engineering, total	13,031	13,097	13,672	13,356	13,711	13,564	13,265	12,968
Education	5,287	4,802	4,934	4,789	5,098	5,143	4,826	4,834
Humanities	5,015	5,561	5,715	5,524	5,594	5,480	5,286	5,145
Professional/other/unknown	2,729	2,734	3,023	3,043	3,019	2,941	3,153	2,989

Source: U.S. National Science Foundation, National Center for Science and Engineering Statistics, "Doctorate Recipients from U.S. Universities: 2018, Data Tables," <https://ncses.nsf.gov/pubs/nsf20301/data-tables/>, accessed January 2020.

Table 847. Employed Scientists and Engineers by Sex, Race/Ethnicity, and Selected Characteristics: 2017

[In thousands (27,273 represents 27,273,000). Scientists and engineers are individuals who have a bachelor's or higher degree, and have an S&E (Science and Engineer) or S&E-related degree or occupation. Data based on various NSF (National Science Foundation) and non-NSF surveys; see <https://ncses.nsf.gov/pubs/nsf19304/technical-notes> for details]

Characteristic	Total [1]	Female	Male	Hispanic or Latino [2]	Asian [3]	Black or African American [3]	White [3]	More than one race [3]
All employed scientists and engineers	27,273	13,002	14,271	2,328	3,546	2,008	18,750	495
Age:								
Under 30 years	4,029	2,273	1,756	481	578	269	2,559	125
30-39 years	7,208	3,571	3,638	672	1,154	572	4,589	185
40-49 years	6,254	3,022	3,231	562	950	496	4,103	94
50-75 years	9,783	4,136	5,647	614	864	671	7,499	90
Employment status:								
Employed, full-time	22,866	10,102	12,764	1,964	3,083	1,772	15,512	407
Employed, part-time	4,407	2,900	1,508	364	463	236	3,239	88
Highest degree attained:								
Bachelor's	15,198	7,197	8,001	1,438	1,655	1,146	10,550	310
Master's	8,236	4,246	3,990	610	1,273	663	5,534	128
Doctorate	1,503	590	913	88	323	69	998	19
Professional	2,336	969	1,367	192	295	130	1,668	38
By occupation:								
S&E occupations	6,769	1,966	4,803	505	1,338	382	4,397	109
Science occupations	5,041	1,697	3,344	362	1,056	320	3,201	78
Engineering occupations	1,728	269	1,459	143	283	62	1,196	31
S&E related occupations	8,271	4,764	3,507	702	1,042	610	5,726	147
Non-S&E related occupations	12,233	6,271	5,962	1,121	1,166	1,016	8,628	239
By employment sector:								
Business or industry	14,541	5,611	8,930	1,189	2,270	873	9,903	241
Federal government	1,287	542	746	120	135	170	816	34
Nonprofit	3,226	2,201	1,026	251	326	297	2,270	67
Self-employed	1,652	777	875	142	137	68	1,274	25
State or local government	1,614	804	809	198	157	214	994	37
Universities and 4-year colleges	2,168	1,166	1,002	147	371	124	1,462	40
Other educational institutions	2,785	1,901	884	282	151	262	2,032	51

[1] Total includes other races, not shown separately. [2] Persons of Hispanic origin may be of any race. [3] Non-Hispanic.

Source: U.S. National Science Foundation, National Center for Science and Engineering Statistics, "Women, Minorities, and Persons with Disabilities in Science and Engineering - Data Tables," <https://ncses.nsf.gov/pubs/nsf19304/data>, accessed April 2019.

Table 848. Science and Engineering (S&E) Degree Holders by Occupation: 2017

[In thousands (21,371 represents 21,371,000). Data represents all workers who attained their highest degree (bachelor's or higher) in an S&E or S&E-related field. Detail may not add to total due to rounding]

Occupation	Total S&E and S&E-related degree holders	Employees by field of highest degree [1]						
		Total S&E fields	Computer and mathematical sciences	Biological, agricultural, and environmental life sciences [2]	Physical and related sciences [3]	Social and related sciences [4]	Engineering	S&E related fields [5]
All occupations	**21,371**	**14,501**	**2,567**	**2,290**	**814**	**5,336**	**3,494**	**6,870**
S&E occupations	**5,467**	**5,085**	**1,437**	**633**	**366**	**679**	**1,970**	**382**
Computer & mathematical scientists	2,545	2,365	1,373	95	62	234	601	180
Computer & information scientists [6]	2,322	2,165	1,255	75	55	202	578	157
Computer engineers—software	662	629	330	4	18	21	256	33
Software developers	542	505	309	11	12	28	144	37
Computer system analysts	258	227	147	11	3	27	39	31
Computer support specialists	160	146	86	10	(S)	19	25	14
Network/computer systems administrators	130	126	81	(S)	3	8	28	4
Mathematical scientists	122	112	47	17	4	30	14	10
Biological, agricultural, & environmental life scientists [6]	577	506	4	416	38	18	30	71
Biological & medical scientists [6]	433	370	3	298	33	11	26	63
Biological scientists [7]	135	132	(S)	114	5	6	(S)	3
Medical scientists (excluding practitioners)	149	105	(S)	81	8	3	13	44
Physical & related scientists [6]	342	330	2	81	217	8	22	12
Chemists, except biochemists	105	102	(S)	26	71	(S)	4	3
Physicists & astronomers	42	41	(S)	(S)	33	(S)	6	1
Social & related scientists [6]	443	416	8	11	2	391	4	27
Psychologists, including clinical	178	170	(S)	3	(S)	166	(S)	8
Postsecondary teachers—social sciences	127	125	1	(S)	(S)	123	(S)	2
Engineers [6]	1,560	1,468	51	30	47	28	1,312	92
Electrical or computer hardware engineers	349	330	21	(S)	7	(S)	297	19
Mechanical engineers	289	274	4	(S)	2	1	265	15
Civil, architectural, or sanitary engineers	247	238	3	5	(S)	1	227	9
Aerospace, aeronautical, or astronautical engineers	113	108	5	(S)	6	(S)	94	5
S&E-related occupations	**6,793**	**1,997**	**307**	**635**	**159**	**366**	**531**	**4,796**
Health-related occupations [6]	4,660	643	18	377	38	192	17	4,017
Diagnosing/treating practitioners [8]	1,228	77	(S)	59	(S)	(S)	5	1,151
Registered nurses, pharmacists, dieticians, therapists, physician assistants, & nurse practitioners	2,385	170	8	106	(S)	52	(S)	2,215
S&E managers	838	523	104	65	39	51	264	315
Medical & health services managers	303	53	(S)	25	9	19	(S)	250
Engineering managers	318	270	21	7	10	12	220	48
Computer & information systems managers	162	150	83	(S)	8	15	41	12
S&E precollege teachers [9]	434	247	56	76	34	68	13	187
S&E technicians & technologists [6]	638	539	111	113	47	42	226	99
Computer programmers	131	123	72	16	(S)	7	25	8
Electrical, electronic, industrial, & mechanical technicians	192	167	19	6	9	10	123	25
Other S&E-related occupations [6]	223	45	18	(S)	(S)	12	11	178
Architects	179	27	3	(S)	(S)	9	11	152
Non-S&E occupations	**9,111**	**7,418**	**823**	**1,022**	**289**	**4,291**	**993**	**1,693**
Non-S&E managers	1,492	1,221	164	167	69	525	297	271
Management-related occupations [6]	1,744	1,456	221	180	42	800	213	288
Accountants, auditors, & other financial specialists	482	436	69	35	6	293	34	46
Personnel, training, & labor relations specialists	259	198	15	19	3	146	15	61
Non-S&E precollege teachers [6]	570	418	41	33	19	316	9	152
Prekindergarten and kindergarten	84	73	(S)	(S)	(S)	63	(S)	11
Elementary	209	163	27	13	8	113	(S)	46
Secondary—other subjects	95	61	4	6	1	45	4	34
Special education—primary & secondary	120	82	2	(S)	(S)	70	(S)	38
Non-S&E postsecondary teachers	143	82	8	4	(S)	61	5	61
Social services & related occupations [6]	661	524	10	23	(S)	483	6	137
Counselors [10]	338	257	(S)	7	(S)	243	(S)	81
Social workers	262	215	(S)	12	(S)	201	1	47
Sales & marketing occupations	1,234	1,025	105	155	38	603	124	209
Arts, humanities, & related occupations	282	252	16	22	11	179	23	30
Other non-S&E occupations [6]	2,985	2,441	258	438	104	1,325	316	544

S Data suppressed for reasons of confidentiality and/or reliability. [1] Includes bachelor's, master's, and doctorate degrees. [2] Biological sciences include biology, ecology, nutritional sciences, pharmacology, zoology, and related fields. [3] Physical sciences include chemistry; earth, atmospheric, and ocean sciences; physics and astronomy; and related fields. [4] Social sciences include economics, political science, psychology, sociology and anthropology, linguistics, geography, history and philosophy of science, and related fields. [5] S&E-related fields include health fields, science and math teacher education, technology and technical fields, architecture, and actuarial science. [6] Includes other occupations not shown separately. [7] Includes botanists, ecologists, zoologists, etc. [8] Includes dentists, optometrists, physicians, psychiatrists, podiatrists, surgeons, and veterinarians. [9] Secondary teachers in computer, mathematics, sciences, and social sciences. [10] Includes educational, vocational, mental health, substance abuse, etc.

Source: U.S. National Science Foundation, Science and Engineering Indicators 2020, *Science and Engineering Labor Force, Supplemental Tables,* NSB-2019-8, September 2019. See also <http://www.nsf.gov/statistics/seind/>.

Table 849. Civilian Employment of Scientists, Engineers, and Related Occupations by Occupation and Industry: 2018

[In thousands (414.4 represents 414,400). As of 2018, the Standard Occupational Classification (SOC) system classifies workers into over 860 detailed occupations. Industry classifications correspond to 2017 North American Industry Classification (NAICS) industrial groups]

Occupation	Total employ- ment, all workers [1]	Wage and salary workers						Self em- ployed [3]
		Mining (NAICS 21) [2]	Con- struction (NAICS 23)	Manu- facturing (NAICS 31–33)	Informa- tion (NAICS 51)	Profes- sional, scientific, technical services (NAICS 54)	Govern- ment	
Computer and information systems.............	414.4	0.9	1.8	29.2	46.9	133.3	25.2	6.2
Architectural and engineering managers.......	192.5	2.1	4.1	67.6	3.4	69.7	17.2	(NA)
Natural science managers....................	63.5	0.2	0.1	6.9	(NA)	24.7	16.5	(NA)
Computer and mathematical scientists [4].......	4,674.4	10.7	17.6	303.2	587.4	1,616.9	278.8	115.2
Computer occupations.....................	4,490.1	10.2	17.5	294.7	580.7	1,573.0	257.2	113.1
Mathematical science occupations............	184.3	0.5	(NA)	8.5	6.7	43.9	21.7	2.1
Surveyors, cartographers, and photogrammetrists.................	61.0	1.3	3.8	0.2	0.3	39.4	10.1	3.1
Engineers [4]...............................	1,779.3	26.7	56.6	620.5	36.2	543.5	206.3	32.6
Aerospace engineers.......................	67.2	(NA)	(NA)	32.0	(NA)	18.8	10.2	0.5
Civil engineers............................	326.8	0.8	34.0	3.8	0.4	178.0	76.8	13.1
Computer hardware engineers..............	64.4	(NA)	(NA)	17.9	3.1	27.5	5.4	2.4
Electrical and electronics engineers..........	330.3	0.8	8.0	113.3	27.8	90.2	29.1	3.4
Industrial engineers [5].....................	311.6	2.2	5.8	208.0	2.4	40.4	5.8	0.5
Mechanical engineers......................	312.9	2.0	5.4	151.7	0.3	87.8	16.0	2.7
Drafters, engineering, and mapping technicians [4].................	701.4	5.8	27.7	215.0	4.5	265.9	87.4	8.5
Engineering technicians, except drafters.....	444.8	4.9	6.3	165.7	3.1	126.1	75.5	2.4
Surveying and mapping technicians...........	56.8	0.4	2.1	0.2	0.2	36.4	8.7	3.0
Life, physical, and social science occupations.................	1,322.7	18.3	1.4	126.5	2.5	341.1	321.8	69.8
Life scientists.............................	332.8	0.1	0.1	29.0	(NA)	102.9	71.8	3.8
Physical scientists........................	270.9	8.4	0.2	43.7	1.2	93.0	74.4	3.3
Social scientists and related occupations.....	314.4	0.1	0.2	0.2	0.6	37.0	89.3	54.9
Life, physical, & social science technicians...	404.6	9.8	0.9	53.5	0.5	108.2	86.4	7.9

NA Not available. [1] Includes other industries not shown separately. [2] Includes oil and gas extraction. [3] Includes unpaid family workers. [4] Includes other occupations not shown separately. [5] Includes health and safety engineers.

Source: U.S. Bureau of Labor Statistics, National Employment Matrix, "Employment Projections," <http://www.bls.gov/emp/tables.htm>, accessed February 2020.

Table 850. Top Metropolitan Areas with the Largest Number of Workers in Science and Engineering Occupations: 2017

[As of May. Ranked for top 20 metro areas with highest number of S&E (science and engineering) workers in 2017. Data are from U.S. Bureau of Labor Statistics' Occupational Employment Statistics Survey. Excludes metropolitan statistical areas where S&E proportions were suppressed. Differences among employment estimates may not be statistically significant; see source for details]

Metropolitan area	Workers employed		Metropolitan workers in S&E occupations as percentage of national total in S&E occupations
	All occupations	S&E occupations	
U.S. total............	142,549,250	6,889,020	100.0
Top 20 total............	44,171,050	2,917,320	42.3
New York-Jersey City-White Plains, NY-NJ metro division............	6,693,930	303,080	4.4
Washington-Arlington-Alexandria, DC-VA-MD-WV metro division............	2,519,220	273,310	4.0
Los Angeles-Long Beach-Glendale, CA metro division............	4,430,840	184,310	2.7
San Jose-Sunnyvale-Santa Clara, CA............	1,089,070	179,220	2.6
Chicago-Naperville-Arlington Heights, IL metro division............	3,662,390	173,730	2.5
Seattle-Bellevue-Everett, WA metro division............	1,647,350	172,730	2.5
Boston-Cambridge-Newton, MA NECTA division [1]............	1,839,740	162,520	2.4
Houston-The Woodlands-Sugar Land, TX............	2,929,400	159,400	2.3
Dallas-Plano-Irving, TX metro division............	2,491,590	157,640	2.3
Atlanta-Sandy Springs-Roswell, GA............	2,619,440	153,360	2.2
San Francisco-Redwood City-South San Francisco, CA metro division............	1,116,390	122,890	1.8
Minneapolis-St. Paul-Bloomington, MN-WI............	1,932,310	122,380	1.8
Denver-Aurora-Lakewood, CO............	1,443,130	109,380	1.6
Phoenix-Mesa-Scottsdale, AZ............	1,980,010	106,750	1.5
Warren-Troy-Farmington Hills, MI metro division............	1,231,590	100,220	1.5
San Diego-Carlsbad, CA............	1,433,340	97,560	1.4
Baltimore-Columbia-Towson, MD............	1,360,320	92,640	1.3
Anaheim-Santa Ana-Irvine, CA metro division............	1,616,210	90,700	1.3
Austin-Round Rock, TX............	996,540	80,860	1.2
Oakland-Hayward-Berkeley, CA metro division............	1,138,240	74,640	1.1

[1] NECTA = New England City and Town Area.

Source: U.S. National Science Foundation, *Science and Engineering Indicators 2020: Science and Engineering Labor Force*, NSB-2019-8, September 2019, and earlier reports. See also <https://ncses.nsf.gov/pubs/nsb20198/>.

Table 851. High Science, Engineering, and Technology Establishments, Business Formations, and Employment by State: 2016

[Employment in thousands (126,753 represents 126,753,000). High science, engineering, and technology (SET) industries are those industries for which employment in technology-oriented occupations accounts for a proportion of that industry's total employment that is at least twice the average for all industries. Includes only private-sector businesses. For a complete list of included industries, see source. Minus sign (-) indicates loss]

| State | All establishments | | High science, engineering, and technology establishments | | | | | |
| | | | Establishments | | Net business formations | | Employment | |
	Total	Employment (1,000)	Total	Percent of all establishments	Total	Percent of all establishments	Total (1,000)	Percent of total employment
United States	**7,743,176**	**126,753**	**714,591**	**9.2**	**9,367**	**0.1**	**15,317**	**12.1**
Alabama	99,422	1,673	7,212	7.3	51	0.1	165	9.9
Alaska	21,032	266	1,772	8.4	41	0.2	39	14.7
Arizona	138,945	2,378	13,065	9.4	327	0.2	256	10.8
Arkansas	65,549	1,024	5,149	7.9	21	(Z)	103	10.1
California	920,062	14,606	98,176	10.7	1,536	0.2	2,032	13.9
Colorado	164,978	2,317	20,726	12.6	137	0.1	342	14.7
Connecticut	89,234	1,534	7,525	8.4	-69	-0.1	202	13.2
Delaware	25,334	400	3,268	12.9	105	0.4	42	10.6
District of Columbia	23,143	527	4,147	17.9	139	0.6	92	17.4
Florida	545,367	8,168	52,807	9.7	1,299	0.2	692	8.5
Georgia	228,064	3,804	23,250	10.2	349	0.2	512	13.5
Hawaii	32,330	528	2,374	7.3	61	0.2	31	5.8
Idaho	45,742	562	3,302	7.2	49	0.1	59	10.5
Illinois	319,063	5,513	29,923	9.4	52	(Z)	702	12.7
Indiana	145,839	2,720	10,722	7.4	131	0.1	254	9.3
Iowa	81,395	1,355	5,043	6.2	64	0.1	122	9.0
Kansas	74,737	1,186	6,462	8.6	79	0.1	156	13.2
Kentucky	91,870	1,603	6,403	7.0	19	(Z)	135	8.4
Louisiana	105,650	1,709	8,644	8.2	-223	-0.2	160	9.4
Maine	41,114	511	2,788	6.8	59	0.1	42	8.1
Maryland	138,265	2,282	17,496	12.7	456	0.3	371	16.2
Massachusetts	177,230	3,255	18,349	10.4	243	0.1	504	15.5
Michigan	220,048	3,805	17,063	7.8	258	0.1	467	12.3
Minnesota	149,878	2,661	13,926	9.3	143	0.1	402	15.1
Mississippi	58,744	939	3,663	6.2	-13	(Z)	67	7.2
Missouri	160,609	2,495	10,810	6.7	378	0.2	298	12.0
Montana	37,527	379	2,830	7.5	9	(Z)	27	7.2
Nebraska	54,193	884	3,689	6.8	25	(Z)	74	8.4
Nevada	64,719	1,165	6,860	10.6	130	0.2	75	6.5
New Hampshire	37,787	594	3,472	9.2	14	(Z)	70	11.8
New Jersey	231,666	3,637	23,699	10.2	12	(Z)	520	14.3
New Mexico	43,678	628	3,571	8.2	-7	(Z)	77	12.2
New York	542,316	8,179	41,983	7.7	611	0.1	827	10.1
North Carolina	226,937	3,795	20,248	8.9	293	0.1	422	11.1
North Dakota	24,554	347	1,548	6.3	-27	-0.1	31	9.0
Ohio	251,781	4,789	20,873	8.3	151	0.1	522	10.9
Oklahoma	93,115	1,361	7,992	8.6	-161	-0.2	157	11.5
Oregon	114,252	1,550	9,371	8.2	217	0.2	179	11.5
Pennsylvania	301,057	5,355	25,359	8.4	175	0.1	617	11.5
Rhode Island	28,632	435	2,241	7.8	–	–	41	9.3
South Carolina	105,808	1,715	7,729	7.3	134	0.1	181	10.6
South Dakota	26,689	358	1,596	6.0	16	0.1	28	7.9
Tennessee	135,123	2,592	9,593	7.1	207	0.2	249	9.6
Texas	578,168	10,431	59,036	10.2	374	0.1	1,385	13.3
Utah	77,389	1,240	8,582	11.1	280	0.4	149	12.0
Vermont	21,145	262	1,627	7.7	17	0.1	23	8.9
Virginia	199,302	3,254	26,415	13.3	519	0.3	575	17.7
Washington	185,624	2,686	17,300	9.3	423	0.2	485	18.1
West Virginia	36,533	559	2,483	6.8	23	0.1	46	8.2
Wisconsin	140,602	2,526	10,445	7.4	230	0.2	289	11.4
Wyoming	20,935	208	1,984	9.5	10	(Z)	19	9.1

– Represents zero. Z Entry amounts to less than .05 percent.

Source: National Science Foundation, Science and Engineering Indicators 2020, "State Indicators," <https://ncses.nsf.gov/indicators/states>, accessed February 2020.

Table 852. Employment and Median Salary of Worker With Highest Degree in Science and Engineering (S&E) Field by Sex and Occupation: 2017

[Rounded to the nearest 1,000. Data are for full-time workers who typically work 35 or more hours weekly in their principal job. Data are from National Science Foundation, National Survey of College Graduates]

Occupation	Total Number	Total Median salary (dollars)	Female Number	Female Percent	Female Median salary (dollars)	Male Number	Male Percent	Male Median salary (dollars)
All occupations	12,315,000	80,000	4,501,000	36.5	60,000	7,814,000	63.5	90,000
S&E	4,643,000	93,000	1,154,000	24.9	80,000	3,488,000	75.1	98,000
Engineers	1,377,000	96,000	207,000	15.0	90,000	1,170,000	85.0	97,000
Computer and mathematical scientists	2,208,000	100,000	490,000	22.2	90,000	1,718,000	77.8	103,000
Biological, agricultural, and other life scientists	464,000	56,000	203,000	43.8	55,000	261,000	56.3	60,000
Physical scientists	278,000	74,000	83,000	29.9	62,000	195,000	70.1	82,000
Social scientists	316,000	75,000	172,000	54.4	71,000	144,000	45.6	84,000
S&E related occupations	1,725,000	80,000	609,000	35.3	60,000	1,117,000	64.8	95,000
Health-related occupations	478,000	56,000	310,000	64.9	56,000	168,000	35.1	53,000
Non-S&E related occupations	5,947,000	62,000	2,738,000	46.0	52,000	3,209,000	54.0	76,000

Source: U.S. National Science Foundation, Science and Engineering Indicators, 2020 *Science and Engineering Labor Force, Supplemental Tables*, NSB-2019-8, September 2019. See also <http://www.nsf.gov/statistics/seind/>.

Table 853. Federal Discretionary Outlays for General Science and Space and Other Technology: 1970 to 2019, and Projections for 2020 and 2021

[In billions of dollars (4.5 represents $4,500,000,000). For fiscal years ending in year shown; see text, Section 8]

Year	Current dollars Total	Current dollars General science and research	Current dollars Space/other technologies	Constant (2012) dollars Total	Constant (2012) dollars General science and research	Constant (2012) dollars Space/other technologies
1970	4.5	0.9	3.6	26.0	5.5	20.6
1980	5.8	1.4	4.5	16.9	4.0	12.9
1990	14.4	2.8	11.6	29.8	5.8	24.0
2000 [1]	18.6	6.2	12.4	26.3	8.7	17.6
2005	23.6	8.8	14.8	27.9	10.4	17.5
2007	24.4	9.1	15.3	27.0	10.1	16.9
2008	26.7	9.5	17.2	28.9	10.3	18.6
2009	28.3	9.9	18.4	30.3	10.6	19.7
2010	30.0	11.6	18.4	31.1	12.1	19.1
2011	29.4	12.3	17.0	29.8	12.5	17.3
2012	28.9	12.3	16.6	28.9	12.3	16.6
2013	28.8	12.4	16.4	28.4	12.2	16.2
2014	28.5	11.9	16.6	27.6	11.5	16.0
2015	29.4	11.7	17.7	28.0	11.1	16.9
2016	30.1	11.9	18.2	28.4	11.2	17.2
2017	30.3	12.2	18.1	28.0	11.3	16.7
2018	31.4	12.3	19.1	28.1	11.0	17.1
2019	32.3	12.8	19.5	28.3	11.2	17.1
2020, projection	34.9	14.0	20.8	30.0	12.1	17.9
2021, projection	37.4	14.3	23.1	31.6	12.1	19.5

[1] Due to the effects of the Credit Reform Act of 1990 on the measurement and classification of Federal credit activities, the discretionary outlays for years prior to 1992 are not strictly comparable to those for 1992 and beyond.

Source: U.S. Office of Management and Budget, *Budget of the U.S. Government, Fiscal Year 2021: Historical Tables*, February 2020. See also <http://www.whitehouse.gov/omb/budget>.

Table 854. Space Launch Events Worldwide: 2000 to 2017

[2,729 represents $2,729,000,000.) Data show all U.S. and international orbital launches. Launch data includes launch failures; launch failures happen when the payload does not reach a usable orbit or is destroyed as the result of a launch vehicle malfunction. In 2017 there were 5 launch failures; these included four government launches and New Zealand's commercial test launch]

Country/region	Non-commercial launches 2000	2010	2015	2017	Commercial launches 2000	2010	2015	2017	Launch revenues for commercial launch events (mil. dol.) 2000	2010	2015	2017
Total	50	51	64	57	35	23	22	33	2,729	2,453	2,150	3,018
United States	21	11	12	8	7	4	8	21	370	307	617	1,731
Russia	23	18	21	16	13	13	5	3	671	826	289	195
Europe	–	–	5	3	12	6	6	8	1,433	1,320	1,066	1,092
New Zealand	–	–	–	–	–	–	–	1	(X)	(X)	(X)	–
China	5	15	19	18	–	–	–	–	(X)	(X)	(X)	(X)
India	–	3	3	5	–	–	2	–	(X)	(X)	66	(X)
Japan	1	2	3	7	–	–	1	–	(X)	(X)	113	(X)
Israel	–	1	–	–	–	–	–	–	(X)	(X)	(X)	(X)
Iran	–	–	1	–	–	–	–	–	(X)	(X)	(X)	(X)
Korea, North	–	–	–	–	–	–	–	–	(X)	(X)	(X)	(X)
Korea, South	–	1	–	–	–	–	–	–	(X)	(X)	(X)	(X)
Multinational	–	–	–	–	3	–	–	–	255	(X)	(X)	(X)

– Represents zero. X Not applicable.

Source: Federal Aviation Administration, *Commercial Space Transportation: 2014 Year in Review*, February 2015, and earlier editions; and *The Annual Compendium of Commercial Space Transportation: 2018*, January 2018, and earlier editions. See also <http://www.faa.gov/about/office_org/headquarters_offices/ast/reports_studies/>.

Section 17
Agriculture

This section presents statistics on farms and farm operators; farm income, expenditures, and debt; farm output, productivity, and marketings; foreign trade in agricultural products; specific crops; livestock, poultry, and their products; and direct marketing to consumers.

The principal sources are the data collected by the National Agricultural Statistics Service (NASS), the Economic Research Service (ERS), and the Foreign Agricultural Service (FAS) of the U.S. Department of Agriculture (USDA) and published in reports or databases. The ERS publishes data on farm assets, debt, and income on the internet at <ers.usda.gov/data-products/farm-income-and-wealth-statistics>. The ERS also provides data on commodity supply and disappearance via commodity outlook reports, yearbooks, and databases, available on the ERS site at <ers.usda.gov/data-products>. Sources of current data on agricultural exports and imports include the Global Agricultural Trade System database provided by the FAS at <apps.fas.usda.gov/gats/> and the "Foreign Agricultural Trade of the United States (FATUS)" data, published by the ERS, available on the ERS site at <ers.usda.gov/data-products/foreign-agricultural-trade-of-the-united-states-fatus>.

The field offices of the NASS collect data on crops, livestock and products, agricultural prices, farm employment, and other related subjects mainly through sample surveys. Information is obtained on crops, livestock, and products pertaining to agricultural production and marketing. State estimates and supporting information are sent to the Agricultural Statistics Board of NASS, which reviews the estimates and issues reports containing state and national data. Among these reports are annual summaries such as *Crop Production, Crop Values, Agricultural Prices,* and *Meat Animals Production, Disposition and Income*. The NASS also provides data through the QuickStats database at <quickstats.nass.usda.gov>.

The USDA conducts the Census of Agriculture every 5 years and collects information concerning all areas of farming and ranching operations, including production expenses, market value of products, and operator characteristics. The information from the 2017 Census of Agriculture is available in print form in the Volume 1, Geographic Area Series; and on the internet at <nass.usda.gov/Publications/AgCensus/2017/>. An evaluation of coverage has been conducted for each census of agriculture since 1945 to provide estimates of the completeness of census farm counts. Beginning with the 1997 Census of Agriculture, census farm counts and totals were statistically adjusted for coverage and reported at the county level. The size of the adjustments varies considerably by state. In general, farms not on the census mail list tended to be small in acreage, production, and sales of farm products.

For more explanation about census mail list compilation, collection methods, coverage measurement, and adjustments, see Appendix A, *2017 Census of Agriculture,* Volume 1, <nass.usda.gov/Publications/AgCensus/2017/>.

Farms and farmland—The definitions of a farm have varied through time. Since 1850, when minimum criteria defining a farm for census purposes first were established, the farm definition has changed nine times. The current definition, first used for the 1974 census, is any place from which $1,000 or more of agricultural products were produced and sold, or normally would have been sold, during the census year.

Acreage designated as "land in farms" consists primarily of agricultural land used for crops, pasture, or grazing. It also includes woodland and wasteland not actually under cultivation or used for pasture or grazing, provided it was part of the farm operator's total operation. Land in farms includes acres set aside under annual commodity acreage programs as well as acres idled by federal conservation programs for places meeting the farm definition. Land in farms is an operating unit concept and includes land owned and operated as well as land rented from others. All grazing land, except land used under government permits on a per-head basis, was included as "land in farms" provided it was part of a farm or ranch.

Farm income—The final agricultural sector output comprises cash receipts from farm marketings of crops and livestock, federal government payments made directly to farmers for farm-related activities, rental value of farm homes, value of farm products consumed in farm homes, and other farm-related income such as machine hire and custom work. Farm marketings represent quantities of agricultural products sold by farmers multiplied by prices received per unit of production at the local market. Information on prices received for farm products is generally obtained by the NASS Agricultural Statistics Board from surveys of firms (such as grain elevators, packers, and processors) purchasing agricultural commodities directly from producers. In some cases, the price information is obtained directly from the producers.

Crops—Estimates of crop acreage and production by the NASS are based on current sample survey data obtained from individual producers and objective yield counts, reports of carlot shipments, market records, personal field observations by field statisticians, and reports from other sources.

Prices received by farmers are marketing year average prices and do not include allowances for outstanding loans, government purchases, deficiency payments or disaster payments. These averages are based on monthly prices weighted by monthly sales during specific periods. All state marketing year average prices are based on individual state marketing years, while U.S. marketing year average prices are based on standard U.S. marketing years for each crop. For a description of how U.S. prices are computed as well as a listing of the crop marketing years, see *Crop Values Annual Summary*.

Value of production is computed by multiplying state prices by each state's production. The U.S. value of production is the sum of state values for all states. Value of production figures should not be confused with cash receipts from farm marketings which relate to sales during a calendar year, irrespective of the year of production.

Livestock—Annual inventory numbers of livestock and estimates of livestock, dairy, and poultry production prepared by the Department of Agriculture are based on information from farmers and ranchers obtained by probability survey sampling methods.

Statistical reliability—For a discussion of statistical collection and estimation, sampling procedures, and measures of statistical reliability pertaining to Department of Agriculture data, see Appendix III.

Table 855. Selected Characteristics of Farms by North American Industry Classification System (NAICS): 2017

[388,522,695 represents $388,522,695,000. See text this section and Appendix III]

Industry	2012 NAICS code [1]	Farms	Land in farms (acres)	Harvested cropland (acres)	Market value of agricultural products sold ($1,000) Total	Crops	Livestock [2]
Total	(X)	**2,042,220**	**900,217,576**	**320,041,858**	**388,522,695**	**193,546,699**	**194,975,996**
Crop production	111	967,090	421,544,023	262,718,038	189,264,224	181,697,779	7,566,445
Oilseed and grain farming	1111	325,033	275,696,715	209,754,358	102,018,657	96,275,715	5,742,943
Soybean farming	11111	105,832	53,532,004	44,561,866	20,411,246	20,077,387	333,859
Oilseed (except soybean) farming	11112	849	1,488,090	1,073,701	251,972	248,984	2,988
Dry pea and bean farming	11113	1,296	1,782,380	1,173,169	321,225	316,886	4,339
Wheat farming	11114	18,312	29,720,570	15,595,523	3,125,617	2,993,054	132,563
Corn farming	11115	133,981	97,079,475	81,479,149	46,437,032	45,435,179	1,001,853
Rice farming	11116	2,680	3,323,806	2,451,234	1,893,094	1,860,141	32,953
Other grain farming	11119	62,083	88,770,390	63,419,716	29,578,471	25,344,085	4,234,387
Vegetable and melon farming	11121	45,165	9,310,059	6,008,800	19,731,533	19,627,511	104,022
Potato farming	111211	2,568	3,189,793	2,516,571	4,605,952	4,587,516	18,435
Other vegetable (except potato) and melon farming	111219	42,597	6,120,266	3,492,229	15,125,582	15,039,994	85,587
Fruit and tree nut farming	1113	95,441	13,357,346	6,173,016	28,336,564	28,211,310	125,254
Orange groves	11131	4,500	1,093,218	562,704	1,589,218	1,563,214	26,004
Citrus (except orange) groves	11132	3,451	513,909	277,376	1,621,780	1,613,949	7,831
Noncitrus fruit and tree nut farming	11133	87,490	11,750,219	5,332,936	25,125,566	25,034,147	91,419
Apple orchards	111331	10,087	2,226,789	472,433	3,518,947	3,512,021	6,926
Grape vineyards	111332	17,949	2,254,802	1,143,044	6,073,378	6,059,901	13,477
Strawberry farming	111333	1,391	137,455	60,565	2,018,159	2,017,404	755
Berry (except strawberry) farming	111334	11,005	1,073,431	254,450	1,359,836	1,355,865	3,971
Tree nut farming	111335	24,174	4,493,273	2,620,517	8,391,403	8,344,887	46,516
Fruit and tree nut combination farming	111336	1,477	250,421	140,631	516,724	510,459	6,265
Other noncitrus fruit farming	111339	21,407	1,314,048	641,296	3,247,118	3,233,609	13,509
Greenhouse, nursery, and floriculture production	1114	45,477	3,934,004	1,364,516	16,496,154	16,460,012	36,142
Food crops grown under cover	11141	4,199	155,700	22,701	2,081,839	2,076,997	4,841
Nursery and floriculture production	11142	41,278	3,778,304	1,341,815	14,414,316	14,383,015	31,301
Nursery and tree production	111421	26,174	3,294,378	1,202,706	8,175,668	8,150,549	25,119
Floriculture production	111422	15,104	483,926	139,109	6,238,648	6,232,466	6,182
Other crop farming	1119	455,974	119,245,899	39,417,348	22,681,315	21,123,231	1,558,084
Tobacco farming	11191	3,757	1,586,381	938,702	1,413,240	1,365,986	47,253
Cotton farming	11192	8,815	15,874,682	11,237,600	6,011,120	5,908,080	103,040
Sugarcane farming	11193	467	1,351,038	940,656	967,695	965,173	2,522
Hay farming	11194	244,035	46,273,222	16,001,743	5,585,232	5,124,522	460,710
All other crop farming	11199	198,900	54,160,576	10,298,647	8,704,028	7,759,469	944,559
Animal production	112	1,075,130	478,673,553	57,323,820	199,258,471	11,848,920	187,409,551
Cattle ranching and farming	1121	692,625	394,097,473	48,045,215	114,809,219	7,935,980	106,873,239
Beef cattle ranching and farming including feedlots	11211	654,875	376,699,018	36,258,728	72,426,397	5,259,911	67,166,486
Beef cattle ranching and farming	112111	641,496	362,543,006	31,777,036	33,370,653	3,454,114	29,916,539
Cattle feedlots	112112	13,379	14,156,012	4,481,692	39,055,744	1,805,797	37,249,947
Dairy cattle and milk production	11212	37,750	17,398,455	11,786,487	42,382,822	2,676,069	39,706,753
Hog and pig farming	1122	23,048	5,793,498	4,308,268	27,143,555	2,386,171	24,757,384
Poultry and egg production	1123	44,260	5,916,544	2,087,155	50,155,733	875,539	49,280,194
Chicken egg production	11231	19,785	1,295,219	371,262	8,905,165	161,201	8,743,964
Broilers and other meat-type chicken production	11232	15,609	3,394,774	1,223,669	31,068,699	482,203	30,586,497
Turkey production	11233	2,517	763,815	410,201	5,972,474	197,628	5,774,846
Poultry hatcheries	11234	264	12,237	878	3,402,867	188	3,402,679
Other poultry production	11239	6,085	450,499	81,145	806,527	34,319	772,208
Sheep and goat farming	1124	92,974	13,975,994	383,580	877,791	49,649	828,143
Sheep farming	11241	46,799	9,952,322	275,661	638,150	37,251	600,899
Goat farming	11242	46,175	4,023,672	107,919	239,641	12,398	227,244
Animal aquaculture	1125	3,981	1,008,935	53,195	1,778,231	26,807	1,751,425
Other animal production	1129	218,242	57,881,109	2,446,407	4,493,942	574,774	3,919,168
Apiculture	11291	10,517	439,719	15,109	357,124	3,590	353,534
Horse and other equine production	11292	157,237	22,695,698	829,208	1,444,757	30,969	1,413,788
Fur-bearing animal and rabbit production	11293	773	30,476	5,662	140,297	2,235	138,062
All other animal production	11299	49,715	34,715,216	1,596,428	2,551,764	537,981	2,013,784

X Not applicable. [1] Based on the North American Industry Classification System (NAICS) 2012; see text, Section 15. [2] Includes poultry and poultry products sold.

Source: U.S. Department of Agriculture, National Agricultural Statistics Service, *2017 Census of Agriculture*, Vol. 1, April 2019. See also <https://www.nass.usda.gov/AgCensus/index.php>.

Table 856. Farms—Number and Acreage: 2000 to 2019

[2,167 represents 2,167,000. As of June. Based on 1974 census definition; for definition of farms and farmland, see text, this section. Data for census years have been adjusted for underenumeration]

Item	Unit	2000	2005	2010	2014	2015	2016	2017	2018	2019
Number of farms..........	1,000	2,167	2,099	2,150	2,082	2,064	2,055	2,042	2,029	2,023
Land in farms..............	Million acres	945	928	916	909	906	903	900	900	897
Average per farm........	Acres	436	442	426	436	439	439	441	443	444

Source: U.S. Department of Agriculture, National Agricultural Statistics Service, *Farm Numbers and Land in Farms, Final Estimates, 2013–2017* and earlier reports; and *Farms and Land in Farms 2019 Summary*, February 2020. See also <http://www.nass.usda.gov/Publications/index.asp>.

Table 857. Farms—Number and Acreage by State: 2010 and 2019

[2,150 represents 2,150,000. See headnote, Table 856]

State	Farms (1,000) 2010	Farms (1,000) 2019	Land in farms (mil. acres) 2010	Land in farms (mil. acres) 2019	Acreage per farm 2010	Acreage per farm 2019	State	Farms (1,000) 2010	Farms (1,000) 2019	Land in farms (mil. acres) 2010	Land in farms (mil. acres) 2019	Acreage per farm 2010	Acreage per farm 2019
United States.....	**2,150**	**2,023**	**915.7**	**897.4**	**426**	**444**	Missouri............	103	95	28.7	27.6	279	290
							Montana............	29	27	60.6	58.0	2,082	2,164
Alabama............	46	39	8.9	8.3	193	214	Nebraska...........	50	46	45.4	44.9	917	982
Alaska..............	1	1	0.9	0.9	1,181	810	Nevada.............	4	3	5.9	6.1	1,579	1,821
Arizona............	18	19	24.8	26.2	1,378	1,379	New Hampshire....	4	4	0.5	0.4	109	105
Arkansas...........	47	42	13.7	14.0	291	331	New Jersey.........	10	10	0.7	0.8	74	76
California..........	79	70	25.5	24.3	322	348	New Mexico........	22	25	43.4	40.0	1,973	1,613
Colorado..........	36	39	31.5	31.8	868	822	New York..........	36	33	7.1	6.9	197	207
Connecticut........	6	6	0.4	0.4	75	69	North Carolina.....	52	46	8.4	8.4	163	182
Delaware..........	3	2	0.5	0.5	200	230	North Dakota.......	31	26	39.5	39.3	1,262	1,506
Florida............	48	47	9.4	9.7	197	205	Ohio..............	75	78	13.8	13.6	184	175
Georgia...........	44	42	9.7	10.2	219	246	Oklahoma..........	83	77	34.7	34.4	417	445
Hawaii............	7	7	1.1	1.1	153	151	Oregon............	37	37	16.2	15.8	439	425
Idaho.............	25	25	11.5	11.5	453	467	Pennsylvania.......	61	53	7.7	7.3	126	139
Illinois............	76	71	26.9	27.0	354	378	Rhode Island.......	1	1	0.1	0.1	56	55
Indiana............	61	56	14.8	14.9	242	266	South Carolina.....	26	25	5.0	4.8	192	195
Iowa..............	89	85	30.6	30.6	343	359	South Dakota......	32	30	43.4	43.2	1,361	1,459
Kansas............	63	59	46.2	45.7	732	781	Tennessee..........	73	70	10.8	10.8	148	155
Kentucky..........	80	75	13.4	12.9	167	172	Texas..............	249	247	131.6	126.5	530	512
Louisiana..........	29	27	8.0	8.0	274	292	Utah..............	18	18	11.0	10.7	629	601
Maine.............	8	8	1.4	1.3	173	171	Vermont...........	7	7	1.2	1.2	172	176
Maryland..........	13	12	2.1	2.0	164	161	Virginia............	47	42	8.2	7.8	176	184
Massachusetts.....	8	7	0.5	0.5	69	69	Washington........	38	36	14.6	14.6	382	410
Michigan..........	53	47	10.0	9.8	187	209	West Virginia.......	22	23	3.6	3.5	161	153
Minnesota.........	77	68	26.3	25.5	342	375	Wisconsin..........	73	65	14.7	14.3	201	220
Mississippi.........	40	35	10.9	10.4	275	301	Wyoming...........	12	12	30.0	29.0	2,586	2,417

Source: U.S. Department of Agriculture, National Agricultural Statistics Service, "Quick Stats," <http://quickstats.nass.usda.gov/>, accessed February 2020. See also <http://www.nass.usda.gov/Statistics_by_Subject/>.

Table 858. Farms by Size and Type of Organization: 1982 to 2017

[2,241 represents 2,241,000. For comments on adjustment, see text, this section]

Size and type of organization	Unit	Not adjusted for coverage 1982	Not adjusted for coverage 1987	Not adjusted for coverage 1992	Adjusted for coverage [1] 1997	Adjusted for coverage [1] 2002	Adjusted for coverage [1] 2007	Adjusted for coverage [1] 2012	Adjusted for coverage [1] 2017
Farms.........................	1,000	2,241	2,088	1,925	2,216	2,129	2,205	2,109	2,042
Land in farms.................	Mil. acres	987	964	946	955	938	922	915	900
Average size of farm......................	Acres	440	462	491	431	441	418	434	441
Farms by size:									
1 to 9 acres..............................	1,000	188	183	166	205	179	233	224	273
10 to 49 acres...........................	1,000	449	412	388	531	564	620	590	583
50 to 179 acres..........................	1,000	712	645	584	694	659	661	634	565
180 to 499 acres.........................	1,000	527	478	428	428	389	368	346	315
500 to 999 acres.........................	1,000	204	200	186	179	162	150	143	133
1,000 to 1,999 acres.....................	1,000	97	102	102	103	99	93	91	88
2,000 acres or more......................	1,000	65	67	71	74	78	80	82	85
Farms by type of organization:									
Family or individual......................	1,000	1,946	1,809	1,653	1,923	1,910	1,906	1,829	1,751
Partnership...............................	1,000	223	200	187	186	130	174	138	130
Corporation...............................	1,000	60	67	73	90	74	96	107	117
Other [2].................................	1,000	12	12	12	17	16	28	36	44

[1] Data have been adjusted for coverage; see text, this section. [2] Cooperative, estate or trust, institutional, etc.

Source: U.S. Department of Agriculture, National Agricultural Statistics Service, *2017 Census of Agriculture*, Vol. 1, April 2019, and earlier reports. See also <https://www.nass.usda.gov/AgCensus/>.

Table 859. Farms—Number and Acreage by Size of Farm: 2012 and 2017

[2,109 represents 2,109,000. Data have been adjusted for coverage; see text, this section]

Size of farm	Number of farms (1,000)		Land in farms (mil. acres)		Cropland harvested (mil. acres)		Percent distribution, 2017		
	2012	2017	2012	2017	2012	2017	Number of farms	All land in farms	Cropland harvested
Total	**2,109**	**2,042**	**914.5**	**900.2**	**315.0**	**320.0**	**100.0**	**100.0**	**100.0**
Under 10 acres	224	273	1.0	1.3	0.3	0.4	13.4	0.1	0.1
10 to 49 acres	590	583	15.1	14.8	4.1	4.1	28.5	1.6	1.3
50 to 69 acres	154	135	8.9	7.8	2.5	2.2	6.6	0.9	0.7
70 to 99 acres	185	163	15.2	13.4	4.4	3.9	8.0	1.5	1.2
100 to 139 acres	166	149	19.3	17.3	5.7	5.2	7.3	1.9	1.6
140 to 179 acres	129	117	20.3	18.4	6.3	5.8	5.7	2.0	1.8
180 to 219 acres	84	74	16.7	14.6	5.6	5.0	3.6	1.6	1.6
220 to 259 acres	64	57	15.1	13.6	5.5	5.0	2.8	1.5	1.6
260 to 499 acres	198	184	70.6	65.8	28.8	27.0	9.0	7.3	8.4
500 to 999 acres	143	133	99.0	92.9	49.5	45.9	6.5	10.3	14.3
1,000 to 1,999 acres	91	88	125.1	120.7	68.7	66.2	4.3	13.4	20.7
2,000 acres or more	82	85	508.2	519.6	133.6	149.4	4.2	57.7	46.7

Source: U.S. Department of Agriculture, National Agricultural Statistics Service, *2017 Census of Agriculture*, Vol. 1, April 2019. See also <https://www.nass.usda.gov/AgCensus/>.

Table 860. Farms—Number, Acreage, and Value by Tenure of Principal Operator and Type of Organization: 2012 and 2017

[2,109 represents 2,109,000. Full owners own all the land they operate. Part owners own a part and rent from others the rest of the land they operate. A principal operator is the person primarily responsible for the on-site, day-to-day operation of the farm or ranch business. Data have been adjusted for coverage; see text, this section]

Item and year	Unit	Total [1]	Tenure of operator			Type of organization		
			Full owner	Part owner	Tenant	Family or individual	Partner-ship	Corpora-tion
NUMBER OF FARMS								
2012	1,000	2,109	1,428	533	148	1,829	138	107
2017	1,000	2,042	1,409	493	140	1,751	130	117
Under 50 acres	1,000	856	740	62	54	779	29	33
50 to 179 acres	1,000	565	419	113	33	499	29	24
180 to 499 acres	1,000	315	167	126	23	262	25	19
500 to 999 acres	1,000	133	45	76	12	101	15	14
1,000 acres or more	1,000	173	37	117	19	110	31	27
LAND IN FARMS								
2012	Mil. acres	915	336	491	87	562	156	131
2017	Mil. acres	900	310	503	87	541	158	140
Value of land and buildings, 2017	Bil. dol.	2,679	907	1,538	234	1,732	451	418
Value of farm products sold, 2017	Bil. dol.	389	142	207	40	182	89	111

[1] Includes other types, not shown separately.

Source: U.S. Department of Agriculture, National Agricultural Statistics Service, *2017 Census of Agriculture*, Vol. 1, April 2019, and earlier reports. See also <https://www.nass.usda.gov/AgCensus/>.

Table 861. Corporate Farms—Characteristics by Type: 2002 to 2017

[139.6 represents 139,600,000. Data have been adjusted for coverage; see text, this section and Appendix III]

Item	Unit	All corpora-tions	Family held corporations			Other corporations		
			Total	1 to 10 stock-holders	11 or more stock-holders	Total	1 to 10 stock-holders	11 or more stock-holders
Farms:								
2002	Number	73,752	66,667	65,017	1,650	7,085	6,010	1,075
2007	Number	96,074	85,837	83,796	2,041	10,237	9,330	907
2012	Number	106,716	95,142	92,834	2,308	11,574	10,438	1,136
2017								
Farms	Number	116,840	104,155	101,851	2,304	12,685	11,541	1,144
Percent distribution	Percent	100.0	89.1	87.2	2.0	10.9	9.9	1.0
Land in farms	Mil. acres	139.6	126.7	119.6	7.1	12.9	10.5	2.4
Average per farm	Acres	1,194	1,216	1,174	3,084	1,016	910	2,090
Value of—								
Land and buildings	Bil. dol.	417.6	378.7	360.8	18.0	38.8	30.0	8.8
Average per farm	$1,000	3,574	3,636	3,542	7,798	3,062	2,601	7,712
Farm products sold	Bil. dol.	111.0	89.1	83.2	5.9	22.0	13.8	8.2
Average per farm	$1,000	950	855	817	2,547	1,733	1,197	7,133

Source: U.S. Department of Agriculture, National Agricultural Statistics Service, *2017 Census of Agriculture*, Vol. 1, April 2019, and earlier reports. See also <https://www.nass.usda.gov/AgCensus/>.

Table 862. Farms—Number, Acreage, and Value by State: 2012 and 2017

[2,109 represents 2,109,000. Data have been adjusted for coverage; see text, this section and Appendix III]

State	Number of farms (1,000) 2012	Number of farms (1,000) 2017	Land in farms (mil. acres) 2012	Land in farms (mil. acres) 2017	Average size of farm (acres) 2012	Average size of farm (acres) 2017	Total value of land and buildings (bil. dol.) 2012	Total value of land and buildings (bil. dol.) 2017	Market value of agricultural products sold and government payments (mil. dol.) 2012	Market value of agricultural products sold and government payments (mil. dol.) 2017
U.S.	2,109	2,042	914.5	900.2	434	441	2,268.5	2,679.0	402,698	397,466
AL.	43	41	8.9	8.6	206	211	23.7	25.6	5,659	6,115
AK.	1	1	0.8	0.8	1,094	858	0.5	0.6	61	73
AZ.	20	19	26.2	26.1	1,312	1,369	16.9	21.2	3,763	3,874
AR.	45	43	13.8	13.9	306	326	36.4	43.9	10,039	9,973
CA.	78	71	25.6	24.5	328	348	160.5	229.4	42,774	45,282
CO.	36	39	31.9	31.8	881	818	40.8	51.2	7,946	7,690
CT.	6	6	0.4	0.4	73	69	4.8	4.8	555	582
DE.	2	2	0.5	0.5	208	228	4.2	4.4	1,284	1,481
FL.	48	48	9.5	9.7	200	204	49.7	57.4	7,742	7,416
GA.	42	42	9.6	10.0	228	235	29.7	34.9	9,397	9,821
HI.	7	7	1.1	1.1	161	155	10.2	10.6	667	572
ID.	25	25	11.8	11.7	474	468	26.1	33.5	7,901	7,697
IL.	75	73	26.9	27.0	359	372	169.8	196.5	17,740	17,531
IN.	59	57	14.7	15.0	251	264	78.8	98.4	11,478	11,450
IA.	89	86	30.6	30.6	345	355	195.6	215.8	31,604	29,639
KS.	62	59	46.1	45.8	747	781	75.3	84.6	18,903	19,292
KY.	77	76	13.0	13.0	169	171	39.5	48.8	5,237	5,865
LA.	28	27	7.9	8.0	281	292	20.2	24.4	3,948	3,350
ME.	8	8	1.5	1.3	178	172	3.4	3.4	773	676
MD.	12	12	2.0	2.0	166	160	14.1	15.6	2,307	2,517
MA.	8	7	0.5	0.5	68	68	5.5	5.4	500	479
MI.	52	48	9.9	9.8	191	205	40.0	48.4	8,834	8,388
MN.	75	69	26.0	25.5	349	371	109.9	123.8	21,748	18,790
MS.	38	35	10.9	10.4	287	298	24.8	28.6	6,622	6,410
MO.	99	95	28.3	27.8	285	291	78.9	94.0	9,489	10,850
MT.	28	27	59.8	58.1	2,134	2,149	46.9	53.2	4,440	3,805
NE.	50	46	45.3	45.0	907	971	107.9	123.9	23,461	22,623
NV.	4	3	5.9	6.1	1,429	1,790	5.5	5.6	767	671
NH.	4	4	0.5	0.4	108	103	2.0	2.2	194	191
NJ.	9	10	0.7	0.7	79	74	9.1	9.9	1,015	1,105
NM.	25	25	43.2	40.7	1,748	1,624	18.7	21.2	2,621	2,646
NY.	36	33	7.2	6.9	202	205	18.7	22.2	5,490	5,428
NC.	50	46	8.4	8.4	168	182	36.5	39.1	12,708	13,008
ND.	31	26	39.3	39.3	1,268	1,492	56.0	67.1	11,332	8,701
OH.	75	78	14.0	14.0	185	179	67.5	86.6	10,293	9,692
OK.	80	79	34.4	34.2	428	435	46.0	59.2	7,386	7,698
OR.	35	38	16.3	16.0	460	424	30.7	38.8	4,970	5,099
PA.	59	53	7.7	7.3	130	137	41.8	47.7	7,487	7,833
RI.	1	1	0.1	0.1	56	55	1.0	0.9	62	59
SC.	25	25	5.0	4.7	197	191	14.8	17.0	3,087	3,064
SD.	32	30	43.3	43.2	1,352	1,443	73.0	89.4	10,454	10,141
TN.	68	70	10.9	10.9	160	155	38.7	42.6	3,679	3,915
TX.	249	248	130.2	127.0	523	511	218.1	243.5	26,020	25,673
UT.	18	18	11.0	10.8	609	587	16.0	19.6	1,840	1,866
VT.	7	7	1.3	1.2	171	175	4.0	4.2	790	787
VA.	46	43	8.3	7.8	180	180	35.8	36.1	3,836	4,021
WA.	37	36	14.7	14.7	396	410	33.9	40.9	9,280	9,803
WV.	21	24	3.6	3.7	168	155	8.9	9.7	814	763
WI.	70	65	14.6	14.3	209	221	57.2	70.2	11,982	11,554
WY.	12	12	30.4	29.0	2,587	2,430	20.6	22.6	1,718	1,502

Source: U.S. Department of Agriculture, National Agricultural Statistics Service, *2017 Census of Agriculture*, Vol. 1, April 2019. See also <https://www.nass.usda.gov/AgCensus/>.

Table 863. Farms—Number, Value of Sales, and Government Payments by Economic Class of Farm: 2012 and 2017

[2,109 represents 2,109,000. Economic class of farm is a combination of market value of agricultural products sold and federal farm program payments. Data have been adjusted for coverage; see text, this section and Appendix III]

Economic class	Number of farms (1,000) 2012, total	Number of farms (1,000) 2017 Total	Number of farms (1,000) 2017 Receiving government payments	Market value of agricultural products sold and government payments (mil. dol.) 2012, total	Market value of agricultural products sold and government payments (mil. dol.) 2017 Total	Market value of agricultural products sold and government payments (mil. dol.) 2017 Agricultural products sold	Market value of agricultural products sold and government payments (mil. dol.) 2017 Government payments
Total.	2,109	2,042	643	402,698	397,466	388,523	8,944
Less than $1,000.	429	472	17	80	97	88	8
$1,000 to $2,499.	237	217	44	393	360	295	65
$2,500 to $4,999.	231	211	47	832	757	629	128
$5,000 to $9,999.	249	234	59	1,769	1,666	1,415	251
$10,000 to $24,999.	272	253	83	4,323	4,041	3,505	536
$25,000 to $49,999.	162	155	67	5,736	5,494	4,915	578
$50,000 to $99,999.	134	126	68	9,575	8,934	8,255	679
$100,000 to $249,999.	142	134	86	23,196	21,730	20,614	1,116
$250,000 to $499,999.	96	89	64	34,463	31,718	30,478	1,241
$500,000 to $999,999.	78	72	54	55,663	50,677	49,011	1,666
$1,000,000 to $2,499,999.	58	56	39	90,534	86,284	84,438	1,846
$2,500,000 to $4,999,999.	15	15	9	50,511	50,087	49,521	567
$5 million or more.	9	9	4	125,624	135,622	135,359	263

Source: U.S. Department of Agriculture, National Agricultural Statistics Service, *2017 Census of Agriculture*, Vol. 1, April 2019.

Table 864. Farms—Number, Acreage, and Value of Sales by Size of Sales: 2012 and 2017

[2,109 represents 2,109,000. Data have been adjusted for coverage; see text, this section and Appendix III]

Market value of agricultural products sold	Farms (1,000)	Acreage Total (mil.)	Acreage Average per farm	Value of sales Total (mil. dol.)	Value of sales Average per farm (dol.)	Percent distribution Farms	Percent distribution Acreage	Percent distribution Value of sales
2012								
Total..........................	2,109	914.5	434	394,644	187,097	100.0	100.0	100.0
Less than $2,500......................	788	118.4	150	380	483	37.4	12.9	0.1
$2,500 to $4,999..................	191	19.6	102	688	3,592	9.1	2.1	0.2
$5,000 to $9,999..................	214	25.4	119	1,522	7,104	10.2	2.8	0.4
$10,000 to $24,999..............	245	59.4	243	3,908	15,954	11.6	6.5	1.0
$25,000 to $49,999..............	153	48.4	316	5,418	35,440	7.2	5.3	1.4
$50,000 to $99,999..............	129	64.0	495	9,251	71,507	6.1	7.0	2.3
$100,000 to $249,999............	139	115.9	835	22,822	164,328	6.6	12.7	5.8
$250,000 to $499,999............	94	121.1	1,288	33,964	361,045	4.5	13.2	8.6
$500,000 to $999,999............	76	129.4	1,704	54,686	719,996	3.6	14.2	13.9
$1,000,000 or more................	79	212.9	2,687	262,006	3,307,109	3.8	23.3	66.4
2017								
Total..........................	2,042	900.2	441	388,523	190,245	100.0	100.0	100.0
Less than $2,500......................	792	103.6	131	404	510	38.8	11.5	0.1
$2,500 to $4,999..................	185	16.1	87	663	3,577	9.1	1.8	0.2
$5,000 to $9,999..................	208	24.7	119	1,478	7,101	10.2	2.7	0.4
$10,000 to $24,999..............	228	50.0	219	3,650	15,994	11.2	5.6	0.9
$25,000 to $49,999..............	144	50.0	347	5,100	35,389	7.1	5.6	1.3
$50,000 to $99,999..............	119	66.3	555	8,478	70,982	5.8	7.4	2.2
$100,000 to $249,999............	131	119.6	914	21,171	161,697	6.4	13.3	5.4
$250,000 to $499,999............	88	126.6	1,441	31,319	356,545	4.3	14.1	8.1
$500,000 to $999,999............	70	131.7	1,889	49,339	707,846	3.4	14.6	12.7
$1,000,000 or more................	77	211.6	2,752	266,922	3,472,604	3.8	23.5	68.7

Source: U.S. Department of Agriculture, National Agricultural Statistics Service, *2017 Census of Agriculture*, Vol. 1, April 2019, and earlier reports. See also <https://www.nass.usda.gov/AgCensus/>.

Table 865. Farmers by Selected Producer Characteristics: 2017

[A producer is a person who is involved in making decisions for the farm operation including decisions about planting, harvesting, livestock management, and marketing. A producer may be the owner, a household member of the owner, hired manager, tenant, renter, or sharecropper. Demographic information was collected for up to four producers per farm. The primary producer is the producer designated as the person who made the most decisions for the farm; if equal decisions were made, the primary was designed as the person who worked off the farm the least. See source for more details]

Characteristics	All producers	Primary producers	Characteristics	All producers	Primary producers
Total.............................	**3,399,834**	**2,042,220**	Primary occupation:		
By sex:			Farming................................	1,416,848	964,477
Male..............................	2,172,373	1,553,220	Other................................	1,982,986	1,077,743
Female..........................	1,227,461	489,000	By place of residence:		
			On farm operated...................	2,530,442	1,562,320
By age:			Not on farm operated...............	869,392	479,900
Under 25 years.....................	50,943	10,518	Days of work off farm:		
25 to 34 years......................	234,496	111,236	None................................	1,311,334	859,347
35 to 44 years......................	390,345	207,348	Any................................	2,088,500	1,182,873
45 to 54 years......................	614,654	351,677	1 to 49 days......................	285,477	172,209
55 to 64 years......................	955,354	580,769	50 to 99 days.....................	151,972	92,576
65 to 74 years......................	757,936	498,595	100 to 199 days...................	282,056	168,777
75 years and older..................	396,106	282,077	200 days or more.................	1,368,995	749,311
Average age........................	57.5	59.4	Years on present farm:		
			2 years or less.....................	201,061	100,947
By race/ethnicity:			3 or 4 years........................	268,316	140,359
American Indian/Alaska Native....	58,199	35,494	5 to 9 years........................	495,022	269,230
Asian..............................	22,016	11,955	10 years or more....................	2,435,435	1,531,684
Black or African American..........	45,508	31,071	Years operating any farm:		
Native Hawaiian or other			5 years or less.....................	474,198	237,838
Pacific Islander.....................	3,018	1,662	6 to 10 years.......................	434,076	234,522
White..............................	3,244,344	1,945,696	11 years or more....................	2,491,560	1,569,860
More than one race reported.......	26,749	16,342	Military service:		
			Never served......................	3,029,215	1,768,912
Hispanic or Latino [1]................	112,451	66,727	Served [2]............................	370,619	273,308

[1] Persons of Hispanic origin may be of any race. [2] Includes producers who currently or previously served on active duty in the U.S. Armed Forces.

Source: U.S. Department of Agriculture, National Agricultural Statistics Service, *2017 Census of Agriculture*, Vol. 1, April 2019. See also <https://www.nass.usda.gov/AgCensus/>.

Table 866. Family Farm Household Income and Wealth: 2014 to 2018, and by Farm Type, 2018

[In dollars, except for number of farms. Based on Agricultural Resource Management Survey (ARMS) Phase III. A family farm is defined as one in which the majority of the ownership of the farm business is held by related individuals. Nearly all farms (98 percent in 2018) are family farms. The farm operator is the person who runs the farm, making the day-to-day management decisions. The operator could be an owner, hired manager, cash tenant, share tenant, and/or a partner. If land is rented or worked on shares, the tenant or renter is the operator. For multiple-operator farms, a principal operator is identified as the individual making most of the day-to-day decisions about the operation. If secondary operators are the spouses of principal operators, both operators are considered part of the principal operator household. Minus sign (-) indicates loss]

Item	2014	2015	2016	2017	2018 Total	2018 ERS farm typology Rural residence farms [1]	2018 ERS farm typology Intermediate farms [2]	2018 ERS farm typology Commercial farms [3]
Number of family farms.................	**2,053,008**	**2,032,300**	**2,027,269**	**1,989,574**	**1,979,368**	**1,069,497**	**742,931**	**166,940**
INCOME PER FAMILY FARM HOUSEHOLD								
Net earnings from farming activities......	31,025	24,740	24,731	21,842	18,425	-2,694	1,914	227,194
Off-farm income of the household.........	103,140	95,140	93,187	89,747	93,786	118,846	62,683	71,654
Earned income........................	71,754	65,814	65,680	61,359	65,596	93,844	29,432	45,561
Unearned income......................	31,386	29,326	27,506	28,387	28,190	25,002	33,251	26,093
Total household income, mean [4].........	134,164	119,880	117,918	111,589	112,210	116,153	64,597	298,847
WEALTH PER FAMILY FARM HOUSEHOLD								
Assets, mean [4]...........................	1,674,467	1,599,151	1,760,480	1,761,623	1,707,669	1,271,800	1,466,598	5,572,883
Farm assets..........................	998,082	1,012,486	1,140,197	1,077,709	1,166,122	650,700	1,070,937	4,891,756
Non-farm assets......................	676,385	586,666	620,283	683,914	541,547	621,100	395,661	681,127
Debt, mean [4]...........................	205,866	190,885	185,679	213,561	160,871	98,182	108,546	795,343
Farm debt............................	101,227	101,430	99,664	106,514	100,805	33,648	64,414	692,992
Non-farm debt........................	104,640	89,454	86,015	107,047	60,066	64,534	44,132	102,351
Net worth, mean [4].......................	1,468,601	1,408,267	1,574,801	1,548,062	1,546,799	1,173,618	1,358,052	4,777,539
Farm net worth........................	896,855	911,055	1,040,533	971,195	1,065,317	617,052	1,006,523	4,198,764
Non-farm net worth....................	571,746	497,211	534,268	576,867	481,481	556,566	351,529	578,776

[1] Farms in which the principal operator is retired or has a major occupation other than farming. [2] Farms with farming as the operator's major occupation, but with less than $350,000 in gross sales. [3] Farms with more than $350,000 in gross sales. [4] For definition of mean see Guide to Tabular Presentation.

Source: U.S. Department of Agriculture, Economic Research Service, "Farm Household Income and Characteristics," <http://www.ers.usda.gov/data-products/farm-household-income-and-characteristics.aspx>, accessed December 2019.

Table 867. Farm Type, Acreage, and Production: 2000 to 2018

[2,166 represents 2,166,000. Based on Agricultural Resource Management Survey (ARMS). The farm typology used by the Economic Research Service was revised in 2013, and has been applied to data beginning in 2011. For more information, see <https://www.ers.usda.gov/publications/pub-details/?pubid=43744>]

Type of farm	Unit	2000	2005	2010	2013	2014	2015	2016	2017	2018
Total farms:										
Number of farms...................	1,000	2,166	2,095	2,193	2,095	2,076	2,059	2,052	2,034	2,021
Total value of production..........	Mil. dol.	177,286	214,010	286,758	383,407	420,251	368,144	353,164	361,648	351,716
Total acres operated...............	Mil.	995	916	912	897	933	850	897	844	812
Acres operated per farm..........	Acres	459	437	416	428	449	413	437	415	402
Commercial farms: [1]										
Number of farms...................	1,000	178	216	264	241	220	212	208	214	208
Total value of production..........	Mil. dol.	121,202	165,267	240,769	296,218	329,903	279,081	273,505	275,649	277,647
Total acres operated...............	Mil.	392	418	482	468	510	439	443	407	424
Acres operated per farm..........	Acres	2,205	1,939	1,829	1,947	2,319	2,066	2,129	1,899	2,036
Intermediate farms: [2]										
Number of farms...................	1,000	668	550	618	695	632	632	617	752	743
Total value of production..........	Mil. dol.	41,813	33,887	30,270	62,494	62,630	61,283	56,277	64,433	54,613
Total acres operated...............	Mil.	392	307	242	257	229	232	255	255	248
Acres operated per farm..........	Acres	587	558	392	370	363	367	414	339	333
Residence farms: [3]										
Number of farms...................	1,000	1,320	1,329	1,311	1,160	1,225	1,215	1,228	1,067	1,069
Total value of production..........	Mil. dol.	14,272	14,856	15,719	24,695	27,717	27,780	23,382	21,565	19,456
Total acres operated...............	Mil.	211	191	187	172	194	179	198	181	140
Acres operated per farm..........	Acres	160	144	143	148	158	147	161	170	131

[1] Data for 2010 and earlier include farms with sales of $250,000 or more. Beginning in 2011, data are for farms with $350,000 or more gross cash farm income and nonfamily farms. [2] Data for 2010 and earlier include small family farms whose operators report farming as their major occupation. Beginning in 2011, data are for farms with less than $350,000 in gross cash farm income and a principal operator whose primary occupation is farming. [3] Data for 2010 and earlier include retirement and residential farms. Beginning in 2011, data are for farms with less than $350,000 in gross cash farm income and where the principal operator is either retired or has a primary occupation other than farming.

Source: U.S. Department of Agriculture, Economic Research Service, "ARMS Farm Financial and Crop Production Practices," <http://www.ers.usda.gov/data-products/arms-farm-financial-and-crop-production-practices.aspx>, accessed February 2020.

Table 868. Farms with Renewable Energy Systems by Type of Farm: 2012

[Farms reporting renewable energy systems on their operation. Based on the 1974 definition of farms and farmland, see text, this section. Farm types are based on the USDA's Economic Research Service typology. Family farms, farms in which the majority of the business is owned by the operator and individuals related to the operator, are classified based on the gross cash farm income (GCFI). GCFI includes sales of crops and livestock, fees for delivering commodities under production contracts, government payments, and farm-related income]

| Energy system | All farms | Small family farms (GCFI less than $350,000) | | | | Mid-sized family farms (GCFI $350,000 to $999,999) | Large-scale family farms (GCFI greater than $1,000,000) | Non-family farms [3] |
| | | Total small family farms | Retirement or off-farm occupation [1] | Farm-occupation farms [2] | | | | |
				Low sales (GCFI less than $150,000)	Moderate sales (GCFI $350,00 to $999,999)			
Number of farms, total	2,109,303	1,861,216	1,423,432	342,440	95,344	118,340	59,537	70,210
Number of farms with any renewable energy system	**57,299**	**48,307**	**34,473**	**10,476**	**3,358**	**4,391**	**2,281**	**2,320**
Percent of all farms	2.7	2.6	2.4	3.1	3.5	3.7	3.8	3.3
By type of system:								
Solar panels	36,331	32,217	23,005	7,464	1,748	1,742	802	1,570
Wind turbines	9,054	6,646	4,460	1,485	701	1,253	713	442
Methane digesters	537	344	258	68	18	32	111	50
Geoexchange systems	9,403	7,809	6,122	1,107	580	906	446	242
Small hydro systems	1,323	1,168	843	275	50	51	21	83
Biodiesel	4,099	3,061	1,958	734	369	547	283	208
Ethanol	2,364	1,623	1,021	338	264	443	211	87
Other	1243	1121	755	305	61	47	9	66
Wind rights leased to others	10,181	6,851	4,402	1,372	1,077	1,893	939	498

[1] Farms in which the principal operator is retired or has a major occupation other than farming. [2] Small family farms with farming as the operator's major occupation. [3] Any farm where the operator and persons related to the operator do not own a majority of the business.

Source: U.S. Department of Agriculture, National Agricultural Statistics Service, *2012 Census of Agriculture, Farm Typology*, Volume 2, January 2015. See also <https://www.nass.usda.gov/AgCensus/>.

Table 869. Sales of Agricultural Products Direct to Consumers: 2007 to 2017

[1,211,270 represents $1,211,270,000. Farm operations who sell directly to consumers for human consumption at roadside stands, farmers' markets, pick-your-own, on-farm stores, and community support agricultural arrangements. Excludes non-edible products such as nursery crops, cut flowers, and wool, but includes livestock sales. Sales of agricultural products by vertically integrated operations through their own processing and marketing operations are also excluded]

| Item | Number of farms with direct sales | | Number of farms with direct and value added sales | Value of direct sales ($1,000) | | Value of direct and value added sales ($1,000) |
	2007	2012	2017 [4]	2007	2012	2017 [4]
Total, all farms with direct sales	**136,817**	**144,530**	**130,056**	**1,211,270**	**1,309,827**	**2,805,310**
Percent of all farms	6.2	6.9	6.4	0.4	0.3	0.7
BY VALUE OF SALES						
$1 to $499	35,440	37,398	30,695	7,217	7,770	6,559
$500 to $999	20,547	20,170	17,318	14,013	13,685	11,615
$1,000 to $4,999	49,957	52,750	43,934	113,960	121,750	101,770
$5,000 to $9,999	13,060	14,452	13,707	88,174	97,308	92,663
$10,000 to $24,999	10,032	11,045	11,669	151,063	164,774	176,745
$25,000 to $49,999	3,903	4,244	5,068	133,328	143,722	172,716
$50,000 or more	3,878	4,471	7,665	703,515	760,819	2,243,242
BY PRIMARY ACTIVITY OF FARM [1,2]						
Oilseed and grains	7,052	8,715	5,143	37,930	63,321	64,610
Vegetables and melons	17,961	23,218	20,013	335,311	420,466	632,095
Fruit and tree nuts	17,161	18,399	19,724	343,878	319,523	1,267,029
Greenhouse and nursery [3]	3,834	6,031	6,105	50,169	59,845	107,661
Beef cattle ranching and farming	35,984	35,980	28,156	141,427	147,315	179,653
Dairy cattle and milk production	3,221	2,982	2,264	52,594	43,546	152,584
Hog and pig farming	5,227	3,897	3,552	18,970	15,970	20,662
Poultry and egg production	8,833	9,999	8,107	54,898	36,782	88,818
Sheep and goat farming	9,127	10,198	9,538	16,613	19,647	32,240

[1] Based on the farms' North American Industry Classification (NAICS) codes, indicating main commodity type produced. [2] Includes other types, not shown separately. [3] Includes floriculture. [4] 2017 data includes value added sales and is not directly comparable to prior data.

Source: U.S. Department of Agriculture, National Agricultural Statistics Service, *2017 Census of Agriculture*, Vol. 1, April 2019, and earlier reports. See also <https://www.nass.usda.gov/AgCensus/>.

Table 870. Organic Agriculture—Number of Farms, Acreage, and Value of Sales, 2008 and 2014, and for Leading States, 2014

[3,164,995 represents $3,164,995,000. Includes all known organic producers that are either certified organic or exempt from certification in the United States (those grossing less than $5,000 annually from organic sales). Organic food must be produced without the use of conventional pesticides, petroleum-based or sewage sludge-based fertilizers, herbicides, pesticides, genetic engineering (biotechnology), antibiotics, growth hormones, or irradiation. Animals raised on an organic operation must be fed organic feed and given access to the outdoors. Land must have no prohibited substances applied to it for at least 3 years before the harvest of an organic crop]

| Year and leading states | Organic farms (number) | Organic land (acres) | Value of sales ($1,000) [1] | | | |
			Total product sales	Crops [2]	Livestock and poultry	Livestock and poultry products
2008...................	14,540	4,077,337	3,164,995	1,942,317	316,470	906,207
2014, U.S. total [3]....	**14,093**	**3,670,560**	**5,454,979**	**3,290,188**	**660,340**	**1,504,452**
California..............	2,805	687,168	2,231,241	1,659,305	271,354	300,582
Washington...........	716	73,841	514,897	386,701	(D)	(D)
Pennsylvania.........	679	97,617	313,456	91,362	112,467	109,627
Oregon................	525	204,166	237,121	127,568	17,630	91,923
Wisconsin.............	1,228	228,605	200,800	48,513	24,908	127,379
Texas.................	234	126,639	199,094	78,169	17,680	103,245
New York.............	917	212,701	164,203	52,698	16,011	95,494
Colorado..............	157	115,116	146,799	52,198	(D)	(D)
Michigan..............	332	58,085	124,612	(D)	(D)	70,698
Iowa..................	612	97,448	102,626	50,741	(D)	(D)

D Data withheld to limit disclosure. [1] Value of sales of commodities; excludes value-added organic products. [2] Includes nursery and greenhouse. [3] Includes other states, not shown separately.

Source: U.S. Department of Agriculture, National Agricultural Statistics Service, *2012 Census of Agriculture: Organic Survey (2014)*, Vol. 3, Special Studies, Part 4, September 2015, and earlier reports. See also <https://www.nass.usda.gov/Surveys/Guide_to_NASS_Surveys/Organic_Production/>.

Table 871. Adoption of Genetically Engineered Crops: 2000 to 2020

[As percent of all crops planted. As of June. Based on June Agricultural Survey conducted by National Agricultural Statistical Services (NASS). Excludes conventionally bred herbicide tolerant varieties. Insect resistant varieties include only those containing bacillus thuringiensis (Bt). The Bt varieties include those that contain more than one gene that can resist different types of insects. Stacked gene varieties include only those varieties containing biotech traits for both herbicide tolerance and insect resistance]

Genetically engineered crop	2000	2005	2010	2013	2014	2015	2016	2017	2018	2019	2020
Corn............................	**25**	**52**	**86**	**90**	**93**	**92**	**92**	**92**	**92**	**92**	**92**
Insect resistant..................	18	26	16	5	4	4	3	3	2	3	3
Herbicide tolerant...............	6	17	23	14	13	12	13	12	10	9	10
Stacked gene....................	1	9	47	71	76	77	76	77	80	80	79
Cotton...........................	**61**	**79**	**93**	**90**	**96**	**94**	**93**	**96**	**94**	**98**	**96**
Insect resistant..................	15	18	15	8	5	5	4	5	3	3	5
Herbicide tolerant...............	26	27	20	15	12	10	9	11	9	6	8
Stacked gene....................	20	34	58	67	79	79	80	80	82	89	83
Soybean.........................	**54**	**87**	**93**	**93**	**94**	**94**	**94**	**94**	**94**	**94**	**94**
Insect resistant..................	(X)	(X)	(X)	(X)	(X)	(X)	(X)	(X)	(X)	(X)	(X)
Herbicide tolerant...............	54	87	93	93	94	94	94	94	94	94	94
Stacked gene....................	(X)	(X)	(X)	(X)	(X)	(X)	(X)	(X)	(X)	(X)	(X)

X Not applicable.

Source: U.S. Department of Agriculture, Economic Research Service, "Adoption of Genetically Engineered Crops in the U.S.," <http://www.ers.usda.gov/data-products/adoption-of-genetically-engineered-crops-in-the-us.aspx>, accessed July 2020.

Table 872. Farm Production Expenses: 2012 and 2017

[2,109 represents 2,109,000. Data have been adjusted for coverage; see text, this section and Appendix III]

| Production expenses | 2012 | | | 2017 | | |
	Farms (1,000)	Expenses (mil. dol.)	Percent of total	Farms (1,000)	Expenses (mil. dol.)	Percent of total
Total..	**2,109**	**328,939**	**100.0**	**2,042**	**326,391**	**100.0**
Fertilizer.......................................	1,012	28,533	8.7	1,025	23,543	7.2
Chemicals.....................................	1,000	16,460	5.0	894	17,585	5.4
Seeds, plants, vines, and trees.................	829	19,493	5.9	703	20,970	6.4
Livestock and poultry...........................	545	41,586	12.6	556	44,934	13.8
Feed...	1,256	75,706	23.0	1,262	62,625	19.2
Gasoline and fuel...............................	1,988	16,573	5.0	1,922	13,474	4.1
Utilities..	1,353	8,262	2.5	1,339	9,009	2.8
Supplies, repairs, and maintenance.............	1,663	18,868	5.7	1,665	19,671	6.0
Farm labor [1]..................................	784	33,461	10.2	709	39,231	12.0
Customwork and custom hauling.................	462	6,611	2.0	428	7,555	2.3
Cash rent for land, buildings and grazing fees...	560	21,001	6.4	482	21,060	6.5
Rent and lease for machinery, equipment, and farm share..	133	2,332	0.7	138	2,424	0.7
Interest expense...............................	784	12,124	3.7	669	12,396	3.8
Property taxes.................................	1,980	7,429	2.3	1,920	9,415	2.9
Medical supplies, veterinary, custom services for livestock..	(NA)	(NA)	(NA)	944	4,446	1.4
Other production expenses [2]...................	1,135	20,501	6.2	849	18,052	5.5

NA Not available. [1] Includes hired and contract labor. [2] Data for 2012 include expenses for medical supplies, veterinary, and custom services for animals. Starting 2017, these data are reported separately.

Source: U.S. Department of Agriculture, National Agricultural Statistics Service, *2017 Census of Agriculture*, Vol. 1, April 2019. See also <https://www.nass.usda.gov/AgCensus/>.

Table 873. Balance Sheet of the Farming Sector: 1990 to 2019

[In billions of dollars, except as indicated (841 represents $841,000,000,000). As of December 31. Balance sheet estimates exclude the personal portion of farm households' assets and debts]

Item	1990	2000	2010	2012	2013	2014	2015	2016	2017	2018	2019
Assets	**841**	**1,203**	**2,171**	**2,638**	**2,768**	**2,931**	**2,880**	**2,914**	**3,006**	**3,027**	**3,075**
Investments and other financial assets	38	57	135	139	86	111	88	78	81	73	87
Investment in cooperatives	(NA)	(NA)	6	7	8	8	7	7	8	7	6
Financial assets and net accounts receivable	(NA)	(NA)	130	132	78	103	80	71	73	65	81
Inventories	97	110	168	182	192	210	187	180	180	173	163
Crops	23	28	57	65	60	62	53	56	57	60	50
Livestock and poultry	71	77	91	96	111	128	118	109	107	97	99
Purchased inputs [1]	3	5	20	21	21	20	16	15	16	16	14
Real estate [2]	619	946	1,660	2,074	2,243	2,365	2,366	2,401	2,473	2,510	2,546
Value of machinery and motor vehicles [3]	86	90	208	244	247	246	240	255	272	271	279
Debt [4]	**131**	**164**	**279**	**298**	**315**	**345**	**357**	**374**	**390**	**402**	**419**
Real estate	68	85	154	173	185	197	209	226	236	246	267
Commercial banks [5]	15	30	51	65	69	73	79	84	88	93	98
Farm Credit System	23	30	72	80	85	89	97	104	107	113	125
Farm Service Agency	7	3	3	4	4	4	5	6	6	7	8
Farmer Mac [6]	(NA)	(NA)	4	4	4	5	5	5	6	7	8
Individuals and others [5]	14	11	10	9	10	13	10	12	13	10	11
Storage facility loans	–	(NA)	1	1	1	1	1	1	1	1	1
Life insurance companies	9	11	12	11	12	12	13	13	15	16	17
Nonreal estate	63	79	125	124	130	148	148	148	154	156	152
Commercial banks [5]	31	45	56	60	64	71	73	73	73	75	70
Farm Credit System	10	17	39	43	44	48	48	49	51	53	53
Farm Service Agency	10	4	4	3	3	4	4	4	4	4	4
Individuals and others [5]	12	13	26	18	20	26	23	22	26	24	25
Equity	**709**	**1,039**	**1,892**	**2,341**	**2,452**	**2,585**	**2,523**	**2,540**	**2,616**	**2,625**	**2,657**
FINANCIAL RATIOS (percent)											
Farm debt/asset ratio	15.60	13.62	12.85	11.28	11.39	11.78	12.39	12.84	12.99	13.28	13.61
Farm debt/equity ratio	18.48	15.77	14.74	12.71	12.86	13.35	14.14	14.73	14.93	15.32	15.76

– Represents or rounds to zero. NA Not available. [1] Purchased inputs represent value of prepaid expenses on supplies such as fertilizer and lime applied, seed, feed and other inputs purchased for next year's production. It also includes the seed, fertilizer, fuel, and other expenses already invested in crops. [2] Includes farmland, buildings and other service structures. Includes farm real estate assets leased from non-operator landlords. [3] Includes automobiles, trucks and farm machinery leased to farm operators. [4] Reflects outstanding agricultural sector debt where it is held rather than where it originated. Excludes debt on operator dwellings and for nonfarm purposes. Sector-level estimates of farm debt report aggregate data by lender type and therefore does not identify who owes the debt. [5] Beginning with 2012, farm sector debt held by savings associations is reported with the commercial bank lender group instead of the individuals and others grouping. [6] The Federal Agricultural Mortgage Corporation (known as Farmer Mac) operates as a federally sponsored enterprise providing a secondary market for agricultural real estate mortgage loans, rural housing mortgage loans, and rural utility cooperative loans.

Source: U.S. Department of Agriculture, Economic Research Service, "U.S. and State Farm Income and Wealth Statistics," <ers.usda.gov/data-products/farm-income-and-wealth-statistics.aspx>, accessed September 2020.

Table 874. Farm Sector Output and Value Added: 1990 to 2019

[In billions of dollars (179.9 represents $179,900,000,000). For definition of value added and explanation of chained dollars, see text, Section 13. Minus sign (-) indicates decrease]

Item	1990	2000	2005	2010	2013	2014	2015	2016	2017	2018	2019
CURRENT DOLLARS											
Farm output	**179.9**	**204.3**	**251.9**	**323.2**	**439.1**	**445.2**	**406.4**	**382.9**	**398.5**	**400.7**	**397.9**
Cash receipts from farm marketings	171.9	197.6	241.4	321.7	404.1	424.9	381.9	366.6	381.9	387.7	392.9
Farm products consumed on farms	0.6	0.3	0.4	0.4	0.5	0.6	0.6	0.5	0.4	0.4	0.4
Other farm income	4.9	8.4	10.2	14.4	23.9	24.0	23.5	20.1	22.2	19.7	19.2
Change in farm finished goods inventories	2.4	-2.0	-0.1	-13.3	10.6	-4.3	0.4	-4.4	-6.0	-7.1	-14.6
Less: Intermediate goods and services consumed	102.1	128.3	147.4	205.6	254.5	277.0	259.0	252.2	258.4	260.5	261.8
Equals: Gross farm value added	**77.8**	**76.0**	**104.5**	**117.6**	**184.6**	**168.1**	**147.4**	**130.6**	**140.1**	**140.3**	**136.1**
Less: Consumption of fixed capital	17.9	22.8	27.5	33.1	40.3	44.4	47.2	47.7	48.0	48.6	49.6
Equals: Net farm value added	**59.8**	**53.2**	**77.0**	**84.6**	**144.4**	**123.7**	**100.2**	**82.9**	**92.1**	**91.7**	**86.4**
Compensation of employees	13.4	19.6	22.0	24.3	28.6	29.1	27.2	29.0	30.9	28.4	30.0
Taxes on production and imports	3.8	4.6	5.3	7.5	8.5	9.9	9.3	8.8	9.4	9.3	10.3
Less: Subsidies to operators	7.6	20.0	20.9	10.5	8.9	7.5	8.6	10.8	9.5	11.8	21.8
Net operating surplus	50.3	48.8	70.5	63.3	116.1	92.2	72.2	55.9	61.3	65.7	67.9
CHAINED (2012) DOLLARS											
Farm output, total	**(NA)**	**(NA)**	**400.8**	**416.1**	**431.4**	**442.6**	**451.7**	**478.6**	**484.2**	**487.2**	**485.4**
Cash receipts from farm marketings	(NA)	(NA)	384.4	415.5	396.5	417.2	420.0	454.4	459.8	466.8	475.1
Farm products consumed on farms	(NA)	(NA)	0.5	0.5	0.5	0.5	0.6	0.6	0.5	0.5	0.5
Other farm income	(NA)	(NA)	17.5	18.6	23.9	27.7	29.3	26.4	28.6	25.0	24.2
Change in farm finished goods inventories	(NA)	(NA)	-0.2	-19.5	9.3	-4.3	0.2	-5.3	-7.3	-8.0	-16.8
Less: Intermediate goods and services consumed	(NA)	(NA)	231.6	251.1	251.3	260.6	257.7	273.0	282.1	277.5	278.0
Equals: Gross farm value added	**(NA)**	**(NA)**	**168.8**	**165.1**	**179.8**	**181.6**	**195.5**	**207.3**	**201.5**	**211.5**	**208.5**
Less: Consumption of fixed capital	(NA)	(NA)	32.0	34.4	39.7	43.0	45.2	45.3	44.8	44.6	44.6
Equals: Net farm value added	**(NA)**	**(NA)**	**139.5**	**131.4**	**140.0**	**138.3**	**150.5**	**164.5**	**158.3**	**170.9**	**167.1**

NA Not available.

Source: U.S. Bureau of Economic Analysis, National Income and Product Accounts, "Table 7.3.5 Farm Sector Output, Gross Value Added, and Net Value Added," and "Table 7.3.6 Real Farm Sector Output, Real Gross Value Added, and Real Net Value Added, Chained Dollars," <bea.gov/itable/>, accessed September 2020.

Table 875. Value Added to Economy by Agricultural Sector: 1990 to 2019

[In billions of dollars (188.5 represents $188,500,000,000). Value of agricultural sector production is the gross value of the commodities and services produced within a year. Net value-added is the sector's contribution to the national economy and is the value of farm sector production minus the value of intermediate goods used. Net farm income is the farm operators' share of income from the sector's production activities. Minus sign (-) indicates decrease]

Item	1990	2000	2010	2012	2013	2014	2015	2016	2017	2018	2019
Value of agricultural production...............	**188.5**	**218.4**	**344.1**	**439.1**	**473.1**	**473.5**	**430.0**	**399.3**	**413.9**	**411.5**	**410.0**
Value of crop production............................	83.2	95.0	168.1	212.9	233.8	206.3	184.3	189.3	187.9	186.2	181.0
Crop cash receipts....................................	80.2	92.5	180.3	231.6	220.9	211.7	187.9	195.8	194.9	195.1	194.6
Cotton..	5.5	2.9	7.5	8.2	6.5	7.1	4.8	5.5	7.6	7.5	7.1
Feed crops...	18.7	20.5	55.1	82.1	70.8	65.9	56.9	55.4	53.9	57.3	59.7
Food grains..	7.5	6.5	14.3	19.3	17.2	16.1	12.3	11.3	11.2	12.1	11.8
Fruits and tree nuts................................	9.4	12.3	21.6	28.1	30.2	32.2	28.4	29.7	30.6	29.2	28.7
Oil crops..	12.3	13.5	36.5	46.9	47.3	42.6	35.5	44.0	41.1	39.5	36.3
Tobacco...	2.7	2.3	1.3	1.3	1.6	1.7	1.6	1.3	1.4	1.2	1.0
Vegetables and melons............................	11.3	15.8	17.4	17.4	19.5	19.0	20.4	19.5	20.5	18.5	19.0
All other crops......................................	12.9	18.6	26.5	28.1	27.8	27.1	28.0	28.9	28.6	29.7	31.0
Home consumption..................................	0.1	0.2	0.1	0.1	0.2	0.2	0.3	0.2	0.2	0.1	0.2
Value of inventory adjustment [1]...............	2.8	2.2	-12.3	-18.8	12.7	-5.6	-3.8	-6.6	-7.1	-9.0	-13.8
Value of livestock production.......................	90.0	99.1	140.2	169.1	181.1	214.3	194.1	165.4	176.9	177.4	176.3
Animals and products cash receipts.............	89.1	99.6	140.9	169.8	183.1	212.3	189.5	162.7	175.6	176.3	176.0
Milk..	20.2	20.6	31.4	37.1	40.3	49.4	35.7	34.5	37.9	35.2	40.5
Meat animals..	51.1	53.0	69.1	88.2	91.6	107.6	98.8	82.7	88.0	87.9	88.3
Miscellaneous livestock...........................	2.5	4.1	5.7	6.3	6.9	6.9	6.7	6.7	6.9	6.9	6.9
Poultry and eggs....................................	15.3	21.9	34.7	38.3	44.4	48.5	48.3	38.8	42.8	46.2	40.4
Home consumption..................................	0.5	0.1	0.3	0.3	0.3	0.3	0.4	0.3	0.3	0.3	0.3
Value of inventory adjustment [1]...............	0.4	-0.6	-0.9	-1.0	-2.4	1.7	4.3	2.4	1.1	0.8	0.0
Farm-related income.................................	15.3	24.4	35.8	57.1	58.2	52.9	51.5	44.5	49.1	47.8	52.6
Forest products sold................................	1.8	0.8	0.5	0.5	0.6	0.6	0.7	0.7	0.7	0.7	0.6
Gross imputed rental value of farm dwellings........	7.2	12.7	15.8	17.9	17.2	16.3	17.1	16.6	17.9	18.7	17.9
Machine hire and custom work....................	1.8	2.2	3.8	3.9	4.4	4.4	4.7	3.6	4.6	3.9	4.1
Other farm income..................................	4.5	8.7	15.7	34.9	36.0	31.5	29.0	23.6	25.8	24.6	30.0
Less: Intermediate product expenses [2]...............	90.7	119.1	189.1	237.4	239.9	255.5	235.7	221.6	228.0	230.1	233.2
Farm origin..	39.5	47.9	82.2	106.3	109.9	117.0	110.1	99.5	104.5	104.9	109.3
Feed purchased.....................................	20.4	24.5	45.4	60.5	62.4	63.7	58.5	55.6	54.5	53.8	59.4
Livestock and poultry purchased.................	14.6	15.9	20.4	24.8	25.5	31.2	30.3	22.1	27.4	29.2	28.7
Seed purchased....................................	4.5	7.5	16.3	20.9	21.9	22.1	21.3	21.8	22.5	21.9	21.2
Manufactured inputs................................	22.0	28.7	50.1	64.8	65.8	67.5	59.1	56.5	56.3	57.9	56.8
Electricity..	2.6	3.0	4.6	5.4	5.5	5.9	5.7	5.6	5.8	6.1	5.7
Fertilizers, lime, and soil conditioners............	8.2	10.0	21.0	28.9	28.3	28.1	25.5	23.5	22.0	23.2	22.3
Pesticides...	5.4	8.5	10.7	14.0	14.6	15.8	14.6	15.2	15.7	15.4	15.5
Petroleum fuel and oils............................	5.8	7.2	13.8	16.5	17.3	17.7	13.2	12.2	12.8	13.2	13.2
Other intermediate expenses [2]..................	29.2	42.5	56.8	66.3	64.2	70.9	66.5	65.6	67.2	67.3	67.1
Machine hire and custom work....................	3.0	4.1	4.3	4.9	4.6	5.9	4.8	4.4	4.6	4.3	5.2
Marketing, storage, and transportation expenses........	4.2	7.5	9.0	9.2	8.0	10.8	9.2	9.7	9.8	11.9	10.1
Repair and maintenance of capital items...........	8.6	10.9	14.6	16.5	17.2	17.8	16.6	15.9	16.6	15.3	15.7
Miscellaneous expenses [2].......................	13.4	19.9	29.0	35.7	34.5	36.5	35.9	35.5	36.3	35.7	36.2
Total insurance premiums [3]......................	3.4	4.8	7.5	10.4	10.6	10.6	10.0	9.6	10.3	9.9	9.9
Less: Contract labor.................................	1.6	2.7	3.9	4.8	4.6	6.4	5.7	6.0	5.9	6.0	6.6
Plus: Net government transactions [4]..................	3.1	15.8	0.9	-1.5	-1.4	-4.6	-2.7	0.3	-1.9	0.1	8.3
Direct government payments [5].....................	9.3	23.2	12.4	10.6	11.0	9.8	10.8	13.0	11.5	13.7	22.4
Property taxes [2]...................................	6.2	7.4	11.5	12.2	12.4	14.3	13.5	12.6	13.5	13.6	14.1
Motor vehicle registration and licensing fees.......	0.4	0.5	0.6	0.7	0.7	0.7	0.7	0.7	0.7	0.7	0.7
Equals: Gross value added.....................	**99.3**	**112.5**	**152.1**	**195.4**	**227.2**	**207.0**	**185.8**	**171.9**	**178.0**	**175.5**	**178.5**
Less: Capital consumption [2].......................	18.1	20.1	17.6	34.3	38.1	50.3	41.4	44.4	36.3	29.9	28.8
Equals: Net value added........................	**81.2**	**92.4**	**134.5**	**161.2**	**189.1**	**156.7**	**144.4**	**127.5**	**141.7**	**145.5**	**149.7**
Less: Factor payments to stakeholders [6]...............	35.0	41.7	57.4	64.8	65.5	64.5	62.8	65.2	66.6	64.2	66.0
Employee compensation [7].........................	12.4	17.9	23.6	27.4	27.7	28.1	26.4	28.4	30.4	28.1	28.5
Net rent paid to operator landlords.................	(NA)	(NA)	2.1	2.6	2.8	4.7	4.7	4.5	4.1	3.7	3.9
Net rent paid to nonoperator landlords..............	9.0	9.2	14.8	18.0	20.0	15.9	15.4	14.9	13.6	11.8	12.9
Total interest expenses..............................	13.5	14.6	16.9	16.9	14.9	15.7	16.4	17.3	18.6	20.6	20.7
Equals: Net farm income........................	**46.3**	**50.7**	**77.1**	**96.4**	**123.7**	**92.2**	**81.6**	**62.3**	**75.1**	**81.3**	**83.7**

NA Not available. [1] A positive value of inventory change represents current-year production not sold by December 31. A negative value is an offset to production from prior years included in current-year sales. [2] Including expenses associated with operator dwellings. [3] Includes federal and private crop and livestock insurance premiums as well as casualty, hail, motor vehicle and all other insurance premiums. [4] Direct government payments minus motor vehicle registration and licensing fees and property taxes. [5] Government payments reflect payments made directly to all recipients in the farm sector, including landlords. The nonoperator landlords share is offset by its inclusion in rental expenses paid to these landlords and thus is not reflected in net farm income or net cash income. [6] Prior to 2008, factor payments to stakeholders only includes net rent paid to nonoperator landlords. [7] Includes hired labor and non-cash employee compensation.

Source: U.S. Department of Agriculture, Economic Research Service, "U.S. and State Farm Income and Wealth Statistics," <http://www.ers.usda.gov/data-products/farm-income-and-wealth-statistics.aspx>, accessed September 2020.

Table 876. Value of Agricultural Production, Income, and Government Payments by State: 2017 and 2018

[In millions of dollars (413,879 represents $413,879,000,000). See headnote, Table 875. Minus sign (-) indicates loss]

State	Value of agricultural production 2017	Value of agricultural production 2018	Net farm income 2017	Net farm income 2018	Government payments, 2018	State	Value of agricultural production 2017	Value of agricultural production 2018	Net farm income 2017	Net farm income 2018	Government payments, 2018
U.S.........	413,879	413,920	75,060	83,777	13,669	MO..........	11,381	10,890	1,669	1,617	580
						MT..........	4,027	4,377	517	1,093	341
AL...........	6,400	6,565	1,492	1,413	105	NE..........	21,911	22,510	2,183	2,590	687
AK...........	52	53	-15	-6	12	NV..........	745	748	83	85	15
AZ...........	4,972	4,669	1,005	928	59	NH..........	283	280	55	57	8
AR...........	9,845	10,034	1,732	1,807	629	NJ..........	1,385	1,335	325	297	10
CA...........	53,722	52,812	15,339	15,597	275	NM..........	3,397	3,187	903	861	112
CO...........	7,997	8,066	1,038	1,259	230	NY..........	5,932	5,685	1,311	1,073	81
CT...........	739	726	161	165	6	NC..........	13,234	12,651	3,010	1,667	106
DE...........	1,548	1,597	598	605	17	ND..........	9,034	9,406	1,166	1,899	739
FL...........	9,030	8,346	3,064	3,061	137	OH..........	10,000	10,415	1,550	2,186	446
GA...........	10,143	10,230	2,700	2,306	326	OK..........	7,649	7,656	1,437	1,783	334
HI...........	782	718	166	142	14	OR..........	5,529	5,591	573	842	118
ID...........	7,997	8,184	1,309	1,753	157	PA..........	8,206	7,887	1,812	1,444	91
IL...........	17,796	18,253	2,240	3,903	1,051	RI..........	90	92	27	30	2
IN...........	11,540	11,686	1,662	2,150	516	SC..........	2,871	2,851	359	275	57
IA...........	28,693	29,497	3,640	5,643	1,184	SD..........	10,041	10,687	1,344	2,574	803
KS...........	16,925	17,280	1,619	2,762	795	TN..........	4,310	4,213	460	325	139
KY...........	6,910	6,950	1,802	1,723	162	TX..........	25,438	25,321	4,119	4,621	850
LA...........	3,488	3,517	890	917	282	UT..........	2,017	1,964	391	474	63
ME...........	764	753	145	144	16	VT..........	889	828	193	148	23
MD...........	2,797	2,683	711	539	39	VA..........	4,499	4,404	795	656	76
MA...........	589	577	69	72	8	WA..........	10,566	10,238	2,556	2,271	197
MI...........	8,151	8,434	831	1,089	232	WV..........	922	900	128	87	12
MN...........	18,088	18,165	2,269	2,860	827	WI..........	12,616	12,032	1,840	2,132	301
MS...........	6,152	6,160	1,548	1,530	366	WY..........	1,785	1,816	238	327	34

Source: U.S. Department of Agriculture, Economic Research Service, "U.S. and State Farm Income and Wealth Statistics," <http://www.ers.usda.gov/data-products/farm-income-and-wealth-statistics.aspx>, accessed February 2020.

Table 877. Farm Income—Cash Receipts From Farm Marketings: 2010 to 2019

[In millions of dollars (321,196 represents $321,196,000,000). Represents gross receipts from commercial market sales as well as net Commodity Credit Corporation loans. The source estimates and publishes individual cash receipt values only for major commodities and major producing states. The U.S. receipts for individual commodities, computed as the sum of the reported states, may understate the value of sales for some commodities, with the balance included in the appropriate category labeled "other" or "miscellaneous." The degree of underestimation in some of the minor commodities can be substantial]

Commodities	2010	2015	2018	2019	Commodities	2010	2015	2018	2019
Total [1]	321,196	377,431	371,425	370,636	Broccoli	727	1,059	739	873
Animals and products	140,871	189,516	176,331	175,993	Carrots	647	820	733	864
Meat animals	69,144	98,806	87,919	88,254	Corn, sweet	952	1,043	864	652
Cattle and calves	51,246	78,253	67,038	66,239	Lettuce	2,213	3,150	2,677	3,491
Hogs	17,898	20,553	20,881	22,015	Lettuce, head	1,058	1,253	1,220	1,960
Dairy products, milk	31,372	35,717	35,242	40,498	Onions	1,050	1,039	887	1,002
Poultry/eggs [1]	34,690	48,292	46,238	40,360	Peppers, bell	592	733	533	558
Broilers	23,692	28,716	31,750	28,314	Tomatoes	2,281	2,603	1,864	1,600
Chicken eggs	6,553	13,763	10,653	7,705	Tomatoes, fresh	1,355	1,221	822	705
Turkeys	4,372	5,708	3,786	4,304	Cantaloupes	305	264	332	303
Miscellaneous animals [1]	5,664	6,701	6,931	6,881	Watermelons	499	488	662	561
Aquaculture	474	468	462	475	Fruits/nuts [1]	21,613	28,447	29,205	28,723
Honey	282	329	339	306	Grapefruit	291	216	208	207
Crops	180,325	187,916	195,094	194,643	Lemons	395	697	716	686
Food grains [1]	14,314	12,296	12,118	11,795	Oranges	1,997	1,963	1,830	1,704
Rice	3,263	2,803	2,518	2,752	Apples	2,311	3,366	2,954	2,746
Wheat	11,021	9,427	9,515	8,954	Cherries	756	838	694	696
Feed crops [1]	55,143	56,930	57,340	59,693	Grapes	4,024	5,914	6,621	5,720
Corn	47,540	47,023	48,596	50,099	Peaches	617	602	511	519
Hay	5,217	6,961	6,924	7,611	Pears	387	494	429	315
Sorghum grain	1,487	1,837	1,051	1,130	Blueberries	644	867	821	935
Cotton	7,465	4,756	7,484	7,115	Cranberries	299	262	246	225
Tobacco	1,336	1,607	1,247	1,004	Raspberries	259	721	367	432
Oil crops [1]	36,544	35,519	39,468	36,317	Strawberries	2,261	2,239	2,416	2,529
Peanuts	824	1,275	1,479	1,150	Almonds	2,903	5,869	5,603	6,094
Soybeans	34,665	33,118	37,037	34,153	Pistachios	1,159	888	2,616	1,939
Sunflower	507	568	377	367	Walnuts	1,028	1,012	917	1,286
Vegetables and melons [1]	17,405	20,359	18,499	18,984	All other crops [1]	26,506	28,001	29,733	31,012
Beans, dry	780	915	959	840	Sugarcane	1,075	1,017	1,031	1,143
Potatoes	3,336	3,708	3,736	3,720	Sugar beets	1,734	1,503	1,365	1,156
Sweet potatoes	472	676	634	588	Floriculture	4,149	4,374	4,766	4,766
Beans, snap	434	414	352	303	Mushrooms	884	1,124	1,067	962

[1] Includes other commodities not shown separately.

Source: U.S. Department of Agriculture, Economic Research Service, "U.S. and State Farm Income and Wealth Statistics," <ers.usda.gov/data-products/farm-income-and-wealth-statistics.aspx>, accessed September 2020.

Table 878. Cash Receipts for Cattle, Corn, Soybeans, and Milk—Total and for Leading States: 2019

[In millions of dollars (66,239 represents $66,239,000,000). See headnote Table 877]

State	Value	State	Value	State	Value	State	Value
Cattle and calves...	**66,239**	**Corn.................**	**50,099**	**Soybeans............**	**34,153**	**Milk..................**	**40,498**
Nebraska...............	10,547	Iowa.....................	8,748	Illinois...................	5,382	California...............	7,341
Texas...................	8,424	Illinois..................	7,712	Iowa.....................	4,459	Wisconsin..............	5,705
Kansas.................	8,391	Nebraska..............	6,277	Minnesota..............	2,897	Idaho...................	2,854
Iowa....................	3,932	Minnesota.............	4,423	Indiana..................	2,768	New York..............	2,847
Colorado...............	3,626	Indiana.................	3,494	Nebraska..............	2,484	Texas...................	2,640

Source: U.S. Department of Agriculture, Economic Research Service, "U.S. and State Farm Income and Wealth Statistics," <http://www.ers.usda.gov/data-products/farm-income-and-wealth-statistics.aspx>, accessed September 2020.

Table 879. Farm Marketings: 2018 and 2019; and Principal Commodities, 2019, by State

[In millions of dollars (371,425 represents 371,425,000,000). See headnote Table 877]

State	2018 Total	2018 Animals and products	2018 Crops	2019 Total	2019 Animals and products	2019 Crops	2019 State rank for total farm marketings and three principal commodities in order of marketing receipts
U.S.........	**371,425**	**176,331**	**195,094**	**370,636**	**175,993**	**194,643**	**Cattle and calves, corn, milk**
AL............	5,785	4,550	1,235	5,229	4,014	1,215	26—Broilers, cattle and calves, chicken eggs
AK............	39	8	31	38	8	31	50—Floriculture, hay, cattle and calves
AZ............	4,156	1,733	2,423	5,042	1,744	3,298	29—Lettuce, milk, cattle and calves
AR............	8,988	5,564	3,425	8,562	5,065	3,497	14—Broilers, soybeans, rice
CA............	49,589	11,812	37,777	50,117	12,339	37,778	1—Milk, almonds, grapes
CO............	7,105	4,699	2,406	7,482	5,012	2,470	19—Cattle and calves, milk, corn
CT............	591	173	418	581	164	417	45—Floriculture, milk, chicken eggs
DE............	1,410	1,132	278	1,256	986	269	39—Broilers, corn, soybeans
FL............	7,315	1,601	5,714	7,667	1,498	6,168	18—Oranges, floriculture, sugarcane
GA............	9,081	6,042	3,038	8,442	5,437	3,004	16—Broilers, cotton lint, chicken eggs
HI............	589	171	419	572	152	420	46—Coffee, macadamia nuts, cattle and calves
ID............	7,476	4,324	3,152	8,153	4,792	3,361	17—Milk, cattle and calves, potatoes
IL............	16,775	2,334	14,441	16,495	2,531	13,964	6—Corn, soybeans, hogs
IN............	10,512	3,796	6,716	10,543	3,731	6,812	10—Corn, soybeans, hogs
IA............	27,363	14,267	13,095	27,536	14,005	13,531	2—Corn, hogs, soybeans
KS............	15,976	9,510	6,466	16,421	9,722	6,699	7—Cattle and calves, corn, soybeans
KY............	5,898	3,373	2,525	5,497	3,104	2,393	24—Broilers, corn, soybeans
LA............	3,110	1,132	1,978	3,033	1,027	2,006	34—Sugarcane, broilers, soybeans
ME............	679	295	384	677	290	388	43—Potatoes, milk, chicken eggs
MD............	2,247	1,369	878	2,176	1,293	883	36—Broilers, corn, soybeans
MA............	441	104	337	438	108	330	47—Cranberries, milk, turkeys
MI............	7,287	3,102	4,185	7,412	3,291	4,121	20—Milk, corn, soybeans
MN............	17,114	7,451	9,663	16,859	7,849	9,010	5—Corn, soybeans, hogs
MS............	5,406	3,381	2,026	5,211	3,063	2,148	27—Broilers, soybeans, cotton lint
MO............	10,071	4,665	5,406	9,396	4,372	5,023	11—Soybeans, cattle and calves, corn
MT............	3,550	1,598	1,951	3,739	1,599	2,140	30—Cattle and calves, wheat, hay
NE............	21,323	11,981	9,343	21,595	11,899	9,695	3—Cattle and calves, corn, soybeans
NV............	665	482	183	709	494	215	42—Cattle and calves, hay, milk
NH............	222	105	117	200	99	101	48—Milk, chicken eggs, turkeys
NJ............	1,107	128	979	1,155	113	1,042	40—Floriculture, blueberries, bell peppers
NM............	2,941	2,228	713	3,180	2,454	726	33—Milk, cattle and calves, pecans
NY............	5,030	3,109	1,921	5,361	3,377	1,983	25—Milk, corn, cattle and calves
NC............	11,067	7,640	3,427	10,688	7,419	3,269	9—Broilers, hogs, turkeys
ND............	7,715	1,274	6,440	7,411	1,199	6,212	21—Soybeans, wheat, corn
OH............	9,073	3,587	5,486	8,491	3,410	5,081	15—Soybeans, corn, milk
OK............	6,722	5,291	1,431	6,763	5,296	1,467	22—Cattle and calves, hogs, broilers
OR............	4,944	1,440	3,504	5,065	1,506	3,559	28—Cattle and calves, milk, hay
PA............	6,703	4,237	2,466	6,690	4,143	2,547	23—Milk, cattle and calves, broilers
RI............	71	23	48	64	21	43	49—Chicken eggs, turkeys, milk
SC............	2,496	1,378	1,119	2,282	1,243	1,038	35—Broilers, corn, cotton lint
SD............	9,045	4,044	5,001	9,025	4,321	4,704	13—Cattles and calves, corn, soybeans
TN............	3,501	1,414	2,087	3,457	1,278	2,179	31—Soybeans, corn, cattle and calves
TX............	21,661	14,269	7,393	21,117	14,356	6,761	4—Cattle and calves, milk, broilers
UT............	1,686	1,201	486	1,818	1,277	541	37—Cattle and calves, milk, hay
VT............	730	550	180	792	611	182	41—Milk, cattle and calves, maple products
VA............	3,546	2,255	1,291	3,370	2,133	1,237	32—Broilers, cattle and calves, milk
WA............	9,435	2,492	6,944	9,333	2,667	6,666	12—Apples, milk, cattle and calves
WV............	688	527	160	639	480	159	44—Cattle and calves, broilers, turkeys
WI............	10,954	7,340	3,614	11,333	7,902	3,431	8—Milk, cattle and calves, corn
WY............	1,547	1,151	396	1,526	1,098	428	38—Cattle and calves, hay, hogs

Source: U.S. Department of Agriculture, Economic Research Service, "U.S. and State Farm Income and Wealth Statistics," <http://www.ers.usda.gov/data-products/farm-income-and-wealth-statistics.aspx>, accessed September 2020.

Table 880. Indexes of Prices Received and Paid by Farmers: 2000 to 2019

[2011=100]

Item	2000	2010	2015	2019	Item	2000	2010	2015	2019
Prices received, all products....	**59**	**87**	**99**	**91**	Livestock and poultry............	71	86	147	102
Crops..............................	54	87	87	86	Seed and plants..................	37	93	125	116
Food grains......................	36	74	76	68	Fertilizer[2]........................	34	77	87	70
Feed grains......................	35	66	63	63	Agricultural chemicals...........	83	100	107	101
Cotton............................	57	81	(NA)	(NA)	Fuels..............................	36	78	64	74
Tobacco..........................	99	99	(NA)	(NA)	Supplies and repairs.............	73	96	106	115
Oil-bearing crops................	40	81	76	69	Autos and trucks.................	103	97	106	106
Fruits and nuts..................	59	89	139	124	Farm machinery..................	57	94	115	124
Commercial vegetables........	77	104	109	122	Building materials................	71	97	107	118
Potatoes and dry beans........	55	82	(NA)	(NA)	Agricultural services.............	72	98	114	117
Animals and products.............	64	86	113	96	Rent...............................	54	93	130	117
Livestock.........................	62	82	120	96					
Dairy products...................	61	81	85	93	Interest...........................	78	92	98	115
Poultry and eggs................	71	102	128	98	Taxes.............................	55	96	110	118
Prices paid, total [1]................	**59**	**90**	**111**	**111**	Wage rates........................	73	99	112	133
Production........................	54	88	112	107					
Feed..............................	45	80	106	103	Parity ratio [3]........................	101	96	90	82

NA Not available. [1] Includes production items, interest, taxes, wage rates, and a family living component. The family living component is the Consumer Price Index for all urban consumers from the Bureau of Labor Statistics. See text, Section 14 and Table 760. [2] Includes lime and soil conditioners. [3] Ratio of prices received by farmers to prices paid.

Source: U.S. Department of Agriculture, National Agricultural Statistics Service, "Quick Stats," <quickstats.nass.usda.gov/>, accessed September 2020.

Table 881. Farm and Marketing Bill Share of the U.S. Food Dollar (Nominal) by Selected Characteristics: 2000 to 2018

[In percent. The food dollar series measures annual expenditures by U.S. consumers on domestically produced food; a food dollar represents the average $1 expenditure. Farm share is measured as the average payment from each food dollar expenditure that farmers receive for their raw food dollar commodities. The food marketing bill is measured as the average value added to the raw food dollar from each consumer food dollar expenditure. Based on input-output data from the Bureau of Labor Statistics and Bureau of Economic Analysis]

Item	2000	2005	2010	2013	2014	2015	2016	2017	2018
SHARE OF FOOD DOLLAR									
Food dollar, total:									
Farm share........................	15.8	15.8	16.4	17.3	17.2	15.5	14.8	14.4	14.6
Marketing bill share.............................	84.2	84.2	83.6	82.7	82.8	84.5	85.2	85.6	85.4
Food at home dollar:									
Farm share........................	22.5	23.6	24.2	25.8	26.2	24.3	23.6	23.1	23.6
Marketing bill share..............	77.5	76.4	75.8	74.2	73.8	75.7	76.4	76.9	76.4
Food away from home dollar:									
Farm share........................	6.2	5.1	5.5	6.1	5.8	4.9	4.4	4.5	4.4
Marketing bill share..............	93.8	94.9	94.5	93.9	94.2	95.1	95.6	95.5	95.6
Food and beverage dollar: [1]									
Farm share........................	13.1	13.2	13.6	14.5	14.5	13.0	12.5	12.2	12.4
Marketing bill share..............	86.9	86.8	86.4	85.5	85.5	87.0	87.5	87.8	87.6
Home food and beverage dollar: [1]									
Farm share........................	18.0	18.9	19.4	20.8	21.2	19.4	18.9	18.4	18.8
Marketing bill share..............	82.0	81.1	80.6	79.2	78.8	80.6	81.1	81.6	81.2
Away food and beverage dollar: [1]									
Farm share........................	5.4	4.5	4.7	5.2	5.1	4.3	4.0	4.0	3.9
Marketing bill share..............	94.6	95.5	95.3	94.8	94.9	95.7	96.0	96.0	96.1
MARKETING BILL COST COMPONENTS									
Primary factors:									
Salary and benefits [2].............	52.9	50.4	49.0	48.5	48.7	50.3	50.6	50.5	50.3
Output taxes [3].....................	7.3	8.0	9.3	8.8	8.8	8.7	8.8	8.8	8.8
Property income [4].................	34.6	35.6	35.9	36.7	36.6	35.9	35.6	35.5	35.7
Imports [5]..........................	5.1	6.0	5.8	5.9	5.9	5.1	5.0	5.2	5.3
Industry groups: [6]									
Farm and agribusiness [7]...........	10.6	10.9	11.6	12.5	12.4	11.0	10.0	9.7	10.0
Food processing..................	18.2	15.8	16.7	15.8	15.3	15.7	15.2	15.4	14.9
Packaging........................	4.2	3.6	2.8	2.6	2.5	2.4	2.4	2.5	2.4
Transportation...................	3.8	3.6	3.3	3.3	3.2	3.4	3.6	3.6	3.4
Wholesale trade..................	9.4	9.2	9.4	9.3	9.1	8.9	9.1	9.0	8.6
Retail trade......................	13.0	13.7	13.9	13.1	12.9	12.6	12.4	12.4	12.3
Food services....................	28.4	30.6	30.2	31.2	32.7	35.0	36.3	36.5	37.4
Energy...........................	4.7	5.5	5.0	5.2	5.1	3.8	3.9	4.1	4.2
Finance and insurance...........	3.8	3.3	3.4	3.3	3.1	3.3	3.3	3.1	3.0
Advertising.......................	2.5	2.5	2.4	2.5	2.5	2.6	2.6	2.6	2.6
Legal and accounting.............	1.5	1.5	1.4	1.3	1.2	1.3	1.3	1.3	1.3

[1] Includes alcoholic beverages and soft drinks. [2] Pre-tax employee wages plus employer and employee costs for employee benefits. [3] Value of excise, sales, property, and severance taxes (less subsidies), customs duties, and other non-tax government fees levied on establishments. [4] Allocated compensation to various owners for services on behalf of a domestic establishment that directs sales to the U.S. food supply. Includes machinery, equipment, structures, natural resources, product inventory, and other tangible or intangible assets. [5] Food and non-food commodities imported from international sources and used by U.S. food supply chain industries producing for the U.S. market. [6] For each industry group, the amount shown excludes value-added contributions to the food dollar that trace back to other supply chain industry groups. For example, the value of energy used by the transportation and packaging industries is deducted from those groups and included with the energy group. [7] Farm and agribusiness value-added contributions from non-farm supply chain industry groups, such as energy, transportation, and financial services, are deducted from the farm share and therefore the industry group series value for farms and agribusiness is smaller than the farm share value of the marketing bill series.

Source: U.S. Department of Agriculture, Economic Research Service, "Food Dollar Series," <http://www.ers.usda.gov/data-products/food-dollar-series.aspx>, accessed June 2020.

Table 882. Agricultural Exports and Import Volume, Selected Commodities: 2000 to 2019

[In thousands (2,380 represents 2,380,000). 1 kiloliter equals 264.17 gallons. Includes Puerto Rico, U.S. territories, and shipments under foreign aid programs. Imports are imports for consumption, see text, Section 28 for definition. Commodity and commodity grouping definitions used are Foreign Agricultural Trade of the United States (FATUS) groupings. See source for details]

Commodity	Unit	2000	2005	2010	2015	2017	2018	2019
EXPORTS								
Red meat and products [1]	Metric tons	2,380	1,909	3,355	3,577	4,698	4,514	4,974
Poultry meat	Metric tons	2,555	2,711	3,401	3,271	3,531	3,636	3,574
Wheat, unmilled	Metric tons	27,568	27,040	27,608	21,258	27,171	22,241	26,935
Wheat flour	Metric tons	743	192	332	309	299	277	279
Rice, paddy, milled	Metric tons	3,241	4,388	4,464	3,880	3,826	3,180	3,625
Feed grains	Metric tons	54,946	50,865	54,504	54,604	58,641	73,852	44,391
Feed grain products	Metric tons	657	3,442	1,081	851	967	921	922
Feeds and fodders [2]	Metric tons	13,065	11,422	19,024	22,725	21,784	22,166	21,214
Fruits and preparations	Metric tons	3,273	3,312	3,750	3,740	3,610	3,428	3,240
Fruit juices	Kiloliters	1,162	1,048	1,112	869	691	579	548
Vegetables, fresh	Metric tons	2,100	2,077	2,140	2,236	2,453	2,421	2,437
Oilcake and meal	Metric tons	6,760	6,905	10,004	11,689	10,839	13,160	12,424
Oilseeds	Metric tons	27,715	26,462	43,282	48,914	56,282	47,194	53,170
Vegetable oils	Metric tons	2,043	1,937	3,544	2,646	2,721	2,527	2,322
Tobacco, unmanufactured	Metric tons	180	154	179	156	144	148	101
Cotton, excluding linters	Metric tons	1,485	3,405	2,956	2,396	3,252	3,576	3,562
IMPORTS								
Red meat and products [1]	Metric tons	1,562	1,759	1,291	1,817	1,735	1,700	1,682
Wheat, excluding seed	Metric tons	1,859	1,298	2,490	2,448	2,800	3,122	1,834
Oats, unmilled	Metric tons	1,696	1,684	1,567	1,672	1,551	1,495	1,477
Biscuits and wafers	Metric tons	427	696	796	1,066	1,387	1,534	1,615
Feeds and fodders [2]	Metric tons	1,224	963	1,423	2,221	1,706	1,839	1,842
Fruits and preparations	Metric tons	8,093	9,242	10,580	13,362	14,139	14,562	14,483
Fruit juices	Kiloliters	3,114	4,149	4,274	4,477	4,718	5,198	4,640
Vegetables, fresh	Metric tons	2,905	3,857	5,472	6,570	7,532	7,856	8,075
Coffee, including products	Metric tons	1,370	1,307	1,390	1,584	1,676	1,643	1,753
Crude rubber and allied gums	Metric tons	1,232	1,169	945	950	972	997	1,010
Tobacco, unmanufactured	Metric tons	216	233	164	155	142	135	131
Wine	Kiloliters	458	726	959	1,157	1,257	1,196	1,271
Malt beverages	Kiloliters	2,346	2,995	3,161	3,675	4,038	4,182	4,270
Oilseeds and oilnuts	Metric tons	951	818	1,223	1,643	1,485	1,409	1,170
Vegetable oils and waxes	Metric tons	1,846	2,386	3,730	4,890	5,531	5,574	5,720
Oilcake and meal	Metric tons	1,254	1,541	1,504	4,020	3,756	3,713	3,990

[1] Includes variety meats. [2] Excluding oilcake and meal.

Source: U.S. Department of Agriculture, Foreign Agricultural Service, "Global Agricultural Trade System," <https://apps.fas.usda.gov/gats/default.aspx>, accessed July 2020.

Table 883. Agricultural Chemical and Fertilizer Exports and General Imports by Type: 2000 to 2019

[In thousands of metric tons (21,480 represents 21,480,000). Metric ton = 1.102 short tons or .984 long tons. Includes Puerto Rico, U.S. territories, and shipments under foreign aid programs. Commodity and commodity grouping definitions used are Foreign Agricultural Trade of the United States (FATUS) groupings. See source for details]

Commodity	2000	2005	2010	2014	2015	2016	2017	2018	2019
GENERAL IMPORTS [1]									
Fertilizers, total	**21,480**	**30,397**	**43,657**	**35,612**	**35,676**	**31,894**	**33,437**	**34,476**	**31,841**
Nitrogen	10,552	17,901	17,171	17,914	18,304	16,134	14,004	12,779	12,036
Potassium	9,324	10,215	10,230	10,646	10,275	8,878	12,288	12,903	11,507
Phosphate	1,592	2,243	16,200	6,965	6,975	6,798	7,028	8,693	8,225
Mixed/organic fertilizer	13	37	56	87	122	83	117	101	73
Agricultural chemicals, total	**58**	**80**	**90**	**100**	**115**	**125**	**141**	**142**	**114**
Herbicides	12	23	15	14	19	27	34	33	21
Fungicides	17	21	25	28	33	35	38	40	35
Insecticides	10	7	1	1	1	1	2	2	1
Other pesticides	19	29	49	57	61	60	68	68	57
EXPORTS									
Fertilizers, total	**21**	**32**	**10,310**	**10,598**	**9,916**	**10,569**	**11,836**	**10,623**	**10,090**
Nitrogen	19	26	1,741	2,564	2,346	2,842	4,001	3,627	3,058
Potassium	–	–	333	96	54	56	83	61	103
Phosphate	2	6	7,820	7,119	6,467	6,660	6,619	6,173	6,338
Mixed/organic fertilizer	–	–	416	819	1,048	1,011	1,134	763	591
Agricultural chemicals, total	**154**	**127**	**146**	**159**	**150**	**156**	**1,170**	**1,151**	**1,155**
Herbicides	60	56	83	84	81	91	117	94	87
Fungicides	14	18	15	24	19	18	19	20	19
Insecticides	62	23	27	27	24	20	–	–	–
Other pesticides	19	29	22	23	26	27	1,035	1,037	1,050

– Represents or rounds to zero. [1] Total shipments arriving in the U.S., including both merchandise that enters consumption channels immediately and merchandise entered into bonded warehouses or Foreign Trade Zones under Customs custody.

Source: U.S. Department of Agriculture, Foreign Agricultural Service, "Global Agricultural Trade System," <http://www.fas.usda.gov/gats>, accessed May 2020.

Table 884. Agricultural Exports and Imports—Value: 1990 to 2017

[In billions of dollars, except percent (16.6 represents $16,600,000,000). Includes Puerto Rico, U.S. territories, and shipments under foreign aid programs. Excludes fish, forest products, distilled liquors, manufactured tobacco, and products made from cotton; but includes raw tobacco, raw cotton, rubber, beer and wine, and processed agricultural products]

Year	Trade balance	Exports, domestic products	Percent of all exports	Imports for con- sumption	Percent of all imports	Year	Trade balance	Exports, domestic products	Percent of all exports	Imports for con- sumption	Percent of all imports
1990.........	16.6	39.5	11.0	22.9	5.0	2011.........	37.5	136.4	10.5	99.0	4.5
2000.........	12.3	51.3	7.2	39.0	3.2	2012.........	38.6	141.6	10.5	102.9	4.6
2005.........	3.9	63.2	7.8	59.3	3.6	2013.........	40.1	144.4	10.5	104.2	4.7
2007.........	18.1	90.0	8.6	71.9	3.7	2014.........	38.1	150.0	10.7	111.8	4.8
2008.........	34.3	114.8	9.8	80.5	3.8	2015.........	19.4	133.1	10.3	113.6	5.2
2009.........	26.8	98.5	10.3	71.7	4.6	2016.........	20.3	134.7	11.0	114.5	5.3
2010.........	34.0	115.8	10.3	81.9	4.3	2017.........	17.4	138.4	10.6	121.0	5.2

Source: U.S. Department of Agriculture, Economic Research Service, "Foreign Agricultural Trade of the United States (FATUS)," <https://www.ers.usda.gov/data-products/foreign-agricultural-trade-of-the-united-states-fatus/>, accessed April 2018.

Table 885. Agricultural Imports—Value by Selected Commodity: 2000 to 2019

[In millions of dollars (38,974 represents $38,974,000,000). For calendar year. Data are imports for consumption; for definition, see text, Section 28. Includes Puerto Rico, U.S. territories, and shipments under foreign aid programs. Excludes fish, forest products, distilled liquors, manufactured tobacco, and products made from cotton; but includes raw tobacco, raw cotton, rubber, beer and wine, and processed agricultural products]

Commodity [1]	Value (mil. dol.)							Percent distribution		
	2000	2005	2010	2015	2017	2018	2019	2000	2010	2019
Total [2].....................	38,974	59,291	81,863	113,633	120,967	128,718	131,040	100.0	100.0	100.0
Cattle, live..................	1,152	1,039	1,575	2,195	1,533	1,586	1,800	3.0	1.9	1.4
Beef and veal...............	2,399	3,651	2,830	6,655	5,257	5,617	5,997	6.2	3.5	4.6
Pork..........................	997	1,281	1,185	1,622	1,734	1,601	1,478	2.6	1.4	1.1
Dairy products..............	1,671	2,686	2,619	3,493	2,826	2,940	3,111	4.3	3.2	2.4
Grains and feeds...........	3,075	4,527	7,788	11,085	12,184	13,663	14,056	7.9	9.5	10.7
Fruits and preparations......	3,851	5,842	9,168	14,047	16,323	17,235	18,136	9.9	11.2	13.8
Vegetables and preparations [3]..	3,958	6,410	9,318	12,063	13,578	14,498	15,123	10.2	11.4	11.5
Sugar and related products..	1,555	2,494	4,047	4,600	4,659	4,661	4,667	4.0	4.9	3.6
Cocoa and products.........	1,404	2,751	4,295	4,860	5,012	4,713	4,978	3.6	5.2	3.8
Coffee and products........	2,700	2,976	4,943	6,303	6,617	6,052	6,098	6.9	6.0	4.7
Rubber, crude natural.......	842	1,552	2,820	1,499	1,768	1,538	1,524	2.2	3.4	1.2
Wine..........................	2,207	3,762	4,279	5,478	6,023	6,334	6,359	5.7	5.2	4.9
Malt beverages..............	2,179	3,096	3,506	4,547	5,084	5,350	5,642	5.6	4.3	4.3
Oilseeds and products.......	1,773	2,998	5,390	8,319	9,222	9,252	8,516	4.5	6.6	6.5

[1] Commodity and commodity grouping definitions used are the Foreign Agricultural Trade of the United States (FATUS) commodity code groupings. See source for more details. [2] Includes other commodities not shown separately. [3] Includes pulses.

Source: U.S. Department of Agriculture, Foreign Agricultural Service, "Global Agricultural Trade System (GATS)," <https://apps.fas.usda.gov/gats/default.aspx>, accessed April 2020.

Table 886. Agricultural Imports—Value by Selected Country of Origin: 2000 to 2019

[In millions of dollars (38,974 represents $38,974,000,000). Data are imports for consumption; for definition, see text, Section 28. Totals include transshipments through Canada, but transshipments are not distributed by country after 1998. See headnote Table 884]

Country	Value (mil. dol.)							Percent distribution		
	2000	2005	2010	2015	2017	2018	2019	2000	2010	2019
Total........................	38,974	59,291	81,863	113,633	120,967	128,718	131,040	100.0	100.0	100.0
Argentina.....................	672	831	1,159	1,536	1,390	1,392	1,355	1.7	1.4	1.0
Australia [1]..................	1,592	2,421	2,307	4,274	3,243	3,209	3,516	4.1	2.8	2.7
Brazil.........................	1,144	1,952	2,894	3,482	3,294	3,340	3,328	2.9	3.5	2.5
Canada.......................	8,661	12,270	16,244	21,821	22,309	23,049	23,628	22.2	19.8	18.0
Chile..........................	1,026	1,521	2,293	2,854	2,887	3,069	2,796	2.6	2.8	2.1
China.........................	812	1,872	3,367	4,356	4,498	4,909	3,625	2.1	4.1	2.8
Colombia.....................	1,123	1,437	1,977	2,428	2,606	2,612	2,666	2.9	2.4	2.0
Costa Rica...................	812	916	1,295	1,484	1,616	1,590	1,544	2.1	1.6	1.2
Ecuador.......................	451	596	869	1,226	1,002	1,077	1,104	1.2	1.1	0.8
European Union [2]..............	8,312	13,426	14,370	20,000	22,063	23,809	24,542	21.3	17.6	18.7
Guatemala....................	710	920	1,387	1,928	2,069	2,186	2,130	1.8	1.7	1.6
India..........................	826	923	1,592	2,670	2,607	2,676	2,649	2.1	1.9	2.0
Indonesia.....................	998	1,702	2,887	2,882	3,710	3,356	3,045	2.6	3.5	2.3
Malaysia......................	353	666	1,729	1,171	991	997	1,025	0.9	2.1	0.8
Mexico........................	5,077	8,331	13,578	21,034	24,568	25,942	28,332	13.0	16.6	21.6
New Zealand [1]..............	1,132	1,712	1,666	2,884	2,589	2,564	2,354	2.9	2.0	1.8
Peru..........................	196	448	974	1,677	1,984	2,229	2,578	0.5	1.2	2.0
Philippines....................	468	568	884	1,146	1,242	1,133	926	1.2	1.1	0.7
Thailand......................	779	1,094	2,034	2,274	2,454	2,671	2,876	2.0	2.5	2.2
Vietnam.......................	200	422	970	1,841	2,402	2,329	2,006	0.5	1.2	1.5
Rest of world.................	3,627	5,264	7,390	10,665	11,442	14,580	15,013	9.3	9.0	11.5

[1] Data is a summarization of component countries. [2] For consistency, data for all years are shown on the basis of 28 countries in the European Union; see footnote 3, Table 1387.

Source: U.S. Department of Agriculture, Foreign Agricultural Service, "Global Agricultural Trade System (GATS)," <https://apps.fas.usda.gov/gats/default.aspx>, accessed April 2020.

Table 887. Selected Farm Products—U.S. and World Production and Exports: 2010 to 2019

[58.9 represents 58,900,000. Metric ton = 1.102 short tons or .984 long tons]

Commodity	Unit	Quantity United States 2010	2015	2019	World 2010	2015	2019	United States as percent of world 2010	2015	2019
PRODUCTION [1]										
Wheat	Mil. metric tons	58.9	56.1	52.3	650.7	738.1	764.1	9.0	7.6	6.8
Corn for grain	Mil. metric tons	315.6	345.5	345.9	849.5	1,015.2	1,112.4	37.2	34.0	31.1
Soybeans	Mil. metric tons	90.7	106.9	96.7	264.7	316.3	337.3	34.2	33.8	28.7
Rice, milled	Mil. metric tons	7.6	6.1	5.9	451.6	477.1	495.7	1.7	1.3	1.2
Cotton	Million bales [2]	18.1	12.9	19.9	117.3	96.2	123.0	15.4	13.4	16.2
EXPORTS [3]										
Wheat [4]	Mil. metric tons	35.1	21.2	26.3	133.0	172.6	190.0	26.4	12.3	13.8
Corn	Mil. metric tons	46.5	48.2	45.6	91.6	120.2	171.2	50.8	40.1	26.6
Soybeans	Mil. metric tons	41.0	52.9	44.9	91.6	132.6	164.6	44.7	39.9	27.3
Rice, milled basis	Mil. metric tons	3.5	3.4	2.9	35.2	40.4	41.4	10.0	8.4	7.1
Cotton	Million bales [2]	14.4	9.2	15.4	34.9	34.7	40.3	41.2	26.4	38.2

[1] Production years vary by commodity. In most cases, includes harvests from July 1 of the year shown through June 30 of the following year. [2] Bales of 480 lb. net weight. [3] Data are for local marketing year beginning in year shown. See source for more information. [4] Includes wheat flour on a grain equivalent.

Source: U.S. Department of Agriculture, Foreign Agricultural Service, "Production, Supply and Distribution Online," <apps.fas.usda.gov/psdonline/app/index.html#/app/home>, accessed September 2020.

Table 888. Percent of U.S. Agricultural Commodity Output Exported: 2008 to 2016

[In percent. All export shares are estimated from export and production values]

Commodity group	2008	2009	2010	2011	2012	2013	2014	2015	2016
Total agriculture	**19.8**	**17.3**	**19.2**	**20.8**	**20.6**	**20.7**	**20.7**	**19.4**	**19.9**
Total food and beverages	19.2	16.8	18.4	19.7	19.8	19.9	20.1	19.1	19.3
Animal foods [1]	9.9	8.8	9.7	11.0	11.3	11.3	10.5	9.5	9.8
Plant foods [2]	30.3	25.4	28.3	29.8	28.3	28.8	31.7	29.6	29.7
Non-manufactured products	26.2	22.0	23.3	23.5	21.3	21.0	22.3	21.3	23.7
Crops	38.4	31.4	34.5	35.4	30.9	31.5	36.3	35.2	36.5
Food grains	76.0	49.5	63.6	80.2	52.9	73.3	59.9	62.0	63.0
Feed grains	26.5	19.9	20.7	21.8	13.4	11.6	20.3	20.4	22.2
Oilseeds	56.6	46.7	52.5	51.4	54.2	47.6	57.8	55.3	53.8
Vegetables and melons	15.8	14.9	16.4	16.5	17.1	16.8	17.6	15.9	17.5
Fruits and tree nuts	37.4	37.4	38.7	40.4	40.1	41.9	42.8	45.2	42.7
Sweeteners	6.5	5.0	6.5	6.3	5.7	5.9	6.6	5.2	3.8
Livestock	0.9	0.9	0.8	0.8	1.0	0.7	0.6	0.5	0.5
Manufactured products	18.8	16.3	18.8	21.3	23.4	24.5	24.4	21.6	19.9
Grain & oilseed milling products	41.2	36.5	45.4	43.8	53.7	59.0	62.8	54.7	49.8
Sugar & confections	14.8	13.8	14.0	16.1	18.0	19.6	20.2	18.7	17.9
Preserved fruit & vegetables	17.0	15.5	17.1	20.1	19.5	19.4	20.5	19.1	18.8
Dairy products	14.6	8.6	12.3	15.5	17.4	22.7	23.7	17.0	14.3
Meat products	32.5	26.5	31.9	39.4	41.3	40.0	38.5	33.1	30.8
Bakery products	4.1	4.1	4.3	5.0	5.6	5.8	5.6	5.3	4.9
Other foods	14.4	13.8	14.9	15.9	19.2	20.0	19.2	18.7	18.2
Beverages	7.6	7.5	9.2	10.4	11.1	13.1	12.7	13.1	11.1

[1] Animal products include red meats, poultry meat and eggs, and dairy products. [2] Plant or crop food products include food grains, vegetable oils, fruits, nuts, vegetables, sweeteners (sugarcane, sugar beets, honey), tropical products (coffee, cocoa, spices), grain and oilseed milling products, sugar and confections, and bakery products.

Source: U.S. Department of Agriculture, Economic Research Service, "U.S. Agricultural Trade," <https://www.ers.usda.gov/topics/international-markets-trade/us-agricultural-trade/>, accessed February 2018.

Table 889. Top 10 U.S. Export Markets for Soybeans, Corn, Wheat, and Poultry: 2019

[In thousands of metric tons (52,279 represents 52,279,000). Commodity and commodity grouping definitions used are the Foreign Agricultural Trade of the United States (FATUS) commodity code groupings. See source for details]

Country	Soybeans	Country	Corn	Country	Wheat [1]	Country	Poultry meat
World, total	**52,279**	**World, total**	**41,449**	**World, total**	**26,935**	**World, total**	**3,574**
China	22,612	Mexico	14,489	Mexico	3,547	Mexico	888
Mexico	5,175	Japan	10,553	Philippines	2,953	Cuba	219
Egypt	2,790	Colombia	3,910	Japan	2,577	Taiwan	208
Japan	2,466	Canada	2,107	Nigeria	2,114	Angola	167
Indonesia	2,429	Korea, South	1,882	Korea, South	1,289	Vietnam	152
Netherlands	2,312	Taiwan	1,187	Taiwan	1,250	Canada	147
Taiwan	1,867	Peru	1,019	Indonesia	1,230	Guatemala	134
Spain	1,596	Guatemala	1,001	Egypt	806	Hong Kong	118
Thailand	1,426	Costa Rica	836	Italy	770	Georgia	116
Bangladesh	1,137	Honduras	674	Yemen	740	Colombia	99
Rest of world	8,468	Rest of world	3,792	Rest of world	9,657	Rest of world	1,326

[1] Unmilled.

Source: U.S. Department of Agriculture, Foreign Agricultural Service, "Global Agricultural Trade System (GATS)," <https://apps.fas.usda.gov/gats/default.aspx>, accessed June 2020.

Table 890. Agricultural Exports—Value by Principal Commodity: 2000 to 2019

[In millions of dollars (51,265 represents $51,265,000,000). Includes Puerto Rico, U.S. territories, and shipments under foreign aid programs. Excludes fish, forest products, distilled liquors, manufactured tobacco, and products made from cotton; but includes raw tobacco, raw cotton, rubber, beer and wine, and processed agricultural products. Commodity and commodity grouping definitions used are the Foreign Agricultural Trade of the United States (FATUS) commodity code groupings. See source for more details]

Commodity	Value (mil. dol.)							Percent distribution		
	2000	2005	2010	2015	2017	2018	2019	2000	2010	2019
Total agricultural exports......	51,265	63,182	115,820	133,057	138,183	139,544	136,650	100.0	100.0	100.0
Animals and animal products [1]....	11,600	12,227	22,340	26,719	28,893	29,602	30,137	22.6	19.3	22.1
Red meat and meat products.....	5,276	4,299	9,336	12,407	14,446	15,282	15,740	10.3	8.1	11.5
Poultry and poultry products......	2,235	3,139	4,806	4,915	5,092	5,141	5,172	4.4	4.1	3.8
Grains and feeds [1]................	13,620	16,364	29,224	31,277	29,799	32,980	28,971	26.6	25.2	21.2
Wheat and products..............	3,578	4,520	7,061	5,977	6,340	5,680	6,532	7.0	6.1	4.8
Corn............................	4,469	4,789	9,792	8,271	9,131	12,462	7,651	8.7	8.5	5.6
Fruits and preparations............	2,743	3,468	5,262	6,285	6,372	6,305	5,971	5.4	4.5	4.4
Nuts and preparations.............	1,322	2,992	4,795	9,058	9,105	9,169	9,701	2.6	4.1	7.1
Vegetables and preparations [2].....	3,112	3,571	5,375	6,995	7,306	6,928	7,190	6.1	4.6	5.3
Oilseeds and products [1]...........	8,584	10,229	27,265	28,319	30,005	26,606	27,395	16.7	23.5	20.0
Soybeans......................	5,258	6,274	18,611	18,862	21,456	17,058	18,663	10.3	16.1	13.7
Vegetable oils and waxes........	1,259	1,656	3,903	3,128	3,124	2,924	2,752	2.5	3.4	2.0
Tobacco, unmanufactured.........	1,204	990	1,168	1,109	1,010	1,049	732	2.3	1.0	0.5
Cotton, excluding linters...........	1,873	3,921	5,734	3,889	5,827	6,550	6,141	3.7	5.0	4.5
Other..............................	7,207	9,421	14,658	19,407	19,867	20,355	20,412	14.1	12.7	14.9

[1] Includes commodities not shown separately. [2] Includes pulses (legumes).

Source: U.S. Department of Agriculture, Foreign Agricultural Service, "Global Agricultural Trade System (GATS)," <https://apps.fas.usda.gov/gats/default.aspx>, accessed July 2020.

Table 891. Agricultural Exports—Value by World Region and Selected Country of Destination: 2000 to 2019

[51,265 represents $51,265,000,000. Includes Puerto Rico, U.S. territories, and shipments under foreign aid programs. Excludes fish, forest products, distilled liquors, manufactured tobacco, and products made from cotton; but includes raw tobacco, raw cotton, rubber, beer and wine, and processed agricultural products]

Country	Value (mil. dol.)							Percent distribution		
	2000	2005	2010	2015	2017	2018	2019	2000	2010	2019
Total agricultural exports [1]......	51,265	63,182	115,820	133,057	138,183	139,544	136,650	100.0	100.0	100.0
Canada............................	7,643	10,619	16,897	20,988	20,608	20,867	20,886	14.9	14.6	15.3
Mexico............................	6,410	9,429	14,585	17,695	18,598	19,090	19,179	12.5	12.6	14.0
Caribbean.........................	1,408	1,913	3,172	3,299	3,527	3,589	3,618	2.7	2.7	2.6
Central America....................	1,121	1,589	2,904	3,728	3,742	4,197	4,336	2.2	2.5	3.2
South America.....................	1,704	1,943	4,240	6,405	6,448	7,643	6,343	3.3	3.7	4.6
Asia, excluding Middle East [2].......	19,877	22,543	49,766	56,477	61,239	56,688	57,374	38.8	43.0	42.0
China [3]..........................	1,716	5,233	17,564	20,230	19,476	9,145	13,860	3.3	15.2	10.1
Indonesia.........................	668	958	2,246	2,190	2,892	3,094	2,858	1.3	1.9	2.1
Japan............................	9,292	7,931	11,784	11,135	11,915	12,925	11,740	18.1	10.2	8.6
Korea, South......................	2,546	2,233	5,307	6,028	6,872	8,313	7,524	5.0	4.6	5.5
Taiwan...........................	1,996	2,301	3,190	3,150	3,317	3,949	3,565	3.9	2.8	2.6
Europe [2].........................	7,654	8,361	11,365	14,096	13,807	15,464	13,569	14.9	9.8	9.9
European Union [4]..................	6,516	7,059	8,925	12,133	11,438	13,502	11,761	12.7	7.7	8.6
Russia............................	580	972	1,132	426	193	231	191	1.1	1.0	0.1
Middle East.......................	2,323	2,844	5,993	5,516	6,083	6,280	5,716	4.5	5.2	4.2
Africa [2]..........................	2,308	2,773	5,725	3,553	3,501	4,540	4,240	4.5	4.9	3.1
Egypt............................	1,050	819	2,095	1,052	770	1,914	1,558	2.0	1.8	1.1
Oceania...........................	490	742	1,389	1,996	1,953	2,036	2,128	1.0	1.2	1.6

[1] Totals include transshipments through Canada, but transshipments are not distributed by country after 2000. [2] Includes areas not shown separately. [3] China includes Macao; however, Hong Kong remains separate economically until 2050 and is not included. [4] For consistency, data for all years are shown on the basis of the 27 countries currently in the European Union plus the United Kingdom (UK). U.S. Department of Agriculture (USDA) is temporarily including the UK and the European Union as EU27 + UK. Although it is officially separated from the EU, the UK estimates remain included within USDA's EU total. See footnote 3, Table 1387.

Source: U.S. Department of Agriculture, Foreign Agricultural Service, "Global Agricultural Trade System (GATS)," <https://apps.fas.usda.gov/gats/default.aspx>, accessed July 2020.

Table 892. Cropland Used for Crops and Acres Harvested: 1990 to 2019

[In millions of acres, except as indicated (341 represents 341,000,000)]

Item	1990	2000	2010	2014	2015	2016	2017	2018	2019 (P)
Cropland used for crops.................	341	345	335	341	337	336	334	338	323
Cropland harvested [1]...........................	310	314	315	318	316	317	313	311	297
Crop failure.............................	6	11	5	10	7	7	9	11	10
Cultivated summer fallow.....................	25	20	14	14	13	12	12	16	15
Cropland idled by all federal programs [2,3].............................	62	31	31	25	24	24	23	23	22
Acres of crops harvested [4]...............	322	325	322	325	323	323	319	317	303

P Preliminary. [1] Land supporting one or more harvested crops. [2] Beginning in 2000, includes only the Conservation Reserve Program; all other federal acreage reduction programs were eliminated by the Federal Agricultural Improvement Act of 1996. [3] Data are for fiscal years. [4] Area in principal crops harvested plus acreages in fruits, vegetables for sale, tree nuts, and other minor crops. Acres are counted twice for land that is double cropped.

Source: U.S. Department of Agriculture, Economic Research Service, *Agricultural Resources and Environmental Indicators*, 2006, and earlier reports; "Major Land Uses," <ers.usda.gov/data-products/major-land-uses.aspx>, accessed September 2020; and Farm Service Agency, "CRP Enrollment and Rental Payments by State, 1986-2019," <fsa.usda.gov/programs-and-services/conservation-programs/reports-and-statistics/index>, accessed September 2020.

Table 893. Cotton, Hay, and Potatoes—Acreage and Production: 2000 to 2019

[13.1 represents 13,100,000. Marketing year beginning January 1 for potatoes, May 1 for hay, and August 1 for cotton. Acreage, production, and yield of all crops periodically revised on basis of census data]

Item	Unit	2000	2005	2010	2015	2017	2018	2019
COTTON								
Acreage harvested	Million	13.1	13.8	10.7	8.1	11.1	10.0	11.6
Yield per acre	Pounds	632	831	812	766	905	882	823
Production	Mil. bales [2]	17.2	23.9	18.1	12.9	20.9	18.4	19.9
Price per unit [1]	Cents/lb.	51.6	49.7	84.6	64.5	71.9	72.3	62.3
Value of production	Mil. dol.	4,260	5,695	7,347	3,989	7,223	6,375	6,013
HAY								
Acreage harvested	Million	60.4	61.6	59.6	54.5	52.8	52.8	52.4
Yield per acre	Tons	2.5	2.4	2.4	2.5	2.4	2.3	2.5
Production	Mil. tons	154	150	145	135	128	124	129
Price per unit [3, 4]	Dol./ton	84.6	98.2	114.0	145.0	142.0	166.0	163.0
Value of production	Mil. dol.	11,557	12,534	14,607	16,568	16,109	17,288	18,161
POTATOES								
Acreage harvested	Million	1.3	1.1	1.0	1.1	1.0	1.0	0.9
Yield per acre	Cwt. [5]	381	390	401	419	432	443	449
Production	Mil. cwt. [5]	514	424	405	449	451	450	423
Price per unit [1]	Dol./cwt. [5]	5.08	7.04	9.20	8.79	9.17	8.9	9.79
Value of production	Mil. dol.	2,590	2,982	3,725	3,942	4,133	4,006	4,138

[1] Marketing year average price. U.S. prices are computed by weighting U.S. monthly prices by estimated monthly marketings and do not include an allowance for outstanding loans and government purchases and payments. [2] Bales of 480 pounds, net weight. [3] Prices are for hay sold baled. [4] Season average prices received by farmers. U.S. prices are computed by weighting state prices by estimated sales. [5] Cwt = hundredweight (100 pounds).

Source: U.S. Department of Agriculture, National Agricultural Statistics Service, "Quick Stats," <http://quickstats.nass.usda.gov/>, accessed September 2020.

Table 894. Horticultural Specialty Crop Operations, Value of Sales, and Total Land Area Used to Grow Horticultural Crops: 2014

[Horticultural specialty operation is defined as any place that produced and sold $10,000 or more of horticultural specialty products. Excludes mushrooms as well as grass seeds, vegetables, and fruits grown in the open. See source for more information]

Item	Operations	Value of sales (1,000)	Total land area [1]			
			Green-houses (1,000 square feet)	Shade structures (1,000 square feet)	Natural shade (acres)	Area in open (acres) [2]
Horticultural specialty crops, total	**23,221**	**13,789,048**	**894,907**	**429,708**	**5,404**	**497,339**
Annual bedding/garden plants	7,964	2,567,534	282,790	17,537	195	7,294
Herbaceous perennial plants	6,291	944,850	31,262	8,857	292	5,397
Potted flowering plants for indoor or patio use	4,059	1,084,274	63,039	21,576	16	1,794
Foliage plants for indoor or patio use	2,644	721,889	40,164	104,013	47	1,828
Cut flowers	1,998	462,098	57,514	11,378	97	15,931
Cut cultivated greens	728	99,040	3,269	166,717	2,159	2,295
Nursery stock sold	8,226	4,266,631	203,861	83,640	2,224	302,202
Propagative material [3]	1,067	695,126	29,492	2,459	94	12,346
Sod, sprigs, or plugs	1,289	1,138,465	707	36	13	55,019
Dried bulbs, corms, rhizomes, and tubers	204	74,014	359	186	8	5,309
Food crops grown under protection	2,521	796,664	84,507	2,366	75	5,330
Transplants for commercial vegetable production [4]	693	371,817	26,638	(D)	(D)	7,618
Vegetable seeds	385	135,122	510	(D)	(D)	32,620
Flower seeds	169	31,607	172	14	(D)	4,869
Aquatic plants	345	20,205	878	45	2	1,274
Cut Christmas trees	3,352	366,632	516	170	29	26,500
Short rotation woody crops	49	1,845	(NA)	(NA)	(NA)	(NA)
Tobacco transplants [5]	183	11,236	(NA)	(NA)	(NA)	(NA)

D Withheld to avoid disclosure. NA Not available. [1] Total land area represents the land utilized on the operation as the area used for horticultural production. Includes volume of stacked benches and stacked pots and the area used to produce multiple crop types. [2] Excludes acres in production for Christmas trees or sod, sprigs, or plugs. [3] Includes cuttings, plug seedlings, liners, tissue cultured plantlets, and prefinished plants. As of 2014, this data includes seedlings for reforestation and may not be comparable to 2009 data. [4] Includes strawberries. [5] Includes transplants grown for sale; excludes transplants for the farmer's own use.

Source: U.S. Department of Agriculture, National Agricultural Statistics Service, *2014 Census of Horticultural Specialties,* Vol. 3, December 2015. See also <http://www.agcensus.usda.gov/Publications/Census_of_Horticulture_Specialties/>.

Table 895. Corn—Acreage, Production, and Value by Leading State: 2017 to 2019

[82,733 represents 82,733,000. One bushel of corn (bu.) = 56 pounds. State value of production is computed by multiplying the state price by its production; acreage harvested and production value for the United States is the sum of state values]

State	Acreage harvested (1,000 acres)			Yield per acre (bu.)			Production (mil. bu.)			Price per unit ($/bu.)			Value of production (mil. dol.)		
	2017	2018	2019	2017	2018	2019	2017	2018	2019	2017	2018	2019	2017	2018	2019
U.S. [1]....	82,733	81,276	81,482	177	176	168	14,609	14,340	13,692	3.36	3.61	3.85	49,568	52,102	52,911
IA.........	12,900	12,750	13,050	202	196	198	2,606	2,499	2,584	3.31	3.59	3.80	8,625	8,971	9,819
IL.........	10,950	10,800	10,200	201	210	181	2,201	2,268	1,846	3.41	3.62	3.85	7,505	8,210	7,108
NE........	9,300	9,300	9,810	181	192	182	1,683	1,786	1,785	3.35	3.58	3.80	5,639	6,392	6,785
MN........	7,630	7,460	7,260	194	182	174	1,480	1,358	1,263	3.18	3.47	3.65	4,707	4,711	4,611
IN.........	5,200	5,120	4,820	180	189	169	936	968	815	3.56	3.78	4.10	3,332	3,658	3,340
KS........	5,200	4,980	6,020	132	129	133	686	642	801	3.28	3.58	3.70	2,251	2,300	2,962
SD........	5,080	4,860	3,910	145	160	145	737	778	567	3.09	3.38	3.70	2,276	2,628	2,098
MO........	3,250	3,330	2,990	170	140	155	553	466	463	3.41	3.68	3.90	1,884	1,716	1,807
OH........	3,150	3,300	2,570	177	187	164	558	617	421	3.61	3.74	4.20	2,013	2,308	1,770
WI.........	2,930	3,170	2,680	174	172	168	510	545	450	3.30	3.52	3.70	1,682	1,919	1,666
ND........	3,230	2,930	3,230	139	153	141	449	448	455	3.04	3.32	3.55	1,365	1,488	1,617
TX........	2,240	1,750	2,150	140	108	133	314	189	286	3.70	4.13	4.30	1,160	781	1,230
KY........	1,220	1,220	1,450	178	175	169	217	214	245	3.69	3.84	4.10	801	820	1,005
MI........	1,890	1,890	1,610	159	153	149	301	289	240	3.46	3.72	4.00	1,040	1,076	960
PA........	920	890	1,060	161	140	153	148	125	162	3.87	4.22	4.40	573	526	714
TN........	710	670	910	171	168	177	121	113	161	3.55	3.76	3.95	431	423	636
CO........	1,300	1,190	1,300	143	130	123	186	155	160	3.37	3.70	3.95	626	572	632
AR........	595	645	725	183	181	175	109	117	127	3.64	3.80	3.90	396	444	495
NC........	840	830	930	142	113	111	119	94	103	4.24	4.39	4.45	506	412	459
MS........	500	460	620	189	185	174	95	85	108	3.68	3.80	4.00	348	323	432

[1] Includes other states, not shown separately.

Source: U.S. Department of Agriculture, National Agricultural Statistics Service, "Quick Stats," <http://quickstats.nass.usda.gov/>, accessed February 2020.

Table 896. Soybeans—Acreage, Production, and Value by Leading State: 2017 to 2019

[89,542 represents 89,542,000. One bushel of soybeans (bu.) = 60 pounds. State value of production is computed by multiplying the state price by its production; value for the United States is the sum of state values]

State	Acreage harvested (1,000 acres)			Yield per acre (bu.)			Production (mil. bu.)			Price per unit ($/bu.)			Value of production (mil. dol.)		
	2017	2018	2019	2017	2018	2019	2017	2018	2019	2017	2018	2019	2017	2018	2019
U.S. [1]...	89,542	87,594	75,021	49	51	47	4,412	4,428	3,558	9.33	8.48	8.75	41,309	37,558	31,203
IL.........	10,550	10,500	9,860	58	64	54	612	667	532	9.60	8.74	9.15	5,874	5,827	4,872
IA.........	9,940	9,830	9,120	57	56	55	567	550	502	9.25	8.46	8.65	5,241	4,657	4,339
MN......	8,090	7,650	6,770	48	49	44	384	375	298	9.17	8.40	8.60	3,524	3,149	2,562
IN........	5,940	5,960	5,360	54	58	51	321	343	273	9.61	8.73	9.10	3,083	2,992	2,488
NE......	5,670	5,590	4,840	58	58	59	326	324	283	9.08	8.20	8.40	2,960	2,659	2,378
MO.....	5,910	5,780	5,010	50	45	46	293	257	230	9.48	8.56	8.90	2,773	2,202	2,051
OH......	5,090	5,020	4,270	50	56	49	252	281	209	9.62	8.69	9.15	2,424	2,443	1,914
KS......	5,110	4,690	4,490	38	43	42	192	202	186	9.00	7.93	8.40	1,725	1,599	1,565
ND......	7,050	6,840	5,450	35	35	32	243	239	174	8.88	7.98	8.10	2,160	1,910	1,413
SD......	5,610	5,580	3,440	43	45	43	241	251	146	8.94	7.97	8.40	2,157	2,001	1,228
AR......	3,500	3,210	2,610	51	51	49	179	162	128	9.77	8.81	9.00	1,744	1,428	1,151
MS......	2,170	2,190	1,630	53	54	50	115	118	82	9.74	8.85	8.90	1,120	1,047	725
KY......	1,940	1,930	1,690	53	51	46	103	98	78	9.70	8.79	9.10	997	865	707
WI......	2,140	2,180	1,700	48	48	47	102	105	80	9.34	8.49	8.55	949	888	683
MI........	2,270	2,310	1,730	43	48	41	96	110	71	9.39	8.53	8.90	906	936	631

[1] Includes other states, not shown separately.

Source: U.S. Department of Agriculture, National Agricultural Statistics Service, "Quick Stats," <http://quickstats.nass.usda.gov/>, accessed February 2020.

Table 897. Wheat—Acreage, Production, and Value by Leading State: 2017 to 2019

[37,555 represents 37,555,000. One bushel of wheat (bu.) = 60 pounds. State value of production is computed by multiplying the price per unit by total production, for each state; value for the United States is the sum of production values for all states]

State	Acreage harvested (1,000 acres)			Yield per acre (bu.)			Production (mil. bu.)			Price per unit ($/bu.)			Value of production (mil. dol.)		
	2017	2018	2019	2017	2018	2019	2017	2018	2019	2017	2018	2019	2017	2018	2019
U.S. [1]......	37,555	39,612	37,162	46	48	52	1,741	1,885	1,920	4.72	5.16	4.55	8,235	9,659	8,837
ND.........	6,260	7,635	6,620	38	48	49	237	363	321	5.74	5.09	4.45	1,361	1,850	1,427
KS.........	6,950	7,300	6,500	48	38	52	334	277	338	4.07	4.93	4.05	1,358	1,368	1,369
MT.........	4,665	5,165	5,175	27	38	42	127	198	219	5.34	5.24	4.65	680	1,036	1,020
WA.........	2,140	2,165	2,205	67	71	65	143	153	143	4.85	5.51	5.55	691	844	792
ID...........	1,109	1,136	1,125	82	92	88	91	104	99	4.64	5.15	5.05	421	538	499
OK.........	2,900	2,500	2,750	34	28	40	99	70	110	3.98	5.10	4.30	392	357	473
CO.........	2,029	1,954	2,000	43	36	49	88	71	98	3.88	4.61	3.95	340	325	387
MN.........	1,135	1,575	1,400	67	59	57	76	93	80	5.76	5.25	4.70	437	488	375
TX..........	2,350	1,750	2,050	29	32	34	68	56	70	3.89	5.17	4.40	265	290	307

[1] Includes other states, not shown separately.

Source: U.S. Department of Agriculture, National Agricultural Statistics Service, "Quick Stats," <http://quickstats.nass.usda.gov/>, accessed February 2020.

Table 898. Commercial Vegetable and Other Specified Crops—Area, Production, and Value: 2017 to 2019

[7 represents 7,000. Except as noted, relates to commercial production for fresh market and processing combined. Includes market garden areas but excludes minor producing acreage in minor producing states. Excludes production for home use in farm and nonfarm gardens. Value is for season or crop year and should not be confused with calendar-year income. Hundredweight (cwt.) is the unit used for fresh market yield and production and is equal to one hundred pounds]

Crop	Area harvested (1,000 acres)			Utilized production [1] (1,000 cwt.)			Value of production [2] (mil. dol.)		
	2017	2018	2019	2017	2018	2019	2017	2018	2019
Artichokes..............	7	7	7	936	1,001	1,008	66	63	79
Asparagus..............	26	22	21	839	775	736	101	88	100
Beans, snap..............	212	214	190	18,040	17,045	16,540	349	352	303
Beans, dry edible..............	2,023	2,016	(NA)	[3] 35,961	[3] 37,494	(NA)	1,006	978	(NA)
Broccoli..............	129	114	112	20,384	17,273	17,440	926	739	873
Cabbage..............	61	54	59	23,795	19,218	21,619	431	408	519
Cantaloupes..............	63	61	53	15,392	14,603	12,706	296	332	303
Carrots..............	76	80	80	30,996	45,757	49,803	696	733	864
Cauliflower..............	46	45	46	9,050	9,493	10,054	416	434	466
Celery..............	32	30	28	16,045	17,500	15,720	322	437	475
Corn, sweet..............	465	474	391	75,369	73,381	62,498	892	864	652
Fresh market..............	(NA)	(NA)	(NA)	23,613	22,548	16,773	689	661	479
Processed..............	(NA)	(NA)	(NA)	51,756	50,833	45,726	203	203	173
Cucumbers..............	117	111	101	18,887	15,421	14,906	392	323	279
Lettuce, head..............	141	120	115	49,396	40,561	41,446	1,775	1,220	1,960
Lettuce, leaf..............	67	66	57	13,675	10,728	12,467	833	556	650
Lettuce, Romaine..............	117	100	88	36,308	29,029	27,212	1,628	901	881
Onions..............	152	130	129	80,561	70,923	68,646	1,042	887	1,002
Peas, green..............	134	131	128	6,012	5,069	5,033	85	65	68
Peppers, bell..............	42	40	38	14,193	12,864	12,090	626	533	558
Pumpkins..............	72	68	61	15,601	15,127	13,221	197	195	180
Spinach..............	65	61	66	8,091	8,103	9,606	471	416	527
Squash..............	46	45	44	7,970	7,250	6,992	236	193	220
Tomatoes..............	311	322	274	240,055	275,627	237,940	1,678	1,864	1,600
Fresh market..............	(NA)	(NA)	(NA)	20,970	19,774	14,215	772	822	705
Processed..............	(NA)	(NA)	(NA)	219,085	255,853	223,725	906	1,042	895
Watermelons..............	108	112	102	40,286	39,149	36,723	594	663	561

NA Not available. [1] Utilized production is the amount of a crop sold plus the quantities used at home or held in storage. It is equal to the difference between the total production and what was harvested but not sold. [2] Fresh market vegetables valued at f.o.b. (free on board) shipping point. Processing vegetables are equivalent returns at packinghouse door. [3] Total production.

Source: U.S. Department of Agriculture, National Agricultural Statistics Service, "Quick Stats," <http://quickstats.nass.usda.gov/>, accessed March 2020.

Table 899. Fruits and Nuts: Utilized Production and Value, 2010 to 2019; and Leading Producing States, 2019

[4,603 represents 4,603,000]

Fruits and nuts	Utilized production [1] (1,000 tons)				Value of utilized production (mil. dol.)				Leading states in order of production, 2019
	2010	2015	2018	2019	2010	2015	2018	2019	
FRUITS									
Apples [2]..............	4,603	4,983	4,937	5,314	2,311	3,350	2,954	2,746	WA, NY, MI
Avocados..............	174	229	184	135	479	433	400	399	CA, FL, HI
Blackberries, cultivated (OR)....	22	26	(NA)	(NA)	33	38	(NA)	(NA)	OR
Blueberries..............	247	330	303	364	644	873	821	935	WA, OR, GA
Cherries, sweet..............	308	334	342	349	716	751	638	660	WA, OR, CA
Cranberries..............	340	423	442	391	299	262	246	225	WI, MA, OR
Dates..............	29	39	40	61	37	61	152	224	CA, AZ
Grapefruit..............	1,238	910	509	604	291	216	208	203	TX, FL, CA
Grapes..............	7,430	7,621	7,596	6,791	4,024	5,914	6,621	5,720	CA, WA
Kiwifruit (CA)..............	33	21	38	51	25	31	56	86	CA
Lemons..............	882	904	888	1,002	395	697	716	731	CA, AZ
Nectarines..............	233	173	120	132	129	158	105	129	CA
Olives (CA)..............	206	179	53	165	137	160	41	130	CA
Oranges..............	8,243	6,353	3,875	5,427	1,997	1,963	1,830	1,765	FL, CA, TX
Peaches..............	1,130	825	638	659	617	606	511	519	CA, SC, GA
Pears..............	813	803	800	725	387	494	429	315	WA, OR, CA
Plums (CA)..............	142	105	106	98	79	105	100	116	CA
Prunes (dried basis) (CA).......	390	319	273	271	176	226	168	136	CA
Raspberries..............	75	145	109	113	259	670	367	432	CA, WA
Strawberries..............	1,426	1,533	1,305	1,125	2,261	2,239	2,416	2,529	CA, FL
Tangerines and mandarins......	596	863	804	1,107	275	468	576	701	CA, FL
NUTS [3]									
Almonds (CA)..............	1,414	1,630	1,864	2,101	2,903	5,869	5,603	6,094	CA
Hazelnuts (OR)..............	28	31	51	44	67	87	92	84	OR
Macadamia nuts (HI)..............	20	24	18	20	30	46	42	49	HI
Pecans..............	147	127	121	128	675	560	422	471	NM, GA, TX
Pistachios (CA)..............	261	135	494	370	1,159	888	2,616	1,939	CA
Walnuts (CA)..............	504	606	679	653	1,028	1,012	917	1,286	CA

NA Not available. [1] Excludes quantities not harvested or not marketed. Utilized production is the amount sold plus the quantities used at home or held in storage. [2] Production in commercial orchards with 100 or more bearing-age trees. [3] In-shell equivalent.

Source: U.S. Department of Agriculture, National Agricultural Statistics Service, *Noncitrus Fruits and Nuts Final Estimates 2007-2012*, October 2014; *Citrus Fruits Final Estimates, 2008-2012*, August 2014; *Citrus Fruits 2020 Summary*, August 2020; and *Noncitrus Fruits and Nuts 2019 Summary*, May 2020. See also <https://www.nass.usda.gov/Data_and_Statistics/index.php>.

Table 900. Tree Nuts—Supply and Use: 2000 to 2018

[In thousands of pounds (shelled) (331,466 represents 331,466,000). Season begins in July for hazelnuts, August for almonds, September for pistachios, and October for pecans. For walnuts, season began in August through 2007; as of 2008, season begins September 1]

Year	Beginning stocks	Marketable production [1]	Imports	Supply, total	Consumption	Exports	Ending stocks
Total nuts:							
2000	331,466	1,127,940	293,047	1,752,452	733,765	780,988	237,699
2010	422,055	2,482,242	485,098	3,389,395	1,195,946	1,786,058	407,391
2016	575,549	3,328,244	697,232	4,601,024	1,571,858	2,381,753	647,413
2017	647,413	3,187,361	738,839	4,573,613	1,642,279	2,395,245	536,089
2018, total [2, 3]	**536,089**	**3,468,514**	**717,170**	**4,721,773**	**1,708,562**	**2,482,620**	**530,590**
Almonds	359,013	2,224,179	32,293	2,583,193	740,833	1,524,042	318,319
Pecans	80,081	(NA)	163,000	347,541	174,541	91,000	82,000
Pistachios	39,548	487,457	1,284	528,289	159,526	303,516	65,247
Hazelnuts	1,401	40,539	16,764	58,704	31,557	20,622	6,524
Walnuts	56,046	595,842	2,556	654,444	177,093	418,850	58,500

NA Not available. [1] Utilized production minus inedibles and noncommercial usage. [2] Includes macadamia nuts, Brazil nuts, cashew nuts, pine nuts, chestnuts, and mixed nuts, not shown separately. [3] Data are preliminary.

Source: U.S. Department of Agriculture, Economic Research Service, "Fruit and Tree Nut Yearbook Tables," <https://www.ers.usda.gov/data-products/fruit-and-tree-nut-data/fruit-and-tree-nut-yearbook-tables/>, accessed November 2019. See also <https://www.ers.usda.gov/data-products/fruit-and-tree-nut-data/>.

Table 901. Honey—Number of Bee Colonies, Yield, and Production: 1990 to 2019

[3,220 represents 3,220,000. Includes only beekeepers with five or more colonies. Colonies were not included if honey was not harvested]

Year	Honey-producing colonies [1] (1,000)	Yield per colony (pounds)	Production (1,000 pounds)	Average price per pound (cents)	Value of production (1,000 dollars)
1990	3,220	61.7	198,674	54	106,688
2000	2,622	84.0	220,286	60	132,865
2005	2,409	72.5	174,614	92	160,994
2010	2,692	65.6	176,462	162	285,692
2014	2,741	65.1	178,310	217	386,933
2015	2,661	58.9	156,705	208	325,946
2016	2,780	58.4	162,246	212	343,962
2017	2,684	55.5	149,025	220	327,855
2018	2,828	54.5	154,008	221	340,358
2019	2,812	55.8	156,922	197	309,136

[1] Honey producing colonies are the maximum number of colonies from which honey was taken during the year. It is possible to take honey from colonies which did not survive the entire year.

Source: U.S. Department of Agriculture, National Agricultural Statistics Service, *Honey–Final Estimates 2013-2017*, June 2019, and earlier editions; and *Honey*, March 2020. See also <http://www.nass.usda.gov/Surveys/Guide_to_NASS_Surveys/Bee_and_Honey>.

Table 902. Vegetables and Dry Edible Beans—Supply and Utilization: 2000 to 2019

[40,556 represents 40,556,000,000. Data for calendar year except where noted. Food availability is a proxy for food consumption. Vegetable data excludes melons]

Item	Unit	2000	2005	2010	2015	2017	2018	2019 (P)
VEGETABLES, FRESH MARKET								
Production	Mil. lbs.	40,556	40,332	38,028	35,983	39,578	36,949	37,628
Imports	Mil. lbs.	5,499	7,783	10,931	13,183	15,006	15,475	16,103
Total supply	Mil. lbs.	47,400	49,606	50,529	50,913	56,361	54,128	55,441
Exports	Mil. lbs.	3,718	3,721	3,388	3,069	3,085	3,146	3,130
Ending stocks [1]	Mil. lbs.	1,266	1,280	1,488	1,685	1,704	1,710	1,415
Domestic availability	Mil. lbs.	41,460	43,864	44,819	45,509	51,080	48,823	50,473
Per capita availability	Lbs.	146.8	148.1	144.9	141.9	157.1	149.2	153.3
VEGETABLES, PROCESSED MARKET [2]								
Production	Mil. lbs.	35,369	33,265	36,570	40,142	33,261	35,663	34,603
Imports	Mil. lbs.	3,581	5,555	6,354	7,192	7,850	8,284	8,399
Total supply	Mil. lbs.	62,174	62,646	71,282	73,264	72,022	72,891	70,894
Exports	Mil. lbs.	4,479	4,889	6,627	10,220	8,914	8,346	7,821
Ending stocks	Mil. lbs.	23,291	20,838	27,999	30,642	28,944	27,892	25,445
Domestic availability	Mil. lbs.	34,404	36,919	36,656	32,402	34,164	36,653	37,628
Per capita availability	Lbs.	121.8	124.6	118.5	101.0	104.7	112.2	114.3
POTATOES, FRESH MARKET								
Utilized production [3]	Mil. lbs.	13,185	12,075	11,342	10,982	11,434	10,791	11,533
Imports	Mil. lbs.	805	788	916	882	1,106	1,073	909
Total supply	Mil. lbs.	13,990	12,863	12,258	11,864	12,540	11,864	12,442
Exports	Mil. lbs.	677	639	856	905	1,204	1,061	1,203
Domestic availability	Mil. lbs.	13,314	12,224	11,402	10,960	11,335	10,803	11,239
Per capita availability	Lbs.	47.1	41.3	36.9	34.2	34.9	33.0	34.1
DRY EDIBLE BEANS								
Production	Mil. lbs.	2,654	2,658	3,180	3,006	3,596	3,775	2,705
Imports	Mil. lbs.	129	225	289	342	335	377	295
Exports	Mil. lbs.	788	564	1,001	947	1,212	919	1,134
Domestic availability	Mil. lbs.	2,170	1,813	2,094	2,300	2,488	2,915	2,268
Per capita availability	Lbs.	7.7	6.1	6.8	7.2	7.7	8.9	6.9

P Preliminary. [1] Applies only to brussel sprouts, onions, and okra. [2] Includes vegetables for canning and freezing. Excludes mushrooms for canning, and potatoes. [3] Crop year utilization for the past season and the current season distributed on a calendar year basis using National Agricultural Statistics Service potato marketing distributions.

Source: U.S. Department of Agriculture, Economic Research Service, "Vegetable and Pulses Yearbook Datasets," accessed April 2020. See also <http://www.ers.usda.gov/data-products/vegetables-and-pulses-data.aspx>.

Table 903. Organic Vegetable, Fruit, and Field Crops—Farms, Production, and Value of Sales: 2016

[Unit column indicates quantity harvested and sales. Includes certified organic producers who have been certified by state or private agencies accredited by the USDA. Organic food must be produced without the use of conventional pesticides, petroleum-based or sewage sludge-based fertilizers, herbicides, pesticides, genetic engineering (biotechnology), antibiotics, growth hormones, or irradiation. Land must have no prohibited substances applied to it for at least 3 years before the harvest of an organic crop. Cwt = hundredweight (100 pounds)]

Commodity	Unit	Farms (number)	Acres harvested (number)	Quantity harvested	Sales Quantity	Sales Value of sales (1,000 dollars)
Vegetables, potatoes, and melons [1,2]		3,121	186,178	(X)	(X)	1,644,431
Beans, snap................	Cwt	538	5,136	(X)	(X)	27,660
Broccoli...................	Cwt	518	7,785	891,931	891,891	70,651
Cabbage, all..............	Cwt	577	1,831	392,151	392,147	19,560
Cantaloupes and muskmelons.........	Cwt	229	1,444	336,004	336,004	14,509
Carrots...................	Cwt	594	9,942	2,365,710	2,365,710	88,349
Cauliflower...............	Cwt	279	2,997	418,428	418,428	32,383
Celery...................	Cwt	138	2,741	1,042,224	1,042,223	37,655
Garlic....................	Cwt	711	1,669	147,286	147,276	28,655
Herbs....................	Pounds	440	1,744	11,465,439	11,465,439	26,992
Lettuce...................	Cwt	819	37,641	3,628,863	3,628,863	277,345
Onions, all...............	Cwt	555	2,574	1,038,112	1,038,104	33,815
Peas, green...............	Tons	332	9,207	16,799	16,799	15,731
Peppers, bell.............	Cwt	675	1,270	259,806	259,805	20,962
Potatoes.................	Cwt	681	17,244	4,668,037	4,667,978	150,579
Spinach..................	Cwt	344	17,547	1,178,182	1,177,948	118,162
Squash...................	Cwt	1,117	6,891	1,084,403	1,084,402	48,280
Sweet corn...............	Cwt	335	11,916	1,525,668	1,525,668	27,215
Sweet potatoes...........	Cwt	285	9,647	2,913,020	2,913,020	100,993
Tomatoes................	Cwt	1,057	12,435	(X)	(X)	174,973
Watermelon..............	Cwt	254	731	146,283	146,283	6,562
Apples, all...............	Pounds	583	15,037	521,256,053	521,191,807	327,423
Grapes, all...............	Tons	712	27,358	149,965	144,403	218,401
Citrus fruits, all..........	Tons	579	12,154	123,318	123,119	122,817
Lemons..................	Tons	252	3,339	38,784	38,784	56,956
Oranges, all.............	Tons	273	5,866	60,630	60,431	41,933
Other fruits and berries [1]..............	(X)	2,366	39,886	(X)	(X)	659,863
Avocado.................	Tons	305	4,025	11,938	11,936	31,412
Peaches.................	Tons	191	2,520	15,775	15,775	27,639
Pears...................	Tons	173	1,963	21,444	21,444	20,804
Plums...................	Tons	151	1,425	5,949	5,949	11,040
Blueberries, cultivated, all.............	Pounds	455	5,359	42,375,017	42,374,189	100,482
Strawberries.............	Cwt	611	6,249	1,493,500	1,490,954	241,621
Tree nuts [1]...............	(X)	345	21,183	(X)	(X)	78,900
Almonds.................	Pounds	76	5,897	6,641,324	6,641,324	32,014
Walnuts, English..........	Tons	186	5,975	5,814	5,814	24,415
Field crops [1].............	(X)	7,403	1,684,047	(X)	(X)	762,613
Barley for grain or seed..............	Bushels	510	51,254	2,717,771	1,937,653	16,866
Corn for grain or seed...........	Bushels	3,275	213,934	25,562,804	18,217,993	163,878
Corn for silage or greenchop...........	Tons	1,109	47,074	726,014	91,733	5,859
Hay, all dry...............	Tons	3,956	490,187	1,432,174	699,350	129,922
Oats for grain or seed..............	Bushels	1,206	50,732	3,051,226	2,097,703	13,343
Soybeans for beans....................	Bushels	1,748	124,591	4,602,376	3,829,144	78,491
Wheat, all................	Bushels	1,139	336,550	10,551,643	8,938,312	107,130

X Not applicable. [1] Includes commodities not shown separately. [2] Vegetable grown in the open.

Source: U.S. Department of Agriculture, National Agricultural Statistics Service, *Certified Organic Survey, 2016 Summary*, September 2017. See also <nass.usda.gov/Surveys/Guide_to_NASS_Surveys/Organic_Production/index.php>.

Table 904. Organic Livestock and Poultry—Farms, Inventory, and Value of Sales: 2016

[Includes all known organic producers that are certified organic. Animals raised on an organic operation must be fed organic feed and given access to the outdoors]

Type of livestock and poultry	Farms (number)	Inventory [1] (number)	Value of sales (dollars)
Milk cows.................	2,559	267,523	57,801,387
Beef cows.................	490	42,554	10,531,380
Other cattle [2].............	3,048	218,268	164,407,528
Hogs and pigs.............	151	14,707	6,891,039
Sheep and lambs..........	102	9,446	1,199,815
Goats and kids...........	70	3,609	227,551
Other livestock [3].........	42	(X)	659,340
Chickens, layers...........	818	15,475,570	2,462,123
Chickens, broilers.........	215	19,437,579	749,929,661
Turkeys..................	103	410,711	83,129,395
Other poultry [4]...........	130	(X)	79,265,683

X Not applicable. [1] As of December 31, 2016. [2] Includes organic bulls, beef calves, replacement milk heifers, etc. [3] Includes organic livestock not listed separately on the report form, such as farm raised bison, deer, rabbits, and fish. [4] Includes organic poultry not listed separately on the report form, including ducks, quail, etc.

Source: U.S. Department of Agriculture, National Agricultural Statistics Service, *Certified Organic Survey, 2016 Summary*, September 2017. See also <nass.usda.gov/Surveys/Guide_to_NASS_Surveys/Organic_Production/index.php>.

Table 905. Meat Supply and Consumption: 2000 to 2019

[In millions of pounds, carcass weight equivalent (82,372 represents 82,372,000,000). Carcass weight equivalent is the weight of the animal minus entrails, head, hide, and internal organs; includes fat and bone. Covers federal and state inspected, and farm slaughtered]

Year and type of meat	Production	Imports	Supply [1]	Exports	Consumption [2]	Ending stocks
RED MEAT AND POULTRY [3]						
2000	82,372	4,144	88,460	9,343	77,073	2,044
2005	86,783	4,856	93,787	9,274	82,328	2,185
2010	91,769	3,459	97,222	13,961	81,147	2,113
2015	94,289	4,875	101,230	14,275	84,593	2,361
2017	99,810	4,515	106,694	16,036	88,242	2,416
2018 (P)	102,071	4,473	108,961	16,805	89,737	2,419
2019 (P)	104,886	4,421	111,725	17,177	92,044	2,504
RED MEATS, TOTAL						
2000	46,299	4,127	51,313	3,760	46,556	996
2005	45,849	4,803	51,805	3,373	47,367	1,066
2010	49,180	3,323	53,617	6,538	45,934	1,145
2015	48,520	4,698	54,408	7,282	45,806	1,320
2017	52,078	4,361	57,743	8,497	48,000	1,246
2018	53,510	4,313	59,069	9,042	48,761	1,266
2019 (P)	55,105	4,275	60,646	9,353	49,963	1,330
Beef: [4]						
2000	26,888	3,032	30,332	2,468	27,338	525
2005	24,787	3,599	29,022	697	27,754	571
2010	26,412	2,298	29,275	2,300	26,390	585
2015	23,760	3,368	27,719	2,267	24,769	683
2017	26,250	2,993	30,000	2,859	26,492	649
2018	26,942	2,998	30,589	3,160	26,767	662
2019 (P)	27,221	3,058	30,940	3,026	27,272	642
Pork:						
2000	18,952	965	20,378	1,287	18,639	453
2005	20,705	1,024	22,239	2,666	19,093	480
2010	22,456	859	23,840	4,223	19,077	541
2015	24,517	1,116	26,191	5,010	20,592	590
2017	25,598	1,116	27,221	5,632	21,034	554
2018	26,330	1,042	27,926	5,877	21,490	559
2019 (P)	27,652	945	29,156	6,321	22,188	646
Veal:						
2000	225	(4)	230	(4)	225	5
2005	165	(4)	169	(4)	164	5
2010	145	(4)	154	(4)	150	4
2015	88	(4)	94	(4)	88	6
2017	80	(4)	95	(4)	78	16
2018	80	(4)	97	(4)	89	8
2019 (P)	79	(4)	87	(4)	81	6
Lamb and mutton:						
2000	234	130	372	5	354	13
2005	191	180	375	9	356	10
2010	168	166	348	16	317	15
2015	155	214	403	4	357	41
2017	150	252	428	6	396	27
2018	158	273	457	6	415	36
2019 (P)	153	272	462	6	422	35
POULTRY, TOTAL [3]						
2000	36,073	16	37,147	5,583	30,516	1,048
2005	40,935	54	41,981	5,902	34,961	1,119
2010	42,589	136	43,605	7,423	35,214	968
2015	45,768	177	46,822	6,994	38,787	1,041
2017	47,732	154	48,950	7,539	40,242	1,170
2018	48,562	160	49,892	7,763	40,976	1,153
2019 (P)	49,781	146	51,080	7,824	42,081	1,175
Broilers:						
2000	30,209	13	31,017	4,918	25,302	798
2005	34,986	42	35,730	5,203	29,617	910
2010	36,515	107	37,238	6,762	29,703	773
2015	39,620	131	40,430	6,321	33,278	832
2017	41,217	126	42,120	6,786	34,478	856
2018	42,145	139	43,140	7,069	35,226	845
2019 (P)	43,435	131	44,411	7,103	36,371	937
Other chicken:						
2000	531	2	541	220	312	9
2005	516	3	522	130	390	2
2010	504	4	510	79	427	4
2015	522	2	527	144	375	8
2017	535	3	546	130	411	5
2018	539	2	546	84	456	6
2019 (P)	528	2	536	81	449	5
Turkeys:						
2000	5,333	1	5,589	445	4,902	241
2005	5,432	9	5,730	570	4,954	206
2010	5,570	25	5,857	581	5,084	192
2015	5,627	45	5,865	529	5,135	201
2017	5,981	25	6,284	622	5,352	310
2018	5,878	19	6,206	611	5,293	303
2019 (P)	5,818	12	6,133	639	5,261	233

P Preliminary. [1] Total supply equals production plus imports plus ending stocks of previous year. [2] Includes shipments to territories. [3] Poultry production is ready-to-cook production; prior to 2001, includes other production (not federally inspected). [4] Veal exports and imports included with beef.

Source: U.S. Department of Agriculture, Economic Research Service, "Livestock and Meat Domestic Data," <ers.usda.gov/data-products/livestock-meat-domestic-data.aspx>, accessed September 2020.

Table 906. Livestock Inventory and Production: 2000 to 2019

[98.2 represents 98,200,000. Production in live weight; includes animals-for-slaughter market, younger animals shipped to other states for feeding or breeding purposes, farm slaughter and custom slaughter consumed on farms where produced, minus livestock shipped into states for feeding or breeding with an adjustment for changes in inventory. Prices are for the marketing year, which for cattle and sheep and lambs starts January 1; for hogs the marketing year starts December 1]

Type of livestock	Unit	2000	2010	2012	2013	2014	2015	2016	2017	2018	2019
ALL CATTLE [1]											
Inventory (number on farms): [2]	Mil.	98.2	94.1	91.2	90.1	88.2	89.2	91.9	93.6	94.3	94.8
Total value	Bil. dol.	67.1	78.3	101.3	102.6	107.9	141.3	129.6	103.8	108.1	97.7
Value per head	Dol.	683	833	1,111	1,139	1,223	1,584	1,410	1,109	1,146	1,031
Production: Quantity	Bil. lb.	43.0	41.4	40.9	40.8	40.3	41.5	42.7	44.2	45.7	44.8
Cattle, price per 100 pounds [3]	Dol.	(NA)	92	121	125	152	147	119	120	115	116
Calves, price per 100 pounds	Dol.	(NA)	117	172	181	261	247	158	168	170	159
Value of production	Bil. dol.	28.5	36.9	48.1	48.6	60.1	60.1	48.6	50.4	49.1	48.2
HOGS AND PIGS [4]											
Inventory (number on farms): [4]	Mil.	59.3	64.7	66.3	66.2	64.8	67.6	69.0	71.3	73.1	75.1
Total value	Bil. dol.	4.3	5.4	8.1	7.7	8.9	9.7	6.6	6.6	7.2	7.4
Value per head	Dol.	72	83	123	116	138	144	96	92	99	98
Production: Quantity	Bil. lb.	25.7	30.3	32.1	32.5	32.1	34.7	35.9	37.0	38.5	40.5
Price per 100 pounds	Dol.	(NA)	54.1	64.2	67.2	76.5	55.3	49.3	53.1	50.2	51.4
Value of production	Bil. dol.	10.8	16.0	20.3	21.6	24.2	18.8	17.4	19.2	18.8	19.8
SHEEP AND LAMBS											
Inventory (number on farms): [2]	Mil.	7.0	5.6	5.4	5.4	5.2	5.3	5.3	5.3	5.3	5.2
Total value	Mil. dol.	669.9	761.1	1,187.7	951.0	982.3	1,127.2	1,071.5	1,067.9	1,071.4	1,061.5
Value per head	Dol.	95	135	221	177	188	214	202	203	204	203
Production: Quantity	Mil. lb.	512	405	(NA)	(NA)	(NA)	(NA)	(NA)	(NA)	(NA)	(NA)
Value of production	Mil. dol.	365.2	442.9	(NA)	(NA)	(NA)	(NA)	(NA)	(NA)	(NA)	(NA)

NA Not available. [1] Includes milk cows. [2] As of January 1. [3] Cattle weighing 500 pounds or more. [4] As of December 1 of preceding year.

Source: U.S. Department of Agriculture, National Agricultural Statistics Service, "Quick Stats," <http://quickstats.nass.usda.gov/>, accessed May 2020. See also *Meat Animals Production, Disposition, and Income Annual Summary*, <http://www.nass.usda.gov/Publications>.

Table 907. Livestock Operations by Size of Herd: 2000 to 2017

[In thousands (1,076 represents 1,076,000). Prior to 2007, an operation is any place having one or more head on hand at any time during the year. Beginning 2007, operations are any place having one or more head on hand on December 31]

Size of herd	2000	2010	2012	2017	Size of herd	2000	2010	2012	2017
CATTLE [1]					**MILK COWS** [2]				
Total operations	**1,076**	**935**	**913**	**883**	**Total operations**	**105**	**63**	**64**	**55**
1 to 49 head	671	635	637	599	1 to 49 head	53	31	34	28
50 to 99 head	186	129	118	119	50 to 99 head	31	16	15	12
100 to 499 head	192	142	130	136	100 head or more	21	16	14	14
500 to 999 head	19	19	17	18					
1,000 head or more	10	11	11	11	**HOGS AND PIGS**				
					Total operations	**87**	**69**	**63**	**66**
BEEF COWS [2]					1 to 99 head	50	49	47	52
Total operations	**831**	**742**	**728**	**729**	100 to 499 head	17	5	4	3
1 to 49 head	655	588	594	577	500 to 999 head	8	3	2	1
50 to 99 head	100	82	71	80	1,000 to 1,999 head	6	4	3	2
100 to 499 head	71	66	57	66	2,000 to 4,999 head	5	5	5	5
500 head or more	6	6	5	6	5,000 or more	2	3	3	4

[1] Includes calves. [2] Included in operations with cattle.

Source: U.S. Department of Agriculture, National Agricultural Statistics Service, *Livestock Operations Final Estimates 2003–2007*, March 2009; and *Farms, Land in Farms, and Livestock Operations 2012 Summary*, February 2013. Beginning with 2012 data, *Census of Agriculture*, Vol. 1, April 2019, and earlier reports. See also <http://www.agcensus.usda.gov/Publications/index.php>.

Table 908. Hogs and Pigs—Number, Production, and Slaughter by Leading State: 2017 to 2019

[73,145 represents 73,145,000. Production in live weight. See headnote Table 906]

State	Number on farms [1] (1,000)			Quantity produced (mil. lb.)			Value of production (mil. dol.)			Commercial slaughter [2] (mil. lb.)	
	2017	2018	2019	2017	2018	2019	2017	2018	2019	2018	2019
U.S. [3]	**73,145**	**75,070**	**78,658**	**36,963**	**38,498**	**40,509**	**19,159**	**18,770**	**19,827**	**35,232**	**37,024**
IA	22,800	23,600	25,000	12,791	14,509	14,456	6,158	6,606	6,652	9,909	11,128
MN	8,500	9,100	9,400	4,442	4,558	4,778	2,238	2,158	2,329	3,246	3,289
NC	9,000	9,200	9,400	4,248	4,162	4,361	2,269	2,078	2,106	(D)	(D)
IL	5,400	5,400	5,450	2,184	2,154	2,196	1,228	1,138	1,184	3,494	3,556
IN	4,000	4,250	4,450	2,198	2,201	2,236	1,092	989	1,030	2,373	2,391
NE	3,600	3,550	3,850	1,379	1,399	1,509	801	778	854	2,216	2,275
MO	3,400	3,650	3,350	1,496	1,208	1,656	850	712	866	2,613	2,562

D Data withheld to limit disclosure. [1] As of December 1. [2] Includes slaughter in federally inspected and other slaughter plants; excludes animals slaughtered on farms. [3] Includes other states, not shown separately.

Source: U.S. Department of Agriculture, National Agricultural Statistics Service, "Quick Stats," <http://quickstats.nass.usda.gov/>, accessed May 2020. See also *Meat Animals Production, Disposition, and Income Annual Summary* and *Livestock Slaughter Annual Summary*, <http://www.nass.usda.gov/Publications>.

Table 909. Cattle and Calves—Number, Production, and Value by Leading State: 2017 to 2020

[94,298 represents 94,298,000. Includes milk cows. See headnote, Table 906]

State	Number on farms [1] (1,000)			Production (mil. lb.)			Value of production (mil. dol.)			Commercial slaughter [2] (mil. lb.)	
	2018	2019	2020	2017	2018	2019	2017	2018	2019	2018	2019
U.S. [3]	94,298	94,805	94,413	44,197	45,677	44,820	50,398	49,148	48,223	44,460	45,012
TX	12,500	13,000	13,000	6,303	6,407	6,181	7,508	7,434	7,257	7,553	7,604
NE	6,800	6,800	6,800	5,292	5,663	5,586	5,791	5,372	5,424	10,484	10,728
KS	6,300	6,400	6,450	4,301	4,420	4,425	4,578	4,477	4,651	9,091	8,643
CA	5,200	5,150	5,200	1,945	2,397	2,312	2,098	2,483	2,427	1,868	2,003
OK	5,100	5,300	5,200	2,451	2,308	2,118	3,048	2,796	2,578	30	33
MO	4,350	4,250	4,350	1,373	1,534	1,446	1,839	1,980	1,881	54	55
IA	4,000	3,950	3,900	2,099	2,180	2,075	2,568	2,555	2,536	(D)	(D)
SD	4,000	4,050	3,900	1,727	1,808	1,720	2,219	2,245	2,123	606	699
WI	3,500	3,450	3,450	1,527	1,503	1,499	1,711	1,611	1,591	1,852	1,895
CO	2,850	2,850	2,800	1,775	1,847	1,861	2,070	1,976	1,796	3,450	3,384
MT	2,550	2,500	2,500	1,150	1,107	1,115	1,326	1,219	1,254	29	29

D Data withheld to limit disclosure. [1] As of January 1. [2] Data cover cattle only. Includes slaughter in federally inspected and other slaughter plants; excludes animals slaughtered on farms. [3] Includes other states, not shown separately.

Source: U.S. Department of Agriculture, National Agricultural Statistics Service, "Quick Stats," <http://quickstats.nass.usda.gov/>, accessed May 2020. See also *Meat Animals Production, Disposition, and Income Annual Summary* and *Livestock Slaughter Annual Summary*, <http://www.nass.usda.gov/Publications>.

Table 910. Milk Cows—Number, Production, and Value by Leading State: 2017 to 2019

[9,406 represents 9,406,000]

State	Number on farms [1] (1,000)			Milk produced on farms [2] (mil. lb.)			Milk produced per milk cow (pounds) [2]			Value of production [3] (mil. dol.)		
	2017	2018	2019	2017	2018	2019	2017	2018	2019	2017	2018	2019
U.S. [4]	9,406	9,398	9,336	215,527	217,568	218,382	22,914	23,150	23,391	38,119	35,409	40,690
CA	1,749	1,734	1,726	39,798	40,404	40,564	22,755	23,301	23,502	6,567	6,376	7,346
WI	1,278	1,274	1,267	30,333	30,579	30,601	23,735	24,002	24,152	5,490	5,046	5,753
NY	624	623	627	14,929	14,882	15,122	23,925	23,888	24,118	2,717	2,485	2,858
ID	600	609	625	14,633	15,146	15,631	24,388	24,870	25,010	2,517	2,378	2,860
TX	515	537	565	12,054	12,860	13,850	23,406	23,948	24,513	2,218	2,173	2,645
PA	525	519	490	10,893	10,657	10,108	20,749	20,534	20,629	2,026	1,790	1,951
MN	458	453	448	9,867	9,868	9,931	21,544	21,784	22,167	1,756	1,628	1,917
MI	427	423	426	11,231	11,171	11,385	26,302	26,409	26,725	1,842	1,664	1,970
NM	329	330	326	8,212	8,285	8,187	24,960	25,106	25,113	1,339	1,218	1,392

[1] Average number during year. Represents cows and heifers that have calved, kept for milk; excluding heifers not yet fresh. [2] Excludes milk sucked by calves. [3] Valued at average returns per 100 pounds of milk in combined marketings of milk and cream. Includes value of milk fed to calves. [4] Includes other states, not shown separately.

Source: U.S. Department of Agriculture, National Agricultural Statistics Service, "Quick Stats," <http://quickstats.nass.usda.gov/>, accessed May 2020. See also *Milk: Production, Disposition, and Income Annual Summary*, <http://www.nass.usda.gov/Publications>.

Table 911. Milk Production and Manufactured Dairy Products: 2000 to 2019

[105 represents 105,000]

Item	Unit	2000	2005	2010	2014	2015	2016	2017	2018	2019
Number of farms with milk cows	1,000	105	78	63	(NA)	(NA)	(NA)	55	(NA)	(NA)
Cows and heifers that have calved, kept for milk [1]	Mil. head	9.2	9.1	9.4	9.2	9.2	9.2	9.1	9.2	9.3
Milk produced on farms	Bil. lb.	167	177	193	206	209	212	216	218	218
Production per cow	1,000 lb.	18.2	19.6	21.1	22.2	22.4	22.8	22.9	23.2	23.4
Milk marketed by producers [2]	Bil. lb.	166	176	192	205	208	211	215	217	217
Value of milk produced	Bil. dol.	20.7	26.9	31.5	49.6	35.9	34.7	38.1	35.4	40.7
Cash receipts from marketing of milk and cream [2]	Bil. dol.	20.6	26.7	31.4	49.4	35.7	34.5	37.9	35.2	40.5
Number of dairy manufacturing plants	Number	1,164	1,088	1,250	1,269	1,273	1,298	1,305	1,275	1,266
Manufactured dairy products:										
Butter (including whey butter)	Mil. lb.	1,256	1,347	1,564	1,855	1,850	1,839	1,847	1,968	1,994
Cheese, total [3]	Mil. lb.	8,258	9,149	10,443	11,512	11,831	12,182	12,640	13,037	13,137
American (excl. full-skim American)	Mil. lb.	3,642	3,808	4,289	4,588	4,694	4,769	5,072	5,254	5,232
Cream and Neufchatel	Mil. lb.	687	715	745	852	876	909	918	915	935
All Italian varieties	Mil. lb.	3,289	3,803	4,416	4,950	5,082	5,304	5,395	5,570	5,671
Cottage cheese—creamed and lowfat	Mil. lb.	735	785	719	668	681	697	675	695	686
Nonfat dry milk [4]	Mil. lb.	1,457	1,210	1,563	1,765	1,822	1,753	1,835	1,778	1,851
Dry whey [5]	Mil. lb.	1,188	1,041	1,013	870	978	955	1,035	999	978
Yogurt, plain and fruit-flavored	Mil. lb.	1,837	3,058	4,181	4,757	4,646	4,458	4,478	4,453	4,376
Ice cream, regular	Mil. gal.	980	960	929	866	897	907	871	852	861
Ice cream, lowfat [6]	Mil. gal.	373	360	415	412	439	436	461	460	465

NA Not available. [1] Average number during year, excluding heifers not yet fresh. [2] Comprises sales to plants and dealers, and retail sales by farmers direct to consumers. [3] Includes varieties not shown separately. [4] Data for 2000 includes dry skim milk for animal feed. [5] Includes animal but excludes modified whey production. [6] Includes freezer-made milkshake in most states.

Source: U.S. Department of Agriculture, National Agricultural Statistics Service, "Quick Stats," <http://quickstats.nass.usda.gov/>, accessed May 2020; *Dairy Products Annual Summary*; *Milk Production, Disposition, and Income Annual Summary*; and *Farms, Land in Farms, And Livestock Operations, Summary*, annual. See also <http://www.nass.usda.gov/Publications/index.asp>.

Table 912. Milk Production and Commercial Use in All Products: 2000 to 2019

[In billions of pounds, milkfat basis (167.4 represents 167,400,000,000) except as noted. Changes have been made to conversion factors used for dairy stocks, trade, and commercial use estimates; data have been revised and are not comparable to data previously shown. See <https://www.ers.usda.gov/data-products/dairy-data/documentation>]

Year	Farm milk supply use			Begin-ning stocks	Imports	Com-mercial supply, total	Commercial use		Ending stocks [1]	Milk price per 100 pounds [2] (dollars)
	Produc-tion	Farm use	Farm market-ings				USDA net removals	Disap-pear-ance		
2000......	167.4	1.3	166.1	5.8	4.5	176.4	0.3	169.5	6.5	12.30
2005......	176.9	1.1	175.8	6.9	7.4	190.2	–	182.6	7.5	15.10
2010......	192.9	1.0	191.9	10.7	4.0	206.6	0.2	196.4	10.1	16.30
2014......	206.0	1.0	205.1	10.3	4.4	219.8	–	209.3	10.4	24.00
2015......	208.5	1.0	207.5	10.4	5.8	223.7	–	211.5	12.3	17.10
2016......	212.5	1.0	211.5	12.3	6.9	230.7	–	218.0	12.7	16.30
2017......	215.5	1.0	214.5	12.7	6.0	233.2	–	219.8	13.4	17.70
2018......	217.6	1.0	216.6	13.4	6.3	236.3	–	222.5	13.8	16.30
2019......	218.4	1.0	217.4	13.8	6.9	238.1	0.2	224.3	13.6	18.60

– Represents or rounds to zero. [1] Includes commercial stocks of butter, cheese, canned milk, dry milk products, whey products, and lactose. [2] Wholesale price received by farmers for all milk delivered to plants and dealers.

Source: U.S. Department of Agriculture, Economic Research Service, "Dairy Data," <ers.usda.gov/data-products/dairy-data.aspx>, accessed June 2020.

Table 913. Chicken, Turkey, and Egg Production: 1990 to 2019

[353 represents 353,000,000. For years ending November 30, except as noted]

Item	Unit	1990	1995	2000	2005	2010	2015	2016	2017	2018	2019
Chickens: [1]											
Number [2]...............	Million	353	388	437	456	457	484	501	515	534	532
Value per head [2]........	Dollars	2.29	2.41	2.44	2.52	3.58	4.38	4.23	4.20	4.32	4.43
Value, total [2].............	Mil. dol.	808	935	1,064	1,150	1,637	2,116	2,115	2,163	2,308	2,362
Number sold............	Million	208	180	218	194	173	199	208	190	191	187
Value of sales...........	Mil. dol.	94	60	64	65	73	105	88	47	49	38
PRODUCTION											
Broiler chickens: [3]											
Number..................	Million	5,864	7,326	8,284	8,872	8,624	8,689	8,777	8,914	9,038	9,177
Weight..................	Bil. lb.	25.6	34.2	41.6	47.9	49.2	53.4	54.3	55.6	56.8	58.3
Production value........	Mil. dol.	8,366	11,762	13,989	20,878	23,692	28,716	25,936	30,232	31,750	28,314
Turkeys: [4]											
Number..................	Million	282	292	270	250	244	233	244	245	238	229
Weight..................	Bil. lb.	6.0	6.8	7.0	7.0	7.1	7.0	7.5	7.5	7.4	7.4
Production value........	Mil. dol.	2,393	2,769	2,828	3,108	4,372	5,708	6,184	4,874	3,786	4,304
Eggs:											
Average number of layers..................	Thousand	270,946	294,350	329,067	345,027	341,505	356,370	369,949	381,175	394,361	399,656
Eggs per layer..........	Number	251	254	257	262	269	276	279	281	279	283
Total production.........	Billion	68.1	74.8	84.7	90.3	91.8	98.3	103.2	107.2	110.1	113.3
In dozens..............	Million	(NA)	(NA)	(NA)	(NA)	(NA)	8,191	8,600	8,937	9,173	9,438
Production value........	Mil. dol.	4,021	3,893	4,359	4,067	6,553	13,763	6,591	7,635	10,653	7,705

NA Not available. [1] Excludes commercial broilers. [2] As of December 1. [3] Young chickens of the heavy breeds and other meat-type birds, to be marketed at 2-5 lbs. live weight and from which no pullets are kept for egg production. Not included in sales of chickens. [4] Data for turkeys are for year ending August 31.

Source: U.S. Department of Agriculture, National Agricultural Statistics Service, "Quick Stats," <http://quickstats.nass.usda.gov/>, accessed May 2020; *Poultry Production and Value Final Estimates 2008-2012*, October 2014, and earlier reports; *Chickens and Eggs Final Estimates 2008-2012*, September 2014, and earlier reports; *Poultry—Production and Value*, annual; and *Chickens and Eggs*, annual. See also <http://www.nass.usda.gov/Publications>.

Table 914. Broiler Chicken and Turkey Production by Leading State: 2017 to 2019

[In millions of pounds, live weight production (55,574 represents 55,574,000,000)]

State	Broiler chickens			Turkeys			State	Broiler chickens			Turkeys		
	2017	2018	2019	2017	2018	2019		2017	2018	2019	2017	2018	2019
U.S. [1].....	55,574	56,798	58,259	7,544	7,423	7,433	MS......	4,743	4,711	4,845	(NA)	(NA)	(NA)
							MO......	1,426	1,466	1,455	614	573	589
AL..........	6,134	6,187	6,240	(NA)	(NA)	(NA)	NC......	6,563	6,901	7,420	1,144	1,196	1,166
AR..........	6,989	7,316	7,429	587	573	576	OH......	526	561	570	281	278	263
CA..........	(NA)	(NA)	(NA)	320	303	254	OK......	1,370	1,319	1,500	(NA)	(NA)	(NA)
DE..........	1,871	1,924	1,935	(NA)	(NA)	(NA)	PA......	1,037	1,141	1,127	205	195	170
FL..........	372	386	358	(NA)	(NA)	(NA)	SC.....	1,799	1,807	1,838	(NA)	(NA)	(NA)
GA..........	8,044	8,168	8,298	(NA)	(NA)	(NA)	SD......	(NA)	(NA)	(NA)	176	177	200
IN..........	(NA)	(NA)	(NA)	792	768	804	TN......	909	940	942	(NA)	(NA)	(NA)
IA..........	(NA)	(NA)	(NA)	485	477	498	TX......	4,103	4,248	4,455	(NA)	(NA)	(NA)
KY..........	1,893	1,972	1,915	(NA)	(NA)	(NA)	UT......	(NA)	(NA)	(NA)	134	(D)	(NA)
MD..........	1,840	1,736	1,833	(NA)	(NA)	(NA)	VA......	1,609	1,673	1,744	459	454	446
MI..........	(NA)	(NA)	(NA)	206	218	233	WV......	336	317	287	111	96	99
MN..........	358	361	390	1,058	1,087	1,104	WI......	226	229	228	(NA)	(NA)	(NA)

NA Not available. D Data withheld to avoid disclosing data for individual operations. Data are included in U.S. total. [1] Includes other states, not shown separately.

Source: U.S. Department of Agriculture, National Agricultural Statistics Service, "Quick Stats," <http://quickstats.nass.usda.gov/>, accessed May 2020. See also *Poultry—Production and Value*, <http://www.nass.usda.gov/Publications>.

Section 18
Forestry, Fishing, and Mining

This section presents data on the area, ownership, production, trade, reserves, and disposition of natural resources, defined here as including forestry, fisheries, and mining and mineral products.

Forestry—This section presents data on the area, ownership, and timber resource of commercial timberland; forestry statistics covering the National Forests and Forest Service cooperative programs; product data for lumber, pulpwood, woodpulp, paper and paperboard; and similar data.

The principal sources of data relating to forests and forest products are *Forest Resources of the United States, 2017*; *U.S. Timber Production, Trade, Consumption, and Price Statistics, 1965 to 2017*; *Land Areas of the National Forest System*, issued annually by the Forest Service of the U.S. Department of Agriculture; *Agricultural Statistics*, issued by the Department of Agriculture; and reports of the Annual Survey of Manufactures issued by the U.S. Census Bureau, see <http://www.census.gov/programs-surveys/asm.html>. Further sources used in this section and issued by the U.S. Census Bureau include the annual *County Business Patterns* reports, and the 2012 and 2017 Economic Census. Additional information is published in the *Paper Industry Annual Statistical Summary* of the American Forest and Paper Association, Washington, DC.

The completeness and reliability of statistics on forests and forest products vary considerably. The data for forest land area and stand volumes are much more reliable for areas that have been recently surveyed than for those for which only estimates are available. In general, more data are available for lumber and other manufactured products such as particle board and softwood panels, etc., than for the primary forest products such as poles and piling and fuelwood.

Fisheries—The principal source of data relating to fisheries is data issued annually by the National Marine Fisheries Service (NMFS), National Oceanic and Atmospheric Administration (NOAA). The NMFS collects and disseminates data on commercial landings of fish and shellfish. Annual reports include quantity and value of commercial landings of fish and shellfish, disposition of landings, and number and kinds of fishing vessels and fishing gear. Reports for the fish-processing industry include annual output for wholesaling, and fish processing establishments and annual and seasonal employment. The principal source for these data is the annual *Fisheries of the United States*. Additional government sources include *Agricultural Statistics*, issued annually by the Department of Agriculture; and *Trout Production* and *Catfish Production*, issued by the National Agricultural Statistics service of the U.S. Department of Agriculture.

Mining and mineral products—This section presents data relating to mineral industries and their products, summary measures of production and employment, and more detailed data on production, prices, imports and exports, consumption, and distribution for specific industries and products. Data on mining and mineral products may also be found in Sections 19,

21, 28, and 30 of this *Abstract*; data on mining employment may be found in Section 12.

Mining comprises the extraction of minerals occurring naturally (coal, ores, crude petroleum, natural gas) and quarrying, well operation, milling, refining and processing, and other preparation customarily done at the mine or well site or as a part of extraction activity. (Mineral preparation plants are usually operated together with mines or quarries.) Exploration for minerals is included as is the development of mineral properties.

The principal governmental sources of these data are the *Minerals Yearbook* and *Mineral Commodity Summaries*, published by the U.S. Geological Survey, U.S. Department of the Interior, and various monthly and annual publications of the Energy Information Administration, U.S. Department of Energy. See text, Section 19, for a list of Department of Energy publications.

Mineral statistics, with principal emphasis on commodity detail, have been collected by the U.S. Geological Survey and the former Bureau of Mines since 1880. Current data in U.S. Geological Survey publications include quantity and value of nonfuel minerals produced, sold, or used by producers, or shipped; quantity of minerals stocked; crude materials treated and prepared minerals recovered; and consumption of mineral raw materials.

The Economic Census, conducted by the Census Bureau at various intervals since 1840, collects data on mineral industries. Beginning with the 1967 census, legislation provides for a census to be conducted every 5 years for years ending in "2" and "7." Data from the 2012 Economic Census have been fully released as of September 2016 through <data.census.gov>. Data from the 2017 Economic Census are being released on a flow basis between September 2019 and December 2021. Economic Census data are based on the North American Industry Classification System (NAICS). The Census provides, for the various types of mineral establishments, information on operating costs, capital expenditures, labor, equipment, and energy requirements in relation to their value of shipments and other receipts.

Table 915. Natural Resource–Related Industries—Establishments, Employees, and Annual Payroll by Industry: 2017 and 2018

[In units as indicated (1,494.8 represents 1,494,800; 96.45 represents $96,450,000,000). Excludes most government employees, railroad employees, and self-employed persons. See source for definitions and statement on reliability of data. An establishment is a single physical location where business is conducted or where services or industrial operations are performed. See Appendix III]

Industry	NAICS Code [1]	Establishments (number)		Number of employees [2] (1,000)		Annual payroll (bil. dol.)	
		2017	2018	2017	2018	2017	2018
Natural resource–related industries, total............	(X)	**67,701**	**67,448**	**1,494.8**	**1,529.4**	**96.4**	**104.8**
Percent of all industries....................................	(X)	0.9	0.9	1.2	1.2	1.4	1.5
Forestry, fishing, hunting, and agriculture support.....	**11**	**23,363**	**23,393**	**164.0**	**164.0**	**7.0**	**7.4**
Forestry and logging..................................	113	8,789	8,690	54.1	54.0	2.5	2.6
Timber tract operations..........................	1131	513	487	3.9	3.7	0.2	0.2
Forest nurseries and gathering forest products...........	1132	187	184	1.1	1.1	0.0	0.0
Logging..............................	1133	8,089	8,019	49.1	49.2	2.2	2.3
Fishing, hunting and trapping........................	114	2,918	2,955	7.2	7.2	0.5	0.5
Fishing............................	1141	2,545	2,570	5.5	5.5	0.4	0.4
Hunting and trapping........................	1142	373	385	1.7	1.7	0.1	0.1
Agriculture and forestry support activities..................	115	11,656	11,748	102.7	102.8	4.1	4.3
Crop production support activities.........................	1151	5,103	5,092	69.7	68.6	2.8	2.9
Animal production support activities.....................	1152	4,758	4,856	20.6	20.8	0.7	0.8
Forestry support activities.........................	1153	1,795	1,800	12.4	13.4	0.6	0.7
Mining, quarrying and oil, and gas extraction............	**21**	**25,732**	**25,593**	**578.1**	**605.7**	**50.6**	**57.2**
Oil and gas extraction..............................	211	6,405	6,277	109.0	107.6	14.1	15.4
Mining (except oil and gas)...............................	212	5,940	5,829	173.2	170.6	12.4	13.7
Coal mining.............................	2121	729	681	50.3	48.6	3.9	4.3
Metal ore mining..............................	2122	300	303	36.8	35.2	3.1	3.3
Nonmetallic mineral mining and quarrying................	2123	4,911	4,845	86.1	86.8	5.4	6.2
Mining support activities..............................	213	13,387	13,487	295.9	327.4	24.1	28.2
Timber–related manufacturing............................	**(X)**	**18,606**	**18,462**	**752.7**	**759.7**	**38.8**	**40.2**
Wood product manufacturing.............................	321	14,552	14,463	407.2	415.2	17.1	17.9
Sawmills and wood preservation...........................	3211	3,281	3,198	87.8	90.5	4.0	4.2
Veneer, plywood and engineered wood product manufacturing.................	3212	1,441	1,459	80.5	81.8	3.8	3.9
Other wood product manufacturing........................	3219	9,830	9,806	238.8	242.9	9.3	9.8
Paper manufacturing..............................	322	4,054	3,999	345.5	344.5	21.8	22.4
Pulp, paper and paperboard mills.........................	3221	406	452	101.1	99.0	8.1	8.2
Converted paper product manufacturing.................	3222	3,648	3,547	244.5	245.6	13.7	14.1

X Not applicable. [1] Data based on North American Industry Classification System (NAICS), 2017. [2] Covers full- and part-time employees who are on the payroll in the pay period including March 12.

Source: U.S. Census Bureau, County Business Patterns, "County Business Patterns by Legal Form of Organization and Employment Size Class for U.S., States, and Selected Geographies," <data.census.gov>, accessed July 2020. See also <census.gov/programs-surveys/cbp.html>.

Table 916. Natural Resource–Related Industries—Establishments, Sales, Payroll, and Employees by Industry: 2017

[400,466 represents $400,466,000,000. Includes only establishments with payroll. Data are based on the 2017 Economic Census, which is subject to nonsampling error. For details on methodology and nonsampling and sampling errors, see Appendix III]

Industry	NAICS code [1]	Establishments (number)	Value of shipments (mil. dol.)	Annual payroll (mil. dol.)	Paid employees [2] (number)
Mining..	21	25,273	400,466	47,500	598,620
Oil & gas extraction.....................................	211	6,409	229,734	12,625	125,129
Mining (except oil & gas)............................	212	5,618	84,169	11,875	170,389
Mining support activities............................	213	13,246	86,562	23,000	303,102
Manufacturing [3]..	31–33	291,586	5,548,797	670,678	11,522,039
Wood product manufacturing......................	321	14,645	107,215	16,814	393,459
Paper manufacturing...............................	322	4,046	186,385	21,277	333,712
Petroleum & coal products manufacturing.......	324	2,116	543,450	11,270	107,931

[1] Data based on North American Industry Classification System (NAICS), 2017. [2] For pay period including March 12. [3] Includes other industries, not shown separately.

Source: U.S. Census Bureau, 2017 Economic Census, "EC1700BASIC: All Sectors: Summary Statistics for the U.S., States, and Selected Geographies: 2017," <data.census.gov>, accessed September 2020.

Table 917. Gross Domestic Product of Natural Resource-Related Industries in Current and Chained (2012) Dollars by Industry: 2010 to 2019

[In billions of dollars (14,992.1 represents $14,992,100,000,000). Data are based on the North American Industry Classification System (NAICS); see text, Section 15. Data include nonfactor charges (capital consumption allowances, indirect business taxes, etc.) as well as factor charges against gross product; corporate profits and capital consumption allowances have been shifted from a company to an establishment basis]

Industry	Current dollars				Chained (2012) dollars			
	2010	2015	2018	2019	2010	2015	2018	2019
All industries, total [1]	**14,992.1**	**18,224.8**	**20,580.2**	**21,427.7**	**15,598.8**	**17,403.8**	**18,638.2**	**19,073.1**
Private industries	12,884.1	15,883.9	18,035.6	18,796.8	13,467.3	15,197.9	16,345.4	16,765.6
Industries covered [2]	**531.7**	**532.5**	**610.6**	**589.1**	**581.9**	**754.6**	**775.5**	**855.1**
Percent of all industries	3.5	2.9	3.0	2.7	3.7	4.3	4.2	4.5
Agriculture, forestry, fishing, and hunting	146.3	180.7	166.5	169.2	193.9	225.8	229.8	240.0
Farms	117.6	146.0	129.6	130.8	165.1	194.4	196.5	206.5
Forestry, fishing, and related activities	28.7	34.6	36.9	38.4	29.1	31.6	32.9	33.7
Mining	305.8	259.9	346.6	320.3	309.3	448.8	467.9	536.2
Oil and gas extraction	188.8	156.5	236.8	210.9	181.7	360.9	388.8	480.0
Mining, except oil and gas	69.5	49.9	60.6	60.4	75.3	62.3	67.5	65.8
Support activities for mining	47.5	53.4	49.3	48.9	52.3	51.0	48.5	48.4
Timber-related manufacturing	79.6	91.9	97.5	99.6	78.7	80.0	77.8	78.9
Wood products	23.3	32.4	40.5	41.4	22.9	25.9	28.7	30.9
Paper products	56.3	59.5	57.0	58.2	55.8	54.1	49.1	48.1

[1] Includes industries not shown separately. [2] Sum of agriculture/forestry/fishing/hunting, mining, and timber-related manufacturing.

Source: U.S. Bureau of Economic Analysis, Industry Economic Data, GDP-by-Industry, "Value Added by Industry" and "Real Value Added by Industry," <http://www.bea.gov/itable/>, accessed July 2020.

Table 918. Timber–Based Manufacturing Industries—Establishments, Shipments, Payroll, and Employees: 2017

[107,606,458 represents $107,606,458,000. Includes only establishments or firms with payroll. See Appendix III]

Industry	NAICS code [1]	Establish-ments (number)	Value of shipments ($1,000)	Annual payroll ($1,000)	Paid employees [2]
Wood product manufacturing	**321**	**14,616**	**107,606,458**	**16,908,009**	**395,951**
Saw mills	321113	2,887	26,199,964	3,516,416	73,584
Wood preservation	321114	413	6,569,108	505,065	10,199
Hardwood veneer and plywood manufacturing	321211	235	3,247,627	539,671	12,935
Softwood veneer and plywood manufacturing	321212	85	4,207,812	703,266	13,843
Engineered wood member (except truss) manufacturing	321213	114	1,985,402	261,958	5,099
Truss manufacturing	321214	800	6,608,190	1,264,743	31,048
Reconstituted wood product manufacturing	321219	204	8,700,022	815,197	13,728
Wood window and door manufacturing	321911	1,114	12,395,209	2,403,660	53,839
Cut stock, resawing lumber, and planing	321912	831	5,872,971	841,120	21,421
Other millwork (including flooring)	321918	1,564	7,332,195	1,260,027	32,882
Wood container and pallet manufacturing	321920	2,721	9,507,080	1,951,616	55,176
Manufactured home (mobile home) manufacturing	321991	244	4,418,468	875,237	21,960
Prefabricated wood building manufacturing	321992	628	3,653,977	703,392	16,173
All other miscellaneous wood product manufacturing	321999	2,776	6,908,433	1,266,641	34,064
Paper manufacturing	**322**	**4,033**	**184,587,048**	**21,256,632**	**335,193**
Pulp mills	322110	32	5,679,217	702,191	8,003
Paper (except newsprint) mills	322121	177	39,460,551	4,070,425	54,782
Newsprint mills	322122	10	1,185,878	147,099	1,825
Paperboard mills	322130	155	30,946,471	2,994,458	35,673
Corrugated and solid fiber box manufacturing	322211	1,231	44,346,333	5,209,061	84,366
Folding paperboard box manufacturing	322212	450	12,517,306	1,949,309	35,473
Other paperboard container manufacturing	322219	289	8,341,043	1,041,282	21,982
Paper bag and coated and treated paper manufacturing	322220	738	20,450,223	2,651,026	45,700
Stationery product manufacturing	322230	381	5,803,949	764,513	16,143
Sanitary paper product manufacturing	322291	132	11,591,603	1,026,473	17,212
All other converted paper product manufacturing	322299	438	4,264,474	700,795	14,034

[1] North American Industry Classification System, 2017. [2] For pay period including March 12.

Source: U.S. Census Bureau, 2017 Economic Census, "EC1700BASIC: All sectors: Summary Statistics for the U.S., States, and Selected Geographies: 2017," <data.census.gov>, accessed May 2020.

Table 919. Timber-Based Manufacturing Industries—Employees, Payroll, and Shipments: 2018

[In thousands (11,714 represents 11,714,000). Based on the Annual Survey of Manufactures, see Appendix III]

Selected industry	NAICS code [1]	All employees			Produc-tion workers, total (1,000)	Value added by manufactures		Value of ship-ments (mil. dol.)
		Number (1,000)	Payroll			Total (mil. dol.)	Per produc-tion worker (dol.)	
			Total (mil. dol.)	Per employee (dol.)				
Manufacturing, all industries [2]	31–33	**11,714**	**695,618**	**59,384**	**8,361**	**2,635,433**	**315,189**	**5,954,927**
Timber-based manufacturing, total	321–322	**735**	**39,267**	**53,415**	**583**	**137,189**	**235,158**	**305,964**
Percent of total manufacturing	(X)	6.3	5.6	(X)	7.0	5.2	(X)	5.1
Wood product manufacturing	321	404	17,589	43,560	325	50,716	155,835	114,845
Sawmills and wood preservation	3211	87	4,300	49,169	74	14,586	196,735	35,429
Veneer, plywood, and engineered wood product	3212	76	3,546	46,525	60	11,284	187,480	25,393
Other wood product	3219	240	9,744	40,577	191	24,845	130,001	54,023
Millwork	32191	108	4,565	42,191	85	12,647	149,654	26,571
Wood container and pallet	32192	53	1,942	36,306	45	4,445	98,207	10,070
All other wood products	32199	78	3,238	41,262	61	7,753	126,388	17,383
Manufactured (mobile) home	321991	24	1,032	42,783	20	2,114	107,958	5,029
Prefabricated wood building	321992	17	790	45,916	12	1,721	141,316	4,192
All other misc. wood product	321999	37	1,415	38,120	30	3,918	132,441	8,162
Paper manufacturing	322	331	21,677	65,426	258	86,473	335,240	191,119
Pulp, paper, and paperboard mills	3221	96	7,950	82,671	77	43,044	560,429	79,335
Pulp mills	32211	9	837	90,853	7	3,533	483,400	6,814
Paper mills	32212	51	3,956	78,108	41	20,388	501,803	38,257
Paperboard mills	32213	36	3,157	86,961	29	19,124	662,435	34,264
Converted paper product	3222	235	13,727	58,373	181	43,429	239,755	111,784
Paperboard container	32221	142	8,465	59,483	110	24,029	218,101	67,966
Paper bag and coated and treated paper	32222	45	2,682	59,215	34	9,508	277,986	21,216
Stationery product	32223	15	740	47,782	13	2,019	161,286	5,831
Other converted paper products	32229	32	1,840	57,375	24	7,872	324,744	16,772

X Not applicable. [1] North American Industry Classification System, 2017; see text, Section 15. [2] Includes other industries, not shown separately.

Source: U.S. Census Bureau, Annual Survey of Manufactures, "Summary Statistics for Industry Groups and Industries in the U.S.: 2018," <http://data.census.gov>, accessed June 2020.

Table 920. Forest Land and Timberland by Type of Owner and Region: 2017

[In thousands of acres (765,493 represents 765,493,000). As of January 1. Data are from the U.S. Forest Service's Forest Inventory and Analysis National Program. Forest land is land at least 10 percent stocked by forest trees of any size, including land that formerly had such tree cover and that will be naturally or artificially regenerated. The minimum area for classification of forest land is 1 acre or strips of timber with a crown width of at least 120 feet wide. Timberland is forest land that is producing or is capable of producing crops of industrial wood and that is not withdrawn from timber utilization by statute or administrative regulation]

Region	Forest land, total	Timberland					State, county, and municipal	Private [1]
		Total	Federal					
			Total	National forest	Bureau of Land Manage-ment lands	Other		
Total	**765,493**	**514,425**	**108,178**	**96,138**	**6,109**	**5,931**	**47,095**	**359,152**
North	175,789	164,894	11,348	10,146	12	1,190	25,650	127,896
Northeast	84,727	78,539	2,852	2,355	0	498	10,102	65,586
North Central	91,062	86,355	8,495	7,792	12	692	15,549	62,310
South	245,513	208,092	16,397	12,258	0	4,138	9,561	182,135
Southeast	89,692	85,754	7,016	5,061	0	1,955	5,618	73,119
South Central	155,821	122,338	9,380	7,197	0	2,183	3,942	109,016
Rocky Mountains	130,641	69,654	47,111	44,206	2,688	217	3,193	19,350
Great Plains	6,797	6,084	1,217	1,051	18	148	265	4,602
Intermountain	123,844	63,569	45,894	43,154	2,670	70	2,927	14,748
Pacific Coast	213,549	71,784	33,323	29,527	3,409	386	8,691	29,771
Alaska	128,735	12,996	4,874	3,848	812	213	4,810	3,313
Pacific Northwest	51,827	41,462	19,200	16,802	2,299	98	3,637	18,625
Pacific Southwest [2]	32,986	17,326	9,249	8,877	297	75	245	7,833

[1] Includes Indian lands. [2] Includes Hawaii.

Source: U.S. Forest Service, National Assessment - Resources Planning Act (RPA), *Forest Resources of the United States, 2017: A Technical Document Supporting the Forest Service 2020 Update of the RPA Assessment,* May 2018. See also <https://www.fia.fs.fed.us/program-features/rpa/>.

Table 921. National Forest System Lands by State: 2019

[In thousands of acres (232,419 represents 232,419,000). As of September 30, 2019. Data do not include Delaware, District of Columbia, Hawaii, Iowa, Maryland, Massachusetts, New Jersey, or Rhode Island]

State	Total lands	National Forest System lands [1]	Other lands [2]	State	Total lands	National Forest System lands [1]	Other lands [2]
United States	**232,419**	**192,994**	**39,425**	Nevada	6,288	5,761	528
Alabama	1,290	671	620	New Hampshire	851	754	97
Alaska	23,932	22,139	1,793	New Mexico	10,249	9,225	1,024
Arizona	11,813	11,179	633	New York	17	16	(Z)
Arkansas	3,549	2,593	955	North Carolina	3,027	1,257	1,770
California	24,288	20,811	3,477	North Dakota	1,103	1,103	(Z)
Colorado	15,960	14,487	1,472	Ohio	856	244	612
Connecticut	(Z)	(Z)	–	Oklahoma	759	400	359
Florida	1,423	1,203	220	Oregon	17,654	15,698	1,956
Georgia	1,796	868	929	Pennsylvania	741	514	227
Idaho	21,714	20,449	1,266	South Carolina	1,381	635	746
Illinois	958	305	653	South Dakota	2,436	2,007	429
Indiana	647	204	443	Tennessee	1,291	723	568
Kansas	109	109	(Z)	Texas	2,002	757	1,245
Kentucky	2,205	818	1,387	Utah	9,205	8,192	1,013
Louisiana	1,032	609	423	Vermont	837	411	426
Maine	94	54	41	Virginia	3,254	1,669	1,586
Michigan	4,887	2,876	2,011	Washington	11,990	9,336	2,654
Minnesota	5,488	2,845	2,642	West Virginia	1,893	1,047	846
Mississippi	2,374	1,191	1,183	Wisconsin	2,003	1,525	478
Missouri	3,093	1,508	1,585	Wyoming	9,726	9,226	500
Montana	19,190	17,195	1,994	Puerto Rico	56	29	27
Nebraska	562	351	211	Virgin Islands	(Z)	(Z)	–

– Represents zero. Z Less than 500 acres. [1] National Forest System is a nationally significant system of federally owned units of forest, range, and related land consisting of national forests, purchase units, national grasslands, land utilization project areas, experimental forest areas, experimental range areas, designated experimental areas, and other land areas; water areas; and interests in lands that are administered by USDA Forest Service or designated for administration through the Forest Service. [2] Other lands are lands within the unit boundaries in private, state, county, and municipal ownership and the federal lands over which the Forest Service has no jurisdiction. Also includes lands offered to the United States and approved for acquisition and subsequent Forest Service administration, but to which title has not yet been accepted by the United States.

Source: U.S. Forest Service, *Land Areas of the National Forest System as of September 30, 2019*, November 2019. See also <https://www.fs.fed.us/land/staff/lar/LAR2019/lar2019index.html>.

Table 922. Timber Volume, Growth, and Removal on Timberland by Species Group and Region: 2016 and 2017

[In millions of cubic feet (1,116,012 represents 1,116,012,000,000). Data are from the U.S. Forest Service's Forest Inventory and Analysis National Program]

Region	2017 Net volume [1]						2016 Net growth and removals of growing stock					
	All timber [2]			Growing stock [3]			Timber growth [4]			Timber removals [5]		
	All species	Soft-woods	Hard-woods	All species	Soft-woods	Hard-woods	All species	Soft-woods	Hard-woods	All species	Soft-woods	Hard-woods
Total	**1,116,012**	**598,873**	**517,139**	**985,238**	**560,526**	**424,712**	**25,009**	**15,468**	**9,542**	**13,041**	**8,901**	**4,140**
North	314,204	68,278	245,926	270,041	60,601	209,440	5,932	1,546	4,386	2,491	654	1,837
Northeast	172,556	41,465	131,091	152,780	37,108	115,672	3,264	917	2,347	1,176	377	799
North Central	141,647	26,813	114,834	117,261	23,494	93,768	2,668	629	2,039	1,315	277	1,038
South	377,781	149,800	227,981	319,088	141,307	177,781	13,764	9,268	4,496	7,859	5,647	2,212
Southeast	167,894	71,539	96,355	142,603	67,540	75,063	6,393	4,285	2,108	3,527	2,736	790
South Central	209,887	78,261	131,626	176,485	73,767	102,717	7,371	4,983	2,388	4,333	2,911	1,422
Rocky Mountains	144,222	128,750	15,472	130,005	119,102	10,903	299	189	109	405	396	8,626
Great Plains	8,476	2,537	5,938	4,487	1,885	2,601	57	-2	59	34	29	6
Intermountain	135,747	126,213	9,534	125,518	117,217	8,301	242	192	50	370	367	3
Pacific Coast	279,805	252,044	27,760	266,104	239,515	26,589	5,015	4,465	550	2,286	2,204	82
Alaska	39,229	35,639	3,590	37,140	33,761	3,379	254	133	121	39	39	(Z)
Pacific Northwest	166,844	153,680	13,163	159,238	146,480	12,758	3,707	3,423	284	1,892	1,811	81
Pacific Southwest [6]	73,732	62,725	11,007	69,726	59,273	10,452	1,054	909	145	355	355	(Z)

Z Less than 500,000. [1] As of January 1. [2] Includes growing stock, live cull and sound dead. [3] Live trees of commercial species meeting specified standards of quality or vigor. Cull trees are excluded. Includes only trees 5.0-inches in diameter or larger at 4 1/2 feet above ground. [4] The net increase in the volume of trees during a specified year. Components include the increment in net volume of trees at the beginning of the specific year surviving to its end, plus the net volume of trees reaching the minimum size class during the year, minus the volume of trees that died during the year, and minus the net volume of trees that became cull trees during the year. [5] The net volume of trees removed from the inventory during a specified year by harvesting, cultural operations such as timber stand improvement, or land clearing. [6] Includes Hawaii.

Source: U.S. Forest Service, National Assessment - Resources Planning Act (RPA), *Forest Resources of the United States, 2017: A Technical Document Supporting the Forest Service 2020 Update of the RPA Assessment,* May 2018. See also <https://www.fia.fs.fed.us/program-features/rpa/>.

Table 923. Timber Removals—Roundwood Product Output by Source and Species Group: 2016

[In millions of cubic feet (13,972 represents 13,972,000,000). Data are from U.S. Forest Service's Forest Inventory and Analysis National Program]

Source and species group	Total	Sawlogs	Pulpwood	Veneer logs	Other products [1]	Fuelwood [2]
Total..............................	**13,972**	**5,521**	**5,368**	**660**	**728**	**1,695**
Softwoods...........................	9,480	4,075	3,640	590	576	599
Hardwoods..........................	4,493	1,446	1,728	69	153	1,096
Growing stock [3].....................	11,650	5,334	4,773	648	563	332
Softwoods...........................	8,393	3,959	3,280	582	423	149
Hardwoods..........................	3,257	1,374	1,493	65	141	183
Other sources [4].....................	2,323	187	596	12	165	1,363
Softwoods...........................	1,086	115	360	8	153	450
Hardwoods..........................	1,236	72	235	4	12	913

[1] Includes poles, pilings, posts, cooperage and miscellaneous products. [2] Downed and dead wood volume left on the ground after trees have been cut on timberland and used for conversion to some form of energy, primarily in residential use. [3] Includes live trees of commercial species meeting specified standards of quality or vigor. Cull trees are excluded. Includes only trees 5.0 inches in diameter or larger at 4.5 feet above the ground. [4] Includes salvable dead trees, rough and rotten trees, trees of noncommercial species, trees less than 5.0 inches in diameter at 4.5 feet above the ground, tops, and roundwood harvested from nonforest land (for example, fence rows).

Source: U.S. Forest Service, National Assessment - Resources Planning Act (RPA), *Forest Resources of the United States, 2017: A Technical Document Supporting the Forest Service 2020 Update of the RPA Assessment,* May 2018. See also <https://www.fia.fs.fed.us/program-features/rpa/>.

Table 924. Timber Products—Production, Foreign Trade, and Consumption by Type of Product: 1990 to 2017

[In millions of cubic feet, roundwood equivalent (15,577 represents 15,577,000,000)]

Type of product	1990	2000	2010	2011	2012	2013	2014	2015	2016	2017
Industrial roundwood:										
Domestic production.............	15,577	15,528	11,006	11,587	12,046	12,547	12,954	13,124	13,329	13,643
Softwoods........................	10,968	10,327	8,235	8,672	9,079	9,399	9,630	9,715	9,925	10,181
Hardwoods.......................	4,609	5,201	2,771	2,914	2,967	3,148	3,324	3,409	3,403	3,463
Imports............................	3,044	4,626	2,488	2,469	2,564	2,838	3,119	3,257	3,615	3,522
Exports............................	2,413	2,039	1,888	2,118	2,073	2,320	2,304	2,214	2,216	2,315
Consumption.....................	16,208	18,115	11,607	11,938	12,537	13,065	13,769	14,167	14,727	14,851
Softwoods........................	11,620	12,830	8,912	9,120	9,681	10,073	10,585	10,931	11,495	11,624
Hardwoods.......................	4,588	5,285	2,695	2,818	2,856	2,992	3,184	3,235	3,233	3,227
Lumber:										
Domestic production.............	7,317	7,384	4,569	5,005	5,219	5,607	5,995	6,065	6,143	6,338
Imports............................	1,905	2,943	1,422	1,403	1,480	1,703	1,915	2,097	2,426	2,328
Exports............................	697	435	389	454	464	519	545	492	527	580
Consumption.....................	8,526	9,892	5,602	5,955	6,234	6,791	7,366	7,670	8,042	8,086
Plywood and veneer:										
Domestic production.............	1,423	1,187	655	651	679	703	693	688	703	729
Imports............................	97	154	161	166	176	205	209	244	263	285
Exports............................	109	51	55	52	57	55	46	39	43	47
Consumption.....................	1,410	1,290	760	765	798	853	856	893	923	967
Pulp products:										
Domestic production.............	5,313	5,881	4,863	4,922	5,088	5,068	5,016	5,056	5,099	5,081
Imports............................	1,038	1,448	880	875	874	902	969	882	896	875
Exports............................	645	776	802	887	864	1,040	1,016	1,009	995	1,013
Consumption.....................	5,705	6,553	4,941	4,911	5,099	4,929	4,969	4,929	5,000	4,943
Logs: [1]										
Imports............................	4	72	20	19	28	26	22	29	24	32
Exports............................	674	422	407	485	432	463	444	363	390	393
Pulpwood chips, exports..........	288	355	235	241	256	242	253	311	262	280
Other industrial timber products: [2]										
Production and consumption....	562	300	277	283	373	463	552	642	732	822
Fuelwood:										
Production and consumption....	2,900	1,622	1,725	1,804	1,882	1,960	2,039	2,117	2,195	2,273

[1] Prior to 2010, pulpwood logs are not included in logs. [2] Includes cooperage logs, poles and piling, fence posts, hewn ties, round mine timbers, box bolts, etc.

Source: U.S. Forest Service, *U.S. Timber Production, Trade, Consumption, and Price Statistics, 1965-2017,* July 2019. See also <https://www.fs.usda.gov/treesearch/pubs/58506>.

Table 925. Selected Timber Products—Imports and Exports: 1990 to 2017

[In million board feet (13,107 represents 13,107,000,000), except as indicated]

Product	Unit	1990	2000	2010	2012	2013	2014	2015	2016	2017
IMPORTS										
Lumber, total..............	Mil. bd. ft.	13,107	20,243	9,769	10,172	11,713	13,170	14,429	16,730	16,058
Softwood..............	Mil. bd. ft.	12,875	19,449	9,468	9,864	11,358	12,729	13,947	16,323	15,704
Hardwood..............	Mil. bd. ft.	232	795	301	308	355	441	482	407	354
From Canada..............	Mil. bd. ft.	11,918	18,616	9,151	9,633	11,044	12,311	13,413	15,555	14,479
Logs, total [1].............	Mil. bd. ft. [2]	23	450	126	176	164	139	139	116	153
Softwood..............	Mil. bd. ft.	13	390	99	136	120	99	97	79	69
Hardwood..............	Mil. bd. ft.	10	59	28	41	44	40	42	37	83
From Canada..............	Mil. bd. ft.	19	426	120	133	161	137	136	114	147
Paper and board [3]............	1,000 tons	12,195	17,356	11,144	10,441	10,967	11,301	10,746	10,512	10,454
Woodpulp..............	1,000 tons	4,893	7,227	6,163	5,599	6,112	6,126	5,872	6,161	6,026
Plywood..............	Mil. sq. ft. [4]	1,687	2,902	3,046	3,339	3,873	3,955	4,609	4,926	5,314
EXPORTS										
Lumber, total..............	Mil. bd. ft.	4,566	2,700	2,425	2,900	3,250	3,387	3,056	3,261	3,585
To: Canada..............	Mil. bd. ft.	658	701	621	634	636	600	533	553	549
Japan..............	Mil. bd. ft.	1,270	325	179	189	207	162	153	130	122
European Union............	Mil. bd. ft.	686	507	209	166	164	196	174	189	173
Softwood..............	Mil. bd. ft.	3,753	1,400	1,347	1,582	1,788	1,734	1,563	1,602	1,700
Hardwood..............	Mil. bd. ft.	813	1,300	1,078	1,318	1,462	1,653	1,493	1,659	1,885
Logs, total [1].............	Mil. bd. ft. [2]	4,213	2,638	2,542	2,698	2,897	2,778	1,742	1,872	1,888
To: Canada..............	Mil. bd. ft. [2]	396	1,350	835	754	641	593	507	464	386
Japan..............	Mil. bd. ft. [2]	2,626	934	425	469	531	478	324	314	303
China..............	Mil. bd. ft. [2]	362	22	780	1,052	1,399	1,385	741	942	1,028
Softwood..............	Mil. bd. ft.	3,994	2,066	2,074	2,280	2,550	2,336	1,411	1,515	1,522
Hardwood..............	Mil. bd. ft.	220	573	468	418	348	442	330	357	366
Paper and board [3]............	1,000 tons	5,163	8,701	8,781	9,036	12,842	12,743	12,326	11,679	12,274
Woodpulp..............	1,000 tons	5,905	6,409	8,265	8,125	8,147	7,901	8,096	8,315	8,367
Plywood..............	Mil. sq. ft. [4]	1,766	916	1,004	1,039	990	832	710	774	859

[1] Prior to 2000, pulpwood logs are not included. [2] Log scale. [3] Includes paper and board products. Excludes hardboard. [4] 3/8 inch basis.

Source: U.S. Forest Service. *U.S. Timber Production, Trade, Consumption, and Price Statistics, 1965-2017*, July 2019. See also <https://www.fs.usda.gov/treesearch/pubs/58506>.

Table 926. Lumber Production and Consumption by Species Group: 1990 to 2017

[In billion board feet (48.1 represents 48,100,000,000), except per capita in board feet. Per capita consumption based on estimated resident population as of July 1]

Item	1990	1995	2000	2005	2010	2011	2012	2013	2014	2015	2016	2017
Production, total..............	**48.1**	**44.9**	**48.6**	**50.9**	**30.5**	**33.3**	**34.8**	**37.3**	**39.8**	**40.3**	**40.8**	**42.2**
By species:												
Softwoods......................	35.8	32.2	36.0	39.8	24.8	26.8	28.3	30.0	31.5	32.0	32.5	33.9
Hardwoods......................	12.3	12.6	12.6	11.2	5.7	6.6	6.5	7.3	8.3	8.3	8.3	8.3
Consumption, total..............	**55.3**	**60.3**	**66.6**	**72.3**	**37.7**	**40.6**	**43.6**	**47.2**	**50.9**	**54.0**	**53.6**	**38.6**
Per capita.......................	221	229	236	244	122	130	139	149	159	168	166	118
By species:												
Softwoods......................	43.6	48.4	54.6	61.6	32.7	35.0	38.0	40.9	43.7	46.8	46.6	32.2
Hardwoods......................	11.7	12.0	11.9	10.6	4.9	5.7	5.6	6.3	7.1	7.2	7.0	6.4

Source: U.S. Forest Service, *U.S. Timber Production, Trade, Consumption, and Price Statistics, 1965-2017*, July 2019. See also <https://www.fs.usda.gov/treesearch/pubs/58506>.

Table 927. Pulpwood Consumption, Woodpulp Production, and Paper and Board Production and Consumption: 1990 to 2017

[In thousands (99,361 represents 99,361,000) except where otherwise indicated]

Item	Unit	1990	2000	2010	2012	2013	2014	2015	2016	2017
Pulpwood consumption.........	1,000 cords [1]	99,361	95,904	89,306	90,744	87,319	86,714	84,979	85,798	84,152
Woodpulp production [2].........	1,000 tons	63,048	62,758	55,343	55,475	54,466	53,367	52,646	52,701	52,701
Paper and board: [3]										
Production.....................	1,000 tons	78,679	94,491	82,968	80,916	80,478	79,488	79,024	78,342	78,445
Consumption [4]................	1,000 tons	85,711	103,147	85,331	82,321	78,603	78,046	77,444	77,175	76,625
Per capita....................	Pounds	686	731	551	524	497	489	482	477	470

[1] One cord equals 128 cubic feet. [2] Includes dissolving and special alpha pulps; excludes defibrated/exploded pulps and screenings. [3] Excludes wet machine board and construction grades. [4] Production plus imports, minus exports.

Source: U.S. Forest Service, *U.S. Timber Production, Trade, Consumption, and Price Statistics, 1965-2017*, July 2019. See also <https://www.fs.usda.gov/treesearch/pubs/58506>.

Table 928. Selected Timber Products—Producer Price Indexes: 1990 to 2019

[1982=100, unless otherwise noted. For information about producer prices, see text, Section 14]

Product	1990	1995	2000	2005	2010	2015	2017	2018	2019
Lumber and wood products..........................	**129.7**	**178.1**	**178.2**	**196.5**	**192.7**	**221.9**	**230.4**	**243.9**	**236.7**
Lumber...	124.6	173.4	178.8	198.6	167.3	199.3	217.2	232.3	210.4
Softwood lumber................................	123.8	178.5	178.6	203.6	160.8	192.7	223.7	241.9	215.4
Softwood cut stock and dimension............	129.7	183.6	195.3	205.1	206.0	199.7	214.2	228.1	204.1
Softwood lumber, not edge worked [1]..........	(NA)	(NA)	(NA)	115.0	85.8	104.9	121.9	131.0	114.4
Softwood lumber, MFPL [1, 2]....................	(NA)	(NA)	(NA)	111.2	111.5	128.3	152.3	171.4	169.2
Hardwood lumber................................	131.0	167.0	185.9	196.6	187.3	221.1	219.6	230.1	215.1
Millwork...	130.4	163.8	176.4	197.2	207.0	237.2	247.6	259.5	263.5
General millwork................................	132.0	165.4	178.0	196.1	211.2	238.0	245.7	251.4	256.9
Prefabricated structural members.............	122.3	163.5	175.1	206.9	185.6	232.6	255.5	299.2	295.6
Plywood...	114.2	165.3	157.6	186.8	176.7	198.9	204.2	230.2	202.9
Softwood veneer and plywood..................	119.6	188.1	173.3	223.5	197.1	234.5	234.8	274.5	222.8
Hardwood veneer and plywood [3]..............	(NA)	(NA)	(NA)	(NA)	103.6	108.6	115.3	123.5	123.9
Other wood products..............................	114.7	143.7	130.5	139.2	142.5	161.4	160.5	169.3	176.6
Wood pallets and pallet containers............	127.6	169.7	178.5	196.3	206.6	242.1	242.2	262.8	281.1
Wood boxes.....................................	119.1	145.0	155.2	164.9	183.0	199.4	201.3	205.4	211.5
Pulp, paper, and allied products....................	**141.2**	**172.2**	**183.7**	**202.6**	**236.9**	**248.8**	**254.6**	**260.0**	**259.4**
Pulp, paper, and products, excl. building paper.....	132.9	163.4	161.4	169.8	206.8	218.4	223.9	229.7	227.3
Woodpulp.......................................	151.3	183.2	145.3	138.0	186.0	181.6	179.3	216.0	174.0
Recyclable paper................................	138.9	371.1	282.5	230.9	421.5	291.8	399.9	276.9	181.2
Paper...	128.8	159.0	149.8	159.6	182.1	189.8	186.4	197.6	200.6
Writing and printing papers.....................	129.1	158.4	146.6	156.1	179.5	183.6	176.7	188.5	197.2
Newsprint.......................................	119.6	161.8	127.5	138.5	125.6	113.6	118.5	138.5	138.8
Paperboard......................................	135.7	183.1	176.7	175.5	224.9	243.1	257.5	273.5	268.1
Converted paper and paperboard products.......	135.2	157.0	162.7	176.1	209.0	228.2	233.8	237.4	241.4
Sanitary paper products, including stock..........	135.3	144.4	146.7	154.6	181.8	182.2	181.4	179.5	182.7
Paper, plastic, and foil bags.....................	156.6	172.4	173.7	210.8	246.0	280.5	279.1	287.0	285.7
Paper boxes and containers.....................	129.9	163.8	172.6	183.7	219.4	247.3	259.5	264.8	269.5
Paperboard fiber drums......................	130.6	150.6	180.6	(NA)	293.4	354.7	391.7	414.9	433.5
Office supplies and accessories................	121.4	134.9	133.8	143.1	159.9	174.0	177.2	186.6	193.7
Die-cut paper & paperboard office supplies [1]....	(NA)	(NA)	(NA)	108.8	125.2	143.8	147.0	150.3	174.0
Fiber cans, tubes, and similar fiber products......	147.8	178.3	205.5	235.2	268.6	283.0	307.6	323.8	331.6
Building paper & building board mill products........	112.2	144.4	138.8	184.9	168.4	186.3	221.3	222.9	200.1
Hardboard, particleboard & fiberboard products. ..	107.5	139.6	132.8	176.9	158.5	175.2	209.1	210.5	188.8

NA Not available. [1] December 2003=100. [2] Made from purchased lumber. [3] December 2005=100.

Source: U.S. Bureau of Labor Statistics, "Producer Price Indexes," <http://www.bls.gov/ppi/>, accessed July 2020.

Table 929. Paper and Paperboard—Production and New Supply: 1990 to 2019

[In millions of short tons (80.55 represents 80,550,000). 1 short ton = 2,000 lbs]

Item	1990	2000	2005	2010	2015	2016	2017	2018	2019
Production, total.............................	**80.55**	**96.05**	**92.61**	**83.70**	**79.80**	**79.15**	**79.17**	**78.87**	**75.38**
Paper, total......................................	39.36	45.52	41.40	35.51	29.60	28.61	27.34	26.25	24.35
Paperboard, total................................	39.42	48.97	49.71	47.46	49.40	49.73	51.07	51.86	50.28
Recycled and unbleached Kraft board........	29.39	37.59	37.64	36.41	39.30	40.11	41.17	41.86	40.44
Recycled....................................	9.03	15.79	15.06	15.05	16.89	17.48	17.86	(NA)	(NA)
Unbleached kraft...........................	20.36	21.80	22.58	21.36	22.41	22.63	23.31	(NA)	(NA)
Semichemical...............................	5.64	5.95	6.41	5.44	4.75	4.42	4.61	4.61	4.48
Bleached kraft..............................	4.26	5.30	5.58	5.62	5.35	5.21	5.29	5.40	5.36
Wet machine board and construction grades........................	1.82	1.56	1.50	0.73	0.80	0.81	0.76	0.76	0.76
New supply, all grades, excluding products......................	**87.68**	**105.02**	**101.81**	**84.16**	**79.99**	**79.46**	**78.94**	**79.41**	**76.13**
Paper, total......................................	49.49	57.13	53.69	40.34	34.43	33.54	31.86	31.38	28.98
Newsprint.......................................	13.41	12.92	10.12	5.00	3.51	3.35	2.91	2.54	2.11
Printing/writing papers.........................	25.46	32.99	31.99	23.73	19.08	18.13	16.79	16.53	14.56
Packaging and industrial converting papers............................	4.72	4.27	4.05	4.18	4.17	4.23	4.36	4.41	4.42
Tissue...	5.90	6.95	7.54	7.43	7.68	7.83	7.80	7.90	7.88
Paperboard, total...............................	36.30	46.02	46.51	43.06	44.77	45.13	46.33	47.29	46.42

NA Not available.

Source: American Forest and Paper Association, Washington, DC, *Paper Industry Annual Statistical Summary* ©.

Table 930. Fishery Products—Domestic Catch, Imports, and Disposition: 1990 to 2018

[Live weight, in millions of pounds (16,349 represents 16,349,000,000)]

Item	1990	1995	2000	2005	2010	2015	2016	2017	2018 (P)
Total supply......	**16,349**	**16,484**	**17,340**	**20,612**	**19,748**	**21,426**	**21,542**	**22,266**	**22,103**
For human food......	12,662	13,584	14,740	18,155	17,560	18,848	18,780	19,805	19,478
For industrial use [1]......	3,687	2,900	2,600	2,457	2,188	2,579	2,762	2,461	2,625
Domestic catch......	**9,404**	**9,788**	**9,069**	**9,707**	**8,231**	**9,718**	**9,572**	**9,916**	**9,385**
For human food......	7,041	7,667	6,912	7,997	6,526	7,750	7,484	8,228	7,500
For industrial use [1]......	2,363	2,121	2,157	1,710	1,705	1,968	2,088	1,688	1,886
Imports [2]......	**6,945**	**6,696**	**8,271**	**10,905**	**11,517**	**11,709**	**11,970**	**12,350**	**12,718**
For human food......	5,621	5,917	7,828	10,158	11,034	11,098	11,295	11,577	11,979
For industrial use [1]......	1,324	779	443	747	483	611	675	773	739
Exports......	**4,627**	**5,166**	**5,758**	**8,420**	**6,129**	**8,771**	**8,675**	**8,921**	**8,468**
For human food......	3,832	4,175	4,587	6,385	5,170	6,936	6,772	6,984	6,674
For industrial use [1]......	795	991	1,171	2,035	959	1,835	1,903	1,938	1,794
Disposition of domestic catch......	**9,404**	**9,788**	**9,069**	**9,707**	**8,231**	**9,718**	**9,572**	**9,916**	**9,385**
Fresh and frozen [3]......	6,501	7,099	6,657	7,776	6,515	7,622	7,509	8,091	7,443
Canned [3]......	751	769	530	563	373	364	186	289	180
Cured......	126	90	119	160	102	65	57	136	139
Reduced to meal, oil, etc......	2,026	1,830	1,763	1,208	1,241	1,667	1,820	1,400	1,623

P Preliminary. [1] Processed into meal, oil, solubles, and shell products, or used as bait and animal food. [2] Includes landings of tuna caught by foreign vessels in American Samoa. [3] Includes for human food, and bait and animal food.

Source: U.S. National Oceanic and Atmospheric Administration, National Marine Fisheries Service, *Fisheries of the United States 2018*, February 2020, and earlier editions. See also <https://www.fisheries.noaa.gov/resource/document/fisheries-united-states-2018-report>.

Table 931. Fisheries—Quantity and Value of Domestic Catch: 1980 to 2018

[In millions of pounds (6,482 represents 6,482,000,000), except as noted]

Year	Quantity [1] (mil. lbs.) Total	For human food	For industrial products [2]	Value (mil. dol.)	Average price per lb. (cents)	Year	Quantity [1] (mil. lbs.) Total	For human food	For industrial products [2]	Value (mil. dol.)	Average price per lb. (cents)
1980......	6,482	3,654	2,828	2,237	34.5	2010......	8,231	6,526	1,705	4,520	54.9
1985......	6,258	3,294	2,964	2,326	37.2	2011......	9,858	7,909	1,949	5,289	53.7
1990......	9,404	7,041	2,363	3,522	37.5	2012......	9,634	7,477	2,157	5,103	53.0
1995......	9,788	7,667	2,121	3,770	38.5	2013......	9,870	8,043	1,827	5,466	55.4
2000......	9,069	6,912	2,157	3,550	39.1	2014......	9,486	7,828	1,658	5,448	57.4
2005......	9,707	7,997	1,710	3,942	40.6	2015......	9,718	7,750	1,968	5,203	53.5
2007......	9,309	7,490	1,819	4,192	45.0	2016......	9,572	7,484	2,088	5,312	55.5
2008......	8,325	6,633	1,692	4,383	52.6	2017......	9,916	8,228	1,688	5,421	54.7
2009......	8,031	6,198	1,833	3,891	48.4	2018 (P)..	9,385	7,500	1,886	5,571	59.4

P Preliminary. [1] Live weight. [2] Processed into meal, oil, solubles, and shell products, or used as bait and animal food.

Source: U.S. National Oceanic and Atmospheric Administration, National Marine Fisheries Service, *Fisheries of the United States 2018*, February 2020, and earlier editions. See also <https://www.fisheries.noaa.gov/resource/document/fisheries-united-states-2018-report>.

Table 932. Domestic Fish and Shellfish Catch and Value by Major Species Caught: 2000 to 2018

[In thousands (9,068,985 represents 9,068,985,000)]

Species	Quantity (1,000 lbs.) 2000	2010	2017	2018 (P)	Value ($1,000) 2000	2010	2017	2018 (P)
Total [1]......	**9,068,985**	**8,230,587**	**9,915,924**	**9,385,368**	**3,549,481**	**4,519,510**	**5,421,425**	**5,571,404**
Fish, total [1]......	**7,689,661**	**6,918,013**	**8,773,469**	**8,240,663**	**1,594,815**	**2,155,593**	**2,541,922**	**2,519,507**
Cod, Atlantic......	25,060	17,714	1,857	2,152	26,384	28,119	4,444	4,777
Cod, Pacific......	530,505	539,635	657,321	512,741	142,330	146,941	156,371	239,092
Flatfish, Atlantic and Pacific [2]......	412,723	624,358	544,866	525,070	109,910	146,243	141,228	153,235
Halibut......	75,190	56,497	26,466	21,929	143,826	206,553	125,785	89,318
Herring, Atlantic......	160,269	144,513	110,804	98,086	9,972	21,275	28,244	25,626
Herring, Pacific......	74,835	108,868	69,116	47,706	12,043	23,308	8,152	6,979
Menhaden......	1,760,498	1,471,803	1,413,104	1,581,578	112,403	107,193	125,495	161,088
Pollock, Alaska......	2,606,802	1,947,580	3,388,620	3,363,901	160,525	282,399	413,273	451,180
Salmon......	628,638	787,740	1,008,198	575,972	270,213	554,816	687,770	598,067
Tuna......	50,779	48,047	54,904	51,684	95,176	108,453	154,392	149,053
Whiting (Atlantic, silver)......	26,855	17,564	11,800	11,393	11,370	10,862	9,009	9,630
Whiting (Pacific, hake)......	452,718	355,272	773,885	686,598	18,809	27,316	60,373	53,705
Shellfish, total [1]......	**1,379,324**	**1,276,366**	**1,108,041**	**1,107,717**	**1,954,666**	**2,341,902**	**2,855,955**	**3,026,945**
Clams......	118,482	88,891	84,883	85,670	153,973	200,657	210,755	244,107
Crabs......	299,006	349,604	274,578	289,021	405,006	572,797	610,377	644,912
Lobsters: American......	83,180	115,433	132,973	146,176	301,300	396,757	552,057	624,228
Oysters......	41,146	28,080	31,805	30,304	90,667	117,590	236,418	258,748
Scallops, sea......	32,747	57,454	51,461	57,880	164,609	455,088	506,531	532,294
Shrimp......	332,486	258,972	283,272	289,178	690,453	413,980	530,977	496,114
Squid, Pacific......	259,508	286,403	137,482	79,730	27,077	70,706	68,635	39,351

P Preliminary. [1] Includes other species not shown separately. [2] Includes flounders, soles, and other flatfish. Excludes halibut.

Source: U.S. National Oceanic and Atmospheric Administration, National Marine Fisheries Service, *Fisheries of the United States 2018*, February 2020, and earlier editions. See also <https://www.fisheries.noaa.gov/resource/document/fisheries-united-states-2018-report>.

Table 933. U.S. Private Aquaculture—Trout and Catfish Production and Value: 1990 to 2019

[67.8 represents 67,800,000. Data are for calendar year and foodsize fish (trout at least 12 inches long; catfish weighing at least three quarters of a pound)]

Item	Unit	1990	1995	2000	2005	2010	2017	2018	2019
TROUT FOODSIZE									
Number sold.............................	Mil.	67.8	60.2	58.4	55.6	38.7	41.0	35.9	32.4
Total weight.............................	Mil. lb.	56.8	55.6	59.0	59.9	45.3	53.9	47.5	43.8
Total value of sales..................	Mil. dol.	64.6	60.8	63.3	63.5	63.2	102.7	91.8	85.8
Avg. price received by processors....	Dol./lb.	1.14	1.09	1.07	1.06	1.40	1.91	1.93	1.96
Percent sold to processors...........	Percent	58.0	68.0	69.7	66.0	63.4	59.4	57.2	54.9
CATFISH FOODSIZE									
Number sold.............................	Mil.	272.9	321.8	420.1	395.6	263.4	199.8	208.6	196.4
Total weight.............................	Mil. lb.	392.4	481.5	633.8	605.5	478.9	330.4	343.6	348.0
Total value of sales..................	Mil. dol.	305.1	378.1	468.8	427.8	375.1	355.4	335.0	362.0
Avg. price received by processors....	Dol./lb.	0.78	0.79	0.74	0.71	0.78	1.08	0.97	1.04

Source: U.S. Department of Agriculture, National Agricultural Statistics Service, *Trout Production*, February 2020, and *Catfish Production*, February 2020. See also <https://www.nass.usda.gov/Publications/Reports_by_Release_Day/index.php>.

Table 934. Supply of Selected Shellfish and Fish Products: 1990 to 2018

[In millions of pounds (734 represents 734,000,000). Totals available for U.S. consumption are supply minus exports plus imports. Round weight is the complete or full weight as caught]

Species	Unit	1990	1995	2000	2005	2010	2015	2016	2017	2018 (P)
Shrimp..................	Heads-off weight	734	832	1,173	1,559	1,739	1,797	1,819	2,053	2,155
Tuna, canned...........	Canned weight	856	875	980	895	834	704	671	670	365
Snow crab..............	Round weight	37	42	122	171	197	239	205	194	74
Clams..................	Meat weight	152	144	133	120	105	105	109	101	103
Salmon, canned [1].....	Canned weight	148	147	95	123	73	101	-11	92	33
American lobster.......	Round weight	95	94	125	144	186	222	230	198	195
Spiny lobster..........	Round weight	89	89	99	83	60	13	28	46	46
Scallops...............	Meat weight	74	62	78	86	85	62	68	71	87
Oysters................	Meat weight	56	63	71	65	57	57	64	66	72
King crab..............	Round weight	19	21	41	78	44	53	50	46	50
Crab meat, canned....	Canned weight	9	12	29	59	66	63	61	64	71

P Preliminary. [1] The method of calculating canned salmon supply does not incorporate annual beginning and ending warehouse stock. Due to the biennial nature of the pink salmon fishery, some salmon canned in one year may be exported in the following year.

Source: U.S. National Oceanic and Atmospheric Administration, National Marine Fisheries Service, *Fisheries of the United States 2018*, February 2020, and earlier editions. See also <https://www.fisheries.noaa.gov/resource/document/fisheries-united-states-2018-report>.

Table 935. Canned, Fresh, and Frozen Fishery Products—Production and Value: 1990 to 2018

[Production in millions of pounds (1,178 represents 1,178,000,000); value in millions of dollars (1,562 represents $1,562,000,000)]

Product	Production (mil. lbs.)					Value (mil. dol.)				
	1990	2000	2010	2017	2018 (P)	1990	2000	2010	2017	2018 (P)
Canned, total.....................	**1,178**	**1,747**	**956**	**856**	**665**	**1,562**	**1,626**	**1,414**	**1,342**	**1,219**
Tuna.................................	581	671	395	334	346	902	856	724	678	776
Salmon...............................	196	171	146	134	66	366	288	356	310	186
Clam products........................	110	127	110	63	64	76	120	98	106	107
Sardines, Maine......................	13	(Z)	(D)	(NA)	(NA)	17	(Z)	(D)	(NA)	(NA)
Shrimp...............................	1	2	(D)	(D)	(D)	3	11	(D)	(D)	(D)
Crab [1].............................	1	(Z)	1	(Z)	(Z)	4	(Z)	8	1	(Z)
Oysters [2]...........................	1	(Z)	(D)	(D)	(D)	1	1	(D)	(D)	(D)
Other................................	275	776	303	324	189	193	350	228	248	150
Fish fillets and steaks [3].........	**441**	**368**	**585**	**800**	**751**	**843**	**823**	**1,486**	**2,177**	**2,189**
Cod..................................	65	56	49	72	62	132	167	131	318	332
Flounder.............................	54	27	32	12	10	154	71	53	50	44
Haddock..............................	7	6	23	11	8	24	24	89	53	42
Ocean perch, Atlantic................	1	(Z)	1	1	2	1	1	3	4	8
Rockfish.............................	33	11	2	3	3	53	25	6	9	9
Pollock, Atlantic....................	12	2	2	10	1	21	4	7	16	3
Pollock, Alaska......................	164	160	290	455	442	174	178	368	583	608
Other................................	105	106	186	235	223	284	353	829	1,146	1,143

P Preliminary. NA Not available. D Figure withheld to avoid disclosure pertaining to a specific organization or individual. Data is included in "other". Z Less than 500,000 pounds or $500,000. [1] Includes crab meat specialties. [2] Includes oyster specialties. [3] Fresh and frozen.

Source: U.S. National Oceanic and Atmospheric Administration, National Marine Fisheries Service, *Fisheries of the United States 2018*, February 2020, and earlier editions. See also <https://www.fisheries.noaa.gov/resource/document/fisheries-united-states-2018-report>.

Table 936. Mineral and Mining Industries—Employment, Hours, and Earnings: 1990 to 2019

[In thousands (680 represents 680,000), except as noted. Industries based on North American Classification System (NAICS) 2017. Based on the Current Employment Statistics Program, see Appendix III]

Industry and item	Unit	1990	1995	2000	2005	2010	2015	2018	2019
All mining: [1]									
All employees..........................	1,000	680	558	520	562	655	760	678	685
Production workers...................	1,000	469	391	383	419	483	550	499	497
Avg. weekly hours..................	Number	46.1	46.8	45.5	46.4	44.8	46.1	47	47
Avg. weekly earnings..............	Dollars	630	711	770	884	1,086	1,238	1,361	1,442
Oil and gas extraction:									
All employees..........................	1,000	190	152	125	126	159	193	142	150
Production workers...................	1,000	84	73	67	72	89	108	79	85
Avg. weekly hours..................	Number	44.4	43.6	41.3	44.3	39.0	43.9	43	44
Avg. weekly earnings..............	Dollars	591	677	802	856	1,066	1,323	1,534	1,655
Coal mining:									
All employees..........................	1,000	136	97	72	74	81	64	52	52
Production workers...................	1,000	110	78	59	61	70	54	44	(NA)
Avg. weekly hours..................	Number	44.7	45.7	45.6	48.5	48.4	45.3	47	(NA)
Avg. weekly earnings..............	Dollars	822	929	945	1,071	1,366	1,386	1,440	(NA)
Metal ore mining:									
All employees..........................	1,000	53	48	38	29	37	42	42	42
Production workers...................	1,000	43	39	29	22	28	(NA)	(NA)	(NA)
Avg. weekly hours..................	Number	42.5	43.4	43.4	44.2	42.5	(NA)	(NA)	(NA)
Avg. weekly earnings..............	Dollars	646	788	871	1,001	1,158	(NA)	(NA)	(NA)
Nonmetallic minerals mining, and quarrying									
All employees..........................	1,000	113	108	115	110	87	92	98	98
Production workers...................	1,000	85	81	87	84	65	(NA)	(NA)	(NA)
Avg. weekly hours..................	Number	45.0	46.3	46.1	45.9	43.8	(NA)	(NA)	(NA)
Avg. weekly earnings..............	Dollars	532	632	722	830	848	(NA)	(NA)	(NA)

NA Not available. [1] Includes other industries not shown separately.

Source: U.S. Bureau of Labor Statistics, Current Employment Statistics, "Employment, Hours, and Earnings—National," <https://www.bls.gov/ces/data.htm>, accessed June 2020.

Table 937. Mine Safety: 2010 to 2019

[In units, as indicated. Calendar year data]

Item	Total			Coal			Metal and non-metal		
	2010	2018	2019	2010	2018	2019	2010	2018	2019
Number of mines.........................	14,283	13,077	12,982	1,941	1,192	1,137	12,342	11,885	11,845
Number of miners........................	362,028	332,272	331,714	136,062	82,857	81,494	225,966	249,415	250,220
Fatalities (number)......................	72	28	27	48	12	12	24	16	15
Fatal injury rate [1]......................	0.024	0.010	0.010	0.038	0.016	0.016	0.013	0.008	0.007
All injury rate [1].........................	2.83	2.05	2.04	3.47	2.88	2.92	2.38	1.74	1.72
Total mining area inspection hours per mine [2]................	63	52	50	259	240	235	23	23	23
Citations and orders [3]................	170,031	97,492	99,386	96,331	46,727	43,635	73,700	50,765	55,751
S&S citations and orders [4] (percent).....	32	20	19	32	21	19	31	20	20
Amount assessed [5] (mil. dol.)...........	162.3	55.0	53.2	110.2	31.9	26.8	52.1	23.1	26.3
Coal production (mil. tons)................	1,086	756	706	1,086	756	706	(X)	(X)	(X)

X Not applicable. [1] Reported injury rates per 200,000 employees. [2] Total Mining Area Time includes: On-site Inspection Time (metal/non-metal), MMU Pit Time (Coal), Outby Area Time (Coal), Surface Area Time (Coal), Citation/Order writing On-Site. On-site inspection hours represent hours entered by Authorized Representatives of the Secretary (AR) for certain inspection activities and task codes. [3] Citations and orders are those not vacated. [4] A violation that "significantly and substantially" contributes to the cause and effect of a coal or other mine safety or health hazard. [5] Government penalties or fines.

Source: U.S. Mine Safety and Health Administration, Office of Program Education and Outreach Services, "Mine Safety and Health At a Glance," <https://www.msha.gov/msha-glance>, accessed August 2020.

Table 938. Mining and Primary Metal Production Indexes: 1990 to 2019

[Index 2012=100]

Industry group	NAICS [1] code	1990	1995	2000	2005	2010	2015	2017	2018	2019
Mining [2]............................	**21**	**92.2**	**89.9**	**88.8**	**84.0**	**87.2**	**113.9**	**110.1**	**123.8**	**132.7**
Oil and gas extraction [2]..............	211	87.7	85.3	82.9	76.0	85.6	134.1	135.0	155.8	172.7
Crude oil and natural gas...........	211111	89.5	86.1	83.0	76.3	85.5	134.2	134.3	154.9	171.8
Coal mining..........................	2121	108.4	106.7	109.4	113.1	106.9	86.9	74.9	73.6	68.8
Metal ore mining.....................	2122	110.3	120.7	117.1	102.0	97.1	99.9	98.0	93.4	93.0
Iron ore.............................	21221	106.6	118.1	118.5	102.1	93.4	85.3	88.7	95.5	90.5
Gold ore and silver ore..............	21222	127.7	136.6	152.2	110.0	99.6	91.9	100.8	88.4	88.0
Copper, nickel, lead, and zinc.......	21223	122.5	140.5	122.6	99.0	96.0	116.8	106.8	105.0	105.0
Oil and gas drilling...................	213111	65.3	49.8	60.2	75.8	71.5	77.3	65.2	75.8	71.0
Primary metal manufacturing [2]......	**331**	**91.3**	**100.5**	**105.0**	**99.1**	**95.1**	**96.8**	**93.7**	**97.6**	**96.9**
Iron and steel........................	3311, 3312	86.0	95.5	99.8	96.6	91.8	91.6	91.7	96.6	96.8
Aluminum............................	3313	99.1	95.6	101.2	103.9	89.0	107.1	102.6	107.0	107.5
Nonferrous metals [2]................	3314	88.7	100.8	90.6	80.4	108.2	98.2	91.3	90.8	88.1

[1] Based on the 2012 North American Industry Classification System (NAICS). [2] Includes other industries not shown separately.

Source: Board of Governors of the Federal Reserve System, "Industrial Production and Capacity Utilization, Statistical Release G.17," <http://www.federalreserve.gov/datadownload/default.htm>, accessed July 2020.

Table 939. Mineral Production: 1990 to 2018

[In units as indicated (1,029.1 represents 1,029,100,000). Data represent production as measured by mine shipments, mine sales, or marketable production. See Appendix IV for information on weights and measures]

Minerals and metals	Unit	1990	2000	2010	2015	2018
FUEL MINERALS						
Coal, total	Mil. short tons	1,029.1	1,073.6	1,084.4	896.9	756.2
Bituminous	Mil. short tons	693.2	574.3	489.5	404.4	357.2
Subbituminous	Mil. short tons	244.3	409.2	514.8	419.5	340.0
Lignite	Mil. short tons	88.1	85.6	78.2	70.9	57.0
Anthracite	Mil. short tons	3.5	4.6	1.8	2.1	1.9
Natural gas (marketed production)	Tril. cu. ft.	18.6	20.2	22.4	28.8	32.8
Petroleum (crude)	Mil. barrels [1]	2,685	2,131	2,002	3,445	4,012
Uranium concentrate (recoverable content)	Mil. lb.	8.9	4.0	4.2	3.3	1.4
NONFUEL MINERALS						
Asbestos (sales)	1,000 metric tons	(D)	5	–	–	–
Barite, primary, sold/used by producers	1,000 metric tons	430	392	662	433	366
Boron minerals, sold or used by producers	1,000 metric tons	1,090	1,070	(D)	(D)	(D)
Bromine, sold or used by producers	1,000 metric tons	177	228	(D)	(D)	(D)
Cement [2]	Mil. metric tons	(NA)	(NA)	66.4	84.4	86.4
Clays	1,000 metric tons	42,900	40,800	25,600	25,500	26,400
Diatomite	1,000 metric tons	631	677	595	832	957
Feldspar	1,000 metric tons	630	790	500	520	550
Fluorspar, finished shipments	1,000 metric tons	64	–	(NA)	(NA)	(NA)
Garnet (industrial)	1,000 metric tons	47	60	53	77	101
Gypsum, crude	Mil. metric tons	15	20	10	19	21
Helium [3]	Mil. cu. meters	65	98	75	71	64
Lime, sold or used by producers [4]	Mil. metric tons	16	20	18	18	18
Mica, scrap/flake, sold or used by producers	1,000 metric tons	109	101	56	33	44
Peat, sales by producers	1,000 metric tons	721	847	628	455	479
Perlite, processed, sold or used	1,000 metric tons	576	672	414	444	[7] 460
Phosphate rock, marketable	Mil. metric tons	46	39	26	27	26
Potash (K2O equivalent), marketable	1,000 metric tons	1,710	1,300	930	740	520
Pumice & pumicite, sold and used	1,000 metric tons	443	1,050	241	310	496
Salt [2]	Mil. metric tons	37	46	43	45	[7] 41
Sand & gravel:						
Construction	Mil. metric tons	829	1,120	807	880	937
Industrial	Mil. metric tons	26	28	32	102	121
Soda ash (sodium carbonate)	1,000 metric tons	9,100	10,200	10,600	11,600	11,900
Stone:						
Crushed and broken	Mil. metric tons	1,110	1,560	1,160	1,340	1,420
Dimension [4]	1,000 metric tons	1,120	1,250	1,670	2,700	2,650
Sulfur: total shipments	1,000 metric tons	11,500	10,700	9,170	9,560	9,690
Talc and pyrophyllite, crude [5]	1,000 metric tons	1,270	851	604	615	[7] 650
Vermiculite concentrate	1,000 metric tons	209	150	100	100	100
METALS						
Aluminum	1,000 metric tons	4,048	3,668	1,726	1,587	891
Copper (recoverable content)	1,000 metric tons	1,590	1,450	1,110	1,380	1,220
Gold (recoverable content)	Metric tons	294	353	231	214	226
Iron ore, usable (gross weight)	Mil. metric tons	57	61	50	46	50
Lead (recoverable content)	1,000 metric tons	484	449	369	370	280
Magnesium metal	1,000 metric tons	139	(D)	(D)	(D)	(D)
Molybdenum, mine	1,000 metric tons	62	41	59	47	41
Nickel ore, refinery byproduct	1,000 metric tons	330	(D)	(D)	(D)	(D)
Palladium metal	Kilograms	5,930	10,300	11,600	12,500	14,300
Platinum metal	Kilograms	1,810	3,110	3,450	3,670	4,160
Silicon (Si content) [6]	1,000 metric tons	418	367	176	411	430
Silver (recoverable content)	Metric tons	2,120	1,860	1,280	1,090	934
Titanium concentrate, (TiO2 content)	1,000 metric tons	(D)	300	200	200	100
Vanadium (recoverable content)	Metric tons	2,310	–	1,060	–	–
Zinc, ore and concentrate	1,000 metric tons	508	796	748	825	824

NA Not available. D Withheld to avoid disclosing individual company data. – Represents or rounds to zero. [1] 42-gallon barrels. [2] Excludes Puerto Rico. [3] Extracted from natural gas. Both grade A and crude helium. [4] Includes Puerto Rico. [5] After 1990, includes only talc. [6] For 2006-2010, ferrosilicon only; silicon metal withheld to avoid disclosing proprietary data. Beginning in 2011, silicon alloys and metal. Beginning 2012, includes statistics for ferrosilicon and silicon metal containing less than 99.9% silicon. [7] Estimated.

Source: Nonfuels, through 1994, U.S. Bureau of Mines; thereafter, U.S. Geological Survey, *Mineral Commodity Summaries 2020*, January 2020, and earlier reports; see also <https://www.usgs.gov/centers/nmic/publications>. Fuels, U.S. Energy Information Administration, *Annual Energy Review 2011,* September 2012, and earlier reports; *Annual Coal Report, 2018*, October 2019; and "Natural Gas Gross Withdrawals and Production," <https://www.eia.gov/naturalgas/data.php>, "Uranium & Nuclear Fuel Summary Production Statistics," <https://www.eia.gov/nuclear/data.php>, and "Crude Oil Production," <https://www.eia.gov/petroleum/data.php>, accessed August 2020.

Table 940. Nonfuel Mineral Commodities—Summary: 2018

[1,570 represents 1,570,000. Except as noted, data are for mine or crude production, and average price or value are in dollars per metric ton]

Mineral	Unit	Mineral disposition				Average price per unit (dollars)	Employ- ment (number)
		Produc- tion	Exports	Net import reliance [1,2] (percent)	Con- sumption, apparent		
Alumina (metal equivalent)........	1,000 metric tons	1,570	288	44	2,800	[3] 592	[21] 31,600
Aluminum........................	1,000 metric tons	891	3,100	49	4,860	[4] 1.15	[21] 31,600
Antimony (contained)............	Metric tons	–	[5] 2,256	84	28,400	[4] 3.88	27
Asbestos.........................	Metric tons	(NA)	–	100	681	1,670	(NA)
Barite............................	1,000 metric tons	366	67	87	2,760	[6] 176	440
Bauxite (metal equiv.)............	1,000 metric tons	(D)	17	>75	(D)	[7] 31	(NA)
Beryllium (contained).............	Metric tons	165	30	18	202	[8] 590	(NA)
Bismuth (contained)..............	Metric tons	–	653	96	1,900	[4] 4.64	(NA)
Boron (B2O3 content)............	1,000 metric tons	(D)	[9] 260	([10])	(D)	[11] 404	1,350
Bromine (contained).............	Metric tons	(D)	[12] 56,200	<25	(D)	[27] 2.21	1,100
Cadmium (contained)............	Metric tons	(D)	[13] 273	<50	(D)	[8,14] 2.89	(NA)
Cement..........................	1,000 metric tons	[15] 86,368	940	14	98,480	[7] 121	12,300
Chromium........................	1,000 metric tons	[16] 143	230	73	538	[7,17] 279	(NA)
Clays............................	1,000 metric tons	[18] 26,400	4,030	([10])	22,800	(NA)	5,470
Cobalt (contained)...............	Metric tons	[19] 2,740	6,960	64	7,580	[4] 37.43	(NA)
Copper (mine, recoverable).....	1,000 metric tons	1,220	253	33	1,820	[4] 2.99	11,700
Diamond, stones (industrial).....	Million carats	–	–	88	1.1	[20] 7.60	(NA)
Diatomite.........................	1,000 metric tons	957	68	([10])	898	[7] 330	370
Feldspar.........................	1,000 metric tons	550	4	24	720	[7] 97	240
Fluorspar........................	1,000 metric tons	(NA)	9	100	450	[7,11] 258	3
Garnet (industrial)...............	Metric tons	101,000	14,200	70	341,000	210	170
Gemstones.......................	Million dollars	[22] 59.5	[23] 1,850	99	25,900	(NA)	1,120
Germanium (contained)..........	Kilograms	(D)	4,880	>50	30,000	[8] 1,543	(NA)
Gold (contained).................	Metric tons	226	474	([10])	160	[24] 1,272	12,200
Graphite (natural)................	Metric tons	–	10,400	100	60,300	[25] 1,520	(NA)
Gypsum (crude)..................	1,000 metric tons	21,100	36	12	42,900	8.3	4,500
Iodine............................	Metric tons	(D)	1,190	>50	(D)	[27] 22.46	60
Iron ore (usable).................	Million metric tons	49,500	1,300	([10])	41,200	93	4,860
Iron and steel scrap (metal).....	Million metric tons	[28] 64.8	17	([10])	52	[7] 323	27,000
Iron and steel slag (metal).......	Million metric tons	17	(Z)	13	17	[7] 26.5	1,500
Lead (contained).................	1,000 metric tons	280	251	30	1,630	[4] 1.1	1,870
Lime.............................	1,000 metric tons	[30] 18,100	422	([10])	18,000	[7,30] 124.6	(NA)
Lithium...........................	Metric tons	(D)	1,660	>50	3,000	17,000	70
Magnesium compounds..........	1,000 metric tons	[26] 405	116	52	840	(NA)	270
Magnesium metal................	1,000 metric tons	(D)	11	<50	(D)	[4] 2.17	400
Manganese (gross weight).......	1,000 metric tons	–	3	100	793	[31] 7.17	(NA)
Mercury [32].....................	Metric tons	(NA)	–	(NA)	(NA)	[33] 1,100	(NA)
Mica, scrap and flake............	Metric tons	44,000	6,000	33	66,100	122	(NA)
Molybdenum (contained)........	Metric tons	41,400	48,400	([10])	31,400	[8] 27.04	940
Nickel (contained) [34]...........	Metric tons	[44] 17,600	76,980	52	259,000	[7] 13,114	(NA)
Niobium (columbium)............	Metric tons	–	955	100	10,100	[8] 21	(NA)
Nitrogen (fixed)-ammonia.........	1,000 metric tons	13,100	281	14	15,200	[35] 281	1,600
Peat.............................	1,000 metric tons	479	37	71	1,670	[7] 25.88	540
Perlite............................	1,000 metric tons	510	16	30	620	[7] 72	130
Phosphate rock..................	1,000 metric tons	25,800	(NA)	2	26,000	70.77	2,000
Platinum-group metals...........	Kilograms	[36] 18,460	[36] 72,200	[37] 74	[36] 149,700	[24,37] 882.66	1,628
Potash (K2O equivalent).........	1,000 metric tons	520	105	92	6,100	[38] 750	900
Pumice and pumicite............	1,000 metric tons	496	11	23	644	[7] 32	140
Salt..............................	1,000 metric tons	41,000	986	30	57,000	[39] 220	4,100
Silicon, metal....................	1,000 metric tons	[40] 430	45	<50	(D)	[4] 1.34	(NA)
Silver (contained)................	Metric tons	934	602	67	6,090	[24] 15.75	961
Soda ash (sodium carbonate)....	1,000 metric tons	11,900	6,960	([10])	4,980	[41] 134.89	2,600
Stone (crushed)..................	Million metric tons	1,420	(Z)	1	1,480	11.86	68,500
Sulfur (all forms).................	1,000 metric tons	9,680	2,502	7	10,400	[42] 70	2,400
Talc..............................	1,000 metric tons	650	273	7	590	226	208
Thallium (contained).............	Kilograms	–	32,353	(NA)	64	(NA)	(NA)
Tin (contained)...................	Metric tons	[19] 11,200	7,817	78	47,000	[4] 9.36	(NA)
Titanium dioxide..................	1,000 metric tons	1,150,000	529,000	([10])	893,000	(NA)	3,050
Tungsten (contained)............	Metric tons	[19] (D)	3,494	>50	(D)	[43] 326	(NA)
Vermiculite.......................	1,000 metric tons	100	14	20	120	[7] 140–575	65
Zinc (contained).................	1,000 metric tons	824	806	([10])	868	[4] 1.32	2,880
Zirconium (ZrO2).................	Metric tons	100,000	79,206	([10])	50,000	[29] 1,290	(NA)

– Represents or rounds to zero. < Less than. > Greater than. D Withheld to avoid disclosing company proprietary data. NA Not available. Z Less than .05 million metric tons or less than half a unit shown. [1] Net imports calculated as imports minus exports and may include adjustments for industry stock changes. [2] Calculated as percent of apparent consumption. [3] Alumina, average value, U.S. imports (f.a.s.). [4] Dollars per pound. [5] Ore and concentrates not included. [6] Estimated price, ground, average value, dollars per ton, ex-works. [7] Dollars per ton. [8] Dollars per kilogram. [9] Boric acid, gross weight. [10] Net exporter. [11] Average value of imports (cost, insurance, and freight, c.i.f.). [12] Elemental bromine and compounds. [13] Unwrought cadmium and powders. [14] Average free market price for 99.95% purity in 10-ton lots; cost, insurance, and freight; global ports. Source: Metal Bulletin. [15] Production for Portland and masonry cement includes cement made from imported clinker; excludes Puerto Rico. [16] Recycling production. [17] Unit value of imported chromite ore; dollars per metric ton gross weight. [18] Excludes attapulgite. [19] Secondary production. [20] Value of imports, dollars per carat. [21] Alumina and aluminum production workers. Source: U.S. Department of Labor, Bureau of Labor Statistics. [22] Natural gemstone production, 9.5 million dollars; laboratory-created (synthetic) gemstone production, 50 million dollars. [23] Includes reexports. [24] Dollars per troy ounce. [25] Price of flake imports (average at foreign ports). Graphite lump/chip (Sri Lankan) price, $1,890 per ton. [26] Magnesium compounds shipments. [27] Average value of imports (c.i.f.), dollars per kilogram. [28] Iron and steel scrap production includes receipts for purchased scrap. Exports excludes rails for rerolling and other uses, and ships, boats, and other vessels for scrapping. [29] Unit value based on annual imports for consumption from Australia, Senegal, and South Africa. [30] Lime production data are sold or used by producers. Price data are for quicklime only. [31] 46% to 48% Mn metallurgical ore, per metric ton unit, contained Mn; cost, insurance, and freight (c.i.f.) value, U.S. ports. [32] Mercury not produced as principal commodity in U.S. since 1992; secondary production (recycled) not reported. [33] Dollars per 76-pound flask. [34] Primary and secondary materials. [35] Dollars per short ton, average, f.o.b. Gulf Coast. [36] Platinum and palladium. [37] Platinum. [38] Dollars per ton of K2O, all products. [39] Vacuum and open pan, bulk, pellets and packaged, f.o.b. mine and plant. [40] Combined for ferrosilicon and silicon metal. [41] Dollars per short ton, f.o.b., mine or plant. [42] Elemental sulfur, f.o.b., mine or plant. [43] A metric ton unit of tungsten trioxide (WO3) contains 7.93 kilograms of tungsten. Platts Metals Week. [44] Mine production only.

Source: U.S. Geological Survey, *Mineral Commodity Summaries 2020*, January 2020. See also <https://www.usgs.gov/centers/nmic/mineral-commodity-summaries>.

Table 941. Selected Fuel and Nonfuel Mineral Products—Average Prices: 1990 to 2019

Year	Nonfuel minerals									Fuels		
	Copper, cathode (cents/ lb.)	Plati– num [1] (dol./troy oz.)	Gold (dol./troy oz.) [2]	Silver (dol./troy oz.) [2]	Lead [3] (cents/ lb.)	Nickel [4] (cents/ lb.)	Tin (New York) [4] (cents/ lb.)	Zinc [5] (cents/ lb.)	Sulfur, crude [6] (dol./ metric ton)	Bituminous coal [7] (dol./ short ton)	Crude petrol– eum [7] (dol./ bbl.)	Natural gas [8] (dol./ 1,000 cu. ft.)
1990.........	123	467	385	4.82	46	402	386	75	80	27.43	20.03	3.03
1995.........	138	425	386	5.15	42	373	416	56	44	25.56	14.62	2.78
2000.........	88	549	280	5.00	44	392	370	56	25	24.15	26.72	4.62
2001.........	77	533	272	4.39	44	270	315	44	10	25.36	21.84	5.72
2002.........	76	543	311	4.62	44	307	292	39	12	26.57	22.51	4.12
2003.........	85	694	365	4.91	44	437	340	41	29	26.57	27.56	5.85
2004.........	134	849	411	6.69	55	627	547	52	33	30.56	36.77	6.65
2005.........	174	900	446	7.34	61	669	483	67	31	36.80	50.28	8.67
2006.........	315	1,144	606	11.61	77	1,100	565	159	33	39.32	59.69	8.61
2007.........	328	1,308	699	13.43	124	1,688	899	154	36	40.80	66.52	8.16
2008.........	319	1,578	874	15.00	120	957	1,129	89	264	51.39	94.04	9.18
2009.........	241	1,208	975	14.69	87	665	837	78	2	55.44	56.35	6.48
2010.........	348	1,616	1,228	20.20	109	989	1,240	102	70	60.88	74.71	6.18
2011.........	406	1,725	1,572	35.28	122	1,038	1,575	106	160	68.50	95.73	5.63
2012.........	367	1,555	1,673	31.22	114	795	1,283	96	124	66.04	94.52	4.73
2013.........	340	1,490	1,415	23.89	110	681	1,352	96	69	60.61	95.99	4.88
2014.........	318	1,388	1,269	19.09	106	765	1,023	107	80	55.99	87.39	5.71
2015.........	256	1,056	1,163	15.72	91	537	756	96	88	51.57	44.39	4.26
2016.........	225	990	1,252	17.20	94	435	839	101	38	48.40	38.29	3.71
2017.........	285	951	1,261	17.07	115	472	937	139	46	55.60	48.05	4.16
2018.........	299	883	1,272	15.75	111	598	936	141	70	59.43	61.40	4.23
2019 [9].......	280	850	1,400	16.20	100	630	860	125	50	(NA)	55.59	3.80

NA Not available. [1] Average annual dealer prices. [2] 99.95 percent purity. [3] North American delivered basis. 1990-2012, North American producer price. Beginning 2013, North American market price. [4] Nickel: London Metal Exchange. Tin: Metals Week composite. [5] Platt's Metals Week price for North American special high grade zinc. Average prices for 1990 are for U.S. high grade zinc. [6] F.o.b. (Free on Board) works. [7] Average value at the point of production or domestic first purchase price. [8] Citygate price. Citygate is a point or measuring station at which a distributing gas utility receives gas from a natural gas pipeline company or transmission system. [9] Estimated.

Source: Nonfuels, through 1994, U.S. Bureau of Mines; thereafter, U.S. Geological Survey, *Mineral Commodity Summaries 2020*, January 2020 and earlier reports. Fuels, U.S. Energy Information Administration, *Monthly Energy Review*, July 2020 and earlier reports; and *Annual Coal Report, 2018*, October 2019 and earlier reports. See also <usgs.gov/centers/nmic/mineral-commodity-summaries> and <eia.gov/totalenergy/data/monthly/>.

Table 942. Value of Domestic Nonfuel Mineral Production by State: 2000 to 2019

[In millions of dollars (39,400 represents $39,400,000,000)]

State	2000	2010	2018 [1]	2019 [1]	State	2000	2010	2018 [1]	2019 [1]
United States [2]........	39,400	66,400	82,200	86,300					
Alabama...................	930	969	1,450	1,690	Montana.............	596	1,140	1,130	1,280
Alaska....................	1,140	3,400	3,440	3,130	Nebraska.............	[3] 84	234	[3] 209	[3] 214
Arizona..................	2,510	6,790	6,690	6,970	Nevada...............	2,980	7,700	7,880	8,190
Arkansas.................	484	709	903	901	New Hampshire......	[3] 57	[3] 94	162	156
California................	3,270	2,890	4,560	4,490	New Jersey..........	[3] 291	[3] 258	295	377
Colorado.................	592	1,850	1,380	1,790	New Mexico..........	786	1,020	1,160	1,090
Connecticut..............	[3] 112	[3] 148	[3] 200	[3] 191	New York............	1,020	1,310	1,790	1,870
Delaware.................	[3] 14	[3] 12	[3] 31	[3] 30	North Carolina......	744	880	[3] 1,210	[3] 1,420
Florida...................	1,820	2,680	3,550	3,370	North Dakota........	35	[3] 70	[3] 136	[3] 58
Georgia..................	1,620	1,430	1,960	2,170	Ohio...............	999	1,170	[3] 1,200	1,400
Hawaii...................	[3] 92	106	141	134	Oklahoma...........	473	702	894	1,070
Idaho....................	358	1,180	[3] 208	[3] 185	Oregon.............	299	312	530	499
Illinois..................	913	924	[3] 1,780	[3] 1,470	Pennsylvania........	[3] 1,250	[3] 1,670	[3] 1,920	[3] 2,100
Indiana...................	695	782	1,060	695	Rhode Island........	[3] 20	[3] 33	[3] 56	[3] 54
Iowa.....................	503	583	[3] 680	[3] 836	South Carolina......	[3] 551	[3] 468	[3] 1,050	[3] 1,140
Kansas...................	629	1,090	[3] 672	[3] 1,070	South Dakota.......	233	258	339	312
Kentucky.................	501	762	[3] 513	[3] 591	Tennessee..........	737	831	1,460	1,420
Louisiana................	325	549	[3] 536	[3] 614	Texas...............	1,950	2,780	6,030	6,470
Maine....................	96	110	[3] 135	[3] 102	Utah................	1,430	4,380	2,940	3,320
Maryland.................	[3] 358	[3] 305	[3] 410	[3] 575	Vermont.............	[3] 67	[3] 121	[3] 104	[3] 95
Massachusetts..........	[3] 200	[3] 233	[3] 340	[3] 289	Virginia.............	710	1,040	1,290	1,520
Michigan.................	1,640	2,190	2,470	2,750	Washington..........	607	712	1,090	869
Minnesota...............	1,460	[3] 4,180	[3] 4,050	[3] 5,300	West Virginia.......	172	272	[3] 263	[3] 332
Mississippi..............	149	198	404	504	Wisconsin...........	[3] 372	509	[3] 2,730	[3] 1,950
Missouri..................	1,370	2,010	2,930	3,050	Wyoming.............	978	1,860	2,410	2,630

[1] Preliminary. [2] Includes data not distributed to States, not shown separately. [3] Partial data only; excludes values withheld to avoid disclosing individual company data.

Source: U.S. Geological Survey, *Minerals Yearbook, 2016*, March 2020, and earlier reports; and *Mineral Commodities Summaries 2020*, January 2020, and earlier reports. See also <http://minerals.er.usgs.gov/minerals/pubs/mcs/>.

Table 943. Net U.S. Imports of Selected Minerals and Metals as Percent of Apparent Consumption: 1980 to 2019

[In percent. Net imports are the difference between imports and exports plus or minus government stockpile and industry stock changes]

Minerals and metals	1980	1990	2000	2005	2010	2015	2017	2018	2019 [1]
Fluorspar	87	91	100	100	100	100	100	100	100
Manganese	98	100	100	100	100	100	100	100	100
Niobium	100	100	100	100	100	100	100	100	100
Strontium	100	100	100	100	100	100	100	100	100
Tantalum	90	86	80	100	100	100	100	100	100
Mica (sheet)	100	100	100	100	100	100	100	100	100
Vanadium	35	(D)	100	100	82	100	100	100	94
Potash	65	68	80	80	83	89	92	92	91
Titanium	(NA)	(NA)	79	71	65	85	92	91	93
Zinc	60	64	72	67	73	81	84	87	87
Barite	44	71	84	84	75	78	88	87	87
Tin	79	71	88	78	73	76	76	78	77
Bauxite [2]	(NA)	98	100	100	100	>75	>75	>75	>75
Platinum	(NA)	(NA)	78	93	91	66	71	74	64
Chromium	67	80	77	68	63	64	70	73	72
Silver	7	(NA)	43	72	65	67	72	67	68
Cobalt	93	84	78	83	81	73	69	64	78
Nickel	76	64	54	48	41	50	51	52	47
Tungsten	53	81	66	68	63	>25	>50	>50	>50
Aluminum	([3])	([3])	33	41	14	41	59	49	22
Palladium	(NA)	(NA)	84	84	49	53	38	41	32
Copper	16	15	37	42	32	32	36	33	35
Iron and steel	13	13	18	15	6	29	26	22	21
Gypsum	21	27	27	27	12	10	10	12	14
Sulfur	14	15	18	24	19	14	4	7	7

D Withheld to avoid disclosure. NA Not available. > Greater than. [1] Preliminary. [2] Includes alumina. [3] Net exporter.

Source: Through 1990, U.S. Bureau of Mines; thereafter, U.S. Geological Survey, *Mineral Commodity Summaries 2020*, January 2020, and earlier reports. See also <http://minerals.usgs.gov/minerals/pubs/mcs/>.

Table 944. Crude Petroleum and Natural Gas Extraction Industry—Establishments, Employees, and Payroll by State: 2018

[11,867,937 represents $11,867,937,000. Based on the North American Classification System (NAICS) 2017. Excludes self-employed individuals, employees of private households, railroad employees, agricultural production employees, and most government employees. See source for definitions and statement on reliability of data. An establishment is a single physical location where business is conducted or where services or industrial operations are performed. See Appendix III]

State	Crude petroleum extraction (NAICS 211120)			Natural gas extraction (NAICS 211130)		
	Establish-ments	Number of employees [1]	Annual payroll ($1,000)	Establish-ments	Number of employees [1]	Annual payroll ($1,000)
United States	**5,160**	**80,770**	**11,867,937**	**1,117**	**26,860**	**3,544,839**
Alabama	14	[2] 70	8,357	7	[2] 199	[2] 24,128
Alaska	19	1,667	359,505	(NA)	(NA)	(NA)
Arizona	4	[2] 6	30	(NA)	(NA)	(NA)
Arkansas	78	924	78,034	18	[2] 285	27,285
California	138	4,196	614,637	22	310	40,935
Colorado	278	4,751	862,940	55	2,127	342,796
Delaware	3	[2] 14	2,139	(NA)	(NA)	(NA)
Florida	17	[2] 100	[2] 6,486	(NA)	(NA)	(NA)
Idaho	4	[2] 5	305	(NA)	(NA)	(NA)
Illinois	134	591	31,944	7	202	25,125
Indiana	30	173	11,800	4	[2] 17	1,053
Kansas	290	1,292	97,919	34	380	34,017
Kentucky	45	206	11,266	20	432	37,767
Louisiana	263	4,333	563,457	82	1,279	139,084
Michigan	50	476	45,535	18	290	20,466
Minnesota	3	[2] 13	[2] 638	(NA)	(NA)	[2] 5,258
Mississippi	53	580	74,352	7	65	(NA)
Missouri	7	[2] 9	1,157	(NA)	(NA)	(NA)
Montana	68	636	67,640	9	[2] 210	[2] 26,493
Nebraska	14	70	4,575	3	[2] 8	[2] 612
Nevada	10	49	5,042	(NA)	(NA)	(NA)
New Mexico	110	2,748	324,796	37	797	73,942
New York	24	88	8,820	3	[2] 17	893
North Dakota	58	2,154	266,609	10	[2] 687	[2] 95,377
Ohio	123	719	38,372	53	886	77,335
Oklahoma	841	9,772	1,256,731	153	3,040	376,248
Pennsylvania	105	764	64,233	62	3,599	619,124
South Dakota	6	37	3,490	(NA)	(NA)	(NA)
Tennessee	4	[2] 27	[2] 3,226	(NA)	(NA)	(NA)
Texas	2,107	42,044	6,811,029	402	8,656	1,194,006
Utah	40	654	67,993	11	444	54,306
Virginia	9	[2] 11	214	5	[2] 242	[2] 21,129
Washington	5	[2] 9	741	(NA)	(NA)	(NA)
West Virginia	92	625	47,285	55	1,495	155,132
Wisconsin	3	7	[2] 558	(NA)	(NA)	(NA)
Wyoming	97	887	104,133	29	1,034	130,970

NA Not available. [1] Covers full- and part-time employees who are on the payroll in the pay period including March 12. [2] Data is flagged for high noise; the value was changed by 5 percent or more to avoid disclosure of data for individual businesses.

Source: U.S. Census Bureau, County Business Patterns, "County Business Patterns by Legal Form of Organization and Employment Size Class for U.S., States, and Selected Geographies," <data.census.gov>, accessed July 2020.

Table 945. Petroleum Industry—Production, Foreign Trade, Reserves, and Refineries: 1990 to 2019

[In units as indicated (2,685 represents 2,685,000,000); mil. bbl.= millions of barrels. For definitions, see source below]

Item	Unit	1990	2000	2005	2010	2015	2017	2018	2019
Crude oil production, total [1]	Mil. bbl.	2,685	2,131	1,892	2,002	3,445	3,413	4,012	4,471
Average price per barrel	Dollars	20	27	50	75	44	48	61	56
Lower 48 states [2]	Mil. bbl.	2,037	1,771	1,577	1,783	3,269	3,233	3,837	4,295
Alaska	Mil. bbl.	647	355	315	219	176	181	175	170
Imports: Crude oil [1, 3]	Mil. bbl.	2,151	3,320	3,696	3,363	2,687	2,909	2,835	2,480
Refined petroleum products	Mil. bbl.	775	874	1,310	942	761	794	794	839
Exports: Crude oil [1]	Mil. bbl.	40	18	12	15	170	423	748	1,087
Proved reserves	Bil. bbl.	26	22	22	23	32	39	44	(NA)
Operable refineries	Number	205	158	148	148	140	141	135	135
Daily capacity (Jan. 1)	1,000 bbl.	15,572	16,512	17,125	17,584	17,967	18,617	18,598	18,802
Refinery input, total	Mil. bbl.	5,325	5,964	6,136	6,345	6,871	7,003	7,137	7,069
Crude oil [1]	Mil. bbl.	4,894	5,514	5,555	5,374	5,909	6,055	6,194	6,045
Hydrocarbon gas liquids	Mil. bbl.	171	139	161	161	189	207	210	208
Other liquids [4]	Mil. bbl.	260	311	420	810	773	741	734	815
Refinery output, total [5]	Mil. bbl.	5,574	6,311	6,497	6,735	7,258	7,409	7,553	7,462
Motor gasoline [6]	Mil. bbl.	2,540	2,910	3,036	3,306	3,560	3,633	3,672	3,683
Jet fuel (kerosene type)	Mil. bbl.	478	588	564	517	580	621	659	656
Distillate fuel oil	Mil. bbl.	1,067	1,310	1,443	1,542	1,819	1,834	1,886	1,875
Residual fuel oil	Mil. bbl.	347	255	229	213	152	156	155	132
Hydrocarbon gas liquids	Mil. bbl.	182	258	209	240	224	229	232	221
Utilization rate	Percent	87	93	91	86	91	91	93	90

NA Not available. [1] Includes lease condensate. [2] Excluding Alaska and Hawaii. [3] Includes imports for the Strategic Petroleum Reserve. [4] Unfinished oils (net), other hydrocarbons, hydrogen, aviation and motor gasoline blending components (net). Beginning 1995, also includes oxygenates (net). [5] Includes other products not shown separately. [6] Finished motor gasoline. Beginning 1995, also includes ethanol blended into motor gasoline.

Source: U.S. Energy Information Administration, "Petroleum & Other Liquids Data," <http://www.eia.gov/naturalgas/data.cfm> and "Monthly Energy Review, Petroleum," <http://www.eia.gov/totalenergy/data/monthly/#petroleum>, accessed August 2020.

Table 946. Crude Oil and Petroleum Products Supply, Disposition, and Ending Stocks: 2019

[In millions of barrels (4,470.5 represents 4,470,500,000). Minus sign (-) indicates decrease]

Commodity	Supply				Disposition				
	Field production [1]	Refinery and blender net production	Imports	Adjustments [2]	Stock change	Refinery and blender net inputs	Exports	Products supplied [3]	Ending stocks
Crude oil	4,470.5	(X)	2,480.2	158.4	-23.0	6,045.3	1,086.8	–	1,067.9
Hydrocarbon gas liquids	1,756.8	221.3	73.7	(X)	28.4	208.4	664.9	1,142.6	211.7
Natural gasoline	202.6	(X)	0.1	(X)	0.1	61.2	61.3	72.5	20.9
Ethane	666.3	1.8	(X)	(X)	7.8	(X)	102.4	557.9	57.4
Propane	578.5	105.1	47.2	(X)	16.0	(X)	397.2	317.7	79.6
Normal butane	156.8	18.5	14.5	(X)	1.9	68.0	102.1	17.8	39.7
Isobutane	152.6	-5.3	4.5	(X)	2.7	79.3	1.8	67.9	11.2
Finished motor gasoline	(X)	3,683.0	29.7	-30.6	0.2	(X)	298.3	3,385.0	26.0
Kerosene-type jet fuel	(X)	655.7	59.9	(X)	-1.1	(X)	81.7	635.1	40.5
Distillate fuel oil [4]	(X)	1,874.7	71.9	25.6	–	(X)	482.1	1,490.1	140.0

– Represents or rounds to zero. X Not applicable. [1] Represents crude oil production on leases, natural gas liquids production at natural gas processing plants, new supply of other hydrocarbons/oxygenates and motor gasoline blending components, fuel ethanol, and distillate fuel oil. [2] Includes an adjustment for crude oil, previously referred to as "Unaccounted For Crude Oil." Also included is an adjustment for motor gasoline blending components, fuel ethanol, and distillate fuel oil. [3] Products supplied is equal to field production, plus refinery and blender net production, plus import, plus adjustments, minus stock change, minus refinery and blender net inputs, minus export. [4] Distillate stocks located in the "Northeast Heating Oil Reserve" are not included.

Source: U.S. Energy Information Administration, Petroleum & Other Liquids, "Supply and Disposition," <http://www.eia.gov/petroleum/>, accessed August 2020.

Table 947. Natural Gas Plant Liquids—Production and Value: 1990 to 2019

[In units, as indicated. Barrels of 42 gallons (569 represents 569,000,000)]

Item	Unit	1990	1995	2000	2005	2010	2015	2017	2018	2019
Field production [1]	Mil. bbl.	569	643	699	627	757	1,220	1,381	1,595	1,757
Pentanes plus	Mil. bbl.	113	122	112	97	101	158	165	184	203
Liquefied petroleum gases	Mil. bbl.	456	521	587	529	656	1,062	1,215	1,411	1,554
Natural gas processed	Tril. cu. ft.	15	17	17	15	16	21	20	22	(NA)

NA Not available. [1] Includes other finished petroleum products, not shown separately.

Source: U.S. Energy Information Administration, "Natural Gas Plant Processing," <https://www.eia.gov/naturalgas/data.php>, and "Natural Gas Plant Field Production," <https://www.eia.gov/petroleum/data.php>; accessed August 2020.

Table 948. Crude Petroleum and Natural Gas—Production and Value for Major Producing States: 2010 to 2019

[In units as indicated (2,002 represents 2,002,000,000 barrels)]

State	Crude petroleum								Natural gas marketed production [1]			
	Quantity (mil. bbl.)				Value (mil. dol.) [2]				Quantity (bil. cu. ft.)			
	2010	2015	2018	2019	2010	2015	2018	2019	2010	2015	2018	2019
Total [3]	2,002	3,448	4,002	4,471	149,555	153,055	245,716	248,517	22,382	28,772	32,823	36,197
Alabama	7	10	6	5	540	432	382	280	223	168	139	(NA)
Alaska [4]	215	170	169	165	15,561	6,970	10,528	9,481	374	344	341	329
Arkansas	6	6	5	5	407	268	294	237	927	1,010	590	530
California	200	201	169	161	14,930	9,185	11,524	10,170	287	237	203	194
Colorado	33	123	171	190	2,406	5,000	10,259	9,654	1,578	1,689	1,831	1,987
Florida	2	2	2	2	(NA)	(NA)	(NA)	(NA)	12	1	1	(NA)
Illinois	9	10	8	8	664	419	516	442	2	2	2	(NA)
Indiana	2	2	2	2	134	99	103	84	7	7	5	(NA)
Kansas	40	45	35	33	2,931	1,963	2,099	1,745	325	284	202	185
Kentucky	3	3	2	3	178	130	140	134	135	96	84	(NA)
Louisiana	68	65	48	46	5,289	3,140	3,206	2,731	2,210	1,805	2,811	3,147
Michigan	7	7	5	5	523	298	356	287	131	108	90	(NA)
Mississippi	24	25	17	17	1,832	1,167	1,092	973	74	58	36	(NA)
Montana	25	29	22	23	1,779	1,153	1,251	1,154	88	51	44	45
Nebraska	2	3	2	2	162	117	121	96	2	(Z)	(Z)	(NA)
New Mexico	66	148	249	329	4,960	6,575	13,952	17,466	1,292	1,245	1,485	1,812
New York	(Z)	(Z)	(Z)	(Z)	(NA)	(NA)	(NA)	(NA)	36	17	12	(NA)
North Dakota	113	430	460	519	7,908	17,796	27,751	27,293	82	471	706	866
Ohio	5	27	23	28	352	1,025	1,380	1,466	78	1,007	2,409	2,605
Oklahoma	70	166	200	212	5,277	7,484	12,562	11,565	1,827	2,500	2,946	3,175
Pennsylvania	3	7	6	7	226	276	386	339	573	4,813	6,211	6,962
Texas	427	1,261	1,609	1,851	32,532	56,671	96,391	101,863	6,715	7,890	7,847	8,998
Utah	25	37	37	37	1,679	1,511	2,110	1,773	432	417	297	275
West Virginia	2	12	12	17	130	390	666	826	265	1,315	1,799	2,156
Wyoming	54	86	88	102	3,670	3,514	5,220	5,261	2,306	1,809	1,640	1,475
Federal offshore	588	564	647	697	(NA)	(NA)	(NA)	(NA)	(NA)	(NA)	(NA)	(NA)
Lower 48 states	1,783	3,272	3,827	4,301	133,789	145,854	234,792	238,596	22,008	28,428	32,482	35,868

Z Less than 500,000. NA Not available. [1] Excludes nonhydrocarbon gases. [2] Crude petroleum production value calculated using production quantity and domestic crude oil first purchase price. [3] Includes other states, not shown separately. State production includes state offshore production, as well as extractions from the Gulf not distributed to states. U.S. level totals shown in Table 945 and Table 950 may contain revisions not carried to state level. [4] Alaska crude oil production and value for North Slope only.

Source: U.S. Energy Information Administration, "Petroleum & Other Liquids Data," <http://www.eia.gov/petroleum/data.cfm> and "Natural Gas Data," <http://www.eia.gov/naturalgas/data.cfm>; accessed September 2020.

Table 949. Crude Oil and Natural Gas—Reserves by State: 2010 to 2018

[23,267 mil. bbl. represents 23,267,000,000 barrels. As of December 31. Proved reserves are estimated quantities of the mineral, which geological and engineering data demonstrate with reasonable certainty, to be recoverable in future years from known reservoirs under existing economic and operating conditions. Based on a sample of operators of oil and gas wells]

Area	2010		2015		2017		2018	
	Crude oil proved reserves (mil. bbl.)	Natural gas (bil. cu. ft.)	Crude oil proved reserves (mil. bbl.)	Natural gas (bil. cu. ft.)	Crude oil proved reserves (mil. bbl.)	Natural gas (bil. cu. ft.)	Crude oil proved reserves (mil. bbl.)	Natural gas (bil. cu. ft.)
United States [1]	23,267	304,625	32,318	307,730	39,160	438,460	43,824	474,821
Alabama	42	2,629	64	2,182	43	1,510	48	1,262
Alaska	3,722	8,838	2,034	4,566	2,016	6,521	2,421	8,811
Arkansas	40	14,178	51	8,339	37	8,267	33	6,740
California	2,938	2,647	2,333	1,832	2,209	1,560	2,296	1,451
Colorado	386	24,119	1,212	17,139	1,528	26,573	1,592	24,114
Florida	18	56	16	–	(NA)	(NA)	(NA)	(NA)
Illinois	64	(NA)	31	(NA)	38	(NA)	(NA)	(NA)
Indiana	8	(NA)	8	(NA)	5	(NA)	(NA)	(NA)
Kansas	295	3,673	337	3,183	304	2,654	330	2,449
Kentucky	15	2,613	10	1,362	8	1,136	9	1,324
Louisiana	424	29,277	424	16,097	418	36,119	412	34,127
Michigan	40	2,919	43	1,386	54	1,489	40	1,490
Mississippi	247	853	158	480	121	350	132	280
Montana	369	944	326	692	302	611	279	593
Nebraska	10	(NA)	17	(NA)	13	(NA)	15	(NA)
New Mexico	823	15,412	1,486	14,364	2,581	19,365	3,240	23,040
New York	(NA)	281	(NA)	104	(NA)	104	(NA)	102
North Dakota	1,814	1,667	5,193	6,203	5,473	8,445	5,895	10,166
Ohio	42	832	62	12,104	47	26,123	80	23,759
Oklahoma	710	26,345	1,262	28,486	1,917	35,491	2,120	37,035
Pennsylvania	22	13,960	13	55,894	11	89,589	8	103,460
Texas	5,674	88,997	11,759	78,866	15,936	105,618	18,043	126,131
Utah	449	6,981	389	3,547	285	3,752	401	3,213
Virginia	(NA)	3,215	(NA)	2,496	(NA)	2,741	(NA)	2,554
West Virginia	17	7,000	12	20,553	9	32,785	7	35,001
Wyoming	567	35,074	725	20,436	943	21,549	1,030	21,343
Federal offshore	4,496	11,765	4,335	7,296	4,789	5,945	5,285	6,285
Lower 48 states	19,545	295,787	30,284	303,164	37,144	431,939	41,403	466,010

– Represents zero. NA Not available. [1] Includes other states, not shown separately.

Source: U.S. Energy Information Administration, "Petroleum & Other Liquids Data," <https://www.eia.gov/petroleum/data.php>; and "Natural Gas Data,"<https://www.eia.gov/naturalgas/data.php>; accessed February 2020.

Table 950. Dry Natural Gas—Supply, Consumption, Reserves, and Marketed Production: 1990 to 2019

[270 represents 270,000. Data are for dry natural gas, plus a small amount of supplemental gaseous fuels. Minus sign (-) indicates debit]

Item	Unit	1990	2000	2005	2010	2015	2017	2018	2019 (P)
Producing wells (year-end)	1,000	270	342	426	488	575	540	523	(NA)
Proved reserves [1]	Bil. cu. ft.	169,346	177,427	204,385	304,625	307,730	438,460	474,821	(NA)
Marketed production [2]	**Bil. cu. ft.**	**18,593.8**	**20,197.5**	**18,927.1**	**22,381.9**	**28,772.0**	**29,203.6**	**32,823.3**	**36,197.1**
Minus: Extraction losses [3]	Bil. cu. ft.	784.1	1,015.5	876.5	1,066.4	1,706.6	1,897.2	2,234.6	2,540.0
Equals: Dry production	Bil. cu. ft.	17,809.7	19,182.0	18,050.6	21,315.5	27,065.5	27,306.3	30,588.7	33,657.0
Plus: Supplemental gas supplies	Bil. cu. ft.	122.8	90.2	63.7	64.6	58.6	65.7	69.3	61.5
Equals: Dry production with supplemental gas	Bil. cu. ft.	17,932.5	19,272.2	18,114.3	21,380.1	27,124.1	27,372.0	30,658.0	33,718.5
Plus: Withdrawals from storage [4]	Bil. cu. ft.	1,933.8	3,498.2	3,056.6	3,274.4	3,099.7	3,590.5	3,999.4	3,652.8
Plus: Imports	Bil. cu. ft.	1,532.3	3,781.6	4,341.0	3,740.8	2,718.1	3,033.2	2,888.8	2,741.6
Plus: Balancing item [5]	Bil. cu. ft.	307.3	-305.7	236.1	115.5	-267.9	-359.6	-175.1	-289.8
Equals: Total supply	Bil. cu. ft.	21,705.8	26,246.3	25,748.0	28,510.7	32,674.0	33,636.1	37,371.2	39,823.2
Minus: Exports	Bil. cu. ft.	85.6	243.7	728.6	1,136.6	1,783.5	3,153.8	3,607.4	4,656.3
Minus: Additions to storage [4]	Bil. cu. ft.	2,433.5	2,684.3	3,001.6	3,291.4	3,638.3	3,336.6	3,675.9	4,152.5
Equals: Consumption, total	**Bil. cu. ft.**	**19,173.6**	**23,333.1**	**22,014.4**	**24,086.8**	**27,243.9**	**27,145.9**	**30,075.3**	**31,014.3**
Lease and plant fuel	Bil. cu. ft.	1,236.4	1,150.9	1,111.5	1,285.6	1,576.4	1,584.0	1,684.2	1,857.3
Pipeline fuel [6]	Bil. cu. ft.	(NA)	642.2	584.0	674.1	678.2	721.9	862.9	889.8
Residential	Bil. cu. ft.	4,391.3	4,996.2	4,826.8	4,782.4	4,612.9	4,412.3	4,996.2	5,000.0
Commercial [7]	Bil. cu. ft.	2,622.7	3,182.5	2,998.9	3,102.6	3,201.7	3,164.5	3,515.1	3,520.9
Industrial	Bil. cu. ft.	(NA)	8,142.2	6,601.2	6,826.2	7,521.9	7,949.4	8,377.5	8,387.6
Vehicle fuel	Bil. cu. ft.	(NA)	12.8	22.9	28.7	39.4	48.2	50.4	51.2
Electric power sector	Bil. cu. ft.	(NA)	5,206.3	5,869.1	7,387.2	9,613.4	9,265.6	10,588.9	11,307.4
World production (dry)	Tril. cu. ft.	73.4	86.8	98.6	113.1	124.7	130.0	(NA)	(NA)
U.S. production (dry)	Tril. cu. ft.	17.8	19.2	18.1	21.3	27.1	27.3	30.6	33.7
U.S. percent of world	Percent	24.3	22.1	18.3	18.8	21.7	21.0	(NA)	(NA)

P Preliminary. NA Not available. [1] Estimated, end of year. [2] Gross withdrawals less gas used for repressuring, quantities vented and flared, and nonhydrocarbon gases removed in treating or processing operations. Includes all quantities of gas used in field and processing plant operations. [3] Volumetric reduction in natural gas resulting from the removal of natural gas plant liquids, which are transferred to petroleum supply. [4] Underground storage. [5] Quantities lost and imbalances in data due to differences among data sources. Since 1980, excludes in-transit shipments that cross U.S.-Canada border (i.e., natural gas delivered to its destination via the other country). [6] Natural gas consumed in the operation of pipelines, primarily in compressors. [7] Includes gas used by local, State, and Federal agencies engaged in nonmanufacturing activities.

Source: U.S. Energy Information Administration, "Natural Gas Data," <http://www.eia.gov/naturalgas/data.cfm>; "Monthly Energy Review, Natural Gas," <http://www.eia.gov/totalenergy/data/monthly/#naturalgas>; and "International Energy Statistics," <https://www.eia.gov/international/overview/world>; accessed September 2020.

Table 951. Unconventional Dry Natural Gas Production and Proved Reserves: 2017 and 2018

[In billions of cubic feet (980 represents 980,000,000,000). For states not listed, no production or reserves were reported]

State	Production Coalbed methane [2] 2017	2018	Production Shale gas [3] 2017	2018	Proved reserves [1] Coalbed methane [2] 2017	2018	Proved reserves [1] Shale gas [3] 2017	2018
United States	**980**	**(D)**	**18,589**	**22,054**	**11,878**	**(D)**	**307,903**	**342,135**
Alabama	62	(D)	(NA)	–	789	(D)	(NA)	–
Alaska	–	(D)	–	–	–	(D)	–	–
Arkansas	1	(D)	618	521	10	(D)	7,090	5,970
California	–	(D)	6	4	–	(D)	62	41
Colorado	338	(D)	97	126	3,275	(D)	1,885	2,727
Florida	–	(D)	(NA)	(NA)	–	(D)	(NA)	(NA)
Kansas	15	(D)	–	–	46	(D)	–	–
Kentucky	(NA)	(D)	(NA)	–	(NA)	(D)	(NA)	–
Louisiana	–	(D)	1,450	2,044	–	(D)	26,484	25,598
Michigan	–	(D)	63	77	–	(D)	942	1,457
Mississippi	–	(D)	2	–	–	(D)	8	–
Montana	–	(D)	18	18	1	(D)	258	221
New Mexico	234	(D)	592	785	3,175	(D)	9,451	13,082
New York	–	(D)	(NA)	(NA)	–	(D)	(NA)	(NA)
North Dakota	–	(D)	664	840	–	(D)	9,984	11,737
Ohio	(NA)	(D)	1,747	2,337	(NA)	(D)	26,468	23,956
Oklahoma	36	(D)	1,290	1,325	318	(D)	22,675	21,396
Pennsylvania	(NA)	(D)	5,365	6,079	(NA)	(D)	89,478	103,388
Texas	8	(D)	5,171	6,392	74	(D)	78,666	100,789
Utah	36	(D)	(NA)	(NA)	438	(D)	(NA)	(NA)
Virginia	99	(D)	4	–	2,465	(D)	66	–
West Virginia	7	(D)	1,486	1,504	89	(D)	34,296	31,748
Wyoming	135	(D)	6	–	1,014	(D)	28	–

– Represents or rounds to zero. D Individual state volumes are withheld to avoid disclosure of operator-level reserves data, due to statistical precision requirements, or due to other data quality reasons. NA Not available. [1] Proved reserves of natural gas as of December 31 of the report year are the estimated quantities which analysis of geological and engineering data demonstrate with reasonable certainty to be recoverable in future years from known reservoirs under existing economic and operating conditions. [2] Methane is generated during coal formation and is contained in the coal microstructure. Typical recovery entails pumping water out of the coal to allow the gas to escape. Methane is the principal component of natural gas. Coal bed methane can be added to natural gas pipelines without any special treatment. [3] Natural gas produced from organic (black) shale formations.

Source: U.S. Energy Information Administration, "Natural Gas Data," <http://www.eia.gov/naturalgas/data.cfm>, accessed February 2020.

Table 952. Coal Production, Supply, Disposition, and Prices: 2000 to 2019

[In millions of short tons (1,073.6 represents 1,073,600,000). 1 short ton = 2,000 lbs]

Item	2000	2005	2010	2015	2017	2018	2019
United States, total production.....	**1,073.6**	**1,131.5**	**1,084.4**	**896.9**	**774.6**	**756.2**	**705.3**
Consumption by sector:							
Total........	1,084.1	1,126.0	1,048.5	798.1	716.9	688.1	587.3
Residential [1].......	0.5	0.4	(NA)	(NA)	(NA)	(NA)	(NA)
Commercial.........	3.7	4.3	3.1	1.5	1.1	1.0	0.9
Industrial..........	94.1	83.8	70.4	58.2	50.8	49.9	47.1
Coke plants.........	28.9	23.4	21.1	19.7	17.5	18.3	17.9
Other industrial plants.........	65.2	60.3	49.3	38.5	33.3	31.6	29.1
Combined heat and power (CHP).........	28.0	25.9	24.6	17.0	13.0	12.2	11.2
Noncombined heat and power.........	37.2	34.5	24.7	21.5	20.3	19.3	17.9
Electric power.........	985.8	1,037.5	975.1	738.4	665.0	637.2	539.4
Year-end coal stocks:							
Total........	140.3	144.3	231.7	238.4	167.0	129.8	158.8
Residential and commercial.........	(NA)	(NA)	0.6	0.4	0.3	0.2	0.2
Industrial..........	6.1	8.2	6.5	6.6	5.0	5.1	5.6
Coke plants.........	1.5	2.6	1.9	2.2	1.7	1.8	2.3
Other industrial plants.........	4.6	5.6	4.5	4.4	3.2	3.3	3.3
Electric power.........	102.3	101.1	174.9	195.5	137.7	102.8	128.5
Producers/distributors.........	31.9	35.0	49.8	35.9	24.0	21.7	24.4
U.S. coal trade:							
Net exports [2].........	46.0	19.5	62.4	62.6	89.2	109.7	86.2
Exports.........	58.5	49.9	81.7	74.0	97.0	115.6	92.9
Steam coal.........	25.7	21.3	25.6	28.0	41.7	54.1	37.7
Metallurgical coal.........	32.8	28.7	56.1	46.0	55.3	61.5	55.1
Coke.........	1.3	1.7	1.5	0.9	1.2	1.2	1.0
Imports.........	12.5	30.5	19.4	11.3	7.8	6.0	6.7
Average delivered price (dollars per short ton) to:							
Electric power sector.........	24.28	31.22	44.27	42.6	39.18	39.16	38.8

NA Not available. [1] Beginning in 2008, residential coal consumption data are not collected by Energy Information Administration. [2] Exports minus imports.

Source: U.S. Energy Information Administration, *Annual Coal Report 2018*, October 2019, and earlier reports; and "Coal Data," <http://www.eia.gov/coal/data.cfm> and "Monthly Energy Review, Coal," <http://www.eia.gov/totalenergy/data/monthly/#coal>, accessed September 2020.

Table 953. Coal and Coke—Summary: 1990 to 2018

[In millions of short tons (1,029 represents 1,029,000,000), except as indicated. Includes coal consumed at mines. Recoverability varies between 40 and 90 percent for individual deposits; 50 percent or more of overall U.S. coal reserve base is believed to be recoverable]

Item	Unit	1990	2000	2005	2010	2015	2016	2017	2018
COAL									
Production, total [1,2]..................	Mil. sh. tons	**1,029**	**1,074**	**1,131**	**1,084**	**897**	**728**	**775**	**756**
Average price per short ton..............	Dollars	21.76	16.78	23.34	35.61	31.81	30.57	33.72	35.99
Anthracite production [2]..................	Mil. sh. tons	3.5	4.6	1.7	1.8	2.1	1.7	1.9	1.9
Bituminous coal and lignite [3].............	Mil. sh. tons	1,026	1,069	1,130	1,083	895	727	773	754
Underground.............................	Mil. sh. tons	425	374	369	337	307	252	273	275
Surface [2]................................	Mil. sh. tons	605	700	763	747	590	476	501	481
Exports..................................	Mil. sh. tons	106	58	50	82	74	60	97	116
Imports..................................	Mil. sh. tons	3	13	30	19	11	10	8	6
Consumption [4]............................	Mil. sh. tons	904	1,084	1,126	1,049	798	731	717	688
Electric power sector [5]..................	Mil. sh. tons	783	986	1,037	975	738	679	665	637
Industrial..............................	Mil. sh. tons	115	94	84	70	58	51	51	50
Number of mines.........................	Number	3,243	1,453	1,415	1,285	853	710	680	679
Daily employment........................	1,000	135	85	79	86	66	52	53	54
Production, by state:									
Alabama.................................	Mil. sh. tons	29	19	21	20	13	10	13	15
Illinois.................................	Mil. sh. tons	60	33	32	33	56	43	48	50
Indiana.................................	Mil. sh. tons	36	28	34	35	34	29	31	35
Kentucky................................	Mil. sh. tons	173	131	120	105	61	43	42	40
Montana.................................	Mil. sh. tons	38	38	40	45	42	32	35	39
Ohio....................................	Mil. sh. tons	35	22	25	27	17	13	9	9
Pennsylvania............................	Mil. sh. tons	71	75	67	59	50	46	49	50
Virginia................................	Mil. sh. tons	47	33	28	22	14	13	13	13
West Virginia...........................	Mil. sh. tons	169	158	154	135	96	80	93	95
Wyoming.................................	Mil. sh. tons	184	339	404	443	376	297	316	304
Other states............................	Mil. sh. tons	187	197	205	159	136	122	123	107
World production.........................	Mil. sh. tons	5,282	5,127	6,644	8,099	8,728	8,160	8,449	(NA)
U.S. percent of world....................	Percent	19.5	20.9	17.0	13.4	10.3	8.9	9.2	(NA)
COKE									
Production................................	Mil. sh. tons	27.6	20.8	16.7	15.0	13.8	11.9	12.9	13.8
Imports..................................	Mil. sh. tons	0.8	3.8	3.5	1.2	0.1	0.2	0.1	0.1
Exports..................................	Mil. sh. tons	0.6	1.1	1.7	1.5	0.9	1.0	1.2	1.2
Consumption [6]............................	Mil. sh. tons	27.8	23.2	18.2	14.8	13.1	11.2	11.8	13.0

NA Not available. [1] Includes bituminous coal, subbituminous coal, lignite, and anthracite. [2] Beginning 2005, includes a small amount of refuse recovery. [3] Includes subbituminous. [4] Includes other categories not shown separately. [5] Electricity-only and combined-heat-and-power (CHP) plants whose primary business is to sell electricity and/or heat to the public. [6] Consumption is calculated as the sum of production and imports minus exports and stock change.

Source: U.S. Energy Information Administration, *Annual Energy Review 2011*, September 2012; *Annual Coal Report 2018*, October 2019; *Quarterly Coal Report*, July 2021; and "International Energy Statistics," <https://www.eia.gov/international/data/world>, accessed September 2020. See also <http://www.eia.gov/totalenergy> and <http://www.eia.gov/coal/annual/>.

Table 954. Demonstrated Coal Reserves by Major Producing State: 2017 and 2018

[Reserves in millions of short tons (474,828 represents 474,828,000,000). As of January 1 the following year. The demonstrated reserve base represents the sum of coal in both measured and indicated resource categories of reliability. Measured resources of coal are estimates that have a high degree of geologic assurance from sample analyses and measurements from closely spaced and geologically well-known sample sites. Indicated resources are estimates based partly from sample and analyses and measurements and partly from reasonable geologic projections]

State	2017 Number of mines	2017 Total reserves	2017 Under-ground	2017 Surface	2018 Number of mines	2018 Total reserves	2018 Under-ground	2018 Surface
United States [1]	**680**	**474,828**	**326,731**	**148,097**	**679**	**473,695**	**326,176**	**147,519**
Alabama	30	3,845	736	3,109	30	3,817	711	3,106
Alaska	1	6,087	5,423	664	1	6,086	5,423	663
Arkansas	3	415	271	144	(NA)	415	271	144
Colorado	7	15,660	10,906	4,754	6	15,635	10,881	4,754
Illinois	18	103,495	87,018	16,477	18	103,398	86,926	16,472
Indiana	18	8,826	8,402	424	18	8,770	8,367	403
Iowa	(NA)	2,189	1,732	457	(NA)	2,189	1,732	457
Kansas	(NA)	970	(NA)	970	(NA)	970	(NA)	970
Kentucky	151	28,172	15,700	12,472	145	28,099	15,638	12,461
Kentucky, Eastern	138	9,423	500	8,924	132	9,395	482	8,914
Kentucky, Western	13	18,749	15,200	3,548	13	18,704	15,156	3,547
Maryland	14	598	557	41	14	596	556	40
Missouri	1	5,984	1,479	4,505	1	5,984	1,479	4,505
Montana	6	118,580	70,856	47,725	6	118,526	70,840	47,686
New Mexico	3	11,755	6,011	5,744	3	11,740	6,007	5,733
North Dakota	5	8,619	(NA)	8,619	5	8,582	(NA)	8,582
Ohio	18	22,831	17,183	5,647	16	22,814	17,170	5,644
Oklahoma	5	1,534	1,221	313	5	1,533	1,221	312
Pennsylvania	153	26,182	22,068	4,114	151	26,087	21,979	4,107
Anthracite [2]	57	7,171	3,840	3,330	50	7,168	3,840	3,328
Bituminous	96	19,012	18,228	784	101	18,918	18,139	779
Tennessee	6	746	495	251	4	745	494	251
Texas	10	11,772	(NA)	11,772	9	11,747	(NA)	11,747
Utah	8	4,938	4,675	263	8	4,912	4,649	262
Virginia	52	1,279	817	463	51	1,256	798	459
Washington	(NA)	1,340	1,332	8	(NA)	1,340	1,332	8
West Virginia	140	30,385	27,265	3,120	155	30,212	27,121	3,091
Wyoming	17	57,724	42,429	15,296	16	57,342	42,424	14,918

NA Not available. [1] Includes other states not shown separately. [2] All of the anthracite mines in the United States are located in northeastern Pennsylvania.

Source: U.S. Energy Information Administration, *Annual Coal Report 2018*, November 2019, and earlier reports. See also <http://www.eia.gov/coal/annual/>.

Table 955. Uranium Concentrate Industry—Summary: 1990 to 2019

[In units as indicated (1.7 represents 1,700,000). See also Section 19, Table 975]

Item	Unit	1990	2000	2005	2010	2015	2016	2017	2018	2019
Exploration and development, surface drilling	Mil. ft.	1.7	1.0	1.7	4.9	0.9	0.8	0.2	(D)	(D)
Expenditures	Mil. dol.	(NA)	5.6	18.1	44.6	28.7	22.3	4.0	(D)	(D)
Mines operated	Number	39	10	10	9	9	9	7	7	6
Underground	Number	27	1	4	4	1	–	–	–	1
Open pit	Number	2	–	–	–	–	–	–	–	–
In situ leaching	Number	7	4	4	4	7	8	6	6	5
Other sources [1]	Number	3	5	2	1	1	1	1	1	–
Mine production	1,000 pounds	5,876	3,123	3,045	4,237	3,711	2,545	1,150	721	174
Underground	1,000 pounds	(D)	(D)	(D)	(D)	(D)	(D)	(D)	(D)	(D)
Open pit	1,000 pounds	1,881	–	–	–	–	–	–	–	–
In situ leaching	1,000 pounds	(D)	2,995	2,681	(D)	(D)	(D)	(D)	(D)	(D)
Other sources [1]	1,000 pounds	3,995	128	(D)	(D)	(D)	(D)	(D)	(D)	(D)
Uranium concentrate production	1,000 pounds	8,886	3,958	2,689	4,228	3,343	2,916	2,443	1,647	174
Concentrate shipments from mills and plants	1,000 pounds	12,957	3,187	2,702	5,137	4,023	3,018	2,277	1,489	190
Employment	Person-years [2]	1,335	627	648	1,073	625	560	424	372	265

– Represents zero. D Data withheld to avoid disclosing figures for individual companies. NA Not available. [1] Includes mine water, mill site cleanup and mill tailings, and well field restoration as sources of uranium. [2] A person-year is defined as one whole year, or fraction thereof, worked by an employee, including contracted man power. 12 months worked is 1 person year.

Source: U.S. Energy Information Administration, through 2002, *Uranium Industry,* annual. Thereafter, *Domestic Uranium Production Report*, May 2020, and earlier reports. See also <http://www.eia.gov/uranium/production/annual/>.

This section presents statistics on fuel resources, energy production and consumption, electric energy, renewable energy, and the electric and gas utility industries. The principal sources are the U.S. Department of Energy's Energy Information Administration (EIA), the Edison Electric Institute, Washington, DC, and the American Gas Association, Arlington, VA. The Department of Energy was created in October 1977 and assumed and centralized the responsibilities of all or part of several agencies including the Federal Power Commission (FPC), the U.S. Bureau of Mines, the Federal Energy Administration, and the U.S. Energy Research and Development Administration. For additional data on transportation, see Section 23; on fuels, see Section 18; and on energy-related housing characteristics, see Section 20.

The EIA, in its *Annual Energy Review*, provides statistics and trend data on energy supply, demand, and prices. Information is included on petroleum and natural gas, coal, electricity, hydroelectric power, nuclear power, solar, wind, wood, and geothermal energy. Due to budget constraints the EIA suspended publication of the *Annual Energy Review* in 2013. Data previously found in the *Annual Energy Review* can now be found in the *Monthly Energy Review*,which presents data on current supply, disposition, and price data for energy resources and monthly publications on petroleum, coal, natural gas, and electric power. Additional EIA reports include the *Electric Power Annual*; *Natural Gas Annual*; *Petroleum Supply Annual*; *U.S. Crude Oil, Natural Gas, and*; *Electric Sales, Revenue, and Price*; *State Energy Consumption, Price, and Expenditure Data*; *Annual Energy Outlook*; *Uranium Marketing Annual Report*; *Domestic Uranium Production Report—Quarterly*; and *International Energy Statistics*. These various reports contain state, national, and international data on the production of electricity, net summer capability of generating plants, fuels used in energy production, energy sales and consumption, and hydroelectric power. The EIA also provides access to regular data updates through its Open Data program. For more information, please refer to the EIA's Open Data program's web site <http://www.eia.gov/opendata/>.

Data on residential energy consumption, expenditures, and conservation activities are available from EIA's Residential Energy Consumption Survey (RECS) and are published every 4 years. The Commercial Buildings Energy Consumption Survey (CBECS), collects information on the stock of U.S. commercial buildings, their energy-related characteristics, and their energy consumption and expenditures. Data on manufacturing energy consumption, use, and expenditures are also collected every 4 years from EIA's Manufacturing Energy Consumption Survey (MECS). Due to the long gaps between the RECS, CBECS, and MECS, tables are rotated in and out of Section 19 in an effort to keep the data as current as possible. The results from these surveys are published at <http://www.eia.gov/consumption/>.

The Edison Electric Institute's annual *Statistical Yearbook of the Electric Power Industry* contains data on the distribution of electric energy by public utilities. The American Gas Association, in its annual yearbook, *Gas Facts*, presents data on gas utilities and financial and operating statistics.

Btu conversion factors—Various energy sources are converted from original units to the thermal equivalent using British thermal units (Btu). A Btu is the amount of energy required to raise the temperature of 1 pound of water 1 degree Fahrenheit (F) at or near 39.2 degrees F. Factors are calculated annually from the latest final annual data available; some are revised as a result.

Electric power industry—In recent years, EIA has restructured the industry categories it once used to gather and report electricity statistics. The electric power industry, previously divided into electric utilities and non-utilities, now consists of the Electric Power Sector, the Commercial Sector, and the Industrial Sector.

The Electric Power Sector is composed of electricity-only and combined-heat-and-power plants (CHPs) whose primary business is to sell electricity, or electricity and heat, to the public.

Electricity-only plants are composed of traditional electric utilities, and nontraditional participants, including energy service providers, power marketers, independent power producers (IPPs), and the portion of CHPs that produce only electricity.

A utility is defined as a corporation, person, agency, authority, or other legal entity or instrumentality aligned with distribution facilities for delivery of electric energy for use primarily by the public. Electric utilities include investor-owned electric utilities, municipal and state utilities, federal electric utilities, and rural electric cooperatives.

An independent power producer is an entity defined as a corporation, person, agency, authority, or other legal entity or instrumentality that owns or operates facilities whose primary business is to produce electricity for use by the public. They are not generally aligned with distribution facilities and are not considered electric utilities.

Combined-heat-and-power producers are plants designed to produce both heat and electricity from a single heat source. These types of electricity producers can be independent power producers or industrial or commercial establishments. As some independent power producers are CHPs, their information is included in the data for the combined-heat-and-power sector.

The Commercial Sector consists of commercial CHPs and commercial electricity-only plants. Industrial CHPs and industrial electricity-only plants make up the Industrial Sector. For more information, please refer to the *Electric Power Annual* web site at <http://www.eia.gov/electricity/annual/>.

Table 956. Utilities—Establishments, Revenue, Payroll, and Employees by Kind of Business: 2017

[577,100 represents $577,100,000,000. Includes only establishments or firms with payroll. Data based on the 2017 Economic Census. See Appendix III]

Kind of business	NAICS code [1]	Establish-ments (number)	Revenue Total (mil. dol.)	Revenue Per paid employee (dol.)	Annual payroll Total (mil. dol.)	Annual payroll Per paid employee (dol.)	Paid employees for pay period including March 12 (number)
Utilities..........................	**22**	**18,913**	**577,100**	**876,541**	**67,667**	**102,777**	**658,384**
Electric power generation, transmission, & distribution..........................	2211	11,496	461,919	888,903	56,541	108,806	519,651
Electric power generation....................	22111	3280	119,266	860,216	15,610	112,590	138,647
Hydroelectric power generation..................	221111	523	3,334	915,503	328	90,185	3,642
Fossil fuel electric power generation............	221112	1711	75,455	992,072	8,193	107,715	76,058
Nuclear electric power generation...............	221113	176	29,014	597,959	6,063	124,959	48,521
Solar electric power generation.................	221114	205	1,801	832,698	222	102,581	2,163
Wind electric power generation.................	221115	454	7,762	1,556,811	511	102,400	4,986
Geothermal electric power generation..........	221116	34	974	801,967	121	99,859	1,214
Biomass electric power generation............	221117	141	906	460,174	163	82,940	1968
Other electric power generation..................	221118	36	21	219,832	9	96,179	95
Electric power transmission, control & distribution..........................	22112	8,216	342,653	899,342	40,931	107,429	381,004
Electric bulk power transmission & control..........................	221121	273	13,772	893,328	1,828	118,571	15,416
Electric power distribution......................	221122	7,943	328,881	899,596	39,103	106,960	365,588
Natural gas distribution........................	2212	2,550	100,586	1,096,344	8,155	88,890	91,747
Water, sewage, & other systems....................	2213	4,867	14,595	310,623	2,970	63,215	46,986
Water supply & irrigation systems.................	22131	4,108	11,759	307,997	2,411	63,152	38,180
Sewage treatment facilities...................	22132	634	1,524	239,375	337	52,977	6,367
Steam & air-conditioning supply...................	22133	125	1,312	537,732	222	90,919	2,439

[1] North American Industry Classification System, 2017; see text, Section 15.

Source: U.S. Census Bureau, 2017 Economic Census, EC1700BASIC, "All Sectors: Summary Statistics for the U.S., States, and Selected Geographies: 2017," <data.census.gov/>, accessed July 2020.

Table 957. Utilities—Employees, Annual Payroll, and Establishments by Utility Type: 2017 and 2018

[67,433 represents $67,433,000,000. Excludes most government employees, railroad employees, and self-employed persons. An establishment is a single physical location where business is conducted or where services or industrial operations are performed. See Appendix III]

Industry	NAICS code [1]	2017 Estab-lish-ments	2017 Number of employ-ees [2]	2017 Annual payroll (mil. dol.)	2017 Average payroll per em-ployee (dol.)	2018 Estab-lish-ments	2018 Number of employ-ees [2]	2018 Annual payroll (mil. dol.)	2018 Average payroll per em-ployee (dol.)
Utilities, total............................	**22**	**18,965**	**644,703**	**67,433**	**104,595**	**19,028**	**646,930**	**70,047**	**108,276**
Electric power generation, transmission and distribution...........	2211	11,515	510,932	56,328	110,245	11,591	509,907	58,082	113,906
Electric power generation...............	22111	3,306	137,075	15,608	113,861	3,497	133,797	15,941	119,144
Hydroelectric power......................	221111	523	3,595	327	91,033	549	4,380	414	94,462
Fossil fuel electric power...............	221112	1,700	75,470	8,277	109,678	1,776	72,019	8,386	116,435
Nuclear electric power..................	221113	178	47,713	5,972	125,163	189	45,657	5,919	129,634
Solar electric power....................	221114	208	2,307	241	104,502	245	2,777	297	106,911
Wind electric power.....................	221115	459	4,629	489	105,634	513	5,634	626	111,078
Geothermal electric power.............	221116	33	1,172	125	106,817	34	1,180	125	105,576
Biomass electric power.................	221117	151	2,039	164	80,465	129	1,942	163	83,782
Other electric power generation.......	221118	54	150	12	77,647	62	[3] 208	13	62,990
Electric power transmission, control & distribution................	22112	8,209	373,857	40,720	108,920	8,094	376,110	42,140	112,043
Electric bulk power transmission & control.................	221121	294	14,026	1,742	124,230	314	16,253	2,070	127,363
Electric power distribution..............	221122	7,915	359,831	38,978	108,323	7,780	359,857	40,070	111,351
Natural gas distribution...................	2212	2,544	89,029	8,211	92,228	2,505	90,698	8,947	98,647
Water, sewage, & other systems.........	2213	4,906	44,742	2,894	64,684	4,932	46,325	3,018	65,156
Water supply & irrigation systems......	22131	4,131	36,836	2,347	63,709	4,180	38,610	2,468	63,910
Sewage treatment facilities..............	22132	652	5,898	353	59,834	624	5,407	325	60,020
Steam & air-conditioning supply........	22133	123	2,008	194	96,815	128	2,308	226	98,038

[1] North American Industry Classification System, 2017; see text, Section 15. [2] Covers full- and part-time employees who are on the payroll in the pay period including March 12. [3] Data is flagged for high noise; the value was changed by 5 percent or more to avoid disclosure of data for individual businesses.

Source: U.S. Census Bureau, County Business Patterns, "County Business Patterns by Legal Form of Organization and Employment Size Class for U.S., States, and Selected Geographies," <data.census.gov>, accessed July 2020. See also <https://www.census.gov/programs-surveys/cbp.html>.

Table 958. Energy Supply and Disposition by Type of Fuel: 1973 to 2019

[In quadrillion British thermal units (Btu) (63.54 represents 63,540,000,000,000,000). For definition of Btu, see source and text, this section]

Year	Production					Renewable energy [4]					Net imports, total [7]	Consumption					Renewable energy, [4] total
	Total [1]	Crude oil [2]	Dry natural gas	Coal [3]	Nuclear electric power	Total [1]	Hydro-electric power [5]	Bio-mass [6]	Solar/photo-voltaic	Wind		Total [1,8]	Petro-leum [9]	Natural gas [10]	Coal	Nuclear electric power	
1973.....	63.54	19.49	22.19	13.99	0.91	4.41	2.86	1.53	(NA)	(NA)	12.58	75.65	34.81	22.51	12.97	0.91	4.41
1975.....	61.30	17.73	19.64	14.99	1.90	4.69	3.15	1.50	(NA)	(NA)	11.71	71.93	32.70	19.95	12.66	1.90	4.69
1980.....	67.15	18.25	19.91	18.60	2.74	5.43	2.90	2.48	(NA)	(NA)	12.10	78.02	34.16	20.24	15.42	2.74	5.43
1985.....	67.66	18.99	16.98	19.33	4.08	6.08	2.97	3.02	(Z)	(Z)	7.58	76.33	30.87	17.70	17.48	4.08	6.08
1990.....	70.67	15.57	18.33	22.49	6.10	6.04	3.05	2.74	0.06	0.03	14.06	84.43	33.50	19.60	19.17	6.10	6.04
1995.....	71.13	13.89	19.08	22.13	7.08	6.56	3.21	3.10	0.07	0.03	17.68	90.93	34.34	22.67	20.09	7.08	6.56
1996.....	72.44	13.72	19.34	22.79	7.09	7.01	3.59	3.16	0.07	0.03	19.02	93.93	35.59	23.08	21.00	7.09	7.01
1997.....	72.42	13.66	19.39	23.31	6.60	7.02	3.64	3.11	0.07	0.03	20.63	94.51	36.07	23.22	21.45	6.60	7.01
1998.....	72.83	13.24	19.61	24.05	7.07	6.49	3.30	2.93	0.07	0.03	22.24	94.92	36.72	22.83	21.66	7.07	6.49
1999.....	71.69	12.45	19.34	23.30	7.61	6.52	3.27	2.97	0.07	0.05	23.48	96.54	37.73	22.91	21.62	7.61	6.51
2000.....	71.27	12.36	19.66	22.74	7.86	6.10	2.81	3.01	0.06	0.06	24.90	98.70	38.15	23.82	22.58	7.86	6.10
2001.....	71.68	12.28	20.17	23.55	8.03	5.16	2.24	2.62	0.06	0.07	26.32	96.06	38.08	22.77	21.91	8.03	5.16
2002.....	70.65	12.16	19.38	22.73	8.15	5.73	2.69	2.71	0.06	0.11	25.72	97.54	38.12	23.51	21.90	8.15	5.73
2003.....	69.88	11.96	19.63	22.09	7.96	5.94	2.79	2.80	0.06	0.11	26.99	97.83	38.71	22.83	22.32	7.96	5.94
2004.....	70.17	11.55	19.07	22.85	8.22	6.06	2.69	3.00	0.06	0.14	29.14	100.00	40.14	22.92	22.47	8.22	6.07
2005.....	69.38	10.97	18.56	23.19	8.16	6.22	2.70	3.10	0.06	0.18	30.20	100.10	40.22	22.57	22.80	8.16	6.23
2006.....	70.68	10.77	19.02	23.79	8.21	6.59	2.87	3.21	0.06	0.26	29.92	99.39	39.73	22.24	22.45	8.21	6.64
2007.....	71.34	10.74	19.79	23.49	8.46	6.51	2.45	3.47	0.07	0.34	29.34	100.89	39.37	23.66	22.75	8.46	6.52
2008.....	73.14	10.61	20.70	23.85	8.43	7.19	2.51	3.87	0.08	0.55	26.02	98.75	36.77	23.84	22.39	8.43	7.17
2009.....	72.59	11.34	21.14	21.62	8.36	7.62	2.67	3.96	0.08	0.72	22.77	93.94	34.78	23.42	19.69	8.36	7.61
2010.....	74.91	11.61	21.81	22.04	8.43	8.31	2.54	4.55	0.09	0.92	21.69	97.52	35.32	24.57	20.83	8.43	8.27
2011.....	78.08	12.00	23.41	22.22	8.27	9.30	3.10	4.70	0.11	1.17	18.38	96.85	34.63	24.95	19.66	8.27	9.20
2012.....	79.23	13.84	24.61	20.68	8.06	8.89	2.63	4.55	0.16	1.34	15.80	94.38	33.84	26.09	17.38	8.06	8.85
2013.....	81.84	15.86	24.86	20.00	8.24	9.42	2.56	4.82	0.22	1.60	12.84	97.12	34.40	26.81	18.04	8.24	9.45
2014.....	87.71	18.60	26.72	20.29	8.34	9.77	2.47	5.02	0.34	1.73	10.97	98.28	34.66	27.38	18.00	8.34	9.74
2015.....	88.25	19.70	28.07	17.95	8.34	9.73	2.32	4.99	0.43	1.78	10.89	97.38	35.37	28.19	15.55	8.34	9.72
2016.....	84.27	18.51	27.58	14.67	8.43	10.42	2.47	5.07	0.57	2.10	11.26	97.33	35.71	28.40	14.23	8.43	10.36
2017.....	88.05	19.53	28.29	15.63	8.42	11.20	2.77	5.10	0.78	2.34	7.51	97.60	36.05	28.06	13.84	8.42	11.08
2018.....	95.62	22.89	31.69	15.36	8.44	11.51	2.66	5.24	0.92	2.48	3.62	101.08	36.88	31.09	13.25	8.44	11.30
2019.....	101.04	25.44	34.89	14.27	8.46	11.64	2.49	5.16	1.04	2.73	-0.71	100.17	36.72	32.10	11.31	8.46	11.46

NA Not available. Z Less than 5 trillion. [1] Includes other types of fuel not shown separately. [2] Includes lease condensate. [3] Beginning 1989, includes waste coal supplied. Beginning 2001, also includes a small amount of refuse recovery. [4] Electricity net generation from conventional hydroelectric power, geothermal, solar, and wind. Consumption of electricity from wood, biomass waste, and alcohol fuels; geothermal heat pump and direct use energy; and solar thermal direct use energy. [5] Conventional hydroelectricity net generation. [6] Organic nonfossil material of biological origin constituting a renewable energy source. [7] Imports minus exports. [8] Includes coal coke net imports and electricity net imports, not shown separately. [9] Petroleum products supplied, including natural gas plant liquids and crude oil burned as fuel. Does not include biofuels that have been blended with petroleum. [10] Excludes supplemental gaseous fuels.

Source: U.S. Energy Information Administration, *Monthly Energy Review*, April 2020. See also <http://www.eia.gov/totalenergy/data/monthly/>.

Energy and Utilities 603

Table 959. Energy Supply and Disposition by Type of Fuel—Estimates, 2019, and Projections, 2020 to 2045

[Quadrillion Btu (102.11 represents 102,110,000,000,000,000) per year. Btu = British thermal unit. For definition of Btu, see source and text, this section. Projections are "reference" or mid-level forecasts. See report for methodology and assumptions used in generating projections]

Type of fuel	2019	Projections					
		2020	2025	2030	2035	2040	2045
Production, total.............	**102.11**	**104.02**	**111.60**	**114.35**	**115.92**	**116.99**	**118.93**
Crude oil and lease condensate......................	25.61	27.47	29.64	29.75	29.68	28.85	28.15
Natural gas plant liquids................................	6.60	7.23	8.38	8.74	8.73	8.60	8.54
Natural gas, dry...	35.03	36.03	39.29	40.93	42.53	43.94	44.98
Coal [1]...	13.57	12.30	10.96	11.15	10.96	10.71	10.64
Nuclear power...	8.44	8.30	7.82	7.12	6.81	6.74	6.70
Renewable energy [2].....................................	11.44	11.86	14.63	15.98	16.51	17.45	19.19
Other [3]...	1.42	0.83	0.88	0.68	0.69	0.71	0.74
Imports, total.................................	**23.46**	**23.87**	**21.47**	**20.35**	**20.35**	**21.06**	**22.35**
Crude oil..	15.55	15.96	14.74	14.41	14.51	15.07	16.22
Petroleum and other liquids [4].........................	4.82	4.87	4.09	3.56	3.56	3.70	3.92
Natural gas..	2.79	2.74	2.45	2.18	2.06	2.07	2.01
Other imports [5]...	0.29	0.31	0.19	0.21	0.22	0.21	0.21
Exports, total.................................	**23.57**	**26.91**	**33.26**	**34.82**	**35.21**	**35.06**	**35.06**
Petroleum and other liquids [6].........................	16.70	19.43	22.20	22.22	22.50	22.27	22.19
Natural gas..	4.48	5.39	8.27	9.94	10.06	10.14	10.16
Coal..	2.38	2.09	2.78	2.66	2.65	2.65	2.71
Consumption, total..........................	**100.00**	**99.59**	**99.58**	**99.55**	**100.79**	**102.72**	**105.96**
Petroleum and other liquids [7].........................	38.04	38.28	37.40	36.84	36.67	36.75	37.53
Natural gas..	32.15	32.20	33.06	32.68	34.05	35.32	36.24
Coal..	11.25	10.26	8.15	8.46	8.28	8.03	7.90
Nuclear power...	8.44	8.30	7.82	7.12	6.81	6.74	6.70
Renewable energy [8].....................................	9.84	10.23	12.86	14.14	14.66	15.57	17.28
Other [9]...	0.28	0.32	0.28	0.31	0.32	0.31	0.31
Net imports of petroleum.....................	**3.67**	**1.39**	**-3.37**	**-4.26**	**-4.42**	**-3.49**	**-2.06**
Prices (2019 dollars per unit):							
Crude oil spot prices (dol. per barrel)							
Brent spot price..........................	63.37	58.51	68.74	75.83	83.33	90.48	97.76
West Texas Intermediate spot price..................	56.26	53.14	64.56	71.34	79.36	85.74	93.35
Natural gas at Henry Hub (dol. per mil. Btu)..........	2.57	2.44	2.84	3.29	3.36	3.44	3.52
Coal minemouth price (dol. per ton) [10]...............	34.30	33.00	34.29	33.55	34.31	36.63	37.50
Electricity price (cents per kWh)......................	10.4	10.2	10.3	10.4	10.3	10.1	10.0

[1] Includes waste coal. [2] Includes grid-connected electricity from conventional hydroelectric power; biomass (including wood and wood waste, and other biomass); landfill gas; biogenic municipal waste; wind; photovoltaic and solar thermal sources; and nonelectric energy from renewable sources, such as active and passive solar systems, and wood. Excludes electricity imports using renewable sources and nonmarketed renewable energy. [3] Includes nonbiogenic municipal waste, hydrogen, methanol, and some domestic inputs to refineries. [4] Includes imports of finished petroleum products, unfinished oils, alcohols, ethers, blending components, and renewable fuels such as ethanol. [5] Includes coal, coal coke (net), and electricity (net). Excludes imports of fuel used in nuclear power plants. [6] Includes crude oil, petroleum products, ethanol, and biodiesel. [7] Includes petroleum-derived fuels and non-petroleum-derived fuels, such as ethanol, biodiesel, and coal-based synthetic liquids. Petroleum coke, which is a solid, is included. Also included are hydrocarbon gas liquids and crude oil consumed as a fuel. [8] Includes grid-connected electricity from wood and wood waste, non-electric energy from wood, and biofuels heat and coproducts used in the production of liquid fuels, but excludes the energy content of the liquid fuels. See also footnote 2. [9] Includes non-biogenic municipal waste, hydrogen, and net electricity imports. [10] Includes reported prices for both open market and captive mines.

Source: U.S. Energy Information Administration, *Annual Energy Outlook 2020*, January 2020. See also <https://www.eia.gov/outlooks/aeo/>.

Table 960. Energy Consumption by End-Use Sector: 1978 to 2019

[Trillion Btu (16,132.9 represents 16,132,900,000,000,000). Btu=British thermal unit. Represents consumption of fossil fuels and renewable energy, plus electricity retail sales and electrical system energy losses. For definition of Btu, see source and text, this section. See Appendix III]

Year	Residential	Commercial [1]	Industrial [2]	Transportation	Year	Residential	Commercial [1]	Industrial [2]	Transportation
1978.........	16,132.9	10,512.1	32,643.0	20,617.1	1999.........	19,554.2	16,376.4	34,691.6	25,916.0
1979.........	15,813.2	10,648.1	33,877.3	20,471.6	2000.........	20,421.8	17,175.5	34,587.2	26,515.5
1980.........	15,753.8	10,578.4	31,993.3	19,696.7	2001.........	20,038.3	17,136.9	32,652.5	26,242.1
1981.........	15,261.9	10,616.0	30,662.4	19,514.1	2002.........	20,786.5	17,345.9	32,590.1	26,807.8
1982.........	15,531.3	10,860.4	27,561.0	19,089.3	2003.........	21,120.0	17,346.3	32,488.6	26,881.0
1983.........	15,425.5	10,938.5	27,372.0	19,176.7	2004.........	21,082.1	17,655.7	33,443.7	27,826.5
1984.........	15,959.9	11,444.0	29,508.4	19,655.6	2005.........	21,613.3	17,853.6	32,374.1	28,260.7
1985.........	16,041.7	11,451.4	28,757.0	20,088.0	2006.........	20,670.9	17,707.4	32,316.8	28,696.8
1986.........	15,975.5	11,606.2	28,224.9	20,788.8	2007.........	21,519.6	18,253.1	32,306.3	28,815.1
1987.........	16,263.7	11,946.1	29,332.0	21,468.9	2008.........	21,668.3	18,402.4	31,261.0	27,421.4
1988.........	17,133.1	12,578.2	30,626.8	22,317.8	2009.........	21,082.1	17,887.8	28,380.2	26,592.2
1989.........	17,790.2	13,196.4	31,281.8	22,478.6	2010.........	21,894.8	18,058.6	30,577.9	26,978.4
1990.........	16,940.5	13,317.5	31,749.3	22,419.0	2011.........	21,381.9	17,981.6	30,880.6	26,598.6
1991.........	17,419.8	13,500.1	31,341.8	22,118.0	2012.........	19,870.1	17,421.5	30,960.5	26,125.8
1992.........	17,355.3	13,441.2	32,512.9	22,415.1	2013.........	21,051.8	17,929.6	31,525.4	26,611.8
1993.........	18,212.1	13,817.0	32,559.2	22,670.8	2014.........	21,445.7	18,264.7	31,690.8	26,868.9
1994.........	18,110.8	14,097.4	33,462.1	23,318.7	2015.........	20,617.7	18,156.9	31,363.8	27,238.1
1995.........	18,517.2	14,690.0	33,908.5	23,811.9	2016.........	20,176.4	18,030.4	31,340.7	27,785.6
1996.........	19,502.4	15,172.0	34,836.4	24,419.3	2017.........	19,882.6	17,899.9	31,805.8	28,014.2
1997.........	18,962.8	15,681.3	35,134.1	24,722.6	2018.........	21,500.6	18,440.5	32,699.5	28,451.0
1998.........	18,952.5	15,967.6	34,779.0	25,224.5	2019.........	21,210.3	18,178.0	32,500.5	28,282.4

[1] Commercial sector fuel use, including use at commercial combined-heat-and-power (CHP) and commercial electricity-only plants. [2] Industrial sector fuel use, including use at industrial combined-heat-and-power (CHP) and industrial electricity-only plants.

Source: U.S. Energy Information Administration, *Monthly Energy Review*, April 2020. See also <http://www.eia.gov/totalenergy/data/monthly/>.

Table 961. Energy Consumption by Mode of Transportation: 2010 to 2017

[27 represents 27,000,000,000,000. Btu = British thermal unit. For conversion rates for each fuel type, see source]

Mode	Trillion Btu			Physical units			
	2010	2015	2017	Unit	2010	2015	2017
AIR [1]							
Aviation gasoline..........................	27	24	25	Mil. gal.	221	196	206
Jet fuel......................................	1,686	1,637	1,739	Mil. gal.	12,492	12,124	12,881
HIGHWAY							
Light duty vehicle, short wheel base & motorcycle [2]...	10,902	11,254	11,464	Mil. gal.	87,215	90,031	91,712
Light duty vehicle, long wheel base [2]...	4,531	4,555	4,683	Mil. gal.	36,251	36,437	37,467
Single-unit 2-axle 6-tire or more truck..................	1,887	1,856	1,950	Mil. gal.	15,097	14,851	15,600
Combination truck [3]......................	3,741	3,611	3,795	Mil. gal.	29,927	28,886	30,364
Bus...	240	279	294	Mil. gal.	1,921	2,228	2,350
TRANSIT [4]							
Electricity..................................	22	23	23	Mil. kWh	6,414	6,668	6,611
Diesel (includes bio-diesel).............	88	80	80	Mil. gal.	633	576	579
Gasoline and other nondiesel fuels [5]..................	12	14	14	Mil. gal.	98	114	113
Compressed natural gas.................	18	22	24	Mil. gal.	126	156	172
RAIL [6]							
Distillate/diesel fuel......................	493	521	494	Mil. gal.	3,557	3,754	3,559
Electricity..................................	2	2	2	Mil. kWh	559	504	490
WATER							
Residual fuel oil..........................	770	503	386	Mil. gal.	5,143	3,358	2,580
Distillate/diesel fuel oil..................	278	335	303	Mil. gal.	2,003	2,417	2,186
Gasoline....................................	146	258	290	Mil. gal.	1,167	2,066	2,323
PIPELINE							
Natural gas................................	695	699	744	Mil. cu. ft.	674,124	678,183	721,518

[1] Includes general aviation and certified carriers, domestic operations only; and fuel used in air taxi operations, but not commuter operations. [2] "Light duty vehicle, short wheel base" includes passenger cars, light trucks, vans and sport utility vehicles with a wheelbase (WB) equal to or less than 121 inches. "Light duty vehicle, long wheel base" includes large passenger cars, vans, pickup trucks, and sport/utility vehicles with wheelbases (WB) larger than 121 inches. [3] A power unit (truck tractor) and one or more trailing units (a semitrailer or trailer). [4] Includes light, heavy, and commuter rail; motor bus; trolley bus; van pools; automated guideway; and demand-responsive vehicles. [5] Includes gasoline, liquefied petroleum gas, liquefied natural gas, methane, ethanol, bunker fuel, kerosene, grain additive, and other fuel. [6] Includes Amtrak and freight service carriers that have an annual operating revenue of $250 million or more.

Source: U.S. Department of Transportation, Bureau of Transportation Statistics, "National Transportation Statistics," <https://www.bts.gov/topics/national-transportation-statistics>, accessed February 2020.

Table 962. Renewable Energy Consumption by Source and Sector: 1990 to 2019

[In trillion Btu (6,040.0 represents 6,040,000,000,000,000). For definition of Btu, see source and text, this section. Renewable energy is obtained from sources that are essentially inexhaustible, unlike fossil fuels of which there is a finite supply]

Source and sector	1990	2000	2010	2015	2017	2018	2019
Consumption, total..................	**6,040.0**	**6,104.2**	**8,267.1**	**9,720.5**	**11,076.5**	**11,301.0**	**11,460.5**
Conventional hydroelectric power [1].........	3,046.4	2,811.1	2,538.5	2,321.2	2,767.0	2,663.1	2,491.8
Geothermal energy [2]....................	170.7	164.4	208.0	211.8	210.2	208.9	209.3
Biomass energy [3].......................	2,735.1	3,008.2	4,505.9	4,983.4	4,979.3	5,031.1	4,984.7
Solar energy [4]...........................	58.8	63.5	91.3	426.9	777.1	915.5	1,042.9
Wind energy [5]...........................	29.0	57.1	923.4	1,777.3	2,342.9	2,482.4	2,731.8
Residential [6]........................	**640.2**	**486.3**	**642.0**	**680.7**	**658.4**	**778.2**	**824.9**
Wood [7]...................................	580.0	420.0	540.5	512.7	425.2	517.3	528.8
Geothermal [2]............................	5.5	8.6	36.8	39.6	39.6	39.6	39.6
Solar [4]...................................	54.7	57.7	64.7	128.3	193.6	221.2	256.5
Commercial [8].......................	**98.4**	**128.3**	**142.4**	**229.9**	**255.2**	**274.1**	**280.2**
Biomass [3]...............................	94.0	119.1	110.9	151.9	156.4	156.5	146.3
Geothermal [2]............................	2.8	7.6	18.5	19.7	19.7	20.0	23.7
Hydroelectric [1]..........................	1.4	1.0	0.8	0.3	2.2	2.1	1.9
Solar energy [4]..........................	0.2	0.6	12.1	56.9	75.6	94.0	106.6
Wind energy [5]..........................	(NA)	(NA)	0.2	1.1	1.3	1.6	1.7
Industrial [9].........................	**1,717.1**	**1,928.2**	**2,343.5**	**2,491.4**	**2,489.6**	**2,486.4**	**2,495.1**
Biomass [3]...............................	1,684.2	1,881.5	2,320.3	2,459.8	2,449.7	2,446.5	2,451.4
Geothermal [2]............................	1.9	4.4	4.2	4.2	4.2	4.2	4.2
Hydroelectric [1]..........................	30.9	42.2	16.3	13.1	12.7	10.5	10.2
Solar energy [4]..........................	(Z)	0.1	2.7	13.7	22.2	24.4	28.4
Wind energy [5]..........................	(NA)	(NA)	(NA)	0.5	0.8	0.9	1.0
Transportation [12]..................	**60.4**	**134.9**	**1,074.8**	**1,334.0**	**1,438.5**	**1,414.7**	**1,410.5**
Fuel ethanol...............................	60.4	134.9	1,041.4	1,109.9	1,155.6	1,152.4	1,160.5
Biodiesel [10].............................	(NA)	(NA)	33.2	190.6	253.3	242.9	231.0
Electric power [11]...................	**3,523.9**	**3,426.5**	**4,064.4**	**4,984.5**	**6,234.8**	**6,347.5**	**6,449.8**
Biomass [3]...............................	316.5	452.8	459.4	524.9	509.5	496.1	447.7
Geothermal [2]............................	160.5	143.8	148.5	148.3	146.7	145.1	141.7
Hydroelectric [1]..........................	3,014.0	2,767.9	2,521.5	2,307.7	2,752.0	2,650.6	2,479.7
Solar [4]...................................	3.8	5.0	11.8	227.9	485.7	575.9	651.4
Wind [5]...................................	29.0	57.1	923.3	1,775.7	2,340.8	2,479.9	2,729.2

NA Not available. Z Less than 500 billion. [1] Power produced from the kinetic energy of falling water. [2] As used at electric power plants, hot water or steam extracted from geothermal reservoirs supplied to steam turbines at electric power plants that drive generators to produce electricity. [3] Wood and wood-derived fuels, municipal solid waste, fuel ethanol, and biodiesel. [4] The radiant energy of the sun, which can be converted into other forms of energy. Solar thermal and photovoltaic electricity net generation and solar thermal direct use energy. [5] Energy present in wind motion that can be converted to mechanical energy for driving pumps, mills, and electric power generators. [6] Living quarters for private households; excludes institutional living quarters. [7] Wood and wood-derived fuels. [8] Service-providing facilities and equipment of businesses, governments, and other private and public organizations. Includes commercial combined-heat-and-power and commercial electricity-only plants. [9] All facilities and equipment used for producing, processing, or assembling goods. Includes industrial combined-heat-and-power and industrial electricity-only plants. [10] Any liquid biofuel suitable as a diesel fuel substitute, additive, or extender. [11] Electricity-only and combined-heat-and-power plants whose primary business is to sell electricity and/or heat to the public. Includes sources not shown separately. [12] Beginning in 2009, includes other renewable diesel fuel and other renewable fuels consumption, not shown separately.

Source: U.S. Energy Information Administration, *Monthly Energy Review*, April 2020. See also <http://www.eia.gov/totalenergy/data/monthly/>.

Table 963. Energy Consumption—End-Use Sector and Selected Source by State: 2018

[In trillions of British thermal units (101,084 represents 101,084,000,000,000,000 Btu), except as indicated. For definition of Btu, see source and text, this section. U.S. totals may not equal sum of states due to independent rounding and/or interstate flows of electricity that are not allocated to the states. For technical notes and documentation, see source <eia.gov/state/seds/seds-technical-notes-complete.php?sid=US>]

State	Total [1,2]	Per capita [3] (mil. Btu)	End-use sector [4]				Source				
			Resi-dential	Com-mercial	Indus-trial [2]	Trans-portation	Petro-leum [5]	Natural gas (dry) [6]	Coal	Hydro-electric power [7]	Nuclear electric power
U.S.	101,084	309	21,474	18,414	32,740	28,456	38,341	31,159	13,250	2,663	8,438
AL	1,955	400	358	264	841	492	547	771	377	101	413
AK	610	830	49	57	334	169	222	346	17	15	–
AZ	1,488	208	407	352	227	502	567	401	331	64	325
AR	1,120	372	235	184	411	289	346	367	304	27	133
CA	7,967	202	1,439	1,509	1,848	3,170	3,668	2,207	33	240	190
CO	1,513	266	360	293	425	436	522	525	284	17	–
CT	753	211	248	193	78	233	327	286	4	5	176
DE	290	301	69	62	86	73	114	99	4	–	–
DC	175	249	42	107	6	20	20	33	(Z)	–	–
FL	4,281	202	1,195	988	489	1,609	1,769	1,511	328	2	306
GA	2,876	274	738	550	770	817	921	760	340	34	359
HI	293	206	34	43	56	160	253	3	14	1	–
ID	553	316	130	91	171	162	188	116	3	100	–
IL	4,012	315	990	823	1,185	1,014	1,292	1,141	705	1	1,026
IN	2,838	424	556	376	1,294	611	771	894	986	2	–
IA	1,616	513	247	198	868	303	436	470	326	8	51
KS	1,134	390	234	222	395	285	359	321	228	(Z)	96
KY	1,744	391	369	268	611	497	626	357	656	40	–
LA	4,403	945	335	269	3,067	732	1,921	1,861	138	11	179
ME	395	295	107	71	108	110	180	48	2	30	–
MD	1,361	226	415	410	104	432	473	313	124	26	157
MA	1,459	212	434	412	151	462	588	453	(Z)	10	46
MI	2,894	290	788	619	722	765	919	1,011	506	14	319
MN	1,914	341	432	378	641	464	625	515	262	10	153
MS	1,193	400	201	157	411	423	483	591	60	–	72
MO	1,848	302	556	428	309	555	641	330	668	8	111
MT	435	410	100	85	132	118	177	91	152	104	–
NE	915	475	168	147	387	212	252	197	264	13	59
NV	727	240	172	153	173	230	271	311	35	17	–
NH	325	240	107	73	42	102	162	51	8	12	105
NJ	2,241	252	586	584	264	806	971	800	17	(Z)	334
NM	703	336	120	123	231	228	269	281	137	1	–
NY	3,854	197	1,174	1,152	393	1,135	1,387	1,394	17	270	449
NC	2,616	252	725	585	566	740	880	599	325	60	440
ND	661	872	76	93	354	139	196	137	407	29	–
OH	3,756	322	924	706	1,206	921	1,158	1,212	718	2	191
OK	1,707	433	307	258	658	484	559	835	171	19	–
OR	1,012	242	247	196	256	314	353	271	17	323	–
PA	3,962	310	965	655	1,403	938	1,249	1,513	644	39	873
RI	197	187	64	48	23	62	88	105	–	(Z)	–
SC	1,672	329	378	275	536	483	555	337	205	27	551
SD	397	452	73	66	158	100	120	96	28	57	–
TN	2,256	333	563	469	578	646	751	404	252	94	378
TX	14,259	498	1,779	1,658	7,282	3,541	7,166	4,564	1,189	10	431
UT	835	265	177	173	218	267	314	254	273	8	–
VT	139	223	48	28	18	45	79	14	–	12	–
VA	2,401	283	610	636	438	717	814	667	149	16	306
WA	2,079	276	479	377	543	680	829	335	61	736	102
WV	833	462	164	115	362	193	227	223	662	17	–
WI	1,886	325	446	378	609	453	570	565	362	22	106
WY	559	967	51	59	330	118	166	175	456	9	–

– Represents zero. Z Less than 500 billion Btu. [1] Includes other sources, not shown separately. [2] U.S. total energy and U.S. industrial sector include net imports of coal coke that are not allocated to the states. [3] Based on estimated resident population as of July 1. [4] End-use sector data include electricity sales and associated electrical system energy losses. [5] Includes fuel ethanol blended into motor gasoline. [6] Includes supplemental gaseous fuels. [7] Conventional hydroelectric power. Does not include pumped-storage hydroelectricity.

Source: U.S. Energy Information Administration, "State Energy Data System," <http://www.eia.gov/state/seds/>, accessed July 2020.

Table 964. Energy-related Carbon Dioxide Emissions by Sector and State: 2016

[In millions of metric tons (5,161.0 represents 5,161,000,000), except percent. Total state CO2 emissions include those from direct fuel use across all sectors as well as primary fuels consumed for electricity generation. Covers emissions released at the location where fossil fuels are consumed. Regarding fuels that are used in one state to generate electricity consumed in another state, emissions are attributed to the state in which the electricity is generated and fuels are combusted. Data are derived from EIA's State Energy Data System]

State	Total carbon dioxide emissions	Percent of carbon dioxide emissions by sector					Per capita
		Commercial	Electric Power	Residential	Industrial	Transpor-tation	
Total [1]	**5,161.0**	**4.5**	**34.8**	**5.8**	**18.2**	**36.7**	**16.0**
Alabama	115.1	1.9	48.0	1.6	18.3	30.1	23.7
Alaska	34.9	5.8	7.9	4.3	48.1	33.9	47.0
Arizona	87.0	3.3	50.9	2.5	5.3	38.0	12.6
Arkansas	62.4	4.7	48.4	2.7	13.2	31.1	20.9
California	361.4	5.2	10.1	6.7	19.1	58.9	9.2
Colorado	89.0	4.4	39.6	8.4	16.0	31.6	16.1
Connecticut	34.3	11.4	20.4	18.3	5.4	44.6	9.6
Delaware	13.3	7.0	26.9	6.3	25.2	34.6	14.0
District of Columbia	2.8	34.1	–	23.2	1.1	41.7	4.0
Florida	230.1	3.2	46.0	0.5	5.2	45.0	11.1
Georgia	136.2	3.4	42.2	5.0	9.8	39.7	13.2
Hawaii	18.4	1.8	35.7	0.2	7.2	55.2	12.9
Idaho	18.4	7.5	6.8	8.9	18.3	58.5	10.9
Illinois	204.1	6.5	32.5	10.8	16.6	33.5	15.9
Indiana	181.9	2.9	46.0	4.2	23.1	23.8	27.4
Iowa	73.1	4.8	33.8	5.6	26.6	29.2	23.4
Kansas	62.1	3.9	40.0	5.4	20.6	30.1	21.3
Kentucky	123.9	2.2	58.6	2.3	10.9	26.0	27.9
Louisiana	209.1	1.0	17.3	0.9	58.2	22.6	44.6
Maine	16.5	9.8	9.1	17.7	9.1	54.2	12.4
Maryland	57.6	8.9	29.8	9.5	3.8	47.9	9.6
Massachusetts	64.2	10.9	16.7	17.7	5.3	49.4	9.4
Michigan	151.8	6.7	36.3	12.3	11.6	33.1	15.3
Minnesota	89.3	7.1	29.6	9.0	19.1	35.1	16.2
Mississippi	68.9	2.3	37.6	2.1	14.8	43.3	23.1
Missouri	117.7	3.6	52.4	4.8	6.9	32.3	19.3
Montana	30.5	4.5	52.4	4.8	12.5	25.8	29.3
Nebraska	48.6	3.7	43.6	4.5	19.7	28.5	25.4
Nevada	36.7	6.2	37.9	6.3	8.7	40.9	12.5
New Hampshire	13.8	10.1	17.2	18.3	5.5	48.9	10.3
New Jersey	110.8	9.1	17.7	12.2	8.6	52.4	12.3
New Mexico	48.4	3.5	47.6	4.3	15.3	29.2	23.2
New York	163.7	13.2	16.9	18.7	5.1	46.1	8.3
North Carolina	120.6	4.4	42.1	4.2	8.6	40.7	11.9
North Dakota	54.3	1.8	53.2	1.7	27.9	15.3	71.8
Ohio	206.3	5.3	39.1	7.8	17.2	30.5	17.7
Oklahoma	96.9	3.1	36.5	3.3	23.5	33.6	24.7
Oregon	38.0	5.6	20.5	6.6	13.5	53.8	9.3
Pennsylvania	217.4	4.9	37.7	8.5	21.0	27.9	17.0
Rhode Island	9.8	8.8	26.4	18.6	6.5	39.7	9.2
South Carolina	71.7	3.0	38.4	2.5	10.6	45.5	14.5
South Dakota	15.0	4.9	17.4	6.3	25.9	45.5	17.4
Tennessee	103.1	3.6	34.8	3.5	15.7	42.3	15.5
Texas	653.8	1.9	31.7	1.7	30.3	34.4	23.4
Utah	58.8	4.5	46.7	6.2	12.5	30.1	19.3
Vermont	6.0	14.3	–	21.8	7.1	56.6	9.6
Virginia	104.2	5.5	32.2	5.5	11.2	45.6	12.4
Washington	78.9	5.5	12.1	6.4	13.9	62.0	10.8
West Virginia	94.6	1.8	72.8	1.7	10.8	12.9	51.7
Wisconsin	95.6	6.2	40.3	9.0	13.6	30.8	16.6
Wyoming	60.7	1.8	66.4	1.4	17.6	12.8	103.7

– Represents zero. [1] For the United States as a whole, see, EIA's *Monthly Energy Review,* Section 12: Environment. The total for all states is different from the national-level estimate because of differing methodologies. These values are unadjusted. See source for details on the data series differences.

Source: U.S. Energy Information Agency, *Energy-Related Carbon Dioxide Emissions by State, 2005-2016,* February 2019. See also <https://www.eia.gov/environment/emissions/state/analysis/>.

Table 965. Energy Expenditures and Average Fuel Prices by Source and Sector: 1980 to 2018

[In millions of dollars (374,350 represents $374,350,000,000), except as indicated. Btu = British thermal units. For definition of Btu, see text, this section. End-use sector and electric utilities exclude expenditures and prices on energy sources such as hydropower, solar, wind, and geothermal. Also excludes expenditures for reported amounts of energy consumed by the energy industry for production, transportation, and processing operations]

Source and sector	1980	1990	2000	2010	2014	2015	2016	2017	2018
EXPENDITURES (mil. dol.)									
Total [1, 2, 3]	**374,350**	**474,652**	**687,711**	**1,214,045**	**1,394,926**	**1,128,068**	**1,038,273**	**1,136,189**	**1,271,064**
Natural gas [4]	51,062	65,278	119,094	161,303	174,398	140,294	127,618	142,084	157,533
Petroleum products	237,679	237,677	359,403	716,865	863,530	623,132	549,322	631,720	742,002
Motor gasoline [5]	124,408	126,558	192,153	376,492	452,821	342,578	310,961	348,456	387,586
Coal	22,607	28,419	27,959	50,245	44,873	36,578	31,694	30,326	29,230
Retail electricity	98,095	176,691	231,578	365,913	389,872	388,344	383,567	387,222	403,427
Residential sector [6]	69,280	110,910	155,299	249,772	264,712	248,045	238,542	246,082	266,963
Commercial sector [2, 3]	47,074	79,602	113,421	177,662	190,720	185,971	178,885	184,764	193,099
Industrial sector [2, 3]	94,316	103,351	140,963	221,454	242,477	186,720	169,456	190,677	212,934
Transportation sector [2]	163,680	180,790	278,028	565,158	697,017	507,332	451,390	514,665	598,069
Motor gasoline [5]	121,809	123,845	189,836	369,433	445,572	329,609	299,361	335,666	373,095
Electric utilities [3]	38,027	40,627	60,053	94,791	95,827	76,352	68,421	69,714	75,621
AVERAGE FUEL PRICES (dol. per mil. Btu)									
All sectors	**6.89**	**8.29**	**10.33**	**18.92**	**21.33**	**17.30**	**15.94**	**17.32**	**18.62**
Residential sector [6]	7.46	11.87	14.21	22.37	23.35	22.93	22.92	23.77	23.30
Commercial sector [3]	7.83	11.87	13.90	20.92	21.43	20.72	20.17	20.86	20.66
Industrial sector [3]	4.72	5.30	6.50	12.13	12.71	9.87	9.00	9.94	10.67
Transportation sector	8.61	8.33	10.77	21.53	26.71	19.15	16.70	18.91	21.74
Electric utilities [3]	1.77	1.48	1.71	2.63	2.80	2.28	2.09	2.21	2.33

[1] Includes other sources not shown separately. [2] There is a discontinuity in this time series between 1988 and 1989 due to the expanded coverage of the use of wood and biomass waste beginning in 1989. [3] There are no direct fuel costs for hydroelectric, geothermal, wind, photovoltaic, or solar thermal energy. [4] Natural gas as it is consumed; includes supplemental gaseous fuels that are commingled with natural gas. [5] Beginning 1995, includes fuel ethanol blended into motor gasoline. [6] There are no direct fuel costs for geothermal, photovoltaic, or solar thermal energy.

Source: U.S. Energy Information Administration, "State Energy Data System (SEDS)," <http://www.eia.gov/state/seds/>, accessed July 2020.

Table 966. Fuel Ethanol and Biodiesel—Summary: 2000 to 2019

[233.1 represents 233,100,000,000,000. Btu=British thermal units. For definition of Btu, see source and text, this section. Minus sign (-) indicates an excess of exports over imports, except where noted]

Fuel	2000	2005	2010	2014	2015	2016	2017	2018	2019
FUEL ETHANOL									
Feedstock [1] (tril. Btu)	233.1	549.5	1,823.5	1,938.0	1,998.0	2,072.2	2,137.9	2,156.3	2,104.2
Production:									
1,000 barrels	38,627	92,961	316,617	340,781	352,553	366,981	379,435	383,127	375,629
Tril. Btu	137.7	331.3	1,127.8	1,212.8	1,254.4	1,305.7	1,349.3	1,361.3	1,335.4
Net imports [2] (1,000 barrels)	116	3,234	-9,115	-18,371	-17,632	-27,002	-31,268	-39,410	-30,527
Stocks [3] (1,000 barrels)	3,400	5,563	17,941	18,739	21,596	19,758	23,043	23,418	22,349
Stock change [4] (1,000 barrels)	-624	-439	1,347	2,315	2,857	-1,838	3,285	375	-989
Consumption:									
1,000 barrels	39,367	96,634	306,155	320,095	332,064	341,817	344,882	343,342	346,091
Tril. Btu	140.3	344.4	1,090.5	1,139.2	1,181.5	1,216.2	1,226.4	1,219.9	1,230.4
BIODIESEL									
Feedstock [5] (tril. Btu)	(NA)	11.7	44.4	165.4	163.4	202.8	206.4	240.3	223.0
Production:									
1,000 barrels	(NA)	2,162	8,177	30,452	30,080	37,327	37,993	44,222	41,054
Tril. Btu	(NA)	11.6	43.8	163.19	161.20	200.04	203.61	236.99	220.01
Net imports (1,000 barrels)	(NA)	1	-2,024	2,604	6,308	14,781	7,146	1,499	1,292
Stocks [6] (1,000 barrels)	(NA)	(NA)	672	3,131	3,943	6,398	4,268	4,662	3,919
Stock change [4] (1,000 barrels)	(NA)	(NA)	-39	-679	813	2,454	-2,130	394	-766
Consumption:									
1,000 barrels	(NA)	2,163	6,192	33,735	35,575	49,653	47,269	45,326	43,112
Tril. Btu	(NA)	11.6	33.2	180.8	190.6	266.1	253.3	242.9	231.0

NA Not available. [1] Total corn and other biomass inputs to the production of undenatured ethanol used for fuel ethanol. [2] Through 2009, data are for fuel ethanol imports only; data for fuel ethanol exports are not available. Beginning in 2010, data are for fuel ethanol imports minus fuel ethanol exports. [3] Stocks are at end of year. [4] A negative number indicates a decrease in stocks. [5] Total vegetable oil and other biomass inputs to the production of biodiesel. [6] Stocks are at end of period. Includes biodiesel stocks at (or in) refineries, pipelines, and bulk terminals. Beginning in 2011, also includes stocks at biodiesel production plants.

Source: U.S. Energy Information Administration, *Monthly Energy Review*, April 2020. See also <http://www.eia.gov/totalenergy/data/monthly/>.

Table 967. Energy Expenditures—End-Use Sector and Selected Source by State: 2018

[In millions of dollars (1,271,064 represents $1,271,064,000,000). End-use sector and electric utilities exclude expenditures on energy sources such as hydroelectric, photovoltaic, solar thermal, wind, and geothermal. Also excludes expenditures for reported amounts of energy consumed by the energy industry for production, transportation, and processing operations. For technical notes and documentation, see source, <https://www.eia.gov/state/seds/seds-technical-notes-complete.php>]

State	Total [1,2]	End-use sector				Source			
		Resi-dential	Com-mercial	Indus-trial [2]	Transpor-tation	Petroleum products [3]	Natural gas [4]	Coal	Electricity sales
U.S.	1,271,064	266,963	193,099	212,934	598,069	742,002	157,533	29,230	403,427
AL.	21,952	4,720	3,190	4,412	9,629	10,948	3,238	957	8,672
AK.	5,925	816	876	663	3,571	4,414	535	113	1,145
AZ.	22,825	5,140	3,795	2,142	11,748	13,342	1,825	809	8,501
AR.	12,510	2,427	1,530	2,623	5,930	6,948	2,049	607	3,846
CA.	138,992	22,860	23,168	15,174	77,790	84,770	14,783	118	41,987
CO.	18,431	3,672	2,776	2,790	9,193	10,899	2,332	470	5,629
CT.	14,145	4,932	2,946	952	5,315	7,407	2,093	18	5,309
DE.	3,734	926	651	483	1,674	2,019	637	11	1,219
DC.	2,146	502	1,179	68	398	447	331	(Z)	1,367
FL.	62,481	15,133	10,549	4,196	32,604	35,864	7,481	965	24,649
GA.	35,706	8,995	5,556	4,693	16,462	18,722	4,583	946	13,453
HI.	6,618	929	1,116	1,058	3,515	4,708	108	47	2,710
ID.	6,917	1,232	740	1,217	3,728	4,391	535	7	1,941
IL.	44,808	10,044	6,834	6,671	21,260	24,489	7,063	1,355	13,473
IN.	30,038	5,865	3,507	7,814	12,852	14,908	5,024	2,448	10,053
IA.	15,603	2,819	1,816	4,607	6,361	8,531	2,545	556	4,566
KS.	12,601	2,744	2,186	2,151	5,520	6,657	1,616	390	4,413
KY.	19,720	3,665	2,465	3,422	10,168	11,768	1,767	1,314	6,473
LA.	35,119	3,570	2,649	17,677	11,223	23,888	5,362	439	6,742
ME.	6,182	1,864	1,033	753	2,532	3,984	421	10	1,660
MD.	19,885	5,330	4,209	1,011	9,336	10,776	2,295	314	7,182
MA.	26,859	8,290	6,394	2,069	10,106	12,976	4,689	1	9,860
MI.	35,988	9,196	5,999	4,867	15,926	18,714	5,813	1,212	11,922
MN.	22,237	4,868	3,529	3,854	9,987	12,316	2,953	582	7,021
MS.	14,394	2,568	1,834	2,193	7,799	8,690	2,197	161	4,593
MO.	23,587	5,797	3,786	2,500	11,504	13,184	2,377	1,211	8,148
MT.	5,077	965	758	642	2,712	3,281	467	308	1,263
NE.	9,215	1,587	1,159	1,945	4,524	5,398	1,022	340	2,792
NV.	10,347	2,057	1,339	1,565	5,386	6,326	1,364	109	3,277
NH.	5,837	1,923	1,078	518	2,319	3,563	484	30	1,880
NJ.	32,961	7,521	6,670	2,386	16,384	18,887	4,996	59	9,991
NM.	8,275	1,312	1,140	1,054	4,769	5,529	703	340	2,229
NY.	60,768	19,001	14,889	3,352	23,527	29,315	10,773	62	22,233
NC.	34,156	8,436	5,262	4,275	16,182	19,104	3,570	1,034	12,797
ND.	6,138	734	771	1,932	2,702	3,923	311	601	1,819
OH.	44,272	10,366	6,451	8,065	19,390	23,105	6,642	1,549	15,074
OK.	17,064	3,276	2,227	2,721	8,841	10,392	2,357	315	5,141
OR.	14,168	2,768	1,967	1,764	7,669	8,613	1,263	41	4,366
PA.	48,478	13,201	6,282	8,572	20,424	26,442	7,979	1,692	14,937
RI.	3,901	1,332	861	341	1,368	1,952	821	–	1,373
SC.	20,351	4,556	2,728	3,249	9,820	11,176	1,870	685	7,900
SD.	4,295	789	587	822	2,097	2,580	447	53	1,282
TN.	27,094	5,651	4,655	3,485	13,302	15,131	2,220	582	9,828
TX.	153,012	20,684	14,000	51,529	66,799	108,343	14,447	2,117	35,247
UT.	10,285	1,708	1,431	1,282	5,864	6,608	1,298	555	2,539
VT.	2,844	961	508	312	1,063	1,815	116	–	837
VA.	30,612	7,341	5,515	2,899	14,858	17,001	3,699	452	11,206
WA.	26,321	4,747	3,482	2,623	15,470	17,218	1,887	148	7,123
WV.	8,768	1,714	1,027	2,059	3,968	5,103	627	1,457	2,930
WI.	22,699	4,907	3,506	4,095	10,191	12,290	3,087	859	7,506
WY.	4,997	526	498	1,658	2,315	3,150	437	787	1,325

– Represents zero. Z Less than $500,000. [1] Total expenditures are the sum of purchases for each source (including electricity sales) less electric power sector purchases of fuel. There are no direct fuel costs for hydroelectric, geothermal, wind, photovoltaic, or solar thermal energy. The U.S. total includes -$269 million for coal coke net imports, which are not allocated to the states. [2] U.S. total includes sources not shown separately, such as electricity imports and exports and coal coke net imports, which are not allocated to the states. [3] Includes fuel ethanol blended into motor gasoline. [4] Includes supplemental gaseous fuels.

Source: U.S. Energy Information Administration, "State Energy Data System," <http://www.eia.gov/state/seds/>, accessed July 2020.

Table 968. Energy Imports and Exports by Type of Fuel: 1980 to 2019

[In quadrillion Btu (12.10 represents 12,100,000,000,000,000 Btu). Btu=British thermal units; for definition, see text, this section]

Type of fuel	1980	1990	1995	2000	2005	2010	2015	2016	2017	2018	2019
Net imports, total [1]	**12.10**	**14.06**	**17.68**	**24.90**	**30.20**	**21.69**	**10.89**	**11.26**	**7.51**	**3.62**	**-0.71**
Coal	-2.39	-2.70	-2.08	-1.21	-0.51	-1.62	-1.60	-1.33	-2.22	-2.69	-2.17
Natural gas (dry)	0.96	1.46	2.74	3.62	3.71	2.69	0.99	0.73	-0.07	-0.68	-1.89
Petroleum [2]	13.50	15.29	16.82	22.31	26.85	20.58	11.29	11.71	9.77	7.07	3.40
Other [3]	0.04	0.01	0.20	0.18	0.14	0.04	0.21	0.15	0.04	-0.07	-0.06
Imports, total	15.80	18.82	22.18	28.87	34.66	29.87	23.79	25.38	25.46	24.83	22.80
Coal	0.03	0.07	0.24	0.31	0.76	0.48	0.26	0.22	0.17	0.12	0.14
Natural gas (dry)	1.01	1.55	2.90	3.87	4.45	3.83	2.79	3.08	3.11	2.96	2.81
Petroleum [2]	14.66	17.12	18.80	24.42	29.20	25.36	20.41	21.70	21.87	21.50	19.58
Other [3]	0.10	0.08	0.24	0.26	0.25	0.19	0.34	0.38	0.31	0.25	0.28
Exports, total	3.69	4.75	4.50	3.96	4.46	8.18	12.90	14.12	17.95	21.21	23.52
Coal	2.42	2.77	2.32	1.53	1.27	2.10	1.85	1.55	2.39	2.81	2.31
Natural gas (dry)	0.05	0.09	0.16	0.25	0.74	1.15	1.80	2.36	3.18	3.64	4.70
Petroleum	1.16	1.82	1.98	2.11	2.34	4.78	9.12	9.99	12.11	14.43	16.18
Other [3]	0.07	0.07	0.05	0.08	0.11	0.15	0.13	0.23	0.27	0.32	0.33

[1] Net imports equals imports minus exports. Minus sign (-) indicates exports are greater than imports. [2] Includes imports into the Strategic Petroleum Reserve. [3] Coal coke, small amounts of electricity transmitted across U.S. borders with Canada and Mexico, and small amounts of biomass fuel.

Source: U.S. Energy Information Administration, *Monthly Energy Review*, April 2020. See also <http://www.eia.gov/totalenergy/>.

Table 969. U.S. Foreign Trade in Natural Gas, Crude Oil, Petroleum Products, and Coal: 1980 to 2019

[985 represents 985,000,000,000 cubic feet. Minus sign (-) indicates trade deficit]

Mineral fuel	Unit	1980	1990	1995	2000	2005	2010	2015	2018	2019 (P)
Natural gas:										
Imports	Bil. cu. ft.	985	1,532	2,841	3,782	4,341	3,741	2,718	2,889	2,742
Exports	Bil. cu. ft.	49	86	154	244	729	1,137	1,784	3,607	4,656
Net trade [1]	Bil. cu. ft.	-936	-1,447	-2,687	-3,538	-3,612	-2,604	-935	719	1,914
Crude oil: [2]										
Imports [3]	Mil. barrels	1,926	2,151	2,639	3,320	3,696	3,363	2,687	2,835	2,480
Exports	Mil. barrels	105	40	35	18	12	15	170	748	1,087
Net trade [1]	Mil. barrels	-1,821	-2,112	-2,604	-3,301	-3,684	-3,348	-2,518	-2,088	-1,393
Petroleum products:										
Imports	Mil. barrels	(NA)	775	586	874	1,310	942	761	794	839
Exports	Mil. barrels	(NA)	273	312	362	414	843	1,560	2,027	2,015
Net trade [1]	Mil. barrels	(NA)	-502	-274	-512	-896	-98	798	1,233	1,177
Coal:										
Imports	Mil. sh. tons	1	3	9	13	30	19	11	6	7
Exports	Mil. sh. tons	92	106	89	58	50	82	74	116	93
Net trade [1]	Mil. sh. tons	91	103	79	46	19	62	63	110	86

P Preliminary. NA Not available. [1] Exports minus imports. [2] Includes lease condensate. [3] Includes Strategic Petroleum Reserve imports.

Source: U.S. Energy Information Administration, *Monthly Energy Review*, May 2020; and "Petroleum and Other Liquids, Imports/Exports," <http://www.eia.gov/petroleum/data.cfm>, accessed June 2020.

Table 970. Crude Oil Imports Into the U.S. by Country of Origin: 1993 to 2019

[In millions of barrels (2,477 represents 2,477,000,000). A barrel contains 42 gallons. Crude oil imports are reported by the Petroleum Administration for Defense (PAD) District in which they are to be processed. A PAD District is a geographic aggregation of the 50 states and D.C. into 5 districts. Includes crude oil imported for storage in the Strategic Petroleum Reserve (SPR). Total Organization of Petroleum Exporting Countries (OPEC) excludes, and non-OPEC includes, petroleum imported into the United States indirectly from members of OPEC, primarily from Caribbean and West European areas, as petroleum products that were refined from crude oil produced by OPEC]

Country of origin	1993	1995	2000	2005	2010	2014	2015	2016	2017	2018	2019
Total imports	**2,477**	**2,639**	**3,320**	**3,696**	**3,363**	**2,681**	**2,687**	**2,873**	**2,909**	**2,835**	**2,480**
OPEC, total [1,2]	**1,346**	**1,303**	**1,663**	**1,758**	**1,662**	**1,097**	**976**	**1,164**	**1,138**	**943**	**541**
Algeria	9	10	(Z)	83	120	2	1	19	24	29	7
Angola	123	131	108	166	140	51	45	58	47	33	12
Iraq	(NA)	(NA)	227	193	152	135	84	154	219	189	121
Kuwait	126	78	96	83	71	113	74	76	53	28	16
Libya	(NA)	(NA)	(NA)	16	16	2	1	4	21	20	22
Nigeria	264	227	320	393	359	21	20	76	113	64	68
Saudi Arabia	468	460	558	527	395	423	384	402	347	318	182
Venezuela	369	420	448	453	333	268	283	271	226	185	29
Non-OPEC, total [2]	**1,131**	**1,336**	**1,657**	**1,938**	**1,701**	**1,584**	**1,712**	**1,709**	**1,771**	**1,893**	**1,940**
Brazil	(NA)	(NA)	2	34	93	53	69	53	72	46	44
Canada	329	380	493	596	719	1,052	1,157	1,181	1,258	1,353	1,391
Colombia	52	75	116	57	124	107	136	162	121	108	116
Ecuador	28	35	46	101	76	78	82	87	75	64	73
Mexico	315	375	480	568	421	285	251	213	222	243	219
Norway	50	94	111	43	9	3	3	13	14	20	17
Russia	(NA)	5	3	73	98	7	14	14	18	27	48
Trinidad and Tobago	20	23	20	23	16	2	3	3	3	3	17
United Kingdom	114	124	106	82	44	3	4	7	9	21	23

NA Not available. Z represents less than 500,000. [1] Countries listed under OPEC and non-OPEC are based on current affiliations. OPEC and non-OPEC totals are based on affiliations for the stated period of time which may differ from current affiliations. Indonesia withdrew from OPEC in January 2009, rejoined in 2016 and withdrew again in December 2016; Angola joined OPEC in January 2007; Ecuador withdrew from OPEC in January 1993, rejoined in November 2007 and withdrew again in January 2020; Gabon terminated its membership in 1995 and rejoined in July 2016; Equatorial Guinea joined OPEC in May 2017; Congo (Republic of) joined OPEC in June 2018; and Qatar withdrew from OPEC in January 2019. [2] Includes countries not shown separately.

Source: U.S. Energy Information Administration, Petroleum & Other Liquids, "U.S. Imports by Country of Origin," <https://www.eia.gov/petroleum/data.php#imports>, accessed June 2020.

Table 971. Crude Oil and Refined Products—Summary: 1980 to 2019

[13,481 represents 13,481,000 bbl. One barrel (bbl.) contains 42 gallons. Data are averages]

Year	Crude oil [1] (1,000 bbl. per day)					Refined oil products (1,000 bbl. per day)			Total oil imports [5] (1,000 bbl. per day)	Crude oil stocks [1,2] (mil. bbl.)	
	Refinery and blender input	Domestic production	Imports		Exports	Domestic demand	Imports	Exports		Total [6]	Strategic reserve [7]
			Total [3]	Strategic reserve [4]							
1980....	13,481	8,597	5,263	44	287	17,056	1,646	258	6,909	466	108
1981....	12,470	8,572	4,396	256	228	16,058	1,599	367	5,996	594	230
1982....	11,774	8,649	3,488	165	236	15,296	1,625	579	5,113	644	294
1983....	11,685	8,688	3,329	234	164	15,231	1,722	575	5,051	723	379
1984....	12,044	8,879	3,426	197	181	15,726	2,011	541	5,437	796	451
1985....	12,002	8,971	3,201	118	204	15,726	1,866	577	5,067	814	493
1986....	12,716	8,680	4,178	48	154	16,281	2,045	631	6,224	843	512
1987....	12,854	8,349	4,674	73	151	16,665	2,004	613	6,678	890	541
1988....	13,246	8,140	5,107	51	155	17,283	2,295	661	7,402	890	560
1989....	13,401	7,613	5,843	56	142	17,325	2,217	717	8,061	921	580
1990....	13,409	7,355	5,894	27	109	16,988	2,123	748	8,018	908	586
1991....	13,301	7,417	5,782	(NA)	116	16,714	1,844	885	7,627	893	569
1992....	13,411	7,171	6,083	10	89	17,033	1,805	861	7,888	893	575
1993....	13,613	6,847	6,787	15	98	17,237	1,833	904	8,620	922	587
1994....	13,866	6,662	7,063	12	99	17,718	1,933	843	8,996	929	592
1995....	13,973	6,560	7,230	(NA)	95	17,725	1,605	855	8,835	895	592
1996....	14,195	6,465	7,508	(NA)	110	18,309	1,971	871	9,478	850	566
1997....	14,662	6,452	8,225	(NA)	108	18,620	1,936	896	10,162	868	563
1998....	14,889	6,252	8,706	(NA)	110	18,917	2,002	835	10,708	895	571
1999....	14,804	5,881	8,731	8	118	19,519	2,122	822	10,852	852	567
2000....	15,067	5,822	9,071	8	50	19,701	2,389	990	11,459	826	541
2001....	15,128	5,801	9,328	11	20	19,649	2,543	951	11,871	862	550
2002....	14,947	5,744	9,140	16	9	19,761	2,390	975	11,530	877	599
2003....	15,304	5,649	9,665	(NA)	12	20,034	2,599	1,014	12,264	907	638
2004....	15,475	5,441	10,088	77	27	20,731	3,057	1,021	13,145	961	676
2005....	15,220	5,184	10,126	52	32	20,802	3,588	1,133	13,714	992	685
2006....	15,242	5,086	10,118	8	25	20,687	3,589	1,292	13,707	984	689
2007....	15,156	5,074	10,031	7	27	20,680	3,437	1,405	13,468	965	697
2008....	14,648	5,000	9,783	19	29	19,498	3,132	1,773	12,915	1,010	702
2009....	14,336	5,357	9,013	56	44	18,771	2,678	1,980	11,691	1,034	727
2010....	14,724	5,484	9,213	(NA)	42	19,180	2,580	2,311	11,793	1,039	727
2011....	14,806	5,667	8,935	(NA)	47	18,887	2,501	2,939	11,436	1,004	696
2012....	14,999	6,518	8,527	(NA)	67	18,487	2,071	3,137	10,598	1,033	695
2013....	15,312	7,493	7,730	(NA)	134	18,967	2,129	3,487	9,859	1,023	696
2014....	15,848	8,787	7,344	(NA)	351	19,100	1,897	3,824	9,241	1,052	691
2015....	16,188	9,439	7,363	(NA)	465	19,534	2,086	4,273	9,449	1,144	695
2016....	16,187	8,839	7,850	(NA)	591	19,687	2,205	4,670	10,055	1,180	695
2017....	16,590	9,352	7,969	(NA)	1,158	19,958	2,175	5,218	10,144	1,084	663
2018....	16,969	10,990	7,768	(NA)	2,048	20,504	2,174	5,553	9,943	1,092	649
2019....	16,562	12,232	6,795	(NA)	2,978	20,464	2,303	5,589	9,093	1,068	635

NA Not available. [1] Includes lease condensate. [2] Crude oil at end of period. Includes commercial and Strategic Petroleum Reserve (SPR) stocks. [3] Includes Strategic Petroleum Reserve. [4] Through 2000, includes imports by SPR only; beginning in 2004, includes imports by SPR, and imports into SPR by others. [5] Crude oil (including Strategic Petroleum Reserve imports) plus refined products. [6] Beginning in 1981, includes stocks of Alaskan crude oil in transit. [7] Crude oil stocks in the Strategic Petroleum Reserve include non-U.S. stocks held under foreign or commercial storage agreements.

Source: U.S. Energy Information Administration, *Monthly Energy Review*, April 2020. See also <http://www.eia.gov/totalenergy/data/monthly/>.

Table 972. Petroleum and Coal Products Corporations—Sales, Net Profit, and Profit Per Dollar of Sales: 2005 to 2019

[956.0 represents $956,000,000,000. Covers North American Industry Classification System (NAICS) 324. Profit rates are averages of quarterly figures at annual rates]

Item	Unit	2005	2010	2012	2013	2014	2015	2016	2017	2018	2019
Sales...................	Bil. dol.	956.0	1,077.1	1,377.4	1,342.5	1,283.8	834.3	681.9	850.1	1,029.3	977.4
Net profit:											
Before income taxes...............	Bil. dol.	120.2	56.0	117.6	79.8	82.3	21.0	1.2	34.0	70.9	30.5
After income taxes.................	Bil. dol.	96.3	54.2	99.0	73.0	74.2	24.0	11.2	48.0	63.3	29.2
Depreciation [1].......................	Bil. dol.	18.6	30.8	29.1	29.2	32.0	33.6	34.6	35.2	34.7	37.2
Profits per dollar of sales:											
Before income taxes...............	Cents	12.6	5.2	8.5	5.9	6.4	2.5	0.2	4.0	6.9	3.1
After income taxes.................	Cents	10.1	5.0	7.2	5.4	5.8	2.9	1.6	5.7	6.2	3.0
Stockholders' equity.................	Bil. dol.	1,263.1	1,826.5	2,057.5	2,194.0	2,286.8	2,160.2	2,102.7	2,183.5	2,328.7	2,399.0

[1] Includes depletion and accelerated amortization of emergency facilities.

Source: U.S. Census Bureau, Quarterly Financial Report (QFR) Manufacturing, Mining, Trade, and Selected Service Industries, "Time Series/Trend Charts," <census.gov/econ/qfr/>, accessed August 2020.

Table 973. Nuclear Power Plants—Number, Capacity, and Generation: 1980 to 2019

[51.8 represents 51,800,000 kilowatts (kW)]

Item	1980	1990	1995	2000	2005	2010	2015	2017	2018	2019 (P)
Operable generating units [1,2]	71	112	109	104	104	104	99	99	98	96
Net summer capacity [2,3] (mil. kW)	51.8	99.6	99.5	97.9	100.0	101.2	98.7	99.6	99.4	98.1
Net generation (bil. kWh)	251.1	576.9	673.4	753.9	782.0	807.0	797.2	805.0	807.1	809.4
Percent of total electricity net generation	11.0	19.0	20.1	19.8	19.3	19.6	19.6	20.0	19.3	19.7
Capacity factor [4] (percent)	56.3	66.0	77.4	88.1	89.3	91.1	92.3	92.3	92.5	93.5

P Preliminary. [1] Total of nuclear generating units holding full-power licenses, or equivalent permission to operate, at the end of the year. Includes units retaining full-power licenses during long, non-routine shutdowns that for a time rendered them unable to generate electricity. [2] As of year-end. [3] Net summer capacity is the peak steady hourly output that generating equipment is expected to supply to system load, exclusive of auxiliary and other power plant, as demonstrated by a test at the time of summer peak demand. [4] Weighted average of monthly capacity factors. Monthly factors are derived by dividing actual monthly generation by the maximum possible generation for the month (number of hours in the month multiplied by the net summer capacity at the end of the month). Please note that as of 2008, the methodology changed; see U.S. Energy Information Administration, *Electric Power Monthly*, Appendix C, under "Average Capacity Factors."

Source: U.S. Energy Information Administration, *Monthly Energy Review*, April 2020. See also <http://www.eia.gov/totalenergy/data/monthly/>.

Table 974. Nuclear Power Plants—Number of Reactors, Net Generation, and Net Summer Capacity by State: 2018

[807,084 represents 807,084,000,000 kilowatt hours (kWh)]

State	Number of reactors	Nuclear net generation Total (mil. kWh)	Percent of total [1]	Nuclear net summer capacity Total (mil. kWh)	Percent of total [2]	State	Number of reactors	Nuclear net generation Total (mil. kWh)	Percent of total [1]	Nuclear net summer capacity Total (mil. kWh)	Percent of total [2]
U.S.	99	807,084	19.3	99.4	9.1	MN	3	14,601	23.7	1.7	9.8
						MS	1	6,919	10.9	1.4	9.5
AL	5	39,463	27.2	5.4	17.8	MO	1	10,655	13.1	1.2	5.6
AZ	3	31,097	27.8	3.9	13.7	NE	1	5,632	15.2	0.8	8.6
AR	2	12,721	18.7	1.8	12.3	NH	1	10,062	58.9	1.3	28.0
CA	2	18,214	9.3	2.2	3.0	NJ	4	31,982	42.6	3.5	20.1
CT	2	16,881	42.8	2.1	21.1	NY	6	42,919	32.4	5.4	13.1
FL	4	29,312	12.0	3.6	6.3	NC	5	42,077	31.3	5.1	15.1
GA	4	34,363	26.6	4.1	11.0	OH	2	18,315	14.5	2.1	7.3
IL	11	98,102	52.2	11.6	25.4	PA	9	83,477	38.8	9.8	20.2
IA	1	4,895	7.7	0.6	3.2	SC	7	52,716	53.1	6.6	27.8
KS	1	9,168	17.7	1.2	7.8	TN	4	36,176	44.4	4.5	21.2
LA	2	17,153	16.8	2.1	9.2	TX	4	41,186	8.6	5.0	4.1
MD	2	14,988	34.2	1.7	11.7	VA	4	29,252	30.6	3.6	12.0
MA	1	4,442	16.3	0.7	5.3	WA	1	9,708	8.3	1.2	3.8
MI	4	30,479	26.3	4.1	13.9	WI	2	10,129	15.4	1.2	7.7

[1] Percent of total electric power generation. See also Table 980. [2] Percent of total net summer capacity. See also Table 980.

Source: U.S. Energy Information Administration, *Electric Power Annual*, and "Electricity: Detailed State Data," <http://www.eia.gov/electricity/data/state/>, accessed January 2020.

Table 975. Uranium Concentrate—Supply, Inventories, and Average Prices: 1990 to 2019

[8.9 represents 8,900,000 pounds (lbs.). Years ending December 31. For additional data on uranium, see Table 939 and Table 955]

Item	Unit	1990	1995	2000	2005	2010	2015	2017	2018	2019
Production [1]	Mil. lbs.	8.9	6.0	4.0	2.7	4.2	3.3	2.4	1.5	0.2
Exports [2]	Mil. lbs.	2.0	9.8	13.6	20.5	23.1	25.7	14.0	13.9	11.7
Imports [2]	Mil. lbs.	23.7	41.3	44.9	65.5	55.3	64.1	42.1	41.5	42.9
Electric plant purchases from domestic suppliers	Mil. lbs.	20.5	22.3	24.3	27.3	16.2	19.6	14.0	11.1	(NA)
Loaded into U.S. nuclear reactors [3]	Mil. lbs.	(NA)	51.1	51.5	58.3	44.3	47.4	45.5	50.4	[5] 43.2
Inventories, total	Mil. lbs.	129.1	72.5	111.3	93.8	111.3	135.5	141.7	130.5	[5] 127.1
At domestic suppliers	Mil. lbs.	26.4	13.7	56.5	29.1	24.7	14.3	17.8	19.3	[5] 14.3
At electric plants	Mil. lbs.	102.7	58.7	54.8	64.7	86.5	121.1	123.9	111.2	[5] 112.8
Average price per pound:										
Purchased imports [4]	Dollars	12.55	10.20	9.84	14.83	47.01	42.96	37.09	35.73	34.77
Domestic purchases	Dollars	15.70	11.11	11.45	13.98	44.88	43.03	38.57	42.98	(D)

D Data withheld. NA Not available. [1] Data are for uranium concentrate, a yellow or brown powder obtained by the milling of uranium ore, processing of in situ leach mining solutions, or as a by-product of phosphoric acid production. [2] Includes transactions by uranium buyers (consumers). Buyer imports and exports prior to 1990 are believed to be small. [3] Does not include any fuel rods removed from reactors and later reloaded into the reactor. [4] For purchases made by U.S. suppliers and by U.S. owners and operators of civilian nuclear power plants. [5] Preliminary.

Source: U.S. Energy Information Administration, through 2010, *Annual Energy Review*; thereafter, *Uranium Marketing Annual Report*, May 2020, and *Monthly Energy Review*, May 2020. See also <http://www.eia.gov/nuclear/>.

Table 976. Renewable Energy Generating Capacity and Generation Projections: 2019 to 2050

[In gigawatts, unless otherwise noted. Reference case projections are business-as-usual trend estimates, given known technology, as well as market, demographic, and technological trends. Based on results from EIA's National Energy Modeling System]

Net summer capacity and generation	Reference case								Annual growth 2019-2050 (percent)
	2019	2020	2025	2030	2035	2040	2045	2050	
ELECTRIC POWER SECTOR [1]									
Total net summer capacity	**232.32**	**259.21**	**363.49**	**425.41**	**444.18**	**486.43**	**565.76**	**613.31**	**3.2**
Conventional hydroelectric power	79.02	79.27	79.31	79.29	79.29	79.29	79.29	79.29	–
Geothermal [2]	2.35	2.46	2.83	3.68	4.71	5.76	6.40	6.86	3.5
Municipal waste [3]	3.60	3.54	6.23	6.33	6.44	6.48	6.59	7.46	2.4
Wood and other biomass [4]	3.14	3.17	3.18	3.18	3.18	3.18	3.18	3.18	–
Solar thermal	1.76	1.76	1.96	1.96	1.96	2.05	2.05	2.05	0.5
Solar photovoltaic [5]	35.65	47.55	109.09	157.86	165.67	202.78	273.80	309.33	7.2
Wind	106.78	121.43	160.02	163.15	164.78	168.72	176.29	186.96	1.8
Offshore wind	0.03	0.03	0.86	9.96	18.16	18.16	18.16	18.16	23.0
Total generation (bil. kWh)	**702.68**	**768.25**	**1,116.75**	**1,295.77**	**1,364.72**	**1,491.26**	**1,702.89**	**1,849.67**	**3.2**
Conventional hydroelectric power	286.85	290.85	290.40	290.09	290.13	289.48	287.05	287.37	–
Geothermal [2]	16.43	16.36	19.68	26.47	34.69	43.06	48.41	52.17	3.8
Biogenic municipal waste [6]	18.62	18.31	41.09	42.37	43.24	44.00	45.42	53.42	3.5
Wood and other biomass	12.56	13.20	13.29	13.52	13.57	13.72	13.82	13.93	0.3
Dedicated plants	12.33	12.98	13.21	13.37	13.42	13.52	13.47	13.76	0.4
Co-firing	0.22	0.22	0.08	0.15	0.16	0.20	0.34	0.17	-0.9
Solar thermal	3.39	3.58	3.61	3.64	3.62	3.87	3.80	3.68	0.3
Solar photovoltaic [5]	69.29	89.75	236.30	364.08	387.16	483.90	664.70	760.16	8.0
Wind	295.43	336.09	509.02	520.17	525.99	539.49	565.97	605.20	2.3
Offshore wind	0.11	0.11	3.36	35.43	66.32	73.73	73.73	73.74	23.4
END-USE SECTORS [7]									
Total net summer capacity	**35.86**	**41.08**	**61.18**	**79.03**	**94.51**	**110.74**	**127.32**	**145.05**	**4.6**
Conventional hydropower	0.24	0.24	0.24	0.24	0.24	0.24	0.24	0.24	–
Geothermal	–	–	–	–	–	–	–	–	(X)
Municipal waste [3]	0.47	0.47	0.47	0.47	0.47	0.47	0.47	0.47	–
Biomass	4.25	4.22	4.63	4.75	4.89	5.01	5.12	5.32	0.7
Solar photovoltaic [5]	30.33	35.58	55.27	73.00	88.33	104.44	120.90	138.43	5.0
Wind	0.57	0.57	0.57	0.58	0.58	0.58	0.59	0.59	0.1
Total generation (bil. kWh)	**69.32**	**75.89**	**101.17**	**124.79**	**145.70**	**167.58**	**190.07**	**214.34**	**3.7**
Conventional hydropower	1.42	1.42	1.42	1.42	1.42	1.42	1.42	1.42	–
Geothermal	–	–	–	–	–	–	–	–	(X)
Municipal waste [3]	3.56	3.56	3.56	3.56	3.56	3.56	3.56	3.56	–
Biomass	22.88	22.74	22.86	23.54	24.33	25.02	25.64	26.34	0.5
Solar photovoltaic [5]	40.68	47.40	72.56	95.49	115.60	136.79	158.65	182.22	5.0
Wind	0.77	0.77	0.78	0.79	0.79	0.80	0.80	0.80	0.1
ALL SECTORS									
Total net summer capacity	**268.17**	**300.29**	**424.66**	**504.45**	**538.70**	**597.17**	**693.09**	**758.36**	**3.4**
Conventional hydropower	79.26	79.51	79.55	79.54	79.54	79.54	79.54	79.54	–
Geothermal	2.35	2.46	2.83	3.68	4.71	5.76	6.40	6.86	3.5
Municipal waste	4.07	4.00	6.70	6.80	6.91	6.95	7.05	7.93	2.2
Wood and other biomass [4]	7.38	7.40	7.80	7.92	8.07	8.19	8.30	8.50	0.5
Solar [5]	67.74	84.89	166.32	232.81	255.95	309.27	396.76	449.82	6.3
Wind	107.38	122.03	161.45	173.69	183.52	187.46	195.03	205.71	2.1
Total generation (bil. kWh)	**772.00**	**844.15**	**1,217.92**	**1,420.56**	**1,510.42**	**1,658.84**	**1,892.95**	**2,064.01**	**3.2**
Conventional hydropower	288.27	292.27	291.82	291.50	291.55	290.90	288.47	288.79	–
Geothermal	16.43	16.36	19.68	26.47	34.69	43.06	48.41	52.17	3.8
Municipal waste	22.18	21.88	44.65	45.93	46.80	47.56	48.98	56.98	3.1
Wood and other biomass	35.44	35.94	36.14	37.06	37.90	38.74	39.46	40.27	0.4
Solar [5]	113.37	140.73	312.47	463.20	506.38	624.56	827.14	946.06	7.1
Wind	296.32	336.97	513.16	556.39	593.10	614.02	640.50	679.74	2.7

– Represents or rounds to zero. X Not applicable. [1] Includes electricity-only and combined heat and power plants that have a regulatory status. [2] Includes both hydrothermal resources and near-field enhanced geothermal systems (EGS). [3] Includes municipal waste, landfill gas, and municipal sewage sludge. [4] Facilities co-firing biomass and coal are classified as coal. [5] Does not include off-grid photovoltaics (PV). [6] Includes biogenic municipal waste, landfill gas, and municipal sludge. [7] Includes combined heat and power plants and electricity-only plants in the commercial and industrial sectors with nonregulatory status, and small on-site generating systems in the residential, commercial, and industrial sectors used primarily for own-use generation, but which many also sell some power to the grid.

Source: U.S. Energy Information Administration, *Annual Energy Outlook 2020*, January 2020. See also <http://www.eia.gov/forecasts/aeo/>.

Table 977. Electricity Net Generation by Sector and Fuel Type: 1990 to 2019

[3,037.8 represents 3,037,800,000,000 kilowatt hours (kWh). Data are for fuels consumed to produce electricity. Also includes fuels consumed to produce useful thermal output at a small number of electric utility combined-heat-and-power (CHP) plants]

Source and sector	Unit	1990	1995	2000	2005	2010	2015	2016	2017	2018	2019
Net generation, total.	**Bil. kWh.**	**3,037.8**	**3,353.5**	**3,802.1**	**4,055.4**	**4,125.1**	**4,077.6**	**4,076.7**	**4,034.3**	**4,178.1**	**4,118.1**
Electric power sector, total..	Bil. kWh.	2,901.3	3,194.2	3,637.5	3,902.2	3,972.4	3,919.3	3,918.1	3,877.5	4,018.0	3,955.8
Commercial sector [1]	Bil. kWh.	5.8	8.2	7.9	8.5	8.6	12.6	12.7	13.1	13.3	13.6
Industrial sector [2]	Bil. kWh.	130.8	151.0	156.7	144.7	144.1	145.7	145.9	143.8	146.8	148.6
Net generation by source, all sectors:											
Fossil fuels, total..	Bil. kWh.	2,103.6	2,293.9	2,692.5	2,909.5	2,883.4	2,727.2	2,654.5	2,536.1	2,657.1	2,580.2
Coal [3]	Bil. kWh.	1,594.0	1,709.4	1,966.3	2,012.9	1,847.3	1,352.4	1,239.1	1,205.8	1,149.5	966.1
Petroleum [4]	Bil. kWh.	126.5	74.6	111.2	122.2	37.1	28.2	24.2	21.4	25.2	18.6
Natural gas [5]	Bil. kWh.	372.8	496.1	601.0	761.0	987.7	1,333.5	1,378.3	1,296.4	1,468.9	1,581.8
Other gases [6]	Bil. kWh.	10.4	13.9	14.0	13.5	11.3	13.1	12.8	12.5	13.5	13.6
Nuclear electric power..	Bil. kWh.	576.9	673.4	753.9	782.0	807.0	797.2	805.7	804.9	807.1	809.4
Hydroelectric pumped storage [7]	Bil. kWh.	-3.5	-2.7	-5.5	-6.6	-5.5	-5.1	-6.7	-6.5	-5.9	-5.3
Renewable energy, total..	Bil. kWh.	357.2	384.8	356.5	357.7	427.4	544.2	609.4	686.6	706.8	720.4
Conventional hydroelectric power.	Bil. kWh.	292.9	310.8	275.6	270.3	260.2	249.1	267.8	300.3	292.5	273.7
Biomass, total.	Bil. kWh.	45.8	56.9	60.7	54.3	56.1	63.6	62.8	62.7	61.8	58.4
Wood [8]	Bil. kWh.	32.5	36.5	37.6	38.9	37.2	41.9	40.9	41.1	40.9	39.9
Waste [9]	Bil. kWh.	13.3	20.4	23.1	15.4	18.9	21.7	21.8	21.6	20.9	18.6
Geothermal.	Bil. kWh.	15.4	13.4	14.1	14.7	15.2	15.9	15.8	15.9	16.0	16.0
Solar [10]	Bil. kWh.	0.4	0.5	0.5	0.6	1.2	24.9	36.1	53.3	63.8	72.2
Wind.	Bil. kWh.	2.8	3.2	5.6	17.8	94.7	190.7	227.0	254.3	272.7	300.1
Other [11]	Bil. kWh.	3.6	4.1	4.8	12.8	12.9	14.0	13.8	13.1	13.0	13.3
Consumption of fuels for electricity generation:											
Coal [3]	Mil. short tons	792.5	860.6	994.9	1,041.4	979.7	739.6	677.4	663.9	636.2	538.5
Petroleum, total.. [12]	Mil. bbl.	218.8	132.6	195.2	206.8	65.1	49.1	43.7	39.1	46.7	34.5
Distillate fuel oil [13]	Mil. bbl.	18.1	19.6	31.7	20.7	14.1	12.4	9.7	9.7	14.2	9.1
Residual fuel oil [13]	Mil. bbl.	190.7	95.5	143.4	141.5	24.0	14.1	11.2	10.4	12.4	9.3
Other liquids [14]	Mil. bbl.	0.4	0.7	1.4	3.0	2.1	2.4	1.5	1.5	2.0	2.0
Petroleum coke.	Mil. short tons	1.9	3.4	3.7	8.3	5.0	4.0	4.3	3.5	3.6	2.8
Natural gas [5]	Bil. cu. ft.	3,691.6	4,737.9	5,691.5	6,036.4	7,680.2	10,016.6	10,170.1	9,508.1	10,831.8	11,550.8
Other gases [6]	Tril. Btu.	111.8	132.5	126.0	109.9	90.1	106.0	73.8	70.7	78.8	78.5
Biomass.	Tril. Btu.	653.5	795.6	825.9	585.3	630.3	719.6	665.1	668.0	659.5	598.9
Wood [8]	Tril. Btu.	442.3	479.9	495.8	355.3	349.5	406.7	360.0	363.6	361.7	345.5
Waste [9]	Tril. Btu.	211.2	315.7	330.1	230.1	280.8	313.0	305.1	304.3	297.8	253.3
Other [11]	Tril. Btu.	36.0	42.0	46.2	173.0	184.4	203.6	198.6	189.7	190.0	191.6

[1] Commercial combined-heat-and-power (CHP) and commercial electricity-only plants. [2] Industrial CHP and industrial electricity-only plants. [3] Anthracite, bituminous coal, subbituminous coal, lignite, waste coal, and coal synfuel. [4] Distillate fuel oil, residual fuel oil, petroleum coke, jet fuel, kerosene, other petroleum, waste oil, and beginning in 2011, propane. [5] Includes a small amount of supplemental gaseous fuels that cannot be identified separately. [6] Blast furnace gas and other manufactured and waste gases derived from fossil fuels. Through 2010, also includes propane. [7] Pumped storage facility production minus energy used for pumping. [8] Wood and wood-derived fuels. [9] Municipal solid waste from biogenic sources, landfill gas, sludge waste, agricultural byproducts, and other biomass. Through 2000, also includes nonrenewable waste (municipal solid waste from non-biogenic sources and tire-derived fuels). [10] Solar thermal and photovoltaic energy. Does not include estimated distributed solar photovoltaic generation, which was 14,139 million kilowatthours in 2015, 18,812 million kilowatthours in 2016, 23,990 million kilowatthours in 2017, and 29,543 million kilowatthours in 2018. [11] Batteries, chemicals, hydrogen, pitch, purchased steam, sulfur, miscellaneous technologies, and beginning 2001, nonrenewable waste (municipal solid waste from nonbiogenic sources, and tire-derived fuels). [12] Fuel oil numbers 1, 2, and 4. For 1990 through 2000, electric utility data also include small amounts of kerosene and jet fuel. [13] Fuel oil numbers 5 and 6. For 1990 through 2000, electric utility data also include a small amount of fuel oil number 4. [14] Jet fuel, kerosene, other petroleum liquids, waste oil, and beginning in 2011, propane.

Source: U.S. Energy Information Administration, *Monthly Energy Review*, April 2020. See also <http://www.eia.gov/totalenergy/data/monthly>.

Table 978. Total Electric Net Summer Capacity for All Sectors by Energy Source: 1990 to 2018

[In million kilowatts (734.1 represents 734,100,000). Data are at end of year. For plants that use multiple sources of energy, capacity is assigned to the predominant energy source]

Source	1990	1995	2000	2005	2010	2015	2016	2017	2018
Net summer capacity, total	**734.1**	**769.5**	**811.7**	**978.0**	**1,039.1**	**1,073.8**	**1,087.1**	**1,100.5**	**1,114.3**
Fossil fuels, total	527.8	554.2	598.9	757.1	782.2	758.5	750.3	748.2	747.8
Coal [1]	307.4	311.4	315.1	313.4	316.8	279.7	266.6	256.5	242.8
Petroleum [2]	77.9	66.6	61.8	58.5	55.6	36.8	34.4	33.3	32.2
Natural gas [3]	140.8	174.5	219.6	383.1	407.0	439.4	446.8	456.0	470.2
Other gases [4]	1.6	1.7	2.3	2.1	2.7	2.5	2.5	2.4	2.5
Nuclear electric power	99.6	99.5	97.9	100.0	101.2	98.7	99.6	99.6	99.4
Hydroelectric pumped storage	19.5	21.4	19.5	21.3	22.2	22.6	22.8	22.8	22.8
Renewable energy, total	86.8	93.9	94.9	98.7	132.6	192.3	212.5	227.0	241.9
Conventional hydroelectric power	73.9	78.6	79.4	77.5	78.8	79.7	79.9	79.8	79.9
Biomass, total	8.1	10.3	10.0	9.8	11.4	14.1	14.0	14.0	13.7
Wood [5]	5.5	6.7	6.1	6.2	7.0	9.0	8.9	8.8	8.7
Waste [6]	2.5	3.5	3.9	3.6	4.4	5.1	5.1	5.1	5.0
Geothermal	2.7	3.0	2.8	2.3	2.4	2.5	2.5	2.5	2.4
Solar [7]	0.3	0.3	0.4	0.4	0.9	23.4	34.7	43.1	51.4
Wind	1.8	1.7	2.4	8.7	39.1	72.6	81.3	87.6	94.4
Other [8]	0.5	0.5	0.5	0.9	0.9	1.8	2.0	2.9	2.3

[1] Coal includes anthracite, bituminous, subbituminous, lignite, and waste coal; coal synfuel and refined coal; and, beginning in 2011, coal-derived synthesis gas. Prior to 2011, coal-derived synthesis gas was included in other gases. [2] Distillate fuel oil, residual fuel oil, petroleum coke, jet fuel, kerosene, other petroleum, waste oil, and, beginning in 2011, synthetic gas and propane. Prior to 2011, synthetic gas and propane were included in other gases. [3] Includes a small amount of supplemental gaseous fuels that cannot be identified separately. [4] Blast furnace gas, propane gas, and other manufactured and waste gases derived from fossil fuels. [5] Wood and wood-derived fuels. [6] Municipal solid waste, landfill gas, sludge waste, agricultural byproducts, other biomass solids, other biomass liquids, and other biomass gases (including digester gases, methane, and other biomass gases). [7] Solar thermal and photovoltaic energy. [8] Batteries, hydrogen, purchased steam, sulfur, tire-derived fuels and other miscellaneous energy sources.

Source: U.S. Energy Information Administration, *Electric Power Annual 2018*, October 2019, and earlier reports. See also <http://www.eia.gov/electricity/annual/>.

Table 979. Electricity—End Use and Average Retail Prices: 1990 to 2018

[2,837.1 represents 2,837,100,000,000. Beginning 2003, the category "other" has been replaced by "transportation," and the categories "commercial" and "industrial" have been redefined. Data represent revenue from electricity retail sales divided by the amount of retail electricity sold (in kilowatt-hours). Prices include state and local taxes, energy or demand charges, customer service charges, environmental surcharges, franchise fees, fuel adjustments, and other miscellaneous charges applied to end-use customers during normal billing operations. Prices do not include deferred charges, credits, or other adjustments, such as fuel or revenue from purchased power, from previous reporting periods. Data are for a census of electric utilities. Beginning in 2000, data also include energy service providers selling to retail customers]

Item	1990	1995	2000	2005	2010	2015	2016	2017	2018
END USE (Billion kilowatt-hours)									
Total end use [1]	**2,837.1**	**3,164.0**	**3,592.4**	**3,811.0**	**3,886.8**	**3,900.2**	**3,902.3**	**3,864.5**	**4,004.2**
Direct use [2]	124.5	150.7	170.9	150.0	131.9	141.2	139.8	141.1	144.1
Retail sales, total [3]	**2,712.6**	**3,013.3**	**3,421.4**	**3,661.0**	**3,754.8**	**3,759.0**	**3,762.5**	**3,723.4**	**3,860.1**
Residential	924.0	1,042.5	1,192.4	1,359.2	1,445.7	1,404.1	1,411.1	1,378.6	1,469.1
Commercial [4]	838.3	953.1	1,159.3	1,275.1	1,330.2	1,360.8	1,367.2	1,352.9	1,381.8
Industrial [5]	945.5	1,012.7	1,064.2	1,019.2	971.2	986.5	976.7	984.3	1,001.6
Transportation [6]	4.8	5.0	5.4	7.5	7.7	7.6	7.5	7.5	7.7
AVERAGE RETAIL PRICES (Cents per kilowatt-hour)									
Total	**6.57**	**6.89**	**6.81**	**8.14**	**9.83**	**10.41**	**10.27**	**10.48**	**10.53**
Residential	7.83	8.40	8.24	9.45	11.54	12.65	12.55	12.89	12.87
Commercial [7]	7.34	7.69	7.43	8.67	10.19	10.64	10.43	10.66	10.67
Industrial [5]	4.74	4.66	4.64	5.73	6.77	6.91	6.76	6.88	6.92
Transportation [6]	(NA)	(NA)	(NA)	8.57	10.56	10.09	9.63	9.68	9.70
Other [8]	6.40	6.88	6.56	(NA)	(NA)	(NA)	(NA)	(NA)	(NA)

NA Not available. [1] The sum of "total retail sales" and "direct use." [2] Use of electricity that is 1) self-generated, 2) produced by either the same entity that consumes the power or an affiliate, and 3) used in direct support of a service or industrial process located within the same facility or group of facilities that house the generating equipment. Direct use is exclusive of station use. [3] Electricity retail sales to ultimate customers reported by electric utilities and, beginning in 2000, other energy service providers. [4] Includes public street and highway lighting, interdepartmental sales, and other sales to public authorities. [5] Beginning 2003, includes agriculture and irrigation. [6] Includes sales to railroads and railways. [7] Beginning 2003, includes public street and highway lighting, interdepartmental sales, and other sales to public authorities. [8] Public street and highway lighting, interdepartmental sales, other sales to public authorities, agriculture and irrigation, and transportation including railroads and railways.

Source: U.S. Energy Information Administration, *Electric Power Annual 2018*, October 2019, and earlier reports. See also <http://www.eia.gov/electricity/>.

Table 980. Electric Power Industry—Net Generation and Net Summer Capacity by State: 2010 to 2018

[4,125.1 represents 4,125,100,000,000. Capacity as of December 31. Covers utilities for public use]

State	Net generation (billion kilowatt-hours)								Net summer capacity (million kilowatts)	
			2018							
			Total [1] (bil. kWh)	Percent from—						
	2010	2017		Petro-leum	Natural gas	Hydro-electric	Nuclear	Coal	2017	2018
United States..........	**4,125.1**	**4,034.3**	**4,174.4**	**0.6**	**35.2**	**7.0**	**19.3**	**27.5**	**1,084.4**	**1,094.7**
Alabama.................	152.2	140.0	145.1	(Z)	40.5	7.7	27.2	21.9	**29.7**	**30.1**
Alaska..................	6.8	6.5	6.2	13.0	47.2	26.6	–	10.1	2.7	2.7
Arizona.................	111.8	105.9	111.9	(Z)	33.2	6.2	27.8	27.5	28.6	28.7
Arkansas...............	61.0	60.8	68.0	0.1	30.3	4.4	18.7	44.1	14.6	14.8
California...............	204.1	206.1	195.3	(Z)	45.9	13.5	9.3	0.1	76.4	75.9
Colorado...............	50.7	53.8	55.4	(Z)	29.6	3.3	–	47.6	16.0	16.6
Connecticut............	33.3	34.6	39.5	0.9	50.7	1.4	42.8	0.8	8.9	9.8
Delaware...............	5.6	7.5	6.2	3.2	86.5	–	–	4.4	3.4	3.4
District of Columbia.....	0.2	0.1	0.1	–	28.7	–	–	–	(Z)	(Z)
Florida.................	229.1	238.4	244.3	0.9	70.4	0.1	12.0	12.4	59.0	57.4
Georgia................	137.6	127.5	129.2	0.3	40.2	2.9	26.6	24.9	36.9	37.0
Hawaii.................	10.8	9.8	9.8	68.9	–	1.0	–	13.4	2.7	2.8
Idaho..................	12.0	17.4	18.2	(Z)	18.0	60.7	–	0.1	5.2	5.2
Illinois.................	201.4	183.6	188.0	(Z)	9.2	0.1	52.2	31.7	45.1	45.6
Indiana.................	125.2	98.9	113.5	0.1	23.6	0.2	–	68.3	25.7	26.7
Iowa...................	57.5	57.9	63.4	0.2	11.6	1.5	7.7	45.1	17.7	18.8
Kansas................	47.9	50.9	51.7	0.1	5.8	0.1	17.7	39.6	16.1	15.6
Kentucky...............	98.2	73.2	78.8	0.1	18.5	5.6	–	75.1	20.1	20.1
Louisiana..............	102.9	97.7	102.1	4.3	60.4	1.2	16.8	11.5	23.7	23.2
Maine..................	17.0	11.3	11.3	1.7	20.7	28.9	–	0.6	4.9	4.9
Maryland...............	43.6	34.1	43.8	0.6	31.6	6.5	34.2	23.0	13.1	14.8
Massachusetts..........	42.8	32.2	27.2	1.7	67.7	4.2	16.3	–	12.1	12.9
Michigan...............	111.6	112.3	115.8	1.0	26.8	1.4	26.3	36.5	29.6	29.7
Minnesota..............	53.7	58.7	61.5	0.1	13.9	1.7	23.7	38.1	16.6	17.0
Mississippi.............	54.5	59.7	63.5	(Z)	78.0	–	10.9	8.3	15.8	14.7
Missouri................	92.3	84.6	81.4	0.1	8.5	1.0	13.1	73.5	21.8	21.1
Montana................	29.8	28.2	28.2	1.6	1.7	40.4	–	47.4	6.2	6.4
Nebraska...............	36.6	35.4	37.0	(Z)	2.6	3.7	15.2	63.0	8.6	9.0
Nevada................	35.1	38.2	39.6	(Z)	67.3	4.7	–	6.3	11.4	11.5
New Hampshire.........	22.2	17.4	17.1	1.0	17.5	7.9	58.9	3.9	4.4	4.5
New Jersey.............	65.7	75.6	75.0	0.5	51.8	(Z)	42.6	1.6	17.8	17.4
New Mexico............	36.3	33.6	32.7	0.1	35.6	0.5	–	41.0	8.3	8.4
New York...............	137.0	128.1	132.5	1.2	38.3	22.4	32.4	0.5	40.1	41.1
North Carolina..........	128.7	128.5	134.2	0.5	32.4	4.9	31.3	23.6	33.0	34.2
North Dakota...........	34.7	41.5	42.6	0.1	2.4	7.5	–	64.6	8.2	8.4
Ohio...................	143.6	119.6	126.2	1.0	35.0	0.2	14.5	46.5	30.0	29.1
Oklahoma..............	72.3	73.7	86.2	(Z)	48.3	2.4	–	17.3	26.7	27.4
Oregon.................	55.1	62.7	64.1	(Z)	28.0	55.3	–	2.3	16.5	16.6
Pennsylvania...........	229.8	213.6	215.4	0.3	35.5	2.0	38.8	20.5	44.1	48.6
Rhode Island...........	7.7	7.6	8.4	0.9	94.3	(Z)	–	–	1.9	2.0
South Carolina.........	104.2	93.1	99.4	0.3	21.8	3.0	53.1	19.6	22.9	23.7
South Dakota...........	10.0	10.9	12.6	0.1	9.3	49.7	–	18.5	4.1	4.2
Tennessee.............	82.3	79.0	81.6	0.2	16.4	12.6	44.4	25.7	21.0	21.3
Texas..................	411.7	452.8	477.4	(Z)	50.2	0.2	8.6	23.4	123.5	122.2
Utah...................	42.2	37.4	39.4	0.1	22.2	2.4	–	65.8	9.0	9.0
Vermont................	6.6	2.1	2.2	0.1	0.1	58.2	–	–	0.7	0.8
Virginia................	73.0	90.4	95.5	1.0	52.5	1.8	30.6	9.7	27.7	29.6
Washington.............	103.5	115.9	116.8	(Z)	9.0	69.3	8.3	4.6	31.0	31.0
West Virginia...........	80.8	73.4	67.2	0.2	2.1	2.7	–	92.3	14.9	14.9
Wisconsin..............	64.3	65.1	65.9	0.2	25.5	3.6	15.4	50.5	17.0	15.5
Wyoming...............	48.1	46.7	46.1	0.1	1.9	2.1	–	86.0	8.6	8.7

– Represents zero. Z Represents less than .05 percent of net electricity generation, or less than .05 million kilowatts summer capacity. [1] Includes other sources not shown separately.

Source: U.S. Energy Information Administration, *Electric Power Annual*, "Data Tables" and "Detailed State Data," <http://www.eia.gov/electricity/annual/>, accessed January 2020.

Table 981. Electric Power Industry—Capability, Peak Load, and Capacity Margin: 1980 to 2016

[558,237 represents 558,237,000 kilowatts (kW). Excludes Alaska and Hawaii. Capability represents the maximum kilowatt output with all power sources available and with hydraulic equipment under actual water conditions, allowing for maintenance, emergency outages, and system operating requirements. Capacity margin is the difference between capability and peak load. Minus sign (-) indicates decrease]

Year	Capability at the time of— Summer peak load (1,000 kW) Amount	Change from prior year	Winter peak load (1,000 kW) Amount	Change from prior year	Noncoincident peak load Summer (1,000 kW)	Winter (1,000 kW)	Capacity margin Summer Amount (1,000 kW)	Percent of capability	Winter Amount (1,000 kW)	Percent of capability
1980	558,237	13,731	572,195	17,670	427,058	384,567	131,179	23.5	187,628	32.8
1985	621,597	17,357	636,475	14,350	460,503	423,660	161,094	25.9	212,815	33.4
1990	685,091	11,775	696,757	11,508	546,331	484,231	138,760	20.3	212,526	30.5
1991	690,915	5,824	703,212	6,455	551,418	485,761	139,497	20.2	217,451	30.9
1992	695,436	4,521	707,752	4,540	548,707	492,983	146,729	21.1	214,769	30.3
1993	694,250	-1,186	711,957	4,205	575,356	521,733	118,894	17.1	190,224	26.7
1994	702,985	8,735	715,090	3,133	585,320	518,253	117,665	16.7	196,837	27.5
1995	714,222	11,237	727,679	12,589	620,249	544,684	93,973	13.2	182,995	25.1
1996	730,376	16,154	737,637	9,958	616,790	554,081	113,586	15.6	183,556	24.9
1997	737,855	7,479	736,666	-971	637,677	529,874	100,178	13.6	206,792	28.1
1998	744,670	6,815	735,090	-1,576	660,293	567,558	84,377	11.3	167,532	22.8
1999	765,744	21,074	748,271	13,181	682,122	570,915	83,622	10.9	177,356	23.7
2000	808,054	42,310	767,505	19,234	678,413	588,426	129,641	16.0	179,079	23.3
2001	788,990	-19,064	806,598	39,093	687,812	576,312	101,178	12.8	230,286	28.6
2002	833,380	44,390	850,984	44,386	714,565	604,986	118,815	14.3	245,998	28.9
2003	856,131	22,751	882,120	31,136	709,375	593,874	146,756	17.1	288,246	32.7
2004	875,870	19,739	864,849	-17,271	704,459	618,701	171,411	19.6	246,148	28.5
2005	882,125	6,255	878,110	13,261	758,876	626,365	123,249	14.0	251,745	28.7
2006	891,226	9,101	899,551	21,441	789,475	640,981	101,751	11.4	258,570	28.7
2007	914,397	23,171	913,650	14,099	782,227	637,905	132,170	14.5	275,745	30.2
2008	909,504	-4,893	927,781	14,131	752,470	643,557	157,034	17.3	284,224	30.6
2009	916,449	6,945	920,002	-7,779	725,958	668,818	190,491	20.8	251,184	27.3
2010	923,559	7,110	935,262	15,260	767,948	651,418	155,611	16.8	283,844	30.3
2011	892,426	-31,133	893,206	-42,056	782,469	648,190	109,957	12.3	245,016	27.4
2012	931,893	39,467	947,156	53,950	767,762	618,570	164,131	17.6	328,586	34.7
2013	944,515	12,622	956,984	9,828	758,953	686,202	185,562	19.6	270,782	28.3
2014	917,167	-27,348	928,477	-28,507	723,411	677,005	193,756	21.1	251,472	27.1
2015	916,439	-728	920,599	-7,878	741,056	636,387	175,383	19.1	284,212	30.9
2016	923,873	7,434	935,447	14,848	768,510	649,538	155,363	16.8	285,909	30.6

Source: Edison Electric Institute, Washington, DC, *Statistical Yearbook of the Electric Power Industry*, annual ©. See also <http://www.eei.org>.

Table 982. Electric Energy Retail Sales by Class of Service and State: 2018

[In billions of kilowatt-hours (3,860.1 represents 3,860,100,000,000). Data include both bundled and unbundled consumers]

State	Total [1]	Residential	Commercial	Industrial	State	Total [1]	Residential	Commercial	Industrial
United States	**3,860.1**	**1,469.1**	**1,381.8**	**1,001.6**	Missouri	82.1	37.5	31.2	13.4
Alabama	90.3	33.1	23.5	33.7	Montana	14.8	5.2	4.9	4.7
Alaska	6.0	2.0	2.6	1.4	Nebraska	30.9	10.4	9.6	11.0
Arizona	78.3	34.7	29.7	14.0	Nevada	37.8	13.4	12.1	12.2
Arkansas	49.6	19.3	12.3	18.1	New Hampshire	11.0	4.6	4.4	2.0
California	255.3	89.1	115.8	49.7	New Jersey	76.0	29.5	38.8	7.4
Colorado	56.5	19.3	21.0	16.0	New Mexico	24.0	6.8	9.0	8.2
Connecticut	28.8	13.1	12.4	3.2	New York	149.9	52.2	76.7	18.1
Delaware	11.8	5.1	4.3	2.4	North Carolina	138.3	61.6	49.3	27.4
District of Columbia	11.4	2.6	8.2	0.2	North Dakota	20.7	5.1	6.8	8.7
Florida	239.0	125.5	96.3	17.1	Ohio	152.9	54.5	47.2	51.2
Georgia	139.9	59.7	47.3	32.7	Oklahoma	64.6	24.1	21.2	19.2
Hawaii	9.3	2.7	3.0	3.6	Oregon	49.3	18.9	16.5	13.9
Idaho	23.8	8.4	6.4	8.9	Pennsylvania	149.0	55.9	43.2	49.2
Illinois	142.7	47.2	50.8	44.1	Rhode Island	7.6	3.1	3.7	0.7
Indiana	104.2	34.6	24.3	45.3	South Carolina	81.8	31.9	22.2	27.7
Iowa	51.2	14.8	12.4	24.0	South Dakota	12.9	5.0	4.9	2.9
Kansas	42.0	14.2	16.2	11.7	Tennessee	102.9	44.4	36.9	21.6
Kentucky	76.6	27.7	20.0	28.9	Texas	424.5	157.3	143.5	123.5
Louisiana	94.2	32.1	24.7	37.4	Utah	31.2	9.7	12.1	9.4
Maine	12.4	4.9	4.4	3.0	Vermont	5.5	2.1	2.0	1.4
Maryland	62.1	28.1	29.5	3.9	Virginia	118.2	48.0	52.3	17.8
Massachusetts	53.3	20.3	26.0	6.7	Washington	90.0	35.3	29.4	25.3
Michigan	104.9	35.1	38.9	30.8	West Virginia	33.6	11.7	7.8	14.2
Minnesota	68.7	22.8	23.4	22.5	Wisconsin	71.0	22.4	24.1	24.4
Mississippi	50.4	19.3	14.5	16.5	Wyoming	16.9	2.7	3.8	10.4

[1] Includes transportation, not shown separately.

Source: U.S. Energy Information Administration, "Electric Sales, Revenue, and Average Price," <http://www.eia.gov/electricity/sales_revenue_price/index.cfm>, accessed January 2020.

Table 983. Electric Energy Average Retail Price by Class of Service and State: 2018

[In cents per kilowatt-hour (kWh). Data include both bundled and unbundled consumers]

State	Total [1]	Resi-dential	Com-mercial	Indus-trial	State	Total [1]	Resi-dential	Com-mercial	Indus-trial
United States	**10.53**	**12.87**	**10.67**	**6.92**	Missouri	9.93	11.34	9.40	7.22
Alabama	9.63	12.18	11.24	6.01	Montana	8.84	10.96	10.11	5.19
Alaska	19.36	21.94	18.58	17.10	Nebraska	9.02	10.70	8.83	7.60
Arizona	10.85	12.77	10.64	6.55	Nevada	8.67	11.85	7.74	6.10
Arkansas	7.78	9.81	7.75	5.64	New Hampshire	17.01	19.69	15.81	13.42
California	16.58	18.84	16.34	13.20	New Jersey	13.23	15.41	12.21	10.07
Colorado	10.02	12.15	10.02	7.47	New Mexico	9.35	12.68	10.02	5.84
Connecticut	18.41	21.20	16.76	13.77	New York	14.83	18.52	14.50	6.02
Delaware	10.55	12.53	9.65	7.95	North Carolina	9.25	11.09	8.58	6.33
District of Columbia	12.03	12.84	11.97	8.30	North Dakota	8.91	10.25	9.10	7.98
Florida	10.31	11.54	9.19	7.67	Ohio	9.94	12.56	10.11	7.01
Georgia	9.62	11.47	9.79	6.00	Oklahoma	8.09	10.30	8.07	5.34
Hawaii	29.18	32.47	29.90	26.10	Oregon	8.85	10.98	8.91	5.86
Idaho	8.17	10.15	7.93	6.47	Pennsylvania	10.10	13.89	8.94	6.84
Illinois	9.60	12.77	9.12	6.80	Rhode Island	18.10	20.55	16.58	15.39
Indiana	9.75	12.26	10.60	7.38	South Carolina	9.66	12.44	10.11	6.10
Iowa	8.92	12.24	9.68	6.45	South Dakota	9.97	11.59	9.62	7.77
Kansas	10.72	13.35	10.66	7.60	Tennessee	9.58	10.71	10.51	5.68
Kentucky	8.52	10.60	9.74	5.68	Texas	8.48	11.20	8.16	5.39
Louisiana	7.71	9.59	8.85	5.35	Utah	8.21	10.41	8.23	5.90
Maine	13.44	16.84	12.51	9.32	Vermont	15.13	18.02	15.24	10.66
Maryland	11.57	13.30	10.43	8.23	Virginia	9.48	11.73	8.32	6.86
Massachusetts	18.50	21.61	17.17	14.89	Washington	8.00	9.75	8.72	4.71
Michigan	11.40	15.45	11.15	7.10	West Virginia	8.72	11.18	9.24	6.40
Minnesota	10.37	13.14	10.38	7.53	Wisconsin	10.58	14.02	10.67	7.33
Mississippi	9.24	11.12	10.43	6.00	Wyoming	8.09	11.29	9.58	6.71

[1] Includes transportation, not shown separately.

Source: U.S. Energy Information Administration, "Electric Sales, Revenue, and Average Price," <http://www.eia.gov/electricity/sales_revenue_price/index.cfm>, accessed January 2020.

Table 984. Total Electric Power Industry—Generation, Sales, Revenue, and Customers: 1990 to 2017

[2,808 represents 2,808,000,000,000 Kilowatt hours (kWh). Sales and revenue are to and from ultimate customers. Commercial and Industrial are not wholly comparable on a year-to-year basis due to changes from one classification to another. Beginning 2003, the Energy Information Administration replaced the "Other" sector with the Transportation sector. The Transportation sector consists entirely of electrified rail and urban transit systems. Data previously reported in "Other" have been relocated to the Commercial sector, except for Agriculture (i.e., irrigation load), which have been relocated to the Industrial sector]

Class	Unit	1990	2000	2005	2010	2013	2014	2015	2016	2017 [1]
Generation [2]	Bil. kWh	2,808	3,802	4,055	4,125	4,066	4,094	4,078	4,079	4,012
Sales [3]	Bil. kWh	2,713	3,421	3,661	3,755	3,752	3,792	3,759	3,762	3,723
Residential or domestic	Bil. kWh	924	1,192	1,359	1,446	1,395	1,407	1,404	1,411	1,379
Percent of total	Percent	34.1	34.9	37.1	38.5	37.2	37.1	37.4	37.5	37.0
Commercial [4]	Bil. kWh	751	1,055	1,275	1,330	1,337	1,352	1,361	1,367	1,353
Industrial [5]	Bil. kWh	946	1,064	1,019	971	985	998	987	977	984
Revenue [3]	Bil. dol.	178.2	233.2	298.0	368.9	375.1	396.3	391.3	386.5	390.3
Residential or domestic	Bil. dol.	72.4	98.2	128.4	166.8	169.1	176.2	177.6	177.1	177.7
Percent of total	Percent	40.6	42.1	43.1	45.2	45.1	44.5	45.4	45.8	45.5
Commercial [4]	Bil. dol.	55.1	78.4	110.5	135.6	137.2	145.3	144.8	142.6	144.2
Industrial [5]	Bil. dol.	44.9	49.4	58.5	65.8	67.9	70.9	68.2	66.1	67.7
Ultimate customers [3]	Million	110.6	127.6	138.4	144.1	146.3	147.4	148.6	150.1	151.8
Residential or domestic	Million	97.1	111.7	120.8	125.7	127.8	128.7	129.8	131.1	132.6
Commercial [4]	Million	12.1	14.3	16.9	17.7	17.7	17.9	18.0	18.1	18.4
Industrial [5]	Million	0.5	0.5	0.7	0.7	0.8	0.9	0.8	0.8	0.8
Avg. kWh used per customer	1,000	24.5	26.8	26.5	26.1	25.5	25.5	25.2	25.1	24.1
Residential	1,000	9.5	10.7	11.3	11.5	10.9	10.9	10.8	10.8	10.3
Commercial [4]	1,000	62.2	73.5	75.4	75.1	75.6	75.7	75.2	75.3	73.3
Avg. annual bill per customer	Dollar	1,612	1,828	2,153	2,560	2,556	2,660	2,628	2,576	2,545
Residential	Dollar	745	879	1,063	1,327	1,321	1,366	1,367	1,351	1,334
Commercial [4]	Dollar	4,562	5,464	6,538	7,661	7,732	8,092	8,008	7,860	7,827
Avg. revenue per kWh sold	Cents	6.6	6.8	8.1	9.8	10.1	10.4	10.4	10.3	10.5
Residential	Cents	7.8	8.2	9.4	11.5	12.1	12.5	12.7	12.6	12.9
Commercial [4]	Cents	7.3	7.4	8.7	10.2	10.3	10.7	10.6	10.4	10.7
Industrial [5]	Cents	4.7	4.6	5.7	6.8	6.9	7.1	6.9	6.8	6.9

[1] Preliminary. [2] Includes batteries, chemicals, hydrogen, pitch, sulfur, purchased steam, and miscellaneous technologies, which are not separately displayed. [3] Includes other types, not shown separately. Data for 1990 are as of December 31; beginning 2000, data are yearly averages. [4] Small light and power. [5] Large light and power.

Source: Edison Electric Institute, Washington, DC, *Statistical Yearbook of the Electric Power Industry*, annual ©. See also <http://www.eei.org>.

Table 985. Revenue and Expense Statistics for Major U.S. Investor-Owned Electric Utilities: 1995 to 2018

[In millions of dollars (199,967 represents $199,967,000,000). Covers investor-owned electric utilities that met any one or more of the following conditions, during each of the last 3 years: 1 million megawatt-hours of total sales, 100 megawatt-hours of annual sales for resale, 500 megawatt-hours of annual power exchange delivered, or 500 megawatt-hours of annual wheeling for others. Missing or erroneous respondent data may result in slight imbalances in some of the expense account subtotals]

Item	1995	2000	2005	2010	2015	2016	2017	2018
Utility operating revenues..........	**199,967**	**233,915**	**265,652**	**285,512**	**282,695**	**282,499**	**286,501**	**293,868**
Electric utility............................	183,655	213,634	234,909	260,119	260,121	261,047	263,265	268,421
Other utility...............................	16,312	20,281	30,743	25,393	22,574	21,451	23,235	25,447
Utility operating expenses..........	**165,321**	**210,250**	**236,786**	**253,022**	**242,728**	**239,037**	**240,041**	**253,944**
Electric utility............................	150,599	191,564	207,830	234,173	228,366	226,457	226,110	238,526
Operation.............................	91,881	132,607	150,645	166,922	149,939	145,077	142,000	163,479
Production.........................	68,983	107,554	120,586	128,831	107,201	100,852	98,859	104,185
Cost of fuel.....................	29,122	32,407	36,106	44,138	34,711	32,621	32,165	33,592
Purchased power.................	29,981	62,608	77,902	67,284	52,970	49,962	49,030	53,060
Other............................	9,880	12,561	6,599	17,409	19,521	18,269	17,664	17,533
Transmission......................	1,425	2,713	5,664	6,948	9,624	10,447	10,804	11,387
Distribution.......................	2,561	3,092	3,502	4,007	4,406	4,734	4,358	4,806
Customer accounts................	3,613	4,239	4,229	5,091	5,184	5,077	4,789	4,969
Customer service.................	1,922	1,826	2,291	4,741	6,445	6,187	5,961	6,019
Sales.............................	348	405	219	185	201	205	213	203
Administrative and general........	13,028	12,768	14,130	17,120	16,878	17,575	17,016	31,911
Maintenance..........................	11,767	12,064	12,033	14,957	16,392	16,982	17,996	17,786
Depreciation.........................	19,885	20,636	17,123	20,951	26,847	30,097	30,323	32,125
Taxes and other......................	27,065	24,479	26,805	31,343	35,188	34,301	35,791	25,136
Other utility.............................	14,722	18,686	28,956	18,849	14,362	12,579	13,931	15,418
Net utility operating income........	**34,646**	**23,665**	**28,866**	**32,490**	**39,968**	**43,462**	**46,460**	**39,924**

Source: U.S. Energy Information Administration, *Electric Power Annual 2018*, January 2020, and earlier reports. See also <http://www.eia.gov/electricity/annual/>.

Table 986. Renewable Energy Net Generation of Electricity by Source and State: 2019

[In millions of kilowatt-hours (273,707 represents 273,707,000,000). Data based on results from the Energy Information Agency's annual survey form EIA-923. For more on net generation, see Table 980]

State	Hydro-electric	Other renewable Total [1]	Other renewable Wind	Other renewable Bio-mass [2]	Other renewable Solar [3]	State	Hydro-electric	Other renewable Total [1]	Other renewable Wind	Other renewable Bio-mass [2]	Other renewable Solar [3]
U.S.......	**273,707**	**481,769**	**300,071**	**58,412**	**107,275**	MO........	764	3,379	2,872	108	399
AL.........	10,839	3,866	(NA)	3,462	404	MT........	9,409	2,400	2,323	20	57
AK.........	1,398	197	154	39	4	NE........	1,160	7,540	7,414	79	47
AZ.........	6,096	8,471	557	232	7,682	NV........	2,233	9,691	324	52	5,547
AR.........	2,719	1,597	(NA)	1,354	243	NH........	1,233	1,931	409	1,392	130
CA.........	40,051	75,960	14,970	5,782	43,801	NJ........	26	4,246	22	805	3,419
CO.........	1,607	12,930	10,926	162	1,842	NM........	133	8,591	6,860	17	1,656
CT.........	522	1,552	13	763	776	NY........	29,541	9,250	4,850	1,895	2,505
DE.........	(NA)	233	5	52	176	NC........	6,207	10,614	523	2,525	7,566
DC.........	(NA)	154	(NA)	55	99	ND........	2,801	10,758	10,754	3	1
FL.........	220	9,093	1	4,497	4,595	OH........	255	3,080	2,029	697	354
GA.........	3,485	7,530	(NA)	5,154	2,376	OK........	1,824	29,273	28,883	310	80
HI.........	70	2,374	595	290	1,381	OR........	29,526	9,319	7,169	1,076	922
ID.........	9,112	3,822	2,657	492	600	PA........	4,040	6,222	3,549	2,098	575
IL.........	131	14,503	13,831	419	253	RI........	4	686	226	208	252
IN.........	194	7,080	6,206	410	464	SC........	2,836	3,543	(NA)	2,418	1,125
IA.........	749	26,955	26,558	221	176	SD........	5,620	3,018	3,015	–	3
KS.........	20	21,619	21,501	61	57	TN........	9,857	1,398	41	930	427
KY.........	4,007	514	(NA)	435	79	TX........	998	91,079	84,429	1,329	5,321
LA.........	1,147	2,448	(NA)	2,206	242	UT........	781	3,930	809	68	2,608
ME.........	3,115	5,015	2,408	2,519	88	VT........	1,198	1,136	384	424	328
MD........	2,205	2,459	577	404	1,478	VA........	1,551	4,783	(NA)	3,803	980
MA........	1,079	4,598	223	1,044	3,331	WA........	66,181	9,578	7,724	1,602	252
MI.........	1,291	8,453	5,813	2,369	271	WV........	1,776	1,749	1,737	–	12
MN.........	887	14,005	11,040	1,351	1,614	WI........	1,993	3,158	1,649	1,358	151
MS.........	(NA)	1,756	(NA)	1,421	335	WY........	820	4,231	4,042	(NA)	189

– Represents or rounds to zero. NA Not available. [1] Includes generation from geothermal energy, not shown separately. [2] Includes wood and wood derived fuels, landfill gas, biogenic municipal solid waste, and other biomass waste. [3] Includes generation from all utility-scale solar and small-scale solar photovoltaic sources.

Source: Energy Information Administration, "Electricity Data Browser," <http://www.eia.gov/electricity/data/browser/>, accessed June 2020.

Table 987. Major Power Outages by Type of Disturbance and Duration: 2019

[Data shown for power outages lasting longer than 42 hours]

Type of disturbance	Month	County and/or state affected	Duration	Number of customers affected [1]
Severe weather............	May	Louisiana, Texas	104 Hours, 10 Minutes	65,844
Severe weather............	June	Collin, Dallas, Denton, Palo Pinto, Tarrant, Ellis, and Williamson counties, Texas	103 Hours, 45 Minutes	558,000
Severe weather............	October	California	103 Hours, 7 Minutes	972,000
Severe weather............	October	Cass, Cameron, Collin, Dallas, Ellis, Erath, Hunt, Kaufman, Lamar, Panola, Rains, Rockwall, Rusk, Tarrant, Van Zandt, and Wood counties, Texas	99 Hours, 45 Minutes	400,000
Fuel supply deficiency....	January	Scott, Illinois	76 Hours, 37 Minutes	(NA)
Severe weather............	January	Washington	76 Hours, 0 Minutes	230,000
Severe weather............	March	Texas	74 Hours, 9 Minutes	54,290
Severe weather............	July	Gloucester county, New Jersey	67 Hours, 25 Minutes	95,600
Severe weather............	August	Oklahoma	66 Hours, 0 Minutes	103,779
Severe weather............	November	Tuscola, Sanilac, Huron, St. Clair, Macomb, Oakland, Wayne, Livingston, Washtenaw, and Monroe counties, Michigan	62 Hours, 0 Minutes	107,000
Severe weather............	July	Wisconsin, Michigan	60 Hours, 5 Minutes	50,000
Severe weather............	November	New York	60 Hours, 0 Minutes	8,000
Severe weather............	January	North Carolina, South Carolina	59 Hours, 30 Minutes	(NA)
Severe weather............	October	Connecticut, Rhode Island, Massachusetts, Vermont, New Hampshire, Maine	56 Hours, 45 Minutes	101,683
Severe weather............	February	Michigan	55 Hours, 35 Minutes	233,000
Severe weather............	July	Bucks and Delaware counties, Pennsylvania	55 Hours, 0 Minutes	165,000
Severe weather............	October	Los Angeles, Orange, Riverside, San Bernardino, Ventura, and Kern counties, California	54 Hours, 57 Minutes	114,402
Severe weather............	February	Ohio, Virginia, West Virginia	54 Hours, 8 Minutes	118,781
Severe weather............	July	Kent, Newaygo, Mecosta, Montcalm, Isabella, Ionia, Allegan, and Barry counties, Michigan	52 Hours, 0 Minutes	160,000
Severe weather............	September	Texas	51 Hours, 30 Minutes	(NA)
Severe weather............	May	Harris county, Texas	50 Hours, 55 Minutes	238,015
Severe weather............	June	Dallas, Denton, Ellis, Collin, Ellis, Hood, Johnson, and Kaufman counties, Texas	49 Hours, 0 Minutes	265,000
Severe weather............	July	Michigan	49 Hours, 0 Minutes	400,000
Severe weather............	July	Collin, Dallas, Denton, Hood, Johnson, and Tarrant counties, Texas	48 Hours, 20 Minutes	57,000
Severe weather............	June	Dallas, Tarrant, Collin, and Denton counties, Texas	45 Hours, 59 Minutes	340,000
Severe weather............	February	California	45 Hours, 40 Minutes	121,000
Severe weather............	November	Connecticut, Maine, Massachusetts, Rhode Island, New Hampshire, Vermont	44 Hours, 15 Minutes	80,066

NA Not available. [1] Number of customers affected are preliminary estimates.

Source: U.S. Energy Information Administration, *Electric Power Monthly*, June 2020. See also <http://www.eia.gov/electricity/monthly/>.

Table 988. Gas Utility Industry—Summary: 1990 to 2018

[54,261 represents 54,261,000. Covers natural, manufactured, mixed, and liquid petroleum gas. Based on a questionnaire mailed to all privately and municipally owned gas utilities in the United States, except those with annual revenues less than $25,000]

Item	Unit	1990	2000	2005	2010	2015	2016	2017	2018
End users [1]........................	1,000	**54,261**	**61,262**	**64,395**	**64,960**	**65,612**	**66,205**	**66,844**	**67,597**
Residential........................	1,000	49,802	56,494	59,569	60,246	60,922	61,496	62,133	62,837
Commercial........................	1,000	4,246	4,610	4,678	4,582	4,559	4,579	4,581	4,630
Industrial............................	1,000	166	157	145	129	120	120	119	119
Other................................	1,000	48	2	2	3	10	10	11	10
Sales [2]............................	Tril. Btu [3]	**9,842**	**9,232**	**8,848**	**7,980**	**7,602**	**7,382**	**7,473**	**8,324**
Residential........................	Tril. Btu	4,468	4,741	4,516	4,371	4,080	3,875	3,944	4,459
Percent of total...............	Percent	45.4	51.4	51.0	54.8	53.7	52.5	52.8	53.6
Commercial........................	Tril. Btu	2,192	2,077	2,056	1,842	1,766	1,693	1,747	1,965
Industrial............................	Tril. Btu	3,010	1,698	1,654	1,209	1,172	1,178	1,194	1,240
Other................................	Tril. Btu	171	715	622	558	584	636	589	659
Revenues [2]....................	Mil. dol.	**45,153**	**59,243**	**96,909**	**72,886**	**60,923**	**55,449**	**61,869**	**67,843**
Residential........................	Mil. dol.	25,000	35,828	55,680	47,231	40,451	37,128	41,046	44,923
Percent of total...............	Percent	55.4	60.5	57.5	64.8	66.4	67.0	66.3	66.2
Commercial........................	Mil. dol.	10,604	13,339	22,653	16,578	14,057	12,440	13,909	15,386
Industrial............................	Mil. dol.	8,996	7,432	13,751	6,437	4,434	4,003	4,725	5,034
Other................................	Mil. dol.	553	2,645	4,825	2,640	1,982	1,878	2,189	2,500
Prices per mil. Btu [3]........	Dollars	**4.59**	**6.42**	**10.95**	**9.13**	**7.99**	**7.51**	**8.28**	**8.15**
Residential........................	Dollars	5.60	7.56	12.33	10.81	9.91	9.58	10.41	10.07
Commercial........................	Dollars	4.84	6.42	11.02	9.00	7.96	7.35	7.96	7.83
Industrial............................	Dollars	2.99	4.38	8.31	5.32	3.78	3.40	3.96	4.06
Gas mains mileage...............	1,000	**1,189**	**1,369**	**1,438**	**1,531**	**1,594**	**1,604**	**1,615**	**1,627**
Field and gathering.................	1,000	32	27	23	19	18	18	18	18
Transmission.......................	1,000	292	297	297	308	301	300	301	302
Distribution........................	1,000	865	1,046	1,118	1,204	1,276	1,286	1,296	1,308
Construction expenditures.......	Mil. dol.	**7,899**	**8,624**	**10,089**	**11,042**	**21,074**	**25,124**	**27,593**	**34,186**
Transmission.......................	Mil. dol.	2,886	1,590	3,368	3,524	6,578	7,559	9,161	12,222
Distribution........................	Mil. dol.	3,714	5,437	5,129	5,674	11,614	13,432	14,878	17,090
Production and storage...........	Mil. dol.	309	138	179	151	135	337	467	1,070
General............................	Mil. dol.	770	1,273	1,070	1,185	1,928	3,187	2,102	2,624
Underground storage..............	Mil. dol.	219	185	343	509	819	607	984	1,180

[1] Annual average. [2] Excludes sales for resale. [3] For definition of Btu (British thermal unit), see text, this section.

Source: American Gas Association, Washington, DC, *Annual Statistics* ©. See also <http://www.aga.org>.

Table 989. Gas Utility Industry—Customers, Sales, and Revenues by State: 2018

[67,597 represents 67,597,000. See headnote, Table 988. For definition of Btu, see text, this section]

State	Customers [1] (1,000) Total	Resi-dential	Sales [2] (tril. Btu) Total	Resi-dential	Revenues [2] (mil. dol.) Total	Resi-dential	State	Customers [1] (1,000) Total	Resi-dential	Sales [2] (tril. Btu) Total	Resi-dential	Revenues [2] (mil. dol.) Total	Resi-dential
U.S.	67,597	62,837	8,324	4,459	67,843	44,923	MO	1,533	1,410	184	118	1,657	1,178
AL	851	779	113	36	1,004	529	MT	313	277	37	23	255	165
AK	148	134	58	19	516	205	NE	514	471	66	39	472	319
AZ	1,310	1,252	69	36	805	539	NV	916	871	67	43	530	387
AR	624	555	61	36	600	412	NH	123	107	15	8	205	125
CA	11,009	10,580	601	417	6,406	4,946	NJ	2,892	2,692	327	245	2,836	2,148
CO	1,939	1,785	213	133	1,451	992	NM	642	593	53	36	360	271
CT	615	555	113	53	1,210	711	NY	4,210	3,915	508	373	5,622	4,471
DE	190	176	20	13	222	152	NC	1,408	1,280	143	76	1,402	887
DC	146	139	14	10	154	117	ND	169	146	41	13	215	91
FL	780	742	51	16	619	334	OH	614	582	70	52	603	466
GA	361	327	72	18	532	222	OK	1,039	946	109	70	819	623
HI	32	29	3	1	108	26	OR	836	752	81	44	729	454
ID	445	403	45	28	288	195	PA	2,627	2,450	295	228	3,078	2,476
IL	3,848	3,600	500	394	3,809	3,101	RI	266	244	29	21	414	321
IN	1,836	1,689	210	143	1,672	1,208	SC	729	669	171	32	1,106	416
IA	1,029	930	158	73	1,011	634	SD	216	191	28	15	182	109
KS	953	870	102	70	908	683	TN	1,298	1,162	167	77	1,313	706
KY	841	757	104	52	877	529	TX	5,030	4,701	1,443	235	7,099	2,586
LA	968	908	106	39	798	441	UT	1,019	951	102	70	837	609
ME	47	35	11	3	143	50	VT	52	46	14	4	116	56
MD	981	926	91	68	983	771	VA	1,258	1,167	134	84	1,311	946
MA	1,629	1,498	235	132	2,991	1,968	WA	1,303	1,194	142	87	1,282	859
MI	3,353	3,117	439	317	3,303	2,506	WV	370	335	43	27	376	258
MN	1,686	1,544	280	146	2,076	1,229	WI	1,950	1,775	298	150	1,930	1,161
MS	516	464	68	25	476	254	WY	132	117	18	10	131	80

[1] Averages for the year. [2] Excludes sales for resale.

Source: American Gas Association, Washington, DC, *Annual Statistics* ©. See also <http://www.aga.org>.

Table 990. Privately Owned Gas Utility Industry—Balance Sheet and Income Account: 1990 to 2018

[In millions of dollars (121,686 represents $121,686,000,000). The gas utility industry consists of pipeline and distribution companies. Excludes operations of companies distributing gas in bottles or tanks]

Item	1990	1995	2000	2005	2010	2015	2016	2017	2018
COMPOSITE BALANCE SHEET									
Assets, total	**121,686**	**141,965**	**165,709**	**196,215**	**220,860**	**262,805**	**286,565**	**300,631**	**324,955**
Total utility plant	112,863	143,636	162,206	207,976	239,718	292,252	315,710	335,599	364,856
Depreciation and amortization	49,483	62,723	69,366	91,794	92,012	104,615	109,089	112,416	120,067
Utility plant (net)	63,380	80,912	92,839	116,183	147,707	187,637	206,621	223,183	244,789
Investment and fund accounts	23,872	26,489	10,846	16,331	7,132	12,202	10,028	10,854	9,202
Current and accrued assets	23,268	18,564	35,691	32,325	27,288	21,309	22,218	23,677	245
Deferred debits [1]	9,576	13,923	24,279	29,574	37,307	40,253	46,355	41,240	44,895
Liabilities, total	**121,686**	**141,965**	**165,709**	**196,215**	**220,860**	**262,805**	**286,565**	**300,631**	**325**
Capitalization, total	74,958	90,581	96,079	120,949	133,414	157,916	172,911	199,086	215,880
Capital stock	43,810	54,402	47,051	62,470	74,157	87,760	96,933	111,722	119,549
Long-term debts	31,148	35,548	48,267	58,264	59,223	70,194	75,826	86,862	96,242
Current and accrued liabilities	29,550	28,272	42,312	34,936	28,564	26,408	28,075	36,216	39,006
Deferred income taxes [2]	11,360	14,393	17,157	24,937	34,401	43,688	50,644	39,708	44,729
Other liabilities and credits	5,818	8,715	10,161	15,393	24,515	34,793	34,935	25,621	25,340
COMPOSITE INCOME ACCOUNT									
Operating revenues, total	**66,027**	**58,390**	**72,042**	**102,018**	**82,315**	**72,298**	**69,605**	**74,040**	**79,560**
Minus: Operating expenses [3]	60,137	50,760	64,988	89,385	71,761	61,229	57,227	61,058	66,249
Operation and maintenance	51,627	37,966	54,602	77,673	57,758	45,746	41,307	43,746	49,608
Federal, state, and local taxes	4,957	6,182	6,163	7,513	7,569	7,872	7,835	9,111	7,794
Equals: Operating income	5,890	7,630	7,053	12,632	10,554	11,069	12,378	12,983	13,311
Utility operating income	6,077	7,848	7,166	12,812	11,045	11,620	12,849	13,359	13,941
Income before interest charges	8,081	9,484	7,589	13,972	12,368	12,049	12,139	13,575	14,363
Net income	4,410	5,139	4,245	9,777	8,619	8,719	8,442	9,808	10,164
Dividends	3,191	4,037	3,239	2,419	2,080	1,487	1,329	1,805	1,236

[1] Includes capital stock discount and expense and reacquired securities. [2] Includes reserves for deferred income taxes. [3] Includes expenses not shown separately.

Source: American Gas Association, Washington, DC, *Annual Statistics* ©. See also <http://www.aga.org>.

Table 991. Sewage Treatment Facilities and Employees: 2017 and 2018

[Beginning 2017, data are based on the North American Industry Classification System (NAICS) 2017; see text, Section 15]

State	Sewage treatment facilities (NAICS 22132)				State	Sewage treatment facilities (NAICS 22132)			
	2017		2018			2017		2018	
	Number of establish-ments	Paid employees	Number of establish-ments	Paid employees		Number of establish-ments	Paid employees	Number of establish-ments	Paid employees
U.S............	**652**	**5,898**	**624**	**5,407**	MO............	**19**	**76**	**19**	**75**
AL..............	15	330	12	333	MT............	7	26	7	23
AK..............	(NA)	(NA)	(NA)	(NA)	NE............	(NA)	(NA)	(NA)	(NA)
AZ..............	20	143	20	146	NV............	(NA)	(NA)	(NA)	(NA)
AR..............	7	64	7	64	NH............	5	20	5	17
CA..............	38	228	38	217	NJ............	11	129	11	142
CO..............	8	70	9	71	NM............	11	(2)	12	165
CT..............	8	62	7	52	NY............	34	497	30	423
DE..............	3	8	4	66	NC............	18	91	17	94
DC..............	(NA)	(NA)	(NA)	(NA)	ND............	(NA)	(NA)	(NA)	(NA)
FL..............	46	523	45	506	OH............	11	249	9	63
GA..............	23	174	22	169	OK............	15	54	21	237
HI..............	19	104	19	99	OR............	10	(1)	10	52
ID..............	6	35	7	36	PA............	48	432	45	414
IL..............	21	201	19	202	RI............	3	(1)	(NA)	(NA)
IN..............	25	281	23	96	SC............	10	81	9	56
IA..............	5	(1)	5	93	SD............	(NA)	(NA)	(NA)	(NA)
KS..............	(NA)	(NA)	(NA)	(NA)	TN............	9	70	7	58
KY..............	6	10	8	53	TX............	69	512	64	410
LA..............	18	176	20	211	UT............	(NA)	(NA)	(NA)	(NA)
ME..............	(NA)	(NA)	(NA)	(NA)	VT............	(NA)	(NA)	(NA)	(NA)
MD..............	5	22	6	54	VA............	7	49	7	56
MA..............	9	109	7	84	WA............	8	71	7	56
MI..............	23	154	20	128	WV............	8	55	7	46
MN..............	12	112	12	102	WI............	7	114	4	13
MS..............	15	160	13	150	WY............	(NA)	(NA)	(NA)	(NA)

NA Not available. [1] 20 to 99 employees. [2] 100 to 249 employees.

Source: U.S. Census Bureau, County Business Patterns, "County Business Patterns by Legal Form of Organization and Employment Size Class for U.S., States, and Selected Geographies," <http://data.census.gov>, accessed July 2020. See also <https://www.census.gov/programs-surveys/cbp.html>.

Section 20
Construction and Housing

This section presents data on the construction industry and on various indicators of its activity and costs; on housing units and their characteristics and occupants; and on the characteristics and vacancy rates for commercial buildings.

The principal source of these data is the U.S. Census Bureau, which issues a variety of current publications, as well as data from the decennial census. Current construction statistics compiled by the Census Bureau appear in its *New Residential Construction* and *New Residential Sales* press releases and web sites at <census.gov/construction/nrc/> and <census.gov/construction/nrs/>. *Construction Spending*, available at <census.gov/construction/c30/c30index.html>, presents data on all types of construction. Reports of the censuses of construction industries (see below) are also issued on various topics.

Other Census Bureau publications include the quarterly *Housing Vacancies and Homeownership*, the quarterly *Survey of Market Absorption*, the biennial *American Housing Survey* (formerly *Annual Housing Survey*), and other reports of the censuses of housing and of construction industries.

Other sources include Dodge Data & Analytics, New York, NY, which presents national and state data on construction contracts; the National Association of Home Builders with data on housing starts; the NATIONAL ASSOCIATION OF REALTORS®, which presents data on existing home sales; the Bureau of Economic Analysis, which presents data on residential fixed assets; the U.S. Energy Information Administration, which provides data on commercial buildings through its periodic sample surveys; and the Federal Financial Institutions Examination Council, which provide data on home loans and home improvement loans.

Censuses and surveys—Censuses of the construction industry were first conducted by the Census Bureau for 1929, 1935, and 1939; beginning in 1967, a census has been taken every 5 years (through 2012, for years ending in "2" and "7"). Release of data from the 2012 Economic Census was completed in 2016. Data from the 2017 Economic Census are being released on a flow basis between September 2019 and December 2021. The construction sector of the Economic Census covers all employer establishments primarily engaged in (1) building construction by general contractors or operative builders; (2) heavy (nonbuilding) construction by general contractors; and (3) construction by special trade contractors. This sector includes construction management and land subdividers and developers. The 2012 census was conducted in accordance with the 2012 North American Industrial Classification System (NAICS). See text, Section 15, Business Enterprise.

The *American Housing Survey* (*Current Housing Reports* Series H-150 and H-170), which began in 1973, provided an annual and ongoing series of data on selected housing and demographic characteristics until 1983. In 1984, the name of the survey was changed from the *Annual Housing Survey*. Currently, national data are collected every other year, and data for selected metropolitan areas are collected on a rotating basis. The supplemental sample of housing units is selected for no more than 30 metropolitan units and combined with the national sample in order to produce metropolitan estimates using the national survey. All samples represent a cross section of the housing stock in their respective areas. Estimates are subject to both sampling and nonsampling errors; caution should therefore be used in making comparisons between years. More information about the survey can be found at <census.gov/programs-surveys/ahs.html>

Data on residential mortgages were collected continuously from 1890 to 1970, except 1930, as part of the decennial census by the Census Bureau. Since 1973, mortgage status data have been presented in the *American Housing Survey*. Data on mortgage activity are covered in Section 25, Banking and Finance.

Housing units—In general, a housing unit is a house, an apartment, a group of rooms or a single room occupied or intended for occupancy as separate living quarters; that is, the occupants live separately from any other individual in the building, and there is direct access from the outside or through a common hall. Transient accommodations, barracks for workers, and institutional-type quarters are not counted as housing units.

Statistical reliability—For a discussion of statistical collection and estimation, sampling procedures, and measures of statistical reliability applicable to Census Bureau data, see Appendix III.

Table 992. Construction—Establishments, Employees, and Payroll by Kind of Business (NAICS Basis): 2016 and 2017

[6,311 represents 6,311,000. Covers establishments with payroll. Excludes most government employees, railroad employees, and self-employed persons. For statement on methodology, see Appendix III]

Kind of business	NAICS code [1]	Establishments		Paid employees [2] (1,000)		Annual payroll (mil. dol.)	
		2016	2017	2016	2017	2016	2017
Construction................................	**23**	**696,733**	**715,641**	**6,311**	**6,533**	**371,256**	**399,209**
Construction of buildings.............................	236	210,469	214,765	1,314	1,328	80,912	85,723
Residential building construction...................	2361	168,202	172,293	664	681	34,416	37,372
New single-family housing construction (except for-sale builders).........................	236115	48,515	49,387	176	171	8,608	8,525
New multifamily housing construction (except for-sale builders).........................	236116	2,885	3,250	34	45	2,573	3,741
New housing for-sale builders....................	236117	12,924	16,152	108	121	8,592	10,093
Residential remodelers...........................	236118	103,878	103,504	346	343	14,643	15,014
Nonresidential building construction...............	2362	42,267	42,472	649	647	46,497	48,351
Industrial building construction..................	23621	3,277	3,183	90	68	5,658	4,457
Commercial and institutional building construction.....................................	23622	38,990	39,289	560	579	40,839	43,894
Heavy and civil engineering construction...........	237	38,477	37,923	942	954	67,508	71,162
Utility system construction.......................	2371	19,315	19,052	552	574	38,307	41,617
Water and sewer line and related structures....	23711	11,107	10,761	166	147	10,592	9,506
Oil and gas pipeline and related structures......	23712	2,126	2,249	164	212	12,842	15,927
Power and communication line and related structures...............................	23713	6,082	6,042	222	215	14,873	16,184
Land subdivision................................	2372	5,063	4,912	26	21	1,830	1,537
Highway, street, and bridge construction..........	2373	9,760	9,673	275	291	21,284	23,016
Other heavy and civil engineering construction...	2379	4,339	4,286	89	68	6,087	4,992
Specialty trade contractors.........................	238	447,787	462,953	4,056	4,251	222,836	242,324
Foundation, structure, and building exterior contractors.................................	2381	90,244	92,984	812	853	41,421	45,444
Poured concrete foundation and structures contractors..................................	23811	19,790	20,771	218	235	11,766	13,173
Structural steel and precast concrete contractors..................................	23812	3,424	3,599	71	77	4,259	4,747
Framing contractors.............................	23813	10,975	11,547	75	83	3,043	3,674
Masonry contractors............................	23814	18,461	18,391	140	140	6,556	6,893
Glass and glazing contractors...................	23815	5,583	5,829	57	62	3,195	3,565
Roofing contractors.............................	23816	18,677	19,396	168	173	8,366	9,207
Siding contractors..............................	23817	7,844	7,832	34	34	1,452	1,516
Other foundation, structure, and building exterior contractors.........................	23819	5,490	5,619	48	48	2,785	2,669
Building equipment contractors...................	2382	178,345	183,959	1,917	1,982	113,799	121,339
Electrical contractors...........................	23821	72,784	74,127	800	835	47,479	51,602
Plumbing, heating, and air-conditioning contractors..................................	23822	98,434	102,455	992	1,016	57,311	60,057
Other building equipment contractors...........	23829	7,127	7,377	125	132	9,009	9,680
Building finishing contractors.......................	2383	111,822	116,349	752	792	35,302	38,583
Drywall and insulation contractors...............	23831	18,148	18,334	229	255	11,729	13,410
Painting and wall covering contractors...........	23832	33,824	35,535	193	187	8,374	8,430
Flooring contractors............................	23833	15,382	16,029	73	77	3,397	3,808
Tile and terrazzo contractors....................	23834	9,489	9,812	54	57	2,450	2,722
Finish carpentry contractors....................	23835	28,165	29,840	136	146	6,147	6,822
Other building finishing contractors..............	23839	6,814	6,799	67	70	3,205	3,390
Other specialty trade contractors..................	2389	67,376	69,661	575	625	32,315	36,957
Site preparation contractors....................	23891	34,498	35,718	330	380	19,095	23,315
All other specialty trade contractors..............	23899	32,878	33,943	244	245	13,220	13,642

[1] Data for 2016 based on North American Industry Classification System (NAICS) 2012; data for 2017 based on NAICS 2017. See text, Section 15. [2] Employees on the payroll for the pay period including March 12.

Source: U.S. Census Bureau, County Business Patterns, CB1600A11 and CB1700CBP, "County Business Patterns by Legal Form of Organization and Employment Size Class for U.S., States, and Selected Geographies," <http://data.census.gov>, accessed December 2019. See also <https://www.census.gov/programs-surveys/cbp.html>.

Table 993. Construction Industries—Establishments, Shipments, Payroll, and Employees: 2017

[1,999,110 represents $1,999,110,000,000. Includes only establishments with payroll]

Industry	2017 NAICS code [1]	Establish-ments (number)	Value of shipments (mil. dol.)	Annual payroll (mil. dol.)	Paid employees [2] Total	Paid employees [2] Construction workers
Construction............................	**23**	**714,939**	**1,999,110**	**398,536**	**6,658,490**	**4,962,903**
Construction of buildings....................	236	214,217	804,780	86,018	1,354,437	858,808
Residential buildings.......................	2361	171,901	342,109	37,329	690,798	448,304
New single-family housing (except for-sale builders)....	236115	48,695	67,247	8,428	172,426	115,386
New multifamily housing (except for-sale builders)......	236116	3,230	48,065	3,689	45,325	24,732
New housing for-sale builders................	236117	17,112	147,319	10,147	133,969	52,134
Residential remodelers.....................	236118	102,864	79,478	15,065	339,078	256,052
Nonresidential buildings....................	2362	42,316	462,672	48,689	663,639	410,504
Industrial buildings.......................	23621	3,203	30,268	5,009	77,248	54,003
Commercial and institutional buildings.........	23622	39,113	432,404	43,680	586,391	356,501
Heavy and civil engineering construction........	237	37,648	308,987	69,870	979,204	753,407
Utility system............................	2371	18,877	152,923	40,789	570,952	460,484
Water and sewer line and related structures.....	23711	10,698	42,167	9,264	146,957	113,903
Oil and gas pipeline and related structures......	23712	2,200	48,940	14,673	200,209	161,083
Power and communication line and related structures...	23713	5,979	61,815	16,852	223,786	185,498
Land subdivision.........................	2372	4,892	8,985	1,550	22,997	9,583
Highway, street, and bridge.................	2373	9,612	124,341	22,771	318,812	236,683
Other heavy and civil engineering............	2379	4,267	22,738	4,760	66,443	46,657
Specialty trade contractors..................	238	463,074	885,342	242,647	4,324,849	3,350,688
Foundation, structure, and building exterior........	2381	92,596	179,076	44,861	864,186	690,868
Poured concrete foundation and structure.......	23811	20,730	52,839	13,106	239,976	205,416
Structural steel and precast concrete..........	23812	3,585	15,267	4,602	78,123	64,235
Framing................................	23813	11,534	16,660	3,666	85,118	71,334
Masonry...............................	23814	18,284	23,488	6,812	141,020	120,549
Glass and glazing........................	23815	5,780	13,892	3,441	60,592	39,017
Roofing................................	23816	19,305	40,887	9,121	177,254	129,596
Siding.................................	23817	7,823	6,742	1,493	35,249	24,146
Other foundation, structure, and building exterior........	23819	5,555	9,302	2,620	46,854	36,575
Building equipment.......................	2382	184,477	414,446	121,854	2,018,230	1,535,639
Electrical and other wiring installation.............	23821	73,888	173,789	51,837	858,047	683,158
Plumbing, heating, and air-conditioning.........	23822	103,273	207,887	60,386	1,028,117	754,501
Other building equipment...................	23829	7,316	32,769	9,631	132,066	97,980
Building finishing.........................	2383	115,790	136,230	38,575	797,785	632,782
Drywall and insulation.....................	23831	18,286	44,122	12,934	244,498	208,827
Painting and wall covering..................	23832	35,426	26,324	8,962	203,938	175,444
Flooring...............................	23833	15,899	18,098	3,800	77,869	51,985
Tile and terrazzo.........................	23834	9,768	9,190	2,663	56,558	44,774
Finish carpentry.........................	23835	29,625	27,358	6,787	144,405	101,206
Other building finishing....................	23839	6,786	11,137	3,428	70,517	50,546
Other specialty trade......................	2389	70,211	155,591	37,357	644,648	491,399
Site preparation.........................	23891	35,386	101,023	23,575	395,285	313,249
All other specialty trade...................	23899	34,825	54,567	13,782	249,363	178,150

[1] North American Industry Classification System, 2017. [2] For pay period including March 12.

Source: U.S. Census Bureau, 2017 Economic Census, "EC1723BASIC: Construction: Summary Statistics for the U.S., States, and Selected Geographies: 2017," <data.census.gov>, accessed May 2020.

Table 994. Value of New Construction Put in Place: 1980 to 2019

[In millions of dollars (273,936 represents $273,936,000,000). Represents value of construction put in place during year; differs from building permit and construction contract data in timing and coverage. Includes installed cost of normal building service equipment and selected types of industrial production equipment (largely site fabricated). Excludes cost of shipbuilding, land, and most types of machinery and equipment. For methodology, see Appendix III]

Year	Total	Private Total	Private Residential buildings	Private Non-residential	Public Total	Public Federal	Public State and local
1980.................	273,936	210,290	100,381	109,909	63,646	9,642	54,004
1990.................	476,778	369,300	191,103	178,197	107,478	12,099	95,379
2000.................	802,756	621,431	346,138	275,293	181,325	14,168	167,157
2005.................	1,116,811	882,651	624,574	258,077	234,160	17,300	216,860
2010.................	812,964	508,998	245,743	263,255	303,966	31,133	272,833
2015.................	1,140,162	846,394	431,769	414,625	293,768	22,548	271,220
2016.................	1,223,671	926,698	479,415	447,283	296,972	22,242	274,731
2017.................	1,279,841	983,302	539,013	444,289	296,539	21,267	275,272
2018.................	1,333,183	1,023,016	557,558	465,457	310,167	21,979	288,188
2019.................	1,365,137	1,030,704	544,449	486,255	334,433	25,263	309,171

Source: U.S. Census Bureau, "Construction Spending," <census.gov/construction/c30/c30index.html>, accessed August 2020.

Table 995. New Privately Owned Housing Units Authorized by State: 2018 and 2019

[1,328.8 represents 1,328,800. Based on the 2014 Universe, which includes approximately 20,100 places in the United States that have building permit systems in 2014]

State	Housing units (1,000) 2018	2019 Total	2019 1-unit [1]	Valuation (mil. dol.) 2018	2019 Total	2019 1-unit [1]	State	Housing units (1,000) 2018	2019 Total	2019 1-unit [1]	Valuation (mil. dol.) 2018	2019 Total	2019 1-unit [1]
U.S.	1,328.8	1,386.0	862.1	271,120	280,534	213,271	MO	16.9	17.5	11.0	3,167	3,389	2,766
AL	14.8	17.7	14.7	3,047	3,545	3,103	MT	5.1	4.8	3.0	870	856	632
AK	1.7	1.7	1.1	429	413	337	NE	7.9	8.0	4.7	1,310	1,325	1,022
AZ	41.7	46.6	34.0	9,728	10,851	9,041	NV	17.6	20.1	13.1	3,401	3,682	2,861
AR	10.2	12.7	7.9	1,829	2,172	1,717	NH	4.4	4.7	2.7	875	1,059	761
CA	113.5	110.2	58.6	27,845	26,583	17,377	NJ	27.9	36.5	11.5	4,220	4,454	2,369
CO	42.6	38.6	24.8	10,231	9,638	7,652	NM	4.8	5.0	4.3	1,038	1,122	1,042
CT	4.8	5.9	2.4	1,112	1,354	765	NY	37.8	45.2	9.4	6,692	7,746	2,938
DE	6.0	6.5	5.6	789	849	752	NC	71.7	71.3	51.6	13,582	13,850	11,743
DC	4.6	5.9	0.2	518	681	40	ND	3.2	2.5	1.8	608	537	449
FL	144.4	154.3	99.8	31,544	33,210	25,774	OH	24.2	23.0	16.1	5,189	5,422	4,570
GA	59.3	53.8	42.9	11,146	10,682	9,343	OK	10.5	12.2	10.4	2,181	2,483	2,275
HI	4.7	4.1	2.5	1,360	1,284	964	OR	20.1	22.0	11.6	4,181	4,447	3,128
ID	15.8	17.7	13.0	3,099	3,401	2,893	PA	23.3	23.5	14.9	4,684	4,677	3,585
IL	21.5	20.5	8.7	4,036	3,726	2,350	RI	1.3	1.4	1.0	260	280	249
IN	21.5	22.3	16.3	4,880	4,988	4,298	SC	35.5	36.0	31.1	8,144	8,007	7,542
IA	11.5	11.9	7.9	2,249	2,500	1,981	SD	5.0	4.4	3.1	854	836	709
KS	9.5	8.0	5.1	1,889	1,683	1,319	TN	37.2	41.4	29.6	7,048	7,876	6,708
KY	13.8	11.8	7.5	2,268	2,136	1,713	TX	192.9	209.9	129.1	34,690	37,413	28,232
LA	15.8	15.8	14.0	3,108	3,136	2,904	UT	25.6	28.8	18.2	5,611	6,454	4,875
ME	4.7	4.8	3.5	959	1,005	833	VT	2.1	1.8	1.0	365	352	258
MD	18.6	18.5	12.1	3,702	3,754	2,734	VA	32.0	32.4	21.1	5,831	5,794	4,669
MA	17.0	17.4	6.3	4,158	3,679	2,095	WA	47.7	48.4	23.3	9,808	10,223	6,850
MI	19.6	20.6	14.6	4,569	4,580	3,823	WV	2.9	3.0	2.6	500	500	455
MN	25.7	28.6	13.7	5,721	6,148	3,882	WI	19.1	17.5	11.3	4,008	3,968	3,213
MS	6.9	7.0	6.2	1,194	1,241	1,162	WY	1.8	1.7	1.5	593	541	518

[1] The 1-unit structure category is a single-family home. It includes fully detached, semi-detached (semi-attached, side-by-side), row houses, and townhouses.

Source: U.S. Census Bureau, Construction Reports, "Building Permits Survey," <census.gov/construction/bps/>, accessed August 2020.

Table 996. Construction Contracts Started—Value of Construction and Floor Space of Buildings by Class of Construction: 2015 to 2019

[689.9 represents $689,900,000,000. Dollar value data includes new construction, additions, and alterations. Square footage data includes new construction and additions; alterations which create no net new square footage are not included]

Year	Total	Residential buildings	Nonresidential buildings Total	Commer-cial [1]	Manu-facturing	Educa-tion [2]	Health	Public	Reli-gious	Social and recrea-tional	Miscel-laneous	Non-building con-struction
VALUE (bil. dol.)												
2015	689.9	273.6	228.9	93.5	25.3	54.7	23.5	8.1	2.1	14.2	7.5	187.4
2016	739.5	297.6	258.4	115.4	20.3	57.0	26.8	9.0	1.8	18.6	9.5	183.5
2017	788.9	307.0	288.5	117.1	26.2	65.2	28.5	9.7	2.2	18.1	21.6	193.4
2018	817.6	330.3	298.1	124.1	32.2	68.9	27.7	9.8	1.8	20.5	13.1	189.2
2019	845.6	329.9	309.1	137.6	31.6	68.0	28.1	10.9	2.3	18.4	12.1	206.6
FLOOR SPACE (mil. sq. ft.)												
2015	3,287	2,240	1,047	664	72	150	73	15	11	41	21	(X)
2016	3,581	2,448	1,133	741	72	148	78	16	10	47	22	(X)
2017	3,832	2,644	1,188	769	71	155	85	20	11	48	30	(X)
2018	4,021	2,836	1,186	760	83	158	81	20	9	49	25	(X)
2019	4,123	2,885	1,237	837	67	156	73	21	8	45	31	(X)

X Not applicable. [1] Includes nonindustrial warehouses. [2] Includes science facilities.

Source: Dodge Data & Analytics (copyright) 1-800-591-4462, as of June 15, 2020 ©.

Table 997. Construction Contracts Started—Value by Region: 2015 to 2019

[In millions of dollars (689,888 represents $689,888,000,000). Includes new construction, additions and alterations]

Region	2015	2016	2017	2018	2019 Total [1]	2019 Residential	2019 Nonresidential
United States	**689,888**	**739,461**	**788,858**	**817,636**	**845,555**	**329,858**	**309,068**
New England	27,530	30,009	30,752	33,474	33,819	10,157	17,250
Middle Atlantic	84,822	85,503	107,893	87,790	86,282	31,100	38,054
East North Central	69,679	78,433	79,734	84,983	89,021	27,331	36,320
West North Central	48,395	54,513	51,445	56,408	65,049	17,625	22,838
South Atlantic	138,444	162,675	176,566	182,493	187,888	92,386	62,758
East South Central	29,717	35,763	34,061	45,570	40,335	17,992	15,653
West South Central	139,888	117,222	120,186	128,867	149,641	51,133	52,556
Mountain	57,946	64,621	61,909	78,672	73,183	37,012	19,535
Pacific	93,467	110,723	126,312	119,381	120,336	45,122	44,105

[1] Includes nonbuilding construction, not shown separately.

Source: Dodge Data & Analytics (copyright) 1-800-591-4462, as of June 15, 2020 ©.

Table 998. Value of Private Construction Put in Place: 2010 to 2019

[In millions of dollars (508,998 represents $508,998,000,000). Represents value of construction put in place during year; differs from building permit and construction contract data in timing and coverage. See Appendix III]

Type of construction	2010	2012	2013	2014	2015	2016	2017	2018	2019
Total private construction [1]	**508,998**	**575,091**	**643,900**	**739,164**	**846,394**	**926,698**	**983,302**	**1,023,016**	**1,030,704**
Residential	245,743	273,730	329,640	377,461	431,769	479,415	539,013	557,558	544,449
New single family	112,569	132,015	170,768	193,600	221,128	242,476	270,163	289,582	279,962
New multifamily	18,395	26,456	37,759	49,221	62,157	73,339	74,011	77,544	80,110
Improvements [2]	114,780	115,260	121,113	134,639	148,484	163,600	194,840	190,432	184,377
Nonresidential	263,255	301,360	314,260	361,704	414,625	447,283	444,289	465,457	486,255
Lodging	11,201	10,197	13,028	16,306	21,436	26,632	28,065	30,453	31,931
Office [1]	24,368	27,448	30,133	38,864	47,864	59,758	59,918	66,835	73,945
General	22,203	25,111	28,419	36,958	46,051	57,524	57,259	64,628	71,702
Financial	2,122	1,945	1,597	1,867	1,669	1,857	2,392	2,049	2,070
Commercial	37,154	44,312	50,947	60,890	64,493	75,514	84,479	82,808	76,432
Automotive [1]	3,546	4,834	4,639	4,830	5,830	7,472	8,127	7,638	6,320
Sales	1,355	2,079	1,956	2,117	2,164	3,113	3,128	3,202	2,022
Service/parts	1,679	2,221	2,313	2,047	2,885	3,367	3,928	3,289	2,599
Parking	511	534	370	666	780	992	1,071	1,148	1,698
Food/beverage	4,605	5,845	6,594	7,230	7,273	8,252	8,155	8,678	9,019
Food	2,027	2,430	2,937	3,447	3,109	3,554	3,231	2,748	3,553
Dining/drinking	1,911	2,436	2,141	2,170	2,589	2,913	3,416	4,027	4,117
Fast food	667	979	1,516	1,613	1,575	1,784	1,508	1,904	1,348
Multi-retail [1]	12,486	14,904	16,686	19,543	20,036	22,404	24,048	20,818	14,166
General merchandise	3,794	3,773	2,942	2,792	2,362	2,659	1,864	2,581	2,216
Shopping center	6,725	7,934	9,806	12,946	13,752	15,713	17,558	14,676	9,123
Shopping mall	1,332	2,288	2,938	2,868	3,035	3,292	3,921	2,861	2,029
Other commercial [1]	4,220	3,934	4,786	4,586	5,225	6,451	5,219	5,494	6,808
Drug store	1,077	765	893	943	535	505	358	255	327
Building supply store	772	493	506	495	586	529	650	593	693
Other stores	1,741	2,069	2,468	2,409	2,881	4,212	3,129	2,777	3,817
Warehouse [1]	5,661	7,047	8,766	13,698	16,850	22,634	29,053	33,056	32,978
General commercial	5,229	6,575	8,107	12,894	15,699	20,323	24,745	27,921	28,178
Ministorage	401	365	472	589	963	2,116	3,932	4,893	4,564
Farm	6,637	7,748	9,476	11,005	9,280	8,303	9,877	7,123	7,141
Health care	29,552	31,429	29,696	28,885	30,939	31,756	33,517	33,962	36,287
Hospital	21,528	21,223	19,199	17,680	19,665	19,773	20,210	20,747	20,738
Medical building	5,276	6,415	7,015	7,167	7,056	8,025	9,229	9,653	10,938
Special care	2,748	3,791	3,482	4,039	4,219	3,958	4,078	3,562	4,611
Educational [1]	13,418	16,625	16,919	16,583	17,688	20,036	21,232	22,346	21,087
Preschool	492	396	420	462	355	515	554	598	652
Primary/secondary	2,585	2,795	2,997	3,599	3,676	3,910	4,574	5,111	4,980
Higher education [1]	8,322	10,809	10,868	10,501	11,932	13,340	12,934	13,657	12,719
Instructional	4,993	5,786	4,928	4,944	5,472	6,101	5,775	5,759	5,537
Dormitory	1,654	2,902	3,924	3,559	3,931	4,604	4,528	4,532	4,480
Sports/recreation	790	709	981	974	1,055	1,146	1,300	1,487	1,254
Other educational [1]	1,687	2,206	2,226	1,656	1,471	1,840	2,393	2,116	1,867
Gallery/museum	1,522	1,407	1,486	1,224	1,038	1,414	1,628	1,573	1,406
Religious	5,237	3,819	3,565	3,380	3,589	3,752	3,586	3,499	3,544
House of worship	4,214	3,143	3,055	2,853	3,029	3,279	3,028	2,956	3,022
Other religious	1,023	675	510	527	561	473	558	543	522
Auxiliary building	795	521	419	391	491	384	508	434	417
Public safety	241	103	125	227	225	105	107	204	227
Amusement and recreation [1]	6,483	6,217	6,916	7,719	10,032	12,588	14,518	15,712	15,139
Theme/amusement park	353	512	670	943	1,213	2,072	2,125	2,054	1,843
Sports	1,596	1,043	1,336	1,889	3,452	4,495	6,071	5,652	4,290
Fitness	1,150	1,251	1,310	1,182	1,192	1,306	1,289	1,835	2,067
Performance/meeting center	565	517	673	657	724	928	1,204	1,950	2,291
Social center	914	614	789	757	869	969	899	1,249	1,514
Movie theater/studio	426	362	618	717	832	1,043	835	976	948
Transportation [1]	9,894	10,883	11,029	12,151	13,563	13,081	14,796	17,880	17,080
Air	259	1,044	921	729	886	2,058	3,458	4,144	4,410
Land	9,503	9,810	9,988	11,035	12,412	10,907	11,041	13,154	11,989
Railroad	8,973	9,279	9,272	10,225	11,653	9,900	10,089	11,204	10,560
Communication	17,689	15,952	17,619	17,105	21,505	22,014	23,571	24,320	22,112
Power	66,117	86,402	81,278	98,206	99,549	102,263	89,774	94,390	107,146
Electricity	48,972	68,967	54,411	69,970	75,169	81,883	65,136	70,422	76,905
Gas	8,297	10,317	10,897	11,033	12,546	14,474	15,745	18,787	17,497
Oil	8,848	7,118	15,970	17,203	11,834	5,906	8,893	5,181	12,744
Sewage and waste disposal	439	597	356	241	375	403	240	408	681
Water supply	717	373	591	573	542	221	277	287	352
Manufacturing	40,607	46,774	51,835	60,139	82,382	78,873	69,970	72,005	79,757
Food/beverage/tobacco	4,000	4,380	5,129	6,607	7,216	7,851	8,447	9,661	6,411
Textile/apparel/leather/furniture	591	171	391	826	639	992	865	528	140
Wood	438	335	761	640	347	469	1,320	1,759	2,115
Paper/printing/publishing	634	1,190	1,056	654	1,035	1,207	1,522	2,444	2,894
Petroleum/coal	11,612	4,777	4,195	5,222	4,428	4,103	3,938	3,557	3,231
Chemical	7,580	10,848	16,095	23,525	37,818	35,841	32,245	30,698	34,379
Plastic/rubber	728	1,686	1,598	2,248	3,317	3,600	3,157	4,257	2,953
Nonmetallic mineral	1,150	857	952	976	1,153	1,434	1,038	660	790
Primary metal	4,738	4,691	4,665	3,968	6,142	4,204	2,823	2,088	3,213
Fabricated metal	1,104	1,726	1,543	847	1,212	2,242	1,972	1,653	1,345
Machinery	1,030	1,631	1,499	1,203	1,938	1,503	903	1,252	1,893
Computer/electronic/electrical	4,614	9,592	7,600	5,133	3,510	1,998	2,141	5,487	8,623
Transportation equipment	1,962	3,869	5,335	7,227	12,639	12,500	8,818	6,765	9,510

[1] Includes other types of construction, not shown separately. [2] Private residential improvement does not include expenditures on rental, vacant, or seasonal properties.

Source: U.S. Census Bureau, "Construction Spending," <census.gov/construction/c30/c30index.html>, accessed August 2020.

Table 999. Value of State and Local Government Construction Put in Place: 2010 to 2019

[In millions of dollars (272,833 represents $272,833,000,000)]

Type of construction	2010	2012	2013	2014	2015	2016	2017	2018	2019
Total construction [1]	**272,833**	**252,378**	**246,955**	**253,712**	**271,220**	**274,731**	**275,272**	**288,188**	**309,171**
Residential	7,576	4,672	4,537	4,128	6,032	5,851	6,233	5,782	5,696
Multifamily	6,536	3,935	3,574	3,444	5,224	5,158	5,911	5,368	5,062
Nonresidential	265,256	247,705	242,418	249,585	265,188	268,879	269,039	282,406	303,474
Office	8,317	6,055	5,220	5,424	5,924	5,693	6,049	6,905	7,776
Commercial [1]	1,456	1,412	1,119	898	1,396	1,710	1,505	1,936	2,303
Automotive	769	942	696	499	852	699	618	982	1,454
Parking	675	799	621	443	807	568	602	899	1,055
Warehouse	286	171	133	184	245	423	403	324	295
Health care	6,193	7,040	6,928	6,174	5,537	5,731	6,372	6,508	6,261
Hospital	4,789	5,522	5,439	4,762	4,276	4,172	4,409	4,726	3,849
Medical building	747	982	970	990	816	919	1,167	1,095	1,648
Special care	657	536	520	422	446	639	795	687	763
Educational [1]	71,948	65,622	60,027	61,176	65,782	69,907	73,992	77,168	82,088
Primary/secondary [1]	44,559	39,389	36,050	35,936	38,221	42,343	46,488	50,226	54,793
Elementary	13,171	11,195	10,580	11,887	10,538	12,820	14,362	15,850	15,794
Middle/junior high	7,029	7,557	7,730	6,781	7,520	8,867	9,557	10,138	10,660
High	24,055	20,276	17,339	16,475	19,765	19,917	21,429	22,772	26,826
Higher education [1]	24,384	23,328	21,790	22,722	25,116	25,004	24,882	24,375	24,519
Instructional	14,138	11,931	11,755	11,948	13,390	13,847	13,815	14,499	14,014
Parking	593	532	398	391	552	534	414	406	729
Administration	357	430	409	528	590	669	540	436	390
Dormitory	3,371	4,435	3,845	3,468	4,130	4,221	3,219	2,779	3,327
Library	662	322	157	279	684	464	511	562	474
Student union/cafeteria	1147	1464	1,378	1,412	1,306	1,306	1,590	1,505	1,587
Sports/recreation	2398	2,356	2,594	2,901	2,885	2,658	3,325	2,750	2,563
Infrastructure	1381	1,735	1,065	1,683	1,570	1,268	1,296	1,407	1,377
Other educational [1]	2,223	2,054	1,500	2,062	1,902	1,887	1,643	1,616	1,999
Library/archive	1386	1,385	1,016	1,079	1,144	1,325	990	1,004	1,372
Public safety [1]	7,586	7,641	6,592	6,414	5,859	5,842	6,216	7,090	7,780
Correctional	4,624	5,126	4,395	4,249	3,619	3,480	3,698	4,222	4,885
Detention	2,789	3,306	2,554	2,171	1,981	1,985	2,071	2,493	2,828
Police/sheriff	1836	1,820	1,841	2,079	1,638	1,496	1,626	1,730	2,057
Other public safety	2,962	2,515	2,197	2,165	2,240	2,362	2,518	2,868	2,895
Fire/rescue	1747	1,627	1,403	1,496	1,561	1,733	2,092	2,358	2,359
Amusement and recreation [1]	9,668	8,876	8,081	8,713	10,048	10,686	11,570	11,909	13,239
Sports	1,819	1,127	1,289	1,856	1,759	1,686	1,614	2,242	3,072
Performance/meeting center	1,841	1,804	1,474	1,780	1,587	1,741	1,926	2,580	2,773
Convention center	1,119	1,316	917	1,154	850	862	1,032	1,562	1,656
Social center	1,561	1,008	1,127	887	1,120	1,223	1,568	1,509	1,872
Neighborhood center	1395	890	1,050	774	1,055	1,040	1,338	1,219	1,617
Park/camp	4,259	4,825	4,098	4,070	5,441	5,795	6,348	5,412	5,038
Transportation	26,493	24,797	25,871	27,757	29,365	27,858	29,286	32,811	37,366
Air [1]	11,897	9,799	9,768	10,821	10,762	10,494	12,297	16,094	17,567
Passenger terminal	6,503	4,992	5,310	4,922	4,969	5,901	7,751	11,172	11,934
Runway	4,710	4,313	3,780	4,980	5,213	3,881	3,819	4,336	4,611
Land [1]	12,954	13,047	13,984	15,106	16,940	15,767	15,444	14,920	17,163
Passenger terminal	3,380	2978	2,946	3,666	4,584	4,494	3,744	3,154	2,133
Mass transit	6,447	7,033	7,189	7,161	7,842	7,067	7,726	7,824	11,016
Railroad	751	850	1,459	1,695	1,666	1,175	1,169	1,486	1,846
Water	1,642	1,952	2,118	1,829	1,663	1,598	1,545	1,796	2,636
Dock/marina	1115	1502	1,583	1,360	1,233	1,261	1,215	1,405	2,362
Dry dock/marine terminal	527	450	536	469	430	337	331	392	275
Power [1]	10,770	9,794	10,951	10,732	10,307	8,511	5,401	4,612	6,312
Electrical	9,972	7,136	8,334	8,946	9,019	7,324	4,599	3,684	5,226
Distribution	3,253	2,046	2,151	3,120	2,623	2,912	2,586	2,253	3,716
Highway and street	81,309	79,722	80,610	84,014	90,810	92,158	88,290	90,405	95,642
Pavement	51,433	47,566	46,282	50,509	54,073	55,279	54,404	57,224	65,034
Lighting	1975	1,738	1,525	1,221	1,520	1,842	1,936	2,301	2,342
Retaining wall	1,250	845	895	878	1,071	873	819	1,451	1,278
Tunnel	810	1359	1,477	1,038	830	1,182	1,119	674	554
Bridge	24,222	27,050	28,811	29,234	31,765	31,031	28,935	27,412	25,354
Toll/weigh	214	338	129	137	210	310	292	312	274
Maintenance building	275	187	373	282	429	510	344	333	288
Rest facility/streetscape	1130	640	1,119	715	910	1,099	441	698	519
Sewage and waste disposal	24,555	20,946	21,037	21,870	23,403	23,169	22,415	23,219	25,013
Sewage/dry waste [1]	13,234	12,077	11,591	12,517	14,009	13,936	13,277	12,994	13,274
Plant	3,755	3,022	2,376	2,565	2,839	2,524	2,660	2,612	2,602
Line/pump station	9,375	8,956	9,072	9,815	10,986	11,174	10,427	10,220	10,512
Waste water	11,321	8,869	9,446	9,353	9,394	9,234	9,138	10,226	11,739
Plant	9,428	7,414	7,861	7,354	7,001	6,935	6,984	7,027	8,425
Line/drain	1,893	1,455	1,585	1,999	2,393	2,298	2,154	3,199	3,315
Water supply	14,420	12,746	12,919	12,731	12,760	13,623	13,701	14,855	15,183
Plant	5,683	4,833	4,358	4,221	4,432	4,373	5,077	5,105	4,863
Well	383	336	480	513	295	355	415	501	689
Line	6,246	5,631	5,777	5,816	6,098	6,264	5,865	6,654	7,227
Pump station	970	633	734	817	642	972	1,015	1,150	1,080
Reservoir	393	639	804	618	401	738	883	857	720
Tank/tower	744	674	765	747	892	922	446	587	605
Conservation and development [1]	2035	2,225	2,500	3,071	3,133	3,270	3,393	3,719	3,120
Dam/levee	783	727	822	1,096	958	976	1,105	1,250	1,114
Breakwater/jetty	675	853	1,022	1,098	1,405	1,479	1,171	1,255	1,113
Dredging	173	184	214	259	301	330	300	272	219

[1] Includes other types of construction, not shown separately.

Source: U.S. Census Bureau, "Construction Spending," <census.gov/construction/c30/c30index.html>, accessed August 2020.

Table 1000. Construction of New Privately Owned Housing Units Started: 1960 to 2019

[In thousands of units (1,252 represents 1,252,000). For composition of regions, see map inside front cover]

Year	Total	1 unit structures	Northeast	Midwest	South	West
1960	1,252	995	221	292	429	309
1970	1,434	813	218	294	612	311
1980	1,292	852	125	218	643	306
1990	1,193	895	131	253	479	329
1995	1,354	1,076	118	290	615	331
1996	1,477	1,161	132	322	662	361
1997	1,474	1,134	137	304	670	363
1998	1,617	1,271	149	331	743	395
1999	1,641	1,302	156	347	746	392
2000	1,569	1,231	155	318	714	383
2001	1,603	1,273	149	330	732	391
2002	1,705	1,359	158	350	782	416
2003	1,848	1,499	163	374	839	472
2004	1,956	1,611	175	356	909	516
2005	2,068	1,716	190	357	996	525
2006	1,801	1,465	167	280	910	444
2007	1,355	1,046	143	210	681	321
2008	906	622	121	135	453	196
2009	554	445	62	97	278	117
2010	587	471	72	98	298	120
2011	609	431	68	101	308	133
2012	781	535	80	128	398	175
2013	925	618	97	150	464	215
2014	1,003	648	110	163	496	235
2015	1,112	715	138	153	556	266
2016	1,174	782	116	182	585	291
2017	1,203	849	111	180	599	313
2018	1,250	876	111	173	630	336
2019	1,290	888	115	169	685	321

Source: U.S. Census Bureau, "New Residential Construction," <census.gov/construction/nrc/historical_data/>, accessed June 2020.

Table 1001. Characteristics of New Privately Owned Single-Family Houses Completed: 2000 to 2019

[Percent distribution, except as noted (1,242 represents 1,242,000). Data are percent distribution of characteristics for all houses completed (includes new houses completed, houses built for sale completed, contractor-built and owner-built houses completed, and houses completed for rent). Percents exclude houses for which characteristics specified were not reported, and are computed using unrounded data]

Characteristic	2000	2010	2018	2019	Characteristic	2000	2010	2018	2019
Total houses (1,000)	**1,242**	**496**	**840**	**903**	Bedrooms	100	100	100	100
Construction type	100	100	100	100	2 or less	11	13	10	11
Site built	94	95	97	97	3	54	52	45	46
Modular	3	2	1	1	4 or more	35	35	45	43
Other	3	2	2	1	Bathrooms	100	100	100	100
Exterior wall material	100	100	100	100	1-1/2 or less	7	8	4	3
Brick	20	23	21	20	2	39	36	31	34
Wood	14	8	5	5	2-1/2 or more	34	32	29	29
Stucco	17	17	25	27	3 baths or more	20	25	36	33
Vinyl siding	39	36	26	25	Heating fuel	100	100	100	100
Fiber cement	(NA)	13	20	21	Gas	70	54	60	56
Other	8	2	2	2	Electricity	27	43	39	43
Floor area	100	100	100	100	Oil [3]	3	1	(NA)	(NA)
Under 1,400 sq. ft.	14	13	7	7	Other [3]	1	2	1	1
1,400 to 1,799 sq. ft.	22	19	16	17	Heating system	100	100	100	100
1,800 to 2,399 sq. ft.	29	27	28	31	Forced air furnace	71	56	58	57
2,400 to 2,999 sq. ft.	17	18	22	21	Electric heat pump	23	38	40	41
3,000 to 3,999 sq. ft.	13	15	19	17	Other	6	5	3	2
4,000 or more	5	7	9	8	Central air-conditioning	100	100	100	100
Average (sq. ft.)	2,266	2,392	2,588	2,509	With	85	88	93	94
Median (sq. ft.)	2,057	2,169	2,386	2,301	Without	15	12	7	6
Number of stories	100	100	100	100	Fireplaces	100	100	100	100
1	47	47	46	48	No fireplace	40	51	56	61
2 or more [1]	52	53	54	52	1 or more	59	49	44	39
Foundation	100	100	100	100	Parking facilities	100	100	100	100
Full or partial basement	37	30	25	23	Garage	89	85	92	91
Slab and other [2]	46	52	60	64	Carport	1	1	1	1
Crawl space	17	18	14	14	No garage or carport	11	13	7	7

NA Not available. [1] Includes houses with 1-1/2 and 2-1/2 stories and split-level houses. [2] Includes raised supports such as pilings and piers, and other types. [3] Beginning in 2014, heating oil and kerosene are included in Other heating fuel.

Source: U.S. Census Bureau and U.S. Department of Housing and Urban Development, "Characteristics of New Housing," <http://www.census.gov/construction/chars/>, accessed June 2020.

Table 1002. Construction Materials—Producer Price Indexes: 2005 to 2019

[1982=100, except as noted. This index, more formally known as the special commodity grouping index for construction materials, covers materials incorporated as integral parts of a building or normally installed during construction and not readily removable. Excludes consumer durables such as kitchen ranges, refrigerators, etc. For discussion of producer price indexes, see text, Section 14]

Commodity	2005	2010	2014	2015	2016	2017	2018	2019
Construction materials	**169.6**	**194.5**	**214.4**	**213.6**	**213.9**	**221.6**	**235.7**	**235.7**
Architectural coatings	203.3	264.1	309.4	302.3	303.0	306.1	320.7	343.5
Plastic construction products	158.8	190.9	211.1	213.1	211.9	217.3	226.1	229.4
Softwood cut stock and dimension	205.1	206.0	207.4	199.7	200.0	214.2	228.1	204.1
Softwood lumber, not edge worked [1]	115.0	85.8	113.4	104.9	108.6	121.9	131.0	114.4
Softwood lumber, made from purchased lumber [1]	111.2	111.5	126.4	128.3	130.5	152.3	171.4	169.2
Hardwood cut stock and dimension	198.4	186.2	275.8	246.6	239.8	250.9	262.9	256.0
Hardwood flooring [2]	168.0	161.2	199.6	195.8	188.5	179.1	184.7	193.8
Millwork	197.2	207.0	232.3	237.2	240.6	247.6	259.5	263.5
Softwood veneer and plywood	223.5	197.1	245.3	234.5	214.5	234.8	274.5	222.8
Hardwood veneer and plywood [3]	(NA)	103.6	108.4	108.6	112.9	115.3	123.5	123.9
Prefabricated wood buildings and components [4]	206.1	215.6	236.4	240.4	243.3	251.6	263.7	270.2
Building paper and building board mill products	184.9	168.4	188.9	186.3	201.0	221.3	222.9	200.1
Pressure and soil pipe and fittings, cast iron	240.8	348.4	390.6	392.9	396.4	384.4	398.5	403.5
Hot rolled steel sheet and strip, incl. tin mill products [5]	125.4	150.7	140.3	115.9	107.2	126.9	149.6	136.0
Hot rolled steel bars, plates, and structural shapes [5]	159.8	192.9	206.8	185.2	164.5	178.7	205.9	205.2
Aluminum extruded and drawn pipe and tube [6]	102.2	98.1	101.1	95.6	90.2	102.2	111.2	107.3
Builders' hardware [7]	179.2	219.4	242.2	244.5	246.8	251.0	256.7	264.0
Plumbing fixtures and fittings	197.6	231.4	252.6	257.1	257.8	262.4	270.2	281.6
Heating equipment	179.9	221.5	243.6	248.2	253.1	255.9	266.5	279.2
Metal doors, sash, and trim	184.9	208.1	228.1	233.6	235.5	243.1	260.1	269.8
Sheet metal products	169.4	191.0	198.6	199.3	197.6	202.3	212.7	218.2
Fabricated structural metal bar joists and concrete reinforcing bars	163.0	176.1	187.9	190.5	194.0	199.5	216.4	214.9
Fabricated metal pipe, tube, and fittings [8]	(NA)	(NA)	101.9	101.5	100.3	100.9	104.9	106.0
Residential electric lighting fixtures, except portable [9]	106.9	121.1	128.1	130.4	131.5	130.2	133.9	145.2
Elevators, escalators, and other lifts	123.5	133.8	143.1	145.4	147.1	151.2	155.0	161.7
Air purification equipment/industrial and commercial fans and blowers	170.9	192.2	211.7	217.3	218.4	220.9	228.6	238.4
Plumbing and heating valves (low pressure) [10]	182.2	249.5	285.8	292.6	296.9	310.8	(NA)	(NA)
Electric switches [11]	101.9	124.4	152.4	153.4	151.0	150.8	149.9	150.4
Wire connectors for electrical circuitry [11]	106.9	132.1	141.8	138.8	132.8	134.6	137.7	139.4
Current-carrying wiring devices not elsewhere classified [12]	(NA)	105.2	112.1	111.3	108.8	109.3	111.3	112.7
Noncurrent-carrying electrical conduit and fittings [6, 13]	106.6	119.2	135.4	134.1	134.1	136.1	141.8	141.5
Other noncurrent-carrying wiring devices [6, 14]	102.3	126.4	135.1	135.6	136.1	138.1	141.7	147.9
Carpets and rugs	145.3	167.5	182.8	184.1	183.9	184.5	193.1	196.0
Resilient (hard surface) floor coverings	169.0	203.2	(NA)	(NA)	(NA)	232.8	236.8	242.5
Flat glass (float, sheet, and plate process)	96.0	88.2	88.8	91.0	97.3	98.5	105.3	107.1
Construction sand, gravel, and crushed stone	195.8	262.2	289.3	299.9	312.6	323.2	334.7	348.7
Cement, hydraulic	176.4	193.5	208.1	223.4	235.2	246.0	252.1	258.1
Concrete products	177.2	210.6	230.3	239.4	247.0	254.1	263.7	271.7
Clay construction products excluding refractories	165.4	179.4	178.1	182.4	184.7	184.5	187.7	189.6
Prepared asphalt and tar roofing and siding products	125.0	218.9	224.5	223.2	221.6	220.5	233.8	243.9
Roofing asphalts, pitches, coatings, and cement	155.0	227.5	265.8	234.3	201.3	210.5	221.4	224.7
Gypsum products	229.6	206.6	290.6	293.1	297.1	322.9	342.6	320.9
Insulation materials	142.2	146.6	182.9	182.6	187.8	189.1	194.7	193.3
Paving mixtures and blocks	156.9	279.4	323.6	313.0	294.6	293.4	313.4	322.6
Cut stone and stone products [4]	145.1	147.8	152.3	156.8	161.6	163.3	168.1	174.9

NA Not available. [1] December 2003=100. [2] June 1984=100. [3] December 2005=100. [4] June 1984=100. [5] June 1982=100. [6] December 2004=100. [7] Includes lock units, key blanks, door and window hardware, cabinet hardware, etc. [8] December 2011=100. [9] June 1998=100. [10] December 1982=100. [11] December 1999=100. [12] June 2006=100. [13] Includes plastic conduit and fittings. [14] Includes boxes, covers, bar hangers, etc.

Source: U.S. Bureau of Labor Statistics, "Producer Price Indexes," <http://www.bls.gov/ppi/data.htm>, accessed May 2020.

Table 1003. Subsidized Apartments Completed by Type of Subsidy: 2015 to 2018

[Data shown for rental apartments in buildings with five units or more. Detail may not sum to totals because of rounding and because more than one subsidy could be selected per unit. Based on sample and subject to sampling variability; see source for details]

Completions and type of subsidy	2015	2016	2017	2018
Total apartments completed	310,000	310,100	346,800	335,600
Subsidized apartments completed	**29,160**	**20,160**	**35,200**	**31,910**
Percent subsidized	9.4	6.5	10.1	9.5
Subsidized by type: [1]				
Section 8	10,680	6,010	12,080	16,570
Housing for Elderly Direct Loan Program	1,163	1,298	(S)	1,790
Low Income Housing Tax Credit (LHITC)	19,190	13,310	21,630	15,020
Federal tax exempt multifamily bond financing	(S)	1,003	2,223	(S)
Other subsidized programs	6,881	6,442	10,080	9,871

S Data estimates do not meet publication standards. [1] Respondents were instructed to select all subsidies that applied to the building.

Source: U.S. Census Bureau, "Survey of Market Absorption of New Multifamily Units, Table Creator," <census.gov/data-tools/demo/soma/soma.html>, accessed July 2020.

Table 1004. Housing Starts and Average Length of Time to Completion of New Privately Owned Single-Family Homes: 1990 to 2019

[895 represents 895,000. For buildings started in permit-issuing places]

Year	Total [1]	Purpose of construction			Region [2]			
		Built for sale	Contractor built	Owner built	North-east	Mid-west	South	West
STARTS (1,000)								
1990	895	529	196	147	104	193	371	226
1995	1,076	712	199	133	102	234	485	256
1997	1,134	784	189	131	111	238	507	278
1998	1,271	882	209	144	122	273	574	303
1999	1,302	912	208	142	126	289	580	308
2000	1,231	871	195	128	118	260	556	297
2001	1,273	919	186	129	111	269	590	303
2002	1,359	999	198	125	118	277	628	336
2003	1,499	1,120	205	127	116	309	686	388
2004	1,611	1,240	198	130	128	306	743	433
2005	1,716	1,358	197	129	138	306	831	441
2006	1,465	1,121	189	119	118	235	757	356
2007	1,046	760	151	104	93	171	540	242
2008	622	408	107	74	63	102	324	133
2009	445	297	83	51	44	76	232	93
2010	471	306	83	55	52	79	247	93
2011	431	287	74	47	41	74	229	86
2012	535	373	82	47	46	92	283	114
2013	618	457	91	45	55	102	326	134
2014	648	460	110	50	51	106	346	145
2015	715	526	109	50	55	107	387	165
2016	782	579	116	49	60	121	421	179
2017	849	635	116	55	62	130	453	204
2018	876	660	119	51	64	123	466	222
2019	888	669	124	55	57	120	497	214
COMPLETION (months)								
1990	6.4	5.9	5.3	10.3	9.3	5.6	5.7	6.9
1995	5.9	5.2	5.8	9.5	7.4	6.0	5.4	6.0
1997	6.0	5.2	5.9	9.8	7.3	6.2	5.6	5.8
1998	6.0	5.4	6.0	9.5	7.1	6.2	5.5	6.1
1999	6.1	5.5	6.4	9.2	7.0	6.4	5.7	6.3
2000	6.2	5.6	6.5	9.2	7.5	6.4	5.9	6.0
2001	6.2	5.6	7.0	9.2	7.6	6.5	5.8	6.3
2002	6.1	5.5	6.6	9.6	7.3	6.4	5.6	6.2
2003	6.2	5.5	6.8	9.9	7.5	6.7	5.7	6.2
2004	6.2	5.7	7.0	9.1	7.3	6.7	5.8	6.3
2005	6.4	5.9	7.6	9.8	7.7	6.6	6.0	6.8
2006	6.9	6.3	7.8	10.7	8.3	7.1	6.3	7.4
2007	7.1	6.5	7.9	10.2	8.5	7.4	6.5	8.0
2008	7.7	6.8	8.5	11.1	8.9	8.2	6.7	9.0
2009	7.9	6.6	8.7	11.9	10.7	8.2	6.7	9.0
2010	6.9	5.8	7.6	11.0	10.1	7.3	5.9	7.3
2011	6.6	5.4	7.7	10.8	8.9	6.9	5.9	6.8
2012	6.0	4.9	7.3	10.5	8.5	6.5	5.2	6.1
2013	6.0	5.0	7.5	11.0	8.4	6.7	5.5	5.6
2014	6.2	5.4	7.5	10.8	8.6	6.9	5.7	6.2
2015	6.3	5.5	7.6	11.1	8.9	7.0	5.8	6.1
2016	6.6	5.8	7.8	11.5	9.6	6.9	6.0	6.7
2017	6.5	5.7	8.1	11.2	9.5	7.2	5.9	6.7
2018	6.7	5.9	8.4	11.4	9.3	7.5	6.0	7.1
2019	7.0	6.1	8.9	12.3	11.1	7.7	6.1	7.7

[1] Includes units built for rent not shown separately. [2] For composition of regions, see map, inside front cover.

Source: U.S. Census Bureau, "New Residential Construction," <http://www.census.gov/construction/nrc/>, accessed June 2020.

Table 1005. Price Indexes of New Single-Family Houses Sold by Region: 1970 to 2019

[2005=100. Based on kinds of homes sold in 2005. Includes value of the lot. For composition of regions, see map, inside front cover]

Year	Total	North-east	Midwest	South	West	Year	Total	North-east	Midwest	South	West
1970	14.9	13.4	17.9	18.2	10.2	2005	100.0	100.0	100.0	100.0	100.0
1975	22.1	19.6	25.4	26.4	15.9	2006	104.7	102.6	102.9	105.4	105.2
1980	38.9	30.2	41.2	44.4	31.9	2007	104.9	101.5	102.8	107.4	102.6
1985	46.2	43.1	48.2	53.9	36.4	2008	99.5	100.8	98.9	103.7	92.7
1990	55.7	58.0	58.6	60.6	46.2	2009	95.1	97.1	96.0	101.1	84.8
1995	64.3	62.3	70.9	70.1	52.7	2010	95.0	101.1	96.9	99.5	85.4
1996	66.0	63.2	72.5	71.2	55.3	2011	94.3	100.0	97.8	99.6	83.1
1997	67.5	65.9	74.3	72.7	56.5	2012	97.6	102.1	101.5	102.7	86.3
1998	69.2	66.1	76.0	74.4	58.4	2013	104.7	108.2	105.3	110.1	94.7
1999	72.8	69.1	79.5	78.1	62.0	2014	110.2	115.2	112.6	115.4	99.5
2000	75.6	73.0	83.5	80.6	64.4	2015	112.9	115.7	116.4	118.3	101.9
2001	77.9	76.7	84.4	82.8	67.1	2016	120.4	121.0	118.7	125.1	113.3
2002	81.4	80.2	86.1	86.3	71.5	2017	126.8	130.5	126.5	131.9	117.9
2003	86.0	84.3	90.6	89.4	78.2	2018	132.4	127.6	128.9	136.2	128.9
2004	92.8	91.6	96.7	94.4	88.2	2019	135.5	127.7	134.1	141.9	127.5

Source: U.S. Census Bureau, "Construction Price Indexes," <http://www.census.gov/construction/cpi/>, accessed June 2020.

Table 1006. New Privately Owned Single-Family Houses Sold by Region and Type of Financing, 2005 to 2019, and by Sales-Price Group, 2019

[In thousands (1,283 represents 1,283,000). Based on a national probability sample of monthly interviews with builders or owners of single-family houses for which building permits have been issued or, for nonpermit areas, on which construction has started. For details, see source and Appendix III. For composition of regions, see map inside front cover]

Year and sales-price group	Total sold	Region				Financing type			
		Northeast	Midwest	South	West	Conventional [1]	FHA insured [2]	VA guaranteed [3]	Cash
2005..........................	1,283	81	205	638	358	1,150	51	28	52
2010..........................	323	31	45	173	74	189	81	35	19
2013..........................	429	31	61	233	105	296	67	36	31
2014..........................	437	28	59	243	108	311	51	38	37
2015..........................	501	24	61	286	130	348	81	42	30
2016..........................	561	32	69	318	142	396	88	48	29
2017..........................	613	40	72	339	163	442	86	49	36
2018..........................	617	32	76	348	160	461	74	43	39
2019..........................	**683**	**30**	**72**	**399**	**182**	**469**	**119**	**52**	**42**
Under $125,000..........	3	(Z)	(Z)	3	(Z)	2	(Z)	(Z)	1
$125,000 to $149,999...	10	(Z)	2	8	(Z)	6	2	1	1
$150,000 to $199,999...	52	1	9	39	3	29	16	3	4
$200,000 to $249,999...	115	1	15	89	10	53	49	8	5
$250,000 to $299,999...	112	2	13	77	19	67	26	10	8
$300,000 to $399,999...	171	6	18	92	55	130	19	14	8
$400,000 to $499,999...	95	6	7	45	38	76	5	10	5
$500,000 to $749,999...	90	8	5	34	43	75	1	7	6
$750,000 and over.......	34	6	2	11	14	30	–	(Z)	3

– Represents zero. Z Less than 500 units. [1] Includes houses reporting other types of financing, not shown separately. [2] Federal Housing Administration. [3] U.S. Department of Veterans Affairs.

Source: U.S. Census Bureau, "Annual Characteristics of New Housing," <https://www.census.gov/construction/chars/>, accessed June 2020.

Table 1007. Median Sales Price of New Privately Owned Single-Family Houses Sold by Region: 1980 to 2019

[In dollars. For definition of median, see Guide to Tabular Presentation. For composition of regions, see map inside front cover. Based on a national probability sample of monthly interviews with builders or owners of single-family houses selected from building permits and a canvassing of areas not requiring permits. For more details, see source]

Year	U.S.	Northeast	Midwest	South	West	Year	U.S.	Northeast	Midwest	South	West
1980.........	64,600	69,500	63,400	59,600	72,300	2013.........	268,900	371,200	255,300	246,600	310,500
1985.........	84,300	103,300	80,300	75,000	92,600	2014.........	288,500	398,000	273,800	264,000	339,000
1990.........	122,900	159,000	107,900	99,000	147,500	2015.........	294,200	442,800	276,700	271,500	348,500
1995.........	133,900	180,000	134,000	124,500	141,000	2016.........	307,800	428,300	277,100	281,400	367,700
2000.........	169,000	227,400	169,700	148,000	196,400	2017.........	323,100	490,400	284,400	291,200	390,000
2005.........	240,900	343,800	216,900	197,300	332,600	2018.........	326,400	484,600	290,900	294,600	410,600
2010.........	221,800	329,900	197,700	196,800	259,300	2019.........	321,500	482,500	289,200	289,000	408,000

Source: U.S. Census Bureau, "Annual Characteristics of New Housing," <https://www.census.gov/construction/chars/>, accessed June 2020.

Table 1008. New Manufactured (Mobile) Homes Placed for Residential Use and Average Sales Price by Region: 1990 to 2019

[195.4 represents 195,400. A mobile home is a moveable dwelling, 8 feet or more wide and 40 feet or more long, designed to be towed on its own chassis, with transportation gear integral to the unit when it leaves the factory, and without need of permanent foundation. Excluded are travel trailers, motor homes, and modular housing. Data are based on a probability sample and subject to sampling variability; see source. For composition of regions, see map inside front cover]

Year	Units placed (1,000)					Average sales price (dollars)				
	Total	Northeast	Midwest	South	West	U.S.	Northeast	Midwest	South	West
1990.............	195.4	18.8	37.7	108.4	30.6	27,800	30,000	27,000	24,500	39,300
1995.............	319.4	15.0	57.5	203.2	43.7	35,300	35,800	35,700	33,300	44,100
2000.............	280.9	14.9	48.7	178.7	38.6	46,400	47,000	47,900	44,300	54,100
2005.............	122.9	9.2	17.1	68.1	28.5	62,600	67,000	60,600	55,700	79,900
2006.............	112.4	7.9	14.5	66.1	23.9	64,300	65,300	59,100	58,900	83,400
2007.............	94.8	7.0	10.8	59.4	17.7	65,400	66,100	64,900	59,900	85,500
2008.............	80.5	5.0	8.2	54.0	13.3	64,700	68,400	65,700	59,600	84,900
2009.............	54.5	3.5	5.3	37.8	7.9	63,100	61,600	65,400	59,300	81,500
2010.............	50.7	3.8	5.8	34.6	6.6	62,800	65,200	60,700	60,000	79,000
2011.............	47.6	3.3	6.3	31.5	6.5	60,500	62,700	60,800	58,400	70,600
2012.............	52.8	3.9	7.9	34.4	6.6	62,200	63,400	60,900	60,100	75,300
2013.............	56.3	4.0	7.5	37.4	7.5	64,000	66,500	62,900	61,200	79,100
2014 [1].............	44.1	3.0	6.8	27.5	6.8	65,300	67,900	60,600	63,000	80,700
2015 [1].............	45.6	3.1	6.6	28.5	7.5	68,000	72,100	60,800	65,100	88,200
2016 [1].............	51.5	3.1	8.2	32.3	7.8	70,600	77,600	61,500	68,500	88,500
2017 [1].............	53.9	3.6	7.7	34.9	7.8	71,900	78,400	65,400	68,200	97,600
2018 [1].............	55.1	4.0	8.6	33.8	8.7	78,500	80,100	72,100	75,700	99,000
2019 [1].............	62.2	4.0	9.0	40.1	9.0	81,900	81,300	72,100	80,600	99,400

[1] Beginning 2014, data not comparable to prior years due to a change in methodology. See source for details.

Source: U.S. Census Bureau, "Manufactured Housing Survey (MHS) Tables," <census.gov/programs-surveys/mhs/data/tables.All.html>, accessed July 2020.

Table 1009. Existing Single-Family Homes Sold and Price by Region: 1990 to 2019

[2,914 represents 2,914,000. Includes existing detached single-family homes and townhomes. Based on data (adjusted and aggregated to regional and national totals) reported by participating real estate multiple listing services. For definition of median, see Guide to Tabular Presentation. See Table 1011 for data on condominiums and cooperatives. For composition of regions, see map inside front cover]

Year	Homes sold (1,000)					Median sales price (dollars)				
	U.S.	Northeast	Midwest	South	West	U.S.	Northeast	Midwest	South	West
1990............	2,914	513	804	1,008	589	97,300	146,200	76,700	86,300	141,200
1995............	3,519	615	940	1,212	752	117,000	146,500	96,500	99,200	153,600
1996............	3,797	656	986	1,283	872	122,600	147,800	102,800	105,000	160,200
1997............	3,964	683	1,004	1,356	921	129,000	152,400	108,900	111,300	169,000
1998............	4,495	745	1,129	1,592	1,029	136,000	157,100	116,300	118,000	179,500
1999............	4,649	728	1,145	1,704	1,072	141,200	160,700	121,600	122,100	189,400
2000............	4,603	715	1,116	1,707	1,065	147,300	161,200	125,600	130,300	199,200
2001............	4,735	710	1,154	1,795	1,076	156,600	169,400	132,300	139,600	211,700
2002............	4,974	730	1,217	1,872	1,155	167,600	190,100	138,300	149,700	234,300
2003............	5,446	770	1,323	2,073	1,280	180,200	220,300	143,700	159,700	254,700
2004............	5,958	821	1,389	2,310	1,438	195,200	254,400	151,500	171,800	289,100
2005............	6,180	838	1,411	2,457	1,474	219,000	281,600	168,300	181,100	340,300
2006............	5,677	787	1,314	2,352	1,224	221,900	280,300	164,800	183,700	350,500
2007............	4,398	587	1,091	1,819	901	217,900	288,100	161,400	178,800	342,500
2008............	3,665	471	882	1,439	873	196,600	271,500	150,500	169,400	276,100
2009............	3,870	480	918	1,460	1,012	172,100	243,200	142,900	155,000	215,400
2010............	3,708	465	859	1,426	958	173,100	243,900	140,800	153,700	220,700
2011............	3,787	449	863	1,471	1,004	166,200	237,500	135,800	149,300	204,500
2012............	4,128	492	1,002	1,605	1,029	177,200	237,200	143,700	158,400	234,300
2013............	4,484	540	1,122	1,775	1,047	197,400	248,900	155,700	174,200	276,400
2014............	4,344	533	1,060	1,789	962	208,900	252,200	164,200	182,900	294,400
2015............	4,646	576	1,162	1,885	1,023	223,900	262,500	175,500	196,400	319,100
2016............	4,838	617	1,222	1,955	1,044	235,500	265,400	184,400	209,200	342,900
2017............	4,892	615	1,222	1,989	1,066	248,800	275,700	196,200	222,700	369,400
2018............	4,742	581	1,192	1,972	997	261,600	289,200	201,700	231,600	388,600
2019............	4,765	581	1,183	2,016	985	274,600	301,900	214,500	241,900	405,200

Source: NATIONAL ASSOCIATION OF REALTORS ®. See also <nar.realtor/research-and-statistics>.

Table 1010. Median Sales Price of Existing Single-Family Homes by Selected Metropolitan Area: 2010 and 2019

[In thousands of dollars (173.1 represents $173,100). Covers existing detached single-family homes and townhouses. Areas are metropolitan statistical areas defined by Office of Management and Budget, though in some areas an exact match is not possible from available data]

Metropolitan area	2010	2019	Metropolitan area	2010	2019
United States, total...............	**173.1**	**274.6**	New Orleans-Metairie, LA........................	159.7	222.0
Allentown-Bethlehem-Easton, PA-NJ............	224.0	207.2	New York-Jersey City-White Plains, NY-NJ....	450.0	386.5
Anaheim-Santa Ana-Irvine, CA...................	546.4	825.0	New York-Newark-Jersey City, NY-NJ-PA.....	393.7	423.9
Atlanta-Sandy Springs-Marietta, GA............	114.8	233.2	Oklahoma City, OK.................................	145.7	158.9
Atlantic City-Hammonton, NJ...................	226.4	210.2	Omaha-Council Bluffs, NE-IA....................	137.3	200.7
Baltimore-Columbia-Towson, MD...............	246.1	299.4	Orlando-Kissimmee-Sanford, FL.................	137.0	276.0
Boston-Cambridge-Newton, MA-NH	357.3	491.9	Philadelphia-Camden-		
Boulder, CO...................................	358.1	618.6	Wilmington, PA-NJ-DE-MD...................	214.9	246.2
Bridgeport-Stamford-Norwalk, CT...............	408.6	445.6	Phoenix-Mesa-Scottsdale, AZ....................	139.2	287.1
Charleston-North Charleston, SC...............	200.5	293.5	Portland-South Portland, ME.....................	218.0	308.5
Chicago-Naperville-Elgin, IL-IN-WI.............	191.4	265.1	Portland-Vancouver-Hillsboro, OR-WA........	237.3	409.3
Cincinnati, OH-KY-IN..........................	128.0	185.6	Providence-Warwick, RI-MA.....................	228.5	311.1
Cleveland-Elyria, OH..........................	114.5	164.1	Raleigh, NC......................................	190.4	291.5
Colorado Springs, CO..........................	195.5	320.5	Reno, NV...	179.5	393.9
Dallas-Fort Worth-Arlington, TX.................	143.8	268.6	Richmond, VA....................................	(NA)	264.0
Deltona-Daytona Beach-Ormond Beach, FL....	115.0	225.0	Riverside-San Bernardino-Ontario, CA........	179.3	378.5
Denver-Aurora-Lakewood, CO...................	232.4	462.1	Sacramento-Roseville-Arden-Arcade, CA.....	184.2	380.0
Des Moines-West Des Moines, IA...............	150.9	214.5	Saint Louis, MO-IL...............................	131.1	187.5
Eugene-Springfield, OR........................	196.3	308.6	Salem, OR..	173.5	310.7
Hartford-West Hartford-East Hartford, CT......	235.8	237.3	Salt Lake City, UT.................................	206.5	355.2
Houston-The Woodlands-Sugar Land, TX......	155.0	245.8	San Diego-Carlsbad, CA.........................	385.7	645.0
Indianapolis-Carmel-Anderson, IN.............	123.3	200.1	San Francisco-Oakland-Hayward, CA.........	525.6	988.0
Las Vegas-Henderson-Paradise, NV............	138.0	306.0	San Jose-Sunnyvale-Santa Clara, CA........	595.0	1,265.0
Little Rock-North Little Rock-Conway, AR.......	132.5	152.5	Seattle-Tacoma-Bellevue, WA..................	295.7	524.7
Los Angeles-Long Beach-Glendale, CA........	323.3	611.2	Tampa-St. Petersburg-Clearwater, FL.........	130.0	245.0
Louisville/Jefferson County, KY-IN.............	134.6	192.7	Trenton, NJ.......................................	250.7	276.3
Madison, WI....................................	217.7	299.2	Tucson, AZ.......................................	156.6	238.9
Memphis, TN-MS-AR...........................	120.2	188.7	Urban Honolulu, HI..............................	607.6	802.5
Miami-Fort Lauderdale-West Palm Beach, FL..	199.9	360.0	Virginia Beach-Norfolk-		
Milwaukee-Waukesha-West Allis, WI............	205.9	268.4	Newport News, VA-NC..........................	205.0	235.0
Minneapolis-St. Paul-Bloomington, MN-WI......	170.6	288.6	Washington-Arlington-		
New Haven-Milford, CT........................	231.0	237.4	Alexandria, DC-VA-MD-WV....................	325.3	440.9

NA Not available.

Source: NATIONAL ASSOCIATION OF REALTORS ®. See also <nar.realtor/research-and-statistics>.

Table 1011. Existing Apartment Condominiums and Cooperatives—Units Sold and Median Sales Price by Region: 1990 to 2019

[272 represents 272,000. Data shown here reflect revisions from prior estimates. For definition of median, see Guide to Tabular Presentation. For composition of regions, see map inside front cover]

Year	Units sold (1,000)					Median sales price (dollars)				
	U.S.	Northeast	Midwest	South	West	U.S.	Northeast	Midwest	South	West
1990	272	73	55	80	64	86,900	107,500	70,200	64,200	114,600
1991	261	76	55	75	55	87,500	104,600	73,900	65,600	114,500
1992	282	88	61	77	56	87,700	100,600	79,000	66,600	117,400
1993	312	98	66	89	59	86,000	96,800	78,900	66,500	112,000
1994	343	108	68	101	66	88,800	97,100	86,200	66,700	118,600
1995	333	108	66	96	63	89,000	92,500	90,700	67,800	114,800
1996	370	120	72	105	73	92,600	95,100	95,200	70,600	119,800
1997	407	134	79	111	83	97,300	98,600	99,100	73,300	128,900
1998	470	157	92	126	95	102,500	100,900	106,400	76,800	137,700
1999	534	182	102	145	105	110,100	109,800	114,600	80,700	143,900
2000	571	197	106	160	108	114,000	108,500	121,700	84,200	149,100
2001	601	203	116	174	108	125,600	121,200	134,800	93,200	160,400
2002	657	221	129	193	114	144,900	143,500	148,600	109,900	187,000
2003	732	250	146	211	125	168,500	178,100	162,600	126,900	222,400
2004	820	292	161	230	137	197,100	214,100	181,000	156,600	258,000
2005	896	331	177	245	143	223,900	245,100	189,100	187,300	283,800
2006	801	299	169	211	122	221,900	249,700	190,900	184,000	264,700
2007	624	126	100	236	162	226,300	256,100	195,200	185,100	263,300
2008	459	103	71	164	121	209,800	252,500	188,200	166,800	218,500
2009	464	105	58	180	121	175,600	232,800	157,100	132,700	162,100
2010	474	95	53	202	124	171,700	242,200	150,500	118,500	154,700
2011	477	89	52	210	126	165,100	237,700	129,000	107,800	176,000
2012	528	104	66	229	129	173,700	240,100	127,800	123,900	196,700
2013	603	118	79	265	141	194,900	250,200	138,300	147,900	249,200
2014	591	112	76	262	141	204,300	254,900	149,300	154,700	273,300
2015	608	115	78	266	149	210,700	249,300	157,900	162,900	294,500
2016	614	116	82	263	153	220,700	256,600	166,200	172,600	321,300
2017	619	116	80	271	152	234,300	271,700	175,200	183,800	345,600
2018	601	110	77	273	141	241,000	284,600	177,600	184,500	361,500
2019	579	106	72	270	131	249,500	294,900	184,400	193,500	369,900

Source: NATIONAL ASSOCIATION OF REALTORS ®. See also <nar.realtor/research-and-statistics>.

Table 1012. New Unfurnished Apartments Completed and Rented in 3 Months by Region: 2015 to 2018

[268.3 represents 268,300. Structures with five or more units, privately financed, nonsubsidized, unfurnished rental apartments. Based on sample and subject to sampling variability; see source for details. For composition of regions, see map, inside front cover]

Year and rent	Number (1,000)					Percent rented in 3 months				
	U.S.	North-east	Midwest	South	West	U.S.	North-east	Midwest	South	West
2015	268.3	32.0	47.4	117.8	71.1	60	63	67	53	66
2016	266.3	30.5	41.0	128.1	66.7	55	49	56	51	64
2017	294.8	42.2	43.9	138.9	69.9	54	55	56	51	61
2018	**277.8**	**36.3**	**39.0**	**125.5**	**77.1**	**54**	**49**	**55**	**53**	**59**
Less than $850	15.8	(S)	2.8	10.3	S	65	87	37	66	90
$850 to $1,049	18.1	0.4	7.1	7.3	3.3	63	93	63	58	72
$1,050 to $1,249	33.3	0.6	9.1	18.0	5.6	60	55	59	56	77
$1,250 to $1,449	40.3	(S)	6.7	23.4	9.2	59	55	55	55	71
$1,450 to $1,649	35.7	2.2	2.9	19.9	10.8	57	73	51	54	59
$1,650 to $1,849	26.6	2.6	1.8	14.9	7.3	52	55	59	51	53
$1,850 to $2,409	21.9	(S)	1.8	9.6	6.0	55	62	54	50	57
$2,050 to $2,249	14.4	2.6	0.8	6.2	4.8	51	55	45	46	56
$2,250 to $2,449	14.2	2.9	(S)	4.3	5.7	52	41	52	51	59
$2,450 or more	57.4	19.2	4.6	11.7	22.0	43	40	50	38	47
Median asking rent (dol.)	1,625	[1] 2,450+	1,261	1,488	1,846	(X)	(X)	(X)	(X)	(X)

X Not applicable. S Data withheld because they did not meet publication standards. [1] Median rent for this region falls within the highest rent range, with no greater specificity available.

Source: U.S. Census Bureau, "Survey of Market Absorption of New Multifamily Units, Table Creator," <https://www.census.gov/programs-surveys/soma/data/tools.html>, accessed August 2020.

Table 1013. Total Housing Inventory for the United States: 2000 to 2019

[In thousands (116,264 represents 116,264,000), except percent. Data for 2000-2009 have been revised based on 2010 estimates. Data for 2010-2019 are based on 2018 estimates. Based on the Current Population Survey/Housing Vacancy Survey and subject to sampling error; see source and Appendix III for details]

Item	2000	2005	2010	2013	2014	2015	2016	2017	2018	2019
All housing units	**116,264**	**125,363**	**131,806**	**133,532**	**134,366**	**135,268**	**136,267**	**137,345**	**138,489**	**139,641**
Vacant	13,680	15,880	18,907	18,224	17,955	17,427	17,390	17,395	16,995	16,761
Year-round vacant	10,315	12,060	14,422	13,769	13,488	13,030	13,024	13,219	13,001	12,904
For rent	2,980	3,763	4,322	3,695	3,434	3,293	3,244	3,400	3,234	3,183
For sale only	1,088	1,468	2,000	1,538	1,453	1,422	1,350	1,258	1,192	1,115
Rented or sold	935	1,073	915	1,075	1,074	1,083	1,059	1,164	1,108	1,092
Held off market	5,313	5,755	7,182	7,461	7,528	7,231	7,372	7,398	7,465	7,513
Occasional use	1,901	1,909	2,264	2,392	2,248	2,020	2,106	2,184	2,117	2,160
Usual residence elsewhere	1,050	1,142	1,266	1,256	1,365	1,356	1,453	1,355	1,366	1,345
Other	2,363	2,703	3,654	3,812	3,918	3,855	3,814	3,858	3,981	4,008
Seasonal [1]	3,364	3,820	4,485	4,455	4,467	4,398	4,363	4,174	3,994	3,857
Total occupied	102,584	109,484	112,899	115,306	116,411	117,841	118,877	119,952	121,493	122,880
Owner	69,223	75,411	75,460	75,075	75,036	75,018	75,395	76,599	78,233	79,323
Renter	33,362	34,073	37,440	40,231	41,375	42,822	43,482	43,354	43,260	43,558
PERCENT DISTRIBUTION										
All housing units	100.0	100.0	100.0	100.0	100.0	100.0	100.0	100.0	100.0	100.0
Vacant	11.8	12.7	14.3	13.6	13.4	12.9	12.8	12.7	12.3	12.0
Total occupied	88.2	87.3	85.7	86.4	86.6	87.1	87.2	87.3	87.7	88.0
Owner	59.5	60.2	57.3	56.2	55.8	55.5	55.3	55.8	56.5	56.8
Renter	28.7	27.2	28.4	30.1	30.8	31.7	31.9	31.6	31.2	31.2

[1] Includes vacant seasonal mobile homes.

Source: U.S. Census Bureau, "Housing Vacancies and Home Ownership," <http://www.census.gov/housing/hvs/>, accessed March 2020.

Table 1014. Occupied Housing Inventory by Age of Householder: 2000 to 2019

[In thousands (102,584 represents 102,584,000). Data for 2000-2009 have been revised based on 2010 estimates. Data for 2010-2019 are based on 2018 estimates. Based on the Current Population Survey/Housing Vacancy Survey; see source for details]

Age of householder	2000	2005	2010	2013	2014	2015	2016	2017	2018	2019
Total	**102,584**	**109,484**	**112,899**	**115,306**	**116,411**	**117,841**	**118,877**	**119,952**	**121,493**	**122,880**
Under 25 years old	5,966	6,614	6,116	6,159	6,161	6,147	6,188	5,965	6,030	5,976
25 to 29 years old	8,199	8,893	9,124	8,777	8,884	9,046	9,122	9,312	9,541	9,580
30 to 34 years old	9,941	9,696	9,568	10,018	10,127	10,132	10,188	10,197	10,243	10,486
35 to 39 years old	11,576	10,648	9,887	9,555	9,738	9,864	10,132	10,394	10,585	10,604
40 to 44 years old	12,016	11,858	10,624	10,408	10,205	10,128	9,011	9,771	9,678	9,986
45 to 49 years old	10,837	11,916	11,798	10,765	10,595	10,608	10,560	10,578	10,501	10,238
50 to 54 years old	9,416	10,716	11,828	11,902	11,770	11,496	11,272	10,931	10,852	10,719
55 to 59 years old	7,457	9,614	10,534	11,373	11,427	11,614	11,733	11,648	11,544	11,602
60 to 64 years old	6,013	7,422	9,431	10,022	10,224	10,538	10,687	11,033	11,317	11,457
65 to 69 years old	5,680	5,968	7,103	8,356	8,765	9,338	9,670	9,807	10,011	10,145
70 to 74 years old	5,421	5,073	5,499	6,205	6,482	6,718	6,974	7,594	8,025	8,383
75 years old and over	10,061	11,066	11,387	11,766	12,032	12,211	12,441	12,723	13,166	13,704

Source: U.S. Census Bureau, "Housing Vacancies and Home Ownership," <http://www.census.gov/housing/hvs/>, accessed March 2020.

Table 1015. Vacancy Rates for Housing Units—Characteristics: 2000 to 2019

[In percent. Rate is the proportion of vacant housing for rent or for sale to the total rental and homeowner supply, which comprises occupied units, units rented or sold and awaiting occupancy, and vacant units available for rent or sale. Based on the Current Population Survey/Housing Vacancy Survey; see source for details. For composition of regions, see map inside front cover]

Characteristic	Rental units					Homeowner units				
	2000	2010	2015	2018	2019	2000	2010	2015	2018	2019
Total units	**8.0**	**10.2**	**7.1**	**6.9**	**6.7**	**1.6**	**2.6**	**1.8**	**1.5**	**1.4**
Northeast	5.6	7.6	5.5	5.3	5.2	1.2	1.7	1.9	1.5	1.3
Midwest	8.8	10.8	7.6	7.5	7.1	1.3	2.6	1.7	1.3	1.2
South	10.5	12.7	8.9	8.6	8.8	1.9	2.8	2.1	1.7	1.7
West	5.8	8.2	5.1	5.0	4.6	1.5	2.7	1.4	1.3	1.1
Units in structure:										
1 unit	7.0	9.2	7.1	6.0	5.6	1.5	2.2	1.7	1.3	1.3
2 units or more	8.7	11.1	7.2	7.7	7.6	4.7	9.2	5.1	4.7	4.3
5 units or more	9.2	11.7	7.4	7.9	8.0	5.8	9.2	4.5	4.0	3.5
Units with:										
3 rooms or fewer	10.3	13.8	9.9	10.2	10.1	10.4	14.8	13.6	9.9	8.7
4 rooms	8.2	10.5	7.0	6.7	6.8	2.9	5.7	4.4	3.3	2.7
5 rooms	6.9	8.9	6.1	5.3	5.2	2.0	3.0	2.2	1.6	1.6
6 rooms or more	5.2	7.1	5.6	5.5	5.1	1.1	1.7	1.2	1.0	1.0

Source: U.S. Census Bureau, "Housing Vacancies and Home Ownership," <http://www.census.gov/housing/hvs/>, accessed March 2020.

Table 1016. Housing Units and Tenure—States: 2018

[138,540 represents 138,540,000. The American Community Survey universe includes the household population and the population living in institutions, college dormitories, and other group quarters. Based on a sample and subject to sampling variability; see Appendix III]

State	Housing units (1,000) Total	Occu-pied	Vacant Total [1]	Vacant For rent only	Vacant For sale only	Vacant For sea-sonal use [2]	Owner-occupied units Total (1,000)	Owner-occupied units Average house-hold size (persons)	Renter-occupied units Total (1,000)	Renter-occupied units Average house-hold size (persons)
United States	**138,540**	**121,520**	**17,020**	**2,909**	**1,206**	**5,435**	**77,708**	**2.71**	**43,812**	**2.48**
Alabama	2,275	1,855	420	68	24	79	1,262	2.63	593	2.44
Alaska	318	255	64	8	4	29	167	2.93	87	2.52
Arizona	3,036	2,614	422	56	30	210	1,694	2.71	920	2.63
Arkansas	1,381	1,156	224	37	16	54	760	2.60	396	2.41
California	14,278	13,072	1,206	247	89	394	7,166	3.03	5,906	2.88
Colorado	2,424	2,177	247	43	15	119	1,418	2.67	759	2.36
Connecticut	1,521	1,378	143	29	14	31	907	2.62	471	2.29
Delaware	439	368	71	7	3	39	261	2.59	107	2.51
District of Columbia	320	287	32	12	2	3	122	2.46	166	2.19
Florida	9,548	7,809	1,738	252	110	917	5,148	2.66	2,661	2.69
Georgia	4,326	3,803	523	109	46	86	2,426	2.76	1,377	2.59
Hawaii	546	455	91	21	5	37	265	3.15	190	2.84
Idaho	736	640	95	11	6	51	453	2.77	187	2.51
Illinois	5,376	4,865	511	113	58	51	3,210	2.68	1,655	2.33
Indiana	2,904	2,599	304	58	24	47	1,792	2.61	807	2.27
Iowa	1,410	1,268	142	27	13	25	904	2.51	364	2.15
Kansas	1,281	1,133	147	34	14	16	750	2.63	384	2.23
Kentucky	1,995	1,733	262	38	18	39	1,168	2.56	565	2.39
Louisiana	2,076	1,737	339	58	22	58	1,138	2.67	600	2.48
Maine	747	570	176	9	7	125	406	2.42	164	1.95
Maryland	2,459	2,216	243	52	25	58	1,483	2.78	733	2.43
Massachusetts	2,915	2,624	291	38	15	137	1,621	2.72	1,004	2.24
Michigan	4,615	3,957	657	59	35	293	2,817	2.56	1,140	2.24
Minnesota	2,456	2,194	261	30	11	142	1,568	2.62	627	2.18
Mississippi	1,333	1,109	224	42	18	34	756	2.62	352	2.57
Missouri	2,806	2,435	371	57	28	89	1,626	2.56	809	2.22
Montana	515	431	84	11	4	41	291	2.49	140	2.19
Nebraska	845	765	80	16	6	16	506	2.60	260	2.17
Nevada	1,269	1,130	139	47	11	35	642	2.75	488	2.52
New Hampshire	638	531	107	7	4	74	379	2.62	152	2.11
New Jersey	3,628	3,250	379	55	35	142	2,079	2.81	1,171	2.46
New Mexico	943	794	149	25	11	47	525	2.65	269	2.46
New York	8,364	7,367	997	151	68	350	3,954	2.73	3,413	2.39
North Carolina	4,685	4,011	674	107	42	208	2,613	2.58	1,399	2.40
North Dakota	378	319	58	15	3	16	199	2.49	120	1.99
Ohio	5,218	4,685	532	95	38	63	3,086	2.54	1,599	2.21
Oklahoma	1,743	1,485	258	48	21	37	972	2.62	513	2.50
Oregon	1,789	1,640	149	28	13	56	1,025	2.59	615	2.36
Pennsylvania	5,713	5,071	642	90	51	179	3,479	2.56	1,592	2.18
Rhode Island	469	407	63	11	5	19	251	2.63	155	2.29
South Carolina	2,318	1,928	390	67	24	133	1,335	2.59	593	2.51
South Dakota	398	345	52	9	4	15	234	2.55	111	2.26
Tennessee	2,992	2,603	389	73	29	72	1,724	2.61	879	2.41
Texas	11,101	9,776	1,325	340	100	242	6,034	3.02	3,742	2.64
Utah	1,109	999	110	20	7	53	704	3.25	295	2.79
Vermont	337	261	76	4	3	55	189	2.39	73	2.05
Virginia	3,539	3,176	363	60	31	82	2,093	2.67	1,082	2.48
Washington	3,148	2,896	253	45	16	89	1,819	2.66	1,077	2.37
West Virginia	894	735	159	15	11	37	533	2.45	202	2.25
Wisconsin	2,711	2,372	339	45	15	195	1,592	2.51	780	2.14
Wyoming	279	230	48	10	3	15	162	2.54	68	2.23

[1] Includes other reasons not shown separately. [2] For seasonal, recreational, or occasional use.

Source: U.S. Census Bureau, 2018 American Community Survey, B25002, "Occupancy Status"; B25003, "Tenure"; B25004, "Vacancy Status"; and B25010, "Average Household Size of Units by Tenure"; <https://data.census.gov/>, accessed November 2019.

Table 1017. Net Stock of Residential Fixed Assets: 1990 to 2019

[In billions of dollars (5,844 represents $5,844,000,000,000). End of year estimates]

Item	1990	1995	2000	2005	2010	2015	2017	2018	2019
Total residential fixed assets	**5,844**	**7,407**	**10,040**	**15,482**	**16,116**	**19,348**	**21,593**	**22,799**	**23,557**
By type of owner and legal form of organization:									
Private	5,702	7,228	9,810	15,150	15,783	18,957	21,167	22,353	23,101
Corporate	63	73	100	151	169	207	233	247	253
Noncorporate	5,640	7,155	9,710	14,999	15,614	18,750	20,933	22,106	22,848
Government	142	179	230	332	333	391	426	446	456
Federal	52	62	75	103	98	107	114	118	120
State and local	90	117	154	229	234	284	312	328	337
By tenure group: [1]									
Owner-occupied	4,184	5,485	7,596	12,053	12,529	15,118	16,922	17,899	18,551
Tenant-occupied	1,634	1,893	2,408	3,377	3,531	4,154	4,582	4,805	4,906

[1] Excludes stocks of other nonfarm residential assets, which consists primarily of dormitories and of fraternity and sorority houses.

Source: U.S. Bureau of Economic Analysis, Fixed Assets Accounts Tables, "Table 5.1 Current-Cost Net Stock of Residential Fixed Assets by Type of Owner, Legal Form of Organization, and Tenure Group," <http://www.bea.gov/iTable/index_FA.cfm>, accessed September 2020.

Table 1018. Homeowner and Rental Vacancy Rates by State: 2019

[In percent. From the Current Population Survey/Housing Vacancy Survey, and includes the civilian noninstitutionalized population, people in noninstitutional group quarters, and military households off post or with families on post (must include 1 household member who is a civilian adult). Based on a sample and subject to sampling variability, see Appendix III]

State	Home-owner vacancy rate	Rental vacancy rate	State	Home-owner vacancy rate	Rental vacancy rate	State	Home-owner vacancy rate	Rental vacancy rate
United States......	**1.4**	**6.7**	Iowa..............	1.0	6.7	North Carolina....	1.3	6.7
			Kansas............	1.3	11.8	North Dakota.....	2.3	11.6
			Kentucky..........	1.1	8.5	Ohio..............	1.2	6.4
Alabama..............	1.9	12.6	Louisiana.........	2.0	10.7	Oklahoma..........	2.4	10.0
Alaska...............	2.0	7.5	Maine.............	1.3	4.1	Oregon............	1.0	5.1
Arizona..............	1.3	5.8	Maryland..........	1.7	8.1	Pennsylvania......	1.2	7.2
Arkansas.............	2.0	9.6	Massachusetts...	0.9	3.6	Rhode Island.....	1.2	3.9
California...........	1.0	4.2	Michigan..........	1.1	6.8	South Carolina. ..	1.3	10.8
Colorado.............	0.7	4.1	Minnesota........	0.7	5.0	South Dakota.....	0.7	9.5
Connecticut..........	1.2	5.6	Mississippi........	1.4	8.7	Tennessee........	1.6	10.1
Delaware.............	1.3	6.3	Missouri..........	1.4	9.3	Texas.............	1.7	9.5
Dist. of Columbia....	1.2	6.0	Montana..........	1.4	5.0	Utah..............	0.9	3.8
Florida..............	1.8	8.4	Nebraska..........	0.9	6.5	Vermont...........	1.3	4.4
Georgia..............	1.8	7.6	Nevada............	2.0	5.8	Virginia..........	1.4	7.0
Hawaii...............	1.6	7.4	New Hampshire..	0.8	4.0	Washington.......	0.9	4.1
Idaho................	1.2	4.5	New Jersey.......	1.4	4.2	West Virginia.....	1.6	5.8
Illinois.............	1.4	7.5	New Mexico......	2.0	7.1	Wisconsin.........	0.9	4.8
Indiana..............	1.6	6.7	New York..........	1.5	5.2	Wyoming..........	1.6	8.1

Source: U.S. Census Bureau, "Housing Vacancies and Home Ownership," <http://www.census.gov/housing/hvs/>, accessed March 2020.

Table 1019. Homeowner and Rental Vacancy Rates by Metropolitan Area: 2019

[In percent. From the Current Population Survey/Housing Vacancy Survey, and includes the civilian noninstitutionalized population, people in noninstitutional group quarters, and military households off post or with families on post (must include 1 household member who is a civilian adult). Data are based on 2010 metropolitan/nonmetropolitan definitions. Subject to sampling error; see source and Appendix III for details]

Metropolitan area	Home-owner vacancy rate	Rental vacancy rate	Metropolitan area	Home-owner vacancy rate	Rental vacancy rate
Inside metropolitan areas..................	**1.3**	**6.5**	Memphis, TN-AR-MS..........	1.4	10.6
Akron, OH.............	1.3	6.2	Miami-Fort Lauderdale-West Palm Beach, FL..........	1.8	7.0
Albany-Schenectady-Troy, NY.................	3.0	12.3	Milwaukee-Waukesha-West Allis, WI..........	0.6	6.6
Albuquerque, NM........	1.9	6.5	Minneapolis-St. Paul-Bloomington, MN-WI..........	0.5	4.1
Allentown-Bethlehem-Easton, PA-NJ..	1.4	4.0	Nashville-Davidson-Murfreesboro-Franklin, TN..........	1.2	8.6
Atlanta-Sandy Springs-Roswell, GA..........	1.3	7.0	New Haven-Milford, CT.......	1.5	8.3
Austin-Round Rock, TX..........	1.8	8.2	New Orleans-Metairie, LA..........	1.8	9.4
Baltimore-Columbia-Towson, MD..............	2.3	8.8	New York-Newark-Jersey City, NY-NJ-PA..........	1.4	4.3
Baton Rouge, LA.........	1.9	10.2	North Port-Bradenton-Sarasota, FL..........	4.0	5.8
Birmingham-Hoover, AL..........	1.5	10.5	Oklahoma City, OK..........	2.7	8.6
Boston-Cambridge-Newton, MA-NH..........	0.8	3.6	Omaha-Council Bluffs, NE-IA..........	0.6	6.3
Bridgeport-Stamford-Norwalk, CT.........	1.8	4.1	Orlando-Kissimmee-Sanford, FL..........	2.5	8.3
Buffalo-Cheektowaga-Niagara Falls, NY......	1.2	6.4	Philadelphia-Camden-Wilmington, PA-NJ-DE-MD.....	1.3	7.1
Cape Coral-Fort Myers, FL..........	2.3	8.5	Phoenix-Mesa-Scottsdale, AZ..........	1.0	5.0
Charleston-N. Charleston-Summerville, SC...	2.2	16.7	Pittsburgh, PA..........	1.2	7.3
Charlotte-Concord-Gastonia, NC-SC..........	1.8	7.6	Portland-Vancouver-Hillsboro, OR-WA..........	0.9	4.4
Chicago-Naperville-Elgin, IL..........	1.5	5.7	Providence-Warwick, RI-MA..........	0.9	4.2
Cincinnati, OH-KY-IN..........	1.1	10.7	Raleigh, NC..........	0.8	7.0
Cleveland-Elyria, OH..........	1.1	3.8	Richmond, VA..........	1.3	9.5
Columbia, SC..........	1.5	9.3	Riverside-San Bernardino-Ontario, CA..........	1.7	4.5
Columbus, OH..........	0.8	4.3	Rochester, NY..........	0.9	5.9
Dallas-Ft. Worth-Arlington, TX..........	1.5	6.9	Sacramento-Roseville-Arden-Arcade, CA..........	0.8	4.2
Dayton, OH..........	2.3	9.6	St. Louis, MO-IL..........	1.2	8.8
Denver-Aurora-Lakewood, CO..........	1.0	4.7	Salt Lake City, UT..........	0.8	5.0
Detroit-Warren-Dearborn, MI..........	1.3	6.2	San Antonio-New Braunfels, TX..........	2.0	10.1
Fresno, CA..........	1.3	6.9	San Diego-Carlsbad, CA..........	0.8	5.8
Grand Rapids-Wyoming, MI..........	0.5	4.5	San Francisco-Oakland-Hayward, CA..........	0.9	3.8
Greensboro-High Point, NC..........	0.7	8.1	San Jose-Sunnyvale-Santa Clara, CA..........	0.5	3.7
Hartford-West Hartford-East Hartford, CT....	0.8	4.3	Seattle-Tacoma-Bellevue, WA..........	1.0	4.4
Houston-The Woodlands-Sugar Land, TX....	1.9	11.4	Syracuse, NY..........	1.3	11.3
Indianapolis-Carmel-Anderson, IN..........	1.5	7.0	Tampa-St. Petersburg-Clearwater, FL..........	1.6	10.7
Jacksonville, FL..........	1.0	5.2	Toledo, OH..........	0.8	10.2
Kansas City, MO-KS..........	1.4	10.0	Tucson, AZ..........	1.5	7.3
Knoxville, TN..........	1.3	7.1	Tulsa, OK..........	1.6	8.5
Las Vegas-Henderson-Paradise, NV.....	2.0	5.5	Urban Honolulu, HI..........	1.8	5.7
Little Rock-North Little Rock-Conway, AR.....	1.7	11.4	Virginia Beach-Norfolk-Newport News, VA..........	2.2	7.1
Los Angeles-Long Beach-Anaheim, CA......	1.1	4.0	Washington-Arlington-Alexandria, DC-VA-MD-WV....	1.1	5.6
Louisville/Jefferson County, KY-IN.............	0.7	10.6	Worcester, MA..........	0.6	2.5

Source: U.S. Census Bureau, "Housing Vacancies and Home Ownership," <https://www.census.gov/housing/hvs/index.html>, accessed March 2020.

Table 1020. Housing Units—Characteristics by Tenure and Region: 2017

[In thousands of units (137,400 represents 137,400,000), except as indicated. As of Fall. Based on the American Housing Survey; see Appendix III. For composition of regions, see map, inside front cover]

Characteristic	Total housing units	Seasonal units	Year-round units — Occupied Total	Owner	Renter	Northeast	Midwest	South	West	Vacant units
Total units	**137,400**	**2,793**	**121,600**	**77,570**	**43,990**	**21,829**	**27,047**	**45,457**	**27,226**	**13,050**
Percent distribution	100.0	2.0	88.5	56.5	32.0	15.9	19.7	33.1	19.8	9.5
Units in structure:										
Single family detached	84,830	1,685	76,830	64,380	12,450	11,676	18,778	29,624	16,752	6,310
Single family attached	10,040	154	8,958	4,735	4,223	2,295	1,763	2,920	1,981	928
2 to 4 units	9,744	133	8,363	1,120	7,243	2,709	1,588	2,306	1,760	1,248
5 to 9 units	6,645	59	5,780	528	5,253	1,004	1,140	2,124	1,512	805
10 to 19 units	6,180	73	5,282	413	4,869	765	1024	2,132	1,361	826
20 or more units	11,496	213	9,543	1,346	8,196	2,879	1,732	2,577	2,354	1,740
Manufactured/mobile home [1]	8,397	477	6,727	4,969	1,758	494	1,016	3,751	1,468	1,192
Year structure built:										
Median year (est.)	1977	1978	1977	1978	1974	(NA)	(NA)	(NA)	(NA)	1975
2016 to 2017	1,007	21	841	621	220	79	130	392	241	145
2010 to 2015	5,772	103	5,113	3,105	2,007	532	844	2,630	1,105	557
2005 to 2009	9,046	232	7,936	5,449	2,487	789	1,350	3,908	1,890	877
2000 to 2004	10,520	248	9,448	6,325	3,123	870	1,834	4,495	2,248	827
1995 to 1999	10,000	154	9,132	6,537	2,596	786	2,023	4,322	2,000	718
1990 to 1994	7,271	153	6,564	4,825	1,739	799	1,507	2,633	1,627	554
1985 to 1989	10,120	239	8,952	5,749	3,203	1,119	1,548	4,059	2,225	934
1980 to 1984	8,851	193	7,736	4,843	2,893	916	1,311	3,521	1,989	922
1970 to 1979	20,460	465	17,950	11,110	6,846	2,386	3,902	7,014	4,651	2,038
1960 to 1969	14,290	254	12,680	8,167	4,518	2,407	2,913	4,524	2,840	1,350
1950 to 1959	14,250	254	12,820	8,436	4,382	2,950	3,325	3,809	2,732	1,182
1940 to 1949	6,617	142	5,740	3,490	2,250	1,346	1,394	1,704	1,297	735
1930 to 1939	4,205	124	3,620	2,012	1,608	1,159	954	881	626	461
1920 to 1929	5,409	66	4,682	2,417	2,265	1,827	1,296	713	847	662
1919 or earlier	9,575	146	8,340	4,483	3,857	3,863	2,717	856	904	1,088
Stories in structure: [2]										
1 story	42,830	1,046	37,750	26,100	11,650	1,497	4,477	20,832	10,945	4,038
2 stories	46,570	725	41,630	26,120	15,510	6,667	11,065	13,432	10,471	4,208
3 stories	29,210	348	26,470	16,940	9,532	8,699	8,816	5,694	3,262	2,395
4 or more stories	10,315	198	8,901	3,360	5,541	4,464	1,671	1,728	1037	1,217
Foundation: [3]										
Full basement	29,130	351	26,950	23,220	3,738	8,952	11,818	4,015	2,168	1,830
Partial building	9,895	126	9,139	7,991	1149	2,612	3,555	1,759	1,214	629
Crawlspace	20,390	461	18,130	14,150	3,988	804	2,759	8,872	5,701	1,796
Concrete slab	33,460	756	29,940	22,610	7,331	1,446	2,184	17,013	9,297	2,766
Equipment:										
With complete facilities [4]	133,000	2,444	120,100	77,220	42,930	21,492	26,759	45,004	26,894	10,380
Lacking complete facilities [4]	4,436	349	1,416	351	1,064	337	294	454	330	2,671
Kitchen sink	136,300	2,643	121,300	77,500	43,760	21,741	26,998	45,368	27,156	12,360
Refrigerator	134,300	2,493	121,100	77,350	43,720	21,743	26,925	45,283	27,124	10,720
Cooking stove or range	133,500	2,487	120,100	76,960	43,130	21,567	26,686	44,938	26,909	10,960
Microwave oven only	863	24	703	271	431	115	210	252	126	136
Dishwasher	95,690	1,487	87,080	62,160	24,920	13,961	18,464	34,034	20,624	7,117
Washing machine	110,500	1,680	102,900	75,210	27,690	16,337	23,134	40,793	22,635	5,966
Clothes dryer	108,700	1,656	101,100	74,340	26,770	15,779	23,005	40,034	22,286	5,894
Main heating equipment:										
Warm-air furnace	88,920	1,474	79,380	53,310	26,070	10,392	22,131	28,557	18,297	8,063
Steam or hot water system	12,250	143	11,100	6,335	4,761	8,061	1,815	589	630	1,011
Electric heat pump	16,260	383	14,130	9,751	4,377	475	919	11,155	1,579	1,744
Built-in electric units	5,667	185	4,925	1,898	3,026	1,426	1,061	781	1,658	557
Floor, wall, or pipeless furnace	6,324	128	5,616	2,481	3,135	843	610	1,438	2,726	579
Room heaters with flue	884	32	740	398	342	165	92	299	184	112
Room heaters without flue	903	37	749	476	273	26	48	589	86	117
Portable electric heaters	2,268	99	2,018	950	1068	53	75	1296	594	150
Stoves	1,527	79	1,348	1081	267	287	215	291	557	100
Fireplaces, with and without inserts	351	31	295	245	51	26	42	112	117	25
Cooking stove	66	5	58	32	26	17	4	21	15	3
None	1,459	160	848	453	395	10	6	164	667	451
Main cooling equipment:										
Central air conditioning	93,840	1,566	84,480	58,680	25,800	8,550	20,386	39,849	15,703	7,794
One or more room units	27,360	384	25,400	12,740	12,660	10,809	5,262	4,825	4,508	1,568
Source of water:										
Public system or private company	(NA)	(NA)	107,800	65,820	41,950	18,478	22,939	41,095	25,257	(NA)
Individual well	(NA)	(NA)	13,530	11,540	1,981	3,319	4,086	4,309	1,811	(NA)
Means of sewage disposal:										
Public sewer	(NA)	(NA)	99,570	58,520	41,050	17,515	22,219	35,725	24,100	(NA)
Septic tank or cesspool	(NA)	(NA)	21,720	18,860	2,858	4,252	4,741	9,643	3,081	(NA)

NA Not available. [1] Includes trailers. Includes width not reported, not shown separately. [2] Excludes mobile homes; includes basements and finished attics. [3] Includes only single family homes (1 unit, attached or detached). [4] A complete kitchen includes sink, refrigerator, oven or burners.

Source: U.S. Census Bureau, "American Housing Survey: AHS Table Creator," <census.gov/programs-surveys/ahs/data.html>, accessed February 2019.

Table 1021. Housing Units by Units in Structure and State: 2018

[In percent, except as indicated (138,540 represents 138,540,000). The American Community Survey universe includes the household population and the population living in institutions, college dormitories, and other group quarters. Based on a sample and subject to sampling variability; see Appendix III]

State	Total housing units (1,000)	Percent of units by units in structures—								
		1-unit detached	1-unit attached	2 units	3 or 4 units	5 or 9 units	10 or 19 units	20 or more units	Mobile homes	Boat, RV, van, etc.
United States......	**138,540**	**61.4**	**5.9**	**3.6**	**4.3**	**4.7**	**4.5**	**9.5**	**6.1**	**0.1**
Alabama.............	2,275	68.3	1.5	2.1	2.9	4.2	3.4	4.2	13.2	0.2
Alaska...............	318	63.0	7.3	5.5	7.3	4.5	2.8	4.8	4.6	0.1
Arizona.............	3,036	64.2	4.6	1.2	3.4	4.1	4.3	7.6	10.3	0.4
Arkansas...........	1,381	69.9	1.7	3.1	3.4	3.4	3.8	3.0	11.4	0.2
California...........	14,278	57.3	7.1	2.5	5.5	6.1	5.2	12.5	3.7	0.1
Colorado............	2,424	61.6	7.0	1.7	3.4	4.5	5.9	11.6	4.2	0.1
Connecticut.........	1,521	58.6	5.3	8.2	9.0	5.4	3.6	9.0	0.9	(Z)
Delaware............	439	57.5	17.0	1.2	2.1	3.2	5.3	4.7	9.0	0.1
District of Columbia..	320	12.5	22.8	3.2	7.5	8.3	9.3	36.1	0.1	0.1
Florida..............	9,548	54.2	6.1	2.1	3.9	5.0	5.8	14.1	8.7	0.1
Georgia.............	4,326	66.3	3.8	2.3	2.8	4.4	4.7	6.8	8.7	0.1
Hawaii...............	546	52.8	9.2	2.1	4.0	6.1	5.3	20.3	0.2	(Z)
Idaho...............	736	72.4	3.3	2.4	4.3	2.6	2.3	3.9	8.5	0.3
Illinois.............	5,376	58.4	5.8	5.8	6.4	6.5	3.9	10.8	2.4	(Z)
Indiana.............	2,904	72.4	3.8	2.5	3.5	4.9	3.6	4.4	4.9	(Z)
Iowa.................	1,410	73.0	4.3	2.3	3.5	3.5	3.7	5.9	3.8	(Z)
Kansas..............	1,281	72.7	4.4	2.4	3.5	4.1	3.9	4.7	4.3	0.1
Kentucky............	1,995	67.5	2.6	2.8	4.4	4.3	3.3	3.1	11.8	(Z)
Louisiana............	2,076	65.6	2.7	4.2	4.0	2.9	2.7	4.8	12.9	0.1
Maine...............	747	69.0	2.1	5.0	5.8	4.1	1.5	4.1	8.3	0.1
Maryland............	2,459	51.2	21.1	1.4	2.2	5.0	8.2	9.6	1.4	(Z)
Massachusetts.......	2,915	51.4	5.5	9.6	10.9	5.9	4.4	11.5	0.8	(Z)
Michigan............	4,615	71.8	4.5	2.3	2.6	4.3	3.6	5.4	5.5	(Z)
Minnesota...........	2,456	66.6	7.3	2.1	2.0	2.3	3.3	13.1	3.3	(Z)
Mississippi..........	1,333	68.6	1.2	2.6	2.9	4.5	2.4	2.4	15.2	0.1
Missouri.............	2,806	69.8	3.6	3.3	4.6	4.0	3.6	4.7	6.3	0.1
Montana............	515	69.4	3.9	2.9	4.3	3.0	2.6	3.7	9.9	0.2
Nebraska............	845	72.0	4.2	1.9	2.6	3.9	4.6	7.3	3.7	(Z)
Nevada.............	1,269	59.6	4.5	1.4	6.5	7.7	5.4	9.5	5.1	0.1
New Hampshire......	638	63.3	5.3	5.4	5.5	4.6	2.9	6.9	6.1	(Z)
New Jersey..........	3,628	53.4	9.6	9.1	5.9	4.7	5.0	11.3	0.9	(Z)
New Mexico.........	943	64.0	3.1	1.9	4.3	2.8	2.2	4.4	16.9	0.3
New York............	8,364	41.8	5.0	10.2	6.8	5.2	4.3	24.4	2.2	(Z)
North Carolina.......	4,685	64.9	4.3	2.1	2.6	4.3	4.2	4.9	12.6	0.1
North Dakota........	378	57.2	5.6	2.0	3.6	3.8	5.0	16.1	6.8	(Z)
Ohio................	5,218	68.4	4.6	4.1	4.4	4.8	4.0	6.0	3.7	(Z)
Oklahoma...........	1,743	73.0	1.9	1.9	2.6	3.8	3.6	3.9	9.1	0.2
Oregon..............	1,789	63.1	4.3	2.5	4.1	4.5	4.1	9.0	7.9	0.4
Pennsylvania........	5,713	57.0	18.6	4.3	4.1	3.2	2.6	6.3	3.9	(Z)
Rhode Island........	469	55.3	3.3	10.5	13.1	4.5	3.7	8.4	1.0	0.1
South Carolina.......	2,318	63.0	3.1	1.9	2.8	4.1	3.4	5.5	15.9	0.1
South Dakota........	398	67.5	3.7	1.6	3.9	3.7	4.4	6.4	8.6	0.1
Tennessee...........	2,992	68.1	3.3	2.6	3.3	4.6	3.7	5.0	9.2	0.1
Texas...............	11,101	64.9	2.5	1.9	3.1	5.0	6.3	9.2	7.0	0.2
Utah................	1,109	67.9	6.5	2.6	4.1	3.6	4.3	7.7	3.2	0.1
Vermont.............	337	67.0	4.4	5.5	6.2	4.4	1.9	4.2	6.4	(Z)
Virginia.............	3,539	61.1	10.9	1.7	2.8	4.7	5.6	8.1	5.2	(Z)
Washington..........	3,148	62.9	4.0	2.3	3.5	4.4	5.0	11.3	6.3	0.2
West Virginia........	894	70.9	2.1	2.0	2.8	2.9	1.8	2.6	14.9	0.1
Wisconsin...........	2,711	66.6	4.1	6.3	3.6	5.0	3.4	7.5	3.4	(Z)
Wyoming............	279	65.7	4.4	2.6	4.5	3.2	2.8	3.7	12.9	0.1

Z Less than .05 percent.

Source: U.S. Census Bureau, 2018 American Community Survey, B25024, "Units in Structure," <https://data.census.gov/>, accessed November 2019.

Table 1022. Housing Units—Size of Units and Lot: 2017

[In thousands (137,400 represents 137,400,000), except as indicated. As of Fall. Based on the American Housing Survey; see Appendix III. For composition of regions, see map inside front cover]

Item	Total housing units	Sea-sonal units	Year-round units Occupied Total	Owner	Renter	North-east	Mid-west	South	West	Vacant units
Total units	**137,400**	**2,793**	**121,600**	**77,570**	**43,990**	**21,829**	**27,047**	**45,457**	**27,226**	**13,050**
Rooms:										
1 room	732	53	530	19	511	127	134	86	183	149
2 rooms	1,474	62	1,181	98	1,083	293	216	259	412	231
3 rooms	11,650	360	9,597	1,145	8,452	2,309	1,926	2,972	2,390	1,692
4 rooms	23,960	878	19,460	6,109	13,350	3,678	4,193	6,891	4,697	3,621
5 rooms	31,320	629	27,560	16,640	10,920	4,256	6,117	11,231	5,957	3,125
6 rooms	28,510	457	25,830	20,070	5,753	4,610	5,625	10,213	5,379	2,227
7 rooms	18,720	194	17,440	15,080	2,359	3,025	4,067	6,549	3,797	1,092
8 or more rooms	21,044	159	19,970	18,403	1,565	3,532	4,770	7,260	4,406	914
Complete bathrooms:										
No bathrooms	339	100	149	32	117	56	30	24	40	90
1 bathroom	46,500	1,128	39,080	13,230	25,840	9,633	9,553	11,818	8,076	6,291
1 and one-half bathrooms	16,070	251	14,430	9,989	4,444	3,693	4,307	4,057	2,374	1,384
2 or more bathrooms	74,493	1,313	67,899	54,313	13,592	8,447	13,159	29,561	16,732	5,285
Square footage of unit:										
Less than 500	3,409	160	2,765	490	2,275	719	528	705	814	484
500 to 749	9,527	292	7,702	1,246	6,457	1,548	1,442	2,553	2,160	1,533
750 to 999	16,510	420	13,810	4,257	9,551	2,422	3,070	5,023	3,294	2,277
1,000 to 1,499	31,570	668	27,730	17,020	10,710	4,236	6,147	10,727	6,620	3,170
1,500 to 1,999	24,340	405	22,200	18,350	3,851	3,228	4,785	8,983	5,207	1,734
2,000 to 2,499	15,670	230	14,550	12,930	1,621	2,409	3,363	5,554	3,227	883
2,500 to 2,999	8,352	124	7,828	7,299	529	1,343	1,712	3,030	1,744	400
3,000 to 3,999	7,875	126	7,333	6,919	414	1,065	1,917	2,828	1,522	417
4,000 or more	3,926	73	3,555	3,260	294	593	922	1,335	705	298
Not reported	16,230	295	14,080	5,784	8,297	4,267	3,164	4,720	1,930	1,855
Median square footage	1,473	1,200	1,500	1,800	974	2,900	3,100	4,500	2,990	1,144
Lot size:										
Single detached and attached units and mobile homes [1]	99,750	2,164	89,490	71,880	17,620	13,899	20,838	35,401	19,349	8,094
Less than one-eighth acre	14,700	358	12,860	8,811	4,053	3,097	2,668	3,511	3,589	1,476
One-eighth to one-quarter acre	33,400	452	30,640	23,670	6,964	2,985	6,695	11,228	9,730	2,311
One-quarter to one-half acre	19,930	395	18,220	15,510	2,718	2,880	5,064	7,763	2,518	1,314
One-half up to one acre	9,455	298	8,369	7,229	1,140	1,662	1,765	4,042	900	787
1 up to 5 acres	15,160	385	13,330	11,370	1,958	2,384	2,767	6,438	1,744	1,439
5 up to 10 acres	3,079	75	2,696	2,412	285	377	839	1,104	376	308
10 or more acres	4,028	201	3,368	2,869	499	518	1,045	1,315	490	459

[1] Does not include cooperatives or condominiums.

Source: U.S. Census Bureau, "American Housing Survey: AHS Table Creator," <census.gov/programs-surveys/ahs/data.html>, accessed February 2019.

Table 1023. Occupied Housing Units—Tenure by Race of Householder: 2003 to 2017

[In thousands (105,842 represents 105,842,000), except percent. As of Fall. Based on the American Housing Survey; see Appendix III]

Race of householder and tenure	2003	2005	2007	2009	2011	2013	2015	2017
ALL RACES [1]								
Occupied units, total	**105,842**	**108,871**	**110,692**	**111,806**	**114,907**	**115,852**	**118,290**	**121,600**
Owner-occupied	72,238	74,931	75,647	76,428	76,091	75,650	74,299	77,570
Percent of occupied	68.3	68.8	68.3	68.4	66.2	65.3	62.8	63.8
Renter-occupied	33,604	33,940	35,045	35,378	38,816	40,201	43,991	43,990
WHITE [2]								
Occupied units, total	**87,483**	**89,449**	**90,413**	**91,137**	**92,820**	**93,284**	**93,748**	**95,320**
Owner-occupied	63,126	65,023	65,554	65,935	65,357	65,088	63,049	65,230
Percent of occupied	72.2	72.7	72.5	72.3	70.4	69.8	67.3	68.4
Renter-occupied	24,357	24,426	24,859	25,202	27,463	28,196	30,699	30,090
BLACK [2]								
Occupied units, total	**13,004**	**13,447**	**13,856**	**13,993**	**14,694**	**15,015**	**16,002**	**16,550**
Owner-occupied	6,193	6,471	6,464	6,547	6,662	6,480	6,665	7,131
Percent of occupied	47.6	48.1	46.7	46.8	45.3	43.2	41.7	43.1
Renter-occupied	6,811	6,975	7,392	7,446	8,033	8,535	9,337	9,421
HISPANIC ORIGIN [3]								
Occupied units, total	**11,038**	**11,651**	**12,609**	**12,739**	**13,841**	**14,675**	**15,620**	**16,500**
Owner-occupied	5,106	5,752	6,364	6,439	6,530	6,897	7,109	7,763
Percent of occupied	46.3	49.4	50.5	50.5	47.2	47.0	45.5	47.0
Renter-occupied	5,931	5,899	6,244	6,300	7,311	7,778	8,511	8,733

[1] Includes other races not shown separately. [2] The 2003 American Housing Survey (AHS) allowed respondents to choose more than one race. Beginning in 2003, data represent householders who selected this race group only and exclude householders reporting more than one race. See also comments on race in the text for Section 1 and the below cited source. [3] Persons of Hispanic origin may be of any race.

Source: U.S. Census Bureau, "American Housing Survey: AHS Table Creator," <census.gov/programs-surveys/ahs/data.html>, accessed February 2019.

Table 1024. Homeownership Rates by Age of Householder and Household Type: 2000 to 2019

[In percent. Represents the proportion of owner households to the total number of occupied households. Based on the Current Population Survey/Housing Vacancy Survey, and includes the civilian noninstitutionalized population, people in noninstitutional group quarters, and military in households off post or with their families on post (must have 1 household member who is a civilian adult). See source and Appendix III for details]

Age of householder and household type	2000	2005	2010	2013	2014	2015	2016	2017	2018	2019
United States..........................	**67.4**	**68.9**	**66.9**	**65.1**	**64.5**	**63.7**	**63.4**	**63.9**	**64.4**	**64.6**
AGE OF HOUSEHOLDER										
Less than 25 years old........................	21.7	25.7	22.8	22.2	21.7	21.8	21.9	22.6	22.7	23.2
25 to 29 years old..............................	38.1	40.9	36.8	34.1	32.7	31.7	30.9	32.1	32.5	32.9
30 to 34 years old..............................	54.6	56.8	51.6	48.1	47.1	45.9	45.4	45.7	47.7	48.0
35 to 39 years old..............................	65.0	66.6	61.9	55.8	56.0	55.3	55.3	56.4	57.6	57.2
40 to 44 years old..............................	70.6	71.7	67.9	65.0	63.2	61.6	62.0	61.8	62.9	63.2
45 to 49 years old..............................	74.7	75.0	72.0	69.6	68.5	68.0	66.7	67.5	68.4	68.2
50 to 54 years old..............................	78.5	78.3	75.0	72.6	72.6	71.8	71.6	71.1	71.7	71.9
55 to 59 years old..............................	80.4	80.6	77.7	75.8	75.4	74.7	74.0	73.8	74.0	73.9
60 to 64 years old..............................	80.3	81.9	80.4	77.6	77.2	76.2	76.1	76.9	76.8	76.6
65 to 69 years old..............................	83.0	82.8	81.6	80.5	80.3	79.3	79.0	79.1	79.3	78.8
70 to 74 years old..............................	82.6	82.9	82.4	82.8	81.6	81.3	81.7	81.4	80.6	80.6
75 years old and over.........................	77.7	78.4	78.9	80.0	78.6	77.2	77.0	76.8	76.6	77.3
Less than 35 years old........................	40.8	43.0	39.1	36.8	35.8	35.0	34.5	35.3	36.2	36.7
35 to 44 years old..............................	67.9	69.3	65.0	60.6	59.7	58.5	58.6	59.0	60.1	60.1
45 to 54 years old..............................	76.5	76.6	73.5	71.2	70.7	70.0	69.3	69.3	70.1	70.1
55 to 64 years old..............................	80.3	81.2	79.0	76.6	76.3	75.4	75.0	75.3	75.4	75.2
65 years and over..............................	80.4	80.6	80.5	80.8	79.9	78.9	78.8	78.7	78.5	78.6
TYPE OF HOUSEHOLD										
Family households:										
Married-couple families........................	82.4	84.2	82.1	80.7	80.3	79.6	80.0	80.1	80.8	81.0
Male householder, no spouse present......	57.5	59.1	56.9	55.3	54.5	53.8	53.7	55.6	56.3	56.1
Female householder, no spouse present...	49.1	51.0	48.6	46.7	46.2	45.9	45.7	46.7	47.9	48.6
Nonfamily households:										
One-person......................................	53.6	55.6	55.3	53.9	53.3	52.2	51.3	51.5	51.8	51.8
Male householder............................	47.4	50.3	51.3	49.8	49.1	48.5	47.2	47.3	47.4	48.5
Female householder..........................	58.1	59.6	58.6	57.2	56.6	55.3	54.6	54.9	55.4	54.6
Two-or-more-persons:										
Male householder............................	38.0	41.7	40.7	39.8	37.7	36.6	36.1	37.2	38.6	39.7
Female householder..........................	40.6	44.7	41.9	41.9	41.4	40.7	38.4	39.4	41.5	40.8

Source: U.S. Census Bureau, "Housing Vacancies and Home Ownership," <http://www.census.gov/housing/hvs/>, accessed March 2020.

Table 1025. Homeownership Rates by State: 2000 to 2019

[In percent. Represents the proportion of owner households to the total number of occupied households. Based on the Current Population Survey/Housing Vacancy Survey, and includes the civilian noninstitutionalized population, people in noninstitutional group quarters, and military in households off post or with their families on post (must have 1 household member who is a civilian adult). See source and Appendix III for details]

State	2000	2005	2010	2015	2018	2019	State	2000	2005	2010	2015	2018	2019
United States.....	**67.4**	**68.9**	**66.9**	**63.7**	**64.4**	**64.6**	Missouri..............	74.2	72.3	71.2	68.5	69.7	69.1
Alabama............	73.2	76.6	73.2	70.0	70.3	70.7	Montana.............	70.2	70.4	68.1	66.4	67.4	68.7
Alaska..............	66.4	66.0	65.7	62.3	63.7	62.6	Nebraska............	70.2	70.2	70.4	68.1	66.4	68.2
Arizona.............	68.0	71.1	66.6	61.7	65.7	65.8	Nevada.............	64.0	63.4	59.7	54.8	57.8	58.2
Arkansas...........	68.9	69.2	67.9	67.1	64.7	65.3	New Hampshire....	69.2	74.0	74.9	71.6	73.4	75.0
California...........	57.1	59.7	56.1	54.3	55.1	54.8	New Jersey.........	66.2	70.1	66.5	64.0	65.0	65.0
Colorado...........	68.3	71.0	68.5	63.6	64.4	64.7	New Mexico.........	73.7	71.4	68.6	66.5	68.0	67.4
Connecticut........	70.0	70.5	70.8	66.5	65.3	64.3	New York..........	53.4	55.9	54.5	51.5	51.0	52.0
Delaware...........	72.0	75.8	74.7	73.3	70.8	73.1	North Carolina......	71.1	70.9	69.5	65.2	65.2	65.1
Dist. of Columbia..	41.9	45.8	45.6	40.4	39.9	40.2	North Dakota........	70.7	68.5	67.1	61.8	61.9	61.4
Florida..............	68.4	72.4	69.3	64.8	65.5	66.0	Ohio................	71.3	73.3	69.7	66.4	67.3	68.2
Georgia.............	69.8	67.9	67.1	62.9	63.8	64.4	Oklahoma...........	72.7	72.9	69.2	67.4	69.5	68.8
Hawaii..............	55.2	59.8	56.1	59.3	59.5	60.0	Oregon..............	65.3	68.2	66.3	61.1	62.0	62.4
Idaho...............	70.5	74.2	72.4	70.0	69.2	70.6	Pennsylvania........	74.7	73.3	72.2	69.6	69.9	69.2
Illinois..............	67.9	70.9	68.8	65.4	66.0	65.1	Rhode Island........	61.5	63.1	62.8	58.9	60.7	63.8
Indiana.............	74.9	75.0	71.2	69.4	69.8	69.5	South Carolina......	76.5	73.9	74.8	67.1	72.0	72.6
Iowa................	75.2	73.9	71.1	68.8	68.9	69.5	South Dakota.......	71.2	68.4	70.6	70.1	69.1	69.5
Kansas.............	69.3	69.5	67.4	64.9	67.3	69.2	Tennessee..........	70.9	72.4	71.0	66.5	68.0	68.8
Kentucky...........	73.4	71.6	70.3	67.9	69.8	69.5	Texas..............	63.8	65.9	65.3	61.9	62.7	62.4
Louisiana...........	68.1	72.5	70.4	63.3	65.7	65.6	Utah................	72.7	73.9	72.5	69.9	72.2	71.9
Maine...............	76.5	73.9	73.8	69.9	71.2	73.8	Vermont.............	68.7	74.2	73.6	71.8	71.4	70.9
Maryland...........	69.9	71.2	68.9	67.1	66.6	68.8	Virginia.............	73.9	71.2	68.7	67.1	66.0	67.6
Massachusetts......	59.9	63.4	65.3	60.5	61.5	61.3	Washington.........	63.6	67.6	64.4	62.6	64.9	63.8
Michigan............	77.2	76.4	74.5	74.6	73.0	73.0	West Virginia........	75.9	81.3	79.0	74.9	74.7	75.6
Minnesota..........	76.1	76.5	72.6	70.1	69.8	71.4	Wisconsin...........	71.8	71.1	71.0	66.6	67.9	66.1
Mississippi.........	75.2	78.8	74.8	70.7	72.5	72.7	Wyoming............	71.0	72.8	73.4	69.9	71.1	71.3

Source: U.S. Census Bureau, "Housing Vacancies and Home Ownership," <https://www.census.gov/housing/hvs/index.html>, accessed March 2020.

Table 1026. Occupied Housing Units—Costs by Region: 2017

[77,570 represents 77,570,000. As of Fall. See headnote, Table 1027, for an explanation of housing costs. Based on the American Housing Survey; see Appendix III. For composition of regions, see map inside front cover]

Category	Number (1,000)					Percent distribution				
	Total units	North-east	Mid-west	South	West	Total units	North-east	Mid-west	South	West
OWNER-OCCUPIED UNITS										
Total	**77,570**	**13,457**	**18,491**	**29,402**	**16,225**	**100.0**	**100.0**	**100.0**	**100.0**	**100.0**
Monthly housing costs:										
Less than $200	1,512	85	201	949	279	1.9	0.6	1.1	3.2	1.7
$200 to $299	3,234	168	641	1,934	492	4.2	1.2	3.5	6.6	3.0
$300 to $399	5,004	386	1,256	2,605	756	6.5	2.9	6.8	8.9	4.7
$400 to $499	5,210	641	1,388	2,336	845	6.7	4.8	7.5	7.9	5.2
$500 to $699	9,446	1,384	2,730	3,636	1,697	12.2	10.3	14.8	12.4	10.5
$700 to $999	11,832	2,068	3,361	4,329	2,074	15.3	15.4	18.2	14.7	12.8
$1,000 to $1,499	15,577	2,814	4,180	5,696	2,888	20.1	20.9	22.6	19.4	17.8
$1,500 to $2,499	16,001	3,272	3,491	5,234	4,005	20.6	24.3	18.9	17.8	24.7
$2,500 or more	9,750	2,641	1,240	2,684	3,184	12.6	19.6	6.7	9.1	19.6
RENTER-OCCUPIED UNITS										
Total	**43,990**	**8,371**	**8,561**	**16,060**	**11,001**	**100.0**	**100.0**	**100.0**	**100.0**	**100.0**
Monthly housing costs:										
Less than $200	1,099	230	274	389	207	2.5	2.7	3.2	2.4	1.9
$200 to $299	1,577	411	353	527	286	3.6	4.9	4.1	3.3	2.6
$300 to $399	1,453	373	306	486	286	3.3	4.5	3.6	3.0	2.6
$400 to $499	1,581	262	411	672	235	3.6	3.1	4.8	4.2	2.1
$500 to $699	5,393	696	1,581	2,339	777	12.3	8.3	18.5	14.6	7.1
$700 to $999	10,189	1,554	2,707	4,105	1,822	23.2	18.6	31.6	25.6	16.6
$1,000 to $1,499	11,224	2,228	1,707	4,134	3,156	25.5	26.6	19.9	25.7	28.7
$1,500 to $2,499	7,137	1,679	619	2,004	2,836	16.2	20.1	7.2	12.5	25.8
$2,500 or more	2,379	640	209	468	1,062	5.4	7.6	2.4	2.9	9.7
No cash rent	1,961	299	395	933	334	4.5	3.6	4.6	5.8	3.0

Source: U.S. Census Bureau, "American Housing Survey: AHS Table Creator," <census.gov/programs-surveys/ahs/data.html>, accessed February 2019.

Table 1027. Occupied Housing Units—Financial Summary by Selected Characteristics of the Householder: 2017

[In thousands of units (121,600 represents 121,600,000), except as indicated. As of Fall. Housing costs include real estate taxes, property insurance, utilities, fuel, water, garbage collection, homeowner association fees, cooperative or condominium fees, mobile home fees, routine maintenance, mortgages, other charges in mortgages, and mortgage insurance. Based on the American Housing Survey; see Appendix III]

Characteristic	Total occupied units	Tenure		Black [1]		Hispanic origin [2]		Elderly [3]		Households below poverty level [4]	
		Owner	Renter	Owner	Renter	Owner	Renter	Owner	Renter	Owner	Renter
Total units [5]	**121,600**	**77,570**	**43,990**	**7,131**	**9,421**	**7,763**	**8,733**	**23,983**	**6,686**	**6,722**	**10,293**
Monthly housing costs:											
Less than $200	2,612	1,512	1,099	254	400	154	137	713	211	569	755
$200 to $299	4,811	3,234	1,577	500	520	305	291	1,536	503	705	1,135
$300 to $399	6,456	5,004	1,453	594	418	539	271	2,645	489	794	643
$400 to $499	6,791	5,210	1,581	456	421	439	217	2,572	382	664	575
$500 to $699	14,839	9,446	5,393	876	1,305	903	858	4,459	841	1,114	1,643
$700 to $999	22,024	11,832	10,189	1,077	2,543	1,062	2,093	4,252	1,352	1,149	2,257
$1,000 to $1,499	26,800	15,577	11,224	1,353	2,208	1,582	2,615	3,838	1,184	959	1,731
$1,500 to $2,499	23,145	16,001	7,137	1,367	1,086	1,818	1,683	2,643	686	505	683
$2,500 or more	12,130	9,750	2,379	655	204	959	285	1,321	486	260	293
Median amount (dol.) [6]	1,036	1,071	991	947	872	1,131	1,056	(NA)	(NA)	1,203	1,426
Monthly housing costs as percent of income: [7]											
Less than 5 percent	3,476	2,984	492	263	106	250	83	761	51	12	32
5 to 9 percent	12,330	10,760	1,569	836	298	870	273	3,364	145	41	36
10 to 14 percent	16,260	13,040	3,215	1,015	563	1,128	565	3,840	209	133	71
15 to 19 percent	17,410	12,660	4,749	975	888	1,169	844	3,309	324	182	114
20 to 24 percent	14,630	9,528	5,100	850	926	875	907	2,338	520	217	191
25 to 29 percent	11,310	6,755	4,553	627	989	717	818	1,845	598	241	452
30 to 34 percent	8,594	4,718	3,876	478	812	588	848	1,553	626	239	496
35 to 39 percent	6,214	3,232	2,982	334	686	384	655	1,163	405	195	363
40 percent or more	27,300	12,938	14,361	1,578	3,484	1,678	3,265	5,509	3,153	4,513	6,825
Median amount (percent) [6,8]	22	19	30	21	33	22	33	(NA)	(NA)	(NA)	(NA)
Median monthly costs (dol.): [6]											
Electricity	106	119	84	121	84	121	85	(NA)	(NA)	(NA)	(NA)
Piped gas	55	60	42	58	44	51	37	(NA)	(NA)	(NA)	(NA)
Fuel oil	100	100	83	108	83	106	83	(NA)	(NA)	(NA)	(NA)

NA Not available. [1] For persons who selected this race group only. [2] Persons of Hispanic origin may be of any race. [3] Householders 65 years old and over. [4] Based on household income of families or of individuals living without relatives. Refers to money income in the 12 months before the survey. Threshold reflects changes in the Consumer Price Index, see source for more information. [5] Include units with no cash rents, not shown separately. [6] For explanation of median, see Guide to Tabular Presentation. [7] Money income before taxes. [8] Excludes households with zero or negative income and those with no cash rent.

Source: U.S. Census Bureau, "American Housing Survey: AHS Table Creator," <census.gov/programs-surveys/ahs/data.html>, accessed February 2019.

Table 1028. Owner-Occupied Housing Units—Value and Costs by State: 2018

[In percent, except as indicated (77,708 represents 77,708,000). The American Community Survey universe includes the household population and excludes the population living in institutions, college dormitories, and other group quarters. Based on a sample and subject to sampling variability; see Appendix III. For definition of median, see Guide to Tabular Presentation]

State	Total (1,000)	Percent of units with value of— $99,999 or less	$100,000 to $199,999	$200,000 or more	Median value (dol.)	Median selected monthly owner costs [1] (dol.)	Selected monthly owner costs as a percent income in the past 12 months [1] Less than 15.0 percent	15.0 to 24.9 percent	25.0 to 29.9 percent	30.0 percent or more
U.S...........	77,708	17.7	25.9	56.4	229,700	1,566	25.7	35.9	10.4	27.6
AL.............	1,262	33.0	33.8	33.2	147,900	1,164	32.6	34.6	8.7	23.5
AK.............	167	11.3	16.7	72.0	276,100	1,895	22.6	36.5	12.2	28.6
AZ.............	1,694	13.9	23.6	62.5	241,100	1,417	26.5	35.8	10.3	26.8
AR.............	760	36.6	36.2	27.2	133,100	1,071	34.4	34.3	8.1	22.7
CA.............	7,166	4.7	5.4	89.9	546,800	2,345	17.6	31.7	12.1	38.0
CO.............	1,418	6.3	9.8	83.8	373,300	1,741	24.4	37.5	10.6	27.1
CT.............	907	5.1	23.0	71.9	277,400	2,056	21.6	36.5	11.2	30.4
DE.............	261	9.8	22.0	68.2	255,300	1,566	24.5	33.7	10.4	30.7
DC.............	122	2.1	2.7	95.2	617,900	2,506	26.3	37.9	9.5	25.9
FL.............	5,148	16.1	25.7	58.2	230,600	1,471	22.7	33.2	10.5	32.8
GA.............	2,426	20.8	32.2	47.0	189,900	1,395	29.5	35.5	9.4	24.9
HI.............	265	2.1	3.5	94.4	631,700	2,354	18.4	30.7	11.7	38.6
ID.............	453	11.8	28.6	59.7	233,100	1,249	26.7	35.4	11.8	25.5
IL.............	3,210	19.2	30.0	50.8	203,400	1,665	25.0	36.9	10.6	27.2
IN.............	1,792	29.2	40.4	30.5	147,300	1,118	35.0	36.4	8.4	19.8
IA.............	904	28.5	37.5	34.0	152,000	1,234	31.1	39.8	9.0	19.8
KS.............	750	29.4	33.7	36.9	159,400	1,364	28.5	39.7	10.0	21.5
KY.............	1,168	31.1	37.3	31.6	148,100	1,164	31.8	36.5	8.1	23.0
LA.............	1,138	26.4	34.8	38.9	167,300	1,254	30.9	33.7	8.9	25.8
ME.............	406	18.2	32.4	49.3	197,500	1,349	26.4	37.4	10.0	25.9
MD.............	1,483	6.2	14.8	79.0	324,800	1,955	24.4	37.7	10.7	27.0
MA.............	1,621	2.7	9.1	88.2	400,700	2,207	21.8	36.3	11.6	30.0
MI.............	2,817	27.3	34.7	38.0	162,500	1,270	31.0	36.8	9.2	22.6
MN.............	1,568	11.1	27.5	61.4	235,400	1,559	27.7	40.4	10.2	21.4
MS.............	756	41.1	33.5	25.4	123,300	1,132	29.6	35.8	9.0	24.9
MO.............	1,626	25.8	36.5	37.7	162,600	1,249	30.8	38.3	9.4	21.1
MT.............	291	13.9	22.5	63.6	249,200	1,413	23.3	35.5	11.6	29.4
NE.............	506	23.6	40.6	35.7	161,800	1,353	29.2	40.8	9.5	20.2
NV.............	642	7.3	15.2	77.6	292,200	1,528	23.7	35.2	10.4	30.0
NH.............	379	8.7	20.3	71.0	270,000	1,892	19.2	39.1	12.2	29.0
NJ.............	2,079	5.0	14.4	80.6	344,000	2,398	18.0	35.2	12.5	34.0
NM.............	525	23.5	34.5	42.0	174,700	1,234	25.7	33.3	10.8	29.2
NY.............	3,954	13.6	20.0	66.4	325,500	2,098	23.7	32.8	10.3	32.6
NC.............	2,613	22.2	33.3	44.4	180,600	1,284	29.7	35.7	9.3	24.7
ND.............	199	21.9	28.5	49.6	198,700	1,425	32.4	39.5	10.5	17.4
OH.............	3,086	28.3	39.0	32.7	151,100	1,248	31.9	36.9	9.3	21.6
OK.............	972	33.8	37.2	28.9	140,000	1,214	30.4	37.3	9.3	22.6
OR.............	1,025	8.0	11.4	80.6	341,800	1,690	20.4	36.8	11.6	30.9
PA.............	3,479	21.0	33.2	45.8	186,000	1,451	27.9	36.8	10.3	24.6
RI.............	251	4.5	18.4	77.1	273,800	1,830	18.7	36.8	11.5	32.8
SC.............	1,335	26.5	31.8	41.7	170,800	1,225	29.3	35.2	9.5	25.5
SD.............	234	24.4	34.5	41.1	171,500	1,301	26.5	40.4	10.8	22.0
TN.............	1,724	22.9	33.9	43.3	177,500	1,228	28.6	36.8	9.9	24.2
TX.............	6,034	23.2	30.6	46.2	186,000	1,603	25.1	36.9	10.3	27.2
UT.............	704	5.5	14.2	80.3	303,300	1,531	24.7	40.1	11.7	23.1
VT.............	189	10.4	29.7	59.9	233,100	1,560	19.6	38.6	11.5	29.9
VA.............	2,093	10.9	21.6	67.4	281,700	1,752	24.9	38.8	10.5	25.4
WA.............	1,819	6.0	11.0	83.0	373,100	1,883	21.6	36.9	12.2	29.0
WV.............	533	41.2	34.3	24.6	121,300	1,001	35.0	33.7	7.8	22.7
WI.............	1,592	16.2	37.6	46.2	188,500	1,387	27.2	39.9	10.2	22.5
WY.............	162	12.6	27.7	59.7	230,500	1,440	25.8	38.4	11.7	23.8

[1] For homes with a mortgage. Selected monthly owner costs are the sum of payments for mortgages, deeds of trust, contracts to purchase, or similar debts on the property (including payments for the first mortgage, second mortgages, home equity loans, and other junior mortgages); real estate taxes; fire, hazard, and flood insurance on the property; utilities; and fuels. It also includes, where appropriate, the monthly condominium fee for condominiums and mobile home costs.

Source: U.S. Census Bureau, 2018 American Community Survey, B25075, "Value"; B25077, "Median Value"; B25088, "Median Selected Monthly Owner Costs by Mortgage Status"; and B25091, "Mortgage Status by Selected Monthly Owner Cost as a Percentage of Household Income in the Past 12 Months"; <https://data.census.gov/>, accessed November 2019. See also <census.gov/programs-surveys/acs/>.

Table 1029. Renter-Occupied Housing Units—Gross Rent by State: 2018

[In percent, except as indicated (43,812 represents 43,812,000). The American Community Survey universe includes the household population, and excludes the population living in institutions, college dormitories, and other group quarters. For definition of median, see Guide to Tabular Presentation. Based on a sample and subject to sampling variability; see Appendix III]

State	Total [1] (1,000)	\$299 or less [2]	\$300 to \$499	\$500 to \$749	\$750 to \$999	\$1,000 or more	Median gross rent (dol.)	Less than 15.0 percent	15.0 to 24.9 percent	25.0 to 29.9 percent	30.0 percent or more
U.S.	**43,812**	**3.8**	**5.3**	**14.5**	**20.1**	**51.4**	**1,058**	**12.1**	**23.9**	**10.8**	**46.2**
AL.	593	6.1	10.0	24.3	24.9	23.8	788	13.6	21.0	10.2	41.1
AK.	87	1.4	3.9	7.2	20.3	58.4	1,177	14.4	24.9	12.1	39.0
AZ.	920	1.9	3.7	14.9	24.1	50.4	1,036	12.0	25.7	11.6	44.0
AR.	396	6.1	10.7	31.3	25.8	17.4	731	14.1	23.6	10.7	41.0
CA.	5,906	2.2	2.6	5.4	10.2	76.6	1,520	10.1	22.1	10.9	51.9
CO.	759	3.5	3.0	8.2	13.7	68.5	1,289	9.9	24.9	11.6	48.9
CT.	471	5.6	4.7	7.1	16.0	62.8	1,171	11.3	22.8	10.7	49.7
DE.	107	4.2	4.5	7.6	21.4	58.2	1,108	13.1	22.0	9.3	49.3
DC.	166	5.9	3.7	5.2	8.3	75.4	1,516	13.1	26.1	11.2	43.8
FL.	2,661	2.4	2.9	8.6	19.1	63.0	1,182	8.1	21.5	11.2	52.8
GA.	1,377	3.4	5.9	15.3	22.0	47.9	1,008	12.3	24.1	9.7	45.7
HI.	190	3.5	2.9	4.7	8.9	73.4	1,613	11.1	21.7	10.4	48.5
ID.	187	3.8	7.8	24.6	26.9	30.9	848	13.5	25.5	10.4	42.1
IL.	1,655	4.4	5.6	15.4	23.0	47.5	995	13.1	24.8	10.9	44.1
IN.	807	4.0	7.2	26.2	31.1	26.1	820	14.0	24.9	10.3	43.0
IA.	364	4.2	10.1	28.8	26.5	24.0	777	17.2	25.2	10.4	39.0
KS.	384	3.3	8.0	25.0	27.5	30.2	840	13.4	26.5	10.7	42.0
KY.	565	6.1	8.8	26.6	26.8	22.4	779	14.8	24.1	10.2	39.3
LA.	600	5.1	7.7	20.2	28.1	29.2	854	12.0	17.8	8.5	48.5
ME.	164	7.1	8.8	20.9	25.6	30.9	839	11.6	22.9	13.2	44.2
MD.	733	4.3	3.5	5.1	10.6	73.1	1,371	10.5	25.6	11.4	47.3
MA.	1,004	6.5	6.8	7.8	11.7	63.7	1,295	11.7	24.0	11.5	46.8
MI.	1,140	5.1	7.0	22.5	28.2	32.1	861	12.9	24.2	10.7	44.7
MN.	627	5.7	6.8	14.9	23.5	44.9	969	13.1	26.3	11.3	43.6
MS.	352	6.1	9.1	26.2	27.0	20.5	777	11.5	21.7	9.4	42.7
MO.	809	3.9	8.7	25.3	27.6	28.6	830	13.9	25.9	10.2	42.3
MT.	140	4.8	9.2	24.9	23.8	28.0	811	15.6	24.6	9.6	39.7
NE.	260	3.7	7.7	25.3	29.0	28.1	830	15.0	28.1	11.1	38.2
NV.	488	1.3	2.4	12.1	22.7	59.0	1,108	10.6	25.4	10.3	48.3
NH.	152	4.0	6.7	8.9	21.7	55.8	1,090	11.8	26.3	11.7	45.4
NJ.	1,171	4.4	3.2	4.5	11.1	74.1	1,336	12.0	23.7	11.1	48.6
NM.	269	5.2	8.2	23.2	23.3	30.4	830	12.3	23.0	9.3	43.4
NY.	3,413	4.9	5.6	9.7	13.3	63.2	1,274	12.9	22.2	10.3	49.1
NC.	1,399	3.6	6.3	21.3	25.0	37.4	900	13.3	24.0	10.5	43.8
ND.	120	3.7	8.0	27.2	29.2	26.6	808	19.5	27.6	9.5	35.4
OH.	1,599	5.4	8.0	28.0	27.6	25.9	797	14.8	25.7	11.1	41.2
OK.	513	4.0	7.6	27.1	27.6	25.2	808	15.2	25.9	9.3	39.0
OR.	615	3.3	3.8	11.4	19.0	58.7	1,130	10.9	24.8	12.0	46.9
PA.	1,592	4.8	6.7	18.2	24.3	40.4	927	13.5	24.2	10.3	44.2
RI.	155	9.7	6.3	10.2	22.3	48.0	998	12.0	25.1	12.7	44.3
SC.	593	4.0	6.5	20.2	24.9	35.2	892	11.8	23.1	10.4	43.2
SD.	111	5.3	12.2	30.9	24.7	19.2	734	16.8	25.6	10.9	37.1
TN.	879	4.9	7.6	22.1	25.4	32.9	861	12.3	23.1	11.0	44.1
TX.	3,742	2.6	3.8	13.1	24.1	51.3	1,046	12.0	24.4	11.1	45.2
UT.	295	2.6	4.2	13.5	24.1	51.5	1,043	12.7	28.6	11.3	41.9
VT.	73	4.5	8.0	13.9	23.7	44.3	969	10.0	26.3	13.1	43.2
VA.	1,082	3.3	4.0	10.0	16.7	61.1	1,215	11.5	25.5	11.0	45.2
WA.	1,077	2.7	3.3	8.6	14.1	67.3	1,316	11.1	26.5	11.8	45.3
WV.	202	6.4	11.4	26.2	23.7	16.1	735	12.8	18.5	9.7	39.9
WI.	780	3.6	6.4	25.1	30.7	30.2	847	15.3	27.2	10.7	41.0
WY.	68	5.5	7.1	24.4	26.6	27.7	818	17.9	24.5	9.9	37.2

[1] Includes units with no cash rent. [2] Includes only units with cash rent. [3] Percent distribution of rental units by gross rent as a percent of household income. Percentage calculated from totals which include units "not computed"; therefore, rows will not total 100 percent.

Source: U.S. Census Bureau, 2018 American Community Survey, B25063, "Gross Rent"; B25064, "Median Gross Rent"; and B25070, "Gross Rent as a Percentage of Household Income in Past 12 Months"; <https://data.census.gov/>, accessed November 2019.

Table 1030. Mortgage Characteristics—Owner-Occupied Units: 2017

[In thousands (77,570 represents 77,570,000). As of Fall. Based on the American Housing Survey; see Appendix III]

Mortgage characteristic	Total owner occupied units	Housing unit characteristics		Household characteristics			
		New construc-tion [1]	Mobile homes	Black [2]	His-panic [3]	Elderly [4]	Below poverty level [5]
ALL OWNERS							
Total.................................	**77,570**	**621**	**4,969**	**7,131**	**7,763**	**23,983**	**6,722**
Mortgages currently on property:							
None, owned free and clear......................	31,380	(S)	(S)	(S)	2,868	(S)	4,279
Reverse mortgage.............................	351	(S)	(S)	(S)	20	(S)	43
Regular or home equity lump sum mortgage(s) [6]...	42,000	(S)	(S)	(S)	4,692	(S)	2,245
1 regular/lump sum mortgage......................	40,100	(S)	(S)	(S)	4,488	(S)	2,177
2 or more regular/lump sum mortgages...........	1,898	(S)	(S)	(S)	203	(S)	67
Regular/home equity lump sum mortgage(s) and home equity line(s) of credit..................	2,246	(S)	(S)	(S)	95	(S)	67
Home equity line(s) of credit.......................	1,593	(S)	(S)	(S)	87	(S)	88
Type of loan: [7, 8]							
Primary regular mortgage [6]....................	44,240	476	1,309	4,266	4,787	7,635	2,312
Secondary regular mortgage [6]....................	1,975	16	8	(S)	213	296	72
Home equity line of credit.......................	3,881	11	44	197	191	1,200	156
OWNERS WITH ONE OR MORE REGULAR OR LUMP SUM HOME EQUITY MORTGAGES							
Total.................................	**44,240**	**476**	**1,309**	**4,266**	**4,787**	**7,635**	**2,312**
Mortgage origination:							
Placed new mortgage(s).........................	43,530	(S)	(S)	(S)	4,622	(S)	(S)
Primary obtained when property acquired.........	26,190	(S)	(S)	(S)	3,238	(S)	(S)
Obtained later................................	17,340	(S)	(S)	(S)	1,384	(S)	(S)
Assumed....................................	287	(S)	(S)	(S)	79	(S)	(S)
Wrap-around.................................	43	(S)	(S)	(S)	19	(S)	(S)
Not reported.................................	373	(S)	(S)	(S)	67	(S)	(S)
Payment plan of primary mortgage:							
Fixed payment, self amortizing.....................	41,710	(S)	(S)	(S)	(S)	(S)	(S)
Payment option..............................	61	(S)	(S)	(S)	(S)	(S)	(S)
Interest only.................................	122	(S)	(S)	(S)	(S)	(S)	(S)
Balloon.....................................	76	(S)	(S)	(S)	(S)	(S)	(S)
Graduated payment mortgage......................	255	(S)	(S)	(S)	(S)	(S)	(S)
Adjustable rate mortgage......................	1,234	(S)	(S)	(S)	(S)	(S)	(S)
Other......................................	573	(S)	(S)	(S)	(S)	(S)	(S)
Interest only adjustable rate......................	13	(S)	(S)	(S)	(S)	(S)	(S)
Not reported.................................	196	(S)	(S)	(S)	(S)	(S)	(S)
Type of mortgage insurance:							
FHA [9]......................................	10,160	(S)	(S)	(S)	1,685	1,309	589
VA...	2,793	(S)	(S)	(S)	283	544	107
RHS/RD [10]..................................	608	(S)	(S)	(S)	60	42	37
Other types.................................	29,040	(S)	(S)	(S)	2,510	5,380	1,435
Not reported.................................	1,634	(S)	(S)	(S)	249	360	144
Reason primary refinanced:							
Units with a refinanced primary mortgage [6].........	14,960	24	212	1,070	1,167	3,076	554
To get a lower interest rate......................	10,100	14	(S)	652	688	1,941	320
To reduce monthly payment......................	3,672	(S)	(S)	312	404	(S)	127
To reduce payment period......................	2,486	(S)	(S)	114	181	(S)	58
To increase payment period......................	432	–	(S)	(S)	42	(S)	15
To receive cash..............................	1,911	–	(S)	(S)	188	(S)	85
To suspend or temporarily reduce payments......	323	–	(S)	(S)	37	95	17
Other reason.................................	1,679	(S)	(S)	114	121	350	62
Cash received in primary mortgage refinance:							
Units receiving refinance cash......................	1,911	–	(S)	(S)	188	(S)	85
Median amount received (dol.)......................	30,000	–	(S)	30,000	30,000	(NA)	(NA)

– Represents or rounds to zero. S Represents estimates that did not meet publication standards. NA Not available. [1] Constructed in the 2016-2017 period. [2] For persons who selected this race group only. [3] Persons of Hispanic origin may be of any race. [4] Householders age 65 years old and over. [5] Those households below the poverty threshold based on household income of families or of individuals living without relatives. Income in the AHS refers to money income in the 12 months before the survey. The threshold is updated every year to reflect changes in the Consumer Price Index. See source for more information. [6] Regular mortgages include all mortgages not classified as home-equity line of credit or reverse. [7] Figures may not add to total because more than one category may apply to a unit. [8] A household can have more than one secondary and/or home-equity credit line. [9] Federal Housing Administration. [10] Rural Housing Service/Rural Development.

Source: U.S. Census Bureau, "American Housing Survey: AHS Table Creator," <census.gov/programs-surveys/ahs/data.html>, accessed February 2019.

Table 1031. Home Purchase Loans by Race/Ethnicity and Sex: 2017

[Amount in millions of dollars (1,156,592 represents $1,156,592,000,000). Includes applications for conventional home-purchase loans 1- to 4- family and manufactured home dwellings. Applicants are only shown in one race and one gender category]

Race/ethnicity and gender	Applications received		Loans originated		Applications approved, not accepted		Applications denied		Applications withdrawn		Files closed for incompleteness	
	Number	Amount (million dollars)	Number	Amount (million dollars)	Number	Amount (million dollars)	Number	Amount (million dollars)	Number	Amount (million dollars)	Number	Amount (million dollars)
Total [1, 2]	**4,141,715**	**1,156,592**	**2,902,072**	**834,108**	**135,283**	**37,607**	**483,643**	**112,339**	**482,130**	**143,668**	**138,587**	**28,870**
White	2,955,150	772,314	2,136,259	575,204	97,242	25,247	305,618	62,909	327,590	91,753	88,441	17,201
Male	992,040	254,573	702,080	184,312	32,539	7,895	112,714	24,832	112,465	31,219	32,242	6,315
Female	653,481	132,927	458,421	97,748	21,420	4,339	79,763	11,980	73,348	15,785	20,529	3,075
Joint (male/female)	1,300,441	382,557	970,187	291,675	43,012	12,948	111,560	25,818	140,484	44,384	35,198	7,732
Black	190,552	36,850	101,772	22,691	6,461	1,124	48,201	6,294	22,336	5,224	11,782	1,518
Male	66,310	13,422	36,794	8,268	2,350	430	15,141	2,137	8,272	2,081	3,753	504
Female	81,854	13,990	43,051	8,505	2,667	400	21,912	2,605	9,399	1,963	4,825	517
Joint (male/female)	40,495	9,171	21,397	5,802	1,394	288	10,261	1,459	4,501	1,148	2,942	474
Hispanic or Latino	318,213	66,930	197,129	45,305	11,201	2,038	55,609	9,080	38,026	8,143	16,248	2,365
Male	144,311	29,783	90,107	19,745	5,077	937	24,610	4,268	17,336	3,757	7,181	1,075
Female	82,185	15,417	50,187	10,249	2,760	445	15,435	2,338	10,044	1,876	3,759	509
Joint (male/female)	90,047	20,639	56,167	14,344	3,311	647	15,003	2,413	10,437	2,471	5,129	763
Asian	313,472	123,015	223,906	86,390	10,428	4,192	27,946	12,577	41,913	16,396	9,279	3,461
Male	137,116	53,109	97,544	36,437	4,523	1,745	11,881	6,344	18,913	7,039	4,255	1,543
Female	68,311	21,514	48,662	15,349	2,261	737	6,612	1,973	8,764	2,827	2,012	628
Joint (male/female)	106,976	47,971	77,031	34,336	3,611	1,696	9,338	4,216	14,043	6,452	2,953	1,271
Native Hawaiian/Other Pacific Islander	10,410	3,106	6,910	2,259	356	89	1,385	294	1,383	379	376	84
Male	4,629	1,524	3,033	1,145	158	41	627	132	639	168	172	39
Female	2,938	677	1,915	465	113	24	418	76	379	89	113	23
Joint (male/female)	2,770	888	1,925	639	84	25	322	84	352	119	87	22
American Indian/Alaska Native	17,711	3,193	8,960	1,897	574	101	4,748	521	1,977	527	1,452	146
Male	7,887	1,428	4,217	887	247	43	1,892	227	931	207	600	63
Female	6,045	1,008	2,960	550	202	34	1,756	163	680	221	447	40
Joint (male/female)	3,411	698	1,633	429	123	24	966	117	329	89	360	37
Two or more minority races	3,302	855	1,941	558	92	24	610	109	511	138	148	25
Male	1,361	359	799	222	37	10	229	50	235	65	61	12
Female	1,262	265	704	171	36	7	268	35	197	44	57	8
Joint (male/female)	651	225	424	162	19	6	105	24	73	28	30	5
Joint [3]	72,441	25,644	51,047	18,565	2,210	763	7,669	2,496	9,078	3,241	2,437	580
Race not available [4]	435,652	146,389	267,817	93,399	13,911	4,488	67,321	22,143	64,713	21,428	21,890	4,931
Male	69,327	20,884	40,653	12,519	2,390	726	12,471	3,949	9,469	2,897	4,344	793
Female	41,895	10,053	24,256	6,137	1,237	289	8,184	1,854	5,890	1,423	2,323	350
Joint (male/female)	75,863	26,000	48,664	17,693	2,429	880	10,186	2,956	10,342	3,597	4,242	874

[1] Total includes those cases in which gender was reported and in those in which gender information was not reported and in those in which gender information was not available. [2] Includes all loans from other race/ethnicities not shown separately. [3] "Joint" means with two applicants, one reported a single designation of "White" and the other applicant reported one or more minority racial designations. [4] "Not available" includes situations in which information was reported as not provided or not applicable.

Source: Bureau of Consumer Financial Protection, Federal Financial Institutions Examination Council, "Home Mortgage Disclosure Act: National Aggregate Reports," <fliec.cfpb.gov/>, accessed August 2019.

Table 1032. Heating Equipment and Fuels for Occupied Units: 2005 to 2017

[108,871 represents 108,871,000. As of Fall. Data for 2005 to 2009 based on population controls from Census 2000. Beginning 2011, data based on Census 2010 controls. Based on American Housing Survey. See Appendix III]

Type of equipment or fuel	Number (1,000)					Percent distribution	
	2005	2011	2013	2015	2017	2015	2017
Occupied units, total.................................	**108,871**	**114,907**	**115,852**	**118,290**	**121,600**	**100.0**	**100.0**
Heating equipment:							
Warm air furnace..	68,275	73,687	74,712	76,207	79,380	64.4	65.3
Steam or hot water.......................................	12,880	12,624	12,448	10,919	11,100	9.2	9.1
Heat pumps...	12,484	13,523	13,526	13,980	14,130	11.8	11.6
Built-in electric units....................................	4,699	4,865	5,064	4,616	4,925	3.9	4.1
Floor, wall, or pipeless furnace.....................	5,102	4,505	4,571	5,963	5,616	5.0	4.6
Room heaters with flue.................................	1,294	932	851	776	740	0.7	0.6
Room heaters without flue............................	1,327	1,094	1,034	647	749	0.5	0.6
Fireplaces, stoves, portable heaters or other.............	2,411	3,208	3,260	4,362	4,076	3.7	3.4
None...	399	468	386	818	848	0.7	0.7
House main heating fuel:							
Electricity...	34,263	40,385	42,041	48,323	52,330	40.9	43.0
Utility gas..	56,317	57,721	58,225	54,791	54,090	46.3	44.5
Bottled, tank, or liquid propane gas...............	6,228	5,415	5,198	4,703	5,074	4.0	4.2
Fuel oil, kerosene, etc..................................	9,929	8,599	7,623	6,654	6,421	5.6	5.3
Coal or coke...	95	79	98	80	89	0.1	0.1
Wood and other fuel.....................................	1,640	2,240	2,280	2,921	2,335	2.5	1.9
None...	398	468	387	818	372	0.7	0.3
Cooking fuel:							
Electricity...	65,297	68,879	69,330	71,262	72,870	60.2	59.9
Gas [1]..	43,316	45,759	46,294	46,386	48,217	39.2	39.7
Other fuel..	51	92	71	200	92	0.2	0.1
None...	206	177	158	441	21	0.4	(Z)

Z Less than 0.05 percent. [1] Includes utility, bottled, tank, and liquid propane gas.

Source: U.S. Census Bureau, "American Housing Survey: AHS Table Creator," <census.gov/programs-surveys/ahs/data.html>, accessed February 2019.

Table 1033. Occupied Housing Units—Housing Amenities and Deficiencies by Selected Characteristics of the Householder: 2017

[In thousands of units (121,600 represents 121,600,000). As of Fall. Based on the American Housing Survey; see Appendix III]

Characteristic	Total occu- pied units	Tenure		Black [1]		Hispanic origin [2]		Elderly [3]		Households below poverty level [4]	
		Owner	Renter	Owner	Renter	Owner	Renter	Owner	Renter	Owner	Renter
Total units........................	**121,600**	**77,570**	**43,990**	**7,131**	**9,421**	**7,763**	**8,733**	**23,983**	**6,686**	**6,722**	**10,293**
Selected amenities:											
Porch, deck, balcony or patio.........	103,700	71,990	31,720	6,277	6,389	6,890	5,862	22,337	4,291	5,966	6,758
Usable fireplace.........................	44,530	38,050	6,482	2,952	1,078	2,760	1,076	11,307	808	2,136	839
Separate dining room...................	59,190	44,900	14,290	4,582	3,362	4,374	3,035	13,896	1,808	3,428	2,974
With 2 or more living rooms or recreation rooms.....................	39,870	35,280	4,594	2,773	741	2,331	623	10,755	610	1,862	618
Garage or carport with home.........	79,840	62,550	17,290	4,893	2,627	5,829	3,484	19,723	2,322	4,571	2,741
Selected deficiencies:											
Signs of mice or rats in last 12 months...................................	15,620	10,260	5,355	914	1,291	728	1,176	3,140	640	987	1,572
Signs of cockroaches in last 12 months...................................	15,300	7,424	7,877	1,092	2,134	1,358	2,342	2,219	904	913	2,305
Holes in floors............................	1,449	654	794	95	201	89	168	179	57	133	254
Open cracks or holes (interior).......	6,600	3,518	3,082	467	790	424	608	909	210	511	968
Broken/peeling paint or plaster (interior)..................................	2,525	1,253	1,272	185	292	165	308	353	104	193	393
No electrical wiring......................	119	76	42	–	3	10	17	10	3	29	32
Exposed wiring...........................	3,267	1,833	1,434	216	311	249	355	631	208	251	390
Rooms without electric outlet.........	2,094	1,091	1,003	131	292	129	193	337	117	199	305
Water leakage from inside structure [5].....................	9,952	5,252	4,699	571	1,148	499	822	1,241	499	427	1,161
Water leakage from outside structure [5]....................	12,320	8,146	4,176	840	920	767	730	2,250	436	745	1,030
Sagging roof [6].........................	1,739	1,256	483	174	67	170	80	338	69	228	171
Missing roof material [6]...............	3,326	2,547	779	378	165	330	109	690	81	334	262
Hole in roof [6]..........................	1,352	921	431	188	102	190	84	252	45	157	168
Missing bricks, siding, or other outside wall material [5]...............	2,556	1,826	730	262	153	229	102	437	65	270	254
Boarded up windows [6]...............	1,061	733	328	81	55	126	74	196	12	149	113
Broken windows [6].....................	3,913	2,799	1,113	332	227	363	191	643	88	386	360
Foundation crumbling or has open crack or hole [6]........................	4,969	3,605	1,364	400	280	411	218	1,029	141	509	383
Units with mold in the last 12 months...................................	3,775	1,721	2,054	220	509	234	482	401	168	272	654

– Represents or rounds to zero. [1] For persons who selected this race group only. [2] Persons of Hispanic origin may be of any race. [3] Householders 65 years old and over. [4] Based on household income of families or of individuals living without relatives. Refers to money income in the 12 months before the survey. Threshold reflects changes in the Consumer Price Index, see source for more information. [5] During the 12 months prior to the survey. [6] Excludes multiunit structures.

Source: U.S. Census Bureau, "American Housing Survey: AHS Table Creator," <census.gov/programs-surveys/ahs/data.html>, accessed February 2019.

Table 1034. Household Energy Consumption and Expenditures by Selected Characteristics: 2015

[118.2 represents 118,200,000. Btu=British thermal units; for definition, see text, Section 19. Includes all primary occupied housing units in the 50 states and the District of Columbia. Vacant housing units, seasonal units, second homes, military houses, and group quarters are excluded. Consumption and expenditures for biomass (wood), coal, district steam, and solar thermal are excluded. Electricity consumption from on-site solar photovoltaic generation (i.e., solar panels) is included. Data from the Residential Energy Consumption Survey (RECS). Data were collected between August 2015 and April 2016]

Characteristic	Total housing units (millions)	Energy consumption				Energy expenditures			
		Total (trillion Btu)	Per household (million Btu)	Per household member (million Btu)	Per square foot (thousand Btu)	Total (billion dollars)	Per household (dollars)	Per household member (dollars)	Per square foot (dollars)
All homes.................	**118.2**	**9,114**	**77.1**	**30.3**	**38.4**	**219.3**	**1,856**	**728**	**0.92**
Region:									
Northeast.................	21.0	1,984	94.4	38.1	45.2	47.7	2,269	915	1.09
Midwest...................	26.4	2,486	94.3	37.8	41.4	46.4	1,760	706	0.77
South......................	44.4	3,064	68.9	27.3	35.6	85.2	1,917	758	0.99
West.......................	26.4	1,581	59.9	22.3	33.4	40.1	1,518	565	0.85
Housing unit type:									
Single-family detached..........	73.9	6,991	94.6	34.6	37.1	161.7	2,188	801	0.86
Single-family attached...........	7.0	491	70.0	28.6	39.5	11.2	1,602	655	0.90
Apartment buildings with 2-4 units.....................	9.4	503	53.5	22.3	52.5	12.5	1,329	555	1.30
Apartment buildings with 5 or more units.................	21.1	724	34.2	17.3	38.8	22.1	1,045	529	1.18
Mobile homes....................	6.8	406	59.8	22.8	50.0	11.9	1,750	666	1.46
Housing tenure:									
Owned...........................	74.5	6,825	91.6	35.4	37.1	159.9	2,146	829	0.87
Single-family...................	66.2	6,347	95.9	36.5	36.5	146.2	2,208	840	0.84
Apartments....................	3.3	175	52.4	26.6	45.5	4.9	1,476	748	1.28
Mobile homes..................	5.0	304	61.1	24.6	49.9	8.8	1,768	712	1.44
Rented [1]........................	43.7	2,289	52.4	21.2	42.7	59.4	1,360	550	1.11
Single-family...................	14.7	1,135	77.4	25.3	41.8	26.7	1,818	594	0.98
Apartments....................	27.2	1,052	38.7	18.2	43.1	29.7	1,090	514	1.22
Mobile homes..................	1.8	103	56.3	18.7	50.2	3.1	1,702	565	1.52
Year of construction:									
Before 1950....................	20.8	1,842	88.7	35.5	44.1	39.5	1,901	762	0.94
1950 to 1959...................	12.6	1,067	84.4	34.5	45.2	23.5	1,861	760	1.00
1960 to 1969...................	12.8	961	75.0	32.0	40.0	22.5	1,756	750	0.94
1970 to 1979...................	18.3	1,290	70.3	27.9	39.8	32.4	1,765	700	1.00
1980 to 1989...................	16.0	1,053	65.7	27.3	35.9	28.0	1,747	725	0.95
1990 to 1999...................	16.8	1,317	78.3	29.1	35.9	32.6	1,937	719	0.89
2000 to 2009...................	17.0	1,328	78.2	28.0	32.7	34.2	2,013	721	0.84
2010 to 2015...................	3.8	257	67.0	23.9	28.5	6.7	1,755	626	0.75
Total square footage: [2]									
Fewer than 1,000...............	26.6	1,072	40.3	19.9	53.8	29.9	1,126	554	1.50
1,000 to 1,499.................	26.1	1,542	59.0	23.2	48.2	41.0	1,569	618	1.28
1,500 to 1,999.................	17.5	1,359	77.8	30.4	44.6	33.5	1,919	750	1.10
2,000 to 2,499.................	14.1	1,268	89.8	32.7	40.3	29.5	2,088	759	0.94
2,500 to 2,999.................	10.8	1,111	102.9	38.5	37.7	24.7	2,282	854	0.84
3,000 or greater...............	23.1	2,762	119.6	40.4	29.4	60.8	2,631	888	0.65
Number of household members:									
1 member......................	28.7	1,591	55.3	55.3	36.6	37.9	1,319	1,319	0.87
2 members.....................	42.7	3,229	75.6	37.8	36.6	79.0	1,849	924	0.90
3 members.....................	19.4	1,643	84.6	28.2	39.9	39.0	2,009	670	0.95
4 members.....................	15.5	1,472	94.9	23.7	40.2	35.3	2,274	569	0.96
5 members.....................	7.2	698	97.1	19.4	42.2	16.8	2,338	468	1.02
6 or more members.............	4.6	481	103.8	15.7	42.0	11.4	2,457	371	0.99
Annual household income:									
Less than $20,000..............	22.9	1,303	57.0	25.9	43.1	32.5	1,421	645	1.08
$20,000 to $39,999.............	27.3	1,882	68.9	29.3	40.7	44.5	1,629	692	0.96
$40,000 to $59,999.............	18.4	1,354	73.6	29.9	38.7	32.7	1,778	723	0.93
$60,000 to $79,999.............	15.2	1,218	80.0	29.9	37.0	29.6	1,940	725	0.90
$80,000 to $99,999.............	9.7	827	85.4	31.5	37.4	19.5	2,014	741	0.88
$100,000 to $119,999...........	8.1	733	90.4	30.6	34.2	17.7	2,187	739	0.83
$120,000 to $139,999...........	5.4	552	101.7	33.7	37.1	13.0	2,396	794	0.87
$140,000 or more...............	11.2	1,244	111.2	36.8	36.0	29.9	2,669	884	0.86
Main heating fuel									
Natural gas.....................	57.7	5,517	95.7	37.0	43.1	108.1	1,875	726	0.84
Electricity......................	40.9	2,096	51.2	20.6	30.5	68.4	1,672	672	1.00
Fuel oil/kerosene...............	5.8	645	111.2	43.6	47.9	16.9	2,919	1,144	1.26
Propane........................	5.0	468	93.4	37.6	37.4	13.3	2,645	1,066	1.06

[1] Rented includes households that occupy their primary housing units without paying rent. [2] Total square footage includes all basements, finished or conditioned (heated or cooled) areas of attics, and conditioned garage space that is attached to the home. Unconditioned and unfinished areas in attics and attached garages are excluded.

Source: U.S. Energy Information Administration, 2015 RECS Survey Data, "Consumption & Energy Expenditures (C&E) Tables," <eia.gov/consumption/residential/index.php>, accessed May 2019.

Table 1035. Household Energy Insecurity By Selected Characteristics: 2015

[In percent, except total units (118.2 represents 118,200,000). Data are from the Residential Energy Consumption Survey (RECS). Energy insecurity defined in this table includes only those issues collected as part of the RECS questionnaire. Other factors, such as energy costs as a percentage of household income, could be considered as household energy insecurity, but are not included here. Respondents may report more than one energy insecurity issue. Data were collected between August 2015 and April 2016. Includes all primary occupied housing units in the 50 states and the District of Columbia. Vacant housing units, seasonal units, second homes, military houses, and group quarters are excluded. For composition of regions, see map inside front cover]

Characteristic	Total housing units (millions)	Percent of households reporting:					
		Any household energy insecurity	Reducing or forgoing food or medicine to pay energy costs	Leaving home at unhealthy temperature	Receiving disconnect or delivery stop notice	Unable to use heating equipment [1]	Unable to use cooling equipment [1]
All homes	**118.2**	**31.3**	**21.4**	**10.8**	**14.6**	**5.2**	**5.8**
Region:							
Northeast	21.0	29.5	19.0	11.9	12.9	6.7	2.9
Midwest	26.4	28.0	18.9	8.3	14.4	4.2	4.2
South	44.4	34.7	24.3	11.3	16.9	6.3	8.8
West	26.4	30.7	20.8	11.7	12.1	3.0	4.9
Housing unit type:							
Single-family detached	73.9	27.1	18.1	8.4	12.9	4.3	5.3
Single-family attached	7.0	34.3	22.9	14.3	15.7	5.7	5.7
Apartment buildings with 2–4 units	9.4	45.7	33.0	18.1	20.2	8.5	5.3
Apartment buildings with 5 or more units	21.1	30.8	21.3	11.4	12.3	2.8	4.3
Mobile homes	6.8	55.9	41.2	23.5	30.9	16.2	16.2
Number of household members:							
1 member	28.7	29.3	18.8	12.9	11.8	4.5	4.5
2 members	42.7	23.9	16.6	8.4	9.6	3.0	4.7
3 members	19.4	35.6	25.3	11.3	16.0	6.2	7.2
4 members	15.5	38.7	28.4	11.0	21.3	7.7	7.1
5 members	7.2	45.8	30.6	12.5	25.0	8.3	8.3
6 or more members	4.6	50.0	28.3	15.2	32.6	13.0	13.0
Annual household income:							
Less than $20,000	22.9	49.8	38.4	20.1	23.1	10.5	10.0
$20,000 to $39,999	27.3	40.3	29.3	13.9	19.8	7.0	8.1
$40,000 to $59,999	18.4	34.2	22.8	10.3	15.8	5.4	5.4
$60,000 to $79,999	15.2	25.7	14.5	7.2	11.8	3.3	5.3
$80,000 to $99,999	9.7	18.6	8.2	4.1	8.2	1.0	2.1
$100,000 to $119,999	8.1	12.3	7.4	3.7	4.9	1.2	1.2
$120,000 to $139,999	5.4	13.0	7.4	5.6	5.6	(S)	(S)
$140,000 or more	11.2	8.0	2.7	2.7	3.6	0.9	1.8
Householder age 60 or older: [2]							
Yes	39.0	20.3	13.1	8.5	6.4	2.3	3.8
No	76.7	36.9	25.7	12.0	18.6	6.4	6.6
Children under age 18 in household:							
Yes	37.7	41.4	28.9	11.7	23.1	7.4	7.7
No	80.5	26.6	18.0	10.4	10.6	4.2	5.0
Ethnicity of householder: [2]							
Hispanic or Latino	15.0	45.3	32.0	16.7	18.7	7.3	8.7
Not Hispanic or Latino	103.2	29.3	20.0	10.0	14.0	4.8	5.3
Race of householder: [2,3]							
White	95.4	28.1	19.1	10.1	12.6	4.4	5.1
Hispanic or Latino	13.8	44.2	30.4	15.9	18.8	6.5	8.7
Not Hispanic or Latino	81.6	25.4	17.2	8.9	11.6	3.9	4.5
Black or African American	13.6	52.2	36.0	16.9	27.9	10.3	10.3
Hispanic or Latino	0.5	60.0	60.0	(S)	(S)	(S)	(S)
Not Hispanic or Latino	13.1	51.9	35.9	16.8	28.2	10.7	10.7
Asian	4.9	20.4	16.3	6.1	4.1	4.1	2.0
American Indian or Alaska Native	1.3	53.8	38.5	(S)	38.5	7.7	15.4
Native Hawaiian or Other Pacific Islander	0.4	75.0	(S)	(S)	(S)	(S)	(S)
More than one race	2.5	44.0	28.0	16.0	24.0	8.0	12.0
Housing tenure: [4]							
Owned	74.5	24.2	15.6	8.1	10.1	4.4	5.1
Rented	43.7	43.5	31.4	15.6	22.2	6.4	6.9

S Data withheld because either the relative standard error was greater than 50% or fewer than 10 cases responded. [1] Includes inability to use equipment because equipment was broken and household could not have it repaired; or electricity, natural gas, or bulk fuel disruption due to lack of payment. [2] A householder is a person in whose name the home is owned or rented. These characteristics refer to the householder that completed the RECS questionnaire. [3] Householders were permitted to select more than one racial category to describe themselves. These householders are only included as "more than one race." [4] Rented includes households that occupy their primary housing units without paying rent.

Source: U.S. Energy Information Administration, 2015 RECS Survey Data, "Housing Characteristics Tables," <eia.gov/consumption/residential/index.php>, accessed May 2019.

Table 1036. Home Remodeling—Number of Households With Work Done by Amount Spent: 2019

[In thousands (2,538 represents 2,538,000), except percent. As of Fall 2019. For work done in the prior 12 months. Based on a household survey and subject to sampling error; see source]

Remodeling project	Total households with work done [1]		Households with work done by outside contractor	Number of households by amount spent		
	Number	Percent of households		Under $1,000	$1,000 to $2,999	Over $3,000
Conversion of garage/attic/basement into living space..............	2,538	1.01	511	423	293	849
Remodel bathroom........................	15,440	6.17	5,099	4,903	2,881	4,446
Remodel kitchen...........................	10,061	4.02	3,384	2,079	1,768	3,929
Remodel bedroom.........................	7,505	3.00	1,455	3,160	891	1,048
Convert room to home office............	3,181	1.27	254	1,789	289	385
Convert room to home theater........	530	0.21	7	251	48	45
Remodel other rooms.....................	6,283	2.51	1,518	2,220	976	1,262
Add bathroom..............................	1,401	0.56	430	193	114	612
Add/extend garage.......................	674	0.27	163	71	34	251
Add other rooms - exterior addition.............	969	0.39	239	8	148	440
Add deck/porch/patio....................	5,526	2.21	1,885	1,461	1,266	1,891
Roofing......................................	9,565	3.82	6,650	1,072	1,495	5,668
Siding - vinyl/metal......................	2,241	0.90	1,205	305	227	1,102
Aluminum windows........................	1,212	0.48	490	83	166	379
Clad-wood/wood windows...............	1,107	0.44	427	188	187	348
Vinyl windows.............................	4,133	1.65	2,363	736	701	1,678
Ceramic tile floors.......................	3,776	1.51	1,450	1,173	763	761
Hardwood floors..........................	5,132	2.05	1,939	1,348	857	1,687
Laminate flooring.........................	5,662	2.26	2,116	1,951	1,445	956
Vinyl flooring..............................	4,402	1.76	1,349	2,016	744	666
Carpeting...................................	6,822	2.73	3,954	1,600	2,350	1,231
Kitchen cabinets..........................	4,838	1.93	1,796	1,018	687	1,527
Kitchen counter tops.....................	5,061	2.02	2,569	1,305	1,235	1,462
Skylights....................................	1,160	0.46	519	302	313	111
Exterior doors.............................	4,972	1.99	2,114	2,338	649	877
Interior doors..............................	3,675	1.47	995	1,815	514	352
Garage doors..............................	3,384	1.35	1,798	1,158	882	304
Concrete or masonry work..............	3,854	1.54	1,953	1,378	541	1,346
Swimming pool - in ground..............	1,013	0.40	433	78	26	356
Ceramic wall tile..........................	2,457	0.98	856	901	260	402

[1] Includes no response and amount unknown.

Source: MRI Survey of the American Consumer. © Courtesy of MRI-Simmons. See also <https://www.mrisimmons.com/>.

Table 1037. Home Improvement Loans by Race/Ethnicity: 2017

[Applications in thousands (1,051.1 represents 1,051,100); values in millions of dollars (351,534.4 represents $351,534,400,000). Includes applications for home improvement loans, 1- to 4- family and manufactured home dwellings. Applicants are categorized by the race of the first person listed on the application unless the 'joint' designation applies]

Item	Unit	Total [1,2]	White, total [1]	Black, total [1]	Asian, total [1]	Joint, total [3]	Hispanic or Latino [4]
Applications received:							
Number...	1,000	1,051.1	729.7	95.9	30.3	14.5	107.1
Amount...	Mil. dol.	351,534.4	296,379.7	9,269.3	6,366.3	2,143.5	15,153.7
Loans originated:							
Number...	1,000	547.0	413.1	34.2	14.4	8.2	42.8
Amount...	Mil. dol.	166,897.4	144,296.1	5,250.0	3,298.7	1,289.0	7,719.7
Applications approved but not accepted:							
Number...	1,000	33.9	23.7	2.1	1.1	0.4	4.0
Amount...	Mil. dol.	7,888.9	6,613.7	177.8	221.8	56.2	329.3
Applications denied:							
Number...	1,000	347.4	210.7	51.4	10.1	4.1	48.6
Amount...	Mil. dol.	40,897.6	28,617.2	2,280.5	1,239.7	420.4	4,049.5
Applications withdrawn:							
Number...	1,000	91.1	61.8	5.8	3.4	1.4	8.2
Amount...	Mil. dol.	130,036.3	113,093.5	1,258.8	1,279.1	282.5	2,251.6
Files closed for incompleteness:							
Number...	1,000	31.6	20.4	2.4	1.4	0.4	3.4
Amount...	Mil. dol.	5,814.1	3,759.2	302.1	327.0	95.5	803.6

[1] Applicants are shown in only one race category. [2] Total includes other races, not shown separately. [3] Joint means one applicant on an application reports a single designation of "White" and the other applicant reports one or more minority racial designations. [4] Persons of Hispanic origin may be of any race.

Source: Bureau of Consumer Financial Protection, Federal Financial Institutions Examination Council, "Home Mortgage Disclosure Act: National Aggregate Reports," <ffiec.cfpb.gov/>, accessed August 2019.

Table 1038. Commercial Buildings—Summary: 2012

[5,557 represents 5,557,000. Includes mall buildings. Building type based on predominant activity in which the occupants were engaged. Based on the Commercial Buildings Energy Consumption Survey (CBECS), a sample survey of building representatives conducted in 2012; subject to sampling variability]

Characteristic	All buildings (1,000)	Total floor-space (mil. sq. ft.)	Total workers in all buildings (1,000)	Mean square foot per building [1] (1,000)	Mean square foot per worker [1]	Mean operating hours per week [1]
All buildings	**5,557**	**87,043**	**88,182**	**15.7**	**987**	**62**
Building floorspace (sq. ft.):						
1,001 to 5,000	2,777	8,036	10,232	2.9	785	56
5,001 to 10,000	1,231	8,910	9,231	7.2	965	62
10,001 to 25,000	882	14,083	14,183	16.0	993	65
25,001 to 50,000	332	11,917	11,327	35.9	1,052	72
50,001 to 100,000	199	13,938	12,354	69.9	1,128	80
100,001 to 200,000	90	12,415	11,310	137.9	1,098	89
200,001 to 500,000	38	10,670	10,347	284.3	1,031	100
Over 500,000	8	7,074	9,196	885.0	769	117
Principal activity within building:						
Education	389	12,237	10,885	31.5	1,124	53
Food sales	177	1,252	1,172	7.1	1,067	121
Food service	380	1,819	3,431	4.8	530	82
Health care	157	4,155	7,613	26.5	546	60
Inpatient	10	2,374	4,281	247.8	555	168
Outpatient	147	1,781	3,333	12.1	535	53
Lodging	158	5,826	3,066	36.9	1,900	165
Mercantile	602	11,330	9,117	18.8	1,243	64
Retail (other than mall)	438	5,439	4,023	12.4	1,352	62
Enclosed and strip malls	164	5,890	5,094	35.9	1,156	69
Office	1,012	15,952	33,756	15.8	473	55
Public assembly	352	5,559	3,108	15.8	1,789	56
Public order and safety	84	1,440	1,854	17.2	776	113
Religious worship	412	4,557	1,940	11.1	2,350	31
Service	619	4,627	4,031	7.5	1,148	56
Warehouse and storage	796	13,032	6,362	16.4	2,048	67
Other	125	2,002	1,611	16.0	1,242	61
Vacant	296	3,256	236	11.0	13,811	8
Number of establishments:						
One	4,205	54,944	52,072	13.1	1,055	64
2 to 5	862	17,756	18,916	20.6	939	65
6 to 10	147	4,425	5,890	30.1	751	77
11 to 20	68	3,704	5,276	54.8	702	70
More than 20	27	3,821	6,028	140.9	634	84
Currently unoccupied	248	2,393	–	9.6	(X)	–
Year constructed:						
Before 1920	362	3,980	3,309	11.0	1,203	48
1920 to 1945	488	6,020	6,003	12.3	1,003	52
1946 to 1959	599	7,381	6,566	12.3	1,124	51
1960 to 1969	639	10,362	9,851	16.2	1,052	61
1970 to 1979	684	10,846	12,536	15.9	865	61
1980 to 1989	915	15,185	17,468	16.6	869	65
1990 to 1999	845	13,803	13,432	16.3	1,028	68
2000 to 2003	375	7,215	7,471	19.2	966	66
2004 to 2007	347	6,524	5,993	18.8	1,089	69
2008 to 2012	303	5,726	5,552	18.9	1,031	76

– Represents zero. X Not applicable. [1] For explanation of mean, see Guide to Tabular Presentation.

Source: U.S. Energy Information Administration, "2012 CBECS Survey Data," <http://www.eia.gov/consumption/commercial/data/2012/>, accessed March 2015.

Manufactures

This section presents summary data for manufacturing as a whole and more detailed information for major industry groups and selected products. The types of measures shown at the different levels include data for establishments, employment and payroll, value and quantity of production and shipments, value added by manufacture, inventories, and various indicators of financial status.

The principal source of these data is the U.S. Census Bureau's Annual Survey of Manufactures. Reports on current activities of industries or current movements of individual commodities are also compiled by such government agencies as the Bureau of Economic Analysis; Bureau of Labor Statistics; the Department of Commerce, International Trade Administration; and by private research or trade associations.

The Census Bureau's *Quarterly Financial Report* publishes up-to-date aggregate statistics on the financial results and position of U.S. corporations. Based upon a sample survey, the QFR presents estimated statements of income and retained earnings, balance sheets, and related financial and operating ratios for manufacturing corporations with assets of $250,000 or over, and mining, wholesale trade and retail trade corporations with assets of $50 million and over or above industry-specific receipt cut-off values. These statistical data are classified by industry and by asset size.

Several private trade associations provide industry coverage for certain sections of the economy.

Censuses and annual surveys—The first census of manufactures covered the year 1809. Between 1809 and 1963, a census was conducted at periodic intervals. Since 1967, it has been conducted every 5 years for years ending in "2" and "7". Results from the 2012 census are presented in this section utilizing the North American Industry Classification System (NAICS). Release of data from the 2012 Economic Census was completed in 2016. The 2017 Economic Census are being released on a flow basis between September 2019 and December 2021. Census data, either directly reported or estimated from administrative records, are obtained for every manufacturing plant with one or more paid employees. For additional information see text, Section 15, Business Enterprise, and the Census Bureau website at <census.gov/programs-surveys/economic-census.html>.

The Annual Survey of Manufactures (ASM), conducted for the first time in 1949, collects data for the years between censuses for the more general measure of manufacturing activity covered in detail by the censuses. The annual survey data are estimates derived from a scientifically selected sample of establishments. The ASM is a sample survey of approximately 50,000 establishments conducted annually, except for years ending in 2 and 7, at which time ASM statistics are included in the manufacturing sector of the Economic Census. In 2017, there were approximately 295,100 active manufacturing establishments. For sample efficiency and cost considerations, the manufacturing population is partitioned into two groups: (1) establishments

eligible to be mailed a questionnaire, defined as the mail stratum, which is comprised of larger single-location manufacturing companies and all manufacturing establishments of multi-location companies, supplemented annually with new large single-location companies from IRS data and new multi-location companies from the Company Organization Survey; and (2) establishments not eligible to be mailed a questionnaire, defined as the nonmail stratum, which includes small- and medium-sized single establishment companies.

Establishments and classification—Each of the establishments covered in the 2017 Economic Census—Manufacturing was classified in accordance with the industry definitions in the 2017 NAICS manual. In NAICS, an industry is generally defined as a group of establishments that have similar production processes. To the extent practical, the system uses supply-based or production-oriented concepts in defining industries. The resulting group of establishments must be significant in terms of number, value added by manufacture, value of shipments, and number of employees. Establishments frequently make products classified both in their industry (primary products) and other industries (secondary products). Industry statistics (employment, payroll, value added by manufacture, value of shipments, etc.) reflect the activities of the establishments, which may make both primary and secondary products. Product statistics, however, represent the output of all establishments without regard for the classification of the producing establishment. For this reason, when relating the industry statistics, especially the value of shipments, to the product statistics, the composition of the industry's output should be considered.

Establishment—An establishment is a single physical location where business is conducted or where services or industrial operations are performed. Data in this sector includes those establishments where manufacturing is performed. A separate report is required for each manufacturing establishment (plant) with one employee or more that is in operation at any time during the year. An establishment not in operation for any portion of the year is requested to return the report form with the proper notation in the "Operational Status" section of the form. In addition, the establishment is requested to report data on any employees, capital expenditures, inventories, or shipment from inventories during the year.

Durable goods—Items with a normal life expectancy of 3 years or more. Automobiles, furniture, household appliances, and mobile homes are common examples.

Nondurable goods—Items which generally last for only a short time (3 years or less). Food, beverages, clothing, shoes, and gasoline are common examples.

Statistical reliability—For a discussion of statistical collection and estimation, sampling procedures, and measures of statistical reliability applicable to Census Bureau data, see Appendix III.

Table 1039. Manufacturing—Contribution to Gross Domestic Product in Current and Real (2012) Dollars by Industry: 2000 to 2019

[In billions of dollars (10,252.3 represents $10,252,300,000,000). Value added GDP is the contribution of each industry's labor and capital to its gross output and to the overall gross domestic product (GDP) of the United States. Value added is equal to an industry's gross output (sales or receipts and other operating income, commodity taxes, and inventory change) minus its intermediate inputs (consumption of goods and services purchased from other industries or imported). Current-dollar value added is calculated as the sum of distributions by an industry to its labor and capital which are derived from the components of gross domestic income]

Industry	NAICS code [1]	2000	2010	2015	2017	2018	2019
CURRENT DOLLARS							
Gross domestic product, total [2]	(X)	**10,252.3**	**14,992.1**	**18,224.8**	**19,519.4**	**20,580.2**	**21,427.7**
Private industries	(X)	8,929.3	12,884.1	15,883.9	17,065.8	18,035.6	18,796.8
Manufacturing	**31–33**	**1,550.2**	**1,797.0**	**2,126.5**	**2,185.1**	**2,321.2**	**2,359.9**
Durable goods	33, 321, 327	924.8	964.3	1,184.0	1,230.7	1,296.4	1,342.7
Wood products	321	28.3	23.3	32.4	38.8	40.5	41.4
Nonmetallic mineral products	327	42.6	38.4	54.5	59.3	61.7	64.0
Primary metals	331	47.0	50.9	59.8	58.1	63.9	64.8
Fabricated metal products	332	121.3	119.9	147.1	149.5	159.8	166.2
Machinery	333	113.1	127.2	152.1	148.1	155.7	160.5
Computer and electronic products	334	225.4	239.8	270.0	280.9	297.3	313.6
Electrical equipment, appliances, and components	335	45.7	50.7	63.5	63.6	66.4	68.3
Motor vehicles, bodies and trailers, and parts	3361–63	137.5	88.7	145.8	158.1	162.4	166.2
Other transportation equipment	3364–66, 69	71.1	120.6	148.6	152.2	161.7	167.2
Furniture and related products	337	33.5	21.8	29.1	29.3	30.2	30.8
Miscellaneous manufacturing	339	59.2	83.0	81.1	92.8	96.8	99.6
Nondurable goods	31, 32 [3]	625.4	832.7	942.5	954.4	1,024.8	1,017.2
Food and beverage and tobacco products	311, 312	163.2	223.2	260.8	264.0	268.9	272.3
Textile mills and textile product mills	313, 314	28.0	15.5	17.9	18.3	18.9	18.7
Apparel and leather and allied products	315, 316	22.2	10.4	9.7	9.3	9.2	9.5
Paper products	322	62.2	56.3	59.5	55.4	57.0	58.2
Printing and related support activities	323	43.7	39.4	40.1	39.8	40.4	41.0
Petroleum and coal products	324	52.7	123.4	144.7	128.3	172.2	142.8
Chemical products	325	187.9	302.6	331.9	362.1	378.1	392.9
Plastics and rubber products	326	65.5	61.8	78.0	77.2	80.1	81.7
CHAINED (2012) DOLLARS							
Gross domestic product, total [2]	(X)	**13,131.0**	**15,598.8**	**17,403.8**	**18,108.1**	**18,638.2**	**19,073.1**
Private industries	(X)	11,384.0	13,467.3	15,197.9	15,843.7	16,345.4	16,765.6
Manufacturing	**31–33**	**1,678.8**	**1,932.6**	**2,037.5**	**2,079.8**	**2,161.3**	**2,177.0**
Durable goods	33, 321, 327	753.1	967.7	1,120.1	1,162.4	1,217.4	1,239.3
Wood products	321	25.4	22.9	25.9	29.7	28.7	30.9
Nonmetallic mineral products	327	49.2	38.7	46.1	47.0	47.7	48.4
Primary metals	331	61.7	50.9	74.2	69.1	67.8	77.3
Fabricated metal products	332	156.0	125.5	134.1	137.6	145.1	142.7
Machinery	333	130.1	132.1	134.1	128.3	135.5	131.9
Computer and electronic products	334	67.6	226.8	284.9	308.5	329.9	348.4
Electrical equipment, appliances, and components	335	54.5	52.7	61.1	62.0	62.4	61.9
Motor vehicles, bodies and trailers, and parts	3361–63	99.7	87.0	122.2	131.3	139.5	142.1
Other transportation equipment	3364–66, 69	95.4	124.3	138.4	139.0	147.0	149.4
Furniture and related products	337	40.1	22.6	27.1	27.0	28.0	26.2
Miscellaneous manufacturing	339	61.0	84.1	77.0	87.6	91.5	90.3
Nondurable goods	31, 32 [3]	967.0	972.3	917.3	916.6	943.1	937.0
Food and beverage and tobacco products	311, 312	225.1	233.3	232.5	232.8	245.5	243.8
Textile mills and textile product mills	313, 314	30.9	16.6	17.1	17.5	17.6	17.0
Apparel and leather and allied products	315, 316	20.0	10.6	9.0	8.4	8.2	8.1
Paper products	322	71.0	55.8	54.1	48.5	49.1	48.1
Printing and related support activities	323	37.7	37.5	37.5	37.0	37.9	37.3
Petroleum and coal products	324	184.7	212.7	200.5	195.9	202.2	190.2
Chemical products	325	289.4	346.5	299.6	308.0	312.8	319.6
Plastics and rubber products	326	77.3	67.6	73.1	73.2	75.0	74.3

X Not applicable. [1] North American Industry Classification System; see text, Section 15. [2] Includes industries, not shown separately. For additional industries, see Table 705. [3] Except NAICS 321 and 327.

Source: U.S. Bureau of Economic Analysis, Industry Data, Gross Domestic Product by Industry, "Value Added by Industry," <http://www.bea.gov/industry/gdpbyind_data.htm>, accessed May 2020.

Table 1040. Manufacturing—Establishments, Employees, and Annual Payroll by Industry: 2017 and 2018

[128,592 represents 128,592,000. Excludes most government employees, railroad employees, and self-employed persons. See Appendix III]

Industry	NAICS code [1]	Establishments 2017	Establishments 2018	Employees (1,000) [2] 2017	Employees (1,000) [2] 2018	Payroll (mil. dol.) 2017	Payroll (mil. dol.) 2018
All industries, total	(X)	**7,860,674**	**7,912,405**	**128,592**	**130,881**	**6,725,347**	**7,097,310**
Manufacturing, total	31–33	**290,936**	**290,092**	**11,722**	**11,913**	**682,640**	**717,859**
Percent of all industries	(X)	3.70	3.67	9.12	9.10	10.15	10.11
Food	311	27,519	27,728	1,544	1,570	68,148	70,745
Beverage and tobacco products	312	9,195	10,113	221	240	11,276	12,175
Textile mills	313	1,993	1,981	97	94	4,117	4,140
Textile product mills	314	5,701	5,749	108	105	4,056	4,115
Apparel manufacturing	315	5,752	5,482	92	85	2,651	2,620
Leather and allied products	316	1,174	1,162	27	26	984	974
Wood products	321	14,552	14,463	407	415	17,051	17,864
Paper	322	4,054	3,999	346	345	21,785	22,361
Printing and related support activities	323	25,256	24,809	444	439	20,827	21,051
Petroleum and coal products	324	2,135	2,106	106	107	10,920	11,279
Chemical	325	13,426	13,615	785	798	63,379	66,424
Plastics and rubber products	326	12,217	12,065	772	786	37,337	39,296
Nonmetallic mineral products	327	15,126	15,076	393	400	21,011	22,069
Primary metal	331	4,287	4,112	371	375	23,496	25,344
Fabricated metal products	332	54,066	55,020	1,398	1,437	74,275	78,747
Machinery	333	23,014	23,060	1,031	1,057	64,432	69,588
Computer and electronic products	334	12,225	12,044	792	781	68,162	69,991
Electrical equipment, appliance and components	335	5,469	5,549	341	345	20,496	21,301
Transportation equipment	336	11,568	11,567	1,536	1,585	101,470	108,513
Furniture and related products	337	14,429	14,581	367	372	15,534	16,128
Miscellaneous	339	27,778	25,811	546	551	31,232	33,133

X Not applicable. [1] Data based on North American Industry Classification System (NAICS) 2017. See text, Section 15. [2] Covers full- and part-time employees who are on the payroll in the pay period including March 12.

Source: U.S. Census Bureau, County Business Patterns, "County Business Patterns by Legal Form of Organization and Employment Size Class for U.S., States, and Selected Geographies," <data.census.gov>, accessed July 2020. See also <census.gov/programs-surveys/cbp.html>.

Table 1041. Manufacturing—Establishments, Employees, and Annual Payroll by State: 2018

[11,913 represents 11,913,000. Excludes most government employees, railroad employees, and self-employed persons. Data are for North American Industry Classification System (NAICS) 2017, codes 31–33. See Appendix III]

State	Establish-ments	Employees (1,000) [1]	Payroll (mil. dol.)	State	Establish-ments	Employees (1,000) [1]	Payroll (mil. dol.)
United States	**290,092**	**11,913**	**717,859**	Missouri	5,680	268	15,040
Alabama	4,145	258	13,820	Montana	1,349	20	996
Alaska	537	12	581	Nebraska	1,753	97	4,854
Arizona	4,336	151	9,591	Nevada	1,872	47	2,760
Arkansas	2,573	163	7,569	New Hampshire	1,796	66	4,200
California	37,433	1,163	83,356	New Jersey	7,291	222	14,769
Colorado	5,155	125	7,751	New Mexico	1,321	26	1,319
Connecticut	3,965	160	11,944	New York	15,112	413	24,529
Delaware	573	30	1,933	North Carolina	8,726	444	23,341
District of Columbia	117	1	54	North Dakota	697	25	1,391
Florida	13,425	319	18,242	Ohio	13,888	684	39,420
Georgia	7,577	389	20,476	Oklahoma	3,392	130	7,230
Hawaii	793	13	560	Oregon	5,518	177	11,183
Idaho	1,904	61	3,620	Pennsylvania	13,463	555	32,537
Illinois	13,051	539	33,415	Rhode Island	1,293	40	2,299
Indiana	8,027	527	29,623	South Carolina	3,859	244	14,087
Iowa	3,491	215	12,187	South Dakota	1,030	45	2,216
Kansas	2,725	163	9,482	Tennessee	5,745	335	18,117
Kentucky	3,687	247	13,401	Texas	20,138	799	51,565
Louisiana	3,156	118	8,733	Utah	3,422	124	7,257
Maine	1,670	50	2,802	Vermont	1,045	30	1,740
Maryland	2,960	99	6,609	Virginia	5,011	239	13,630
Massachusetts	6,360	226	17,451	Washington	6,988	265	18,318
Michigan	12,385	603	35,263	West Virginia	1,115	48	2,795
Minnesota	7,103	310	18,989	Wisconsin	8,749	468	26,835
Mississippi	2,109	148	7,254	Wyoming	582	10	726

[1] Covers full- and part-time employees who are on the payroll in the pay period including March 12.

Source: U.S. Census Bureau, County Business Patterns, "County Business Patterns by Legal Form of Organization and Employment Size Class for U.S., States, and Selected Geographies," <data.census.gov>, accessed July 2020. See also <https://www.census.gov/programs-surveys/cbp.html>.

Table 1042. Manufactures—Summary by Selected Industry: 2018

[Employee data in thousands (11,713.8 represents 11,713,800); financial data in millions of dollars (695,618 represents $695,618,000,000), except as noted. Based on data from the Annual Survey of Manufactures]

Industry based on shipments	2017 NAICS code [1]	All employees			Produc-tion workers [2] (1,000)	Value added by manufac-tures [3] (mil. dol.)	Value of ship-ments [4] (mil. dol.)
		Number [2] (1,000)	Payroll				
			Total (mil. dol.)	Per employee (dol.)			
Manufacturing, total [5]............................	**31–33**	**11,713.8**	**695,618**	**59,384**	**8,361.4**	**2,635,433**	**5,954,927**
Food [5]..	311	1,498.5	68,773	45,895	1,214.3	300,768	786,991
Grain and oil seed milling..................	3112	54.6	3,389	62,116	42.3	21,243	85,317
Sugar and confectionery products...........	3113	84.0	3,966	47,233	64.6	16,372	37,906
Fruit and vegetable preserving and specialty food........	3114	159.9	7,742	48,423	132.5	36,103	74,018
Dairy products.............................	3115	150.4	8,066	53,633	111.7	38,164	117,145
Animal slaughtering and processing.........	3116	499.3	19,999	40,053	439.5	68,833	216,792
Bakeries and tortilla........................	3118	264.2	10,887	41,204	199.7	40,089	69,535
Beverage and tobacco products.............	312	221.0	11,728	53,075	124.0	97,869	156,193
Beverage...................................	3121	207.3	10,795	52,069	113.7	58,594	108,733
Textile mills................................	313	91.2	4,033	44,218	73.6	11,500	28,158
Textile product mills........................	314	103.1	4,009	38,872	79.2	10,813	22,786
Apparel [5].................................	315	79.4	2,554	32,151	63.8	5,401	9,874
Cut and sew apparel........................	3152	60.8	1,987	32,683	48.9	4,270	7,626
Leather and allied products..................	316	25.1	967	38,544	19.4	2,037	4,530
Wood products [5]...........................	321	403.8	17,589	43,560	325.4	50,716	114,845
Sawmills and wood preservation.............	3211	87.4	4,300	49,169	74.1	14,586	35,429
Paper.......................................	322	331.3	21,677	65,426	257.9	86,473	191,119
Pulp, paper, and paperboard mills...........	3221	96.2	7,950	82,671	76.8	43,044	79,335
Converted paper products...................	3222	235.2	13,727	58,373	181.1	43,429	111,784
Printing and related support activities.......	323	420.0	20,801	49,533	305.5	50,580	83,754
Petroleum and coal products................	324	109.0	11,576	106,225	71.4	133,167	684,976
Chemical [5]................................	325	757.4	60,189	79,469	477.8	416,494	765,145
Basic chemical.............................	3251	147.0	13,440	91,419	93.0	101,222	228,449
Pharmaceutical and medicine...............	3254	241.5	20,968	86,828	141.1	160,901	215,109
Soap, cleaning compound, and toilet preparation........	3256	100.2	6,221	62,095	63.7	50,283	84,766
Plastics and rubber products................	326	770.7	37,759	48,991	599.1	125,286	251,098
Plastics products...........................	3261	636.9	30,467	47,835	494.0	101,816	203,500
Rubber product.............................	3262	133.8	7,293	54,494	105.1	23,470	47,598
Nonmetallic mineral products................	327	401.1	21,700	54,103	312.1	74,406	130,548
Glass and glass product....................	3272	93.5	5,022	53,716	74.4	16,473	27,586
Cement and concrete products..............	3273	180.5	9,682	53,636	144.2	32,942	61,000
Primary metal [5]...........................	331	368.0	24,136	65,583	290.4	96,177	255,087
Iron and steel mills and ferroalloy...........	3311	86.4	7,522	87,070	69.4	38,911	105,185
Foundries..................................	3315	117.1	6,391	54,552	94.1	17,333	31,286
Fabricated metal products [5]...............	332	1,400.6	77,612	55,412	1,058.3	206,818	375,880
Forging and stamping.......................	3321	104.3	5,828	55,881	80.4	16,051	34,489
Architectural and structural metals..........	3323	359.1	19,338	53,853	261.4	49,826	98,151
Machine shops, turned product and screw, nut, and bolt.............................	3327	372.5	20,524	55,098	292.5	45,943	72,831
Coating, engraving, heat treating, and allied activities...............................	3328	123.1	6,105	49,602	99.4	17,619	27,817
Machinery [5]...............................	333	1,063.6	67,583	63,541	690.6	198,634	395,951
Agriculture, construction, and mining machinery..........	3331	187.5	11,341	60,476	130.8	40,010	91,506
Industrial machinery........................	3332	110.5	8,768	79,318	61.9	20,165	36,517
HVAC and commercial refrigeration equipment...........	3334	133.5	6,671	49,978	95.8	23,419	44,033
Metalworking machinery....................	3335	148.0	9,090	61,401	106.5	20,622	33,766
Computer and electronic products [5]........	334	842.7	69,170	82,080	401.5	189,380	324,264
Computer and peripheral equipment.........	3341	40.7	3,261	80,144	16.3	10,825	21,638
Communications equipment.................	3342	90.0	7,914	87,914	39.4	19,980	34,871
Semiconductor and other electronic component..........	3344	266.0	20,712	77,853	163.6	53,413	99,952
Navigational, measuring, medical, and control instruments.............................	3345	427.1	36,232	84,823	171.5	102,516	163,014
Electrical equipment, appliance, and component [5].........	335	347.6	20,516	59,027	236.9	66,609	132,679
Electrical equipment........................	3353	115.6	7,141	61,775	74.1	21,509	43,698
Other electrical equipment and component..............	3359	137.4	8,465	61,593	91.7	25,787	51,394
Transportation equipment [5]................	336	1,563.3	106,156	67,906	1,128.3	368,970	1,007,683
Motor vehicle..............................	3361	217.9	16,930	77,691	181.6	80,915	352,927
Motor vehicle parts.........................	3363	588.5	32,300	54,883	454.1	88,594	268,961
Aerospace product and parts...............	3364	402.8	36,902	91,613	231.1	148,743	262,942
Ship and boat building......................	3366	133.7	8,293	62,052	91.8	20,527	36,543
Furniture and related products [5]...........	337	386.0	16,324	42,290	295.5	42,742	77,832
Miscellaneous [5]...........................	339	530.4	30,765	58,002	336.3	100,592	155,532
Medical equipment and supplies............	3391	268.8	17,781	66,146	166.0	63,646	93,383

[1] North American Industrial Classification System, 2017; see text, Section 15. [2] Includes all full-time and part-time employees on payrolls of operating manufacturing establishments. All employees represents the average of production workers plus all other employees for the payroll period ended nearest the 12th of March. [3] Adjusted value added; takes into account (a) value added by merchandising operations (that is, difference between the sales value and cost of merchandise sold without further manufacture, processing, or assembly), plus (b) net change in finished goods and work-in-process inventories between beginning and end of year. [4] This item covers the received or receivable net selling values, "free on board" (FOB) plant (exclusive of freight and taxes), of all products shipped as well as all miscellaneous receipts. In the case of multiunit companies, the manufacturer was requested to report the value of products transferred to other establishments of the same company at full economic or commercial value. [5] Includes industries not shown separately.

Source: U.S. Census Bureau, Annual Survey of Manufactures, "Annual Survey of Manufactures: Summary Statistics for Industry Groups and Industries in the U.S.: 2018," April 2020, <data.census.gov/>, accessed July 2020. See also <https://www.census.gov/programs-surveys/asm.html>.

Table 1043. Manufactures—Summary by State: 2016

[Employment data in thousands (11,112.8 represents 11,112,800); financial data in millions of dollars (643,406 represents $643,406,000,000). Based on data from the 2016 Annual Survey of Manufactures. Data are for North American Industry Classification System (NAICS) 2012 codes 31–33. Sum of state totals may not add to U.S. total due to independent rounding. See Appendix III]

State	All employees [1]			Production workers [1]		Value added by manufactures [2]		Value of shipments [3] (mil. dol.)
	Number (1,000)	Payroll Total (mil. dol.)	Per employee (dol.)	Number (1,000)	Wages (mil. dol.)	Total (mil. dol.)	Per production worker (dol.)	
United States	**11,112.8**	**643,406**	**57,898**	**7,733.2**	**364,985**	**2,408,996**	**311,515**	**5,354,694**
Alabama	234.8	12,256	52,195	176.7	7,884	46,264	261,855	131,012
Alaska	12.2	590	48,431	10.2	442	2,212	217,420	6,003
Arizona	136.9	9,142	66,753	82.4	3,990	29,122	353,384	55,065
Arkansas	145.7	6,657	45,679	116.8	4,721	25,096	214,939	55,731
California	1,119.9	73,011	65,194	706.4	34,022	255,636	361,891	493,165
Colorado	121.1	7,373	60,896	79.1	3,713	26,020	329,156	50,853
Connecticut	155.1	10,968	70,731	88.0	4,730	32,663	371,311	56,376
Delaware	25.4	1,455	57,216	17.9	816	5,870	327,905	16,558
District of Columbia	1.3	58	46,270	0.8	34	213	262,593	330
Florida	270.2	15,473	57,271	180.0	7,959	57,038	316,950	104,865
Georgia	352.0	18,119	51,482	265.7	11,282	71,133	267,687	166,678
Hawaii	11.5	568	49,359	7.1	312	2,093	292,744	5,686
Idaho	55.8	3,186	57,123	41.2	1,945	9,195	223,155	20,968
Illinois	538.2	30,952	57,511	371.0	17,266	111,573	300,764	252,503
Indiana	476.4	26,341	55,290	357.5	17,133	102,353	286,302	241,539
Iowa	203.8	10,913	53,538	148.0	6,563	43,511	294,086	105,663
Kansas	154.7	8,626	55,762	110.9	5,318	33,892	305,605	83,920
Kentucky	230.8	12,487	54,110	178.6	8,550	45,084	252,440	128,159
Louisiana	113.9	8,008	70,298	80.1	4,925	47,821	596,800	156,874
Maine	49.7	2,657	53,453	36.0	1,734	8,093	224,915	15,169
Maryland	91.8	6,051	65,923	56.3	2,754	22,769	404,720	41,214
Massachusetts	224.0	15,416	68,821	131.0	6,678	46,717	356,565	84,735
Michigan	555.0	32,361	58,307	398.9	19,868	103,771	260,112	261,293
Minnesota	297.8	16,961	56,961	197.1	8,984	56,929	288,836	117,397
Mississippi	130.5	6,329	48,483	103.1	4,324	21,760	211,095	56,801
Missouri	245.4	(S)	(NA)	182.9	9,029	50,314	275,121	118,828
Montana	16.7	888	53,170	11.2	522	3,175	282,553	9,396
Nebraska	92.9	4,496	48,367	70.7	2,986	19,005	268,741	53,112
Nevada	41.4	2,311	55,887	27.8	1,312	8,702	313,493	16,682
New Hampshire	65.6	4,137	63,109	39.5	1,845	11,562	292,986	20,658
New Jersey	210.3	13,237	62,946	139.9	6,818	45,823	327,608	90,605
New Mexico	21.7	1,253	57,626	14.7	707	4,936	335,788	12,674
New York	395.1	23,105	58,474	261.2	12,404	79,496	304,332	148,469
North Carolina	411.1	20,701	50,362	303.8	12,424	109,824	361,536	210,018
North Dakota	22.9	1,181	51,672	16.9	752	4,923	291,086	13,050
Ohio	642.9	36,033	56,044	460.8	22,047	129,554	281,162	312,532
Oklahoma	121.2	6,469	53,370	89.1	4,024	22,705	254,923	56,775
Oregon	160.1	9,543	59,598	108.9	5,222	27,846	255,597	57,315
Pennsylvania	522.2	29,380	56,260	362.0	17,290	105,636	291,806	217,753
Rhode Island	36.1	2,148	59,526	23.7	1,145	5,607	236,153	11,344
South Carolina	213.1	11,641	54,638	159.8	7,513	44,029	275,528	109,000
South Dakota	44.1	2,040	46,256	32.5	1,263	7,882	242,575	17,441
Tennessee	309.0	16,329	52,852	228.5	10,236	66,937	292,939	149,126
Texas	725.3	44,620	61,523	493.7	24,678	216,626	438,788	523,118
Utah	114.5	6,541	57,124	75.8	3,562	23,250	306,881	48,428
Vermont	27.4	1,542	56,230	18.6	864	4,205	225,578	8,788
Virginia	222.8	12,504	56,118	156.9	7,374	57,359	365,564	99,131
Washington	253.5	16,567	65,362	165.5	9,067	60,007	362,491	142,700
West Virginia	44.9	2,594	57,750	32.0	1,623	11,341	354,612	23,851
Wisconsin	435.9	23,662	54,280	310.1	13,931	78,972	254,671	168,601
Wyoming	8.4	603	71,954	6.1	403	2,452	404,175	6,742

NA Not available. S Withheld because estimate did not meet publication standards. [1] Includes all full-time and part-time employees on the payrolls of operating manufacturing establishments during the pay period that included March 12. Included are employees on paid sick leave, paid holidays, and paid vacations; not included are proprietors and partners of unincorporated businesses. [2] Value added is derived by subtracting the cost of materials, supplies, containers, fuel, purchased electricity, and contract work from the value of shipments (products manufactured plus receipts for services rendered). The result of this calculation is adjusted by the addition of value added by merchandising operations (i.e., the difference between the sales value and the cost of merchandise sold without further manufacture, processing, or assembly) plus the net change in finished goods and work-in-process between the beginning and end of year inventories. [3] Includes extensive and unmeasurable duplication from shipments between establishments in the same industry classification.

Source: U.S. Census Bureau, Annual Survey of Manufactures, "Geographic Area Statistics for All Manufacturing by State: 2016 and 2015," December 2017, <data.census.gov/>, accessed August 2018. See also <https://www.census.gov/programs-surveys/asm.html>.

Table 1044. Manufacturing Industries—Employees by Industry: 1990 to 2019

[Annual averages of monthly figures (132,011 represents 132,011,000). Covers all full- and part-time employees who worked during, or received pay for, any part of the pay period including the 12th of the month. Minus sign (-) indicates decrease. See also head note, Table 663]

Industry	2017 NAICS code [1]	All employees (1,000)					Percent change		
		2000	2010	2017	2018	2019	1990-2000	2000-2010	2010-2019
All industries	(X)	**132,011**	**130,345**	**146,608**	**148,908**	**150,939**	**20.5**	**-1.3**	**15.8**
Manufacturing	31–33	**17,263**	**11,528**	**12,439**	**12,688**	**12,840**	**-2.4**	**-33.2**	**11.4**
Percent of all industries	(X)	13.1	8.8	8.5	8.5	8.5	-19.1	-32.4	-3.8
Durable goods	(X)	10,877	7,064	7,741	7,946	8,059	1.3	-35.1	14.1
Wood products [2]	321	615	342	397	406	409	13.3	-44.4	19.5
Sawmills & wood preservation	3211	134	82	92	92	92	-9.6	-38.5	12.2
Nonmetallic mineral products [2]	327	554	371	410	417	422	4.9	-33.1	13.7
Cement & concrete products	3273	234	170	192	194	199	20.1	-27.4	17.1
Primary metals [2]	331	622	362	371	380	385	-9.7	-41.7	6.3
Iron & steel mills & ferroalloy production	3311	135	87	82	84	86	-27.7	-35.9	-0.1
Steel products from purchased steel	3312	73	52	56	57	58	4.0	-28.7	10.3
Alumina & aluminum production	3313	101	54	58	59	60	-7.3	-46.3	10.7
Foundries	3315	217	112	117	120	119	1.4	-48.4	6.7
Fabricated metal products [2]	332	1,753	1,282	1,425	1,470	1,492	8.9	-26.9	16.4
Architectural & structural metals	3323	428	321	373	392	401	20.0	-25.0	24.8
Machine shops & threaded products	3327	365	313	353	363	365	18.4	-14.4	16.7
Coating, engraving, & heat treating metals	3328	175	122	136	140	142	22.7	-30.0	16.1
Machinery [2]	333	1,457	996	1,079	1,117	1,126	3.3	-31.6	13.1
Agricultural, construction, & mining machinery	3331	222	208	206	218	221	-2.8	-6.4	6.3
HVAC & commercial refrigeration equipment	3334	194	125	130	133	138	17.7	-35.9	10.6
Metalworking machinery	3335	274	155	180	182	180	2.5	-43.3	15.9
Turbine & power transmission equipment	3336	111	92	97	98	100	-2.4	-17.6	8.5
Other general purpose machinery	3339	344	226	261	272	276	2.4	-34.4	22.0
Computer & electronic products [2]	334	1,820	1,095	1,039	1,054	1,081	-4.3	-39.9	-1.3
Computer & peripheral equipment	3341	302	158	156	157	163	-17.8	-47.8	3.4
Communications equipment	3342	239	117	87	85	84	7.0	-50.8	-28.9
Semiconductors & electronic components	3344	676	369	362	369	377	17.8	-45.4	2.1
Electronic instruments	3345	488	406	401	410	424	-23.2	-16.7	4.4
Electrical equipment & appliances [2]	335	591	360	386	400	405	-6.7	-39.2	12.7
Electrical equipment	3353	210	136	138	141	147	-13.9	-35.1	8.0
Other electrical equipment & components	3359	191	119	137	147	150	-2.3	-37.8	26.6
Transportation equipment [2]	336	2,057	1,333	1,643	1,702	1,734	-3.6	-35.2	30.1
Motor vehicles	3361	291	153	219	234	237	7.4	-47.6	55.4
Motor vehicle bodies & trailers	3362	183	107	155	165	166	40.8	-41.4	54.7
Motor vehicle parts	3363	840	419	589	600	596	28.6	-50.1	42.2
Aerospace products & parts	3364	517	478	488	508	534	-38.5	-7.5	11.8
Ship & boat building	3366	154	125	135	139	142	-11.3	-19.1	14.0
Furniture & related products [2]	337	680	357	395	393	388	13.0	-47.5	8.7
Household & institutional furniture	3371	441	223	249	247	243	10.7	-49.3	8.9
Miscellaneous manufacturing	339	728	567	595	608	618	6.2	-22.1	9.0
Medical equipment & supplies	3391	305	303	311	318	325	7.7	-0.7	7.2
Other miscellaneous manufacturing	3399	423	264	284	290	293	5.1	-37.6	11.0
Nondurable goods	(X)	6,386	4,464	4,699	4,742	4,781	-8.2	-30.1	7.1
Food manufacturing [2]	311	1,553	1,451	1,598	1,621	1,643	3.0	-6.6	13.3
Fruit & vegetable preserving & specialty	3114	197	173	174	175	173	-9.5	-12.6	0.5
Dairy products	3115	136	130	146	151	156	-5.9	-4.2	19.4
Animal slaughtering & processing	3116	507	489	513	522	531	18.6	-3.5	8.6
Bakeries & tortilla manufacturing	3118	306	277	311	312	316	4.9	-9.7	14.1
Textile mills [2]	313	378	119	113	112	109	-23.1	-68.5	-8.7
Fabric mills	3132	192	53	53	53	52	-29.0	-72.2	-2.8
Textile product mills [2]	314	230	119	116	116	113	-2.5	-48.2	-4.8
Textile furnishings mills	3141	129	57	52	52	50	1.3	-55.7	-11.6
Apparel [2]	315	484	157	119	114	110	-46.4	-67.6	-29.6
Cut & sew apparel	3152	380	124	96	91	87	-49.3	-67.4	-29.8
Paper & paper products	322	605	395	366	366	365	-6.6	-34.7	-7.4
Pulp, paper, & paperboard mills	3221	191	112	97	95	96	-19.7	-41.3	-14.2
Converted paper products	3222	413	282	269	270	269	1.1	-31.7	-4.8
Printing & related support activities	323	807	488	440	432	425	-0.2	-39.6	-12.9
Petroleum & coal products	324	123	114	115	115	115	-19.4	-7.5	0.5
Chemicals [2]	325	980	787	824	835	850	-5.3	-19.8	8.0
Basic chemicals	3251	188	142	151	151	153	-24.4	-24.5	7.5
Pharmaceuticals & medicines	3254	274	277	293	297	306	32.4	0.9	10.5
Soaps, cleaning compounds, & toiletries	3256	129	102	107	109	110	-2.4	-20.6	8.0
Plastics & rubber products [2]	326	951	625	717	730	737	15.3	-34.3	18.0
Plastics products	3261	737	502	581	593	599	19.2	-31.9	19.4
Rubber products	3262	214	123	136	137	138	3.5	-42.5	11.9
Miscellaneous nondurable goods manufacturing [2]	312,6	276	211	291	301	314	-21.4	-23.5	48.6
Beverages	3121	175	167	251	262	275	1.2	-4.5	64.8

X Not applicable. [1] Based on the North American Industry Classification System, 2017 (NAICS); see text, this section and Section 15. [2] Includes other industries, not shown separately.

Source: U.S. Bureau of Labor Statistics, Current Employment Statistics, "Employment, Hours, and Earnings—National," <http://www.bls.gov/ces/data.htm>, accessed March 2020.

Table 1045. Manufacturing—Value of Imports and Exports by Commodity: 2016

[In thousands of dollars (22,933,334 represents $22,933,334,000). Values are based on manufacturing data from the Annual Survey of Manufacturers and administrative records from official U.S. import and export merchandise trade statistics]

Commodity description	Product code [1]	Value of product shipments [2]	Total export value of goods [3]	General import value of goods [4]
Food manufacturing:				
Dog and cat food	311111	22,933,334	1,315,436	750,587
Other animal food	311119	32,310,895	1,633,277	552,029
Soybean and other oilseed products	311224	31,282,491	6,470,490	6,770,328
Fruit and vegetable canning products	311421	25,481,320	2,992,732	5,659,242
Fluid milk products	311511	33,320,569	259,924	59,719
Cheese products	311513	40,139,943	1,209,024	1,259,170
Animal (except poultry) slaughtering products	311611	87,629,077	14,721,102	8,533,537
Meat processed from carcasses	311612	50,661,463	(NA)	75,688
Poultry processing products	311615	61,740,224	3,892,349	519,487
Commercial bakery products	311812	30,589,439	(NA)	(NA)
Beverage and tobacco product manufacturing:				
Soft drinks	312111	35,464,262	1,042,512	2,817,168
Brewery products	312120	30,518,887	2,779,377	4,940,274
Tobacco products	312230	41,360,631	1,155,877	1,413,967
Wood product manufacturing:				
Sawmill products	321113	22,332,560	3,594,972	6,821,382
Paper manufacturing:				
Paper (except newsprint) mill products	322121	38,387,992	2,387,662	3,523,186
Paperboard mill products	322130	28,456,285	4,749,078	1,974,937
Corrugated and solid fiber boxes	322211	37,137,108	1,541,479	456,034
Paper bags and coated and treated paper	322220	20,496,725	5,066,946	3,499,012
Printing and related support activities manufacturing:				
Commercial printing products (except screen and books)	323111	63,006,196	2,975,117	3,448,871
Petroleum and coal products manufacturing:				
Petroleum refinery products	324110	367,379,559	66,138,901	41,757,855
Chemical manufacturing:				
Petrochemicals	325110	49,724,229	1,962,962	1,161,965
Other basic inorganic chemicals	325180	27,160,725	12,087,142	9,063,331
Ethyl alcohol	325193	25,171,720	2,052,938	474,199
All other basic organic chemical manufacturing	325199	71,734,847	30,009,159	32,781,551
Plastics materials and resins	325211	75,842,384	27,410,887	12,529,935
Pharmaceutical preparations	325412	151,058,524	28,369,122	76,867,073
Biological products (except diagnostic)	325414	27,776,154	19,053,878	20,053,806
Paints and coatings	325510	27,445,132	2,688,799	1,043,696
Soaps and other detergents	325611	22,433,822	1,474,230	1,005,264
Toilet preparations	325620	36,599,913	9,059,348	8,408,216
Plastics and rubber products manufacturing:				
All other plastics products	326199	91,168,720	11,139,675	19,174,669
Nonmetallic mineral product manufacturing:				
Ready-mix concrete	327320	28,910,513	4,133	1,188
Primary metal manufacturing:				
Iron and steel mill products and ferroalloys	331110	75,671,972	11,693,601	24,284,212
Fabricated metal product manufacturing:				
Fabricated structural metal products	332312	27,415,851	1,022,136	3,990,190
Machine shops	332710	35,017,553	(NA)	(NA)
Machinery manufacturing:				
Farm machinery and equipment	333111	22,568,333	6,607,460	7,145,733
Construction machinery	333120	24,010,377	10,958,135	16,189,841
Air-conditioning and warm air heating equipment and commercial and industrial refrigeration equipment	333415	31,113,498	5,513,311	10,004,731
Other engine equipment	333618	23,203,303	10,431,523	11,859,221
Computer and electronic product manufacturing:				
Semiconductors and related devices	334413	45,729,550	42,932,709	45,535,817
Electromedical and electrotherapeutic apparatus	334510	26,291,936	10,217,928	10,747,574
Search, detection, navigation, guidance, aeronautical, and nautical systems and instruments	334511	40,690,878	3,958,648	7,571,485
Transportation equipment manufacturing:				
Automobiles	336111	123,557,447	47,654,237	168,796,384
Light truck and utility vehicles	336112	190,316,687	9,834,772	18,359,171
Heavy duty trucks	336120	26,779,308	5,259,339	10,645,150
Motor vehicle gasoline engines and engine parts	336310	31,209,958	9,731,596	18,415,781
Motor vehicle electrical and electronic equipment	336320	23,457,092	7,035,692	20,087,287
Motor vehicle transmission and power train parts	336350	39,919,280	2,901,242	8,637,523
Motor vehicle seating and interior trim	336360	31,773,837	2,451,721	7,802,656
Motor vehicle metal stampings	336370	35,529,192	1,587,182	665,764
Other motor vehicle parts	336390	65,150,150	16,318,203	36,476,598
Aircraft	336411	120,974,701	4,546,595	13,844,272
Aircraft engines and engine parts	336412	39,652,987	2,267,804	19,039,796
Other aircraft parts and auxiliary equipment	336413	40,570,416	5,983,217	16,508,498
Guided missiles and space vehicles	336414	23,130,420	1,509,744	2,264
Ships and ship repair	336611	23,417,674	1,366,634	493,378
Miscellaneous manufacturing:				
Surgical and medical instruments	339112	41,039,499	16,998,378	13,476,651
Surgical appliances and supplies	339113	30,630,740	11,014,731	14,101,341

NA Not available. [1] Based on North American Industry Classification (NAICS) product codes. [2] Includes total value of all products produced and shipped by all producers. For selected products, this can represent value of receipts, value of production, or value of work done. [3] Exports measure total physical movement of merchandise out of the U.S. to foreign countries whether such merchandise is exported from within the U.S. Customs territory, from a U.S. Customs bonded warehouse, or a U.S. Foreign Trade Zone. [4] Imports include commodities of foreign origin as well as goods of domestic origin returned to the U.S. with no change in condition or after having been processed and/or assembled in other countries.

Source: U.S. Census Bureau, *Manufacturing and International Trade Report: 2016*, February 2018. See also <https://www.census.gov/foreign-trade/index.html>.

Table 1046. Manufacturing Industries—Average Weekly Hours and Average Weekly Overtime Hours of Production Workers: 2000 to 2019

[Covers all full- and part-time employees who worked during, or received pay for, any part of the pay period including the 12th of the month]

Industry	2017 NAICS code [1]	Average weekly hours of production workers					Average weekly overtime hours of production workers				
		2000	2010	2015	2018	2019	2000	2010	2015	2018	2019
Total................................	31–33	41.3	41.1	41.8	42.2	41.6	4.7	3.8	4.3	4.6	4.3
Durable goods.......................	(X)	41.8	41.4	42.1	42.5	42.0	4.8	3.8	4.3	4.7	4.3
Wood products.....................	321	41.0	39.1	41.3	41.9	41.5	4.1	3.0	4.1	5.0	5.1
Nonmetallic mineral products.....	327	41.6	41.7	42.4	44.2	43.8	6.1	4.7	4.9	6.2	5.7
Primary metals....................	331	44.2	43.7	43.8	44.6	43.8	6.5	5.7	6.5	6.7	6.2
Fabricated metal products.........	332	41.9	41.4	42.3	42.2	41.7	4.9	3.8	4.3	4.4	4.1
Machinery..........................	333	42.3	42.1	41.9	42.7	42.4	5.1	3.9	4.0	4.7	4.0
Computer and electronic products...................	334	41.4	40.9	40.9	40.9	40.5	4.6	2.9	3.0	3.2	2.5
Electrical equipment and appliances.........................	335	41.6	41.1	42.2	42.6	41.4	3.7	3.6	4.2	4.5	3.8
Transportation equipment.........	336	43.3	42.9	43.7	44.4	43.4	5.6	4.7	5.3	5.8	5.5
Furniture and related products....	337	39.2	38.5	39.8	39.3	39.4	3.5	2.3	3.1	2.6	2.7
Miscellaneous manufacturing.....	339	39.0	38.7	40.1	39.5	39.7	3.1	2.7	3.1	3.2	2.8
Nondurable goods.................	(X)	40.3	40.8	41.4	41.6	41.1	4.5	3.8	4.3	4.4	4.2
Food manufacturing................	311	40.1	40.7	41.0	42.0	41.5	4.9	4.5	4.5	4.9	4.7
Textile mills.......................	313	41.4	41.2	42.5	42.3	43.5	4.8	3.3	5.2	5.0	4.7
Textile product mills...............	314	38.7	39.0	37.0	39.3	37.8	3.4	2.4	2.5	2.6	2.2
Apparel............................	315	35.7	36.6	38.2	37.7	37.0	2.1	1.1	2.0	2.6	2.0
Paper and paper products.........	322	42.8	42.9	43.0	43.1	42.1	5.7	4.9	4.8	5.5	4.8
Printing and related support activities.........................	323	39.2	38.2	39.8	39.3	38.8	3.7	2.2	3.1	3.1	2.8
Petroleum and coal products......	324	42.7	43.0	45.2	45.6	48.3	6.5	6.4	7.8	9.9	12.3
Chemicals..........................	325	42.2	42.2	42.6	42.1	41.8	5.0	3.6	4.5	3.8	3.8
Plastics and rubber products......	326	40.8	41.9	42.4	42.1	41.0	3.9	4.0	4.5	4.3	4.0
Misc. nondurable manufacturing..	329	40.5	37.8	38.0	37.7	36.1	5.4	2.3	3.2	2.6	2.3

X Not applicable. [1] Based on the North American Industry Classification System (NAICS), 2017; see text, this section and Section 15.

Source: U.S. Bureau of Labor Statistics, Current Employment Statistics, "Employment, Hours, and Earnings — National," <https://www.bls.gov/ces/data/home.htm>, accessed April 2020.

Table 1047. Indexes of Employment and Hours of All Persons in Manufacturing: 2010 to 2019

[2007=100. Based on Current Employment Statistics and supplemented with Current Population Survey. Employment and hours of all persons include those of paid employees, the self employed (partners and proprietors), and unpaid family workers. See text, Section 12]

Industry	NAICS code [1]	Employment					Hours				
		2010	2015	2017	2018	2019	2010	2015	2017	2018	2019
Food manufacturing..............	311	97.4	102.6	108.5	110.0	111.1	97.6	103.2	110.1	112.9	112.4
Beverage and tobacco products......................	312	93.2	115.5	135.8	137.1	144.0	87.0	109.1	126.0	133.1	130.2
Textile mills........................	313	71.3	68.8	64.2	64.5	62.7	73.2	72.1	63.8	67.4	68.8
Textile product mills..............	314	72.5	74.0	74.2	71.6	69.8	76.6	71.5	76.4	72.7	68.2
Apparel manufacturing...........	315	72.4	63.9	55.1	51.5	50.1	72.3	64.9	53.3	51.0	47.8
Leather and allied products.....	316	83.2	84.2	86.8	79.3	83.9	82.8	86.2	81.6	78.6	82.6
Wood product manufacturing. ..	321	66.6	72.9	76.8	79.2	80.4	67.7	76.1	80.8	83.7	85.5
Paper and paper products.......	322	86.4	81.4	80.3	80.3	79.8	87.2	81.9	79.7	81.0	78.7
Printing and related support activities.........................	323	79.7	71.8	70.0	68.2	67.5	79.0	72.6	71.2	69.0	68.0
Petroleum and coal products....	324	99.0	98.1	99.3	101.0	99.7	95.7	100.3	100.5	105.3	108.6
Chemical manufacturing.........	325	91.5	94.2	96.5	97.9	99.3	92.6	94.5	95.2	97.0	99.0
Plastics and rubber products....	326	82.2	90.7	94.4	96.1	97.3	82.8	93.1	96.9	97.8	97.1
Nonmetallic mineral products. ..	327	75.2	80.0	83.0	82.6	84.4	74.4	78.2	82.3	84.7	85.1
Primary metal products..........	331	79.7	86.5	81.3	83.3	84.0	81.8	88.4	82.4	87.7	86.7
Fabricated metal products.......	332	82.4	92.9	90.7	93.3	94.6	81.3	94.1	91.3	93.8	93.9
Machinery manufacturing........	333	83.6	94.1	90.4	93.3	94.2	84.2	93.2	91.8	94.0	94.1
Computer and electronic products.........................	334	86.2	82.4	81.6	82.6	84.9	87.6	84.0	83.1	82.9	84.6
Electrical equipment and appliances.......................	335	83.8	88.9	91.1	93.1	94.7	83.9	91.0	95.0	95.5	93.8
Transportation equipment.......	336	78.1	93.5	96.3	99.5	101.0	79.2	96.8	99.7	103.5	102.8
Furniture and related products..	337	67.7	72.2	74.4	74.4	72.3	66.5	73.4	75.2	75.4	74.2
Miscellaneous manufacturing. ..	339	87.2	91.9	91.1	92.4	95.0	87.5	95.0	95.0	95.0	95.9

[1] North American Industry Classification System; see text, Section 15.

Source: U.S. Bureau of Labor Statistics, Labor Productivity and Costs, "LPC Tables and Charts," <http://www.bls.gov/lpc/tables.htm>, accessed August 2020.

Table 1048. Average Hourly Earnings of Production Workers in Manufacturing Industries by State: 2016 to 2019

[In dollars. Data are based on the North American Industry Classification System (NAICS), 2017. Based on the Current Employment Statistics Program. Covers full- and part-time employees who received pay for any part of the pay period including the 12th of the month. Excludes proprietors, self-employed, unpaid family or volunteer workers, farm workers, and domestic workers. See source, and Appendix III]

State	2016	2017	2018	2019	State	2016	2017	2018	2019
United States........	**20.44**	**20.90**	**21.54**	**22.15**	Montana.................	18.59	19.31	20.94	20.60
Alabama...............	19.37	19.89	20.10	19.93	Nebraska..............	17.57	18.52	19.12	19.98
Alaska................	22.18	21.61	20.21	21.27	Nevada................	19.13	19.51	19.75	20.61
Arizona...............	17.61	17.50	19.49	20.36	New Hampshire.......	20.67	21.57	21.64	22.48
Arkansas..............	15.86	16.09	17.40	18.48	New Jersey...........	21.22	21.59	22.10	23.68
California..............	21.88	22.46	23.16	23.96	New Mexico...........	16.85	17.39	18.09	19.59
Colorado..............	28.66	27.52	26.91	27.70	New York..............	19.51	20.55	22.05	22.83
Connecticut...........	26.72	25.01	26.85	27.20	North Carolina.........	17.39	17.74	18.27	18.40
Delaware..............	17.61	19.17	19.14	20.13	North Dakota..........	20.14	19.94	19.77	20.99
Florida................	21.00	21.47	21.76	23.29	Ohio..................	20.58	21.05	21.52	21.72
Georgia...............	18.17	18.44	18.92	19.59	Oklahoma.............	18.62	18.94	19.00	18.94
Hawaii................	21.40	20.49	20.63	22.19	Oregon................	19.95	20.67	21.70	22.66
Idaho.................	18.57	18.31	18.37	18.80	Pennsylvania..........	19.29	20.34	20.78	21.60
Illinois................	20.25	20.22	21.30	21.89	Rhode Island..........	18.22	19.00	19.15	19.59
Indiana...............	18.53	19.58	20.19	20.96	South Carolina........	19.23	19.07	19.30	20.52
Iowa..................	18.66	19.37	19.68	20.60	South Dakota..........	18.59	18.75	18.80	19.48
Kansas................	19.01	19.15	19.95	20.71	Tennessee.............	18.07	18.72	19.51	19.76
Kentucky..............	20.41	20.30	20.45	20.78	Texas.................	21.41	21.72	21.87	21.89
Louisiana.............	22.11	21.88	22.01	22.57	Utah..................	20.32	20.69	20.83	21.23
Maine.................	21.28	22.18	22.48	22.50	Vermont...............	20.15	21.09	21.17	21.00
Maryland..............	19.01	19.94	20.32	20.34	Virginia...............	18.94	18.90	19.10	19.47
Massachusetts........	22.83	23.69	24.57	25.03	Washington............	26.42	27.38	28.43	29.16
Michigan..............	20.50	20.76	21.32	22.22	West Virginia..........	19.83	21.14	21.38	21.51
Minnesota.............	20.03	20.76	21.71	22.77	Wisconsin.............	19.62	20.25	20.56	21.49
Mississippi............	20.33	20.58	20.54	20.77	Wyoming..............	21.99	22.78	23.94	25.76
Missouri...............	20.23	21.02	21.10	21.55	Puerto Rico............	12.27	12.60	12.37	12.50

Source: U.S. Bureau of Labor Statistics, Current Employment Statistics, "Employment, Hours, and Earnings – National," <http://www.bls.gov/ces/data.htm>; and "Employment, Hours, and Earnings – State and Metro Area," <http://www.bls.gov/sae/data.htm>; accessed April 2020.

Table 1049. Manufacturing Full-Time Equivalent (FTE) Employees and Wages by Industry: 2000 to 2019

[123,384 represents 123,384,000. Based on National Income and Product Account tables. Full-time equivalent employees equals the number of employees on full-time schedules plus the number of employees for part-time schedules converted to full-time basis]

Industry	2012 NAICS code [1]	Full-time equivalent (FTE) employees (1,000)				Wage and salary accruals per FTE worker (dol.)			
		2000	2010	2018	2019	2000	2010	2018	2019
Domestic industries, total...........	(X)	**123,384**	**120,519**	**138,895**	**140,917**	**39,166**	**52,939**	**64,111**	**66,148**
Manufacturing..............................	31–33	**16,948**	**11,223**	**12,389**	**12,515**	**43,957**	**59,997**	**71,316**	**72,735**
Percent of all industries...................	(X)	13.7	9.3	8.9	8.9	112.2	113.3	111.2	110.0
Durable goods............................	(X)	10,713	6,900	7,795	7,888	46,573	63,311	75,655	77,095
Wood products...........................	321	602	333	398	398	30,351	38,149	48,145	49,812
Nonmetallic mineral products..........	327	549	357	411	412	39,021	50,628	61,195	62,518
Primary metals..........................	331	611	353	371	379	45,836	61,058	73,585	73,712
Fabricated metal products..............	332	1,735	1,249	1,432	1,453	37,766	51,445	60,277	61,152
Machinery...............................	333	1,427	975	1,095	1,105	46,612	62,656	74,161	75,028
Computer and electronic products......	334	1,779	1,079	1,039	1,059	70,449	96,001	127,671	129,378
Electrical equipment, appliances, and components...............................	335	583	351	391	393	40,241	59,438	70,177	72,565
Motor vehicles, bodies and trailers, and parts..................................	3361–3363	1,301	666	990	987	48,754	57,922	64,613	65,757
Other transportation equipment........	3364–3365	740	645	692	725	53,294	79,421	96,937	98,080
Furniture and related products..........	337	671	345	384	375	29,571	39,980	48,339	49,824
Miscellaneous manufacturing..........	339	715	547	592	602	38,744	56,903	69,117	70,784
Nondurable goods........................	(X)	6,235	4,322	4,594	4,627	39,464	54,706	63,953	65,302
Food and beverage and tobacco products.................................	311–312	1,728	1,561	1,812	1,843	33,956	44,711	52,371	52,857
Textile mills and textile product mills. ..	313–314	588	230	220	212	29,013	39,110	47,125	48,751
Apparel and leather and allied products.................................	315	539	179	137	131	24,198	38,244	45,661	47,607
Paper products..........................	322	598	382	354	354	45,834	61,586	71,419	72,497
Printing and related support activities..	323	757	472	419	412	39,142	45,783	52,868	53,585
Petroleum and coal products...........	324	120	109	112	112	62,998	97,162	119,356	123,814
Chemical products.......................	325	967	775	820	838	61,314	84,813	98,811	101,719
Plastics and rubber products...........	326	938	615	720	725	35,624	47,778	56,190	56,924

X Not applicable. [1] North American Industry Classification System, 2012; see text, Section 15.

Source: U.S. Bureau of Economic Analysis, National Income and Product Accounts, "Table 6.5D. Full-Time Equivalent Employees by Industry," and "Table 6.6D. Wages and Salaries Per Full-Time Equivalent Employee by Industry," <bea.gov/itable/>, accessed August 2020.

Table 1050. Manufacturers' Shipments, Inventories, and New Orders: 1995 to 2019

[In billions of dollars (3,480 represents $3,480,000,000,000), except ratio. Data are not seasonally adjusted, except ratios as noted. Based on the Manufacturers' Shipments, Inventories, and Orders (M3) survey. See source for details]

Year	Shipments	Inventories (December 31) [1]	Ratio of inventories to shipments [2]	New orders	Unfilled orders (December 31)
1995	3,480	415	1.41	3,427	443
1996	3,597	421	1.40	3,567	485
1997	3,835	433	1.36	3,780	508
1998	3,900	439	1.37	3,808	492
1999	4,032	453	1.34	3,957	501
2000	4,209	470	1.37	4,161	545
2001	3,970	417	1.33	3,869	506
2002	3,915	412	1.30	3,823	476
2003	4,015	398	1.20	3,976	503
2004	4,309	429	1.17	4,289	555
2005	4,742	461	1.14	4,764	652
2006	5,016	509	1.22	5,090	796
2007	5,319	547	1.22	5,397	946
2008	5,469	529	1.42	5,452	995
2009	4,424	491	1.29	4,206	825
2010	4,911	538	1.28	4,896	870
2011	5,492	589	1.29	5,512	953
2012	5,697	607	1.30	5,710	1,015
2013	5,810	612	1.29	5,827	1,077
2014	5,888	623	1.34	5,926	1,162
2015	5,519	619	1.44	5,439	1,130
2016	5,355	615	1.37	5,293	1,115
2017	5,605	643	1.36	5,579	1,136
2018	6,000	666	1.35	5,994	1,180
2019	6,034	686	1.40	5,958	1,154

[1] Inventories are stated at current cost. [2] Ratio based on December seasonally adjusted inventory data.

Source: U.S. Census Bureau, Manufacturers' Shipments, Inventories, and Orders, "Historical Data," <http://www.census.gov/manufacturing/m3/historical_data/index.html>, accessed April 2020.

Table 1051. Ratios of Manufacturers' Inventories to Shipments and Unfilled Orders to Shipments by Industry Group: 2000 to 2019

[Based on the Manufacturers' Shipments, Inventories, and Orders (M3) survey. Ratio based on December seasonally adjusted inventory and unfilled orders data. See source for details]

Industry	2012 NAICS code [1]	2000	2010	2015	2016	2017	2018	2019
INVENTORIES-TO-SHIPMENTS RATIO								
All manufacturing industries	**(X)**	**1.37**	**1.28**	**1.44**	**1.37**	**1.36**	**1.35**	**1.40**
Durable goods	(X)	1.56	1.62	1.75	1.66	1.64	1.61	1.74
Wood products	321	1.41	1.39	1.33	1.27	1.26	1.37	1.29
Nonmetallic mineral products	327	1.26	1.52	1.28	1.28	1.27	1.35	1.33
Primary metals	331	1.77	1.58	1.92	1.71	1.70	1.69	1.77
Fabricated metals	332	1.56	1.58	1.72	1.65	1.61	1.62	1.60
Machinery	333	2.05	1.86	2.21	2.16	2.07	2.14	2.20
Computers and electronic products	334	1.47	1.59	1.75	1.65	1.66	1.57	1.58
Electrical equipment, appliances, and components	335	1.41	1.47	1.65	1.59	1.67	1.73	1.72
Transportation equipment	336	1.42	1.64	1.72	1.58	1.59	1.45	1.81
Furniture and related products	337	1.36	1.18	1.14	1.17	1.22	1.20	1.17
Miscellaneous products	339	1.83	1.72	1.67	1.79	1.67	1.76	1.80
Nondurable goods	(X)	1.13	0.99	1.12	1.09	1.08	1.08	1.06
Food products	311	0.86	0.79	0.85	0.83	0.82	0.80	0.80
Beverages and tobacco products	312	1.50	1.65	1.78	1.85	2.00	1.99	2.00
Textile mills	313	1.54	1.24	1.33	1.26	1.29	1.39	1.37
Textile product mills	314	1.87	1.65	1.70	1.58	1.57	1.49	1.56
Apparel	315	1.91	1.63	2.31	2.14	2.04	1.98	1.95
Leather and allied products	316	1.88	1.77	2.12	1.77	1.83	1.98	1.84
Paper products	322	1.11	0.97	1.03	1.04	0.99	1.01	1.00
Printing	323	0.78	0.77	0.78	0.81	0.84	0.84	0.78
Petroleum and coal products	324	0.68	0.74	0.86	0.77	0.76	0.74	0.73
Basic chemicals	325	1.35	1.23	1.37	1.39	1.36	1.36	1.33
Plastics and rubber products	326	1.24	1.21	1.27	1.27	1.31	1.38	1.35
UNFILLED ORDERS-TO-SHIPMENTS RATIO								
All manufacturing industries	**(X)**	**4.02**	**6.11**	**7.32**	**7.07**	**6.77**	**6.57**	**6.65**
Durable goods	(X)	4.02	6.11	7.32	7.07	6.77	6.57	6.65
Primary metals	331	1.52	1.91	1.58	1.46	1.45	1.46	1.60
Fabricated metals	332	2.13	2.81	2.72	2.66	2.60	2.61	2.63
Machinery	333	2.66	3.81	3.54	3.64	3.52	3.59	3.46
Computers and electronic products	334	4.24	5.93	5.74	5.87	5.46	5.38	5.47
Electrical equipment, appliances, and components	335	1.83	1.95	2.01	1.97	1.96	1.85	1.89
Transportation equipment	336	8.06	13.92	16.52	15.46	15.30	14.31	15.01
Furniture and related products	337	1.29	1.40	1.54	1.51	1.51	1.48	1.47

X Not applicable. [1] Based on the North American Industry Classification System, 2012; see text, this section and Section 15.

Source: U.S. Census Bureau, Manufacturers' Shipments, Inventories, and Orders, "Historical Data," <http://www.census.gov/manufacturing/m3/historical_data/index.html>, accessed April 2020.

Table 1052. Value of Manufacturers' Shipments, Inventories, and New Orders by Industry: 2000 to 2019

[In billions of dollars (4,209 represents $4,209,000,000,000). Data are not seasonally adjusted. Based on the Manufacturers' Shipments, Inventories, and Orders (M3) survey. See source for details]

Industry	2017 NAICS code [1]	2000	2010	2015	2017	2018	2019
SHIPMENTS							
All manufacturing industries	(X)	**4,209**	**4,911**	**5,519**	**5,605**	**6,000**	**6,034**
Durable goods	(X)	2,374	2,281	2,772	2,814	3,017	3,043
Wood products	321	94	69	98	109	112	110
Nonmetallic mineral products	327	97	90	118	126	131	135
Primary metals	331	157	231	228	222	255	245
Fabricated metals	332	268	295	349	361	393	404
Machinery	333	292	316	378	369	391	396
Computers and electronic products	334	511	328	299	304	323	334
Electrical equipment, appliances, and components	335	125	110	125	128	136	140
Transportation equipment	336	640	636	949	959	1,032	1,032
Furniture and related products	337	75	60	74	76	78	81
Miscellaneous products	339	115	145	153	159	165	165
Nondurable goods	(X)	1,835	2,631	2,747	2,791	2,982	2,991
Food products	311	435	654	774	797	807	812
Beverages and tobacco products	312	112	130	155	148	151	151
Textile mills	313	52	30	29	29	30	29
Textile product mills	314	34	21	25	25	27	27
Apparel	315	60	13	11	11	12	11
Leather and allied products	316	10	5	5	5	5	5
Paper products	322	165	172	185	184	193	194
Printing	323	104	83	81	78	79	82
Petroleum and coal products	324	235	628	508	537	657	637
Basic chemicals	325	449	705	737	744	784	804
Plastics and rubber products	326	178	189	237	233	237	237
INVENTORIES (as of December 31)							
All manufacturing industries	(X)	**470**	**538**	**619**	**643**	**666**	**686**
Durable goods	(X)	298	313	381	386	405	424
Wood products	321	10	8	11	12	12	12
Nonmetallic mineral products	327	10	11	13	14	15	15
Primary metals	331	22	31	33	33	36	35
Fabricated metals	332	34	40	47	50	54	53
Machinery	333	49	52	64	65	68	69
Computers and electronic products	334	63	42	41	41	42	42
Electrical equipment, appliances, and components	335	15	14	16	17	19	19
Transportation equipment	336	69	90	128	124	128	146
Furniture and related products	337	8	6	7	8	8	8
Miscellaneous products	339	18	20	22	23	23	24
Nondurable goods	(X)	172	225	238	256	261	262
Food products	311	32	44	53	54	53	54
Beverages and tobacco products	312	14	18	23	24	25	25
Textile mills	313	6	3	3	3	3	3
Textile product mills	314	5	3	3	3	3	3
Apparel	315	9	2	2	2	2	2
Leather and allied products	316	2	1	1	1	1	1
Paper products	322	15	14	16	16	16	16
Printing	323	6	5	5	5	5	5
Petroleum and coal products	324	13	43	28	38	36	38
Basic chemicals	325	52	73	80	85	89	88
Plastics and rubber products	326	18	19	24	25	27	26
NEW ORDERS							
All manufacturing industries	(X)	**4,161**	**4,896**	**5,439**	**5,579**	**5,994**	**5,958**
Durable goods	(X)	2,327	2,265	2,692	2,788	3,012	2,967
Wood products	321	94	(NA)	(NA)	(NA)	(NA)	(NA)
Nonmetallic mineral products	327	97	(NA)	(NA)	(NA)	(NA)	(NA)
Primary metals	331	154	244	223	224	258	246
Fabricated metals	332	270	304	345	366	399	404
Machinery	333	295	334	370	375	394	392
Computers and electronic products	334	436	270	251	260	280	284
Electrical equipment, appliances, and components	335	126	110	124	129	136	141
Transportation equipment	336	663	638	935	963	1,059	1,008
Furniture and related products	337	75	60	75	76	78	82
Miscellaneous products	339	117	(NA)	(NA)	(NA)	(NA)	(NA)
Nondurable goods	(X)	1,835	2,631	2,747	2,791	2,982	2,991

NA Not available. X Not applicable. [1] Based on the North American Industry Classification System, 2017; see text, this section and Section 15.

Source: U.S. Census Bureau, Manufacturers' Shipments, Inventories, and Orders, "Annual Benchmark Data and Benchmark Procedures," <http://www.census.gov/manufacturing/m3/index.html>, and "Historical Data," <http://www.census.gov /manufacturing/m3/historical_data/index.html>; accessed August 2020.

Table 1053. Value of Manufacturers' Shipments, Inventories, and New Orders by Market Grouping: 2000 to 2019

[In billions of dollars (4,209 represents $4,209,000,000,000). Data are not seasonally adjusted. Based on the Manufacturers' Shipments, Inventories, and Orders (M3) survey. See source for details]

Market grouping	2000	2010	2014	2015	2016	2017	2018	2019
SHIPMENTS								
All manufacturing industries	**4,209**	**4,911**	**5,888**	**5,519**	**5,355**	**5,605**	**6,000**	**6,034**
Consumer goods	1,501	2,059	2,508	2,256	2,184	2,331	2,528	2,540
Consumer durable goods	391	323	436	462	477	476	513	522
Consumer nondurable goods	1,109	1,735	2,072	1,795	1,708	1,855	2,015	2,017
Aircraft and parts	112	147	211	210	208	209	217	181
Defense aircraft and parts	25	63	58	55	50	53	55	53
Nondefense aircraft and parts	87	84	153	155	158	156	163	128
Construction materials and supplies	445	444	547	554	555	582	615	627
Motor vehicles and parts	471	401	600	638	647	652	707	728
Computers and related products	110	42	27	26	24	23	22	21
Information technology industries	400	270	263	258	255	270	294	304
Nondefense capital goods	808	728	906	878	833	870	928	909
Excluding aircraft	758	675	804	774	728	767	816	831
Defense capital goods	67	130	111	110	112	125	140	152
INVENTORIES (as of December 31)								
All manufacturing industries	**470**	**538**	**623**	**619**	**615**	**643**	**666**	**686**
Consumer goods	128	169	181	179	185	193	194	198
Consumer durable goods	26	21	27	28	27	28	29	30
Consumer nondurable goods	102	148	155	152	158	165	165	168
Aircraft and parts	36	55	72	79	75	76	77	93
Defense aircraft and parts	9	12	12	12	11	13	13	13
Nondefense aircraft and parts	27	43	60	67	63	63	64	79
Construction materials and supplies	49	52	64	62	63	67	73	71
Motor vehicles and parts	22	22	33	34	33	34	36	37
Computers and related products	8	4	4	4	3	4	4	4
Information technology industries	51	36	35	36	35	37	38	39
Nondefense capital goods	127	135	166	172	163	168	176	192
Excluding aircraft	107	100	117	116	112	117	123	126
Defense capital goods	17	21	20	21	21	23	23	24
NEW ORDERS								
All manufacturing industries	**4,161**	**4,896**	**5,926**	**5,439**	**5,293**	**5,579**	**5,994**	**5,958**
Consumer goods	1,502	2,059	2,508	2,256	2,185	2,331	2,528	2,540
Consumer durable goods	393	323	436	462	477	476	513	523
Consumer nondurable goods	1,109	1,735	2,072	1,795	1,708	1,855	2,015	2,017
Aircraft and parts	131	155	291	200	193	215	232	156
Defense aircraft and parts	31	63	56	51	55	54	64	58
Nondefense aircraft and parts	99	91	235	149	137	161	168	98
Construction materials and supplies	447	451	547	554	556	586	620	626
Motor vehicles and parts	468	403	605	639	648	654	708	727
Computers and related products	108	40	27	27	25	24	22	21
Information technology industries	410	273	257	255	257	272	297	304
Nondefense capital goods	831	748	977	858	810	883	935	870
Excluding aircraft	768	685	805	761	727	774	821	827
Defense capital goods	80	137	108	105	120	122	151	160

Source: U.S. Census Bureau, Manufacturers' Shipments, Inventories, and Orders, "Historical Data," <http://www.census.gov/manufacturing/m3/historical_data/index.html>, accessed May 2020.

Table 1054. Finances and Profits of Manufacturing Corporations: 2005 to 2019

[In billions of dollars (5,411 represents $5,411,000,000,000). Data exclude estimates for corporations with less than $250,000 in assets at time of sample selection]

Item	2005 [1]	2010 [2]	2012 [3]	2013 [3]	2014 [3]	2015 [3]	2016 [3]	2017 [4]	2018 [4]	2019 [4]
Net sales	5,411	5,756	6,668	6,743	6,903	6,433	6,249	6,552	6,971	6,843
Net operating profit	359	420	508	497	538	516	502	530	572	528
Net profit:										
Before taxes	524	584	676	722	745	612	649	681	720	649
After taxes	401	478	564	601	609	506	541	549	636	588
Cash dividends	179	180	212	242	259	275	276	290	312	314
Net income retained in business	222	298	353	359	350	231	265	259	324	273

[1] Based on the North American Industry Classification System, 2002. [2] Based on the North American Industry Classification System, 2007. [3] Based on the North American Industry Classification System, 2012. [4] Based on the North American Industry Classification System, 2017.

Source: U.S. Census Bureau, Quarterly Financial Report (QFR) Manufacturing, Mining, Trade, and Selected Service Industries, "Time Series/Trend Charts," <census.gov/econ/qfr/>, accessed August 2020.

Table 1055. Manufacturing Corporations—Selected Finances: 2000 to 2019

[In billions of dollars (4,548 represents $4,548,000,000,000). Data are not necessarily comparable from year to year due to changes in accounting procedures, industry classifications, sampling procedures, etc.; for details, see source. Through 2000 based on Standard Industrial Classification code; beginning 2001, based on North American Industry Classification System; see text, Section 15. Minus sign (-) indicates loss]

| Year | All manufacturing corporations | | | Durable goods | | | Nondurable goods | | |
| | | Profits [1] | | | Profits [1] | | | Profits [1] | |
	Sales	Before taxes	After taxes	Sales	Before taxes	After taxes	Sales	Before taxes	After taxes
2000.	4,548	381	275	2,457	191	132	2,091	190	144
2001 [2]	4,295	83	36	2,321	-69	-76	1,974	152	112
2002.	4,216	195	135	2,261	46	22	1,956	150	113
2003.	4,397	306	237	2,283	118	88	2,114	188	149
2004.	4,934	447	348	2,537	200	157	2,397	248	192
2005.	5,411	524	401	2,731	211	161	2,681	313	240
2006.	5,783	605	470	2,910	249	193	2,873	356	278
2007.	6,060	603	443	3,016	247	159	3,044	356	283
2008.	6,374	388	266	2,970	98	43	3,405	290	223
2009.	5,110	361	286	2,427	84	55	2,683	276	232
2010.	5,756	584	478	2,708	287	232	3,048	297	245
2011.	6,486	722	594	2,927	335	284	3,558	387	310
2012.	6,668	676	564	3,102	303	260	3,567	373	304
2013.	6,743	722	601	3,178	358	294	3,566	365	308
2014.	6,903	745	609	3,342	378	308	3,561	367	301
2015.	6,433	612	506	3,367	324	265	3,065	289	241
2016.	6,249	649	541	3,320	333	273	2,929	316	268
2017.	6,552	681	549	3,403	373	273	3,149	308	276
2018.	6,971	720	636	3,611	399	356	3,359	321	280
2019.	6,843	649	588	3,563	361	331	3,280	288	256

[1] Beginning 1998, profits before and after income taxes reflect inclusion of minority stockholders' interest in net income before and after income taxes. [2] Beginning 2001, data reported based on the North American Industry Classification System.

Source: U.S. Census Bureau, Quarterly Financial Report (QFR) Manufacturing, Mining, Trade, and Selected Service Industries, "Time Series/Trend Charts," <census.gov/econ/qfr/>, accessed August 2020.

Table 1056. Motor Vehicle Manufactures—Summary by Selected Industry: 2018

[56,891 represents $56,891,000,000. Based on the Annual Survey of Manufactures; see Appendix III]

| Industry | 2017 NAICS code [1] | All employees [2] | | | Produc- tion workers [2] | Value of product ship- ments [3] (mil. dol.) |
| | | Number | Payroll | | | |
			Total (mil. dol.)	Payroll per employee (dol.)		
Motor vehicle manufacturing, total	**3361-3363**	**962,931**	**56,891**	**59,081**	**762,210**	**672,890**
Motor vehicle, total	3361	217,911	16,930	77,691	181,592	352,927
Automobile and light duty motor vehicle	33611	189,975	15,056	79,252	158,474	321,553
Automobile	336111	81,872	6,672	81,495	63,073	104,987
Light truck and utility vehicle	336112	108,103	8,384	77,554	95,401	216,566
Heavy duty truck	33612	27,936	1,874	67,077	23,118	31,374
Motor vehicle body and trailer	3362	156,503	7,662	48,956	126,518	51,002
Motor vehicle body	336211	47,533	2,375	49,964	37,863	15,057
Truck trailer	336212	38,060	1,708	44,881	31,745	12,085
Motor home	336213	13,713	650	47,420	10,591	5,469
Travel trailer and camper	336214	57,197	2,928	51,199	46,319	18,391
Motor vehicle parts	3363	588,517	32,300	54,883	454,100	268,961
Motor vehicle gasoline engine and engine parts	33631	63,329	4,144	65,434	49,016	39,966
Motor vehicle electrical and electronic equipment	33632	59,840	3,166	52,906	44,685	25,285
Motor vehicle steering and suspension	33633	35,564	1,996	56,119	25,069	16,035
Motor vehicle brake system	33634	23,907	1,253	52,430	18,105	12,114
Motor vehicle transmission and power train parts	33635	74,616	4,750	63,665	58,349	41,493
Motor vehicle seating and interior trim	33636	72,902	3,477	47,691	57,318	30,196
Motor vehicle metal stamping	33637	104,937	5,904	56,261	83,267	37,833
Other motor vehicle parts	33639	153,420	7,610	49,600	118,292	66,040

[1] North American Industry Classification System, 2017; see text, Section 15. [2] Includes all full-time and part-time employees on the payrolls of operating manufacturing establishments during any part of the pay period that included the 12th of the month specified on the report form. Included are employees on paid sick leave, paid holidays, and paid vacations; not included are proprietors and partners of unincorporated businesses. [3] Includes extensive and unmeasurable duplication from shipments between establishments in the same industry classification.

U.S. Census Bureau, Annual Survey of Manufactures, "Annual Survey of Manufactures: Summary Statistics for Industry Groups and Industries in the U.S.: 2018," <data.census.gov/>, accessed July 2020.

Table 1057. Motor Vehicle Manufactures—Employees, Payroll, and Shipments by Major Producing State: 2016

[14,770,141 represents $14,770,141,000. Industry based on the 2012 North American Industry Classification System (NAICS); see text, Section 15. See footnote 3, Table 1056 for information regarding shipments. Based on the Annual Survey of Manufactures; see Appendix III]

State	Motor vehicle manufacturing (NAICS 3361)			Motor vehicle parts manufacturing (NAICS 3363)		
	Employees	Payroll ($1,000)	Value of shipments ($1,000)	Employees	Payroll ($1,000)	Value of shipments ($1,000)
United States [1]	197,666	14,770,141	344,359,096	539,878	29,406,642	260,812,268
Alabama	11,221	930,298	29,538,857	27,427	1,266,510	16,777,419
Arizona	80	7,093	(D)	2,240	129,737	2,790,091
Arkansas	(4)	(D)	(D)	4,858	214,338	1,742,582
California	7,203	679,296	5,971,811	14,479	770,921	6,436,684
Colorado	41	3,375	(D)	1,324	96,253	336,653
Florida	1,235	76,618	432,609	3,423	173,457	1,184,213
Georgia	(8)	(D)	(D)	14,904	723,335	8,898,694
Illinois	9,860	647,386	(D)	30,189	1,440,266	10,489,757
Indiana	17,179	1,272,255	36,133,016	54,670	3,145,356	24,544,473
Iowa	56	3,410	45,968	4,665	225,117	1,396,331
Kentucky	24,050	1,784,246	32,012,789	33,993	1,691,990	16,397,671
Louisiana	(NA)	(NA)	(NA)	389	(D)	146,272
Maine	(NA)	(NA)	(NA)	(4)	(D)	133,389
Maryland	(3)	(D)	(D)	625	48,253	292,905
Massachusetts	(3)	(D)	(D)	989	58,016	438,633
Michigan	36,707	2,830,551	66,265,067	112,573	6,695,090	54,312,932
Minnesota	(7)	(D)	(D)	2,164	103,025	760,695
Mississippi	(9)	(D)	(D)	5,166	244,611	2,540,537
Missouri	13,662	1,106,336	(D)	11,642	539,784	4,813,210
Nebraska	(3)	(D)	35,445	3,946	200,365	1,300,132
Nevada	(3)	(D)	(D)	231	(D)	77,732
New Hampshire	(NA)	(NA)	(NA)	1,699	71,783	395,470
New Jersey	32	2,529	(D)	801	43,351	300,165
New Mexico	(NA)	(NA)	(NA)	(3)	(D)	27,451
New York	32	1,849	20,793	9,435	805,371	5,322,539
North Carolina	(8)	(D)	(D)	17,247	893,800	9,605,501
North Dakota	(4)	(D)	(D)	821	40,724	200,471
Ohio	21,361	1,539,530	43,240,528	69,830	4,162,332	33,863,209
Oregon	(6)	(D)	(D)	1,400	71,024	421,552
Pennsylvania	(7)	(D)	(D)	8,240	363,153	3,311,449
South Carolina	(9)	(D)	(D)	14,315	839,611	9,042,030
South Dakota	(5)	(D)	(D)	775	35,025	222,918
Tennessee	8,348	640,678	15,815,996	40,142	2,063,339	21,614,749
Texas	8,415	675,798	28,401,053	15,282	744,214	7,799,885
Utah	(2)	(D)	(D)	3,995	174,184	2,141,784
Virginia	(7)	(D)	(D)	5,094	243,350	1,494,564
Washington	(5)	(D)	(D)	2,588	122,846	924,603
West Virginia	(4)	(D)	(D)	2,859	155,844	3,076,616
Wisconsin	(8)	(D)	(D)	9,644	463,819	3,520,006
Wisconsin	(NA)	(NA)	(NA)	(3)	(D)	7,261

D Withheld to avoid disclosing data on individual companies. NA Not available. [1] Includes states not shown separately. [2] Employee class size of 0 to 19. [3] Employee class size of 20 to 99. [4] Employee class size of 100 to 249. [5] Employee class size of 250 to 499. [6] Employee class size of 500 to 999. [7] Employee class size of 1,000 to 2,499. [8] Employee class size of 2,500 to 4,999. [9] Employee class size of 5,000 to 9,999.

Source: U.S. Census Bureau, Annual Survey of Manufactures, "Geographic Area Statistics: Statistics for All Manufacturing by State: 2016 and 2015," December 2017, <data.census.gov/>, accessed July 2018.

Table 1058. General Aviation Airplane Shipments and Billings: 1990 to 2019

[2,008 represents $2,008,000,000. Data are for U.S. manufactured airplanes. Totals may not add up due to rounding]

Type of airplane	1990	2000	2010	2015	2016	2017	2018	2019
Airplane units shipped (number)	**1,144**	**2,816**	**1,334**	**1,592**	**1,531**	**1,599**	**1,746**	**1,771**
Total piston	695	1,913	746	783	718	786	829	883
Single-engine	608	1,810	679	740	685	745	771	825
Multi-engine	87	103	67	43	33	41	58	58
Total turbine	449	903	588	809	813	813	917	888
Turboprop	281	315	224	420	411	409	444	385
Business jet	168	588	364	389	402	404	473	503
Factory net billings (mil. dol.)	**2,008**	**8,558**	**7,875**	**11,982**	**11,560**	**10,641**	**11,598**	**13,972**
Total piston	92	446	368	477	505	434	466	513
Single-engine	68	(NA)	(NA)	(NA)	(NA)	(NA)	(NA)	(NA)
Multi-engine	24	(NA)	(NA)	(NA)	(NA)	(NA)	(NA)	(NA)
Total turbine	1,916	8,112	7,506	11,506	11,055	10,207	11,132	13,459
Turboprop	644	934	724	1,282	1,180	1,032	1,151	1,006
Business jet	1,272	7,178	6,782	10,224	9,875	9,175	9,981	12,453

NA Not available.

Source: General Aviation Manufacturers Association, *2019 Databook* ©, 2020, and earlier reports. See also <www.gama.aero>.

Table 1059. Pharmaceutical Preparations—Value of Shipments: 2010 to 2016

[In millions of dollars (117,282 represents $117,282,000,000). Data are from the Annual Survey of Manufactures (ASM) and based on the North American Industry Classification System (NAICS). The ASM is conducted annually, except for years ending in 2 and 7, at which time ASM data are included in the manufacturing sector of the Economic Census]

Product description	Product code	2010	2011	2012	2013	2014	2015	2016
Pharmaceutical preparations.................	325412	117,282	128,060	115,776	120,032	137,663	146,661	151,059
Affecting neoplasms, endocrine system, and metabolic disease.......................	3254121	27,335	28,181	24,432	27,019	26,101	25,888	27,429
Acting on the central nervous system and sense organs....	3254124	27,102	28,500	24,154	25,334	27,966	30,889	33,614
Acting on the cardiovascular system.........................	3254127	10,537	11,205	7,796	12,317	13,807	13,492	15,798
Acting on the respiratory system.........................	325412A	14,237	20,525	19,241	13,108	13,705	13,751	12,464
Acting on the digestive system or genito-urinary system.....	325412D	8,633	8,197	7,500	4,581	5,286	5,318	4,786
Acting on the skin........................	325412G	4,160	3,601	2,986	2,624	2,771	4,531	4,343
Vitamin, nutrient, and hematinic preparations.................	325412L	8,669	9,796	9,298	8,103	10,665	10,995	11,958
Affecting parasitic and infective diseases (excl. diagnostic).......................	325412P	8,464	8,978	8,355	15,634	28,032	33,215	30,451
Preparations for veterinary use (excl. diagnostic) [1]...........	325412T	2,698	2,883	2,920	2,411	2,328	1,582	1,540
In vivo diagnostic substances.......................	325412V	1,951	2,309	2,692	2,504	1,259	1,318	2,018
Other pharmaceutical preparation manufacturing [2]..........	325412W	3,494	3,885	6,402	6,397	5,744	5,682	6,659
In-vitro diagnostic substances manufacturing..............	325413	11,133	11,468	11,580	11,978	11,180	11,742	11,884
Biological product (excl. diagnostic) manufacturing........	325414	23,793	23,372	23,959	23,987	23,075	26,729	27,776
Blood and blood derivatives, for human use..................	3254141	2,664	2,785	6,238	6,746	5,297	5,093	5,403
Vaccines, toxoids, and antigens, excluding allergens, for human use.........................	3254144	9,114	7,245	6,344	6,355	6,987	8,114	8,484
Other biologics (excl. diagnostic) for human use..............	3254147	7,576	8,799	6,619	5,785	5,573	6,336	6,375
Biological products (excl. diagnostic) for veterinary, industrial, and all other miscellaneous uses.....	325414A	4,063	3,912	4,326	4,599	4,672	6,546	6,881
Biological product (excl. diagnostic) manufacturing, total [2]...	325414W	376	631	433	501	546	640	633

[1] Including medicinal premixes and medicated pet care products; excluding pet flea and tick products. [2] Not specified by kind.

Source: U.S. Census Bureau, Annual Survey of Manufactures, "Value of Products Shipments: Value of Shipments for Product Classes: 2016 and 2015," <data.census.gov>, accessed April 2018, and earlier releases.

Table 1060. Household Appliances Manufacturing—Value of Shipments: 2010 to 2016

[In millions of dollars (3,676 represents $3,676,000,000). Data are from the Annual Survey of Manufacturers (ASM) and are based on the North American Industry Classification System (NAICS). The ASM is conducted annually, except for years ending in 2 and 7, at which time ASM data are included in the manufacturing sector of the Economic Census]

Product description	Product code	2010	2011	2012	2013	2014	2015	2016
Household cooking appliance manufacturing.....................	335221	3,676	3,729	4,369	4,419	4,472	4,768	4,865
Electric household ranges, ovens, and surface cooking units & equipment..................	3352211	1,839	1,836	2,494	2,376	2,452	2,618	2,601
Gas household ranges, ovens, and surface cooking units & equipment..................	3352213	1,131	1,168	1,156	1,223	975	1,039	1,111
Other household ranges and cooking equipment..............	3352215	698	719	700	801	1,012	1,069	1,121
Other household cooking appliance manufacturing..............	335221W	7	6	18	19	33	41	32
Household refrigerator and home freezer manufacturing........	335222	3,495	3,530	3,497	3,364	3,824	4,095	4,451
Household refrigerators (incl. combination refrigerator-freezers).................	3352221	(D)	2,884	2,966	2,931	(D)	3,751	(D)
Household laundry equipment manufacturing....................	335224	3,491	3,531	3,553	3,529	3,497	3,526	3,845
Other major household appliance manufacturing.................	335228	3,729	3,902	4,385	4,318	4,610	4,882	4,854
Household water heaters, electric, for permanent installation.......................	3352281	611	671	957	815	898	861	1,116
Household water heaters, except electric.......................	3352283	964	1,064	1,251	1,144	1,253	1,433	1,293
All other misc. household appliances (including parts)........	3352285	2,139	2,152	2,161	2,317	2,437	2,587	2,445
Other major household appliance manufacturing [1].............	335228W	15	15	16	42	22	–	–

D Data withheld to avoid disclosing data of individual companies. – Rounds to zero. [1] Not specified by kind.

Source: U.S. Census Bureau, Annual Survey of Manufactures, "Value of Products Shipments: Value of Shipments for Product Classes: 2016 and 2015," <data.census.gov>, accessed April 2018, and earlier releases.

Table 1061. Communications Equipment Manufacturing—Value of Shipments: 2010 to 2016

[In millions of dollars (8,793 represents $8,793,000,000). Data are from the Annual Survey of Manufacturers (ASM) and are based on the North American Industry Classification System (NAICS). The ASM is conducted annually, except for years ending in 2 and 7, at which time ASM data are included in the manufacturing sector of the Economic Census]

Product description	Product code	2010	2011	2012	2013	2014	2015	2016
Telephone apparatus manufacturing.............................	334210	8,793	8,590	7,171	7,539	6,535	6,384	5,722
Telephone switching and switchboard equipment.............	3342101	1,366	1,161	654	1,368	1,333	1,355	1,207
Carrier line equipment and non-consumer modems..........	3342104	2,521	2,802	2,310	1,728	1,860	1,966	2,062
Wireline voice and data network equipment....................	3342107	4,179	3,889	3,348	3,621	2,530	2,293	1,738
Other telephone apparatus manufacturing.....................	334210W	728	739	859	822	812	771	715
Radio and television broadcast and wireless communications equipment.........................	334220	27,592	27,161	26,345	26,379	23,066	22,565	22,316
Broadcast, studio, and related electronic equipment...........	3342202	3,484	3,205	2,335	2,025	1,923	2,028	1,892
Wireless networking equipment................................	3342203	2,224	1,728	2,093	2,262	1,528	1,430	2,304
Radio station equipment.......................................	3342205	12,210	11,309	9,761	9,936	9,140	8,729	8,721
Other communications systems and equipment..............	3342209	8,556	9,545	10,571	10,582	9,142	9,094	8,170
Other radio and television broadcast and wireless communications equipment.	334220W	(S)	(S)	1,586	1,574	1,334	1,283	1,229
Other communications equipment manufacturing...............	334290	4,871	5,008	4,663	4,909	4,923	3,922	3,496
Alarm systems (incl. electric sirens and horns)...............	3342901	1,394	1,561	2,015	2,177	1,951	1,606	1,516
Vehicular and pedestrian traffic control equipment............	3342902	2,585	2,543	1,595	1,739	1,995	1,522	1,242
Intercommunications systems (incl. inductive paging systems)...	3342903	358	342	562	465	450	321	337
Other communications equipment [2]...........................	334290W	534	563	491	528	527	473	401
External modems, consumer...................................	3344184	637	597	232	260	180	[1] 112	97

S Estimates do not meet publication standards. [1] Sampling error exceeds 40 percent. [2] Not specified by kind.

Source: U.S. Census Bureau, Annual Survey of Manufactures, "Value of Products Shipments: Value of Shipments for Product Classes: 2016 and 2015," <data.census.gov>, accessed April 2018, and earlier releases.

Table 1062. Computers and Peripheral Equipment Manufacturing—Value of Shipments: 2010 to 2016

[In millions of dollars (17,731 represents $17,731,000,000). Data are from the Annual Survey of Manufacturers (ASM) and are based on the North American Industry Classification System (NAICS). The ASM is conducted annually, except for years ending in 2 and 7, at which time ASM data are included in the manufacturing sector of the Economic Census]

Product description	Product code	2010	2012	2013	2014	2015	2016
Electronic computers manufacturing.........................	334111	17,731	8,116	7,878	8,918	9,172	8,951
Host computers, multiusers (mainframes, servers, etc.).......................	3341111	12,443	4,769	4,559	5,464	5,724	5,372
Single user computers, microprocessor-based..............	3341117	4,584	2,550	2,534	2,531	2,557	2,678
Other computers (array, analog, hybrid, and special-use computers)........	334111D	426	456	446	517	380	389
Other electronic computer [2]................................	334111W	[1] 278	341	340	407	511	511
Computer storage devices manufacturing.....................	334112	8,425	8,619	9,072	8,138	7,441	6,631
Computer storage devices [3]................................	3341121	7,697	6,948	7,092	6,359	5,962	5,258
Parts, attachments, and accessories for computer storage devices..........	3341124	649	1,616	1,920	1,699	1,417	1,302
Other computer storage device manufacturing [2]..................	334112W	79	56	60	80	63	71
Computer terminal and other computer peripheral equipment manufacturing.........	334118	(NA)	10,634	10,691	8,974	8,350	7,180
Computer terminals (excluding point-of-sale and funds-transfer devices, parts, attachments, and accessories)...............	3341181	(NA)	353	514	579	664	556
Parts, attachments, and accessories for computer terminals (excluding point-of-sale and funds-transfer devices).............	3341182	(NA)	20	22	70	96	127
All other miscellaneous computer peripheral (input/output) equipment [3].....	3341183	(NA)	7,041	6,232	4,721	3,992	3,452
Parts, subassemblies, and accessories for computer peripheral equipment [3]...	3341184	(NA)	1,445	2,287	2,412	2,417	1,855
Point-of-sale terminals and fund-transfer devices........................	3341185	(NA)	906	855	592	568	541
Parts and attachments for point-of-sale terminals and fund-transfer devices...	3341186	(NA)	284	135	97	80	82
Other computer terminal and other computer peripheral equipment [2]........	334118W	(NA)	585	645	503	534	567
Magnetic and optical recording media........................	334613	532	321	[1] 233	452	446	345
Software and other prerecorded compact disc, tape, and record reproducing...	334614	(NA)	2,670	2,525	2,291	2,301	2,144
Software reproducing...	3346141	(NA)	684	649	648	613	665
Reproduction of recording media.............................	3346142	(NA)	1,904	1,749	1,554	1,596	1,364

NA Not available. [1] Sampling error exceeds 40 percent. [2] Not specified by kind. [3] Excluding parts, attachments, digital cameras, accessories, etc.

Source: U.S. Census Bureau, Annual Survey of Manufactures, "Value of Products Shipments: Value of Shipments for Product Classes: 2016 and 2015," <data.census.gov>, accessed April 2018, and earlier releases.

Table 1063. Semiconductors, Electronic Components, and Other Electronic Component Manufacturing Equipment—Value of Shipments: 2010 to 2016

[In millions of dollars (9,083 represents $9,083,000,000). Data are from the Annual Survey of Manufacturers (ASM) and are based on the North American Industry Classification System (NAICS). The ASM is conducted annually, except for years ending in 2 and 7, at which time ASM data are included in the manufacturing sector of the Economic Census]

Product description	Product code	2010	2012	2013	2014	2015	2016
Semiconductor machinery manufacturing	333242	(NA)	9,765	8,795	6,970	5,816	5,412
Semiconductor machinery manufacturing	333295	9,083	(NA)	(NA)	(NA)	(NA)	(NA)
Electron tube manufacturing	334411	1,287	(NA)	(NA)	(NA)	(NA)	(NA)
Bare printed circuit board manufacturing	334412	4,977	4,773	4,449	4,121	4,166	3,867
Semiconductors and related device manufacturing	334413	58,474	47,211	43,411	45,443	45,810	45,730
Integrated circuit packages	3344131	39,784	33,611	29,360	31,073	30,693	32,017
Transistors	3344134	637	542	539	285	317	422
Diodes and rectifiers	3344137	398	286	215	243	291	316
Other semiconductor devices (incl. chips, wafers, & heat sinks)	334413A	14,875	10,524	11,316	12,517	13,077	11,582
Other semiconductor and related device [1]	334413W	2,780	2,249	1,981	1,325	1,431	1,392
Electronic capacitor manufacturing	334414	916	(NA)	(NA)	(NA)	(NA)	(NA)
Electronic resistor manufacturing	334415	563	(NA)	(NA)	(NA)	(NA)	(NA)
Capacitor, resistor, coil, transformer, and other inductor manufacturing	334416	1,743	3,522	3,323	3,343	3,458	3,433
Capacitors for electronic circuitry	3344161	(NA)	1,025	916	946	1,160	1,174
Resistors for electronic circuitry	3344162	(NA)	433	382	402	340	279
Electronic coils, transformers, and other inductors	3344163	(NA)	1,977	1,936	1,889	1,847	1,882
Other capacitor, resistor, coil, transformer, & other inductor [1]	334416W	(NA)	86	90	106	112	98
Electronic connector manufacturing	334417	4,639	5,393	5,488	5,157	5,536	5,432
Printed circuit assembly, electronic assembly manufacturing	334418	18,497	16,383	16,947	15,820	16,912	15,688
External modems, consumer	3344184	637	232	260	180	[2] 112	97
Printed circuit assemblies, loaded boards and modules	334418B	16,673	15,134	15,757	14,776	15,852	14,631
Other printed circuit assembly, electronic assembly	334418W	1,188	1,017	930	864	948	960
Other electronic component manufacturing	334419	9,072	10,717	10,684	11,340	11,648	10,435
Crystals, filters, piezoelectric, & other related electronic devices	3344191	879	992	937	880	932	703
Electron tubes and parts, excluding glass blanks	3344192	(NA)	1,154	927	952	905	774
Transducers, incl. electrical-electronic input/output transducers	3344194	1,177	626	789	943	904	710
Switches, mechanical, for electronic circuitry	3344197	1,121	981	973	997	993	934
Microwave components and devices (excl. antennae, tubes, etc.)	334419A	1,248	1,807	1,684	1,707	1,663	1,605
All other miscellaneous electronic components	334419E	3,856	4,212	4,508	4,840	5,182	4,729
Other electronic component manufacturing [1]	334419W	791	946	866	1,022	1,069	980

NA Not available. [1] Not specified by kind. [2] Sampling error exceeds 40 percent.

Source: U.S. Census Bureau, Annual Survey of Manufactures, "Value of Products Shipments: Value of Shipments for Product Classes: 2016 and 2015," <data.census.gov>, accessed April 2018, and earlier releases.

Table 1064. Beverage Manufacturing Industry—Brewery, Distillery, and Winery Establishments and Employment: 2009 to 2018

[Beverage manufacturer data are from the Quarterly Census of Employment and Wages (QCEW). Covers North American Industry Classification System (NAICS) 31212, 31213, 31214, and 31211]

Industry characteristic	2009	2010	2011	2012	2013	2014	2015	2016	2017	2018
Establishments (number):										
Breweries	482	527	638	843	1,167	1,616	2,190	2,843	3,509	4,156
Wineries	2,456	2,616	2,771	2,978	3,201	3,560	3,848	4,083	4,343	4,643
Distilleries	132	145	184	243	306	424	558	675	805	964
Soft drink and ice manufacturing	1,854	1,845	1,808	1,802	1,830	1,864	1,858	1,969	2,053	2,065
Employment (number):										
Breweries	25,058	24,864	26,707	29,309	34,519	40,101	48,401	58,580	68,148	77,911
Wineries	40,100	40,830	42,231	45,351	48,386	52,879	57,003	60,436	64,212	67,832
Distilleries	7,189	7,252	7,625	8,001	8,872	10,579	11,075	12,207	13,759	15,839
Soft drink and ice manufacturing	96,018	94,225	92,889	94,576	93,854	93,333	94,334	102,793	104,743	103,124
Average weekly wages (in dollars):										
Breweries	1,401	1,321	1,266	1,226	1,140	1,129	1,163	969	906	866
Wineries	770	773	792	808	789	803	833	846	861	871
Distilleries	1,311	1,352	1,417	1,550	1,430	1,415	1,462	1,362	1,300	1,279
Soft drink and ice manufacturing	884	938	962	955	952	980	1,020	1,028	1,044	1,079

Source: U.S. Bureau of Labor Statistics, Quarterly Census of Employment and Wages, QCEW Databases, "State and County Wages," <http://www.bls.gov/cew/home.htm>, accessed March 2020

Section 22
Wholesale and Retail Trade

This section presents statistics relating to the distributive trades, specifically wholesale trade and retail trade. Data shown for the trades are classified by kind of business and cover sales, establishments, employees, payrolls, and other items. The principal sources of these data are from the U.S. Census Bureau and include the 2012 and 2017 Economic Censuses, annual and monthly surveys, and the County Business Patterns program. These data are supplemented by several tables from trade associations, such as the National Automobile Dealers Association.

Data on wholesale and retail trade also appear in several other sections. For instance, labor force employment and earnings data appear in Section 12, Labor Force, Employment, and Earnings; gross domestic product of the industry (Table 705) appears in Section 13, Income, Expenditures, Poverty, and Wealth; and financial data (several tables) from the quarterly *Statistics of Income Bulletin*, published by the Internal Revenue Service, appear in Section 15, Business Enterprise.

Censuses—Censuses of wholesale trade and retail trade have been taken at various intervals since 1929. Beginning with the 1967 Economic Census, legislation provides for a census to be conducted every 5 years (for years ending in "2" and "7"). The industries covered in the censuses and surveys of business are defined in the North American Industry Classification System (NAICS). Retail trade refers to places of business primarily engaged in retailing merchandise to the general public; and wholesale trade, to establishments primarily engaged in selling goods to other businesses and normally operating from a warehouse or office that have little or no display of merchandise. Census Bureau tables in this section primarily utilize the 2012 or 2017 NAICS codes. NAICS codes are reviewed every 5 years to identify areas for revision, so that the classification system can keep pace with the changing economy. For information on this system and how it affects the comparability of wholesale and retail statistics historically, see text, Section 15, Business Enterprise, and especially the Census Bureau Web site at <census.gov/eos/www/naics>.

The 2012 and 2017 Economic Censuses have three series of publications for these two sectors: 1) subject series with reports such as product lines and establishment and firm sizes, 2) geographic reports with individual reports for each state, and 3) industry series with individual reports for industry groups. Release of data from the *2012 Economic Census* was completed in 2016. Data from the *2017 Economic Census* are being released on a flow basis between September 2019 and December 2021. For information on these series, see the Census Bureau Web site at <census.gov/programs-surveys/economic-census.html>.

Current surveys—Current sample surveys conducted by the Census Bureau cover various aspects of wholesale and retail trade. Its *Monthly Retail Trade and Food Services* release at <census.gov/retail/index.html> contains monthly estimates of sales, inventories, and inventory/sales ratios for the United States, by kind of business. Annual figures on retail sales, year-end inventories, purchases, accounts receivable, and gross margins by kind of business are located on the Census Bureau Web site at <census.gov/programs-surveys/arts.html>.

Statistics from the Census Bureau's monthly wholesale trade survey include national estimates of sales, inventories, and inventory/sales ratios for merchant wholesalers excluding manufacturers' sales branches and offices. Data are presented by major summary groups "durable and nondurable," and 4-digit NAICS industry groups. Merchant wholesalers excluding manufacturers' sales branches and offices are those wholesalers who take title to the goods they sell (e.g., jobbers, exporters, importers, industrial distributors). These data, based on reports submitted by a sample of firms, appear in the *Monthly Wholesale Trade Report*. This report, along with monthly sales, inventories, and inventories/sales ratios, also provides data on annual sales, inventories, and year-end inventories/sales ratios. The *Annual Wholesale Trade Report* provides data on merchant wholesalers excluding manufacturer sales branches and offices as well as summary data for all merchant wholesalers. This report also provides separate data for manufacturer sales branches and offices, and electronic markets, agents, brokers, and commission merchants. Included in the *Annual Wholesale Trade Report* are data on annual sales, year-end inventories, inventories/sales ratios, operating expenses, purchases, and gross margins. Data are presented by major summary groups "durable and nondurable" and 4-digit NAICS industry groups. These reports are available on the Census Bureau Web site at <census.gov/econ/wholesale.html>.

E-commerce—Electronic commerce (or e-commerce) is the sale of goods and services over the internet and extranet, electronic data interchange (EDI) network, electronic mail, or other online systems. Payment may or may not be made online. E-commerce data are collected in four separate Census Bureau surveys. These surveys use different measures of economic activity such as shipments for manufacturing, sales for wholesale and retail trade, and revenues for service industries. Data can be found at <census.gov/programs-surveys/e-stats.html>. Consequently, measures of total economic and e-commerce activity vary by economic sector, are conceptually and definitionally different, and therefore, are not additive. This edition has several tables on e-commerce sales, such as Tables 1068, 1078, and 1079 in this section; and Table 1299 in Section 27, Accommodation, Food Services, and Other Services.

Statistical reliability—For a discussion of statistical collection and estimation, sampling procedures, and measures of statistical reliability applicable to Census Bureau data, see Appendix III.

Table 1065. Wholesale and Retail Trade—Establishments, Sales, Payroll, and Employees: 2017

[8,735 represents $8,735,000,000,000. Covers establishments with payroll. Based on data from the Economic Census; see Appendix III]

Kind of business	2017 NAICS code [1]	Establishments	Sales (billion dollars)	Annual payroll (billion dollars)	Paid employees (1,000)
Wholesale trade	**42**	**408,333**	**8,735**	**427**	**6,242**
Wholesale trade, durable goods	423	240,906	3,688	252	3,547
Wholesale trade, nondurable goods	424	129,714	4,344	160	2,397
Wholesale electronic markets and agents and brokers	425	37,713	703	14	298
Retail trade	**44–45**	**1,064,087**	**4,950**	**442**	**15,939**
Motor vehicle and parts dealers	441	118,882	1,168	91	2,003
Furniture and home furnishings stores	442	50,664	113	14	466
Electronics and appliance stores	443	30,440	91	10	332
Building material and garden equipment and supplies dealers	444	75,054	347	39	1,285
Food and beverage stores	445	150,238	721	72	3,176
Health and personal care stores	446	94,666	319	34	1,039
Gasoline stations	447	115,369	475	19	943
Clothing and clothing accessories stores	448	143,534	255	32	1,791
Sporting goods, hobby, book, and music stores	451	45,054	81	10	539
General merchandise stores	452	53,777	690	68	2,793
Miscellaneous store retailers	453	109,019	110	17	774
Nonstore retailers	454	77,390	579	35	797

[1] North American Industrial Classification System, 2017; see text, Section 15.

Source: U.S. Census Bureau, "EC1700BASIC: All Sectors: Summary Statistics for the U.S., States, and Selected Geographies: 2017," <data.census.gov>, accessed July 2020.

Table 1066. Wholesale Trade—Nonemployer Firms and Receipts by Industry Type: 2018

[37,977,982 represents $37,977,982,000. Includes only firms subject to federal income tax. Nonemployers are businesses with no paid employees. Each distinct business income tax return filed by a nonemployer business is counted as a firm]

Industry type	2017 NAICS code [1]	Firms Total	Corporations [2]	Individual proprietorships [3]	Partnerships [4]	Receipts ($1,000)
Wholesale trade, total	**42**	**399,400**	**69,141**	**301,616**	**28,643**	**37,977,982**
Durable goods merchant wholesalers	**423**	**188,494**	**36,829**	**137,014**	**14,651**	**19,255,513**
Motor vehicle and motor vehicle parts and supplies merchant wholesalers	4231	16,851	3,379	12,389	1,083	2,358,008
Furniture and home furnishing merchant wholesalers	4232	12,242	1,881	9,554	807	1,079,378
Lumber and other construction materials merchant wholesalers	4233	6,911	1,399	4,849	663	857,844
Professional and commercial equipment and supplies merchant wholesalers	4234	10,931	2,254	7,600	1,077	1,216,243
Metal and mineral (except petroleum) merchant wholesalers	4235	2,578	605	1,771	202	385,063
Household appliance and electrical and electronic goods merchant wholesalers	4236	8,914	2,654	5,413	847	1,099,707
Hardware and plumbing and heating equipment and supplies merchant wholesalers	4237	4,072	963	2,738	371	446,402
Machinery, equipment, and supplies merchant wholesalers	4238	17,404	4,726	11,014	1,664	2,420,676
Miscellaneous durable goods merchant wholesalers	4239	108,591	18,968	81,686	7,937	9,392,192
Nondurable goods merchant wholesalers	**424**	**144,944**	**24,634**	**109,098**	**11,212**	**13,821,559**
Paper and paper product merchant wholesalers	4241	4,630	874	3,481	275	452,172
Drugs and druggists' sundries merchant wholesalers	4242	2,819	632	1,897	290	266,078
Apparel, piece goods, and notions merchant wholesalers	4243	26,150	3,929	20,464	1,757	1,816,166
Grocery and related products merchant wholesalers	4244	27,507	5,333	19,963	2,211	4,015,983
Farm product raw material merchant wholesalers	4245	5,810	607	4,827	376	641,880
Chemical and allied products merchant wholesalers	4246	3,210	929	1,935	346	419,767
Petroleum and petroleum products merchant wholesalers	4247	2,223	443	1,540	240	303,042
Beer, wine, and distilled alcoholic beverage merchant wholesalers	4248	6,313	960	4,367	986	558,835
Miscellaneous nondurable goods merchant wholesalers	4249	66,282	10,927	50,624	4,731	5,347,636
Wholesale electronic markets and agents and brokers	**425**	**65,962**	**7,678**	**55,504**	**2,780**	**4,900,910**
Business to business electronics markets	42511	9,184	1,291	7,361	532	851,411
Wholesale trade agents and brokers	42512	56,778	6,387	48,143	2,248	4,049,499

[1] North American Industry Classification System, 2017; see text, Section 15. [2] A legally incorporated business under state laws. [3] Also referred to as "sole proprietorship," an unincorporated business with a sole owner. Includes self-employed persons. [4] An unincorporated business where two or more persons join to carry on a trade or business with each having a shared financial interest in the business.

Source: U.S. Census Bureau, Nonemployer Statistics, "All Sectors: Nonemployer Statistics for the U.S., States, Counties, Metropolitan Areas, and Combined Statistical Areas; and by Legal Form of Organization and Sales, Value of Shipments, or Revenue Size for Selected Geographies: 2018," <data.census.gov>, accessed May 2020.

Table 1067. Wholesale Trade—Establishments, Employees, and Payroll: 2017 and 2018

[409.7 represents 409,700. Covers establishments with payroll. Excludes self-employed individuals, employees of private households, railroad employees, agricultural production employees, and most government employees. For statement on methodology, see Appendix III]

Kind of business	NAICS code [1]	Establishments (1,000)		Employees [2] (1,000)		Payroll (bil. dol.)	
		2017	2018	2017	2018	2017	2018
Wholesale trade, total.....................	**42**	**409.7**	**403.6**	**6,115**	**6,164**	**434.3**	**450.5**
Merchant wholesalers, durable goods......................	423	239.8	236.6	3,460	3,498	256.5	268.9
Motor vehicle and motor vehicle parts and supply merchant wholesalers......................	4231	23.8	23.5	407	408	22.7	24.1
Furniture and home furnishing merchant wholesalers......	4232	13.2	12.9	170	167	10.6	10.5
Lumber and other construction materials merchant wholesalers......................	4233	17.6	17.6	248	258	14.8	15.9
Professional and commercial equipment and supplies merchant wholesalers......................	4234	35.6	35.4	640	643	60.3	62.5
Metal and mineral (except petroleum) merchant wholesalers......................	4235	9.7	9.6	151	151	9.8	10.4
Household appliances and electrical and electronic goods merchant wholesalers....................	4236	29.2	28.6	517	521	51.8	54.2
Hardware, plumbing and heating equipment and supplies merchant wholesalers......................	4237	19.7	19.6	248	253	16.1	17.2
Machinery, equipment, and supplies merchant wholesalers......................	4238	58.7	57.6	759	771	51.9	54.9
Miscellaneous durable goods merchant wholesalers.......	4239	32.3	31.9	321	326	18.4	19.1
Merchant wholesalers, nondurable goods....................	424	129.7	128.0	2,364	2,382	162.3	165.9
Paper and paper product merchant wholesalers...........	4241	9.8	9.3	148	150	9.1	9.2
Drugs and druggists' sundries merchant wholesalers......	4242	10.3	10.4	305	307	38.8	38.3
Apparel, piece goods and notions merchant wholesalers..	4243	15.6	15.0	201	197	13.0	12.7
Grocery and related product merchant wholesalers........	4244	35.5	35.5	834	858	46.0	48.1
Farm product raw material merchant wholesalers..........	4245	6.3	6.2	65	61	3.8	3.6
Chemical and allied products merchant wholesalers.......	4246	12.4	12.4	159	162	12.5	13.1
Petroleum and petroleum products merchant wholesalers......................	4247	6.4	6.3	100	100	7.9	8.2
Beer, wine, and distilled alcoholic beverages...........	4248	4.5	4.6	205	202	12.7	13.2
Miscellaneous nondurable goods merchant wholesalers...	4249	28.9	28.5	347	344	18.7	19.5
Wholesale electronic markets and agents and brokers......	425	40.2	39.0	291	284	15.5	15.7

[1] Data based on North American Industry Classification System (NAICS) 2017. See text, Section 15. [2] Covers full- and part-time employees who are on the payroll in the pay period including March 12.

Source: U.S. Census Bureau, County Business Patterns, "County Business Patterns by Legal Form of Organization and Employment Size Class for U.S., States, and Selected Geographies," <data.census.gov/>, accessed July 2020. See also <https://www.census.gov/programs-surveys/cbp.html>.

Table 1068. Merchant Wholesale Trade Sales—Total and E-Commerce: 2018

[5,939,422 represents $5,939,422,000,000. Covers only businesses with paid employees. Excludes manufacturers' sales branches and offices. Based on the Annual Wholesale Trade Survey; see Appendix III]

Kind of business	NAICS code [1]	Value of sales (mil. dol.)		E-commerce as percent of total sales	Percent distribution of E-commerce sales
		Total	E-commerce		
Total merchant wholesale trade.....................	**42**	**5,939,442**	**1,674,992**	**28.2**	**100.0**
Durable goods........................	**423**	**2,858,725**	**705,921**	**24.7**	**42.1**
Motor vehicles, parts and supplies.....................	4231	465,029	181,287	39.0	10.8
Furniture and home furnishings.....................	4232	91,775	19,741	21.5	1.2
Lumber and other construction materials.....................	4233	149,492	(S)	(S)	(S)
Professional and commercial equipment and supplies.................	4234	510,129	143,533	28.1	8.6
Computers and peripheral equipment and software..............	42343	262,537	62,940	24.0	3.8
Medical, dental, and hospital equipment and supplies..............	42345	148,373	60,178	40.6	3.6
Metals and minerals (except petroleum).....................	4235	182,985	16,326	8.9	1.0
Household appliances and electrical and electronic goods...........	4236	617,028	215,735	35.0	12.9
Hardware, plumbing and heating equipment.....................	4237	150,362	25,859	17.2	1.5
Machinery, equipment and supplies.....................	4238	444,647	54,009	12.1	3.2
Miscellaneous durable goods.....................	4239	247,278	38,361	15.5	2.3
Nondurable goods.....................	**424**	**3,080,717**	**969,071**	**31.5**	**57.9**
Paper and paper products.....................	4241	96,765	(S)	(S)	(S)
Drugs and druggists' sundries.....................	4242	691,227	(S)	(S)	(S)
Apparel, piece goods and notions.....................	4243	160,654	40,150	25.0	2.4
Groceries and related products.....................	4244	667,008	196,563	29.5	11.7
Farm product raw materials.....................	4245	197,438	16,832	8.5	1.0
Chemical and allied products.....................	4246	133,097	13,950	10.5	0.8
Petroleum and petroleum products.....................	4247	713,310	73,887	10.4	4.4
Beer, wine, and distilled alcoholic beverages.....................	4248	154,434	11,507	7.5	0.7
Miscellaneous nondurable goods.....................	4249	266,784	41,341	15.5	2.5

S Figure does not meet publication standards. [1] North American Industry Classification System, 2012. See text, Section 15.

Source: U.S. Census Bureau, "Annual Report for Wholesale Trade: 2018," <https://www.census.gov/programs-surveys/awts/data/tables.html>, accessed February 2020.

Table 1069. Merchant Wholesalers' Sales and Inventories by Kind of Business: 2010 to 2018

[In billions of dollars (4,337.4 represents $4,337,400,000,000), except ratios. Inventories and inventories/sales ratios, as of December, not seasonally adjusted. Excludes manufacturers' sales branches and offices. Data adjusted using final results of the 2012 Economic Census. Based on data from the Annual Wholesale Trade Survey and the Monthly Wholesale Trade Survey; see Appendix III]

Kind of business	NAICS code [1]	2010	2013	2014	2015	2016	2017	2018
SALES								
Merchant wholesalers	**42**	**4,337.4**	**5,370.6**	**5,564.2**	**5,292.4**	**5,222.0**	**5,549.0**	**5,939.4**
Durable goods	**423**	**1,999.2**	**2,461.0**	**2,556.6**	**2,520.1**	**2,504.9**	**2,674.1**	**2,858.7**
Motor vehicles, parts, and supplies	4231	303.0	401.6	415.0	430.2	426.0	447.7	465.0
Furniture and home furnishings	4232	57.4	71.6	76.7	79.6	83.7	89.0	91.8
Lumber and other construction materials	4233	86.5	105.0	111.5	117.6	128.7	138.0	149.5
Professional, commercial equipment and supplies	4234	397.8	425.5	437.9	449.3	461.0	478.8	510.1
Computer, peripheral equipment and software	42343	220.1	224.6	228.8	231.9	232.7	242.1	262.5
Medical, dental, and hospital equipment and supplies	42345	(NA)	(NA)	(NA)	126.4	135.2	140.3	148.4
Metals and minerals (except petroleum)	4235	138.4	173.8	184.7	156.7	138.2	157.6	183.0
Household appliances and electrical and electronic goods	4236	391.2	510.9	535.8	549.1	542.2	587.4	617.0
Hardware, plumbing, heating equipment and supplies	4237	96.1	117.3	124.5	129.1	134.4	140.8	150.4
Machinery, equipment, and supplies	4238	305.3	404.2	421.3	398.2	382.3	406.5	444.6
Miscellaneous durable goods	4239	223.7	251.1	249.4	210.2	208.4	228.2	247.3
Nondurable goods	**424**	**2,338.1**	**2,909.5**	**3,007.5**	**2,772.3**	**2,717.1**	**2,875.0**	**3,080.7**
Paper and paper products	4241	86.0	92.0	95.9	95.8	95.9	96.6	96.8
Drugs and druggists' sundries	4242	415.9	486.8	540.1	604.4	643.3	661.5	691.2
Apparel, piece goods, and notions	4243	137.0	156.2	162.4	165.5	161.8	161.1	160.7
Grocery and related products	4244	491.3	576.8	611.5	629.1	630.3	653.4	667.0
Farm product raw materials	4245	188.3	270.7	254.9	219.1	203.0	196.3	197.4
Chemical and allied products	4246	102.7	124.4	128.8	117.8	111.7	121.6	133.1
Petroleum and petroleum products	4247	591.0	818.5	834.5	552.5	476.8	581.8	713.3
Beer, wine, and distilled alcoholic beverages	4248	111.3	130.0	130.7	136.5	143.7	148.4	154.4
Miscellaneous nondurable goods	4249	214.5	254.1	248.7	251.6	250.4	254.2	266.8
INVENTORIES								
Merchant wholesalers	**42**	**444.3**	**545.3**	**577.7**	**585.0**	**596.8**	**614.7**	**655.0**
Durable goods	**423**	**256.1**	**324.4**	**346.3**	**346.5**	**347.0**	**361.3**	**394.4**
Motor vehicles, parts, and supplies	4231	40.3	49.7	53.7	60.8	60.9	60.6	64.9
Furniture and home furnishings	4232	8.6	10.6	11.2	11.8	12.1	12.5	13.4
Lumber and other construction materials	4233	10.2	12.3	13.1	13.9	15.4	16.5	18.9
Professional, commercial equipment and supplies	4234	33.0	39.0	42.6	42.0	43.8	45.9	49.9
Computer, peripheral equipment and software	42343	13.0	14.4	15.9	15.0	15.1	16.5	18.1
Medical, dental, and hospital equipment and supplies	42345	(NA)	(NA)	(NA)	16.2	17.0	17.8	19.5
Metals and minerals (except petroleum)	4235	23.0	29.7	33.2	27.3	25.9	29.5	34.5
Household appliances and electrical and electronic goods	4236	35.3	45.4	47.3	49.6	49.4	51.7	54.6
Hardware, plumbing, heating equipment and supplies	4237	16.8	19.4	21.2	22.1	22.5	23.7	26.2
Machinery, equipment, and supplies	4238	64.2	89.7	95.3	92.0	88.8	91.6	100.8
Miscellaneous durable goods	4239	24.8	28.5	28.8	27.1	28.2	29.2	31.1
Nondurable goods	**424**	**188.2**	**221.0**	**231.4**	**238.5**	**249.8**	**253.4**	**260.6**
Paper and paper products	4241	7.6	8.5	8.9	8.9	9.0	9.2	9.4
Drugs and druggists' sundries	4242	38.9	48.9	57.3	64.2	66.3	66.4	66.9
Apparel, piece goods, and notions	4243	20.1	23.8	25.3	27.5	26.4	26.1	26.6
Grocery and related products	4244	27.3	32.8	35.7	37.2	38.3	39.0	40.5
Farm product raw materials	4245	28.4	27.7	27.9	24.7	27.3	28.5	30.1
Chemical and allied products	4246	9.4	11.6	12.1	11.8	12.1	12.7	13.4
Petroleum and petroleum products	4247	22.8	25.1	19.0	17.7	23.4	22.0	20.1
Beer, wine, and distilled alcoholic beverages	4248	10.7	13.6	14.2	14.4	15.1	16.0	16.3
Miscellaneous nondurable goods	4249	23.0	29.1	31.0	32.0	31.9	33.4	37.3
INVENTORIES/SALES RATIO								
Merchant wholesalers	**42**	**1.02**	**1.02**	**1.04**	**1.11**	**1.14**	**1.11**	**1.10**
Durable goods	**423**	**1.28**	**1.32**	**1.35**	**1.37**	**1.39**	**1.35**	**1.38**
Motor vehicles, parts, and supplies	4231	1.33	1.24	1.29	1.41	1.43	1.35	1.40
Furniture and home furnishings	4232	1.49	1.48	1.46	1.48	1.45	1.40	1.46
Lumber and other construction materials	4233	1.18	1.17	1.17	1.18	1.20	1.20	1.27
Professional, commercial equipment and supplies	4234	0.83	0.92	0.97	0.93	0.95	0.96	0.98
Computer, peripheral equipment and software	42343	0.59	0.64	0.69	0.65	0.65	0.68	0.69
Medical, dental, and hospital equipment and supplies	42345	(NA)	(NA)	(NA)	1.3	1.3	1.3	1.3
Metals and minerals (except petroleum)	4235	1.66	1.71	1.80	1.74	1.87	1.87	1.88
Household appliances and electrical and electronic goods	4236	0.90	0.89	0.88	0.90	0.91	0.88	0.88
Hardware, plumbing, heating equipment and supplies	4237	1.75	1.65	1.70	1.71	1.67	1.68	1.74
Machinery, equipment, and supplies	4238	2.10	2.22	2.26	2.31	2.32	2.25	2.27
Miscellaneous durable goods	4239	1.11	1.14	1.15	1.29	1.35	1.28	1.26
Nondurable goods	**424**	**0.80**	**0.76**	**0.77**	**0.86**	**0.92**	**0.88**	**0.85**
Paper and paper products	4241	0.88	0.93	0.93	0.93	0.94	0.96	0.97
Drugs and druggists' sundries	4242	0.93	1.00	1.06	1.06	1.03	1.00	0.97
Apparel, piece goods, and notions	4243	1.47	1.53	1.56	1.66	1.63	1.62	1.66
Grocery and related products	4244	0.56	0.57	0.58	0.59	0.61	0.60	0.61
Farm product raw materials	4245	1.51	1.02	1.10	1.13	1.34	1.45	1.52
Chemical and allied products	4246	0.91	0.93	0.94	1.01	1.08	1.05	1.01
Petroleum and petroleum products	4247	0.39	0.31	0.23	0.32	0.49	0.38	0.28
Beer, wine, and distilled alcoholic beverages	4248	0.97	1.04	1.09	1.06	1.05	1.08	1.06
Miscellaneous nondurable goods	4249	1.07	1.14	1.24	1.27	1.28	1.31	1.40

NA Not available. [1] North American Industry Classification System, 2012. See text, Section 15.

Source: U.S. Census Bureau, "Annual Report for Wholesale Trade: 2018," <https://www.census.gov/programs-surveys/awts.html>, accessed February 2020.

Table 1070. Wholesale and Retail Trade—Establishments, Employees, and Payroll by State: 2017 and 2018

[6,115 represents 6,115,000. Covers establishments with payroll. Excludes self-employed individuals, employees of private households, railroad employees, agricultural production employees, and most government employees. Data based on North American Industry Classification System (NAICS), 2017. See text, Section 15. For statement on methodology, see Appendix III]

State	Wholesale trade (NAICS 42)						Retail trade (NAICS 44, 45)					
	Establishments		Employees [1] (1,000)		Annual payroll (mil. dol.)		Establishments		Employees [1] (1,000)		Annual payroll (mil. dol.)	
	2017	2018	2017	2018	2017	2018	2017	2018	2017	2018	2017	2018
U.S.........	409,656	403,648	6,115	6,164	434,322	450,454	1,064,449	1,050,175	15,706	15,683	444,392	457,384
AL............	5,250	5,154	76	74	4,241	4,331	17,987	17,787	227	228	5,927	6,124
AK............	753	737	9	9	559	570	2,489	2,465	34	34	1,097	1,132
AZ............	6,540	6,533	96	98	6,249	6,520	17,931	17,564	318	324	9,445	10,084
AR............	3,377	3,326	50	50	2,571	2,684	10,919	10,781	140	140	3,656	3,672
CA............	58,878	58,226	840	840	70,197	72,849	108,276	106,420	1,681	1,697	54,669	56,982
CO............	7,225	7,172	101	104	7,652	8,345	18,892	18,687	276	280	8,445	8,919
CT............	4,097	4,006	76	75	6,498	6,294	12,462	12,145	186	182	5,705	5,858
DE............	1,157	1,155	17	16	1,735	1,667	3,678	3,636	58	57	1,565	1,585
DC............	405	387	4	4	334	355	1,783	1,699	22	22	696	711
FL............	31,283	30,949	319	326	19,012	20,539	74,530	73,672	1,081	1,079	30,080	31,156
GA............	13,102	12,972	206	216	13,178	14,549	34,160	34,071	476	478	12,533	13,004
HI............	1,620	1,583	19	19	1,012	1,017	4,681	4,641	70	71	2,200	2,245
ID............	2,169	2,149	33	33	1,877	1,977	6,131	6,127	82	83	2,405	2,489
IL............	18,097	17,750	328	326	25,094	26,002	38,142	37,533	611	592	16,190	16,541
IN............	7,609	7,476	121	123	7,529	7,778	21,343	20,944	332	327	8,568	8,829
IA............	5,038	4,998	70	70	3,862	4,007	11,461	11,444	180	180	4,568	4,674
KS............	4,436	4,330	63	62	3,823	3,814	10,074	9,866	148	148	3,798	3,819
KY............	4,279	4,184	72	72	3,899	4,280	15,035	14,870	217	217	5,637	5,689
LA............	5,337	5,275	74	74	4,171	4,389	16,614	16,255	231	225	6,041	6,076
ME............	1,540	1,529	19	18	1,060	1,077	6,238	6,130	81	81	2,302	2,318
MD............	5,433	5,369	89	90	6,261	6,441	17,920	17,541	292	288	8,418	8,482
MA............	7,567	7,427	146	148	13,413	13,930	24,129	23,486	372	357	11,232	11,447
MI............	10,917	10,643	184	184	12,636	12,784	34,228	33,785	460	461	12,476	12,823
MN............	7,949	7,801	140	140	11,332	11,548	18,819	18,524	304	304	8,311	8,471
MS............	2,711	2,685	37	38	1,912	2,025	11,547	11,425	141	138	3,384	3,417
MO............	7,625	7,420	125	131	7,236	7,707	20,730	20,416	311	308	8,240	8,203
MT............	1,600	1,574	16	16	802	809	4,742	4,648	58	58	1,626	1,694
NE............	3,201	3,168	41	41	2,450	2,429	7,132	7,034	109	109	2,894	2,966
NV............	3,120	3,127	38	41	2,259	2,619	8,689	8,620	143	147	4,213	4,419
NH............	1,830	1,794	25	25	1,896	1,996	6,023	5,919	97	97	2,847	2,895
NJ............	13,859	13,689	272	276	25,929	26,171	31,354	30,809	462	455	13,847	14,081
NM............	1,747	1,704	19	20	1,019	1,088	6,333	6,261	92	93	2,518	2,590
NY............	30,560	29,805	357	354	26,400	26,517	78,497	77,043	925	918	27,945	28,527
NC............	11,722	11,481	192	192	13,871	13,915	34,954	34,506	491	495	12,755	13,102
ND............	1,739	1,721	22	21	1,276	1,341	3,258	3,163	49	49	1,460	1,486
OH............	13,678	13,483	234	234	14,807	15,098	35,550	34,906	563	557	14,727	15,001
OK............	4,623	4,559	58	59	3,209	3,409	12,991	12,881	179	177	4,704	4,802
OR............	5,336	5,227	78	78	5,390	5,511	14,336	14,171	207	210	6,104	6,265
PA............	14,299	14,001	254	251	18,365	18,197	42,608	42,001	660	656	17,522	17,972
RI............	1,312	1,301	22	21	1,608	1,462	3,797	3,675	49	48	1,472	1,449
SC............	5,020	4,999	72	74	4,336	4,495	17,757	17,612	247	248	6,182	6,405
SD............	1,566	1,554	19	18	1,001	1,006	3,875	3,830	53	53	1,368	1,412
TN............	6,867	6,743	117	119	7,277	7,725	22,629	22,567	318	317	8,610	8,813
TX............	33,359	33,010	516	524	35,957	38,276	80,629	80,437	1,294	1,306	36,685	38,140
UT............	3,687	3,685	54	59	3,380	3,731	9,942	10,050	155	156	4,498	4,640
VT............	790	767	11	11	634	644	3,232	3,142	38	38	1,127	1,139
VA............	6,943	6,866	105	107	7,170	7,678	26,798	26,524	425	426	11,516	11,825
WA............	9,191	9,018	136	137	9,159	9,709	21,710	21,538	338	343	11,143	11,524
WV............	1,411	1,400	18	18	906	938	5,963	5,852	82	82	2,013	2,058
WI............	6,973	6,935	123	122	7,452	7,753	18,880	18,533	311	314	8,183	8,532
WY............	829	801	7	7	428	455	2,571	2,539	29	30	850	899

[1] Covers full- and part-time employees who are on the payroll in the pay period including March 12.

Source: U.S. Census Bureau, County Business Patterns, "County Business Patterns by Legal Form of Organization and Employment Size Class for U.S., States, and Selected Geographies," <data.census.gov>, accessed July 2020.

[1,064.4 represents 1,064,400. Covers establishments with payroll. Excludes self-employed individuals, employees of private households, railroad employees, agricultural production employees, and most government employees. For statement on methodology, see Appendix III]

Kind of business	NAICS code [1]	Establishments (1,000)		Employees (1,000) [2]		Payroll (bil. dol.)	
		2017	2018	2017	2018	2017	2018
Retail trade, total.............................	44–45	1,064.4	1,050.2	15,706	15,683	444.4	457.4
Motor vehicle and parts dealers.........................	441	118.9	118.4	2,016	2,011	92.9	94.5
Automobile dealers...................................	4411	47.1	46.9	1,332	1,334	70.3	71.0
New car dealers....................................	44111	21.6	21.6	1,178	1,181	63.8	64.4
Used car dealers...................................	44112	25.5	25.3	154	154	6.5	6.6
Other motor vehicle dealers.........................	4412	13.8	13.7	151	152	6.7	7.0
Recreational vehicle dealers......................	44121	2.7	2.7	46	48	2.3	2.5
Motorcycle and boat and other motor vehicle dealers [3].......	44122	11.1	11.0	105	104	4.4	4.4
Motorcycle, ATV, and all other motor vehicle dealers........	441228	6.9	6.8	72	71	2.8	2.9
Automotive parts, accessories, and tire stores............	4413	57.9	57.8	533	525	15.9	16.5
Automotive parts and accessories stores................	44131	37.6	37.6	361	351	9.2	9.6
Tire dealers.......................................	44132	20.3	20.2	173	174	6.7	6.9
Furniture and home furnishing stores....................	442	50.6	49.8	461	469	14.6	15.1
Furniture stores.....................................	4421	23.6	23.2	209	209	7.9	8.2
Home furnishings stores..............................	4422	27.0	26.7	252	260	6.7	7.0
Floor covering stores..............................	44221	11.2	10.9	70	72	3.1	3.3
Other home furnishings stores [3]...................	44229	15.8	15.8	181	189	3.6	3.7
Window treatment stores.........................	442291	1.8	1.9	7	7	0.3	0.3
Electronics and appliance stores.......................	443	30.5	27.5	321	308	10.3	9.8
Household appliance stores...........................	443141	7.3	6.8	61	57	2.3	2.3
Electronics stores...................................	443142	23.1	20.7	260	252	8.1	7.6
Building material & garden equipment & supplies dealers.......	444	75.1	74.6	1,305	1,361	40.1	42.0
Building material & supplies dealers [3]................	4441	57.5	57.1	1,147	1,205	35.4	37.0
Home centers....................................	44411	6.0	6.0	[5]689	[5]736	[5]17.2	[5]17.6
Hardware stores....................................	44413	15.0	15.3	145	146	3.7	3.9
Lawn & garden equipment & supplies stores [3]..........	4442	17.6	17.5	158	156	4.8	5.0
Nursery, garden center, and farm supply stores...........	44422	13.6	13.6	129	128	3.7	3.9
Food & beverage stores...............................	445	150.2	150.3	3,130	3,087	72.1	74.0
Grocery stores.......................................	4451	93.4	93.5	2,798	2,752	65.1	66.6
Supermarkets & grocery (except convenience) stores.......	44511	64.9	64.1	2,668	2,625	62.7	64.1
Convenience stores..................................	44512	28.4	29.4	130	127	2.4	2.5
Specialty food stores................................	4452	22.4	22.2	161	160	3.2	3.4
Beer, wine, & liquor stores [4].........................	4453	34.5	34.6	170	175	3.8	4.0
Health & personal care stores [3].......................	446	97.4	93.5	1,014	1,038	35.4	36.3
Pharmacies & drug stores............................	44611	48.0	44.4	664	690	26.4	26.8
Cosmetics, beauty supplies, & perfume stores............	44612	17.2	17.5	166	163	3.1	3.3
Optical goods stores.................................	44613	12.2	12.1	83	84	2.3	2.5
Gasoline stations....................................	447	112.9	112.7	944	974	19.5	20.0
Gasoline stations with convenience stores................	44711	98.6	99.1	794	825	15.9	16.6
Other gasoline stations...............................	44719	14.2	13.6	150	149	3.6	3.5
Clothing & clothing accessories stores..................	448	143.2	139.6	1,758	1,702	32.3	33.0
Clothing stores [3]...................................	4481	96.2	94.2	1,393	1,343	23.9	24.6
Men's clothing stores..............................	44811	6.9	6.6	55	52	1.5	1.5
Women's clothing stores...........................	44812	32.9	31.9	343	305	5.4	5.4
Children's & infants' clothing stores.................	44813	6.9	6.4	75	69	1.0	1.0
Family clothing stores.............................	44814	28.9	28.9	735	732	12.1	12.7
Shoe stores...	4482	24.7	23.4	243	240	4.1	4.1
Jewelry, luggage, & leather goods stores [3].............	4483	22.3	22.0	122	120	4.4	4.4
Jewelry stores....................................	44831	21.3	21.1	116	114	4.1	4.1
Sporting goods, hobby, musical instrument, & book stores.......	451	45.1	43.9	535	526	10.1	10.2
Sporting goods/hobby/musical instrument stores [3]..............	4511	37.6	36.8	452	456	8.8	8.9
Sporting goods stores.............................	45111	21.4	20.9	241	246	5.4	5.3
Hobby, toy, and game stores.......................	45112	8.5	8.5	144	144	2.2	2.3
Book stores and news dealers [3].....................	4512	7.5	7.1	[5]83	[5]70	1.3	1.3
Book stores.......................................	451211	6.5	6.1	[5]79	[5]67	1.2	1.2
General merchandise stores............................	452	53.7	53.8	2,703	2,665	65.1	66.7
Department stores...................................	4522	4.4	4.1	477	456	9.7	9.2
General merchandise stores...........................	4523	49.4	49.6	2,226	2,209	55.4	57.5
Warehouse clubs and supercenters....................	452311	8.2	8.1	1,793	1,770	48.4	50.3
All other general merchandise stores..................	452319	41.2	41.6	433	440	7.0	7.3
Miscellaneous store retailers [3].......................	453	109.2	108.2	758	760	17.0	17.9
Florists...	4531	12.7	12.4	57	56	1.1	1.1
Office supplies, stationery, and gift stores...............	4532	27.3	26.3	217	206	4.1	4.3
Office supplies and stationery stores.................	45321	5.7	5.4	70	60	1.4	1.5
Gift, novelty, and souvenir stores....................	45322	21.7	20.9	147	146	2.7	2.8
Used merchandise stores.............................	4533	20.4	19.7	200	203	3.8	4.0
Other miscellaneous store retailers [3].................	4539	48.9	49.9	284	296	8.0	8.5
Pet and pet supplies stores.........................	45391	10.0	10.1	114	120	2.5	2.7
Nonstore retailers [3]................................	454	77.6	78.0	762	779	34.9	37.8
Electronic shopping & mail-order houses.................	4541	41.5	42.5	534	557	25.6	28.4
Direct selling establishments.........................	4543	32.4	31.7	187	181	7.9	8.0
Fuel dealers..	45431	8.3	8.0	75	73	3.5	3.7

[1] Data based on North American Industry Classification System (NAICS), 2017. See text, Section 15. [2] Covers full- and part-time employees who are on the payroll in the pay period including March 12. [3] Includes other kinds of business, not shown separately. [4] Includes government employees. [5] Data is flagged for high noise; the value was changed by 5 percent or more to avoid disclosure of data for individual businesses.

Source: U.S. Census Bureau, County Business Patterns, "County Business Patterns by Legal Form of Organization and Employment Size Class for U.S., States, and Selected Geographies," <data.census.gov>, accessed July 2020.

Table 1072. Retail Trade—Nonemployer Firms and Receipts by Industry Type: 2018

[92,223,301 represents $92,223,301,000. See headnote, Table 1066]

Industry type	2017 NAICS code [1]	Firms				Receipts ($1,000)
		Total	Corpora- tions [2]	Individual proprietor- ships [3]	Partner- ships [4]	
Retail trade, total............................	**44–45**	**2,103,399**	**120,311**	**1,903,857**	**79,231**	**92,223,301**
Motor vehicle & parts dealers..........................	441	166,570	15,656	143,859	7,055	18,085,703
Furniture & home furnishings stores...................	442	38,370	4,741	30,935	2,694	2,496,779
Electronics and appliance stores.......................	443	23,325	3,154	19,053	1,118	1,352,950
Building material & garden equipment & supplies dealers......	444	34,430	3,578	29,068	1,784	2,373,993
Building material & supplies dealers.................	4441	22,976	2,850	18,795	1,331	1,817,534
Food & beverage stores..............................	445	96,867	11,277	78,509	7,081	7,311,232
Grocery stores..................................	4451	37,000	4,638	30,245	2,117	3,147,052
Specialty food stores............................	4452	49,967	4,942	41,157	3,868	2,712,864
Health & personal care stores.......................	446	169,899	7,776	157,716	4,407	4,491,513
Gasoline stations...................................	447	7,477	1,616	5,247	614	1,041,751
Clothing & clothing accessories stores................	448	179,730	10,349	160,041	9,340	6,696,482
Clothing stores..................................	4481	133,026	7,448	117,670	7,908	4,751,440
Jewelry, luggage, and leather goods stores.........	4483	41,750	2,428	38,155	1,167	1,652,176
Sporting goods, hobby, musical instrument, & book stores.....	451	76,610	5,016	67,156	4,438	3,401,296
Book stores and news dealer.....................	4512	12,645	637	11,483	525	449,070
General merchandise stores..........................	452	33,345	1,939	30,072	1,334	1,546,393
Miscellaneous store retailers........................	453	271,204	20,638	235,096	15,470	13,112,995
Office supplies, stationery, and gift stores.........	4532	45,198	3,427	39,188	2,583	1,754,204
Nonstore retailers..................................	454	1,005,572	34,571	947,105	23,896	30,312,214
Electronic shopping & mail-order houses...........	4541	176,762	12,780	155,082	8,900	9,571,485
Direct selling establishments.....................	4543	811,504	20,184	777,714	13,606	20,057,259

[1] North American Industry Classification System, 2017; see text, Section 15. [2] A legally incorporated business under state laws. [3] Also referred to as "sole proprietorship," an unincorporated business with a sole owner. Includes self-employed persons. [4] An unincorporated business where two or more persons join to carry on a trade or business with each having a shared financial interest in the business.

Source: U.S. Census Bureau, Nonemployer Statistics, "All Sectors: Nonemployer Statistics for the U.S., States, Counties, Metropolitan Areas, and Combined Statistical Areas; and by Legal Form of Organization and Sales, Value of Shipments, or Revenue Size for Selected Geographies: 2018," <data.census.gov>, accessed May 2020.

Table 1073. Retail Industries—Employees, Average Weekly Hours, and Average Hourly Earnings: 2010 to 2019

[Annual averages of monthly figures (14,446 represents 14,446,000). Covers all full- and part-time employees who worked during, or received pay for, any part of the pay period including the 12th of the month]

Industry	2017 NAICS code [1]	Employees (1,000)			Average weekly hours [2]			Average hourly earnings [2] (dol.)		
		2010	2015	2019	2010	2015	2019	2010	2015	2019
Retail trade, total [3]..........................	**44,45**	**14,446**	**15,611**	**15,644**	**30.2**	**30.1**	**30.3**	**13.25**	**14.83**	**16.62**
Motor vehicle and parts dealers [3]....................	441	1,629	1,929	2,035	36.5	37.5	37.2	17.06	18.93	21.02
Automobile dealers............................	4411	1,012	1,239	1,300	36.7	37.6	37.5	18.22	20.34	22.85
Auto parts, accessories, and tire stores...........	4413	489	545	571	36.9	37.7	37.1	14.54	15.88	16.88
Furniture and home furnishings stores..............	442	438	467	473	29.1	30.7	30.2	15.25	16.79	18.86
Electronics and appliance stores [3]..................	443	523	523	477	31.6	37.4	34.8	16.84	21.91	23.12
Electronics stores................................	443142	466	466	430	31.3	37.8	35.0	17.04	22.57	23.54
Building material and garden supply stores [3]........	444	1,133	1,235	1,296	33.9	32.0	32.8	14.12	15.15	17.72
Building material and supplies dealers............	4441	1,006	1,085	1,141	34.2	31.7	32.9	14.14	15.21	17.87
Lawn and garden equip. and supplies stores.....	4442	127	150	155	31.6	34.0	32.0	13.98	14.73	16.53
Food and beverage stores [3].........................	445	2,808	3,062	3,078	29.0	28.4	28.6	12.03	12.71	13.77
Grocery stores...................................	4451	2,461	2,682	2,688	29.0	28.5	28.7	12.12	12.76	13.75
Supermarkets and other grocery stores.........	44511	2,323	2,523	2,529	28.9	28.4	28.6	12.27	12.91	13.89
Convenience stores............................	44512	138	159	160	31.3	30.8	29.2	9.43	10.41	11.31
Specialty food stores............................	4452	211	227	227	29.7	27.8	27.3	11.13	12.42	14.25
Beer, wine, and liquor stores....................	4453	136	153	163	27.2	26.1	28.4	11.89	12.02	13.46
Health and personal care stores [3]..................	446	981	1,034	1,052	29.4	28.8	29.6	16.99	17.31	19.47
Pharmacies and drug stores.....................	44611	715	721	696	29.3	28.9	29.1	17.59	17.87	20.92
Gasoline stations [3].................................	447	819	905	945	30.7	30.7	30.8	10.25	10.99	12.11
Gasoline stations with convenience stores........	44711	719	799	843	30.4	30.5	30.6	9.99	10.76	11.85
Clothing and clothing accessories stores [3].........	448	1,353	1,354	1,299	21.2	21.7	22.1	11.59	12.87	15.92
Clothing stores.................................	4481	1,040	1,006	974	20.1	20.2	20.5	10.91	12.12	15.28
Shoe stores....................................	4482	182	212	196	23.3	24.0	25.4	11.80	14.01	15.88
Jewelry, luggage, and leather goods stores........	4483	131	136	130	28.1	30.0	30.3	15.56	15.46	19.55
Sporting goods, hobby, book, and music stores [3]..	451	579	623	550	23.4	24.5	24.7	11.69	13.74	14.80
Sporting goods and musical instrument stores....	4511	459	538	471	23.8	24.6	25.6	11.82	13.92	14.89
Book stores and news dealers....................	4512	120	86	79	22.0	24.0	18.8	11.10	12.58	14.03
General merchandise stores........................	452	2,998	3,131	3,043	31.7	29.3	30.0	10.98	12.03	14.69
Miscellaneous store retailers [3].....................	453	762	828	834	28.0	28.9	27.7	12.50	13.75	14.49
Florists.......................................	4531	69	63	58	22.4	27.4	26.4	11.05	11.66	13.61
Office supplies, stationary, and gift stores........	4532	303	281	240	27.1	27.8	25.0	13.06	15.31	14.59
Used merchandise stores........................	4533	125	171	178	29.5	30.1	28.4	10.72	11.20	12.73
Other miscellaneous store retailers..............	4539	264	314	358	29.8	29.4	29.3	13.07	14.34	15.46
Pet and pet supplies stores....................	45391	99	114	124	27.4	28.8	29.0	12.83	14.09	14.41
Nonstore retailers [3]...............................	454	425	519	563	36.3	36.5	35.1	17.83	22.42	20.79
Electronic shopping and mail-order houses.......	4541	250	346	387	35.9	36.5	33.9	18.34	23.92	20.58

[1] Based on the North American Industry Classification System (NAICS), 2017; see text, this section and Section 15. [2] Data shown for production and nonsupervisory employees. [3] Includes other kind of businesses, not shown separately.

Source: U.S. Bureau of Labor Statistics, Current Employment Statistics, "Employment, Hours, and Earnings—National," <http://www.bls.gov/ces/data.htm>, accessed March 2020.

Table 1074. Retail Trade—Sales by Kind of Business: 2000 to 2018

[In billions of dollars (2,983.3 represents $2,983,300,000,000). Data have been adjusted using final results of the 2012 Economic Census]

Kind of business	NAICS code [1]	2000	2010	2014	2015	2016	2017	2018
Retail sales, total.	**44, 45**	**2,983.3**	**3,818.0**	**4,639.4**	**4,726.0**	**4,853.0**	**5,053.2**	**5,269.5**
GAFO, total [2]	(X)	862.7	1,114.4	1,238.7	1,258.2	1,261.6	1,272.5	1,302.2
Motor vehicle and parts dealers	441	796.2	742.9	1,020.9	1,094.1	1,140.6	1,172.4	1,191.3
Automobile dealers	4411	687.8	621.2	875.6	940.5	981.5	1,008.2	1,022.9
New car dealers	44111	630.1	549.5	785.1	842.1	875.6	896.0	908.5
Used car dealers	44112	57.7	71.7	90.4	98.3	105.9	112.2	114.4
Other motor vehicle dealers	4412	45.0	43.8	59.5	64.4	68.7	73.5	76.6
Auto parts, accessories, and tire stores	4413	63.4	77.9	85.8	89.3	90.4	90.6	91.9
Furniture and home furnishings stores	442	91.2	85.2	99.7	106.6	110.4	113.0	116.9
Furniture stores	4421	50.6	46.7	53.3	57.3	58.9	59.6	61.6
Home furnishings stores	4422	40.6	38.5	46.4	49.3	51.5	53.5	55.3
Electronics and appliance stores [3]	443	90.4	99.6	105.2	103.7	99.0	98.6	100.2
Electronics stores	443142	77.8	84.1	88.1	86.5	81.8	82.2	83.8
Building materials, garden equipment, and supply stores	444	229.0	260.6	318.4	331.6	348.7	365.6	381.3
Food and beverage stores [3]	445	444.8	580.5	669.2	685.4	699.3	725.1	745.7
Grocery stores	4451	402.5	520.8	599.6	613.2	623.9	647.8	665.1
Supermarkets and other grocery (except convenience) stores	44511	381.4	498.0	573.8	587.8	597.0	619.6	634.0
Beer, wine and liquor stores	4453	28.5	41.4	48.3	50.6	53.2	55.2	58.0
Health and personal care stores [3]	446	155.2	260.4	299.3	315.2	327.2	333.3	347.5
Pharmacies and drug stores	44611	130.9	222.2	250.5	263.5	272.3	277.4	288.8
Gasoline stations	447	249.8	448.3	538.8	444.0	422.8	459.5	503.9
Clothing and clothing accessory stores [3]	448	167.7	213.3	250.4	255.8	260.1	260.6	268.2
Clothing stores [3]	4481	118.1	158.3	183.1	187.1	189.9	190.8	194.7
Shoe stores	4482	22.9	27.2	33.5	34.5	36.2	35.7	38.1
Jewelry, luggage, and leather goods stores	4483	26.7	27.8	33.8	34.1	34.0	34.0	35.4
Sporting goods, hobby, musical instrument, and book stores [3]	451	67.6	78.2	83.8	85.7	86.5	84.2	81.2
Sporting goods stores	45111	25.3	37.4	44.7	46.3	47.3	45.1	43.9
Hobby, toy, and game stores	45112	16.9	15.8	17.4	18.0	18.3	18.1	16.8
General merchandise stores [3]	452	404.2	603.8	667.2	674.9	675.4	687.1	706.3
Department stores	4521	232.5	184.8	168.1	164.0	152.6	144.7	141.6
Discount department stores	452112	136.2	119.9	107.5	105.1	97.9	94.4	95.7
Other general merchandise stores	4529	171.8	419.0	499.1	510.9	522.8	542.5	564.7
Warehouse clubs and supercenters	45291	139.6	368.0	433.3	441.7	449.9	465.3	484.1
Miscellaneous store retailers [3]	453	106.7	104.2	115.9	119.4	121.6	124.5	130.1
Office supplies, stationery, and gift stores	4532	41.7	34.3	32.4	31.5	30.2	29.0	29.4
Office supplies and stationery stores	45321	22.7	18.8	15.8	14.7	13.3	12.3	11.6
Gift, novelty, and souvenir stores	45322	18.9	15.5	16.6	16.8	16.9	16.6	17.8
Used merchandise stores	4533	9.8	11.8	16.2	17.0	17.4	18.4	18.8
Nonstore retailers [3]	454	180.5	341.0	470.9	509.7	561.4	629.2	696.8
Electronic shopping and mail-order houses	4541	113.8	263.5	386.1	434.0	488.8	551.3	611.7
Direct selling establishments	4543	58.1	71.0	78.3	68.9	65.4	70.7	77.4
Fuel dealers	45431	26.7	35.5	39.6	29.8	23.9	26.7	31.0

X Not applicable. [1] North American Industry Classification System, 2012; see text, Section 15. [2] GAFO (General Merchandise, Apparel, Furniture, and Office Supplies) represents stores classified in the following NAICS codes: 442, 443, 448, 451, 452, and 4532. [3] Includes other kinds of businesses, not shown separately.

Source: U.S. Census Bureau, "Annual Retail Trade Survey (ARTS) Tables," <https://www.census.gov/programs-surveys/arts/data/tables.html>, accessed February 2020.

Table 1075. Retail Trade Corporations—Sales, Net Profit, and Profit Per Dollar of Sales: 2018 and 2019

[3,080.7 represents $3,080,700,000,000. Represents 2017 North American Industry Classification System (NAICS) groups 44 and 45. Profit rates are averages of quarterly figures at annual rates. Covers corporations with assets of $50,000,000 or more]

Item	Unit	Total retail trade		Food and beverage stores (NAICS 445)		Clothing & general merchandise stores (NAICS 448, 452)		All other retail stores	
		2018	2019	2018	2019	2018	2019	2018	2019
Sales	Bil. dol.	3,080.7	3,181.0	475.2	493.3	991.8	1,034.3	1,613.8	1,653.3
Net profit:									
Before income taxes	Bil. dol.	114.8	137.8	8.8	12.5	35.3	48.0	70.6	77.3
After income taxes	Bil. dol.	89.2	110.9	6.8	9.8	25.3	37.3	57.1	63.8
Profits per dollar of sales:									
Before income taxes	Cents	3.7	4.3	1.9	2.5	3.6	4.6	4.4	4.7
After income taxes	Cents	2.9	3.5	1.4	2.0	2.6	3.6	3.5	3.9
Stockholders' equity	Bil. dol.	2,155.1	2,398.5	252.6	281.3	707.9	707.4	1,194.6	1,409.9

Source: U.S. Census Bureau, Quarterly Financial Report (QFR) Manufacturing, Mining, Trade, and Selected Service Industries, "Time Series/Trend Charts," <census.gov/econ/qfr/>, accessed August 2020.

Table 1076. Retail Trade—Estimated Per Capita Sales by Selected Kind of Business: 2000 to 2018

[Estimates are shown in dollars and are based on data from the Annual Retail Trade Survey and the Census Bureau's Population Estimates Program. Based on estimated resident population estimates as of July 1. Data have been adjusted using final results of the 2012 Economic Census. For additional information, see source and Appendix III]

Kind of business	NAICS code [1]	2000	2005	2010	2015	2016	2017	2018
Retail, total.	**44–45**	**10,573**	**12,484**	**12,343**	**14,739**	**15,027**	**15,549**	**16,130**
Total excluding motor vehicle and parts dealers	44–45, ex 441	7,751	9,478	9,942	11,327	11,495	11,941	12,483
Motor vehicle and parts dealers	441	2,822	3,006	2,402	3,412	3,532	3,607	3,647
Furniture and home furnishings stores	442	323	369	275	332	342	348	358
Electronics and appliance stores	443	320	359	322	323	307	303	307
Building material and garden equipment and supplies dealers	444	812	1,086	842	1,034	1,080	1,125	1,167
Food and beverage stores	445	1,576	1,721	1,877	2,138	2,166	2,231	2,283
Health and personal care stores	446	550	711	842	983	1,013	1,026	1,064
Gasoline stations	447	885	1,282	1,449	1,385	1,309	1,414	1,543
Clothing and clothing accessories stores	448	594	680	690	798	805	802	821
Sporting goods, hobby, musical instrument, and book stores	451	240	255	253	267	268	259	248
General merchandise stores	452	1,433	1,788	1,952	2,105	2,091	2,114	2,162
Miscellaneous store retailers	453	378	363	337	372	376	383	398
Nonstore retailers	454	640	865	1,102	1,590	1,738	1,936	2,133

[1] North American Industry Classification System, 2012; see text, Section 15.

Source: U.S. Census Bureau, "Annual Retail Trade Survey (ARTS) Tables," <https://www.census.gov/programs-surveys/arts/data/tables.html>, accessed February 2020.

Table 1077. Retail Trade—Merchandise Inventories and Inventory/Sales Ratios by Kind of Business: 2016 to 2019

[Inventories in billions of dollars (613.2 represents $613,200,000,000). As of Dec. 31. Estimates exclude food services. Includes warehouses. Adjusted for seasonal variations. Sales data also adjusted for holiday and trading-day differences. Based on data from the Monthly Retail Trade Survey, Annual Retail Trade Survey, and administrative records; see Appendix III]

Kind of business	2012 NAICS code [1]	Inventories				Inventory/sales ratio			
		2016	2017	2018	2019	2016	2017	2018	2019
Retail inventories, total [2]	**44–45**	**613.2**	**627.8**	**656.9**	**663.7**	**1.49**	**1.45**	**1.51**	**1.44**
Total excluding motor vehicle and parts dealers	44–45 ex 441	399.6	408.3	423.4	431.5	1.27	1.22	1.26	1.21
Motor vehicle and parts dealers	441	213.5	219.5	233.6	232.2	2.17	2.21	2.31	2.21
Furniture, home furnishings, electronics, and appliance stores	442, 443	27.5	28.1	28.2	27.6	1.60	1.56	1.58	1.55
Building material and garden equipment and supplies dealers	444	52.3	54.5	57.8	61.3	1.78	1.73	1.80	1.87
Food and beverage stores	445	46.9	48.3	49.8	51.3	0.80	0.78	0.80	0.79
Clothing and clothing accessories stores	448	52.3	52.2	53.5	52.7	2.40	2.40	2.41	2.33
General merchandise stores	452	83.1	80.5	82.6	81.5	1.49	1.38	1.40	1.37
Department stores	4521	28.2	26.2	25.1	23.2	2.31	2.22	2.20	2.11

[1] North American Industry Classification System, 2012; see text, Section 15. [2] Includes other kind of businesses, not shown separately.

Source: U.S. Census Bureau, Monthly Retail Trade Report, "Retail Inventories and Inventories/Sales Ratios," <http://www.census.gov/retail/index.html>, accessed April 2020.

Table 1078. Retail Trade Sales—Total and E-Commerce by Kind of Business: 2018

[5,269,468 represents $5,269,468,000,000. Covers retailers with and without payroll. Based on the Annual Retail Trade Survey; see Appendix III]

Kind of business	NAICS code [1]	Value of sales (mil. dol.)		E-commerce as percent of total sales	Percent distribution of E-commerce sales
		Total	E-commerce		
Retail trade, total	**44-45**	**5,269,468**	**519,635**	**9.9**	**100.0**
Motor vehicle and parts dealers	441	1,191,321	35,348	3.0	6.8
Furniture and home furnishings stores	442	116,895	1,533	1.3	0.3
Electronics and appliance stores	443	100,205	2,056	2.1	0.4
Building material and garden equipment and supplies stores	444	381,313	2,795	0.7	0.5
Food and beverage stores	445	745,736	4,837	0.6	0.9
Health and personal care stores	446	347,454	744	0.2	0.1
Gasoline stations	447	503,925	(S)	(S)	(S)
Clothing and clothing accessories stores	448	268,163	10,981	4.1	2.1
Sporting goods, hobby, book, and music stores	451	81,179	2,617	3.2	0.5
General merchandise stores	452	706,298	(S)	(S)	(S)
Miscellaneous store retailers	453	130,130	(S)	(S)	(S)
Nonstore retailers	454	696,849	453,584	65.1	87.3
Electronic shopping and mail-order houses	4541	611,743	451,635	73.8	86.9

S Data do not meet publication standards because of high sampling variability or poor response quality. [1] North American Industry Classification System, 2012; see text, Section 15.

Source: U.S. Census Bureau, "Annual Retail Trade Survey (ARTS) Tables," <https://www.census.gov/programs-surveys/arts/data/tables.html>, accessed February 2020.

Table 1079. Electronic Shopping and Mail-Order Houses—Total and E-Commerce Sales by Merchandise Line: 2017 and 2018

[551,298 represents $551,298,000,000. Represents 2012 North American Industry Classification System code 4541, which comprises establishments primarily engaged in retailing all types of merchandise using nonstore means including catalogs, toll-free telephone numbers, and electronic media, such as interactive television or computer. Covers businesses with and without paid employees. Based on the Annual Retail Trade Survey; see Appendix III]

Merchandise lines	2017			2018		
	Value of sales (million dollars)		E-commerce as percent of total sales	Value of sales (million dollars)		E-commerce as percent of total sales
	Total	E-commerce		Total	E-commerce	
Total	**551,298**	**398,415**	**72.3**	**611,743**	**451,635**	**73.8**
Books (includes audio books and e-books)	16,933	15,414	91.0	19,853	18,022	90.8
Clothing and clothing accessories (includes footwear)	75,021	67,737	90.3	84,162	76,187	90.5
Computer and communications equipment & related products (includes cell phones)	24,862	22,222	89.4	28,746	25,880	90.0
Computer software (including video game)	16,164	15,486	95.8	20,366	19,545	96.0
Drugs, health aids, beauty aids	144,519	36,432	25.2	149,267	38,391	25.7
Electronics and appliances	49,024	45,384	92.6	55,353	51,488	93.0
Food, beer, and wine	14,923	13,088	87.7	16,092	14,147	87.9
Furniture and home furnishings	52,612	48,663	92.5	61,339	57,922	94.4
Jewelry	8,974	7,112	79.3	9,962	7,878	79.1
Audio and video recordings [1]	10,284	9,591	93.3	11,532	10,729	93.0
Office equipment and supplies	10,832	9,005	83.1	12,137	10,497	86.5
Sporting goods	18,807	16,928	90.0	21,713	19,008	87.5
Toys, hobby goods, and games	17,563	16,357	93.1	19,312	18,117	93.8
Other merchandise [2]	75,429	62,398	82.7	85,004	69,977	82.3
Nonmerchandise receipts [3]	15,351	12,598	82.1	16,905	13,847	81.9

[1] Includes purchased downloads. [2] Includes other merchandise such as collectibles, souvenirs, auto parts and accessories, hardware, and lawn and garden equipment and supplies. [3] Includes auction commissions, shipping and handling, customer training, customer support, and advertising.

Source: U.S. Census Bureau, "Annual Retail Trade Survey (ARTS) Tables," <https://www.census.gov/programs-surveys/arts/data/tables.html>, accessed February 2020.

Table 1080. Franchised New Car Dealerships—Summary: 2000 to 2019

[In units as indicated (8.8 represents 8,800,000)]

Item	Unit	2000	2005	2010	2013	2014	2015	2016	2017	2018	2019
Dealerships [1]	Number	20,490	19,898	16,181	16,170	16,396	16,545	16,708	16,802	16,753	16,682
Sales	Bil. dol.	(NA)	(NA)	(NA)	797	868	938	996	1,003	1,026	1,027
New light duty vehicle sales	Millions	(NA)	16.9	11.6	15.5	16.4	17.4	17.5	17.1	17.2	17.1
New cars sold	Millions	8.8	7.7	5.6	7.6	7.7	7.5	6.9	6.1	5.3	4.8
New light trucks sold	Millions	(NA)	9.3	5.9	7.9	8.7	9.9	10.6	11.1	11.9	12.3
Average retail new vehicle selling price	Dollars	(NA)	(NA)	30,079	32,035	32,824	33,456	34,449	34,670	35,608	36,824
Used vehicles sold	Millions	20.5	19.7	15.3	17.4	(NA)	14.1	14.2	14.4	14.4	14.9
Employment	1,000	1,114	1,138	892	998	1,041	1,085	1,118	1,130	1,132	1,134
Annual payroll	Bil. dol.	46.1	51.5	42.4	53.5	57.4	61.8	64.9	65.3	66.5	68.8
Average dealer pretax profits as percent of sales	Percent	(NA)	(NA)	(NA)	2.6	2.6	2.7	2.5	2.3	2.2	2.3
Inventory: [2]											
Domestic: [3]											
Total	Millions	3.2	3.0	1.7	1.9	1.9	1.9	2.1	1.9	2.1	1.9
Days' supply	Days	68	70	60	77	71	72	74	70	76	67
Imported: [3]											
Total	Millions	0.5	0.6	0.5	1.6	1.7	1.7	1.9	1.9	1.8	1.7
Days' supply	Days	50	52	55	53	54	53	54	56	54	50

NA Not available. [1] Light-duty new vehicle dealerships, as of December 31. [2] Annual average. [3] Classification based on location of automobile production (i.e., automobiles manufactured by foreign companies but produced in the U.S., Canada, and Mexico are classified as domestic).

Source: National Automobile Dealers Association, <www.nada.org>. *NADA Data 2019: Annual Financial Profile of America's Franchised New-Car Dealerships*, annual ©.

Table 1081. New Motor Vehicle Sales and Car Production: 1990 to 2019

[In thousands (14,137 represents 14,137,000). Data are primarily from "Ward's Automotive Reports" published by Ward's Communications, Southfield, MI]

Type of vehicle	1990	2000	2010	2013	2014	2015	2016	2017	2018	2019
New motor vehicle sales	**14,137**	**17,812**	**11,773**	**15,883**	**16,860**	**17,846**	**17,866**	**17,551**	**17,701**	**17,480**
New-car sales	9,300	8,778	5,636	7,586	7,708	7,517	6,873	6,081	5,304	4,715
Domestic	6,897	6,762	3,791	5,433	5,610	5,595	5,146	4,593	4,087	3,544
Import	2,403	2,016	1,844	2,153	2,098	1,922	1,727	1,488	1,217	1,171
New-truck sales	4,837	9,034	6,137	8,296	9,152	10,329	10,993	11,470	12,398	12,765
Light	4,560	8,572	5,919	7,944	8,744	9,879	10,592	11,055	11,910	12,238
Domestic	3,957	7,720	5,020	6,704	7,384	8,097	8,436	8,652	9,159	9,623
Import	603	852	899	1,239	1,360	1,782	2,156	2,404	2,751	2,615
Heavy	278	462	218	353	408	449	401	415	488	527
Domestic-car production	**6,231**	**5,471**	**2,731**	**4,369**	**4,253**	**4,163**	**3,917**	**3,033**	**2,785**	**2,512**

Source: U.S. Bureau of Economic Analysis, National Economic Accounts, "Supplemental Information & Additional Data: Motor Vehicles," <https://www.bea.gov/data/gdp/gross-domestic-product#supp>, accessed March 2020.

Table 1082. Food and Alcoholic Beverage Expenditures by Sales Outlet: 2000 to 2018

[In millions of dollars (295,066 represents $295,066,000,000). In constant dollars (1988=100). Includes taxes and tips. Data are shown for final purchasers including individuals and households, government (food assistance programs, Medicare/Medicaid inpatient meals, expensed meals), and businesses (expensed meals) for final use by individuals and households (including food assistance programs)]

Sales outlet	2000	2005	2010	2014	2015	2016	2017	2018
Food at home..................................	295,066	323,583	330,104	342,192	342,938	353,041	366,834	379,939
Grocery stores............................	199,081	198,339	195,127	199,625	202,184	208,262	216,695	223,803
Convenience stores......................	7,167	5,625	5,588	6,334	6,151	6,617	7,016	6,815
Other food stores.........................	7,825	8,448	8,016	8,465	8,525	8,826	8,884	9,012
Warehouse clubs and supercenters........	31,354	58,072	70,292	73,731	74,315	76,742	78,922	81,718
Mass merchandisers......................	6,516	6,585	6,085	5,043	4,873	4,601	4,447	4,464
Other stores and foodservice..............	29,520	32,778	32,717	35,752	33,316	33,744	35,728	38,382
Mail order and home delivery..............	10,648	10,891	9,355	9,791	9,739	10,352	11,168	12,086
Direct selling by farmers, manufacturers, and wholesalers.........................	2,187	1,800	1,905	2,543	2,794	2,843	2,903	2,543
Home production and donations...........	767	1,044	1,019	908	1,041	1,055	1,070	1,116
Food away from home (FAFH)..............	287,324	325,941	331,166	367,521	382,185	390,424	399,963	410,847
Full-service restaurants....................	100,586	115,925	114,118	131,460	137,786	139,468	141,936	149,139
Limited-service restaurants...............	93,964	110,908	114,508	128,250	136,007	141,478	147,637	150,175
Drinking places...........................	1,461	1,828	1,999	1,870	1,911	2,077	2,227	2,288
Hotels and motels........................	15,568	13,383	12,172	15,187	15,646	15,967	16,118	15,427
Retail stores and vending.................	13,396	15,323	16,151	17,748	16,580	16,197	16,532	17,059
Recreational places.......................	12,245	12,412	11,224	12,760	13,308	13,674	14,105	14,911
Schools and colleges......................	23,019	27,457	32,221	30,694	30,940	31,087	30,685	30,970
Other FAFH sales, not elsewhere classified...............................	9,117	10,169	9,670	9,766	10,112	10,421	10,623	10,756
Food furnished and donated...............	17,968	18,536	19,104	19,786	19,894	20,056	20,099	20,122
Alcohol at home.............................	41,685	44,951	49,620	56,997	57,567	58,811	60,907	63,161
Liquor stores..............................	18,093	20,008	22,743	25,774	26,944	28,098	28,992	29,993
Food stores...............................	11,546	12,187	13,396	15,853	16,125	16,349	16,907	17,200
All other..................................	12,045	12,757	13,481	15,371	14,497	14,364	15,008	15,969
Alcohol away from home.....................	32,755	34,070	32,889	37,171	38,929	40,366	41,701	43,392
Eating and drinking places.................	26,059	27,689	26,834	30,099	31,589	32,814	33,969	35,618
Hotels and motels.........................	3,500	3,066	2,917	3,640	3,779	3,885	3,933	3,781
All other..................................	3,195	3,316	3,138	3,431	3,560	3,667	3,799	3,993

Source: U.S. Department of Agriculture, Economic Research Service, "Food Expenditure Series," <https://www.ers.usda.gov/data-products/food-expenditure-series/>, accessed January 2020.

This section presents data on civil air transportation, both passenger and cargo, and on water transportation, including inland waterways, oceanborne commerce, the merchant marine, cargo, and vessel tonnages.

This section also presents statistics on revenues, passenger and freight traffic volume, and employment in various revenue-producing modes of the transportation industry, including motor vehicles, trains, and pipelines. Data are also presented on highway mileage and finances, motor vehicle travel, accidents, and registrations; and characteristics of public transit, railroads, and pipelines.

The principal source of transportation data is the annual *National Transportation Statistics* publication of the U.S. Bureau of Transportation Statistics. Principal sources of water transportation data is provided by the Corps of Engineers of the Department of Army. In addition, the U.S. Census Bureau in its Commodity Flow Survey (part of the Economic Census, taken every 5 years through 2017, for years ending in "2" and "7") provides data on the type, weight, and value of commodities shipped by manufacturing establishments in the United States, by means of transportation, origin, and destination. Release of data from the 2012 Economic Census was completed in 2016. The 2017 Economic Census is being released on a flow basis between September 2019 and December 2021. This census was conducted in accordance with the 2017 North American Industry Classification System (NAICS). See text, Section 15, Business Enterprise, for a discussion of the Economic Census and NAICS.

The Bureau of Transportation Statistics (BTS) was established within the U.S. Department of Transportation (DOT) in 1992 to collect, report, and analyze transportation data. BTS products include reports to Congress, the Secretary of Transportation, and stakeholders in the nation's transportation community. These stakeholders include: federal agencies, state and local governments, metropolitan planning organizations, universities, the private sector, and the general public. Congress requires, by congressional mandate laid out in 49 U.S.C. 111 (1), the BTS to report on transportation statistics to the President and Congress. *The Transportation Statistics Annual Report* (TSAR), provides a data overview of U.S. transportation issues, located at <bts.gov/tsar>. The BTS publication *National Transportation Statistics* (NTS), a companion report to the TSAR, has more comprehensive and longer time-series data. NTS presents information on the U.S. transportation system, including its physical components, safety record, economic performance, energy use, and environmental impacts. The BTS publication *State Transportation Statistics* presents a statistical profile of transportation in the 50 states and the District of Columbia. This profile includes infrastructure, freight movement and passenger travel, system safety, vehicles, transportation-related economy and finance, energy usage, and the environment.

The principal compiler of data on public roads and on operation of motor vehicles is the U.S. Department of Transportation's (DOT) Federal Highway Administration (FHWA). These data appear in FHWA's annual *Highway Statistics* and other publications.

The U.S. National Highway Traffic Safety Administration (NHTSA), through its *Traffic Safety Facts Annual Report Tables*, </cdan.nhtsa.gov/tsftables/tsfar.htm#>, and Fatality and Injury Reporting System Tool (FIRST), <cdan.dot.gov/query>, presents descriptive statistics about traffic crashes of all severities, from those that result in property damage to those that result in the loss of life. The tool compiles motor vehicle crash data from the Fatality Analysis Reporting System (FARS), the General Estimates System (GES), and Crash Report Sampling System (CRSS). Other publications and reports can be found at the National Center for Statistics and Analysis (NCSA), Publications and Data Request, located on the internet at <crashstats.nhtsa.dot.gov/#/>. DOT's Federal Railroad Administration (FRA), Office of Safety Analysis presents railroad safety information, including accidents and incidents, inspections, and highway-rail crossing data at its "Safety Database," located at <safetydata.fra.dot.gov/officeofsafety>.

Civil aviation—Federal promotion and regulation of civil aviation have been carried out by the Federal Aviation Administration (FAA) and the Civil Aeronautics Board (CAB). The CAB promoted and regulated the civil air transportation industry within the United States and between the United States and foreign countries. The Board granted licenses to provide air transportation service, approved or disapproved proposed rates and fares, and approved or disapproved proposed agreements and corporate relationships involving air carriers. In December 1984, the CAB ceased to exist as an agency. Some of its functions were transferred to the DOT, as outlined below. The responsibility for investigation of aviation accidents resides with the National Transportation Safety Board.

The Office of the Secretary, DOT aviation activities include: negotiation of international air transportation rights, selection of U.S. air carriers to serve capacity controlled international markets, oversight of international rates and fares, maintenance of essential air service to small communities, and consumer affairs. DOT's Bureau of Transportation Statistics (BTS) handles aviation information functions formerly assigned to CAB. Prior to BTS, the Research and Special Programs Administration handled these functions.

The principal activities of the FAA include: the promotion of air safety; controlling the use of navigable airspace; prescribing regulations dealing with the competency of airmen, airworthiness of aircraft, and air traffic control; operation of air route traffic control centers, airport traffic control towers, and flight service stations; the design, construction, maintenance, and inspection of navigation, traffic control, and communications equipment; and the development of general aviation.

The CAB published monthly and quarterly financial and traffic statistical data for the certificated route air carriers. BTS continues these publications, including both certificated and noncertificated (commuter) air carriers. The FAA annually publishes data on the use of airway facilities; data related to the location of airmen, aircraft, and airports; the volume of activity in the field of nonair carrier (general aviation) flying; and aircraft production and registration.

General aviation comprises all civil flying (including such commercial operations as small demand air taxis, agriculture application, powerline patrol, etc.) but excludes certificated route air carriers, supplemental operators, large-aircraft commercial operators, and commuter airlines.

Air carriers and service—The CAB previously issued "certificates of public convenience and necessity" under Section 401 of the Federal Aviation Act of 1958 for scheduled and nonscheduled (charter) passenger services and cargo services. It also issued certificates under Section 418 of the Act to cargo air carriers for domestic all-cargo service only. The DOT Office of the Secretary now issues the certificates under a "fit, willing, and able" test of air carrier operations. Carriers operating only a 60-seat-or-less aircraft are given exemption authority to carry passengers, cargo, and mail in scheduled and nonscheduled service under Part 298 of the DOT (formerly CAB) regulations. Exemption authority carriers who offer scheduled passenger service to an essential air service point must meet the "fit, willing, and able" test.

Vessel shipments, entrances, and clearances—Shipments by dry cargo vessels comprise shipments on all types of watercraft, except tanker vessels; shipments by tanker vessels comprise all types of cargo, liquid and dry, carried by tanker vessels. A vessel is reported as entered only at the first port which it enters in the United States, whether or not cargo is unloaded at that port.

A vessel is reported as cleared only at the last port at which clearance is made to a foreign port, whether or not it takes on cargo. Army and Navy vessels entering or clearing without commercial cargo are not included in the figures.

Units of measurement—Cargo (or freight) tonnage and shipping weight both represent the gross weight of the cargo including the weight of containers, wrappings, crates, etc.; however, shipping weight excludes lift and cargo vans and similar substantial outer containers. Other tonnage figures generally refer to stowing capacity of vessels, 100 cubic feet being called 1 ton. Gross tonnage comprises the space within the frames and the ceiling of the hull, together with those closed-in spaces above deck available for cargo, stores, passengers, or crew, with certain minor exceptions. Net or registered tonnage is the gross tonnage less the spaces occupied by the propelling machinery, fuel, crew quarters, master's cabin, and navigation spaces. Net tonnage represents space available for cargo and passengers. The net tonnage capacity of a ship may bear little relation to weight of cargo. Deadweight tonnage is the weight in long tons required to depress a vessel from light water line (that is, with only the machinery and equipment on board) to load line. It is, therefore, the weight of the cargo, fuel, etc., which a vessel is designed to carry with safety.

Federal-aid highway systems—The Intermodal Surface Transportation Efficiency Act (ISTEA) of 1991 eliminated the historical Federal-Aid Highway Systems and created the National Highway System (NHS) and other federal-aid highway categories. The final NHS was approved by Congress in December of 1995 under the National Highway System Designation Act.

Functional systems—Roads and streets are assigned to groups according to the character of service intended. The functional systems are (1) arterial highways that generally handle the long trips, (2) collector facilities that collect and disperse traffic between the arterials and the lower systems, and (3) local roads and streets that primarily serve direct access to residential areas, farms, and other local areas.

Regulatory bodies—The Federal Energy Regulatory Commission (FERC) is an independent agency that regulates the interstate transmission of electricity, natural gas, and oil. FERC also reviews proposals to build liquefied natural gas (LNG) terminals and interstate natural gas pipelines, and licenses hydropower projects. The Energy Policy Act of 2005 gave FERC additional responsibilities such as regulating the transmission and wholesale sales of electricity in interstate commerce.

The Surface Transportation Board (STB) was created in the Interstate Commerce Commission Termination Act of 1995, Pub. L. No.104-88, 109 Stat. 803 (1995) (ICCTA), and is the successor agency to the Interstate Commerce Commission. The STB is an economic regulatory agency that Congress charged with the fundamental missions of resolving railroad rate and service disputes and reviewing proposed railroad mergers. The STB makes decisions independently, although it is administratively affiliated with the Department of Transportation.

The STB serves as both an adjudicatory and a regulatory body. The agency has jurisdiction over railroad rate and service issues and rail restructuring transactions (mergers, line sales, line construction, and line abandonment); certain trucking company, moving van, and noncontiguous ocean shipping company rate matters; certain intercity passenger bus company structure, financial, and operational matters; and rates and services of certain pipelines not regulated by the Federal Energy Regulatory Commission. Other ICC regulatory functions were either eliminated or transferred to the Federal Highway Administration or the Bureau of Transportation Statistics within DOT.

Class I Railroads are regulated by the STB and subject to the Uniform System of Accounts and required to file annual and periodic reports. Railroads are classified based on their annual operating revenues. The class to which a carrier belongs is determined by comparing its adjusted operating revenues for 3 consecutive years to the following scale: Class I, $250 million or more; Class II, $20 million to $250 million; and Class III, $0 to $20 million. Operating revenue dollar ranges are indexed for inflation.

Postal Service—The U.S. Postal Service provides mail processing and delivery services within the United States. The Postal Accountability and Enhancement Act of 2006 was the first major legislative change to the Postal Service since 1971 when the Postal Reorganization Act of 1970 created the Postal Service as an independent establishment of the Federal Executive Branch. The Act of 2006 changed the way the U.S. Postal Service operates and conducts business. Now annual rate increases for market dominant products are linked to the Consumer Price Index and the Postal Service has more flexibility for pricing competitive products, enabling it to respond to dynamic market conditions and changing customer needs.

Revenue and cost analysis describes the Postal Service's system of attributing revenues and costs to classes of mail and service. This system draws primarily upon probability sampling techniques to develop estimates of revenues, volumes, and weights, as well as costs by class of mail and special service. The costs attributed to classes of mail and special services are primarily incremental costs that vary in response to changes in volume; they account for roughly 60 percent of the total costs of the Postal Service. The balance represents "institutional costs." Statistics on revenues, volume of mail, and distribution of expenditures are presented in the Postal Service's annual reports *Public Cost and Revenue Analysis* and *Annual Report to Congress*.

Statistical reliability—For a discussion of statistical collection and estimation, sampling procedures, and measures of statistical reliability applicable to Census Bureau data, see Appendix III.

Table 1083. Transportation-Related Components of U.S. Gross Domestic Product: 2005 to 2018

[In billions of dollars (1,242.7 represents $1,242,700,000,000), except percent. For explanation of chained dollars, see text, Section 13. Minus sign (-) indicates a decrease]

Item	2005	2010	2015	2016	2017	2018
CURRENT DOLLARS						
Total transportation-related final demand [1]	**1,242.7**	**1,344.7**	**1,671.5**	**1,670.6**	**1,733.8**	**1,852.9**
Total gross domestic product (GDP)	13,036.6	14,992.1	18,224.8	18,715.0	19,519.4	20,580.2
Transportation as a percent of GDP	9.5	9.0	9.2	8.9	8.9	9.0
Personal consumption of transportation	955.3	961.8	1,162.5	1,161.7	1,231.9	1,311.8
Motor vehicles and parts	410.0	344.5	474.2	483.6	502.2	521.5
Motor vehicle fuels, lubricants, and fluids	261.4	312.1	289.7	259.2	290.3	328.1
Transportation services	283.9	305.2	398.6	418.9	439.4	462.2
Gross private domestic investment	186.7	145.7	320.3	306.1	297.8	318.8
Transportation structures	7.1	9.9	13.6	13.1	14.8	17.0
Transportation equipment	179.6	135.8	306.7	293.0	283.0	301.8
Net exports of transportation-related goods and service [2]	-133.2	-75.9	-143.1	-141.8	-144.7	-154.4
Exports (+)	206.9	255.6	359.1	356.0	367.7	382.4
Civilian aircraft, engines, and parts	55.9	71.9	119.5	120.9	121.0	130.7
Automotive vehicles, engines, and parts	98.4	112.0	151.9	150.4	157.9	158.8
Transport	52.6	71.7	87.7	84.7	88.8	92.9
Imports (-)	340.1	331.5	502.2	497.8	512.4	536.8
Civilian aircraft, engines, and parts	25.8	31.3	55.2	50.0	51.4	55.5
Automotive vehicles, engines, and parts	238.7	225.6	350.0	350.8	359.2	373.1
Transport	75.6	74.6	97.0	97.0	101.8	108.2
Government transportation-related purchases	236.8	301.3	321.6	326.5	336.2	354.0
Federal purchases [3]	29.9	38.5	40.6	41.0	42.5	45.0
State and local purchases [3]	191.0	238.1	267.8	272.3	280.2	295.0
Defense-related purchases [4]	15.9	24.7	13.2	13.2	13.5	14.0
CHAINED (2012) DOLLARS						
Total transportation-related final demand [1]	**1,584.5**	**1,497.0**	**1,757.1**	**1,783.0**	**1,794.1**	**1,849.1**
Total gross domestic product (GDP)	14,912.5	15,598.8	17,403.8	17,688.9	18,108.1	18,638.2
Transportation as a percent of GDP	10.6	9.6	10.1	10.1	9.9	9.9
Personal consumption of transportation	1,206.3	1,086.8	1,282.1	1,316.0	1,352.5	1,385.8
Motor vehicles and parts	435.1	360.0	471.7	486.3	511.1	533.1
Motor vehicle fuels, lubricants, and fluids	419.5	406.0	421.8	424.7	421.7	420.6
Transportation services	351.7	320.8	388.6	405.0	419.7	432.1
Gross private domestic investment	200.3	151.7	306.0	289.0	276.6	295.0
Transportation structures	8.2	10.2	12.8	12.0	13.3	14.9
Transportation equipment	192.1	141.5	293.2	277.0	263.3	280.1
Net exports of transportation-related goods and service [2]	-147.5	-80.9	-154.1	-157.9	-165.6	-175.0
Exports (+)	248.5	272.3	353.1	352.1	357.8	366.7
Civilian aircraft, engines, and parts	73.2	76.6	110.7	110.3	106.2	112.1
Automotive vehicles, engines, and parts	106.7	115.9	150.4	150.1	157.1	156.9
Transport	68.6	79.8	92.0	91.7	94.5	97.7
Imports (-)	396.0	353.2	507.2	510.0	523.4	541.7
Civilian aircraft, engines, and parts	36.9	36.1	52.8	47.5	48.2	51.4
Automotive vehicles, engines, and parts	264.5	237.0	360.7	364.3	374.5	388.9
Transport	94.6	80.1	93.7	98.2	100.7	101.4
Government transportation-related purchases	328.6	327.1	312.8	317.6	317.7	320.2
Federal purchases [3]	35.1	39.9	38.8	38.7	39.2	40.1
State and local purchases [3]	273.8	260.3	260.9	265.5	264.9	266.5
Defense-related purchases [4]	19.7	26.9	13.1	13.4	13.6	13.6

[1] Sum of total personal consumption of transportation, total gross private domestic investment, net exports of transportation-related goods and services, and total government transportation-related purchases. [2] Exports minus imports. [3] Federal purchases and state and local purchases are the sum of consumption expenditures and gross investment. [4] Defense-related purchases are the sum of transportation of material and travel.

Source: U.S. Bureau of Transportation Statistics, "National Transportation Statistics," <https://www.bts.gov/product/national-transportation-statistics>, accessed February 2020.

Table 1084. Employment in Transportation and Warehousing: 2000 to 2019

[In thousands (4,401 represents 4,401,000). Annual average of monthly figures. Based on Current Employment Statistics program; see Appendix III]

Industry	NAICS code [1]	2000	2010	2013	2014	2015	2016	2017	2018	2019
Transportation and warehousing	**48–49**	**4,401**	**4,179**	**4,486**	**4,649**	**4,859**	**5,004**	**5,178**	**5,426**	**5,618**
Air transportation	481	614	458	444	444	459	478	492	497	503
Rail transportation	482	206	183	196	200	204	184	182	182	175
Water transportation	483	56	62	65	67	66	66	65	65	66
Truck transportation	484	1,406	1,251	1,383	1,418	1,453	1,448	1,457	1,496	1,531
Transit and ground passenger	485	376	436	456	474	485	490	495	495	499
Pipeline transportation	486	46	42	45	47	50	50	49	50	51
Scenic and sightseeing	487	28	27	29	31	33	35	35	35	36
Support activities	488	546	553	609	637	663	678	701	729	754
Couriers and messengers	492	605	528	544	577	613	645	676	740	816
Warehousing and storage	493	518	638	716	755	834	932	1,027	1,139	1,188

[1] North American Industry Classification System 2017, see text, Sections 12 and 15.

Source: U.S. Bureau of Labor Statistics, Current Employment Statistics, "Employment, Hours, and Earnings—National," <http://www.bls.gov/ces/data.htm/>, accessed March 2020.

Table 1085. Transportation and Warehousing—Establishments, Employees, and Payroll by Industry: 2017 and 2018

[Employment in thousands (4,866.3 represents 4,866,300); payroll in millions of dollars ($245,135.0 represents $245,135,000,000). Covers establishments with payroll. Excludes self-employed individuals, railroad employees, and most government employees. For statement on methodology, see Appendix III. County Business Patterns excludes rail transportation (NAICS 482) and the Postal Service (NAICS 491)]

Industry	NAICS code [1]	Establishments		Paid employees (1,000) [2]		Annual payroll (mil. dol.)	
		2017	2018	2017	2018	2017	2018
Transportation & warehousing.................	**48–49**	**237,308**	**244,800**	**4,866.3**	**5,031.8**	**245,135.0**	**262,456.6**
Air transportation.........................	481	4,441	4,414	470.4	479.6	39,966.0	41,816.6
Scheduled air transportation.................	4811	2,247	2,201	430.4	437.5	36,324.0	37,748.6
Scheduled passenger air transportation.............	481111	1,872	1,846	421.2	429.3	35,658.2	37,111.0
Scheduled freight air transportation.................	481112	375	355	9.2	8.2	665.8	637.6
Nonscheduled air transportation.................	4812	2,194	2,213	40.0	42.1	3,642.0	4,068.0
Water transportation.........................	483	1,668	1,646	61.8	61.5	5,191.1	5,293.0
Deep sea, coastal, & Great Lakes water transportation.........................	4831	1,076	1,048	41.5	42.1	3,678.8	3,779.0
Inland water transportation.................	4832	592	598	20.3	19.4	1,512.3	1,514.0
Inland water freight transportation.................	483211	314	327	17.3	16.3	1,339.0	1,340.9
Inland water passenger transportation.................	483212	278	271	3.0	3.1	173.3	173.1
Truck transportation.........................	484	126,986	134,769	1,465.0	1,514.3	71,922.7	77,505.0
General freight trucking.................	4841	76,833	84,662	973.9	1,019.2	48,012.8	52,236.9
General freight trucking, local.................	48411	31,490	33,134	192.7	205.5	8,561.8	9,529.1
General freight trucking, long distance.................	48412	45,343	51,528	781.2	813.7	39,451.1	42,707.7
Specialized freight trucking.................	4842	50,153	50,107	491.2	495.1	23,909.8	25,268.1
Used household & office goods moving.................	48421	8,417	8,282	98.0	97.3	3,614.9	3,661.2
Specialized freight (except used goods) trucking, local.................	48422	30,872	30,702	220.7	222.0	11,176.3	11,760.6
Specialized freight (except used goods) trucking, long-distance.................	48423	10,864	11,123	172.4	175.7	9,118.7	9,846.3
Transit & ground passenger transportation.................	485	20,397	20,415	514.7	512.8	15,188.6	16,302.8
Urban transit systems.................	4851	1,002	746	59.1	55.3	2,772.1	2,776.3
Mixed mode systems.................	485111	36	41	0.7	0.8	27.3	30.3
Commuter rail.................	485112	16	18	3.7	3.8	318.0	336.0
Bus and other motor vehicle mode systems.........	485113	760	629	52.6	49.3	2,331.8	2,325.3
Other.................	485119	190	58	2.1	1.5	95.0	84.7
Interurban & rural bus transportation.................	4852	806	655	20.6	18.9	666.0	627.5
Taxi & limousine service.................	4853	7,887	8,028	81.0	73.1	2,934.8	3,432.4
Taxi service.................	48531	3,266	3,222	44.0	35.8	1,886.2	2,314.6
Limousine service.................	48532	4,621	4,806	37.0	37.3	1,048.7	1,117.9
School & employee bus transportation.................	4854	4,275	4,349	224.3	234.8	5,131.4	5,631.2
Charter bus industry.................	4855	1,273	1,287	32.1	32.9	1,032.1	1,103.6
Other transit & ground passenger transportation......	4859	5,154	5,350	97.6	97.6	2,652.3	2,731.8
Special needs transportation.................	485991	3,333	3,514	74.2	75.2	2,019.7	2,075.2
Pipeline transportation.................	486	3,712	3,440	51.4	47.8	6,140.3	5,785.8
Pipeline transportation of crude oil.................	4861	802	777	13.4	12.8	1,483.8	1,516.2
Pipeline transportation of natural gas.................	4862	2,176	1,976	29.5	26.3	3,649.0	3,199.3
Other pipeline transportation.................	4869	734	687	8.5	8.7	1,007.5	1,070.3
Scenic & sightseeing transportation.................	487	2,898	2,938	29.6	29.8	1,136.3	1,201.4
Scenic & sightseeing transportation, land.................	4871	738	761	11.5	11.7	386.7	391.2
Scenic & sightseeing transportation, water...........	4872	1,817	1,908	14.5	14.6	575.4	636.0
Scenic & sightseeing transportation, other.................	4879	343	269	3.6	3.5	174.2	174.3
Support activities for transportation.................	488	45,946	45,792	718.3	742.8	36,867.1	40,382.7
Support activities for air transportation.................	4881	6,099	6,138	200.0	210.2	8,677.0	9,471.3
Airport operations.................	48811	2,205	2,198	114.4	122.8	3,563.8	3,891.1
Air traffic control.................	488111	192	200	1.3	1.3	98.2	104.6
Other support activities for air transportation.........	48819	3,894	3,940	85.5	87.4	5,113.2	5,580.3
Support activities for rail transportation.................	4882	1,543	1,502	40.9	42.0	2,073.6	2,285.0
Support activities for water transportation.................	4883	2,681	2,625	90.8	96.3	6,704.7	7,198.2
Port and harbor operations.................	48831	335	354	9.0	11.1	503.2	733.5
Marine cargo handling.................	48832	480	464	58.7	62.7	4,514.1	4,799.9
Navigational services to shipping.................	48833	1,032	1,020	13.6	15.0	1,056.3	1,198.2
Other support activities for water transportation.....	48839	834	787	9.5	7.4	631.1	466.6
Support activities for road transportation.................	4884	12,505	12,600	104.5	104.5	3,622.4	3,847.4
Motor vehicle towing.................	48841	9,211	9,307	62.3	64.0	2,321.6	2,484.3
Freight transportation arrangement.................	4885	21,395	21,173	265.2	271.9	15,167.2	16,708.6
Other support activities for transportation.................	4889	1,723	1,754	16.9	17.9	622.2	872.1
Couriers & messengers.................	492	14,359	14,467	641.6	676.0	28,982.0	30,932.5
Couriers.................	4921	9,906	9,985	588.4	620.5	27,124.6	28,897.0
Local messengers & local delivery.................	4922	4,453	4,482	53.2	55.5	1,857.4	2,035.6
Warehousing & storage.................	493	16,901	16,919	913.6	967.4	39,741.0	43,236.8

[1] Data based on 2017 North American Industry Classification System (NAICS). See text, Section 15. [2] Covers full- and part-time employees who are on the payroll in the pay period including March 12.

Source: U.S. Census Bureau, County Business Patterns, "County Business Patterns by Legal Form of Organization and Employment Size Class for U.S., States, and Selected Geographies," <data.census.gov>, accessed July 2020. See also <https://www.census.gov/programs-surveys/cbp.html>.

Table 1086. Transportation Sector—Estimated Revenue by Kind of Business: 2010 to 2018

[In millions of dollars (660,440 represents $660,440,000,000). For taxable employer firms. Estimates have been adjusted to results of the 2012 Economic Census. Based on the Service Annual Survey; see Appendix III]

Kind of business	NAICS code [1]	2010	2015	2016	2017	2018
Transportation and warehousing (excl. 482 and 491)	**4849y**	**660,440**	**876,498**	**879,220**	**918,981**	**991,615**
Air transportation [2]	481	148,419	200,161	199,396	209,725	225,785
Scheduled passenger air transportation	481111	126,902	174,099	172,268	180,421	194,101
Nonscheduled chartered passenger air transportation	481211	10,499	13,709	13,785	14,314	14,867
Water transportation [2]	483	37,392	44,003	42,806	42,231	45,950
Deep sea freight transportation	483111	9,281	8,443	7,656	6,167	6,426
Deep sea passenger transportation	483112	14,393	18,593	19,692	21,421	24,020
Coastal and great lakes freight transportation	483113	6,254	7,509	6,872	6,505	6,784
Inland water freight transportation	483211	6,879	8,652	7,742	7,179	7,679
Truck transportation	484	197,963	263,249	259,531	272,784	294,489
General freight trucking, local	48411	19,902	26,426	26,453	27,919	30,545
General freight trucking, long-distance, truckload	484121	77,474	101,884	101,243	107,161	118,521
General freight trucking, long-distance, less than truckload	484122	31,698	41,221	40,739	43,210	46,755
Used household and office goods moving	48421	12,361	15,897	16,169	16,295	17,047
Specialized freight (except used goods) trucking, local	48422	28,465	38,828	37,399	39,745	41,522
Specialized freight (except used goods) trucking, long-distance	48423	28,063	38,993	37,528	38,454	40,099
Transit and ground passenger transportation [2]	485	26,900	34,031	35,809	39,842	42,508
Urban transit systems	4851	4,460	5,596	5,901	6,047	6,339
Interurban and rural bus transportation	4852	1,037	1,146	1,154	1,155	1,147
Taxi service	48531	2,225	2,678	(S)	5,624	(S)
Limousine service	48532	3,554	4,564	4,338	4,185	4,303
School and employee bus transportation	4854	8,628	10,939	11,482	12,528	13,023
Charter bus industry	4855	2,888	3,439	3,513	3,669	3,828
Pipeline transportation [2]	486	33,069	43,764	44,459	46,676	52,820
Pipeline transportation of crude oil	4861	5,004	10,004	10,158	10,621	12,680
Pipeline transportation of natural gas	4862	21,831	25,230	25,612	27,275	30,641
Pipeline transportation of refined petroleum products	48691	5,993	8,227	8,403	8,510	9,231
Scenic and sightseeing transportation [2]	487	2,545	3,666	3,581	3,477	3,601
Scenic and sightseeing transportation, land	4871	903	1,084	1,121	1,151	1,261
Scenic and sightseeing transportation, water	4872	1,236	1,906	1,767	1,636	1,717
Support activities for transportation [2]	488	125,423	177,816	177,591	180,727	194,773
Airport operations	48811	5,699	7,936	8,283	(S)	8,492
Other support activities for air transportation	48819	15,072	16,826	17,983	16,327	17,083
Support activities for rail transportation	4882	3,945	5,781	6,299	6,403	6,682
Port and harbor operations	48831	1,856	2,809	2,770	2,846	3,063
Marine cargo handling	48832	7,572	10,782	10,393	10,531	10,946
Navigational services to shipping	48833	2,886	3,503	3,417	3,498	3,609
Motor vehicle towing	48841	5,040	6,016	6,220	6,648	6,996
Freight transportation arrangement	4885	77,359	116,044	113,784	117,508	128,850
Couriers and messengers	492	63,855	78,424	82,976	88,780	95,366
Couriers and express delivery services	4921	60,917	74,117	78,110	82,771	88,701
Local messengers and local delivery	4922	2,938	4,307	4,866	6,009	6,665
Warehousing and storage	493	24,874	31,384	33,071	34,739	36,323
General warehousing and storage	49311	15,966	19,486	20,619	21,827	22,945
Refrigerated warehousing and storage	49312	4,083	(S)	(S)	4,931	5,199
Farm product warehousing and storage	49313	698	786	798	811	850
Other warehousing and storage	49319	4,127	6,698	6,995	7,170	7,329

S Estimate does not meet publication standards. [1] 2010 data are based on 2007 North American Industry Classification System (NAICS). Beginning 2013, data are based on 2012 NAICS; see text, this section and Section 15. [2] Includes other kinds of business not shown separately.

Source: U.S. Census Bureau, Service Annual Survey, "Service Annual Survey Latest Data (NAICS-basis): 2018," <https://www.census.gov/programs-surveys/sas/data.html>, accessed April 2020.

Table 1087. Transportation and Warehousing—Establishments, Revenue, Payroll, and Employees by Industry: 2017

[895,225 represents $895,225,000,000. For establishments with payroll. Based on the 2017 Economic Censuses. Paid employees for pay period including March 12. See Appendix III]

Industry type	NAICS code [1]	Number of establish- ments	Revenue (mil. dol.)	Annual payroll (mil. dol.)	Paid employees (1,000)
Transportation and warehousing total	**48–49**	**237,095**	**895,225**	**242,145**	**4,954.9**
Air transportation	481	4,450	208,830	39,652	508.3
Water transportation	483	1,643	43,009	5,083	62.7
Truck transportation	484	126,803	290,531	71,121	1,480.1
Transit and ground passenger transportation	485	20,267	44,040	15,320	535.2
Pipeline transportation	486	3,688	47,193	5,980	52.6
Scenic and sightseeing transportation	487	2,865	4,162	1,157	32.0
Support activities for transportation	488	45,956	128,966	35,943	729.5
Couriers and messengers	492	14,467	90,408	28,164	633.1
Warehousing and storage	493	16,956	38,086	39,726	921.3

[1] Data based on the 2017 North American Industry Classification System (NAICS); see text, Section 15.

Source: U.S. Census Bureau, 2017 Economic Census, EC1748BASIC, "Transportation and Warehousing: Summary Statistics for the U.S., States, and Selected Geographies: 2017," <data.census.gov/>, accessed July 2020.

Table 1088. Transportation and Warehousing—Nonemployer Establishments and Receipts by Kind of Business: 2010 to 2018

[1,021.2 represents 1,021,200. Includes only firms subject to federal income tax. Nonemployers are businesses with no paid employees. Data originate chiefly from administrative records of the Internal Revenue Service; see Appendix III]

Kind of business	NAICS code [1]	Establishments (1,000)			Receipts (mil. dol.)		
		2010	2017	2018	2010	2017	2018
Transportation and warehousing............	**48–49**	**1,021.2**	**2,205.6**	**2,572.4**	**60,746**	**99,482**	**117,316**
Air transportation............................	481	19.1	22.4	24.0	1,219	1,486	1,586
Water transportation........................	483	6.6	7.0	7.7	490	590	620
Truck transportation.........................	484	490.3	621.4	682.6	42,485	62,357	71,325
General freight trucking...................	4841	445.1	572.1	626.5	39,277	58,575	67,062
General freight trucking, local.........	48411	168.7	194.9	210.7	12,144	17,386	19,578
General freight trucking, long-distance........	48412	276.4	377.2	415.9	27,133	41,189	47,484
Specialized freight trucking..........................	4842	45.2	49.3	56.1	3,207	3,782	4,263
Transit and ground passenger transportation....	485	218.4	1,099.6	1,327.5	7,463	21,938	29,257
Urban transit system.................................	4851	1.1	2.6	2.4	39	71	77
Interurban and rural bus transportation..........	4852	1.5	2.4	2.5	67	80	86
Taxi and limousine service.........................	4853	176.4	973.8	1,196.3	6,107	19,137	25,892
School and employee bus transportation........	4854	6.9	6.9	7.1	191	201	219
Charter bus industry...............................	4855	3.8	4.3	4.4	172	209	219
Other transit and ground passenger transportation..................................	4859	28.7	109.8	114.9	887	2,240	2,763
Pipeline transportation..........................	486	0.9	1.3	1.5	76	91	107
Scenic and sightseeing transportation............	487	4.9	6.3	6.6	163	236	252
Support activities for transportation................	488	105.2	169.6	143.6	4,624	7,070	7,378
Couriers and messengers..........................	492	166.6	262.1	361.7	3,772	5,085	6,121
Warehousing and storage..........................	493	9.2	15.9	17.2	455	628	671

[1] 2010 data based on the 2007 North American Industry Classification System (NAICS); and beginning 2017 data based on 2017 NAICS.

Source: U.S. Census Bureau, Nonemployer Statistics, "All Sectors: Nonemployer Statistics for the U.S., States, Counties, Metropolitan Areas, and Combined Statistical Areas; and by Legal Form of Organization and Sales, Value of Shipments, or Revenue Size for Selected Geographies: 2018," <data.census.gov/>, accessed May 2020.

Table 1089. Transportation System Mileage Within the United States: 1985 to 2018

[3,864 represents 3,864,000. Numbers, except where indicated]

System	Unit	1985	1990	1995	2000	2005	2010	2015	2017	2018
Highway [1]......................	1,000	3,864	3,867	3,912	3,936	3,996	4,067	4,155	4,165	4,177
Class 1 rail [2]...................	Number	145,764	119,758	108,264	99,250	95,830	95,700	93,628	93,150	92,837
Amtrak [2]........................	Number	24,000	24,000	24,000	23,000	22,007	21,178	21,358	21,407	21,407
Transit: [3]										
Commuter rail [4]..............	Number	3,574	4,132	4,160	5,209	7,118	7,630	7,697	7,815	(NA)
Heavy rail [5]....................	Number	1,293	1,351	1,458	1,558	1,622	1,617	1,643	1,653	(NA)
Light rail [6]....................	Number	384	483	568	834	1,188	1,497	1,893	2,030	(NA)
Navigable channels [7].........	Number	25,000	25,000	25,000	25,000	25,000	25,000	25,000	25,000	25,000
Oil pipeline [8]...................	Number	(NA)	(NA)	(NA)	(NA)	166,760	181,986	208,618	215,867	218,696
Gas pipeline [9].................	1,000	1,641	1,871	2,028	2,115	2,287	2,427	2,509	2,542	2,558

NA Not available. [1] All public road and street mileage in the 50 states and the District of Columbia. Beginning in 1998, approximately 43,000 miles of Bureau of Land Management Roads are excluded. [2] Data represent miles of road owned (aggregate length of road, excluding yard tracks, sidings, and parallel lines). Portions of Class I freight railroads, Amtrak, and Commuter rail networks share common trackage. Amtrak data represent miles of road operated. [3] Transit system length is measured in directional route-miles; see source. [4] Urban passenger train service for short-distance travel between a central city and adjacent suburb. Does not include rapid rail transit or light rail service. [5] Also known as subway, elevated (railway), or metropolitan railway (metro). [6] A streetcar-type vehicle operated on city streets. Beginning in 2011, "Light rail" includes light rail, street car rail, and hybrid rail. [7] Estimated sums of domestic waterways which include rivers, bays, channels, and the inner route of the Southeast Alaskan Islands, but does not include the Great Lakes or deep ocean traffic. Beginning in 2007, includes waterways connecting the Great Lakes and the St. Lawrence Seaway inside the U.S. [8] Includes trunk and gathering lines for crude-oil pipeline. Oil pipeline data has been discontinued for years prior to 2001. [9] Excludes service pipelines.

Source: U.S. Bureau of Transportation Statistics, "National Transportation Statistics," <https://www.bts.gov/content/system-mileage-within-united-states>, accessed February 2020.

Table 1090. U.S. Aircraft, Vehicles, and Other Conveyances: 2000 to 2018

[Number, or in thousands (225,821 represents 225,821,000), as indicated]

Mode	2000	2010	2012	2013	2014	2015	2016	2017	2018
AIR									
Air carrier [1]	7,826	7,185	6,914	6,740	6,761	6,876	7,077	7,196	7,475
General aviation [2] (active fleet)	217,533	223,370	209,034	199,927	204,408	210,030	211,793	211,757	211,749
HIGHWAY, REGISTERED VEHICLES (1,000s)									
Total registered vehicles	225,821	250,070	253,639	255,877	260,351	263,610	268,799	272,481	273,602
Light duty vehicle, short wheel base [3]	133,621	190,203	183,172	184,497	187,555	189,618	192,775	193,672	192,856
Motorcycle	4,346	8,010	8,455	8,405	8,418	8,601	8,679	8,715	8,666
Light duty vehicle, long wheel base [4]	79,085	40,242	50,589	51,513	52,600	53,299	54,870	56,881	57,854
Trucks [5]	5,926	8,217	8,190	8,126	8,329	8,456	8,747	9,337	10,328
Truck, combination	2,097	2,553	2,469	2,471	2,577	2,747	2,752	2,892	2,906
Bus	746	846	765	865	872	889	976	983	992
TRANSIT									
Motor bus	58,578	63,108	61,245	66,823	62,449	63,573	63,270	63,759	63,284
Light rail cars [6]	1,306	2,096	2,348	2,842	2,444	2,478	2,553	2,557	2,729
Heavy rail cars [7]	10,311	11,510	10,469	10,380	10,551	10,737	10,775	10,705	10,763
Trolley bus	652	571	570	560	537	611	601	539	571
Commuter rail cars and locomotives	5,497	6,768	6,938	7,150	7,177	7,151	7,190	7,129	7,023
Demand responsive	22,087	33,555	31,929	31,433	31,359	32,490	33,225	33,012	33,253
Other [8]	7,705	18,066	16,996	17,793	17,994	18,601	17,042	18,104	17,803
RAIL									
Class I, freight cars	560,154	397,730	380,641	373,838	371,642	330,996	315,227	306,268	293,742
Class I, locomotive	20,028	23,893	24,707	25,033	25,916	26,574	26,716	26,547	26,086
Nonclass I freight cars	132,448	101,755	92,742	88,122	(NA)	(NA)	(NA)	(NA)	(NA)
Car companies' and shippers' freight cars	688,194	809,544	842,802	873,679	(NA)	(NA)	(NA)	(NA)	(NA)
Amtrak, passenger train car	1,894	1,274	2,090	1,447	1,419	1,428	1,402	1,405	1,403
Amtrak, locomotive	378	282	485	418	428	423	434	419	431
WATER									
Non-self-propelled vessels [9]	31,372	30,265	32,394	32,047	31,171	31,748	33,212	32,808	32,828
Self-propelled vessels [10]	9,293	9,618	10,139	9,921	9,210	9,043	9,462	9,344	9,310
Ocean-going self-propelled vessels (1,000 gross tons and over) [11]	282	221	198	187	179	170	169	176	182
Recreational boats (1,000s)	12,782	12,439	12,102	12,013	11,804	11,867	11,862	11,962	11,853

NA Not available. [1] Air carrier aircraft are those carrying passengers or cargo for hire under 14 CFR 121 and 14 CFR 135. [2] Includes air taxi aircraft. [3] Data for 2000-06 are for passenger cars. Beginning 2007, data are for Light Duty Vehicles Short Wheel Base—passenger cars, light trucks, vans and sport utility vehicles with a wheelbase of 121 inches or less. [4] Data for 2000-06 are for 2-axle, 4-tire vehicles other than passenger cars, motorcycles, and buses. Beginning 2007, data are for Light Duty Vehicles Long Wheel Base—large passenger cars, vans, pickup trucks, and sport/utility vehicles with wheelbases larger than 121 inches. [5] Includes trucks on a single frame with at least 2 axles and 6 tires. [6] Fixed rail streetcar or trolley, for example. [7] Metro, subway, or rapid transit, for example. [8] Includes Alaska railroad, automated guideway transit, cable car, ferry boat, inclined plane, monorail, and vanpool. [9] Includes dry-cargo barges, tank barges, and railroad-car floats. [10] Includes dry-cargo and/or passenger, offshore supply vessels, railroad-car ferries, tankers, and towboats. [11] 2000-06 data include private and government owned vessels of 1,000 gross tons or more. Beginning 2007, data are reported only for privately owned vessels of 1,000 gross tons or more. 2009 data include privately owned vessels of 10,000 deadweight tons or more, not including the Great Lakes vessels.

Source: U.S. Bureau of Transportation Statistics, "National Transportation Statistics," <https://www.bts.gov/topics/national-transportation-statistics>, accessed July 2020.

Table 1091. Transportation Shipments by Mode: 2012 to 2045

[16,996 represents 16,996,000,000. All truck, rail, water, and pipeline movements that involve more than one mode, including exports and imports that change mode at international gateways, are included in multiple modes & mail to avoid double counting. Data do not include imports and exports that pass through the United States from a foreign origin to a foreign destination by any mode]

Mode	2012 Total	2012 Domestic	2012 Exports	2012 Imports	2016 [1] Total	2016 [1] Domestic	2016 [1] Exports	2016 [1] Imports	2045 [2] Total	2045 [2] Domestic	2045 [2] Exports	2045 [2] Imports
WEIGHT (millions of tons)												
Total	**16,996**	**14,895**	**933**	**1,169**	**17,686**	**15,762**	**887**	**1,037**	**25,521**	**20,932**	**2,330**	**2,259**
Truck	10,098	9,893	115	90	11,086	10,882	101	103	14,836	14,226	304	306
Rail	1,625	1,481	57	87	1,575	1,418	66	90	1,926	1,588	112	226
Water	959	502	77	380	798	519	131	148	1,186	609	203	373
Air, air and truck	11	2	5	4	11	2	4	4	41	4	19	18
Multiple modes and mail [3]	1,361	309	627	425	1,354	322	505	528	2,941	431	1,482	1,028
Pipeline	2,901	2,672	50	179	2,823	2,589	72	162	4,559	4,058	205	296
Other and unknown	42	37	2	3	39	29	9	1	32	16	5	11
VALUE (billions of 2012 dollars)												
Total	**17,729**	**13,965**	**1,545**	**2,219**	**18,142**	**14,341**	**1,542**	**2,259**	**37,064**	**22,469**	**6,511**	**8,084**
Truck	10,929	10,251	366	311	11,225	10,532	347	347	18,682	16,219	1,244	1,219
Rail	582	411	63	109	621	445	65	111	1,080	646	157	278
Water	631	270	73	288	527	279	98	151	1,031	340	281	411
Air, air and truck	1,067	135	461	472	1,081	132	447	502	5,221	324	2,544	2,354
Multiple modes and mail [3]	3,246	1,746	552	947	3,315	1,784	487	1,044	8,981	3,393	2,123	3,465
Pipeline	1,233	1,150	13	70	1,282	1,169	31	81	1,744	1,546	88	110
Other and unknown	40	1	17	22	91	1	67	23	325	–	76	248

– Represents zero. [1] The 2016 data are provisional estimates that are based on selected modal and economic trend data. [2] Freight Analysis Framework forecasts. [3] Multiple modes and mail also includes some air movements.

Source: U.S. Department of Transportation, Bureau of Transportation Statistics, *Transportation Statistics Annual Report 2018*, February 2019. See also <https://www.bts.gov/TSAR>.

Table 1092. Shipment Characteristics by Mode of Transportation: 2012 and 2017

[13,852,143 represents $13,852,143,000,000, unless otherwise noted. For business establishments in mining, manufacturing, wholesale trade, and selected retail and services industries. 2017 industries classified by the 2012 North American Industry Classification System (NAICS). 2012 industries classified by 2007 NAICS. Selected auxiliary establishments are also included. Based on the Commodity Flow Survey, conducted as part of the Economic Census; see Appendix III]

Mode of transportation	Value (mil. dol.)		Tons (1,000)		Ton-miles (mil.)		Average miles per shipment	
	2012	2017	2012	2017	2012	2017	2012	2017
All modes..................	13,852,143	14,366,611	11,299,409	12,478,849	2,969,506	3,130,697	630	633
Single modes..................	11,900,364	11,642,939	10,905,518	11,496,515	2,697,418	2,399,208	262	222
Truck [1]....................	10,132,229	10,490,038	8,060,166	8,925,313	1,247,717	1,301,054	227	188
For-hire truck..............	6,504,636	7,257,437	4,298,693	5,568,811	1,050,942	1,142,613	508	325
Private truck................	3,627,592	3,232,602	3,761,472	3,356,501	196,775	158,441	58	46
Rail.......................	473,070	203,432	1,628,537	1,156,760	1,211,481	842,716	805	554
Water.....................	301,554	145,179	575,996	561,634	192,866	175,829	908	225
Great Lakes................	218,927	59,246	424,542	288,697	118,742	119,297	275	256
Inland water................	59,878	80,426	72,987	202,146	22,130	28,337	1,157	215
Deep sea..................	424	733	31,403	55,564	10,959	20,778	347	290
Multiple waterways.............	(NA)	4,774	(NA)	15,228	(NA)	7,417	(NA)	(S)
Air (includes truck and air)......	450,575	408,772	4,845	5,745	5,810	6,853	1,295	1,437
Pipeline [2].................	542,936	395,517	635,975	847,063	(S)	(S)	(S)	(S)
Multiple modes................	1,950,753	2,720,518	357,047	856,355	271,832	731,363	922	890
Parcel, U.S. Postal Service or courier........................	1,688,242	2,037,533	28,490	36,040	22,716	27,182	922	890
Truck and rail................	224,833	459,933	213,814	650,615	169,524	577,100	988	1,140
Truck and water.................	29,035	178,624	56,720	81,063	48,568	43,228	1,562	994
Rail and water................	7,976	21,485	55,570	75,996	29,170	70,177	1,073	1,306
Other multiple modes............	668	22,944	2,452	12,642	1,853	13,676	(S)	1,429
Other and unknown modes..	1,026	3,153	36,844	125,979	256	126	(S)	1

NA Not available. S Data do not meet publication standards due to high sampling variability or other reasons. [1] Truck as a single mode includes shipments that went by private truck only, for-hire truck only, or a combination of private truck and for-hire truck. [2] Commodity Flow Survey data exclude shipments of crude oil.

Source: U.S. Department of Transportation, Bureau of Transportation Statistics, and U.S. Census Bureau, Commodity Flow Survey, "CFS Preliminary Report: Shipment Characteristics by Mode of Transportation: 2017," <data.census.gov>, accessed August 2019. See also <https://www.census.gov/programs-surveys/cfs.html>.

Table 1093. Hazardous Shipments—Value, Tons, and Ton-Miles: 2012 and 2017

[2,334,425 represents $2,334,425,000,000. For business establishments in mining, manufacturing, wholesale trade, and selected retail industries. Data cover industries classified by the 2012 North American Industry Classification System (NAICS). Also includes auxiliary establishments of multi-establishment companies. Due to definitional and processing changes made each survey year, any data comparisons between one CFS survey and another should be made with caution, see Methodology. Based on the Commodity Flow Survey, conducted as part of the Economic Census; see Appendix III]

Mode of transportation and class of material	Value (mil. dol.)		Tons (1,000)		Ton-miles (mil.)		Average miles per shipment	
	2012	2017	2012	2017	2012	2017	2012	2017
All modes..........................	2,334,425	1,680,231	2,580,153	2,967,965	307,524	382,472	114	189
Single modes..................	2,304,743	1,612,129	2,552,868	2,889,521	275,628	307,204	68	72
Truck [1]........................	1,466,021	1,091,250	1,531,405	1,814,848	96,559	126,800	56	63
For-hire truck..................	870,893	567,599	882,288	932,658	62,018	92,146	150	153
Private truck, company-owned.............	595,128	523,651	649,117	882,190	34,541	34,655	33	28
Rail.........................	79,222	39,040	110,988	90,387	84,850	61,669	808	640
Water........................	217,816	137,109	283,561	304,189	54,902	60,934	212	72
Air (includes truck and air)..................	4,380	4,817	261	251	271	201	1,120	1,333
Pipeline [2]......................	537,304	339,912	626,652	679,846	(S)	(S)	(S)	(S)
Multiple modes [3].......................	29,682	68,101	27,285	78,444	31,896	75,268	654	947
Parcel, U.S. Postal Service or courier.......	10,294	13,475	305	345	178	236	650	949
Class of Material..........................	2,334,425	1,680,231	2,580,153	2,967,965	307,524	382,472	114	189
Class 1, Explosives........................	18,397	14,936	4,045	3,290	1,012	1,011	840	1,046
Class 2, Gases............................	125,054	114,845	164,794	227,616	33,157	28,880	57	210
Class 3, Flammable and combustible liquid........	2,016,681	1,373,803	2,203,490	2,466,634	204,573	269,803	93	100
Class 4, Flammable solid; spontaneously combustible material; dangerous when wet material........	5,415	5,308	11,321	28,210	5,804	7,614	565	478
Class 5, Oxidizers and organic peroxides...	7,562	9,753	12,025	14,978	5,479	5,827	437	204
Class 6, Toxic materials and infectious substances........	15,196	13,298	7,612	6,358	3,607	3,838	513	828
Class 7, Radioactive materials...............	12,288	6,945	(S)	427	39	42	34	63
Class 8, Corrosive materials................	75,850	79,322	125,287	151,007	37,784	45,704	264	273
Class 9, Miscellaneous hazardous material..........	57,981	62,020	51,006	69,444	16,068	19,753	530	944

S Data do not meet publication standards. [1] Truck as a single mode includes shipments that went by private truck only, for-hire truck only, or a combination of private truck and for-hire truck. [2] Commodity Flow Survey Data exclude shipments of crude oil. [3] Includes other modes not shown.

Source: U.S. Department of Transportation, Bureau of Transportation Statistics, and U.S. Census Bureau, and 2017 Commodity Flow Survey, CF1700H01, "Hazardous Materials Series: HazMat Shipment Characteristics by Mode for the United States: 2017 and 2012," and CF1700H02, "Hazardous Materials Series: HazMat Shipment Characteristics by Hazardous Class or Division for the United States: 2017 and 2012," <data.census.gov>, accessed July 2020. See also <census.gov/programs-surveys/cfs.html>.

Table 1094. Transportation Accidents, Deaths, and Injuries: 2000 to 2018

[6,394 represents 6,394,000]

Mode	Unit	Accidents			Deaths			Injuries		
		2000	2010	2018	2000	2010	2018	2000	2010	2018
Air, total.............	Number	1,985	1,507	1,348	764	477	394	359	278	272
Air carrier [1].............	Number	56	30	30	92	2	1	31	17	25
Commuter [2].............	Number	12	6	2	5	–	–	7	2	–
On-demand [3].............	Number	80	30	41	71	17	12	12	3	17
General aviation.............	Number	1,837	1,441	1,275	596	458	381	309	256	230
Land:										
Highway crashes [4].............	1,000	6,394	5,419	6,734	41.9	33.0	36.6	3,194	2,248	2,709
Passenger car occupants.............	1,000	4,926	5,350	6,658	20.7	12.5	12.8	2,057	1,256	1,512
Motorcyclists.............	1,000	69	96	109	2.9	4.5	5.0	58	82	82
Light truck occupants.............	1,000	3,208	3,775	4,670	11.5	9.8	9.9	886	737	921
Large truck occupants.............	1,000	438	276	531	0.8	0.5	0.9	31	20	39
Bus occupants.............	1,000	56	54	65	–	–	–	17	18	15
Pedestrians.............	1,000	(NA)	(NA)	(NA)	4.8	4.3	6.3	78	70	75
Pedalcyclists.............	1,000	(NA)	(NA)	(NA)	0.7	0.6	0.9	51	52	47
Other.............	1,000	(NA)	(NA)	(NA)	0.6	0.7	0.8	15	13	20
Railroad [5].............	Number	14,024	10,032	10,046	937	735	831	11,643	8,379	8,196
Highway-rail grade crossing [6]......	Number	607	453	583	425	261	262	1,219	888	840
Transit [7].............	Number	24,261	3,492	7,040	295	222	251	56,697	25,376	22,522
Waterborne [8].............	Number	13,143	9,889	6,773	716	821	684	(NA)	3,770	2,967
Recreational boating [9].............	Number	7,740	4,604	4,145	701	672	633	4,355	3,153	2,511
Pipeline:		380	586	636	38	22	8	81	108	90
Hazard liquid.............	Number	146	350	405	1	1	–	4	3	2
Gas.............	Number	234	236	231	37	21	8	77	105	88

– Represents or rounds to zero. NA Not available. [1] See footnote 1, Table 1101. Injuries classified as serious. [2] See footnote 2, Table 1101. Injuries classified as serious. [3] See footnote 3, Table 1101. Injuries classified as serious. [4] Highway crashes often involve more than one motor vehicle, and hence "total highway crashes" is smaller than the sum of the components. Data on deaths are from U.S. National Highway Traffic Safety Administration and are based on deaths within 30 days of the accident. Includes only police reported crashes. For more details, see Table 1134. [5] Accidents and incidents resulting from freight and passenger rail operations including commuter rail. Grade crossing accidents are also included when classified as a train accident. Deaths and injuries exclude those in highway-rail grade crossing accidents involving motor vehicles. Injury figures also include occupational illness. [6] Accidents and incidents occurring at highway-rail crossings resulting from freight and passenger rail operations including commuter rail. Public highway-rail grade crossing incidents, fatalities, and injuries involving motor vehicles are excluded and counted under Highway. Highway-rail grade crossing injuries, except train occupants, are also counted under Highway. [7] Includes motor bus, commuter rail, heavy rail, light rail, demand response, van pool, and automated guideway. Starting with 2002, only injuries requiring immediate medical treatment away from the scene now qualify as reportable. [8] To include vessel-related deaths and injuries include those involving damage to vessels, such as collisions or groundings. Totals include deaths and injuries not related to vessel casualties, not shown separately. [9] Covers occurrences involving a vessel or its equipment that results in 1) a death; 2) an injury that requires medical treatment beyond first aid; 3) damage to a vessel and other property, totaling to more than $2,000 or complete loss of a vessel; or 4) the disappearance of the vessel under circumstances that indicate death or injury. Federal regulations (33 CFR 173-4) require the operator of any vessel that is numbered or used for recreational purposes to submit an accident report.

Source: U.S. Bureau of Transportation Statistics, "National Transportation Statistics," <bts.gov/topics/national-transportation-statistics>, accessed May 2020.

Table 1095. On-Time Flight Arrivals and Departures at Major U.S. Airports: 2019

[In percent. All U.S. airlines with 1 percent or more of total U.S. domestic scheduled airline passenger revenues are required to report on-time data. based on gate arrival and departure times for operations of U.S. major airlines. A flight is considered on time if it operated within 15 minutes of the scheduled time shown in the carrier's computerized reservation system. See source for data on individual airlines]

Airport	Code	On-time arrivals				On-time departures			
		1st quarter	2nd quarter	3rd quarter	4th quarter	1st quarter	2nd quarter	3rd quarter	4th quarter
Total, all airports [1].............	**(X)**	**78.3**	**76.9**	**79.6**	**82.0**	**79.4**	**77.6**	**80.1**	**82.4**
Atlanta, Hartsfield-Jackson Intl.............	ATL	85.5	82.9	85.3	86.7	83.7	79.3	82.3	85.7
Baltimore/Washington Intl.............	BWI	81.8	79.4	81.8	85.7	78.0	74.9	77.0	78.9
Boston, Logan Intl.............	BOS	73.6	72.0	75.9	75.9	75.1	76.3	78.4	78.4
Charlotte, Douglas.............	CLT	83.0	78.2	82.4	85.0	81.9	74.3	78.3	83.0
Chicago, Midway Intl.............	MDW	75.0	77.5	83.3	84.2	63.4	67.6	75.4	75.3
Chicago, O'Hare.............	ORD	71.4	72.6	73.3	81.4	71.4	73.0	73.9	81.9
Dallas-Fort Worth Intl.............	DFW	76.6	70.7	80.7	80.1	77.2	69.3	77.8	79.3
Denver Intl.............	DEN	78.6	75.0	78.4	81.1	76.3	72.7	76.6	78.4
Detroit, Metro Wayne County.............	DTW	82.4	82.9	82.9	86.5	81.4	82.7	82.4	85.5
Fort Lauderdale-Hollywood Intl.............	FLL	78.1	75.4	72.6	80.1	77.7	74.3	72.5	80.8
Houston, George Bush Intercontinental.....	IAH	80.5	73.6	76.3	81.4	83.1	74.2	78.1	83.3
Las Vegas, McCarran Intl.............	LAS	77.7	77.8	83.3	81.7	77.4	76.3	81.5	80.9
Los Angeles Intl.............	LAX	77.0	79.0	82.5	81.7	78.2	78.4	81.8	81.7
Miami Intl.............	MIA	82.1	78.7	78.4	84.9	81.7	76.9	75.9	86.0
Minneapolis-St. Paul Intl.............	MSP	80.3	83.7	84.1	85.4	80.7	84.7	84.7	85.3
New York, JFK Intl.............	JFK	79.5	75.9	75.0	82.8	80.9	78.5	75.9	84.1
New York, La Guardia.............	LGA	69.8	68.4	69.7	74.1	74.4	73.6	74.5	78.2
Newark Intl.............	EWR	69.3	63.9	67.5	69.7	75.1	69.9	71.1	74.4
Orlando Intl.............	MCO	79.6	75.2	75.0	82.9	78.9	73.6	74.0	81.3
Philadelphia Intl.............	PHL	83.0	75.9	76.8	82.2	83.8	77.1	77.2	83.7
Phoenix, Sky Harbor Intl.............	PHX	79.8	79.5	83.3	82.6	79.3	76.8	81.7	81.5
Portland Intl.............	PDX	81.4	82.2	84.8	84.0	85.7	86.5	87.6	86.8
Salt Lake City Intl.............	SLC	82.1	84.9	86.8	86.1	83.7	86.1	86.7	87.3
San Diego Intl.............	SAN	77.9	78.8	82.6	81.7	79.5	78.7	84.2	82.9
San Francisco Intl.............	SFO	65.5	74.2	72.7	76.4	72.1	78.1	76.5	78.3
Seattle-Tacoma Intl.............	SEA	79.4	80.0	79.0	80.8	82.1	83.7	80.9	82.2
Tampa, Tampa Intl.............	TPA	80.4	77.0	78.1	83.9	80.6	77.5	80.3	84.7
Washington, Reagan National.............	DCA	77.2	77.5	77.9	82.0	78.7	78.6	79.2	82.7
Washington/Dulles.............	IAD	82.2	78.5	79.4	84.7	84.0	81.8	80.5	86.1

X Not applicable. [1] Includes other airports not shown separately.

Source: U.S. Department of Transportation, Bureau of Transportation Statistics, "TranStats," <transtats.bts.gov>, accessed June 2020.

Table 1096. Airline Fuel Consumption and Fuel Costs: 2000 to 2019

[20,373 represents 20,373,000,000. Data shown are aggregated for scheduled and unscheduled service on U.S. carriers with over $20 million in revenue per year]

Year	Total fuel consumption (million gallons)	Total fuel cost (million dollars)	Cost per gallon (dollars)	Domestic service Consumption (million gallons)	Domestic service Cost (million dollars)	Domestic service Cost per gallon (dollars)	International service Consumption (million gallons)	International service Cost (million dollars)	International service Cost per gallon (dollars)
2000	20,373	16,448	0.81	14,865	11,708	0.79	5,508	4,739	0.86
2010	17,298	39,350	2.27	11,257	25,571	2.27	6,042	13,779	2.28
2015	17,349	32,196	1.86	10,929	20,006	1.83	6,421	12,190	1.90
2016	17,668	25,742	1.46	11,374	16,636	1.46	6,295	9,106	1.45
2017	18,029	30,630	1.70	11,588	19,728	1.70	6,441	10,902	1.69
2018	18,731	40,504	2.16	12,148	26,121	2.15	6,599	14,383	2.18
2019	19,191	38,521	2.01	12,537	25,129	2.00	6,659	13,392	2.01

Source: U.S. Bureau of Transportation Statistics, "Airline Fuel Cost and Consumption," <https://www.transtats.bts.gov/fuel.asp>, accessed February 2020.

Table 1097. Top 50 Airports in 2018—Passengers Enplaned: 2017 and 2018

[In thousands (855,920 represents 855,920,000), except rank. For calendar year. Intl = international. Airports ranked by total passengers enplaned on U.S. carrier scheduled domestic and international service and foreign carrier scheduled international service from the U.S.]

Airport city and code	2017 Rank	2017 Total	2018 Rank	2018 Total	Airport city and code	2017 Rank	2017 Total	2018 Rank	2018 Total
All U.S. airports	(X)	855,920	(X)	898,245	Washington, DC (IAD)	26	11,023	25	11,638
Total, top 50 [1]	(X)	726,184	(X)	759,148	Washington, DC (DCA)	24	11,506	26	11,367
Atlanta, GA (ATL)	1	50,271	1	51,871	Chicago, IL (MDW)	27	10,908	27	10,673
Los Angeles, CA (LAX)	2	41,232	2	42,737	Tampa, FL (TPA)	29	9,548	28	10,372
Chicago, IL (ORD)	3	38,593	3	39,905	Portland, OR (PDX)	30	9,435	29	9,804
Dallas/Fort Worth, TX (DFW)	4	31,816	4	32,799	Honolulu, HI (HNL)	28	9,726	30	9,577
Denver, CO (DEN)	5	29,809	5	31,365	Nashville, TN (BNA)	33	6,900	31	7,821
New York, NY (JFK)	6	29,528	6	30,605	Dallas, TX (DAL)	31	7,593	32	7,819
San Francisco, CA (SFO)	7	26,900	7	27,849	Austin-Bergstrom, TX (AUS)	34	6,809	33	7,713
Seattle-Tacoma, WA (SEA)	9	22,614	8	24,010	St. Louis, MO (STL)	32	7,194	34	7,615
Las Vegas, NV (LAS)	8	23,209	9	23,693	Houston, TX (HOU)	35	6,539	35	7,052
Orlando, FL (MCO)	12	21,565	10	23,196	San Jose, CA (SJC)	37	6,130	36	7,029
Newark, NJ (EWR)	11	21,571	11	22,819	Oakland, CA (OAK)	36	6,413	37	6,684
Charlotte-Douglas, NC (CLT)	10	22,011	12	22,281	New Orleans, LA (MSY)	38	6,022	38	6,581
Phoenix, AZ (PHX)	13	21,185	13	21,637	Raleigh, NC (RDU)	39	5,691	39	6,257
Houston, TX (IAH)	15	19,603	14	21,167	Sacramento, CA (SMF)	41	5,341	40	5,907
Miami, FL (MIA)	14	20,708	15	21,065	Kansas City, MO (MCI)	40	5,627	41	5,790
Boston, MA (BOS)	16	18,759	16	20,017	Santa Ana, CA (SNA)	42	5,083	42	5,198
Minneapolis-St. Paul, MN (MSP)	17	18,406	17	18,359	San Antonio, TX (SAT)	44	4,382	43	4,844
Fort Lauderdale, FL (FLL)	19	15,816	18	17,618	Cleveland, OH (CLE)	43	4,446	44	4,701
Detroit, MI (DTW)	18	17,036	19	17,436	Pittsburgh, PA (PIT)	47	4,326	45	4,668
Philadelphia, PA (PHL)	21	14,269	20	15,279	Indianapolis, IN (IND)	46	4,341	46	4,652
New York, NY (LGA)	20	14,606	21	15,079	Fort Myers, FL (RSW)	45	4,364	47	4,604
Baltimore, MD (BWI)	22	12,945	22	13,339	Cincinnati, OH (CVG)	49	3,792	48	4,269
Salt Lake City, UT (SLT)	23	11,615	23	12,225	San Juan, PR (SJU)	48	4,160	49	4,009
San Diego, CA (SAN)	25	11,139	24	12,176	Columbus, OH (CMH)	50	3,677	50	3,975

X Not applicable. [1] The 2017 totals for the top 50 airports will not sum to total top 50 because some top 50 airports in 2018 were not in the top 50 in 2017.

Source: U.S. Bureau of Transportation Statistics, "National Transportation Statistics," <https://www.bts.gov/topics/national-transportation-statistics>, accessed January 2020.

Table 1098. Consumer Complaints Filed Against U.S. Airlines: 2000 to 2019

[Calendar year data. Represents complaints filed by consumers to the U.S. Department of Transportation (DOT), Aviation Consumer Protection Division, regarding service problems with air carriers. See source for data on individual airlines]

Complaint category	2000	2005	2010	2014	2015	2016	2017	2018	2019
Total	20,564	6,900	10,988	15,539	20,175	17,908	18,156	15,544	15,332
Flight problems [1]	8,698	1,942	3,337	4,974	6,434	6,179	6,078	4,517	4,756
Baggage	2,753	1,586	1,938	2,667	3,133	2,770	2,745	2,728	2,565
Ticketing/boarding [2]	1,405	679	1,510	2,256	2,695	2,115	2,194	1,908	1,823
Customer service [3]	4,074	800	1,345	1,708	2,276	1,934	1,781	1,618	1,703
Refunds	803	530	730	1,156	1,573	1,361	1,359	1,329	1,568
Fares [4]	708	219	465	916	1,813	1,363	2,022	1,542	1,033
Disability [5]	612	430	572	784	944	865	850	827	905
Oversales [6]	759	284	544	514	648	597	511	409	376
Discrimination [7]	(NA)	100	143	68	65	95	98	97	107
Advertising	42	45	77	130	163	124	80	57	61
Animals	1	3	8	2	3	1	1	2	2
Other [8]	684	282	319	364	428	504	437	510	433

NA Not available. [1] Cancellations, delays, and other deviations from schedule. [2] Errors in reservations and ticketing; and problems in making reservations, obtaining tickets, and boarding (except oversales). Prior to 1998, includes disability complaints. [3] Unhelpful employees, inadequate meals or cabin service, treatment of delayed passengers. [4] Incorrect or incomplete information about fares, discount fare conditions, and availability, etc. [5] Civil rights complaints by air travelers with disabilities. Prior to 2000, included in ticketing/boarding. [6] All bumping problems, whether or not airline complied with DOT regulations. [7] Civil rights complaints by air travelers (other than disability) based on factors such as race, religion, national origin or sex. [8] Frequent flyer, smoking, tours credit, cargo problems, security, airport facilities, claims for bodily injury, and others not classified above.

Source: U.S. Department of Transportation, Aviation Consumer Protection Division, *Air Travel Consumer Report*, February 2020, and earlier reports. See also <https://www.transportation.gov/airconsumer>.

Table 1099. U.S. Airline Carrier Delays, Cancellations, and Diversions: 2000 to 2019

[5,683.0 represents 5,683,000. For calendar year. See headnote, Table 1095]

Item	2000	2010	2012	2013	2014	2015	2016	2017	2018	2019
Total operations	**5,683.0**	**6,450.1**	**6,096.8**	**6,369.5**	**5,819.8**	**5,819.1**	**5,617.7**	**5,674.6**	**7,213.4**	**7,422.0**
NUMBER (1,000)										
Delayed departures [1]	1,131.7	1,111.9	991.8	1,229.3	1,193.2	1,055.5	952.2	1,012.5	1,304.2	1,359.6
Delayed arrivals [2]	1,356.0	1,174.9	1,015.2	1,269.3	1,240.5	1,063.4	964.2	1,029.5	1,352.7	1,389.3
Cancellations [3]	187.5	113.3	78.9	96.0	127.0	89.9	65.9	82.7	116.6	134.9
Diversions [4]	14.3	15.5	12.5	14.2	14.4	15.2	13.7	12.5	17.9	18.9
PERCENT										
Delayed departures [1]	19.9	17.2	16.3	19.3	20.5	18.1	17.0	17.8	18.1	18.3
Delayed arrivals [2]	23.9	18.2	16.7	19.9	21.3	18.3	17.2	18.1	18.8	18.7
Cancellations [3]	3.3	1.8	1.3	1.5	2.2	1.5	1.2	1.5	1.6	1.8
Diversions [4]	0.3	0.2	0.2	0.2	0.2	0.3	0.2	0.2	0.2	0.3

[1] Late departures departed 15 minutes or more after the scheduled departure time. [2] Late arrivals arrived 15 minutes or more after the scheduled arrival time. [3] A cancelled flight is one that was not operated, but was listed in a carrier's computer reservation system within seven days of the scheduled departure. [4] A diverted flight is one that left from the scheduled departure airport but flew to a destination point other than the scheduled destination point.

Source: U.S. Bureau of Transportation Statistics, "National Transportation Statistics," <https://www.bts.gov/topics/national-transportation-statistics>, accessed May 2020.

Table 1100. Commuter/Regional Airline Operations Summary: 2010 to 2018

[In units as indicated (164.1 represents 164,100,000). Calendar year data. Commuter/regional airlines primarily operate aircraft of 75 passengers or less and 18,000 pounds of payload capacity serving short haul and small community markets. Represents operations within all of North America by U.S. regional carriers. As of 2014, "operating carriers" is defined as those certificate holders operating scheduled passenger service under 14 CFR Parts 135 or 121 with capacities of fewer than 100 seats. As of 2015, Part 380 public charter operations are excluded. Averages are means. For definition of mean, see Guide to Tabular Presentation]

Item	Unit	2010	2014	2015	2016	2017	2018
Passenger certificated carriers operating	Number	66	65	64	67	65	66
Passengers enplaned	Millions	164.1	157.6	156.6	154.9	153.3	159.1
Average passengers enplaned per carrier	1,000	2,486.4	2,424.0	2,446.3	2,312.2	2,358.3	2,410.0
Revenue passenger miles (RPM)	Billions	76.6	75.1	74.8	75.5	74.5	77.8
Average RPMs per carrier	Millions	1,160.9	1,155.5	1,168.0	1,126.3	1,146.0	1,178.8
Available seat miles	Billions	100.1	94.0	92.8	94.8	94.6	98.0
Average load factor	Percent	76.6	79.9	80.6	79.6	78.8	79.4
Departures completed	Millions	4.69	4.11	3.87	3.81	3.68	3.86
Airports served	Number	673	607	615	622	619	630
Average trip length	Miles	467	477	478	488	487	489
Average seating capacity (seats)	Number	56	58	61	62	64	63
Fleet flying hours	1,000	5,048	4,522	4,302	4,255	4,137	4,346

Source: Regional Airline Association, *2019 Annual Report* ©, and previous editions. See also <http://www.raa.org/>.

Table 1101. U.S. Air Carrier Aircraft Accidents: 2000 to 2018

[For years ending December 31. See source for more details]

Item	Unit	2000	2010	2014	2015	2016	2017	2018 (P)
Air carrier accidents, all services [1]	Number	56	30	31	29	30	32	30
Fatal accidents	Number	3	1	–	–	–	–	1
Fatalities	Number	92	2	–	–	–	–	1
Aboard	Number	92	2	–	–	–	–	1
Rates per 100,000 flight hours:								
Accidents	Rate	0.31	0.17	0.18	0.16	0.16	0.17	0.16
Fatal accidents	Rate	0.02	0.01	–	–	–	–	0.01
Commuter air carrier accidents [2]	Number	12	6	3	5	8	6	2
Fatal accidents	Number	1	–	–	1	2	–	–
Fatalities	Number	5	–	–	1	8	–	–
Aboard	Number	5	–	–	1	6	–	–
Rates per 100,000 flight hours:								
Accidents	Rate	3.25	1.91	0.90	1.39	2.12	1.53	0.48
Fatal accidents	Rate	0.27	–	–	0.28	0.53	–	–
On-demand air taxi accidents [3]	Number	80	30	35	38	30	44	41
Fatal accidents	Number	22	6	8	7	7	8	6
Fatalities	Number	71	17	20	27	19	16	12
Aboard	Number	68	17	20	27	19	16	12
Rates per 100,000 flight hours:								
Accidents	Rate	2.04	0.96	0.96	1.07	0.86	1.25	1.07
Fatal accidents	Rate	0.56	0.19	0.22	0.20	0.20	0.23	0.16
General aviation accidents [4]	Number	1,837	1,441	1,222	1,211	1,269	1,233	1,275
Fatal accidents	Number	345	271	255	230	213	203	225
Fatalities	Number	596	458	422	378	386	331	381
Aboard	Number	585	455	412	375	379	331	378
Rates per 100,000 flight hours:								
Accidents	Rate	6.57	6.63	6.23	5.85	5.93	5.67	5.88
Fatal accidents	Rate	1.21	1.24	1.30	1.10	0.98	0.94	1.03

– Represents zero. P Preliminary. [1] U.S. air carriers operating aircraft with 10 or more seats, under 14 CFR 121. [2] All scheduled service of U.S. air carriers operating aircraft with fewer than 10 seats, under 14 CFR 135. [3] All nonscheduled service of U.S. air carriers operating aircraft with fewer than 10 seats, under 14 CFR 135. [4] U.S. civil registered aircraft not operated under 14 CFR 121 or 135.

Source: U.S. National Transportation Safety Board, Investigations Data and Stats, "Review of Accident Data—2018 Preliminary Aviation Statistics," <https://www.ntsb.gov/investigations/data/Pages/Data_Stats.aspx>, accessed January 2020.

Table 1102. Airports, Aircraft, and Airmen: 1990 to 2019

[As of December 31 or for years ending December 31]

Item	1990	2000	2010	2015	2016	2017	2018	2019
AIRPORTS								
Airports, total [1]	**17,490**	**19,281**	**19,802**	**(NA)**	**19,536**	**19,655**	**19,627**	**19,636**
Public [1]	5,589	5,317	5,175	(NA)	5,136	5,104	5,099	5,080
Percent with lighted runways	71.4	75.9	(NA)	(NA)	(NA)	(NA)	(NA)	(NA)
Percent with paved runways	70.7	74.3	(NA)	(NA)	(NA)	(NA)	(NA)	(NA)
Private	11,901	13,964	14,353	(NA)	14,112	14,263	14,528	14,556
Percent with lighted runways	7.0	7.2	(NA)	(NA)	(NA)	(NA)	(NA)	(NA)
Percent with paved runways	31.5	32.0	(NA)	(NA)	(NA)	(NA)	(NA)	(NA)
Military	(NA)	(NA)	274	(NA)	288	288	305	308
Certificated [2]	680	651	551	(NA)	531	526	523	522
General aviation	16,810	18,630	19,251	(NA)	19,005	19,129	19,116	19,117
AIRCRAFT								
Active air carrier fleet [3]	**6,083**	**7,826**	**7,185**	**6,876**	**7,077**	**7,196**	**7,397**	**(NA)**
Fixed wing	6,072	8,010	(NA)	(NA)	(NA)	(NA)	(NA)	(NA)
Helicopter [4]	11	39	(NA)	(NA)	(NA)	(NA)	(NA)	(NA)
General aviation fleet [5]	**198,000**	**217,533**	**223,370**	**210,030**	**211,793**	**211,757**	**211,749**	**(NA)**
Fixed-wing	184,500	183,276	176,272	164,293	166,168	167,082	167,561	(NA)
Turbojet	4,100	7,001	11,484	13,440	13,751	14,217	14,596	(NA)
Turboprop	5,300	5,762	9,369	9,712	9,779	9,949	9,925	(NA)
Piston	175,200	170,513	155,419	141,141	142,638	142,916	143,040	(NA)
Rotorcraft	6,900	7,150	10,102	10,506	10,577	10,511	9,990	(NA)
Other	6,600	6,700	5,684	4,941	4,986	4,692	4,114	(NA)
Gliders	(X)	2,041	1,899	1,870	1,789	1,747	1,772	(NA)
Lighter than air	(X)	4,660	3,785	3,071	3,197	2,945	2,343	(NA)
Experimental	(X)	20,407	29,662	27,922	27,585	26,921	27,531	(NA)
AIRMAN CERTIFICATES HELD								
Pilot, total	**702,659**	**625,581**	**627,588**	**590,039**	**584,362**	**609,306**	**633,317**	**664,565**
Female	40,515	36,757	42,218	39,287	39,187	42,694	46,463	52,740
Student [6]	128,663	93,064	119,119	122,729	128,501	149,121	167,804	197,665
Recreational	87	340	212	190	175	153	144	127
Sport	(X)	(X)	3,682	5,482	5,889	6,097	6,246	6,467
Airplane:								
Private	299,111	251,561	202,020	170,718	162,313	162,455	163,695	161,105
Commercial	149,666	121,858	123,705	101,164	96,081	98,161	99,880	100,863
Air transport	107,732	141,596	142,198	154,730	157,894	159,825	162,145	164,947
Rotorcraft only	9,567	7,775	15,377	15,566	15,518	15,355	15,033	14,248
Glider only	7,833	9,387	21,275	19,460	17,991	18,139	18,370	19,143
Flight instructor certificates	63,775	80,931	96,473	102,628	104,382	106,692	108,564	113,445
Instrument ratings	297,073	311,944	318,001	304,329	302,572	306,652	311,017	314,168
Remote pilots [7]	(NA)	(NA)	(X)	(X)	20,362	69,166	106,321	160,302
Nonpilot [8]	**492,237**	**547,453**	**686,717**	**728,329**	**652,943**	**671,222**	**688,002**	**714,201**
Mechanic	344,282	344,434	331,989	342,528	279,435	286,268	292,002	301,087
Repairmen	(X)	38,208	41,267	39,363	34,411	35,040	35,382	36,294
Parachute rigger	10,094	10,477	8,407	8,846	5,851	6,192	6,430	6,800
Ground instructor	66,882	72,326	75,205	70,957	65,053	66,423	67,784	69,991
Dispatcher	11,000	16,340	20,691	23,754	19,758	20,664	21,465	22,598
Flight navigator	1,290	570	174	102	67	64	58	40
Flight attendant	(X)	(X)	159,946	200,319	212,607	222,037	231,355	245,699
Flight engineer	58,687	65,098	49,038	42,460	35,761	34,534	33,526	31,692

NA Not available. X Not applicable. [1] Includes civil and joint-use civil-military airports, heliports, STOL (short takeoff and landing) ports, and seaplane bases in the U.S. and its territories. Sole-use military airports are included beginning in 2007. Public airports are under public agency control; private airports are owned by a private individual or corporation. [2] Certificated airports serve air-carriers with aircraft seating more than 9 passengers. As of 2005, the Federal Aviation Administration (FAA) no longer certificates military airports. [3] Air-carrier aircraft carry passengers or cargo for hire under 14 CFR 121 (large aircraft—more than 30 seats) and 14 CFR 135 (small aircraft—30 seats or fewer). Beginning in 1990, the number of aircraft is the monthly average reported in use for the last three months of the year. Prior to 1990, it was the number of aircraft reported in use during December of a given year. [4] 2000 change in helicopters due to estimating methods. [5] Beginning 1995, excludes commuters. [6] Beginning 2010, duration of validity for student pilot certificates for pilots under age 40 increased from 36 to 60 months. [7] Remote pilot certification started in August 2016. These numbers are not included in the pilot totals. [8] All certificates on record. No medical examination required.

Source: Prior to 2000: *FAA Statistical Handbook of Aviation*, annual. Thereafter: U.S. Bureau of Transportation Statistics, "National Transportation Statistics," <https://www.bts.gov/topics/national-transportation-statistics>, accessed August 2020. U.S. Federal Aviation Administration, "U.S. Civil Airmen Statistics" and "General Aviation and Air Taxi (Part 135) Activity Surveys," <http://www.faa.gov/data_research/aviation_data_statistics/>, accessed August 2020.

Table 1103. Passenger Airline Revenues from Fares, Fees, and Services; and Expenses and Profits: 2017 to 2019

[In millions of dollars (175,337 represents $175,337,000,000). Data shown for U.S. scheduled passenger airlines. Data for 2017 are compiled from 23 reporting airlines; 2018-2019 data are compiled from 21 airlines]

Item	2017	2018	2019 (P)	Item	2017	2018	2019 (P)
Total operating revenue [1]	**175,337**	**187,474**	**196,215**	Landing fees	3,056	3,211	3,340
Passenger fares, scheduled/charter	130,491	138,982	145,173	Maintenance materials	2,438	2,208	2,473
Cargo	2,985	3,522	3,196	Transport-related [2]	19,009	21,493	22,463
Baggage fees	4,576	5,072	5,760	Other [4]	31,656	33,760	34,264
Reservation change fees	2,856	2,858	2,841	**Operating profit**	**21,444**	**17,646**	**20,768**
Transport-related [2]	28,694	28,474	29,382	Operating margin (percent) [5]	12	9	11
Other [3]	5,735	8,566	9,776	Nonoperating income/expense [6]	-2,298	-2,483	-1,548
Total operating expenses	**153,893**	**169,828**	**175,446**	Pre-tax income	19,146	15,163	19,221
Fuel	26,241	34,460	32,814	Income tax benefit/expense	-3,851	-3,388	-4,458
Labor	53,556	56,104	60,333	Other income/expense	–	–	–
Rentals	8,887	9,098	9,722	Net income	15,295	11,775	14,763
Depreciation and amortization	9,051	9,495	10,037	Net margin (percent) [7]	9	6	8

P Preliminary – Represents or rounds to zero. [1] Based on U.S. Department of Transportation accounting standards. Total operating revenues are overstated by code share revenues, which are included in both mainline transport-related revenues and code share passenger revenues. Code share revenues are expensed out in the mainline transport-related expense to allow a true operating profit (loss). This reporting may understate all components of operating revenue, including passenger revenue, as a percent of total operating revenue. [2] Includes in-flight onboard sales, code share revenues, and revenues and expenses from associated businesses (aircraft maintenance, fuel sales, restaurants, vending machines). [3] Includes pet transportation, sale of frequent flyer award miles to airline business partners, standby passenger fees, and public service revenues subsidy. [4] Includes purchase of materials such as passenger food and purchase of services such as advertising, communication, insurance, outside flight equipment maintenance, and traffic commissions. [5] Operating profit or loss as a percent of operating revenue. [6] Interest on long-term debt and capital leases, other interest expense, foreign exchange gains and losses, capital gains and losses, and other income and expenses. [7] Net income or loss as a percent of operating revenue.

Source: U.S. Department of Transportation, Bureau of Transportation Statistics, "2019 Annual and 4th Quarter U.S. Airline Financial Data," and earlier releases, <https://www.bts.gov/statistical-releases>, accessed May 2020.

Table 1104. Worldwide Airline Accidents and Fatalities by World Region: 2018

[Number, except departures in thousands (38,087 represents 38,087,000). Regions are Regional Aviation Safety Group (RASG) regions]

Region	Departures (1,000)	Accidents	Accident rates [1]	Fatal accidents	Fatalities
World	**38,087**	**98**	**2.6**	**11**	**514**
Africa (AFI)	1,441	4	2.8	2	21
Asia and Pacific (APAC)	12,445	20	1.6	3	241
Europe (EUR) [2]	9,299	26	2.8	2	72
Middle East (MID)	1,327	3	2.3	1	66
Americas (PA)	13,576	45	3.3	3	114

– Represents zero. [1] Number of accidents per million departures of scheduled commercial operations that involve the transportation of passengers, cargo and mail for remuneration or hire. [2] RASG EUR includes Algeria, Morocco, and Tunisia.

Source: International Civil Aviation Organization, Montreal, Canada, *State of Global Aviation Safety, ICAO Safety Report 2019 Edition* ©, <http://www.icao.int/safety/Pages/Safety-Report.aspx>.

Table 1105. Water Transportation System Summary: 2000 to 2016

[12.8 represents 12,800,000. Data compiled from U.S. Army Corps of Engineers, Department of Homeland Security/Coast Guard, and Bureau of Transportation Statistics publications; see source for details]

Item or characteristic	Unit	2000	2010	2013	2014	2016
U.S.-flag privately owned merchant fleet [1]	Number	282	221	187	179	(NA)
Recreational boats	Millions	12.8	12.4	12.0	11.8	11.9
Lock chambers	Number	276	239	239	239	239
Lock sites	Number	230	193	193	193	193
Average age of locks	Years	50.2	59.5	62.5	63.5	(NA)
Waterway facilities (including cargo handling docks)	Number	9,309	8,060	8,231	8,229	8,227
Ports (handling over 250,000 tons)	Number	197	178	182	183	181
Miles of navigable waterways	Number	25,000	25,000	25,000	25,000	25,000
U.S. flag vessels:						
Total vessels [2]	Number	41,354	40,512	39,999	40,082	41,328
Barge/non-self-propelled vessels	Number	33,152	31,412	31,081	31,043	32,354
Self-propelled vessels	Number	8,202	9,078	8,918	9,039	8,974
U.S. flag vessels by age:						
Under 6 years old	Percent	19.6	18.5	19.3	17.7	(NA)
6 to 10 years old	Percent	9.2	11.5	12.1	14.1	(NA)
11 to 15 years old	Percent	5.1	17.0	14.3	12.4	(NA)
16 to 20 years old	Percent	19.6	8.7	13.6	15.1	(NA)
21 to 25 years old	Percent	18.3	4.2	7.7	8.3	(NA)
25 years old and over	Percent	27.7	39.3	32.6	31.9	(NA)

NA Not available. [1] Includes only oceangoing self-propelled, cargo-carrying vessels of 1,000 gross tons and above. [2] Includes unclassified vessels.

Source: U.S. Department of Transportation, Bureau of Transportation Statistics, *Transportation Statistics Annual Report 2018*, February 2019. See also <https://www.bts.dot.gov/product/transportation-statistics-annual-report>.

Table 1106. Ferry Operators, Vessels, Terminals, Route Distance, and Boarding Counts by State and Island Area: 2015

[Data from the 2016 National Census of Ferry Operators (NCFO). States without ferry operations are omitted. Ferry operations included within the scope of the NCFO were those providing itinerant, fixed route, common carrier passenger and/or vehicle ferry service; and railroad car float operations. Also includes operations providing international services to or from at least one U.S. terminal. Not included within the scope of the ferry census were operations that were exclusively nonitinerant, such as excursion services (e.g. whale watches, casino boats, day cruises, dinner cruises, etc.)]

State and area	Business operators	Vessels in service	Terminals	Route segment distance (nautical miles) [1]	Boarding counts Passengers	Boarding counts Vehicles
Total...................	**163**	**609**	**560**	**20,042.4**	**118,868,511**	**25,000,034**
U.S. total..................	157	585	537	19,358.2	118,311,065	24,796,601
Alabama....................	1	3	4	11.4	248,166	80,782
Alaska......................	6	18	41	12,492.5	906,851	268,862
Arizona.....................	–	–	1	3.1	–	–
Arkansas...................	1	5	1	0.7	34,502	17,250
California..................	12	54	47	1,048.6	8,923,100	566,073
Connecticut...............	4	15	9	83.9	2,034,954	776,343
Delaware...................	1	1	3	14.2	400,000	189,160
Florida.....................	6	19	18	23.4	798,570	248,276
Georgia....................	3	9	8	55.3	899,972	–
Hawaii.....................	1	4	3	32.0	–	–
Illinois.....................	6	29	16	19.3	2,136,032	801,717
Iowa.......................	–	–	3	6.5	32,844	2,831
Kentucky...................	5	11	15	5.9	428,053	463,752
Louisiana..................	3	15	16	6.0	1,978,521	905,425
Maine......................	7	23	32	324.9	1,730,675	278,884
Maryland...................	4	22	21	91.2	898,914	250,000
Massachusetts.............	9	45	23	439.0	5,681,996	638,158
Michigan...................	10	22	31	1,461.7	1,065,364	1,147,176
Minnesota..................	1	2	1	270.0	5,639	–
Mississippi.................	2	5	4	22.4	61,304	910
Missouri....................	3	5	6	252.3	60,508	103,777
Montana....................	2	3	6	0.5	3,473	4,022
New Hampshire.............	1	1	2	13.0	10,000	–
New Jersey................	6	48	14	87.0	5,035,614	140,000
New York..................	12	53	60	335.7	43,557,550	1,733,475
North Carolina.............	6	37	29	252.1	2,500,990	821,244
Ohio.......................	2	8	7	125.4	1,467,807	28,983
Oklahoma..................	1	3	4	16.1	10,338	–
Oregon.....................	2	3	7	2.2	1,065,475	412,522
Pennsylvania...............	1	2	2	(NA)	2,319	600
Rhode Island...............	5	10	11	189.3	201,634	26,024
South Carolina.............	1	2	5	53.0	358,785	–
Tennessee.................	1	6	4	1.7	93,440	73,000
Texas......................	4	17	8	9.3	6,393,436	2,259,084
Utah.......................	1	1	2	7.7	7,022	2,546
Vermont....................	2	13	4	13.5	(D)	(D)
Virginia....................	6	12	17	76.2	2,649,150	955,233
Washington................	12	44	40	1,345.3	26,081,154	11,145,634
Wisconsin..................	7	15	12	165.9	546,913	454,858
Puerto Rico................	1	9	5	82.0	–	–
Virgin Islands..............	5	15	14	434.0	287,046	79,755
British Columbia...........	(X)	(X)	3	167.2	236,638	74,671
Ontario....................	(X)	(X)	1	1.0	33,762	49,007

X Not applicable. NA Not available. D Data withheld to avoid individual disclosure. – Represents zero. [1] Interstate segment route nautical miles are assigned to the state of the origin terminal.

Source U.S. Department of Transportation, Bureau of Transportation Statistics, *2016 Highlights of Ferry Operations in the United States*, October 2017. See also <https://www.bts.gov/NCFO>.

Table 1107. Freight Carried on Major U.S. Waterways: 2000 to 2018

[In millions of short tons (3.1 represents 3,100,000). One short ton equals 2,000 pounds]

Waterway	2000	2005	2010	2014	2015	2016	2017	2018
Atlantic Intracoastal Waterway............	3.1	2.7	2.9	2.4	2.6	2.3	2.3	2.4
Great Lakes..................................	187.5	169.4	129.5	132.3	123.7	118.2	125.4	122.2
Gulf Intracoastal Waterway.................	113.8	116.1	116.2	126.1	118.9	111.7	111.2	110.4
Mississippi River system [1]...............	715.5	678.0	663.2	718.6	684.4	680.9	702.1	692.3
Mississippi River main stem..............	515.6	464.6	483.2	536.2	521.1	526.3	552.3	557.6
Ohio River system [2]......................	274.4	280.1	245.2	246.0	223.1	204.7	202.1	198.0
Columbia River.............................	55.2	51.5	54.7	61.7	54.7	61.3	63.4	67.1
Snake River.................................	6.7	5.3	3.4	4.4	3.6	3.4	3.5	3.9

[1] Main channels and all tributaries of the Mississippi, Illinois, Missouri, and Ohio Rivers. [2] Main channels and all navigable tributaries and embayments of the Ohio, Tennessee, and Cumberland Rivers.

Source: U.S. Army Corps of Engineers, *Waterborne Commerce of the United States, 2017*, December 2018, and earlier reports; and "Ports and Waterways - Webtool," <https://www.iwr.usace.army.mil/About/Technical-Centers/WCSC-Waterborne-Commerce-Statistics-Center/>, accessed August 2020.

Table 1108. Top 30 U.S. Ports by Tons of Traffic: 2018

[In thousands of short tons (44,778 represents 44,778,000), except rank. One short ton equals 2,000 lbs. For calendar year. Represents tons of cargo shipped from or received by the specified port. Excludes cargo carried on general ferries; coal and petroleum products loaded from shore facilities directly onto bunkers of vessels for fuel; and amounts of less than 100 tons of government-owned equipment in support of Corps of Engineers projects]

Port name	Rank	Total	Domestic	Foreign Total	Foreign Inbound	Foreign Outbound
Baltimore, MD.	14	44,778	7,271	37,507	13,445	24,062
Baton Rouge, LA.	8	82,235	47,150	35,085	6,284	28,800
Beaumont, TX.	4	100,244	38,398	61,847	27,617	34,229
Charleston, SC.	30	24,823	2,039	22,784	14,145	8,639
Cincinnati-Northern KY, Ports of.	18	38,534	38,534	–	–	–
Corpus Christi, TX.	5	93,468	24,244	69,225	21,719	47,506
Duluth-Superior, MN and WI.	20	35,102	26,785	8,317	613	7,704
Freeport, TX.	28	25,446	4,547	20,899	8,004	12,894
Houston, TX.	2	268,930	77,847	191,083	73,863	117,220
Huntington-Tristate [1].	21	34,245	34,245	–	–	–
Lake Charles, LA.	12	56,908	27,842	29,066	16,894	12,172
Long Beach, CA.	7	86,536	10,347	76,189	53,588	22,601
Los Angeles, CA.	10	67,806	7,972	59,834	39,643	20,192
Mobile, AL.	11	58,636	22,119	36,516	19,105	17,411
New Orleans, LA.	6	93,333	49,522	43,811	18,402	25,409
New York, NY and NJ.	3	140,282	46,650	93,632	74,890	18,741
Pascagoula, MS.	23	27,358	9,836	17,522	8,833	8,689
Philadelphia, PA.	25	26,656	10,468	16,188	15,137	1,052
Plaquemines, LA, Port of.	13	56,850	31,114	25,736	6,606	19,130
Port Arthur, TX.	17	39,852	10,872	28,980	9,190	19,790
Port Everglades, FL.	29	25,022	13,376	11,647	8,137	3,510
Richmond, CA.	24	27,255	8,856	18,399	13,503	4,896
Savannah, GA.	16	41,274	1,136	40,138	22,513	17,625
Seattle, WA.	26	26,046	5,642	20,404	10,127	10,277
South Louisiana, LA, Port of.	1	275,513	133,976	141,537	38,253	103,284
St. Louis, MO and IL.	19	37,427	37,427	–	–	–
Tampa, FL.	22	31,006	18,790	12,217	8,053	4,164
Texas City, TX.	15	42,682	17,199	25,483	5,795	19,688
Valdez, AK.	27	25,808	25,558	250	–	250
Virginia, VA, Port of.	9	71,774	4,571	67,203	12,802	54,402

– Represents or rounds to zero. [1] The Port of Huntington is the largest inland shipping port in the United States. Port operations occur in Ashland, KY; Ironton, OH; and Huntington, WV.

Source: U.S. Army Corps of Engineers, Waterborne Commerce Statistics Center, Ports & State Data, "Tonnage for Selected U.S. Ports in 2018," <https://www.iwr.usace.army.mil/About/Technical-Centers/WCSC-Waterborne-Commerce-Statistics-Center/>, accessed June 2020.

Table 1109. Top 30 U.S. Ports/Waterways Ranked by Container Traffic: 2018

[In thousands of twenty-foot equivalent units (TEUs) (40,189.4 represents 40,189,400). For calendar year. For the 30 leading ports/waterways in total TEUs. A TEU is a measure of containerized cargo capacity equal to one standard 20-foot length by 8-foot width by 8-foot, 6 inch height container. Does not include empty foreign containers]

Port/waterway name	Rank	Total loaded	Domestic loaded Total [1]	Domestic loaded Inbound	Domestic loaded Outbound	Foreign loaded Total	Foreign loaded Inbound	Foreign loaded Outbound
Total U.S. [2]	(X)	**40,189.4**	**5,118.4**	**1,908.4**	**1,908.4**	**36,372.6**	**24,081.5**	**12,291.1**
Anchorage, AK.	19	274.2	349.4	207.4	66.8	–	–	–
Baltimore, MD.	15	713.2	12.2	6.5	4.3	702.4	478.0	224.4
Boston, MA.	22	219.3	–	–	–	219.3	144.9	74.5
Camden-Gloucester, NJ.	27	102.2	42.1	13.6	20.1	68.5	68.2	0.3
Charleston, SC.	8	1,803.1	–	–	–	1,803.1	1,022.1	781.0
Chester, PA.	26	135.0	–	–	–	135.0	97.0	37.9
Gulfport, MS.	24	159.2	–	–	–	159.2	79.4	79.7
Honolulu, HI.	11	835.7	1,098.4	490.3	304.1	41.3	25.7	15.6
Houston, TX.	5	2,251.6	–	–	–	2,251.6	1,209.4	1,042.3
Jacksonville, FL.	14	774.5	447.6	54.1	349.2	371.1	257.5	113.6
Juneau, AK.	28	92.1	131.9	69.3	22.8	–	–	–
Kahului, HI.	29	89.5	143.2	75.0	14.5	–	–	–
Ketchikan, AK.	30	89.0	145.0	22.2	66.8	–	–	–
Long Beach, CA.	2	5,595.7	275.8	31.2	185.5	5,379.0	4,104.1	1,274.9
Los Angeles, CA.	1	6,627.3	142.4	11.8	130.6	6,484.9	4,897.6	1,587.3
Miami, FL.	12	803.7	–	–	–	803.7	456.6	347.2
Mobile, AL.	20	269.6	–	–	–	269.6	142.2	127.4
New Orleans, LA.	17	400.2	–	–	–	400.2	122.8	277.4
New York (NJ-NY), NY.	3	5,282.5	59.1	26.8	27.3	5,228.4	3,755.6	1,472.8
Oakland, CA.	7	1,812.6	178.8	25.9	90.6	1,696.0	949.7	746.3
Palm Beach, FL.	25	137.0	–	–	–	137.0	23.5	113.5
Philadelphia, PA.	18	376.6	11.7	4.6	4.3	367.6	285.5	82.1
Port Everglades, FL.	13	795.0	–	–	–	795.0	365.8	429.2
Port of Virginia, VA.	6	2,205.6	12.9	4.6	6.5	2,194.6	1,301.9	892.7
San Juan, PR.	16	691.2	489.8	369.3	67.7	254.1	215.8	38.3
Savannah, GA.	4	3,386.9	–	–	–	3,386.9	2,027.4	1,359.5
Seattle, WA.	10	1,315.3	372.1	66.9	145.0	1,103.5	702.4	401.0
Tacoma, WA.	9	1,552.2	356.8	68.0	211.9	1,272.2	767.0	505.2
Wilmington, DE.	23	201.1	–	–	–	201.1	177.5	23.5
Wilmington, NC.	21	229.7	–	–	–	229.7	114.5	115.2

– Represents or rounds to zero. X Not applicable. [1] Includes empty TEUs, not shown separately. [2] Includes other ports/waterways not shown separately.

Source: U.S. Army Corps of Engineers, Waterborne Commerce Statistics Center, "Waterborne Container Traffic," <https://www.iwr.usace.army.mil/About/Technical-Centers/WCSC-Waterborne-Commerce-Statistics-Center/>, accessed June 2020.

Table 1110. Highway Mileage—Urban and Rural by Ownership: 1990 to 2018

[In thousands (3,880 represents 3,880,000). As of December 31. Includes Puerto Rico beginning 2000]

Type and control of roadways	1990	2000	2005	2010	2014	2015	2016	2017	2018
Total mileage [1]	**3,880**	**3,951**	**4,012**	**4,084**	**4,194**	**4,171**	**4,157**	**4,184**	**4,195**
Urban mileage.......................	757	859	1,023	1,103	1,215	1,223	1,226	1,235	1,241
Under state control...............	96	112	144	(NA)	172	174	173	172	173
Under local control [1]...........	661	746	874	(NA)	1,036	1,042	1,044	1,054	1,060
Under federal control [2]........	(NA)	(NA)	4	(NA)	8	7	8	8	8
Rural mileage........................	3,123	3,092	2,989	2,980	2,978	2,949	2,931	2,949	2,955
Under state control...............	703	664	637	(NA)	616	612	612	613	612
Under local control [1]..........	2,242	2,311	2,228	(NA)	2,209	2,198	2,186	2,180	2,184
Under federal control [2]........	178	117	123	(NA)	154	139	133	156	159

NA Not available. [1] Includes state park, state toll, other state agency, other local agency, and other roadways not identified by ownership. [2] Includes roadways in federal parks, forest, and reservations that are not part of the state and local highway system.

Source: U.S. Federal Highway Administration, "Highway Statistics 2018," and earlier reports, <http://www.fhwa.dot.gov/policyinformation/statistics.cfm>, accessed April 2020.

Table 1111. Highway Mileage—Functional Systems and Urban/Rural Status by State: 2018

[As of December 31. For definition of functional systems, see text, this section]

State	Total	Functional systems					Urban	Rural
		Interstate	Other freeways and expressways	Arterial	Collector	Local		
United States......	**4,195,274**	**48,741**	**18,659**	**404,436**	**816,273**	**2,907,165**	**1,240,601**	**2,954,672**
Alabama.............	100,962	1,004	29	9,688	22,206	68,036	29,039	71,923
Alaska................	17,050	1,080	–	1,571	3,289	11,110	3,315	13,735
Arizona..............	66,782	1,169	233	5,972	8,251	51,157	26,381	40,400
Arkansas............	102,622	749	174	7,403	20,971	73,325	17,255	85,367
California............	175,589	2,456	1,919	27,060	32,499	111,655	104,315	71,275
Colorado............	88,975	952	352	8,905	16,211	62,554	20,815	68,160
Connecticut.........	21,556	346	279	2,724	3,407	14,799	15,865	5,691
Delaware............	6,461	41	56	627	1,134	4,602	3,626	2,835
District of Columbia..	1,514	12	15	270	156	1,061	1,514	–
Florida...............	123,099	1,495	750	12,992	15,554	92,308	86,519	36,580
Georgia..............	128,397	1,247	177	14,358	22,731	89,883	52,248	76,149
Hawaii...............	4,475	55	34	794	743	2,850	2,831	1,645
Idaho................	56,347	616	141	4,209	10,710	40,672	6,388	49,959
Illinois...............	145,976	2,185	166	14,167	22,747	106,711	49,756	96,219
Indiana..............	96,962	1,287	314	8,942	22,827	63,592	30,326	66,636
Iowa.................	114,745	789	–	9,910	31,590	72,456	12,727	102,018
Kansas..............	142,200	874	595	8,558	34,076	98,097	14,385	127,815
Kentucky............	80,180	944	462	5,568	16,980	56,227	15,153	65,027
Louisiana............	61,416	943	97	5,952	10,353	44,072	17,615	43,801
Maine................	22,815	366	18	2,112	5,958	14,360	3,216	19,599
Maryland............	32,269	480	378	3,634	5,398	22,378	18,708	13,561
Massachusetts......	36,763	572	333	6,433	4,556	24,868	30,573	6,190
Michigan............	122,164	1,238	697	14,324	24,657	81,249	37,996	84,169
Minnesota...........	139,591	913	255	13,309	30,667	94,447	22,325	117,266
Mississippi..........	77,477	832	64	7,577	15,849	53,155	13,064	64,413
Missouri.............	132,094	1,380	1,620	8,920	25,210	94,964	24,496	107,598
Montana.............	73,573	1,192	–	6,173	16,159	50,049	4,251	69,322
Nebraska............	95,262	483	462	7,712	20,850	65,754	8,023	87,239
Nevada..............	48,458	620	53	3,516	6,062	38,208	10,288	38,170
New Hampshire......	16,171	225	83	1,662	2,648	11,553	5,065	11,105
New Jersey..........	38,919	432	488	5,896	4,436	27,667	33,473	5,447
New Mexico.........	77,605	999	12	5,649	8,747	62,198	11,177	66,428
New York............	113,533	1,742	997	13,594	20,719	76,481	49,646	63,886
North Carolina.......	107,348	1,306	892	10,103	17,347	77,701	41,477	65,872
North Dakota........	88,050	571	–	5,991	12,317	69,171	2,898	85,152
Ohio.................	123,014	1,574	915	10,600	23,315	86,610	47,495	75,519
Oklahoma...........	116,065	932	207	8,360	25,730	80,835	18,822	97,243
Oregon..............	79,266	730	64	7,025	18,754	52,693	15,211	64,055
Pennsylvania........	120,590	1,862	918	12,910	20,029	84,871	48,270	72,320
Rhode Island........	6,013	70	92	852	898	4,102	4,654	1,359
South Carolina......	77,992	851	128	7,371	14,940	54,702	22,863	55,129
South Dakota........	82,501	679	309	6,126	19,011	56,376	3,413	79,089
Tennessee..........	96,116	1,201	187	9,225	18,224	67,278	31,818	64,298
Texas................	314,648	3,459	1,523	33,123	66,882	209,660	108,979	205,668
Utah.................	48,913	937	58	3,814	8,387	35,717	11,370	37,543
Vermont.............	14,253	320	18	1,339	3,154	9,422	1,502	12,751
Virginia..............	75,369	1,119	444	8,857	15,689	49,260	26,614	48,754
Washington..........	80,653	764	1,034	7,523	17,329	54,004	24,258	56,394
West Virginia........	38,850	555	15	3,483	8,642	26,155	6,659	32,191
Wisconsin...........	115,609	879	545	12,264	23,545	78,377	23,907	91,701
Wyoming............	29,666	913	3	3,681	12,039	13,030	2,851	26,814
Puerto Rico..........	18,359	301	56	1,609	1,688	14,705	15,168	3,191

– Represents zero.

Source: U.S. Federal Highway Administration, "Highway Statistics 2018," <http://www.fhwa.dot.gov/policyinformation/statistics.cfm>, accessed April 2020.

Table 1112. Bridge Inventory—Total, Area, and Condition: 2012 to 2019, and by State, 2019

[Based on the National Bridge Inventory program; for details, see source]

State and year	Number of bridges	Bridge deck area (square meters)	Bridge condition [1]					
			Number			Percent		
			Good	Fair	Poor	Good	Fair	Poor
2012	607,380	358,547,072	287,194	262,878	57,049	47.3	43.3	9.4
2013	607,751	362,428,004	287,581	265,456	54,492	47.3	43.7	9.0
2014	610,749	365,542,771	287,701	269,734	52,905	47.1	44.2	8.7
2015	611,845	369,109,088	289,158	271,690	50,917	47.3	44.4	8.3
2016	614,387	371,463,919	291,412	274,306	48,559	47.4	44.6	7.9
2017	615,002	374,362,285	288,030	279,270	47,619	46.8	45.4	7.7
2018	616,096	390,438,601	283,316	285,676	47,054	46.0	46.4	7.6
U.S. total, 2019	**617,084**	**393,265,002**	**279,582**	**291,339**	**46,163**	**45.3**	**47.2**	**7.5**
Alabama	16,162	9,892,013	6,740	8,768	654	41.7	54.3	4.0
Alaska	1,595	745,016	706	744	145	44.3	46.6	9.1
Arizona	8,320	5,875,021	5,098	3,085	137	61.3	37.1	1.6
Arkansas	12,902	6,807,904	6,598	5,678	626	51.1	44.0	4.9
California	25,771	30,105,500	13,707	10,267	1,797	53.2	39.8	7.0
Colorado	8,785	5,059,489	3,550	4,769	466	40.4	54.3	5.3
Connecticut	4,336	3,439,401	1,256	2,805	275	29.0	64.7	6.3
Delaware	879	1,018,350	248	603	28	28.2	68.6	3.2
District of Columbia	244	566,541	60	174	10	24.6	71.3	4.1
Florida	12,518	17,673,167	8,279	3,878	361	66.1	31.0	2.9
Georgia	14,940	10,336,351	6,796	7,703	441	45.5	51.6	3.0
Hawaii	1,138	1,324,476	297	761	80	26.1	66.9	7.0
Idaho	4,493	1,761,438	1,282	2,916	295	28.5	64.9	6.6
Illinois	26,825	13,515,434	13,084	11,334	2,407	48.8	42.3	9.0
Indiana	19,284	8,241,996	7,892	10,226	1,166	40.9	53.0	6.0
Iowa	24,043	8,844,910	9,319	10,149	4,575	38.8	42.2	19.0
Kansas	24,934	8,713,392	13,468	10,186	1,280	54.0	40.9	5.1
Kentucky	14,394	6,550,521	4,908	8,444	1,042	34.1	58.7	7.2
Louisiana	12,884	16,646,743	6,244	4,939	1,701	48.5	38.3	13.2
Maine	2,461	1,265,300	748	1,399	314	30.4	56.8	12.8
Maryland	5,402	5,447,959	1,783	3,346	273	33.0	61.9	5.1
Massachusetts	5,233	4,141,999	1,371	3,393	469	26.2	64.8	9.0
Michigan	11,244	6,458,784	4,304	5,723	1,217	38.3	50.9	10.8
Minnesota	13,346	7,169,808	8,085	4,630	631	60.6	34.7	4.7
Mississippi	17,019	9,961,961	10,682	4,853	1,484	62.8	28.5	8.7
Missouri	24,494	10,746,879	10,228	12,119	2,147	41.8	49.5	8.8
Montana	5,278	2,061,357	1,602	3,296	380	30.4	62.4	7.2
Nebraska	15,332	4,352,306	7,996	5,980	1,356	52.2	39.0	8.8
Nevada	2,029	1,861,886	1,009	994	26	49.7	49.0	1.3
New Hampshire	2,502	1,148,375	1,323	966	213	52.9	38.6	8.5
New Jersey	6,786	7,481,037	1,825	4,432	529	26.9	65.3	7.8
New Mexico	4,014	2,087,121	1,517	2,277	220	37.8	56.7	5.5
New York	17,540	13,305,353	6,348	9,447	1,745	36.2	53.9	9.9
North Carolina	18,407	10,092,890	7,087	9,606	1,714	38.5	52.2	9.3
North Dakota	4,329	1,322,727	2,352	1,515	462	54.3	35.0	10.7
Ohio	27,167	14,084,569	16,101	9,609	1,457	59.3	35.4	5.4
Oklahoma	23,138	8,846,492	10,174	10,612	2,352	44.0	45.9	10.2
Oregon	8,211	5,093,961	2,850	4,935	426	34.7	60.1	5.2
Pennsylvania	22,911	13,170,292	7,330	12,080	3,501	32.0	52.7	15.3
Rhode Island	779	792,393	138	467	174	17.7	59.9	22.3
South Carolina	9,419	7,008,451	4,130	4,494	795	43.8	47.7	8.4
South Dakota	5,821	1,816,258	1,940	2,890	991	33.3	49.6	17.0
Tennessee	20,226	10,314,556	8,777	10,562	887	43.4	52.2	4.4
Texas	54,432	51,499,656	27,958	25,749	725	51.4	47.3	1.3
Utah	3,063	1,968,376	1,419	1,578	66	46.3	51.5	2.2
Vermont	2,818	937,146	1,494	1,256	68	53.0	44.6	2.4
Virginia	13,933	10,199,966	4,670	8,656	607	33.5	62.1	4.4
Washington	8,300	7,165,450	4,307	3,609	384	51.9	43.5	4.6
West Virginia	7,291	3,819,429	1,861	3,899	1,531	25.5	53.5	21.0
Wisconsin	14,249	7,027,520	7,271	5,952	1,026	51.0	41.8	7.2
Wyoming	3,114	1,313,851	943	1,956	215	30.3	62.8	6.9
Puerto Rico	2,315	2,177,549	422	1,609	284	18.2	69.5	12.3

[1] Good: pavement and bridge infrastructure that is free of significant defects, and has a condition that does not adversely affect its performance. Fair: pavement and bridge infrastructure that has isolated surface defects or functional deficiencies on pavements; or minor deterioration of bridge elements. Poor: pavement and bridge infrastructure that is exhibiting advanced deterioration and conditions that impact structural capacity.

Source: U.S. Federal Highway Administration, Office of Bridges and Structures, "Bridge Condition by Highway System 2019," and earlier editions, <https://www.fhwa.dot.gov/bridge/britab.cfm>, accessed May 2020.

Table 1113. Funding for Highways and Disposition of Highway–User Revenue: 1990 to 2018

[In millions of dollars (75,444 represents $75,444,000,000). Data compiled from reports of state and local authorities]

Type	1990	2000	2010	2013	2014	2015	2016	2017	2018
Total receipts	**75,444**	**131,115**	**220,977**	**(NA)**	**252,642**	**241,063**	**267,941**	**(NA)**	**237,833**
Current income	69,880	119,815	187,960	(NA)	222,515	218,812	248,789	(NA)	216,154
Highway-user revenues	44,346	81,335	93,830	(NA)	106,423	113,454	111,296	(NA)	121,325
Other taxes and fees	19,827	31,137	80,220	(NA)	97,838	85,434	118,366	(NA)	72,859
Investment income, other receipts	5,707	7,342	13,910	(NA)	18,253	19,924	19,126	(NA)	21,970
Bond issue proceeds [1]	5,564	11,301	33,017	(NA)	30,127	22,251	19,152	(NA)	21,679
Funds drawn from or placed in reserves [2,3]	-36	-8,418	-15,664	(NA)	-14,213	-5,868	-48,940	(NA)	6,666
Total funds available	75,408	122,697	205,313	(NA)	238,429	235,195	219,001	(NA)	244,498
Total disbursements	**75,408**	**122,697**	**205,313**	**(NA)**	**238,429**	**235,195**	**219,001**	**(NA)**	**244,498**
Current disbursements	72,457	117,592	193,034	(NA)	204,976	207,537	204,617	(NA)	228,609
Capital outlay	35,151	61,323	100,175	(NA)	105,452	106,539	106,780	(NA)	117,025
Maintenance and traffic services	20,365	30,636	48,773	(NA)	51,593	51,817	49,749	(NA)	59,139
Administration and research	6,501	10,020	16,165	(NA)	16,137	16,930	19,706	(NA)	19,437
Highway law enforcement and safety	7,235	11,031	18,080	(NA)	19,629	20,165	17,850	(NA)	21,205
Interest on debt	3,205	4,583	9,842	(NA)	12,164	12,087	10,532	(NA)	11,802
Bond retirement [1]	2,951	5,105	12,279	(NA)	33,453	27,658	14,384	(NA)	15,890

NA Not available. [1] Amounts shown represent Federal payments to territories, and Federal expenditures in territories for highways and mass transit. [2] Proceeds and redemptions of short-term notes and refunding issues are excluded. [3] Negative numbers indicate that funds were placed in reserves.

Source: U.S. Federal Highway Administration, "Highway Statistics 2018," and earlier reports, <fhwa.dot.gov/policyinformation/statistics.cfm>, accessed August 2020.

Table 1114. State Motor Fuel Tax and Related Receipts, 2015 to 2018; and Gasoline Tax Rates, 2018

[667 represents $667,000,000. Federal tax rate is 18.4 cents a gallon. This table includes revenues from state taxes on all motor-vehicle fuels and related receipts due to motor-fuel taxation and administration. In many states, however, the tax on special fuels (fuels other than gasoline and gasohol) is applicable only to the amount used on the highways. For the states that apply the tax to all fuel sold, the revenue and refunds covering the nonhighway portion of these special fuels have been excluded]

State	Adjusted total receipts (million dollars)				Tax rate, [1]	State	Adjusted total receipts (million dollars)				Tax rate, [1]
	2015	2016	2017	2018	2018		2015	2016	2017	2018	2018
AL	667	670	672	644	18.00	MO	680	698	700	706	17.00
AK	32	30	29	31	8.00	MT	210	208	193	244	32.25
AZ	657	689	718	719	18.00	NE	332	349	357	374	28.90
AR	437	486	473	482	21.50	NV	579	624	665	701	24.00
CA	5,485	4,809	4,587	6,153	41.70	NH	180	184	185	187	23.83
CO	606	649	670	682	22.00	NJ	542	560	545	535	37.10
CT	869	746	719	799	25.00	NM	284	284	290	305	17.00
DE	117	124	129	131	23.00	NY	1,654	1,639	1,653	1,604	24.95
DC	25	25	26	135	23.50	NC	1,913	1,924	1,914	1,963	35.35
FL	2,452	2,586	2,685	2,750	27.50	ND	207	195	190	194	23.00
GA [2]	1,026	1,605	1,740	1,801	26.80	OH	1,819	1,837	1,871	1,861	28.00
HI	84	85	82	82	16.00	OK	455	138	161	163	20.00
ID	238	309	324	335	33.00	OR	601	620	629	620	34.00
IL	1,215	1,260	1,251	1,268	19.00	PA	2,991	3,344	3,533	3,872	57.60
IN	828	837	848	826	30.00	RI	144	151	150	152	34.00
IA	491	656	705	637	31.70	SC	566	597	606	677	20.00
KS	447	454	448	465	24.00	SD	171	187	187	185	30.00
KY	849	748	759	763	24.60	TN	863	900	914	1,100	25.00
LA	595	616	629	598	20.00	TX	3,445	3,490	3,560	3,682	20.00
ME	243	244	252	250	30.00	UT	362	418	482	496	29.40
MD	911	996	1,063	1,068	35.30	VT	122	117	119	120	30.46
MA	755	766	764	769	24.00	VA	773	889	927	923	16.20
MI	987	993	1,342	1,444	26.30	WA	1,198	1,419	1,632	1,701	49.40
MN	879	912	923	942	28.50	WV	383	359	358	403	35.70
MS	398	433	425	413	18.40	WI	993	1,017	1,034	1,054	30.90
						WY	168	162	168	166	24.00

[1] State gasoline tax rates in cents per gallon. In effect July 1. Includes other miscellaneous tax (environmental, etc.). [2] Beginning 2014, Georgia receipts includes special fuel and use tax.

Source: U.S. Federal Highway Administration, "Highway Statistics 2018," and earlier reports, <http://www.fhwa.dot.gov/policyinformation/statistics.cfm>, accessed April 2020.

Table 1115. Public Obligations for Highways—Changes in Indebtedness During the Year: 2000 to 2018

[In millions of dollars (56,264 represents $56,264,000,000). Table summarizes state indebtedness from all state bond issues, including the toll facility issues and the state issues for local roads. This table is compiled from reports of state authorities. Table also summarizes the change in status of the highway obligations of local governments, including toll authorities]

Item	2000	2005	2010	2014	2015	2016	2017	2018
STATE GOVERNMENT								
Obligations outstanding, beginning of year.........	56,264	82,476	138,798	201,462	211,692	216,516	217,090	139,481
Obligations issued...................................	9,067	19,784	26,895	30,402	29,155	20,103	34,186	26,394
Obligations retired...................................	3,897	14,072	11,143	19,311	22,909	16,991	23,355	11,334
Obligations outstanding, end of year...............	61,434	88,187	154,550	212,553	217,938	219,628	227,921	154,541
LOCAL GOVERNMENT [1,2]								
Obligations outstanding, beginning of year.........	34,904	44,406	65,679	(NA)	51,377	78,923	79,109	(NA)
Bonds outstanding, beginning of year.............	34,229	43,403	63,891	(NA)	48,262	75,524	75,506	(NA)
Bonds outstanding, end of year..................	34,949	46,168	67,707	(NA)	49,189	75,867	76,419	(NA)
Obligations outstanding, end of year...............	35,557	47,170	69,794	(NA)	52,579	79,552	80,148	(NA)

NA Not available. [1] Short-term notes data not shown. The data are included in beginning and ending year obligations. [2] Local government reporting is on a biennial basis with even-numbered years optional; therefore, data for some states is estimated in non-reporting years.

Source: U.S. Federal Highway Administration, "Highway Statistics 2018," and earlier reports, <https://www.fhwa.dot.gov/policyinformation/statistics.cfm>, accessed May 2020.

Table 1116. State Disbursements for Highways by State: 2000 to 2018

[In millions of dollars (89,832 represents $89,832,000,000). Comprises disbursements from current revenues or loans for construction, maintenance, interest and principal payments on highway bonds, transfers to local units, and miscellaneous. Includes transactions by state toll authorities. Data exclude amounts allocated for collection expenses, nonhighway purposes, and mass transit]

State	2000	2005	2010	2014	2015	2016	2017	2018
United States.............	**89,832**	**116,517**	**145,944**	**164,620**	**168,242**	**162,673**	**168,666**	**177,582**
Alabama.....................	1,246	1,519	1,781	2,285	2,281	1,948	1,963	2,273
Alaska......................	501	643	756	1,173	1,185	1,277	(NA)	1,122
Arizona.....................	2,040	2,458	2,663	2,388	3,388	2,574	3,158	2,765
Arkansas...................	817	1,078	1,376	2,022	1,473	1,535	1,901	1,860
California...................	6,750	8,308	19,961	14,350	12,162	11,620	11,001	15,837
Colorado....................	1,392	1,652	2,249	2,571	2,632	2,975	2,081	2,225
Connecticut................	1,304	1,434	1,761	1,943	2,097	2,325	1,975	1,947
Delaware...................	595	1,104	1,353	1,291	984	1,984	1,717	1,702
District of Columbia........	244	327	582	386	413	384	607	571
Florida......................	4,208	7,369	7,867	8,538	9,635	11,231	10,390	11,356
Georgia.....................	1,567	2,070	2,926	2,743	3,017	3,223	4,796	4,450
Hawaii......................	272	506	460	397	568	402	702	385
Idaho.......................	492	608	959	808	853	965	790	1,025
Illinois......................	3,447	4,201	(NA)	6,331	6,783	6,907	6,350	6,317
Indiana.....................	1,932	2,235	2,839	2,613	2,636	2,684	3,360	3,072
Iowa........................	1,494	1,392	1,888	2,025	2,183	2,181	2,341	2,404
Kansas.....................	1,206	1,394	1,571	1,727	1,806	1,573	1,200	1,333
Kentucky...................	1,651	1,723	2,528	2,946	3,013	3,232	2,525	2,565
Louisiana...................	1,301	1,387	2,457	1,774	2,698	1,865	2,177	2,293
Maine.......................	488	616	684	(NA)	988	1,052	1,159	1,164
Maryland....................	1,599	2,049	2,255	2,785	3,395	3,052	3,673	4,380
Massachusetts..............	3,524	3,196	2,923	(NA)	(NA)	(NA)	4,364	(NA)
Michigan....................	2,748	3,561	3,484	3,419	3,111	3,883	3,659	3,794
Minnesota..................	1,692	2,131	2,625	2,997	3,486	3,365	3,071	3,316
Mississippi.................	1,039	1,081	1,345	1,413	1,200	1,209	1,365	1,245
Missouri....................	1,818	2,069	2,814	3,421	2,364	2,248	2,422	2,446
Montana....................	474	664	778	764	783	763	698	712
Nebraska...................	745	876	1,409	1,555	1,595	1,770	1,721	1,793
Nevada.....................	651	865	1,007	779	867	1,218	1,250	1,273
New Hampshire.............	387	389	793	722	858	609	642	658
New Jersey.................	4,503	7,119	5,201	(NA)	7,146	6,423	8,545	6,834
New Mexico................	1,162	911	1,163	1,018	1,142	885	956	1,442
New York...................	5,307	9,638	7,711	11,391	9,821	9,926	9,735	9,597
North Carolina..............	2,621	3,698	3,646	4,414	4,324	4,424	5,334	6,128
North Dakota...............	385	456	559	880	950	800	838	493
Ohio........................	3,351	4,040	4,520	5,151	5,838	5,529	5,343	5,345
Oklahoma...................	1,417	1,163	2,040	2,005	2,669	3,318	3,018	2,783
Oregon.....................	1,010	1,628	1,522	2,223	2,265	1,372	2,571	(NA)
Pennsylvania...............	4,517	4,567	8,835	8,200	8,592	9,930	10,091	11,529
Rhode Island...............	256	407	540	(NA)	(NA)	611	473	488
South Carolina..............	970	1,360	1,899	1,864	1,555	1,441	1,709	2,082
South Dakota...............	466	466	532	651	625	579	541	509
Tennessee..................	1,440	1,718	2,076	1,987	1,879	1,899	1,959	2,235
Texas.......................	5,665	8,918	9,365	19,682	21,222	15,105	15,372	13,866
Utah........................	1,072	986	2,303	1,482	1,622	1,412	1,571	2,006
Vermont....................	287	310	436	532	568	536	552	568
Virginia.....................	2,678	3,384	3,334	5,316	5,235	5,761	5,691	7,449
Washington................	1,871	2,625	4,149	4,802	5,489	4,407	5,159	4,981
West Virginia...............	1,170	1,425	1,327	1,315	1,227	1,413	1,295	2,315
Wisconsin..................	1,663	2,363	2,702	3,316	3,547	3,409	3,071	3,200
Wyoming...................	396	429	605	594	635	515	506	513

NA Not available.

Source: U.S. Federal Highway Administration, "Highway Statistics 2018," and earlier reports, <https://www.fhwa.dot.gov/policyinformation/statistics.cfm>, accessed July 2020.

Table 1117. Federal Highway Trust Fund—Receipts, Expenditures, and Balance: 1960 to 2018

[In billions of dollars (2.54 represents $2,540,000,000). For fiscal year ending September 30. Established as part of the Federal Aid Highway Act of 1956]

Year	Receipts	Expenditures	Balance	Year	Receipts	Expenditures	Balance
1960.	2.54	2.94	0.12	2009.	37.32	37.57	8.88
1970.	5.47	4.38	2.61	2010.	44.89	32.01	20.74
1980.	7.65	9.21	11.00	2011.	32.01	37.32	14.32
1990.	13.45	14.38	9.63	2012.	37.64	41.15	9.73
2000.	30.35	27.00	22.55	2013.	37.70	42.92	3.77
2004.	29.79	31.97	10.81	2014.	52.50	43.79	11.38
2005.	32.91	33.12	10.59	2015.	41.83	42.95	9.04
2006.	33.70	33.91	9.01	2016.	88.27	44.79	51.44
2007.	34.31	34.98	8.11	2017.	36.11	44.98	41.44
2008.	39.36	37.01	10.03	2018.	37.93	45.13	32.61

Source: U.S. Federal Highway Administration, "Highway Statistics 2018," <https://www.fhwa.dot.gov/policyinformation/statistics.cfm>, accessed April 2020.

Table 1118. Federal Highway Trust Fund Receipts from Highway Users by State: 2018

[In thousands of dollars (42,613,967 represents $42,613,697,000). For fiscal year ending September 30. Federal Highway Trust Fund receipts are reported by the U.S. Department of the Treasury. Payments into the Fund attributable to highway users in each State are estimated by the Federal Highway Administration]

State	Total	Highway account						Mass transit account	
		Motor fuel			Other				
		Motor fuel, total	Gasoline	Special fuels	Federal use tax	Trucks and trailers	Tires	Gasoline	Special fuels
Total.	42,613,967	31,167,814	22,154,928	9,012,886	1,247,084	4,337,216	540,036	4,121,645	1,200,172
Alabama.	835,043	604,516	416,104	188,412	26,070	90,668	11,289	77,411	25,089
Alaska.	99,539	68,920	40,520	28,400	3,930	13,667	1,702	7,538	3,782
Arizona.	862,314	630,410	447,488	182,922	25,310	88,026	10,960	83,250	24,358
Arkansas.	528,637	371,350	230,595	140,755	19,476	67,735	8,434	42,899	18,743
California.	4,102,153	3,090,564	2,393,778	696,786	96,412	335,310	41,750	445,332	92,785
Colorado.	681,361	500,198	359,595	140,603	19,455	67,662	8,425	66,898	18,723
Connecticut.	383,785	292,966	235,012	57,954	8,019	27,889	3,473	43,721	7,717
Delaware.	120,106	92,689	76,453	16,236	2,246	7,813	973	14,223	2,162
Dist. of Columbia.	23,009	18,327	16,297	2,030	281	977	122	3,032	270
Florida.	2,281,578	1,733,278	1,372,867	360,411	49,869	173,438	21,595	255,405	47,993
Georgia.	1,525,073	1,113,804	788,158	325,646	45,058	156,708	19,512	146,627	43,364
Hawaii.	105,416	83,139	72,270	10,869	1,504	5,230	651	13,445	1,447
Idaho.	259,559	184,717	120,122	64,595	8,938	31,085	3,870	22,347	8,602
Illinois.	1,514,552	1,096,451	754,752	341,699	47,280	164,434	20,474	140,412	45,501
Indiana.	1,072,910	764,123	498,209	265,914	36,794	127,964	15,933	92,686	35,410
Iowa.	560,569	393,764	244,475	149,289	20,657	71,841	8,945	45,482	19,880
Kansas.	402,841	291,477	200,295	91,182	12,617	43,879	5,464	37,262	12,142
Kentucky.	722,452	518,819	347,883	170,936	23,652	82,258	10,242	64,719	22,762
Louisiana.	662,033	481,069	335,104	145,965	20,197	70,242	8,746	62,342	19,437
Maine.	207,548	148,337	97,884	50,453	6,981	24,279	3,023	18,210	6,718
Maryland.	708,776	538,169	425,682	112,487	15,564	54,131	6,740	79,193	14,979
Massachusetts.	685,717	529,256	436,698	92,558	12,807	44,541	5,546	81,242	12,325
Michigan.	1,210,630	916,682	719,739	196,943	27,250	94,774	11,801	133,898	26,225
Minnesota.	787,747	573,616	402,196	171,420	23,719	82,491	10,271	74,823	22,827
Mississippi.	581,806	413,959	269,003	144,956	20,057	69,756	8,686	50,045	19,303
Missouri.	992,416	719,359	497,173	222,186	30,743	106,921	13,313	92,493	29,587
Montana.	198,901	137,519	80,391	57,128	7,905	27,491	3,423	14,956	7,607
Nebraska.	343,623	237,681	139,179	98,502	13,629	47,401	5,902	25,893	13,117
Nevada.	363,504	264,595	185,308	79,287	10,971	38,155	4,751	34,474	10,558
New Hampshire.	168,336	130,539	108,975	21,564	2,984	10,377	1,292	20,273	2,871
New Jersey.	1,060,798	803,431	631,241	172,190	23,825	82,862	10,317	117,434	22,929
New Mexico.	406,907	279,008	157,736	121,272	16,780	58,359	7,266	29,345	16,149
New York.	1,644,277	1,212,188	882,527	329,661	45,614	158,641	19,753	164,183	43,898
North Carolina.	1,311,459	977,800	735,631	242,169	33,508	116,538	14,510	136,855	32,248
North Dakota.	197,709	131,937	66,146	65,791	9,103	31,660	3,942	12,306	8,761
Ohio.	1,575,965	1,144,824	796,677	348,147	48,172	167,537	20,860	148,212	46,360
Oklahoma.	718,473	497,137	291,514	205,623	28,451	98,951	12,321	54,232	27,381
Oregon.	520,005	373,456	250,462	122,994	17,018	59,188	7,370	46,595	16,378
Pennsylvania.	1,515,183	1,105,723	780,567	325,156	44,991	156,473	19,483	145,215	43,298
Rhode Island.	92,848	71,245	57,920	13,325	1,844	6,412	798	10,775	1,774
South Carolina.	850,285	621,822	441,842	179,980	24,903	86,611	10,784	82,199	23,966
South Dakota.	178,094	123,679	73,562	50,117	6,935	24,118	3,003	13,685	6,674
Tennessee.	1,016,459	746,084	536,111	209,973	29,053	101,044	12,581	99,737	27,960
Texas.	4,821,402	3,441,159	2,260,151	1,181,008	163,412	568,329	70,764	420,473	157,265
Utah.	414,102	293,276	187,528	105,748	14,632	50,889	6,336	34,887	14,082
Vermont.	84,210	63,023	47,923	15,100	2,089	7,267	905	8,915	2,011
Virginia.	1,163,015	863,349	641,448	221,901	30,704	106,784	13,296	119,333	29,549
Washington.	792,339	588,227	437,136	151,091	20,906	72,709	9,053	81,324	20,120
West Virginia.	300,101	208,286	123,602	84,684	11,717	40,752	5,074	22,995	11,277
Wisconsin.	772,010	561,203	391,402	169,801	23,495	81,712	10,174	72,815	22,611
Wyoming.	186,392	120,664	51,597	69,067	9,557	33,237	4,138	9,599	9,197

Source: U.S. Federal Highway Administration, "Highway Statistics 2018," <fhwa.dot.gov/policyinformation/>, accessed May 2020.

Table 1119. Motor Vehicle Distance Traveled by Type of Vehicle: 1970 to 2018

[1,110 represents 1,110,000,000,000. The travel data by vehicle type and stratification of trucks are estimated by the Federal Highway Administration (FHWA)]

Year	Vehicle miles of travel (bil.) [1]					Average miles traveled per vehicle (1,000) [1]				
	Total [2]	Light duty vehicle short WB [3]	Buses [4]	Light duty vehicle long WB [3]	Trucks [5,6]	Total [2]	Light duty vehicle short WB [3]	Buses [4]	Light duty vehicle long WB [3]	Trucks [5,6]
1970	1,110	920	4.5	123	62	10.0	10.0	12.0	8.7	13.6
1975	1,328	1,040	6.1	201	81	9.6	9.3	13.1	9.8	15.2
1980	1,527	1,122	6.1	291	108	9.5	8.8	11.5	10.4	18.7
1985	1,775	1,256	4.5	391	124	10.0	9.4	7.5	10.5	20.6
1990	2,144	1,418	5.7	575	146	11.1	10.3	9.1	11.9	23.6
1995	2,423	1,438	6.4	790	178	11.8	11.2	9.4	12.0	26.5
2000	2,747	1,967	14.8	491	262	12.2	11.0	19.8	14.6	29.1
2001	2,796	1,987	13.0	512	272	11.9	10.7	17.3	14.7	28.9
2002	2,856	2,036	13.3	520	276	12.2	11.1	17.5	14.3	29.4
2003	2,890	2,051	13.4	528	286	12.2	11.1	17.2	14.8	30.3
2004	2,965	2,083	13.5	569	284	12.2	11.0	17.0	15.2	29.7
2005	2,989	2,096	13.2	581	285	12.1	11.0	16.3	14.8	28.8
2006	3,014	2,048	14.0	633	301	12.0	10.5	17.1	16.3	29.1
2007	3,031	2,104	14.5	587	304	11.9	10.7	17.4	15.0	28.3
2008	2,977	2,025	14.8	605	311	11.6	10.3	17.6	15.3	28.6
2009	2,957	2,016	14.4	617	288	11.6	10.4	17.1	15.3	26.3
2010	2,967	2,026	13.8	623	287	11.9	10.7	16.3	15.5	26.6
2011	2,950	2,046	13.8	604	268	11.7	11.2	20.7	12.0	26.1
2012	2,969	2,063	14.8	601	269	11.7	11.3	19.3	11.9	25.3
2013	2,988	2,074	15.2	603	275	11.7	11.2	17.5	11.7	26.0
2014	3,026	2,072	16.0	638	279	11.6	11.0	18.3	12.1	25.6
2015	3,095	2,148	16.2	632	280	11.7	11.3	18.3	11.9	25.0
2016	3,174	2,192	16.3	658	288	11.8	11.4	16.7	12.0	25.0
2017	3,212	2,221	17.2	657	298	11.8	11.5	17.5	11.5	24.3
2018	3,240	2,233	18.3	664	305	11.8	11.6	18.4	11.5	23.0

[1] Beginning with 2000 data, FHWA updated data using an enhanced methodology implemented in March 2011. Prior to 2000, "Light Duty Vehicles Short WB" were categorized as "Cars"; and "Light Duty Vehicles Long WB" were categorized as "Vans, pickups, sport utility vehicles." [2] Motorcycles included with "Cars" through 1994; thereafter in total, not shown separately. [3] Light Duty Vehicles Short WB—passenger cars, light trucks, vans and sport utility vehicles with a wheelbase (WB) equal to or less than 121 inches. Light Duty Vehicles Long WB—large passenger cars, vans, pickup trucks, and sport/utility vehicles with WB larger than 121 inches. [4] Includes school buses. [5] Includes combination trucks. [6] Beginning in 2000: Single-Unit—single frame trucks that have 2-axles and at least 6 tires or a gross vehicle weight rating exceeding 10,000 lbs.

Source: U.S. Federal Highway Administration, "Highway Statistics 2018," and earlier reports, <http://www.fhwa.dot.gov/policyinformation/statistics.cfm>, accessed April 2020.

Table 1120. Licensed Drivers, Total and as a Percent of Age Group, by Age: 2000 to 2018

[Licensed drivers in thousands (190,625 represents 190,625,000). Percentages are computed using Census Bureau data]

Age or range	Licensed drivers (1,000)							Licensed drivers as percent of age group [1]		
	2000	2010	2014	2015	2016	2017	2018	2010	2017	2018
Total	190,625	210,115	214,092	218,084	221,712	225,346	227,558	83.5	85.1	85.5
Under 16 years old [2]	27	398	62	65	63	77	43	4.7	1.9	1.0
16 years old	1,470	1,213	1,022	1,065	1,121	1,100	1,066	28.1	26.0	25.8
17 years old	2,331	2,028	1,881	1,920	1,973	1,990	1,976	46.1	46.3	46.6
18 years old	2,839	2,731	2,540	2,550	2,619	2,629	2,630	60.7	62.0	60.9
19 years old	3,077	3,187	2,986	2,990	3,040	3,049	3,040	69.5	71.6	71.3
20 to 24 years old	15,966	17,468	17,579	17,630	17,710	17,611	17,519	80.9	79.6	80.1
20 years old	3,140	3,426	3,221	3,224	3,250	3,253	3,249	75.8	76.1	76.0
21 years old	3,172	3,474	3,341	3,368	3,390	3,365	3,355	79.8	77.9	78.2
22 years old	3,182	3,483	3,536	3,532	3,547	3,528	3,506	81.7	79.8	80.9
23 years old	3,247	3,515	3,683	3,688	3,691	3,667	3,645	83.7	81.2	82.1
24 years old	3,225	3,571	3,799	3,818	3,832	3,797	3,764	84.0	82.8	83.0
25 to 29 years old	17,586	18,431	18,710	19,266	19,723	20,076	20,186	87.3	85.9	85.7
30 to 34 years old	19,155	17,849	18,651	19,120	19,472	19,755	19,979	89.4	89.9	90.3
35 to 39 years old	21,059	18,161	17,512	18,088	18,649	19,194	19,603	90.0	90.4	90.9
40 to 44 years old	21,093	19,178	18,351	18,107	17,852	17,897	18,043	91.8	91.1	91.5
45 to 49 years old	19,154	20,814	18,910	18,988	19,221	19,345	19,198	91.7	92.2	92.5
50 to 54 years old	16,868	20,628	20,587	20,488	20,186	19,831	19,445	92.5	92.7	93.1
55 to 59 years old	12,760	18,440	19,750	20,068	20,304	20,502	20,539	93.8	93.2	93.6
60 to 64 years old	9,915	15,858	17,102	17,647	18,076	18,677	19,042	94.3	93.4	93.7
65 to 69 years old	8,386	11,468	14,014	14,788	15,417	15,626	15,942	92.2	92.8	93.3
70 to 74 years old	7,468	8,231	9,818	10,232	10,653	11,705	12,252	88.7	91.1	91.4
75 to 79 years old	5,911	6,158	6,634	6,834	7,151	7,581	8,054	84.1	86.7	86.9
80 to 84 years old	3,511	4,464	4,405	4,521	4,606	4,723	4,936	77.7	79.2	80.6
85 and over	2,050	3,411	3,577	3,716	3,877	3,980	4,065	62.1	61.5	62.1

[1] Calculated based on Census Bureau population estimates for the population aged 14 and over; see <https://www.census.gov/data/tables/time-series/demo/popest/2010s-national-detail.html>. [2] Percent of age group data based on Census Bureau population estimates for 14- and 15-year olds.

Source: U.S. Federal Highway Administration, "Highway Statistics 2018," and earlier reports, <https://www.fhwa.dot.gov/policyinformation/statistics.cfm>, accessed April 2020.

Table 1121. State Motor Vehicle Registrations, 1990 to 2018; and Motorcycle Registrations and Licensed Drivers, 2018

[In thousands (188,798 represents 188,798,000). Motor vehicle registrations cover publicly, privately, and commercially owned vehicles. Some states did not provide complete current registration data. Table displays estimates by FHWA, transaction data, or previous year data; see source and earlier editions for more information. For uniformity, data have been adjusted to a calendar-year basis as registration years in states differ; figures represent net numbers where possible. See also Table 1122]

| State | Motor vehicle registrations [1] | | | | | | 2018 | | Motor-cycle registra-tions [2], in 2018 | Licensed drivers in 2018 |
	1990	2000	2010	2015	2016	2017	Total	Auto-mobile		
U.S.	188,798	221,475	242,061	255,009	260,120	263,766	264,936	111,242	8,637	227,558
AL	3,744	3,960	4,654	5,285	5,359	4,944	5,190	2,161	109	3,999
AK	477	594	710	783	763	773	772	183	32	536
AZ	2,825	3,795	4,320	5,470	5,620	5,800	5,636	2,392	170	5,285
AR	1,448	1,840	2,073	2,680	2,717	2,744	2,726	921	91	2,145
CA	21,926	27,698	31,014	28,595	29,379	29,953	30,199	15,066	809	27,039
CO	3,155	3,626	4,180	4,814	4,926	5,070	5,165	1,798	191	4,245
CT	2,623	2,853	3,082	2,755	2,755	2,736	2,792	1,307	88	2,606
DE	526	630	799	936	976	943	980	433	28	787
DC	262	242	212	319	333	342	348	210	4	528
FL	10,950	11,781	14,373	15,532	16,018	16,373	16,909	7,966	585	15,369
GA	5,489	7,155	7,702	7,937	8,037	8,238	8,309	3,557	203	7,169
HI	771	738	904	1,209	1,201	1,224	1,236	509	31	948
ID	1,054	1,178	1,325	1,788	1,776	1,773	1,813	599	67	1,253
IL	7,873	8,973	10,079	10,249	9,962	10,557	10,269	4,478	320	8,715
IN	4,366	5,571	5,698	5,822	5,917	5,919	5,940	2,249	251	4,589
IA	2,632	3,106	3,313	3,447	3,484	3,555	3,497	1,242	194	2,260
KS	2,012	2,296	2,436	2,539	2,553	2,622	2,589	975	95	2,149
KY	2,909	2,826	3,589	4,041	4,118	4,192	4,267	1,722	101	3,033
LA	2,995	3,557	4,086	3,787	3,791	3,793	3,771	1,389	114	3,425
ME	977	1,024	1,054	1,049	1,055	1,043	1,074	391	51	1,041
MD	3,607	3,848	4,557	4,009	4,055	4,239	4,087	1,922	118	4,408
MA	3,726	5,265	5,334	4,902	4,902	4,896	4,893	2,183	169	4,945
MI	7,209	8,436	9,286	8,037	8,076	8,260	8,128	3,024	258	7,154
MN	3,508	4,630	4,848	5,033	5,129	5,441	5,163	1,977	242	3,391
MS	1,875	2,289	2,016	2,041	2,039	2,029	2,039	825	28	2,058
MO	3,905	4,580	5,153	5,406	5,531	5,430	5,345	2,102	154	4,273
MT	783	1,026	926	1,448	1,504	1,557	1,552	453	294	806
NE	1,384	1,619	1,802	1,925	1,896	1,909	1,906	683	56	1,420
NV	853	1,220	1,362	2,242	2,324	2,379	2,440	1,074	75	1,983
NH	946	1,052	1,203	1,222	1,244	1,240	1,267	507	79	1,162
NJ	5,652	6,390	6,628	5,786	5,790	5,905	5,905	2,754	151	6,343
NM	1,301	1,529	1,612	1,760	1,762	1,682	1,764	656	60	1,458
NY	10,196	10,235	10,255	10,284	10,730	10,465	11,093	4,713	389	12,194
NC	5,162	6,223	5,743	7,740	8,075	7,882	8,022	3,394	188	7,509
ND	630	694	736	852	856	1,005	861	240	39	561
OH	8,410	10,467	9,801	10,152	10,278	10,399	10,504	4,604	410	8,033
OK	2,649	3,014	3,357	2,859	3,601	3,608	3,570	1,296	129	2,504
OR	2,445	3,022	3,050	3,479	3,675	3,961	3,809	1,489	133	2,931
PA	7,971	9,260	9,991	10,205	10,356	10,312	10,355	4,424	372	8,991
RI	672	760	782	843	845	842	844	412	28	757
SC	2,521	3,095	3,661	4,046	4,206	4,286	4,341	1,830	117	3,846
SD	704	793	926	986	1,132	1,141	1,149	359	120	638
TN	4,444	4,820	5,114	5,446	5,542	5,635	5,590	2,285	179	5,422
TX	12,800	14,070	17,194	21,478	21,391	21,766	21,837	8,248	348	17,370
UT	1,206	1,628	2,655	2,150	2,235	2,272	2,288	937	84	2,031
VT	462	515	567	624	585	591	589	218	31	565
VA	4,938	6,046	6,149	7,046	7,109	7,321	7,409	3,268	195	5,929
WA	4,257	5,116	4,683	6,489	6,812	7,025	6,917	2,965	236	5,910
WV	1,225	1,442	1,436	1,555	1,644	1,631	1,633	560	59	1,137
WI	3,815	4,366	4,968	5,142	5,229	5,272	5,347	2,088	336	4,288
WY	528	586	663	784	825	790	808	204	29	419

[1] Automobiles, trucks, and buses (excludes motorcycles). Excludes vehicles owned by military services. [2] Private and commercial, excluding publicly-owned.

Source: U.S. Federal Highway Administration, "Highway Statistics 2018," and earlier reports, <http://www.fhwa.dot.gov/policyinformation/statistics.cfm>, accessed April 2020.

Table 1122. State Motor Vehicle Registrations: 2000 to 2018

[In thousands (221,475 represents 221,475,000). Information obtained from state authorities; see source. For motorcycles; see Table 1121]

Type	2000	2010	2013	2014	2015	2016	2017	2018
All motor vehicles	221,475	242,061	247,417	251,933	255,009	260,120	263,766	264,936
Private and commercial	217,567	237,784	243,487	247,849	250,967	255,972	259,623	260,788
Publicly owned	3,908	4,277	3,985	4,084	4,042	4,148	4,142	4,148
Automobiles	133,621	130,892	113,676	113,899	112,864	112,961	111,177	111,242
Private and commercial	132,247	129,434	112,128	112,261	111,412	111,491	109,750	109,814
Publicly owned	1,374	1,458	1,548	1,638	1,453	1,471	1,427	1,429
Buses	746	846	865	872	889	976	983	992
Private and commercial	314	347	361	467	466	568	572	576
Publicly owned	432	499	503	405	423	409	411	417
Trucks [1]	87,108	110,322	132,931	137,162	141,256	146,182	151,605	152,702
Private and commercial	85,005	108,003	130,998	135,121	139,090	143,913	149,301	150,398
Publicly owned	2,103	2,319	1,934	2,041	2,166	2,269	2,304	2,303

[1] Includes panel, delivery, personal, passenger vans, minivans, pickups, and utility vehicles.

Source: U.S. Federal Highway Administration, "Highway Statistics 2018," and earlier reports, <http://www.fhwa.dot.gov/policyinformation/statistics.cfm>, accessed April 2020.

Table 1123. Domestic Motor Fuel Consumption by Type of Vehicle: 1970 to 2018

[Consumption in billions (92.3 represents 92,300,000,000 gallons). See Table 1119. Comprises all fuel types used for propulsion of vehicles under state motor fuels laws. Excludes federal purchases for military use. Minus sign (-) indicates decrease]

Year	Annual fuel consumption (bil. gal.) [1]						Average miles per gallon [1]				
	All vehi-cles [2]	Annual percent change [3]	Light duty vehicle short WB [4]	Buses [5]	Light duty vehicle long WB [4]	Trucks [6, 7]	All vehi-cles [2]	Light duty vehicle short WB [4]	Buses [5]	Light duty vehicle long WB [4]	Trucks [6, 7]
1970......	92.3	4.8	67.8	0.8	12.3	11.3	12.0	13.5	5.5	10.0	5.5
1980......	115.0	-5.9	70.2	1.0	23.8	20.0	13.3	16.0	6.0	12.2	5.4
1990......	130.8	-0.8	69.8	0.9	35.6	24.5	16.4	20.3	6.4	16.1	6.0
2000......	162.5	0.7	88.9	2.2	28.9	42.0	16.9	22.1	6.7	17.0	6.2
2001......	163.5	0.6	87.8	1.9	30.1	43.0	17.1	22.6	6.8	17.0	6.3
2002......	168.7	3.2	91.5	1.9	30.8	43.3	17.0	22.3	6.9	16.9	6.4
2003......	170.0	0.8	91.6	1.9	31.3	44.8	17.0	22.4	7.1	16.9	6.4
2004......	173.5	2.1	93.4	1.9	33.8	44.4	17.1	22.3	7.1	16.9	6.4
2005......	174.8	0.7	93.2	1.9	34.4	44.5	17.2	22.5	7.1	16.9	6.4
2006......	175.0	0.1	88.6	2.0	37.0	46.4	17.2	23.1	7.1	17.1	6.5
2007......	176.2	0.7	89.6	2.0	36.9	47.2	17.2	22.9	7.2	17.1	6.4
2008......	170.8	-3.1	85.6	2.1	34.9	47.7	17.4	23.7	7.2	17.3	6.5
2009......	168.1	-1.6	85.7	2.0	35.7	44.3	17.6	23.5	7.2	17.3	6.5
2010......	170.4	1.4	86.8	1.9	36.3	45.0	17.4	23.3	7.2	17.2	6.4
2011......	168.5	-1.1	88.4	1.9	35.3	42.4	17.5	23.2	7.1	17.1	6.3
2012......	168.6	0.1	88.6	2.1	35.1	42.4	17.6	23.3	7.2	17.1	6.4
2013......	169.7	0.6	88.6	2.1	35.2	46.8	17.6	23.4	7.2	17.2	6.4
2014......	173.3	2.2	89.3	2.2	37.3	44.0	17.5	23.2	7.2	17.1	6.3
2015......	172.9	-0.2	90.0	2.2	36.4	43.7	17.9	23.9	7.3	17.3	6.4
2016......	176.9	2.3	91.5	2.2	37.8	44.9	17.9	24.0	7.3	17.4	6.4
2017......	178.0	0.6	91.7	2.4	37.5	46.0	18.1	24.2	7.3	17.5	6.5
2018......	178.1	0.1	91.6	2.5	37.2	46.4	18.2	24.4	7.3	17.9	6.6

[1] See footnote 1, Table 1119. [2] Motorcycles included with Light Duty Vehicles Short WB through 1994; thereafter in total, not shown separately. [3] Change from immediate prior year. [4] Light Duty Vehicles Short WB—passenger cars, light trucks, vans and sport utility vehicles with a wheelbase (WB) equal to or less than 121 inches. Light Duty Vehicles Long WB—large passenger cars, vans, pickup trucks, and sport/utility vehicles with WB larger than 121 inches. [5] Includes school buses. [6] Includes combination trucks. [7] Beginning 2000: Single-Unit—single frame trucks that have 2-axles and at least 6 tires or a gross vehicle weight rating over 10,000 lbs.

Source: U.S. Federal Highway Administration, "Highway Statistics 2018," and earlier reports, <http://www.fhwa.dot.gov/policyinformation/statistics.cfm>, accessed May 2020.

Table 1124. Alternative Fuel Vehicles—Models Available and Refueling Stations by Vehicle Fuel Type: 1995 to 2019

[Data gathered as close to September 30 as possible. The Energy Policy Act of 1992 defines alternative fuels and allows the U.S. Department of Energy (DOE) to add to the list of alternative fuels if the fuel is substantially nonpetroleum, yields substantial energy security benefits, and offers substantial environmental benefits]

Fuel type	1995	2000	2005	2010	2015	2017	2018	2019
MODELS AVAILABLE								
Total.................	**13**	**37**	**29**	**36**	**141**	**111**	**128**	**(NA)**
Propane [1]......................	–	2	–	–	10	9	7	(NA)
Compressed natural gas (CNG) [1]..............	10	15	5	1	17	8	9	(NA)
Ethanol (E85)....................	–	8	24	34	84	45	54	(NA)
Methanol (M85)..................	2	–	–	–	–	–	–	(NA)
Electric vehicle [2]...............	1	12	–	1	27	46	56	(NA)
Hydrogen........................	–	–	–	–	3	3	2	(NA)
REFUELING STATIONS								
Total.................	**4,677**	**5,205**	**5,164**	**6,912**	**39,963**	**60,053**	**70,562**	**87,557**
Propane..........................	3,299	3,268	2,995	2,647	3,594	3,541	3,341	3,185
Compressed Natural Gas (CNG)..............	1,065	1,217	787	841	1,563	1,697	1,659	1,591
LNG (Liquid Natural Gas)........................	(NA)	44	40	39	111	131	137	119
Biodiesel [3].....................	–	2	304	644	721	702	681	613
Ethanol (E85)....................	37	113	436	2,142	2,990	3,322	3,617	3,781
Methanol (M85)..................	88	3	–	–	–	–	–	–
Electric vehicle [4]...............	188	558	588	541	30,945	50,627	61,067	78,207
Hydrogen........................	(NA)	(NA)	14	58	39	64	60	61

– Represents zero. NA Not available. [1] Dedicated and bi-fuel vehicles. [2] Electric vehicles include plug-in hybrid-electric vehicles but do not include neighborhood electric vehicles, low-speed electric vehicles, or two-wheeled electric vehicles. [3] Stations selling biodiesel blends less than B20 are only included in the 2005-2007 station counts. [4] Beginning 2011, electric stations are counted by the plug rather than by the geographical location. This is different from the other fuels, which count only the geographical location regardless of how many dispensers or nozzles are on site.

Source: U.S. Department of Energy, Office of Energy Efficiency and Renewable Energy, *Transportation Energy Data Book*, Edition 38, January 2020. See also <https://tedb.ornl.gov/>.

Table 1125. Traffic Fatalities—Number and Rate by State: 2000 to 2018

[For deaths within 30 days of the accident]

State	2000	2010	2017	2018	Fatality rate [1] 2010	2018	State	2000	2010	2017	2018	Fatality rate [1] 2010	2018
U.S.	**41,945**	**32,999**	**37,473**	**36,560**	**1.11**	**1.13**	MO	1,157	821	932	921	1.16	1.20
AL	996	862	948	953	1.34	1.34	MT	237	189	186	182	1.69	1.43
AK	106	56	79	80	1.17	1.46	NE	276	190	228	230	0.98	1.10
AZ	1,036	759	998	1,010	1.27	1.53	NV	323	257	311	330	1.16	1.17
AR	652	571	525	516	1.70	1.41	NH	126	128	102	147	0.98	1.07
CA	3,753	2,720	3,884	3,563	0.84	1.02	NJ	731	556	624	564	0.76	0.73
CO	681	450	648	632	0.96	1.17	NM	432	349	380	391	1.38	1.43
CT	341	320	281	294	1.02	0.93	NY	1,460	1,201	1,006	943	0.92	0.76
DE	123	101	119	111	1.13	1.09	NC	1,557	1,320	1,412	1,437	1.29	1.19
DC	48	24	31	31	0.67	0.84	ND	86	105	116	105	1.27	1.07
FL	2,999	2,444	3,116	3,133	1.25	1.41	OH	1,366	1,080	1,179	1,068	0.97	0.93
GA	1,541	1,247	1,540	1,504	1.12	1.14	OK	650	668	657	655	1.40	1.44
HI	132	113	107	117	1.13	1.07	OR	451	317	439	506	0.94	1.37
ID	276	209	245	231	1.32	1.30	PA	1,520	1,324	1,137	1,190	1.32	1.17
IL	1,418	927	1,090	1,031	0.88	0.96	RI	80	67	84	59	0.81	0.74
IN	886	754	916	858	1.00	1.05	SC	1,065	809	989	1,037	1.65	1.83
IA	445	390	330	318	1.24	0.96	SD	173	140	129	130	1.58	1.34
KS	461	431	461	404	1.44	1.26	TN	1,307	1,032	1,024	1,041	1.47	1.28
KY	820	760	782	724	1.58	1.46	TX	3,779	3,023	3,732	3,642	1.29	1.29
LA	938	721	770	768	1.59	1.53	UT	373	253	273	260	0.95	0.81
ME	169	161	173	137	1.11	0.93	VT	76	71	69	68	0.98	0.93
MD	588	496	558	501	0.88	0.84	VA	929	740	839	820	0.90	0.96
MA	433	347	347	360	0.64	0.54	WA	631	460	563	546	0.80	0.88
MI	1,382	942	1,031	974	0.97	0.95	WV	411	315	304	294	1.64	1.51
MN	625	411	358	381	0.73	0.63	WI	799	572	613	588	0.96	0.89
MS	949	641	685	664	1.61	1.63	WY	152	155	123	111	1.66	1.06

[1] Deaths per 100 million vehicle miles traveled.

Source: U.S. National Highway Traffic Safety Administration, "Traffic Safety Facts Annual Report Tables," <https://cdan.nhtsa.gov/tsftables/tsfar.htm>, and "Fatality Analysis Reporting System," <http://www.nhtsa.gov/FARS>; accessed July 2020.

Table 1126. Motor Vehicle Occupants and Nonoccupants Killed and Injured: 1990 to 2018

[Injuries in thousands (3,206 represents 3,206,000). For deaths within 30 days of the accident. Beginning 2016, data for persons injured are not comparable to previous years due to a new data collection system. The National Automotive Sampling System (NASS) GES (General Estimates System) was replaced with the Crash Report Sampling System (CRSS). See <crashstats.nhtsa.dot.gov/Api/Public/ViewPublication/812509> for details]

Year	Total	Occupants Total	Passenger cars	Light trucks [1]	Large trucks [1]	Buses	Other/unknown [2]	Motorcycle occupants [3]	Nonoccupants Total	Pedestrian	Pedalcyclist	Other/unknown [2]
KILLED												
1990	44,599	33,890	24,092	8,601	705	32	460	3,244	7,465	6,482	859	124
2000	41,945	33,451	20,699	11,526	754	22	450	2,897	5,597	4,763	693	141
2005	43,510	33,070	18,512	13,037	804	58	659	4,576	5,864	4,892	786	186
2006	42,708	32,119	17,925	12,761	805	27	601	4,837	5,752	4,795	772	185
2007	41,259	30,527	16,614	12,458	805	36	614	5,174	5,558	4,699	701	158
2008	37,423	26,791	14,646	10,816	682	67	580	5,312	5,320	4,414	718	188
2009	33,883	24,526	13,135	10,312	499	26	554	4,469	4,888	4,109	628	151
2010	32,999	23,371	12,491	9,782	530	44	524	4,518	5,110	4,302	623	185
2011	32,479	22,510	12,014	9,302	640	55	499	4,630	5,339	4,457	682	200
2012	33,782	23,017	12,361	9,418	697	39	502	4,986	5,779	4,818	734	227
2013	32,893	22,483	12,037	9,186	695	54	511	4,692	5,718	4,779	749	190
2014	32,744	22,307	11,947	9,103	656	44	557	4,594	5,843	4,910	729	204
2015	35,484	23,899	12,763	9,878	665	49	544	5,029	6,556	5,494	829	233
2016	37,806	25,276	13,508	10,279	815	64	610	5,337	7,193	6,080	853	260
2017	37,473	25,127	13,477	10,186	878	43	543	5,229	7,117	6,075	806	236
2018	36,560	24,221	12,775	9,922	885	43	596	4,985	7,354	6,283	857	214
INJURED (1,000)												
1990	3,206	2,935	2,360	499	40	33	4	84	186	105	75	7
2000	3,194	3,001	2,057	886	31	17	10	58	135	78	51	6
2005	2,709	2,504	1,580	874	28	12	10	88	118	65	45	8
2006	2,583	2,383	1,479	860	23	10	11	88	112	61	44	7
2007	2,499	2,272	1,383	845	23	13	8	103	124	70	43	10
2008	2,356	2,130	1,308	773	24	16	9	96	130	69	52	9
2009	2,224	2,017	1,219	762	16	13	7	89	117	59	51	7
2010	2,248	2,036	1,256	737	20	18	5	82	130	70	52	8
2011	2,227	2,019	1,244	733	23	14	6	82	126	69	48	9
2012	2,369	2,140	1,330	766	25	12	6	93	136	76	49	10
2013	2,319	2,105	1,299	753	25	24	5	89	125	66	48	11
2014	2,343	2,125	1,294	784	27	14	6	92	125	65	50	10
2015	2,455	2,241	1,382	809	30	12	8	89	125	70	45	10
2016 [4]	3,062	2,791	1,690	1,035	36	25	5	104	166	86	64	16
2017 [4]	2,745	2,523	1,529	937	40	12	5	89	133	71	50	12
2018 [4]	2,710	2,491	1,511	921	39	15	5	82	137	75	47	15

[1] See footnotes 2 and 3, Table 1128. [2] Includes combination trucks. [3] Includes mopeds, three wheel motorcycles, off-road motorcycles, etc. [4] Beginning 2016, data are not comparable to previous years due to a new data collection system. Numbers are not actual counts but estimates of actual counts.

Source: U.S. National Highway Traffic Safety Administration, "Traffic Safety Facts Annual Report Tables," <cdan.nhtsa.gov/tsftables/tsfar.htm>, accessed July 2020. See also <nhtsa.gov/research>.

Table 1127. Fatal Motor Vehicle Accidents—National Summary: 2000 to 2018

[Based on data from the Fatality Analysis Reporting System (FARS). FARS gathers data on accidents that result in loss of human life. FARS is operated and maintained by National Highway Traffic Safety Administration's (NHTSA), National Center for Statistics and Analysis (NCSA). FARS data are gathered on motor vehicle accidents that occurred on a roadway customarily open to the public, resulting in the death of a person within 30 days of the accident. Collection of these data depend on the use of police, hospital, medical examiner/coroner, and Emergency Medical Services reports; state vehicle registration, driver licensing, and highway department files; and vital statistics documents and death certificates. See source for further detail]

Item	2000	2010	2013	2014	2015	2016	2017	2018
Fatal crashes, total..........	**37,526**	**30,296**	**30,202**	**30,056**	**32,538**	**34,748**	**34,560**	**33,654**
One vehicle involved..........	21,117	18,221	18,156	17,930	18,902	20,264	19,714	19,116
Two or more vehicles involved..........	16,409	12,075	12,046	12,126	13,636	14,484	14,846	14,538
Occupants involved..........	94,325	69,383	68,171	67,358	74,556	78,813	78,232	75,824
Drivers involved..........	57,280	44,599	44,803	44,671	49,163	52,399	52,752	51,490
Persons killed in fatal crashes [1]..........	**41,945**	**32,999**	**32,893**	**32,744**	**35,484**	**37,806**	**37,473**	**36,560**
Occupants..........	33,451	23,371	22,483	22,307	23,899	25,276	25,127	24,221
Drivers..........	22,914	16,864	16,520	16,470	17,615	18,717	18,816	18,250
Passengers..........	10,451	6,451	5,896	5,766	6,213	6,485	6,237	5,915
Other..........	86	56	67	71	71	74	74	56
Motorcyclists..........	2,897	4,518	4,692	4,594	5,029	5,337	5,229	4,985
Nonoccupants..........	5,597	5,110	5,718	5,843	6,556	7,193	7,117	7,354
Pedestrians..........	4,763	4,302	4,779	4,910	5,494	6,080	6,075	6,283
Pedalcyclists..........	693	623	749	729	829	853	806	857
Other..........	141	185	190	204	233	260	236	214
Occupants killed by vehicle type:								
Passenger cars..........	20,699	12,491	12,037	11,947	12,763	13,508	13,477	12,775
Mini-compact (95 inches)..........	1,113	171	(NA)	(NA)	135	131	145	176
Subcompact (95 to 99 inches)..........	3,660	1,259	(NA)	(NA)	1,018	885	949	859
Compact (100 to 104 inches)..........	7,022	3,977	(NA)	(NA)	3,532	3,454	3,475	3,252
Intermediate (105 to 109) inches..........	5,204	4,244	(NA)	(NA)	4,621	4,696	5,148	4,801
Full-size (110 to 114) inches..........	2,287	1,993	(NA)	(NA)	2,353	2,418	2,478	2,482
Largest (115 inches and over)..........	897	685	(NA)	(NA)	796	835	912	794
Unknown..........	516	162	(NA)	(NA)	308	1,089	370	411
Motorcycles and other motorized cycles..........	2,897	4,518	4,692	4,594	5,029	5,337	5,229	4,985
Motorcycles..........	2,783	4,281	4,356	4,270	4,696	4,971	4,784	4,569
Other motorized cycles..........	114	237	336	324	333	366	445	416
Light trucks [2]..........	11,526	9,782	9,186	9,103	9,878	10,279	10,186	9,922
Pickup..........	6,003	4,486	4,175	4,249	4,470	4,446	4,307	4,253
Utility..........	3,358	3,942	3,831	3,800	4,213	4,462	4,610	4,534
Van..........	2,129	1,346	1,142	1,021	1,128	1,240	1,175	1,077
Other..........	36	8	38	33	67	131	94	58
Large trucks [3]..........	754	530	695	656	665	815	878	885
Buses..........	22	44	54	44	49	64	43	43
Other/unknown vehicles..........	450	524	511	557	544	610	543	596
Persons killed, and distribution by highest driver BAC in the crash [6]..........	41,945	32,999	32,893	32,744	35,484	37,806	37,473	36,560
0.00 percent..........	62	64	63	64	65	65	66	66
0.01 to 0.07 percent..........	6	5	6	5	5	5	5	5
0.08 percent and over..........	32	31	31	30	29	29	29	29
Drivers in fatal crashes by BAC [6]..........	57,280	44,599	44,803	44,671	49,163	52,399	52,752	51,490
0.00 percent..........	42,643	33,190	33,478	33,438	37,529	40,005	40,478	39,541
0.01 to 0.07 percent..........	2,376	1,812	1,850	1,837	1,964	2,041	1,920	1,939
0.08 percent and over..........	12,261	9,598	9,475	9,396	9,670	10,353	10,354	10,011
Fatalities per 100,000 resident population:								
Under 5 years old..........	3.70	2.00	1.98	1.71	1.90	2.01	2.03	1.74
5 to 9 years old..........	3.55	1.74	1.67	1.72	1.73	1.88	1.58	1.64
10 to 15 years old..........	5.65	2.71	2.37	2.27	2.46	2.66	2.50	2.08
16 to 20 years old..........	29.38	15.44	13.86	14.12	14.85	15.20	14.72	13.58
21 to 24 years old..........	27.02	19.49	18.14	17.85	18.91	20.07	18.79	18.20
25 to 34 years old..........	17.29	13.47	13.44	13.40	14.40	15.51	15.07	14.73
35 to 44 years old..........	15.08	11.09	10.87	10.48	11.63	12.40	12.50	12.09
45 to 54 years old..........	13.79	11.32	11.35	11.34	12.32	12.54	12.71	12.34
55 to 64 years old..........	13.61	10.94	11.12	11.01	11.91	12.61	12.85	12.73
65 to 74 years old..........	15.29	10.96	10.93	10.43	11.42	12.06	11.12	11.52
75 years old and over..........	23.29	16.80	15.23	15.02	15.36	16.47	16.82	15.47
Fatalities per 100 million VMT [4]..........	1.53	1.11	1.10	1.08	1.15	1.19	1.17	1.13
Fatalities per 100,000 licensed drivers..........	22.00	15.71	15.50	15.29	16.27	17.05	16.63	16.07
VMT per registered vehicle [4]..........	12,657	11,531	11,096	11,011	11,002	11,020	11,061	10,908
Fatalities per 100,000 registered vehicles..........	19.33	12.82	12.21	11.92	12.61	13.13	12.90	12.31
Fatal crashes per 100 million VMT [4]..........	1.37	1.02	1.01	0.99	1.05	1.09	1.08	1.04
Fatalities per 100,000 resident population..........	14.87	10.67	10.41	10.28	11.06	11.70	11.52	11.17
Vehicle miles traveled (VMT) (bil.)..........	2,747	2,967	2,988	3,026	3,095	3,174	3,212	3,240
Licensed drivers (1,000)..........	190,625	210,115	212,160	214,092	218,084	221,712	225,346	227,558
Registered vehicles (1,000) [5]..........	217,028	257,312	269,294	274,805	281,312	288,034	290,387	297,043

NA Not available. [1] Deaths within 30 days of the accident. Starting with 1995, total does not include motorcyclist data. [2] Trucks with a gross vehicle weight rating of 10,000 pounds or less, including pickups, vans, truck-based station wagons, and utility vehicles. [3] Trucks with a gross vehicle weight rating of over 10,000 pounds. [4] VMT = vehicle miles of travel. [5] Data on motor vehicle registrations for 2011 and beyond are not strictly comparable to data for prior years due to methodology changes. See source for details. [6] BAC = blood alcohol concentration. NHTSA estimates alcohol involvement when test results are unknown. Includes crashes in which there was no driver present.

Source: National Highway Traffic Safety Administration, *Traffic Safety Facts, 2017*, and earlier reports; "Traffic Safety Facts Annual Report Tables," <https://cdan.nhtsa.gov/tsftables/tsfar.htm> accessed July 2020; and "Fatality Analysis Reporting System," <nhtsa.gov/FARS>, accessed July 2020.

Table 1128. Vehicles Involved in Crashes by Vehicle Type, Rollover Occurrence, and Crash Severity: 2018

[Excludes motorcycles. Beginning 2016, data for injury and property damage only crashes are not comparable to previous years due to a new data collection system. The National Automotive Sampling System (NASS) General Estimates System (GES) was replaced with the Crash Report Sampling System (CRSS). See <crashstats.nhtsa.dot.gov/Api/Public/ViewPublication/812509> for details]

Crash severity by vehicle type	Total	Rollover occurrence				
		Yes			No	
	Number	Number	Percent		Number	Percent
Vehicles involved in all crashes [1]......	**11,940,000**	**234,000**	**2.0**		**11,706,000**	**98.0**
Passenger cars......	6,658,000	89,000	1.3		6,569,000	98.7
Light trucks: [2]						
Pickup......	1,563,000	52,000	3.3		1,511,000	96.7
Utility......	2,484,000	65,000	2.6		2,419,000	97.4
Van......	597,000	6,000	1.1		590,000	98.9
Other......	26,000	1,000	3.4		26,000	96.6
Large truck [3]......	531,000	19,000	3.7		512,000	96.3
Bus......	65,000	(Z)	0.6		65,000	99.4
Other/unknown......	16,000	2,000	10.9		14,000	89.1
Fatal crashes......	**46,757**	**7,488**	**16.0**		**39,269**	**84.0**
Passenger cars......	20,333	2,467	12.1		17,866	87.9
Light trucks: [2]						
Pickup......	8,652	1,853	21.4		6,799	78.6
Utility......	8,927	1,990	22.3		6,937	77.7
Van......	2,081	254	12.2		1,827	87.8
Other......	115	38	33.0		77	67.0
Large truck [3]......	4,862	592	12.2		4,270	87.8
Bus......	234	13	5.6		221	94.4
Other/unknown......	1,553	281	18.1		1,272	81.9
Injury crashes......	**3,409,000**	**134,000**	**3.9**		**3,275,000**	**96.1**
Passenger cars......	1,960,000	55,000	2.8		1,905,000	97.2
Light trucks: [2]						
Pickup......	436,000	29,000	6.6		407,000	93.4
Utility......	707,000	37,000	5.2		670,000	94.8
Van......	166,000	3,000	2.1		163,000	97.9
Other......	6,000	1,000	10.1		5,000	89.9
Large truck [3]......	112,000	8,000	6.8		105,000	93.2
Bus......	15,000	(Z)	1.9		15,000	98.1
Other/unknown......	7,000	1,000	14.0		6,000	86.0

Z less than 500 or 0.05 percent. [1] Includes property-only crashes, not shown separately. [2] Light trucks of 10,000 pounds gross vehicle weight rating or less, including pickups, vans, truck-based station wagons and utility vehicles. [3] Large trucks over 10,000 pounds gross vehicle weight rating.

Source: U.S. National Highway Traffic Safety Administration, "Traffic Safety Facts Annual Report Tables," <cdan.nhtsa.gov/tsftables/tsfar.htm>, accessed July 2020. See also <nhtsa.gov/research>.

Table 1129. Distracted Drivers—Crashes, Road Fatalities, and Injuries: 2010 to 2018

["Distraction" is defined as a specific type of inattention that occurs when drivers divert their attention from the driving task to focus on some other activity instead. "Distraction" is a subset of "inattention" (which also includes fatigue and physical and emotional conditions of the driver). For more information, including revision in coding of "distracted driving," see appendix in source report]

Description	2010	2013	2014	2015	2016	2017	2018
FATAL CRASHES [1]							
Total......	30,196	30,202	30,056	32,538	34,748	34,560	33,654
Drivers involved......	44,440	44,574	44,583	48,613	51,914	52,274	51,490
Fatalities......	32,885	32,719	32,675	35,092	37,461	37,133	36,560
Crashes involving driver distraction [2]......	**2,993**	**2,923**	**2,972**	**3,242**	**3,157**	**2,935**	**2,628**
Percent......	10	10	10	10	9	9	8
Involving cell phone use......	366	411	387	453	444	401	349
Percent......	12	14	13	14	14	14	13
Drivers involved......	2,912	2,959	3,000	3,263	3,210	2,994	2,688
Percent......	7	7	7	7	6	6	5
Fatalities......	3,092	3,154	3,179	3,477	3,450	3,166	2,841
Percent......	9	10	10	10	9	9	8
INJURY CRASHES (ESTIMATED) [3]							
Total......	1,542,000	1,591,000	1,648,000	1,715,000	2,116,000	1,889,000	1,894,000
People injured......	2,239,000	2,313,000	2,343,000	2,455,000	3,062,000	2,745,000	2,710,000
In crashes involving driver distraction......	416,000	424,000	430,000	393,000	445,000	435,000	400,000
Percent of total......	19	18	18	16	15	16	15
In crashes involving cell phone use......	24,000	34,000	34,000	30,000	34,000	31,000	33,000
Percent of total distracted......	6	8	8	8	8	7	8

[1] Data from NHTSA's Fatality Analysis Reporting System (FARS). [2] For multiple-vehicle crashes, the crash was reported as a distracted-driving crash if at least one driver was reported as distracted. In some of these multiple-vehicle crashes, multiple drivers were reported as distracted. [3] Data for 2010 to 2015 are from the National Automotive Sampling System (NASS) General Estimates System (GES). Beginning 2016, data are from the Crash Report Sampling System (CRSS). CRSS estimates and NASS GES estimates are not comparable due to different sample designs. See <http://www.nhtsa.gov/crash-data-systems/crash-report-sampling-system-crss> for details.

Source: U.S. National Highway Traffic Safety Administration, *Distracted Driving, 2018*, April 2020, and earlier reports. See also <https://crashstats.nhtsa.dot.gov> and <https://www.nhtsa.gov/risky-driving/distracted-driving>.

Table 1130. Traffic Fatalities by State and Highest Driver Blood Alcohol Concentration (BAC) in the Crash: 2018

[A crash is a police-reported event that produces injury and/or property damage, involves a vehicle in transport and occurs on a trafficway or while the vehicle is in motion after running off the trafficway. A positive blood alcohol concentration (BAC level of .01 grams per deciliter and higher) indicates that alcohol was consumed by the person tested, and the incident is alcohol related or alcohol involved; a BAC level of .08 g/dL or more indicates that the person was alcohol impaired]

State	Traffic fatalities, total [1]	Traffic fatalities not involving alcohol (BAC=.00)		Alcohol involved driving fatalities (BAC=.01–.07)		Alcohol impaired driving fatalities (BAC=.08 or more)		Total fatalities involving alcohol (BAC=.01 or more)	
		Number	Percent	Number	Percent	Number	Percent	Number	Percent
United States [2]	**36,560**	**24,075**	**66**	**1,878**	**5**	**10,511**	**29**	**12,389**	**34**
Alabama	953	654	69	49	5	246	26	295	31
Alaska	80	44	55	7	9	29	36	36	45
Arizona	1,010	655	65	50	5	285	28	334	33
Arkansas	516	343	66	38	7	134	26	172	33
California	3,563	2,322	65	166	5	1,069	30	1,235	35
Colorado	632	411	65	31	5	188	30	219	35
Connecticut	294	162	55	17	6	115	39	132	45
Delaware	111	76	68	8	7	28	25	35	32
District of Columbia	31	21	66	2	5	9	29	11	34
Florida	3,133	2,175	69	135	4	814	26	950	30
Georgia	1,504	1,054	70	72	5	375	25	447	30
Hawaii	117	71	61	10	9	35	30	45	38
Idaho	231	165	72	8	4	58	25	66	28
Illinois	1,031	653	63	66	6	309	30	375	36
Indiana	858	587	68	39	5	227	26	266	31
Iowa	318	218	68	13	4	85	27	98	31
Kansas	404	306	76	9	2	88	22	96	24
Kentucky	724	552	76	31	4	137	19	169	23
Louisiana	768	516	67	35	5	216	28	251	33
Maine	137	88	64	8	6	42	30	49	36
Maryland	501	346	69	32	6	122	24	154	31
Massachusetts	360	214	59	24	7	120	33	145	40
Michigan	974	649	67	56	6	267	27	323	33
Minnesota	381	251	66	20	5	105	28	126	33
Mississippi	664	466	70	35	5	163	25	198	30
Missouri	921	639	69	39	4	240	26	279	30
Montana	182	95	52	8	4	79	43	87	48
Nebraska	230	152	66	12	5	66	29	78	34
Nevada	330	220	67	22	7	87	26	110	33
New Hampshire	147	92	63	7	5	48	33	55	37
New Jersey	564	404	72	35	6	125	22	159	28
New Mexico	391	251	64	30	8	108	28	138	35
New York	943	580	61	53	6	307	33	361	38
North Carolina	1,437	952	66	61	4	421	29	482	34
North Dakota	105	72	68	4	4	29	27	33	32
Ohio	1,068	724	68	45	4	294	28	340	32
Oklahoma	655	477	73	33	5	145	22	179	27
Oregon	506	321	63	31	6	153	30	184	36
Pennsylvania	1,190	801	67	53	4	334	28	387	33
Rhode Island	59	34	57	5	8	20	34	25	43
South Carolina	1,037	702	68	44	4	291	28	335	32
South Dakota	130	80	62	5	4	45	35	50	38
Tennessee	1,041	752	72	46	4	243	23	289	28
Texas	3,642	1,965	54	235	6	1,439	40	1,673	46
Utah	260	190	73	9	3	61	23	70	27
Vermont	68	45	66	8	12	15	23	23	34
Virginia	820	534	65	45	6	240	29	285	35
Washington	546	351	64	30	5	166	30	195	36
West Virginia	294	223	76	14	5	57	19	71	24
Wisconsin	588	353	60	36	6	199	34	235	40
Wyoming	111	72	64	6	5	34	30	40	36
Puerto Rico	308	160	52	24	8	123	40	147	48

[1] Total fatalities include those in which there was no driver or motorcycle rider present. [2] U.S. total excludes Puerto Rico.

Source: U.S. National Highway Traffic Safety Administration, "Traffic Safety Facts Annual Report Tables," <https://cdan.nhtsa.gov/tsftables/tsfar.htm>, accessed July 2020. See also <nhtsa.gov/research>.

Table 1131. Alcohol Involvement for Drivers in Fatal Crashes: 2000 to 2018

[BAC = blood alcohol concentration. See headnote, Table 1130. NHTSA estimates alcohol involvement when alcohol test results are unknown, see source for more information]

Age, sex, and vehicle type	2000 Total drivers in fatal crashes	2000 Percent with .08% BAC or greater	2010 Total drivers in fatal crashes	2010 Percent with .08% BAC or greater	2015 Total drivers in fatal crashes	2015 Percent with .08% BAC or greater	2017 Total drivers in fatal crashes	2017 Percent with .08% BAC or greater	2018 Total drivers in fatal crashes	2018 Percent with .08% BAC or greater
Total drivers involved in fatal crashes [1]	**57,280**	**21**	**44,599**	**22**	**49,163**	**20**	**52,752**	**20**	**51,490**	**19**
Drivers by age group:										
Under 16 years old	320	10	159	6	155	9	145	7	126	8
16 to 20 years old	8,024	18	4,505	18	4,258	16	4,327	15	4,061	15
21 to 24 years old	5,950	32	4,608	34	5,014	28	5,070	27	4,777	27
25 to 34 years old	11,739	28	8,567	30	9,994	27	11,006	26	10,738	25
35 to 44 years old	11,132	26	7,333	25	7,768	23	8,284	23	8,110	21
45 to 54 years old	8,234	18	7,517	21	7,915	19	8,186	19	7,863	19
55 to 64 years old	4,766	12	5,577	14	6,525	14	7,316	15	7,261	15
65 to 74 years old	3,134	8	2,902	8	3,794	9	4,148	9	4,218	10
75 years old and over	3,147	4	2,688	4	2,762	6	3,151	6	3,098	7
Drivers by sex:										
Male	41,795	24	32,079	24	35,850	22	38,028	21	37,062	21
Female	14,790	13	11,859	15	12,382	14	13,673	14	13,269	14
Drivers by vehicle type:										
Passenger cars	27,661	24	17,710	24	19,689	21	21,133	20	20,175	21
Light trucks [2]	20,393	22	17,385	22	18,762	21	19,878	20	19,663	19
Large trucks [3]	4,948	1	3,456	1	4,020	2	4,746	3	4,786	3
Motorcycles	2,971	32	4,647	28	5,126	26	5,375	27	5,108	25

[1] Includes age and sex unknown, and other and unknown types of vehicles. [2] See footnote 2, Table 1128. [3] See footnote 3, Table 1128.

Source: U.S. National Highway Traffic Safety Administration, "Traffic Safety Facts Annual Report Tables," <https://cdan.nhtsa.gov/tsftables/tsfar.htm>, accessed July 2020. See also <nhtsa.gov/research>.

Table 1132. Fatalities by Highest Driver Blood Alcohol Concentration (BAC) in the Crash: 2000 to 2018

[A motor vehicle crash is alcohol impaired if at least one driver involved in the crash is determined to have a BAC of .08 gram per deciliter (g/dl) or higher. Thus, any fatality that occurs in an alcohol impaired crash is considered an alcohol impaired driving fatality. A person is considered to be legally impaired with a BAC of .08 g/dl or more. See source for more information]

Item	2000	2005	2010	2014	2015	2016	2017	2018
Total fatalities [1]	**41,945**	**43,510**	**32,999**	**32,744**	**35,484**	**37,806**	**37,473**	**36,560**
BAC=.00								
Number	26,082	27,423	21,005	20,913	23,165	24,762	24,580	24,075
Percent	62.2	63.0	63.7	63.9	65.3	65.5	65.6	65.9
BAC=.01–.07								
Number	2,422	2,404	1,771	1,800	1,930	1,984	1,876	1,878
Percent	5.8	5.5	5.4	5.5	5.4	5.2	5.0	5.1
Alcohol impaired driving fatalities:								
BAC=.08 or more								
Number	13,324	13,582	10,136	9,943	10,280	10,967	10,908	10,511
Percent	31.8	31.2	30.7	30.4	29.0	29.0	29.1	28.8

[1] Total fatalities include those in which there was no driver or motorcycle rider present.

Source: U.S. National Highway Traffic Safety Administration, "Traffic Safety Facts Annual Report Tables," <https://cdan.nhtsa.gov/tsftables/tsfar.htm>, accessed July 2020. See also <nhtsa.gov/research>.

Table 1133. Motor Vehicle Crashes by Crash Severity: 2000 to 2018

[6,394 represents 6,394,000. A crash is a police-reported event that produces injury and/or property damage, involves a vehicle in transport, and occurs on a trafficway or while the vehicle is in motion after running off the trafficway. A fatal crash involves at least 1 person dying within 30 days of the crash. Beginning 2016, data for injury and property damage crashes are not comparable to previous years due to a new data collection system. The National Automotive Sampling System (NASS) General Estimates System (GES) was replaced with the Crash Report Sampling System (CRSS). See <https://crashstats.nhtsa.dot.gov/Api/Public/ViewPublication/812509> for details]

Item	2000	2010	2012	2013	2014	2015	2016 [1]	2017 [1]	2018 [1]
Crashes (1,000)	**6,394**	**5,419**	**5,615**	**5,687**	**6,064**	**6,296**	**6,821**	**6,453**	**6,734**
Fatal	37.5	30.3	31.0	30.2	30.1	32.5	34.7	34.6	33.7
Nonfatal injury	2,070	1,542	1,634	1,591	1,648	1,715	2,116	1,889	1,894
Property damage only	4,286	3,847	3,950	4,066	4,387	4,548	4,670	4,530	4,807
Percent of total crashes:									
Fatal	0.6	0.6	0.6	0.5	0.5	0.5	0.5	0.5	0.5
Nonfatal injury	32.4	28.5	29.1	28.0	27.2	27.2	31.0	29.3	28.1
Property damage only	67.0	71.0	70.3	71.5	72.3	72.2	68.5	70.2	71.4

[1] Beginning 2016, injury and property damage only data are not comparable to previous years due to a new data collection system. Numbers are not actual counts but estimates of actual counts.

Source: U.S. National Highway Traffic Safety Administration, "Traffic Safety Facts Annual Report Tables," <https://cdan.nhtsa.gov/tsftables/tsfar.htm>, accessed July 2020. See also <nhtsa.gov/research>.

Table 1134. Motor Vehicle Crashes—Number and Deaths: 2000 to 2018

[6,394 represents 6,394,000. Beginning 2016, data for injury and property damage crashes are not comparable to previous years due to a new data collection system. The National Automotive Sampling System (NASS) General Estimates System (GES) was replaced with the Crash Report Sampling System (CRSS). See <https://crashstats.nhtsa.dot.gov/Api/Public/ViewPublication/812509> for details]

Item	Unit	2000	2010	2013	2014	2015	2016	2017	2018
CRASHES									
Total [1,2]	1,000	6,394	5,419	5,687	6,064	6,296	6,821	6,453	6,734
Fatal	1,000	38	30	30	30	33	35	35	34
Injury [2]	1,000	2,070	1,542	1,591	1,648	1,715	2,116	1,889	1,894
Property damage only [2]	1,000	4,286	3,847	4,066	4,387	4,548	4,670	4,530	4,807
DEATHS									
Deaths within 30 days of crash	Number	41,945	32,999	32,893	32,744	35,484	37,806	37,473	36,560
Occupants	Number	33,451	23,371	22,483	22,307	23,899	25,276	25,127	24,221
Passenger cars	Number	20,699	12,491	12,037	11,947	12,763	13,508	13,477	12,775
Light trucks [3]	Number	11,526	9,782	9,186	9,103	9,878	10,279	10,186	9,922
Large trucks [3]	Number	754	530	695	656	665	815	878	885
Buses	Number	22	44	54	44	49	64	43	43
Other/unknown	Number	450	524	511	557	544	610	543	596
Motorcycle riders [4]	Number	2,897	4,518	4,692	4,594	5,029	5,337	5,229	4,985
Nonoccupants	Number	5,597	5,110	5,718	5,843	6,556	7,193	7,117	7,354
Pedestrians	Number	4,763	4,302	4,779	4,910	5,494	6,080	6,075	6,283
Pedalcyclist	Number	693	623	749	729	829	853	806	857
Other/unknown	Number	141	185	190	204	233	260	236	214
TRAFFIC DEATH RATES [5]									
Per 100 million vehicle miles	Rate	1.5	1.1	1.1	1.1	1.2	1.2	1.2	1.1
Per 100,000 licensed drivers	Rate	22.0	15.7	15.5	15.3	16.3	17.1	16.6	16.1
Per 100,000 registered vehicles	Rate	19.3	12.8	12.2	11.9	12.6	13.1	12.9	12.3
Per 100,000 resident population	Rate	14.9	10.7	10.4	10.3	11.1	11.7	11.5	11.2

[1] Covers police-reported accidents in which at least one person dies within 30 days of the crash; or no one dies but at least one person is injured; or no one is injured but property damage has occurred. [2] Beginning 2016, injury and property damage only data are not comparable to previous years due to a new data collection system. Numbers are not actual counts but estimates of actual counts. [3] See footnotes 2 and 3 in Table 1128. [4] Includes motor scooters, minibikes, and mopeds. [5] Based on 30-day definition of traffic deaths.

Source: U.S. National Highway Traffic Safety Administration, "Traffic Safety Facts Annual Report Tables," <https://cdan.nhtsa.gov/tsftables/tsfar.htm>, accessed July 2020. See also <nhtsa.gov/research>.

Table 1135. Licensed Drivers and Number in Fatal Accidents by Age and Sex: 2018

[227,558 represents 227,558,000]

Age group	Licensed drivers (1,000)			Drivers in fatal accidents			Accident rates per number of drivers [1]	
	Total	Male	Female	Total	Male	Female	Male	Female
Total	**227,558**	**112,480**	**115,079**	**50,252**	**36,983**	**13,250**	**32.9**	**11.5**
19 years old and under	8,756	4,431	4,324	3,113	2,074	1,038	46.8	24.0
Under 16 years old	43	21	22	126	88	38	416.1	173.9
16 years old	1,066	525	541	356	224	132	42.7	24.4
17 years old	1,976	989	987	663	417	246	42.1	24.9
18 years old	2,630	1,340	1,290	924	621	302	46.3	23.4
19 years old	3,040	1,556	1,485	1,044	724	320	46.5	21.6
20 to 24 years old	17,519	8,876	8,643	5,851	4,237	1,613	47.7	18.7
20 years old	3,249	1,658	1,590	1,074	758	316	45.7	19.9
21 years old	3,355	1,706	1,649	1,211	875	335	51.3	20.3
22 years old	3,506	1,775	1,731	1,222	876	346	49.4	20.0
23 years old	3,645	1,842	1,803	1,204	878	326	47.7	18.1
24 years old	3,764	1,895	1,869	1,140	850	290	44.9	15.5
25 to 29 years old	20,186	10,099	10,088	5,778	4,261	1,514	42.2	15.0
30 to 34 years old	19,979	9,953	10,026	4,960	3,650	1,309	36.7	13.1
35 to 39 years old	19,603	9,725	9,877	4,304	3,183	1,120	32.7	11.3
40 to 44 years old	18,043	8,956	9,087	3,806	2,863	941	32.0	10.4
45 to 49 years old	19,198	9,550	9,648	4,003	3,044	957	31.9	9.9
50 to 54 years old	19,445	9,665	9,779	3,860	2,949	910	30.5	9.3
55 to 59 years old	20,539	10,134	10,405	4,023	3,079	942	30.4	9.1
60 to 64 years old	19,042	9,328	9,713	3,238	2,434	800	26.1	8.2
65 to 69 years old	15,942	7,759	8,183	2,397	1,758	639	22.7	7.8
70 to 74 years old	12,252	5,963	6,289	1,821	1,334	486	22.4	7.7
75 to 79 years old	8,054	3,878	4,176	1,310	891	419	23.0	10.0
80 to 84 years old	4,936	2,315	2,621	925	635	290	27.4	11.1
85 and over	4,065	1,847	2,218	863	591	272	32.0	12.3

[1] Per 100,000 male or female licensed drivers. Rates for drivers 19 years old and under are likely overstated because of a higher proportion of unlicensed drivers.

Source: U.S. Federal Highway Administration, "Highway Statistics 2018," <https://www.fhwa.dot.gov/policyinformation/>; and National Highway Traffic Safety Administration, "Fatality and Injury Reporting System Tool," <cdan.dot.gov/query>; accessed September 2020.

Table 1136. Speeding-Related Traffic Fatalities by Road Type and State: 2018

[Speeding consists of exceeding the posted speed limit or driving too fast for the road conditions or any speed-related violation charged (racing, driving above speed limit, speed greater than reasonable, exceeding special speed limit)]

| State | Traffic fatalities, total | Speeding-related fatalities by roadway function class | | | | | | | |
| | | Total [2] | Interstate | | Non-interstate | | | | |
			Rural	Urban	Freeway and expressway	Other principal arterial	Minor arterial	Collector	Local
United States [1]	36,560	9,378	491	862	396	2,343	1,968	1,757	1,481
Alabama....................	953	262	16	18	–	48	54	90	36
Alaska.....................	80	42	9	6	–	6	6	14	1
Arizona....................	1,010	285	38	25	22	57	74	34	31
Arkansas..................	516	131	6	9	–	37	23	19	37
California..................	3,563	927	39	133	117	259	153	121	105
Colorado..................	632	210	12	15	7	69	50	31	26
Connecticut...............	294	90	–	14	11	15	25	12	13
Delaware..................	111	33	–	2	5	5	3	12	6
District of Columbia.......	31	15	–	1	–	–	1	–	13
Florida....................	3,133	303	6	11	11	89	61	39	42
Georgia...................	1,504	267	4	29	5	53	69	59	48
Hawaii....................	117	51	–	6	–	26	19	–	–
Idaho.....................	231	46	2	2	–	14	8	8	12
Illinois....................	1,031	434	22	55	–	113	105	82	57
Indiana...................	858	188	14	11	–	44	34	61	24
Iowa......................	318	62	10	5	–	11	11	13	12
Kansas....................	404	94	13	7	4	17	10	14	29
Kentucky..................	724	111	9	4	1	27	22	32	15
Louisiana.................	768	136	6	17	1	30	22	33	27
Maine....................	137	42	1	1	–	8	9	17	6
Maryland.................	501	123	2	18	5	27	32	16	18
Massachusetts............	360	95	–	16	2	23	26	13	14
Michigan..................	974	245	5	30	13	44	61	52	40
Minnesota................	381	113	5	9	–	21	42	25	9
Mississippi...............	664	48	–	4	–	7	7	18	12
Missouri..................	921	367	19	25	24	82	80	74	63
Montana..................	182	67	8	1	1	22	6	13	16
Nebraska.................	230	29	8	–	–	3	6	7	5
Nevada...................	330	92	6	5	5	27	27	10	11
New Hampshire...........	147	71	6	7	–	18	10	8	22
New Jersey...............	564	114	1	6	9	42	25	8	23
New Mexico...............	391	132	8	5	–	45	18	29	26
New York.................	943	274	13	10	18	75	28	14	116
North Carolina............	1,437	327	10	32	6	149	30	33	67
North Dakota.............	105	40	6	–	–	15	5	9	5
Ohio......................	1,068	290	9	24	9	39	46	92	64
Oklahoma.................	655	147	4	12	6	27	31	38	29
Oregon...................	506	110	4	–	–	37	30	30	9
Pennsylvania..............	1,190	455	23	33	22	89	108	92	88
Rhode Island..............	59	27	1	5	5	6	2	–	8
South Carolina............	1,037	447	44	25	9	90	211	19	49
South Dakota.............	130	52	7	1	5	15	9	7	8
Tennessee................	1,041	167	3	15	2	30	43	38	36
Texas.....................	3,642	990	50	136	64	268	164	220	87
Utah......................	260	70	5	6	–	30	10	10	8
Vermont..................	68	25	4	–	–	2	5	8	6
Virginia...................	820	241	8	23	3	51	56	67	25
Washington...............	546	179	8	23	–	48	39	40	18
West Virginia..............	294	88	4	9	–	16	17	27	15
Wisconsin.................	588	186	5	11	4	53	32	41	39
Wyoming..................	111	38	8	–	–	14	3	8	5
Puerto Rico...............	308	82	12	6	2	17	18	21	6

– Represents zero. [1] U.S. totals do not include Puerto Rico. [2] Includes fatalities that occurred on roads for which the type was unknown.

Source: U.S. National Highway Traffic Safety Administration, "Traffic Safety Facts Annual Report Tables," <https://cdan.nhtsa.gov/tsftables/tsfar.htm>, accessed July 2020. See also <nhtsa.gov/research>.

Table 1137. Roadway Traffic Congestion by Urbanized Area: 2017

[16,736 represents 16,736,000. Various federal, state, and local information sources were used to develop the database with the primary source being the Federal Highway Administration's Highway Performance Monitoring System]

Urbanized area	Daily vehicle miles of travel (1,000)		Annual person hours of delay		Annual congestion cost [1]		
	Freeway	Arterial streets	Total hours (1,000)	Per auto commuter [2]	Delay and fuel cost (million dollars)	Per person (dollars) [2]	Fuel wasted (gal. per person) [2]
101 Urban Areas, average [3].............	**16,736**	**15,485**	**74,303**	**66**	**1,502**	**1,324**	**26**
Akron, OH.............................	6,191	4,498	15,352	37	312	681	17
Albany-Schenectady, NY..................	6,470	5,523	17,489	49	356	736	21
Albuquerque, NM.......................	5,547	7,760	23,302	44	474	936	20
Allentown, PA-NJ.......................	5,585	5,324	18,068	38	369	653	16
Atlanta, GA............................	55,427	54,375	237,405	77	4,754	1,653	31
Austin, TX.............................	15,552	14,037	68,187	66	1,368	1,391	25
Baltimore, MD.........................	31,098	19,243	93,815	59	1,897	1,046	22
Birmingham, AL........................	12,334	9,132	22,877	40	461	819	16
Boston, MA-NH-RI......................	44,199	41,908	189,426	80	3,829	1,580	31
Bridgeport-Stamford, CT-NY..............	10,497	5,956	38,789	57	785	991	22
Buffalo, NY............................	6,796	9,959	31,977	48	652	965	23
Charleston-North, Charleston, SC..........	4,398	6,998	21,087	51	425	948	22
Charlotte, NC-SC.......................	16,721	14,359	50,641	57	1,015	1,269	22
Chicago, IL-IN.........................	60,644	74,827	352,759	73	7,150	1,431	30
Cincinnati, OH-KY-IN...................	19,442	14,116	64,061	52	1,301	1,110	25
Cleveland, OH.........................	18,958	13,290	56,070	46	1,144	970	23
Colorado Springs, CO...................	5,412	5,640	17,883	43	362	785	19
Columbus OH..........................	17,182	13,137	51,381	50	1,041	1,054	21
Dallas-Fort, Worth-Arlington, TX...........	71,557	47,773	224,883	67	4,511	1,272	25
Dayton, OH...........................	7,964	6,311	17,377	32	353	601	13
Denver-Aurora, CO.....................	26,961	23,413	107,463	61	2,177	1,163	25
Detroit, MI............................	34,296	46,371	165,339	61	3,352	1,129	25
El Paso, TX-NM........................	6,786	6,731	22,711	41	458	794	17
Fresno, CA............................	4,462	5,339	19,311	40	396	779	19
Grand Rapids, MI.......................	6,107	7,873	19,417	41	394	716	16
Hartford, CT...........................	11,328	7,800	27,436	50	557	881	20
Honolulu, HI...........................	6,488	3,267	36,378	64	753	1,374	29
Houston, TX...........................	59,793	48,044	247,440	75	4,982	1,508	31
Indianapolis, IN........................	15,336	16,898	43,003	48	876	813	22
Jackson, MS...........................	5,039	6,377	10,999	42	220	684	13
Jacksonville, FL........................	13,537	9,625	34,792	46	698	893	15
Kansas City, MO-KS....................	24,488	13,778	48,328	47	974	837	15
Las Vegas -Henderson, NV..............	12,787	16,510	67,761	51	1,377	932	20
Los Angeles-Long Beach-Anaheim, CA....	133,061	117,129	971,478	119	19,490	2,676	35
Louisville-Jefferson Co., KY-IN..............	10,536	7,760	29,392	46	595	726	18
Memphis, TN-MS-AR....................	10,000	14,320	28,015	48	565	651	18
Miami, FL..............................	46,868	53,296	265,947	69	5,367	1,412	34
Milwaukee, WI.........................	12,550	16,089	42,146	46	862	864	23
Minneapolis-St Paul, MN-WI..............	32,969	25,956	103,695	56	2,078	980	18
Nashville-Davidson, TN..................	21,128	14,619	52,249	58	1,055	1,217	26
New Haven, CT.........................	7,695	4,182	15,574	45	316	767	18
New Orleans, LA.......................	7,024	9,349	55,833	58	1,127	1,208	26
New York-Newark, NY-NJ-CT..............	124,035	106,014	811,609	92	16,466	1,947	38
Oklahoma City, OK.....................	11,995	10,737	43,448	50	874	842	21
Omaha, NE-IA.........................	6,571	6,500	19,117	38	388	674	17
Orlando, FL............................	16,405	18,899	63,205	57	1,275	1,103	22
Oxnard, CA............................	2,091	3,145	9,548	34	193	709	11
Philadelphia, PA-NJ-DE-MD..............	39,913	46,597	194,655	62	3,967	1,203	26
Phoenix-Mesa, AZ......................	32,587	40,584	163,247	62	3,300	1,089	26
Pittsburgh, PA.........................	11,593	14,523	51,370	46	1,052	908	21
Portland, OR-WA.......................	14,717	14,738	88,009	66	1,806	1,305	31
Providence, RI-MA......................	12,201	10,588	36,273	48	736	828	19
Raleigh, NC...........................	10,593	12,468	27,243	42	546	794	16
Richmond, VA..........................	13,280	10,264	24,461	35	490	641	17
Riverside-San Bernardino, CA..............	26,237	13,554	107,411	70	2,154	1,288	20
Sacramento, CA........................	17,750	13,064	76,437	59	1,557	1,118	24
Salt Lake City-West Valley City, UT.........	9,521	9,755	29,739	45	612	833	25
San Antonio, TX........................	24,890	16,751	69,982	51	1,407	964	22
San Diego, CA.........................	41,237	21,102	148,503	64	2,960	1,584	24
San Francisco-Oakland, CA..............	39,755	20,843	253,838	103	5,175	2,619	39
San Jose, CA..........................	18,250	14,127	126,774	81	2,577	1,643	32
Seattle, WA............................	30,675	27,622	167,384	78	3,405	1,541	31
St Louis, MO-IL........................	32,408	19,150	71,481	46	1,442	898	19
Tampa-St Petersburg, FL.................	17,361	31,509	85,860	50	1,730	987	20
Toledo, OH-MI.........................	4,362	4,748	15,407	40	313	757	21
Tucson, AZ............................	3,972	10,272	32,305	52	655	831	20
Tulsa, OK.............................	8,541	8,090	25,228	46	508	732	17
Virginia Beach, VA......................	12,882	14,932	40,510	46	812	758	15
Washington, DC-VA-MD..................	46,139	43,718	247,811	102	5,010	2,015	38
Worcester, MA.........................	6,916	5,825	14,173	43	287	823	17

[1] Value of extra time (delay) and the extra fuel consumed by vehicles traveling at slower speeds. Fuel cost per gallon is the average price for each state. [2] Per auto commuter data are based on estimated commuters in the urban area. [3] Includes additional areas not shown below.

Source: Texas A&M Transportation Institute, College Station, Texas, *Urban Mobility Report 2019*, August 2019, revised ©. See also <http://mobility.tamu.edu>.

Table 1138. Commuting to Work by Transportation Method and State: 2018

[In percent, except as indicated. Workers in thousands (154,609 represents 154,609,000). For workers 16 years old and over. The American Community Survey universe includes the household population and the population living in institutions, college dormitories, and other group quarters. Based on a sample and subject to sampling variability; see Appendix III]

| State | Total workers (1,000) | Car, truck, or van | | Public transportation [1] | Walking | Taxi, motorcycle, bicycle or other means | Working at home | Mean travel time to work (minutes) |
		Drove alone	Car-pooled					
U.S.	**154,609**	**76.3**	**9.0**	**4.9**	**2.6**	**1.9**	**5.3**	**27.1**
AL.	2,068	86.3	7.9	0.3	1.1	1.0	3.5	25.2
AK.	355	68.0	12.3	1.2	7.8	5.5	5.3	19.1
AZ.	3,175	76.1	11.0	1.7	1.7	2.7	6.8	25.7
AR.	1,301	82.6	10.4	0.4	1.5	1.3	3.7	21.7
CA.	18,530	73.8	10.0	4.9	2.6	2.6	6.0	30.2
CO.	2,963	74.9	8.6	2.8	3.0	2.2	8.6	25.9
CT.	1,793	77.9	8.1	4.4	2.6	1.2	5.7	26.8
DE.	453	79.6	9.1	2.2	2.4	1.1	5.7	26.4
DC.	378	34.2	5.1	34.4	13.3	6.8	6.1	30.9
FL.	9,609	79.1	9.4	1.7	1.4	2.4	6.2	28.0
GA.	4,891	79.4	9.4	2.0	1.5	1.8	5.9	29.0
HI.	707	67.3	14.7	5.7	3.7	3.2	5.4	27.6
ID.	795	79.7	8.9	0.8	2.5	1.9	6.2	21.0
IL.	6,192	72.7	8.3	9.4	2.8	1.7	5.1	29.4
IN.	3,175	82.9	8.9	0.9	1.9	1.5	3.9	23.9
IA.	1,589	81.6	8.1	1.0	3.0	1.2	5.1	19.5
KS.	1,435	82.0	9.3	0.5	2.2	1.3	4.8	19.7
KY.	1,965	82.4	9.4	1.0	2.0	1.2	4.1	23.5
LA.	1,994	82.7	9.0	1.2	1.8	1.9	3.4	26.3
ME.	666	77.8	9.9	0.6	4.1	1.7	6.0	24.1
MD.	3,066	74.3	8.8	7.9	2.1	1.6	5.2	33.3
MA.	3,559	69.8	7.4	10.2	5.1	2.2	5.3	30.5
MI.	4,616	82.0	8.9	1.4	2.3	1.3	4.1	24.7
MN.	2,923	77.7	8.4	3.6	2.8	1.5	6.1	23.8
MS.	1,217	85.5	8.9	0.3	1.4	1.4	2.6	25.0
MO.	2,891	82.2	8.4	1.3	2.0	1.2	4.8	24.0
MT.	515	74.9	9.5	0.8	5.5	2.1	7.3	18.6
NE.	986	82.1	8.7	0.6	2.5	1.1	5.1	18.8
NV.	1,427	78.3	10.5	2.9	1.8	2.4	4.2	24.9
NH.	714	80.8	7.4	0.9	2.6	1.5	6.9	27.6
NJ.	4,398	70.9	8.2	11.7	2.6	2.0	4.7	32.4
NM.	875	79.3	11.2	1.1	1.8	1.5	5.1	23.0
NY.	9,311	53.1	6.3	28.0	6.0	2.1	4.5	34.0
NC.	4,859	80.6	9.3	1.0	1.8	1.2	6.0	24.8
ND.	399	82.2	8.7	0.7	3.4	1.2	3.7	17.7
OH.	5,524	82.4	8.2	1.6	2.2	1.2	4.4	23.6
OK.	1,777	82.5	9.5	0.5	2.0	1.4	4.1	22.1
OR.	1,995	71.7	9.5	4.2	3.9	3.2	7.5	23.8
PA.	6,136	75.6	8.5	5.8	3.5	1.5	5.1	27.2
RI.	520	81.3	8.1	2.2	3.4	1.2	3.7	25.0
SC.	2,303	81.4	9.4	0.6	2.1	1.5	5.0	25.1
SD.	448	81.1	8.8	0.3	2.8	0.9	6.2	17.3
TN.	3,093	83.1	9.0	0.6	1.3	1.3	4.7	25.4
TX.	13,337	80.7	9.8	1.3	1.5	1.5	5.2	26.7
UT.	1,514	75.7	11.1	2.2	2.4	1.6	6.9	22.0
VT.	324	75.4	9.0	0.9	5.2	2.1	7.5	23.6
VA.	4,221	76.7	9.1	4.5	2.2	1.9	5.6	28.7
WA.	3,660	71.0	9.8	7.0	3.7	2.1	6.5	28.4
WV.	727	83.3	8.6	0.9	2.6	1.3	3.4	26.5
WI.	2,957	81.7	7.5	1.5	2.9	1.5	4.8	22.0
WY.	285	75.8	10.2	1.2	4.3	2.3	6.2	16.2
PR.	981	84.2	7.9	1.8	2.1	1.8	2.3	30.3

[1] Excluding taxicabs.

Source: U.S. Census Bureau, 2018 American Community Survey, B08006, "Sex of Workers by Means of Transportation to Work," and DP03, "Selected Economic Characteristics," <http://data.census.gov/>, accessed January 2020.

Table 1139. Use of Ride Hailing Services by Age Group: 2017

[Data from the 2017 National Household Travel Survey. Approximately 8% of the U.S. population used a ride-hailing service (services such as Uber and Lyft) at least once in the last 30 days. Age groups are based on Pew Research Center definitions]

Item	Millennials, aged 21 to 36	Generation X, aged 37 to 52	Baby Boomers, aged 53 to 71	Matures, aged 72 and over
Used ride-hailing service (percent)	19	10	5	2
Total respondents (millions) [2]	**8.6**	**6.3**	**6.9**	**1.4**
Used public transit and ride hailing	4.8	2.1	1.1	0.1
Used public transit but not ride hailing	3.8	4.2	5.8	1.3

[1] Data shown for metropolitan statistical areas with populations of 3 million or more people.

Source: U.S. Department of Transportation, Federal Highway Administration, *Changing Attitudes and Transportation Choices, 2017 National Household Travel Survey*, February 2019. See also <https://nhts.ornl.gov/>.

Table 1140. Passenger Transit Industry—Summary: 1990 to 2018

[16,053 represents $16,053,000,000. Includes Puerto Rico. Includes aggregate information for all transit systems in the United States. Excludes nontransit services such as taxicab, school bus, unregulated jitney (a small bus or automobile that transports passengers on a route for a small fare), sightseeing bus, intercity bus, and special application mass transportation systems (e.g., amusement parks, airports, island, and urban park ferries). Includes active vehicles only]

Item	Unit	1990	2000	2010	2015	2016	2017	2018
Operating systems	Number	5,078	6,000	7,088	6,752	6,719	6,770	6,704
Motor bus systems	Number	2,688	2,262	1,206	1,163	1,232	1,226	1,241
Revenue vehicles, active	Number	93,430	131,089	174,425	183,601	179,021	181,652	181,541
Motor bus	Number	58,714	75,013	66,239	72,075	71,956	72,338	71,743
Commuter rail	Number	4,982	5,498	6,927	7,216	7,350	7,290	7,184
Demand response [1]	Number	16,471	33,080	68,621	71,299	68,059	69,316	70,093
Heavy rail	Number	10,567	10,311	11,510	10,737	10,775	10,705	10,763
Surface rail (light rail, street car)	Number	910	1,327	2,104	2,423	2,498	2,502	2,663
Trolley bus	Number	610	652	571	611	601	539	571
Other	Number	1,176	5,208	18,453	19,240	17,782	18,962	18,524
Operating funding, total	Mil. dol.	16,053	24,243	39,117	48,367	50,634	50,807	52,278
Agency funds	Mil. dol.	6,786	11,004	14,675	18,105	18,394	18,457	18,845
Passenger funding	Mil. dol.	5,891	8,746	12,556	15,727	15,848	15,929	16,031
Other	Mil. dol.	895	2,258	2,119	2,378	2,546	2,528	2,814
Government funds [2]	Mil. dol.	9,267	13,239	24,442	30,262	32,240	32,350	33,433
Directly generated [3]	Mil. dol.	([4])	1,959	2,549	3,242	3,418	3,484	3,196
Local	Mil. dol.	5,327	5,319	8,458	11,812	12,491	12,866	13,857
State	Mil. dol.	2,971	4,967	9,761	11,197	12,274	11,673	11,867
Federal	Mil. dol.	970	994	3,675	4,011	4,057	4,327	4,513
Operating expense	Mil. dol.	15,742	22,646	37,755	45,353	47,409	47,544	49,482
Vehicle operations	Mil. dol.	6,653	10,111	17,009	19,388	19,998	19,902	20,760
Maintenance	Mil. dol.	4,631	6,445	9,797	12,237	13,017	13,327	13,404
General administration	Mil. dol.	3,450	3,329	5,731	7,300	7,909	7,543	8,154
Purchased transportation	Mil. dol.	1,008	2,761	5,218	6,427	6,484	6,772	7,165
Capital expenditures	Mil. dol.	(NA)	9,587	17,824	19,696	19,943	20,185	21,772
Vehicle-miles operated	Million	3,242	4,081	5,455	5,509	5,654	5,696	5,719
Motor bus	Million	2,130	2,315	2,413	2,428	2,483	2,502	2,532
Trolley bus	Million	14	15	12	11	12	11	11
Heavy rail	Million	537	595	666	695	696	704	705
Surface rail (light rail, street car)	Million	24	53	94	114	120	127	128
Commuter rail	Million	213	271	345	374	376	378	377
Demand response [1]	Million	306	759	1,694	1,617	1,692	1,705	1,702
Other	Million	18	74	232	271	275	270	264
Trips taken	Million	8,799	9,363	10,218	10,599	10,459	10,152	9,953
Motor bus	Million	5,677	5,678	5,256	5,199	5,054	4,793	4,707
Trolley bus	Million	126	122	99	90	94	83	77
Heavy rail	Million	2,346	2,632	3,550	3,860	3,848	3,816	3,724
Surface rail (light rail, street car)	Million	175	320	457	529	550	555	543
Commuter rail	Million	328	413	464	495	504	503	505
Demand response [1]	Million	68	105	190	223	211	207	204
Other	Million	79	93	202	204	199	195	192
Avg. fare per trip	Dollars	(NA)	0.93	1.23	1.50	1.52	1.56	1.62
Employees, number (avg.) [5]	1,000	273	360	394	433	436	432	436
Salaries and wages, employee	Mil. dol.	7,226	10,400	14,286	15,913	16,739	16,688	16,947
Fringe benefits, employee	Mil. dol.	3,986	5,413	10,342	11,992	13,034	12,729	13,477

NA Not available. [1] This operation (also called paratransit or dial-a-ride) is comprised of passenger cars, vans or small buses operating in response to calls from passengers or their agents to the transit operator, who then dispatches a vehicle to pick up the passengers and transport them to their destinations. [2] Represents the sum of federal, state, and local assistance, and that portion of directly generated funds that accrue from tax collections, toll transfers from other sectors of operations, and bond proceeds. [3] These are any funds generated from taxes controlled by the transit agency. [4] Funds data are included in local government data through 1993. [5] Through 1990, represents employee equivalents of 2,080 hours = one employee; beginning 1995, equals actual employees.

Source: American Public Transportation Association, Washington, DC, *Public Transportation Fact Book*, annual ©. See also <https://www.apta.com/research-technical-resources/research-reports>.

Table 1141. Top Twenty Cities—Public Transit Savings for Daily Commuters: 2020

[Individuals who use public transportation for their daily commute can save on average $9,848 annually based on the February 28, 2020 national average gas price and the national unreserved monthly parking rate. On a per month basis, transit riders can save on average $821 per month versus driving. See source report and other monthly "Transit Savings" releases for information and methodology on how savings are calculated. The cities with the highest transit ridership are ranked in order of their transit savings based on the purchase of a monthly public transit pass and factoring in local gas prices and the local monthly unreserved parking rate]

City	Savings (dollars) Monthly	Savings (dollars) Annual	City	Savings (dollars) Monthly	Savings (dollars) Annual
New York	1,218	14,618	Minneapolis	859	10,306
San Francisco	1,113	13,356	Denver	846	10,152
Boston	1,068	12,810	Baltimore	842	10,105
Seattle	998	11,979	Washington, DC	823	9,837
Philadelphia	989	11,866	Pittsburgh	810	9,716
Chicago	979	11,753	Cleveland	801	9,613
Honolulu	972	11,669	Miami	773	9,279
Los Angeles	958	11,497	Las Vegas	773	9,278
San Diego	911	10,936	Atlanta	767	9,200
Portland	891	10,691	Dallas	752	9,029

Source: American Public Transportation Association, Media Center, Press Releases ©. See also <https://www.apta.com/news-publications/public-transportation-facts/>.

Table 1142. Characteristics of Rail Transit by Transit Authority: 2018

[9,364.8 represents $9,364,800,000]

Mode and transit agency	Metro area served	Directional route–miles [1,2]	Grade crossings	Number of stations	Fare revenues earned (mil. dol.)	Total operating expenses (mil. dol.)	Unlinked passenger trips (million)
Total [3]	(X)	**12,566.4**	**6,580**	**3,448**	**9,364.8**	**18,144.3**	**4,775.1**
Heavy rail	(X)	**1,659.8**	**93**	**1,054**	**5,542.5**	**9,075.8**	**3,724.4**
Chicago Transit Authority	Chicago	207.8	33	145	314.1	617.9	225.9
Greater Cleveland Regional Transit Authority	Cleveland	38.1	–	18	7.8	35.2	6.3
Los Angeles County Metropolitan Transportation Authority, Metro	Los Angeles	31.9	–	16	32.3	171.7	43.8
Maryland Transit Administration	Baltimore	29.4	1	14	11.5	63.8	8.9
Massachusetts Bay Transportation Authority	Boston	76.3	–	54	223.4	301.6	163.5
Metropolitan Atlanta Rapid Transit Authority	Atlanta	96.1	–	38	80.3	203.9	65.1
Miami-Dade Transit	Miami	49.8	47	23	15.1	99.3	19.2
MTA New York City Transit	New York	493.7	5	472	3,503.3	5,069.0	2,628.4
Port Authority Trans-Hudson Corporation	New York	28.6	5	13	190.5	446.0	89.7
Port Authority Transit Corporation	Philadelphia	31.5	2	13	26.4	54.7	10.8
San Francisco Bay Area Rapid Transit District	San Francisco	218.3	–	45	474.8	644.1	127.9
Southeastern Pennsylvania Transportation Authority	Philadelphia	74.9	–	75	113.0	200.7	94.0
Staten Island Rapid Transit Operating Authority, MTA Staten Island Railway	New York	28.6	–	21	8.7	59.5	8.1
Washington Metropolitan Area Transit Authority	Washington	234.2	–	91	536.5	1,044.4	229.2
Alternativa de Transporte Integrado ATI	San Juan, PR	20.6	–	16	5.0	64.0	3.8
Light rail	(X)	**1,576.8**	**1,838**	**923**	**511.1**	**2,329.8**	**487.0**
Missouri-Illinois Metropolitan District Metro	St. Louis	91.1	39	37	14.2	80.2	13.6
Central Puget Sound Regional Transit Authority	Seattle	40.4	37	16	41.6	115.6	24.5
Charlotte Area Transit System	Charlotte	23.3	39	26	4.0	21.4	5.8
Greater Cleveland Regional Transit Authority	Cleveland	30.4	25	34	2.8	12.1	1.6
Dallas Area Rapid Transit	Dallas	182.4	136	64	26.0	191.5	28.9
Denver Regional Transportation District	Denver	115.2	39	54	37.6	122.3	25.3
Los Angeles County Metropolitan Transportation Authority, Metro	Los Angeles	171.9	197	79	49.1	377.4	66.4
Maryland Transit Administration (MTA)	Baltimore	57.6	44	33	7.2	44.0	7.4
Massachusetts Bay Transportation Authority	Boston	51.0	53	74	81.4	213.7	56.8
Metro Transit	Minneapolis	44.3	109	37	26.7	73.0	25.0
Harris County, Texas (Metro)	Houston	43.6	165	63	5.3	79.3	19.0
New Jersey Transit Corporation	Newark	46.5	39	41	20.2	120.4	21.0
Niagara Frontier Transportation Authority	Buffalo	12.4	8	14	5.0	25.6	4.5
Port Authority of Allegheny County	Pittsburgh	49.6	51	30	9.7	66.8	7.7
Sacramento Regional Transit District	Sacramento	84.9	137	43	13.0	70.9	10.4
San Diego Metropolitan Transit System	San Diego	108.4	96	54	39.4	90.3	37.0
San Francisco Municipal Railway	San Francisco	64.4	24	9	40.0	221.1	49.8
Santa Clara Valley Transportation Authority	San Jose	81.0	11	64	8.0	128.6	8.5
Hampton Roads Transit	Hampton	14.8	40	11	1.6	10.6	1.4
Metropolitan Transportation District of Oregon	Portland	118.9	212	44	48.3	150.7	38.9
Utah Transit Authority	Salt Lake City	93.9	145	56	18.1	71.4	17.9
Valley Metro Rail, Inc.	Phoenix	50.8	192	40	11.9	43.0	15.8
Commuter rail [3]	(X)	**8,861.6**	**3,581**	**1,288**	**3,256.2**	**6,424.6**	**500.9**
Alaska Railroad Corporation	Anchorage	959.9	147	8	25.7	49.9	0.2
Altamont Corridor Express	San Jose	166.5	175	10	9.8	19.2	1.4
Central Florida Commuter Rail	Orlando	63.5	94	12	1.8	35.2	0.8
Central Puget Sound Regional Transit Authority	Seattle	163.8	63	12	16.7	52.2	4.6
Connecticut Department of Transportation	Hartford	101.2	–	9	2.3	31.7	0.7
Dallas Area Rapid Transit	Dallas	72.3	45	10	8.7	29.5	2.0
Denver Regional Transportation District	Denver	58.7	29	9	24.8	53.8	7.6
Maryland Transit Administration	Baltimore	400.4	1	42	52.5	161.0	9.3
Massachusetts Bay Transportation Authority	Boston	776.1	304	140	229.1	371.9	32.9
Metro Transit	Minneapolis	77.9	36	7	2.6	16.2	0.8
MTA Metro-North Railroad	New York	545.7	133	112	740.3	1,258.6	91.9
MTA Long Island Rail Road	New York	638.2	365	125	740.6	1,482.5	105.5
New Jersey Transit Corporation	New York	1,001.8	319	166	561.7	1,017.0	87.1
North County Transit District	San Diego	82.2	27	8	5.0	16.6	1.4
Northeast Illinois Regional Commuter Railroad Corporation,	Chicago	975.0	503	243	370.0	762.0	68.4
Northern Indiana Commuter Transport District	Chicago	151.2	138	19	22.8	51.2	3.4
Northern New England Passenger Rail Authority	Boston	224.6	103	12	10.5	23.2	0.6
Peninsula Corridor Joint Powers Board: Caltrain	San Francisco	153.7	54	32	97.1	127.4	18.5
Pennsylvania Department of Transportation	Philadelphia	144.4	–	12	37.8	48.6	1.5
Regional Transportation Authority	Nashville	62.8	48	6	1.0	4.5	0.3
Rio Metro Regional Transit District	Albuquerque	193.1	95	15	2.0	31.8	0.8
Sonoma-Marin Area Rail Transit District	Bay Area, CA	85.8	73	10	3.3	23.9	0.6
South Florida Regional Transportation Authority	Miami	142.2	–	18	13.1	96.2	4.3
Southeastern Pennsylvania Transportation Authority	Philadelphia	446.9	287	155	144.7	303.7	32.2
Southern California Regional Rail Authority	Los Angeles	825.6	458	62	82.7	235.0	14.2
Utah Transit Authority	Salt Lake City	174.5	65	15	7.4	43.4	5.1
Virginia Railway Express	Washington	173.6	19	19	42.2	78.5	4.6

– Represents zero. X Not applicable. [1] Vehicles operated in maximum services (VOMS) include directly operated (DO) and Purchase Transportation (PT) by mode. [2] The mileage in each direction over which public transportation vehicles travel while in revenue service. The mileage is computed without regard to the number of traffic lanes or rail tracks existing in the right-of-way. [3] Includes hybrid and streetcar rail, not shown separately. Excludes commuter-type services operated independently by Amtrak.

Source: U.S. Department of Transportation, Federal Transit Administration, National Transit Database, Annual Data Tables, "Transit Way Mileage," "Federal Funding Allocation," "Metrics," and "Transit Stations," <transit.dot.gov/ntd/ntd-data>, accessed September 2020.

Table 1143. Household Daily Travel Trips and Trip Length by Trip Purpose: 1969 to 2017

[Data based on the National Household Travel Survey (NHTS), which asks each participating household to report all travel by household members on a randomly assigned 24-hour single travel day using any mode of transportation including walking. Data for 2017 may not be comparable to previous years due to change in survey methodology; see source for details]

Trip characteristic	1969	1977	1983	1990	1995	2001	2009	2017
Daily person trips per person...........................	2.0	2.9	2.9	3.8	4.3	4.1	3.8	3.4
Daily person miles of travel (PMT) per person.........	19.5	26.0	25.1	34.9	38.7	36.9	36.1	39.0
Daily vehicle trips per driver........................	2.3	2.3	2.4	3.3	3.6	3.4	3.0	2.7
Daily vehicle miles of travel (VMT) per driver..........	20.6	19.5	18.7	28.5	32.1	32.7	29.0	28.5
Average person trip length (miles).....................	9.7	8.9	8.7	9.5	9.1	10.0	9.8	11.6
Average vehicle trip length (miles)....................	8.9	8.3	7.9	8.9	9.1	9.9	9.7	10.5
AVERAGE ANNUAL PERSON TRIPS PER HOUSEHOLD BY TRIP PURPOSE								
All purposes................................	(NA)	(NA)	2,628	3,262	3,828	3,581	3,466	3,140
To/from work................................	(NA)	(NA)	537	539	676	565	541	546
Work related business........................	(NA)	(NA)	62	38	100	109	106	51
Shopping....................................	(NA)	(NA)	474	630	775	707	725	580
Other family/personal errands.................	(NA)	(NA)	456	854	981	863	748	628
School/church...............................	(NA)	(NA)	310	304	337	351	333	341
Social/recreation............................	(NA)	(NA)	728	874	953	952	952	866
Other.......................................	(NA)	(NA)	61	22	6	30	61	128
AVERAGE PERSON TRIP LENGTH BY TRIP PURPOSE (miles)								
All purposes................................	(NA)	(NA)	8.7	9.5	9.1	10.0	9.7	11.6
To/from work................................	(NA)	(NA)	8.5	10.7	11.6	12.1	11.8	12.2
Work related business........................	(NA)	(NA)	21.8	28.2	20.3	28.3	20.0	27.4
Shopping....................................	(NA)	(NA)	5.4	5.4	6.1	7.0	6.5	7.9
Other family/personal errands.................	(NA)	(NA)	7.3	8.6	7.6	7.8	7.0	7.9
School/church...............................	(NA)	(NA)	4.9	5.4	6.0	6.0	6.3	7.0
Social/recreation............................	(NA)	(NA)	12.3	13.2	11.3	11.4	10.7	11.4
Other.......................................	(NA)	(NA)	8.2	10.3	22.8	43.1	51.5	50.4
AVERAGE ANNUAL VEHICLE TRIPS PER HOUSEHOLD								
All purposes................................	1,396	1,442	1,486	2,077	2,321	2,171	2,068	1,865
To/from work................................	445	423	414	448	553	479	457	450
Shopping....................................	213	268	297	431	501	459	468	372
Other family/personal errands.................	195	215	272	579	626	537	500	434
Social/recreation............................	312	320	335	460	427	441	436	410
AVERAGE VEHICLE TRIP LENGTH (miles)								
All purposes................................	8.9	8.4	7.9	8.9	9.1	9.9	9.7	10.5
To/from work................................	9.4	9.0	8.6	11.0	11.8	12.1	12.2	12.8
Shopping....................................	4.4	5.0	5.3	5.1	5.6	6.7	6.4	7.9
Other family/personal errands.................	6.5	6.7	6.7	7.4	6.9	7.5	7.1	7.7
Social/recreation............................	13.1	10.3	10.6	11.8	11.2	11.9	11.2	11.8

NA Not available.

Source: U.S. Department of Transportation, Federal Highway Administration, *Summary of Travel Trends 2017, National Household Travel Survey*, July 2018. See also <https://nhts.ornl.gov/>.

Table 1144. Federal Transit Administration (FTA) Funding Allocations by State: 2019 and 2020

[In millions of dollars (11,417.7 represents $11,417,700,000). For fiscal years ending September 30. Data shown are apportionments and allocations for formula and discretionary programs]

State	2019	2020	State	2019	2020	State	2019	2020	State	2019	2020
Total [1]...	11,417.7	9,908.7	ID.........	32.3	29.7	MO.......	110.1	107.8	PA........	458.6	446.0
AL........	62.2	61.0	IL.........	633.6	614.0	MT........	24.3	24.8	RI........	42.7	44.0
AK........	60.5	56.7	IN.........	98.2	100.5	NE........	31.6	29.7	SC........	57.1	56.1
AZ........	232.1	132.8	IA.........	46.9	46.6	NV........	71.7	70.0	SD........	19.1	19.8
AR........	36.6	37.3	KS.........	41.1	40.2	NH........	19.7	19.7	TN........	98.7	98.0
CA........	2,070.4	1,462.4	KY.........	61.5	60.5	NJ........	664.2	652.5	TX........	579.9	487.6
CO........	134.7	133.7	LA.........	72.6	71.2	NM........	58.2	55.4	UT........	92.2	89.0
CT........	189.8	187.0	ME.........	39.1	35.6	NY........	1,597.4	1,547.8	VT........	14.9	12.1
DE........	31.6	29.3	MD.........	393.1	269.3	NC........	135.2	137.3	VA........	181.7	185.2
DC........	213.2	198.6	MA........	557.5	394.8	ND........	18.0	17.9	WA........	484.7	277.3
FL........	410.2	405.6	MI.........	152.0	152.9	OH........	203.1	200.7	WV.......	29.0	29.4
GA........	214.9	210.2	MN........	127.3	127.3	OK........	56.5	54.3	WI.......	92.3	91.9
HI........	47.2	47.8	MS........	33.9	33.7	OR........	186.8	116.7	WY.......	14.5	14.7

[1] Includes data for Island Areas of the U.S. and unallocated funds, not shown separately. Does not include oversight funds.

Source: U.S. Department of Transportation, Federal Transit Administration, "FTA Allocations for Formula and Discretionary Programs by State FY1998-2020," <https://www.transit.dot.gov/funding/apportionments/funding-state>, accessed May 2020.

Table 1145. Commuters by Commuting Time to Work for Top Metropolitan Statistical Areas: 2018

[146,358 represents 146,358,000, except percent. For workers 16 years and over who did not work at home. Covers any mode of travel. Based on a sample, subject to sampling variability]

Metropolitan Statistical Area	Total commuters (1,000)	Percent over 35 minutes	Commuters by commuting time								
			Less than 10 minutes	10 to 14 minutes	15 to 19 minutes	20 to 24 minutes	25 to 29 minutes	30 to 34 minutes	35 to 44 minutes	45 to 59 minutes	60 or more minutes
United States................	**146,358**	**25.1**	**17,592**	**19,129**	**22,215**	**20,909**	**9,563**	**20,272**	**10,515**	**12,328**	**13,835**
Atlanta-Sandy Springs-Roswell, GA.......	2,715	36.2	181	259	331	357	166	437	254	341	389
Baltimore-Columbia-Towson, MD..........	1,337	33.6	98	127	172	189	93	209	125	145	179
Boston-Cambridge-Newton, MA-NH......	2,446	37.1	217	251	285	286	136	365	234	303	370
Charlotte-Concord-Gastonia, NC-SC.....	1,188	26.3	115	141	169	177	89	184	103	118	93
Chicago-Naperville-Elgin, IL-IN-WI.......	4,455	36.7	363	446	501	542	278	691	435	553	646
Dallas-Ft. Worth-Arlington, TX..........	3,541	28.1	299	406	488	512	246	597	313	369	311
Denver-Aurora-Lakewood, CO............	1,467	27.4	114	155	212	223	107	253	134	161	108
Detroit-Warren-Dearborn, MI.............	1,928	25.9	169	229	279	299	151	302	172	180	148
Houston-The Woodlands-Sugar Land, TX....	3,132	31.4	237	308	417	431	199	557	273	363	347
Los Angeles-Long Beach-Anaheim, CA...	6,078	32.2	413	616	825	818	347	1,099	497	620	842
Miami-Ft. Lauderdale-West Palm Beach, FL....	2,815	30.7	172	255	357	414	187	564	254	294	317
Minneapolis-St. Paul-Bloomington, MN-WI....	1,837	22.7	188	229	270	300	163	268	168	147	102
New York-Newark-Jersey City, NY-NJ-PA....	9,258	44.6	621	761	885	1,008	491	1,366	852	1,179	2,094
Orlando-Kissimmee-Sanford, FL..........	1,184	29.8	86	118	151	189	89	198	119	141	92
Philadelphia-Camden-Wilmington, PA-NJ-DE-MD....	2,808	32.3	255	297	360	378	186	426	254	320	334
Phoenix-Mesa-Scottsdale, AZ..............	2,101	24.9	206	253	309	340	162	308	177	185	160
Pittsburgh, PA........................	1,086	26.5	133	133	157	146	81	148	98	104	87
Portland-Vancouver-Hillsboro, OR-WA....	1,167	25.1	120	135	179	180	83	176	95	109	89
Riverside-San Bernardino-Ontario, CA. ..	1,889	32.6	176	231	254	264	100	248	119	162	335
St. Louis, MO-IL......................	1,325	24.0	145	155	193	212	105	197	123	116	79
San Diego-Carlsbad, CA.................	1,540	22.5	120	195	254	262	109	253	113	120	114
San Francisco-Oakland-Hayward, CA. ...	2,254	39.7	134	222	282	264	121	337	199	276	419
Seattle-Tacoma-Bellevue, WA...........	1,921	34.3	146	177	231	265	135	307	184	222	253
Tampa-St. Petersburg-Clearwater, FL.....	1,335	27.0	132	159	191	189	91	213	106	137	117
Washington-Arlington-Alexandria, DC-VA-MD-WV....	3,145	41.9	179	245	345	368	197	491	326	443	550

Source: U.S. Census Bureau, 2018 American Community Survey, B08134, "Means of Transportation to Work by Travel Time to Work," <data.census.gov/>, accessed May 2020.

Table 1146. Commuters Who Ride Bicycles or Walk to Work—Selected Large Cities: 2016

[Covers cities with the highest percent of commuters who walk or bike to work, based on the American Community Survey. Data are weighted 5-year averages for 2012-2016]

Leading cities	Walking			Leading cities	Bicycling		
	Percent of commuters who walk to work	Percent male	Percent female		Percent of commuters who bike to work	Percent male	Percent female
Boston......................	14.8	47.3	52.7	Portland, OR...............	6.5	64.0	36.0
Washington, DC.............	13.3	50.1	49.9	Minneapolis................	4.3	65.3	34.7
San Francisco..............	10.6	52.2	47.8	Washington, DC.............	4.3	61.0	39.0
Seattle.....................	10.1	56.9	43.1	San Francisco..............	4.1	68.7	31.3
New York City..............	10.0	48.5	51.5	Seattle.....................	3.8	70.2	29.8
Philadelphia................	8.2	46.4	53.6	Oakland....................	3.1	62.3	37.7
Minneapolis................	7.2	52.7	47.3	Tucson.....................	2.9	67.5	32.5
Baltimore..................	6.7	47.2	52.8	Denver.....................	2.3	70.7	29.3
Chicago....................	6.7	49.8	50.2	Boston.....................	2.1	71.5	28.5
Portland, OR...............	6.0	52.8	47.2	Philadelphia................	2.1	62.9	37.1
Cleveland..................	5.3	55.8	44.2	Sacramento................	2.1	64.8	35.2
Milwaukee.................	5.0	47.7	52.3	Chicago....................	1.6	71.5	28.5
Atlanta....................	4.6	59.0	41.0	Albuquerque................	1.5	73.4	26.6
Denver....................	4.5	55.8	44.2	Austin.....................	1.4	70.7	29.3
Miami.....................	4.2	52.9	47.1	Los Angeles................	1.2	80.1	19.9
Oakland...................	4.0	45.8	54.2	Fresno.....................	1.1	75.0	25.0
Detroit....................	3.7	53.5	46.5	New York City..............	1.1	73.5	26.5
Los Angeles................	3.5	51.2	48.8	Long Beach................	1.0	71.3	28.7
Tucson....................	3.3	56.2	43.8	Miami.....................	1.0	77.0	23.0
Sacramento................	3.1	51.7	48.3	Milwaukee.................	1.0	70.0	30.0
San Diego.................	3.1	60.4	39.6	San Diego.................	1.0	75.4	24.6
Columbus, OH..............	3.0	55.7	44.3	Mesa......................	0.9	70.7	29.3
Virginia Beach.............	2.6	66.4	33.6	San Jose...................	0.9	76.0	24.0
Long Beach................	2.5	49.1	50.9	Atlanta....................	0.8	80.2	19.8
Austin....................	2.3	53.7	46.3	Baltimore..................	0.8	72.2	27.8

Source: League of American Bicyclists, *Bicycling and Walking in the United States: 2018 Benchmarking Report* ©. See also <http://bikeleague.org/benchmarking-report/>.

Table 1147. Truck Transportation—Revenue and Equipment Inventory: 2013 to 2018

[In millions of dollars (245,520 represents $245,520,000,000), except where noted. For all employer firms regardless of tax status. Covers NAICS 484. Estimates have been adjusted to the results of the 2012 Economic Census. Data are based on the 2012 North American Industry Classification System (NAICS); see text, this section and Section 15]

Item	2013	2014	2015	2016	2017	2018
Total operating revenue	245,520	263,875	263,249	259,531	272,784	294,489
Total motor carrier revenue	(NA)	(NA)	244,353	240,542	253,629	275,673
Revenue by commodities handled:						
Agricultural products	(NA)	(NA)	27,834	28,893	28,324	30,913
Grains, alcohol, and tobacco products	(NA)	(NA)	9,545	9,649	10,022	10,250
Stone, nonmetallic minerals, and metallic ores	(NA)	(NA)	17,867	17,399	19,429	21,559
Coal and petroleum products	(NA)	(NA)	15,733	14,579	13,852	14,136
Pharmaceutical and chemical products	(NA)	(NA)	12,685	12,105	12,687	12,539
Wood products, textiles, and leathers	(NA)	(NA)	15,990	15,927	18,287	19,881
Base metal and machinery	(NA)	(NA)	24,038	22,305	23,529	25,350
Electronic, motorized vehicles, and precision instruments	(NA)	(NA)	11,809	11,374	13,200	14,587
Used household and office goods	(NA)	(NA)	12,755	13,139	13,754	14,747
New furniture and miscellaneous manufactured products	(NA)	(NA)	17,536	17,219	18,465	20,827
Other goods	(NA)	(NA)	78,561	77,953	82,080	90,884
Hazardous materials	(NA)	(NA)	16,469	15,562	15,988	16,885
Inventory of revenue-generating equipment (1,000):						
Trucks	223	228	165	171	188	198
Owned and/or leased with drivers	201	203	149	154	170	178
Leased without drivers	(S)	(S)	16	17	18	20
Truck-tractors	761	817	569	579	625	638
Owned and/or leased with drivers	666	717	493	503	544	547
Leased without drivers	95	100	76	76	81	91
Trailers	1,772	1,858	1,426	1,468	1,498	1,593
Owned and/or leased with drivers	1,577	1,677	1,268	1,299	1,362	1,451
Leased without drivers	195	181	158	169	136	142

S Estimate does not meet publication standards. NA Not available.

Source: U.S. Census Bureau, Service Annual Survey, "Service Annual Survey Latest Data (NAICS-basis): 2018," <https://www.census.gov/programs-surveys/sas/data.html>, accessed July 2020.

Table 1148. Crude Oil, Fuel Ethanol and Biodiesel Movements by Rail: 2010 to 2019

[In thousands of barrels (23,788 represents 23,788,000). Crude oil movements on railroads to and from Canada, within the 50 States and the District of Columbia (including interstate and intrastate). Estimates based on data from the Surface Transportation Board and other information]

Item	2010	2011	2012	2013	2014	2015	2016	2017	2018	2019
Crude oil	23,788	42,370	152,047	296,064	382,034	318,782	175,701	139,805	201,293	250,250
Intra-U.S. movements	23,712	41,371	138,024	259,194	316,276	275,218	142,587	87,190	113,977	140,844
U.S. exports to Canada	55	256	6,217	7,391	12,605	4,414	–	102	180	–
U.S. imports from Canada	21	743	7,807	29,479	53,153	39,149	33,114	52,513	87,136	109,406
Fuel ethanol	208,061	219,324	207,870	202,412	211,692	220,877	237,259	253,874	258,954	246,905
Biodiesel	2,606	6,387	7,892	7,950	9,473	8,332	12,226	11,706	13,653	13,054

– Represents zero.

Source: U.S. Energy Information Administration, Petroleum & Other Liquids, "Movements of Crude Oil and Selected Products by Rail," <http://www.eia.gov/petroleum/data.cfm>, accessed June 2020.

Table 1149. Petroleum Pipeline Companies—Characteristics: 1980 to 2018

[173 represents 173,000. Covers pipeline companies operating in interstate commerce and subject to the jurisdiction of the Federal Energy Regulatory Commission]

Item	Unit	1980	1990	2000	2010	2014	2015	2016	2017	2018
Miles of pipeline, total	1,000	173	168	152	148	161	165	166	168	172
Gathering lines	1,000	36	32	18	10	15	16	15	15	16
Trunk lines	1,000	136	136	134	138	146	149	152	154	156
Total deliveries	Mil. barrel	10,600	11,378	14,450	13,518	16,170	18,148	18,504	19,331	21,779
Crude oil	Mil. barrel	6,405	6,563	6,923	7,204	9,289	10,865	10,730	11,421	13,216
Products	Mil. barrel	4,195	4,816	7,527	6,314	6,881	7,283	7,785	7,911	8,562
Total trunk line traffic	Bil. barrel miles	3,405	3,500	3,508	3,565	4,193	4,589	4,771	5,135	5,556
Crude oil	Bil. barrel miles	1,948	1,891	1,602	1,634	2,059	2,339	2,499	2,775	3,126
Products	Bil. barrel miles	1,458	1,609	1,906	1,931	2,134	2,250	2,272	2,359	2,430
Carrier property value	Mil. dol.	19,752	25,828	29,648	45,380	84,910	93,485	99,565	111,862	122,370
Operating revenues	Mil. dol.	6,356	7,149	7,483	11,219	19,281	22,019	23,100	25,427	29,035
Net income	Mil. dol.	1,912	2,340	2,705	4,582	9,573	6,689	10,542	13,856	16,522

Source: Endeavor Business Media, *Oil & Gas Journal*, annual ©. See also <http://www.ogj.com/>.

Table 1150. Pipelines—Mileage and Incident Summary: 2005 to 2018

[In miles except where indicated (1,245,463 represents $1,245,463,000)]

Year	Pipeline mileage								Pipeline incidents [2]	
	Natural gas systems			Hazardous liquid or carbon dioxide systems						
	Distri-bution [1]	Trans-mission	Gathering	Total [3]	Petro-leum/ refined products	Highly volatile liquids	Crude oil	CO2 or other	Number of incidents	Total cost as reported ($1,000)
2005.......	1,962,351	300,468	23,754	166,760	62,899	51,284	48,732	3,846	719	1,245,463
2006.......	2,022,474	300,324	20,898	166,719	61,905	52,533	48,453	3,827	639	151,984
2007.......	2,025,731	301,066	20,042	169,846	62,091	54,382	49,488	3,884	610	153,772
2008.......	2,075,191	303,181	20,663	173,789	61,599	57,024	50,963	4,203	659	564,831
2009.......	2,086,689	304,560	20,376	175,965	61,803	57,233	52,737	4,192	627	179,070
2010.......	2,102,483	304,810	19,621	181,986	64,800	57,980	54,631	4,560	586	1,692,502
2011.......	2,121,305	305,069	19,277	183,580	64,130	58,599	56,100	4,735	588	426,129
2012.......	2,137,962	303,393	16,532	186,221	64,042	59,861	57,463	4,840	571	229,843
2013.......	2,149,818	302,880	17,377	192,412	63,351	62,768	61,087	5,190	618	368,913
2014.......	2,169,370	301,823	17,530	199,793	61,766	65,792	66,943	5,276	706	321,320
2015.......	2,189,585	301,165	17,776	208,621	62,634	67,676	73,055	5,241	712	349,959
2016.......	2,210,358	300,346	17,858	212,108	62,461	68,727	75,710	5,195	634	377,370
2017.......	2,223,701	300,694	18,110	215,993	62,369	69,161	79,211	5,237	647	339,175
2018.......	2,238,701	301,578	17,960	218,917	62,710	70,267	80,719	5,206	636	1,098,073

[1] Includes main and estimated service mileage. [2] Includes serious and significant incidents. Serious incidents include a fatality or injury requiring in-patient hospitalization. Significant incidents include serious incidents; those with $50,000 or more in total costs; highly volatile liquid releases of 5 barrels or more, or other liquid releases of 50 barrels or more; and liquid releases resulting in an unintentional fire or explosion. [3] Beginning 2010, includes fuel grade ethanol, not shown separately.

Source: U.S. Department of Transportation, Pipeline and Hazardous Materials Safety Administration, "Pipeline Mileage and Facilities" and "Pipeline Incidents: 20 Year Trends," <https://www.phmsa.dot.gov/data-and-statistics/pipeline/data-and-statistics-overview>, accessed February 2020.

Table 1151. U.S. Postal Service Rates for Letters and Postcards: 1991 to 2020

[In dollars. For 1st class retail mail. Prior to 2013, international rates exclude Canada and Mexico]

Domestic mail date of rate change	Letters		Post-cards	Express mail— first 1/2 pound [1]	International air mail date of rate change	Letters	Post-cards
	First ounce	Each added ounce					
1991 (Feb. 3).................	0.29	0.23	0.19	9.95	**First 1/2 ounce**		
1995 (Jan. 1).................	0.32	0.23	0.20	10.75	1991 (Feb. 3).............	0.50	0.40
1999 (Jan. 10)................	0.33	0.22	0.20	11.75	1995 (July 9).............	0.60	0.40
2001 (Jan. 7).................	0.34	0.21	0.20	12.25	1999 (Jan. 10)............	0.60	0.50
2001 (July 1).................	0.34	0.23	0.21	12.45	**First ounce [2]**		
2002 (June 30)...............	0.37	0.23	0.23	13.65	2001 (Jan. 7).............	0.80	0.70
2006 (Jan. 8).................	0.39	0.24	0.24	14.40	2006 (Jan. 8).............	0.84	0.75
2007 (May 14)................	0.41	0.17	0.26	16.25	2007 (May 14)............	0.90	0.90
2008 (May 12)................	0.42	0.17	0.27	[3] 12.60	2008 (May 12)............	0.94	0.94
2009 (May 11)................	0.44	0.17	0.28	[4] 13.05	2009 (May 11)............	0.98	0.98
2010 (Jan. 4).................	0.44	0.17	0.28	[5] 13.65	2010 (no change)........	0.98	0.98
2011 (Apr. 17)................	0.44	0.20	0.29	[6] 13.25	2011 (no change)........	0.98	0.98
2012 (Jan. 22)................	0.45	0.20	0.32	[7] 12.95	2012 (Jan. 22)...........	1.05	1.05
2013 (Jan. 27)................	0.46	0.20	0.33	[8] 14.10	2013 (Jan. 27)...........	1.10	1.10
2014 (Jan. 26)................	0.49	0.21	0.34	[9] 16.95	2014 (Jan. 26)...........	1.15	1.15
2015 (May 31)................	0.49	0.22	0.35	[9] 16.95	2015 (May 31)...........	1.20	1.20
2016 (Apr. 10)................	0.47	0.21	0.34	[10] 22.95	2016 (Apr. 10)...........	1.15	1.15
2017 (Jan. 22)................	0.49	0.21	0.34	[11] 23.75	2017 (no change)........	1.15	1.15
2018 (Jan. 21)................	0.50	0.21	0.35	[12] 24.70	2018 (no change)........	1.15	1.15
2019 (Jan. 27)................	0.55	0.15	0.35	[13] 25.50	2019 (no change)........	1.15	1.15
2020 (Jan. 26)................	0.55	0.15	0.35	[14] 26.35	2020 (Jan. 26)...........	1.20	1.20

[1] On May 12, 2008, the Postal Service initiated a zoned pricing structure for Express Mail. [2] International letter prices after the first ounce vary according to the price group that is applicable to each destination country. [3] Prices increased on May 12, 2008. Prices range from $12.60 to zones 1 and 2 to $19.50 to zone 8. [4] Prices increased on January 18, 2009. Prices range from $13.05 to zones 1 and 2 to $21.20 to zone 8. [5] Prices range from $13.65 to zones 1 and 2 to $22.20 to zone 8. [6] Prices changed on January 2, 2011. Prices range from $13.25 to zones 1 and 2 to $26.65 to zone 8. [7] Prices range from $12.95 to zones 1 and 2 to $28.00 to zone 8. [8] Prices range from $14.10 to zones 1 and 2 to $30.60 to zone 8. [9] Beginning January 2014, the Postal Service implemented a Zone 9. Prices range from $16.95 to zones 1 and 2 to $38.05 to zone 9. [10] Prices range from $22.95 to zones 1 and 2 to $38.05 to zone 9. [11] Prices range from $23.75 to zones 1 and 2 to $39.40 to zone 9. [12] Prices range from $24.70 to zones 1 and 2 to $40.95 to zone 9. [13] Prices range from $25.50 to zones 1 and 2 to $47.70 to zone 9. [14] Prices range from $26.35 to zones 1 and 2 to $50.60 to zone 9.

Source: U.S. Postal Service, *Domestic Rate History*, July 2009; and "Price List Notice 123," <http://pe.usps.com/text/dmm300/Notice123.htm>, accessed January 2020.

Table 1152. U.S. Postal Service—Summary: 1990 to 2019

[166,301 represents 166,301,000,000 except as indicated. For years ending September 30. Includes Puerto Rico and all Island Areas]

Item	1990	2000	2010	2015	2017	2018	2019
Offices, stations, and branches (number)...	**40,067**	**38,060**	**36,222**	**35,520**	**35,005**	**34,772**	**34,613**
Post offices.	28,959	27,876	27,077	26,615	26,410	26,365	26,362
Stations and branches.	11,108	10,184	9,145	8,905	8,595	8,407	8,251
Delivery points (mil.)	**(NA)**	**135.9**	**150.9**	**155.0**	**157.3**	**158.6**	**159.9**
Residential.	(NA)	123.9	137.5	142.1	144.5	145.8	147.2
City.	(NA)	76.1	80.5	82.0	82.9	83.3	83.7
P.O. Box.	(NA)	15.9	15.7	15.9	16.0	16.0	16.0
Rural/highway contract.	(NA)	31.9	41.2	44.2	45.7	46.6	47.4
Business.	(NA)	12.1	13.3	12.8	12.8	12.8	12.8
Pieces of mail handled (mil.)	**166,301**	**207,882**	**170,859**	**154,321**	**149,590**	**146,402**	**142,570**
First-class mail [1, 2].	89,270	103,526	77,592	62,599	58,834	56,712	54,943
Periodicals (formerly 2nd class).	10,680	10,365	7,269	5,838	5,301	4,994	4,635
Marketing Mail (formerly Standard A) [2].	63,725	90,057	81,841	80,030	78,329	77,270	75,653
U.S. Postal Service.	538	363	438	356	322	293	285
Free for the blind.	35	47	68	46	45	43	34
Shipping and package services [2, 3, 6].	(X)	(X)	3,057	4,539	5,758	6,149	6,165
Express mail [2, 3, 5].	59	71	43	36	30	28	26
Package services (formerly Standard B).	663	1,128	657	566	620	642	622
Priority mail [2, 3, 4].	518	1,223	779	1,007	1,045	1,085	1,097
International economy mail (surface) [3].	166	79	([3])	([3])	([3])	([3])	([3])
International, airmail or total [3, 7].	632	1,021	594	913	1,001	941	855
Employees, total (1,000).	**843**	**901**	**672**	**622**	**644**	**634**	**633**
Career.	**761**	**788**	**584**	**492**	**503**	**497**	**497**
Headquarters.	2	2	3	3	3	3	3
Headquarters support.	6	6	5	4	4	3	3
Inspection Service.	4	4	2	2	2	2	2
Inspector General.	(X)	1	1	1	1	1	1
Field Career.	749	775	573	482	493	487	487
Postmasters.	27	26	23	15	14	14	14
Supervisors/managers.	43	39	28	24	25	26	26
Professional, administrative, and technical.	10	10	6	4	5	5	5
Clerks.	290	282	157	126	128	122	122
Mail handlers.	51	61	49	38	39	38	37
City carriers.	236	241	192	164	167	168	166
Motor vehicle operators.	7	9	7	7	8	8	9
Rural carriers.	42	57	67	67	69	71	73
Special delivery messengers.	2	(X)	(X)	(X)	(X)	(X)	(X)
Building and equipment maintenance.	33	42	37	31	31	30	30
Vehicle maintenance.	5	6	5	5	5	5	5
Other [8].	1	2	(X)	(X)	(X)	(X)	(X)
Non-career.	**83**	**114**	**88**	**130**	**141**	**137**	**136**
Casuals.	27	30	7	2	1	1	1
Transitional.	(X)	13	16	–	–	–	–
Rural part-time.	43	58	52	51	60	59	58
Relief/leave replacements.	12	12	11	5	2	2	2
Non-bargaining temporary.	(Z)	1	2	(Z)	(Z)	(Z)	(Z)
Compensation and employee benefits (mil. dol.).	34,214	49,532	48,909	47,278	45,634	46,525	47,519
Avg. salary per employee (dol.) [9].	37,570	50,103	72,099	(NA)	(NA)	(NA)	(NA)
Pieces of mail per employee (1,000).	197	231	254	248	232	231	225
Operating postal revenue (million dollars)...	**39,201**	**64,476**	**67,052**	**68,928**	**69,636**	**70,660**	**71,154**
Mail revenue.	**37,891**	**62,285**	**63,262**	**65,548**	**65,876**	**66,872**	**67,258**
First-class mail [1, 2].	24,023	35,516	32,111	28,412	25,689	24,948	24,434
Periodicals (formerly 2nd class).	1,509	2,171	1,879	1,589	1,375	1,277	1,194
Marketing Mail (formerly Standard A) [2].	8,082	15,193	16,728	17,646	16,626	16,512	16,359
Shipping and Package Services [2, 3, 6].	(X)	(X)	10,156	15,061	19,529	21,467	22,787
Express mail [2, 3, 5].	630	996	829	779	766	752	716
Package Services (formerly Standard B).	919	1,912	1,531	810	803	824	822
Priority mail [2, 3, 4].	1,555	4,837	5,455	7,664	8,717	9,342	9,730
International economy mail (surface) [3].	222	180	([3])	([3])	([3])	([3])	([3])
International, airmail or total [3, 7].	941	1,477	2,388	2,702	2,614	2,630	2,466
Service revenue.	**1,310**	**2,191**	**3,790**	**3,380**	**3,760**	**3,788**	**3,896**
Certified [10].	310	385	791	669	672	678	654
Insurance [10].	47	109	128	90	74	79	78
Money orders.	155	235	182	159	147	147	148
Other [10].	592	1,342	2,635	2,462	2,867	2,884	3,016
Operating expenses (million dollars) [11]...	**40,490**	**62,992**	**75,426**	**73,641**	**72,436**	**74,696**	**80,119**

– Represents zero. NA Not available. X Not applicable. Z Fewer than 500. [1] Items mailed at 1st class rates and weighing 11 ounces or less. [2] Beginning 2010, Express Mail, Priority Mail, First-Class Parcels, and Standard Parcels are not included in Mail categories but reclassified under Shipping and Package Services. [3] "Volume" and "Mailing & Shipping Revenue" restructured for the "Postal Accountability and Enhancement Act (PAEA) of 2006." Some categories eliminated. [4] Provides 2 to 3 day delivery service. [5] Overnight delivery of packages weighing up to 70 pounds. [6] Beginning 2010, also includes Package Services. [7] Airmail only, for 2005 and earlier. Beginning 2010, total international, including all international revenues and pieces formerly included in First-Class Mail, Standard Mail, and Package Services. [8] Includes discontinued operations, area offices, and nurses. Beginning 2010, nurses are included with clerks. [9] For career bargaining unit employees. Includes fringe benefits. [10] Beginning 2000, return receipt revenue broken out from registry, certified, and insurance and included in "other." [11] Shown in year in which obligation was incurred.

Source: U.S. Postal Service, *FY2019 Annual Report to Congress,* 2020, and earlier reports, and unpublished data. See also <https://about.usps.com/strategic-planning/future-postal-service/publications.htm>.

Section 24
Information and Communications

This section presents statistics on the various information and communications media: publishing, including newspapers, periodicals, books, and software; motion pictures, sound recordings, broadcasting, and telecommunications; computers, and internet access and use; and information services, such as libraries.

Information industry—The U.S. Census Bureau's *Service Annual Survey* provides estimates of revenues and expenses of firms in the information sector. Data are based on the North American Industry Classification System (NAICS). The information sector comprises establishments engaged in the following: (1) producing and distributing information and cultural products, (2) providing the means to transmit or distribute these products as well as data or communications, and 3) processing data.

The main components of the information sector include the publishing industries, including software publishing, and both traditional publishing and publishing exclusively on the internet; the motion picture and sound recording industries; the broadcasting industries, including traditional broadcasting and broadcasting over the internet; the telecommunications industries; and web search portals, data processing industries, and information services.

Telecommunications encompasses wired (including broadband internet service), wireless (including mobile), and satellite telecommunications. Broadcasting covers radio, television, and cable and other subscription programming. Internet publishing and broadcasting, and web search portals are grouped together.

Service Annual Survey data from 1998 to 2003 are based on the 1997 NAICS; 2004 to 2012 data are based variously on 2002 and 2007 NAICS; beginning in 2013, data are all based on 2012 NAICS, with data for various previous years revised to accommodate the new NAICS codes. Major revisions in many communications industries affect the comparability of these data. For detailed information about NAICS, see <census.gov/eos/www/naics/>. See also the text in Section 15, Business Enterprise.

The 1997 Economic Census was the first to cover the new information sector of the economy. The census, conducted every 5 years, for the years ending in "2" and "7," provides information on the number of establishments, receipts, payroll, and paid employees for the United States and various geographic levels in the U.S., including the U.S. territories. Data covered in this edition of the *Statistical Abstract of the U.S.* come from the 2017 Economic Census. Data from the 2017 Economic Census are being released on a flow basis between September 2019 and December 2021.

The Bureau of Economic Analysis recently began producing statistics to measure the digital economy. The BEA is developing a digital economy satellite account to provide economic measures on the infrastructure that enables a digital economy, electronic commerce transactions, and the content that users of the digital economy create and access (digital media). Currently, the BEA covers only services that are primarily digital, and excludes goods and services that have a non-digital component. Thus, a service such as ride-sharing, which uses the internet to connect services, is not included since a major component (the ride) is not digital. The BEA is working on expanding coverage of the digital economy.

The Federal Communications Commission (FCC), established in 1934, regulates interstate and international communications by radio, television, wire, satellite, and cable across the entire U.S. Large carriers and holding companies file annual financial reports, which are publicly available. The FCC has jurisdiction over interstate and foreign communication services but not over intrastate or local services. Also, the gross operating revenues of the telephone carriers reporting publicly available data annually to the FCC are estimated to cover about 90 percent of the revenues of all U.S. telephone companies. Data are not comparable with Census Bureau's *Service Annual Survey* because of coverage and different accounting practices for those telephone companies which report to the FCC.

Reports filed by the broadcasting industry cover all radio and television stations operating in the United States. Private radio services represent the largest and most diverse group of licensees regulated by the FCC. These services provide voice, data communications, point-to-point, and point-to-multipoint radio communications for fixed and mobile communicators. Major users of these services are small businesses, the aviation industry, the maritime trades, the land transportation industry, the manufacturing industry, state and local public safety and governmental authorities, emergency medical service providers, amateur radio operators, and personal radio operations (CB and the General Mobile Radio Service). The FCC also licenses entities as private and common carriers. Private and common carriers provide fixed and land mobile communications service on a for-profit basis.

Statistics on publishing are available from the Census Bureau and various private agencies. Editor & Publisher Co., Irvine, CA, provides annual data on the number and circulation of daily and Sunday newspapers in its *Data Book*. Data on public libraries are from the Institute of Museums and Library Services. The Pew Research Center in Washington D.C. collects data on media use, including the internet and social media, and of mobile electronic devices, among the general public. MRI-Simmons (launched as a joint venture under GfK in 2019) also collects data on internet use, and use of other traditional media.

Statistical reliability—For a discussion of statistical collection and estimation, sampling procedures, and measures of statistical reliability applicable to Census Bureau data, see Appendix III.

Table 1153. Information Industries—Type of Establishment, Employees, and Payroll: 2018

[Employees in thousands (3,600.9 represents 3,600,900); payroll in millions of dollars (385,211 represents $835,211,000,000). Excludes self-employed individuals, employees of private households, railroad employees, agricultural production employees, and most government employees. For more information, see source and Appendix III]

| Industry | NAICS code [1] | Establishments | | | | Employ- ees [6] (1,000) | Annual payroll (mil. dol.) |
		Total [2]	Corpora- tions [3]	Individual proprietor- ships [4]	Non- profits [5]		
Information industries..............................	**51**	**157,766**	**129,198**	**5,430**	**5,667**	**3,600.9**	**385,211**
Publishing industries (except internet)...............	511	29,662	24,317	1,393	703	1,015.9	133,413
Newspaper, periodical, book, and directory.........	5111	15,474	12,065	982	678	343.7	22,198
Newspaper publishers..............................	51111	6,693	5,315	482	157	153.1	7,283
Periodical publishers..............................	51112	4,976	3,786	275	295	84.4	7,130
Book publishers..................................	51113	2,413	1,846	136	201	73.1	5,822
Directory and mailing list publishers...............	51114	719	610	27	4	14.4	1,061
Other publishers..................................	51119	673	508	62	21	18.7	902
Greeting card publishers.........................	511191	118	101	9	(NA)	13.7	593
All other publishers..............................	511199	555	407	53	20	5.0	309
Software publishers.................................	5112	14,188	12,252	411	25	672.3	111,215
Motion picture and sound recording industries.......	512	26,880	21,703	1,267	635	336.7	19,665
Motion picture and video industries.................	5121	23,174	18,825	999	550	313.1	17,231
Motion picture and video production...............	51211	15,251	12,909	617	260	132.2	12,301
Motion picture and video distribution...............	51212	358	260	17	16	2.9	268
Motion picture and video exhibition.................	51213	4,630	3,080	268	258	147.5	2,170
Motion picture theaters (except drive-ins)........	512131	4,428	2,972	217	257	146.2	2,144
Drive-in motion picture theaters.................	512132	202	108	51	(NA)	1.3	26
Postproduction and other motion picture and video industries.............................	51219	2,935	2,576	97	16	30.5	2,492
Teleproduction and other post- production services.................................	512191	2,714	2,399	84	10	29.6	2,416
Other motion picture and video industries........	512199	221	177	13	6	0.9	76
Sound recording industries...........................	5122	3,706	2,878	268	85	23.6	2,434
Music publishers..................................	51223	743	554	66	7	5.5	511
Sound recording studios...........................	51224	1,894	1,526	147	16	5.8	330
Record production and distribution..................	51225	654	492	39	9	9.5	1,433
Other sound recording industries...................	51229	415	306	16	53	2.7	161
Broadcasting (except internet)........................	515	8,063	5,394	286	1,200	254.4	23,276
Radio and television broadcasting....................	5151	7,361	4,961	272	1,038	203.8	16,103
Radio broadcasting................................	51511	5,258	3,486	211	753	87.3	5,585
Radio networks..................................	515111	762	454	20	198	11.4	1,255
Radio stations..................................	515112	4,496	3,032	191	555	75.9	4,329
Television broadcasting............................	51512	2,103	1,475	61	285	116.5	10,518
Cable and other subscription programming.........	5152	702	433	14	162	50.6	7,173
Telecommunications.................................	517	63,342	55,255	1,230	250	1,129.1	84,807
Wired and wireless telecommunications carriers...	5173	59,241	51,965	998	242	1,068.6	78,799
Wired telecommunications carriers.................	517311	32,164	31,012	226	233	738.2	58,941
Wireless telecommunications carriers (except satellite).................................	517312	27,077	20,953	772	9	330.3	19,858
Satellite telecommunications.........................	5174	410	318	35	3	8.3	963
Other telecommunications...........................	5179	3,691	2,972	197	5	52.2	5,045
Telecommunications resellers....................	517911	2,040	1,641	85	(NA)	23.8	1,628
All other telecommunications.....................	517919	1,651	1,331	112	4	28.5	3,417
Data processing, hosting, and related services.....	518	17,526	14,453	580	533	546.9	57,689
Other information services...........................	519	12,293	8,076	674	2,346	317.9	66,361
News syndicates....................................	51911	398	348	11	18	6.6	602
Libraries and archives...............................	51912	2,263	137	46	2,054	26.3	839
Internet publishing and broadcasting and web search portals..............................	51913	8,335	6,669	423	230	275.9	64,155
All other information services........................	51919	1,297	922	194	44	9.2	765

NA Not available. [1] 2017 North American Industry Classification System; see text, this section and Section 15. [2] Includes other types of establishments, not shown separately. [3] Includes C- and S-Corporations. [4] An unincorporated business with a sole owner. [5] An organization that does not distribute surplus funds to its owners or shareholders, but instead uses surplus funds to help pursue its goals. Most non-profit organizations are exempt from income taxes. [6] For employees on the payroll for the pay period including March 12.

Source: U.S. Census Bureau, County Business Patterns, "County Business Patterns by Legal Form of Organization and Employment Size Class for U.S., States, and Selected Geographies: 2018," <https://data.census.gov/>, accessed July 2020. See also <https://www.census.gov/programs-surveys/cbp.html>.

Table 1154. Information Industries—Establishments, Revenue, Payroll, and Employees by Kind of Business: 2017

[1,594,628 represents $1,594,628,000,000. For establishments with payroll. Based on the 2017 Economic Census; see Appendix III]

Kind of business	2017 NAICS code [1]	Establishments	Receipts [2] (mil. dol.)	Annual payroll (mil. dol.)	Paid employees (1,000)
Information............................	**51**	**154,096**	**1,594,628**	**361,755**	**3,720**
Publishing industries (except internet)................	511	29,940	360,239	121,424	1,042
Newspaper publishers............................	51111	7,251	26,819	8,064	194
Periodical publishers.............................	51112	5,274	27,179	6,811	91
Book publishers................................	51113	2,433	28,992	5,549	80
Software publishers.............................	5112	13,573	266,821	98,571	638
Motion picture & sound recording industries..........	512	25,749	103,670	18,182	342
Motion picture & video industries.................	5121	22,063	90,121	15,845	315
Sound recording industries [3]...................	5122	3,686	13,548	2,336	27
Music publishers............................	51223	705	4,677	512	7
Record production and distribution..............	51225	681	7,333	1,321	10
Broadcasting (except internet)......................	515	8,267	164,057	22,841	276
Radio broadcasting............................	51511	5,444	20,643	5,617	94
Television broadcasting........................	51512	2,117	55,960	10,538	121
Cable & other subscription programming............	5152	706	87,455	6,686	60
Telecommunications..............................	517	60,530	620,383	82,719	1,143
Wired telecommunications carriers................	517311	30,352	322,238	56,981	741
Wireless telecommunications carriers (except satellite)............	517312	22,451	253,022	19,330	310
Satellite telecommunications....................	5174	442	5,545	907	9
Other telecommunications.......................	5179	7,285	39,578	5,501	83
Data processing, hosting, and related services.......	518	17,748	175,519	59,957	603
Other information services [3].....................	519	11,862	170,759	56,633	313
Internet publishing & broadcasting and web search portals........	51913	8,064	164,106	54,456	266

[1] North American Industry Classification System, 2017; see text, this section and Section 15. [2] Includes value of sales, shipments, receipts, or revenue. [3] Includes other kinds of businesses not shown separately.

Source: U.S. Census Bureau, 2017 Economic Census, "EC1751BASIC: Information: Summary Statistics for the U.S., States, and Selected Geographies: 2017," <https://data.census.gov/>, accessed June 2020.

Table 1155. Information Industries—Establishments, Employees, and Payroll by State: 2018

[Annual payroll in millions of dollars (385,211 represents $385,211,000,000). Based on Census Bureau's County Business Patterns and Nonemployer Statistics programs. Data based on 2017 North American Industry Classification System (NAICS) code 51]

State	Establishments	Annual payroll (mil. dol.)	Paid employees [1]	Nonemployer establishments	State	Establishments	Annual payroll (mil. dol.)	Paid employees [1]	Nonemployer establishments
U.S.........	**157,766**	**385,211**	**3,600,900**	**358,505**	MO.........	2,738	4,132	59,377	4,770
AL...........	1,852	2,019	34,290	3,141	MT.........	689	442	8,541	1,057
AK...........	416	458	6,546	509	NE.........	969	1,392	20,959	1,326
AZ...........	2,598	3,974	58,569	6,311	NV.........	1,467	1,316	20,185	3,696
AR...........	1,178	1,582	20,985	1,788	NH.........	779	1,381	16,538	1,367
CA...........	26,339	119,090	688,789	69,518	NJ.........	3,875	9,313	89,932	10,791
CO...........	3,763	8,931	96,624	7,938	NM.........	842	585	11,728	1,638
CT...........	1,778	4,009	41,292	4,047	NY.........	12,096	36,706	303,133	33,513
DE...........	585	472	6,695	1,204	NC.........	4,025	7,169	92,398	8,927
DC...........	812	2,858	23,828	1,504	ND.........	356	472	6,906	458
FL...........	9,603	14,118	176,404	25,881	OH.........	4,298	6,699	100,197	9,100
GA...........	4,893	12,587	134,591	12,310	OK.........	1,569	1,532	28,181	2,821
HI...........	562	531	8,550	1,267	OR.........	2,436	3,193	39,611	5,276
ID...........	829	689	12,817	1,644	PA.........	5,656	10,364	114,306	10,690
IL...........	6,102	11,641	129,798	11,829	RI.........	444	520	6,696	1,009
IN...........	2,450	2,864	45,296	4,618	SC.........	1,691	2,459	39,713	3,686
IA...........	1,643	1,831	30,886	2,188	SD.........	473	354	7,319	631
KS...........	1,407	2,342	31,233	2,154	TN.........	2,912	3,154	49,481	7,875
KY...........	1,819	1,507	31,023	2,877	TX.........	10,920	22,690	268,074	26,542
LA...........	1,590	1,305	23,253	3,501	UT.........	1,813	4,126	54,209	4,313
ME...........	806	656	11,190	1,360	VT.........	502	544	7,946	918
MD...........	2,535	4,545	52,175	6,870	VA.........	4,070	10,541	101,802	8,216
MA...........	3,825	15,081	122,207	8,305	WA.........	3,989	26,555	146,972	7,778
MI...........	4,233	5,581	71,143	8,438	WV.........	660	447	9,193	916
MN...........	2,771	5,289	63,769	5,493	WI.........	2,616	4,331	57,690	4,223
MS...........	1,071	641	13,848	1,553	WY.........	421	191	4,012	720

[1] Number of paid employees for pay period including March 12.

Source: U.S. Census Bureau, County Business Patterns and Nonemployer Statistics, "2018 CBP and NES Combined Report," <census.gov/programs-surveys/cbp.html> and <census.gov/programs-surveys/nonemployer-statistics.html>, accessed July 2020.

Table 1156. Digital Economy—Value Added, Gross Output, and Employment by Industry: 2010 to 2018

[In billions of dollars (1,232.0 represents $1,232,000,000,000), except as noted. Estimates are based on goods and services that are primarily digital. BEA includes in its definition of the digital economy: (1) infrastructure, or the basic physical materials and organizational arrangements that support the existence and use of computer networks and the digital economy; primarily information and communications technology (ICT) goods and services; (2) electronic commerce (e-commerce), the remote sale of goods and services over computer networks; and (3) priced digital services, the computing and communication services performed for a fee charged to the consumer. Industries are based on 2012 North American Classification System (NAICS). For more information on defining and measuring the digital economy, see <https://www.bea.gov/data/special-topics/digital-economy>]

Industry	Value added (bil. dol.) [1]			Gross output (bil. dol.) [1]			Employees (1,000)		
	2010	2017	2018	2010	2017	2018	2010	2017	2018
All industries	**1,232.0**	**1,740.5**	**1,849.3**	**1,970.0**	**2,785.6**	**2,973.3**	**7,033**	**8,647**	**8,849**
Private industries	**1,218.4**	**1,729.5**	**1,837.5**	**1,956.1**	**2,774.4**	**2,961.2**	**6,868**	**8,527**	**8,724**
Agriculture and mining	0.3	0.4	0.5	0.3	0.4	0.5	2	2	2
Utilities	0.4	0.5	0.5	0.4	0.5	0.5	3	3	3
Construction	0.2	0.4	0.4	0.2	0.4	0.4	2	5	5
Manufacturing	183.3	187.4	197.2	273.7	251.6	265.8	848	776	790
Wholesale trade	206.5	308.7	316.1	337.6	560.9	583.0	1,424	1,673	1,667
Retail trade	66.4	144.2	158.4	95.9	238.2	262.9	660	1,309	1,399
Transportation and warehousing	0.7	0.8	1.0	0.7	0.8	1.0	9	10	12
Information	516.0	698.8	746.7	885.1	1,198.8	1,283.0	1,769	1,871	1,878
Publishing, except internet (includes software)	104.6	174.2	193.7	152.0	218.0	238.6	445	640	662
Motion picture and sound recording	31.5	29.2	31.9	44.7	48.6	53.6	128	133	137
Broadcasting and telecommunications	305.5	344.7	351.2	569.0	685.6	705.5	979	845	817
Data processing, internet publishing, and other information services	74.4	150.7	169.9	119.3	246.6	285.3	217	252	263
Finance, insurance, real estate, rental, and leasing	6.2	7.5	7.9	6.2	7.5	7.9	63	60	62
Professional and business services	220.4	358.4	385.3	330.6	483.1	522.8	1,713	2,439	2,516
Educational services, health care, and social assistance	12.0	15.1	15.9	16.2	21.1	22.0	220	237	245
Arts, entertainment, recreation, accommodation, and food services	0.4	0.6	0.7	0.4	0.6	0.7	7	8	9
Other services, except government	5.6	6.5	6.8	8.8	10.1	10.6	147	135	138
Government	13.6	11.0	11.8	13.8	11.3	12.1	165	120	124
Federal	6.2	5.3	5.7	6.1	5.3	5.7	64	51	52
State and local	7.4	5.7	6.2	7.7	6.0	6.5	102	69	72
Private goods-producing industries	183.8	188.2	198.1	274.2	252.5	266.7	852	783	797
Private services-producing industries	1,034.6	1,541.2	1,639.4	1,681.9	2,521.9	2,694.4	6,016	7,744	7,927

[1] These estimates are based on data valued in producers' prices and exclude transportation costs and wholesale and retail trade markups, with the exception of retail trade markups associated with e-commerce transactions.

Source: U.S. Bureau of Economic Analysis, Special Topics: Digital Economy, "Data for 2005-2018," <https://www.bea.gov/data/special-topics/digital-economy>, accessed August 2020.

Table 1157. Digital Economy—Value Added and Gross Output by Commodity: 2005 to 2018

[In billions of dollars (13,036.6 represents $13,036,600,000,000). Estimates are based on goods and services that are primarily digital. See headnote, Table 1156]

Commodity	Value added (GDP) [1,2]				Gross output [2]			
	2005	2010	2017	2018	2005	2010	2017	2018
BILLION DOLLARS								
Total U.S. economy	13,036.6	14,992.1	19,519.4	20,580.2	23,512.9	26,422.4	34,495.4	36,593.3
Digital economy, total	**948.4**	**1,232.0**	**1,740.5**	**1,849.3**	**1,634.6**	**1,970.0**	**2,785.6**	**2,973.3**
Digital-enabling infrastructure	278.7	321.2	404.0	435.7	503.5	462.9	523.3	562.2
Hardware	163.9	171.6	177.1	187.4	337.8	270.9	256.6	272.3
Software	114.8	149.6	226.9	248.3	165.7	192.1	266.7	289.9
E-commerce	168.4	269.2	444.9	465.8	256.5	422.7	783.8	830.3
Business-to-business	135.0	204.9	304.3	311.4	205.6	331.4	552.3	574.5
Business-to-consumer	33.4	64.3	140.6	154.4	50.9	91.3	231.5	255.8
Priced digital services	501.3	641.6	891.5	947.8	874.6	1,084.4	1,478.5	1,580.9
Cloud services, paid	25.0	41.2	63.9	68.9	32.8	62.1	99.7	110.0
All other priced digital services	476.3	600.4	827.7	878.8	841.8	1,022.3	1,378.9	1,470.9
Addendum:								
Digital goods	130.6	131.3	128.4	131.8	291.0	211.0	177.7	184.2
Digital services	817.8	1,100.8	1,612.0	1,717.5	1,343.6	1,759.0	2,608.0	2,789.1
PERCENT								
Total U.S. economy	100.0	100.0	100.0	100.0	100.0	100.0	100.0	100.0
Digital economy	**7.3**	**8.2**	**8.9**	**9.0**	**7.0**	**7.5**	**8.1**	**8.1**
Infrastructure	2.1	2.1	2.1	2.1	2.1	1.8	1.5	1.5
E-commerce	1.3	1.8	2.3	2.3	1.1	1.6	2.3	2.3
Priced digital services	3.8	4.3	4.6	4.6	3.7	4.1	4.3	4.3
Addendum:								
Digital goods	1.0	0.9	0.7	0.6	1.2	0.8	0.5	0.5
Digital services	6.3	7.3	8.3	8.3	5.7	6.7	7.6	7.6

[1] Value added by commodity is prepared by (1) calculating ratios of commodity output to total industry output for each industry and digital commodity, (2) applying these ratios to each industry's value added, and (3) aggregating the result by digital commodity. [2] These estimates are based on data valued in producers' prices and exclude transportation costs and wholesale and retail trade markups, with the exception of retail trade markups associated with e-commerce transactions.

Source: U.S. Bureau of Economic Analysis, Special Topics: Digital Economy, "Data for 2005-2018," <https://www.bea.gov/data/special-topics/digital-economy>, accessed August 2020.

Table 1158. Information Sector Services—Estimated Revenue and Expenses: 2016 to 2018

[In millions of dollars (1,489,380 represents $1,489,380,000,000). For all employer firms regardless of tax status. Estimates have been adjusted to the results of the 2012 Economic Census and are based on the 2012 North American Industry Classification System (NAICS). Based on the Service Annual Survey and administrative data; see Appendix III]

Industry	NAICS code	Operating revenue			Operating expenses		
		2016	2017	2018	2016	2017	2018
Information industries	51	**1,489,380**	**1,533,015**	**1,630,015**	**1,125,430**	**1,166,487**	**1,202,973**
Publishing industries (except internet)	511	308,469	322,323	342,459	218,279	226,643	245,813
Newspaper publishers	51111	25,247	25,685	24,654	23,611	24,083	23,221
Periodical publishers	51112	28,237	28,258	27,266	23,123	23,390	21,253
Book publishers	51113	27,744	28,045	26,927	17,260	17,571	16,725
Directory and mailing list publishers	51114	7,775	6,468	6,654	6,676	5,208	5,512
Greeting card publishers	511191	3,351	3,705	3,740	(S)	(S)	(S)
All other publishers	511199	1,318	1,310	1,258	790	781	825
Software publishers	5112	214,797	228,852	251,960	144,662	153,360	175,967
Motion picture and sound recording industries	512	103,222	101,738	109,969	73,328	73,309	72,315
Motion picture and video production and distribution [1]	5121x	66,862	64,410	69,911	45,572	44,251	42,856
Motion picture and video exhibition	51213	16,539	15,980	17,590	13,050	13,294	13,158
Teleproduction and other postproduction services	512191	5,885	6,001	5,751	4,823	4,912	4,446
Other motion picture and video industries	512199	379	443	475	299	291	317
Record production	51221	388	391	388	302	294	325
Integrated record production/distribution	51222	6,259	7,246	7,932	5,836	6,623	7,480
Music publishers	51223	5,247	5,594	6,124	2,152	2,331	2,356
Sound recording studios	51224	1,095	1,099	1,185	869	865	922
Other sound recording industries	51229	568	574	613	425	448	455
Broadcasting (except internet)	515	159,259	160,814	168,843	111,860	112,064	118,411
Radio networks	515111	7,089	7,641	8,063	5,296	5,623	5,978
Radio stations	515112	12,807	12,359	12,438	11,029	10,727	10,405
Television broadcasting	51512	57,855	57,487	62,843	47,184	46,045	50,578
Cable and other subscription programming	5152	81,508	83,327	85,499	48,351	49,669	51,450
Telecommunications	517	627,970	617,045	630,683	484,716	484,752	467,287
Wired telecommunications carriers	5171	326,119	315,390	311,465	263,017	262,293	249,981
Wireless telecommunications carriers (except satellite)	5172	259,231	257,778	272,046	188,918	189,092	181,197
Satellite telecommunications	5174	7,208	6,947	7,070	5,634	5,432	5,511
Telecommunications resellers	517911	19,035	19,454	20,024	12,664	12,461	12,383
All other telecommunications	517919	16,377	17,476	20,078	14,483	15,474	18,215
Data processing, hosting, and related services	518	135,525	152,277	169,480	117,863	129,063	138,100
Other information services	519	154,935	178,818	208,581	119,384	140,656	161,047
News syndicates	51911	2,043	1,860	1,877	1,711	1,515	1,498
Libraries and archives	51912	2,460	2,741	2,771	2,364	2,495	2,524
Internet publishing and broadcasting, and Web search portals	51913	148,020	171,787	201,231	113,376	134,661	154,886
Other information services	51919	2,412	2,430	2,702	1,933	1,985	(S)

S Data does not meet publication standards. [1] Includes NAICS 51211 (Motion Picture and Video Production) and NAICS 51212 (Motion Picture and Video Distribution).

Source: U.S. Census Bureau, Service Annual Survey, "Service Annual Survey Latest Data (NAICS-basis): 2018," <https://www.census.gov/programs-surveys/sas/data.html>, accessed February 2020.

Table 1159. Audience Use of Media by Type: 2019

[In percent, except total population (250,323 represents 250,323,000). As of Fall 2019. For persons age 18 and over. Represents the percent of persons using each media type during an average week, except as noted. Based on a sample and subject to sampling error]

Audience characteristic	Total population (1,000)	TV viewing [1]	TV prime time viewing [1]	Cable/ pay TV viewing [2]	Radio listening	Newspaper reading [3]	Internet use
Total	**250,323**	**89.43**	**78.25**	**88.98**	**20.09**	**35.14**	**86.29**
18 to 24 years old	29,506	78.89	59.72	81.60	20.75	27.15	97.49
25 to 34 years old	45,047	84.33	70.46	82.76	22.90	29.76	96.31
35 to 44 years old	40,822	88.66	76.64	86.14	22.02	28.27	95.21
45 to 54 years old	41,742	91.00	81.14	91.14	22.12	33.36	91.06
55 to 64 years old	41,882	93.58	85.80	93.22	20.26	39.73	82.67
65 years old and over	51,325	95.93	88.53	95.73	13.91	47.61	63.06
Male	120,931	89.16	77.57	88.80	19.98	34.54	86.53
Female	129,392	89.69	78.89	89.15	20.19	35.70	86.08
White only	181,982	89.97	79.76	89.53	19.66	36.05	87.13
Black only	30,521	91.07	77.80	90.96	23.25	42.43	82.21
Other races/multiple classifications	37,821	85.55	71.37	84.73	19.62	24.88	85.57
Employed:							
Full time	128,304	89.04	77.35	88.32	22.63	33.08	94.94
Part time	33,148	84.42	70.02	86.74	20.95	33.34	91.66
Not employed	88,871	91.87	82.63	90.77	16.10	38.78	71.81
Household income:							
Less than $50,000	84,323	88.11	76.19	87.25	20.40	35.58	73.41
$50,000 to $74,999	41,667	90.39	78.51	89.08	20.25	35.70	87.98
$75,000 to $149,999	77,818	90.17	79.95	89.95	21.03	34.35	93.18
$150,000 or more	46,515	89.74	78.92	90.40	17.80	35.15	96.63

[1] Includes broadcast and cable TV. [2] In the past 7 days. [3] One or more issues over a 28-day period.

Source: © Fall 2019, MRI Survey of the American Consumer. Courtesy of MRI-Simmons. See also <https://www.mrisimmons.com/>.

Table 1160. Utilization and Number of Selected Media: 2000 to 2018

[100.2 represents 100,200,000]

Media	Unit	2000	2005	2010	2012	2013	2014	2015	2016	2017	2018
Households with—											
Telephones [1]	Millions	100.2	107.0	114.0	116.9	118.4	119.9	122.2	122.6	122.1	124.2
Telephone service [1]	Percent	94.1	92.9	95.5	95.8	95.7	96.1	96.3	96.3	95.8	96.0
Landline households with											
wireless telephone [2]	Percent	(X)	42.4	58.1	52.5	49.5	44.7	41.6	40.2	37.8	36.3
Wireless-only [2]	Percent	(X)	7.3	26.6	35.8	39.4	44.0	47.4	49.3	52.5	54.9
Total broadcast stations [3,4]	Number	(NA)	27,354	30,630	30,470	30,432	30,592	31,032	32,397	33,006	33,342
Radio stations	Number	(NA)	13,660	14,619	15,196	15,358	15,432	15,480	15,516	15,503	15,508
AM stations	Number	4,685	4,757	4,782	4,738	4,727	4,705	4,684	4,669	4,639	4,619
FM commercial	Number	5,892	6,231	6,526	6,598	6,612	6,652	6,701	6,746	6,744	6,754
FM educational	Number	(NA)	2,672	3,311	3,860	4,019	4,075	4,095	4,101	4,120	4,135
Television stations [3]	Number	1,663	1,750	1,781	1,781	1,784	1,785	1,782	1,778	1,767	1,761
Commercial	Number	1,288	1,370	1,390	1,386	1,388	1,390	1,387	1,384	1,377	1,373
UHF TV band	Number	721	782	1,022	1,028	1,030	1,032	1,031	1,033	1,013	1,006
VHF TV band	Number	567	588	368	358	358	358	356	351	364	367
Educational	Number	(NA)	380	391	395	396	395	395	394	390	388
UHF TV band	Number	(NA)	254	284	288	289	289	289	289	276	270
VHF TV band	Number	(NA)	126	107	107	107	106	106	105	114	118
Broadband subscribers: [5]											
Total fixed broadband [6]	Millions	6.8	47.8	84.5	92.5	96.0	98.2	102.2	105.7	108.2	110.9
25 Mbps/3 Mbps [7]	Millions	(NA)	(NA)	(NA)	(NA)	(NA)	42.7	54.3	62.9	73.3	82.0
Mobile wireless [8]	Millions	(NA)	(NA)	97.5	170.1	197.4	240.0	273.7	299.3	312.8	330.5
Residential fixed broadband [6]	Millions	5.2	44.0	76.9	84.4	87.6	89.5	93.4	96.6	98.8	101.3
25 Mbps/3 Mbps [7]	Millions	(NA)	(NA)	(NA)	(NA)	(NA)	40.9	51.8	59.5	68.9	75.8
Residential mobile wireless	Millions	(NA)	(NA)	72.5	131.4	159.2	201.2	229.1	241.4	253.1	267.2

NA Not available. X Not applicable. [1] As of November. Based on Current Population Survey. Source: Federal Communications Commission, prior to 2011, *Telephone Subscribership in the United States*, December 2011, and earlier reports. Beginning 2012, *Universal Service Monitoring Report, 2019,* and earlier reports. See also <https://www.fcc.gov/general/federal-state-joint-board-monitoring-reports>. [2] For January to June. Based on National Health Interview Survey. For families living in the same housing unit. Source: U.S. National Center for Health Statistics, *Wireless Substitution: Early Release of Estimates From the National Health Interview Survey, January–June 2018,* December 2018, and earlier reports. [3] As of December 31. Source: Federal Communications Commission, "Broadcast Station Totals," <https://www.fcc.gov/media/broadcast-station-totals>, accessed June 2020. [4] Includes Class A UHF and VHF, UHF and VHF Low Power TV, UHF and VHF Translators, FM Translators and Boosters, and Low Power FM stations. [5] As of December. Internet access over 200 kilobits per second in at least one direction. Based on FCC Form 477. Source: Federal Communications Commission, Wireline Competition Bureau, *Internet Access Services: Status as of December 31, 2018,* September 2020, and previous reports. [6] Includes aDSL, sDSL, cable modem, fiber-to-the-premises, satellite, fixed wireless, and power line/other. [7] Internet download and upload speeds, measured in megabits per second (Mbps). [8] Data prior to 2008 not shown due to reporting instruction changes on FCC Form 477.

Source: Compiled from sources mentioned in footnotes.

Table 1161. Publishing Industries—Estimated Revenue by Source and Media Type: 2010 to 2018

[In millions of dollars (260,795 represents $260,795,000,000). 2010 data based on the 2007 North American Industry Classification System (NAICS); beginning 2013, data based on 2012 NAICS. See text, this section and Section 15, and Appendix III]

Source of revenue and media type	2010	2015	2016	2017	2018
Publishing industries (except internet), NAICS 511 [1]	**260,795**	**293,771**	**308,469**	**322,323**	**342,459**
Newspaper publishers, NAICS 51111	33,360	26,550	25,247	25,685	24,654
Subscription and sales	8,491	8,877	8,849	9,041	8,887
Advertising space	20,378	14,729	13,628	13,619	12,334
Printing services	1,214	1,103	1,076	1,137	1,132
Distribution services	1,268	613	546	536	447
All other operating revenue	2,009	1,228	1,148	1,352	1,854
Print newspapers	26,973	18,993	17,714	17,463	16,434
Online newspapers	1,614	4,572	4,721	5,138	4,738
Other media newspapers	282	(S)	(S)	59	(S)
Periodical publishers, NAICS 51112	31,876	28,314	28,237	28,258	27,266
Subscription and sales	10,764	10,108	9,861	(S)	8,999
Advertising space	13,938	14,496	14,425	(S)	(S)
Print periodicals	20,587	16,818	16,550	(S)	(S)
Online periodicals	3,402	6,569	6,582	6,594	7,054
Other media periodicals	713	(S)	(S)	(S)	(S)
Book publishers, NAICS 51113 [1]	27,735	27,676	27,744	28,045	26,927
Textbooks	8,596	11,696	10,166	9,866	8,791
Children's books	3,189	1,898	2,853	2,971	2,952
General reference books	637	(S)	(S)	(S)	255
Professional, technical, and scholarly books	5,131	6,419	6,999	(S)	(S)
Adult trade books	6,626	5,171	5,420	5,373	5,177
Print books	19,890	16,620	16,552	16,137	13,849
Online books	3,297	7,505	7,753	(S)	(S)
Other media books	992	1,388	1,429	(S)	(S)
Directory and mailing list publishers, NAICS 51114 [1]	11,987	8,214	7,775	6,468	6,654
Subscription and sales	2,067	2,994	2,975	2,152	3,055
Advertising space	9,226	4,322	3,761	3,606	2,706
Print directories, databases, and other information collections	7,360	3,175	2,608	(S)	2,076
Online directories, databases, and other information collections	3,507	3,646	3,599	3,036	3,425
Greeting card publishers operating revenue, NAICS 511191	3,829	3,457	3,351	3,705	3,740

S Figure does not meet publication standards. [1] Includes other industries or revenue sources not shown separately.

Source: U.S. Census Bureau, Service Annual Survey, "Service Annual Survey Latest Data (NAICS-basis): 2018," and previous data releases, <https://www.census.gov/programs-surveys/sas/data.html>, accessed February 2020.

Table 1162. Daily and Sunday Newspapers—Number and Circulation: 1970 to 2018

[Circulation in millions (62.1 represents 62,100,000). Number of newspapers as of February 1 the following year, except as noted. Circulation figures as of 6-month period ended primarily September 30 of year shown. Covers all 50 States and D.C. For English language newspapers only]

Type	1970	1980	1990	2000	2005	2010	2013 [3]	2014 [3]	2015 [3]	2016 [3]	2017 [3]	2018 [3]
NUMBER												
Total daily newspapers [1]	1,748	1,745	1,611	1,480	1,452	(NA)	1,395	1,331	1,338	1,286	1,277	1,279
Morning	334	387	559	766	817	(NA)	980	953	972	939	947	925
Evening	1,429	1,388	1,084	727	645	(NA)	444	402	389	369	356	354
Sunday newspapers	586	736	863	917	914	(NA)	934	923	904	866	857	840
NET PAID CIRCULATION (mil.)												
Total daily newspapers [1]	62.1	62.2	62.3	55.8	53.3	(NA)	40.7	40.4	34.9	33.4	29.2	25.7
Morning	25.9	29.4	41.3	46.8	46.1	(NA)	37.0	36.8	31.6	30.4	26.2	23.0
Evening	36.2	32.8	21.0	9.0	7.2	(NA)	3.7	3.7	3.3	3.1	3.0	2.7
Sunday newspapers	49.2	54.7	62.6	59.4	55.3	(NA)	43.3	42.8	40.0	37.8	33.2	29.3
PER CAPITA CIRCULATION [2]												
Total daily newspapers [1]	0.30	0.27	0.25	0.20	0.18	(NA)	0.13	0.13	0.11	0.10	0.09	0.08
Morning	0.13	0.13	0.17	0.17	0.16	(NA)	0.12	0.12	0.10	0.09	0.08	0.07
Evening	0.18	0.14	0.08	0.03	0.02	(NA)	0.01	0.01	0.01	0.01	0.01	0.01
Sunday newspapers	0.24	0.24	0.25	0.21	0.19	(NA)	0.14	0.13	0.12	0.12	0.10	0.09

NA Not available. [1] All-day newspapers are counted in both morning and evening rows but only once in total. Circulation is divided equally between morning and evening. [2] Based on U.S. Census Bureau estimated resident population as of July 1 of year shown. [3] Number of newspapers as of January 1 of following year.

Source: Editor & Publisher, *Editor & Publisher Newspaper DataBook* ©, annual. See also <http://www.editorandpublisher.com/>.

Table 1163. Daily and Sunday Newspapers—Number and Circulation: Total, 1997 to 2018, and by State, 2018

[Circulation in thousands (56,728 represents 56,728,000). Number of newspapers as of February 1 the following year, except as noted. Circulation as of 6-month period ended primarily September 30 of year shown. Covers the 50 states and D.C. For English language newspapers only]

State	Daily Number	Daily Circulation [1] Net paid (1,000)	Daily Circulation [1] Per capita [2]	Sunday Number	Sunday Net paid circulation [1] (1,000)	State	Daily Number	Daily Circulation [1] Net paid (1,000)	Daily Circulation [1] Per capita [2]	Sunday Number	Sunday Net paid circulation [1] (1,000)
1997	1,509	56,728	0.21	903	60,484	IN	67	719	0.11	29	777
1998	1,489	56,182	0.20	898	60,066	IA	33	321	0.10	13	305
1999	1,483	55,979	0.20	905	59,894	KS	30	219	0.08	11	170
2000	1,480	55,773	0.20	917	59,421	KY	21	284	0.06	14	307
2001	1,468	55,578	0.19	913	59,090	LA	18	232	0.05	13	254
2002	1,457	55,186	0.19	913	58,780	ME	7	108	0.08	5	95
2003	1,456	55,185	0.19	917	58,495	MD	9	213	0.04	8	340
2004	1,457	54,626	0.19	915	57,753	MA	30	633	0.09	16	651
2005	1,452	53,345	0.18	914	55,270	MI	47	670	0.07	24	744
2006	1,437	52,329	0.18	907	53,175	MN	22	586	0.10	14	787
2007	1,422	50,742	0.17	907	51,246	MS	17	161	0.05	15	163
2008	1,408	48,598	0.16	902	49,115	MO	36	388	0.06	16	388
2009	1,397	46,278	0.15	919	46,895	MT	11	133	0.13	8	153
2010	(NA)	(NA)	(NA)	(NA)	(NA)	NE	15	218	0.11	6	196
2011	1,381	44,243	0.14	899	48,301	NV	5	241	0.08	5	276
2012	1,425	43,154	0.14	980	44,612	NH	10	105	0.08	7	108
2013 [3]	1,395	40,712	0.13	934	43,292	NJ	17	460	0.05	16	652
2014 [3]	1,331	40,420	0.13	923	42,751	NM	14	157	0.07	10	161
2015 [3]	1,338	34,901	0.11	904	40,014	NY	55	3,366	0.17	39	3,936
2016 [3]	1,286	33,419	0.10	866	37,771	ND	44	579	0.06	36	651
2017 [3]	1,277	29,185	0.09	857	33,160	ND	10	103	0.14	7	102
						OH	81	1,113	0.10	46	1,231
Total, 2018 [3]	1,279	25,705	0.08	840	29,273	OK	33	309	0.08	26	330
AL	22	186	0.04	16	214	OR	16	293	0.07	11	310
AK	8	98	0.13	4	89	PA	70	1,167	0.09	41	1,386
AZ	12	285	0.04	10	403	RI	5	77	0.07	2	79
AR	25	253	0.08	14	256	SC	16	268	0.05	14	315
CA	69	2,178	0.06	49	2,846	SD	11	84	0.10	4	55
CO	28	418	0.07	14	503	TN	25	424	0.06	18	466
CT	18	279	0.08	14	357	TX	66	1,100	0.04	64	1,562
DE	2	73	0.08	2	89	UT	6	174	0.05	6	274
DC	3	473	0.67	2	483	VT	8	52	0.08	4	37
FL	37	1,159	0.05	33	1,598	VA	20	2,174	0.26	17	1,415
GA	29	435	0.04	23	494	WA	20	534	0.07	16	657
HI	6	183	0.13	5	198	WV	17	175	0.10	11	174
ID	12	130	0.07	9	213	WI	32	470	0.08	20	525
IL	56	1,183	0.09	27	1,437	WY	8	62	0.11	6	61

NA Not available. [1] Circulation figures based on the principal community served by a newspaper, which is not necessarily the same location as the publisher's office. [2] Per capita based on estimated resident population as of July 1 of year shown. [3] Number of newspapers as of January 1 of following year.

Source: Editor & Publisher, *Editor & Publisher Newspaper DataBook* ©, annual. See also <http://www.editorandpublisher.com/>.

Table 1164. Software Publishers—Estimated Revenue, Expenses, and Inventories by Type: 2013 to 2018

[In millions of dollars (181,734 represents $181,734,000,000). For all employer firms regardless of tax status. Data are based on the 2012 North American Industry Classification System (NAICS), and cover NAICS 5112. Estimates are adjusted to the 2012 Economic Census where applicable. See text, this section, and Section 15, Business Enterprise. See also Appendix III]

Item	2013	2014	2015	2016	2017	2018
Operating revenue	**181,734**	**193,822**	**198,341**	**214,797**	**228,852**	**251,960**
By source:						
System software publishing [1]	59,447	61,352	55,269	57,728	62,297	72,021
Operating system software	19,813	19,127	18,991	19,897	21,247	23,387
Network software	17,614	18,163	12,894	14,243	15,044	19,810
Database management software	12,737	13,364	13,838	13,913	14,294	14,647
Development tools and programming languages software	4,185	4,264	2,366	2,297	2,188	2,235
Application software publishing [1]	68,088	75,125	88,933	96,142	101,459	114,012
General business productivity and home use applications	32,173	35,803	41,503	45,285	50,094	55,637
Cross-industry application software	17,973	18,713	25,074	26,746	26,227	29,017
Vertical market application software	9,726	11,350	11,186	12,293	13,745	14,782
Utilities application software	3,142	3,164	2,327	2,604	2,526	3,465
Other services [1]	(NA)	57,345	54,139	60,927	65,096	65,927
Custom application design and development	6,192	5,667	3,483	3,659	3,824	5,177
Information technology technical consulting services	6,560	6,516	6,170	7,318	9,115	9,262
Resale of computer hardware and software	6,602	8,609	8,145	8,792	8,398	9,365
Information technology-related training services	2,004	1,947	2,958	3,558	3,427	3,375
By software sales type:						
System software	59,447	61,352	55,269	57,728	62,297	72,021
Personal computer software	16,119	15,469	14,738	15,601	15,967	15,471
Enterprise or network software	26,096	26,651	24,020	26,266	29,426	38,144
Mainframe computer software	12,205	13,485	9,883	9,851	11,466	12,258
Other system software	5,027	5,747	6,628	6,010	5,438	6,148
Application software	68,088	75,125	88,933	96,142	101,459	114,012
Personal computer software	22,360	23,107	22,300	24,881	26,128	30,981
Enterprise or network software	34,937	38,555	44,269	46,569	49,593	56,441
Mainframe computer software	1,541	1,619	5,014	5,142	4,542	(S)
Other application software	(S)	(S)	17,350	19,550	21,196	(S)
Operating expenses, total [1, 2]	**117,706**	**128,834**	**132,400**	**144,662**	**153,360**	**175,967**
Gross annual payroll	57,019	61,306	60,596	64,682	70,576	81,622
Employer's cost for fringe benefits	14,215	15,310	16,277	17,435	19,080	(S)
Temporary staff and leased employee expense	3,663	3,922	3,240	3,699	4,009	5,060
Expensed equipment, materials, parts, and supplies	(S)	(S)	2,365	2,269	2,569	(S)
Expensed purchases of software	956	1,222	1,537	1,932	2,092	(S)
Purchased software reproduction	442	526	734	738	688	814
Depreciation and amortization charges	7,011	7,856	8,718	10,076	10,138	12,855
Inventories at end of year, total	**(S)**	**3,961**	**3,697**	**3,551**	**3,397**	**3,925**
Finished goods	(S)	1,912	2,388	2,303	2,123	2,944
Works-in-process	(S)	1,273	932	859	930	778
Materials, supplies, fuel, etc	(S)	(S)	377	389	(S)	203

NA Not available. S Data do not meet publication standards. [1] Includes other sources of revenue and types of expenses, not shown separately. [2] The 2018 Service Annual Survey consolidated and eliminated several expense items. For more information, see <https://www.census.gov/programs-surveys/sas/newsroom/updates/Changes_to_Detailed_Operating_Expense_Items.html>.

Source: U.S. Census Bureau, Service Annual Survey, "Service Annual Survey Latest Data (NAICS-basis): 2018," <https://www.census.gov/programs-surveys/sas/data.html>, accessed February 2020.

Table 1165. Internet Publishing and Broadcasting, and Web Search Portals—Estimated Revenue and Expenses: 2013 to 2018

[In millions of dollars (96,951 represents $96,951,000,000). For all employer firms regardless of tax status. Data are based on the 2012 North American Industry Classification System (NAICS). Covers NAICS 51913. Estimates are adjusted to the 2012 Economic Census. See text, Section 15, and Appendix III]

Item	2013	2014	2015	2016	2017	2018
Operating revenue	**96,951**	**109,414**	**125,868**	**148,020**	**171,787**	**201,231**
Source of revenue:						
Publishing and broadcasting of content on the internet	30,765	34,079	34,966	39,750	44,369	51,161
Licensing of rights to use intellectual property	3,782	4,133	(S)	2,925	(S)	(S)
Online advertising space	49,805	54,670	74,893	89,759	105,049	123,411
All other operating revenue	12,599	16,532	13,268	15,586	19,061	23,179
Revenue by type of customer:						
Household consumers and individual users	25,125	31,741	39,224	45,341	52,325	(S)
Business firms, nonprofit organizations, and government	71,826	77,673	86,644	102,679	119,462	(S)
Operating expenses	**74,525**	**89,128**	**100,541**	**113,376**	**134,661**	**154,886**

S Data do not meet publication standards.

Source: U.S. Census Bureau, Service Annual Survey, "Service Annual Survey Latest Data (NAICS-basis): 2018," <https://www.census.gov/programs-surveys/sas/data.html>, accessed February 2020.

Table 1166. Motion Picture and Sound Recording Industries—Estimated Revenue and Sources of Revenue: 2010 to 2018

[In millions of dollars (90,108 represents $90,108,000,000). For all employer firms regardless of tax status. Data for 2010 are based on the 2007 North American Industry Classification System (NAICS); beginning 2013, data are based on the 2012 NAICS. Covers NAICS 512. Estimates have been adjusted to the results of the 2012 Economic Census. See text, this section, and Section 15, Business Enterprise. See also Appendix III]

Kind of business and revenue source	2010	2015	2016	2017	2018
Operating revenue, total...................	**90,108**	**98,982**	**103,222**	**101,738**	**109,969**
Motion picture and video industries........................	**77,520**	**86,119**	**89,665**	**86,834**	**93,727**
Motion picture and video production and distribution [1,2].....................	59,411	64,434	66,862	64,410	69,911
Domestic licensing of rights to motion picture films....	13,113	14,583	13,772	12,986	12,405
Domestic licensing of rights to television programs....	10,767	13,316	14,225	13,534	15,071
International licensing of rights to motion picture films....	8,623	7,759	7,602	6,341	6,374
International licensing of rights to television programs....	3,010	3,691	3,842	3,452	3,395
Sale of audiovisual works for wholesale, retail, and rental markets.............	10,619	7,602	7,102	5,897	5,757
Motion picture and video exhibition, NAICS 51213 [1].............	12,869	15,787	16,539	15,980	17,590
Admissions to feature film exhibitions.............	8,731	9,597	10,026	9,685	10,335
Food and beverage sales.............	3,615	4,940	5,306	5,099	5,638
Postproduction services and other motion picture and video industries, NAICS 51219 [1].............	5,240	5,898	6,264	6,444	6,226
Audiovisual postproduction services.............	3,125	3,387	3,663	3,661	3,867
Motion picture film laboratory services.............	428	(S)	(S)	94	144
Duplication and copying services.............	1,158	238	250	(S)	(S)
Sound recording industries.............	**11,803**	**11,905**	**12,601**	**13,939**	**15,241**
Integrated record production and distribution, NAICS 51222 [1].............	6,991	5,765	6,259	7,246	7,932
Licensing revenue.............	(NA)	471	503	566	618
Sales of recordings.............	5,475	4,608	4,972	5,764	6,338
Music publishers, NAICS 51223 [1].............	3,964	5,054	5,247	5,594	6,124
Licensing of rights to use musical compositions.............	3,205	4,162	4,307	4,509	4,865
Print music.............	280	266	259	291	250
Sound recording studios, NAICS 51224 [1].............	848	1,086	1,095	1,099	1,185
Studio recording.............	627	773	747	675	650

NA Not available. S Data do not meet publication standards. [1] Includes other sources of revenue not shown separately. [2] Includes NAICS 51211 (Motion Picture and Video Production) and NAICS 51212 (Motion Picture and Video Distribution).

Source: U.S. Census Bureau, Service Annual Survey, "Service Annual Survey Latest Data (NAICS-basis): 2018," and "Service Annual Survey Historical Tables," <https://www.census.gov/programs-surveys/sas/data.html>, accessed February 2020.

Table 1167. Recorded Music Industry—Estimated Retail Volume and Value: 2000 to 2019

[1,079.2 represents 1,079,200,000. Data are net after returns. Formats with no retail value equivalent included at wholesale value. Based on reports of Recording Industry Association of America member companies who distribute about 85 percent of the music sold in the U.S.]

Medium	2000	2005	2010	2014	2015	2016	2017	2018	2019
VOLUME (million units)									
Total [1].............	**1,079.2**	**1,301.9**	**1,739.5**	**1,458.2**	**1,255.5**	**970.1**	**742.6**	**532.3**	**453.3**
Physical [2].............	**1,079.2**	**748.8**	**267.7**	**154.6**	**135.1**	**115.5**	**105.7**	**70.5**	**67.3**
Compact disk, album [3].............	942.5	705.4	253.0	138.7	117.1	97.6	87.7	52.0	46.5
Compact disk, single.............	34.2	2.8	1.0	0.9	0.4	0.1	0.1	(Z)	(Z)
Vinyl LP/EP (long play/extended play)........	2.2	1.0	4.2	10.3	13.7	14.8	15.6	16.7	19.1
Vinyl single.............	4.8	2.3	0.3	0.5	0.5	0.4	0.4	0.3	0.3
Music video [4].............	18.2	33.8	9.1	4.1	3.1	2.5	1.9	1.4	1.3
Digital [5].............	**(NA)**	**554.4**	**1,473.3**	**1,311.4**	**1,131.2**	**877.3**	**672.2**	**508.7**	**446.4**
Download single.............	(NA)	366.9	1,177.4	1,154.4	986.3	743.0	553.5	399.8	335.3
Download album.............	(NA)	13.6	85.8	114.2	106.8	85.1	66.4	49.7	40.2
Mobile [6].............	(NA)	170.0	188.5	26.6	21.9	22.6	14.3	10.0	8.6
Paid subscription [7].............	(NA)	1.3	1.5	7.7	10.8	22.7	35.3	46.9	60.4
VALUE (million dollars) [13]									
Total.............	**14,323.7**	**12,289.9**	**7,013.8**	**6,694.7**	**6,710.8**	**7,578.7**	**8,796.6**	**9,846.1**	**11,111.6**
Physical [2].............	**14,323.7**	**11,195.0**	**3,663.7**	**2,121.8**	**1,862.2**	**1,552.3**	**1,495.5**	**1,154.8**	**1,148.3**
Compact disk, album [3].............	13,214.5	10,520.2	3,389.4	1,776.2	1,445.0	1,130.8	1,057.3	698.4	614.5
Compact disk, single.............	142.7	10.9	2.9	3.6	1.2	0.3	1.5	0.2	0.2
Vinyl LP/EP (long play/extended play)........	27.7	14.2	88.9	243.8	333.4	355.4	388.5	419.2	497.6
Vinyl single.............	26.3	13.2	2.3	5.5	5.8	4.9	6.1	5.3	6.8
Music video [4].............	281.9	602.2	177.6	89.7	70.4	56.9	38.6	27.6	27.7
Digital [5].............	**(NA)**	**1,094.9**	**3,161.4**	**4,383.2**	**4,645.7**	**5,811.5**	**7,069.0**	**8,405.8**	**9,687.0**
Download single.............	(NA)	363.3	1,336.4	1,355.3	1,185.2	900.2	678.5	490.4	414.8
Download album.............	(NA)	135.7	872.4	1,117.9	1,064.4	868.6	668.5	499.7	394.5
Mobile [6].............	(NA)	421.6	448.0	66.3	54.6	56.3	35.5	25.0	21.4
Paid subscription [7].............	(NA)	149.2	212.4	770.3	1,156.7	2,244.2	3,500.6	4,656.0	5,934.4
Limited tier paid subscription [8].............	(NA)	(NA)	(NA)	(NA)	(NA)	263.4	591.6	747.1	829.5
SoundExchange distributions [9].............	(NA)	20.4	249.2	773.4	802.6	883.9	652.0	952.8	908.2
On-demand streaming [10].............	(NA)	(NA)	(NA)	283.8	372.0	489.4	658.6	759.5	908.1
Other ad-supported streaming [11].............	(NA)	(NA)	(NA)	(NA)	(NA)	81.3	261.8	251.4	251.1
Synchronization royalties [12].............	**(NA)**	**(NA)**	**188.7**	**189.7**	**202.9**	**214.8**	**232.1**	**285.5**	**276.3**

Z Represents less than 50,000. NA Not available. [1] Total volume excludes paid digital subscriptions. [2] Includes other media (DVD audio, super audio CD, and cassettes), not shown separately. [3] Prior to 2006, includes DualDisc. [4] Includes DVD video. [5] Includes kiosks, music video downloads, and, beginning 2016, value for other digital music licensing, not shown separately. [6] Master ringtones and ringbacks; prior to 2013, also included music videos, full length downloads, and other mobile. [7] Streaming, tethered, and other paid subscription services not operating under statutory licenses. Volume is annual average number of subscribers. [8] Includes streaming services with interactivity limitations by availability, device restriction, catalog limitations, on demand access, or other factors. [9] SoundExchange is a nonprofit organization that collects and distributes digital performance royalties on behalf of recording artists and master rights owners. [10] Advertising supported audio and music video services not operating under statutory licenses. [11] Includes revenues from services paid directly that are not distributed by SoundExchange and not included in other streaming categories. [12] Include fees and royalties from synchronization of sound recordings with other media. [13] In 2016, accounting standards updated.

Source: Recording Industry Association of America, Washington, D.C., Facts & Research, *Year-End 2019 RIAA Music Revenues Report* ©, <https://www.riaa.com/reports/>, accessed March 2020.

Table 1168. Radio and Television Broadcasting—Estimated Revenue and Expenses: 2013 to 2018

[In millions of dollars (5,703 represents $5,703,000,000). For all employer firms regardless of tax status. Based on the 2012 North American Industry Classification System (NAICS). See text, this section, and Section 15, Business Enterprise]

Item	2013	2014	2015	2016	2017	2018
RADIO NETWORKS (NAICS 515111)						
Total operating revenue	**5,703**	**6,011**	**6,509**	**7,089**	**7,641**	**8,063**
National/regional/local air time	961	1,005	1,467	1,596	1,801	1,934
Public and non-commercial programming services	421	427	367	395	415	448
All other operating revenue	4,321	4,579	4,675	5,098	5,425	5,681
RADIO STATIONS (NAICS 515112)						
Total operating revenue	**12,523**	**12,397**	**12,445**	**12,807**	**12,359**	**12,438**
National/regional/local air time	10,558	10,437	10,667	11,037	10,583	10,664
Public and non-commercial programming services	689	685	711	659	750	760
All other operating revenue	1,276	1,275	1,067	1,111	1,026	1,014
TELEVISION BROADCASTING (NAICS 51512)						
Total operating revenue	**44,782**	**49,911**	**50,577**	**57,855**	**57,487**	**62,843**
National/regional/local air time	34,240	37,274	35,711	39,451	37,050	41,021
Public and non-commercial programming services	2,121	2,246	2,122	2,180	2,002	2,246
All other operating revenue	8,421	10,391	12,744	16,224	18,435	19,576
RADIO AND TELEVISION BROADCASTING (NAICS 5151)						
Operating expenses, total [1]	**50,974**	**54,769**	**58,349**	**63,509**	**62,395**	**66,961**
Gross annual payroll	13,740	14,856	14,759	15,038	15,169	15,131
Employer's cost for fringe benefits	2,483	2,619	2,915	2,946	2,906	(S)
Temporary staff and leased employee expense	475	545	645	511	(S)	(S)
Expensed equipment, materials, parts, and supplies	(S)	(S)	413	473	471	(S)
Expensed purchases of software	198	204	238	252	244	(S)
Broadcast rights and music license fees	15,053	15,649	16,489	14,153	14,457	11,756
Network compensation fees (networks only)	590	821	1,606	2,082	2,350	2,820
Depreciation and amortization charges	2,834	3,395	3,297	3,411	3,505	4,844
All other operating expenses	(S)	(S)	17,987	24,643	22,850	28,442

S Figure does not meet publication standards. [1] The 2018 Service Annual Survey consolidated and eliminated several expense items. For more information, see <https://www.census.gov/programs-surveys/sas/newsroom/updates/Changes_to_Detailed_Operating_Expense_Items.html>.

Source: U.S. Census Bureau, Service Annual Survey, "Service Annual Survey Latest Data (NAICS-basis): 2018," <https://www.census.gov/programs-surveys/sas/data.html>, accessed February 2020.

Table 1169. Cable and Other Subscription Programming—Estimated Revenue and Expenses: 2013 to 2018

[In millions of dollars (68,405 represents $68,405,000,000). For all employer firms regardless of tax status. Based on the 2012 North American Industry Classification System. Covers NAICS 5152. See text, this section and Section 15, and Appendix III]

Item	2013	2014	2015	2016	2017	2018
Operating revenue, total	**68,405**	**72,473**	**78,931**	**81,508**	**83,327**	**85,499**
Advertising and program revenue [1]	39,273	42,266	48,811	50,715	52,160	55,078
Air time	24,734	26,039	26,264	26,745	26,907	25,900
All other operating services revenue	4,398	4,168	3,856	4,048	4,260	4,521
Operating expenses, total [2]	**40,731**	**44,080**	**46,359**	**48,351**	**49,669**	**51,450**
Gross annual payroll	5,966	6,151	6,979	7,265	7,566	7,372
Employer's cost for fringe benefits	1,200	1,308	1,395	1,434	1,622	(S)
Temporary staff and leased employee expense	225	277	238	272	306	340
Expensed equipment, materials, parts, and supplies	(S)	(S)	145	145	177	(S)
Expensed purchases of software	109	126	153	178	220	(S)
Program and production costs	20,798	21,779	23,100	24,494	24,349	24,243
Depreciation and amortization charges	4,445	4,911	4,957	4,983	5,667	6,797
All other operating expenses	(S)	(S)	9,392	9,580	9,762	10,608

S Estimate does not meet publication standards. [1] Licensing of rights to broadcast specialty programming protected by copyright. [2] See footnote 1, Table 1168.

Source: U.S. Census Bureau, Service Annual Survey, "Service Annual Survey Latest Data (NAICS-basis): 2018," <https://www.census.gov/programs-surveys/sas/data.html>, accessed February 2020.

Table 1170. Wired and Wireless Telecommunications Carriers—Estimated Revenue: 2010 to 2018

[In millions of dollars (281,149 represents $281,149,000,000). For all employer firms regardless of tax status. Data for 2010-2012 are based on the 2007 North American Industry Classification System (NAICS); beginning 2013, data are based on the 2012 NAICS. Covers NAICS 5171 Wired Telecommunications Carriers and NAICS 5172 Wireless Telecommunications Carriers (except satellite). Estimates have been adjusted to the results of the 2012 Economic Census. See text, this section and Section 15, and Appendix III]

Revenue source	2010	2012	2013	2014	2015	2016	2017	2018
Wired telecommunications carriers operating revenue	**281,149**	**285,663**	**288,647**	**296,792**	**306,384**	**326,119**	**315,390**	**311,465**
Fixed local telephony	43,765	35,990	31,201	30,395	18,790	19,394	17,087	15,165
Fixed long-distance telephony	19,964	18,068	16,447	15,478	(S)	18,812	(S)	20,401
Fixed all distance	2,640	1,894	1,249	1,131	2,003	1,951	1,587	2,761
Carrier services	18,183	17,663	16,386	18,588	21,489	(S)	13,254	14,279
Private network services	21,069	20,496	19,929	19,429	17,463	17,607	(S)	7,598
Internet access services	51,588	63,069	70,146	73,048	78,354	87,254	88,714	95,786
Internet telephony	9,874	12,530	12,976	13,013	11,709	11,289	10,244	9,583
Telecommunications network installation services	503	399	504	654	897	818	842	1,293
Reselling services for telecommunications equipment, retail	1,696	1,273	1,305	1,143	1,628	1,477	1,466	802
Rental of telecommunications equipment	687	472	484	592	563	1,701	4,458	6,923
Repair and maintenance services for telecommunications equipment	373	638	566	904	974	(S)	858	(S)
Subscriber line charges	3,289	3,988	3,555	3,430	3,230	3,223	2,896	2,784
Basic programming package	52,634	55,594	58,569	60,034	61,091	63,659	59,733	60,321
Premium programming package	20,367	21,752	21,181	21,124	23,258	24,394	22,978	22,180
Pay-per-view	3,303	3,200	(S)	3,086	2,893	2,898	2,782	1,986
Air time	4,843	(S)	(S)	5,021	5,722	6,344	5,607	6,451
Rental and reselling services for program distribution equipment	7,840	10,707	11,558	12,132	14,220	13,861	12,049	11,001
Installation services for connections to program distribution networks	1,081	1,245	1,360	1,658	(S)	(S)	(S)	(S)
Website hosting services	291	140	134	178	568	(S)	(S)	(S)
All other operating revenue	17,159	12,058	13,345	15,754	20,764	31,271	33,544	28,931
Wireless telecommunications carrier operating revenue [1]	**199,235**	**225,397**	**233,123**	**251,766**	**254,406**	**259,231**	**257,778**	**272,046**
Messaging (paging) services	921	554	(S)	(S)	3,722	2,962	(S)	2,217
Mobile telephony	58,238	54,716	62,015	59,890	46,480	45,754	(S)	47,477
Mobile long distance	3,387	(D)	(D)	4,184	2,916	2,446	2,530	2,484
Mobile all distance	(S)	65,493	59,666	54,093	47,092	(S)	37,722	40,031
Internet access services	(S)	62,878	66,274	77,373	90,944	97,500	96,257	90,949
Telecommunications network installation services	(S)	172	196	207	207	242	192	(S)
Reselling services for telecommunications equipment, retail	18,754	23,682	24,690	35,483	41,370	44,459	46,767	57,730
Rental of telecommunications equipment	333	342	433	489	(S)	(S)	4,714	6,768
Repair and maintenance services for telecommunications equipment	1,219	(D)	(D)	2,232	2,308	2,343	1,861	1,684
All other operating revenue	11,492	12,694	13,723	17,277	15,824	16,891	18,092	22,518

S Data do not meet publication standards. D Estimate in table is withheld to avoid disclosing data of individual companies; data are included in higher level totals. [1] Excludes satellite telecommunications.

Source: U.S. Census Bureau, Service Annual Survey, "Service Annual Survey Latest Data (NAICS-basis): 2018," and "Service Annual Survey Historical Tables," <https://www.census.gov/programs-surveys/sas/data.html>, accessed February 2020.

Table 1171. Telecommunications Industry Revenue by Service Type: 2010 to 2018

[Revenue in millions of dollars (446,386 represents $446,386,000,000). Data are based on carrier Form 499-A filings to the Federal Communications Commission, and are the basis for establishing Universal Service Fund (USF) program collections]

Category	Revenue (mil. dol.)						
	2010	2013	2014	2015	2016	2017	2018
Total reported revenue.........................	446,386	494,981	497,303	515,598	509,679	504,516	507,474
Non-telecommunications revenue.......................	173,228	251,892	268,804	301,121	311,404	321,597	337,212
Total telecommunications revenue.................	**273,158**	**243,088**	**228,499**	**214,477**	**198,276**	**182,918**	**170,262**
Local service and payphone revenue.............	**102,847**	**93,105**	**90,969**	**90,495**	**87,162**	**83,572**	**77,048**
Local exchange...	43,878	32,922	30,537	28,410	25,900	23,208	20,771
Pay telephone...	197	359	322	286	271	269	265
Local private line......................................	26,809	29,632	31,222	32,191	30,472	30,272	26,906
Voice over internet protocol (VoIP) local...............	8,234	10,103	11,136	11,968	14,398	14,428	14,503
Other local..	3,032	1,746	1,450	1,493	1,510	1,749	1,710
Federal and State USF support.........................	4,880	5,991	5,786	6,137	6,016	5,904	5,994
Subscriber line charges...............................	7,481	5,968	5,511	5,175	4,787	4,431	4,049
Access..	8,336	6,384	5,006	4,836	3,809	3,312	2,850
Mobile service revenue.............................	**111,643**	**98,160**	**86,996**	**75,262**	**65,636**	**56,952**	**52,890**
Toll service revenue...............................	**50,006**	**42,837**	**41,450**	**39,678**	**36,342**	**34,075**	**31,885**
Operator..	3,585	3,064	2,699	2,351	1,876	1,844	1,810
VoIP toll..	1,943	4,999	5,139	5,238	3,447	3,768	3,925
Non-operator switched toll.............................	25,189	18,346	17,354	16,261	14,850	11,841	11,068
Long distance private line.............................	14,344	12,542	12,293	12,778	13,353	13,316	12,850
Other long distance....................................	4,945	3,886	3,965	3,050	2,816	3,306	2,233
Universal service surcharges.....................	**8,662**	**8,986**	**9,083**	**9,041**	**9,135**	**8,319**	**8,438**

Source: U.S. Federal Communications Commission, *Universal Service Monitoring Report, 2019,* February 2020. See also <https://www.fcc.gov/general/federal-state-joint-board-monitoring-reports>.

Table 1172. Data Processing, Hosting, and Related Services—Estimated Revenue and Expenses: 2013 to 2018

[In millions of dollars (116,040 represents $116,040,000,000). For all employer firms regardless of tax status. Data are based on the 2012 North American Industry Classification System (NAICS), and cover NAICS 518. Estimates have been adjusted to the results of the 2012 Economic Census. See text, Section 15, and Appendix III]

Item	2013	2014	2015	2016	2017	2018
Total operating revenue........................	**116,040**	**120,450**	**129,957**	**135,525**	**152,277**	**169,480**
Data processing, information technology infrastructure provisioning, and hosting services....................	85,252	86,546	(S)	95,233	107,574	122,040
Information technology design and development services...........	3,223	4,141	6,725	6,451	(S)	(S)
Information technology technical support services....................	3,311	4,023	4,344	4,102	4,159	(S)
Information technology technical consulting services................	5,214	5,421	3,802	3,860	(S)	(S)
Information and document transformation services..................	3,020	2,827	2,470	(S)	2,687	(S)
Software publishing....................................	(S)	(S)	2,797	(S)	(S)	3,954
Reselling of computer hardware and software........................	(S)	(S)	2,554	2,540	3,196	(S)
All other operating revenue............................	13,178	14,138	18,870	(S)	(S)	(S)
Total operating expenses.......................	**105,748**	**112,709**	**124,786**	**117,863**	**129,063**	**138,100**
Gross annual payroll..................................	41,929	46,756	46,212	48,544	52,864	57,246
Employer's cost for fringe benefits......................	7,020	8,172	(S)	9,499	10,388	(S)
Temporary staff and leased employee expense......................	3,262	3,372	(S)	2,383	(S)	(S)
Expensed equipment, materials, parts, and supplies................	(S)	(S)	(S)	3,026	(S)	(S)
Expensed purchases of software........................	2,854	3,361	(S)	2,995	3,467	(S)
Depreciation and amortization charges..................	9,173	9,478	(S)	11,135	13,625	16,183
All other operating expenses...........................	(S)	(S)	(S)	40,281	43,089	(S)

S Data do not meet publication standards.

Source: U.S. Census Bureau, Service Annual Survey, "Service Annual Survey Latest Data (NAICS-basis): 2018," <https://www.census.gov/programs-surveys/sas/data.html>, accessed February 2020.

Table 1173. Cellular Telecommunications Industry: 2000 to 2019

[In units as indicated (109.5 represents 109,500,000). Calendar year data, except as noted. Based on a survey sent to facilities-based commercial mobile radio service providers, including cellular, personal communications services, advanced wireless service, mobile WiMAX, and enhanced special mobile radio (ESMR) systems. Beginning 2000, the number of operational systems differs from that reported for previous periods as a result of the consolidated operation of ESMR systems in a broader service area instead of by a city-to-city basis]

Item	Unit	2000	2005	2010	2015	2016	2017	2018	2019
Wireless subscriber connections [1]	Millions	109.5	207.9	296.3	377.9	395.9	400.2	421.8	442.5
Wireless penetration [2]	Percent	38.0	69.0	94.2	115.7	120.6	120.7	126.6	132.7
Cell sites [3]	Number	104,288	183,689	253,086	307,626	308,334	323,448	349,344	395,562
Employees	Number	184,449	233,067	250,393	235,818	216,537	207,324	205,855	188,639
Service revenue	Mil. dol.	52,466	113,538	159,930	191,949	188,524	179,091	182,779	187,362
Capital investment [4]	Mil. dol.	89,624	199,025	310,015	462,605	488,997	514,625	542,033	571,125
Average monthly revenue per unit [5]	Dollars	48.55	50.65	47.53	44.65	41.50	38.66	37.85	36.86
Voice minutes, annual reported	Billions	258.9	1,495.5	2,241.3	2,881.0	2,751.0	2,180.0	2,389.3	3,078.3
Voice minutes, monthly [6]	Minutes	248.0	716.0	683.0	670.0	606.0	471.0	495.0	606.0
Wireless data usage (megabytes), annual	Billions	(NA)	(NA)	388.0	9,649.9	13,719.0	15,678.3	28,584.7	37,059.6
Number of text messages [7]	Billions	(Z)	9.8	187.7	156.7	132.7	128.5	141.0	138.4
Number of MMS [7, 8]	Billions	(NA)	0.2	4.3	19.8	25.7	26.0	31.0	36.5

NA Not available. Z Entry less than half the unit of measurement shown. [1] Number of active wireless devices. Does not represent individual subscribers. [2] Number of active wireless devices divided by total U.S. population (including U.S. territories). [3] The basic geographic unit for wireless telecommunications coverage. [4] Beginning 2005, cumulative capital investment figure reached by summing the incremental capital investment in year shown with cumulative capital investment of prior year. [5] As of December 31. [6] Derived, based on minutes divided by reported devices. [7] Number of messages in final month of survey (December). [8] Multimedia Messaging Service.

Source: CTIA-The Wireless Association, Washington, DC, *Annual Wireless Industry Survey* ©.

Table 1174. Landline and Wireless Telephone Status of Adults by Selected Characteristics: 2010 to 2019

[In percent. Data cover 6-month period from January to June. Estimates are preliminary. Based on interviews of a sample of the civilian noninstitutionalized population conducted for the National Health Interview Survey (NHIS). The 2016 NHIS implemented a new sample design. The 2019 NHIS implemented a redesigned questionnaire and changes in weighting methodology, both of which may impact comparisons between estimates for 2019 and earlier years. See source for details]

Telephone status and characteristics	2010	2012	2013	2014	2015	2016	2017	2018	2019
Adults by household telephone status:									
Landline only (no wireless)	10.9	7.8	6.9	7.0	6.2	5.8	4.8	4.1	2.5
Landline with wireless	62.2	56.1	52.8	47.3	43.9	42.1	39.6	37.4	37.2
Wireless mostly [1]	17.7	17.6	17.7	16.6	16.3	16.6	16.3	16.8	(NA)
Wireless only	24.9	34.0	38.0	43.1	46.7	49.0	52.0	55.2	59.2
Without any telephone	1.7	1.9	2.2	2.4	3.1	2.9	3.4	3.2	1.0
Other [2]	0.3	0.2	0.1	0.2	0.1	0.1	0.1	0.1	0.1
Children in wireless telephone only households	29.0	40.6	45.4	52.1	55.3	59.4	62.3	64.9	70.5
ADULTS IN WIRELESS ONLY HOUSEHOLDS [5]									
Total	(NA)	(NA)	(NA)	(NA)	(NA)	(NA)	(NA)	(NA)	58.4
Sex:									
Male	26.2	35.2	39.7	44.3	48.2	50.3	53.2	56.4	59.6
Female	23.7	32.9	36.5	41.9	45.3	47.8	51.0	54.1	57.4
Age:									
18 to 24 years	39.9	49.5	54.3	57.8	59.4	62.7	64.2	65.0	66.5
25 to 29 years	51.3	60.1	65.6	69.3	71.3	72.1	73.3	77.3	80.2
30 to 34 years	40.4	55.1	59.9	64.9	67.8	69.8	74.4	77.3	78.3
35 to 44 years	27.0	39.1	44.5	52.5	56.6	60.0	63.9	65.7	70.9
45 to 64 years	16.9	25.8	29.8	35.7	40.8	43.3	47.1	50.7	55.6
65 and over years	5.4	10.5	12.6	15.7	19.3	21.1	23.9	29.2	30.9
Race/ethnicity:									
White only, non-Hispanic	22.7	30.4	35.1	39.6	43.2	45.0	48.0	51.6	56.0
Black only, non-Hispanic	28.5	37.7	39.4	44.9	48.1	49.2	52.5	55.6	54.3
Asian only, non-Hispanic	18.8	33.4	35.2	41.3	47.9	51.4	53.1	53.8	55.5
Other race or multiple race, non-Hispanic	(NA)	(NA)	(NA)	(NA)	(NA)	(NA)	(NA)	(NA)	64.3
Hispanic or Latino, any race	34.7	46.5	49.9	56.1	59.2	63.7	66.3	69.1	71.2
Education:									
Some high school or less	28.6	36.4	41.7	46.6	49.0	52.1	54.8	58.7	58.1
High school graduate or GED [3]	23.6	33.9	37.2	43.3	46.7	48.4	51.5	56.5	57.2
Some post-high school, no degree	26.5	36.7	40.6	45.6	49.0	50.8	55.1	56.0	60.1
4-year college degree or higher	22.7	30.1	34.5	39.0	43.5	46.5	48.6	51.9	58.1
Family poverty status: [4]									
Poor	39.3	51.8	54.7	59.1	59.3	63.1	67.5	67.1	67.1
Near poor	32.9	42.3	47.5	50.8	54.4	54.0	61.6	62.8	62.2
Not poor	21.7	30.7	35.3	40.8	45.7	48.2	50.3	53.4	57.4
Home ownership status:									
Owned or home being bought	15.5	23.2	27.2	32.9	37.2	39.0	42.9	46.8	50.2
Renting	47.1	58.2	61.5	64.6	67.0	69.7	70.7	74.4	75.1
Other arrangement	34.9	37.7	42.6	52.2	52.8	52.0	64.8	60.0	61.6

NA Not available. [1] Wireless mostly is for adults living in households with both landline and cellular telephones but in which all families receive all or almost all calls on cell phones. [2] Other includes unknown cellular telephone or unknown landline status. [3] GED is General Educational Development high school equivalency diploma. [4] Based on the U.S. Census Bureau's poverty thresholds by household income and size. "Poor" persons have incomes below the poverty threshold. "Near poor" persons have incomes of 100% to less than 200% of the poverty threshold. "Not poor" persons have incomes of 200% of the poverty threshold or greater. [5] Through 2018, data are for adults who live in households without a landline telephone. Beginning 2019, data are for "wireless only adults" who have their own wireless cellular telephone and who live in a household without a landline telephone.

Source: U.S. National Center for Health Statistics, *Wireless Substitution: Early Release of Estimates From the National Health Interview Survey, January–June 2019*, May 2020, and earlier reports. See also <https://www.cdc.gov/nchs/nhis/releases.htm>.

Table 1175. Average Annual Telephone Service Expenditures by All Consumer Units: 2001 to 2018

[In dollars except percent distribution. Based on the Consumer Expenditure Survey. Expenditures reported are direct out-of-pocket expenditures. A consumer unit is defined as members of a household related by blood, marriage, adoption, or some other legal arrangement; a single person living alone or sharing a household with others, but who is financially independent; or two or more persons living together who share responsibility for at least two out of the three major types of expenses: food, housing, and other expenses]

Year	Average annual expenditures (dollars)				Percent distribution			
	Total telephone services	Residential and other telephone services [1]	Cellular phone service	Other services [2]	Total telephone services	Residential and other telephone services [1]	Cellular phone service	Other services [2]
2001	914	686	210	19	100.0	75.1	23.0	2.1
2002	957	641	294	22	100.0	67.0	30.7	2.3
2003	956	620	316	20	100.0	64.9	33.1	2.1
2004	990	592	378	20	100.0	59.8	38.2	2.0
2005	1,048	570	455	23	100.0	54.4	43.4	2.2
2006	1,087	542	524	21	100.0	49.9	48.2	1.9
2007	1,110	482	608	20	100.0	43.4	54.8	1.8
2008	1,127	467	643	17	100.0	41.4	57.0	1.5
2009	1,162	434	712	17	100.0	37.3	61.2	1.4
2010	1,178	401	760	17	100.0	34.1	64.5	1.4
2011	1,226	381	826	20	100.0	31.1	67.3	1.6
2012	1,239	359	862	19	100.0	28.9	69.6	1.5
2013	1,271	358	913	(NA)	100.0	28.2	71.8	(NA)
2014	1,315	353	963	(NA)	100.0	26.8	73.2	(NA)
2015	1,347	324	1,023	(NA)	100.0	24.1	75.9	(NA)
2016	1,431	307	1,124	(NA)	100.0	21.5	78.5	(NA)
2017	1,356	238	1,118	(NA)	100.0	17.6	82.4	(NA)
2018	1,407	220	1,188	(NA)	100.0	15.6	84.4	(NA)

NA Not available. [1] Beginning 2013, data are shown for residential telephone, phone cards, VoIP (Voice over Internet Protocol), and pay phone services combined. Prior to 2013, data are shown for residential and pay telephone services only. [2] Phone cards, pager services, and for 2007-2012, VoIP.

Source: U.S. Bureau of Labor Statistics, Consumer Expenditure Survey, unpublished data; and "Annual Calendar Year Tables," <http://www.bls.gov/cex/home.htm>, accessed February 2020.

Table 1176. Electronic Device Ownership by Device Type and Owner Characteristics: 2019

[In percent. Based on a January 8-February 7, 2019 survey of 1,502 adults age 18 and older. Surveys are conducted in English and Spanish, on landline and cellular telephones]

Owner characteristic	Any cellular telephone	Smart-phone	Cellphone, not smart-phone	Tablet computer	Computer [1]
Total	**96**	**81**	**15**	**52**	**74**
SEX					
Men	98	84	14	50	**76**
Women	95	79	16	54	73
RACE/ETHNICITY					
White, non-Hispanic	96	82	14	53	82
Black, non-Hispanic	98	80	17	58	58
Hispanic	96	79	17	43	57
AGE					
18 to 29 years	99	96	4	46	80
30 to 49 years	99	92	6	57	78
50 to 64 years	95	79	17	55	75
65 years and older	91	53	39	42	62
EDUCATION					
Less than high school	92	66	25	33	36
High school graduate	96	72	24	43	60
Some college	96	85	11	56	82
College or higher	98	91	7	61	93
HOUSEHOLD INCOME					
Less than $30,000	95	71	23	36	54
$30,000 to $49,999	96	78	18	51	74
$50,000 to $74,999	98	90	8	52	89
$75,000 and over	100	95	5	68	92
METRO STATUS					
Urban	97	83	13	49	73
Suburban	96	83	13	58	80
Rural	95	71	24	49	69

[1] Desktop or laptop computer.

Source: Pew Research Center ©, "Mobile Fact Sheet," <http://www.pewinternet.org/fact-sheet/mobile/>, accessed August 2019; and unpublished data.

Table 1177. Computer and Internet Use by Selected Characteristics: 2018

[In thousands (281,779 represents 281,779,000), except percent. Based on the American Community Survey. Data are based on a sample and are subject to sampling variability. Due to changes in the ACS questionnaire, use caution when comparing data on computer and internet use before and after 2016. For more information, see <https://www.census.gov/programs-surveys/acs/methodology/content-test.html>]

Characteristic	Population with computer in household [1]				No computer in household	
	With broadband internet subscription [2]		No internet subscription [3]			
	Number	Percent	Number	Percent	Number	Percent
Total household population.............	**281,779**	**88.3**	**20,257**	**6.3**	**16,449**	**5.2**
AGE						
Under 18 years.................................	66,936	91.5	4,360	6.0	1,790	2.4
18 to 64 years.................................	176,090	90.3	12,026	6.2	6,691	3.4
65 years and over.............................	38,753	76.1	3,871	7.6	7,968	15.7
RACE AND ETHNICITY						
White alone.....................................	205,633	89.0	13,305	5.8	11,493	5.0
Black or African American alone..............	32,718	82.2	3,878	9.7	3,187	8.0
American Indian and Alaska Native alone........	2,056	76.0	323	11.9	320	11.8
Asian alone....................................	17,019	94.3	641	3.6	364	2.0
Native Hawaiian/Other Pacific Islander alone....	510	84.1	57	9.3	39	6.4
Some other race alone.........................	13,664	85.5	1,540	9.6	761	4.8
Two or more races.............................	10,179	92.6	514	4.7	286	2.6
Hispanic or Latino origin [4]...................	50,208	85.6	5,446	9.3	2,980	5.1
White alone, not Hispanic or Latino..............	172,905	89.8	9,671	5.0	9,429	4.9
EDUCATIONAL ATTAINMENT						
Household population age 25 and over.........	190,003	86.9	14,033	6.4	14,077	6.4
Less than high school graduate................	17,415	70.1	3,023	12.2	4,348	17.5
High school graduate/some college [5].............	103,910	85.5	8,771	7.2	8,463	7.0
Bachelor's degree or higher.....................	68,678	95.0	2,239	3.1	1,265	1.8
EMPLOYMENT STATUS						
Civilian population age 16 and over............	221,852	87.5	16,292	6.4	14,821	5.8
In labor force.................................	149,776	91.6	9,122	5.6	4,349	2.7
Employed....................................	142,855	91.8	8,522	5.5	3,980	2.6
Unemployed.................................	6,921	87.6	600	7.6	369	4.7
Not in labor force..............................	72,076	80.0	7,170	8.0	10,472	11.6

[1] Includes desktop or laptop; smartphone; tablet or other portable wireless computer; or some other type of computer. [2] Paid internet access services via cable, fiber optic, or DSL; a cellular data plan (smartphone or mobile phone); satellite; or a fixed wireless subscription. [3] Includes those who accessed the internet without a subscription and also those with no internet access at all. [4] Persons of Hispanic or Latino origin may be of any race. [5] Includes persons with high school equivalency, and with associate's degree.

Source: U.S. Census Bureau, 2018 American Community Survey, S2802 "Types of Internet Subscriptions by Selected Characteristics," <https://data.census.gov/>, accessed February 2020.

Table 1178. Percent of Households with a Computer and Paid Internet Subscription by State: 2018

[In percent. Survey respondents could select more than one type of computer and more than one type of internet subscription. Household computer can include desktop or laptop; smartphone; tablet or other portable wireless computer; or some other type of computer. Based on the American Community Survey. Please note that although the ACS includes people living in group quarters, computer and internet use data were not collected from group quarters. See also headnote Table 1177]

State	Total households with computer	Type of internet subscription			State	Total households with computer	Type of internet subscription		
		Dial-up internet service	Broadband internet service [1]	No paid internet service [2]			Dial-up internet service	Broadband internet service [1]	No paid internet service [2]
U.S.......	**91.8**	**0.3**	**91.8**	**7.9**	MO........	90.7	0.3	90.5	9.2
AL.........	87.2	0.4	89.9	9.7	MT.........	89.9	0.6	92.1	7.3
AK.........	95.6	0.3	91.0	8.7	NE.........	91.7	0.5	92.9	6.6
AZ.........	93.2	0.3	91.8	7.9	NV.........	93.6	0.2	91.1	8.7
AR.........	88.6	0.3	86.0	13.7	NH.........	93.8	0.4	94.2	5.4
CA........	94.4	0.2	93.3	6.5	NJ.........	93.0	0.2	93.8	6.0
CO........	94.5	0.3	94.0	5.8	NM........	87.9	0.4	86.3	13.3
CT.........	92.3	0.3	93.6	6.2	NY.........	91.0	0.2	92.6	7.2
DE.........	92.9	0.2	94.6	5.2	NC.........	91.0	0.2	90.8	8.9
DC.........	92.7	0.1	91.9	8.1	ND.........	90.3	0.2	88.1	11.7
FL.........	93.3	0.2	90.7	9.1	OH.........	90.6	0.3	92.3	7.4
GA.........	91.7	0.2	90.5	9.3	OK.........	90.6	0.3	89.5	10.2
HI.........	91.6	0.2	92.7	7.1	OR.........	94.4	0.4	92.6	7.0
ID.........	93.8	0.4	91.5	8.0	PA.........	89.6	0.5	92.9	6.7
IL.........	91.5	0.3	92.2	7.5	RI.........	89.7	0.2	94.0	5.8
IN.........	90.5	0.3	90.5	9.2	SC.........	90.3	0.2	89.4	10.4
IA.........	90.5	0.5	91.6	8.0	SD.........	89.7	0.2	90.7	9.1
KS.........	92.1	0.3	90.9	8.8	TN.........	89.3	0.2	91.1	8.7
KY.........	88.7	0.4	91.0	8.6	TX.........	92.4	0.2	90.6	9.3
LA.........	87.4	0.2	88.2	11.6	UT.........	96.3	0.3	93.0	6.7
ME.........	90.3	0.7	92.1	7.2	VT.........	91.7	0.7	89.1	10.2
MD.........	93.2	0.2	93.8	6.0	VA.........	91.9	0.3	92.4	7.3
MA........	92.5	0.2	94.2	5.6	WA........	94.7	0.2	94.4	5.3
MI.........	91.1	0.3	91.4	8.3	WV........	86.2	0.4	90.0	9.6
MN........	92.5	0.5	93.1	6.5	WI.........	90.4	0.5	92.6	6.8
MS........	86.5	0.2	87.0	12.8	WY........	93.1	0.3	91.1	8.7

[1] Broadband internet service includes access via cable, fiber optic, or DSL; a cellular data plan; satellite; or a fixed wireless subscription. [2] Includes households accessing the internet without a subscription and also households with no internet access.

Source: U.S. Census Bureau, 2018 American Community Survey, B28003, "Presence of a Computer and Type of Internet Subscription in Household," <https://data.census.gov/>, accessed February 2020.

Table 1179. Internet Access by Location and Selected User Characteristics: 2019

[In percent, except as noted (250,323 represents 250,323,000). For persons aged 18 and over. As of Fall 2019. Based on sample and subject to sampling error]

Characteristic	Total adults (1,000)	Accessed the internet (percent)					Wireless internet connection from home [1] (percent)
		At home	At work	At school or library	At another place	Using a cellphone or smart-phone	
Total adults [2].............................	**250,323**	**85.0**	**47.9**	**13.2**	**37.5**	**82.0**	**83.3**
Age:							
18 to 34 years old.............	74,553	93.2	58.5	23.8	47.4	96.1	87.9
35 to 54 years old.............	82,564	90.6	63.1	12.5	41.8	91.7	87.9
55 years old and over.............	93,207	73.4	26.1	5.3	25.8	62.1	75.5
Sex:							
Male.............	120,931	85.1	51.2	11.7	38.0	81.3	83.8
Female.............	129,392	84.9	44.9	14.6	37.0	82.6	82.7
Census region: [3]							
Northeast.............	44,254	87.3	50.4	11.8	41.4	82.5	85.9
South.............	95,401	82.9	46.6	12.8	35.9	81.4	80.4
Midwest.............	52,452	82.7	47.2	13.2	30.9	79.5	82.3
West.............	58,216	88.7	48.9	14.8	43.1	84.7	86.7
Household size:							
1 to 2 persons.............	116,426	78.9	39.4	9.0	32.6	72.3	76.7
3 to 4 persons.............	91,498	90.3	56.7	16.6	42.2	90.1	89.6
5 or more persons.............	42,399	90.2	52.5	17.2	40.9	91.1	87.7
Presence of child in household.............	94,442	91.5	58.2	15.4	42.2	92.7	89.1
Marital status:							
Never married.............	72,137	88.2	52.5	23.5	43.7	89.4	82.5
Married.............	131,898	87.8	50.7	9.3	38.0	83.6	88.9
Other [4].............	54,588	74.6	36.6	9.8	29.1	69.9	70.4
Education:							
Graduated college plus.............	80,743	95.4	66.9	16.8	49.3	92.1	94.6
Attended college.............	70,570	89.3	51.7	16.6	38.5	86.3	87.9
Did not attend college.............	99,010	73.4	29.8	7.8	27.2	70.6	70.7
Employment status:							
Employed full-time.............	128,304	91.9	77.7	11.8	43.3	93.1	89.3
Employed part-time.............	33,148	89.3	58.4	24.6	41.8	88.6	86.7
Occupation of employed:							
Professional.............	37,369	96.5	87.8	23.1	49.9	96.9	96.2
Management/business/financial.............	26,665	95.3	91.0	9.9	50.4	95.4	95.4
Sales/office.............	32,530	91.5	80.2	14.6	43.2	93.6	90.8
Natural resources/construction/maintenance. ..	14,116	86.3	55.3	5.8	33.3	85.6	80.5
Other.............	50,772	87.0	55.4	12.7	36.6	87.9	80.8
Sector of employment:							
Business.............	82,022	91.5	73.7	11.2	44.3	92.4	88.0
Government.............	23,136	93.6	83.0	24.6	46.7	94.8	93.5
Other.............	41,657	89.1	65.9	12.3	38.1	89.2	86.3
Household income:							
Less than $50,000.............	84,323	72.2	25.1	12.3	26.8	68.0	65.7
$50,000 to $74,999.............	41,667	87.5	42.1	12.4	34.0	82.3	86.3
$75,000 to $149,999.............	77,818	91.5	60.7	14.0	42.7	89.7	93.1
$150,000 or more.............	46,515	94.9	73.1	14.3	51.4	94.1	95.7

[1] Excludes cellphone access. [2] Includes other labor force status not shown separately. [3] For composition of regions, see map inside front cover. [4] Includes separated, divorced, and widowed, and persons engaged to be married.

Source: © Fall 2019, MRI Survey of the American Consumer. Courtesy of MRI-Simmons. See also <https://www.mrisimmons.com/>.

Table 1180. Internet Activities by Sex and Age: 2019

[In percent. Covers population age 15 and over. Based on the November 2019 Computer and Internet Use supplement to the Current Population Survey, for the National Telecommunications and Information Administration's Digital Nation research project]

Activity conducted online or via the internet	Total	By sex		By age			
		Male	Female	15 to 24 years old	25 to 44 years old	45 to 64 years old	65 years and over
Uses the internet, any location.............	**81.1**	**81.2**	**81.0**	**85.0**	**86.1**	**82.4**	**68.0**
Interact with household equipment.............	17.5	18.6	16.6	10.9	23.7	17.7	11.2
Offer services for sale.............	7.6	8.1	7.2	6.8	9.8	7.6	4.0
Video or voice calls, or conferencing.............	50.8	49.2	52.2	64.1	60.3	45.2	28.6
Post or upload blog posts, videos, or other original content.............	16.7	16.4	17.0	25.8	20.8	13.2	6.0
Request services provided by other people.............	33.8	34.1	33.5	33.8	44.3	30.6	18.5
Search for a job.............	20.5	20.4	20.5	34.5	26.3	15.2	4.8
Shop, make travel reservations, or use other consumer services.............	72.2	70.7	73.5	66.6	78.8	73.1	62.3
Stream or download music, radio, podcasts, etc......	55.9	57.0	54.9	77.8	68.0	46.8	26.8
Take class or participate in job training.............	20.1	19.5	20.6	29.8	25.1	17.0	6.2
Telecommute.............	23.8	25.6	22.0	11.7	33.2	28.1	8.4
Use email.............	90.3	89.4	91.1	90.0	93.6	90.1	84.1
Use financial services such as banking, investing, paying bills.............	69.9	69.4	70.4	56.8	80.8	71.8	56.9
Use social networks.............	73.7	70.1	77.2	87.9	82.4	68.0	52.8
Use text messaging or instant messaging.............	92.3	91.5	92.9	96.2	97.1	92.7	77.8
Use internet to sell goods.............	11.3	12.0	10.7	10.2	14.2	11.1	7.0
Watch videos.............	74.3	76.2	72.6	89.5	86.0	68.1	47.5

Source: U.S. Department of Commerce, National Telecommunications and Information Administration, "Digital Nation Data Explorer," <www.ntia.doc.gov/category/data-central>, accessed June 2020.

Table 1181. Home Internet Access—Broadband and Smartphone Only Service by Selected Characteristics: 2016 to 2019

[In percent. Based on a survey of 4,535 adults conducted in April and November 2016 (sampling error plus or minus 1.7 percentage points); a survey of 2,002 adults conducted in January 2018; and a survey of 1,502 adults conducted January 8-February 7, 2019 (sampling error plus or minus 2.8 percentage points). Surveys were conducted in English and Spanish on landline and cellular telephones]

Characteristic	Internet broadband service in the home			Internet via smartphone only [1]		
	2016	2018	2019	2016	2018	2019
Total..........	**72**	**65**	**73**	**12**	**20**	**17**
SEX						
Male..........	74	66	73	12	20	17
Female..........	70	64	73	12	19	16
RACE/ETHNICITY						
White, non-Hispanic..........	77	72	79	9	14	12
Black, non-Hispanic..........	65	57	66	15	24	23
Hispanic..........	55	47	61	23	35	25
AGE						
18 to 29 years..........	78	67	77	17	28	22
30 to 49 years..........	80	70	77	13	24	18
50 to 64 years..........	72	68	79	11	16	14
65 years and older..........	51	50	59	7	10	12
EDUCATION						
Less than high school graduate..........	30	24	46	27	39	32
High school graduate..........	61	56	59	15	22	24
Some college..........	80	68	77	12	21	16
College graduate..........	90	85	93	5	10	4
HOUSEHOLD INCOME						
Less than $30,000..........	52	45	56	21	31	26
$30,000 to $49,999..........	72	67	72	12	22	20
$50,000 to $74,999..........	82	79	87	10	14	10
$75,0000 and over..........	92	87	92	5	9	6
METRO STATUS						
Urban..........	73	67	75	12	22	17
Suburban..........	74	70	79	12	17	13
Rural..........	62	58	63	14	17	20
PARENTAL STATUS						
Parent of minor child..........	79	(NA)	(NA)	12	(NA)	(NA)
Not parent of minor child..........	69	(NA)	(NA)	12	(NA)	(NA)

NA Not available. [1] Persons without traditional home broadband internet service who own a smartphone that can access the internet.

Source: Pew Research Center ©, "Internet/Broadband Fact Sheet," <http://www.pewinternet.org/fact-sheet/internet-broadband/>, accessed June 2019; and unpublished data.

Table 1182. Adult Internet Users and Home Internet Connection by Selected Characteristics: 2000 to 2019

[In percent. Covers persons age 18 and over who use the internet at a workplace, school, home, or anywhere else, on at least an occasional basis. Based on telephone surveys of persons with landline telephones unless otherwise noted. Beginning 2011, surveys include interviews conducted in English and Spanish. Data for 2019 are from January-February 2019 interviews of 1,502 persons, including 1,200 cellphone users. Data for 2018 are from January 2018 interviews of 2,002 persons, including 1,502 cellphone users. Data for 2016 are from November 2016 interviews with 3,015 persons, including 2,258 cellphone users. Data for 2015 are from July 2015 interviews with 2,001 persons, including 1,300 cellphone users. Data for 2010 are from interviews with 2,252 persons, including 744 cellphone users]

Characteristic	Adult internet users							All adults, by type of home connection, 2019	
	2000	2005	2010	2015	2016	2018	2019	Broadband	Dial-up
Total adults..........	**53**	**69**	**79**	**87**	**90**	**89**	**90**	**73**	**2**
Sex:									
Male..........	56	70	79	87	90	89	90	73	2
Female..........	51	67	79	87	90	88	91	73	1
Race/ethnicity:									
White, non-Hispanic..........	55	70	80	87	90	89	92	79	1
Black, non-Hispanic..........	42	54	71	84	86	87	85	66	1
Hispanic..........	48	73	82	84	90	88	86	61	2
Age:									
18 to 29 years old..........	72	82	95	97	99	98	100	77	1
30 to 49 years old..........	62	80	87	97	96	97	97	77	1
50 to 64 years old..........	48	68	78	80	89	87	88	79	1
65 years old and over..........	15	28	42	65	67	66	73	59	3
Education:									
Less than high school..........	19	35	52	68	71	65	71	46	1
High school graduate [1]..........	41	59	67	77	84	84	84	59	2
Some college..........	69	80	90	93	94	93	95	77	1
College graduate or higher..........	79	88	96	97	98	97	98	93	1
Annual household income:									
Less than $30,000..........	35	50	63	78	81	81	82	56	2
$30,000 to $49,999..........	61	74	84	87	91	93	93	72	1
$50,000 to $74,999..........	74	86	89	94	96	97	97	87	2
$75,000 or more..........	81	91	95	97	98	98	98	92	1

[1] Includes those with a GED certificate.

Source: Pew Research Center, Pew Internet & American Life Project Surveys © conducted September-December 2000, September and December of 2005, May 2010, July 2015, November 2016, January 2018, and January-February 2019. See also <http://www.pewinternet.org>.

Table 1183. Teen Electronic Device Ownership and Social Media Use by Selected Characteristics: 2018

[In percent. Based on responses from 1,058 parents of teenagers and 743 teenagers age 13 to 17 participating in a survey conducted by NORC at the University of Chicago, March 7 to April 10, 2018. Margin of error for results at 95% level of confidence for parents is 4.5 percentage points and for teens 5.0 percentage points. Multiple responses were allowed]

Characteristic	Device ownership [1]				Social media platform use				
	Smart-phone	Cellphone but not smart-phone	Desktop or laptop	Gaming console	YouTube	Instagram	Snapchat	Facebook	Twitter
Total	**95**	**29**	**88**	**84**	**85**	**72**	**69**	**51**	**32**
SEX									
Male	93	27	89	92	89	69	67	49	33
Female	97	31	88	75	81	75	72	53	32
RACE/ETHNICITY									
White, non-Hispanic	94	25	90	87	86	73	72	48	33
Black, non-Hispanic	94	32	89	78	79	72	77	57	29
Hispanic [2]	95	34	82	81	85	72	64	58	36
AGE									
13 to 14 years	94	26	88	86	84	63	63	47	24
15 to 17 years	95	30	88	82	86	78	74	54	38
HOUSEHOLD INCOME									
Less than $30,000	93	38	75	85	86	74	77	70	40
$30,000 to $74,999	93	28	89	82	84	72	71	56	30
$75,000 and over	97	24	96	84	85	71	64	36	30

[1] Percent of US teens who say they have or have access at home to the listed device. [2] Persons of Hispanic origin may be of any race.

Source: Pew Research Center, *Teens, Social Media & Technology 2018,* May 2018 ©. See also <http://www.pewinternet.org>.

Table 1184. Households Using Electronics, Internet Devices, and Cell Phones by Type and Household Income: 2015

[In millions (118.2 represents 118,200,000). Based on the Residential Energy Consumption Survey. Includes single-family homes, units in multifamily buildings, and mobile homes. Excludes secondary homes, vacant, seasonal and vacation homes, group quarters, and common areas of apartment buildings. Data may not sum to totals due to rounding]

Item	Households by income (millions)								
	Total	Less than $20,000	$20,000 to $39,999	$40,000 to $59,999	$60,000 to $79,999	$80,000 to $99,000	$100,000 to $119,999	$120,000 to $139,999	$140,000 or more
Total households	**118.2**	**22.5**	**27.2**	**18.6**	**15.4**	**9.7**	**8.1**	**5.4**	**11.2**
TELEVISION AND VIDEO									
Number of televisions:									
0	3.1	0.9	1.0	0.4	0.3	(B)	(B)	(B)	(B)
1	30.0	8.7	7.0	4.2	3.8	1.5	1.7	0.9	2.2
2	39.1	7.5	9.6	6.4	4.9	3.4	2.5	1.8	2.9
3 or more	46.0	5.4	9.6	7.6	6.4	4.5	3.8	2.7	6.0
Hours TV used per weekday: [1]									
Less than 1 hour	3.7	0.9	0.8	0.5	0.5	0.2	0.3	(B)	0.5
1 to 3 hours	29.7	4.2	5.7	4.3	4.4	2.6	2.7	1.9	4.0
4 to 6 hours	43.0	6.6	9.2	6.9	6.0	4.1	3.1	2.4	4.6
7 to 10 hours	21.5	4.6	5.8	3.9	2.4	1.7	1.3	0.6	1.3
More than 10 hours	17.2	5.4	4.7	2.6	1.9	0.9	0.6	0.4	0.6
Hours TV used per weekend day: [1]									
Less than 1 hour	3.1	1.0	0.8	0.4	0.4	(B)	0.2	(B)	(B)
1 to 3 hours	20.2	3.7	4.0	2.6	3.0	1.9	1.5	1.1	2.6
4 to 6 hours	38.4	5.7	8.6	5.9	5.0	3.4	3.0	2.1	4.7
7 to 10 hours	30.4	5.3	7.0	5.4	4.1	2.6	2.3	1.3	2.4
More than 10 hours	23.0	6.1	5.7	4.0	2.7	1.6	1.0	0.7	1.2
Number of cable or satellite TV boxes: [2]									
1	34.0	4.2	6.8	6.3	4.7	3.3	2.8	1.8	4.2
2 or more	20.0	1.6	3.3	3.0	2.9	2.5	1.9	1.7	3.1
Number of internet streaming devices:									
1	24.9	3.0	4.6	4.1	3.7	2.2	2.5	1.3	3.5
2 or more	9.0	0.5	1.4	1.5	1.1	1.2	0.7	0.8	1.8
COMPUTERS AND PHONES									
Number of desktop computers:									
1	41.3	5.2	9.2	6.7	5.4	3.8	3.3	2.6	5.0
2 or more	8.0	(NA)	1.1	(NA)	(NA)	(NA)	(NA)	(NA)	1.5
Number of laptop computers:									
1	44.6	6.2	10.1	8.2	6.7	4.6	3.3	1.7	3.8
2	21.2	1.8	3.3	3.2	3.6	2.1	2.1	1.9	3.3
3 or more	9.6	0.7	0.9	0.9	1.1	0.8	1.2	0.9	3.0
Number of tablets and e-readers:									
1	38.2	5.2	9.1	6.9	5.5	3.9	2.8	1.8	3.0
2	19.1	1.6	2.6	2.9	2.7	1.9	2.0	1.5	3.8
3 or more	10.5	0.4	1.1	1.1	1.7	1.1	1.3	1.1	2.5
Number of smartphones:									
1	28.4	5.8	8.0	5.6	3.7	2.1	1.4	0.8	1.1
2	37.6	4.0	6.5	6.3	5.9	4.1	3.3	2.6	4.9
3 or more	23.9	2.5	3.6	3.1	3.2	2.4	2.7	1.7	4.6

B Data withheld due to relative standard error being greater than 50 percent or fewer than 10 cases responded. NA Not available. [1] Data shown for primary television. [2] Cable and satellite boxes with digital video recorder (DVR).

Source: U.S. Energy Information Administration, Residential Energy Consumption Survey—2015 Data, "Table HC4.5 Electronics in U.S. Homes by Household Income, 2015," <https://www.eia.gov/consumption/residential/data/2015/>, accessed June 2017.

Table 1185. Social Media—Use of Social Networking Sites Among Adult Internet Users: 2019

[In percent. Based on a survey of 1,502 adults age 18 and older living in all 50 states and DC, conducted January 8-February 7, 2019 in English and Spanish on landline and cellular telephones. Margin of error for results for the total sample is plus or minus 2.85 percentage points]

Characteristic	Social media platform							
	Facebook	Instagram	LinkedIn	Pinterest	Snapchat	Twitter	WhatsApp	YouTube
Total....................	**69**	**37**	**27**	**28**	**24**	**22**	**20**	**73**
SEX								
Male........................	63	31	29	15	24	24	21	78
Female......................	75	43	24	42	24	21	19	68
RACE/ETHNICITY								
White, non-Hispanic...........	70	33	28	33	22	21	13	71
Black, non-Hispanic...........	70	40	24	27	28	24	24	77
Hispanic origin [1]...........	69	51	16	22	29	25	42	78
AGE								
18 to 29 years...............	79	67	28	34	62	38	23	91
30 to 49 years...............	79	47	37	35	25	26	31	87
50 to 64 years...............	68	23	24	27	9	17	16	70
65 years and over............	46	8	11	15	3	7	3	38
EDUCATION								
High school graduate or less........	61	33	9	19	22	13	18	64
Some college................	75	37	26	32	29	24	14	79
College graduate or higher.........	74	43	51	38	20	32	28	80
INCOME								
Under $30,000...............	69	35	10	18	27	20	19	68
$30,000 to $74,999..........	72	39	26	27	26	20	16	75
$75,000 and over............	74	42	49	41	22	31	25	83
METRO STATUS								
Urban.......................	73	46	33	30	29	26	24	77
Suburban....................	69	35	30	30	20	22	19	74
Rural.......................	66	21	10	26	20	13	10	64

[1] Persons of Hispanic origin may be of any race.

Source: Pew Research Center, Fact Tank, "Share of U.S. adults using social media, including Facebook, is mostly unchanged since 2018," April 2019 ©. See also <http://www.pewinternet.org/>.

Table 1186. Public Libraries—Selected Characteristics: 2017

[Total operating income in thousands of dollars (13,236,542 represents $13,236,542,000). Data are generally for the fiscal year ending in June; see source for reporting periods. Based on a census of all public libraries in the 50 states and the District of Columbia. See source for details]

Population of service area	Number of—		Operating income			Paid staff [4]		Avg. number of public use internet computers per stationary outlet [6]
				Source (percent)				
	Public libraries [1]	Stationary outlets [2]	Total [3] ($1,000)	State government	Local government	Total FTE	Librarians with ALA-MLS [5]	
Total...................	**9,045**	**16,557**	**13,236,542**	**6.7**	**85.9**	**142,131**	**33,620**	**18.1**
Less than 1,000........	935	940	39,592	7.0	76.5	715	42	4.6
1,000 to 2,499..........	1,461	1,477	123,355	5.2	78.0	2,090	155	6.4
2,500 to 4,999..........	1,263	1,299	207,312	5.5	79.1	3,191	394	8.2
5,000 to 9,999..........	1,494	1,638	493,074	6.5	83.4	6,832	1,267	12.3
10,000 to 24,999.......	1,757	2,230	1,336,468	5.9	86.6	16,316	3,945	15.8
25,000 to 49,999.......	989	1,755	1,583,276	6.3	86.9	17,874	4,567	18.8
50,000 to 99,999.......	578	1,576	1,642,031	7.4	86.4	17,987	4,477	22.1
100,000 to 249,999....	366	2,024	2,036,440	7.3	86.3	22,510	5,180	22.7
250,000 to 499,999....	112	1,186	1,563,570	7.1	87.5	16,295	3,935	25.3
500,000 to 999,999....	55	1,071	1,900,057	7.2	85.8	18,184	4,234	29.4
1,000,000 or more.....	35	1,361	2,311,366	5.7	85.0	20,136	5,424	33.3

[1] A public library is the administrative entity, the agency, that provides public library services. Of the 9,045 public libraries in the 50 States and DC, 7,320 were single-outlet and 1,725 were multiple-outlet libraries. There are 8,870 central library outlets, 7,687 branch library outlets, and 672 bookmobiles. [2] The sum of central and branch libraries. [3] Total includes income from the federal government (0.4%) and other sources (7.1%), not shown separately. [4] Full-time equivalents. Forty hours per week equals 1 FTE. [5] Librarians with master's degrees from a graduate library education program accredited by the American Library Association (ALA). Total librarians, including those without ALA-MLS, is 49,576. [6] The average per stationary outlet was calculated by dividing the total number of public use internet computers in central and branch outlets by the total number of such outlets.

Source: Institute of Museum and Library Services, Public Libraries Survey, *Supplementary Tables, Public Libraries Survey, Fiscal Year 2017*, June 2019. See also <https://www.imls.gov/research-evaluation/data-collection/public-libraries-survey>.

Table 1187. Number of Public Libraries and Library Services by State: 2017

[1,317,654 represents 1,317,654,000. Data are generally for the fiscal year ending in June; see source documentation for reporting periods. Based on a census of all public libraries that meet the definition of a Federal State Cooperative System (FSCS) Public Library, which can have one or more outlets (central, branch, bookmobile, or books-by-mail-only) that provide direct service to the public]

State	Number of public libraries [1]	Visits		Circulation				Average number of public use internet computers [3]
		Library visits (1,000s)	Per capita visits [2]	Total circulation (1,000s)	Per capita circulation of materials [2]	Children's circulation (1,000s)	Children's circulation as percent of total circulation	
United States........	9,045	1,317,654	4.2	2,163,539	6.9	766,459	35.4	18.1
Alabama................	218	14,578	3.2	19,919	4.3	6,766	34.0	17.4
Alaska.................	61	3,364	5.2	4,680	7.3	1,490	31.8	11.7
Arizona................	90	24,589	3.5	45,352	6.6	12,427	27.3	33.3
Arkansas..............	60	10,358	3.9	13,900	5.3	3,919	28.1	12.0
California.............	184	151,059	3.8	208,171	5.3	85,182	40.9	20.9
Colorado..............	113	31,976	5.9	62,439	11.5	21,350	34.2	24.6
Connecticut...........	181	20,036	5.9	24,804	7.6	9,132	35.3	18.7
Delaware..............	21	4,118	4.3	5,546	5.8	1,775	32.0	32.7
District of Columbia....	1	3,593	5.2	4,293	6.2	1,519	35.4	38.5
Florida................	81	66,753	3.3	99,660	4.9	31,821	31.9	31.5
Georgia...............	63	28,816	2.7	35,453	3.4	15,921	44.9	24.1
Hawaii................	1	4,135	2.9	5,906	4.1	2,359	39.9	11.3
Idaho.................	102	8,029	5.6	15,618	11.0	6,557	42.0	13.4
Illinois................	622	66,175	5.7	107,710	9.3	41,948	38.8	20.2
Indiana................	236	31,849	5.2	70,761	11.6	21,293	30.1	19.7
Iowa..................	535	17,233	5.6	25,213	8.3	9,060	35.8	9.1
Kansas...............	319	13,734	5.5	24,534	9.8	9,574	39.0	10.1
Kentucky.............	119	17,909	4.0	29,539	6.7	9,271	31.4	24.6
Louisiana.............	67	17,211	3.7	21,469	4.6	4,739	22.1	17.0
Maine.................	228	6,673	5.8	8,467	7.3	3,109	36.7	7.9
Maryland..............	24	26,090	4.4	56,357	9.5	23,038	40.9	27.3
Massachusetts........	368	40,456	6.0	54,673	8.1	20,050	36.7	14.4
Michigan..............	397	46,053	4.7	77,583	7.9	25,017	32.2	19.0
Minnesota............	137	23,357	4.2	48,990	8.9	19,489	39.7	16.0
Mississippi............	52	8,582	2.9	7,189	2.4	2,314	32.2	11.8
Missouri...............	148	26,129	4.8	51,981	9.5	17,157	33.0	13.5
Montana..............	82	4,215	4.3	5,973	6.0	1,998	33.5	11.1
Nebraska.............	235	7,726	4.9	12,395	7.9	5,783	46.6	11.4
Nevada...............	22	9,685	3.3	18,414	6.2	6,038	32.8	16.4
New Hampshire........	222	7,016	5.3	10,425	7.9	3,613	34.6	6.7
New Jersey............	286	41,874	4.8	51,596	6.0	20,391	39.4	19.6
New Mexico...........	87	7,019	4.7	9,321	6.2	2,658	28.5	15.2
New York..............	756	100,012	5.2	127,223	6.6	41,037	32.3	19.7
North Carolina.........	81	32,621	3.2	49,231	4.9	21,643	44.0	19.6
North Dakota..........	74	2,159	3.2	3,592	5.3	1,342	37.3	9.4
Ohio..................	251	71,896	6.3	170,443	14.9	52,515	30.7	20.0
Oklahoma.............	119	13,491	4.2	23,661	7.3	6,686	28.3	15.0
Oregon................	131	20,260	5.7	54,031	15.2	12,182	22.6	13.8
Pennsylvania..........	453	42,252	3.4	61,830	5.0	22,272	35.9	13.1
Rhode Island..........	48	5,669	5.4	6,049	5.7	1,847	30.5	20.9
South Carolina........	42	14,568	3.1	23,924	5.1	8,705	36.4	22.0
South Dakota..........	111	3,700	4.7	5,929	7.6	2,422	40.5	7.9
Tennessee.............	186	19,397	3.0	26,992	4.2	9,394	34.8	19.9
Texas.................	540	70,302	2.8	117,268	4.6	46,981	40.0	25.2
Utah..................	74	15,327	5.1	33,801	11.4	15,072	44.2	17.8
Vermont...............	162	3,585	6.2	3,932	7.4	1,732	40.3	6.7
Virginia...............	92	34,563	4.2	65,985	7.9	24,967	37.8	21.6
Washington............	62	37,988	5.3	84,405	11.7	26,610	31.5	20.1
West Virginia..........	97	5,231	2.8	6,510	3.5	2,030	31.2	8.0
Wisconsin.............	381	30,877	5.3	55,712	9.6	20,416	36.7	13.8
Wyoming..............	23	3,367	5.8	4,691	8.0	1,846	39.4	12.0

[1] A public library is the administrative entity, the agency, that provides public library services. Of the 9,045 public libraries in the 50 States and DC, 7,320 were single-outlet libraries and 1,725 were multiple-outlet libraries. There are 8,870 central library outlets, 7,687 branch library outlets, and 672 bookmobiles. Excludes 168 libraries that do not meet the criteria in the FSCS public library definition but that qualify as public libraries under state law. [2] Per capita rate based on total unduplicated population of legal service area given by the state library agency of each state. [3] The average per stationary outlet was calculated by dividing the total number of public use Internet computers in central and branch outlets by the total number of such outlets.

Source: Institute of Museum and Library Services, Public Libraries Survey, *Supplementary Tables, Public Libraries Survey, Fiscal Year 2017,* June 2019. See also <https://www.imls.gov/research-evaluation/data-collection/public-libraries-survey>.

Table 1188. Public Library Holdings by Type by State: 2017

[In thousands (715,019 represents 715,019,000). Data are generally for the fiscal year ending in June; see source for reporting periods. Based on a census of all public libraries conducted by Institute of Museum and Library Services. Covers only libraries that meet the definition of a Federal State Cooperative System (FSCS) public library. State data comparisons should be made with caution because of differences in reporting periods and adherence to survey definitions. Data are not subject to sampling error; census results may contain nonsampling error]

| | Type of holding (1,000) | | | | | | | |
| | Print | | Electronic materials | | Audio | | Video | |
State	Print materials [1]	Current print serial subscriptions	Electronic books [2]	Electronic collections [3]	Physical units	Download-able units [4]	Physical units	Download-able units [4]
United States...........	**715,019**	**1,574.2**	**463,489**	**417.4**	**43,568**	**258,582**	**65,904**	**16,140**
Alabama...................	8,808	8.5	4,460	14.4	435	1,590	674	113
Alaska....................	2,083	4.2	1,056	3.3	113	823	276	15
Arizona...................	7,586	17.4	4,378	3.6	592	4,535	1,049	285
Arkansas..................	6,079	9.3	1,426	3.5	257	1,488	526	75
California.................	62,110	86.7	13,595	4.1	3,329	17,262	5,317	723
Colorado..................	9,517	21.4	2,815	15.2	811	2,277	1,407	216
Connecticut...............	12,942	18.8	2,026	8.4	776	1,079	1,159	23
Delaware..................	1,434	3.6	497	0.2	114	122	254	18
District of Columbia......	1,049	2.7	29	0.1	21	13	85	1
Florida...................	28,148	42.6	5,202	7.2	1,880	18,368	3,509	371
Georgia...................	16,219	13.3	772	4.1	534	300	1,022	123
Hawaii....................	2,922	2.7	82	0.1	114	27	170	–
Idaho.....................	4,221	5.0	515	5.4	227	323	358	1
Illinois..................	39,946	91.3	21,831	15.2	2,836	7,855	3,582	492
Indiana...................	21,370	43.3	8,637	23.8	1,445	2,948	2,177	224
Iowa......................	11,698	26.1	14,590	8.4	658	6,748	1,116	23
Kansas....................	8,780	13.2	32,882	20.8	500	7,712	964	55
Kentucky..................	8,919	14.8	12,955	6.9	519	2,867	932	275
Louisiana.................	11,737	22.1	3,164	4.3	472	1,588	1,208	205
Maine.....................	5,921	8.8	2,091	13.8	239	1,240	417	74
Maryland..................	10,729	19.0	1,550	1.0	918	1,150	1,080	127
Massachusetts.............	29,788	42.6	18,452	25.6	1,532	5,220	2,098	518
Michigan..................	27,948	45.4	8,404	2.1	1,946	4,830	2,669	493
Minnesota.................	13,773	24.9	5,230	7.7	841	901	1,094	4
Mississippi...............	5,484	4.7	626	2.7	201	95	377	32
Missouri..................	15,700	25.6	4,119	2.6	936	1,311	1,264	144
Montana...................	2,505	3.8	1,432	0.2	114	968	213	8
Nebraska..................	5,475	9.9	4,423	6.2	234	2,473	370	8
Nevada....................	3,915	5.6	655	1.3	301	803	591	62
New Hampshire.............	5,660	10.2	4,774	5.1	283	3,887	494	47
New Jersey................	25,712	313.5	6,243	10.0	1,573	4,214	2,303	1,017
New Mexico................	4,083	6.4	685	4.7	207	415	359	59
New York..................	68,129	134.7	28,446	26.0	3,533	6,074	5,320	262
North Carolina...........	15,527	20.3	6,418	7.6	667	1,003	844	153
North Dakota..............	2,188	3.5	885	2.1	92	800	132	33
Ohio......................	39,581	90.0	81,436	21.1	3,368	33,758	5,487	3,882
Oklahoma..................	6,423	73.1	3,456	4.2	371	792	577	58
Oregon....................	8,940	13.6	7,071	4.2	637	4,349	949	106
Pennsylvania..............	24,238	47.1	26,462	15.4	2,115	46,996	2,037	3,296
Rhode Island..............	3,461	4.7	2,594	2.0	152	878	260	33
South Carolina...........	8,637	25.9	1,722	2.5	437	1,530	735	80
South Dakota..............	2,752	4.0	1,244	6.5	129	510	156	9
Tennessee.................	11,262	31.6	21,178	14.8	565	9,472	769	575
Texas.....................	38,322	40.8	10,300	35.8	1,946	5,661	3,114	499
Utah......................	6,404	9.4	1,647	4.5	616	1,663	667	133
Vermont...................	2,613	4.9	226	8.6	126	113	210	–
Virginia..................	16,308	20.9	9,780	4.1	951	5,201	1,305	299
Washington................	12,696	37.5	3,852	2.3	1,055	1,359	1,504	151
West Virginia.............	4,947	5.5	3,799	1.7	198	14,230	345	220
Wisconsin.................	18,084	36.0	62,895	20.1	1,492	18,498	2,156	503
Wyoming...................	2,246	3.3	482	1.9	159	263	221	17

– Rounds to zero. [1] Includes books, and non-serial government documents. [2] E-books include digital documents digitized by the library, licensed or not; and non-serial government documents. [3] An electronic collection is a collection of electronically stored data or unit records (facts, bibliographic data, abstracts, texts, photographs, music, video, etc.) with a common user interface and software for the retrieval and use of the data. Electronic collections do not have a circulation period. [4] Downloadable units are items for which permanent or temporary access rights have been acquired. For items with a finite number of simultaneous users, the number of units equals the number of simultaneous users (equivalent to purchasing multiple copies of a single title). For items with unlimited simultaneous users, the number of units equals the number of titles acquired.

Source: Institute of Museum and Library Services, Public Libraries Survey, *Supplementary Tables, Public Libraries Survey, Fiscal Year 2017*, June 2019. See also <https://www.imls.gov/research-evaluation/data-collection/public-libraries-survey>.

Banking, Finance, and Insurance

This section presents data on the nation's finances, various types of financial institutions, money and credit, securities, insurance, and real estate. The primary sources of these data are publications of several departments of the federal government, especially the U.S. Treasury Department, and independent agencies such as the Federal Deposit Insurance Corporation, the Board of Governors of the Federal Reserve System, and the Securities and Exchange Commission. National data on insurance are available primarily from private organizations, such as the American Council of Life Insurers and the National Association of Insurance Commissioners.

Financial Accounts of the United States—The Federal Reserve Board brings together statistics on all of the major forms of financial instruments to present an economy-wide view of asset and liability relationships in the Financial Accounts of the United States. The accounts relate borrowing and lending to one another and to the nonfinancial activities that generate income and production. Each claim outstanding is included simultaneously as an asset of the lender and as a liability of the debtor. The accounts also indicate the balance between asset totals and liability totals over the economy as a whole. Several publications of the Federal Reserve Board contain information on these financial accounts: Summary data on flows and outstandings in the statistical release *Financial Accounts of the United States* (quarterly); and concepts and organization of the accounts in *Financial Accounts Guide* <federalreserve.gov/apps/fof/>. Data are also available on the Federal Reserve Board's website at <federalreserve.gov/releases/z1/>.

Survey of Consumer Finances (SCF)—The Federal Reserve Board, in cooperation with the Treasury Department, sponsors this survey, which is conducted every 3 years to provide detailed information on the finances of U.S. families. Among the topics covered are the balance sheet, pension, income, and other demographic characteristics of U.S. families. The survey also gathers information on the use of financial institutions. Since 1992, data for the SCF have been collected by NORC at the University of Chicago. Information on the survey is available on the Federal Reserve Board's website at <federalreserve.gov/econres/scfindex.htm>.

Banking system—Banks in this country are organized under the laws of both the states and the federal government and are regulated by several bank supervisory agencies. National banks are supervised by the Comptroller of the Currency. *Reports of Condition and Income*, commonly known as call reports, have been collected from national banks since 1863. Summaries of these reports are published in the Comptroller's *Annual Report*, which also presents data on the structure of the national banking system.

The Federal Reserve System was established in 1913 to exercise central banking functions, some of which are shared with the U.S. Treasury. It includes national banks and state banks that voluntarily join the system. Statements of state bank members are consolidated by the Federal Reserve Board with data for national banks collected by the Comptroller of the Currency

into totals for all member banks of the system. Balance sheet data for member banks and other commercial banks are available on the Federal Reserve Board's website at <federalreserve.gov/data.htm>.

The Federal Deposit Insurance Corporation (FDIC), established in 1933, insures each depositor up to $250,000. Major item balance sheet and income data for all insured financial institutions are published in the *FDIC Quarterly Banking Profile*. This publication is also available on the internet at <fdic.gov/bank/analytical/qbp/>. Quarterly financial information for individual institutions is available through the FDIC and Federal Financial Institutions Examination Council websites at <fdic.gov> and <ffiec.gov>.

Credit unions—Federally chartered credit unions are under the supervision of the National Credit Union Administration (NCUA). State-chartered credit unions are supervised by the respective state supervisory authorities. The NCUA publishes comprehensive program and statistical information on all federal and federally insured state credit unions in the *Annual Report of the National Credit Union Administration*.

Other credit agencies—Insurance companies, finance companies dealing primarily in installment sales financing, and personal loan companies represent important sources of funds for the credit market. Statistics on loans, investments, cash, etc., of life insurance companies are published principally by the American Council of Life Insurers in its *Life Insurers Fact Book*. Consumer credit data are available on the Federal Reserve Board's website at <federalreserve.gov/data.htm>. Government corporations and credit agencies make available credit of specified types or to specified groups of private borrowers, either by lending directly or by insuring or guaranteeing loans made by private lending institutions. Data on operations of government credit agencies, along with other government corporations, are available in reports of individual agencies.

Securities—The Securities and Exchange Commission (SEC) was established in 1934 to protect the interests of the public and investors against malpractices in the securities and financial markets and to provide the fullest possible disclosure of information regarding securities to the investing public.

Data on the securities industry and securities transactions are also available from a number of private sources. The Securities Industry and Financial Markets Association (SIFMA), New York, NY, <sifma.org/>, publishes the *SIFMA Fact Book*. The Investment Company Institute, Washington, DC, <ici.org/>, publishes a reference book, research newsletters, and a variety of research reports that examine the industry, its shareholders, or industry issues. The annual *Investment Company Fact Book* is a guide to trends and statistics observed in the investment company industry. Institute research reports provide a detailed examination of shareholder demographics and other aspects of fund ownership.

Among the many sources of data on stock and bond prices and sales are the New York Stock Exchange, New York, NY, <nyse.com/>; NASDAQ, Washington,

DC, <nasdaq.com/>; and Global Financial Data, Los Angeles, CA, <globalfinancialdata.com/>.

Insurance—Insuring companies, which are regulated by the various states or the District of Columbia, are classified as either life or property. Both life and property insurance companies may underwrite health insurance. Insuring companies, other than those classified as life, are permitted to underwrite one or more property lines provided they are so licensed and have the necessary capital or surplus. There are a number of published sources for statistics on the various classes of insurance—life, health, fire, marine, and casualty. Organizations representing certain classes of insurers publish reports for these classes. The American Council of Life Insurers publishes statistics on life insurance purchases, ownership, benefit payments, and assets in its *Life Insurers Fact Book*.

Statistical reliability—For a discussion of statistical collection, estimation, and sampling procedures and measures of reliability applicable to data from the Census Bureau and the Federal Reserve Board's Survey of Consumer Finances, see Appendix III.

Table 1189. Gross Domestic Product in Finance, Insurance, Real Estate, Rental and Leasing Industries in Current and Chained (2012) Dollars: 2000 to 2019

[In billions of dollars, except percent (743 represents $743,000,000,000). Represents value added by industry. For definition of gross domestic product and explanation of chained dollars, see text, Section 13, Income]

Industry	2012 NAICS code [1]	Current dollars				Chained (2012) dollars			
		2000	2010	2018	2019	2000	2010	2018	2019
Finance & insurance, total..............	**52**	**743**	**1,004**	**1,567**	**1,628**	**905**	**1,078**	**1,165**	**1,204**
Percent of gross domestic product......	(X)	7.2	6.7	7.6	7.6	6.9	6.9	6.3	6.3
Federal Reserve banks, credit intermediation, and related activities..........	521, 522	320	418	623	646	362	444	394	403
Securities, commodity contracts, & investments..................	523	133	196	313	329	173	232	220	227
Insurance carriers & related activities......	524	275	373	609	630	341	385	560	587
Funds, trusts, & other financial vehicles. ..	525	15	17	23	23	18	20	17	17
Real estate & rental & leasing, total....	**53**	**1,232**	**1,939**	**2,734**	**2,864**	**1,546**	**1,987**	**2,374**	**2,412**
Percent of gross domestic product......	(X)	12.0	12.9	13.3	13.4	11.8	12.7	12.7	12.6
Real estate..................	531	1,096	1,779	2,503	2,622	1,374	1,823	2,140	2,171
Rental & leasing services and lessors of intangible assets..............	532, 533	136	160	231	242	175	164	237	244

X Not applicable. [1] Data based on the 2012 North American Industry Classification System (NAICS). See text, Section 15.

Source: U.S. Bureau of Economic Analysis, "Value Added by Industry" and "Real Value Added by Industry," <http://www.bea.gov/iTable/index_industry_gdpIndy.cfm>, accessed May 2020.

Table 1190. Finance, Insurance, Real Estate, and Rental and Leasing—Establishments, Revenue, Payroll, and Employees by Kind of Business: 2017

[4,340 represents $4,340,000,000,000. For establishments with payroll. Based on the 2017 Economic Censuses; see Appendix III]

Kind of business	2017 NAICS code [1]	Establishments (number)	Revenue (bil. dol.)	Annual payroll (bil. dol.)	Paid employees (1,000)
Finance & insurance [2].................	**52**	**475,780**	**4,340**	**638.8**	**6,500**
Monetary authorities—central bank........................	521	57	117	2.3	19
Credit intermediation & related activities...................	522	192,924	1,287	230.9	2,944
Security, commodity contracts, & like activity..............	523	102,555	596	195.1	954
Insurance carriers & related activities.....................	524	180,244	2,340	210.6	2,583
Real estate & rental & leasing..........................	**53**	**410,820**	**674**	**113.4**	**2,195**
Real estate..........................	531	350,913	469	84.6	1,644
Rental & leasing services......................	532	57,147	158	24.9	515
Lessors of other nonfinancial intangible assets...........	533	2,760	47	4.0	37

[1] Based on the North American Industry Classification System (NAICS); see text, Section 15. [2] Total does not include NAICS 525, Funds, trusts, and other financial vehicles.

Source: U.S. Census Bureau, "EC1700BASIC: All Sectors: Summary Statistics for the U.S., States, and Selected Geographies: 2017," <data.census.gov>, accessed July 2020.

Table 1191. Finance and Insurance—Nonemployer Establishments and Receipts by Kind of Business: 2010 to 2018

[716.8 represents 716,800. Includes only firms subject to federal income tax. Nonemployers are businesses with no paid employees. Data originate chiefly from administrative records of the Internal Revenue Service; see Appendix III]

Kind of business	NAICS code [1]	Establishments (1,000)			Receipts (mil. dol.)		
		2010	2015	2018	2010	2015	2018
Finance and insurance.........................	**52**	**716.8**	**718.5**	**755.4**	**50,626**	**55,329**	**63,410**
Credit intermediation & related activities........................	522	53.3	45.8	46.2	2,790	3,134	3,365
Depository credit intermediation......................	5221	6.2	5.9	6.2	181	214	257
Nondepository credit intermediation............................	5222	21.8	22.1	22.4	1,554	1,864	1,988
Activities related to credit intermediation......................	5223	25.3	17.8	17.6	1,056	1,056	1,120
Securities, commodity contracts, & related activities...........	523	273.4	272.2	300.1	29,202	30,204	36,323
Securities & commodity contracts intermediation and brokerage........................	5231	29.8	27.6	27.9	4,969	4,812	5,818
Investment banking and securities dealing..................	52311	7.2	7.4	7.9	1,748	1,389	1,899
Securities brokerage..........................	52312	18.6	17.0	16.0	2,589	2,914	3,326
Commodity contracts dealing........................	52313	1.1	1.0	2.0	236	175	281
Commodity contracts brokerage.......................	52314	2.9	2.2	2.0	397	334	312
Securities & commodity exchanges...................	5232	1.9	1.8	1.0	660	354	369
Other financial investment activities....................	5239	241.7	242.7	271.2	23,573	25,038	30,136
Insurance carriers & related activities........................	524	390.1	400.5	409.0	18,634	21,991	23,722
Insurance carriers..............................	5241	2.7	1.8	1.9	185	172	182
Agencies & other insurance-related activities...............	5242	387.4	398.7	407.2	18,449	21,819	23,539
Insurance agencies & brokerages............................	52421	270.5	279.0	290.2	13,854	16,340	17,538
Other insurance related activities........................	52429	116.9	119.8	117.0	4,595	5,479	6,001

[1] Data for 2010 are based on 2007 North American Industry Classification System (NAICS); data for 2015 are based on 2012 NAICS; and beginning 2017, data based on 2017 NAICS. For more information, see text, Section 15.

Source: U.S. Census Bureau, Nonemployer Statistics, "All Sectors: Nonemployer Statistics for the U.S., States, Counties, Metropolitan Areas, and Combined Statistical Areas; and by Legal Form of Organization and Sales, Value of Shipments, or Revenue Size for Selected Geographies: 2018," <data.census.gov>, accessed May 2020.

Table 1192. Finance and Insurance—Establishments, Employees, and Payroll: 2016 and 2017

[477.0 represents 477,000. Covers establishments with payroll. Employees are for the week including March 12. Excludes most government employees, railroad employees, and self-employed persons. For statement on methodology, see Appendix III]

Kind of business	NAICS code [1]	Establishments (1,000)		Employees (1,000)		Payroll (bil. dol.)	
		2016	2017	2016	2017	2016	2017
Finance & insurance, total [2]	**52**	**477.0**	**478.2**	**6,337**	**6,408**	**611.7**	**643.7**
Monetary authorities—central bank	521	0.1	0.1	19	20	2.3	2.3
Credit intermediation & related activities	522	192.1	193.9	2,838	2,884	220.8	232.2
Depository credit intermediation [2]	5221	118.9	118.9	1,954	1,968	144.1	153.6
Commercial banking	52211	91.6	92.0	1,552	1,568	120.9	130.1
Savings institutions	52212	8.7	7.6	121	106	8.6	7.6
Credit unions	52213	18.5	19.3	279	292	14.4	15.7
Nondepository credit intermediation [2]	5222	44.6	45.9	597	603	55.0	52.6
Real estate credit	522292	14.7	14.8	259	262	26.1	25.6
Activities related to credit intermediation	5223	28.7	29.0	287	313	21.8	26.0
Security, commodity contracts & like activity [2]	523	102.0	103.2	907	904	184.1	197.0
Security & commodity contracts intermediation & brokerage [2]	5231	44.6	28.9	410	361	84.3	84.5
Securities brokerage	52312	39.3	23.3	298	244	49.9	45.8
Other financial investment activities [2]	5239	57.4	74.2	490	537	98.5	111.2
Portfolio management	52392	23.6	42.8	282	342	72.2	84.5
Insurance carriers & related activities	524	181.5	180.1	2,565	2,596	203.5	211.6
Insurance carriers [2]	5241	35.3	31.9	1,574	1,544	138.6	141.1
Direct life insurance carriers	524113	8.3	8.6	366	340	37.5	37.2
Direct health & medical insurance carriers	524114	6.7	5.4	567	538	44.7	44.5
Direct property & casualty insurance carriers	524126	15.2	13.1	548	576	47.7	51.0
Agencies & other insurance-related activities [2]	5242	146.2	148.2	991	1,052	64.9	70.6
Insurance agencies & brokerages	52421	134.4	136.4	711	725	47.6	49.6

[1] Data for 2016 based on North American Industry Classification System (NAICS) 2012; data for 2017 based on NAICS 2017. See text, Section 15. [2] Includes other kinds of businesses, not shown separately.

Source: U.S. Census Bureau, County Business Patterns, "County Business Patterns by Legal Form of Organization and Employment Size Class for U.S., States, and Selected Geographies," <http://data.census.gov>, accessed December 2019. See also <https://www.census.gov/programs-surveys/cbp.html>.

Table 1193. Revenues of Finance and Insurance Industries: 2010 to 2018

[In billions of dollars (3,495.7 represents $3,495,700,000,000). Covers taxable employer firms only. Based on Service Annual Survey. Estimates have been adjusted to the results of the 2012 Economic Census. See Appendix III]

Kind of business	NAICS code [1]	2010	2014	2015	2016	2017	2018
Finance & insurance, total	**52**	**3,495.7**	**3,948.4**	**4,101.7**	**4,266.4**	**4,499.5**	**4,766.9**
Monetary authorities—central bank	521	88.2	114.2	113.5	112.2	116.8	113.1
Credit intermediation & related activities	522	1,161.3	1,075.0	1,104.8	1,167.2	1,234.3	1,335.7
Commercial banking	52211	407.9	384.7	391.5	423.1	453.0	500.5
Savings institutions	52212	48.2	(D)	(D)	38.7	40.9	44.3
Credit unions	52213	47.7	49.9	53.4	58.5	64.1	72.1
Other depository credit intermediation	52219	0.9	(D)	(D)	1.0	1.1	1.1
Credit card issuing	52221	81.5	83.6	85.1	89.8	96.4	105.0
Sales financing	52222	89.5	97.3	104.9	112.8	119.7	128.7
Other nondepository credit intermediation	52229	416.6	338.3	342.0	348.5	360.5	382.3
Mortgage & nonmortgage loan brokers	52231	6.3	7.2	9.5	11.1	11.2	11.3
Financial transactions processing, reserve, and clearinghouse activities	52232	52.7	62.4	65.0	67.5	70.9	73.3
Other activities related to credit intermediation	52239	9.8	15.3	16.3	16.1	16.5	17.2
Securities, commodity contracts, and other financial investment activities	523	497.6	582.5	586.5	594.2	630.9	655.4
Investment banking and securities dealing	52311	119.6	105.9	107.3	108.8	116.5	119.8
Securities brokerage	52312	114.8	136.5	135.6	137.5	147.7	148.2
Commodity contracts dealing	52313	6.9	7.8	7.9	7.2	7.0	7.6
Commodity contracts brokerage	52314	6.2	5.3	5.1	5.0	5.0	5.0
Securities and commodity exchanges	5232	10.1	10.0	10.5	11.3	11.2	12.1
Miscellaneous intermediation	52391	17.2	22.2	22.5	23.2	26.6	32.3
Portfolio management	52392	172.3	227.2	227.2	227.4	242.1	250.1
Investment advice	52393	25.7	40.8	44.3	45.8	47.4	51.1
All other financial investment activities	52399	24.9	26.6	26.0	28.0	27.6	29.3
Insurance carriers & related activities	524	1,748.6	2,176.9	2,296.9	2,392.8	2,517.6	2,662.7
Direct life, health, medical insurance carriers	52411	1,060.7	1,298.9	1,378.8	1,435.0	1,506.6	1,596.7
Other direct insurance carriers	52412	441.6	521.2	544.3	561.9	587.9	620.9
Reinsurance carriers	52413	45.7	55.0	55.8	58.3	61.4	63.8
Insurance agencies & brokerages	52421	98.4	120.1	130.0	134.4	138.8	145.6
Other insurance-related activities	52429	102.1	181.6	188.0	203.2	222.9	235.8

D Estimate in table is withheld to avoid disclosing data of individual companies; data are included in higher level totals. [1] Data for 2010 are based on the 2007 North American Industry Classification System (NAICS); beginning 2013, data are based on 2012 NAICS. See text, this section and Section 15 for more information.

Source: U.S. Census Bureau, Service Annual Survey, "Service Annual Survey Latest Data (NAICS-basis): 2018" and "Service Annual Survey Historical Survey Tables," <https://www.census.gov/programs-surveys/sas/data.html>, accessed December 2019.

Table 1194. Financial Accounts of the United States—Financial Assets of Nonfinancial and Financial Institutions by Holder Sector: 2000 to 2019

[In billions of dollars (95,900 represents $95,900,000,000,000). As of Dec. 31]

Sector	2000	2005	2010	2013	2014	2015	2016	2017	2018	2019
All sectors	**95,900**	**134,958**	**165,264**	**199,434**	**211,679**	**215,035**	**226,181**	**245,165**	**244,929**	**271,357**
DOMESTIC NONFINANCIAL										
Households[1]	34,489	47,009	55,611	68,557	73,116	74,543	78,394	85,587	85,380	95,610
Nonfinancial business	11,264	14,549	15,884	18,547	19,832	21,348	23,002	24,342	25,445	27,627
Nonfinancial corporations	9,792	11,953	12,155	14,016	14,858	15,976	17,086	17,998	18,575	20,246
Nonfinancial noncorporate	1,473	2,597	3,728	4,531	4,974	5,372	5,917	6,344	6,871	7,381
Federal government	565	655	1,638	1,733	1,881	2,133	2,338	2,287	2,593	2,602
State and local government	1,673	2,340	2,773	2,809	2,844	2,867	3,042	3,100	2,978	3,050
DOMESTIC FINANCIAL										
Monetary authority	636	879	2,452	4,217	4,918	4,821	4,734	4,731	4,236	4,501
Private depository institutions	7,496	11,092	13,644	15,777	16,804	17,265	17,963	18,834	19,193	20,049
U.S.-chartered depository institutions	6,323	9,435	11,443	12,681	13,597	14,114	14,820	15,318	15,633	16,330
Foreign banking offices in U.S.	691	889	1,244	1,999	2,041	1,900	1,798	2,085	2,050	2,090
Banks in U.S.-affiliated areas	62	107	82	80	88	85	92	88	91	96
Credit unions	421	661	876	1,016	1,078	1,166	1,254	1,342	1,419	1,533
Property-casualty insurance companies	1,059	1,718	1,868	2,064	2,134	2,142	2,224	2,388	2,412	2,704
Life insurance companies	3,250	4,631	5,635	6,551	6,929	6,895	7,248	7,747	7,566	8,573
Private pension funds	4,283	5,391	6,604	8,398	8,675	8,567	9,052	9,961	9,691	10,883
Defined benefit plans	1,785	2,251	2,836	3,415	3,427	3,400	3,433	3,447	3,454	3,474
Defined contribution plans	2,497	3,140	3,768	4,984	5,248	5,167	5,619	6,514	6,237	7,409
Federal government retirement funds	2,007	2,479	3,133	3,515	3,605	3,704	3,792	3,906	3,979	4,150
State and local government employee retirement funds	3,322	4,695	6,169	7,438	7,778	8,089	8,332	8,678	8,979	9,328
Money market mutual funds[2]	1,845	2,027	2,804	2,733	2,749	2,742	2,731	2,848	3,038	3,634
Mutual funds[2]	5,119	6,865	9,030	12,333	13,151	12,897	13,616	15,899	14,670	17,660
Closed-end funds	143	276	238	279	289	263	265	277	251	278
Exchange-traded funds	66	301	992	1,675	1,975	2,101	2,525	3,401	3,371	4,396
Government-sponsored enterprises (GSE)[3]	1,965	2,822	6,722	6,361	6,400	6,488	6,685	6,819	6,926	7,110
Agency- and GSE-backed mortgage pools[4]	2,493	3,548	1,147	1,574	1,649	1,775	1,933	2,127	2,293	2,407
Asset-backed securities issuers	1,509	3,499	2,343	1,510	1,423	1,347	1,231	1,168	1,160	1,210
Finance companies[5]	1,241	1,880	1,814	1,736	1,745	1,605	1,539	1,540	1,470	1,506
Real estate investment trusts	65	306	302	663	725	659	675	754	821	927
Security brokers and dealers	2,020	3,569	3,504	3,408	3,255	3,044	3,022	3,097	3,359	3,469
Holding companies[6]	841	1,500	2,894	3,623	3,745	3,608	3,853	3,858	3,841	4,013
Other financial business[7]	984	1,299	1,123	920	921	1,016	1,260	1,314	1,370	1,375
Rest of the world	7,565	11,630	16,940	23,012	25,138	25,117	26,726	30,502	29,906	34,295

[1] Includes nonprofit organizations. [2] Open-end investment companies including variable annuity money market funds or mutual funds. [3] Federal Home Loan Banks, Federal National Mortgage Association (Fannie Mae), Federal Home Loan Mortgage Corporation (Freddie Mac), Federal Agriculture Mortgage Corporation, Farm Credit System, the Financing Corporation, and the Resolution Funding Corporation. The Student Loan Marketing Association (Sallie Mae), was included until it was fully privatized in 2004. [4] Government National Mortgage Association, Federal National Mortgage Association, Federal Home Loan Mortgage Corporation, Federal Agriculture Mortgage Corporation, and Farmers Home Administration pools. Also includes agency- and GSE-backed mortgage pool securities that are used as collateral for agency- and GSE-backed collateralized mortgage obligations (CMOs) and privately issued CMOs. Excludes Federal Financing Bank holdings of pool securities, which are included with federal government mortgages and other loans and advances. [5] Includes retail captive finance companies and mortgage companies. [6] Parent-only bank holding companies, savings and loan holding companies and security holding companies that file Federal Reserve Board form FR Y-9LP, FR Y-9SP, or FR Y-2320. [7] Includes funding subsidiaries, custodial accounts for reinvested collateral of securities lending operations, Federal Reserve lending facilities, and funds associated with the Public-Private Investment Program (PPIP).

Source: Board of Governors of the Federal Reserve System, "Financial Accounts of the United States, Z.1," <https://www.federalreserve.gov/data.htm>, accessed April 2020.

Table 1195. Financial Accounts of the United States—Debt Securities and Debt Loans Outstanding By Sector: 2000 to 2019

[In billions of dollars (28,608 represents $28,608,000,000,000). As of December 31. Represents credit market debt owed by sectors shown. Some sectors only borrow/lend through debt securities or loans, but not both]

Item	2000	2005	2010	2013	2014	2015	2016	2017	2018	2019
Total debt outstanding	**28,608**	**43,466**	**55,253**	**59,778**	**62,034**	**63,685**	**66,191**	**69,150**	**72,161**	**75,465**
Total debt securities [1]	**16,395**	**24,760**	**33,952**	**37,762**	**39,091**	**40,049**	**41,629**	**43,241**	**45,097**	**47,352**
Domestic nonfinancial	8,114	11,425	17,952	21,854	22,872	24,012	25,172	25,940	27,436	28,874
Nonprofit and household sector	138	217	271	235	228	220	217	219	216	213
Nonfinancial corporate business	2,698	2,985	3,961	4,811	5,138	5,551	5,838	6,159	6,299	6,558
Federal government	4,090	5,585	10,529	13,705	14,441	15,166	16,008	16,455	17,865	19,040
State and local governments [2]	1,189	2,638	3,192	3,103	3,065	3,076	3,109	3,107	3,056	3,064
Financial sectors	7,577	12,126	13,924	13,258	13,352	13,284	13,656	13,957	14,295	14,748
U.S.-chartered depository institutions	99	134	585	350	314	301	277	223	247	236
Foreign banking offices in U.S.	2	1	88	57	46	43	49	38	41	46
Government-sponsored enterprises (GSE)	1,826	2,592	6,435	6,200	6,276	6,369	6,563	6,716	6,797	6,975
Agency- and GSE-backed mortgage pools	2,493	3,548	1,147	1,574	1,649	1,775	1,933	2,127	2,293	2,407
Asset-backed securities issuers	1,516	3,503	2,343	1,510	1,423	1,347	1,231	1,168	1,160	1,210
Finance companies	743	966	1,188	1,078	1,080	953	886	835	879	850
Real estate investment trusts	65	217	145	355	403	396	417	439	470	540
Brokers and dealers	41	62	130	112	124	131	129	186	184	174
Holding companies	290	482	1,241	1,403	1,394	1,213	1,376	1,449	1,402	1,448
Other financial business	503	620	622	618	644	755	793	776	821	861
Rest of the world	703	1,209	2,076	2,649	2,867	2,753	2,801	3,344	3,367	3,730
Total loans [3]	**12,214**	**18,706**	**21,301**	**22,016**	**22,943**	**23,636**	**24,562**	**25,909**	**27,064**	**28,113**
Domestic nonfinancial	10,981	16,987	19,535	19,934	20,594	21,183	22,004	23,329	24,438	25,473
Financial sectors	1,099	1,602	1,596	1,761	1,934	1,978	2,052	2,038	2,027	1,954
Rest of the world	134	116	170	321	415	474	506	541	599	686

[1] Includes open market paper, Treasury securities, agency- and GSE-backed securities, municipal securities, and corporate and foreign bonds. [2] Excludes employee retirement funds. [3] Includes depository loans not elsewhere classified, other loans and advances, mortgages, and consumer credit.

Source: Board of Governors of the Federal Reserve System, "Financial Accounts of the United States, Z.1," <https://www.federalreserve.gov/data.htm>, accessed April 2020.

Table 1196. Financial Accounts of the United States—Financial Assets and Liabilities of Foreign Sector: 2000 to 2019

[In billions of dollars (7,565 represents $7,565,000,000,000). As of December 31. Minus sign (-) indicates loss]

Type of instrument	2000	2005	2010	2013	2014	2015	2016	2017	2018	2019
Total financial assets	**7,565**	**11,630**	**16,940**	**23,012**	**25,138**	**25,117**	**26,726**	**30,502**	**29,906**	**34,295**
Special Drawing Rights allocations	6	7	54	54	51	49	47	50	49	49
Net interbank assets	49	-42	-68	292	258	198	54	158	207	122
U.S. checkable deposits and currency	236	300	390	591	674	707	767	848	928	986
U.S. time deposits	226	223	308	445	499	480	551	565	601	597
Money market fund shares	11	23	70	106	105	108	93	93	111	130
Security repurchase agreements	91	736	641	824	924	903	972	1,003	940	1,025
Debt securities, excluding negotiable certificates of deposit	2,335	4,980	8,252	9,587	10,174	10,337	10,661	11,342	11,178	12,102
Open market (commercial) paper	114	157	102	101	108	104	141	135	124	127
Treasury securities	1,021	1,984	4,459	5,793	6,158	6,146	6,003	6,211	6,265	6,698
Agency- and GSE-backed securities [1]	348	1,006	1,096	884	900	916	992	1,012	1,078	1,181
Municipal securities	8	29	72	76	81	87	94	101	101	103
U.S. corporate bonds	843	1,804	2,523	2,733	2,928	3,083	3,432	3,882	3,610	3,993
Nonfinancial business loans	117	163	162	140	171	208	203	376	733	831
U.S. corporate equities	1,483	2,118	3,213	5,205	5,921	5,501	5,783	7,019	6,511	8,179
Mutual fund shares	149	163	263	553	617	601	694	829	799	1,030
Trade receivables	70	122	203	224	237	247	254	300	333	337
Life insurance reserves	–	1	6	4	11	6	17	20	10	12
Pension entitlements	–	–	1	2	5	3	4	4	15	15
Foreign direct investment in U.S. [2]	2,783	2,818	3,422	4,948	5,457	5,731	6,586	7,844	7,432	8,821
Miscellaneous assets (insurance receivables)	7	19	22	36	36	39	40	50	59	60
Total liabilities	**4,562**	**6,889**	**9,630**	**11,455**	**11,688**	**11,211**	**11,619**	**13,904**	**12,733**	**14,200**
U.S. official reserve assets [3]	57	54	121	133	119	106	106	112	115	118
U.S. private deposits	803	1,165	1,304	951	828	591	501	756	789	762
Security repurchase agreements	–	381	664	692	709	789	905	873	915	1,154
Debt securities	703	1,209	2,076	2,649	2,867	2,753	2,801	3,344	3,367	3,730
Commercial paper	121	87	173	266	275	329	270	362	368	417
Bonds	582	1,122	1,903	2,384	2,592	2,424	2,531	2,982	2,999	3,313
Loans	134	116	170	321	415	474	506	541	599	686
Depository institution loans n.e.c. [4,5]	84	85	149	289	381	441	475	487	552	631
Other loans and advances	50	31	21	32	34	34	32	54	46	55
Trade credit and advances	47	46	65	71	66	66	69	77	79	64
Life insurance reserves	22	49	68	52	48	51	75	98	67	73
Pension entitlements	6	16	33	28	21	21	15	19	78	76
U.S. direct investment abroad [2]	2,694	3,638	4,810	6,254	6,320	6,059	6,412	7,829	6,453	7,259
Miscellaneous liabilities	96	215	319	303	297	299	228	255	273	279

– Represents or rounds to zero. [1] GSE = Government-sponsored enterprises. [2] Direct investment is valued on a market value basis. [3] Excludes monetary gold. [4] N.e.c. = not elsewhere classified. [5] Beginning with 2010, includes loans to foreign non-depository financial institutions.

Source: Board of Governors of the Federal Reserve System, "Financial Accounts of the United States, Z.1," <https://www.federalreserve.gov/data.htm>, accessed April 2020.

Table 1197. Financial Accounts of the United States—Assets of Households and Nonprofit Organizations: 2000 to 2019

[In billions of dollars (34,489 represents $34,489,000,000,000). As of December 31. See also Table 758]

Type of instrument	Total (billion dollars)							Percent distribution		
	2000	2005	2010	2015	2017	2018	2019	2000	2010	2019
Total financial assets...............	**34,489**	**47,009**	**55,611**	**74,543**	**85,587**	**85,380**	**95,610**	**100.0**	**100.0**	**100.0**
Foreign deposits........................	48	64	67	32	39	40	34	0.1	0.1	–
Checkable deposits and currency.........	398	359	515	1,205	1,325	1,402	1,263	1.2	0.9	1.3
Time and savings deposits...............	3,067	4,880	6,405	8,403	9,261	9,664	10,162	8.9	11.5	10.6
Money market fund shares................	1,296	1,262	1,658	1,551	1,619	1,800	2,148	3.8	3.0	2.2
Debt securities.......................	2,041	3,161	5,183	4,659	4,517	5,179	5,514	5.9	9.3	5.8
Treasury securities..................	548	263	1,043	1,031	1,145	1,716	1,961	1.6	1.9	2.1
Agency and GSE-backed securities [1]....	577	369	225	497	460	648	721	1.7	0.4	0.8
Municipal securities.................	476	1,701	1,912	1,901	1,887	1,859	1,894	1.4	3.4	2.0
Corporate and foreign bonds............	441	828	2,002	1,231	1,024	956	938	1.3	3.6	1.0
Loans [2].............................	558	759	955	985	903	883	891	1.6	1.7	0.9
Mortgages............................	96	127	132	99	82	69	57	0.3	0.2	0.1
Consumer credit (student loans).........	–	–	71	45	35	31	28	–	0.1	–
Corporate equities [3]...................	7,074	8,088	8,565	13,688	18,110	16,656	21,076	20.5	15.4	22.0
Mutual fund shares....................	2,558	3,409	4,702	6,958	8,655	7,961	9,683	7.4	8.5	10.1
Trade receivables....................	124	153	184	241	250	255	259	0.4	0.3	0.3
Life insurance reserves...............	839	1,136	1,273	1,511	1,627	1,659	1,766	2.4	2.3	1.8
Pension entitlements [4].................	11,030	14,521	18,293	23,450	25,919	25,904	27,996	32.0	32.9	29.3
Equity in noncorporate business..........	5,020	8,473	6,906	10,778	12,169	12,732	13,542	14.6	12.4	14.2
Miscellaneous assets....................	437	744	905	1,082	1,193	1,245	1,275	1.3	1.6	1.3

– Represents or rounds to zero. [1] GSE = government-sponsored enterprises. [2] Includes other instruments not shown separately. [3] Directly held corporate equities, including closed-end fund, exchange-traded fund, and real estate investment trust shares. [4] Includes public and private defined benefit and defined contribution plans and annuities, including those in IRAs and at life insurance companies. Excludes social security.

Source: Board of Governors of the Federal Reserve System, "Financial Accounts of the United States, Z.1," <https://www.federalreserve.gov/data.htm>, accessed April 2020.

Table 1198. Financial Assets Held by Families by Type of Asset: 2013 and 2016

[Median value in thousands of constant 2016 dollars (21.9 represents $21,900). All dollar figures are adjusted to 2016 dollars using the "current methods" version of the consumer price index for all urban consumers published by U.S. Bureau of Labor Statistics. Families include one-person units; for definition of family, see text, Section 1. Based on Survey of Consumer Finances; see Appendix III]

Age of family head and family income	Any financial asset [1]	Trans-action accounts [2]	Certifi-cates of deposit	Savings bonds	Stocks [3]	Pooled invest-ment funds [4]	Retire-ment accounts [5]	Life insur-ance [6]	Other man-aged [7]
PERCENT OF FAMILIES OWNING ASSET									
2013, total..................	94.5	93.2	7.8	10.0	13.8	8.2	49.2	19.2	5.2
2016, total..................	**98.5**	**98.0**	**6.5**	**8.6**	**13.9**	**10.0**	**52.1**	**19.4**	**5.5**
Under 35 years old..........	98.1	97.7	2.4	5.8	10.0	4.8	42.2	9.3	1.4
35 to 44 years old...........	97.9	97.3	4.7	10.2	11.4	6.9	56.7	12.6	1.7
45 to 54 years old...........	99.0	98.5	4.6	9.3	14.6	9.9	59.8	18.4	2.6
55 to 64 years old...........	98.6	98.0	6.7	8.6	15.5	12.6	59.3	23.4	6.4
65 to 74 years old...........	98.9	98.6	10.5	9.7	15.2	13.3	49.8	29.7	12.5
75 years old and over........	98.4	97.8	14.5	9.1	19.6	15.6	40.8	29.5	12.6
Percentiles of income: [8]									
Less than 20.................	95.2	94.2	2.9	2.7	3.9	1.6	11.3	12.2	2.1
20 to 39.9...................	97.4	96.3	5.1	5.1	6.0	3.2	33.6	15.9	3.9
40 to 59.9...................	99.7	99.4	6.3	8.6	10.5	5.4	53.1	19.5	3.7
60 to 79.9...................	100.0	99.9	6.7	11.3	13.8	12.5	75.2	22.7	6.7
80 to 89.9...................	100.0	99.8	11.5	15.0	25.1	17.6	82.2	22.3	8.6
90 to 100....................	100.0	100.0	11.5	15.8	45.9	37.3	91.9	31.0	13.3
MEDIAN VALUE [9]									
2013, total..................	21.9	4.2	16.5	1.0	27.8	82.5	60.8	8.2	103.1
2016, total..................	**23.5**	**4.5**	**20.0**	**1.0**	**25.0**	**114.0**	**60.0**	**8.5**	**110.0**
Under 35 years old..........	6.0	2.6	4.0	0.5	5.0	10.3	12.3	3.0	50.0
35 to 44 years old...........	17.0	3.8	7.7	0.6	12.0	55.9	37.0	6.0	22.0
45 to 54 years old...........	35.0	4.1	10.0	0.8	25.0	100.0	82.6	9.6	70.0
55 to 64 years old...........	59.3	5.4	20.0	2.0	45.0	270.0	120.0	15.0	165.0
65 to 74 years old...........	59.5	8.0	25.0	1.0	55.0	300.0	126.0	9.6	140.0
75 years old and over........	63.0	10.0	40.0	4.8	70.0	155.0	120.0	7.5	100.0

[1] Includes other types of financial assets, not shown separately. [2] Checking, savings, and money market deposit accounts, money market mutual funds, call or cash accounts at brokerages, and prepaid debit cards. [3] Covers only publicly traded stocks that are directly held by families—that is, corporate equities not held as part of a managed investment account or mutual fund. [4] Excludes money market mutual funds and indirectly held mutual funds and includes all other types of directly held pooled investment funds, such as traditional open-ended and closed-end mutual funds, real estate investment trusts, and hedge funds. [5] The tax-deferred retirement accounts consist of IRAs, Keogh accounts, and certain employer-sponsored accounts. Employer-sponsored accounts include 401(k), 403(b), and thrift saving accounts from current or past jobs; other current job plans from which loans or withdrawals can be made; and accounts from past jobs from which the family expects to receive the account balance in the future. [6] The value of such policies according to their current cash value, not their death benefit. [7] Includes personal annuities and trusts with an equity interest and managed investment accounts. [8] Percentiles of income distribution in 2016 dollars: 20th: $25,300; 40th: $43,500; 60th: $69,500; 80th: $111,400; 90th: $177,100. Percentile: A value on a scale of zero to 100 that indicates the percent of a distribution that is equal to or below it. [9] Median value of financial asset for families holding such assets.

Source: Board of Governors of the Federal Reserve System, 2016 Survey of Consumer Finances, Changes in U.S. Family Finances From 2013 to 2016: Evidence from the Survey of Consumer Finances, Federal Reserve Bulletin, Vol. 103, No. 3, September 2017. See also <federalreserve.gov/econres/scfindex.htm>.

Table 1199. Financial Accounts of the United States—Liabilities of Households and Nonprofit Organizations: 2000 to 2019

[In billions of dollars (7,407 represents $7,407,000,000,000). As of December 31. Minus sign (-) indicates decrease. See also Table 758]

Type of instrument	Total (billion dollars)							Percent distribution		
	2000	2005	2010	2015	2017	2018	2019	2000	2010	2019
Total liabilities.................	7,407	12,259	14,035	14,537	15,545	16,028	16,576	100.0	100.0	100.0
Debt securities (municipal securities).......	138	217	271	220	219	216	213	1.9	1.9	1.3
Loans.................	7,102	11,816	13,465	13,945	14,929	15,399	15,936	95.9	95.9	96.1
Home mortgages [1].................	4,817	8,940	9,992	9,577	10,049	10,316	10,610	65.0	71.2	64.0
Consumer credit....................	1,741	2,321	2,647	3,411	3,828	4,010	4,191	23.5	18.9	25.3
Depository institution loans, not elsewhere classified [2]	61	36	214	281	299	333	346	0.8	1.5	2.1
Other loans and advances.................	354	352	414	437	488	463	500	4.8	3.0	3.0
Commercial mortgages....................	129	168	198	239	265	277	289	1.7	1.4	1.7
Trade payables....................	148	203	274	341	364	378	391	2.0	2.0	2.4
Deferred and unpaid life insurance premiums.................	20	23	25	32	33	35	37	0.3	0.2	0.2

[1] Includes loans made under home equity lines of credit and home equity loans secured by junior liens. [2] Includes loans extended by the Federal Reserve to financial institutions such as domestic hedge funds through the Term Asset-Backed Securities Loan Facility (TALF).

Source: Board of Governors of the Federal Reserve System, "Financial Accounts of the United States, Z.1," <https://www.federalreserve.gov/data.htm>, accessed April 2020.

Table 1200. Financial Debt Held by Families by Type of Debt: 2013 and 2016

[Median debt in thousands of constant 2016 dollars (62.3 represents $62,300). See headnote, Table 1198]

Age and race of family head and family income	Any debt	Secured by residential property		Installment loans [2]	Credit card balances [3]	Lines of credit not secured by residential property	Other [4]
		Primary residence [1]	Other				
PERCENT OF FAMILIES HOLDING DEBT							
2013, total....................	74.5	42.9	5.2	47.2	38.1	1.9	6.6
2016, total.................	**77.1**	**41.9**	**5.6**	**50.2**	**43.9**	**1.8**	**5.4**
Under 35 years old..................	81.0	28.3	2.3	67.5	45.4	1.9	4.0
35 to 44 years old..................	86.2	50.1	6.7	64.2	49.1	2.6	5.9
45 to 54 years old..................	86.6	53.5	6.4	55.2	52.3	2.2	8.2
55 to 64 years old..................	77.1	49.0	8.8	44.9	41.4	1.9	7.0
65 to 74 years old..................	70.1	38.8	5.8	33.7	42.1	1.1	3.7
75 years old and over..................	49.8	26.5	2.7	19.3	26.2	(B)	1.5
White, non-Hispanic..................	77.5	46.4	6.5	49.3	42.1	1.8	5.1
Black or African-American, non-Hispanic..................	77.1	31.9	2.7	54.2	47.8	2.5	5.9
Hispanic or Latino..................	74.0	31.5	3.3	46.0	49.6	(B)	4.7
Other or multiple race..................	77.9	37.8	6.2	53.8	44.1	1.9	7.1
Percentiles of income: [5]							
Less than 20..................	57.9	14.1	0.7	35.8	29.0	1.2	2.5
20 to 39.9..................	70.4	26.1	1.6	44.4	41.7	1.4	3.3
40 to 59.9..................	84.3	40.7	2.5	57.1	53.0	2.1	5.3
60 to 79.9..................	88.2	59.3	7.0	60.3	52.8	2.4	7.0
80 to 89.9..................	89.0	70.9	12.2	61.3	51.5	1.7	8.4
90 to 100..................	80.6	67.3	19.9	45.5	34.4	2.3	9.0
MEDIAN DEBT [6]							
2013, total....................	62.3	118.6	92.8	15.1	2.4	4.5	4.1
2016, total.................	**59.8**	**111.0**	**100.0**	**17.1**	**2.3**	**3.0**	**5.0**
Under 35 years old..................	39.3	119.0	37.0	21.0	1.4	0.6	2.0
35 to 44 years old..................	93.7	140.0	127.5	20.5	2.5	5.0	4.0
45 to 54 years old..................	89.9	125.0	85.0	17.8	2.8	5.0	7.0
55 to 64 years old..................	69.0	96.1	110.0	13.8	2.8	3.5	8.0
65 to 74 years old..................	42.0	79.0	96.0	12.4	2.5	1.2	5.0
75 years old and over..................	20.6	50.1	100.0	9.8	2.1	(B)	9.0
White, non-Hispanic..................	74.1	115.0	116.0	17.0	2.7	3.0	7.5
Black or African-American, non-Hispanic..................	31.1	78.9	19.2	18.6	1.4	0.9	2.5
Hispanic or Latino..................	30.0	99.0	55.8	15.7	1.7	(B)	2.0
Other or multiple race..................	56.7	150.0	78.5	16.3	2.3	1.2	7.0

B Base figure too small. [1] Debt secured by residential property consists of first-lien and junior-lien mortgages and home equity lines of credit secured by the primary residence. [2] Consumer loans that typically have fixed payments and a fixed term. Examples are automobile loans, student loans, and loans for furniture, appliances, and other durable consumer goods. [3] Balances exclude purchases made after the most recent bill was paid. [4] Includes loans on insurance policies, loans against pension accounts, borrowing on margin accounts, and unclassified loans. [5] See footnote 8, Table 1198. [6] Median amount of financial debt for families holding such debts.

Source: Board of Governors of the Federal Reserve System, 2016 Survey of Consumer Finances, Changes in U.S. Family Finances From 2013 to 2016: Evidence from the Survey of Consumer Finances, Federal Reserve Bulletin, Vol. 103, No. 3, September 2017. See also <federalreserve.gov/econres/scfindex.htm>.

Table 1201. Debt Held by Families—Percent Distribution by Type and Purpose of Debt: 2010 to 2016

[See headnote, Table 1198]

Type and purpose of debt	2010	2013	2016	Type and purpose of debt	2010	2013	2016
TYPE OF DEBT				**PURPOSE OF DEBT**			
Total...............................	**100.0**	**100.0**	**100.0**	**Total**..................................	**100.0**	**100.0**	**100.0**
Secured by residential property:				Primary residence:			
Primary residence..................	74.1	73.8	69.4	Purchase............................	69.5	70.5	66.7
Other.................................	9.8	9.0	9.4	Improvement........................	1.9	1.7	1.5
Lines of credit not secured				Other residential property...........	10.5	10.2	10.3
by residential property.............	1.0	0.7	1.1	Investments, except real estate.....	2.0	1.0	1.5
Installment loans......................	11.1	13.1	16.0	Vehicles...............................	4.7	5.1	6.3
Credit card balances..................	2.9	2.4	2.6	Goods and services..................	5.7	4.4	4.9
Other...................................	1.1	1.1	1.5	Education.............................	5.2	6.6	8.2
				Other.................................	0.4	0.5	0.5

Source: Board of Governors of the Federal Reserve System, 2016 Survey of Consumer Finances, *Changes in U.S. Family Finances From 2013 to 2016: Evidence from the Survey of Consumer Finances*, Federal Reserve Bulletin, Vol. 103, No. 3, September 2017. See also <federalreserve.gov/econres/scfindex.htm>.

Table 1202. Ratios of Debt Payments to Family Income: 2010 to 2016

[In percent. See headnote, Table 1198]

Family characteristic	Ratio of debt payments to family income						Percent of debtors with—					
	Aggregate [1]			Median for debtors [2]			Ratios above 40 percent			Any payment 60 days or more past due		
	2010	2013	2016	2010	2013	2016	2010	2013	2016	2010	2013	2016
All families..............	**14.7**	**12.0**	**10.8**	**18.2**	**15.9**	**14.7**	**13.9**	**11.0**	**9.1**	**10.8**	**9.3**	**7.5**
Under 35 years old..........	17.0	14.9	14.1	16.4	13.7	13.1	11.6	8.1	8.5	10.4	11.6	10.6
35 to 44 years old..........	18.4	13.6	15.2	20.9	16.1	16.0	16.4	9.8	8.7	15.7	11.4	10.5
45 to 54 years old..........	16.2	13.9	11.7	19.2	18.6	16.2	15.6	12.0	8.5	12.6	12.0	6.9
55 to 64 years old..........	12.5	11.1	9.1	17.6	16.4	15.1	13.1	14.0	10.9	8.4	6.4	5.7
65 to 74 years old..........	11.3	8.8	7.9	17.0	14.2	13.7	12.1	12.2	8.5	6.1	4.7	4.5
75 years old and over.......	6.8	5.8	6.0	14.1	10.6	12.5	11.9	10.0	9.9	3.2	2.7	2.8
Percentiles of income: [3]												
Less than 20.................	23.5	15.5	16.2	16.3	12.8	11.9	26.1	23.2	21.6	21.2	16.1	13.9
20 to 39.9...................	16.9	14.8	14.6	17.5	15.3	15.6	18.7	18.4	13.3	15.2	14.3	11.1
40 to 59.9...................	19.5	16.2	15.3	20.0	16.4	14.4	15.5	11.1	8.3	10.2	10.0	9.1
60 to 79.9...................	19.3	16.7	15.7	20.4	17.9	16.1	11.0	6.1	4.2	8.8	7.3	4.4
80 to 89.9...................	18.1	16.5	15.4	19.3	18.5	16.3	5.4	3.9	4.2	5.4	4.1	2.9
90 to 100....................	9.4	7.3	6.2	13.1	11.8	11.3	2.9	1.8	1.5	2.1	1.0	0.8
Percentiles of net worth: [3]												
Less than 25.................	19.2	16.7	13.2	13.6	12.2	9.9	14.9	12.3	8.3	22.2	21.1	16.7
25 to 49.9...................	19.3	16.9	16.1	21.3	18.0	17.2	15.4	13.8	10.7	13.3	10.4	8.9
50 to 74.9...................	19.2	16.8	16.9	20.8	17.8	17.7	14.1	10.2	9.9	6.8	5.0	3.9
75 to 89.9...................	15.9	14.1	13.3	16.7	15.4	14.9	11.0	7.7	7.8	2.0	1.8	1.9
90 to 100....................	8.8	6.4	5.5	13.4	11.3	11.2	11.0	7.9	6.3	1.2	1.0	0.4
Owner occupied.............	16.1	13.1	11.7	22.2	19.7	18.9	17.1	14.0	11.5	8.7	6.5	5.0
Renter occupied or other. ..	7.0	6.6	6.7	6.8	6.8	6.5	5.0	4.2	3.9	16.6	15.9	13.1

[1] The aggregate measure is the ratio of total debt payments to total income for all families. [2] The median is the median of the distribution of ratios calculated for individual families with debt. [3] Percentiles of income distribution in 2016 dollars: 20th: $25,300; 40th: $43,500; 60th: $69,500; 80th: $111,400; 90th: $177,100. Percentiles of distribution of net worth in 2016 dollars: 25th: $10,300; 50th: $97,300; 75th: $369,100; 90th: $1,186,300.

Source: Board of Governors of the Federal Reserve System, 2016 Survey of Consumer Finances, *Changes in U.S. Family Finances From 2013 to 2016: Evidence from the Survey of Consumer Finances*, Federal Reserve Bulletin, Vol. 103, No. 3, September 2017. See also <federalreserve.gov/econres/scfindex.htm>.

Table 1203. Household Debt-Service Payments and Financial Obligations as a Percent of Disposable Personal Income: 1990 to 2019

[As of end of year (4th quarter), seasonally adjusted. Mortgage debt service ratio (DSR) is defined as the total quarterly required mortgage payments divided by total quarterly disposable personal income. The consumer DSR is defined as the total quarterly required consumer debt payments divided by total quarterly disposable personal income. The financial obligations ratio adds automobile lease payments, rental payments on tenant-occupied property, homeowners' insurance, and property tax payments to the debt service ratio]

Year	Financial obligations ratio	Household debt service ratio			Year	Financial obligations ratio	Household debt service ratio		
		Total	Mortgage	Consumer			Total	Mortgage	Consumer
1990............	16.96	11.60	6.18	5.42	2013............	15.36	10.07	4.86	5.21
2000............	17.06	12.06	5.72	6.34	2014............	15.19	9.85	4.56	5.30
2005............	17.26	12.59	6.49	6.10	2015............	15.52	9.92	4.48	5.44
2009............	17.15	11.96	6.54	5.42	2016............	15.69	10.04	4.38	5.65
2010............	16.08	10.98	5.95	5.03	2017............	15.41	9.88	4.25	5.63
2011............	15.64	10.45	5.44	5.01	2018............	15.12	9.74	4.19	5.56
2012............	14.89	9.83	4.95	4.88	2019............	15.08	9.73	4.12	5.61

Source: Board of Governors of the Federal Reserve System, "Household Debt Service and Financial Obligations Ratios," <https://www.federalreserve.gov/data.htm>, accessed April 2020.

Table 1204. FDIC-Insured Financial Institutions—Number and Assets by State and Island Area: 2019

[In billions of dollars, except as indicated (18,735.0 represents $18,735,000,000,000). As of December 31. Includes data from U.S. banks and U.S. branches of foreign banks that have insured deposits. Information is obtained primarily from the Federal Financial Institutions Examination Council (FFIEC) Call Reports and the Office of Thrift Supervision's Thrift Financial Reports. Data are based on the location of each reporting institution's main office. Reported data may include assets located outside of the reporting institution's home state]

State or Island Area	Number of institutions	Assets by asset size of bank				State or Island Area	Number of institutions	Assets by asset size of bank			
		Total	Less than $100 mil.	$100 mil. to $1 bil.	Greater than $1 bil.			Total	Less than $100 mil.	$100 mil. to $1 bil.	Greater than $1 bil.
Total.......	5,186	18,735.0	68.5	1,088.0	17,578.5	NE...........	165	82.4	3.3	30.0	49.1
AL...........	110	261.0	2.0	22.6	236.4	NV...........	19	265.1	0.1	3.7	261.4
AK...........	5	6.8	–	1.4	5.4	NH...........	18	11.5	0.1	7.7	3.7
AZ...........	14	31.2	0.2	4.2	26.9	NJ...........	66	164.3	0.1	17.0	147.2
AR...........	87	112.9	0.9	19.8	92.1	NM...........	34	12.6	0.2	9.4	3.0
CA...........	149	868.1	0.5	35.0	832.6	NY...........	144	1,210.8	0.5	33.7	1,176.6
CO...........	75	60.2	0.8	12.8	46.6	NC...........	46	2,386.3	0.6	9.9	2,375.9
CT...........	35	118.8	0.1	9.5	109.2	ND...........	74	34.9	1.6	10.8	22.5
DE...........	21	1,006.3	0.1	2.8	1,003.4	OH...........	180	3,352.1	3.1	35.4	3,313.5
DC...........	3	1.4	–	1.4	–	OK...........	198	137.2	4.0	38.7	94.5
FL...........	104	204.1	0.8	28.1	175.1	OR...........	16	34.6	–	5.7	28.8
GA...........	160	147.9	1.4	32.9	113.7	PA...........	141	242.2	0.6	36.2	205.4
HI...........	8	55.0	–	1.4	53.6	RI...........	8	177.2	0.1	0.5	176.7
ID...........	11	6.4	–	3.3	3.1	SC...........	47	40.2	0.6	14.3	25.3
IL...........	415	528.0	7.5	67.7	452.8	SD...........	62	3,257.4	1.1	9.0	3,247.3
IN...........	102	107.7	1.0	23.0	83.7	TN...........	139	142.8	1.4	37.0	104.4
IA...........	273	91.7	4.6	49.3	37.8	TX...........	420	545.6	5.5	95.1	445.0
KS...........	227	75.3	5.2	33.2	36.9	UT...........	39	751.4	0.2	6.6	744.6
KY...........	141	60.5	1.7	28.7	30.2	VT...........	11	5.4	0.1	4.2	1.1
LA...........	114	82.3	1.2	29.3	51.7	VA...........	71	771.6	0.4	19.1	752.1
ME...........	26	29.9	0.3	5.0	24.7	WA...........	41	84.6	0.4	7.5	76.8
MD...........	41	42.4	0.1	11.0	31.3	WV...........	49	36.4	0.6	9.6	26.2
MA...........	113	412.4	0.4	31.9	380.1	WI...........	190	118.8	2.0	46.5	70.4
MI...........	91	70.2	1.1	21.3	47.8	WY...........	30	9.3	0.3	9.0	–
MN...........	281	79.6	6.6	42.8	30.2	GU...........	3	2.4	–	0.5	1.9
MS...........	71	111.1	0.6	14.5	95.9	FM...........	1	0.2	–	0.2	–
MO...........	248	175.4	3.7	50.7	121.1	PR...........	4	69.5	–	–	69.5
MT...........	44	41.1	1.1	6.7	33.3	VI...........	1	0.3	–	0.3	–

– Represents or round zero. GU—Guam, FM—Federated States of Micronesia, PR—Puerto Rico, VI—Virgin Islands.

Source: U.S. Federal Deposit Insurance Corporation, "Statistics on Depository Institutions (SDI)," <https://www.fdic.gov/bank/statistical/index.html>, accessed March 2020.

Table 1205. FDIC-Insured Financial Institutions—Income and Selected Measures of Financial Condition: 2000 to 2019

[In billions of dollars, except as indicated (511.9 represents $511,900,000,000). Includes Island Areas. Includes foreign branches of U.S. banks. Minus sign (-) indicates decrease]

Item	2000	2005	2010	2014	2015	2016	2017	2018	2019
INCOME									
Interest income.........................	511.9	522.2	536.9	469.8	478.5	515.8	572.3	661.1	705.5
Interest expense........................	276.6	205.1	106.9	47.1	46.9	54.4	73.1	119.8	158.7
Net interest income..................	235.3	317.0	430.0	422.7	431.6	461.4	499.0	541.3	546.7
Provisions for loan losses..............	32.1	29.8	158.0	29.8	37.1	48.1	51.1	50.0	55.0
Noninterest income.....................	165.6	223.4	235.7	247.9	253.3	253.6	255.2	266.1	264.4
Noninterest expense....................	242.3	317.4	391.8	422.8	416.9	423.6	442.9	459.3	465.9
Income taxes...........................	43.6	64.6	38.4	68.2	70.6	75.9	97.8	61.0	61.0
Net income attributable to bank............	81.5	133.8	85.5	152.2	163.4	170.5	164.1	236.8	233.1
PERFORMANCE RATIOS									
Return on assets (percent)[1].....................	1.14	1.28	0.65	1.01	1.04	1.04	0.97	1.35	1.29
Return on equity (percent)[2].....................	13.53	12.43	5.85	9.01	9.29	9.27	8.60	11.98	11.40
Net interest margin (percent)[3]................	3.77	3.47	3.76	3.14	3.08	3.13	3.25	3.40	3.36
Net charge-offs (bil. dol.)[4]................	26.32	31.59	187.64	39.56	37.28	42.42	46.81	47.50	52.12
Net charge-offs to loans and leases, total (percent)...	0.59	0.49	2.55	0.49	0.44	0.47	0.50	0.48	0.52
Net charge-off rate, credit card loans (percent)...	4.36	4.74	10.08	3.12	2.92	3.16	3.61	3.75	3.82
CONDITION RATIOS									
Equity capital to assets (percent)...............	8.49	10.28	11.15	11.15	11.24	11.10	11.22	11.25	11.32
Noncurrent assets plus other real estate owned to assets (percent)[5]	0.71	0.50	3.11	1.20	0.97	0.86	0.72	0.60	0.55

[1] Net income (including securities transactions and nonrecurring items) as a percentage of average total assets. [2] Net income as a percentage of average total equity capital. [3] Interest income less interest expense as a percentage of average earning assets (i.e. the profit margin a bank earns on its loans and investments). [4] Total loans and leases charged off (removed from balance sheet because of uncollectibility), less amounts recovered on loans and leases previously charged off. [5] Noncurrent assets: the sum of loans, leases, debt securities and other assets that are 90 days or more past due, or in nonaccrual status, plus other real estate owned, primarily foreclosed property.

Source: U.S. Federal Deposit Insurance Corporation, *Quarterly Banking Profile*, Fourth Quarter 2019, and earlier reports; and "QBP Time Series Spreadsheets, Annual Income," <https://www.fdic.gov/bank/analytical/qbp/>, accessed April 2020.

Table 1206. FDIC-Insured Financial Institutions—Assets, and Liabilities: 2000 to 2019

[In billions of dollars, except as indicated (7,463 represents $7,463,000,000,000). As of December 31. Includes Island Areas. Excludes insured branches of foreign banks. Includes foreign branches of U.S. banks]

Item	2000	2005	2010	2014	2015	2016	2017	2018	2019
Number of financial institutions									
reporting.................................	**9,904**	**8,833**	**7,658**	**6,509**	**6,182**	**5,913**	**5,670**	**5,406**	**5,177**
Assets, total [1]..........................	**7,463**	**10,879**	**13,319**	**15,554**	**15,968**	**16,780**	**17,415**	**17,943**	**18,645**
Net loans and leases [1]...................	4,572	6,641	7,144	8,187	8,721	9,183	9,597	10,027	10,394
Real estate loans [1]..................	2,396	4,140	4,267	4,171	4,375	4,603	4,774	4,887	5,049
1-4 family residential mortgages............	1,340	2,042	1,900	1,842	1,904	1,995	2,064	2,119	2,202
Nonfarm nonresidential....................	525	826	1,071	1,150	1,232	1,324	1,391	1,444	1,516
Construction and development.............	197	450	321	238	275	313	338	350	362
Home equity loans.......................	151	534	637	492	465	434	411	376	342
Multifamily residential real estate..........	117	188	213	297	344	383	404	431	459
Commercial and industrial loans............	1,086	1,086	1,184	1,715	1,837	1,932	2,009	2,165	2,203
Loans to individuals [1]....................	672	949	1,316	1,418	1,498	1,589	1,678	1,743	1,837
Credit cards and related plans.............	266	396	702	718	756	800	865	903	942
Other loans to individuals..................	406	553	614	700	741	790	813	839	896
Auto loans...........................	(NA)	(NA)	(NA)	385	415	442	450	455	484
Loans to depository institutions..............	118	162	109	101	98	88	87	84	75
Lease financing receivables.................	167	139	102	114	116	127	130	133	132
Less: Reserve for losses....................	71	77	231	123	119	122	124	125	124
Securities.................................	1,361	1,893	2,668	3,219	3,354	3,560	3,632	3,723	3,982
Domestic office assets.....................	6,702	9,825	11,693	13,866	14,408	15,177	15,714	16,150	16,840
Foreign office assets......................	760	1,054	1,626	1,688	1,560	1,603	1,702	1,793	1,805
Liabilities and capital, total [1].............	**7,463**	**10,879**	**13,319**	**15,554**	**15,968**	**16,780**	**17,415**	**17,943**	**18,645**
Deposits...................................	4,915	7,141	9,423	11,764	12,190	12,895	13,399	13,866	14,535
Foreign office deposits....................	707	921	1,550	1,393	1,282	1,246	1,318	1,253	1,315
Domestic office deposits...................	4,208	6,221	7,873	10,371	10,908	11,649	12,081	12,613	13,220
Interest-bearing deposits.................	3,437	5,004	6,184	7,518	7,908	8,497	8,832	9,478	10,060
Noninterest-bearing deposits..............	771	1,217	1,689	2,852	3,000	3,152	3,250	3,135	3,160
Equity capital.............................	633	1,119	1,511	1,741	1,801	1,869	1,958	2,023	2,114

NA Not available. [1] Includes other items not shown separately.

Source: U.S. Federal Deposit Insurance Corporation, "FDIC Quarterly Banking Profile," <https://www.fdic.gov/bank/analytical/qbp/>, accessed September 2020.

Table 1207. FDIC-Insured Financial Institutions by Asset Size: 2019

[17,491.5 represents $17,491,500,000,000. Includes Island Areas. Includes foreign branches of U.S. banks]

Item	Unit	Total	Less than $100 mil.	$100 mil. to $1 bil.	$1 bil. to $10 bil.	Greater than $10 bil.
COMMERCIAL BANKS						
Institutions reporting.................................	Number	4,518	1,022	2,832	539	125
Assets, total..	Billion dollars	17,491.5	60.7	937.5	1,437.3	15,055.9
Deposits..	Billion dollars	13,614.2	50.9	788.0	1,171.0	11,604.4
Net income attributable to bank......................	Billion dollars	217.8	0.6	11.7	18.8	186.8
Percentage of banks losing money..................	Percent	3.17	7.53	2.19	0.56	0.80
Return on assets.....................................	Percent	1.29	0.99	1.29	1.36	1.28
Return on equity......................................	Percent	11.34	7.36	11.14	11.51	11.35
Net charge-offs to loans and leases................	Percent	0.49	0.23	0.15	0.23	0.55
Noncurrent assets plus other real estate owned to assets.................................	Percent	0.52	0.94	0.72	0.59	0.50
Equity capital to assets..............................	Percent	11.35	13.59	11.74	11.95	11.26
SAVINGS INSTITUTIONS						
Institutions reporting.................................	Number	659	133	394	117	15
Assets, total..	Billion dollars	1,153.9	7.7	150.5	316.6	679.0
Deposits..	Billion dollars	921.0	5.7	119.4	244.8	551.2
Net income attributable to bank......................	Billion dollars	15.3	0.1	2.0	3.1	10.1
Percentage of banks losing money..................	Percent	6.53	21.05	3.55	0.85	(NA)
Return on assets.....................................	Percent	1.36	1.19	1.33	1.03	1.51
Return on equity......................................	Percent	12.41	6.04	9.82	8.22	15.84
Net charge-offs to loans and leases................	Percent	0.91	0.04	0.08	0.11	1.76
Noncurrent assets plus other real estate owned to assets.................................	Percent	1.02	0.93	0.61	0.47	1.36
Equity capital to assets..............................	Percent	10.84	19.79	13.71	12.44	9.36

NA Not available.

Source: U.S. Federal Deposit Insurance Corporation, "Statistics on Depository Institutions," <https://www5.fdic.gov/sdi/main.asp>, accessed March 2020.

Table 1208. FDIC-Insured Financial Institutions—Deposit Insurance Fund (DIF) Indicators: 2010 to 2019

[In billions of dollars, except as indicated (7,888 represents $7,888,000,000,000). As of December 31. Includes Island Areas. Includes insured branches of foreign banks. Minus sign (-) indicates decrease]

Item	2010	2011	2012	2013	2014	2015	2016	2017	2018	2019
Number of institutions reporting..........	7,667	7,366	7,092	6,821	6,518	6,191	5,922	5,679	5,415	5,186
Domestic deposits, total [1].................	7,888	8,782	9,475	9,825	10,408	10,953	11,693	12,130	12,659	13,262
Estimated insured deposits [2]............	6,302	6,973	7,405	5,998	6,196	6,519	6,917	7,156	7,525	7,818
DIF balance............................	-7	12	33	47	63	73	83	93	103	113
Reserve ratio [3]......................	-0.12	0.17	0.45	0.79	1.01	1.11	1.20	1.30	1.36	1.41
Number of problem institutions..........	884	813	651	467	291	183	123	95	60	51
Assets of problem institutions............	390.0	319.4	232.7	152.7	86.7	46.8	27.6	13.9	48.5	46.2
Number of failed institutions..............	157	92	51	24	18	8	5	8	–	4
Assets of failed institutions...............	92.1	34.9	11.6	6.0	2.9	6.7	0.3	5.1	–	0.2

– Represents zero. [1] Excludes foreign office deposits, which are uninsured. [2] In general, insured deposits are total domestic deposits minus estimated uninsured deposits. Prior to September 30, 2009, insured deposits included deposits in accounts of $100,000 or less. Beginning September 30, 2009, insured deposits include deposits in accounts of $100,000 to $250,000 that are covered by a temporary increase in the FDIC's standard maximum deposit insurance amount. The Dodd-Frank Wall Street Reform and Consumer Protection Act of July 21, 2010 (Dodd-Frank) made permanent the standard maximum deposit insurance amount of $250,000. The Dodd-Frank Act also provided unlimited coverage for noninterest bearing transaction accounts for two years beginning December 31, 2010, and ending December 31, 2012. [3] DIF balance as percent of DIF-insured deposits.

Source: U.S. Federal Deposit Insurance Corporation, *Quarterly Banking Profile*, Fourth Quarter 2019, and earlier reports. See also <https://www.fdic.gov/bank/analytical/qbp/index.html>.

Table 1209. FDIC-Insured Financial Institutions—Number of Offices and Deposits by State: 2019

[12,813 represents $12,813,000,000,000. As of June 30. Includes insured U.S. branches of foreign banks. The term "offices" includes both main offices and branches. "Banking office" is defined to include all offices and facilities that actually hold deposits, and does not include loan production offices, computer centers, and other nondeposit installations, such as automated teller machines (ATMs). Several institutions have designated home offices that do not accept deposits; these have been included to provide a more complete listing of all offices. The figures for each geographical area only include deposits of offices located within that area. Based on the Summary of Deposits survey]

State	Number of offices	Total deposits (bil. dol.)	State	Number of offices	Total deposits (bil. dol.)	State	Number of offices	Total deposits (bil. dol.)
Total [1].....	86,367	12,813	IA..............	1,509	90	NC............	2,249	365
			KS.............	1,439	76	ND............	423	29
U.S...........	86,002	12,731	KY.............	1,599	84	OH............	3,528	369
AL..............	1,456	108	LA.............	1,434	106	OK............	1,338	92
AK..............	121	12	ME............	463	32	OR............	944	80
AZ..............	1,157	142	MD............	1,446	150	PA............	4,015	416
AR..............	1,332	71	MA............	2,137	408	RI.............	252	31
CA..............	6,734	1,460	MI.............	2,426	227	SC............	1,193	89
CO..............	1,445	143	MN............	1,667	236	SD............	457	692
CT..............	1,129	140	MS............	1,133	55	TN............	2,031	160
DE..............	261	379	MO............	2,279	170	TX............	6,400	878
DC..............	211	53	MT............	382	24	UT............	512	575
FL..............	4,816	603	NE............	1,074	67	VT............	235	14
GA..............	2,252	256	NV............	492	279	VA............	2,224	335
HI..............	269	45	NH............	409	35	WA............	1,670	165
ID..............	469	27	NJ............	2,810	343	WV............	608	34
IL..............	4,217	500	NM............	455	32	WI............	1,919	151
IN..............	1,966	138	NY............	4,795	1,745	WY............	220	16

[1] Includes outlying areas not shown separately.

Source: U.S. Federal Deposit Insurance Corporation, "Summary of Deposits, Reference Tables," <https://www5.fdic.gov/sod/sodSummary.asp?barItem=3>, accessed July 2020.

Table 1210. U.S. Banking Offices of Foreign Banks—Summary: 2000 to 2019

[In billions of dollars (1,358 represents $1,358,000,000,000), except as indicated. As of December. The U.S. offices of foreign banking organizations consist of U.S. branches and agencies of foreign banks and bank subsidiaries of foreign banking organizations. Foreign-owned institutions are those owned by a bank located outside of the United States and its affiliated insular areas. Bank subsidiaries of foreign banking organizations are U.S. commercial banks of which more than 25 percent are owned by a foreign banking organization or where the relationship is reported as being a controlling relationship by the filer of the FR Y-10 (Report of Changes in Organizational Structure) report form. Covers the U.S. offices of foreign banking organizations that are located in the 50 states and the District of Columbia; excludes offices located in Puerto Rico, American Samoa, Guam, the Virgin Islands and other U.S.-affiliated insular areas]

Item	2000	2005	2010	2015	2016	2017	2018	2019	Share [1] 2000	Share [1] 2010	Share [1] 2019
Assets.....................	1,358	2,123	2,838	3,539	3,515	3,776	3,739	3,845	18.9	20.4	19.3
Loans, total..................	557	802	960	1,416	1,444	1,484	1,560	1,590	13.5	13.7	14.9
Business loans............	308	276	326	580	584	568	602	604	25.0	25.1	24.5
Deposits....................	770	1,162	1,752	2,029	1,962	2,032	2,036	2,163	16.5	18.3	14.8

[1] Foreign owned banks plus U.S. branches and offices of foreign banks as percent of all banks in the United States.

Source: Board of Governors of the Federal Reserve System, Structure and Share Data for U.S. Banking Offices of Foreign Entities, "Share Data for U.S. Offices of Foreign Banks," <https://www.federalreserve.gov/releases/iba/default.htm>, accessed June 2020.

Table 1211. Federal and State-Chartered Credit Unions—Summary: 2000 to 2019

[43,883 represents 43,883,000. As of December 31. Federal data include District of Columbia, Puerto Rico, Guam, and Virgin Islands. Excludes state-insured, privately insured, and noninsured state-chartered credit unions and corporate central credit unions, which have mainly other credit unions as members]

Year	Operating credit unions		Number of failed institu- tions [1]	Members (1,000)		Assets (mil. dol.)		Loans outstanding (mil. dol.)		Savings (mil. dol.)	
	Federal	State		Federal	State	Federal	State	Federal	State	Federal	State
2000......	6,336	3,980	29	43,883	33,705	242,881	195,363	163,851	137,485	210,188	169,053
2009......	4,714	2,840	31	49,604	40,333	482,684	402,069	311,154	261,285	408,832	343,835
2010......	4,589	2,750	29	50,081	40,447	500,075	414,395	306,276	258,555	427,603	358,877
2011......	4,447	2,647	16	50,743	41,093	525,633	436,121	308,845	262,640	449,316	378,093
2012......	4,272	2,547	22	51,797	42,043	557,119	464,612	322,675	275,066	474,903	402,948
2013......	4,105	2,449	17	52,499	43,762	571,326	490,588	343,780	301,440	485,500	424,587
2014......	3,927	2,346	15	53,355	45,870	596,145	525,942	373,387	338,938	499,683	451,107
2015......	3,764	2,257	16	54,284	48,369	628,012	576,266	404,729	382,288	522,109	493,892
2016......	3,608	2,177	14	56,598	50,205	670,124	622,354	444,516	424,591	559,825	532,759
2017......	3,499	2,074	10	59,036	52,261	718,287	660,530	490,115	467,175	594,662	564,807
2018......	3,376	1,999	8	61,272	54,891	753,546	699,853	532,693	510,860	625,464	594,269
2019......	3,283	1,953	2	63,087	57,299	803,000	763,708	561,199	546,791	670,912	648,838

[1] A failed institution is defined as a credit union which has ceased operation because it was involuntarily liquidated or merged with assistance from the National Credit Union Share Insurance Fund.

Source: National Credit Union Administration, *National Credit Union Administration 2019 Annual Report,* February 2020, and earlier reports; and "5300 Call Report Aggregate Financial Performance Report," December 2019, <https://www.ncua.gov/analysis/credit-union-corporate-call-report-data>. See also <https://www.ncua.gov/news/annual-reports>.

Table 1212. Noncash Payments by Method of Payment: 2015 and 2018

[143.6 represents 143,600,000,000. Estimates are based on survey data from the Federal Reserve Payments Survey, which is conducted every three years and updated with a smaller supplemental annual data collection between the triennial studies. The Study combines information gathered in three related survey efforts. Some estimates are based on data collected in the Depository and Financial Institutions Payments Survey (DFIPS), which was sent to a nationally representative, stratified random sample of depository and financial institutions. Other estimates are based on data collected in the Networks, Processors, and Issuers Payments Surveys (NPIPS) through a set of surveys of payment networks, processors, and card issuers. Finally, some estimates are from data collected in the Check Sample Survey (CSS), which are based on the information from a random sample of checks processed by a selected number of large commercial banks. ATM withdrawals are excluded here]

Method of payment [1]	Transactions (billions)		Value (trillion dollars)		Average value per transaction (dollars)	
	2015	2018 (P)	2015	2018 (P)	2015	2018 (P)
Total noncash payments..........................	**143.6**	**174.2**	**86.8**	**97.0**	**604**	**557**
Total card payments.................................	**101.5**	**131.2**	**5.5**	**7.1**	**54**	**54**
Debit cards..	67.8	86.4	2.5	3.1	36	36
Non-prepaid..	56.6	72.7	2.2	2.7	38	38
Prepaid..	11.2	13.8	0.3	0.3	26	25
General purpose [2]............................	4.3	6.0	0.1	0.2	35	32
Private label [3].................................	4.4	5.5	0.1	0.1	16	18
Electronic benefits transfer (EBT)...................	2.6	2.2	0.1	0.1	29	26
Credit cards...	33.7	44.7	3.1	4.0	91	89
General purpose [2]...............................	31.0	40.9	2.8	3.6	90	89
Private label [3]....................................	2.7	3.8	0.2	0.3	93	89
Automated clearinghouse (ACH) [4]...................	**23.9**	**28.5**	**52.1**	**64.2**	**2,177**	**2,250**
Network [5]...	19.3	22.9	41.6	51.3	2,159	2,234
Credit transfers...................................	8.0	9.5	26.8	33.4	3,333	3,512
Debit transfers....................................	11.3	13.4	14.9	17.8	1,321	1,328
On-us [6]...	4.6	5.6	10.4	12.9	2,249	2,315
Credit transfers...................................	2.0	2.4	5.7	7.5	2,922	3,154
Debit transfers....................................	2.7	3.2	4.7	5.5	1,761	1,697
Checks..	**18.1**	**14.5**	**29.2**	**25.8**	**1,609**	**1,779**
Interbank...	13.6	11.0	21.3	19.0	1,564	1,725
On-us [6]..	4.5	3.5	7.9	6.8	1,746	1,949

P Preliminary. [1] ATM withdrawals are not included in the data. [2] Cards issued by depository institutions and processed over card networks. They carry a network brand from one of the four major card networks or from smaller or regional networks and can be used wherever that network card is accepted, regardless of merchant or merchant type. [3] Cards issued by merchants and processed over proprietary networks. They are accepted only by the sponsoring merchant. [4] The Automated Clearing House (ACH) is an electronic funds transfer system that processes financial transactions for consumers, businesses, and governments. The ACH provides many payment services, including payroll, direct deposit, tax payments and refunds, and consumer bills. [5] Network ACH payments are mainly passed between two depository institutions (interbank payments). Some depository institutions send all ACH transfers to ACH operators; ACH network payments also include a small portion of payments that are received by the same depository institution that sent them. [6] On-us payments are those payment processed by a depository institution between their own customers internally.

Source: Board of Governors of the Federal Reserve System *The 2019 Federal Reserve Payments Study: Initial Data Release*, accessed April 2020. See also <https://www.federalreserve.gov/paymentsystems/fr-payments-study.htm>.

Table 1213. Debit Cards: Holders, Number, Transactions, and Volume: 2000 and 2010, and Projections, 2018

[160 represents 160,000,000]

Type of debit card	Cardholders (mil.)			Number of cards (mil.)			Number of point-of-sale transactions (mil.)			Purchase volume (bil. dol.)		
	2000	2010	2018 (P)	2000	2010	2018 (P)	2000	2010	2018 (P)	2000	2010	2018 (P)
Total [1]	**160**	**185**	**209**	**235**	**4,008**	**5,357**	**9,571**	**49,281**	**84,585**	**342**	**1,825**	**3,321**
Bank [2]	137	164	192	137	516	752	5,290	36,879	62,717	210	1,387	2,452
EFT networks [3]	159	184	206	223	281	321	2,979	7,239	14,313	100	262	569
Private label prepaid [4]	(NA)	(NA)	(NA)	(NA)	3,447	5,004	1,280	5,125	7,284	31	172	283
ACH network [5]	11	13	31	11	13	32	22	39	270	1	3	17

NA Not available. P Projected. [1] Cardholders may hold more than one type of card. Bank cards and electronic funds transfer (EFT) cards are the same pieces of plastic that carry multiple brands. The total card figure shown does not include any duplication. [2] Visa and MasterCard debit cards, including prepaid cards. Beginning 2006, includes Interlink & MasterCard PIN debit. [3] Cards issued by financial institution members of regional and national switches such as Star, Interlink (for 2000), Pulse, Nyce, etc. EFT = Electronic funds transfer. [4] Prepaid cards without the Visa, MasterCard, American Express, or Discover logos. [5] ACH = Automated clearing house. Retail cards such as those issued by Target, Nordstrom, etc.

Source: The Nilson Report, Carpinteria, CA, twice-monthly newsletter. © Used by permission.

Table 1214. Credit Cards: Holders, Number, Purchase Volume, and Debt: 2000 and 2010, and Projections, 2018

[159 represents 159,000,000]

Type of credit card	Cardholders (mil.)			Number of cards (mil.)			Credit card purchase volume (bil. dol.)			Credit card debt outstanding (bil. dol.)		
	2000	2010	2018 (P)	2000	2010	2018 (P)	2000	2010	2018 (P)	2000	2010	2018 (P)
Total [1]	**159**	**152**	**180**	**1,425**	**877**	**1,123**	**1,242**	**2,061**	**3,936**	**680**	**811**	**1,125**
Visa	93	100	124	255	240	338	487	809	1,956	268	332	471
MasterCard	86	75	97	200	171	231	281	479	811	212	240	310
Store	114	95	110	597	318	392	120	138	182	92	92	131
Oil company	76	38	27	98	35	32	45	47	56	5	6	6
Discover	36	41	44	50	55	57	69	106	139	48	50	73
American Express	23	34	36	33	49	54	221	476	772	50	90	120
The rest [2]	7	6	16	192	9	19	18	5	20	5	1	15

P Projected. [1] Cardholders may hold more than one type of card. [2] Includes Universal Air Travel Plan (UATP), medical cards, automobile rental, and miscellaneous cards.

Source: The Nilson Report, Carpinteria, CA, twice-monthly newsletter. © Used by permission.

Table 1215. Consumer Credit by Type of Holder: 2000 to 2019

[In billions of dollars (1,741 represents $1,741,000,000,000). As of December 31. Not seasonally adjusted]

Type of holder	2000	2005	2010	2012	2013	2014	2015	2016	2017	2017	2019
Total	**1,741**	**2,321**	**2,647**	**2,914**	**3,091**	**3,313**	**3,411**	**3,644**	**3,828**	**4,010**	**4,191**
Nonprofit organizations [1]	–	–	71	58	52	48	45	41	35	31	28
Nonfinancial corporate business	81	60	44	45	39	39	38	40	39	39	39
Federal government [2]	60	90	364	622	736	846	950	1,049	1,146	1,236	1,320
U.S.-chartered depository institutions	616	816	1,186	1,215	1,271	1,343	1,428	1,532	1,612	1,682	1,771
Credit unions	184	229	226	244	266	303	342	380	418	469	482
Asset-backed securities issuers	528	610	50	50	49	50	46	53	38	18	14
Finance companies	234	517	705	680	679	684	561	549	541	534	537
Memo:											
Credit card loans [3]	702	857	839	840	855	888	907	968	1,022	1,053	1,093
Auto loans	581	823	713	809	878	957	1,000	1,075	1,113	1,153	1,196
Student loans [4]	–	–	855	1,055	1,146	1,236	1,320	1,408	1,490	1,569	1,643
Other consumer credit [5]	458	641	239	209	213	232	184	193	203	235	258

– Represents or rounds to zero. [1] Student loans originated under the Federal Family Education Loan Program. Asset of the households and nonprofit organizations sector. [2] Includes loans originated by the Department of Education under the Federal Direct Loan Program and Perkins Loans, as well as Federal Family Education Loan Program loans that the government purchased from depository institutions, finance companies, and nonprofit and educational institutions, and loans in default. [3] Revolving credit that also includes overdraft plans on checking accounts and other loans without a fixed repayment schedule. [4] Includes student loans held by nonprofit organizations, the federal government, depository institutions, and finance companies. Data begin in 2006. [5] Prior to 2006, includes student loans.

Source: Board of Governors of the Federal Reserve System, "Financial Accounts of the United States, Z.1," <https://www.federalreserve.gov/data.htm>, accessed April 2020.

Table 1216. Consumer Credit Outstanding and Finance Rates: 2000 to 2019

[In billions of dollars (1,717 represents $1,717,000,000,000), except percent. Covers most short- and intermediate-term credit extended to individuals, excluding loans secured by real estate. Estimated amounts of seasonally adjusted credit outstanding as of end of year; finance rates are annual averages]

Type of credit	2000	2005	2010	2013	2014	2015	2016	2017	2018	2019
Total	**1,717**	**2,291**	**2,647**	**3,091**	**3,312**	**3,410**	**3,643**	**3,829**	**4,011**	**4,191**
Revolving	683	830	839	854	888	907	969	1,023	1,055	1,094
Nonrevolving [1]	1,034	1,461	1,808	2,237	2,424	2,503	2,675	2,806	2,956	3,097
FINANCE RATES (percent)										
Commercial banks:										
New automobiles (48 months)	9.34	7.07	6.21	4.43	4.24	4.19	4.30	4.61	5.03	5.39
Personal loans (24 months)	13.90	12.06	10.87	10.20	10.23	9.75	9.69	10.13	10.32	10.32
Credit card plans, all accounts	15.78	12.51	13.78	11.91	11.87	12.09	12.35	12.89	14.22	15.05
Credit card plans, accounts assessed interest	14.92	14.55	14.26	12.95	13.19	13.66	13.56	14.44	16.05	16.98
Finance companies:										
New automobiles [2]	(NA)	(NA)	4.70	4.68	4.89	5.13	5.05	5.36	6.13	6.41

NA Not available. [1] Comprises automobile loans and all other loans not included in revolving credit, such as loans for mobile homes, education, boats, trailers, or vacations. These loans may be secured or unsecured. [2] Covers most of the captive and non-captive finance companies. Amount of finance weighted.

Source: Board of Governors of the Federal Reserve System, Data Releases, Household Finances, "Consumer Credit-G.19" <http://www.federalreserve.gov/econresdata/statisticsdata.htm>, accessed May 2020.

Table 1217. Bank Account Status of Households by Selected Characteristics: 2015 and 2017

[In percent, except total households (127,538 represents 127,538,000). A household is 'unbanked' if no one in the household has a checking or savings account at an insured bank. An 'underbanked' household is one that had a bank account but also used the following products or services from an alternative financial services (AFS) provider in the past 12 months: money orders, check cashing, international remittances, payday loans, refund anticipation loans, rent-to-own services, pawn shop loans, or auto title loans. A 'fully banked' household is one that has a bank account and has not used an AFS in the past 12 months. Data collected through a Federal Deposit Insurance Corporation (FDIC)-sponsored supplement to the Current Population Survey]

Characteristic	Total households (1,000)		Unbanked households		Banked households					
					Underbanked		Fully banked		Underbanked status unknown	
	2015	2017	2015	2017	2015	2017	2015	2017	2015	2017
Total households	**127,538**	**129,276**	**7.0**	**6.5**	**19.9**	**18.7**	**68.0**	**68.4**	**5.0**	**6.3**
RACE/ETHNICITY [1]										
White	85,428	85,599	3.1	3.0	15.6	14.1	76.6	77.1	4.7	5.7
Black	17,961	18,201	18.2	16.9	31.1	30.4	45.5	45.8	5.2	6.9
Asian	6,275	6,792	4.0	2.5	21.0	17.5	67.2	69.2	7.8	10.8
Hispanic	16,106	16,655	16.2	14.0	29.3	28.9	48.9	49.7	5.6	7.4
Other	1,767	2,030	(NA)	12.8	(NA)	28.0	(NA)	55.8	(NA)	3.3
AGE										
15 to 24 years	6,648	6,625	13.1	10.0	29.4	29.3	52.1	56.5	5.5	4.2
25 to 34 years	21,005	20,997	10.6	8.5	24.5	23.1	60.8	62.5	4.0	5.9
35 to 44 years	21,640	21,532	8.9	7.8	22.7	22.2	63.1	63.6	5.3	6.5
45 to 54 years	23,773	23,277	6.7	6.9	21.1	19.3	67.5	67.1	4.8	6.7
55 to 64 years	23,981	24,484	5.8	5.9	18.5	17.8	70.9	70.3	4.8	6.0
65 years or more	30,491	32,361	3.1	3.9	13.0	11.6	78.1	77.5	5.8	7.0
EDUCATION										
No high school diploma	13,802	12,461	23.2	22.4	25.9	24.3	46.4	46.3	4.5	7.0
High school diploma	33,239	33,334	9.7	9.4	22.2	20.3	62.9	63.7	5.3	6.5
Some college	37,512	37,355	5.5	5.1	22.0	20.8	67.7	67.8	4.8	6.3
College degree	42,985	46,127	1.1	1.3	14.5	14.4	79.1	78.3	5.2	6.1
EMPLOYMENT STATUS										
Employed	78,152	79,436	5.0	4.5	21.4	20.4	68.7	68.8	5.0	6.3
Unemployed	3,869	3,433	23.0	19.9	24.8	23.9	48.6	51.4	3.7	4.8
Not in labor force	45,517	46,407	9.2	9.0	17.1	15.4	68.5	69.0	5.3	6.6
FAMILY INCOME										
Less than $15,000	18,046	15,997	25.6	25.7	24.3	20.9	45.1	47.7	4.9	5.7
$15,000 to $30,000	21,392	19,842	11.8	12.3	23.6	22.4	59.5	58.3	5.1	7.0
$30,000 to $50,000	25,336	25,610	5.0	5.1	23.7	22.8	66.2	65.4	5.1	6.8
$50,000 to $75,000	23,003	23,763	1.6	1.5	20.2	19.7	73.0	72.8	5.1	6.0
At least $75,000	39,761	44,064	0.5	0.6	13.4	13.3	81.3	79.9	4.9	6.2
DISABILITY STATUS										
Disabled, age 25 to 64	11,497	11,297	17.6	18.1	28.4	24.7	49.7	52.2	4.3	5.0
Not disabled, age 25 to 64	78,902	78,993	6.5	5.7	20.6	19.9	68.1	68.0	4.8	6.4
HOUSING TENURE										
Homeowner	80,685	82,241	2.3	2.3	15.4	14.2	77.4	77.2	4.9	6.3
Non-homeowner	46,853	47,035	15.2	14.0	27.7	26.5	51.8	53.1	5.3	6.4
REGION										
Northeast	22,699	22,776	6.3	6.0	19.3	17.9	67.9	69.0	6.4	7.2
Midwest	27,625	27,719	5.7	5.4	17.5	15.8	72.5	73.3	4.3	5.5
South	48,382	49,360	8.7	7.7	21.6	21.0	65.0	65.1	4.7	6.2
West	28,832	29,420	5.9	6.0	19.9	18.2	68.9	69.1	5.3	6.7

NA Not available. [1] Households are categorized into racial/ethnic classification as follows: if the householder is black, the household is classified as "black" regardless of whether the householder is also Hispanic or any other race. If the householder is not identified as black and is identified as Hispanic, the household is classified as "Hispanic." If the householder is identified as white and not any other race and not Hispanic, then the household is classified as "white." If the householder is identified as Asian and not black or Hispanic, then the household is classified as "Asian." All other households are listed as "other".

Source: Federal Deposit Insurance Corporation, Division of Depositor and Consumer Protection, *2017 FDIC National Survey of Unbanked and Underbanked Households*, October 2018. See also <economicinclusion.gov/surveys/>.

Table 1218. Mortgage Debt Outstanding by Type of Property and Holder: 2000 to 2019

[In billions of dollars (6,767 represents $6,767,000,000,000). As of December 31]

Type of property and holder	2000	2005	2010	2013	2014	2015	2016	2017	2018	2019
MORTGAGES BY TYPE										
Total	**6,767**	**12,115**	**13,894**	**13,340**	**13,486**	**13,876**	**14,328**	**14,884**	**15,417**	**16,014**
Home [1]	5,125	9,449	10,523	9,957	9,936	10,074	10,275	10,578	10,862	11,168
Multifamily residential	404	674	863	939	1,009	1,117	1,235	1,355	1,471	1,593
Commercial	1,152	1,887	2,354	2,259	2,344	2,477	2,593	2,714	2,839	2,996
Farm	85	105	154	185	197	209	226	236	246	257
Total liabilities	**6,767**	**12,115**	**13,894**	**13,340**	**13,486**	**13,876**	**14,328**	**14,884**	**15,417**	**16,014**
Household sector	4,946	9,108	10,190	9,700	9,681	9,816	10,014	10,313	10,593	10,899
Nonfinancial business	1,737	2,861	3,527	3,426	3,573	3,825	4,077	4,329	4,598	4,893
Nonfinancial corporate business	356	768	674	439	402	475	460	500	549	601
Nonfinancial noncorporate business	1,381	2,093	2,853	2,986	3,172	3,350	3,618	3,829	4,049	4,292
Real estate investment trusts	84	145	176	214	231	235	236	242	226	221
Total assets	**6,767**	**12,115**	**13,894**	**13,340**	**13,486**	**13,876**	**14,328**	**14,884**	**15,417**	**16,014**
Household sector	96	127	132	122	113	99	92	82	69	57
Nonfinancial corporate business	44	68	28	27	29	53	30	32	34	35
Nonfinancial noncorporate business	23	36	42	35	34	42	40	43	46	50
Federal government	76	77	107	115	117	116	120	120	123	124
State and local governments	136	171	222	222	221	226	239	242	224	221
Private depository institutions	2,503	4,337	4,583	4,392	4,531	4,778	5,071	5,283	5,443	5,661
U.S.-chartered depository institutions	2,350	4,055	4,195	3,983	4,091	4,297	4,538	4,698	4,818	4,985
Foreign banking offices in U.S.	17	21	35	31	38	51	68	77	78	81
Banks in U.S.-affiliated areas	16	35	36	32	30	26	26	26	24	23
Credit unions	120	226	317	346	372	405	439	481	523	572
Property-casualty insurance companies	2	3	4	8	10	13	15	18	20	21
Life insurance companies	236	286	319	366	388	431	465	507	568	612
Private pension funds	12	10	26	22	24	22	22	27	29	32
State and local government retirement funds	22	11	11	6	8	8	15	7	12	12
Government-sponsored enterprises (GSE)	264	589	5,021	4,878	4,870	4,920	5,027	5,194	5,334	5,511
Agency- and GSE-backed mortgage pools	2,493	3,548	1,147	1,574	1,649	1,775	1,933	2,127	2,293	2,407
Asset-backed securities issuers	604	2,163	1,963	1,201	1,094	1,016	894	846	852	850
Finance companies	238	541	244	157	148	159	138	124	115	117
Real estate investment trusts	18	147	45	215	247	218	228	235	255	305
HOME MORTGAGES [1]										
Total liabilities	**5,125**	**9,449**	**10,523**	**9,957**	**9,936**	**10,074**	**10,275**	**10,578**	**10,862**	**11,168**
Household sector	4,817	8,940	9,992	9,478	9,453	9,577	9,761	10,049	10,316	10,610
Nonfinancial corporate business	14	31	14	10	11	13	15	16	17	17
Nonfinancial noncorporate business	294	477	518	469	472	484	498	514	529	541
Total assets	**5,125**	**9,449**	**10,523**	**9,957**	**9,936**	**10,074**	**10,275**	**10,578**	**10,862**	**11,168**
Household sector	87	118	124	112	102	91	80	70	59	49
Nonfinancial corporate business	21	41	17	16	17	32	18	19	20	21
Nonfinancial noncorporate business	9	13	15	13	13	15	14	16	17	18
Federal government	16	13	24	26	27	28	30	29	29	29
State and local governments	69	88	114	114	114	117	123	125	115	114
U.S.-chartered depository institutions	1,556	2,730	2,616	2,386	2,390	2,434	2,510	2,557	2,586	2,639
Foreign banking offices in U.S.	–	–	1	1	3	2	1	1	2	1
Banks in U.S.-affiliated areas	9	16	20	19	17	16	15	15	14	13
Credit unions	120	226	317	346	372	405	439	481	523	572
Life insurance companies	7	7	9	12	15	19	23	25	32	34
Private pension funds	8	1	2	1	1	1	1	1	1	1
State and local government retirement funds	7	4	4	2	3	3	5	2	4	4
Government-sponsored enterprises (GSE)	210	454	4,691	4,546	4,538	4,571	4,645	4,776	4,884	5,023
Agency- and GSE-backed mortgage pools	2,426	3,446	1,075	1,424	1,475	1,569	1,685	1,826	1,949	2,026
Asset-backed securities issuers	385	1,671	1,315	793	700	603	518	475	467	443
Finance companies	187	490	170	115	105	123	107	95	87	85
Real estate investment trusts	8	128	9	31	44	46	60	65	73	95
Memo:										
Home equity loans included above [2]	408	918	929	703	673	642	601	570	533	501
U.S.-chartered depository institutions	308	701	783	596	568	533	495	460	420	384
Credit unions	41	76	88	72	74	76	78	84	89	93
Asset-backed securities issuers	10	43	23	12	10	8	6	6	6	6
Finance companies	49	98	34	23	21	25	21	19	17	17

– Represents zero. [1] Mortgages on one- to four-family properties, including mortgages on farm houses. [2] Loans made under home equity lines of credit and home equity loans secured by junior liens. Excludes home equity loans held by individuals.

Source: Board of Governors of the Federal Reserve System, "Financial Accounts of the United States, Z.1," <https://www.federalreserve.gov/data.htm>, accessed April 2020.

Table 1219. Mortgage Originations and Delinquency and Foreclosure Rates: 2000 to 2019

[In percent, except as indicated (1,139 represents $1,139,000,000,000). Covers one- to four-family residential nonfarm mortgage loans. Mortgage origination is the making of a new mortgage, including all steps taken by a lender to attract and qualify a borrower, process the mortgage loan, and place it on the lender's books. Based on the National Delinquency Survey, which covers 45 million loans on one- to four-unit properties, representing between 80 to 85 percent of all 'first-lien' residential mortgage loans outstanding. Loans surveyed were reported by approximately 120 lenders, including mortgage bankers, commercial banks, and thrifts]

Item	2000	2005	2010	2013	2014	2015	2016	2017	2018	2019
MORTGAGE ORIGINATIONS										
Total (bil. dol.)	**1,139**	**2,908**	**1,698**	**1,845**	**1,261**	**1,679**	**2,051**	**1,710**	**1,250**	**2,173**
Purchase (bil. dol.)	905	1,512	530	734	759	903	1,052	1,110	873	1,272
Refinance (bil. dol.)	234	1,397	1,168	1,111	502	776	999	600	377	901
DELINQUENCY RATES [1]										
Total	**4.4**	**4.5**	**9.3**	**6.7**	**5.9**	**5.1**	**4.7**	**4.8**	**4.4**	**4.2**
Conventional loans [2]	(NA)	3.6	8.8	5.9	5.1	4.4	3.9	3.9	3.5	3.2
Prime conventional loans	2.3	2.3	6.5	3.9	3.4	3.0	2.8	(NA)	(NA)	(NA)
Subprime conventional loans	11.9	10.8	25.9	21.0	19.1	16.5	14.9	(NA)	(NA)	(NA)
Federal Housing Administration loans	9.1	12.5	12.8	10.6	9.7	9.0	8.6	9.0	8.8	8.7
Veterans Administration loans	6.8	7.0	7.5	5.8	5.2	4.5	4.1	4.1	4.0	4.0
FORECLOSURE RATES										
Total loans in foreclosure process [3]	**1.2**	**1.0**	**4.6**	**3.2**	**2.5**	**2.0**	**1.6**	**1.3**	**1.0**	**0.9**
Conventional loans [2]	(NA)	0.9	4.8	3.2	2.4	1.9	1.5	1.2	0.9	0.7
Prime conventional loans	0.4	0.4	3.5	2.2	1.5	1.2	0.9	(NA)	(NA)	(NA)
Subprime conventional loans	9.4	3.3	14.5	11.1	9.8	8.3	7.2	(NA)	(NA)	(NA)
Federal Housing Administration loans	1.7	2.3	3.5	3.6	2.8	2.6	2.2	1.8	1.7	1.6
Veterans Administration loans	1.2	1.1	2.4	5.8	1.5	1.4	1.2	1.0	0.9	0.9
Loans entering foreclosure process [4]	**1.5**	**1.6**	**5.0**	**2.5**	**1.8**	**1.6**	**1.3**	**1.1**	**1.0**	**0.9**
Conventional loans [2]	(NA)	1.5	5.1	2.3	1.6	1.4	1.1	0.9	0.8	0.7
Prime conventional loans	0.6	0.7	4.0	1.6	1.1	1.0	0.7	(NA)	(NA)	(NA)
Subprime conventional loans	9.2	5.6	12.9	8.2	6.1	5.2	4.7	(NA)	(NA)	(NA)
Federal Housing Administration loans	2.3	3.4	4.7	3.3	2.5	2.5	2.2	1.9	2.0	1.8
Veterans Administration loans	1.5	1.5	3.3	1.9	1.4	1.4	1.3	1.1	1.1	1.0

NA Not available. [1] Number of loans delinquent 30 days or more as a percent of mortgage loans serviced in survey. Annual average of quarterly figures, not seasonally adjusted. Delinquency rate does not include loans in the process of foreclosure. [2] Conventional loans include any non-government (FHA or VA) loans. The prime and subprime criteria used in the National Delinquency Survey are based on survey participants' reporting of what they consider to be their prime or subprime servicing portfolio, since internal servicing guidelines vary. Participants who service both prime and subprime loans report the results of each separately for maximum precision in the classification. [3] Percent of loans in the foreclosure process at year-end, not seasonally adjusted. [4] Percent of loans entering foreclosure process at year-end, not seasonally adjusted.

Source: Mortgage Bankers Association of America, Washington, DC, "MBA Mortgage Originations Estimates," and National Delinquency Survey, <mba.org/>, and unpublished data ©.

Table 1220. Delinquency Rates and Charge-Off Rates on Loans at Insured Commercial Banks: 2000 to 2019

[In percent. Annual averages of quarterly figures, not seasonally adjusted. Delinquent loans are those past due 30 days or more and still accruing interest as well as those in nonaccrual status. They are measured as a percentage of end-of-period loans. Charge-offs, which are the value of loans removed from the books and charged against loss reserves, are measured, net of recoveries, as a percentage of average loans and annualized. Includes only U.S.-chartered commercial banks]

Type of loan	2000	2005	2010	2014	2015	2016	2017	2018	2019
DELINQUENCY RATES									
Total loans	**2.20**	**1.57**	**6.96**	**3.00**	**2.34**	**2.10**	**1.85**	**1.62**	**1.48**
Real estate	1.87	1.37	9.69	4.83	3.62	2.80	2.31	1.97	1.63
Residential [1, 2]	2.08	1.55	10.81	7.20	5.64	4.46	3.71	3.12	2.51
Commercial [2, 3]	1.48	1.07	8.53	1.87	1.23	0.90	0.77	0.72	0.68
Consumer	3.55	2.81	4.15	2.22	2.00	2.07	2.23	2.29	2.34
Credit cards	4.51	3.70	4.90	2.23	2.14	2.26	2.48	2.52	2.58
Other	2.98	2.23	3.32	2.21	1.88	1.90	1.99	2.07	2.10
Leases	1.62	1.28	1.89	0.75	0.77	1.01	1.00	1.01	1.18
Business	2.30	1.51	3.46	0.80	0.87	1.57	1.34	1.03	1.12
Agricultural production	2.54	1.30	3.04	0.91	0.84	1.22	1.53	1.70	1.87
Farmland [2]	2.30	1.59	3.57	1.71	1.55	1.75	2.01	2.15	2.29
CHARGE-OFF RATES									
Total loans	**0.66**	**0.54**	**2.66**	**0.49**	**0.42**	**0.46**	**0.47**	**0.46**	**0.49**
Real estate	0.09	0.06	2.15	0.20	0.13	0.06	0.03	0.01	0.01
Residential [1, 2]	0.12	0.08	2.11	0.29	0.21	0.10	0.04	(Z)	-0.01
Commercial [2, 3]	0.05	0.05	2.34	0.07	0.04	0.01	0.02	0.01	0.03
Consumer	2.32	2.74	5.90	1.92	1.75	1.91	2.18	2.24	2.28
Credit cards	4.30	4.83	9.43	3.16	2.93	3.15	3.56	3.64	3.70
Other	1.13	1.38	2.05	0.77	0.68	0.78	0.90	0.88	0.91
Leases	0.31	0.58	0.72	0.08	0.18	0.24	0.17	0.17	0.21
Business	0.76	0.26	1.71	0.22	0.24	0.43	0.36	0.28	0.35
Agricultural production	0.27	0.07	0.77	0.04	0.05	0.21	0.21	0.24	0.23
Farmland [2]	0.04	0.04	0.43	0.04	0.01	0.03	0.05	0.04	0.08

Z Represents less than .005%. [1] Residential real estate loans include loans secured by one- to four-family properties, including home equity lines of credit. [2] Booked in domestic offices only. [3] Commercial real estate loans include construction and land development loans, loans secured by multifamily residences, and loans secured by nonfarm, nonresidential real estate, only.

Source: Board of Governors of the Federal Reserve, Data Releases, Bank Assets and Liabilities, "Charge-Off and Delinquency Rates on Loans and Leases at Commercial Banks," <http://www.federalreserve.gov/releases/chargeoff/>, accessed April 2020.

Table 1221. Money Stock: 2000 to 2019

[In billions of dollars (1,089 represents $1,089,000,000,000). As of December. Seasonally adjusted averages of daily figures]

Item	2000	2005	2010	2013	2014	2015	2016	2017	2018	2019
M1, total	**1,089**	**1,374**	**1,836**	**2,664**	**2,941**	**3,095**	**3,342**	**3,612**	**3,751**	**4,005**
Currency [1]	531	725	919	1,161	1,253	1,340	1,422	1,526	1,627	1,713
Travelers' checks [2]	8.3	7.2	4.7	3.5	2.9	2.5	2.2	1.9	1.7	(NA)
Demand deposits [3]	311	324	517	1,034	1,200	1,238	1,371	1,489	1,495	1,609
Other checkable deposits [4]	239	318	396	466	485	515	548	595	628	684
M2, total	**4,914**	**6,669**	**8,790**	**11,016**	**11,670**	**12,336**	**13,210**	**13,852**	**14,368**	**15,402**
M1	1,089	1,374	1,836	2,664	2,941	3,095	3,342	3,612	3,751	4,005
Non-M1 components of M2	3,826	5,294	6,954	8,352	8,730	9,241	9,867	10,240	10,617	11,396
Retail money funds	900	698	687	652	632	654	692	704	813	995
Savings deposits (including money market deposit accounts)	1,880	3,602	5,332	7,129	7,575	8,176	8,824	9,124	9,277	9,819
Commercial banks	1,425	2,777	4,413	6,109	6,498	7,031	7,564	7,825	7,941	8,463
Thrift institutions	454	825	919	1,020	1,078	1,144	1,260	1,299	1,337	1,356
Small time deposits [5]	1,046	994	934	570	523	412	352	411	526	583
Commercial banks	701	647	664	426	391	302	250	300	420	457
Thrift institutions	345	347	271	144	132	110	101	111	106	126

NA Not available. [1] Currency outside U.S. Treasury, Federal Reserve Banks and the vaults of depository institutions. [2] Outstanding amount of U.S. dollar-denominated travelers' checks of nonbank issuers. Travelers' checks issued by depository institutions are included in demand deposits. [3] Demand deposits at domestically chartered commercial banks, U.S. branches and agencies of foreign banks, and Edge Act corporations (excluding those amounts held by depository institutions, the U.S. government, and foreign banks and official institutions) less cash items in the process of collection and Federal Reserve float. [4] Negotiable order of withdrawal (NOW) and automatic transfer service (ATS) balances at domestically chartered commercial banks, U.S. branches and agencies of foreign banks, Edge Act corporations, and thrift institutions, credit union share draft balances, and demand deposits at thrift institutions. [5] Small-denomination time deposits are those issued in amounts of less than $100,000. All Individual Retirement Account (IRA) and Keogh account balances at commercial banks and thrift institutions are subtracted from small time deposits.

Source: Board of Governors of the Federal Reserve System, Data Releases, Money Stock and Reserve Balances, "Money Stock Measures – H.6," weekly releases, <http://www.federalreserve.gov/releases/h6/>, accessed January 2020.

Table 1222. Volume of Debt Markets by Type of Security: 2000 to 2019

[In billions of dollars (2,604 represents $2,604,000,000,000). Covers debt markets as represented by the source]

Type of security	2000	2005	2010	2015	2016	2017	2018	2019
NEW ISSUE VOLUME [1]								
Total	**2,604**	**5,809**	**7,339**	**6,819**	**7,469**	**7,561**	**7,445**	**8,190**
Municipal	198	407	433	405	452	449	347	426
U.S. Treasury securities [2]	313	746	2,320	2,123	2,169	2,224	2,685	2,935
Federal agency debt [3]	447	635	1,362	645	928	731	649	989
Mortgage-backed securities [4]	780	2,764	2,013	1,801	2,044	1,935	1,875	2,116
Asset-backed securities [5]	240	474	126	333	325	550	517	306
Corporate debt [6]	627	783	1,086	1,511	1,550	1,671	1,372	1,417
AVERAGE DAILY TRADING VOLUME								
Total	**357.6**	**918.6**	**893.7**	**728.7**	**775.5**	**763.7**	**816.1**	**895.0**
Municipal	8.8	16.9	13.3	8.6	10.6	10.8	11.6	11.5
U.S. Treasury securities [2]	206.5	554.5	528.2	490.0	519.1	505.2	547.8	593.6
Federal agency debt [3, 7]	72.8	78.8	11.2	4.5	5.4	4.1	3.5	4.1
Mortgage-backed securities [4, 7]	69.5	251.8	320.6	193.0	206.6	209.1	218.1	247.6
Non-agency mortgaged-back securities [8]	(NA)	(NA)	(NA)	3.1	2.9	2.5	2.4	2.7
Corporate [6]	(NA)	16.6	20.5	27.9	29.6	30.6	31.2	33.9
Asset-backed securities [5]	(NA)	(NA)	(NA)	1.4	1.3	1.4	1.4	1.5
VOLUME OF SECURITIES OUTSTANDING								
Total	**16,175**	**24,677**	**33,913**	**38,526**	**39,755**	**41,040**	**42,862**	**44,982**
Municipal [9]	1,481	3,099	3,965	3,830	3,876	3,890	3,835	3,855
U.S. Treasury securities [2]	2,952	4,170	8,853	13,192	13,908	14,469	15,608	16,673
Federal agency debt [3]	1,854	2,616	2,539	1,995	1,972	1,935	1,842	1,826
Mortgage-backed securities [4]	4,119	7,218	9,258	8,895	9,023	9,305	9,732	10,308
Asset-backed securities [5]	702	1,281	1,508	1,377	1,392	1,458	1,616	1,678
Money market instruments [10]	1,614	1,644	1,058	941	885	966	996	1,045
Corporate debt [11]	3,454	4,649	6,732	8,296	8,699	9,018	9,233	9,598

NA Not available. [1] Covers only long-term issuance. [2] Marketable public debt. [3] Beginning with 2004, Sallie Mae (Student Loan Marketing Association) has been excluded due to privatization. [4] Includes Government National Mortgage Association (GNMA), Federal National Mortgage Association (FNMA), and Federal Home Loan Mortgage Corporation (FHLMC) mortgage-backed securities (MBS), and collateralized mortgage obligations (CMOs), and CMBS, and private-label MBS/CMOs. [5] Excludes mortgage-backed assets. Includes auto, credit card, home equity loans, manufacturing, student loan and other. Collateralized debt obligations are included. [6] Includes nonconvertible corporate debt, Yankee bonds, and MTNs (Medium-Term Notes), but excludes federal agency debt and certificates of deposit. [7] Primary dealer trading volume through March 2010 for federal agency debt and through May 2011 for mortgage-backed securities. After those dates, data from FINRA Trace. [8] Includes mortgage securities issued by private institutions, such as subsidiaries of investment banks, banks, financial institutions, non-bank mortgage lenders, and home builders. [9] Due to the change in underlying sourcing from the Federal Reserve, municipal securities outstanding has been restated from 2004 onward and revised upward by about $840 billion. [10] Commercial paper, bankers acceptances, and large time deposits. [11] Debt obligations of U.S. financial and nonfinancial corporations including bonds, notes, debentures, mandatory convertible securities, long-term debt, private mortgage-backed securities, and unsecured debt. Includes bonds issued both in the United States and in foreign countries, but not bonds issued in foreign countries by foreign subsidiaries of U.S. corporations. Recorded at book value.

Source: The Securities Industry and Financial Markets Association, New York, NY ©. Based on data supplied by Bloomberg, Dealogic, Thomson Reuters Eikon, Thomson Reuters SDC, U.S. Treasury, Fannie Mae (FNMA), Freddie Mac (FHLMC), Ginnie Mae (GNMA), Farmer Mac, Farm Credit, FHLB, Federal Reserve Bank of New York, Municipal Securities Rulemaking Board, and FINRA Trace (Financial Industry Regulatory Authority Trade Reporting and Compliance Engine). See also <https://www.sifma.org/>.

Table 1223. Bond Yields: 2000 to 2019

[Percent per year. Annual averages of daily figures]

Type	2000	2005	2010	2013	2014	2015	2016	2017	2018	2019
U.S. Treasury, constant maturities: [1]										
1-year	6.11	3.62	0.32	0.13	0.12	0.32	0.61	1.20	2.33	2.05
2-year	6.26	3.85	0.70	0.31	0.46	0.69	0.83	1.40	2.53	1.97
3-year	6.22	3.93	1.11	0.54	0.90	1.02	1.00	1.58	2.63	1.94
5-year	6.16	4.05	1.93	1.17	1.64	1.53	1.33	1.91	2.75	1.95
7-year	6.20	4.15	2.62	1.74	2.14	1.89	1.63	2.16	2.85	2.05
10-year	6.03	4.29	3.22	2.35	2.54	2.14	1.84	2.33	2.91	2.14
20-year	6.23	4.64	4.03	3.12	3.07	2.55	2.22	2.65	3.02	2.40
High-grade municipal bonds (Standard & Poor's) [2]	5.77	4.29	4.16	3.96	3.78	3.48	3.07	3.36	3.53	3.38

[1] Yields on actively traded non-inflation-indexed issues adjusted to constant maturities. Yields are based on closing indicative prices quoted by secondary market participants. [2] Source: U.S. Council of Economic Advisors, *Economic Indicators*, monthly, <https://www.govinfo.gov/app/collection/econi>, accessed March 2020.

Source: Except as noted, Board of Governors of the Federal Reserve System, "H15, Selected Interest Rates," <https://www.federalreserve.gov/releases/h15/>, accessed March 2020.

Table 1224. Securities Industry—Financial Summary: 2000 to 2016

[In billions of dollars, except as indicated (349.5 represents $349,500,000,000). Minus sign (-) indicates loss]

Type	2000	2005	2010	2011	2012	2013	2014	2015	2016
Number of firms	7,258	6,016	4,907	4,708	4,761	4,555	4,380	4,247	4,135
Revenues, total	**349.5**	**332.5**	**262.0**	**245.8**	**264.4**	**272.5**	**279.4**	**275.7**	**278.7**
Commissions	54.1	46.8	47.0	47.7	40.6	40.1	39.5	37.3	34.3
Trading/investment gains	70.8	30.7	31.2	10.2	26.9	21.2	21.6	16.4	21.8
Underwriting profits	18.7	19.9	24.4	22.9	27.9	32.0	33.5	30.7	26.9
Margin interest	24.5	13.3	5.0	6.2	7.2	7.1	8.2	8.4	8.9
Mutual fund sales	19.4	20.7	18.8	19.4	20.1	21.6	22.8	22.1	20.4
Other	161.9	201.2	135.5	139.3	141.7	150.4	153.9	160.7	166.5
Expenses, total	**310.4**	**311.3**	**224.0**	**228.9**	**229.9**	**243.8**	**253.9**	**250.9**	**251.2**
Interest expense	131.9	140.2	22.4	20.3	20.6	16.6	15.9	16.1	23.7
Compensation	95.2	88.8	102.1	102.4	104.7	110.0	114.5	115.8	113.9
Commissions/clearance paid	15.5	18.6	24.0	25.4	24.2	25.1	25.7	25.1	23.1
Other	67.8	63.6	75.5	80.8	80.4	92.2	97.7	93.8	90.5
Net income, pretax	**39.1**	**21.2**	**38.0**	**16.8**	**34.6**	**28.6**	**25.6**	**24.8**	**27.5**
Pre-tax profit margin (percent)	11.2	6.4	14.5	6.9	13.1	10.5	9.2	9.0	9.9
Pre-tax return on equity (percent)	31.1	13.1	17.1	7.5	14.7	12.0	10.5	10.2	11.3
Assets	2,866	5,215	4,757	4,662	4,892	4,591	4,440	4,051	3,906
Liabilities	2,728	5,051	4,526	4,444	4,658	4,348	4,197	3,806	3,665
Ownership equity	138	164	231	218	234	243	243	245	241

Source: U.S. Securities and Exchange Commission, "Select Market Data Fiscal 2017," and earlier reports, <https://www.sec.gov/reports>, accessed September 2018.

Table 1225. Total Returns of Stocks, Bonds, and Treasury Bills: 1980 to 2019

[Average annual percent change. Stock return data are based on the Standard & Poor's 500 index. Minus sign (-) indicates loss]

Period	Stocks				Treasury bills, total return	Bonds (10-year), total return
	Total return before inflation	Capital gains	Dividends and reinvestment	Total return after inflation		
1980 to 1989	17.55	12.59	4.40	11.85	9.13	13.01
1990 to 1999	18.21	15.31	2.51	14.85	4.95	8.02
2000 to 2009	-0.45	-2.73	2.27	-3.39	2.74	6.63
2001	-11.89	-13.04	1.32	-13.68	3.32	5.53
2002	-22.10	-23.37	1.65	-23.91	1.61	15.37
2003	28.68	26.38	1.82	26.31	1.03	0.46
2004	10.88	8.99	1.73	7.38	1.43	4.61
2005	4.91	3.00	1.85	1.45	3.30	3.09
2006	15.80	13.62	1.91	11.97	4.97	2.21
2007	5.49	3.53	1.89	1.35	4.52	10.54
2008	-37.00	-38.49	1.88	-37.10	1.24	20.23
2009	26.25	23.45	2.44	23.11	0.15	-9.50
2010	15.06	12.78	2.02	13.36	0.03	7.26
2011	2.96	–	2.96	0.83	0.06	16.89
2012	16.00	13.41	2.29	14.02	0.08	2.77
2013	32.39	29.60	2.15	30.43	0.05	-8.56
2014	13.69	11.39	2.06	12.83	0.03	10.74
2015	1.32	-0.73	2.05	0.58	0.06	11.27
2016	11.96	9.53	2.22	9.68	0.33	-5.40
2017	21.83	19.41	2.03	19.30	0.95	2.81
2018	-4.38	-6.24	1.98	-6.37	2.00	0.34
2019	31.49	28.88	2.02	28.55	2.09	9.28

– Represents or rounds to zero.

Source: Global Financial Data, Los Angeles, CA, "GFD Guide to Total Returns," <www.globalfinancialdata.com>, and unpublished data ©.

Table 1226. New Security Issues of Corporations by Type of Offering: 2010 to 2019

[In billions of dollars (1,025 represents $1,025,000,000,000). Represents gross proceeds of issues maturing in more than one year. Figures are the principal amount or the number of units multiplied by the offering price. Excludes secondary offerings, employee stock plans, investment companies other than closed-end, intracorporate transactions, Yankee bonds, and private placements listed. Stock data include ownership securities issued by limited partnerships]

Type of offering	2010	2015	2018	2019	Type of offering	2010	2015	2018	2019
Total [1].............	**1,025**	**1,664**	**1,549**	**1,737**	Nonfinancial...........	498	888	651	867
					Financial...............	396	723	876	885
Bonds, total....................	894	1,611	1,526	1,752	Stocks, total [2]..........	131	174	131	169
Sold in the U.S...............	880	1,511	1,489	1,626	Nonfinancial...........	61	111	88	102
Sold abroad..................	14	100	38	125	Financial...............	70	63	44	66

[1] Total reflects the sum of the gross issuance of bonds and the gross proceeds of stocks in the domestic market. [2] Gross proceeds of stocks in all markets.

Source: Board of Governors of the Federal Reserve System, "New Security Issues, U.S. Corporations," <https://www.federalreserve.gov/data/corpsecure/current.htm>, April 2020.

Table 1227. Equities, Corporate Bonds, and Municipal and Treasury Securities—Holdings and Net Purchases by Type of Investor: 2000 to 2019

[In billions of dollars (18,216 represents $18,216,000,000,000). Holdings as of December 31. Minus sign (-) indicates net sales]

Type of investor	Holdings					Net purchases				
	2000	2010	2015	2018	2019	2000	2010	2015	2018	2019
EQUITIES [1]										
Total [2]......................	**18,216**	**24,079**	**37,132**	**43,913**	**54,906**	**16.7**	**41.1**	**-124.7**	**-138.0**	**-333.3**
Household sector [3].................	7,074	8,565	13,688	16,656	21,076	-400.8	-202.1	-123.0	-89.7	233.6
State and local governments.............	97	89	122	138	173	6.0	-3.4	-3.4	-3.4	-3.4
Property-casualty insurance companies......................	195	224	334	392	498	1.1	-5.2	-1.5	20.8	4.0
Life insurance companies.................	338	408	546	538	619	-5.6	43.3	27.0	-44.4	-29.4
Private pension funds.....................	1,823	1,778	2,220	2,364	2,912	64.4	38.7	-29.3	-98.4	-115.3
Federal government retirement funds. ..	57	145	240	292	370	5.2	6.1	–	-21.7	-5.2
State and local government retirement funds.....................................	1,299	1,723	2,250	2,532	2,999	11.6	-67.4	22.6	-27.6	-92.9
Mutual funds.............................	3,911	5,873	8,625	9,657	11,891	233.3	69.0	58.1	-120.5	-213.2
Exchange-traded funds...................	66	753	1,710	2,669	3,486	42.4	80.1	173.5	210.4	165.9
Brokers and dealers......................	77	117	167	148	167	20.2	-23.0	-18.4	-19.9	-22.8
Rest of the world [4].....................	1,483	3,213	5,501	6,511	8,179	197.1	129.6	-191.4	96.4	-211.4
CORPORATE & FOREIGN BONDS										
Total [2]......................	**4,748**	**11,088**	**11,799**	**12,660**	**14,250**	**343.8**	**-15.5**	**280.9**	**345.1**	**477.4**
Household sector [3].................	441	2,002	1,231	956	938	95.4	-196.0	-237.8	-5.0	-116.4
U.S.-chartered depository institutions....	312	551	507	452	499	46.9	-98.2	-12.0	-37.9	44.0
Foreign banking offices in U.S............	55	238	173	150	135	7.6	-9.4	-10.8	-0.6	-29.2
Property-casualty insurance companies......................	192	348	452	534	628	7.4	24.3	19.2	56.7	40.4
Life insurance companies.................	1,189	2,074	2,429	2,711	3,119	54.2	85.8	92.4	123.7	134.5
Private pension funds.....................	263	446	691	835	981	-76.9	27.6	5.8	83.0	62.0
State and local government retirement funds.....................................	314	427	558	415	468	4.2	12.0	37.2	-2.0	31.5
Mutual funds.............................	361	1,224	1,737	2,017	2,359	-39.2	211.5	55.8	115.2	135.4
Exchange-traded funds...................	–	78	242	420	544	–	18.7	37.2	33.6	93.7
Rest of the world [4].....................	843	2,523	3,083	3,610	3,993	168.3	-36.8	334.9	-20.2	100.1
MUNICIPAL SECURITIES [5]										
Total [2]......................	**1,473**	**3,798**	**4,052**	**3,973**	**4,141**	**23.6**	**115.6**	**15.8**	**-57.9**	**19.5**
Household sector [3].................	476	1,912	1,901	1,859	1,894	17.8	76.8	-40.1	-8.8	-50.5
U.S.-chartered depository institutions....	117	255	508	499	472	3.4	30.3	45.4	-40.9	-28.4
Property-casualty insurance companies......................	189	370	358	292	300	-13.8	-24.0	10.2	-37.7	-5.2
Money market funds......................	242	388	236	143	134	32.5	-53.1	-28.8	8.4	-8.9
Mutual funds.............................	273	490	604	694	833	-20.5	33.0	16.2	22.1	107.6
TREASURY SECURITIES										
Total [2]......................	**4,031**	**10,513**	**15,263**	**17,691**	**19,308**	**-274.0**	**1,645.3**	**724.4**	**1,411.2**	**1,176.6**
Household sector [3].................	548	1,043	1,031	1,716	1,961	-195.5	282.2	326.7	612.8	322.2
State and local governments.............	317	630	668	684	663	6.4	15.7	6.8	-62.0	-45.3
Monetary authority......................	512	1,021	2,676	2,338	2,544	33.7	244.9	-15.6	-243.3	100.0
U.S.-chartered depository institutions....	97	218	435	570	704	-36.4	93.0	14.8	87.3	125.4
Life insurance companies.................	60	161	206	204	207	-6.4	20.7	7.2	-28.8	-4.4
Private pension funds.....................	111	202	287	406	476	-9.3	46.0	-13.1	59.9	52.7
Federal government retirement funds. ..	739	1,277	1,715	2,039	2,150	22.9	77.2	91.6	309.3	110.5
State and local governments retirement funds........................	179	154	175	373	410	-19.8	3.4	-22.2	57.7	30.2
Money market funds......................	94	342	486	873	1,037	-13.2	-72.4	53.4	170.6	163.0
Mutual funds.............................	113	417	827	1,146	1,305	7.5	129.8	155.3	69.7	114.4
Rest of the world [4].....................	1,021	4,459	6,146	6,265	6,698	-75.2	740.4	42.7	114.8	180.6

– Represents or rounds to zero. [1] Includes shares of exchange-traded funds, closed-end funds, and real estate investment trusts. Excludes mutual fund shares of open-end investment companies; see Table 1233. [2] Includes other types not shown separately. [3] Includes nonprofit organizations. [4] Holdings and net purchases of U.S. issues by foreign residents. [5] Includes loans.

Source: Board of Governors of the Federal Reserve System, "Financial Accounts of the United States, Z.1," <https://www.federalreserve.gov/data.htm>, accessed April 2020.

Table 1228. Foreign Securities Held by U.S. Residents: 2010 to 2018

[In billions of dollars (6,763 represents $6,763,000,000,000). Estimates for end of calendar year. See also Table 1305]

Country	Total			Equities			Long-term and short-term debt		
	2010	2015	2018	2010	2015	2018	2010	2015	2018
Total holdings [1]	**6,763**	**9,455**	**11,297**	**4,647**	**6,756**	**7,900**	**2,116**	**2,699**	**3,397**
Australia	323	296	333	150	139	174	174	157	158
Belgium	35	68	52	29	56	39	7	12	13
Bermuda	160	217	236	134	187	200	25	30	36
Brazil	235	116	169	194	66	139	41	50	29
Canada	695	705	981	409	325	468	287	380	514
Cayman Islands	366	1,217	1,742	166	915	1,287	200	302	455
China [2]	102	108	159	101	103	152	2	5	8
Curacao [3]	(NA)	70	37	(NA)	67	35	(NA)	3	1
France	366	474	563	244	327	383	122	146	180
Germany	299	378	402	207	283	306	92	95	96
Hong Kong	135	136	171	133	129	160	2	7	10
India	91	130	176	86	120	164	5	10	12
Ireland	132	498	503	101	422	421	31	77	81
Israel	64	80	65	45	63	47	19	17	18
Italy	66	107	115	51	73	77	14	34	38
Japan	519	822	1,010	450	690	760	69	131	250
Jersey	42	92	101	21	80	85	21	12	16
Korea, South	148	171	213	122	139	191	26	32	23
Luxembourg	100	128	139	33	41	72	68	87	66
Mexico	109	148	146	77	56	61	32	91	85
Netherlands	233	404	456	120	250	270	112	154	186
Norway	56	58	61	23	22	33	33	36	28
Russia	62	40	57	56	32	47	7	8	9
Singapore	64	99	89	56	81	54	8	18	35
South Africa	78	63	91	70	54	77	8	9	14
Spain	87	115	139	66	90	104	22	25	34
Sweden	122	138	144	63	86	90	59	51	54
Switzerland	327	420	458	319	407	428	8	13	30
Taiwan	95	108	158	94	108	158	(Z)	(Z)	(Z)
United Kingdom	1,001	1,240	1,360	626	897	927	375	343	433

NA Not available. Z Less than $500 million. [1] Includes other countries, not shown separately. [2] Excludes Hong Kong, Macau, and Taiwan. [3] Separate reporting for Curacao began with the 2013 survey. In previous years, data were reported as part of Netherlands Antilles.

Source: U.S. Department of Treasury, "Securities (C): Annual Cross-U.S. Border Portfolio Holdings, U.S. Claims on Foreigners from Holdings of Foreign Securities," <https://www.treasury.gov/resource center/data-chart-center/tic/Pages/shcreports.aspx>, accessed November 2019.

Table 1229. U.S. Securities Held by Foreign Residents: 2010 and 2019

[In billions of dollars (10,691 represents $10,691,000,000,000). Estimates as of June. Long-term securities include all forms of equity and all debt securities with an original term-to-maturity of over one year]

Region and country	U.S. securities, total [1]		U.S. equities [2]		U.S Treasury long-term securities		Long-term corporate debt	
	2010	2019	2010	2019	2010	2019	2010	2019
Total [3]	**10,691**	**20,534**	**2,814**	**8,630**	**3,343**	**5,903**	**2,493**	**3,943**
Australia	118	344	74	262	14	33	22	36
Belgium	408	780	19	58	31	175	342	515
Bermuda	249	349	44	111	42	49	91	134
Brazil	169	322	2	5	132	309	2	1
British Virgin Islands	85	178	42	112	4	27	22	23
Canada	424	1,262	298	956	29	99	80	184
Cayman Islands	743	1,877	290	1,084	36	134	303	524
China, mainland [4]	1,611	1,543	127	189	1,108	1,109	11	14
Denmark	49	138	26	100	5	17	14	20
France	194	373	115	177	15	114	52	60
Germany	195	396	57	191	46	69	65	120
Hong Kong	293	397	33	110	60	190	16	55
India	41	168	1	4	21	161	3	(Z)
Ireland	356	1,081	77	456	27	224	130	251
Israel	37	114	13	65	8	38	3	7
Italy	41	101	13	35	21	40	3	18
Japan	1,393	2,280	224	596	737	1,065	130	260
Korea, South	122	366	13	153	34	111	9	52
Kuwait	80	287	45	197	13	38	7	21
Luxembourg	622	1,623	172	663	49	183	302	640
Netherlands	247	421	152	284	22	46	57	73
Norway	136	452	90	309	14	98	25	45
Saudi Arabia	125	289	36	93	68	130	9	14
Singapore	176	363	91	180	47	133	28	33
Sweden	81	236	49	180	14	49	11	6
Switzerland	397	813	162	450	87	195	110	117
Taiwan	228	626	12	68	149	172	18	117
Thailand	38	104	1	11	12	68	1	3
United Arab Emirates	86	160	44	101	17	38	8	8
United Kingdom	798	1,776	324	1,002	72	286	369	422

Z Less than $500 million. [1] Includes short-term debt and other long-term debt. [2] Includes common and preferred stock, all types of investment company shares (open-end funds, closed-end funds, money market mutual funds, and hedge funds), interests in limited partnerships, and other equity interests that may not involve stocks or shares. [3] Includes other countries not shown separately. [4] Excludes Hong Kong, Macau, and Taiwan.

Source: U.S. Department of Treasury, "Securities (c): Annual Cross-U.S. Border Portfolio Holdings: Foreign Residents' Portfolio Holdings of U.S. Securities," <http://www.treasury.gov/resource-center/data-chart-center/tic/Pages/fpis.aspx>, accessed May 2020.

Table 1230. Stock Prices and Yields: 2000 to 2019

[Closing values as of end of December, except as noted]

Index	2000	2005	2010	2015	2017	2018	2019
STOCK PRICES							
Standard & Poor's indices: [1]							
S&P 500 composite (1941–43 = 10)	1,320	1,248	1,257	2,044	2,674	2,507	3,231
S&P 400 MidCap Index (1982 = 100)	517	738	907	1,399	1,901	1,663	2,063
S&P 600 SmallCap Index (Dec. 31, 1993 = 100)	220	351	416	672	936	845	1,021
S&P 500 Citigroup Value Index (Dec. 31, 1974 = 35)	636	648	590	876	1,127	1,000	1,286
S&P 500 Citigroup Growth Index (Dec. 31, 1974 = 35)	688	597	659	1,164	1,533	1,512	1,953
Russell indices: [2]							
Russell 1000 (Dec. 31, 1986 = 130)	700	679	697	1,132	1,482	1,384	1,784
Russell 2000 (Dec. 31, 1986 = 135)	484	673	784	1,136	1,536	1,349	1,668
Russell 3000 (Dec. 31, 1986 = 140)	726	723	749	1,206	1,583	1,472	1,892
N.Y. Stock Exchange common stock index:							
Composite (Dec. 31, 2002 = 5000)	6,946	7,754	7,964	10,143	12,809	11,374	13,913
Yearly high	7,165	7,868	7,983	11,255	12,886	11,378	13,944
Yearly low	6,095	6,903	6,356	9,510	12,809	11,272	11,190
American Stock Exchange Composite Index (Dec. 29, 1995 = 550)	898	1,759	2,208	2,149	2,662	2,292	2,553
NASDAQ Composite Index (Feb. 5, 1971 = 100)	2,471	2,205	2,653	5,007	6,903	6,635	8,973
Nasdaq-100 (Jan. 31, 1985 = 125)	2,342	1,645	2,218	4,593	6,396	6,330	8,733
Industrial (Feb. 5, 1971 = 100)	1,483	1,860	2,184	4,101	5,514	5,401	6,808
Banks (Feb. 5, 1971 = 100)	1,939	3,078	1,847	2,853	3,988	3,274	3,969
Computers (Oct. 29, 1993 = 200)	1,295	992	1,372	2,606	4,060	3,911	5,879
Transportation (Feb. 5, 1971 = 100)	1,160	2,438	2,562	3,334	5,075	4,605	5,292
Telecommunications (Oct. 29, 1993 = 200)	463	184	226	251	339	349	389
Biotech (Oct. 29, 1993 = 200)	1,085	790	970	3,540	3,357	3,044	3,787
Dow Jones Averages:							
Composite (65 stocks)	3,317	3,638	4,033	5,978	8,310	7,710	9,386
Industrial (30 stocks)	10,787	10,718	11,578	17,425	24,719	23,327	28,538
Transportation (20 stocks)	2,947	4,196	5,107	7,509	10,612	9,170	10,901
Utility (15 stocks)	412	405	405	578	723	713	879
COMMON STOCK YIELDS (percent)							
Standard & Poor's Composite Index (500 stocks): [3]							
Dividend-price ratio [4]	1.15	1.83	1.98	2.2	1.84	2.20	1.87
Earnings-price ratio [5]	3.63	5.36	6.04	4.64	3.89	4.60	4.19

[1] Standard & Poor's Indices are market-value weighted and are chosen for market size, liquidity, and industry group representation. The S&P 500 index represents 500 large publicly-traded companies. The S&P MidCap Index tracks mid-cap companies. The S&P SmallCap Index consists of 600 domestic small-cap stocks. [2] The Russell 1000 and 3000 indices show respectively the 1000 and 3000 largest capitalization stocks in the United States. The Russell 2000 index shows the 2000 largest capitalization stocks in the United States after the first 1000. [3] Source: U.S. Council of Economic Advisors, *Economic Indicators*, monthly. [4] Aggregate cash dividends (based on latest known annual rate) divided by aggregate market value based on Wednesday closing prices. Averages of monthly figures. [5] Averages of quarterly ratios which are ratio of earnings (after taxes) for 4 quarters ending with particular quarter- to-price index for last day of that quarter.

Source: Except as noted, Global Financial Data, Los Angeles, CA, <http://www.globalfinancialdata.com/> ©.

Table 1231. Stock Ownership by Age of Head of Family and Family Income: 2010 to 2016

[Median value in thousands of constant (2016) dollars (32.1 represents $32,100). All dollar figures are adjusted to 2016 dollars using the "current methods" version of the consumer price index for all urban consumers published by U.S. Bureau of Labor Statistics. Families include one-person units; for definition of family, see text, Section 1. Based on Survey of Consumer Finance; see Appendix III. For definition of median, see Guide to Tabular Presentation]

Age of family head and family income (constant (2016) dollars)	Families having direct or indirect stock holdings [1] (percent)			Median value among families with holdings			Stock holdings share of group's financial assets (percent)		
	2010	2013	2016	2010	2013	2016	2010	2013	2016
All families	**49.9**	**48.8**	**51.9**	**32.1**	**37.1**	**40.0**	**47.0**	**51.7**	**53.4**
Under 35 years old	39.8	38.6	41.1	7.7	7.3	7.8	39.3	46.5	40.2
35 to 44 years old	50.1	53.9	55.7	21.9	24.2	21.9	50.5	53.7	50.0
45 to 54 years old	58.0	54.9	57.4	41.8	45.4	50.8	48.6	56.2	55.0
55 to 64 years old	59.7	57.2	57.5	61.9	61.1	80.0	48.3	51.6	56.0
65 to 74 years old	45.6	49.2	50.4	85.0	121.1	94.5	44.2	49.2	50.2
75 years old and over	42.0	34.5	48.9	60.8	82.7	100.0	44.6	50.3	54.2
Percentiles of income: [2]									
Less than 20	12.5	11.4	11.6	5.9	6.2	6.0	40.5	31.7	39.8
20 to 39.9	30.5	26.4	32.5	7.8	10.7	10.0	31.3	33.2	33.1
40 to 59.9	51.7	49.7	51.8	13.2	14.4	15.0	37.5	41.7	38.3
60 to 79.9	68.1	69.5	73.6	24.6	28.9	32.4	41.6	43.9	45.3
80 to 89.9	82.6	81.6	85.3	64.0	71.1	81.2	44.4	49.7	49.3
90 to 100	90.6	93.0	94.7	295.7	290.4	363.4	50.9	56.1	57.9

[1] Indirect holdings are those in pooled investment trusts, retirement accounts and other managed assets. [2] See footnote 8, Table 1198.

Source: Board of Governors of the Federal Reserve System, 2016 Survey of Consumer Finances, *Changes in U.S. Family Finances From 2013 to 2016: Evidence from the Survey of Consumer Finances*, Federal Reserve Bulletin, Vol. 103, No. 3, September 2017. See also <federalreserve.gov/econres/scfindex.htm>.

Table 1232. Transaction Activity in Equities, Options, and Security Futures, 2000 to 2016, and by Exchange, 2016

[In billions of dollars (36,275 represents $36,275,000,000,000). Market value of all sales of equities and options listed on an exchange or subject to last-sale reporting. Also reported are the value of such options that were exercised and the value of single-stock futures that were delivered. Excludes options and futures on indexes]

Year and exchange	Market value of sales			
	Total	Equity trading	Option trading	Option exercises and futures deliveries
2000	36,275	35,557	485	233
2004	27,876	27,158	223	495
2005	34,568	33,223	350	995
2006	43,941	41,798	531	1,611
2007	66,136	63,064	861	2,211
2008	82,012	78,653	1,096	2,264
2009	59,850	57,566	710	1,574
2010	64,008	61,146	725	2,137
2011	70,100	66,683	923	2,494
2012	59,371	55,620	938	2,813
2013	62,899	59,515	752	2,633
2014	69,979	66,354	762	2,863
2015	74,148	70,790	720	2,638
2016, total	**72,494**	**69,264**	**647**	**2,583**
BATS (Better Alternative Trading System) Exchange, Inc	5,067	4,743	65	260
BATS Y-Exchange, Inc	2,522	2,522	–	–
BOX Options Exchange LLC	79	–	16	63
C2 Options Exchange, Inc	50	–	10	40
Chicago Board Options Exchange, Inc	504	–	102	402
The Chicago Stock Exchange, Inc	583	583	–	–
EDGA Exchange, Inc	1,611	1,611	–	–
EDGX Exchange, Inc	4,836	4,808	6	22
FINRA, Inc. [1]	23,783	23,783	–	–
International Securities Exchange, LLC	453	–	91	362
Investors' Exchange LLC	406	406	–	–
ISE Mercury, LLC	4	–	1	3
Miami International Securities Exchange, LLC	–	–	–	–
Securities Exchange, LLC	172	–	34	138
NASDAQ OMX BX	1,660	1,637	5	19
NASDAQ OMX PHLX	1,342	719	125	498
The Nasdaq Stock Market LLC	11,313	11,081	47	185
National Stock Exchange	8	8	–	–
New York Stock Exchange, Inc	8,621	8,621	–	–
NYSE Amex LLC	345	36	63	246
NYSE Arca, Inc	9,053	8,707	70	277
OneChicago, LLC	19	–	–	19

– Represents or rounds to zero. [1] Financial Industry Regulatory Authority.

Source: U.S. Securities and Exchange Commission, "Select SEC and Market Data, Fiscal 2017," <http://www.sec.gov/about.shtml>, accessed September 2018.

Table 1233. Mutual Fund Shares—Holdings and Net Purchases by Type of Investor: 2000 to 2019

[In billions of dollars (5,119.4 represents $5,119,400,000,000). Holdings as of Dec. 31. A mutual fund is an open-end investment company that continuously issues and redeems shares that represent an interest in a pool of financial assets. Excludes money market funds and exchange-traded funds. Minus sign (-) indicates net sales]

Type of investor	Holdings					Net purchases				
	2000	2010	2015	2018	2019	2000	2010	2015	2018	2019
Total	**5,119.4**	**9,029.8**	**12,897.2**	**14,669.8**	**17,659.5**	**295.2**	**395.9**	**98.9**	**-63.3**	**210.1**
Households, nonprofit organizations	2,557.9	4,701.7	6,958.5	7,960.8	9,682.9	82.1	260.0	92.4	-25.1	244.9
Nonfinancial corporate business	118.0	185.7	248.2	271.0	311.9	0.3	7.5	12.3	-9.8	-9.8
State and local governments	32.2	46.0	64.8	75.9	91.5	1.1	1.2	1.2	1.2	1.2
U.S.-chartered depository institutions	15.0	45.0	53.0	52.1	61.7	2.5	-5.8	-0.9	-5.9	-1.9
Credit unions	2.3	1.5	1.9	2.5	3.3	-0.7	-0.3	-0.1	0.4	0.3
Property-casualty insurance companies	3.0	11.4	19.1	21.3	29.1	0.5	-0.7	0.7	-1.1	2.6
Life insurance companies	632.8	1,117.4	1,397.4	1,402.7	1,599.7	57.6	28.2	-30.8	-87.0	-85.3
Private pension funds	1,246.1	2,220.2	3,088.1	3,619.1	4,301.3	106.9	55.4	-8.6	10.8	-10.0
State and local government retirement funds	362.5	438.4	465.6	465.3	548.4	51.5	-6.1	30.8	24.5	-6.1
Rest of the world	149.5	262.5	600.6	799.0	1,029.7	-6.7	56.5	1.8	28.7	74.4

Source: Board of Governors of the Federal Reserve System, "Financial Accounts of the United States, Z.1," <https://www.federalreserve.gov/data.htm>, accessed April 2020.

Table 1234. Household Ownership of Mutual Funds by Age and Income: 2009 and 2019

[In percent. Ownership includes money market, stock, bond, and hybrid mutual funds, variable annuities, and mutual funds owned through Individual Retirement Accounts (IRAs), Keoghs, and employer-sponsored retirement plans. In 2019, an estimated 58,500,000 households own mutual funds. A mutual fund is an open-end investment company that continuously issues and redeems shares that represent an interest in a pool of financial assets]

Age of household head [1]	Percent distribution of all households owning mutual funds, 2019 [3]	As a percent of all households within each group		Household income [2]	Percent distribution of all households owning mutual funds, 2019 [3]	As a percent of all households within each group	
		2009	2019 [3]			2009	2019 [3]
Total........................	**100**	**45**	**46**	Less than $25,000......	4	10	10
Less than 35 years old......	17	35	36	$25,000 to $34,999....	3	22	18
35 to 44 years old............	20	51	56	$35,000 to $49,999....	8	42	28
45 to 54 years old............	20	57	54	$50,000 to $74,999....	17	53	45
55 to 64 years old............	21	49	50	$75,000 to $99,999....	16	71	57
65 years old and over........	22	34	37	$100,000 and over.....	52	79	78

[1] Age is based on the sole or co-decision maker for household saving and investing. [2] Total reported is household income before taxes in prior year. [3] Starting in 2014, the survey was revised to include a dual frame random digit dial (RDD) sample design of landline and cellular telephone numbers. See source for details.

Source: Investment Company Institute. Holden, Sarah, Daniel Schrass, and Michael Bogdan. 2019. "Ownership of Mutual Funds, Shareholder Sentiment, and Use of the Internet, 2019." ICI Research Perspective 25, no. 8 (November). See also <ici.org/pdf/per25-08.pdf>.

Table 1235. Characteristics of Mutual Fund Owners: 2019

[In percent, except as indicated. The 2019 data are based on responses from 1,821 households owning mutual funds. Interviews were conducted with the person most knowledgeable about the household's investments and savings. Prior to 2014, the annual mutual fund shareholder survey was conducted via landline telephones only; starting in 2014, the survey was expanded and is based on a dual frame sample of landline and cellular telephone numbers. Mutual fund ownership includes holdings of money market, stock, bond, and hybrid mutual funds; and funds owned through variable annuities, Individual Retirement Accounts (IRAs), Keoghs, and employer-sponsored retirement plans. A mutual fund is an open-end investment company that continuously issues and redeems shares that represent an interest in a pool of financial assets. For definition of median, see Guide to Tabular Presentation]

Characteristic	Total	Age [1]				Household income [2]			
		Under 35 years	35 to 54 years	55 to 64 years	65 years and over	Less than $50,000	$50,000 to $99,000	$100,000 to $149,000	$150,000 or more
Median age [1] (years)........................	51	29	45	60	72	56	52	49	51
Median household income [2] (dol.)............	100,000	87,500	112,000	110,000	80,000	34,100	72,300	119,300	200,000
Median household financial assets [3] (dol.)...	250,000	53,000	225,000	450,000	400,000	62,500	170,000	300,000	538,000
Own an IRA..	65	63	60	70	73	57	63	59	78
Household with defined contribution retirement plan(s) [4]...........................	84	80	92	89	67	73	83	88	89
401(k) plan...	74	76	82	80	52	60	73	77	81
403(b), state, local, or federal government plan..................................	34	24	40	35	32	24	32	39	39
Median mutual fund assets (dol.)..............	150,000	30,000	130,000	300,000	300,000	40,000	100,000	125,000	400,000
Own:									
Equity funds......................................	88	87	90	89	85	84	84	90	93
Bond funds..	45	39	44	49	49	35	43	48	50

[1] See Table 1234, footnote 1. [2] See Table 1234, footnote 2. [3] Includes assets in employer-sponsored retirement plans but excludes value of primary residence. [4] For definition of defined contribution plan, see headnote, Table 583.

Source: Investment Company Institute. Schrass, Daniel, and Michael Bogdan. 2019. "Profile of Mutual Fund Shareholders, 2019." ICI Research Report (December) ©. See also <ici.org/pdf/rpt_19_profiles19.pdf>.

Table 1236. Mutual Funds—Summary: 2000 to 2019

[6,956 represents $6,956,000,000,000. Number of funds and assets as of December 31. A mutual fund is an open-end investment company that continuously issues and redeems shares that represent an interest in a pool of financial assets. Excludes data for funds that invest in other mutual funds. Minus sign (-) indicates net redemptions]

Type of fund	Unit	2000	2005	2010	2014	2015	2016	2017	2018	2019
Number of funds, total......................	**Number**	**8,134**	**7,967**	**7,546**	**7,934**	**8,121**	**8,073**	**7,966**	**8,094**	**7,945**
Equity funds....................................	Number	4,359	4,566	4,508	4,647	4,762	4,751	4,705	4,766	4,651
Hybrid funds....................................	Number	506	480	495	674	726	727	740	784	774
Bond funds......................................	Number	2,232	2,052	1,891	2,086	2,152	2,174	2,139	2,176	2,156
Money market funds, taxable [1]..........	Number	703	592	442	364	336	319	299	287	284
Money market funds, tax-exempt [2]......	Number	334	277	210	163	145	102	83	81	80
Net assets, total............................	**Bil. dol.**	**6,956**	**8,889**	**11,831**	**15,877**	**15,658**	**16,353**	**18,765**	**17,710**	**21,292**
Equity funds....................................	Bil. dol.	3,933	4,885	5,596	8,314	8,150	8,577	10,305	9,228	11,376
Hybrid funds....................................	Bil. dol.	361	621	842	1,379	1,341	1,400	1,547	1,384	1,579
Bond funds......................................	Bil. dol.	817	1,356	2,589	3,459	3,412	3,648	4,065	4,061	4,704
Money market funds, taxable [1]..........	Bil. dol.	1,611	1,690	2,474	2,464	2,500	2,598	2,716	2,892	3,494
Money market funds, tax-exempt [2]......	Bil. dol.	234	336	330	261	255	130	131	145	138
Net new cash flow:.........................	**Bil. dol.**	**390**	**254**	**-281**	**106**	**-98**	**-223**	**179**	**-187**	**454**
Equity funds....................................	Bil. dol.	315	124	-24	25	-76	-258	-159	-257	-362
Hybrid funds....................................	Bil. dol.	-37	43	36	30	-19	-42	-28	-91	-49
Bond funds......................................	Bil. dol.	-48	25	232	44	-25	107	260	2	312
Money market funds..........................	Bil. dol.	159	62	-525	6	21	-30	107	159	553

[1] Funds invest in short-term, high-grade securities sold in the money market. [2] Funds invest in municipal securities with relatively short maturities.

Source: Investment Company Institute. 2020. *Investment Company Fact Book: A Review of Trends and Activities in the U.S. Investment Company Industry.* © Washington, DC: Investment Company Institute. See also <www.icifactbook.org>.

Table 1237. Retirement Assets by Type of Asset: 2000 to 2019

[In billions of dollars, except as indicated (11,556 represents $11,556,000,000,000). As of December 31]

Item	2000	2005	2010	2014	2015	2016	2017	2018	2019
Retirement assets, total...............	**11,556**	**14,386**	**17,951**	**23,958**	**23,990**	**25,374**	**28,827**	**28,047**	**32,599**
IRA assets [1]...............	2,629	3,425	5,029	7,292	7,477	8,015	9,439	9,250	11,025
Bank and thrift deposits [2]...............	250	278	461	506	523	561	548	568	558
Life insurance companies [3]...............	202	301	311	365	380	393	413	426	460
Mutual funds...............	1,262	1,780	2,418	3,524	3,493	3,707	4,279	3,994	4,816
Other assets [1,4]...............	916	1,067	1,840	2,897	3,081	3,354	4,200	4,262	5,190
Traditional [1]...............	2,407	3,034	4,340	6,225	6,387	6,824	8,018	7,850	9,350
Roth [1]...............	78	156	355	600	625	697	842	850	1,020
SEP and SAR-SEP [1,5]...............	134	193	265	367	364	382	453	430	515
SIMPLE [1,6]...............	10	42	69	100	101	112	127	120	140
Defined contribution plans...............	2,958	3,739	4,767	6,497	6,452	6,909	7,900	7,671	9,049
401(k) plans...............	1,738	2,393	3,119	4,406	4,377	4,741	5,486	5,330	6,395
Other private-sector defined contribution plans [7].....	500	413	464	514	483	498	550	510	570
403(b) plans...............	519	622	723	877	870	893	986	963	1,079
Thrift Savings Plan [8]...............	92	168	272	440	458	495	557	559	654
457 plans...............	110	143	189	261	263	282	321	309	351
Private-sector defined benefit plans...............	2,020	2,262	2,481	3,003	2,861	2,935	3,238	3,072	3,514
State and local government defined benefit plans.....	2,340	2,761	2,946	3,730	3,679	3,820	4,306	4,168	4,779
Federal defined benefit plans [9]...............	705	912	1,168	1,445	1,519	1,603	1,695	1,796	1,910
Annuities [10]...............	904	1,287	1,559	1,992	2,003	2,091	2,249	2,091	2,322
Memo:									
Mutual fund retirement assets...............	2,545	3,656	4,920	7,218	7,121	7,547	8,809	8,168	9,939
Percent of total retirement assets...............	22	25	27	30	30	30	31	29	30
Percent of all mutual funds...............	37	41	42	45	45	46	47	46	47

[1] Data for 2018 and 2019 are estimated. [2] Includes Keogh deposits. [3] Annuities held by IRAs, excluding variable annuity mutual fund IRA assets, which are included in mutual funds. [4] Excludes mutual fund assets held through brokerage accounts, which are included in mutual funds. [5] Simplified Employee Pension (SEP) IRAs and salary reduction (SAR) IRAs. [6] Savings Incentive Match Plan for Employees (SIMPLE) IRAs. [7] Includes Keoghs and other defined contribution plans (profit-sharing, thrift-savings, stock bonus, and money purchase) without 401(k) features. [8] Federal Employees Retirement System (FERS) Thrift Savings Plan (TSP) as reported by the Federal Reserve Board. [9] Federal pension plans include U.S. Treasury security holdings of the civil service retirement and disability fund, the military retirement fund, the judicial retirement funds, the Railroad Retirement Board, and the foreign service retirement and disability fund. These plans also include securities held in the National Railroad Retirement Investment Trust. [10] Annuities include all fixed and variable annuities held outside of retirement plans and IRAs.

Source: Investment Company Institute. 2020. "The US Retirement Market, First Quarter 2020" (June) ©. For the most up-to-date figures about the fund industry, please visit <https://www.ici.org/research/stats>.

Table 1238. Pension Funds—Summary: 2000 to 2019

[In billions of dollars (9,611 represents $9,611,000,000,000). As of end of year. Covers private pension funds, state and local government employee retirement funds, and federal government retirement funds in defined benefit plans and defined contribution plans (including 401(k) type plans). Excludes social security trust funds; see Table 578]

Item	2000	2005	2010	2013	2014	2015	2016	2017	2018	2019
Total financial assets [1]...............	**9,611**	**12,565**	**15,906**	**19,352**	**20,058**	**20,360**	**21,176**	**22,546**	**22,649**	**24,360**
Money market fund shares...............	104	143	195	212	211	208	223	221	223	233
Debt securities [1]...............	2,058	2,371	2,927	3,479	3,764	3,792	3,961	4,100	4,562	5,044
Treasury securities [2]...............	1,029	1,225	1,633	1,998	2,127	2,176	2,337	2,370	2,818	3,037
Agency- and GSE (government-sponsored enterprises)-backed securities...............	374	514	334	264	290	268	277	312	378	435
Corporate and foreign bonds...............	578	583	881	1,127	1,257	1,262	1,249	1,317	1,264	1,464
Corporate equities...............	3,178	3,931	3,646	4,708	4,808	4,711	4,912	5,744	5,188	6,281
Mutual fund shares...............	1,609	2,213	2,659	3,415	3,620	3,554	3,770	4,368	4,084	4,850
Miscellaneous assets [1]...............	2,443	3,769	6,366	7,415	7,522	7,965	8,172	7,829	8,451	7,785
Unallocated insurance contracts [3]...............	462	533	626	676	672	652	671	698	686	736
Contributions receivable...............	73	45	91	79	76	91	100	119	131	147
Claims of pension fund on sponsor [4]...............	1,734	2,965	4,984	5,867	5,948	6,411	6,498	5,988	6,536	5,720
Pension entitlements (liabilities) [5]...............	**9,699**	**12,658**	**16,049**	**19,534**	**20,250**	**20,537**	**21,323**	**22,667**	**22,756**	**24,470**
Memo:										
Defined benefit plan funded status:										
Pension entitlements, total...............	**6,798**	**8,959**	**11,534**	**13,657**	**14,082**	**14,436**	**14,808**	**15,156**	**15,525**	**15,912**
Funded by assets [6]...............	5,065	5,994	6,549	7,790	8,134	8,025	8,310	9,168	8,989	10,193
Unfunded...............	1,734	2,965	4,984	5,867	5,948	6,411	6,498	5,988	6,536	5,720
Household retirement assets, total [7]...............	**13,434**	**17,601**	**22,924**	**28,621**	**29,906**	**30,417**	**31,836**	**34,454**	**34,108**	**(NA)**
Defined benefit plans...............	6,798	8,959	11,534	13,657	14,082	14,436	14,808	15,156	15,525	15,912
Defined contribution plans...............	2,901	3,699	4,515	5,877	6,169	6,101	6,515	7,511	7,231	8,558
Individual retirement plans (IRAs) [8]...............	2,629	3,425	5,029	6,819	7,292	7,477	8,015	9,105	8,715	(NA)
Annuities at life insurance companies [9]...............	1,106	1,518	1,846	2,268	2,363	2,403	2,497	2,682	2,637	(NA)

NA Not available. [1] Includes other types of assets not shown separately. [2] Includes both marketable and nonmarketable government securities. [3] Assets of pension plans held at life insurance companies. [4] Unfunded defined benefit pension entitlements. [5] Actuarial value of accrued pension entitlements in defined benefit plans and assets of defined contribution plans. These liabilities are assets of the household sector. [6] Total defined benefit financial assets plus nonfinancial assets less claims of pension fund on sponsor. [7] Households' retirement assets in tax-deferred accounts, including employer sponsored pension plans, individual retirement accounts (IRAs), Roth IRAs, and annuities. [8] IRA assets are not included in above assets or entitlements. [9] Excludes annuities held in IRAs at life insurance companies.

Source: Board of Governors of the Federal Reserve System, "Financial Accounts of the United States, Z.1," <https://www.federalreserve.gov/data.htm>, accessed April 2020.

Table 1239. Private Pension Fund Assets by Type, and Liabilities: 2000 to 2019

[In billions of dollars (4,283 represents $4,283,000,000,000). As of December 31. Covers private defined benefit plans and defined contribution plans (including 401(k) type plans). Minus sign (-) indicates overfunding]

Type of instrument	2000	2005	2010	2014	2015	2016	2017	2018	2019
Total financial assets [1]	**4,283**	**5,391**	**6,604**	**8,675**	**8,567**	**9,052**	**9,961**	**9,691**	**10,883**
Money market fund shares	84	90	142	156	153	158	159	162	165
Debt securities [1]	596	665	867	1,210	1,176	1,232	1,391	1,511	1,770
Treasury securities	111	111	202	305	287	304	351	406	476
Agency and GSE-backed securities [2]	194	245	181	168	158	168	194	225	267
Corporate and foreign bonds	263	286	446	694	691	720	804	835	981
Corporate equities	1,823	2,288	1,778	2,284	2,220	2,330	2,713	2,364	2,912
Mutual fund shares	1,246	1,727	2,220	3,175	3,088	3,358	3,892	3,619	4,301
Miscellaneous assets [1]	387	518	1,524	1,768	1,853	1,901	1,720	1,942	1,636
Unallocated insurance contracts [3]	362	405	466	527	506	542	560	537	577
Pension entitlements (liabilities) [4]	**4,323**	**5,430**	**6,641**	**8,711**	**8,603**	**9,089**	**9,998**	**9,728**	**10,920**
Funded status of defined benefit plans:									
Pension entitlements	1,826	2,290	2,872	3,464	3,436	3,469	3,484	3,491	3,511
Funded by assets [5]	2,020	2,321	2,435	2,959	2,827	2,887	3,189	3,026	3,465
Unfunded	-193	-30	437	504	609	582	295	465	46
Defined benefit plan assets	1,785	2,251	2,836	3,427	3,400	3,433	3,447	3,454	3,474
Defined contribution plan assets	2,497	3,140	3,768	5,248	5,167	5,619	6,514	6,237	7,409

[1] Includes other types of assets not shown separately. [2] GSE=Government-sponsored enterprises. [3] Assets of private pension plans held at life insurance companies (e.g., GICs, variable annuities). [4] Actuarial value of accrued pension entitlements in defined benefit plans and assets of defined contribution plans. [5] Total defined benefit financial assets plus nonfinancial assets less claims of pension fund on sponsor.

Source: Board of Governors of the Federal Reserve System, "Financial Accounts of the United States, Z.1," <https://www.federalreserve.gov/data.htm>, accessed April 2020.

Table 1240. Public Employee Retirement Systems—Assets and Liabilities: 2000 to 2019

[In billions of dollars (3,322 represents $3,322,000,000,000). As of December 31. Includes claims of sponsor (unfunded pension entitlements). Minus sign (-) indicates overfunding]

Type of instrument	2000	2005	2010	2014	2015	2016	2017	2018	2019
STATE AND LOCAL GOVERNMENT EMPLOYEE RETIREMENT PLANS									
Total financial assets [1]	**3,322**	**4,695**	**6,169**	**7,778**	**8,089**	**8,332**	**8,678**	**8,979**	**9,328**
Debt securities [1]	721	740	765	910	881	893	955	989	1,098
Treasury securities	179	163	154	199	175	219	289	373	410
Agency and GSE-backed securities [2]	179	261	144	113	101	100	109	144	158
Corporate and foreign bonds	314	289	427	551	558	515	499	415	468
Corporate equities	1,299	1,530	1,723	2,284	2,250	2,322	2,707	2,532	2,999
Mutual fund shares	363	486	438	445	466	412	476	465	548
Miscellaneous assets [1]	846	1,852	3,150	4,033	4,385	4,577	4,434	4,884	4,563
Claims of pension fund on sponsor [3]	717	1,596	2,855	3,723	4,075	4,222	4,017	4,446	4,088
Pension entitlements (liabilities) [4]	**3,369**	**4,749**	**6,275**	**7,934**	**8,230**	**8,443**	**8,763**	**9,049**	**9,401**
Funded status of defined benefit plans:									
Pension entitlements	3,058	4,358	5,801	7,452	7,754	8,042	8,323	8,614	8,906
Funded by assets [5]	2,340	2,761	2,946	3,730	3,679	3,820	4,306	4,168	4,819
Unfunded [3]	717	1,596	2,855	3,723	4,075	4,222	4,017	4,446	4,088
Defined benefit plan assets	3,011	4,304	5,695	7,297	7,614	7,931	8,238	8,544	8,833
Defined contribution plan assets	311	391	474	482	476	401	440	435	495
FEDERAL GOVERNMENT EMPLOYEE RETIREMENT FUNDS									
Total financial assets [1]	**2,007**	**2,479**	**3,133**	**3,605**	**3,704**	**3,792**	**3,906**	**3,979**	**4,150**
Debt securities [1]	740	966	1,295	1,644	1,736	1,837	1,754	2,062	2,177
Treasury securities [6]	739	951	1,277	1,623	1,715	1,814	1,730	2,039	2,150
Corporate equities	57	113	145	240	240	261	324	292	370
Claims of pension fund on sponsor [7]	1,210	1,399	1,692	1,721	1,727	1,694	1,676	1,624	1,586
Pension entitlements (liabilities) [8]	**2,007**	**2,479**	**3,133**	**3,605**	**3,704**	**3,792**	**3,906**	**3,979**	**4,150**
Funded status of defined benefit plans:									
Pension entitlements	1,915	2,311	2,860	3,166	3,246	3,297	3,349	3,420	3,495
Funded by assets [9]	705	912	1,168	1,445	1,519	1,603	1,673	1,796	1,909
Unfunded [7]	1,210	1,399	1,692	1,721	1,727	1,694	1,676	1,624	1,586
Defined benefit plan assets [10]	1,915	2,311	2,860	3,166	3,246	3,297	3,349	3,420	3,495
Defined contribution plan assets [11]	92	168	272	440	458	495	557	559	654

[1] Includes other types of instruments not shown separately. [2] GSE=Government sponsored enterprises. [3] Unfunded defined benefit pension entitlements. [4] Actuarial value of projected pension entitlements. These liabilities are assets of the household sector. [5] Total defined benefit financial assets plus nonfinancial assets less claims of pension fund on sponsor. [6] Comprised primarily of nonmarketable Treasury securities. [7] Unfunded defined benefit pension entitlements. [8] Actuarial value of projected pension entitlements in defined benefit plans and assets of defined contribution plans. These liabilities are assets of the household sector. [9] Total defined benefit financial assets less defined benefit claims of pension fund on sponsor. [10] Includes the Civil Service Retirement and Disability Fund, Railroad Retirement Board, judicial retirement fund, Military Retirement Fund, Foreign Service Retirement and Disability Fund, and National Railroad Retirement Investment Trust. [11] Thrift Savings Plan.

Source: Board of Governors of the Federal Reserve System, "Financial Accounts of the United States, Z.1," <https://www.federalreserve.gov/data.htm>, accessed April 2020.

Table 1241. Life Insurance in Force and Purchases in the United States—Summary: 1990 to 2019

[389 represents 389,000,000. As of December 31 or calendar year, as applicable. Covers life insurance with life insurance companies, and beginning in 2003, also with fraternal benefit societies. Data represents all life insurance in force on lives of U.S. residents whether issued by U.S. or foreign companies]

Year	Number of policies, total (millions)	Life insurance in force — Value (bil. dol.)			Life insurance purchases [1] — Number (1,000)			Life insurance purchases [1] — Amount (bil. dol.)		
		Total [2]	Individual	Group	Total	Individual	Group	Total	Individual	Group
1990.......	389	9,393	5,391	3,754	28,791	14,199	14,592	1,529	1,070	459
2000.......	369	15,953	9,376	6,376	34,882	13,345	21,537	2,515	1,594	921
2005.......	373	18,399	9,970	8,263	34,519	11,407	23,112	2,836	1,796	1,040
2010.......	284	18,426	10,484	7,831	28,621	10,123	18,498	2,809	1,673	1,135
2011.......	286	19,219	10,994	8,120	27,177	10,309	16,867	2,832	1,673	1,160
2012.......	272	19,321	11,215	8,012	27,063	10,306	16,757	2,800	1,679	1,121
2013.......	275	19,662	11,365	8,215	25,264	9,929	15,336	2,779	1,640	1,139
2014.......	278	20,115	11,826	8,209	27,147	9,440	17,707	2,759	1,590	1,168
2015.......	281	20,779	12,342	8,361	28,315	10,305	18,010	2,877	1,647	1,229
2016.......	291	20,316	11,992	8,246	27,523	11,005	16,518	2,874	1,685	1,190
2017.......	289	20,416	11,927	8,411	28,035	10,478	17,557	3,027	1,712	1,316
2018.......	267	19,571	12,120	7,367	27,748	10,289	17,459	2,972	1,728	1,244
2019.......	259	19,834	12,388	7,358	31,356	10,118	21,238	3,042	1,803	1,239

[1] Excludes revivals, increases, dividend additions, and reinsurance acquired. Includes long-term credit insurance (life insurance on loans of more than 10 years' duration). [2] Includes other types of policies not shown separately such as credit.

Source: American Council of Life Insurers, Washington, DC, *Life Insurers Fact Book*, annual ©.

Table 1242. U.S. Life Insurance Companies—Summary: 2000 to 2019

[811.5 represents $811,500,000,000. As of December 31 or calendar year, as applicable. Covers domestic and foreign business of U.S. companies. Includes annual statement data for companies that primarily are health insurance companies. Beginning in 2005, includes also fraternal benefit societies]

Item	Unit	2000	2005	2010	2014	2015	2016	2017	2018	2019
U.S. companies [1]	**Number**	**1,269**	**1,119**	**917**	**830**	**814**	**797**	**781**	**773**	**761**
Income [2]	**Bil. dol.**	**811.5**	**779.0**	**862.6**	**999.4**	**1,064.7**	**985.8**	**973.4**	**1,008.2**	**1,094.4**
Life insurance premiums	Bil. dol.	130.6	142.3	104.6	138.3	155.9	119.3	141.8	150.2	156.6
Annuity considerations [3]	Bil. dol.	306.7	277.1	293.6	361.6	333.0	326.8	294.9	279.3	347.5
Health insurance premiums	Bil. dol.	105.6	118.3	172.7	158.4	159.9	164.0	170.5	185.4	188.1
Investment and other [4]	Bil. dol.	268.5	241.4	291.6	341.1	416.0	375.7	366.3	393.3	402.2
Payments under life insurance and annuity contracts	Bil. dol.	375.2	365.7	365.6	443.8	447.7	443.0	490.1	536.9	530.3
Payments to life insurance beneficiaries	Bil. dol.	44.1	53.0	58.4	67.9	74.3	76.0	77.1	79.7	78.4
Surrender values under life insurance [5]	Bil. dol.	27.2	39.2	35.8	27.8	28.8	30.2	33.2	35.3	34.1
Surrender values under annuity contracts [5, 6]	Bil. dol.	214.0	190.3	184.1	256.7	247.2	238.0	279.4	319.1	310.4
Policyholder dividends	Bil. dol.	20.0	17.9	15.9	16.7	18.5	18.4	17.7	18.4	18.2
Annuity payments [6]	Bil. dol.	68.7	63.9	70.1	73.8	77.8	79.1	81.6	83.4	88.1
Matured endowments	Bil. dol.	0.6	0.6	0.6	0.4	0.4	0.4	0.5	0.4	0.4
Other payments	Bil. dol.	0.6	0.7	0.7	0.7	0.7	0.7	0.6	0.7	0.7
Health insurance benefit payments	Bil. dol.	78.8	79.6	122.5	113.6	115.3	119.8	126.7	132.2	141.6
BALANCE SHEET										
Assets	**Bil. dol.**	**3,182**	**4,482**	**5,311**	**6,406**	**6,478**	**6,772**	**7,183**	**6,993**	**7,567**
Mortgage-backed securities	Bil. dol.	(NA)	(NA)	631	567	556	568	568	576	564
Government bonds	Bil. dol.	364	590	413	479	496	522	547	475	485
Corporate securities	Bil. dol.	2,238	3,136	3,271	4,133	4,150	4,313	4,627	4,441	4,887
Bonds	Bil. dol.	1,241	1,850	1,700	2,061	2,150	2,257	2,365	2,441	2,589
Stocks	Bil. dol.	997	1,285	1,570	2,072	2,001	2,056	2,262	2,000	2,298
Mortgages	Bil. dol.	237	295	327	395	437	472	514	565	615
Real estate	Bil. dol.	36	33	28	32	44	47	43	39	42
Policy loans	Bil. dol.	102	110	127	133	135	135	137	137	134
Other	Bil. dol.	204	319	515	666	659	715	749	760	841
Interest earned on assets [7]	Percent	7.05	4.90	4.33	4.61	4.81	4.50	4.28	4.72	4.57
Obligations and surplus funds [8]	Bil. dol.	3,182	4,482	5,311	6,406	6,478	6,772	7,183	6,993	7,567
Policy reserves	**Bil. dol.**	**2,712**	**3,360**	**4,098**	**4,956**	**5,025**	**5,232**	**5,542**	**5,375**	**5,788**
Annuities [9]	Bil. dol.	1,875	2,189	2,660	3,299	3,320	3,467	3,701	3,554	3,880
Group	Bil. dol.	960	758	863	1,050	1,022	1,053	1,129	1,079	1,179
Individual	Bil. dol.	881	1,415	1,780	2,228	2,276	2,391	2,548	2,449	2,675
Supplementary contracts [10]	Bil. dol.	34	16	17	22	23	23	24	25	26
Life insurance	Bil. dol.	742	1,029	1,224	1,423	1,463	1,500	1,563	1,574	1,650
Health insurance	Bil. dol.	96	141	214	234	242	264	279	247	257
Liabilities for deposit-type contracts [11]	Bil. dol.	21	456	420	468	470	495	530	524	572
Capital and surplus	Bil. dol.	188	256	319	368	383	398	413	419	441

NA Not available. [1] Includes life insurance companies that sell accident and health insurance. [2] Premiums are net of reinsurance business and fluctuate with reinsurance activities as well as sale changes. [3] Beginning 2005, excludes certain deposit-type funds from income due to codification. [4] Investment represents gross investment income. [5] "Surrender values" include annuity withdrawals of funds. [6] Beginning 2005, excludes payments under deposit-type contracts. [7] Net rate. [8] Includes other obligations not shown separately. [9] Beginning 2005, excludes reserves for guaranteed interest contracts (GICs). [10] Data for 2000 include reserves for contracts with and without life contingencies; beginning 2005, includes only reserves for contracts with life contingencies. [11] Policyholder dividend accumulations for all years. Beginning 2005, also includes liabilities for guaranteed interest contracts, supplementary contracts without life contingencies, and premium and other deposits.

Source: American Council of Life Insurers, Washington, DC, *Life Insurers Fact Book*, annual ©.

Table 1243. Automobile Insurance—Average Expenditures Per Insured Vehicle by State: 2014 to 2017

[In dollars. Average expenditure equals total premiums written divided by liability car-years. A car-year is equal to 365 days of insured coverage for a single vehicle. The average expenditures for automobile insurance in a state are affected by a number of factors, including the underlying rate structure, the coverages purchased, the deductibles and limits selected, the types of vehicles insured, and the distribution of driver characteristics. The National Association of Insurance Commissioners does not rank state average expenditures and does not endorse any conclusions drawn from these data]

State	2014	2015	2016	2017	State	2014	2015	2016	2017
U.S.	**866**	**889**	**935**	**1,005**	MO	724	745	791	869
AL	695	723	769	857	MT	695	692	707	785
AK	884	872	859	930	NE	663	682	708	767
AZ	837	844	891	994	NV	970	990	1,026	1,141
AR	729	736	772	848	NH	751	775	802	824
CA[1]	815	841	893	957	NJ[4]	1264	1,266	1,309	1,350
CO	821	858	935	1,050	NM	749	762	781	870
CT	1,032	1,049	1,086	1,168	NY	1205	1,235	1,302	1,350
DE	1,126	1,146	1,160	1,221	NC	644	655	700	706
DC[2]	1,192	1,202	1,247	1,334	ND	630	638	639	660
FL	1,141	1,185	1,260	1,357	OH	683	703	727	778
GA	840	896	966	1,127	OK	808	826	851	895
HI	752	763	782	803	OR	819	828	877	961
ID	572	574	600	679	PA	858	878	918	961
IL	775	804	837	897	RI	1106	1,147	1,194	1,301
IN	642	667	692	744	SC	825	854	923	1,020
IA	586	599	628	674	SD	601	616	648	693
KS	689	698	714	766	TN	725	737	760	821
KY	783	802	839	896	TX	906	934	1,009	1,097
LA	1,193	1,232	1,302	1,444	UT	766	784	824	890
ME	607	618	650	667	VT	665	680	692	763
MD	1,001	1,017	1,077	1,149	VA	743	751	786	820
MA[3]	1,036	1,059	1,097	1,137	WA	872	884	924	994
MI	1,227	1,231	1,271	1,359	WV	871	855	870	913
MN	773	788	808	840	WI	646	665	688	731
MS	797	827	859	930	WY	669	657	678	742

[1] The California Department of Insurance performs a rigorous set of tests on the data each year to ensure accuracy. The tests are not completed until after the publication of the source report. [2] The District of Columbia is entirely urban. As such, results are not directly comparable to states with large rural areas. [3] Data incorporates Safe Driver Plan credits and surcharges. [4] New Jersey is predominantly urban. Results are not directly comparable to states with large rural areas. Historically, New Jersey has paid two to four times the national average in dividends to policyholders, and at times this has been as high as six times the national average, which reduces the average expenditure for New Jersey consumers.

Source: National Association of Insurance Commissioners (NAIC), Kansas City, MO, *Auto Insurance Database Report*, annual ©. Reprinted with permission of the NAIC. Further reprint or distribution strictly prohibited without prior written permission of the NAIC.

Table 1244. Renters and Homeowners Insurance—Average Premiums by State: 2017

[In dollars. Average premium equals premiums divided by exposure per house-years. A house-year is equal to 365 days of insured coverage for a single dwelling and is the standard measurement for homeowners insurance. The National Association of Insurance Commissioners does not rank state average expenditures and does not endorse any conclusions drawn from these data]

State	Renters[1]	Home-owners[2]	State	Renters[1]	Home-owners[2]	State	Renters[1]	Home-owners[2]	State	Renters[1]	Home-owners[2]
U.S.	**180**	**1,211**	ID	153	730	MO	173	1,285	PA	158	931
AL	235	1,433	IL	167	1,056	MT	146	1,174	RI	182	1,551
AK	166	959	IN	174	1,000	NE	143	1,481	SC	188	1,269
AZ	178	825	IA	144	964	NV	178	755	SD	123	1,202
AR	212	1,373	KS	172	1,584	NH	149	972	TN	199	1,196
CA	182	1,008	KY	168	1,109	NJ	165	1,192	TX[3]	232	1,893
CO	159	1,495	LA	235	1,968	NM	187	1,017	UT	151	692
CT	192	1,479	ME	149	882	NY	194	1,309	VT	155	918
DE	159	833	MD	161	1,037	NC	157	1,086	VA	152	999
DC	158	1,235	MA	194	1,488	ND	120	1,253	WA	163	854
FL	188	1,951	MI	182	942	OH	175	862	WV	188	940
GA	219	1,267	MN	140	1,348	OK	236	1,885	WI	134	779
HI	185	1,102	MS	258	1,537	OR	163	677	WY	147	1,156

[1] Based on the HO-4 renters insurance policy for tenants. Includes broad named-peril coverage for the personal property of tenants. [2] Based on the HO-3 homeowner package policy for owner-occupied dwellings, 1–4 family units. Provides "all risks" coverage (except those specifically excluded in the policy) on buildings, broad named-peril coverage on personal property, and is the most common package written. [3] The Texas Insurance Commissioner promulgates residential policy forms which are similar but not identical to the standard forms.

Source: National Association of Insurance Commissioners (NAIC), Kansas City, MO, *Dwelling Fire, Homeowners Owner-Occupied, and Homeowners Tenant and Condominium/Cooperative Unit Owners Insurance* ©. Reprinted with permission of the NAIC. Further reprint or distribution strictly prohibited without prior written permission of the NAIC.

Table 1245. Real Estate and Rental and Leasing—Nonemployer Establishments and Receipts by Kind of Business: 2010 to 2018

[2,343.1 represents 2,343,100. Includes only firms subject to federal income tax. Nonemployers are businesses with no paid employees. Data originate chiefly from administrative records of the Internal Revenue Service; see Appendix III]

Kind of business	NAICS code [1]	Establishments (1,000)			Receipts (mil. dol.)		
		2010	2015	2018	2010	2015	2018
Real estate & rental & leasing, total..........................	**53**	**2,343.1**	**2,635.8**	**2,876.3**	**209,549**	**259,768**	**289,866**
Real estate....................	531	2,262.2	2,552.5	2,790.4	203,065	252,450	282,014
Lessors of real estate............................	5311	989.3	1,156.2	1,219.7	135,015	158,624	172,191
Offices of real estate agents & brokers.........................	5312	641.6	694.7	797.9	25,502	38,904	45,732
Activities related to real estate........................	5313	631.3	701.6	772.8	42,549	54,922	64,091
Rental & leasing services................................	532	78.9	80.2	83.0	6,288	7,024	7,552
Automotive equipment rental & leasing....................	5321	18.3	18.6	21.1	990	1,171	1,296
Consumer goods rental.......................	5322	18.3	19.1	18.7	779	887	830
General rental centers........................	5323	4.8	6.5	7.2	409	519	618
Commercial/industrial equipment rental & leasing..............	5324	37.5	36.0	36.0	4,109	4,448	4,808
Lessors of other nonfinancial intangible assets..................	533	2.0	3.1	2.8	197	293	299

[1] Data for 2010 based on 2007 North American Industry Classification System (NAICS); data for 2015 based on 2012 NAICS; data for 2018 based on 2017 NAICS. For more information, see text, Section 15.

Source: U.S. Census Bureau, Nonemployer Statistics, "All Sectors: Nonemployer Statistics for the U.S., States, Counties, Metropolitan Areas, and Combined Statistical Areas; and by Legal Form of Organization and Sales, Value of Shipments, or Revenue Size for Selected Geographies: 2018," <data.census.gov>, accessed May 2020.

Table 1246. Real Estate and Rental and Leasing—Establishments, Employees, and Payroll: 2016 and 2017

[390.5 represents 390,500. Covers establishments with payroll. Data for 2016 based on the North American Industry Classification System (NAICS) 2012; data for 2017 based on NAICS 2017; see text, section 15, Business Enterprise. Employees are for the week including March 12. Most government employees are excluded. For statement on methodology, see Appendix III]

Kind of business	NAICS code	Establishments (1,000)		Employees (1,000)		Payroll (bil. dol.)	
		2016	2017	2016	2017	2016	2017
Real estate & rental & leasing, total..........................	**53**	**390.5**	**406.6**	**2,111.4**	**2,148.0**	**110.5**	**115.7**
Real estate....................	531	334.3	349.3	1,563.0	1,606.9	82.5	86.4
Lessors of real estate............................	5311	127.1	129.9	576.6	587.4	26.7	28.1
Offices of real estate agents & brokers.........................	5312	110.9	122.2	306.5	324.1	20.4	20.8
Activities related to real estate [1]............................	5313	96.3	97.2	679.9	695.4	35.4	37.6
Residential property managers..........................	531311	49.4	49.7	439.4	448.2	18.8	19.7
Rental & leasing services................................	532	53.7	54.5	512.4	502.6	24.3	25.2
Automotive equipment rental & leasing......................	5321	16.4	16.4	167.1	160.8	7.0	7.0
Passenger car rental & leasing........................	53211	10.7	10.5	101.2	104.1	3.9	4.2
Truck, utility trailer & RV rental & leasing................	53212	5.7	5.9	65.9	56.7	3.2	2.9
Consumer goods rental [1]...........................	5322	19.6	19.6	146.2	135.2	5.1	4.8
Consumer electronics and appliances rental.................	53221	6.8	7.0	39.8	33.3	1.3	1.2
Other consumer goods rental..........................	53228	(NA)	12.6	(NA)	102.0	(NA)	3.7
Video tape & disc rental..........................	532282	(NA)	1.7	(NA)	11.3	(NA)	0.2
Home health equipment rental......................	532283	(NA)	2.7	(NA)	28.8	(NA)	1.2
Recreational goods rental.........................	532284	(NA)	2.3	(NA)	10.3	(NA)	0.4
General rental centers........................	5323	2.8	3.0	19.6	20.5	0.8	0.9
Commercial/industrial equipment rental & leasing [1]..........	5324	14.9	15.5	179.5	186.0	11.4	12.4
Construction, transportation, and mining equipment.........	53241	5.1	5.3	62.7	63.8	4.6	5.1
Lessors of other nonfinancial intangible assets..................	533	2.6	2.8	36.0	38.6	3.7	4.1

NA Not available. [1] Includes industries not shown separately.

Source: U.S. Census Bureau, County Business Patterns, "County Business Patterns by Legal Form of Organization and Employment Size Class for U.S., States, and Selected Geographies," <http://data.census.gov>, accessed December 2019. See also <https://www.census.gov/programs-surveys/cbp.html>.

Table 1247. Real Estate and Rental and Leasing Services—Revenue by Kind of Business: 2013 to 2018

[In millions of dollars (523,255 represents $523,255,000,000). Covers taxable and tax-exempt employer firms. Data are based on the 2012 North American Industry Classification System (NAICS). See text, this section and Section 15. Estimates have been adjusted using the results of the 2012 Economic Census. Based on Service Annual Survey; see Appendix III]

Kind of business	NAICS code	2013	2014	2015	2016	2017	2018
Real estate and rental and leasing, total....................	**53**	**523,255**	**564,613**	**602,846**	**636,015**	**668,219**	**707,520**
Real estate [1]....................	531	351,972	380,860	410,457	439,880	463,158	484,439
Lessors of residential buildings and dwellings..................	53111	91,448	98,130	105,318	111,469	116,345	118,414
Lessors of nonresidential buildings (excl. miniwarehouses)...	53112	100,759	107,747	114,499	119,560	124,733	129,709
Offices of real estate agents and brokers.........................	5312	75,928	84,199	92,869	102,395	108,378	117,420
Real estate property managers........................	53131	50,670	55,574	59,429	65,408	69,193	72,555
Offices of real estate appraisers.....................	53132	5,734	5,464	5,881	6,571	6,545	6,154
Rental and leasing services [1]........................	532	135,753	145,799	152,544	154,604	159,914	173,748
Passenger car rental.....................	532111	25,957	27,295	28,194	29,334	30,024	31,806
Passenger car leasing........................	532112	8,136	8,610	9,050	9,472	10,230	11,327
Truck, trailer, and recreational vehicle rental and leasing.....	53212	15,941	16,933	18,082	19,172	19,799	22,458
Consumer electronics and appliances rental..................	53221	6,809	7,462	7,991	8,049	8,055	8,449
Construction/transportation/mining equipment rental and leasing..................	53241	32,837	36,285	36,201	34,426	37,741	41,845
Lessors of other nonfinancial intangible assets..................	533	35,530	37,954	39,845	41,531	45,147	49,333

[1] Includes other kinds of business, not shown separately.

Source: U.S. Census Bureau, Service Annual Survey, "Service Annual Survey Latest Data (NAICS-basis): 2018," <https://www.census.gov/programs-surveys/sas/data.html>, accessed December 2019.

Section 26
Arts, Recreation, and Travel

This section presents data on the arts, entertainment, and recreation economic sector of the economy, and personal recreational activities, the arts and humanities, and domestic and foreign travel.

Arts, entertainment, and recreation industry—The U.S. Census Bureau surveys—County Business Patterns, Economic Census, Nonemployer Statistics, and Service Annual Survey—provide data on the arts, entertainment, and recreation sector. The County Business Patterns' annual data include number of establishments, number of employees, first quarter and annual payrolls, and number of establishments by employment size class. The Economic Census, conducted every five years for the years ending in '2' and '7', provides information on the number of establishments, receipts, payroll, and paid employees for the United States and various geographic levels. Data from the 2012 Economic Census have been fully released on <data.census.gov>. Data from the 2017 Economic Census are being released on a flow basis between September 2019 and December 2021. Nonemployer Statistics is an annual tabulation of economic data by industry for active businesses that are subject to federal income tax and that do not have paid employees. The Service Annual Survey provides estimates of operating revenue of taxable firms and revenues and expenses of firms exempt from federal taxes for industries in this sector of the economy. See Appendix III for more details.

Recreation and leisure activities—Data on the participation in various recreation and leisure time activities are based on several sample surveys. Data on the public's involvement with arts events and activities are published by the National Endowment for Arts (NEA). The NEA's Survey of Public Participation in the Arts remains the largest periodic study of arts participation in the United States. The most recent data are from the 2017 survey. Data on participation in fishing, hunting, and other forms of wildlife associated recreation are published periodically by the U.S. Department of Interior, Fish and Wildlife Service in The National Survey of Fishing, Hunting, and Wildlife-Associated Recreation. The most recent data are from the 2016 survey. Data on participation in various sports recreation activities are published by the National Sporting Goods Association. MRI-Simmons (launched as joint venture under GfK in 2019) also conducts periodic surveys on sports and leisure activities, as well as other topics.

Parks and recreation—The Department of the Interior has responsibility for administering the national parks. The National Park Service publishes information on visits to national park areas in its annual report, *National Park Statistical Abstract*. Additional data regarding acreage and visits for each area administered by the service can be found at <irma.nps.gov/Stats/>. Statistics for state parks are compiled by the National Association of State Park Directors in its annual *Statistical Report of State Park Operations*.

Travel—Statistics on arrivals and departures to the United States, cities and states visited by overseas travelers, and tourism sales and employment, are reported by the International Trade Administration (ITA), Office of Travel & Tourism Industries (OTTI). Data on domestic travel and travel expenditures are published by the research department of the U.S. Travel Association. Other data on household transportation characteristics are in Section 23, Transportation.

Statistical reliability—For a discussion of statistical collection and estimation, sampling procedures, and measures of statistical reliability applicable to Census Bureau data, see Appendix III.

Table 1248. Arts, Entertainment, and Recreation Services—Estimated Revenue: 2010 to 2018

[In millions of dollars (188,117 represents $188,117,000,000). For taxable and tax-exempt employer firms. Data for 2010 are based on the 2007 North American Industry Classification System (NAICS); beginning 2013, data are based on 2012 NAICS. Selected estimates have been adjusted using the results of the 2012 Economic Census. Based on the Service Annual Survey, see Appendix III]

Kind of business	NAICS Code	2010	2014	2015	2016	2017	2018
Arts, entertainment, and recreation.............	71	188,117	223,154	237,482	249,736	266,877	281,034
Performing arts, spectator sports, and related industries.....................................	711	80,461	96,483	104,698	110,408	119,277	127,403
Performing arts companies.............................	7111	13,814	14,332	15,263	15,967	17,127	18,037
Sports teams and clubs...............................	711211	21,442	26,668	28,979	31,232	34,309	36,106
Racetracks..	711212	6,951	7,238	7,596	7,558	7,839	7,869
Other spectator sports................................	711219	3,344	3,358	3,520	3,662	3,701	3,769
Promoters of performing arts, sports, and similar events..	7113	16,312	22,020	24,538	26,168	28,587	31,024
Agents and managers for artists, athletes, entertainers and other public figures..............	7114	5,358	6,674	7,322	7,868	8,045	8,759
Independent artists, writers, and performers.......	7115	13,240	16,193	17,480	17,953	19,669	21,839
Museums, historical sites, and similar institutions. ..	712	14,241	15,900	15,168	15,191	17,167	16,773
Amusement, gambling, and recreation industries. ..	713	93,415	110,771	117,616	124,137	130,433	136,858
Amusement and theme parks........................	71311	10,205	14,694	16,252	17,144	17,945	19,171
Amusement arcades...................................	71312	1,627	1,680	1,823	2,028	2,426	2,703
Casinos (except casino hotels)......................	71321	15,367	17,094	18,323	18,868	19,159	19,846
Other gambling industries............................	71329	8,065	9,513	9,600	10,251	11,737	12,644
Golf courses and country clubs.....................	71391	19,788	21,224	21,821	22,432	22,940	23,698
Skiing facilities...	71392	2,265	2,530	2,571	2,973	3,367	3,560
Marinas..	71393	3,604	4,203	4,291	4,377	4,606	4,972
Fitness and recreational sports centers.............	71394	22,311	26,673	28,319	30,456	31,920	32,987
Bowling centers..	71395	3,007	3,403	3,629	3,831	3,966	4,209
All other amusement and recreation industries.....	71399	7,176	9,757	10,987	11,777	12,367	13,068

Source: U.S. Census Bureau, Service Annual Survey, "Service Annual Survey Latest Data (NAICS-basis): 2018," <https://www.census.gov/programs-surveys/sas/data.html>, accessed February 2020.

Table 1249. Arts, Entertainment, and Recreation—Establishments, Revenue, Payroll, and Employees by Kind of Business: 2017

[265,620 represents $265,620,000,000). Definition of paid employees varies among NAICS sectors. Data are based on the 2017 Economic Census which is subject to nonsampling error. For details on survey methodology, sampling and nonsampling errors, see Appendix III]

Kind of business	NAICS code [1]	Number of establishments	Revenue (mil. dol.)	Annual payroll (mil. dol.)	Paid employees (1,000)
Arts, entertainment, and recreation, total..	71	142,938	265,620	82,256	2,390
Performing arts, spectator sports, and related industries [2].............................	711	53,613	119,507	41,237	489
Performing arts companies.............................	7111	8,836	16,157	4,552	121
Spectator sports..	7112	3,900	46,201	21,624	130
Promoters of performing arts, sports and similar events..	7113	8,072	29,367	4,984	167
Agents and managers for artists, athletes, entertainers and other public figures....................	7114	4,111	7,868	2,408	22
Independent artists, writers, and performers...........	7115	28,694	19,914	7,669	49
Museums, historical sites, and similar institutions [2]......................................	712	7,557	19,631	5,414	158
Amusement, gambling, and recreation industries [2]......................................	713	81,768	126,481	35,605	1,743
Amusement parks and arcades........................	7131	4,317	21,392	5,140	226
Gambling industries...................................	7132	3,038	25,584	4,469	135
Other amusement and recreation services..	7139	74,413	79,505	25,996	1,383

[1] Based on 2017 North American Industry Classification System (NAICS); see text, this section and section 15. [2] Includes other industries not shown separately.

Source: U.S. Census Bureau, 2017 Economic Census, EC1771BASIC, "Arts, Entertainment, and Recreation: Summary Statistics for the U.S., States, and Selected Geographies: 2017," <http://data.census.gov/>, accessed August 2020.

Table 1250. Arts, Entertainment, and Recreation—Nonemployer Establishments and Receipts by Kind of Business (NAICS Basis): 2010 to 2018

[Firms in thousands (1,154.0 represents 1,154,000); receipts in millions of dollars (26,756 represents $26,756,000,000). Includes only firms subject to federal income tax. Nonemployers are businesses with no paid employees but with annual receipts of $1,000 or more]

Kind of business	NAICS code [1]	Firms (1,000)			Receipts (mil. dol.)		
		2010	2015	2018	2010	2015	2018
Arts, entertainment, and recreation.	**71**	**1,154.0**	**1,341.7**	**1,513.7**	**26,756**	**34,549**	**40,346**
Performing arts, spectator sports, and related industries.	711	1,004.9	1,177.3	1,351.2	21,053	27,590	32,897
Performing arts companies.	7111	61.2	93.8	90.1	1,249	1,832	2,033
Spectator sports.	7112	151.9	169.8	213.9	2,515	3,242	3,887
Promoters of performing arts, sports, and similar events.	7113	45.0	55.9	68.2	1,699	2,467	2,861
Agents/managers for artists, athletes, and other public figures.	7114	36.3	38.5	36.9	1,300	1,678	1,872
Independent artists, writers, and performers.	7115	710.3	819.2	942.0	14,290	18,371	22,244
Museums, historical sites, and similar institutions.	712	5.8	6.5	6.1	95	122	125
Amusement, gambling, and recreation industries.	713	143.4	158.0	156.5	5,607	6,837	7,323
Amusement parks and arcades.	7131	4.7	4.3	4.2	251	248	260
Gambling industries.	7132	10.2	10.5	11.9	1,185	1,325	1,559
Other amusement and recreation services.	7139	128.5	143.2	140.4	4,171	5,265	5,505

[1] Data for 2010 are based on 2007 North American Industry Classification System; 2015 data are based on the 2012 NAICS; 2018 data are based on the 2017 NAICS. See text, Section 15.

Source: U.S. Census Bureau, Nonemployer Statistics, "NES Datasets," <https://www.census.gov/programs-surveys/nonemployer-statistics/data/datasets.html>, accessed May 2020.

Table 1251. Arts, Entertainment, and Recreation—Establishments, Employees, and Payroll by Kind of Business (NAICS Basis): 2017 and 2018

[Employees in thousands (2,368.9 represents 2,368,900); payroll in millions of dollars (84,169 represents $84,169,000,000). Covers establishments with paid employees. Excludes self-employed individuals, employees of private households, railroad employees, agricultural production employees, and most government employees. For statement on methodology, see Appendix III]

Kind of business	NAICS code [1]	Establishments		Employees [2] (1,000)		Payroll (mil. dol.)	
		2017	2018	2017	2018	2017	2018
Arts, entertainment, & recreation.	**71**	**143,396**	**147,122**	**2,368.9**	**2,435.6**	**84,169**	**88,195**
Performing arts, spectator sports.	711	54,245	56,503	508.3	524.8	42,972	45,179
Performing arts companies.	7111	9,066	9,216	125.0	122.7	4,689	4,916
Theater companies & dinner theaters.	71111	3,276	3,392	68.4	67.5	2,151	2,284
Dance companies.	71112	632	656	10.1	10.6	297	310
Musical groups & artists.	71113	4,857	4,935	39.1	38.0	1,902	2,025
Other performing arts companies.	71119	301	233	7.4	6.6	339	297
Spectator sports.	7112	4,139	4,103	127.3	131.8	22,129	23,422
Sports teams & clubs.	711211	944	878	74.6	78.4	19,923	21,168
Racetracks.	711212	608	570	36.8	37.7	1,220	1,273
Other spectator sports.	711219	2,587	2,655	15.9	15.7	986	981
Promoters of performing arts, sports, & similar events.	7113	8,104	8,120	184.2	194.8	5,207	5,516
Promoters of performing arts, sports, & similar events with facilities.	71131	3,524	3,552	150.2	157.8	3,564	3,782
Promoters of performing arts, sports, & similar events without facilities.	71132	4,580	4,568	34.0	37.0	1,643	1,734
Agents/managers for artists, athletes, and other public figures.	7114	4,150	4,268	21.6	22.4	2,521	2,687
Independent artists, writers, & performers.	7115	28,786	30,796	50.2	53.1	8,425	8,638
Museums, historical sites, & similar institutions.	712	7,654	7,736	154.4	157.8	5,330	5,531
Museums.	71211	5,270	5,284	97.4	96.6	3,468	3,494
Historical sites.	71212	1,036	1,104	9.5	12.5	271	372
Zoos & botanical gardens.	71213	650	668	39.1	40.9	1,302	1,378
Nature parks & other similar institutions.	71219	698	680	8.4	7.8	289	288
Amusement, gambling, & recreation industries.	713	81,497	82,883	1,706.2	1,752.9	35,867	37,485
Amusement parks & arcades.	7131	4,349	3,880	213.2	229.1	4,814	5,335
Amusement & theme parks.	71311	499	472	164.4	162.6	4,127	4,231
Amusement arcades.	71312	3,850	3,408	48.8	66.4	687	1,104
Gambling industries.	7132	3,059	3,094	141.6	134.8	4,825	4,712
Casinos (except casino hotels).	71321	292	276	89.4	82.9	3,092	3,007
Other gambling industries.	71329	2,767	2,818	52.2	51.9	1,733	1,705
Other amusement & recreation services.	7139	74,089	75,909	1,351.4	1,389.1	26,228	27,438
Golf courses & country clubs.	71391	10,853	10,711	302.3	301.2	9,287	9,507
Skiing facilities.	71392	364	337	71.1	69.3	912	921
Marinas.	71393	3,669	3,732	26.8	29.0	1,051	1,178
Fitness & recreational sports centers.	71394	36,525	37,758	727.2	757.4	10,577	11,159
Bowling centers.	71395	3,616	3,651	71.7	69.2	1,105	1,131
All other amusement & recreation industries.	71399	19,062	19,720	152.3	163.1	3,296	3,543

[1] Data based on 2017 North American Industry Classification System (NAICS) see text, this section and Section 15. [2] For employees on the payroll for the period including March 12.

Source: U.S. Census Bureau, County Business Patterns, "All Sectors: County Business Patterns by Legal Form of Organization and Employment Size Class for U.S., States, and Selected Geographies," <http://data.census.gov/>, accessed August 2020.

Table 1252. Arts and Culture Production—Real Value Added In Chained (2009) Dollars and Employment by Industry: 2010 to 2017

[Value in millions of dollars (676,495 represents $676,495,000,000); employment in thousands (4,716 represents 4,716,000)]

Industry	2010	2013	2014	2015	2016	2017
REAL VALUE ADDED, CHAINED (2012) DOLLARS (Million dollars)						
Total	**676,495**	**713,345**	**726,389**	**758,422**	**798,287**	**827,490**
Core arts and cultural production	**136,818**	**151,323**	**159,039**	**159,832**	**158,854**	**163,183**
Performing arts	52,727	60,103	63,292	62,136	61,702	63,784
Performing arts companies	12,461	12,534	12,887	12,104	12,444	12,341
Promoters of performing arts and similar events	9,616	11,811	12,704	11,623	12,466	12,928
Agents/managers for artists	3,035	3,948	4,185	3,906	4,099	4,232
Independent artists, writers, and performers	27,606	31,807	33,510	34,543	32,657	34,250
Museums	5,696	7,711	7,939	6,583	6,864	6,919
Design services [1]	69,793	75,281	79,324	82,493	81,536	83,823
Advertising	26,950	26,559	27,572	28,535	28,507	29,448
Architectural services	14,157	16,426	17,593	18,590	18,861	19,841
Landscape architectural services	2,161	2,411	2,516	2,520	2,478	2,495
Interior design services	7,230	8,606	9,370	10,016	9,317	9,152
Industrial design services	1,286	1,616	1,698	1,779	1,662	1,537
Graphic design services	6,940	7,443	7,819	8,203	8,099	7,999
Computer systems design	2,081	2,881	3,105	3,375	3,745	4,234
Photography and photofinishing services	8,355	8,386	8,594	8,404	7,806	8,272
Fine arts education	2,789	2,011	2,132	2,127	2,137	2,113
Education services	5,856	6,218	6,358	6,570	6,669	6,609
Supporting arts and cultural production	**519,072**	**543,498**	**547,932**	**578,660**	**619,375**	**644,496**
Art support services [1]	101,813	97,540	97,307	97,599	98,138	98,714
Rental and leasing	5,337	4,226	4,119	4,632	4,838	4,736
Grant-making and giving services	776	773	793	858	848	881
Unions	1,080	1,145	1,109	1,131	1,108	1,193
Government	94,332	91,140	91,016	90,708	91,067	91,578
Information services [1]	321,680	353,116	356,089	385,127	424,152	445,641
Publishing	77,184	79,652	79,977	83,541	88,702	92,691
Motion pictures	77,513	70,848	70,279	74,973	75,034	75,199
Sound recording	12,563	10,998	11,437	12,881	13,707	14,429
Broadcasting	121,194	133,595	128,527	133,492	134,416	132,463
Manufacturing [1]	15,177	15,036	15,616	14,813	14,645	14,840
Jewelry and silverware manufacturing	3,281	2,424	3,016	2,391	2,324	2,592
Printed goods manufacturing	7,035	7,131	6,834	6,342	6,179	5,999
Musical instruments manufacturing	721	702	671	642	675	646
Custom architectural woodwork & metalwork manufacturing	2,139	2,532	2,548	2,644	2,680	2,719
Construction	15,366	10,718	11,015	11,855	13,072	13,689
Wholesale and transportation industries	30,566	32,177	32,353	33,349	33,021	33,894
Retail industries	34,557	35,023	35,699	36,603	37,936	39,820
All other industries	**20,637**	**18,530**	**19,395**	**19,991**	**20,370**	**20,219**
EMPLOYMENT (1,000s)						
Total	**4,716**	**4,801**	**4,888**	**4,974**	**5,064**	**5,108**
Core arts and cultural production	**1,012**	**1,100**	**1,152**	**1,181**	**1,215**	**1,241**
Performing arts	241	261	278	280	290	300
Performing arts companies	108	111	115	116	119	122
Promoters of performing arts and similar events	78	87	97	99	105	112
Agents/managers for artists	10	12	12	13	14	15
Independent artists, writers, and performers	45	51	54	53	52	51
Museums	118	129	135	138	145	149
Design services [1]	483	519	538	554	563	567
Advertising	131	159	169	172	174	175
Architectural services	117	119	125	131	136	140
Landscape architectural services	30	29	32	33	32	32
Interior design services	28	32	35	37	39	42
Industrial design services	12	14	14	17	17	19
Graphic design services	58	59	60	60	61	61
Computer systems design	17	20	21	22	23	24
Photography and photofinishing services	84	78	74	72	69	66
Fine arts education	88	103	109	115	121	126
Education services	81	88	91	95	96	99
Supporting arts and cultural production	**3,539**	**3,551**	**3,580**	**3,633**	**3,685**	**3,704**
Art support services [1]	1,284	1,246	1,244	1,241	1,241	1,250
Rental and leasing	38	24	21	20	20	19
Grant-making and giving services	7	8	9	9	9	9
Unions	18	23	22	24	21	24
Government	1,218	1,188	1,189	1,185	1,188	1,195
Information services [1]	1,198	1,257	1,273	1,311	1,348	1,346
Publishing	337	317	315	323	319	312
Motion pictures	347	357	358	380	413	410
Sound recording	17	16	16	16	17	17
Broadcasting	405	443	448	441	439	431
Manufacturing [1]	171	176	175	175	175	173
Jewelry and silverware manufacturing	21	27	26	26	25	23
Printed goods manufacturing	91	83	80	77	75	73
Musical instruments manufacturing	9	10	10	10	10	10
Custom architectural woodwork & metalwork manufacturing	29	34	33	36	38	39
Construction	127	98	104	113	122	128
Wholesale and transportation industries	197	206	203	205	205	207
Retail industries	561	568	580	588	594	600
All other industries	**166**	**149**	**156**	**160**	**164**	**163**

[1] Includes other services or goods manufacturing, not shown separately.

Source: U.S. Bureau of Economic Analysis, "Arts and Cultural Production Satellite Account," <https://www.bea.gov/data/special-topics/arts-and-culture>, accessed March 2020.

Table 1253. Arts and Cultural Production—Summary by State: 2017

[In millions of dollars (877,809 represents $877,809,000,000), except employment (5,108 represents 5,108,000). Arts and cultural production is defined narrowly to include creative artistic activity; the goods and services produced by it; the goods and services produced in the support of it; and the construction of buildings in which it is taking place]

State	Total arts and cultural production industries [1]			Core arts and cultural production industries			Supporting arts and cultural production industries		
	Value added (mil. dol.) [2]	Employ-ment (1,000)	Compen-sation (mil. dol.)	Value added (mil. dol.) [2]	Employ-ment (1,000)	Compen-sation (mil. dol.)	Value added (mil. dol.) [2]	Employ-ment (1,000)	Compen-sation (mil. dol.)
Total..............	877,809	5,108	404,854	179,010	1,241	81,559	676,695	3,704	311,967
Alabama............	4,875	47	2,532	718	9	350	3,891	36	2,055
Alaska..............	1,370	12	922	123	2	64	1,201	10	836
Arizona.............	9,677	87	4,976	1,897	19	876	7,397	65	3,899
Arkansas...........	2,946	34	1,595	505	6	241	2,275	26	1,277
California..........	230,293	764	95,869	48,212	181	20,575	179,500	565	73,822
Colorado...........	15,632	103	7,586	3,019	(D)	(D)	12,222	75	5,971
Connecticut........	9,341	59	4,798	1,899	(D)	(D)	7,097	41	3,705
Delaware...........	1,029	9	494	216	3	97	740	6	358
Dist. of Columbia...	11,833	55	7,405	3,049	15	1,538	8,682	40	5,801
Florida.............	36,937	261	16,537	8,794	67	3,436	26,888	184	12,498
Georgia............	24,407	152	11,499	4,674	32	2,000	19,073	115	9,173
Hawaii..............	2,606	22	1,368	731	7	346	1,787	14	981
Idaho...............	2,014	21	1,055	286	4	139	1,643	16	872
Illinois.............	30,348	224	15,154	7,329	(D)	(D)	22,035	157	11,177
Indiana............	8,357	87	4,466	1,359	(D)	(D)	6,554	68	3,621
Iowa...............	4,237	43	2,307	663	9	334	3,343	32	1,868
Kansas.............	4,370	46	2,639	603	8	309	3,564	37	2,238
Kentucky...........	4,970	53	2,725	775	9	355	3,926	41	2,240
Louisiana..........	5,943	53	2,812	992	11	458	4,665	40	2,229
Maine..............	1,554	17	846	385	4	181	1,090	12	626
Maryland..........	11,720	81	6,055	2,325	20	1,146	9,000	58	4,710
Massachusetts.....	25,805	141	12,446	5,372	45	2,901	19,807	91	9,190
Michigan...........	13,915	121	7,566	3,228	33	1,688	9,993	83	5,528
Minnesota.........	12,209	98	6,565	2,600	26	1,276	9,131	69	5,048
Mississippi........	2,481	26	1,248	274	3	128	2,065	21	1,059
Missouri...........	10,015	92	5,080	2,315	(D)	(D)	7,296	65	3,785
Montana...........	1,596	16	883	315	3	140	1,221	12	716
Nebraska..........	2,943	29	1,556	648	8	316	2,149	20	1,177
Nevada............	8,738	41	2,864	1,959	11	705	6,615	29	2,065
New Hampshire. ..	2,658	23	1,522	456	5	239	2,100	17	1,228
New Jersey........	23,016	138	11,425	4,033	32	1,805	18,257	100	9,244
New Mexico........	2,673	27	1,466	366	4	175	2,212	21	1,245
New York..........	119,972	483	47,294	30,297	161	13,735	88,160	312	32,656
North Carolina.....	15,349	124	7,931	2,975	28	1,410	11,745	92	6,216
North Dakota.......	1,455	14	856	151	2	74	1,243	12	752
Ohio...............	19,164	177	9,993	4,274	(D)	(D)	14,072	128	7,599
Oklahoma..........	4,386	42	2,306	777	7	371	3,370	33	1,834
Oregon.............	8,111	68	4,370	1,712	17	842	6,134	49	3,388
Pennsylvania......	25,787	177	11,666	4,799	52	2,568	20,049	118	8,625
Rhode Island.......	1,998	18	1,042	388	5	202	1,540	13	803
South Carolina.....	5,835	54	3,004	1,026	(D)	(D)	4,542	40	2,394
South Dakota......	1,229	15	743	175	3	86	995	11	631
Tennessee.........	14,192	91	5,972	4,015	(D)	(D)	9,760	64	4,097
Texas..............	46,566	375	24,018	9,202	77	4,276	35,444	284	18,767
Utah...............	7,214	64	3,497	1,221	15	570	5,804	47	2,837
Vermont............	1,043	11	572	265	3	141	740	7	412
Virginia............	17,922	123	8,322	2,999	27	1,457	14,355	92	6,571
Washington........	44,303	167	19,494	2,703	(D)	(D)	41,035	137	17,819
West Virginia.......	1,559	17	914	114	2	58	1,354	15	813
Wisconsin..........	10,119	97	5,834	1,662	19	811	8,006	74	4,818
Wyoming..........	1,099	12	764	135	2	56	930	10	692

D Withheld to avoid disclosing data on individual companies. [1] Includes all other industries not shown separately. [2] Nominal; not adjusted for inflation.

Source: U.S. Bureau of Economic Analysis, "Arts and Cultural Production Satellite Account," <https://www.bea.gov/data/special-topics/arts-and-culture>, accessed March 2020.

Table 1254. Broadway Shows and Tours—Selected Data: 1990 to 2019

[In units, as indicated (282 represents $282,000,000). For season ending in year shown, except as indicated]

Item	Unit	1990	1995	2000	2005	2010	2015	2016	2017	2018	2019
Broadway shows:											
New productions......................	Number	39	34	36	39	39	37	39	45	33	38
Attendance..........................	Millions	8.0	9.0	11.4	11.5	11.9	13.1	13.3	13.3	13.8	14.8
Playing weeks [1, 2].....................	Number	1,070	1,120	1,464	1,494	1,464	1,626	1,648	1,580	1,624	1,737
Gross ticket sales................ [3]	Mil. dol.	282	406	603	769	1,020	1,365	1,373	1,449	1,697	1,829
Broadway road tours: [3]											
Attendance..........................	Millions	11.1	9.9	11.4	12.9	15.9	13.7	14.0	13.9	17.0	18.5
Playing weeks......................	Number	944	882	854	1,027	1,250	953	1,014	983	1,125	1,188
Gross ticket sales..................	Mil. dol.	367	547	553	706	947	957	981	1,007	1,416	1,633

NA Not available. [1] All shows (new productions and holdovers from previous seasons). [2] Eight performances constitute one playing week. [3] North American Tours include U.S. and Canadian companies.

Source: The Broadway League, New York, NY ©. See also <http://www.broadwayleague.com>.

Table 1255. Arts and Humanities—Selected Federal Aid Programs: 1990 to 2018

[In millions of dollars (170.8 represents $170,800,000), except as indicated. For fiscal year ending September 30. FY2010 includes funds from the American Recovery and Reinvestment Act]

Type of fund and program	1990	1995	2000	2005	2010	2015	2016	2017	2018
National Endowment for the Arts:									
Funds available [1]	170.8	152.1	85.2	108.8	153.1	127.1	132.7	129.5	124.3
Program appropriation [2]	152.3	138.1	79.6	99.5	138.7	116.6	118.4	119.2	120.7
Grants awarded (number) [3]	4,252	3,534	1,906	2,161	2,731	2,346	2,446	2,509	2,306
Funds obligated [4,5]	157.6	147.9	83.5	104.4	141.1	118.4	124.4	128	121.7
National Endowment for the Humanities:									
Funds available [1]	140.6	152.3	102.6	119.8	146.6	129.8	130.1	128.7	134.4
Program appropriation	114.2	125.7	82.7	99.9	125.7	108.1	109.8	111.2	113.4
Matching funds [6]	26.3	25.7	15.1	15.9	14.3	10.9	10.9	10.7	11.3
Grants awarded (number) [3]	2,195	1,871	1,230	1,174	1,204	822	920	813	697
Funds obligated [4,5]	141.0	151.8	100.0	117.8	142.7	121.5	121.9	120.7	116.1
Education programs	16.3	19.2	13.0	14.6	16.0	13.8	13.5	13.3	10.3
State partnership	29.6	32.0	30.6	36.9	49.1	42.6	43.9	46.5	47.2
Research grants	22.5	22.2	6.9	7.1	12.5	10.1	10.1	10.1	9.4
Fellowships	15.3	16.5	6.1	8.9	6.8	7.0	5.8	5.8	5.9
Challenge [7]	14.6	13.8	10.8	12.7	10.5	7.8	8.8	6.9	4.8
Public programs	25.4	25.8	11.8	14.4	19.4	17.6	13.9	14.4	13.4
Digital Humanities	(NA)	(NA)	(NA)	(NA)	4.9	4.7	4.7	4.7	4.8
Preservation and access	17.5	22.2	20.7	22.4	22.6	17.1	15.7	15.4	20.3

NA Not available. [1] Includes other program funds not shown separately. Excludes administrative funds. [2] FY1990–FY1996 include Regular Program Funds, Treasury Funds, Challenge Grant Funds, and Policy, Planning, and Research Funds. FY1997 includes Regular Program Funds, Matching Grant Funds, and Policy, Research and Technology Funds. FY1998–FY 2000 includes Regular Program Funds and Matching Grant Funds. [3] Excludes cooperative agreements and interagency agreements. [4] Includes obligations for new grants, supplemental awards on previous years' grants, cooperative agreements, and interagency agreements. Excludes obligations funded with administrative funds. [5] Beginning with 1997 data, the grantmaking structure changed from discipline-based categories to thematic ones. [6] Represents federal funds obligated only upon receipt or certification by endowment of matching nonfederal gifts. Funds for matching grants are not allocated by program area because they are awarded on a grant-by-grant basis. [7] Program designed to stimulate new sources and higher levels of giving to institutions for the purpose of guaranteeing long-term stability and financial independence. Program currently requires a match of at least 3 private dollars to each federal dollar.

Source: U.S. National Endowment for the Arts, unpublished data; and U.S. National Endowment for the Humanities, unpublished data.

Table 1256. State Arts Agency Legislative Appropriations: 2019 and 2020

[In thousands of dollars (359,878 represents $359,878,000). For fiscal year ending June 30 in most states. The National Assembly of State Arts Agencies (NASAA) is the membership organization of the nations' state and jurisdictional arts agencies. Legislative appropriations include funds designated to the state arts agency by state legislatures. These include line items, which are not controlled by the agency but passed through to designated entities. State arts agencies also receive monies from other sources including other state funds, the federal government (primarily the National Endowment for the Arts), private funds, and legislative earmarks. Minus sign (-) indicates decrease in spending]

State	Legislative appropriations including line items 2019, revised	Legislative appropriations including line items 2020, enacted	Percent change, 2019 to 2020	State	Legislative appropriations including line items 2019, revised	Legislative appropriations including line items 2020, enacted	Percent change, 2019 to 2020	State	Legislative appropriations including line items 2019, revised	Legislative appropriations including line items 2020, enacted	Percent change, 2019 to 2020
U.S.	**359,878**	**494,241**	**37.3**	LA	2,131	2,070	-2.9	OR	2,449	4,083	66.7
AL	5,459	5,829	6.8	ME	947	1,007	6.3	PA [6]	10,464	10,474	0.1
AK	704	704	0.1	MD	21,747	23,409	7.6	RI	3,165	2,670	-15.6
AZ [1]	2,000	2,200	10.0	MA	16,155	18,180	12.5	SC [7]	4,216	11,820	180.4
AR	1,426	1,426	–	MI	10,000	9,000	-10.0	SD	931	1,006	8.1
CA	24,883	53,583	115.3	MN	39,275	40,741	3.7	TN	7,176	7,958	10.9
CO	2,000	2,023	1.2	MS	1,595	1,719	7.8	TX	5,043	15,165	200.7
CT [10]	5,219	5,500	5.4	MO	6,459	6,571	1.7	UT [8]	3,590	5,333	48.6
DE	3,206	3,813	18.9	MT [10]	516	525	1.7	VT	718	724	0.8
DC	31,199	34,155	9.5	NE [10]	1,484	1,509	1.7	VA [10]	3,704	3,837	3.6
FL [2]	7,404	24,638	232.8	NV	1,826	1,840	0.8	WA	1,633	2,169	32.8
GA [3]	1,211	1,517	25.3	NH	499	805	61.5	WV	880	880	–
HI	5,952	6,945	16.7	NJ	16,405	16,405	–	WI [9]	763	790	3.5
ID	841	885	5.2	NM	1,322	1,332	0.8	WY	1,039	1,039	–
IL [4]	12,914	63,397	390.9	NY [5]	45,334	45,274	-0.1	AS	85	116	36.5
IN	4,000	3,920	-2.0	NC [5]	9,103	8,278	-9.1	GU	361	439	21.6
IA [10]	1,367	1,467	7.3	ND [10]	782	809	3.4	MP	586	535	-8.8
KS	189	500	165.1	OH	14,654	17,178	17.2	PR	8,034	11,033	37.3
KY	1,709	1,729	1.2	OK	2,799	2,913	4.0	VI	325	375	15.4

– Represents zero. [1] Arizona: The SAA's FY2019 appropriations were drawn from interest on the state's rainy-day fund and were nonrecurring; the FY2020 appropriations were drawn from the state's general fund and are nonrecurring. [2] Florida: Funding for the division suffered a 71.1% reduction for FY2019 due to the state legislature's decision to not fund a large portion of designated grants for organizations. [3] Georgia: The Georgia Council for the Arts appropriation includes one-time funding of $100,000 in FY2019. [4] Illinois: The Illinois Arts Council Agency was allocated $50 million in one-time appropriations for capital projects. The Agency is awaiting action from the governor's office before distributing funds over multiple years. [5] North Carolina: The state had not enacted an FY2020 budget at the time of data collection. In such a case, state law requires that agencies operate using the same funding level as the prior year. [6] Pennsylvania: Total legislative appropriation includes an administrative allocation for the Pennsylvania Council on the Arts. [7] South Carolina: For FY2020, the South Carolina Arts Commission received a line item of $7,000,000 for the Community Foundation of Greenville. [8] Utah: The agency's appropriation does not include state support for the Fine Arts Outreach POPS program and the Beverley Taylor Sorenson Arts Learning Program, which are administered by agencies other than the SAA. [9] Wisconsin: FY2020 legislative appropriation figure does not include an additional $23,700 to match Partnership Agreement funds from the National Endowment for the Arts. The additional appropriation was pending legislative action at the time of data collection. [10] Figure reflects state arts agency (SAA) appropriation only and does not include appropriation to the state's cultural endowment.

Source: National Assembly of State Arts Agencies, *State Arts Agency Revenues, Fiscal Year 2020* ©, February 2020. See also <http://www.nasaa-arts.org>.

Table 1257. Attendance/Participation Rates for Various Arts Activities by Selected Characteristics: 2017

[In percent. For persons 18 years old and over. Represents attendance at least once in the prior twelve months. Excludes elementary and high school performances]

Item	Adult popu-lation	Jazz concert	Classical music concert	Musicals	Non-musical plays	Art muse-ums/ galleries	Craft/ visual art festivals	Parks/ historic build-ings [1]
Total............................	**100.0**	**8.6**	**8.6**	**16.5**	**9.4**	**23.7**	**23.8**	**28.3**
Sex:								
Male............................	48.2	8.7	6.8	12.8	8.2	21.1	19.5	26.6
Female..........................	51.8	8.5	10.3	19.9	10.5	26.2	27.8	29.9
Race and ethnicity:								
White alone.....................	63.9	9.2	10.4	20.2	11.6	26.7	29.6	33.2
African American alone.........	11.8	12.1	3.9	10.1	7.7	17.1	12.7	18.6
Hispanic........................	16.0	5.8	5.5	9.7	4.0	16.2	12.8	17.1
Asian...........................	5.9	3.9	8.5	9.4	4.8	26.2	13.2	24.9
Other alone.....................	2.4	[2] 6.3	[2] 5.5	11.5	[2] 7.0	22.1	20.8	27.4
Age:								
18 to 24 years old..............	12.0	8.6	8.0	16.0	8.9	24.0	18.9	24.6
25 to 34 years old..............	17.8	8.8	7.5	15.1	8.0	25.3	24.4	29.2
35 to 44 years old..............	16.2	8.2	7.5	17.0	8.8	27.3	22.3	32.0
45 to 54 years old..............	16.9	8.6	8.2	15.1	10.0	23.4	24.2	31.1
55 to 64 years old..............	16.9	9.7	9.0	17.9	9.7	21.6	26.4	27.8
65 to 74 years old..............	11.9	9.2	11.5	20.2	11.4	23.6	29.1	28.9
75 years old and older..........	8.1	5.8	10.1	13.6	9.8	17.3	18.2	18.0
Education:								
Grade school....................	3.7	(S)	(S)	[2] 1.8	(S)	[2] 3.1	[2] 4.5	6.2
Some high school................	6.7	[2] 2.6	(S)	[2] 4.0	[2] 2.2	6.7	8.1	8.8
High school graduate............	29.4	4.6	3.7	8.2	4.2	10.4	14.8	17.1
Some college....................	28.0	8.0	7.2	16.2	8.2	23.0	25.1	27.1
College graduate................	20.7	13.7	14.7	26.1	16.0	39.5	34.3	42.7
Graduate school.................	11.5	17.5	21.9	34.0	21.6	49.0	40.9	53.9

[1] Visiting historic parks or monuments or touring buildings or neighborhoods for the historic or design value. [2] Interpret data with caution.

Source: U.S. National Endowment for the Arts, *US Patterns of Arts Participation: A Full Report from the 2017 Survey of Public Participation in the Arts*, December 2019. See also <https://www.arts.gov/publications/state-level-estimates-arts-participation-patterns-2017-2018>.

Table 1258. Personal Participation in Various Arts or Creative Activities and Reading by Selected Characteristics: 2017

[In percent. Represents creating or performing or reading at least once in the prior 12 months. Based on the 2017 household survey of Public Participation in the Arts. Data are subject to sampling error; see source]

Item	Art-making activities				Took art lessons or classes	Reading				
	Any art-making [1]	Perform-ing art [1]	Visual art [2]	Creative art [3]		Any books	Novels or short stories	Poetry	Listen to audio-books	Read any books using electronic devices
Total......................	**53.7**	**40.0**	**32.7**	**6.5**	**9.5**	**52.7**	**41.8**	**11.7**	**16.5**	**23.5**
Sex:										
Male.........................	49.8	35.5	26.3	5.8	7.4	44.3	33.0	8.7	14.2	19.2
Female.......................	57.3	44.2	38.8	7.3	11.5	60.5	50.0	14.5	18.6	27.5
Race and ethnicity:										
White alone..................	58.2	41.2	37.6	7.6	9.9	59.6	48.1	11.4	17.8	25.9
African American alone.......	49.3	43.4	21.7	5.6	11.2	46.5	30.8	15.3	13.4	21.3
Hispanic.....................	44.6	36.1	24.6	3.9	5.6	32.2	26.8	9.7	11.5	15.4
Asian alone..................	37.8	29.4	23.1	3.2	10.5	44.8	36.1	12.6	19.7	25.8
Other alone..................	62.6	44.9	38.0	9.2	15.7	53.7	39.6	14.2	21.2	19.0
Age:										
18 to 24 years old...........	64.7	46.1	37.2	11.7	19.2	47.3	38.7	17.5	17.1	25.7
25 to 34 years old...........	64.7	45.8	36.5	9.2	10.5	52.6	42.6	12.3	20.3	25.9
35 to 44 years old...........	50.4	38.5	31.9	7.1	9.8	53.6	42.4	11.4	18.5	26.3
45 to 54 years old...........	51.4	38.7	29.8	4.3	8.1	50.5	38.3	9.9	16.8	25.1
55 to 64 years old...........	49.4	37.2	31.0	5.0	7.7	53.6	41.8	10.6	15.3	22.0
65 to 74 years old...........	55.2	38.9	34.2	4.4	6.4	57.2	46.8	10.3	13.2	19.4
75 years old and older. ...	37.0	33.5	27.1	3.1	4.7	55.4	42.9	11.0	9.1	14.2

[1] Includes singing, dancing, playing a musical instrument, or acting. [2] Includes painting, drawing, sculpting, or making prints; photography; videography; animation, digital art, computer graphics, or video games; pottery, ceramics, or jewelry; doing leatherwork, metalwork, or woodwork; weaving, crocheting, quilting, needleworking, knitting, or sewing; and scrapbooking, origami, or other paper-based art. [3] Includes through email, websites, or social media.

Source: U.S. National Endowment for the Arts, *U.S. Patterns of Arts Participation: A Full Report from the 2017 Survey of Public Participation in the Arts*, December 2019. See also <https://www.arts.gov/publications/state-level-estimates-arts-participation-patterns-2017-2018>.

Table 1259. Outdoor Recreation Sector Gross Output by Activity: 2012 to 2017

[In millions of current dollars (691,782 represents $691,782,000,000)]

Activity	2012	2013	2014	2015	2016	2017
Total outdoor recreation	**691,782**	**709,072**	**725,728**	**730,955**	**741,630**	**778,487**
Total core outdoor recreation	**342,735**	**358,561**	**368,355**	**377,843**	**386,701**	**408,053**
Conventional outdoor recreation	214,386	225,790	231,538	235,600	241,433	253,955
Bicycling	3,182	3,341	3,454	3,342	3,840	4,011
Boating/fishing	32,428	33,413	34,434	35,757	37,050	39,878
Canoeing	124	123	130	136	142	153
Kayaking	580	595	616	661	738	805
Fishing (excludes boating)	4,863	5,007	5,171	5,353	5,337	5,346
Sailing	1,824	1,906	2,027	2,148	2,282	2,372
Other boating	25,037	25,781	26,489	27,458	28,552	31,202
Climbing/hiking/tent camping	5,588	5,910	6,171	6,170	6,327	6,361
Equestrian	9,307	10,031	11,106	11,487	12,315	14,174
Hunting/shooting/trapping	11,371	13,342	12,918	13,942	13,807	15,060
Motorcycling/ATVing	17,154	17,680	17,996	18,134	18,082	19,553
Recreational flying	2,870	2,957	3,069	2,727	2,747	2,888
RVing	26,710	29,388	31,524	31,980	33,974	36,095
Snow activities	10,638	10,754	11,135	10,770	10,670	11,304
Skiing	2,929	2,996	3,260	3,438	3,439	3,593
Snowboarding	2,534	2,646	2,820	2,979	3,068	3,225
Other snow activities (includes snowmobiling) [1]	5,175	5,112	5,055	4,352	4,162	4,486
Other conventional outdoor recreation activities	18,331	18,856	19,026	18,206	18,620	19,669
Multi-use apparel and accessories (conventional) [2]	76,807	80,117	80,705	83,085	84,001	84,963
Other outdoor recreation	128,349	132,772	136,817	142,243	145,268	154,099
Amusement parks/water parks	13,206	13,246	13,609	14,708	15,805	17,765
Festivals/sporting events/concerts	20,560	21,326	22,660	24,156	25,656	27,153
Field sports	5,232	5,352	5,665	5,983	6,256	6,416
Game areas (includes golfing and tennis)	32,082	33,316	32,945	33,674	34,917	36,011
Guided tours/outfitted travel	25,481	26,275	27,770	27,387	25,769	28,403
Productive activities (includes gardening)	10,703	11,288	11,749	12,322	12,792	13,484
Other outdoor recreation activities [3]	14,722	15,195	15,931	17,405	17,411	17,891
Multi-use apparel and accessories (other) [2]	6,362	6,775	6,489	6,608	6,663	6,977
Supporting outdoor recreation	**349,046**	**350,511**	**357,372**	**353,112**	**354,929**	**370,433**
Construction	9,385	9,429	9,936	11,696	12,956	13,197
Local trips [4]	71,515	72,417	72,354	64,665	62,214	66,300
Travel and tourism [5]	234,570	233,694	239,182	239,604	241,213	251,064
Food and beverages	38,079	32,197	33,699	36,283	38,145	39,281
Lodging	49,531	51,543	51,805	55,703	58,250	59,378
Shopping and souvenirs	40,398	41,746	43,215	43,161	43,558	44,975
Transportation	106,561	108,208	110,464	104,457	101,260	107,431
Government expenditures	33,576	34,971	35,900	37,147	38,546	39,873
Federal Government	3,947	4,247	4,011	4,036	4,247	4,313
State and local government	29,629	30,724	31,889	33,111	34,299	35,560

[1] Dog mushing, sleighing, snowmobiling, snow shoeing, and snow tubing. [2] Backpacks, bug spray, coolers, general outdoor clothing, GPS equipment, hydration equipment, lighting, sports racks, sunscreen, watches, and other miscellaneous gear and equipment. [3] Agritourism, augmented reality games, beachgoing, disc golf, hot springs soaking, kite flying, model airplane/rocket/UAV, paintball, photography, stargazing/astronomy, swimming, therapeutic programs, water polo, and yard sports. [4] Trip expenses less than 50 miles away from home, including food and beverages, lodging, shopping and souvenirs, and transportation. [5] Expenses for travel at least 50 miles away from home.

Source: U.S. Bureau of Economic Analysis, Satellite Accounts, *Outdoor Recreation Satellite Account, U.S. and Prototype for States, 2017*, September 2019. See also <https://www.bea.gov/data/special-topics/outdoor-recreation>.

Table 1260. Personal Consumption Expenditures for Recreation: 1990 to 2019

[In billions of dollars (314.7 represents $314,700,000,000), except percent. Represents market value of purchases of goods and services by individuals and nonprofit institutions]

Type of product or service	1990	2000	2005	2010	2015	2018	2019
Total recreation expenditures	**314.7**	**633.7**	**805.2**	**884.4**	**1,045.6**	**1,209.7**	**1,277.9**
Percent of total personal consumption [1]	8.3	9.4	9.2	8.7	8.5	8.6	8.8
Video and audio equipment, computers, and related services	81.1	181.2	240.0	275.5	313.9	361.8	386.5
Video and audio equipment	43.7	79.9	101.4	83.2	77.5	84.6	93.4
Information processing equipment	9.6	44.1	68.4	95.0	111.6	143.4	157.1
Services related to video and audio goods and computers	27.8	57.2	70.2	97.3	124.8	133.8	135.9
Sports and recreational goods and related services	74.2	146.0	184.1	177.4	226.3	257.0	272.5
Sports and recreational vehicles	16.6	34.9	49.1	35.8	52.0	62.8	68.0
Other sporting and recreational goods	55.4	106.8	130.0	137.2	168.6	187.8	197.9
Maintenance and repair of recreational vehicles and sports equipment	2.1	4.2	4.9	4.4	5.6	6.4	6.6
Membership clubs, sports centers, parks, theaters, and museums	49.7	91.9	117.9	146.1	177.7	208.9	218.2
Membership clubs and participant sports centers	14.3	26.4	34.3	40.9	49.6	56.5	58.7
Amusement parks, campgrounds, and related services	19.2	31.1	33.6	40.1	54.2	65.9	68.9
Admissions to specified spectator amusements	14.4	30.6	43.7	58.7	65.4	76.9	80.2
Motion picture theaters	5.1	8.6	9.7	12.3	13.3	14.3	13.8
Live entertainment, excluding sports	4.5	10.4	18.3	26.7	28.9	35.0	37.2
Spectator sports	4.8	11.6	15.7	19.7	23.1	27.6	29.1
Museums and libraries	1.9	3.8	6.4	6.5	8.4	9.7	10.4
Magazines, newspapers, books, and stationery	47.3	81.0	85.0	74.8	77.0	94.6	103.2
Gambling	23.7	67.6	96.1	109.4	125.7	141.8	147.0
Pets, pet products, and related services	18.8	39.7	57.2	76.2	98.4	114.7	118.4
Photographic goods and services	16.7	19.7	17.7	15.2	15.9	16.9	17.0
Package tours [2]	3.2	6.7	7.2	9.8	10.9	14.0	15.0

[1] See Table 713. [2] Consists of tour operators' and travel agents' margins. Purchases of travel and accommodations included in tours are accounted for separately in other personal consumption expenditures categories.

Source: U.S. Bureau of Economic Analysis, National Income and Product Accounts Tables, "Table 2.5.5. Personal Consumption Expenditures by Function," <http://www.bea.gov/iTable/index_nipa.cfm>, accessed August 2020.

Table 1261. Expenditures Per Consumer Unit for Entertainment and Reading: 1985 to 2018

[Data are annual averages. In dollars, except as indicated. Based on the Consumer Expenditure Survey (CES). For description of survey, see text, Section 13; also see headnote, Table 722. For composition of regions, see map, inside front cover]

Year and characteristic	Entertainment and reading		Entertainment					Reading
	Total	Percent of total expenditures	Total	Fees and admissions	Audio and visual equipment and services	Other supplies, equipment & services [1]		Reading
1985..........................	1,311	5.6	1,170	320	371	479		141
1990..........................	1,575	5.6	1,422	371	454	597		153
1995..........................	1,775	5.5	1,612	433	542	637		163
2000..........................	2,009	5.3	1,863	515	622	727		146
2001..........................	2,094	5.3	1,953	526	660	767		141
2002..........................	2,218	5.5	2,079	542	692	845		139
2003..........................	2,187	5.4	2,060	494	730	835		127
2004..........................	2,348	5.4	2,218	528	788	903		130
2005..........................	2,514	5.4	2,388	588	888	912		126
2006..........................	2,493	5.2	2,376	606	906	863		117
2007..........................	2,816	5.7	2,698	658	987	1,053		118
2008..........................	2,951	5.8	2,835	616	1,036	1,183		116
2009..........................	2,803	5.7	2,693	628	975	1,090		110
2010..........................	2,604	5.4	2,504	581	954	970		100
2011..........................	2,687	5.4	2,572	594	977	1,001		115
2012..........................	2,714	5.3	2,605	614	979	1,011		109
2013..........................	2,584	5.1	2,482	569	964	949		102
2014..........................	2,831	5.3	2,728	636	1,051	1,041		103
2015..........................	2,956	5.3	2,842	652	1,084	1,106		114
2016..........................	3,031	5.3	2,913	681	1,085	1,146		118
2017..........................	3,313	5.5	3,203	750	985	1,468		110
2018, total..........	**3,334**	**5.4**	**3,226**	**766**	**1,030**	**1,430**		**108**
Age of reference person:								
Under 25 years old................	1,444	4.5	1,409	412	460	536		35
25 to 34 years old.................	2,613	4.6	2,547	635	851	1,062		66
35 to 44 years old.................	3,679	5.2	3,572	1,140	1,098	1,333		107
45 to 54 years old.................	4,052	5.4	3,952	1,047	1,207	1,698		100
55 to 64 years old.................	3,856	5.8	3,755	748	1,138	1,870		101
65 years old and older............	3,123	6.1	2,958	500	1,028	1,430		165
65 to 74 years old...............	3,978	7.1	3,801	594	1,102	2,105		177
75 years old and over...........	1,911	4.4	1,763	368	924	472		148
Hispanic or Latino origin of reference person:								
Hispanic.........................	2,338	4.3	2,282	459	858	965		56
Non-Hispanic....................	3,489	5.6	3,373	814	1,056	1,503		116
Race of reference person: [2]								
White, and all other races [2].........	3,650	5.8	3,531	818	1,061	1,652		119
Asian...........................	2,594	3.6	2,519	1,237	713	570		75
Black...........................	1,637	3.7	1,585	273	949	363		52
Region of residence:								
Northeast.......................	3,256	4.9	3,117	922	1,081	1,114		139
Midwest........................	3,756	6.4	3,630	708	1,031	1,891		126
South..........................	2,859	5.0	2,778	648	996	1,134		81
West...........................	3,810	5.6	3,696	901	1,044	1,751		114
Size of consumer unit:								
One person......................	1,916	5.3	1,822	377	723	722		94
Two or more persons.............	3,919	5.5	3,805	927	1,157	1,721		114
Two persons....................	4,024	6.1	3,897	760	1,142	1,995		127
Three persons..................	3,611	5.0	3,519	787	1,192	1,540		92
Four persons...................	3,907	4.8	3,793	1,378	1,153	1,262		114
Five persons or more...........	4,067	5.1	3,969	1,136	1,169	1,664		98
Income before taxes:								
Quintiles of income:								
Lowest 20 percent..............	1,437	5.4	1,369	228	584	557		68
Second 20 percent.............	2,278	5.7	2,183	271	829	1,083		95
Third 20 percent...............	2,631	5.1	2,542	463	974	1,106		89
Fourth 20 percent..............	3,610	5.2	3,494	814	1,140	1,539		116
Highest 20 percent.............	6,703	5.6	6,532	2,050	1,621	2,861		171
Education:								
Less than a high school graduate........	1,164	3.8	1,138	90	601	447		26
High school graduate.............	1,835	4.8	1,776	177	797	803		59
High school graduate with some college........	2,574	5.3	2,492	440	936	1,115		82
Associate's degree...............	4,035	6.8	3,951	615	1,093	2,244		84
Bachelor's degree................	4,033	5.6	3,912	964	1,186	1,762		121
Master's, professional, or doctoral degree.......	5,017	5.3	4,808	1,777	1,258	1,773		209

[1] Includes pets, toys, hobbies, and playground equipment, and other entertainment supplies, equipment, and services. [2] All other races includes Native Hawaiian or other Pacific Islander, American Indian or Alaska Native, and approximately 1 percent reporting more than one race.

Source: U.S. Bureau of Labor Statistics, Consumer Expenditure Survey, "Annual Calendar Year Tables, 2018," <https://www.bls.gov/cex/tables.htm#annual>, accessed February 2020.

Table 1262. Adult Participation in Selected Leisure Activities by Frequency: 2019

[In thousands (19,971 represents 19,971,000), except percent. For Fall 2019. Percent is based on total projected population of 250,323,000. Based on sample and subject to sampling error; see source]

Activity	Participated in the last 12 months [1]		Two or more times a week		Once a week		Two to three times a month		Once a month	
	Number (1,000)	Percent	Number (1,000)	Percent	Number (1,000)	Percent	Number (1,000)	Percent	Number (1,000)	Percent
Adult education courses	19,971	8.0	4,405	1.8	2,178	0.9	1,635	0.7	1,433	0.6
Aquarium attendance	14,689	5.9	205	0.1	128	0.1	26	(Z)	273	0.1
Attend a state or county fair	34,133	13.6	629	0.3	544	0.2	398	0.2	783	0.3
Attend art galleries or shows	17,749	7.1	245	0.1	217	0.1	737	0.3	1,615	0.7
Attend auto shows	14,130	5.6	235	0.1	235	0.1	307	0.1	758	0.3
Attend classical music/opera performances	9,019	3.6	132	0.1	196	0.1	293	0.1	901	0.4
Attend country music performances	16,041	6.4	198	0.1	67	(Z)	419	0.2	759	0.3
Attend dance performances	9,462	3.8	222	0.1	77	(Z)	242	0.1	435	0.2
Attend other music performances [2]	27,791	11.1	292	0.1	372	0.2	849	0.3	2,307	0.9
Attend rock music performances	25,412	10.2	345	0.1	33	(Z)	658	0.3	1,750	0.7
Baking	54,858	21.9	7,438	3.0	6,741	2.7	11,418	4.6	8,958	3.6
Barbecuing	65,996	26.4	7,934	3.2	10,063	4.0	13,479	5.4	9,526	3.8
Billiards/pool	14,554	5.8	783	0.3	798	0.3	1,177	0.5	1,764	0.7
Bird watching	10,557	4.2	3,481	1.4	755	0.3	1,180	0.5	952	0.4
Board games	39,984	16.0	2,534	1.0	3,782	1.5	5,599	2.2	8,011	3.2
Chess	8,768	3.5	1,164	0.5	463	0.2	728	0.3	595	0.2
Cooking for fun	48,409	19.3	17,332	6.9	6,701	2.7	6,575	2.6	3,519	1.4
Crossword puzzles	24,278	9.7	8,813	3.5	3,237	1.3	2,521	1.0	1,525	0.6
Dance/go dancing	19,201	7.7	2,331	0.9	1,006	0.4	1,743	0.7	1,860	0.7
Dining out	130,262	52.0	22,626	9.0	27,625	11.0	30,765	12.3	17,596	7.0
Entertain friends or relatives at home	80,237	32.1	5,148	2.1	7,981	3.2	14,697	5.9	17,191	6.9
Fantasy sports league	11,382	4.6	2,682	1.1	2,170	0.9	534	0.2	791	0.3
Furniture refinishing	10,757	4.3	361	0.1	302	0.1	469	0.2	1,186	0.5
Genealogy	10,512	4.2	1,124	0.5	751	0.3	629	0.3	758	0.3
Go to bars/night clubs	44,388	17.7	2,074	0.8	4,535	1.8	8,271	3.3	6,944	2.8
Go to beach	75,219	30.1	3,097	1.2	2,147	0.9	5,915	2.4	6,149	2.5
Go to live theater	29,811	11.9	136	0.1	277	0.1	906	0.4	2,796	1.1
Go to museums	37,880	15.1	262	0.1	257	0.1	1,372	0.6	3,934	1.6
Home decoration and furnishing	25,551	10.2	934	0.4	1,222	0.5	2,255	0.9	4,067	1.6
Karaoke	9,693	3.9	338	0.1	245	0.1	602	0.2	984	0.4
Painting, drawing	22,260	8.9	4,080	1.6	1,971	0.8	2,112	0.8	2,830	1.1
PC/computer games (play offline with software)	16,201	6.5	8,195	3.3	1,349	0.5	801	0.3	652	0.3
PC/computer games (play online)	29,299	11.7	16,994	6.8	1,851	0.7	1,949	0.8	1,178	0.5
Photo album/scrap book	9,538	3.8	657	0.3	422	0.2	881	0.4	1,095	0.4
Photography	22,934	9.2	5,259	2.1	2,349	0.9	3,114	1.2	2,290	0.9
Picnic	20,735	8.3	533	0.2	808	0.3	1,460	0.6	2,306	0.9
Play bingo	12,702	5.1	861	0.3	854	0.3	623	0.3	807	0.3
Play cards	42,275	16.9	3,862	1.5	3,927	1.6	5,563	2.2	6,233	2.5
Play musical instrument	18,489	7.4	6,578	2.6	2,018	0.8	1,703	0.7	838	0.3
Reading books	76,808	30.7	38,360	15.3	7,218	2.9	6,154	2.5	5,552	2.2
Sudoku puzzles	20,704	8.3	7,458	3.0	2,105	0.8	1,930	0.8	2,068	0.8
Tailgating	9,478	3.8	130	0.1	185	0.1	582	0.2	340	0.1
Trivia games	16,075	6.4	3,728	1.5	1,506	0.6	1,192	0.5	1,652	0.7
Video/electronic games (console)	23,862	9.5	10,849	4.3	2,427	1.0	2,669	1.1	1,500	0.6
Video/electronic games (portable)	11,892	4.8	5,698	2.3	896	0.4	819	0.3	384	0.2
Woodworking	11,782	4.7	1,828	0.7	1,074	0.4	1,624	0.7	1,509	0.6
Word games	27,357	10.9	11,877	4.7	3,391	1.4	2,229	0.9	1,265	0.5
Zoo attendance	29,560	11.8	92	(Z)	177	0.1	739	0.3	1,665	0.7

Z Represents less than 0.05. [1] Includes those participating less than once a month, not shown separately. [2] Excluding country and rock.

Source: MRI Survey of the American Consumer.© Courtesy of MRISimmons. See also <https://www.mrisimmons.com/>.

Table 1263. Selected Recreational Activities: 1990 to 2019

[18,719 represents 18,719,000]

Activity	Unit	1990	2000	2005	2010	2015	2016	2017	2018	2019
Golf facilities [1]	Number	12,846	15,489	16,052	15,890	15,204	15,014	14,794	14,613	14,300
Tennis players: [2]	1,000	(NA)	(NA)	(NA)	18,719	17,963	18,079	17,683	17,841	17,681
Skiing: [3]										
Skier & snowboarder visits [4]	Million	50.0	52.2	56.9	59.8	53.6	52.8	54.8	53.3	59.3
Operating resorts	Number	591	503	492	471	470	463	481	472	476

NA Not available. [1] Source: National Golf Foundation, Jupiter, FL. [2] Source: Tennis Industry Association, Hilton Head Island, SC. Based on a nationwide telephone survey of households, in which all household members ages 6 and up are enumerated, with data on tennis participation collected for each person. Data prior to 2007 is not available due to new methodology being implemented after 2007. [3] Source: National Ski Areas Association, Lakewood, CO. ©. [4] Represents one person visiting a ski area for all or any part of a day or night, and includes full-and half-day, night, complimentary, adult, child, season, and other types of tickets. Data are estimated and are for the season ending in the year shown.

Source: Compiled from sources listed in footnotes.

Table 1264. Amusement Park Attendance at Top 15 U.S. Facilities: 2010 to 2019

[In thousands (16,972 represents 16,972,000). Covers gated (entry ticket required) commercial theme and amusement parks with annual attendance of one million or more. Ranked for top 15 parks in 2019. Excludes water parks]

Park name	Location	Attendance				
		2010	2015	2017	2018	2019
Magic Kingdom, Walt Disney World	Lake Buena Vista, FL	16,972	20,492	20,450	20,859	20,963
Disneyland	Anaheim, CA	15,980	18,278	18,300	18,666	18,666
Disney's Animal Kingdom	Lake Buena Vista, FL	9,886	10,922	12,500	13,750	13,888
EPCOT, Walt Disney World	Lake Buena Vista, FL	10,825	11,798	12,200	12,444	12,444
Disney's Hollywood Studios	Lake Buena Vista, FL	9,603	10,828	10,722	11,258	11,483
Universal Studios at Universal Orlando	Orlando, FL	5,925	9,585	10,198	10,708	10,922
Universal's Islands of Adventure	Orlando, FL	5,949	8,792	9,549	9,788	10,375
Disney's California Adventure	Anaheim, CA	6,278	9,383	9,574	9,861	9,861
Universal Studios Hollywood	Universal City, CA	5,040	7,097	9,056	9,147	9,147
SeaWorld Orlando	Orlando, FL	5,100	4,777	3,962	4,594	4,640
Knott's Berry Farm	Buena Park, CA	3,600	3,867	4,034	4,115	4,238
Busch Gardens	Tampa, FL	4,200	4,252	3,961	4,139	4,180
Cedar Point	Sandusky, OH	3,051	3,507	3,604	3,676	3,731
Six Flags Magic Mountain	Valencia, CA	2,600	3,104	3,500	3,592	3,610
Kings Island	Kings Island, OH	3,112	3,335	3,469	3,486	3,521

Source: Themed Entertainment Association and AECOM, *2019 Theme Index and Museum Index: The Global Attractions Attendance Report* ©, and previous reports. See also <aecom.com/theme-index/> and <teaconnect.org/Resources/Theme-Index/index.cfm>.

Table 1265. Reading in Print, Electronic, and Audio Formats Among Adults: 2016 and 2019

[In percent. Data shown for adults aged 18 years and older who read at least one book in the formats shown during the previous 12 months. Based on telephone surveys conducted March 7-April 4, 2016 among a nationally representative sample of 1,520 adults, and January 8-February 7, 2019 among a nationally representative sample of 1,502 adults]

Characteristic	2016				2019			
	Total	Print	E-book	Audio-book	Total	Print	E-book	Audio-book
Total	**73**	**65**	**28**	**14**	**72**	**65**	**25**	**20**
SEX								
Male	68	61	27	14	67	60	24	17
Female	77	70	29	14	76	70	27	22
RACE/ETHNICITY								
White, non-Hispanic	76	70	31	15	76	70	27	22
Black, non-Hispanic	69	63	23	11	65	58	19	13
Hispanic	58	48	18	12	59	54	20	15
AGE								
18 to 29 years	80	72	35	16	81	73	34	23
30 to 49 years	73	65	32	15	72	76	28	27
50 to 64 years	70	64	24	15	67	74	22	16
65 years and older	67	61	19	9	68	65	17	8
EDUCATION								
Less than high school	45	38	11	12	32	25	5	6
High school graduate	62	55	19	9	61	55	15	12
Some college	81	74	32	14	75	70	26	17
College graduate	86	79	41	20	90	82	41	34
HOUSEHOLD INCOME								
Less than $30,000	65	59	19	9	62	56	18	14
$30,000 to $49,000	74	68	26	16	67	63	19	13
$50,000 to $74,999	75	69	33	19	78	71	28	27
$75,000 and higher	81	73	40	16	86	78	38	30
METRO STATUS								
Urban	75	69	29	17	75	68	27	23
Suburban	73	64	30	14	74	68	27	19
Rural	66	61	22	10	66	58	20	18

Source: Pew Research Center, *Book Reading 2016*, September 2016 ©; and unpublished data. See also <http://www.pewinternet.org/>.

Table 1266. Leisure Time Use on Weekends and Holidays by Type of Activity and Selected Demographic Characteristics: 2019

[Data are based on interviews of approximately 9,400 individuals age 15 years and over who reported their activities for a single 24-hour period. Respondents engaging in more than one activity at a time reported only their primary activity; except for child care, secondary activities were not reported]

Selected characteristics	Average hours per day spent on all leisure and sports activities			Percent distribution of leisure time on weekends and holidays						
	All days (hours)	Weekdays (hours)	Weekends and holidays (hours)	Sports, exercise, recrea-tion	Socializing, communi-cating	Watching TV	Reading	Relaxing, thinking	Playing games, using computers for leisure	Other [1]
Total, 15 years old and over	**5.19**	**4.64**	**6.44**	**5.3**	**15.1**	**52.2**	**4.7**	**5.7**	**7.9**	**9.3**
Sex:										
Men	5.53	4.86	7.11	6.3	13.2	53.0	3.8	5.8	9.1	8.7
Women	4.86	4.45	5.81	4.1	17.4	51.1	5.5	5.5	6.4	10.2
Age:										
15 to 19 years	5.34	4.73	6.71	8.5	14.8	40.2	2.2	3.9	18.3	11.9
20 to 24 years	4.91	4.46	5.94	10.8	15.2	44.1	1.7	3.2	16.3	8.9
25 to 34 years	4.28	3.61	5.84	6.5	18.3	44.0	2.1	5.0	11.8	12.3
35 to 44 years	3.99	3.31	5.53	6.3	18.3	49.7	3.6	6.0	6.7	9.4
45 to 54 years	4.38	3.62	6.18	4.7	15.2	51.1	4.9	7.6	4.2	12.1
55 to 64 years	5.45	4.96	6.58	3.8	14.7	58.2	4.6	6.2	3.6	9.0
65 to 74 years	7.10	6.93	7.51	2.9	12.3	60.3	8.0	5.2	4.9	6.3
75 years and over	7.67	7.39	8.33	1.9	10.7	63.6	8.5	6.6	4.8	3.8
Race/ethnicity:										
White	5.20	4.65	6.48	5.6	15.6	51.5	5.1	4.9	7.9	9.4
Black	5.49	4.94	6.75	3.9	12.0	58.2	1.6	10.1	6.7	7.6
Asian	3.99	3.50	5.21	6.1	16.3	41.8	4.2	4.0	14.4	13.1
Hispanic origin [2]	4.59	4.10	5.75	3.8	21.0	49.7	1.7	7.7	7.3	8.5
Employment status:										
Employed	4.18	3.47	5.82	6.0	17.4	48.8	3.6	5.2	7.9	11.3
Full-time workers	4.01	3.22	5.84	6.5	17.6	49.3	3.3	5.0	6.7	11.5
Part-time workers	4.79	4.37	5.75	4.3	16.2	46.4	4.5	6.1	12.0	10.4
Not employed	6.91	6.66	7.48	4.4	12.2	56.6	5.9	6.4	7.9	6.8
Weekly earnings: [3]										
$0 to $650	4.12	3.54	5.40	5.7	16.9	53.9	2.0	5.0	8.5	8.0
$651 to $1,000	4.35	3.50	6.25	5.3	18.1	50.2	3.5	5.1	8.0	9.6
$1,001 to $1,620	4.05	3.17	5.91	5.9	16.8	50.1	2.9	3.7	6.3	14.4
$1,621 and higher	3.83	2.96	6.12	9.0	17.8	45.1	4.7	4.1	5.4	14.1
Presence and age of children:										
No household children under age 18	5.74	5.25	6.88	4.8	13.2	55.2	5.4	5.5	7.3	8.7
Household children under age 18	4.13	3.49	5.62	6.6	19.4	45.0	2.7	6.0	9.3	10.9
Children age 13 to 17, none younger	4.61	3.95	5.99	5.5	18.0	47.6	3.7	2.2	12.0	10.9
Children age 6 to 12, none younger	4.09	3.46	5.69	6.7	19.7	42.5	2.8	7.0	9.5	11.6
Youngest child under age 6	3.88	3.23	5.32	7.3	20.3	45.3	2.1	8.1	7.3	10.0
Educational attainment, age 25 and over:										
Less than a high school diploma	5.98	5.49	7.06	3.0	19.0	55.1	2.0	10.8	3.8	6.4
High school graduates, no college	5.73	5.28	6.77	2.5	13.1	59.7	3.7	8.0	5.9	6.8
Some college or associate degree	5.29	4.76	6.53	4.3	14.7	55.1	4.1	5.2	6.7	9.6
Bachelor's degree and higher	4.56	3.93	6.04	6.6	15.9	48.0	7.8	3.8	6.3	11.4

[1] Includes other leisure and sports activities, not elsewhere classified, and travel related to leisure and sports activities. [2] People of Hispanic origin may be of any race. [3] These values are based on usual weekly earnings. The earnings data are limited to wage and salary workers (both incorporated and unincorporated self-employed workers are excluded). Each earnings range represents approximately 25 percent of full-time wage and salary workers who held only one job.

Source: U.S. Bureau of Labor Statistics, *American Time Use Survey, 2019*, USDL 20-1275, June 2020. See also <http://www.bls.gov/tus/>.

Table 1267. Characteristics of Selected Spectator Sports: 1990 to 2019

[54,824 represents 54,824,000]

Sport	Unit	1990	1995	2000	2005	2010	2015	2017	2018	2019
Baseball, major leagues: [1]										
Regular season attendance........	1,000	54,824	50,469	72,749	74,926	73,054	73,760	72,670	69,625	68,495
National League..................	1,000	24,492	25,110	39,851	41,644	40,890	38,903	38,307	37,251	37,902
American League..................	1,000	30,332	25,359	32,898	33,282	32,164	34,857	34,364	32,375	30,593
Playoffs attendance [2]...........	1,000	479	533	1,314	1,191	1,210	1,420	1,399	1,258	1,345
World Series attendance...........	1,000	209	286	277	168	244	215	347	239	305
Basketball: [3, 4]										
NCAA—Men's college:										
Teams........................	Number	768	866	937	984	1,027	1,067	1,068	1,071	1,074
Attendance....................	1,000	28,741	28,225	28,949	30,940	32,632	32,382	32,781	31,277	31,401
NCAA—Women's college:										
Teams........................	Number	782	864	958	1,018	1,048	1,084	1,092	1,093	1,097
Attendance [5].................	1,000	2,777	4,962	8,825	9,903	11,160	11,367	11,496	11,514	11,058
NCAA—Men's college football: [4]										
Teams........................	Number	534	600	624	618	644	666	666	669	669
Attendance....................	1,000	35,330	35,638	39,059	43,487	49,671	49,058	47,622	46,985	47,538
National Hockey League: [6]										
Regular season attendance........	1,000	12,580	9,234	18,800	(NA)	20,996	21,533	21,545	22,174	22,187
Playoffs attendance..............	1,000	1,356	1,329	1,525	(NA)	1,702	1,701	1,606	1,518	1,575
Professional rodeo: [7]										
Rodeos.........................	Number	754	739	688	662	570	624	650	644	(NA)
Performances....................	Number	2,159	2,217	2,081	1,940	1,671	1,663	1,711	1,682	(NA)
Members........................	Number	5,693	6,894	6,255	6,127	5,323	4,782	4,885	4,618	(NA)
Permit-holders..................	Number	3,290	3,835	3,249	2,701	1,881	1,784	1,734	1,694	(NA)
Total prize money................	Mil. dol.	18.2	24.5	32.3	36.6	39.9	46.3	48.2	49.0	(NA)

NA Not available. [1] Source: Major League Baseball (previously, The National League of Professional Baseball Clubs), New York, NY, National League Green Book ©; and The American League of Professional Baseball Clubs, New York, NY, American League Red Book ©. [2] Beginning 1995, two rounds of playoffs were played. Prior years had one round. [3] Season beginning in year shown. [4] Source: National Collegiate Athletic Association, Indianapolis, IN ©. [5] Attendance for women's basketball includes doubleheaders with men's teams beginning with the 1997 season, if attendance was taken by halftime of the women's game. [6] For season ending in year shown. Source: National Hockey League, Montreal, Quebec ©. In September 2004, franchise owners locked out their players upon the expiration of the collective bargaining agreement. The entire season was cancelled in February 2005. [7] Source: Professional Rodeo Cowboys Association, Colorado Springs, CO, Official Professional Rodeo Media Guide, annual ©.

Source: Compiled from sources listed in footnotes.

Table 1268. Adult Attendance at Sports Events by Frequency: 2019

[In thousands (240 represents 240,000), except percent. For Fall 2019. Percent is based on total projected population of 250,323,000. Data not comparable to previous years. Based on a survey and subject to sampling error; see source]

Event	Attend regularly Number (1,000)	Attend regularly Per-cent	Attend on occasion [1] Number (1,000)	Attend on occasion [1] Per-cent	Event	Attend regularly Number (1,000)	Attend regularly Per-cent	Attend on occasion [1] Number (1,000)	Attend on occasion [1] Per-cent
Alpine skiing and ski jumping...	240	0.10	561	0.22	Gymnastics.....................	128	0.05	652	0.26
Auto racing – NASCAR.........	302	0.12	1,286	0.51	High school sports............	3,196	1.28	6,448	2.58
Auto racing – other.............	649	0.26	2,063	0.82	Horse racing (track or OTB)...	296	0.12	1,152	0.46
Baseball:					Ice hockey:				
College.........................	236	0.09	1,300	0.52	NHL regular season.........	774	0.31	3,834	1.53
Pro (MLB) regular season. . . .	1,315	0.53	11,062	4.42	NHL playoffs and Stanley				
Pro (MLB) playoffs/					Cup finals...................	280	0.11	940	0.38
World Series..................	588	0.2	1,955	0.78	Lacrosse (MLL)...............	190	0.08	348	0.14
Basketball:					Marathon, triathlon & other				
College.........................	926	0.37	4,337	1.73	endurance events............	272	0.11	477	0.19
NCAA tournament.............	250	0.10	995	0.40	Mixed martial arts (other)......	103	0.04	469	0.19
Pro (NBA) regular season. . . .	525	0.21	3,505	1.40	Motorcycle racing.............	81	0.03	623	0.25
Pro (NBA) playoffs.............	491	0.20	1417	0.57	Olympics – Summer...........	136	0.05	485	0.19
Pro (WNBA)....................	210	0.08	612	0.24	Olympics – Winter.............	207	0.08	385	0.15
Bicycle racing..................	158	0.06	506	0.20	Poker..........................	123	0.05	351	0.14
Bowling........................	154	0.06	666	0.27	Rodeo.........................	265	0.11	1,222	0.49
Boxing.........................	180	0.07	699	0.28	Soccer:				
Bull riding (Pro)................	162	0.06	557	0.22	MLS..........................	278	0.11	1,780	0.71
Equestrian events..............	278	0.11	836	0.33	World Cup....................	224	0.09	679	0.27
Extreme sports – Summer.....	15	0.01	167	0.07	Men's national team..........	74	0.03	392	0.16
Extreme sports – Winter........	126	0.05	354	0.14	Women's national team......	54	0.02	520	0.21
Figure skating..................	127	0.05	329	0.13	Tennis:				
Fishing.........................	191	0.08	669	0.27	Men's.........................	44	0.02	827	0.33
Football:					Women's.......................	111	0.04	732	0.29
College.........................	1,860	0.74	7,858	3.14	Track & field....................	131	0.05	427	0.17
Pro (NFL) Monday, Thursday					Truck and tractor				
or Sunday night games......	521	0.21	3,266	1.30	pull/mud racing...............	176	0.07	699	0.28
NFL weekend games...........	566	0.23	4,017	1.60	Ultimate Fighting				
NFL playoffs/Super Bowl......	256	0.10	1,182	0.47	Championship (UFC).........	134	0.05	354	0.14
Golf:					Volleyball (Pro beach).........	186	0.07	386	0.15
PGA............................	219	0.09	1,093	0.44	Wrestling:				
LPGA..........................	46	0.02	324	0.13	WWE..........................	225	0.09	865	0.35
Other golf......................	33	0.01	281	0.11	Other Pro......................	223	0.09	682	0.27

[1] Attended at least once during last 12 months.

Source: MRI Survey of the American Consumer. © Courtesy of MRISimmons. See also <https://www.mrisimmons.com/>.

Table 1269. Participation in NCAA Sports by Sex: 2018 to 2019

[For the academic year ending in 2019]

Sport	Males			Females		
	Teams	Athletes	Average squad	Teams	Athletes	Average squad
Total..........	**9,351**	**284,191**	**(X)**	**10,783**	**221,042**	**(X)**
Baseball...........	951	36,011	37.9	(X)	(X)	(X)
Basketball.........	1,086	18,816	17.3	1,101	16,509	15.0
Bowling [2].......	3	35	11.7	83	783	9.4
Cross country [1]...	997	14,303	14.3	1,072	15,624	14.6
Equestrian [1,2,3]..	7	11	1.6	50	1,395	27.9
Fencing [1]........	35	661	18.9	43	703	16.3
Field hockey.......	(X)	(X)	(X)	278	6,119	22.0
Football...........	672	73,712	109.7	(X)	(X)	(X)
Golf [1]...........	838	8,485	10.1	700	5,436	7.8
Gymnastics.........	16	333	20.8	83	1,542	18.6
Ice hockey.........	150	4,323	28.8	106	2,531	23.9
Lacrosse...........	386	14,603	37.8	519	12,452	24.0
Rifle [1]..........	23	146	6.3	29	194	6.7
Rowing [2].........	57	2,340	41.1	148	7,294	49.3
Rugby [2,3]........	3	164	54.7	17	530	31.2
Sailing [1,2]......	22	417	19.0	(X)	(X)	(X)
Sand volleyball....	(X)	(X)	(X)	76	1,312	17.3
Skiing [1].........	32	431	13.5	35	388	11.1
Soccer.............	837	25,499	30.5	1,038	28,310	27.3
Softball...........	(X)	(X)	(X)	998	20,419	20.5
Squash [2,3].......	33	503	15.2	31	405	13.1
Swimming/diving [1].	444	9,799	22.1	560	12,980	23.2
Synchronized swimming [3]..	(X)	(X)	(X)	3	47	15.7
Tennis.............	749	7,785	10.4	904	8,596	9.5
Track, indoor......	734	26,173	35.7	826	27,981	33.9
Track, outdoor [1].	834	28,914	34.7	928	30,326	32.7
Volleyball.........	148	2,355	15.9	1,069	17,780	16.6
Water polo.........	49	1,072	21.9	64	1,217	19.0
Wrestling [3]......	245	7,300	29.8	4	49	12.3

X Not applicable. [1] Co-ed sport. [2] Sport recognized by the NCAA but does not have an NCAA men's championship. [3] Sport recognized by the NCAA as an emerging sport for women.

Source: The National Collegiate Athletic Association (NCAA), Indianapolis, IN, *NCAA Sports Sponsorship and Participation Rates Report* ©, November 2019. See also <http://www.ncaapublications.com/>.

Table 1270. Participation in High School Athletic Programs by Sex: 1980 to 2019

[For academic years. Data based on number of state associations reporting and may underrepresent the number of schools with and participants in athletic programs]

Year	Participants [1]		Sex and sport	Most popular sports, 2018–2019 [2]	
	Males	Females		Schools	Participants
1980 to 1981..........	3,503,124	1,853,789	MALE		
1985 to 1986..........	3,344,275	1,807,121	Football (11-player)...............	14,247	1,006,013
1990 to 1991..........	3,406,355	1,892,316	Track & field (outdoor)............	17,052	605,354
1995 to 1996..........	3,634,052	2,367,936	Basketball.........................	18,617	540,769
2000 to 2001..........	3,921,069	2,784,154	Baseball...........................	16,170	482,740
2002 to 2003..........	3,988,738	2,856,358	Soccer.............................	12,552	459,077
2003 to 2004..........	4,038,253	2,865,299	Cross country......................	15,632	269,295
2004 to 2005..........	4,110,319	2,908,390	Wrestling..........................	10,843	247,441
2005 to 2006..........	4,206,549	2,953,355	Tennis.............................	9,809	159,314
2006 to 2007..........	4,321,103	3,021,807	Golf...............................	13,590	143,200
2007 to 2008..........	4,372,115	3,057,266	Swimming & diving..................	7,704	136,638
2008 to 2009..........	4,422,662	3,114,091	FEMALE		
2009 to 2010..........	4,455,740	3,172,637	Track & field (outdoor)............	17,012	488,267
2010 to 2011..........	4,494,406	3,173,549	Volleyball.........................	16,572	452,808
2011 to 2012..........	4,484,987	3,207,533	Basketball.........................	18,210	399,067
2012 to 2013..........	4,490,854	3,222,723	Soccer.............................	12,107	394,105
2013 to 2014..........	4,527,994	3,267,664	Softball (fast pitch)..............	15,877	362,038
2014 to 2015..........	4,519,312	3,287,735	Cross country......................	15,435	219,345
2015 to 2016..........	4,541,959	3,324,306	Tennis.............................	10,290	189,436
2016 to 2017..........	4,563,238	3,400,297	Swimming & diving..................	8,007	173,088
2017 to 2018..........	4,565,580	3,415,306	Competitive spirit squads.........	7,214	161,358
2018 to 2019..........	4,534,758	3,402,733	Lacrosse...........................	2,877	99,750

[1] Participants are counted in each sport in which they participate. [2] Ten most popular sports for each gender, ranked by number of participants.

Source: National Federation of State High School Associations, Indianapolis, IN, *The 2018–19 High School Athletics Participation Survey* ©. Reprinted with permission of the National Federation of State High School Associations. See also <http://www.nfhs.org/>.

Table 1271. Participants in Selected Sports Activities: 2016

[In thousands (293,474 represents 293,474,000). Data are based on an online survey of 34,000 individuals. The questionnaire asked the heads of households and up to three other household members who were at least seven years of age to indicate their age, the sports in which they participated in 2016, and the number of days of participation in 2016. A participant is defined as an individual seven years of age or older who participates in a sport more than once a year; selected fitness activities required participation of 6 or more days during the year. See source for methodology]

Activity	Total (number)	Sex		Age (years)								Household income (dollars)						
		Male	Female	7-17	18-24	25-34	35-44	45-54	55-64	65-74	75 and over	Under 25,000	25,000-34,999	35,000-49,999	50,000-74,999	75,000-99,999	100,000-149,999	150,000 and over
Total persons age 7 and older [1]	293,474	143,950	149,524	45,700	31,220	44,137	40,590	43,188	40,878	36,135	11,625	64,858	29,347	37,271	49,010	35,510	41,380	36,097
Aerobic exercising [1]	45,591	16,413	29,179	3,616	4,680	9,548	7,736	6,823	6,440	5,671	1,077	7,350	3,768	5,144	8,336	5,728	7,607	7,659
Archery, target	8,311	5,274	3,037	2,618	1,340	1,266	1,190	988	623	252	36	1,930	531	921	1,314	924	1,262	1,428
Backpacking [2]	12,555	7,600	4,955	2,354	1,713	2,873	2,419	1,918	906	321	53	2,387	1,206	1,137	1,972	1,759	2,111	1,985
Baseball	12,179	9,501	2,678	5,811	1,382	2,113	1,489	920	342	122	–	1,084	576	1,100	1,867	2,498	2,840	2,214
Basketball	24,762	18,621	6,142	9,569	4,452	4,494	3,404	1,910	726	206	–	4,012	1,965	2,879	4,010	3,689	4,731	3,478
Bicycle riding [1]	36,188	21,007	15,181	10,458	2,955	4,923	5,138	5,193	4,521	2,548	452	5,828	2,723	3,919	6,414	4,594	6,489	6,221
Billiards/pool	21,250	13,966	7,284	2,120	3,497	5,011	3,870	3,272	2,211	996	274	4,319	1,977	2,503	3,956	2,536	2,887	3,071
Boating, motor/power	14,412	7,998	6,414	2,003	1,560	1,889	2,180	2,496	2,466	1,577	241	1,837	1,036	1,517	2,534	2,069	2,441	2,978
Bowling	34,691	18,666	16,024	7,818	4,309	6,881	5,725	5,089	2,939	1,472	458	6,312	3,175	4,287	6,057	3,768	5,400	5,693
Camping [3]	40,410	21,865	18,545	7,989	4,281	7,927	7,354	5,923	4,255	2,287	395	7,261	4,132	5,094	7,234	5,719	6,752	4,218
Cheerleading	3,709	559	3,150	2,553	483	409	125	139	–	–	–	414	262	326	863	575	538	730
Dart throwing	9,504	6,017	3,487	1,114	1,398	2,071	1,950	1,710	895	271	95	1,759	862	1,165	1,775	1,220	911	1,811
Exercise walking [1]	105,700	46,028	59,672	7,688	8,918	15,373	15,705	19,772	18,365	15,339	4,540	22,568	10,378	13,438	18,537	12,054	14,704	14,022
Exercise with equipment [1]	57,100	27,710	29,390	4,035	6,984	10,920	8,862	9,801	7,920	6,773	1,805	9,055	4,960	7,247	10,976	6,936	8,229	9,699
Fishing, fresh water	28,921	19,614	9,306	5,095	2,671	3,469	4,580	5,720	3,650	3,047	689	5,615	3,422	4,105	5,241	3,321	3,220	3,997
Fishing, salt water	9,116	6,658	2,458	1,254	574	1,658	1,420	1,611	1,489	816	294	1,372	849	1,157	1,339	1,293	1,675	1,430
Football, tackle	7,899	7,157	742	4,580	999	1,190	782	263	85	–	–	1,116	480	701	1,220	1,565	1,835	983
Golf	18,472	13,757	4,715	1,517	1,209	2,751	3,198	3,188	3,234	2,568	808	1,516	797	1,798	2,922	2,718	4,065	4,656
Gymnastics	6,115	1,645	4,469	3,722	612	877	462	218	70	142	13	407	325	619	1,041	1,138	1,535	1,049
Hiking	42,927	21,694	21,234	5,394	4,683	8,618	7,297	7,380	5,743	3,350	462	6,994	3,524	5,344	8,021	5,237	6,832	6,975
Hockey, ice	3,366	2,680	686	1,065	512	772	511	318	189	–	–	290	59	259	616	552	787	803
Hunting with bow & arrow	5,843	4,188	1,655	768	781	1,513	1,240	824	502	197	19	1,506	390	689	978	772	766	740
Hunting with firearms	18,027	14,815	3,212	1,657	1,740	2,902	3,309	3,808	2,663	1,646	302	3,229	1,777	2,673	3,123	1,938	2,464	2,822
In-line roller skating	4,600	2,024	2,576	2,303	602	847	466	251	112	19	–	548	390	675	822	688	753	725
Kayaking	9,617	4,533	5,084	1,505	1,205	2,187	1,514	1,300	1,297	513	97	1,138	323	1,122	1,712	1,316	1,954	2,052
Lacrosse	2,947	1,933	1,014	1,540	419	500	254	179	55	–	–	190	281	254	369	833	383	638
Mountain biking, off road	5,741	4,119	1,622	919	652	1,602	1,212	807	398	152	–	1,131	229	452	980	931	1,047	971
Muzzleloading	2,727	2,405	322	226	463	439	342	593	320	307	37	579	228	436	510	371	257	345
Paintball games	5,320	3,832	1,488	2,004	1,070	1,145	826	234	41	–	–	473	430	574	820	1,040	918	1,064
Running/jogging [1]	44,946	23,808	21,137	8,873	7,378	10,513	8,482	5,323	2,913	1,204	261	6,510	3,375	5,383	8,041	6,586	8,096	6,957
Skateboarding	5,400	3,802	1,598	2,797	1,115	944	351	119	73	–	–	626	463	555	987	755	1,064	950
Skiing, alpine	5,791	3,492	2,299	1,299	1,631	1,065	779	880	825	313	–	277	167	453	574	869	940	2,512
Skiing, cross country	2,335	1,338	998	354	284	467	409	341	372	107	–	437	1	240	130	408	450	671
Snowboarding	4,000	2,575	1,425	1,032	685	1,399	474	236	153	22	–	428	168	373	810	676	696	850
Soccer	14,053	9,263	4,790	7,670	1,930	2,302	1,452	484	191	24	–	1,007	720	1,582	2,347	2,587	3,466	2,346
Softball	9,634	5,130	4,504	4,007	988	1,468	1,305	1,005	618	243	–	740	708	890	1,429	1,681	1,832	2,355
Swimming [1]	45,618	21,679	23,939	12,763	3,840	5,894	6,321	5,840	5,541	4,318	1,102	5,179	3,579	5,747	7,834	6,360	8,303	8,616
Table tennis/ping pong	10,242	5,708	4,534	2,319	1,570	2,208	1,344	1,296	804	582	119	1,083	772	708	1,638	1,693	2,132	2,217
Target shooting, live ammunition	20,446	14,392	6,055	1,790	1,965	4,557	3,686	3,392	2,888	1,862	307	2,764	1,691	2,945	3,804	2,806	3,343	3,094
Target shooting, airgun	5,033	3,949	1,084	1,148	752	1,028	681	703	342	310	70	609	497	672	942	765	876	671
Tennis	12,643	6,776	5,867	2,750	1,614	2,601	2,382	1,627	1,003	551	115	971	811	936	2,135	2,233	2,690	2,884
Volleyball	10,697	4,604	6,093	4,696	1,631	1,943	1,259	822	270	39	–	957	759	936	1,568	2,246	2,732	1,499
Water skiing	3,571	1,882	1,688	914	550	889	633	354	192	39	–	348	103	301	305	580	841	1,092
Weightlifting [1]	35,569	23,153	12,416	2,901	5,182	7,939	6,549	5,729	4,033	2,746	489	5,318	2,926	4,346	6,939	4,632	5,740	5,668
Workout at club [1]	37,800	17,846	19,954	2,773	5,623	8,590	5,783	5,743	4,339	3,928	1,021	4,838	2,639	4,200	6,909	5,033	6,565	7,616
Wrestling	2,984	2,381	604	1,463	451	626	244	184	17	–	–	520	122	322	540	650	401	428
Yoga	30,320	7,227	23,093	2,294	4,757	8,187	5,481	4,341	3,059	1,822	378	6,057	2,083	4,023	5,239	3,614	4,478	4,825

– Represents zero. [1] Participant engaged in activity at least six times in the year. [2] Includes wilderness camping. [3] Vacation/overnight.

Source: National Sporting Goods Association, Mt. Prospect, IL, *Sports Participation in the United States, 2017 Edition* ©. See also <https://www.nsga.org/research/nsga-research-offerings/>.

Table 1272. Consumer Purchases of Sporting Goods by Consumer Characteristics: 2016

[Shown as percent of dollar purchases. Data are based on an online survey of over 15,000 households]

| Characteristic | Total | Footwear | | | | | Equipment | | | | |
		Cross-train/ fitness shoes	Gym shoes/ sneakers	Hiking shoes/ boots	Jog-ging/ running shoes	Walking shoes	Bi-cycles	Fitness trackers/ pedo-meters	Golf club sets	Hand-guns	Rod/ reel combi-nation
Total..........................	100.0	100.0	100.0	100.0	100.0	100.0	100.0	100.0	100.0	100.0	100.0
Age of user:											
Under 14 years old..............	17.7	4.4	11.2	3.2	4.2	3.5	9.4	1.4	1.1	–	2.7
14 to 17 years old...............	5.2	4.4	8.3	4.5	5.4	3.4	5.7	1.5	2.3	0.4	2.7
18 to 24 years old...............	9.7	10.9	12.7	5.5	9.9	5.2	7.1	9.1	3.9	3.5	6.5
25 to 34 years old...............	13.7	20.2	17.0	12.5	17.4	11.6	16.3	18.1	14.0	16.0	14.3
35 to 44 years old...............	12.6	18.8	14.0	20.0	21.7	15.6	13.9	16.5	24.0	15.5	16.2
45 to 64 years old...............	26.2	32.3	23.5	40.0	32.6	35.4	42.7	41.6	38.0	40.1	36.6
65 years old and over..........	14.9	9.0	13.3	14.3	8.8	25.3	4.9	11.8	16.7	24.5	21.0
Sex of user:											
Male........................	49.2	48.2	43.7	62.4	52.9	45.9	60.3	38.5	85.0	83.7	81.5
Female......................	50.8	51.8	56.3	37.6	47.1	54.1	39.7	61.5	15.0	16.3	18.5
Annual household income:											
Under $15,000....................	11.6	4.9	5.3	6.6	5.2	7.4	3.3	5.2	3.2	3.7	6.3
$15,000 to $24,999.............	10.5	3.7	6.5	5.5	3.9	6.7	4.2	4.0	0.5	3.2	6.8
$25,000 to $34,999.............	10.0	5.8	9.0	6.3	5.1	8.3	4.4	5.6	6.5	7.0	11.6
$35,000 to $49,999.............	12.7	9.2	11.1	11.0	8.5	10.6	5.3	8.0	4.9	11.6	11.6
$50,000 to $74,999.............	16.7	16.2	17.5	13.2	16.9	17.2	11.9	18.8	20.2	17.1	18.7
$75,000 to $99,999.............	12.1	16.0	13.1	13.1	15.0	13.9	14.0	15.3	14.9	14.8	12.8
$100,000 to $149,999...........	14.1	21.8	17.3	19.6	20.3	20.2	23.2	20.6	37.1	16.8	13.6
$150,000 and over.............	12.3	22.4	20.2	24.7	25.1	15.7	33.7	22.5	12.7	25.8	18.6
Education of household head:											
Less than high school...........	11.7	1.1	1.2	0.7	0.8	1.4	0.5	0.9	0.7	0.5	1.8
High school...................	29.0	9.7	13.4	9.2	9.8	12.8	10.7	7.3	7.8	11.0	20.2
Some college....................	28.6	19.8	30.2	21.8	22.5	24.3	18.3	21.4	18.1	25.8	29.4
College graduate................	30.7	69.4	55.2	68.3	66.9	61.5	70.5	70.4	73.4	62.7	48.6

– Represents or rounds to zero.

Source: National Sporting Goods Association, Mt. Prospect, IL, *Sporting Goods Market: 2017 Edition* ©. See also <https://www.nsga.org/research/nsga-research-offerings/>.

Table 1273. National Park Service—Summary: 1990 to 2019

[In units as indicated (986 represents $986,000,000). For year ending September 30, except as noted. Covers all States, the District of Columbia, and the U.S. territories of American Samoa, Guam, Puerto Rico, and the U.S. Virgin Islands]

Item	1990	1995	2000	2005	2010	2017	2018	2019
FINANCES (mil. dol.): [1]								
Expenditures reported.........................	986	1,445	1,833	2,451	3,239	3,119	3,245	(NA)
Salaries and wages....................	459	633	799	984	1,237	1,197	1,195	(NA)
Improvements, maintenance.................	160	234	299	361	531	588	606	(NA)
Construction.........................	109	192	215	381	443	223	228	(NA)
Other.................................	259	386	520	725	1,028	1,111	1,227	(NA)
Funds available.........................	1,506	2,225	3,316	4,218	5,402	5,559	6,366	(NA)
Appropriations......................	1,053	1,325	1,881	2,425	2,848	3,343	3,804	(NA)
Other [2].............................	453	900	1,435	1,793	2,554	2,152	2,515	(NA)
Revenue from operations................	79	106	234	286	387	546	551	(NA)
RECREATION VISITS (millions): [3]								
All areas............................	258.7	269.6	285.9	273.5	281.3	330.9	318.2	327.5
National parks [4]......................	57.7	64.8	66.1	63.5	64.6	85.5	85.9	89.8
National monuments....................	23.9	23.5	23.8	20.9	23.0	26.3	22.2	22.4
National historical, commemorative, archaeological [5]......................	57.5	56.9	72.2	74.9	80.0	96.5	93.2	95.4
National parkways......................	29.1	31.3	34.0	31.7	28.6	31.4	29.8	30.2
National recreation areas [4].............	47.2	53.7	50.0	46.8	49.0	52.1	51.0	52.1
National seashores and lakeshores........	23.3	22.5	22.5	21.7	22.2	23.3	21.0	22.9
National Capital Parks [6].....................	7.5	5.5	4.1	3.1	2.5	3.3	3.2	3.0
Recreation overnight stays (millions)........	17.6	16.8	15.4	13.5	14.4	14.8	14.0	13.8
In commercial lodgings [7].....................	3.9	3.8	3.7	3.4	3.5	4.9	4.5	4.5
In Park Service campgrounds..............	7.9	7.1	5.9	5.2	5.5	6.2	6.0	6.0
In backcountry.........................	1.7	2.2	1.9	1.7	1.8	2.1	1.9	1.9
Other [8]............................	4.2	3.7	3.8	3.2	3.7	1.6	1.6	1.4
LAND (1,000 acres): [9]								
Total............................	76,362	77,355	78,153	79,048	80,527	81,008	81,041	81,090
Parks.........................	46,089	49,307	49,785	49,910	50,662	50,749	50,752	50,678
Recreation areas.....................	3,344	3,353	3,388	3,391	3,418	3,400	3,425	3,155
Other.........................	26,929	24,695	24,980	25,747	26,447	26,859	26,864	2,619
Acquisition, net............................	21	27	186	17	23	282	33	49

[1] Financial data are those associated with the National Park System. Certain other functions of the National Park Service (principally the activities absorbed from the former Heritage Conservation and Recreation Service in 1981) are excluded. [2] Includes funds carried over from prior years. [3] For calendar year. Includes other types of areas, not shown separately. [4] For 1990, combined data for North Cascades National Park and two adjacent National Recreation Areas are included in National Parks total. [5] Includes National Battlefields, National Battlefield Parks, National Historic Sites, National Historical Parks, National Memorials, National Military Parks, National Preserves, and National Reserves. [6] For 1990 to 1996, data are for National Capital Parks combined. Beginning 1997, data are summed for National Capital Parks East and National Capital Parks Central (also known as National Mall and Memorial Parks). [7] Beginning in 2011, includes concessioner lodging and campgrounds. [8] Prior to 2011, includes concessioner campgrounds. [9] Federal land only, as of December 31. Federal land acreages, in addition to National Park Service administered lands, also include lands within national park system area boundaries but under the administration of other agencies. Year-to-year changes in the federal lands figures includes changes in the acreages of these other lands and hence often differ from "net acquisition."

Source: U.S. National Park Service, *National Park Statistical Abstract 2018*, April 2019, and earlier reports; unpublished data; and "National Park Service Visitor Use Statistics, National Reports," <https://irma.nps.gov/Stats/Reports/National>, accessed September 2020.

Table 1274. National Park Service (NPS) Visits and Acreage by State: 2019

Table 1274. National Park Service (NPS) Visits and Acreage by State: 2019

State	Recreation visits [1]	Gross area acres	Federal land — NPS fee acres [2]	Federal land — NPS less than fee acres [3]	Federal land — Other federal fee acres [4]	Nonfederal land — Other public acres [5]	Nonfederal land — Private acres
Total [6]	327,516,623	85,103,543	80,026,780	352,206	710,663	1,395,840	2,618,055
Alabama	1,219,216	22,747	17,540	203	13	3,288	1,702
Alaska	3,218,301	54,653,962	52,455,708	103,093	8	372,384	1,722,770
Arizona	12,463,772	2,947,211	2,658,192	94	75,949	56,833	156,142
Arkansas	3,227,883	104,982	98,348	3,428	20	2,749	438
California	39,620,672	8,210,924	7,649,874	22,427	12,454	352,118	174,050
Colorado	7,761,213	738,668	665,260	4,276	42,456	303	26,374
Connecticut	38,700	7,782	5,846	1,055	–	874	6
Delaware	(NA)	904	890	6	–	2	6
District of Columbia	39,687,383	8,625	8,476	8	6	134	2
Florida	12,009,271	2,638,605	2,474,850	1,350	44,486	101,784	16,135
Georgia	8,206,285	67,524	39,956	167	1,461	17,754	8,186
Hawaii	4,929,610	371,494	360,111	1	22	11,228	132
Idaho	617,646	806,298	511,963	1,226	273,488	9,058	10,562
Illinois	197,816	115	12	–	–	17	85
Indiana	2,413,129	15,575	10,781	538	–	3,419	836
Iowa	191,269	2,713	2,670	–	–	42	1
Kansas	109,729	11,628	462	271	–	56	10,838
Kentucky	1,752,796	97,504	94,483	137	–	838	2,046
Louisiana	661,300	27,000	21,145	–	–	2,779	3,075
Maine	3,448,899	182,007	157,737	11,204	24	10,646	2,395
Maryland	6,854,872	74,059	41,473	5,816	395	23,731	2,645
Massachusetts	10,003,220	59,500	33,336	1,029	44	21,920	3,172
Michigan	2,702,015	718,190	632,302	673	46	58,515	26,654
Minnesota	1,099,282	301,352	139,816	3,193	142	98,659	59,542
Mississippi	7,031,781	119,301	105,079	5,229	–	72	8,920
Missouri	3,629,384	83,545	54,576	9,168	–	14,070	5,732
Montana	5,547,209	1,274,133	1,214,193	1,850	6,137	1,464	50,489
Nebraska	305,112	66,569	6,462	485	845	435	58,343
Nevada	5,756,090	801,172	797,613	–	2,508	44	1,008
New Hampshire	31,759	21,190	13,696	1,556	5,772	162	5
New Jersey	4,588,966	99,598	35,683	140	3,208	59,050	1,517
New Mexico	2,139,674	483,504	472,664	5	25	4,656	6,153
New York	21,013,245	97,419	34,111	3,903	148	19,988	39,271
North Carolina	18,895,659	410,459	366,881	12,272	20,782	3,289	7,235
North Dakota	714,979	72,568	71,192	256	151	122	847
Ohio	2,613,089	34,555	20,290	1,462	84	8,482	4,237
Oklahoma	1,431,731	10,241	10,011	9	189	5	27
Oregon	1,237,602	203,385	196,197	1,404	4,976	295	513
Pennsylvania	10,153,809	116,509	53,460	3,043	387	19,593	40,026
Rhode Island	59,419	331	5	–	–	–	326
South Carolina	1,655,573	32,564	32,339	63	16	51	96
South Dakota	3,928,433	296,584	148,007	122,326	–	78	26,173
Tennessee	9,979,139	389,245	359,252	1,714	9,665	4,203	14,410
Texas	5,834,681	1,260,150	1,204,850	1,133	1,932	11,185	41,050
Utah	15,285,200	2,117,689	2,097,901	833	1,142	12,819	4,994
Vermont	45,979	23,237	9,836	3,927	8,809	544	120
Virginia	22,815,596	371,635	306,435	7,161	24,866	7,144	26,029
Washington	8,776,096	1,967,552	1,834,634	2,165	100,222	12,798	17,733
West Virginia	1,652,243	92,697	65,843	371	386	6,893	19,205
Wisconsin	559,746	133,757	61,835	11,353	802	47,619	12,148
Wyoming	7,431,294	2,396,431	2,345,654	177	48,462	497	1,640

– Represents or rounds to zero. [1] See footnote 1, Table 1275. [2] See footnote 2, Table 1275. [3] See footnote 3, Table 1275. [4] See footnote 4, Table 1275. [5] See footnote 5, Table 1275. [6] Includes Island Areas of the U.S., not shown separately.

Source: U.S. National Park Service, Land Resources Division, unpublished data; and "National Park Service Visitor Use Statistics, National Reports," <https://irma.nps.gov/Stats/Reports/National>, accessed September 2020.

Table 1275. National Park Service (NPS) Visits and Acreage by Type of Area: 2019

[Includes data for four areas in Virgin Islands, and one area in each Puerto Rico, American Samoa, and Guam]

Type of area	Recreation visits [1]	Gross area acres	Federal land — NPS fee acres [2]	Federal land — NPS less than fee acres [3]	Federal land — Other federal fee acres [4]	Non-federal land — Other public acres [5]	Non-federal land — Private acres
Total [6]	327,516,619	85,103,543	80,026,780	352,206	710,663	1,395,840	2,618,055
National historic sites	8,850,017	31,804	20,085	856	42	374	10,448
National historical parks	34,732,138	198,710	142,821	4,202	565	29,597	21,525
National memorials	37,653,264	10,564	9,664	3	46	60	792
National monuments	22,406,247	1,992,189	1,826,688	14,727	23,474	8,562	118,738
National parks	89,815,063	52,408,264	50,678,486	222,549	45,735	572,712	888,781
National parkways	30,186,057	182,285	161,996	9,134	128	404	10,624
National recreation areas	52,110,142	3,712,388	3,154,703	24,831	245,758	112,313	174,782
National seashores	20,273,975	596,931	404,612	14,947	61,226	106,820	9,326

[1] Recreation visit represents the entry of a person onto lands or waters administered by the NPS for recreational purposes, excluding government personnel, through traffic, tradespeople, and persons residing within park boundaries. [2] Complete Federal ownership of all rights in the land. [3] Federal ownership of some rights in the land. [4] Tracts under the administration of another federal agency (e.g., U.S. Forest Service, Department of the Army, etc.). Bureau of Land Management tracts are also identified as Other Fee (Federal) until they are withdrawn for NPS use; then status changes to Fee (Federal). [5] Non-federal tracts owned by the state, county, and/or other municipalities, including quasi-public entities. [6] Includes other types of areas, not shown separately.

Source: U.S. National Park Service, Land Resources Division, unpublished data; and "National Park Service Visitor Use Statistics," <https://irma.nps.gov/Stats/Reports/National>, accessed September 2020.

Table 1276. State Parks and Recreation Areas by State: 2018

[In units as indicated (18,553 represents 18,553,000). For year ending June 30. Data are shown as reported by state park directors. In some states, the park agency has forests, fish and wildlife areas, and/or other areas under its control. In other states, the park agency is responsible for state parks only]

State	Acreage (1,000)	Visitors (1,000) [1]	Total revenue generated ($1,000)	Operating expenditures ($1,000)	Revenue share of operating expenditures
United States.............	**18,553**	**813,216**	**1,391,600**	**2,849,225**	**48.8**
Alabama.................	48	4,815	38,195	41,663	91.7
Alaska..................	3,387	3,686	3,809	13,393	28.4
Arizona.................	64	3,190	20,362	22,298	91.3
Arkansas...............	55	7,108	28,389	63,432	44.8
California..............	1,647	81,043	132,154	617,211	21.4
Colorado...............	1,580	14,777	85,246	63,105	135.1
Connecticut............	210	9,134	5,230	16,296	32.1
Delaware...............	26	5,893	19,730	28,432	69.4
Florida.................	721	28,179	66,068	82,520	80.1
Georgia................	83	9,003	33,664	49,311	68.3
Hawaii.................	33	11,348	4,321	12,650	34.2
Idaho..................	59	5,696	11,794	18,057	65.3
Illinois................	483	38,527	7,221	49,840	14.5
Indiana................	171	16,765	66,757	62,969	106.0
Iowa...................	116	14,492	5,310	19,940	26.6
Kansas.................	33	6,884	10,689	13,970	76.5
Kentucky...............	44	6,505	52,713	87,915	60.0
Louisiana..............	43	1,772	10,916	29,033	37.6
Maine..................	98	2,804	5,348	9,106	58.7
Maryland...............	140	14,095	11,971	65,813	18.2
Massachusetts..........	354	27,292	17,568	84,025	20.9
Michigan...............	303	31,277	64,370	67,532	95.3
Minnesota..............	284	9,737	29,319	100,784	29.1
Mississippi.............	24	1,200	9,798	13,970	70.1
Missouri...............	160	22,142	14,507	54,673	26.5
Montana................	46	2,663	2,469	10,667	23.1
Nebraska...............	170	10,894	35,286	25,961	135.9
Nevada.................	151	3,888	6,576	18,569	35.4
New Hampshire..........	232	1,177	25,077	23,182	108.2
New Jersey.............	455	17,438	13,989	40,450	34.6
New Mexico.............	192	5,010	6,124	16,053	38.1
New York...............	4,318	72,032	107,004	225,675	47.4
North Carolina..........	235	19,078	11,043	43,967	25.1
North Dakota...........	35	1,497	3,867	17,062	22.7
Ohio...................	175	42,831	32,026	73,698	43.5
Oklahoma..............	62	9,903	22,905	28,518	80.3
Oregon.................	113	54,421	31,261	65,612	47.6
Pennsylvania...........	295	38,338	25,917	105,761	24.5
Rhode Island...........	10	8,928	5,444	11,872	45.9
South Carolina.........	77	8,731	30,684	31,112	98.6
South Dakota...........	103	7,734	27,865	22,944	121.5
Tennessee..............	226	40,477	42,924	96,391	44.5
Texas..................	640	8,772	49,995	81,724	61.2
Utah...................	153	5,728	25,368	19,764	128.4
Vermont................	74	987	11,491	7,289	157.7
Virginia................	74	9,443	24,818	45,781	54.2
Washington.............	122	36,745	49,852	74,250	67.1
West Virginia...........	151	6,865	22,701	43,176	52.6
Wisconsin..............	158	17,749	18,487	21,375	86.5
Wyoming...............	120	4,525	2,979	10,438	28.5

[1] Includes day and overnight visitors.

Source: National Association of State Park Directors, Raleigh NC, *Statistical Report of State Park Operations: 2017-2018, Annual Information Exchange for the Period of July 1, 2017 through June 30, 2018* ©, September 2019. See also <http://www.stateparks.org/>.

Table 1277. Participants in Wildlife-Related Recreation Activities: 2016

[In thousands (39,553 represents 39,553,000). For persons 16 years old and over engaging in activity at least once in 2016. Based on survey and subject to sampling error; see source for details]

Participant	Number	Days of participation	Trips	Participant	Number	Days of participation
Total sportspersons [1]	**39,553**	**643,362**	**530,167**	**Wildlife watchers** [1]	**86,042**	**(X)**
Total anglers	35,754	459,341	383,296	Away from home [2]	23,720	386,045
Freshwater	30,137	383,192	322,266	Observe wildlife	19,583	308,769
Excluding Great Lakes	29,490	372,660	311,237	Photograph wildlife	13,721	151,559
Great Lakes	1,824	13,440	11,029	Feed wildlife	4,869	70,846
Saltwater	8,320	75,392	61,030	Around the home [3]	81,128	(X)
				Observe wildlife	43,829	(X)
Total hunters	11,453	184,021	146,871	Photograph wildlife	30,473	(X)
Big game	9,208	132,665	88,561	Feed wildlife	59,083	(X)
Small game	3,505	38,306	31,772	Visit public parks	11,359	(X)
Migratory birds	2,353	15,621	14,548	Maintain plantings or		
Other animals	1,315	13,275	11,989	natural areas	11,024	(X)

X Not applicable. [1] Detail does not add to total due to multiple responses and nonresponse. [2] Persons taking a trip of at least 1 mile from home for activity. [3] Activity within 1 mile of home.

Source: U.S. Fish and Wildlife Service, *2016 National Survey of Fishing, Hunting, and Wildlife Associated Recreation*, April 2018. See also <https://wsfrprograms.fws.gov/Subpages/NationalSurvey/2016_Survey.html>.

Table 1278. Expenditures for Wildlife-Related Recreation Activities: 2016

[46,115 represents $46,115,000,000. For persons 16 years old and over. Based on survey and subject to sampling error; see source]

Expenditure item	Fishing			Hunting			Wildlife watching		
		Spenders			Spenders			Spenders	
	Expenditures (mil. dol.)	Number (1,000)	Percent of anglers	Expenditures (mil. dol.)	Number (1,000)	Percent of hunters	Expenditures [1] (mil. dol.)	Number (1,000)	Percent [2]
Total, all items [3]	**46,115**	**32,511**	**91**	**26,190**	**10,992**	**96**	**75,867**	**63,578**	**74**
Total trip-related	21,730	31,260	87	9,196	9,984	87	11,588	20,235	85
Food and lodging	7,849	27,127	76	3,114	9,065	79	6,068	17,058	72
Food	4,759	26,867	75	2,507	9,053	79	3,810	16,955	71
Lodging	3,090	8,625	24	607	1,775	16	2,258	6,331	27
Transportation	5,049	26,337	74	3,184	9,047	79	4,229	19,018	80
Public	543	2,852	8	193	912	8	1,233	3,052	13
Private	4,506	25,622	72	2,991	8,937	78	2,996	17,766	75
Other trip costs	8,832	26,212	73	2,898	3,664	32	1,291	8,609	36
Equipment expenditures:									
Equipment	7,431	22,393	63	7,384	8,413	73	64,279	57,496	67
Auxiliary equipment	3,164	4,522	13	2,019	4,436	39	1,044	6,669	8
Special equipment [4]	10,483	2,291	6	[5] 3,353	[5] 396	[5] 3	41,934	3,037	4
Other expenditures:									
Magazines and books	147	3,142	9	166	1,130	10	237	7,022	8
Land leasing and ownership	2,359	1,019	3	2,899	1,845	16	4,196	1,195	1
Membership dues and contributions	214	1,741	5	182	1,403	12	3,817	10,076	12
Plantings	(X)	(X)	(X)	[5] 165	[5] 1,020	[5] 9	946	7,289	8
Licenses, stamps, tags, and permits	587	15,647	44	826	8,668	76	(X)	(X)	(X)

X Not applicable. [1] Information on trip-related expenditures for wildlife watching was collected for away-from-home participants only. Equipment and other expenditures for wildlife watching are base on information collected from both away-from-home and around-the-home participants. [2] Based on away-from-home participants for trip-related expenditures. For equipment and other expenditures the percent of wildlife-watching participants is based on total participants. [3] Total not adjusted for multiple responses or nonresponse. [4] Special equipment includes boats, campers, cabins, trail bikes, etc. [5] Estimate based on a sample size of 10 to 29.

Source: U.S. Fish and Wildlife Service, *2016 National Survey of Fishing, Hunting, and Wildlife Associated Recreation*, April 2018. See also <https://wsfrprograms.fws.gov/Subpages/NationalSurvey/2016_Survey.html>.

Table 1279. Tribal Gaming Revenues: 2010 to 2018

[Revenue in millions of dollars (26,503 represents $26,503,000,000). For year ending September 30]

Region	2010		2015		2016		2017		2018	
	Operations (number)	Revenue	Operations (number)	Revenue	Operations (number)	Revenue	Operations (number)	Revenue	Operations (number)	Revenue
Total [1]	**422**	**26,503**	**474**	**29,882**	**484**	**31,196**	**494**	**32,404**	**501**	**33,720**
Portland	50	2,655	52	3,022	53	3,177	52	3,384	55	3,663
Sacramento	62	6,794	71	7,881	70	8,381	74	8,996	73	9,279
Phoenix	48	2,539	53	2,808	57	2,932	59	3,038	59	3,141
St. Paul [2]	119	4,452	134	4,829	93	4,511	92	4,587	95	4,796
Rapid City [3]	(X)	(X)	(X)	(X)	39	373	39	363	36	369
Tulsa	65	1,769	68	2,207	69	2,295	72	2,391	73	2,466
Oklahoma City	51	1,583	65	2,142	66	2,265	69	2,312	72	2,480
Washington DC	27	6,711	31	6,994	37	7,261	37	7,333	38	7,525

X Not applicable. [1] Regions formerly were numbered I to VI, as follows: Portland (Region I): Alaska, Idaho, Oregon, and Washington. Sacramento (Region II): California, and Northern Nevada. Phoenix (Region III): Arizona, Colorado, New Mexico, and Southern Nevada. St Paul (Region IV): Iowa, Michigan, Minnesota, Montana, North Dakota, Nebraska, South Dakota, Wisconsin, and Wyoming. Tulsa (Eastern part of Region V): Kansas, and Eastern Oklahoma. Oklahoma City (Western part of Region V): Western Oklahoma, and Texas. Washington (Region VI): Alabama, Connecticut, Florida, Louisiana, Mississippi, North Carolina, and New York. See footnote 2 regarding St. Paul region. [2] Through FY2015, St. Paul region covers Iowa, Michigan, Minnesota, Montana, North Dakota, Nebraska, South Dakota, Wisconsin, and Wyoming. Beginning FY2016, St. Paul region covers Indiana, Iowa, Michigan, Minnesota, Nebraska, and Wisconsin. Also known as Region IV. [3] Rapid City region data begins with data for FY2016, and covers North Dakota, South Dakota, Montana, and Wyoming.

Source: National Indian Gaming Commission, *Gross Gaming Revenues 2014-2018*, September 2019, and earlier reports; and *Gross Gaming Revenues by Region 2017 and 2018*, September 2019, and earlier reports.

Table 1280. Real Tourism Output: 2005 to 2018

[In millions of dollars (708,427 represents $708,427,000,000)]

Commodity	Direct output (current dollars)			Real output (chained 2012 dollars)		
	2005	2010	2018	2005	2010	2018
Total	**708,427**	**719,896**	**1,088,880**	**868,593**	**804,376**	**1,061,271**
Traveler accommodations	125,130	138,439	215,808	133,572	144,413	191,786
Food and beverage services	107,579	91,912	141,159	132,840	96,933	122,105
Domestic passenger air transportation services	96,991	107,155	162,799	130,150	121,118	162,697
International passenger air transportation services	30,398	38,308	51,498	41,671	43,212	52,360
Passenger rail transportation services	1,307	1,842	2,364	1,565	1,853	2,277
Passenger water transportation services	9,084	12,560	18,813	7,879	12,176	17,873
Intercity bus transportation	1,636	1,248	1,363	2,151	1,312	1,295
Intercity charter bus transportation	1,737	1,826	2,797	2,283	1,918	2,657
Intracity mass transit	3,667	3,740	6,731	4,726	4,036	5,928
Taxicab and ride sharing service	3,840	4,053	5,031	4,950	4,374	4,432
Scenic and sightseeing transportation services	2,464	2,379	3,801	2,801	2,432	3,358
Automotive vehicle rental	23,862	23,646	34,429	28,644	22,352	36,634
Other vehicle rental	761	623	737	883	623	719
Automotive repair services	12,272	10,848	13,233	15,186	11,256	11,977
Parking lots and garages	2,194	2,319	2,880	3,078	2,579	2,457
Highway tolls	704	686	981	987	762	837
Travel arrangement and reservation services	31,456	33,355	50,766	33,213	33,681	49,843
Motion pictures and performing arts	14,519	13,831	21,276	16,954	14,243	18,638
Spectator sports	5,076	4,245	5,653	6,290	4,375	4,643
Participant sports	11,370	9,945	16,089	12,149	10,109	14,507
Gambling	37,721	43,769	56,094	44,348	46,078	51,283
All other recreation and entertainment	18,693	15,607	17,119	22,202	16,737	15,966
Gasoline	56,492	63,994	123,318	90,266	83,434	159,449
Shopping	109,474	93,565	134,140	133,508	101,500	135,087

Source: U.S. Bureau of Economic Analysis, "Travel and Tourism Satellite Accounts 1998-2018," <https://www.bea.gov/data/specialtopics/travel-and-tourism>, accessed August 2020.

Table 1281. Chain–Type Price Indexes for Direct Tourism Output: 2000 to 2018

[Index numbers, 2012=100. For explanation of chain-type price indexes, see text, Section 13]

Tourism goods and services group	2000	2005	2010	2014	2015	2016	2017	2018
All tourism goods and services	**74.5**	**81.6**	**89.0**	**102.1**	**98.4**	**97.5**	**99.7**	**102.6**
Traveler accommodations	86.3	93.7	95.9	105.2	108.5	111.2	111.9	112.5
Food and beverage services	70.4	81.0	94.8	104.6	107.5	110.2	112.7	115.6
Domestic passenger air transportation services	82.9	74.5	88.5	102.8	99.9	97.6	98.3	100.1
International passenger air transportation services	57.7	72.9	88.7	104.6	98.3	94.1	93.8	98.4
Passenger rail transportation services	74.4	83.6	99.4	99.0	98.1	100.2	103.5	103.8
Passenger water transportation services	145.3	115.3	103.2	100.5	100.4	104.0	105.0	105.3
Intercity bus transportation	64.0	76.1	95.2	100.5	100.4	104.1	105.0	105.3
Intercity charter bus transportation	64.0	76.1	95.2	100.5	100.5	104.1	105.0	105.3
Intracity mass transit	62.1	77.6	92.7	105.6	107.9	109.7	111.6	113.5
Taxicab and ride sharing service	62.1	77.6	92.7	105.6	107.8	109.7	111.6	113.5
Scenic and sightseeing transportation services	75.2	88.0	97.8	102.9	105.3	107.8	110.6	113.2
Automotive vehicle rental	76.6	83.3	105.8	107.5	99.0	91.6	91.9	94.0
Other vehicle rental	87.1	86.2	100.0	103.3	103.1	105.8	103.5	102.4
Automotive repair services	69.5	80.8	96.4	103.1	104.8	106.5	108.5	110.5
Parking lots and garages	57.0	71.3	89.9	106.1	108.8	111.8	114.6	117.2
Highway tolls	57.0	71.3	89.9	106.1	108.8	111.8	114.6	117.2
Travel arrangement and reservation services	107.4	94.7	99.0	101.0	101.6	101.5	101.3	101.9
Motion pictures and performing arts	71.4	85.6	97.1	103.0	105.3	109.1	111.8	114.2
Spectator sports	64.0	80.7	97.0	105.7	113.2	117.0	119.6	121.8
Participant sports	86.8	93.6	98.4	103.1	103.7	105.4	107.8	110.9
Gambling	75.0	85.1	95.0	103.1	103.2	104.5	106.8	109.4
All other recreation and entertainment	78.5	84.2	93.2	100.7	102.5	104.2	106.6	107.2
Gasoline	41.3	62.6	76.7	93.3	68.0	60.2	68.1	77.3
Shopping	74.0	82.0	92.2	100.6	97.1	95.9	97.4	99.3

Source: U.S. Bureau of Economic Analysis, "Travel and Tourism Satellite Accounts 1998-2018," <https://www.bea.gov/data/specialtopics/travel-and-tourism>, accessed August 2020.

Table 1282. Travel Forecast Summary: 2016 to 2022

[In units as indicated (18,707 represents $18,707,000,000,000)]

Indicator	Unit	2016	2017	2018	2019 (P)	2020 (P)	2021 (P)	2022 (P)
Real GDP	Bil. dol.	18,707	19,485	20,494	21,357	22,115	22,955	23,857
Unemployment rate	Percent	4.9	4.4	3.9	3.6	3.5	3.7	3.8
Consumer price index (CPI) [1]	Percent	240.0	245.1	251.1	256.3	261.1	265.9	271.2
Travel price index (TPI) [1]	Percent	273.1	279.4	286.5	289.0	293.2	298.5	303.8
Total travel expenditures in U.S.	Bil. dol.	994.1	1,037.7	1,089.0	1,118.7	1,160.6	1,209.4	1,257.7
U.S. residents	Bil. dol.	838.5	881.9	932.7	959.7	996.3	1,038.3	1,079.6
International visitors [2]	Bil. dol.	155.6	155.8	156.3	159.0	164.4	171.1	178.1
Total international visitors to the U.S.	Millions	76.4	76.9	79.6	79.8	82.2	84.9	87.8
Overseas arrivals to the U.S. [3]	Millions	38.1	38.9	39.9	40.6	42.0	43.5	45.0
Total domestic person trips [4]	Millions	2,206.6	2,247.9	2,291.1	2,330.8	2,369.2	2,411.2	2,457.5
Business	Millions	454.7	456.3	463.6	470.4	477.0	484.9	493.7
Leisure	Millions	1,751.9	1,791.5	1,827.5	1,860.5	1,892.2	1,926.3	1,963.8

P Projected. [1] 1982-1984=100. [2] Excludes international traveler spending on medical, educational, and cross-border/seasonal work-related activities or international passenger fares on U.S. airlines. [3] Subject to revision as updated visitation statistics are released by the Department of Commerce. [4] One person on one trip 50 miles or more, one way, away from home or including one or more nights away from home.

Source: U.S. Travel Association, *Travel Forecast Summary Table*, July 2019 ©. See also <https://www.ustravel.org/research>.

Table 1283. Tourism Sales and Employment by Industry Segment: 2000 to 2018

[Sales in millions of dollars (605,059 represents $605,059,000,000); employment in thousands (6,238 represents 6,238,000). Direct tourism-related sales comprise all output purchased directly by visitors (e.g., traveler accommodations, passenger air transportation, souvenirs). Direct tourism-related employment comprises all jobs where the workers are engaged in the production of direct tourism-related sales (output), such as hotel staff, airline pilots, and souvenir sellers]

Tourism commodity group	2000	2005	2010	2015	2016	2017	2018
DIRECT TOURISM SALES (OUTPUT) (mil. dol.)							
All tourism goods and services[1]	**605,059**	**708,427**	**719,896**	**961,448**	**969,794**	**1,014,844**	**1,088,880**
Traveler accommodations	108,663	125,130	138,439	194,119	201,631	207,405	215,808
Food and beverage services	91,630	107,579	91,912	130,022	133,415	134,387	141,159
Domestic passenger air transportation services	91,875	96,991	107,155	142,715	142,709	150,064	162,799
Gasoline	37,053	56,492	63,994	92,668	87,150	100,885	123,318
Shopping	96,746	109,474	93,565	130,437	125,841	127,639	134,140
DIRECT TOURISM EMPLOYMENT (1,000)							
All tourism goods and services[1]	**6,238**	**5,910**	**4,914**	**5,688**	**5,789**	**5,835**	**5,925**
Traveler accommodations	1,422	1,372	1,310	1,460	1,481	1,513	1,538
Vacation home rentals	16	16	17	14	13	13	13
Food and beverage services	1,702	1,745	1,323	1,662	1,684	1,652	1,665
Air transportation services	638	538	483	530	540	569	582
Rail transportation services	11	9	9	10	10	9	9
Water transportation services	28	31	33	37	39	39	42
Intercity bus transportation	23	20	18	18	18	19	18
Intercity charter bus transportation	32	23	19	19	19	19	19
Intracity mass transit	82	75	54	55	59	63	62
Taxicab and ride sharing service	14	10	9	8	7	7	6
Scenic and sightseeing transportation services	30	26	25	27	27	28	28
Automotive vehicle rental	121	104	80	98	100	102	104
Automotive repair services	98	87	71	73	76	76	76
Parking lots and garages	21	30	31	36	36	36	38
Toll highways	3	5	3	4	5	5	5
Travel arrangement and reservation services	284	213	175	184	196	198	199
Motion pictures and performing arts	81	76	54	56	58	56	59
Spectator sports	36	46	35	40	42	42	46
Participant sports	248	255	191	220	238	249	263
Gambling	140	155	154	130	131	137	137
All other recreation and entertainment	105	100	77	65	67	67	71
Petroleum refineries	8	7	6	9	9	9	9
Wholesale trade and transportation services	167	156	119	162	162	160	162
Gasoline service stations	140	122	107	163	171	178	189
Shopping	460	425	325	391	387	376	375
All other industries	112	97	77	81	80	79	80

[1] Includes groups not shown separately.

Source: U.S. Bureau of Economic Analysis, "Travel and Tourism Satellite Accounts 1998-2018," <https://www.bea.gov/data/specialtopics/travel-and-tourism>, accessed August 2020.

Table 1284. Top States and Cities Visited by Overseas Travelers: 2000 to 2018

[25,975 represents 25,975,000. Excludes visitors from Canada and Mexico. Includes travelers for business and pleasure, international travelers in transit through the United States, and students. Excludes travel by international personnel and international businessmen employed in the United States. Beginning 2006, the statistical policy for visitation estimates of international visitation requires a minimum sample of 400 respondents. States and cities are ranked by the latest overseas visitors data and may not reflect revisions for previous years]

State and other area	Overseas visitors (1,000)				City/MSA	Overseas visitors (1,000)			
	2000	2010	2015	2018		2000	2010	2015	2018
Total[1,2]	**25,975**	**26,363**	**38,700**	**39,883**	New York-White Plains-Wayne, NY-NJ	5,714	8,462	10,132	10,557
New York	5,922	8,647	10,385	10,804	Miami-Miami Beach-Kendall, FL	2,935	3,111	5,509	5,137
Florida	6,026	5,826	9,667	9,377	Los Angeles-Long Beach-Glendale, CA	3,533	3,348	4,857	5,073
California	6,364	5,615	8,139	8,531	Orlando-Kissimmee-Sanford, FL	3,013	2,715	4,718	4,351
Nevada	2,364	2,504	3,505	3,243	San Francisco, CA[3]	2,831	2,636	3,632	3,522
Hawaiian Islands	2,727	2,135	3,021	3,183	Las Vegas-Paradise, NV	2,260	2,425	3,409	3,103
Texas	1,169	1,028	1,789	1,938	Honolulu, HI	2,234	1,634	2,380	2,588
Massachusetts	1,429	1,292	1,789	1,835	Washington (DC Metro Area), DC-MD-VA	1,481	1,740	2,135	2,038
Illinois	1,377	1,186	1,708	1,619	Boston-Quincy, MA	1,325	1,186	1,609	1,651
Guam	1,325	1,318	1,505	1,615	Chicago-Joliet-Naperville, IL	1,351	1,134	1,620	1,524
Arizona	883	765	1,044	1,169	San Diego-Carlsbad-San Marcos, CA	701	765	1,159	1,133
New Jersey	909	975	994	1,109	Fort Lauderdale, FL[4]	(X)	(X)	902	969
Pennsylvania	649	923	1,029	1,013	Houston-Sugar Land-Baytown, TX	442	448	864	889
Georgia	805	817	998	838	Santa Ana-Anaheim-Irvine, CA	494	369	610	774
Washington	468	501	852	798	Flagstaff, AZ	(B)	501	672	742
Utah	(B)	475	595	718	Seattle-Bellevue-Everett, WA	416	475	783	730
Colorado	519	343	461	550	Atlanta-Sandy Springs-Marietta, GA	701	712	837	710
North Carolina	416	343	491	546	Dallas-Plano-Irving, TX	494	343	545	638
Louisiana	(X)	(X)	518	499	Philadelphia, PA	390	633	680	638

X Not applicable (not ranked). [1] Total overseas travelers; includes other states and cities, not shown separately. [2] A person is counted in each area visited, but only once in the total. [3] San Francisco-San Mateo-Redwood City, CA. [4] Fort Lauderdale-Pompano Beach-Deerfield Beach, FL.

Source: U.S. Department of Commerce, International Trade Administration, National Travel and Tourism Office, "2018 U.S. Travel and Tourism Statistics (Inbound), Overseas Visitation Estimates," <https://travel.trade.gov/outreachpages/inbound.general_information.inbound_overview.asp>, accessed April 2020.

Table 1285. Domestic and International Travel Expenditures by State: 2017

[In millions of dollars (1,037,677 represents $1,037,677,000,000). Shows aggregate spending by foreign visitors and by U.S. residents on domestic overnight trips and day trips of 50 miles or more, one way, away from home]

State	Total (mil. dol.)	Percent distribution	Rank	State	Total (mil. dol.)	Percent distribution	Rank	State	Total (mil. dol.)	Percent distribution	Rank
U.S. total.....	1,037,677	100.0	(X)	KS.........	7,662	0.7	35	ND.........	2,914	0.3	46
				KY.........	9,711	0.9	31	OH.........	20,375	2.0	16
AL.........	9,761	0.9	30	LA.........	12,691	1.2	25	OK.........	8,122	0.8	34
AK.........	2,727	0.3	48	ME.........	4,166	0.4	43	OR.........	12,330	1.2	26
AZ.........	20,257	2.0	17	MD.........	17,703	1.7	20	PA.........	26,393	2.5	8
AR.........	7,058	0.7	37	MA.........	22,870	2.2	13	RI.........	2,160	0.2	51
CA.........	139,940	13.5	1	MI.........	22,291	2.1	14	SC.........	14,640	1.4	22
CO.........	20,129	1.9	18	MN.........	14,588	1.4	23	SD.........	2,855	0.3	47
CT.........	11,822	1.1	27	MS.........	6,467	0.6	38	TN.........	20,771	2.0	15
DE.........	2,202	0.2	50	MO.........	14,665	1.4	21	TX.........	72,483	7.0	4
DC.........	13,201	1.3	24	MT.........	4,573	0.4	41	UT.........	9,148	0.9	32
FL.........	98,578	9.5	2	NE.........	5,141	0.5	39	VT.........	2,557	0.2	49
GA.........	29,619	2.9	7	NV.........	41,485	4.0	5	VA.........	25,639	2.5	10
HI.........	25,926	2.5	9	NH.........	4,209	0.4	42	WA.........	19,140	1.8	19
ID.........	4,789	0.5	40	NJ.........	23,060	2.2	12	WV.........	4,021	0.4	44
IL.........	39,733	3.8	6	NM.........	7,181	0.7	36	WI.........	11,822	1.1	27
IN.........	11,737	1.1	29	NY.........	79,133	7.6	3	WY.........	3,392	0.3	45
IA.........	8,706	0.8	33	NC.........	24,928	2.4	11	Other [1]....	10,207	1.0	(X)

X Not applicable. [1] This category includes foreign visitor spending in U.S. territories, and Canadian and Mexican visitor spending in the U.S. Those dollars are not represented in state totals.

Source: U.S. Travel Association, Washington, DC, *Impact of Travel on State Economies 2018* ©, March 2019. See also <http://www.ustravel.org/research>.

Table 1286. Average Cost of Airfare for Domestic Routes: 1995 to 2019

[In dollars, except percent. Fares based on domestic itinerary fares. Itinerary fares consist of round-trip fares unless the customer does not purchase a return trip. In that case, the one-way fare is included. Fares are based on the total ticket value, which consists of the price charged by the airlines plus any additional taxes and fees levied by an outside entity at the time of purchase. Fares include only the price paid at the time of the ticket purchase and do not include other fees paid at the airport or onboard the aircraft. Averages do not include frequent-flyer or "zero fares" or a few abnormally high reported fares]

Year	Current dollars			Constant (2020) dollars [1]		
		Percent change			Percent change	
	Average fare	From previous year	Cumulative from 1995	Average fare	From previous year	Cumulative from 1995
1995.....................	292	(NA)	(NA)	495	(NA)	(NA)
2000.....................	339	4.7	16.0	508	1.3	2.7
2005.....................	307	0.6	5.2	406	-2.7	-17.9
2010.....................	336	8.3	15.0	398	6.5	-19.6
2012.....................	375	3.0	28.3	422	0.9	-14.9
2013.....................	384	2.5	31.5	426	1.0	-14.0
2014.....................	396	3.2	35.6	432	1.5	-12.7
2015.....................	379	-4.3	29.8	413	-4.4	-16.6
2016.....................	350	-7.6	19.9	377	-8.7	-23.9
2017.....................	347	-0.9	18.8	366	-3.0	-26.1
2018.....................	350	0.7	19.7	360	-1.7	-27.4
2019.....................	355	1.5	21.4	358	-0.3	-27.6

NA Not available. [1] Rate calculated using Bureau of Labor Statistics Consumer Price Index.

Source: U.S. Department of Transportation, Bureau of Transportation Statistics, Air Fares, "National Level Fares since 1995—Annual," <https://www.bts.gov/air-fares>, accessed August 2020.

Table 1287. Top 20 U.S. Gateway Airports for Nonstop International Air Travel Passengers: 2019

[243,947 represents 243,947,000. International passengers are residents of any country traveling nonstop to and from the United States on U.S. and foreign carriers. The data cover all passengers arriving and departing from U.S. airports on nonstop commercial international flights with 60 seats or more]

Gateway airport	Airport code	Passengers, (1,000)	Gateway airport	Airport code	Passengers, (1,000)
Total, all airports........................	(X)	243,947	Dallas-Ft. Worth, TX....................	DFW	9,269
Total, top 20 airports.....................	(X)	216,873	Fort Lauderdale, FL....................	FLL	8,540
Top 20, percentage of total..............	(X)	88.9	Washington (Dulles), VA................	IAD	8,307
			Boston, MA............................	BOS	7,882
New York (JFK), NY........................	JFK	33,936	Orlando, FL...........................	MCO	7,057
Los Angeles, CA...........................	LAX	25,402	Seattle-Tacoma, WA....................	SEA	5,513
Miami, FL.................................	MIA	21,271	Honolulu, HI..........................	HNL	5,279
San Francisco, CA.........................	SFO	15,038	Philadelphia, PA......................	PHL	3,972
Newark, NJ................................	EWR	14,193	Detroit, MI...........................	DTW	3,724
Chicago (O'Hare), IL......................	ORD	13,800	Las Vegas, NV.........................	LAS	3,545
Atlanta, GA...............................	ATL	12,455	Charlotte, NC.........................	CLT	3,520
Houston (G. Bush), TX.....................	IAH	10,938	Minneapolis-St. Paul, MN..............	MSP	3,232

X Not applicable.

Source: U.S. Department of Transportation, Research and Innovative Technology Administration, Bureau of Transportation Statistics, Office of Airline Information, "T-100 International Segment data," <http://www.transtats.bts.gov/Fields.asp?Table_ID=261>, accessed September 2020.

Table 1288. International Travel: 2005 to 2019

[In thousands (63,502 represents 63,502,000), except percent. U.S. travelers cover residents of the United States, its territories and possessions. International travelers to the U.S. include travelers for business and pleasure, and excludes travel by international personnel and international businessmen employed in the United States. Some traveler data revised since originally issued]

Item and area	2005	2010	2013	2014	2015	2016	2017	2018	2019
U.S. TRAVELERS TO FOREIGN COUNTRIES BY WORLD REGION OF DESTINATION [1]									
Total	63,502	61,061	61,344	68,185	74,191	80,226	87,555	92,587	99,745
Canada	14,390	11,871	11,478	11,523	12,669	13,895	14,280	14,440	14,994
Mexico	20,325	20,683	20,851	25,882	28,733	31,194	34,947	36,373	39,942
Total overseas [2]	28,787	28,507	29,015	30,780	32,789	35,137	38,327	41,774	44,808
Percent of overseas travelers to...									
Europe	41.6	34.4	34.6	35.1	34.7	35.7	37.8	39.3	38.5
Caribbean	18.0	21.7	24.8	24.0	23.9	23.2	23.3	21.9	22.0
Asia	21.1	19.7	18.8	18.5	18.5	18.8	18.0	17.9	17.6
Central America	6.1	6.7	6.9	7.7	7.9	7.9	7.2	6.9	7.1
South America	8.2	8.4	7.3	7.4	7.2	7.2	6.5	6.7	7.1
Middle East	3.8	6.4	5.9	5.6	5.8	5.0	4.8	4.9	5.0
Africa	2.0	3.4	2.9	2.9	2.9	2.8	2.7	2.8	3.2
Oceania	2.9	2.1	1.9	1.9	2.0	2.0	2.0	2.0	2.2
INTERNATIONAL TRAVELERS TO U.S. BY VISITOR REGION OF RESIDENCE									
Total	49,206	60,010	71,643	75,379	77,774	76,407	77,187	79,746	79,256
Canada	14,862	20,176	23,407	23,014	20,699	19,287	20,493	21,475	20,723
Mexico	12,665	13,472	14,547	17,070	18,374	18,991	17,788	18,387	18,140
Total overseas [2]	21,679	26,363	33,689	35,296	38,700	38,129	38,906	39,883	40,393
Europe	10,313	11,985	13,571	14,269	15,790	14,831	14,974	15,424	15,706
Asia	6,198	7,020	9,516	9,833	10,946	11,538	12,137	11,874	12,250
South America	1,820	3,250	5,330	5,533	5,699	5,407	5,556	6,027	5,733
Caribbean	1,135	1,201	1,235	1,339	1,479	1,587	1,671	1,793	1,921
Oceania	737	1,095	1,572	1,592	1,768	1,661	1,632	1,687	1,641
Central America	696	760	882	943	1,077	1,187	1,168	1,283	1,360
Middle East	527	736	1,110	1,254	1,369	1,342	1,182	1,197	1,216
Africa	252	316	471	533	573	576	586	598	567

NA Not available. [1] A person is counted in each area visited but only once in the total. [2] "Overseas" excludes Canada and Mexico.

Source: U.S. Department of Commerce, International Trade Administration, National Travel and Tourism Office, "Arrivals Data - Country of Residence (COR)," <https://travel.trade.gov/view/m-2017-I-001/index.asp>, and "2019 U.S. Travel and Tourism Statistics (U.S. Resident Outbound)," <https://travel.trade.gov/outreachpages/outbound.general_information.outbound_overview.asp>; accessed September 2020.

Table 1289. International Travel Payments: 2000 to 2019

[In millions of dollars (86,184 represents $86,184,000,000)]

Year	Travel and passenger fare (mil. dol.)						U.S. net travel and passenger receipts (mil. dol.)
	Payments by U.S. travelers			Receipts from international visitors			
	Total	Travel payments [1, 2]	Air transport [3]	Total	Travel receipts [1, 2]	Air transport [3]	
2000	86,184	65,787	20,397	120,384	100,187	20,197	34,200
2001	79,661	60,730	18,931	103,914	86,733	17,181	24,253
2002	76,381	59,942	16,439	98,160	81,869	16,291	21,779
2003	79,128	61,884	17,244	95,423	80,332	15,091	16,295
2004	94,237	74,024	20,213	110,319	92,387	17,932	16,082
2005	101,419	79,988	21,431	122,079	101,470	20,609	20,660
2006	106,848	84,206	22,642	126,778	105,140	21,638	19,930
2007	112,788	89,235	23,553	144,224	119,037	25,187	31,436
2008	119,837	92,545	27,292	164,718	133,761	30,957	44,881
2009	102,953	81,421	21,532	146,005	119,902	26,103	43,052
2010	110,049	86,623	23,426	167,997	137,010	30,987	57,948
2011	116,447	89,700	26,747	187,630	150,867	36,763	71,183
2012	129,903	100,338	29,565	200,996	161,632	39,364	71,093
2013	130,149	98,120	32,029	218,497	177,484	41,013	88,348
2014	140,558	105,668	34,890	235,989	191,918	44,071	95,431
2015	150,042	114,548	35,494	249,183	206,936	42,247	99,141
2016	160,959	123,549	37,410	245,991	206,650	39,341	85,032
2017	173,760	134,868	38,892	251,544	210,655	40,889	77,784
2018	186,506	144,463	42,043	256,145	214,680	41,465	69,639
2019, preliminary	195,583	152,321	43,262	254,229	213,482	40,747	58,646

[1] Covers purchases of goods and services by U.S. persons traveling abroad and by foreign travelers in the United States for business or personal reasons. These goods and services include food, lodging, recreation, gifts, entertainment, local transportation in the country of travel, and other items incidental to a foreign visit. [2] Covers business travel, including expenditures by border, seasonal, and other short-term workers; and personal travel, including health-related and education-related travel, along with spending on day-trips (less than one night). [3] Fares received for the transport of nonresidents by U.S. air carriers between the United States and foreign countries and between two foreign points, and the transport of U.S. residents by foreign air carriers between the United States and foreign countries.

Source: U.S. Department of Commerce, International Trade Administration, National Travel and Tourism Office, "Annual Visitor Spending (1960-Present)," <https://travel.trade.gov/research/reports/recpay/index.asp>, accessed April 2020.

Table 1290. Inbound Crossings for Top 5 U.S.-Canadian and U.S.-Mexican Border Land Passenger Gateways: 2019

[26,733 represents 26,733,000]

Item and gateway	Entering the U.S. (1,000)	Item and gateway	Entering the U.S. (1,000)
All U.S.-Canadian land gateways: [1]		**All U.S.-Mexican land gateways:** [1]	
Personal vehicles	26,733	Personal vehicles	73,085
Personal vehicle passengers	51,177	Personal vehicle passengers	136,890
Buses	77	Buses	152
Bus passengers	1,713	Bus passengers	2,153
Train passengers	285	Train passengers	10
Pedestrians	523	Pedestrians	49,176
Top five gateways:		**Top five gateways:**	
Personal vehicles:		Personal vehicles:	
Buffalo-Niagara Falls, NY	4,858	San Ysidro, CA	14,979
Detroit, MI	4,475	El Paso, TX	10,528
Blaine, WA	3,961	Otay Mesa, CA	6,584
Port Huron, MI	1,462	Laredo, TX	5,110
Champlain-Rouses Point, NY	1,018	Calexico, CA	4,985
Personal vehicle passengers:		Personal vehicle passengers:	
Buffalo-Niagara Falls, NY	10,515	San Ysidro, CA	25,845
Blaine, WA	7,708	El Paso, TX	18,703
Detroit, MI	7,560	Otay Mesa, CA	11,372
Port Huron, MI	2,986	Laredo, TX	10,374
Champlain-Rouses Point, NY	2,300	Brownsville, TX	9,416
Pedestrians:		Pedestrians:	
Buffalo-Niagara Falls, NY	385	San Ysidro, CA	10,799
Sumas, WA	60	El Paso, TX	7,626
Point Roberts, WA	28	Laredo, TX	3,790
International Falls-Ranier, MN	10	Calexico, CA	3,708
Calais, ME	8	Otay Mesa, CA	3,567

[1] Data reflect all personal vehicles and buses, passengers, and pedestrians entering the U.S.-Canadian border and U.S.-Mexican border, regardless of nationality.

Source: U.S. Department of Transportation, Bureau of Transportation Statistics, "Border Crossing / Entry Data," <https://www.bts.gov/content/border-crossingentry-data>, accessed September 2020.

Table 1291. Foreign Tourists Admitted by Country of Citizenship: 2000 to 2018

[In thousands (30,511 represents 30,511,000). For years ending September 30. Represents non-U.S. citizens admitted to the country for a temporary period of time, for pleasure (tourists). Includes nonimmigrant admission classes B2 (temporary visitors for pleasure), GMT (Commonwealth of the Northern Marianas Islands visa waiver program–temporary visitors for pleasure, Guam or Northern Mariana Islands), and WT (visa waiver program–temporary visitors for pleasure)]

Country and region	2000 [1]	2010	2015	2018	Country and region	2000 [1]	2010	2015	2018
All countries [2]	**30,511**	**35,131**	**61,017**	**64,820**	Thailand	76	48	72	**77**
Europe [3]	**11,806**	**11,741**	**13,552**	**14,269**	Turkey	93	74	143	125
Austria	182	166	181	175	United Arab Emirates	36	8	28	28
Belgium	254	227	244	249	**Africa** [3]	**327**	**274**	**540**	**565**
Czechia	44	58	87	110	Egypt	44	34	73	69
Denmark	150	244	281	286	Nigeria	27	62	170	178
Finland	95	106	128	122	South Africa	114	63	99	104
France [4]	1,113	1,371	1,658	1,790	**Oceania** [3]	**748**	**1,047**	**1,545**	**1,609**
Germany	1,925	1,599	1,786	1,759	Australia	535	843	1,245	1,275
Greece	60	54	57	74	New Zealand	170	191	281	317
Hungary	58	49	68	86	**North America** [3, 6]	**6,501**	**12,754**	**30,038**	**31,664**
Iceland	27	35	48	67	Canada [7]	277	87	9,977	10,341
Ireland	325	406	402	492	Mexico	3,972	11,010	17,904	18,679
Italy	626	924	1,052	1,155	**Caribbean**	**1,404**	**999**	**1,226**	**1,485**
Netherlands [4]	559	598	596	674	Bahamas, The	24	250	229	268
Norway	144	197	273	248	Dominican Republic	195	219	295	435
Poland	116	103	146	177	Haiti	72	90	126	130
Portugal	86	120	151	181	Jamaica	240	180	249	298
Russia	74	134	242	207	Trinidad and Tobago	133	129	163	164
Spain	370	692	846	991	**Central America**	**792**	**657**	**930**	**1,159**
Sweden	321	330	505	463	Costa Rica	172	143	202	285
Switzerland	400	315	409	368	El Salvador	175	105	150	196
United Kingdom [4]	4,671	3,768	3,991	4,143	Guatemala	177	159	209	246
Asia [3]	**7,853**	**6,254**	**9,826**	**10,689**	Honduras	87	101	156	**203**
China [5]	656	482	1,950	2,205	Nicaragua	47	38	56	67
India	253	490	921	1,064	Panama	106	94	136	137
Indonesia	62	44	84	92	**South America** [3]	**2,867**	**2,785**	**5,484**	**5,967**
Israel	319	253	340	365	Argentina	515	375	713	1,040
Japan	4,946	3,252	3,350	3,129	Bolivia	48	31	55	66
Korea, South	606	896	1,564	2,185	Brazil	706	976	2,222	2,186
Malaysia	64	37	59	62	Chile	194	119	298	392
Pakistan	47	39	87	94	Colombia	411	455	854	906
Philippines	163	179	255	311	Ecuador	122	169	351	432
Saudi Arabia	67	36	138	95	Peru	190	162	269	291
Singapore	131	72	97	94	Uruguay	66	35	70	78
Taiwan	(NA)	183	344	385	Venezuela	570	423	560	478

[1] Due to the expiration of the Visa Waiver Program during May-October 2000, data for business and pleasure not available separately. [2] Total includes visitors of unknown country of citizenship. [3] Total includes other countries, not shown separately. [4] As of 2005, includes overseas territories; see source for details. [5] Prior to 2005, data for China includes Taiwan. As of 2005, data for China includes Hong Kong and Macau. [6] The majority of short-term admissions from Canada and Mexico are excluded. [7] Beginning in 2014, the number of admissions greatly exceeds totals reported in previous years due to a more complete count of Canadian air and sea admissions.

Source: U.S. Department of Homeland Security, Office of Immigration Statistics, "2018 Yearbook of Immigration Statistics," and earlier reports, <https://www.dhs.gov/immigration-statistics/yearbook>, accessed February 2020.

Section 27
Accommodation, Food Services, and Other Services

This section presents statistics relating to services other than those covered in the previous sections on wholesale and retail trade, transportation, communications, financial services, and recreation services. Data shown for services are classified by kind of business and cover sales or receipts, establishments, employees, payrolls, and other items.

The principal sources of these data are from the U.S. Census Bureau and include the 2012 and 2017 Economic Censuses, Service Annual Survey, and the County Business Patterns program.

Data on these services also appear in several other sections. For instance, labor force employment and earnings data appear in Section 12, Labor Force, Employment, and Earnings; gross domestic product of the industry (Table 705) appears in Section 13, Income, Expenditures, Poverty, and Wealth; and financial data (several tables) from the quarterly *Statistics of Income Bulletin*, published by the Internal Revenue Service, appear in Section 15, Business Enterprise.

Censuses—Limited coverage of the service industries started in 1933. Beginning with the 1967 Economic Census, legislation provides for a census to be conducted every 5 years (for years ending in "2" and "7"). For more information on the most current census, see the Census Bureau's Economic Census website at <census.gov/programs-surveys/economic-census. html>. The industries covered in the censuses and surveys of business are defined in the North American Industry Classification System (NAICS). For information on NAICS, see the Census website at <census.gov/eos/www/naics/>.

In general, the 2012 and 2017 Economic Censuses have three series of publications for these sectors: 1) subject series with reports such as product lines, and establishment and firm sizes, 2) geographic reports with individual reports for each state, and 3) industry series with individual reports for industry groups.

Release of data from the 2012 Economic Census was completed in 2016. Data from the 2017 Economic Census are being released on a flow basis between September 2019 and December 2021.

Current surveys—The Service Annual Survey provides annual estimates of nationwide receipts for selected personal, business, leasing and repair, amusement and entertainment, social and health, and other professional service industries in the United States. For selected social, health, and other professional service industries, separate estimates are developed for receipts of taxable firms and revenue and expenses for firms and organizations exempt from federal income taxes. Several service sectors from this survey are covered in other sections of this publication. The estimates for tax exempt firms in these industries are derived from a sample of employer firms only. Estimates obtained from annual and monthly surveys are based on sample data and are not expected to agree exactly with results that would be obtained from a complete census of all establishments. Data include estimates for sampling units not reporting. Data are released in the *Quarterly Services Report* and the *Annual Services Report* at <census.gov/services/index.html>.

Statistical reliability—For a discussion of statistical collection and estimation, sampling procedures, and measures of statistical reliability applicable to Census Bureau data, see Appendix III.

Table 1292. Selected Service-Related Industries—Establishments, Sales, Payroll, and Employees by Kind of Business: 2017

[1,880,518,146 represents $1,880,518,146,000. Covers only establishments with payroll. Based on the 2017 Economic Census; for statement on methodology, see Appendix III]

Kind of business	NAICS code [1]	Establish-ments, (number)	Sales or receipts ($1,000)	Annual payroll ($1,000)	Paid employees [2] (number)
Professional, scientific, and technical services..................	54	912,404	1,880,518,146	731,868,965	9,181,261
Professional, scientific, and technical services................	541	912,404	1,880,518,146	731,868,965	9,181,261
Management of companies and enterprises......................	55	59,210	171,760,052	369,369,649	3,660,929
Administrative and support and waste management and remediation services..	56	420,417	1,015,820,401	485,271,662	12,655,377
Administrative and support services..........................	561	395,218	916,730,459	462,112,073	12,226,132
Waste management and remediation services...............	562	25,199	99,089,942	23,159,589	429,245
Accommodation and food services.............................	72	728,615	957,866,229	268,518,167	14,197,096
Accommodation...	721	68,290	266,341,855	62,493,279	2,136,338
Food services and drinking places..............................	722	660,325	691,524,374	206,024,888	12,060,758
Other services (except public administration)..................	81	561,572	553,839,745	135,781,747	3,771,508
Repair and maintenance..	811	218,257	185,092,480	52,223,988	1,309,338
Personal and laundry services..................................	812	236,149	111,747,568	35,752,207	1,498,438
Religious, grantmaking, civic, professional, and similar organizations...	813	107,166	256,999,697	47,805,552	963,732

[1] North American Industrial Classification System, 2017; see text, Section 15. [2] For employees on the payroll during the pay period including March 12.

Source: U.S. Census Bureau, 2017 Economic Census, "EC1700BASIC: All Sectors: Summary Statistics for the U.S., States, and Selected Geographies: 2017," <data.census.gov>, accessed April 2020.

Table 1293. Selected Service-Related Industries—Nonemployer Establishments and Receipts by Kind of Business: 2016 to 2018

[3,441 represents 3,441,000. Includes only firms subject to federal income tax. Nonemployers are businesses with no paid employees. Data originate chiefly from administrative records of the Internal Revenue Service; see Appendix III]

Kind of business	NAICS code [1]	Firms (1,000)			Receipts (mil. dol.)		
		2016	2017	2018	2016	2017	2018
Professional, scientific, and technical services.............	**54**	**3,441**	**3,535**	**3,727**	**159,177**	**166,944**	**178,373**
Professional, scientific, and technical services [2]................	541	3,441	3,535	3,727	159,177	166,944	178,373
Legal services..	5411	286	290	293	19,566	20,432	21,060
Accounting, tax preparation, bookkeeping, and payroll services...	5412	370	373	382	10,146	10,428	10,984
Architectural, engineering, and related services...............	5413	227	230	237	11,475	11,924	12,570
Specialized design services.......................................	5414	231	238	254	8,779	9,171	10,106
Computer systems design and related services...............	5415	303	309	316	14,931	15,306	16,098
Management, scientific and technical consulting..............	5416	758	800	889	36,820	39,543	43,792
Scientific research and development services..................	5417	43	48	51	1,492	1,575	1,706
Advertising, public relations, and related services............	5418	150	158	169	8,273	8,700	9,230
Administrative and support and waste management and remediation services..	**56**	**2,083**	**2,143**	**2,522**	**47,214**	**50,102**	**59,169**
Administrative and support services [2]...........................	561	2,064	2,124	2,502	45,726	48,497	57,460
Office administrative services..................................	5611	245	266	295	4,336	4,748	5,343
Business support services......................................	5614	221	215	233	6,220	6,334	6,791
Services to buildings and dwellings..........................	5617	1,270	1,301	1,582	25,946	27,540	34,114
Waste management and remediation services...............	562	18	19	20	1,488	1,605	1,709
Accommodation and food services.........................	**72**	**383**	**403**	**460**	**17,628**	**18,580**	**18,744**
Accommodation...	721	73	79	112	3,875	4,077	4,554
Food services and drinking places..............................	722	310	323	348	13,753	14,503	14,190
Special food services..	7223	189	200	221	5,248	5,555	5,952
Drinking places (alcoholic beverages)........................	7224	25	25	25	1,591	1,600	1,592
Restaurants and other eating places.........................	7225	97	98	101	6,914	7,348	6,645
Full-service restaurants......................................	722511	42	43	45	3,363	3,603	3,134
Limited-service eating places................................	722513	35	34	34	2,967	3,053	2,784
Other services (except public administration)................	**81**	**3,680**	**3,740**	**2,978**	**100,380**	**104,780**	**90,820**
Repair and maintenance [2]...	811	747	753	559	28,948	29,895	25,241
Automotive repair and maintenance...........................	8111	329	331	313	14,878	15,269	14,893
Personal and household goods repair and maintenance.....	8114	324	331	176	9,784	10,319	6,704
Personal and laundry services [2]..................................	812	2,721	2,776	2,221	68,042	71,490	62,312
Personal care services..	8121	1,334	1,335	1,299	31,963	33,487	35,236
Hair, nail, and skin care services.............................	81211	1,088	1,098	1,123	26,909	28,270	30,647
Beauty salons...	812112	731	733	750	16,588	17,214	18,752
Death care services...	8122	17	17	16	906	900	881
Drycleaning and laundry services.............................	8123	30	29	25	1,748	1,739	1,661
Other personal services...	8129	1,340	1,395	882	33,425	35,365	24,534
Religious, grantmaking, civic, professional, and similar organizations...	813	212	211	198	3,391	3,395	3,268

[1] Data for 2016, based on North American Industry Classification System (NAICS), 2012; beginning 2017, based on NAICS 2017. See text, Section 15. [2] Includes other kinds of business not shown separately.

Source: U.S. Census Bureau, Nonemployer Statistics, "All Sectors: Nonemployer Statistics for the U.S., States, Counties, Metropolitan Areas, and Combined Statistical Areas; and by Legal Form of Organization and Sales, Value of Shipments, or Revenue Size for Selected Geographies: 2018," <data.census.gov>, accessed May 2020.

Table 1294. Selected Service-Related Industries—Establishments, Employees, and Payroll by Industry: 2017 and 2018

[In thousands (914.7 represents 914,700); payroll in billions of dollars (747.1 represents $747,100,000,000). Covers establishments with paid employees. Excludes self-employed individuals, employees of private households, railroad employees, agricultural production employees, and most government employees; see source for NAICS and other exclusions. For statement on methodology, see Appendix III]

Industry	NAICS code [1]	Establishments (1,000)		Employees [2] (1,000)		Annual payroll (bil. dol.)	
		2017	2018	2017	2018	2017	2018
Professional, scientific, & technical services	**54**	**914.7**	**921.5**	**8,905.5**	**9,111.7**	**747.1**	**801.7**
Professional, scientific, & technical services	541	914.7	921.5	8,905.5	9,111.7	747.1	801.7
Legal services	5411	186.5	185.6	1,153.0	1,148.5	107.5	111.0
Offices of lawyers	54111	173.0	171.9	1,063.7	1,061.7	102.6	105.8
Accounting, tax preparation, bookkeeping, and payroll services	5412	133.4	134.4	1,147.5	1,152.7	65.2	69.9
Offices of certified public accountants	541211	56.7	56.2	503.8	512.7	38.9	42.2
Tax preparation services	541213	30.0	31.0	177.7	162.1	2.1	2.2
Architectural, engineering, & related services [3]	5413	113.9	114.3	1,506.6	1,534.7	125.6	135.9
Architectural services	54131	22.0	22.1	174.0	177.2	14.3	14.8
Engineering services	54133	61.9	61.9	1,083.8	1,102.6	96.1	104.9
Specialized design services [3]	5414	32.9	33.7	119.3	122.1	7.2	7.5
Graphic design services	54143	15.6	15.8	54.0	53.4	3.1	3.1
Computer systems design & related services [3]	5415	143.6	140.6	1,826.3	1,890.0	177.8	190.7
Custom computer programming services	541511	66.9	65.7	839.6	886.2	82.3	90.6
Computer systems design services	541512	58.7	58.2	762.7	780.7	75.4	78.9
Management, scientific, & technical consulting services [3]	5416	175.5	181.8	1,266.9	1,331.2	108.0	116.8
Management consulting services	54161	139.7	146.2	1,048.1	1,107.8	90.9	98.8
Environmental consulting services	54162	10.2	10.0	85.9	86.8	5.9	6.1
Scientific research & development services	5417	18.7	18.9	751.2	772.3	91.1	100.6
Research & development in the physical engineering & life sciences	54171	16.8	16.9	706.5	734.7	88.1	97.6
Advertising & related services [3]	5418	38.0	38.0	485.3	484.1	33.8	36.1
Advertising agencies	54181	13.7	13.7	191.7	187.9	16.8	17.8
Public relations agencies	54182	8.5	8.5	54.7	55.9	5.4	5.9
Other professional, scientific, & technical services	5419	72.1	74.2	649.4	676.1	30.9	33.2
Veterinary services	54194	31.8	31.9	368.9	379.5	14.0	15.1
Management of companies and enterprises	**55**	**56.4**	**54.7**	**3,462.5**	**3,528.9**	**370.8**	**393.6**
Administrative and support and waste management and remediation services	**56**	**419.8**	**418.9**	**11,897.1**	**12,287.8**	**482.0**	**512.1**
Administrative & support services [3]	561	394.5	393.3	11,489.6	11,862.1	458.0	487.2
Employment services	5613	53.2	53.7	6,505.4	6,771.4	273.2	293.4
Temporary help services	56132	37.2	37.7	3,483.2	3,522.5	114.4	119.2
Business support services [3]	5614	32.0	31.2	811.2	812.2	29.0	30.2
Telephone call centers	56142	5.2	5.2	457.3	456.4	12.2	13.0
Collection agencies	56144	3.9	3.7	134.2	135.2	5.6	5.6
Travel arrangement & reservation services	5615	22.6	18.2	213.4	221.6	12.9	14.4
Travel agencies	56151	15.7	11.3	96.0	99.1	6.2	7.2
Investigation & security services	5616	25.4	25.6	954.7	988.9	29.4	30.9
Investigation, guard, & armored car services	56161	14.5	14.5	811.5	843.3	22.3	23.5
Security systems services	56162	11.0	11.1	143.2	145.6	7.2	7.4
Services to buildings & dwellings [3]	5617	200.3	204.3	1,947.9	1,990.5	56.7	60.1
Landscaping services	56173	104.3	106.3	663.8	681.0	25.6	27.5
Waste management & remediation services	562	25.3	25.6	407.5	425.7	23.9	24.9
Waste collection	5621	11.8	11.8	215.8	223.6	12.7	12.8
Waste treatment & disposal	5622	2.7	2.6	57.9	58.8	3.8	3.9
Remediation & other waste management services	5629	10.9	11.2	133.8	143.3	7.4	8.2
Accommodation & food services	**72**	**726.2**	**733.1**	**14,088.2**	**14,345.1**	**274.5**	**291.4**
Accommodation	721	68.4	69.1	2,111.4	2,121.4	62.7	65.8
Traveler accommodation [3]	7211	58.8	59.5	2,054.3	2,063.5	60.8	63.8
Hotels (except casino hotels) & motels	72111	53.9	54.7	1,610.0	1,617.1	45.4	47.6
RV (recreational vehicle) parks & recreational camps	7212	7.5	7.6	46.6	48.2	1.6	1.7
Rooming & boarding houses	7213	2.0	1.9	10.5	9.7	0.3	0.3
Food services & drinking places	722	657.8	664.1	11,976.8	12,223.8	211.9	225.6
Drinking places (alcoholic beverages)	7224	40.2	40.1	369.5	371.8	6.6	6.9
Restaurants and other eating places	7225	572.7	579.3	10,778.9	11,028.4	186.5	198.9
Full-service restaurants	722511	250.9	253.9	5,495.6	5,579.1	108.0	114.1
Limited-service restaurants	722513	251.0	253.8	4,449.8	4,629.4	65.5	71.5
Cafeterias, grill buffets, and buffets	722514	5.8	5.7	107.6	107.4	1.6	1.7
Snack and nonalcoholic beverage bars	722515	65.0	65.9	725.8	712.6	11.4	11.6
Other services (except public administration)	**81**	**764.8**	**766.8**	**5,535.0**	**5,595.7**	**180.9**	**189.0**
Repair & maintenance [3]	811	218.7	217.8	1,284.1	1,303.5	53.0	55.4
Automotive repair & maintenance	8111	162.6	162.3	909.9	925.9	33.3	34.8
Personal & household goods repair & maintenance	8114	21.6	21.2	74.4	73.0	2.5	2.5
Personal & laundry services [3]	812	236.0	239.3	1,464.6	1,504.4	36.4	39.1
Personal care services	8121	133.9	136.6	707.0	737.5	15.5	16.8
Death care services	8122	21.0	20.7	143.2	135.4	5.1	5.1
Drycleaning & laundry services	8123	33.9	33.2	288.5	283.9	7.8	8.2
Religious/grantmaking/civic/professional [4]	813	310.2	309.6	2,786.3	2,787.8	91.5	94.5
Religious organizations	8131	186.5	185.8	1,690.4	1,693.7	37.6	38.4
Grantmaking & giving services	8132	20.2	20.7	193.8	196.0	12.0	12.6
Social advocacy organizations	8133	18.0	18.4	178.9	185.9	8.5	9.2
Civic & social organizations	8134	26.6	25.7	235.4	218.7	5.4	5.2
Business/professional/labor/political [4]	8139	58.9	59.0	487.8	493.6	28.0	29.0
Labor unions [4]	81393	13.9	13.7	144.8	145.9	5.7	5.9

[1] Data based on North American Industry Classification System (NAICS) 2017. See text, section 15. [2] Includes employees on the payroll for the pay period including March 12. [3] Includes other kinds of business, not shown separately. [4] Also includes other similar organizations.

Source: U.S. Census Bureau, County Business Patterns, "County Business Patterns by Legal Form of Organization and Employment Size Class for U.S., States, and Selected Geographies," <data.census.gov>, accessed July 2020.

Table 1295. Employed Persons in Service Industries by Sex, Race, and Hispanic Origin and by Industry: 2019

[19,606 represents 19,606,000. Civilian noninstitutionalized population 16 years and older. Based on the Current Population Survey (CPS); see text, Section 1, and Appendix III. For information on employees in other sectors, see Table 647 and Table 665]

Industry	NAICS code [1]	Total employed (1,000)	Percent of total				
			Female	White	Black [2]	Asian [2]	Hispanic or Latino [3]
Professional and business services......	**54-56**	**19,606**	**41.3**	**77.4**	**10.0**	**9.6**	**16.0**
Professional and technical services......	**54**	**12,808**	**42.6**	**77.2**	**7.4**	**13.0**	**9.2**
Legal services......	5411	1,747	56.6	84.8	7.3	5.3	11.7
Accounting, tax preparation, bookkeeping, and payroll services......	5412	1,219	60.9	79.7	7.9	9.9	10.7
Architectural, engineering, and related services......	5413	1,818	25.9	83.7	6.1	7.7	8.7
Specialized design services......	5414	472	57.2	81.6	6.8	8.3	9.7
Computer systems design and related services......	5415	3,703	27.8	66.1	8.1	23.5	7.4
Management, scientific, and technical consulting services......	5416	1,693	42.0	77.2	8.4	12.5	8.2
Scientific research and development services......	5417	607	46.6	73.6	6.6	17.7	9.4
Advertising, public relations, and related services......	5418	649	51.3	82.6	8.1	6.2	12.5
Veterinary services......	54194	410	82.4	92.8	3.4	2.3	6.3
Other professional, scientific, and technical services [4]......	5419	489	59.5	82.5	7.8	7.4	12.2
Management, administrative, and waste services......	**55-56**	**6,799**	**39.0**	**77.9**	**14.8**	**3.2**	**28.8**
Management of companies and enterprises......	55	200	44.9	87.7	7.3	2.1	15.0
Employment services......	5613	899	53.0	70.5	19.6	5.8	19.2
Business support services......	5614	707	60.6	70.5	21.0	4.4	17.0
Travel arrangement and reservation services......	5615	279	59.6	78.8	9.0	9.8	12.2
Investigations and security services......	5616	811	22.7	66.9	26.4	3.2	18.4
Services to buildings and dwellings [5]......	5617	1,603	56.2	80.1	12.8	1.9	41.3
Landscaping services......	56173	1,408	10.5	87.5	7.4	1.0	42.7
Other administrative and support services......	5611,2,9	364	44.6	80.7	12.0	4.5	20.8
Waste management and remediation services......	562	528	17.3	78.7	14.6	2.9	21.9
Accommodation and food services......	**72**	**11,200**	**52.8**	**73.0**	**13.9**	**7.7**	**27.0**
Accommodation......	721	1,489	57.6	67.3	17.9	9.0	28.8
Traveler accommodation......	7211	1,385	58.7	65.6	18.8	9.6	30.2
Recreational vehicle parks and camps, and rooming and board houses......	7212,3	104	43.9	90.2	5.8	0.7	10.8
Food services and drinking places......	722	9,711	52.1	73.9	13.2	7.5	26.8
Restaurants and other food services [6]......	722, excl. 7224	9,462	52.0	73.6	13.4	7.6	27.1
Drinking places, alcoholic beverages......	7224	249	54.7	84.2	6.8	2.4	14.7
Other services......	**81**	**7,617**	**53.9**	**77.7**	**10.6**	**8.4**	**19.9**
Other services (except private households)......	81	6,796	49.4	77.4	10.4	9.0	17.3
Repair and maintenance......	811	2,099	13.3	84.6	7.9	4.2	24.4
Automotive repair and maintenance [7]......	8111	1,253	9.9	86.1	7.1	2.9	24.8
Car washes......	811192	167	15.1	78.3	17.0	2.8	37.6
Electronic and precision equipment repair and maintenance......	8112	150	20.1	68.6	12.2	14.4	18.3
Commercial and industrial machinery and equipment repair and maintenance......	8113	319	10.7	85.7	7.7	3.6	24.0
Personal and household goods repair and maintenance [8]......	8114	197	31.5	90.0	2.6	6.6	16.3
Footwear and leather goods repair......	81143	12	(B)	(B)	(B)	(B)	(B)
Personal and laundry services......	812	2,691	72.9	69.1	11.4	16.6	17.4
Barber shops......	812111	150	27.0	62.5	29.0	6.0	28.4
Beauty salons......	812112	1,045	90.4	76.3	12.0	8.5	17.4
Nail salons and other personal care services......	812113, 81219	600	78.3	44.8	6.2	46.4	9.4
Drycleaning and laundry services......	8123	275	49.8	65.5	14.0	17.0	31.9
Funeral homes, cemeteries, and crematories......	8122	114	33.0	88.3	7.8	1.7	7.6
Other personal services......	8129	507	65.7	82.4	10.4	4.3	17.9
Membership associations and organizations......	813	2,006	55.6	81.2	11.7	3.7	9.8
Religious organizations......	8131	1,012	47.5	84.5	9.2	3.7	9.1
Civic, social, advocacy organizations, grantmaking and giving services......	8132,3,4	740	67.1	76.4	15.2	4.0	10.5
Labor unions......	81393	80	43.1	76.6	17.2	3.4	21.1
Business, professional, political, and similar organizations [9]......	8139	174	59.5	84.7	9.0	2.8	5.3
Private households......	814	821	91.0	79.8	12.6	3.7	41.3

B Base less than 50,000. [1] Based on the North American Industry Classification System, 2012; see Section 15. [2] The Current Population Survey (CPS) allows respondents to choose more than one race. Data represent persons who selected this race group only and exclude persons reporting more than one race. See also comments on race in text for Section 1. [3] Persons of Hispanic origin may be of any race. [4] Excludes NAICS 54194 (veterinary services). [5] Excludes NAICS 56173 (landscaping services). [6] Excludes NAICS 7224 (drinking places, alcoholic beverages). [7] Excludes NAICS 811192 (car washes). [8] Excludes NAICS 81143 (footwear and leather goods repair). [9] Excludes NAICS 81393 (labor unions).

Source: U.S. Bureau of Labor Statistics, CPS Tables, "Employed persons by detailed industry, sex, race, and Hispanic or Latino ethnicity," <http://www.bls.gov/cps/tables.htm>, accessed February 2020.

Table 1296. Selected Service-Related Industries—Establishments, Employees, and Annual Payroll by State: 2018

[Employees in thousands (9,112 represents 9,112,000); payroll in millions of dollars (801,736 represents $801,736,000,000). Covers establishments with paid employees. Excludes most government employees, railroad employees, and self-employed persons. Data are from Census Bureau's County Business Patterns program. For statement on methodology, see Appendix III]

State	Professional, scientific, and technical services (NAICS 54) [1]			Administrative and support and waste management and remediation services (NAICS 56) [1]			Accommodation and food services (NAICS 72) [1]		
	Establish-ments	Employ-ees [2] (1,000)	Annual payroll (mil. dol.)	Establish-ments	Employ-ees [2] (1,000)	Annual payroll (mil. dol.)	Establish-ments	Employ-ees [2] (1,000)	Annual payroll (mil. dol.)
United States	**921,521**	**9,112**	**801,736**	**418,868**	**12,288**	**512,059**	**733,134**	**14,345**	**291,362**
Alabama	9,456	105	7,996	4,443	155	4,811	9,143	190	3,002
Alaska	1,959	18	1,358	1,145	21	1,071	2,187	26	752
Arizona	18,467	157	12,055	8,718	289	10,663	13,288	312	6,299
Arkansas	6,003	39	2,220	2,791	65	1,690	5,998	109	1,717
California	130,204	1,242	133,324	45,650	1,618	80,335	91,245	1,781	42,102
Colorado	26,856	201	17,818	9,341	264	12,899	14,310	299	6,534
Connecticut	9,134	105	10,349	5,354	87	4,046	8,839	145	3,325
Delaware	3,128	31	3,215	1,522	29	1,090	2,240	43	895
District of Columbia	5,840	104	14,108	1,091	32	1,521	2,754	75	2,297
Florida	80,627	532	38,283	37,476	1,882	83,952	42,951	997	20,634
Georgia	30,007	281	22,774	12,808	390	13,838	21,531	452	7,731
Hawaii	3,413	23	1,579	1,889	64	2,336	3,895	113	3,586
Idaho	4,881	34	2,083	2,601	45	1,503	3,948	68	1,138
Illinois	38,599	394	37,168	17,024	521	18,966	28,953	544	11,065
Indiana	12,982	129	9,383	7,625	219	6,904	13,625	284	4,605
Iowa	6,531	56	3,482	3,830	85	3,029	7,312	125	2,028
Kansas	7,138	67	4,314	3,740	86	3,007	6,256	120	1,880
Kentucky	8,100	75	4,133	4,183	123	3,431	8,259	182	2,859
Louisiana	12,300	98	6,639	4,831	109	4,226	9,945	217	4,067
Maine	3,544	23	1,499	2,253	24	786	4,283	56	1,319
Maryland	20,870	282	26,140	8,423	217	9,007	12,232	247	5,146
Massachusetts	21,874	306	36,611	11,123	208	10,369	17,812	313	7,482
Michigan	21,689	287	23,221	11,446	368	12,352	20,762	403	7,221
Minnesota	16,580	186	15,403	7,711	182	7,354	11,989	246	4,722
Mississippi	4,689	31	1,642	2,341	58	1,566	5,649	132	2,242
Missouri	14,088	164	12,018	7,508	178	6,044	12,919	270	4,668
Montana	3,921	18	984	1,898	19	598	3,571	52	964
Nebraska	4,679	39	2,490	2,782	69	2,555	4,578	79	1,268
Nevada	9,220	61	3,995	4,557	123	4,161	6,944	321	9,848
New Hampshire	3,644	36	2,897	2,434	59	2,719	3,842	62	1,306
New Jersey	28,566	327	31,570	14,211	353	14,864	21,780	327	7,086
New Mexico	4,646	57	4,262	1,927	35	1,295	4,441	95	1,747
New York	61,859	651	65,270	27,472	679	41,080	55,035	819	21,679
North Carolina	25,001	227	17,840	13,278	294	10,011	21,757	449	7,518
North Dakota	1,837	16	1,042	1106	13	474	2,086	37	665
Ohio	23,777	258	18,599	13,460	407	14,510	24,324	479	7,661
Oklahoma	9,887	78	5,073	4,528	109	4,348	8,429	163	2,623
Oregon	12,737	97	7,664	6,005	107	3,963	11,796	189	4,001
Pennsylvania	29,952	332	27,543	15,859	333	12,800	28,974	490	8,661
Rhode Island	3,040	24	1,630	1,796	25	943	3,152	52	1,156
South Carolina	11,060	100	6,798	6,141	274	8,796	10,953	234	4,011
South Dakota	1,994	13	680	1,161	11	358	2,508	41	719
Tennessee	11,463	122	8,624	7,235	272	8,942	13,722	298	5,363
Texas	71,548	738	63,414	29,341	997	40,626	58,135	1,237	22,925
Utah	11,224	94	5,911	4,651	159	5,982	6,063	127	2,285
Vermont	2,094	12	859	1,179	9	313	1,991	34	683
Virginia	31,211	483	46,303	10,973	267	11,789	18,387	370	6,826
Washington	22,458	212	19,435	10,150	159	7,752	18,035	297	7,245
West Virginia	2,754	25	1,354	1,470	35	1,101	3,593	69	1,146
Wisconsin	11,503	114	8,086	7,267	153	5,007	14,905	251	4,058
Wyoming	2,487	10	598	1,120	7	276	1,808	28	601

[1] North American Industry Classification System, 2017. See text, section 15. [2] For employees on the payroll for the pay period including March 12.

Source: U.S. Census Bureau, County Business Patterns, CB1800CBP, "County Business Patterns by Legal Form of Organization and Employment Size Class for U.S., States, and Selected Geographies," <https://data.census.gov>, accessed July 2020.

Table 1297. Professional, Scientific, and Technical Services—Estimated Revenue by Kind of Business: 2010 to 2018

[In millions of dollars (1,293,795 represents $1,293,795,000,000). For taxable employer firms. Estimates have been adjusted to the results of the 2012 Economic Census. Based on the Service Annual Survey and administrative data; see Appendix III]

Kind of business	NAICS code [1]	2010	2014	2015	2016	2017	2018
Professional, scientific, and technical services (except notaries) [2,3]	**54**	**1,293,795**	**1,549,333**	**1,605,848**	**1,681,097**	**1,779,191**	**1,871,029**
Offices of lawyers	54111	231,608	251,745	260,956	267,823	286,978	287,299
Other legal services	54119	11,228	13,193	14,092	14,527	14,782	15,516
Offices of certified public accountants	541211	68,702	84,586	91,321	97,590	101,493	106,251
Tax preparation services	541213	5,740	6,657	7,099	7,011	7,274	7,665
Payroll services	541214	25,748	32,803	35,097	31,187	31,126	30,912
Other accounting services	541219	15,742	20,733	22,498	24,349	26,705	26,977
Architectural services	54131	26,849	31,967	34,864	37,547	39,882	42,708
Landscape architectural services	54132	3,021	3,211	3,357	3,560	3,794	4,031
Engineering services	54133	191,660	217,178	225,517	230,737	241,951	253,641
Drafting services	54134	602	1,046	1,134	1,044	1,116	1,205
Building inspection services	54135	1,856	2,416	2,590	2,680	2,856	3,141
Surveying and mapping services [4]	5413z	7,534	9,871	9,130	8,356	8,817	9,578
Testing laboratories	54138	14,057	16,257	17,190	17,203	18,303	19,092
Drafting, building inspection, and mapping services [5]	5413x	9,992	13,333	12,854	12,080	12,789	13,924
Interior design services	54141	6,594	9,479	10,351	10,559	10,689	11,171
Industrial design services	54142	1,308	1,827	1,941	1,839	2,094	2,147
Graphic design services	54143	7,378	8,157	8,761	9,348	9,700	9,743
Other specialized design services	54149	945	1,506	1,562	1,553	1,538	1,533
All other design services [6]	5414y	2,253	3,333	3,503	3,392	3,632	3,680
Computer systems design and related services	5415	283,362	347,637	348,245	372,584	397,985	431,159
Management consulting services [7]	54161	138,955	193,290	199,868	211,358	217,133	227,409
Environmental consulting services	54162	12,554	13,018	12,789	12,884	12,732	13,952
Other scientific and technical consulting services	54169	18,779	27,821	29,409	29,830	30,827	32,292
Research and development in physical, engineering and life sciences	54171	73,067	86,013	92,803	100,644	114,792	125,419
Research and development in social sciences and humanities	54172	1,848	2,293	2,168	2,230	2,197	2,180
Advertising agencies	54181	30,870	37,563	39,815	42,682	47,550	53,704
Public relations agencies	54182	9,515	11,405	11,863	13,614	12,628	13,949
Media buying agencies	54183	5,107	7,165	7,503	7,751	7,343	7,832
Media representatives	54184	2,992	3,311	3,296	3,365	3,236	3,431
Outdoor advertising	54185	7,089	7,159	7,248	7,299	7,376	7,217
Direct mail advertising	54186	10,140	10,226	10,126	10,611	10,308	10,277
Advertising material distribution services	54187	3,616	3,475	3,976	3,922	3,666	3,659
Other services related to advertising	54189	11,964	13,369	13,630	14,580	15,295	15,939
All other advertising [8]	5418y	15,580	16,844	17,606	18,502	18,961	19,598
Marketing research and public opinion polling	54191	16,531	17,695	17,769	18,867	18,161	19,150
Photography studios, portrait	541921	4,180	3,952	4,109	4,042	4,114	4,198
Commercial photography	541922	1,590	1,908	1,757	1,821	1,856	2,031
Translation and interpretation services	54193	3,740	3,654	3,627	3,927	4,187	4,739
Veterinary services	54194	27,033	33,390	35,421	38,719	41,805	42,150
All other professional, scientific, and technical services	54199	10,291	12,357	12,966	13,454	16,902	17,732

[1] Data for 2010 are based on the 2007 North American Industry Classification System (NAICS); beginning 2013, data are based on 2012 NAICS. See text Section 15 for more information. [2] Data prior to 2011 have been restated to reflect comparable data on the 2007 NAICS basis for more detailed levels within this aggregate. [3] Excludes NAICS 54112 (Offices of Notaries). [4] Includes NAICS 54136 (Geophysical Surveying and Mapping Services) and NAICS 54137 (Surveying and Mapping Services, except Geophysical Services). [5] Includes NAICS 54134 (Drafting Services), NAICS 54135 (Building Inspection Services), NAICS 54136 (Geophysical Surveying and Mapping Services), and NAICS 54137 (Surveying and Mapping (except Geophysical) Services). [6] Includes NAICS 54142 (Industrial Design Services) and NAICS 54149 (Other Specialized Design Services). [7] A portion of NAICS 54161 (Management Consulting Services) moved to NAICS 56131 (Employment Placement Agencies and Executive Search Services) with the 2007 NAICS update. Data prior to 2011 have been restated to reflect comparable data on the 2007 NAICS basis. [8] Includes NAICS 54187 (Advertising Material Distribution Services) and NAICS 54189 (Other Services Related to Advertising).

Source: U.S. Census Bureau, Service Annual Survey, "Service Annual Survey Latest Data (NAICS-basis): 2018" and "Service Annual Historical Survey Tables," <https://www.census.gov/programs-surveys/sas/data.html>, accessed February 2020.

Table 1298. Administrative and Support and Waste Management and Remediation Services—Estimated Revenue by Kind of Business: 2010 to 2018

[In millions of dollars (614,178 represents $614,178,000,000). For taxable and tax-exempt employer firms. Estimates have been adjusted to results of the 2012 Economic Census. Based on the Service Annual Survey and administrative data; see Appendix III]

Kind of business	NAICS code [1]	2010	2014	2015	2016	2017	2018
Administrative and support and waste management and remediation services [2]	**56**	**614,178**	**769,796**	**816,393**	**886,254**	**952,050**	**1,023,027**
Administrative and support services [2]	**561**	**535,359**	**683,527**	**728,883**	**793,515**	**854,277**	**918,174**
Office administrative services	5611	39,193	49,552	50,806	50,902	50,205	52,618
Facilities support services	5612	25,592	25,773	27,218	27,839	29,839	33,692
Employment placement agencies & executive search services [3]	56131	14,336	18,236	19,186	21,126	22,724	25,977
Temporary help services	56132	99,329	136,727	153,477	173,436	185,144	191,719
Professional employer organizations	56133	90,081	135,918	146,510	164,277	189,332	203,698
Document preparation services	56141	3,130	3,320	3,400	3,702	3,956	3,869
Telephone answering services	561421	2,167	1,982	2,086	2,244	2,278	2,406
Telemarketing bureaus and other contact centers	561422	14,729	18,269	18,626	19,827	19,255	21,295
Private mail centers	561431	2,107	2,491	2,626	2,752	2,996	3,153
Other business service centers (including copy shops)	561439	6,619	5,920	5,896	6,513	6,304	5,815
Collection agencies	56144	11,660	11,945	11,537	11,542	11,674	11,893
Credit bureaus	56145	6,604	8,084	9,330	10,180	11,136	11,642
Repossession services	561491	844	760	769	878	975	1,001
Court reporting and stenotype services	561492	2,252	2,175	2,240	2,379	2,496	2,583
All other business support services	561499	8,199	6,997	7,018	7,464	7,809	7,465
Travel agencies	56151	12,203	14,313	15,052	16,904	19,006	21,108
Tour operators	56152	5,125	5,826	6,084	6,128	6,742	7,432
Convention and visitors bureaus	561591	1,387	1,876	2,010	2,192	2,364	2,530
All other travel arrangement and reservation services	561599	12,846	16,393	17,640	18,307	20,059	21,577
Investigation services	561611	4,404	5,133	5,323	5,617	5,905	6,114
Security guards and patrol services	561612	20,820	23,604	24,012	26,113	28,053	29,834
Armored car services	561613	2,291	2,191	2,247	2,387	2,362	2,476
Security systems services (except locksmiths)	561621	13,833	17,861	19,045	20,726	21,941	23,598
Locksmiths	561622	1,542	1,767	1,803	1,963	2,124	2,215
Exterminating and pest control services	56171	9,444	11,525	11,929	12,713	14,292	16,239
Janitorial services	56172	34,559	40,015	41,676	43,935	44,569	49,416
Landscaping services	56173	47,674	63,570	67,549	75,061	81,188	91,554
Carpet and upholstery cleaning services	56174	2,746	3,446	3,537	3,795	3,857	3,973
Other services to buildings and dwellings	56179	4,758	6,609	7,141	7,746	8,145	9,207
Packaging and labeling services	56191	5,397	6,875	7,474	7,749	8,103	8,581
Convention and trade show organizers	56192	10,016	12,920	13,050	14,109	14,658	15,446
All other support services	56199	19,472	21,454	22,586	23,009	24,786	28,048
Waste management and remediation services	**562**	**78,819**	**86,269**	**87,510**	**92,739**	**97,773**	**104,853**
Solid waste collection	562111	36,431	39,409	39,503	41,804	44,069	47,836
Hazardous waste collection	562112	2,096	2,899	3,225	3,475	3,511	3,703
Other waste collection	562119	1,271	1,508	1,703	1,724	1,813	2,006
Hazardous waste treatment and disposal	562211	6,221	8,019	7,915	8,536	9,106	8,925
Solid waste landfill	562212	4,798	5,782	5,778	6,348	6,490	6,695
Solid waste combustors and incinerators	562213	(S)	2,517	(S)	(S)	(S)	(S)
Other nonhazardous waste treatment and disposal	562219	481	480	509	378	440	453
Remediation services	56291	16,422	14,940	15,532	16,867	17,805	19,492
Materials recovery facilities	56292	5,092	5,722	5,285	5,388	5,898	6,546
Septic tank and related services	562991	2,351	3,101	3,563	4,142	4,374	4,804
All other miscellaneous waste management services	562998	1,442	1,892	1,947	1,707	1,864	1,880

S Figure does not meet publication standards. [1] Data for 2010 are based on the 2007 North American Industry Classification System (NAICS); beginning 2013, data are based on 2012 NAICS. See text Section 15 for more information. [2] Data prior to 2011 have been restated to reflect comparable data on the 2007 NAICS basis for more detailed levels within this aggregate. [3] Includes 2002 NAICS 561310 (Employment Placement Agencies) and a portion of 2002 NAICS 541612 (Human Resources and Executive Search Consulting Services).

Source: U.S. Census Bureau, Service Annual Survey, "Service Annual Survey Latest Data (NAICS-basis): 2018" and "Service Annual Survey Historical Survey Tables," <https://www.census.gov/programs-surveys/sas/data.html>, accessed February 2020.

Table 1299. Selected Service Industries Revenue—Total and from Electronic Sources: 2017 and 2018

[15,338,892 represents $15,338,892,000,000. Data shown for service businesses with paid employees. Revenues from electronic sources include revenues from customers entering orders directly on a firm's Website or mobile application, entering orders directly on third party Websites or mobile applications, and entering orders via any other electronic system (such as private networks, dedicated lines, kiosks, etc.). Based on the Service Annual Survey, see Appendix III]

Kind of business	NAICS code [1]	Total revenue (million dollars)		Electronic sources revenue (million dollars)		Electronic sources revenue as a percent of total revenue	
		2017	2018	2017	2018	2017	2018
Selected service industries, total...............	(X)	**15,338,892**	**16,195,954**	**997,735**	**1,151,736**	**6.5**	**7.1**
Utilities [2]..	22	579,388	599,744	(S)	(S)	(S)	(S)
Selected transportation and warehousing [3]........	4849y	918,981	991,615	174,351	175,100	19.0	17.7
Air transportation...	481	209,725	225,785	92,792	93,082	44.2	41.2
Water transportation.......................................	483	42,231	45,950	9,615	11,065	22.8	24.1
Truck transportation.......................................	484	272,784	294,489	30,529	30,508	11.2	10.4
Transit and ground passenger transportation.......	485	39,842	42,508	(S)	(S)	(S)	(S)
Pipeline transportation...................................	486	46,676	52,820	(S)	(S)	(S)	(S)
Scenic and sightseeing transportation................	487	3,477	3,601	1,157	1,199	33.3	33.3
Support activities for transportation..................	488	180,727	194,773	14,709	14,708	8.1	7.6
Information...	51	1,533,015	1,630,015	313,280	356,564	20.4	21.9
Publishing industries (except internet)...............	511	322,323	342,459	98,009	117,510	30.4	34.3
Motion picture and sound recording industries.....	512	101,738	109,969	8,731	10,619	8.6	9.7
Broadcasting (except internet).........................	515	160,814	168,843	(S)	2,754	(S)	1.6
Telecommunications.......................................	517	617,045	630,683	(S)	(S)	(S)	(S)
Data processing, hosting, and related services....	518	152,277	169,480	17,555	18,464	11.5	10.9
Other information services..............................	519	178,818	208,581	128,225	151,910	71.7	72.8
Finance and insurance [4]................................	52	4,499,547	4,766,939	188,036	(S)	4.2	(S)
Activities related to credit intermediation...........	5223	98,610	101,708	17,433	19,335	17.7	19.0
Securities and commodity contracts intermediation and brokerage............................	5231	276,143	280,648	17,037	16,582	6.2	5.9
Real estate and rental and leasing.....................	53	668,219	707,520	41,730	(S)	6.2	(S)
Rental and leasing services.............................	532	159,914	173,748	23,896	25,983	14.9	15.0
Selected professional, scientific, and technical services [5]..	54	1,821,160	1,914,440	58,854	68,859	3.2	3.6
Computer systems design and related services....	5415	397,985	431,159	25,964	25,897	6.5	6.0
Administrative and support and waste management and remediation services.............	56	952,050	1,023,027	58,965	64,501	6.2	6.3
Travel arrangement and reservation services.......	5615	48,171	52,647	21,800	21,445	45.3	40.7
Educational services [6]..................................	61	67,808	71,159	11,071	11,395	16.3	16.0
Health care and social assistance.....................	62	2,545,317	2,652,544	7,778	8,254	0.3	0.3
Arts, entertainment, and recreation...................	71	266,877	281,034	29,599	35,288	11.1	12.6
Accommodation and food services [7]................	72	929,333	979,205	79,687	90,317	8.6	9.2
Other services (except public administration) [8]....	81	557,197	578,712	30,569	34,308	5.5	5.9
Repair and maintenance.................................	811	175,122	182,249	4,180	(S)	2.4	(S)
Personal and laundry services.........................	812	111,202	117,821	5,815	6,933	5.2	5.9
Religious, grantmaking, civic, professional, and similar organizations....................................	813	270,873	278,642	20,574	22,800	7.6	8.2

X Not applicable. S Data do not meet publication standards. [1] North American Industry Classification System (NAICS), 2012; see text Section 15. [2] Excludes government owned utilities. [3] Excludes NAICS 482 (Rail Transportation) and NAICS 491 (Postal Service). [4] Excludes NAICS 525 (Funds, Trusts, and Other Financial Vehicles). [5] Excludes NAICS 54112 (Offices of Notaries). [6] Excludes NAICS 6111 (Elementary and Secondary Schools), NAICS 6112 (Junior Colleges), and NAICS 6113 (Colleges, Universities, and Professional Schools). [7] Prior to 2016, NAICS sector 72 was collected and published by the Annual Retail Trade Report. [8] Excludes NAICS 81311 (Religious Organizations), NAICS 81393 (Labor Unions and Similar Labor Organizations), NAICS 81394 (Political Organizations), and NAICS 814 (Private Households).

Source: U.S. Census Bureau, Service Annual Survey, "Service Annual Survey Latest Data (NAICS-basis): 2018," <https://www.census.gov/programs-surveys/sas/data.html>, accessed February 2020.

Table 1300. Accommodation and Food Services Revenue by Kind of Business: 2013 to 2018

[In millions of dollars (737,177 represents $737,177,000,000). Based on data from the Service Annual Survey, see headnote Table 1298. Prior to 2016, data collected and published by the Annual Retail Trade Report; see <https://census.gov/retail/arts/historic_releases.html>]

Kind of business	NAICS code [1]	2013	2014	2015	2016	2017	2018
Accommodation and food services, total.....	**72**	**737,177**	**781,828**	**840,745**	**887,451**	**929,333**	**979,205**
Accommodation..	721	205,978	218,444	231,082	243,975	252,176	262,193
Hotels (except casino hotels) and motels..........	72111	142,890	153,699	164,964	175,507	180,591	187,703
Casino hotels...	72112	54,981	56,133	57,010	58,931	61,358	63,655
Other traveler accommodations......................	72119	1,823	2,037	2,264	2,340	2,463	2,625
RV (recreation vehicle) parks and recreational camps..................................	7212	4,942	5,128	5,413	5,787	6,254	6,624
Rooming and boarding houses........................	7213	1,342	1,447	1,431	1,410	1,510	1,586
Food services and drinking places..................	722	531,199	563,384	609,663	643,476	677,157	717,012
Food services contractors.............................	72231	37,685	39,271	42,049	44,683	45,595	47,156
Caterers..	72232	7,459	7,652	8,191	8,668	9,039	9,380
Mobile food services....................................	72233	822	986	1,138	1,405	1,607	1,908
Drinking places (alcoholic beverages).............	7224	19,796	19,956	20,971	23,348	25,398	27,139
Full-service restaurants................................	722511	232,900	250,216	269,741	279,735	291,232	307,716
Limited-service restaurants...........................	722513	193,009	202,213	219,699	233,937	248,963	264,622
Cafeterias, grill buffets, and buffets................	722514	6,401	6,230	7,043	7,323	7,779	8,271
Snack and nonalcoholic beverage bars............	722515	33,127	36,860	40,831	44,337	47,544	50,820

[1] North American Industry Classification System (NAICS), 2012; see text, Section 15.

Source: U.S. Census Bureau, Service Annual Survey, "Service Annual Survey Latest Data (NAICS-basis): 2018," <https://www.census.gov/programs-surveys/sas/data.html>, accessed February 2020.

Table 1301. Other Services—Estimated Revenue for Employer Firms by Kind of Business: 2014 to 2018

[In millions of dollars (482,548 represents $482,548,000,000). For taxable and tax exempt employer firms. Estimates have been adjusted to results of the 2012 Economic Census. Based on the Service Annual Survey; see Appendix III]

Kind of business	NAICS code [1]	2014	2015	2016	2017	2018
Other services (except public administration) [2]	**81**	**482,548**	**498,951**	**517,395**	**557,197**	**578,712**
Repair and maintenance	811	157,449	162,955	169,788	175,122	182,249
General automotive repair	811111	46,655	47,718	49,954	50,867	53,940
Automotive exhaust system repair	811112	727	774	788	815	854
Automotive transmission repair	811113	2,369	2,313	2,319	2,362	2,501
Other automotive mechanical and electrical repair and maintenance	811118	2,053	2,054	2,136	2,043	2,076
Automotive body, paint, interior repair and maintenance	811121	30,244	32,009	34,646	36,684	37,274
Automotive glass replacement shops	811122	3,729	4,196	4,591	4,517	4,713
Automotive oil change and lubrication shops	811191	5,122	5,336	5,762	6,268	6,584
Car washes	811192	7,609	8,031	8,747	9,450	10,533
All other automotive repair and maintenance	811198	1,916	1,964	2,092	2,334	2,596
Consumer electronics repair and maintenance	811211	1,640	1,653	1,617	1,431	1,466
Computer and office machine repair and maintenance	811212	5,014	4,962	5,085	4,976	4,811
Communication equipment repair and maintenance	811213	3,015	3,145	3,350	3,349	3,559
Other electronic and precision equipment repair and maintenance	811219	6,727	7,187	7,199	7,186	7,609
Commercial and industrial machinery and equipment (except automotive and electronic) repair and maintenance	8113	33,679	34,270	33,795	35,047	35,763
Home and garden equipment and appliance repair and maintenance	81141	2,780	2,808	2,937	2,870	2,802
Reupholstery and furniture repair	81142	1,085	1,173	1,204	1,183	1,235
Footwear and leather goods repair	81143	217	230	230	221	230
Other personal and household goods repair and maintenance	81149	2,868	3,132	3,336	3,519	3,703
Personal and laundry services	812	96,608	101,406	105,884	111,202	117,821
Barber shops	812111	692	748	818	949	1,227
Beauty shops	812112	20,866	21,348	22,279	22,693	23,818
Nail salons	812113	3,834	4,415	5,032	5,612	6,435
Diet and weight reducing centers	812191	1,569	1,456	1,533	1,567	1,758
Other personal care services	812199	6,033	6,661	7,420	8,518	9,530
Funeral homes and funeral services	81221	13,733	14,476	14,792	15,124	14,784
Cemeteries and crematories	81222	3,646	3,782	3,996	4,095	4,145
Coin-operated laundries and drycleaners	81231	4,003	4,021	4,119	4,236	4,475
Dry-cleaning and laundry services (except coin-operated)	81232	7,956	7,908	7,842	8,056	8,134
Linen supply	812331	5,610	6,075	6,175	6,239	6,603
Industrial launders	812332	7,718	7,982	8,494	8,645	9,377
Pet care (except veterinary) services	81291	4,206	4,768	5,340	6,165	7,065
Photofinishing	81292	1,839	1,844	1,720	1,770	1,775
Parking lots and garages	81293	8,315	9,033	8,907	9,368	9,669
All other personal services	81299	6,588	6,889	7,417	8,159	9,026
Religious, grantmaking, civic, professional, and similar organizations [3]	813	228,491	234,590	241,723	270,873	278,642
Grantmaking and giving services	8132	114,180	117,547	119,414	139,127	142,811
Social advocacy organizations	8133	28,253	28,693	30,633	32,615	34,096
Civic and social organizations	8134	17,143	17,864	18,186	19,753	20,499
Business, professional, labor, political, and similar organizations [4]	8139	68,915	70,486	73,490	79,378	81,236

[1] Data based on 2012 NAICS. See section 15, Business Enterprise. [2] Excludes NAICS 8131 (Religious Organizations), NAICS 81393 (Labor Unions and Similar Labor Organizations), NAICS 81394 (Political Organizations), and NAICS 814 (Private Households). [3] Excludes NAICS 8131 (Religious Organizations), NAICS 81393 (Labor Unions and Similar Labor Organizations), and NAICS 81394 (Political Organizations). [4] Excludes NAICS 81393 (Labor Unions and Similar Labor Organizations) and NAICS 81394 (Political Organizations).

Source: U.S. Census Bureau, Service Annual Survey, "Service Annual Survey Latest Data (NAICS-basis): 2018," <https://www.census.gov/programs-surveys/sas/data.html>, accessed February 2020.

Table 1302. National Nonprofit Associations—Number by Type: 1980 to 2020

[Data compiled during last few months of year previous to year shown and the beginning months of year shown]

Type	1980	1990	2000	2005	2010 [1]	2015	2018	2019	2020
Total	**14,726**	**22,289**	**21,840**	**22,720**	**23,983**	**23,891**	**24,146**	**24,242**	**24,414**
Trade, business, commercial	3,118	3,918	3,880	3,789	3,761	3,487	3,576	3,571	3,670
Agriculture and environment	677	940	1,103	1,170	1,442	1,421	1,393	1,441	1,484
Legal, governmental, public admin., military	529	792	790	868	913	894	958	977	977
Scientific, engineering, technical	1,039	1,417	1,302	1,354	1,563	1,507	1,567	1,570	1,564
Educational	[2] 2,376	1,291	1,297	1,318	1,444	1,344	1,365	1,436	1,438
Cultural	([2])	1,886	1,786	1,733	1,717	1,610	1,655	1,658	1,657
Social welfare	994	1,705	1,829	2,072	2,673	3,166	3,018	2,950	2,979
Health, medical	1,413	2,227	2,495	2,982	3,481	4,069	4,350	4,283	4,293
Public affairs	1,068	2,249	1,776	1,854	1,734	1,601	1,509	1,459	1,463
Fraternal, nationality, ethnic	435	573	525	550	461	398	405	405	398
Religious	797	1,172	1,123	1,147	1,056	964	968	992	1,000
Veteran, hereditary, patriotic	208	462	835	774	585	545	541	550	566
Hobby, avocational	910	1,475	1,330	1,433	1,374	1,287	1,268	1,353	1,341
Athletic sports	504	840	717	762	946	899	884	863	904
Labor unions	235	253	232	208	188	162	160	215	168
Chambers of Commerce [3]	105	168	143	135	142	125	116	106	105
Greek and non-Greek letter societies	318	340	296	349	305	294	316	317	313
Fan clubs	(NA)	581	381	314	198	118	97	96	94

NA Not available. [1] Beginning in 2007, there was an increase in the number of associations due to an increase in newly discovered and established associations. [2] Data for cultural associations included with educational associations. [3] National and binational. Includes trade and tourism organizations.

Source: Gale, Cengage Learning. *Encyclopedia of Associations: National Organizations* © 2020 Gale, a part of Cengage, Inc. Reproduced by permission. See <www.cengage.com/permissions>.

Section 28
Foreign Commerce and Aid

This section presents data on the flow of goods, services, and capital between the United States and other countries; changes in official reserve assets of the United States; international investments; and foreign assistance programs.

The Bureau of Economic Analysis publishes current figures on U.S. international transactions and the U.S. international investment position in its monthly *Survey of Current Business* and in an interactive database on the internet at <apps.bea.gov/iTable/>. Statistics for the foreign aid programs are presented by the Agency for International Development (USAID) in its annual *U.S. Overseas Loans and Grants*.

The principal source of merchandise import and export data is the U.S. Census Bureau. Current data are presented monthly in *U.S. International Trade in Goods and Services Report* Series FT 900, as well as in the "USA Trade Online" database, at <usatrade.census.gov/>. The *Guide to Foreign Trade Statistics*, found on the Census Bureau website at <census.gov/foreign-trade/guide/index.html>, lists the Census Bureau's monthly and annual products and services in this field. In addition, the International Trade Administration and the Bureau of Economic Analysis present summary as well as selected commodity and country data for U.S. foreign trade on their websites: <trade.gov/trade-data-analysis> and <bea.gov/data/economic-accounts/international>, respectively. The merchandise trade data published by the Bureau of Economic Analysis in the *Survey of Current Business* and on the web include balance of payments adjustments to the Census Bureau data. The U.S. Treasury Department's *Monthly Treasury Statement of Receipts and Outlays of the United States Government* contains information on import duties. The International Trade Commission, U.S. Department of Agriculture (agricultural products), U.S. Department of Energy (mineral fuels, like petroleum and coal), and the U.S. Geological Survey (minerals) release various reports and specialized products on U.S. trade.

International accounts—The international transactions tables (Tables 1303, 1306, and 1307) show, for given time periods, the transfer of goods, services, grants, and financial assets and liabilities between the United States and the rest of the world. The international investment position table (Table 1305) presents, for specific dates, the value of U.S. investments abroad and of foreign investments in the United States. The movement of foreign and U.S. capital as presented in the balance of payments is not the only factor affecting the total value of foreign investments. Among the other factors are changes in the valuation of assets or liabilities, including changes in prices of securities, defaults, expropriations, and write-offs.

Direct investment abroad means the ownership or control, directly or indirectly, by one person of 10 percent or more of the voting securities of an incorporated business enterprise or an equivalent interest in an unincorporated business enterprise. Direct investment position is the value of U.S. parents' claims on the equity of and receivables due from foreign affiliates, less foreign affiliates' receivables due from their U.S. parents. Income consists of

parents' shares in the earnings of their affiliates plus net interest received by parents on intercompany accounts, less withholding taxes on dividends and interest.

Foreign aid—Foreign assistance is divided into three major categories—grants (military supplies and services and other grants), credits, and other assistance (through net accumulation of foreign currency claims from the sale of agricultural commodities). *Grants* are transfers for which no payment is expected (other than a limited percentage of the foreign currency "counterpart" funds generated by the grant), or which at most involve an obligation on the part of the receiver to extend aid to the United States or other countries to achieve a common objective. *Credits* are loan disbursements or transfers under other agreements which give rise to specific obligations to repay, over a period of years, usually with interest. All known returns to the U.S. government stemming from grants and credits (reverse grants, returns of grants, and payments of principal) are taken into account in net grants and net credits, but no allowance is made for interest or commissions. *Other assistance* represents the transfer of U.S. farm products in exchange for foreign currencies (plus, since enactment of Public Law 87-128, currency claims from principal and interest collected on credits extended under the farm products program), less the government's disbursements of the currencies as grants, credits, or for purchases. The net acquisition of currencies represents net transfers of resources to foreign countries under the agricultural programs, in addition to those classified as grants or credits.

Exports—Export statistics consist of goods valued at more than $2,500 per commodity shipped by individuals and organizations (including exporters, freight forwarders, and carriers) from the U.S. to other countries. The Census Bureau compiles export data primarily from three sources: Shipper's Export Declaration documents filed with Customs and Border Protection and sent to the Census Bureau (3 percent of all transactions), data in electronic form submitted directly by exporters and their agents (63 percent); and special computer tapes from Canada for U.S. exports to Canada (34 percent). Estimates are made for low-value exports by country of destination, and based on bilateral trade patterns. They include U.S. exports under mutual security programs and exclude shipments to U.S. Armed Forces for their own use.

The value reported in the export statistics is generally equivalent to a free alongside ship (f.a.s.) value at the U.S. port of export, based on the transaction price, including inland freight, insurance, and other charges incurred in placing the merchandise alongside the carrier at the U.S. port of exportation. This value, as defined, excludes the cost of loading merchandise aboard the exporting carrier and also excludes freight, insurance, and any other charges or transportation and other costs beyond the U.S. port of exportation. The country of destination is defined as the country of ultimate destination or country where the merchandise is to be consumed, further processed, or manufactured, as known to the shipper at the time of exportation. When ultimate destination is not known, the shipment is statistically credited to the last country to which the shipper knows the merchandise will be shipped in the same form as exported.

Statistics for U.S. exports to Canada are based on import documents filed with Canadian agencies and forwarded to the U.S. Census Bureau under a 1987 data exchange agreement. Under this agreement, each country eliminated most cross-border export documents; maintains detailed statistics on cross-border imports; exchanges monthly files of cross-border import statistics; and publishes exchanged statistics in place of previously compiled export statistics.

Prior to 1989, exports were based on Schedule B, Statistical Classification of Domestic and Foreign Commodities Exported from the United States. Beginning in 1989, Schedule B classifications are based on the Harmonized System and coincide with the Standard International Trade Classification, Revision 3. This revision will affect the comparability of most export series beginning with the 1989 data for commodities.

Imports—Import statistics consist of goods valued at more than $2,000 per commodity shipped by individuals and organizations (including importers and customs brokers) into the U.S. from other countries. The Census Bureau compiles import data from records filed with Customs and Border Protection, usually within 10 days after the merchandise enters the United States. Estimates are made for low-value shipments by country of origin, based on previous bilateral trade patterns and periodically updated. Country of origin is defined as country where the merchandise was grown, mined, or manufactured. If country of origin is unknown, country of shipment is reported. Statistics for over 95 percent of all commodity transactions are compiled from records filed electronically with Customs and forwarded as computer tape files to the U.S. Census Bureau. Statistics for other transactions are compiled from

hard-copy documents filed with Customs and forwarded on a flow basis for U.S. Census Bureau processing.

Data on import values are presented on two valuations bases in this section: the c.i.f. (cost, insurance, and freight) and the customs import value (as appraised by the U.S. Customs Service in accordance with legal requirements of the Tariff Act of 1930, as amended). This latter valuation, primarily used for collection of import duties, frequently does not reflect the actual transaction value.

Imports are classified either as "General imports" or "Imports for consumption." *General imports* are a combination of entries for immediate consumption, entries into customs bonded warehouses, and entries into U.S. Foreign Trade Zones, thus generally reflecting total arrivals of merchandise. *Imports for consumption* are a combination of entries for immediate consumption, withdrawals from warehouses for consumption, and entries of merchandise into U.S. customs territory from U.S. Foreign Trade Zones, thus generally reflecting the total of the commodities entered into U.S. consumption channels.

Beginning in 1989, import statistics are based on the Harmonized Tariff Schedule of the United States, which coincides with import Standard International Trade Classification, Revision 3. This revision will affect the comparability of most import series beginning with the 1989 data.

Area coverage—Except as noted, the geographic area covered by the export and import trade statistics is the United States Customs area (includes the 50 states, the District of Columbia, and Puerto Rico), the U.S. Virgin Islands (effective January 1981), and U.S. Foreign Trade Zones (effective July 1982).

Statistical reliability—For a discussion of statistical collection and estimation, sampling procedures, and measures of statistical reliability applicable to Census Bureau data, see Appendix III.

Table 1303. U.S. International Transactions by Type of Transaction: 2000 to 2019

[In millions of dollars (1,486,120 represents $1,486,120,000,000). Minus sign (-) indicates debits. N.i.e. is not indicated elsewhere]

Type of transaction	2000	2005	2010	2013	2014	2015	2016	2017	2018	2019
Exports of goods and services and income receipts	**1,486,120**	**1,893,153**	**2,687,457**	**3,250,758**	**3,379,101**	**3,236,349**	**3,235,442**	**3,542,008**	**3,792,867**	**3,805,938**
Exports of goods and services	1,082,963	1,291,503	1,872,320	2,313,237	2,392,268	2,279,743	2,237,923	2,387,391	2,539,383	2,528,262
Goods	784,940	913,016	1,290,279	1,593,708	1,635,563	1,511,381	1,457,393	1,557,003	1,676,950	1,652,437
General merchandise	778,718	906,104	1,271,972	1,559,363	1,612,611	1,489,795	1,436,552	1,535,249	1,654,735	1,632,679
Foods, feeds, and beverages	47,871	58,955	107,719	136,163	143,721	127,721	130,515	132,761	133,129	131,103
Industrial supplies and materials	171,108	236,812	388,561	492,422	500,677	418,141	387,600	459,380	537,038	526,843
Capital goods except automotive	357,000	358,426	447,839	534,757	551,758	539,805	520,001	533,696	563,375	548,111
Automotive vehicles, parts, and engines	80,356	98,406	112,008	152,661	159,812	151,894	150,398	157,867	158,836	162,468
Consumer goods except food and automotive	89,305	115,228	164,909	188,093	198,398	197,318	193,258	197,190	205,524	205,028
Other general merchandise	33,078	38,276	50,938	55,268	58,246	54,917	54,781	54,357	56,833	59,127
Net exports of goods under merchanting	159	1,330	411	461	299	261	300	210	270	435
Nonmonetary gold	6,063	5,582	17,896	33,883	22,654	21,325	20,542	21,544	21,945	19,323
Services	298,023	378,487	582,041	719,529	756,705	768,362	780,530	830,388	862,433	875,825
Manufacturing services on physical inputs owned by others	(NA)	(NA)	(NA)	(NA)	(NA)	(NA)	(NA)	(NA)	(NA)	(NA)
Maintenance and repair services n.i.e.	4,423	6,652	13,111	15,720	17,978	19,847	21,587	23,239	27,948	27,868
Transport [1]	49,462	58,377	76,357	89,999	90,687	84,434	81,779	86,342	93,251	91,092
Travel (for all purposes including education) [2]	96,872	93,423	130,315	170,979	180,265	192,602	192,868	193,834	196,465	193,315
Construction	1,993	1,489	2,951	2,213	2,070	2,759	1,690	2,053	2,948	3,189
Insurance services	3,631	7,566	14,854	15,768	16,277	15,464	16,249	18,223	17,904	16,238
Financial services	29,192	47,405	86,512	109,794	119,933	114,951	114,762	128,035	132,420	135,698
Charges for the use of intellectual property n.i.e.	43,476	64,466	94,968	113,824	116,380	111,151	112,981	118,147	118,875	117,401
Telecommunications, computer, and information services	12,250	15,568	26,556	36,325	38,629	41,427	43,122	47,657	49,653	55,657
Other business services [3]	38,217	56,846	99,595	122,166	132,240	141,421	153,089	167,270	177,261	189,441
Personal, cultural, and recreational services n.i.e. [4,5]	9,351	11,114	17,612	20,888	22,551	24,220	23,626	25,664	23,759	23,372
Government goods and services n.i.e.	9,156	15,582	19,210	21,852	19,693	20,087	18,777	19,924	21,949	22,555
Primary income receipts [6]	365,612	536,294	723,223	811,561	845,926	825,100	857,091	997,524	1,108,472	1,135,691
Investment income	361,217	531,498	717,292	804,948	839,423	818,521	851,489	991,177	1,101,820	1,128,966
Compensation of employees	4,395	4,796	5,931	6,613	6,503	6,578	6,329	6,347	6,652	6,725
Secondary income (current transfer) receipts [6]	37,545	65,356	91,915	125,960	140,907	131,507	139,700	157,094	145,012	141,984
Imports of goods and services and income payments	**1,888,038**	**2,642,385**	**3,119,466**	**3,587,611**	**3,746,930**	**3,643,704**	**3,630,307**	**3,907,277**	**4,242,560**	**4,286,163**
Imports of goods and services	1,452,650	2,008,045	2,375,407	2,760,066	2,876,412	2,771,004	2,719,092	2,901,181	3,119,320	3,105,127
Goods	1,231,722	1,695,820	1,938,950	2,294,247	2,385,480	2,273,249	2,207,195	2,356,345	2,557,251	2,516,767
General merchandise	1,225,780	1,691,201	1,924,446	2,276,499	2,370,016	2,260,659	2,189,041	2,343,660	2,546,058	2,504,815
Foods, feeds, and beverages	46,489	69,072	92,492	116,003	126,805	128,762	131,010	138,825	148,331	151,560
Industrial supplies and materials	303,768	533,686	610,268	686,673	675,567	492,483	441,793	508,645	580,696	525,864
Capital goods except automotive	347,706	382,833	450,406	558,971	598,759	607,160	593,614	642,884	694,656	681,051
Automotive vehicles, parts, and engines	194,954	238,715	225,641	309,573	329,498	350,049	350,847	359,118	372,368	376,804
Consumer goods except food and automotive	284,634	412,734	485,121	532,876	558,700	596,417	584,900	603,470	648,441	655,930
Other general merchandise	48,229	54,161	60,519	72,402	80,688	85,789	86,876	90,739	101,566	113,607
Nonmonetary gold	5,942	4,618	14,504	17,748	15,464	12,590	18,154	12,685	11,193	11,953
Services	220,927	312,225	436,456	465,819	490,932	497,755	511,898	544,836	562,069	588,359
Manufacturing services on physical inputs owned by others	(NA)	(NA)	(NA)	(NA)	(NA)	(NA)	(NA)	(NA)	(NA)	(NA)
Maintenance and repair services n.i.e.	2,316	2,730	5,857	6,674	6,732	8,084	7,595	6,796	7,133	7,823
Transport [1]	58,526	78,796	88,394	94,434	99,810	99,557	92,391	96,515	106,303	107,458
Travel (for all purposes including education) [2]	64,174	74,112	85,166	91,119	96,248	102,664	109,155	117,992	126,008	134,594
Construction	1,447	1,295	2,578	2,583	2,314	3,012	1,768	1,950	3,151	1,327
Insurance services	11,284	28,710	63,452	52,993	52,760	49,842	52,070	50,889	43,735	51,547
Financial services	16,445	21,971	27,215	29,284	32,770	32,594	32,672	36,649	39,249	40,350
Charges for the use of intellectual property n.i.e.	16,139	24,127	31,116	35,295	37,562	35,178	41,974	44,405	43,933	42,733
Telecommunications, computer, and information services	14,128	18,404	29,421	35,868	38,461	38,815	39,720	43,091	42,558	43,720
Other business services [3]	20,306	32,076	65,903	84,024	90,716	95,119	100,505	106,991	107,834	113,584
Personal, cultural, and recreational services n.i.e. [3]	1,645	2,550	5,393	8,205	9,323	11,358	12,544	17,530	19,190	21,140
Government goods and services n.i.e. [4,7]	14,516	27,454	31,960	25,341	24,236	21,531	21,503	22,047	22,975	24,083
Primary income payments [6]	350,980	492,108	553,311	616,041	645,623	639,724	660,798	739,731	857,298	899,347
Investment income	339,107	475,701	539,783	600,831	629,675	623,031	643,482	722,836	840,180	880,562
Compensation of employees	11,873	16,407	13,528	15,210	15,948	16,693	17,316	16,895	17,117	18,785
Secondary income (current transfer) payments [6]	84,408	142,232	190,749	211,504	224,885	232,976	250,417	266,365	265,943	281,689
Capital transfer receipts and other credits	**42**	**15,473**	**9**	**20**	**49**	**67**	**76**	**19,200**	**3,286**	**67**

See footnotes at end of table.

Table 1303. U.S. International Transactions by Type of Transaction: 2000 to 2019-Continued.

See headnote on page 811.

Type of transaction	2000	2005	2010	2013	2014	2015	2016	2017	2018	2019
Capital transfer payments and other debits	**4,259**	**14,523**	**6,900**	**6,578**	**6,584**	**8,006**	**6,682**	**6,805**	**7,482**	**6,311**
Net U.S. acquisition of financial assets [8]	**587,682**	**562,996**	**958,737**	**649,753**	**866,702**	**197,359**	**335,233**	**1,188,188**	**358,971**	**440,751**
Direct investment assets	186,371	52,591	349,829	392,796	387,528	302,072	299,814	405,375	-151,298	188,469
Equity	170,011	42,287	338,294	334,706	344,914	292,455	325,722	392,160	-218,115	173,537
Debt instruments	16,360	10,304	11,535	58,090	42,614	9,618	-25,908	13,215	66,817	14,932
Portfolio investment assets	159,713	267,290	199,620	481,298	582,676	160,410	36,283	569,375	335,263	46,570
Equity and investment fund shares	106,714	186,684	79,150	287,432	431,625	196,922	21,743	139,940	171,300	-191,306
Debt securities [9]	52,999	80,606	120,469	193,866	151,051	-36,511	14,541	429,435	163,963	237,876
Other investment assets	241,308	257,210	407,454	-221,242	-99,920	-258,831	-2,955	215,127	170,017	201,053
Other equity	1,438	1,138	1,907	2,030	2,058	2,098	1,746	1,506	1,329	1,367
Currency and deposits	(NA)	82,879	150,249	-126,959	-160,480	-191,472	-91,039	173,372	106,078	132,600
Loans	(NA)	171,906	249,255	-106,118	64,326	-67,754	85,434	34,827	61,431	66,116
Insurance technical reserves	(NA)	(NA)	(NA)	(NA)	(NA)	(NA)	(NA)	(NA)	(NA)	(NA)
Trade credit and advances	680	1,286	6,043	9,805	-5,824	-1,702	903	5,422	1,179	970
Reserve assets	290	-14,094	1,835	-3,099	-3,583	-6,292	2,090	-1,690	4,989	4,659
Special drawing rights	722	-4,511	31	22	23	9	684	78	156	237
Reserve position in the International Monetary Fund	-2,308	-10,200	1,293	-3,438	-3,849	-6,485	1,348	-1,812	4,824	4,271
Other reserve assets	1,876	617	511	317	243	185	58	44	10	150
Net U.S. incurrence of liabilities [8]	**1,066,074**	**1,277,056**	**1,391,042**	**1,052,068**	**1,109,443**	**503,468**	**706,693**	**1,546,281**	**758,291**	**797,960**
Direct investment liabilities	349,124	142,345	264,039	288,131	251,857	511,434	474,388	366,996	261,480	351,629
Equity	258,438	116,476	207,842	211,769	146,073	426,321	374,243	302,046	344,269	290,311
Debt instruments	90,686	25,869	56,197	76,362	105,784	85,114	100,145	64,950	-82,789	61,318
Portfolio investment liabilities	441,966	832,037	820,434	511,987	697,607	213,910	231,265	790,796	303,075	179,980
Equity and investment fund shares	193,600	89,258	178,952	-62,642	154,311	-187,306	-139,700	149,633	156,916	-244,069
Debt securities [9]	248,366	742,779	641,481	574,629	543,296	401,216	370,965	641,163	146,159	424,049
Other investment liabilities	274,984	302,673	306,569	251,949	159,979	-221,876	1,040	388,489	193,736	266,350
Financial derivatives, net [10]	**(NA)**	**(NA)**	**-14,076**	**2,222**	**-54,335**	**-27,035**	**7,827**	**23,998**	**-20,404**	**-38,340**
Statistical discrepancy [11]	**-72,257**	**34,223**	**-7,481**	**-56,681**	**77,278**	**82,151**	**37,838**	**18,779**	**34,165**	**90,921**
Balance on current account (exports less imports)	**-401,918**	**-749,232**	**-432,009**	**-336,854**	**-367,819**	**-407,355**	**-394,865**	**-365,269**	**-449,693**	**-480,226**
Balance on goods and services	-369,686	-716,542	-503,087	-446,829	-484,144	-491,261	-481,169	-513,791	-579,937	-576,865
Balance on goods	-446,783	-782,804	-648,671	-700,539	-749,917	-761,868	-749,801	-799,343	-880,301	-864,331
Balance on services	77,096	66,262	145,584	253,710	265,773	270,607	268,632	285,552	300,364	287,466
Balance on primary income	14,632	44,186	169,911	195,520	200,303	185,376	197,021	257,793	251,174	236,344
Balance on secondary income	-46,863	-76,876	-98,834	-85,545	-83,978	-101,470	-110,716	-109,272	-120,931	-139,705
Balance on capital account	**-4,217**	**950**	**-6,891**	**-6,559**	**-6,535**	**-7,940**	**-6,606**	**12,394**	**-4,196**	**-6,244**
Net lending/borrowing from current- and capital-account transactions [12]	**-406,135**	**-748,283**	**-438,900**	**-343,412**	**-374,354**	**-415,295**	**-401,471**	**-352,875**	**-453,890**	**-486,470**
Net lending/borrowing from financial-account transactions [12]	**-478,392**	**-714,059**	**-446,381**	**-400,093**	**-297,076**	**-333,144**	**-363,633**	**-334,095**	**-419,724**	**-395,549**

– Represents zero. NA Not available. [1] Includes passenger fares. [2] All travel purposes include 1) business travel, including expenditures by border, seasonal, and other short-term workers and 2) personal travel, including health-related and education-related travel. [3] Includes audiovisual services, artistic-related services, educational services delivered online, remotely provided telemedicine services, and services associated with museums and other cultural, sporting gambling, and recreational activities, except those acquired from the host economy by diplomatic and military personnel; and [4] Includes goods and services supplied by and to embassies, consulates, and military bases; goods and services acquired from the host economy by diplomatic and military personnel; and payments include U.S. government and to governments that are not included in other service categories. [5] Includes transfers under U.S. military sales contracts. [6] Secondary income (current transfer) receipts and transfers, and other current transfers. [7] Includes direct defense expenditures. [8] Excluding financial derivatives. [9] Includes transactions in U.S. Treasury and other U.S. securities. [10] Transactions for U.S. government and private transfers, such as U.S. government grants and pensions, fines and penalties, withholding taxes, personal transfers (remittances), insurance-related financial derivatives are only available as a net value equal to transactions for assets less transactions for liabilities. A positive value represents net U.S. cash payments arising from derivatives contracts, and a negative value represents net U.S. cash receipts. [11] The statistical discrepancy is the difference between total debits and total credits recorded in the current, capital, and financial accounts. In the current and capital accounts, credits and debits are labeled in the table. In the financial account, an acquisition of an asset or a repayment of a liability is a debit, and an incurrence of a liability or a disposal of an asset is a credit. [12] Net lending means that U.S. residents are net suppliers of funds to foreign residents, and net borrowing means the opposite. Net lending or net borrowing can be computed from current- and capital-account transactions or from financial-account transactions. The two amounts differ by the statistical discrepancy.

Source: U.S. Bureau of Economic Analysis, International Economic Accounts, "Table 1.2. U.S. International Transactions, Expanded Detail," <bea.gov/international/index.htm>, accessed July 2020.

Table 1304. U.S. Government Reserve Assets: 1990 to 2018

[In billions of dollars (83.3 represents $83,300,000,000). As of end of year]

Type	1990	2000	2010	2011	2012	2013	2014	2015	2016	2017	2018
Total	**83.3**	**67.6**	**132.4**	**148.0**	**150.2**	**144.6**	**130.1**	**117.6**	**117.3**	**123.3**	**125.8**
Gold stock	11.1	11.0	11.0	11.0	11.0	11.0	11.0	11.0	11.0	11.0	11.0
Special drawing rights	11.0	10.5	56.8	55.0	55.1	55.2	51.9	49.7	48.9	51.9	50.8
Reserve position in IMF [1]	52.2	14.8	12.5	30.1	34.2	30.8	25.2	17.6	18.4	17.6	22.0
Foreign currencies	9.1	31.2	52.1	51.9	49.9	47.6	41.9	39.2	39.0	42.8	41.9

[1] International Monetary Fund.

Source: Data prior to 2005, U.S. Department of the Treasury, *Treasury Bulletin*. Beginning in 2005, Board of Governors of the Federal Reserve System, "International Summary Statistics," January 2020 and earlier releases, <https://www.federalreserve.gov/data.htm>.

Table 1305. U.S. International Investment Position by Type of Investment: 2010 to 2019

[In billions of dollars (-2,511 represents -$2,511,000,000,000). Estimates as of end of 4th quarter. Minus sign (-) indicates loss or deficit]

Type of investment	2010	2014	2015	2016	2017	2018	2019
U.S. net international investment position	**-2,511**	**-6,944**	**-7,460**	**-8,129**	**-7,622**	**-9,674**	**-11,051**
Net international investment position excluding financial derivatives	-2,621	-7,030	-7,515	-8,187	-7,660	-9,716	-11,071
Financial derivatives other than reserves, net	110	86	54	58	38	42	20
U.S. assets	**21,769**	**24,884**	**23,432**	**24,031**	**27,772**	**25,234**	**29,153**
Assets excluding financial derivatives	18,116	21,632	20,989	21,811	26,212	23,784	27,362
Financial derivatives other than reserves, gross positive fair value	3,652	3,252	2,443	2,220	1,561	1,450	1,790
By functional category:							
Direct investment at market value	5,486	7,242	7,057	7,403	8,923	7,444	8,799
Equity	4,621	6,060	5,812	6,186	7,684	6,149	7,485
Debt instruments	866	1,183	1,245	1,217	1,239	1,295	1,314
Portfolio investment	7,160	9,704	9,570	10,011	12,571	11,434	13,376
Equity and investment fund shares	4,900	6,771	6,756	7,146	9,118	7,900	9,459
Debt securities	2,260	2,934	2,814	2,865	3,453	3,534	3,917
Financial derivatives other than reserves, gross positive fair value	3,652	3,252	2,443	2,220	1,561	1,450	1,790
Over-the-counter contracts	3,622	3,182	2,400	2,184	1,497	1,409	1,755
Exchange-traded contracts	31	70	44	37	64	41	35
Other investment [1]	4,981	4,251	3,978	3,991	4,267	4,458	4,673
Currency and deposits	2,767	1,807	1,633	1,572	1,774	1,854	2,011
Loans	2,110	2,337	2,238	2,309	2,377	2,484	2,541
Trade credit and advances	51	47	45	45	51	52	53
Reserve assets	489	434	384	406	450	449	514
Monetary gold	368	315	277	300	338	334	396
Special drawing rights	57	52	50	49	52	51	51
Reserve position in the International Monetary Fund	12	25	18	18	18	22	26
Other reserve assets	52	42	39	39	43	42	41
U.S. liabilities	**24,280**	**31,828**	**30,892**	**32,161**	**35,395**	**34,908**	**40,203**
Liabilities excluding financial derivatives	20,738	28,662	28,503	29,998	33,871	33,501	38,433
Financial derivatives other than reserves, gross negative fair value	3,542	3,167	2,389	2,162	1,523	1,408	1,770
By functional category:							
Direct investment at market value	4,099	6,379	6,729	7,511	8,815	8,402	10,547
Equity	2,928	4,896	5,110	5,823	7,076	6,725	8,764
Debt instruments	1,171	1,483	1,619	1,687	1,739	1,676	1,783
Portfolio investment	11,869	16,922	16,646	17,360	19,398	18,844	21,390
Equity and investment fund shares	3,546	6,643	6,209	6,570	7,942	7,539	9,220
Debt securities	8,323	10,279	10,437	10,790	11,457	11,305	12,170
Financial derivatives other than reserves, gross negative fair value	3,542	3,167	2,389	2,162	1,523	1,408	1,770
Over-the-counter contracts	3,512	3,101	2,346	2,122	1,461	1,366	1,738
Exchange-traded contracts	30	66	43	40	62	41	32
Other investment	4,769	5,361	5,128	5,128	5,658	6,255	6,496
Currency and deposits	2,365	2,891	2,947	2,967	3,228	3,257	3,459
Loans	2,238	2,264	1,970	1,945	2,197	2,750	2,782
Trade credit and advances	112	155	162	168	183	199	206
Special drawing rights allocations	54	51	49	47	50	49	49

[1] Includes value of other equity, not shown separately.

Source: U.S. Bureau of Economic Analysis, International Economic Accounts, International Investment Position, "Table 1.2 U.S. Net International Investment Position at the End of the Period, Expanded Detail," <http://www.bea.gov/iTable/index_ita.cfm>, accessed September 2020. See also <http://www.bea.gov/international/index.htm>.

Table 1306. International Service Transactions by Selected Type of Service and Selected Country: 2000 to 2019

[In millions of dollars (298,023 represents $298,023,000,000). Country data are based on information available from U.S. reporting sources. In some instances, the statistics may not necessarily reflect the ultimate foreign transactor. For the June 2020 data release, the Bureau of Economic Analysis has revised all International Transactions data to incorporate a number of changes including new services categories, new classifications, and improved methodologies. For details, see <https://apps.bea.gov/scb/2020/04-april/0420-international-annual-revision-preview.htm>. N.i.e. is not included elsewhere]

Type of service and country	Exports				Imports			
	2000	2010	2018	2019	2000	2010	2018	2019
Services, total	**298,023**	**582,041**	**862,433**	**875,825**	**220,927**	**436,456**	**562,069**	**588,359**
TYPE OF SERVICE								
Maintenance and repair services n.i.e. [1]	4,423	13,111	27,948	27,868	2,316	5,857	7,133	7,823
Transport [2]	49,462	76,357	93,251	91,092	58,526	88,394	106,303	107,458
Sea transport	11,554	16,308	19,019	18,222	21,787	28,022	33,292	32,670
Air transport [2]	34,971	55,877	69,086	68,047	33,598	56,617	69,158	70,995
Passenger	21,445	31,506	41,261	40,143	21,316	38,667	46,540	47,771
Travel [2]	96,872	130,315	196,465	193,315	64,174	85,166	126,008	134,594
Business	38,023	38,171	38,250	37,192	18,940	19,115	19,129	18,865
Personal	58,849	92,145	158,215	156,124	45,235	66,051	106,879	115,729
Health related	1,033	879	1,132	1,180	240	366	677	717
Education related	9,695	18,365	42,603	44,046	2,117	5,957	11,419	11,654
Construction	1,993	2,951	2,948	3,189	1,447	2,578	3,151	1,327
Insurance services	3,631	14,854	17,904	16,238	11,284	63,452	43,735	51,547
Direct insurance	628	4,348	1,920	1,479	1,683	4,470	3,653	3,573
Reinsurance	3,002	9,046	14,371	13,145	9,601	57,511	38,248	44,597
Financial services [2]	29,192	86,512	132,420	135,698	16,445	27,215	39,249	40,350
Explicitly charged and other financial services [2]	23,385	79,295	113,679	116,305	11,326	17,067	32,022	33,212
Credit card and credit-related services	(NA)	10,569	25,704	28,462	(NA)	3,862	9,387	10,567
Financial management services	(NA)	23,889	46,231	45,879	(NA)	3,112	9,600	9,221
Charges for the use of intellectual property n.i.e. [2]	43,476	94,968	118,875	117,401	16,139	31,116	43,933	42,733
Franchises and trademarks licensing fees	(NA)	19,349	25,192	26,988	(NA)	4,757	4,594	4,601
License to use outcomes of research & development [3]	(NA)	37,561	49,268	47,811	(NA)	19,422	25,043	24,021
License to reproduce/distribute computer software	(NA)	35,906	39,796	37,954	(NA)	5,192	11,256	11,981
License to reproduce/distribute audiovisual products	(NA)	2,152	4,619	4,649	(NA)	1,745	3,040	2,130
Telecommunications, computer, and information services	12,250	26,556	49,653	55,657	14,128	29,421	42,558	43,720
Telecommunications services	5,266	10,921	9,045	7,825	6,167	8,077	5,897	5,105
Computer services	4,393	10,124	30,905	36,828	7,666	19,665	34,075	34,519
Information services	2,591	5,510	9,703	11,005	295	1,680	2,585	4,095
Other business services	38,217	99,595	177,261	189,441	20,306	65,903	107,834	113,584
Research and development services	7,123	22,165	46,977	49,614	3,370	22,593	34,828	33,772
Professional and management consulting services	17,640	48,657	93,339	105,070	10,763	29,380	52,471	55,695
Technical, trade-related, and other business services [4]	13,455	28,774	36,945	34,756	6,173	13,930	20,535	24,116
Personal, cultural, and recreational services [5]	9,351	17,612	23,759	23,372	1,645	5,393	19,190	21,140
Government goods and services n.i.e. [6]	9,156	19,210	21,949	22,555	14,516	31,960	22,975	24,083
AREA AND COUNTRY								
Canada	25,184	57,288	68,937	67,748	19,802	28,518	38,033	38,550
Europe [7]	109,786	221,283	333,835	345,229	97,268	178,884	232,643	245,414
European Union [7]	94,671	184,990	271,487	279,002	84,323	150,251	196,016	208,326
Euro Area [7, 8]	57,578	114,783	170,734	178,704	52,102	95,907	118,748	130,753
France	10,413	17,926	21,936	22,406	11,357	17,746	19,497	20,440
Germany	15,974	26,541	35,953	36,637	16,676	31,356	33,065	34,918
Italy	5,611	8,394	9,651	9,618	6,529	8,982	11,253	12,116
Netherlands	6,963	13,569	20,203	20,492	5,884	8,846	13,570	15,116
United Kingdom	32,562	55,811	80,418	78,329	26,801	44,481	62,185	62,345
Latin America, other Western Hemisphere [7]	57,711	113,715	160,493	158,226	44,959	102,534	114,444	123,245
Brazil	6,748	18,418	26,802	24,562	1,486	5,895	6,699	6,795
Mexico	16,285	23,730	33,056	32,928	11,435	15,891	27,927	29,813
Africa	6,209	11,875	15,221	14,742	3,395	7,745	9,673	9,546
Middle East	9,476	21,531	34,061	34,178	5,438	18,011	17,154	17,235
Asia and Pacific [7]	85,649	153,674	247,373	253,170	48,811	99,659	148,588	154,289
Australia	6,396	16,096	23,071	22,030	2,731	6,073	8,323	8,641
China	5,497	20,518	57,060	56,537	3,109	11,493	19,112	20,140
Hong Kong	3,977	5,836	13,757	14,234	3,878	7,381	11,172	11,568
India	3,047	9,898	23,210	24,333	1,777	15,257	28,874	29,738
Japan	37,169	43,519	46,656	50,052	17,085	25,064	35,350	35,825
Korea, South	7,023	16,618	23,199	23,973	5,222	9,530	10,046	10,611
Singapore	6,515	10,664	22,720	23,690	2,472	5,214	9,904	10,247
Taiwan	5,581	9,921	10,741	11,037	3,181	5,724	7,494	7,359
International organizations and unallocated	4,008	2,674	2,512	2,531	1,254	1,105	1,534	80

NA Not available. [1] Covers maintenance and repair services by residents of country on goods owned by residents of another country. Excludes transportation equipment, construction, and computer maintenance and repair. [2] Includes other types not shown separately. [3] Includes patents, industrial processes, and trade secrets. [4] Includes construction, architectural and engineering services, waste treatment, operational leasing, trade-related, and other business services. [5] Includes audiovisual services, artistic-related services, educational services delivered online, remotely provided telemedicine services, and services associated with museums and other cultural, sporting gambling, and recreational activities, except those acquired by customers traveling outside their country of residence. [6] See footnote 4, Table 1303. Exports include transfers under U.S. military sales contracts; imports include direct defense expenditures. [7] Includes countries not shown separately. [8] Euro area refers to European Union member countries that have adopted the Euro as the common currency. Data for each year cover only member countries in that year.

Source: U.S. Bureau of Economic Analysis, International Economic Accounts, International Transactions, "Table 3.1. U.S. International Trade in Services," and "Table 3.3. U.S. International Trade in Services by Area and Country, Not Seasonally Adjusted Detail," <http://www.bea.gov/international/index.htm>, accessed September 2020.

Table 1307. U.S. Balances on International Transactions by Area and Selected Country: 2018 and 2019

[In millions of dollars (-449,693 represents -$449,693,000,000). Country data are based on information available from U.S. reporting sources. In some instances, the statistics may not necessarily reflect the ultimate foreign transactor. For the June 2020 data release, the Bureau of Economic Analysis has revised all International Transactions data to incorporate a number of changes including new services categories, new classification of certain services and transactions, and improved methodologies. For more information and details, see <https://apps.bea.gov/scb/2020/04-april/0420-international-annual-revision-preview.htm>. Minus sign (-) indicates debits]

Area or country	2018, balance on—				2019, balance on—			
	Current account	Goods	Services	Primary income [1]	Current account	Goods	Services	Primary income [1]
All areas	**-449,693**	**-880,301**	**300,364**	**251,174**	**-480,226**	**-864,331**	**287,466**	**236,344**
Canada	18,270	-23,893	30,904	12,402	4,408	-31,866	29,199	7,976
Europe	22,427	-201,300	101,192	126,521	17,763	-222,654	99,815	150,771
European Union	25,960	-169,466	75,471	115,179	39,323	-179,480	70,676	148,499
Euro Area [2]	-35,608	-152,919	51,986	63,897	-13,942	-159,872	47,951	97,606
Germany	-79,692	-68,495	2,888	-14,191	-79,588	-67,921	1,719	-13,882
Italy	-31,814	-32,026	-1,602	2,468	-34,043	-33,613	-2,499	2,840
Netherlands	92,142	23,690	6,633	61,597	103,679	21,033	5,376	76,396
United Kingdom	79,244	5,432	18,233	50,725	75,942	5,653	15,984	53,265
Latin America, other Western Hemisphere	56,350	-42,540	46,049	96,327	10,781	-55,417	34,982	84,316
Brazil	31,931	9,280	20,104	2,203	32,411	11,910	17,768	2,951
Mexico	-96,033	-84,346	5,129	-1,015	-123,646	-107,267	3,115	-2,716
Africa	-19,663	-9,887	5,548	5,076	-14,907	-3,545	5,196	4,796
Middle East	-4,299	-7,160	16,907	-5,364	12,748	13,556	16,943	-9,099
Asia and Pacific	-521,259	-595,790	98,785	7,039	-509,389	-564,841	98,881	-10,896
Australia	40,752	15,369	14,748	11,356	39,390	15,296	13,389	11,040
China	-408,943	-417,988	37,948	-24,476	-338,020	-344,239	36,398	-24,453
Hong Kong	41,027	31,395	2,585	6,604	35,672	26,298	2,665	6,303
India	-29,233	-21,035	-5,664	4,566	-31,108	-23,344	-5,405	4,964
Japan	-78,681	-67,520	11,307	-24,479	-85,494	-69,735	14,227	-31,582
Singapore	58,037	6,368	12,816	38,743	52,058	4,948	13,443	33,466
Korea, South	-6,931	-17,693	13,153	-759	-11,168	-20,773	13,362	-2,792
Taiwan	-25,449	-14,583	3,247	-12,549	-33,987	-22,463	3,678	-13,698
International organizations and unallocated	-1,520	270	978	9,174	-1,630	435	2,450	8,480

[1] Primary income consists of investment income and compensation of employees. [2] Euro area refers to European Union member countries that have adopted the Euro as the common currency. For the 2018 and 2019 data, this includes the countries that had adopted the Euro as of January 1, 2018: Austria, Belgium, Cyprus, Estonia, Finland, France, Germany, Greece, Ireland, Italy, Latvia, Luxembourg, Malta, Netherlands, Portugal, Slovakia, Slovenia, and Spain.

Source: U.S. Bureau of Economic Analysis, International Transactions, "Table 1.3. U.S. International Transactions, Expanded Detail by Area and Country," <bea.gov/iTable/>, accessed September 2020.

Table 1308. Employment of Majority-Owned U.S. Affiliates of Foreign Companies by State: 2010 to 2017

[In thousands (5,435.4 represents 5,435,400). Covers full-time and part-time employees on the payroll, generally at the end of the fiscal year. A U.S. majority-owned affiliate is a U.S. business enterprise in which a foreign entity has a direct or indirect voting interest greater than 50 percent]

State and other area	2010	2015	2016	2017	State and other area	2010	2015	2016	2017
Total	**5,435.4**	**6,822.8**	**7,155.5**	**7,357.7**	Montana	6.3	6.8	7.5	7.8
					Nebraska	23.9	31.4	30.7	31.4
Alabama	81.9	104.6	111.1	113.9	Nevada	39.0	47.8	48.7	49.8
Alaska	14.1	16.3	18.6	18.1	New Hampshire	39.3	41.2	44.7	44.9
Arizona	77.0	104.4	108.4	113.6	New Jersey	222.9	270.7	281.4	284.7
Arkansas	35.9	46.1	45.6	46.4	New Mexico	15.3	16.9	17.8	18.1
California	584.0	734.2	772.1	802.8	New York	398.9	477.9	495.2	493.9
Colorado	80.9	105.0	111.9	113.1	North Carolina	194.7	252.6	264.6	279.2
Connecticut	100.9	102.6	104.4	108.6	North Dakota	11.5	13.0	12.5	12.8
Delaware	26.7	25.2	27.1	25.5	Ohio	210.2	257.7	266.5	272.8
District of Columbia	22.4	23.5	22.8	23.1	Oklahoma	38.6	49.6	51.9	50.7
Florida	232.9	331.2	366.4	368.1	Oregon	43.0	60.6	58.9	60.6
Georgia	189.5	228.9	246.3	259.3	Pennsylvania	261.3	291.4	303.5	309.2
Hawaii	26.8	36.7	37.7	37.3	Rhode Island	26.1	25.5	25.9	26.4
Idaho	13.4	15.6	15.2	16.8	South Carolina	108.4	134.6	139.6	145.5
Illinois	252.7	321.7	348.6	353.0	South Dakota	7.2	11.9	12.5	12.6
Indiana	136.0	189.7	196.0	203.0	Tennessee	117.2	164.2	178.0	182.2
Iowa	44.9	59.9	59.3	58.2	Texas	451.4	588.5	607.2	622.7
Kansas	54.5	56.1	58.2	60.8	Utah	31.4	42.6	47.0	48.2
Kentucky	89.2	120.2	133.5	138.8	Vermont	11.1	11.0	10.5	10.1
Louisiana	56.1	67.5	69.1	70.0	Virginia	147.8	180.6	186.9	194.9
Maine	30.3	34.3	34.3	34.8	Washington	94.4	113.3	120.0	127.7
Maryland	101.6	116.9	120.0	120.1	West Virginia	28.7	29.4	28.4	28.1
Massachusetts	187.3	203.0	215.5	216.6	Wisconsin	77.5	97.3	104.6	107.6
Michigan	145.4	243.3	251.5	270.3	Wyoming	7.8	7.2	8.0	7.7
Minnesota	90.7	113.9	123.7	133.9	Puerto Rico	21.9	24.0	25.0	24.0
Mississippi	26.8	37.4	37.3	39.9	Other U.S. areas	13.9	24.2	([2])	25.1
Missouri	81.7	109.8	116.7	128.6	Foreign	2.3	([1])	([1])	5.1

[1] 2,500 to 4,999 employees. [2] 10,000 to 24,999 employees.

Source: U.S. Bureau of Economic Analysis, International Economic Accounts, "Direct Investment and Multinational Enterprises (MNEs)," <http://www.bea.gov/iTable/index_MNC.cfm>, accessed December 2019.

Table 1309. New Foreign Direct Investment in the U.S. by Industry of U.S. Business Enterprise and Country of Ultimate Beneficial Owner: 2018 and 2019

[In millions of dollars (312,455 represents $312,455,000,000). Data shown are first year expenditures by foreign direct investors to acquire, establish, or expand U.S. businesses. First year expenditures include those expenditures in the calendar year in which the transaction occurred. A U.S. business enterprise is categorized as "acquired" if a foreign entity acquired a 10 percent or more voting interest in an incorporated U.S. business, or an equivalent interest of an unincorporated U.S. affiliate. A U.S. business enterprise is categorized as "established" if a foreign entity or existing U.S. affiliate of a foreign entity establishes a new legal entity in the U.S. in which the foreign entity owns 10 percent or more of the new business enterprise's voting interest, or an equivalent interest if unincorporated. An existing U.S. affiliate is categorized as "expanded" if it expands its operations to include a new facility where business is conducted and the expansion has a projected total cost of more than $3 million]

Industry and country	2018 Total	2018 U.S. businesses acquired	2018 U.S. businesses established	2018 U.S. businesses expanded	2019 Total	2019 U.S. businesses acquired	2019 U.S. businesses established	2019 U.S. businesses expanded
Total¹	**312,455**	**303,334**	**4,880**	**4,241**	**194,662**	**190,651**	**2,503**	**1,507**
INDUSTRY²								
Manufacturing	202,476	199,883	1,056	1,537	78,180	76,477	701	1,001
Wholesale trade	5,466	5,326	134	6	4,568	4,485	80	3
Retail trade	14,195	14,157	37	2	3,367	3,346	20	2
Information	18,837	18,503	328	6	18,965	18,862	95	9
Finance and insurance	7,409	7,012	352	44	13,088	12,585	(D)	(D)
Real estate and rental and leasing	22,828	20,030	1,285	1,513	6,246	5,892	332	22
Professional, scientific, and technical services	10,045	9,226	778	41	23,574	23,377	172	26
Other industries	31,198	29,196	910	1,092	46,673	45,627	(D)	(D)
COUNTRY³								
Canada	36,610	34,452	543	1,615	35,717	34,755	446	516
Europe¹	228,294	224,612	1,667	2,015	103,776	102,674	455	647
France	20,324	19,300	18	1,006	15,653	15,288	4	361
Germany	(D)	(D)	152	254	21,613	21,483	97	33
Ireland	(D)	(D)	3	2	3,327	(D)	4	(D)
Netherlands	3,146	3,118	28	–	861	835	(D)	(D)
Switzerland	24,725	24,116	(D)	(D)	7,435	7,408	(D)	(D)
United Kingdom	20,217	19,950	191	76	40,359	40,151	115	93
Latin America/other Western Hemisphere	13,813	13,483	(D)	(D)	22,904	22,816	(D)	(D)
South and Central America	(D)	(D)	(D)	–	1,128	1,081	(D)	(D)
Other Western Hemisphere¹	(D)	(D)	(D)	(D)	21,776	21,734	(D)	(D)
Bermuda	(D)	(D)	3	–	(D)	(D)	(D)	–
Caribbean Islands (British)	7	–	7	(D)	15	(D)	(D)	(D)
Africa	–	–	–	–	(D)	(D)	(D)	–
Middle East	2,038	(D)	100	(D)	1,951	(D)	(D)	(D)
Asia and Pacific¹	31,384	28,582	2,386	416	29,735	28,476	942	316
Australia	2,167	2,144	(D)	(D)	4,192	4,158	32	2
China	2,293	1,634	654	5	585	553	(D)	–
Hong Kong	2,199	2,175	25	–	(D)	30	(D)	–
Japan	16,361	14,994	1,023	344	17,828	16,714	813	301
Singapore	3,851	(D)	(D)	–	856	852	4	–
South Korea	1,189	1,108	18	63	4,095	4,077	9	9

– Represents zero. D Suppressed to avoid disclosure of data of individual companies. ¹ Includes other countries not shown separately. ² Based on 2012 North American Industry Classification System (NAICS); see text, Section 15. ³ Country of ultimate beneficial owner (UBO). The UBO is the entity proceeding up a U.S. affiliate's ownership chain, beginning with the foreign parents, which is not owned more than 50 percent by another entity.

Source: U.S. Bureau of Economic Analysis, International Economic Accounts, "Direct Investment and Multinational Enterprises," <bea.gov/iTable/index_MNC.cfm>, accessed September 2020.

Table 1310. Foreign Direct Investment Position in the United States on a Historical-Cost Basis: by Selected Country, 2000 to 2019, and by Industry, 2019

[In millions of dollars (1,256,867 represents $1,256,867,000,000). Foreign direct investment is defined as the ownership or control, directly or indirectly, by one foreign entity of 10 percent or more of the voting interest of a U.S. business enterprise. As used here, "entity" is synonymous with "person," used in a broad legal sense that includes any individual, branch, partnership, association, trust, corporation, or government. Data are based on surveys of U.S. affiliates of foreign companies]

Country	All industries total				2019			
	2000	2010	2015	2018	Total [1]	Manufacturing	Wholesale trade	Finance and insurance [2]
All countries	1,256,867	2,280,044	3,354,907	4,127,175	4,458,362	1,785,688	467,238	549,691
Canada	114,309	192,463	323,207	442,802	495,720	71,733	19,273	76,436
Europe [3]	887,014	1,659,774	2,306,254	2,794,561	2,871,431	1,318,188	254,549	339,391
Austria	3,007	4,532	7,159	12,392	13,964	6,091	(D)	(D)
Belgium	14,787	69,565	88,121	64,661	65,918	52,979	2,743	(D)
Denmark	4,025	7,772	14,509	20,654	23,870	6,717	10,388	(D)
Finland	8,875	4,943	6,471	14,464	14,826	10,659	2,236	(D)
France	125,740	189,763	233,547	268,169	282,226	120,986	25,749	50,812
Germany	122,412	203,077	281,295	328,124	372,879	142,623	50,562	43,343
Ireland	25,523	24,097	55,861	265,004	225,517	89,350	5,599	8,217
Italy	6,576	20,142	27,709	30,749	32,811	11,298	2,151	(D)
Luxembourg	58,930	170,309	350,772	312,976	297,052	209,569	7,226	(D)
Netherlands	138,894	234,408	298,782	462,303	487,079	246,975	50,761	50,806
Norway	2,665	10,478	20,641	26,007	24,221	(D)	20,701	(D)
Spain	5,068	43,095	67,349	83,379	86,796	12,418	265	(D)
Sweden	21,991	38,780	44,961	49,546	52,683	42,413	-325	(D)
Switzerland	64,719	180,642	241,008	295,783	300,393	164,086	2,998	86,683
United Kingdom	277,613	400,435	522,954	496,622	505,088	167,230	71,082	64,346
Latin America and other Western Hemisphere	53,691	62,130	123,846	153,638	193,786	51,145	8,153	25,171
South and Central America [3]	13,384	17,943	25,261	32,025	35,072	9,146	1,770	997
Brazil	882	1,357	142	2,514	4,617	1,142	-146	663
Mexico	7,462	10,970	15,262	21,050	21,526	5,093	1,341	208
Venezuela	792	3,122	4,186	1,673	1,705	(D)	22	-1
Other Western Hemisphere [3]	40,307	44,187	98,585	121,613	158,714	41,999	6,383	24,174
Bermuda	18,336	365	-7,323	28,018	56,279	(D)	-19	195
Netherlands Antilles	3,807	2,819	(X)	(X)	(X)	(X)	(X)	(X)
U.K. Islands, Caribbean	15,191	38,477	101,725	83,555	90,554	26,262	5,883	24,416
Africa	2,700	2,265	4,310	5,652	9,823	(D)	(D)	5
Middle East [3]	6,506	16,808	17,582	29,329	29,076	(D)	(D)	842
Israel	3,012	8,714	6,865	13,982	14,566	9,519	455	(D)
Asia and Pacific [3]	192,647	346,605	579,708	701,193	858,527	328,760	176,670	107,846
Australia	18,775	35,632	65,259	63,070	80,974	19,759	(D)	4,916
China	(NA)	3,300	14,714	33,543	37,685	6,221	6,357	469
Hong Kong	1,493	4,440	10,981	13,159	14,110	2,812	2,909	-54
India	(NA)	4,102	9,639	5,127	5,009	2,301	10	(D)
Japan	159,690	255,012	401,835	493,763	619,259	276,449	112,474	92,630
Singapore	5,087	21,517	21,585	18,267	21,060	7,110	1,675	(D)
South Korea	3,110	15,746	39,784	56,612	61,822	7,863	47,009	589
Taiwan	3,174	4,642	6,889	10,512	11,099	4,133	2,651	-46

D Suppressed to avoid disclosure of data of individual companies. NA Not available. X Not applicable. [1] Includes other industries, not shown separately. [2] Excludes depository institutions. [3] Includes other countries, not shown separately.

Source: U.S. Bureau of Economic Analysis, International Economic Accounts, "Direct Investment and Multinational Enterprises," <bea.gov/iTable/index_MNC.cfm>, accessed September 2020.

Table 1311. U.S. Majority-Owned Affiliates of Foreign Companies—Assets, Sales, Employment, Value, Exports, and Imports by Industry of Affiliate: 2016

[In billions of dollars (13,627 represents $13,627,000,000,000), except as indicated. A majority-owned U.S. affiliate is a U.S. business enterprise in which a foreign entity ("entity" is used here in a broad legal sense including any individual, branch, partnership, association, trust, corporation, or government) has a direct or indirect voting interest greater than 50 percent]

Industry	NAICS code [2]	Total assets	Sales	Employment (1,000)	Employee compensation	Gross property, plant, and equipment	Merchandise exports	Merchandise imports
All industries	(X)	13,627	4,029	7,156	581	2,393	353	630
Manufacturing [1]	31-33	2,754	1,669	2,558	234	1,025	208	245
Petroleum and coal products	324	287	185	44	11	263	18	26
Chemicals	325	949	359	374	50	221	44	52
Machinery	333	165	104	230	22	28	21	13
Transportation equipment	336	387	429	575	46	196	57	90
Wholesale trade	42	903	1,083	683	64	365	132	361
Retail trade	44-45	132	200	705	28	75	2	19
Information	51	425	162	306	28	127	1	0
Finance and insurance	52	7,862	388	413	74	116	(D)	(Z)
Real estate and rental and leasing	53	233	34	66	5	142	(D)	(D)
Professional, scientific, and technical services	54	250	137	393	45	27	1	0
Other industries	(X)	1,070	355	2,031	104	514	8	(D)

X Not applicable. D Suppressed to avoid disclosure of data of individual companies. Z Less than $500,000,000. [1] Includes other industries not shown separately. [2] Based on the North American Industry Classification System (NAICS); see text, Section 15.

Source: U.S. Bureau of Economic Analysis, International Economic Accounts, "Foreign Direct Investment in the United States," <http://www.bea.gov/international/di1fdiop.htm>, accessed January 2020.

Table 1312. U.S. Direct Investment Position Abroad, Capital Outflows, and Income by Industry of Foreign Affiliates: 2000 to 2019

[In millions of dollars (1,316,247 represents $1,316,247,000,000). U.S. investment abroad is the ownership or control by one U.S. person (in the broad legal sense to include any individual, partnership, corporation, or other form of organization) of 10 percent or more of the voting securities of an incorporated foreign business enterprise or an equivalent interest in an unincorporated foreign business enterprise]

Industry	2000	2005	2010	2015	2017	2018	2019
DIRECT INVESTMENT POSITION ON A HISTORICAL-COST BASIS							
All industries, total [1]	1,316,247	2,241,656	3,741,910	5,289,071	6,097,690	5,801,025	5,959,592
Mining	72,111	109,280	172,819	180,418	162,908	155,221	154,267
Manufacturing [1]	343,899	430,737	518,321	693,847	806,448	773,622	903,664
Food	23,497	27,638	47,704	81,914	93,903	85,335	87,576
Chemicals	75,807	106,975	111,327	151,369	139,746	143,276	214,170
Primary and fabricated metals	21,644	23,013	18,674	34,506	44,856	47,273	48,886
Machinery	22,229	26,433	41,285	45,932	55,776	50,598	75,629
Computer and electronic products	59,909	50,773	72,935	97,641	144,946	128,682	143,167
Electrical equipment, appliances, and components	10,005	15,449	19,941	17,591	18,033	17,057	18,094
Transportation equipment	49,887	50,739	49,636	62,087	87,292	83,105	87,453
Wholesale trade	93,936	132,915	168,722	225,217	255,235	229,232	238,632
Information	52,345	102,848	126,063	198,689	240,143	292,184	284,224
Depository institutions (banking)	40,152	66,707	118,585	118,271	124,044	124,671	135,374
Finance and insurance	217,086	463,981	734,859	719,608	781,180	835,500	847,075
Professional, scientific, and technical services	32,868	57,164	81,874	117,646	140,179	150,492	154,099
Holding companies (nonbank)	(NA)	710,386	1,584,903	2,686,477	3,176,645	2,843,122	2,804,997
FINANCIAL OUTFLOWS [INFLOWS(-)] WITHOUT CURRENT-COST ADJUSTMENT							
All industries, total [1]	142,627	15,369	277,779	264,359	327,781	-194,412	93,552
Mining	2,174	12,015	11,884	416	-11,233	-3,756	-2,807
Manufacturing [1]	43,002	28,121	33,320	43,502	82,886	46,199	63,370
Food	2,014	1,171	5,341	4,449	6,725	2,985	1,865
Chemicals	3,812	3,911	7,614	6,470	13,846	10,462	31,804
Primary and fabricated metals	1,233	-703	546	503	3,466	1,891	1,533
Machinery	2,659	2,077	4,229	3,110	5,202	1,632	3,392
Computer and electronic products	17,303	3,607	6,772	6,440	27,956	13,979	6,098
Electrical equipment, appliances, and components	2,100	1,662	1,743	1,545	1,748	838	988
Transportation equipment	7,814	-250	-380	11,282	7,995	5,700	4,777
Wholesale trade	11,938	12,517	15,487	9,495	12,624	-19,350	18,339
Information	16,531	2,831	8,777	13,488	16,316	52,178	2,716
Depository institutions	-1,274	-4,751	-4,811	-6,448	-4,600	-2,840	7,233
Finance and insurance	21,659	13,079	21,887	15,632	37,081	76,342	-1,114
Professional, scientific, and technical services	5,441	-2,055	2,774	5,121	-3,013	12,136	2,306
Holding companies (nonbank)	(NA)	-66,351	169,743	161,310	169,924	-368,620	-26,838
INCOME WITHOUT CURRENT-COST ADJUSTMENT [2]							
All industries, total [1]	133,692	271,877	417,605	433,333	518,653	543,960	532,724
Mining	13,164	24,559	29,138	3,541	11,495	16,815	12,934
Manufacturing [1]	42,230	46,896	61,240	67,102	89,883	85,780	80,986
Food	2,681	3,558	4,322	4,149	4,732	4,361	4,240
Chemicals	11,552	13,056	14,088	18,114	24,831	24,356	25,659
Primary and fabricated metals	1,536	1,815	1,349	1,721	2,642	3,042	2,916
Machinery	2,257	2,253	4,465	3,495	5,691	5,882	4,361
Computer and electronic products	8,860	7,714	11,440	10,868	20,041	17,380	16,807
Electrical equipment, appliances, and components	1,079	1,703	1,653	1,461	1,785	1,749	1,489
Transportation equipment	4,107	1,936	6,471	10,632	9,699	10,672	8,105
Wholesale trade	14,198	24,494	24,538	19,129	23,036	25,186	25,164
Information	-964	10,832	12,229	14,756	15,043	20,330	17,493
Depository institutions	2,191	164	1,328	3,521	7,467	7,970	8,965
Finance and insurance	15,210	27,911	35,143	45,760	43,766	54,985	51,734
Professional, scientific, and technical services	3,548	9,272	8,856	11,145	12,365	10,531	15,532
Holding companies (nonbank)	(NA)	109,566	220,101	233,272	274,507	284,677	275,289

NA Not available. [1] Includes other industries, not shown separately. [2] Prior to 2006, income is shown net of withholding taxes. Beginning 2006, income is shown gross of withholding taxes.

Source: U.S. Bureau of Economic Analysis, International Economic Accounts, "Direct Investment and Multinational Enterprises," <http://www.bea.gov/iTable/index_MNC.cfm>, accessed September 2020.

Table 1313. U.S. Direct Investment Position Abroad on a Historical-Cost Basis by Selected Country: 2000 to 2019

[In millions of dollars (1,316,247 represents $1,316,247,000,000). U.S. investment abroad is the ownership or control by one U.S. person (in the broad legal sense to include any individual, partnership, corporation, or other form of organization) of 10 percent or more of the voting securities of an incorporated foreign business enterprise or an equivalent interest in an unincorporated foreign business enterprise. Negative position can occur when a U.S. parent company's liabilities to the foreign affiliate are greater than its equity in and loans to the foreign affiliate]

Country	2000	2005	2010	2015	2016	2017	2018	2019
All countries.................	1,316,247	2,241,656	3,741,910	5,289,071	5,518,644	6,097,690	5,801,025	5,959,592
Canada........................	132,472	231,836	295,206	361,954	355,394	371,274	368,498	402,255
Europe [1].....................	687,320	1,210,679	2,034,559	3,075,567	3,302,727	3,654,095	3,475,989	3,571,710
Austria.........................	2,872	11,236	11,485	6,508	7,566	7,987	6,740	7,643
Belgium........................	17,973	49,306	43,975	48,096	49,692	53,645	61,271	63,157
Czechia........................	1,228	2,729	5,268	6,343	4,896	4,844	4,515	4,815
Denmark.......................	5,270	6,914	11,802	15,794	16,909	12,107	9,498	8,992
Finland.........................	1,342	1,950	1,597	1,258	2,538	2,513	3,268	3,745
France..........................	42,628	60,526	78,320	81,274	72,926	78,632	68,035	83,826
Germany.......................	55,508	100,473	103,319	120,519	129,985	132,595	137,148	148,259
Greece..........................	795	1,884	1,775	1,007	1,017	1,198	1,399	938
Hungary........................	1,920	2,795	4,237	7,625	7,392	6,672	6,597	6,114
Ireland..........................	35,903	55,173	158,851	337,831	399,885	457,301	410,636	354,940
Italy.............................	23,484	24,528	27,137	30,869	30,573	27,617	33,080	34,900
Luxembourg...................	27,849	79,937	272,206	599,001	646,508	703,066	726,121	766,099
Netherlands...................	115,429	240,205	514,689	829,693	816,667	929,746	810,238	860,528
Norway.........................	4,379	8,533	28,541	31,697	28,657	26,901	26,145	25,556
Poland..........................	3,884	5,575	13,152	11,872	11,260	12,266	11,744	10,403
Portugal........................	2,664	2,138	2,612	1,971	2,288	2,372	2,513	2,425
Russia..........................	1,147	9,363	10,040	10,259	14,357	13,786	14,071	14,439
Spain...........................	21,236	50,197	52,390	36,075	36,651	35,482	35,425	40,793
Sweden.........................	25,959	30,153	23,275	32,593	34,722	36,896	41,024	38,787
Switzerland....................	55,377	100,692	119,891	171,342	185,329	252,231	253,253	228,968
Turkey..........................	1,826	2,563	4,155	3,798	3,726	4,074	3,903	3,333
United Kingdom..............	230,762	351,513	501,247	632,327	747,425	815,059	796,564	851,414
Latin America and other Western Hemisphere..........	266,576	379,582	752,788	902,642	893,558	1,008,741	948,789	911,869
South America [1]............	84,220	73,311	136,598	129,303	133,272	138,996	137,089	142,823
Argentina....................	17,488	10,103	11,747	14,624	14,273	15,219	9,522	10,698
Brazil.........................	36,717	30,882	66,963	56,847	67,922	77,486	79,032	81,731
Chile..........................	10,052	11,127	30,747	28,134	28,141	25,793	25,986	25,084
Colombia....................	3,693	4,292	6,181	7,750	7,884	7,669	8,055	8,264
Ecuador......................	832	941	1,283	913	981	715	722	619
Peru..........................	3,130	5,542	7,196	7,573	4,541	5,700	5,765	7,470
Venezuela...................	10,531	8,934	10,255	9,825	5,113	3,174	2,185	2,228
Central America [1].........	73,841	82,496	97,752	112,690	109,314	111,631	107,172	113,246
Costa Rica..................	1,716	1,598	1,827	1,642	1,335	1,546	1,597	1,521
Honduras....................	399	821	936	1,274	1,283	1,330	850	1,281
Mexico.......................	39,352	73,687	85,751	101,326	98,421	100,169	95,873	100,888
Panama......................	30,758	4,826	5,156	4,447	4,472	4,821	5,075	5,272
Other Western Hemisphere [1]....	108,515	223,775	518,438	660,650	650,972	758,114	704,527	655,800
Barbados....................	2,141	3,881	7,524	14,084	20,910	21,736	39,802	45,382
Bermuda.....................	60,114	113,222	265,524	303,244	311,363	401,435	333,843	262,418
Dominican Republic.......	1,143	815	1,432	1,079	1,469	2,009	2,162	2,604
U.K. Islands, Caribbean........	33,451	83,164	191,680	303,438	282,111	286,601	282,937	300,505
Africa [1]....................	11,891	22,756	54,816	52,004	49,926	50,403	44,378	43,193
Egypt..........................	1,998	5,475	12,599	14,068	10,545	11,095	10,781	11,000
Nigeria.........................	470	1,105	5,058	5,872	4,252	4,844	4,501	5,469
South Africa..................	3,562	3,969	6,017	6,926	7,398	8,058	7,313	7,812
Middle East [1]............	10,863	21,115	34,431	49,802	49,123	74,509	75,240	75,205
Israel...........................	3,735	7,978	9,464	10,251	11,615	28,160	27,715	28,543
Saudi Arabia.................	3,661	3,830	7,436	10,025	10,164	10,702	10,884	10,826
United Arab Emirates.......	683	2,285	4,935	16,205	13,699	16,881	17,437	17,153
Asia and Pacific [1].......	207,125	375,689	570,111	847,102	867,916	938,668	888,133	955,361
Australia.......................	34,838	75,669	125,421	160,061	167,791	169,749	163,999	162,400
China...........................	11,140	19,016	58,996	92,150	97,458	105,146	109,332	116,203
Hong Kong....................	27,447	36,415	41,264	69,367	69,287	79,048	79,797	81,883
India............................	2,379	7,162	24,666	35,361	40,121	45,160	42,444	45,883
Indonesia......................	8,904	8,603	10,558	15,717	15,049	13,866	10,240	12,151
Japan...........................	57,091	81,175	113,523	106,932	124,039	117,134	113,254	131,793
Malaysia.......................	7,910	11,097	11,791	15,765	10,069	11,767	10,867	10,849
New Zealand..................	4,271	5,191	6,724	11,427	12,042	12,384	11,667	12,018
Philippines....................	3,638	6,522	5,399	5,992	6,412	6,926	6,922	6,940
Singapore.....................	24,133	76,390	102,778	253,277	243,165	293,452	254,670	287,951
South Korea...................	8,968	19,760	26,233	38,608	39,278	40,237	39,021	39,105
Taiwan.........................	7,836	14,356	22,188	15,295	15,510	16,484	16,562	17,353
Thailand.......................	5,824	10,252	12,999	17,942	18,386	15,578	16,952	17,738

[1] Includes other countries, not shown separately.

Source: U.S. Bureau of Economic Analysis, International Economic Accounts, "Direct Investment and Multinational Enterprises," <bea.gov/iTable/index_MNC.cfm>, accessed September 2020.

Table 1314. U.S. Foreign Economic and Military Aid by Major Recipient Country: 2000 to 2018

[In millions of dollars (17,111.9 represents $17,111,900,000). For years ending September 30. Annual figures are for obligations. Total aid may not add due to rounding]

Region/country	2000	2010	2015	2017	2018 Total	2018 Economic aid	2018 Military aid
Total [1]	**17,111.9**	**48,398.0**	**49,362.8**	**47,836.5**	**46,821.2**	**33,103.5**	**13,717.7**
Middle East & North Africa [1]	**6,799.2**	**8,829.2**	**10,679.1**	**11,318.4**	**11,434.7**	**4,971.4**	**6,463.3**
Egypt	2,076.1	1,603.1	1,567.3	370.5	1,247.9	233.7	1,014.2
Iraq	1.2	2,092.4	1,547.6	1,581.9	1,180.7	863.6	317.2
Israel	3,863.4	2,837.6	3,293.3	3,225.2	3,128.4	10.8	3,117.6
Jordan	448.3	765.8	1,512.6	1,502.9	1,652.4	1,161.7	490.7
Lebanon	35.0	158.7	506.9	511.4	725.8	518.6	207.2
Morocco	51.1	56.4	108.6	529.1	156.8	56.2	100.6
Syria	–	22.4	913.6	891.0	835.1	835.1	–
Tunisia	7.1	21.2	123.2	223.7	224.2	147.5	76.7
West Bank/Gaza [2]	122.0	686.9	556.8	399.1	87.1	87.1	–
Yemen	57.2	122.4	176.8	653.0	648.4	643.0	5.4
Sub-Saharan Africa [1]	**2,025.1**	**8,434.7**	**11,456.6**	**12,831.0**	**12,181.7**	**11,451.3**	**730.4**
Angola	105.4	99.9	58.3	75.9	50.7	50.1	0.6
Botswana	0.9	52.0	44.1	42.6	57.7	57.0	0.6
Burkina Faso	18.1	33.3	34.0	81.7	98.2	84.3	13.9
Chad	4.1	184.4	108.7	116.4	128.1	118.9	9.2
Congo, Democratic Republic of	32.6	366.2	469.7	494.3	706.6	703.4	3.3
Ethiopia	277.6	832.1	809.9	1,104.5	875.7	875.2	0.5
Ghana	66.8	110.1	290.2	184.3	151.7	148.1	3.5
Kenya	93.5	573.3	940.0	1,092.6	828.4	767.2	61.2
Lesotho	2.1	33.3	29.2	52.4	79.1	79.1	–
Liberia	22.4	179.8	770.9	212.4	100.1	98.6	1.5
Madagascar	27.4	58.2	155.6	111.9	110.7	110.1	0.6
Malawi	44.4	173.2	244.0	304.5	272.5	271.3	1.1
Mali	43.7	125.6	206.5	230.7	223.2	221.9	1.2
Mozambique	82.1	299.0	338.4	579.1	324.3	323.5	0.8
Namibia	15.5	89.4	43.4	54.7	60.0	60.0	(Z)
Nigeria	112.6	408.5	591.5	851.6	822.1	807.2	14.9
Rwanda	39.0	173.6	246.0	170.5	200.0	199.0	1.0
Senegal	37.4	657.0	118.5	197.2	232.6	228.0	4.6
Somalia	13.9	156.2	252.7	583.8	742.2	506.8	235.4
South Africa	56.8	467.2	354.3	509.7	549.8	549.1	0.7
South Sudan [3]	–	–	848.9	924.2	789.1	761.6	27.5
Sudan	51.0	893.9	233.5	269.2	257.8	257.8	–
Tanzania	44.5	422.6	592.5	624.1	583.8	580.5	3.3
Uganda	76.2	423.8	591.3	742.9	729.4	656.7	72.7
Zambia	35.4	264.5	244.9	418.4	273.4	272.9	0.4
Zimbabwe	20.9	217.4	188.4	195.0	228.8	228.8	–
Latin America & Caribbean [1]	**2,301.2**	**4,347.6**	**3,945.3**	**2,535.1**	**2,518.8**	**2,260.7**	**258.1**
Bolivia	241.1	91.7	56.0	2.3	1.9	1.9	–
Colombia	1,168.6	795.4	839.6	515.7	528.1	430.1	98.0
El Salvador	34.9	62.2	331.9	118.2	95.4	88.6	6.8
Guatemala	71.8	153.5	137.8	257.6	241.6	217.6	23.9
Haiti	84.5	1,366.2	501.6	308.0	252.1	246.9	5.2
Honduras	41.8	39.7	133.5	180.9	122.4	112.3	10.1
Mexico	43.9	718.2	581.5	290.0	236.6	202.3	34.3
Peru	204.2	203.7	301.7	123.1	129.0	119.6	9.4
Asia [1]	**1,163.2**	**15,178.4**	**11,299.6**	**8,751.8**	**8,883.4**	**3,575.8**	**5,307.6**
Afghanistan	54.1	10,873.2	8,130.2	5,731.0	5,958.0	978.8	4,979.2
Bangladesh	78.3	184.6	225.4	261.0	558.9	543.6	15.4
Cambodia	27.5	72.2	84.9	96.1	152.4	152.0	0.4
India	188.0	117.2	113.0	103.0	107.0	105.4	1.6
Indonesia	242.3	309.3	220.4	276.8	91.9	73.0	18.9
Mongolia	25.8	38.1	12.3	23.9	45.5	40.7	4.8
Nepal	22.6	66.8	263.5	192.8	146.2	136.9	9.2
Pakistan	23.8	2,681.7	1,141.1	845.6	437.3	422.1	15.3
Philippines	82.2	200.9	262.4	154.9	341.8	220.4	121.4
Sri Lanka	10.5	81.5	30.6	76.1	56.4	46.5	9.9
Oceania [1]	**164.7**	**209.7**	**229.3**	**229.2**	**292.6**	**291.6**	**1.0**
Micronesia, Federated States of	81.0	90.1	112.8	125.0	119.5	119.4	0.1
Central Asia [1]	**1,461.9**	**2,143.2**	**1,140.6**	**1,076.1**	**1,182.2**	**811.3**	**370.9**
Armenia	104.2	54.6	52.3	31.7	27.8	27.2	0.6
Georgia	112.4	229.4	109.0	96.4	142.2	97.6	44.6
Kazakhstan	53.4	331.4	106.5	30.6	30.2	21.1	9.2
Kyrgyzstan	47.3	128.3	61.4	61.7	62.6	62.1	0.5
Moldova	48.6	294.0	47.7	49.7	39.5	37.7	1.9
Russia	708.6	505.7	314.9	167.8	159.8	159.8	–
Ukraine	199.5	314.7	268.1	510.5	556.1	260.9	295.3
Eastern Europe [1]	**1,045.3**	**707.5**	**316.4**	**426.8**	**473.5**	**313.0**	**160.5**
Kosovo	–	35.0	52.2	101.6	54.6	43.1	11.5
Poland	84.8	221.2	11.1	11.2	4.9	3.2	1.7
Western Europe	**24.0**	**77.7**	**116.0**	**233.9**	**276.0**	**177.9**	**98.1**

– Represents zero. Z Represents less than $500,000. [1] Includes other countries, not shown separately, and aid not assigned to specific countries within their parent regions. [2] See footnote 6, Table 1352. [3] South Sudan seceded from Sudan in July 2011.

Source: U.S. Agency for International Development, *U.S. Overseas Loans and Grants: Obligations and Loan Authorizations, July 1, 1945–September 30, 2018*, and earlier reports. See also <https://explorer.usaid.gov/reports.html>.

Table 1315. U.S. Foreign Economic and Military Aid Programs: 1980 to 2018

[In millions of dollars (9,682 represents $9,682,000,000). For years ending September 30. Total foreign aid programs are the sum of economic and military assistance. Major components in recent years include U.S. Agency for International Development (USAID), U.S. Department of Agriculture (USDA), U.S. Department of State, and U.S. Department of Treasury. Annual figures are in obligations]

Year and world region	Total foreign assistance	Military assistance	Economic assistance, by funding agency					
			Total	USAID	USDA	State Department	Treasury Department	Other U.S. agencies
1980	9,682	2,110	7,572	4,062	1,437	459	1,478	137
1985	18,107	5,780	12,327	8,132	2,052	431	1,548	164
1990	16,003	4,959	11,044	6,964	1,643	590	1,469	377
1995	15,556	4,290	11,266	7,281	1,284	132	1,781	788
2000	17,112	5,149	11,963	5,907	1,936	2,278	1,110	731
2005	35,461	9,071	26,390	14,160	2,208	4,674	1,240	4,108
2007	39,726	13,973	25,754	10,371	1,806	5,594	1,476	6,507
2008	46,747	16,457	30,290	9,800	2,755	8,969	1,217	7,550
2009	46,643	14,801	31,842	11,810	2,614	11,263	1,638	4,518
2010	48,398	14,853	33,546	12,056	2,562	11,558	2,245	5,124
2011	49,133	18,621	30,512	10,552	1,999	10,613	2,034	5,314
2012	50,062	17,861	32,202	11,288	2,028	12,629	2,829	3,429
2013	45,673	13,808	31,865	11,776	1,675	11,190	2,672	4,552
2014	43,108	10,483	32,626	10,853	1,728	13,922	2,735	3,387
2015	49,363	14,993	34,370	13,183	1,679	13,403	2,642	3,462
2016	49,093	14,669	34,425	12,411	1,979	14,024	2,286	3,725
2017	47,837	12,548	35,288	14,436	2,074	13,630	1,846	3,302
2018, total	**46,821**	**13,718**	**33,104**	**13,473**	**2,210**	**13,230**	**1,558**	**2,633**
Asia	8,883	5,308	3,576	2,023	148	1,202	52	151
Eurasia	1,182	371	811	469	41	123	4	175
Eastern Europe	474	161	313	201	–	97	8	8
Latin America and Caribbean	2,519	258	2,261	1,028	120	969	8	135
Middle East and North Africa	11,435	6,463	4,971	3,359	277	1,251	–	84
Oceania	293	1	292	11	(Z)	8	(Z)	273
Sub-Saharan Africa	12,182	730	11,451	3,502	1,554	5,449	211	735
Western Europe	276	98	178	20	(Z)	158	–	(Z)
Canada	24	(Z)	24	–	(Z)	–	–	24
World, not specified [1]	9,555	328	9,227	2,861	71	3,972	1,275	1,048

– Represents zero. Z indicates a value less than $500,000. [1] Includes U.S. Government loan and grant assistance not assigned to a specific country that could not be assigned to a region "not specified," including assistance to international financial institutions, international organizations and global programs.

Source: U.S. Agency for International Development, *U.S. Overseas Loans and Grants: Obligations and Loan Authorizations, July 1, 1945–September 30, 2018*, and earlier reports. See also <https://explorer.usaid.gov/reports.html>.

Table 1316. U.S. International Trade in Goods by Related Parties: 2010 to 2019

[In millions of dollars (1,900,587 represents $1,900,587,000,000). "Related party trade" is trade by U.S. companies with their subsidiaries abroad as well as trade by U.S. subsidiaries of foreign companies with their parent companies]

Country and commodity	NAICS code [2]	2010	2015	2017	2018	2019
IMPORTS FOR CONSUMPTION						
Total imports	(X)	1,900,587	2,227,237	2,327,153	2,549,379	2,501,880
Related party trade, imports, total [1]	**(X)**	**922,340**	**1,113,211**	**1,140,822**	**1,247,479**	**1,230,494**
Mexico	(X)	135,989	207,923	215,030	238,636	246,854
Canada	(X)	138,210	148,471	153,477	163,294	165,066
Japan	(X)	94,001	101,753	107,553	112,353	111,320
Germany	(X)	54,005	83,616	79,405	87,925	88,497
China	(X)	107,007	131,390	123,735	125,531	87,163
Ireland	(X)	27,980	35,350	43,832	49,966	52,290
Transportation equipment	336	179,675	276,328	290,886	299,835	306,659
Chemicals	325	134,018	152,484	155,282	185,089	191,530
Computer & electronic products	334	203,829	221,761	214,678	217,178	188,002
Machinery, except electrical	333	53,722	81,871	86,505	99,234	99,994
Oil & gas	211	80,046	53,351	53,989	69,749	67,627
Electrical equipment, appliances & components	335	33,496	50,007	53,418	57,583	58,320
EXPORTS						
Total exports	(X)	1,122,567	1,286,172	1,308,395	1,413,168	1,392,664
Related party trade, domestic exports, total [1]	**(X)**	**311,693**	**382,910**	**410,613**	**449,513**	**457,827**
Canada	(X)	85,861	91,863	97,367	103,247	97,989
Mexico	(X)	49,612	78,123	75,518	81,597	77,426
China	(X)	13,396	22,196	28,549	27,253	27,732
Netherlands	(X)	15,032	17,309	19,490	23,755	24,836
Japan	(X)	16,690	17,702	19,479	22,410	23,261
United Kingdom	(X)	11,200	13,798	14,953	18,434	19,617
Transportation equipment	336	55,466	86,973	93,529	94,090	101,770
Chemicals	325	64,361	79,695	77,796	83,839	85,592
Oil & gas	211	4,316	5,362	17,708	32,915	45,293
Computer & electronic products	334	42,795	38,524	37,739	39,684	39,758
Machinery, except electrical	333	32,318	34,338	36,709	39,719	39,482
Petroleum & coal products	324	23,367	24,271	29,370	32,885	26,505

X Not applicable. [1] Includes other countries and other commodities, not shown separately. [2] Based on the North American Industry Classification System (NAICS); see text, Section 15.

Source: U.S. Census Bureau, "NAICS Related Party Database," <https://relatedparty.ftd.census.gov/>, accessed June 2020. See also <https://www.census.gov/foreign-trade/index.html>.

Table 1317. U.S. International Trade in Goods and Services: 2000 to 2019

[In millions of dollars (-369,686 represents -$369,686,000,000). Data are presented on a balance of payments basis and will not agree with the following merchandise trade tables in this section. Additionally, all data were revised due to updates to classifications and change in methodology and will not necessarily be comparable with data previously presented. See source for more information. Minus sign (-) indicates deficit]

Category	2000	2010	2015	2016	2017	2018	2019
TRADE BALANCE							
Total	**-369,686**	**-503,087**	**-491,261**	**-481,169**	**-513,791**	**-579,937**	**-576,865**
Goods	-446,783	-648,671	-761,868	-749,801	-799,343	-880,301	-864,331
Services	77,096	145,584	270,607	268,632	285,552	300,364	287,466
Maintenance and repair services, n.i.e. [1]	2,107	7,254	11,763	13,992	16,443	20,815	20,045
Transport [2]	-9,064	-12,037	-15,123	-10,612	-10,173	-13,052	-16,366
Travel for all purposes [3]	32,698	45,149	89,938	83,713	75,862	70,457	58,721
Construction [4]	546	373	-253	-78	103	-203	1,862
Insurance services	-7,653	-48,598	-34,378	-35,821	-32,666	-25,831	-35,309
Financial services	12,747	59,297	82,357	82,090	91,386	93,171	95,348
Charges for the use of intellectual property, n.i.e. [1,5]	27,337	63,852	75,973	71,007	73,742	74,942	74,668
Telecommunications, computer, and information services	-1,878	-2,865	2,612	3,402	4,566	7,095	11,937
Other business services [6]	17,911	33,692	46,302	52,584	60,279	69,427	75,857
Personal, cultural, recreational services [7]	7,706	12,219	12,862	11,082	8,134	4,569	2,232
Government goods and services, n.i.e. [1,8]	-5,360	-12,750	-1,444	-2,726	-2,123	-1,026	-1,528
EXPORTS							
Total	**1,082,963**	**1,872,320**	**2,279,743**	**2,237,923**	**2,387,391**	**2,539,383**	**2,528,262**
Goods	784,940	1,290,279	1,511,381	1,457,393	1,557,003	1,676,950	1,652,437
Services	298,023	582,041	768,362	780,530	830,388	862,433	875,825
Maintenance and repair services, n.i.e. [1]	4,423	13,111	19,847	21,587	23,239	27,948	27,868
Transport [2]	49,462	76,357	84,434	81,779	86,342	93,251	91,092
Travel for all purposes [3]	96,872	130,315	192,602	192,868	193,834	196,465	193,315
Construction [4]	1,993	2,951	2,759	1,690	2,053	2,948	3,189
Insurance services	3,631	14,854	15,464	16,249	18,223	17,904	16,238
Financial services	29,192	86,512	114,951	114,762	128,035	132,420	135,698
Charges for the use of intellectual property, n.i.e. [1,5]	43,476	94,968	111,151	112,981	118,147	118,875	117,401
Telecommunications, computer, and information services	12,250	26,556	41,427	43,122	47,657	49,653	55,657
Other business services [6]	38,217	99,595	141,421	153,089	167,270	177,261	189,441
Personal, cultural, recreational services [7]	9,351	17,612	24,220	23,626	25,664	23,759	23,372
Government goods and services, n.i.e. [1,8]	9,156	19,210	20,087	18,777	19,924	21,949	22,555
IMPORTS							
Total	**1,452,650**	**2,375,407**	**2,771,004**	**2,719,092**	**2,901,181**	**3,119,320**	**3,105,127**
Goods	1,231,722	1,938,950	2,273,249	2,207,195	2,356,345	2,557,251	2,516,767
Services	220,927	436,456	497,755	511,898	544,836	562,069	588,359
Maintenance and repair services, n.i.e. [1]	2,316	5,857	8,084	7,595	6,796	7,133	7,823
Transport [2]	58,526	88,394	99,557	92,391	96,515	106,303	107,458
Travel for all purposes [3]	64,174	85,166	102,664	109,155	117,972	126,008	134,594
Construction [4]	1,447	2,578	3,012	1,768	1,950	3,151	1,327
Insurance services	11,284	63,452	49,842	52,070	50,889	43,735	51,547
Financial services	16,445	27,215	32,594	32,672	36,649	39,249	40,350
Charges for the use of intellectual property, n.i.e. [1,5]	16,139	31,116	35,178	41,974	44,405	43,933	42,733
Telecommunications, computer, and information services	14,128	29,421	38,815	39,720	43,091	42,558	43,720
Other business services [6]	20,306	65,903	95,119	100,505	106,991	107,834	113,584
Personal, cultural, recreational services [7]	1,645	5,393	11,358	12,544	17,530	19,190	21,140
Government goods and services, n.i.e. [1,8]	14,516	31,960	21,531	21,503	22,047	22,975	24,083

[1] N.i.e. means not included elsewhere. [2] Includes passenger fares. [3] All travel purposes include 1) business travel, including expenditures by border, seasonal, and other short-term workers and 2) personal travel, including health-related and education-related travel. [4] Construction covers the services provided to create, renovate, repair, or extend buildings, land improvements, and civil engineering constructions, such as roads and bridges. Construction exports exclude inputs purchased by foreign contractors for projects in the U.S. Construction imports include inputs purchased abroad by U.S. contractors. See source for more detail. [5] Includes charges for the use of proprietary rights, such as patents, trademarks, and copyrights, and charges for licenses to use, reproduce and/or distribute intellectual property. [6] Consists of research and development services, professional and management consulting services (including advertising and market research), and technical, trade-related, and other business services. [7] This service category consists of three subcategories: 1) Audiovisual services, which covers production of audiovisual content, end-user rights to use audiovisual content, and outright sales and purchases of audiovisual originals; 2) artistic-related services, which includes the services provided by performing artists, authors, composers, and other visual artists; set, costume, and lighting design; presentation and promotion of performing arts and other live entertainment events; and fees to artists and athletes for performances, sporting events, and similar events; and 3) other personal, cultural, and recreational services, which includes services such as education services delivered online, remotely provided telemedicine services, and services associated with museum and other cultural, sporting gambling, and recreational activities, except those acquired by customers traveling outside their country of residence. See source for more information. [8] Includes goods and services supplied by and to embassies, military bases, and international organizations; goods and services acquired by diplomatic and military personnel in the host economy; and services supplied by and to governments not included in other categories of services.

Source: U.S. Bureau of Economic Analysis, "International Economic Accounts: Trade in Goods and Services," <https://www.bea.gov/data/economic-accounts/international#trade>, accessed June 2020.

Table 1318. U.S. Freight Gateways—Value of Shipments: 2019

[In billions of dollars (4,140.7 represents $4,140,700,000,000), except as indicated. For the top 40 gateways ranked by value of shipments]

Port	Rank	Total trade	Exports	Imports	Exports as a percent of total
Total U.S. merchandise trade	(X)	**4,140.7**	**1,643.2**	**2,497.5**	**39.7**
Top 40 gateways	(X)	3,276.4	1,241.5	2,034.8	37.9
As a percent of total	(X)	79.1	75.6	81.5	(X)
Los Angeles, CA	1	278.2	31.9	246.2	11.5
Laredo, TX	2	231.5	95.0	136.5	41.1
Chicago, IL	3	217.1	50.4	166.7	23.2
Newark, NJ	4	195.2	16.9	178.2	8.7
JFK International Airport, NY	5	187.3	85.7	101.6	45.8
Houston, TX	6	157.3	92.8	64.5	59.0
Detroit, MI	7	149.0	79.2	69.8	53.1
New Orleans, LA	8	132.2	67.8	64.3	51.3
Los Angeles International Airport, CA	9	118.3	54.9	63.4	46.4
Savannah, GA	10	108.1	29.9	78.2	27.7
Port Huron, MI	11	99.9	46.5	53.4	46.5
Long Beach, CA	12	92.9	31.2	61.8	33.5
Charleston, SC	13	90.6	40.1	50.5	44.2
Buffalo-Niagara Falls, NY	14	79.6	41.1	38.5	51.6
El Paso, TX	15	79.0	31.7	47.3	40.2
Norfolk-Newport News, VA	16	74.8	24.8	50.0	33.1
Cleveland, OH	17	66.5	41.0	25.5	61.6
San Francisco International Airport, CA	18	61.7	29.7	32.0	48.2
Atlanta, GA	19	60.6	21.9	38.7	36.1
Dallas-Fort Worth, TX	20	59.2	24.3	34.9	41.0
Miami International Airport, FL	21	58.7	35.8	22.9	61.0
Baltimore, MD	22	58.5	15.0	43.6	25.6
Anchorage, AK	23	57.2	20.7	36.6	36.1
Oakland, CA	24	51.1	20.3	30.9	39.6
Otay Mesa, CA	25	49.1	16.9	32.2	34.4
Tacoma, WA	26	48.7	8.0	40.8	16.3
New York, NY	27	42.9	32.3	10.6	75.2
Hidalgo, TX	28	36.7	13.2	23.6	35.8
Corpus Christi, TX	29	34.5	28.7	5.8	83.3
Philadelphia, PA	30	30.5	4.9	25.7	15.9
Santa Teresa, NM	31	30.5	14.1	16.4	46.2
Eagle Pass, TX	32	29.7	7.5	22.2	25.1
Seattle, WA	33	27.3	8.5	18.8	31.1
Jacksonville, FL	34	27.2	6.6	20.6	24.3
Champlain-Rouses Point, NY	35	26.6	10.7	15.9	40.3
Miami, FL	36	26.6	10.0	16.6	37.6
Nogales, AZ	37	26.2	10.5	15.7	40.1
Pembina, ND	38	25.8	12.8	13.0	49.6
Blaine, WA	39	25.7	14.1	11.6	55.0
Seattle-Tacoma International Airport, WA	40	23.9	14.5	9.4	60.5

X Not applicable.

Source: U.S. Census Bureau, Foreign Trade Division, "USA Trade Online," <usatrade.census.gov/>, accessed September 2020.

Table 1319. U.S. Agricultural Exports by State: 2000 to 2018

[In millions of dollars (51,258 represents $51,258,000,000). Calendar year. Export estimates based on U.S. farm cash receipts. Export values are calibrated such that the sum of state export estimates for a commodity equals the total U.S. export value for the commodity]

State	2000	2010	2015	2017	2018	State	2000	2010	2015	2017	2018
U.S.	**51,258**	**115,806**	**133,016**	**138,127**	**138,916**	MO	1,348	3,485	3,611	4,072	3,939
						MT	503	1,077	1,182	1,231	1,196
AL	576	1,135	1,217	1,310	1,349	NE	2,299	5,335	6,479	6,349	6,802
AK	6	11	15	17	17	NV	66	111	135	132	137
AZ	486	1,070	1,283	1,513	1,467	NH	33	65	86	89	85
AR	1,308	3,190	3,135	3,182	3,013	NJ	247	399	546	575	544
CA	6,855	15,355	22,844	22,657	23,305	NM	322	682	750	780	752
CO	893	1,511	1,650	1,763	1,866	NY	501	1,225	1,453	1,432	1,459
CT	132	214	297	292	276	NC	1,844	3,391	3,573	3,663	3,470
DE	131	241	260	265	263	ND	1,228	3,691	3,817	4,400	4,246
FL	1,883	2,963	3,494	3,449	3,146	OH	1,461	3,407	3,708	3,672	3,682
GA	1,303	2,588	2,846	2,853	2,865	OK	817	1,541	1,511	1,817	1,810
HI	151	308	367	360	308	OR	800	1,353	1,870	1,996	2,007
ID	718	1,488	1,860	2,003	2,076	PA	700	1,615	2,038	2,040	2,056
IL	3,109	7,464	8,034	8,067	8,488	RI	13	32	33	36	34
IN	1,710	4,299	4,706	4,755	4,649	SC	398	809	808	793	864
IA	3,471	9,368	9,987	10,367	10,647	SD	1,209	2,964	3,702	3,627	3,560
KS	1,953	4,667	4,163	4,829	4,882	TN	552	1,241	1,522	1,516	1,472
KY	1,276	1,515	2,100	2,118	2,222	TX	2,697	6,325	5,739	6,889	6,883
LA	614	1,510	1,566	1,476	1,443	UT	163	330	432	459	430
ME	144	237	248	252	247	VT	49	140	188	191	187
MD	338	565	670	708	669	VA	541	875	1,052	1,093	1,094
MA	106	198	210	209	206	WA	1,313	2,801	3,477	3,676	3,615
MI	910	2,355	2,855	2,792	2,827	WV	60	115	144	162	160
MN	2,206	6,113	6,339	6,955	6,943	WI	922	2,412	2,869	2,956	2,979
MS	750	1,784	1,840	1,979	1,936	WY	147	235	304	311	339

Source: U.S. Department of Agriculture, Economic Research Service, "State Export Data," <https://www.ers.usda.gov/data-products/state-export-data/>, accessed November 2019.

Table 1320. U.S. Exports and General Imports of Merchandise by Customs District: 2010 to 2019

[In billions of dollars (1,278.5 represents $1,278,500,000,000). Exports are f.a.s. (free alongside ship) value basis; imports are on customs-value basis. General imports are a combination of entries for immediate consumption, entries into customs bonded warehouses, and entries into U.S. Foreign Trade Zones. These data may differ from those in Table 1316, Table 1323, and Table 1324. For methodology, see Foreign Trade Statistics in Appendix III]

Customs district	Exports					General imports				
	2010	2015	2017	2018	2019	2010	2015	2017	2018	2019
Total [1]	1,278.5	1,503.3	1,547.2	1,665.7	1,643.2	1,913.9	2,248.8	2,339.6	2,537.7	2,497.5
Anchorage, AK	14.5	18.7	19.8	21.8	21.2	16.2	16.9	17.2	19.2	17.0
Baltimore, MD	14.7	15.6	16.3	17.3	15.4	28.8	36.8	38.9	43.4	44.4
Boston, MA	8.2	7.4	8.8	9.1	8.7	19.2	25.2	21.7	24.1	25.6
Buffalo, NY	40.6	47.3	42.5	42.3	41.1	39.2	41.6	40.0	40.1	39.5
Charleston, SC	19.5	31.7	31.1	34.5	40.3	29.4	47.2	44.9	49.0	49.8
Chicago, IL	35.8	46.6	48.0	52.5	50.7	125.6	155.2	175.5	199.3	204.7
Cleveland, OH	25.4	34.1	41.1	46.5	51.2	69.2	95.8	101.6	105.6	100.0
Columbia-Snake, OR	12.3	12.1	14.2	15.2	13.7	12.2	12.3	13.7	14.3	13.5
Dallas-Fort Worth, TX	18.1	21.9	24.5	24.3	25.4	38.4	52.0	51.3	52.5	54.2
Detroit, MI	113.2	120.5	130.0	132.8	129.5	106.0	124.7	134.5	137.4	133.5
Duluth, MN	2.6	5.0	4.7	5.0	4.3	6.8	8.9	9.1	11.0	9.8
El Paso, TX	29.3	41.9	40.6	44.0	46.1	44.1	56.9	61.3	66.9	69.4
Great Falls, MT	17.4	14.3	13.1	14.2	16.1	26.9	24.2	26.2	28.8	29.1
Honolulu, HI	7.4	13.9	11.8	12.0	3.4	4.6	4.1	3.8	4.4	4.4
Houston-Galveston, TX	94.5	109.2	109.1	141.0	150.5	116.9	86.2	83.0	92.6	85.3
Laredo, TX	81.4	121.7	126.1	134.2	127.4	104.2	163.5	176.4	191.8	197.2
Los Angeles, CA	105.1	114.1	128.5	130.4	121.4	242.7	279.5	302.4	325.6	306.5
Miami, FL	58.9	58.6	59.2	61.6	60.7	36.6	48.2	48.5	49.9	49.1
Milwaukee, WI	0.1	0.3	0.4	0.4	0.3	0.9	1.0	1.0	1.3	1.0
Minneapolis, MN	2.6	2.6	2.1	2.1	2.0	13.6	12.6	14.4	14.5	14.8
Mobile, AL	8.7	10.6	10.6	10.3	9.4	20.8	22.8	22.9	24.0	24.9
New Orleans, LA	69.1	84.1	95.5	107.3	104.5	125.3	115.2	122.0	130.9	113.7
New York, NY	136.3	143.8	136.3	145.0	135.2	190.6	226.5	227.8	247.3	245.9
Nogales, AZ	8.9	14.9	12.4	12.7	14.1	17.4	21.7	21.0	19.8	22.5
Norfolk, VA	21.1	28.8	27.1	24.7	24.9	23.9	34.4	34.0	35.3	36.1
Ogdensburg, NY	16.2	17.2	16.5	19.0	18.6	27.8	29.3	27.8	29.6	28.4
Pembina, ND	21.3	25.7	27.8	30.0	27.8	14.7	17.3	17.1	20.5	20.1
Philadelphia, PA	14.3	15.8	16.8	18.5	19.7	56.9	56.0	57.8	59.9	61.2
Port Arthur, TX	6.5	12.2	17.6	26.4	30.6	26.4	14.3	13.2	16.1	10.6
Portland, ME	4.4	4.3	5.1	5.1	5.0	9.8	14.0	12.7	13.8	13.7
Providence, RI	0.3	0.2	0.3	0.4	0.4	5.8	8.6	8.5	8.9	10.3
San Diego, CA	16.2	22.7	23.3	25.8	25.3	32.4	47.4	45.7	47.8	50.3
San Francisco, CA	47.1	47.8	54.7	55.7	60.9	60.6	70.0	78.2	86.8	80.3
San Juan, PR	19.7	17.3	13.0	14.0	16.3	19.4	20.1	18.7	26.8	24.7
Savannah, GA	41.0	47.6	49.1	54.2	57.4	68.0	101.1	106.7	119.0	123.2
Seattle, WA	58.5	87.9	79.8	78.6	68.3	52.6	66.9	69.3	76.6	74.3
St. Albans, VT	3.3	2.1	2.2	2.5	2.5	6.9	9.3	7.8	8.4	8.7
St. Louis, MO	1.0	1.6	2.0	1.3	0.7	11.5	17.3	16.6	19.3	18.5
Tampa, FL	14.4	14.7	11.0	11.9	11.4	16.4	25.6	29.0	30.2	32.1
Virgin Islands, U.S.	1.9	0.1	1.0	0.9	0.9	10.5	0.1	1.2	1.5	0.9
Washington, DC	6.0	5.1	5.9	7.4	7.6	8.2	7.1	6.9	8.3	10.1
Wilmington, NC	5.3	5.1	6.0	7.5	7.5	12.8	13.6	11.8	17.0	19.3

[1] Totals include the following special districts, not shown separately: vessels under their own power or afloat, low valued imports and exports, and mail shipments. Totals may also include data for two or more Customs Districts that have been combined and published under an arbitrary designation, as a solution to disclosure situations.

Source: U.S. Census Bureau, U.S. Foreign Trade Division, "USA Trade Online," <https://usatrade.census.gov/>, accessed July 2020.

Table 1321. U.S. Exports of Goods by State of Origin: 2005 to 2019

[In millions of dollars (901,082 represents $901,082,000,000), except as indicated. Data are on a Census Basis. Exports are on a f.a.s. (free alongside ship) value basis and are based on origin of movement]

State	2005	2010	2011	2012	2013	2014	2015	2016	2017	2018	2019 Total	2019 Rank
Total¹	901,082	1,278,495	1,482,508	1,545,821	1,578,517	1,621,874	1,503,328	1,451,460	1,547,195	1,665,688	1,643,161	(X)
United States	853,292	1,208,081	1,416,625	1,478,314	1,509,865	1,551,164	1,436,224	1,385,513	1,481,701	1,595,073	1,569,907	(X)
Alabama	10,879	15,495	17,928	19,577	19,301	19,450	19,322	20,471	21,798	21,417	20,800	23
Alaska	3,613	4,155	5,259	4,543	4,528	5,111	4,620	4,350	4,941	4,834	4,990	40
Arizona	14,947	15,721	17,885	18,405	19,478	21,247	22,654	22,004	20,918	22,516	24,669	19
Arkansas	3,871	5,219	5,611	7,615	7,161	6,866	5,871	5,722	6,234	6,449	6,232	36
California	116,690	143,208	159,421	161,757	168,192	173,869	165,360	163,261	171,193	178,163	174,026	2
Colorado	6,773	6,726	7,338	8,170	8,545	8,364	7,950	7,569	8,054	8,331	8,097	33
Connecticut	9,750	16,029	16,233	15,871	16,427	15,963	15,242	14,394	14,792	17,404	16,243	26
Delaware	2,535	4,945	5,516	5,114	5,327	5,267	5,408	4,517	4,565	4,704	4,407	42
District of Columbia	823	1,483	1,041	2,014	2,708	940	1,088	1,331	1,483	2,724	3,690	43
Florida	33,444	55,399	65,010	66,223	60,482	58,439	53,903	52,036	54,897	57,246	55,995	7
Georgia	20,657	28,899	34,863	36,039	37,578	39,413	38,596	35,673	37,222	40,617	41,252	12
Hawaii	1,032	684	884	732	599	1,447	1,896	795	952	659	454	51
Idaho	3,273	5,157	5,913	6,120	5,789	5,138	4,302	4,877	3,863	4,028	3,434	44
Illinois	36,169	50,061	64,903	68,158	66,213	68,394	63,369	59,862	65,288	65,471	59,724	6
Indiana	21,594	28,764	32,332	34,399	34,216	35,589	33,819	34,653	37,747	39,321	39,283	13
Iowa	7,373	10,880	13,317	14,622	13,903	15,112	13,238	12,330	13,422	14,370	13,221	28
Kansas	6,736	9,900	11,623	11,684	12,459	12,022	10,689	10,155	11,244	11,582	11,659	31
Kentucky	14,961	19,346	20,119	22,132	25,412	27,757	27,637	29,192	30,919	31,808	32,991	16
Louisiana	19,404	41,371	54,971	62,869	63,247	64,770	48,679	48,367	56,865	67,197	63,700	4
Maine	2,332	3,162	3,422	3,048	2,687	2,811	2,762	2,863	2,712	2,836	2,724	46
Maryland	7,138	10,167	10,863	11,745	11,747	12,228	10,052	9,656	9,317	12,104	13,055	29
Massachusetts	22,052	26,305	27,871	25,614	26,812	27,384	25,289	25,893	27,561	27,146	26,130	18
Michigan	37,849	44,851	51,064	57,051	59,400	57,573	53,945	54,752	59,921	58,011	55,802	8
Minnesota	14,736	18,904	20,732	20,827	20,760	21,398	20,013	19,201	20,692	22,681	22,188	21
Mississippi	4,021	8,224	10,939	11,794	12,415	11,485	10,849	10,505	10,985	11,588	11,859	30
Missouri	10,514	12,925	14,161	13,903	12,958	14,190	13,647	13,935	14,289	14,529	13,406	27
Montana	715	1,393	1,592	1,576	1,506	1,545	1,404	1,360	1,616	1,666	1,685	48
Nebraska	3,003	5,821	7,588	7,455	7,393	7,890	6,664	6,381	7,210	7,947	7,453	34
Nevada	3,941	5,913	7,990	10,261	8,701	7,692	8,667	9,766	12,162	11,093	8,976	32
New Hampshire	2,557	4,368	4,307	3,488	3,511	4,233	4,001	4,143	5,148	5,306	5,829	39
New Jersey	21,107	32,131	38,172	37,286	36,612	36,587	32,063	31,164	34,258	35,301	35,675	14
New Mexico	2,543	1,543	2,096	2,958	2,726	3,802	3,782	3,616	3,696	3,899	4,679	41
New York	51,841	69,685	84,999	81,338	86,407	88,834	83,125	76,691	78,190	84,728	75,653	3
North Carolina	19,507	24,918	27,067	28,839	29,347	31,420	30,202	30,183	32,620	32,765	34,336	15
North Dakota	1,192	2,532	3,393	4,310	4,402	5,513	4,027	5,294	6,148	7,800	6,977	35
Ohio	35,110	41,505	46,458	48,819	51,048	52,641	51,262	49,330	50,071	54,393	53,229	9
Oklahoma	4,322	5,354	6,228	6,579	6,920	6,308	5,251	5,046	5,363	6,112	6,143	37
Oregon	12,407	17,684	18,317	18,388	18,634	20,889	20,057	21,772	21,894	22,332	23,599	20
Pennsylvania	22,334	34,943	41,103	38,852	41,181	40,411	39,439	36,453	38,640	41,158	42,722	10
Rhode Island	1,268	1,949	2,289	2,366	2,164	2,388	2,133	2,278	2,391	2,405	2,675	47
South Carolina	13,960	20,336	24,733	25,115	26,341	29,773	31,021	31,324	32,202	34,627	41,462	11
South Dakota	948	1,259	1,462	1,557	1,582	1,578	1,421	1,218	1,356	1,430	1,357	50
Tennessee	19,174	25,948	30,016	31,143	32,474	33,251	32,617	31,476	33,233	32,717	31,076	17
Texas	129,346	206,992	251,104	264,665	277,716	285,559	248,780	231,527	265,068	315,835	328,864	1
Utah	6,067	13,808	18,968	19,260	16,111	12,224	13,308	12,078	11,583	14,390	17,339	25
Vermont	4,672	4,278	4,275	4,139	4,027	3,670	3,176	2,993	2,776	2,920	3,021	45
Virginia	12,238	17,169	18,125	18,227	17,866	19,391	17,801	16,311	16,508	18,341	17,843	24
Washington	33,078	53,345	64,800	75,654	81,630	90,558	86,375	79,562	76,351	77,871	60,310	5
West Virginia	3,161	6,443	9,039	11,407	8,732	7,597	5,833	5,045	7,110	8,223	5,937	38
Wisconsin	14,961	19,800	22,069	23,119	23,110	23,426	22,442	21,036	22,305	22,719	21,668	22
Wyoming	671	983	1,219	1,439	1,351	1,757	1,175	1,099	1,196	1,357	1,367	49

X Not applicable. ¹ Includes other areas, not shown separately, and exports with an unknown state or area of origin.

Source: U.S. Census Bureau, Foreign Trade Division, "USA Trade Online," <https://usatrade.census.gov/>, accessed June 2020. See also <http://www.census.gov/foreign-trade/data/index.html>.

Table 1322. Value of State Exports to Top Trading Countries by State: 2019

[In millions of dollars (1,643,161 represents $1,643,161,000,000). Data are on a f.a.s. (free alongside ship) value basis. Exports are based on origin of movement]

	Total	Canada	Mexico	China	Japan	United Kingdom	Germany	South Korea	Nether-lands
United States [1]	**1,643,161**	**292,633**	**256,570**	**106,447**	**74,376**	**69,078**	**60,112**	**56,539**	**51,108**
Alabama	20,800	3,918	2,233	2,317	773	379	3,140	531	460
Alaska	4,990	582	23	855	679	17	219	1,083	350
Arizona	24,669	2,199	8,187	1,087	807	831	744	472	783
Arkansas	6,232	1,536	745	191	372	140	100	123	97
California	174,026	16,696	27,965	15,848	11,887	5,263	6,439	9,199	6,409
Colorado	8,097	1,445	1,059	524	399	243	280	542	331
Connecticut	16,243	1,952	811	1,262	402	1,452	2,542	475	775
Delaware	4,407	579	164	464	193	542	224	244	75
District of Columbia	3,690	14	10	2	4	519	13	2	8
Florida	55,995	4,363	3,323	1,361	1,155	1,894	1,830	818	1,016
Georgia	41,252	5,992	3,518	2,365	1,487	1,540	2,776	996	1,332
Hawaii	454	16	1	21	94	10	3	76	2
Idaho	3,434	943	258	209	229	111	49	102	91
Illinois	59,724	15,630	9,304	2,915	1,974	1,632	3,309	1,109	1,199
Indiana	39,283	13,243	5,671	2,022	2,111	1,063	1,406	764	1,397
Iowa	13,221	3,850	2,087	760	943	315	513	338	302
Kansas	11,659	1,923	2,194	553	1,031	463	508	395	152
Kentucky	32,991	7,794	2,200	2,098	940	3,553	1,197	649	1,127
Louisiana	63,700	2,942	8,427	4,929	2,658	1,928	340	3,630	2,999
Maine	2,724	1,411	51	134	72	64	58	66	67
Maryland	13,055	1,653	405	529	1,028	550	331	202	707
Massachusetts	26,130	2,975	1,941	2,370	1,505	2,743	1,834	952	1,329
Michigan	55,802	23,117	11,160	3,240	1,446	904	2,047	1,402	439
Minnesota	22,188	4,748	2,428	2,125	1,521	556	1,126	1,007	452
Mississippi	11,859	2,735	1,429	457	366	159	219	99	531
Missouri	13,406	4,940	2,296	598	478	331	475	428	231
Montana	1,685	741	54	96	72	41	33	212	16
Nebraska	7,453	1,592	1,734	341	818	66	158	467	122
Nevada	8,976	1,163	772	514	300	207	336	168	122
New Hampshire	5,829	860	409	294	345	159	992	61	211
New Jersey	35,675	7,185	2,860	1,834	1,486	2,543	1,547	987	1,350
New Mexico	4,679	128	2,388	803	280	29	62	129	22
New York	75,653	16,492	3,136	2,850	1,811	5,315	3,094	1,234	1,141
North Carolina	34,336	6,658	3,778	3,250	1,110	832	898	603	1,077
North Dakota	6,977	6,132	229	19	37	26	58	5	7
Ohio	53,229	20,707	6,882	3,240	1,544	2,198	1,440	1,082	940
Oklahoma	6,143	1,581	820	212	284	200	568	105	258
Oregon	23,599	3,360	530	7,193	1,587	276	503	1,354	333
Pennsylvania	42,722	11,198	4,242	2,544	2,317	2,433	1,541	1,067	1,822
Rhode Island	2,675	592	188	156	78	68	141	58	24
South Carolina	41,462	4,010	2,198	6,495	2,267	2,069	4,488	755	1,051
South Dakota	1,357	525	316	75	75	23	44	37	9
Tennessee	31,076	7,060	4,166	2,096	2,091	1,010	1,119	726	1,315
Texas	328,864	28,533	108,586	10,922	11,260	9,618	4,535	16,577	11,595
Utah	17,339	1,391	762	575	839	8,752	401	426	486
Vermont	3,021	1,194	47	187	61	94	98	195	84
Virginia	17,843	3,076	1,044	1,196	457	929	725	513	522
Washington	60,310	8,566	2,512	8,987	7,205	1,859	1,762	2,514	1,299
West Virginia	5,937	1,528	120	373	258	99	190	236	447
Wisconsin	21,668	6,754	3,282	1,373	704	805	760	545	452
Wyoming	1,367	225	46	24	70	3	3	54	7

[1] Total includes data for Puerto Rico and the Virgin Islands, not shown separately. Total also includes exports to unknown partners and to countries not shown separately..

Source: U.S. Census Bureau, Foreign Trade Division, "USA Trade Online," <usatrade.census.gov/>, accessed September 2020. See also <census.gov/foreign-trade/statistics/state/index.html>.

Table 1323. U.S. Exports, Imports, and Trade Balance by Country: 2005 to 2019

[In millions of dollars (901,082 represents $901,082,000,000). Data reflect trade between foreign countries and the U.S., Puerto Rico, the U.S. Virgin Islands, and U.S. Foreign Trade Zones. Data are shown on a Census Basis. Country totals include exports of special category commodities, if any. Minus sign (-) denotes an excess of imports over exports]

Country	Exports, domestic and foreign					General imports					Merchandise trade balance				
	2005	2010	2015	2018	2019	2005	2010	2015	2018	2019	2005	2010	2015	2018	2019
Total [1]	901,082	1,278,495	1,503,328	1,665,688	1,643,161	1,673,455	1,913,857	2,248,811	2,537,729	2,497,531	-772,373	-635,362	-745,483	-872,041	-854,371
Afghanistan	262	2,151	479	1,227	758	67	85	24	29	39	195	2,066	455	1,199	719
Algeria	1,106	1,194	1,876	1,261	1,000	10,446	14,518	3,372	4,618	2,480	-9,340	-13,324	-1,496	-3,357	-1,480
Angola	929	1,293	1,166	525	535	8,484	11,940	2,806	2,698	955	-7,555	-10,646	-1,640	-2,173	-420
Antigua and Barbuda	190	158	678	520	478	4	5	5	5	11	186	153	671	516	468
Argentina	4,122	7,392	9,362	9,908	8,151	4,584	3,803	3,951	4,834	4,917	-462	3,589	5,411	5,074	3,235
Armenia	65	113	50	46	53	46	75	62	54	55	19	38	-12	-8	-2
Aruba	559	540	1,168	614	526	2,920	19	55	31	20	-2,361	521	1,113	583	506
Australia	15,589	21,805	25,032	25,334	25,990	7,342	8,583	10,886	10,081	10,845	8,246	13,222	14,147	15,253	15,146
Austria	2,544	2,429	4,024	3,564	5,709	6,103	6,835	11,312	13,573	13,162	-3,558	-4,407	-7,288	-10,009	-7,453
Azerbaijan	132	253	478	314	374	45	1,989	507	505	26	87	-1,736	-29	-191	348
Bahamas, The	1,787	3,178	2,387	3,021	3,350	700	815	453	481	411	1,087	2,363	1,934	2,539	2,939
Bahrain	351	1,235	1,271	2,042	1,407	432	420	902	991	1,050	-81	815	368	1,052	357
Bangladesh	320	576	943	2,082	2,339	2,693	4,294	5,990	6,102	6,681	-2,373	-3,718	-5,048	-4,020	-4,342
Barbados	395	397	595	584	568	32	43	68	55	42	363	355	527	528	526
Belarus	35	133	59	132	125	345	175	158	397	380	-310	-41	-99	-264	-255
Belgium	18,691	25,458	34,174	31,410	34,726	13,023	15,552	19,487	17,176	20,165	5,668	9,906	14,687	14,234	14,561
Belize	218	289	285	407	406	98	120	75	226	57	119	169	210	180	349
Benin	72	463	631	254	267	1	(Z)	5	19	9	72	462	626	235	258
Bermuda	490	637	601	611	577	87	22	109	18	21	403	614	492	593	556
Bolivia	219	508	932	560	552	293	680	1,006	486	455	-74	-172	-75	74	97
Botswana	67	48	39	82	104	178	170	212	461	275	-111	-121	-173	-379	-171
Brazil	15,372	35,418	31,641	39,409	42,853	24,436	23,958	27,474	31,214	30,844	-9,064	11,460	4,167	8,194	12,009
British Virgin Islands	125	146	260	823	581	34	19	16	20	5	91	127	243	803	576
Brunei	50	124	133	266	288	563	12	19	98	41	-513	112	114	168	246
Bulgaria	268	171	289	370	463	454	260	598	986	910	-186	-89	-308	-616	-447
Cambodia	70	154	391	446	514	1,767	2,301	3,026	3,806	5,357	-1,697	-2,147	-2,635	-3,361	-4,843
Cameroon	117	132	225	193	200	158	297	132	219	330	-41	-165	93	-26	-130
Canada	211,899	249,256	280,855	299,732	292,633	290,384	277,637	296,305	318,521	319,428	-78,486	-28,380	-15,450	-18,790	-26,795
Chad	54	90	57	51	85	1,498	2,044	1,303	479	133	-1,444	-1,954	-1,247	-428	-48
Chile	5,134	10,907	15,449	15,312	15,728	6,664	7,017	8,777	11,385	10,393	-1,531	3,889	6,672	3,928	5,335
China	41,192	91,911	115,873	120,289	106,447	243,470	364,953	483,202	539,243	451,651	-202,278	-273,042	-367,328	-418,954	-345,204
Colombia	5,462	12,068	16,302	15,114	14,746	8,849	15,659	14,079	13,753	14,166	-3,387	-3,592	2,223	1,361	580
Congo, Rep. of	104	254	249	100	106	1,623	3,316	304	433	563	-1,519	-3,062	-55	-332	-457
Congo, Dem. Rep. of	65	93	136	78	132	264	528	154	50	22	-199	-434	-18	28	110
Costa Rica	3,599	5,178	6,045	6,470	6,219	3,415	8,697	4,489	4,891	5,147	183	-3,519	1,556	1,579	1,072
Cote d'Ivoire	124	163	266	309	279	1,198	1,177	1,028	1,248	924	-1,074	-1,014	-761	-938	-645
Croatia	159	312	332	615	711	364	336	577	466	548	-206	-24	-245	150	163
Cuba	369	363	186	271	286	(Z)	(Z)	(Z)	1	3	369	363	186	270	284
Curacao [2]	(X)	134	521	719	399	(X)	(X)	335	105	71	(X)	(X)	186	614	327
Cyprus	84	134	102	132	204	31	32	32	68	73	54	102	70	65	131
Czechia	1,054	1,411	1,977	3,003	2,790	2,193	2,450	4,489	4,993	5,525	-1,139	-1,039	-2,512	-1,990	-2,734
Denmark	1,918	2,132	2,203	2,608	3,195	5,144	6,012	7,760	8,857	11,010	-3,226	-3,879	-5,557	-6,249	-7,815
Djibouti	48	123	145	111	151	1	3	35	48	120	46	120	109	63	31
Dominican Republic	4,719	6,579	7,115	8,953	9,194	4,604	3,672	4,668	5,304	5,553	115	2,908	2,447	3,649	3,641
Ecuador	1,964	5,409	5,818	5,903	5,535	5,759	7,451	7,467	6,738	6,954	-3,795	-2,042	-1,649	-835	-1,418
Egypt	3,159	6,833	4,759	5,052	5,484	2,091	2,238	1,406	2,480	3,154	1,068	4,594	3,353	2,572	2,331
El Salvador	1,854	2,434	3,249	3,391	3,369	1,989	2,206	2,532	2,510	2,480	-134	228	717	881	889
Equatorial Guinea	281	272	162	139	214	1,561	2,214	163	580	328	-1,280	-1,942	-1	-440	-114
Ethiopia	456	773	1,555	1,308	1,014	62	128	310	445	572	394	645	1,245	863	442
Fiji	28	44	57	105	103	169	179	203	220	247	-141	-135	-146	-115	-144
Finland	2,254	2,180	1,560	1,881	1,768	4,342	3,884	4,510	7,162	6,384	-2,088	-1,704	-2,951	-5,281	-4,616
France	22,259	26,970	30,026	36,589	37,718	33,842	38,355	47,809	52,443	57,593	-11,583	-11,386	-17,782	-15,854	-19,875
French Polynesia	112	122	120	288	651	60	53	43	36	51	52	69	77	252	600
Gabon	99	243	204	113	129	2,816	2,212	337	288	120	-2,716	-1,969	-133	-175	10

See footnotes at end of table.

Table 1323. U.S. Exports, Imports, and Trade Balance by Country: 2005 to 2019 — Continued.

See headnote on page 827.

Country	Exports, domestic and foreign 2005	2010	2015	2018	2019	General imports 2005	2010	2015	2018	2019	Merchandise trade balance 2005	2015	2018	2019
Georgia	214	301	340	478	769	194	198	181	190	153	20	159	287	616
Germany	34,184	48,155	49,979	57,758	60,112	84,751	82,450	124,888	125,784	127,507	-50,567	-74,909	-68,026	-67,395
Ghana	337	989	950	769	840	158	273	309	581	943	179	641	187	-103
Gibraltar	163	1,494	1,979	1,358	1,259	5	1	2	(Z)	16	159	1,978	1,358	1,243
Greece	1,192	1,106	726	1,084	1,442	884	798	1,357	1,606	1,513	309	-631	-521	-71
Grenada	82	71	90	119	118	6	8	9	15	14	77	81	104	104
Guatemala	2,835	4,477	5,821	6,639	6,811	3,137	3,523	4,121	4,208	3,988	-302	1,700	2,431	2,823
Guyana	177	291	368	541	672	120	299	431	253	132	57	-63	288	540
Haiti	710	1,209	1,141	1,414	1,242	447	551	950	990	1,061	262	190	423	181
Honduras	3,254	4,606	5,216	5,594	5,440	3,749	3,933	4,760	4,693	4,824	-495	457	901	616
Hong Kong	16,351	26,570	37,183	37,311	30,783	8,892	4,296	6,802	6,274	4,734	7,459	30,381	31,037	26,048
Hungary	1,023	1,290	1,715	1,750	1,914	2,561	2,491	5,719	5,063	5,310	-1,538	-4,004	-3,312	-3,396
Iceland	512	325	415	670	555	269	201	317	430	483	243	99	241	72
India	7,919	19,249	21,453	33,191	34,288	18,804	29,533	44,783	54,282	57,694	-10,886	-23,330	-21,091	-23,406
Indonesia	3,054	6,948	7,118	8,171	7,733	12,014	16,478	19,605	20,829	20,147	-8,960	-12,487	-12,658	-12,414
Iran	96	211	282	426	77	174	95	11	70	1	-79	271	356	75
Iraq	1,374	1,643	1,973	1,312	1,190	9,054	12,143	4,353	11,872	7,025	-7,680	-2,380	-10,560	-5,835
Ireland	8,447	7,276	8,931	10,744	9,058	28,733	33,848	39,351	57,450	61,894	-20,286	-30,421	-46,706	-52,836
Israel	9,737	11,295	13,539	13,709	14,405	16,830	20,985	24,495	21,777	19,508	-7,093	-10,956	-8,068	-5,103
Italy	11,524	14,220	16,212	22,844	23,839	31,009	28,514	44,221	54,699	57,263	-19,485	-28,008	-31,856	-33,424
Jamaica	1,701	1,661	1,716	2,611	2,479	376	328	306	379	391	1,325	1,410	2,233	2,088
Japan	54,681	60,472	62,388	75,149	74,376	138,004	120,552	131,445	142,242	143,566	-83,323	-69,058	-67,093	-69,189
Jordan	644	1,172	1,360	1,581	1,493	1,267	974	1,492	1,814	2,170	-623	-132	-232	-677
Kazakhstan	538	730	510	729	740	1,101	1,872	816	1,392	1,226	-563	-1,142	-663	-486
Kenya	573	375	943	365	401	348	311	573	643	667	225	64	-278	-266
Korea, South	27,572	38,821	43,484	56,310	56,539	43,781	48,875	71,775	74,244	77,470	-16,210	-28,291	-17,934	-20,931
Kuwait	1,975	2,775	2,741	2,974	3,171	4,335	5,382	4,685	2,088	1,418	-2,360	-1,944	886	1,753
Kyrgyzstan	31	79	32	17	21	5	4	5	7	5	27	27	10	16
Laos	10	13	25	16	17	4	59	45	142	148	6	-21	-126	-131
Latvia	178	345	267	510	552	362	193	303	726	815	-185	-36	-216	-263
Lebanon	466	2,009	1,286	1,328	1,004	86	84	93	109	150	379	1,193	1,219	854
Liberia	69	191	136	197	114	91	180	45	62	67	-22	91	135	47
Libya	84	666	231	244	412	1,590	2,117	155	1,404	1,503	-1,506	76	-1,160	-1,091
Liechtenstein	20	29	35	49	18	296	213	310	304	326	-276	-274	-255	-308
Lithuania	390	628	528	706	934	634	637	1,060	1,268	1,108	-244	-532	-561	-174
Luxembourg	711	1,440	1,394	1,084	1,922	389	451	639	553	636	323	755	531	1,286
Macau	102	225	542	602	572	1,249	141	122	102	104	-1,147	420	499	468
Madagascar	28	116	55	117	67	324	108	320	892	846	-295	-265	-775	-779
Malawi	28	37	37	17	23	116	72	61	57	80	-87	-24	-40	-57
Malaysia	10,461	14,079	12,278	12,952	13,192	33,685	25,901	33,972	39,354	40,567	-23,224	-21,694	-26,402	-27,375
Malta	194	457	491	201	143	283	262	241	186	171	-89	249	15	-28
Marshall Islands	75	91	54	290	105	17	12	29	21	11	58	25	269	95
Martinique	35	297	133	248	135	22	23	37	12	13	13	95	236	122
Mauritania	86	84	88	88	91	1	195	173	13	5	85	-85	75	86
Mexico	120,248	163,665	236,460	265,945	256,570	170,109	229,986	296,433	344,272	357,971	-49,861	-59,973	-78,327	-101,401
Mongolia	22	116	69	121	193	144	12	17	10	25	-122	52	111	168
Morocco	481	1,948	1,625	3,000	3,496	446	686	1,012	1,553	1,583	35	613	1,447	1,913
Mozambique	63	224	264	183	196	12	65	96	113	137	51	168	71	60
Namibia	112	110	128	206	194	130	195	85	119	144	-17	43	86	50
Nepal	25	28	36	56	122	111	61	87	99	91	-87	-51	-43	31
Netherlands	26,468	34,740	40,212	48,560	51,108	14,862	19,055	16,844	24,513	29,719	11,606	23,368	24,047	21,389
New Zealand	2,592	2,820	3,631	4,060	3,948	3,155	2,764	4,293	4,188	4,114	-563	-662	-128	-166
Nicaragua	625	981	1,267	1,629	1,652	1,181	2,008	3,189	3,580	3,884	-555	-1,921	-1,951	-2,232
Niger	79	49	72	62	93	66	27	4	29	47	13	67	32	46
Nigeria	1,620	4,061	3,431	2,687	3,200	24,239	30,516	1,916	5,616	4,610	-22,620	1,516	-2,929	-1,410
North Macedonia[3]	32	33	31	41	39	48	37	203	353	283	-17	-173	-311	-244
Norway	1,942	3,100	3,570	5,424	3,894	6,776	6,950	4,763	6,786	6,511	-4,834	-1,192	-1,362	-2,618

See footnotes at end of table.

Table 1323. U.S. Exports, Imports, and Trade Balance by Country: 2005 to 2019-Continued.

See headnote on page 827.

Country	Exports, domestic and foreign					General imports					Merchandise trade balance				
	2005	2010	2015	2018	2019	2005	2010	2015	2018	2019	2005	2010	2015	2018	2019
Oman	571	1,105	2,355	2,415	1,937	555	773	907	1,275	1,160	16	332	1,448	1,140	777
Pakistan	1,252	1,901	1,838	2,852	2,648	3,253	3,509	3,701	3,710	3,922	-2,002	-1,608	-1,863	-858	-1,274
Panama	2,162	6,066	7,669	6,733	7,534	327	381	408	420	452	1,835	5,685	7,261	6,313	7,083
Papua New Guinea	55	186	208	87	95	58	97	91	90	70	-3	89	117	-3	25
Paraguay	896	1,810	1,492	2,256	2,108	52	62	163	131	162	844	1,748	1,329	2,126	1,946
Peru	2,309	6,750	8,724	9,695	9,668	5,119	5,243	5,056	7,886	6,144	-2,810	1,506	3,668	1,809	3,524
Philippines	6,895	7,377	7,903	8,716	8,642	9,250	7,982	10,232	12,592	12,778	-2,355	-605	-2,329	-3,875	-4,136
Poland	1,268	2,983	3,715	5,358	5,955	1,949	2,964	5,611	8,013	8,377	-681	19	-1,896	-2,655	-2,421
Portugal	1,132	1,058	942	1,573	1,716	2,329	2,142	3,271	3,886	3,893	-1,197	-1,084	-2,328	-2,313	-2,178
Qatar	987	3,160	4,222	4,428	6,457	448	466	1,354	1,571	1,695	539	2,693	2,868	2,857	4,763
Romania	609	730	754	1,114	949	1,208	1,008	2,150	2,609	2,381	-599	-278	-1,396	-1,495	-1,432
Russia	3,962	5,994	7,087	6,658	5,784	15,307	25,691	16,372	20,851	22,260	-11,344	-19,697	-9,286	-14,193	-16,475
Rwanda	11	31	14	25	19	6	21	46	67	46	4	9	-31	-42	-27
Saudi Arabia	6,805	11,506	19,792	13,597	14,486	27,193	31,413	22,083	24,066	13,405	-20,387	-19,907	-2,292	-10,469	1,082
Senegal	141	219	199	289	197	4	5	72	127	131	138	214	127	162	65
Serbia	(X)	104	126	166	151	(X)	164	273	322	340	(X)	-60	-146	-156	-189
Sierra Leone	38	61	77	71	78	9	29	40	57	30	29	32	38	15	48
Singapore	20,466	29,009	28,481	32,881	31,218	15,110	17,428	18,272	26,524	26,398	5,356	11,581	10,209	6,357	4,820
Sint Maarten [2]	(X)	(X)	741	677	689	(X)	(X)	52	96	130	(X)	(X)	690	581	559
Slovakia	150	256	380	289	389	961	1,073	2,300	4,160	5,149	-811	-817	-1,920	-3,870	-4,760
Slovenia	234	328	346	322	344	413	465	678	847	963	-179	-137	-332	-525	-619
South Africa	3,907	5,632	5,457	5,531	5,368	5,886	8,220	7,323	8,466	7,800	-1,979	-2,589	-1,866	-2,935	-2,432
Spain	6,839	10,355	10,310	13,064	15,207	8,615	8,554	14,133	17,208	16,787	-1,776	1,802	-3,823	-4,144	-1,579
Sri Lanka	198	179	362	371	390	2,083	1,748	2,891	2,669	2,749	-1,885	-1,569	-2,529	-2,298	-2,359
Suriname	246	362	444	388	376	165	191	146	86	83	80	171	297	302	293
Sweden	3,715	4,740	3,939	4,471	4,368	13,821	10,497	9,910	10,991	12,130	-10,106	-5,757	-5,971	-6,520	-7,763
Switzerland	10,718	20,704	22,154	22,172	17,896	13,000	19,137	31,431	41,091	44,644	-2,282	1,567	-9,277	-18,919	-26,748
Syria	155	503	3	51	9	324	429	7	6	6	-169	74	-3	45	3
Taiwan	21,614	26,050	25,826	30,480	31,294	34,826	35,847	40,911	45,732	54,253	-13,211	-9,797	-15,085	-15,252	-22,959
Tajikistan	29	57	19	14	11	241	1	31	1	2	-212	56	-12	14	9
Tanzania	96	163	173	332	333	34	43	105	97	130	63	121	68	235	203
Thailand	7,257	8,976	11,229	12,521	13,299	19,890	22,694	28,622	31,863	33,447	-12,633	-13,717	-17,393	-19,342	-20,148
Togo	28	158	312	649	438	7	9	14	13	13	21	149	298	636	425
Trinidad and Tobago	1,417	1,925	2,512	2,118	2,801	7,891	6,613	4,320	3,672	3,426	-6,474	-4,688	-1,808	-1,554	-626
Tunisia	261	573	602	597	461	264	405	546	649	470	-3	167	56	-52	-9
Turkey	4,239	10,538	9,520	10,254	10,033	5,182	4,207	7,886	10,307	10,631	-943	6,331	1,633	-53	-598
Turkmenistan	215	40	81	31	28	135	48	56	12	16	80	-8	25	19	12
Uganda	63	94	88	88	104	26	58	64	69	80	37	36	24	19	24
Ukraine	533	1,349	862	2,487	2,355	1,098	1,078	852	1,352	1,296	-565	271	11	1,135	1,059
United Arab Emirates	8,120	11,662	23,001	19,497	19,975	1,468	1,145	2,474	4,999	4,347	6,651	10,517	20,527	14,498	15,627
United Kingdom	38,568	48,410	56,095	66,454	69,078	51,033	49,305	58,057	60,697	63,219	-12,445	-1,395	-1,962	5,757	5,858
Uruguay	357	975	1,295	1,384	1,617	732	235	605	508	519	-376	740	690	876	1,097
Uzbekistan	74	101	138	297	506	96	68	10	18	34	-22	33	128	278	471
Venezuela	6,421	10,645	8,344	6,074	1,289	33,978	32,707	15,564	13,194	1,933	-27,557	-22,063	-7,221	-7,120	-644
Vietnam	1,193	3,706	7,101	9,676	10,860	6,631	14,868	38,015	49,159	66,630	-5,438	-11,162	-30,914	-39,483	-55,769
Yemen	219	398	158	191	270	279	181	48	2	5	-60	216	110	189	265
Zambia	29	56	84	195	99	32	30	47	190	83	-3	27	37	6	16
Zimbabwe	46	68	38	34	40	94	59	67	75	47	-49	9	-29	-42	-7

X Not applicable. Z Entry would amount to less than half the unit of measurement shown. [1] Includes additional countries, not shown separately. [2] The Netherlands Antilles dissolved on October 10, 2010. Curacao and Sint Maarten became autonomous territories of the Kingdom of the Netherlands. [3] In June 2018, The Republic of Macedonia agreed to change its name to the Republic of North Macedonia. The agreement became effective February 2019.

Source: U.S. Census Bureau, "USA Trade Online," <usatrade.census.gov/>, accessed September 2020. See also U.S. International Trade in Goods and Services, Series FT-900, <census.gov/foreign-trade/Press-Release/ft900_index.html>.

Table 1324. U.S. Exports and General Imports by Selected Commodity Groups: 2017 to 2019

[In millions of dollars (1,547,195 represents $1,547,195,000,000). All data are presented on a Census basis. For methodology, see Foreign Trade Statistics in Appendix III]

Selected commodity	Exports			General imports		
	2017	2018	2019	2017	2018	2019
Total [1]	**1,547,195**	**1,665,688**	**1,643,161**	**2,339,591**	**2,537,729**	**2,497,531**
Manufactured goods [2]	1,095,908	1,159,423	1,125,554	2,019,347	2,179,214	2,158,690
Agricultural commodities [2]	138,174	139,533	136,642	120,983	128,771	131,183
Food and live animals [3]	99,075	103,849	100,343	105,876	113,314	115,916
Live animals other than fish	906	954	977	2,812	2,743	3,009
Meat and preparations	18,026	18,958	19,226	8,870	9,253	9,681
Cereals and preparations	22,470	24,918	20,971	9,600	10,666	10,997
Vegetables and fruits	22,520	22,067	22,496	34,519	36,722	37,651
Coffee, tea, cocoa, and spices	3,025	3,026	2,994	14,042	13,116	13,429
Feeding stuff for animals	11,033	12,524	11,903	2,878	3,293	3,320
Crude materials except fuels [3]	76,466	77,161	74,045	33,881	36,738	34,288
Hides, skins, and furskins, raw	1,888	1,459	1,048	100	56	46
Oil seeds and oleaginous fruits	23,270	19,379	20,735	1,046	1,022	977
Crude rubber	2,727	2,710	2,216	3,320	3,147	3,120
Cork and wood	7,536	7,608	6,126	8,659	8,791	7,375
Pulp and waste paper	8,605	9,207	8,322	3,160	3,739	3,424
Textile fibers including waste	7,711	8,475	7,966	1,286	1,397	1,318
Crude fertilizers	2,751	3,016	2,687	2,607	3,288	3,031
Metalliferous ores and metal scrap	18,866	21,931	21,592	7,982	9,174	9,017
Mineral fuels and lubricants [3]	137,920	190,843	197,836	194,790	232,741	200,900
Coal, coke, and briquettes	10,183	12,451	10,169	966	871	918
Petroleum products and preparations	104,975	149,661	156,553	181,672	219,489	189,075
Gas, natural and manufactured	22,576	28,339	30,679	9,887	10,129	9,012
Animal and vegetable oils [3]	2,744	2,533	2,498	6,804	6,704	6,086
Animal oil and fat	689	692	813	269	308	339
Fixed vegetable fats and oil, crude	1,814	1,595	1,455	6,332	6,150	5,492
Chemicals and related products [3]	194,633	209,043	209,235	221,547	258,398	267,834
Organic chemicals	34,027	38,402	36,010	43,810	51,255	49,305
Inorganic chemicals	11,297	11,529	10,731	10,553	12,093	11,816
Dyeing, tanning, and coloring materials	7,568	7,670	7,209	4,019	4,465	4,302
Medicinal and pharmaceutical products	45,040	47,756	52,429	99,799	119,401	134,186
Fertilizers	3,002	3,121	3,101	5,593	6,648	6,555
Plastics in primary forms	32,867	36,184	35,517	15,498	17,675	15,627
Plastics in nonprimary forms	13,256	13,829	13,369	10,452	11,653	11,607
Manufactured goods by material	106,573	110,903	103,834	255,463	276,916	257,399
Leather and leather manufactures	1,026	926	775	1,431	1,505	1,275
Rubber manufactures	8,979	9,430	9,360	20,832	22,671	22,656
Cork and wood manufactures	2,007	2,008	1,935	11,553	12,826	10,997
Paper and paperboard	15,474	16,084	14,726	16,126	17,708	17,064
Textile yarn, fabric	12,182	12,353	11,945	28,301	30,340	29,975
Nonmetallic mineral manufactures	13,180	12,851	11,742	45,632	48,578	43,322
Iron and steel	14,730	14,115	12,124	36,881	39,278	31,821
Nonferrous metals	14,292	16,831	15,117	41,994	45,214	42,297
Manufactures of metals	24,703	26,305	26,110	52,711	58,796	57,991
Machinery and transport equipment	502,267	518,989	507,604	1,013,177	1,069,905	1,058,554
Power generating machinery	34,776	35,955	36,425	68,349	74,739	78,329
Specialized industrial machinery	44,991	48,128	45,251	49,139	54,481	56,980
Metalworking machinery	4,880	5,306	4,814	10,406	11,375	11,108
General industrial machinery	59,357	62,215	60,793	97,979	108,437	107,525
Office machinery	19,636	19,417	17,710	123,906	137,172	125,745
Telecommunications equipment	21,559	21,015	19,612	167,533	163,283	152,633
Electrical machinery	78,453	80,224	79,291	175,478	189,077	186,750
Road vehicles	116,907	116,541	120,066	285,988	295,928	300,662
Transport equipment	121,707	130,188	123,642	34,399	35,415	38,821
Miscellaneous manufactured articles [3]	119,792	126,598	126,715	380,412	404,904	405,375
Prefabricated buildings	2,357	2,524	2,399	13,764	14,866	13,309
Furniture	6,297	6,323	5,969	49,984	53,656	50,611
Travel goods	635	715	668	10,841	11,509	10,673
Apparel and clothing accessories	3,008	3,223	3,217	88,198	91,896	92,417
Footwear	859	985	1,133	25,634	26,544	27,091
Scientific and controlling equipment	47,174	51,062	51,205	56,669	61,294	64,501
Photographic equipment	6,390	6,540	6,573	14,425	14,994	15,079
Miscellaneous commodities [4]	62,566	66,807	64,632	102,672	111,674	123,520
Re-exports	**238,801**	**252,521**	**250,497**	**(X)**	**(X)**	**(X)**

X Not applicable. [1] Total exports including re-exports (exports of foreign merchandise). [2] Manufactured goods is based on the North American Industry Classification System (NAICS) and Agricultural commodities is based on the Harmonized System commodities specified by the U.S. Department of Agriculture definition. All other commodity detail is based on Standard International Trade Classification (SITC). [3] Includes other commodities, not shown separately. [4] Includes special transactions, coin, nonmonetary gold, and the low value estimate.

Source: U.S. Census Bureau, *U.S. International Trade in Goods and Services, Annual Revision for 2019*, Series FT-900, June 2020. See also <http://www.census.gov/foreign-trade/Press-Release/ft900_index.html>.

Table 1325. Domestic Exports and Imports for Consumption of Merchandise by Selected NAICS Product Category: 2005 to 2019

[In millions of dollars (799,957 represents $799,957,000,000). Includes nonmonetary gold. For methodology, see Foreign Trade Statistics in Appendix III. NAICS = North American Industry Classification System; see text, Section 15. N.e.c. = Not elsewhere classified]

Product category	2005	2010	2015	2017	2018	2019
Domestic exports, total.	**799,957**	**1,122,567**	**1,286,172**	**1,308,395**	**1,413,168**	**1,392,664**
Agricultural, forestry, and fishery products.	37,109	65,753	69,766	75,862	74,316	70,452
Agricultural products, total.	30,683	58,023	60,200	65,931	64,367	61,590
Livestock and livestock products.	1,118	1,539	2,032	1,825	1,921	1,916
Forestry products, n.e.c.	1,686	2,181	2,354	2,636	2,712	1,973
Fish, fresh or chilled, and other marine products.	3,622	4,011	5,180	5,471	5,315	4,974
Mining, total.	12,629	26,394	34,188	62,929	97,022	113,886
Oil and gas.	4,547	9,248	19,802	45,005	75,954	94,791
Minerals and ores.	8,082	17,146	14,386	17,924	21,068	19,095
Manufacturing, total.	708,205	952,360	1,110,979	1,095,908	1,159,423	1,125,554
Food and kindred products.	28,937	50,902	61,982	62,616	64,862	64,969
Beverages and tobacco products.	3,423	5,339	8,476	7,141	7,787	7,291
Textiles and fabrics.	8,483	7,833	9,001	8,435	8,656	8,388
Textile mill products.	2,344	2,583	2,793	2,791	2,761	2,649
Apparel and accessories.	4,075	3,070	3,104	2,827	3,047	3,042
Leather and allied products.	2,300	2,421	3,041	2,930	2,977	2,872
Wood products.	4,463	5,075	6,812	7,584	7,664	6,707
Paper products.	16,640	22,962	23,321	23,522	24,569	22,852
Printed, publishing, & similar products.	5,526	6,021	5,088	4,799	4,633	4,540
Petroleum and coal products.	17,979	61,010	78,168	83,077	103,144	93,171
Chemicals.	114,821	171,365	182,411	181,506	195,037	195,596
Plastics and rubber products [1].	18,784	24,262	29,970	29,908	31,358	30,500
Nonmetallic mineral products [1].	6,663	9,226	10,699	11,048	11,388	10,759
Primary metal products.	27,455	49,725	51,694	52,183	54,165	46,997
Fabricated metal products.	23,370	32,690	41,602	39,435	41,803	42,235
Machinery, except electrical.	97,001	126,023	123,736	116,766	124,483	119,121
Computers and electronic products [1].	122,744	121,121	119,879	114,813	116,073	112,256
Electrical equipment, appliances, and components [1].	26,457	31,035	46,671	44,177	46,168	45,884
Transportation equipment [1].	144,985	176,337	252,299	251,092	258,298	254,546
Furniture and fixtures.	2,844	3,979	4,960	4,695	4,817	4,679
Miscellaneous manufactured commodities.	28,909	39,381	45,271	44,562	45,730	46,500
Newspapers, books, & other published matter, n.e.c.	960	851	(NA)	(NA)	(NA)	(NA)
Special classification provisions.	41,055	77,210	71,239	73,696	82,406	82,773
Waste and scrap.	10,389	29,420	17,548	18,187	20,546	19,498
Used or second-hand merchandise.	2,570	4,711	12,432	13,033	15,514	16,229
Goods returned or reimported.	65	30	32	49	35	42
Special classification provision, n.e.c.	28,030	43,049	41,228	42,427	46,312	47,004
Imports for consumption, total.	**1,664,625**	**1,900,587**	**2,227,237**	**2,327,153**	**2,549,379**	**2,501,880**
Agricultural, forestry, and fishery products.	30,761	42,686	56,308	62,351	63,335	63,765
Agricultural products, total.	15,818	24,017	33,435	37,193	37,934	38,497
Livestock and livestock products.	3,277	4,116	6,124	6,179	6,303	6,600
Forestry products, n.e.c.	2,250	3,356	2,380	2,733	2,611	2,619
Fish, fresh or chilled, and other marine products.	9,416	11,198	14,369	16,245	16,488	16,049
Mining, total.	192,115	235,401	115,949	124,828	150,884	129,950
Oil and gas.	185,621	228,066	109,006	119,142	144,298	123,850
Minerals and ores.	6,494	7,335	6,943	5,686	6,586	6,100
Manufacturing, total.	1,372,004	1,550,204	1,948,837	2,029,354	2,209,809	2,173,075
Food and kindred products.	29,779	41,039	58,434	60,856	67,277	68,529
Beverages and tobacco products.	12,849	15,515	21,201	23,557	25,004	26,387
Textiles and fabrics.	7,450	6,525	8,570	8,112	8,729	8,201
Textile mill products.	13,508	15,825	20,752	21,572	23,084	23,513
Apparel and accessories.	74,478	75,411	89,281	84,083	89,032	89,660
Leather and allied products.	26,559	30,859	40,163	37,725	39,550	39,455
Wood products.	23,654	11,364	17,107	20,160	21,508	18,351
Paper products.	22,094	21,029	20,304	19,782	22,024	21,218
Printed, publishing, & similar products.	5,599	5,324	5,532	5,554	5,864	5,887
Petroleum and coal products.	81,359	102,169	67,950	63,844	81,190	73,484
Chemicals.	131,936	187,576	217,099	221,438	256,684	262,885
Plastics and rubber products.	28,072	34,364	49,836	52,293	58,463	59,263
Nonmetallic mineral products.	18,445	16,075	21,799	22,991	25,337	24,053
Primary metal products.	64,666	79,617	85,118	91,863	96,390	85,997
Fabricated metal products.	41,026	46,712	67,397	68,820	77,333	75,894
Machinery, except electrical.	109,619	104,832	156,908	168,546	188,125	188,462
Computers and electronic products.	269,921	324,379	372,260	398,795	420,790	390,722
Electrical equipment, appliances, and components.	55,179	68,465	101,912	110,880	123,205	122,811
Transportation equipment.	251,386	239,870	375,354	385,242	404,771	415,903
Furniture and fixtures.	25,096	25,702	36,874	41,889	45,440	42,479
Miscellaneous manufactured commodities.	79,329	97,554	114,987	121,352	130,012	129,923
Newspapers, books, & other published matter, n.e.c.	128	35	(NA)	(NA)	(NA)	(NA)
Special classification provisions.	69,617	72,261	106,143	110,620	125,350	135,091
Waste and scrap.	3,207	5,261	5,089	6,230	6,875	6,548
Used or second-hand merchandise.	6,026	6,403	13,159	11,711	13,170	13,120
Goods returned or reimported.	37,024	40,992	66,960	71,085	82,884	92,403
Special classification provision, n.e.c.	23,359	19,605	20,935	21,593	22,421	23,019

NA Not available. [1] Beginning 2009, export statistics for certain commodity classifications related to the aircraft industry are subject to suppression and have been aggregated in a manner that prevents the disclosure of confidential information.

Source: U.S. Census Bureau, Foreign Trade Division, USA Trade Online, <https://usatrade.census.gov/>, accessed July 2020. See also U.S. International Trade in Goods and Services, Series FT-900, <http://www.census.gov/foreign-trade/data/index.html>.

Table 1326. Knowledge- and Technology-Intensive Products Exports and Imports by World Region and Country: 2005 to 2018

[In billions of dollars (4,759.9 represents $4,759,900,000,000). Knowledge- and technology-intensive products include high research and development (R&D) intensive and medium-high R&D intensive products classified by the Organisation for Economic Co-operation and Development. High R&D intensive products include aircraft; pharmaceuticals; and computer, electronic, and optical products. Medium-high R&D intensive products include weapons and ammunition; motor vehicles; medical and dental instruments; machinery and equipment; chemicals and chemical products; electrical equipment; and railroad, military vehicles, and transport. World exports do not equal imports due to statistical errors in reporting of trade data and lack of trade data for sub-Sahara African countries. Data are primarily from Oxford Economics, special tabulations (2019) of Global Trade Databank]

Region and country	2005	2010	2011	2012	2013	2014	2015	2016	2017	2018
EXPORTS										
World [1]	**4,759.9**	**6,582.7**	**7,491.7**	**7,499.6**	**7,707.6**	**7,955.3**	**7,377.7**	**7,318.8**	**8,058.9**	**8,587.8**
North America	791.9	995.1	1,103.3	1,161.3	1,173.9	1,219.9	1,190.2	1,154.2	1,208.1	1,271.8
Canada	146.0	136.9	151.9	159.4	155.6	159.7	156.4	154.2	153.6	159.9
Mexico	125.4	182.8	203.4	222.7	234.6	254.5	257.9	252.9	276.3	302.7
United States	**520.4**	**675.4**	**748.0**	**779.1**	**783.7**	**805.7**	**775.9**	**747.0**	**778.2**	**809.3**
Central & South America [2]	59.8	81.7	97.9	97.6	102.3	88.3	78.4	78.1	84.6	87.0
Brazil	38.1	46.3	54.4	53.8	58.9	46.8	43.3	46.3	49.8	53.3
Europe	2,351.3	2,922.9	3,391.3	3,247.5	3,396.8	3,499.0	3,142.6	3,183.2	3,475.0	3,670.6
European Union [2,3]	2,198.4	2,694.0	3,116.9	2,966.2	3,110.9	3,209.3	2,877.7	2,920.5	3,186.3	3,359.2
France	254.3	296.6	327.5	317.8	323.9	323.9	287.5	288.8	310.4	336.4
Germany	640.9	793.0	933.5	900.4	927.1	961.6	865.8	872.8	955.5	1,023.8
United Kingdom	212.1	206.5	233.9	228.6	232.2	257.7	245.5	234.4	244.7	252.8
Other Europe	152.9	228.9	274.3	281.3	285.9	289.7	264.9	262.8	288.7	311.4
Middle East	50.4	106.0	125.1	172.7	185.1	191.2	135.1	124.1	168.8	119.0
Asia [2]	1,486.9	2,453.1	2,746.9	2,791.8	2,822.8	2,930.7	2,807.7	2,755.4	3,098.5	3,414.1
China [4]	394.0	832.7	966.7	1,006.3	1,046.1	1,131.1	1,112.8	1,062.6	1,196.2	1,344.7
India	22.4	56.2	74.0	75.0	86.5	86.7	80.3	81.1	91.1	108.3
Indonesia	18.2	27.9	33.5	33.6	33.3	33.2	28.5	29.6	31.5	34.1
Japan	443.2	550.0	580.9	570.6	504.1	487.1	442.6	461.9	495.7	525.1
Malaysia	85.1	100.9	104.2	102.5	103.5	108.5	99.9	97.9	112.4	132.3
Philippines	31.3	24.5	22.0	33.3	34.3	38.3	40.2	38.2	47.2	47.5
Singapore	93.5	222.0	242.2	243.3	245.4	245.7	229.4	221.8	238.5	258.7
South Korea	210.6	344.5	390.2	378.8	399.5	410.3	393.6	369.1	428.1	444.0
Taiwan	123.1	174.0	193.6	187.1	193.3	203.4	190.1	191.0	219.5	230.6
Thailand	58.5	100.0	109.4	117.0	120.7	123.8	117.1	118.6	130.9	140.0
Vietnam	3.7	13.5	22.0	34.8	47.2	53.3	65.1	75.1	98.4	139.1
Oceania [2]	19.5	23.9	27.2	28.6	26.8	26.2	23.7	23.7	23.9	25.3
Australia	15.6	19.8	22.3	23.6	21.9	21.2	18.9	19.1	19.3	20.7
IMPORTS										
World [1]	**4,880.0**	**6,677.7**	**7,621.8**	**7,652.6**	**7,864.3**	**8,093.1**	**7,580.8**	**7,669.4**	**8,416.0**	**9,046.2**
North America	1,127.7	1,322.3	1,479.9	1,580.6	1,608.8	1,686.7	1,719.7	1,693.5	1,798.8	1,936.5
Canada	178.0	207.3	231.7	242.2	243.5	244.7	231.9	225.7	241.8	254.8
Mexico	134.0	181.9	204.5	219.7	230.1	240.1	242.7	238.0	250.3	271.6
United States	**815.6**	**933.1**	**1,043.7**	**1,118.7**	**1,135.2**	**1,201.9**	**1,245.1**	**1,229.7**	**1,306.7**	**1,410.1**
Central & South America [2]	132.8	269.0	333.8	342.9	348.2	326.0	284.0	245.7	263.6	290.4
Brazil	43.6	107.2	130.8	130.1	138.7	130.8	103.9	87.0	90.5	111.9
Europe	2,200.4	2,759.1	3,177.3	2,970.2	3,074.2	3,172.1	2,850.2	2,918.9	3,217.4	3,388.5
European Union [2,3]	1,961.4	2,379.4	2,696.9	2,474.9	2,570.1	2,694.7	2,465.4	2,524.0	2,762.4	2,923.9
France	237.5	295.2	341.6	316.4	318.9	318.9	288.1	297.4	318.3	333.1
Germany	389.8	507.1	586.5	542.1	552.2	580.2	529.4	537.7	603.0	660.1
United Kingdom	256.7	267.8	295.4	270.7	283.0	328.0	313.5	305.6	312.0	319.8
Other Europe [2]	239.0	379.6	480.4	495.3	504.1	477.4	384.9	394.9	455.0	464.6
Middle East	130.2	222.4	253.4	309.2	334.7	360.3	307.6	286.1	408.7	367.3
Asia [2]	1,204.2	1,987.7	2,246.1	2,304.6	2,365.0	2,416.0	2,297.5	2,405.0	2,586.4	2,921.6
China [4]	461.8	812.6	924.6	931.1	989.1	1,025.7	950.9	1,045.2	1,061.2	1,207.5
India	42.6	100.1	121.1	125.9	122.9	125.4	129.9	127.7	148.8	209.8
Indonesia	23.5	64.1	78.8	87.8	80.9	75.9	67.4	65.3	72.8	87.2
Japan	178.4	232.0	264.3	275.2	264.5	268.8	249.3	253.4	269.9	294.8
Malaysia	75.3	97.9	103.2	105.6	108.2	109.3	95.8	95.1	108.0	119.3
Philippines	32.3	33.3	25.0	34.5	35.0	35.4	41.8	51.2	57.8	64.4
Singapore	71.1	166.9	177.7	183.5	183.7	180.3	166.7	165.6	180.3	203.7
South Korea	110.2	170.0	187.4	181.2	187.1	195.2	195.2	191.5	219.7	229.6
Taiwan	102.1	130.1	139.9	128.9	131.9	135.2	126.6	132.7	146.1	158.3
Thailand	57.4	85.0	99.5	116.0	111.4	104.4	99.4	99.3	107.9	115.3
Vietnam	14.7	37.7	47.2	55.6	68.2	75.3	91.1	97.0	120.9	133.0
Oceania [2]	84.8	117.2	131.3	145.1	133.3	132.1	121.7	120.2	141.2	141.8
Australia	70.8	103.2	114.8	127.5	114.6	111.0	102.7	101.2	120.0	119.6

[1] World total does not include all countries and economies due to limitations in data availability. [2] Includes other countries not shown separately. [3] Data are not available for EU member Luxembourg. [4] Includes Hong Kong but, excludes bilateral flows between mainland China and Hong Kong.

Source: National Science Foundation, *Science and Engineering Indicators 2020, Production and Trade of Knowledge- and Technology-Intensive Industries, Supplemental Tables*, NSB-2020-5, January 2020. See also <https://ncses.nsf.gov/pubs/nsb20205/data#supplemental-tables>.

Table 1327. Exporting Firms and Revenue, Employees, and Payroll by Country and Area of Export Destination: 2014

[33,036,935 represents $33,036,935,000,000. Covers nonfarm employer firms with paid employees. A company or firm is a business consisting of one or more domestic establishments that the reporting firm specified under its ownership or control. Data were compiled from two Census Bureau data products, the 2014 Profile of U.S. Importing and Exporting Companies and the 2014 Annual Survey of Entrepreneurs. Excludes firms without reported sales, payroll, and employment; non-employer firms; firms operating primarily in out of scope industries, such as crop and animal production; and firms located in Puerto Rico and other Island Areas]

Export destination	Firms (number)	Revenue (mil. dol.)	Export revenue (mil. dol.)	Paid employees (1,000)	Annual payroll (mil. dol.)
All firms with and without exports......................	5,437,782	33,036,935	1,593,012	115,129	5,640,983
Firms with exports [1]......................................	**183,439**	**18,726,634**	**1,593,012**	**41,367**	**2,585,583**
Australia..	26,047	9,094,380	23,459	15,029	1,122,439
Austria...	4,964	3,912,745	20,918	6,166	525,658
Belgium..	9,791	6,544,309	26,297	9,608	774,267
Brazil..	14,863	8,379,882	39,861	14,073	1,025,895
Canada...	70,936	14,797,648	290,071	30,821	1,918,882
Chile..	12,245	7,890,198	15,062	13,099	908,350
China..	27,292	9,687,754	160,409	17,262	1,188,211
Colombia...	11,344	7,767,439	24,397	11,806	860,604
France...	17,692	7,736,831	48,623	13,941	1,009,770
Germany..	25,540	9,578,466	47,619	17,453	1,244,802
Hong Kong..	19,953	8,121,675	44,700	14,027	1,044,024
India..	14,637	8,155,963	14,623	14,264	1,050,460
Italy..	15,060	7,419,636	21,455	11,788	881,439
Japan..	22,405	9,462,453	66,592	16,533	1,189,041
Malaysia...	10,916	6,255,066	13,018	9,902	747,884
Mexico...	43,314	11,728,934	226,835	21,095	1,404,870
Netherlands..	15,804	8,361,018	38,331	14,065	1,021,324
Saudi Arabia.......................................	8,930	5,836,188	15,475	9,289	686,547
Singapore..	17,096	7,879,007	26,101	13,030	993,388
South Korea..	18,217	7,932,405	37,525	12,914	956,678
Spain..	10,474	6,236,271	32,233	10,168	770,541
Switzerland..	9,465	5,223,332	22,487	9,536	748,359
Taiwan...	14,659	7,414,200	26,664	11,058	852,190
United Arab Emirates...............................	13,470	7,390,577	17,975	12,820	878,927
United Kingdom.....................................	35,249	10,440,985	52,405	19,219	1,452,752
APEC (Asia-Pacific Economic Cooperation)...........	138,425	17,311,670	986,037	37,172	2,349,030
ASEAN (Association of Southeast Asian Nations)......	31,462	9,984,971	69,936	18,661	1,277,471
European Union.....................................	72,662	14,004,167	319,520	27,367	1,886,698
LAFTA (Latin American Free Trade Area)..............	62,793	12,959,214	347,289	24,719	1,637,559
OECD [2]..	147,350	17,794,292	1,025,069	38,594	2,429,459
OPEC [3]..	29,286	10,020,895	63,620	17,862	1,201,791

[1] Includes other countries, not shown separately. [2] Organisation for Economic Cooperation and Development. [3] Organization of Petroleum Exporting Countries.

Source: U.S. Census Bureau, Annual Survey of Entrepreneurs (ASE), "U.S. Exporting Firms: 2014 Tables," <census.gov/programs-surveys/ase/data/tables.2014.html>, accessed May 2018. See also <census.gov/programs-surveys/ase/about.html>

Table 1328. U.S. Exporting and Importing Companies by Employment-Size Class: 2010 and 2017

[Value in millions of dollars (1,140,406 represents $1,140,406,000,000). Data include all companies that can be linked to import and/or export transactions. Trade values are taken from the transactions used to compile the official U.S. Trade statistics; company information is taken from the Census Bureau Business Register. For information on data limitations, see Technical Documentation in source]

Employment-size class and company type	Number		Known value [1] (mil. dol.)		Percent of—			
					Number		Known value	
	2010	2017	2010	2017	2010	2017	2010	2017
EXPORTERS								
All companies, total..........	**293,988**	**290,142**	**1,140,406**	**1,377,324**	**100.0**	**100.0**	**100.0**	**100.0**
By employment-size:								
1 to 19 employees...............	112,572	105,239	82,739	81,652	38.3	36.3	7.3	5.9
20 to 49 employees.............	30,984	29,701	45,037	46,096	10.5	10.2	3.9	3.3
50 to 99 employees.............	15,179	14,791	43,710	39,618	5.2	5.1	3.8	2.9
100 to 249 employees...........	11,581	11,870	59,349	88,605	3.9	4.1	5.2	6.4
250 to 499 employees..........	4,336	4,808	46,254	68,055	1.5	1.7	4.1	4.9
500 or more employees.........	6,490	7,287	755,466	917,670	2.2	2.5	66.2	66.6
Unknown [2]......................	112,846	116,446	107,851	135,628	38.4	40.1	9.5	9.8
IMPORTERS								
All companies, total..........	**181,648**	**218,585**	**1,679,522**	**2,032,453**	**100.0**	**100.0**	**100.0**	**100.0**
By employment-size:								
1 to 19 employees...............	77,796	89,862	112,664	140,076	42.8	41.1	6.7	6.9
20 to 49 employees.............	18,487	21,378	71,093	77,753	10.2	9.8	4.2	3.8
50 to 99 employees.............	9,472	10,885	58,075	65,475	5.2	5.0	3.5	3.2
100 to 249 employees...........	7,820	9,103	96,080	106,014	4.3	4.2	5.7	5.2
250 to 499 employees..........	3,174	3,867	69,812	105,875	1.7	1.8	4.2	5.2
500 or more employees.........	5,013	5,896	1,148,183	1,395,946	2.8	2.7	68.4	68.7
Unknown [2]......................	59,886	77,594	123,616	141,315	33.0	35.5	7.4	7.0

[1] Known value is defined as the portion of U.S. total exports and general imports that could be matched to specific companies. Export values are on f.a.s. or "free alongside ship" basis. [2] Includes missing employment data, nonemployers, and companies that reported annual payroll but did not report any employees on their payroll.

Source: U.S. Census Bureau, *Profile of U.S. Importing and Exporting Companies 2016-2017*, September 2019, and earlier reports. See also <http://www.census.gov/foreign-trade/statistics/press-release/>.

Table 1329. Export and Import Value Indexes—Selected Countries: 2014 to 2018

[Indexes in U.S. dollars, 2000=100. Values are the current value of exports/imports converted to U.S. dollars and expressed as a percentage of the average for the base period]

Country	Export value index					Import value index				
	2014	2015	2016	2017	2018	2014	2015	2016	2017	2018
United States	**207.3**	**192.2**	**185.6**	**197.8**	**213.1**	**191.6**	**183.9**	**178.7**	**191.3**	**207.4**
Australia	375.7	293.9	301.4	361.9	402.5	331.3	291.5	274.4	319.8	329.1
Belgium	251.3	211.2	211.9	229.1	248.4	256.2	212.1	214.2	230.9	254.2
Canada	172.2	148.2	141.0	152.1	162.9	193.8	175.7	168.7	181.0	192.2
France	177.7	154.9	153.4	163.8	178.1	200.8	168.8	167.9	183.0	198.9
Germany	271.5	240.9	242.4	263.1	283.5	243.4	211.9	212.8	234.5	259.2
Greece	307.2	243.6	240.2	278.5	336.8	192.2	140.1	140.2	162.6	191.1
Ireland	156.8	159.7	169.5	177.9	213.5	161.1	151.2	159.5	183.0	211.4
Italy	220.3	190.0	192.0	211.0	227.3	198.7	172.1	170.4	189.8	209.8
Japan	144.0	130.4	134.6	145.7	154.0	214.0	170.8	160.1	176.9	197.2
Korea, South	332.4	305.8	287.6	333.0	351.1	327.5	272.0	253.1	298.2	333.5
Netherlands	289.1	245.3	245.4	280.4	311.2	270.8	235.2	230.0	263.9	296.1
Norway	240.9	173.0	147.2	168.3	202.8	260.1	222.2	209.7	236.3	251.8
Spain	282.3	245.5	252.2	277.9	300.2	230.4	200.2	199.6	226.0	249.1
Sweden	189.4	161.1	160.3	175.9	190.9	223.1	190.4	194.0	212.1	234.1
Switzerland	386.6	360.0	376.3	(NA)	(NA)	334.1	306.7	327.3	(NA)	(NA)
United Kingdom	177.2	161.4	143.7	154.9	171.0	198.7	180.4	183.4	185.3	194.1

NA Not available.

Source: World Bank, "World Development Indicators" database ©, <data.worldbank.org/>, accessed September 2020.

Table 1330. U.S. Trade with China—Leading Commodity Imports and Exports: 2010 to 2019

[In billions of dollars (365.0 represents $365,000,000,000), except as noted]

Commodity	NAICS code [1]	2010	2015	2017	2018	2019	2018-2019 percent change
IMPORTS FROM CHINA [2]							
Total imports [3]	(X)	**365.0**	**483.2**	**505.2**	**539.2**	**451.7**	**-16.2**
Communications equipment	3342	33.0	67.4	78.2	77.5	64.6	-16.7
Computer equipment	3341	57.2	57.8	58.5	59.6	52.9	-11.3
Misc. manufactured commodities	3399	34.2	35.3	35.9	38.0	36.6	-3.6
Apparel	3152	26.6	27.9	24.6	24.8	22.2	-10.2
Plastics products	3261	7.2	12.1	13.7	16.0	15.7	-2.0
Household appliances and misc. machines	3352	10.0	15.0	14.5	16.5	15.6	-5.1
Household and institutional furniture and kitchen cabinets	3371	11.6	15.9	18.3	19.8	15.0	-24.2
Footwear	3162	15.7	17.1	14.1	13.9	13.3	-4.3
Motor vehicle parts	3363	6.7	13.3	13.5	15.4	12.6	-17.7
Electrical equipment and components	3359	7.1	11.3	12.8	15.3	12.1	-20.7
EXPORTS TO CHINA							
Total exports [3]	(X)	**85.8**	**107.2**	**120.1**	**109.7**	**94.1**	**-14.2**
Aerospace products and parts	3364	5.7	15.1	15.7	17.7	9.9	-44.5
Oilseeds and grains	1111	11.3	13.0	13.6	3.8	8.3	118.4
Semiconductors and other electronic components	3344	6.1	5.3	5.1	5.8	7.8	35.2
Motor vehicles	3361	3.2	8.3	9.5	6.0	6.7	11.2
Navigational, measuring, electromedical, and control instruments	3345	3.5	4.8	4.8	5.2	5.0	-5.3
Industrial machinery	3332	2.0	2.2	3.2	4.3	4.3	-0.1
Basic chemicals	3251	4.1	4.4	4.8	4.7	3.9	-16.7
Pharmaceuticals and medicines	3254	0.8	2.1	3.0	3.4	3.8	12.0
Resin, synthetic rubber, artificial and synthetic fibers and filaments	3252	4.3	3.7	4.1	4.2	3.4	-20.1
Oil and gas	2111	(Z)	1.0	6.7	7.0	2.7	-61.8

X Not applicable. Z Less than $500,000. [1] Based on the North American Industry Classification System (NAICS); see text, Section 15. [2] Imports classified as general imports. For definition of General Imports, see Text, this section. [3] Includes items not shown separately.

Source: U.S. International Trade Commission, "Interactive Tariff and Trade DataWeb," <dataweb.usitc.gov/>, accessed September 2020.

Table 1331. U.S. Trade with Canada and Mexico—Leading Commodity Imports and Exports: 2010 to 2019

[In billions of dollars (277.6 represents $277,600,000,000), except as noted]

Commodity	NAICS code [1]	2010	2015	2017	2018	2019	2018-2019 percent change
IMPORTS FROM CANADA [2]							
Total imports [3]................................	(X)	**277.6**	**296.3**	**299.1**	**318.5**	**319.4**	**0.3**
Oil & gas.............................	2111	66.3	55.0	58.8	69.4	70.3	1.3
Motor vehicles...........................	3361	36.5	43.4	44.8	41.1	41.4	0.7
Motor vehicle parts......................	3363	12.1	14.4	13.1	14.1	13.7	-2.5
Petroleum & coal products...............	3241	14.5	12.0	11.1	12.4	12.7	2.1
Aerospace products & parts.............	3364	6.4	10.7	8.6	9.3	10.2	9.8
Nonferrous metal (except aluminum) production and processing...........	3314	10.3	9.4	8.7	9.0	10.1	11.4
Basic chemicals.........................	3251	7.4	6.4	6.4	7.0	6.4	-8.3
Other general purpose machinery.........	3339	3.6	4.6	5.0	5.8	6.0	4.2
Pharmaceuticals and medicines.........	3254	4.4	5.6	4.1	5.3	5.8	10.4
Alumina and aluminum production and processing....	3313	6.2	5.9	6.9	6.7	5.6	-15.6
EXPORTS TO CANADA							
Total exports [3].............................	(X)	**206.8**	**234.1**	**234.2**	**247.7**	**241.7**	**-2.4**
Motor vehicles...........................	3361	20.7	25.0	27.8	27.7	28.7	3.6
Motor vehicle parts......................	3363	19.5	17.1	19.1	18.0	17.2	-4.6
Oil & gas.............................	2111	5.2	10.5	9.9	12.6	12.7	0.8
Petroleum & coal products...............	3241	5.9	10.1	9.2	12.9	10.7	-16.4
Aerospace products & parts.............	3364	4.7	7.2	7.1	8.1	8.4	3.7
Other general purpose machinery.........	3339	6.2	6.8	6.6	7.3	7.5	3.2
Agriculture, construction, and mining machinery.......	3331	7.4	6.9	7.2	7.9	7.0	-12.3
Motor vehicle bodies & trailers............	3362	2.5	6.4	6.5	7.1	6.6	-6.6
Basic chemicals.........................	3251	6.1	6.3	6.4	6.6	6.5	-2.3
Plastics products........................	3261	4.9	5.9	6.1	6.3	6.2	-1.8
IMPORTS FROM MEXICO [2]							
Total imports [3].............................	(X)	**230.0**	**296.4**	**312.7**	**344.3**	**358.0**	**4.0**
Motor vehicles...........................	3361	27.5	50.0	57.5	64.5	70.7	9.7
Motor vehicle parts......................	3363	23.6	43.9	45.1	49.4	50.5	2.3
Computer & peripheral equipment.........	3341	13.2	17.1	20.2	26.6	27.9	4.8
Electrical equipment.....................	3353	6.8	10.5	10.9	11.5	12.7	10.4
Audio & video equipment.................	3343	16.5	14.5	12.1	11.2	12.4	10.9
Oil & gas.............................	2111	29.7	12.5	10.1	14.2	12.1	-15.0
Navigational, measuring, electromedical, and control instruments..............	3345	5.0	8.4	9.0	9.4	9.7	3.1
Communications equipment...............	3342	14.1	13.3	12.5	11.6	9.1	-20.8
Other electrical equipment and components............	3359	4.2	6.5	8.0	9.0	9.0	0.1
Fruits and tree nuts......................	1113	2.4	4.7	6.5	6.6	7.6	15.1
EXPORTS TO MEXICO							
Total exports [3].............................	(X)	**131.8**	**186.0**	**187.2**	**204.5**	**195.7**	**-4.3**
Petroleum & coal products...............	3241	12.0	15.4	21.7	29.3	28.3	-3.3
Motor vehicle parts......................	3363	12.6	17.6	16.0	16.4	16.5	1.0
Basic chemicals.........................	3251	7.0	8.3	9.2	10.1	9.3	-7.6
Resin, synthetic rubber, artificial and synthetic fibers and filaments....................	3252	6.2	7.9	7.9	8.7	7.8	-10.6
Engines, turbines, & power transmission equipment...	3336	3.3	5.2	6.4	7.4	7.2	-3.8
Plastics products........................	3261	4.2	6.5	6.4	6.8	6.3	-7.4
Oil & gas.............................	2111	2.0	3.0	4.8	5.7	6.1	6.5
Oilseeds & grains........................	1111	4.5	4.9	5.6	6.0	6.0	-0.4
Other electrical equipment and components............	3359	2.9	5.7	5.4	5.6	5.3	-6.1
Other fabricated metal products........................	3329	3.1	4.8	4.7	5.1	4.8	-4.7

X Not applicable. [1] Based on the North American Industry Classification System (NAICS); see text, Section 15. [2] Imports classified as general imports. For definition of general imports, see Text, this section. [3] Includes items not shown separately.

Source: U.S. International Trade Commission, "Interactive Tariff and Trade DataWeb," <dataweb.usitc.gov/>, accessed September 2020.

Table 1332. U.S. Trade in Processed Foods By Commodity: 2000 to 2019

[Includes Puerto Rico, U.S. territories, and shipments under foreign aid programs. Metric ton = 1.102 short tons or .984 long tons]

Product category	Units	2000	2010	2015	2018	2019
Processed foods imports, total [1,2]	**Metric tons**	**11,054,749**	**16,834,276**	**20,871,014**	**24,277,340**	**24,556,864**
Beer and wine	Kiloliters	2,771,174	4,078,532	4,752,894	5,294,387	5,446,239
Beer	Kiloliters	2,331,185	3,146,395	3,658,196	4,163,153	4,236,913
Wine	Kiloliters	439,989	932,137	1,094,698	1,131,234	1,209,326
Distilled spirits and other alcoholic beverages	Kiloliters	47,708	36,640	96,825	117,982	147,901
Chocolate and confectionery [2]	Metric tons	858,136	1,362,569	1,445,896	1,637,904	1,719,613
Chocolate	Metric tons	525,437	820,017	857,595	957,508	1,018,268
Sugar confectionery	Metric tons	293,105	499,236	552,216	646,082	666,967
Condiments and sauces	Metric tons	351,000	569,652	688,589	813,941	863,090
Fats and oils [2]	Metric tons	1,698,793	3,518,341	4,518,987	5,146,849	5,245,158
Olive oil	Metric tons	203,960	275,435	312,317	339,626	346,931
Soybean oil	1,000 kilograms	35,949	53,697	141,979	164,973	169,443
Vegetable oils (excl. soybean)	Metric tons	1,427,711	3,075,082	3,911,059	4,407,006	4,478,611
Food preparations [2]	Metric tons	1,111,342	2,052,605	2,610,736	3,011,398	2,994,295
Baking inputs, mixes, and types of dough [3]	Metric tons	682,340	1,097,081	1,449,035	1,725,776	1,757,036
Non-alcoholic beverages [2]	Kiloliters	3,689,991	5,552,744	6,316,792	7,268,213	6,720,732
Bottled drinks [4]	Kiloliters	555,954	1,222,531	1,853,009	2,122,146	2,152,766
Juices	Kiloliters	3,134,037	4,330,213	4,463,783	5,146,067	4,567,966
Pasta and processed cereals [2]	Metric tons	517,471	881,572	1,117,843	1,443,914	1,519,541
Breakfast cereals and other breakfast products	Metric tons	113,024	277,763	345,427	711,030	735,690
Pasta	Metric tons	316,886	367,974	453,293	473,755	495,790
Prepared/preserved meats	Metric tons	197,083	143,248	183,471	196,410	208,720
Prepared/preserved seafood	Metric tons	876,402	1,283,775	1,302,087	1,451,405	1,428,052
Processed fruit	Metric tons	865,350	1,422,793	2,013,971	2,080,606	1,931,560
Processed vegetables and pulses [2]	Metric tons	1,695,961	2,455,785	2,814,411	3,266,761	3,270,763
Frozen potato products [5]	Metric tons	527,642	725,033	836,770	1,054,750	1,030,340
Processed/prepared dairy products [2]	Metric tons	245,530	230,269	332,609	357,087	370,178
Cheese	Metric tons	188,707	138,539	197,768	176,201	179,326
Cream & powdered/condensed milk	Metric tons	18,897	33,250	43,062	49,318	44,657
Ice cream	Metric tons	9,151	30,263	24,253	29,239	29,264
Yogurt and dairy drinks	Liters	23,060	11,197	766,532	938,472	1,814,124
Snack foods	Metric tons	627,030	1,126,307	1,392,480	1,940,461	2,025,131
Baked snack foods [6]	Metric tons	480,515	899,781	1,203,116	1,718,155	1,824,556
Mixes of nuts and fruit [7]	Metric tons	92,782	156,182	97,200	108,845	97,856
Potato chips	Metric tons	23,758	40,569	49,443	56,857	56,863
Prepared peanuts and peanut butter	Metric tons	29,976	29,774	42,721	56,605	45,856
Spices	Metric tons	192,577	300,902	373,529	411,444	428,074
Syrups and sweeteners [2]	Metric tons	1,106,543	866,613	1,109,099	1,249,424	1,281,462
Fructose and fructose syrup	Metric tons	66,513	92,496	128,660	96,304	107,186
Glucose and glucose syrup	Metric tons	113,647	217,058	250,667	254,413	308,857
Processed foods exports, total [2]	**Metric tons**	**10,908,071**	**17,719,580**	**19,634,075**	**20,172,948**	**19,625,269**
Beer and wine	Kiloliters	526,828	703,995	1,037,531	1,036,027	880,980
Beer	Kiloliters	262,305	320,694	623,417	694,986	530,899
Wine	Kiloliters	264,523	383,301	414,114	341,041	350,081
Distilled spirits and other alcoholic beverages	Kiloliters	23,884	23,969	47,166	33,059	23,278
Chocolate and confectionery [2]	Metric tons	302,600	420,212	507,548	515,520	495,152
Chocolate	Metric tons	192,742	303,757	359,697	360,187	353,148
Sugar confectionery	Metric tons	98,043	108,527	139,194	147,516	134,861
Condiments and sauces	Metric tons	363,963	638,943	1,035,365	958,049	969,230
Fats and oils [2]	Metric tons	1,998,801	3,356,665	2,388,023	2,322,152	2,143,736
Soybean oil	1,000 kilograms	586,786	1,656,926	957,404	1,105,341	956,258
Vegetable oils (excl. soybean)	Metric tons	1,044,199	1,066,611	916,581	672,326	662,679
Food preparations [2]	Metric tons	2,492,061	3,397,278	4,475,534	4,959,599	4,920,091
Baking inputs, mixes, and types of dough [3]	Metric tons	1,904,460	2,280,017	3,247,709	3,727,548	3,682,873
Non-alcoholic beverages [2]	Kiloliters	1,661,547	1,617,263	1,540,424	1,129,503	1,099,923
Bottled drinks [4]	Kiloliters	487,448	636,964	752,004	615,835	628,397
Juices	Kiloliters	1,174,098	980,299	788,420	513,668	471,526
Pasta and processed cereals [2]	Metric tons	683,017	983,674	812,351	743,043	758,684
Breakfast cereals and other breakfast products	Metric tons	265,399	568,666	447,769	418,107	414,205
Pasta	Metric tons	102,295	181,765	208,630	174,235	176,216
Prepared/preserved meats	Metric tons	313,841	643,614	733,100	758,065	656,775
Prepared/preserved seafood	Metric tons	434,173	457,886	499,510	463,022	412,402
Processed fruit	Metric tons	388,844	571,165	619,759	512,772	488,595
Processed vegetables and pulses [2]	Metric tons	1,272,076	1,679,157	2,376,787	2,387,309	2,392,902
Frozen potato products [5]	Metric tons	568,709	790,640	1,047,741	1,079,769	1,163,799
Processed/prepared dairy products [2]	Metric tons	398,655	1,179,545	1,441,155	1,764,597	1,628,358
Cheese	Metric tons	47,760	173,327	316,885	347,505	356,526
Cream & powdered/condensed milk	Metric tons	114,847	466,853	612,493	777,019	757,226
Ice cream	Metric tons	41,652	35,680	69,668	74,735	72,370
Snack foods	Metric tons	490,079	784,168	1,026,988	1,009,997	1,001,660
Baked snack foods [6]	Metric tons	274,577	476,137	658,300	662,348	684,102
Mixes of nuts and fruit [7]	Metric tons	72,748	160,303	187,305	159,157	141,269
Potato chips	Metric tons	106,040	86,510	90,800	93,113	97,357
Prepared peanuts and peanut butter	Metric tons	36,713	61,218	90,583	95,379	78,932
Soups	1,000 kilograms	97,212	140,420	172,054	191,792	255,913
Syrups and sweeteners [2]	Metric tons	726,427	2,525,583	2,386,299	2,342,997	2,197,729
Fructose and fructose syrup	Metric tons	322,904	1,395,278	1,339,450	1,382,958	1,292,452
Glucose and glucose syrup	Metric tons	209,686	738,966	521,434	458,352	423,719
Molasses	Kiloliters	199,070	203,841	61,713	28,197	39,275

[1] Imports for consumption. Excludes merchandise entered into bonded warehouses of Foreign Trade Zones under Customs custody; see source for details. [2] Includes commodities not shown separately. [3] Includes pudding. [4] Includes soda, juice mixes, beer, milk-based drinks, etc. [5] Includes French fries. [6] Pastries, pretzels, corn chips, etc. [7] Includes packaged and microwaveable popcorn.

Source: U.S. Department of Agriculture, Foreign Agricultural Service, "Global Agricultural Trade System," <https://apps.fas.usda.gov/gats/default.aspx>, accessed August 2020.

Section 29
Puerto Rico and the Island Areas

This section presents summary economic and social statistics for Puerto Rico, the U.S. Virgin Islands, Guam, American Samoa, and the Northern Mariana Islands. Primary sources include the decennial censuses of population and housing and the annual Puerto Rico Community Survey conducted by the U.S. Census Bureau; County Business Patterns and other Census Bureau publications and databases; and the *National Vital Statistics Reports* (NSVR) series, issued by the National Center for Health Statistics.

Jurisdiction—The United States gained jurisdiction over these areas as follows: the islands of Puerto Rico and Guam, surrendered by Spain in December 1898, were ceded to the United States by the Treaty of Paris, ratified in 1899. Puerto Rico became a commonwealth on July 25, 1952, thereby achieving a high degree of local autonomy under its own constitution. The U.S. Virgin Islands, comprising approximately 50 islands and cays, was purchased by the United States from Denmark in 1917. American Samoa, a group of seven islands, was acquired in accordance with a convention among the United States, Great Britain, and Germany, ratified in 1900 (Swains Island was annexed in 1925). By an agreement approved by the United Nations Security Council and the United States, the Northern Mariana Islands, previously under Japanese mandate, was administered by the United States between 1947 and 1986 under the United Nations trusteeship system. The Northern Mariana Islands became a U.S. commonwealth in 1986.

Censuses—Because characteristics of Puerto Rico and the Island Areas differ, the presentation of census data for them is not uniform. The 1960 Census of Population covered all the territories listed above except the Northern Mariana Islands (their census was conducted in April 1958 by the Office of the High

Commissioner of the Trust Territory of the Pacific Islands), while the 1960 Census of Housing excluded American Samoa. The 1970, 1980, 1990, 2000, and 2010 censuses of population and housing covered all five areas. Beginning in 1967, Congress authorized the Economic Censuses, to be taken at 5-year intervals, for years ending in "2" and "7." Prior economic censuses were conducted in Puerto Rico for 1949, 1954, 1958, and 1963 and in Guam and the U.S. Virgin Islands for 1958 and 1963. In 1967, the census of construction industries was added for the first time in Puerto Rico; in 1972, the U.S. Virgin Islands and Guam were covered; and in 1982, the Economic Census was taken for the first time for the Northern Mariana Islands. Agricultural censuses have been conducted with increasing regularity in Puerto Rico since 1910, in the U.S. Virgin Islands since 1917, and in Guam and American Samoa since 1920; the first agricultural census in the Northern Mariana Islands was conducted in 1970.

Puerto Rico Community Survey—The Puerto Rico Community Survey (PRCS) began in 2005 and was an important element in the Census Bureau's re-engineered 2010 census plan. The American Community Survey (ACS) is the equivalent of the PRCS for the United States (50 states and District of Columbia). The PRCS collects and produces population and housing information every year instead of every 10 years. About 36,000 households are surveyed each year from across every municipio in Puerto Rico.

Information in other sections—In addition to the statistics presented in this section, other data on Puerto Rico and the island areas are included in many tables showing distribution by states in various sections of the *Abstract*. See "Puerto Rico" and "Island Areas of the U.S." in the Index.

Selected Island Areas of the United States

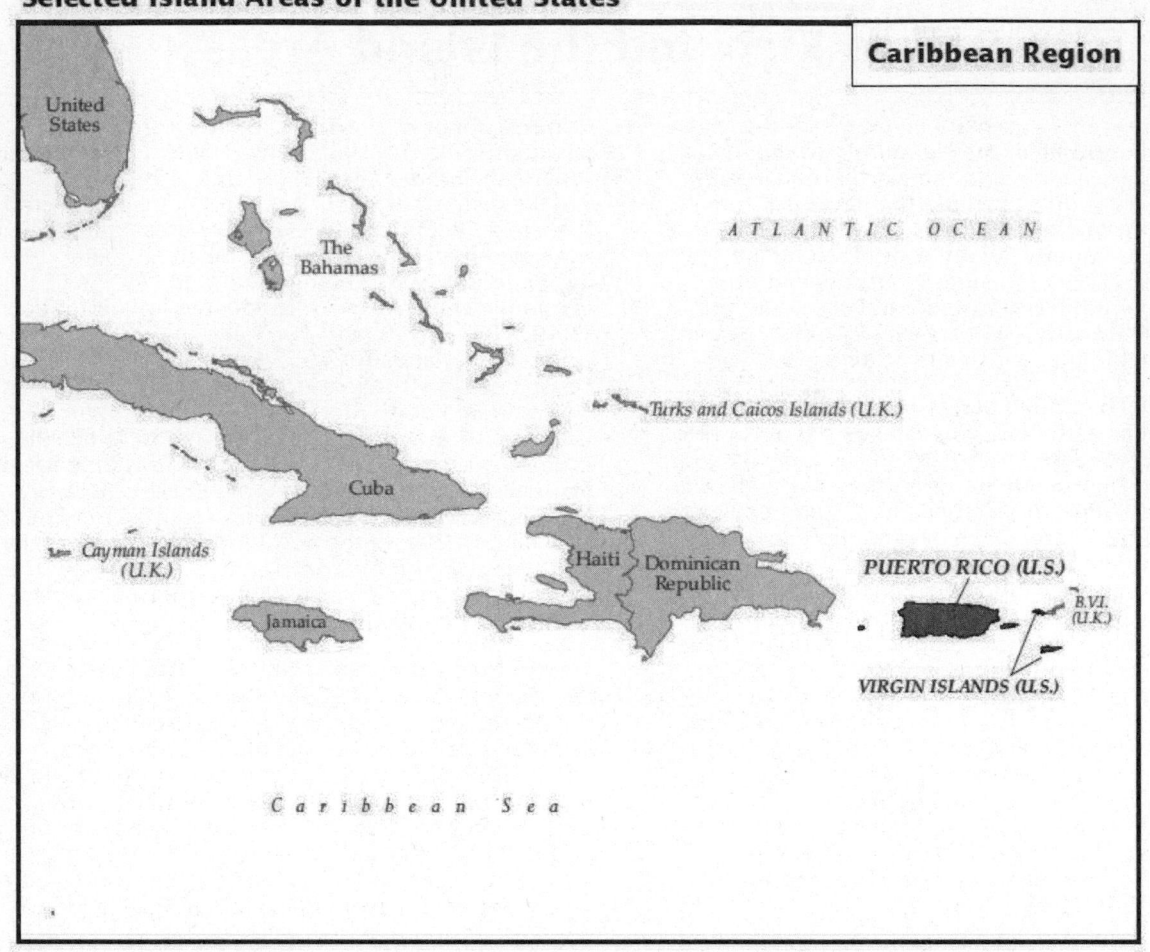

Caribbean Region

United States

ATLANTIC OCEAN

The Bahamas

Turks and Caicos Islands (U.K.)

Cuba

Cayman Islands (U.K.)

Haiti Dominican Republic

Jamaica

PUERTO RICO (U.S.)

B.V.I. (U.K.)

VIRGIN ISLANDS (U.S.)

Caribbean Sea

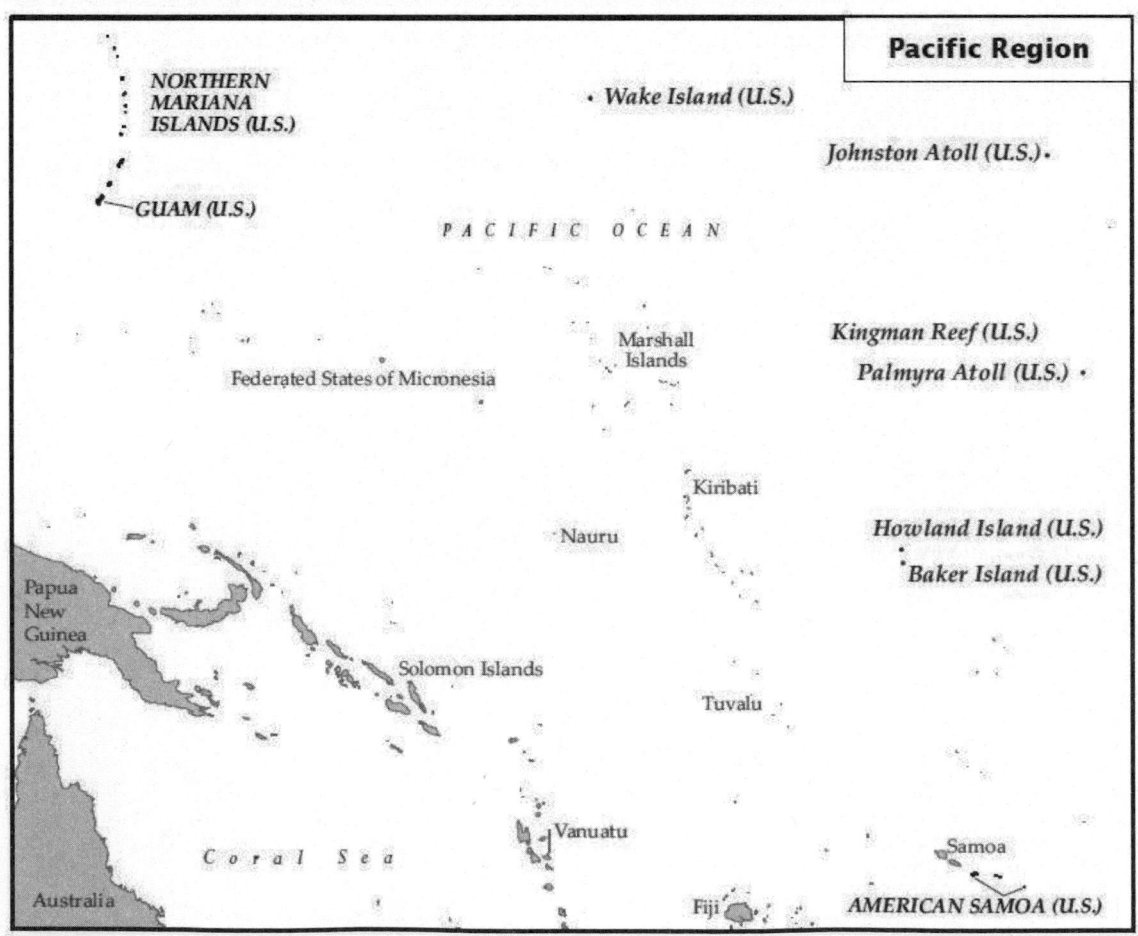

Pacific Region

NORTHERN MARIANA ISLANDS (U.S.)

Wake Island (U.S.)

Johnston Atoll (U.S.)

GUAM (U.S.)

PACIFIC OCEAN

Federated States of Micronesia

Marshall Islands

Kingman Reef (U.S.)

Palmyra Atoll (U.S.)

Kiribati

Nauru

Howland Island (U.S.)

Baker Island (U.S.)

Papua New Guinea

Solomon Islands

Tuvalu

Vanuatu

Samoa

Coral Sea

Australia

Fiji

AMERICAN SAMOA (U.S.)

Table 1333. Estimated and Projected Resident Population of Puerto Rico and Island Areas: 2000 to 2040

[In thousands (58 represents 58,000). Population as of July 1. Population data generally are de facto figures for the present territory. Data are adjusted to the 2010 Census of Population. See text, Section 30, for general comments regarding the data. For details of methodology, coverage, and reliability, see source]

Area	2000	2005	2010	2015	2018	2019	2020	Projected 2030	2035	2040
American Samoa...............	58	57	56	53	51	50	49	43	39	36
Guam...........................	155	160	163	166	168	168	168	169	168	166
Northern Mariana Islands......	70	68	55	53	52	52	51	48	47	44
Puerto Rico....................	3,811	3,822	3,722	3,473	3,295	3,240	3,189	2,809	2,631	2,449
Virgin Islands..................	109	108	108	108	107	107	106	100	95	90

Source: U.S. Census Bureau, "International Data Base (IDB)," <https://www.census.gov/data-tools/demo/idb/informationGateway.php>, accessed April 2020.

Table 1334. Births, Deaths, and Infant Deaths for Puerto Rico and the Island Areas: 2000 to 2018

[Births, deaths, and infant deaths by place of residence. Rates for 2000 and 2010 based on population enumerated as of April 1; for other years, on population estimated as of July 1]

Area and year	Births Number	Rate [1]	Deaths Number	Rate [2]	Infant deaths Number	Rate [3]
Puerto Rico:						
2000.........................	59,333	15.6	28,365	7.4	574	9.7
2010.........................	42,153	11.3	29,153	7.8	341	8.1
2015.........................	31,157	9.0	28,085	8.1	218	7.0
2017.........................	24,310	7.3	30,777	9.2	163	6.7
2018.........................	21,424	6.7	(NA)	(NA)	(NA)	(NA)
Guam:						
2000.........................	3,766	24.2	648	4.2	22	5.8
2010.........................	3,416	21.4	857	5.4	48	14.1
2015.........................	3,366	20.8	985	6.1	47	14.0
2017.........................	3,297	19.7	990	5.9	24	7.3
2018.........................	3,165	18.9	(NA)	(NA)	(NA)	(NA)
Virgin Islands:						
2000.........................	1,564	14.4	641	5.9	21	13.4
2010.........................	1,600	15.1	715	6.7	13	(B)
2015.........................	1,325	12.8	673	6.5	4	(B)
2017.........................	(NA)	(NA)	707	6.6	10	(B)
2018.........................	(NA)	(NA)	(NA)	(NA)	(NA)	(NA)
American Samoa:						
2000.........................	1,731	30.0	219	3.8	11	(B)
2010.........................	1,234	22.2	224	4.0	14	(B)
2015.........................	1,078	19.8	303	5.6	10	(B)
2017.........................	977	19.0	304	5.9	12	(B)
2018.........................	(NA)	(NA)	(NA)	(NA)	(NA)	(NA)
Northern Marianas:						
2000.........................	1,431	20.5	136	2.0	11	(B)
2010.........................	1,072	20.0	174	3.3	4	(B)
2015.........................	427	8.2	223	4.3	5	(B)
2017.........................	363	6.9	232	4.4	8	(B)
2018.........................	566	10.9	(NA)	(NA)	(NA)	(NA)

B Base figure too small to meet statistical standards of reliability. NA Not available. [1] Birth rates are births per 1,000 women of child-bearing age. [2] Death rates are deaths per 1,000 population. [3] Infant death rates are infant deaths (under 1 year old) per 1,000 live births.

Source: U.S. National Center for Health Statistics, National Vital Statistics Reports (NVSR), *Births: Final Data for 2018*, Vol. 68, No. 13, November 2019, and earlier reports; and *Deaths: Final Data for 2017*, Vol. 68, No. 9, June 2019, and earlier reports. See also <http://www.cdc.gov/nchs/nvss.htm>.

Table 1335. Public Elementary and Secondary Schools by Island Area: 2017

[Enrollment and staff are for Fall of year shown. Revenues and expenditures are for school year ending in year shown]

Item	Puerto Rico	Guam	U.S. Virgin Islands	American Samoa	Northern Marianas
Enrollment..	346,096	30,112	10,868	12,620	[2] 10,638
Elementary (pre-kindergarten to grade 8 and ungraded).......	238,807	20,227	7,427	8,877	[2] 7,340
Secondary (grades 9 to 12 and ungraded).....................	107,289	9,885	3,441	3,743	[2] 3,298
Total staff (Fall)..	39,301	3,852	2,238	[1] 1,869	[2] 876
School district staff.....................................	1,644	332	75	[1] 186	[2] 98
School staff..	31,570	3,226	1,668	[1] 1,364	[2] 679
Teachers...	28,039	2,202	1,066	[1] 971	[2] 417
Student support staff.....................................	1,607	126	63	[1] 218	[2] 22
Other support services staff..............................	4,480	168	432	[1] 101	[2] 77
Revenues, total [4] ($1,000)...............................	2,819,791	332,552	193,314	73,876	87,683
Current expenditures [5] ($1,000)..........................	2,789,459	298,340	171,521	65,490	87,920
Per pupil [5] (dollars)...................................	7,639	9,700	13,000	[1] 3,481	[3] 5,886

[1] 2006 data. [2] 2013 data. [3] 2014 data. [4] Includes federal, territorial, local, and private revenues. [5] Includes current expenditures only, and excludes capital expenditures, interest on school debt, community services, private school programs, adult education, and other expenditures not directly allocable to public school operations.

Source: U.S. National Center for Education Statistics, *Digest of Education Statistics*, "Advance Release of Selected 2019 Digest Tables," <http://www.nces.ed.gov/programs/digest/>, accessed July 2020.

Table 1336. Puerto Rico—Selected Social, Demographic, and Housing Characteristics: 2010 and 2018

[The Puerto Rico Community Survey universe includes the household population and the population living in institutions, college dormitories, and other group quarters. Based on a sample and subject to sampling variability; see text, this section and Appendix III]

Characteristic	2010 Number	2010 Percent	2018 Number	2018 Percent
Total population..........	**3,722,133**	**100.0**	**3,195,153**	**100.0**
SEX				
Male..........	1,785,266	48.0	1,520,415	47.6
Female..........	1,936,867	52.0	1,674,738	52.4
AGE				
Under 5 years..........	223,247	6.0	125,796	3.9
5 to 9 years..........	236,531	6.4	167,470	5.2
10 to 14 years..........	268,378	7.2	181,046	5.7
15 to 19 years..........	284,254	7.6	210,051	6.6
20 to 24 years..........	264,790	7.1	222,760	7.0
25 to 34 years..........	482,756	13.0	381,445	11.9
35 to 44 years..........	487,539	13.1	396,979	12.4
45 to 54 years..........	486,273	13.1	422,128	13.2
55 to 59 years..........	219,460	5.9	214,899	6.7
60 to 64 years..........	223,184	6.0	211,363	6.6
65 to 74 years..........	313,604	8.4	361,819	11.3
75 to 84 years..........	170,712	4.6	217,779	6.8
85 years and over..........	61,405	1.6	81,618	2.6
MARITAL STATUS				
Males 15 years and over..........	**1,410,023**	**100.0**	**1,276,876**	**100.0**
Never married..........	566,489	40.2	563,590	44.1
Married, not separated..........	610,584	43.3	493,596	38.7
Separated..........	39,169	2.8	27,331	2.1
Widowed..........	39,752	2.8	44,857	3.5
Divorced..........	154,029	10.9	147,502	11.6
Females 15 years and over..........	**1,583,954**	**100.0**	**1,443,965**	**100.0**
Never married..........	523,558	33.1	540,924	37.5
Married, not separated..........	601,632	38.0	489,977	33.9
Separated..........	50,458	3.2	35,566	2.5
Widowed..........	171,416	10.8	164,077	11.4
Divorced..........	236,890	15.0	213,421	14.8
HOUSEHOLDS				
Total households..........	**1,319,448**	**100.0**	**1,179,637**	**100.0**
Family households (families)..........	966,123	73.2	791,354	67.1
With own children under 18 years..........	405,933	30.8	268,032	22.7
Married-couple families..........	557,851	42.3	438,070	37.1
With own children under 18 years..........	200,406	15.2	114,276	9.7
Male householder, no spouse present..........	82,129	6.2	82,218	7.0
With own children under 18 years..........	39,285	3.0	34,827	3.0
Female householder, no spouse present..........	326,143	24.7	271,066	23.0
With own children under 18 years..........	166,242	12.6	118,929	10.1
Nonfamily households..........	353,325	26.8	388,283	32.9
Householder living alone..........	306,036	23.2	335,367	28.4
65 years and over..........	125,754	9.5	166,543	14.1
Average household size..........	2.79	(X)	2.68	(X)
Average family size..........	3.28	(X)	3.32	(X)
DISABILITY STATUS				
Total civilian noninstitutionalized population..........	**3,695,636**	**100.0**	**3,171,580**	**100.0**
With a disability..........	726,334	19.7	675,318	21.3

X Not applicable.

Source: U.S. Census Bureau, 2018 Puerto Rico Community Survey, DP02PR, "Selected Social Characteristics in Puerto Rico," and DP05, "Demographic and Housing Estimates," <data.census.gov>, accessed May 2020. See also <http://census.gov/programs-surveys/acs/about/puerto-rico-community-survey.html>.

Table 1337. Puerto Rico—Owner and Renter Occupied Housing by Household Type: 2018

[The Puerto Rico Community Survey universe includes the household population and the population living in institutions, college dormitories, and other group quarters. Based on a sample and subject to sampling variability; see text, this section and Appendix III]

Household type	Owner occupied	Renter occupied	Household type	Owner occupied	Renter occupied
Total households..........	**793,791**	**385,846**			
Family households..........	**559,199**	**232,155**	Householder 15 to 34 years..........	9,371	44,820
Married-couple family..........	361,943	76,127	Householder 35 to 64 years..........	86,373	65,137
Householder 15 to 34 years..........	12,571	19,330	Householder 65 years and over....	55,381	9,984
Householder 35 to 64 years..........	209,408	45,130	**Nonfamily households**..........	**234,592**	**153,691**
Householder 65 years and over.....	139,964	11,667	Householder living alone..........	206,540	128,827
Other family..........	197,256	156,028	Householder 15 to 34 years..........	5,815	18,791
Male householder, no wife present..	46,131	36,087	Householder 35 to 64 years..........	83,045	61,173
Householder 15 to 34 years..........	5,250	12,772	Householder 65 years and over....	117,680	48,863
Householder 35 to 64 years..........	27,831	19,237	Householder not living alone..........	28,052	24,864
Householder 65 years and over....	13,050	4,078	Householder 15 to 34 years..........	2,932	9,857
Female householder,			Householder 35 to 64 years..........	17,504	12,222
no husband present..........	151,125	119,941	Householder 65 years and over....	7,616	2,785

Source: U.S. Census Bureau, 2018 Puerto Rico Community Survey, B25011, "Tenure by Household Type and Age of Householder," <data.census.gov/>, accessed May 2020. See also <http://census.gov/programs-surveys/acs/about/puerto-rico-community-survey.html>.

Table 1338. Puerto Rico—School Enrollment and Educational Attainment by Level: 2005 to 2018

[The Puerto Rico Community Survey universe includes the household population and the population living in institutions, college dormitories, and other group quarters. Based on a sample and subject to sampling variability; see text, this section and Appendix III]

Item	2005	2010	2014	2015	2016	2017	2018
EDUCATIONAL ENROLLMENT							
Population 3 years and over enrolled in school.....	1,138,768	995,743	921,168	892,872	846,874	804,711	742,847
Nursery school, preschool..........................	69,731	55,298	55,250	52,792	48,916	45,061	35,928
Kindergarten..	52,261	45,366	37,899	37,989	36,227	33,751	27,389
Elementary school (grades 1-8)...................	486,546	414,233	362,625	340,580	320,223	307,128	289,314
High school (grades 9-12).........................	242,548	213,581	187,227	189,446	179,748	168,446	153,451
College or graduate school........................	287,682	267,265	278,167	272,065	261,760	250,325	236,765
EDUCATIONAL ATTAINMENT							
Population 25 years and over.......................	2,431,653	2,444,933	2,400,677	2,382,526	2,372,197	2,343,675	2,288,030
Less than 9th grade.................................	547,055	484,138	398,760	391,558	370,922	370,702	336,242
9th to 12th grade, no diploma....................	269,039	262,682	229,019	210,220	207,689	188,871	178,663
High school graduate (includes equivalency)......	588,130	623,709	669,936	647,581	657,523	653,789	644,702
Some college, no degree...........................	290,283	317,797	292,524	314,431	298,426	285,018	276,042
Associate's degree..................................	231,848	212,186	223,726	228,508	237,746	242,776	241,678
Bachelor's degree...................................	377,437	389,954	417,133	424,255	433,120	428,558	430,692
Graduate or professional degree..................	127,861	154,467	169,579	165,973	166,771	173,961	180,011
Percent high school graduate or higher..............	66.4	69.5	73.8	74.7	75.6	76.1	77.5
Percent bachelor's degree or higher................	20.8	22.3	24.4	24.8	25.3	25.7	26.7

Source: U.S. Census Bureau, 2018 Puerto Rico Community Survey, DP02PR, "Selected Social Characteristics in Puerto Rico," <data.census.gov>, accessed May 2020. See also <http://census.gov/programs-surveys/acs/about/puerto-rico-community-survey.html>.

Table 1339. Puerto Rico—Agricultural Summary: 1993 to 2018

[1 cuerda = 0.97 acre]

All farms	Unit	1993	1998	2002	2007	2012	2018
Farms.................................	Number	22,350	19,951	17,659	15,745	13,159	8,230
Farm land..........................	Cuerdas	826,893	865,478	690,687	557,530	584,988	487,775
Average size of farm.............	Cuerdas	37.0	43.4	39.1	35.4	44.5	59.3
Approximate land area............	Cuerdas	2,254,365	2,254,365	2,254,365	2,254,365	2,254,365	2,254,365
Proportion in farms...............	Percent	36.7	38.4	30.6	24.7	25.9	21.6
Farms by size:							
Less than 10 cuerdas.............	Number	10,413	7,759	7,943	7,502	5,129	2,213
10 to 19 cuerdas.................	Number	4,475	4,473	3,847	3,545	2,859	1,853
20 to 49 cuerdas.................	Number	3,966	4,023	3,228	2,680	2,872	1,950
50 to 99 cuerdas.................	Number	1,723	1,792	1,282	865	940	952
100 to 174 cuerdas...............	Number	820	809	590	524	563	579
175 to 259 cuerdas..............	Number	366	421	281	207	401	330
260 cuerdas or more.............	Number	587	674	488	422	395	353
Tenure of operator:							
Operators..........................	Number	22,350	19,951	17,659	15,745	13,159	8,230
Full owners......................	Number	17,759	15,620	13,693	11,402	9,362	5,474
Part owners......................	Number	2,218	2,207	2,330	1,918	1,069	948
Tenants...........................	Number	2,373	2,124	1,636	2,425	2,728	1,808
Average size of farm by operator:							
Full owners......................	Cuerdas	27	29	27	25	29	41
Part owners......................	Cuerdas	92	112	96	83	134	115
Tenants...........................	Cuerdas	63	76	61	46	61	87
Farms by type of organization:							
Individual or family...............	Number	19,911	17,887	15,843	13,958	11,938	6,886
Partnership.......................	Number	288	211	162	49	117	77
Corporation.......................	Number	382	437	595	575	738	1,147
Other.............................	Number	1,769	1,416	1,059	1,163	366	120
Farms by value of sales:							
Less than $1,000.................	Number	4,456	3,307	3,977	4,442	2,973	2,885
$1,000 to $2,499.................	Number	4,591	3,633	3,471	2,771	2,015	814
$2,500 to $4,499.................	Number	4,593	3,900	3,044	2,428	1,986	778
$5,000 to $7,499.................	Number	2,566	2,408	1,575	1,206	1,209	621
$7,500 to $9,999.................	Number	1,248	1,233	1,087	882	771	403
$10,000 to $19,999...............	Number	2,115	2,366	1,781	1,497	1,521	781
$20,000 to $39,999...............	Number	1,071	1,247	1,062	1,030	968	648
$40,000 to $59,999...............	Number	348	405	375	281	394	303
$60,000 or more.................	Number	1,362	1,452	1,287	1,208	1,322	997

Source: U.S. Department of Agriculture, National Agricultural Statistics Service (NASS), *2017 Census of Agriculture: Puerto Rico (2018), Island and Regional Data*, Geographic Area Series, Volume 1: Part 52, June 2020. See also <nass.usda.gov/Publications/AgCensus/2017/index.php>.

Table 1340. Puerto Rico—Farms and Market Value of Agricultural Products Sold: 2018

[For market value, 485,053 represents $485,053,000]

Type of product	Number of farms	Market value ($1,000)	Average value per farm (dol.)	Type of product	Number of farms	Market value ($1,000)	Average value per farm (dol.)
Total............................	**8,230**	**485,053**	**58,937**	Horticultural specialties.........	303	34,853	115,027
Crops.................................	3,877	242,419	(NA)	Grasses and other crops.......	282	11,482	40,716
Coffee............................	1,363	4,773	3,502	Livestock, poultry, and their			
Pineapples......................	90	2,977	33,077	products.........................	3,074	242,634	78,931
Plantains........................	1,353	42,272	31,243	Cattle and calves...............	2,305	37,689	16,351
Bananas.........................	801	10,830	13,521	Poultry and poultry products. ..	409	20,095	49,131
Grains............................	317	74,399	234,698	Dairy products....................	281	172,208	612,840
Root crops or tubers..............	770	8,706	11,306	Hogs and pigs....................	423	6,215	14,694
Fruits and coconuts..............	858	18,594	21,672	Aquaculture......................	37	136	3,686
Vegetables and melons [1].......	750	33,533	44,711	Other..............................	490	6,290	12,837

NA Not available. [1] Includes hydroponic crops.

Source: U.S. Department of Agriculture, National Agricultural Statistics Service (NASS), *2017 Census of Agriculture: Puerto Rico (2018), Island and Regional Data*, Geographic Area Series, Volume 1: Part 52, June 2020. See also <nass.usda.gov/Publications/AgCensus/2017/index.php>.

Table 1341. Puerto Rico—Merchandise Imports and Exports: 1980 to 2019

[In millions of dollars (9,018 represents $9,018,000,000). Data shown is trade for the San Juan, Puerto Rico Customs District. Imports are imports for consumption; see text, Section 28]

Item	1980	1990	2000	2010	2012	2013	2014	2015	2016	2017	2018	2019
Imports..........	9,018	16,200	27,006	39,766	45,407	43,811	42,768	42,288	45,833	41,950	52,896	46,588
From U.S......	5,345	10,792	15,172	20,641	19,808	20,314	20,848	22,882	25,151	23,160	26,994	23,560
From other....	3,673	5,408	11,834	19,125	25,599	23,497	21,920	19,406	20,682	18,789	25,902	23,028
Exports..........	6,576	20,402	43,191	67,347	58,646	61,632	66,746	70,621	71,976	64,278	62,525	64,344
To U.S..........	5,643	17,915	38,335	47,630	42,308	44,229	49,194	53,281	56,136	51,287	48,508	48,052
To other.......	933	2,487	4,856	19,717	16,337	17,404	17,552	17,339	15,840	12,991	14,018	16,292

Source: U.S. Census Bureau, Foreign Trade Division, *U.S. Trade with Puerto Rico and U.S. Possessions* (FT 895), 2019 and earlier reports; *U.S. Merchandise Trade: Selected Highlights* (FT 920), December 2011 and earlier reports; and "USA Trade Online," <usatrade.census.gov/>, accessed July 2020.

Table 1342. Puerto Rico—Business Summary by Industry: 2016 and 2017

[Payroll in millions of dollars (17,315.9 represents $17,315,900,000). Covers establishments with payroll. Excludes self-employed individuals, employees of private households, railroad employees, agricultural production employees, and most government employees. For statement on methodology, see Appendix III]

Industry	NAICS code [1]	Establishments 2016	Establishments 2017	Paid employees [2] 2016	Paid employees [2] 2017	Annual payroll (mil. dol.) 2016	Annual payroll (mil. dol.) 2017
Total, all industries.................	**(X)**	**43,620**	**43,688**	**677,974**	**676,266**	**17,315.9**	**17,228.6**
Agriculture, forestry, fishing and hunting..........	11	14	12	172	123	1.4	1.1
Mining, quarrying, and oil and gas extraction.....	21	43	39	516	477	10.7	9.1
Utilities...................................	22	26	29	344	342	21.7	20.7
Construction..............................	23	1,773	1,734	24,510	20,481	527.9	471.4
Manufacturing............................	31–33	1,730	1,749	73,706	74,237	2,885.2	2,854.2
Wholesale trade.........................	42	1,986	1,956	29,568	29,782	1,129.0	1,099.4
Retail trade..............................	44–45	9,569	9,326	130,558	130,091	2,388.4	2,363.6
Transportation and warehousing..................	48–49	988	995	14,312	15,053	414.8	441.5
Information...............................	51	681	703	18,019	17,542	749.7	747.5
Finance and insurance.............................	52	1,814	1,758	31,708	32,227	1,432.4	1,468.6
Real estate and rental and leasing...............	53	1,581	1,633	10,414	11,935	257.5	294.4
Professional, scientific, and technical services. ..	54	4,327	4,442	32,389	33,232	1,218.9	1,273.3
Management of companies and enterprises......	55	102	107	7,129	6,690	341.3	320.3
Administrative, support, waste management and remediation services........................	56	1,928	1,954	77,062	74,818	1,469.2	1,462.5
Educational services........................	61	920	841	40,866	40,406	853.9	803.3
Health care and social assistance.................	62	7,646	7,682	84,261	83,975	2,065.3	2,043.9
Arts, entertainment, and recreation.................	71	452	468	3,543	4,042	71.4	73.3
Accommodation and food services...............	72	4,434	4,706	79,246	82,139	1,100.3	1,128.5
Other services (except public administration). ...	81	3,313	3,289	18,841	18,171	363.8	342.7
Industries not classified............................	99	293	265	810	503	12.9	9.3

X Not applicable. [1] Data for 2016 based on the North American Industry Classification System (NAICS) 2012; data for 2017 based on NAICS 2017. See text, Section 15. [2] Covers full- and part-time employees who are on the payroll in the pay period including March 12.

Source: U.S. Census Bureau, County Business Patterns, "County Business Patterns by Legal Form of Organization and Employment Size Class for U.S., States, and Selected Geographies," <http://data.census.gov>, accessed December 2019. See also <https://www.census.gov/programs-surveys/cbp.html>.

Table 1343. Guam, Virgin Islands, Northern Mariana Islands, and American Samoa—Economic Summary by Sector: 2017

[Sales and payroll in millions of dollars (8,465 represents $8,465,000,000). Data for establishments with annual payroll. Based on the 2017 Economic Census of Island Areas; see Appendix III]

Kind of business	Guam	Virgin Islands	Northern Mariana Islands	American Samoa	Kind of business	Guam	Virgin Islands	Northern Mariana Islands	American Samoa
Total: [1]					Paid employees [2]	3,074	872	797	293
Establishments........	3,508	2,419	1,742	511	Retail trade:				
Sales..................	8,465	5,836	3,616	1,080	Establishments........	680	489	332	190
Annual payroll..........	1,630	1,018	420	144	Sales..................	2,064	1,205	460	292
Paid employees [2]....	60,539	30,506	22,652	8,767	Annual payroll..........	223	128	45	23
Construction:					Paid employees [2]....	10,073	6,118	2,910	1,759
Establishments........	358	137	108	33	Professional, scientific,				
Sales..................	662	146	146	34	& technical services:				
Annual payroll..........	168	47	34	9	Establishments......	256	254	112	25
Paid employees [2].....	5,501	1,298	2,803	562	Sales..................	336	240	53	18
Manufacturing:					Annual payroll..........	116	59	14	5
Establishments........	58	52	46	46	Paid employees [2]....	2,723	1,134	899	231
Sales..................	96	175	49	390	Accommodation &				
Annual payroll..........	25	26	10	36	food services:				
Paid employees [2].....	942	601	523	2,506	Establishments........	557	304	206	52
Wholesale trade:					Sales..................	1,083	520	341	35
Establishments........	228	62	88	23	Annual payroll..........	267	150	72	7
Sales..................	1,016	527	350	125	Paid employees [2]....	15,121	6,737	4,710	800
Annual payroll........	88	47	14	5					

[1] Includes other industries, not shown separately. [2] For pay period including March 12.

Source: U.S. Census Bureau, Economic Census of the Island Areas, Table IA1700BASIC01, "Geographic Area Series: Summary Statistics for American Samoa, Commonwealth of the Northern Mariana Islands, Guam, Puerto Rico, and U.S. Virgin Islands: 2017," <data.census.gov/>, accessed April 2020.

Table 1344. Virgin Islands—Business Summary by Industry: 2016 and 2017

[Payroll in thousands of dollars (986,079 represents $986,079,000). Covers establishments with payroll. Excludes self-employed individuals, employees of private households, railroad employees, agricultural production employees, and most government employees. For statement on methodology, see Appendix III]

Industry	NAICS code [1]	Establishments 2016	Establishments 2017	Paid employees [2] 2016	Paid employees [2] 2017	Annual payroll ($1,000) 2016	Annual payroll ($1,000) 2017
Total, all industries......................	(X)	**2,528**	**2,517**	**29,598**	**29,823**	**986,079**	**971,148**
Agriculture, forestry, fishing and hunting................	11	1	(NA)	([3])	(NA)	(D)	(NA)
Mining, quarrying, and oil and gas extraction..........	21	3	3	([3])	([4])	(D)	(S)
Utilities...	22	5	5	47	43	2,841	2,828
Construction..	23	154	150	1,348	1,401	50,231	66,491
Manufacturing..	31-33	46	46	585	650	26,002	37,243
Wholesale trade..	42	60	60	630	675	27,245	29,471
Retail trade...	44-45	508	499	6,262	6,222	137,206	130,704
Transportation and warehousing........................	48-49	113	115	1,749	1,787	54,015	54,768
Information...	51	45	46	720	741	34,554	32,488
Finance and insurance..................................	52	119	120	1,118	1,090	67,835	64,828
Real estate and rental and leasing......................	53	204	196	1,127	1,052	44,865	41,759
Professional, scientific, and technical services........	54	225	229	918	1,205	54,375	80,213
Management of companies and enterprises...........	55	7	7	84	88	5,343	4,991
Administrative, support, waste management and remediation services.............................	56	155	161	2,142	1,889	86,377	53,848
Educational services..................................	61	33	32	643	637	18,595	18,127
Health care and social assistance......................	62	248	239	3,116	3,268	140,516	136,205
Arts, entertainment, and recreation.....................	71	51	48	609	686	14,455	13,921
Accommodation and food services.....................	72	305	315	7,239	7,157	182,638	169,139
Other services (except public administration)..........	81	222	228	1,200	1,123	36,372	31,011
Industries not classified...............................	99	24	17	46	54	918	887

X Not applicable. D Withheld to avoid disclosing data for individual companies; data are included in total. NA Not available. S Withheld because data did not meet publication standards. [1] Data for 2016 based on the North American Industry Classification System (NAICS) 2012; data for 2017 based on NAICS 2017. See text, Section 15. [2] Covers full- and part-time employees who are on the payroll in the pay period including March 12. [3] 0 to 19 employees. [4] 20 to 99 employees.

Source: U.S. Census Bureau, County Business Patterns, "County Business Patterns by Legal Form of Organization and Employment Size Class for U.S., States, and Selected Geographies," <http://data.census.gov>, accessed December 2019. See also <https://www.census.gov/programs-surveys/cbp.html>.

Table 1345. Guam—Business Summary by Industry: 2016 and 2017

[Payroll in thousands of dollars (1,522,834 represents $1,522,834,000). Covers establishments with payroll. Excludes self-employed individuals, employees of private households, railroad employees, agricultural production employees, and most government employees. For statement on methodology, see Appendix III]

Industry	NAICS code [1]	Establishments		Paid employees [2]		Annual payroll ($1,000)	
		2016	2017	2016	2017	2016	2017
Total, all industries.................	**(X)**	**3,504**	**3,567**	**59,032**	**60,058**	**1,522,834**	**1,609,731**
Agriculture, forestry, fishing and hunting............	11	3	(NA)	([3])	(NA)	78	(NA)
Mining, quarrying, and oil and gas extraction......	21	1	(NA)	([3])	(NA)	(D)	(NA)
Utilities.................	22	4	4	66	65	2,863	3,094
Construction..........	23	357	355	5,696	4,996	141,633	153,993
Manufacturing..........	31-33	52	55	885	805	22,090	20,140
Wholesale trade..........	42	205	209	3,007	3,087	80,716	87,543
Retail trade..........	44-45	683	697	9,930	10,149	230,025	233,510
Transportation and warehousing..........	48-49	92	89	2,649	2,714	100,471	107,618
Information..........	51	50	48	1,247	1,770	46,428	73,026
Finance and insurance..........	52	127	128	2,161	2,236	95,677	97,117
Real estate and rental and leasing..........	53	278	288	2,188	2,469	57,487	59,740
Professional, scientific, and technical services....	54	261	252	2,718	2,698	117,701	118,143
Management of companies and enterprises.......	55	8	8	75	83	3,263	3,144
Administrative, support, waste managment and remediation services..........	56	166	179	4,314	4,530	92,250	92,501
Educational services..........	61	63	61	1,249	1,287	27,130	27,104
Health care and social assistance..........	62	211	218	4,363	4,677	175,057	195,114
Arts, entertainment, and recreation..........	71	71	76	1,209	1,204	22,005	23,243
Accommodation and food services..........	72	522	554	14,643	14,739	247,552	252,588
Other services (except public administration)......	81	284	283	2,411	2,374	57,266	58,859
Industries not classified..........	99	66	60	214	168	3,002	3,004

X Not applicable. D Withheld to avoid disclosing data for individual companies; data are included in total. NA Not available. [1] Data for 2016 based on the North American Industry Classification System (NAICS) 2012; data for 2017 based on NAICS 2017. See text, Section 15. [2] Covers full- and part-time employees who are on the payroll in the pay period including March 12. [3] 0 to 19 employees.

Source: U.S. Census Bureau, County Business Patterns, "County Business Patterns by Legal Form of Organization and Employment Size Class for U.S., States, and Selected Geographies," <http://data.census.gov>, accessed December 2019. See also <https://www.census.gov/programs-surveys/cbp.html>.

Table 1346. Northern Marianas—Business Summary by Industry: 2016 and 2017

[Payroll in thousands of dollars (362,360 represents $362,360,000). Covers establishments with payroll. Excludes self-employed individuals, employees of private households, railroad employees, agricultural production employees, and most government employees. For statement on methodology, see Appendix III]

Industry	NAICS code [1]	Establishments		Paid employees [2]		Annual payroll ($1,000)	
		2016	2017	2016	2017	2016	2017
Total, all industries.................	**(X)**	**1,759**	**1,782**	**18,374**	**21,296**	**362,360**	**425,090**
Agriculture, forestry, fishing and hunting............	11	1	3	([3])	13	(D)	231
Mining, quarrying, and oil and gas extraction......	21	1	(NA)	([4])	(NA)	(D)	(NA)
Utilities.................	22	4	4	([5])	([5])	(D)	(S)
Construction..........	23	96	111	1,399	2,334	29,205	31,378
Manufacturing..........	31-33	45	45	550	477	9,255	8,468
Wholesale trade..........	42	92	89	762	778	13,230	14,321
Retail trade..........	44-45	349	350	2,577	2,775	42,260	46,280
Transportation and warehousing..........	48-49	53	59	1,057	1,191	20,754	23,613
Information..........	51	22	20	397	452	10,967	11,726
Finance and insurance..........	52	48	49	285	298	8,009	8,240
Real estate and rental and leasing..........	53	161	166	662	689	9,665	11,246
Professional, scientific, and technical services....	54	110	104	534	471	13,306	13,844
Management of companies and enterprises.......	55	6	6	37	45	977	1,160
Administrative, support, waste management and remediation services..........	56	162	159	1,655	1,768	25,422	27,442
Educational services..........	61	61	61	391	341	7,235	8,548
Health care and social assistance..........	62	45	44	1,016	1,066	36,553	39,249
Arts, entertainment, and recreation..........	71	57	56	500	434	8,158	7,344
Accommodation and food services..........	72	202	210	5,255	6,792	102,829	145,072
Other services (except public administration)......	81	162	160	636	688	9,729	10,471
Industries not classified..........	99	82	84	202	209	2,363	2,499

X Not applicable. D Withheld to avoid disclosing data for individual companies; data are included in total. NA Not available. S Withheld because estimate did not meet publication standards. [1] Data for 2016 based on the North American Industry Classification System (NAICS) 2012; data for 2017 based on NAICS 2017. See text, Section 15. [2] Covers full- and part-time employees who are on the payroll in the pay period including March 12. [3] 0 to 19 employees. [4] 20 to 99 employees. [5] 250 to 499 employees.

Source: U.S. Census Bureau, County Business Patterns, "County Business Patterns by Legal Form of Organization and Employment Size Class for U.S., States, and Selected Geographies," <http://data.census.gov>, accessed December 2019. See also <https://www.census.gov/programs-surveys/cbp.html>.

Table 1347. American Samoa—Business Summary by Industry: 2016 and 2017

[Payroll in thousands of dollars (144,226 represents $144,226,000). Covers establishments with payroll. Excludes self-employed individuals, employees of private households, railroad employees, agricultural production employees, and most government employees. For statement on methodology, see Appendix III]

Industry	NAICS code [1]	Establishments 2016	Establishments 2017	Paid employees [2] 2016	Paid employees [2] 2017	Annual payroll ($1,000) 2016	Annual payroll ($1,000) 2017
Total, all industries.................................	(X)	504	517	8,506	8,203	144,226	124,651
Agriculture, forestry, fishing and hunting..........	11	2	(NA)	([3])	(NA)	(D)	(NA)
Construction...	23	33	31	502	441	8,512	8,037
Manufacturing...	31-33	40	43	3,190	2,946	51,017	33,085
Wholesale trade.......................................	42	26	24	268	264	5,785	5,014
Retail trade..	44-45	172	177	1,515	1,530	21,398	21,506
Transportation and warehousing....................	48-49	27	24	343	330	4,893	4,816
Information..	51	7	6	185	163	4,253	4,426
Finance and insurance...............................	52	11	15	109	105	2,685	2,645
Real estate and rental and leasing................	53	15	15	80	83	1,270	1,175
Professional, scientific, and technical services...	54	26	24	169	171	5,355	5,514
Management of companies and enterprises.....	55	2	3	([3])	11	(D)	101
Administrative, support, waste management and remediation services.........................	56	21	22	119	173	1,868	2,027
Educational services..................................	61	5	5	168	147	1,994	2,000
Health care and social assistance.................	62	16	16	([4])	([4])	(D)	(S)
Arts, entertainment, and recreation................	71	1	(NA)	([3])	(NA)	(D)	(NA)
Accommodation and food services................	72	44	51	576	671	7,176	6,833
Other services (except public administration)....	81	47	46	384	342	4,982	4,946
Industries not classified..............................	99	9	11	29	33	306	496

X Not applicable. D Withheld to avoid disclosing data for individual companies; data are included in total. NA Not available. S Withheld because estimate did not meet publication standards. [1] Data for 2016 based on the North American Industry Classification System (NAICS) 2012; data for 2017 based on NAICS 2017. See text, Section 15. [2] Covers full- and part-time employees who are on the payroll in the pay period including March 12. [3] 0 to 19 employees. [4] 500 to 999 employees.

Source U.S. Census Bureau, County Business Patterns, "County Business Patterns by Legal Form of Organization and Employment Size Class for U.S., States, and Selected Geographies," <http://data.census.gov>, accessed December 2019. See also <https://www.census.gov/programs-surveys/cbp.html>.

Table 1348. Occupational Employment and Average Annual Wages in Guam, Puerto Rico, and Virgin Islands: 2019

[The Occupational Employment Survey (OES) program conducts a semiannual mail survey designed to produce estimates of employment and wages for specific occupations. Excludes self-employed persons. For more details on the survey, see <https://www.bls.gov/oes/oes_emp.htm>]

Selected occupation	SOC code [1]	Guam Employment	Guam Average annual wages [2]	Puerto Rico Employment	Puerto Rico Average annual wages [2]	Virgin Islands Employment	Virgin Islands Average annual wages [2]
Total, all occupations [3].............................	(X)	63,630	36,930	865,160	29,670	34,420	45,970
Management occupations.............................	11	5,240	70,670	39,000	76,660	3,270	87,130
Business and financial operations...................	13	2,720	55,230	43,170	40,770	1,640	58,190
Computer and mathematical occupations...........	15	700	52,680	12,110	42,880	370	60,060
Architecture and engineering........................	17	1,100	62,420	14,410	55,260	240	62,070
Life, physical, and social sciences..................	19	470	56,910	6,760	46,090	330	53,120
Community and social services......................	21	850	44,530	15,440	29,760	380	47,560
Legal occupations....................................	23	310	74,820	4,610	65,200	290	108,300
Educational instruction and library occupations.....	25	4,550	44,870	63,560	35,330	2,290	45,490
Arts, design, entertainment, sports, and media.....	27	720	38,250	6,120	35,200	170	45,680
Healthcare practitioner and technical occupations...	29	2,180	68,210	50,620	36,280	1,360	71,450
Healthcare support....................................	31	980	29,020	14,680	20,130	620	30,220
Protective service occupations......................	33	2,560	37,470	53,830	25,460	2,470	37,540
Food preparation and serving related occupations...	35	7,230	21,230	69,940	19,180	3,580	28,120
Buildings and grounds cleaning and maintenance.......................................	37	3,350	21,990	39,720	20,330	1,520	28,950
Personal care and service occupations..............	39	1,480	22,590	8,830	21,380	430	33,100
Sales and related occupations.......................	41	5,660	24,900	103,140	23,210	3,380	34,240
Office and administrative support....................	43	9,350	30,950	138,140	25,750	4,650	37,530
Farming, fishing, and forestry........................	45	170	27,470	1,700	23,280	(NA)	(NA)
Construction and extraction..........................	47	4,610	32,110	28,170	22,050	2,370	55,530
Installation, maintenance, and repair................	49	3,260	35,460	30,780	26,700	1,690	45,830
Production occupations...............................	51	1,860	30,140	57,630	24,330	780	43,620
Transportation and material moving.................	53	4,280	27,460	62,810	22,430	2,590	33,270

X Not applicable. NA Not available. [1] Office of Management and Budget's Standard Occupational Classification (SOC) is used to define occupations. SOC categorizes workers into one of over 800 detailed occupations, which are classified into 23 major occupational groups. [2] Annual wages have been calculated by multiplying the hourly mean wage by a "year-round, full-time" hours figure of 2,080 hours; for those occupations where there is not an hourly mean wage published, the annual wage has been directly calculated from the reported survey data. [3] Estimates do not sum to the total because the total may include data for occupations not shown separately. See source for more information.

Source: U.S. Bureau of Labor Statistics, "Occupational Employment Statistics," <http://www.bls.gov/oes/current/oessrcst.htm>, accessed April 2020.

This section presents statistics for the world as a whole and for many countries on a comparative basis with the United States. Data are shown for population, births and deaths, social and economic indicators, finances, agriculture, energy, climate, science and technology, communications, and military affairs.

Statistics for individual countries may be found primarily in official national publications, generally in the form of yearbooks, issued by most countries in their own national languages and expressed in their own customary units of measure. For a listing of selected publications, see Appendix I table under international statistical abstracts from a foreign agency.

For international comparisons, the United Nations Statistics Division compiles data as submitted by member countries and issues a number of summary publications, generally in English and French. Among these are the annual *Statistical Yearbook; Demographic Yearbook; Population and Vital Statistics Report; International Trade Statistics Yearbook; Energy Statistics Yearbook; Industrial Commodity Statistics Yearbook; National Accounts Statistics;* and the *Monthly Bulletin of Statistics*. Specialized agencies of the United Nations also issue international summary publications on various topics, including agricultural, labor, health, and trade statistics. Among these are *Food Outlook* and the *Statistical Pocketbook* issued by the Food and Agriculture Organization (FAO); *World Employment and Social Outlook* issued by the International Labor Organization (ILO); *World Health Statistics* issued by the World Health Organization (WHO); and the *Handbook of Statistics* issued by the Conference on Trade and Development (UNCTAD).

The U.S. Census Bureau publishes estimates and projections of key demographic measures for countries and regions of the world in its International Data Base at <census.gov/programs-surveys/international-programs.html>.

The International Monetary Fund (IMF), the World Bank, and the Organisation for Economic Co-operation and Development (OECD) also compile international statistics. The IMF publishes a series of reports related to financial data. These include *World Economic Outlook, Global Financial Stability Report*, and *Fiscal Monitor*. The World Bank publishes many reports on a wide range of topics related to international development. Three of their flagship statistical publications are *World Development Report, World Development Indicators*, and *Global Economic Prospects*. The OECD also produces numerous statistical publications in fields including economics, health, and education. Among these are the *Economic Outlook; National Accounts of OECD Countries; Science, Technology and Innovation Outlook; International Migration Outlook; Employment Outlook*; and *Education at a Glance.*

Statistical coverage and country classifications— Problems of space and availability of data limit the number of countries and the extent of statistical coverage shown. The lists of countries and territories included in individual tables are generally based on source publications and databases, as cited.

In the last three decades several important changes took place in the status of the world's nations. In 1991, the Soviet Union broke up into 15 independent countries: Armenia, Azerbaijan, Belarus, Estonia, Georgia, Kazakhstan, Kyrgyzstan, Latvia, Lithuania, Moldova, Russia, Tajikistan, Turkmenistan, Ukraine, and Uzbekistan.

Germany was reunified in 1990, when the German Democratic Republic (former East Germany) joined the Federal Republic of Germany (former West Germany) to form a single country. On January 1, 1993, Czechoslovakia was succeeded by two independent countries: the Czech Republic, now known as Czechia, and Slovakia.

Following the breakup of the Socialist Federal Republic of Yugoslavia in 1992, the United States recognized Bosnia and Herzegovina, Croatia, Slovenia, and Macedonia as independent countries. Serbia and Montenegro, both former republics of Yugoslavia, became independent of one another on May 31, 2006. This separation is reflected in the population estimates of Table 1352. On February 17, 2008, Kosovo declared its independence from Serbia. In 2019, Macedonia formally adopted the name Republic of North Macedonia.

The Treaty of Maastricht created the European Union (EU) in 1992 with 12 member countries. The EU is not a state intended to replace existing states, but it is more than just an international organization. Its member states have set up common institutions to which they delegate some of their sovereignty so that decisions on specific matters of joint interest can be made democratically at a European level. This pooling of sovereignty is also called "European integration." The EU has grown in size with successive waves of accessions in 1995, 2004, 2007, and 2013. The 27 current members of the EU are: Austria, Belgium, Bulgaria, Croatia, Cyprus, Czechia, Denmark, Estonia, Finland, France, Germany, Greece, Hungary, Ireland, Italy, Latvia, Lithuania, Luxembourg, Malta, the Netherlands, Poland, Portugal, Romania, Slovakia, Slovenia, Spain, and Sweden. In June 2016, the electorate of the United Kingdom voted to withdraw from the EU. The withdrawal became official in January of 2020.

In 1992, the EU decided to establish an economic and monetary union (EMU), with the introduction of a single European currency managed by a European Central Bank. The single currency—the euro—became a reality on January 1, 2002, when euro notes and coins replaced national currencies in 12 of the then 15 countries of the European Union (Austria, Belgium, Finland, France, Germany, Greece, Ireland, Italy, Luxembourg, the Netherlands, Portugal, and Spain). Since then, 13 additional countries have acceded to EU membership, but Cyprus, Estonia, Latvia, Lithuania, Malta, Slovakia, and Slovenia have been the only new members of the EU to adopt the euro as the national currency. In total, the euro is the official currency of 19 of the 27 EU member countries.

Elsewhere in the world, Eritrea announced its independence from Ethiopia in April 1993 and was subsequently recognized as an independent nation by the United States. In the South Pacific, the Marshall Islands, Micronesia, and Palau gained independence from the United States in 1991. In May of 2002, Timor-Leste won independence from Indonesia. The Netherlands Antilles dissolved on October 10, 2010. As a result, Curaçao and Sint Maarten became autonomous territories of the Netherlands. As of July 2011, Sudan and South Sudan became separate countries. And, in 2018, Swaziland was officially renamed Eswatini.

The population estimates and projections used in Tables 1349 through 1353, 1355, and 1356 were prepared by the U.S. Census Bureau. For each country, available data on population by age and sex, fertility, mortality, and international migration were evaluated and, where necessary, adjusted for inconsistencies and errors in the data. Comprehensive population projections were made by the cohort-component method based on an assessment of probable future trends.

Economic associations—The Organisation for European Economic Co-operation (OEEC) was originally a regional grouping of Western European countries established in 1948 for the purpose of harmonizing national economic policies and conditions. It was succeeded on September 30, 1961 by the Organisation for Economic Co-operation and Development (OECD). As of 2020, the 37 member nations of the OECD are Australia, Austria, Belgium, Canada, Chile, Colombia, Czechia, Denmark, Estonia, Finland, France, Germany, Greece, Hungary, Iceland, Ireland, Israel, Italy, Japan, Latvia, Lithuania, Luxembourg, Mexico, the Netherlands, New Zealand, Norway, Poland, Portugal, Slovak Republic, Slovenia, South Korea, Spain, Sweden, Switzerland, Turkey, the United Kingdom, and the United States. Additionally, Colombia has been invited to join and its accession is imminent.

Quality and comparability of the data—The quality and comparability of the data presented here are affected by a number of factors:

1 The year for which data are presented may not be the same for all subjects for a particular country or for a given subject for different countries, though the data shown are the most recent available. All such variations have been noted. The data shown are for calendar years except as otherwise specified.

2 The statistical bases, methods of estimating, methods of data collection, extent of coverage, precision of definition, scope of territory, and margins of error may vary for different items within a particular country, and for like items for different countries. Footnotes and headnotes to the tables describe some of the major coverage qualifications attached to the figures; considerably more detail is presented in the source publications. Many of the measures shown are merely rough indicators of magnitude.

3 Figures shown in this section for the United States may not always agree with figures shown in the preceding sections. Discrepancies may be attributable to the use of differing original sources, differences in the definition of geographic limits (the 50 states, continental U.S. only, or the U.S. including certain outlying areas and possessions), or to possible adjustments made to the U.S. figures in order to make them more comparable with figures from other countries.

International comparisons of national accounts data—To compare national accounts data for different countries, it is necessary to convert each country's data into a common unit of currency, usually the U.S. dollar. The market exchange rates, which often are used in converting national currencies, do not necessarily reflect the relative purchasing power in the various countries. It is necessary that the goods and services produced in different countries be valued consistently if the differences observed are meant to reflect real differences in the volumes of goods and services produced. The use of purchasing power parities (see Tables 1364, 1365, and 1371) instead of exchange rates is intended to achieve this objective.

The method used to present the data shown in Table 1371 is to construct volume measures directly by revaluing the goods and services sold in different countries at a common set of international prices. By dividing the ratio of the gross domestic products of two countries expressed in their own national currencies by the corresponding ratio calculated at constant international prices, it is possible to derive the implied purchasing power parity (PPP) between the two currencies concerned. PPPs show how many units of currency are needed in one country to buy the same amount of goods and services that one unit of currency will buy in the other country. For further information, see *National Accounts of OECD Countries, Main Aggregates*, issued annually by the Organisation for Economic Co-operation and Development (OECD), Paris, France.

International Standard Industrial Classification—The original version of the International Standard Industrial Classification of All Economic Activities (ISIC) was adopted in 1948. A number of countries have utilized ISIC as the basis for devising their industrial classification schemes. Substantial comparability has been attained among the industrial classification schemes of many countries, including the United States, by ensuring that national classification categories correspond to ISIC categories. The United Nations, the International Labour Organization, the Food and Agriculture Organization, and other international bodies use ISIC in publishing and analyzing statistical data. Revisions of ISIC were issued in 1958, 1968, 1989, 2002, and 2008.

Table 1349. Total World Population and Population Projections: 1980 to 2050

[4,445.4 represents 4,445,400,000. As of midyear]

Year	Population (mil.)	Average annual [1] Growth rate (percent)	Average annual [1] Population change (mil.)	Year	Population (mil.)	Average annual [1] Growth rate (percent)	Average annual [1] Population change (mil.)
1980	4,445.4	1.81	81.38	**2020**	**7,684.3**	**1.03**	**79.82**
1990	5,285.7	1.56	83.03	2025	8,077.0	0.92	74.71
1995	5,691.9	1.40	80.23	2030	8,440.0	0.82	69.59
2000	6,081.8	1.26	76.90	2035	8,779.3	0.74	65.26
2005	6,468.7	1.23	79.77	2040	9,097.4	0.67	61.07
2010	6,877.8	1.17	81.09	2045	9,393.8	0.60	56.36
2015	7,285.2	1.10	80.58	2050	9,665.3	(NA)	(NA)

NA Not available. [1] Represents change from year shown to immediate succeeding year.

Source: U.S. Census Bureau, "International Data Base (IDB)," <https://www.census.gov/programs-surveys/international-programs/data/tools.html>, accessed March 2020.

Table 1350. World Population by Continent: 1970 to 2050

[In millions, except percent (3,713.5 represents 3,713,500,000). As of midyear. For geographic classification of individual countries, see source]

Year	World	Africa	North America [1]	South America	Asia	Europe	Oceania
1970	3,713.5	366.8	320.0	190.3	2,159.2	657.9	19.2
1980	4,445.4	479.5	370.8	239.7	2,637.7	695.2	22.5
1990	5,285.7	632.7	423.0	295.4	3,182.4	725.9	26.2
2000	6,081.8	807.0	485.7	346.3	3,681.7	730.8	30.2
2010	6,877.8	1,040.8	539.5	391.5	4,130.1	740.5	35.3
2020	**7,684.3**	**1,339.5**	**589.3**	**425.5**	**4,539.6**	**749.3**	**41.1**
2030	8,440.0	1,696.0	632.9	457.5	4,861.2	746.6	45.8
2040	9,097.4	2,098.9	665.6	477.7	5,070.4	735.4	49.5
2050	9,665.3	2,533.6	688.1	486.5	5,188.0	716.4	52.6
PERCENT DISTRIBUTION							
1970	100.0	9.9	8.6	5.1	58.1	17.7	0.5
1980	100.0	10.8	8.3	5.4	59.3	15.6	0.5
1990	100.0	12.0	8.0	5.6	60.2	13.7	0.5
2000	100.0	13.3	8.0	5.7	60.5	12.0	0.5
2010	100.0	15.1	7.8	5.7	60.0	10.8	0.5
2020	**100.0**	**17.4**	**7.7**	**5.5**	**59.1**	**9.8**	**0.5**
2030	100.0	20.1	7.5	5.4	57.6	8.8	0.5
2040	100.0	23.1	7.3	5.3	55.7	8.1	0.5
2050	100.0	26.2	7.1	5.0	53.7	7.4	0.5

[1] Data for North America include Central America and Caribbean area.

Source: U.S. Census Bureau, "International Data Base (IDB)," <https://www.census.gov/programs-surveys/international-programs/data/tools.html>, accessed March 2020.

Table 1351. Population and Population Change by Development Status: 1950 to 2050

[2,557.6 represents 2,557,600,000. As of midyear. Minus sign (-) indicates decrease. "Less developed" countries include all of Africa, all of Asia except Japan, the Transcaucasian and Central Asian republics, all of Latin America and the Caribbean, and all of Oceania except Australia and New Zealand. For details on classification of individual countries, see source]

Year	Number (millions) World	Number (millions) Less developed countries	Number (millions) More developed countries	Percent of world Less developed countries	Percent of world More developed countries
POPULATION					
1950	2,557.6	1,750.6	807.1	68.4	31.6
1960	3,043.0	2,132.3	910.8	70.1	29.9
1970	3,713.5	2,709.8	1,003.6	73.0	27.0
1980	4,445.4	3,363.7	1,081.7	75.7	24.3
1990	5,285.7	4,138.6	1,147.1	78.3	21.7
2000	6,081.8	4,888.2	1,193.6	80.4	19.6
2010	6,877.8	5,639.9	1,237.9	82.0	18.0
2020	7,684.3	6,408.6	1,275.7	83.4	16.6
2030	8,440.0	7,143.4	1,296.6	84.6	15.4
2040	9,097.4	7,795.7	1,301.8	85.7	14.3
2050	9,665.3	8,371.2	1,294.1	86.6	13.4
POPULATION CHANGE					
1950 to 1960	485.4	381.7	103.7	78.6	21.4
1960 to 1970	670.4	577.6	92.9	86.2	13.8
1970 to 1980	731.9	653.9	78.1	89.3	10.7
1980 to 1990	840.3	774.8	65.4	92.2	7.8
1990 to 2000	796.1	749.6	46.5	94.2	5.8
2000 to 2010	796.0	751.7	44.3	94.4	5.6
2010 to 2020	806.5	768.7	37.8	95.3	4.7
2020 to 2030	755.8	734.8	20.9	97.2	2.8
2030 to 2040	657.4	652.3	5.1	99.2	0.8
2040 to 2050	567.9	575.5	-7.6	101.3	-1.3

Source: U.S. Census Bureau, "International Data Base (IDB)," <https://www.census.gov/programs-surveys/international-programs/data/tools.html>, accessed March 2020.

Table 1352. Population and Land Area by Country or Territory: 2000 to 2020 and Projected 2025

[6,081,773 represents 6,081,773,000. Covers countries or territories with populations of 5,000 or more in 2020. Population estimates were derived from information available as of December 2019. See text of this section for general comments concerning the data. For details of methodology, coverage, and reliability, see source. Minus sign (-) indicates decrease]

Country or territory	Mid-year population (1,000)				Popula-tion rank, 2020	Annual growth rate [1], 2010 to 2020	Popula-tion per sq. mile, 2020	Land area [2], (sq. mile)
	2000	2010	2020	2025 (P)				
World................	**6,081,773**	**6,877,807**	**7,684,292**	**8,077,007**	(X)	1.1	151	50,894,326
Afghanistan.................	22,461	29,121	36,644	41,117	39	2.3	146	251,827
Albania...................	3,158	2,987	3,075	3,105	136	0.3	291	10,578
Algeria...................	30,638	35,950	42,973	45,841	35	1.8	47	919,595
Andorra...................	65	85	86	85	200	0.1	474	181
Angola...................	15,657	22,641	32,522	38,467	43	3.6	68	481,354
Antigua and Barbuda..............	75	87	98	104	197	1.2	574	171
Argentina.................	37,336	41,358	45,479	47,334	32	1.0	43	1,056,642
Armenia.................	3,100	3,072	3,021	2,961	137	-0.2	277	10,889
Australia.................	18,836	21,840	25,466	27,026	55	1.5	9	2,966,153
Austria.................	8,113	8,448	8,859	8,987	97	0.5	278	31,832
Azerbaijan................	8,463	9,302	10,206	10,534	90	0.9	320	31,903
Bahamas, The..............	283	310	338	349	179	0.8	87	3,865
Bahrain.................	655	1,180	1,505	1,580	154	2.4	5,129	293
Bangladesh..............	128,735	146,616	162,651	170,281	8	1.0	3,236	50,259
Barbados................	274	286	295	297	182	0.3	1,774	166
Belarus.................	10,033	9,680	9,478	9,325	94	-0.2	121	78,340
Belgium.................	10,264	10,866	11,721	12,038	80	0.8	1,003	11,690
Belize.................	252	327	400	433	176	2.0	45	8,805
Benin.................	6,677	9,179	12,865	15,202	74	3.4	301	42,711
Bhutan.................	606	700	782	820	165	1.1	53	14,824
Bolivia.................	8,195	9,947	11,640	12,463	81	1.6	28	418,265
Bosnia and Herzegovina..............	3,806	3,885	3,836	3,787	130	-0.1	194	19,763
Botswana................	1,655	1,978	2,317	2,484	144	1.6	11	218,816
Brazil.................	174,315	195,834	211,716	218,259	7	0.8	66	3,227,096
Brunei.................	325	395	464	499	174	1.6	228	2,033
Bulgaria.................	7,909	7,391	6,967	6,728	106	-0.6	166	41,888
Burkina Faso..............	11,430	15,634	20,835	23,600	61	2.9	197	105,715
Burma.................	46,641	51,415	56,590	58,787	25	1.0	224	252,321
Burundi.................	6,282	9,140	11,866	14,026	77	2.6	1,197	9,915
Cabo Verde..............	430	509	583	619	173	1.4	375	1,557
Cambodia................	12,351	14,454	16,927	18,038	69	1.6	248	68,153
Cameroon................	15,837	20,900	27,745	31,816	51	2.8	152	182,514
Canada.................	31,100	34,207	37,694	39,095	38	1.0	11	3,511,023
Central African Republic..............	3,980	4,845	5,991	6,638	113	2.1	25	240,535
Chad.................	8,118	11,990	16,877	19,676	71	3.4	35	486,180
Chile.................	15,175	16,760	18,187	18,765	65	0.8	63	287,187
China.................	1,268,302	1,336,681	1,394,016	1,407,007	1	0.4	387	3,600,947
Colombia................	38,910	44,205	49,085	51,195	30	1.1	122	401,044
Comoros................	545	706	846	906	163	1.8	981	863
Congo, Republic of.............	2,939	4,238	5,293	5,948	121	2.2	40	131,854
Congo, Democratic Republic of........	52,922	72,742	101,780	119,066	15	3.4	116	875,312
Costa Rica..............	3,883	4,516	5,098	5,353	123	1.2	259	19,714
Cote d'Ivoire..............	16,686	21,719	27,481	30,639	52	2.4	224	122,782
Croatia.................	4,390	4,417	4,228	4,125	127	-0.4	196	21,612
Cuba.................	11,147	11,262	11,059	10,938	83	-0.2	261	42,402
Cyprus.................	920	1,103	1,267	1,330	157	1.4	355	3,568
Czechia.................	10,269	10,551	10,702	10,697	85	0.1	359	29,825
Denmark.................	5,337	5,547	5,869	5,995	115	0.6	358	16,384
Djibouti.................	669	741	922	1,017	162	2.2	103	8,950
Dominica................	71	73	74	74	202	0.2	256	290
Dominican Republic..............	8,231	9,433	10,500	10,978	88	1.1	563	18,656
Ecuador.................	12,446	14,791	16,905	17,868	70	1.3	158	106,889
Egypt.................	65,504	81,239	104,124	115,502	14	2.5	271	384,345
El Salvador..............	5,825	5,967	6,481	6,647	109	0.8	810	8,000
Equatorial Guinea..............	491	651	836	936	164	2.5	77	10,831
Eritrea.................	3,884	5,365	6,081	6,411	112	1.3	156	38,996
Estonia.................	1,380	1,303	1,229	1,183	158	-0.6	75	16,366
Eswatini................	1,032	1,019	1,104	1,143	160	0.8	166	6,643
Ethiopia.................	62,891	82,066	108,113	122,146	13	2.8	255	423,388
Fiji.................	805	876	936	956	161	0.7	133	7,056
Finland.................	5,169	5,355	5,572	5,631	116	0.4	47	117,304
France.................	61,255	64,941	67,848	68,860	21	0.4	274	247,270
Gabon.................	1,199	1,628	2,231	2,515	145	3.2	22	99,486
Gambia, The..............	1,357	1,755	2,174	2,369	146	2.1	556	3,907
Georgia.................	4,819	4,903	4,930	4,930	125	0.1	183	26,911
Germany.................	82,184	81,644	80,160	79,226	19	-0.2	595	134,623
Ghana.................	18,981	23,571	29,340	32,610	49	2.2	334	87,851
Greece.................	10,926	11,400	10,607	10,418	86	-0.4	210	50,443
Grenada................	102	108	113	115	190	0.5	851	133
Guatemala................	11,283	14,209	17,153	18,551	68	1.9	415	41,374
Guinea.................	7,780	9,571	12,527	14,375	76	2.7	132	94,872
Guinea-Bissau..............	1,208	1,516	1,927	2,187	151	2.4	177	10,857
Guyana.................	785	746	750	781	166	0.1	10	76,004
Haiti.................	8,279	9,553	11,068	11,750	82	1.5	1,040	10,641
Honduras................	6,367	7,991	9,235	9,797	95	1.5	214	43,201
Hungary.................	10,147	9,992	9,772	9,615	93	-0.2	282	34,598
Iceland.................	281	318	351	367	178	1.0	9	38,707
India.................	1,006,300	1,173,108	1,326,093	1,396,046	2	1.2	1,155	1,147,956
Indonesia................	214,091	243,423	267,026	276,746	4	0.9	382	699,451

See footnotes at end of table.

Country or territory	Mid-year population (1,000)				Popula-tion rank, 2020	Annual growth rate [1], 2010 to 2020	Popula-tion per sq. mile, 2020	Land area [2], (sq. mile)
	2000	2010	2020	2025 (P)				
Iran	66,482	75,035	84,923	88,969	17	1.2	144	591,352
Iraq	22,847	29,095	38,873	42,971	36	2.9	230	168,868
Ireland	3,822	4,623	5,177	5,418	122	1.1	195	26,596
Israel	6,097	7,368	8,675	9,305	98	1.6	1,045	8,300
Italy	57,784	60,749	62,403	62,591	23	0.3	549	113,568
Jamaica	2,811	2,839	2,809	2,791	140	-0.1	672	4,182
Japan	126,776	127,579	125,507	123,386	11	-0.2	892	140,728
Jordan	4,785	6,800	10,821	11,311	84	4.6	316	34,287
Kazakhstan	15,687	17,085	19,092	19,809	64	1.1	18	1,042,360
Kenya	30,922	41,765	53,528	59,466	27	2.5	244	219,746
Kiribati	85	99	112	118	191	1.2	357	313
Korea, North	22,785	24,326	25,643	26,242	54	0.5	552	46,490
Korea, South	46,841	49,258	51,835	52,566	28	0.5	1,385	37,421
Kosovo	1,700	1,815	1,933	1,999	150	0.6	460	4,203
Kuwait	1,972	2,543	2,994	3,169	138	1.6	435	6,880
Kyrgyzstan	4,937	5,410	5,965	6,219	114	1.0	81	74,055
Laos	5,397	6,368	7,447	7,972	101	1.6	84	89,112
Latvia	2,368	2,115	1,881	1,773	153	-1.2	78	24,034
Lebanon	3,834	4,492	5,470	5,397	118	2.0	1,385	3,950
Lesotho	1,916	1,920	1,969	1,971	149	0.3	168	11,720
Liberia	2,847	3,817	5,073	5,812	124	2.8	136	37,189
Libya	5,064	6,367	6,891	7,462	107	0.8	10	679,362
Liechtenstein	33	36	39	41	213	0.8	634	62
Lithuania	3,489	3,089	2,731	2,573	141	-1.2	113	24,201
Luxembourg	438	509	628	681	169	2.1	629	998
Madagascar	15,712	20,847	26,956	30,183	53	2.6	120	224,534
Malawi	11,129	15,183	21,197	24,958	60	3.3	584	36,324
Malaysia	23,151	28,275	32,652	34,683	42	1.4	257	126,895
Maldives	300	396	392	389	177	-0.1	3,406	115
Mali	10,844	14,514	19,553	22,637	62	3.0	42	471,118
Malta	394	417	457	471	175	0.9	3,748	122
Marshall Islands	53	66	78	83	201	1.7	1,115	70
Mauritania	2,501	3,205	4,005	4,425	128	2.2	10	397,955
Mauritius	1,186	1,294	1,379	1,412	156	0.6	1,760	784
Mexico	99,775	114,061	128,650	134,829	10	1.2	171	750,561
Micronesia, Federated States of	108	107	102	99	194	-0.5	378	271
Moldova	4,180	3,732	3,364	3,177	133	-1.0	265	12,699
Monaco	32	31	31	32	217	0.1	40,067	1
Mongolia	2,461	2,783	3,168	3,301	135	1.3	5	599,831
Montenegro	623	623	610	597	171	-0.2	117	5,194
Morocco	28,171	31,852	35,562	37,137	40	1.1	206	172,317
Mozambique	18,498	23,012	30,098	34,209	47	2.7	99	303,623
Namibia	1,878	2,183	2,630	2,879	142	1.9	8	317,874
Nauru	10	9	10	10	223	0.5	1,207	8
Nepal	23,487	26,664	30,328	31,566	46	1.3	548	55,348
Netherlands	15,930	16,574	17,280	17,572	67	0.4	1,321	13,086
New Zealand	3,802	4,269	4,925	5,204	126	1.4	48	102,138
Nicaragua	4,866	5,604	6,203	6,494	111	1.0	134	46,328
Niger	10,746	15,611	22,772	27,360	58	3.8	47	489,076
Nigeria	125,581	165,905	214,028	242,557	6	2.6	609	351,649
North Macedonia	2,017	2,080	2,126	2,137	147	0.2	216	9,820
Norway	4,492	4,891	5,467	5,682	119	1.1	47	117,484
Oman	2,432	2,968	3,635	3,981	131	2.0	30	119,499
Pakistan	148,400	188,339	233,501	257,222	5	2.2	785	297,637
Palau	19	21	22	22	219	0.4	122	177
Panama	2,900	3,411	3,894	4,118	129	1.3	136	28,703
Papua New Guinea	4,813	6,065	7,259	7,823	102	1.8	42	174,850
Paraguay	5,418	6,376	7,192	7,603	104	1.2	47	153,399
Peru	25,797	28,948	31,915	33,283	44	1.0	65	494,209
Philippines	76,452	93,137	109,181	117,446	12	1.6	948	115,124
Poland	38,654	38,616	38,282	37,754	37	-0.1	326	117,474
Portugal	10,361	10,663	10,303	10,201	89	-0.3	292	35,317
Qatar	640	1,719	2,444	2,563	143	3.5	546	4,473
Romania	22,447	21,959	21,303	20,872	59	-0.3	240	88,761
Russia	147,054	142,527	141,722	140,139	9	-0.1	22	6,323,482
Rwanda	8,047	9,923	12,712	13,851	75	2.5	1,335	9,524
Saint Kitts and Nevis	46	50	54	55	208	0.8	534	101
Saint Lucia	153	161	166	169	187	0.3	712	234
Saint Vincent and the Grenadines	108	104	101	100	195	-0.3	675	150
Samoa	176	192	204	210	185	0.6	187	1,089
San Marino	27	31	34	35	215	0.8	1,453	24
Sao Tome and Principe	141	176	211	227	184	1.8	567	372
Saudi Arabia	21,362	27,963	34,173	37,038	41	2.0	41	830,000
Senegal	9,469	12,323	15,736	17,581	72	2.4	212	74,336
Serbia	7,604	7,345	7,012	6,846	105	-0.5	234	29,913
Seychelles	79	88	96	99	198	0.8	546	176
Sierra Leone	3,809	5,246	6,625	7,500	108	2.3	240	27,653
Singapore	4,063	5,140	6,210	6,733	110	1.9	22,684	274
Slovakia	5,400	5,426	5,441	5,406	120	(Z)	293	18,573
Slovenia	2,011	2,084	2,103	2,094	148	0.1	270	7,780
Solomon Islands	434	559	685	747	167	2.0	63	10,805
Somalia	7,501	9,768	11,757	13,274	78	1.9	49	242,216

See footnotes at end of table.

Table 1352. Population and Land Area by Country or Territory: 2000 to 2020 and Projected 2025-Continued.

See headnote on page 850.

Country or territory	Mid-year population (1,000)				Popula-tion rank, 2020	Annual growth rate [1], 2010 to 2020	Popula-tion per sq. mile, 2020	Land area [2], (sq. mile)
	2000	2010	2020	2025 (P)				
South Africa	44,913	51,123	56,464	59,108	26	1.0	120	468,909
South Sudan [3]	6,366	9,765	10,561	13,302	87	0.8	42	248,777
Spain	40,589	46,506	50,016	51,415	29	0.7	260	192,657
Sri Lanka	19,041	21,084	22,889	23,563	57	0.8	917	24,954
Sudan [3]	27,634	34,984	45,562	51,818	31	2.6	63	718,723
Suriname	464	546	610	637	172	1.1	10	60,232
Sweden	8,924	9,432	10,202	10,587	91	0.8	64	158,431
Switzerland	7,277	7,770	8,404	8,666	100	0.8	544	15,443
Syria	16,457	22,225	19,398	24,271	63	-1.4	270	71,771
Taiwan	22,185	23,127	23,603	23,642	56	0.2	1,895	12,456
Tajikistan	6,230	7,487	8,874	9,510	96	1.7	162	54,637
Tanzania	33,193	44,288	58,553	66,905	24	2.8	171	342,009
Thailand	62,902	66,720	68,977	69,588	20	0.3	350	197,256
Timor-Leste	767	1,088	1,384	1,539	155	2.4	241	5,743
Togo	4,992	6,587	8,608	9,741	99	2.7	410	20,998
Tonga	100	106	106	105	193	(Z)	383	277
Trinidad and Tobago	1,252	1,229	1,209	1,184	159	-0.2	611	1,980
Tunisia	9,546	10,526	11,721	12,115	79	1.1	195	59,985
Turkey	65,970	74,687	82,018	84,544	18	0.9	276	297,157
Turkmenistan	4,385	4,941	5,529	5,800	117	1.1	30	181,441
Tuvalu	10	10	11	12	222	0.8	1,130	10
Uganda	23,192	31,002	43,253	50,872	34	3.3	568	76,101
Ukraine	49,014	45,768	43,923	42,888	33	-0.4	196	223,681
United Arab Emirates	3,231	8,380	9,992	10,756	92	1.8	310	32,278
United Kingdom	59,140	62,348	65,761	67,244	22	0.5	704	93,410
United States	**282,162**	**309,326**	**332,639**	**344,234**	**3**	**0.7**	**94**	**3,532,614**
Uruguay	3,220	3,301	3,388	3,432	132	0.3	50	67,574
Uzbekistan	25,042	27,866	30,565	31,824	45	0.9	186	164,248
Vanuatu	191	245	298	323	180	2.0	63	4,706
Venezuela	24,249	28,705	28,645	31,786	50	(-Z)	84	340,561
Vietnam	79,178	89,571	98,721	102,459	16	1.0	825	119,719
Yemen	17,236	23,210	29,884	32,822	48	2.5	147	203,850
Zambia	9,984	13,042	17,427	20,105	66	2.9	61	287,028
Zimbabwe	12,047	12,722	14,546	16,031	73	1.3	97	149,362
TERRITORIES AND DEPENDENCIES								
American Samoa	58	56	49	46	211	-1.2	647	76
Anguilla	11	15	18	20	220	2.0	515	35
Aruba	90	105	119	126	189	1.3	1,718	69
Bermuda	63	68	72	73	203	0.5	3,441	21
Cayman Islands	38	50	62	68	205	2.1	608	102
Cook Islands	16	11	9	8	224	-2.9	94	91
Curacao [4]	134	143	151	154	188	0.5	883	171
Faroe Islands	46	49	52	53	209	0.5	96	538
French Polynesia	236	269	295	305	181	0.9	200	1,478
Gaza Strip [5]	1,128	1,503	1,918	2,121	152	2.4	13,800	139
Gibraltar	27	29	30	30	218	0.2	10,945	3
Greenland	57	58	58	57	206	(Z)	(Z)	836,330
Guam	155	163	168	170	186	0.3	802	210
Guernsey	62	65	67	68	204	0.4	2,226	30
Hong Kong	6,656	7,029	7,250	7,297	103	0.3	17,500	414
Isle of Man	76	84	90	93	199	0.8	410	221
Jersey	87	93	101	104	196	0.8	2,257	45
Macau	432	568	614	630	170	0.8	56,837	11
Montserrat	4	5	5	6	227	0.5	136	39
New Caledonia	211	252	290	307	183	1.4	41	7,056
Northern Mariana Islands	70	55	51	50	210	-0.7	282	182
Puerto Rico	3,811	3,722	3,189	2,980	134	-1.5	931	3,424
Saint Barthelemy	7	7	7	7	226	-0.4	738	10
Saint Helena	7	8	8	8	225	0.3	52	152
Saint Martin	28	30	33	33	216	0.7	1,561	21
Saint Pierre and Miquelon	6	6	5	5	228	-1.1	57	93
Sint Maarten [4]	31	38	44	47	212	1.5	3,340	13
Turks and Caicos Islands	19	43	56	61	207	2.6	153	366
Virgin Islands, British	23	30	37	41	214	2.3	641	58
Virgin Islands, U.S	109	108	106	104	192	-0.2	791	134
Wallis and Futuna	15	15	16	16	221	0.3	289	55
West Bank [5]	1,947	2,404	2,900	3,153	139	1.9	1,332	2,178
Western Sahara	336	492	652	736	168	2.8	6	102,703

P Projected. X Not applicable. Z Less than 0.05 percent or less than 1 person per square mile. [1] Computed by the exponential method. For explanation of average annual percent change, see Guide to Tabular Presentation. [2] Data converted from square kilometers to square miles. [3] Sudan and South Sudan became separate countries in July 2011. [4] The Netherlands Antilles dissolved on October 10, 2010. Curacao and Sint Maarten became autonomous territories of the Kingdom of the Netherlands. [5] The Gaza Strip and West Bank are Israeli occupied with interim status subject to Israeli/Palestinian negotiations. The final status is yet to be determined.

Source: U.S. Census Bureau, "International Data Base (IDB)," <https://www.census.gov/programs-surveys/international-programs/about/idb.html>, accessed March 2020.

Table 1353. Net Migration by Country: 2000 to 2019

[Net number of migrants is the difference between the number of migrants entering and those leaving a country in a year. A positive figure is known as net immigration and a negative figure as net emigration. Population as of midyear]

Country	Net number of migrants					Net number of migrants per 1,000 population				
	2000	2010	2015	2018	2019	2000	2010	2015	2018	2019
Algeria.............	-18,996	-33,074	-36,379	-36,242	-36,400	-0.6	-0.9	-0.9	-0.9	-0.9
Armenia.............	-27,156	-18,493	-17,727	-17,014	-16,788	-8.8	-6.0	-5.8	-5.6	-5.5
Australia............	107,364	172,096	180,916	229,660	217,482	5.7	7.9	7.7	9.3	8.7
Austria.............	17,282	21,289	48,180	38,251	34,961	2.1	2.5	5.6	4.4	4.0
Bahrain.............	2,259	20,569	17,627	16,677	16,317	3.5	17.4	13.1	11.6	11.1
Bangladesh..........	-616,639	-605,524	-601,379	-481,548	-481,578	-4.8	-4.1	-3.9	-3.0	-3.0
Belgium.............	25,146	69,215	66,472	60,168	58,120	2.5	6.4	5.9	5.2	5.0
Brazil..............	-43,579	-41,125	-28,596	-27,150	-27,339	-0.3	-0.2	-0.1	-0.1	-0.1
Burma..............	-68,097	-153,216	-61,662	-82,878	-80,801	-1.5	-3.0	-1.1	-1.5	-1.4
Canada.............	165,139	253,474	211,934	216,555	214,622	5.3	7.4	5.9	5.8	5.7
China..............	-329,758	-454,472	-601,694	-595,416	-597,536	-0.3	-0.3	-0.4	-0.4	-0.4
Colombia............	-299,999	-30,060	-29,912	-29,865	-30,152	-7.7	-0.7	-0.6	-0.6	-0.6
Congo, Dem. Rep. of...	-65,623	-43,645	28,532	-99,311	-93,661	-1.2	-0.6	0.3	-1.0	-1.0
Cote d'Ivoire..........	-167	3,692	34,726	33,876	33,853	--	0.2	1.4	1.3	1.3
Cuba...............	-29,316	-38,966	-63,135	-49,913	-45,457	-2.6	-3.5	-5.6	-4.5	-4.1
Czechia.............	6,572	15,615	24,802	24,792	24,814	0.6	1.5	2.3	2.3	2.3
Denmark............	9,501	17,085	42,548	24,690	20,445	1.8	3.1	7.5	4.3	3.5
Dominican Republic....	-34,160	-19,997	-24,371	-26,983	-27,872	-4.2	-2.1	-2.4	-2.6	-2.7
Egypt..............	-36,682	-59,304	-55,378	-43,742	-39,693	-0.6	-0.7	-0.6	-0.4	-0.4
El Salvador..........	-66,001	-71,065	-40,832	-21,398	-26,353	-11.3	-11.9	-6.6	-3.4	-4.1
Eritrea.............	-35,270	-14,324	-90,141	-78,395	-74,467	-9.1	-2.7	-15.5	-13.1	-12.4
Ethiopia............	-81,758	4,103	55,826	-12,321	-22,130	-1.3	0.1	0.6	-0.1	-0.2
France.............	71,669	72,084	72,544	72,080	72,344	1.2	1.1	1.1	1.1	1.1
Germany............	166,833	30,208	100,259	119,882	119,667	2.0	0.4	1.2	1.5	1.5
Ghana.............	-93,007	-52,328	-53,182	-48,617	-47,094	-4.9	-2.2	-2.0	-1.7	-1.6
Guatemala..........	-129,418	-21,171	-43,240	-40,127	-34,746	-11.5	-1.5	-2.8	-2.4	-2.1
Haiti..............	-29,640	-46,048	121,613	-21,361	-21,311	-3.6	-4.8	11.9	-2.0	-2.0
India..............	-60,378	-58,655	-50,068	-51,873	-52,462	-0.1	-0.1	(NA)	(NA)	(NA)
Indonesia...........	-338,263	-296,976	-296,953	-296,950	-296,728	-1.6	-1.2	-1.2	-1.1	-1.1
Iran...............	-124,322	-20,259	-10,391	-17,435	-21,838	-1.9	-0.3	-0.1	-0.2	-0.3
Iraq...............	(NA)	92,814	-20,909	-13,766	-13,314	(NA)	3.2	-0.6	-0.4	-0.4
Ireland.............	24,997	(NA)	20,010	20,019	19,981	6.5	(NA)	4.1	4.0	3.9
Israel..............	59,206	15,326	18,030	18,029	18,041	9.7	2.1	2.2	2.1	2.1
Italy...............	170,464	307,390	253,606	221,598	210,692	3.0	5.1	4.1	3.6	3.4
Jamaica............	-19,253	-36,476	-28,300	-26,349	-26,335	-6.9	-12.9	-10.1	-9.4	-9.4
Jordan.............	-17,992	(NA)	326,721	(NA)	(NA)	-3.8	(NA)	33.8	(NA)	(NA)
Korea, South........	7,963	82,261	137,755	125,460	121,344	0.2	1.7	2.7	2.4	2.4
Kyrgyzstan..........	-23,254	-54,538	-29,571	-29,539	-29,540	-4.7	-10.1	-5.2	-5.1	-5.0
Lebanon............	14,494	-51,392	-6,803	-245,894	-365,397	3.8	-11.4	-1.1	-40.3	-62.5
Lithuania...........	-4,362	-84,107	-18,085	-16,899	-16,547	-1.3	-27.2	-6.3	-6.1	-6.0
Mali...............	-84,038	-54,573	-76,933	-71,139	-73,286	-7.8	-3.8	-4.6	-3.9	-3.9
Mexico.............	-517,835	-41,062	-204,518	-227,986	-235,539	-5.2	-0.4	-1.7	-1.8	-1.9
Moldova............	-40,506	-37,840	-34,298	-31,833	-31,121	-9.7	-10.1	-9.7	-9.3	-9.2
Morocco............	-119,444	-67,527	-67,217	-66,605	-66,567	-4.2	-2.1	-2.0	-1.9	-1.9
Mozambique.........	-92,491	-92,509	-48,552	-44,263	-47,207	-5.0	-4.0	-1.8	-1.6	-1.6
Nepal..............	-154,075	-65,059	-56,783	-74,591	-84,091	-6.6	-2.4	-2.0	-2.5	-2.8
Netherlands.........	53,844	34,308	33,048	32,930	33,056	3.4	2.1	2.0	1.9	1.9
New Zealand........	-12,586	10,460	57,107	49,090	44,179	-3.3	2.5	12.6	10.3	9.1
Niger..............	-14,937	-16,392	30,034	-3,808	-15,806	-1.4	-1.1	1.6	-0.2	-0.7
Nigeria.............	-2,512	-53,090	-256,849	-42,725	-43,823	--	-0.3	-1.4	-0.2	-0.2
Norway.............	9,704	42,359	37,756	28,204	24,993	2.2	8.7	7.3	5.3	4.6
Pakistan............	1,248,047	-92,286	-439,879	-172,442	-187,557	8.4	-0.5	-2.1	-0.8	-0.8
Peru...............	-83,324	-97,555	-77,026	-64,856	-60,718	-3.2	-3.4	-2.5	-2.1	-1.9
Philippines..........	-97,858	-267,302	-211,087	-201,197	-197,865	-1.3	-2.9	-2.1	-1.9	-1.8
Puerto Rico..........	(NA)	-53,776	-64,769	-52,813	-48,831	(NA)	-14.5	-18.7	-16.0	-15.1
Qatar..............	21,149	135,443	49,142	27,205	21,251	33.1	78.8	22.4	11.5	8.8
Russia.............	326,460	240,870	240,696	241,609	241,306	2.2	1.7	1.7	1.7	1.7
Rwanda............	-175,185	-23,320	-139,824	-6,216	-14,455	-21.8	-2.4	-12.3	-0.5	-1.2
Saudi Arabia.........	12,603	454,674	156,109	135,012	145,288	0.6	16.3	5.0	4.1	4.3
Senegal............	-37,120	-24,523	-22,222	-20,879	-20,451	-3.9	-2.0	-1.6	-1.4	-1.3
Singapore...........	68,670	86,200	79,726	75,849	74,578	16.9	16.8	14.1	12.7	12.2
Somalia............	49,429	-117,215	-90,133	-63,051	-54,053	6.6	-12.0	-8.5	-5.6	-4.7
Spain..............	389,654	126,961	400,094	369,983	360,204	9.6	2.7	8.3	7.5	7.3
Sri Lanka...........	5,903	-49,969	-29,772	-29,124	-28,875	0.3	-2.4	-1.4	-1.3	-1.3
Sudan.............	(NA)	-347,740	46,489	80,205	-19,958	(NA)	-9.9	1.2	1.9	-0.5
Sweden............	24,542	49,991	53,125	53,117	53,139	2.8	5.3	5.4	5.3	5.3
Switzerland..........	20,886	65,034	38,497	38,479	38,488	2.9	8.4	4.7	4.6	4.6
Syria..............	(NA)	-54,451	-1,282,968	649,628	350,058	(NA)	-2.5	-69.7	36.6	18.8
Taiwan.............	5,546	21,970	20,839	20,250	20,041	0.3	1.0	0.9	0.9	0.9
Tanzania............	58,752	-9,301	-27,565	-24,953	-24,504	1.8	-0.2	-0.5	-0.5	-0.4
Tunisia.............	-9,546	-21,473	-21,988	-18,311	-17,085	-1.0	-2.0	-2.0	-1.6	-1.5
Turkey.............	-88,400	-127,714	171,535	-361,595	-357,619	-1.3	-1.7	2.2	-4.5	-4.4
Uganda............	-52,878	-262,589	-171,172	-420,372	-170,260	-2.3	-8.5	-4.7	-10.4	-4.1
Ukraine............	-115,673	16,019	-99,966	199,983	200,041	-2.4	0.4	-2.3	4.6	4.6
United Arab Emirates...	134,043	70,559	40,817	60,633	68,907	41.5	8.4	4.4	6.3	7.0
United Kingdom........	159,087	162,729	162,784	162,763	162,937	2.7	2.6	2.5	2.5	2.5
United States.........	**(NA)**	**(NA)**	**1,026,377**	**981,502**	**1,007,320**	**(NA)**	**(NA)**	**3.2**	**3.0**	**3.1**
Uzbekistan...........	-66,611	-79,139	-69,204	-63,350	-61,198	-2.7	-2.8	-2.4	-2.1	-2.0
Venezuela...........	-41,466	-38,464	-85,450	-1,958,089	-610,376	-1.7	-1.3	-2.8	-66.0	-21.3
Vietnam............	-30,088	-33,141	-28,305	-26,201	-25,453	-0.4	-0.4	-0.3	-0.3	-0.3
Zimbabwe............	-93,488	-174,798	-145,696	-102,141	-87,663	-7.8	-13.7	-10.9	-7.3	-6.1

-- Represents or rounds to zero. NA Not available.

Source: U.S. Census Bureau, "International Data Base (IDB)," <https://www.census.gov/programs-surveys/international-programs/data/tools.html>, accessed April 2020.

Table 1354. Foreign or Foreign-Born Population in Selected OECD Countries: 2000 to 2018

[28,052 represents 28,052,000. In Australia, Israel, Mexico, and the United States, the data refer to residents who are foreign born. In the European countries, Japan, and South Korea, data represent the legal nationality or citizenship status of residents. Data are based on censuses, population registers, and residence permits. For details about data methodology for individual countries, see source]

Country	2000	2005	2010	2013	2014	2015	2016	2017	2018
United States	28,052	34,258	38,453	40,738	41,344	42,391	43,290	43,739	44,525
Australia	4,412	4,877	5,881	6,409	6,570	6,730	6,912	7,140	7,343
Austria	694	774	884	1,004	1,066	1,146	1,268	1,342	1,396
Belgium	897	871	1,058	1,257	1,268	1,277	1,333	1,367	1,389
Denmark	259	268	330	375	397	423	463	485	506
France	3,259	(NA)	3,821	4,084	4,200	4,335	4,400	4,556	4,617
Germany	7,344	6,717	6,695	7,214	7,634	8,153	9,108	10,039	10,624
Greece	274	533	840	768	687	707	686	538	(NA)
Ireland	(NA)	(NA)	575	550	555	564	607	567	594
Israel [1]	1,944	1,961	1,878	1,835	1,821	1,817	1,818	1,812	(NA)
Italy	1,341	2,402	3,648	4,388	4,921	5,014	5,027	5,047	5,144
Japan	1,556	1,974	2,185	2,034	2,066	2,122	2,232	2,383	2,562
Korea, South	210	511	1,003	986	1,092	1,143	1,162	1,172	(NA)
Mexico	493	612	961	991	940	1,007	1,007	(NA)	(NA)
Netherlands	652	699	735	796	816	847	901	972	1,041
Norway	179	213	334	449	483	512	538	559	568
Portugal	191	449	454	417	401	395	389	398	422
Spain	924	3,731	5,403	5,073	4,677	4,454	4,418	4,419	4,572
Sweden	482	481	603	667	695	739	783	852	897
Switzerland	1,369	1,495	1,680	1,825	1,887	1,947	1,994	2,030	2,054
Turkey	(NA)	(NA)	167	279	457	518	650	816	919
United Kingdom	2,208	2,857	4,524	4,941	5,154	5,592	5,951	6,137	5,991

NA Not available. [1] See footnote 2, Table 1357.

Source: Organisation for Economic Co-operation and Development (OECD), 2020, "International Migration Database," OECD International Migration Statistics (database) ©, <http://dx.doi.org/10.1787/data-00342-en>, accessed July 2020.

Table 1355. Youth and Elderly Population Distribution by Country: 2020 and 2025

[Percent of total population, as of mid-year. Covers countries with 11 million or more population in 2020]

Country	2020 Under 15 years old	2020 65 years old and over	2025 (P) Under 15 years old	2025 (P) 65 years old and over	Country	2020 Under 15 years old	2020 65 years old and over	2025 (P) Under 15 years old	2025 (P) 65 years old and over
World	25.3	9.5	24.6	10.6	Korea, South	12.8	15.9	12.3	20.0
Afghanistan	40.6	2.7	39.7	2.8	Madagascar	38.9	3.5	36.9	3.9
Algeria	29.6	6.2	27.9	7.4	Malawi	45.9	2.7	45.0	2.7
Angola	47.8	2.3	46.6	2.4	Malaysia	26.8	6.9	25.2	8.5
Argentina	24.0	12.1	23.1	13.0	Mali	47.7	3.0	46.5	3.1
Australia	18.7	15.9	18.2	17.2	Mexico	26.0	7.7	24.6	9.1
Bangladesh	26.5	6.8	25.0	7.9	Morocco	27.0	7.1	25.4	8.7
Belgium	17.2	19.2	16.9	20.5	Mozambique	45.6	2.9	44.3	2.9
Benin	45.6	2.4	45.2	2.5	Nepal	28.4	5.7	26.3	6.7
Bolivia	30.3	5.7	28.1	6.5	Netherlands	16.1	19.8	16.1	21.7
Brazil	21.1	9.2	19.7	10.9	Niger	50.6	2.7	49.4	2.7
Burkina Faso	43.6	3.2	41.1	3.2	Nigeria	41.7	3.3	40.1	3.4
Burma	26.0	6.0	24.2	7.3	Pakistan	36.0	4.4	34.2	5.0
Burundi	43.8	3.1	42.1	3.4	Peru	25.4	8.0	24.0	9.3
Cambodia	30.2	4.6	28.2	5.3	Philippines	32.4	4.9	30.8	5.5
Cameroon	42.3	3.1	41.3	3.2	Poland	14.8	18.7	14.1	21.7
Canada	16.0	19.0	15.5	21.5	Romania	14.1	17.6	13.4	19.4
Chad	47.4	2.4	45.4	2.5	Russia	17.2	15.5	16.3	18.0
Chile	19.8	11.8	19.0	14.1	Rwanda	40.0	2.6	36.5	3.1
China	17.3	12.3	16.9	14.2	Saudi Arabia	24.8	3.6	22.1	4.6
Colombia	23.3	8.4	21.9	10.3	Senegal	40.4	3.1	38.3	3.4
Congo, Dem. Rep.	46.4	2.5	45.5	2.5	Somalia	42.4	2.3	41.5	2.8
Cote d'Ivoire	38.5	2.8	35.7	3.0	South Africa	27.9	6.1	26.7	6.8
Cuba	16.3	15.8	16.1	17.7	Spain	15.0	18.5	14.0	19.9
Ecuador	25.8	8.1	24.0	9.4	Sri Lanka	23.1	10.6	21.2	12.6
Egypt	33.6	4.4	33.3	5.0	Sudan	42.0	3.0	39.9	3.3
Ethiopia	39.8	3.4	38.3	3.7	Syria	33.5	4.5	32.4	4.3
France	18.4	20.5	17.8	22.0	Taiwan	12.4	15.7	12.1	19.4
Germany	12.9	23.0	13.1	25.0	Tanzania	42.7	3.1	41.0	3.2
Ghana	37.4	4.4	36.3	4.8	Thailand	16.4	11.8	15.9	14.6
Guatemala	33.7	4.7	31.3	5.3	Tunisia	25.3	8.9	24.1	10.8
Guinea	41.2	3.9	40.8	4.1	Turkey	23.4	8.4	21.5	9.9
Haiti	31.2	4.3	28.9	4.7	Uganda	48.2	2.4	46.8	2.4
India	26.3	6.7	24.8	7.7	Ukraine	16.2	17.0	15.5	19.1
Indonesia	23.9	7.8	22.2	9.4	United Kingdom	17.6	18.5	17.3	19.6
Iran	24.1	5.9	23.0	7.2	United States	18.5	16.9	18.0	18.9
Iraq	37.0	3.3	34.1	3.7	Uzbekistan	23.2	5.9	22.2	7.6
Italy	13.4	22.1	13.0	23.4	Venezuela	25.7	8.2	24.7	9.4
Japan	12.5	29.2	11.7	30.7	Vietnam	22.6	6.9	20.9	8.9
Kazakhstan	26.1	8.4	24.3	10.2	Yemen	37.7	2.9	34.0	3.4
Kenya	38.7	3.1	35.1	3.5	Zambia	45.7	2.3	45.0	2.3
Korea, North	20.5	9.7	20.2	11.1	Zimbabwe	38.3	4.5	38.3	4.5

P Projected.

Source: U.S. Census Bureau, "International Data Base (IDB)," <https://www.census.gov/programs-surveys/international-programs/about/idb.html>, accessed March 2020.

Table 1356. Births, Deaths, and Life Expectancy by Country or Territory: 2020 and 2025

[Covers countries with 12 million or more population in 2020]

Country or territory	Crude birth rate [1] 2020	Crude birth rate [1] 2025 (P)	Crude death rate [2] 2020	Crude death rate [2] 2025 (P)	Expectation of life at birth (years) 2020	Expectation of life at birth (years) 2025 (P)	Infant mortality rate [3] 2020	Infant mortality rate [3] 2025 (P)	Total fertility rate per woman [4] 2020	Total fertility rate per woman [4] 2025 (P)
World............	**18.1**	**17.1**	**7.7**	**7.7**	**70.5**	**71.6**	**30.8**	**27.4**	**2.42**	**2.38**
Afghanistan............	36.7	33.6	12.7	11.5	52.8	54.8	104.3	93.7	4.82	4.34
Algeria.................	20.0	16.5	4.4	4.5	77.5	78.4	17.6	14.8	2.59	2.39
Angola.................	42.7	40.8	8.5	7.4	61.3	63.3	62.3	54.0	5.96	5.63
Argentina.............	16.0	15.1	7.4	7.5	77.8	78.7	9.0	7.9	2.21	2.14
Australia...............	12.4	12.1	6.9	7.3	82.7	82.9	3.1	3.1	1.74	1.73
Bangladesh............	18.1	17.1	5.5	5.7	74.2	75.3	28.3	23.5	2.11	2.06
Benin..................	42.1	40.0	8.4	7.5	61.4	63.4	58.7	51.6	5.53	5.33
Brazil..................	13.6	13.0	6.9	7.2	74.7	75.9	15.9	13.6	1.73	1.71
Burkina Faso...........	35.1	31.1	8.2	7.1	62.7	64.6	52.0	45.8	4.51	3.90
Burma.................	17.0	15.5	7.2	7.3	69.3	70.8	31.7	26.6	2.07	1.95
Cambodia..............	21.3	18.9	7.3	7.0	65.9	67.6	43.7	37.9	2.39	2.25
Cameroon..............	36.3	34.3	8.1	7.2	62.3	64.6	51.5	44.9	4.66	4.39
Canada................	10.2	10.0	7.9	8.6	83.4	83.7	4.3	4.1	1.57	1.59
Chad..................	41.7	38.6	10.0	8.8	58.3	60.4	68.6	61.1	5.68	5.13
Chile..................	13.1	12.2	6.5	7.0	79.4	80.1	6.2	5.6	1.77	1.74
China..................	11.6	9.9	8.2	8.8	76.1	76.9	11.4	10.0	1.60	1.60
Colombia..............	15.4	14.3	5.6	6.1	76.6	77.6	12.3	10.6	1.94	1.87
Congo, Dem. Rep......	41.0	38.8	8.4	7.4	61.0	63.0	64.5	55.8	5.77	5.42
Cote d'Ivoire............	29.1	27.1	7.9	7.2	61.3	63.6	59.1	50.9	3.67	3.33
Ecuador................	17.0	15.7	5.2	5.4	77.5	78.4	15.0	12.9	2.09	1.97
Egypt..................	27.2	23.6	4.4	4.3	73.7	74.9	17.1	14.3	3.29	3.01
Ethiopia................	31.6	29.0	5.9	5.4	67.5	69.3	35.8	30.4	4.14	3.77
France.................	11.9	11.4	9.6	9.9	82.2	82.6	3.2	3.1	2.06	2.00
Germany...............	8.6	8.5	12.1	12.7	81.1	81.6	3.3	3.2	1.47	1.51
Ghana.................	29.6	28.1	6.6	6.2	68.2	69.8	32.1	27.6	3.90	3.72
Guatemala.............	23.3	21.1	4.9	4.9	72.4	73.6	21.8	18.7	2.72	2.47
Guinea.................	36.1	35.0	8.4	7.7	63.2	65.0	52.4	45.8	4.92	4.75
India..................	18.2	17.0	7.3	7.3	69.7	71.2	35.4	29.8	2.35	2.25
Indonesia..............	15.4	14.6	6.6	6.9	73.7	74.9	20.4	17.2	2.04	1.96
Iran...................	16.3	13.8	5.3	5.6	74.5	75.2	14.9	13.3	1.94	1.90
Iraq...................	25.7	23.3	3.9	3.9	72.6	73.9	19.5	16.5	3.39	3.03
Italy...................	8.4	8.3	10.7	11.2	82.5	82.9	3.2	3.1	1.47	1.50
Japan.................	7.3	7.0	10.2	10.9	86.0	87.2	1.9	1.7	1.43	1.46
Kazakhstan............	16.4	14.0	8.2	8.0	72.0	73.3	17.9	15.3	2.16	2.03
Kenya.................	27.2	25.3	5.2	4.8	69.0	70.7	29.8	25.2	3.43	3.09
Korea, North...........	14.5	13.6	9.4	9.6	71.6	72.9	20.0	16.9	1.92	1.87
Korea, South...........	8.2	8.2	6.8	8.1	82.6	82.8	3.0	2.9	1.29	1.34
Madagascar............	29.9	27.2	6.2	5.7	67.3	68.9	37.8	32.6	3.78	3.39
Malawi................	40.1	38.4	7.2	6.1	63.2	66.1	39.5	33.6	5.31	5.03
Malaysia...............	18.3	17.2	5.3	5.6	75.9	76.9	11.4	9.9	2.43	2.33
Mali...................	42.2	39.5	9.0	7.9	61.6	63.6	64.0	55.8	5.72	5.26
Mexico................	17.6	16.3	5.4	5.7	76.7	77.6	10.7	9.4	2.19	2.11
Morocco...............	17.9	16.4	6.6	6.7	73.3	74.5	18.2	15.3	2.31	2.22
Mozambique...........	38.6	36.1	11.0	9.3	55.9	58.9	64.7	56.7	4.97	4.58
Nepal.................	18.1	16.7	5.7	5.8	71.8	73.2	25.1	21.1	1.96	1.82
Netherlands............	11.0	11.0	9.2	9.8	81.7	82.2	3.5	3.4	1.77	1.76
Niger..................	47.5	46.2	10.2	9.0	59.3	61.3	67.7	60.1	7.00	6.53
Nigeria................	34.6	33.1	9.1	8.2	60.4	62.7	59.8	52.3	4.72	4.39
Pakistan...............	27.4	25.1	6.2	5.7	69.2	70.7	52.3	43.8	3.60	3.25
Peru...................	17.0	15.7	6.2	6.4	74.7	75.8	16.7	14.3	2.04	1.94
Philippines.............	22.9	21.8	6.0	6.1	70.0	71.0	20.0	18.0	2.92	2.78
Poland.................	8.9	8.0	10.6	11.2	78.3	79.1	4.3	4.0	1.38	1.43
Romania...............	8.5	8.0	12.0	12.2	76.0	77.0	8.7	7.7	1.38	1.43
Russia.................	10.0	8.9	13.4	13.2	71.9	73.2	6.5	6.0	1.60	1.60
Rwanda................	27.9	24.4	6.1	5.6	65.1	66.9	28.0	24.2	3.52	3.04
Saudi Arabia...........	14.7	13.0	3.4	3.7	76.2	77.1	11.3	9.7	1.95	1.79
Senegal................	31.8	29.4	7.6	7.0	63.2	65.0	45.7	40.3	4.04	3.69
South Africa...........	19.2	17.6	9.3	9.2	64.8	66.1	27.8	23.3	2.22	2.13
Spain..................	8.7	8.4	9.3	9.6	82.0	82.4	3.2	3.1	1.51	1.54
Sri Lanka..............	14.2	13.2	6.5	6.9	77.5	78.4	7.8	7.0	2.01	1.94
Sudan.................	33.8	33.0	6.5	5.9	66.5	68.2	41.8	36.2	4.72	4.41
Syria..................	23.8	21.3	4.5	4.0	73.7	74.9	16.5	13.8	2.90	2.64
Taiwan................	8.0	7.6	7.9	8.7	80.6	81.2	4.2	4.0	1.14	1.17
Tanzania...............	34.6	33.1	7.1	6.5	63.9	65.7	36.4	31.3	4.59	4.30
Thailand...............	10.7	10.1	8.3	8.9	75.6	76.6	8.6	7.7	1.54	1.56
Turkey................	14.8	13.6	6.1	6.5	75.7	76.7	15.8	13.3	1.96	1.88
Uganda................	42.3	38.9	5.3	4.6	68.2	70.0	32.6	27.5	5.54	5.08
Ukraine................	9.6	8.7	14.0	13.8	72.9	74.2	7.4	6.7	1.56	1.58
United Kingdom........	11.9	11.3	9.5	9.7	81.1	81.6	4.1	3.9	1.86	1.84
United States.........	**12.4**	**12.1**	**8.3**	**8.5**	**80.3**	**81.1**	**5.3**	**5.0**	**1.84**	**1.84**
Uzbekistan.............	16.1	14.5	5.4	5.6	74.8	75.9	16.3	14.0	1.74	1.72
Venezuela.............	17.9	16.5	7.5	6.6	71.0	74.7	27.9	13.5	2.26	2.16
Vietnam...............	14.5	13.0	6.0	6.2	74.4	75.6	15.7	13.3	1.77	1.74
Yemen................	25.8	22.9	5.6	5.3	66.9	68.6	41.9	35.7	3.20	2.72
Zambia................	40.4	38.8	11.6	10.4	53.6	55.5	56.0	49.4	5.49	5.24
Zimbabwe.............	33.6	32.0	9.3	8.1	62.3	64.7	30.3	26.0	3.93	3.84

P Projection. [1] Number of births during 1 year per 1,000 persons (based on midyear population). [2] Number of deaths during 1 year per 1,000 persons (based on midyear population). [3] Number of deaths of children under 1 year of age per 1,000 live births in a calendar year. [4] Average number of children that would be born if all women lived to the end of childbearing age, based on birth rates for each specified year.

Source: U.S. Census Bureau, "International Data Base (IDB)," <https://www.census.gov/programs-surveys/international-programs/about/idb.html>, accessed March 2020.

Table 1357. Life Expectancy at Birth and at Age 65 by Sex—Selected Countries: 2010 and 2018

Country	Life expectancy at birth (years)				Life expectancy at age 65 (years)			
	Females		Males		Females		Males	
	2010	2018	2010	2018	2010	2018	2010	2018
United States	**81.0**	**81.2**	**76.2**	**76.2**	**20.3**	**20.7**	**17.7**	**18.1**
Australia	84.0	84.9	79.5	80.7	21.8	22.6	18.9	19.9
Austria	83.5	84.1	77.8	79.4	21.4	21.6	17.9	18.5
Belgium	83.0	83.9	77.5	79.4	21.3	21.9	17.6	18.6
Canada	83.3	84.1	78.8	79.9	21.5	22.1	18.4	19.4
Czechia	80.9	82.0	74.5	76.2	19.0	19.8	15.5	16.2
Denmark	81.4	82.9	77.2	79.1	19.7	20.7	17.0	18.0
Finland	83.5	84.5	76.9	79.1	21.5	22.0	17.5	18.6
France	85.3	85.9	78.3	79.7	23.4	23.8	18.9	19.7
Germany	83.0	83.3	78.0	78.6	20.9	21.1	17.8	18.0
Greece	83.3	84.4	78.0	79.3	21.0	21.9	18.2	19.1
Hungary	78.6	79.6	70.7	72.7	18.2	18.5	14.1	14.6
Iceland	84.1	84.5	79.8	81.3	21.5	21.7	18.3	20.0
Ireland	83.1	84.1	78.5	80.5	20.8	21.6	17.7	19.1
Israel [2]	83.6	84.8	79.7	80.9	21.2	22.1	18.9	19.7
Italy	84.7	85.6	79.5	81.2	22.1	22.8	18.3	19.6
Japan	86.3	[1] 87.3	79.6	[1] 81.1	[1] 23.8	[1] 24.4	18.7	[1] 19.6
Korea, South	83.6	85.7	76.8	79.7	21.2	22.8	16.8	18.7
Mexico	77.0	[3] 77.9	71.1	[3] 72.2	18.5	[1] 18.7	16.6	[1] 16.8
Netherlands	83.0	83.4	78.9	80.3	21.0	21.1	17.7	18.7
New Zealand	82.7	83.5	78.9	80.0	21.0	21.7	18.5	19.5
Norway	83.3	84.5	79.0	81.1	21.2	21.7	18.0	19.4
Poland	80.7	81.7	72.2	73.7	19.5	20.1	15.1	15.8
Portugal	83.2	84.5	76.8	78.3	21.0	22.0	17.2	18.2
Russia	74.9	77.8	63.1	67.8	16.5	18.1	12.1	13.8
Slovenia	83.1	84.4	76.4	78.5	21.0	21.8	16.8	17.8
Spain	85.5	86.3	79.2	80.7	22.9	23.5	18.6	19.5
Sweden	83.6	84.3	79.6	80.9	21.2	21.6	18.3	19.2
Switzerland	84.9	85.7	80.3	81.9	22.5	23.0	19.0	20.2
Turkey	76.8	81.0	71.8	75.6	16.0	19.4	14.0	16.2
United Kingdom	82.6	83.1	78.6	79.5	20.8	21.1	18.2	18.9

[1] Data are for 2017. [2] The statistical data for Israel are supplied by and under the responsibility of the relevant Israeli authorities. The use of such data by the OECD is without prejudice to the status of the Golan Heights, East Jerusalem and Israeli settlements in the West Bank under the terms of international law. [3] Provisional.

Source: Organisation for Economic Co-operation and Development (OECD), 2020, "OECD Health Data: Health Status," OECD Health Statistics (database) ©, <http://dx.doi.org/10.1787/data-00546-en>, accessed July 2020.

Table 1358. Percent of the Adult Population Considered to Be Obese: 2000 to 2018

[Obesity rates are defined as the percentage of the population with a Body Mass Index (BMI) over 30 kg/m ^{2}. The BMI is a single number that evaluates an individual's weight status in relation to height (weight/height ^{2}). Obesity estimates derived from health examinations are generally higher and more reliable than those coming from self-reports because they preclude any misreporting of people's height and weight. However, health examinations are only conducted regularly in a few countries. For more information on methods, see source]

Country	2000	2005	2010	2014	2015	2016	2017	2018
OBESITY, MEASURED								
United States	**30.9**	**(NA)**	**36.1**	**38.2**	**(NA)**	**40.0**	**(NA)**	**(NA)**
Australia	(NA)	(NA)	(NA)	[1] 27.9	(NA)	(NA)	30.4	(NA)
Canada	(NA)	23.7	25.4	(NA)	[1] 28.1	(NA)	26.3	(NA)
Colombia	(NA)	13.8	16.5	(NA)	18.7	(NA)	(NA)	(NA)
Czechia	14.0	17.0	21.0	(NA)	(NA)	(NA)	(NA)	(NA)
Finland	22.5	(NA)	(NA)	(NA)	(NA)	(NA)	26.8	(NA)
Ireland	(NA)	(NA)	(NA)	(NA)	23.0	(NA)	23.0	(NA)
Japan	2.9	3.9	3.5	3.9	3.7	4.2	4.4	4.0
Korea, South	(NA)	3.5	4.1	4.3	5.3	5.5	5.4	5.9
Luxembourg	16.3	18.6	22.5	22.6	(NA)	(NA)	(NA)	(NA)
Mexico	24.2	30.2	(NA)	(NA)	(NA)	33.1	(NA)	36.1
New Zealand	(NA)	(NA)	(NA)	29.9	30.7	31.6	32.2	32.2
United Kingdom	21.2	23.2	26.1	25.6	26.9	26.2	28.7	27.7
OBESITY, SELF-REPORTED								
United States	**21.8**	**25.1**	**28.2**	**29.6**	**30.2**	**30.2**	**31.0**	**31.6**
Brazil	(NA)	(NA)	15.0	16.8	17.0	18.9	18.9	(NA)
Canada	(NA)	15.2	17.5	19.6	[1] 19.2	19.7	19.8	19.7
Denmark	9.5	11.4	13.4	14.9	(NA)	(NA)	16.8	(NA)
Estonia	14.1	(NA)	16.9	19.5	(NA)	19.2	(NA)	19.1
Finland	11.2	14.1	15.6	18.3	[1] 18.8	[1] 19.0	[1] 19.0	[1] 20.0
France	9.0	(NA)	12.9	15.3	15.2	(NA)	15.4	(NA)
Germany	(NA)	13.6	(NA)	16.4	(NA)	(NA)	16.3	(NA)
Israel [2]	(NA)	(NA)	15.7	17.8	(NA)	[1] 16.6	14.7	(NA)
Italy	8.6	9.9	10.3	10.3	9.8	10.4	10.6	10.7
Korea, South	(NA)	(NA)	2.0	2.6	2.8	3.2	3.4	4.3
Netherlands	9.4	10.7	11.4	[1] 13.3	12.8	13.6	13.4	14.4
Russia	17.3	19.4	19.9	[1] 23.0	22.3	22.1	22.4	22.7
Sweden	9.2	10.9	11.3	12.2	12.3	13.0	13.1	14.1
Turkey	(NA)	(NA)	16.9	19.9	(NA)	19.6	(NA)	(NA)

NA Not available. [1] Break in series or difference in methodology. [2] See footnote 2, Table 1357.

Source: Organisation for Economic Co-operation and Development (OECD), 2020, "OECD Health Data: Non-medical Determinants of Health," OECD Health Statistics (database) ©, <http://dx.doi.org/10.1787/data-00546-en>, accessed July 2020.

Table 1359. Daily Tobacco Consumption by Country and Sex: 2000 to 2018

[Daily smokers as percent of population aged over 15. Covers only tobacco forms consumed by smoking]

Country	Total 2000	Total 2010	Total 2017	Total 2018	Females 2000	Females 2010	Females 2017	Females 2018	Males 2000	Males 2010	Males 2017	Males 2018
United States.......	19.1	15.1	10.5	10.3	17.3	13.6	9.5	9.1	21.2	16.7	11.5	11.5
Brazil...............	(NA)	14.1	10.1	(NA)	(NA)	11.7	7.5	(NA)	(NA)	16.8	13.2	(NA)
Canada.............	(NA)	16.3	12.0	11.3	(NA)	13.7	10.0	9.7	(NA)	19.0	14.2	12.8
Costa Rica.........	12.5	8.2	4.7	4.2	6.1	4.4	3.2	3.1	18.7	11.8	6.2	5.4
Czechia.............	(NA)	22.8	18.4	21.1	(NA)	16.5	14.5	17.9	(NA)	29.3	22.6	24.5
Estonia.............	30.3	26.2	(NA)	17.2	20.0	18.7	(NA)	12.9	45.0	36.8	(NA)	23.4
France..............	27.0	29.7	26.9	25.4	21.0	26.6	24.2	22.9	33.0	33.1	29.8	28.2
Ireland.............	(NA)	(NA)	18.0	17.0	(NA)	(NA)	17.0	15.0	(NA)	(NA)	20.0	19.0
Israel [2]...........	24.1	18.5	16.9	(NA)	15.4	12.6	12.8	(NA)	34.0	24.8	21.3	(NA)
Italy...............	24.4	23.1	19.9	19.2	17.4	17.1	15.0	15.1	31.9	29.6	25.1	23.5
Japan...............	27.0	19.5	17.7	17.8	11.5	8.4	7.2	8.1	47.4	32.2	29.4	29.0
Korea...............	(NA)	22.9	17.5	17.5	(NA)	5.2	3.5	4.5	(NA)	40.8	31.6	30.5
Luxembourg.........	(NA)	18.3	16.0	14.5	(NA)	15.7	14.0	13.4	(NA)	20.9	18.1	15.7
Mexico..............	[1] 12.4	(NA)	[1] 7.6	(NA)	[1] 6.4	(NA)	[1] 3.6	(NA)	[1] 20.5	(NA)	[1] 12.0	(NA)
Netherlands........	32.0	[1] 20.9	16.8	15.5	29.0	[1] 18.8	14.1	13.4	35.0	[1] 23.1	19.5	17.8
New Zealand.......	25.0	13.8	13.1	13.1	25.0	(NA)	12.6	11.9	25.0	(NA)	15.1	14.3
Norway.............	32.0	19.0	11.0	12.0	32.0	19.0	10.0	11.0	31.0	19.0	12.0	12.0
Russia..............	34.9	(NA)	[1] 27.5	26.7	12.6	(NA)	[1] 13.9	13.7	62.2	(NA)	[1] 45.9	44.7
Sweden.............	18.9	13.6	10.4	10.1	21.0	12.5	10.3	9.2	16.8	14.7	10.5	11.0
United Kingdom.....	27.0	20.0	16.8	16.6	25.0	20.0	15.0	16.2	29.0	21.0	18.7	17.0

NA Not available. [1] Break in series or difference in methodology. [2] See footnote 2, Table 1357.

Source: Organisation for Economic Co-operation and Development (OECD), 2020, "OECD Health Data: Non-medical Determinants of Health," OECD Health Statistics (database) ©, <http://dx.doi.org/10.1787/data-00546-en>, accessed July 2020.

Table 1360. Road Traffic Fatalities by Country: 2000 to 2018

[Fatalities include any person killed immediately or dying within 30 days as a result of an injury accident. For countries that do not apply the threshold of 30 days, conversion coefficients are estimated so that comparisons on the basis of the 30 day-definition can be made]

Country	2000	2010	2015	2017	2018	Country	2000	2010	2015	2017	2018
United States......	41,945	32,999	35,485	37,133	[2] 36,750	Ireland.............	415	212	162	[2] 157	[2] 143
						Israel [3]...........	516	375	356	364	316
Albania.............	280	353	270	222	213	Italy...............	7,061	4,114	3,428	3,378	3,325
Australia...........	1,817	1,353	1,204	1,223	1,137	Japan..............	10,410	5,828	4,885	4,431	4,166
Austria.............	976	552	479	414	409	Korea, South......	10,236	5,505	4,621	4,185	3,781
Azerbaijan..........	596	925	894	750	722	Latvia.............	588	218	188	136	151
Belarus.............	1,594	1,190	664	589	549	Lithuania..........	641	299	242	191	173
Belgium.............	1,470	850	762	609	604	Mexico.............	5,224	5,032	3,490	2,919	(NA)
Bosnia-						Moldova...........	406	452	298	302	274
Herzegovina.....	(NA)	362	341	298	277	Netherlands.......	1,166	640	621	613	678
Bulgaria............	1,012	776	708	682	611	New Zealand......	462	375	318	378	377
Canada.............	2,904	2,238	1,882	[2] 1,841	(NA)	Poland.............	6,294	3,907	2,938	2,831	2,862
China...............	(NA)	65,225	58,022	63,772	(NA)	Portugal...........	1,857	937	593	602	(NA)
Croatia.............	655	426	348	331	317	Romania...........	2,499	2,377	1,893	1,951	1,867
Czechia.............	1,486	802	738	577	656	Russia.............	29,594	26,567	23,114	19,088	18,214
Finland.............	396	272	270	238	[2] 234	Slovakia...........	648	353	310	276	260
France..............	8,079	3,992	3,461	3,448	3,248	Spain..............	5,776	2,478	1,689	1,830	1,806
Georgia.............	500	685	602	517	459	Sweden............	591	[1] 266	259	252	324
Germany............	7,503	3,648	3,459	3,180	3,275	Switzerland........	592	327	253	230	233
Greece.............	2,037	1,258	793	731	[2] 700	Turkey.............	5,510	4,045	[1] 7,530	7,427	6,675
Hungary............	1,200	740	644	625	633	United Kingdom...	3,580	1,905	1,804	1,856	[2] 1,837
India...............	78,911	134,513	146,133	147,913	(NA)						

NA Not available. [1] Break in series. [2] Estimated or provisional. [3] See footnote 2, Table 1357.

Source: International Transport Forum (ITF) / Organisation for Economic Co-operation and Development (OECD), 2020, "Road accidents," ITF Transport Statistics (database) ©, <https://doi.org/10.1787/g2g55585-en>, accessed June 2020. See also <itf-oecd.org/>.

Table 1361. Suicide Rates by Sex and Country: 2017

[Deaths due to intentional self-harm per 100,000 persons. Rates are standardized]

Country	Total	Men	Women	Country	Total	Men	Women
United States............	14.5	23.2	6.4	Ireland [2].................	9.3	15.0	3.9
Australia.................	12.8	19.5	6.3	Israel [3]..................	5.5	8.8	2.5
Austria..................	12.4	20.9	5.0	Italy [1]..................	5.5	9.2	2.2
Belgium [1]...............	15.9	23.6	8.8	Japan....................	14.9	21.7	8.4
Brazil....................	6.4	10.6	2.6	Korea, South.............	23.0	35.1	12.8
Canada..................	11.0	16.6	5.5	Lithuania................	24.4	43.9	8.5
Chile....................	10.7	18.8	3.4	Luxembourg [1]...........	7.2	11.0	3.5
Colombia................	5.7	9.9	1.9	Mexico..................	5.5	9.6	1.9
Costa Rica..............	5.7	9.2	2.2	Netherlands [1]...........	10.6	14.7	6.6
Czechia.................	12.4	20.8	5.0	Norway..................	11.6	15.8	7.4
Estonia.................	16.1	27.5	6.8	Poland..................	11.1	20.1	2.8
Finland.................	14.6	22.0	7.5	Portugal.................	8.8	14.4	4.2
France [1]...............	12.3	20.2	5.5	Spain...................	7.0	10.9	3.6
Germany................	9.5	15.3	4.4	Sweden.................	11.4	16.2	6.7
Greece [1]...............	4.0	7.0	1.4	Switzerland [1]...........	11.2	17.3	5.6
Hungary................	15.1	26.1	6.5	Turkey [1]................	2.6	4.1	1.1
Iceland.................	9.7	17.7	1.3	United Kingdom [1]........	7.3	11.4	3.3

[1] 2016 data. [2] 2015 data. [3] See footnote 2, Table 1357.

Source: Organisation for Economic Co-operation and Development (OECD), 2020, "Health Status," OECD Health Statistics database ©, <http://dx.doi.org/10.1787/data-00540-en>, accessed July 2020.

Table 1362. Health Expenditures by Country: 1990 to 2019

[In percent. GDP = gross domestic product]

Country	Total expenditures on health (percent of GDP)					Public (government) expenditures on health (percent of total)				
	1990	2000	2010	2018	2019 [1]	1990	2000	2010	2018	2019 [1]
United States	**11.3**	**12.5**	**16.3**	**16.9**	**17.0**	**40.2**	**44.2**	**48.5**	**84.7**	**84.8**
Australia	6.5	7.6	8.4	9.3	9.3	66.2	68.4	68.6	66.7	67.4
Austria	7.7	9.2	10.2	10.3	10.4	74.4	75.5	74.6	74.7	75.2
Belgium	7.1	8.0	10.2	10.3	10.3	(NA)	74.6	76.1	75.8	76.0
Canada	8.4	8.2	10.7	10.8	10.8	74.3	70.0	70.1	70.4	70.4
Chile	(NA)	7.0	6.8	9.1	9.1	(NA)	53.3	59.0	60.3	59.3
Czechia	3.7	5.7	6.9	7.6	7.8	97.1	89.8	83.3	83.0	83.3
Denmark	8.0	8.1	10.3	10.1	10.0	82.4	83.1	83.9	83.9	83.8
Finland	7.3	7.1	9.1	9.0	9.1	80.0	72.4	76.8	76.9	77.2
France	8.0	9.6	11.2	11.3	11.2	76.0	78.9	76.3	83.6	83.7
Germany [2]	8.0	9.9	11.1	11.5	11.7	75.4	78.1	83.2	84.6	85.0
Greece	6.1	7.2	9.5	7.7	7.8	54.1	61.6	68.9	58.7	59.2
Iceland	7.4	9.0	8.5	8.5	8.8	86.2	80.6	80.4	82.4	82.9
Ireland	5.6	5.9	10.5	6.9	6.8	73.2	77.5	76.2	73.9	74.3
Israel [3]	6.5	6.8	7.0	7.5	7.5	(NA)	63.1	62.8	64.7	64.7
Italy	7.0	7.6	8.9	8.7	8.7	81.3	72.6	78.5	73.9	74.1
Japan	5.8	7.2	9.2	11.0	11.1	77.6	80.4	81.9	84.1	84.3
Korea, South	3.6	3.9	5.9	7.6	8.0	40.1	53.9	60.9	59.9	60.8
Luxembourg	5.1	5.9	7.0	5.3	5.4	93.1	82.0	84.9	84.1	84.5
Mexico	(NA)	4.4	6.0	5.5	5.5	(NA)	45.2	48.6	50.8	50.5
Netherlands	7.0	7.7	10.2	10.0	10.0	71.2	69.0	83.4	82.1	82.7
New Zealand	6.7	7.5	9.6	9.2	9.3	82.4	78.0	81.2	79.2	79.5
Norway	7.1	7.7	8.9	10.0	10.5	82.8	81.7	84.7	85.3	85.4
Poland	4.3	5.3	6.4	6.3	6.3	90.9	68.9	71.7	71.5	71.9
Portugal	5.5	8.4	9.8	9.4	9.6	64.9	70.5	69.8	61.5	61.2
Spain	6.1	6.8	9.1	9.0	9.0	78.4	71.4	74.4	70.4	70.8
Sweden	7.2	7.4	8.3	10.9	10.9	79.6	85.5	82.4	85.1	85.2
Switzerland	7.9	9.4	10.3	11.9	12.1	(NA)	58.1	64.3	64.4	64.5
Turkey	2.5	4.6	5.1	4.2	4.4	59.9	61.7	78.0	77.4	78.3
United Kingdom	5.1	7.3	10.0	10.0	10.3	84.3	76.4	81.8	77.8	77.8

NA Not available. [1] Data are estimated or provisional. [2] Data prior to 1991 are for former West Germany. [3] See footnote 3, Table 1363.

Source: Organisation for Economic Co-operation and Development (OECD), 2020, "Health expenditure and financing: Health expenditure indicators," OECD Health Statistics (database) ©, <http://dx.doi.org/10.1787/data-00349-en>, accessed July 2020.

Table 1363. Physicians and Inpatient Hospital Care—Selected Countries: 2000 to 2018

Country	Practicing physicians per 1,000 population				Acute (curative) inpatient hospital care							
					Beds per 1,000 population				Average length of stay (days)			
	2000	2010	2017	2018	2000	2010	2017	2018	2000	2010	2017	2018
United States	**2.3**	**2.4**	**2.6**	**2.6**	**3.0**	**2.7**	**[2]2.5**	**(NA)**	**5.8**	**5.4**	**5.5**	**(NA)**
Australia	2.5	(NA)	[1]3.7	[1]3.8	(NA)	(NA)	(NA)	(NA)	6.1	5.0	4.1	(NA)
Austria	3.9	4.8	5.2	5.2	6.9	6.2	5.5	5.4	7.6	6.6	6.4	6.3
Belgium	2.8	2.9	3.1	3.1	[2]6.2	[2]5.5	[2]5.0	[2]5.0	8.2	7.2	6.6	6.6
Canada	[1]2.0	[1]2.3	[1]2.7	[1]2.7	3.5	2.1	2.0	2.0	7.2	7.7	7.4	7.5
Czechia	[2]3.4	3.6	(NA)	[1]4.0	[2]5.8	[2]4.8	4.1	4.1	7.9	6.6	5.8	5.8
Denmark	2.9	3.7	4.1	4.2	[2]4.3	[2]3.4	2.5	2.4	3.8	(NA)	(NA)	(NA)
Estonia	2.9	3.2	3.5	3.5	[2]6.0	3.8	3.5	3.4	7.3	5.5	6.1	6.1
Finland	2.5	[1]3.0	(NA)	(NA)	[2]3.9	3.4	2.8	2.8	[2]6.9	7.0	6.4	6.4
France	[1]3.0	[1]3.0	3.2	3.2	4.1	3.5	3.1	3.0	5.6	5.8	5.4	5.4
Germany	3.3	3.7	4.3	4.3	6.8	6.2	6.0	(NA)	10.1	8.1	7.5	(NA)
Hungary	[1]2.7	[2]2.9	3.3	3.4	[2]6.2	4.5	4.3	4.3	7.1	5.8	5.5	5.4
Ireland	(NA)	(NA)	3.3	3.3	2.8	2.5	2.8	2.8	6.4	6.0	5.9	5.9
Israel [3]	3.5	3.3	3.1	3.2	2.9	2.4	2.2	2.2	7.1	5.2	5.1	5.0
Italy	[1]3.4	[1]3.8	4.0	4.0	[2]4.2	3.0	2.6	2.6	7.0	6.7	6.9	7.0
Japan	1.9	2.2	(NA)	2.5	9.8	8.1	7.8	7.8	24.8	18.2	16.2	16.1
Korea, South	1.3	2.0	2.3	2.4	4.6	6.4	7.1	7.1	11.0	10.0	7.6	7.5
Latvia	2.9	3.1	3.2	3.3	[2]6.1	3.5	3.3	3.2	8.5	6.2	6.0	6.0
Lithuania	3.6	4.0	4.6	4.6	[1]7.6	[1]6.1	[1]5.4	[1]5.3	9.2	7.1	6.5	6.5
Netherlands	(NA)	(NA)	3.6	[2]3.7	[2]3.2	[2]2.9	2.8	[2]2.7	9.0	5.6	5.0	[1]5.1
New Zealand	2.2	2.6	[1]3.3	[1]3.4	(NA)	[2]2.8	[2]2.7	[2]2.6	4.4	6.1	5.0	(NA)
Norway	3.4	4.1	4.7	4.8	[2]3.8	[2]3.8	[2]3.2	[2]3.1	6.0	6.3	6.0	6.0
Poland	2.2	2.2	2.4	(NA)	5.2	[2]5.0	4.9	4.7	(NA)	7.3	6.6	6.5
Portugal	(NA)	(NA)	(NA)	(NA)	3.7	3.3	3.3	3.3	9.4	8.6	8.9	9.0
Russia	4.6	5.0	4.0	4.1	(NA)	(NA)	(NA)	(NA)	13.5	10.8	9.3	9.1
Slovenia	2.2	2.4	3.1	3.2	[2]5.2	[2]4.3	[2]4.2	[2]4.1	7.1	5.5	6.6	6.7
Spain	3.1	3.8	3.9	4.0	2.9	[2]2.5	2.5	[1]2.5	7.1	6.4	6.0	[1]6.0
Sweden	3.0	3.8	4.3	(NA)	[2]3.1	[2]2.5	[2]2.0	[2]2.0	6.6	5.8	5.6	5.5
Switzerland	(NA)	3.8	4.3	4.3	5.3	[2]4.1	3.7	3.6	9.3	[2]7.8	7.0	6.9
Turkey	(NA)	(NA)	(NA)	(NA)	(NA)	2.7	2.8	2.8	5.6	4.0	4.1	4.1
United Kingdom	2.0	2.7	2.8	2.8	(NA)	(NA)	(NA)	(NA)	(NA)	6.1	5.9	5.9

NA Not available. [1] Estimated or provisional. [2] Break in series or difference in methodology. [3] The statistical data for Israel are supplied by and under the responsibility of the relevant Israeli authorities. The use of such data by the OECD is without prejudice as to the status of the Golan Heights, East Jerusalem and Israeli settlements in the West Bank under the terms of international law.

Source: Organisation for Economic Co-Operation and Development (OECD), 2020, "Health care resources," OECD Health Statistics (database) ©, <http://dx.doi.org/10.1787/data-00541-en>; and "Health care utilisation," OECD Health Statistics (database) ©, <http://dx.doi.org/10.1787/data-00542-en>; accessed July 2020.

Table 1364. Gross National Income (GNI) by Country: 2010 and 2019

[For total GNI, 65,206,143 represents $65,206,143,000,000. GNI is the sum of value added by all resident producers, plus any product taxes (less subsidies) not included in the valuation of output, plus net receipts of primary income from abroad]

Country	Gross national income [1]				GNI on purchasing power parity basis [2]			
	Total (mil. dol.)		Per capita (dol.)		Total (mil. dol.)		Per capita (dol.)	
	2010	2019	2010	2019	2010	2019	2010	2019
World [3]	65,206,143	88,781,543	9,420	11,570	88,779,060	134,984,258	12,826	17,591
United States	15,154,199	21,584,413	48,990	65,760	15,126,736	21,624,996	48,900	65,880
Algeria	161,030	170,722	4,480	3,970	470,024	496,317	13,060	11,530
Angola	75,764	97,005	3,240	3,050	139,022	203,209	5,950	6,390
Argentina	378,137	503,116	9,270	11,200	711,419	991,401	17,440	22,060
Australia	1,027,320	1,392,773	46,630	54,910	832,246	1,307,711	37,770	51,560
Austria	414,883	455,396	49,610	51,300	354,517	524,255	42,390	59,060
Bangladesh	118,314	316,235	800	1,940	389,104	845,446	2,640	5,190
Belgium	511,504	543,718	46,950	47,350	441,038	628,537	40,480	54,730
Brazil	1,887,920	1,926,332	9,650	9,130	2,712,167	3,134,970	13,860	14,850
Bulgaria	51,339	65,620	6,940	9,410	107,688	166,588	14,560	23,880
Canada	1,512,537	1,742,831	44,480	46,370	1,337,096	1,910,034	39,320	50,810
Chile	183,354	284,504	10,750	15,010	288,017	457,580	16,880	24,140
China	5,801,888	14,554,341	4,340	10,410	12,325,778	23,403,179	9,210	16,740
Colombia	254,125	327,716	5,620	6,510	467,552	762,426	10,340	15,150
Croatia	60,435	60,641	14,070	14,910	82,052	120,055	19,100	29,520
Czechia	201,913	234,718	19,280	22,000	268,605	433,854	25,640	40,660
Denmark	339,645	367,945	61,220	63,240	242,632	357,320	43,740	61,410
Dominican Republic	51,644	86,880	5,330	8,090	106,666	196,350	11,000	18,280
Ecuador	65,933	105,643	4,390	6,080	134,421	199,871	8,950	11,500
Egypt	196,207	270,172	2,370	2,690	772,380	1,185,110	9,330	11,810
Ethiopia	33,248	95,111	380	850	89,796	257,834	1,020	2,300
Finland	266,033	273,699	49,600	49,580	211,782	282,683	39,490	51,210
France	2,851,169	2,843,038	43,850	42,400	2,390,316	3,379,236	36,760	50,390
Germany	3,643,117	4,033,546	44,550	48,520	3,251,502	4,795,663	39,760	57,690
Ghana	30,547	67,508	1,230	2,220	72,468	167,736	2,920	5,510
Greece	307,604	217,766	27,660	20,320	306,865	335,971	27,590	31,350
Guatemala	39,586	76,503	2,780	4,610	93,394	146,880	6,550	8,850
Hong Kong, China	236,168	381,678	33,620	50,840	352,799	492,466	50,230	65,600
Hungary	131,922	157,734	13,190	16,140	206,069	319,981	20,610	32,750
India	1,505,735	2,910,840	1,220	2,130	5,173,299	9,507,241	4,190	6,960
Indonesia	612,254	1,097,223	2,530	4,050	2,002,210	3,229,573	8,280	11,930
Iraq	136,160	225,739	4,580	5,740	382,580	443,347	12,860	11,280
Ireland	204,646	307,422	44,880	62,210	165,548	336,252	36,300	68,050
Israel	226,091	391,874	29,660	43,290	215,667	381,509	28,290	42,140
Italy	2,243,489	2,077,674	37,850	34,460	2,081,078	2,687,761	35,110	44,580
Japan	5,562,858	5,263,515	43,440	41,690	4,596,531	5,654,422	35,890	44,780
Kazakhstan	121,367	163,117	7,440	8,810	272,722	445,227	16,710	24,050
Kenya	40,445	91,824	960	1,750	96,815	232,294	2,300	4,420
Korea, South	1,104,402	1,743,709	22,290	33,720	1,575,220	2,245,536	31,790	43,430
Malaysia	232,945	357,979	8,260	11,200	560,108	916,168	19,860	28,680
Mexico	1,031,499	1,203,618	9,040	9,430	1,720,422	2,526,977	15,080	19,810
Morocco	96,295	118,058	2,930	3,190	204,980	284,422	6,240	7,680
Myanmar	42,923	75,186	850	1,390	164,058	278,800	3,240	5,160
Netherlands	895,636	922,129	53,900	53,200	751,121	1,038,101	45,210	59,890
New Zealand	129,187	209,792	29,690	42,670	129,222	209,985	29,700	42,710
Nigeria	339,100	407,928	2,140	2,030	705,437	1,039,633	4,450	5,170
Norway	432,970	441,210	88,560	82,500	286,646	372,280	58,630	69,610
Oman	56,276	76,282	18,500	15,330	135,387	142,211	44,510	28,590
Pakistan	184,039	331,616	1,030	1,530	724,600	1,129,050	4,040	5,210
Panama	26,429	63,468	7,260	14,950	50,866	129,953	13,960	30,600
Peru	127,971	219,157	4,410	6,740	261,705	414,710	9,020	12,760
Philippines	222,746	415,750	2,370	3,850	588,001	1,102,794	6,260	10,200
Poland	485,874	577,290	12,770	15,200	775,271	1,242,060	20,380	32,710
Portugal	242,755	237,025	22,960	23,080	279,259	365,570	26,410	35,600
Puerto Rico	62,977	70,178	16,920	21,970	75,214	77,400	20,210	24,240
Qatar	118,091	179,583	63,620	63,410	219,767	266,701	118,390	94,170
Romania	174,972	244,497	8,640	12,630	339,699	616,613	16,780	31,860
Russia	1,425,184	1,651,559	9,980	11,260	2,836,589	4,147,418	19,860	28,270
Saudi Arabia	514,152	782,868	18,750	22,850	1,431,868	1,692,868	52,220	49,400
Singapore	228,092	339,861	44,930	59,590	378,119	524,842	74,480	92,020
Slovak Republic	93,827	105,346	17,400	19,320	132,884	183,678	24,650	33,680
South Africa	317,112	353,529	6,190	6,040	587,541	739,744	11,470	12,630
Spain	1,484,708	1,430,849	31,880	30,390	1,455,146	1,991,316	31,240	42,300
Sri Lanka	48,796	87,694	2,410	4,020	164,224	288,411	8,110	13,230
Sweden	511,828	574,299	54,580	55,840	406,623	589,329	43,360	57,300
Switzerland	606,981	733,126	77,570	85,500	439,966	620,733	56,230	72,390
Tanzania	31,207	60,816	720	1,080	88,300	152,045	2,050	2,700
Thailand	308,010	505,186	4,580	7,260	849,520	1,289,400	12,640	18,520
Turkey	754,130	801,438	10,430	9,610	1,250,657	2,287,043	17,290	27,410
Ukraine	136,703	141,637	2,980	3,370	372,635	578,032	8,120	13,750
United Arab Emirates	285,541	424,764	33,400	43,470	554,579	686,307	64,860	70,240
United Kingdom	2,614,105	2,831,800	41,650	42,370	2,284,297	3,210,887	36,390	48,040
Uzbekistan	39,017	60,396	1,370	1,800	146,732	248,452	5,140	7,400
Vietnam	110,302	244,944	1,250	2,540	356,506	747,220	4,050	7,750

[1] Gross national income calculated using the World Bank Atlas conversion factor; for details, see source. [2] For explanation of purchasing power parity (PPP), see headnote, Table 1365. [3] Includes other countries not shown separately.

Source: The World Bank, Washington, DC, "World Development Indicators" database ©, <https://data.worldbank.org/data-catalog/world-development-indicators>, accessed August 2020.

Table 1365. Real Gross Domestic Product (GDP) Per Capita and Per Employed Persons by Country: 1960 to 2019

[U.S. figures based on the System of National Income and Product Accounts (NIPA) from the Bureau of Economic Analysis. Data for all other countries are based on the 1993 or 2008 United Nations System of National Accounts (SNA). Per capita data based on total resident population. Real GDP is a macroeconomic measure of the size of an economy adjusted for price changes and inflation. Employment data include people serving in the armed forces. Real dollars are calculated based on 2019 Purchasing Power Parities (PPPs). PPPs are currency conversion rates used to convert GDP expressed in different currencies to a common value (U.S. dollars in this case). A PPP for a given country is the number of national currency units needed to buy the specific basket of goods and services that one dollar will buy in the United States. See text, this section]

REAL GDP PER CAPITA (2019 U.S. dollars)

Country	1960	1970	1980	1990	2000	2005	2010	2014	2015	2016	2017	2018	2019
United States	20,271	27,127	33,345	42,065	52,176	56,577	56,538	59,554	60,836	61,386	62,440	63,871	64,747
Canada	16,745	23,054	30,947	36,106	43,146	46,633	46,829	49,645	49,572	49,548	50,507	50,821	51,017
Australia	18,008	24,347	28,064	33,318	41,745	46,345	48,755	51,140	51,566	52,118	52,570	53,161	53,295
Japan	6,723	16,381	22,644	33,385	36,987	38,945	39,234	40,987	41,554	41,841	42,819	43,045	43,434
South Korea	1,860	3,288	6,241	13,205	23,959	29,881	35,885	39,613	40,511	41,540	42,679	43,639	44,346
Singapore	6,329	12,164	24,820	38,965	57,925	64,751	80,538	90,004	90,943	92,151	94,397	95,899	94,910
Austria	15,032	22,478	31,730	38,960	48,286	51,317	53,870	55,002	54,940	55,481	56,462	57,547	58,175
Belgium	14,958	22,830	31,127	37,000	44,834	48,291	49,877	50,799	51,532	52,030	52,817	53,359	53,899
Czechia	(NA)	15,106	21,301	24,484	26,163	31,826	35,001	35,947	37,781	38,633	40,207	41,214	42,184
Denmark	19,259	27,725	33,525	41,074	51,471	54,182	53,490	54,777	55,665	57,025	57,813	58,903	59,993
Finland	12,546	19,285	26,075	34,095	41,295	46,360	47,486	46,556	46,655	47,782	49,148	49,883	50,301
France	14,420	22,241	29,200	35,343	41,645	43,664	44,210	44,981	45,320	45,696	46,631	47,363	47,887
Germany[1]	18,503	26,028	33,892	38,250	44,700	45,766	48,985	52,134	52,583	53,324	54,434	55,100	55,288
Ireland	9,384	13,586	18,717	25,898	46,817	55,496	51,715	56,024	60,184	61,697	66,000	70,513	73,572
Italy	13,781	22,638	30,630	38,000	44,718	45,972	44,314	41,441	41,804	42,416	43,188	43,616	43,838
Netherlands	18,328	26,468	32,523	38,179	49,657	51,798	54,485	54,646	55,470	56,385	57,684	58,838	59,624
Norway	16,647	23,172	34,755	43,149	58,500	63,357	62,828	63,889	64,501	64,621	65,590	65,999	66,302
Spain	7,142	14,692	21,396	28,028	36,129	39,461	38,792	37,388	38,852	39,996	41,056	41,837	42,485
Sweden	17,737	26,249	30,294	35,872	42,785	47,846	50,561	52,013	53,741	54,351	54,917	55,490	55,551
United Kingdom	15,757	19,626	24,072	31,458	39,107	43,833	43,232	45,360	46,062	46,591	47,151	47,495	47,871

REAL GDP PER EMPLOYED PERSON (2019 U.S. dollars)

Country	1960	1970	1980	1990	2000	2005	2010	2014	2015	2016	2017	2018	2019
United States	52,738	67,104	74,240	86,190	106,022	117,127	124,160	128,041	129,924	130,113	131,234	133,345	134,594
Canada	45,344	60,420	68,192	74,822	88,262	91,942	92,458	97,558	97,293	97,228	98,412	99,344	98,898
Australia	45,374	56,934	65,219	72,028	89,051	94,353	97,124	103,429	103,633	104,752	104,869	104,892	104,361
Japan	13,276	31,242	44,861	63,846	71,557	75,983	76,396	78,767	79,397	79,054	79,989	78,936	78,742
South Korea	6,727	10,962	17,293	31,128	52,942	63,065	73,992	77,623	78,948	80,563	82,127	84,010	84,767
Singapore	21,216	38,943	54,889	82,152	111,423	131,919	135,549	140,915	142,075	145,212	151,797	155,908	154,673
Austria	30,995	51,746	68,756	84,521	103,628	109,662	110,580	110,995	111,450	112,309	113,217	113,997	114,484
Belgium	39,002	59,038	81,166	95,889	111,855	118,442	121,253	124,428	125,852	126,128	126,471	126,602	126,424
Czechia	(NA)	29,476	42,203	46,762	55,087	65,866	72,325	73,886	76,714	77,364	79,496	80,672	82,184
Denmark	41,800	56,434	68,284	80,164	99,753	105,505	106,441	110,779	111,832	113,557	114,067	115,162	116,505
Finland	25,235	38,912	52,806	68,876	92,945	100,545	102,089	100,672	101,295	103,573	105,675	104,768	104,797
France	33,332	54,172	71,076	86,993	98,931	104,611	106,843	109,227	110,212	110,708	112,092	112,923	113,037
Germany[1]	36,167	53,687	68,563	76,459	91,876	95,948	97,443	100,311	101,107	102,100	103,215	103,376	103,047
Ireland	24,051	36,341	52,575	74,808	104,879	117,453	125,069	134,513	140,779	140,726	147,736	154,900	158,913
Italy	32,956	60,756	80,646	95,067	104,619	108,771	106,037	103,468	103,597	103,533	104,047	104,034	103,703
Netherlands	44,598	61,690	76,040	83,929	96,405	101,360	103,119	105,628	106,683	107,375	108,095	108,239	108,257
Norway	38,981	54,763	72,894	88,940	113,257	126,383	120,620	121,847	123,647	124,604	126,014	125,582	124,929
Spain	17,717	37,010	63,392	78,264	88,822	88,510	93,781	97,813	98,801	99,669	99,893	100,029	99,921
Sweden	36,298	53,379	58,818	66,755	88,263	99,507	105,624	106,458	109,543	110,148	110,104	110,793	111,515
United Kingdom	34,161	44,155	54,038	67,307	84,159	92,165	93,237	95,694	96,285	96,714	97,580	97,723	98,013

NA Not available. [1] Prior to 1991, data are for the former West Germany.

Source: The Conference Board, Inc., "Total Economy Database™," June 2020 (original version). © The Conference Board 2020.

Table 1366. Sectoral Contributions to Gross Value Added: 2010 and 2019

[In percent. According to the 2008 System of National Accounts (SNA) and the International Standard Industrial Classification (ISIC), Revision 4 (2008), with some exceptions, value added is estimated at basic prices and includes financial intermediation services indirectly measured (FISIM). Value added represents an industry's contribution to national GDP and is calculated as the difference between production and intermediate inputs. Value added comprises labor costs, consumption of fixed capital, indirect taxes less subsidies, and net operating surplus and mixed income. Selected data are estimated or provisional; see source for details]

| Country | Agriculture [1] | | Industry [2] | | | | Services | |
| | | | Total | | Manufacturing | | | |
	2010	2019	2010	2019	2010	2019	2010	2019
United States [3]	1.1	[5] 0.9	16.4	[5] 14.7	12.4	[5] 11.6	78.9	[5] 80.2
Australia	2.4	[6] 2.2	20.4	[6] 18.9	7.9	[6] 6.0	69.3	[6] 70.8
Austria	1.4	1.3	22.2	21.9	18.5	18.7	69.9	70.0
Belgium	0.9	0.5	17.9	16.0	14.9	13.5	75.7	78.2
Chile [4]	3.9	3.9	32.3	24.5	11.7	11.0	57.3	64.1
China [4]	9.6	7.4	40.1	32.0	(NA)	(NA)	43.7	53.4
Czechia	1.7	2.1	29.9	29.6	23.4	24.9	61.5	62.4
Denmark	1.4	1.4	18.4	17.9	12.7	15.0	75.8	74.6
Estonia	3.6	3.3	21.9	19.2	15.6	14.8	68.8	70.6
Finland	2.8	2.7	23.4	20.5	19.4	17.0	67.3	69.4
France	1.8	1.8	13.8	13.5	11.5	11.0	78.4	78.9
Germany	0.9	0.9	25.5	24.2	21.9	21.6	69.2	69.3
Greece	3.3	4.2	11.2	14.8	8.2	10.9	81.1	78.2
Hungary	3.6	4.1	25.7	24.1	21.5	21.5	66.5	65.2
Ireland	1.0	1.0	24.1	34.9	21.4	33.2	73.3	61.1
Italy	2.0	2.2	18.7	19.6	15.8	16.6	73.7	73.9
Japan [7]	1.1	[6] 1.2	23.7	[6] 23.5	20.9	[6] 20.8	70.4	[6] 69.6
Korea	2.4	[6] 2.0	32.5	[6] 31.4	30.2	[6] 29.2	60.1	[6] 60.7
Mexico	3.4	[6] 3.6	25.7	[6] 24.9	16.3	[6] 18.4	62.9	[6] 63.6
Netherlands	2.0	1.8	16.7	14.9	11.7	12.3	76.1	78.3
Norway	1.8	2.2	33.7	26.1	8.1	7.0	59.2	65.0
Poland	2.9	2.5	24.7	25.1	17.7	19.2	63.9	64.7
Portugal	2.2	2.4	16.8	17.4	13.2	13.5	75.1	75.8
Slovak Republic	1.8	2.8	25.2	24.5	20.1	20.7	64.3	64.9
Slovenia	2.2	2.3	24.1	26.7	20.1	23.2	67.4	65.2
South Africa	2.6	2.1	26.3	25.4	14.4	13.2	67.2	68.7
Spain	2.6	2.9	16.3	15.8	12.4	12.2	72.1	74.8
Sweden	1.9	1.6	21.3	18.2	16.7	14.7	71.2	73.4
Switzerland	0.7	0.7	21.6	21.0	19.5	19.3	72.7	73.0
United Kingdom	0.7	0.7	15.4	13.3	10.6	9.6	78.4	79.8

NA Not available. [1] Includes forestry, fishing, and hunting sectors. [2] Includes energy. [3] Value added is estimated at factor cost for U.S. [4] Value added is estimated at producer's prices. [5] Data is for 2017. [6] Data is for 2018. [7] Value added is estimated approximately at market prices for Japan.

Source: Organisation for Economic Co-operation and Development (OECD), 2020, "National Accounts at a Glance," OECD National Accounts Statistics (database) ©, <http://dx.doi.org/10.1787/data-00369-en>, accessed July 2020.

Table 1367. Index of Industrial Production by Country: 2000 to 2019

[Annual averages of monthly data. Industrial production indexes generally measure output in the manufacturing, mining, electric, gas, and water utilities sectors. Minus sign (-) indicates decrease]

| Country | Index (2015=100) | | | | | | | Annual percent change | | | | |
	2000	2005	2010	2015	2017	2018	2019	2010 to 2011	2014 to 2015	2015 to 2016	2017 to 2018	2018 to 2019
United States	91.5	95.6	90.4	100.0	100.3	104.3	105.1	3.1	-1.0	-2.0	3.9	0.8
Australia	74.4	79.6	88.6	100.0	103.1	107.1	109.6	0.8	1.7	1.9	3.8	2.3
Austria	70.1	82.2	90.6	100.0	107.6	112.7	113.2	5.9	2.1	2.4	4.8	0.4
Belgium	71.2	83.9	97.0	100.0	107.2	108.7	114.0	4.7	-0.7	4.5	1.4	4.8
Brazil	83.8	97.8	112.2	100.0	95.9	96.9	95.8	0.4	-8.2	-6.4	1.0	-1.1
Canada	96.8	100.0	89.9	100.0	105.5	109.7	109.2	4.8	-0.4	0.1	3.9	-0.5
Chile	70.1	87.7	88.5	100.0	99.0	101.8	102.6	5.4	0.7	0.0	2.8	0.8
Czechia	60.5	78.9	87.1	100.0	110.1	113.5	113.2	5.9	4.3	3.4	3.0	-0.2
Denmark	109.8	115.7	98.6	100.0	106.3	108.4	111.3	1.1	0.1	4.2	2.0	2.7
Finland	99.9	105.6	106.6	100.0	107.5	111.2	113.5	1.7	-0.9	4.1	3.5	2.0
France	109.3	110.5	100.1	100.0	102.7	103.3	103.5	2.5	1.7	0.6	0.6	0.2
Germany	80.4	85.9	90.4	100.0	104.5	105.7	101.2	8.5	1.1	1.5	1.2	-4.2
Greece	140.2	135.2	113.2	100.0	106.9	108.8	(NA)	-5.9	1.0	2.6	1.8	(NA)
Hungary	58.2	76.1	82.2	99.7	105.8	109.8	115.7	5.6	7.0	0.8	3.8	5.3
India	42.9	[2] 57.8	87.9	100.0	108.9	114.5	115.3	4.8	2.5	5.2	5.2	0.7
Ireland	42.9	57.2	63.0	100.0	99.5	94.6	97.3	-0.4	36.9	1.8	-5.0	2.8
Italy	127.7	121.8	107.8	99.7	105.5	106.2	105.0	0.8	1.0	2.1	0.6	-1.1
Japan	106.1	108.9	102.8	100.0	102.8	103.9	101.2	-2.8	-1.2	0.2	1.0	-2.6
Korea, South	49.4	66.5	92.5	100.0	104.8	106.3	106.3	6.0	-0.3	2.2	1.5	0.0
Mexico [1]	92.5	96.8	100.0	109.8	[3] 109.1	(NA)	(NA)	(NA)	(NA)	(NA)	(NA)	(NA)
Netherlands	95.9	100.2	106.9	100.0	102.5	103.1	102.4	-0.5	-3.4	1.4	0.7	-0.8
New Zealand	87.0	98.4	97.3	100.0	103.3	104.7	106.1	-2.8	1.5	1.5	1.3	1.4
Norway	121.6	116.4	102.5	100.0	98.5	96.7	92.5	-5.0	1.5	-1.2	-1.8	-4.4
Poland	47.4	62.0	83.4	100.0	109.6	116.1	120.9	6.7	4.9	2.8	5.9	4.2
Russia	61.6	81.4	89.1	100.0	105.5	109.2	111.8	5.0	-0.8	1.8	3.5	2.3
Spain	124.0	127.1	105.6	100.0	105.1	105.4	106.2	-1.5	3.2	1.9	0.3	0.7
Sweden	101.2	110.0	102.6	100.0	106.2	108.7	110.3	2.7	3.7	1.8	2.4	1.5
Switzerland	83.4	82.3	96.4	100.0	105.0	110.7	115.5	1.9	-1.7	0.0	5.4	4.4
Turkey	43.8	59.6	69.4	100.0	112.8	114.0	113.3	15.4	6.1	3.4	1.1	-0.6
United Kingdom	109.8	106.6	100.9	100.0	103.2	103.6	102.6	0.0	1.0	1.1	0.4	-1.0

NA Not available. [1] Including construction. [2] Break in series. [3] Estimated.

Source: Organisation for Economic Co-operation and Development (OECD), 2020, "Key short-term indicators," Main Economic Indicators (database) ©, <http://dx.doi.org/10.1787/data-00039-en>, accessed July 2020.

Table 1368. Selected Indexes of Manufacturing Productivity, Unit Labor Costs, Employment, and Hours Worked by Country: 2000 to 2018

[2010=100. Data for all countries are prepared according to the System of National Accounts (SNA) 2008 or its European counterpart, the European System of Accounts 2010 (ESA 2010). Data refer to all employed persons (including employees, self-employed, and unpaid family workers). Minus sign (-) indicates decrease]

Index	United States	Australia	Canada	France	Germany	Italy	Japan	Netherlands	South Korea	Sweden	United Kingdom
REAL VALUED ADDED PER HOUR WORKED (PRODUCTIVITY)											
2000	58.3	80.9	91.8	75.0	79.0	90.8	75.7	76.0	48.9	67.6	70.2
2010	100.0	100.0	100.0	100.0	100.0	100.0	100.0	100.0	100.0	100.0	100.0
2015	97.8	105.9	109.0	111.3	106.0	108.2	109.4	109.2	107.6	106.1	101.0
2017	98.7	105.0	113.9	116.2	113.6	112.6	113.1	116.9	118.4	108.4	102.7
2018	100.6	105.8	115.5	117.1	113.6	113.5	113.6	120.4	125.8	110.9	102.0
Average annual percent change:											
2000-2007	6.5	2.9	1.6	3.9	4.0	1.5	4.0	4.4	8.9	5.9	4.7
2010-2017	0.5	0.9	2.1	2.6	3.6	3.0	3.0	2.7	2.9	3.5	1.0
2017-2018	1.9	0.8	1.4	0.7	(Z)	0.8	0.4	3.0	6.3	2.2	-0.6
HOURLY LABOR COSTS (national currency basis)											
2000	72.4	65.2	74.9	73.0	82.2	72.0	101.9	74.6	46.1	70.6	63.7
2010	100.0	100.0	100.0	100.0	100.0	100.0	100.0	100.0	100.0	100.0	100.0
2015	109.8	121.1	114.8	111.9	112.4	111.3	102.7	110.6	117.3	117.4	110.8
2017	114.3	123.2	117.1	116.4	118.1	112.6	105.0	115.9	127.2	121.2	112.3
2018	116.6	127.9	121.3	119.1	120.8	114.7	108.5	118.7	138.5	127.3	116.7
Average annual percent change:											
2000-2007	4.0	5.2	3.6	3.2	2.2	3.0	-0.5	3.5	9.7	4.4	5.1
2010-2017	1.8	2.6	1.9	2.4	2.2	1.9	0.4	1.3	3.5	2.2	2.1
2017-2018	2.1	3.9	3.5	2.3	2.3	1.9	3.3	2.4	8.9	5.0	3.9
REAL HOURLY COMPENSATION, CPI DEFLATED (national currency basis)											
2000	91.7	87.7	91.4	86.5	95.9	89.2	99.2	91.1	63.0	81.9	78.2
2010	100.0	100.0	100.0	100.0	100.0	100.0	100.0	100.0	100.0	100.0	100.0
2015	101.0	108.1	105.7	106.0	104.9	103.6	99.1	101.3	106.8	113.4	99.8
2017	101.6	106.5	104.6	108.9	108.0	103.6	101.0	104.4	112.5	113.8	97.7
2018	101.3	108.5	105.9	109.4	108.6	104.3	103.3	105.1	120.8	117.3	99.2
Average annual percent change:											
2000-2007	1.2	2.0	1.3	1.3	0.6	0.7	-0.1	1.3	6.6	2.8	3.3
2010-2017	0.1	0.4	0.3	1.3	0.9	0.7	(Z)	-0.1	1.6	1.3	(Z)
2017-2018	-0.4	1.9	1.3	0.4	0.5	0.7	2.3	0.7	7.3	3.0	1.6
UNIT LABOR COSTS, (national currency basis)											
2000	124.2	80.7	81.5	97.3	104.0	79.2	134.6	98.2	94.2	104.5	90.7
2010	100.0	100.0	100.0	100.0	100.0	100.0	100.0	100.0	100.0	100.0	100.0
2015	112.3	114.4	105.4	100.5	106.1	102.9	93.9	101.2	109.0	110.7	109.7
2017	115.8	117.3	102.8	100.1	103.9	100.0	92.8	99.2	107.4	111.8	109.4
2018	116.0	120.9	105.0	101.7	106.3	101.1	95.5	98.6	110.1	114.8	114.4
Average annual percent change:											
2000-2007	-2.4	2.3	2.0	-0.7	-1.8	1.5	-4.3	-0.9	0.7	-1.4	0.5
2010-2017	1.3	1.6	-0.1	-0.2	-1.3	-1.0	-2.6	-1.3	0.6	-1.2	1.0
2017-2018	0.2	3.0	2.1	1.6	2.3	1.1	2.8	-0.6	2.5	2.7	4.6
REAL VALUE ADDED PER EMPLOYED PERSON											
2000	58.4	82.8	93.2	75.8	81.2	98.1	76.4	77.1	52.3	67.7	70.8
2010	100.0	100.0	100.0	100.0	100.0	100.0	100.0	100.0	100.0	100.0	100.0
2015	98.8	106.1	108.7	111.4	107.2	107.5	110.8	110.4	104.0	103.8	101.7
2017	99.9	104.3	112.6	114.9	113.8	113.4	114.7	117.9	111.3	108.3	102.9
2018	102.2	104.5	115.5	114.8	113.6	114.3	114.3	121.0	116.5	110.9	101.4
Average annual percent change:											
2000-2007	6.3	2.5	1.4	3.6	3.9	1.3	4.4	4.1	7.8	5.8	4.5
2010-2017	1.0	0.8	2.1	2.6	4.1	3.2	3.9	3.0	2.4	3.9	1.2
2017-2018	2.3	0.3	2.6	0.0	-0.2	0.8	-0.4	2.7	4.7	2.4	-1.4
ALL EMPLOYED PERSONS											
2000	148.8	110.0	129.9	125.8	109.8	109.8	114.7	118.9	103.8	124.5	151.4
2010	100.0	100.0	100.0	100.0	100.0	100.0	100.0	100.0	100.0	100.0	100.0
2015	106.7	89.4	99.7	95.2	105.2	92.0	94.9	95.8	111.0	94.1	101.1
2017	107.7	88.2	100.6	94.3	106.4	93.4	95.6	97.2	110.0	94.6	102.4
2018	109.5	89.8	100.1	94.4	108.2	94.7	97.0	99.1	108.7	95.2	104.2
Average annual percent change:											
2000-2007	-2.7	-1.0	-0.8	-1.4	-0.8	(-Z)	-1.2	-1.4	0.3	-1.2	-4.1
2010-2017	0.6	-1.8	(Z)	-1.3	0.5	-1.3	-0.7	-0.7	1.8	-0.9	(Z)
2017-2018	1.6	1.8	-0.5	0.1	1.7	1.4	1.4	1.9	-1.2	0.6	1.8
HOURS WORKED OF ALL EMPLOYED PERSONS											
2000	149.0	112.7	131.7	127.0	112.8	118.6	115.8	120.6	111.0	124.7	152.5
2010	100.0	100.0	100.0	100.0	100.0	100.0	100.0	100.0	100.0	100.0	100.0
2015	107.8	89.6	99.5	95.3	106.3	91.4	96.1	96.8	107.3	92.1	101.8
2017	109.0	87.6	99.4	93.2	106.5	94.0	97.0	98.1	103.4	94.5	102.6
2018	111.2	88.7	100.0	92.6	108.1	95.4	97.6	99.6	100.6	95.3	103.6
Average annual percent change:											
2000-2007	-2.8	-1.4	-1.0	-1.7	-0.9	-0.2	-0.8	-1.7	-0.7	-1.2	-4.2
2010-2017	1.1	-1.9	0.1	-1.2	1.1	-1.1	0.1	-0.4	1.3	-0.5	0.2
2017-2018	2.0	1.2	0.7	-0.6	1.5	1.4	0.6	1.6	-2.7	0.8	1.0

Z less than 0.05 percent.

Source: The Conference Board, Inc., International Labor Comparisons Program, "International Comparisons of Manufacturing Productivity and Unit Labor Cost Trends, 2018," December 2019, <https://www.conference-board.org/ilcprogram>. © The Conference Board 2020.

Table 1369. Indexes of Hourly Compensation Costs for Employees in Manufacturing by Country: 2000 to 2016

[United States=100. Compensation costs include pay for time worked (base wages and salaries, overtime pay, bonuses and premiums paid each pay period, and cost of living adjustments), directly-paid benefits (pay for leave time, irregular bonuses, and pay in kind), employer social insurance expenditures (legally required, private, and contractual social benefit costs), and labor-related taxes (minus subsidies). Data are adjusted for exchange rates. Regional averages are trade-weighted to account for differences in countries' relative importance to total world trade in manufactured goods. See source for details]

Area or country	2000	2010	2014	2015	2016	Area or country	2000	2010	2014	2015	2016
United States..........	100	100	100	100	100	Hungary..............	12	24	26	22	22
						Ireland..............	66	117	117	95	93
ILC economies [1].......	78	90	93	82	80	Israel................	49	55	62	58	58
OECD [2]................	82	96	97	85	84	Italy................	67	97	102	86	83
Europe...............	82	103	108	91	88	Japan [6].............	100	91	73	62	68
Euro Area [3].........	83	112	118	98	95	Mexico..............	14	13	13	12	10
Eastern Europe [4].....	13	28	29	25	25	Netherlands.........	85	111	114	93	89
East Asia ex-Japan [5]..	35	44	54	51	50	New Zealand........	36	59	73	61	61
Argentina [6].............	33	37	48	53	43	Norway.............	98	165	170	135	125
Australia.............	67	114	124	102	98	Philippines..........	4	5	6	6	5
Austria...............	88	115	123	103	101	Poland..............	14	24	27	23	22
Belgium..............	105	146	152	127	121	Portugal............	24	35	34	29	28
Brazil...............	17	29	28	20	20	Singapore...........	47	56	72	68	69
Canada..............	73	99	93	81	77	Slovakia............	10	31	35	29	30
Czechia..............	14	33	32	27	27	South Korea.........	39	51	64	60	59
Denmark.............	89	139	143	118	116	Spain...............	50	77	76	62	60
Estonia..............	10	27	34	29	30	Sweden.............	94	123	135	110	107
Finland..............	79	116	122	102	99	Switzerland.........	108	147	175	161	155
France...............	85	112	119	99	97	Taiwan [6]............	29	24	26	25	25
Germany..............	101	126	134	112	111	Turkey..............	(NA)	18	17	15	16
Greece...............	40	65	52	42	40	United Kingdom......	83	83	89	82	73

NA Not available. [1] ILC (International Labor Comparisons) economies refers to the 35 national economies included in ILC compensation comparisons, excluding China and India that are not strictly comparable with each other or with data for other countries. Data for 2000 excludes Turkey. [2] Organisation for Economic Co-operation and Development; see text, this section. Includes only those countries that are also ILC economies. [3] Euro Area includes Austria, Belgium, Estonia, Finland, France, Germany, Greece, Ireland, Italy, the Netherlands, Portugal, Slovakia and Spain. [4] Czechia, Estonia, Hungary, Poland, and Slovakia. [5] South Korea, Philippines, Singapore, and Taiwan. Excludes Japan. [6] Except for Argentina, Japan, and Taiwan, data relate to manufacturing as defined by the International Standard Industrial Classification of All Economic Activities (ISIC) Revision 4.

Source: The Conference Board, Inc., International Labor Comparisons program, "International Comparisons of Hourly Compensation Costs in Manufacturing, 2016," April 2018, <https://www.conference-board.org/ilcprogram/compensation>. © The Conference Board 2020.

Table 1370. Annual Percent Change in Labor Productivity and Hours Worked by Country: 2002 to 2019

[Annual percent change for period shown. Labor productivity growth refers to the growth in gross domestic product (GDP) per hour worked. Data are derived from The Conference Board Total Economy Database. Regional labor productivity growth rates are aggregated using shares in nominal PPP converted GDP; regional hours growth is weighted using total hours shares. Growth rates are the averages of yearly growth rates. Minus sign (-) indicates decrease]

Country	Labor productivity		Total hours worked		Country	Labor productivity		Total hours worked	
	2002-2007	2010-2019	2002-2007	2010-2019		2002-2007	2010-2019	2002-2007	2010-2019
Advanced economies [1]........	1.9	1.1	0.7	0.8	Czechia...............	4.3	1.6	0.5	0.7
United States.......	2.2	0.8	0.6	1.5	Estonia...............	6.1	2.5	1.7	1.1
Japan................	1.3	1.1	0.1	0.2	Hungary..............	4.7	1.1	-1.0	1.6
					Latvia................	8.2	3.0	1.2	-0.5
European Union (EU-15, old) [2]......	1.2	0.8	0.9	0.6	Lithuania.............	6.4	2.8	1.8	0.6
Austria..............	2.0	0.8	0.4	0.7	Malta................	1.7	2.4	0.8	3.1
Belgium..............	1.4	0.5	1.0	1.1	Poland...............	3.5	3.4	1.0	0.2
Denmark.............	1.4	1.6	0.3	0.2	Romania..............	8.6	3.7	-2.0	-0.6
Finland.............	2.3	0.9	0.9	0.3	Slovak Republic.......	5.8	2.4	1.0	0.6
France...............	1.2	0.9	0.6	0.4	Slovenia..............	3.9	1.7	0.6	0.1
Germany..............	1.2	1.1	0.1	0.9	European Union (EU-28, enlarged) [4]...	1.6	1.1	0.8	0.5
Greece...............	2.2	-0.7	1.8	-1.4	Addenda:				
Ireland..............	2.3	3.3	2.9	1.3	Other advanced economies [1]..........	2.9	1.8	1.1	1.1
Italy................	-0.1	0.3	1.1	-0.1	Australia..............	1.3	1.0	2.2	1.6
Luxembourg...........	1.4	0.4	2.8	2.7	Canada...............	1.0	0.9	1.6	1.2
Netherlands........	1.4	0.6	0.5	0.9	Hong Kong............	4.5	2.3	1.1	0.6
Portugal.............	1.3	0.9	-0.2	-0.1	Iceland...............	4.4	1.0	0.8	1.7
Spain................	0.5	1.0	2.9	0.0	Israel................	1.6	1.4	2.0	2.3
Sweden..............	2.8	1.1	0.5	1.3	New Zealand.........	1.5	0.7	2.3	2.2
United Kingdom....	2.0	0.5	0.7	1.4	Norway...............	1.6	0.5	0.8	1.0
European Union (EU-13, new) [3]....	4.8	2.7	0.3	0.2	Singapore............	4.6	2.9	2.6	1.9
Bulgaria.............	3.7	2.9	2.5	-0.6	South Korea..........	5.2	2.8	0.0	0.4
Croatia..............	2.9	2.0	2.0	-1.0	Switzerland...........	1.4	1.1	1.0	0.7
Cyprus..............	1.8	0.6	2.5	0.6	Taiwan................	4.1	2.2	1.6	1.3

[1] "Advanced" includes the U.S., EU-15, Japan, and "other advanced" economies. [2] Referring to membership of the European Union until April 30, 2004. [3] Referring to membership of the European Union as of January 1, 2007. [4] Referring to all 28 members of the European Union as of 2019. See text, this section.

Source: The Conference Board, New York, NY, "The Conference Board Total Economy Database™," June 2020 (original version). © The Conference Board 2020.

Table 1371. Comparative Price Levels—Selected OECD Countries: May 2020

[Purchasing power parities (PPPs) are rates of currency conversion that eliminate the differences in price levels between countries. Comparative price levels are defined as the ratios of PPPs to exchange rates. The PPPs are given in national currency units per U.S. dollar. This table should be read vertically. Each column shows the number of specified monetary units needed in each of the countries listed to buy the same representative basket of consumer goods and services. In each case the representative basket costs a hundred units in the country whose currency is specified. For example, in May 2020, an item that costs $1.00 in the United States would cost $1.05 (U.S. dollars) in Japan]

Country	United States (USD)	Australia (AUD)	Canada (CAD)	Chile (Chilean peso)	France (EUR)	Germany (EUR)	Italy (EUR)	Japan (JPY)	Korea (KRW)	Mexico (MXN)	Spain (EUR)	Turkey (TRY)	United Kingdom (GBP)
United States	100	99	108	163	110	116	122	96	126	218	132	287	103
Australia [1]	101	100	108	165	110	117	123	96	128	220	133	290	104
Austria	91	90	97	148	99	105	110	87	115	197	119	260	93
Belgium	93	92	100	151	102	107	113	89	117	202	122	266	95
Canada	93	92	100	152	102	108	113	89	118	203	122	267	96
Chile	61	61	66	100	67	71	74	59	78	134	81	176	63
Colombia	39	39	42	64	43	46	48	38	50	86	52	113	41
Czechia	58	57	62	94	63	67	70	55	73	126	76	166	59
Denmark	113	112	121	184	124	131	137	108	143	246	148	324	116
Estonia	66	66	71	108	72	77	80	63	84	144	87	190	68
Finland	101	100	108	164	110	116	122	96	127	219	132	289	104
France	91	91	98	149	100	106	111	87	115	199	120	262	94
Germany	86	86	93	141	95	100	105	83	109	188	114	248	89
Greece	68	67	73	111	74	79	83	65	86	148	89	195	70
Hungary	49	49	53	80	54	57	60	47	62	107	65	141	51
Iceland	110	109	119	180	121	128	134	106	140	241	145	317	114
Ireland	106	105	114	172	116	122	128	101	134	230	139	304	109
Israel [1][2]	117	116	126	191	128	135	142	112	148	255	154	336	120
Italy	82	82	88	134	90	95	100	79	104	179	108	237	85
Japan	105	104	113	171	115	121	127	100	132	228	138	301	108
Korea, South	79	78	85	129	87	92	96	76	100	172	104	227	81
Latvia	62	62	67	102	68	72	76	59	79	136	82	179	64
Lithuania	55	55	60	90	61	64	67	53	70	121	73	159	57
Luxembourg	105	104	113	171	115	121	127	100	132	228	138	301	108
Mexico	46	45	49	75	50	53	56	44	58	100	60	132	47
Netherlands	95	94	102	154	104	110	115	90	120	206	125	272	97
New Zealand [1]	97	96	104	158	106	112	118	93	123	212	128	279	100
Norway	108	107	116	175	118	125	131	103	136	234	142	309	111
Poland	47	46	50	76	51	54	57	45	59	102	61	134	48
Portugal	71	70	76	115	77	82	86	68	89	154	93	203	73
Slovak Republic	66	65	71	108	72	76	80	63	84	144	87	190	68
Slovenia	70	69	75	114	76	81	85	67	88	152	92	200	72
Spain	76	75	82	124	83	88	92	73	96	166	100	218	78
Sweden	96	95	103	157	105	111	117	92	122	210	127	277	99
Switzerland	134	133	144	219	147	155	163	128	170	293	177	386	138
Turkey	35	35	37	57	38	40	42	33	44	76	46	100	36
United Kingdom	97	96	104	158	106	113	118	93	123	212	128	279	100

[1] Estimates based on quarterly consumer prices. [2] The statistical data for Israel are supplied by and under the responsibility of the relevant Israeli authorities. The use of such data by the OECD is without prejudice to the status of the Golan Heights, East Jerusalem and Israeli settlements in the West Bank under the terms of international law.

Source: Organisation for Economic Co-operation and Development (OECD), 2020 "Prices: Comparative Price Levels," Main Economic Indicators (database) ©, <http://dx.doi.org/10.1787/data-00536-en>, accessed July 2020.

Table 1372. Indexes of Living Costs Abroad by Selected City: 2019

[As of January 2019. Washington, DC=100. Indexes compare the costs in dollars of representative goods and services (excluding housing and education) purchased at the foreign location and the cost of comparable goods and services in the Washington, DC area. The indexes are place-to-place comparisons at specific times and currency exchange rates. They cannot be used for measuring cost changes over time at a foreign location. Since the indexes reflect only the expenditure pattern and living costs of American families, they are not comparable to the living costs of foreign nationals living in their own country. Survey dates show month/day/year]

Country/territory	City	Survey date	Local index [1]	Country/territory	City	Survey date	Local index [1]
Algeria	Algiers	12/13/2015	88	Kyrgyzstan	Bishkek	4/26/2016	112
Angola	Luanda	9/27/2015	184	Laos	Vientiane	1/15/2014	127
Argentina	Buenos Aires	6/14/2017	143	Latvia	Riga	5/11/2014	143
Armenia	Yerevan	11/22/2015	140	Lebanon	Beirut	12/17/2014	130
Australia	Canberra	4/16/2015	147	Liberia	Monrovia	10/31/2017	155
Austria	Vienna	12/3/2013	176	Libya	Tripoli	1/5/2007	116
Azerbaijan	Baku	1/5/2015	156	Lithuania	Vilnius	12/7/2014	105
Bahamas	Nassau	4/11/2016	160	Luxembourg	(X)	6/8/2015	140
Bangladesh	Dhaka	7/1/2015	130	Macedonia	Skopje	7/8/2015	82
Belarus	Minsk	11/2/2016	84	Madagascar	Antananarivo	1/13/2016	156
Belgium	Brussels	3/23/2015	132	Malawi	Lilongwe	3/12/2014	132
Belize	Belmopan	3/20/2014	131	Malaysia	Kuala Lumpur	12/29/2016	93
Bolivia	La Paz	6/7/2017	122	Mali	Bamako	2/12/2014	154
Bosnia-Herzegovina	Sarajevo	2/23/2015	102	Mauritania	Nouakchott	4/4/2018	119
Botswana	Gaborone	11/5/2014	129	Mexico	Mexico City	2/24/2018	105
Brazil	Sao Paulo	3/19/2018	162	Moldova	Chisinau	5/1/2012	122
Bulgaria	Sofia	8/11/2017	138	Mongolia	Ulaanbaatar	4/6/2014	141
Burma	Rangoon	12/1/2015	90	Montenegro	Podgorica	9/14/2015	116
Burundi	Bujumbura	12/2/2014	128	Morocco	Casablanca	12/27/2017	121
Cambodia	Phnom Penh	2/15/2016	121	Mozambique	Maputo	5/17/2017	122
Cameroon	Yaounde	5/11/2015	143	Nepal	Kathmandu	3/17/2014	109
Canada	Ottawa	9/26/2017	139	Netherlands	The Hague	4/21/2014	159
Chad	Ndjamena	7/20/2017	137	New Zealand	Wellington	2/8/2016	126
Chile	Santiago	9/7/2015	134	Nicaragua	Managua	2/1/2017	122
China	Beijing	5/26/2016	139	Niger	Niamey	5/16/2016	135
Colombia	Bogota	12/15/2014	138	Nigeria	Abuja	5/9/2016	153
Costa Rica	San Jose	1/26/2016	146	Norway	Oslo	1/25/2016	153
Cote d'Ivoire	Abidjan	2/23/2015	142	Oman	Muscat	1/22/2017	116
Croatia	Zagreb	6/15/2016	108	Pakistan	Islamabad	11/14/2016	96
Cuba	Havana	12/26/2014	137	Panama	Panama City	12/31/2015	127
Cyprus	Nicosia	9/17/2014	148	Papua New Guinea	Port Moresby	1/22/2015	170
Czechia	Prague	3/31/2017	101	Paraguay	Asuncion	11/26/2015	116
Dem. Rep. of Congo	Kinshasa	7/20/2016	178	Peru	Lima	6/5/2015	138
Denmark	Copenhagen	5/4/2015	160	Philippines	Manila	4/19/2015	115
Djibouti	Djibouti City	2/11/2014	155	Poland	Warsaw	7/31/2012	131
Dominican Republic	Santo Domingo	4/20/2017	134	Portugal	Lisbon	2/9/2018	127
Ecuador	Quito	4/13/2016	157	Qatar	Doha	9/9/2015	133
Egypt	Cairo	3/13/2006	96	Romania	Bucharest	1/10/2018	100
El Salvador	San Salvador	11/1/2016	119	Russia	Moscow	2/6/2017	155
Equatorial Guinea	Malabo	8/24/2016	136	Rwanda	Kigali	8/16/2017	142
Eritrea	Asmara	4/12/2015	184	Samoa	(X)	6/20/2011	137
Estonia	Tallinn	7/21/2015	138	Saudi Arabia	Riyadh	6/2/2014	141
Ethiopia	Addis Ababa	11/30/2016	149	Senegal	Dakar	9/17/2014	179
Fiji	Suva	2/6/2017	121	Serbia	Belgrade	3/28/2016	97
Finland	Helsinki	2/3/2015	133	Sierra Leone	Freetown	5/14/2014	155
France	Paris	2/19/2015	162	Singapore	(X)	11/7/2016	127
Gabon	Libreville	10/21/2015	153	Slovakia	Bratislava	7/27/2016	116
Georgia	Tbilisi	7/27/2014	130	Slovenia	Ljubljana	3/18/2016	139
Germany	Berlin	3/1/2017	135	South Africa	Pretoria	10/23/2014	128
Ghana	Accra	7/26/2017	127	Spain	Madrid	3/2/2017	123
Greece	Athens	10/22/2013	150	Sri Lanka	Colombo	3/4/2015	98
Guatemala	Guatemala City	2/10/2014	125	Sudan	Khartoum	10/11/2017	141
Guyana	Georgetown	9/29/2017	139	Sweden	Stockholm	5/13/2010	185
Haiti	Port-au-Prince	3/23/2016	147	Switzerland	Geneva	11/17/2015	169
Honduras	Tegucigalpa	3/14/2017	126	Syria	Damascus	10/13/2010	116
Hong Kong	(X)	8/1/2017	142	Taiwan	Taipei	12/29/2015	126
Hungary	Budapest	11/22/2017	102	Tajikistan	Dushanbe	4/7/2016	117
Iceland	Reykjavik	6/12/2017	150	Tanzania	Dar es Salaam	10/14/2014	147
India	New Delhi	4/21/2016	105	Thailand	Bangkok	3/10/2015	122
Indonesia	Jakarta	11/17/2015	107	Tunisia	Tunis	1/9/2014	121
Iraq	Baghdad	7/21/2004	74	Turkey	Istanbul	3/9/2014	129
Ireland	Dublin	12/4/2014	147	Uganda	Kampala	2/8/2017	114
Israel	Tel Aviv	3/4/2014	153	Ukraine	Kyiv	10/28/2015	130
Italy	Rome	11/8/2016	146	United Arab Emirates	Dubai	3/15/2018	130
Jamaica	Kingston	3/31/2016	118	United Kingdom	London	9/11/2014	220
Japan	Tokyo City	2/18/2014	180	Uruguay	Montevideo	10/19/2017	132
Jordan	Amman	3/12/2013	140	Uzbekistan	Tashkent	2/15/2017	143
Kazakhstan	Astana	4/3/2018	108	Venezuela	Caracas	9/4/2014	173
Kenya	Nairobi	5/4/2017	120	Vietnam	Hanoi	2/28/2017	98
Korea, South	Seoul	10/24/2017	145	Yemen	Sanaa	4/25/2009	92
Kosovo	Pristina	8/16/2009	129	Zambia	Lusaka	6/15/2014	143
Kuwait	Kuwait City	3/26/2017	113	Zimbabwe	Harare	10/12/2017	154

X Not applicable. [1] The local index measures living costs for private American citizens and excludes special price advantages available only to U.S. government employees. The local index is a comparison of prices at the foreign post and in Washington, DC, with the price ratios weighted by the expenditure pattern of American employees living at the foreign post. This is the index most appropriate for use by business firms and other private organizations to establish cost-of-living allowances for their American employees stationed abroad.

Source: U.S. Department of State, Bureau of Administration, "Indexes of Living Costs Abroad, Quarters Allowances, and Hardship Differentials," January 2019, <https://aoprals.state.gov/content.asp?content_id=186&menu_id=81>.

Table 1373. Percent of Consumer Expenditures Spent on Food, Alcohol, and Tobacco Consumed at Home by Selected Country: 2018

Country/territory	Food [1]	Alcoholic beverages and tobacco	Country/territory	Food [1]	Alcoholic beverages and tobacco	Country/territory	Food [1]	Alcoholic beverages and tobacco
United States..........	**6.4**	**1.7**	France................	13.2	3.7	Nigeria..................	59.0	1.0
Algeria..................	37.3	1.0	Georgia.............	32.3	3.4	Norway.................	11.7	4.1
Argentina...............	28.3	1.9	Germany..............	10.7	3.2	Pakistan...............	39.5	1.1
Australia.................	9.3	3.5	Ghana................	41.3	1.0	Peru....................	26.3	2.4
Austria...................	9.8	3.2	Greece..............	17.1	4.9	Philippines.............	42.0	1.4
Bahrain.................	13.2	0.4	Honduras..........	32.8	4.7	Portugal...............	16.6	3.2
Bangladesh.............	53.5	1.9	Hong Kong.........	14.7	1.2	Romania...............	27.3	5.7
Belarus................	32.3	7.2	Hungary.............	18.2	7.3	Russia..................	28.0	7.4
Belgium.................	13.4	4.3	India.................	29.8	2.4	Saudi Arabia............	20.6	0.6
Bolivia..................	29.1	2.1	Indonesia.............	31.7	7.2	Serbia.................	25.6	7.0
Bosnia-Herzegovina. ..	30.7	9.2	Iran..................	27.9	0.6	Singapore..............	6.9	1.9
Brazil...................	15.7	1.5	Iraq..................	30.1	4.2	Slovakia...............	18.4	5.0
Bulgaria.................	19.3	5.0	Ireland..............	9.0	5.8	Slovenia...............	14.6	5.1
Cambodia...............	42.3	2.2	Israel...............	16.2	2.9	South Africa............	21.4	4.9
Canada..................	9.1	3.3	Italy.................	14.2	4.1	South Korea............	13.8	2.7
Chile....................	16.0	2.9	Japan................	16.0	2.3	Spain..................	12.1	3.5
China...................	21.6	2.5	Jordan..............	29.6	4.6	Sweden................	12.4	3.4
Colombia................	19.2	3.0	Kazakhstan.........	44.9	1.7	Switzerland............	9.2	3.6
Costa Rica..............	25.7	1.2	Kenya...............	52.9	4.1	Taiwan.................	14.7	2.3
Croatia..................	23.0	2.3	Kuwait..............	19.2	0.2	Thailand...............	24.3	3.4
Czechia.................	16.3	8.0	Latvia...............	17.3	7.9	Tunisia................	21.9	3.2
Denmark................	11.5	3.4	Lebanon.............	20.7	1.2	Turkey.................	21.8	3.4
Dominican Republic. ..	26.8	3.8	Lithuania............	21.2	5.9	Ukraine................	42.2	7.7
Ecuador................	26.2	0.8	Malaysia............	21.5	1.8	United Arab Emirates. ..	13.7	0.4
Egypt...................	33.3	4.7	Mexico..............	23.4	2.8	United Kingdom.........	8.1	3.2
El Salvador.............	26.5	0.5	Morocco.............	34.0	1.4	Uruguay...............	18.6	1.3
Ethiopia.................	56.6	3.8	Netherlands.........	11.4	3.3	Venezuela..............	19.1	3.8
Finland.................	11.5	4.3	New Zealand.......	13.4	4.8	Vietnam................	38.8	2.3

[1] Includes nonalcoholic beverages.

Source: U.S. Department of Agriculture, Economic Research Service, International Consumer and Food Industry Trends, "Data on expenditures on food and alcoholic beverages in selected countries," <https://www.ers.usda.gov/topics/international-markets-us-trade/international-consumer-and-food-industry-trends/>, accessed July 2019.

Table 1374. Gross Government Assets and Liabilities as a Percent of GDP by Country: 2010 to 2021

[Percent of nominal gross domestic product. The general government sector is a consolidation of accounts for the central, state, and local governments plus social security. Table includes data for two scenarios of the COVID-19 pandemic]

Country	General government gross financial liabilities as a percent of GDP				General government gross financial assets as a percent of GDP			
	2010	2019	2021, single hit [1]	2021, double hit [1]	2010	2019	2021, single hit [1]	2021, double hit [1]
United States.............	**95.2**	**108.5**	**133.0**	**139.9**	**25.0**	**23.1**	**23.1**	**23.1**
Australia...................	25.1	45.8	57.7	65.8	43.0	54.6	53.6	56.1
Austria.....................	96.3	94.7	107.2	113.1	44.9	45.2	46.9	46.9
Belgium....................	108.7	121.6	135.3	147.8	26.4	34.7	34.7	34.7
Canada.....................	86.4	94.5	104.8	110.1	55.2	72.7	72.7	72.7
Czechia....................	46.2	38.5	46.4	52.3	37.4	28.8	28.8	28.8
Denmark....................	53.4	47.1	57.4	64.6	56.7	53.2	52.6	55.0
Estonia.....................	11.8	13.1	27.3	32.3	46.0	37.1	40.0	41.5
Finland.....................	55.7	73.0	81.7	82.6	119.5	135.7	133.4	133.4
France.....................	100.1	124.2	142.2	151.7	45.8	46.5	47.4	47.9
Germany...................	88.2	69.3	85.3	95.9	41.5	40.3	46.2	49.0
Greece.....................	129.7	200.6	214.8	228.8	37.1	55.4	49.7	54.5
Hungary....................	87.3	84.5	99.2	105.2	26.1	30.3	30.3	30.3
Ireland.....................	84.6	72.0	87.5	96.5	36.6	28.1	29.5	29.5
Israel [2]...................	70.6	61.7	80.1	86.6	6.5	3.5	3.5	3.5
Italy.......................	125.6	156.2	176.3	191.8	25.5	29.2	27.1	30.4
Japan......................	186.6	225.3	247.7	256.9	78.7	99.4	99.4	99.4
Latvia......................	50.9	44.0	52.4	57.9	36.7	33.4	32.9	32.9
Lithuania...................	45.6	44.9	57.4	62.0	32.8	31.1	31.1	31.1
Luxembourg................	28.4	29.4	39.5	41.2	77.9	76.6	76.6	76.6
Netherlands................	69.5	62.1	78.6	85.6	36.3	30.7	30.7	30.7
New Zealand...............	37.0	36.5	53.0	58.4	35.3	35.1	33.4	34.8
Poland.....................	61.2	63.9	79.3	86.6	34.2	26.7	26.7	26.7
Portugal....................	106.7	137.6	151.2	157.8	33.4	37.6	37.5	35.9
Slovak Republic...........	48.7	63.4	78.5	84.7	19.2	21.3	21.3	21.3
Slovenia...................	47.9	86.6	103.5	108.0	47.5	60.3	63.6	63.6
Spain......................	67.6	117.1	137.4	150.4	28.8	34.4	36.0	37.6
Sweden....................	47.3	46.7	60.7	63.4	70.3	84.4	84.4	85.6
Switzerland................	42.8	40.0	46.7	50.5	34.7	50.0	50.0	50.0
United Kingdom..........	89.8	116.1	136.2	148.6	37.2	34.3	34.3	34.3

[1] Preliminary. Given the level of uncertainty caused by the COVID-19 pandemic, the OECD Economic Outlook (EO107) presents two scenarios for each country and economy. One scenario in which a second outbreak occurs in most economies towards the end of 2020 (double-hit scenario) and an alternative scenario where the second outbreak is avoided (single-hit scenario). [2] See footnote 2, Table 1371.

Source: Organisation for Economic Co-operation and Development (OECD), 2020, "OECD Economic Outlook No. 107 - Single-hit scenario (Edition 2020/1)" and "OECD Economic Outlook No. 107 - Double-hit scenario (Edition 2020/1)," OECD Economic Outlook: Statistics and Projections (database) ©, <https://www.oecd-ilibrary.org/economics/data/oecd-economic-outlook-statistics-and-projections_eo-data-en>, accessed August 2020.

Table 1375. Percent Distribution of Tax Receipts by Country and Tax Type: 2010 to 2018

Country	Total [1]	Taxes on income and profits [2]			Social security contributions			Taxes on goods and services [5]		
		Total [3]	Individual	Corporate	Total [4]	Employees	Employers	Total [3]	General consumption taxes [6]	Taxes on specific goods, services [7]
United States:										
2010	100.0	42.3	34.8	7.5	26.1	11.6	13.1	18.1	8.4	7.2
2018 [8]	100.0	45.1	40.7	4.4	25.1	11.3	12.5	17.6	8.3	7.1
Australia:										
2010	100.0	56.5	38.6	17.9	0.0	0.0	0.0	29.0	13.8	11.9
2017 [9]	100.0	58.8	40.3	18.5	0.0	0.0	0.0	26.0	12.5	9.8
Canada:										
2010	100.0	46.6	35.0	10.5	14.9	5.9	8.4	24.0	14.0	8.5
2018 [8]	100.0	48.8	36.5	11.1	14.0	5.6	7.9	23.4	14.2	7.6
Chile:										
2010	100.0	38.1	6.8	20.4	6.8	6.6	0.3	51.2	38.5	9.8
2018 [8]	100.0	35.8	6.7	22.1	6.9	6.7	0.2	53.3	40.2	9.3
Czechia:										
2010	100.0	20.2	10.2	10.0	44.8	9.1	28.2	33.2	20.5	10.8
2018 [8]	100.0	22.0	12.2	9.8	44.1	9.1	28.3	32.1	21.7	8.8
France:										
2010	100.0	22.6	17.0	5.5	38.3	9.2	26.0	24.8	16.7	7.4
2018 [8]	100.0	25.1	20.6	4.6	34.9	8.2	24.3	25.0	15.9	8.3
Germany:										
2010	100.0	28.5	24.3	4.3	39.2	17.2	18.5	29.5	20.0	8.4
2018 [8]	100.0	32.8	27.2	5.6	37.7	17.0	17.5	26.2	18.2	6.6
Greece:										
2010	100.0	22.0	12.5	7.9	34.2	18.4	15.8	38.2	22.8	11.9
2017 [9]	100.0	22.8	16.0	5.0	29.6	17.4	12.2	39.3	21.3	11.7
Italy:										
2010	100.0	32.7	26.9	5.5	31.1	5.6	21.5	26.3	14.5	9.1
2018 [8]	100.0	31.0	25.6	4.5	31.1	5.8	20.9	28.3	14.8	9.9
Japan:										
2010	100.0	30.2	18.6	11.6	41.1	17.8	18.6	18.7	9.6	7.2
2017 [9]	100.0	30.7	18.8	11.8	39.9	17.7	18.4	21.0	13.0	6.6
Korea, South:										
2010	100.0	28.0	14.2	13.8	23.3	9.5	10.4	33.7	17.5	15.1
2018 [8]	100.0	34.1	18.4	15.7	25.4	10.9	11.6	26.3	15.3	9.4
Turkey:										
2010	100.0	21.3	14.0	7.3	24.9	9.4	13.7	47.7	21.7	24.1
2018 [8]	100.0	24.2	15.4	8.7	30.0	11.3	16.8	40.5	19.8	19.2
United Kingdom:										
2010	100.0	37.7	28.6	9.1	18.9	7.5	10.9	30.8	18.7	10.7
2018 [8]	100.0	35.8	27.2	8.6	19.1	7.3	11.1	32.0	21.0	9.8

[1] Includes property taxes, employer payroll taxes other than social security contributions, and miscellaneous taxes, not shown separately. [2] Includes taxes on capital gains. [3] Includes other taxes, not shown separately. [4] Includes contributions of self-employed persons, not shown separately. [5] Taxes on the production, extraction, sale, transfer, leasing or delivery of goods, and the rendering of services. [6] Primarily value-added and sales taxes. [7] For example, excise taxes on alcohol, tobacco, and gasoline. [8] Data are provisional/estimates. [9] Data for 2018 are not available.

Source: Organisation for Economic Co-operation and Development (OECD), 2020, "Revenue Statistics: Comparative tables," OECD Tax Statistics (database) ©, <http://dx.doi.org/10.1787/data-00262-en>, accessed June 2020.

Table 1376. Household Tax Burden by Country: 2019

[As percent of gross wage earnings of the average worker. The tax burden reflects income tax plus employee social security contributions less cash benefits]

Country	Single person without children	One-earner married couple with two children	Country	Single person without children	One-earner married couple with two children
OECD average [1]	25.91	20.48	Italy	31.59	24.96
			Japan	22.38	21.01
United States	**24.01**	**12.17**	Korea, South	15.32	13.17
Australia	23.65	23.65	Latvia	28.69	20.20
Austria	33.21	25.64	Lithuania	36.11	36.11
Belgium	39.29	27.27	Luxembourg	29.93	18.44
Canada	23.18	18.67	Mexico	10.84	10.84
Chile	7.05	7.00	Netherlands	29.70	28.46
Czechia	24.99	7.18	New Zealand	18.77	18.77
Denmark	35.56	31.55	Norway	27.31	27.31
Estonia	16.03	11.35	Poland	25.01	20.34
Finland	30.03	30.03	Portugal	26.93	16.17
France [2]	27.32	20.84	Slovak Republic	24.19	14.49
Germany	39.31	21.33	Slovenia	34.51	26.15
Greece	26.10	26.59	Spain	21.39	14.47
Hungary	33.50	22.71	Sweden	24.66	24.66
Iceland	28.73	21.70	Switzerland	17.43	10.86
Ireland	25.89	15.74	Turkey	28.47	26.51
Israel [3]	18.34	18.34	United Kingdom	23.33	22.72

[1] As of 2019, the Organisation for Economic Co-operation and Development (OECD) was comprised of the 36 member countries shown. See text, this section. [2] Figures correspond to tax calculations that are based on the tax legislation relating to the income earned in the selected year. [3] See footnote 2, Table 1371.

Source: Organisation for Economic Co-operation and Development (OECD), 2020, "Taxing Wages: Comparative tables," OECD Tax Statistics (database) ©, <http://dx.doi.org/10.1787/data-00265-en>, accessed June 2020.

Table 1377. Household Net Saving Rates by Country: 2000 to 2018

[As a percentage of household disposable income. Household savings are estimated by subtracting household consumption expenditure from household disposable income, plus the change in net equity of households in pension funds. Households include households plus nonprofit institutions serving households. Net saving rates are measured after deducting consumption of fixed capital (depreciation), with respect to assets used in enterprises operated by households, as well as owner-occupied dwellings. The household saving rate is calculated as the ratio of household savings to household disposable income (plus the change in net equity of households in pension funds). Minus sign (-) indicates an excess of expenditures over income]

Country	2000	2005	2010	2012	2013	2014	2015	2016	2017	2018
United States...............	5.0	3.3	6.8	9.1	6.6	7.6	7.9	7.0	7.2	8.0
Australia [1]...................	2.0	0.3	8.4	7.5	7.9	8.0	6.1	5.1	3.8	3.0
Austria.....................	10.6	11.1	9.6	8.9	7.1	7.3	6.7	7.7	7.3	7.7
Belgium....................	11.5	10.2	9.3	7.9	6.6	6.4	5.5	5.4	5.2	4.8
Canada....................	5.4	1.6	4.4	4.9	4.9	3.7	4.2	1.7	2.0	1.5
Chile......................	(NA)	12.1	7.9	10.6	10.7	10.6	9.6	10.7	9.8	9.6
Denmark..................	-5.7	-4.3	1.8	0.1	2.3	-2.9	3.9	5.6	6.6	6.6
Finland...................	2.6	0.5	3.3	0.4	0.9	–	-0.5	-1.4	-1.2	-0.8
France....................	8.7	8.5	10.5	10.0	8.5	8.9	8.3	8.2	[2] 8.1	[2] 8.4
Germany..................	9.3	10.6	10.3	9.7	9.3	9.8	10.1	10.2	10.4	11.0
Greece....................	-1.4	-2.9	-6.9	[2] -10.9	[2] -16.4	[2] -13.8	[2] -15.5	[2] -17.0	[2] -16.9	[2] -15.1
Hungary..................	4.5	7.5	5.9	5.0	6.8	7.5	7.3	7.0	6.6	6.9
Ireland...................	-3.9	1.5	7.7	6.5	4.8	3.3	3.9	3.2	6.0	5.8
Italy......................	7.4	8.9	3.9	1.5	3.3	3.7	2.9	3.0	2.6	2.5
Japan.....................	8.9	3.7	3.9	2.9	0.6	0.1	1.4	3.3	2.6	4.3
Latvia....................	-9.8	-6.9	-2.4	-15.7	-16.5	-13.7	-8.9	-5.0	-5.1	-2.6
Lithuania................	(NA)	-0.2	[3] 4.8	-0.7	-1.3	-3.5	-3.4	-0.8	-3.6	-5.1
Luxembourg.............	9.3	10.7	15.3	14.4	14.6	15.2	15.1	13.7	16.1	16.0
Mexico...................	(NA)	6.0	14.5	14.6	12.2	14.2	15.1	13.8	13.0	10.8
New Zealand [1].........	-2.4	-5.3	2.2	1.0	0.6	-0.6	-0.2	–	0.1	[2] -0.3
Norway...................	4.3	9.7	4.0	7.1	7.4	8.2	10.3	7.3	6.7	6.5
Poland....................	11.0	2.2	2.4	-1.1	-0.1	-0.4	-0.4	1.5	0.3	[2] -1.0
Portugal.................	6.1	2.8	1.6	2.1	1.6	-1.4	-1.2	-1.3	-2.2	[2] -2.2
Slovak Republic.........	4.6	0.8	2.6	1.9	0.8	1.4	3.1	3.0	2.5	3.1
Spain.....................	6.6	4.3	5.1	2.2	4.0	2.3	3.2	3.0	1.3	1.7
Sweden...................	1.4	3.6	10.0	13.0	13.4	13.9	12.1	13.9	13.3	15.4
United Kingdom..........	5.0	3.5	7.3	4.3	3.5	4.1	4.7	1.7	-0.3	0.4

– Represents or rounds to zero. NA Not available. [1] Data refer to fiscal year. [2] Data are estimates. [3] Break in series.

Source: Organisation for Economic Co-operation and Development (OECD), 2020, "National Accounts at a Glance," OECD National Accounts Statistics (database) ©, <http://dx.doi.org/10.1787/data-00369-en>, accessed June 2020.

Table 1378. Insurance and Pensions by Country: 2018

[169,914 represents $169,914,000,000]

Country	Insurance					Pensions [2]	
	Investment assets (mil. U.S. dollars) [1]	Direct gross premiums (percent of GDP)	Total gross premiums (mil. U.S. dollars)		Gross claims payments (mil. U.S. dollars)	Investment assets (mil. U.S. dollars)	Benefits paid (percent of GDP)
			Life	Non-life			
United States...............	(NA)	11.3	1,139,513	1,492,771	1,492,707	27,549,363	6.5
Australia....................	169,914	4.1	34,664	35,328	60,590	1,921,756	6.4
Austria.....................	138,560	4.5	6,543	15,337	17,209	(NA)	0.2
Belgium....................	346,637	6.1	18,437	15,266	28,966	(NA)	0.2
Canada....................	566,231	4.5	26,213	60,799	43,761	2,524,309	3.4
Denmark..................	497,500	11.1	28,664	12,312	27,837	677,088	0.7
Estonia....................	2,064	3.6	275	817	593	4,978	(Z)
Finland...................	77,842	1.9	5,156	(NA)	5,470	151,947	1.5
France....................	2,886,616	10.6	186,967	151,741	279,259	(NA)	(NA)
Germany..................	1,934,263	6.4	106,802	228,866	187,607	267,557	0.2
Greece....................	17,858	2.0	2,220	2,265	(NA)	1,584	(NA)
Hungary..................	9,449	2.4	1,742	2,025	2,236	7,968	0.1
Iceland....................	1,110	2.5	54	598	492	38,796	5.3
Ireland...................	(NA)	12.2	36,272	10,006	44,150	125,746	(NA)
Israel [3]..................	131,065	5.0	10,016	8,544	10,797	203,224	(NA)
Italy......................	924,288	7.7	122,310	41,470	113,945	197,817	0.4
Japan.....................	(NA)	7.8	302,966	99,808	326,888	1,693,428	(NA)
Korea, South.............	974,882	10.5	102,507	90,303	109,235	455,985	2.5
Lithuania................	1,521	1.9	293	744	535	3,739	0.1
Luxembourg.............	220,590	34.5	22,523	2,016	14,350	1,853	0.2
Mexico...................	62,955	2.3	12,672	15,578	14,307	194,031	0.4
Netherlands..............	475,194	9.3	14,136	71,621	87,960	1,536,269	(NA)
Norway...................	193,921	5.1	12,291	9,702	14,016	(NA)	0.2
Poland....................	48,001	2.8	6,009	11,202	11,743	47,987	(NA)
Portugal.................	55,525	5.8	9,188	5,680	11,718	44,543	0.4
Slovenia..................	7,623	4.7	621	2,242	1,973	3,595	0.2
Spain.....................	330,231	5.1	34,263	44,315	56,995	173,285	0.4
Sweden...................	511,935	8.5	37,087	11,957	17,798	470,566	(NA)
Switzerland..............	457,035	8.4	30,835	38,621	90,144	(NA)	5.3
Turkey....................	12,175	1.3	1,801	9,532	5,706	(NA)	0.1
United Kingdom..........	9,987,138	13.1	336,122	132,998	480,539	2,809,112	(NA)

NA Not available or not applicable. Z Less than 0.05 percent. [1] Includes total investment assets of direct insurance companies (excludes re-insurance). [2] Includes public and private autonomous pension funds of all types (occupational and personal, mandatory and voluntary). [3] See footnote 2, Table 1371.

Source: Organisation for Economic Co-operation and Development (OECD), 2020, Insurance Statistics (database) ©, <http://www.oecd.org/daf/fin/insurance/oecdinsurancestatistics.htm>; and Global Pension Statistics (database) ©, <http://www.oecd.org/daf/fin/private-pensions/globalpensionstatistics.htm>; accessed July 2020.

Table 1379. Inflation—Annual Percent Changes in Consumer Prices by Country: 2010 to 2019

[Percent change from previous year. Inflation as measured by the consumer price index reflects the annual percent change in the cost to the average consumer of acquiring a basket of goods and services that may be fixed or adjusted at specified intervals, such as yearly. For general comments concerning the data, see text, this section. For additional qualifications of the data for individual countries, see source. Minus sign (-) indicates decrease]

Country	2010	2015	2017	2018	2019	Country	2010	2015	2017	2018	2019
World [1]	3.3	1.4	2.2	2.5	2.3	Kenya	4.0	6.6	8.0	4.7	(NA)
United States	1.6	0.1	2.1	2.4	1.8	Korea, South	2.9	0.7	1.9	1.5	0.4
Afghanistan	2.2	-0.7	5.0	0.6	2.3	Malaysia	1.6	2.1	3.9	0.9	0.7
Australia	2.9	1.5	1.9	1.9	1.6	Mexico	4.2	2.7	6.0	4.9	3.6
Austria	1.8	0.9	2.1	2.0	1.5	Mongolia	10.0	5.7	4.3	6.8	7.3
Bangladesh	8.1	6.2	5.7	5.5	5.6	Morocco	1.0	1.6	0.8	1.9	0.2
Belarus	7.7	13.5	6.0	4.9	5.6	Netherlands	1.3	0.6	1.4	1.7	2.6
Brazil	5.0	9.0	3.4	3.7	3.7	New Zealand	2.3	0.3	1.9	1.6	1.6
China	3.2	1.4	1.6	2.1	2.9	Nigeria	13.7	9.0	16.5	12.1	11.4
Colombia	2.3	5.0	4.3	3.2	3.5	Norway	2.4	2.2	1.9	2.8	2.2
Croatia	1.0	-0.5	1.1	1.5	0.8	Pakistan	12.9	2.5	4.1	5.1	10.6
Czechia	1.5	0.3	2.5	2.1	2.8	Peru	1.5	3.5	2.8	1.3	2.1
Denmark	2.3	0.5	1.1	0.8	0.8	Philippines	3.8	0.7	2.9	5.2	2.5
Egypt	11.3	10.4	29.5	14.4	(NA)	Poland	2.6	-0.9	2.1	1.8	2.2
El Salvador	1.2	-0.7	1.0	1.1	0.1	Portugal	1.4	0.5	1.4	1.0	0.3
Ethiopia	-27.8	9.6	10.7	13.8	15.8	Romania	6.1	-0.6	1.3	4.6	3.8
France	1.5	(Z)	1.0	1.9	1.1	Russia	6.8	15.5	3.7	2.9	4.5
Germany	1.1	0.5	1.5	1.7	1.4	Saudi Arabia	5.3	1.2	-0.8	2.5	-2.1
Ghana	10.7	17.1	12.4	7.8	7.2	Singapore	2.8	-0.5	0.6	0.4	0.6
Greece	4.7	-1.7	1.1	0.6	0.3	South Africa	4.1	4.5	5.2	4.5	4.1
Haiti	4.8	6.7	10.7	12.5	(NA)	Spain	1.8	-0.5	2.0	1.7	0.7
Honduras	4.7	3.2	3.9	4.3	4.4	Sri Lanka	6.2	3.8	7.7	2.1	3.5
India	12.0	5.9	2.5	4.9	7.7	Sweden	1.2	(-Z)	1.8	2.0	1.8
Indonesia	5.1	6.4	3.8	3.2	3.0	Switzerland	0.7	-1.1	0.5	0.9	0.4
Iran	10.1	12.5	8.0	18.0	39.9	Thailand	3.2	-0.9	0.7	1.1	0.7
Ireland	-0.9	-0.3	0.3	0.5	0.9	Tunisia	3.3	4.4	5.3	7.3	6.7
Israel	2.7	-0.6	0.2	0.8	0.8	Turkey	8.6	7.7	11.1	16.3	15.2
Italy	1.5	(Z)	1.2	1.1	0.6	Ukraine	9.4	48.7	14.4	11.0	7.9
Japan	-0.7	0.8	0.5	1.0	0.5	United Kingdom	2.5	0.4	2.6	2.3	1.7
Jordan	4.8	-0.9	3.3	4.5	0.8	Vietnam	9.2	0.6	3.5	3.5	2.8

NA Not available. Z Less than 0.05 percent. [1] Includes other countries not shown separately.

Source: The World Bank, Washington, DC, World Development Indicators database, "Inflation, consumer prices (annual %)" ©, <http://data.worldbank.org/data-catalog/world-development-indicators>, accessed July 2020.

Table 1380. Unemployment Rates by Country: 2000 to 2019

[Annual averages. The standardized unemployment rates shown here are calculated as the number of unemployed persons as a percentage of the civilian labor force. The unemployed are persons of working age who, in the reference period, are without work, are available for work, and have taken specific steps to find work]

Country	2000	2005	2010	2012	2013	2014	2015	2016	2017	2018	2019
OECD, total [1]	(NA)	(NA)	8.4	8.0	7.9	7.4	6.9	6.4	5.9	5.5	5.4
EU-28	(NA)	8.9	9.6	10.4	10.8	10.2	9.4	8.5	7.6	6.8	6.3
United States	4.0	5.1	9.6	8.1	7.4	6.2	5.3	4.9	4.4	3.9	3.7
Australia	6.3	5.0	5.2	5.2	5.7	6.1	6.1	5.7	5.6	5.3	5.2
Austria	3.5	5.6	4.8	4.9	5.3	5.6	5.7	6.0	5.5	4.8	4.5
Belgium	7.0	8.4	8.3	7.5	8.4	8.5	8.5	7.8	7.1	5.9	5.4
Canada	6.8	6.8	8.1	7.3	7.1	6.9	6.9	7.0	6.3	5.8	5.7
Chile	9.7	9.2	8.2	6.4	5.9	6.4	6.2	6.5	6.7	7.0	7.0
Czechia	8.8	7.9	7.3	7.0	7.0	6.1	5.0	4.0	2.9	2.2	2.0
Denmark	4.6	4.8	7.7	7.8	7.4	6.9	6.3	6.0	5.8	5.1	5.0
Estonia	14.6	8.0	16.7	10.0	8.6	7.4	6.2	6.8	5.8	5.4	4.4
Finland	9.8	8.4	8.4	7.7	8.2	8.7	9.4	8.8	8.6	7.4	6.7
France	(NA)	8.5	8.9	9.4	9.9	10.3	10.4	10.0	9.4	9.0	8.4
Germany	7.8	11.2	7.0	5.4	5.2	5.0	4.6	4.1	3.7	3.4	3.1
Greece	11.4	10.0	12.7	24.4	27.5	26.5	24.9	23.5	21.5	19.3	17.3
Hungary	6.4	7.2	11.2	11.0	10.2	7.7	6.8	5.1	4.2	3.7	3.4
Iceland	(NA)	2.5	7.5	6.0	5.4	4.9	4.0	3.0	2.7	2.7	3.5
Ireland	4.3	4.3	14.5	15.4	13.7	11.9	9.9	8.4	6.7	5.7	5.0
Israel [2]	8.8	9.0	6.6	6.9	6.2	5.9	5.2	4.8	4.2	4.0	3.8
Italy	10.6	7.7	8.4	10.7	12.1	12.7	11.9	11.7	11.2	10.6	10.0
Japan	4.7	4.4	5.1	4.4	4.0	3.6	3.4	3.1	2.8	2.4	2.4
Korea, South	4.4	3.8	3.7	3.2	3.1	3.5	3.6	3.7	3.7	3.8	3.8
Latvia	(NA)	10.0	19.5	15.1	11.9	10.8	9.9	9.6	8.7	7.4	6.3
Lithuania	(NA)	8.3	17.8	13.4	11.8	10.7	9.1	7.9	7.1	6.2	6.3
Luxembourg	(NA)	4.5	4.4	5.1	5.8	5.9	6.7	6.3	5.5	5.6	5.6
Mexico	2.5	3.6	5.3	4.9	4.9	4.8	4.3	3.9	3.4	3.3	3.5
Netherlands	2.9	5.9	5.0	5.8	7.2	7.4	6.9	6.0	4.8	3.8	3.4
New Zealand	6.2	3.8	6.2	6.4	5.8	5.4	5.4	5.1	4.7	4.3	4.1
Norway	3.3	4.4	3.5	3.1	3.4	3.5	4.3	4.7	4.2	3.8	3.7
Poland	16.1	17.8	9.6	10.1	10.3	9.0	7.5	6.2	4.9	3.8	3.3
Portugal	4.0	7.6	10.8	15.5	16.2	13.9	12.4	11.1	8.9	7.0	6.5
Slovak Republic	18.8	16.3	14.4	14.0	14.2	13.2	11.5	9.7	8.1	6.5	5.8
Spain	13.9	9.2	19.9	24.8	26.1	24.4	22.1	19.6	17.2	15.3	14.1
Sweden	(NA)	7.5	8.6	8.0	8.1	8.0	7.4	7.0	6.7	6.4	6.8
Switzerland	(NA)	(NA)	4.8	4.5	4.7	4.8	4.8	4.9	4.8	4.7	4.4
Turkey	(NA)	(NA)	10.7	8.2	8.7	9.9	10.2	10.8	10.8	10.9	13.7
United Kingdom	5.6	4.7	7.8	7.9	7.5	6.1	5.3	4.8	4.3	4.0	3.7

NA Not available. [1] For OECD membership listing, see Section 30 introduction. [2] See footnote 2, Table 1371.

Source: Organisation for Economic Co-operation and Development (OECD), 2020, "Labour Force Statistics: Summary tables," OECD Employment and Labour Market Statistics (database) ©, <http://dx.doi.org/10.1787/data-00286-en>, accessed July 2020.

Table 1381. Labor Force, Employment, and Unemployment by Country: 1990 to 2018

[Labor force and employment in thousands (125,840 represent 125,840,000)]

Country and indicator	1990	2000	2005	2010	2011	2012	2013	2014	2015	2016	2017	2018
LABOR FORCE (1,000s)												
United States	125,840	142,583	149,321	153,889	153,616	154,975	155,389	155,922	157,130	159,187	160,319	162,075
Australia	8,443	9,495	10,400	11,626	11,813	11,976	12,145	12,275	12,517	12,691	12,971	13,283
Canada	14,048	15,634	17,054	18,177	18,350	18,551	18,776	18,857	19,011	19,173	19,384	19,526
France	(NA)	(NA)	26,957	27,925	27,926	28,294	28,376	28,367	28,442	28,596	28,775	28,767
Germany	(NA)	38,342	39,724	40,586	41,045	41,151	41,536	41,778	41,987	42,867	43,017	43,085
Italy	(NA)	(NA)	24,027	24,305	24,425	24,957	25,014	25,247	25,248	25,508	25,684	25,727
Japan	(NA)	(NA)	(NA)	65,526	65,106	64,731	64,913	65,154	65,320	65,856	66,395	67,477
Netherlands	(NA)	(NA)	8,269	8,677	8,674	8,812	8,886	8,846	8,884	8,920	8,994	9,097
Sweden	(NA)	(NA)	(NA)	4,931	4,999	5,040	5,093	5,161	5,204	5,253	5,355	5,435
United Kingdom	(NA)	28,962	30,224	31,637	31,883	32,173	32,435	32,705	32,983	33,288	33,452	33,729
EMPLOYMENT LEVEL (1,000s)												
United States	118,793	136,891	141,730	139,064	139,869	142,469	143,929	146,305	148,834	151,436	153,337	155,761
Australia	7,856	8,899	9,877	11,021	11,213	11,350	11,457	11,531	11,760	11,967	12,247	12,580
Canada	12,961	14,683	16,035	16,889	17,153	17,371	17,630	17,741	17,889	18,026	18,357	18,588
France	(NA)	(NA)	24,636	25,421	25,436	25,617	25,537	25,528	25,560	25,789	26,146	26,227
Germany	(NA)	35,338	35,328	37,757	38,644	38,926	39,355	39,688	40,038	41,092	41,397	41,615
Italy	(NA)	(NA)	22,157	22,256	22,351	22,262	21,948	22,031	22,210	22,502	22,763	22,964
Japan	(NA)	(NA)	(NA)	62,431	62,372	62,245	62,715	63,170	63,463	64,120	64,782	66,088
Netherlands	(NA)	(NA)	7,779	8,241	8,241	8,296	8,239	8,186	8,270	8,381	8,556	8,747
Sweden	(NA)	(NA)	(NA)	4,511	4,614	4,643	4,688	4,756	4,823	4,894	5,003	5,096
United Kingdom	(NA)	27,375	28,760	29,140	29,289	29,601	29,961	30,679	31,202	31,655	31,976	32,349
UNEMPLOYMENT LEVEL (1,000s)												
United States	7,047	5,692	7,591	14,825	13,747	12,506	11,460	9,617	8,296	7,751	6,982	6,314
Australia	587	596	523	605	600	626	688	744	757	724	724	703
Canada	1,087	951	1,019	1,288	1,197	1,180	1,146	1,116	1,122	1,147	1,027	938
France	1,890	2,136	2,321	2,504	2,490	2,677	2,839	2,839	2,882	2,807	2,629	2,540
Germany	(NA)	3,004	4,396	2,829	2,401	2,225	2,181	2,090	1,949	1,775	1,620	1,470
Italy	(NA)	(NA)	1,870	2,049	2,074	2,695	3,066	3,216	3,038	3,006	2,921	2,763
Japan	1,282	2,916	2,479	3,095	2,734	2,486	2,198	1,984	1,857	1,736	1,613	1,389
Netherlands	(NA)	(NA)	490	436	433	516	647	660	614	539	438	350
Sweden	(NA)	(NA)	(NA)	420	385	397	405	405	381	359	352	339
United Kingdom	(NA)	1,587	1,464	2,497	2,594	2,572	2,474	2,026	1,781	1,633	1,476	1,380
UNEMPLOYMENT RATE (percent)												
United States	5.6	4.0	5.1	9.6	8.9	8.1	7.4	6.2	5.3	4.9	4.4	3.9
Australia	6.9	6.3	5.0	5.2	5.1	5.2	5.7	6.1	6.1	5.7	5.6	5.3
Canada	7.7	6.1	6.0	7.1	6.5	6.4	6.1	5.9	5.9	6.0	5.3	4.8
France	(NA)	(NA)	8.6	9.0	8.9	9.5	10.0	10.0	10.1	9.8	9.1	8.8
Germany	(NA)	7.8	11.1	7.0	5.8	5.4	5.3	5.0	4.6	4.1	3.8	3.4
Italy	(NA)	(NA)	7.8	8.4	8.5	10.8	12.3	12.7	12.0	11.8	11.4	10.7
Japan	(NA)	(NA)	(NA)	4.7	4.2	3.8	3.4	3.0	2.8	2.6	2.4	2.1
Netherlands	(NA)	(NA)	5.9	5.0	5.0	5.9	7.3	7.5	6.9	6.0	4.9	3.8
Sweden	(NA)	(NA)	(NA)	8.5	7.7	7.9	8.0	7.8	7.3	6.8	6.6	6.2
United Kingdom	(NA)	5.5	4.8	7.9	8.1	8.0	7.6	6.2	5.4	4.9	4.4	4.1

NA Not available.

Source: The Conference Board, Inc., *Business Cycle Indicators*, 2019 . © The Conference Board 2020 . For more information see <https://www.conference-board.org/data/bci.cfm>.

Table 1382. Youth Educational Enrollment and Employment Status by Country: 2009 and 2019

[Percent of total youth population for selected age groups]

Country	2009 15 to 29 year olds: In education, total	2009 15 to 29 year olds: Not in education Employed	2009 15 to 29 year olds: Not in education Not employed	2009 20 to 24 year olds: In education, total	2009 20 to 24 year olds: Not in education Employed	2009 20 to 24 year olds: Not in education Not employed	2019 15 to 29 year olds: In education, total	2019 15 to 29 year olds: Not in education Employed	2019 15 to 29 year olds: Not in education Not employed	2019 20 to 24 year olds: In education, total	2019 20 to 24 year olds: Not in education Employed	2019 20 to 24 year olds: Not in education Not employed
OECD average....	46.2	38.3	15.5	41.6	39.8	18.7	47.1	39.9	13.0	45.2	39.8	15.2
United States.....	45.7	37.4	16.9	38.7	41.2	20.1	44.1	43.2	12.7	38.5	46.7	14.8
Australia.....	43.9	43.7	12.3	39.9	48.5	11.6	47.4	42.2	10.4	46.7	42.3	11.0
Canada.......	43.2	43.5	13.4	37.9	46.6	15.5	43.5	45.3	11.3	43.5	44.0	12.6
Denmark.....	57.9	33.3	8.8	50.6	37.3	12.1	54.9	33.4	11.6	52.7	34.6	12.7
Finland.......	54.4	33.6	12.0	49.3	35.7	15.1	54.8	34.2	11.0	51.3	35.8	12.9
France........	44.6	39.7	15.6	40.0	40.0	20.0	48.6	35.9	15.4	42.9	37.7	19.5
Germany.....	52.4	36.0	11.6	48.5	37.8	13.7	53.7	38.0	8.2	55.5	35.7	8.8
Greece.......	44.2	39.2	16.6	48.0	34.1	17.8	54.8	25.6	19.6	59.0	18.9	22.0
Hungary......	48.1	34.1	17.7	49.2	29.9	20.9	42.3	44.4	13.3	41.0	43.5	15.5
Ireland........	37.7	43.7	18.6	34.2	45.0	20.8	50.3	38.7	11.0	44.6	42.4	13.0
Israel.........	42.0	29.3	28.7	28.5	34.0	37.5	44.4	42.7	12.9	28.9	53.0	18.2
Italy.........	45.3	33.5	21.2	42.3	32.9	24.8	47.6	28.8	23.7	43.2	28.3	28.5
Latvia........	45.7	34.1	20.2	37.9	34.8	27.3	47.3	42.7	10.0	47.5	38.6	13.9
Lithuania.....	56.0	32.6	11.4	51.4	32.7	15.9	49.8	38.8	11.3	51.3	34.2	14.5
Mexico.......	34.5	41.2	24.4	25.8	46.7	27.4	37.6	41.7	20.7	30.8	46.3	22.9
Netherlands..	54.1	38.9	7.0	52.5	39.6	7.9	55.7	37.4	6.9	58.6	34.0	7.4
Norway.......	45.6	46.4	8.0	41.6	49.0	9.4	46.5	45.6	7.9	47.4	43.9	8.7
Poland........	50.7	35.1	14.2	54.3	29.2	16.4	42.5	45.0	12.5	42.0	44.0	14.0
Portugal......	42.3	44.9	12.8	37.9	46.3	15.7	48.7	39.8	11.5	42.9	41.8	15.3
Slovenia......	58.2	32.7	9.0	62.9	25.7	11.4	52.5	38.1	9.4	55.9	35.4	8.7
Spain.........	36.8	40.6	22.6	35.3	38.8	25.9	51.3	30.4	18.3	50.8	27.3	21.9
Sweden......	51.0	38.0	11.0	39.0	44.5	16.5	53.2	39.8	7.0	50.4	40.7	9.0
Switzerland...	46.7	42.6	10.7	44.7	44.3	10.9	49.4	43.3	7.3	47.9	44.1	8.1
Turkey........	29.5	30.9	39.6	23.9	30.0	46.1	40.5	30.7	28.8	34.0	32.7	33.3
United Kingdom....	40.4	43.9	15.7	31.5	49.3	19.1	36.3	51.5	12.3	34.8	51.6	13.6

Source: Organisation for Economic Co-operation and Development (OECD), 2020, "Indicator A2: Transition from education to work: Where are today's youth," Education at a Glance 2020: OECD Indicators, OECD Publishing ©, <https://doi.org/10.1787/bd3a6fb1-en>, accessed September 2020.

Table 1383. Educational Performance and Attainment by Country: 2018 and 2019

Country	2018 Student mean scores in reading, science, and mathematics proficiency [1]: Reading scale	Mathematics scale	Science scale	2019 Educational attainment of adult population 25 to 64 years old (percent): Below upper secondary	Upper secondary and vocational	Tertiary [2]
United States....................	505.4	478.2	502.4	9.2	42.5	48.3
Australia........................	502.6	491.4	503.0	17.1	35.7	47.1
Austria.........................	484.4	498.9	489.8	14.4	51.8	33.8
Belgium........................	492.9	508.1	498.8	21.3	38.0	40.7
Canada........................	520.1	512.0	518.0	8.1	32.5	59.4
Colombia.......................	412.3	390.9	413.3	43.3	32.9	23.8
Czechia........................	490.2	499.5	496.8	6.2	69.5	24.2
Denmark........................	501.1	509.4	492.6	18.4	41.2	40.4
France..........................	492.6	495.4	493.0	19.6	42.5	37.9
Germany........................	498.3	500.0	503.0	13.3	56.8	29.9
Greece.........................	457.4	451.4	451.6	26.0	42.1	31.9
Ireland.........................	518.1	499.6	496.1	16.3	36.4	47.3
Israel [3].......................	470.4	463.0	462.2	12.9	36.8	50.2
Italy...........................	476.3	486.6	468.0	37.8	42.5	19.6
Japan..........................	503.9	527.0	529.1	(NA)	(NA)	[4] 52.7
Korea, South...................	514.1	525.9	519.0	11.3	38.7	50.0
Mexico.........................	420.5	408.8	419.2	60.2	21.5	18.3
Netherlands....................	484.8	519.2	503.4	20.4	39.2	40.4
New Zealand...................	505.7	494.5	508.5	19.3	41.6	39.1
Norway.........................	499.5	501.0	490.4	17.5	38.4	44.1
Poland.........................	511.9	515.6	511.0	7.4	60.6	32.0
Portugal........................	491.8	492.5	491.7	47.8	25.9	26.3
Spain..........................	(NA)	481.4	483.3	38.7	22.7	38.6
Sweden........................	505.8	502.4	499.4	16.4	39.7	44.0
Switzerland.....................	483.9	515.3	495.3	11.0	44.6	44.4
Turkey.........................	465.6	453.5	468.3	58.3	19.7	22.0
United Kingdom.................	503.9	501.8	504.7	19.9	32.9	47.2

NA Not available. [1] Proficiency scores are based on the Program for International Student Assessment (PISA), an international standardized test which takes place in three-year cycles. PISA tests are administered to a nationally representative sample of fifteen-year-old students in each country. [2] Tertiary education entails completion of an advanced course of study or research program leading to an associate's, bachelor's, master's, or doctorate degree, usually 2 years or longer in duration. [3] See footnote 2, Table 1371. [4] Includes data from another category.

Source: Organisation for Economic Co-operation and Development (OECD), 2020, "Education at a glance: Educational Attainment and Labour-force Status," OECD Education Statistics (database) ©, <http://dx.doi.org/10.1787/889e8641-en>; and "Annex B1. Results (tables)" in PISA 2018 Results (Volume 1), OECD Publishing ©, <https://doi.org/10.1787/5f07c754-en>; accessed September 2020.

Table 1384. World Supply and Utilization of Major Crops and Livestock: 2010 to 2020

[In millions of units (225.8 represents 225,800,000). For major crops, data are for marketing or trade year ending in year shown, unless otherwise indicated. For livestock and dairy, data are for calendar year]

Commodity	2010	2014	2015	2016	2017	2018	2019	2020 [1]
Wheat:								
Area harvested (hectares)	225.8	220.0	221.3	224.0	222.4	218.7	215.5	216.7
Production (metric tons)	688.2	716.6	730.4	738.1	756.3	763.0	730.8	764.4
Exports (metric tons)	135.3	162.5	161.9	171.7	182.4	184.0	175.4	185.8
Consumption (metric tons)	651.0	691.3	700.5	713.1	734.5	740.6	732.2	744.2
Ending stocks (metric tons)	204.1	197.7	222.8	245.0	263.0	284.1	279.8	295.8
Corn:								
Area harvested (hectares)	158.8	188.0	188.9	188.1	194.8	191.5	191.8	192.4
Production (metric tons)	834.0	1,027.0	1,057.8	1,015.1	1,127.5	1,078.6	1,123.3	1,113.5
Exports (metric tons)	92.7	130.8	128.4	145.2	142.3	152.8	171.9	174.9
Consumption (metric tons)	832.3	950.6	975.4	1,001.6	1,062.7	1,091.2	1,126.2	1,120.8
Ending stocks (metric tons)	131.6	214.7	279.8	312.4	352.2	341.3	320.1	312.9
Rice, milled:								
Area harvested (hectares)	155.9	162.3	162.4	160.5	163.3	162.9	162.4	160.5
Production (metric tons)	441.0	481.3	482.7	477.1	491.3	494.7	496.5	494.3
Exports (metric tons)	31.8	44.2	42.8	40.2	48.1	47.6	43.4	42.5
Consumption (metric tons)	435.5	472.2	473.1	467.9	477.2	480.6	483.8	488.4
Ending stocks (metric tons)	96.6	127.8	135.2	142.5	150.3	164.1	176.8	181.3
Coarse grains: [2]								
Area harvested (hectares)	307.7	331.0	332.9	326.0	338.1	328.4	330.7	332.2
Production (metric tons)	1,124.0	1,313.7	1,346.4	1,303.7	1,418.9	1,359.6	1,397.0	1,406.5
Exports (metric tons)	118.8	165.2	173.9	185.3	182.3	189.2	203.8	209.3
Consumption (metric tons)	1,124.5	1,238.3	1,281.5	1,270.4	1,382.2	1,374.9	1,420.4	1,410.2
Ending stocks (metric tons)	182.7	251.2	316.0	349.3	386.1	370.8	347.4	343.7
Oilseeds:								
Area harvested (hectares)	235.7	261.0	267.4	265.5	268.3	281.1	282.8	279.7
Production (metric tons)	447.2	503.4	538.7	524.2	573.8	582.3	599.9	575.2
Exports (metric tons)	107.6	133.8	147.2	153.0	170.0	176.3	170.3	178.9
Consumption (metric tons)	425.4	494.2	520.8	526.7	554.7	573.0	580.6	590.8
Ending stocks (metric tons)	77.4	81.0	95.3	93.4	108.7	116.6	131.4	114.5
Coffee, green:								
Production (60 kg bags)	129.8	160.1	153.8	152.9	161.7	158.6	174.9	166.9
Exports (60 kg bags)	106.3	128.9	123.6	133.4	133.5	131.1	140.9	132.3
Consumption (60 kg bags)	138.3	142.4	145.7	152.8	153.9	159.7	165.0	163.9
Ending stocks (60 kg bags)	28.8	41.2	43.1	34.4	35.3	31.0	35.7	35.1
Sugar, centrifugal:								
Production (metric tons)	153.2	176.0	177.6	165.0	174.1	194.3	179.7	166.2
Exports (metric tons)	48.3	58.0	55.0	53.9	59.0	64.3	56.0	54.1
Consumption (metric tons)	154.1	165.7	168.0	169.3	170.6	173.3	172.6	171.6
Ending stocks (metric tons)	28.0	44.8	48.8	44.5	42.6	52.2	54.0	44.4
Cotton:								
Area harvested (hectares)	30.2	32.9	33.9	30.8	29.8	33.8	33.4	35.0
Production (480 lb. bales)	103.1	120.4	119.2	96.2	106.7	124.0	118.7	123.0
Exports (480 lb. bales)	35.8	41.0	36.0	34.7	37.9	41.6	41.1	39.8
Consumption (480 lb. bales)	119.5	110.0	112.5	113.5	116.4	122.9	120.4	102.8
Ending stocks (480 lb. bales)	46.2	99.9	106.7	90.2	80.3	80.9	80.5	100.6
Beef:								
Beef cow beginning stocks (head)	202.9	207.8	200.5	201.6	205.0	205.9	205.7	206.3
Production (metric tons) [3]	56.9	57.6	57.6	58.0	59.2	60.7	61.7	61.5
Exports (metric tons) [3]	7.4	9.6	9.1	9.0	9.5	10.1	10.9	10.7
Consumption (metric tons) [3]	55.6	55.3	55.5	56.3	57.2	58.7	59.6	59.6
Ending stocks (metric tons) [3]	0.6	0.6	0.6	0.6	0.5	0.5	0.5	0.5
Pork:								
Sow beginning stocks (head)	79.3	78.9	76.3	74.5	74.0	73.0	66.3	55.5
Production (metric tons) [3]	102.9	111.4	111.8	111.3	112.0	112.9	102.0	94.3
Exports (metric tons) [3]	5.9	6.8	7.1	8.2	8.1	8.2	9.3	10.5
Consumption (metric tons) [3]	102.5	110.5	111.2	110.8	111.4	112.2	100.9	93.4
Ending stocks (metric tons) [3]	0.6	0.7	0.7	0.6	0.6	0.7	0.9	0.9
Chicken (meat): [4]								
Beginning stocks (metric tons)	0.5	0.6	0.6	0.7	0.7	0.8	0.7	0.8
Production (metric tons)	77.8	87.4	90.2	91.1	92.7	94.5	99.0	100.5
Exports (metric tons)	8.9	10.5	10.3	10.8	11.0	11.3	11.9	11.7
Consumption (metric tons)	76.2	85.4	88.4	89.6	90.7	92.6	97.1	98.5
Ending stocks (metric tons)	0.5	0.6	0.7	0.7	0.8	0.7	0.8	0.8
Dairy:								
Dairy cows beginning stocks (head)	229.2	238.9	238.0	237.7	238.3	240.9	241.8	244.6
Milk production (metric tons) [5]	513.8	570.9	585.9	595.4	612.1	625.4	635.3	648.0
Milk exports (metric tons) [5]	0.7	1.3	1.5	1.8	1.8	1.7	1.9	2.0
Milk consumption (metric tons) [5]	513.5	570.6	585.4	594.9	611.6	624.8	634.7	647.4

[1] Preliminary. [2] Coarse grains include corn, barley, sorghum, oats, rye, millet, and mixed grains but exclude trade in barley malt, millet, and mixed grains. [3] Carcass weight equivalent (CWE). [4] Weight in ready-to-eat equivalent meat. [5] Includes milk from cows as well as other bovines.

Source: U.S. Department of Agriculture, Foreign Agricultural Service, "Production, Supply and Distribution Online," <http://www.fas.usda.gov/psdonline/>, accessed June 2020.

Table 1385. World Crop Production Summary: 2018 to 2020

[In millions of metric tons (730.8 represents 730,800,000). Data are for marketing or trade year. Data for 2019-2020 are preliminary]

Country	Wheat		Coarse grains [1]		Rice (milled)		Oilseeds [2]		Cotton	
	2018–2019	2019–2020	2018–2019	2019–2020	2018–2019	2019–2020	2018–2019	2019–2020	2018–2019	2019–2020
World	**730.8**	**764.4**	**1,397.0**	**1,406.5**	**496.5**	**494.3**	**599.9**	**575.2**	**118.7**	**123.0**
Total foreign	679.5	712.1	1,019.1	1,047.2	489.4	488.4	469.2	468.2	100.3	103.1
United States	**51.3**	**52.3**	**377.9**	**359.3**	**7.1**	**5.9**	**130.7**	**107.0**	**18.4**	**19.9**
Canada	32.2	32.3	26.2	28.5	–	–	27.7	25.1	–	–
Mexico	3.0	3.2	33.4	30.4	0.2	0.2	1.3	1.1	1.7	1.6
Russia	71.7	73.6	35.0	40.5	0.7	0.7	18.7	21.7	–	–
Ukraine	25.1	29.2	44.5	46.5	–	–	22.7	24.0	–	–
European Union [3]	(4)	(4)	(4)	(4)	(4)	(4)	(4)	(4)	1.7	2.0
China	131.4	133.6	264.5	268.2	148.5	146.7	60.0	62.6	27.8	27.3
India	99.9	103.6	43.2	47.5	116.5	117.9	35.5	37.2	25.8	30.5
Indonesia	–	–	12.0	11.9	34.2	33.5	14.1	14.4	–	–
Pakistan	25.1	24.3	6.6	7.4	7.3	7.2	3.8	3.3	7.6	6.2
Thailand	–	–	5.7	5.3	20.3	18.0	1.0	1.1	–	–
Argentina	19.5	19.5	59.2	56.8	0.8	0.8	61.0	55.1	1.1	1.4
Brazil	5.4	5.2	104.3	104.6	7.1	7.4	123.9	129.1	13.0	13.2
Australia	17.6	15.2	11.5	10.4	–	–	3.1	2.6	2.2	0.6
South Africa	1.9	1.5	12.4	16.7	–	–	2.0	2.1	0.2	0.1
Turkey	19.0	18.5	13.3	14.5	0.6	0.6	3.4	3.2	3.8	3.5
All others	227.8	252.4	347.2	358.1	153.1	155.3	91.1	85.6	15.4	16.7

– Represents zero. [1] Includes corn, barley, sorghum, oats, rye, millet, and mixed grains. [2] Includes soybean, cottonseed, peanut (in shell), sunflower seed, and rapeseed for individual countries. Copra and palm kernel are added to world totals. [3] U.S. Department of Agriculture (USDA) is temporarily including the United Kingdom (UK) and the European Union as EU27 + UK. Although it is officially separated from the EU, the UK estimates remain included within USDA's EU total. [4] Indicates no reported or insignificant production.

Source: U.S. Department of Agriculture, Foreign Agricultural Service, *World Agricultural Production*, June 2020. See also <fas.usda.gov/data/world-agricultural-production>.

Table 1386. Meat Production by Type and Country: 2018 and 2019

[In thousands of metric tons (60,690 represents 60,690,000). Carcass weight equivalent basis for beef, veal, and pork. Chicken weight based on ready-to-cook equivalent basis]

Country	Beef and veal [1]		Country	Pork		Country	Chicken [2]	
	2018	2019		2018	2019		2018	2019
World	**60,690**	**61,675**	**World**	**112,932**	**101,969**	**World**	**94,517**	**99,039**
United States	**12,256**	**12,381**	China	54,040	42,550	**United States**	**19,361**	**19,941**
Brazil	9,900	10,200	EU27 + UK [3]	24,082	23,935	China	11,700	13,750
EU27 + UK [3]	8,003	7,900	**United States**	**11,943**	**12,542**	Brazil	13,355	13,690
China	6,440	6,670	Brazil	3,763	3,975	EU27 + UK [3]	12,260	12,460
India	4,240	4,305	Russia	3,155	3,321	Russia	4,684	4,671
Argentina	3,050	3,120	Vietnam	2,811	2,380	India	4,062	4,350
Australia	2,306	2,432	Canada	1,955	2,020	Mexico	3,485	3,600
Mexico	1,980	2,030	Philippines	1,601	1,585	Thailand	3,170	3,300
Pakistan	1,800	1,820	Mexico	1,321	1,408	Argentina	2,068	2,171
Russia	1,357	1,369	Korea, South	1,329	1,364	Turkey	2,157	2,138
Others	9,358	9,448	Others	6,932	6,889	Others	18,215	18,968

[1] May include meat of other bovines. [2] Excludes chicken paws. [3] See footnote 3, Table 1387.

Source: U.S. Department of Agriculture, Foreign Agricultural Service, "Production, Supply and Distribution Online," <http://apps.fas.usda.gov/psdonline>, accessed June 2020.

Table 1387. Meat Consumption by Type and Country: 2018 and 2019

[In thousands of metric tons (58,671 represents 58,671,000). Carcass weight equivalent basis for beef, veal, and pork. Chicken weight based on ready-to-cook equivalent meat]

Country	Beef and veal [1]		Country	Pork		Country	Chicken [2]	
	2018	2019		2018	2019		2018	2019
World	**58,671**	**59,621**	**World**	**112,166**	**100,904**	**World**	**92,638**	**97,125**
United States	**12,180**	**12,407**	China	55,295	44,866	**United States**	**16,184**	**16,700**
China	7,808	8,826	EU27+UK [3]	21,258	20,400	China	11,595	13,902
Brazil	7,925	7,929	**United States**	**9,748**	**10,064**	EU27+UK [3]	11,537	11,636
EU27+UK [3]	8,071	7,911	Russia	3,202	3,360	Brazil	9,671	9,865
India	2,729	2,811	Brazil	3,043	3,116	Russia	4,785	4,724
Argentina	2,568	2,374	Japan	2,774	2,714	Mexico	4,301	4,473
Mexico	1,902	1,906	Vietnam	2,811	2,420	India	4,059	4,347
Pakistan	1,753	1,771	Mexico	2,116	2,153	Japan	2,761	2,801
Russia	1,790	1,753	Korea, South	2,001	2,011	Thailand	2,354	2,459
Japan	1,298	1,319	Philippines	1,883	1,806	Argentina	1,955	2,021
Others	10,647	10,614	Others	8,035	7,994	Others	23,436	24,197

[1] May include meat of other bovines. [2] Excludes chicken paws. [3] U.S. Department of Agriculture (USDA) is temporarily including the United Kingdom (UK) and the European Union (EU) as EU27 + UK. Although it is officially separated from the EU, the UK estimates remain included within USDA's EU total. European Union-27: Austria, Belgium, Bulgaria, Croatia, Cyprus, Czech Republic, Denmark, Estonia, Finland, France, Germany, Greece, Hungary, Ireland, Italy, Latvia, Lithuania, Luxembourg, Malta, Netherlands, Poland, Portugal, Romania, Slovakia, Slovenia, Spain, and Sweden.

Source: U.S. Department of Agriculture, Foreign Agricultural Service, "Production, Supply and Distribution Online," <http://apps.fas.usda.gov/psdonline>, accessed June 2020.

Table 1388. Wheat, Rice, and Corn—Exports and Imports of Leading Countries: 2010 to 2020

[In thousands of metric tons (22,293 represents 22,293,000). Wheat data represent trade years ending in June of year shown; corn data represent trade years ending in September of year shown; rice data represent trade years ending in December of year shown. Countries listed are the ten leading exporters or importers in 2020]

Leading country	Exports			Leading country	Imports		
	2010	2019	2020 (P)		2010	2019	2020 (P)
WHEAT				**WHEAT**			
EU27+UK [1]	22,293	23,310	36,500	Egypt	10,500	12,347	13,300
Russia	18,556	35,838	33,500	Indonesia	5,364	10,934	10,800
United States	**24,143**	**26,069**	**26,400**	Turkey	3,218	6,494	10,500
Canada	18,992	24,476	22,800	Philippines	3,197	7,546	7,200
Ukraine	9,337	16,019	20,500	Brazil	6,691	7,442	7,100
Argentina	5,255	12,680	13,600	Bangladesh	3,353	5,100	6,700
Australia	13,764	9,835	9,500	Algeria	5,167	7,515	6,500
Turkey	4,363	6,215	6,400	Japan	5,502	5,726	5,600
Kazakhstan	7,871	8,780	5,800	Mexico	3,196	4,861	5,200
Mexico	839	526	1,100	Nigeria	3,990	4,585	5,200
RICE				**RICE**			
India	2,228	9,790	10,500	Philippines	2,400	2,900	2,500
Thailand	9,047	7,562	7,000	China	366	2,800	2,300
Vietnam	6,734	6,581	6,700	EU27+UK [1]	1,235	2,159	2,200
Pakistan	4,000	4,550	4,400	Cote d'Ivoire	840	1,400	1,350
United States	**3,868**	**3,135**	**3,100**	Nigeria	2,000	1,800	1,200
China	619	2,720	3,000	Iran	1,520	1,400	1,100
Burma	700	2,700	2,200	Iraq	1,188	1,220	1,100
Uruguay	808	809	800	Saudi Arabia	1,069	1,425	1,100
Brazil	430	954	600	**United States**	**562**	**981**	**1,070**
Guyana	298	496	485	Malaysia	907	1,000	1,000
CORN				**CORN**			
United States	**49,696**	**49,194**	**47,000**	EU27+UK [1]	2,758	25,209	21,500
Brazil	8,623	38,807	37,000	Mexico	8,298	16,658	17,300
Argentina	16,973	32,879	36,000	Japan	15,971	16,047	16,000
Ukraine	5,072	30,321	32,000	Korea, South	8,461	10,856	11,400
EU27+UK [1]	1,569	3,629	4,500	Vietnam	1,600	11,000	11,000
Paraguay	1,359	2,559	2,500	Egypt	5,832	9,367	9,900
South Africa	1,586	1,183	2,500	Iran	4,300	9,000	9,000
Burma	300	1,500	1,300	China	1,296	4,483	7,000
Canada	186	1,719	1,100	Colombia	3,651	6,048	6,200
Mexico	642	718	700	Algeria	2,569	4,816	4,800

P Preliminary. [1] See footnote 3, Table 1387.

Source: U.S. Department of Agriculture, Foreign Agricultural Service, "Production, Supply and Distribution Online," <http://www.fas.usda.gov/psdonline>, accessed June 2020.

Table 1389. World Production of Major Mineral Commodities: 2015 to 2018

[Units are as noted. Th. represents thousand, mil. represents million, and bil. represents billion]

Commodity	Unit	2015	2016	2017	2018	Leading producers, 2018
MINERAL FUELS						
Coal	mil. short tons	8,728	8,160	8,449	(NA)	China, India, United States [7]
Dry natural gas	bil. cubic feet	124,611	125,740	130,751	(NA)	United States, Russia, Iran [7]
Natural gas plant liquids	mil. barrels [1]	3,696	3,764	3,873	4,080	United States, Saudi Arabia, Canada
Petroleum, crude	mil. barrels [1]	29,471	29,497	29,600	30,270	United States, Russia, Saudi Arabia
NONMETALLIC MINERALS						
Barite	th. metric tons	8,250	7,440	8,670	9,180	China, India, Morocco
Cement, hydraulic	mil. metric tons	4,070	4,150	4,080	4,050	China, India, Vietnam
Fluorspar	th. metric tons	5,820	5,760	5,880	6,720	China, Mexico, Mongolia
Nitrogen in ammonia	mil. metric tons	142	144	142	144	China, Russia, United States
Phosphate rock, marketable	mil. metric tons	261	263	270	249	China, Morocco/Western Sahara, U.S.
Potash, marketable	mil. metric tons	40	39	42	43	Canada, Russia, Belarus
Salt	mil. metric tons	277	274	288	286	China, United States, India
Sulfur	mil. metric tons	78	79	80	79	China, United States, Russia
METALS						
Aluminum, metal content	mil. metric tons	58	59	60	64	China, India, Russia
Bauxite, gross weight	mil. metric tons	298	282	308	327	Australia, China, Guinea
Chromium (chromite), gross weight	th. metric tons	36,500	34,400	35,700	43,100	South Africa, Turkey, Kazakhstan
Copper, metal content [2]	th. metric tons	19,100	20,100	20,000	20,400	Chile, Peru, China
Gold, metal content	metric tons	3,120	3,180	3,230	3,300	China, Australia, Russia
Iron ore, gross weight [3]	mil. metric tons	2,310	2,340	2,430	2,460	Australia, Brazil, China
Lead, metal content [2]	th. metric tons	5,000	4,750	4,580	4,560	China, Australia, Peru
Magnesium [4]	th. metric tons	970	989	1,040	996	China, Russia, Israel
Manganese ore, metal content	th. metric tons	17,000	15,700	17,300	18,900	South Africa, Australia, Gabon
Nickel, metal content [2]	th. metric tons	2,180	2,040	2,160	2,400	Indonesia, Philippines, Russia
Steel, raw	mil. metric tons	1,620	1,630	1,690	1,810	China, India, Japan
Tantalum concentrates [2]	Metric tons	1,490	1,540	1,810	1,890	Congo, Dem. Rep. of; Rwanda, Brazil
Tin, metal content [2]	th. metric tons	341	288	313	318	China, Indonesia, Burma
Titanium (Ilmenite concentrate) [2,5]	th. metric tons	9,540	9,550	9,090	6,870	China, South Africa, Australia
Tungsten [2,6]	th. metric tons	84	80	82	81	China, Vietnam, Mongolia
Vanadium [2,6]	th. metric tons	88	75	77	71	China, Russia, South Africa
Zinc, metal content [2]	th. metric tons	13,500	12,700	12,500	12,500	China, Peru, Australia

NA Not available. [1] 42-gallon barrels. [2] Mine output. [3] Includes iron ore concentrates and agglomerates. [4] Primary production; excludes U.S. production. [5] World production includes U.S. production of rutile and ilmenite. [6] Content of ore and concentrate. [7] Leading producers in 2017.

Source: Mineral fuels, U.S. Energy Information Administration, "International Energy Statistics", <eia.gov/international/data/world>, accessed August 2020. Nonmetallic minerals and metals, U.S. Geological Survey, *Minerals Yearbook*, annual; *Mineral Commodity Summaries*, annual; and "Commodity Statistics and Information," <usgs.gov/centers/nmic/commodity-statistics-and-information>, accessed August 2020.

Table 1390. Net Electricity Generation by Energy Source and Country: 2017

[24,343.6 represents 24,343,600,000,000. kWh = kilowatt hours. Ranked for top 40 countries]

Country	Total [1] (bil. kWh)	Amount Fossil fuels [2]	Amount Hydro-electricity	Amount Nuclear	Amount Non-hydro renew-ables [3]	Percent distribution Fossil fuels [2]	Percent distribution Hydro-electricity	Percent distribution Nuclear	Percent distribution Non-hydro renew-ables [3]
World, total [4]	**24,343.6**	**15,627.2**	**4,006.1**	**2,484.5**	**2,266.6**	**64.2**	**16.5**	**10.2**	**9.3**
China	6,266.2	4,397.6	1,145.5	232.8	502.0	70.2	18.3	3.7	8.0
United States	**4,058.3**	**2,536.1**	**300.3**	**805.0**	**423.4**	**62.5**	**7.4**	**19.8**	**10.4**
India	1,438.2	1,155.8	125.0	34.8	122.5	80.4	8.7	2.4	8.5
Russia	1,034.4	658.2	183.2	190.1	3.8	63.6	17.7	18.4	0.4
Japan	986.8	770.7	82.5	11.6	125.1	78.1	8.4	1.2	12.7
Canada	640.5	117.2	388.6	95.1	39.6	18.3	60.7	14.9	6.2
Germany	618.3	325.3	20.0	72.2	203.1	52.6	3.2	11.7	32.8
Brazil	577.9	100.4	367.2	14.9	95.5	17.4	63.5	2.6	16.5
France	534.1	59.1	49.4	381.8	45.8	11.1	9.2	71.5	8.6
Korea, South	530.6	369.7	2.8	141.3	18.1	69.7	0.5	26.6	3.4
Saudi Arabia	327.0	326.8	–	–	0.2	100.0	–	–	–
United Kingdom	318.3	151.9	5.9	63.9	97.6	47.7	1.8	20.1	30.7
Mexico	305.1	244.0	31.7	10.6	18.8	80.0	10.4	3.5	6.2
Iran	289.6	267.9	14.9	6.4	0.4	92.5	5.1	2.2	0.1
Turkey	283.1	196.6	57.8	–	28.6	69.5	20.4	–	10.1
Italy	280.7	175.8	35.7	–	69.8	62.6	12.7	–	24.9
Spain	259.9	118.6	18.5	55.6	68.6	45.6	7.1	21.4	26.4
Taiwan	249.5	216.5	5.4	21.6	6.9	86.8	2.2	8.6	2.8
Australia	244.5	204.5	16.0	–	24.2	83.6	6.6	–	9.9
Indonesia	241.3	209.3	18.4	–	13.6	86.7	7.6	–	5.6
South Africa	236.4	213.3	0.9	15.1	8.7	90.2	0.4	6.4	3.7
Egypt	182.3	166.0	13.3	–	3.1	91.0	7.3	–	1.7
Thailand	177.1	146.6	9.4	–	21.1	82.8	5.3	–	11.9
Vietnam	173.3	102.7	70.2	–	0.4	59.3	40.5	–	0.2
Sweden	161.0	1.7	64.7	63.1	31.6	1.0	40.2	39.2	19.6
Poland	160.6	136.8	2.6	–	21.5	85.2	1.6	–	13.4
Malaysia	156.0	128.6	26.3	–	1.2	82.4	16.9	–	0.7
Norway	146.5	2.6	141.1	–	3.4	1.8	96.3	–	2.3
Ukraine	145.7	54.5	8.9	80.4	1.9	37.4	6.1	55.2	1.3
Argentina	138.4	90.7	39.5	5.7	2.7	65.6	28.5	4.1	2.0
United Arab Emirates	126.5	125.7	–	–	0.8	99.4	–	–	0.6
Pakistan	126.1	84.2	27.6	8.1	6.1	66.8	21.9	6.4	4.8
Netherlands	111.4	88.9	0.1	3.3	19.2	79.8	0.1	2.9	17.2
Venezuela	103.9	39.6	64.2	–	0.1	38.1	61.8	–	0.1
Kazakhstan	97.6	86.0	11.1	–	0.5	88.1	11.4	–	0.5
Philippines	90.0	66.9	9.5	–	13.6	74.3	10.6	–	15.1
Iraq	82.3	80.8	1.4	–	0.1	98.2	1.8	–	0.1
Czechia	81.0	44.9	1.9	26.8	7.9	55.4	2.3	33.1	9.7
Belgium	80.9	24.0	0.3	40.2	16.8	29.6	0.3	49.7	20.8
Chile	76.2	41.9	20.9	–	13.5	54.9	27.4	–	17.7

– Represents or rounds to zero. [1] Electricity generated from fossil fuels, and hydroelectric, nuclear, geothermal, solar, wind, tidal, biomass, and waste energy resources. Includes negative values from hydroelectric pumped storage. [2] Electricity generated from coal, oil, and gas resources. [3] Electricity generated from geothermal, solar, wind, tidal and wave, biomass, and waste resources. [4] Includes countries not shown separately.

Source: U.S. Energy Information Administration, "International Energy Statistics," <https://www.eia.gov/international/data/world>, accessed March 2020.

Table 1391. World Primary Energy Production by Region and Type: 1980 to 2017

[In quadrillion Btu (294.7 represents 294,700,000,000,000,000). Btu = British thermal unit. For Btu conversion factors, see source]

Region and type	1980	1990	1995	2000	2005	2010	2015	2016	2017
World total	**294.7**	**358.5**	**367.0**	**398.9**	**460.3**	**518.3**	**569.2**	**564.6**	**574.9**
REGION									
North America	83.0	91.5	95.8	98.4	98.4	102.1	117.0	112.8	116.7
United States [1]	**67.1**	**70.7**	**71.1**	**71.3**	**69.4**	**74.9**	**88.3**	**84.3**	**88.2**
Central and South America	12.1	16.9	21.5	26.2	28.3	31.3	33.8	33.6	32.3
Europe	41.5	48.7	49.4	50.7	49.1	46.1	44.1	43.7	42.9
Eurasia [2]	61.6	77.7	54.5	55.6	67.9	72.5	76.8	77.5	80.2
Middle East	42.3	40.9	48.3	57.5	66.3	72.2	83.0	87.8	87.8
Africa	17.2	21.5	23.9	27.3	34.1	36.7	32.8	31.7	33.3
Asia and Oceania	37.0	61.2	73.7	83.1	116.2	157.4	181.9	177.4	181.6
TYPE OF FUEL									
Petroleum [3]	133.1	136.2	141.8	156.4	169.7	173.0	187.4	188.4	188.7
Dry natural gas	54.8	75.7	80.3	89.3	102.1	116.9	129.6	130.9	136.1
Coal	78.5	99.9	91.7	95.4	124.9	154.2	168.5	158.0	161.8
Nuclear, renewables, and other	28.4	46.6	53.2	57.9	63.7	74.1	83.6	87.3	88.3

[1] Includes biomass, geothermal, and solar energy produced in the United States and not used for generating electricity. [2] Prior to 1992, data were for the former U.S.S.R. [3] Includes crude oil, lease condensate, and natural gas plant liquids.

Source: U.S. Energy Information Administration, "International Energy Statistics," <https://www.eia.gov/international/data/world>, accessed March 2020.

Table 1392. World Primary Energy Consumption by Region and Type: 1980 to 2017

[In quadrillion Btu (293.5 represents 293,500,000,000,000,000). Btu = British thermal unit. For Btu conversion factors, see source]

Region and type	1980	1990	1995	2000	2005	2010	2015	2016	2017
World, total...................	**293.5**	**359.0**	**367.9**	**402.3**	**465.1**	**523.8**	**570.1**	**574.2**	**582.5**
REGION									
North America......................	91.4	99.9	108.5	118.0	121.0	118.9	120.0	120.0	120.7
United States [1]...................	**78.0**	**84.4**	**90.9**	**98.7**	**100.1**	**97.5**	**97.4**	**97.3**	**97.7**
Central and South America.............	11.1	14.8	17.6	21.1	23.5	27.1	29.8	29.0	29.0
Europe............................	75.0	79.4	77.7	81.7	86.5	85.0	81.0	82.2	83.0
Eurasia [2].........................	52.1	66.2	43.5	39.6	42.1	44.6	44.8	44.5	46.1
Middle East.......................	5.9	11.0	13.8	17.8	23.5	30.1	35.5	36.1	37.2
Africa............................	6.7	9.7	10.7	12.1	14.7	16.9	19.3	19.4	19.9
Asia and Oceania..................	51.5	77.8	96.0	112.0	153.9	201.4	239.7	243.0	246.6
TYPE OF FUEL									
Petroleum [3].......................	132.1	136.5	142.0	156.9	171.7	178.6	191.2	191.7	194.7
Dry natural gas....................	53.9	75.1	81.3	89.6	102.6	119.4	130.1	132.7	137.3
Coal..............................	79.2	101.1	91.8	98.3	128.1	154.3	168.4	166.1	163.8
Nuclear, renewables, and other.......	28.3	46.3	52.8	57.5	62.8	71.5	80.4	83.7	86.6

[1] Includes biomass, geothermal, and solar energy consumed in the United States and not used for generating electricity. [2] Prior to 1992, data were for the former U.S.S.R. [3] Includes all refined petroleum products.

Source: U.S. Energy Information Administration, "International Energy Statistics," <https://www.eia.gov/international/data/world>, accessed March 2020.

Table 1393. Energy Consumption by Country: 2010 to 2017

[In quadrillion Btu (523.84 represents 523,840,000,000,000,000). Btu = British thermal units. Total primary energy consumption includes the consumption of petroleum, dry natural gas, coal, and net nuclear, hydroelectric, and non-hydroelectric renewable electricity. For data qualifications for countries and Btu conversion factors, see source]

Country	Total (quad. Btu)				Country	Total (quad. Btu)			
	2010	2015	2016	2017		2010	2015	2016	2017
World, total [1]........	**523.84**	**570.05**	**574.23**	**582.46**	Kuwait...................	1.40	1.65	1.67	1.59
United States..........	**97.52**	**97.38**	**97.33**	**97.71**	Libya....................	0.90	0.62	0.60	0.57
Algeria.................	1.78	2.35	2.33	2.40	Malaysia.................	2.97	3.33	3.30	3.51
Argentina...............	3.57	3.90	3.90	3.87	Mexico..................	7.52	7.77	7.94	7.93
Australia................	5.53	5.74	5.91	6.13	Morocco.................	0.68	0.79	0.78	0.82
Austria.................	1.52	1.44	1.47	1.49	Netherlands.............	4.28	3.82	3.89	3.92
Azerbaijan..............	0.59	0.62	0.61	0.59	New Zealand............	0.84	0.89	0.91	0.92
Bahrain.................	0.59	0.69	0.69	0.72	Nigeria.................	0.83	1.57	1.58	1.54
Bangladesh..............	0.95	1.28	1.38	1.42	Norway.................	1.85	1.90	1.92	1.89
Belarus.................	1.12	0.95	0.94	0.96	Oman...................	0.89	1.17	1.15	1.14
Belgium................	2.82	2.49	2.64	2.66	Pakistan................	2.61	2.96	3.12	3.18
Brazil..................	11.72	12.95	12.51	12.57	Paraguay...............	0.44	0.47	0.53	0.52
Bulgaria................	0.74	0.79	0.75	0.77	Peru...................	0.86	1.05	1.10	1.12
Burma..................	0.24	0.38	0.43	0.52	Philippines.............	1.21	1.62	1.73	1.83
Canada.................	13.84	14.83	14.71	15.02	Poland.................	3.96	4.00	4.13	4.35
Chile...................	1.26	1.40	1.48	1.50	Portugal................	1.11	1.04	1.08	1.07
China..................	109.36	137.28	137.42	138.69	Qatar..................	1.25	2.05	2.03	2.16
Colombia...............	1.30	1.73	1.72	1.66	Romania................	1.45	1.36	1.37	1.41
Czechia................	1.79	1.68	1.66	1.75	Russia.................	30.73	31.41	31.16	32.83
Denmark...............	0.83	0.72	0.74	0.74	Saudi Arabia............	8.81	10.65	10.46	11.00
Ecuador................	0.60	0.69	0.68	0.71	Serbia..................	0.68	0.64	0.66	0.64
Egypt..................	3.51	3.73	3.77	4.01	Singapore...............	2.93	3.29	3.49	3.63
Finland................	1.30	1.19	1.22	1.21	Slovakia................	0.78	0.71	0.71	0.74
France.................	11.00	10.44	10.28	10.31	South Africa............	5.66	5.63	5.63	5.67
Germany...............	14.06	13.72	13.84	14.01	Spain..................	6.20	5.64	5.74	5.74
Greece.................	1.32	1.13	1.12	1.16	Sweden................	2.22	2.15	2.17	2.23
Hong Kong.............	1.34	1.28	1.31	1.32	Switzerland.............	1.31	1.21	1.18	1.17
Hungary...............	1.03	0.98	1.00	1.04	Syria..................	1.03	0.42	0.39	0.39
India..................	21.70	28.38	29.48	30.48	Taiwan.................	4.64	4.69	4.79	4.67
Indonesia..............	6.24	7.01	7.07	7.16	Thailand...............	4.41	5.18	5.40	5.52
Iran...................	9.22	10.78	11.17	11.60	Trinidad and Tobago. ..	0.96	0.98	0.88	0.90
Iraq...................	1.36	1.43	1.77	1.87	Turkey.................	4.51	5.75	5.97	6.44
Ireland................	0.63	0.60	0.63	0.64	Turkmenistan...........	1.03	1.76	1.75	1.74
Israel.................	0.94	1.04	1.07	1.06	Ukraine................	5.17	3.85	3.89	3.63
Italy..................	7.68	6.77	6.72	6.79	United Arab Emirates...	3.63	4.65	4.72	4.67
Japan..................	21.51	19.56	19.61	19.48	United Kingdom........	9.19	8.36	8.77	8.22
Kazakhstan.............	3.17	3.29	3.46	3.58	Uzbekistan.............	1.94	1.96	1.72	1.80
Korea, North...........	0.69	0.33	0.37	0.33	Venezuela..............	3.11	3.06	2.70	2.49
Korea, South...........	10.94	11.97	12.18	12.43	Vietnam................	1.96	2.82	3.11	3.24

[1] Includes countries not shown separately.

Source: U.S. Energy Information Administration, "International Energy Statistics," <https://www.eia.gov/international/data/world>, accessed March 2020.

Table 1394. World Energy Consumption by Region and Energy Source: 2018, and Projections, 2020 to 2050

[In quadrillion Btu (620.0 represents 620,000,000,000,000,000). Btu = British thermal units. For Btu conversion factors, see source. Energy totals include net imports of coal coke and electricity generated from biomass in the United States. The electricity portion of the national consumption values consists of generation for domestic use plus an adjustment for electricity trade based on a fuel's share of total generation in the exporting country. OECD = Organisation for Economic Co-operation and Development; see text, this section]

| Region and energy source | 2018 | Projections | | | | | | | | Average annual percent change 2018-2050 |
		2020	2025	2030	2035	2040	2045	2050	
World, total................	**620.0**	**635.0**	**664.9**	**705.2**	**747.2**	**794.9**	**853.7**	**910.7**	**1.21**
OECD, total [1]................	249.4	250.3	252.8	257.2	261.4	268.2	276.5	286.8	0.44
OECD Americas................	125.2	125.5	125.1	125.6	126.6	129.7	133.3	138.1	0.31
United States................	**99.8**	**99.8**	**99.0**	**98.8**	**98.9**	**100.7**	**103.0**	**106.0**	**0.19**
OECD Europe................	83.3	84.3	85.9	88.6	90.1	92.8	95.8	99.3	0.55
OECD Asia................	40.9	40.5	41.8	43.1	44.6	45.7	47.4	49.4	0.59
Non-OECD, total................	370.6	384.7	412.1	447.9	485.8	526.7	577.2	623.9	1.64
Non-OECD Europe and Eurasia..	49.1	48.9	48.2	49.7	50.7	51.5	53.1	54.3	0.32
Non-OECD Asia................	227.4	239.1	259.6	285.6	313.7	344.5	382.8	416.4	1.91
China................	149.1	156.7	166.2	175.7	185.7	195.5	208.9	217.9	1.19
India................	35.2	37.4	44.9	55.9	69.3	83.7	102.3	120.3	3.92
Middle East................	37.3	38.7	41.6	45.0	48.1	50.8	54.1	57.8	1.37
Africa................	24.5	25.5	28.1	31.4	35.3	39.9	45.1	51.4	2.34
Non-OECD Americas................	32.3	32.5	34.6	36.3	38.0	40.0	42.1	44.0	0.98
Liquids................	198.9	203.3	206.9	210.7	215.6	222.9	232.3	242.5	0.62
Natural gas................	138.2	139.9	145.2	153.8	164.5	175.3	187.6	198.9	1.14
Coal................	160.1	156.7	155.6	155.8	157.7	161.0	168.4	179.2	0.35
Nuclear................	28.0	28.7	29.5	32.2	33.4	34.8	36.1	37.9	0.95
Other................	94.8	106.3	127.7	152.8	176.1	200.8	229.3	252.2	3.10

[1] For full membership listing of the Organisation for Economic Co-operation and Development (OECD), see introductory text, this section. For purposes of this report, Lithuania is included in Non-OECD Europe and Eurasia despite joining the OECD in 2018.

Source: U.S. Energy Information Administration, *International Energy Outlook 2019*, September 2019. See also <https://www.eia.gov/outlooks/ieo/>.

Table 1395. World Daily Crude Oil Production by Major Producing Country: 1980 to 2019

[In thousands of barrels per day (59,558 barrels represents 59,558,000 barrels). Includes lease condensate. Ranked for top 40 countries, as of current year]

Country	1980	1990	2000	2005	2010	2015	2016	2017	2018	2019
World, total [1]................	**59,558**	**60,498**	**68,527**	**73,869**	**74,894**	**80,762**	**80,848**	**81,096**	**82,923**	**82,275**
United States................	**8,597**	**7,355**	**5,822**	**5,184**	**5,484**	**9,439**	**8,839**	**9,352**	**10,990**	**12,229**
Russia................	(X)	(X)	6,479	9,043	9,694	10,253	10,551	10,580	10,759	10,847
Saudi Arabia................	9,900	6,410	8,404	9,550	8,900	10,168	10,461	10,134	10,425	9,824
Iraq................	2,514	2,040	2,571	1,878	2,399	4,045	4,444	4,454	4,613	4,730
Canada................	1,435	1,553	1,977	2,369	2,741	3,677	3,679	3,977	4,343	4,404
China................	2,114	2,774	3,249	3,609	4,078	4,278	3,983	3,821	3,773	3,825
United Arab Emirates................	1,709	2,117	2,368	2,535	2,570	3,149	3,243	3,174	3,216	3,414
Iran................	1,662	3,088	3,696	4,139	4,080	3,293	4,151	4,469	4,255	2,963
Kuwait................	1,656	1,175	2,078	2,529	2,300	2,784	2,905	2,753	2,846	2,891
Brazil................	182	631	1,269	1,634	2,055	2,437	2,515	2,622	2,587	2,788
Nigeria................	2,055	1,810	2,165	2,627	2,408	2,171	1,871	1,946	1,915	1,954
Kazakhstan................	(X)	(X)	718	1,288	1,525	1,653	1,595	1,777	1,856	1,863
Mexico................	1,936	2,553	3,104	3,423	2,621	2,302	2,187	1,981	1,852	1,703
Qatar................	472	406	742	978	1,451	1,498	1,496	1,500	1,458	1,520
Angola................	150	475	746	1,239	1,909	1,802	1,770	1,666	1,593	1,448
Norway................	486	1,630	3,222	2,698	1,871	1,610	1,648	1,618	1,517	1,437
Algeria................	1,106	1,180	1,214	1,692	1,540	1,429	1,348	1,306	1,259	1,259
Libya................	1,787	1,375	1,410	1,651	1,710	484	466	897	1,039	1,184
United Kingdom................	1,622	1,820	2,275	1,649	1,233	893	933	911	1,000	1,026
Oman................	282	685	970	774	865	981	1,004	970	979	971
Colombia................	126	440	691	526	786	1,003	886	854	863	886
Venezuela................	2,168	2,137	3,155	2,565	2,410	2,500	2,277	2,007	1,486	877
Azerbaijan................	(X)	(X)	280	433	1,035	848	834	791	798	778
Indonesia................	1,577	1,462	1,428	1,059	945	786	832	802	770	737
India................	182	660	646	665	751	761	735	734	709	667
Egypt................	595	873	768	623	636	686	654	630	639	631
Malaysia................	283	619	690	726	638	654	667	648	647	604
Ecuador................	204	285	395	532	486	543	548	531	517	531
Argentina................	491	483	761	704	626	532	511	479	489	507
Australia................	380	575	722	456	479	322	290	263	284	361
Congo, Republic of................	65	165	280	229	340	238	198	245	340	330
Thailand................	–	44	110	183	242	248	258	240	228	228
Vietnam................	–	50	316	358	299	333	302	271	242	222
Turkmenistan................	(X)	(X)	142	183	178	243	231	245	244	210
Gabon................	175	270	315	266	246	213	211	199	196	202
Ghana................	2	–	7	6	7	102	98	151	173	201
South Sudan................	(X)	(X)	(X)	(X)	(X)	153	152	150	126	178
Equatorial Guinea................	–	–	168	363	298	250	227	188	172	156
Chad................	–	–	–	177	123	123	114	128	132	128
Brunei................	235	150	193	188	131	115	109	101	100	110

X Not applicable. – Represents zero or rounds to zero. [1] Includes countries not shown separately.

Source: U.S. Energy Information Administration, "International Energy Statistics," <https://www.eia.gov/international/data/world>, accessed April 2020.

Table 1396. World Dry Natural Gas Production by Major Producing Country: 1980 to 2018

[In billions of cubic feet (53,378 represents 53,378,000,000,000). Ranked for top 30 countries in 2017]

Country	Dry natural gas production								
	1980	1990	2000	2005	2010	2015	2016	2017	2018 (P)
World, total [1]	**53,378**	**73,387**	**86,770**	**98,598**	**113,108**	**124,659**	**126,054**	**130,018**	**(NA)**
United States	**19,403**	**17,810**	**19,182**	**18,051**	**21,316**	**27,065**	**26,592**	**27,306**	**30,589**
Russia	(X)	(X)	19,335	21,224	21,458	21,531	21,750	22,453	23,576
Iran	250	818	2,127	3,655	5,161	6,526	7,083	7,577	7,920
Qatar	184	222	1,028	1,617	4,121	5,794	5,869	5,875	5,967
Canada	2,759	3,849	6,470	6,561	5,390	5,489	5,554	5,618	(NA)
China	505	508	962	1,763	3,278	4,632	5,007	5,359	5,839
Norway	917	976	1,867	3,072	3,756	4,139	4,115	4,375	4,281
Saudi Arabia	334	1,077	1,759	2,516	3,096	3,614	3,739	3,859	3,928
Australia	313	723	1,159	1,266	1,859	2,373	3,068	3,717	4,317
Algeria	411	1,787	2,940	3,151	2,988	2,933	3,312	3,302	3,291
Turkmenistan	(X)	(X)	1,642	2,225	1,466	2,831	2,692	2,735	2,749
Indonesia	654	1,602	2,237	2,001	2,917	2,571	2,533	2,546	2,563
Malaysia	56	501	1,465	1,977	2,171	2,240	2,214	2,454	2,454
United Arab Emirates	200	780	1,355	1,659	1,811	2,125	2,157	2,190	2,200
Uzbekistan	(X)	(X)	1,992	2,108	2,123	1,967	1,823	1,840	1,955
Egypt	30	286	646	1,501	2,166	1,565	1,497	1,796	2,017
Netherlands	3,398	2,687	2,572	2,773	3,126	1,907	1,840	1,601	1,335
Nigeria	38	131	440	791	1,024	1,594	1,475	1,571	1,609
United Kingdom	1,323	1,754	3,826	3,118	2,111	1,460	1,471	1,487	1,441
Argentina	280	630	1,321	1,611	1,416	1,285	1,387	1,445	1,524
Pakistan	286	482	856	1,088	1,400	1,388	1,379	1,379	1,291
Thailand	–	208	658	837	1,278	1,406	1,384	1,363	1,336
Trinidad and Tobago	81	177	493	1,094	1,499	1,389	1,274	1,297	1,378
Mexico	900	903	1,297	1,513	1,769	1,426	1,296	1,115	1,086
India	51	399	719	1,056	1,848	1,103	1,092	1,114	1,122
Oman	28	99	322	705	957	1,057	1,076	1,103	1,178
Bangladesh	50	162	343	494	711	949	1,039	1,043	1,041
Venezuela	517	761	961	828	697	918	972	956	957
Brazil	42	97	257	345	523	829	840	947	877
Kazakhstan	(X)	(X)	314	428	621	749	751	791	830

P Preliminary. NA Not available. X Not applicable. – Represents zero. [1] Includes countries not shown separately.

Source: U.S. Energy Information Administration, "International Energy Statistics," <https://www.eia.gov/international/data/world>, accessed September 2020.

Table 1397. World Coal Production by Major Producing Country: 1980 to 2017

[In thousands of short tons (4,158,801 represents 4,158,801,000). Coal includes anthracite, bituminous, subbituminous, metallurgical and lignite. Ranked for top 30 countries, as of current year]

Country	Coal production								
	1980	1990	2000	2005	2010	2014	2015	2016	2017
World, total [1]	**4,158,801**	**5,281,983**	**5,126,951**	**6,644,453**	**8,099,273**	**8,982,413**	**8,735,612**	**8,156,080**	**8,358,234**
China	683,587	1,189,725	1,525,800	2,607,124	3,779,212	4,270,260	4,129,851	3,708,155	3,797,961
India	127,989	239,035	372,518	481,825	578,216	713,454	747,074	761,662	790,476
United States	**829,700**	**1,029,076**	**1,073,612**	**1,131,498**	**1,084,368**	**1,000,049**	**896,941**	**728,364**	**774,610**
Australia	115,196	225,491	338,103	408,505	467,823	555,812	556,120	554,764	552,320
Indonesia	627	13,165	87,498	188,495	303,316	504,965	508,789	502,871	508,438
Russia	(X)	(X)	264,912	311,823	329,258	393,765	409,701	423,095	449,579
South Africa	126,898	192,684	247,138	270,055	280,403	288,695	278,003	276,239	278,113
Germany	(X)	(X)	226,047	226,993	202,286	205,597	203,612	193,593	193,039
Poland	253,517	237,082	178,247	174,987	146,257	150,374	149,147	143,996	139,486
Kazakhstan	(X)	(X)	82,548	91,258	122,278	125,647	118,299	113,620	116,806
Colombia	4,590	22,562	42,044	65,107	82,021	97,640	94,300	99,772	98,590
Turkey	20,531	52,280	69,741	64,309	80,908	75,094	67,025	80,473	84,486
Canada	40,442	75,323	76,239	72,582	74,835	76,079	68,267	67,606	67,642
Mongolia	5,818	7,889	5,715	8,285	27,793	29,061	26,432	38,687	54,543
Czechia	(X)	(X)	71,829	68,372	60,857	51,651	51,168	49,949	49,298
Serbia	(X)	(X)	(X)	(X)	41,861	33,081	41,696	42,373	43,879
Vietnam	5,732	5,100	12,797	37,581	49,422	45,290	45,927	42,469	42,149
Greece	25,571	57,205	70,423	76,498	62,303	56,047	50,977	35,977	41,208
Bulgaria	33,304	34,916	29,136	27,222	32,413	34,467	39,528	34,426	37,784
Romania	38,762	42,090	32,281	34,288	34,312	25,976	28,101	25,344	28,387
Ukraine	(X)	(X)	68,787	66,537	63,558	50,630	37,990	39,261	26,639
Korea, North	33,367	36,542	24,802	26,522	35,452	33,985	30,303	34,238	20,826
Thailand	1,681	13,711	19,605	23,014	20,126	19,821	16,701	18,716	17,922
Laos	–	3	253	408	808	1,288	5,284	14,590	14,961
Philippines	363	1,370	1,491	3,487	7,330	8,379	8,133	12,358	13,153
Mozambique	–	–	26	36	39	7,551	7,274	6,819	12,983
Mexico	3,405	7,642	12,505	14,854	16,870	16,961	16,831	13,853	12,981
Hungary	28,688	19,654	15,469	10,549	10,045	10,528	10,208	10,159	8,768
Kosovo	(X)	(X)	(X)	(X)	9,534	7,941	9,084	9,701	8,350
Bosnia and Herzegovina	(X)	(X)	8,200	6,356	7,047	6,798	6,666	7,167	7,861

– Represents zero. X Not applicable. [1] Includes other countries not shown separately.

Source: U.S. Energy Information Administration, "International Energy Statistics," <https://www.eia.gov/international/data/world>, accessed March 2020.

Table 1398. Carbon Dioxide Emissions From Consumption of Fossil Fuels by Country: 1980 to 2017

[In millions of metric tons of carbon dioxide (19,286 represents 19,286,000,000). Ranked for top 25 countries, as of most recent year shown. Includes carbon dioxide emissions from the consumption of petroleum, natural gas, coal, and the flaring of natural gas]

Region/country	1980	1990	2000	2005	2010	2014	2015	2016	2017
World, total [1]	**19,286**	**22,717**	**24,368**	**28,875**	**32,521**	**35,437**	**35,505**	**35,281**	**35,545**
China	1,665	2,667	3,523	6,106	8,779	10,701	10,512	10,502	10,419
United States	**4,751**	**5,039**	**5,862**	**5,991**	**5,586**	**5,414**	**5,267**	**5,175**	**5,133**
India	275	559	924	1,171	1,606	2,094	2,180	2,237	2,312
Russia	(X)	(X)	1,539	1,597	1,736	1,737	1,742	1,690	1,782
Japan	911	1,113	1,200	1,252	1,122	1,183	1,139	1,139	1,117
Germany	(X)	(X)	821	822	839	821	830	835	821
Iran	119	216	322	452	568	645	641	631	676
Korea, South	146	251	428	482	570	613	627	611	637
Saudi Arabia	177	208	291	405	502	599	625	611	631
Canada	412	413	545	589	539	565	569	541	558
Indonesia	85	158	268	317	423	471	509	500	531
Brazil	186	244	355	380	474	556	623	522	530
South Africa	230	331	396	448	481	473	476	474	477
Turkey	70	139	205	232	299	357	379	396	449
France	537	407	410	423	456	408	413	411	417
Australia	192	247	345	370	384	384	399	408	416
United Kingdom	591	549	574	591	524	464	452	475	416
Mexico	214	243	386	424	397	400	414	411	406
Italy	399	434	446	473	446	375	385	383	376
Thailand	34	84	158	237	280	334	337	344	349
Poland	344	314	270	278	321	308	313	327	347
Taiwan	70	119	238	267	272	318	322	330	325
Spain	214	237	319	383	337	300	316	310	322
United Arab Emirates	30	79	116	140	218	261	286	289	289
Kazakhstan	(X)	(X)	171	217	265	272	270	280	289

X Not applicable. [1] Includes other countries not shown separately.

Source: U.S. Energy Information Administration, "International Energy Statistics," <https://www.eia.gov/international/data/world>, accessed March 2020.

Table 1399. Average Temperatures and Precipitation—Selected International Cities

[In degrees Fahrenheit, except as noted. Data are generally based on a standard 30-year period; for details, see source. Minus sign (-) indicates degrees below zero]

City	January					July				
	Average high	Average low	Warmest	Coldest	Average precipitation (inches)	Average high	Average low	Warmest	Coldest	Average precipitation (inches)
Amsterdam, Netherlands	41	34	57	3	3.1	69	55	90	39	2.9
Athens, Greece	55	44	70	28	1.9	89	73	108	61	0.2
Baghdad, Iraq	58	38	75	25	1.1	110	78	122	61	–
Bangkok, Thailand	89	71	95	54	0.4	90	78	99	72	6.2
Beijing, China	34	17	54	1	0.2	86	72	104	63	8.8
Berlin, Germany	35	26	58	-11	(NA)	73	56	95	41	(NA)
Bogota, Colombia	66	43	84	27	1.9	64	47	82	32	1.8
Brasilia, Brazil	81	64	95	54	(NA)	79	52	97	37	(NA)
Buenos Aires, Argentina	85	64	104	44	4.2	58	41	88	23	2.3
Cairo, Egypt	65	49	86	32	0.2	93	72	108	63	–
Frankfurt, Germany	38	30	56	-4	1.8	75	57	97	38	2.4
Geneva, Switzerland	39	29	57	-2	2.2	77	56	96	41	2.8
Hong Kong, China	67	58	79	43	1.1	89	81	97	70	14.3
Istanbul, Turkey	46	37	64	16	3.7	82	66	100	50	0.7
Jakarta, Indonesia	83	75	92	72	(NA)	88	74	92	67	(NA)
Karachi, Pakistan	76	55	93	39	0.3	89	83	109	68	3.5
Lagos, Nigeria	82	79	93	64	(NA)	79	76	88	70	(NA)
London, England	45	36	61	15	2.4	72	56	93	45	1.8
Madrid, Spain	51	32	68	14	1.8	90	61	104	46	0.4
Manila, Philippines	86	71	95	61	0.8	88	76	99	70	15.9
Mexico City, Mexico	70	45	86	26	0.3	74	56	86	37	5.1
Montreal, Canada	21	7	52	-31	2.8	79	61	93	43	3.4
Moscow, Russia	21	11	46	-33	1.4	71	55	95	41	3.2
Nairobi, Kenya	77	58	88	45	1.8	71	54	85	43	0.5
New Delhi, India	68	48	85	32	0.9	93	81	111	70	7.9
Paris, France	43	34	59	1	(NA)	75	58	95	41	(NA)
Rio De Janeiro, Brazil	91	74	109	64	5.3	81	64	102	52	1.8
Rome, Italy	55	39	64	19	3.2	83	66	100	55	0.6
Seoul, Korea	33	21	55	-1	(NA)	82	71	97	55	(NA)
Singapore, Singapore	85	73	100	66	9.4	86	76	99	70	5.9
Sydney, Australia	79	65	109	49	4.0	62	44	80	32	2.5
Tel Aviv, Israel	62	46	84	32	(NA)	87	69	100	50	(NA)
Tokyo, Japan	48	35	66	25	2.0	82	71	95	55	5.3
Toronto, Canada	28	15	59	-24	1.9	79	60	99	45	2.8

– Represents zero. NA Not available.

Source: U.S. National Oceanic and Atmospheric Administration, *Climates of the World*. See also <https://library.noaa.gov/Research-Tools/Subject-Guides/weathersites>.

Table 1400. Telephones, Mobile Cellular Phones, and Internet Use by Country: 2018

[For data qualifications for individual countries, see source]

Country	Fixed telephone subscriptions per 100 people [1]	Cellphone subscriptions per 100 people [2]	Internet users (as percent of population) [3]	Country	Fixed telephone subscriptions per 100 people [1]	Cellphone subscriptions per 100 people [2]	Internet users (as percent of population) [3]
United States....	**33.6**	**129.0**	**(NA)**	Kazakhstan.......	18.3	142.3	78.9
Algeria............	9.9	111.7	49.0	Korea, South.....	50.6	129.7	96.0
Austria............	42.4	123.5	87.5	Latvia............	13.8	107.3	83.6
Azerbaijan........	16.9	103.9	79.8	Lithuania........	15.2	163.9	79.7
Brazil.............	18.3	98.8	70.4	Luxembourg......	45.3	132.2	97.1
Bulgaria..........	15.9	118.9	64.8	Malaysia.........	20.4	134.5	81.2
Cambodia.........	0.5	119.5	40.0	Mexico...........	17.2	95.2	65.8
Colombia..........	14.0	129.9	64.1	Mongolia.........	11.7	133.2	47.2
Croatia...........	32.6	105.6	75.3	Montenegro......	27.5	180.7	71.5
Cyprus............	36.1	138.9	84.4	Morocco..........	6.1	124.2	64.8
Czechia...........	14.2	119.1	80.7	Norway...........	10.5	107.2	96.5
Egypt.............	8.0	95.3	46.9	Poland...........	17.3	134.7	77.5
France............	59.4	108.4	82.0	Portugal..........	49.5	115.6	74.7
Georgia...........	15.1	136.4	62.7	Romania.........	18.8	116.2	70.7
Germany..........	51.1	129.3	89.7	Russia...........	20.7	157.4	80.9
Greece...........	48.3	115.7	73.0	Saudi Arabia......	16.0	122.6	93.3
Haiti..............	0.1	57.5	32.5	Singapore........	34.8	148.8	88.2
Indonesia........	3.1	119.3	39.9	Spain............	41.7	116.0	86.1
Iran..............	37.3	108.5	70.0	Sweden..........	24.0	126.8	92.1
Iraq..............	7.0	95.0	75.0	Thailand.........	4.2	180.2	56.8
Ireland............	38.0	103.2	84.5	Turkey............	14.1	97.3	71.0
Israel.............	38.2	127.7	83.7	Ukraine...........	14.4	127.8	62.6
Italy..............	33.6	137.5	74.4	United Kingdom..	47.5	118.4	94.9
Japan.............	49.9	141.4	91.3	Vietnam..........	4.5	147.2	70.3

[1] Refers to the sum of active number of analogue fixed telephone lines, voice-over-IP (VoIP) subscriptions, fixed wireless local loop (WLL) subscriptions, ISDN voice-channel equivalents and fixed public payphones. [2] Subscriptions to a public mobile telephone service that provide access to the public switched telephone network (PSTN) using cellular technology. Includes number of postpaid subscriptions and active prepaid accounts. Applies to all mobile cellular subscriptions that offer voice communications. Excludes subscriptions via data cards or USB modems, subscriptions to public mobile data services, private trunked mobile radio, telepoint, radio paging, and telemetry services. [3] Internet users are individuals who have used the internet (from any location) in the last 3 months. The internet can be used via a computer, mobile phone, personal digital assistant, games machine, digital TV etc.

Source: The World Bank, Washington, DC, "World Development Indicators" database ©, <http://data.worldbank.org/data-catalog/world-development-indicators>, accessed September 2020.

Table 1401. Global Telecommunications Indicators: 2000 to 2018

[975 represents 975,000,000]

Indicators	2000	2005	2010	2013	2014	2015	2016	2017	2018
NUMBER (million)									
Fixed telephone subscriptions [1].......................	975	1,244	1,229	1,142	1,091	1,046	1,008	978	942
Mobile cellular subscriptions [2].........................	738	2,206	5,296	6,662	6,999	7,182	7,509	7,750	7,858
Fixed broadband internet subscriptions [3].............	(NA)	220	532	690	727	840	915	1,025	1,065
PERCENT OF POPULATION									
Internet users [4]...	6.7	15.7	28.8	36.8	39.9	41.7	44.7	49.7	(NA)
PER 100 INHABITANTS									
Fixed telephone subscriptions [1].......................	15.9	19.3	17.7	15.8	15.0	14.2	13.5	13.0	12.8
Mobile cellular subscriptions [2].........................	12.0	33.8	76.1	92.4	96.0	97.4	100.7	102.8	106.4
Fixed broadband internet subscriptions [3].............	(NA)	3.7	7.8	9.8	10.2	11.5	12.4	13.7	14.5

NA Not available. [1] Refers to the sum of active number of analogue fixed telephone lines, voice-over-IP (VoIP) subscriptions, fixed wireless local loop (WLL) subscriptions, ISDN voice-channel equivalents and fixed public payphones. [2] Subscriptions to a public mobile telephone service that provide access to the public switched telephone network (PSTN) using cellular technology. Includes number of postpaid subscriptions and active prepaid accounts. Applies to all mobile cellular subscriptions that offer voice communications. Excludes subscriptions via data cards or USB modems, subscriptions to public mobile data services, private trunked mobile radio, telepoint, radio paging, and telemetry services. [3] Internet users are individuals who have used the internet (from any location) in the last 3 months. The internet can be used via a computer, mobile phone, personal digital assistant, games machine, digital TV etc. [4] Refers to fixed subscriptions to high-speed access to the public internet (a TCP/IP connection), at downstream speeds equal to, or greater than, 256 kbit/s. Includes cable modem, DSL, fiber-to-the-home/building, other fixed (wired)-broadband subscriptions, satellite broadband and terrestrial fixed wireless broadband. Excludes subscriptions that have access to data communications (including the internet) via mobile-cellular networks.

Source: The World Bank, Washington, DC, "World Development Indicators" database ©, <http://data.worldbank.org/data-catalog/world-development-indicators>, accessed September 2020.

Table 1402. Patents by Country: 2018

[Includes only U.S. patents granted to residents of areas outside of the United States and its territories. For information on types of patents, see <https://www.uspto.gov/patents-getting-started/general-information-concerning-patents>. Countries are in rank order. See also Table 811 and Table 812]

Country	Total [1]	Utility (inventions)	Designs	Country	Total [1]	Utility (inventions)	Designs
Total....................	**178,184**	**163,347**	**13,853**	Sweden...................	3,177	2,807	359
				Switzerland.............	2,987	2,669	312
Japan.......................	49,702	47,566	2,014	Australia.................	1,986	1,656	286
Korea, South..............	21,817	19,780	1,967	Finland..................	1,563	1,444	110
Germany....................	17,326	16,033	1,196	Austria..................	1,489	1,403	83
China.......................	16,759	14,488	2,262	Belgium..................	1,383	1,276	96
Taiwan......................	11,742	10,933	793	Denmark..................	1,271	1,122	98
United Kingdom...........	7,599	6,616	943	Singapore................	1,064	989	74
Canada.....................	7,181	6,518	634	Spain....................	973	873	96
France.....................	7,062	6,469	563	Hong Kong...............	952	693	258
India.......................	4,329	4,225	103	Saudi Arabia............	690	686	4
Israel......................	4,219	3,996	191	Ireland..................	656	635	21
Italy.......................	3,386	2,802	557	Norway...................	638	602	36
Netherlands...............	3,220	2,700	200	Other countries.........	5,013	4,366	597

[1] Includes patents for botanical plants and reissues, not shown separately.

Source: U.S. Patent and Trademark Office, "General Patent Statistics Reports Available for Viewing," <http://www.uspto.gov/web/offices/ac/ido/oeip/taf/reports_stco.htm>, accessed February 2020.

Table 1403. Foreign Currency Exchange Rates by Country: 2014 to 2019

[Foreign currency units per U.S. dollar. Data are yearly averages]

Country	Currency	2014	2015	2016	2017	2018	2019
Afghanistan................	Afghani	59.77	63.65	70.65	71.09	73.60	77.58
Algeria.....................	Dinar	84.24	104.88	114.43	115.88	117.41	119.40
Argentina..................	Peso	8.45	9.62	15.36	17.23	28.17	48.19
Australia...................	Dollar	1.15	1.35	1.40	1.36	1.34	1.44
Bahrain.....................	Dinar	0.39	0.40	0.40	0.40	0.40	0.38
Brazil......................	Real	2.45	3.47	3.63	3.32	3.66	3.95
Canada.....................	Dollar	1.15	1.33	1.38	1.35	1.30	1.33
Cayman Islands...........	Dollar	0.88	0.89	0.89	0.88	0.83	0.83
China.......................	Renminbi (yuan)	6.39	6.49	6.91	7.03	6.62	6.91
Denmark....................	Krone	5.84	6.99	7.00	6.86	6.32	6.67
Egypt.......................	Pound	7.40	8.04	10.46	18.59	17.81	16.81
Euro Zone.................	Euro	0.78	0.94	0.94	0.92	0.85	0.89
Hong Kong.................	Dollar	8.07	8.06	8.07	8.11	7.84	7.84
Hungary....................	Forint	242.08	290.64	293.08	285.58	270.44	290.71
Iceland.....................	Krona	121.57	137.47	126.26	111.23	116.38	122.57
India.......................	Rupee	63.47	66.77	69.96	67.81	68.42	70.39
Iraq........................	Dinar	1,228.79	1,231.23	1,236.45	1,241.68	1,193.48	1,191.25
Israel......................	New Shekel	3.72	4.05	4.00	3.75	3.60	3.56
Japan.......................	Yen	110.10	125.91	113.14	116.67	110.42	109.01
Lebanon....................	Pound	1,591.28	1,588.88	1,593.64	1,593.97	1,511.68	1,510.29
Mexico.....................	Peso	13.84	16.51	19.44	19.68	19.23	19.25
Morocco....................	Dirham	8.83	10.21	10.28	10.23	9.39	9.61
New Zealand..............	Dollar	1.26	1.49	1.49	1.47	1.45	1.52
Norway.....................	Kroner	6.56	8.39	8.75	8.61	8.14	8.80
Qatar.......................	Riyal	3.79	3.79	3.79	3.85	3.64	3.64
Russia......................	Ruble	40.12	63.66	69.69	60.69	62.85	64.69
Saudi Arabia..............	Riyal	3.90	3.90	3.90	3.90	3.75	3.75
Singapore..................	Dollar	1.32	1.43	1.44	1.44	1.35	1.36
South Africa...............	Rand	11.29	13.28	15.32	13.86	13.26	14.45
South Korean..............	Won	1,098.23	1,179.13	1,211.12	1,178.59	1,100.59	1,165.70
Sweden.....................	Krona	7.14	8.78	8.91	8.89	8.70	9.46
Switzerland................	Franc	0.95	1.00	1.03	1.02	0.98	0.99
Taiwan......................	Dollar	31.57	33.09	33.59	31.68	30.15	30.90
Thailand....................	Baht	33.84	35.68	36.78	35.37	32.32	31.03
Tunisia.....................	Dinar	1.77	2.04	2.24	2.51	2.71	2.93
Turkey......................	New Lira	2.28	2.83	3.15	3.79	4.85	5.69
United Arab Emirates.....	Dirham	3.82	3.82	3.82	3.82	3.67	3.67
United Kingdom...........	Pound	0.63	0.68	0.77	0.81	0.75	0.78

Source: U.S. Internal Revenue Service, "Yearly Average Currency Exchange Rates," <https://www.irs.gov/individuals/international-taxpayers/yearly-average-currency-exchange-rates>, accessed April 2020.

Table 1404. Foreign Stock Market Indices: 1980 to 2019

[As of year end. The DAX-30 index is a total return index that includes dividends, whereas the other foreign indices are price indices that exclude dividends]

Year	London FTSE 100	Tokyo Nikkei 225	Hong Kong Hang Seng	Germany DAX-30	Paris CAC-40	Dow Jones Europe STOXX 50
1980	647	7,116	1,477	481	(X)	(X)
1985	1,413	13,113	1,752	1,366	(X)	(X)
1990	2,144	23,849	3,025	1,398	1,518	835
1995	3,689	19,868	10,073	2,254	1,872	1,538
2000	6,223	13,786	15,096	6,434	5,926	4,557
2005	5,619	16,111	14,876	5,408	4,715	3,349
2010	5,900	10,229	23,035	6,914	3,805	2,586
2014	6,566	17,451	23,605	9,806	4,273	3,004
2015	6,242	19,034	21,914	10,743	4,637	3,100
2016	7,143	19,114	22,001	11,481	4,862	3,011
2017	7,688	22,765	29,919	12,918	5,313	3,178
2018	6,728	20,015	25,846	10,559	4,731	2,760
2019	7,542	23,657	28,190	13,249	5,978	3,403

X Not applicable.

Source: Global Financial Data, Los Angeles, CA ©, <http://www.globalfinancialdata.com>.

Table 1405. Research and Development (R&D) Expenditures by Sector and Country: 2018

[Total and per capita expenditures in millions of dollars (1,447,828 represents $1,447,828,000,000). Gross domestic expenditure on R&D (GERD) may include financing from abroad. Selected data are preliminary or estimated. For methodological information for individual countries, see source. GDP = gross domestic product]

Country	Gross domestic expenditure on R&D (GERD)			Percent of GERD performed by:			
	Total (million current PPP U.S. dollars) [1]	Per capita (million current PPP U.S. dollars) [1]	Percent of GDP	Government sector	Business enterprise sector	Higher education sector	Private non-profit sector
OECD total [2]	1,447,828	1,072	2.4	9.9	70.6	17.1	2.4
EU-28 [2]	464,876	905	2.0	10.9	66.3	21.9	0.9
EU-15 [3]	426,691	1,043	2.2	10.8	66.5	21.7	0.9
United States [4]	**581,553**	**1,776**	**2.8**	**10.4**	**72.6**	**12.8**	**4.2**
Austria	15,786	1,786	3.1	7.1	69.9	22.4	0.5
Belgium	15,992	1,399	2.7	9.9	69.8	19.7	0.6
Canada	29,003	783	1.6	6.9	50.9	41.7	0.5
Chile	1,621	86	0.3	12.6	33.6	47.4	6.4
China	468,062	335	2.1	15.2	77.4	7.4	(NA)
Colombia	2,125	44	0.3	7.8	36.9	31.5	23.8
Czechia	8,287	780	1.9	16.4	61.9	21.5	0.2
Denmark	10,054	1,735	3.0	3.0	64.3	32.4	0.3
Estonia	675	512	1.4	11.4	42.3	44.5	1.7
Finland	7,504	1,360	2.8	8.3	65.7	25.2	0.8
France	68,441	1,017	2.2	12.5	65.4	20.5	1.6
Germany	141,300	1,704	3.1	13.5	68.9	17.6	(NA)
Greece	3,844	358	1.2	22.4	48.2	28.4	1.1
Hungary	4,734	484	1.5	10.9	75.6	12.7	(NA)
Iceland	416	1,179	2.0	4.2	64.3	31.5	(NA)
Ireland	4,100	844	1.0	4.9	70.9	24.1	(NA)
Israel [5]	17,670	1,990	4.9	1.5	88.3	9.3	0.9
Italy	36,893	610	1.4	12.4	63.3	22.8	1.5
Japan	171,294	1,355	3.3	7.8	79.4	11.6	1.3
Korea, South	98,451	1,908	4.5	10.1	80.3	8.2	1.4
Latvia	378	196	0.6	22.8	24.9	52.4	(NA)
Lithuania	945	337	0.9	22.2	41.8	35.9	(NA)
Luxembourg	860	1,413	1.2	23.8	55.8	20.4	(NA)
Mexico	8,054	65	0.3	26.2	22.1	50.6	1.1
Netherlands	21,463	1,246	2.2	5.8	67.1	27.2	(NA)
Norway	7,406	1,394	2.1	13.9	51.5	34.6	(NA)
Poland	14,622	381	1.2	1.9	66.1	31.7	0.3
Portugal	4,787	465	1.4	5.3	51.4	41.6	1.6
Romania	2,857	147	0.5	30.6	59.3	9.8	0.2
Russia	41,505	283	1.0	34.4	55.6	9.7	0.3
Singapore	10,531	1,867	1.8	11.5	60.7	27.7	(NA)
Slovak Republic	1,487	273	0.8	21.2	54.1	24.3	0.4
Slovenia	1,568	757	2.0	13.5	74.2	11.9	0.3
Spain	23,553	504	1.2	16.8	56.5	26.4	0.3
Sweden	18,162	1,785	3.3	3.6	71.0	25.3	0.1
Taiwan	43,343	1,837	3.5	10.7	80.3	8.9	0.1
Turkey	23,966	294	1.0	9.2	60.4	30.3	(NA)
United Kingdom	53,953	812	1.7	6.6	67.6	23.6	2.2

NA Not available or not applicable. [1] Purchasing power parities (PPPs) are currency conversion rates used to convert different currencies to a common value (U.S. dollars in this case). See introductory text, this section. [2] For full membership listing of the Organisation for Economic Co-operation and Development (OECD) and the European Union-28, see introductory text, this section. [3] European Union-15: Austria, Belgium, Denmark, Finland, France, Germany, Greece, Ireland, Italy, Luxembourg, Netherlands, Portugal, Spain, Sweden, and United Kingdom. [4] Excludes all or most capital expenditures. [5] Excludes defense expenditures. The statistical data for Israel are supplied by and under the responsibility of the relevant Israeli authorities. The use of such data by the OECD is without prejudice to the status of the Golan Heights, East Jerusalem and Israeli settlements in the West Bank under the terms of international law.

Source: Organisation for Economic Co-cooperation and Development (OECD), 2020, "Main Science and Technology Indicators," OECD Science, Technology and R&D Statistics (database) ©, <http://dx.doi.org/10.1787/data-00182-en>, accessed August 2020.

Table 1406. Development Assistance Outlays by Donor Country: 2017 and 2018

[147,169 represents $147,169,000,000 except percent. Official development assistance (ODA) includes concessional loans and grants made by donor governments to developing countries and to multilateral institutions such as the United Nations or the World Bank]

	Official development assistance (ODA)					2018	
	2017		2018				
Country	Net disbursements (mil. current U.S. dollars)	Percent of GNI [1]	Net disbursements (mil. current U.S. dollars)	Percent of GNI [1]	Percent of total DAC [2] ODA	Multilateral ODA (mil. current U.S. dol.)	Net private grants (mil. current U.S. dol.)
DAC countries total [2]...	147,169	0.31	150,059	(NA)	100.0	44,838	42,070
United States...............	34,732	0.18	33,787	(NA)	22.5	3,852	36,285
Australia......................	3,036	0.23	3,149	(NA)	2.1	599	(NA)
Austria......................	1,251	0.30	1,167	(NA)	0.8	684	(NA)
Belgium......................	2,196	0.45	2,348	(NA)	1.6	1,012	(NA)
Canada......................	4,305	0.26	4,641	(NA)	3.1	1,147	2,869
Denmark......................	2,448	0.74	2,577	(NA)	1.7	780	11
Finland......................	1,084	0.42	984	(NA)	0.7	508	(NA)
France......................	11,331	0.43	12,840	(NA)	8.6	5,474	(NA)
Germany......................	25,005	0.67	25,670	(NA)	17.1	6,212	1,363
Greece......................	314	0.16	290	(NA)	0.2	252	–
Hungary......................	149	0.11	285	(NA)	0.2	156	(NA)
Ireland......................	838	0.32	934	(NA)	0.6	404	433
Italy......................	5,858	0.30	5,098	(NA)	3.4	2,958	23
Japan......................	11,463	0.23	10,064	(NA)	6.7	3,965	522
Korea, South............	2,201	0.14	2,423	(NA)	1.6	624	(NA)
Luxembourg...............	424	1.00	473	(NA)	0.3	130	(NA)
Netherlands...............	4,958	0.60	5,617	(NA)	3.7	1,871	(NA)
New Zealand............	450	0.23	556	(NA)	0.4	93	(NA)
Norway......................	4,125	0.99	4,258	(NA)	2.8	1,028	(NA)
Poland......................	679	0.13	759	(NA)	0.5	521	(NA)
Portugal......................	381	0.18	388	(NA)	0.3	256	10
Slovak Republic............	119	0.13	138	(NA)	0.1	105	(NA)
Spain......................	2,560	0.19	2,590	(NA)	1.7	1,882	–
Sweden......................	5,563	1.02	6,000	(NA)	4.0	2,163	(NA)
Switzerland...............	3,147	0.47	3,097	(NA)	2.1	766	552
United Kingdom............	18,103	0.70	19,462	(NA)	13.0	7,123	(NA)

– Represents or rounds to zero. NA Not available. [1] Gross national income. See headnote, Table 1364. [2] Development Assistance Committee (DAC) of the Organisation for Economic Co-operation and Development (OECD) is comprised of 29 developed countries, not all shown above, and European Union institutions, not shown separately.

Source: Organisation for Economic Co-operation and Development (OECD), 2020, "Detailed aid statistics: Official and private flows," OECD International Development Statistics (database) ©, <http://dx.doi.org/10.1787/data-00072-en>, accessed September 2020.

Table 1407. Net Flow of Financial Resources to Developing Countries and Multilateral Organizations by Donor Country: 2000 to 2018

[134,228 represents $134,228,000,000. Net flow covers official and private loans, grants, development assistance, and technical assistance, minus amortization on loans. Military flows are excluded. GNI = gross national income. Minus sign (-) indicates net inflow]

Country	Amount (million dollars)				Percent of GNI			
	2000	2010	2015	2018	2000	2010	2015	2018
DAC countries total [1]............	134,228	512,792	316,043	292,004	0.54	1.25	0.72	0.58
United States......................	25,252	216,950	38,520	50,784	0.25	1.48	0.21	0.24
Australia......................	1,891	14,531	13,840	398	0.51	1.23	1.15	0.03
Austria......................	1,135	6,372	4,692	2,443	0.61	1.70	1.25	0.54
Belgium......................	2,281	7,896	3,635	3,946	1.00	1.68	0.79	0.73
Canada......................	6,483	22,642	3,718	8,886	0.95	1.46	0.24	0.53
Czechia......................	16	228	263	129	0.03	0.13	0.16	0.06
Denmark......................	2,176	4,794	2,931	5,724	1.39	1.52	0.97	1.59
Finland......................	1,087	4,312	-48	2,297	0.91	1.78	-0.02	0.84
France......................	5,557	35,198	1,234	12,632	0.41	1.35	0.05	0.44
Germany......................	12,331	41,637	47,627	47,097	0.66	1.24	1.39	1.15
Greece......................	229	761	-85	261	0.20	0.26	-0.04	0.12
Hungary......................	(NA)	114	156	1,100	(NA)	0.09	0.13	0.81
Iceland......................	9	29	40	77	0.10	0.26	0.24	0.30
Ireland......................	740	2,695	1,228	1,368	0.93	1.57	0.54	0.46
Italy......................	10,846	9,608	15,621	7,378	1.01	0.47	0.86	0.35
Japan......................	11,423	48,249	37,908	53,667	0.24	0.86	0.83	1.05
Korea......................	44	11,834	12,318	12,615	0.01	1.17	0.89	0.73
Luxembourg......................	129	411	363	473	0.73	1.07	0.95	0.98
Netherlands......................	6,947	13,013	68,160	14,696	1.85	1.67	8.91	1.61
New Zealand......................	142	426	621	556	0.32	0.32	0.37	0.28
Norway......................	1,437	5,876	4,565	4,262	0.87	1.41	1.12	0.94
Poland......................	29	378	499	976	0.02	0.08	0.11	0.17
Portugal......................	4,622	162	520	921	4.45	0.07	0.27	0.40
Slovak Republic............	6	74	85	138	0.03	0.09	0.10	0.13
Slovenia......................	(NA)	59	156	236	(NA)	0.13	0.37	0.44
Spain......................	23,471	10,340	22,041	14,452	4.25	0.74	1.84	1.01
Sweden......................	3,952	5,127	10,365	6,639	1.76	1.10	2.05	1.19
Switzerland......................	1,765	23,444	6,518	18,902	0.64	4.01	0.94	2.67
United Kingdom......................	10,230	25,632	18,553	18,950	0.72	1.12	0.70	0.68

NA Not available. [1] The OECD Development Assistance Committee (DAC) is comprised of the above-listed member countries plus the EU.

Source: Organisation for Economic Co-operation and Development (OECD), 2020, "Detailed aid statistics: Official and private flows," OECD International Development Statistics (database) ©, <http://dx.doi.org/10.1787/data-00072-en>, accessed July 2020.

Table 1408. External Debt by Developing Country: 2000 to 2018

[In millions of U.S. dollars (9,763 represents $9,763,000,000). Total external debt is debt owed to nonresidents repayable in foreign currency, goods, or services. Total external debt is the sum of public, publicly guaranteed, and private nonguaranteed long-term debt, use of International Monetary Fund (IMF) credit, and short-term debt. Short-term debt includes all debt having an original maturity of one year or less and interest in arrears on long-term debt]

Country	2000	2010	2015	2018	Country	2000	2010	2015	2018
Angola	9,763	26,600	56,272	54,563	Laos	2,531	6,554	11,642	15,588
Argentina	150,063	126,642	176,575	280,516	Lebanon	10,075	47,822	67,707	79,345
Azerbaijan	1,585	7,258	13,450	16,212	Mexico	152,558	245,906	426,905	452,991
Bangladesh	15,603	26,881	36,309	52,124	Mongolia	960	5,928	21,940	29,377
Belarus	2,620	28,412	38,258	38,844	Morocco	20,790	27,296	43,070	49,041
Bosnia and Herzegovina	2,791	14,289	13,917	15,824	Mozambique	6,681	6,150	13,863	15,218
Brazil	242,512	352,364	543,397	557,823	Nigeria	32,374	15,484	29,273	47,047
Bulgaria	12,009	50,635	40,115	39,874	Pakistan	33,026	62,975	66,712	90,957
China	145,874	734,639	1,325,925	1,962,304	Papua New Guinea	2,325	5,987	20,387	17,718
Colombia	34,329	64,153	114,623	134,940	Paraguay	3,106	15,903	16,125	15,806
Costa Rica	4,692	8,154	23,589	27,819	Peru	28,834	42,154	67,185	66,697
Cote d'Ivoire	12,060	11,704	11,386	15,660	Philippines	58,456	65,358	76,495	78,824
Dominican Republic	4,618	13,499	26,727	33,905	Russia	146,665	417,852	467,699	453,938
Ecuador	17,175	15,378	28,389	45,019	Serbia [1]	11,573	32,907	31,301	34,339
Egypt	29,233	36,776	49,847	98,705	South Africa	25,435	108,392	138,078	179,306
El Salvador	4,535	11,496	15,571	17,486	Sri Lanka	9,250	21,684	43,925	52,626
Ethiopia	5,516	7,286	21,021	28,027	Sudan [2]	16,076	22,323	21,426	21,596
Georgia	1,826	8,790	14,375	17,118	Tanzania	7,188	8,892	15,278	18,585
Ghana	6,743	8,360	20,105	23,316	Thailand	79,830	106,358	131,819	169,241
Guatemala	3,948	15,043	20,378	22,349	Tunisia	11,355	22,581	27,245	34,661
India	101,131	290,428	478,834	521,391	Turkey	116,799	300,869	399,949	445,139
Indonesia	144,049	198,278	307,754	379,664	Ukraine	13,915	124,527	117,456	114,512
Jamaica	4,828	14,193	14,113	16,307	Uzbekistan	4,948	7,802	14,059	17,630
Jordan	11,063	17,073	25,739	32,045	Venezuela	49,458	116,966	160,909	154,898
Kazakhstan	12,890	119,151	153,398	156,921	Vietnam	12,841	44,936	77,829	108,096
Kenya	6,147	8,856	19,767	31,511	Zambia	5,811	4,384	11,917	19,116

[1] Data from 2000 to 2005 are for Serbia and Montenegro. In June 2006, Serbia and Montenegro became separate countries; beginning 2006, data exclude Montenegro. Data from 2008 onward exclude Kosovo, which declared independence that year. [2] South Sudan declared independence July 2011.

Source: The World Bank, Washington, DC, "External debt stocks, total," World Development Indicators (database) ©, <http://data.worldbank.org/data-catalog/world-development-indicators>, accessed July 2020.

Table 1409. Foreign Direct Investment Flows in Selected Countries: 2010 to 2019

[In millions of dollars (210,554 represents $210,554,000,000). Data are converted to U.S. dollars using the yearly average exchange rate]

Country	Inflows					Outflows				
	2010	2015	2017	2018	2019	2010	2015	2017	2018	2019
United States	**210,544**	**481,502**	**291,898**	**268,441**	**260,939**	**296,334**	**279,471**	**321,822**	**-68,407**	**147,798**
Australia	36,442	28,274	42,289	60,425	(NA)	19,803	-10,220	3,320	3,634	(NA)
Austria	-21,694	-7,577	10,018	-627	3,382	-14,065	-1,783	6,677	2,600	9,756
Belgium	132,604	-70,573	5,149	17,722	9,706	60,335	57,563	33,528	26,503	19,707
Brazil	77,687	49,961	66,585	59,802	71,989	22,060	-11,643	19,040	-16,336	15,515
Canada	28,399	43,853	26,518	43,450	50,326	34,721	67,467	78,338	49,869	76,594
Chile	(NA)	20,491	6,519	7,021	11,437	(NA)	15,543	5,526	278	7,937
China	243,703	242,489	166,084	235,365	155,815	57,954	174,391	138,293	143,027	97,703
Czechia	6,147	465	9,518	9,477	7,809	1,168	2,488	7,557	5,277	4,813
Denmark	-12,559	2,237	2,033	-2,633	1,212	-1,407	7,536	7,976	-3,259	16,265
Estonia	1,509	36	1,917	1,474	3,044	167	182	873	49	1,967
Finland	7,359	2,109	2,858	-3,889	10,044	10,189	-16,080	-738	11,453	6,470
France	13,891	45,355	29,812	37,286	43,569	48,158	53,206	41,271	102,408	29,754
Germany	65,646	30,534	60,225	73,524	36,358	125,453	99,003	103,865	78,764	98,698
Greece	330	1,268	3,477	3,971	4,631	1,558	1,578	168	477	438
Hungary	-37,104	-28,167	2,088	-73,460	4,564	-41,085	-31,123	-176	-76,698	2,454
Iceland	(NA)	670	-3,058	-394	-239	(NA)	-29	-3,224	80	515
Indonesia	13,771	16,641	20,579	20,563	23,429	2,664	5,937	2,077	8,053	3,380
Ireland	42,807	217,820	52,722	-28,073	78,234	22,350	168,443	-2,043	723	18,100
Italy	9,179	19,631	23,996	32,865	26,569	32,657	21,640	24,478	32,673	24,934
Japan	-1,252	-2,251	10,976	9,856	14,548	56,276	128,698	164,658	143,142	226,573
Korea, South	8,117	3,076	12,699	13,299	(NA)	26,821	18,490	51,044	45,232	(NA)
Latvia	420	734	667	995	790	20	68	132	190	-161
Lithuania	1,020	1,054	1,027	1,093	975	42	369	68	671	153
Luxembourg	222,023	606,573	89,660	-524,457	-249,214	205,556	713,734	250,750	-452,093	-285,465
Netherlands	135,774	329,916	82,615	-276,218	85,731	210,620	397,500	132,054	-265,203	135,388
New Zealand	-61	-309	2,429	1,945	5,426	716	-59	227	425	-183
Norway	17,043	-2,515	-5,922	226	(NA)	23,238	30,947	-7,415	11,405	(NA)
Poland	12,799	11,819	9,507	15,577	11,865	6,148	1,928	1,878	934	671
Portugal	2,913	7,628	7,517	6,790	8,235	-9,456	5,225	-948	502	-470
Russia	31,668	11,858	25,954	13,228	31,735	41,116	27,090	34,153	35,820	22,530
Slovak Republic	1,770	106	4,008	1,183	2,449	946	6	1,323	234	153
Slovenia	106	1,675	896	1,368	910	-19	267	338	267	135
Spain	(NA)	8,557	38,724	44,982	12,406	(NA)	41,917	52,238	27,058	24,134
Sweden	141	8,395	14,252	3,858	20,573	20,364	13,045	25,512	16,818	22,820
Switzerland	28,750	75,289	107,321	-53,150	-21,741	85,718	88,759	30,144	60,781	11,098
Turkey	9,086	18,978	11,020	12,983	8,381	1,469	4,813	2,623	3,607	2,844
United Kingdom	58,180	39,189	101,290	65,285	59,126	48,075	-66,827	117,605	41,415	31,474

NA Not available.

Source: Organisation for Economic Co-operation and Development (OECD), 2020, "Benchmark definition, 4th edition (BMD4): Foreign direct investment: financial flows, main aggregates," OECD International Direct Investment Statistics (database) ©, <http://dx.doi.org/10.1787/data-00741-en>, accessed June 2020.

Table 1410. International Transaction Balances, Reserve Assets, and Trade in Relation to Gross Domestic Product (GDP) by Country: 2018 and 2019

[In millions of U.S. dollars (-490,991 represents -$490,991,000,000), except as noted. Minus sign (-) indicates deficit]

Country	Current account balance		Reserve assets [1]		Goods and services trade balance		Exports as percent of GDP		Imports as percent of GDP	
	2018	2019	2018	2019	2018	2019	2018	2019	2018	2019
United States........	**-490,991**	**-498,350**	**114,757**	**118,438**	**-638,214**	**(NA)**	**12.2**	**(NA)**	**15.3**	**(NA)**
Afghanistan...........	-3,897	-3,799	7,306	7,427	-6,374	-5,752	8.3	7.8	41.0	37.9
Albania..............	-1,010	-1,165	3,830	3,627	-2,079	-2,094	31.5	31.5	45.3	45.2
Argentina............	-27,276	-3,462	63,964	42,193	-11,122	9,833	14.3	17.3	16.4	15.1
Armenia..............	-1,165	-1,118	2,259	2,850	-1,950	-1,967	37.7	38.5	53.4	52.9
Australia.............	-29,264	7,122	51,048	56,364	5,980	35,874	21.8	24.1	21.4	21.6
Austria..............	10,799	11,714	11,653	9,906	16,952	16,596	55.8	55.7	52.0	52.0
Azerbaijan...........	6,051	4,365	6,666	7,043	7,779	5,917	54.1	49.2	37.6	36.9
Bangladesh..........	-7,593	-3,087	31,453	32,013	-23,685	-18,496	14.8	15.3	23.4	21.4
Belgium..............	-7,348	-6,512	17,487	17,835	-886	874	82.6	81.7	82.8	81.6
Bolivia..............	-1,820	-1,362	7,178	4,374	-2,068	-2,643	26.0	25.0	31.1	31.4
Brazil...............	-41,540	-49,452	371,934	353,588	7,195	-6,104	14.9	14.3	14.5	14.7
Bulgaria.............	3,492	2,742	27,045	25,920	1,713	2,326	65.9	63.6	63.3	60.1
Cambodia............	-2,992	-4,207	13,373	17,033	-420	-372	61.6	61.1	63.3	62.5
Canada..............	-42,993	-34,194	83,926	85,297	-33,619	-29,307	32.1	31.6	34.0	33.3
China...............	25,499	141,336	3,091,881	3,127,494	106,707	164,986	19.1	18.4	18.3	17.3
Colombia............	-13,047	-13,800	47,359	51,974	-15,925	-20,421	15.9	15.9	20.7	22.2
Costa Rica...........	-1,999	-1,545	7,501	8,937	160	869	33.5	33.8	33.2	32.3
Croatia..............	1,028	1,456	19,991	20,771	-515	-338	50.5	51.1	51.3	51.7
Cyprus..............	-1,067	-1,655	351	353	196	-97	73.1	71.1	72.3	71.5
Czechia.............	1,190	-867	142,151	149,464	15,660	15,023	78.5	75.5	72.1	69.4
Denmark.............	24,781	27,581	68,200	63,577	21,508	23,434	55.6	55.9	49.6	49.1
Ecuador.............	-1,335	-79	1,896	1,866	-1,240	43	22.6	23.4	23.8	23.3
El Salvador..........	-1,226	-558	3,512	4,379	-5,122	-4,890	28.8	29.5	48.4	47.6
Estonia.............	612	690	745	1,414	1,080	1,253	74.3	72.6	70.7	68.6
Finland..............	-4,571	-2,060	8,284	9,020	-2,746	1,308	38.6	40.0	39.6	39.5
France..............	-19,014	-18,549	66,103	69,725	-29,018	-26,593	31.7	31.8	32.8	32.8
Georgia.............	-1,193	-901	3,290	3,506	-1,872	-1,575	50.6	54.0	61.2	62.9
Germany.............	293,073	274,847	59,173	59,185	243,346	224,495	47.4	47.0	41.3	41.1
Greece..............	-6,249	-2,928	2,918	2,950	-570	-20	36.1	37.2	36.4	37.2
Guatemala...........	595	1,854	12,299	14,447	-7,835	-8,034	18.2	17.7	28.9	28.2
Honduras............	-1,284	-163	4,741	5,711	-4,574	-4,046	41.8	40.2	60.8	56.4
Hong Kong, China....	13,514	22,740	424,534	441,248	-773	6,487	188.4	177.3	188.6	175.5
Hungary.............	139	-1,247	30,068	30,288	6,906	5,917	84.9	83.3	80.6	79.7
Iceland..............	792	1,404	6,239	6,685	776	1,143	47.5	45.3	44.5	40.6
India................	-65,599	-26,894	374,425	432,378	-100,378	-77,474	19.9	18.7	23.6	21.4
Indonesia............	-30,633	-30,387	117,425	125,339	-11,022	-5,466	21.0	18.4	22.0	18.9
Iraq.................	34,370	15,675	60,752	(NA)	18,002	-5,190	44.0	37.1	35.9	39.3
Ireland..............	40,901	-36,374	4,975	5,439	126,823	55,879	122.3	126.8	89.2	112.4
Israel...............	9,277	14,051	115,266	126,008	1,585	(NA)	29.4	(NA)	29.0	(NA)
Italy................	51,525	58,933	51,331	55,341	49,891	61,478	31.5	31.6	29.1	28.5
Korea, South.........	77,467	59,971	398,780	403,705	79,172	48,324	41.6	39.8	37.0	36.9
Latvia...............	-211	-176	4,098	4,155	-64	28	61.5	59.9	61.7	59.8
Lithuania............	818	2,298	5,531	4,800	1,038	3,034	75.6	78.1	73.7	72.5
Luxembourg..........	3,333	3,095	847	945	25,542	25,590	211.6	208.8	175.5	172.8
Mexico..............	-23,004	-2,444	171,445	177,177	-22,824	-674	39.3	39.1	41.2	39.1
Mongolia............	-1,903	-2,162	2,780	3,239	-728	-427	58.5	61.3	64.0	64.4
Montenegro..........	-943	-837	1,203	1,529	-1,314	-1,170	42.9	44.1	66.7	65.4
Morocco.............	-6,205	-4,915	23,550	25,330	-12,406	-10,904	38.7	39.1	49.3	48.3
Namibia.............	-387	-284	2,150	2,049	-1,354	-1,466	36.3	35.8	46.4	47.7
Netherlands..........	99,065	92,805	13,195	13,331	100,466	97,500	84.3	82.5	73.3	71.8
Norway..............	31,138	16,066	63,146	66,946	25,221	7,072	38.4	36.9	32.6	35.2
Pakistan.............	-18,859	-7,143	9,175	13,421	-34,915	-28,379	9.0	10.1	20.1	20.3
Philippines...........	-8,773	-464	71,040	79,824	-40,706	-44,940	30.2	28.3	41.9	40.3
Poland..............	-5,820	2,776	111,656	117,196	20,126	31,136	55.5	55.8	52.0	50.5
Portugal.............	917	-236	9,159	6,272	1,001	130	43.7	43.8	43.3	43.8
Qatar...............	16,652	4,229	29,070	37,651	36,750	25,246	53.6	50.2	34.4	36.4
Romania.............	-10,503	-11,384	37,856	36,931	-7,250	-9,646	41.6	40.4	44.6	44.2
Russia..............	113,733	64,608	381,575	443,970	165,296	128,375	30.5	28.3	20.6	20.8
Saudi Arabia.........	70,606	49,842	496,156	499,143	104,121	78,491	39.9	36.0	26.7	26.1
Serbia...............	-2,459	-3,536	12,033	13,496	-4,310	-4,499	50.8	51.9	59.3	60.7
Singapore............	64,114	63,139	287,466	279,240	106,096	103,754	177.7	173.5	149.3	145.6
Slovak Republic.......	-2,760	-3,019	3,923	5,617	2,130	1,092	96.2	93.1	94.2	92.1
Slovenia............	3,073	3,525	802	860	4,715	4,911	84.8	84.4	76.0	75.3
South Africa..........	-13,384	-10,667	46,478	48,920	1,266	1,768	29.9	29.9	29.6	29.4
Spain...............	27,307	27,724	59,030	60,944	38,526	39,362	35.1	34.9	32.4	32.0
Sweden.............	9,665	20,783	55,386	49,354	12,414	18,765	45.7	47.0	43.4	43.5
Switzerland..........	57,857	86,167	744,167	804,004	86,211	88,789	66.1	66.0	53.9	53.4
Thailand.............	28,457	37,911	199,297	216,817	44,768	49,920	64.9	59.7	56.0	50.6
Turkey..............	-20,745	8,691	72,867	78,532	-8,463	13,836	29.5	31.6	30.6	29.8
Uganda.............	-2,302	-2,333	3,359	(NA)	-2,146	-2,506	15.2	19.4	21.7	26.7
Ukraine.............	-4,367	-1,322	19,818	24,083	-11,415	-12,040	45.2	41.2	53.9	49.0
United Kingdom.......	-110,231	-106,886	159,872	158,376	-39,738	-33,053	30.6	31.5	32.0	32.7
Uruguay.............	54	419	15,552	14,499	1,202	1,355	21.0	21.7	19.0	19.3
Uzbekistan...........	-3,594	-3,246	12,441	12,843	-5,313	-6,151	28.0	31.2	38.6	41.8
Zambia..............	-342	242	1,569	1,449	270	2	37.0	35.0	36.0	35.0

NA Not available. [1] Reserve assets are comprised of special drawing rights and reserve position in International Monetary Fund (IMF), and foreign exchange holdings. Gold holdings are excluded.

Source: The World Bank, Washington, DC, "World Development Indicators" database ©, <http://data.worldbank.org/data-catalog/world-development-indicators>, accessed July 2020.

Table 1411. International Tourism Arrivals, Expenditures, and Receipts—Leading Countries: 2000 to 2018

[Arrivals at national borders in thousands of non-resident tourists (689,646 represents 689,646,000). Expenditures and receipts in millions of current U.S. dollars (453,356 represents $453,356,000,000). Expenditures are money spent by foreign tourists while traveling inside the country shown and include prepayment for goods or services in destination country. Expenditures are money spent by tourists from a given country of origin while traveling outside their home country. Data exclude receipts and expenditures for international transport. Ranked for top 50 countries in tourist arrivals as of 2018. Sources and collection methods differ, thus caution should be used in comparing data across countries]

Country	Arrivals (1,000)					Expenditures (mil. dol.)					Receipts (mil. dol.)				
	2000	2005	2010	2015	2018	2000	2005	2010	2015	2018	2000	2005	2010	2015	2018
World [1]	689,646	823,378	973,772	1,227,874	1,441,953	453,356	666,689	873,292	1,195,904	1,407,802	500,653	717,414	970,465	1,219,533	1,444,904
France	77,190	74,988	76,647	84,452	89,322	22,537	31,347	38,297	39,521	47,764	32,857	43,937	46,459	58,326	65,358
Spain	46,403	55,914	52,677	68,175	82,773	5,969	15,169	16,926	17,429	26,670	31,528	51,959	58,348	62,449	81,250
United States	51,238	49,206	60,010	77,774	79,746	65,786	79,990	86,623	114,550	144,465	100,188	101,469	137,010	206,936	214,680
China	31,229	46,809	55,664	56,886	62,900	13,114	21,759	54,880	249,831	277,345	16,231	29,296	45,814	44,969	40,386
Italy	41,181	36,513	43,626	50,732	61,567	15,686	22,362	26,902	24,425	30,004	27,498	35,310	38,432	39,433	49,066
Turkey	9,586	20,273	31,364	39,478	45,768	1,713	3,104	5,194	5,368	4,595	7,636	19,191	22,585	26,616	25,220
Mexico	20,641	21,915	23,290	32,093	41,313	5,499	7,600	7,255	10,098	11,230	8,294	11,803	11,992	17,734	22,526
Germany	18,983	21,500	26,875	34,970	38,881	52,829	74,167	77,566	77,468	95,199	18,611	29,111	34,557	36,895	42,895
Thailand	9,579	11,567	15,936	29,923	38,178	2,772	3,803	5,627	7,718	12,352	7,483	9,576	20,104	41,246	60,225
United Kingdom	23,212	28,039	28,295	34,436	36,316	41,862	66,166	60,716	68,116	68,888	22,413	32,948	34,715	50,904	48,515
Japan	4,757	6,728	8,611	19,737	31,192	31,884	37,565	27,950	15,974	20,197	3,373	12,430	13,224	24,968	42,093
Austria	17,982	19,952	22,004	26,728	30,816	6,232	9,316	10,120	9,329	11,940	9,899	16,243	18,751	18,292	23,233
Greece	13,096	14,765	15,007	23,599	30,123	4,558	3,038	2,853	2,259	2,582	9,221	13,336	12,478	15,665	18,821
Hong Kong, China	8,814	14,773	20,085	26,686	29,263	12,502	13,305	17,357	23,059	26,498	5,868	10,171	21,689	35,795	35,268
Malaysia	10,222	16,431	24,577	25,721	25,832	2,075	3,711	8,324	10,708	12,168	5,011	8,846	18,152	17,666	19,607
Russia	21,169	22,201	22,281	33,729	24,551	8,848	16,972	26,693	34,932	34,271	3,429	5,870	8,830	8,420	11,486
United Arab Emirates	3,907	7,126	(NA)	17,472	21,286	(NA)	(NA)	(NA)	(NA)	(NA)	(NA)	(NA)	(NA)	(NA)	(NA)
Canada	19,627	18,771	16,219	17,971	21,134	12,438	18,021	29,977	30,271	33,581	10,778	13,651	15,830	16,531	21,978
Poland	17,400	15,200	12,470	16,728	19,622	3,315	5,547	8,569	7,939	9,721	5,677	6,304	9,575	10,474	14,040
Netherlands	10,003	10,012	10,883	15,007	18,780	12,191	13,724	19,044	18,038	22,702	7,197	8,770	11,653	13,171	18,640
Macao, China	5,197	9,014	11,926	14,308	18,493	(NA)	412	800	1,227	1,411	(NA)	(NA)	22,276	30,981	40,358
Hungary	2,649	9,979	9,510	14,316	17,552	1,651	2,277	2,404	1,830	2,639	3,733	4,120	5,587	5,320	6,887
India	(NA)	3,919	5,776	13,284	17,423	2,690	6,187	10,490	14,838	21,319	3,460	7,493	14,490	21,013	28,568
Croatia	5,831	7,743	9,111	12,683	16,645	568	754	832	755	1,693	2,758	7,370	8,069	8,833	11,855
Portugal	5,599	5,769	6,756	11,723	16,186	2,228	3,049	3,905	3,695	5,486	5,244	7,674	10,004	12,875	19,807
Indonesia	5,064	5,002	7,003	10,407	15,810	3,197	3,584	6,395	7,292	8,772	4,975	4,522	6,958	10,761	14,110
Vietnam	2,140	3,477	5,050	7,944	15,498	(NA)	(NA)	(NA)	(NA)	(NA)	(NA)	(NA)	(NA)	(NA)	(NA)
Korea, South	5,322	6,023	8,798	13,232	15,347	7,132	15,406	18,766	25,270	31,973	6,834	5,798	10,263	14,798	15,319
Saudi Arabia	6,585	8,037	10,850	17,994	15,334	4,535	9,087	21,135	19,346	16,644	(NA)	4,626	6,712	10,130	13,791
Singapore	6,062	7,079	9,161	12,051	14,673	4,669	10,070	18,700	23,658	25,346	5,142	6,209	14,178	16,617	20,416
Ukraine	6,431	17,631	21,203	12,428	14,104	470	2,805	3,742	5,101	7,899	394	3,125	3,788	1,082	1,445
Denmark	3,535	9,587	9,425	10,424	12,749	425	6,850	9,082	8,918	10,485	3,671	5,293	5,704	6,685	9,097
Morocco	4,278	5,843	9,288	10,177	12,289	224	612	1,203	1,402	2,007	2,039	4,610	6,702	6,260	7,775
Bahrain	3,869	6,313	11,952	9,670	12,045	425	414	506	4,342	2,717	573	920	1,362	2,705	3,689
Romania	5,264	5,839	7,498	9,331	11,720	216	923	1,637	2,059	4,307	359	1,051	1,136	1,711	2,770
Belarus	60	91	119	4,386	11,502	1,072	448	622	901	1,058	93	253	440	729	883
Egypt	5,116	8,244	14,051	9,139	11,196	2,525	1,629	2,240	3,442	2,667	4,345	6,851	12,528	6,065	11,615
Ireland	6,646	7,333	7,134	9,528	10,926	1,276	6,073	7,069	5,695	7,390	2,615	4,781	4,085	4,786	6,164
Czechia	4,773	6,336	6,334	8,707	10,611	2,085	2,405	4,252	4,772	5,972	2,973	4,813	7,172	6,056	7,454
South Africa	5,872	7,369	8,074	8,904	10,472	5,419	3,374	5,595	2,998	3,402	2,677	7,516	9,085	8,259	8,989
Switzerland	7,821	7,229	8,628	9,305	10,362	538	8,801	11,173	16,294	18,335	6,652	10,047	14,721	16,936	16,976
Bulgaria	2,785	4,837	6,047	7,099	9,273	6,388	1,309	826	1,116	1,868	1,074	2,412	3,343	3,154	4,479
Australia	4,931	5,499	5,790	7,449	9,246	9,429	11,749	22,558	29,190	36,866	9,375	16,750	28,472	34,269	45,098
Belgium	6,457	6,747	7,186	8,355	9,119	408	14,948	18,862	13,654	18,481	6,592	9,845	11,393	7,865	8,901
Kazakhstan	1,683	4,365	4,097	6,430	8,789	2,495	753	1,273	2,867	2,687	356	701	1,005	1,632	2,255
Kuwait	1,944	3,474	5,208	6,941	8,508	263	4,532	6,434	12,381	14,318	98	165	289	500	458
Tunisia	5,058	6,378	7,828	5,359	8,299	8,048	374	547	696	864	1,682	2,143	2,645	1,381	1,741
Sweden	3,828	4,883	5,183	6,482	7,440	668	10,014	12,126	14,410	18,056	4,064	6,554	8,336	11,307	14,926
Iran	(NA)	(NA)	2,938	5,237	7,295	1,642	3,724	9,655	8,992	(NA)	467	791	2,438	4,388	(NA)
Philippines	1,992	2,623	3,520	5,361	7,168	(NA)	3,018	5,487	11,343	11,863	2,156	2,287	2,645	5,272	8,255

NA Not available. [1] Includes other countries not shown separately.

Source: The World Bank, Washington, DC, "World Development Indicators" database ©, <http://data.worldbank.org/data-catalog/world-development-indicators>, accessed July 2020.

Table 1412. Military Expenditures as a Percent of GDP by Country: 2019

[Military expenditures compares spending on defense programs for the most recent year available as a percent of gross domestic product (GDP), calculated on an exchange rate basis]

Country	Expenditures (percent of GDP)	Rank [1]	Country	Expenditures (percent of GDP)	Rank [1]	Country	Expenditures (percent of GDP)	Rank [1]
United States [2]	3.4	19	France [2]	1.8	58	Niger	1.8	62
Afghanistan	1.2	100	Georgia	2.0	50	Nigeria	0.5	149
Albania [2]	1.3	96	Germany [2]	1.4	87	Norway [2]	1.8	63
Algeria	6.0	3	Greece [2]	2.3	41	Oman	8.8	1
Angola	1.6	69	Guinea	2.0	51	Pakistan	4.0	11
Argentina	0.7	130	Honduras	1.6	73	Peru	1.2	106
Armenia	4.9	7	Hungary [2]	1.2	99	Philippines	1.0	118
Australia	1.9	54	India	2.4	37	Poland [2]	2.0	52
Austria	0.7	131	Indonesia	0.7	135	Portugal [2]	1.5	77
Azerbaijan	4.0	10	Iran [2]	3.8	16	Romania [2]	2.0	47
Bahrain	3.7	17	Iraq	3.5	18	Russia	3.9	14
Bangladesh	1.3	91	Ireland	0.3	155	Rwanda	1.2	107
Belarus	1.2	101	Israel	5.3	6	Saudi Arabia	8.0	2
Belgium	0.9	122	Italy [2]	1.2	97	Senegal [2]	1.5	84
Bolivia	1.4	85	Jamaica	1.6	74	Serbia	2.2	43
Botswana	2.8	30	Japan	0.9	123	Singapore	3.2	24
Brazil	1.5	78	Jordan	4.7	8	Slovakia [2]	1.7	64
Brunei	3.3	21	Kazakhstan	1.1	113	Slovenia [2]	1.0	115
Bulgaria [2]	3.3	22	Kenya	1.3	92	South Africa	1.0	119
Burkina Faso	2.4	36	Korea, South	2.7	33	South Sudan	3.4	20
Cambodia	2.3	38	Kuwait	5.6	5	Spain [2]	0.9	124
Cameroon	1.1	110	Kyrgyzstan	1.5	81	Sri Lanka	1.9	56
Canada [2]	1.3	90	Latvia [2]	2.0	49	Sudan	1.6	76
Chad	2.2	42	Lebanon	4.2	9	Sweden	1.1	114
Chile	1.8	60	Liberia	0.5	147	Switzerland	0.7	139
China	1.9	55	Lithuania [2]	2.0	48	Taiwan	1.7	66
Colombia	3.2	23	Madagascar	0.6	143	Tanzania	1.3	94
Congo, Rep. of	2.7	32	Malaysia	1.0	116	Thailand	1.3	95
Croatia [2]	1.7	67	Mali	2.7	34	Togo	3.1	26
Czechia [2]	1.2	109	Mauritania	2.8	31	Tunisia	2.6	35
Denmark	1.3	89	Mexico	0.5	148	Turkey [2]	1.9	57
Ecuador	2.3	39	Montenegro [2]	1.7	68	Uganda	2.1	46
Egypt	1.2	103	Morocco	3.1	25	Ukraine	3.9	15
El Salvador	1.2	104	Namibia	3.0	27	United Kingdom [2]	2.1	45
Estonia [2]	2.1	44	Nepal	1.6	75	Uruguay	2.0	53
Ethiopia	0.6	142	Netherlands [2]	1.4	88	Zambia	1.2	108
Finland	1.5	80	New Zealand	1.5	83	Zimbabwe	0.7	141

[1] Based on a list of 158 countries for which data is available. Not all countries are shown. [2] Data are estimated.

Source: Central Intelligence Agency, *The World Factbook*, <https://www.cia.gov/library/publications/the-world-factbook/index.html>, accessed August 2020.

Table 1413. Terrorism Incidents, Fatalities, Injuries, and Hostages Taken for Top Countries and Perpetrator Groups: 2018

[Data shown for top 10 countries and top 5 perpetrator groups of attacks in 2018. An incident is deemed "terrorist" if it conforms to Title 22, Section 2656f, of the U.S. Code; includes only violent acts carried out by non-state actors. Based on data collected by the Global Terrorism Trends and Analysis Center (GTTAC) established by the Development Services Group, Inc. (DSG) and supported by the Terrorism, Transnational Crime and Corruption Center operated by the Schar School of Policy and Government at George Mason University. Any assessments and descriptions, including those regarding the nature of the incidents or the factual circumstances thereof, are offered only as part GTTAC's analytic work and may not reflect the views of the U.S. Government. Data collection methodology significantly differs from that of previous reports. Caution should be used when comparing statistics over time. See source for details]

Country and perpetrator group	Total incidents	Deaths Total	Deaths Average fatality rate per incident	Injuries Total	Injuries Average injury rate per incident	Kidnapped/ hostages taken
Worldwide total	8,093	32,836	4.1	22,651	2.8	3,534
By country:						
Afghanistan	1,294	9,961	7.7	7,039	5.4	1,111
Syria	871	3,875	4.5	2,631	3.0	240
Iraq	765	1,520	2.0	1,829	2.4	140
India	671	917	1.4	784	1.2	107
Nigeria	546	3,331	6.1	1,190	2.2	375
Somalia	526	2,063	3.9	1,317	2.5	109
Philippines	350	483	1.4	635	1.8	45
Pakistan	329	766	2.3	1,130	3.4	7
Yemen	224	3,038	13.6	1,095	4.9	45
Cameroon	207	615	3.0	254	1.2	328
By perpetrator:						
Taliban	1,079	8,509	7.9	4,943	4.6	1,082
Islamic State in Iraq and Syria (ISIS)	647	3,585	5.5	1,761	2.7	325
Al-Shabaab	535	2,062	3.9	1,278	2.4	107
Boko Haram [1]	220	1,311	6.0	927	4.2	267
Communist Party of the Philippines/ New People's Army (CPP/NPA)	194	170	0.9	233	1.2	28

[1] Local sources do not always differentiate between Boko Haram and ISIS-West Africa.

Source: U.S. State Department, Bureau of Counterterrorism, *Annex of Statistical Information: Country Reports on Terrorism 2018*, October 2019. See also <https://www.state.gov/country-reports-on-terrorism-2/>.

Guide to Sources of Statistics, State Statistical Abstracts, and Foreign Statistical Abstracts

Alphabetically arranged, this guide contains references to important primary sources of statistical information for the United States and other countries. Secondary sources have been included if the information contained in them is presented in a particularly convenient form or if primary sources are not readily available. Nonrecurrent publications presenting compilations or estimates for years later than 2005, or types of data not available in regular series, are also included. Data are also available in press releases.

Valuable information may also be found in state reports and foreign statistical abstracts, which are included at the end of this appendix, and in reports for particular commodities, industries, or similar segments of our economic and social structures, many of which are not included here.

Publications listed under each subject are divided into two main groups: "U.S. Government" and "Nongovernment." The location of the publisher of each report is given except for federal agencies located in Washington, DC. Most federal publications may be purchased from the Superintendent of Documents, U.S. Government Printing Office, Washington, DC, tel. 1-866-512-1800, or at <http://bookstore.gpo.gov>. In some cases, federal publications may be obtained from the issuing agency.

Appendix I Table: Sources of Statistics, State Statistical Abstracts, and Foreign Statistical Abstracts

Title	Frequency	Paper	Internet PDF	Internet Other *Formats*
U.S. GOVERNMENT				
Administrative Office of the United States Courts				
http://www.uscourts.gov				
Calendar Year Reports on Authorized Wiretaps (state and federal)	Annual		X	X
Federal Court Management Statistics	Quarterly		X	X
Federal Judicial Caseload Statistics	Annual			X
Judicial Business of the United States Courts	Annual		X	X
Statistical Tables for the Federal Judiciary	Semiannual		X	
Agency for International Development				
http://www.usaid.gov				
U.S. Overseas Loans and Grants: Obligations and Loan Authorizations	Annual		X	X
Army Corps of Engineers				
http://www.usace.army.mil				
Waterborne Commerce of the United States Waterways and Harbors	Annual		X	X
Board of Governors of the Federal Reserve System				
http://www.federalreserve.gov				
Assets and Liabilities of Commercial Banks in the United States H.8	Weekly		X	X
Consumer Credit G.19	Monthly		X	X
Federal Reserve Bulletin	Periodic	X	X	X
Financial Accounts of the United States Z.1	Quarterly	X	X	X
Foreign Exchange Rates H.10	Weekly			X
Industrial Production and Capacity Utilization G.17	Monthly		X	X
Money Stock Measures H.6	Weekly		X	X
Survey of Consumer Finances	Triennial		X	X
Bureau of Economic Analysis				
http://www.bea.gov				
Arts and Cultural Production Satellite Accounts	Ongoing		X	X
Health Care Satellite Account	Ongoing		X	X
Industry Economic Accounts: Digital Economy	Ongoing		X	X
International Economic Accounts	Ongoing		X	X
National Economic Accounts	Ongoing		X	X
Regional Economic Accounts	Ongoing		X	X
Survey of Current Business	Monthly	X	X	X
Travel and Tourism Satellite Accounts	Ongoing		X	X
Bureau of Justice Statistics				
http://www.bjs.gov/				
2018 Update On Prisoner Recidivism: A 9-Year Follow-Up Period (2005-2014)	Periodic		X	X
Background Checks for Firearm Transfers	Annual		X	X
Capital Punishment	Annual		X	X
Census of Problem-Solving Courts	Periodic		X	X
Census of Publicly Funded Forensic Crime Laboratories	Periodic		X	X
Census of State and Federal Correctional Facilities, 2005, October 2008	Periodic		X	X
Civil Rights Complaints in U.S. District Courts, 1990-2006, August 2008	Periodic	X	X	X
Civil Trial Cases and Verdicts in Large Counties, 2005, September 2009	Periodic	X	X	X
Compendium of Federal Justice Statistics, 2009, December 2011	Periodic	X	X	X
Crimes Against the Elderly, 2003-2013, November 2014	Periodic		X	X
Criminal Victimization	Annual		X	X
Family Violence Statistics	Periodic	X	X	X
Federal Law Enforcement Officers	Periodic		X	X
Felony Defendants in Large Urban Counties, 2009, December 2013	Biennial		X	X
HIV in Prisons, 2015, August 2017	Periodic		X	X

See footnotes at end of table.

Title	Frequency	Paper	Internet PDF	Internet Other Formats
Homicide in the U.S. Known to Law Enforcement, 1992 to 2011, December 2013	Periodic		X	X
Immigration Offenders in the Federal Criminal Justice System, 2010, July 2012	Periodic		X	X
Indicators of School Crime and Safety	Annual		X	X
Intimate Partner Violence, 1993-2011, November 2013	Periodic	X	X	X
Prison and Jail Inmates at Midyear	Annual		X	X
Jails in Indian Country, 2016, December 2017	Annual		X	X
Justice Expenditure and Employment Extract Series	Annual			X
Local Police Departments, 2013: Personnel, Policies, and Practices, May 2015	Periodic		X	X
Prisoners	Annual		X	X
Probation and Parole in the United States, 2016, April 2018	Annual		X	X
Publicly Funded Forensic Crime Laboratories: Resources and Services, 2014, November 2016	Periodic		X	X
Prosecutors in State Courts, 2007, December 2011	Biennial		X	X
Rape and Sexual Assault Victimization Among College-Age Females, 1995-2013	Periodic		X	X
Sheriffs' Offices Personnel, 1993-2013, June 2016	Periodic	X	X	X
Sourcebook of Criminal Justice Statistics	Periodic		X	X
Survey of State Criminal History Information Systems, 2014, December 2015	Biennial	X	X	X
Survey of State Procedures Related to Firearm Sales, 2005, November 2006	Periodic	X	X	X
Tribal Crime Data Collection Activities	Annual		X	X
Victims of Identity Theft	Periodic		X	X
Bureau of Labor Statistics http://www.bls.gov				
100 Years of U.S. Consumer Spending: Data for the Nation, New York City, and Boston, Report 991	Periodic	X	X	
College Enrollment and Work Activity of High School Graduates	Annual		X	X
Compensation and Working Conditions	Periodic		X	X
Consumer Expenditure Survey, Integrated Diary and Interview Survey data	Annual		X	X
Consumer Price Index (CPI) Detailed Report	Monthly		X	X
Consumer Prices	Monthly		X	X
Contingent and Alternative Employment Arrangements	Periodic		X	X
Employer Costs for Employee Compensation	Quarterly		X	X
Employment and Earnings	Monthly		X	X
Employment and Wages	Annual		X	X
Employment Characteristics of Families	Annual		X	X
Employment Cost Index	Quarterly		X	X
The Employment Situation	Monthly		X	X
Geographic Profile of Employment and Unemployment	Annual		X	X
Metropolitan Area Employment and Unemployment	Monthly		X	X
Monthly Labor Review	Monthly		X	X
National Compensation Survey	Annual		X	X
Occupational Employment and Wages	Annual		X	X
Occupational Injuries and Illnesses	Annual		X	X
Occupational Projections Data	Biennial		X	X
Producer Price Index (PPI) Detailed Report	Monthly		X	X
Productivity and Costs by Industry	Annual		X	X
Real Earnings	Monthly		X	X
Regional and State Employment and Unemployment	Monthly		X	X
Relative Importance of Components in the Consumer Price Indexes	Annual		X	X
U.S. Import and Export Price Indexes	Monthly		X	X
Union Membership	Annual		X	X
Usual Weekly Earnings of Wage and Salary Workers	Quarterly		X	X
Work Experience of the Population	Annual		X	X
Bureau of Land Management http://www.blm.gov				
Public Land Statistics	Annual		X	
Census Bureau http://www.census.gov				
2012 Economic Census, Bridge Between 2012 NAICS and 2007 NAICS Report	Quinquennial			X
2012 Economic Census, Company Statistics Series, Survey of Business Owners	Quinquennial			X
2012 Economic Census, Comparative Statistics	Quinquennial			X
2017 Economic Census, Industry/Geography	Quinquennial			X
America's Families and Living Arrangements	Annual			X
Annual Business Survey	Annual			X
Annual Revision of Monthly Retail and Food Services: Sales and Inventories	Annual		X	X
Annual Revision of Monthly Wholesale Distributors: Sales and Inventories	Annual		X	X
Annual Survey of Entrepreneurs	Annual		X	X
Annual Survey of Manufactures	Annual		X	
Census of Governments	Quinquennial		X	
Census of Population and Housing Decennial (2010, most recent)	Decennial	X	X	X
Computer and Internet Access in the United States: 2016	Biennial		X	X
Consumer Income and Poverty, P60, and Household Economic Studies, P70	Periodic	X	X	
County Business Patterns	Annual		X	X
Current Construction Reports: New Residential Construction and New Residential Sales	Monthly		X	X
Current Construction Reports: Value of Construction Put in Place, C30	Monthly		X	X
Current Housing Reports, American Housing Survey for Selected Metropolitan Areas, H170	Biennial			X
Current Housing Reports, American Housing Survey for the United States, H150	Biennial			X
Current Housing Reports, Housing Vacancies and Homeownership, H111	Quarterly			X
Current Housing Reports, Survey of Market Absorption of New Multifamily Units (SOMA)	Quarterly		X	X
Current Housing Reports, Who Can Afford to Buy a Home in 2009, H121	Periodic	X	X	X
Current Population Reports (Series P20 and P23)	Periodic		X	X
Economic Census of Island Areas	Quinquennial			X

See footnotes at end of table.

Appendix I Table: Sources of Statistics, State Statistical Abstracts, and Foreign Statistical Abstracts-Continued.

See headnote on page 889.

Title	Frequency	Paper	Internet	
			PDF	Other Formats
Fertility of American Women in the United States	Annual			X
Health Insurance Coverage in the United States	Annual		X	X
Income and Poverty in the United States	Annual		X	X
International Data Base	Annual			X
International Population Reports (Series P95)	Periodic		X	
Manufacturing and International Trade Report: 2016	Annual		X	X
Manufacturer's Shipments, Inventories, and Orders	Monthly		X	X
Manufacturer's Shipments, Inventories, and Orders: 1992-2018	Annual			X
New York City Housing and Vacancy Survey	Triennial			X
Nonemployer Statistics	Annual			X
Population Estimates and Projections	Annual			X
Quarterly Financial Report for Manufacturing, Mining, and Trade Corporations	Quarterly		X	X
Service Annual Survey Report	Annual			X
Survey of Plant Capacity Utilization	Quarterly			X
U.S. International Trade in Goods and Services (FT900)	Annual		X	X
U.S. Trade with Puerto Rico and U.S. Possessions (FT 895)	Annual		X	
Centers for Disease Control and Prevention, Atlanta, Georgia http://www.cdc.gov				
Morbidity and Mortality Weekly Report	Weekly	X	X	X
National Health Interview Survey	Ongoing		X	X
National Immunization Survey (NIS) – Children (19-35 months)	Annual		X	X
Surveillance for Foodborne Disease Outbreaks	Annual		X	
Centers for Medicare and Medicaid Services (CMS) http://www.cms.gov				
CMS Program Statistics	Annual		X	X
Trustees Report	Annual	X	X	X
Central Intelligence Agency http://www.cia.gov				
World Factbook	Annual		X	X
Coast Guard (See Department of Homeland Security)				
Council of Economic Advisers http://www.whitehouse.gov/cea				
Economic Indicators	Monthly	X	X	X
Economic Report of the President	Annual	X	X	X
Department of Agriculture, Economic Research Service http://www.ers.usda.gov				
Amber Waves	Monthly		X	X
America's Diverse Family Farms	Annual	X	X	X
Cotton and Wool Yearbook	Annual			X
Feed Grains Yearbook	Annual		X	X
Food Availability (Per Capita) Data System	Ongoing			X
Food Expenditures	Annual			X
Fruit and Tree Nut Yearbook	Annual		X	X
Household Food Security in the United States	Annual		X	X
Oil Crops Yearbook	Annual		X	X
Rice Yearbook	Annual			X
Situation and Outlook Reports. Issued for: agricultural exports, feed, fruit and tree nuts, livestock and poultry, oil crops, rice, sugar and sweeteners, vegetables, wheat, and world agriculture	Periodic	X	X	X
Structure and Finances of U.S. Farms: Family Farm Report	Periodic	X	X	X
Sugar and Sweeteners Yearbook	Annual			X
Vegetable and Pulses Yearbook	Annual		X	X
World Agricultural Supply and Demand Estimates	Monthly	X	X	X
Department of Agriculture, Food and Nutrition Service http://www.fns.usda.gov/fns/				
Characteristics of Supplemental Nutrition Assistance Program Households	Annual	X	X	
WIC Participant and Program Characteristics	Biennial	X	X	
Department of Agriculture, Foreign Agricultural Service http://www.fas.usda.gov				
Livestock and Poultry World Markets and Trade	Semiannual	X	X	
Department of Agriculture, National Agricultural Statistics Service http://www.nass.usda.gov				
Agricultural Chemical Usage	Periodic			X
Agricultural Statistics	Annual	X	X	
Catfish Production	Semiannual	X	X	X
Cattle	Semiannual	X	X	X
Census of Agriculture	Quinquennial	X	X	X
Census of Agriculture: Organic Survey	Periodic		X	X
Cherry Production	Annual	X	X	X
Chickens and Eggs	Monthly	X	X	X
Citrus Fruits	Annual	X	X	X
Cranberries	Annual	X	X	X
Crop Production	Monthly	X	X	X
Crop Progress	Weekly	X	X	X
Crop Values	Annual	X	X	X
Dairy Products	Monthly	X	X	X
Farm Labor	Semiannual	X	X	X
Farms and Land in Farms	Annual	X	X	X
Floriculture Crops	Annual	X	X	X
Agricultural Land Values	Annual	X	X	X

See footnotes at end of table.

Appendix I Table: Sources of Statistics, State Statistical Abstracts, and Foreign Statistical Abstracts-Continued.

See headnote on page 889.

Title	Frequency	Paper	Internet PDF	Internet Other Formats
Livestock Slaughter	Monthly	X	X	X
Meat Animals Production, Disposition, and Income	Annual	X	X	X
Milk Production	Monthly	X	X	X
Milk Production, Disposition, and Income	Annual	X	X	X
Noncitrus Fruits and Nuts	Semiannual	X	X	X
Poultry Yearbook	Annual	X	X	X
Stock Reports. Stocks of grain, peanuts, potatoes, and rice	Periodic	X	X	X
Trout Production	Annual	X	X	X
Turkey Hatchery	Monthly	X	X	X
Turkeys Raised	Annual	X	X	X
Usual Planting and Harvesting Dates	Periodic	X	X	X
Vegetables	Periodic	X	X	X
Weekly Weather and Crop Bulletin	Weekly	X	X	
Winter Wheat and Rye Seedlings	Annual	X	X	X
Winter Wheat Seedlings	Annual	X	X	X
Department of Agriculture, Natural Resources Conservation Service				
http://www.nrcs.usda.gov				
National Resources Inventory	Periodic		X	X
Department of Defense				
http://www.dod.gov				
Base Structure Report				
A Summary of the Real Property Inventory	Annual		X	X
Demographics Report, Profile of the Military Community	Annual		X	X
Department of Defense, Defense Manpower Data Center				
https://www.dmdc.osd.mil/appj/dwp/dwp_reports.jsp				
Personnel Statistics	Periodic		X	X
Department of Defense, Defense Security Cooperation Agency				
http://www.dsca.mil/resources/dsca-historical-facts-book-fiscal-year-series				
Historical Facts Book & Fiscal Year Series	Annual		X	
Department of Education				
http://www.ed.gov				
Annual Report for Federal Student Aid	Annual		X	
Annual Report on Teacher Quality	Annual		X	
Federal Campus-Based Programs Data Book	Annual			X
Federal Pell Grant Program, End of Year Report	Annual		X	X
Department of Energy				
https://energy.gov				
Transportation Energy Data Book	Annual		X	X
Department of Health and Human Services				
http://www.hhs.gov				
Health Care Fraud and Abuse Control Program Annual Report	Annual	X	X	
Profile of Older Americans	Annual	X	X	X
Department of Homeland Security				
https://www.dhs.gov				
Budget in Brief	Annual	X	X	
Entry/Exit Overstay Report	Annual		X	
Department of Homeland Security, Coast Guard				
https://www.uscg.mil				
State of the Coast Guard	Annual	X	X	
Department of Homeland Security, Office of Immigration Statistics				
http://www.dhs.gov/immigration-statistics				
Yearbook of Immigration Statistics	Annual	X	X	X
Department of Housing and Urban Development				
http://www.hud.gov				
National Housing Market Summary	Quarterly		X	X
Department of Justice				
https://www.justice.gov				
Asset Forfeiture Fund Report to Congress	Annual		X	X
Department of Justice, Bureau of Alcohol, Tobacco, Firearms and Explosives				
http://www.atf.gov				
Firearms Commerce in the U.S. [Annual Firearms Manufacturing and Export Report]	Annual		X	
Firearms Trace Data (by State)	Annual		X	
Department of Labor				
http://www.dol.gov				
Agency Financial Report	Annual	X	X	
Annual Performance Report	Annual	X	X	
Health Insurance Coverage Bulletin	Periodic		X	X
Retirement Bulletins	Periodic		X	X
Department of State				
http://www.state.gov				
Country Reports on Terrorism	Annual		X	X
United States Contributions to International Organizations	Annual		X	X
Annex of Statistical Information: Country Reports on Terrorism	Annual		X	X
Department of Transportation				
http://www.dot.gov				
Air Travel Consumer Report	Monthly	X	X	
Annual U.S Domestic Average Itinerary Fare in Current and Constant Dollars	Annual			X

See footnotes at end of table.

Appendix I Table: Sources of Statistics, State Statistical Abstracts, and Foreign Statistical Abstracts-Continued.

See headnote on page 889.

Title	Frequency	Paper	Internet PDF	Internet Other Formats
National Transportation Statistics	Quarterly		X	X
Transportation Statistics Annual Report	Annual	X	X	
U.S. International Air Passenger and Freight Statistics	Quarterly	X	X	X
Department of the Treasury, Alcohol and Tobacco Tax and Trade Bureau http://www.ttb.gov				
Tobacco Products Monthly Statistical Releases	Monthly	X	X	
Department of the Treasury, Bureau of the Fiscal Service https://www.fiscal.treasury.gov				
Combined Statement of Receipts, Outlays, and Balances	Annual	X	X	X
Financial Report of the United States Government	Annual	X	X	X
Monthly Statement of the Public Debt of the United States	Monthly	X	X	X
Monthly Treasury Statement of Receipts and Outlays of the United States Government	Monthly	X	X	X
Treasury Bulletin	Quarterly	X	X	X
Department of Veterans Affairs http://www.va.gov				
Annual Benefits Report	Annual		X	
Annual Performance Plan and Report	Annual		X	
Compensation and Pension Data by County	Annual			X
Employment and Training Administration http://www.doleta.gov				
Unemployment Insurance Weekly Claims	Weekly		X	X
Energy Information Administration http://www.eia.gov				
Annual Coal Report	Annual		X	X
Annual Energy Outlook	Annual	X	X	X
Electric Power Annual	Annual		X	X
Electric Power Monthly	Monthly		X	X
Electric Sales, Revenue and Average Price	Annual		X	X
International Energy Outlook	Annual	X	X	X
International Energy Statistics portal	Ongoing		X	X
Monthly Energy Review	Monthly		X	X
Petroleum Marketing Monthly	Monthly		X	X
Petroleum Supply Annual	Annual		X	X
Petroleum Supply Monthly	Monthly		X	X
Quarterly Coal Report	Quarterly		X	X
Residential Energy Consumption Survey	Quadrennial		X	X
State Electricity Profiles	Annual		X	X
State Energy Data System Reports	Annual		X	X
U.S. Crude Oil and Natural Gas Proved Reserves	Annual		X	X
Weekly Coal Production	Weekly			X
Environmental Protection Agency http://www.epa.gov				
Air Quality Statistics Report	Annual		X	X
Clean Watersheds Needs Survey	Quadrennial		X	
Drinking Water Infrastructure Needs Survey and Assessment	Quadrennial		X	
National Water Quality Inventory Report to Congress	Periodic			X
Toxics Release Inventory National Analysis	Annual		X	X
UST Performance Measures	Semi-Annual		X	
Export-Import Bank of the United States http://www.exim.gov				
Annual Report	Annual	X	X	
Report to the U.S. Congress on Global Export Credit Competition and the Export-Import Bank of the United States	Annual	X	X	
Farm Credit Administration https://www.fca.gov/				
Annual Report on the Farm Credit System	Annual	X	X	
Federal Bureau of Investigation https://ucr.fbi.gov/				
Crime in the United States	Annual		X	X
Hate Crime Statistics	Annual		X	X
Law Enforcement Officers Killed and Assaulted	Annual		X	X
Federal Communications Commission http://www.fcc.gov				
Annual Assessment of the Status of Competition in the Market for the Delivery of Video Programming	Annual		X	X
International Telecommunications Traffic and Revenue Data Report	Periodically		X	X
Internet Access Services	Semi-Annual		X	X
Report on Cable Industry Prices	Periodically		X	X
Voice Telephone Services Report	Semi-Annual		X	X
Federal Deposit Insurance Corporation http://www.fdic.gov				
Annual Report	Annual	X	X	X
FDIC Survey of Unbanked and Underbanked Households	Biennial		X	X
FDIC Quarterly	Quarterly	X	X	X
Historical Bank Data	Annual			X
Quarterly Banking Profile	Quarterly		X	X
Statistics on Banking	Quarterly			X
Summary of Deposits	Annual			X

See footnotes at end of table.

Title	Frequency	Paper	Internet PDF	Internet Other Formats
Federal Highway Administration				
http://www.fhwa.dot.gov				
Highway Statistics	Annual	X	X	X
Federal Railroad Administration				
http://safetydata.fra.dot.gov/OfficeofSafety/default.aspx				
Railroad Safety Statistics	Annual	X	X	
Fish and Wildlife Service				
http://www.fws.gov				
National Survey of Fishing, Hunting, and Wildlife Associated Recreation	Quinquennial	X	X	
Forest Service				
http://www.fs.fed.us				
An Analysis of the Timber Situation in the United States 1952-2050	Periodic	X	X	
Land Areas of the National Forest System	Annual	X	X	X
RPA Assessment Tables	Periodic	X	X	X
U.S. Timber Production, Trade, Consumption, and Price Statistics	Biennial	X	X	
General Services Administration				
http://www.gsa.gov				
Federal Real Property Profile	Annual		X	X
Geological Survey				
http://www.usgs.gov				
Estimated Use of Water in the United States	Quinquennial	X	X	X
Mineral Commodity Summaries	Annual	X	X	
Mineral Industry Surveys	Monthly/ Quarterly		X	X
Minerals Yearbook	Annual	X	X	X
Internal Revenue Service				
https://www.irs.gov/statistics				
Corporation Income Tax Returns	Annual	X	X	X
Individual Income Tax Returns	Annual	X	X	X
IRS Data Book	Annual	X	X	X
Statistics of Income Bulletin	Quarterly	X	X	X
International Trade Administration, National Travel and Tourism Office				
https://travel.trade.gov				
U.S. Travel and Tourism Statistics	Annual		X	X
International Trade Commission				
http://www.usitc.gov				
Interactive Tariff and Trade Dataweb	Ongoing			X
Recent Trends in U.S. Services Trade	Annual	X	X	
Library of Congress				
http://www.loc.gov				
Annual Report	Annual	X	X	
Maritime Administration				
http://www.marad.dot.gov				
Annual Report to Congress	Annual	X	X	
Fleet Statistics	Annual			X
U.S. Waterborne Foreign Trade	Annual			X
Vessel Calls	Annual		X	X
Mine Safety and Health Administration				
http://www.msha.gov				
Informational Reports by Mining Industry: Coal, Metallic Minerals, Nonmetallic Minerals (except stone and coal), Sand and Gravel, and Stone	Annual		X	X
Mine Injuries and Worktime	Quarterly	X	X	X
National Aeronautics and Space Administration				
http://www.nasa.gov				
Annual Procurement Report	Annual	X	X	
National Center for Education Statistics				
http://nces.ed.gov				
After the Post-9/11 GI Bill: A Profile of Military Service Members and Veterans Enrolled in Undergraduate and Graduate Education	Periodic		X	X
Career and Technical Education Programs in Public School Districts	Annual	X	X	X
Characteristics of Private Schools in the United States	Annual	X	X	X
The Condition of Education	Annual	X	X	X
Digest of Education Statistics	Annual	X	X	X
Enrollment in Postsecondary Institutions, Graduation Rates, and Financial Statistics	Annual		X	
Indicators of School Crime and Safety	Annual	X	X	X
National Teacher and Principal Survey	Periodic		X	X
Profile and Financial Aid Estimates of Graduate Students	Quadrennial		X	X
Programs and Services for High School English Learners in Public School Districts	Annual		X	X
The Nation's Report Card: Civics	Periodic	X	X	
The Nation's Report Card: Economics	Periodic	X	X	
The Nation's Report Card: Geography	Periodic	X	X	
The Nation's Report Card: U.S. History	Periodic	X	X	
The Nation's Report Card: Mathematics	Periodic	X	X	
The Nation's Report Card: Reading	Periodic	X	X	
The Nation's Report Card: Science	Periodic	X	X	
The Nation's Report Card: Writing	Periodic	X	X	
Trends in Undergraduate Nonfederal Grant and Scholarship Aid by Demographic and Enrollment Characteristics	Quadrennial		X	X

See footnotes at end of table.

Title	Frequency	Paper	Internet PDF	Internet Other Formats
Trends in Pell Grant Receipt and the Characteristics of Pell Grant Recipients	Quadrennial		X	X
Projections of Education Statistics	Annual	X	X	X
Status and Trends in the Education of Racial and Ethnic Groups	Irregular	X	X	X
Trends in High School Dropout and Completion Rates in the United States	Annual		X	X
National Center for Health Statistics http://www.cdc.gov/nchs				
Health, United States	Annual	X	X	X
National Health Statistics Reports	Periodic	X	X	
National Vital Statistics Reports	Periodic	X	X	
Vital and Health Statistics:				
Series 3: Analytical and Epidemiological Studies	Irregular	X	X	
Series 11: Health and Nutrition Examination Survey Statistics	Irregular	X	X	
Series 13: Data on Health Resources Utilization	Irregular	X	X	
Series 20: Data on Mortality	Irregular	X	X	
Series 21: Data on Natality, Marriage, and Divorce	Irregular	X	X	
Series 23: Data from the National Survey of Family Growth	Irregular	X	X	
National Credit Union Administration http://www.ncua.gov				
Annual Report	Annual	X	X	
Call Report Quarterly Summary Reports	Quarterly		X	
National Endowment for the Arts https://www.arts.gov/				
Annual Report	Annual	X	X	
Appropriations Request	Annual	X	X	
National Endowment for the Humanities http://www.neh.gov				
Annual Report	Annual	X	X	
Appropriations Request	Annual	X	X	
National Guard Bureau http://www.nationalguard.mil				
Posture Statement	Annual		X	
National Highway Traffic Safety Administration http://www.nhtsa.gov				
Traffic Safety Facts	Annual	X	X	
National Oceanic and Atmospheric Administration http://www.noaa.gov				
Climatic Data for the World	Monthly			X
Comparative Climatic Data	Annual		X	X
Daily Normals of Temperature, Precipitation, Heating Degree Days (HDD), and Cooling Degree Days (CDD)	Periodic			X
Fisheries of the United States	Annual	X	X	
Hourly Precipitation Data. Monthly with annual summary; for each state	Monthly		X	X
Local Climatological Data. Monthly with annual summary; for major cities	Monthly		X	X
Monthly Normals of Temperature, Precipitation, Heating Degree Days (HDD), and Cooling Degree Days (CDD)	Periodic			X
Our Living Oceans	Periodic	X	X	
Storm Data	Monthly		X	
Tornado Summaries	Monthly			X
U.S. Climate Normals	Decennial	X	X	X
National Park Service http://www.nps.gov				
National Park Statistical Abstract	Annual	X	X	
National Science Foundation http://www.nsf.gov/statistics				
Academic Institutional Profiles	Annual			X
Academic Research and Development Expenditures	Annual		X	X
Characteristics of Doctoral Scientists and Engineers in the United States	Biennial		X	X
Characteristics of Recent Science/Engineering Graduates	Biennial		X	X
Doctorate Recipients from U.S. Universities	Annual		X	X
Federal Funds for Research and Development	Annual		X	X
Federal Research and Development Funding by Budget Function	Annual		X	X
Federal Science and Engineering Support to Universities, Colleges, and Nonprofit Institutions	Annual		X	X
Graduate Students and Postdoctorates in Science and Engineering	Annual		X	X
National Patterns of Research and Development Resources	Annual		X	X
Research and Development in Industry	Annual		X	X
Science and Engineering Degrees	Biennial		X	X
Science and Engineering Degrees, by Race/Ethnicity of Recipients	Biennial		X	X
Science and Engineering Doctorate Awards	Annual		X	X
Science and Engineering Indicators	Biennial	X	X	X
Science and Engineering State Profiles	Annual			X
Science Resources Statistics Info Briefs (various topics)	Frequent	X	X	X
Scientific and Engineering Research Facilities at Universities and Colleges	Biennial		X	X
Women, Minorities, and Persons with Disabilities in Science and Engineering	Biennial		X	X
National Transportation Safety Board http://www.ntsb.gov				
Review of U.S. Civil Aviation Accidents	Annual		X	X
Office of Juvenile Justice and Delinquency Prevention http://ojjdp.gov				

See footnotes at end of table.

Appendix I Table: Sources of Statistics, State Statistical Abstracts, and Foreign Statistical Abstracts-Continued.

See headnote on page 889.

Title	Frequency	Paper	Internet	
			PDF	Other *Formats*
Highlights of the National Youth Gang Survey	Annual	X	X	X
Juvenile Arrests	Annual	X	X	X
Juvenile Offenders and Victims	Periodic	X	X	X
Office of Management and Budget				
http://www.whitehouse.gov/omb				
The Budget of the United States Government	Annual	X	X	X
Office of Personnel Management				
http://www.opm.gov				
Common Characteristics of the Government	Annual		X	
Demographic Profile of the Federal Workforce	Biennial		X	
Executive Branch Retirement Statistics	Annual		X	
Office of the Clerk, U.S. House of Representatives				
http://clerk.house.gov				
Statistics of the Presidential and Congressional Election	Biennial	X	X	
Patent and Trademark Office				
http://www.uspto.gov				
All Technologies (Utility Patents)	Annual	X	X	X
Patent Counts by Country/State and Year	Annual	X		X
Patenting Trends in the United States	Annual	X		X
Railroad Retirement Board				
https://secure.rrb.gov				
Annual Report	Annual	X	X	
Quarterly Benefit Statistics	Quarterly	X	X	
Securities and Exchange Commission				
http://www.sec.gov/about.shtml				
Select SEC and Market Data	Annual		X	
Small Business Administration				
http://www.sba.gov				
Loan Program Performance Reports	Annual		X	
Quarterly Bulletin	Quarterly		X	X
Small Business Lending in the United States	Annual	X	X	X
Small Business Economy	Annual		X	X
Small Business Profiles for States and Territories	Annual		X	
Social Security Administration				
http://www.ssa.gov				
Annual Statistical Report on the Social Security Disability Insurance Program	Annual	X	X	X
Annual Statistical Supplement to the Social Security Bulletin	Annual	X	X	X
Congressional Statistics	Annual	X	X	X
Fast Facts & Figures about Social Security	Annual	X	X	X
Income of the Population 55 and over	Biennially	X	X	X
OASDI Beneficiaries by State and County	Annual	X	X	X
Social Security Bulletin	Quarterly	X	X	X
SSI Annual Statistical Report	Annual	X	X	X
SSI Recipients by State and County	Annual	X	X	X
Substance Abuse and Mental Health Services Administration				
http://www.samhsa.gov				
Behavioral Health Barometer, United States	Annual	X	X	
National Mental Health Services Survey (N-MHSS)	Annual	X	X	X
National Survey on Drug Use and Health (NSDUH)	Annual	X	X	
National Survey on Substance Abuse Treatment Services (N-SSATS)	Annual	X	X	X
U.S. Copyright Office				
http://www.copyright.gov				
Annual Report	Annual	X	X	
U.S. Equal Employment Opportunity Commission				
https://www.eeoc.gov				
Enforcement and Litigation Statistics	Ongoing		X	X
U.S. Health Resources & Services Administration				
https://www.hrsa.gov				
Health Center Data Program	Ongoing		X	X
U.S. Sentencing Commission				
https://www.ussc.gov/				
Sourcebook of Federal Sentencing Statistics	Annual		X	X
NONGOVERNMENT				
Aerospace Industries Association, Arlington, VA				
http://www.aia-aerospace.org				
Aerospace Industry Year-End Review and Forecast	Annual		X	
Economic Impact Study of the U.S. Aerospace and Defense Industry	Annual		X	
Quarterly Trade Bulletin	Quarterly		X	
U.S. Aerospace Manufacturing Update	Quarterly		X	
Airlines for America, Washington, DC				
http://www.airlines.org				
American Council of Life Insurers, Washington, DC				
http://www.acli.com				
Life Insurers Fact Book	Annual		X	
American Dental Association, Chicago, IL				
http://www.ada.org				

See footnotes at end of table.

Appendix I Table: Sources of Statistics, State Statistical Abstracts, and Foreign Statistical Abstracts-Continued.

See headnote on page 889.

Title	Frequency	Paper	Internet PDF	Internet Other Formats
Survey of Dental Practice	Annual			X
American Forest and Paper Association, Washington, DC				
http://www.afandpa.org				
Monthly Exports/Imports Report	Monthly		X	
Monthly Statistics of Paper, Paperboard and Wood Pulp	Monthly		X	X
Paper Industry Annual Capacity and Fiber Consumption	Annual		X	
Paper Industry Annual Statistical Summary	Annual		X	
American Gas Association, Washington, DC				
http://www.aga.org				
Gas Facts	Annual	X	X	
American Iron and Steel Institute, Washington, DC				
http://www.steel.org				
Annual Statistical Report	Annual	X	X	
American Medical Association, Chicago, IL				
http://www.ama-assn.org				
State Medical Licensure Statistics and License Requirements	Annual	X		X
American Osteopathic Association, Chicago, IL				
http://www.osteopathic.org				
Osteopathic Medical Profession Report	Annual		X	
American Public Transportation Association, Washington, DC				
http://www.apta.com				
Public Transportation Fact Book	Annual		X	X
American Society for Aesthetic Plastic Surgery				
https://www.surgery.org				
Cosmetic Surgery National Data Bank Statistics	Annual		X	
Association of American Medical Colleges				
https://www.aamc.org				
Physician Specialty Data Report	Biennial	X	X	
State Physician Workforce Data Book	Biennial	X	X	
Association of American Railroads, Washington, DC				
http://www.aar.org				
Analysis of Class I Railroads	Annual	X	X	X
Freight Commodity Statistics	Annual	X	X	X
Railroad Facts	Annual	X	X	
Berman Jewish Data Bank, Storrs, CT				
http://www.jewishdatabank.org				
Jewish Population in the United States	Annual		X	X
Bloomberg BNA, Washington, DC				
https://www.bloombergindustry.com				
BNA's Labor and Employment Outlook Report	Annual	X		
BNA's Job Absence and Turnover Report	Quarterly	X		
Directory of U.S. Labor Organizations	Annual	X		
Source Book on Collective Bargaining	Annual	X		
Union Membership and Earnings Data Book	Annual	X		
Brookings Institution, Washington, DC				
https://www.brookings.edu				
Vital Statistics on Congress	Biennial		X	X
Chronicle of Higher Education, Inc., Washington, DC				
https://chronicle.com				
Almanac of Higher Education	Annual	X		X
College Board, New York, NY				
https://www.collegeboard.org/				
Suite of Assessments Annual Report	Annual		X	
cmdty® by barchart, Chicago, IL				
https://www.barchart.com/cmdty				
Commodity Indexes	Ongoing		X	X
cmdty Yearbook®	Annual	X		X
CRB Infotech	Monthly			X
End of Day Data	Daily			X
Conference Board, New York, NY				
http://www.conference-board.org				
Business Cycle Indicators	Monthly		X	X
International Comparisons of Annual Labor Force Statistics	Annual		X	X
International Comparisons of Hourly Compensation Costs for Production Workers in Manufacturing	Annual		X	X
International Comparisons of Manufacturing Productivity and Unit Labor Cost Trends	Annual		X	X
Performance: Productivity, Employment, and Growth in the World's Economies	Irregular		X	
Congressional Quarterly (CQ) Press, Washington, DC				
https://us.sagepub.com/en-us/nam/cqpress				
America Votes	Biennial	X		
Consumer Technology Association, Arlington, VA				
https://www.cta.tech/				
U.S. Consumer Technology Sales and Forecasts	Semiannual		X	
Council of State Governments, Lexington, KY				

See footnotes at end of table.

Title	Frequency	Paper	Internet PDF	Internet Other Formats
http://www.csg.org				
Book of the States	Annual	X	X	
Credit Union National Association, Washington, DC				
http://www.cuna.org				
Operating Ratios and Spreads	Quarterly	X	X	
Dodge Data & Analytics, New York, NY				
https://www.construction.com				
Construction Potentials Bulletin	Monthly		X	
Dow Jones and Company, New York, NY				
http://www.dowjones.com/				
Wall Street Journal	Daily	X		X
Curated Experiences Group, Fountain Valley, CA				
http://www.editorandpublisher.com				
Editor and Publisher	Monthly	X		X
Newspaper Databook	Annual	X		X
Edison Electric Institute, Washington, DC				
http://www.eei.org				
Statistical Yearbook of the Electric Power Industry	Annual	X	X	X
Euromonitor International, London, England				
http://www.euromonitor.com				
Consumer Lifestyles in the US	Annual	X	X	
Federal National Mortgage Association, Washington, DC				
http://www.fanniemae.com				
Annual Report on Form 10-K	Annual		X	
Food and Agriculture Organization of the United Nations, Rome, Italy				
http://www.fao.org				
World Fertilizer Trends and Outlook	Annual		X	
FAO Statistical Yearbook: World Food and Agriculture	Annual	X	X	
FAO Yearbook: Fishery and Aquaculture Statistics	Periodic	X	X	X
Yearbook of Forest Products	Annual	X	X	
General Aviation Manufacturers Association, Washington, DC				
http://www.gama.aero				
General Aviation Aircraft Shipment Report	Quarterly		X	
General Aviation Statistical Databook & Industry Outlook	Annual		X	
Giving USA Foundation, Chicago, IL				
http://www.givingusa.org/				
Giving USA	Annual	X	X	X
Guttmacher Institute, New York, NY				
http://www.guttmacher.org				
Perspectives on Sexual and Reproductive Health	Quarterly		X	
Health Forum, an American Hospital Association Company, Chicago, IL				
http://www.ahadataviewer.com/				
AHA Annual Survey Data Base	Annual			X
AHA Hospital Statistics	Annual	X		X
IHS Global, Inc., Englewood, CO				
http://www.janes.com				
IHS Jane's All the World's Aircraft: Development & Production	Annual	X		X
IHS Jane's Defence: C4ISR & Mission Systems	Annual	X		X
IHS Jane's Fighting Ships	Annual	X		X
IHS Jane's Flight Avionics	Annual	X		X
IHS Jane's Land Warfare Platforms: Armoured Fighting Vehicles	Annual	X		X
IHS Jane's Land Warfare Platforms: Logistics, Support & Unmanned	Annual	X		X
IHS Jane's Simulation & Training Systems	Annual	X		X
IHS Jane's Space Systems & Industry	Annual	X		X
IHS Jane's Weapons: Air-Launched	Annual	X		X
IHS Jane's Weapons: Infantry	Annual	X		X
Independent Petroleum Association of America, Washington, DC				
http://www.ipaa.org				
IPAA Oil & Gas Producing Industry in Your State	Annual	X	X	
U.S. Petroleum Statistics	Annual	X	X	
Infobase Publishing, New York, NY				
http://www.worldalmanac.com				
The World Almanac and Book of Facts	Annual	X		
Information Today, Inc., Medford, NJ				
http://www.infotoday.com				
American Library Directory	Annual	X		X
Library and Book Trade Almanac (formerly The Bowker Annual)	Annual	X		
Institute for Criminal Justice Ethics, New York, NY				
https://www.jjay.cuny.edu/institute-criminal-justice-ethics				
Criminal Justice Ethics	Thrice yearly	X	X	
Insurance Information Institute, New York, NY				
http://www.iii.org				
The I.I.I. Insurance Fact Book	Annual	X	X	X
Inter-American Development Bank, Washington, DC				
http://www.iadb.org				

See footnotes at end of table.

See headnote on page 889.

Title	Frequency	Paper	Internet PDF	Internet Other Formats
Annual Report	Annual	X	X	
Development in the Americas	Annual	X	X	X
International Air Transport Association, Montreal, Canada and Geneva, Switzerland				
http://www.iata.org				
World Air Transport Statistics	Annual	X	X	X
International City Management Association, Washington, DC				
http://www.icma.org				
ICMA Chief Administrative Officers Salary & Compensation Survey	Annual		X	
Municipal Year Book	Annual		X	
International Labour Organization, Geneva, Switzerland				
http://www.ilo.org				
Yearbook of Labour Statistics	Annual	X		X
International Monetary Fund, Washington, DC				
http://www.imf.org				
Annual Report	Annual	X	X	X
Balance of Payments Statistics	Monthly	X	X	X
Direction of Trade Statistics	Quarterly	X		X
Government Finance Statistics Yearbook	Annual	X	X	X
International Financial Statistics	Monthly	X	X	X
International Telecommunication Union, Geneva, Switzerland				
http://www.itu.int/home/index.html				
ITU Yearbook of Statistics	Annual	X	X	
World Telecommunication/ICT Indicators	Annual	X	X	X
Investment Company Institute, Washington, DC				
http://www.ici.org				
Investment Company Fact Book	Annual		X	X
Joint Center for Housing Studies of Harvard University, Cambridge, MA				
http://www.jchs.harvard.edu				
The State of the Nation's Housing	Annual		X	X
Media Source, Inc., New York, NY				
https://www.mediasourceinc.com				
Library Journal	Semimonthly	X		X
School Library Journal	Monthly	X		X
National Academy of Social Insurance, Washington, DC				
http://www.nasi.org				
Workers Compensation: Benefits, Coverage, and Costs	Annual	X	X	
National Association of Home Builders, Washington, DC				
http://www.nahb.org				
HousingEconomics.com (online subscription)	Ongoing			X
National Association of Latino Elected and Appointed Officials, Los Angeles, CA				
http://www.naleo.org				
National Directory of Latino Elected Officials	Annual		X	X
National Association of Realtors, Chicago, IL				
https://www.nar.realtor				
Economist's Outlook	Daily			X
NAR Member Profile	Annual	X	X	X
NAR Profile of Home Buyer and Sellers	Annual	X	X	
National Association of State Budget Officers, Washington, DC				
http://www.nasbo.org				
Fiscal Survey of the States	Semiannual	X	X	
State Expenditure Report	Annual	X	X	
National Association of State Park Directors, Raleigh, NC				
https://www.stateparks.org				
Statistical Report of State Park Operations: Annual Information Exchange	Annual	X	X	
National Catholic Educational Association, Arlington, VA				
http://www.ncea.org				
The Annual Financial Report	Biennial	X	X	
U.S. Catholic Elementary and Secondary Schools: The Annual Statistical Report on Schools, Enrollment and Staffing	Annual	X	X	
National Education Association, Washington, DC				
http://www.nea.org				
Rankings & Estimates: Rankings of the States and Estimates of School Statistics	Annual	X	X	
National Fire Protection Association, Quincy, MA				
http://www.nfpa.org				
National Fire Protection Association (NFPA) Journal	Bimonthly	X		X
National Golf Foundation, Jupiter, FL				
http://www.ngf.org				
Golf Facilities in the U.S.	Annual	X	X	
National Restaurant Association, Washington, DC				
http://www.restaurant.org				
Restaurant Industry 2020	Recurring		X	
Restaurant Industry Pocket Factbook	Annual	X	X	X
Restaurant Operations Report	Recurring	X	X	
Restaurant Performance Index	Monthly		X	
Restaurant Trendmapper (online subscription)	Ongoing			X

See footnotes at end of table.

Appendix I Table: Sources of Statistics, State Statistical Abstracts, and Foreign Statistical Abstracts-Continued.

See headnote on page 889.

Title	Frequency	Paper	Internet PDF	Internet Other Formats
State of the Industry	Annual	X	X	
National Safety Council, Itasca, IL				
http://www.nsc.org				
Injury Facts	Annual	X	X	
National Sporting Goods Association, Mount Prospect, IL				
http://www.nsga.org				
Sporting Goods Market	Annual	X	X	
Sports Participation in the U.S.	Annual	X	X	
Organisation for Economic Cooperation and Development, Paris, France				
http://www.oecd-ilibrary.org/				
CO2 Emissions From Fuel Combustion	Annual	X	X	X
Coal Information	Annual	X	X	X
Digital Economy Outlook	Biennial	X	X	X
Education at a Glance: OECD Indicators	Annual	X	X	X
Electricity Information	Annual	X	X	X
Energy Prices and Taxes	Quarterly	X	X	
Environmental Outlook	Periodic	X	X	X
Financial Accounts	Annual	X	X	X
Financial Balance Sheets	Annual	X	X	X
General Government Accounts	Annual	X	X	X
Geographical Distribution of Financial Flows to Developing Countries	Annual	X	X	X
International Migration Outlook	Annual	X	X	X
International Trade by Commodity Statistics	Ongoing	X	X	X
Issue 1: Main Aggregates	Annual	X	X	X
Issue 2: Detailed Tables	Annual	X	X	X
ITF Transport Outlook	Annual	X	X	X
Main Economic Indicators	Monthly	X	X	X
Main Science and Technology Indicators	Semiannual	X	X	X
National Accounts at a Glance	Annual	X	X	X
National Accounts of OECD Countries	Annual	X	X	X
Natural Gas Information	Annual	X	X	
Nuclear Energy Data	Annual	X	X	X
OECD Communications Outlook	Biennial	X	X	X
OECD Economic Outlook	Semiannual	X	X	X
OECD Economic Surveys	Periodic	X	X	X
OECD Employment Outlook	Annual	X	X	X
OECD Factbook	Annual	X	X	X
OECD-FAO Agricultural Outlook	Annual	X	X	X
OECD Health Statistics	Annual			X
OECD Insurance Statistics	Annual	X	X	X
OECD International Development Statistics	Annual			X
OECD Quarterly International Trade Statistics	Quarterly	X	X	X
OECD Review of Fisheries: Policies and Summary Statistics	Annual	X	X	X
OECD Science, Technology, and Innovation Outlook	Biennial	X	X	X
OECD Science, Technology and R&D Statistics	Ongoing			X
OECD Society at a Glance	Biennial	X	X	X
OECD Territorial Reviews	Periodic	X	X	X
Oil Information	Annual	X	X	
Oil, Gas, Coal, and Electricity Quarterly Statistics	Quarterly	X	X	X
Pensions at a Glance	Biennial	X	X	X
PISA (OECD Programme for International Student Assessment)	Periodic	X	X	X
Quarterly National Accounts	Quarterly	X	X	X
Revenue Statistics	Ongoing			X
Taxing Wages	Annual	X	X	X
Uranium: Resources Production and Demand	Biennial	X	X	X
World Energy Balances	Annual	X	X	
World Energy Outlook	Annual	X	X	
World Energy Statistics	Annual	X	X	
Endeavor Business Media, Nashville, TN				
https://www.endeavorbusinessmedia.com				
Offshore	Monthly	X	X	X
Oil and Gas Journal	Weekly	X	X	X
Pew Research Center				
http://www.pewinternet.org				
Book Reading	Periodic		X	X
Home Broadband	Periodic		X	X
Libraries and Learning	Periodic		X	X
Social Media Update	Periodic		X	X
Technology Device Ownership	Periodic		X	X
Teens, Social Media & Technology	Periodic		X	X
Puerto Rico Planning Board, San Juan, PR				
http://www.jp.gobierno.pr				
Construction Industry	Periodic	X		
Economic Report to the Governor	Annual	X	X	X
External Trade Statistics	Annual	X	X	
Income and Production	Annual	X	X	
Statistical Appendix-Economic Report to the Governor	Annual	X	X	X
PWxyz, LLC, New York, NY				
http://www.publishersweekly.com				
Publishers Weekly	Weekly	X		X

See footnotes at end of table.

Title	Frequency	Paper	Internet PDF	Internet Other Formats
Radio Advertising Bureau, Dallas, TX http://www.rab.com				
Why Radio: Fact Sheets	Ongoing			X
Regional Airline Association, Washington, DC http://www.raa.org				
Regional Airlines Association Annual Report	Annual		X	
Securities Industry and Financial Markets Association, New York, NY http://www.sifma.org				
SIFMA Fact Book	Annual	X		X
U.S. Foreign Activity Report	Quarterly		X	X
Standard and Poor's Financial Services LLC, New York, NY http://www.standardandpoors.com				
Analyst's Handbook	Monthly	X		X
Corporation Records: Corporate Description	Monthly	X	X	X
Corporation Records: Daily News	Daily	X	X	X
Daily Stock Price Records	Quarterly			X
United Nations Conference on Trade and Development, Geneva, Switzerland http://www.unctad.org				
Development and Globalization: Facts and Figures	Periodic	X	X	X
Handbook of Statistics	Annual	X	X	X
United Nations Statistics Division, New York, NY https://unstats.un.org/home				
Demographic Yearbook (Series R)	Annual	X	X	
Energy Balances and Electricity Profiles (Series W)	Annual	X	X	
Energy Statistics Yearbook (Series J)	Annual	X	X	
Industrial Commodity Statistics Yearbook: Production Statistics	Annual	X	X	
International Trade Statistics Yearbook (Series G)	Annual	X	X	
Monthly Bulletin of Statistics (Series Q)	Monthly	X	X	
National Accounts Statistics: Analysis of Main Aggregates	Annual	X		
National Accounts Statistics (Series X)	Annual	X	X	
Population and Vital Statistics Report (Series A)	Quarterly	X	X	
Statistical Yearbook	Annual	X	X	
World Statistics Pocketbook (Series V)	Annual	X	X	
The World's Women: Progress in Statistics	Quinquennial	X	X	
University of Michigan, Institute for Social Research, Inter-University Consortium for Political and Social Research, Ann Arbor, MI http://www.icpsr.umich.edu/icpsrweb/ICPSR/studies/8475				
American National Election Studies Cumulative Data File	Biennial			X
Warren Communications News, Washington, DC http://www.warren-news.com				
Television and Cable Factbook	Ongoing			X
World Bank Group, Washington, DC http://www.worldbank.org				
Atlas of Global Development	Periodic	X	X	
Global Development Finance	Annual	X	X	X
The Little Data Book	Annual	X	X	
World Development Indicators	Annual	X		X
World Health Organization, Geneva, Switzerland http://www.who.int/en/				
World Health Statistics Report	Annual	X	X	
World Trade Organization, Geneva, Switzerland http://www.wto.org				
World Trade Statistical Review	Annual	X	X	X
STATE STATISTICAL ABSTRACTS FROM UNIVERSITIES				
Pennsylvania State University, Pennsylvania State Data Center, Middletown, PA http://pasdc.hbg.psu.edu				
Pennsylvania Abstract: A Statistical Fact Book	Annual	X	X	X
State University of New York: Nelson A. Rockefeller Institute of Government, Nelson A. Rockefeller Institute of Government, Albany, NY http://www.rockinst.org				
New York State Statistical Yearbook	Annual	X	X	X
University of Florida: Bureau of Economic and Business Research, Gainesville, FL http://www.bebr.ufl.edu				
Florida Statistical Dashboards	Ongoing			X
University of Georgia: Selig Center for Economic Growth, Athens, GA http://www.terry.uga.edu/selig				
Georgia Economic Outlook	Annual	X	X	X
University of Kansas: Institute for Policy and Social Research, Lawrence, KS http://www.ipsr.ku.edu/ksdata/ksah				
Kansas Statistical Abstract	Annual		X	X
University of Missouri-Columbia: Economic and Policy Analysis Research Center, Columbia, MO http://eparc.missouri.edu				
Missouri Statistical Data Archive (online)	Ongoing		X	
University of Oklahoma: Center for Economic and Management Research, Norman, OK				

See footnotes at end of table.

Appendix I Table: Sources of Statistics, State Statistical Abstracts, and Foreign Statistical Abstracts-Continued.

See headnote on page 889.

Title	Frequency	Paper	Internet PDF	Internet Other Formats
http://www.ou.edu/content/price/centersresearch/cemr/cemr_publications.html Oklahoma Statistical Abstract	Annual	X		
STATE STATISTICAL ABSTRACT FROM AN ASSOCIATION				
Texas State Historical Association, Austin, TX http://texasalmanac.com Texas Almanac	Biennial	X	X	X
STATE STATISTICAL ABSTRACTS FROM STATE AGENCIES				
Hawaii State Department of Business, Economic Development & Tourism, Honolulu, HI http://dbedt.hawaii.gov/economic/databook State of Hawaii Data Book	Annual		X	X
Maryland State Data Center, Maryland Department of Planning, Baltimore, MD http://www.mdp.state.md.us/msdc Maryland Statistical Abstract	Annual		X	
Maryland Statistical Handbook	Periodic		X	
Mississippi Secretary of State http://www.sos.ms.gov 2016-2020 Mississippi Blue Book	Quadrennial	X	X	
South Carolina, Revenue and Fiscal Affairs Office, Columbia, SC http://abstract.sc.gov South Carolina Statistical Abstract	Ongoing			X
INTERNATIONAL STATISTICAL ABSTRACTS FROM A FOREIGN AGENCY				
Austria **Statistik Austria, Vienna** http://www.statistik.at/web_en Statistisches Jahrbuch Österreichs	Annual	X	X	X
Belgium **Statistics Belgium, Brussels** http://statbel.fgov.be/en Key Figures: Statistical Overview of Belgium	Annual	X	X	X
Czechia **Czech Statistical Office, Praha** http://www.czso.cz Statistical Yearbook of the Czech Republic, 2017	Annual	X	X	X
Denmark **Statistics Denmark, Copenhagen** http://www.dst.dk/en Statistical Yearbook (Discontinued)	Annual		X	
Finland **Statistics Finland, Helsinki** http://www.stat.fi/index_en.html Statistical Yearbook of Finland	Annual	X		
France **National Institute of Statistics and Economic Studies, Paris** http://www.insee.fr/en Tableaux de l'Economie Francaise	Annual		X	X
Germany **Statistisches Bundesamt, Wiesbaden** https://www.destatis.de/EN/Homepage.html Statistisches Jahrbuch: Deutschland und Internationales	Annual		X	
Greece **Hellenic Statistical Authority, Pireus** http://www.statistics.gr/en/home Greece in Figures	Quarterly	X	X	
Hungary **Hungarian Central Statistical Office, Budapest** http://www.ksh.hu Statistical Yearbook of Hungary	Annual	X	X	X
Ireland **Central Statistics Office, Cork** http://www.cso.ie/en Statistical Yearbook of Ireland	Annual			X
Italy **Italian National Institute of Statistics, Rome** http://www.istat.it/en Annuario Statistico Italiano	Annual	X	X	X
Japan **Statistics Bureau, Ministry of Internal Affairs and Communications, Tokyo** http://www.stat.go.jp/english/data/index.html Japan Statistical Yearbook	Annual	X	X	X
Korea, South **Statistics Korea, Daejeon** http://kostat.go.kr/eng Korea Statistical Yearbook	Annual	X		

See footnotes at end of table.

Title	Frequency	Paper	Internet	
			PDF	Other *Formats*
Luxembourg **Service Central de la Statistique et des Etudes Economiques, Luxembourg** http://www.statistiques.public.lu/fr/acteurs/statec/index.html Annuaire statistique du Luxembourg	Annual	X	X	
Mexico **Instituto Nacional de Estadistica y Geografia, Aguascalientes** http://www.inegi.org.mx/ Anuario Estadístico de los Estados Unidos Mexicanos, 2016	Annual		X	X
Netherlands **Statistics Netherlands, The Hague** https://www.cbs.nl/nl-nl Trends in the Netherlands	Annual		X	X
New Zealand **Statistics New Zealand, Wellington** http://www.stats.govt.nz New Zealand Official Yearbook	Biennial		X	X
Poland **Central Statistical Office of Poland, Warsaw** http://stat.gov.pl/en/intrastat Concise Statistical Yearbook of Poland Statistical Yearbook of the Republic of Poland	Annual Annual	X X	X X	
Portugal **Statistics Portugal, Lisbon** https://www.ine.pt Statistical Yearbook of Portugal	Annual	X	X	X
Russia **Russian Federation Federal State Statistics Service, Moscow** http://www.gks.ru Russia in Figures	Annual			X
Slovakia **Statistical Office of the Slovak Republic, Bratislava** http://slovak.statistics.sk Statistical Yearbook of the Slovak Republic	Annual	X	X	X
Spain **Instituto Nacional de Estadistica, Madrid** http://www.ine.es/en/welcome_en.htm Statistical Yearbook of Spain	Annual	X	X	
Switzerland **Federal Statistical Office, Neuchâtel** https://www.bfs.admin.ch/bfs/en/home.html Statistisches Jahrbuch der Schweiz	Annual	X		
Turkey **Turkish Statistical Institute, Ankara** http://www.turkstat.gov.tr Turkey's Statistical Yearbook Turkey in Statistics	Annual Annual	X X	X X	X X
United Kingdom **Office for National Statistics, London** http://www.ons.gov.uk Annual Abstract of Statistics, 2011 (Discontinued)	Annual		X	

Source: ProQuest research.

Guide to State Statistical Abstracts

This bibliography includes the most recent statistical abstracts for states published since 2008, plus those that will be issued in 2020. For some states, a near equivalent has been listed in substitution for, or in addition to, a statistical abstract. All sources contain statistical tables on a variety of subjects for the state as a whole, its component parts, or both. Internet sites also contain statistical data.

Alabama

University of Alabama, Center for Business and Economic Research, Box 870221, Tuscaloosa, AL 35487-0221. 205-348-6191. Fax: 205-348-2951. Internet site <http://cber.culverhouse.ua.edu>.
Alabama Economic Outlook. Annual. Print.

Alaska

Department of Commerce, Community and Economic Development, P.O. Box 110804, Juneau, AK 99811. 907-465-2510. Fax: 907-465-3767. Internet site <http://commerce.alaska.gov/web/ded/>.
The Alaska Economic Performance Report, 2013. Online.
Alaska's Economic Report. Quarterly. Online.

Arizona

University of Arizona, Economic and Business Research Center, Eller College of Management, 1130 East Helen Street, McClelland Hall, Room 103, P.O. Box 210108, Tucson, AZ 85721-0108. 520-621-2155. Internet site <https://azeconomy.org/>.
Arizona's Economy. Quarterly. Online.

Arkansas

University of Arkansas at Little Rock, Arkansas Economic Development Institute, 2801 South University Avenue, Little Rock, AR 72204-1099. 501-569-8519. Internet site <http://youraedi.com/>.
Arkansas State and County Economic Data, 2017. Annual. Print and Online.
Arkansas Personal Income Handbook. Annual. Print and Online.

California

Department of Finance, 915 L Street, Sacramento, CA 95814. 916-445-3878. Internet site <http://www.dof.ca.gov/>.
Finance Bulletin. Monthly. Online.

Colorado

Colorado Department of Local Affairs, Division of Local Government, State Demography Office, 1313 Sherman Street, Room 521, Denver, CO 80203. 303-864-7720. Fax: 303-353-0751. Internet site <http://dola.colorado.gov/demog-cms/content/region-profiles>.
2017 Region Profiles and Reports. Online.

Connecticut

Connecticut Department of Economic and Community Development, 450 Columbus Boulevard, Hartford, CT 06103. 860-500-2300. Internet site <http://profiles.ctdata.org/>.
Connecticut Town Profiles, 2019. Recurring. Online.

Delaware

Delaware Economic Development Office, 99 Kings Highway, Dover, DE 19901-7305. 302-739-4271. Fax: 302-739-5749. Internet site <http://business.delaware.gov>.
Delaware Data Book, 2017. Online.

District of Columbia

Office of the City Administrator, John A. Wilson Building, 1350 Pennsylvania Avenue, NW, Suite 521, Washington, DC 20004. 202-478-9200. Fax: 202-727-9878. Internet site <http://opendata.dc.gov/>.
Open Data Catalog. Online.

Florida

University of Florida, Bureau of Economic and Business Research, P.O. Box 117148, Gainesville, FL 32611. 352-392-0171. Fax: 888-534-2404. Internet site <http://bebr.ufl.edu/data>.
Florida Statistical Dashboards. Online.

Georgia

University of Georgia, Terry College of Business, Selig Center for Economic Growth, E201 Ivester Hall, 650 S. Lumpkin St., Athens, GA 30602-6269. 706-542-5073. Internet site <http://www.terry.uga.edu/about/centers-institutes/selig>.
Georgia Economic Outlook, 2019. Annual. Online.

University of Georgia, Carl Vinson Institute of Government, 201 N. Milledge Avenue, Athens, GA 30602. 706-542-2736. Fax: 706-542-9301. Internet site <https://cviog.uga.edu/>.
The Georgia County Guide, 2020. Annual. Print.

Hawaii

Hawaii State Department of Business, Economic Development & Tourism, Research and Economic Analysis Division, Statistics and Data Support Branch, P.O. Box 2359, Honolulu, HI 96804. 808-586-2355. Internet site <http://dbedt.hawaii.gov/economic/databook/>.
2019 State of Hawaii Data Book. Annual. Online.

Idaho

University of Idaho Extension, 875 Perimeter Drive. MS 2338, Moscow, ID 83844-2338. 208-885-5883. Internet site <http://indicatorsidaho.org/>.
Indicators Idaho. Online.

Illinois

University of Illinois, Institute of Government and Public Affairs, 1007 W. Nevada Street, Urbana, IL 61801, MC-037. 217-333-3340. Fax: 217-244-4817. Internet site <http://igpa.uillinois.edu/>.

Indiana

Indiana University, Kelley School of Business, Indiana Business Research Center, 1309 E. 10th Street, Suite 4048, Bloomington, IN 47405. 812-855-5507. Internet site <http://stats.indiana.edu/>.
STATS Indiana. Online.

Iowa

Iowa State University of Science and Technology: Community Indicators Program, 17 East Hall, Ames, IA 50010. 515-294-9903. Fax: 515-294-0592. Internet site <http://icip.iastate.edu/>.
Community Indicators. Online.

State Library of Iowa, State Data Center, Ola Babcock Miller Building, 1112 East Grand, Des Moines, IA 50319-0233. 800-248-4483. Fax: 515-242-6543. Internet site <http://iowadatacenter.org>.

Kansas

University of Kansas, Institute for Policy and Social Research, 1541 Lilac Lane, 607 Blake Hall, Lawrence, KS 66045-3129. 785-864-3701. Fax: 785-864-3683. Internet site <http://ipsr.ku.edu/ksdata/ksah/>.
Kansas Statistical Abstract, 2018. Online.

Kentucky

Kentucky Cabinet for Economic Development, Old Capitol Annex, 300 West Broadway, Frankfort, KY 40601. 800-626-2930. Fax:502-564-3256. Internet site <http://thinkkentucky.com/>.

Louisiana

Louisiana State Census Data Center, Office of Electronic Services, 1201 N. Third Street, Suite 7-210, Baton Rouge, LA 70802. 225-342-7000. Internet site <https://louisiana.gov/demographics-and-geography/>.

Maine

Department of Administrative and Financial Services, 78 State House Station, Augusta, ME 04333. 207-624-7800. Fax: 207-624-7804. Internet site <http://maine.gov/portal/about_me/statistics.html>.

Maryland

Maryland Department of Planning, 301 W. Preston Street, Suite 1101, Baltimore, MD 21201. 410-767-3219. Internet site <http://mdp.state.md.us/msdc/>.
2018 Maryland Statistical Handbook. Annual. Online.

Massachusetts

MassCHIP, Massachusetts Department of Public Health, 250 Washington Street, Boston, MA 02108-4619. 617-624-5670. Internet site <http://mass.gov/dph/masschip>. Instant Topics. Online.

Michigan

Michigan Economic Development Corporation, 300 N. Washington Square, Lansing, MI 48913. 1-888-522-0103. Internet site <http://michiganbusiness.org>.

Minnesota

Minnesota Department of Employment and Economic Development, 1st National Bank Building, 332 Minnesota Street, Suite E200, Saint Paul, MN 55101-1351. 800-657-3858. Internet site <mn.gov/deed/data/>.
Compare Minnesota: Profiles of Minnesota's Economy & Population. Online.

Minnesota State Demographic Center, 658 Cedar Street, Room 300, Saint Paul, MN 55155. 651-296-2557. Internet site <http://demography.state.mn.us/>.

Mississippi

Mississippi Secretary of State, 401 Mississippi Street, Jackson, MS 39201. 601-359-1350. Internet site <http://sos.ms.gov/Education-Publications/Pages/Blue-Book-2016-2020.aspx>.
2016-2020 Mississippi Blue Book. Quadrennial. Online.

Missouri

University of Missouri—Columbia, Economic and Policy Analysis Research Center, 10 Professional Building, Columbia, MO 65211. 573-882-4805. Fax: 573-882-5563. Internet site <http://eparc.missouri.edu/>.
Missouri Statistical Data Archive. Online.

Montana

Montana Department of Commerce, Census and Economic Information Center, 301 S. Park Avenue, Helena, MT 59620-0533. 406-841-2742. Fax: 406-841-2871. Internet site <http://ceic.mt.gov/>.

Nebraska

Nebraska Department of Economic Development, P.O. Box 94666, 301 Centennial Mall South, Lincoln, NE 68509-4666. 800-426-6505. Fax: 402-471-3778. Internet site <https://opportunity.nebraska.gov/>.

Nevada

Nevada Department of Administration, Budget Division, 209 East Musser Street, Room 200, Carson City, NV 89701-4298. 775-684-0222. Fax: 775-684-0260. Internet site <http://budget.nv.gov/>.

New Hampshire

New Hampshire State Data Center, Governor Hugh J. Gallen State Office Park, Johnson Hall, 3rd Floor, 107 Pleasant Street, Concord, NH 03301-8501. 603-271-2155. Fax: 603-271-2615. Internet site <https://nh.gov/osi/data-center/>.

New Jersey

State of New Jersey Department of Labor and Workforce Development, Bureau of Labor Market Information, 1 John Fitch Plaza, P.O. Box 110, Trenton, NJ 08625-0110. 609-292-2582. Fax: 609-633-9240. Internet site <http://lwd.dol.state.nj.us/labor/lpa/LMI_index.html>.
Labor Market Information. Online.

New Mexico

University of New Mexico, Bureau of Business and Economic Research, 400 Cornell Dr NE, Albuquerque, NM 87106. 505-277-6626. Fax: 505-277-2773. Internet site <http://bber.unm.edu/>.
New Mexico's Economy: Current Situation and Outlook. Annual. Online.

New York

Nelson A. Rockefeller Institute of Government, 411 State Street, Albany, NY 12203-1003. 518-443-5522. Fax: 518-443-5788. Internet site <rockinst.org/>.
New York State Statistical Yearbook, 2015. Annual. Print and Online.

North Carolina

Office of State Budget and Management, MSC 20320, Raleigh, NC 27699-0320. 919-807-4700. Internet site <http://osbm.nc.gov/>.
State Comparisons. Online.

North Dakota

University of North Dakota, Nistler College of Business and Public Administration, Gamble Hall Room 110, 293 Centennial Drive, Stop 8098, Grand Forks, ND 58202-8098. 701-777-2135. Fax: 701-777-2019. Internet site <http://business.und.edu/>.

Ohio

Office of Research, Ohio Development Services Agency, 77 South High Street, Columbus, OH 43215-6130. 614-466-2116. Internet site <https://development.ohio.gov>.
Research Products and Services. Updated continuously.
Ohio County Trends. Online.

Oklahoma

University of Oklahoma, Center for Economic and Management Research, Michael F. Price College of Business, 307 West Brooks, Room 3, Norman, OK 73019-4004. 405-325-2931. Fax: 405-325-7688. Internet site <http://ou.edu/price/centersresearch/cemr.html>.
Statistical Abstract of Oklahoma, Annual. Print.

Oregon

Secretary of State, Archives Division, Archives Bldg., 800 Summer Street NE, Salem, OR 97310. 503-373-0701 ext.1. Fax: 503-378-4118. Internet site <http://arcweb.sos.state.or.us/>.
Oregon Blue Book. 2019-2020. Biennial. Online.

Pennsylvania

Pennsylvania State Data Center, Institute of State and Regional Affairs, Penn State Harrisburg, 777 West Harrisburg Pike, Middletown, PA 17057-4898. 717-948-6336. Fax: 717-948-6754. Internet site <http://pasdc.hbg.psu.edu>.
Pennsylvania Statistical Abstract, 2019. Print and electronic.

Rhode Island

Rhode Island Department of Labor and Training, Labor Market Information, 1511 Pontiac Avenue, Cranston, RI 02920. 401-462-8740. Fax: 401-462-8766. Internet site <http://dlt.ri.gov/lmi/>.
State of the State: A Statistical Profile of Rhode Island's Cities and Towns. Online.

South Carolina

South Carolina Revenue and Fiscal Affairs Offices, Health and Demographics Section, 1000 Assembly Street, Suite 402, Columbia, SC 29201. 803-898-9940. Internet site <http://abstract.sc.gov>.
South Carolina Statistical Abstract. Ongoing. Online.

South Dakota

South Dakota State University, Rural Life and Census Data Center, Box 504, Brookings, SD 57007. 605-688-4899. Internet site <http://sdstate.edu/soc/rlcdc/index.cfm>.
Preliminary Population Projections 2010-2035. Online.
South Dakota State and Demographic Profiles 2008. Online.

Tennessee

Tennessee State Data Center, 916 Volunteer Blvd., 716 Stokely Management Center, Knoxville, TN 37996-0570. 865-974-6070. Fax: 865-974-3100. Internet site <http://tndata.utk.edu/>.

Texas

Texas State Historical Association, 3001 Lake Austin Blvd., Suite 3.116, Austin, TX 78703. 512-471-2600. Fax: 512-473-8691. Internet site <http://www.tshaonline.org/publications/books/3196>.
Texas Almanac, 2018-2019. Biennial. Print and Online.

Texas State Data Center and Office of the State Demographer, Institute for Demographic and Socioeconomic Research (IDSER), 501 W. César E. Chavez Blvd., San Antonio, TX 78207-4415. 210-458-6543. Fax: 210-458-6541. Internet site <https://texasalmanac.com/>.

Utah

The University of Utah, Thomas S. Monson Center, 411 East South Temple Street, Salt Lake City, UT 84111. 801-585-5618. Internet site <gardner.utah.edu/economics-and-public-policy/economic-report-to-the-governor/>.
2020 Economic Report to the Governor. Annual. Online.

Vermont

Department of Labor, Labor Market Information, P.O. Box 488, Montpelier, VT 05601-0488. 802-828-4202. Fax: 802-828-4050. Internet site <http://vtlmi.info/>.
Vermont Economic-Demographic Profile, 2020. Annual. Online.

Virginia

University of Virginia, Weldon Cooper Center for Public Service, 2400 Old Ivy Road, P.O. Box 400206, Charlottesville, VA 22904-4206. 434-982-5522. Fax: 434-982-5524. Internet site <http://coopercenter.org/>.
Virginia Population Estimates. Online.
Virginia Population Projections. Online.

Washington

Washington State Office of Financial Management, Forecasting Division, P.O. Box 43113, Olympia, WA 98504-3113. 360-902-0599. Internet site <ofm.wa.gov/>.
Washington State Data Book, 2019. Biennial. Online.

West Virginia

West Virginia University, John Chambers College of Business and Economics, Bureau of Business and Economic Research, P.O. Box 6527, Morgantown, WV 26506-6025. 304-293-7831. Internet site <http://be.wvu.edu/bber/index.htm >.
West Virginia County Data Profile 2019. Annual. Online.
West Virginia Economic Outlook, 2019-2023. Annual. Online.

Wisconsin

Wisconsin Legislative Reference Bureau, One East Main Street, Suite 200, Madison, WI 53703. 608-266-0341. Internet site <http://legis.wisconsin.gov/lrb/>.
2019-2020 Wisconsin Blue Book. Biennial. Online.

Wyoming

Department of Administration and Information, Economic Analysis Division, 2800 Central Avenue, Cheyenne, WY 82002-0060. 307-777-7504. Fax: 307-632-1819. Internet site <http://eadiv.state.wy.us/>.
The Equality State Almanac, 2010. Annual. Online.
Wyoming and County Profiles, 2019. Annual. Online.

Metropolitan and Micropolitan Statistical Areas: Concepts, Components, and Population

The United States Office of Management and Budget (OMB) defines metropolitan and micropolitan statistical areas according to published standards that are applied to U.S. Census Bureau data. The general concept of a metropolitan or micropolitan statistical area is that of a core area containing a substantial population nucleus, together with adjacent communities having a high degree of economic and social integration with that core. Currently defined metropolitan and micropolitan statistical areas are based on application of 2010 standards (which appeared in the Federal Register on June 28, 2010) to 2010 decennial census data. OMB regularly updates metropolitan and micropolitan statistical area definitions. Data presented in this appendix use definitions effective as of September 2018.

Standard definitions of metropolitan areas were first issued in 1949 by the then Bureau of the Budget (predecessor of OMB), under the designation "standard metropolitan area" (SMA). The term was changed to "standard metropolitan statistical area" (SMSA) in 1959 and to "metropolitan statistical area" (MSA) in 1983. The term "metropolitan area" (MA) was adopted in 1990 and referred collectively to metropolitan statistical areas (MSAs), consolidated metropolitan statistical areas (CMSAs), and primary metropolitan statistical areas (PMSAs). The term "core-based statistical area" (CBSA) became effective in 2000 and refers collectively to metropolitan and micropolitan statistical areas.

OMB has been responsible for the official metropolitan areas since they were first defined, except for the period 1977 to 1981, when they were the responsibility of the Office of Federal Statistical Policy and Standards, U.S. Department of Commerce. The standards for defining metropolitan areas were modified in 1958, 1971, 1975, 1980, 1990, 2000, and 2010.

Defining Metropolitan and Micropolitan Statistical Areas—The 2010 standards provide that each CBSA must contain at least one urban area of 10,000 or more population. Each metropolitan statistical area must have at least one urbanized area of 50,000 or more inhabitants. Each micropolitan statistical area must have at least one urban cluster of at least 10,000 but less than 50,000 population.

Under the standards, the county (or counties) in which at least 50 percent of the population resides within urban areas of 10,000 or more population, or that contain at least 5,000 people residing within a single urban area of 10,000 or more population, is identified as a "central county" (counties). Additional "outlying counties" are included in the CBSA if they meet specific requirements of commuting to or from the central counties. Counties or equivalent entities form the geographic "building blocks" for metropolitan and micropolitan statistical areas throughout the United States and Puerto Rico.

If specific criteria are met, a metropolitan statistical area containing a single core with a population of 2.5 million or more may be subdivided to form smaller groupings of counties referred to as "metropolitan divisions."

As of September 2018, there are 384 metropolitan statistical areas and 542 micropolitan statistical areas in the United States. In addition, there are 8 metropolitan statistical areas and 4 micropolitan statistical areas in Puerto Rico.

Principal Cities and Metropolitan and Micropolitan Statistical Area Titles—The largest city in each metropolitan or micropolitan statistical area is designated a "principal city." Additional cities qualify if specific requirements are met concerning population size and employment. The title of each metropolitan or micropolitan statistical area consists of the names of up to three of its principal cities in order of descending population size and the name of each state into which the metropolitan or micropolitan statistical area extends. Titles of metropolitan divisions also typically are based on principal city names, but in certain cases consist of county names.

Defining New England City and Town Areas—Cities and towns are the primary units of local government in the six New England states, where counties, unlike elsewhere, have little or no official governmental functions. The 2010 standards provide for a set of geographic areas that are defined using cities and towns in the New England states. The New England city and town areas (NECTAs) are defined using the same criteria as metropolitan and micropolitan statistical areas and are identified as either metropolitan or micropolitan, based, respectively, on the presence of either an urbanized area of 50,000 or more population or an urban cluster of at least 10,000 but less than 50,000 population. If the specific criteria are met, a NECTA containing a single core with a population of at least 2.5 million may be subdivided to form smaller groupings of cities and towns referred to as New England city and town area divisions.

Changes in Definitions Over Time—Changes in the definitions of these statistical areas since the 1950 census have consisted chiefly of (1) the recognition of new areas as they reached the minimum required city or urbanized area population and (2) the addition of counties (or cities and towns in New England) to existing areas as new decennial census data showed them to qualify.

In some instances, formerly separate areas have been merged, components of an area have been transferred from one area to another, or components have been dropped from an area. The large majority of changes are based on decennial census data; however, Census Bureau data serve as the basis for intercensal updates in specific circumstances.

Because of these historical changes in geographic definitions, users must be cautious in comparing data for these statistical areas from different dates. For some purposes, comparisons of data for areas as defined at given dates may be appropriate; for other purposes, it may be preferable to maintain consistent area definitions. Historical metropolitan area definitions are available for 1950, 1960, 1963, 1970, 1973, 1981, 1983, 1990, 1993, and 1999.

Excluding Tables 22 through 24 in the Population section, Table 626 in the Labor Force section, Table 719 in the Income section, and the tables that follow in this appendix, the tables presenting data for metropolitan areas in this edition of the Statistical Abstract may be based on earlier metropolitan area definitions. See the Census Bureau website at <https://www.census.gov/programs-surveys/metro-micro.html> for information on historical delineations and component counties.

Table A. Metropolitan Statistical Areas and Components—Population: 2019

[In thousands (172 represents 172,000). Population as of July 2019. Metropolitan Statistical Areas defined by the U.S. Office of Management and Budget as of September 2018. All Metropolitan Statistical Areas are arranged alphabetically]

Metropolitan Statistical Area ~~Metropolitan Division ~~~~Component county	Popu- lation, 2019 (1,000)
Abilene, TX	**172**
Callahan County, TX	14
Jones County, TX	20
Taylor County, TX	138
Akron, OH	**703**
Portage County, OH	162
Summit County, OH	541
Albany, GA	**147**
Dougherty County, GA	88
Lee County, GA	30
Terrell County, GA	9
Worth County, GA	20
Albany-Lebanon, OR	**130**
Linn County, OR	130
Albany-Schenectady-Troy, NY	**880**
Albany County, NY	306
Rensselaer County, NY	159
Saratoga County, NY	230
Schenectady County, NY	155
Schoharie County, NY	31
Albuquerque, NM	**918**
Bernalillo County, NM	679
Sandoval County, NM	147
Torrance County, NM	15
Valencia County, NM	77
Alexandria, LA	**152**
Grant Parish, LA	22
Rapides Parish, LA	130
Allentown-Bethlehem-Easton, **PA-NJ**	**844**
Warren County, NJ	105
Carbon County, PA	64
Lehigh County, PA	369
Northampton County, PA	305
Altoona, PA	**122**
Blair County, PA	122
Amarillo, TX	**265**
Armstrong County, TX	2
Carson County, TX	6
Oldham County, TX	2
Potter County, TX	117
Randall County, TX	138
Ames, IA	**123**
Boone County, IA	26
Story County, IA	97
Anchorage, AK	**396**
Anchorage Municipality, AK	288
Matanuska-Susitna Borough, AK	108
Ann Arbor, MI	**368**
Washtenaw County, MI	368
Anniston-Oxford, AL	**114**
Calhoun County, AL	114
Appleton, WI	**238**
Calumet County, WI	50
Outagamie County, WI	188
Asheville, NC	**463**
Buncombe County, NC	261
Haywood County, NC	62
Henderson County, NC	117
Madison County, NC	22
Athens-Clarke County, GA	**214**
Clarke County, GA	128
Madison County, GA	30
Oconee County, GA	40
Oglethorpe County, GA	15
Atlanta-Sandy **Springs-Alpharetta, GA**	**6,020**
Barrow County, GA	83
Bartow County, GA	108
Butts County, GA	25
Carroll County, GA	120
Cherokee County, GA	259
Clayton County, GA	292
Cobb County, GA	760
Coweta County, GA	149
Dawson County, GA	26
DeKalb County, GA	759
Douglas County, GA	146
Fayette County, GA	114

Metropolitan Statistical Area ~~Metropolitan Division ~~~~Component county	Popu- lation, 2019 (1,000)
Forsyth County, GA	244
Fulton County, GA	1,064
Gwinnett County, GA	936
Haralson County, GA	30
Heard County, GA	12
Henry County, GA	235
Jasper County, GA	14
Lamar County, GA	19
Meriwether County, GA	21
Morgan County, GA	19
Newton County, GA	112
Paulding County, GA	169
Pickens County, GA	33
Pike County, GA	19
Rockdale County, GA	91
Spalding County, GA	67
Walton County, GA	95
Atlantic City-Hammonton, NJ	**264**
Atlantic County, NJ	264
Auburn-Opelika, AL	**165**
Lee County, AL	165
Augusta-Richmond County, **GA-SC**	**609**
Burke County, GA	22
Columbia County, GA	157
Lincoln County, GA	8
McDuffie County, GA	21
Richmond County, GA	203
Aiken County, SC	171
Edgefield County, SC	27
Austin-Round **Rock-Georgetown, TX**	**2,227**
Bastrop County, TX	89
Caldwell County, TX	44
Hays County, TX	230
Travis County, TX	1,274
Williamson County, TX	591
Bakersfield, CA	**900**
Kern County, CA	900
Baltimore-Columbia-Towson, **MD**	**2,800**
Anne Arundel County, MD	579
Baltimore County, MD	827
Carroll County, MD	168
Harford County, MD	255
Howard County, MD	326
Queen Anne's County, MD	50
Baltimore city, MD	593
Bangor, ME	**152**
Penobscot County, ME	152
Barnstable Town, MA	**213**
Barnstable County, MA	213
Baton Rouge, LA	**855**
Ascension Parish, LA	127
Assumption Parish, LA	22
East Baton Rouge Parish, LA	440
East Feliciana Parish, LA	19
Iberville Parish, LA	33
Livingston Parish, LA	141
Pointe Coupee Parish, LA	22
St. Helena Parish, LA	10
West Baton Rouge Parish, LA	26
West Feliciana Parish, LA	16
Battle Creek, MI	**134**
Calhoun County, MI	134
Bay City, MI	**103**
Bay County, MI	103
Beaumont-Port Arthur, TX	**393**
Hardin County, TX	58
Jefferson County, TX	252
Orange County, TX	83
Beckley, WV	**116**
Fayette County, WV	42
Raleigh County, WV	73
Bellingham, WA	**229**
Whatcom County, WA	229
Bend, OR	**198**
Deschutes County, OR	198
Billings, MT	**182**
Carbon County, MT	11

Metropolitan Statistical Area ~~Metropolitan Division ~~~~Component county	Popu- lation, 2019 (1,000)
Stillwater County, MT	10
Yellowstone County, MT	161
Binghamton, NY	**239**
Broome County, NY	190
Tioga County, NY	48
Birmingham-Hoover, AL	**1,090**
Bibb County, AL	22
Blount County, AL	58
Chilton County, AL	44
Jefferson County, AL	659
St. Clair County, AL	90
Shelby County, AL	218
Bismarck, ND	**129**
Burleigh County, ND	96
Morton County, ND	31
Oliver County, ND	2
Blacksburg-Christiansburg, **VA**	**168**
Giles County, VA	17
Montgomery County, VA	99
Pulaski County, VA	34
Radford city, VA	18
Bloomington, IL	**172**
McLean County, IL	172
Bloomington, IN	**169**
Monroe County, IN	148
Owen County, IN	21
Bloomsburg-Berwick, PA	**83**
Columbia County, PA	65
Montour County, PA	18
Boise City, ID	**749**
Ada County, ID	482
Boise County, ID	8
Canyon County, ID	230
Gem County, ID	18
Owyhee County, ID	12
Boston-Cambridge-Newton, **MA-NH**	**4,873**
Boston, MA	**2,032**
Norfolk County, MA	707
Plymouth County, MA	521
Suffolk County, MA	804
Cambridge-Newton- **Framingham, MA**	**2,401**
Essex County, MA	789
Middlesex County, MA	1,612
Rockingham County-Strafford **County, NH**	**440**
Rockingham County, NH	310
Strafford County, NH	131
Boulder, CO	**326**
Boulder County, CO	326
Bowling Green, KY	**179**
Allen County, KY	21
Butler County, KY	13
Edmonson County, KY	12
Warren County, KY	133
Bremerton-Silverdale-Port **Orchard, WA**	**271**
Kitsap County, WA	271
Bridgeport-Stamford-Norwalk, **CT**	**943**
Fairfield County, CT	943
Brownsville-Harlingen, TX	**423**
Cameron County, TX	423
Brunswick, GA	**119**
Brantley County, GA	19
Glynn County, GA	85
McIntosh County, GA	14
Buffalo-Cheektowaga, NY	**1,128**
Erie County, NY	919
Niagara County, NY	209
Burlington, NC	**170**
Alamance County, NC	170
Burlington-South Burlington, **VT**	**220**
Chittenden County, VT	164
Franklin County, VT	49
Grand Isle County, VT	7
California-Lexington Park, MD	**114**

See footnotes at end of table.

Table A. Metropolitan Statistical Areas and Components—Population: 2019 -Continued.

See headnote on page 911.

Metropolitan Statistical Area ~~Metropolitan Division ~~~~Component county	Population, 2019 (1,000)
St. Mary's County, MD	114
Canton-Massillon, OH	**398**
Carroll County, OH	27
Stark County, OH	371
Cape Coral-Fort Myers, FL	**771**
Lee County, FL	771
Cape Girardeau, MO-IL	**97**
Alexander County, IL	6
Bollinger County, MO	12
Cape Girardeau County, MO	79
Carbondale-Marion, IL	**136**
Jackson County, IL	57
Johnson County, IL	12
Williamson County, IL	67
Carson City, NV	**56**
Carson City, NV	56
Casper, WY	**80**
Natrona County, WY	80
Cedar Rapids, IA	**273**
Benton County, IA	26
Jones County, IA	21
Linn County, IA	227
Chambersburg-Waynesboro, PA	**155**
Franklin County, PA	155
Champaign-Urbana, IL	**226**
Champaign County, IL	210
Piatt County, IL	16
Charleston, WV	**257**
Boone County, WV	21
Clay County, WV	9
Jackson County, WV	29
Kanawha County, WV	178
Lincoln County, WV	20
Charleston-North Charleston, SC	**802**
Berkeley County, SC	228
Charleston County, SC	411
Dorchester County, SC	163
Charlotte-Concord-Gastonia, NC-SC	**2,637**
Anson County, NC	24
Cabarrus County, NC	216
Gaston County, NC	225
Iredell County, NC	182
Lincoln County, NC	86
Mecklenburg County, NC	1,110
Rowan County, NC	142
Union County, NC	240
Chester County, SC	32
Lancaster County, SC	98
York County, SC	281
Charlottesville, VA	**219**
Albemarle County, VA	109
Fluvanna County, VA	27
Greene County, VA	20
Nelson County, VA	15
Charlottesville city, VA	47
Chattanooga, TN-GA	**565**
Catoosa County, GA	68
Dade County, GA	16
Walker County, GA	70
Hamilton County, TN	368
Marion County, TN	29
Sequatchie County, TN	15
Cheyenne, WY	**100**
Laramie County, WY	100
Chicago-Naperville-Elgin, IL-IN-WI	**9,459**
Chicago-Naperville-Evanston, IL	**7,123**
Cook County, IL	5,150
DuPage County, IL	923
Grundy County, IL	51
McHenry County, IL	308
Will County, IL	691
Elgin, IL	**766**
DeKalb County, IL	105
Kane County, IL	532
Kendall County, IL	129
Gary, IN	**703**
Jasper County, IN	34
Lake County, IN	485

Metropolitan Statistical Area ~~Metropolitan Division ~~~~Component county	Population, 2019 (1,000)
Newton County, IN	14
Porter County, IN	170
Lake County-Kenosha County, IL-WI	**866**
Lake County, IL	697
Kenosha County, WI	170
Chico, CA	**219**
Butte County, CA	219
Cincinnati, OH-KY-IN	**2,221**
Dearborn County, IN	49
Franklin County, IN	23
Ohio County, IN	6
Union County, IN	7
Boone County, KY	134
Bracken County, KY	8
Campbell County, KY	94
Gallatin County, KY	9
Grant County, KY	25
Kenton County, KY	167
Pendleton County, KY	15
Brown County, OH	43
Butler County, OH	383
Clermont County, OH	206
Hamilton County, OH	817
Warren County, OH	235
Clarksville, TN-KY	**308**
Christian County, KY	70
Trigg County, KY	15
Montgomery County, TN	209
Stewart County, TN	14
Cleveland, TN	**125**
Bradley County, TN	108
Polk County, TN	17
Cleveland-Elyria, OH	**2,048**
Cuyahoga County, OH	1,235
Geauga County, OH	94
Lake County, OH	230
Lorain County, OH	310
Medina County, OH	180
Coeur d'Alene, ID	**166**
Kootenai County, ID	166
College Station-Bryan, TX	**265**
Brazos County, TX	229
Burleson County, TX	18
Robertson County, TX	17
Colorado Springs, CO	**746**
El Paso County, CO	720
Teller County, CO	25
Columbia, MO	**208**
Boone County, MO	180
Cooper County, MO	18
Howard County, MO	10
Columbia, SC	**838**
Calhoun County, SC	15
Fairfield County, SC	22
Kershaw County, SC	67
Lexington County, SC	299
Richland County, SC	416
Saluda County, SC	20
Columbus, GA-AL	**321**
Russell County, AL	58
Chattahoochee County, GA	11
Harris County, GA	35
Marion County, GA	8
Muscogee County, GA	196
Stewart County, GA	7
Talbot County, GA	6
Columbus, IN	**84**
Bartholomew County, IN	84
Columbus, OH	**2,122**
Delaware County, OH	209
Fairfield County, OH	158
Franklin County, OH	1,317
Hocking County, OH	28
Licking County, OH	177
Madison County, OH	45
Morrow County, OH	35
Perry County, OH	36
Pickaway County, OH	58
Union County, OH	59
Corpus Christi, TX	**429**
Nueces County, TX	362

Metropolitan Statistical Area ~~Metropolitan Division ~~~~Component county	Population, 2019 (1,000)
San Patricio County, TX	67
Corvallis, OR	**93**
Benton County, OR	93
Crestview-Fort Walton Beach-Destin, FL	**285**
Okaloosa County, FL	211
Walton County, FL	74
Cumberland, MD-WV	**97**
Allegany County, MD	70
Mineral County, WV	27
Dallas-Fort Worth-Arlington, TX	**7,573**
Dallas-Plano-Irving, TX	**5,082**
Collin County, TX	1,035
Dallas County, TX	2,636
Denton County, TX	887
Ellis County, TX	185
Hunt County, TX	99
Kaufman County, TX	136
Rockwall County, TX	105
Fort Worth-Arlington-Grapevine, TX	**2,491**
Johnson County, TX	176
Parker County, TX	143
Tarrant County, TX	2,103
Wise County, TX	70
Dalton, GA	**145**
Murray County, GA	40
Whitfield County, GA	105
Danville, IL	**76**
Vermilion County, IL	76
Daphne-Fairhope-Foley, AL	**223**
Baldwin County, AL	223
Davenport-Moline-Rock Island, IA-IL	**379**
Henry County, IL	49
Mercer County, IL	15
Rock Island County, IL	142
Scott County, IA	173
Dayton-Kettering, OH	**808**
Greene County, OH	169
Miami County, OH	107
Montgomery County, OH	532
Decatur, AL	**153**
Lawrence County, AL	33
Morgan County, AL	120
Decatur, IL	**104**
Macon County, IL	104
Deltona-Daytona Beach-Ormond Beach, FL	**668**
Flagler County, FL	115
Volusia County, FL	553
Denver-Aurora-Lakewood, CO	**2,967**
Adams County, CO	517
Arapahoe County, CO	657
Broomfield County, CO	70
Clear Creek County, CO	10
Denver County, CO	727
Douglas County, CO	351
Elbert County, CO	27
Gilpin County, CO	6
Jefferson County, CO	583
Park County, CO	19
Des Moines-West Des Moines, IA	**699**
Dallas County, IA	93
Guthrie County, IA	11
Jasper County, IA	37
Madison County, IA	16
Polk County, IA	490
Warren County, IA	51
Detroit-Warren-Dearborn, MI	**4,320**
Detroit-Dearborn-Livonia, MI	**1,749**
Wayne County, MI	1,749
Warren-Troy-Farmington Hills, MI	**2,570**
Lapeer County, MI	88
Livingston County, MI	192
Macomb County, MI	874
Oakland County, MI	1,258
St. Clair County, MI	159

See footnotes at end of table.

Table A. Metropolitan Statistical Areas and Components—Population:
2019-Continued.

See headnote on page 911.

Metropolitan Statistical Area ~~Metropolitan Division ~~~~Component county	Popu- lation, 2019 (1,000)
Dothan, AL	**149**
Geneva County, AL	26
Henry County, AL	17
Houston County, AL	106
Dover, DE	**181**
Kent County, DE	181
Dubuque, IA	**97**
Dubuque County, IA	97
Duluth, MN-WI	**289**
Carlton County, MN	36
Lake County, MN	11
St. Louis County, MN	199
Douglas County, WI	43
Durham-Chapel Hill, NC	**644**
Chatham County, NC	74
Durham County, NC	321
Granville County, NC	60
Orange County, NC	148
Person County, NC	39
East Stroudsburg, PA	**170**
Monroe County, PA	170
Eau Claire, WI	**169**
Chippewa County, WI	65
Eau Claire County, WI	105
El Centro, CA	**181**
Imperial County, CA	181
Elizabethtown-Fort Knox, KY	**154**
Hardin County, KY	111
Larue County, KY	14
Meade County, KY	29
Elkhart-Goshen, IN	**206**
Elkhart County, IN	206
Elmira, NY	**83**
Chemung County, NY	83
El Paso, TX	**844**
El Paso County, TX	839
Hudspeth County, TX	5
Enid, OK	**61**
Garfield County, OK	61
Erie, PA	**270**
Erie County, PA	270
Eugene-Springfield, OR	**382**
Lane County, OR	382
Evansville, IN-KY	**315**
Posey County, IN	25
Vanderburgh County, IN	181
Warrick County, IN	63
Henderson County, KY	45
Fairbanks, AK	**97**
Fairbanks North Star Borough, AK	97
Fargo, ND-MN	**246**
Clay County, MN	64
Cass County, ND	182
Farmington, NM	**124**
San Juan County, NM	124
Fayetteville, NC	**527**
Cumberland County, NC	336
Harnett County, NC	136
Hoke County, NC	55
Fayetteville-Springdale-Rogers, AR	**535**
Benton County, AR	279
Madison County, AR	17
Washington County, AR	239
Flagstaff, AZ	**143**
Coconino County, AZ	143
Flint, MI	**406**
Genesee County, MI	406
Florence, SC	**205**
Darlington County, SC	67
Florence County, SC	138
Florence-Muscle Shoals, AL	**148**
Colbert County, AL	55
Lauderdale County, AL	93
Fond du Lac, WI	**103**
Fond du Lac County, WI	103
Fort Collins, CO	**357**
Larimer County, CO	357
Fort Smith, AR-OK	**250**

Metropolitan Statistical Area ~~Metropolitan Division ~~~~Component county	Popu- lation, 2019 (1,000)
Crawford County, AR	63
Franklin County, AR	18
Sebastian County, AR	128
Sequoyah County, OK	42
Fort Wayne, IN	**413**
Allen County, IN	379
Whitley County, IN	34
Fresno, CA	**999**
Fresno County, CA	999
Gadsden, AL	**102**
Etowah County, AL	102
Gainesville, FL	**329**
Alachua County, FL	269
Gilchrist County, FL	19
Levy County, FL	42
Gainesville, GA	**204**
Hall County, GA	204
Gettysburg, PA	**103**
Adams County, PA	103
Glens Falls, NY	**125**
Warren County, NY	64
Washington County, NY	61
Goldsboro, NC	**123**
Wayne County, NC	123
Grand Forks, ND-MN	**101**
Polk County, MN	31
Grand Forks County, ND	69
Grand Island, NE	**76**
Hall County, NE	61
Howard County, NE	6
Merrick County, NE	8
Grand Junction, CO	**154**
Mesa County, CO	154
Grand Rapids-Kentwood, MI	**1,077**
Ionia County, MI	65
Kent County, MI	657
Montcalm County, MI	64
Ottawa County, MI	292
Grants Pass, OR	**87**
Josephine County, OR	87
Great Falls, MT	**81**
Cascade County, MT	81
Greeley, CO	**324**
Weld County, CO	324
Green Bay, WI	**323**
Brown County, WI	265
Kewaunee County, WI	20
Oconto County, WI	38
Greensboro-High Point, NC	**772**
Guilford County, NC	537
Randolph County, NC	144
Rockingham County, NC	91
Greenville, NC	**181**
Pitt County, NC	181
Greenville-Anderson, SC	**920**
Anderson County, SC	203
Greenville County, SC	524
Laurens County, SC	67
Pickens County, SC	127
Gulfport-Biloxi, MS	**418**
Hancock County, MS	48
Harrison County, MS	208
Jackson County, MS	144
Stone County, MS	18
Hagerstown-Martinsburg, MD-WV	**288**
Washington County, MD	151
Berkeley County, WV	119
Morgan County, WV	18
Hammond, LA	**135**
Tangipahoa Parish, LA	135
Hanford-Corcoran, CA	**153**
Kings County, CA	153
Harrisburg-Carlisle, PA	**578**
Cumberland County, PA	253
Dauphin County, PA	278
Perry County, PA	46
Harrisonburg, VA	**135**
Rockingham County, VA	82
Harrisonburg city, VA	53

Metropolitan Statistical Area ~~Metropolitan Division ~~~~Component county	Popu- lation, 2019 (1,000)
Hartford-East Hartford-Middletown, CT	**1,205**
Hartford County, CT	892
Middlesex County, CT	162
Tolland County, CT	151
Hattiesburg, MS	**169**
Covington County, MS	19
Forrest County, MS	75
Lamar County, MS	63
Perry County, MS	12
Hickory-Lenoir-Morganton, NC	**370**
Alexander County, NC	37
Burke County, NC	90
Caldwell County, NC	82
Catawba County, NC	160
Hilton Head Island-Bluffton, SC	**222**
Beaufort County, SC	192
Jasper County, SC	30
Hinesville, GA	**81**
Liberty County, GA	61
Long County, GA	20
Homosassa Springs, FL	**150**
Citrus County, FL	150
Hot Springs, AR	**99**
Garland County, AR	99
Houma-Thibodaux, LA	**208**
Lafourche Parish, LA	98
Terrebonne Parish, LA	110
Houston-The Woodlands-Sugar Land, TX	**7,066**
Austin County, TX	30
Brazoria County, TX	374
Chambers County, TX	44
Fort Bend County, TX	812
Galveston County, TX	342
Harris County, TX	4,713
Liberty County, TX	88
Montgomery County, TX	607
Waller County, TX	55
Huntington-Ashland, WV-KY-OH	**356**
Boyd County, KY	47
Carter County, KY	27
Greenup County, KY	35
Lawrence County, OH	59
Cabell County, WV	92
Putnam County, WV	56
Wayne County, WV	39
Huntsville, AL	**472**
Limestone County, AL	99
Madison County, AL	373
Idaho Falls, ID	**152**
Bonneville County, ID	119
Butte County, ID	3
Jefferson County, ID	30
Indianapolis-Carmel-Anderson, IN	**2,075**
Boone County, IN	68
Brown County, IN	15
Hamilton County, IN	338
Hancock County, IN	78
Hendricks County, IN	170
Johnson County, IN	158
Madison County, IN	130
Marion County, IN	965
Morgan County, IN	70
Putnam County, IN	38
Shelby County, IN	45
Iowa City, IA	**173**
Johnson County, IA	151
Washington County, IA	22
Ithaca, NY	**102**
Tompkins County, NY	102
Jackson, MI	**159**
Jackson County, MI	159
Jackson, MS	**595**
Copiah County, MS	28
Hinds County, MS	232

See footnotes at end of table.

Table A. Metropolitan Statistical Areas and Components—Population: 2019-Continued.

See headnote on page 911.

Metropolitan Statistical Area ~~Metropolitan Division ~~~~Component county	Popu- lation, 2019 (1,000)
Holmes County, MS	17
Madison County, MS	106
Rankin County, MS	155
Simpson County, MS	27
Yazoo County, MS	30
Jackson, TN	**179**
Chester County, TN	17
Crockett County, TN	14
Gibson County, TN	49
Madison County, TN	98
Jacksonville, FL	**1,560**
Baker County, FL	29
Clay County, FL	219
Duval County, FL	958
Nassau County, FL	89
St. Johns County, FL	265
Jacksonville, NC	**198**
Onslow County, NC	198
Janesville-Beloit, WI	**163**
Rock County, WI	163
Jefferson City, MO	**151**
Callaway County, MO	45
Cole County, MO	77
Moniteau County, MO	16
Osage County, MO	14
Johnson City, TN	**204**
Carter County, TN	56
Unicoi County, TN	18
Washington County, TN	129
Johnstown, PA	**130**
Cambria County, PA	130
Jonesboro, AR	**134**
Craighead County, AR	110
Poinsett County, AR	24
Joplin, MO	**180**
Jasper County, MO	121
Newton County, MO	58
Kahului-Wailuku-Lahaina, HI	**167**
Maui County, HI	167
Kalamazoo-Portage, MI	**265**
Kalamazoo County, MI	265
Kankakee, IL	**110**
Kankakee County, IL	110
Kansas City, MO-KS	**2,158**
Johnson County, KS	602
Leavenworth County, KS	82
Linn County, KS	10
Miami County, KS	34
Wyandotte County, KS	165
Bates County, MO	16
Caldwell County, MO	9
Cass County, MO	106
Clay County, MO	250
Clinton County, MO	20
Jackson County, MO	703
Lafayette County, MO	33
Platte County, MO	104
Ray County, MO	23
Kennewick-Richland, WA	**300**
Benton County, WA	204
Franklin County, WA	95
Killeen-Temple, TX	**460**
Bell County, TX	363
Coryell County, TX	76
Lampasas County, TX	21
Kingsport-Bristol, TN-VA	**307**
Hawkins County, TN	57
Sullivan County, TN	158
Scott County, VA	22
Washington County, VA	54
Bristol city, VA	17
Kingston, NY	**178**
Ulster County, NY	178
Knoxville, TN	**869**
Anderson County, TN	77
Blount County, TN	133
Campbell County, TN	40
Knox County, TN	470
Loudon County, TN	54
Morgan County, TN	21
Roane County, TN	53
Union County, TN	20
Kokomo, IN	**83**

Metropolitan Statistical Area ~~Metropolitan Division ~~~~Component county	Popu- lation, 2019 (1,000)
Howard County, IN	83
La Crosse-Onalaska, WI-MN	**137**
Houston County, MN	19
La Crosse County, WI	118
Lafayette, LA	**489**
Acadia Parish, LA	62
Iberia Parish, LA	70
Lafayette Parish, LA	244
St. Martin Parish, LA	53
Vermilion Parish, LA	60
Lafayette-West Lafayette, IN	**233**
Benton County, IN	9
Carroll County, IN	20
Tippecanoe County, IN	196
Warren County, IN	8
Lake Charles, LA	**210**
Calcasieu Parish, LA	203
Cameron Parish, LA	7
Lake Havasu City-Kingman, AZ	**212**
Mohave County, AZ	212
Lakeland-Winter Haven, FL	**725**
Polk County, FL	725
Lancaster, PA	**546**
Lancaster County, PA	546
Lansing-East Lansing, MI	**550**
Clinton County, MI	80
Eaton County, MI	110
Ingham County, MI	292
Shiawassee County, MI	68
Laredo, TX	**277**
Webb County, TX	277
Las Cruces, NM	**218**
Doña Ana County, NM	218
Las Vegas-Henderson- Paradise, NV	**2,267**
Clark County, NV	2,267
Lawrence, KS	**122**
Douglas County, KS	122
Lawton, OK	**126**
Comanche County, OK	121
Cotton County, OK	6
Lebanon, PA	**142**
Lebanon County, PA	142
Lewiston, ID-WA	**63**
Nez Perce County, ID	40
Asotin County, WA	23
Lewiston-Auburn, ME	**108**
Androscoggin County, ME	108
Lexington-Fayette, KY	**517**
Bourbon County, KY	20
Clark County, KY	36
Fayette County, KY	323
Jessamine County, KY	54
Scott County, KY	57
Woodford County, KY	27
Lima, OH	**102**
Allen County, OH	102
Lincoln, NE	**336**
Lancaster County, NE	319
Seward County, NE	17
Little Rock-North Little Rock-Conway, AR	**742**
Faulkner County, AR	126
Grant County, AR	18
Lonoke County, AR	73
Perry County, AR	10
Pulaski County, AR	392
Saline County, AR	122
Logan, UT-ID	**142**
Franklin County, ID	14
Cache County, UT	128
Longview, TX	**287**
Gregg County, TX	124
Harrison County, TX	67
Rusk County, TX	54
Upshur County, TX	42
Longview, WA	**111**
Cowlitz County, WA	111
Los Angeles-Long Beach-Anaheim, CA	**13,215**

Metropolitan Statistical Area ~~Metropolitan Division ~~~~Component county	Popu- lation, 2019 (1,000)
Anaheim-Santa Ana-Irvine, CA	**3,176**
Orange County, CA	3,176
Los Angeles-Long Beach-Glendale, CA	**10,039**
Los Angeles County, CA	10,039
Louisville/Jefferson County, KY-IN	**1,265**
Clark County, IN	118
Floyd County, IN	79
Harrison County, IN	41
Washington County, IN	28
Bullitt County, KY	82
Henry County, KY	16
Jefferson County, KY	767
Oldham County, KY	67
Shelby County, KY	49
Spencer County, KY	19
Lubbock, TX	**322**
Crosby County, TX	6
Lubbock County, TX	311
Lynn County, TX	6
Lynchburg, VA	**264**
Amherst County, VA	32
Appomattox County, VA	16
Bedford County, VA	79
Campbell County, VA	55
Lynchburg city, VA	82
Macon-Bibb County, GA	**230**
Bibb County, GA	153
Crawford County, GA	12
Jones County, GA	29
Monroe County, GA	28
Twiggs County, GA	8
Madera, CA	**157**
Madera County, CA	157
Madison, WI	**665**
Columbia County, WI	58
Dane County, WI	547
Green County, WI	37
Iowa County, WI	24
Manchester-Nashua, NH	**417**
Hillsborough County, NH	417
Manhattan, KS	**130**
Geary County, KS	32
Pottawatomie County, KS	24
Riley County, KS	74
Mankato, MN	**102**
Blue Earth County, MN	68
Nicollet County, MN	34
Mansfield, OH	**121**
Richland County, OH	121
McAllen-Edinburg-Mission, TX	**869**
Hidalgo County, TX	869
Medford, OR	**221**
Jackson County, OR	221
Memphis, TN-MS-AR	**1,346**
Crittenden County, AR	48
DeSoto County, MS	185
Marshall County, MS	35
Tate County, MS	28
Tunica County, MS	10
Fayette County, TN	41
Shelby County, TN	937
Tipton County, TN	62
Merced, CA	**278**
Merced County, CA	278
Miami-Fort Lauderdale- Pompano Beach, FL	**6,166**
Fort Lauderdale-Pompano Beach-Sunrise, FL	**1,953**
Broward County, FL	1,953
Miami-Miami Beach-Kendall, FL	**2,717**
Miami-Dade County, FL	2,717
West Palm Beach-Boca Raton-Boynton Beach, FL	**1,497**
Palm Beach County, FL	1,497
Michigan City-La Porte, IN	**110**

See footnotes at end of table.

Table A. Metropolitan Statistical Areas and Components—Population: 2019-Continued.

See headnote on page 911.

Metropolitan Statistical Area ~~Metropolitan Division ~~~~Component county	Population, 2019 (1,000)
LaPorte County, IN	110
Midland, MI	**83**
Midland County, MI	83
Midland, TX	**183**
Martin County, TX	6
Midland County, TX	177
Milwaukee-Waukesha, WI	**1,575**
Milwaukee County, WI	946
Ozaukee County, WI	89
Washington County, WI	136
Waukesha County, WI	404
Minneapolis-St. Paul-Bloomington, MN-WI	**3,640**
Anoka County, MN	357
Carver County, MN	105
Chisago County, MN	57
Dakota County, MN	429
Hennepin County, MN	1,266
Isanti County, MN	41
Le Sueur County, MN	29
Mille Lacs County, MN	26
Ramsey County, MN	550
Scott County, MN	149
Sherburne County, MN	97
Washington County, MN	262
Wright County, MN	138
Pierce County, WI	43
St. Croix County, WI	91
Missoula, MT	**120**
Missoula County, MT	120
Mobile, AL	**430**
Mobile County, AL	413
Washington County, AL	16
Modesto, CA	**551**
Stanislaus County, CA	551
Monroe, LA	**200**
Morehouse Parish, LA	25
Ouachita Parish, LA	153
Union Parish, LA	22
Monroe, MI	**151**
Monroe County, MI	151
Montgomery, AL	**373**
Autauga County, AL	56
Elmore County, AL	81
Lowndes County, AL	10
Montgomery County, AL	226
Morgantown, WV	**139**
Monongalia County, WV	106
Preston County, WV	33
Morristown, TN	**143**
Grainger County, TN	23
Hamblen County, TN	65
Jefferson County, TN	54
Mount Vernon-Anacortes, WA	**129**
Skagit County, WA	129
Muncie, IN	**114**
Delaware County, IN	114
Muskegon, MI	**174**
Muskegon County, MI	174
Myrtle Beach-Conway-North Myrtle Beach, SC-NC	**497**
Brunswick County, NC	143
Horry County, SC	354
Napa, CA	**138**
Napa County, CA	138
Naples-Marco Island, FL	**385**
Collier County, FL	385
Nashville-Davidson-- Murfreesboro--Franklin, TN	**1,934**
Cannon County, TN	15
Cheatham County, TN	41
Davidson County, TN	694
Dickson County, TN	54
Macon County, TN	25
Maury County, TN	96
Robertson County, TN	72
Rutherford County, TN	332
Smith County, TN	20
Sumner County, TN	191
Trousdale County, TN	11

Metropolitan Statistical Area ~~Metropolitan Division ~~~~Component county	Population, 2019 (1,000)
Williamson County, TN	238
Wilson County, TN	145
New Bern, NC	**124**
Craven County, NC	102
Jones County, NC	9
Pamlico County, NC	13
New Haven-Milford, CT	**855**
New Haven County, CT	855
New Orleans-Metairie, LA	**1,271**
Jefferson Parish, LA	432
Orleans Parish, LA	390
Plaquemines Parish, LA	23
St. Bernard Parish, LA	47
St. Charles Parish, LA	53
St. James Parish, LA	21
St. John the Baptist Parish, LA	43
St. Tammany Parish, LA	260
New York-Newark-Jersey City, NY-NJ-PA	**19,216**
Nassau County-Suffolk County, NY	**2,834**
Nassau County, NY	1,357
Suffolk County, NY	1,477
Newark, NJ-PA	**2,168**
Essex County, NJ	799
Hunterdon County, NJ	124
Morris County, NJ	492
Sussex County, NJ	140
Union County, NJ	556
Pike County, PA	56
New Brunswick-Lakewood, NJ	**2,380**
Middlesex County, NJ	825
Monmouth County, NJ	619
Ocean County, NJ	607
Somerset County, NJ	329
New York-Jersey City-White Plains, NY-NJ	**11,835**
Bergen County, NJ	932
Hudson County, NJ	672
Passaic County, NJ	502
Bronx County, NY	1,418
Kings County, NY	2,560
New York County, NY	1,629
Putnam County, NY	98
Queens County, NY	2,254
Richmond County, NY	476
Rockland County, NY	326
Westchester County, NY	968
Niles, MI	**153**
Berrien County, MI	153
North Port-Sarasota-Bradenton, FL	**837**
Manatee County, FL	403
Sarasota County, FL	434
Norwich-New London, CT	**265**
New London County, CT	265
Ocala, FL	**366**
Marion County, FL	366
Ocean City, NJ	**92**
Cape May County, NJ	92
Odessa, TX	**166**
Ector County, TX	166
Ogden-Clearfield, UT	**684**
Box Elder County, UT	56
Davis County, UT	355
Morgan County, UT	12
Weber County, UT	260
Oklahoma City, OK	**1,409**
Canadian County, OK	148
Cleveland County, OK	284
Grady County, OK	56
Lincoln County, OK	35
Logan County, OK	48
McClain County, OK	40
Oklahoma County, OK	797
Olympia-Lacey-Tumwater, WA	**291**
Thurston County, WA	291
Omaha-Council Bluffs, NE-IA	**949**
Harrison County, IA	14

Metropolitan Statistical Area ~~Metropolitan Division ~~~~Component county	Population, 2019 (1,000)
Mills County, IA	15
Pottawattamie County, IA	93
Cass County, NE	26
Douglas County, NE	571
Sarpy County, NE	187
Saunders County, NE	22
Washington County, NE	21
Orlando-Kissimmee-Sanford, FL	**2,608**
Lake County, FL	367
Orange County, FL	1,393
Osceola County, FL	376
Seminole County, FL	472
Oshkosh-Neenah, WI	**172**
Winnebago County, WI	172
Owensboro, KY	**119**
Daviess County, KY	102
Hancock County, KY	9
McLean County, KY	9
Oxnard-Thousand Oaks-Ventura, CA	**846**
Ventura County, CA	846
Palm Bay-Melbourne-Titusville, FL	**602**
Brevard County, FL	602
Panama City, FL	**175**
Bay County, FL	175
Parkersburg-Vienna, WV	**89**
Wirt County, WV	6
Wood County, WV	84
Pensacola-Ferry Pass-Brent, FL	**503**
Escambia County, FL	318
Santa Rosa County, FL	184
Peoria, IL	**401**
Fulton County, IL	34
Marshall County, IL	11
Peoria County, IL	179
Stark County, IL	5
Tazewell County, IL	132
Woodford County, IL	38
Philadelphia-Camden-Wilmington, PA-NJ-DE-MD	**6,102**
Camden, NJ	**1,243**
Burlington County, NJ	445
Camden County, NJ	506
Gloucester County, NJ	292
Montgomery-Bucks-Chester, PA	**1,984**
Bucks County, PA	628
Chester County, PA	525
Montgomery County, PA	831
Philadelphia, PA	**2,151**
Delaware County, PA	567
Philadelphia County, PA	1,584
Wilmington, DE-MD-NJ	**724**
New Castle County, DE	559
Cecil County, MD	103
Salem County, NJ	62
Phoenix-Mesa-Chandler, AZ	**4,948**
Maricopa County, AZ	4,485
Pinal County, AZ	463
Pine Bluff, AR	**88**
Cleveland County, AR	8
Jefferson County, AR	67
Lincoln County, AR	13
Pittsburgh, PA	**2,318**
Allegheny County, PA	1,216
Armstrong County, PA	65
Beaver County, PA	164
Butler County, PA	188
Fayette County, PA	129
Washington County, PA	207
Westmoreland County, PA	349
Pittsfield, MA	**125**
Berkshire County, MA	125
Pocatello, ID	**95**
Bannock County, ID	88
Power County, ID	8
Portland-South Portland, ME	**539**

See footnotes at end of table.

Table A. Metropolitan Statistical Areas and Components—Population: 2019-Continued.

See headnote on page 911.

Metropolitan Statistical Area ~~Metropolitan Division ~~~~Component county	Population, 2019 (1,000)
Cumberland County, ME	295
Sagadahoc County, ME	36
York County, ME	208
Portland-Vancouver-Hillsboro, OR-WA	**2,492**
Clackamas County, OR	418
Columbia County, OR	52
Multnomah County, OR	813
Washington County, OR	602
Yamhill County, OR	107
Clark County, WA	488
Skamania County, WA	12
Port St. Lucie, FL	**489**
Martin County, FL	161
St. Lucie County, FL	328
Poughkeepsie-Newburgh-Middletown, NY	**679**
Dutchess County, NY	294
Orange County, NY	385
Prescott Valley-Prescott, AZ	**235**
Yavapai County, AZ	235
Providence-Warwick, RI-MA	**1,625**
Bristol County, MA	565
Bristol County, RI	48
Kent County, RI	164
Newport County, RI	82
Providence County, RI	639
Washington County, RI	126
Provo-Orem, UT	**648**
Juab County, UT	12
Utah County, UT	636
Pueblo, CO	**168**
Pueblo County, CO	168
Punta Gorda, FL	**189**
Charlotte County, FL	189
Racine, WI	**196**
Racine County, WI	196
Raleigh-Cary, NC	**1,391**
Franklin County, NC	70
Johnston County, NC	209
Wake County, NC	1,112
Rapid City, SD	**142**
Meade County, SD	28
Pennington County, SD	114
Reading, PA	**421**
Berks County, PA	421
Redding, CA	**180**
Shasta County, CA	180
Reno, NV	**476**
Storey County, NV	4
Washoe County, NV	472
Richmond, VA	**1,292**
Amelia County, VA	13
Charles City County, VA	7
Chesterfield County, VA	353
Dinwiddie County, VA	29
Goochland County, VA	24
Hanover County, VA	108
Henrico County, VA	331
King and Queen County, VA	7
King William County, VA	17
New Kent County, VA	23
Powhatan County, VA	30
Prince George County, VA	38
Sussex County, VA	11
Colonial Heights city, VA	17
Hopewell city, VA	23
Petersburg city, VA	31
Richmond city, VA	230
Riverside-San Bernardino-Ontario, CA	**4,651**
Riverside County, CA	2,471
San Bernardino County, CA	2,180
Roanoke, VA	**313**
Botetourt County, VA	33
Craig County, VA	5
Franklin County, VA	56
Roanoke County, VA	94
Roanoke city, VA	99
Salem city, VA	25
Rochester, MN	**222**
Dodge County, MN	21
Fillmore County, MN	21

Metropolitan Statistical Area ~~Metropolitan Division ~~~~Component county	Population, 2019 (1,000)
Olmsted County, MN	158
Wabasha County, MN	22
Rochester, NY	**1,070**
Livingston County, NY	63
Monroe County, NY	742
Ontario County, NY	110
Orleans County, NY	40
Wayne County, NY	90
Yates County, NY	25
Rockford, IL	**336**
Boone County, IL	54
Winnebago County, IL	283
Rocky Mount, NC	**146**
Edgecombe County, NC	51
Nash County, NC	94
Rome, GA	**98**
Floyd County, GA	98
Sacramento-Roseville-Folsom, CA	**2,364**
El Dorado County, CA	193
Placer County, CA	398
Sacramento County, CA	1,552
Yolo County, CA	221
Saginaw, MI	**191**
Saginaw County, MI	191
St. Cloud, MN	**202**
Benton County, MN	41
Stearns County, MN	161
St. George, UT	**178**
Washington County, UT	178
St. Joseph, MO-KS	**125**
Doniphan County, KS	8
Andrew County, MO	18
Buchanan County, MO	87
DeKalb County, MO	13
St. Louis, MO-IL [1]	**2,803**
Bond County, IL	16
Calhoun County, IL	5
Clinton County, IL	38
Jersey County, IL	22
Macoupin County, IL	45
Madison County, IL	263
Monroe County, IL	35
St. Clair County, IL	260
Franklin County, MO	104
Jefferson County, MO	225
Lincoln County, MO	59
St. Charles County, MO	402
St. Louis County, MO	994
Warren County, MO	36
St. Louis city, MO	301
Salem, OR	**434**
Marion County, OR	348
Polk County, OR	86
Salinas, CA	**434**
Monterey County, CA	434
Salisbury, MD-DE	**416**
Sussex County, DE	234
Somerset County, MD	26
Wicomico County, MD	104
Worcester County, MD	52
Salt Lake City, UT	**1,233**
Salt Lake County, UT	1,160
Tooele County, UT	72
San Angelo, TX	**122**
Irion County, TX	2
Sterling County, TX	1
Tom Green County, TX	119
San Antonio-New Braunfels, TX	**2,551**
Atascosa County, TX	51
Bandera County, TX	23
Bexar County, TX	2,004
Comal County, TX	156
Guadalupe County, TX	167
Kendall County, TX	47
Medina County, TX	52
Wilson County, TX	51
San Diego-Chula Vista-Carlsbad, CA	**3,338**
San Diego County, CA	3,338

Metropolitan Statistical Area ~~Metropolitan Division ~~~~Component county	Population, 2019 (1,000)
San Francisco-Oakland-Berkeley, CA	**4,732**
Oakland-Berkeley-Livermore, CA	**2,825**
Alameda County, CA	1,671
Contra Costa County, CA	1,154
San Francisco-San Mateo-Redwood City, CA	**1,648**
San Francisco County, CA	882
San Mateo County, CA	767
San Rafael, CA	**259**
Marin County, CA	259
San Jose-Sunnyvale-Santa Clara, CA	**1,991**
San Benito County, CA	63
Santa Clara County, CA	1,928
San Luis Obispo-Paso Robles, CA	**283**
San Luis Obispo County, CA	283
Santa Cruz-Watsonville, CA	**273**
Santa Cruz County, CA	273
Santa Fe, NM	**150**
Santa Fe County, NM	150
Santa Maria-Santa Barbara, CA	**446**
Santa Barbara County, CA	446
Santa Rosa-Petaluma, CA	**494**
Sonoma County, CA	494
Savannah, GA	**393**
Bryan County, GA	40
Chatham County, GA	289
Effingham County, GA	64
Scranton--Wilkes-Barre, PA	**554**
Lackawanna County, PA	210
Luzerne County, PA	317
Wyoming County, PA	27
Seattle-Tacoma-Bellevue, WA	**3,980**
Seattle-Bellevue-Kent, WA	**3,075**
King County, WA	2,253
Snohomish County, WA	822
Tacoma-Lakewood, WA	**905**
Pierce County, WA	905
Sebastian-Vero Beach, FL	**160**
Indian River County, FL	160
Sebring-Avon Park, FL	**106**
Highlands County, FL	106
Sheboygan, WI	**115**
Sheboygan County, WI	115
Sherman-Denison, TX	**136**
Grayson County, TX	136
Shreveport-Bossier City, LA	**395**
Bossier Parish, LA	127
Caddo Parish, LA	240
De Soto Parish, LA	27
Sierra Vista-Douglas, AZ	**126**
Cochise County, AZ	126
Sioux City, IA-NE-SD	**145**
Woodbury County, IA	103
Dakota County, NE	20
Dixon County, NE	6
Union County, SD	16
Sioux Falls, SD	**268**
Lincoln County, SD	61
McCook County, SD	6
Minnehaha County, SD	193
Turner County, SD	8
South Bend-Mishawaka, IN-MI	**324**
St. Joseph County, IN	272
Cass County, MI	52
Spartanburg, SC	**320**
Spartanburg County, SC	320
Spokane-Spokane Valley, WA	**569**
Spokane County, WA	523
Stevens County, WA	46
Springfield, IL	**207**
Menard County, IL	12
Sangamon County, IL	195
Springfield, MA	**697**
Franklin County, MA	70
Hampden County, MA	466

See footnotes at end of table.

Table A. Metropolitan Statistical Areas and Components—Population: 2019-Continued.

See headnote on page 911.

Metropolitan Statistical Area ~~Metropolitan Division ~~~~Component county	Popu- lation, 2019 (1,000)
Hampshire County, MA	161
Springfield, MO	**470**
Christian County, MO	89
Dallas County, MO	17
Greene County, MO	293
Polk County, MO	32
Webster County, MO	40
Springfield, OH	**134**
Clark County, OH	134
State College, PA	**162**
Centre County, PA	162
Staunton, VA	**123**
Augusta County, VA	76
Staunton city, VA	25
Waynesboro city, VA	23
Stockton, CA	**762**
San Joaquin County, CA	762
Sumter, SC	**140**
Clarendon County, SC	34
Sumter County, SC	107
Syracuse, NY	**649**
Madison County, NY	71
Onondaga County, NY	461
Oswego County, NY	117
Tallahassee, FL	**387**
Gadsden County, FL	46
Jefferson County, FL	14
Leon County, FL	294
Wakulla County, FL	34
Tampa-St. Petersburg- **Clearwater, FL**	**3,195**
Hernando County, FL	194
Hillsborough County, FL	1,472
Pasco County, FL	554
Pinellas County, FL	975
Terre Haute, IN	**186**
Clay County, IN	26
Parke County, IN	17
Sullivan County, IN	21
Vermillion County, IN	15
Vigo County, IN	107
Texarkana, TX-AR	**149**
Little River County, AR	12
Miller County, AR	43
Bowie County, TX	93
The Villages, FL	**132**
Sumter County, FL	132
Toledo, OH	**642**
Fulton County, OH	42
Lucas County, OH	428
Ottawa County, OH	41
Wood County, OH	131
Topeka, KS	**232**
Jackson County, KS	13
Jefferson County, KS	19
Osage County, KS	16
Shawnee County, KS	177
Wabaunsee County, KS	7
Trenton-Princeton, NJ	**367**
Mercer County, NJ	367
Tucson, AZ	**1,047**
Pima County, AZ	1,047
Tulsa, OK	**999**
Creek County, OK	72
Okmulgee County, OK	38
Osage County, OK	47
Pawnee County, OK	16
Rogers County, OK	92
Tulsa County, OK	652
Wagoner County, OK	81
Tuscaloosa, AL	**252**
Greene County, AL	8
Hale County, AL	15
Pickens County, AL	20

Metropolitan Statistical Area ~~Metropolitan Division ~~~~Component county	Popu- lation, 2019 (1,000)
Tuscaloosa County, AL	209
Twin Falls, ID	**111**
Jerome County, ID	24
Twin Falls County, ID	87
Tyler, TX	**233**
Smith County, TX	233
Urban Honolulu, HI	**975**
Honolulu County, HI	975
Utica-Rome, NY	**290**
Herkimer County, NY	61
Oneida County, NY	229
Valdosta, GA	**147**
Brooks County, GA	15
Echols County, GA	4
Lanier County, GA	10
Lowndes County, GA	117
Vallejo, CA	**448**
Solano County, CA	448
Victoria, TX	**100**
Goliad County, TX	8
Victoria County, TX	92
Vineland-Bridgeton, NJ	**150**
Cumberland County, NJ	150
Virginia Beach-Norfolk-Newport **News, VA-NC**	**1,769**
Camden County, NC	11
Currituck County, NC	28
Gates County, NC	12
Gloucester County, VA	37
Isle of Wight County, VA	37
James City County, VA	77
Mathews County, VA	9
Southampton County, VA	18
York County, VA	68
Chesapeake city, VA	245
Franklin city, VA	8
Hampton city, VA	135
Newport News city, VA	179
Norfolk city, VA	243
Poquoson city, VA	12
Portsmouth city, VA	94
Suffolk city, VA	92
Virginia Beach city, VA	450
Williamsburg city, VA	15
Visalia, CA	**466**
Tulare County, CA	466
Waco, TX	**274**
Falls County, TX	17
McLennan County, TX	257
Walla Walla, WA	**61**
Walla Walla County, WA	61
Warner Robins, GA	**185**
Houston County, GA	158
Peach County, GA	28
Washington-Arlington- **Alexandria, DC-VA-MD-WV**	**6,280**
Frederick-Gaithersburg- **Rockville, MD**	**1,310**
Frederick County, MD	260
Montgomery County, MD	1,051
Washington-Arlington- **Alexandria, DC-VA-MD-WV**	**4,970**
District of Columbia, DC	706
Calvert County, MD	93
Charles County, MD	163
Prince George's County, MD	909
Arlington County, VA	237
Clarke County, VA	15
Culpeper County, VA	53
Fairfax County, VA	1,148
Fauquier County, VA	71
Loudoun County, VA	414
Madison County, VA	13
Prince William County, VA	470

Metropolitan Statistical Area ~~Metropolitan Division ~~~~Component county	Popu- lation, 2019 (1,000)
Rappahannock County, VA	7
Spotsylvania County, VA	136
Stafford County, VA	153
Warren County, VA	40
Alexandria city, VA	159
Fairfax city, VA	24
Falls Church city, VA	15
Fredericksburg city, VA	29
Manassas city, VA	41
Manassas Park city, VA	17
Jefferson County, WV	57
Waterloo-Cedar Falls, IA	**169**
Black Hawk County, IA	131
Bremer County, IA	25
Grundy County, IA	12
Watertown-Fort Drum, NY	**110**
Jefferson County, NY	110
Wausau-Weston, WI	**163**
Lincoln County, WI	28
Marathon County, WI	136
Weirton-Steubenville, WV-OH	**116**
Jefferson County, OH	65
Brooke County, WV	22
Hancock County, WV	29
Wenatchee, WA	**121**
Chelan County, WA	77
Douglas County, WA	43
Wheeling, WV-OH	**139**
Belmont County, OH	67
Marshall County, WV	31
Ohio County, WV	41
Wichita, KS	**640**
Butler County, KS	67
Harvey County, KS	34
Sedgwick County, KS	516
Sumner County, KS	23
Wichita Falls, TX	**151**
Archer County, TX	9
Clay County, TX	10
Wichita County, TX	132
Williamsport, PA	**113**
Lycoming County, PA	113
Wilmington, NC	**298**
New Hanover County, NC	234
Pender County, NC	63
Winchester, VA-WV	**141**
Frederick County, VA	89
Winchester city, VA	28
Hampshire County, WV	23
Winston-Salem, NC	**676**
Davidson County, NC	168
Davie County, NC	43
Forsyth County, NC	382
Stokes County, NC	46
Yadkin County, NC	38
Worcester, MA-CT	**947**
Windham County, CT	117
Worcester County, MA	831
Yakima, WA	**251**
Yakima County, WA	251
York-Hanover, PA	**449**
York County, PA	449
Youngstown-Warren- **Boardman, OH-PA**	**536**
Mahoning County, OH	229
Trumbull County, OH	198
Mercer County, PA	109
Yuba City, CA	**176**
Sutter County, CA	97
Yuba County, CA	79
Yuma, AZ	**214**
Yuma County, AZ	214

[1] The portion of Sullivan city in Crawford County, Missouri, is legally part of the St. Louis, MO-IL Metropolitan Statistical Area. The estimate shown here for the St. Louis, MO-IL Metropolitan Statistical Area does not include this area.

Source: U.S. Census Bureau, 2019 Population Estimates, <census.gov/programs-surveys/metro-micro/data/tables.html>.

Table B. Micropolitan Statistical Areas and Components—Population: 2019

[In thousands (43 represents 43,000). Population as of July 2019. Micropolitan Statistical Areas defined by the U.S. Office of Management and Budget as of September 2018. All Micropolitan Statistical Areas are arranged alphabetically]

Micropolitan Statistical Area ~~Component county	Population, 2019 (1,000)
Aberdeen, SD	**43**
Brown County, SD	39
Edmunds County, SD	4
Aberdeen, WA	**75**
Grays Harbor County, WA	75
Ada, OK	**38**
Pontotoc County, OK	38
Adrian, MI	**98**
Lenawee County, MI	98
Alamogordo, NM	**67**
Otero County, NM	67
Albemarle, NC	**63**
Stanly County, NC	63
Albert Lea, MN	**30**
Freeborn County, MN	30
Albertville, AL	**97**
Marshall County, AL	97
Alexander City, AL	**51**
Coosa County, AL	11
Tallapoosa County, AL	40
Alexandria, MN	**38**
Douglas County, MN	38
Alice, TX	**52**
Duval County, TX	11
Jim Wells County, TX	40
Alma, MI	**41**
Gratiot County, MI	41
Alpena, MI	**28**
Alpena County, MI	28
Altus, OK	**25**
Jackson County, OK	25
Americus, GA	**35**
Schley County, GA	5
Sumter County, GA	30
Amsterdam, NY	**49**
Montgomery County, NY	49
Andrews, TX	**19**
Andrews County, TX	19
Angola, IN	**35**
Steuben County, IN	35
Arcadia, FL	**38**
DeSoto County, FL	38
Ardmore, OK	**58**
Carter County, OK	48
Love County, OK	10
Arkadelphia, AR	**22**
Clark County, AR	22
Ashland, OH	**53**
Ashland County, OH	53
Ashtabula, OH	**97**
Ashtabula County, OH	97
Astoria, OR	**40**
Clatsop County, OR	40
Atchison, KS	**16**
Atchison County, KS	16
Athens, OH	**65**
Athens County, OH	65
Athens, TN	**54**
McMinn County, TN	54
Athens, TX	**83**
Henderson County, TX	83
Atmore, AL	**37**
Escambia County, AL	37
Auburn, IN	**43**
DeKalb County, IN	43
Auburn, NY	**77**
Cayuga County, NY	77
Augusta-Waterville, ME	**122**
Kennebec County, ME	122
Austin, MN	**40**
Mower County, MN	40
Bainbridge, GA	**26**
Decatur County, GA	26
Baraboo, WI	**64**
Sauk County, WI	64
Bardstown, KY	**46**
Nelson County, KY	46
Barre, VT	**58**
Washington County, VT	58
Bartlesville, OK	**52**
Washington County, OK	52

Micropolitan Statistical Area ~~Component county	Population, 2019 (1,000)
Batavia, NY	**57**
Genesee County, NY	57
Batesville, AR	**55**
Independence County, AR	38
Sharp County, AR	17
Bay City, TX	**37**
Matagorda County, TX	37
Beatrice, NE	**22**
Gage County, NE	22
Beaver Dam, WI	**88**
Dodge County, WI	88
Bedford, IN	**45**
Lawrence County, IN	45
Beeville, TX	**33**
Bee County, TX	33
Bellefontaine, OH	**46**
Logan County, OH	46
Bemidji, MN	**47**
Beltrami County, MN	47
Bennettsville, SC	**26**
Marlboro County, SC	26
Bennington, VT	**35**
Bennington County, VT	35
Berlin, NH	**32**
Coos County, NH	32
Big Rapids, MI	**43**
Mecosta County, MI	43
Big Spring, TX	**37**
Howard County, TX	37
Big Stone Gap, VA	**41**
Wise County, VA	37
Norton city, VA	4
Blackfoot, ID	**47**
Bingham County, ID	47
Bluefield, WV-VA	**106**
Bland County, VA	6
Tazewell County, VA	41
Mercer County, WV	59
Blytheville, AR	**41**
Mississippi County, AR	41
Bogalusa, LA	**46**
Washington Parish, LA	46
Bonham, TX	**36**
Fannin County, TX	36
Boone, NC	**56**
Watauga County, NC	56
Borger, TX	**21**
Hutchinson County, TX	21
Bozeman, MT	**114**
Gallatin County, MT	114
Bradford, PA	**41**
McKean County, PA	41
Brainerd, MN	**95**
Cass County, MN	30
Crow Wing County, MN	65
Branson, MO	**56**
Taney County, MO	56
Breckenridge, CO	**31**
Summit County, CO	31
Brenham, TX	**36**
Washington County, TX	36
Brevard, NC	**34**
Transylvania County, NC	34
Brookhaven, MS	**34**
Lincoln County, MS	34
Brookings, OR	**23**
Curry County, OR	23
Brookings, SD	**35**
Brookings County, SD	35
Brownsville, TN	**17**
Haywood County, TN	17
Brownwood, TX	**38**
Brown County, TX	38
Bucyrus-Galion, OH	**41**
Crawford County, OH	41
Burley, ID	**45**
Cassia County, ID	24
Minidoka County, ID	21
Burlington, IA-IL	**46**
Henderson County, IL	7
Des Moines County, IA	39
Butte-Silver Bow, MT	**35**

Micropolitan Statistical Area ~~Component county	Population, 2019 (1,000)
Silver Bow County, MT	35
Cadillac, MI	**49**
Missaukee County, MI	15
Wexford County, MI	34
Calhoun, GA	**58**
Gordon County, GA	58
Cambridge, MD	**32**
Dorchester County, MD	32
Cambridge, OH	**39**
Guernsey County, OH	39
Camden, AR	**29**
Calhoun County, AR	5
Ouachita County, AR	23
Campbellsville, KY	**37**
Green County, KY	11
Taylor County, KY	26
Cañon City, CO	**48**
Fremont County, CO	48
Carlsbad-Artesia, NM	**58**
Eddy County, NM	58
Carroll, IA	**20**
Carroll County, IA	20
Cedar City, UT	**55**
Iron County, UT	55
Cedartown, GA	**43**
Polk County, GA	43
Celina, OH	**41**
Mercer County, OH	41
Central City, KY	**31**
Muhlenberg County, KY	31
Centralia, IL	**37**
Marion County, IL	37
Centralia, WA	**81**
Lewis County, WA	81
Charleston-Mattoon, IL	**61**
Coles County, IL	51
Cumberland County, IL	11
Chillicothe, OH	**77**
Ross County, OH	77
Clarksburg, WV	**92**
Doddridge County, WV	8
Harrison County, WV	67
Taylor County, WV	17
Clarksdale, MS	**22**
Coahoma County, MS	22
Clearlake, CA	**64**
Lake County, CA	64
Cleveland, MS	**31**
Bolivar County, MS	31
Clewiston, FL	**42**
Hendry County, FL	42
Clinton, IA	**46**
Clinton County, IA	46
Clovis, NM	**49**
Curry County, NM	49
Coffeyville, KS	**32**
Montgomery County, KS	32
Coldwater, MI	**44**
Branch County, MI	44
Columbus, MS	**59**
Lowndes County, MS	59
Columbus, NE	**33**
Platte County, NE	33
Concord, NH	**151**
Merrimack County, NH	151
Connersville, IN	**23**
Fayette County, IN	23
Cookeville, TN	**114**
Jackson County, TN	12
Overton County, TN	22
Putnam County, TN	80
Coos Bay, OR	**64**
Coos County, OR	64
Cordele, GA	**22**
Crisp County, GA	22
Corinth, MS	**37**
Alcorn County, MS	37
Cornelia, GA	**45**
Habersham County, GA	45
Corning, NY	**95**
Steuben County, NY	95
Corsicana, TX	**50**

See footnotes at end of table.

Table B. Micropolitan Statistical Areas and Components—Population: 2019-Continued.

See headnote on page 918.

Micropolitan Statistical Area ~~Component county	Population, 2019 (1,000)	Micropolitan Statistical Area ~~Component county	Population, 2019 (1,000)	Micropolitan Statistical Area ~~Component county	Population, 2019 (1,000)
Navarro County, TX	50	Elko County, NV	53	Kearny County, KS	4
Cortland, NY	**48**	Eureka County, NV	2	**Gardnerville Ranchos, NV**	**49**
Cortland County, NY	48	**Ellensburg, WA**	**48**	Douglas County, NV	49
Coshocton, OH	**37**	Kittitas County, WA	48	**Georgetown, SC**	**63**
Coshocton County, OH	37	**Emporia, KS**	**36**	Georgetown County, SC	63
Craig, CO	**13**	Chase County, KS	3	**Gillette, WY**	**61**
Moffat County, CO	13	Lyon County, KS	33	Campbell County, WY	46
Crawfordsville, IN	**38**	**Enterprise, AL**	**52**	Crook County, WY	8
Montgomery County, IN	38	Coffee County, AL	52	Weston County, WY	7
Crescent City, CA	**28**	**Escanaba, MI**	**36**	**Glasgow, KY**	**54**
Del Norte County, CA	28	Delta County, MI	36	Barren County, KY	44
Crossville, TN	**61**	**Española, NM**	**39**	Metcalfe County, KY	10
Cumberland County, TN	61	Rio Arriba County, NM	39	**Glenwood Springs, CO**	**78**
Cullman, AL	**84**	**Eufaula, AL-GA**	**27**	Garfield County, CO	60
Cullman County, AL	84	Barbour County, AL	25	Pitkin County, CO	18
Cullowhee, NC	**58**	Quitman County, GA	2	**Gloversville, NY**	**53**
Jackson County, NC	44	**Eureka-Arcata, CA**	**136**	Fulton County, NY	53
Swain County, NC	14	Humboldt County, CA	136	**Granbury, TX**	**62**
Danville, KY	**55**	**Evanston, WY**	**20**	Hood County, TX	62
Boyle County, KY	30	Uinta County, WY	20	**Grand Rapids, MN**	**45**
Lincoln County, KY	25	**Fairfield, IA**	**18**	Itasca County, MN	45
Danville, VA	**100**	Jefferson County, IA	18	**Grants, NM**	**27**
Pittsylvania County, VA	60	**Fairmont, MN**	**20**	Cibola County, NM	27
Danville city, VA	40	Martin County, MN	20	**Great Bend, KS**	**26**
Dayton, TN	**33**	**Fairmont, WV**	**56**	Barton County, KS	26
Rhea County, TN	33	Marion County, WV	56	**Greeneville, TN**	**69**
Decatur, IN	**36**	**Fallon, NV**	**25**	Greene County, TN	69
Adams County, IN	36	Churchill County, NV	25	**Greensburg, IN**	**27**
Defiance, OH	**38**	**Faribault-Northfield, MN**	**67**	Decatur County, IN	27
Defiance County, OH	38	Rice County, MN	67	**Greenville, MS**	**44**
Del Rio, TX	**49**	**Farmington, MO**	**67**	Washington County, MS	44
Val Verde County, TX	49	St. Francois County, MO	67	**Greenville, OH**	**51**
Deming, NM	**24**	**Fergus Falls, MN**	**59**	Darke County, OH	51
Luna County, NM	24	Otter Tail County, MN	59	**Greenwood, MS**	**38**
DeRidder, LA	**37**	**Fernley, NV**	**58**	Carroll County, MS	10
Beauregard Parish, LA	37	Lyon County, NV	58	Leflore County, MS	28
Dickinson, ND	**32**	**Findlay, OH**	**76**	**Greenwood, SC**	**71**
Billings County, ND	1	Hancock County, OH	76	Greenwood County, SC	71
Stark County, ND	31	**Fitzgerald, GA**	**17**	**Grenada, MS**	**21**
Dixon, IL	**34**	Ben Hill County, GA	17	Grenada County, MS	21
Lee County, IL	34	**Forest City, NC**	**67**	**Guymon, OK**	**20**
Dodge City, KS	**34**	Rutherford County, NC	67	Texas County, OK	20
Ford County, KS	34	**Forrest City, AR**	**25**	**Hailey, ID**	**24**
Douglas, GA	**51**	St. Francis County, AR	25	Blaine County, ID	23
Atkinson County, GA	8	**Fort Dodge, IA**	**36**	Camas County, ID	1
Coffee County, GA	43	Webster County, IA	36	**Hannibal, MO**	**39**
Dublin, GA	**64**	**Fort Leonard Wood, MO**	**53**	Marion County, MO	29
Johnson County, GA	10	Pulaski County, MO	53	Ralls County, MO	10
Laurens County, GA	48	**Fort Madison-Keokuk,**		**Harrison, AR**	**45**
Treutlen County, GA	7	**IA-IL-MO**	**58**	Boone County, AR	37
DuBois, PA	**79**	Hancock County, IL	18	Newton County, AR	8
Clearfield County, PA	79	Lee County, IA	34	**Hastings, NE**	**31**
Dumas, TX	**21**	Clark County, MO	7	Adams County, NE	31
Moore County, TX	21	**Fort Morgan, CO**	**29**	**Hays, KS**	**29**
Duncan, OK	**43**	Morgan County, CO	29	Ellis County, KS	29
Stephens County, OK	43	**Fort Payne, AL**	**72**	**Heber, UT**	**76**
Durango, CO	**56**	DeKalb County, AL	72	Summit County, UT	42
La Plata County, CO	56	**Fort Polk South, LA**	**47**	Wasatch County, UT	34
Durant, OK	**48**	Vernon Parish, LA	47	**Helena, MT**	**82**
Bryan County, OK	48	**Frankfort, IN**	**32**	Jefferson County, MT	12
Dyersburg, TN	**37**	Clinton County, IN	32	Lewis and Clark County, MT	69
Dyer County, TN	37	**Frankfort, KY**	**74**	**Helena-West Helena, AR**	**18**
Eagle Pass, TX	**59**	Anderson County, KY	23	Phillips County, AR	18
Maverick County, TX	59	Franklin County, KY	51	**Henderson, NC**	**45**
Easton, MD	**37**	**Fredericksburg, TX**	**27**	Vance County, NC	45
Talbot County, MD	37	Gillespie County, TX	27	**Hereford, TX**	**19**
Edwards, CO	**55**	**Freeport, IL**	**44**	Deaf Smith County, TX	19
Eagle County, CO	55	Stephenson County, IL	44	**Hermiston-Pendleton, OR**	**90**
Effingham, IL	**34**	**Fremont, NE**	**37**	Morrow County, OR	12
Effingham County, IL	34	Dodge County, NE	37	Umatilla County, OR	78
El Campo, TX	**42**	**Fremont, OH**	**59**	**Hillsdale, MI**	**46**
Wharton County, TX	42	Sandusky County, OH	59	Hillsdale County, MI	46
El Dorado, AR	**39**	**Gaffney, SC**	**57**	**Hilo, HI**	**202**
Union County, AR	39	Cherokee County, SC	57	Hawaii County, HI	202
Elizabeth City, NC	**53**	**Gainesville, TX**	**41**	**Hobbs, NM**	**71**
Pasquotank County, NC	40	Cooke County, TX	41	Lea County, NM	71
Perquimans County, NC	13	**Galesburg, IL**	**50**	**Holland, MI**	**118**
Elk City, OK	**22**	Knox County, IL	50	Allegan County, MI	118
Beckham County, OK	22	**Gallup, NM**	**71**	**Hood River, OR**	**23**
Elkins, WV	**29**	McKinley County, NM	71	Hood River County, OR	23
Randolph County, WV	29	**Garden City, KS**	**40**	**Hope, AR**	**30**
Elko, NV	**55**	Finney County, KS	36	Hempstead County, AR	22

See footnotes at end of table.

Microplitan Statistical Area ~~Component county	Population, 2019 (1,000)
Nevada County, AR	8
Houghton, MI	**38**
Houghton County, MI	36
Keweenaw County, MI	2
Hudson, NY	**59**
Columbia County, NY	59
Huntingdon, PA	**45**
Huntingdon County, PA	45
Huntington, IN	**37**
Huntington County, IN	37
Huntsville, TX	**73**
Walker County, TX	73
Huron, SD	**20**
Beadle County, SD	18
Jerauld County, SD	2
Hutchinson, KS	**62**
Reno County, KS	62
Hutchinson, MN	**36**
McLeod County, MN	36
Indiana, PA	**84**
Indiana County, PA	84
Indianola, MS	**25**
Sunflower County, MS	25
Iron Mountain, MI-WI	**30**
Dickinson County, MI	25
Florence County, WI	4
Jackson, OH	**32**
Jackson County, OH	32
Jackson, WY-ID	**36**
Teton County, ID	12
Teton County, WY	23
Jacksonville, IL	**39**
Morgan County, IL	34
Scott County, IL	5
Jacksonville, TX	**53**
Cherokee County, TX	53
Jamestown, ND	**21**
Stutsman County, ND	21
Jamestown-Dunkirk-Fredonia, NY	**127**
Chautauqua County, NY	127
Jasper, AL	**64**
Walker County, AL	64
Jasper, IN	**55**
Dubois County, IN	43
Pike County, IN	12
Jefferson, GA	**73**
Jackson County, GA	73
Jennings, LA	**31**
Jefferson Davis Parish, LA	31
Jesup, GA	**30**
Wayne County, GA	30
Juneau, AK	**32**
Juneau City and Borough, AK	32
Kalispell, MT	**104**
Flathead County, MT	104
Kapaa, HI	**72**
Kauai County, HI	72
Kearney, NE	**56**
Buffalo County, NE	50
Kearney County, NE	6
Keene, NH	**76**
Cheshire County, NH	76
Kendallville, IN	**48**
Noble County, IN	48
Kennett, MO	**29**
Dunklin County, MO	29
Kerrville, TX	**53**
Kerr County, TX	53
Ketchikan, AK	**14**
Ketchikan Gateway Borough, AK	14
Key West, FL	**74**
Monroe County, FL	74
Kill Devil Hills, NC	**37**
Dare County, NC	37
Kingsville, TX	**31**
Kenedy County, TX	(Z)
Kleberg County, TX	31
Kinston, NC	**56**
Lenoir County, NC	56
Kirksville, MO	**30**

Microplitan Statistical Area ~~Component county	Population, 2019 (1,000)
Adair County, MO	25
Schuyler County, MO	5
Klamath Falls, OR	**68**
Klamath County, OR	68
Laconia, NH	**61**
Belknap County, NH	61
La Grande, OR	**27**
Union County, OR	27
LaGrange, GA-AL	**103**
Chambers County, AL	33
Troup County, GA	70
Lake City, FL	**72**
Columbia County, FL	72
Lamesa, TX	**13**
Dawson County, TX	13
Laramie, WY	**39**
Albany County, WY	39
Las Vegas, NM	**32**
Mora County, NM	5
San Miguel County, NM	27
Laurel, MS	**84**
Jasper County, MS	16
Jones County, MS	68
Laurinburg, NC	**35**
Scotland County, NC	35
Lawrenceburg, TN	**44**
Lawrence County, TN	44
Lebanon, MO	**36**
Laclede County, MO	36
Lebanon, NH-VT	**217**
Grafton County, NH	90
Sullivan County, NH	43
Orange County, VT	29
Windsor County, VT	55
Levelland, TX	**23**
Hockley County, TX	23
Lewisburg, PA	**45**
Union County, PA	45
Lewisburg, TN	**34**
Marshall County, TN	34
Lewistown, PA	**46**
Mifflin County, PA	46
Lexington, NE	**26**
Dawson County, NE	24
Gosper County, NE	2
Liberal, KS	**21**
Seward County, KS	21
Lincoln, IL	**29**
Logan County, IL	29
Lock Haven, PA	**39**
Clinton County, PA	39
Logansport, IN	**38**
Cass County, IN	38
London, KY	**148**
Clay County, KY	20
Knox County, KY	31
Laurel County, KY	61
Whitley County, KY	36
Los Alamos, NM	**19**
Los Alamos County, NM	19
Ludington, MI	**29**
Mason County, MI	29
Lufkin, TX	**87**
Angelina County, TX	87
Lumberton, NC	**131**
Robeson County, NC	131
Macomb, IL	**30**
McDonough County, IL	30
Madison, IN	**32**
Jefferson County, IN	32
Madisonville, KY	**45**
Hopkins County, KY	45
Magnolia, AR	**23**
Columbia County, AR	23
Malone, NY	**50**
Franklin County, NY	50
Malvern, AR	**34**
Hot Spring County, AR	34
Manitowoc, WI	**79**
Manitowoc County, WI	79
Marietta, OH	**60**
Washington County, OH	60

Microplitan Statistical Area ~~Component county	Population, 2019 (1,000)
Marinette, WI-MI	**63**
Menominee County, MI	23
Marinette County, WI	40
Marion, IN	**66**
Grant County, IN	66
Marion, NC	**46**
McDowell County, NC	46
Marion, OH	**65**
Marion County, OH	65
Marquette, MI	**67**
Marquette County, MI	67
Marshall, MN	**25**
Lyon County, MN	25
Marshall, MO	**23**
Saline County, MO	23
Marshalltown, IA	**39**
Marshall County, IA	39
Martin, TN	**33**
Weakley County, TN	33
Martinsville, VA	**63**
Henry County, VA	51
Martinsville city, VA	13
Maryville, MO	**22**
Nodaway County, MO	22
Mason City, IA	**50**
Cerro Gordo County, IA	42
Worth County, IA	7
Mayfield, KY	**37**
Graves County, KY	37
Maysville, KY	**17**
Mason County, KY	17
McAlester, OK	**44**
Pittsburg County, OK	44
McComb, MS	**39**
Pike County, MS	39
McMinnville, TN	**41**
Warren County, TN	41
McPherson, KS	**29**
McPherson County, KS	29
Meadville, PA	**85**
Crawford County, PA	85
Menomonie, WI	**45**
Dunn County, WI	45
Meridian, MS	**99**
Clarke County, MS	16
Kemper County, MS	10
Lauderdale County, MS	74
Mexico, MO	**25**
Audrain County, MO	25
Miami, OK	**31**
Ottawa County, OK	31
Middlesborough, KY	**26**
Bell County, KY	26
Milledgeville, GA	**53**
Baldwin County, GA	45
Hancock County, GA	8
Minden, LA	**38**
Webster Parish, LA	38
Mineral Wells, TX	**29**
Palo Pinto County, TX	29
Minot, ND	**76**
McHenry County, ND	6
Renville County, ND	2
Ward County, ND	68
Mitchell, SD	**23**
Davison County, SD	20
Hanson County, SD	3
Moberly, MO	**25**
Randolph County, MO	25
Montrose, CO	**48**
Montrose County, CO	43
Ouray County, CO	5
Morehead City, NC	**69**
Carteret County, NC	69
Morgan City, LA	**49**
St. Mary Parish, LA	49
Moscow, ID	**40**
Latah County, ID	40
Moses Lake, WA	**98**
Grant County, WA	98
Moultrie, GA	**46**
Colquitt County, GA	46

See footnotes at end of table.

Table B. Micropolitan Statistical Areas and Components—Population: 2019-Continued.

See headnote on page 918.

Micropolitan Statistical Area ~~Component county	Popu- lation, 2019 (1,000)
Mountain Home, AR	**42**
Baxter County, AR	42
Mountain Home, ID	**28**
Elmore County, ID	28
Mount Airy, NC	**72**
Surry County, NC	72
Mount Gay-Shamrock, WV	**32**
Logan County, WV	32
Mount Pleasant, MI	**70**
Isabella County, MI	70
Mount Pleasant, TX	**46**
Camp County, TX	13
Titus County, TX	33
Mount Sterling, KY	**47**
Bath County, KY	13
Menifee County, KY	6
Montgomery County, KY	28
Mount Vernon, IL	**38**
Jefferson County, IL	38
Mount Vernon, OH	**62**
Knox County, OH	62
Murray, KY	**39**
Calloway County, KY	39
Muscatine, IA	**43**
Muscatine County, IA	43
Muskogee, OK	**68**
Muskogee County, OK	68
Nacogdoches, TX	**65**
Nacogdoches County, TX	65
Natchez, MS-LA	**50**
Concordia Parish, LA	19
Adams County, MS	31
Natchitoches, LA	**38**
Natchitoches Parish, LA	38
Newberry, SC	**38**
Newberry County, SC	38
New Castle, IN	**48**
Henry County, IN	48
New Castle, PA	**86**
Lawrence County, PA	86
New Philadelphia-Dover, OH	**92**
Tuscarawas County, OH	92
Newport, OR	**50**
Lincoln County, OR	50
Newport, TN	**36**
Cocke County, TN	36
New Ulm, MN	**25**
Brown County, MN	25
Nogales, AZ	**46**
Santa Cruz County, AZ	46
Norfolk, NE	**48**
Madison County, NE	35
Pierce County, NE	7
Stanton County, NE	6
North Platte, NE	**36**
Lincoln County, NE	35
Logan County, NE	1
McPherson County, NE	(Z)
North Vernon, IN	**28**
Jennings County, IN	28
North Wilkesboro, NC	**68**
Wilkes County, NC	68
Norwalk, OH	**58**
Huron County, OH	58
Oak Harbor, WA	**85**
Island County, WA	85
Ogdensburg-Massena, NY	**108**
St. Lawrence County, NY	108
Oil City, PA	**51**
Venango County, PA	51
Okeechobee, FL	**42**
Okeechobee County, FL	42
Olean, NY	**76**
Cattaraugus County, NY	76
Oneonta, NY	**59**
Otsego County, NY	59
Ontario, OR-ID	**55**
Payette County, ID	24
Malheur County, OR	31
Opelousas, LA	**82**
St. Landry Parish, LA	82
Orangeburg, SC	**86**

Micropolitan Statistical Area ~~Component county	Popu- lation, 2019 (1,000)
Orangeburg County, SC	86
Oskaloosa, IA	**22**
Mahaska County, IA	22
Othello, WA	**20**
Adams County, WA	20
Ottawa, IL	**147**
Bureau County, IL	33
LaSalle County, IL	109
Putnam County, IL	6
Ottawa, KS	**26**
Franklin County, KS	26
Ottumwa, IA	**35**
Wapello County, IA	35
Owatonna, MN	**37**
Steele County, MN	37
Oxford, MS	**54**
Lafayette County, MS	54
Ozark, AL	**49**
Dale County, AL	49
Paducah, KY-IL	**96**
Massac County, IL	14
Ballard County, KY	8
Livingston County, KY	9
McCracken County, KY	65
Pahrump, NV	**47**
Nye County, NV	47
Palatka, FL	**75**
Putnam County, FL	75
Palestine, TX	**58**
Anderson County, TX	58
Pampa, TX	**23**
Gray County, TX	22
Roberts County, TX	1
Paragould, AR	**45**
Greene County, AR	45
Paris, TN	**32**
Henry County, TN	32
Paris, TX	**50**
Lamar County, TX	50
Parsons, KS	**20**
Labette County, KS	20
Payson, AZ	**54**
Gila County, AZ	54
Pearsall, TX	**20**
Frio County, TX	20
Pecos, TX	**16**
Loving County, TX	(Z)
Reeves County, TX	16
Pella, IA	**33**
Marion County, IA	33
Peru, IN	**36**
Miami County, IN	36
Picayune, MS	**56**
Pearl River County, MS	56
Pierre, SD	**21**
Hughes County, SD	18
Stanley County, SD	3
Pinehurst-Southern Pines, NC	**101**
Moore County, NC	101
Pittsburg, KS	**39**
Crawford County, KS	39
Plainview, TX	**33**
Hale County, TX	33
Platteville, WI	**51**
Grant County, WI	51
Plattsmouth, NY	**80**
Clinton County, NY	80
Plymouth, IN	**46**
Marshall County, IN	46
Point Pleasant, WV-OH	**56**
Gallia County, OH	30
Mason County, WV	27
Ponca City, OK	**44**
Kay County, OK	44
Pontiac, IL	**36**
Livingston County, IL	36
Poplar Bluff, MO	**56**
Butler County, MO	42
Ripley County, MO	13
Portales, NM	**19**
Roosevelt County, NM	19

Micropolitan Statistical Area ~~Component county	Popu- lation, 2019 (1,000)
Port Angeles, WA	**77**
Clallam County, WA	77
Port Lavaca, TX	**21**
Calhoun County, TX	21
Portsmouth, OH	**75**
Scioto County, OH	75
Pottsville, PA	**141**
Schuylkill County, PA	141
Price, UT	**20**
Carbon County, UT	20
Prineville, OR	**24**
Crook County, OR	24
Pullman, WA	**50**
Whitman County, WA	50
Quincy, IL-MO	**75**
Adams County, IL	65
Lewis County, MO	10
Raymondville, TX	**21**
Willacy County, TX	21
Red Bluff, CA	**65**
Tehama County, CA	65
Red Wing, MN	**46**
Goodhue County, MN	46
Rexburg, ID	**53**
Fremont County, ID	13
Madison County, ID	40
Richmond, IN	**66**
Wayne County, IN	66
Richmond-Berea, KY	**107**
Estill County, KY	14
Madison County, KY	93
Rio Grande City-Roma, TX	**65**
Starr County, TX	65
Riverton, WY	**39**
Fremont County, WY	39
Roanoke Rapids, NC	**69**
Halifax County, NC	50
Northampton County, NC	19
Rochelle, IL	**51**
Ogle County, IL	51
Rockingham, NC	**45**
Richmond County, NC	45
Rockport, TX	**24**
Aransas County, TX	24
Rock Springs, WY	**42**
Sweetwater County, WY	42
Rolla, MO	**45**
Phelps County, MO	45
Roseburg, OR	**111**
Douglas County, OR	111
Roswell, NM	**65**
Chaves County, NM	65
Ruidoso, NM	**20**
Lincoln County, NM	20
Russellville, AR	**85**
Pope County, AR	64
Yell County, AR	21
Ruston, LA	**47**
Lincoln Parish, LA	47
Rutland, VT	**58**
Rutland County, VT	58
Safford, AZ	**39**
Graham County, AZ	39
St. Marys, GA	**55**
Camden County, GA	55
St. Marys, PA	**30**
Elk County, PA	30
Salem, OH	**102**
Columbiana County, OH	102
Salina, KS	**60**
Ottawa County, KS	6
Saline County, KS	54
Sandpoint, ID	**46**
Bonner County, ID	46
Sandusky, OH	**74**
Erie County, OH	74
Sanford, NC	**62**
Lee County, NC	62
Sault Ste. Marie, MI	**37**
Chippewa County, MI	37
Sayre, PA	**60**
Bradford County, PA	60

See footnotes at end of table.

Micropolitan Statistical Area ~~Component county	Population, 2019 (1,000)
Scottsbluff, NE	**38**
Banner County, NE	1
Scotts Bluff County, NE	36
Sioux County, NE	1
Scottsboro, AL	**52**
Jackson County, AL	52
Scottsburg, IN	**24**
Scott County, IN	24
Searcy, AR	**79**
White County, AR	79
Sedalia, MO	**42**
Pettis County, MO	42
Selinsgrove, PA	**40**
Snyder County, PA	40
Selma, AL	**37**
Dallas County, AL	37
Seneca, SC	**80**
Oconee County, SC	80
Seneca Falls, NY	**34**
Seneca County, NY	34
Sevierville, TN	**98**
Sevier County, TN	98
Seymour, IN	**44**
Jackson County, IN	44
Shawano, WI	**45**
Menominee County, WI	5
Shawano County, WI	41
Shawnee, OK	**73**
Pottawatomie County, OK	73
Shelby, NC	**98**
Cleveland County, NC	98
Shelbyville, TN	**50**
Bedford County, TN	50
Shelton, WA	**67**
Mason County, WA	67
Sheridan, WY	**30**
Sheridan County, WY	30
Show Low, AZ	**111**
Navajo County, AZ	111
Sidney, OH	**49**
Shelby County, OH	49
Sikeston, MO	**38**
Scott County, MO	38
Silver City, NM	**27**
Grant County, NM	27
Snyder, TX	**17**
Scurry County, TX	17
Somerset, KY	**65**
Pulaski County, KY	65
Somerset, PA	**73**
Somerset County, PA	73
Sonora, CA	**54**
Tuolumne County, CA	54
Spearfish, SD	**26**
Lawrence County, SD	26
Spencer, IA	**16**
Clay County, IA	16
Spirit Lake, IA	**17**
Dickinson County, IA	17
Starkville, MS	**59**
Oktibbeha County, MS	50
Webster County, MS	10
Statesboro, GA	**80**
Bulloch County, GA	80
Steamboat Springs, CO	**26**
Routt County, CO	26
Stephenville, TX	**43**
Erath County, TX	43
Sterling, CO	**22**
Logan County, CO	22
Sterling, IL	**55**
Whiteside County, IL	55
Stevens Point, WI	**71**
Portage County, WI	71
Stillwater, OK	**82**
Payne County, OK	82
Storm Lake, IA	**20**
Buena Vista County, IA	20
Sturgis, MI	**61**
St. Joseph County, MI	61
Sulphur Springs, TX	**37**
Hopkins County, TX	37
Summerville, GA	**25**

Micropolitan Statistical Area ~~Component county	Population, 2019 (1,000)
Chattooga County, GA	25
Sunbury, PA	**91**
Northumberland County, PA	91
Susanville, CA	**31**
Lassen County, CA	31
Sweetwater, TX	**15**
Nolan County, TX	15
Tahlequah, OK	**49**
Cherokee County, OK	49
Talladega-Sylacauga, AL	**80**
Talladega County, AL	80
Taos, NM	**33**
Taos County, NM	33
Taylorville, IL	**32**
Christian County, IL	32
The Dalles, OR	**27**
Wasco County, OR	27
Thomaston, GA	**26**
Upson County, GA	26
Thomasville, GA	**44**
Thomas County, GA	44
Tiffin, OH	**55**
Seneca County, OH	55
Tifton, GA	**41**
Tift County, GA	41
Toccoa, GA	**26**
Stephens County, GA	26
Torrington, CT	**180**
Litchfield County, CT	180
Traverse City, MI	**151**
Benzie County, MI	18
Grand Traverse County, MI	93
Kalkaska County, MI	18
Leelanau County, MI	22
Troy, AL	**33**
Pike County, AL	33
Truckee-Grass Valley, CA	**100**
Nevada County, CA	100
Tullahoma-Manchester, TN	**105**
Coffee County, TN	57
Franklin County, TN	42
Moore County, TN	6
Tupelo, MS	**166**
Itawamba County, MS	23
Lee County, MS	85
Pontotoc County, MS	32
Prentiss County, MS	25
Ukiah, CA	**87**
Mendocino County, CA	87
Union, SC	**27**
Union County, SC	27
Union City, TN	**30**
Obion County, TN	30
Urbana, OH	**39**
Champaign County, OH	39
Uvalde, TX	**27**
Uvalde County, TX	27
Van Wert, OH	**28**
Van Wert County, OH	28
Vermillion, SD	**14**
Clay County, SD	14
Vernal, UT	**36**
Uintah County, UT	36
Vernon, TX	**13**
Wilbarger County, TX	13
Vicksburg, MS	**45**
Warren County, MS	45
Vidalia, GA	**36**
Montgomery County, GA	9
Toombs County, GA	27
Vincennes, IN	**37**
Knox County, IN	37

Micropolitan Statistical Area ~~Component county	Population, 2019 (1,000)
Vineyard Haven, MA	**17**
Dukes County, MA	17
Wabash, IN	**31**
Wabash County, IN	31
Wahpeton, ND-MN	**22**
Wilkin County, MN	6
Richland County, ND	16
Wapakoneta, OH	**46**
Auglaize County, OH	46
Warren, PA	**39**
Warren County, PA	39
Warrensburg, MO	**54**
Johnson County, MO	54
Warsaw, IN	**79**
Kosciusko County, IN	79
Washington, IN	**33**
Daviess County, IN	33
Washington, NC	**47**
Beaufort County, NC	47
Washington Court House, OH	**29**
Fayette County, OH	29
Watertown, SD	**34**
Codington County, SD	28
Hamlin County, SD	6
Watertown-Fort Atkinson, WI	**85**
Jefferson County, WI	85
Wauchula, FL	**27**
Hardee County, FL	27
Waycross, GA	**55**
Pierce County, GA	19
Ware County, GA	36
Weatherford, OK	**29**
Custer County, OK	29
West Plains, MO	**40**
Howell County, MO	40
West Point, MS	**19**
Clay County, MS	19
Whitewater, WI	**104**
Walworth County, WI	104
Williston, ND	**38**
Williams County, ND	38
Willmar, MN	**43**
Kandiyohi County, MN	43
Wilmington, OH	**42**
Clinton County, OH	42
Wilson, NC	**82**
Wilson County, NC	82
Winfield, KS	**35**
Cowley County, KS	35
Winnemucca, NV	**17**
Humboldt County, NV	17
Winona, MN	**50**
Winona County, MN	50
Wisconsin Rapids-Marshfield, WI	**73**
Wood County, WI	73
Woodward, OK	**24**
Ellis County, OK	4
Woodward County, OK	20
Wooster, OH	**116**
Wayne County, OH	116
Worthington, MN	**22**
Nobles County, MN	22
Yankton, SD	**23**
Yankton County, SD	23
Zanesville, OH	**86**
Muskingum County, OH	86
Zapata, TX	**14**
Zapata County, TX	14

Z Represents less than 500.

Source: U.S. Census Bureau, 2019 Population Estimates, <census.gov/programs-surveys/metro-micro/data/tables.html>.

Introduction—The data presented in this *Statistical Abstract* come from not only federal statistical bureaus and other organizations that collect and issue statistics as their principal activity, but also governmental administrative and regulatory agencies, private research bodies, trade associations, insurance companies, health associations, private organizations, and philanthropic foundations. Consequently, the data vary considerably as to reference periods, definitions of terms and, for ongoing series, the number and frequency of time periods for which data are available.

The statistics presented were obtained and tabulated by various methods. Some statistics are based on complete enumerations or censuses while others are based on samples. Some information is extracted from records kept for administrative or regulatory purposes (such as school enrollment, hospital records, securities registration, financial accounts, social security records, and income tax returns), while other information is obtained explicitly for statistical purposes through surveys.

Each set of data relates to a group of individuals or units of interest referred to as the *target universe,* or *target population*, or simply as the *universe* or *population*. Tables may present data obtained for all population units, *a census*, or data obtained for only a portion, or *sample*, of the population units.

Prior to data collection, the target universe is clearly defined. For example, if data are to be collected for the universe of households in the United States, it is necessary to define a "household." The target universe may not be completely tractable. Cost and other considerations may restrict data collection to a *survey universe* based on an available list. This list is called a *survey frame, sampling frame,* or *survey sample.*

When data are based on a sample, the sample is usually a scientifically selected *probability sample.* This is a sample selected from a list or sampling frame in such a way that every possible sample has a known chance of selection and usually each unit selected can be assigned a number, greater than zero and less than or equal to one, representing its likelihood or probability of selection.

For large-scale sample surveys, the probability sample of units is often selected as a multistage sample. The first stage of a multistage sample is the selection of a probability sample of large groups of population members, referred to as primary sampling units (PSUs). For example, in a national multistage household sample, PSUs are often counties or groups of counties. The second stage of a multistage sample is the selection, within each PSU selected at the first stage, of smaller groups of population units, referred to as secondary sampling units. In subsequent stages of selection, smaller and smaller nested groups are chosen until the ultimate sample of population units is obtained. To qualify a multistage sample as a probability sample, all stages of sampling must be carried out using probability sampling methods.

Prior to selection at each stage of a multistage (or a single stage) sample, a list of the sampling units or sampling frame for that stage must be obtained. For example, for the first stage of selection of a national household sample, a list of the counties and county groups that form the PSUs must be compiled. For the final stage of selection, lists of households, and sometimes persons within the households, have to be compiled in the field. For surveys of economic entities and for the economic censuses, the U.S. Census Bureau generally uses a frame constructed from the Bureau's Business Register. The Business Register contains all establishments with payroll in the United States, including small single-establishment firms as well as larger firms with multiple establishments.

Wherever the quantities in a table refer to an entire universe, but are constructed from data collected in a sample survey, the table quantities are referred to as *sample estimates*. In constructing a sample estimate, an attempt is made to come as close as is feasible to the corresponding universe quantity that would be obtained from a complete census of the universe. Estimates based on a sample will, however, generally differ from the hypothetical census figures. Two classifications of errors are associated with estimates based on sample surveys:

1 *Sampling error*—the error arising from the use of a sample, rather than a census, to estimate population quantities.

2 *Nonsampling error*—those errors arising from nonsampling sources. Nonsampling errors can include mistakes made in data collection or data processing, misunderstandings of the interviewer or the respondent, and data entry errors. As discussed below, the magnitude of the sampling error for an estimate can usually be estimated from the sample data; however, the magnitude of the nonsampling error for an estimate can rarely be estimated. Consequently, actual error in an estimate exceeds the error that can be estimated.

The particular sample used in a survey is only one of a large number of possible samples of the same size which could have been selected using the same sampling procedure. Estimates derived from the different samples would, in general, differ from each other. The *standard error* (SE) is a measure of the variation among the estimates derived from all possible samples. The standard error is the most commonly used measure of the sampling error of an estimate. Valid estimates of the standard errors of survey estimates can usually be calculated from the data collected in a probability sample. For convenience, the standard error is sometimes expressed as a percent of the estimate and is called the relative standard error or *coefficient of variation* (CV). For example, an estimate of 200 units with an estimated standard error of 10 units has an estimated CV of 5 percent.

A sample estimate and an estimate of its standard error or CV can be used to construct interval estimates that have a prescribed confidence that the interval includes the average of the estimates derived from all possible samples with a known probability. To illustrate, if all possible samples were selected under essentially the same general conditions, and using the same sample design, and if an estimate and its estimated standard error were calculated from each sample, then: 1) approximately 68 percent of the intervals from one standard error below the estimate to one standard error above the estimate would include the average estimate derived from all possible samples; 2) approximately 90 percent of the intervals from 1.6 standard errors below the estimate to 1.6 standard errors above the estimate would include the average estimate derived from all possible samples; and 3) approximately 95 percent of the intervals from two standard errors below the estimate to two standard errors above the estimate would include the average estimate derived from all possible samples.

Thus, for a particular sample, one can say with the appropriate level of confidence (e.g., 90 percent or 95 percent) that the average of all possible samples is included in the constructed interval. Example of a confidence interval: an estimate is 200 units with a standard error of 10 units. An approximately 90 percent confidence interval (plus or minus 1.6 standard errors) is from 184 to 216.

All surveys and censuses are subject to nonsampling errors. Nonsampling errors arise from a variety of factors, including total nonresponse (no usable data obtained for a sampled unit), partial or item nonresponse (only a portion of a response may be usable), inability or unwillingness on the part of respondents to provide correct information, difficulty interpreting questions, mistakes in recording or keying data, errors of collection or processing, and coverage problems (overcoverage and undercoverage of the target universe). Nonresponse errors usually, but not always, result in an understatement of sampling errors and thus an overstatement of the precision of survey estimates. Estimating the magnitude of nonsampling errors would require special experiments or access to independent data. Organizations seldom attempt to measure nonsampling errors.

Nearly all types of nonsampling errors that affect surveys also occur in complete censuses. Since surveys can be conducted on a smaller scale than censuses, nonsampling errors can presumably be controlled more tightly. Relatively more funds and effort can perhaps be expended toward eliciting responses, detecting and correcting response error, and reducing processing errors. As a result, survey results can sometimes be more accurate than census results.

To reduce nonsampling errors, most surveys use computer-assisted telephone or personal interviewing (CATI or CAPI). The computer-assisted data collection method employs computer software and programs that guide the interviewer through the questionnaire to keep the survey consistent across all respondents, and can automatically route the interviewer to appropriate questions based on answers to previous questions. Often the computer program determines if responses are within an allowable range, and checks for consistency against other data collected during the interview. Capturing a survey on a computer also aids in the complete and accurate transfer of data to the organization's data system. Once collected, survey organizations run automated reviews and edits of data, and impute and weight data items.

Adjustments of sample estimates are often made, frequently for nonresponse, both total and partial. These adjustments are *imputations*. Imputation for total nonresponse is usually made by substituting for the questionnaire responses of the nonrespondents the "average" questionnaire responses of the respondents. These imputations usually are made separately within various groups of sample members, formed by attempting to place respondents and nonrespondents together that have similar characteristics. Imputation for item nonresponse is usually made by substituting for a missing item the response to that item of a respondent having characteristics that are similar to those of the nonrespondent.

For an estimate calculated from a sample survey, the *total error* in the estimate is composed of the sampling error, which can usually be estimated from the sample, and the nonsampling error, which usually cannot be estimated from the sample. The total error present in a population quantity obtained from a complete census is composed of only nonsampling errors. Ideally, estimates of the total error associated with data presented in the *Statistical Abstract* tables would be available; however, due to the unavailability of estimates of nonsampling errors, only estimates of the levels of sampling errors, in terms of estimated standard errors or coefficients of variation, are available. To obtain estimates of the estimated standard errors from the sample of interest, see the source cited at the end of each table.

Source of Additional Material: The Federal Committee on Statistical Methodology (FCSM) is an interagency committee dedicated to improving the quality of federal statistics, online at <https://nces.ed.gov/FCSM /index.asp>. See also information available on the Census Bureau website at <https://www.census.gov/ about/policies/quality/guidelines.html>.

Principal data sources—Beginning below are brief descriptions of over 30 of the sample surveys and censuses that provide a substantial portion of the data contained in this *Abstract*.

U.S. DEPARTMENT OF AGRICULTURE, National Agricultural Statistics Service

Census of Agriculture

Universes, Frequency, and Types of Data: Complete count of U.S. farms and ranches conducted once every 5 years, with data at the national, state, and county level. The survey includes any place from which $1,000 or more of agricultural products were produced and sold, or normally would have been sold, during the census year. The census collects data on all commodities produced in the U.S. as well as detailed information on land use and ownership, operator characteristics (such as race, gender, age, tenure on farm, and operating arrangement), production practices, and income and expenditures.

Type of Data Collection Operation: Data collection is by mailing questionnaires to all farmers and ranchers. Producers can return their forms by mail or utilize a census form online. Nonrespondents are contacted by telephone and correspondence follow-ups. Collection is supplemented by electronic data reporting on the internet, and personal enumeration for special classes of records in census operations. Personal enumeration (interviewing) involves the use of both Computer-Assisted Telephone Interview (CATI) and Computer-Assisted Personal Interview (CAPI) data collection instruments. The response rate for the 2012 Census was 74.6 percent, and for the 2017 Census, 71.8 percent.

Imputation Procedures: Computer editing determined the best value to impute for reported responses that were deemed unreasonable and for required responses that were absent. If an item could not be calculated directly from other current responses, the edit determined whether acreage, production, or inventory items had been reported for that farm on a recent NASS crop or livestock survey. For producers who had not changed in five years, demographics such as race and gender were taken from the previous census. Administrative data from the Farm Service Agency were used for a few items, such as Conservation Reserve Program acreage. When deterministic edit logic and previously reported data sources were unable to provide a current value, data from a reporting farm of similar type, size, and location were considered. In cases where automated imputation was unable to provide a consistent report, the record was referred to an analyst for resolution.

Estimates of Sampling Error: NASS uses statistical methodology to correct for undercoverage (farms not reached in the original mailing), nonresponse (people not returning their census questionnaires), and misclassification (whether an operation is correctly classified as a farm or not). The uncertainty these adjustments introduce causes the exact numbers to be unknown; however, the uncertainty can be quantified. This measure of relative reliability is known as the coefficient of variation. In the 2017 Census results, NASS is publishing a measure of uncertainty with all estimates at the national, state, and county level, increasing transparency and data usability.

Nonsampling Errors: Nonsampling errors are embedded in the census process that cannot be directly measured as part of the design of the census but must be contained to ensure an accurate count. Extensive efforts were made to compile a complete and accurate mail list for the census, to elicit response to the census, to design an understandable report form with clear instructions, to minimize processing errors through the use of quality control measures, to reduce matching error associated with the capture-recapture estimation process, and to minimize error associated with identification of a respondent as a farm operation (referred to as classification error). The weight adjustment and tabulation processes recognize the presence of nonsampling errors; however, it is assumed that these errors are small and that, in total, the net effect is zero. The positive errors cancel the negative errors.

Sources of Additional Material: U.S. Department of Agriculture (NASS), 2017 Census of Agriculture, *Appendix A Census of Agriculture Methodology*, and *Appendix B General Explanation and Census of Agriculture Report Form*, online at <https://www.nass.usda.gov/Publications/AgCensus/2017/index.php> and

<https://www.nass.usda.gov/Surveys/Guide_to_NASS_Surveys/Census_of_Agriculture/index.php>.

June Area Survey

Universe, Frequency, and Types of Data: The annual June Area survey utilizes an area sampling frame, and is designed to account for every acre of land, all agricultural activities, and land uses within segment boundaries. Data are collected annually from all states (except Alaska), on crop acreage, grain stocks, cattle inventory, hog inventory, sheep inventory, poultry inventory, land values, cash rents, farm numbers, and sales. The survey also serves to measure list incompleteness and is subsampled for multiple frame surveys.

Data Collection and Imputation Procedures: Stratified probability sample of about 11,000 land area units of about 1 sq. mile (range from 0.1 sq. mile in cities to several sq. miles in open grazing areas). All farm operators within the boundaries of selected segments are interviewed. The JAS typically conducts over 35,000 interviews each year. Approximately 20 percent of the sample is replaced annually. Data collection for the June Area survey is completed entirely by personal interview during the 1st two weeks in June. Imputation is based on enumerator observation or data reported by respondents having similar agricultural characteristics.

Estimates of Sampling Error: Estimated CVs range from 1 to 2 percent for regional estimates and 3 to 6 percent for state estimates of major crop acres and livestock Inventories.

Nonsampling Errors: Steps taken to minimize nonsampling errors include comprehensive interviewer training, validation, and verification of processing systems, application of detailed computer edits, and evaluation of the data via analysis tools.

Sources of Additional Material: U.S. Department of Agriculture, National Agricultural Statistics Service, *Area Frame Design for Agricultural Surveys*, June 2009, online at <https://www.nass.usda.gov/Publications/Methodology_and_Data_Quality/index.php>; and <https://www.nass.usda.gov/Surveys/Guide_to_NASS_Surveys/June_Area/index.php>.

Objective Yield Surveys

Universe, Frequency, and Types of Data: Monthly forecasts and end-of-season estimates of planted and harvested acres, yield, and production of winter wheat, corn for grain, soybeans, fall potatoes, and upland cotton. All acres for harvest as grain in the leading producing states are eligible for this survey. Survey samples are selected from participants in the March Crops/Stocks Survey or the June Agricultural Survey, and include only the top producing states that together produce the majority of a given crop in the U.S.

Data Collection Operation: Random location of plots in probability sample. Field work begins April 25 for winter wheat and July 25 for all the other crops. Sample units are visited at the end of each month during the growing season. Enumerators count and measure plant characteristics in sample fields. Production is measured from plots at harvest. Harvest loss is measured from post harvest gleanings.

Estimates of Sampling Error: CVs for national estimates of production are about 2 to 3 percent.

Nonsampling Errors: In addition to above, replicated sampling procedures are used to monitor effects of changes in survey procedures.

Sources of Additional Material: U.S. Department of Agriculture, National Agricultural Statistics Service, Statistical Methods Branch, *The Yield Forecasting Program of NASS,* May 2012, online at <https://www.nass.usda.gov/Publications/ Methodology_and_Data_Quality/index.php> and <https://www.nass.usda.gov/Surveys/ Guide_to_NASS_Surveys/Objective_Yield/index. php>.

U.S. BUREAU OF JUSTICE STATISTICS (BJS)

National Crime Victimization Survey (NCVS)

Universe, Frequency, and Types of Data: Annual survey of U.S. household members age 12 and older to obtain data on criminal victimization for the compilation of annual estimates. The 2018 NCVS data file includes 151,055 household interviews; 73% of eligible households completed an interview. Within participating households, 242,928 persons completed an interview in 2018, representing an 82% response rate among eligible persons from responding households. Survey excludes victimizations occurring outside of the U.S. The NCVS covers nonfatal personal crime and household property crime victimization, and the characteristics of crimes and victims. Nonfatal personal crimes include rape or sexual assault, robbery, aggravated and simple assault, and personal larceny (purse-snatching, pick-pocketing). Household property crimes include burglary and trespassing, motor vehicle theft, and other types of theft. The survey covers crimes that are both reported and not reported to the police. The survey excludes homicide, arson, and commercial crimes. The survey collects data on the characteristics of the crime, the offender, and of the survey respondent.

Data Collection and Imputation Procedures: Eligible household members age 12 and older are interviewed every 6 months for a total of 7 interviews. Households stay in the sample for about 3 1/2 years. New households rotate into the sample on an ongoing basis. Personal interviews are used in the first interview; subsequent interviews are conducted either in person or by telephone. Survey respondents provide information about their crime victimization experiences during the past 6 months, and their personal characteristics. NCVS data include both person and household weights to provide estimates of the population and households represented by each person and each household in the sample. Weights are designed to adjust data to known population totals and to compensate for survey nonresponse and other aspects of the complex sample design. Please note, beginning 2017, NCVS utilized new household weighting adjustments that resulted in 2017 NCVS household estimates being about 8 percent lower than the previous year. Users should exercise caution when comparing trends in household property crimes over time.

Estimates of Sampling Error: To generate standard errors around victimization and incidence estimates from the NCVS, the U.S. Census Bureau produces generalized variance function (GVF) parameters for BJS. To generate standard errors around prevalence estimates, BJS used direct variance estimation methods. The GVFs and direct variance estimation methods take into account aspects of the NCVS complex sample design and represent the curve fitted to a selection of individual standard errors based on the Balanced Repeated Replication (BRR) technique. The BJS determined that the estimated 2018 victimization rate per 1,000 persons age 12 and older for violent crime has a standard error of 1.30, and for property crime a standard error of 1.94. The source report provides standard errors by detailed type of crime and victim characteristics.

Nonsampling Errors: These include respondent recall errors, including reporting incidents for other than the reference period; interviewer coding and processing errors; and possible mistaken reporting or classifying of events.

Sources of Additional Material: U.S. Bureau of Justice Statistics, *Criminal Victimization, 2018,* and the BJS website.

U.S. BUREAU OF LABOR STATISTICS

Consumer Expenditure Survey (CE)

Universe, Frequency and Types of Data: The Consumer Expenditure Survey (CE) is a nationwide household survey on family expenditures for goods and services. The CE also collects information on amount and sources of family income, changes in assets and liabilities, and demographic and economic characteristics of family members. The CE has two components: a quarterly interview survey, and a weekly diary survey. Estimates covering 12-month periods are released twice a year. Samples are national probability samples of households that are representative of the civilian noninstitutional population. The CE interviews approximately 16,800 households each year.

Type of Data Collection Operation: Both the Interview Survey and the Diary survey are conducted primarily by personal visit, with some telephone interviewing. The Interview Survey is a panel rotation survey. Each panel is interviewed for four quarters and then dropped from the survey. The measurement unit is the set of eligible individuals constituting a consumer unit (CU). The CU is defined as 1) all members in a housing unit who make up a family (includes foster children); 2) a person living alone or sharing a household with others, or living as a roomer in a private home or other lodging (includes hotel or motel), but who is financially independent; or 3) two or more unrelated persons living together who pool their income to make joint expenditure decisions. Students living in university-sponsored housing are also included in the sample as separate consumer units. The Census Bureau selects a sample of approximately 12,000 addresses per year to participate in the Diary Survey; approximately 6,900 households provide usable diaries (two 1-week diaries per household). For the Interview Survey, approximately 12,000 addresses are contacted each quarter. One-fourth of the addresses that are contacted each quarter are new to the survey. Approximately 6,900 households provide usable interviews.

Data Collection and Imputation Procedures: For the Interview Survey, data are collected by personal interview with each consumer unit interviewed once per quarter. The Interview Survey is designed to collect information that respondents can recall for the past 3 months or longer regarding large or recurring expenditures. For the Diary Survey, respondents record all their expenditures in a self-reporting diary for two consecutive 1-week periods. The Diary Survey is designed to pick up small, frequently purchased items which can be difficult to recall over a long period of time. These items include food, beverages, and household and personal care products and services. Data for the Interview Survey and the Diary Survey are collected and processed separately. The Census Bureau collects data, and performs field editing, coding, checks for consistency, and other quality control measures. The BLS performs additional review and editing procedures, including allocating and imputing data for incomplete or missing variables and data items.

Estimates of Sampling Error: Standard errors measure the uncertainty in the survey estimates caused by the fact that a random sample of consumer units from across the United States is used instead of every consumer unit in the nation. Beginning with the release of 2012 data, standard errors are not issued separately but are included in the combined expenditure, share, and standard error tables.

Nonsampling Errors: Nonsampling errors can be attributed to many sources, such as differences in the interpretation of questions, inability or unwillingness of the respondent to provide correct information, mistakes in recording or coding the data obtained, and other errors of collection, response, processing, coverage, and estimation for missing data. The full extent of nonsampling error is unknown.

Sources of Additional Material: Bureau of Labor Statistics website <http://www.bls.gov/cex>; and "BLS Handbook of Methods," <http://www.bls.gov/opub/hom/cex/home.htm>.

Consumer Price Index (CPI)

Universe, Frequency, and Types of Data: The Consumer Price Index (CPI) is a measure of the average change over time in the prices paid by urban consumers for a market basket of consumer goods and services. The CPI is derived from a monthly survey. The CPI reflects spending patterns of two population groups: all urban consumers (CPI-U), and urban wage earners and clerical workers (CPI-W). The all urban consumer group represents approximately 93 percent of the total U.S. population. The CPI-W population represents about 29 percent of the total U.S. population and is a subset of the CPI-U population. Not included in the CPI are the spending patterns of people living in rural non-metropolitan areas, farm families, Armed Forces personnel, and those in institutions such as prisons and mental hospitals. The BLS calculates CPI indexes for the U.S., the census regions and divisions, urban areas by population size, and selected metropolitan and local areas. The CPI covers over 200 item categories of consumer purchases in eight major groups: food and

beverages, housing, apparel, transportation, medical care, recreation, education and communication, and other goods and services. Included within these major groups are selected government-charged user fees, such as water and sewerage charges and motor vehicle registration.

Data Collection Operation: BLS data collectors, called economic assistants, visit or call thousands of retail stores, service establishments, rental units, and doctors' offices, all over the United States, to obtain information on the prices of thousands of items used for the CPI. Prices are collected each month for approximately 80,000 items in 75 urban areas across the country from about 6,000 housing units and approximately 22,000 retail and service establishments. The BLS also collects rents from about 50,000 landlords and tenants; rent information is collected every 6 months. The CPI also covers price quotes from a small percentage of online outlets.

Imputation Procedures: The CPI uses imputation for missing information, which can be due to refusals of responses, inability to collect data for some other reason (the item may be out of season), and the inability to make a satisfactory estimate of the quality change. For noncomparable substitutions, an estimate of constant-quality price change is made by imputation.

Estimates of Sampling Error: The CPI is a statistical estimate that is subject to sampling error because it is based upon a sample of retail prices and not the complete universe of all prices. BLS calculates and publishes estimates of the 1-month, 2-month, 6-month, and 12-month percent change standard errors annually for the CPI-U by expenditure item. These standard error estimates can be used to construct confidence intervals for hypothesis testing. For the latest data, including information on how to use the estimates of standard error, see <https://www.bls.gov/cpi/tables/variance-estimates/home.htm>.

Nonsampling Errors: The total nonsampling error of the CPI results from errors in the type of data collected, the methods of collection, the data processing routines, and the estimation processes. The cumulative nonsampling error can be much greater than the sampling error. These errors occur for a variety of reasons, including logistical lags in conducting surveys, and difficulties in defining basic concepts and their operational implementation. Highly trained personnel ensure the comparability of quality of items from period to period; collection procedures are extensively documented, and recurring audits are conducted. The CPI program has an ongoing research and evaluation program in order to identify and implement improvements in the index.

Sources of Additional Material: U.S. Bureau of Labor Statistics, <https://www.bls.gov/cpi/overview.htm>; and "BLS Handbook of Methods," Chapter 17, <https://www.bls.gov/opub/hom/pdf/cpihom.pdf>.

Current Employment Statistics (CES) Program

Universe, Frequency, and Types of Data: Monthly survey of approximately 145,000 businesses and government agencies representing approximately 697,000 worksites drawn from a sampling frame of Unemployment Insurance (UI) tax accounts covering roughly 10.2 million establishments, about 97 percent of all employment within the scope of the CES. The active CES sample includes approximately one-third of all nonfarm payroll employees in the 50 states and the District of Columbia. A semiannual update is performed each summer to select units from the population of business openings and other units not previously eligible for selection. The CES collects data on employment, hours, and earnings at detailed industry levels. The CES series are estimates of nonfarm wage and salary jobs, not of employed persons; an individual with 2 jobs is counted twice by the payroll survey. The CES excludes employees in agriculture and private households, and the self-employed.

Type of Data Collection Operation: The BLS uses various collection techniques. Data collection centers (DCCs) perform initial enrollment of each firm via telephone, collect the data for several months via Computer Assisted Telephone Interviewing (CATI), and, where possible, transfer respondents to a self-reporting mode such as touch-tone data entry (TDE), facsimile, or internet collection. Very large, multi-establishment firms are often enrolled via personal visit, and thereafter report data via electronic data interchange (EDI). These firms provide electronic files to BLS that include data from all their worksites. All firms with 1,000 or more employees are asked to participate in the survey, as is a sample of firms across all employment sizes. When firms are rotated into the sample, they are retained for 2 years or more. Each month, respondents extract the employment, hours, and earnings data from their payroll records and submit it to the BLS. Data are collected for the pay period that includes the 12th of each month. BLS staff prepare national estimates of employment, hours, and earnings. State agencies cooperate with the BLS to develop state and metropolitan area estimates.

Microdata Review: The CES program tests all respondent data, collectively known as microdata, in order to generate accurate, timely, and relevant monthly employment estimates. These tests, also called microdata screening tests, compare all new data reported by survey respondents to the respondent's historically reported data. Data that fail these microdata screening tests are then reviewed by analysts to determine whether the microdata should be used in the estimation of employment, hours, and earnings. Detailed information is available online under "Technical Notes for the Current Employment Statistics Survey" at <http://www.bls.gov/web/empsit/cestn.htm>.>

Estimates of Sampling Errors: The magnitude of sampling error, or variance, is directly related to the size of the sample and the percentage of universe coverage achieved by the sample. The establishment survey sample covers over one-third of total universe employment; this yields a relatively small variance on the total nonfarm estimates. Information on measurements of error associated with sample estimates are available online under "Technical Notes for the Current Employment Statistics Survey" at <https://www.bls.gov/web/empsit/cestn.htm>.

Total Error: The benchmark error is used as a proxy measure of total error for the CES survey, and it represents the difference between two employment estimates derived from separate statistical processes (the CES sample process, and the Unemployment Insurance administrative process), and thus reflects the sum of the errors present in each program. For total nonfarm employment over the past 10 years, absolute percentage benchmark error has averaged 0.2 percent, with an absolute range from less than 0.05 percent to 0.7 percent.

Sources of Additional Material: U.S. Bureau of Labor Statistics, "BLS Handbook of Methods," Chapter 2, <https://www.bls.gov/opub/hom/pdf/ces-20110307.pdf>; and Current Employment Statistics, "Technical Notes," <http://www.bls.gov/web/empsit/cestn.htm>.

National Compensation Survey (NCS)

Universe, Frequency, and Types of Data: The NCS is an establishment-based survey that provides comprehensive measures of 1) employer costs for employee compensation, including wages and salaries, and benefits, 2) compensation trends, and 3) the availability of and/or employee participation in employer-provided benefits, with an emphasis on health insurance and retirement benefits. The NCS includes establishments in private industry and in state and local government; major exclusions are workers in federal and quasi-federal agencies, military personnel, agricultural workers, workers in private households, the self-employed, and unpaid workers. The NCS releases data through the quarterly Employment Cost Index and the Employer Costs for Employee Compensation, and annual reports on employee benefits, with data shown by various employer and/or employee characteristics, including industry, occupational group, labor union status, and other characteristics.

Sample Selection: The total sample is selected in two stages, one for establishments, and one for occupations within the sample of establishments. The establishment sample has three rotation groups, one for private industry, one for state and local government, and one for the aerospace industry. Government establishments are rotated approximately every 10 years, and all others are rotated every 3 years (except during the government rotation year). Field economists use a probability selection of occupations method to select jobs to sample, then match employees with those jobs, and classify workers according to their duties rather than specific job title. NCS data releases include the number of establishments and occupations covered in the survey.

Data Collection and Imputation Procedures: BLS field economists use personal visits, mail, telephone, and email, to obtain data from NCS survey respondents; they do not use paper and online surveys, but rather use conversational interviews and descriptive documents. Updated data are collected quarterly. Imputation is done for individual benefits. To address the problems of nonresponse and missing data, the NCS adjusts the weights of the remaining establishments and imputes missing values; missing values for an initially responding establishment are replaced by values from the original interview after accounting for the rate of change for workers in similar establishments; missing values for an item are replaced by values derived from establishments with similar characteristics.

Estimates of Sampling Error: NCS uses standard errors to evaluate published series. A discussion of sampling and nonsampling errors, as well as web-based links to more detailed data on the reliability of estimates from the NCS, are available online at <https://www.bls.gov/opub/hom/ncs/calculation.htm>.

Nonsampling Errors: Data collection and processing errors are mitigated primarily through quality assurance programs that include the use of data collection reinterviews, observed interviews, computer edits of the data, and a systematic professional review of the data.

Sources of Additional Material: Bureau of Labor Statistics, Handbook of Methods, "National Compensation Measures," <https://www.bls.gov/opub/hom/ncs/home.htm>.

Producer Price Index (PPI)

Universe, Frequency, and Types of Data: Monthly survey of producing companies to determine price changes of all commodities and services produced in the United States for sale in commercial transactions. Price changes are from the perspective of the seller. Covers nearly all industries in the goods-producing sectors, including agriculture, fishing, forestry, mining, and manufacturing, and over 70 percent of the service sector's output as measured by revenue reported in the Economic Census. Domestic production of goods for the military is included, as are goods shipped between establishments owned by the same company. The BLS releases each month about 10,000 PPIs for individual products and groups of products. PPIs are organized into three main sets: (1) Final demand-Intermediate demand (FD-ID) indexes, (2) commodity indexes, and (3) indexes for the net output of industries and their products.

Type of Data Collection Operation: PPIs are based on selling prices reported by establishments of all sizes selected by probability sampling, with the probability of selection proportionate to employment size. Individual items and services from these firms are chosen by disaggregation, a process to select items based on their proportionate value to the manufacturer's overall revenue; further steps involve the item's characteristics. BLS periodically updates the PPI sample of survey respondents to reflect current conditions when the structure, membership, technology, or product mix of an industry shifts significantly, and to spread reporting burden among smaller firms. Results of these resampling efforts are incorporated into the PPI with the release of data for January and July. Participation in the PPI program is voluntary. The BLS encourages companies to supply actual transaction prices at the time of shipment to minimize the use of list prices. Each month approximately 100,000 prices are solicited from roughly 25,000 establishments. Establishments report prices via a secure website.

Data Collection and Imputation Procedures: Prices are effective on the Tuesday of the week containing the 13th day of the month. Missing prices are estimated by using prices received for similar products or services. The current standard base period for most commodity-oriented PPI series is 1982, but many indexes that began after 1982 are based on the month of their introduction. The FD-ID indexes typically have a reference base of November 2009 = 100. All unadjusted PPIs are routinely subject to revision only once, 4 months after their original publication, to reflect late reports and corrections by company respondents. Once revised, indexes are considered final.

Estimates of Sampling Error: The Producer Price Index (PPI) program began publishing variance estimates in 2016 based on data for 2015. PPI intends to publish variance estimates on an annual basis. The median absolute value of the percent change is provided as the reference statistic and the corresponding median standard error is provided as the measure of variance. Reports on variance methodology and estimates are available online at <https://www.bls.gov/ppi/ppivariance.htm>.

Nonsampling Errors: Nonsampling error occurs in many forms, but whatever the form, nonsampling error does not affect the spread of the sample estimates. Nonsampling error can, however, cause the estimate to be consistently higher (or lower) than the true population estimate. When this occurs, it is called the bias of a sample estimate. The PPI program, along with other programs at BLS, analyzes estimates for the presence of bias and mitigates nonsampling error by conducting research into the population of interest, by clearly documenting data collection procedures, and by performing quality checks throughout the collection process.

Sources of Additional Material: U.S. Bureau of Labor Statistics, PPI overview available online at <https://www.bls.gov/ppi/ppiover.htm>, methodology online at <http://www.bls.gov/ppi/methodology.htm>; and more information at <https://www.bls.gov/ppi/ppi_variance_methodology.htm>.

BOARD OF GOVERNORS OF THE FEDERAL RESERVE SYSTEM

Survey of Consumer Finances (SCF)

Universe, Frequency, and Types of Data: Triennial sample survey of families on their finances. The 2016 Survey of Consumer Finances was the most recent survey available for coverage in this *Statistical Abstract.* The survey collects detailed data on the composition of family balance sheets, pensions, income, the terms of loans, and relationships with financial institutions. It also gathers information on the employment history and pension rights of the survey respondent and the spouse or partner of the respondent. Data include respondent demographic characteristics. In this survey a given household is divided into a primary economic unit (the family), and everyone else in the household. The primary economic unit is the economically dominant single person or couple (married or cohabitating) and all other persons in the household who are financially interdependent with the economically dominant person or couple. The primary economic unit is used as the reference family. To stay up-to-date with new developments in family finances, the SCF underwent a redesign in 2016. Despite the changes, the core questionnaire remains comparable with earlier surveys. The goals of the redesign were to improve the collection of data on new developments key to family finances, improve coordination and integration with other household surveys and administrative data sources, reduce respondent burden, and generally improve upon the quality of data collected.

Type of Data Collection Operation: The SCF employs a sample design consisting of two parts: a standard, geographically based random sample and a special list sample that oversamples relatively wealthy families under strict rules to provide confidentiality and give potential respondents the right to refuse participation. Weights are used to combine information from the two samples to make estimates for the full population. In the 2016 survey, 6,254 families were interviewed, and in the 2013 survey, 6,026 were interviewed. Of the 6,254 interviews completed for the 2016 SCF, 4,754 were from the area-probability sample, and 1,500 were from the list sample; for 2013, 4,568 were from the area-probability sample, and 1,458 were from the list sample. In both the 2013 and 2016 surveys, about 65 percent of the households selected for the area-probability sample and about a third of the list sample completed interviews.

Data Collection and Imputation Procedures: National Opinion Research Center (NORC) at the University of Chicago has collected data for the survey since 1992. The majority of interviews for the SCF are conducted in person. Interviews are conducted via telephone if more convenient for respondents. Adjustments for nonresponse are made through multiple imputations of unanswered questions and through weighting adjustments based on data used in the sample design for families that refused participation.

Estimates of Sampling Error: The SCF attempts to reduce sampling error by designing the sample to reduce important sources of variability. Sampling error is estimated using replication methods. Replication methods draw samples, called replicates, from the set of actual respondents, and compute weights for all cases in each of the replicates.

Nonsampling Errors: Proper training and monitoring of interviewers, careful design of questionnaires, and systematic editing of the resulting data were used to control for nonsampling errors.

Sources of Additional Material: Board of Governors of the Federal Reserve System, "Changes in U.S. Family Finances from 2013 to 2016: Evidence from the Survey of Consumer Finances," *Federal Reserve Bulletin*, September 2017, <https://www.federalreserve.gov/econres/scfindex.htm>.

U.S. CENSUS BUREAU

Economic Census

Universe, Frequency, and Types of Data: Conducted every 5 years to obtain data on number of establishments, number of employees, payroll, total sales/shipments/receipts/revenue, and other industry-specific statistics from nearly 4 million businesses of all sizes. Data are shown by North American Industry Classification code. The universe is all establishments with paid employees in most industries (exclusions include agriculture, forestry, fishing and hunting, rail transportation, postal service, schools and colleges, religious organizations, private households, and public administration). The sample frame comes from the Census Bureau's Business Register. All establishments of multi-establishment firms are included; single-establishment firms are included based on certain criteria. (Nonemployer Statistics,

discussed separately, covers establishments without paid employees.) The most recent Economic Census is for 2017. Results for the 2017 Economic Census are being released on a flow basis from September 2019 through December 2021. Businesses included in the Economic Census (EC) are required by law under Title 13, Section 224, to respond to the survey. Section 9 of the same law makes the information collected confidential.

Type of Data Collection Operation: Beginning with the 2017 EC, businesses used a secure online portal to respond to the survey. Business were mailed instructions for completing the survey online. For 2017, the Economic Census used approximately 800 versions of the survey that were tailored for particular industries and industry groups. The EC also includes a non-sampled component; data for selected small single-establishment firms were collected from administrative data from the Census Bureau and other government agencies.

Imputation Procedures: Imputation is used for replacing missing data due to nonresponse. The primary sources for obtaining or deriving data for imputation are administrative data from the Census Bureau or other government agency, the establishment's other reported or administrative data, 2012 Census data, and another 2017 survey.

Sampling Error: Estimates of basic data items, such as receipts, sales, payroll, employment, and inventories, included in the 2017 Economic Census First Look and Geographic Area Series publications are computed from all in-scope establishments in the country and therefore are not subject to sampling error. For those establishments that were not sampled or did not respond, missing data items were either imputed or filled in with administrative data from other government agencies.

Nonsampling Errors: Nonsampling errors may be attributed to an inability to identify all cases in the actual universe; definition and classification difficulties; differences in interpretation of questions; errors in recording or coding data; and other errors of collection, response, coverage, processing, and estimation for missing or misreported data. Nonsampling error is not measured, but the Census Bureau employs quality control measures to reduce the effects of errors.

Sources of Additional Material: U.S. Census Bureau, <https://www.census.gov/EconomicCensus>.

American Community Survey (ACS)

Universe, Frequency, and Types of Data: The American Community Survey is conducted every month, every year. The survey is sent to a sample of about 3.54 million households in the U.S. and 36,000 households in Puerto Rico, per year, to obtain data about demographic, social, economic, and housing characteristics of housing units and the people residing in them. It covers the household population and, beginning in 2006, also includes the group quarter population living in correctional facilities, skilled-nursing homes, military barracks, college residence halls, and other group quarters. Sampling frames are drawn from the Census Bureau's Master Address File.

Sample Selection: Housing unit address sampling is performed twice a year. First-phase of sampling defines the universe for the second stage of sampling through two steps. First, all addresses that were eligible for the second-phase sampling within the past four years are excluded from eligibility. This ensures that no address is in the sample more than once in any 5-year period. The second step is to select a 20 percent systematic sample of "new" units, i.e. those units that have never appeared on a previous Master Address File (MAF) extract. All new addresses are systematically assigned to either the current year or to one of four back-samples. This procedure maintains five equal partitions of the universe. The second-phase sampling is done on the current year's partition and results in approximately 3,540,000 housing unit addresses in the U.S. and 36,000 in Puerto Rico (PR).

Group quarter sampling is performed separately from the housing unit sampling. The sampling begins with separating the small (15 persons or fewer) and the large (more than 15 persons) group quarters. The target sampling rate for both groups is a 2.5% sample of the group quarters population. Data are collected from approximately 20,000 group quarters and 195,000 sample residents per year.

Data Collection Procedures: The data collection operation for housing units (HUs) consists of four modes: internet, mail, telephone, and personal visit. For most housing units, the first phase includes a mailed request to respond by internet, followed later by an option to complete a paper questionnaire and return it by mail. If no response is received by mail or internet, the Census Bureau follows up with computer-assisted telephone interviewing (CATI) when a telephone number is available. If a telephone interview is not successful, then the ACS attempts a personal visit and interview. Mailable addresses with neither a response to the mail-out nor a telephone interview are sampled at a rate of 1 in 2, 2 in 5, or 1 in 3 based on the expected rate of completed interviews at the tract level. Unmailable addresses are sampled at a rate of 2 in 3. Those addresses selected through this process are assigned to field representatives (FRs), who visit the addresses, verify their existence, determine their occupancy status, and conduct interviews.

Collection of group quarters data is conducted primarily through FR interviews. Field representatives' methods include completing the questionnaire while speaking to the resident in person or over the telephone, or leaving paper questionnaires for residents to complete for themselves and then pick up later. This last option is used for data collection in federal prisons. If needed, a personal interview can be conducted with a proxy, such as a relative or guardian.

Imputation Procedures: The Census Bureau uses two principal methods to impute missing or inconsistent data: assignment and allocation. Assignment involves looking at other data as reported by the respondent to fill in missing responses. For example, if sex is unknown but the respondent reported giving birth, the assignment is female. Hot-deck allocation uses a statistical method to supply missing or inconsistent responses from other housing units or survey respondents with similar characteristics.

Estimates of Sampling Error: The data in the ACS products are estimates and can vary from the actual values that would have been obtained by conducting a census of the entire population. The estimates from the chosen sample addresses can also vary from those that would have been obtained from a different set of addresses. This variation causes uncertainty, which can be measured using statistics such as standard errors, margins of error, and confidence intervals. All ACS estimates are accompanied by margins of errors or confidence intervals to assist users.

Nonsampling Errors: Other types of errors may occur during any of the various complex operations used to select, collect, and process survey data. An important goal of the ACS is to minimize the amount of nonsampling error introduced through coverage issues in the sample list, nonresponse from sample housing units, and transcribing or editing data. One way of accomplishing this is by finding additional sources of addresses, following up on nonrespondents, and maintaining quality control systems.

Sources of Additional Material: U.S. Census Bureau, American Community Survey, online at <http://www.census.gov/programs-surveys/acs/>; and American Community Survey Accuracy of the Data documents available on the internet at <http://www.census.gov/programs-surveys/acs/methodology.html>.

American Housing Survey (AHS)

Universe, Frequency, and Types of Data: Conducted biennially in odd numbered years to obtain data on occupied or vacant housing units in the United States (group quarters are excluded). This *Statistical Abstract* presents data from the 2017 AHS. The AHS provides information on a wide range of "core" housing subjects, including size and composition of the nation's housing inventory, vacancies, fuel usage, physical condition of housing units, characteristics of occupants, equipment breakdowns, home improvements, mortgages and other housing costs, persons eligible for and beneficiaries of assisted housing, home values, and characteristics of recent movers. Beginning 2011, the AHS includes topical supplements. For the 2017 survey, the AHS topics include commuting to work, evictions, delinquent payment and notices, and emergency and disaster preparedness. In 2015 AHS, the Department of Housing and Urban Development (HUD) and the Census Bureau selected a integrated national sample that includes a representative sample of the nation, and oversamples of the top 15 metro areas and HUD-assisted housing units. Beginning in 2015, the total sample size is about 115,000 housing units. The 2017 AHS sample comprised of 114,860 housing units, including 45,285 units in top 15 metropolitan areas, 29,981 housing units in an additional 10 metropolitan areas, and 5,202 units in a subsidized-renter oversample.

Type of Data Collection Operation: Census Bureau interviewers visit or telephone the household occupying each housing unit in the sample. For unoccupied units, they obtain information from landlords, rental agents, or neighbors. Housing units participating in the AHS are scientifically selected to represent a cross section of all housing in the nation. The same basic sample of housing units is interviewed every two years until a new sample is selected. The U.S. Census Bureau updates the sample by adding newly constructed housing units and units discovered through coverage improvement efforts. Each housing unit in the AHS sample represents itself and between 450 to 4,000 other units.

Estimates of Sampling Error: Error from sampling reflects how estimates from a sample vary from the actual value if all housing units had been interviewed under the same conditions. The AHS provides documentation for users to use to calculate sampling errors. See source website under Technical Documentation, "Accuracy of the Data."

Nonsampling Errors: These may arise from a variety of factors, including errors in coverage, nonresponse, missing response, and inaccurate responses, and processing errors. The AHS takes numerous steps to minimize these types of errors.

Sources of Additional Material: U.S. Census Bureau, "American Housing Survey, Methodology and other Technical Documentation," <https://www.census. gov/programs-surveys/ahs/tech-documentation. html>; and <https://www.census.gov/programs-surveys/ahs/about/methodology.html>.

Annual Survey of Public Employment and Payroll, and Census of Governments

Universe, Frequency, and Types of Data: A sample survey is conducted annually except in years ending in '2' and '7', when a census of all state and local governments is done. Covers employees of all agencies of the 50 state governments, the District of Columbia, and about 90,500 local governments (i.e., counties, municipalities, townships, special districts, and school districts). For the annual survey, a sample is selected from the Census of Governments; the typical sample contains approximately 11,000 state and local governments. The survey measures the number of state and local government employees and their gross payrolls for the pay period including March 12. The annual survey provides state and local government data on full-time and part-time employment, full-time equivalent employment, and payroll statistics by governmental function. The census obtains data on how governments are organized, employment and payroll, and government finances. Through 2014, the survey also collected data for federal government employees.

Type of Data Collection Operations: Most state governments provide data from central payroll records for all or most of their agencies and institutions. Data for agencies and institutions for the remaining state governments and all local governments are obtained by an online collection instrument. Some elementary and secondary school system data are supplied by special arrangements with the state government.

Editing Procedures: Editing ensures survey data are accurate, complete, and consistent. Efforts are made at all phases of collection, processing, and tabulation to minimize errors. Edits are built into the internet data collection instrument and the data entry programs. Post collection edits consist primarily of two types: consistency, and a ratio of the current years reported value to the prior year's value.

Imputation Procedures: For general purpose governments, school districts, and special districts not responding to the survey, imputations were based on recent historical data from either a prior year annual survey or the most recent Census of Governments, as available. These data were adjusted by a growth rate that was determined by the growth of units that were similar (in size, geography, and type of government) to the nonrespondent. If no recent historical data were available, imputations were based on the data from a randomly selected donor that was similar to the nonrespondent.

Estimates of Sampling Error: Census data are not subject to sampling and do not contain sampling error. Data from the annual survey are subject to sampling error. The estimated coefficients of variation (CVs), which are provided for each estimate in data tables available online, are an estimate of this sampling variability. The CVs are expressed as percentages. The CV is the ratio of the standard error to the expectation of the estimate. State government employment and payroll data are not subject to sampling error. Consequently, state and local government aggregates for individual states are more reliable statistically than the local government only estimates.

Nonsampling Errors: Sample data are subject to nonsampling errors such as inability to obtain data for every variable from all units in the sample, inaccuracies in classification, response errors, misinterpretation of questions, mistakes in keying and coding, and coverage errors. These same errors may be evident in census collections and may affect the Census of Governments data used to adjust the sample during the estimation phase and used in the imputation process.

Sources of Additional Material: Census Bureau, Annual Survey of Public Employment and Payroll (ASPEP), <https://www.census.gov/programs-surveys/apes/technical-documentation.html>.

Annual Survey of State and Local Government Finances

Universe, Frequency, and Types of Data: In the years ending in "2" and "7," the Census Bureau conducts a census of the entire universe of all 50 state governments, the District of Columbia, and approximately 90,000 local governments (counties, cities, townships, special districts, and school districts). In intervening years, the Bureau conducts an annual survey of a sample of state and local governments. The survey collects data on government revenue (including taxes, charges, interest, and other earnings), expenditures by function and accounting category, debt, and financial assets by type. Data are published about 24 months after data collection. Revisions are made for the next 2 years.

Type of Data Collection Operations: Data are collected via mail canvass, internet, and central collection from State sources. Collection methods vary by state and type of government. Reviews of government accounting records provide data for most state government agencies and some of the largest and most complex county and municipal governments. Twenty-seven states have central collection arrangements with the Census Bureau; these states get special mailings for all or specific types of government units within that state. In some cases, data could be obtained from state Comprehensive Annual Financial Reports. Data edits were built into the internet data collection instrument and data entry programs, and include consistency edits, historical and current year ratio edits, and balance checks.

Imputation Procedures: Imputations for nonresponding general purpose governments are based on recently reported historical data from either a prior year annual survey or the most recent census, adjusted by a growth rate. If no historical data are available, or the unit has not responded in over five years, data from a randomly selected similar unit are adjusted by the ratio of the populations of the non-responding and randomly selected donor governments. The imputations for non-responding special districts are done similarly. If prior year reported data are available, the prior year data for the non-respondent are adjusted by a growth rate that is determined from reporting units that are similar to the non-respondent.

Estimates of Sampling Error: State government financial statistics result from a complete canvass of all state government agencies, and therefore do not have an associated measure of sampling error. Data from local governments come from a sample of local governments, and are subject to sampling variability. Data files include the coefficients of variation that can be used to derive the standard error of the estimates.

Nonsampling Errors: The estimates are subject to inaccuracies in classification, response, and processing. Efforts were made at all phases of collection, processing, and tabulation to minimize errors. Data are also subject to errors from imputations for missing data, errors from misreported data, errors from miscoding, and difficulties in identifying every unit that should be included in the report. Every effort was made to keep such errors to a minimum through examining, editing, and tabulating the data reported by government officials.

Sources of Additional Material: Census Bureau, State and Local Government Finances, <https://www.census.gov/programs-surveys/gov-finances/technical-documentation.html>.

Annual Survey of Manufactures (ASM)

Universe, Frequency, and Types of Data: The Annual Survey of Manufactures is a sample survey of approximately 50,000 manufacturing establishments conducted annually, except for years ending in '2' and '7' when the survey is included in the Economic Census, for all manufacturing establishments having one or more paid employees. Sample selection is currently made from the 2012 Economic Census - Manufacturing universe, which contains approximately 294,600 active manufacturing establishments. The purpose of the ASM is to provide key intercensal measures of manufacturing activity, products, and location for the public and private sectors. The ASM provides statistics on employment, payroll, worker hours, payroll supplements, cost of materials, value added by manufacturing, capital expenditures, inventories, and energy consumption. It also provides estimates of value of shipments for 1,390 seven-digit NAICS product classes.

Type of Data Collection Operation: The ASM mails out instructions for responding to the survey via an online tool. Firms not responding receive follow up mailings and telephone calls. About 15,600 establishments are selected with certainty, and the remaining establishments are selected with

probability proportional to a composite measure of establishment size. The sample universe is updated from two sources: Internal Revenue Service administrative records are used to include new single-establishment manufacturers, and the Company Organization Survey identifies new establishments of companies with multiple establishments.

Imputation Procedures: The primary sources for imputing data missing due to nonresponse are administrative data, other data reported by the establishment, and data reported in previous surveys or other census surveys. Sampled establishments that did not report product data are assigned products in a hot-deck imputation process. In this process the products from a similar establishment (called the donor) are assigned to the establishment missing the product data (the recipient).

Estimates of Sampling Error: Statistics for the industry groups and industries, and product shipments include estimated relative standard errors. Relative standard errors vary by industry and product category.

Nonsampling Errors: Includes errors due to collection, reporting, and transcription errors, many of which are corrected through computer and clerical checks.

Sources of Additional Material: Census Bureau, Annual Survey of Manufactures Methodology, <http://www.census.gov/programs-surveys/asm/technical-documentation/methodology.html>.

Decennial Census of Population and Housing

Universe, Frequency, and Types of Data: Mandated by the U.S. Constitution, the Decennial Census has made a complete count of the U.S. population every 10 years since 1790. The Census obtains data on the number and characteristics of people in the United States and its outlying territories, and also counts Federally affiliated Americans overseas. The 2010 Census asked information on name, gender, age, race, ethnicity, relationship to householder, and whether the respondent owns or rents their home.

Data Collection and Imputation Procedures: In 1980, 1990, and 2000, mail questionnaires were used extensively with personal interviews in the remainder. The Census employed extensive telephone and personal follow-ups for nonrespondents. From 1940 to 2000, the Census used long and short form questionnaires. The 2010 Census used a single questionnaire that contained 10 questions. Detailed information that was asked on the long form questionnaire was moved to the annual American Community Survey. For the 2010 Census, 130 million households received a census form. Questionnaires were mailed and hand-delivered, and for nonresponding households, census workers made personal visits to conduct a census count. Imputations, which were needed most often when an entry for a given item was missing, included three general procedures known as assignments, allocations, and substitution, which all in one form or another use values or entries that were consistent for the person or housing unit in question.

Estimates of Sampling Error: Sampling errors for data are estimated for all items collected by sample and vary by characteristic and geographic area. The coefficients of variation (CVs) for national and state estimates are generally very small.

Nonsampling Errors: Since 1950, evaluation programs have been conducted to provide information on the magnitude of some sources of nonsampling errors such as response bias and undercoverage in each census. Results from the evaluation program for the 1990 census indicated that the estimated net undercoverage amounted to about 1.61 percent of the total resident population. Census 2000 had a national overcount of 0.49 percent (0.20 percent standard error) for the household population. For the 2010 Census, the Census Coverage Measurement Program found a net overcount of 0.01 percent (0.14 percent standard error) of the resident population.

Sources of Additional Material: U.S. Census Bureau, *The Coverage of Population in the 1980 Census,* PHC80-E4; *Content Reinterview Study: Accuracy of Data for Selected Population and Housing Characteristics as Measured by Reinterview,* PHC80-E2; *1980 Census of Population,* Vol. 1, (PC80-1), Appendixes B, C, and D. *Content Reinterview Survey: Accuracy of Data for Selected Population and Housing Characteristics as Measured by Reinterview,* 1990, CPH-E-1; *Effectiveness of Quality Assurance, CPH-E-2; Programs to Improve Coverage in the 1990 Census,* 1990, CPH-E-3. Documentation regarding the 2010 Census is available online at <https://www.census.gov/newsroom/releases/archives/2010_census/press-kits/> and <https://www.census.gov/programs-surveys/decennial-census/technical-documentation.html>. General information is available at <https://www.census.gov/programs-surveys/decennial-census.html>.

County Business Patterns

Universe, Frequency, and Types of Data: County Business Patterns is an annual series that contains data on number of establishments, number of employees, and first quarter and annual payrolls, by detailed industry and geographic level. Data cover over 6 million single-unit establishments and 1.8 million multi-unit establishments, and are available by geographic area (state, county, and metropolitan areas), 6-digit NAICS industry, legal form of organization (U.S. and state only), and employment size class. Most industries are covered; excluded are crop and animal production; rail transportation; U.S. Postal Service; pension, health, welfare, and vacation funds; trusts, estates, and agency accounts; private households; and public administration. CBP also excludes most establishments reporting government employees.

Type of Data Collection Operation: Most basic data items are extracted from the Census Bureau's Business Register, a database of all known employer companies. The Company Organization Survey provides individual establishment data for companies that operate 2 or more units (multi-establishment companies). Data for single establishment companies are obtained from various Census Bureau programs, such as the Economic Census, Annual Survey of Manufactures, and Current Business Surveys, as well as from administrative records of the Internal Revenue Service, the Social Security Administration, and the Bureau of Labor Statistics.

Estimates of Sampling Error: Payroll and employment data are not subject to sampling error.

Nonsampling Errors: The data are subject to nonsampling errors, such as inability to identify all cases in the universe; definition and classification difficulties; differences in interpretation of questions; errors in recording or coding the data obtained; and estimation of employers who reported too late to be included in the tabulations and for records with missing or misreported data. Employment data are missing from approximately 6.5 percent of incoming administrative payroll records. Missing employment and payroll data are imputed by examining employment and payroll patterns for various time periods.

Sources of Additional Material: U. S. Census Bureau, County Business Patterns, online at <http://www.census.gov/programs-surveys/cbp/about.html> and <http://www.census.gov/programs-surveys/cbp/technical-documentation/methodology.html>.

Current Population Survey (CPS)

Universe, Frequency, and Types of Data: Nationwide monthly sample of approximately 60,000 households designed primarily to produce national and state estimates of labor force and other characteristics of the civilian noninstitutionalized population 15 years of age and older, including sex, age, race, marital status, educational attainment, and family structure. In addition to the monthly survey, each March the CPS produces the Annual Social and Economic (ASEC) Supplement, which contains the basic monthly demographic and labor force data covered by the CPS, plus additional data on numerous other topics, including work experience, income, health insurance coverage, poverty, receipt of noncash benefits, and geographic mobility.

Type of Data Collection Operation: Multistage probability sample that currently includes 60,000 households from 824 sample areas. Sample size increased in some states to improve data reliability for those areas on an average annual basis. A continual sample rotation system is used. Households are in sample for 4 months, out for 8 months, and in for 4 more. The CPS questionnaire is a computerized document that is administered by Census Bureau field representatives across the country through both personal and telephone interviews. One person, usually the person who owns or rents the housing unit, generally responds for all eligible members in a household regarding activities during the prior week (the week including the 12th of the month).

Imputation Procedures: The CPS makes imputations for missing and inconsistent data items. The CPS uses 3 imputation methods for item nonresponse: relational imputation, which infers the missing value from other characteristics on the person's record or within the household; longitudinal edits for most of the labor force edits, as appropriate; and "hot deck" allocation, a method of assigning a missing value from a record with similar characteristics, which is the hot deck. Hot decks are defined by variables such as age, race, and sex.

Estimates of Sampling Error: Sufficient sample is allocated to maintain, at most, a 1.9 percent coefficient of variation on national monthly estimates of unemployment, assuming a 6 percent unemployment rate. This translates into a change of 0.2 percentage point in the unemployment rate being significant at a 90 percent confidence level. For each of the 50 States and for the District of Columbia, the design maintains a coefficient of variation of at most 8 percent on the annual average estimate of unemployment, assuming a 6 percent unemployment rate.

Nonsampling Errors: Nonsampling errors in surveys can be attributed to many sources. The full extent of nonsampling error is unknown, but special studies have been conducted to quantify some sources of nonsampling error in the CPS. The CPS employs numerous measures to reduce nonsampling error.

Sources of Additional Material: U.S. Census Bureau and Bureau of Labor Statistics, *Current Population Survey: Design and Methodology*, (Technical Paper 66), online at <http://www.census.gov/prod/2006pubs/tp-66.pdf>; and internet site <http://www.census.gov/programs-surveys/cps/technical-documentation.html>.

Foreign Trade—Export Statistics

Universe, Frequency, and Types of Data: Export statistics cover goods valued at more than $2,500 per commodity shipped by individuals and organizations (including exporters, freight forwarders, and carriers) from the U.S. to other countries. Data are compiled in terms of commodity classification, quantities, values, shipping weights, method of transportation (air or vessel), state of (movement) origin, customs district, customs port, country of destination, and whether contents are domestic goods or reexports. Transactions are classified under approximately 8,000 different products leaving the United States. Data cover about 240 U.S. trading partners. Data are continuously compiled and processed. Documents are collected as shipments depart, and processed on a flow basis. Reports summarize shipments made during calendar months, quarters, and years. Statistics are reported monthly approximately 35 days after the end of the reference month and on a year-to-date basis.

Type of Data Collection Operation: A full compilation (i.e., a "census") is taken of commodity exports, plus U.S. Census Bureau estimates of low-valued exports and Bureau of Economic Analysis (BEA) estimates of trade in services. Statistics for exported goods transactions are compiled from three sources: Shipper's Export Declaration documents filed with Customs and Border Protection (CBP) and sent to the U.S. Census Bureau (3 percent of all transactions), comparable data in electronic form submitted directly by exporters and their agents (63 percent), and special computer tapes from Canada for U.S. exports to Canada (34 percent). Estimates are made for low-value exports by country of destination, and based on bilateral trade patterns. Statistics for U.S. exports to Canada are based on import documents filed with Canadian agencies and forwarded to the U.S. Census Bureau under a 1987 data exchange agreement. Under this agreement, each country eliminated most cross-border export documents; maintains detailed statistics on cross-border imports; exchanges monthly files of cross-border import statistics; and publishes exchanged statistics in place of previously compiled export statistics.

Estimates of Sampling Error: Not applicable.

Nonsampling Errors: The goods data are a complete enumeration of electronic export information (EEI) reported in the automated export system (AES) and are not subject to sampling errors, but they are subject to several types of nonsampling errors. Quality assurance procedures are performed at every stage of collection, processing and tabulation; however the data are still subject to several types of nonsampling errors. The most significant of these include reporting errors, undocumented shipments, timeliness, data capture errors, and errors in the estimation of low-valued transactions.

Sources of Additional Material: Foreign Trade Statistics Overview, <http://www.census.gov/foreign-trade/about/index.html>.

Foreign Trade—Import Statistics

Universe, Frequency, and Types of Data: The import statistics consist of goods valued at more than $2,000 per commodity shipped by individuals and organizations (including importers and customs brokers) into the U.S. from other countries. Data are compiled in terms of commodity classification, quantities, values, shipping weights, methods of transportation (air or vessel), duties collected, unit prices, and market share, country of origin, customs district, customs port, import charges and duties. Commodities are compiled under the Harmonized Tariff Schedules of the United States containing more than 18,000 import commodity codes. Data cover about 240 U.S. trading partners. Data are continuously compiled and processed. Documents are collected as shipments arrive and processed on a flow basis. Reports summarize shipments made during calendar months and years. Statistics are reported monthly approximately 35 days after the end of the reference month and on a year-to-date basis.

Type of Data Collection Operation: A full compilation (i.e., a census) is taken of import shipments, plus U.S. Census Bureau estimates of low-valued imports and Bureau of Economic Analysis (BEA) estimates of trade in services. Statistics for imported goods shipments are compiled from the records filed with Customs and Border Protection (CBP), usually within 10 days after the merchandise enters the United States. Estimates are made for low-value shipments by country of origin, based on previous bilateral trade patterns and periodically updated. Statistics for over 95 percent of all commodity transactions are compiled from records filed electronically with CBP and forwarded as computer tape files to the U.S. Census Bureau. Statistics for other transactions are compiled from hard-copy documents filed with CBP and forwarded on a flow basis for U.S. Census Bureau processing.

Estimates of Sampling Error: Not applicable.

Nonsampling Errors: The goods data are a complete enumeration of documents collected by the U.S. Customs and Border Protection and are not subject to sampling errors, but they are subject to several types of nonsampling errors. The most significant of these include reporting errors, undocumented shipments, timeliness, data capture errors, and errors in the estimation of low-valued transactions. Quality assurance procedures are performed at every stage of collection, processing, and tabulation.

Sources of Additional Material: Foreign Trade Statistics Overview, online at <http://www.census.gov/foreign-trade/about/index.html>.

Monthly and Annual Retail Trade Survey

Universe, Frequency, and Types of Data: The size of the Monthly Retail Trade Survey (MRTS) sample is approximately 13,000 employer firms. Data cover sales at retail stores and inventories held by retail stores. Statistics are available at the national level only. The Annual Retail Trade Survey (ARTS) uses a sample of approximately 16,500 employer firms in the retail trade sector and electronic commerce sales, and requests data on sales, sales taxes, inventories, purchases, operating expenses, and other financial items. Annual data are published at the industry level, using the North American Industry Classifcation System.

Data Collection and Imputation Procedures: Firms for the retail trade surveys come from the Economic Census and the Census Bureau's Business Register. Data are collected by mail questionnaire and the internet, with telephone follow-ups for nonrespondents. Imputation is made for each nonresponse item and each item failing edit checks. For both unit and item nonresponse, a missing value is replaced by a predicted value obtained from an appropriate model for nonresponse. This imputation uses survey data and administrative data as input. In any given month, imputed data amount to about 30 percent of the total monthly retail and food services sales estimate and about 32 percent of the total retail end-of-month inventory estimate. For the annual survey, imputed data amount to about 8 percent of the total retail sales and food services estimate and about 10 percent of the total retail end-of-year inventory estimate. Additional information about the imputation rates for published estimates are available upon request.

Estimates of Sampling Error: Estimated CVs and standard errors are released with monthly reports available online at <http://www.census.gov/retail/index.html#mrts>. Annual data releases include measures of sampling variability.

Nonsampling Errors: Nonsampling errors are difficult to measure and can be attributed to many sources: the inclusion of erroneous units in the survey (overcoverage), the exclusion of eligible units from the survey (undercoverage), nonresponse, misreporting, mistakes in recording and coding responses, misinterpretation of questions, and other errors of collection, response, coverage, or processing. Although nonsampling errors are not measured directly, the Census Bureau employs quality control procedures throughout the process to minimize these types of errors.

Sources of Additional Material: Census Bureau, Monthly and Annual Retail Trade, <http://www.census.gov/retail/index.html>, <http://www.census.gov/retail/how_surveys_are_collected.html>, and <https://www.census.gov/programs-surveys/arts/technical-documentation/methodology.html>.

Survey of Construction

Universe, Frequency, and Types of Data: The Survey of Construction provides current national and regional statistics on starts, completions, and characteristics of new, privately-owned single-family and multifamily housing units and on sales of new single-family houses. Data collected include start and completion dates, sales date, sales price (single-family houses only), and the physical characteristics of housing units. Survey data are available monthly and annually for housing starts since 1959, for new home sales since 1963, and for completions since 1968. Reported data are for building or sales activity taking place during the applicable reference period. Monthly data collection begins the first day after the reference month and continues through the 7th working day.

Type of Data Collection Operation: A multistage probability sample of approximately 900 permit-issuing jurisdictions in the U.S. was selected. Each month in each of these permit offices, field representatives list and select a sample of permits for which to collect data. To obtain data in areas where building permits are not required, a multistage probability sample of over 80 land areas (census tracts or subsections of census tracts) is selected. All roads in these areas are canvassed and data are collected on all new residential construction found. Sampled buildings are followed up until they are completed (and sold, if for sale), or abandoned. Permits for 1- to 4-unit buildings are sampled at an overall rate of 1 in 50. All permits authorizing buildings with 5 or more housing units in the sampled permit offices are selected.

Data Collection and Processing: Data are obtained by telephone and/or field visit each month. Contact continues until the project is either completed or abandoned. If a single-family home is not sold by the time of completion, the project is followed until the sale occurs. Each month, interviews are required for about half of the buildings currently being followed up. Nonresponse/undercoverage adjustment factors are used to account for late reported data. Each month, housing starts, completions, and sales estimates derived from this survey are adjusted by the total numbers of authorized housing units (obtained from the Building Permits Survey) to develop national and regional estimates. Estimates are adjusted to reflect variations by region and type of construction, and to account for late reports and houses started or sold before a permit has been issued. Reported data are seasonally adjusted.

Estimates of Sampling Error: Data are subject to sampling errors. Estimates of the standard errors have been computed from the sample data for selected statistics. They are presented in the source tables in the form of average relative standard errors (RSEs). The relative standard error equals the standard error divided by the estimated value to which it refers.

Nonsampling Errors: Nonsampling errors are attributable to definition problems, differences in interpretation of questions, incorrect reporting, inability to obtain information about all cases in the sample, and processing errors. Although not measured directly, the Census Bureau employs quality control procedures to minimize nonsampling errors.

Sources of Additional Material: Census Bureau, Survey of Construction, online at <https://www.census.gov/econ/overview/co0400.html>.

Nonemployer Statistics

Universe, Frequency, and Types of Data: Nonemployer statistics are an annual tabulation of economic data by industry for active businesses without paid employees or payroll, that are subject to federal income taxes, and that have receipts of $1,000 or more ($1 or more for the construction sector). Excluded are corporations and partnerships with over $1 million in receipts (except for service-type industries, maximum is $2 million). Maximum receipts for sole proprietorships depends on industry classification. Data showing the number of firms and receipts by industry are available for the U.S., states, counties, and metropolitan areas. Most types of businesses covered by the Census Bureau's economic statistics programs are included in the nonemployer statistics. Tax-exempt and agricultural-production businesses are excluded from nonemployer statistics.

Data Collection and Processing: The universe of nonemployer firms is created annually as a byproduct of the Census Bureau's Business Register processing for employer establishments. If a business is active but without paid employees, then it becomes part of the potential nonemployer universe. Industry classification and receipts are available for each potential nonemployer business. These data are obtained primarily from the annual business income tax returns of the Internal Revenue Service (IRS). The potential nonemployer universe undergoes a series of complex processing, editing, and analytical review procedures at the Census Bureau to distinguish nonemployers from employers, and to correct and complete data items used in creating the data tables.

Estimates of Sampling Error: Data are tabulated from administrative records, and are not subject to sampling error.

Nonsampling Errors: The data are subject to nonsampling errors, such as inability to identify all cases that should be included, difficulties with definitions and classification, errors in recording or coding data, and other coverage and processing errors. The improper inclusion of possible employer establishments in the nonemployer universe is a primary source of nonsampling error. The Census Bureau takes several steps to identify and remove these establishments from the nonemployer universe.

Sources of Additional Material: U. S. Census Bureau, Nonemployer Statistics, <https://www.census.gov/programs-surveys/nonemployer-statistics/technical-documentation.html>.

Service Annual Survey (SAS)

Universe, Frequency, and Types of Data: The U.S. Census Bureau conducts the Service Annual Survey (SAS) to provide nationwide estimates of revenues and expenses for most traditional service industries. Estimates are summarized by industry classification based on the North American Industry Classification System (NAICS). Service industries covered by the Service Annual Survey include all or part of the following NAICS sectors: Utilities (NAICS 22), Transportation and Warehousing (NAICS 48-49); Information (NAICS 51); Finance and Insurance (NAICS 52); Real Estate and Rental and Leasing (NAICS 53); Professional, Scientific, and Technical Services (NAICS 54); Administrative and Support and Waste Management and Remediation Services (NAICS 56); Educational Services (NAICS 61); Health Care and Social Assistance (NAICS 62); Arts, Entertainment, and Recreation (NAICS 71); Accommodation and Food Services (NAICS 72); and

Other Services, except Public Administration (NAICS 81). Covers taxable firms and firms exempt from Federal income taxes.

Type of Data Collection Operation: Questionnaires are mailed in January and request annual data for the prior year. Estimates are published approximately 12 months after the initial survey mailing. The Service Annual Survey estimates are developed from a probability sample of approximately 78,000 employer firms, and administrative records for nonemployers. Service Annual Survey uses a probability sample that is periodically reselected from a universe of firms having paid employees. The sample includes firms of all sizes and covers both taxable firms and firms exempt from federal income taxes. Updates to the sample are made on a quarterly basis to account for new and closed businesses. Firms without paid employees, or nonemployers, are included in the estimates through imputation and/or administrative records data provided by other federal agencies.

Estimates of Sampling Error: Estimates are based on a sample and subject to sampling error. The most recent Service Annual Survey results, including coefficients of variations (CVs), can be found on the internet at <https://www.census.gov/programs-surveys/sas/data/tables.html>. Additional information regarding sampling error may also be found online at <https://www.census.gov/programs-surveys/sas/technical-documentation/methodology.html>.

Nonsampling Errors: For both unit and item nonresponse, a missing value is replaced by a predicted value obtained from an appropriate model for nonresponse. The imputation uses survey data and administrative data as input.

Sources of Additional Material: U.S. Census Bureau, "Service Annual Survey," <https://www.census.gov/programs-surveys/sas/about.html>.

Annual Business Survey

Universe, Frequency, and Types of Data: The survey is conducted by the U.S. Census Bureau and the National Science Foundation's National Center for Science and Engineering Statistics. The survey began in 2017, and replaces several surveys, including the Census Bureau's Survey of Business Owners, and the Annual Survey of Entrepreneurs. The survey covers all nonfarm employers filing 941, 944, or 1120 tax forms with receipts of $1,000 or more. In 2017, the survey sampled approximately 850,000 employer businesses; the survey plans to sample approximately 300,00 businesses each year, 2018 to 2021. The survey collects data on the number of employer firms, sales and receipts, payroll, and employment by sex, race, ethnicity, and veteran status. Data are tabulated by business owner sex, race, ethnicity, and veteran status. The survey also collects data on research and development, innovation, and technology. The survey may also include new topics of relevance to the business community. Data are available for the U.S., and by state, metropolitan statistical area, and county, and economic place levels.

Data Collection: Businesses selected for the survey receive an initial letter about the survey and instructions for accessing the survey on the internet. Survey response is required by law. Additional data are collected electronically from the Economic Census and government administrative records, and are combined with survey data. Data results are available by business owner characteristics. Business ownership is defined as having 51 percent or more of the stock or equity in the business and is categorized by firms classifiable by sex, race, ethnicity, and veteran status and firms unclassifiable by sex, race, ethnicity, and veteran status. Businesses could be tabulated in more than one racial group.

Nonresponse and Imputation: Historical data and imputation methods were used to adjust for nonresponse. If available, historical data from the Survey of Business Owners and the Annual Survey of Entrepreneurs were substituted for missing data to determine the sex, ethnicity, race, and veteran status of the business owner or majority business owners. When historical data were not available, the sex, ethnicity, race and veteran status were imputed from donor respondents in the same sampling frame with similar characteristics (industry, legal form of organization, geography). Sampling variability estimates are adjusted to account for nonresponse. Overall, imputed data accounted for approximately 27.9 percent of the firm count estimates by sex, ethnicity, race, and veteran status and approximately 34.6 percent of the estimates for receipts.

Sampling Error: The estimated relative standard errors and estimated standard errors presented in the ABS data tables estimate the sampling variability, and thus measure the precision with which an estimate from the particular sample selected for this survey approximates the average result of all possible samples. Relative standard errors and standard errors are applicable only to those published cells in which sample cases are tabulated. A relative standard error is an expression of the standard error as a percent of the quantity being estimated. For the *Characteristics of Businesses* and *Characteristics of Business Owners* datasets, some data are expressed as percentages with standard errors rather than relative standard errors.

Nonsampling Errors: While explicit measures of the effects of nonsampling errors are not available, adjustments are made to the published relative standard errors to account for errors associated with imputation of missing data. The Census Bureau makes every effort to detect and correct important operational and data errors during processing, editing, analysis, and estimation phases of the survey life cycle.

Sources of Additional Materials: U.S. Census Bureau, Annual Business Survey, <https://www.census.gov/programs-surveys/abs.html> and <https://www.census.gov/programs-surveys/abs/technical-documentation/methodology.html>

Survey of Business Owners, and Annual Survey of Entrepreneurs (ASE)

Discontinued: The Survey of Business Owners and the Annual Survey of Entrepreneurs (ASE) have been discontinued and replaced with the Annual Business Survey (see above). The most recent Survey of Business Owners covers data for 2012. The most recent Annual Survey of Entrepreneurs covers data for 2016.

U.S. DEPARTMENT OF EDUCATION National Center for Education Statistics

Integrated Postsecondary Education Data Survey (IPEDS), Completions

Universe, Frequency, and Types of Data: The IPEDS annually collects institution-level data from postsecondary institutions across the U.S. on tuition and fees, number and types of degrees and certificates conferred, number of students applying and enrolled, number of employees, financial statistics, graduation rates, student financial aid, and academic libraries. The survey consists of 12 components are administered across the fall, winter, and spring reporting seasons. Submission of data to IPEDS is mandatory for any institution that participates in or is an applicant for participation in any federal financial assistance program authorized by Title IV of the Higher Education Act of 1965. IPEDS response rates for each component are nearly 100 percent. Close to 7,000 institutions participate in the survey each year.

Type of Data Collection Operation: The IPEDS collects data via the internet. As respondents enter data online, the data collection system automatically calculates totals, averages, and percentages, and compares the responses with the previous year's submission for the same institution to ensure the data are consistent. The system also compares data with other related values to ensure consistency of reporting within each survey component and across the data collection program. If data are still missing, analysts conduct imputations to complete the database.

Imputation Procedures: Missing data are imputed by using data of similar institutions. With the exception of the Institutional Characteristics component, all items collected in each component are eligible for imputation. Within the Institutional Characteristics component, only cost of attendance and other institutional charges data are eligible for imputation. IPEDS applies a single imputation method for both unit and item nonresponse. The Nearest Neighbor procedure identifies data related to the key statistics of interest for each component (the distance measure), then uses those data to identify a responding institution similar to the nonresponding institution and uses the respondent's data as a substitute for the nonrespondent's missing items.

Estimates of Sampling Error: Not applicable.

Edit Procedures: The internet-based survey instrument contains edit checks to detect major reporting errors. The system automatically generates percentages and totals for each collection component and compared current responses to data reported the previous year. As edit checks run, they prompt survey respondents to correct any errors detected by the system. If accurate data fails the edit checks, the survey respondents either confirm the response or explain why the data appears to be out of the expected data range. The system requires all edit checks to be confirmed or explained. In some cases, respondents can contact IPEDS for assistance. IPEDS staff also review data for additional errors and contact respondents for verification.

Sources of Additional Material: U.S. Department of Education, National Center for Education Statistics, IPEDS Technical/Methodological reports, online at <http://nces.ed.gov/pubsearch/getpubcats. asp?sid=010>.

National Household Education Surveys (NHES) Program

Universe, Frequency, and Types of Data: The National Household Education Surveys Program is a system of surveys of the noninstitutionalized civilian population of the United States. NHES surveys have been conducted periodically since 1991 and have varying universes of interest depending on the particular survey. Some surveys are recurring, others are fielded as 1-time surveys. Currently, the four main topics NHES surveys cover are young children's care and education before school, participation in adult training and education, parent involvement in their children's education, and home schooling. Specific topics covered by each survey are at the NHES website <http://nces.ed.gov/nhes>. Surveys fielded as part of NHES, each universe, and the years they were fielded include:

1 Early Childhood Program Participation—Surveys of parents of a representative sample of children from birth through grade 3, with the specific age groups varying by survey year (1991, 1995, 1999, 2001, 2005, 2012, 2016, and 2019).

2 School Readiness—Interviews with parents of a representative sample of 3-7 year-old children (1993 and 1999) and of 3-6 year old children, not yet in kindergarten (2007).

3 Before- and After-School Programs and Activities—Interviews with parents of a representative sample of students in grades K through 8 (1999, 2001, and 2005).

4 School Safety and Discipline—Interviews with a representative sample of students in grades 6-12, their parents, and the parents of a representative sample of students in grades 3-12 (1993).

5 Parent and Family Involvement in Education—Surveys of parents of a representative sample of children age three through grade 12 or in grades K through 12 depending on the survey year (1996, 1999, 2003, 2007, 2012, 2016, and 2019). Separate questionnaires are administered for children enrolled in public and private schools, and for children who are home schooled.

6 Adult Education—Interviews with a representative sample of civilian, noninstitutionalized persons aged 16 and older who were not enrolled in grade 12 or below (1991, 1995, 1999, 2001, 2003, and 2005).

7 Civic Involvement—Interviews with representative samples of parents, youth, and adults (1996 and 1999).

8 Household Library Use—Interviews with a representative sample of U.S. households (1996).

9 Adult Training and Education Survey—Covers adults age 16 to 65 who are not enrolled in high school, focusing on nondegree credentials and work experience programs (2016).

Data Collection Operation: NHES typically fields 2 to 3 topical surveys at a time, although the number has varied across its administrations. Surveys are administered in English and in Spanish. From 1991 to 2007, the NHES used telephone interviews to collect data. In 2012, the NHES switched to a mail survey, and samples were developed using household address information for all 50 states and the District of Columbia. The 2019 NHES mailed invitations to participate in the survey; data were collected using an internet-based survey instrument. Both of the 2016 and 2019 NHES samples were selected using a 2-stage address-based sampling frame. Black and Hispanic American households were sampled at a higher rate than other households. The 2016 and 2019 NHES fielded the Parent and Family Involvement in Education Survey, and the Early Childhood Program Participation survey.

Estimates of Sampling Error: Reports presenting NHES data include tables on standard errors.

Nonsampling Errors: For each NHES survey, efforts are made to prevent nonsampling errors and errors from bias from occurring and to compensate for them, where possible. For instance, during the survey design phase, cognitive interviews are conducted to assess respondents' knowledge of the survey topics, their comprehension of questions and terms, and the sensitivity of items.

Sources of Additional Material: Please see the NHES website at <http://nces.ed.gov/nhes>; and technical notes and related methodological information in individual NHES reports available online at <https://nces.ed.gov/pubsearch/getpubcats.asp?sid=004>.

U.S. DEPARTMENT OF JUSTICE, FEDERAL BUREAU OF INVESTIGATION

Uniform Crime Reporting (UCR) Program

Universe, Frequency, and Types of Data: Monthly reports on the number of criminal offenses that become known to law enforcement agencies. More than 18,000 city, university and college, county, state, tribal, and federal law enforcement agencies are eligible to contribute data to the FBI. The UCR Program collects information regarding the violent crimes of murder and nonnegligent manslaughter, rape, robbery, and aggravated assault as well as the property crimes of burglary, larceny-theft, motor vehicle theft, and arson. (Although the FBI classifies arson as a property crime, it does not estimate arson data because of variations in the level of participation by the reporting agencies. Consequently, arson is not included in the property crime estimate.) The program also collects arrest data for the offenses listed above plus 20 offenses that include all other crimes except traffic violations.

Type of Data Collection Operation: The UCR Program consists of four data collections: The National

Incident-Based Reporting System (NIBRS), the Summary Reporting System (SRS), the Law Enforcement Officers Killed and Assaulted (LEOKA) Program, and the Hate Crime Statistics Program. The SRS will be phased out; by January 1, 2021, data will be collected via the NIBRS only. Currently in development, but with no major data releases as of publication of this *Statistical Abstract*, is a new collection of data on the use of force by law enforcement; the National Use-of-Force Data Collection began accepting data January 2019. Crime statistics are based on reports of crime data submitted either directly to the FBI by contributing law enforcement agencies or through cooperating state UCR Programs. States with UCR programs collect data directly from individual law enforcement agencies and forward reports, prepared in accordance with UCR standards, to the FBI. UCR program participation is voluntary. Beginning with the 2013 data collections, all data must be submitted electronically, and after July 2013, the UCR Program no longer accepted paper submissions or the electronic submission of documents (i.e., Portable Document Format files).

Data Quality Procedures: The FBI's Crime Statistics Management Unit staff initially review the data to determine adherence to UCR policy, conformance to UCR definitions and principles, and consistency with established statistical methodologies and norms. Before the information is entered into the national database, the CSMU staff use edit functions to ensure that the data meet established standards. If staff find errors or anomalies, they obtain verification and/or correction from the submitting agency/state UCR Program. After the data pass through this first series of checks, the data are uploaded into the national database. Data then undergo a series of multi-layered processes to check for reasonableness, quality, and validity. FBI staff contact data contributors to clarify data submissions that do not pass data quality checks.

Estimates of Sampling Error: Not applicable.

Nonsampling Errors: Due to computer problems, changes in records management systems, personnel shortages, or a number of other reasons, some agencies cannot provide data for publication.

Sources of Additional Material: U.S. Department of Justice, Federal Bureau of Investigation, <https://www.fbi.gov/services/cjis/ucr>; and *Crime in the United States*, annual, *Hate Crime Statistics*, annual, and *Law Enforcement Officers Killed and Assaulted*, annual, <https://www.fbi.gov/services/cjis/ucr/publications>.

U.S. INTERNAL REVENUE SERVICE, TAX STATISTICS

Corporation Income Tax Returns

Universe, Frequency, and Types of Data: Annual study of unaudited corporation income tax returns, Forms 1120, 1120-F, 1120-L, 1120-PC, 1120-REIT, 1120-RIC, and 1120S, filed by corporations or businesses legally defined as corporations. The IRS Statistics of Income (SOI) Division collects data on corporations by size, industry, total assets, business receipts, deductions, liabilities, net income, income tax liability, tax credits, and other financial data. SOI aggregates these data for C corporations and passthrough entities, such as S

corporations. The target population consists of all returns of active corporations organized for profit that are required to file one of the 1120 forms that are part of the SOI study.

Type of Data Collection Operation: For the 2017 tax year, the target sample was approximately 116,660 corporate tax returns (including inactive and non-eligible corporations), allocated to sample classes which are based on type of return, and either size of total assets alone or both size of total assets and a measure of income. Sampling rates for sample classes varied from 0.25 percent to 100 percent. The total realized sample for 2017, including inactive and noneligible corporations, is 120,098 returns.

Data Collection and Imputation Procedures: Data processing for SOI begins with information already extracted for IRS administrative purposes; over 100 items available from the Business Master File system are checked and corrected as necessary. SOI extracts some 2,500 additional data items from corporate tax returns during processing. After data capture, data go through hundreds of tests for consistency and error resolution. If missing data items are from the balance sheet, then imputation procedures are used. If data for a whole return are missing because the return is unavailable to SOI during the data capture process, imputation procedures are also used in certain cases. Beginning with the Tax Year 2012 sample, only the largest returns with incomplete balance sheets are subject to a balance sheet imputation procedure. The IRS's Statistics of Income (SOI) division performs imputation on an ad hoc basis only.

Estimates of Sampling Error: Statistics of Income reports do not directly present the standard error. Instead, the ratio of the standard error to the estimate itself is presented in percentage form. This ratio is called the coefficient of variation (CV). The user of SOI data may multiply an estimate by its CV to recreate the standard error and to construct confidence intervals. Estimated CVs for are published in the Statistics of Income, *Corporation Complete Report.*

Nonsampling Errors: These may include coverage errors, processing errors, and nonresponse errors.

Sources of Additional Material: U.S. Internal Revenue Service, Statistics of Income, *Corporation Income Tax Returns*, <http://www.irs.gov/uac/SOI-Tax-Stats-Corporation-Tax-Statistics>.

Individual Income Tax Returns

Universe, Frequency, and Types of Data: Annual study of unaudited individual income tax returns, Forms 1040, 1040A, and 1040EZ, filed by U.S. citizens and residents. Data provided on various financial characteristics by size of adjusted gross income, marital status, and by taxable and nontaxable returns.

Type of Data Collection Operation: For 2017 tax year, data cover a stratified probability sample of 352,316 returns selected from a total of 153,575,872 returns received during the calendar year 2018. These are mostly returns filed for the 2017 tax year, but might they also include a few for other tax years that the IRS received during the 2018 calendar year. All tax returns were classified into one of 4 subpopulations, strata, and each strata was sampled at a rate of 0.10 percent to 100 percent. All data were captured and processed electronically.

Data Collection and Imputation Procedures: Computer selection of sample of tax return records. Data adjusted and imputed during editing for incorrect, missing, or inconsistent entries to ensure consistency with other entries on return. Adjustments and imputations are based on prior-year data and other available information.

Estimates of Sampling Error: Coefficients of variation and confidence intervals are provided along with the data tables at the website indicated below.

Nonsampling Errors: Processing errors and errors can arise from the use of tolerance checks for the data.

Sources of Additional Material: U.S. Internal Revenue Service, Statistics of Income, *Individual Income Tax Returns* (Publication 1304), annual, <https://www.irs.gov/statistics/soi-tax-stats-individual-income-tax-returns-publication-1304-complete-report>, and <https://www.irs.gov/statistics/soi-tax-stats-individual-income-tax-return-form-1040-statistics>.

U.S. NATIONAL CENTER FOR HEALTH STATISTICS (NCHS)

National Health Interview Survey (NHIS)

Universe, Frequency, and Types of Data: Since 1957, the NHIS has been a continuous data collection covering the civilian noninstitutional population to obtain information on demographic characteristics, health conditions, injuries, impairments, use of health services, health behaviors, and other health topics. Excluded are persons in long-term care institutions, correctional facilities, and U.S. nationals living abroad; active-duty armed forces personnel are also excluded unless at least one other family member is a civilian eligible for the survey. The NHIS aims to have a sample size (completed interviews) of approximately 35,000 households containing about 87,500 persons. The annual response rate is approximately 65-70 percent of eligible households in the sample.

Type of Data Collection Operation: Trained interviewers from the U.S. Census Bureau visit each selected household and administer the NHIS in person using computer assisted personal interviewing. Follow-up interviews may be conducted via telephone. The core questionnaire remains largely the same each year and has 4 main components: the Household Composition section, the Family Core, the Sample Child Core, and the Sample Adult Core. The Household component collects limited demographic information on all of the individuals living in the household. The Family component collects additional demographic information on each member from each family in the house and collects data on topics such as health status and limitations, injuries, healthcare access and utilization, and health insurance. From each family, one sample adult and one sample child (if any children are present) are randomly selected for data collection. Because some health issues are different for children and adults, the Sample Child Core and the Sample Adult Core questionnaires differ in some items but both collect basic information on health status, health care services, and health behaviors. All eligible adults in a family

had the same chance of being selected as the sample adult. A feature of the current sample design is that adults age 65 and older who are black, Hispanic, or Asian have an increased chance of being selected as the sample adult, relative to adults under age 65 and adults age 65 and older who are not black, Hispanic, or Asian. Core questions remain consistent. The NHIS also uses supplements to ask questions on current health topics that change.

Imputation Procedures: The computer assisted personal interviewing program incorporates range and consistency checks of the data. Some missing data items (e.g., race, ethnicity) are imputed using a hot deck imputation value. Sequential regression models are used to create multiple imputation files for family income. Unit nonresponse is compensated for by an adjustment to the survey weights. Since 2004, imputation has been performed for injury and poisoning episodes for which the respondent did not provide sufficient information to determine a month, day, and year of occurrence.

Estimates of Sampling Error: Because NHIS data are based on a sample of the population, they are subject to sampling error. Standard errors appear with the data to indicate the reliability of the estimates. Analysts at NCHS generally use the software package SUDAAN® with Taylor series linearization methods to produce standard error estimates and hypothesis test results (such as p values).

Nonsampling Errors: Nonsampling errors such as response errors, defective sample frames, nonresponse, and undercoverage, are difficult quantities to measure, but every effort is made to minimize such errors at each step of the NHIS operation.

Sources of Additional Material: National Center for Health Statistics, National Health Interview Survey, online at <http://www.cdc.gov/nchs/nhis/about_nhis.htm>. See also <http://www.cdc.gov/nchs/nhis/methods.htm>.

National Survey of Family Growth (NSFG)

Universe, Frequency, and Types of Data: The National Survey of Family Growth (NSFG) gathers information on family life and planning, marriage and divorce, pregnancy, infertility, use of contraception, and general and reproductive health. The NSFG also collects data on sexual behavior and attraction, and sexual orientation. The NSFG began in 1973 as a periodic survey of women age 15-44 among the civilian noninstitutionalized population. In 2002, the NSFG included men age 15-44. In 2015 the age range covered became 15-49. Beginning 2006, the program switched from periodic surveys to continuous interviewing. The 2011-2013 NSFG conducted in-person interviews with 5,601 women and 4,815 men. The response rates were 72.8 percent for all respondents, 73.4 percent for women, and 72.1 percent for men. The 2013-2015 NSFG included 5,699 interviews with women and 4,506 interviews with men; response rates were 71.2 percent for women and 67.1 percent for men.

Type of Data Collection Operation: Survey participation is voluntary. Only one person is interviewed in a selected household. Signed consent is required for minors age 15-17. The NSFG collects data by employing female interviewers to conduct personal interviews using computer-assisted personal interviewing (CAPI). Selected data items are also collected using audio computer-assisted self-interviewing (ACASI). In ACASI, the respondent listens to the questions through headphones, reads them on the screen, or both, and enters the response directly into the computer. This method avoids asking the respondent to give his or her answers to the interviewer, and it has been found to yield more complete reporting of sensitive behaviors.

Imputation Procedures: Imputation is the process of assigning answers to cases with missing data. In the NSFG, item imputation is performed on approximately 600 "recoded variables," or "recodes," rather than all of the thousands of variables in the data set. The purposes of imputation are to make the data more complete, more consistent, easier to use, and to reduce bias caused by differential failure to respond. Imputation is done in two ways for the 2013-2015 NSFG, logical and regression imputation. Regression imputation uses a regression equation to estimate a value for a case with missing data. Regression imputation was used to assign most of the imputed values. Logical imputation uses a subject-matter expert to assign a value based on the value of other variables for the case with missing data. Recodes involving imputation did not exceed 2 percent of values imputed.

Data Quality: Standard errors are generally released along with data in NCHS reports. The NSFG utilizes the following to maintain high quality data: 1) questionnaire design work, 2) consistency checks built into the interview to enable the interviewer to resolve problems in the field, 3) evaluation of monthly data files to find and correct survey instrument problems, and 4) extensive interviewer training. The source website has numerous documents discussing the survey sample design and collection methods, sample error estimation design, examples of variance estimation, and other methodological issues under National Survey of Family Growth, "Questionnaires, Datasets, and Related Documentation," for each cycle of the NSFG online at <https://www.cdc.gov/nchs/nsfg/nsfg_questionnaires.htm>

Sources of Additional Material: National Center for Health Statistics, National Survey of Family Growth, online at <http://www.cdc.gov/nchs/nsfg/about_nsfg.htm>.

National Vital Statistics System

Universe, Frequency, and Types of Data: Annual data on births, deaths, marriages, divorces, and fetal deaths in the United States. Legal authority for the registration of these events resides individually with the 50 States, 2 cities (Washington, DC, and New York City), and 5 territories (Puerto Rico, the Virgin Islands, Guam, American Samoa, and the Commonwealth of the Northern Mariana Islands). These jurisdictions are responsible for maintaining registries of vital events and for issuing copies of birth, marriage, divorce, and death certificates.

Type of Data Collection Operation: Mortality data are based on a complete file of death records, except 1972, based on 50 percent sample. Natality statistics 1951-1971, are based on 50 percent sample of birth certificates, except a 20 percent to 50 percent sample in 1967, received by NCHS.

Data Collection and Imputation Procedures: Reports are based on records from registration offices of the jurisdictions listed above. Data pertaining to causes of death are classified and coded according to the International Classification of Diseases (ICD).

Estimates of Sampling Error: For recent years, there is no sampling for these files; the files are based on 100 percent of certificates registered. Generally more than 99 percent of the births and deaths occurring in this country are registered.

Nonsampling Errors: The NCHS checks electronic files for completeness, valid coding of items, inconsistencies in data items, and other problems or errors. The NCHS investigates items that effect the quality and completeness of data, and registration areas are asked to verify counts or determine the nature of data discrepancies, in order to resolve and correct data.

Sources of Additional Material: U.S. National Center for Health Statistics, *Vital Statistics of the United States*, Vol. I and Vol. II, annual 1980 to 2003, and the *National Vital Statistics Reports*. See the NCHS website at <http://www.cdc.gov/nchs/nvss/index.htm>.

National Highway Traffic Safety Administration (NHTSA)

Fatality Analysis Reporting System (FARS)

Universe, Frequency, and Types of Data: FARS is a census of all fatal motor vehicle traffic crashes that occur throughout the United States, including the District of Columbia and Puerto Rico, on roadways customarily open to the public. The crash must be reported to the state/jurisdiction, and is classified as fatal if a directly related fatality occurs within thirty days of the crash.

Data Collection and Imputation Procedures: NHTSA has a cooperative agreement with an agency in each State government to provide specific information in a standard format on fatal crashes occurring in the State. State analysts extract data from state documents and enter the data into a standardized electronic database. State documents include police accident reports, death certificates, state vehicle registration files, coroner/medical examiner reports, vital statistics, and other records. Computerized edit checks monitor the accuracy, consistency, and completeness of the data. The FARS incorporates a sophisticated mathematical multiple imputation procedure to develop a probability distribution of missing blood alcohol concentration (BAC) levels in the database for drivers, pedestrians, and cyclists.

Estimates of Sampling Error: Since this is census data, there are no sampling errors.

Nonsampling Errors: FARS represents a census of all police-reported crashes and captures all data reported at the state level. FARS data undergo a rigorous quality control process to prevent inaccurate reporting. However, these data are highly dependent on the accuracy of the police accident reports. Errors or omissions within police accident reports may not be detected.

Sources of Additional Material: Fatality Analysis Reporting System (FARS), online at <http://www.nhtsa.gov/FARS>.

Weights and Measures

U.S. Customary/Metric Conversion Table

[Conversions provided in the table are approximate]

Symbol	When you know U.S. customary	Multiply by	To find metric	Symbol
in	inches	2.54	centimeters	cm
ft	feet	30.48	centimeters	cm
yd	yards	0.91	meters	m
mi	miles	1.61	kilometers	km
in^2	square inches	6.45	square centimeters	cm^2
ft^2	square feet	0.09	square meters	m^2
yd^2	square yards	0.84	square meters	m^2
mi^2	square miles	2.59	square kilometers	km^2
	acre	0.41	hectare	ha
oz	ounces	28.35	grams	g
lb	pounds	0.45	kilograms	kg
oz (troy)	troy ounces	31.1	grams	g
	short tons (2,000 lb)	0.91	metric tons	t
	long tons (2,240 lb)	1.02	metric tons	t
fl oz	fluid ounces	29.57	milliliters	mL
c	cups	0.24	liters	L
pt	pints	0.47	liters	L
qt	quarts	0.95	liters	L
gal	gallons	3.79	liters	L
ft^3	cubic feet	0.03	cubic meters	m^3
yd^3	cubic yards	0.76	cubic meters	m^3
°F	degrees Fahrenheit (subtract 32)	0.55	degrees Celsius	°C

Symbol	When you know metric	Multiply by	To find U.S. customary	Symbol
cm	centimeters	0.39	inches	in
cm	centimeters	0.03	feet	ft
m	meters	1.09	yards	yd
km	kilometers	0.62	miles	mi
cm^2	square centimeters	0.16	square inches	in^2
cm^2	square centimeters	10.76	square feet	ft^2
m^2	square meters	1.2	square yards	yd^2
km^2	square kilometers	0.39	square miles	mi^2
ha	hectare	2.47	acre	
g	grams	0.04	ounces	oz
kg	kilograms	2.20	pounds	lb
g	grams	0.04	troy ounces	oz (troy)
t	metric tons	1.1	short tons (2,000 lb)	
t	metric tons	0.98	long tons (2,240 lb)	
mL	milliliters	0.03	fluid ounces	fl oz
L	liters	4.23	cups	c
L	liters	2.11	pints	pt
L	liters	1.06	quarts	qt
L	liters	0.26	gallons	gal
m^3	cubic meters	35.31	cubic feet	ft^3
m^3	cubic meters	1.31	cubic yards	yd^3
°C	degrees Celsius (after multiplying, add 32)	1.8	degrees Fahrenheit	°F

Source: National Institute of Standards and Technology (NIST), Weights and Measures Division. See <https://www.nist.gov/pml/weights-and-measures/metric-si/unit-conversion>

Index

[NOTE: Index citations refer to **table** numbers, not **page** numbers]

Note: Index citations refer to **table** numbers, not **page** numbers

---

Note: Index citations refer to **table** numbers, not **page** numbers

---

Note: Index citations refer to **table** numbers, not **page** numbers

Note: Index citations refer to **table** numbers, not **page** numbers

---

Note: Index citations refer to **table** numbers, not **page** numbers

Note: Index citations refer to **table** numbers, not **page** numbers

Book, periodical, and music stores, 665, 673, 1071, 1072, 1073
Book publishing industry, 772, 1153, 1158, 1161
Bookkeeping. (See Accounting, tax preparation, bookkeeping, and payroll services.)
Books (see also Book publishing industry, Libraries and Reading), 1079, 1161, 1188
Boots. (See Footwear.)
Borders, Canada and Mexico, 411, 1290
Border Patrol activities, 562, 563
Boron, 939, 940
Bosnia and Herzegovina. (See Foreign countries.)
Botox, 199
Botswana. (See Foreign countries.)
Botulism, 203
Bowling, 1268, 1269, 1271
Bowling center industry, 1248, 1251
Boxing, 1268
Brazil. (See Foreign countries.)
Bread, 763, 768
Breastfeeding, 106
Breweries, 1064
Bridges, 1112
Broadband, 1160, 1177, 1178, 1181, 1182, 1401
Broadcasting industry:
　Capital, 814
　Earnings, 665, 788, 1153, 1154
　Employees, 665, 788, 1153, 1154
　Establishments, 788, 1153, 1154
　Finances, 780, 1158
　Gross domestic product, 705
　Multinational companies, 828, 829
　Number of stations, 1160
　Productivity, 673
　Receipts, revenue, 780, 788, 1154, 1158
Broadway and off-Broadway shows, 1254
Broccoli, 248, 877, 898
Broilers (see also Poultry), 772, 877, 905, 913, 914
Bromine, 939, 940
Bronchitis, 212
Brunei. (See Foreign countries.)
Buddhist population. (See Religion.)
Budget, federal:
　Debt, 509
　Outlays, 508, 510, 511, 512
　Receipts, 508, 514
　Tax expenditures, 516
　Taxes, 514
Building construction:
　Earnings, 665
　Employees, 665, 992
　Occupational safety, 696
Building materials, and garden supplies stores:
　Earnings, 665, 788, 1073
　Electronic commerce, 1068, 1078
　Employees, 665, 788, 1065, 1071, 1073
　Establishments, 788, 1065, 1071, 1072
　Inventories, 1053, 1077
　Nonemployers, 1072
　Price indexes, 1002
　Productivity, 673
　Sales, 788, 1053, 1065, 1068, 1072, 1074, 1076, 1077, 1078
Building permits. (See Construction industry, and Housing and housing units.)

Buildings (see also Construction industry, and Housing and housing units):
　Characteristics of, 1038
　Construction value, 994, 996, 998, 999
　Federal, 536
　Fires and property loss, 402, 405, 436
　Floor space, 536, 996, 1038
Bulgaria. (See Foreign countries.)
Bullying, 337, 340
Burglaries, 335, 343, 344, 345, 346, 349, 359, 360
Burkina Faso. (See Foreign countries.)
Burma. (See Foreign countries.)
Burundi. (See Foreign countries.)
Buses and bus transportation. (See Passenger transit industry, and Motor vehicles.)
Business cycles, 818
Business enterprises (see also individual types of business and industry):
　Age of firms, 798
　Age of owner, 792
　American Indian- and Alaska Native- owned businesses, 801, 808
　Asian- owned businesses, 801, 806
　Bankruptcies filed, 809, 810
　Births and deaths of, 799, 851
　Black- owned businesses, 801, 805
　Capital, 814, 815, 816
　Corporations, partnerships, and proprietorships, 778, 780, 781, 782, 783, 1066, 1072
　Employees, 671, 790, 791, 795, 796, 797, 799, 803, 804, 805, 806, 807, 808, 827, 851, 1295, 1327, 1328
　Establishments, 671, 788, 789, 790, 791, 792, 793, 796, 797, 799, 801, 1328
　Expansions and contractions, 799
　Finances, 778, 781, 782, 783, 784, 785, 823, 824, 825, 828, 829, 1054, 1055, 1075
　Firms, 795, 796, 797, 799, 803, 804, 805, 806, 807, 808, 1327
　Flow of funds, 1194, 1195
　Foreign investment in the U.S., 1308, 1309, 1310
　Foreign trade, 1327, 1328
　Franchises, 794
　High technology, 851
　Hispanic- owned businesses, 801, 804
　Leading indicators, 819
　Loans to minority- operated small businesses, 800
　Minority- owned, 803, 804, 805, 806, 807, 808
　Multinational companies, 826, 827, 828, 829
　Native Hawaiian, Other Pacific Islander- owned business, 801, 807
　Patents, 811, 812, 1402
　Payroll, 790, 791, 795, 796, 797
　Profits, 823, 824, 825, 1054, 1055, 1075
　Sales, shipments, receipts, 1050, 1052, 1053, 1055, 1075
　Small business, 795, 796, 797, 800
　Startups, 798
　Veteran–owned, 801
　Women- owned businesses, 801, 802
Business management, degrees, 325, 328, 329, 330, 331
Butane, 946
Butter, 249, 768, 911

Note: Index citations refer to **table** numbers, not **page** numbers

C

Note: Index citations refer to **table** numbers, not **page** numbers

---

Note: Index citations refer to **table** numbers, not **page** numbers

Note: Index citations refer to **table** numbers, not **page** numbers

Computers and electronic product manufacturing:
  Capital, 814
  Earnings, 665, 1042, 1049
  Employees, 665, 1040, 1042, 1044, 1049
  Establishments, 1040
  Foreign trade, 1325, 1330, 1331
  Gross domestic product, 705, 1039
  Industrial production index, 821
  Inventories, 1051, 1052, 1053
  Multinational companies, 828, 829
  Productivity, 673
  Prices, 776
  Research and development, 836
  Shipments, 1042, 1051, 1052, 1053, 1062,
    1063
Condensed and evaporated milk, 249
Congestion, traffic, 1137
Congo (Brazzaville). (See Foreign countries.)
Congo (Kinshasa). (See Foreign countries.)
Congress, U.S.:
  Apportionment of, 461
  Asian members, 464
  Bills, acts, resolutions, 466, 467
  Black members, 464
  Campaign finances, 475, 476
  Composition of, 462, 463, 465
  Congressional districts, 460
  Hispanic members, 464
  Seniority, 463
  Time in session, 466
  Women members, 464
  Votes cast, 448, 450, 458, 459, 460
Connecticut. (See State data.)
Construction industry (see also Building
    construction, and Highways):
  Building permits, 995
  Capital, 793, 814, 816
  Construction contracts, 996, 997
  Earnings, 663, 665, 676, 677, 788, 802, 803, 804,
    805, 806, 807, 808, 993, 1343
  Employees, 650, 651, 652, 654, 663, 664, 665,
    671, 788, 791, 796, 802, 803, 804, 805,
    806, 807, 808, 849, 992, 993, 1343
  Establishments, 671, 788, 789, 791, 792, 793,
    796, 801, 802, 803, 804, 805, 806, 807, 808,
    992, 993, 1343
  Finances, 780, 783
  Gross domestic product, 705
  Hires and separations, 669, 670
  Hours, 663
  Nonemployers, 789
  Occupational safety, 694, 696
  Profits, 825
  Residential, 995, 998, 999, 1000, 1001, 1003,
    1005
  Shipments, receipts, 780, 783, 788, 789, 802,
    803, 804, 805, 806, 807, 808
  Unions, 699
  Value, of, 994, 996, 998, 999
Construction machinery, manufacturing:
  Earnings, 665, 1042
  Employees, 665, 1042
  Productivity, 673
  Shipments, 1042

Construction materials. (See Building materials.)
Consumers:
  Consumer complaints, 358, 361, 1098
  Consumer goods, 217, 772
  Credit, 784, 785, 1197, 1199, 1200, 1203, 1212,
    1214, 1215, 1216, 1220
  Expenditures:
    Entertainment, 713, 722, 725, 726, 1260,
      1261
    Education, 713, 722, 725, 726, 773
    Food, 713, 722, 723, 725, 726, 727, 773, 881
    Health insurance, 149, 713
    Housing, 713, 722, 723, 725, 726, 727, 773
    Medical care, 143, 144, 145, 146, 149, 150,
      713, 722, 723, 725, 726, 727, 773
    Metropolitan areas, 723
    Pets, 713, 1260
    Reading material, 713, 722, 725, 726, 773,
      1260, 1261, 1265
    Sporting goods, 773, 1260, 1272, 1278
    Transportation, 713, 722, 723, 725, 726, 727,
      773
Consumer price indexes, 760, 761, 762, 763
  Foreign countries, 1372, 1379
  Medical care, 148, 761, 762, 763
  Purchasing power of the dollar, 760
Consumption. (See individual commodities, and
    Personal consumption expenditures.)
Contraception, use of, 101, 104
Contract employees, 648
Convenience stores. (See Food and beverage
    stores.)
Copper:
  Consumption, 940, 943
  Foreign trade, 940, 943
  Prices, 772, 776, 777, 940, 941
  Production and value, 939, 940, 1389
Copyrights, registration, 813
Corn:
  Acreage, 895, 898, 903, 1384
  Consumption, 248, 249, 1384
  Farm marketings, sales, 877, 878, 903
  Foreign trade, 887, 889, 890, 1324, 1384, 1388
  Genetically engineered, 871
  Prices, 772, 776, 895
  Production, 887, 895, 898, 903, 1384
  Supply and disappearance, 1384
Coronavirus disease 2019 (COVID- 19), 120, 179
Corporations:
  Bonds, 1222
  Capital, 787
  Dividend payments, 823
  Finances, 778, 779, 781, 782, 783, 785, 786,
    787, 1054, 1055, 1075, 1193, 1194, 1233
  Manufacturing, 1054, 1055
  Nonfinancial, 785
  Philanthropy, 612
  Profits, 778, 823, 824, 825, 1054, 1055, 1075
  Receipts, 778, 783
  Sales, 783, 1054, 1055, 1075
  Taxes:
    Corporate income tax, 482, 483, 496, 498,
      823
    Returns, 778, 779, 787

Note: Index citations refer to **table** numbers, not **page** numbers

Note: Index citations refer to **table** numbers, not **page** numbers

Note: Index citations refer to **table** numbers, not **page** numbers

Note: Index citations refer to **table** numbers, not **page** numbers

Note: Index citations refer to **table** numbers, not **page** numbers

Elections:
    Campaign finances, 475, 476
    Congressional, 448, 450, 458, 459, 460
    Gubernatorial, 469
    Hispanic origin officials, 473
    Political action committees (PAC), 474, 476
    Presidential, 448, 450, 454, 455, 456, 457
    State legislatures, 470, 471, 472
    Voter registration, 451, 452, 453
    Voter turnout, 448, 449, 450, 451, 452, 453
    Votes cast, 452, 454, 455, 456, 457, 458, 459,
        460, 469
    Voting- age population, 448, 450, 451, 452
    Women in public office, 472
Electric light and power industry (see also Electricity,
        and Utilities):
    Customers, 984, 988
    Emissions, 422, 423
    Finances, 985
    General capacity, 978, 980, 981
    Industrial production index, 821
    Peak load, 981
    Water use, 977, 978
Electric vehicles and fueling stations, 1124
Electrical engineering, 846, 849
Electrical equipment, appliances, and components
        manufacturing (see also Computers and
        electronic product manufacturing):
    Capital, 814
    Earnings, 665, 1042, 1049
    Employees, 665, 1040, 1042, 1044, 1049
    Establishments, 1040
    Foreign trade, 1325, 1330, 1331
    Gross domestic product, 705, 1039
    Industrial production index, 821
    Inventories, 1051, 1052
    Productivity, 673
    Research and development, 836
    Shipments, 1042, 1051, 1052, 1060, 1062, 1063
    Toxic chemical releases, 430
Electricity (see also Electric light and power
        industry):
    Capability, 978, 980, 981
    Cogeneration of, 977
    Consumption, 959, 961, 963, 982, 984
    Expenditures, 725, 726, 967
    Foreign countries, 1390
    Hydroelectric power, 958, 978, 986, 1390
    Nuclear, 958, 959, 963, 973, 974, 978, 1390
    Price indexes, 763, 773
    Prices, 765, 772, 959, 979, 983
    Production, 959, 977, 980, 984, 1390
    Renewable sources, 958, 959, 962, 976, 977, 978,
        986, 1390
    Residential, 982, 984
    Sales, 982, 984
    Service, class of, 979, 982, 983
    Weather- related outages, 987
Electronic benefits transfer cards, 1212
Electronic commerce (e- commerce):
    Business sales, 1068, 1078, 1079
    Consumer sales, 1079
    Nonemployer, 1072
    Output, 1156, 1157
    Retail trade, 1078, 1079

Revenue, 1299
Services, 1299
Value added, 1156, 1157
Wholesale, 1068
Electronic goods:
    Foreign trade, 1324
    Ownership, devices, sales, 772, 1079, 1176, 1183,
        1184
Electronic instruments manufacturing, 665, 673
Electronic medical records, 177
Electronic shopping and mail order houses, 665,
    673, 1074, 1079
Electronics and appliance stores:
    Earnings, 665, 788, 1073
    Electronic commerce, 1078
    Employees, 665, 788, 1065, 1071, 1073
    Establishments, 788, 1065, 1071, 1072
    Productivity, 673
    Sales, 788, 1065, 1072, 1074, 1076, 1078
Elevation, extreme and mean by state, 414
El Salvador. (See Foreign countries.)
Emergency medicine, departments, 189, 190, 193
Emergency shelters, 609
Emissions. (See Air pollution.)
Emphysema, 123, 124, 212
Employee benefits, 169, 170, 504, 689, 690, 691,
    692, 769
Employees. (See Business enterprise, and individual
    industries.)
Employment. (See Labor Force.)
Employment service industry, 665, 1294
Endangered species, 447
Energy (see also Electric light and power industry,
        and various fuel types):
    Air pollutant emissions, 420, 421, 422, 423, 424,
        964, 1398
    Consumption, 958, 960, 962, 963, 966, 1392
        End- use sector, 960, 963
        Foreign countries, 1392, 1393, 1394
        Renewable sources, 958, 959, 962, 977, 978,
            986
        Source, 958, 959, 963
        Transportation, 961
    Electric, 956, 957, 963, 965, 967, 973, 974, 975,
        976, 977, 978, 979, 980, 981, 982, 983, 984,
        985, 986
    End- use sector, 960, 963, 967
    Expenditures, 965, 967, 1038
    Federal outlays, 481, 512
    Price indexes:
        Consumer, 761, 762, 763
        Producer, 772
    Prices, 765, 965, 979
    Renewable energy systems on farms, 868
Engineering and architectural services:
    Earnings, 665
    Employees, 665, 849, 1294, 1295
    Establishments, 1293, 1294
    Nonemployers, 1293
    Receipts, 1293, 1297
Engineers and scientists (see also individual fields):
    Characteristics, 841, 847
    Degrees conferred, 328, 329, 330, 331, 842,
        843, 844, 845, 846

Note: Index citations refer to **table** numbers, not **page** numbers

Note: Index citations refer to **table** numbers, not **page** numbers

Housing, rental value, 875
Income, 866, 867, 874, 875, 876, 877, 879
Inventories, change in, 874
Labor expenses, 875
Machinery and motor vehicles, 873, 875
Mortgage loans, 1218
Number of farms, 855, 856, 857, 858, 859, 860, 862, 863, 864, 870
Organic, 870, 903, 904
Parity ratio, 880
Partnerships, 858, 860, 1339
Prices, 880, 893, 906
Renewable energy systems, 868
Sales direct to consumers, 869
Taxes, 874, 880
Value of land and buildings, 860, 861, 862, 873
Water use, 419
Farmers, characteristics, 865
Fat, consumption, 250, 251
Fatalities. (See Accidents and fatalities.)
Federal aid to education, 252, 315, 481
Elementary and secondary education, 252
Higher education institutions, 252
Research and development, 830, 832, 839
Science and engineering, 838
Federal aid to state and local government, 480, 481, 482
Federal budget. (See Expenditures of U.S. government.)
Federal debt, 509, 1222
Federal employee's retirement trust fund. (See under Government.)
Federal government. (See Government.)
Federal government finances. (See Receipts, and Expenditures of U.S. government.)
Federal Housing Administration, mortgage loans, 1030, 1219
Federal Transit Administration, 1144
Federal trust funds, 514, 515
Federal Highway Trust Fund, 1117, 1118
Feed. (See Grain.)
Feedstock, 966
Feldspar, 939, 940
Female householders. (See Households or families.)
Female population. (See Women.)
Fencing, 1269
Fentanyl, 135
Fertility rates, 84, 85, 89
Fertilizers:
    Farm expenditures for, 875
    Foreign trade, 883, 1324
    Prices, 772, 880
Fetal deaths (neonatal), 116, 117
Fiber, dietary, 250, 251
Fibers, 770, 772
Field hockey, 1269
Figs, 899
Fiji. (See Foreign countries.)
Filberts (hazelnuts), 899, 900
Filling stations. (See Gasoline stations.)
Finance and insurance industry:
    Capital, 793, 814, 816, 1226
    Earnings, 663, 665, 676, 677, 788, 802, 803, 804, 805, 806, 807, 808, 1190, 1192, 1193
    Electronic commerce, 1299

Employees, 654, 663, 664, 665, 671, 788, 791, 796, 802, 803, 804, 805, 806, 807, 808, 1190, 1192
Establishments, 671, 788, 789, 791, 792, 793, 796, 801, 802, 803, 804, 805, 806, 807, 808, 1190, 1191, 1192
Finances, 780, 783, 1194, 1195, 1312
Foreign investments in U.S., 1309, 1310
Gross domestic product, 705, 709
Hires and separations, 669, 670
Hours, 663
Multinational companies, 826, 828, 829, 1312
Nonemployers, 789, 1191
Occupational safety, 694, 696
Profits, 824, 825
Sales or receipts, 780, 783, 788, 789, 793, 802, 803, 804, 805, 806, 807, 808, 1190, 1191
Union membership, 699
Finance companies, 1194, 1195
    Consumer credit, 1215, 1216
    Corporate funds, 786
Financial crime, 362, 371, 372
Financial institutions. (See Banks, commercial; Credit unions; and Savings institutions.)
Finland. (See Foreign countries.)
Fire departments and personnel, 403, 404
Firearms:
    Deaths from, 123, 124, 131, 132, 364
    Sales of, 365, 366, 1272
    TSA screenings, 568
    Use in crimes, 351, 354, 363, 364, 373, 398
    Use in hunting, sports, 1271
Fires, 402, 405, 438
    Property loss, 402, 405
Firms. (See Business enterprise, and individual types of businesses and industries.)
Fish (see also individual species):
    Aquaculture, 877, 933
    Canning and preserving, 934, 935
    Catch, quantity, value, 930, 931, 932
    Consumer expenditures, 725, 726
    Consumption, 249
    Foreign trade, 930, 1325
    Prices, 763, 772, 777, 931
    Production and value, processed products, 933, 935
    Sales, 933
    Supply, 930, 934
Fishing, commercial, 930, 931, 932, 935
Fishing, recreational, 1268, 1271, 1277, 1278
Fishing and hunting industry, 802, 803, 804, 805, 806, 807, 808, 915, 1271
Floods, 436, 439, 446
Florida. (See State data.)
Florists, 665, 673, 1071, 1073
Flounder, 932, 935
Flour, 249, 768, 772
Flu (influenza), 121, 122, 123, 124, 125, 126, 207
Fluorspar, 939, 940, 943
Food (see also individual commodities):
    Commercial vegetables, 898
    Consumption, 248, 249, 250, 251
    Expenditures, 713, 722, 723, 725, 726, 727, 728, 1082, 1373
    Fish products, 763, 772, 930, 931, 932, 933, 934, 935

Note: Index citations refer to **table** numbers, not **page** numbers

Note: Index citations refer to **table** numbers, not **page** numbers

Note: Index citations refer to **table** numbers, not **page** numbers

---

Note: Index citations refer to **table** numbers, not **page** numbers

Note: Index citations refer to **table** numbers, not **page** numbers

---

Note: Index citations refer to **table** numbers, not **page** numbers

Employment, 323, 503, 506
Enrollment, 254, 255, 256, 259, 260, 296, 297,
  298, 299, 300, 301, 302, 303, 304, 305, 320, 841
Expenditures, 253
Faculty, 296, 322, 323, 324
Federal funding, 252
Finances, 253, 320
Financial aid, 315, 316, 317, 318, 319
Foreign- born students, 300, 303, 841
Foreign languages, 304
Housing population, 71
Libraries, 334
Number, 296, 297
Online course enrollment, 333
Price indexes, 321, 763
Research and development, 830, 832, 838, 839,
  1405
Salary offers, college graduates, 325
State appropriations, 320
Tuition and fees, 310, 312, 319
Voluntary financial support, 316, 318, 319
Highways:
  Accidents, 1094, 1125, 1126, 1127, 1128,
    1129, 1131, 1133, 1134, 1135, 1136
  Bridge inventory and condition, 1112
  Debt, state and local government, 1115
  Distracted driving, 1129
  Employees, government, 503, 506
  Expenditures:
    Local government, 484, 485, 501
    State and local government, 482, 483, 484,
      485, 490
    State government, 484, 485, 496, 499
    U.S. government, 481
  Funding, 1113, 1117, 1118
  Federal- aid systems, 1110
  Interstate highways, 1111
  Mileage, 1089, 1110, 1111
  Motor fuel consumption, 961, 1123
  Motor fuel tax, 1114, 1118
  Transit savings, 1141
  Types of roads, 1110, 1111
  Value of new construction, 998, 999
Hiking, 1271
Hindu population. (See Religions.)
Hispanic or Latino origin population, 6, 8, 10,
    11, 12, 14, 20, 37, 38, 43
  Adoption, 604
  Age and/or sex, 8, 10, 11, 12, 38
  AIDS and/or HIV, 205, 206
  Births and birth rates, 6, 84, 85, 86, 87, 89,
    90, 91, 94, 95, 96, 97
  Body weight, 228, 229
  Breastfeeding, 106
  Bullying, student, 340, 341
  Business owners, 804
  Cancer, 201
  Child care, 601, 605
  Children, 10, 11, 12, 38, 69, 243
  College costs, 309, 311
  College enrollment, 275, 292, 297, 298,
    300, 301, 302, 333
  Congress, members of, 464
  Consumer expenditure, 725
  Contraceptive use, 101, 104
  Criminal victimizations, 350, 355, 359, 363
  Deaths, 6, 112, 114, 119, 122, 127, 130,
    132, 134

Dental care visits, 232
Degrees conferred, 327, 845
Disability status, 306
Educational attainment, 37, 38, 261, 262, 263,
  264, 292, 298
Elderly, 10, 11, 12, 749
Elected officials, 464, 473
Elections, voter registration and turnout, 451
Families, characteristics, 37, 38, 67, 73
Food stamp participants, 574, 600
Foreign- born populations, 38, 42, 43, 620
Foster care, 604
Grandparents living with grandchildren, 67, 70
Hate crimes, 355
Health insurance coverage, 157, 164, 165, 166
Health and dental care visits, 186, 187, 190
Heart disease, deaths, 122, 127
High school dropouts, 38, 275, 292, 294, 295
Household or family characteristics, 38, 62, 67,
  73
Housing, 37, 1023, 1027, 1030, 1033
Immunization of children, 241
Income:
  Family, 37, 38, 734, 735, 736
  Household, 729, 730, 732
  Persons, 573, 739, 742, 743
Internet access/use, 1177, 1181, 1182, 1185
Jail inmates, 393, 394
Labor force and employment, 618, 619, 620,
    624, 627, 631, 680, 699
  Displaced workers, 643
  Earnings, 264, 505, 680, 685, 687
  Educational attainment, 624, 627, 640, 653,
    660
  Employed, 38, 505, 619, 620, 624, 627, 636,
    639, 640, 647, 653, 654
  Industry, 654, 1295
  Job search, 656
  Multiple job holders, 639
  Unemployed, 38, 619, 620, 627, 655, 656,
    660
  Union membership, 699
Leisure time use, 1266
Life expectancy, 108, 109
Living arrangements, 69, 79
Marital status, 59, 63, 73
Maternal mortality, 119
Minimum wage workers, 685
Migration, 6
Murders, 352
Nurses, 647
Occupation, 37, 280, 647, 653
Pension plan coverage, 573
Physical activity, 230
Poverty, 37, 38, 747, 748, 749, 751, 752
Projections, 12, 14
Public assistance, 573, 574, 600, 606
Schools and education:
  College costs, 309, 311
  Homeschooled, 286
  Parent participation, 274
  Preprimary school, 267, 275
  School enrollment, 258, 275, 292, 295,
    300, 301, 627
  Teachers, 280, 281, 282, 647
Sexual activity and identity, 101, 102, 103, 104
States, 20
Suicides, deaths, 122, 130, 546

Note: Index citations refer to **table** numbers, not **page** numbers

Note: Index citations refer to **table** numbers, not **page** numbers

---

Note: Index citations refer to **table** numbers, not **page** numbers

Note: Index citations refer to **table** numbers, not **page** numbers

Influenza and pneumonia, 121, 122, 123, 124,
125, 126, 203, 207
Inhalants, persons using, 223
Injuries (see also Accidents, and Occupational
safety), 216, 217, 405, 436, 1094, 1126
  Crime victimization, 349
  Industrial, 693, 694, 696, 697, 937
Inmates (see also Prisoners), 392, 393, 394
Installment loans (see also Loans and mortgages),
1200, 1201, 1216
Institutional care facilities (see also Hospitals, and
Nursing and residential care facilities), 71, 153,
180, 191, 192, 195, 196
Instruments and related products, manufacturing:
  Earnings, 665
  Employees, 665
  Foreign trade, 776, 777, 1324, 1325
  Productivity, 673
Insurance. (See individual forms of insurance.)
Insurance agents, brokers, and services:
  Earnings, 1192
  Employees, 1192
  Establishments, 1192
  Finances, 1193, 1227
  Foreign countries, 1378
  Gross domestic product, 1189
  Prices, 763
Insurance carriers:
  Capital, 814
  Earnings, 665, 1190, 1192
  Employees, 665, 1190, 1192
  Establishments, 1190, 1191, 1192
  Finances, 1193, 1194
  Gross domestic product, 1189
  Nonemployers, 1191
  Receipts, 1190, 1191
Insurance, government. (See Social insurance.)
Insurance, medical care, 141, 142, 145, 146
Intellectual property, 569, 712, 759
Intentional self- harm. (See Suicide.)
Interest:
  Payments, federal government, 512
  Persons receiving income, 573
  Receipts, by source:
    Individual income tax returns, 520
    National and personal income component, 714
Intermediate goods, price indexes, producer, 771,
772
Internal revenue collections (see also Tax receipts),
517
Internal waterways, traffic, 1107
International affairs:
  Charitable organizations, 612
  Commerce, 1320, 1323, 1326, 1329, 1341
  Development aid, 1406, 1407
  Federal outlays, 512
  Foreign investments in U.S., 1229, 1305, 1308,
  1309, 1310
  International transactions, U.S., 1303, 1304, 1305,
  1306, 1307
  U.S. government aid, 1314, 1315
  U.S. investments, 1228, 1303, 1312, 1313
International data (See Foreign countries, or World
summary statistics.)

International investment position, U.S., 1303, 1305,
1312, 1313
International mail (U.S. postal), 1151, 1152
Internet:
  Access and use, 1159, 1160, 1177, 1178,
  1179, 1180, 1181, 1184, 1185, 1262, 1400,
  1401
  Connection type, 1177, 1178, 1181, 1182
  Crime, 358
Internet publishing and broadcasting:
  Earnings, 665, 1153
  Employees, 665, 1153
  Establishments, 1153
  Finances, 1158, 1165
  Revenue, 1158, 1165
Internet service providers, Web search portals, data
processing:
  Earnings, 665, 788, 1153
  Employees, 665, 788, 1153
  Establishments, 788, 1153
  Finances, 1158, 1172
  Revenue, 788, 1158, 1172
Interracial married couples, 63
Inventories (see also commodities), 702, 1050,
1051, 1052, 1053, 1069, 1077, 1080
Investments (see also Capital stocks, and Securities):
  Foreign, in U.S., 1229, 1305, 1308, 1309, 1310
  Private domestic, gross, 702, 703, 707, 774, 817
  U.S. government obligations, 1206
  U.S. international, 1228, 1303, 1305, 1312,
  1313
Iodine, 940
Iowa. (See State data.)
Iran. (See Foreign countries.)
Iraq. (See Foreign countries.)
Ireland. (See Foreign countries.)
Iron (see also Steel):
  Foreign trade, 940, 943, 1324
  Mining industry, 673, 938
  Prices, 772, 938, 940
  Production, 939, 940, 1389
Iron and steel mills (see also Primary metal
manufacturing):
  Earnings, 665, 1042
  Employees, 665, 1042, 1044
  Shipments, 1042
Iron and steel products, 776, 777, 938, 939, 940,
943, 1324
Irrigation, 419
Islamic population. (See Religions.)
Island Areas of the U.S.:
  Agriculture, 1339, 1340
  Area, 406
  Births, 85, 1334
  Business summary, 1342, 1343, 1344, 1345,
  1346, 1347
  Climate (Puerto Rico), 441, 442, 443, 444
  Commerce, 1341
  Deaths, 118, 1334
  Education, 1335, 1338
  Employees, 1342, 1343, 1344, 1345, 1346,
  1347, 1348
  Establishments, 1342, 1343, 1344, 1345, 1346,
  1347

Note: Index citations refer to **table** numbers, not **page** numbers

Note: Index citations refer to **table** numbers, not **page** numbers

Note: Index citations refer to **table** numbers, not **page** numbers

---

Note: Index citations refer to **table** numbers, not **page** numbers

Lung disease. (See Pulmonary or respiratory disease.)
Luxembourg. (See Foreign countries.)
Lyme disease, 203, 204

M

Macadamia nuts, 899
Macedonia. (See Foreign countries.)
Machine tools, 763, 772
Machinery manufacturing:
  Capital, 814
  Earnings, 665, 1042, 1049
  Employees, 665, 1040, 1042, 1044, 1049
  Establishments, 1040
  Foreign trade, 776, 777, 1045, 1316, 1324
  Gross domestic product, 705, 1039
  Industrial production index, 821
  Inventories, 1051, 1052
  Multinational companies, 828, 829
  Price indexes, 776, 777
  Productivity, 673
  Research and development, 836
  Shipments, 1042, 1045, 1051, 1052
  Toxic chemical releases, 430
Madagascar. (See Foreign countries.)
Magnesium, 939, 940, 1389
Mail, 1151, 1152
Mail order houses (including electronic shopping):
  Earnings, 665, 1073
  Employees, 665, 1071, 1073
  Establishments, 1071, 1072
  Productivity, 673
  Sales, 1072, 1074, 1078, 1079
Maine. (See State data.)
Malaria, 203
Malawi. (See Foreign countries.)
Malaysia. (See Foreign countries.)
Maldives. (See Foreign countries.)
Male householders. (See Households or families.)
Mali. (See Foreign countries.)
Malignant neoplasms. (See Cancer.)
Malt beverages (see also Beverages), 763, 882, 885
Malta. (See Foreign countries.)
Mammography testing, 219
Managed care health plans, 160
Management of companies and enterprises:
  Capital, 814, 816
  Earnings, 665, 676
  Employees, 647, 665, 671, 788, 791, 796, 802, 803, 804, 805, 806, 807, 808, 1292, 1294, 1295
  Establishments, 671, 788, 791, 792, 793, 796, 801, 802, 803, 804, 805, 806, 807, 808, 1292, 1293, 1294
  Finances, 780, 783
  Gross domestic product, 705
  Occupational safety, 694
  Profits, 788, 825
  Sales, receipts, 780, 783, 802, 803, 804, 805, 806, 807, 808, 1292, 1293
Managers. (See Proprietors.)
Mandatory minimum sentencing, 387

Manganese, 940, 943, 1389
Manufacturing industry (see also individual industries):
  Capital, 793, 814, 816
  Construction value, 998
  Earnings, 663, 665, 676, 677, 788, 802, 803, 804, 805, 806, 807, 808, 1042, 1048, 1049, 1064, 1343
  Economic indicators, 819
  Employees, 652, 654, 663, 664, 665, 671, 788, 791, 796, 802, 803, 804, 805, 806, 807, 808, 1040, 1041, 1042, 1043, 1044, 1047, 1049, 1064, 1343
  Establishments, 671, 788, 789, 791, 792, 793, 796, 801, 802, 803, 804, 805, 806, 807, 808, 1040, 1041, 1064, 1343
  Finances, 780, 783, 1054, 1055, 1312
  Foreign countries, 1368, 1369
  Foreign investments in U.S., 1309, 1310
  Foreign trade, 1045
  Gross domestic product, 705, 709, 1039
  Hires and separations, 669, 670
  Hours, 663, 1046, 1047
  Industrial production index, 821, 1047
  Inventories, 820, 1050, 1051, 1052, 1053
  Investment abroad, 1312
  Island areas of the United States, 1342, 1343
  Multinational companies, 826, 828, 829
  Nonemployers, 789
  Occupational safety, 694, 696
  Research and development, 836
  Productivity, 673, 674, 821, 822, 1047, 1368
  Profits, 824, 825, 1054, 1055
  Sales, shipments, receipts, 780, 783, 788, 789, 802, 803, 804, 805, 806, 807, 808, 820, 1042, 1043, 1045, 1050, 1051, 1052, 1053, 1054, 1055, 1056, 1057, 1059, 1060, 1061, 1062, 1063
  State data, 1041, 1043, 1048
  Toxic chemical releases, 430
  Union membership, 699
  Value added, 1042, 1043
Margarine, 768
Marijuana (see also Drugs, illegal), 223, 224, 377
Marine Corps, 541
Marital status, 59, 60, 139
  Asian population, 59, 73
  Black, African American population, 59, 63, 73
  Computer use, 1179
  Couples with or without own household, 62
  Elderly, 34, 60, 73
  Employed persons, 629, 630, 632
  Foreign- born population, 41
  Hispanic origin population, 59, 63
  Householder status, 62, 64
  Internet access, 1179
  Interracial, 63
  Labor force participation rates, 628, 629, 630, 631
  Male householder, 62, 64
  Same- sex couple households, 73, 75
  Unmarried partners, 73, 74, 75
  Women in the labor force, 628, 629, 630, 631
Marriages (see also Marital status), 83, 136, 137, 138, 139

Note: Index citations refer to **table** numbers, not **page** numbers

Note: Index citations refer to **table** numbers, not **page** numbers

Note: Index citations refer to **table** numbers, not **page** numbers

---

Note: Index citations refer to **table** numbers, not **page** numbers

---

Note: Index citations refer to **table** numbers, not **page** numbers

Note: Index citations refer to **table** numbers, not **page** numbers

---

Note: Index citations refer to **table** numbers, not **page** numbers

Note: Index citations refer to **table** numbers, not **page** numbers

---

Note: Index citations refer to **table** numbers, not **page** numbers

Note: Index citations refer to **table** numbers, not **page** numbers

Q

Qatar. (See Foreign countries.)
Quarries. (See Mining industries.)
Quicksilver (mercury), 940

R

Rabies, 203
Race (See individual race categories.)
Radio broadcasting industry (see also Broadcasting, and Telecommunications):
    Earnings, 665, 1153, 1154
    Employees, 665, 1153, 1154
    Establishments, 1153, 1154
    Finances, 1158, 1168
    Productivity, 673
    Revenue, 1154, 1158, 1168
    Stations, 1160
Radiologists, 174
Radio listening, 1159
Rail transportation industry (see also Railroads):
    Capital, 814
    Earnings, 665
    Employees, 665, 1084, 1085
    Establishments, 1085
    Foreign trade, 1091
    Gross domestic product, 705
    Shipments, 1091, 1092, 1148
Railroad employees' retirement funds, 571
Railroads:
    AMTRAK, 1089, 1090
    Energy consumption, 961
    Mileage owned and operated, 1089
    Occupational safety, 1094
    Passenger traffic and revenue, 1142, 1290
    Shipments, 1091, 1092, 1148
    Vehicles, 1090
Rainfall, selected cities, 1399
Rankings:
    Airport traffic, 1097, 1287
    Amusement parks, 1264
    Cities:
        Commuting, 1146
        Population, 22, 25, 40
        Residential property tax, 492
        Science and engineering employment, 850
    Countries:
        Agricultural exports and imports, 1388
        Consumption of beef, pork, poultry, 1387
        Military expenditures, 1412
        Population, 1352
    Federal R&D obligations to higher education, 839
    Freight gateways, 1318
    Port traffic, 1108, 1109
    State:
        Exports, 1321
        Farm marketings, 879
        Foreign trade, 1321
        Personal income per capita, 717
        Population, 16, 22
        Public elementary/secondary school finances, 269
        Travel expenditures, 1285

Rape, 335, 343, 344, 345, 346, 349, 350, 357, 371, 372, 547
Raspberries, 877, 899
Raw materials. (See Crude materials.)
Reading (see also Books, and Libraries), 722, 725, 726, 1258, 1261, 1262, 1265, 1266
    E- book readers, 1265
    Literacy, 1383
Real estate (see also Housing), 754
Real estate and rental and leasing industry:
    Capital, 793, 814, 816
    Earnings, 663, 665, 676, 788, 794, 802, 803, 804, 805, 806, 807, 808, 1190, 1246, 1247
    Electronic commerce, 1299
    Employees, 647, 654, 663, 665, 671, 788, 791, 794, 802, 803, 804, 805, 806, 807, 808, 1190, 1246
    Establishments, 671, 788, 789, 791, 792, 793, 801, 802, 803, 804, 805, 806, 807, 808, 1190, 1245, 1246
    Finances, 780, 783
    Gross domestic product, 705, 709, 1189
    Hires and separations, 669, 670
    Hours, 663
    Multinational companies, 828, 829
    Nonemployers, 789, 1245
    Occupational safety, 694
    Productivity, 673
    Profits, 825
    Sales, receipts, 780, 783, 788, 789, 802, 803, 804, 805, 806, 807, 808, 1190, 1245
Real estate investment trust (REITs), 1194, 1218
Receipts (see also Tax receipts, and individual industries):
    American Indian, Alaska Native- owned businesses, 808
    Asian- owned businesses, 806
    Black- owned businesses, 805
    Corporations, partnerships, and proprietorships, 778, 779, 780, 781, 782, 783, 787, 1066
    Hispanic- or Latino- owned businesses, 804
    International transactions, 1303
    Minority- owned businesses, 803, 804, 805, 806, 807, 808
    Native Hawaiian, Other Pacific Islander- owned businesses, 807
Revenue, government (see also individual governmental units):
    Local governments, 483, 500
    State and local governments combined, 479, 482, 483, 488, 489
    State governments, 483, 496, 497
    Tax collections, 498
    United States government, 482, 508, 514, 517
Recreation (see also Arts, recreation, and travel, and Sports):
    Activities, 230, 1254, 1257, 1258, 1262, 1263, 1264, 1266, 1271, 1273, 1276
    Art, 1257, 1258
    Building construction, value, 996, 998, 999
    Consumer expenditures, 713, 1260, 1261, 1272, 1278
    Consumer price indexes, 763, 773
    Employment and expenditures, government, 503, 506, 512
    Leisure, 1258, 1262, 1266

Note: Index citations refer to **table** numbers, not **page** numbers

---

Note: Index citations refer to **table** numbers, not **page** numbers

Running/jogging, 1271
Rural population, 24, 27
Russell, stock index, 1230
Russia. (See Foreign countries.)
Rwanda. (See Foreign countries.)

S

Safety and security measures, 339, 937
Saint Kitts and Nevis. (See Foreign countries.)
Saint Lucia. (See Foreign countries.)
Saint Vincent and the Grenadines. (See Foreign countries.)
Salaries and wages. (See Earnings.)
Sales. (See individual commodities and industries.)
Sales workers, 647
Salmon, 932, 934, 935
Salmonellosis, 203, 247
Salt (common), production/value, 939, 940, 1389
Samoa. (See Foreign countries.)
Samoa, American. (See Island areas of the U.S.)
Samoan population, 1333
San Marino. (See Foreign countries.)
Sand and gravel industry (see also Mining industry), 772, 939
Sanitation. (See Refuse collection, and Sewage treatment.)
Sao Tome and Principe. (See Foreign countries.)
Sardines, 935
SAT scores, 314
Saudi Arabia. (See Foreign countries.)
Savings:
    Credit unions, 1211
    Deposits, 711, 1197
    Gross savings, sources and uses, 707
    Personal, 707, 714
    Rates, 1377
Savings banks. (See Savings institutions.)
Savings bonds, 1198
Savings institutions:
    Consumer credit, 1215
    Debt held by families, 1201
    Earnings, 1192
    Employees, 1192
    Establishments, 1192, 1206
    Finances, 1193, 1194, 1207, 1208, 1218, 1221
    Individual Retirement Accounts (IRAs), 1237
Saw logs, 924, 925
Saw mills, 915, 918, 919
Scallops, 932, 934
Scenic and sightseeing transportation industry, 665, 1084, 1085, 1086, 1087, 1088
Schools (see also Education):
    Boards, elected officials, 473
    Bullying, 337, 340, 341
    Career and technology programs, 289
    Districts, 477, 478
    Dress code, 339
    Fundraising, 274
    Homeschooling, 286
    Lunch and breakfast programs, 597
    Number, 277, 278, 287, 288, 296, 297
    Parent participation, 269
    Parent Teacher Association (PTA), 274
    Parent Teacher Organization, 274

Safety and security, 339
Special education, 238, 239
Start times, 285
States, 288
Types, 278, 287, 288
Volunteers, 274
Weapons, 338
Science, literacy, 1383
Scientific instruments. (See Instruments.)
Scientific research. (See Research and development.)
Scientists and engineers (see also individual fields):
    Characteristics, 841, 847
    Degrees conferred, 328, 329, 330, 331, 842, 843, 844, 845, 846
    Earnings, 852
    Employment, 647, 849, 850, 852
    Non U.S. citizens, 842
    Occupation, 849
    School enrollment, 841
Scrap metal. (See individual commodities, and Municipal waste and Solid Waste.)
Seafood, 932, 934, 935
Securities (see also individual types of securities):
    Foreign holdings, 1196, 1229, 1303, 1305
    Government, 487, 784, 785, 1196, 1222, 1229
    Held by life insurance, 1242
    Holdings of banks, 784, 785, 1206
    Holdings of individuals and businesses, 1197
    New issues, 1222, 1226
    Prices, indexes, yields, and issues, 1223, 1230
    Sales, stocks and bonds, 1222
    Savings of individuals, 711
    State and local government, 479, 487, 784, 785, 1222
Securities, commodity contracts, and investments industry:
    Capital, 814
    Earnings, 665, 1190, 1192
    Electronic commerce, 1299
    Employees, 665, 1190, 1192
    Establishments, 1190, 1191, 1192
    Finances, 1193, 1194, 1195, 1224
    Gross domestic product, 1189
    Nonemployers, 1191
    Profits, 1224
    Receipts, 1190, 1191
Seeds, 875
Self- employed, 636, 637, 849
Semiconductors (see also Computer and electronic product components), 1063
Senators, U.S., 458, 462, 463, 464, 465, 466
Senegal. (See Foreign countries.)
Septicemia, 122, 123, 124, 125
Serbia. (See Foreign countries.)
Service industries (see also specific sectors):
    Capital, 793, 814, 816
    Earnings, 665, 676, 677, 794, 802, 803, 804, 805, 806, 807, 808, 1292, 1343
    Electronic commerce, 1299
    Employees, 173, 654, 664, 665, 788, 791, 794, 796, 802, 803, 804, 805, 806, 807, 808, 1292, 1294, 1295, 1342, 1343
    Establishments, 789, 791, 792, 793, 794, 796, 801, 802, 803, 804, 805, 806, 807, 808, 1292, 1293, 1294, 1342, 1343

Note: Index citations refer to **table** numbers, not **page** numbers

Note: Index citations refer to **table** numbers, not **page** numbers

Social services, 665
Social welfare (see also Public aid, and individual programs):
  Charitable contributions, 612
  Employees (government), 503, 506
  Federal government outlays, 512, 513
  Program participation, 574
  State and local government, 482, 483, 490
  State government, 496, 499, 501
  Volunteers, 611
Social workers, 283
Sodium carbonate, 939, 940
Soft drinks (see also Beverages), 763, 772, 1064
Softball, 1269, 1270, 1271
Software publishing industry (see also Publishing):
  Earnings, 665, 1153, 1154
  Employees, 665, 1153, 1154
  Establishments, 1153, 1154
  Finances, 1154, 1158, 1164
  Productivity, 673
  Research and development, 836
  Revenue, 1158, 1164
Solar energy, 958, 962, 976, 977, 978, 986
Solid waste:
  Disposal, 414, 425, 426, 427
  Expenditures, 485, 490, 499, 501
  Industry, 428
  Landfills, 425, 426, 427
  Recycling, 425, 426, 427
Solomon Islands. (See Foreign countries.)
Somalia. (See Foreign countries.)
South Africa. (See Foreign countries.)
South Carolina. (See State data.)
South Dakota. (See State data.)
South Korea. (See Foreign countries.)
Soybeans:
  Acreage, 896, 903
  Farm marketings, sales, 877, 878, 903
  Foreign trade, 887, 889, 890
  Genetically engineered, 871
  Prices, 772, 896
  Production, 887, 896, 903
Space industry, commercial, 854
Space research and technology, federal outlays, 512, 853
Spain. (See Foreign countries.)
Spanish speakers, 56, 58, 266, 284
Special education, 238, 239
Specialty trade contractors, 665, 992, 993
Speeding, 1136
Spices, 763
Spinach, 248, 898, 903
Sporting and athletic goods, 217, 763, 772, 1079, 1272
Sporting goods, hobby, book, and music stores:
  Earnings, 665, 788, 1065, 1073
  Electronic commerce, 1078
  Employees, 665, 788, 1065, 1071, 1073
  Establishments, 788, 1065, 1071, 1072
  Nonemployers, 1072
  Productivity, 673
  Sales, 788, 1065, 1072, 1074, 1076, 1078

Sports (see also Sporting and athletic goods), 1262, 1263, 1266, 1267, 1268, 1269, 1270
  NCAA, 1267, 1268, 1269
  Volunteers, 611
Sports associations, 1302
Sports industry, 1248, 1250, 1251
Spot market price index, 770
Spotted fever, 203
Squash (NCAA), 1269
Squash (vegetable), 248, 898, 903
Squid, 932
Sri Lanka. (See Foreign countries.)
Standard & Poor's (S&P), 1230
Startups, firms, 798
State and local governments, combined data (see also individual governmental units):
  Debt, 482, 483, 486, 490
  Highways, 484, 485, 1115
  Employees, 502, 503, 506, 507
    Benefits, 504
  Employer costs, 690
  Expenditures, 320, 479, 482, 483, 484, 485, 487, 488, 490, 712
    By type, 482, 483, 484, 490
    Capital outlay, 484, 485
    Construction, value, 999
    Hospitals and medical care, 144, 146, 195, 490
  Federal aid, 480, 481, 510
  Finances, 479, 481, 482, 483, 488, 489
  Flow of funds, 1194, 1195
  Governmental units, 477
  Gross domestic product, 705
  Hospitals, 195, 198
  Mortgage holdings, 1218
  Payrolls, 502, 503
  Purchases of goods and services, 702, 703, 704
  Receipts by source, 479, 482, 483, 489
  Retirement systems, 581, 1194, 1227, 1233, 1237, 1238
  Securities issued, 487
  Treasury securities holdings, 1227
  Women holding public office, 472
State and regional data:
  Agriculture, 857, 862, 876, 878, 879
  AIDS and/or HIV, 204, 205
  Alcohol use, 224
  Altitudes, 414
  American Indian, Alaska Native population, 21
  Area, 406
  Arts, funding and production, 1253, 1256
  Asian population, 21
  Asset forfeiture, 370
  Automobile insurance expenditures, 1243
  Average pay, 679
  Bankruptcies, 810
  Births and birth rates, 17, 85, 92, 99
  Black, African American population, 21
  Blood alcohol concentration (BAC), 1130
  Border crossings, 1290
  Border lengths, 411
  Bridge inventory and condition, 1112
  Building permits, 995
  Buildings, federally owned, 536
  Cancer, 202
  Charter schools, 288

Note: Index citations refer to **table** numbers, not **page** numbers

Note: Index citations refer to **table** numbers, not **page** numbers

Note: Index citations refer to **table** numbers, not **page** numbers

Note: Index citations refer to **table** numbers, not **page** numbers

---

Note: Index citations refer to **table** numbers, not **page** numbers

---

Note: Index citations refer to **table** numbers, not **page** numbers

Turks and Caicos Islands. (See Foreign countries.)
Tuvalu. (See Foreign countries.)
Typhoid fever, 203

U

Uganda (See Foreign countries.)
Ukraine (See Foreign countries.)
Ulcers, 213
Unemployment. (See Labor force, unemployed
    workers.)
Unemployment insurance:
    Beneficiaries, 573, 587, 588, 662
    Coverage, workers and earnings, 587, 588
    Government finances, 482, 496, 514, 515
    Payments, 570, 571, 572, 587, 588
Union membership, 698, 699, 700
United Arab Emirates. (See Foreign countries.)
United Kingdom. (See Foreign countries.)
United States securities (see also Debt), 1195,
    1196, 1197, 1206, 1222, 1223, 1227, 1229
Universities. (See Education, higher education
    institutions.)
Unpaid work, 633, 688, 710
Uranium (see also Nuclear power), 939, 955, 975
Urban population (see also Cities, and Metropolitan
    statistical areas), 27, 82
Urban transit systems, 1085, 1089, 1141
Uruguay. (See Foreign countries.)
Utah. (See State data.)
Utilities (see also Electric light and power industry,
    and Gas utility industry.):
    Capital, 814, 816, 988, 990
    Consumer expenditures, 713, 722
    Customers and bills, 984, 988, 989
    Earnings, 663, 665, 676, 788, 802, 803, 804, 805,
        806, 807, 808, 956, 957
    Electric, 976, 981
    Employees, 654, 663, 665, 788, 791, 802, 803,
        804, 805, 806, 807, 808, 956, 957, 991
    Establishments, 788, 789, 791, 957
    Expense, 985
    Finances, 780, 783, 990
    Gross domestic product, 705
    Gas, 988, 989, 990
    Government employees and payroll, 503
    Hours, 663
    Income, 985
    Industrial production index, 821
    Industry, 788, 956, 957, 981
    Investor owned, 985
    Multinational companies, 828, 829
    Net generation, 981, 984
    Net summer capacity, 976, 980, 981
    Nonemployers, 789
    Occupational safety, 694, 696
    Price indexes, 762, 763
    Productivity, 673
    Profits, 824, 825
    Revenue, 956, 984, 985, 988, 989
    Sales, receipts, 780, 783, 788, 789, 802, 803,
        804, 805, 806, 807, 808, 989
    Sewage treatment, 957, 991
    State and local government expenditures, 483,
        484, 485, 490, 496, 499, 501

States, 980, 982, 983
Water, 957
Uzbekistan. (See Foreign countries.)

V

Vacancy rates, housing, 1013, 1015, 1016, 1018,
    1019, 1022
Vaccination, 207, 240, 241
Vanadium, 939, 943, 1389
Vanuatu. (See Foreign countries.)
Vaping (Electronic cigarette use), 245
Veal (see also Beef, and Meat and meat products), 249,
    772, 905, 1386, 1387
Vegetable oils. (See Oils.)
Vegetables (see also individual commodities):
    Acreage, 898, 903
    Consumer expenditures, 722, 725, 726
    Consumption, 248, 902
    Farm marketings, sales, 869, 875, 877, 903
    Foreign trade, 882, 885, 888, 890, 902, 1324
    Organic, 903
    Prices, 763, 772, 776, 777, 880
    Production, 898, 902, 903
Vehicles. (See Motor vehicles.)
Veneer, wood products, 915, 918, 919
Venezuela. (See Foreign countries.)
Vermiculite, 939, 940
Vermont. (See State data.)
Vessels. (See Ships.)
Veterans:
    Characteristics, 551, 554, 555
    Employment, 532, 621
    Number, 550, 553, 551
    Pensions and other benefits:
        Beneficiaries, 552, 553, 573
        Service- connected compensation, 552, 553
        Disbursements, 537, 553, 571, 572
        Federal aid to state and local governments, 481
        Federal payments, 512, 513, 570, 571, 572
Veterans Affairs, Dept. of:
    Expenditures, 141, 144, 147, 552, 553, 570,
        571, 572
    Home loans, 1219
    Mental health treatment facilities, 181, 182
Veterinary services, 1294, 1295, 1297
Vetoed bills, Congressional, 467
Victimizations, criminal, 349, 350, 353, 354,
    355, 356, 358, 359, 360, 363, 364
Vietnam. (See Foreign countries.)
Violent crime, (see also Crime), 335, 343, 344, 345,
    346, 347, 348, 349, 351, 352, 354, 363, 364,
    371, 372
Virgin Islands. (See Island areas of the U.S.)
Virginia. (See State data.)
Visa holders, doctorates, 842
Visa overstays, 565
Visual and performing arts, degrees, 328, 329,
    330, 331
Vital statistics. (See Births and birth rates, Deaths
    and death rates, Divorces, and Marriages.)
Vitamins, 250
Vocational rehabilitation, 141, 608
Volleyball, 1268, 1269, 1270, 1271
Volunteer activities, 274, 611

Note: Index citations refer to **table** numbers, not **page** numbers

Votes:
  Congressional, 448, 450, 458, 459, 460
  Early voting, 449
  Gubernatorial, 469
  Presidential, 448, 450, 454, 455, 456, 457
  Votes cast, 448, 449, 450, 451, 452, 453
  Voting- age population, 448, 450, 451, 452

W

Wage earners. (See Labor force, and individual
  industries.)
Wages and wage rates. (See Earnings.)
Walnuts, 877, 899, 900, 903
Warehouse clubs and superstores, 1071, 1074
Warehousing and storage industry:
  Capital, 814
  Earnings, 665, 1087
  Employees, 665, 1038, 1084, 1085, 1087
  Establishments, 1038, 1085, 1087, 1088
  Gross domestic product, 705
  Revenue, 1086, 1088
Washing machines, homes with, 1020
Washington. (See State data.)
Waste management & remediation services, 788,
  814, 1293, 1294, 1295, 1298
Wastepaper, 772, 928
Wastewater treatment, 956, 957, 991
Watches. (See Clocks and watches.)
Water (see also Wastewater treatment, and Water
  transportation industry):
  Area, 1, 406, 415
  Consumption, 419
  Freight, 1107, 1318
  Lakes, 407, 408, 409
  Pollution, 429, 434
  Public supply, 419, 1020
  Vessels, 1090, 1105
Water polo, 1269
Water transportation industry:
  Accidents and deaths, 1094
  Capital, 814
  Earnings, 665, 1087
  Employees, 503, 665, 1084, 1085, 1087
  Establishments, 1085, 1087, 1088
  Ferry operators, 1106
  Foreign trade, 1091, 1108, 1109
  Freight, 1107, 1108, 1109, 1318
  Fuel consumption, 961
  Gross domestic product, 705
  Outlays, 512
  Shipments, 1091, 1092
  Revenue, 1086, 1088
Water utility, 485, 725, 726, 763, 956, 957
Water, sewage and other systems, 485, 665, 956,
  957, 991
Waterborne commerce, 1107, 1108, 1109
Watermelons, 248, 877, 898
Waterways, 1105, 1107
Wealth:
  Business, 759
  Families, 756, 757
  Family farms, 866
  Government, 759
  Households, 759
  Millionaires, 754, 755

Persons, 753, 754, 755
Weather, 436, 439, 440, 441, 442, 443, 444, 445,
  446, 987, 1399
Weight, 228, 231
Weightlifting, 1268, 1271
Welfare services. (See Public aid, assistance; Social
  welfare; and individual programs.)
West Bank. (See Foreign countries.)
West Nile virus, 203
West Virginia. (See State data.)
Western Sahara. (See Foreign countries.)
Wetlands, 416, 418
Wheat:
  Acreage, 897, 903, 1384
  Farm marketings, sales, 877, 903
  Foreign trade, 882, 887, 889, 890, 1384, 1388
  Price indexes, 772, 776
  Prices, 897
  Production, 887, 897, 903, 1384, 1385
  Supply and disappearance, 1384
Wheat flour, 249
Whiting, 932
Wholesale trade:
  Capital, 793, 814, 816
  Earnings, 663, 665, 676, 788, 802, 803, 804, 805,
    806, 807, 808, 1065, 1343
  Electronic commerce, 1068
  Employees, 654, 663, 665, 671, 788, 791, 796,
    802, 803, 804, 805, 806, 807, 808, 1065, 1067,
    1070, 1342, 1343
  Establishments, 671, 788, 789, 791, 792, 793, 796,
    801, 802, 803, 804, 805, 806, 807, 808, 1065,
    1066, 1067, 1070, 1342, 1343
  Finances, 780, 783, 1312
  Foreign investments in U.S., 1309, 1310
  Gross domestic product, 705, 709
  Hires and separations, 669, 670
  Hours, 663
  Inventories, 820, 1069
  Multinational companies, 826, 828, 829, 1312
  Nonemployers, 789, 1066
  Occupational safety, 694, 696
  Productivity, 673
  Profits, 824, 825
  Sales, receipts, 780, 783, 788, 789, 802, 803,
    804, 805, 806, 807, 808, 820, 1065, 1066,
    1068, 1069, 1343
Whooping cough (pertussis), 203
Wildfires, 404, 438
Wildlife, 447, 1277, 1278
Wind:
  Energy sources, 958, 962, 976, 977, 978, 986
  Average speed, 444
Wine (see also Alcoholic beverages), 763, 882, 885
Wineries, 1064
Wisconsin. (See State data.)
Women:
  Abortions, 105
  Age, 7, 9
  AIDS and/or HIV, 205, 206
  American Indian, Alaska Native population, 8
  Asian population, 8
  Births and birth rates, 83, 84, 85, 86, 87, 88, 89,
    90, 91, 92, 93, 94, 95, 96, 97, 98, 99, 100
    Births to unmarried women, 91, 92, 95, 96, 97,
    100

Note: Index citations refer to **table** numbers, not **page** numbers

Note: Index citations refer to **table** numbers, not **page** numbers

Note: Index citations refer to **table** numbers, not **page** numbers